October 29–November 2, 2012
Maui, Hawaii, USA

Association for
Computing Machinery

Advancing Computing as a Science & Profession

CIKM'12

The Proceedings of the 21st ACM International Conference on Information and Knowledge Management

Co-located with:

CIKM 2012

Sponsored by:

ACM SIGIR & ACM SIGWEB

Volume 1

Association for Computing Machinery

Advancing Computing as a Science & Profession

The Association for Computing Machinery
2 Penn Plaza, Suite 701
New York, New York 10121-0701

ISBN: 978-1-4503-1156-4 (Digital)

ISBN: 978-1-4503-2010-8 (Print)

Additional copies may be ordered prepaid from:

ACM Order Department
PO Box 30777
New York, NY 10087-0777, USA

Phone: 1-800-342-6626 (USA and Canada)
+1-212-626-0500 (Global)
Fax: +1-212-944-1318
E-mail: acmhelp@acm.org
Hours of Operation: 8:30 am – 4:30 pm ET

Printed in the USA

CIKM 2012 Chair's Welcome

On behalf of the organizing committee, it is my genuine honor and great pleasure to welcome you to the 21st ACM International Conference on Information and Knowledge Management (CIKM 2012) in Maui, Hawaii! I hope this conference proves to be both interesting and beneficial.

Since its inception, the CIKM conference has provided a unique international forum for the presentation, discussion and dissemination of research findings in data management, information retrieval and knowledge management. The purpose of the conference is to identify challenging problems facing the development of future knowledge and information systems and to shape future research directions though the publication of high quality, applied and theoretical research findings. The conference has been a leading forum in which experts from academic, industry and the public sector gather to exchange ideas, research achievements and technical developments in multidisciplinary research areas.

As one of the world's most recognized conferences in the field, this year's CIKM conference has received a record high number of submissions in the history of CIKM, as can be seen from the following statistics:

- 1492 abstracts submitted
- 1088 full papers, 229 posters, and 70 demo papers submitted
- 146 papers accepted for presentation as full papers (13.4% acceptance rate) and 157 papers were accepted for short papers (27.8% cumulative acceptance rate)

The increased number of submissions alone is a great demonstration of the lively research areas that contribute to the CIKM area. In addition, CIKM 2012 will host 15 workshops on cutting-edge areas of research and a dedicated Industry Event featuring leading industrial practitioners. We are grateful to all authors who chose to submit their work to CIKM 2012 and are very excited by the final program.

CIKM values interdisciplinary research and we are proud to present three keynote speakers for the main conference (Dr. Ricardo Baeza-yates, Prof. William Cohen, and Prof. Jeffrey S. Vitter) and four keynote speakers for the Industry Event (Drs. Eric Brill, Raghu Ramakrishnan, Tom Malloy, and Xuedong Huang), all of whom will give presentations that cross discipline boundaries. I deeply appreciate their time and commitment to deliver their speeches and share their cutting-edge research experiences and insightful comments in their research topics.

Putting together CIKM 2012 program represents a huge amount of team effort on behalf of many people. The dedication and support of the Organizing Committee members helped overcome obstacles to deliver a successful conference program on time. First of all, the contributions to the technical program were selected by a renowned program committee headed by our three program chairs, Guy Lebanon, Mohammed Zaki, and Haixun Wang. I am grateful to them for all their hard work in managing such a complex reviewing task and to their senior program committee members, program committee members and additional reviewers who freely gave their time, effort and intelligence to the difficult task of selecting which contributions would form the program. I am also very grateful to Wolfgang Gatterbauer, who monitored and managed the process of editing the proceedings to meet very tight production schedules.

I am also grateful to Evgeniy Gabrilovich and Dou Shen to put together an excellent Industry Event; Dimitrios Gunopulos and Alin Dobra to organize and manage the workshop program;

Amelie Marian and Paul N. Bennett to manage the demonstrations track; Arvin Agah and Deng Cai to handle poster papers; Qi He, Prem Melville, and Yilong Yin who were great publicity chairs; Yi Chang and Ya Zhang who actively seek sponsorship and whose hard work allowed us to award grants to several student attendees; and Peter Scheuermann who organized the Best Paper Awards committee. The local arrangement team has been superbly led by Lipyeow Lim and Debasis Bhattacharya, who have made a huge effort into every aspect of the conference. Our treasures, Bo Luo and Eun K Park, have worked hard to set up the registration site and monitor the registration process. Finally, I value the effort of Jong Cheol Jeong (webmaster).

In addition, I would like to express my appreciation to all of our sponsors: Microsoft Research, eBay, Yahoo! Labs, IBM Research, Yandex, Adobe, Google, and Rakuten. All their generous sponsorship and support made this conference successful and possible. I would also like to thank the sponsoring ACM SIGs, SIGIR and SIGWEB, and their respective chairs, James Allan (AIGIR) and Simon Harper (SIGWEB), as well as Charles Nicholas (CIKM Liaison), for their advice and support.

Finally, I would like to thank the CIKM Steering Committee for their vote of confidence in us and their consistent support and guidance, in particular, our special thanks to Eun K Park and David Grossman. It is a great honor and pleasure to accept the responsibilities and challenges of general chair. I hope that attendees find the technical program to be interesting and productive towards their research endeavors. I hope that you all take full advantage of these opportunities for professional development and that the conference will provide you with a valuable opportunity to share ideas with other researchers and practitioners from institutions around the world. I further hope that the conference will be stimulating, informative, enjoyable, and a fulfilling experience to all who attend it.

Enjoy the CIKM 2012 conference and your stay in Maui, Hawaii!

Xuewen Chen
ACM CIKM 2012 General Chair
Wayne State University, USA

Program Committee Chairs' Welcome

Welcome to the 21st ACM International Conference on Information and Knowledge Management (CIKM). Over the past two decades, CIKM has been serving as a leading forum for researchers from the database, information retrieval, and knowledge management communities. The purpose of the conference is to disseminate the challenges and solutions for the next generation of knowledge and information systems, and to shape future research directions through the publication of high-quality research papers, both theoretical and applied. This year's call for papers attracted 1088 submissions from all over the world. The program committee accepted 146 full papers (13.4%), and an additional 157 short papers (27.8% cumulative acceptance rate).

We thank and acknowledge everyone who made this strong technical program possible. We thank the authors for submitting their best work for consideration to CIKM. Our unreserved gratitude is to the program committee and external reviewers, who worked extremely hard to provide high quality reviews and feedback on the submissions. The senior program committee members deserve much recognition for their meta-reviews and ensuring a smooth reviewing workflow. We would like to thank the general chair, Prof. Xue-wen Chen, in assembling an excellent organizing team, who have put together a strong and exciting program including the invited talks, papers, posters, workshops and demos. Thanks are also due to Joonseok Lee and Seungyeon Kim who helped administer the IR track. Finally, we would like to thank all our corporate sponsors for their generous support.

We hope that you will find this program interesting and thought-provoking. Please enjoy the conference and the opportunity to network with friends and colleagues from around the world.

Guy Lebanon
CIKM12 IR Track Chair
Georgia Institute of Technology

Haixun Wang
CIKM12 DB Track Chair
Microsoft Research Asia

Mohammed J. Zaki
CIKM12 KM Track Chair
Rensselaer Polytechnic Institute

Table of Contents (Volume 1)

Session 3 – IR Track: Evaluation Methodologies

Session 4 – IR Track: Social Media Search

Session 5 – KM Track: Link and Graph Mining

Session 6 – IR Track: Language Technologies

Session 7 – DB Track: Graph and Knowledge Base

Session 8 – DB Track: Temporal, Spatial and Multimedia Databases

Session 9 – KM Track: Matrix Methods and Anomaly Detection

Session 10 – KM Track: Social Networks

Session 11 – IR Track: Advertising

Session 12 – IR Track: System Architecture, Distributed IR, Scalability

Session 13 – KM Track: Advertisement and Products

Session 14 – KM Track: Clustering

Session 15 – IR Track: Recommendation Systems

Session 16 – IR Track: Digital Libraries and Citation Analysis

Session 17 – KM Track: Text Mining

Session 18 – IR Track: Formal Retrieval Models and Learning to Rank

Session 19 – DB Track: Probabilistic and Uncertain Data

Session 20 – DB Track: Top-k and Nearest Neighbor Queries

Session 21 – KM Track: Spatial and Temporal Methods

Table of Contents (Volume 2)

Session 25 – IR Track: Topic Modeling and Content and Sentiment Analysis

Session 26 – DB Track: Query Processing, Optimization and Performance

Session 27 – KM Track: Classification and Semantic Methods

Session 28 – IR Track: Multimedia and User Feedback

Session 29 – DB Track: Emerging and Advanced Topics

Session 30 – KM Track: Novel Applications

Session 31 – IR Track: Social Networks

Knowledge Management Short Paper Session

Table of Contents (Volume 3)

Databases Short Paper Session

Knowledge Management Poster Session

Information Retrieval Poster Session

Databases Poster Session

Knowledge Management Demonstration Session

Information Retrieval Demonstration Session

Databases Demonstration Session

Workshop Summaries

CIKM 2012 Conference Organization

General Conference Chair: Xuewen Chen *(Wayne State University, USA)*

DB Track Program Chair: Haixun Wang *(Microsoft Research Asia, China)*

IR Track Program Chair: Guy Lebanon *(Georgia Institute of Technology, USA)*

KM Track Program Chair: Mohammed J. Zaki *(Rensselaer Polytechnic Institute, USA)*

Workshop Chairs: Dimitrios Gunopulos *(University of Athens, Greece)*
Alin Dobra *(University of Florida, USA)*

Poster Chairs: Arvin Agah *(University of Kansas, USA)*
Deng Cai *(Zhejiang University, USA)*

Demonstration Chairs: Amelie Marian *(Rutgers University, USA)*
Paul N. Bennett *(Microsoft Research, USA)*

Industry Chairs: Evgeniy Gabrilovich *(Google, USA)*
Dou Shen *(CityGrid Media, USA)*

Local Chairs: Lipyeow Lim *(University of Hawaii, USA)*
Debasis Bhattacharya *(University of Hawaii, USA)*

Publicity Chairs: Qi He *(IBM Research, USA)*
Prem Melville *(IBM Research, USA)*
Yilong Yin *(Shandong University, China)*

Sponsorship Chairs: Yi Chang *(Yahoo!, USA)*
Ya Zhang *(Shanghai Jiaotong University, China)*

Proceedings Chair: Wolfgang Gatterbauer *(Carnegie Mellon University, USA)*

Award Chair: Peter Scheuermann *(Northwestern University, USA)*

Treasure: Bo Luo *(University of Kansas, USA)*
Eun K Park *(California State University, Chico, USA)*

Webmaster: Jong Cheol Jeong *(University of Kansas, USA)*

Steering Committee Chair: David Grossman *(Illinois Institute of Technology, US)*

Steering Committee: Charles Clarke *(University of Waterloo, Canada)*
Alberto Leander *(Federal University of Minas Gerais, Brazil)*
Charles Nicholas *(University of Maryland Baltimore County, US)*
E.K. Park *(City University of New York, US)*
Philip S. Yu *(University of Illinois at Chicago, US)*

CIKM 2012 DB Track Senior Program Committee

CIKM 2012 DB Track Program Committee

Sunil Prabhakar, *Purdue University, USA*
Anish Das Sarma, *Google Research, USA*
Atish Das Sarma, *eBay Research Labs, USA*
Bin Shao, *Microsoft Research Asia, China*
Kyuseok Shim, *Seoul National University, Korea*
Nan Tang, *Qatar Computing Research Institute, Qatar*
Frank Tompa, *University of Waterloo, Canada*
Stratis Viglas, *University of Edinburgh, UK*
Daisy Zhe Wang, *University of Florida, USA*
Guoren Wang, *North Eastern University, China*
Sean Wang, *Fudan University, China*
Zhongyuan Wang, *Microsoft Research Asia, China*
Raymond Wong, *HKUST, Hong Kong*
Yinghui Wu, *University of California, Santa Barbara, USA*
Yanghua Xiao, *Fudan University, China*
Ke Yi, *Hong Kong University of Science and Technology, HK*
Ge Yu, *Northeastern University, China*
Xiangliang Zhang, *KAUST, Saudi Arabia*
Baihua Zheng, *Singapore Management University, Singapore*
Aoying Zhou, *East China Normal University, China*
Xuan Zhou, *Renmin University of China, China*
Kenny Zhu, *SJTU, China*
Lei Zou, *Peking University, China*

CIKM 2012 IR Track Senior Program Committee

Eugene Agichstein, *Emory University, USA*
Ram Akella, *University of California, Santa Cruz, USA*
Nicholas Belkin, *Rutgers University, USA*
Paul Bennett, *Microsoft, USA*
Ben Carterette, *University of Dellaware, USA*
Yi Chang, *Yahoo, USA*
Olivier Chapelle, *Yahoo, USA*
Kevyn Collins-Thompson, *Microsoft, USA*
Fernando Diaz, *Yahoo, USA*
Evgeniy Gabrilovich, *Google, USA*
Sreenivas Gollapudi, *Microsoft, USA*
Qi He, *IBM Almaden Research Center, USA*
Arun Iyengar, *IBM T.J. Watson Research Center, USA*
Rong Jin, *Michigan State University, USA*
Gareth Jones, *Dublin City University, Ireland*
Yehuda Koren, *Yahoo, USA*
Oren Kurland, *Technion, Israel*
Mounia Lalmas, *Yahoo, USA*
Hang Li, *Microsoft, USA*
R. Manmatha, *University of Massachusetts, USA*
Paul McNamee, *Johns Hopkins University, USA*
Donald Metzler, *University of Southern California, USA*
Peter Mika, *Yahoo, USA*
Wolfgang Nejdl, *Leibniz Universitat Hannover, Germany*
Bo Pang, *Yahoo, USA*
Tetsuya Sakai, *Microsoft, USA*
Luo Si, *Purdue University, USA*
Fabrizio Silvestri, *Istituto di Scienzae Tecnologie dell'Informazione, Italy*
Torsten Suel, *Polytechnic Institute of New York University, USA*
Andrew Trotman, *University of Otago, New Zealand*
Jun Wang, *UCL, UK*
Ji-Rong Wen, *Microsoft, USA*
Ryen White, *Microsoft, USA*
Emine Yilmaz, *Microsoft, USA*
Elad Yom-Tov, *Yahoo, USA*
Hongyuan Zha, *Georgia Tech, USA*
Min Zhang, *Tsinghua University, USA*
Yi Zhang, *University of California Santa Cruz, USA*

CIKM 2012 IR Track Program Committee

Nima Asadi, *University of Maryland, USA*
Javed Aslam, *Northeastern University, USA*
Giuseppe Attardi, *Universita di Pisa, Italy*
Leif Azzopardi, *University of Glasgow, UK*
Jing Bai, *Microsoft Corporation, USA*
Suhrid Balakrishnan, *AT&T Research, USA*
Niranjan Balasubramanian, *University of Massachusetts Amherst, USA*
Krisztian Balog, *Norwegian University of Science and Technology, Norway*
Luca Becchetti, *Universita di Roma - La Sapienza, Italy*
Alejandro Bellogin, *Universidad Autonoma de Madrid, Spain*
Jiang Bian, *Yahoo Labs, USA*
Bodo Billerbeck, *Microsoft Bing, USA*
Roi Blanco, *Yahoo! Research Barcelona, Spain*
Edward Bortnikov, *Yahoo! Labs, USA*
Wray Buntine, *National ICT Australia Limited, Australia*
David Carmel, *IBM, USA*
Marc-Allen Cartright, *University of Massachusetts Amherst, USA*
Pablo Castells, *Universidad autonoma de madrid, Spain*
Carlos Castillo, *Yahoo! Research Barcelona, Spain*
James Caverlee, *Texas A&M, USA*
Yu Chen, *Microsoft Research Asia, China*
Zheng Chen, *Microsoft Research Asia, China*
Xueqi Cheng, *Chinese Academy of Sciences, China*
Tat-Seng Chua, *NUS, Singapore*
Charlie Clarke, *University of Waterloo, Canada*
Ingemar Cox, *University college london, UK*
Bin Cui, *Peking University, China*
Shane Culpepper, *RMIT, Australia*
Ludovic Denoyer, *LIP6, France*

Zhicheng Dou, *Microsoft Research Asia, China*
Greg Druck, *Yahoo!, USA*
Georges Dupret, *Yahoo!, USA*
Koji Eguchi, *Kobe University, Japan*
Carsten Eickhoff, *Tech Univ Delft, Netherlands*
Li Fan, *Yahoo, USA*
Hui Fang, *University of Delaware, USA*
Ayman Farahat, *Yahoo, USA*
Henry Feild, *University of Massachusetts, USA*
Nicola Ferro, *University of Padova, Italy*
Dennis Fetterly, *MSR, USA*
Luanne Freund, *University of British Columbia, Canada*
Ingo Frommholz, *University of Bedfordshire, UK*
Bin Gao, *Microsoft Research Asia, China*
Roberto Grossi, *Universita di Pisa, Italy*
Jiafeng Guo, *Chinese Academy of Sciences, China*
Maxim Gurevich, *Google, USA*
Cathal Gurrin, *Dublin City University, Ireland*
Claudia Hauff, *Delft University of Technology, Netherlands*
Ben He, *Graduate University of CAS, China*
Djoerd Hiemstra, *University of Twente, Netherlands*
Katja Hofmann, *Universiteit Van Amsterdam, Netherlands*
Steven Hoi, *Nanyang Technological University, Singapore*
Vivian Hu, *York University, Canada*
Yunhua Hu, *Microsoft Research Asia, China*
Minlie Huang, *Tsinghua University, China*
Xuanjing Huang, *Fudan University, China*
Jagadeesh Jagarlamudi, *University of Maryland, USA*
Tamas Jambor, *University college london, UK*
Heng Ji, *City University of New York, USA*
Vanja Josifovski, *Yahoo Labs, USA*
Jaap Kamps, *University of Amsterdam, Netherlands*
Evangelos Kanoulas, *Google Zurich, Swiss*
Tapas Kanungo, *Microsoft, USA*
Gabriella Kazai, *Microsoft Research, USA*
Jinyoung Kim, *University of Massachusetts, USA*
Sang-Wook Kim, *Hanyang University, South Korea*
Irwin King, *Chinese University of Hong Kong,*
Noam Koenigstein, *Tel Aviv University, Israel*
Marijn Koolen, *University of Amsterdam, Netherlands*
Alexander Kotov, *Emory University, USA*
Eyal Krikon, *Technion, Israel*
Neal Lathia, *Cambridge University, UK*
Dawn Lawrie, *Loyola University, USA*
Daniel Lemire, *Universite de Quebec a Montreal, Canada*
Wen Li, *Delft University of Technology, Netherlands*
Xiaoming Li, *Peking University, China*
Hongfei Lin, *Dalian Univ. of Technology, China*
Yi Liu, *Google Research, USA*
Alexander Loser, *TU Berlin, German*
Yue Lu, *Twitter, USA*
Yuanhua Lv, *University of Illinois at Urbana-Champaign, USA*
Yosi Mass, *IBM Research Lab at Haifa, Israel*
James Mayfield, *Johns Hopkins University, USA*
Richard Mccreadie, *University of Glasgow, UK*
Qiaozhu Mei, *University of Michigan, USA*
Edgar Meij, *University of Amsterdam, Netherlands*
Jun Miao, *York University, Canada*
Natasa Milic-Frayling, *Microsoft Research, USA*
Prasenjit Mitra, *Penn State University, USA*
Dunja Mladenic, *Jozef Stefan Institute, Slovenia*
Alistair Moffat, *University of Melbourne, Australia*
Jian-Yun Nie, *Univeristy of Montreal, Canada*
Chikashi Nobata, *Yahoo Labs, USA*
Giorgio Di Nunzio, *University of Padova, Italy*
Arlindo Oliveira, *Instituto Superior Tecnico / INESC-ID, Portugal*
Virgil Pavlu, *Northeastern University, USA*
Fuchun Peng, *Microsoft, USA*
Raffaele Perego, *ISTI - CNR, Italy*
Benjamin Piwowarski, *University of Glasgow, Scotland*
Vassilis Plachouras, *Presans, France*
Tamara Polajnar, *University of Glasgow, UK*
Jeffrey Pound, *University of Waterloo, Canada*
Tao Qin, *Microsoft Research Asia, China*
Baojun Qiu, *eBay, USA*
Filip Radlinski, *Microsoft Research Cambridge, UK*
Davood Rafiei, *University of Alberta, Canada*
Jan Ramon, *K.U. Leuven, Belgium*
Edie Rasmussen, *University of British Columbia, Canada*
Srihari Reddy, *Google, USA*
Maarten de Rijke, *University of Amsterdam, Netherlands*
Haggai Roitman, *IBM, USA*
Stevan Rudinac, *Delft University of Technology, Netherlands*
Scott Sanner, *NICTA & ANU, Australia*

Rodrygo Santos, *University of Glasgow, UK*
Carlos Scheidegger, *AT&T Research, USA*
Ralf Schenkel, *Max-Planck-Institut Informatik, German*
Yue Shi, *delft university of technology, Netherlands*
Milad Shokouhi, *Microsoft Research, USA*
Mark Smucker, *University of Waterloo, Canada*
Ian Soboroff, *NIST, USA*
Zhong Su, *IBM Research China, China*
Venkata Subramaniam, *IBM Research India, India*
Krysta Svore, *Microsoft Research, USA*
Lei Tang, *Yahoo Labs, USA*
Paul Thompson, *Dartmouth Medical School, USA*
Hamed Valizadegan, *University of Pittsburgh, USA*
Emre Velipasaoglu, *Yahoo!, USA*
Rossano Venturini, *ISTI - CNR, Italy*
Vishwa Vinay, *Microsoft Research, USA*
Arjen de Vries, *Centrum Wiskunde & Informatica, Netherlands*
Xiaojun Wan, *Peking University, China*
Lidan Wang, *University of Maryland, USA*
Xin-Jin Wang, *Microsoft Research Asia, China*
Xuanhui Wang, *Yahoo Labs, USA*
Rob Warren, *University of Waterloo, Canada*
Takashi Washio, *Osaka University, Japan*
Ingmar Weber, *Yahoo! Labs, USA*
Wouter Weerkamp, *University of Amsterdam, Netherlands*
Tong Wei, *Carnegie Mellon University, USA*
Xing Wei, *Google, USA*
Lei Wu, *University of Pittsburgh, USA*
Hongbo Xu, *Chinese Academy of Sciences, China*
Jun Xu, *Microsoft Research Asia, China*
Zenglin Xu, *Purdue University, USA*
Ismet Zeki Yalniz, *University of Massachusetts Amherst, USA*
Tianbao Yan, *Michigan State University, USA*
Christopher Yang, *Drexel University, USA*
Jie Yang, *Yahoo research, USA*
Shuang-Hong Yang, *Georgia Institute of Technology, USA*
Wai Yee, *Orbitz LLC, USA*
Xing Yi, *University of Massachusetts Amherst, USA*
Yisong Yue, *Carnegie Mellon University, USA*
De-Chuan Zhan, *Nanjin University, China*
Dan Zhang, *Purdue University, USA*
Dell Zhang, *Birkbeck College, UK*
Dongyan Zhao, *Peking University, China*
Jun Zhao, *National Laboratory of Pattern Recognition, China*
Le Zhao, *Carnegie Mellon University, USA*
Yang Zhou, *Yahoo! lab, USA*
Guido Zuccon, *University of Glasgow, UK*

CIKM 2012 KM Track Senior Program Committee

Michael Berthold, *University of Konstanz, Germany*
Ming-Syan Chen, *National Taiwan University, Taiwan*
David W-L. Cheung, *University of Hong Kong, Hong Kong*
Chris Ding, *University of Texas at Arlington, USA*
Minos Garofalakis, *Technical University of Crete, Greece*
Jiawei Han, *University of Illinois at Urbana-Champaign, USA*
David Jensen, *University of Massachusetts, Amherst*
Thorsten Joachims, *Cornell University, USA*
George Karypis, *University of Minnesotta, USA*
Hans-Peter Kriegel, *University of Munich, Germany*
Bing Liu, *University of Illinois Chicago, USA*
Huan Liu, *Arizona State University, USA*
Wagner Meira, Jr., *Federal University of Minas Gerais, Brazil*
Srinivasan Pathasarathy, *Ohio State University, USA*
Dino Pedreschi, *University of Pisa, Italy*
Thomas Seidl, *RWTH Aachen, Germany*
Philip Yu, *University of Illinois at Chicago, USA*

CIKM 2012 KM Track Program Committee

Naoki Abe, *IBM TJ Watson Research Center, USA*
Muhammad Abulaish, *King Saud University, Saudi Arabia*
Evrim Acar, *University of Copenhagen, Denmark*
Ankit Agrawal, *Northwestern University, USA*
Luca Aiello, *University of Torino, Italy*
Reda Alhajj, *University of Calgary, Canada*
Hisham Al-Mubaid, *University of Houston, USA*
Hiroki Arimura, *Hokkaido University, Japan*
Ira Assent, *Aarhus University, Denmark*
Antonio Badia, *University of Louisville, USA*
Ricardo Baeza-Yates, *Yahoo! Research, Spain*
James Bailey, *University of Melbourne, Australia*
Roberto Bayardo, *Google, USA*
Tanya Berger-Wolf, *University of Illinois at Chicago, USA*
Michele Berlingerio, *IBM, USA*
Michael Berry, *University of Tennessee, USA*
Francesco Bonchi, *Yahoo! Research, Spain*
Christian Borgelt, *European Center for Soft Computing, Spain*
Christos Boutsidis, *IBM TJ Watson Research Center, USA*
Bin Cao, *Hong Kong University of Science and Technology, Hong Kong*
Cornelia Caragea, *Pennsylvania State University, USA*
Loic Cerf, *Federal University of Minas Gerais, Brazil*
Keith Chan, *Hong Kong Polytechnic University, Hong Kong*
Philip Chan, *Florida Institute of Technology, USA*
Vineet Chaoji, *Yahoo! Research, India*
Nitesh Chawla, *University of Notre Dame, USA*
Jake Chen, *Indiana University Purdue University Indianapolis, USA*
Ye Chen, *Microsoft, USA*
Hong Cheng, *Chinese University of Hong Kong,*
Tao Cheng, *Microsoft, USA*
Yun Chi, *NEC Labs, USA*
Alfredo Cuzzocrea, *University of Calabria, Italy*
Wei Ding, *University of Massachusetts, Boston, USA*
Chabane Djeraba, *University of Lille, France*
Alin Dobra, *University of Florida, USA*
Petros Drineas, *Rensselaer Polytechnic Institute, USA*
Frank Eichinger, *SAP Research, Germany*
Hongliang Fei, *University of Kansas,*
Hakan Ferhatosmanoglu, *Ohio State University, USA*
Samah Fodeh, *Yale University, USA*
Thomas Gaertner, *University of Bonn, Germany*
Gemma Garriga, *INRIA, France*
Carlotta George, *Carlotta Domeniconi George Mason University, USA*
Rayid Ghani, *Accenture, USA*
Amol Ghoting, *IBM TJ Watson Research Center, USA*
Fosca Giannotti, *ISTI CNR, Italy*
C. Lee Giles, *The Pennsylvania State University, USA*

CIKM 2012 External Reviewers

Jaafar Abdallah, *University of Louisville*
Artur Abdullin, *University of Louisville*
Andrea Albarelli, *Ca'Foscari University of Venice*
Mohammad Allaho, *Pennsylvania State University*
Mshabab Alrizah, *Pennsylvania State University*
Rabaa Alzaidy, *Pennsylvania State University*
Kevin Amaral, *University of Massachusetts Boston*
Rajul Anand, *Wayne State University*
Jordi Atserias, *Yahoo*
Muzammil Baig, *University of South Australia*
Krishnakumar Balasubramanian, *Georgia Tech*
Yubin Bao, *Northeastern University*
Nicola Barbieri, *University of Calabria*
Christian Beecks, *RWTH Aachen University*
Michael Behrisch, *University of Konstanz*
Julien Blanchard, *University of Nantes*
Sam Blasiak, *George Mason University*
Francesca Bonin, *Trinity College Dublin*
Matthias Bracht, *Karlsruhe Institute of Technology*
Igo Brilhante, *Federal University of Ceara*
Ivan Brugere, *University of Minnesota*
Berkant Cambazoglu, *Yahoo*
Xin Cao, *Nanyang Technological University*
Luigi Caro, *University of Torino*
Mario Cataldi, *University of Torino*
Eugenio Cesario, *ICAR-CNR*
Muhammad Cheema, *UNSW*
Xi Chen, *University of Minnesota*
Yang Chen, *University of Florida*
Ying-Ju Chen, *National Taiwan University*
Yu-Fen Chen, *National Taiwan University*
Chen Cheng, *Chinese University of Hong Kong*
Wei Cheng, *University of North Carolina, Chapel Hill*
Yu Cheng, *Northwestern University*
Chiraz Cherif, *University Manouba*
Ping Chi, *Pennsylvania State University*
Nai-Hui Chia, *Pennsylvania State University*
Shih-Chuan Chiu, *Academica Sinica*
Xiang Ci, *Renmin University of China*
Cathal Coffey, *National University of Maynooth*
Carmela Comito, *University of Calabria*
Chaoran Cui, *Shandong University of Finance and Economics*
Hanbo Dai, *Singapore Management University*
Bhavana Dalvi, *Carnegie Mellon University*
Xuan-Hong Dang, *Aarhus University*
Jerome David, *INRIA*
Elena Demidova, *L3S Research Center*
Wei Dong, *Singapore Management University*
Greg Drzadzewski, *University of Waterloo*
Wouter Duivesteijn, *Leiden University*
Dora Erdos, *Boston University*
Yulei Fan, *Renmin University of China*
Sergiy Fefilatyev, *University of South Florida*
Shi Feng, *Northeastern University*
Wei Feng, *Tsinghua University*
Greg Ference, *Pennsylvania State University*
Laura Ferrari, *IBM Research*
Renato Fileto, *University of Florianopolis*
Fabian Fischer, *University of Konstanz*
Francesco Folinoi, *ICAR-CNR*
Philippe Fournier-Viger, *University of Moncton*
Lizhen Fu, *Renmin University of China*
Johannes Fuchs, *University of Konstanz*
Fabio Fumarola, *University of Bari*
Esther Galbrun, *University of Helsinki*
Clint George, *University of Florida*
Nikos Giatrakos, *University of Piraeus*
Aris Gkoulalas-Divanis, *IBM research Ireland*
Sean Goldberg, *University of Florida*
Daniel Golovin, *Google Inc.*
Eduardo Goncalves, *Fluminense Federal University*
Jagadeesh Gorla, *University College London*
Bluma Gottesman, *Polytechnic Institute of New York University*
Swapna Gottipati, *Singapore Management University*
Justin Graber, *Kansas University*
Quanquan Gu, *University of Illinois, Urbana Champaign*
Yu Gu, *Northeastern University*
Ziyu Guan, *University of California, Santa Barbara*
Alexandre Guitton, *University Blaise Pascal*
Tias Guns, *Katholieke University Leuven*
Lei Guo, *Shandong University of Finance and Economics*
WANG Guoping, *National University of Singapore*
Zhen Hai, *Nanyang Technological University*

Tarek Hamrouni, *Institut Superieur des Arts Multimedias de la Manouba*
Mounira Harzallah, *University of Nantes*
Basheer Hawwash, *University of Louisville*
Yuxiong He, *Microsoft Research*
Joyce Ho, *University of Texas*
Dzung Hong, *Purdue*
Leong Hou, *University of Macau*
Hao Hu, *University of Science and Technology*
Wei Hu, *Tsinghua University*
Xia Hu, *Arizona State University*
Yajie Hu, *University of Miami*
Shanshan Huang, *Shandong University of Finance and Economics*
Shunping Huang, *University of North Carolina, Chapel Hill*
Hui-Ju Hung, *Academia Sinica*
Zheng Huo, *Renmin University of China*
Dino Ienco, *IRSTEA*
Patricia Iglesias, *Karlsruhe Institute of Technology*
Roberto Interdonato, *University of Calabria*
Rohit Jain, *Purdue*
Nandish Jayaram, *University of Texas, Arlington*
Yi Jia, *Kansas University*
Lili Jiang, *Tsinghua University*
Ruoyi Jiang, *Adometry Inc.*
Yexi Jiang, *Florida International University*
Ning Jin, *Amazon Inc.*
Anthony Kakas, *University of Cyprus*
Andrey Kan, *University of Melbourne*
Andrew Kane, *University of Waterloo*
Anuj Karpatne, *University of Minnesota*
Jaya Kawale, *University of Minnesota*
Mehdi Kaytoue, *LIRIS Lyon*
Fabian Keller, *Karlsruhe Institute of Technology*
Holger Kiefhaber, *SAP Inc.*
Kibaek Kim, *Northwestern University*
Seungyeon Kim, *Georgia Tech*
Arno Knobbe, *Leiden University*
Tobias Koetter, *University of Konstanz*
John Korecki, *University of South Florida*
Yue Kou, *Northeastern University*
Milos Krstajic, *University of Konstanz*
Mayank Lahiri, *Facebook Inc.*
Philippe Lamarre, *LIRIS Lyon*
Chao Lan, *Kansas University*
Thuc Le, *University of South Australia*
Jihwan Lee, *Purdue*
Joonseok Lee, *Georgia Tech*
Remi Lehn, *Universiy of Nantes*
Johannes Leveling, *Dublin City University*
Hui Li, *Guizhou University*
Jianxin Li, *Swinburne University of Technology*
Jingxuan Li, *Florida International University*
Kun Li, *University of Florida*
Lei Li, *Florida International University*
Yang Li, *University of California, Santa Barbara*
Yuxuan Li, *University of Melbourne*
Zhenhui Li, *University of Illinois Urbana Champaign*
Shuang Lin, *University of Florida*
Su-Chen Lin, *National Taiwan University*
Yu-Chieh Lin, *National Taiwan University*
France Liroz, *INRIA & Lirmm - University of Montpellier*
Bo Liu, *Guangdong University of Technology*
Bo Liu, *Facebook*
Hao Liu, *Hokkaido University*
Lin Liu, *University of South Australia*
Wei Liu, *University of Melbourne*
Xingjie Liu, *Pennsylvania State University*
Yi Liu, *University of North Carolina, Chapel Hill*
Yunzhong Liu, *Arizona State University*
Henry Lo, *University of Massachusetts Boston*
Cheng LONG, *Hong Kong University of Science and Technology*
Gaelle Loosli, *University Blaise Pascal*
Vanessa Lopez, *IBM Research*
Ruxia Ma, *Renmin University of China*
Youzhong Ma, *Renmin University of China*
Claudia Marinica, *Lina Polytech Nantes*
Fabrizio Marozzo, *University of Calabria*
Luiz Merschmann, *Ouro Preto Federal University*
Barbora Micenkova, *Aarhus University*
Meenakshi Mishra, *Kansas University*
Luyi Mo, *The University of Hong Kong*
Samaneh Moghaddam, *Simon Fraser University*
Vineeth Mohan, *Wayne State University*
Pierre-Nicolas Mougel, *INSA-Lyon*
Yang Mu, *University of Massachusetts Boston*
Prashanth Mundkur, *Nokia Inc.*
Franco Nardini, *ISTI-CNR*
Hoang Nguyen, *Karlsruhe Institute of Technology*
Tiezheng Nie, *Northeastern University*
Siegfried Nijssen, *Katholieke University Leuven*

Weike Pan, *University of Science and Technology*
Odysseas Papapetrou, *Technical University of Crete*
Luca Pappalardo, *University of Pisa*
Joseph Paul, *University of Massachusetts Boston*
Peng PENG, *Hong Kong University of Science and Technology*
Yu PENG, *Hong Kong University of Science and Technology*
Fabien Picarougne, *Lina Polytech Nantes*
Yoann Pitarch, *Aalborg University*
Giovanni Ponti, *ENEA*
Romila Pradhan, *Purdue*
Xu Pu, *Tsinghua University*
Chiara Pulice, *University of Calabria*
Minghui Qiu, *Singapore Management University*
Chedy Raissi, *INRIA*
Parikshit Ram, *Georgia Tech*
Karthik Raman, *Cornell University*
Huzefa Rangwala, *George Mason University*
Mathieu Roche, *University Montpellier 2*
Christian Rohrdantz, *University of Konstanz*
Ji Rong, *Microsoft*
Massimo Ruffolo, *ICAR-CNR*
Diego Saez-Trumper, *Pompeu Fabra University*
Rabie Saidi, *University Blaise Pascal*
Esin saka, *Microsoft Inc.*
Sarowar Sattar, *University of South Australia*
Rossano Schifanella, *University of Torino*
Matthias Schubert, *University of Munich*
D. Sculley, *Google Inc.*
Marian Scuturici, *LIRIS Lyon*
Chaofeng Sha, *Fudan University*
Yi Shan, *Arizona State University*
Chao Shen, *Florida International University*
Chih-Ya Shen, *National Taiwan University*
Wei Shen, *Tsinghua University*
Zhitao Shen, *UNSW*
Yingjie Shi, *Renmin University of China*
Pannaga Shivaswamy, *Cornell University*
Arlei Silva, *Federal University of Minas Gerais*
Claudio Silvestri, *Ca'Foscari University of Venice*
Ruben Sipos, *Cornell University*
Afroza Sultana, *University of Texas, Arlington*
Huan Sun, *University of California, Santa Barbara*
Jiankai Sun, *Shandong University of Finance and Economics*
Sabina Surdu, *LIRIS Lyon*
Adith Swaminathan, *Cornell University*
Chih-Hua Tai, *National Taiwan University*
Lei Tang, *Yahoo Labs*
Liang Tang, *Florida International University*
Andrada Tatu, *University of Konstanz*
Gabriele Tolomei, *CNR*
Paolo Trunfio, *Universiy of Calabria*
Patrick Valduriez, *INRIA & Lirmm - University of Montpellier*
Bhanukiran Vinzamuri, *Wayne State University*
Dawei Wang, *University of Massachusetts Boston*
Fei Wang, *The University of Hong Kong*
Jiantao Wang, *Renmin University of China*
Quan Wang, *Peking University*
Weibo Wang, *University of North Carolina, Chapel Hill*
Xufei Wang, *Arizona State University*
Yu Wang, *Emory University*
Franz Wanner, *University of Konstanz*
Tim Weninger, *University of Illinois Urbana-Champaign*
Tim Weninger, *University of Illinois Urbana-Champaign*
Yinghui Wu, *University of California, Santa Barbara*
Zhiping Wu, *University of Waterloo*
Wei Xiang, *University of Science and Technology*
Yusheng Xie, *Northwestern University*
Takehiro Yamamoto, *Kyoto University*
Yusuke Yamamoto, *Kyoto University*
Kaige Yan, *Kansas University*
Shengqi Yang, *University of California, Santa Barbara*
Xuan Yang, *The University of Hong Kong*
Peifeng Yin, *Pennsylvania State University*
Ji Yoon, *IBM Research Ireland*
Chung-Hsien Yu, *University of Massachusetts Boston*
Guoxian Yu, *George Mason University*
Kui Yu, *University of Massachusetts Boston*
Weiren Yu, *UNSW*
Xiao Yu, *University of Illinois Urbana Champaign*
Quan Yuan, *Nanyang Technological University*
Man-ching Yuen, *Chinese University of Hong Kong*
Jintao Zhang, *Kansas University*
Jinzeng Zhang, *Renmin University of China*
Kunpeng Zhang, *Northwestern University*
Wenjie Zhang, *UNSW*
Xiaojian Zhang, *Renmin University of China*

Yansong Zhang, *Renmin University of China*
Ying Zhang, *UNSW*
Zhishan Zhang, *University of North Carolina, Chapel Hill*
Xiang Zhao, *UNSW*
Erheng Zhong, *Hong Kong University of Science and Technology*
Xiang Zhong, *University of Wisconsin-- Madison*
Dong Zhou, *Trinity College Dublin*
Jiayu Zhou, *Arizona State Univerisity*
Ke Zhou, *Georgia Tech*
Mu Zhou, *University of South Florida*
Rui Zhou, *Swinburne University of Technology*
Tom Zhou, *Chinese University of Hong Kong*
Yun Zhou, *University of Melbourne*
Ke Zhu, *UNSW*
Yin Zhu, *Hong Kong University of Science and Technology*
Albrecht Zimmermann, *Katholieke University Leuven*
Bo Zong, *University of California, Santa Barbara*

CIKM 2012 Sponsors & Supporters

Sponsors:

SIGIR
Special Interest Group
on Information Retrieval

sig web

Gold Supporter:

Microsoft
Research

Silver Supporters:

ebay
Research Labs

YAHOO! LABS

Bronze Supporters:

IBM Research

Google

Rakuten

Yandex

Adobe

User Engagement:The Network Effect Matters!

Ricardo Baeza-Yates, Mounia Lalmas
Yahoo! Labs Barcelona
Barcelona, Spain
{rbaeza,mounia}@acm.org

ABSTRACT

In the online world, user engagement refers to the quality of the user experience that emphasizes the positive aspects of the interaction with a web application and, in particular, the phenomena associated with wanting to use that application longer and frequently. This definition is motivated by the observation that successful web applications are not just used, but they are engaged with. Users invest time, attention, and emotion into them.

Online providers aim not only to engage users with each service, but across all services in their network. They spend increasing effort to direct users to various services (e.g. using hyperlinks to help users navigate to and explore other services), to increase user traffic between their services. Nothing is known for users engaging across such a network of Web sites, something we call **networked user engagement**. We address this problem by combining techniques from web analytics and mining, information retrieval evaluation, and existing works on user engagement coming from the domains of information science, multimodal human computer interaction and cognitive psychology. In this way, we can combine insights from big data with deep analysis of human behavior in the lab or through crowd-sourcing experiments.

This work was mainly done in collaboration with Janette Lehmann and Georges Dupret from Yahoo! Labs, as well as Elad Yom-Tov from Microsoft Research.

Categories and Subject Descriptors

H.1.2 [**User/Machine Systems**]: Human information processing

General Terms

Human Factors, Measurement.

Keywords

User engagement, network of services, Web sites, metrics.

CIKM'12, October 29–November 2, 2012, Maui, HI, USA.
ACM 978-1-4503-1156-4/12/10.

1. CONTENTS

User engagement is measured in many ways, through methods of self-reporting (e.g., questionnaires), observer methods (e.g., facial expression analysis, speech analysis, desktop actions, etc.), neuro-physiological signal processing methods (e.g., respiratory and cardiovascular accelerations and decelerations, muscle spasms, etc.), and from a web analytics perspective (through online behavior metrics that assess users' depth of engagement with a site). These methods represent various tradeoffs between scale of data and depth of understanding (for instance, surveys are small-scale but deep, whereas clicks are large-scale but shallow in understanding). However, little work has been done to integrate these various measures into a coherent understanding of engagement success.

The presentation comprises three parts:

1) First, we define user engagement, list its many characteristics as identified in the research and analytic literature, and discuss through real examples the challenges associated with measuring user engagement [1, 2].

2) Second, we describe recent data-driven approaches looking at user engagement through the development of new measures that allow for a better representation of how users engage with and across different web services, what we call networked user engagement [5, 6].

3) Finally, we describe how emerging research directions looking at affect and cognition as well as graph related measures are providing additional insights into measuring networked user engagement [3, 4].

2. CONCLUSIONS

This research line is a first step forward to fully understand user engagement in the context of the Web. This work also shows the need and importance of combining different points of view coming from different disciplines. This way of thinking is crucial to many areas, going beyond the Web and will in time lead to a new genre of computational social sciences that transcend specific applications on the Internet.

3. REFERENCES

[1] S. Attfield, G. Kazai, M. Lalmas and B. Piwowarski. Towards a science of user engagement (position paper). WSDM Workshop on User Modeling for Web Applications, Hong Kong, China, 9 February 2011.

[2] J. Lehmann, M. Lalmas, E. Yom-Tov and G. Dupret. Models of User Engagement. In *20th conference on User Modeling, Adaptation, and Personalization.* Montreal, Canada, 2012, 164–175.

[3] J. Lehmann, M. Lalmas, and R. Baeza-Yates. User Engagement: The Network Effect Matters!. Submitted, 2012.

[4] L. McCay-Peet, M. Lalmas and V. Navalpakkam. On Saliency, Affect and Focused Attention. In *ACM SIGCHI Conference on Human Factors in Computing Systems (CHI)*, Austin, Texas, ACM Press, 2012, 541–550.

[5] E. Yom-Tov, M. Lalmas, G. Dupret, R. Baeza-Yates, P. Donmez, J. Lehmann. The effect of links on networked user engagement (poster). In *WWW 2012 (Companion Volume)*, Lyon, France, Apr 2012, 641–642.

[6] E. Yom-Tov, M. Lalmas, R. Baeza-Yates, G. Dupret, J. Lehmann, P. Donmez. Networked User Engagement. Submitted, 2012.

Short Biography

Ricardo Baeza-Yates is VP of Yahoo! Research for Europe, Middle East and Latin America, leading the labs at Barcelona, Spain and Santiago, Chile, since 2006, as well as supervising the lab in Haifa, Israel, since 2008. He is also part time Professor at the Dept. of Information and Communication Technologies of the Universitat Pompeu Fabra in Barcelona, Spain, since 2005. Until 2005 he was Professor and Director of the Center for Web Research at the Department of Computer Science of the Engineering School of the University of Chile (currently in a leave of absence).

He obtained a Ph.D. from the University of Waterloo, Canada, in 1989. Before he obtained two masters (M.Sc. CS & M.Eng. EE) and the electrical engineering degree from the University of Chile, Santiago. He is co-author of the best-seller Modern Information Retrieval textbook, published in 1999 by Addison-Wesley with a second enlarged edition in 2011, as well as co-author of the 2nd edition of the Handbook of Algorithms and Data Structures, Addison-Wesley, 1991; and co-editor of Information Retrieval: Algorithms and Data Structures, Prentice-Hall, 1992, among more than 400 other publications.

He has received the Organization of American States award for young researchers in exact sciences (1993) and the CLEI Latin American distinction for contributions to computer science in the region (2009). In 2003 he was the first computer scientist to be elected to the Chilean Academy of Sciences. During 2007 he was awarded the Graham Medal for innovation in computing, given by the University of Waterloo to distinguished ex-alumni. In 2009 he was named ACM Fellow and in 2011 IEEE Fellow.

Learning Similarity Measures Based on Random Walks

[Extended Abstract]

William W. Cohen
Machine Learning Department
Carnegie Mellon University
Pittsburgh, Pennsylvania
wcohen@cs.cmu.edu

ABSTRACT

We describe a novel learnable proximity measure based on personalized PageRank (also known as "random walk with reset"). Instead of introducing one weight per edge label, as in most prior work, we introduce one weight for each edge label *sequence*. We show that this approach is advantageous for a number of real-world tasks, including querying graph databases, recommendation tasks, and inference in large, noisy knowledge bases.

Categories and Subject Descriptors

H.4 [**Information Systems Applications**]: Miscellaneous

Keywords

personalized PageRank, learning

1. OVERVIEW

The scientific literature can be represented as a graph of documents, terms, and meta-data, with edges corresponding to containment of a term in a document, authorship of a document by a person, and so on. One popular way of querying such a graph is via queries based on proximity measures, such as personalized PageRank, also known as Random Walk with Restart (RWR).

We describe a novel learnable proximity measure based on RWR. Instead of introducing one weight per edge label, as in most prior work, we introduce one weight for each edge label sequence. In this model proximity is defined by a weighted combination of simple "random walk experts", each corresponding to conducting a random walk constrained to follow a particular sequence of labeled edges.

Experiments on several tasks using graphs based on literature from two subdomains of biology show that the new learning method significantly outperforms the prior methods. We extend the method to support two additional types of experts to model intrinsic properties of entities: "query-independent experts", which generalize the PageRank measure, and "popular entity experts" which allow rankings to be adjusted for particular entities that are especially important.

We also present experiments in which we use this approach to learn relationships in the ontology of NELL, a wide-coverage, large-scale information extraction system for web data. We show that these types of learnable "proximity measures" are general enough to accurately model a significant number of real-world relations, and that they outperform an alternative technique that learns to model relations based on more traditional logical rules.

Acknowledgements

This is joint work with Ni Lao (now at Google Research) and Tom Mitchell. Parts of this work were supported by NIH under grant R01GM081293, by NSF under grant IIS0811562, by DARPA under awards FA8750-08-1-0009 and AF8750-09-C-0179, and by a gift from Google.

CIKM'12, October 29–November 2, 2012, Maui, HI, USA.
ACM 978-1-4503-1156-4/12/10.

Compressed Data Structures with Relevance

(Invited Keynote)

Jeffrey Scott Vitter
The University of Kansas
Lawrence, KS 66047 USA
jsv@ku.edu

ABSTRACT

We describe recent breakthroughs in the field of compressed data structures, in which the data structure is stored in a compressed representation that still allows fast answers to queries. We focus in particular on compressed data structures to support the important application of pattern matching on massive document collections. Given an arbitrary query pattern in textual form, the job of the data structure is to report all the locations where the pattern appears. Another variant is to report all the documents that contain at least one instance of the pattern. We are particularly interested in reporting only the most relevant documents, using a variety of notions of relevance. We discuss recently developed techniques that support fast search in these contexts as well as under additional positional and temporal constraints.

Categories and Subject Descriptors

E.4 [**Data**]: Coding and Information Theory—*data compaction and compression*; F.2.2 [**Analysis of Algorithms and Problem Complexity**]: Nonnumerical Algorithms and Problems—*pattern matching*; H.3.1 [**Information Storage and Retrieval**]: Content Analysis and Indexing—*indexing methods*; H.3.2 [**Information Storage and Retrieval**]: Information Storage—*file organization*; H.3.3 [**Information Storage and Retrieval**]: Information Search and Retrieval—*search process.*

General Terms

Algorithms, Design, Performance, Theory.

Keywords

Compressed data structure, compression, data compression, entropy, external memory, index, pattern matching, search.

1. Introduction

The field of compressed data structures began over 20 years ago [9] with the goal of achieving fast query time while using a compressed representation. The challenge is to construct a compressed representation of the input data — substantially smaller than the original input size, ideally about the size of the input data in entropy-compressed format — so that it can be queried directly without need for decompression, yet still provide the same functionality and speed as traditional data structures.

In this invited presentation, we focus on the ubiquitous problem of searching for a query pattern in a massive document collection. Web search engines such as Google support word-based search using the well-known inverted index: For each word in the document collection, the inverted index maintains a list of locations where the word appears. The search for a particular word involves a simple ordered search of the inverted index. However, in many applications, we are interested in searching for a query pattern that is not in word form — such as a partial word, multiword phrase, or more generally an arbitrary sequence of characters. In fact, in some document collections, there may be no natural notion of "word" at all; examples include collections of DNA sequences, protein data, music scores, Asian languages, and other heterogeneous sources.

In all those cases, we must use an alternative to inverted indexes. Suffix trees and suffix arrays provide the desired functionality, but for massive document collections they use an unacceptably large amount of space: A document collection containing n characters from an alphabet Σ occupies $n \log |\Sigma|$ bits.[1] However, a suffix tree or suffix array built on that document collection requires $O(n \log n)$ bits, which in practice is typically a factor of 4–15 times larger. And compared with the size of the documents in *compressed* format, the space blow-up is even more severe.

Theoretical breakthroughs just over a dozen years ago led to the development of a new generation of space-efficient search indexes. The *compressed suffix array* [5, 6, 14, 15, 4, 16] and the *FM-index* [1, 2, 3, 10] achieve high-order entropy space compression, and their query time is proportional to the query pattern size (in units of computer words) plus the product of the output size and polylog n. Moreover, these new indexes are *self-indexing* in that they can reconstruct any part of the original document collection in a random-access manner, and thus the document collection becomes redundant and can be discarded. The net effect is that the document collection can be completely replaced by a much smaller index structure.

The output of all locations where a query pattern occurs may be unmanageably large, and it is often more helpful to report only the documents that contain the query pattern

[1]We assume for simplicity that $|\Sigma|$ is a power of 2.

CIKM'12, October 29–November 2, 2012, 2012 Maui, HI, USA.
ACM 978-1-4503-1156-4/12/10.

rather than all the matching locations within those documents. It is even more meaningful to report only the *most relevant* documents that contain the query pattern. We can define relevance in various ways — such as by the frequency of the pattern in the document, or perhaps by how close the pattern is to other instances, or as in Google by the static notion of the document's PageRank.

The *document indexing* problem, for a query pattern and query parameter k, is to find the top-k most relevant documents containing the pattern; in the absolute version, we find those documents that have a relevance value of at least k. We discuss recent advances [11, 7, 13, 17] in the standard RAM model as well as in the external memory model [19], when the data collection and the index are too massive to fit into the internal memory of a computer and must instead be stored externally, such as on disk. We give algorithmic paradigms in these models for efficient indexing, including dealing with approximations, and illustrate some biological applications.

In summary, inverted indexes have well-known strengths: They are relatively easy to implement using small amounts of memory space. They can be readily adapted for efficient implementation in external memory. They allow dynamic updates and distributed operations. And they are easily tuned for top-k applications. However, they are inherently word-based and cannot readily handle searches for arbitrary patterns. Nor are they self-indexing. An ongoing challenge in the field is to simultaneously achieve the many advantages inverted indexes offer as well as the important features of self-indexing and the ability to search for general patterns. In this presentation, we discuss several exciting developments toward answering that challenge.

For more details, the reader is referred to surveys on indexing for massive string data [12, 8] as well as to recent papers with several co-authors, which can be found on the author's web page [18].

2. Acknowledgments

Support was provided in part by National Science Foundation grants CCF–0621457 and CCF–1017623. Thanks go to Wing-Kai Hon, Rahul Shah, and Cheng Sheng for helpful comments.

3. References

[1] P. Ferragina and G. Manzini. Opportunistic data structures with applications. In *Proc. IEEE Symp. on Foundations of Computer Science*, volume 41, pages 390–398, November 2000.

[2] P. Ferragina and G. Manzini. Indexing compressed texts. *Journal of the ACM*, 52(4):552–581, 2005.

[3] L. Foschini, R. Grossi, A. Gupta, and J. S. Vitter. When indexing equals compression: Experiments on suffix arrays and trees. *ACM Transactions on Algorithms*, 2(4):611–639, 2006. Conference versions in *SODA 2004* and *DCC 2004*.

[4] R. Grossi, A. Gupta, and J. S. Vitter. High-order entropy-compressed text indexes. In *Proc. ACM-SIAM Symp. on Discrete Algorithms*, January 2003.

[5] R. Grossi and J. S. Vitter. Compressed suffix arrays and suffix trees with applications to text indexing and string matching. In *Proc. ACM Symp. on Theory of Computing*, volume 32, pages 397–406, May 2000.

[6] R. Grossi and J. S. Vitter. Compressed suffix arrays and suffix trees with applications to text indexing and string matching. *SIAM Journal on Computing*, 35(32):378–407, 2005.

[7] W.-K. Hon, R. Shah, and J. S. Vitter. Space-efficient framework for top-k string retrieval problems. In *Proc. IEEE Symp. on Foundations of Computer Science*, Atlanta, October 2009.

[8] W.-K. Hon, R. Shah, and J. S. Vitter. Compression, indexing, and retrieval for massive string data. In *Proc. Symp. on Combinatorial Pattern Matching*, volume 6129 of *LNCS*, pages 260–274. Springer, June 2010. Invited keynote paper.

[9] G. Jacobson. Succinct static data structures. Technical Report CMU-CS-89-112, Dept. of Computer Science, Carnegie-Mellon University, January 1989.

[10] V. Mäkinen and G. Navarro. Implicit compression boosting with applications to self-indexing. In *Proc. Intl. Symp. on String Processing Information Retrieval*, volume 4726 of *LNCS*, pages 229–241. Springer, October 2007.

[11] S. Muthukrishnan. Efficient Algorithms for Document Retrieval Problems. In *Proc. ACM-SIAM Symp. on Discrete Algorithms*, pages 657–666, 2002.

[12] G. Navarro and V. Mäkinen. Compressed full-text indexes. *ACM Computing Surveys*, 39(1):article 2, 2007.

[13] G. Navarro and Y. Nekrich. Top-k document retrieval in optimal time and linear space. In *Proc. ACM-SIAM Symp. on Discrete Algorithms*, pages 1066–1077, January 2012.

[14] K. Sadakane. Compressed text databases with efficient query algorithms based on the compressed suffix array. In *Proc. Intl. Symp. on Algorithms and Computation*, volume 1969 of *LNCS*, pages 410–421. Springer, December 2000.

[15] K. Sadakane. New text indexing functionalities of the compressed suffix arrays. *Journal of Algorithms*, 48(2):294–313, 2003.

[16] K. Sadakane. Compressed suffix trees with full functionality. *Theory of Computing Systems*, 41(4):589–607, 2007.

[17] R. Shah, C. Sheng, S. V. Thankachan, and J. S. Vitter. On optimal top-k string retrieval, July 2012. arXiv:1207.2632v1 [cs.DS].

[18] J. S. Vitter. Online publication library, `http://www.ittc.ku.edu/~jsv/Papers/catalog/`.

[19] J. S. Vitter. *Algorithms and Data Structures for External Memory*. Foundations and Trends in Theoretical Computer Science. Now Publishers, Hanover, MA, 2008.

LogUCB: An Explore-Exploit Algorithm For Comments Recommendation*

Dhruv Mahajan
Microsoft Research India
Bangalore
dhrumaha@microsoft.com

Rajeev Rastogi
Amazon
Bangalore, India
rastogi@amazon.com

Charu Tiwari
Yahoo! Labs
Bangalore, India
charu@yahoo-inc.com

Adway Mitra
CSA Department, IISc
Bangalore, India
adway@csa.iisc.ernet.in

ABSTRACT

The highly dynamic nature of online commenting environments makes accurate ratings prediction for new comments challenging. In such a setting, in addition to *exploiting* comments with high predicted ratings, it is also critical to *explore* comments with high uncertainty in the predictions. In this paper, we propose a novel *upper confidence bound* (UCB) algorithm called LogUCB that balances exploration with exploitation when the average rating of a comment is modeled using logistic regression on its features. At the core of our LogUCB algorithm lies a novel variance approximation technique for the Bayesian logistic regression model that is used to compute the UCB value for each comment. In experiments with a real-life comments dataset from Yahoo! News, we show that LogUCB with bag-of-words and topic features outperforms state-of-the-art explore-exploit algorithms.

Categories and Subject Descriptors

I.2.6 [**Computing Methodologies**]: Learning

General Terms

Algorithms, Experimentation

Keywords

logistic regression, explore-exploit, comment ratings, upper confidence bound

1. INTRODUCTION

User generated content in the form of comments has witnessed an explosive growth on the web. Web sites like Yahoo! and YouTube allow users to comment on diverse content like news articles and videos. These "crowd-sourced" comments are highly engaging because they reflect the views and opinions of real users, and are a means for users to discuss and debate controversial issues. Furthermore, comments can be informative, and are an effective gauge of public sentiment on a topic.

However, a key challenge with user generated comments is that a single news article on a major event can easily trigger thousands of comments. Clearly, it is unrealistic to expect that users will sift through the copious comments for an article. A more realistic scenario is that a user will look through the first K comments that are presented to him/her, and ignore the remaining comments. Fortunately, most commenting environments allow users to provide feedback on comments shown to them – users can give a *thumbs-up* rating to indicate that they like, or a *thumbs-down* rating to express dislike for a comment. Thus, our goal in this paper is to develop algorithms that leverage past comment ratings to rank an article's comments so that the top K comments have the highest chance of being liked by the user.

Recommender systems have been extensively studied in the research literature – these systems use collaborative filtering, content-based filtering, or hybrid approaches to recommend items to users. Traditional collaborative filtering techniques rely on either item-item/user-user similarity models [26], or matrix factorization models [22] that multiply user- and item-specific factors for ratings prediction. A shortcoming of classical collaborative filtering approaches is that they cannot predict ratings for new users or items (referred to as the *cold-start problem*). Content-based filtering methods alleviate the cold-start problem by building predictive models based on user and item features like age, gender, and category. But they do not consider user- or item-specific parameters learnt from past ratings. Recently proposed hybrid approaches [2, 1, 4] combine collaborative filtering with content-based filtering by simultaneously incorporating features and user/item-centric parameters in models – this allows them to predict ratings more accurately for both existing user-item pairs as well as new pairs (through features). The top K items with the highest predicted ratings are then recommended to the user.

Commenting environments are highly dynamic with new comments and articles arriving continuously. These new comments have zero or few user ratings, and constantly changing content that may have little overlap with previous comments. Furthermore, of the users who view comments, only a small fraction typically rate comments causing training data to be extremely sparse. In such a scenario, even models that exploit features and past ratings in-

*Work done while the authors were at Yahoo!.

CIKM'12, October 29–November 2, 2012, Maui, HI, USA.

formation may be unable to make accurate predictions, and there may be a high degree of uncertainty in the predicted ratings of new comments. Consequently, simply ranking comments based on their predicted rating scores may lead to poor comments being ranked high and good comments being ranked low because of inaccuracies in their rating estimates. Thus, a strategy that only *exploits* user comments with high predicted ratings may be suboptimal, and it is important to also *explore* comments with low predicted ratings but high uncertainty since their true ratings may be much higher.

Our comments recommendation problem is an instance of the well-known *exploitation-exploration* tradeoff that has been studied extensively in the context of the *multi-armed bandits* problem [12, 6]. Given a set of arms with unknown rewards, the objective in bandit problems is to select arms in successive trials (one per trial) so that the expected total reward over a finite number of trials is maximized. In our comments setting, comments correspond to arms and the ratings they receive are the rewards. Existing bandit algorithms [6, 16, 7] balance exploration and exploitation to achieve optimal rewards. Exploration gathers information to refine the expected reward estimates for seemingly suboptimal arms while exploitation selects arms with high reward estimates based on past observations.

A popular class of bandit algorithms are the *upper confidence bound* (UCB) algorithms [6, 16, 7] – these compute an upper confidence bound for each arm which is essentially a high-probability upper bound on the expected reward. The UCB for an arm is computed by combining the current reward estimate with the uncertainty in the estimate. In each trial, the arm with the highest UCB value is then selected. Thus, the selected arms either have a high reward estimate (and so should be exploited more to increase the total reward) or high uncertainty (and so should be explored more since the arm could potentially give a high reward). In recent work, [16] proposes a UCB-based bandit algorithm LINUCB that estimates the reward of each arm through a linear regression on features. Leveraging textual and other informative features help to overcome data sparsity and improve the accuracy of reward estimates. The authors compute the variance in the reward estimated by the linear model and use it to determine the UCB for each arm. Such bandit algorithms that utilize context information (e.g., features) are called *contextual bandits*.

In this paper, we propose a UCB-based contextual bandit algorithm LOGUCB that estimates average ratings for comments using *logistic regression* on features. Logistic regression is better suited for modeling thumbs-up/down style binary ratings data compared to linear regression. Unlike linear regression, it ensures that average ratings lie in the fixed range [0, 1], and so estimates have bounded variance (between 0 and 1). Moreover, logistic regression models are more robust to outliers [8]. We adopt a Bayesian approach to estimate average ratings for comments and the variance in the estimates. Since logistic regression models are more complex, the mean rating estimates and variance are not available in closed form, and need to be approximated. Similar to UCB-type algorithms, we combine the rating estimate (exploitation) with the variance in the estimate (exploration) to compute a UCB for each comment, and select the top-K comments with the highest UCBs.

Our main contributions can be summarized as follows:

1) We propose a novel UCB-based algorithm called LOGUCB that balances exploration with exploitation when the average rating of a comment is a logistic sigmoid function of its features. Our LOGUCB algorithm for recommending comments consists of the following core modules: (1) A global logistic regression model that uses past comments to compute a global prior on feature weights, (2) A per-article Bayesian logistic regression model that incorporates the global prior and additional slack variables per comment – in the beginning when ratings data is sparse, the model relies on past comments and comment features for rating prediction; but once a comment has sufficient ratings, the model makes a smooth transition and uses empirical rating estimates, and (3) An explore-exploit module that combines the predicted rating with uncertainty in the prediction to determine the comments recommended to the user.

2) To compute the UCB for each comment, we assume a Bayesian setting and employ a host of approximation techniques to efficiently estimate the mean rating and associated variance. Our variance approximation technique for the Bayesian logistic regression model is novel and lies at the core of our LOGUCB algorithm – this is a key technical contribution of our work.

3) In addition to the words in each comment, we also include a comment's *Latent Dirichlet Allocation* (LDA) topics [10] as features to further improve rating prediction accuracy.

4) We conduct an extensive experimental study on a real-life dataset containing comments for Yahoo! News articles. Our experimental results indicate that our per-article logistic regression models incorporating global priors and leveraging bag-of-words and topic features predict ratings with higher accuracy compared to simple baselines. Furthermore, our LOGUCB explore-exploit algorithm outperforms state-of-the-art techniques like LINUCB.

2. SYSTEM MODEL AND PROBLEM DEFINITION

Each online article has an associated set of user generated comments. Every time an article is viewed by a user, our system selects K comments for the article to display to the user. The user then assigns one of two ratings to a (random) subset of the K comments shown to him/her: (1) A *thumbs-up* rating if the user likes the comment, or (2) A *thumbs-down* rating to express dislike for the comment. The user can also post additional comments for the article. Thus, the comments for an article and the ratings for each comment are highly dynamic.

Consider an article a at time t. We denote the set of comments posted by users for article a at time t by $C(t)$ and the number of comments in $C(t)$ at time t by $N(t)$. Thus, $N(t) = |C(t)|$. Each comment $i \in C(t)$ has an associated M-dimensional feature vector $\mathbf{x}_i$. The M feature values for a comment are computed based on its content and include word occurrence frequency, comment length, presence of numeric values or special symbols like exclamation marks, etc.

We will use binary 0/1 values for ratings with a 1 corresponding to a thumbs-up, and a 0 to a thumbs-down. We will denote by $n_i(t)$ the total number of 0/1 ratings provided by users for comment i at time t – of these, the number of 0 and 1 ratings are denoted by $n_i^-(t)$ and $n_i^+(t)$, respectively. Furthermore, we will represent the vector of observed ratings for comment i by $\mathbf{y}_i(t)$ and the jth rating for comment i by y_{ij}. Finally, we will use $\mathbf{X}(t) = \{\mathbf{x}_i\}$ and $\mathbf{Y}(t) = \{\mathbf{y}_i(t)\}$ to denote the feature and rating vectors, respectively, for all the comments of article a in $C(t)$.

Let μ_i be the expected rating of comment i, that is, $\mu_i = E[y_{ij}]$. Note that μ_i for comment i is unknown. At time t, our comments recommendation system only has access to the comments $C(t)$ and rating information $\mathbf{Y}(t)$ for the comments – based on these, it tries to identify the K best comments with the highest expected ratings, and recommends them to users. These comments with high likeli-

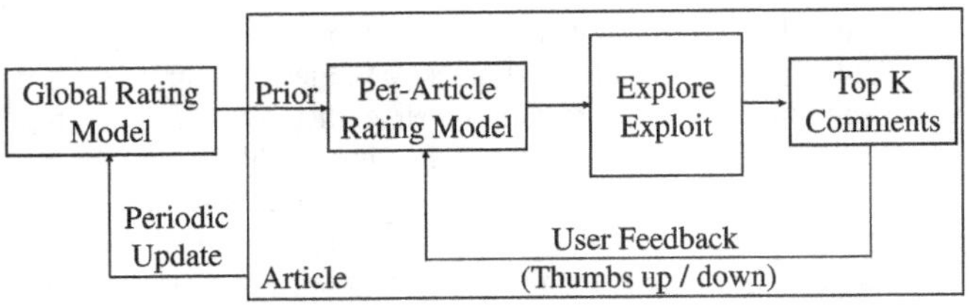

Figure 1: LOGUCB Components.

hoods of getting a thumbs-up are precisely the ones that the average user will like, and thus will lead to increased user satisfaction.

Comments Recommendation Problem: Let article a be viewed at times $t_1, t_2, t_3 \ldots$. At each time t_l, the problem is to select K comments from $C(t_l)$ to recommend such that the total expected number of thumbs-up ratings received until time t_l is maximum, that is, $\sum_{i \in C(t_l)} \sum_{j=1}^{n_i(t_l)} E[y_{ij}]$ is maximum. □

As mentioned earlier, our comments recommendation problem above has a natural mapping to the *multi-armed bandit* problem with comments as arms, and ratings as the corresponding rewards.

3. LOGUCB ALGORITHM COMPONENTS

LOGUCB is a novel UCB-style contextual bandit algorithm that employs logistic regression on comment features to model the expected rating for a comment. For each article a, LOGUCB trains a separate logistic regression model. We consider a Bayesian setting in our work because the priors on model parameters help to regularize them while the posteriors provide a natural method to compute the variance of estimated ratings.

Below, we give a brief description of the different modules of our LOGUCB algorithm shown in Figure 1.

Global Rating Model: A newly posted article has very few comment ratings initially. Consequently, the per-article model that we train can lead to overfitting due to data sparseness issues. To address this, we learn a global logistic regression model by pooling comments and user ratings data across past articles. The global model is used to initialize the parameters of the per-article model. When training data is insufficient, the per-article model parameters shrink to the global parameters. Hence, the global model provides a good backoff estimate that helps to improve predictive accuracy for new articles. The global model is updated periodically (every few days).

Per-Article Rating Model: For an article a, a per-article logistic regression model is learnt at regular time intervals; at time t, our training procedure uses the features $\mathbf{X}(t)$ and ratings $\mathbf{Y}(t)$ for comments in $C(t)$ as training data. The rationale for having a local per-article model is that once an article has a sufficient number of comments with ratings, the local model can provide better rating estimates than the global model for both existing as well as unseen comments. This is because it can capture article-specific feature-rating correlations, and deviations of the article from the average behavior captured by the global model – these deviations could be due to new article content never seen before, dynamically changing user sentiment, etc.

As mentioned earlier, when an article is new and has very little training data (cold-start scenario), our per-article model falls back to the global model and prediction accuracy is not adversely impacted. Furthermore, as the article collects more training data, the per-article model parameters start deviating to incorporate the article-specific comments and ratings. Finally, as each comment acquires more ratings, predictions become comment-specific based on the actual ratings the comment receives as opposed to its features. This is enabled by including a per-comment slack variable which helps to fill in the residuals not captured by the features. Thus, as the training data for a comment grows, our per-article model makes a smooth transition from feature-based predictions to comment-specific ones.

We should point out here that we don't include user features in our model because only a small fraction of users rate comments – as a result, (user, comment) ratings data is extremely sparse. Furthermore, in many cases, it is difficult to accurately identify users because they may not be logged in, or user cookie information is unreliable. Finally, even if we could identify users, certain information they may have provided in their profiles (e.g., age, salary, etc.) may be inaccurate, or they may have not been very active in terms of browsing or searching. In case reliable user features are available, these can be easily incorporated into our model to enable greater personalization.

Explore-Exploit: The explore-exploit module is responsible for selecting the K best comments to be displayed when a user views an article. Specifically, it uses the posterior estimates for the per-article model to obtain mean rating and variance estimates for each comment. These are subsequently combined to compute UCBs for each comment and the top-K comments with the highest UCB values are finally recommended to the user. Thus, LOGUCB exploits comments with high predicted ratings and explores the ones with high uncertainty in the predictions. The user rating feedback is incorporated into the training data for the article and used to further improve the per-article model.

Note that it is possible that the top-K comments with the highest UCBs may contain very similar or redundant comments – exploring/exploiting such comments can be wasteful. Recently, there has been some work [21, 25] on extending multi-armed bandit problems to select multiple arms per trial. However, the modeling assumption is that the K selected arms correspond to the K ranked results for a search query and at most one arm (corresponding to the first relevant result) gives a reward. Our comments scenario is somewhat different since ratings are determined by logistic regression and a user can give ratings to multiple comments in a single view. In this paper, we do not address the problem of diverse recommendations although LOGUCB can be used in conjunction with techniques such as *Maximal Marginal Relevance* (MMR) [11] (with UCB values substituted for relevance scores) to ensure comments diversity. Extending our comments recommendation framework to address diversity is left as future work.

The goal of bandit algorithms is to minimize the *regret*, that is, the difference between the expected reward of the algorithm and the optimal expected reward. In [16], LINUCB is shown to have an $\tilde{O}(\sqrt{T})$ regret over T trials for a fixed set of arms – this assumption, however, does not hold in our dynamic comments environment. Since logistic regression models are much more complex, formally proving regret bounds for LOGUCB is difficult and we do not focus on this in our work. However, logistic models are a natural choice (compared to linear models) for modeling binary ratings data, and in our experiments, we empirically show that our LOGUCB algorithm outperforms LINUCB.

In the following sections, we will provide a detailed description on each of the above three modules. For notational convenience, we will drop the argument t indicating time from $C(t)$, $\mathbf{Y}(t)$, etc. when it is clear from context.

4. GLOBAL MODEL

We start by describing our global probabilistic model and training procedure. We denote the comments (belonging to older articles) used for training the global model by C^g, and the corresponding features and ratings for the comments by $\mathbf{X}^g$ and $\mathbf{Y}^g$, respectively.

4.1 Model Specification

Since our ratings y_{ij} are binary, we assume that they come from a Bernoulli distribution with probability equal to the mean rating μ_i. Further, we model μ_i as a logistic function of the linear projection of the comment feature vector $\mathbf{x}_i$. Hence,

$$y_{ij} \sim \text{Bernoulli}(\mu_i) \quad (1)$$

$$\mu_i = \sigma(\mathbf{w}^\top \mathbf{x}_i) = \frac{1}{1+\exp(-\mathbf{w}^\top \mathbf{x}_i)} \quad (2)$$

where $\mathbf{w}$ is an M-dimensional weight parameter that captures the preferences of an average user for the different content features, and $\sigma(\cdot)$ is the logistic sigmoid function.

Data Likelihood: Given our ratings generation model, the likelihood of observations $\mathbf{y}_i$ for comments i is given by:

$$P(\mathbf{Y}^g|\mathbf{w}) = \prod_{i\in C^g} P(\mathbf{y}_i|\mathbf{w}) = \prod_{i\in C^g} \mu_i^{n_i^+}(1-\mu_i)^{n_i^-} \quad (3)$$

Prior over w: We also assume a standard prior Gaussian distribution with zero mean and κ^2 variance over the weight vector $\mathbf{w}$:

$$P(\mathbf{w}) = N(\mathbf{w}|\mathbf{0},\kappa^2) = \frac{1}{\sqrt{2\pi}\kappa}\exp(-\frac{\mathbf{w}^\top\mathbf{w}}{2\kappa^2}) \quad (4)$$

Posterior Distribution of w: Using Bayes rule, the posterior distribution of $\mathbf{w}$ can be written as the product of the likelihood (in Equation (3)) and prior (in Equation (4)):

$$P(\mathbf{w}|\mathbf{Y}^g) \propto P(\mathbf{Y}^g|\mathbf{w})P(\mathbf{w})$$

4.2 Model Training

The goal of our model training procedure is to find the mode, also known as the *maximum-a-posteriori* (MAP) estimate, of the posterior distribution of $\mathbf{w}$. To find the mode $\mathbf{w}^g_{\text{map}}$, we minimize the negative log of the posterior, that is,

$$\mathbf{w}^g_{\text{map}} = \arg\min_{\mathbf{w}} -\sum_{i\in C^g}(n_i^+\log(\mu_i)+n_i^-\log(1-\mu_i)) + \frac{1}{2\kappa^2}\mathbf{w}^\top\mathbf{w}$$

We use the standard iterative conjugate gradient descent [18] algorithm to obtain $\mathbf{w}^g_{\text{map}}$.

5. PER-ARTICLE MODEL

As discussed earlier in Section 3, we learn a per-article model specifically for article a with the comments C of the article as training data. The set C contains N comments with features and ratings **X** and **Y**, respectively.

5.1 Model Specification

As in the global model, we assume that the rating y_{ij} for a comment i comes from a Bernoulli distribution and the mean rating μ_i is a logistic function. However, it is possible that the comment feature space and/or the logistic model are incapable of predicting the rating correctly even if sufficient observations are available. Hence, the mean rating estimate $\hat{\mu}_i$ has a bias which is independent of the training data size. Thus, in addition to $\mathbf{w}^\top\mathbf{x}_i$, we add a per-comment slack variable z_i to our model for μ_i.

$$\mu_i = \sigma(\mathbf{w}^\top\mathbf{x}_i + z_i) = \frac{1}{1+\exp(-(\mathbf{w}^\top\mathbf{x}_i+z_i))} \quad (5)$$

We will use $\mathbf{z}$ to denote the vector of slack variables, that is, $\mathbf{z} = [z_1, z_2, \ldots, z_N]^\top$.

Prior over $(\mathbf{w},\mathbf{z})$: We assume a Gaussian prior over the weight vector $\mathbf{w}$ with mean equal to the MAP estimate, $\mathbf{w}^g_{\text{map}}$, of our global model and variance κ_w^2. Thus, $P(\mathbf{w}) = N(\mathbf{w}|\mathbf{w}^g_{\text{map}},\kappa_w^2)$. Observe that this prior provides backoff estimates from the global model when an article is new and has very few comments.

We also place a zero-mean Gaussian prior on each z_i. Thus, $P(\mathbf{z}) = N(\mathbf{z}|\mathbf{0},\kappa_z^2)$. Note that if a comment i has no ratings in the training data, then z_i is zero because of the prior and μ_i is predicted using the projection $\mathbf{w}^\top\mathbf{x}_i$ only. On the other hand, if the comment has many ratings, then data likelihood dominates the prior and we precisely estimate the bias z_i. Thus, our prediction reduces to the empirical rating estimate based only on the fraction of thumbs-ups.

Posterior Distribution of $(\mathbf{w},\mathbf{z})$: Using Bayes rule, the posterior distribution of $(\mathbf{w},\mathbf{z})$ can be written as

$$P((\mathbf{w},\mathbf{z})|\mathbf{Y}) \propto P(\mathbf{Y}|\mathbf{w},\mathbf{z})P(\mathbf{w})P(\mathbf{z})$$
$$\propto \prod_{i\in C}\mu_i^{n_i^+}(1-\mu_i)^{n_i^-}N(\mathbf{w}|\mathbf{w}^g_{\text{map}},\kappa_w^2)N(\mathbf{z}|\mathbf{0},\kappa_z^2) \quad (6)$$

5.2 Model Training

Observe that the likelihood involves logistic functions and the priors are Gaussians. Hence, a closed form does not exist for the posterior distribution. A popular technique is to approximate the posterior of $(\mathbf{w},\mathbf{z})$ by a Gaussian distribution using the Laplace approximation [19]. The mean of the Gaussian is approximated by the mode $(\mathbf{w}_{\text{map}},\mathbf{z}_{\text{map}})$ of the true posterior, while the inverse of the covariance matrix $\mathbf{S}$ is approximated by the Hessian matrix which comprises the second order derivatives of the negative log likelihood at the mode. Thus, the posterior $P((\mathbf{w},\mathbf{z})|\mathbf{Y})$ is approximated as $N((\mathbf{w},\mathbf{z})|(\mathbf{w}_{\text{map}},\mathbf{z}_{\text{map}}),\mathbf{S})$.

The mode $(\mathbf{w}_{\text{map}},\mathbf{z}_{\text{map}})$ can be found by minimizing $L = -\log P((\mathbf{w},\mathbf{z})|\mathbf{Y})$, the negative log of the posterior. Thus,

$$(\mathbf{w}_{\text{map}},\mathbf{z}_{\text{map}}) = \arg\min_{(\mathbf{w},\mathbf{z})} -\sum_{i\in C}(n_i^+\log(\mu_i)+n_i^-\log(1-\mu_i)) + \frac{1}{2\kappa_w^2}(\mathbf{w}-\mathbf{w}^g_{\text{map}})^\top(\mathbf{w}-\mathbf{w}^g_{\text{map}}) + \frac{1}{2\kappa_z^2}\mathbf{z}^\top\mathbf{z}$$

We use the standard iterative conjugate gradient descent algorithm to minimize L where the gradients are given by

$$\frac{\partial L}{\partial \mathbf{w}} = -\sum_{i\in C}(n_i^+(1-\mu_i)-n_i^-\mu_i)\mathbf{x}_i + \frac{1}{\kappa_w^2}(\mathbf{w}-\mathbf{w}^g_{\text{map}})$$

$$\frac{\partial L}{\partial \mathbf{z}} = -\sum_{i\in C}(n_i^+(1-\mu_i)-n_i^-\mu_i) + \frac{1}{\kappa_z^2}\mathbf{z}$$

Next, we derive the equations for the covariance matrix $\mathbf{S}$ which is obtained by inverting the $M+N$-dimensional Hessian matrix.

$$\mathbf{S}^{-1} = \frac{\partial^2 L}{\partial(\mathbf{w},\mathbf{z})^2}\Big|_{(\mathbf{w}_{\text{map}},\mathbf{z}_{\text{map}})} \quad (7)$$

Data: New article a, Global comments set C^g;
Variance for priors $\kappa, \kappa_w, \kappa_z$;
Explore-exploit parameter α;

begin
  Train global model to find MAP estimate $\mathbf{w}^g_{\text{map}}$;
  Initialize comment set C for a to $\emptyset$;
  Initialize per-article model for a using priors for $(\mathbf{w}, \mathbf{z})$;
  for *each user viewing article* a **do**
    for *each comment* $i \in C$ **do**
      Estimate the expected rating $\hat{\mu}_i$ and its variance σ_i^2 using the per-article model;
      Set $\text{UCB}_i \longleftarrow \hat{\mu}_i + \alpha\sigma_i$;
    end
    Select top-K comments with the highest UCBs to show to user;
    Add new comments to C and update (features, ratings) information $(\mathbf{X}, \mathbf{Y})$ based on user feedback;
    Retrain per-article model if sufficient number of new ratings are added to $\mathbf{Y}$;
  end
end

Algorithm 1: The LOGUCB Algorithm.

where,

$$\frac{\partial^2 L}{\partial(\mathbf{w},\mathbf{z})^2} = \begin{pmatrix} \frac{\partial^2 L}{\partial \mathbf{w}^2} & \frac{\partial^2 L}{\partial \mathbf{w}\partial \mathbf{z}} \\ \frac{\partial^2 L}{\partial \mathbf{z}\partial \mathbf{w}} & \frac{\partial^2 L}{\partial \mathbf{z}^2} \end{pmatrix} = \begin{pmatrix} \frac{1}{\kappa_w^2}\mathbf{I}_{M\times M} + \mathbf{XPX^T} & \mathbf{XP} \\ \mathbf{PX^T} & \frac{1}{\kappa_z^2}\mathbf{I}_{N\times N} + \mathbf{P} \end{pmatrix}$$

Above, $\mathbf{P}$ is a $N \times N$ diagonal matrix, where $\mathbf{P}[i,i] = n_i\mu_i(1-\mu_i)$. The overall time complexity of computing the covariance matrix $\mathbf{S}$ is $O(M^2N + (M+N)^3)$. Here, $O((M+N)^3)$ is the time complexity of inverting the $M+N-$dimensional Hessian. If the number of dimensions $M+N$ is large, then we simply use the diagonal approximation of the Hessian. The complexity of finding the inverse then reduces to $O(M+N)$ and the overall time complexity for computing the covariance becomes $O(MN)$. Thus, model training can be achieved in a matter of a few seconds for thousands of dimensions and comments (see Section 7.5).

6. EXPLORE-EXPLOIT

Our LOGUCB algorithm (see Algorithm 1) adopts a UCB-based approach to handle the exploitation-exploration trade-off for our logistic regression rating prediction model. For each comment i, it uses Bayesian estimation methods to compute the mean rating estimate $\hat{\mu}_i$ and its variance σ_i^2. Specifically, $\hat{\mu}_i$ and σ_i^2 are chosen as the predictive mean and variance, respectively, of the mean rating μ_i over the posterior of the per-article model. Now, by Chebyshev's inequality, it follows that for an appropriate choice of α, $|\mu_i - \hat{\mu}_i| \le \alpha\sigma_i$ holds with high probability ($\ge 1 - \frac{1}{\alpha^2}$). Thus, $\hat{\mu}_i + \alpha\sigma_i$ is a UCB on μ_i, and our algorithm selects the comments with the top-K UCB values to show to users. We collect the user feedback (thumbs-up/down ratings) on the displayed comments as well as any new comments posted by the user. Clearly, since only a small fraction of users typically rate comments, the estimated model parameters will not change (by much) often. Consequently, we keep collecting new observations until we have a sufficient number of new ratings – we then perform a periodic batch update of the per-article model parameters (as in [16]). Below, we present approximation techniques for computing the mean rating estimate $\hat{\mu}_i$ and its variance σ_i^2. The method for estimating $\hat{\mu}_i$ is from [19] while the approximation scheme for σ_i^2 is novel.

Mean Rating Prediction: Following the Bayesian approach, we predict the mean rating μ_i by its posterior predictive mean, that is, the expectation of μ_i with respect to the posterior of model parameters $(\mathbf{w}, \mathbf{z})$ conditional on observed data. Thus,

$$\hat{\mu}_i = \int \mu_i P((\mathbf{w},\mathbf{z})|\mathbf{Y}) d\mathbf{w}d\mathbf{z} \approx \int \sigma(\mathbf{w}^\top \mathbf{x}_i + z_i) N((\mathbf{w},\mathbf{z})|(\mathbf{w}_{\text{map}}, \mathbf{z}_{\text{map}}), \mathbf{S}) d\mathbf{w}d\mathbf{z}$$

Substituting $t = \mathbf{w}^\top \mathbf{x}_i + z_i$ in the above equation, we get

$$\hat{\mu}_i \approx \int \sigma(t) N(t|\mu_t, \vartheta_t^2) dt$$

where $\mu_t = \begin{bmatrix} \mathbf{w}_{\text{map}} \\ \mathbf{z}_{\text{map}} \end{bmatrix}^\top \begin{bmatrix} \mathbf{x}_i \\ \mathbf{u}_i \end{bmatrix}$ and $\vartheta_t^2 = \begin{bmatrix} \mathbf{x}_i \\ \mathbf{u}_i \end{bmatrix}^\top \mathbf{S} \begin{bmatrix} \mathbf{x}_i \\ \mathbf{u}_i \end{bmatrix}$ for $\mathbf{u}_i = [\mathbf{0}_{i-1}\ \mathbf{1}\ \mathbf{0}_{N-i}]^\top$.

Note that the above integral over t represents the convolution of a Gaussian with a logistic function, and cannot be solved analytically. However, as pointed out in [19], the logistic function $\sigma(t)$ can be approximated well by the scaled probit function $\phi(\lambda t)$, where $\phi(t) = \int_{-\infty}^{t} N(\theta|0,1)d\theta$. The parameter λ is found by making the slopes of the two functions same at the origin, which gives $\lambda^2 = \frac{\pi}{8}$. Now, the convolution of a probit with a Gaussian can be expressed in terms of another probit function. Specifically,

$$\hat{\mu}_i \approx \int \phi(\lambda t) N(t|\mu_t, \vartheta_t^2) dt = \phi\left(\frac{\mu_t}{\sqrt{\lambda^{-2} + \vartheta_t^2}}\right) \approx \sigma\left(\frac{\mu_t}{\sqrt{1 + \frac{\pi\vartheta_t^2}{8}}}\right) \quad (8)$$

The computational complexity to predict the mean rating is $O((M+N)^2)$ which is the number of steps needed to compute ϑ_t^2. However, if $\mathbf{S}$ is approximated by a diagonal matrix, then the time complexity reduces to $O(M+N)$. Note that the inverse computation needed to compute $\mathbf{S}$ is done only once (when the per-article model is trained) for all the comments.

Variance of Mean Rating Estimate: The variance σ_i^2 is given by the predictive variance of the mean rating μ_i which is

$$\begin{aligned} \sigma_i^2 &= E_{(\mathbf{w},\mathbf{z})}[\mu_i^2|\mathbf{Y}] - E_{(\mathbf{w},\mathbf{z})}[\mu_i|\mathbf{Y}]^2 \\ &= \int \sigma^2(\mathbf{w}^\top \mathbf{x}_i + z_i) N((\mathbf{w},\mathbf{z})|(\mathbf{w}_{\text{map}}, \mathbf{z}_{\text{map}}), \mathbf{S}) d\mathbf{w}d\mathbf{z} - \hat{\mu}_i^2 \\ &= \int \sigma^2(t) N(t|\mu_t, \vartheta_t^2) dt - \hat{\mu}_i^2 \end{aligned}$$

Above, the final equation is obtained by substituting $t = \mathbf{w}^\top \mathbf{x}_i + z_i$, and μ_t and ϑ_t are as defined earlier.

Again, the convolution of a Gaussian with a squared logistic function cannot be solved analytically. However, we observe empirically that a squared logistic function $\sigma^2(t)$ can be approximated well by a scaled and translated probit $\phi(\lambda(t+\gamma))$ (as opposed to only a scaled probit for the logistic function). We minimize the squared error between the two functions to empirically find the values of parameters λ and γ, which gives $\lambda = 0.703$ and

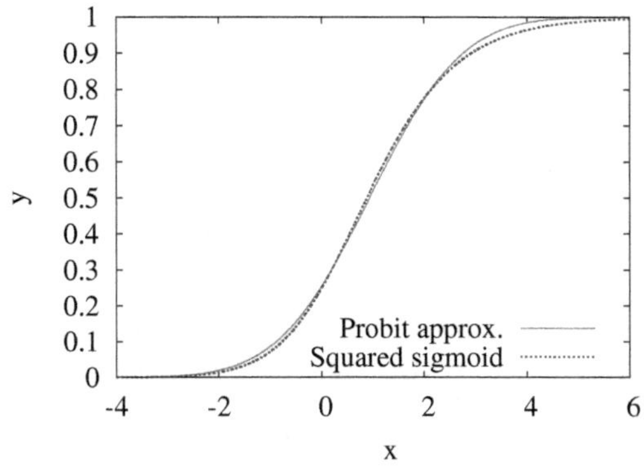

Figure 2: Probit approximation of σ^2.

$\gamma = -0.937$. The similarity between the squared logistic and probit functions for this choice of parameters is shown in Figure 2. The root mean square error is 0.0053 with a maximum error of 0.02. Again, since the convolution of a probit with a Gaussian can be expressed in terms of another probit function, we have,

$$\begin{aligned} \sigma_i^2 &\approx \int \phi(\lambda(t+\gamma))N(t|\mu_t,\vartheta_t^2)dt - \hat{\mu}_i^2 \\ &= \phi(\frac{\mu_t+\gamma}{\sqrt{(\lambda^{-2}+\vartheta_t^2)}}) - \hat{\mu}_i^2 \\ &\approx \sigma^2(\frac{\mu_t+\gamma}{\sqrt{1+\vartheta_t^2\lambda^2}} - \gamma) - \hat{\mu}_i^2 \end{aligned} \quad (9)$$

Note that the variance σ_i^2 above is the difference between the squares of two sigmoids and is thus upper bounded by 1. However, such a bound does not hold for the variance of linear regression models. Thus, the UCB values for LogUCB are more accurate compared to LinUCB [16].

We should also point out here that [23] presents an alternate variance estimation method for logistic regression which computes the variance of the Taylor approximation of μ_i (that ignores higher-order terms in the Taylor expansion of μ_i). However, since the probit approximates the squared logistic function so closely (see Figure 2), we expect our variance estimate to be more accurate.

7. EXPERIMENTAL RESULTS

In this section, we perform multiple experiments that demonstrate the effectiveness of our proposed methods on a real-life comments dataset from Yahoo! News. Our first experiment shows that our per-article logistic regression models incorporating global priors and leveraging bag-of-words and topic features have higher predictive accuracy compared to other models such as linear regression. In our second experiment, we show that our LogUCB algorithm outperforms state-of-the-art explore-exploit methods. Finally, we report the running times of our per-article model training and rating prediction procedures.

7.1 Dataset

We obtain the comments rating data between March and June, 2011 from Yahoo! News. The ratings for different comments are available in terms of the number of thumbs-ups and thumbs-downs given by different users. Note that no ground truth per-comment mean rating μ_i is available. Hence, in order to reliably evaluate the performance of our algorithms, we only consider the comments that receive at least 10 ratings and assume that the ground truth mean rating μ_i is the same as the empirical mean given by the fraction of thumbs-ups. In our experiments, we consider 780 articles with 408, 643 comments and a total of 16.8 million ratings.

We randomly select 70% of the articles and consider their comments as the global comments set C^g used to train the global model. Another 5% of the articles are used as a validation set to learn parameters of the different models. The remaining 198 articles are used to train per-article models for the model accuracy and explore-exploit experiments.

7.2 Features

We consider two different types of features.

Bag of words: The text of each comment is cleaned using standard techniques like lower-casing, removal of stop-words, etc. For the articles used to train the global model, we prune all words with very low (present in less than 10 comments) and high (present in greater than 50% of the comments) frequencies. The final vocabulary consists of approximately 9,000 words. On the other hand, for articles on which we train a per-article model, the low frequency threshold for pruning words is set to a lower value of 3 – this is because there are a lot fewer comments per article. We consider both L_2 normalized *tf* and *tf-idf* as feature values for words in each comment. The *tf* feature values give slightly better performance – so all the results are shown using them.

Topics: *Latent Dirichlet Allocation* (LDA) [10, 13] is a topic model that represents each document as a mixture of (latent) topics, where each topic is a probability distribution over words. LDA clusters co-occurring words into topics, and is able to overcome data sparsity issues by learning coarse-grained topic-rating correlations. We compute topic assignments to words in a comment using Gibbs sampling as described in [13], and use the topic distribution for a comment as feature values. The topic-word distributions are first learnt on the global comments set, and subsequently used to assign topics to the comments of each article. In our experiments, we set the default number of topics to 50.

We also considered a number of other per-comment features like (1) the fraction of positive and negative sentiment words where the sentiment of a word is obtained using Senti-WordNet[1], (2) number of special characters like question marks (?) or exclamations (!), and (3) total number of words, fraction of non-stop words, and fraction of upper-case words. However, none of these features had an effect on model performance.

7.3 Model Accuracy Experiments

In this experiment, we compare the mean rating prediction accuracy of different models.

7.3.1 Experimental Setup

Models Compared: We compare the following variants of our per-article model as well as other state-of-the-art models.

- *Global:* This is our global logistic regression model described in Section 4 trained on the comments set C^g. The features comprise the (unpruned) words in C^g and LDA topics.
- *PA1:* This is our per-article logistic regression model described in Section 5 with slack variables z_i set to zero and no global prior. It is trained on the article's comments, and features consist of the words in the article's comments and LDA topics.
- *PA2:* This is the same as *PA1* but uses the global prior and so has additional features corresponding to the words in C^g. We consider

[1] *http://sentiwordnet.isti.cnr.it/.*

Baselines	Training Size (%)				
	5%	10%	25%	50%	75%
Global	0.68	0.68	0.68	0.68	0.68
PA1	0.64	0.66	0.68	0.72	0.73
PA2	**0.68**	**0.69**	**0.72**	**0.74**	**0.76**
LinReg	0.64	0.66	0.68	0.72	0.73

Table 1: AUC scores for different models in Section 8.3.1

Training Size (%)	# Topics			
	0	25	50	100
5%	0.66	0.67	**0.68**	0.68
10%	0.68	0.68	**0.69**	0.69
25%	0.71	0.70	**0.72**	0.72

Table 2: AUC scores for $PA2$ for different number of topics.

this model to measure the impact of the global prior on prediction accuracy.

• *LinReg:* This is a linear model, $\mu_i = \mathbf{w}^\top \mathbf{x}_i$, to predict the mean rating scores. As in [16], we use ridge regression to solve for the coefficients $\mathbf{w}$. We choose a simple linear model since this is the underlying model for the state-of-the-art feature-based LinUCB explore-exploit algorithm [16]. The model is trained on an article's comments with the comment words and LDA topics as features.

Note that we do not consider models with slack variables since they mainly impact the rating estimates of training comments and not test comments. However, as shown later, slack variables do lead to performance improvements in an explore-exploit setting where there is no separate notion of test data. The variance parameters κ for the global model, and κ_w and κ_z for the per-article models are tuned using the validation set.

Evaluation Methodology: For model comparisons, the (non-global) comments in each of the 198 articles are further split into training comments (75%) and test comments (25%). The training comments for each article are used to train the per-article models *PA1*, *PA2*, and *LinReg*, and the test comments are used to measure the accuracy of all 4 models.

Evaluation Metric: Since we are looking to recommend comments with high mean rating scores to users, we are primarily concerned about the rating prediction accuracy for comments with extreme mean rating values. Furthermore, we want the predicted ratings for comments at the two extremes to be well separated. We use the *Area Under the Receiver Operating Characteristic (ROC) Curve* (AUC) metric to evaluate the predictive performance of the various models.

AUC is a popular measure of classifier accuracy on data with binary labels. We only choose test comments i with extreme mean ratings $\mu_i < 0.25$ and $\mu_i > 0.75$. Further, we assign positive labels to test comments with $\mu_i > 0.75$ and negative labels to comments with $\mu_i < 0.25$. The AUC is then computed based on the correctly and incorrectly classified comments for different classification thresholds on the predicted mean rating. We finally report the average AUC over all the articles. Note that a higher AUC value implies better predictive performance. Also, a random or constant rating prediction yields an AUC of 0.5 irrespective of the number of positive and negative examples in the test set.

7.3.2 Experimental Results

Our results show that both the global prior and per-article model are critical for achieving high prediction accuracy. Table 1 shows the AUC scores for the models discussed in Section 7.3.1 for different training set sizes. First, note that the global model (*Global*) has an AUC score greater than 0.5 and so significantly outperforms a model that makes random predictions. This clearly shows that a global model learned by pooling the articles together is useful. Furthermore, the two per-article models (*PA1, PA2*) provide better rating estimates than *Global* when sufficient training data is available. This is because per-article models are able to effectively capture article-specific feature-rating correlations involving new article content. However, since *PA1* does not use the global prior, it overfits and performs worse than *Global* when the article is new and hence training data is sparse. Introducing the global prior in the per-article model *PA2* ensures better predictive performance than both *Global* and *PA1* at all the training set sizes. Note that the AUC scores of the linear *LinReg* model are similar to those of *PA1* but lower than *PA2* because of the global prior. However, as we show later, *PA1* (and *PA2*) outperforms *LinReg* in an explore-exploit setting due to better variance estimates.

Table 2 shows the AUC scores of the *PA2* model for different number of LDA topics and training set sizes. In general, the bag-of-words feature (corresponding to 0 topics) turns out to be the most important for our models. Topic features help to improve the performance of our models when training sets are small. This is because topics are essentially clusters of words that frequently co-occur, and using them as features allows us to overcome data sparsity issues by generalizing correlations between a few topic words and ratings to the other words within the topic. For large training set sizes and number of topics beyond 50, however, we didn't see an improvement in AUC scores on adding topic features. We should point out here that all the observations made above (Tables 1 and 2) are statistically significant using the one-sided paired t-test with significance level 0.01.

7.4 Explore-Exploit Experiments

In this experiment, we compare the total expected number of thumbs-up ratings for different explore-exploit algorithms.

7.4.1 Experimental Setup

Explore-Exploit Schemes Compared: We consider the following context-free (without features) as well as contextual (with features) bandit schemes for evaluation.

• *Random:* This policy chooses the top-K comments randomly.

• *UCB1:* This is a context-free UCB-based policy from [6]. In round t, the mean rating μ_i for a comment i is estimated as the current fraction of thumbs-ups the comment has received so far. The confidence interval for the estimate is given by $\sqrt{\frac{2\log t}{n_i(t)}}$, where $n_i(t)$ is the total number of ratings received by the comment until round t.

• *ϵ-greedy1:* This context-free policy chooses a random comment to show with probability ϵ, and with probability $1-\epsilon$, chooses the comment with the highest current fraction of thumbs-ups. To obtain the top-K comments, we repeat the process K times (each time excluding the comments that have already been selected).

• *ϵ-greedy2:* This is the contextual version of *ϵ-greedy* discussed above. With probability $1-\epsilon$, it chooses the comment with the highest predicted mean rating given by the per-article logistic regression model with global prior and slack variables (see Equation (8)).

• *LinUCB:* This algorithm represents the state-of-the-art and uses the *LinReg* model to obtain the mean rating estimate $\hat{\mu}_i$. Similar to

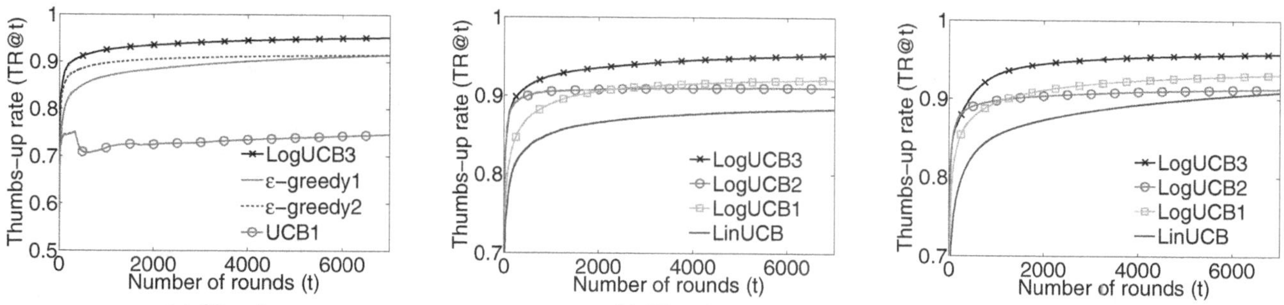

(a) $K = 1$ (b) $K = 1$ (c) $K = 10$

Figure 3: Performance of different explore-exploit algorithms.

our formulation, in [16], a closed form confidence bound is computed based on the predictive variance of the mean rating.

- *LogUCB1:* This is our LOGUCB algorithm (Algorithm 1) with per-article model *PA1* (without global prior) used for rating prediction.
- *LogUCB2:* This is our LOGUCB algorithm with per-article model *PA2* (with slack variables set to 0) used for rating prediction.
- *LogUCB3:* This is our full LOGUCB algorithm (Algorithm 1) with non-zero slack variables.

The parameters ϵ for ϵ-*greedy1* and ϵ-*greedy2*, and α for *LinUCB* and *LogUCB* variants are tuned using the validation set. Also, since *PA2* has a large number of features, we use the diagonal approximation of the Hessian in *LogUCB2* and *LogUCB3* for computing the covariance (see Section 5.2).

Evaluation Methodology: For evaluating the different explore-exploit schemes, the train-test split is not needed and we use all the comments of the 198 articles. Further, we evaluate performance using an offline simulation over 7000 rounds with new comment arrivals for an article following a poisson distribution. For a given explore-exploit algorithm, in each round t, the simulator takes the top-K comments chosen by the algorithm. For each of the K comments, it generates a binary thumbs-up/down rating from a Bernoulli distribution with probability given by the ground truth mean rating of the comment. These ratings are then provided to the algorithm as feedback, and the underlying models and mean rating estimates are appropriately updated at the end of the round.

Evaluation Metrics: We define the *Thumbs-up rate at round t* (TR@t) as the fraction of thumbs-up ratings received until round t. We use TR@t to evaluate the different explore-exploit algorithms since it is a good proxy for the total expected number of thumbs-up ratings that the algorithms are trying to maximize.

7.4.2 Experimental Results

Figure 3 plots TR@t values for the different explore-exploit algorithms discussed in Section 7.4.1 as a function of the number of rounds t.

Figure 3(a) compares the different context-free schemes with our logistic regression-based schemes for $K = 1$. Note that $K = 1$ corresponds to the standard single-slot multi-armed bandit problem. We do not present the curve for *Random* since it performs significantly worse than the other schemes with TR@t values below 0.65. Observe that ϵ-*greedy2* performs significantly better than ϵ-*greedy1* and *UCB1* when the number of rounds is small. This clearly shows that using the predictions of our feature-based logistic model in the exploit phase is more useful than empirical estimates of ratings in either ϵ-*greedy1* or *UCB1*. When the number of rounds become large and empirical estimates of ratings become reliable, the performance of ϵ-*greedy1* and ϵ-*greedy2* are comparable. Also, note that *LogUCB3* consistently outperforms ϵ-*greedy2*. Thus, the UCB value which includes model variance in *LogUCB3* is a better exploration strategy than the random one in ϵ-*greedy2*.

# Comments	25	50	100	250	500	1000
Time (seconds)	0.87	0.92	1.0	1.13	1.28	1.63

Table 3: Training time for per-arcticle model $PA2$.

Figures 3(b) and 3(c) compare the different variants of our LOG UCB algorithm and LINUCB for $K = 1$ and $K = 10$, respectively. Observe that *LogUCB3* has a higher thumbs-up rate than both *LogUCB1* and *LogUCB2* – this can be attributed to more accurate rating estimates due to the use of slack variables in *LogUCB3*. Initially, when there are very few user ratings, *LogUCB2* does better than *LogUCB1* due to the global prior. However, the diagonal approximation for computing covariance causes its thumbs-up rate to fall below that of *LogUCB1* as the rounds progress. Finally, *LogUCB3* and the other *LogUCB* variants outperform *LinUCB* since as mentioned earlier, logistic regression has bounded mean rating and variance estimates (between 0 and 1), and is thus better suited for modeling binary ratings data. Again, it is worth mentioning here that the difference in performance of the various schemes in Figure 3 was found to be statistically significant with significance level 0.01.

7.5 Running Time Experiments

Table 3 depicts the total time (in seconds) taken by the *LogUCB3* algorithm to train the per-article model and compute UCB values as the number of comments is increased from 25 to 1000. The running times are measured on a machine with 2 × 2.5 GHz Xeon processors and 16 GB of RAM.

In our experiments, we found that more than 90% of the time is spent on computing the MAP estimates $\mathbf{w}_{map}$ and $\mathbf{z}_{map}$ (see Section 5.2). Observe that model training and UCB computation are extremely fast and take only 1.63 seconds for 1000 comments. This is because we use the previous MAP estimates as the starting point in our conjugate gradient descent algorithm and the number of new ratings between two successive model updates is generally small – this causes the algorithm to converge within a few iterations. Moreover, gradient computations are also quick because comment feature vectors are sparse (comments are short with very few words). This is also the reason why computing the covariance (see Section 5.2) and the UCB values (mean ratings in Equation (8) and variance in Equation (9)) takes only 26 and 148 msec, respectively, for all 1000 comments. Thus, our per-article models can be trained at frequent time intervals to give accurate rating estimates. We should also point out here that compared to 1.63 seconds taken by *LogUCB3*, *LinUCB* takes 0.95 sec to train models and compute UCB values for 1000 comments.

8. RELATED WORK

Recommender Systems: Recommender systems have been studied extensively in the literature. Popular methods predict user-item ratings based on neighborhoods defined using similarities between users/items [26], latent factors found using user-item matrix factorization [22], and generalizations of matrix factorization that model latent factors using regression on user/item features [1, 4] or item LDA topics [2]. However, these methods focus only on estimating ratings, and not on balancing the exploitation-exploration tradeoff which is so critical in our setting due to the dynamic nature of comments. Furthermore, due to fewer comment ratings per article, the feature weight and slack variable parameters in our per-article models both contribute to variance in the mean rating estimate – so we place Gaussian priors on both parameters (instead of only slack variables as is done in [1, 2]). Note that although our modeling framework currently models an average user, it can be easily extended to make personalized recommendations if user features are available.

Explore-Exploit: There exists a large body of work on the multi-armed bandit problem [12, 6, 15, 5, 16, 7]. Context-free bandit algorithms [6, 15, 5] such as ϵ-greedy and UCB assume that no side information is available and that arms are independent of each other. Such algorithms have been shown to achieve the lower bound of $O(\ln T)$ on the regret [15] (here, T is the number of trials). [3] develops a Bayesian solution and extends several existing bandit schemes to a dynamic set of items with short lifetimes, delayed feedback, and non-stationary reward distributions. However, the above methods assume that arms are independent, and hence do not model the correlation between the comments of a given article.

Contextual bandit algorithms [16, 7] assume that side information (e.g., features) is also available. LinRel [7] and LinUCB [16] are UCB-based algorithms that assume the reward of an arm is linearly dependent on its features. The algorithms have been shown to have an $\tilde{O}(\sqrt{T})$ regret for a fixed set of arms; however, in our problem setting, arms are dynamic. Furthermore, linear regression is not suitable for modeling binary ratings data, and cannot ensure that the average rating lies in the range $[0, 1]$.

Pandey et. al [20] assume that dependencies among arms can be described by a generative model on clusters of arms. However, these clusters are assumed to be known beforehand and each arm belongs to exactly one cluster. In contrast, our framework does not assume any clustering of comments. Instead, the dependencies among comments are effectively captured by our logistic regression model with comment features.

User Generated Content: Recently, analysis of user generated content has been an active area of research [24, 17, 28, 27, 11, 4, 14]. [11] uses different user, textual, and network features to analyze the credibility of tweets on twitter. [27] extends LDA [10] to model the generation of blog posts, authorship, as well as comments on the posts. [28] proposes a variant of supervised LDA [9] called the Topic-Poisson model to identify which blog posts will receive a high volume of comments. However, these methods do not focus on recommending comments to users. [14] uses an SVM regressor on different features such as unigrams, review length etc. to determine how helpful a review is. The helpfulness is defined as the fraction of users who found the review to be helpful. [24] analyzes the dependencies between comments, their ratings, and different topic categories. An SVM classifier is used to estimate the ratings of new or unrated comments. However, none of these methods employ an explore-exploit strategy, and are thus inadequate for ranking dynamic comments.

9. CONCLUSIONS AND FUTURE WORK

In this paper, we proposed a novel UCB-based explore-exploit algorithm called LogUCB for recommending comments to users. LogUCB uses a logistic regression model on word and topic features to predict the average rating for a comment. At its core, LogUCB relies on a novel variance approximation technique under a Bayesian setting to derive the upper confidence bounds used to select comments. In experiments with a real-life comments dataset from Yahoo! News, LogUCB outperforms other state-of-the-art context-free and feature-based explore-exploit methods like LinUCB. Directions for future work include extending our LogUCB algorithm to ensure diversity of the K recommended comments, and proving formal regret bounds for our LogUCB algorithm.

10. REFERENCES

[1] Deepak Agarwal and Bee-Chung Chen. Regression-based latent factor models. In *SIGKDD*, pages 19–28, 2009.

[2] Deepak Agarwal and Bee-Chung Chen. flda: matrix factorization through latent dirichlet allocation. In *WSDM*, pages 91–100, 2010.

[3] Deepak Agarwal, Bee-Chung Chen, and Pradheep Elango. Explore/exploit schemes for web content optimization. In *ICDM*, 2009.

[4] Deepak Agarwal, Bee-Chung Chen, and Bo Pang. Personalized recommendation of user comments via factor models. In *EMNLP*, pages 571–582, July 2011.

[5] R. Agrawal. Sample mean based index policies with o(log n) regret for the multi-armed bandit problem. *Advances in Applied Probability*, pages 1054–1078, 1995.

[6] Peter Auer, Nicolò Cesa-Bianchi, and Paul Fischer. Finite-time analysis of the multiarmed bandit problem. *Mach. Learn.*, 47:235–256, May 2002.

[7] Peter Auer and M. Long. Using confidence bounds for exploitation-exploration trade-offs. *JMLR*, 3:2002, 2002.

[8] Chris Bishop. *Pattern Recognition and Machine Learning*. Springer-Verlag, 2006.

[9] David Blei and Jon McAuliffe. Supervised topic models. In *NIPS*, 2008.

[10] David M. Blei, Andrew Y. Ng, Michael I. Jordan, and John Lafferty. Latent dirichlet allocation. *JMLR*, 3:2003, 2003.

[11] Carlos Castillo, Marcelo Mendoza, and Barbara Poblete. Information credibility on twitter. In *WWW*, pages 675–684, 2011.

[12] J. C. Gittins. Bandit Processes and Dynamic Allocation Indices. *Journal of the Royal Statistical Society. Series B (Methodological)*, 41(2):148–177, 1979.

[13] T. L. Griffiths and M. Steyvers. Finding scientific topics. *PNAS*, 101(Suppl. 1):5228–5235, April 2004.

[14] Soo-Min Kim, Patrick Pantel, Tim Chklovski, and Marco Pennacchiotti. Automatically assessing review helpfulness. In *EMNLP*, pages 423–430, 2006.

[15] Tze L. Lai and Herbert Robbins. Asymptotically efficient

adaptive allocation rules. *Advances in Applied Mathematics*, 6(1):4–22, 1985.

[16] Lihong Li, Wei Chu, John Langford, and Robert E. Schapire. A contextual-bandit approach to personalized news article recommendation. In *WWW*, pages 661–670, 2010.

[17] Yue Lu, ChengXiang Zhai, and Neel Sundaresan. Rated aspect summarization of short comments. In *WWW*, pages 131–140, 2009.

[18] David Luenberger and Yinyu Ye. *Linear and Nonlinear programming*. Springer, 2008.

[19] D J C MacKay. The evidence framework applied to classification networks. *Neural Computation*, 4(5), 1992.

[20] Sandeep Pandey, Deepayan Chakrabarti, and Deepak Agarwal. Multi-armed bandit problems with dependent arms. In *ICML*, 2007.

[21] Filip Radlinski, Robert Kleinberg, and Thorsten Joachims. Learning diverse rankings with multi-armed bandits. In *ICML*, pages 784–791, New York, NY, USA, 2008.

[22] Ruslan Salakhutdinov and Andriy Mnih. Bayesian probabilistic matrix factorization using markov chain monte carlo. In *ICML*, pages 880–887, 2008.

[23] Andrew Schein and Lyle Ungar. Active learning for logistic regression: An evaluation. *Machine Learning*, 69(3), 2007.

[24] Stefan Siersdorfer, Sergiu Chelaru, Wolfgang Nejdl, and Jose San Pedro. How useful are your comments?: analyzing and predicting youtube comments and comment ratings. In *WWW*, pages 891–900, 2010.

[25] Aleksandrs Slivkins, Filip Radlinski, and Sreenivas Gollapudi. Learning optimally diverse rankings over large document collections. In *ICML*, pages 983–990. Omnipress, 2010.

[26] Jun Wang, Arjen P. de Vries, and Marcel J. T. Reinders. Unifying user-based and item-based collaborative filtering approaches by similarity fusion. In *SIGIR*, pages 501–508, 2006.

[27] Tae. Yano, William. Cohen, and Noah A. Smith. Predicting response to political blog posts with topic models. In *NAACL-HLT*, 2009.

[28] Tae. Yano and Noah A. Smith. What's worthy of comment? content and comment volume in political blogs with topic models. In *ICWSM*, 2010.

DQR: A Probabilistic Approach to Diversified Query Recommendation

Ruirui Li† Ben Kao† Bin Bi‡ Reynold Cheng† Eric Lo§

†The University of Hong Kong ‡University of California, Los Angeles §Hong Kong Polytechnic University

†{rrli, kao, ckcheng}@cs.hku.hk ‡bbi@cs.ucla.edu §ericlo@comp.polyu.edu.hk

ABSTRACT

Web search queries issued by casual users are often short and with limited expressiveness. Query recommendation is a popular technique employed by search engines to help users refine their queries. Traditional similarity-based methods, however, often result in redundant and monotonic recommendations. We identify five basic requirements of a query recommendation system. In particular, we focus on the requirements of redundancy-free and diversified recommendations. We propose the DQR framework, which mines a search log to achieve two goals: (1) It clusters search log queries to extract query concepts, based on which recommended queries are selected. (2) It employs a probabilistic model and a greedy heuristic algorithm to achieve recommendation diversification. Through a comprehensive user study we compare DQR against five other recommendation methods. Our experiment shows that DQR outperforms the other methods in terms of relevancy, diversity, and ranking performance of the recommendations.

Categories and Subject Descriptors

H.2.8 [**Database Management**]: Database Applications—*Data mining*

Keywords

Query recommendation, query concept, diversification

1. INTRODUCTION

The effectiveness of keyword-based search engines, such as Google and Bing, depends largely on the ability of a user to formulate proper queries that are both *expressive* and *selective*. An expressive query clearly and unambiguously describes a user's search intent, while a selective query results in a relatively small set of matching documents. Properly formulated queries bring users directly to the desired information, which make search engines powerful tools for tapping into the wealth of knowledge accessible through the world-wide-web. In practice, translating human thoughts into concise sets of keywords to form queries is never straightforward [3]. This is particularly true for search engine users, who are mostly untrained casual users. In many cases, casual users have very limited background knowledge about the information they are searching for. To assist users in formulating queries, modern search engines are equipped with machine intelligence. This includes techniques like automatic query completion [8] and query recommendation [6, 12, 15, 16]. For the latter, given a user query, a search engine deduces the search intent of the user and recommends a set of queries that are more expressive and selective than the original user input. Our goal is to study the various properties and requirements of a query recommendation system and to propose a novel approach to achieve the desired requirements.

Web search queries are usually very short, typically with only one or two keywords each [21]. Short queries lead to two issues. First, they are often *ambiguous*. For example, the query "Jaguar" can refer to a big cat, an automobile brand-name, or an operating system. In [18], it is reported that up to 23.6% of web search queries are ambiguous. Ambiguity weakens the expressiveness of queries because the search engine may not get the users' hidden search intents. This causes poor retrieval results.

The second issue is that short queries are often not specific enough. For example, a user issuing the query "Disney" may really be interested only in "Disney Pictures". Without knowing the hidden intent, a search engine would return web pages on Disney's theme parks, stores, and cartoon characters in addition to those on the film-making studios. Although there is no ambiguity in the meaning of the keyword "Disney", it is too general a query for the search engine to pinpoint the specific information the user is interested.

In recent years, research has been carried out to tackle the problems of query ambiguity and weak selectivity. One prominent approach is query recommendation. Given a query, e.g., "Jaguar", a search engine provides a list of recommended queries such as "Jaguar Cat", "Jaguar Car", and "Jaguar Mac". This helps the user refine his query by picking the most relevant recommendation.

Many of existing query-recommendation techniques are based on query similarity. Given an input query $\tilde{q}$, a recommender system suggests a set of queries that it has frequently seen and which are the most similar to $\tilde{q}$. The various similarity-based methods differ in the way they measure query similarity. The rationale behind this approach is that similar queries reflect the same or similar search intent, and it is likely that the search intent is more properly expressed by the frequently seen queries, which are the results of the collective wisdom of the community. We observe that similarity-based methods are not always the best approach. This is because queries that are the most similar to $\tilde{q}$ tend to be similar among themselves. This may lead to *redundancy* and *monotonicity* in the recommendation.

Recommendation redundancy refers to the situation where some

CIKM'12, October 29–November 2, 2012, Maui, HI, USA.

recommended queries are of equivalent meaning, describing almost the same search intent. For example, consider the input query "Recommendation" and two recommended queries returned by the Bing search engine: "Letter of recommendation examples" and "Recommendation letter samples". Obviously, the recommended queries refer to the same information and they are likely to give very similar search results. They are thus redundant.

Recommendation monotonicity refers to the situation where the recommended queries all refer to search intents of a common predominant interpretation of the input query keywords. For example, consider the input query "Jaguar", the recommendation {"Jaguar parts", "Jaguar sedan", "Jaguar used car", "Jaguar dealer"} all follow the interpretation of "Jaguar as an automobile manufacturer". The recommendation is thus monotonic and it could miss out the real search intent of the user, such as "Jaguar as an animal".

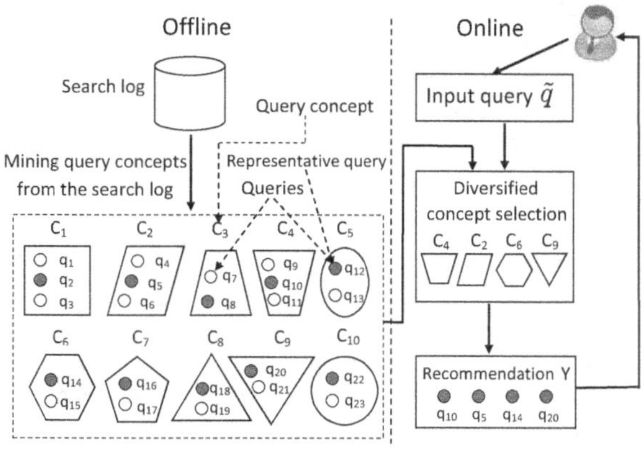

Figure 1: The DQR framework

We propose that a good query recommender should go beyond pure similarity and towards providing redundancy-free and diversified recommendations. To avoid redundancy, we highlight the notion of *query concept* (see Figure 1). In our model, a query concept is a set of queries that reflect the same or similar search intent. For example, the queries "Letter of recommendation examples" and "Recommendation letter sample" both describe the same search intent and therefore they should belong to the same query concept. An important pre-processing step of our query recommendation system is to group (previously seen) queries into query concepts. Given an input query $\tilde{q}$, our system first selects and ranks a small set of relevant concepts. A representative query from each of the selected concepts is then extracted. These extracted queries form a list Y of ranked recommended queries. Through query concept selection, we are able to avoid recommendation redundancy. This is because only one (representative) query from each relevant concept is returned to the user. Other redundant queries, which belong to the same concept, are not extracted.

To diversify recommendation, the concept selection component (Figure 1) employs a probabilistic model whose goal is to maximize the likelihood that the recommended concepts (or equivalently their representative queries) cover as many hidden search intents and interpretations of the input query keywords as possible. For example, the recommendation Y_1: {"Jaguar Cat", "Jaguar Car ", "Jaguar Mac", "Jaguar NFL"} is superior to the recommendation Y_2: {"Jaguar Parts", "Jaguar Dealer", "Jaguar sedan", "Jaguar used cars"}, because Y_1 covers more interpretations of the query keyword "Jaguar". It is therefore more likely that at least one of the recommended queries is relevant to the hidden search intent of the user.

To extract query concepts and to construct the probabilistic model for recommendation diversification, we mine search logs. A search

UserID	Query String	Time	Clicked URL
193661	maps	2006-05-13 13:16:32	maps.yahoo.com
193661	maps	2006-05-13 13:16:32	maps.google.com
2356008	map search	2006-03-14 07:35:04	maps.google.com
2356008	map search	2006-03-14 07:35:04	maps.yahoo.com
16462215	map search	2006-03-31 10:34:32	www.mapquest.com
93537	driving directions	2006-03-22 23:34:40	www.mapquest.com
366529	driving directions	2006-04-04 20:03:50	www.randmcnally.com
1965790	rand mcnally	2006-03-01 07:21:40	www.randmcnally.com

Table 1: Sample AOL search log records

log contains historical records, each of which registers the details of a web search conducted by a user. Table 1 shows some sample records extracted from the AOL search engine's search log [17][1]. Each record includes a query string, an anonymous user ID by whom the query was formulated, a query submission time, and the URL subsequently clicked by the user (if done). To distinguish user queries for which recommendations are to be made from those historical queries recorded in the search log, we call the former *input queries* (denoted by $\tilde{q}$) and the latter *log queries* or simply queries.

Before we proceed to describe the details of our approach, let us enumerate the properties that a good query recommendation system should observe:

[Relevancy] Recommended queries should be semantically relevant to the user search query.

[Redundancy Free] The recommendation should not contain redundant queries that repeat similar search intents.

[Diversity] The recommendation should cover search intents of different interpretations of the keywords given in the input query.

[Ranking] Highly relevant queries should be ranked first ahead of less relevant ones in the recommendation list.

[Efficiency] Query recommendation provides online help. Therefore, recommendation algorithms should achieve fast response times.

Here we summarize the major contributions of our work:

(1) We study the main features that a query recommender should possess. These include relevancy, redundancy-free, diversity, ranking, and real-time response. Our approach, called DQR, is the first to address all the 5 requirements.

(2) We highlight the notion of query concept to tackle the recommendation redundancy problem. We propose a clustering method to achieve query concept construction.

(3) We propose a concept-based probabilistic query recommendation model, which considers both the requirements of relevancy and diversity.

(4) We present a comprehensive empirical evaluation of our approach against a number of recommendation methods using real search engine datasets. The results show that our approach is both highly effective and efficient in suggesting relevant and diversified recommendations.

2. RELATED WORK

Query recommendation is an active research topic. In this section we give a brief account of some representative works on general web search recommendation techniques (Section 2.1). Since our approach uses concept extraction to avoid recommendation redundancy and we aim to achieve recommendation diversification, we highlight some related work on recommendation diversification (Section 2.2) and concept mining (Section 2.3).

2.1 Query Recommendation

There are a number of studies on search-log-based query recommendation methods [2, 4, 6]. Many of these studies derive click-through bipartite graphs (CTBG) from search logs to measure

[1]Each log record is associated with many fields. We are displaying only those fields that are of our interest.

query similarity. The set of queries (Q) and the set of clicked URLs (D) in a search log form two disjoint sets of vertices in a CTBG. An edge connects a query $q \in Q$ and an URL $d \in D$ if q and d appear together in a log record. Figure 2 shows the CTBG derived from the search log shown in Table 1. Assuming that the URLs a user clicked reflect his search intent, queries that share more clicked URLs are considered more similar.

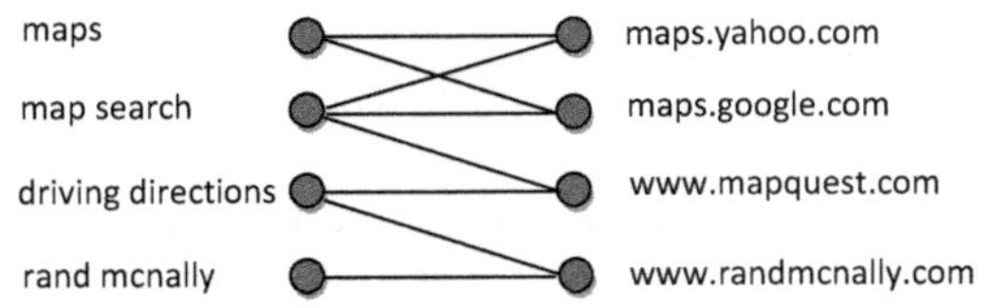

Figure 2: A click-through bipartite graph

Based on a similarity measure, queries are clustered. For example, in [2], each query is associated with a term vector that is derived from the contents of the web pages referred to by its clicked URLs. The similarity of two queries is given by the cosine similarity of the queries' term vectors. The k-means algorithm is then applied to cluster the queries. Given an input query $\tilde{q}$, the cluster C to which $\tilde{q}$ belongs is determined. Queries in the cluster are then ranked and the highly ranked queries are returned in the recommendation. In [4], a similar cluster-based recommendation approach is proposed, except that an agglomerative clustering method applied on the CTBG is used instead of k-means. In [21], the similarity of two queries is measured by a combination of the clicked URLs they share as well as the keywords shared by their query strings. A density-based clustering algorithm (DBSCAN) is then applied to form query clusters. Our approach is in sharp contrast to the above methods. Although we also cluster queries, the purpose is not to recommend queries that are in the same cluster of the input query. Instead, each cluster forms one *query concept* and only one representative query from each cluster (concept) is considered in the recommendation procedure to avoid redundancy.

Some studies apply various probabilistic models for query recommendation. For example, in [12, 15, 16], a *query graph* is constructed from a search log in which vertices represent queries in the log. An edge connecting two queries is weighted by a *transition probability*, which is related to the similarity of the two queries. A *hitting time algorithm*, which performs a random walk, is then executed on the graph. The hitting time $h(q_j|q_i)$ is the expected number of steps it takes to reach a query vertex q_j from a starting vertex q_i. In [12], given an input query $\tilde{q}$, queries q_j's with the smallest hitting times $h(q_j|\tilde{q})$ are recommended. One weakness of the hitting time approach is that query graphs are huge. For example, the query graph derived from the AOL search log [17] is about 100 GB. Typically, either a depth-first search or a breadth-first search on the query graph is executed to obtain a reduced graph for the execution of the hitting time algorithm. This is computationally expensive and it works against the real-time requirement of query recommendation.

2.2 Diversified Recommendation

In [7], Carbonell et al. introduce Maximal Marginal Relevance (MMR) as a technique to diversify results in traditional document retrieval systems. Given a keyword query, MMR selects relevant documents incrementally. When a relevant document d is selected, MMR updates the relevancy of each remaining document d' by computing a penalty, which is based on the similarity between d and d'. The next relevant document picked by MMR is then based on the updated relevancy scores. By doing so, MMR favors documents that are not only relevant to the query, but are also not so similar to those that have already been included in the retrieval result. In [15], Ma et al. study diversified query recommendation. Similar to MMR, a recommendation list is constructed incrementally. They employ a reversed hitting time algorithm to ensure that the next query selected for recommendation is not very similar to those that have already been selected. Like other hitting-time-based algorithms, their method suffers from high computational cost in processing huge query graphs. Our approach is similar to that of [15] in that we also construct the recommendation list incrementally. However, we pick recommended queries at the query concept levels to avoid recommendation redundancy. Also, instead of using query graphs, we propose a probabilistic model that allows recommendations to be determined much more efficiently to satisfy the real-time requirement.

2.3 Concept Mining

In traditional IR, concepts are often extracted from unstructured text collections to improve retrieval accuracy. Techniques such as LSI [9] are often employed. However, the literature on mining query concepts from search log queries remains sparse.

In [6], Cao et al. propose CACB, which employs a one-pass clustering algorithm to cluster search log queries into query concepts. In Section 4.1 we will give the details of this clustering algorithm, point out its potential weaknesses, and propose a method to improve the clustering results. In [11], Fonseca et al. extract query concepts from *query relation graphs* (QRGs). The idea is to first identify user sessions from the search log (e.g., based on the queries' submission times). Search log queries that frequently co-occur in the same sessions are considered highly associated, and so they are connected by an edge in the QRG. Subsets of queries that are strongly connected in the QRG are taken as query concepts.

3. NOTATIONS AND PROBLEM STATEMENT

A search log R consists of a number of log records. Given a log record $r \in R$, we use r^q, r^u, r^t, and r^d to denote the query, the user who issued the query, the query submission time, and the clicked URL of that record, respectively. We use Q, U, and D to denote the set of all unique queries, the set of all unique user ID's, and the set of all unique clicked URLs, respectively, in the search log.

Given an input query $\tilde{q}$ issued by a user u, we say that a recommended query q *matches* $\tilde{q}$ if user u finds q relevant to his search intent. Note that this concept of matching is subjective to the user, and there could be more than one query matching $\tilde{q}$. Without referring to a particular user, we use e_q to denote the event that *an arbitrary user* finds q matching his input query $\tilde{q}$. Similarly, given a set of recommended queries $Y \subseteq Q$, we use e_Y to denote the event that *at least one* query in Y matches $\tilde{q}$. We use $p(e_q)$ and $p(e_Y)$ to denote the probabilities of the corresponding events.

PROBLEM STATEMENT 1. ***(Diversified Query Recommendation)*** *Given an input query $\tilde{q}$ and an integer m, the diversified query recommendation problem is to find a set $Y \subseteq Q$ of m queries that maximizes the probability $p(e_Y)$.*

4. THE DQR APPROACH

The diversified query recommendation problem is a difficult one. First, the number of queries in Q is huge. For example, there are more than 10 million queries in the AOL dataset. Even picking, say, $m = 10$ recommended queries from Q involves a huge search space. Second, it is not apparent how the probability $p(e_Y)$ is estimated. To strike a balance between efficiency and recommendation quality, we propose a heuristic approach called DQR. DQR consists of an offline component and an online component. Figure 1 shows the framework. For the offline component, queries in the search log are clustered. Each cluster forms a query concept. For the online component, given an input query $\tilde{q}$, DQR employs a probabilistic model to find a set Y_c of m query concepts. For each concept $C_i \in Y_c$, a representative query q_i is selected from the cluster of C_i. These m selected queries, one from each concept in Y_c, form the recommendation Y. In this section we first discuss our offline concept mining algorithm (Section 4.1), followed by our probabilistic model for online concept selection and recommendation construction (Section 4.2).

4.1 Concept Mining

We group similar queries in the search log to form query concepts. This step is done for two purposes. First, as we have explained in the introduction, by recommending at most one query from each cluster, we avoid recommendation redundancy. Second, the number of query concepts is much smaller than the number of queries in a search log ($|Q|$). Selecting m query concepts (for recommendation) thus involves a much smaller search space than the problem of selecting m queries out of Q. This allows the online recommendation process to be done efficiently enough to satisfy the real-time requirement of the recommendation problem.

To cluster queries, we need a similarity measure. We use the set of URLs as the features of queries. Each query $q_i \in Q$ is thus represented by a $|D|$-dimensional vector $\overrightarrow{q_i}$. More specifically, given a query q_i and an URL d_j, we follow [10] and assign the *user-frequency-inverse-query-frequency* (UF-IQF) score as the component weight of q_i for dimension d_j. This weight, $w'(q_i, d_j)$, is given by the formula:

$$w'(q_i, d_j) = N_u(q_i, d_j) \times \log(|Q|/N_q(d_j)), \quad (1)$$

where $N_u(q_i, d_j)$ is the number of unique users who have issued query q_i and subsequently clicked URL d_j, and $N_q(d_j)$ is the number of queries that led to the clicking of URL d_j:

$$N_u(q_i, d_j) = |\{u \in U | \exists r \in R, r^u = u, r^q = q_i, r^d = d_j\}|,$$
$$N_q(d_j) = |\{q \in Q | \exists r \in R, r^q = q, r^d = d_j\}|.$$

We further normalize the weights to $w(q_i, d_j)$ by

$$w(q_i, d_j) = \frac{w'(q_i, d_j)}{\sqrt{\sum_{d_k \in D} w'(q_i, d_k)^2}}. \quad (2)$$

The *distance*, $d(q_i, q_j)$, between two queries q_i and q_j is measured by the Euclidean distance of their normalized vectors. We also use $s(q_i, q_j)$ to denote a similarity measure of the queries:

$$d(q_i, q_j) = ||\overrightarrow{q_i} - \overrightarrow{q_j}||, \qquad s(q_i, q_j) = 1 - d(q_i, q_j)/\sqrt{2}. \quad (3)$$

Before we describe our clustering algorithm, let us point out two requirements: (1) *Adaptability*: The clustering algorithm should be able to automatically determine the number of clusters in a search log, since this number is unknown beforehand. (2) *Efficiency*: The algorithm has to be efficient because the number of queries in the search log is huge.

With these requirements k-means, for example, is not suitable. Not only does it require the number of concepts be known, it also requires numerous iterations through the search log queries during the clustering process. As an example, we have applied k-means to cluster the queries in the AOL search log. The algorithm did not terminate in two days.

In view of the efficiency requirement, a one-pass clustering algorithm is proposed in [6]. The algorithm maintains a set of clusters $\mathcal{C}$ (initially $\mathcal{C} = \emptyset$). The algorithm then scans the search log queries. For each query q_i, the algorithm locates the cluster $C \in \mathcal{C}$ that is the "*closest*" to q_i. If adding q_i to C does not violate a *compactness requirement* of C, q_i is added to C; otherwise, q_i forms a cluster by itself and this new cluster is added to $\mathcal{C}$.

This one-pass algorithm, although very efficient, is highly sensitive to the order in which log queries are scanned. As a simple example, Figure 3(a) shows three queries and their pairwise distances. Suppose we impose the following compactness requirement: "the average pairwise distance of queries in a cluster $\leq$ 0.5". Then, if the queries are scanned in the order q_1, q_2, q_3, the clustering result is $\mathcal{C}_1 = \{\{q_1, q_2\}, \{q_3\}\}$. Note that q_3 is not added to the cluster $\{q_1, q_2\}$ because doing so will violate the compactness requirement. We observe that a better clustering result is $\mathcal{C}_2 = \{\{q_1\}, \{q_2, q_3\}\}$ because q_2 is closer to q_3 than it is to q_1. It is easy to see that $\mathcal{C}_2$ can be obtained by scanning the queries in a different order: q_2, q_3, q_1.

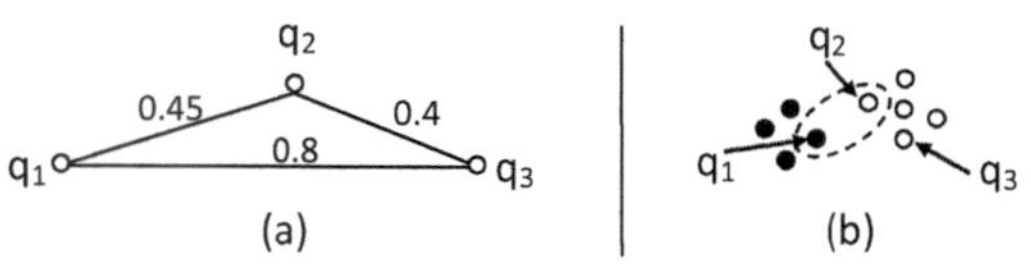

Figure 3: Clustering example

Figure 3(b) further illustrates this problem when the one-pass algorithm is applied to cluster a number of queries. We note that if the compactness requirement is set too loose, the one-pass algorithm runs the risk of putting two far points (e.g., q_1 and q_2) into the same cluster, leading to sub-optimal clustering. By limiting to one pass through the data, the algorithm cannot rectify the clustering result. This argues for a more stringent compactness requirement. However, if the requirement is too stringent, we will end up with a large number of very small clusters, which is not desirable either. Our solution is to use hierarchical clustering: we start with a very stringent compactness requirement to make sure that only points that are very close among themselves form a cluster. We then merge these clusters by gradually relaxing the compactness requirement. Algorithm 1 shows our clustering method.

Given a query cluster C, we use the diameter measure ($L(C)$) proposed in [22] as our cluster compactness measure:

$$L(C) = \sqrt{\frac{\sum_{q_i \in C} \sum_{q_j \in C} (||\overrightarrow{q_i} - \overrightarrow{q_j}||)^2}{|C|(|C| - 1)}}. \quad (4)$$

We use $\mu(C)$ to represent the centroid of cluster C. Our algorithm maintains a set of clusters $\mathcal{C}$ and the set of their centroids, $\mathcal{P} = \{\mu(C) | C \in \mathcal{C}\}$. It also maintains a compactness requirement $L(C) \leq L \; \forall C \in \mathcal{C}$, where L is a compactness bound that changes from 0 (initially) to L_{max} with an increment step of L_δ across iterations of the algorithm. Initially, each query $q_i \in Q$ forms a cluster $\{q_i\}$ by itself. This is equivalent to having a compactness requirement of $L(C) = 0$ for each cluster. In each iteration of the algorithm, we group the centroids (in $\mathcal{P}$) using the one-pass algorithm of [6] with the compactness bound L. If a set of centroids are grouped together by the one-pass algorithm, we merge their corresponding clusters to form a bigger cluster. At the end of an iteration, we update the set of cluster centroids ($\mathcal{P}$), increase the compactness bound L by L_δ, and repeat until L exceeds the maximum bound L_{max}. Figure 4 illustrates our clustering algorithm.

We have argued that a query clustering algorithm should not execute too many iterations because the number of log queries are typically huge. By controlling the value of the compactness bound increment L_δ, we can control the number of clustering iterations,

Algorithm 1: Clustering Algorithm

Input: query set $Q = \{q_1, q_2, ..., q_{|Q|}\}$, increment step L_δ and compactness threshold L_{max}
Output: a set of clusters $\mathcal{C} = \{C_i | C_i \subset Q\}$

Initialization: $\mathcal{C} \leftarrow \{\{q_i\} | q_i \in Q\}$; $\mathcal{P} \leftarrow Q$; $L \leftarrow 0$;
repeat
  $CP \leftarrow \emptyset$; //clustering points in $\mathcal{P}$
  foreach $p_i \in \mathcal{P}$ **do**
    if $CP = \emptyset$ **then**
      $CP \leftarrow \{\{p_i\}\}$;
    else
      $C^* \leftarrow \arg\min_{C \in CP} d(\mu(C), p_i)$;
      if $L(C^* \cup \{p_i\}) \leq L$ **then**
        $C^* \leftarrow C^* \cup \{p_i\}$;
      else
        $CP \leftarrow CP \cup \{\{p_i\}\}$;
  // Merge clusters
  Update $\mathcal{C} \leftarrow \{X | X = \cup_{C \in \mathcal{C}, \mu(C) \in A} C, \; A \in CP\}$;
  Update $\mathcal{P} = \{p_i | p_i = \mu(C_i), C_i \in \mathcal{C}\}$;
  $L = L + L_\delta$;
until $L > L_{max}$;
return $\mathcal{C}$

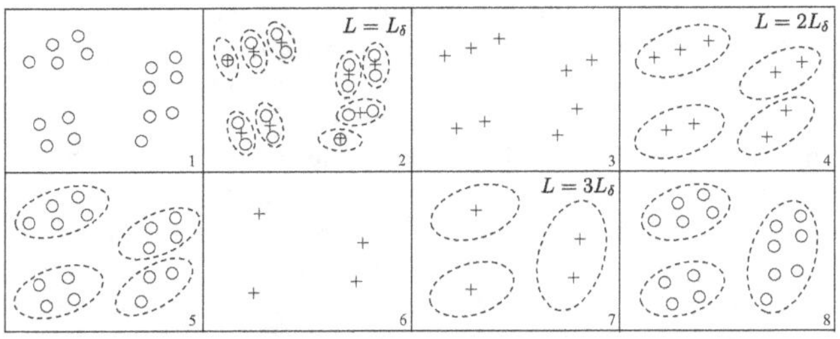

Figure 4: Clustering illustration: (1) Some queries. (2) Grouped with bound $L = L_\delta$. (3) Cluster centroids. (4) Centroids grouped with $L = 2L_\delta$. (5) Merged query clusters. (6) Centroids of the merged clusters. (7) Centroids grouped with $L = 3L_\delta$. (8) Merged query clusters.

and thus the clustering efficiency. We remark that the choice of the maximum bound L_{max} is more of an engineering effort. One way to determine a "good" L_{max} is to perform a user study on the recommender's effectiveness under a few values of L_{max}. Fortunately, our experiment results show that our DQR approach gives very good performance over a wide range of L_{max} values so it is not critical that an optimal value of L_{max} be found.

4.2 Query Recommendation

Let $\mathcal{C}$ be the set of query concepts extracted from the search log. Given an input query $\tilde{q}$, we construct a list of recommended queries Y with a two-step process. First, we use a probabilistic model to select a set $Y_c \subseteq \mathcal{C}$ of m recommended query concepts. Then, Y is constructed by selecting a representative query from each of the concepts in Y_c.

Recall that in Section 3 we defined the notion of a recommended query q *matches* a user input query $\tilde{q}$. Since the first step of our recommendation procedure operates at the query concept level, we extend our notion of *matching* to the concept level as well. In particular, given a user u who has issued an input query $\tilde{q}$, we say that a query concept $C \in \mathcal{C}$ matches $\tilde{q}$ if user u finds some queries in C relevant to his search intent. We use e_C to denote the event that an arbitrary user u finds C matches $\tilde{q}$. Note that, depending on the perspective of the user, there could be more than one concept C matching $\tilde{q}$. Furthermore, given a set $Y_c \subseteq \mathcal{C}$ of query concepts we use e_{Y_c} to denote the event that an arbitrary user u finds some concepts in Y_c matching $\tilde{q}$. With these notations, the first step (concept selection) of our two-step recommendation procedure can be performed as followed:

[Concept Selection] Given an input query $\tilde{q}$, let $C_{\tilde{q}} \in \mathcal{C}$ be the query concept $\tilde{q}$ belongs[2]. Since the user has expressed his search intent with the input query $\tilde{q}$, the concept $C_{\tilde{q}}$ is deemed relevant to the user's search intent. To recommend queries selected from other concepts, our heuristic algorithm finds a set $Y_c \subseteq \mathcal{C} - \{C_{\tilde{q}}\}$ of m query concepts such that $p(e_{Y_c} | e_{C_{\tilde{q}}})$ is maximized. To better explain the model and the algorithm, we first give a few definitions.

After a user issues a query q to a search engine, he may click a set of URLs, s, returned by the search engine. We use I: $q \rightarrow s$ to denote such an interaction, which is captured by a set of records in the search log. For example, the first two records in the search log shown in Table 1 shows that a user issued the query "maps" and subsequently clicked two URLs: *maps.yahoo.com* and *maps.google.com*. We call s the *click-set* of the interaction I. Note that records that constitute an interaction all share the same user ID, query string, and query-submission time. We use $\mathcal{I}$ to denote the set of all such interactions found in the search log R. We use CS to denote the set of all click-sets found in R.

For example, from the log in Table 1, we get four queries:

$$Q = \left\{ \begin{array}{ll} q_1 = \text{"maps"}, & q_2 = \text{"map search"}, \\ q_3 = \text{"driving directions"}, & q_4 = \text{"rand mcnally"} \end{array} \right\},$$

three click-sets:

$$CS = \left\{ \begin{array}{l} s_1 = \{\texttt{maps.yahoo.com, maps.google.com}\}, \\ s_2 = \{\texttt{www.mapquest.com}\}, \quad s_3 = \{\texttt{www.randmcnally.com}\} \end{array} \right\}$$

and six interactions:

$$\mathcal{I} = \left\{ \begin{array}{lll} q_1 \rightarrow s_1, & q_2 \rightarrow s_1, & q_2 \rightarrow s_2 \\ q_3 \rightarrow s_2, & q_3 \rightarrow s_3, & q_4 \rightarrow s_3 \end{array} \right\}.$$

There are $\binom{|\mathcal{C}|-1}{m}$ or $O(|\mathcal{C}|^m)$ ways of picking m concepts into the set Y_c out of the pool of query concepts $\mathcal{C} - \{C_{\tilde{q}}\}$. Enumerating them to find the one that maximizes $p(e_{Y_c} | e_{C_{\tilde{q}}})$ is too inefficient. Instead, we apply a greedy strategy and construct the set Y_c incrementally.

Let Y'_c (which is initially empty) be a set of concepts our algorithm has picked so far. We want to add more concepts to Y'_c (one concept at a time) until the selection contains m concepts. At each step, our greedy heuristic picks the concept $C \in \mathcal{C} - \{C_{\tilde{q}}\} - Y'_c$ that maximizes the probability increment:

$$\Delta(Y'_c, C, C_{\tilde{q}}) = p(e_{Y'_c \cup \{C\}} | e_{C_{\tilde{q}}}) - p(e_{Y'_c} | e_{C_{\tilde{q}}}).$$

To estimate this value, we make one reasonable assumption: we assume that the search intent of a user, who issues a query q to a search engine, is truly reflected by the URLs he would click when presented with the search results of q. This has two implications:

IMPLICATION 1. *Given concepts C_a and C_b, and a click-set s, we have $p(e_{C_b} | e_s, e_{C_a}) = p(e_{C_b} | e_s)$, where e_s represents the event that the user clicks the URLs in s. That is, knowing that concept C_a matches the input query $\tilde{q}$ does not add more information to estimating $p(e_{C_b})$ given that we already know the user would click the click-set s.*

[2] If $\tilde{q}$ has previously appeared in the search log, we simply look up which concept in $\mathcal{C}$ contains $\tilde{q}$. If $\tilde{q}$ is a new query previously unseen, we find the query $q_\star \in Q$ whose content (such as the keywords contained in the query strings) is the most similar to that of $\tilde{q}$ and use the concept $q_\star$ belongs as $C_{\tilde{q}}$.

IMPLICATION 2. *Given two concepts C_a, C_b and a click-set s, we have $p(e_{C_a}, e_{C_b}|e_s) = p(e_{C_a}|e_s)p(e_{C_b}|e_s)$. That is, the event of C_a matching $\tilde{q}$ and the event of C_b matching $\tilde{q}$ are conditionally independent given e_s.*

With the conditional independence assumption, we derive $p(e_{Y'_c}|e_{C_{\tilde{q}}})$ (and likewise for $p(e_{Y'_c \cup \{C\}}|e_{C_{\tilde{q}}})$) by marginalizing the probability across all click-sets in CS:

$$p(e_{Y'_c}|e_{C_{\tilde{q}}}) = \sum_{s \in CS} p(e_{Y'_c}|e_s, e_{C_{\tilde{q}}})p(e_s|e_{C_{\tilde{q}}}), = \sum_{s \in CS} p(e_{Y'_c}|e_s)p(e_s|e_{C_{\tilde{q}}}). \quad (5)$$

Then,

$$\Delta(Y'_c, C, C_{\tilde{q}}) = \sum_{s \in CS} p(e_{Y'_c \cup \{C\}}|e_s)p(e_s|e_{C_{\tilde{q}}}) - \sum_{s \in CS} p(e_{Y'_c}|e_s)p(e_s|e_{C_{\tilde{q}}}), = \sum_{s \in CS} \{p(e_{Y'_c \cup \{C\}}|e_s) - p(e_{Y'_c}|e_s)\} p(e_s|e_{C_{\tilde{q}}}). \quad (6)$$

Since $p(e_{Y'_c}|e_s) = 1 - \prod_{C_j \in Y'_c}(1 - p(e_{C_j}|e_s))$, we have

$$\begin{aligned} & p(e_{Y'_c \cup \{C\}}|e_s) - p(e_{Y'_c}|e_s) \\ =& \left\{1 - (1 - p(e_C|e_s)) \prod_{C_j \in Y'_c} (1 - p(e_{C_j}|e_s))\right\} - \left\{1 - \prod_{C_j \in Y'_c} (1 - p(e_{C_j}|e_s))\right\}, \\ =& \left\{\prod_{C_j \in Y'_c} (1 - p(e_{C_j}|e_s))\right\} - \left\{(1 - p(e_C|e_s)) \prod_{C_j \in Y'_c} (1 - p(e_{C_j}|e_s))\right\}, \\ =& p(e_C|e_s) \prod_{C_j \in Y'_c} (1 - p(e_{C_j}|e_s)). \end{aligned} \quad (7)$$

Substituting Equation (7) into Equation (6), we get

$$\Delta(Y'_c, C, C_{\tilde{q}}) = \sum_{s \in CS} \left\{p(e_s|e_{C_{\tilde{q}}})p(e_C|e_s) \prod_{C_j \in Y'_c} (1 - p(e_{C_j}|e_s))\right\}. \quad (8)$$

To evaluate the right-hand side of Equation (8) we need to estimate $p(e_s|e_{C_{\tilde{q}}})$, $p(e_C|e_s)$, and $p(e_{C_j}|e_s)$. To do so, we consider the set of interactions recorded in the search log. Note that $p(e_s|e_{C_{\tilde{q}}})$ is the probability that a user would click the click-set s if he finds the concept $C_{\tilde{q}}$ relevant to his search intent. We estimate this probability by counting the number of interactions in $\mathcal{I}$ that involve some query of the cluster $C_{\tilde{q}}$ (we denote this number by $(NI(C_{\tilde{q}}))$), and the number of those interactions that involve click-set s (denoted by $NI(C_{\tilde{q}}, s)$). We then approximate the probability $p(e_s|e_{C_{\tilde{q}}})$ by the fraction $NI(C_{\tilde{q}}, s)/NI(C_{\tilde{q}})$. Formally,

$$p(e_s|e_{C_{\tilde{q}}}) \approx \frac{NI(C_{\tilde{q}}, s)}{NI(C_{\tilde{q}})} = \frac{|\{(I : q \to s) \in \mathcal{I} \text{ s.t. } q \in C_{\tilde{q}}\}|}{|\{(I : q \to s') \in \mathcal{I} \text{ s.t. } q \in C_{\tilde{q}} \text{ and } s' \in CS\}|}.$$

Similarly, $p(e_{C_j}|e_s)$ is estimated by

$$p(e_{C_j}|e_s) \approx \frac{NI(C_j, s)}{NI(s)} = \frac{|\{(I : q \to s) \in \mathcal{I} \text{ s.t. } q \in C_j\}|}{|\{(I : q' \to s) \in \mathcal{I} \text{ s.t. } q' \in Q\}|}.$$

Note that the computation of all these probabilities can be done offline. With these quantities, the online estimation of $\Delta(Y'_c, C, C_{\tilde{q}})$ can be done efficiently (see Section 5.5.4). Finally, the concept C that gives the largest $\Delta(Y'_c, C, C_{\tilde{q}})$ is added to the set Y'_c. We repeat this process until Y'_c contains m concepts. Algorithm 2 summaries the procedure.

Algorithm 2: Diversified Concept Recommendation

Input: $m, C_{\tilde{q}}, \mathcal{C}$
Output: a concept list $Y_c =< C_1, C_2, \cdots, C_m >$
$\mathcal{X} \leftarrow \mathcal{C} - \{C_{\tilde{q}}\}$; $Y'_c \leftarrow \emptyset$
for $i \leftarrow 1$ **to** m **do**
  $C_i \leftarrow \arg\max_{C \in \mathcal{X}} \Delta(Y'_c, C, C_{\tilde{q}})$
  $Y'_c \leftarrow Y'_c \cup \{C_i\}$
  $\mathcal{X} \leftarrow \mathcal{X} - \{C_i\}$
return Y'_c

With the m concepts selected, the next step of DQR is to pick one representative query from each concept to form the recommendation list Y. We pick representative queries by popularity votes. More specifically, given a concept C, its representative query is the one that is issued by the largest number of distinct users in the search log among all the queries in C. For example, from the search log of Table 1, we see that the query "maps search" has been issued by two distinct users, while the query "maps" has been issued by just one. The former is therefore more popular. Finally, the queries in Y are ranked according to the order in which their corresponding concepts are selected into the set Y'_c, e.g., if a concept is added to Y'_c first, then its representative query will be ranked first in Y.

5. EXPERIMENTS

In this section we present the experimental results for evaluating our DQR method. We first briefly describe the datasets used in Section 5.1. Then we describe five other recommendation methods against which we compare DQR in Section 5.2. In Section 5.3 we compare the recommendations made by the various methods for an example input query to highlight the differences of the methods. Finally, in Section 5.4, we give a comprehensive analysis of the various methods with a user study.

5.1 Data Sets

Our experiments were done on two real datasets: (1) AOL is a search log collected from the *AOL* search engine [17], and (2) SOGOU is the search log of the Chinese search engine *Sogou*[3]. We follow the method employed in [13, 20] to clean the data. This involves: (1) removing non-alpha-numerical characters from query strings except for '.' (dot) and '␣' (space), (2) removing redundant space characters, and (3) removing queries that appear only once in the search log. (These queries are likely typos.) Similarly, we applied the cleaning steps to the SOGOU dataset except that we retain Chinese characters in SOGOU queries. Table 2 shows the statistics of the datasets.

Dataset		$\lvert Q \rvert$	$\lvert D \rvert$	$\lvert U \rvert$	$\lvert R \rvert$
AOL	Raw	10,154,742	1,632,788	657,426	36,389,567
	Cleaned	2,516,156	1,346,752	491,720	16,895,112
SOGOU	Raw	5,630,793	15,951,255	10,679,392	51,537,377
	Cleaned	3,599,539	14,504,373	10,328,952	49,506,111

Table 2: Dataset statistics

5.2 Recommendation Algorithms

Besides our DQR method, we have implemented five other query recommendation methods for the comparison study.

[3]Available at http://www.sogou.com/labs/dl/q-e.html.

[SR (Similarity-based Ranking)] Given an input query $\tilde{q}$, we first find the log query $q_\star \in Q$ whose query string is the most similar to that of $\tilde{q}$. (Since a search log typically consists of a large number of queries, it is very likely that $\tilde{q}$ already exists in Q. This is true especially for frequently asked queries [6, 12, 16]. In this case, $q_\star = \tilde{q}$.) The top m queries $q \in Q - \{q_\star\}$ with the smallest distances $d(q, q_\star)$ (see Equation 3) are put into the recommendation list Y. These queries are sorted in increasing value of $d(q, q_\star)$. SR is purely similarity-based method. It considers recommendation relevancy but does not consider redundancy or diversity.

[MMR (Maximal Marginal Relevance)] The second recommendation method adopts the idea of MMR from [7]. The recommendation set Y is constructed incrementally. Initially, $Y = \emptyset$. Recommended queries are added to Y one at a time. Given a Y that contains some $k < m$ queries, we define the *marginal relevance* score $MR(q)$ of each query $q \in Q - Y$ by

$$MR(q) = \lambda \cdot s(q, q_\star) - (1 - \lambda) \cdot \max_{q' \in Y} s(q, q'), \qquad (9)$$

where $0 \leq \lambda \leq 1$ is a constant parameter[4] and $s(q_i, q_j)$ measures the similarity of two queries q_i and q_j (Equation 3). The MR score thus favors queries that are similar to the input query (represented by $q_\star$) but penalizes those that are similar to some query q' that is already selected and put in Y. The query q that gives the highest $MR(q)$ score is added to Y. The process repeats until Y contains m recommended queries. The queries in Y are sorted according to the order in which they are added to Y. MMR considers both recommendation relevancy and diversity. However, it does not operate at the concept level and does not consider redundancy.

[CACB (Context-Aware Concept-Based Method)] CACB, proposed in [6], is based on search sessions. CACB first scans the search log to identify user search sessions. Queries are considered to be in the same session if they are issued by the same user and their submission times all fall within a small window. (In many studies a window size of about 30 minutes is used.) Moreover, CACB clusters log queries using the one-pass algorithm proposed in [6] (see Section 4.1) to derive query concepts. Given a user search session W, CACB extracts the sequence of queries issued in W. These queries are then mapped to their query concepts to form a concept sequence. For example, let $q_1 \rightarrow q_2 \rightarrow q_3 \rightarrow q_4$ be the query sequence found in a session. This sequence is transformed to $C_1 \rightarrow C_2 \rightarrow C_3 \rightarrow C_4$, where C_i is the concept q_i belongs. If successive concepts in the concept sequence are the same, they are merged. For example, if $C_2 = C_3$, then the concept sequence becomes $C_1 \rightarrow C_2 \rightarrow C_4$.

Given an input query $\tilde{q}$, CACB first finds the concept $C_{\tilde{q}}$ that $\tilde{q}$ belongs. It then selects the top m concepts that follow $C_{\tilde{q}}$ most frequently according to the concept sequences derived from the search log. Finally, the most popular query from each such selected concept is put into the recommendation list Y.

Like DQR, CACB uses query concepts and thus it combats recommendation redundancy. However, it does not consider diversity. Moreover, its one-pass clustering algorithm, as we have explained, may give low-quality result in concept extraction.

[DQR-ND (DQR with No Diversity)] DQR-ND is exactly the same as DQR except that it does not consider diversity. When picking a concept C to be included into the concept set Y_c, DQR-ND maximizes the following objective function:

$$\Delta_{ND}(Y_c', C, C_{\tilde{q}}) = \sum_{s \in CS} p(e_s | e_{C_{\tilde{q}}}) p(e_C | e_s). \qquad (10)$$

[4]In our experiments, we set $\lambda = 0.4$, which gives the best overall performance for MMR over a wide range of λ values we tested.

Comparing Equation 10 with Equation 8, we see that the term $\prod_{C_j \in Y_c'} (1 - p(e_{C_j} | e_s))$ is removed. So, the concepts already selected in Y_c' are not taken into account. We compare the performance of DQR and DQR-ND to evaluate the effectiveness of our probabilistic model in achieving recommendation diversity.

[DQR-OPC (DQR with One Pass Clustering)] DQR-OPC also follows the same framework of DQR except that it extracts query concepts by employing the one-pass clustering algorithm proposed in [6] instead of Algorithm1 we proposed. We compare the performance of DQR and DQR-OPC to evaluate the effectiveness of our clustering algorithm in query concept extraction.

Table 3 summarizes the features of the various methods.

Method	Consider redundancy	Consider diversity	Remarks
SR	✗	✗	No query concepts
MMR	✗	✓	No query concepts
CACB	✓	✗	One-pass clustering
DQR-ND	✓	✗	
DQR-OPC	✓	✓	One-pass clustering
DQR	✓	✓	

Table 3: Features of the recommendation methods

5.3 A Recommendation Example

We illustrate the differences of the recommendation methods by comparing their recommendation lists for the query "yahoo" using the AOL dataset. Table 4 shows the results. In the table, we also show the recommendation made by Google Search[5]. We remark that a direct comparison against Google search is difficult because we do not have Google's log or the details of Google's recommendation algorithm. Nonetheless, Google's recommendation serves as an interesting reference.

The first thing we notice from Table 4 is that many queries recommended by SR and MMR are "typo queries"[6], while there are no typo queries recommended by CACB, DQR-ND, or DQR. The reason is that the latter three methods employ query concept mining and recommend only representative queries from relevant concepts. Since a representative query is the most popular one within its concept, it is unlikely a typo. The list recommended by DQR-OPC also contains some typo queries, showing that the one-pass clustering algorithm is less than perfect in extracting query concepts. The results show the importance of mining query concepts for recommender systems in avoiding typo queries.

Next we observe that queries recommended by SR are all relevant to the input query, but they are all redundant. This shows the weakness of a pure similarity-based recommender that does not perform concept extraction. The list recommended by MMR, which does not operate at the concept level either, also contains redundancy. By properly clustering queries into concepts, the lists recommended by DQR-ND and DQR are redundancy-free. Minor redundancy is also found in the lists of CACB and DQR-OPC, such as "myspace" and "myspace.com"; and "yahoo search engine" and "yahoo search". This shows that the one-pass clustering algorithm sometimes fails to group redundant queries into the same concept.

If we remove redundant queries from MMR's list, MMR's recommendation is quite diverse. For example, the queries "yahoo web messenger", "yahoo maps", "yahoo canada" and "yahoo finance" cover different aspects of "yahoo". This emphasis of diversity, however, could overshoot at times. For example, "play 13" and "minnesotajaycees" do not seem relevant to the input query. CACB

[5]The recommendation made by Google varies with time. The list shown is the one we obtained at the time of writing.

[6]Although we have removed queries that appear only once in the log to remove typo queries, the typo queries shown in Table 4 are quite common and so are not removed by our cleaning procedure.

Rank	SR	MMR	CACB	DQR-ND	DQR-OPC	DQR	Google
1	www yahoo	www yahoo	google	yahoo.com	yahoo.c om	yahoo.com	yahoo login
2	yahoo.con	wwwyahoo.om	myspace	yahoo mail	yahoo.m	yahoo mail	yahoo sign up
3	www yahoo.com	y yahoo	msn	yahoo search	yahoo.c	yahoo groups	yahoo email
4	www.yahoo	yahoo web messenger	ebay	sign in yahoo id	messenger.yahoo.com	yahoo maps	yahoo messenger download
5	www.yahoo.comhttp	play 13	yahoo.com	yahoo maps	mail.yahoo.com	yahoo games	yahoo news
6	www.yahoo com	yahoo maps	hotmail	yahoo groups	yahoomaps.com	yahoo instant messenger	yahoo weather
7	yahoo.comhttp	minnesotajaycees	mapquest	yahoo games	yahoo.com	yahoo finance	yahoo messenger
8	www.yahoo.com	yahoo canada	craigslist	yahoo instant messenger	yahoo search engine	yahoo people search	yahoo groups
9	http yahoo.com	yahoo.com chat rooms	myspace.com	yahoo finance	my yahoo	yahoo dictionary	
10	yahoo.vcom	yahoo finance	ask jeeves	yahoo news	yahoo search	yahoo news	

Table 4: Top 10 queries recommended by the 6 methods for the input query "yahoo"

offers a very interesting list. Most of the recommended queries do not match the user's search intent ("yahoo"). However, those queries point to other interesting sources that are similar to yahoo services. Recall that CACB's objective is to *predict* a user's next query, the recommendation it makes does not necessarily has to be relevant to the user's input query.

DQR's recommendation is very diversified. This diversity is weakened in DQR-ND. For example, "yahoo search" is a key function of "yahoo.com", and "sign in yahoo id" is a step of logging into "yahoo mail". They thus cover the same aspects. By applying Equation 8, DQR considers the concepts that are already in the set Y_c when it adds more concepts to Y_c. This further diversifies the recommendation and allows DQR to replace the query "sign in yahoo id" by, e.g., "yahoo dictionary" in its recommendation.

Google only recommended 8 queries among which we see some redundancy, e.g., "yahoo messenger download" and "yahoo messenger" are similar. This example shows that DQR is able to give a better recommendation despite it was trained with a much smaller search log.

5.4 User Study

To evaluate the performances of the recommendation methods, we carried out a user study using the `AOL` dataset. We invited 12 people to judge the recommendations given by the six methods. We selected 60 test queries from the `AOL` search log that we thought the judges could comprehend. These queries are listed in [1]. We then randomly divided the 12 judges into two groups of 6 each. The 60 test queries were also randomly divided into two groups of 30 queries each. Each group of 6 judges were assigned 30 test queries. For each test query, each judge was presented with the recommendation given by a particular recommendation method. The judges were asked to evaluate the recommendations presented to them. We followed the user study procedure employed in [12] in assigning a set of recommendations to each judge to evaluate. Table 5 shows this assignment. The set of 30 queries were further randomly divided into 6 sets: Query-Set-1 to Query-Set-6, each containing 5 queries. The entry marked with a ► in Table 5, for example, shows that Judge No. 3 was presented with the recommendations given by the MMR method for the queries of Query-Set-6. Note that the judges were not told which methods were used to generate the recommendations. The evaluation assignment (Table 5) ensured that each judge evaluated recommendations that cover all 30 queries and all 6 methods. Also, no judge evaluated more than one recommendation (given by different methods) of the same query. This is purposely done to avoid bias induced by the evaluation order.

	SR	MMR	CACB	DQR-ND	DQR-OPC	DQR
Judge1	QuerySet1	QuerySet2	QuerySet3	QuerySet4	QuerySet5	QuerySet6
Judge2	QuerySet6	QuerySet1	QuerySet2	QuerySet3	QuerySet4	QuerySet5
Judge3	QuerySet5	► QuerySet6	QuerySet1	QuerySet2	QuerySet3	QuerySet4
Judge4	QuerySet4	QuerySet5	QuerySet6	QuerySet1	QuerySet2	QuerySet3
Judge5	QuerySet3	QuerySet4	QuerySet5	QuerySet6	QuerySet1	QuerySet2
Judge6	QuerySet2	QuerySet3	QuerySet4	QuerySet5	QuerySet6	QuerySet1

Table 5: Evaluation assignment

To evaluate a recommendation, a judge was given an evaluation form. Table 6 shows an example. On the form, the judge was shown the test query (e.g., "interview") and a ranked list of 10 recommended queries (e.g., "interview preparation"). For each recommended query, the judge had to label it with a relevancy score: irrelevant (0), partially relevant (1), and relevant (2). Also, for those partially relevant or relevant recommended queries, the judge had to group them so that queries sharing the same search intent are put into the same group. An example evaluation done by a judge is indicated in Table 6 by ✓ marks. For example, the evaluation shows that the judge found four search intents from the recommendation that are relevant to the test query "interview". In particular, the judge regarded the recommended queries "interview questions" and "interview answers" to be of the same search intent.

Query: "interview"	Relevance			Latent Search Intents									
interview preparation	0	1	2✓	I_1✓	I_2	I_3	I_4	I_5	I_6	I_7	I_8	I_9	I_{10}
types of interview	0	1	2✓	I_1	I_2✓	I_3	I_4	I_5	I_6	I_7	I_8	I_9	I_{10}
interview questions	0	1	2✓	I_1	I_2	I_3✓	I_4	I_5	I_6	I_7	I_8	I_9	I_{10}
interview answers	0	1	2✓	I_1	I_2	I_3✓	I_4	I_5	I_6	I_7	I_8	I_9	I_{10}
interview techniques	0	1	2✓	I_1	I_2	I_3	I_4✓	I_5	I_6	I_7	I_8	I_9	I_{10}
interview tips	0	1	2✓	I_1	I_2	I_3	I_4✓	I_5	I_6	I_7	I_8	I_9	I_{10}
interview skills	0	1	2✓	I_1	I_2	I_3	I_4✓	I_5	I_6	I_7	I_8	I_9	I_{10}
job interview tips	0	1	2✓	I_1	I_2	I_3	I_4✓	I_5	I_6	I_7	I_8	I_9	I_{10}
working hours	0✓	1	2	I_1	I_2	I_3	I_4	I_5	I_6	I_7	I_8	I_9	I_{10}
admission	0✓	1	2	I_1	I_2	I_3	I_4	I_5	I_6	I_7	I_8	I_9	I_{10}

Table 6: An example evaluation form

5.5 Results

We compare the quality of the recommendations given by the six methods in terms of *relevancy*, *diversity* and *ranking performance*. The results shown in this section are those for the `AOL` dataset. We have also conducted a similar study on the `SOGOU` dataset. The conclusions drawn for `SOGOU` is very similar to those of `AOL`. Due to space limitation, we report the results on `SOGOU` in [1].

5.5.1 Relevancy Performance

Table 7 shows the statistics of the relevancy scores the methods received. The first three rows show the score label distributions. The row $N_{1,2}$ shows the average number of partially relevant (score 1) or relevant (score 2) recommended queries in an evaluation. (Recall that there are 10 recommended queries on each evaluation form. See Table 6). The row $S_{1,2}$ shows the average score of non-irrelevant recommended queries and the row $S_{0,1,2}$ shows the average score of all the recommended queries.

Relevancy score	SR	MMR	CACB	DQR-ND	DQR-OPC	DQR
0 (irrelevant)	11%	35%	48%	14%	12%	14%
1 (partially relevant)	31%	28%	28%	23%	27%	24%
2 (relevant)	58%	37%	24%	63%	61%	62%
$N_{1,2}$	8.9	6.5	5.2	8.6	8.8	8.6
$S_{1,2}$	1.65	1.57	1.47	1.73	1.70	1.72
$S_{0,1,2}$	1.47	1.02	0.76	1.50	1.50	1.48

Table 7: Relevancy performance

From the results, we see that SR receives very good relevancy scores. In particular, its recommendations contain the least percentage of irrelevant queries (score 0) among all the six methods. This is not surprising because SR only recommends queries that are the most similar to input queries. About 1/3 of MMR's recommended queries are irrelevant, and there are only slightly more than 1/3 of them are considered straightly relevant by the judges. This shows that MMR sacrifices too much relevancy to achieve diversity. The relevancy scores of CACB are even lower. As we have explained, the objective of CACB is to predict the next query a user is likely to issue following his current input query in a user session. Since the search intent of a user could drift over a session, CACB's recommendation does not necessarily have to be relevant to the original input query. This explains CACB's low relevancy scores even though its recommendations are sometimes interesting (Table 4). The relevancy scores of the three DQR methods are very good and are comparable to that of SR. In particular, more than 60% of their recommended queries are rated straightly relevant. These ratings are even better than SR's. The reason is that queries recommended by the DQR-based methods are representatives of query concepts. These representative queries are usually better-worded, more expressive and noise-free. Therefore, it is more likely that the judges found them straightly relevant. Among the three methods, DQR-ND gets slightly more '2' scores (63%). This is because DQR-ND focuses more on similarity than diversity. DQR-OPC has slightly fewer '2' scores (61%) because the one-pass clustering algorithm sometimes gives inferior concept extraction. Overall, the relevancy performance of DQR is very good. For example, on average, 8.6 out of the 10 recommended queries ($N_{1,2}$) DQR made are considered either partially relevant or relevant to the judges.

5.5.2 Diversity Performance

Next, we analyze how well the recommendations made by the various methods cover distinct relevant search intents. Recall that a judge had to group non-irrelevant recommended queries on an evaluation form into distinct search intents. We define the measure *Intent-Coverage@k* (or *IC@k* for short) [23] as the number of search intents so identified among the top k recommended queries on an evaluation form. For example, consider Table 6, we have *IC*@4 equals 3 because three search intents were identified by the judge from the top 4 recommended queries given. Note that irrelevant queries are ignored and *IC@k* is upper-bounded by k. Figure 5 shows the average Intent-Coverage of the recommendations made by the six methods as k varies from 1 to 10.

From the figure, we see that SR has a low intent coverage. Even though most of SR's recommended queries are relevant, they are highly redundant and cover only a few search intents. Although CACB's recommendations tend to cover different aspects, however, they suffer from low relevancy. Therefore, the number of relevant distinct search intents given by CACB is small. This explains its low *IC@k* scores. MMR, which focuses on diversification, has a larger intent coverage than CACB. However, many of its recommended queries are irrelevant, which keeps MMR's *IC@k* scores low. DQR gives the best intent coverage. This shows that the probabilistic model DQR uses in diversifying recommended queries works very well. For example, its score at $k = 10$ shows that on average the 10 recommended queries given by DQR cover 7 distinct relevant search intents. DQR-ND, which does not employ Equation 8 to improve recommendation diversity has lower *IC@k* scores than DQR. Fortunately, DQR-ND uses Algorithm 1 to form query concepts, and selects relevant concepts from which representative queries are obtained to compose recommendation lists. With high-quality concepts formed, representative queries recommended to a user tend to distinguish among themselves. This results in a reasonably good intent coverage. The importance of high-quality query concepts in diversified query recommendation is further reflected by the performance of DQR-OPC. From Figure 5, we see that DQR-OPC has lower *IC@k* scores than those of DQR-ND and DQR. This is because, in some cases, the one-pass clustering algorithm fails to put queries that cover the same search intent into the same cluster. This may result in DQR-OPC recommending representative queries which, although come from different clusters, indeed are covering the same search intent.

5.5.3 Ranking Performance

Next, we analyze how well the methods rank the recommended queries. Intuitively, relevant queries should be ranked higher in the recommendation list. We consider two ranking measures, namely, *Normalized Discounted Cumulative Gain* (NDCG) [5, 14] and *Mean Reciprocal Rank* (MRR) [19]. The *NDCG@k* score is defined as:

$$NDCG@k = Z_k \sum_{i=1}^{k} \frac{(2^{l_i} - 1)}{\log(i+1)}, \tag{11}$$

where l_i is the relevancy score (0, 1, or 2) of the ith-ranked recommended query, and Z_k is a normalization factor so chosen such that the optimal ranking's *NGCG@k* score is 1. Intuitively, the *NDCG@k* score summarizes the relevancy scores of the k highest-ranked recommended queries in such a way that a relevant query contributes more to the score if the query is ranked higher in the commendation list.

Given an input query $\tilde{q}$, let $Y(\tilde{q})$ be a ranked list of recommended queries determined by a recommendation method. We use $rank_j(Y(\tilde{q}))$ to denote the rank of the jth relevant query (score 2) in $Y(\tilde{q})$[7]. For example, if the 1st and 2nd recommended queries in $Y(\tilde{q})$ are not relevant but the 3rd and the 4th are, then $rank_1(Y(\tilde{q})) = 3$ and $rank_2(Y(\tilde{q})) = 4$. (If $Y(\tilde{q})$ contains fewer than j relevant queries, $rank_j(Y(\tilde{q}))$ is defined as ∞.) We extend the MRR score proposed in [19] to the *MRR@h* score, which is defined as:

$$MRR@h = \sum_{j=1}^{h} \frac{1}{rank_j(Y(\tilde{q}))}. \tag{12}$$

Essentially, the *MRR@h* score summarizes the ranks of the first h relevant queries in the recommendation list $Y(\tilde{q})$ — A larger score indicates that the first h relevant queries are ranked higher in the list. Note that *MRR@h* is bounded by $H_h = \sum_{i=1}^{h} 1/i$, which is the h-th harmonic number.

Figures 6 and 7 show the *NDCG@k* and *MRR@h* scores of the recommendation methods. In Figure 7, the optimal values (i.e., H_h) are also shown for reference. From the figures, we see that CACB and MMR give relatively poor ranking performance. This is because many of their recommended queries are not relevant and these queries are sometimes ranked high in the recommendation lists, pushing the relevant ones down the lists. The three DQR-based methods generally give better ranking scores than SR. In particular, their *MRR@h* scores are always higher than those of SR. This is due to the fact that they use query concepts and recommend representative queries. These representative queries give high-quality recommendations which lead to more relevant (score 2) top-ranked recommended queries than SR does. Finally, we see that the ranking scores of DQR-OPC is slightly lower than those of DQR and DQR-ND. This is due to the less-than-perfect clustering achieved by the one-pass algorithm, which occasionally leads

[7]We have also considered counting both partially relevant queries (score 1) and relevant queries (score 2) as well. The conclusion drawn is similar so we skip the details of this alternative.

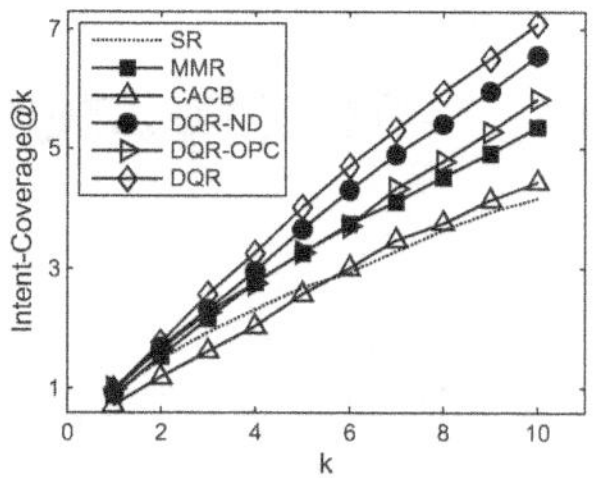

Figure 5: Intent-Coverage

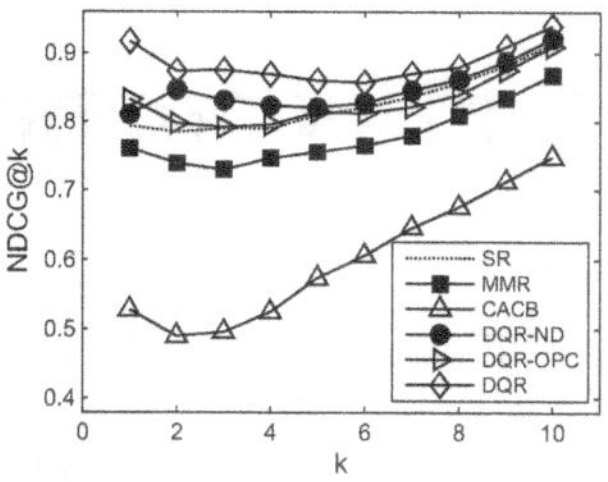

Figure 6: NDCG

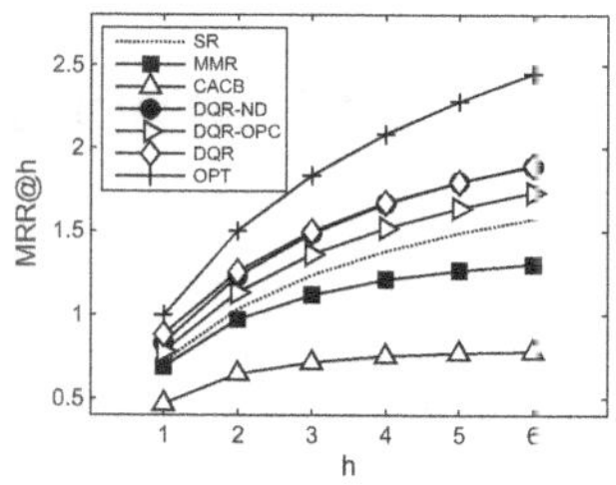

Figure 7: MRR

to the recommendation of irrelevant concepts at the top of the recommendation lists.

5.5.4 *Efficiency*

Recall that the DQR method constructs the selected concept set Y_c incrementally. Specifically, it iterates m times where m is the number of recommended queries, and in each iteration the concept C with the largest $\Delta(Y_c', C, C_{\tilde{q}})$ is picked. To determine $\Delta(Y_c', C, C_{\tilde{q}})$ a sum over the set of all clicked-sets CS is computed (Equation 8). This might sound computationally expensive. Fortunately, the values $p(e_s|e_{C_{\tilde{q}}})$ and $p(e_C|e_s)$ are 0 for most concepts C and click-sets s. An index can be built offline to help DQR identify the few non-zero terms of the summation during online query recommendation. The recommendation can thus be done very efficiently. For example, we tested the efficiency performance of DQR written in Java on a Core 2 Duo 2.83GHz PC. In the experiment, 1000 test queries were randomly picked from the search log as input queries. The maximum and the average processing times were 630ms and 51ms, respectively.

6. CONCLUSIONS

In this paper we investigated the problem of recommending queries to better capture the search intents of search engine users. We identified five important requirements of a query recommendation system, namely, relevancy, redundancy-free, diversity, ranking-performance, and efficiency. We discussed the weaknesses of existing recommendation methods and proposed DQR. DQR mines a search log to extract query concepts based on which recommendations are made. DQR also employs a probabilistic model to achieve recommendation diversification. Through a comprehensive user study, we showed that DQR performed very well w.r.t. a number of measures that cover the five requirements of a recommender system.

Acknowledgments

This project was supported by HKU Research Grant 201011159070. Reynold Cheng was supported by the Research Grants Council of Hong Kong (GRF Project 711309E). We would like to thank the anonymous reviewers for their insightful comments.

7. REFERENCES

[1] `http://www.cs.hku.hk/research/techreps/document/TR-2012-06.pdf`.

[2] R. A. Baeza-Yates, C. A. Hurtado, and M. Mendoza. Query recommendation using query logs in search engines. In *EDBT Workshops*, 2004.

[3] R. Baraglia, C. Castillo, D. Donato, F. M. Nardini, R. Perego, and F. Silvestri. Aging effects on query flow graphs for query suggestion. In *CIKM*, 2009.

[4] D. Beeferman and A. L. Berger. Agglomerative clustering of a search engine query log. In *KDD*, 2000.

[5] C. J. C. Burges, T. Shaked, E. Renshaw, A. Lazier, M. Deeds, N. Hamilton, and G. N. Hullender. Learning to rank using gradient descent. In *ICML*, 2005.

[6] H. Cao, D. Jiang, J. Pei, Q. He, Z. Liao, E. Chen, and H. Li. Context-aware query suggestion by mining click-through and session data. In *KDD*, 2008.

[7] J. G. Carbonell and J. Goldstein. The use of mmr, diversity-based reranking for reordering documents and producing summaries. In *SIGIR*, 1998.

[8] P.-A. Chirita, C. S. Firan, and W. Nejdl. Personalized query expansion for the web. In *SIGIR*, 2007.

[9] S. C. Deerwester, S. T. Dumais, T. K. Landauer, G. W. Furnas, and R. A. Harshman. Indexing by latent semantic analysis. *JASIS*, 41(6), 1990.

[10] H. Deng, I. King, and M. R. Lyu. Entropy-biased models for query representation on the click graph. In *SIGIR*, 2009.

[11] B. M. Fonseca, P. B. Golgher, B. Pôssas, B. A. Ribeiro-Neto, and N. Ziviani. Concept-based interactive query expansion. In *CIKM*, 2005.

[12] J. Guo, X. Cheng, G. Xu, and H. Shen. A structured approach to query recommendation with social annotation data. In *CIKM*, 2010.

[13] J. Guo, X. Cheng, G. Xu, and X. Zhu. Intent-aware query similarity. In *CIKM*, 2011.

[14] K. Järvelin and J. Kekäläinen. Cumulated gain-based evaluation of IR techniques. *ACM Trans. Inf. Syst.*, 20(4), 2002.

[15] H. Ma, M. R. Lyu, and I. King. Diversifying query suggestion results. In *AAAI*, 2010.

[16] Q. Mei, D. Zhou, and K. W. Church. Query suggestion using hitting time. In *CIKM*, 2008.

[17] G. Pass, A. Chowdhury, and C. Torgeson. A picture of search. In *Infoscale*, 2006.

[18] M. Sanderson. Ambiguous queries: test collections need more sense. In *SIGIR*, 2008.

[19] E. M. Voorhees. The TREC-8 question answering track report. In *TREC*, 1999.

[20] X. Wang and C. Zhai. Learn from web search logs to organize search results. In *SIGIR*, 2007.

[21] J.-R. Wen, J.-Y. Nie, and H. Zhang. Clustering user queries of a search engine. In *WWW*, 2001.

[22] T. Zhang, R. Ramakrishnan, and M. Livny. BIRCH: An efficient data clustering method for very large databases. In *SIGMOD Conference*, 1996.

[23] X. Zhu, J. Guo, X. Cheng, P. Du, and H. Shen. A unified framework for recommending diverse and relevant queries. In *WWW*, 2011.

Dynamic Covering for Recommendation Systems

Ioannis Antonellis
oDesk
antonell@cs.stanford.edu

Anish Das Sarma
Google Research
anish.dassarma@gmail.com

Shaddin Dughmi
Microsoft Research
shaddin@gmail.com

ABSTRACT

In this paper, we identify a fundamental algorithmic problem that we term *succinct dynamic covering* (SDC), arising in many modern-day web applications, including ad-serving and online recommendation systems such as in eBay, Netflix, and Amazon. Roughly speaking, SDC applies two restrictions to the well-studied Max-Coverage problem [14]: Given an integer k, $\mathcal{X} = \{1, 2, \ldots, n\}$ and $\mathcal{I} = \{S_1, \ldots, S_m\}$, $S_i \subseteq \mathcal{X}$, find $\mathcal{J} \subseteq \mathcal{I}$, such that $|\mathcal{J}| \leq k$ and $(\bigcup_{S \in \mathcal{J}} S)$ is as large as possible. The two restrictions applied by SDC are: (1) *Dynamic:* At query-time, we are given a *query* $Q \subseteq \mathcal{X}$, and our goal is to find $\mathcal{J}$ such that $Q \bigcap (\bigcup_{S \in \mathcal{J}} S)$ is as large as possible; (2) *Space-constrained:* We don't have enough space to store (and process) the entire input; specifically, we have $o(mn)$, and maybe as little as $O((m+n)polylog(mn))$ space. A solution to SDC maintains a small data structure, and uses this datastructure to answer *most* dynamic queries with high accuracy. We call such a scheme a *Coverage Oracle*.

We present algorithms and complexity results for coverage oracles. We present deterministic and probabilistic near-tight upper and lower bounds on the approximation ratio of SDC as a function of the amount of space available to the oracle. Our lower bound results show that to obtain constant-factor approximations we need $\Omega(mn)$ space. Fortunately, our upper bounds present an explicit tradeoff between space and approximation ratio, allowing us to determine the amount of space needed to guarantee certain accuracy.

Categories and Subject Descriptors

H.0 [**Information Systems**]: General

General Terms

Algorithms

Keywords

dynamic covering, recommendation systems, max-coverage problem

1. INTRODUCTION

The explosion of data and applications on the web over the last decade have given rise to many new data management challenges. This paper identifies a fundamental subproblem inherent in several Web applications, including online recommendation systems, and serving advertisements on webpages. Let us begin with a motivating example.

EXAMPLE 1.1. *Consider the online movie rental and streaming website, Netflix [3], and one of their users Alice. Based on Alice's movie viewing (and rating) history, Netflix would like to recommend new movies to Alice for watching. (Indeed, Netflix threw open a million-dollar challenge on significantly improving their movie recommendations [4].) Conceivably, there are many ways of devising algorithms for recommendation ranging from data mining to machine learning techniques, and indeed there has been a great deal of such work on providing personalized recommendations (see [6] for a survey). Regardless of the specific technique, an important subproblem that arises is finding users "similar" to Alice, i.e., finding users who have independently or in conjunction viewed (and liked) movies seen (and liked) by Alice.*

Abstractly speaking, we are given a universal set *of all Netflix movies, and Netflix users identified by the* subset *of movies they have viewed (and liked or disliked). Given a specific user Alice, we are interested in finding (say k) other users, who together* cover *a large set of Alice's likes and dislikes. Note that for each user, the set of movies that need to be covered is different, and therefore the covering cannot be performed* statically, *independent of the user. In fact, Netflix* dynamically *provides movie recommendations as users rate movies in a particular genre (say comedy), or request movies in specific languages, or time periods. Providing recommendations at interactive speed, based on user queries (such as a particular genre), rules out computationally-expensive processing over the entire Netflix data, which is very large.*[1] *Therefore, we are interested in* approximately *solving the aforementioned covering problem based on a* subset *of the data.*

[1]Netflix currently has over 10 millions users, over 100,000 movies, and obviously some of the popular movies have been viewed by many users, and movie buffs have rated a large number of movies; Netflix owns over 55 million discs.

The main challenge that arises is to statically *identify a* subset *of the data that would provide good approximations to the covering problem for any* dynamic *user query.*

Note that very similar challenges arise in other recommendation systems, e.g., Alice visits an online shopping website like eBay [2] or Amazon [1], and the website is interested in recommending products to her based on her current query for a particular brand or product, and her prior purchasing (and viewing) history.

The example above can be formulated as an instance of a simple algorithmic covering problem, generalizing the NP-hard optimization problem *max k-cover* [14]. The input to this problem is an integer k, a set $\mathcal{X} = \{1, \ldots, n\}$, a family $\mathcal{I} \subseteq 2^{\mathcal{X}}$ of subsets of $\mathcal{X}$, and *query* $Q \subseteq X$. Here $(\mathcal{X}, \mathcal{I})$ is called a *set system*, $\mathcal{X}$ is called the *ground set* of the set-system, and members of $\mathcal{X}$ are called *elements* or *items*. We make no assumptions on how the set system is represented in the input, though the reader can think of the obvious representation by a $n \times m$ bipartite graph for intuition. This $n \times m$ bipartite graph can be stored in $O(nm)$ bits, which is in fact information-theoretically optimal for storing an arbitrary set system on n items and m sets. The objective of the problem is to return $\mathcal{J} \subseteq \mathcal{I}$ with $|\mathcal{J}| \leq k$ that collectively cover as much of Q as possible. Since this problem is a generalization of max k-cover, it is NP-hard. Nevertheless, absent any additional constraints this problem can be approximated in polynomial time by a straightforward adaptation of the greedy algorithm for max k-cover [2], which attains a constant factor $\frac{e}{e-1}$ approximation in $O(mn)$ time [16]. However, we further constrain the problem as follows, rendering new techniques necessary.

From the above example, we identify two properties that we require of any system that solves this covering problem:

1. **Space Constrained:** We need to (statically) preprocess the set system $(\mathcal{X}, \mathcal{I})$ and store a small sketch (much smaller than $O(mn)$), in the form of a *data structure*, and discard the original representation of $(\mathcal{X}, \mathcal{I})$. This can be thought of as a form of lossy compression. We do not require the data structure to take any particular form; it need only be a sequence of bits that allows us to extract information about the original set system $(\mathcal{X}, \mathcal{I})$. For instance, any statistical summary, a subgraph of the bipartite graph representing the set system, or other representation is acceptable.

2. **Dynamic**: The query Q is not known a-priori, but arrives *dynamically*. More precisely: Q arrives *after* the data structure is constructed and the original data discarded. It is at that point that the data structure must be used to compute a solution $\mathcal{J}$ to the covering problem.

We call this covering problem (formalized in the next section) the *Succinct Dynamic Covering* (SDC) problem. Moreover, we call a solution to SDC a *Coverage Oracle*. A coverage oracle consists of a *static stage* that constructs a datastructure, and a *dynamic stage* that uses the datastructure to answer queries.

[2]The greedy algorithm for max k-cover, adapted to our problem, is simple: Find the set in $\mathcal{I}$ covering as many uncovered items in Q as possible, and repeat this k times. This can clearly be implemented in $O(mn)$ time, and has been shown to yield a $e/(e-1)$ approximation.

Next we briefly present another, entirely different, Web application that also needs to confront SDC . In addition, we note that there are several other applications facing similar covering problems, including gene identification [13], searching domain-specific aggregator sites like Yelp [5], topical query decomposition [9], and search-result diversification [10, 12].

EXAMPLE 1.2. *Online advertisers bid on (1) webpages matching relevancy criteria and (2) typically target a certain user demographic. Advertisements are served based on a combination of the two criterion above. When a user visits a particular webpage, there is usually no precise information about the users' demographic, i.e., age, location, interests, gender, etc. Instead, there is a range of possible values for each of these attributes, determined based on the search query the user issued or session information. Ad-servers therefore attempt to pick a set of advertisements that would be of interest (i.e., "cover") a large number of users; the user demographic that needs to be covered is determined by the page on which the advertisement is being placed, the user query, and session information. Therefore, ad-serving is faced with the SDC problem. The space constraint arises because the set system consisting of all webpages, and each user identified by the set of webpages visited by the user is prohibitively large to store in memory and process in real-time for every single page view. The dynamic aspect arises because each user view of each page is associated with a different user demographic that needs to be covered.*

1.1 Contributions and Outline

Next we outline the main contributions of this paper.

- In Section 3 we formally define the succinct dynamic covering (SDC) problem, and summarize our results.
- In Section 4 we present a randomized coverage oracle for SDC . The oracle is presented as a function of the available space, thus allowing us to tradeoff space for accuracy based on the specific application. Unfortunately, the approximation ratio of this oracle degrades rapidly as space decreases; However, the next section shows that this is in fact unavoidable.
- In Section 5 we present a lowerbound on the best possible approximation attainable as a function of the space allowed for the datastructure. This lowerbound essentially matches the upperbound of Section 4, though with the caveat that the lowerbound is for oracles that do not use randomization. We expect the lowerbound to hold more generally for randomized oracles, though we leave this as an open question.

Related work is presented next, and future directions are presented in Section 6. To maintain the flow of the paper, we defer some of the longer proofs of our results to Appendix A, with brief sketches appearing in the main body of the paper.

2. RELATED WORK

Our study of the tradeoff between space and approximation ratio is in the spirit of the work of Thorup and Zwick [19] on *distance oracles*. They considered the problem of compressing a graph G into a small datastructure, in such a way that the datastructure can be used to approximately answer queries for the distance between pairs of nodes in G. Similar to our results, they showed matching upper and lower bounds on the space needed for compressing the graph subject to preserving a certain approximation ratio. Moreover, similarly to our upperbounds for SDC, their distance oracles benefit from a speedup at query time as approximation ratio is sacrificed for space.

Previous work has studied the set cover problem under streaming models. One model studied in [8, 15] assumes that the sets are known in advance, only elements arrive online, and, the algorithms do not know in advance which subset of elements will arrive. An alternative model assumes that elements are known in advance and sets arrive in a streaming fashion [18]. Our work differs from these works in that SDC operates under a storage budget, so all sets cannot be stored; moreover, SDC needs to provide a good cover for *all* possible dynamic query inputs.

Another related area is that of nearest neighbor search. It is easy to see that the SDC problem with $k = 1$ corresponds to nearest neighbor search using the dot product similarity measure, i.e., $sim_{dot}(x, y) = \frac{dot(x,y)}{n}$. However, following from a result from Charikar [11], there exists no locality sensitive hash function family for the dot product similarity function. Thus, there is no hope that signature schemes (like minhashing for the Jaccard distance) can be used for SDC .

3. SDC

We start by defining the succinct dynamic covering (SDC) problem in Section 3.1. Then, in Section 3.2 we summarize the main technical results achieved by this paper.

3.1 Problem Definition

We now formally define the SDC problem.

DEFINITION 3.1 (SDC). *Given an offline input consisting of a set system $(\mathcal{X}, \mathcal{I})$ with n* elements *(a.k.a* items*) $\mathcal{X}$ and m* sets *$\mathcal{I}$, and an integer $k \geq 1$, devise a* coverage oracle *such that given a dynamic* query *$Q \subseteq \mathcal{X}$, the oracle finds a $\mathcal{J} \subseteq \mathcal{I}$ such that $|\mathcal{J}| \leq k$ and $(\bigcup_{S \in \mathcal{J}} S) \bigcap Q$ is as large as possible.*

DEFINITION 3.2 (COVERAGE ORACLE). *A* Coverage Oracle *for SDC consists of two stages:*

1. **Static Stage:** *Given integers m,n,k, and set system $(\mathcal{X}, \mathcal{I})$ with $|\mathcal{X}| = n$ and $|\mathcal{I}| = m$, build a datastructure $\mathcal{D}$.*
2. **Dynamic Stage:** *Given a dynamic* query *$Q \subseteq \mathcal{X}$, use $\mathcal{D}$ to return $\mathcal{J} \subseteq \mathcal{I}$ with $|\mathcal{J}| \leq k$ as a solution to SDC.*

Note that our two constraints on a solution for SDC are illustrated by the two stages above. (1) We are interested in building an offline data structure $\mathcal{D}$, and only use $\mathcal{D}$ to answer queries. Typically, we want to maintain a *small* data structure, certainly $o(mn)$, and maybe as little as $O((m + n)polylog(mn))$ or even $O(m + n)$. Therefore, we cannot store the entire set system. (2) Unlike the traditional max-coverage problem where the entire set of elements $\mathcal{X}$ need to be covered, in SDC we are given queries dynamically. Therefore, we want a coverage oracle that returns good solutions for all queries.

Given the space limitation of SDC, we cannot hope to exactly solve SDC (for all dynamic input queries). The goal of this paper is to explore *approximate* solutions for SDC, given a specific space constraint on the offline data structure $\mathcal{D}$. We define the *approximation ratio* of an oracle as the worst-case, taken over all inputs, of the ratio between the coverage of Q by the optimal solution and the coverage of Q by the output of the oracle. We allow the approximation ratio to be a function of n, m, and k, and denote it by $\alpha(n, m, k)$.

More precisely, given a coverage oracle $\mathcal{A}$, if on inputs $k, \mathcal{X}, \mathcal{I}, Q$ (where implicitly $n = |\mathcal{X}|$ and $m = |\mathcal{I}|$) the oracle $\mathcal{A}$ returns $\mathcal{J} \subseteq \mathcal{I}$, we denote the size of the coverage as $\mathcal{A}(k, \mathcal{X}, \mathcal{I}, Q) := |(\bigcup_{S \in \mathcal{J}} S) \bigcap Q|$. Similarly, we denote the coverage of the optimal solution by $OPT(k, \mathcal{X}, \mathcal{I}, Q) := \max\{|(\bigcup_{S \in \mathcal{J}^*} S) \bigcap Q| : \mathcal{J}^* \subseteq \mathcal{I}, |\mathcal{J}^*| \leq k\}$. We then express the *approximation ratio* $\alpha(n, m, k)$ as follows.

$$\alpha(n, m, k) = \max \frac{OPT(k, \mathcal{X}, \mathcal{I}, Q)}{\mathcal{A}(k, \mathcal{X}, \mathcal{I}, Q)}$$

Where the maximum above is taken over set systems $(\mathcal{X}, \mathcal{I})$ with $|\mathcal{X}| = n$ and $|\mathcal{I}| = m$, and queries $Q \subseteq \mathcal{X}$.

We will also be concerned with *randomized* coverage oracles. Note that, when we devise randomized coverage oracle, we use randomization only in the static stage; i.e. in the construction of the datastructure. We then let the *expected approximation ratio* be the worst case *expected* performance of the oracle as compared to the optimal solution.

$$\alpha(n, m, k) = \max \left(\mathbf{E} \left[\frac{OPT(k, \mathcal{X}, \mathcal{I}, Q)}{\mathcal{A}(k, \mathcal{X}, \mathcal{I}, Q)} \right] \right) \quad (1)$$

The expectation in the above expression is over the random coins flipped by the static stage of the oracle, and the maximization is over $\mathcal{X}, \mathcal{I}, Q$ as before. We elaborate on this benchmark in Section 4.

We study the space-approximation tradeoff; i.e., how the (expected) approximation ratio improves as the amount of space allowed for $\mathcal{D}$ is increased. In our lowerbounds, we are not specifically concerned with the time taken to compute the datastructure or answer queries. Therefore, our lowerbounds are purely *information-theoretic*: we calculate the amount of information we are required to store if we are to guarantee a specific approximation ratio, independent of computational concerns. Our lowerbounds are particularly novel and striking in that *they assume nothing* about the datastructure, which may be an arbitrary sequence of bits. We establish our lowerbounds via a novel application of the probabilistic method that may be of independent interest.

Even though we focus on space vs approximation, and not on runtime, fortunately the coverage oracles in our upperbounds can be implemented efficiently (both static and dynamic stage). Moreover, using our upperbounds to trade approximation for space yields, as a side-effect, an improvement in runtime when answering a query. In particular, observe that if no sparsification of the data is done up-front, then answering each query using the standard greedy approximation algorithm for max k-cover [16] takes $O(mn)$ time. Our oracles, presented in Section 4, spends $O(mn)$ time up-front building a data structure of size $O(b)$, where b is a parameter of the oracle between n and nm. In the dynamic stage, however, answering a query now takes $O(b)$, since we use the greedy algorithm for max k-cover on a "sparse" set system. Therefore, the dynamic stage becomes

Table 1: Summary of SDC results giving the approximation-ratio, space constraint on coverage oracle, and whether the nature of the bound: upper bound (UB) or lower bound (LB) and deterministic (Det.) or randomized (Rand.)

Approximation Ratio	Storage	Bound
$O\left(\min\left(\frac{m}{k}, \sqrt{\frac{n}{k}}\right)\right)$	$\widetilde{O}(n)$	Det. UB
$O\left(\min\left(\frac{m^\epsilon}{\sqrt{k}}, \sqrt{\frac{n}{k}}\right)\right)$	$\widetilde{O}(nm^{1-2\epsilon})$	Rand. UB
$\Omega\left(\min\left(\frac{m^{\epsilon-\delta_1}}{k\sqrt{k}}, \frac{n^{1/2-\delta_2}}{k\sqrt{k}}\right)\right)$	$\widetilde{O}(nm^{1-2\epsilon})$	Det. LB

faster as we decrease size of the data structure. In fact, this increase in speed is not restricted to an algorithmic speedup as described above. It is likely that there will also be speedup due to architectural reasons, since a smaller amount of data needs to be kept in memory. Therefore, trading off approximation for space yields an incidental speedup in runtime which bodes well for the dynamic nature of the queries.

3.2 Summary of results

Table 1 summarizes the main results obtained in this paper for SDC input with n elements, m sets, and integer $k \geq 1$. The lower bound in the table is for any nonnegative constants δ_1, δ_2 not both 0, and the randomized upperbound is parameterized by ϵ with $0 \leq \epsilon \leq 1/2$. The upper and lower bounds are developed in Sections 4 and 5 respectively.

4. UPPER BOUNDS

In this section, we show a coverage oracle that trades off space and approximation ratio. We designate a trade-off parameter ϵ, where $0 \leq \epsilon \leq 1/2$. For any such ϵ, we get an $O\left(\frac{\min(m^\epsilon, \sqrt{n})}{\sqrt{k}}\right)$-approximate coverage oracle that stores $\widetilde{O}(nm^{1-2\epsilon})$ bits. Therefore, setting a small value of ϵ achieves a better approximation ratio, at the expense of storage space. As is common practice, we use $\widetilde{O}()$ to denote suppressing polylogarithmic factors in n and m; this is reasonable when the guarantees are super-polylogarithmic, as is the case here.

The oracle we show is randomized, in the sense that the static stage flips some random coins. The datastructure constructed is a random variable in the internal coin flips of the static stage of the oracle. We measure the *expected approximation ratio* (a.k.a approximation ratio, when clear from context) of the oracle, as defined in Equation (1). For every fixed query Q independent of the random coins used in constructing the datastructure, this ratio is attained in expectation. In other words, our adversarial model is that of an *oblivious adversary*: someone trying to fool our oracle may choose any query they like, but their choice cannot depend on knowledge of the random choices made in constructing the datastructure.

In Section 5 we will see that our oracle attains a space-approximation tradeoff that is essentially optimal when compared with oracles that are deterministic. In other words, no deterministic oracle can do substantially better. We leave open the questions of whether a better randomized oracle is possible, and whether an equally good deterministic oracle exists.

4.1 Main Result and Roadmap

The following theorem states the main result of this section.

THEOREM 4.1. *For every ϵ with $0 \leq \epsilon \leq 1/2$, there is a randomized coverage oracle for SDC that achieves an $O\left(\frac{\min(m^\epsilon, \sqrt{n})}{\sqrt{k}}\right)$ approximation and stores $\widetilde{O}(nm^{1-2\epsilon})$ bits.*

The remainder of this section, leading up to the above result, is organized as follows. Before proving Theorem 4.1, to build intuition we show in Section 4.2 (Remark 4.2) a much simpler deterministic oracle, with a much weaker approximation guarantee. Then, we prove Theorem 4.1 in two parts. First, in Section 4.3, we show a randomized coverage oracle that stores $\widetilde{O}(nm^{1-2\epsilon})$ bits and achieves an $O(m^\epsilon/\sqrt{k})$ approximation in expectation. Then, in Section 4.4, we show a deterministic oracle that achieves a $O(\sqrt{n}/\sqrt{k})$ approximation and stores $\widetilde{O}(n)$ bits. Combining the two oracles into one in the obvious way yields Theorem 4.1.

4.2 Simple Deterministic Oracle

REMARK 4.2. *There is a simple deterministic oracle that attains a m/k approximation with $\widetilde{O}(n)$ space. The static stage proceeds as follows: Given set system $(\mathcal{X}, \mathcal{I})$, for each $i \in \mathcal{X}$ we "remember" one set $S \in \mathcal{I}$ with $i \in S$ (breaking ties arbitrarily). In other words, for each $S \in \mathcal{I}$ we define $\widehat{S} \subseteq S$ such that $\left\{\widehat{S} : S \in \mathcal{I}\right\}$ is a partition of $\mathcal{X}$. We then store the "sparsified" set system $\left(\mathcal{X}, \widehat{\mathcal{I}} = \left\{\widehat{S} : S \in \mathcal{I}\right\}\right)$. It is clear that this can be done in linear time by a trivial greedy algorithm. Moreover, $(\mathcal{X}, \widehat{\mathcal{I}})$ can be stored in $\widetilde{O}(n)$ space as a $n \times m$ bipartite graph with n edges.*

The dynamic stage is straightforward: given a query Q, we simply return the indices of the k sets in $\widehat{\mathcal{I}}$ that collectively cover as much of Q as possible. It is clear that this gives a m/k approximation. Moreover, since $\widehat{\mathcal{I}}$ is a partition of $\mathcal{X}$, it can be accomplished by a trivial greedy algorithm in polynomial time.

Next we use randomization to show a much better, and much more involved, upperbound that trades off approximation and space.

4.3 An $O(m^\epsilon/\sqrt{k})$ Approximation with $\widetilde{O}(nm^{1-2\epsilon})$ Space

Consider the set system $(\mathcal{X}, \mathcal{I})$, where $\mathcal{X}$ is the set of items and $\mathcal{I}$ is the family of sets. We assume without loss that each item is in some set. We define a randomized oracle for building a datastructure, which is a "sparsified" version of $(\mathcal{X}, \mathcal{I})$. Namely, for every $S \in \mathcal{I}$ we define $\widehat{S} \subseteq S$, and store the set system $\left(\mathcal{X}, \widehat{\mathcal{I}} = \left\{\widehat{S}\right\}_{S \in \mathcal{I}}\right)$. We require that $(\mathcal{X}, \widehat{\mathcal{I}})$ can be stored in $\widetilde{O}(nm^{1-2\epsilon})$ space. We construct the datastructure in two stages, as follows.

- Label all items in $\mathcal{X}$ "uncovered" and all sets in $\mathcal{I}$ "unchosen"
- Stage 1: While there exists an unchosen set $S \in \mathcal{I}$ containing at least $\frac{n}{m^\epsilon \sqrt{k}}$ uncovered items
  - Let $\widehat{S}$ be the set of uncovered items in S.

- Relabel all items in $\widehat{S}$ as "covered" and "significant"
- Relabel S as "chosen" and "significant"

- Stage 2: For every remaining "unchosen" set S
  - Choose $\frac{n}{m^{2\epsilon}}$ "uncovered" items $\widehat{S} \subseteq S$ uniformly at random from the uncovered items in S (if fewer than $\frac{n}{m^{2\epsilon}}$ such items, then let $\widehat{S}$ be all of them).
  - Relabel each item in $\widehat{S}$ as "covered" and "insignificant"
  - Relabel S as "chosen" and "insignificant"
- Label every uncovered item as "uncovered" and "insignificant"

When presented with a query $Q \subseteq \mathcal{X}$, we use the stored datastructure $(\mathcal{X}, \widehat{\mathcal{I}})$ in the obvious way: namely, we find $\widehat{S_1}, \ldots, \widehat{S_k} \in \widehat{\mathcal{I}}$ maximizing $|(\bigcup_{i=1}^k \widehat{S_i}) \bigcap Q|$, and return the name of the corresponding original sets $S_1, \ldots, S_k$. However, this problem cannot be solved exactly in polynomial time in general. Nevertheless, we can instead use the greedy algorithm for max-k-cover to get a constant-factor approximation [16]; this will not affect our asymptotic guarantee on the approximation ratio. The following two lemmas complete the proof that the above oracle achieves an $O(m^\epsilon/\sqrt{k})$ approximation with $\widetilde{O}(nm^{1-2\epsilon})$ space.

LEMMA 4.3. *The datastructure $(\mathcal{X}, \widehat{\mathcal{I}})$ can be stored using $\widetilde{O}(nm^{1-2\epsilon})$ bits.*

The proof of the above lemma, appearing in Appendix A.1, shows that $(\mathcal{X}, \widehat{\mathcal{I}})$ can be stored as a bipartite graph with a small number of edges, by accounting for the edges created in each stage of our algorithm.

LEMMA 4.4. *For every query Q, the oracle returns sets $S_1, \ldots, S_k$ such that*

$$\mathbf{E}[|(\bigcup_{i=1}^{k} S_i) \bigcap Q|] \geq \frac{|(\bigcup_{i=1}^k S_i^*) \bigcap Q|}{O(m^\epsilon/\sqrt{k})}$$

for any $S_1^*, \ldots, S_k^* \in \mathcal{I}$.

Note that $S_1, \ldots, S_k$ are random variables in the internal coin-flips of the static stage that constructs the datastructure. The expectation in the statement of the lemma is over these random coins. The proof of the lemma, appearing in Appendix A.1, distinguishes two cases depending on whether the majority of the items covered by the optimal solution appears in significant or insignificant sets.

4.4 An $O(\sqrt{n/k})$ Approximation with $\widetilde{O}(n)$ Space

This coverage oracle is similar to the one in the previous section, though is much simpler. Moreover, it is deterministic. Indeed, we construct the datastructure by the following greedy algorithm that resembles the greedy algorithm for max-k-cover

- Label all items in $\mathcal{X}$ "uncovered" and all sets in $\mathcal{I}$ "unchosen"
- While there are unchosen sets
  - Find the unchosen set $S \in \mathcal{I}$ containing the most uncovered items
  - Let $\widehat{S}$ be the set of uncovered items in S.
  - Relabel all items in $\widehat{S}$ as "covered"
  - Relabel S as "chosen"

Observe that $\widehat{\mathcal{I}}$ is a partition of $\mathcal{X}$. When presented with a query $Q \subseteq \mathcal{X}$, we use the datastructure $(\mathcal{X}, \widehat{\mathcal{I}} = \{\widehat{S} : S \in \mathcal{I}\})$ in the obvious way. Namely, we find the sets $\widehat{S_1}, \ldots, \widehat{S_k} \in \widehat{\mathcal{I}}$ maximizing $|(\bigcup_{i=1}^k \widehat{S_i}) \bigcap Q|$, and output the corresponding non-sparse sets $S_1, \ldots, S_k$. This can easily be done in polynomial time by using the obvious greedy algorithm, since $\widehat{\mathcal{I}}$ is a partition of $\mathcal{X}$.

Note that the oracle described above is very similar to the oracle from Section 4.2: The dynamic stage is identical. The static stage, however, needs to build the partition using a specific greedy ordering – as opposed to the arbitrary ordering used in Section 4.2. The following two Lemmas complete the proof that the oracle achieves an $O(\sqrt{n/k})$ approximation with $\widetilde{O}(n)$ space.

LEMMA 4.5. *The datastructure $(\mathcal{X}, \widehat{\mathcal{I}})$ can be stored using $\widetilde{O}(n)$ bits*

PROOF. Observe that each item is contained in exactly one $\widehat{S} \in \widehat{\mathcal{I}}$. Therefore, the bipartite graph representing the set system $(\mathcal{X}, \widehat{\mathcal{I}})$ has at most n edges. This establishes the Lemma. □

LEMMA 4.6. *For every query Q, the oracle returns sets $S_1, \ldots, S_k$ with*

$$|(\bigcup_{i=1}^{k} S_i) \bigcap Q| \geq \frac{|(\bigcup_{i=1}^k S_i^*) \bigcap Q|}{O(\sqrt{n/k})}$$

for any $S_1^*, \ldots, S_k^* \in \mathcal{I}$.

The full proof of the lemma, appearing in Appendix A.1, considers two cases based on whether the majority of the elements covered by an optimal choice are in big or small sets.

5. LOWER BOUNDS

This section develops lower bounds for the SDC problem. We consider deterministic oracles that store a datastructure of size $b(n, m, k)$ for set systems with n items, m sets, maximum number of allowed sets k. Moreover, we assume that $n \leq b(n, m, k) \leq nm$, since no nontrivial positive result is possible when $b(n, m, k) = o(n)$, and a perfect approximation ratio of 1 is possible when $b(n, m, k) = \Omega(nm)$.

5.1 Main Result and Roadmap

The main result of this section is stated in the following theorem, which says that our randomized oracle in the previous section achieves a space-approximation tradeoff that essentially matches the best possible for any deterministic oracle.

THEOREM 5.1. *Consider any deterministic oracle that stores a datastructure of size at most $b(n, m, k)$ bits, where $n \leq b(n, m, k) \leq nm$. Let $\epsilon(n, m, k)$ be such that $b(n, m, k) =$*

$nm^{1-2\epsilon(n,m,k)}$. *When* $m^{\epsilon(n,m,k)} \le \sqrt{n}$, *the oracle does not attain an approximation ratio of* $O(\frac{m^{\epsilon(n,m,k)-\delta}}{k\sqrt{k}})$ *for any constant* $\delta > 0$. *Moreover, when* $\sqrt{n} \le m^{\epsilon(n,m,k)}$ *the oracle does not attain an approximation ratio of* $O(\frac{n^{1/2-\delta}}{k\sqrt{k}})$ *for any* $\delta > 0$.

The proof of the theorem above is somewhat involved. Therefore, to simplify the presentation we prove in Section 5.2 a slight simplification of Theorem 5.1 that captures all the main ideas: Our simplification sets $k = 1$, and proves the $O(\frac{m^{\epsilon(n,m,k)-\delta}}{k\sqrt{k}})$ approximation ratio, for $m^{\epsilon(n,m,k)} \le \sqrt{n}$. Then, in Section 5.3 we prove the approximation ratio for the case of $\sqrt{n} \le m^{\epsilon(n,m,k)}$, still maintaining $k = 1$. Finally, in Section 5.4, we demonstrate how to modify our proofs for any k, yielding Theorem 5.1.

We fix $\delta > 0$. For the remainder of the section, we use b and ϵ as shorthand for $b(n,m,k)$ and $\epsilon(n,m,k)$, respectively. We let $\alpha(n,m,k)$ be the approximation ratio of the oracle, and use α as shorthand. Observe that $0 \le \epsilon \le 1/2$.

5.2 Proof of a Simpler Lowerbound

We simplify Theorem 5.1 by assuming $k = 1$ and $m^{\epsilon} \le \sqrt{n}$. The result is the following proposition, stated using the shorthand notation described above.

PROPOSITION 5.2. *Fix* $k = 1$ *and parameter* ϵ *with* $0 \le \epsilon \le 1/2$. *Assume* $m^{\epsilon} \le \sqrt{n}$. *Consider any deterministic oracle that stores a datastructure of size at most* $b = nm^{1-2\epsilon}$ *bits. The oracle does not attain an approximation ratio of* $O(m^{\epsilon-\delta})$ *for any constant* $\delta > 0$.

We assume the approximation ratio α attained by the oracle is $O(m^{\epsilon-\delta})$ and derive a contradiction. The proof uses the probabilistic method (see [7]). We begin by defining a distribution on set systems, and then go on to show that this distribution "fools" a small coverage oracle with positive probability.

5.2.1 Defining a Distribution D on Set Systems

We will show that there is a set system $(\mathcal{X}, \mathcal{I})$ and a query Q that forces the algorithm to output a set $S \in \mathcal{I}$ that is not within α from optimal. We use the probabilistic method. Namely, we exhibit a distribution D over set systems $(\mathcal{X}, \mathcal{I})$ such that, for every deterministic oracle storing a datastructure of size b, there exists with non-zero probability a query Q for which the oracle outputs a set of approximation worse than α. To show this, we draw two set systems i.i.d from D, and show that with non-zero probability both the following hold: the two set systems are not distinguished by the coverage oracle, and moreover there exists a query Q that requires that the algorithm return different answers for the two set systems for a $O(m^{\epsilon-\delta})$ approximation.

We define D as follows. Given the ground set $\mathcal{X} = \{1,\ldots,n\}$, we let $\mathcal{I} = \{A_i\}_{i=1}^m$ and draw $A_1,\ldots,A_m$ i.i.d as follows: We let A_i be a subset of $\mathcal{X}$ of size $nm^{-\epsilon}$ drawn uniformly at random.

5.2.2 Sampling twice from D and collisions

Next, we draw two set systems $(\mathcal{X}, \mathcal{I} = \{A_i\}_{i=1}^m)$ and $(\mathcal{X}, \mathcal{I}' = \{A'_i\}_{i=1}^m)$ i.i.d from D, as discussed above. First, we lowerbound the probability that $(\mathcal{X}, \mathcal{I})$ and $(\mathcal{X}, \mathcal{I}')$ are not distinguished by the coverage oracle. We call such an occurence a "Collision". The following result, proved in Appendix A.2, lower bounds the probability of a collision.

LEMMA 5.3. *The probability that the same datastructure is stored for* $(\mathcal{X}, \mathcal{I})$ *and* $(\mathcal{X}, \mathcal{I}')$ *is at least* 2^{-b}.

5.2.3 Fooling Queries and Candidates

Next, we lowerbound the probability that a query Q exists requiring two different answers for $(\mathcal{X}, \mathcal{I})$ and $(\mathcal{X}, \mathcal{I}')$ in order to get the desired $\alpha = O(m^{\epsilon-\delta})$ approximation. We call such a query Q a *fooling query*. We define a set of queries that are "candidates" for being a fooling query: A set $Q \subseteq \mathcal{X}$ is called a *candidate query* if $Q = A_i \bigcup A'_{i'}$ for some $i \ne i'$. In other words, a query is a candidate if it is the union of a set from $(\mathcal{X}, \mathcal{I})$ and a set from $(\mathcal{X}, \mathcal{I}')$ with different indices.

Ideally, candidate $Q = A_i \bigcup A'_{i'}$ would be a fooling query by forcing the oracle to output i for $(\mathcal{X}, \mathcal{I})$ and i' for $(\mathcal{X}, \mathcal{I}')$ in order to guarantee the desired approximation. However, this need not be the case: consider for instance the case when, for some $j \ne i, i'$, both A_j and A'_j have large intersection with Q, making it ok to output j for both. We will show that the probability that none of the candidate queries is a fooling query is strictly less than 2^{-b} when n and m are sufficiently large. Doing so would complete the proof: collision occurs with probability $\ge 2^{-b}$, and a fooling query exists with probability $> 1 - 2^{-b}$, and therefore both occur simultaneously with positive probability. This would yield the desired contradiction.

5.2.4 The Probability that None of the Candidates is Fooling is Small

We now upperbound the probability that none of the candidates is a fooling query. Observe that if candidate $Q = A_i \bigcup A'_{i'}$ is not a fooling query, then there exists $A \in \mathcal{I} \bigcup \mathcal{I}' \setminus \{A_i, A'_{i'}\}$ with $|A \bigcap Q| \ge nm^{-\epsilon}/\alpha$. Therefore one of the following must be true:

1. There exists $A \in \mathcal{I} \bigcup \mathcal{I}' \setminus \{A_i, A'_{i'}\}$ with $|A \bigcap A_i| \ge nm^{-\epsilon}/2\alpha = \Omega(nm^{-2\epsilon+\delta})$.

2. There exists $A \in \mathcal{I} \bigcup \mathcal{I}' \setminus \{A_i, A'_{i'}\}$ with $|A \bigcap A'_{i'}| \ge nm^{-\epsilon}/2\alpha = \Omega(nm^{-2\epsilon+\delta})$.

Therefore, if none of the candidates were fooling queries, then there are many "pairs" of sets in $\mathcal{I} \bigcup \mathcal{I}'$ that have an intersection substantially larger than the expected size of $nm^{-2\epsilon}$. This seems very unlikely. Indeed, the remainder of this proof will demonstrate just that.

If none of the candidates are fooling queries, then by examining (1) and (2) above we deduce the following. There exists [3] a set of pairs $P \subseteq (\mathcal{I} \bigcup \mathcal{I}') \times (\mathcal{I} \bigcup \mathcal{I}')$ such that:

1. $|P| \ge m - 2 = \Omega(m)$

2. The undirected graph with nodes $\mathcal{I} \bigcup \mathcal{I}'$ and edges P is bipartite. Moreover, every node in the left part has degree at most 1. Thus P is acyclic.

[3]Consider constructing P as follows: For candidate query $Q = A_1 \bigcup A'_2$, find the set in $\mathcal{I} \bigcup \mathcal{I}' \setminus \{A_1, A'_2\}$ with a large intersection with one of A_1 or A'_2 as in (1) or (2). Say for instance we find that A_7 has a large intersection with A_1. We include (A_1, A_7) in P, mark both A_1 and A_7 as "touched", and designate A_1 a "left" node and A_7 a "right" node. Then, we repeat the process with some candidate $Q' = A_i \bigcup A'_{i'}$ for some "untouched" A_i and $A'_{i'}$. We keep repeating until there are no such candidates. Throughout this greedy process, we mark at most two members of $\mathcal{I} \bigcup \mathcal{I}'$ as "touched" for every pair we include in P. Note that some A_i may be "touched" more than once. As long as there are at least 2 untouched sets in each of $\mathcal{I}$ and $\mathcal{I}'$, the algorithm may continue.

3. If $(B,C) \in P$ then $|B \bigcap C| \geq \Omega(nm^{-2\epsilon+\delta})$

We now proceed to bound the probability of existence of such a P, and in the process also bound the probability that none of the candidate queries are fooling. Recall that members of $\mathcal{I} \bigcup \mathcal{I}'$ are drawn i.i.d from the uniform distribution on subsets of $\mathcal{X}$ of size $nm^{-\epsilon}$. For every pair $(B,C) \in \mathcal{I} \bigcup \mathcal{I}'$, we let $\mathcal{R}(B,C) = |B \bigcap C|$ denote the size of their intersection. It is easy to see the random variables $\{\mathcal{R}(B,C)\}_{B,C \in \mathcal{I} \bigcup \mathcal{I}'}$ are pairwise independent. Therefore, any acyclic set of pairs is mutually independent, by basic probability theory. Thus, if we fix a particular P satisfying (1) and (2), the probability that P satisfies condition (3) is at most

$$\prod_{(B,C)\in P} \mathbf{Pr}[\mathcal{R}(B,C) \geq \Omega(nm^{-2\epsilon+\delta})]$$

We now want to estimate the probability that the intersection of B and C is a factor $\Omega(m^{\delta})$ more than its expectation of $nm^{-2\epsilon}$. Therefore, we consider an indicator random variable Y_i for each $i \in \mathcal{X}$, designating wheter $i \in B \cap C$. If Y_i were independent, we could use Chernoff bounds to bound the probability that $\mathcal{R}(B,C)$ is large. Fortunately, it is easy to see that the Y_i's are negatively-correlated: i.e., for any $L \subseteq \{1,\ldots,n\}$, we have $\mathbf{Pr}[\bigwedge_{i\in L} Y_i = 1] \leq \prod_{i \in L} \mathbf{Pr}[Y_i = 1]$. Therefore, by the result of [17], if we "pretend" that they are independent by approximating their joint-distribution by i.i.d bernoulli random variables, we can still use Chernoff Bounds to bound the upper-tail probability. Therefore, using Chernoff bounds[4] we deduce that the probability that the intersection of B and C is a factor $\Omega(m^{\delta})$ more than the expectation of $nm^{-2\epsilon}$ is at most $2^{-(\Omega(m^{\delta})-1)nm^{-2\epsilon}} \leq 2^{-\Omega(nm^{-2\epsilon+\delta})}$. Therefore, the probability that the fixed P satisfies condition (3) is at most

$$\prod_{(B,C)\in P} 2^{-\Omega(nm^{-2\epsilon+\delta})} \leq (2^{-\Omega(nm^{-2\epsilon+\delta})})^{|P|} \leq 2^{-\Omega(nm^{1-2\epsilon+\delta})}$$

Now, we can sum over all possible choices for P satisfying (1) and (2) to get a bound on the existence of a P satisfying (1), (2) and (3). It is easy to see that there are at most m^m choices for P that satify (1) and (2). Using the union bound, we get the following bound on the existence of such a P.

$$m^m \cdot 2^{-\Omega(nm^{1-2\epsilon+\delta})} \leq 2^{m\log m - \Omega(nm^{1-2\epsilon+\delta})} \leq 2^{-\Omega(nm^{1-2\epsilon+\delta})}$$

Where the last inequality follows by simple algebraic manipulation from our assumption that $m^{\epsilon} \leq \sqrt{n}$ and $\delta > 0$, when n and m are sufficiently large. Recall that, by our previous discussion, this expression also upperbounds the probability that none of the candidate queries are fooling queries. But, when n and m are sufficiently large, this is strictly smaller than $2^{-b} = 2^{-nm^{1-2\epsilon}}$. Thus, by our previous discussion, this completes the proof of Proposition 5.2.

5.3 Modifying the proof for the case $\sqrt{n} \leq m^{\epsilon}$

We maintain the assumption that $k = 1$, and extend Proposition 5.2 for the case when $\sqrt{n} \leq m^{\epsilon}$; the proof of the following result is similar to that of Proposition 5.2, and appears in Appendix A.2.

PROPOSITION 5.4. *Fix $k = 1$ and parameter ϵ with $0 \leq \epsilon \leq 1/2$. Assume $\sqrt{n} \leq m^{\epsilon}$. Consider any deterministic oracle that stores a datastructure of size at most $b = nm^{1-2\epsilon}$ bits. The oracle does not attain an approximation ratio of $O(n^{1/2-\delta})$ for any constant $\delta > 0$.*

5.4 Modifying the proof for arbitrary k

In this section, we generalize Proposition 5.2 to arbitrary k. The generalization of Proposition 5.4 to arbitrary k is essentially identical, and therefore we leave it as an exercise for the reader. We now state the generalization of Proposition 5.2 to arbitrary k, the proof of which again follows Proposition 5.2 and appears in Appendix A.2.

PROPOSITION 5.5. *Let parameter ϵ be such that $0 \leq \epsilon \leq 1/2$. Assume $m^{\epsilon} \leq \sqrt{n}$. Consider any deterministic oracle that stores a datastructure of size at most $b = nm^{1-2\epsilon}$ bits. The oracle does not attain an approximation ratio of $O(\frac{m^{\epsilon-\delta}}{k\sqrt{k}})$ for any constant $\delta > 0$.*

6. CONCLUSIONS AND FUTURE WORK

This paper introduced and studied a fundamental problem, called SDC, arising in many large-scale Web applications. A summary of results obtained by the paper appear in Table 1 (Section 3.2). The main specific open question that arises is whether there is a deterministic oracle that is as good as the randomized oracle proposed in Section 4. More generally, a detailed analysis of practical subclasses of SDC seems to hold promise.

7. REFERENCES

[1] Amazon. *www.amazon.com.*

[2] eBay. *www.ebay.com.*

[3] Netflix. *http://www.netflix.com.*

[4] Netflix Prize. *http://www.netflixprize.com.*

[5] Yelp. *www.yelp.com.*

[6] Gediminas Adomavicius and Er Tuzhilin. Toward the next generation of recommender systems: A survey of the state-of-the-art and possible extensions. *IEEE TKDE*, 17, 2005.

[7] N. Alon and J. Spencer. *The Probabilistic Method.* John Wiley, 1992.

[8] Y. Azar ÁÍÄ N. Alon ÁÍÄ B. Awerbuch. The online set cover problem. In *STOC*, 2003.

[9] Francesco Bonchi, Carlos Castillo, Debora Donato, and Aristides Gionis. Topical query decomposition. In *KDD*, 2008.

[10] Jaime G. Carbonell and Jade Goldstein. The use of mmr, diversity-based reranking for reordering documents and producing summaries. In *SIGIR*, 1998.

[11] M. Charikar. Similarity estimation techniques from rounding algorithms. In *STOC*, 2002.

[12] Harr Chen and David R. Karger. Less is more: probabilistic models for retrieving fewer relevant documents. In *SIGIR*, 2006.

[13] Nello Cristianini and Matthew W. Hahn. *Introduction to Computational Genomics.* Cambridge Unversity Press, 2006.

[4]We use the following version of the Chernoff Bound: Let $X_1,\ldots,X_n$ be independent bernoulli random variables, and let $X = \sum_i X_i$. If $\mathbf{E}[X] = \mu$ and $\Delta > 2e - 1$, then $\mathbf{Pr}[X > (1+\Delta)\mu] \leq 2^{-\Delta\mu}$.

[14] M. R. Garey and D. S. Johnson. Computers and Intractability. *W. H. Freeman and Company*, 1979.

[15] YJ. Naor and N. Buchbinder. Online primal-dual algorithms for covering and packing problems. In *ESA*, 2005.

[16] G. L. Nemhauser, L. A. Wolsey, and M. L. Fisher. An analysis of approximations for maximizing submodular set functions – I. *Mathematical Programming*, 14(3):265–294, 1978.

[17] Alessandro Panconesi and Aravind Srinivasan. Randomized distributed edge coloring via an extension of the chernoff-hoeffding bounds. *SIAM J. Comput.*, 26(2):350–368, 1997.

[18] B. Saha and L. Getoor. On maximum coverage in the streaming model and application to multi-topic blog-watch. In *SDM*, 2009.

[19] Mikkel Thorup and Uri Zwick. Approximate distance oracles. *J. ACM*, 52(1):1–24, 2005.

APPENDIX

A. PROOFS

A.1 Upper Bound Proofs

Proof of Lemma 4.3: We store the set system as a bipartite graph representing the containment relation between items and sets. To show that the bipartite graph can be stored in the required space, it suffices to show that $(\mathcal{X}, \widehat{\mathcal{I}})$ is "sparse"; namely, that the total number of edges $(x, \widehat{S}) \in \mathcal{X} \times \widehat{\mathcal{I}}$ such that $x \in \widehat{S}$ is $O(nm^{1-2\epsilon})$. We account for the edges created in stages 1 and 2 separately.

1. Every significant item is connected to a single set. This creates at most n edges.
2. For every insignificant set, we store $\leq nm^{-2\epsilon}$ items, creating at most $mnm^{-2\epsilon} = nm^{1-2\epsilon}$ edges.

□

Proof of Lemma 4.4: We fix an optimal choice for $S_1^*, \ldots, S_k^* \in \mathcal{I}$, and denote $OPT = |(\bigcup_{i=1}^k S_i^*) \bigcap Q|$. Since, by construction, $\widehat{S} \subseteq S$ for all $S \in \mathcal{I}$, it suffices to show that the output of the oracle satisfies $|(\bigcup_{i=1}^k \widehat{S}_i) \bigcap Q| \geq \frac{OPT}{O(m^\epsilon/\sqrt{k})}$ in expectation. Moreover, since the dynamic stage algorithm finds a constant factor approximation to $\max\{|(\bigcup_{i=1}^k \widehat{S}_i) \bigcap Q| : \widehat{S_1}, \ldots, \widehat{S_k} \in \widehat{\mathcal{I}}\}$, it is sufficient to show that there *exists* $S_1, \ldots, S_k \in \mathcal{I}$ with $\mathbf{E}[|(\bigcup_{i=1}^k \widehat{S}_i) \bigcap Q|] \geq \frac{OPT}{O(m^\epsilon/\sqrt{k})}$.

We distinguish two cases, based on whether most of the items $(\bigcup_{i=1}^k S_i^*) \bigcap Q$ covered by the optimal solution are in significant or insignificant sets. We use the "significant" and "insignificant" designation as used in the static stage algorithm. Moreover, we refer to $\widehat{S} \in \widehat{\mathcal{I}}$ as significant (insignificant, resp.) when the corresponding $S \in \mathcal{I}$ is significant (insignificant, resp.).

1. **At least half of $(\bigcup_{i=1}^k S_i^*) \bigcap Q$ are significant items:** Notice that, by construction, there are at most $m^\epsilon\sqrt{k}$ significant sets in $\widehat{\mathcal{I}}$. Moreover, the significant items are precisely those covered by the significant sets of $\widehat{\mathcal{I}}$, and those sets form a partition of the significant items. Therefore, by the pigeonhole principle, there are there are some $\widehat{S_1}, \ldots, \widehat{S_k} \in \widehat{\mathcal{I}}$ such that $\bigcup_{i=1}^k \widehat{S}_i$ contains at least an $\frac{k}{m^\epsilon\sqrt{k}} = \frac{\sqrt{k}}{m^\epsilon}$ fraction of the significant items in $(\bigcup_{i=1}^k S_i^*) \bigcap Q$. This gives the desired $O(m^\epsilon/\sqrt{k})$ approximation.
2. **At least half of $(\bigcup_{i=1}^k S_i^*) \bigcap Q$ are insignificant items:** In this case, at least half the items $(\bigcup_{i=1}^k S_i^*) \bigcap Q$ covered by the optimal solution are contained in the insignificant members of $\{S_1^*, \ldots, S_k^*\}$. Recall that any insignificant set in $\mathcal{I}$ contains at most $\frac{n}{m^\epsilon\sqrt{k}}$ insignificant items. Therefore, the algorithm includes each element of an insignificant S_i^* in $\widehat{S_i^*}$ with probability at least $\frac{n}{m^{2\epsilon}} / \frac{n}{m^\epsilon\sqrt{k}}$, which is at least $\sqrt{k}/m^\epsilon$. Thus, every insignificant item in $(\bigcup_{i=1}^k S_i^*)$ is in $(\bigcup_{i=1}^k \widehat{S_i^*})$ with probability at least $\sqrt{k}/m^\epsilon$. This gives that the expected size of $(\bigcup_{i=1}^k \widehat{S_i^*}) \bigcap Q$ is at least $\frac{OPT}{O(m^\epsilon/\sqrt{k})}$. Taking $S_i = S_i^*$ completes the proof.

□

Proof of Lemma 4.6: Fix an optimal choice of $S_1^*, \ldots, S_k^*$, and denote $OPT = |(\bigcup_{i=1}^k S_i^*) \bigcap Q|$. Recall that the oracle finds $\widehat{S_1}, \ldots, \widehat{S_k} \in \widehat{\mathcal{I}}$ maximizing $|(\bigcup_{i=1}^k \widehat{S}_i) \bigcap Q|$, and then outputs the corresponding original sets $S_1, \ldots, S_k$.

It suffices to show that there are some $\widehat{S}_1, \ldots, \widehat{S}_k \in \widehat{\mathcal{I}}$ with $|(\bigcup_{i=1}^k \widehat{S}_i) \bigcap Q| \geq OPT/O(\sqrt{n/k})$. We distinguish two cases, based on whether most of $(\bigcup_{i=1}^k S_i^*) \bigcap Q$ are in big or small sets in $\widehat{\mathcal{I}}$.

Recall that $\widehat{\mathcal{I}}$ forms a partition of $\mathcal{X}$. We say $\widehat{S} \in \widehat{\mathcal{I}}$ is "significant" if $|\widehat{S}| \geq \sqrt{n/k}$, otherwise $\widehat{S}$ is "insignificant". Similarly, we say an item $i \in \mathcal{X}$ is "significant" if it falls in a significant set in $\widehat{\mathcal{I}}$, otherwise it is "insignificant". Notice that there are at most $\frac{n}{\sqrt{n/k}} = \sqrt{nk}$ significant sets.

First, we consider the case where at least half the items in $(\bigcup_{i=1}^k) S_i^* \bigcap Q$ are significant. Since there at most $\sqrt{nk}$ significant sets in $\widehat{\mathcal{I}}$, by the pigeonhole principle there are k of them that collectively cover a $k/\sqrt{nk} = \sqrt{k/n}$ fraction of all significant items in $(\bigcup_{i=1}^k S_i^*) \bigcap Q$. This would guarantee the $O(\sqrt{n/k})$ approximation, as needed.

Next, we consider the case where at least half of $(\bigcup_{i=1}^k S_i^*) \bigcap Q$ are insignificant. By examining the greedy algorithm of the static stage, it is easy to see that each $S \in \mathcal{I}$ contains at most $\sqrt{n/k}$ insignificant items. Therefore, there are at most $k \cdot \sqrt{n/k} = \sqrt{nk}$ insignificant items in $(\bigcup_{i=1}^k S_i^*)$. Therefore we deduce that $OPT = |(\bigcup_i S_i^*) \bigcap Q| \leq 2\sqrt{kn}$. Since the optimal covers $O(\sqrt{kn})$ items in Q, it suffices for a $O(\sqrt{n/k})$ approximation to show that there are $\widehat{S}_1, \ldots, \widehat{S}_k \in \widehat{\mathcal{I}}$ that collectively cover k items of Q. It is easy to see that this is indeed the case, since $\widehat{\mathcal{I}}$ is a partition of $\mathcal{X}$. This completes the proof. □

A.2 Lower Bound Proofs

A.2.1 Proof of Lemma 5.3

There are 2^b possible datastructures. Let p_i denote the probability that, when presented with random $(\mathcal{X}, \mathcal{I}) \sim D$, the oracle stores the i'th datastructure. We can write this probability of "collision" of the two i.i.d samples $(\mathcal{X}, \mathcal{I})$ and $(\mathcal{X}, \mathcal{I}')$ as $\sum_{i=1}^{2^b} p_i^2$. However, since $\sum_i p_i = 1$, this expression is minimized when $p_i = 2^{-b}$ for all i. Plugging into the above expression gives a lowerbound of 2^{-b}, as required. □

A.2.2 *Proof of Proposition 5.4*

Instead of replicating almost the entire proof of Proposition 5.2, we instead point out the key changes necessary to yield a proof of 5.4 and leave the rest as an easy excercise for the reader.

The proof proceeds almost identically to the proof of Proposition 5.2, with the following main changes:

- **Modifications to Section 5.2.1**: When defining D, we let each A_i be a subset of $\mathcal{X}$ of size $\sqrt{n}$ instead of $nm^{-\epsilon}$.
- We perform similar calculations throughout, accomodating the above modification to the size of A_i.
- **Modifications to Section 5.2.4**: We eventually arrive at an upper bound of $2^{-mn^{\delta}}$ on the probability that none of the candidate queries are fooling. Using the assumption $m^{\epsilon} \geq \sqrt{n}$ and the fact that $b = nm^{1-2\epsilon}$, a simple algebraic manipulation shows that this bound is stricly less than 2^{-b}. This completes the proof, as before.

A.2.3 *Proof of Proposition 5.5*

The proof of Proposition 5.5 follows the outline of the proof of Proposition 5.2. The necessary modifications to the proof of Proposition 5.2 are as follows:

- **Modifications to Section 5.2.1**: We define distribution D as before, except that we let each A_i be a subset of $\mathcal{X}$ of size $nm^{-\epsilon}\sqrt{k}$.
- **Modifications to Section 5.2.2**: Instead of sampling from D twice, we sample $2k+1$ times to get set systems $(\mathcal{X}, \mathcal{I}^1), (\mathcal{X}, \mathcal{I}^2), \ldots, (\mathcal{X}, \mathcal{I}^{2k+1})$. This changes the probability of collision of Lemma 5.3 to 2^{-2kb}. Here, collision means that all $2k+1$ samples from D are stored as the same datastructure by the static stage of the oracle.
- **Modifications to Section 5.2.3**: We now define a *fooling query* analogously for general k: A query Q is fooling if there is no single index i such that returning the i'th set gives a good approximation for all the set systems $(\mathcal{X}, \mathcal{I}^1), \ldots (\mathcal{X}, \mathcal{I}^{2k+1})$.

  Moreover, we analogously define *candidate queries*: We use A^a_b to denote the b'th set in set system $(\mathcal{X}, \mathcal{I}^a)$. We say $Q \subseteq \mathcal{X}$ is a candidate if $Q = A^{\ell_1}_{i_1} \bigcup A^{\ell_2}_{i_2} \bigcup \ldots \bigcup A^{\ell_{k+1}}_{i_{k+1}}$, where indices $\ell_1, \ldots, \ell_{k+1}$ are distinct, and indices $i_1, \ldots, i_k$ are distinct. In other words, Q is a fooling query if it is the union of $k+1$ sets from $k+1$ distinct set systems and $k+1$ distinct indices in those set systems.
- **Modifications to Section 5.2.4**: Similarly, if a candidate $Q = A^{\ell_1}_{i_1} \bigcup \ldots \bigcup A^{\ell_{k+1}}_{i_{k+1}}$ is not a fooling query, then there is some $A \in (\mathcal{I}^1 \bigcup \ldots \mathcal{I}^{2k+1}) \setminus \left\{A^{\ell_j}_{i_j}\right\}_j$ with $|A \bigcap Q| \geq nm^{-\epsilon}/\alpha$. Therefore, for one of the components $A^{\ell_j}_{i_j}$ of Q we have that $|A \bigcap A^{\ell_j}_{i_j}| \geq nm^{-\epsilon}/k\alpha$. Plugging in the approximation ratio $\alpha = m^{\epsilon-\delta}/k\sqrt{k}$ we have that $|A \bigcap A^{\ell_j}_{i_j}| \geq nm^{-2\epsilon+\delta}\sqrt{k}$. It is not too hard to see that we can construct P similarly with
  1. $|P| \geq k(m-k) = \Omega(km)$.[5]
  2. The undirected graph with nodes $\mathcal{I} \bigcup \mathcal{I}'$ and edges P is bipartite. Moreover, every node in the left part has degree at most 1. Thus P is acyclic.
  3. If $(B, C) \in P$ then $|B \bigcap C| \geq \Omega(nm^{-2\epsilon+\delta}\sqrt{k})$

  Continuing with the remaining calculations in this section almost identically gives a bound of $2^{-\Omega(knm^{1-2\epsilon+\delta})}$ on the probability of existance of a fixed P. The number of such P is at most $(km)^{km}$, therefore a similar calculation gives a bound of

  $$2^{-\Omega(knm^{1-2\epsilon+\delta})} = 2^{-\Omega(kbm^{\delta})}$$

  on the *existence* of any such P. As before, this completes the proof.

Acknowledgements

We thank Philip Bohannon, Hector Garcia-Molina, Ashwin Machavanajhhala, Tim Roughgarden, and Elad Verbin for insightful discussions.

[5]This is not true when k is almost equal to m. However, the theorem becomes trivially true when $k > m^{1/6}$, so we can without loss assume that k is not too large.

MEET: A Generalized Framework for Reciprocal Recommender Systems

Lei Li
School of Computing and Information Sciences
Florida International University
Miami, FL 33199
lli003@cs.fiu.edu

Tao Li
School of Computing and Information Sciences
Florida International University
Miami, FL 33199
taoli@cs.fiu.edu

ABSTRACT

Reciprocal recommender systems refer to systems from which users can obtain recommendations of other individuals by satisfying preferences of both parties being involved. Different from the traditional user×item recommendation, reciprocal recommenders focus on the preferences of both parties simultaneously, as well as some special properties in terms of "reciprocal". In this paper, we propose MEET – a generalized fra*M*ework for r*E*ciprocal r*E*commenda*T*ion, in which we model the correlations of users as a bipartite graph that maintains both *local* and *global* "reciprocal" utilities. The *local* utility captures users' mutual preferences, whereas the *global* utility manages the overall quality of the entire reciprocal network. Extensive empirical evaluation on two real-world data sets (online dating and online recruiting) demonstrates the effectiveness of our proposed framework compared with existing recommendation algorithms. Our analysis also provides deep insights into the special aspects of reciprocal recommenders that differentiate them from user×item recommender systems.

Categories and Subject Descriptors: H.3.3[Information Search and Retrieval]: Information filtering

General Terms: Algorithms, Design, Experimentation

Keywords: Reciprocal Recommender, Global and Local Regularization, Bipartite Graph

1. INTRODUCTION

Recommender systems have been intensively studied in both academia and industry, following a paradigm of providing a target user with a list of items that the user might prefer, i.e., the user×item recommendation. In recent years, a special class of recommender systems – reciprocal recommenders – have emerged, and are tailored for applications that focus on recommending people to people, in which the preferences of both parties involved in the recommendation need to be satisfied. For instance, in an online recruiting system, a job seeker would search jobs that match his/her preference, e.g., the special skills and the salary; and a recruiter might seek suitable candidates to fulfil the job requirement. Other illustrative examples of reciprocal recommenders include online dating services, online mentoring systems, customer-to-customer marketplaces, etc.

Obviously, the major challenge of reciprocal recommender systems is how to satisfy the needs of both users in a recommended match. This requires modeling *the bilateral relations between users* by considering the double-sided preferences. However, simply considering the bilateral relations is *insufficient* in the reciprocal community. In practice, reciprocal recommenders, such as online dating and online recruiting, possess special characteristics differentiating them from traditional user×item recommender systems. Figure 1 illustrates some challenges in these systems. We summarize the challenges as follows:

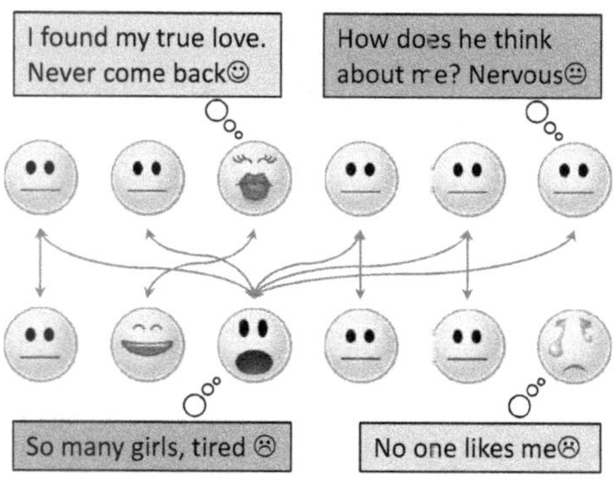

Figure 1: A toy example in an online dating system.

- *Reciprocity*: The success of a match *depends on the double-sided preference*, not solely on the user who receives the recommendation. This is the key feature of a reciprocal recommender.
- *Limitedness*: In traditional recommenders, an item can be preferred by a great amount of users. However, in reciprocal recommenders, people have *limited availability* towards other people, e.g., a boy cannot date with ten girls simultaneously.
- *Passiveness*: In reciprocal recommenders, a lot of users with limited engagement activities passively receive messages from other users. To maintain a vibrant community and further attract more users, it is imperative to consider the *passiveness* of users.

CIKM'12, October 29–November 2, 2012, Maui, HI, USA.

- *Sparsity*: Users in reciprocal communities would probably not return to the system if they find their preference. Therefore, different from traditional recommenders where users often have a long consumption history, the *data sparsity* issue in a reciprocal recommender needs more careful consideration.

The aforementioned challenges are essential to a successful reciprocal recommender system. Previous studies either focus on handling the main reciprocity of the recommender, or delve into a specific issue that exists in reciprocal recommenders. Little research work has been proposed to address the challenges in a principled and unified manner. In our work, we model the bilateral relations of users as a bipartite graph that maintains both *local* and *global* utilities in a reciprocal community. The *local* utility captures users' mutual preferences by considering *reciprocity*, *limitedness* and *passiveness*, whereas the *global* utility manages the overall quality of the entire reciprocal network in order to resolve the *sparsity* problem. The bipartite graph is constructed based on the users' self-descriptive and preference features, and then is refined by users' interactive activities.

In summary, the contribution of our work is three-fold:

1. We propose a *generalized* reciprocal recommendation framework, in which various challenges (e.g., *reciprocity*, *limitedness*, *passiveness* and *sparsity*) in reciprocal recommenders can be effectively addressed;

2. We define a novel quality metric (Set Vitality) to *intentionally evaluate the vitality of the recommended list* by considering the interaction histories of users;

3. We perform empirical evaluation on two real-world reciprocal data sets to demonstrate the effectiveness of our proposed framework.

The rest of the paper is organized as follows. Section 2 presents a brief summary of prior work relevant to reciprocal recommenders. In Section 3, we formalize the problem. Section 4 presents an overview of the generalized framework. In Section 5, we describe the feature space generally used in reciprocal recommenders. We then present the algorithmic details of our framework in Section 6, and discuss the generalization in Section 7. Empirical evaluation of our method compared with different baselines is reported in Section 8. Finally Section 9 concludes the paper.

2. RELATED WORK

Reciprocal recommenders provide platforms for people to achieve a win-win situation. A couple of interesting methods have been proposed to address issues of reciprocal recommendation from both mathematical and practical perspectives. In the following, we highlight the previous research that are most related to our work.

In mathematics, reciprocal recommendation can be modeled as the well-known stable marriage problem [10], which aims at finding an optimal matching between two sets of elements given a set of preferences for each element. Similar problems include stable roommates and college admissions problem. In our problem setting, we do not require to provide an optimal matching for any pair of users, as we need to consider other properties of a reciprocal recommender, e.g., to enhance the vitality of the entire reciprocal network.

In practice, reciprocity in a recommender system refers to the bilateral relations between people. This reciprocity is often considered in social matching in a broader sense [19]. Several existing methods [2, 13] focus on people-to-people recommendation in social networks, in which people have a dual role as both "users" and "items". Although the reciprocity is emphasized in these methods, they failed to consider other important properties of a reciprocal recommender, as we discussed in Section 1.

Pizzato *et al.* analyzed the characteristics of reciprocal recommenders in detail [15], by providing a comparison of the reciprocal recommender against traditional recommender systems. However, they did not address all the concerns of the reciprocal recommender in a unified way. In their follow-up works [1, 16, 17], they focused on how to capture the bilateral preference of users and presented different strategies to model the reciprocity between users in an online dating environment. Beside the online dating, there are a couple of works focusing on other reciprocal domains, e.g., online recruiting [21] and expertise management [18, 12]. Unfortunately, the special issues of reciprocal recommendation are not properly handled in previous works. These issues render the recommender not effective (as demonstrated in the experiment). Different from these previous works, in our study we shed light on not only the bilateral correlations between users, but also the *passiveness* and *limitedness* of users, and the *sparsity* of the reciprocal network, and provide a unified solution for reciprocal recommenders.

Reciprocity has also been investigated in Information Retrieval (IR) community. In [6] the problem of match-making is modeled as the retrieval and ranking of candidate matches for a given user. To this end, a series of features are initially extracted from user profiles, and then the correlation between the queries and the candidate is formalized in a feature level. The ranking function is learned via gradient boosted decision tree [9] over the extracted features. Our problem setting is more general than theirs since the search can be regarded as an explicit recommendation process.

3. PROBLEM STATEMENT

In this section we formally state our problem. We consider the reciprocal recommendation scenario consisting of two sets of users $\mathcal{U}$ and $\mathcal{V}$, in which each user maintains a self-description, $\mathcal{F}^s$, about himself/herself and a preference, $\mathcal{F}^p$, towards users in the other set. For example, in an online dating system, the two sets of users correspond to men and women; in an online recruiting system, they correspond to recruiters and job seekers. $\mathcal{F}^s$ and $\mathcal{F}^p$ are composed of a set of descriptive attributes, which might be scalar, categorical or free texts. Given a user $u \in \mathcal{U}$, our goal is to recommend u a list of users $\mathcal{Q}_u \subset \mathcal{V}$ such that $\mathcal{F}^p_u$ of u and $\mathcal{F}^p_v$ of any $v \in \mathcal{Q}_u$ are both satisfied, i.e., the *reciprocity*.

DEFINITION 1. AN OPTIMAL MATCH: *Given two users $u \in \mathcal{U}$ and $v \in \mathcal{V}$, the pair (u,v) is said to be an optimal match* iff *$\mathcal{F}^s_u$ maximally satisfies $\mathcal{F}^p_v$ and $\mathcal{F}^s_v$ maximally satisfies $\mathcal{F}^p_u$.*

Ideally, we expect that all the recommended pairs (u, v) are optimal matches. However in practice, the optimality cannot be fully achieved. In general, the capacity of a user receiving and responding recommendations in the scenario of reciprocal recommenders is quite dissimilar to the one of traditional user×item recommenders. For example, a boy cannot date with ten girls simultaneously. Therefore, in reciprocal recommenders, it is imperative to consider the limited capacity of users, i.e., the *limitedness.*

DEFINITION 2. AVAILABILITY: *Given a budget b, a user $u \in \mathcal{U}$ is said to be available if the number of recommendations that u receives is less than b within a time range t. We use $\tau(u)$ to indicate the number of times that u has been recommended to other users within t, e.g., one week.*

DEFINITION 3. A SUCCESSFUL MATCH: *Given two users $u \in \mathcal{U}$ and $v \in \mathcal{V}$, the pair (u,v) is said to be a successful match* iff *$\mathcal{F}_u^s$ suboptimally satisfies $\mathcal{F}_v^p$ and $\mathcal{F}_v^s$ suboptimally satisfies $\mathcal{F}_u^p$,* w.r.t. *the availability of u and v. We denote a successful match as $u \cong_b v$ or $v \cong_b u$.*

A user-oriented recommender should be capable of getting all users involved in an interactive community. In practice, a user might often interact with other users through different channels. For example, in an online recruiting system, a job seeker often sends resumes to recruiters and a recruiter often makes interviews with job seekers. Similarly, in an online dating system, people often send messages to whom they prefer. However, there are still a great number of users that passively receive such interactions from other users, i.e., the *passiveness*, which to some extent violates the reciprocal property of the entire community. Therefore, we need to consider the *passiveness* of a user in order to enrich the vitality of the reciprocal community.

DEFINITION 4. VITALITY: *Given a user u and his/her interactive activities with other users, u is said to be vital if the average number of u's interactions, $avg(|u_{\leftrightarrow}|)$, reaches the average number of interactions within the entire reciprocal community.*

In a reciprocal recommender system, a vital user is possible to improve the engagement of passive users, e.g., by sending messages to a shy boy to ask him for a date. By recommending passive users to vital users and vice versa, the overall vitality of the recommendation community would increase to some extent. It is possible that considering the vitality of users might deviate the definition of a successful match. However, the success of a recommendation is not solely determined by the match. The engagement of users after receiving the recommendation is also an important indicator to a successful recommendation.

We are expected that all the recommendations are successful matches in a reciprocal recommender, by considering both the bilateral preferences of individuals and the vitality of users. We now define our technical problem of reciprocal recommendation as follows.

PROBLEM (Reciprocal Recommendation): *Given a user $u \in \mathcal{U}$ (or $v \in \mathcal{V}$) and a budget b (the availability), recommend for u (or v) a list of users $\mathcal{Q}_u \subset \mathcal{V}$ (or $\mathcal{Q}_v \subset \mathcal{U}$), such that $\forall\ v \in \mathcal{Q}_u$ (or $u \in \mathcal{Q}_u$), $u \cong_b v$ (or $v \cong_b u$), and also the vitality of u (or v) should have potential to increase.*

The essence of reciprocal recommendation, including *reciprocity, limitedness* and *passiveness*, has been well captured in the above problem formation. We will discuss our solution to the problem of *reciprocal recommendation* in Section 6.

4. FRAMEWORK OVERVIEW

Figure 2 shows an overview of our proposed reciprocal recommendation framework, *MEET*. It consists of three interrelated components:

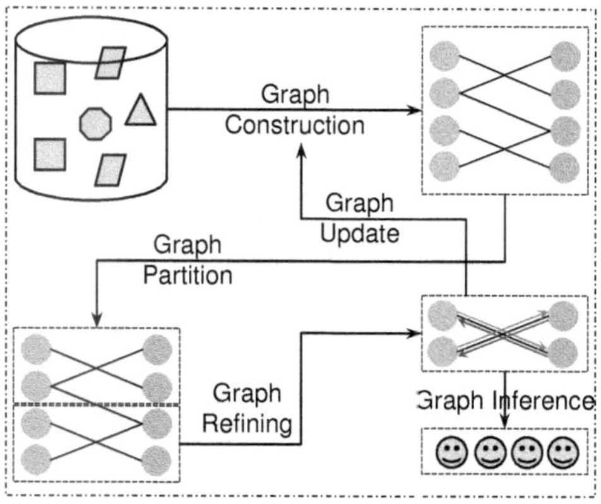

Figure 2: An overview of *MEET*.

Graph Construction and Updating (Section 5 and 6.3): The reciprocal community is represented as a bipartite graph based on the bilateral preference of users. *MEET* automatically analyzes the feature space of users and calculates the relevance between users from different sets. In addition, *MEET* treats the profiles of users who have successfully obtained their preferred information (e.g., jobs or friends) as the basis to learn the weights of features, and consequently improves the quality of the generated bipartite graph.

Bipartite Graph Partition (Section 6.1): To provide reasonable results and expedite the recommendation process, *MEET* first partitions the bipartite graph into different pieces, and then performs the recommendation on subgraphs. The subgraphs obtained by graph partition contain more specialized structures of the community, and therefore provide an elegant base for further inference.

Recommendation Inference (Section 6.2): Besides the relevance between users, *MEET* also considers the interactive activities within the community, and refines the subgraph based on such information. In each refined bipartite subgraph, the recommendation problem is modeled as an optimization problem, and the result is obtained by performing the inference over different sets of users.

5. BILATERAL FEATURES

In our problem setting, the profile of a user is composed of two types of features: a self-description, $\mathcal{F}^s$, and a preference, $\mathcal{F}^p$. Given a user $u \in \mathcal{U}$, we are interested in finding a relevant user $v \in \mathcal{V}$, such that (u,v) is a successful match. In Definition 3, we relax the condition of the perfect reciprocal match and allow partial matches of the users' preferences. By *relevance*, we mean that $\mathcal{F}_v^s$ matches $\mathcal{F}_u^p$, and meanwhile, $\mathcal{F}_u^s$ matches $\mathcal{F}_v^p$. Therefore, the *relevance* includes two components, $rel(u \sim v)$ and $rel(v \sim u)$. Here, the *relevance* cannot be regarded as the affinity between users, but a quantitative measure that describes how matchable the two users from different user sets are. Both $rel(u \sim v)$ and $rel(v \sim u)$ are calculated using the same set of attribute-value pairs for any user pair, and hence the *relevance* is comparable.

To calculate the relevance, we consider three groups of features that we believe have the predictive power of rele-

Table 1: Bilateral features in an online dating system. Features with the prefix "match" are all the preference features, whereas the others are the self-description features.

scalar		categorical					free text
birth_year	match_min_age	sex	dating_status	marriage	avatar	match_avatar	self_character
height	match_max_age	location	valid_mobile	children	match_certified	match_location	match_character
income	match_min_height	sublocation	house_status	nation	match_marriage	match_sublocation	
	match_max_height	education	auto_status	belief	match_education		
		industry	honest_level	access_photo	match_edu_more		

vance, including scalar features, categorical features and free texts. The features used in online dating data set are listed in Table 1. For scalar features, we first categorize them into different ranges, e.g., the length of working experience includes 0-3 years, 3-5 years, 5-10 years and 10- years. We then encode these ranges as binary features, e.g., if a user's working experience falls into the range of 0-3 years, then this feature (0-3 years) would be set to true (1), and all other ranges would be set to false (0). With categorical attributes, we use the same strategy of dealing with working experiences ranges. For free text features, we transform the text into an l_2-normalized TF.IDF-based term vector, and then combine this vector with the vector obtained based on other types of attributes. We can also specify the importance of each attribute. Finally, $rel(u \sim v)$ or $rel(v \sim u)$ is computed using the cosine similarity of the two corresponding vectors.

Once we obtain the relevance scores of both $rel(u \sim v)$ and $rel(v \sim u)$, we integrate these two scores as the final relevance between u and v, described in Eq.(1):

$$rel(u,v) = rel(u \sim v) \cdot rel(v \sim u). \quad (1)$$

We use the product of these two scores instead of the linear combination to eliminate the condition of unilateral preference, e.g., a job position is preferred by an applicant but the applicant is not suitable for this job. In addition, the relevance model is simplified since no parameter is involved.

6. RECOMMENDATION METHODOLOGY

In *MEET*, a reciprocal network is represented by a bipartite graph based on the mutual relevance of users. The recommendation is achieved by first partitioning the graph into multiple subgraphs, and then performing label inference on a specific subgraph with respect to the target user.

6.1 Community Specialization

A reciprocal community involves two different sets of users interacting with each other. It is intuitive to represent the community as a bipartite graph, where each set of users can be denoted as a set of nodes in the graph, and the relevances between users can be described by the edges in the bipartite graph. Note that the relevance quantifies the degree of match between two users, and hence the edges in the graph are not directional. The relevance score is filtered by a threshold θ to reduce the probability of a dense graph. A toy example can be found in Figure 1.

The recommendation can be achieved by analyzing the properties of the bipartite graph and the special characteristics of the target user. However in practice, the number of users involved in such a bilateral community might be large, which renders direct analysis on the entire bipartite graph inefficient. Taking into account the scalability issue, we propose to simultaneously separate the two sets of users in the graph into several groups, such that within each subgraph, the focus of users are more specialized, e.g., users that are all in the community of engineering in an online recruiting system. In this way, the generated subgraph contains less users with more similar preferences.

A simple way of partitioning the data into groups is to categorize the data by the attributes. However, the data considered in our problem setting is not fully structured, with text descriptions involved. Even if the text description can be transformed to quantitative values, the values of other attributes might be missing, which results in the difficulty of attribute selection for partitioning. The way we represent the data as a bipartite graph and use graph-partitioning methods to regroup users helps resolve the issues mentioned above.

Formally, given a bipartite graph $\mathbb{G} = (\mathcal{U}, \mathcal{V}, E, \mathbf{w})$ where $\mathbf{w} : E \rightarrow \mathbb{R}$, our goal is to partition the vertex sets $\mathcal{U}$ and $\mathcal{V}$ into k disjoint clusters, i.e., $\mathcal{U} = \{\mathcal{U}_1, \mathcal{U}_2, \cdots, \mathcal{U}_k\}$ and $\mathcal{V} = \{\mathcal{V}_1, \mathcal{V}_2, \cdots, \mathcal{V}_k\}$. Clearly the "best" clustering would correspond to a partitioning of the graph such that the crossing edges between clusters have minimum weight, denoted as *cut*,

$$cut(\mathcal{U}_1 \cup \mathcal{V}_1, \cdots, \mathcal{U}_k \cup \mathcal{V}_k) = \min_{G_1, \cdots, G_k} cut(G_1, \cdots, G_k), \quad (2)$$

where $G_1, \cdots, G_k$ is any k-partitioning of the graph $\mathbb{G}$.

The problem defined in Eq.(2) is essentially a co-clustering problem, which can be solved by many existing methods [5, 20]. In this paper, we will not focus on how to resolve the co-clustering problem. We employ a graph partitioning method [4] as the solution. The method proposes a spectral co-clustering algorithm that uses the second left and right singular vectors of an appropriately scaled user-user matrix to yield good bi-partitions, which is essentially suitable to our partitioning task.

By partitioning, we can obtain a list of subgraphs that embrace specialized information about each small reciprocal community, which can be well explained under different real-world cases. Let us take the online recruiting system as an example. For each subgraph, it may represent different areas of work, e.g., *computer engineering*, *chemical engineering* and *finance*. Such a subgraph characterizes the special properties of the area of work, and therefore provides us a reasonable and effective base to perform reciprocal recommendation.

6.2 Local Recommendation

Given a specialized community represented by a bipartite subgraph, our goal is to recommend for each user an attractive list of users from the other user set. By considering the characteristics of the reciprocal recommendation, we employ the bipartite graph inference to obtain the recommendation result. Besides the relevance between users, we have the interactive activities, e.g., messages and chatting in online dating, and adding favorite jobs and sending interviews to applicants in online recruiting. We also take into account the availability of the users. We refine the bipartite subgraph based on these information. After refinement, each vertex has its vertex attribute, i.e., the availability, and also has two sets of edges, including the relevance edges and the activity edges. The relevance edge is undirected, and the activity edge is directed, indicating which vertex is the initiator of the activity.

A natural question is why we do not consider the activity information when partitioning the bipartite graph. Within the reciprocal community, not all the users have sufficient activities; if we incorporate the activities into the partitioning process, the generated results might isolate users with few activities from more active users, which may render the recommendation for these inactive users not reasonable.

6.2.1 Bipartite Graph Preliminaries

Formally in our problem setting, a bipartite graph $\mathbb{G}^* = (\mathcal{U}, \mathcal{V}, E_r, E_a, \mathbf{w}_r, \mathbf{w}_a)$ consists of two sets of vertices, $\mathcal{U}$ and $\mathcal{V}$, and two sets of edges, $E_r, E_a \subseteq \mathcal{U} \times \mathcal{V}$. Each edge in E_r is an undirected pair of nodes weighted by $rel(u,v)$, i.e., $\mathbf{w}_r : \mathcal{U} \times \mathcal{V} \rightarrow \mathbb{R}_r$. Each edge in E_a is an ordered pair of nodes $[u,v]$ representing the activity connection from u to v, weighted by the ratio of the activities toward the end node and all the activities of the initial node, i.e., $\mathbf{w}_a : \mathcal{U} \times \mathcal{V} \rightarrow \mathbb{R}_a$. Given a vertex v in $\mathbb{G}^*$ (either $v \in \mathcal{U}$ or $v \in \mathcal{V}$), the in-degree $p(v)$ and out-degree $q(v)$ are defined as

$$p(v) = \sum_{\{u|[u,v]\in E_a\}} w_a(u,v), \quad q(v) = \sum_{\{u|[v,u]\in E_a\}} w_a(v,u).$$

Let $\mathcal{H}(\mathbb{G}^*)$ denote the space of functions $f : \mathcal{U}, \mathcal{V} \rightarrow \mathbb{R}$, which assigns a real value $f(v)$ to each vertex v.

6.2.2 Inference on Bipartite Graph

Given a bipartite graph representing the relevance structure of the reciprocal network, a simple solution to the recommendation is to select top relevant users that directly link to a given user as the recommended result. However, the specific properties (availability and vitality) of users in a reciprocal community would be ignored if we follow such a simple paradigm. For example, a job seeker u has been recommended to multiple job recruiters; if we recommend u to a new job recruiter v, then u will have little chance to respond v, even if they are relevant in some sense. In such a situation, it would be more reasonable to recommend for v other job seekers who are similar to u, which is essentially collaborative filtering. Yet, both directional and non-directional information on the bipartite graph cannot be easily incorporated into traditional collaborative filtering algorithms. A much more natural solution to this problem is to perform graph inference on the bipartite graph to obtain the recommendation list.

Our inference paradigm is motivated by [23], in which the graph inference is performed on a directed bipartite graph to solve the problem of classification. The problem setting in their method is similar to ours. However, they only consider the directional information within the bipartite graph, i.e., the in-degree and out-degree of nodes, but fail to consider the rationality of the connectivity between nodes, i.e., why the two nodes are connected with each other, which is essential in the problem of reciprocal recommendation. In our work, we explicitly model the rationality of the connectivity of nodes as the relevance between users, by which the connectivity can be naturally explained, and the final recommendation result is more reasonable and explainable.

Formally, if two distinct vertices u_1 and u_2 in $\mathcal{U}$ are co-linked by vertex v in $\mathcal{V}$, it indicates that the properties of both u_1 and u_2 are likely to be similar, e.g., both job seekers are similar in profile-wise since they are all preferred by the same job recruiter. The co-linkage strength induced by v between u_1 and u_2 can be measured by

$$c_v(u_1,u_2) = w_r(u_1,v) \cdot w_r(u_2,v) \cdot \frac{w_a(v,u_1)w_a(v,u_2)}{q(v)}. \quad (3)$$

With such a similarity measure, we not only consider the interactive activities of users ($w_a(v,u_1)$ and $w_a(v,u_2)$), but also emphasize the relevance between users ($w_r(u_1,v)$ and $w_r(u_2,v)$). It can be naturally understood in the context of online dating. If two boys are simultaneously contacted by a girl, then it indicates that both boys have similar characteristics that are preferred by the girl. Moreover, the more girls contact both boys, the more significant the similarity. A natural question arising in this context is why the similarity measure is further normalized by out-degree of v. It can be easily interpreted if we use the previous example. A girl who sends messages to a lot of boys may not have clear preference on what boy characteristics, and therefore the induced similarity of two boys by this girl is not significant.

In Eq.(3), we penalize the influence of active users by normalizing the similarity score using $q(v)$. It should be clarified that the vitality of the community cannot be reflected by flooded messages without definite purposes. The way we formalize the similarity considers the importance of dedicated users, e.g., if a girl is interested in a boy, she will not send too many messages to other boys but focus on building the relationship with this boy. Such an observation is beneficial to construct a vibrant reciprocal community.

Let f denote a function defined on one vertex set $\mathcal{U}$. Then the inference cost of function f can be measured by the following functional:

$$\Omega_{\mathcal{U}}(f) = \frac{1}{2} \sum_{u_1,u_2\in\mathcal{U}} \sum_{v\in\mathcal{V}} \frac{1}{\tau(v)} c_v(u_1,u_2) \left(\frac{f(u_1)}{\sqrt{p(u_1)}} - \frac{f(u_2)}{\sqrt{(p(u_2))}} \right)^2. \quad (4)$$

In Eq.(4), we penalize large differences in function values for vertices in $\mathcal{U}$. Notice that the function values are normalized by in-degrees of the corresponding vertices. In the context of online dating, the explanation is similar to the one given before. Many girls will prefer a handsome and successful man, which does not mean that these girls have similar preferences over the characteristics of the man. However, if two girls are sending messages to a boy without handsome appearance and strong background, it is likely to express a common interest of both girls. We also consider the availability of users using the reverse of $\tau(u)$. If the user has been recommended to other users many times within a time range, e.g., one week, then the possibility of this user being recommended to the target user should be small.

Similarly, the inference cost of function f on the vertex set $\mathcal{V}$ can be measured by:

$$\Omega_{\mathcal{V}}(f) = \frac{1}{2} \sum_{v_1,v_2\in\mathcal{V}} \sum_{u\in\mathcal{U}} \frac{1}{\tau(u)} c_u(v_1,v_2) \left(\frac{f(v_1)}{\sqrt{p(v_1)}} - \frac{f(v_2)}{\sqrt{(p(v_2))}} \right)^2. \quad (5)$$

Convexly combining together the two cost functionals Eq.(4) and Eq.(5), we can obtain an inference cost measure of function f over the bipartite graph $\mathbb{G}^*$:

$$\Omega_\gamma(f) = \gamma \cdot \Omega_{\mathcal{U}}(f) + (1-\gamma) \cdot \Omega_{\mathcal{V}}(f), \quad \text{s.t. } 0 \leq \gamma \leq 1, \quad (6)$$

where the parameter γ indicates the relative importance between $\Omega_{\mathcal{U}}(f)$ and $\Omega_{\mathcal{V}}(f)$.

6.2.3 Recommendation by Regularization

$\Omega_\gamma(f)$ captures the inference cost of labeling nodes in a bipartite graph. For recommendation, the intuitive idea is to minimize the inference cost, since we want to find the set of users closely relevant yet not recommended to the target user, by making use of the co-linkage of nodes. Besides the inference, we have additional information about users in reciprocal communities, i.e., the interactive activities, which can be regarded as a user's engagement profile for recommendation. Formally, given a user in $u \in \mathcal{U}$, we can define a function y in $\mathcal{H}(\mathbb{G}^*)$ in which $y(v \in \mathcal{V}) = 1$ if vertex v has interaction with u, or 0 if v has never interacted with u. Then the recommendation problem can be regarded as the problem of finding a function f, which infers new vertices for u while reproducing the target function y to a sufficient degree of accuracy [22, 7]. A formalization of this idea leads to the following optimization problem:

$$f^* = \arg\min_{f \in \mathcal{H}(\mathbb{G}^*)} \{\Omega_\gamma(f) + \mu \|f - y\|^2\}, \quad (7)$$

where $\mu > 0$ is the regularization parameter. The first component measures the inference cost of function f, and the second component indicates the closeness of f with respect to the given function y. The trade-off between these two competitive terms is captured by μ. The solution of Eq.(7) can be found in [22].

After obtaining the result of $f^*(u)$ for user u, we can take $\text{sign} f^*(u)$ to select the vertices in $\mathcal{V}$ whose labels are 1, and then rank the selected users based on the mutual relevance of users, i.e., $rel(u, v)$. The final recommendation result is obtained by selecting the top ranked ones without considering the users who have already interacted with u and the users whose availabilities exceed the availability budget b. Further, if the target user is a vital user, then the recommended list will be ranked via the vitality of users in an ascend order; otherwise, the list will be ranked in a descend order of the vitality. In this way, the engagement of passive users is possible to be improved to some extent.

6.3 Feature Weighting

In the context of reciprocal recommendation, e.g., online dating and online recruiting, users will not return to the system during a long time period if they obtain their preferred friends or jobs. In this case, the system will not recommend them any further information. However, such users' profiles are good indicators showing that the recommendation of the system is successful, and therefore they have great potential to improve the quality of the reciprocal network. In *MEET*, we filter out the profiles of these "successful" users, and then analyze their properties in order to facilitate the construction of the bipartite graph.

Specifically, we use feature weighting algorithms to capture the relative importance among different user features. Feature weighting has already been extensively explored [3, 8]. In our framework, we choose the Passive-Aggressive (PA) algorithm [3] to learn the weights for different features. The goal of PA is to change the model as little as possible to correct for any mistakes and low-confidence predictions it encounters, with the following optimization:

$$\mathbf{w}_{t+1} \leftarrow \underset{\mathbf{w}}{\text{argmin}} \frac{1}{2} \|\mathbf{w}_t - \mathbf{w}\|^2, \text{s.t. } y_i(\mathbf{w} \cdot \mathbf{x}_t) \geq 1. \quad (8)$$

Updates occur when the inner product does not exceed a fixed confidence margin, i.e., $y_t(\mathbf{w}_t \cdot \mathbf{x}_t) < 1$. The closed-form update for all examples is as follows:

$$\mathbf{w}_{t+1} \leftarrow \mathbf{w}_t + \alpha_t y_t \mathbf{x}_t, \quad (9)$$

where $\alpha_t = \max\{\frac{1 - y_t(\mathbf{w}_t \cdot \mathbf{x}_t)}{\|\mathbf{x}_t\|^2}, 0\}$. (Please refer to [3] for more details.) The PA algorithm has been successfully applied in practice because the updates explicitly incorporate the notion of classification confidence. Once we obtain the weights for each feature in the feature repository, we feed them into the relevance model described in Section 5, and then use the refined relevance to construct the bipartite graph.

7. DISCUSSION

The reciprocal recommendation framework we propose is quite general. In this section, we show the connections and differences between our framework and various existing methods for reciprocal recommendation. The methods discussed in this section include gradient boosted decision trees (GBDTs) [6], reciprocal recommender for online dating (RECON) [15] and content-collaborative reciprocal recommender (CCR) [1].

GBDTs and *MEET*: GBDTs considers the relevance between the query and the candidate by integrating the matching attributes and post-presentation (activities) features into a unified feature vector. Based on this vector, GBDTs calculates the relevance score between two single users. *MEET* considers a more general problem – recommendation, in which a user might have no definite preference on the information and therefore no explicit query is specified. Also the post-presentation features might not be available to new users. Moreover, *MEET* formalizes the reciprocal community as a dynamic network, whereas in GBDTs, the users are treated individually.

RECON and *MEET*: RECON calculates the compatibility scores between users from different sets by considering the self-description attributes and the activities. However, it fails to consider the other special characteristics of reciprocal recommendation, e.g., the *sparsity*, the *limitedness* and the *passiveness*. In such sense, RECON can be regarded as a special case of our proposed generalized framework.

CCR and *MEET*: CCR computes the users' similarity based on the content of user profiles, and then performs recommendation from collaborative-wise. It considers the a single-step diffusion of "like" and "dislike" of users towards other users. Such a diffusion is also incorporated into *MEET* by the inference on the refined bipartite graph. Therefore, CCR can also be treated as a special case of *MEET*.

8. EXPERIMENTAL EVALUATION

8.1 Real-world Data

Online Dating Data: This data set is collected from a dating web site from Oct, 2008 to Mar, 2011, with anonymized user information. The original feature space is described in

Table 1. We transform the features using the strategy described in Section 5, and then calculate the user relevance based on the new feature space. We set $\mathcal{U}$ as the male set and $\mathcal{V}$ as the female set. The statistics of this data set is depicted in Table 2(a).

Table 2: Statistics of two data sets.

(a) Online Dating

Male (u)	344,552
Female (v)	203,843
# of $\mathcal{F}_u^s$	528
# of $\mathcal{F}_u^p$	506
# of $\mathcal{F}_v^s$	506
# of $\mathcal{F}_v^p$	528
Activities	8,599,013

(b) Online Recruiting

Job Seekers (u)	199,999
Recruiters (v)	46,629
# of $\mathcal{F}_u^s$	860
# of $\mathcal{F}_u^p$	928
# of $\mathcal{F}_v^s$	928
# of $\mathcal{F}_v^p$	860
Activities	664,943

Online Recruiting Data: This data set is provided by Xiamen Talent Service Center[1], a popular online recruiting platform in China. We collected the profiles and activities for anonymized users from Jan, 2008 to Oct, 2011. The feature set is not listed due to the space limit. We set $\mathcal{U}$ as the job seeker set and $\mathcal{V}$ as the recruiter set. We use the same strategy to process this data set. The statistics of the data after processing is described in Table 2(b).

8.1.1 Experimental Setup

For experiments, we split the two data sets into training and testing sets. Each set includes two sets of users, associated with their interactive activities. Since a reciprocal recommender system may suffer from the *sparsity* problem, we treat users who do not have activities within 3 continued months as "successful" users and feed their profiles into the learning module for feature weighting. These profiles will not be included in the bipartite graph. Table 3 summarizes the details of training and testing datasets for both online dating and online recruiting data.

Table 3: Statistics of training and testing datasets.

(a) Online Dating

	training	testing
Male	293,470	51,082
Female	168,329	35,514
Activities	6,735,210	1,863,803
Successful	26,380	-

(b) Online Recruiting

	training	testing
Job Seekers	176,423	23,576
Recruiters	39,850	6,779
Activities	493,128	171,815
Successful	10,458	-

8.1.2 Evaluation Metrics

For each user in the testing set, we recommend top ranked users (top@10, top@20 and top@30) to the user at each week of the testing range. Within the testing set, each user has a series of activities, e.g., sending messages to other users. Based on such activities, we use different evaluation metrics to verify the quality of the recommended user list.

Set Evaluation: For comparison, we compute the averaged precision and recall based on users' activities over weeks. Specifically, the ground truth of a user u's activities, including who have been clicked or contacted by u, is denoted by M, and the recommended user list by algorithms is denoted by N. Then the precision (P) and recall (R) can be computed as

$$P = \frac{M \cap N}{N}, \quad R = \frac{M \cap N}{M}. \tag{10}$$

We then compute the F_1-score of the recommendation results, i.e., $F_1 = \frac{2PR}{P+R}$.

Ranking Evaluation: We employ Normalized Discount Cumulative Gain (NDCG) to evaluate the ranking quality of the recommended list based on a user's actual activity sequence. NDCG at position n is defined as

$$NDCG@n = N(n) \times \sum_{i=1}^{n} \frac{2^{r_i} - 1}{\log_2(i+1)}, \tag{11}$$

where $N(n)$ is the NDCG at n of the ideal ranking list, and r_i is the relevance rating of item at rank i. In our scenario, $r_i = 1$ if the user has clicked on or contacted with the recommended users and 0 otherwise.

Vitality Evaluation: The vitality of a user is an important feature within the reciprocal community. It defines how active the user is, e.g., how often the user sends messages to other users. By explicitly considering the vitality for recommendation, a vital user improve the engagement of other passive users, which renders the reciprocal network more healthy and energetic. To measure how active that users within the recommended list are, we define the *set vitality* measurement as the *average activeness* of all the users in the list. Specifically, given a recommended user set $\mathcal{S}$, associated with each user's interactive activities $u_{i\leftrightarrow}$, the *set vitality* of $\mathcal{S}$ is calculated as

$$f_a(\mathcal{S}) = \frac{1}{|\mathcal{S}|} \sum_{u_i \in \mathcal{S}} \frac{1}{|V_{u_i}|} \sum_{v_j} \frac{|u_{i\to j}|}{|u_{i\leftrightarrow j}|}, \tag{12}$$

where V_{u_i} is the set of users that have been clicked or contacted by u_i, $|u_{i\to j}|$ denotes the number of clicks on v_j by u_i and messages that u_i has sent to v_j and $|u_{i\leftrightarrow j}|$ represents the total number of interactions between u_i and v_j.

8.2 Experiment Results

In this subsection, we first evaluate the effects of local recommendation (recommending users within a bipartite subgraph) and global recommendation (recommending users within the entire bipartite graph); We then investigate the impact of different reciprocal properties to the recommendation result; Further, we demonstrate the effectiveness of our framework on improving the vitality of the reciprocal network. We also provide comprehensive comparisons with recently published approaches discussed in Section 7.

8.2.1 Parameter Setting

In our framework, there are several parameters for tuning, including the availability threshold b, the relevance threshold θ to construct the bipartite graph, the number of clusters k in Section 6.1, the importance factor γ in Section 6.2.2 and the regularization parameter μ in Section 6.2.3. For b, we empirically set it as 30 for online dating and 50 for online recruiting. For θ, we empirically set it as 0.01 for both online dating and online recruiting data. For k, we empirically set it as 10 for online dating and 20 for online recruiting. We will evaluate the performance of the algorithm with different k in the next section. To explore the effect of the parameters γ and μ towards the recommendation result, we use F_1-score as the evaluation metric to compare the quality of

[1] http://www.xmrc.com.cn.

the recommended list (top@10, top@20 and top@30). Note that the optimal parameter setting is obtained by *performing cross-validation on the training data.*

Figure 3 shows the performance curve with different parameter settings. We first empirically fix μ as 0.1 and evaluate γ. Figure 3(a) shows the F_1-score measured as a function of γ. The optimal value of γ for online dating is obtained when $\gamma = 0.5$, meaning that the two sets of users have approximately equal importance towards the development of the online dating environment. However, for the online recruiting dataset, the optimal γ is 0.7, indicating that within the online recruiting system, the inference cost of recommendation for job seekers is dominating. Such an observation is consistent with the actual situation since in practice the number of job seekers is superior to recruiters. We then fix γ as 0.5 for online dating and 0.7 for online recruiting, and evaluate the changing of μ. Figure 3(b) shows the F_1-score measured as a function of μ. The best result is achieved when $\mu = 0.1$. In the following experiments, we set μ as 0.1, γ as 0.5 for online dating and γ as 0.7 for online recruiting.

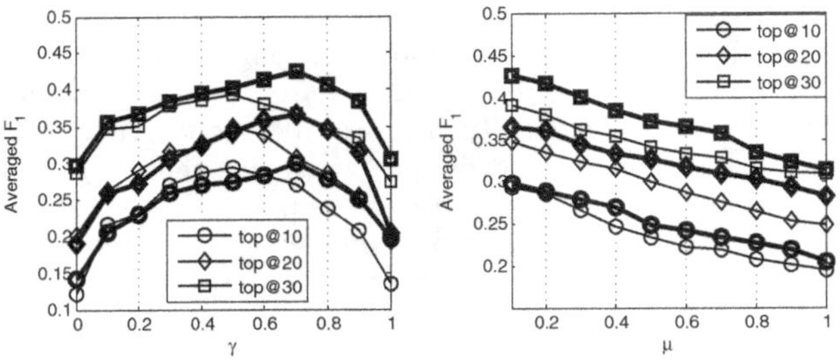

(a) $\mu = 0.1$ (b) $\gamma = 0.5(0.7)$

Figure 3: Parameter Tuning. Remark: thinner – online dating; thicker – online recruiting.

8.2.2 Local V.S. Global Recommendation

For reciprocal recommendation, our proposed framework first partitions the bipartite graph into multiple subgraphs (with specialized information), and then recommends users to the target user within the specific subgraph that embraces this target user. Such a paradigm can not only expedite the recommendation (since we only consider partial bipartite graph), but also improve the quality of the recommendation list. In the experiment, we choose different values of k (the number of clusters defined in Section 6.1) and compare the results with the one using the entire bipartite graph (Global, for short). The comparison is reported in Figure 4.

With different k, the performance of our proposed framework varies. *MEET* achieves the optimal performance when $k = 20$ for online recruiting dataset. *By partitioning the entire bipartite graph into multiple subgraphs, the information within each subgraph is more specialized, and therefore the reciprocity within each subgraph becomes considerably dense.* However, the performance on online dating is not quite sensitive to the number of clusters k. When $k = 10$, the results are slightly better than the other settings. The reason behind this might be that the populations within the online dating community are more general, whereas the ones within the online recruiting community are mostly related to some specific areas. Another interesting finding is that the overall performance of local recommendation is better than the one of global recommendation, especially for online recruiting. This could benefit from the fact that *the local presentation of the reciprocal network could help specialize the local community, and therefore facilitate the candidate matching within particular domains.*

8.2.3 Effects of Reciprocal Properties

In our generalized framework, we comprehensively consider the special properties of reciprocal recommendation, i.e., *reciprocity, limitedness, passiveness* and *sparsity*. To examine the influence of different properties on the recommendation results, we evaluate several alternatives of *MEET* as follows:

- $MEET^1$: Do not consider *reciprocity, passiveness, limitedness* and *sparsity*, i.e., to drop the term $\frac{1}{\tau(v)}c_v(u_1, u_2)$ in Eq.(4) and Eq.(5) and do not perform feature weight learning process;
- $MEET^2$: In Eq.(4) and Eq.(5), only consider the relevance between users, i.e., to drop the term $\frac{1}{\tau(v)}$ and the term $\frac{w_a(v,u_1)w_a(v,u_2)}{q(v)}$ in Eq.(3);
- $MEET^3$: In Eq.(3), do not consider the passiveness of users, i.e., to drop the term $\frac{w_a(v,u_1)w_a(v,u_2)}{q(v)}$;
- $MEET^4$: In Eq.(4) and Eq.(5), do not consider the availability of users, i.e., to drop the term $\frac{1}{\tau(v)}$;
- $MEET^5$: Do not perform the feature weight learning process.

We compare these alternatives with the comprehensive *MEET* in terms of F_1-score and NDCG. Figure 5 shows the comparison results on two datasets.

It is evident that the generalized model *MEET* significantly outperforms the alternatives from both accuracy and ranking perspective. The reason behind this is quite straightforward: in the generalized model, *the special characteristics of reciprocal community are well captured*, rendering the recommendation results derived from such unified model more reasonable. Besides this, we observe that: (1) The *reciprocity* is the dominant aspect in the reciprocal network, since only considering the relevance between users can significantly improve the quality of the recommendation results; and (2) The *limitedness, passiveness* and *sparsity* are also important properties of the reciprocal community, by which the performance of *MEET* can achieve slight improvement.

8.2.4 Comparison with Existing Methods

Our proposed framework is designated to reciprocal recommendation, which cannot be easily tackled by traditional collaborative filtering approaches. To verify this claim, we choose two recently published collaborative filtering methods [11, 14] as our baselines. [11] (CFIF for short) proposed treating the data as indication of positive and negative preference associated with vastly varying confidence levels, which is a pure collaborative filtering approach. [14] (OCCF for short) exploited the rich user information available in community-based interactive information systems, and incorporated user information into modeling the recommendation. For this method, we use the neighborhood model as the baseline. We also implement GBDTs [6], RECON [15] and CCR [1] (in Section 7) for comparison. We

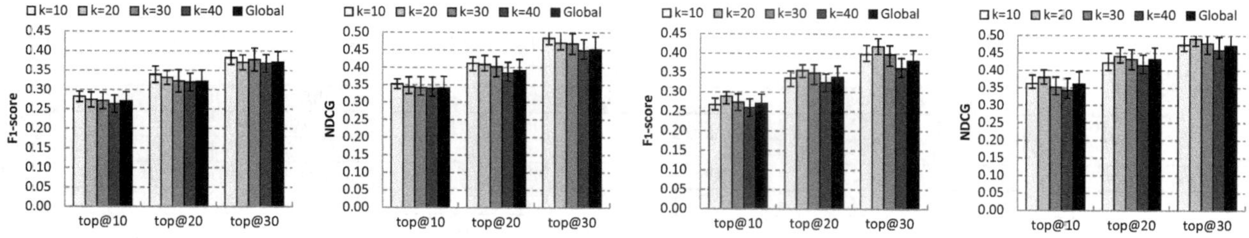

(a) F1 on online dating. (b) NDCG on online dating. (c) F1 on recruiting. (d) NDCG on recruiting.

Figure 4: Performance comparison of local recommendation with different k and global recommendation.

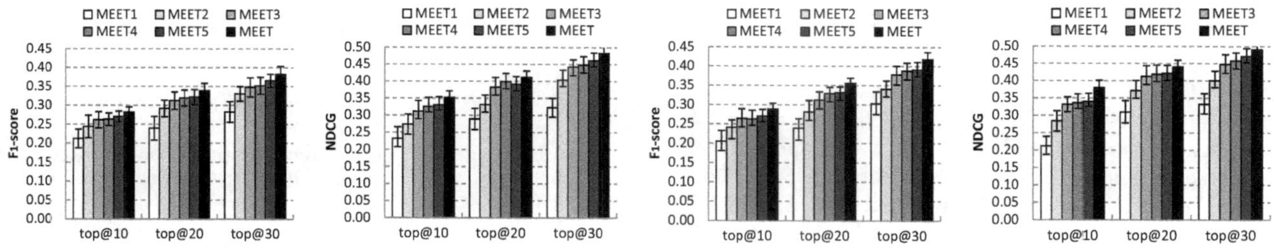

(a) F_1 on online dating. (b) NDCG on online dating. (c) F_1 on recruiting. (d) NDCG on recruiting.

Figure 5: Performance comparison of different alternatives of *MEET*.

use F_1-score and NDCG to compare these algorithms with *MEET* for both online dating and online recruiting datasets. The feature set used in the baselines are identical to the one in our proposed method, and also the parameters in the baselines are optimally tuned.

The results are shown in Table 4. It is evident that *MEET* significantly outperforms the baselines on both F_1-score and NDCG. The two collaborative filtering based methods cannot effectively handle the reciprocal task. We investigated the recommendation results of both methods and found that users in most recommended matches are relevant. However, there are two reasons that both users in a match have *few or even no interactions*: (1) *The recommended user has been recommended to multiple users, and therefore he/she has limited availability*; and (2) *Both users are not vital, and hence they do not contact with each other.* The three reciprocal methods being compared can slightly improve the recommendation performance; however, they only focus on different aspects of the reciprocal community. Instead, *MEET* provides a comprehensive overview of the reciprocal network, and therefore achieves the best.

8.2.5 Vitality Evaluation

The recommended user list provided by *MEET* exhibits a great vitality, which is originated from the sparkle that we intentionally consider the *passiveness* of users. We assume that passive users can be spurred by active users, and formalize the activeness of users in Eq.(3). Such activeness is beneficial to construct an energetic reciprocal network, in which users are willing to proactively contact with each other, and therefore improve the vitality of the network.

To evaluate the vitality of the recommended results, we use the *set vitality* measurement defined in Eq.(12), and compare *MEET* with GBDTs, RECON and CCR. These three methods consider the interactive activities of users from different perspectives. We also compare *MEET* with an alternative $MEET^3$ that does not consider the passiveness of users. Note that the recommended list are ranked based on the activeness of users. The ranking quality of the recommended list has been verified in Section 8.2.4, and therefore we put our concern on the overall vitality of the list. We report the comparison results in Table 5.

Table 5: Evaluation on the set vitality of the recommended results. (Bold indicates the best performance. * indicates the statistical significance at $p < 0.01$.)

	top@10	top@20	top@30
GBDTs	0.3513	0.3306	0.3027
RECON	0.3629	0.3430	0.3085
CCR	0.3731	0.3325	0.2964
$MEET^3$	0.3515	0.3276	0.2909
MEET	**0.4639***	**0.4517***	**0.4425***

From the comparison, we observe that the set vitality of results from different methods varies a lot. Since our framework explicitly formalizes the interaction between users into Eq.(3), it achieves the best performance. An interesting phenomenon is that when the number of recommended results increases, most methods show a decreasing trend in terms of the *set vitality*. Take CCR as an example for further analysis. CCR generates the results by considering the users who have interactions with users that are similar to the target user (based on the profile). The user ranking is based on the reciprocal interests. When recommending more users to the target user, the reciprocal interests of users with lower rankings will decrease significantly, and therefore the set vitality of the recommended list deceases. Comparatively, in our framework, we prefer dedicated users, i.e., *the users who have a lot of interactions with several other users but do not send flooded messages.* Based on this intuition, *MEET* outperforms other candidates.

Table 4: Comparison with existing methods. (Bold indicates the best performance. * indicates the statistical significance at $p < 0.01$.)

Methods	Online Dating						online recruiting					
	top@10		top@20		top@30		top@10		top@20		top@30	
	F_1	NDCG	F_1	NDCG	F_1	NDCG	F_1	NDCG	F_1	NDCG	F_1	NDCG
CFIF	0.2307	0.3069	0.2918	0.3534	0.3206	0.4417	0.2301	0.3174	0.3121	0.3813	0.3481	0.4036
OCCF	0.2415	0.3134	0.3059	0.3670	0.3385	0.4498	0.2485	0.3320	0.3219	0.3929	0.3569	0.4127
GBDTs	0.2607	0.3146	0.3106	0.3881	0.3475	0.4662	0.2567	0.3592	0.3304	0.4131	0.3718	0.4432
RECON	0.2523	0.3221	0.3027	0.3672	0.3503	0.4530	0.2604	0.3608	0.3247	0.4025	0.3839	0.4507
CCR	0.2309	0.3250	0.3389	0.3724	0.3428	0.4621	0.2431	0.3745	**0.3573**	0.3987	0.3912	0.4729
MEET	**0.2823***	**0.3521***	0.3390	**0.4118***	**0.3826***	**0.4836***	**0.2890***	**0.3799**	0.3560	**0.4405***	**0.4181***	**0.4904***

9. CONCLUDING REMARKS

In this paper, we study the problem of reciprocal recommendation. We comprehensively investigate the special properties of a reciprocal community, including *reciprocity*, *limitedness*, *passiveness* and *sparsity*. We propose a generalized reciprocal framework, *MEET*, in which the aforementioned properties are seamlessly integrated. Specifically, *MEET* first constructs a bipartite graph based on the mutual relevance of users, and then performs graph inference on the resulted subgraphs to obtain the recommendation list for individuals. The inference model formalizes the properties of the reciprocal network and elegantly casts the recommendation as an optimization problem.

Bilateral reciprocal recommendation discussed in our work might not cover all possible reciprocal recommendation tasks in a broader perspective. For example, friend recommendations on Facebook and colleague recommendations on LinkedIn exhibit different characteristics, since the recommendation activities on these two platforms might involve multiple parties instead of two. In the future, we plan to expand our reciprocal framework to tackle more reciprocal tasks.

ACKNOWLEDGEMENT

The work is partially supported by NSF grants DMS-0915110 and CNS-1126619 and DHS grants 2009-ST-062-000016 and 2010-ST-062-000039. We would like to thank Xiamen University and Xiamen Talent Service Center for providing us with the online recruiting data set used in the paper.

10. REFERENCES

[1] J. Akehurst, I. Koprinska, K. Yacef, L. Pizzato, J. Kay, and T. Rej. Ccr-a content-collaborative reciprocal recommender for online dating. In *Proc. of IJCAI*, pages 2199–2204, 2011.

[2] X. Cai, M. Bain, A. Krzywicki, W. Wobcke, Y. Kim, P. Compton, and A. Mahidadia. Collaborative filtering for people to people recommendation in social networks. *Advances in Artificial Intelligence*, pages 476–485, 2011.

[3] K. Crammer, O. Dekel, J. Keshet, S. Shalev-Shwartz, and Y. Singer. Online passive-aggressive algorithms. *The Journal of Machine Learning Research*, 7:551–585, 2006.

[4] I.S. Dhillon. Co-clustering documents and words using bipartite spectral graph partitioning. In *Proc. of SIGKDD*, pages 269–274. ACM, 2001.

[5] I.S. Dhillon, S. Mallela, and D.S. Modha. Information-theoretic co-clustering. In *Proc. of SIGKDD*, pages 89–98. ACM, 2003.

[6] F. Diaz, D. Metzler, and S. Amer-Yahia. Relevance and ranking in online dating systems. In *Proc. of SIGIR*, pages 66–73, 2010.

[7] C. Ding, R. Jin, T. Li, and H.D. Simon. A learning framework using greenąŕs function and kernel regularization with application to recommender system. In *Proc. of SIGKDD*, pages 260–269. ACM, 2007.

[8] M. Dredze, K. Crammer, and F. Pereira. Confidence-weighted linear classification. In *Proc. of ICML*, pages 264–271, 2008.

[9] J.H. Friedman. Greedy function approximation: a gradient boosting machine. *Annals of Statistics*, pages 1189–1232, 2001.

[10] D. Gale and L.S. Shapley. College admissions and the stability of marriage. *American Mathematical*, 69(1):9–15, 1962.

[11] Y. Hu, Y. Koren, and C. Volinsky. Collaborative filtering for implicit feedback datasets. In *Proc. of ICDM*, pages 263–272. IEEE, 2008.

[12] M. Karimzadehgan and C.X. Zhai. Constrained multi-aspect expertise matching for committee review assignment. In *Proc. of CIKM*, pages 1697–1700. ACM, 2009.

[13] Y. Kim, A. Mahidadia, P. Compton, X. Cai, M. Bain, A. Krzywicki, and W. Wobcke. People recommendation based on aggregated bidirectional intentions in social network site. *Knowledge Management and Acquisition for Smart Systems and Services*, pages 247–260, 2011.

[14] Y. Li, J. Hu, C.X. Zhai, and Y. Chen. Improving one-class collaborative filtering by incorporating rich user information. In *Proc. of CIKM*, pages 959–968. ACM, 2010.

[15] L. Pizzato, T. Rej, T. Chung, I. Koprinska, and J. Kay. Recon: a reciprocal recommender for online dating. In *Proc. of Recommender Systems*, pages 207–214. ACM, 2010.

[16] L. Pizzato, T. Rej, K. Yacef, I. Koprinska, and J. Kay. Finding someone you will like and who won't reject you. *User Modeling, Adaption and Personalization*, pages 269–280, 2011.

[17] L.A. Pizzato and C. Silvestrini. Stochastic matching and collaborative filtering to recommend people to people. In *Proc. of Recommender Systems*, pages 341–344. ACM, 2011.

[18] D. Richards, M. Taylor, and P. Busch. Expertise recommendation: A two-way knowledge communication channel. In *Proc. of ICAAS*, pages 35–40. IEEE, 2008.

[19] L. Terveen and D.W. McDonald. Social matching: A framework and research agenda. *ACM Transactions on Computer-Human Interaction*, 12(3):401–434, 2005.

[20] F. Wang, T. Li, X. Wang, S. Zhu, and C. Ding. Community discovery using nonnegative matrix factorization. *Data Mining and Knowledge Discovery*, 22(3): 493-521.

[21] X. Yi, J. Allan, and W.B. Croft. Matching resumes and jobs based on relevance models. In *Proc. of SIGIR*, pages 809–810. ACM, 2007.

[22] D. Zhou, O. Bousquet, T.N. Lal, J. Weston, and B. Schölkopf. Learning with local and global consistency. *Advances in neural information processing systems*, 16:321–328, 2004.

[23] D. Zhou, B. Schölkopf, and T. Hofmann. Semi-supervised learning on directed graphs. *Advances in neural information processing systems*, pages 1633–1640, 2005.

Social Contextual Recommendation

Meng Jiang†§, Peng Cui†§, Rui Liu§, Qiang Yang¶, Fei Wang‡
Wenwu Zhu†§, Shiqiang Yang†§

†Beijing Key Laboratory of Networked Multimedia
§Department of Computer Science and Technology, Tsinghua University, Beijing, China
‡Healthcare Transformation Group, IBM T J Watson Research Center, USA
¶Department of Computer Science and Engineering, Hong Kong University of Science and Technology
jm06@mails.tsinghua.edu.cn, cuip@tsinghua.edu.cn, lr09@mails.tsinghua.edu.cn
feiwang03@gmail.com, qyang@cse.ust.uk, wwzhu@tsinghua.edu.cn, yangshq@tsinghua.edu.cn

ABSTRACT

Exponential growth of information generated by online social networks demands effective recommender systems to give useful results. Traditional techniques become unqualified because they ignore social relation data; existing social recommendation approaches consider social network structure, but social context has not been fully considered. It is significant and challenging to fuse social contextual factors which are derived from users' motivation of social behaviors into social recommendation. In this paper, we investigate social recommendation on the basis of psychology and sociology studies, which exhibit two important factors: individual preference and interpersonal influence. We first present the particular importance of these two factors in online item adoption and recommendation. Then we propose a novel probabilistic matrix factorization method to fuse them in latent spaces. We conduct experiments on both Facebook style bidirectional and Twitter style unidirectional social network datasets in China. The empirical result and analysis on these two large datasets demonstrate that our method significantly outperform the existing approaches.

Categories and Subject Descriptors

H.3.3 [**Information Search and Retrieval**]: Information Filtering; J.4 [**Computer Applications**]: Social and Behavioral Sciences

General Terms

Algorithms, Experimentation

Keywords

Social Recommendation, Individual Preference, Interpersonal Influence, Matrix Factorization

CIKM'12, October 29–November 2, 2012, Maui, HI, USA.

1. INTRODUCTION

Users on social networks generate large volume of information and urge recommender systems to provide useful results. Traditional techniques typically based on collaborative filtering become unqualified in solving the social recommendation problem because they ignore social relation or interaction data. Recently, Ma et al. [20, 21] propose a framework of social recommender systems that utilize the social relation data, from which friendships and trust relationships are exploited to regularize the latent user space, but social contextual information has not been fully considered. It is significant and challenging to discover social contextual factors from contextual information and fuse them into social recommendation.

Figure 1 shows the entire social contextual information which can be derived from links on social networks. Users intend to judge received items from its content and sender. For example in Twitter, when a user receives a tweet that is posted by one of his friends (the sender), he usually reads its content to see whether the item is interesting. We can get this knowledge from item content and user-item interaction information. He also cares about who the sender is and whether the sender is a close friend or authoritative. If more than one of friends send him the same tweet, he may read it more attentively. This knowledge can be learnt from social relation and user-user interaction information. Both of these aspects are important for the user to decide whether to adopt (e.g. retweet, comment) the item. The above can be summarized as two contextual factors: (1) individual preference and (2) interpersonal influence.

Besides the experiential assumptions, psychology and sociology studies have proved that individual preference and interpersonal influence affect users' decisions on information adoption. In Bond's work[5], it is indicated that individuals are to some extent influenced by others' behaviors, rather than making decisions independently (i e. purely preference driven). In [25], web-based experiments are designed for music adoption prediction in an artificial music market. This work demonstrates that the introduction of interpersonal influence into the preference driven decision process (as is the case in real social networks) makes user behaviors more complex and thus increases the unpredictability of the item adoption. Therefore, only when individual preference and interpersonal influence are properly incorporated into recommendation, the unpredictability can be reduced and the recommendation performance can be improved accordingly.

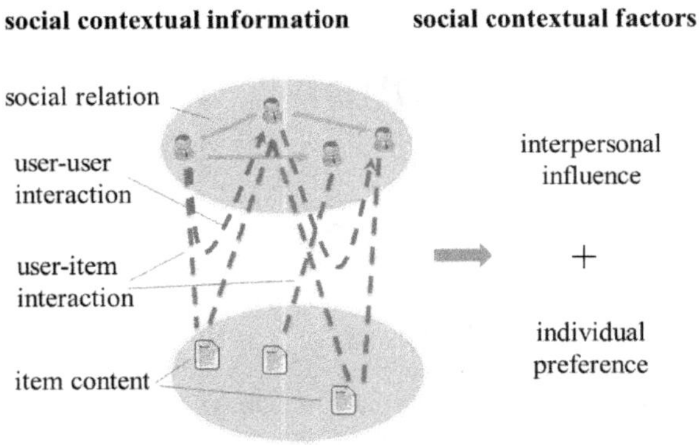

Figure 1: From Social Contextual Information to Social Contextual Factors

To address this problem, we propose a social contextual recommendation framework (as shown in Figure 2) based on a probabilistic matrix factorization method to incorporate individual preference and interpersonal influence to improve the accuracy of social recommendation. More specifically, we factorize the user-item interaction matrix into two intermediated latent matrices: user-item influence matrix and user-item preference matrix, which are generated from three objective latent matrices: user latent feature matrix, item latent feature matrix, and user-user influence matrix. Moreover, as we can partially observe individual preference and interpersonal influence based on historical user-item and user-user interaction data, we further utilize the observed contextual factors to compute the three objective latent matrices.

We've conducted experiments on two real social network datasets. One is collected from Renren (`www.renren.com`), a Facebook style website in China; and the other is collected from Tencent Weibo[1](`t.qq.com`), a Twitter style website in China. The two datasets represent two typical social network datasets, one for bidirectional social relations, and the other for unidirectional social relations. We show that social contextual factors can greatly boost the performance of recommender systems on social network data, and our method greatly outperforms the previous algorithms by a large margin. We attribute this result to the incorporation of complete social contextual factors from both individual and interpersonal sides, and experiments verify this conclusion.

This paper is organized as follows. Related work is introduced in section 2. We introduce the effectiveness of two contextual factors with studies on social datasets in section 3. Our social contextual model is formulated in section 4 and experimental results are reported in section 5. Conclusion comes in section 6.

2. RELATED WORKS

In this section, we review several major approaches to recommendation methods. Collaborative filtering and content-based filtering have been widely used to help users find out the most valuable information. With the emerge of social networks, researchers design trust-based [22, 23, 11] and influence-based [16, 17, 10, 7] methods to take use of the power coming from user relationships for recommendation. Matrix factorization methods have been proposed for social recommendation due to their efficiency to dealing with large datasets. Although there are some mixture models of these methods, it is valuable to understand social recommendation from users' motivation of item adoption.

Collaborative filtering methods have broad applications, which are divided into two categories, i.e. memory-based and model-based. In the memory based methods, item-based approaches [26, 14] calculate the similarity between all users based on their ratings of items. Si et al. [27] combine collaborative filtering and content-based filtering [1] which selects items based on the correlation between the contents of items and preferences of users. The model-based methods learn a model based on patterns recognized in the ratings of users using Bayesian networks and other clustering techniques [6, 8, 19]. Collaborative filtering only requires the information about user interactions, but it is not able to make full use of the graph-based social relations and rich social knowledge including user profiles and detailed item descriptions.

Recently, several matrix factorization methods [18, 13, 14] have been proposed for collaborative filtering. The matrix approximations all focus on representing the user-item rating matrix with low-dimensional latent vectors [24, 15, 12]. Recognizing that influence is a subtle force that governs the dynamics of social networks [16, 17], influence-based recommendation [10] involves interpersonal influence brought by senders and receivers into social recommendation cases. Trust-based approaches [22, 23, 11] exploit the trust network among users and make recommendations based on the ratings of users who are directly or indirectly trusted. SoRec [20] is proposed as a probabilistic factor analysis framework which fuses the users' tastes and their trusted friends' favors together. Yang et al. [30] propose that information contained in user-service interactions can help predict friendship propagations and vice versa. They use data from both user-item interactions and user-user relations. Aiming at improving recommender systems by incorporating users' social network information in both friend network and trust network, Ma et al. [21] propose a matrix factorization framework with social regularization. But this work only constrains user feature vectors from interpersonal side but ignores users' individual side, which makes the framework lack of complete contextual information to further improve the recommendation accuracy. However, it is still an open issue about what factors motivate user adoption on recommended items and how can they be effectively integrated to further improve the accuracy of social recommendation.

From psychological and sociological views, Bandura [2] gives a social cognitive theory of mass communication and argues that communication systems operate through two pathways. In the direct pathway, they promote changes by informing, enabling, motivating, and guiding participants to get what they prefer. In the socially mediated pathway, media influences participants to social networks and communities that provide natural incentives and personalized guidance. More previously, Benjamin [3] shows the similar opinion that factors such as cognition, feeling, taste, interest and interpersonal relationship develop the structure of social behaviors and interactions. On the social web, these two factors exactly represent individual preference and interpersonal influence, which motivate us to propose a social contextual recommendation framework to incorporate them by analyzing both user motivation and application mecha-

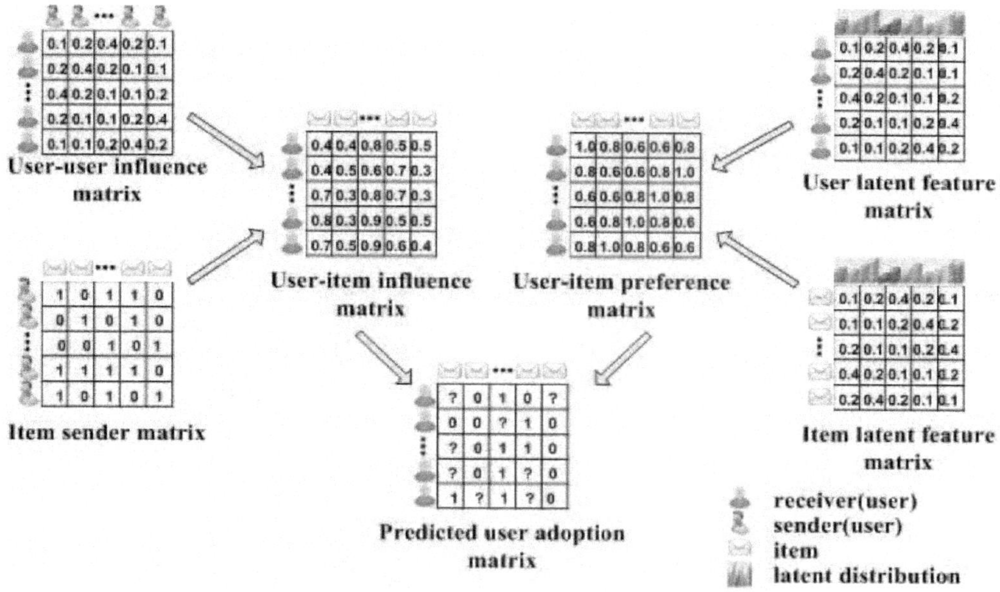

Figure 2: An illustrator on social contextual recommendation framework. Receiver is the user who receives the item (e.g., post, retweet, etc.) and sender is the receiver's friend or followed user who generated the item.

nism to recommender systems for social networks. In our paper, we incorporate both individual preference and interpersonal influence in a principled manner.

3. SOCIAL CONTEXTUAL FACTORS

In this section, we will demonstrate the existence and significance of social contextual factors (including individual preference and interpersonal influence) for social recommendation on real large datasets.

Given an item, the behavior of user adoption depends on individual preference to understand whether the user likes it or not, and interpersonal influence to tell whether the user has tight relationships with the item senders (e.g. the followed users who generate or retweet the tweet in Twitter) or not. Based on historical data, we apply LDA [4] on the web post (e.g. tweet) content and extract topic-level distributions of items. From user behavior history, we summarize how much user u likes item a with a naïve preference measurement as

$$P_u(a) = T_a \cdot \left(\frac{1}{|A(u,a)|} \sum_{a' \in A(u,a)} T_{a'}\right) \tag{1}$$

where $A(u,a)$ is the set of items adopted by user u excluding a, and T_a is the topic distribution of item a.

To describe interpersonal influence from user-user interactions on social web, we calculate the percentage of recommended items adopted by u from the item a:

$$I_u(a) = \frac{1}{|V(u,a)|} \sum_{v \in V(u,a)} \frac{|\mathcal{S}(u,v) \cap \mathcal{A}(u)|}{|\mathcal{S}(u,v)|} \tag{2}$$

where $V(u,a)$ is the set of senders who send item a to user u, $\mathcal{S}(u,v)$ is the set of items sent from v to u, and $\mathcal{A}(u)$ is the set of items that u adopts.

We classify the items into adopted and refused ones according to user behaviors, and plot the pairs (u, a) as points

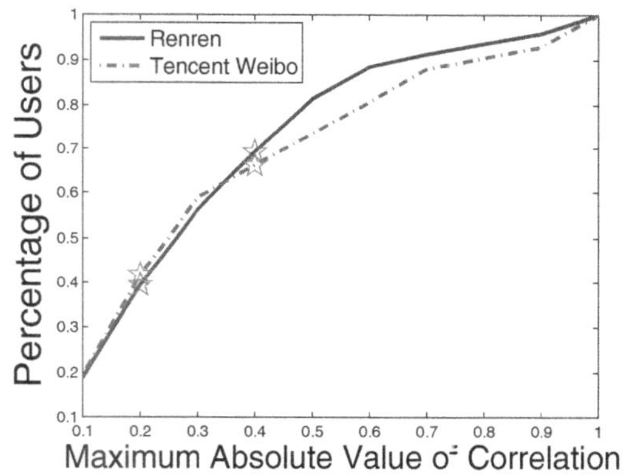

Figure 4: Percentage of Users vs. Correlation Between Preference and Influence

w.r.t. individual preference $P_u(a)$ and interpersonal influence $I_u(a)$ in Figure 3, which shows that users intend to adopt items with better preference scores and from higher influential friends or followers in both Facebook and Twitter style networks.

In order to demonstrate that individual preference and interpersonal influence are not only effective but also complementary social contextual factors, we calculate their correlations in social recommendation cases. We use P and I for each user to denote preference and influence of his adopted items. The Pearson correlation is defined as

$$\rho_{P,I} = \frac{cov(P,I)}{\sigma_P \sigma_I} = \frac{E[(P-\mu_P)(I-\mu_I)]}{\sigma_P \sigma_I} \tag{3}$$

The correlation is 1 or -1 in the case of perfect positive or negative linear relationship, and zero if preference and influence are uncorrelated. In Figure 4, the absolute correlation values of more than 40% users are less than 0.2 and the

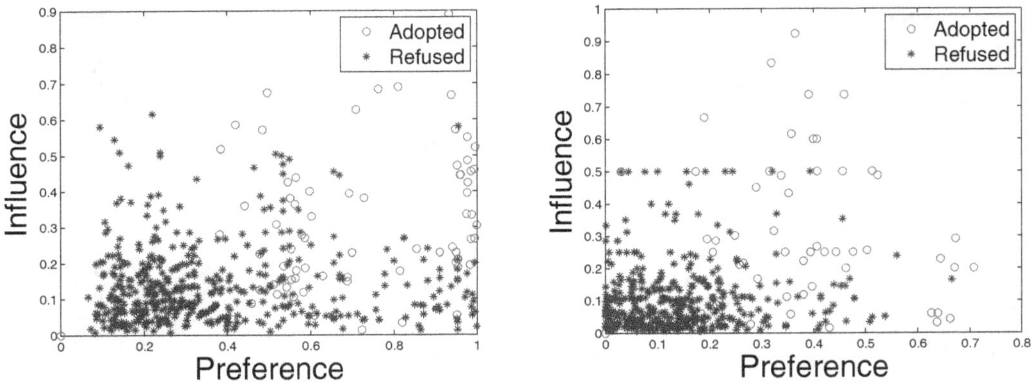

Figure 3: Comparison of Individual Preference and Interpersonal Influence on Adopted and Refused Items: (a) Renren Dataset (b) Tencent Weibo Dataset

values of around 70% are less than 0.4. Thus we conclude that individual preference and interpersonal influence can be applied as two complementary social contextual factors in recommendation.

4. SOCIAL CONTEXTUAL MODEL

In this section, we will introduce details of our social contextual recommendation model. First, we formally define the problem of social recommendation. Suppose that we have M users with the i-th user denoted as u_i, and N items with the j-th item denoted as p_j.

We denote the information adoption matrix as $\mathbf{R} \in \{0,1\}^{M\times N}$, with its (i,j)-th entry

$$R_{ij} = \begin{cases} 1 & \text{if } u_i \text{ adopted } p_j \\ 0 & \text{otherwise} \end{cases} \quad (4)$$

Then the social recommendation problem is converted to predicting the unobserved entries in the information adoption matrix $\mathbf{R}$ based on the observed entries and other factors.

In our model, we suppose that whether a user adopts an item on social networks is determined by three aspects: (1) what's the item (e.g. descriptive contents)? (2) what items does the user like? and (3) who are the senders?

Let $\mathbf{U} \in \mathbb{R}^{k\times M}$ be the latent user feature matrix, $\mathbf{V} \in \mathbb{R}^{k\times N}$ be the latent item feature matrix. $\mathbf{S} \in \mathbb{R}^{M\times M}$ is the interpersonal influence matrix, with each entry S_{ij} representing the degree of influence user u_i has on user u_j. It should be noted that $S_{ij} > 0$ if and only if u_i is the friend of u_j in social network services such as Facebook and Renren, or is followed by u_j in microbloggings such as Twitter and Tencent Weibo. $\mathbf{G} \in \mathbb{R}^{N\times M}$ is the item sender matrix, with entry $G_{ij} = 1$ meaning that u_j sends the item p_i and vice versa. With these denotations and the assumption that users can only receive items from their friends as social networks usually do ($G_{ii} = 0$), the social recommendation problem is to find out $\mathbf{U}, \mathbf{V}, \mathbf{S}$ so that $((\mathbf{S}\mathbf{G}^\top) \odot (\mathbf{U}^\top\mathbf{V}))$ can well approximate the observed entries in $\mathbf{R}$ without overfitting, where $\odot$ is the Hadamard Product.

In our case, we know the contents of items, user behaviors over the items, and the interactions between users. From these historical data, we can derive the item content representation, individual preference, and interpersonal influence. We compute the user-user preference similarity matrix $\mathbf{W} \in \mathbb{R}^{M\times M}$, item-item content similarity matrix $\mathbf{C} \in \mathbb{R}^{N\times N}$, and user-user interaction matrix $\mathbf{F} \in \mathbb{R}^{M\times M}$ as

$$\begin{aligned} W_{i,j} &= \frac{\sum_{a\in\mathcal{A}(u_i)} P_{u_i}(a)}{|\mathcal{A}(u_i)|} \cdot \frac{\sum_{a'\in\mathcal{A}(u_j)} P_{u_j}(a')}{|\mathcal{A}(u_j)|} && (5) \\ C_{i,j} &= T_{a_i} \cdot T_{a_j} && (6) \\ F_{i,j} &= |\mathcal{S}(u_i,u_j) \cap \mathcal{A}(u_i)| && (7) \end{aligned}$$

Though the accuracy of similarity matrices $\mathbf{W}$ and $\mathbf{C}$ depends on LDA performing on previous data, it is fair towards competing methods in experiments to share these matrices.

With the hypothesis that the similarities in observed spaces are consistent with the latent spaces, we regularize the three latent spaces by observed matrices (social contextual factors) in that: (1) the users that are similar in hidden user space have similar preferences (derived from preference similarity matrix); (2) the items that are similar in hidden item space have similar descriptive contents (derived from content similarity matrix); (3) high interpersonal influence in the hidden influence space generates frequent interpersonal interactions; (4) the product of user hidden space and item hidden space corresponds to the users' individual preference on the items; (5) the product of interpersonal influence and individual preference is proportional to the probability of item adoptions.

As the model performance is evaluated by root mean square error (RMSE) on the test set, we adopt a probabilistic linear model with Gaussian observation noise as in [24]. Here we define the conditional distribution over the observed entries in $\mathbf{R}$ as:

$$P(\mathbf{R}|\mathbf{S},\mathbf{U},\mathbf{V},\sigma_R^2) = \prod_{i=1}^{M}\prod_{j=1}^{N} \mathcal{N}(\mathbf{R}_{ij}|\mathbf{S}_i\mathbf{G}_j^\top \odot \mathbf{U}_i^\top\mathbf{V}_j, \sigma_R^2) \quad (8)$$

By incorporating the social contextual factors, we define

the posterior distribution as

$$P(\mathbf{S},\mathbf{U},\mathbf{V}|\mathbf{R},\mathbf{G},\mathbf{W},\mathbf{C},\mathbf{F},\Omega) \tag{9}$$
$$= \frac{P(\mathbf{R},\mathbf{W},\mathbf{C},\mathbf{F},\mathbf{G}|\mathbf{S},\mathbf{U},\mathbf{V},\Omega)P(\mathbf{S},\mathbf{U},\mathbf{V}|\Omega)}{P(\mathbf{R},\mathbf{G},\mathbf{W},\mathbf{C},\mathbf{F},\Omega)}$$
$$\propto P(\mathbf{R}|\mathbf{S},\mathbf{U},\mathbf{V},\Omega)P(\mathbf{W}|\mathbf{U},\Omega)P(\mathbf{C}|\mathbf{V},\Omega)P(\mathbf{F}|\mathbf{S},\Omega)$$
$$P(\mathbf{S}|\Omega)P(\mathbf{U}|\Omega)P(\mathbf{V}|\Omega)$$
$$= \prod_{i,j}\mathcal{N}(R_{ij}|\mathbf{S}_i\mathbf{G}_j^\top \odot \mathbf{U}_i^\top\mathbf{V}_j,\sigma_R^2)\prod_{p,q}\mathcal{N}(W_{pq}|\mathbf{U}_p^\top\mathbf{U}_q,\sigma_W^2)$$
$$\prod_{m,n}\mathcal{N}(C_{mn}|\mathbf{V}_m^\top\mathbf{V}_n,\sigma_C^2)\prod_{s,t}\mathcal{N}(F_{st}|S_{st},\sigma_F^2)$$
$$\prod_{x}\mathcal{N}(\mathbf{S}_x|0,\sigma_S^2)\prod_{y}\mathcal{N}(\mathbf{U}_y|0,\sigma_U^2)\prod_{z}\mathcal{N}(\mathbf{V}_z|0,\sigma_V^2)$$

where Ω denotes that zero-mean spherical Gaussian priors [28] are placed on latent feature vectors and observed matrices. Then

$$\ln P(\mathbf{S},\mathbf{U},\mathbf{V}|\mathbf{R},\mathbf{G},\mathbf{M},\mathbf{C},\mathbf{F},\Omega) \tag{10}$$
$$\propto -\frac{1}{2\sigma_R^2}\sum_{i,j}(R_{ij}-\mathbf{S}_i\mathbf{G}_j^\top \odot \mathbf{U}_i^\top\mathbf{V}_j)^2$$
$$-\frac{1}{2\sigma_W^2}\sum_{p,q}(W_{pq}-\mathbf{U}_p^\top\mathbf{U}_q)^2$$
$$-\frac{1}{2\sigma_C^2}\sum_{m,n}(C_{pq}-\mathbf{V}_p^\top\mathbf{V}_q)^2-\frac{1}{2\sigma_F^2}\sum_{s,t}(F_{st}-S_{st})^2$$
$$-\frac{1}{2\sigma_S^2}\sum_x\mathbf{S}_x^\top\mathbf{S}_x-\frac{1}{2\sigma_U^2}\sum_y\mathbf{U}_y^\top\mathbf{U}_y-\frac{1}{2\sigma_V^2}\sum_z\mathbf{V}_z^\top\mathbf{V}_z$$

Maximizing the posterior distribution is equivalent to minimizing the sum-of-squared errors function with hybrid quadratic regularization terms:

$$\mathcal{J} = ||\mathbf{R}-\mathbf{S}\mathbf{G}^\top \odot \mathbf{U}^\top\mathbf{V}||_F^2+\alpha||\mathbf{W}-\mathbf{U}^\top\mathbf{U}||_F^2 \tag{11}$$
$$+\beta||\mathbf{C}-\mathbf{V}^\top\mathbf{V}||_F^2+\gamma||\mathbf{S}-\mathbf{F}||_F^2$$
$$+\delta||\mathbf{S}||_F^2+\eta||\mathbf{U}||_F^2+\lambda||\mathbf{V}||_F^2$$

where $\alpha=\frac{\sigma_R^2}{\sigma_W^2},\beta=\frac{\sigma_R^2}{\sigma_C^2},\gamma=\frac{\sigma_R^2}{\sigma_F^2},\delta=\frac{\sigma_R^2}{\sigma_S^2},\eta=\frac{\sigma_R^2}{\sigma_U^2},\lambda=\frac{\sigma_R^2}{\sigma_V^2}$, and $||.||_F$ is the Frobenius norm.

We can adopt a block coordinate descent scheme to solve the problem. That is, starting from some random initialization on $\mathbf{S},\mathbf{U},\mathbf{V}$, we solve each of them alternatively with the other two matrices fixed and proceed step by step until convergence. As the objective is obviously lower bounded by 0 and the alternating gradient search procesure will reduce it monotonically, the algorithm is guaranteed to be convergent. In this paper, we use the gradient search method to solve the problem. Specifically, the gradients of the objective with respect to the variables are

$$\frac{\partial\mathcal{J}}{\partial\mathbf{S}} = 2\Big(-\mathbf{R}(\mathbf{G}\odot\mathbf{V}^\top\mathbf{U})+(\mathbf{S}\mathbf{G}^\top\odot\mathbf{U}^\top\mathbf{V})\mathbf{G}$$
$$+\gamma(\mathbf{S}-\mathbf{F})+\delta\mathbf{S}\Big) \tag{12}$$
$$\frac{\partial\mathcal{J}}{\partial\mathbf{U}} = 2\Big(-\mathbf{V}\mathbf{R}^\top+\mathbf{V}(\mathbf{G}\mathbf{S}^\top\odot\mathbf{V}^\top\mathbf{U})-2\alpha\mathbf{U}\mathbf{W}$$
$$+2\alpha\mathbf{U}\mathbf{U}^\top\mathbf{U}+\eta\mathbf{U}\Big) \tag{13}$$
$$\frac{\partial\mathcal{J}}{\partial\mathbf{V}} = 2\Big(-\mathbf{U}\mathbf{R}+\mathbf{U}(\mathbf{S}\mathbf{G}^\top\odot\mathbf{U}^\top\mathbf{V})-2\beta\mathbf{V}\mathbf{C}$$
$$+2\beta\mathbf{V}\mathbf{V}^\top\mathbf{V}+\lambda\mathbf{V}\Big) \tag{14}$$

Thus, we apply the following gradient based approach on our social contextual model in Algorithm 1. $\mathcal{J}$ decreases the fastest in the direction of gradients during each iteration and the sequence $(\mathcal{J}^{(t)})$ converges to the desired minimum.

Algorithm 1 Social Contextual Model Gradient Algorithm

Require: $0 < \alpha_S^{(t)},\alpha_U^{(t)},\alpha_V^{(t)} < 1$, $t=0$. Initialization $\mathcal{J}^{(0)}=\mathcal{J}(\mathbf{S}^{(0)},\mathbf{U}^{(0)},\mathbf{V}^{(0)})$.
Ensure: $\mathcal{J}^{(0)}\geq 0$, $\mathcal{J}^{(t+1)}<\mathcal{J}^{(t)}$
for $t=1,2,\cdots$ **do**
  Calculate $\frac{\partial\mathcal{J}}{\partial\mathbf{S}}^{(t-1)}, \frac{\partial\mathcal{J}}{\partial\mathbf{U}}^{(t-1)}, \frac{\partial\mathcal{J}}{\partial\mathbf{V}}^{(t-1)}$
  $\mathbf{S}^{(t)}=\mathbf{S}^{(t-1)}-\alpha_S^{(t-1)}\cdot\frac{\partial\mathcal{J}}{\partial\mathbf{S}}^{(t-1)}$
  $\mathbf{U}^{(t)}=\mathbf{U}^{(t-1)}-\alpha_U^{(t-1)}\cdot\frac{\partial\mathcal{J}}{\partial\mathbf{U}}^{(t-1)}$
  $\mathbf{V}^{(t)}=\mathbf{V}^{(t-1)}-\alpha_V^{(t-1)}\cdot\frac{\partial\mathcal{J}}{\partial\mathbf{V}}^{(t-1)}$
  $\mathcal{J}^{(t)}\leftarrow\mathcal{J}(\mathbf{S}^{(t)},\mathbf{U}^{(t)},\mathbf{V}^{(t)})$
end for

Our model can be applied in the real system to deal with incrementally increasing data. It has been proved both storage and computational efficient by solving the smoothly evolved factorized matrices in [29].

5. EXPERIMENTS

5.1 Datasets Description

We collect data from Renren, a typical social networking service that enables users to put on their profiles and add friends. One of the most popular actions on Renren is sharing blogs, photos and external video links (denoted as items in the paper). After an item is shared by a user, the item will be sent to the user's friends and appear in his friends' pages in real time. We crawled relationships and shared items of nearly 1 million users from February 2007 to December 2009. The statistics of Renren dataset are summarized in Table 1.

Meanwhile, we crawled data from Tencent Weibo, which allows users to follow any other user and receive messages from those followed users. Like Twitter, it also empowers users to spread information by forwarding the messages. We crawled tweets, retweets and user lists during January 2011 from more than 100 thousand users. The statistics of Tencent Weibo dataset are summarized in Table 2.

In Figure 5, we show the characteristics of Renren and Tencent Weibo datasets by plotting curve (a) the number of users with respect to the number of shared or forwarded posts (calculated by $\sum_i G_{ij}$ for user u_j) and curve (b) the

Table 1: Statistics of Renren Dataset

Value	Description
939,363	user number
1,625,689	sharing item number
5,829,368	sharing behavior number

Table 2: Statistics of Tencent Weibo Dataset

Value	Description
163,661	user number
529,615	tweet number
1,566,609	forward number

number of posts with respect to the number of users who share or forward them (calculated by $\sum_j G_{ij}$ for post p_i). We can see that all the four figures follow power law distributions, which reflect that user behaviors are always very sparse on social networks. Calculated with user number, item number and adoption number, the density of Renren dataset is 0.59%, and the density of Tencent Weibo dataset is 0.09%. The sparsity problem is very serious in our case.

5.2 Experimental Settings

We design our experiments based on two user tasks [9]: (1) annotation in context (2) find good items. The first task requires the recommender to generate predictions for the items that the user is reading. The second task requires a more direct focus on actual recommendation and provides users with a ranked list of recommended items, along with predictions for how much the users would like them.

Different from those static held-out experiments on datasets without time information, the recommendation on social items, e.g. tweets, should be evaluated in a temporal setting. For example, given an item and a user, the interpersonal influence that the user receives at t_1 on the item may be different from that the user receives at a later time t_2, if new friends (or followers) share (or retweet) the item during the time $t_2 - t_1$. Moreover, as we do not have any information about when the user is online, we can not decide which items the user actually reads. Thus, here we use online sessions to represent the time when the user is online, and we suppose the user will read all the items received from his relationships during the online session time. Given a user, we randomly select a number of online session candidates with the session width being 15 items. And we select the candidates that include at least 2 adopted items as valid online sessions. Then based on the valid online sessions, we design the temporal social recommendation experiments as shown in Figure 6. We arbitrarily select a time to divide the dataset into the training and testing parts. Our model learns interpersonal influence matrix and latent features of users and items from the training set. Meanwhile, we generate valid online sessions from the testing set as testing cases. Then we conduct all baseline algorithms and our method on these test cases. Although the estimation of online session cannot be guaranteed to be perfect, the experiment settings are fair for all the comparative algorithms and the proposed one. Thus, it is adequate to demonstrate the advantages and characteristics of the methods.

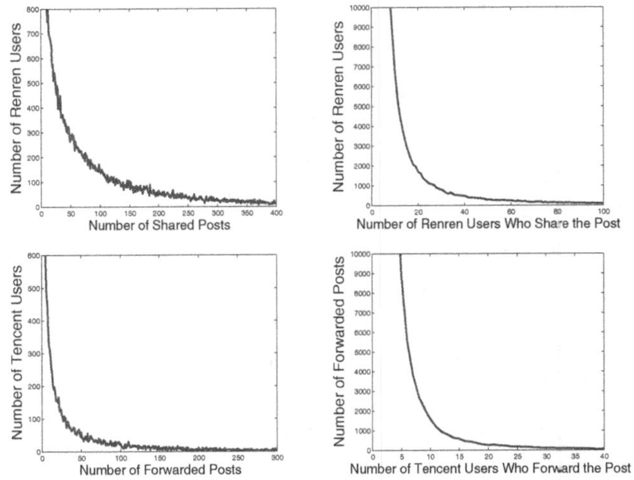

Figure 5: Characteristics of Renren (a)(b) and Tencent Weibo (c)(d) Datasets

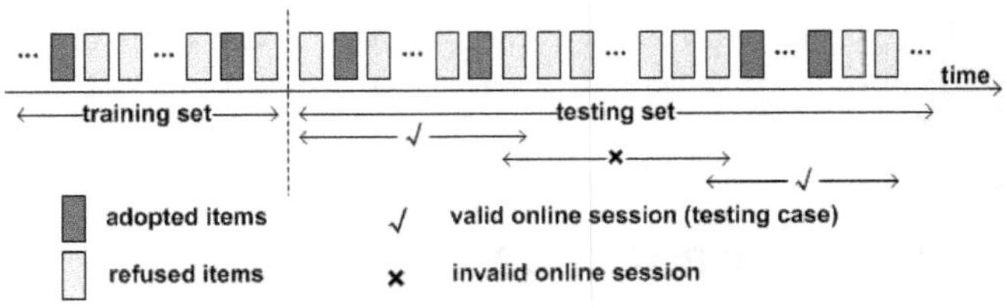

Figure 6: An Illustrator on Experiment Settings

5.3 Comparative Algorithms

We implement the following baselines for comparison with our social contextual model (Context MF).

- Content-based [1]: This method recommends similar items with ones that the receiver has shared or forwarded before. It only uses adopted items' content.
- Item CF [26]: The standard item-based collaborative filtering assumes that users like what their close friends or followers like. It only uses user-item interaction information.
- FeedbackTrust [23]: This method improves the basic trust-based recommendation algorithm [22] with users feedback. It is accurate to compute users' correlations in trust network, but only interactions between users.
- Influence-based [10]: This method estimates influence as social utility based on a gradient ascent algorithm. It uses information of user interactions through items, but fails to discover individual correlations between users and items.
- SoRec [20]: This method jointly analyzes social network data and user-item data by extracting a common latent factor from the shared mode, using *Probabilistic Matrix Factorization*. It does not take into account influence from user interactions.
- SoReg [21]: This method designs a matrix factorization objective function with *Social Regularization* to constraint social recommendation. It considers tastes

of all the friends when estimates the user latent features, but both user and item features should be regularized with respect to individual preference on items.

Meanwhile, we implement different configurations of our model to demonstrate the effectiveness of our proposed algorithm.

- Influence MF: This method uses only one kind of social contextual factors (interpersonal influence) in our social recommendation model. The adjusted function to minimize is

$$\mathcal{J} = ||\mathbf{R} - \mathbf{S}\mathbf{G}^\top||_F^2 + \gamma||\mathbf{S} - \mathbf{F}||_F^2 + \delta||\mathbf{S}||_F^2 \quad (15)$$

- Preference MF: This method only uses individual preference for the matrix factorization model. The degenerated function is

$$\mathcal{J} = ||\mathbf{R} - \mathbf{U}^\top\mathbf{V}||_F^2 + \alpha||\mathbf{W} - \mathbf{U}^\top\mathbf{U}||_F^2 + \beta||\mathbf{C} - \mathbf{V}^\top\mathbf{V}||_F^2 + \eta||\mathbf{U}||_F^2 + \lambda||\mathbf{V}||_F^2 \quad (16)$$

5.4 Evaluation Measures

Error Metrics: To measure the prediction quality of our proposed approach in comparison with other collaborative filtering and matrix factorization algorithms, we use two popular metrics, the Mean Absolute Error (MAE) and the Root Mean Square Error (RMSE). The metrics MAE is defined as

$$MAE = \frac{1}{|\mathcal{R}|}\sum_{R_{ij}\in\mathcal{R}} |\mathbf{R_{ij}} - \mathbf{S_i}\mathbf{G_j}^\top \odot \mathbf{U_i}^\top\mathbf{V_j}| \quad (17)$$

where R_{ij} denotes the information adoption value (0 or 1) given to j-th item by user u_i. The metrics RMSE is defined as

$$RMSE = \sqrt{\frac{1}{|\mathcal{R}|}\sum_{R_{ij}\in\mathcal{R}} (\mathbf{R_{ij}} - \mathbf{S_i}\mathbf{G_j}^\top \odot \mathbf{U_i}^\top\mathbf{V_j})^2} \quad (18)$$

Therefore, a smaller MAE or RMSE value means a better performance.

Precision on Top K Recommendation: Precision is defined as the ratio of adopted items to number of items recommended. Precision represents the probability that a recommended item is adopted. Recommendation algorithms are often evaluated by Precision@K [26], which is more important w.r.t. precision, because the recommendation space is limited and only the top k recommended items make sense in real recommendation applications. Here we range K value from 2 to 10.

Ranking Coefficients: Compared to the absolute value prediction accuracy, the predicted order accuracy is more important in real recommendation scenarios. Here we use two ranking-based evaluation methods to evaluate the performance: Kendall's ranking coefficient $\hat{\tau}$ and Spearman's $\hat{\rho}$. They start by defining the following intuitive statistics: the number of ranking order switches, which means how many of the pairs in the test data are ordered incorrectly by the model.

$$T = \sum_{i<j} 1(s_i > s_j) \quad (19)$$

The weighted sum of order switches, which weighs the incorrect ordered pairs by the ranking difference:

$$R = \sum_{i<j}(j-i)\cdot 1(s_i > s_j). \quad (20)$$

These two measures are transformed linearly into the range [-1,1], where 1 corresponds to perfect model performance (T,$R = 0$) and -1 corresponds to making all possible errors, thus attaining perfect reverse ranking. Thus after we re-scale T and R, we have the non-parametric correlation prevalent data analysis tools:

$$\hat{\tau} = 1 - \frac{4T}{n(n-1)} \quad (21)$$

$$\hat{\rho} = 1 - \frac{12R}{n(n-1)(n-1)} \quad (22)$$

T-test: An algorithm that gives higher probabilities on adopted items than refused items will better help the recommender systems. In order to demonstrate the distinguish ability, for each method, a group of T-tests are conducted to compare numerical gaps between good recommendations and bad ones. When T is higher, the classification is more accurate on whether user adoption will happen or not.

5.5 Parameter Settings

Here we focus on parameter settings. We investigate the performance when the parameters change, and implement algorithms of our model and all baselines with these parameters.

Tradeoff Parameters: The tradeoff parameters α, β, γ, δ, η and λ in our model play the role of adjusting the strengths of different terms in the objective function Equation (11). To balance the components in this function, these parameters are proportional to $\frac{1}{||\mathbf{W}-\mathbf{U}^\top\mathbf{U}||_F^2}$, $\frac{1}{||\mathbf{C}-\mathbf{V}^\top\mathbf{V}||_F^2}$, $\frac{1}{||\mathbf{S}-\mathbf{F}||_F^2}$, $\frac{1}{||\mathbf{S}||_F^2}$ and $\frac{1}{||\mathbf{V}||_F^2}$. Taking the scales of **S**, **U**, **V**, **F**, **W** and **C** into account (Table 1 and 2), we scan orders of magnitude and try different combinations of parameters as shown in Table 3. We use the second row for Renren dataset and the third row for Tencent Weibo dataset. Although they are not the perfect ones, the following experiments demonstrate they are adequate. We tune parameters following the same way as *Context MF* for *Preference MF* and *Influence MF*. We also find the best configurations while applying original versions of competing methods on our real datasets to make sure comparisons are fair.

Number of Hidden Features: We train **U**, **V** to find the proper number of hidden features k for users and items. If k is too small, the recommender system cannot make a distinction between any users or items. If k is too large, users and items will be too unique for the system to calculate their similarities and the complexity will considerably increase.

Thus, we conduct experiments with k ranging from 3 to 80 on both Renren and Tencent Weibo datasets. The results are shown in Figure 7, from which we can find that with the hidden feature number k increasing, RMSE reduces gradually. It shows obviously that when $k > 60$ on both datasets, RMSE decreases rather slow. Considering the recommendation effect and time efficiency, we choose $k = 60$ as the latent space dimension in our experiments.

Number of Iterations: In Figure 8, we can observe that both RMSE and the objective function value $\mathcal{J}$ decrease

Table 3: Tradeoff Parameters on Renren (a) and Tencent Weibo (b) Datasets (60 Hidden Features and 60 Iterations)

α,η	β	γ,δ	λ	MAE	RMSE
Renren Dataset					
10^{-4}	10^{-7}	10^{-6}	10^{-5}	0.2452	0.3139
$\mathbf{10^{-3}}$	$\mathbf{10^{-6}}$	$\mathbf{10^{-5}}$	$\mathbf{10^{-4}}$	**0.2416**	**0.3086**
10^{-2}	10^{-5}	10^{-4}	10^{-3}	0.2431	0.3115
10^{-1}	10^{-4}	10^{-3}	10^{-2}	0.2676	0.3392
Tencent Weibo Dataset					
10^{-3}	10^{-6}	10^{-5}	10^{-4}	0.1613	0.2529
10^{-2}	10^{-5}	10^{-4}	10^{-3}	0.1539	0.2432
$\mathbf{10^{-1}}$	$\mathbf{10^{-4}}$	$\mathbf{10^{-3}}$	$\mathbf{10^{-2}}$	**0.1514**	**0.2348**
1	10^{-3}	10^{-2}	10^{-1}	0.1795	0.2767

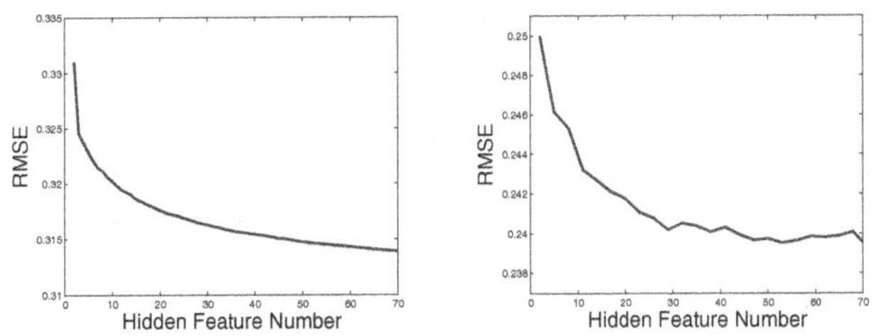

Figure 7: RMSE vs. Hidden Feature Number on Renren (a) and Tencent Weibo (b) Datasets (60 Iterations)

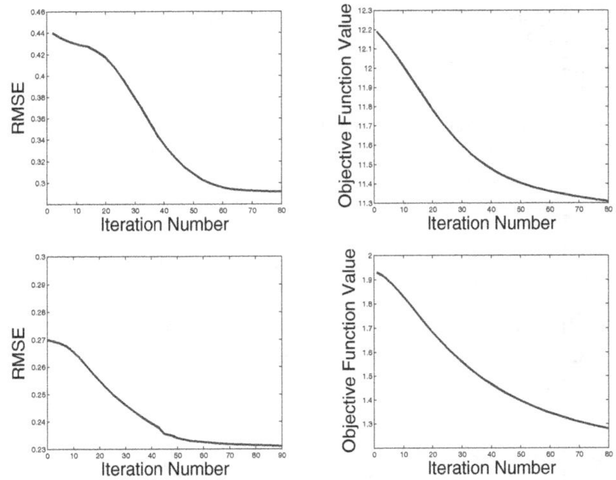

Figure 8: RMSE and Objective Function Value $\mathcal{J}$ vs. Iteration Number on Renren (a)(b) and Tencent Weibo (c)(d) Datasets (60 Hidden Features)

gradually with the number of iterations increasing. It shows that, by incorporating effective regularizers, our method successfully avoids the overfitting problem which often occurs in gradient algorithms. On both datasets, it is better to run 60 iterations in order to reach a converged result with an acceptable time cost.

5.6 Recommendation Performance

We evaluate each algorithm with the accuracy measured as MAE, RMSE and ranking coefficients. As shown in Table 4, our social contextual model, which recommends items based on matrix factorization algorithm with social contextual factors, provides reasonably accurate recommendations that are much better than baselines. On Renren and Tencent Weibo datasets, we decrease the prediction error by 19.1% and 12.8% on MAE, by 24.2% and 20.7% on RMSE over *SoReg*, a state-of-the-art algorithm with social regularization.

It should be noted that *Preference MF* and *Influence MF* achieve better performance than *SoRec*, which demonstrates the effectiveness of introducing either individual preference or interpersonal influence. The large improvement margin achieved by *Context MF* over both *Preference MF* and *Influence MF* demonstrates the importance of incorporating complete contextual information from both individual and interpersonal sides for social recommendation. Moreover, the fact that our proposed *Context MF* performs better than *SoReg* proves the effectiveness of incorporating the two social contextual factors from users' motivations on item adoption, instead of adding average-based or individual-based regularization to user latent vectors [21].

Table 4: Recommendation Performance on Two Datasets (Renren and Tencent Weibo)

Method	MAE	RMSE	$\hat{\tau}$	$\hat{\rho}$
Renren Dataset				
Content-based [1]	0.3842	0.4769	0.5409	0.5404
Item CF [26]	0.3601	0.4513	0.5896	0.5988
FeedbackTrust [23]	0.3764	0.4684	0.5433	0.5469
Influence-based [10]	0.3859	0.4686	0.5394	0.5446
SoRec [20]	0.3276	0.4127	0.6168	0.6204
SoReg [21]	0.2985	0.3537	0.7086	0.7140
Influence MF	0.3102	0.3771	0.6861	0.7006
Preference MF	0.3032	0.3762	0.6937	0.7036
Context MF	**0.2416**	**0.3086**	**0.7782**	**0.7896**
Tencent Weibo Dataset				
Content-based [1]	0.2576	0.3643	0.7728	0.7777
Item CF [26]	0.2375	0.3372	0.7867	0.8049
FeedbackTrust [23]	0.2830	0.3887	0.7094	0.7115
Influence-based [10]	0.2651	0.3813	0.7163	0.7275
SoRec [20]	0.2256	0.3325	0.7973	0.8064
SoReg [21]	0.1997	0.2962	0.8390	0.8423
Influence MF	0.2183	0.3206	0.8179	0.8258
Preference MF	0.2111	0.3088	0.8384	0.8453
Context MF	**0.1514**	**0.2348**	**0.8570**	**0.8685**

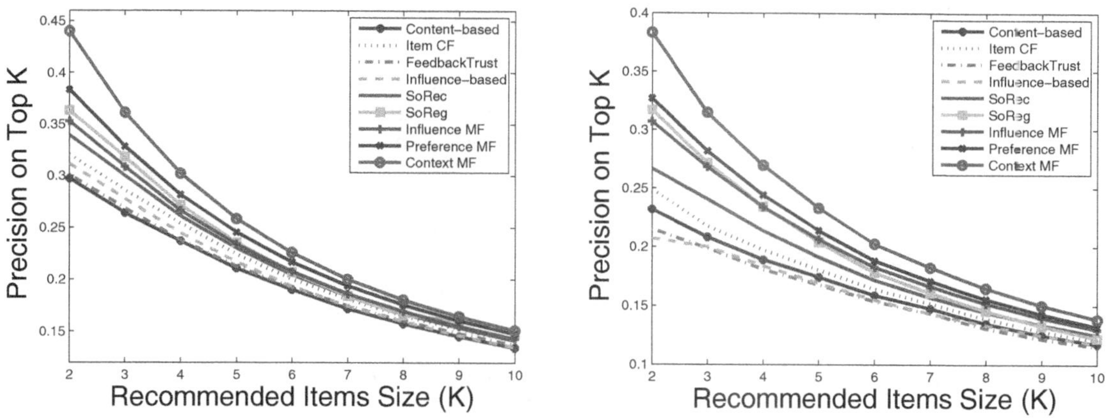

Figure 9: Top K Precision Curve on Renren (a) and Tencent Weibo (b) Datasets

We draw the precision curve on top K recommendations in Figure 9. The performance increases regularly as we decreases the size of recommended items. Compared with baselines, our top 5 precision increases by 21.7% and top 10 precision increases by 10.8% on Renren dataset. The top 5 precision increases by 12.3% and top 10 precision increases by 6.85% on Tencent Weibo dataset. The advantage of our method is much more obvious when K is small. As the user adoption behavior is very sparse, it is difficult to distinguish excellent methods when K is rather large. That's why all the baseline algorithms tend to converge as K becomes larger.

To compare the distinguish-ability of our method with baselines, we report average and variance of prediction and T-test results in Table 5. Our model gives the highest T (1.78 and 1.26 times of the best baseline on Renren and Tencent Weibo datasets), which shows the social contextual model has better distinguish-ability compared with baselines.

We conduct 100 parameter-fixed experiments to test the stability of our model with different random starts. As shown in Table 6, the low variances of MAE and RMSE (less than 0.001) show that our algorithm not only performs well on both social networking and microblogging datasets, but also runs without big fluctuation.

Table 5: T Statistics on Two Datasets (Renren and Tencent Weibo)

Method	Adopted	Refused	T-test
Renren Dataset			
Content-based [1]	0.7019(0.046)	0.6653(0.052)	1.055
Item CF [26]	0.3596(0.001)	0.2679(0.001)	1.342
FeedbackTrust [23]	0.3632(0.082)	0.343(0.080)	1.060
Influence-based [10]	0.6413(0.004)	0.5898(0.004)	1.087
SoRec [20]	0.4733(0.010)	0.3465(0.003)	1.366
SoReg [21]	0.5234(0.012)	0.3356(0.007)	1.560
Influence MF	0.3505(0.015)	0.2131(0.006)	1.645
Preference MF	0.1324(0.028)	0.0555(0.015)	2.384
Context MF	0.4556(0.095)	0.1074(0.019)	**4.244**
Tencent Weibo Dataset			
Content-based	0.4173(0.048)	0.2764(0.029)	1.509
Item CF	0.6374(0.004)	0.2436(0.001)	2.617
FeedbackTrust	0.7920(0.019)	0.6096(0.009)	1.299
Influence-based	0.8004(0.019)	0.3918(0.007)	2.043
SoRec	0.4949(0.004)	0.0580(0.004)	8.532
SoReg	0.5523(0.003)	0.0602(0.006)	9.1744
Influence MF	0.5222(0.012)	0.0620(0.005)	8.423
Preference MF	0.5758(0.015)	0.0517(0.001)	11.13
Context MF	0.8115(0.020)	0.0580(0.001)	**13.99**

Table 6: Stability of Performance on Renren and Tencent Weibo Datasets (60 Hidden Features and 60 Iterations)

Renren Dataset					
	MAE	RMSE	$\hat{\tau}$	$\hat{\rho}$	T
$\overline{x}$	0.2416	0.3086	0.7783	0.7897	4.2437
σ	0.0001	0.0001	0.0006	0.0006	0.5545
Tencent Dataset					
	MAE	RMSE	$\hat{\tau}$	$\hat{\rho}$	T
$\overline{x}$	0.1514	0.2348	0.8571	0.8686	13.989
σ	0.0001	0.0002	0.0002	0.0001	1.8962

6. CONCLUSIONS

We conducted extensive experiments on two large real-world social network datasets, and showed that social contextual information can greatly boost the performance of recommendation on these social network data. In particular, we have gained increases of 24.2% and 20.7% in prediction accuracy and 21.7% and 12.3% in recommendation Precision@K upon previous approaches on these social networks, respectively. Also, the proposed algorithm is general and can be easily adapted according to different real-world recommendation scenarios.

7. ACKNOWLEDGMENTS

This work is supported by the Natural Science Foundation of China (No.60933013, No.61003097), 973 Program (No.2011CB302206), National Significant Science and Technology Projects of China (No.2011ZX01042-001-002) and

Tsinghua-Tencent Joint Lab for Internet Innovation Technologies.

8. REFERENCES

[1] M. Balabanovic and Y. Shoham. Fab: content-based, collaborative recommendation. *Communications of the ACM*, 40:66–72, March 1997.

[2] A. Bandura. Social cognitive theory of mass communication. *Media Psychology*, 2001.

[3] L. S. Benjamin. Structural analysis of social behavior. *Psychological Review*, 1974.

[4] D. M. Blei, A. Y. Ng, and M. I. Jordan. Latent dirichlet allocation. *Journal of Machine Learning Research*, 3:993–1022, March 2003.

[5] R. Bond and P. B. Smith. Culture and conformity: a meta-analysis of studies using asch's (1952b, 1956) line judgment task. *Psychological Bulletin*, 119:111–137, January 1996.

[6] Y. Chen and J. Canny. Recommending ephemeral items at web scale. *In Proceedings of the 34th International ACM SIGIR Conference on Research and Development in Information Retrieval (SIGIR)*, pages 1013–1022, 2011.

[7] P. Cui, F. Wang, S. Liu, M. Ou, S. Yang, and L. Sun. Who should share what? item-level social influence prediction for users and posts ranking. *In Proceedings of the 34th International ACM SIGIR Conference on Research and Development in Information Retrieval (SIGIR)*, pages 185–194, 2011.

[8] M. Harvey, M. J. Carman, I. Ruthven, and F. Crestani. Bayesian latent variable models for collaborative item rating prediction. *In Proceedings of CIKM*, pages 699–708, 2011.

[9] J. L. Herlocker, J. A. Konstan, L. G. Terveen, and J. T. Riedl. Evaluating collaborative filtering recommender systems. *ACM Transactions on Information Systems (TOIS)*, 22:5–53, January 2004.

[10] J. Huang, X. Cheng, J. Guo, H. Shen, and K. Yang. Social recommendation with interpersonal influence. *In Proceedings of the 19th European Conference on Artificial Intelligence (ECAI)*, pages 601–606, 2010.

[11] M. Jamali and M. Ester. Trustwalker: a random walk model for combining trust-based and item-based recommendation. *In Proceedings of the 15th ACM SIGKDD International Conference on Knowledge Discovery and Data Mining (KDD)*, pages 397–406, 2009.

[12] D. Kong, C. Ding, and H. Huang. Robust nonnegative matrix factorization using l21-norm. *In Proceedings of CIKM*, pages 673–682, 2011.

[13] Y. Koren. Factorization meets the neighborhood: a multifaceted collaborative filtering model. *In Proceeding of the 14th ACM SIGKDD International Conference on Knowledge Discovery and Data Mining (KDD)*, pages 426–434, 2008.

[14] Y. Koren. Collaborative filtering with temporal dynamics. *In Proceeding of the 15th ACM SIGKDD International Conference on Knowledge Discovery and Data Mining (KDD)*, 2009.

[15] Y. Koren, R. Bell, and C. Volinsky. Matrix factorization techniques for recommender systems. *Computer*, 42:30–37, 2009.

[16] J. Leskovec, A. Singh, and J. Kleinberg. Patterns of influence in a recommendation network. *Lecture Notes in Computer Science*, 3918:380–389, 2006.

[17] L. Liu, J. Tang, J. Han, M. Jiang, and S. Yang. Mining topic-level influence in heterogeneous networks. *In Proceedings of CIKM*, pages 199–208, 2010.

[18] N. N. Liu, M. Zhao, and Q. Yang. Probabilistic latent preference analysis for collaborative filtering. *In Proceedings of CIKM*, pages 759–766, 2009.

[19] Q. Liu, E. Chen, H. Xiong, C. Ding, and J. Chen. Enhancing collaborative filtering by user interest expansion via personalized ranking. *IEEE Transactions on Systems, Man, and Cybernetics - Part B (TSMCB)*, 42(1):218–233, February 2012.

[20] H. Ma, H. Yang, M. R. Lyu, and I. King. Sorec: Social recommendation using probabilistic matrix factorization. *In Proceedings of CIKM*, pages 931–940, 2008.

[21] H. Ma, D. Zhou, C. Liu, M. R. Lyu, and I. King. Recommender system with social regularization. *In Proceedings of the 4th ACM International Conference on Web Search and Data Mining (WSDM)*, pages 287–296, 2011.

[22] P. Massa and P. Avesani. Trust-aware recommender systems. *In Proceedings of the 2007 ACM Conference on Recommender Systems (RecSys)*, 2007.

[23] S. Moghaddam, M. Jamali, M. Ester, and J. Habibi. Feedbacktrust: using feedback effects in trust-based recommendation systems. *In Proceedings of the 3rd ACM Conference on Recommender Systems (RecSys)*, pages 269–272, 2009.

[24] R. Salakhutdinov and A. Mnih. Probabilistic matrix factorization. *Neural Information Processing Systems (NIPS)*, 2007.

[25] M. J. Salganik. Experimental study of inequality and unpredictability in an artificial cultural market. *Science*, 311:854–856, 2006.

[26] B. Sarwar, G. Karypis, J. Konstan, and J. Reidl. Item-based collaborative filtering recommendation algorithms. *In Proceedings of the 10th International Conference on World Wide Web (WWW)*, pages 285–295, 2001.

[27] L. Si and R. Jin. Unified filtering by combining collaborative filtering and content-based filtering via mixture model and exponential model. *In Proceedings of CIKM*, pages 156–157, 2004.

[28] M. E. Tipping and C. M. Bishop. Probabilistic principal component analysis. *Journal of the Royal Statistical Society, Series B*, 61:611–622, 1999.

[29] F. Wang, H. Tong, and C.-Y. Lin. Towards evolutionary nonnegative matrix factorization. *In Proceedings of the 25th AAAI Conference on Artificial Intelligence (AAAI)*, pages 501–506, 2011.

[30] S.-H. Yang, B. Long, A. Smola, N. Sadagopan, Z. Zheng, and H. Zha. Like like alike: joint friendship and interest propagation in social networks. *In Proceedings of the 20th International Conference on World Wide Web (WWW)*, 2011.

Mining High Utility Itemsets without Candidate Generation

Mengchi Liu[†‡] Junfeng Qu[†*]

[†]State Key Lab of Software Engineering, School of Computer, Wuhan University, Wuhan 430072, China

[‡]School of Computer Science, Carleton University, Ottawa K1S 5B6, Canada

mengchi@scs.carleton.ca cocoqjf@gmail.com

ABSTRACT

High utility itemsets refer to the sets of items with high utility like profit in a database, and efficient mining of high utility itemsets plays a crucial role in many real-life applications and is an important research issue in data mining area. To identify high utility itemsets, most existing algorithms first generate candidate itemsets by overestimating their utilities, and subsequently compute the exact utilities of these candidates. These algorithms incur the problem that a very large number of candidates are generated, but most of the candidates are found out to be not high utility after their exact utilities are computed. In this paper, we propose an algorithm, called HUI-Miner (High Utility Itemset Miner), for high utility itemset mining. HUI-Miner uses a novel structure, called utility-list, to store both the utility information about an itemset and the heuristic information for pruning the search space of HUI-Miner. By avoiding the costly generation and utility computation of numerous candidate itemsets, HUI-Miner can efficiently mine high utility itemsets from the utility-lists constructed from a mined database. We compared HUI-Miner with the state-of-the-art algorithms on various databases, and experimental results show that HUI-Miner outperforms these algorithms in terms of both running time and memory consumption.

Categories and Subject Descriptors

H.2.8 [**Database Applications**]: Data mining

General Terms

Algorithms, Experimentation, Performance

Keywords

High utility itemset, mining algorithm

*Corresponding author.

CIKM'12, October 29–November 2, 2012, Maui, HI, USA.

1. INTRODUCTION

The rapid development of database techniques facilitates the storage and usage of massive data from business corporations, governments, and scientific organizations. How to obtain valuable information from various databases has received considerable attention, which results in the sharp rise of related research topics. Among the topics, the high utility itemset mining problem is one of the most important, and it derives from the famous frequent itemset mining problem [7, 8].

Mining frequent itemsets is to identify the sets of items that appear frequently in transactions in a database. The frequency of an itemset is measured with the support of the itemset, i.e., the number of transactions containing the itemset. If the support of an itemset exceeds a user-specified minimum support threshold, the itemset is considered as frequent. Most frequent itemset mining algorithms employ the downward closure property of itemsets [4]. That is, all supersets of an infrequent itemset are infrequent, and all subsets of a frequent itemset are frequent. The property provides the algorithms with a powerful pruning strategy. In the process of mining frequent itemsets, once an infrequent itemset is identified, the algorithms no longer check all supersets of the itemset. For example, for a database with n items, after the algorithms identify an infrequent itemset containing k items, there is no need to check all of its supersets, i.e., $2^{(n-k)} - 1$ itemsets.

Mining of frequent itemsets only takes the presence and absence of items into account. Other information about items is not considered, such as the independent utility of an item and the context utility of an item in a transaction. Typically, in a supermarket database, each item has a distinct price/profit, and each item in a transaction is associated with a distinct count which means the quantity of the item one bought. Consider the database in Fig. 1. There are seven items in the utility table and seven transactions in the transaction table in the database. To calculate support, an algorithm only makes use of the information of the first two columns in the transaction table, the information of both the utility table and the other columns in the transaction table are discarded. However, an itemset with high support may have low utility, or vice versa. For example, the support and utility of itemset {bc} appearing in T1, T2, and T6 are 3 and 18 respectively(See Section 2.1 for utility computation), and those of itemset {de}

Item	a	b	c	d	e	f	g
Utility	1	2	1	5	4	3	1

(a) Utility table

Tid	Transaction	Count
T1	{ b, c, d, g }	{ 1, 2, 1, 1 }
T2	{ a, b, c, d, e }	{ 4, 1, 3, 1, 1 }
T3	{ a, c, d }	{ 4, 2, 1 }
T4	{ c, e, f }	{ 2, 1, 1 }
T5	{ a, b, d, e }	{ 5, 2, 1, 2 }
T6	{ a, b, c, f }	{ 3, 4, 1, 2 }
T7	{ d, g }	{ 1, 5 }

(b) Transaction table

Figure 1: Database

appearing in T2 and T5 are 2 and 22. In some applications, such as market analysis, one may be more interested in the utility rather than support of itemsets. Traditional frequent itemset mining algorithms cannot evaluate the utility information about itemsets.

Like frequent itemsets, itemsets with utilities not less than a user-specified minimum utility threshold are generally valuable and interesting, and they are called "high utility itemsets". To mine all high utility itemsets from a database is very intractable, because the downward closure property of itemsets no longer holds for high utility itemsets. When items are appended to an itemset one by one, the support of the itemset monotonously decreases or remains unchanged, but the utility of the itemset varies irregularly. For example, for the database in Fig. 1, the supports of {a}, {ab}, {abc}, and {abcd} are 4, 3, 2, and 1, but the utilities of these itemsets are 16, 26, 21, and 14, respectively. Suppose the threshold is 20, and then high utility {abc} contains both high utility {ab} and low utility {a}. Therefore, the pruning strategy used in the frequent itemset mining algorithms becomes invalid.

Recently, a number of high utility itemset mining algorithms have been proposed [25, 18, 14, 5, 23, 22]. Most of the algorithms adopt a similar framework: firstly, generate candidate high utility itemsets from a database; secondly, compute the exact utilities of the candidates by scanning the database to identify high utility itemsets. However, the algorithms often generate a very large number of candidate itemsets and thus are confronted with two problems: (1) excessive memory requirement for storing candidate itemsets; (2) a large amount of running time for generating candidates and computing their exact utilities. When the number of candidates is so large that they cannot be stored in memory, the algorithms will fail or their performance will be degraded due to thrashing.

To solve these problems, we propose in this paper an algorithm for high utility itemset mining. The contributions of the paper are as follows:

1. A novel structure, called *utility-list*, is proposed. A utility-list stores not only the utility information about an itemset but also the heuristic information about whether the itemset should be pruned or not.

2. An efficient algorithm, called *HUI-Miner* (*High Utility Itemset Miner*), is developed. Different from previous algorithms, HUI-Miner does not generate candidate high utility itemsets. After constructing the initial utility-lists from a mined database, HUI-Miner can mine high utility itemsets from these utility-lists.

3. Extensive experiments on various databases were performed to compare HUI-Miner with the state-of-the-art algorithms. Experimental results that show HUI-Miner outperforms these algorithms are reported.

After the related background is stated in Section 2, the paper is organized according to the three points aforementioned in Section 3, 4, and 5. Our work is summarized in Section 6.

2. BACKGROUND

In the section, we first give the formal description of the high utility itemset mining problem and subsequently introduce the previous solutions to the problem.

2.1 Problem Definition

Let $\mathcal{I}=\{i_1, i_2, i_3, \ldots, i_n\}$ be a set of items and DB be a database composed of a utility table and a transaction table. Each item in $\mathcal{I}$ has a utility value in the utility table. Each transaction T in the transaction table has a unique identifier (*tid*) and is a subset of $\mathcal{I}$, in which each item is associated with a count value. An itemset is a subset of $\mathcal{I}$ and is called a k-itemset if it contains k items.

DEFINITION 1. *The external utility of item i, denoted as eu(i), is the utility value of i in the utility table of DB.*

DEFINITION 2. *The internal utility of item i in transaction T, denoted as iu(i, T), is the count value associated with i in T in the transaction table of DB.*

DEFINITION 3. *The utility of item i in transaction T, denoted as u(i, T), is the product of iu(i, T) and eu(i), where* $u(i, T) = iu(i, T) \times eu(i)$.

For example, in Fig. 1, eu(e) = 4, iu(e, T5) = 2, and u(e, T5)= iu(e, T5) × eu(e) = 2 × 4 = 8.

DEFINITION 4. *The utility of itemset X in transaction T, denoted as u(X, T), is the sum of the utilities of all the items in X in T in which X is contained, where* $u(X, T) = \sum_{i \in X \wedge X \subseteq T} u(i, T)$.

DEFINITION 5. *The utility of itemset X, denoted as u(X), is the sum of the utilities of X in all the transactions containing X in DB, where* $u(X) = \sum_{T \in DB \wedge X \subseteq T} u(X, T)$.

For example, in Fig. 1, u({ae}, T2) = u(a, T2) + u(e, T2) = 4 × 1 + 1 × 4 = 8, and u({ae}) = u({ae}, T2) + u({ae}, T5) = 8 + 13 = 21.

DEFINITION 6. *The utility of transaction T, denoted as tu(T), is the sum of the utilities of all the items in T, where* $tu(T) = \sum_{i \in T} u(i, T)$*, and the total utility of DB is the sum of the utilities of all the transactions in DB.*

Fig. 2 shows the utility of each transaction, for example, tu(T1) = u(b, T1) + u(c, T1) + u(d, T1) + u(g, T1) = 2 + 2 + 5 + 1 = 10. The total utility of the database in Fig. 1 is 98. An itemset X is *high utility* if u(X) is not less than a user-specified minimum utility threshold denoted as *minutil*,

Tid	T1	T2	T3	T4	T5	T6	T7
TU	10	18	11	9	22	18	10

Figure 2: Transaction Utility

or the product of a minutil and the total utility of a mined database if the minutil is a percentage. Given a database and a minutil, the high utility itemset mining problem is to discover from the database all the itemsets whose utilities are not less than the minutil.

2.2 Related Work

Before the high utility itemset mining problem was formally proposed [25] as above, a variation of the problem had been studied, namely the problem of extracting share frequent itemsets [6, 13, 12] that invariably defines the external utility of each item as 1. The ZP [6], ZSP [6], FSH [13], ShFSH [12], and DCG [11] algorithms for share frequent itemset mining can also be used to mine high utility itemsets. Since the downward closure property cannot be directly applied, Liu et al. proposed an important property [17] for pruning the search space of the high utility itemset mining problem.

DEFINITION 7. *The transaction-weighted utility of itemset X in DB, denoted as twu(X), is the sum of the utilities of all the transactions containing X in DB, where* $twu(X) = \sum_{T \in DB \wedge X \subseteq T} tu(T)$.

PROPERTY 1. *If twu(X) is less than a given "minutil", all supersets of X are not high utility.*
Rationale. If $X \subseteq X'$, *then* $u(X') \leq twu(X') \leq twu(X) <$ *minutil.*

Itemset	{a}	{b}	{c}	{d}	{e}	{f}	{g}
TWU	69	68	66	71	49	27	10

Figure 3: Transaction-Weighted Utility

Fig. 3 shows the transaction-weighted utilities of all 1-itemsets. For example, itemset {f} is contained in T4 and T6, and thus twu({f}) = tu(T4) + tu(T6) = 9 + 18 = 27. If a minutil is equal to 30, all supersets of {f} are not high utility according to Property 1. The Two-Phase algorithm [18, 17] first adopts Property 1 to prune the search space. Afterwards, the isolated items discarding strategy (IIDS) is proposed [14], and the strategy can be incorporated in the above algorithms to improve their performance, for example, the FUM [14] and DCG+ [14] algorithms outperform ShFSH and DCG, respectively.

ZP, ZSP, FSH, ShFSH, DCG, Two-Phase, FUM, and DCG+ mine high utility itemsets as the famous Apriori algorithm [4] mines frequent itemsets. Given a database, firstly, all 1-itemsets are candidate high utility itemsets. After scanning the database, the algorithms eliminate unpromising 1-itemsets and generate 2-itemsets from the remaining 1-itemsets as candidate high itemsets. After the second scan over the database, unpromising 2-itemsets are eliminated and 3-itemsets as candidates are generated from the remaining 2-itemsets.. The procedure is performed repeatedly until there is no generated candidate itemset. Finally, these algorithms, except for DCG and DCG+, compute the exact utilities of all remaining candidates by an additional database scan to identify high utility itemsets (DCG and DCG+ compute exact utility in each database scan.). Besides the two problems mentioned in Section 1, these algorithms suffer from the level-wise mining problems as well, e.g., repeated database scans.

The algorithms based on the FP-Growth algorithm [9] show better performance. These algorithms include IHUPTWU [5], UP-Growth [23], and UP-Growth+ [22]. Firstly, they transform a mined database into a prefix-tree, and the tree maintains the utility information about itemsets. Secondly, for each item of the tree, if it is estimated to be valuable, namely there is likely to be high utility itemsets containing the item, the algorithms construct a conditional prefix-tree for the item. Thirdly, the algorithms recursively process all conditional prefix-trees to generate candidate high utility itemsets. Finally, the algorithms scan the database again to compute the exact utilities of all candidates for identifying high utility itemsets. Reducing the numbers of both database scans and candidate itemsets, these algorithms outperform the Apriori-based algorithms. Even so, compared with the number of resultant high utility itemsets, these algorithms still generate a large number of candidate itemsets in most cases, and it is very costly to both generate these candidates and compute their exact utilities.

There are also a number of studies that focus on the problem of mining an approximate set of all high utility itemsets [10, 24] or a condensed set of all high utility itemsets [20, 21]. In this study, the problem of mining the complete set of all high utility itemsets from a database is discussed.

3. UTILITY-LIST STRUCTURE

To mine high utility itemsets, many previous algorithms directly perform on an original database. Although FP-Growth-based algorithms generate candidate itemsets from prefix-trees, they have to compute the exact utilities of candidates by scanning the database. In the section, we propose a utility-list structure to maintain the utility information about a database.

3.1 Initial Utility-Lists

In our HUI-Miner algorithm, each itemset holds a utility-list. Initial utility-lists storing the utility information about a mined database can be constructed by two scans of the database. Firstly, the transaction-weighted utilities of all items are accumulated by a database scan. If the transaction-weighted utility of an item is less than a given minutil, the item is no longer considered according to Property 1 in the subsequent mining process. For the items whose transaction-weighted utilities exceed the minutil, they are sorted in transaction-weighted-utility-ascending order. For the database in Fig. 1, suppose the minutil is 30, and then the algorithm no longer takes items f and g into consideration after the first database scan. The remaining items are sorted: e<c<b<a<d.

DEFINITION 8. *A transaction is considered as "revised" after (1) all the items whose transaction-weighted utilities are less than a given minutil are deleted from the transaction; (2) the remaining items are sorted in transaction-weighted-utility-ascending order.*

When scanning the database again, the algorithm revises

Tid	Item	Util.	Item	Util.	item	Util.	item	Util.	item	Util.	TU
T1	c	2	b	2	d	5					9
T2	e	4	c	3	b	2	a	4	d	5	18
T3	c	2	a	4	d	5					11
T4	e	4	c	2							6
T5	e	8	b	4	a	5	d	5			22
T6	c	1	b	8	a	3					12
T7	d	5									5

Figure 4: Database View

each transaction for constructing initial utility-lists. The database view in Fig. 4 lists all revised transactions derived from the database in Fig. 1. From here on, the following convention holds in the remainder of this paper:

CONVENTION 1. *A transaction is considered as revised, and all the items in an itemset are sorted in transaction-weighted-utility-ascending order, when mentioned.*

DEFINITION 9. *Given an itemset X and a transaction (or itemset) T with $X \subseteq T$, the set of all the items after X in T is denoted as T/X.*

For example, consider the view in Fig. 4, T2/{eb} = {ad} and T2/{c} = {bad}.

DEFINITION 10. *The remaining utility of itemset X in transaction T, denoted as $ru(X, T)$, is the sum of the utilities of all the items in T/X in T, where $ru(X, T) = \sum_{i \in (T/X)} u(i, T)$.*

Each element in the utility-list of itemset X contains three fields: *tid, iutil,* and *rutil.*

- Field tid indicates a transaction T containing X.
- Field iutil is the utility of X in T, i.e., u(X, T).
- Field rutil is the remaining utility of X in T, i.e., ru(X, T).

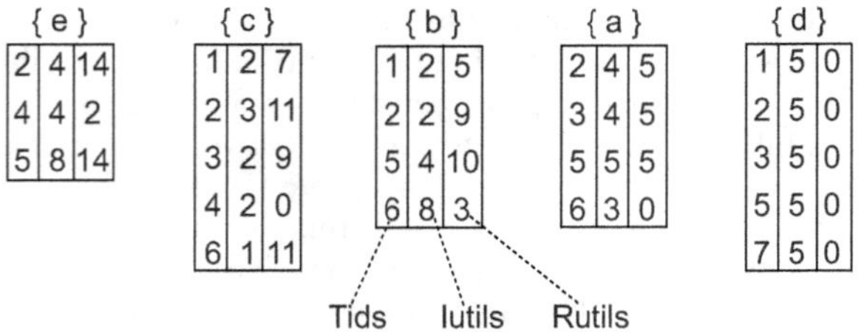

Figure 5: Initial Utility-Lists

During the second database scan, the algorithm constructs the initial utility-lists showed in Fig. 5. For example, consider the utility-list of itemset {c}. In T1, u({c}, T1) = 2, ru({c}, T1) = u(b, T1) + u(d, T1) = 2 + 5 = 7, and thus element <1, 2, 7> is in the utility-list of {c} (<x, y, z> means <tid, iutil, rutil>, and 1 represents T1 for simplicity.). In T2, u({c}, T2) = 3, ru({c}, T2) = u(b, T2) + u(a, T2) + u(d, T2) = 2 + 4 + 5 = 11, and thus element <2, 3, 11> belongs to the utility-list of {c} as well. The rest can be figured out in the same manner.

3.2 Utility-Lists of 2-Itemsets

No need for database scan, the utility-list of 2-itemset $\{xy\}$ can be constructed by the intersection of the utility-list of $\{x\}$ and that of $\{y\}$. The algorithm identifies common transactions by comparing the tids in the two utility-lists. Suppose the lengths of the utility-lists are m and n respectively, and then $(m + n)$ comparisons at most are enough for identifying common transactions, because all tids in a utility-list are ordered. The identification process is actually a 2-way comparison. For example, the tid comparison between the utility-lists of itemsets {e} and {c} in Fig. 5 is demonstrated in Fig. 6(a).

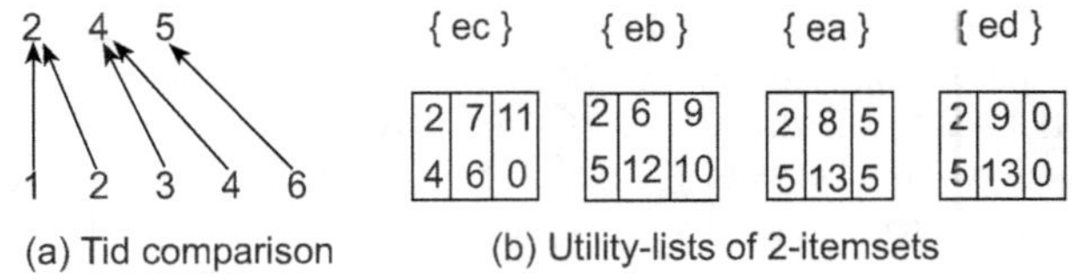

Figure 6: Constructing Utility-Lists of 2-Itemsets

For each common transaction t, the algorithm will generate an element E and append it to the utility-list of $\{xy\}$. The tid field of E is the tid of t. The iutil of E is the sum of the iutils associated with t in the utility-lists of $\{x\}$ and $\{y\}$. Suppose x is before y, and then the rutil of E is assigned as the rutil associated with t in the utility-list of $\{y\}$.

Fig. 6(b) depicts the utility-lists of all the 2-itemsets with itemset {e} as prefix. For example, to construct the utility-list of itemset {eb}, the algorithm intersects the utility-list of {e}, i.e., {<2, 4, 14>, <4, 4, 2>, <5, 8, 14>}, and that of {b}, i.e., {<1, 2, 5>, <2, 2, 9>, <5, 4, 10>, <6, 8, 3>}, which results in {<2, 6, 9>, <5, 12, 10>}. One can observe from the database view in Fig. 4 that itemset {eb} only appears in T2 and T5. In T2, u({eb}, T2) = u(e, T2) + u(b, T2) = 2 + 4 = 6, and ru({eb}, T2) = u(a, T2) + u(d, T2) = 4 + 5 = 9. Similarly, in T5, the utility of {eb} is 8 + 4 = 12, and the remaining utility of {eb} is 5 + 5 = 10.

3.3 Utility-Lists of k-Itemsets (k≥3)

To construct the utility-list of k-itemset $\{i_1 \cdots i_{(k-1)} i_k\}$ (k≥3), we can directly intersect the utility-list of $\{i_1 \cdots i_{(k-2)} i_{(k-1)}\}$ and that of $\{i_1 \cdots i_{(k-2)} i_k\}$ as we do to construct the utility-list of a 2-itemset. For example, to construct the utility-list of {eba}, we can intersect the utility-list of {eb} and that of {ea} in Fig. 6(b), and the resultant utility-list is depicted in Fig. 7(a). Itemset {eba} does appear in T2 and T5 in the database view in Fig. 4, and however the utilities of the itemset in T2 and T5 are 10 and 17 rather than 14 and 25, respectively.

The reason for miscalculating the utility of {eba} in T2 is that the sum of the utilities of both {eb} and

Figure 7: Utility-Lists of 3-Itemsets

Algorithm 1: *Construct* Algorithm

```
   Input: P.UL, the utility-list of itemset P;
          Px.UL, the utility-list of itemset Px;
          Py.UL, the utility-list of itemset Py.
   Output: Pxy.UL, the utility-list of itemset Pxy.
1  Pxy.UL = NULL;
2  foreach element Ex ∈ Px.UL do
3      if ∃Ey∈Py.UL and Ex.tid==Ey.tid then
4          if P.UL is not empty then
5              search such element E∈P.UL that
               E.tid==Ex.tid;
6              Exy=<Ex.tid, Ex.iutil+Ey.iutil-E.iutil,
               Ey.rutil>;
7          else
8              Exy=<Ex.tid, Ex.iutil+Ey.iutil, Ey.rutil>;
9          end
10         append Exy to Pxy.UL;
11     end
12 end
13 return Pxy.UL;
```

{ea} in T2 contains the utility of {e} in T2 twofold. Generally, to calculate the utility of $\{i_1 \cdots i_{(k-2)} i_{(k-1)} i_k\}$ in T, the following formula holds: u($\{i_1 \cdots i_{(k-2)} i_{(k-1)} i_k\}$, T) = u($\{i_1 \cdots i_{(k-2)} i_{(k-1)}\}$, T) + u($\{i_1 \cdots i_{(k-2)} i_k\}$, T) - u($\{i_1 \cdots i_{(k-2)}\}$, T).

Therefore, the iutil of the element associated with T2 in the utility-list of {eba} is: u({eba}, T2) = u({eb}, T2) + u({ea}, T2) - u({e}, T2) = 6 + 8 - 4 = 10. That associated with T5 is: u({eba}, T5) = u({eb}, T5) + u({ea}, T5) - u({e}, T5) = 12 + 13 - 8 = 17. The values of u({eb}, T), u({ea}, T), and u({e}, T) can be accessed from the utility-lists of {eb}, {ea}, and {e}, respectively.

Suppose itemsets *Px* and *Py* are the combinations of itemset *P* with items *x* and *y* (*x* is before *y*.), respectively, and *P.UL*, *Px.UL*, and *Py.UL* are the utility-lists of itemsets *P*, *Px*, and *Py*. Algorithm 1 shows how to construct the utility-list of itemset *Pxy*. The utility-list of a 2-itemset is constructed when *P.UL* is empty, namely when *P* is empty, and the utility-list of a *k*-itemset (k≥3) is constructed when *P.UL* is not empty. Note that element *E* in line 5 can always be found out when *P.UL* is not empty, because the tid sets in both *Px.UL* and *Py.UL* are subsets of the tid set in *P.UL*. The utility-lists of all the itemsets with {eb} as prefix constructed by Algorithm 1 are showed in Fig. 7(b).

Thus far, we have illustrated how to construct the utility-list of an itemset. When does HUI-Miner construct the utility-list of an itemset and how does HUI-Miner judge whether or not the utility-list of an itemset should be constructed, which will be illuminated in the next section.

4. HIGH UTILITY ITEMSET MINER

After constructing the initial utility-lists from a database, the HUI-Miner algorithm can efficiently mine all high utility itemsets from the utility-lists as the Eclat algorithm mines frequent itemsets [26]. In the section, the search space of HUI-Miner is first introduced, and subsequently we propose a pruning strategy for the algorithm. Finally, the HUI-Miner algorithm and a number of implementation details are presented.

4.1 Search Space

The search space of the high utility itemset mining problem can be represented as a set-enumeration tree [19]. Given a set of items $\mathcal{I} = \{i_1, i_2, i_3, \ldots, i_n\}$ and a total order on all items (suppose $i_1 < i_2 < \cdots < i_n$), a set-enumeration tree representing all itemsets can be constructed as follows. Firstly, the root of the tree is created; secondly, the n child nodes of the root representing n 1-itemsets are created, respectively; thirdly, for a node representing itemset $\{i_s \cdots i_e\}$ $(1 \leq s \leq e < n)$, the $(n-e)$ child nodes of the node representing itemsets $\{i_s \cdots i_e i_{(e+1)}\}$, $\{i_s \cdots i_e i_{(e+2)}\}$, ..., $\{i_s \cdots i_e i_n\}$ are created. The third step is done repeatedly until all leaf nodes are created. For example, given $\mathcal{I}$ = {e, c, b, a, d} and $e < c < b < a < d$, a set-enumeration tree representing all itemsets of $\mathcal{I}$ is depicted in Fig. 8.

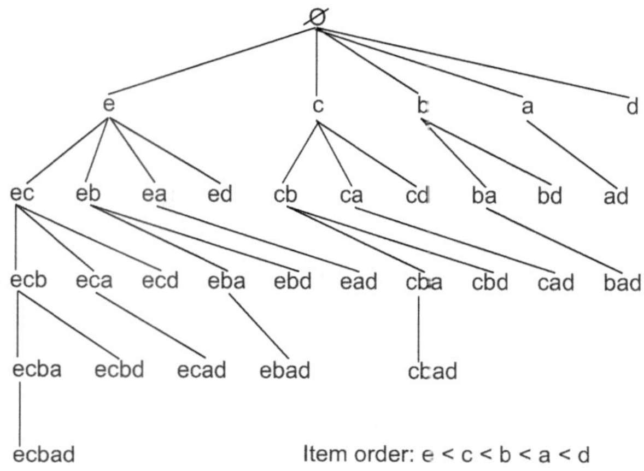

Figure 8: Set-Enumeration Tree

DEFINITION 11. *Given a set-enumeration tree, an itemset represented by a node is called an extension of an itemset represented by an ancestor node of the node. For an itemset containing k items, its extension containing (k+i) items is called an i-extension of the itemset.*

PROPERTY 2. *If X' is an extension of X, (X'–X)=(X'/X).*
Rationale. Any extension of X is a combination of X with the item(s) after X.

For example, in Fig. 8, itemsets {eba} and {ebd} are the 1-extensions of {eb}, and {ebad} is the 2-extension of {eb}. Starting from the root of a set-enumeration tree, for an itemset, HUI-Miner first checks all of its 1-extensions by constructing their utility-lists. After identifying and outputting high utility itemsets from the extensions, HUI-Miner recursively processes promising extensions one by one and gives up the others. The question is: what are "promising" extensions?

4.2 Pruning Strategy

Exhaustive search can discover all high utility itemsets but is excessively time-consuming, because the numbers of items are large for many databases. For a database with n items, exhaustive search has to check 2^n itemsets.

To reduce the search space, we can exploit the iutils and rutils in the utility-list of an itemset. The sum of all the iutils in the utility-list of an itemset is the utility of the itemset according to Definition 5, and thus the itemset is high utility if the sum exceeds a given minutil. The sum of all the iutils and rutils in the utility-list provides HUI-Miner with the key information about whether the itemset should be pruned or not.

LEMMA 1. *Given the utility-list of itemset X, if the sum of all the iutils and rutils in the utility-list is less than a given "minutil", any extension X' of X is not high utility.*

PROOF. For $\forall$ *transaction* $t \supseteq X'$:

$$\because X' \text{ is an extension of } X \implies (X' - X) = (X'/X)$$
$$X \subset X' \subseteq t \implies (X'/X) \subseteq (t/X)$$

$$\begin{aligned} \therefore u(X', t) &= u(X,t) + u((X'-X),t) \\ &= u(X,t) + u((X'/X),t) \\ &= u(X,t) + \sum_{i \in (X'/X)} u(i,t) \\ &\leq u(X,t) + \sum_{i \in (t/X)} u(i,t) \\ &= u(X,t) + ru(X,t), \end{aligned}$$

suppose $id(t)$ denotes the tid of transaction t, $X.tids$ denotes the tid set in the utility-list of X, and $X'.tids$ that in X', then:

$$\because X \subset X' \implies X'.tids \subseteq X.tids$$

$$\begin{aligned} \therefore \; u(X') &= \sum_{id(t) \in X'.tids} u(X', t) \\ &\leq \sum_{id(t) \in X'.tids} (u(X,t) + ru(X,t)) \\ &\leq \sum_{id(t) \in X.tids} (u(X,t) + ru(X,t)) \\ &< minutil. \end{aligned}$$

□

For example, consider the utility-lists in Fig. 6(b). Itemset {ec} should be pruned because the sum of all the iutils and rutils in its utility-list, i.e., 24, is less than the minutil, i.e., 30. Therefore, there is no need to check the 7 extensions of itemset {ec} (see Fig. 8).

4.3 HUI-Miner Algorithm

Algorithm 2 shows the pseudo-code of HUI-Miner. For each utility-list X in *ULs* (the second parameter), if the sum of all the iutils in X exceeds *minutil*, and then the extension associated with X is high utility and outputted. According to Lemma 1, only when the sum of all the iutils and rutils in X exceeds *minutil* should it be processed further. When the initial utility-lists are constructed from a database, they are sorted and processed in transaction-weighted-utility-ascending order (see Section 3.1). Therefore, all the utility-lists in *ULs* are ordered as the initial utility-lists are. To explore the search space, the algorithm intersects X and each utility-list Y after X in *ULs*. Suppose X is the utility-list of itemset Px and Y that of itemset Py, and then *construct*($P.UL$, X, Y) in line 8 is to construct the utility-list of itemset Pxy as stated in Algorithm 1. Finally, the set of utility-lists of all the 1-extensions of itemset Px is recursively processed. Given a database and a minutil,

Algorithm 2: *HUI-Miner* Algorithm

Input: $P.UL$, the utility-list of itemset P, initially empty;
ULs, the set of utility-lists of all P's 1-extensions;
minutil, the minimum utility threshold.

Output: all the high utility itemsets with P as prefix.

```
1  foreach utility-list X in ULs do
2      if SUM(X.iutils)≥minutil then
3          output the extension associated with X;
4      end
5      if SUM(X.iutils)+SUM(X.rutils)≥minutil then
6          exULs = NULL;
7          foreach utility-list Y after X in ULs do
8              exULs = exULs+Construct(P.UL, X, Y);
9          end
10         HUI-Miner(X, exULs, minutil);
11     end
12 end
```

after the initial utility-lists *IULs* are constructed, *HUI-Miner*(∅, IULs, minutil) can mine all high utility itemsets.

4.4 Implementation Details

The sums of the iutils and rutils in the utility-list of an itemset can be computed by scanning the utility-list. To avoid utility-list scan, in the process of constructing a utility-list, HUI-Miner simultaneously accumulates the iutils and rutils in the utility-list. In addition, there is also no need to bind each itemset to its utility-list. The itemsets represented by all child nodes of a node in a set-enumeration tree have the same prefix itemset. Therefore, for a 1-extension, its extended item can be separated from its prefix itemset. We slightly modify the utility-list structure when implementing HUI-Miner. For example, the utility-lists in Fig. 7(b) are implemented as those showed in Fig. 9. The first line in a utility-list stores the extended item and the sums of the iutils and rutils, and the prefix itemset is stored independently.

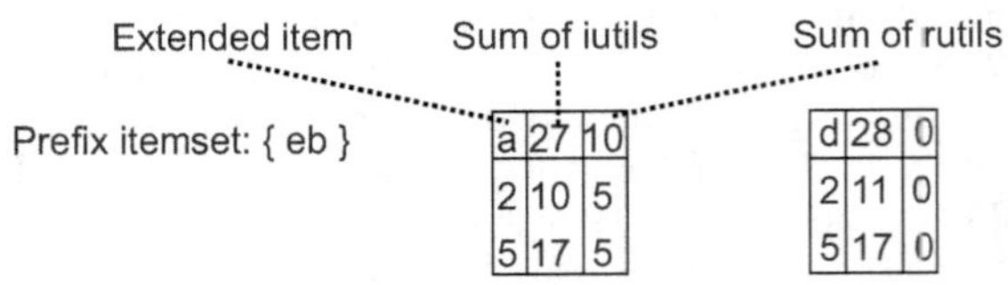

Figure 9: Utility-List Implementation

Another important detail is the processing order of items. In previous algorithms, such as IHUPTWU and UP-Growth, items are sorted in transaction-weighted-utility-descending order, which can reduce the size of prefix-trees used in these algorithms. However, IHUPTWU and UP-Growth process items in transaction-weighted-utility-ascending order. The processing order of items can result in the decrease in the explored scope of the search space and thus speed an algorithm up [15]. HUI-Miner adopts utility-lists as data structure, and the size of utility-lists is constant, no matter what order items are sorted in. Therefore, in HUI-Miner, items are sorted in transaction-weighted-utility-ascending order, and more important, processed in the same order.

Database	Size(kB)	#Trans	#Items	AvgLen	MaxLen
Accidents	59663	340183	468	33.8	51
Chain	63573	1112949	46086	7.3	170
Chess	591	3196	75	37	37
Kosarak	49859	990002	41270	8.1	2498
Mushroom	963	8124	119	23	23
Retail	6076	88162	16470	10.3	76
T10I4D100K	6144	100000	870	10.1	29
T40I10D100K	23796	100000	942	39.6	77

Figure 10: Statistical Information about Databases

5. EXPERIMENTS

To evaluate the performance of HUI-Miner, we have done extensive experiments on various databases, in which HUI-Miner is compared with the state-of-the-art mining algorithms. In this section, experimental results are reported and discussed.

5.1 Experimental Setup

Besides HUI-Miner, our experiments include the following algorithms: IHUPTWU (the fastest one among the algorithms proposed in [5]), UP-Growth [23], and UP-Growth+ [22]. The main procedure of IHUPTWU has been introduced in Section 2.2. On the basis of IHUPTWU, UP-Growth incorporates four strategies to lessen the estimated utilities of candidate itemsets and thus reduces the number of candidates. UP-Growth+, an improved UP-Growth algorithm, can generate fewer candidate itemsets than UP-Growth for a mining task. The less the number of candidate itemsets is, the less the costs of the generation and utility computation of candidates are. The three state-of-the-art algorithms had been proven to be superior to other algorithms, such as Two-Phase [18], ShFSM [12], DCG [11], FUM [14], and DCG+ [14]. Further, we optimized the three algorithms by transforming a mined database into a database view similar to that in Fig. 4. The view is implemented in memory, which can not only reduce the size of the database but also speed utility computation up.

The four algorithms were implemented in C++ language, used the same libraries, and were compiled using g++ (version 4.3.2). The experiments were performed on a 2.83GHz PC machine (Intel Core2 Q9500) with 4GB of memory, running on a Debian (Linux 2.6.26) operating system.

Eight databases were used in our experiments. Database *chain* was downloaded from NU-MineBench 2.0 [2], in which transaction records taken from a major grocery store chain in California are contained. The other databases were downloaded from FIMI Repository [1]. Databases *accidents*, *chess*, *kosarak*, *mushroom*, and *retail* are real. Synthetic databases *T10I4D100K* and *T40I10D100K* were generated by IBM Quest Synthetic Data Generation Code. Other than *chain*, the other databases do not provide item utility (external utility) and item count for each transaction (internal utility). Like the performance evaluation of previous algorithms [5, 23, 22], external utilities for items are generated between 0.01 and 10 using a log-normal distribution and internal utilities for items are generated randomly ranging from 1 to 10. Fig. 10 shows the statistical information about these databases, including the size on disk, the number of transactions, the number of distinct items, the average number of items in a transaction, and the maximal number of items in the longest transaction(s).

5.2 Running Time

The running time of the four algorithms on all databases is depicted in Fig. 11. Running time was recorded by the "time" command, and it contains input time, CPU time, and output time. The output results of the four algorithms are the same for a mining task, and they were written to "/dev/null". We terminated a mining task, once its running time exceeds 10000 seconds.

When measuring running time, we varied the minutil for each database. The lower the minutil is, the larger the number of high utility itemsets is, and thus the more the running time is. For example, for database *chain* in Fig. 11(b), when the minutils are 0.004% and 0.009%, the numbers of high utility itemsets are 18480 and 4578, and the running times of HUI-Miner are 580.9 seconds and

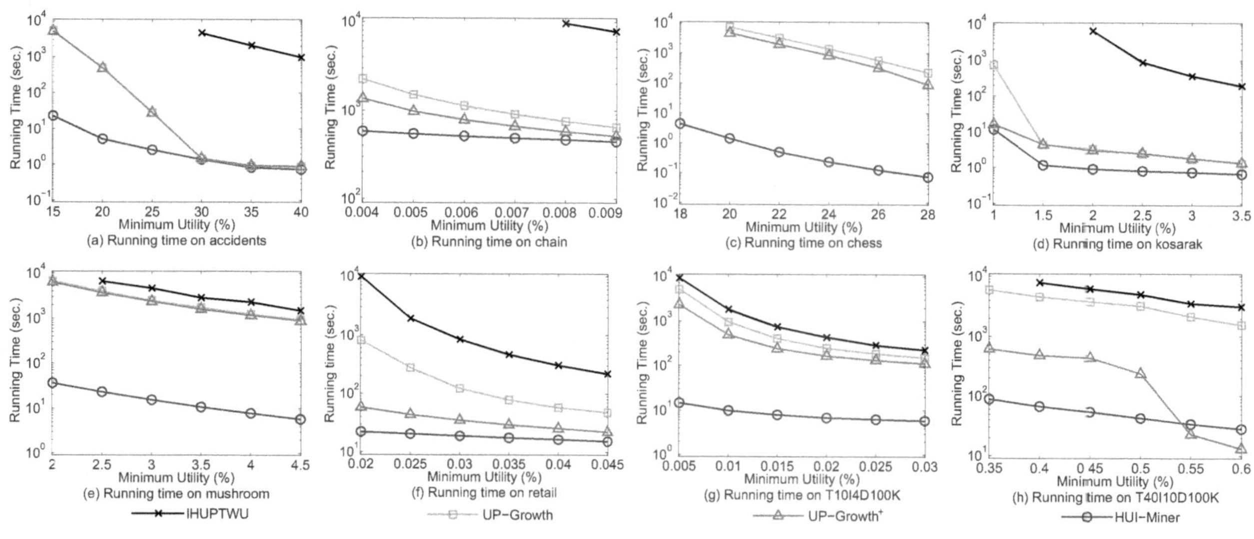

Figure 11: Running Time

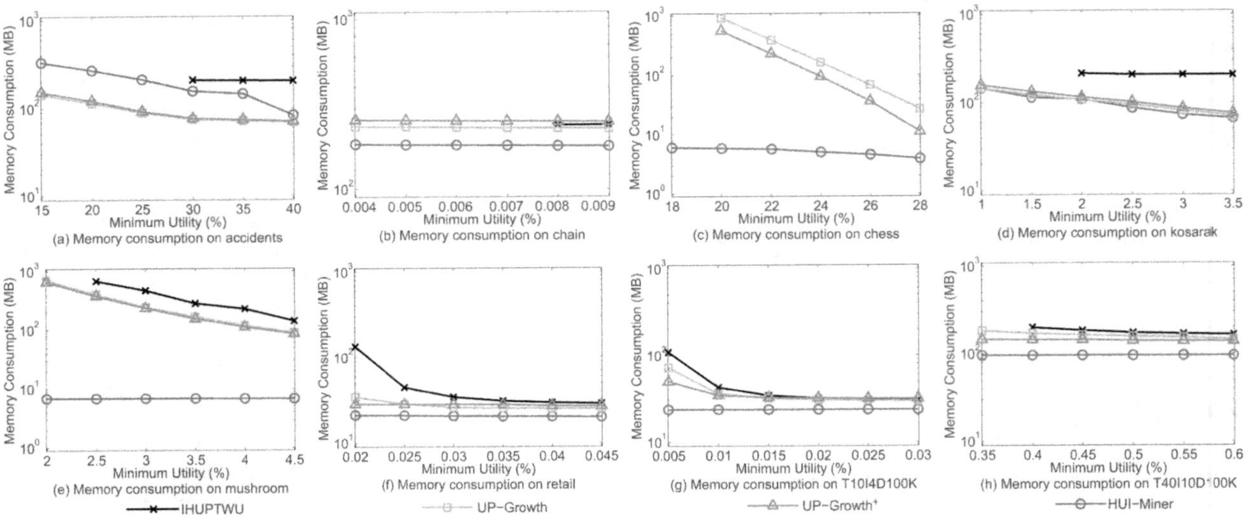

Figure 12: Memory Consumption

445.1 seconds, respectively. In addition, the curve for UP-Growth almost totally overlaps the curve for UP-Growth+ in Fig. 11(a); the running time of IHUPTWU for any minutil exceeds 10000 seconds for database *chess*, and thus there is no curve for IHUPTWU in Fig. 11(c).

For almost all databases and minutils, HUI-Miner performs the best. HUI-Miner is almost two orders of magnitude faster than the other algorithms for dense databases. For example, the running times of HUI-Miner and UP-Growth+ are 35.8 seconds and 6302.3 seconds for database *mushroom* in Fig. 11(e), when the minutil is 2%. In Fig. 11(h), HUI-Miner is slower than UP-Growth+ for high minutils, and we found out in this case that UP-Growth+ generates very few candidate itemsets (only 2007 candidates when the minutil is 0.6%); however, for low minutils, HUI-Miner is even an order of magnitude faster than UP-Growth+ (UP-Growth+ generates 178128 candidates when the minutil is 0.35%.). For most sparse databases, the performance superiority of HUI-Miner becomes very significant when the minutil decreases. For example, for *retail* in Fig. 11(f), the running times of HUI-Miner and IHUPTWU are 15.3 seconds and 219.1 seconds when the minutil is 0.045%, while their running times are 22.2 seconds and 9758.0 seconds when the minutil is reduced to 0.02%.

5.3 Memory Consumption

Fig. 12 shows the peak memory consumption of the four algorithms on all databases, in which each subfigure corresponds to a subfigure in Fig. 11. Peak memory consumption was recorded by the "massif" tool of the "valgrind" software [3].

Except for database *accidents* in Fig. 12(a), HUI-Miner always consumes less memory than the other algorithms. The reason is that these algorithms have to consume a very large amount of memory to store candidate high utility itemsets during their mining processes, while HUI-Miner does not. Generally, the memory consumption of these algorithms is proportional to the number of candidate itemsets they generate. For example, for database *T10I4D100K*, IHUPTWU generates 3826202 candidate itemsets and consumes 109.0 MB of memory while UP-Growth+ generates 1007150 candidate itemsets and consumes 50.22 MB of memory, when the minutil is 0.005%. The number of high utility itemsets is only 313509 for the mining task. HUI-Miner neither generates nor stores candidate itemsets, and thus it consumes only 23.62 MB of memory.

Another observation is that UP-Growth+ consumes more memory than UP-Growth in some cases, for example, in Fig. 12(b) and (d), although UP-Growth+ always generates fewer candidate itemsets than UP-Growth. It is because that each node in the prefix-trees used in UP-Growth+ holds more information than that in the prefix-trees used in UP-Growth [22]. When a database is sparse and large, the size of a corresponding prefix-tree is relatively large, while the number of candidate itemsets is relatively small. For example, the size of sparse database *kosarak* is 49859KB, but the numbers of candidate itemsets are only 80 and 74 for UP-Growth and UP-Growth+ when the minutil is 1.5%.

5.4 Processing Order of Items

The processing order of items significantly influences the performance of a high utility itemset mining algorithm [5]. As IHUPTWU, UP-Growth, and UP-Growth+ do, HUI-Miner processes items in transaction-weighted-utility-ascending order (see Section 4.4). To get the knowledge of the performance difference for different processing orders, we tested the running time of HUI-Miner on condition that items are processed in transaction-weighted-utility-

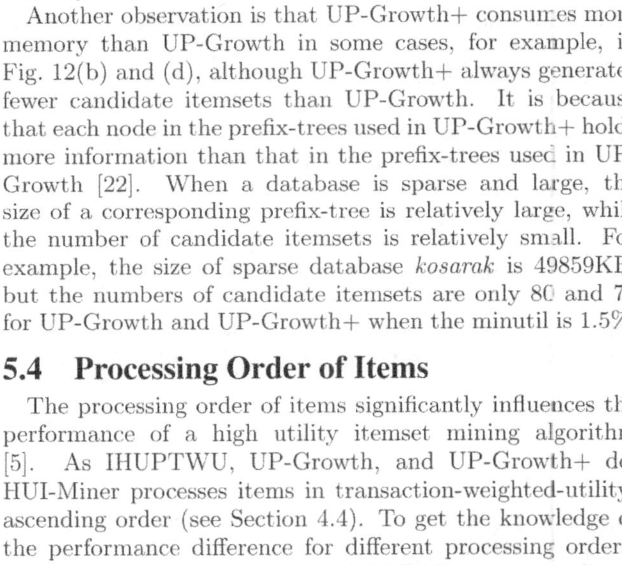

Figure 13: Different Item Orders

Accidents	15%	20%	25%	30%	35%	40%
IHUPTWU	2953047	978170	378955	163363	74144	35113
UP-Growth	184239	18761	1215	34	1	0
UP-Growth+	178732	18192	1193	34	1	0
HUI	280	0	0	0	0	0
Chain	0.004%	0.005%	0.006%	0.007%	0.008%	0.009%
IHUPTWU	43971025	9478232	739627	558254	429745	345648
UP-Growth	124509	82403	61215	48198	39637	33656
UP-Growth+	72560	51523	40725	33966	29274	25868
HUI	18480	12244	9040	6920	5585	4578
Chess	18%	20%	22%	24%	26%	28%
IHUPTWU	453506887	283147997	181541329	118826006	79065869	53468011
UP-Growth	50226806	22578752	9891125	4242057	1786383	702604
UP-Growth+	31670472	13725409	5795829	2464762	957940	273424
HUI	34870	4872	230	0	0	0
Kosarak	1%	1.5%	2%	2.5%	3%	3.5%
IHUPTWU	---	---	246648	35740	14244	6979
UP-Growth	27864	80	38	31	18	12
UP-Growth+	660	74	38	31	18	12
HUI	48	20	15	10	8	8
Mushroom	2%	2.5%	3%	3.5%	4%	4.5%
IHUPTWU	29593409	17342263	11985059	7396747	5981219	3741959
UP-Growth	17594549	10295610	6383808	4361711	3122163	2349568
UP-Growth+	16681744	9602355	6145020	4037680	2942177	2246587
HUI	3583596	1879818	1059350	640404	400137	256988
Retail	0.02%	0.025%	0.03%	0.035%	0.04%	0.045%
IHUPTWU	3280836	695675	308951	170144	111500	79647
UP-Growth	304128	112917	55037	35925	27208	22436
UP-Growth+	27917	21047	17006	14279	12329	10781
HUI	8723	6026	4377	3340	2676	2212
T10I4D100K	0.005%	0.01%	0.015%	0.02%	0.025%	0.03%
IHUPTWU	3826202	802793	335849	197697	133848	105685
UP-Growth	2155382	421526	188067	115329	85544	70147
UP-Growth+	1007150	226448	114948	78282	61451	51523
HUI	313509	81562	51457	40898	34092	29176
T40I10D100K	0.35%	0.4%	0.45%	0.5%	0.55%	0.6%
IHUPTWU	4214124	2229232	1752536	1410616	1240654	1105830
UP-Growth	1703398	1298224	1079166	912479	759925	541878
UP-Growth+	178128	141242	127305	71366	5342	2007
HUI	20448	4618	328	147	28	19

Figure 14: Number of Candidate Itemsets & Number of Resultant High Utility Itemsets

descending order, lexicographic order, and transaction-weighted-utility-ascending order, respectively. Fig. 13 shows the experimental results on databases *accidents* and *retail*.

As we can see, the transaction-weighted-utility-ascending order leads to the best performance. The reason is that the processing order of items is capable of reducing the number of sets of utility-lists for a mining task. To comprehend the reason in depth, one can consult the related work in [15, 16].

5.5 Discussion

From above experiments, we can observe that HUI-Miner outperforms the state-of-the-art algorithms.

To mine high utility itemsets, almost all existing algorithms first generate candidate high utility itemsets and subsequently compute the exact utility of each candidate to identify high utility itemsets. To improve performance, previous studies focus on how to reduce the number of candidates, which can lead to the decrease in the costs of both candidate generation and utility computation.

Fig. 14 shows the number of candidate itemsets the three algorithms generate and the number of resultant high utility itemsets. For database *kosarak*, when the minutils are 1% and 1.5%, the times of candidate generation are so much ($\gg$100000 seconds) that we had to terminate the two tests. From Fig. 11, Fig. 12, and Fig. 14, one can observe that the number of candidate itemsets generated by an algorithm is proportional to the running time and memory consumption of the algorithm. The state-of-the-art algorithms have been able to efficiently reduce the number of candidates. However, the number is still far larger than the number of resultant high utility itemsets in most cases. For example, IHUPTWU, UP-Growth, and UP-Growth+ generate 558254, 48198, and 33966 candidate itemsets, when the minutil is 0.007% for database *chain*, but the number of resultant high utility itemsets is only 6920.

Using the utility-list structure, the HUI-Miner algorithm can mine high utility itemsets without candidate generation. The distinct advantage of HUI-Miner is that it avoids the costly candidate generation and utility computation. For the above example, IHUPTWU, UP-Growth, and UP-Growth+ have to process 551334 (= 558254 − 6920), 41278 (= 48198 − 6920), and 27046 (= 33966 − 6920) candidate itemsets, respectively. These algorithms not only generate these itemsets but also compute their exact utilities on 1112949 transactions. However, these itemsets are discarded finally. The potential advantage of HUI-Miner is that a large amount of memory is saved. For example, the size of database *mushroom* is only 0.92MB, but UP-Growth and UP-Growth+ generate 17594549 and 16681744 candidate itemsets, and consume 699.9 MB and 658.7MB of memory, respectively (when the minutil is 2%.) and a large amount of memory is used to store candidate itemsets. Although the algorithms can be modified to swap candidate itemsets to disk, the disk space requirement is also considerable, and moreover, the algorithms' performance will be degraded.

6. CONCLUSION

In this paper, we have proposed a novel data structure, utility-list, and developed an efficient algorithm, HUI-Miner, for high utility itemset mining. Utility-lists provide not only utility information about itemsets but also important pruning information for HUI-Miner. Previous algorithms have to process a very large number of candidate itemsets during their mining processes. However, most candidate itemsets are not high utility and are discarded finally. HUI-Miner can mine high utility itemsets without candidate generation, which avoids the costly generation and utility computation of candidates. We have studied the performance of HUI-Miner in comparison with the state-of-the-art algorithms on various databases. Experimental results show that HUI-Miner gains significant performance improvement over these algorithms in terms of both running time and memory consumption.

7. ACKNOWLEDGMENTS

The authors would like to thank anonymous reviewers. Their helpful comments and suggestions have improved the quality of the paper.

8. REFERENCES

[1] Frequent Itemset Mining Dataset Repository. `http://fimi.ua.ac.be/`, 2012.

[2] NU-MineBench: A Data Mining Benchmark Suite. `http://cucis.ece.northwestern.edu/projects/DMS/MineBench.html`, 2012.

[3] Valgrind: A GPL'd System for Debugging and Profiling Linux Programs. `http://valgrind.org/`, 2012.

[4] R. Agrawal and R. Srikant. Fast algorithms for mining association rules in large databases. In *Proc. Int'l Conf. Very Large Data Bases*, pages 487–499, 1994.

[5] C. F. Ahmed, S. K. Tanbeer, B.-S. Jeong, and Y.-K. Lee. Efficient tree structures for high utility pattern mining in incremental databases. *IEEE Transactions on Knowledge and Data Engineering*, 21(12):1708–1721, 2009.

[6] B. Barber and H. J. Hamilton. Extracting share frequent itemsets with infrequent subsets. *Data Mining and Knowledge Discovery*, 7(2):153–185, 2003.

[7] A. Ceglar and J. F. Roddick. Association mining. *ACM Computing Surveys*, 38(2), 2006.

[8] J. Han, H. Cheng, D. Xin, and X. Yan. Frequent pattern mining: Current status and future directions. *Data Mining and Knowledge Discovery*, 15(1):55–86, 2007.

[9] J. Han, J. Pei, Y. Yin, and R. Mao. Mining frequent patterns without candidate generation: A frequent-pattern tree approach*. *Data Mining and Knowledge Discovery*, 8(1):53–87, 2004.

[10] J. Hu and A. Mojsilovic. High-utility pattern mining: A method for discovery of high-utility item sets. *Pattern Recognition*, 40(11):3317 – 3324, 2007.

[11] Y.-C. Li, J.-S. Yeh, and C.-C. Chang. Direct candidates generation: A novel algorithm for discovering complete share-frequent itemsets. In *Proc. Fuzzy Systems and Knowledge Discovery*, pages 551–560, 2005.

[12] Y.-C. Li, J.-S. Yeh, and C.-C. Chang. Efficient algorithms for mining share-frequent itemsets. In *Proc. World Congress of Int'l. Fuzzy Systems Association*, pages 534–539, 2005.

[13] Y.-C. Li, J.-S. Yeh, and C.-C. Chang. A fast algorithm for mining share-frequent itemsets. In *Proc. Asia-Pacific Web Conf.*, pages 417–428, 2005.

[14] Y.-C. Li, J.-S. Yeh, and C.-C. Chang. Isolated items discarding strategy for discovering high utility itemsets. *Data & Knowledge Engineering*, 64(1):198–217, 2008.

[15] G. Liu, H. Lu, W. Lou, Y. Xu, and J. X. Yu. Efficient mining of frequent patterns using ascending frequency ordered prefix-tree. *Data Mining and Knowledge Discovery*, 9(3):249–274, 2004.

[16] G. Liu, H. Lu, J. X. Yu, W. Wang, and X. Xiao. Afopt: An efficient implementation of pattern growth approach. In *Proc. IEEE Int'l Conf. Data Mining Workshop Frequent Itemset Mining Implementations*, 2003.

[17] Y. Liu, W.-K. Liao, and A. Choudhary. A fast high utility itemsets mining algorithm. In *Proc. Utility-Based Data Mining Workshop*, pages 90–99, 2005.

[18] Y. Liu, W.-K. Liao, and A. N. Choudhary. A two-phase algorithm for fast discovery of high utility itemsets. In *Proc. Pacific-Asia Conf. Knowledge Discovery and Data Mining*, pages 689–695, 2005.

[19] R. Rymon. Search through systematic set enumeration. In *Proc. Int'l Conf. Principles of Knowledge Representation and Reasoning*, pages 539–550, 1992.

[20] A. Soulet and B. Crémilleux. Adequate condensed representations of patterns. *Data Mining and Knowledge Discovery*, 17:94–110, 2008.

[21] A. Soulet, C. Raïssi, M. Plantevit, and B. Crémilleux. Mining dominant patterns in the sky. In *Proc. IEEE Int'l Conf. Data Mining*, pages 655 –664, 2011.

[22] V. S. Tseng, B.-E. Shie, C.-W. Wu, and P. S. Yu. Efficient algorithms for mining high utility itemsets from transactional databases. *IEEE Transactions on Knowledge and Data Engineering*, 2012, doi: 10.1109/TKDE.2012.59.

[23] V. S. Tseng, C.-W. Wu, B.-E. Shie, and P. S. Yu. Upgrowth: An efficient algorithm for high utility itemset mining. In *Proc. ACM SIGKDD Int'l Conf. Knowledge Discovery and Data Mining*, pages 253–262, 2010.

[24] C. W. Wu, P. Fournier-Viger, P. S. Yu, and V. S. Tseng. Efficient mining of a concise and lossless representation of high utility itemsets. In *Proc. IEEE Int'l Conf. Data Mining*, pages 824 –833, 2011.

[25] H. Yao, H. J. Hamilton, and C. J. Butz. A foundational approach to mining itemset utilities from databases. In *Proc. SIAM Int'l Conf. Data Mining*, 2004.

[26] M. J. Zaki. Scalable algorithms for association mining. *IEEE Transactions on Knowledge and Data Engineering*, 12(3):372–390, 2000.

A General Framework to Encode Heterogeneous Information Sources for Contextual Pattern Mining

Weishan Dong[†], Wei Fan[‡] [*], Lei Shi[♯], Changjin Zhou[†], and Xifeng Yan[§]
[†]IBM Research – China
[‡]Huawei Noah's Ark Lab
[♯]Institute of Software, Chinese Academy of Sciences
[§]University of California at Santa Barbara
{dongweis,zhoucj}@cn.ibm.com, wei.fan@gmail.com, shil@ios.ac.cn, xyan@cs.ucsb.edu

ABSTRACT

Traditional pattern mining methods usually work on single data sources. However, in practice, there are often multiple and heterogeneous information sources. They collectively provide contextual information not available in any single source alone describing the same set of objects, and are useful for discovering hidden *contextual patterns*. One important challenge is to provide a general methodology to mine contextual patterns easily and efficiently. In this paper, we propose a general framework to encode contextual information from multiple sources into a coherent representation—Contextual Information Graph (CIG). The complexity of the encoding scheme is linear in both time and space. More importantly, CIG can be handled by any single-source pattern mining algorithms that accept taxonomies without any modification. We demonstrate by three applications of the contextual association rule, sequence and graph mining, that contextual patterns providing rich and insightful knowledge can be easily discovered by the proposed framework. It enables Contextual Pattern Mining (CPM) by reusing single-source methods, and is easy to deploy and use in real-world systems.

Categories and Subject Descriptors

H.2.8 [**Database Management**]: Database Applications—*Data Mining*

Keywords

Heterogeneous sources, contextual pattern mining

1. INTRODUCTION

Today's explosion in data does not only grow in the number of examples, but also grow in the number of available information sources describing related set of objects. Traditional frequent pattern mining methods for association rules [1, 8], sequences [2, 19], and graphs [20, 11] usually work on single information sources. The target objects of interest are simply a set of transactions, sequences composed of time-stamped elements, or labeled graphs. However, in reality, there are usually multiple heterogeneous information sources describing the contexts or related attributes of the target objects. These sources provide important contextual information not available from any single source alone, but can be useful to understand the data and discover interesting knowledge [13]. For example, in a crime scene analysis case, on Mondays, vehicle thefts happened more frequently in areas with high population density. Interestingly, the same type of crimes on Saturdays happened more frequently in low population density areas. Here the contextual information, i.e., the population density, from census data feeds but not available in the crime database, played an important role to extract useful crime patterns. Another example is that, in the epidemic spread characterization scenario, the location contexts such as the relative position to a river supplying drinking water, can be extracted from the map data source. Sequential patterns indicating that most people with diarrhea symptoms had visited downstream areas before getting sick can be discovered. A probable water-borne transmission and the source of contamination can therefore be inferred. Such insightful patterns cannot be found only by analyzing people's symptoms without utilizing the location contextual information of their movements. Most traditional data mining methods do not consider the contextual information from the heterogeneous sources, but focus on finding patterns explicitly appearing in a single source. Therefore, they are not directly applicable to these problems.

However, simply joining multiple data sources into a single dataset does not work either; it is well known that joining multiple sources not only results in an unnecessarily huge dataset but also leads to the loss of information at the same time (the semantics represented by the linkages between information sources) [5, 7]. Multi-relational data mining (MRDM) [4, 5] can be applied to mine multiple sources. However, in a real-world system, such as a modern enterprise's data analytics platform or a commercial business intelligence product, it is usually expensive to deploy a new set of algorithms, as it often involves intensive testing and requires a lot of engineering effort. Yet, another practitioners' concern recently raised from real-world applications of mining multiple sources is the "ease of use" [14].

[*]Part of this work was done when the author was in IBM T.J.Watson Research Center.

CIKM'12, October 29–November 2, 2012, Maui, HI, USA.

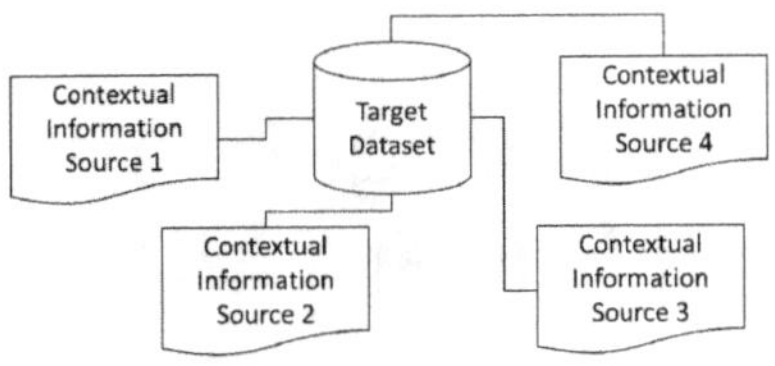

Figure 1: Star Schema of Information Sources

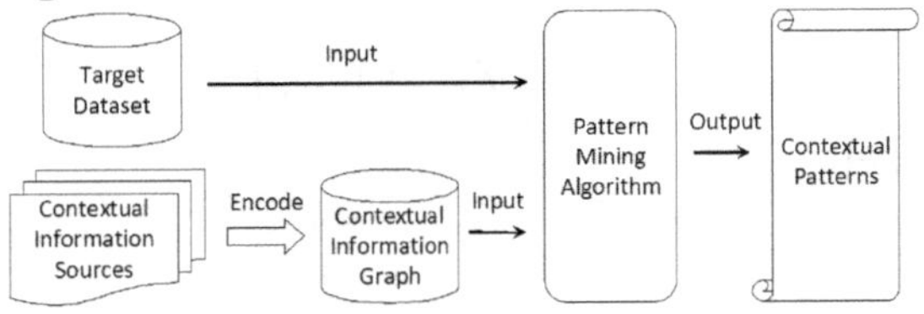

Figure 2: Contextual Pattern Mining

In this paper, we answer the question that: given a set of traditional single-source pattern mining algorithms, how to non-intrusively and maximally reuse them for discovering insightful patterns across multiple heterogeneous sources? In real-world applications, one of the most common ways in which multiple information sources relate to each other is the star schema, which consists of a target dataset and a number of heterogeneous contextual information sources. The target dataset is a main information source of objects that are of primary interest, where the primary key identifies the *target objects* (a target object can be a transaction, a sequence, or a graph in the dataset), and several foreign keys identify the *identities* inside a target object (an identity can be an item inside a transaction or sequence, or a label of graph vertex or edge). The contextual information sources provide auxiliary information about all or a subset of objects in the target dataset, where the primary key is linked to a foreign key (possibly via predicates, Section 2.3) in the target dataset. These information sources contain the features (either constant or dynamic over time) of the identities inside the target objects, which provides rich context for mining insightful patterns of target objects. Figure 1 is an example of star schema of a target dataset and four contextual information sources. We define patterns discovered from such multiple sources as *contextual patterns*:

DEFINITION 1 (CONTEXTUAL PATTERN). *A pattern of the target objects, which contains the information explicitly appearing in the target dataset and the information implicitly represented across the contextual information sources.*

Apparently, contextual patterns can only be mined by collectively considering the target dataset and the contextual information sources. Figure 2 illustrates the flow of the proposed Contextual Pattern Mining (CPM) concept. As shown, the idea of CPM is quite different from the traditional MRDM approaches, although sharing the same objective. By solving the problem from a new perspective, CPM outperforms the traditional MRDM approaches, in terms of non-intrusiveness, ease of use, and efficiency. More details can be found in Section 6. The main challenge of CPM is how to effectively encode multiple sources of contextual information before running a traditional single-source pattern mining method, so that contextual patterns can be easily discovered. In this paper, we propose the Contextual Information Graph (CIG) encoding framework to solve this problem. An example of CIG in the crime analysis scenario is given in Figure 3. It encodes the population densities (POPDEN) as well as the ratios of male to female (RMF) of census tracts where the crime had happened. With CIG, a

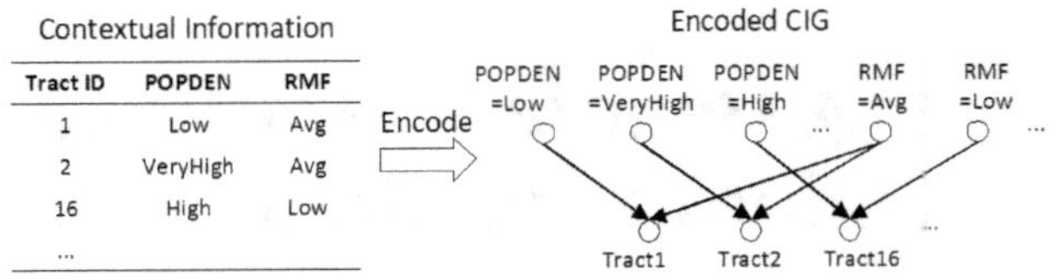

Figure 3: Contextual Information Graph (CIG)

single-source pattern mining algorithm accepting taxonomy as an additional input can be applied to the target crime history dataset. We also show that simply joining contextual information to the target dataset does not work, and can result in a large number of redundant patterns (Section 5). The advantages of the proposed CIG encoding framework include: (1) Generality. CIG supports mining all the three types of popular frequent patterns: itemset/association rule, sequence, and graph. (2) Efficiency and scalability. With the HashSet and HashMap data structure, both the time and space complexities of CIG encoding are linear. The Knowledge-to-Identity path query on CIG in pattern mining stage (Section 2.2) is constant in time. (3) Robustness. CIG is capable of handling missing values, dynamically changing values, and multiple values on contextual features. (4) No information loss. CIG encoding is a one-to-one mapping of the contextual information sources.

2. ENCODING FRAMEWORK

In most cases, frequent pattern mining deals with discrete features [7]. In this paper, we assume all the contextual information (including time information) is in discrete feature values, or has been discretized according to some criterions. To effectively conduct Contextual Pattern Mining (CPM), we encode all available contextual information by a CIG, which is a labeled DAG (Directed Acyclic Graph) with labels associated only with its vertices. Let U denote the set of contextual information, V denote the set of identities, and E denote the set of linkages between U and V.

DEFINITION 2 (CONTEXTUAL INFORMATION GRAPH). *A Contextual Information Graph (CIG) is a labeled bipartite directed graph $G = (U, V, E)$, s.t. (1) $\forall u, v \in U \cup V, \ell(u) \neq \ell(v)$ if $u \neq v$, and (2) $\forall$ edge $(u, v) \in E, u \in U, v \in V$, where ℓ is the label function of the vertices in G.*

An example is given in Figure 3. Available contextual information collected from census data feeds consists of two features (POPDEN and RMF) for each identity (census tract). Here U is the set of all possible combinations of a feature and its value (vertices in the upper half of the CIG), where one vertex stands for a combination. V is the set of all identities (vertices in the lower half of the CIG), where one vertex stands for an identity. The meaning of a vertex is shown by its label displayed aside. The directed edges from a vertex in U to a vertex in V denote the linkages between the identities and the feature values, which constitute set E. As can be seen, the first condition in Definition 2 means that in a CIG $G = (U, V, E)$, the label of a vertex is unique that only one vertex in U stands for a specific feature value and only one vertex in V stands for a specific identity. The second condition means that the linkages exist only between the identities and the feature values, and are represented by directed edges from a feature value to an identity.

2.1 Encoding Algorithm

Algorithm 1 summarizes the CIG encoding procedure. For some applications, contextual information is not fixed, and

Algorithm 1 CIG Encoding

Input: A set of contextual information sources $\mathcal{S}$.
Output: A CIG $G = (U, V, E)$.
1: $U \leftarrow \emptyset; V \leftarrow \emptyset; E \leftarrow \emptyset$;
2: **foreach** contextual information source $s \in \mathcal{S}$
3:    **foreach** state of identity i at time t, $i_t \in s$
4:       insert a vertex v to V, $\ell(v) \leftarrow i_t$;
5:       **foreach** combination of feature F and its value X, $(F = X) \in i_t$
6:          vertex $u \leftarrow$ search in U with $\ell(u) = (F = X)$;
7:          **if** u is not found **then**
8:             insert a vertex u to U, $\ell(u) \leftarrow (F = X)$;
9:          insert a directed edge (u, v) to E;
10: **return** $G = (U, V, E)$;

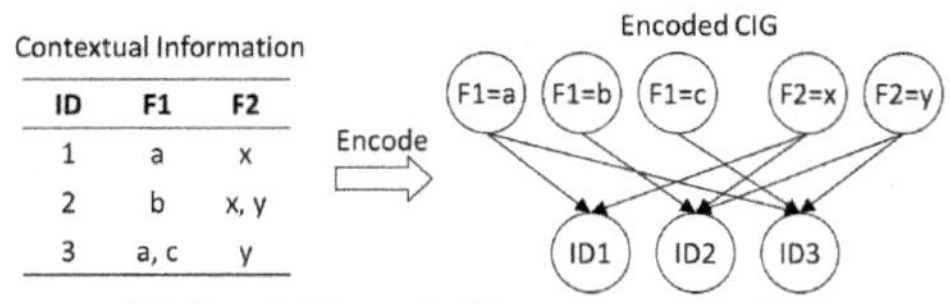

Figure 4: CIG of Fixed Contextual Information

can be changing over time. For example, temperature of an outdoor location varies over time, and traffic flow of a road may change between working hours and midnight. Therefore, on line 3, if the features of an identity change over time, a vertex indicating the state at a specific discrete time frame will be created. In reality, multiple values for one feature can exist. In this case, the algorithm reads every possible combination of the feature and its values, and creates separate vertices. Figure 4 is an example of encoding *fixed* contextual information from one source into a CIG. ID indicates the identities. F1 and F2 are two multi-valued features. The labels of vertices are shown inside. Figure 5 encodes *dynamic* contextual information from one source. The only difference in the CIG is that an identity state vertex is defined by its ID together with a time stamp. When encoding multiple sources, the resulting CIG is the union of several small CIGs, each is constructed from one source.

2.2 Contextual Pattern Mining

As shown in Figure 2, we propose to perform Contextual Pattern Mining in two steps: (1) construct a CIG from the contextual information sources, and (2) apply a single-source pattern mining algorithm to discover contextual patterns. The single-source pattern mining algorithm can be implemented based on an existing Generalized Pattern Mining (GPM) algorithm [16, 6, 17, 9, 3] with only minor modification or even no change at all. GPM algorithms accept a taxonomy of the identities besides reading a target dataset as primary input, and can mine generalized patterns across different levels of the taxonomy. A taxonomy describes the concept hierarchies (ontologies) of identities, typically appearing as a tree with great depth or forest structures. In most cases, a taxonomy is defined by human knowledge and constructed manually. Figure 6 is an example of a taxonomy of items. In a taxonomy, all the leaf nodes are specific identities appearing in target objects. The non-leaf nodes are virtual concepts defined by human knowledge. A directed edge from a higher level concept to a lower level concept, or from a concept to an identity indicates the conceptual generalization, i.e., reversely *is-a* semantics. For instance, in Figure 6, concept *Outerwear* generalizes identities *Jacket* and *Ski Pants*, thus *Jacket is-a Outerwear*, and *Ski Pants is-a Outerwear*. With this taxonomy, generalized association rule mining [16, 6] can discover rules like "*Outerwear* $\Rightarrow$ *Hiking Boots*" from a

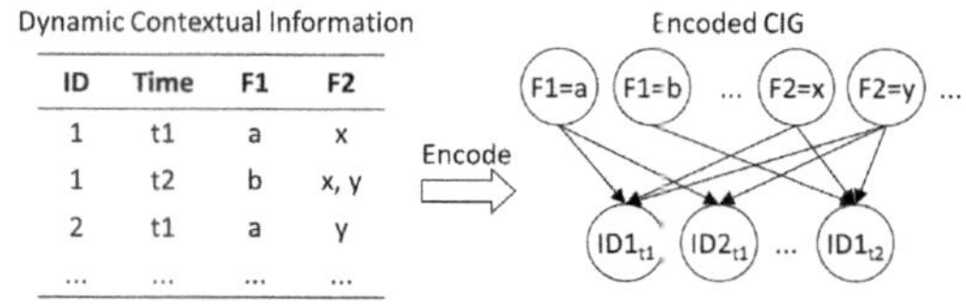

Figure 5: CIG of Dynamic Contextual Information

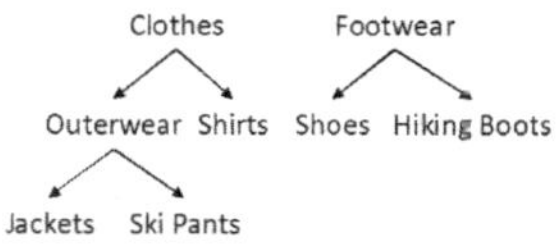

Figure 6: Taxonomy of Items (adopted from [16])

dataset of item purchase transactions, meaning that the customers bought *Outerwear* also bought *Hiking Boots*. However, specialized rules only at identity (item) level, such as "*Jacket* $\Rightarrow$ *Hiking Boots*" and "*Ski Pants* $\Rightarrow$ *Hiking Boots*", may not be frequent or confident. Generalized sequential pattern mining [17] and generalized graph mining [9, 3] work in similar ways.

CIG is different from taxonomy in the following aspects: (1) A CIG can be automatically constructed with Algorithm 1, whereas defining a taxonomy heavily requires involving human knowledge in most cases. (2) In a CIG $G = (U, V, E)$, there is no edge connecting two vertices in U, i.e., no linkage exists between the vertices representing contextual information. However, in a taxonomy, such linkages define relationships between two concepts. (3) In a typical taxonomy of a tree (or forest) structure, vertices representing identities have in-degree $= 1$. Whereas in a CIG $G = (U, V, E)$, vertices in V representing identities have $1 \leq$ in-degree $\leq |U|$. (4) We can regard both contextual information and concepts as knowledge. It can be proven that if a path exists in a CIG that starts from a vertex representing knowledge and ends at a vertex representing an identity, it always contains only one edge. But in a taxonomy, such paths can contain multiple edges. Generally, we call such a path the Knowledge-to-Identity (KI) path.

DEFINITION 3 (KNOWLEDGE-TO-IDENTITY (KI) PATH). *Given a CIG $G = (U, V, E)$, a KI path exists from knowledge $(F = X)$ to identity i iff.* $\exists(u, v) \in E$, *s.t.* $\ell(u) = (F = X), \ell(v) = i, u \in U, v \in V$. *We denote it by* $(F = X) \rhd i$.

In existing GPM algorithms, the KI path is usually referred as the antecedent-descendant relationship on a taxonomy. In most cases, the KI path query is the only necessary interface that a GPM algorithm interacts with a taxonomy [16, 6, 17, 9, 3]. To be specific, a GPM algorithm only needs to know the followings to mine generalized patterns, all of which are essentially KI path queries: (1) Given an identity, identify all the antecedents, i.e., concepts generalizing the identity. (2) Given a concept, identify all the descendants, i.e., lower level concepts and identities specializing the concept. (3) Given a concept and an identity, check if there exits a path connecting them. We can see that as long as these KI path queries can be done on CIG, a GPM algorithm can accept a CIG by blindly treating it as a taxonomy, and the output will be contextual patterns

This is a favorable characteristic: We can conduct CPM by non-intrusively leveraging traditional GPM algorithms, with an appropriate way of encoding new information that GPM algorithms cannot directly handle. And indeed, performing the KI path queries on CIG is straightforward (Section 2.4). We can find that CPM can be done with a relatively small cost. With the CIG encoding, existing single-source GPM algorithms can be reused to the maximum level. One thing should be noticed is that, if the GPM algorithm applied only accepts tree (or forest) structured taxonomies, it may need minor changes so that a general DAG structured CIG can be processed. In this case, the time complexity bounds of a GPM algorithm [16, 6, 17, 9, 3] does not change if replacing a taxonomy input by a CIG. This is because in a general sense, KI path query on either a taxonomy or a CIG shares the same time complexity if the taxonomy and the CIG are isomorphic. Besides, since CIG is a bipartite graph, KI path queries on it can be highly efficient (Section 2.4). It is also feasible to combine a taxonomy to a CIG, so that the algorithm can discover contextual patterns and traditional generalized patterns simultaneously. However in this case, KI path queries are essentially done on a DAG not necessarily being bipartite. Such KI path queries become the general graph reachability queries. Labeling and indexing methods [18] can be employed to accelerate the queries. Specific CPM algorithms for mining contextual association rules, sequences, and graphs will be presented in Section 4.

2.3 Indirect Contextual Information

In some cases, contextual information may not be directly linked to identities, but via *predicates*. Take the crime scene analysis as example. To study the factors contributing to crime, contextual information such as location features, need to be considered. The location of a crime is usually represented by GPS coordinate in IT systems of police departments. However, environmental contexts, such as population densities of the communities and types of the buildings nearby, do not directly relate to the GPS location. In this case, a *predicate* defining a relationship between two identities is needed to correlate available information. Specifically, in the crime example, spatial predicates (e.g., *within*, *close_to*) [10] can define spatial relationships between a GPS location identity and the contextual identities (community, building, etc.). The computation of predicates is usually done externally (e.g., by a computation engine or a lookup table), but a predicate itself can still be directly represented in the target dataset. Table 1 illustrates an example of a target dataset relating to contextual identities via predicates. Consider each target object has a feature F1. The values of F1 include predicates $p_1(\cdot)$ and $p_2(\cdot)$. Using the crime example, F1 could denote the spatial features derived from GPS coordinates, and p_1 and p_2 may stand for *within* and *close_to* relationships, respectively. ID1 and ID2 that relate to target objects via p_1 and p_2 could stand for a community and a building, respectively. CPM treats an instantiated predicate (in the above example, p_1(ID1) or p_2(ID2)) as a whole to be one item. It works by simply defining the following.

DEFINITION 4. *Given a CIG G and a predicate $p(\cdot)$, $p(F = X) \rhd p(i)$ on G iff. $(F = X) \rhd i$ on G.*

For example, given the CIG in Figure 4 and the dataset in Table 1, we have p_1(F1=a) $\rhd$ p_1(ID1), p_1(F2=x) $\rhd$ p_1(ID1), p_2(F1=b) $\rhd$ p_2(ID2), and p_2(F2=x) $\rhd$ p_2(ID2). By doing so, CPM can deal with predicates as well as ordinary identities.

2.4 Implementation & Complexity Analyses

In our implementation, a HashSet is used to store the vertices $U \cup V$ given a CIG $G = (U, V, E)$. One HashMap is used to store the directed edges E, where each key is a vertex $u \in U$, and its mapped value is a HashSet of all its descendant vertices on G, defined by $\{v | v \in V, (u, v) \in E\}$. Another HashMap representing the reverse edges is also maintained, where each key is a vertex $v \in V$, and its mapped value is a HashSet of all its antecedents, defined by $\{u | u \in U, (u, v) \in E\}$. These two HashMaps are built simultaneously on line 9 in Algorithm 1.

Table 1: Dataset Relating Contexts via Predicates

	F1
TargetObj1	p_1(ID1)
TargetObj2	p_1(ID1), p_2(ID2)
...	...

Time Complexities: On HashSet/HashMap, it is known that any insertion or search operation is $O(1)$ asymptotically, assuming there is no collision. In practice, this is usually true, especially when sufficiently large capacity of the HashSet/HashMap is available as compared to the total number of elements (keys) to be stored. In this case, in Algorithm 1, line 4 (vertex insertion), line 6 (vertex search) and line 9 (edge insertion) are all constant in time. The time complexity of Algorithm 1 is thus $O(\sum_{\forall s \in S} \sum_{\forall i_t \in s} \sum_{\forall (F=X) \in i_t}$ $O(|E|)$, linear to the amount of information encoded[1]. The worst case of HashSet/HashMap operations is $O(n)$ only if, in the extreme case, that all hashes collide for the total n elements in the HashSet/HashMap. Figure 7 demonstrates a simple example of Hash collision. Therefore, in most cases, the time complexity of CIG encoding is linear. Only once scanning of all the contextual information is sufficient to construct CIG. Because CIG is always a bipartite graph, KI path query is equivalent to edge search. Given a constructed CIG, assuming no collision, searching all descendants or antecedents of a vertex and searching an edge defined by two specified vertices in the HashMaps, are all constant in time. Similarly, the worst cases are $O(|U|)$, $O(|V|)$, and $O(|U|+d)$, respectively, where d is the max degree of vertices in U. In a word, any KI path query on CIG is constant in time in most cases, where there is no hash collision.

Space Complexities: A HashSet/HashMap typically has space complexity of $O(n)$, where n is the number of elements stored. In our case, the HashSet for vertices has $O(|U \cup V|) = O(|U|+|V|)$ space complexity. We can also infer that the two HashMaps have $O(|U|+|E|)$ and $O(|V|+|E|)$ space complexities, respectively. Therefore, the overall space complexity of a CIG is $O(|U| + |V| + |E|)$.

3. EXPERIMENTS

In this section, we experimentally validate the linear time and space complexities of CIG encoding and the constant time complexity of KI path query. All the experiments are done on a machine with Intel Core2 2.66GHz CPU and 2GB memory, using Java programming with the initial capacity of 16 and the load factor of 0.75 for HashSet/HashMap. The results are shown in Table 2 and Figure 8, which are obtained on the contextual information used in Section 4.

[1]When the information source is a typical flat table of M rows and N columns, this complexity is $O(M \cdot N)$, and $|E| = M \cdot N$.

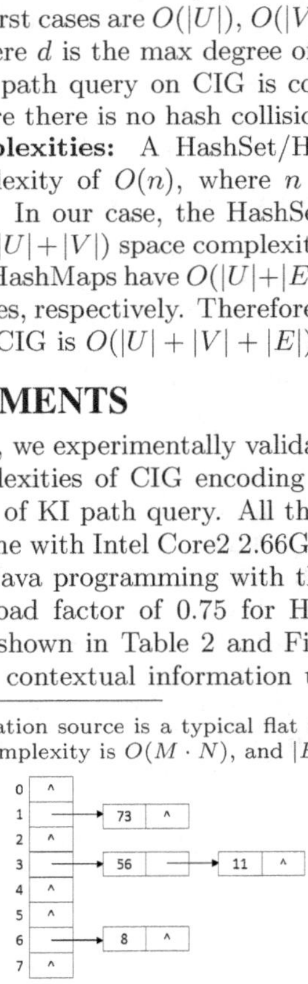

Figure 7: HashSet of Capacity 8. Keys $\{8, 56, 11, 73\}$ stored with hash function x mod 8. 56 and 11 collide.

Table 2: Results of Time and Space Complexities

$\|U\|$	$\|V\|$	$\|E\|$	CIG encoding CPU time (ms)	CIG memory usage (KB)	KI path query CPU time (ms)*
7	10	20	0.99	1.832	23.82
10	14	28	1.14	1.844	23.86
9	237	237	4.39	10.465	17.11
13	298	298	5.20	13.324	23.40
15	400	400	6.95	17.9	16.26
15	269	430	7.15	14.116	18.71
14	459	459	7.51	20.472	17.19
15	347	592	9.32	18.758	26.16
16	479	853	10.65	26.56	21.27
16	572	1043	13.63	32.082	19.31

*Total CPU time of 10,000 random KI path queries.

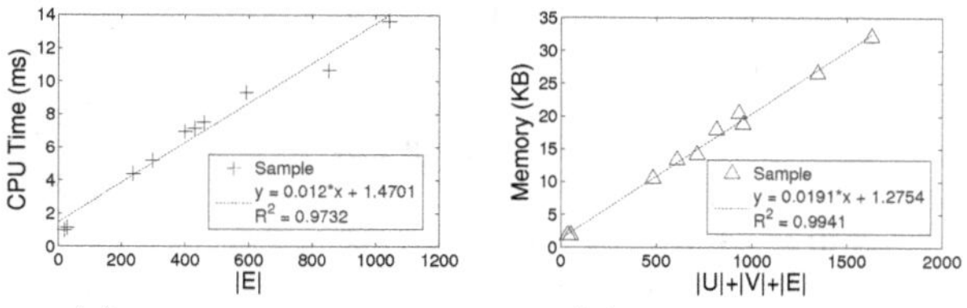

(a) Time Complexity (b) Space Complexity

Figure 8: Linear Complexities of CIG Encoding

The contextual data is represented by the integer type to eliminate the effects of varying hash code calculation time and storage size caused by data types like string. We can find that the CPU time of CIG encoding is linear to $|E|$, and the storage (space) of CIG is linear to $(|U| + |V| + |E|)$. Two linear equations fitting the samples are also shown in Figure 8. Both have the R square highly close to 1, indicating the linearities. To verify the constant time complexity of KI path queries, in each test, we randomly generate KI path queries 10^4 times and report the total CPU time. It is shown from Table 2 that the KI path query is efficient and only costs nearly constant time in the order of 20ms across all tests, in spite of the data change. In summary, all the results are consistent with the analyses in Section 2.4.

4. CASE STUDIES

Applications of specific contextual pattern mining algorithms to three case studies are given in this section.

4.1 Contextual Association Rule Mining

Data Overview: The first case study is on the real crime history of the City of Spokane, WA, USA. Contextual association rule mining is conducted to find crime patterns. Totally 816 crime incidents of 3 general types, *Drugs* (167 incidents), *Vehicle Theft* (552 incidents), and *Robbery* (97 incidents), reported in the northeast city (covering 10 census tracts) during Jan 2009 to Mar 2010, constitute the target dataset. The day of week on which the incident happened and its general type are included in pattern mining as normal attributes. The geometries of the census tracts and 23 major streets in the area are also used to derive spatial features for each incident, including *within* a tract and *close_to* a street (distance < 500 feet). A sample of the target dataset in transaction format is given in Table 3 (tid indicates id of transaction/incident). Figure 9 is a map overview of the data. The US Census Bureau data is involved as a contextual information source. Population density (per sq mi) and ratio of male to female are considered as contexts. Because these two features, according to the domain knowledge, can influence the distribution of crime occurrences. The tracts' features are summarized in Table 4. A CIG that encodes the POPDEN and RMF is constructed for CPM. A portion of the CIG is shown in Figure 3. A simple taxonomy of "every street *is-a Road*" is also combined as part of the CIG.

Table 3: Sample Crime Target Dataset

tid	items
4	Wednesday, Drugs, within(Tract26), close_to(Trent Av)
251	Thursday, Robbery, within(Tract16), close_to(Garland Av)
266	Friday, Vehicle Theft, within(Tract1), close_to(Freya St), close_to(Wellesley Av)

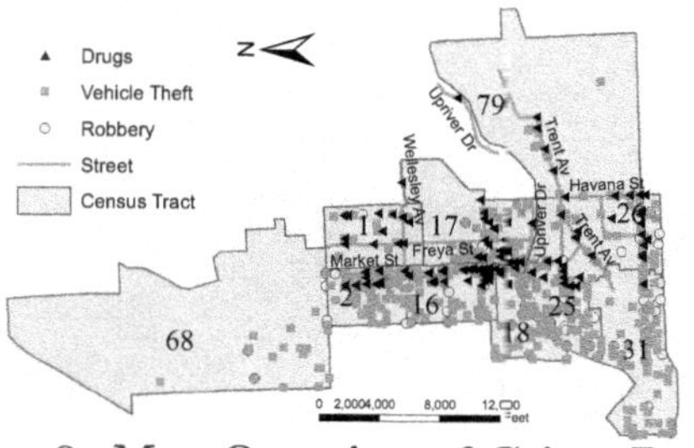

Figure 9: Map Overview of Crime Dataset

Contextual Association Rule Mining: The contextual association rule mining is summarized in Algorithm 2. As in the generalized association rule mining [16], first the transactions are expanded with the contextual information related to items using KI path queries on the CIG, where an item can be a predicate or an identity. Duplicate features expanded, if any, are removed. For example, after expansion, Table 3 will become Table 5. Then frequent itemsets are enumerated and pruned as in typical generalized association rule mining. Any itemsets containing an item $\triangleright$ the other are pruned to prevent generating itemsets like {within(Tract26), within(POPDEN=Low)} and {close_to(Trent Av), close_to(Road)}. Such itemsets indicate the correlation between an item and its context, which can be frequent but provide redundant knowledge already represented in the CIG. It can be proven that only pruning 2-itemsets is sufficient (Lemmas 1 and 2 in [16]) to eliminate such redundant patterns.

Algorithm 2 Contextual Association Rule Mining

Input: Target transactions $\mathcal{D}$; CIG G; Minimum support (min_sup); Minimum confidence (min_conf).
Output: Contextual association rule set $\mathcal{C}$.

```
foreach item i in each row of D
    expand the row with all the contexts ▷i on G, removing
    any duplicates, to construct D';
find all candidate 2-itemsets from D';
foreach candidate 2-itemset {i1, i2}
    if i1 ▷ i2 or i2 ▷ i1 then prune this 2-itemset;
continue to find all frequent itemsets using min_sup ;
C ← find all confident association rules using min_conf ;
return C;
```

Results: We use min_sup = 2% and min_conf = 80%. No pattern about *Robbery* can be found, which indicates the randomness of these crimes. If only the crime target dataset is regarded as input without other information, only 12 rules including the following two can be found (support and confidence are shown in brackets, $\wedge$ indicates "AND"):

within(Tract18) $\wedge$ close_to(Upriver Dr) $\Rightarrow$ Vehicle Theft (2.2%, 90%)
within(Tract68) $\Rightarrow$ Vehicle Theft (6.4%, 88.1%)

If the taxonomy of streets is further involved, 20 rules (including the above 12) can be found, corresponding to the output of typical generalized association rule mining. Below list two new rules. Both can be verified in Figure 9.

within(Tract79) $\Rightarrow$ close_to(Road) (2.3%, 86.4%)
Drugs $\Rightarrow$ close_to(Road) (16.5%, 80.8%)

If the CIG encoding POPDEN and RMF features is further involved for CPM, 212 rules (including the above 20) can be found, including the followings

Table 4: Features of Census Tracts

ID	POPDENSITY*	RATIO_MF*	POPDEN	RMF
1	954.447	1.02	Low	Avg
2	6381.73	0.96	VeryHigh	Avg
16	4715.44	0.88	High	Low
17	2879.07	0.96	Avg	Avg
18	4426.01	0.88	High	Low
25	6027.64	0.98	VeryHigh	Avg
26	569.551	1.10	Low	High
31	1060.55	1.17	Low	High
68	717.115	0.95	Low	Avg
79	543.256	1.10	Low	High

*Original numerical data. Discretized POPDEN & RMF are used for CPM.

Table 5: Samples of Expanded Crime Target Dataset

tid	items
4	Wednesday, Drugs, within(Tract26), close_to(Trent Av), within(RMF=High), within(POPDEN=Low), close_to(Road)
251	Thursday, Robbery, within(Tract16), close_to(Garland Av), within(RMF=Low), within(POPDEN=High), close_to(Road)
266	Friday, Vehicle Theft, within(Tract1), close_to(Freya St), close_to(Wellesley Av), within(RMF=Avg), within(POPDEN=Low), close_to(Road)

$$\text{Saturday} \wedge \text{within(POPDEN=Low)} \wedge \text{within(RMF=High)} \Rightarrow \text{Vehicle Theft} \ \ (3.7\%, 81.1\%)$$

$$\text{Monday} \wedge \text{within(POPDEN=VeryHigh)} \Rightarrow \text{Vehicle Theft} \ \ (2.5\%, 80\%)$$

$$\text{Drugs} \wedge \text{within(RMF=High)} \Rightarrow \text{close\_to(Road)} \ \ (4.3\%, 83.3\%)$$

$$\text{Drugs} \wedge \text{within(RMF=Low)} \Rightarrow \text{close\_to(Road)} \ \ (5.3\%, 89.6\%)$$

These results show that, on Saturdays, *Vehicle Theft* crimes are more probable to occur in tracts with POPDEN=Low and RMF=High. However, on Mondays, tracts with POPDEN=VeryHigh have more chance to report such type of crimes. For *Drugs* crimes, RMF=High or Low can increase the probability of reporting the incidents near a road. Meanwhile, no pattern of *Drugs* and RMF=Avg can be discovered. The detected rules reveal the hidden patterns of the crimes and provide extra insights.

4.2 Contextual Sequential Pattern Mining

Data Overview: The dataset is from the IEEE VAST Challenge 2011 Mini-Challenge 1. It contains 1,023,077 microblogs collected during Apr 30–May 20, 2011 (21 days), each has GPS coordinates, date, and author id. With text analysis, each microblog is tagged with 34 candidate epidemic keywords as its features, include: fever, diarrhea, cough, ache, etc. Among all, two keywords, fever and diarrhea, are used to derive two sequence datasets. The fever dataset consists of all microblogs from authors who sent at least one message tagged by *fever*. The diarrhea dataset consists of all microblogs from authors who sent at least one message tagged by *diarrhea*. There are 40,472 microblogs sent by 2,786 authors in the fever dataset, and 16,353 microblogs sent by 1,196 authors in the diarrhea dataset. For each author, a sequence of microblogs s/he sent is constructed. Each microblog is an element (itemset) of a sequence. The statistics of lengths and number of distinct dates of sequences in the two datasets are summarized in Table 6. It can be seen that in both datasets, on average, an author sent at least one microblog every two days. We can say that the sequences reflect the general movements of the people. Studying these sequences can help conduct some reasonable characterization on the spreads of fever and diarrhea.

Figure 11 shows the city map, which serves as the contextual information source for this case study. There are 13 districts, 6 water bodies (a river and 5 lakes) and 13 hospitals in the city. The river flowing from north to southwest, is known as part of the drinking water supply system. Using the map, the spatial features *within*(·) and *close_to*(·) (distance < 1km) are derived for microblogs. A sample sequence in the fever dataset is shown in Tables 7. Sequences in the diarrhea dataset are similar and omitted. Importantly,

Table 6: Statistics of Sequences in The Two Datasets

Sequence Length	Fever	Diarrhea	*#Distinct Date*	Fever	Diarrhea
Range	[10, 18]	[9, 15]	Range	[7, 15]	[6, 14]
Mean	14.527	13.673	Mean	10.528	10.299

Table 7: A Sample Sequence in Fever Dataset

author	date	items
42	2011-4-30	within(Lakeside)
42	2011-5-3	within(Uptown)
	...	...
42	2011-5-18	within(Downtown), close_to(Vastopolis City Hospital)
42	2011-5-19	fever, within(Eastside)
	...	...

features of the districts including their relative orientations to the river (up/mid/downstream) and to the entire region (north/south/east/west/center) (Table 8), are involved as contextual information and encoded by a CIG (Figure 10). A taxonomy indicating that "every hospital *is-a Hospital*" is also combined as part of the CIG.

Contextual Sequential Pattern Mining: The contextual sequential pattern mining is summarized in Algorithm 3. With the same CIG, we apply Algorithm 3 once to the fever dataset and once to the diarrhea dataset, to find unique patterns for each. Similar to the contextual association rule mining, first the sequences are expanded via KI path queries on the CIG. Redundant patterns here refer to those sequences with an element (itemset) containing both an item and its contexts. Such an element rephrases the linkage information already represented the CIG, but provides nothing useful for new pattern discovery. Patterns with such elements are pruned during mining the sequences. Three additional time constraints are implemented: window-size, min-gap, and max-gap [16]. Explicitly, we set windows-size = 0 day, enforcing that all the items in an element must occur within the same day, but not necessarily from the same microblog. Min-gap and max-gap determine the minimum and the maximum time difference between two consecutive elements, respectively. We set min-gap = 0 day. Considering the frequency of people sending microblogs and the intuition that short term activities affect people's health more, we set max-gap = 2 days. It indicates that an element can occur at most 2 days before the next element. The dates of microblogs are also regarded as items in pattern mining.

Algorithm 3 Contextual Sequential Pattern Mining

Input: Target sequences $\mathcal{D}$; CIG G; min_sup .
Output: Contextual sequential pattern set $\mathcal{C}$.
foreach item i in each element of each sequence in $\mathcal{D}$
  expand the element with all the contexts $\rhd i$ on G, removing any duplicates, to construct $\mathcal{D}'$;
$C \leftarrow$ find frequent sequences from $\mathcal{D}'$ using min_sup , pruning any sequences with an element containing items i_1 and i_2, s.t. $i_1 \rhd i_2$ **or** $i_2 \rhd i_1$;
return C;

Results on Fever Dataset: We use min_sup = 40%. Since we are interested in knowing where the people visited before they mentioned fever, sequences ending with *fever* are selected and analyzed. Without the contextual information, traditional sequence mining only finds four patterns as below (support shown in brackets):

$$\text{2011-05-18} \wedge \text{fever} \ \ (49.0\%) \tag{1}$$

$$\text{2011-05-19} \wedge \text{fever} \ \ (44.1\%) \tag{2}$$

$$\text{2011-05-18} \rightarrow \text{fever} \ \ (51.9\%) \tag{3}$$

$$\text{within(Downtown)} \rightarrow \text{fever} \ \ (48.0\%) \tag{4}$$

Patterns (1) and (2) are sequences of only one element (a 2-itemset). Patterns (1)–(3) indicate that people mentioned fever mostly on May 18 and 19. These imply the fever outbreak may start from May 18. Pattern (4) implies that the

Table 8: Features of Districts

District ID	Relative Orientation (RO)
Villa	north, west, south
Westside	downstream, north, west, south
Riverside	upstream, north
Suburbia	north, east
Smogtown	downstream, south, west
Plainville	downstream, midstream, south, west
Downtown	midstream, center
Uptown	upstream, center
Southville	south
Lakeside	south, east
Cornertown	north, west
Northville	midstream, north
Eastside	east

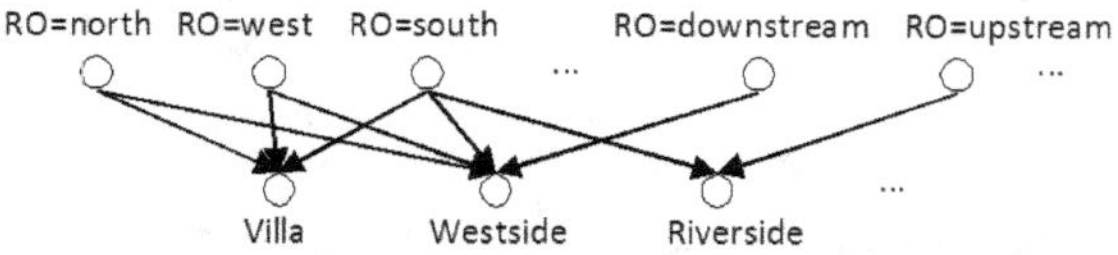

Figure 10: CIG Encoding Contexts from Table 8

ground zero location for fever could be Downtown because people mentioned fever just after they visited Downtown in the last two days. However, as shown below, this is far from the whole picture. CPM with the contextual information of districts' features finds four additional patterns ("RO=" omitted in *within*(·)):

$$\text{within(midstream)} \rightarrow \text{fever} \ (55.5\%) \quad (5)$$

$$\text{within(center)} \rightarrow \text{fever} \ (62.6\%) \quad (6)$$

$$\text{2011-05-18} \wedge \text{within(center)} \rightarrow \text{fever} \ (41.2\%) \quad (7)$$

$$\text{within(midstream)} \wedge \text{within(center)} \rightarrow \text{fever} \ (49.1\%) \quad (8)$$

These imply that not just the people who visited Downtown, but more precisely, the ones who visited the central and midstream areas would mention fever. CPM also finds patterns that start with *fever* and end with *close_to(Hospital)*:

$$\text{fever} \rightarrow \text{close\_to(Hospital)} \ (47.2\%) \quad (9)$$

$$\text{fever} \rightarrow \text{2011-05-20} \wedge \text{close\_to(Hospital)} \ (41.1\%) \quad (10)$$

$$\text{fever} \wedge \text{within(center)} \rightarrow \text{close\_to(Hospital)} \ (40.0\%) \quad (11)$$

It is revealed that, after the people got fever (especially in the city center), they went to hospitals on May 20. These additional insights can be vital for government and medical agency. They could collect relevant information from the hospitals to understand the medical nature of the epidemic, and take actions to control the disease spread.

Results on Diarrhea Dataset: We use a larger min_sup = 80%, as it is observed that people's movements in this dataset are not as random as in the fever dataset. Similarly, sequences ending with *diarrhea* are analyzed. Traditional sequence mining without the contextual information cannot find any pattern. In contrast, CPM finds the followings (only closed patterns [19] are shown here to save space):

$$\text{within(west)} \wedge \text{within(south)} \rightarrow \text{diarrhea} \ (88.0\%) \quad (12)$$

$$\text{2011-05-19} \wedge \text{within(west)} \wedge \text{within(south)} \rightarrow \text{diarrhea} \ (85.8\%) \quad (13)$$

$$\text{within(downstream)} \wedge \text{within(west)} \wedge \text{within(south)} \rightarrow \text{diarrhea} \ (83.9\%) \quad (14)$$

$$\text{2011-05-19} \wedge \text{within(downstream)} \wedge \text{within(west)} \wedge \text{within(south)} \rightarrow \text{diarrhea} \ (82.0\%) \quad (15)$$

These imply that people mentioned diarrhea mostly after visiting the southwest and downstream areas on May 19. If instead using min_sup = 40% as on the fever dataset, a pattern indicating the diarrhea outbreak started and lasted after May 18, i.e., on May 19–20, can also be found:

$$\text{2011-05-18} \rightarrow \text{diarrhea} \ (44.1\%) \quad (16)$$

However, still no pattern like "diarrhea → close_to(Hospital)" is detected, suggesting the patients with diarrhea did not go to hospitals for treatment although they felt sick.

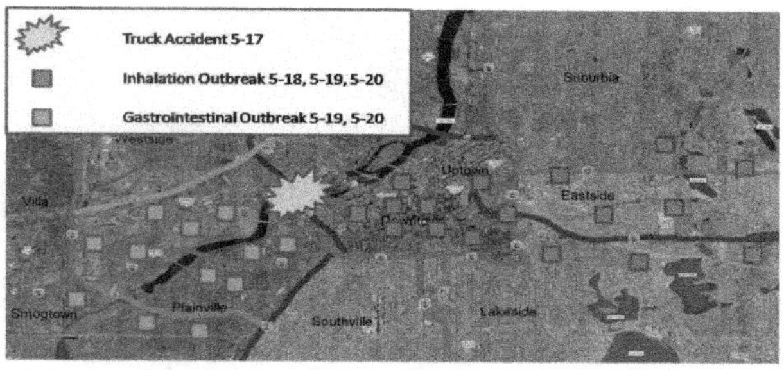

Figure 11: Ground Truth of Epidemic Spreads

Ground Truth: The ground truth provided by the Challenge committees is summarized in Figure 11. The ground zero location is a bridge over the river at the joint of midstream and downstream. On May 17, a truck carrying food contaminated by harmful spores had an accident there. The spores were dispersed into the air and the river, spread through wind and water current, and led to the outbreaks of inhalation and gastrointestinal diseases. Fever and diarrhea are two major symptoms, respectively. Due to the different incubation periods, the inhalation disease first outbreak on May 18 in Downtown, Uptown, and part of Plainville (revealed by patterns (5)–(8)). The disease also dispersed to the wide east on May 19–20 by west wind, but with much lower density. The gastrointestinal disease then outbreak on May 19 in downstream/southwest areas (revealed by patterns (12)–(15)). Unlike the *diarrhea* microblogs, the *fever* microblogs were collected in almost everywhere of the city, which makes the movement pattern noisy. Many people with the inhalation disease went to different hospitals on May 20 (revealed by patterns (9)–(11)). But people with the gastrointestinal disease never did, which is also verified by our results. In conclusion, CPM draws a complete and accurate picture of the epidemic outbreaks, and provides useful clues to infer the correct ground zero location.

4.3 Contextual Graph Mining

Data Overview: The dataset comes from the IEEE InfoVis 2007 Contest. It contains 20,204 US movies (2000–2006). For each movie, at least one director, one cinematographer and the first ten billed actors and actresses (at most 20 acting persons) are given with names. Movies are classified into 20 genres. Multiple genres are allowed. On average, one movie has 1.75 genres. IMDB and Netflix ratings, including the average rating score and the number of votes are also available. The movie collaboration graph is defined as such: a vertex represents a person, and an edge between two persons indicates they collaborate in at least one movie. We create two collaboration graph series: (1) by movie release year, and (2) by movie genre. Frequent subgraphs are mined on the two series, respectively. As graph mining cannot be done on the entire collaboration graph with up to 50,000 vertices and a million edges, we truncate the graphs by only considering the most popular (POP) and the best rated (BEST) movies, and also the persons that perform at least a certain number of movies. For example, in the Action movies, only the top 10 movies in the *number of user ratings* ranking (POP) and the top 10 movies in the *average rating score* ranking (BEST) are selected, respectively. The resulting four series of collaboration graphs are listed in Tables 9–10. Sample graph data is shown in Figure 12. Contextual information is defined over vertices (persons) by their acting preferences. For each person, all genres of the

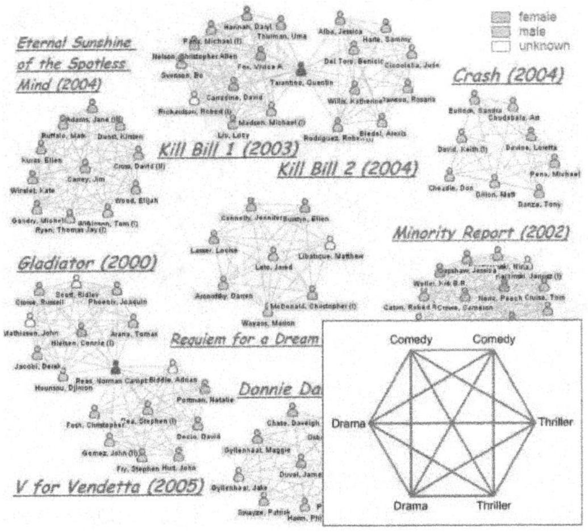

Figure 12: POP *Drama* Movies & CPM Result

Table 9: Movie Collaboration Graphs by Year

Year	Type	#vertex	#edge	Year	Type	#vertex	#edge
2000& 2001	POP	503	7299	2000& 2001	BEST	205	1790
2002& 2003	POP	546	10697	2002& 2003	BEST	357	5725
2004& 2005	POP	465	9509	2004	BEST	255	2108
				2005	BEST	428	8126

movies s/he has performed are collected. The top genres determined by either a large count or a large relative ratio are chosen as the person's acting genres. A CIG encoding the genre features of persons is shown in Figure 13.

Contextual Graph Mining: First we define the contextual subgraph isomorphism by conceptually extending the generalized subgraph isomorphism [9, 3]. We denote the vertex set of a graph g by $V(g)$, and the edge set by $E(g)$. A graph g is a contextual subgraph of another graph g' if there exits a contextual subgraph isomorphism from g to g'.

DEFINITION 5 (CONTEXTUAL SUBGRAPH ISOMORPHISM). *Given a CIG G, a contextual subgraph isomorphism is an injective function* $\phi : V(g) \to V(g')$, *s.t.* (1) $\forall u \in V(g), \ell(u) = \ell'(\phi(u))$ *or* $\ell(u) \rhd \ell'(\phi(u))$ *on G, and* (2) $\forall (u,v) \in E(g)$, $(\phi(u),\phi(v)) \in E(g')$, $\ell(u,v) = \ell'(\phi(u),\phi(v))$ *or* $\ell(u,v) \rhd \ell'(\phi(u),\phi(v))$ *on G, where* ℓ *and* ℓ' *are the label functions of* g *and* g', *respectively.*

The contextual graph mining is shown in Algorithm 4. Similar to the contextual association rule and sequence mining, here the over-generalized graph patterns [9, 3] need to be pruned: If a graph pattern *gp* is a contextual subgraph of a graph pattern *gp'* ($gp \neq gp'$) and their supports are identical, then *gp* is an over-generalized pattern.

Algorithm 4 Contextual Graph Mining

Input: Target graphs $\mathcal{D}$; CIG G; min_sup .
Output: Contextual graph pattern set $\mathcal{C}$.
1: find frequent contextual graphs with single vertex in $\mathcal{D}$;
2: expand the graphs by adding vertices or edges (labels can be contexts encoded in G) to generate new patterns;
3: insert those frequent (using min_sup) and non over-generalized patterns to $\mathcal{C}$;
4: **return** C;

Results: We apply a traditional graph mining algorithm, gSpan [20], a generalized graph mining algorithm, Taxogram [3], and CPM (Algorithm 4) to the movie graphs using min_sup = 100%: gSpan runs without any additional information, thus only finds subgraphs consisting of specific persons; Taxogram runs with a taxonomy that, for each person,

Table 10: Movie Collaboration Graphs by Genre

POP.Genre	#vertex	#edge	BEST.Genre	#vertex	#edge
Action	91	561	Action	70	432
Animation	63	223	Adventure	60	339
Comedy	77	396	Animation	35	115
Drama	94	482	Comedy	94	484
Horror	83	395	Crime	95	518
Musical	70	316	Documentary	60	416
Mystery	103	595	Drama	80	416
Romance	90	500	Fantasy	72	385
Sci-Fi	123	1240	Family	48	169
Thriller	101	632	Mystery	134	1078
War	97	607	Romance	84	461
			Sci-Fi	99	717
			Thriller	89	595
			War	80	485

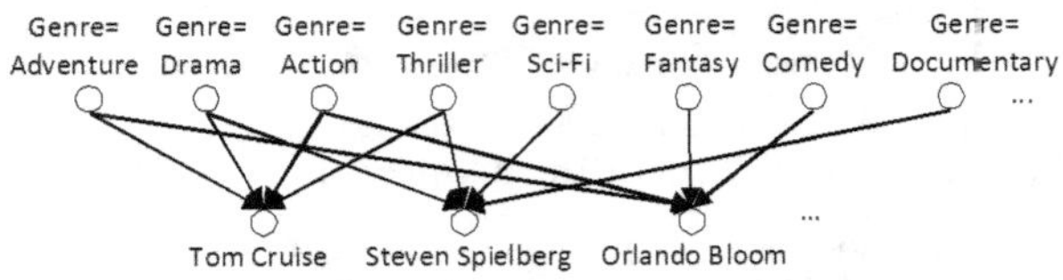

Figure 13: CIG Encoding Persons' Genre Contexts

a concept defined by his/her primary genre (with the largest relative ratio) is associated; CPM runs with the CIG in Figure 13. Results are summarized in Table 11. On the four graph series, gSpan only finds two subgraphs in total, suggesting that there is few consistent collaboration patterns at specific person level. By generalizing persons with the primary genre, Taxogram finds more patterns. With more contextual information available, CPM achieves the best results in name of the patterns discovered. It finds patterns more than 10 times of Taxogram in almost all graph series including several interesting ones: First, POP movies tends to have more common collaboration patterns than BEST movies in either the temporal investigation or the horizontal by-genre comparison. This suggests that there exists some common actor "flavor ingredient" to attract audience through advertising, across the years and the genres. In contrast, there are fewer common patterns for BEST movies. Every top-ranked movie may has its own reason for success. We further checked the discovered patterns among POP movies of different genres. In the 66 subgraphs with the largest size of 6, most are with the mixed person genre of Drama, Comedy and Thriller (Figure 12). This suggests that to produce a popular movie, there should at least have movie stars in these three genres to play to the gallery.

5. DISCUSSIONS

One may ask why simply joining the contextual information to the target dataset and then running a traditional single-source pattern mining algorithm does not work for CPM. The reason is two-fold: (1) The join can generate replicated contextual features for one target object, which makes the joined dataset contain redundancy and can result in meaningless patterns. For example, in Section 4.1, directly joining the *Road* information to the third row (tid=266) of Table 3 can generate two close_to(Road) predicates. If this occurs frequently in the crime target dataset, itemsets like {close_to(Road), close_to(Road)} can become frequent. But such patterns are meaningless. (2) The join will cause information loss that, the linkages between identities and the contextual information are removed. Again, take the case study in Section 4.1 as an example. Even if with removing the data redundancy caused by the join and Table 5 is obtained, itemsets like {within(Tract26), within(POPDEN=Low)} and {close_to(Trent Av), close_to(Road)} can be generated and frequent. However, such patterns reveals nothing new

Table 11: Collaboration Graph Mining Results

Graph Series	Type	Algorithm	#Patterns by Subgraph Size				
			2	3	4	5	6
By Year	POP	gSpan	2	0	0	0	0
		Taxogram	6	18	41	7	12
		CPM	49	497	3807	OoM*	OoM*
	BEST	gSpan	0	0	0	0	0
		Taxogram	2	7	35	272	1497
		CPM	27	187	966	OoM*	OoM*
By Genre	POP	gSpan	0	0	0	0	0
		Taxogram	3	4	4	1	0
		CPM	10	44	121	152	66
	BEST	gSpan	0	0	0	0	0
		Taxogram	3	8	6	0	0
		CPM	7	20	44	77	0

*Out of memory due to too many patterns discovered

Table 12: CPM vs. "Simple Join"

Dataset	Algorithm	CPU time (s)	#itemsets	#rules
crime	CPM	13.891	431	212
	Simple Join	14.016	822	1563

Dataset	Algorithm	CPU time (s)	Total #patterns	#patterns end with symptom
fever with min_sup =40%	CPM	152.672	659	9
	Simple Join	175.828	1334	12
diarrhea with min_sup =80%	CPM	14.266	537	15
	Simple Join	14.422	543	15
diarrhea with min_sup =40%	CPM	190.938	6877	68
	Simple Join	367.422	12932	76

but the known correlation between an item and its related feature, which is already represented in the CIG. It is a common issue among association rule, sequence, and graph mining. It is known that, if a small pattern, e.g., a meaningless 2-itemset in the above two cases, is frequent, it is bound to enlarge the search space by growing to larger patterns [16, 17, 9, 3], which inevitably leads to the generation of a huge number of redundant or over-generalized patterns. A feasible way to handle this is to post-process all the patterns after they are generated, by filtering the result with additional information. However, one may need to enumerate nearly all possible patterns due to its NP-completeness, which makes it intractable, especially when min_sup is small. Previous study [16] has shown that, not generating useless patterns in the earliest stage can make the algorithm 100 times faster than post-processing. On the other hand, the proposed CPM approach can avoid all these issues.

Table 12 shows the comparisons between CPM and running traditional pattern mining on the datasets simply joined with the contextual information (denoted by "Simple Join"). We can see that, with same parameters, "Simple Join" always costs more CPU time and finds a lot more patterns. However, none of the extra patterns is useful or provides new insight. The larger the dataset is and the smaller min_sup is, the more obvious that CPM is advantageous. In the case study of Section 4.3, graph mining without pruning over-generalized patterns yields little difference and thus is not shown here. Because the CIG is bipartite, a large number of over-generalized patterns can exist only when there are many specified patterns. However, from Table 11 we can see that, with min_sup = 100%, only 2 specified subgraph patterns, both of which contain 2 vertices, can be found (the first row, gSpan result). The largest possible number of over-generalized patterns of the two 2-vertex subgraphs is: (the number of contexts of one vertex) $\times$ (the number of contexts of the other) $-$ 1. In this specific case study, this number is small. Therefore, no significant difference can be observed between CPM and "Simple Join" here. However, we should keep in mind that, generally, pruning over-generalized contextual graph patterns is needed, especially when the number of specialized patterns is large.

There are two ways of handling missing values in CPM. Suppose feature F to be encoded has missing value. One way is to insert a vertex with label ($F = null$) to the CIG and CPM works. This may make ($F = null$) appear in the final patterns, which makes sense and is needed in some cases. The other way is to ignore all missing values when constructing the CIG, then they will not be considered in pattern mining. It is possible that the identities are not the same among different contextual information sources, which is not a problem for CIG encoding. As can be seen in Algorithm 1, CIG encoding can also be done incrementally. Whenever new contextual information sources are available, given a previously constructed CIG, new information can be encoded without re-encoding the previous information sources. The effects of different discretization methods to CIG encoding include the followings. Given a fixed size of identities $|V|$, a fine granularity of feature discretization can increase $|U|$ and $|E|$ of a CIG $G = (U, V, E)$, which can enlarge the search space for pattern mining because the number of frequent combinations can increase, and vice versa. Nonetheless, the linear time and space complexities of CIG encoding do not change at all.

6. RELATED WORK

Previous studies on frequent pattern mining mainly focus on mining from a single source. The most typical pattern mining methods include itemset/association rule mining [1, 8], sequential pattern mining [2, 19], and graph mining [20, 11]. In this paper, we propose the CPM approach that appropriately utilizes available contextual information from multiple sources for pattern discovery. The goals of CPM and multi-relational data mining (MRDM) approaches proposed to discover patterns involving multiple tables (relations) [4, 5] are similar, but they have different focuses: (1) CPM addresses to involve contextual information by non-intrusively utilizing existing single-source pattern mining methods, i.e., with a two-step "CIG encoding + pattern mining". The CIG encoding works with different types of pattern mining methods (itemset/assocaiton rule, sequence, and graph), and can be seen as a unified pre-processing step, given that the contextual information sources link to the target dataset in a star schema. Because the encoding is efficient, with an efficient single-source pattern mining method implementation, the two-step strategy of CPM can be efficient and implemented with limited effort. This is especially meaningful for systems that already have a suite of single-source pattern mining algorithms seeking a quick and cheap enabling technique to collectively mine new information sources. On the other hand, implementing and deploying new algorithms is usually far more expensive in real-world systems. (2) Typical MRDM approaches solves the similar problem but in an intrusive way. To be specific, implementing MRDM approaches usually cannot reuse existing single-source pattern mining algorithms, especially when joining multiple tables is not considered a good solution. MRDM approaches based on inductive logic programming (ILP) [12, 4] can be applied to a general class of data mining problems and do not restrict to star schema of tables. Nonetheless, due to the generality, ILP based approaches can often be far less efficient in specific tasks compared with CPM. For example, WARMR [4] can be seen as a generalized algorithm for mining itemsets and sequences. Previous work [5] has pointed out that due to its general-purpose nature, WARMR does not fully exploit the properties of the specific patterns compared with traditional itemset and sequence mining algorithms [1, 2] and their GPM versions [16, 17]. On the other hand, CPM based on the proposed CIG encoding framework works directly with the GPM algorithms designed for specific tasks, including association rule mining (Section 4.1), sequence mining (Section 4.2), and graph mining (Section 4.3). Therefore, we can infer that in most cases, the proposed CPM approach can have better efficiency than ILP based approaches when solving a same problem.

A different MRDM approach recently proposed is RMiner [15]. It is designed to mine the MCCS (Maximal Connected Complete Subgraph) pattern in the K-partite graph representation of a MRD (multi-relational database). First, multiple (say, K) tables in a MRD is converted into a K-partite graph. Then RMiner runs on the graph to find patterns in the form of MCCS. The differences between the proposed CPM approach and RMiner include: (1) CPM searches patterns of classical forms (itemset/association rule, sequence, and subgraph) in a space defined by the CIG and the target dataset (of transactions, sequences and graphs). RMiner searches MCCS patterns which is far different from classical forms, and on the K-partite graph defining its search space. (2) The proposed CIG encoding only encodes contextual information into a graph, which is always bipartite. The target dataset of transactions, sequences, or graphs is not changed a bit. In contrast, RMiner runs on the K-partite graph which actually encodes the entire MRD of all the K tables. Although both CPM and RMiner work with graph representations of information, they are significantly different. More fundamentally, RMiner has a different objective with traditional MRDM approaches that it finds interesting (defined by the maximum entropy model) pattern of co-occurring attributes [15], whereas CPM finds similar patterns to traditional MRDM approaches.

To obtain contextual patterns, other alternatives may also exist to the proposed CPM approach. However, they require either significant intrusive modifications to the pattern mining algorithms or the development of new algorithms, so that the contextual information can be handled appropriately. The CPM approach proposed in this paper, i.e., "CIG encoding + pattern mining", is the shortest path and the cheapest way so far we can find. As long as the applied GPM algorithms accept a general DAG structured CIG, no modification is required and CPM can be done transparently to the end users. This makes the system much easier to use, and little engineering effort is required.

7. CONCLUSIONS

With a growing number of information sources describing properties of related objects in today's big data challenge, we propose a general framework to encode contextual information from multiple sources via the Contextual Information Graph (CIG) for Contextual Pattern Mining (CPM). The main objective is the capability to reuse the existing single-source pattern methods without any modification and with high efficiency and ease. The proposed approach discovers more predictive, insightful, and interesting patterns that traditional pattern mining algorithms cannot find. The CIG encoding does not introduce any additional computational cost to the pattern mining process, except the pre-processing of the contextual data, which has linear time and space complexities. Missing values, multiple values, and dynamically changing contextual information can also be handled. We demonstrate through case studies that, the mining of all the three major types of contextual patterns, i.e., association rule, sequence, and graph, are well supported by our framework. Experiments and case studies on real-world datasets demonstrate that contextual patterns containing richer information and more useful insights are discovered by CPM, which is both efficient and easy to use; on the other hand, traditional methods cannot discover most of these interesting patterns.

8. REFERENCES

[1] R. Agrawal and R. Srikant. Fast algorithms for mining association rules. In *VLDB*, pages 487–499, 1994.

[2] R. Agrawal and R. Srikant. Mining sequential patterns. In *ICDE*, pages 3–14, 1995.

[3] A. Cakmak and G. Ozsoyoglu. Taxonomy-superimposed graph mining. In *EDBT*, pages 217–228, 2008.

[4] L. Dehaspe and H. Toivonen. Discovery of frequent datalog patterns. *Data Mining and Knowledge Discovery*, 3(1):7–36, 1999.

[5] S. Džeroski. Multi-relational data mining: an introduction. *SIGKDD Explorations*, 5(1):1–16, 2003.

[6] J. Han and Y. Fu. Discovery of multiple-level association rules from large databases. In *VLDB*, pages 420–431, 1995.

[7] J. Han, M. Kamber, and J. Pei. *Data mining: concepts and techniques, 3rd ed.* Morgan Kaufmann, 2006.

[8] J. Han, J. Pei, and Y. Yin. Mining frequent patterns without candidate generation. In *ACM SIGMOD Record*, volume 29, pages 1–12, 2000.

[9] A. Inokuchi. Mining generalized substructures from a set of labeled graphs. In *ICDM*, pages 415–418, 2004.

[10] K. Koperski and J. Han. Discovery of spatial association rules in geographic information databases. In *Advances in spatial databases*, pages 47–66, 1995.

[11] J. Leskovec, J. Kleinberg, and C. Faloutsos. Graphs over time: densification laws, shrinking diameters and possible explanations. In *KDD*, pages 177–187, 2005.

[12] S. Muggleton. Inductive logic programming. *New generation computing*, 8(4):295–318, 1991.

[13] K. Olsen and A. Malizia. Automated personal assistants. *Computer*, pages 112–111, 2011.

[14] D. Page and M. Craven. Biological applications of multi-relational data mining. *SIGKDD Explorations*, 5(1):69–79, 2003.

[15] E. Spyropoulou and T. De Bie. Interesting multi-relational patterns. In *ICDM*, pages 675–684, 2011.

[16] R. Srikant and R. Agrawal. Mining generalized association rules. In *VLDB*, pages 407–419, 1995.

[17] R. Srikant and R. Agrawal. Mining sequential patterns: Generalizations and performance improvements. In *EDBT*, pages 1–17. Springer, 1996.

[18] H. Wang, H. He, J. Yang, P. Yu, and J. Yu. Dual labeling: Answering graph reachability queries in constant time. In *ICDE*, pages 1–12, 2006.

[19] J. Wang, J. Han, and C. Li. Frequent closed sequence mining without candidate maintenance. *IEEE Trans. on Knowl. and Data Eng.*, 19(8):1042–1056, 2007.

[20] X. Yan and J. Han. gSpan: Graph-based substructure pattern mining. In *ICDM*, pages 721–724, 2002.

Incorporating Occupancy into Frequent Pattern Mining for High Quality Pattern Recommendation

Linpeng Tang[13]*, Lei Zhang[23]*, Ping Luo[3] and Min Wang[3]
[1] Shanghai Jiao Tong University ,[2] University of Science and Technology of China ,[3] HP Labs China
{Linpeng.tang, lei.zhang7, ping.luo, min.wang6}@hp.com

ABSTRACT

Mining interesting patterns from transaction databases has attracted a lot of research interest for more than a decade. Most of those studies use *frequency*, the number of times a pattern appears in a transaction database, as the key measure for pattern interestingness. In this paper, we introduce a new measure of pattern interestingness, *occupancy*. The measure of occupancy is motivated by some real-world pattern recommendation applications which require that any interesting pattern X should occupy a large portion of the transactions it appears in. Namely, for any supporting transaction t of pattern X, the number of items in X should be close to the total number of items in t. In these pattern recommendation applications, patterns with higher occupancy may lead to higher recall while patterns with higher frequency lead to higher precision. With the definition of occupancy we call a pattern *dominant* if its occupancy is above a user-specified threshold. Then, our task is to identify the *qualified* patterns which are both frequent and dominant. Additionally, we also formulate the problem of *mining top-k qualified patterns*: finding the qualified patterns with the top-k values of any function (e.g. weighted sum of both occupancy and support).

The challenge to these tasks is that the *monotone* or *anti-monotone* property does not hold on occupancy. In other words, the value of occupancy does not increase or decrease monotonically when we add more items to a given itemset. Thus, we propose an algorithm called DOFIA (DOminant and Frequent Itemset mining Algorithm), which explores the upper bound properties on occupancy to reduce the search process. The tradeoff between bound tightness and computational complexity is also systematically addressed. Finally, we show the effectiveness of DOFIA in a real-world application on print-area recommendation for Web pages, and also demonstrate the efficiency of DOFIA on several large synthetic data sets.

Categories and Subject Descriptors

H.2.8 [**Database Management**]: Database Applications—*Data Mining*

*This work was done when Linpeng and Lei were visiting HP Labs China.

CIKM'12, October 29–November 2, 2012, Maui, HI, USA.

Keywords

Frequent pattern mining, Constraint-based mining, Frequent and Dominant pattern, DOFIA

1. INTRODUCTION

Frequent pattern mining has been attracting abundant research interest for over a decade. Most of those studies use *frequency*, namely the number of times a pattern appears in a transaction database, as the key measure for pattern interestingness. In this paper we introduce a new measure, *occupancy*, which considers the degree that a pattern occupies the items in its supporting transactions. Specifically, we prefer the pattern that occupies a large portion of the transactions it appears in. This new measure of occupancy is motivated by some real-world applications of pattern recommendation and we describe two of the such applications below.

The first application is on print-area recommendation for Web pages. We often find that the printout generated by a Web browser's print function is far from satisfactory since it usually contains a large portion of irrelevant content (e.g., navigation menu, advertisements, and related links). To solve this problem, HP provides *Smart Print*[1] that contains a user-friendly interface so that a user can easily select her interested print areas. Such selections are stored in print logs with user consent. If we view each content clip (a selected content area) as an item and all the selected clips by a user on a given Web page as a transaction of items, the print log data from all users form a transaction database. Our task is to recommend an itemset (i.e., a set of content clips) in a given Web page to users based on this database. Naturally, the itemset we recommend should occur frequently to reflect the interests of most users. Equally important is the completeness of the itemset: it should occupy a large portion of the transactions it appears in so that the user would not feel that the recommendation is missing too much relevant content.

Another motivating application is on investment portfolio recommendation. Assume that we have a transaction database that contains a large set of *high-quality and diversified* investment portfolios. Each transaction represents the set of financial assets (e.g., stocks, bonds,funds etc.) owned by an experienced investor. Our goal is to mine the "interesting patterns" (i.e., high-quality and diversified patterns) from the database to recommend to new investors. Similarly, we prefer the investment patterns that appear frequently in the database. More importantly, a good investment portfolio usually works as an entirety to achieve investment balance and reduce risks. So we would expect that a good investment pattern should cover a large portion of the transactions in which it appears. For example, we have two patterns X, Y of equal fre-

[1] A Web browser extension, www.hp.com/go/smartprint

quency. If X covers 90% assets of its supporting transactions while Y only covers 30%, it is natural to consider X as a much better investment pattern. Thus, the occupancy of a pattern is very critical to this application.

The commonality of the above two applications is that the set of items in each transaction *works as an entirety for a task* and thus making occupancy as important a factor as frequency for recommending interesting patterns. In these applications, occupancy becomes another pattern interestingness measure which is an indispensable complement to frequency (or support): we consider a pattern interesting if it is not only frequent, but also as complete as possible in its supporting transactions. Intuitively, the support of a recommended pattern correlates to the recommendation precision while its occupancy is related to the recommendation recall.

We show that the value of occupancy does not increase or decrease monotonically when we add more items to a given itemset. As a result, previous techniques for pruning the search space for frequent itemset mining based on the anti-monotonicity of support do not apply in our setting. We explore the properties for the upper bounds of occupancy and quality (the weighted sum of support and occupancy) for various patterns and use the upper bound to prune the search process for high-efficient qualified pattern mining. The contributions of our work can be summarized as follows:

• We introduce a new interestingness measure *occupancy* for pattern mining problems. It is an indispensable complement to the widely-studied measure of support when the items in a transaction serve as a whole for certain tasks. We formulate the problem of mining top-k qualified patterns which maximize any increasing function of support and occupancy. In this study the weighted sum of support and occupancy is adopted as a show case.

• We propose an algorithm called DOFIA (DOminant and Frequent Itemset mining Algorithm) to solve the problem of qualified pattern mining. In DOFIA, we explore the properties on the upper bound of occupancy for the patterns to prune the search process for high-efficient pattern mining. Specifically, we propose two upper bounds on occupancy for any given itemset X and its supersets in the search tree. The first bound is computationally efficient, while the second is proved to be the tightest bound with certain input constraint. We also show techniques to achieve tradeoff between these two bounds.

• We demonstrate the importance of applying occupancy measure in pattern recommendation applications and the effectiveness of DOFIA through a real-world application of print-area recommendation for Web pages using real data. We show the introduction of occupancy results in significant improvement on the quality of the recommendation and the high performance of DOFIA in finding the top quality patterns.

• We systematically evaluate the efficiency of DOFIA on some large synthetic data sets. Specifically, we evaluate the impact on the efficiency of the algorithm by varying the transaction database (i.e., the number of transactions, the average length of transactions, etc.), the parameter settings (i.e., α, β, etc.), and the different strategies used in DOFIA.

The rest of the paper is organized as follows. We first present the formulation of the problem in Section 2. In Section 3 we give the overview of the proposed algorithm DOFIA. The details of DOFIA, especially on how to calculate the upper bounds on occupancy and quality, are discussed in Section 4. We report the empirical study to show the effectiveness and efficiency of DOFIA in Sections 5 and 6. We present the related works in Section 7 and conclude the paper in Section 8.

2. PRELIMINARIES AND PROBLEM FORMULATION

In this section we first give some preliminaries in pattern mining and propose the definitions of occupancy. Then, we formulate the qualified pattern mining problems which consider both support and occupancy.

2.1 Definitions and Notations

A transaction database is a set of transactions, where each *transaction* is a set of items. Let $\mathcal{I}$ be the complete set of distinct items and $\mathcal{T}$ be the complete set of transactions. Any non-empty set of items is called an *itemset* and any set of transactions is called a *transaction set*. The transactions that contain all the items in an itemset X are the *supporting transactions* of X, denoted as $\mathcal{T}_X$. The *frequency* of an itemset X (denoted as $freq(X)$) is the number of transactions in $\mathcal{T}_X$. The definitions of support and frequent itemset are adopted from [1].

In the motivating applications in Section 1, the itemset we intend to find should occupy a large portion of the transactions in which it appears. We can calculate the occupancy degree as follows. For an itemset X we identify all its supporting transactions $\mathcal{T}_X$. For each transaction $t \in \mathcal{T}_X$ we calculate the ratio of $\frac{|X|}{|t|}$. We then aggregate these ratios to compute a single value of occupancy for X. In this paper we focus on the average of these ratios while other aggregate functions such as *quantile* or *min* may also be considered. The definition of occupancy is given as follows.

Definition 1 (Occupancy): Formally, the *occupancy* of an itemset X is defined as

$$\phi(X) = average(\{\frac{|X|}{|t|} : t \in \mathcal{T}_X\}),$$

where $average()$ is the average function of all the values in the set. ■

Then, we can use two different average functions, *harmonic average* and *arithmetic average*, in the above definition. Due to space limitations, we only consider the harmonic average in this paper, but similar techniques can also be employed when considering arithmetic average [2].

Definition 2 (Harmonic occupancy): The harmonic average of a set of numbers A is $HAverage(A) = \frac{|A|}{\sum_{a \in A} \frac{1}{a}}$. The *harmonic occupancy* of an itemset X is defined as

$$\phi_H(X) = HAverage(\{\frac{|X|}{|t|} : t \in \mathcal{T}_X\}) = \frac{|\mathcal{T}_X||X|}{\sum_{t \in \mathcal{T}_X} |t|}$$ ■

It is clear that the occupancy of an itemset X is the average ratio of the occurrences of the items in X to the number of the items in the transaction it appears in. The high value of the occupancy indicates that besides the items in X there are only a small number of items left inside the supporting transactions of X. Let us take the transaction database in Table 1[3] as an example. We calculate the harmonic occupancy of the two itemsets $I_1 = \{2, 7, 14, 20\}$ and $I_2 = \{2, 7, 14, 15, 20\}$ as follows. The supporting transactions of I_1 are $\{t_1, t_2, t_3, t_4, t_7, t_8, t_9\}$ while the supporting transactions of I_2 are $\{t_1, t_2, t_4\}$.

$$\phi_H(I_1) = \frac{4 \times 7}{12 + 8 + 5 + 11 + 4 \times 3} \approx 0.54$$

$$\phi_H(I_2) = \frac{5 \times 3}{12 + 8 + 11} \approx 0.48$$

[2]The comparison on effectiveness between harmonic and arithmetic average is out of the scope of this paper.

[3]This is a real world example taken from the HP's print log database.

Table 1: The transaction database of example 1

Trans No.	Length	Items
t_1	12	1 2 4 7 8 9 10 14 15 16 20 21
t_2	8	2 5 7 9 12 14 15 20
t_3	5	2 7 13 14 20
t_4	11	1 2 4 5 7 8 14 15 18 20 21
t_5	6	2 3 7 11 14 21
t_6	12	1 2 5 6 7 9 12 14 15 17 19 21
t_7	4	2 7 14 20
t_8	4	2 7 14 20
t_9	4	2 7 14 20
t_{10}	3	2 14 20

One may think that the itemset containing more items leads to a bigger value of occupancy. However, it is not always true. Consider itemsets I_1 and I_2. Even though $I_1 \subsetneq I_2$, we have $\phi_H(I_1) > \phi_H(I_2)$. The reason is that I_2 only appears in large transactions where it only occupies a small fraction, while I_1 appears in many smaller transactions where it occupies a large fraction. Thus, occupancy does not always increase monotonically when we add more items to an itemset. Similarly, we can show that occupancy does not always decrease monotonically when we add more items to an itemset either. This non-monotonic property of occupancy is in contrast to that of support in frequent pattern mining.

Definition 3 (Dominant Itemset): For a given minimum occupancy threshold β $(0 < \beta \leq 1)$, X is said to be *dominant* if $\phi(X) \geq \beta$. ■

With the definition of support and occupancy we can measure the *quality* of an itemset by combining these two factors.

Definition 4 (Quality): The *quality* of an itemset X is defined as $q(X) = \sigma(X) + \lambda\phi(X)$, where $\sigma(\cdot)$ denotes the (relative) support of a transaction, occupancy weight $0 \leq \lambda < +\infty$ is a user defined parameter to capture the relative importance of support and occupancy. ■

Here we use the weighted sum of support and occupancy as the quality. But it should be noted that any other functions, such as the harmonic average (similar to the F1 score), the sum of logarithms (similar to block size proposed in [8]) can be used to combine the two values of support and occupancy. Additionally, the proposed algorithms in this paper are independent of this function.

Definition 5 (Qualified Itemset): For a given minimum support threshold α and a minimum occupancy threshold β $(0 < \alpha, \beta \leq 1)$, X is said to be *qualified* if $\sigma(X) \geq \alpha$ and $\phi(X) \geq \beta$. ■

2.2 Problem Formulation

Some pattern recommendation applications require that interesting patterns should be both frequent and dominant. On one hand, if a pattern X is frequent it means that there are enough cases such a pattern appears in the transaction database. Thus, it improves the recommendation precision. On the other hand, if X is dominant it indicates that the recommendation of X is complete enough. Thus, it guarantees the recommendation recall. Therefore, with the definition of support and occupancy, we formulate the problem of mining qualified patterns as follows.

Mining Qualified Patterns. This task is to find all the qualified patterns (which are both frequent and dominant) in a transaction database for the given support threshold α and the occupancy threshold β.

Additionally, among all the qualified patterns we also aim to find the pattern with the maximal quality value for recommendation. Formally, it can be formulated as follows.

Table 2: The transaction database of example 2

Trans No.	Items
t_1	b c
t_2	a b
t_3	a b c
t_4	a b d
t_5	a b c d

Top Qualified Pattern. The top qualified pattern X is defined as the qualified pattern with the maximal quality value:

$$\underset{X:\sigma(X)\geq\alpha,\phi(X)\geq\beta}{\arg\max} \quad (\sigma(X) + \lambda\phi(X)) \tag{1}$$

Note that there may be multiple top qualified patterns if there are ties in the maximum quality values.

There are three parameters in the definition of the top qualified pattern, namely α, β, λ. If there is no itemset that is both frequent and dominant with respect to α, β, the top qualified pattern does not exist and a valid algorithm will not output any result since no non-empty pattern exists that meets the quality requirements. Parameter λ, the occupancy weight, is a user defined parameter to capture the relative importance of support and occupancy.

In the rest of the paper, we will primarily focus on mining top (i.e., $k = 1$) qualified pattern first. We then show that the solution to top qualified pattern mining can be easily extended to solve the problem of mining top-k qualified patterns for $k > 1$.

2.3 Discussion

One may think that dominant patterns with high occupancy usually contain a large number of items and thus methods based on *Maximal Frequent Itemset* mining may be adopted for finding top-k qualified patterns. (An itemset X is a maximal frequent itemset if X is frequent and no superset of X is frequent [6]). Given a support threshold we can get multiple maximal frequent itemsets, among which we can select the one with the largest number of items as the top qualified pattern. Is this a valid algorithm for mining top qualified pattern? The answer is "no" for the following reasons.

First, in methods based on mining maximal frequent itemsets, the number of items in a pattern is used as a measure in pattern selection. Compared with the concept of occupancy, this is actually the *absolute* size of an itemset while occupancy is the *relative* size of an itemset to the number of items in its supporting transactions. Thus, it is possible that the maximal frequent itemsets selected by such methods have very low occupancy, even lower than the minimal occupancy threshold, thus leading to a low recall in recommendation. For example, when $\alpha = 0.3$, $I_2 = \{2, 7, 14, 15, 20\}$ is a maximal frequent itemset for the transaction database in Table 1. However, its occupancy is much lower than its subset $I_1 = \{2, 7, 14, 20\}$ as described earlier. Secondly, in mining top qualified pattern a weighted sum of both support and occupancy is used as the interestingness measure, which may lead to better recommendation performance compared to the patterns selected by methods based on maximal frequent itemsets. The experimental results in Section 5 further validate our analysis here.

In the next section we will present our algorithm for the top qualified pattern mining problem.

3. OVERVIEW OF DOFIA

The straightforward solution to the pattern mining problem is to first generate all the frequent itemsets, calculate the occupancy value for each frequent itemset, and then select the qualified itemset with maximum quality value. In this section we will show how

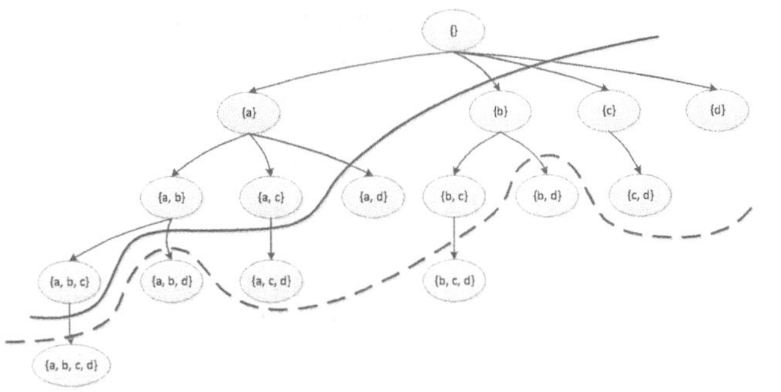

Figure 1: The lexicographic subset tree for the transaction database in Table 2. The solid line shows the search space of DOFIA, while the dashed line shows the search space for frequent pattern mining. $\alpha = 0.4, \beta = 0.3, \lambda = 1$.

the properties on occupancy and quality measures can be injected deeply into the search process and greatly prune the search space.

Pattern mining algorithms usually adopt the *lexicographic subset tree* to guide the search process. See Figure 1 as an example for four items a, b, c, d. The top element in the tree is the empty set and each lower level l contains all the l-itemsets (itemsets with exactly l items). The l-itemsets are ordered lexicographically on each level. Generating children in this manner enumerates all the distinct itemsets to be considered without redundancy. As there are 4 items, there are in total $2^4 = 16$ itemsets for consideration. Thus, in the lexicographic subset tree there are 16 nodes, each of which corresponds to an itemset.

Frequent pattern mining usually leverages the *monotonic decreasing* property of support values when adding more items to a given itemset. That is, if an itemset X is not frequent then all the supersets of X are not frequent either. Thus, the traversal in the tree is to find a cut (the dashed line in Figure 1) such that all the nodes (itemsets) above the cut are frequent, and all the nodes below the line are infrequent.

In this section we will show how to explore the properties on occupancy and quality to further prune the search space in the search tree. Specifically, given the root of a subtree we can estimate the upper bounds of the occupancy and quality values for all the nodes in this subtree. In other words, the occupancy and quality of any node in the given subtree will be no bigger than its upper bounds, respectively. If the upper bound on the occupancy is smaller than the occupancy threshold β, this subtree should be pruned. Also, we can maintain the current biggest quality value in the search process so far, denoted by $q*$, and all subtrees with the upper bounds less than $q*$ should be pruned.

Take the subtree with the root $\{b\}$ in Figure 1 as an example. We can give an upper bound of the quality for all the nodes in the subtree, including $\{b\}, \{bc\}, \{bd\}, \{bcd\}$. Assume we have already found $\{ac\}$ is the node with the highest quality 1.467 so far, which is bigger than the upper bound for the subtree rooted at $\{b\}$. Thus, subtree $\{b\}$ can be pruned. The solid line (which is above the dashed one) in Figure 1 is the cut line for pruning the search space for mining top qualified pattern. In this example, the search space when using only the frequency constraint for pruning has 12 nodes while the search space of DOFIA has only 5 nodes. The search space is greatly reduced by pruning using the upper bounds for occupancy and quality.

In Figure 1 the children of a node in the subset tree are ordered lexicographically on each level. It is worth mentioning that the order of these children also affects the algorithm efficiency. Ideally, we prefer to visit the nodes with the bigger quality values as early as possible since the big quality value can be used to prune the nodes whose quality upper bounds are less than it. On the other hand, we hope that the proposed upper bounds for occupancy and quality are as close as possible to the ground-truth values for a given subtree, which also helps to prune the search space. We consider two kinds of orders for the children of a node, i.e. the ascending and descending order of itemset support. Some experiments show that usually the ascending support order is more efficient than the other one (at least on the transaction databases used in the experiments). It seems the "fail first principle" applies in this case. The analysis on this observation is omitted.

Algorithm 1: DOFIA_DFS

```
input : the current Node currentNode, the top qualified pattern so
        far bestNode
if currentNode.quality > bestNode.quality then
    bestNode ← currentNode;
for node ∈ currentNode.children do
    supp ← node.support;
    occu ← the occupancy bound on the subtree rooted at node;
    qual ← the quality bound on the subtree rooted at node;
    if (supp ≥ α) ∧ (occu ≥ β) ∧ (qual ≥ bestNode.quality)
    then
        DOFIA_DFS(node, bestNode);
```

Algorithm 1 is the pattern mining process of a Depth-First-Search (DFS) with the pruning techniques. Note that since each node in the search tree uniquely corresponds to an itemset, we use the terms "node" and "itemset" interchangeably here. At $currentNode$ we first compare its quality with the top qualified node found so far. Then, we check any child, denoted by $node$, of $currentNode$. If $node$ is not frequent, or its occupancy upper bound is smaller than β, or its quality upper bound is smaller than the current maximal quality value, then $node$ is pruned. Otherwise, we recursively check $node$.

So far we have omitted the most challenging part in the algorithm: how to compute the upper bounds on occupancy and quality. Since the pruning of the search process is at the cost of computing these upper bounds, they should be computed efficiently. We describe its details in the next section.

4. THE UPPER BOUNDS OF OCCUPANCY AND QUALITY

In this section we will show how to efficiently compute the upper bounds of the harmonic occupancy and its quality. First, We give an overview of these upper bounds in Section 4.1.

4.1 Overview of the Upper Bounds

We give the notations which will be widely used in this study as follows. For any subtree, let X be the itemset for the subtree root (the root itemset), Y be the itemset including all the new items which will be extended in all the descendants of this subtree (the extension itemset). For example, for the subtree root $X = \{b\}$ in Figure 1 there are two new items c, d which appear in the descendants. Thus, $Y = \{cd\}$. With the extension itemset Y, we can get the following two vectors EL (Extension Length vector) and TL (Transaction Length vector) such that $\mathsf{EL}(i) = |t_i \cap Y|$ and $\mathsf{TL}(i) = |t_i|$, where t_i is any transaction in $\mathcal{T}_X$. For example, for the root set $X = \{ab\}$ with extension set $Y = \{cd\}$, the supporting transactions are $\mathcal{T}_X = \langle t_2, t_3, t_4, t_5 \rangle$, and thus $\mathsf{EL} = \langle |t_2 \cap Y|, |t_3 \cap Y|, |t_4 \cap Y|, |t_5 \cap Y| \rangle = \langle 0, 1, 1, 2 \rangle$, and $\mathsf{TL} = \langle |t_2|, |t_3|, |t_4|, |t_5| \rangle = \langle 2, 3, 3, 4 \rangle$. Furthermore, we will use u to denote the frequency of an itemset W in the subtree rooted at X, and v to denote how many items are in W aside from the items in X, i.e. $v = |W - X|$. These notations are summarized in Table 3.

Furthermore, we will frequently need to sort EL, TL. For a vector V (V is EL or TL in our case), $\mathsf{V}^{\uparrow}$ ($\mathsf{V}^{\downarrow}$) is the vector obtained by sorting V in ascending (descending) order. So $\mathsf{EL}^{\downarrow}(1)$ will be the largest value in EL, and $\mathsf{TL}^{\uparrow}(i)$ will be the i-th smallest value in TL.

Table 3: Notations used by Section 3

X	The itemset for the root of a subtree
Y	The extension itemset for the corresponding subtree
W	Any itemset in the subtree X, $X \subseteq W \subseteq (X \cup Y)$
u	u often denotes $\lvert\mathcal{T}_W\rvert$
v	v often denotes $\lvert W - X\rvert$
EL	The Extension Length vector, $\mathsf{EL}(i) = \lvert t_i \cap Y\rvert$ where $t_i \in \mathcal{T}_X$
TL	The Transaction Length vector, $\mathsf{TL}(i) = \lvert t_i\rvert$ where $t_i \in \mathcal{T}_X$
$\mathsf{V}^{\uparrow}, \mathsf{V}^{\downarrow}$	vector V sorted by ascending/descending order

We aim to estimate the occupancy and quality upper bounds of all the nodes in the subtree of X. In other words, the occupancy (quality) of any node in the subtree of X will be less than this occupancy (quality) upper bound. The basic idea is briefly described as follows.

First, we assume that we know the frequency u of any itemset $W \subseteq (X \cup Y)$ in the subtree of X. Then, we will propose $F(u, |X|, \mathsf{EL}, \mathsf{TL})$ such that

$$\phi(W) \leq F(u, |X|, \mathsf{EL}, \mathsf{TL}), \tag{2}$$

It is worth mentioning that the computation of F only involves $u, |X|, \mathsf{EL}, \mathsf{TL}$. Using more detailed information in $\mathcal{T}_X$ would surely lead to better bounds, but it would also make the computation more costly. Also note that here F is dependent on u, the frequency of W.

Then, we will show $F(u, |X|, \mathsf{EL}, \mathsf{TL})$ is not increasing with the increase of u, namely

$$F(u + 1, |X|, \mathsf{EL}, \mathsf{TL}) \leq F(u, |X|, \mathsf{EL}, \mathsf{TL}) \tag{3}$$

We call Equation 3 the *anti-monotonicity* property of the occupancy upper bound with respect to u.

Since it is required that W be frequent, its frequency u should not be less than the minimum frequency threshold $freq_{min}$, the minimal integer which is not smaller than $\alpha \cdot |\mathcal{T}|$. Thus, we have the following theorem.

Theorem 1 (Occupancy Upper Bound): For any itemset W in the subtree of X

$$\phi(W) \leq F(freq_{min}, |X|, \mathsf{EL}, \mathsf{TL}), \tag{4}$$

Proof: The conclusion holds if $F(u, |X|, \mathsf{EL}, \mathsf{TL})$ satisfies Inequalities (2) and (3). ∎

Note that in Theorem 1 it is not required to know the frequency of W. Thus, this is the occupancy upper bound of any node in the subtree of X. Next, for the upper bound of quality we also have

Theorem 2 (Quality Upper Bound): For any itemset W in the subtree of X

$$q(W) \leq \max_{freq_{min} \leq u' \leq |\mathcal{T}_X|} \left(\frac{u'}{|\mathcal{T}|} + \lambda F(u', |X|, \mathsf{EL}, \mathsf{TL})\right) \tag{5}$$

Proof: For any W in the subtree of X with the frequency u,

$$q(W) = \frac{u}{|\mathcal{T}|} + \phi(W) \leq \frac{u}{|\mathcal{T}|} + \lambda F(u, |X|, \mathsf{EL}, \mathsf{TL}), \tag{6}$$

Then, the conclusion holds if $F(u, |X|, \mathsf{EL}, \mathsf{TL})$ satisfies Inequality (2). ∎

Theorem 2 gives the quality upper bound of any node in the subtree of X. It should be noted that the result is independent of the function to combine support and occupancy. Any other functions can be used here and the quality upper bounds can be computed in similar ways.

In the following we will propose the F functions which satisfy Inequalities (2) and (3) for the harmonic occupancy.

4.2 The Upper Bounds of the Harmonic Occupancy

For harmonic occupancy we will propose two instances of F which satisfy Inequalities (2) and (3). We will show that the first F is more efficient, however, less tight than the second one. We also theoretically prove that the second F gives the tightest upper bound if only the values of $|X|, \mathsf{EL}, \mathsf{TL}$ are used for the computation. Finally, we show how to achieve the tradeoff between the bound tightness and computational efficiency.

4.2.1 The Efficient Upper Bound $F(u, |X|, \mathsf{EL}, \mathsf{TL})$

We propose $F(u, |X|, \mathsf{EL}, \mathsf{TL})$ function as follows.

$$F(u, |X|, \mathsf{EL}, \mathsf{TL}) = \frac{u|X| + u\mathsf{EL}^{\downarrow}(u)}{\sum_{i=1}^{u} \mathsf{TL}^{\uparrow}(i)}, \tag{7}$$

Next, We propose Properties 1 and 2 to show that the F function in Equation (7) satisfies Inequalities (2) and (3).

Property 1: For any itemset W in the subtree of X, let u be the frequency of W. Then, the occupancy of W satisfies that

$$\phi_H(W) \leq F(u, |X|, \mathsf{EL}, \mathsf{TL}) \tag{8}$$

Proof: Let's consider the harmonic occupancy of W.

$$\phi_H(W) = \frac{u|W|}{\sum_{t \in \mathcal{T}_W} |t|} \tag{9}$$

$$= \frac{u|X| + u|W - X|}{\sum_{t \in \mathcal{T}_W} |t|} \tag{10}$$

$$\leq \frac{u|X| + u\mathsf{EL}^{\downarrow}(u)}{\sum_{t \in \mathcal{T}_W} |t|} \tag{11}$$

$$\leq \frac{u|X| + u\mathsf{EL}^{\downarrow}(u)}{\sum_{i=1}^{u} \mathsf{TL}^{\uparrow}(i)} \tag{12}$$

Note that Inequality (11) is due to the fact that since $|\mathcal{T}_W| = u$, there are at least u transactions whose extension lengths are not smaller than $|W - X|$, and so $|W - X|$ can be no larger than the smallest of these u lengths. ∎

Property 2: $F(u + 1, |X|, \mathsf{EL}, \mathsf{TL}) \leq F(u, |X|, \mathsf{EL}, \mathsf{TL})$. ∎

Proof:

$$F(u + 1, |X|, \mathsf{EL}, \mathsf{TL}) \tag{13}$$

$$= \frac{(u + 1)|X| + (u + 1)\mathsf{EL}^{\downarrow}(u + 1)}{\sum_{i=1}^{u+1} \mathsf{TL}^{\uparrow}(i)} \tag{14}$$

$$\leq \frac{u(|X| + \mathsf{EL}^{\downarrow}(u)) + (|X| + \mathsf{EL}^{\downarrow}(u))}{(\sum_{i=1}^{u} \mathsf{TL}^{\uparrow}(i)) + \mathsf{TL}^{\uparrow}(u + 1)} \tag{15}$$

$$\leq \frac{u|X| + u\mathsf{EL}^{\downarrow}(u)}{\sum_{i=1}^{u} \mathsf{TL}^{\uparrow}(i)} \tag{16}$$

$$= F(u, |X|, \mathsf{EL}, \mathsf{TL}) \tag{17}$$

Inequality (15) comes from $\mathsf{EL}^{\downarrow}(u+1) \leq \mathsf{EL}^{\downarrow}(u)$. Inequality (16) comes from the property that for any $a_1, a_2 \geq 0$ and $b_1, b_2 > 0$, $\frac{a_1}{b_1} \geq \frac{a_2}{b_2} \Rightarrow \frac{a_1}{b_1} \geq \frac{a_1+a_2}{b_1+b_2}$. It is easy to check that $\frac{u(|X|+\mathsf{EL}^{\downarrow}(u))}{\sum_{i=1}^{u} \mathsf{TL}^{\uparrow}(i)} \geq \frac{|X|+\mathsf{EL}^{\downarrow}(u)}{\mathsf{TL}^{\uparrow}(u+1)}$, so Inequality (16) follows.

With Properties 1 and 2 we can also easily prove that the results in Theorems 1 and 2 hold for $F(u, |X|, \mathsf{EL}, \mathsf{TL})$. Then, Algorithm 2 gives the pseudo code for computing the quality upper bound in Theorem 2 with $F(u, |X|, \mathsf{EL}, \mathsf{TL})$.

The complexity of Algorithm 2 is $O(n + \mathsf{TL}^{\downarrow}(1))$. We first use the time of $O(n + \mathsf{TL}^{\downarrow}(1))$ for sorting EL, TL with *counting sort algorithm*, and then $O(n)$ time for the loop in Line 5.

Note that if any other function is used in the *quality* definition to combine support and occupancy we can substitute the equation of $u/|\mathcal{T}| + \lambda \cdot occu$ in Line 9 with the used function to get the right answer.

Algorithm 2: The quality upper bound based on $F(u, |X|, \mathsf{EL}, \mathsf{TL})$

```
input : the root set X, the extension set Y, the corresponding two
        vectors EL, TL and n = |T_X|.
output: qual, the quality upper bound of any itemset in the subtree
        rooted at X.
1 sort EL by descending order;
2 sort TL by ascending order;
3 sum ← 0;
4 qual ← −∞;
5 for u ← 1 to n do
6     sum ← sum + TL(u);
7     if u ≥ freq_min then
8         occu ← (u|X| + u · EL(u))/sum;
9         qual ← max(qual, u/|T| + λ · occu);
```

4.2.2 The "Tightest" Upper Bound $F'(u, v, |X|, \mathsf{EL}, \mathsf{TL})$

As mentioned before, $F(u, |X|, \mathsf{EL}, \mathsf{TL})$ has the parameter u, frequency for any itemset W in the subtree of X. Using a new parameter $v = |W \cap Y| = |W - X|$, i.e., the number of items in W aside from those in X, we may obtain a stronger upper bound.

Property 3: Let

$$F'(u, v, |X|, \mathsf{EL}, \mathsf{TL}) = \frac{u|X| + u \cdot v}{\min_{l_1, \cdots, l_u, \mathsf{EL}(l_i) \geq v} \sum_{i=1}^{u} \mathsf{TL}^{\uparrow}(l_i)} \tag{18}$$

Then for any itemset W in the subtree of X with $|\mathcal{T}_W| = u$ and $|W \cap Y| = v$, we have $\phi_H(W) \leq F'(u, v, |X|, \mathsf{EL}, \mathsf{TL})$.

Furthermore, for any itemset W' in the subtree of X with $|\mathcal{T}_{W'}| = u$ (and no constraint on $|W' \cap Y|$), we have

$$\phi_H(W') \leq \max_{0 \leq v \leq \mathsf{EL}^{\downarrow}(u)} F'(u, v, |X|, \mathsf{EL}, \mathsf{TL}) \tag{19}$$

$$\triangleq F'(u, |X|, \mathsf{EL}, \mathsf{TL}) \tag{20}$$

Proof: For any itemset W as described in Property 3, we have

$$\phi_H(W) = \frac{u|W|}{\sum_{t \in \mathcal{T}_W} |t|} \tag{21}$$

$$= \frac{u|W \cap (\mathcal{I} - Y)| + u|W \cap Y|}{\sum_{t \in \mathcal{T}_W} |t|} \tag{22}$$

$$= \frac{u|X| + uv}{\sum_{t \in \mathcal{T}_W} |t|} \tag{23}$$

Note that $\mathcal{T}_W$ are the supporting transactions of W and $|\mathcal{T}_W| = u$. Since $X \subset W$, by the anti-monotonicity of frequent itemsets, $\mathcal{T}_W \subseteq \mathcal{T}_X$. Since $|W \cap Y| = v$, for any $t \in \mathcal{T}_W$, $|t \cap Y| \geq |W \cap Y| = v$. Combining these two factors, $\sum_{t \in \mathcal{T}_W} |t| \geq \min_{l_1, \cdots, l_u, \mathsf{EL}(l_i) \geq v} \sum_{i=1}^{u} \mathsf{TL}^{\uparrow}(l_i)$. Thus,

$$\phi_H(W) = \frac{u|X| + uv}{\sum_{t \in \mathcal{T}_W} |t|} \leq \frac{u|X| + uv}{\min_{l_1, \cdots, l_u, \mathsf{EL}(l_i) \geq v} \sum_{i=1}^{u} \mathsf{TL}^{\uparrow}(l_i)}$$

For any itemsets W' in the subtree with $|\mathcal{T}_{W'}| = u$, it must be the case that $0 \leq |W' \cap Y| \leq \mathsf{EL}^{\downarrow}(u)$. We unify the bounds $F'(u, v, |X|, \mathsf{EL}, \mathsf{TL})$ over v and then have

$$\phi_H(W') \leq \max_{0 \leq v \leq \mathsf{EL}^{\downarrow}(u)} F'(u, v, |X|, \mathsf{EL}, \mathsf{TL})$$ ■

Property 4: $F'(u+1, |X|, \mathsf{EL}, \mathsf{TL}) \leq F'(u, |X|, \mathsf{EL}, \mathsf{TL})$. Here, the definition of $F'(u, |X|, \mathsf{EL}, \mathsf{TL})$ is given in Equation (20). ■

Proof: By the definition of $F'(u, v, |X|, \mathsf{EL}, \mathsf{TL})$, similar to the proof of Inequality (16), we have

$$F'(u+1, v, |X|, \mathsf{EL}, \mathsf{TL}) \leq F'(u, v, |X|, \mathsf{EL}, \mathsf{TL})$$

for any u, v.

Since $\mathsf{EL}^{\downarrow}(u+1) \leq \mathsf{EL}^{\downarrow}(u)$, we have

$$F'(u+1, |X|, \mathsf{EL}, \mathsf{TL}) \tag{24}$$

$$= \max_{0 \leq v \leq \mathsf{EL}^{\downarrow}(u+1)} F'(u+1, v, |X|, \mathsf{EL}, \mathsf{TL}) \tag{25}$$

$$\leq \max_{0 \leq v \leq \mathsf{EL}^{\downarrow}(u+1)} F'(u, v, |X|, \mathsf{EL}, \mathsf{TL}) \tag{26}$$

$$\leq \max_{0 \leq v \leq \mathsf{EL}^{\downarrow}(u)} F'(u, v, |X|, \mathsf{EL}, \mathsf{TL}) \tag{27}$$

$$= F'(u, |X|, \mathsf{EL}, \mathsf{TL}) \tag{28}$$

■

With Properties 3 and 4 we can also easily prove that Theorems 1 and 2 also hold for $F'(u, |X|, \mathsf{EL}, \mathsf{TL})$.

Remark 1: The Functions of F and F' proposed in Property 1 and Property 3 can be both improved by a small technique. If $|t \cap Y| = |Y|$ for some $t \in \mathcal{T}_X$, then $Y \subseteq t$. Thus, t is a supporting transaction for any W in the subtree of X. This observation can further improve the two bounds above. We omit details because it would make the formulae too complicated. ■

Algorithm 3: The quality upper bound based on $F'(u, v, |X|, \mathsf{EL}, \mathsf{TL})$

```
input : the root set X, the extension set Y, the corresponding two
        vectors EL, TL and n = |T_X|.
output: qual, the quality upper bound of any itemset in the subtree
        rooted at X.
sort ⟨EL, TL⟩ by ascending order of TL;
sum ← 0;
qual ← −∞;
for v ← 0 to EL↓(freq_min) do
    u ← 0;
    for i ← 1 to n do
        if EL(i) ≥ v then
            u ← u + 1;
            sum ← sum + TL(i);
            if u ≥ freq_min then
                occu ← (u|X| + u · v)/sum;
                qual ← max(qual, u/|T| + λ · occu);
```

Algorithm 3 shows the pseudo code for computing the quality upper bound based on $F'(u, v, |X|, \mathsf{EL}, \mathsf{TL})$. The time complexity

Quality Upper Bound	Complexity
F	$O(n+\mathsf{TL}^{\downarrow}(1))$
F'	$O(\mathsf{TL}^{\downarrow}(1)+n\cdot\mathsf{EL}^{\downarrow}(1))$
$\hat{F}$	$O(\mathsf{TL}^{\downarrow}(1)+mn)$

Table 4: The complexity of different estimation methods of quality upper bound

is $O(n+\mathsf{TL}^{\downarrow}(1)+n\cdot\mathsf{EL}^{\downarrow}(freq_{min}))$, in which $O(n+\mathsf{TL}^{\downarrow}(1))$ is for sorting the transactions (with counting sort algorithm) and $O(n\cdot\mathsf{EL}^{\downarrow}(freq_{min}))$ for the double loop in Line 4 and Line 6.

Also, we theoretically prove that F' is the tightest upper bound if only the values of $|X|$, EL and TL are used in the computation. Namely, we have the following theorem and its proof is omitted.

Theorem 3: $F'(u,|X|,\mathsf{EL},\mathsf{TL})$ is the tightest upper bound for harmonic occupancy of any node in the subtree of X with u supporting transactions if we only use the values of $|X|$, EL, TL to compute the bound. ∎

Corollary 1: $\max_{1\leq u\leq|\mathcal{T}_X|}\left(\frac{u}{|\mathcal{T}|}+\lambda F'(u,|X|,\mathsf{EL},\mathsf{TL})\right)$ is the tightest upper bound of the harmonic quality (harmonic occupancy used inside) of any node in the subtree of X if we only use the values of $|X|$, EL, TL to compute the bound. ∎

4.2.3 Tradeoff Between Bound Tightness and Computational Efficiency

We have proposed two quality bounds based on harmonic occupancy so far. Their complexity is summarized in Table 4.2.3. Although F' is provably tighter than F, when $\mathsf{EL}^{\downarrow}(1)$ is large, it can also take much more time than F and possibly becomes the computing bottleneck. To alleviate this situation, we propose a new technique that achieves balance between the bound tightness and computational efficiency. The basic idea is as follows. Instead of enumerating every possible value of EL in the range of $[0,\mathsf{EL}^{\downarrow}(freq_{min})]$, we split this large interval into m smaller intervals $[v_0,v_1-1],\cdots,[v_{m-1},v_m-1]$ $(v_0=0,v_m=\mathsf{EL}^{\downarrow}(freq_{min})+1)$.

For each interval $[v_{k-1},v_k-1]$, using the assumption that $v_{k-1}\leq|W-X|<v_k$, we obtain a tighter bound on occupancy in Property 5. In the end, we unify the m bounds and get a final result. The time complexity for computing such a quality bound is $O(n+\mathsf{TL}^{\downarrow}(1)+mn)$. Using a proper value for m, we achieve the tradeoff between the efficiency and effectiveness of the bound. The complexity for these three methods are summarized in Table 4.

Property 5: For any itemset W in the subtree of X, let u be the frequency of W. Assume $v_k\leq|W-X|<v_{k+1}$, then the harmonic occupancy of W satisfies that

$$\phi_H(W)\leq\frac{u|X|+u\min(\mathsf{EL}^{\downarrow}(u),v_{k+1}-1)}{\min_{l_1,\cdots,l_u,\mathsf{EL}(l_i)\geq v_k}\sum_{i=1}^{u}\mathsf{TL}^{\uparrow}(l_i)} \tag{29}$$

where t_{l_i} is any supporting transaction of X. ∎

The proof is omitted here. Then, we have the following theorems.

Theorem 4: Let $u'=freq_{min}$ be the minimum frequency threshold. For any integers $0=v_0<v_1<\cdots<v_m=\mathsf{EL}^{\downarrow}(u')+1$,

$$\hat{F}(u',|X|,\mathsf{EL},\mathsf{TL})=\max_{0\leq k<m}\hat{F}(u',v_k,v_{k+1},|X|,\mathsf{EL},\mathsf{TL})$$

is the upper bound on harmonic occupancy for any frequent W in the subtree of X. And

$$\max_{u'\leq u\leq|\mathcal{T}_X|}\frac{u}{|\mathcal{T}|}+\lambda\hat{F}(u,|X|,\mathsf{EL},\mathsf{TL})$$

is the upper bound on quality for any such W. ∎

5. EVALUATION ON EFFECTIVENESS

In this section we evaluate the effectiveness of occupancy in a real-world application of print-area recommendation. Here, assume that we have the log database which records how previous users clipped the Web pages from a Web site. Each transaction refers a set of content clips selected on a Web page. Given a Web page from the same Web site, we aim to recommend the informative clips for this Web page. More specifically, let $\mathcal{I}$ be the complete set of distinct clips in the database. For a given Web page we can get a set $Q\subseteq\mathcal{I}$ of clips which are included in this Web page (how to determine Q is omitted). Thus, our task is to select a subset of Q for the clip recommendation. By mining top qualified itemset the recommended itemset is the one $F\subseteq Q$ which has the maximal quality value among the qualified itemsets (for a given support threshold α and a occupancy threshold β).

To show the effectiveness of the proposed method we manually labeled the ground-truth of print-areas on the 2000 Web pages from the 100 major print-worthy Web sites (20 pages for each Web site).

We compare the proposed solution with the maximal frequent itemset based method (introduced in Section 2.3). Specifically, we can first generate all the maximal frequent itemsets and among them select the one with the largest number of items for recommendation.

For the 20 Web pages from a Web site, we use leave-one-out cross validation to evaluate the recommendation accuracy, i.e. we iteratively select one page as query and the log data on the left 19 Web pages are used to generate the transaction database for recommendation. A recommendation result actually refers to a set of content clips on the given Web page. Thus, we can evaluate its effectiveness by calculating the overlap area between the recommended clips and the ground truth on the query page. Then, with the overlap area we can calculate the precision P, recall R and $F1$ score of the recommendation in terms of area size. Specifically

$$P=\frac{|A_G\cap A_R|}{|A_R|},\ R=\frac{|A_G\cap A_R|}{|A_G|},\ F1=2\times\frac{P\times R}{P+R}, \tag{30}$$

Where A_G is the clipping region of ground truth, A_R is the clipping region of the recommendation result and $|\ldots|$ denotes the region size. If the precision is less than 1, it means that we need to remove some areas from the recommendation. If the recall is less than 1, it indicates that we need to add some contents to get the exact clipping areas. Then, we can average these these performance values over the 2000 Web pages to get the average performance.

The experiments in this section try to answer the following questions: (1) Does the concept of occupancy help to improve the recommendation performance compared with the baseline method? (2) How does the occupancy weight λ affect the recommendation performance?

The results of the baseline method are summarized in Table 5. The results of DOFIA are show in Table 6. Each entry in Tables 5 and 6 is the arithmetic average of the values (precision, recall and $F1$) over the 2000 Web pages. Since the $F1$ value is the harmonic average of precision and recall, the average $F1$ value over all those Web pages may be less than the average values of both precision and recall. For example, as shown in Table 6 when $\lambda=0$ the average $F1$ value is 79.79%, which is smaller than the corresponding average values of precision and recall.

Note that for the baseline method, the maximal $F1$ score is 90.56% (when $\alpha=0.1$), while DOFIA achieves a maximal $F1$ score of 93.8% (when $\lambda=6.0$). So the improvement on recommendation accuracy is clear.

The role of λ in DOFIA to this application is quite interesting. Intuitively, λ represents the emphasis we put on occupancy. A higher emphasis on occupancy is expected to lead to a better recall.

Such is indeed the case—when λ increases from 0.0 to around 5.0, recommendation recall increases significantly for the models. Interestingly, recommendation precision increases at the same time. The main reason is that with the increase of λ the quality value (considering both support and occupancy) may lead to better patterns whose area intersection with the ground truth have both better precision and better recall (see Equation (30)). However, when λ is too large, the performance of DOFIA deteriorates. Too much emphasis on occupancy tends to find patterns with a very small support just above the threshold α and the recommendation quality will naturally drop greatly.

6. EVALUATION ON EFFICIENCY

In this section we present the empirical evaluation on the efficiency of the proposed algorithm DOFIA over the large synthetic data sets. Specifically, we compare its running time with the baseline method to our problem. Here, the baseline method is to find all frequent itemsets first, compute the occupancy and quality for them, and then output top-k qualified ones. The implementation of MAFIA [6] includes a fast algorithm for frequent pattern mining, which is adopted in this comparison. We use MAFIA to find all the closed frequent itemsets, compute their quality values in the search process, and use a priority queue to maintain the top-k qualified itemsets. In practice, we find that the time to compute quality values and maintain the priority queue is actually negligible compared to the search process, so in the experiments below, we only show the time MAFIA used to find all the closed frequent itemsets, which is a lower bound for the time spent by the baseline. To abuse the notation a little bit, we still call the baseline method MAFIA. Our method, DOFIA, leverages the properties in Section 3 to further prune the search space, thus may achieve better efficiency.

The data sets used in this section are generated with the IBM synthetic data generator for itemset patterns [2]. We evaluate the efficiency on the data sets with different characteristics. The main parameters to generate the data include N: the number of transactions, L: the average length of transactions, I: the number of distinct items, PL: the average length of patterns, PN: the number of patterns. In our experiments, the default parameters for data generation are $N = 50000, I = 1000, L = 20, I = 1000, PL = 5, PN = 100$. In Section 6.1, We will adjust one parameter while fixing all the others to generate a series of data sets and show the efficiency changes. Only experiments on N and L are presented, and other parameters do not have much impact on running time of the algorithms when their values are within a reasonable range.

In addition, we also check the performance changes with different settings of problem parameters, including: the frequency threshold, α; the occupancy threshold, β; the number of top qualified itemsets we are searching for, k. The default values for these parameters are $\alpha = 0.005, \beta = 0.5, \lambda = 5, k = 5$. Similarly, we will adjust one parameter while fixing all the others to see the efficiency changes.

Table 5: The recommendation performance of the maximum frequent itemsets based method

α	P(%)	R(%)	F1(%)
0.0	85.85	96.02	88.74
0.05	90.28	92.2	89.81
0.1	90.6	92.84	**90.56**
0.2	90.65	92.12	90.05
0.3	89.5	91.02	88.88
0.4	87.11	87.57	85.48
0.5	82.0	81.75	79.06

Table 6: The recommendation performance (α = 0.05 and $\beta = 0.1$)

λ	P(%)	R(%)	F1(%)
0.0	90.04	82.15	79.79
0.5	89.67	92.84	88.78
1.0	90.77	94.74	91.3
2.0	91.63	95.96	92.81
4.0	92.65	96.31	93.6
5.0	92.81	96.3	93.64
6.0	93.23	96.19	**93.8**
8.0	93.23	95.95	93.7
10.0	93.34	95.84	93.71
$+\infty$	91.27	91.62	89.82
Average	91.76	93.91	91.12

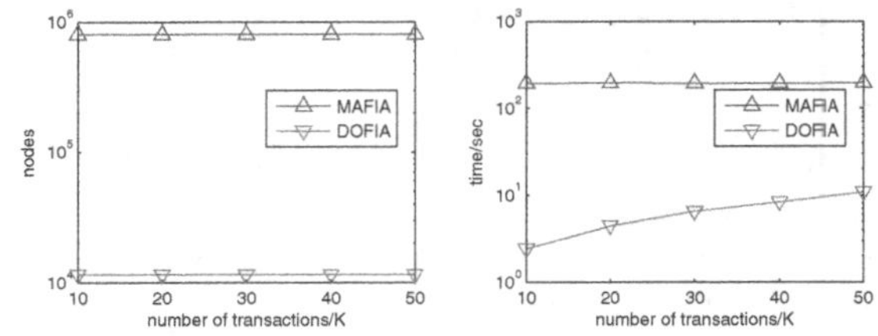

(a) Number of Nodes (b) Running Time

Figure 2: The effects of the number of transactions on MAFIA and DOFIA

Finally, we will compare the tradeoff between computational efficiency and bound tightness. By default, we use the upper bounds proposed in Section 4.2.1.

The experiments were performed on a Windows 7 laptop with quad core Intel i5-540M processor and 4 GB of main memory.

6.1 Evaluation on Different Databases

The number of transactions. Here, we generate a database of $N = 10000$ transactions and scale it up by vertical concatenation of the database. The results are shown in Figure 2, including the running time and the number of nodes in the subset tree searched by MAFIA and DOFIA. Note that in this experiments we only duplicate the database to increase its size. Thus, the number of nodes visited in the subset tree are expected to stay unchanged. As can be seen from Figure 2(a), DOFIA only searches about 1.4% nodes of those searched by MAFIA. With respect to running time, DOFIA's running time grows linearly, from 2.45 seconds for 10000 transactions to 10.34 seconds for 50000 transactions. What is interesting is that MAFIA's running time remains stable when the number of transactions grows. After careful investigation, we think it is due to the extreme efficiency of bit operators used extensively by MAFIA. However, since it takes MAFIA about 195 seconds to run the experiment for each data set, DOFIA is still much faster.

The average length of transactions. Here, we vary the average length of transactions. With the number of items growing in each transaction, the length of interesting patterns also grows. So we expect an exponentially growing number of frequent itemsets. Without proper pruning, MAFIA obviously cannot handle such cases. As shown in Figure 3, although it is faster than DOFIA when $L = 10$, it becomes very slow as L grows larger, taking more than 10^6 seconds when $L \geq 25$. On the hand, with the help of efficient pruning on occupancy and quality, DOFIA's running time grows smoothly, from 1.22 seconds for $L = 10$ to 5.88 seconds for $L = 30$.

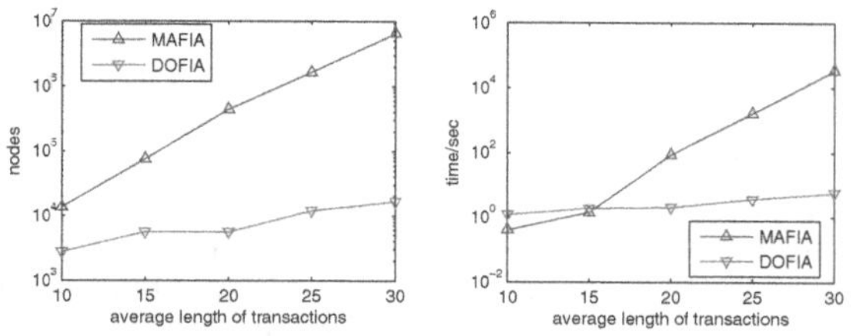

(a) Number of Nodes (b) Running Time

Figure 3: The effects of the average length of transactions on MAFIA and DOFIA

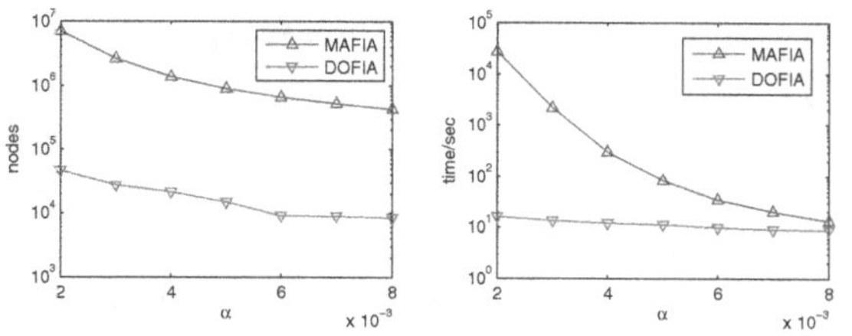

(a) Number of Nodes (b) Running Time

Figure 4: The effects of the minimum frequency threshold on MAFIA and DOFIA

6.2 Evaluation on Different Problem Settings

The frequency threshold. In practice, it is often desirable to have a low frequency threshold in order to detect more diverse patterns. However, with the lowering of frequency also comes the problem of too many frequent patterns and long running time. As seen in Figure 4, although MAFIA is just a little slower than DOFIA when frequency threshold $\alpha = 0.8\%$, it running time grows quickly with the decrease on α, and takes longer than 10000 seconds when $\alpha = 0.2\%$. On the other hand, DOFIA remains relatively efficient even at very low frequency threshold, due to the pruning on occupancy and quality.

The occupancy threshold. As shown in Figure 5, with the decrease of the occupancy threshold β, the running time and the number of the visited nodes increases moderately for DOFIA. As beta β decreases from 0.5 to 0.1, the number of nodes searched increases by 40.6% and the running time increases by 11.1%. One might expect that the increase in running time is exponential, but since we are doing the top-k qualified search, the most qualified nodes DOFIA has encountered helps a lot in reducing the search space, even if we set a low value in occupancy threshold. This observation gives us a lot of flexibility in choosing a proper value for β.

The occupancy weight parameter. The occupancy weight parameter λ reflects the priority we put on occupancy. Here, we empirically test DOFIA's performance when we vary λ. As can be seen from Figure 6, with the increase of λ from 0 to 2, the number of nodes visited by DOFIA increased by 80%, and the running time increased by 17%. The increase is mainly due to the fact that when λ is small the quality is dominated by its support, thus the high-frequency itemset with a small number of items will be output very fast. When λ becomes larger, it has to visit much more itemsets with high occupancy. When $\lambda > 1$, the number of nodes visited and running time converges because occupancy is already playing the major role here, and thus the increase on λ has little effect on the behavior of the algorithm.

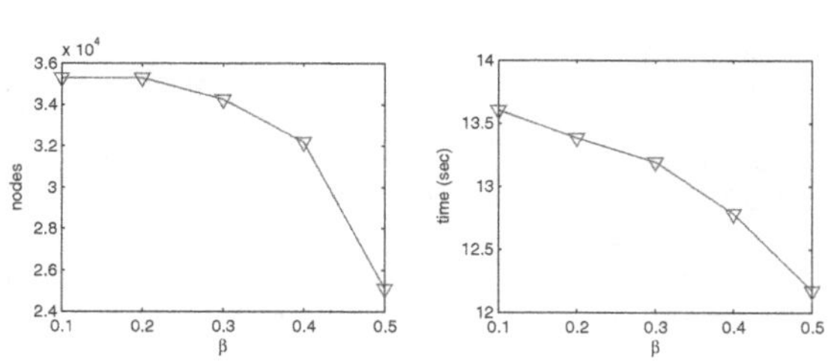

(a) Number of Nodes (b) Running Time

Figure 5: The effects of the minimum occupancy threshold on DOFIA

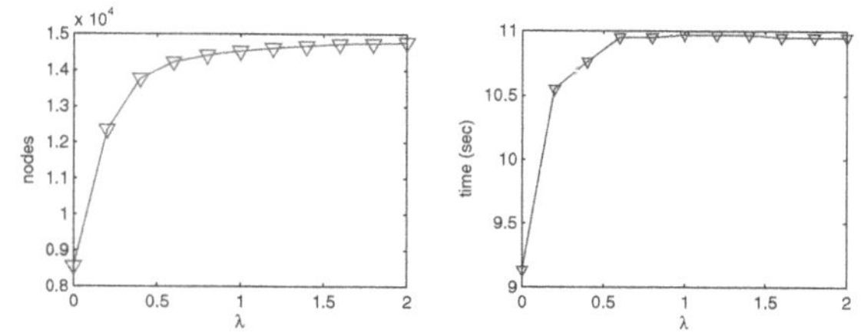

(a) Number of Nodes (b) Running Time

Figure 6: The effects of the occupancy weight parameter on DOFIA

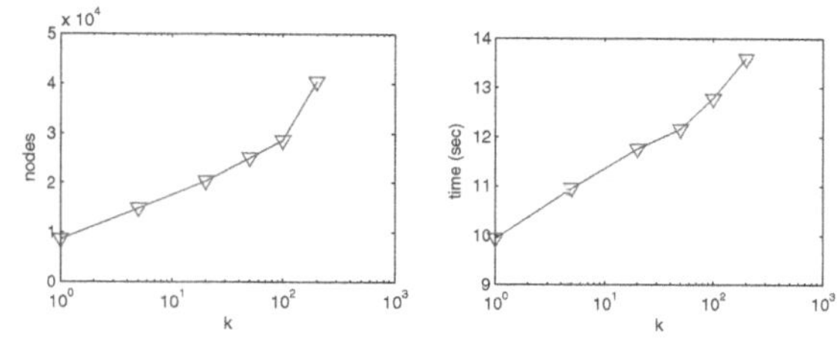

(a) Number of Nodes (b) Running Time

Figure 7: The effects of top-k on DOFIA

Top k. In practice, we often want to mine more than just the top few qualified patterns. With more patterns we can even do ranking on these patterns and find a set of diverse and high-quality itemsets. Here, we increase k to check the performance of DOFIA. As can be seen from Figure 7, though the number nodes grows about 300% when k increases from 1 to 200, the running time only increases moderately by about 40%.

6.3 Tradeoff between Bound Tightness and Computational Efficiency

In section 4.2.3 we proposed a technique that achieves tradeoff between bound tightness and computational efficiency. Specifically, instead of enumerating each possible value of $|W \cap Y|$ in the range of $[0, \mathsf{EL}^{\downarrow}(freq_{min})]$ as F' does, we suggest to split the large interval into smaller intervals $[v_0, v_1 - 1], \cdots, [v_{K-1}, v_K - 1], (v_0 = 0, v_K = \mathsf{EL}^{\downarrow}(freq_{min}) + 1)$.

Figure 8 shows the effect of this technique in one of our synthetic data sets. The x-axis shows the "interval length", i.e. $v_i - v_{i-1}$ and the y-axis shows the number of nodes searched and the running time in the two figures respectively. As can be seen, smaller the interval length, tighter the bound and fewer the nodes searched. In the case where the interval length is 1, only 60% nodes are searched compared to the case where the interval length is 13. However, the shortest running time does not occur when the bound is tightest, since the computation is too costly. In this case, the algorithm is fastest when the interval length is 7.

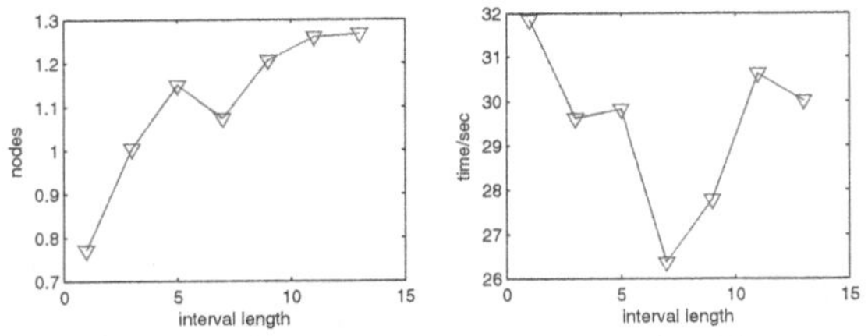

(a) Number of Nodes (b) Running Time

Figure 8: Tradeoff between computing efficiency and bound tightness

7. RELATED WORKS

Frequent pattern mining [1] has been well recognized to be fundamental to many important data mining tasks. There is a great amount of work that studies efficient mining of frequent patterns [11, 9, 6, 12], and we refer to [10] as a recent review on this field. These algorithms can be classified into mining frequent patterns [11, 9], frequent maximal patterns [6], and frequent closed patterns [12]. To reduce the number of frequent patterns some interestingness measures and constraints are proposed [13, 4, 5, 8] along with algorithms to implement them efficiently. Recently, graphical models[16] and compression[15] have also been proposed to approximate the frequent itemset with a minimal number of rules or patterns.

The concept of *occupancy* proposed in this paper can be viewed as a new interesting measure and constraint. It can be seen as the *relative size* of a pattern to its supporting transactions rather than the *absolute size* of it, and might be more meaningful in many applications. After proposing the concept of occupancy, we then formulate the problem of mining top-k qualified patterns which maximize the weighted sum of support and occupancy. Empirical tests on web print recommendation shows that the top qualified patterns can significantly improve the recommendation results when the weight on occupancy is chosen properly.

One work very similar to the spirits of ours is [17], where Wang et al. formulated the problem of finding the top-k frequent itemsets with their sizes no smaller than a threshold. Here we should note the difference between our work and theirs. First, [17] used the absolute size of an itemset as a constraint, while we use occupancy, the relative size of an itemset to its supporting transactions. As argued before, in many cases occupancy might be a more reasonable constraint. Besides, since occupancy is a normalized value, it also makes the tuning easier. Second, [17] tried to find the top-k frequent itemset, so frequency was used as the quality measure. In our work we define quality as the weighted sum of support and occupancy, which might be more appropriate. In another work [8], Gade et al. proposed to maximize the product of itemset size and its frequency. Again, occupancy might be a better measure than absolute itemset size. Recent works [7, 14] have also proposed methods to deal with complex constraints constructed from primitives. In those works, the primitives are required to be monotonic/anti-monotonic/convex, none of which is a property of occupancy. But in might be an interesting work to extend these frameworks to handle occupancy properly.

Different from many other constraints proposed, occupancy is not *anti-monotonic*, *monotonic*, *convertible*, and *succinct* [8], thus, no previous methods can be leveraged.

8. CONCLUSION

In this study, motivated by the pattern recommendation applications we introduce a new measure of pattern interestingness *occupancy* and formulate the problem of mining top-k qualified patterns. To solve this problem, we explore the upper bound properties on occupancy and propose DOFIA that injects these properties deeply into the search process. We propose two upper bounds, in which the first one is more efficient and the second one is theoretically proved to be tightest with certain input constraints. We show the effectiveness of occupancy in the real-world application of print-area recommendation for Web pages. Finally, on large synthetic data we demonstrate that DOFIA significantly outperforms the baseline method in terms of efficiency. It is worth mentioning that the concept of occupancy can be extended to sequential pattern mining [3] and graph mining [18], and thus is useful in many pattern mining applications.

9. REFERENCES

[1] R. Agrawal, T. Imielinski, and A. Swami. Mining association rules between sets of items in large databases. In *Proceedings of the ACM SIGMOD*, 1993.

[2] R. Agrawal, H. Mannila, R. Srikant, H. Toivonen, and A. I. Verkamo. Advances in knowledge discovery and data mining. chapter Fast discovery of association rules, pages 307–328. American Association for Artificial Intelligence, Menlo Park, CA, USA, 1996.

[3] R. Agrawal and R. Srikant. Mining sequential patterns. In *Proceedings of the 11th ICDE*, 1995.

[4] F. Bonchi, F. Giannotti, A. Mazzanti, and D. Pedreschi. Exante: Anticipated data reduction in constrained pattern mining. *Knowledge Discovery in Databases: PKDD 2003*, 2003.

[5] F. Bonchi and C. Lucchese. On closed constrained frequent pattern mining. In *Data Mining, 2004. ICDM'04. Fourth IEEE International Conference on*, pages 35–42. IEEE, 2004.

[6] D. Burdick, M. Calimlim, and J. Gehrke. Mafia: A maximal frequent itemset algorithm for transactional databases. In *Proceedings of the 17th ICDE*, 2001.

[7] L. Cerf, J. Besson, C. Robardet, and J.-F. Boulicaut. Closed patterns meet n-ary relations. *ACM Trans. Knowl. Discov. Data*, 3(1):3:1–3:36, Mar. 2009.

[8] K. Gade, J. Wang, and G. Karypis. Efficient closed pattern mining in the presence of tough block constraints. In *Proceedings of the tenth ACM SIGKDD international conference on Knowledge discovery and data mining*, pages 138–147. ACM, 2004.

[9] K. Gouda and M. Zaki. Genmax: An efficient algorithm for mining maximal frequent itemsets. *Data Mining and Knowledge Discovery*, 2005.

[10] J. Han, H. Cheng, D. Xin, and X. Yan. Frequent pattern mining: current status and future directions. *Data Mining and Knowledge Discovery*, 2007.

[11] J. Han, P. Jian, and Y. Yin. Mining frequent patterns without candidate generation. In *Proceedings of ACM SIGMOD*, 2000.

[12] N. Pasquier, Y. Bastide, R. Taouil, and L. Lakhal. Discovering frequent closed itemsets for association rules. In *Proceedings of the 7th International Conference on Database Theory*, 1999.

[13] J. Pei, J. Han, and L. Lakshmanan. Mining frequent itemsets with convertible constraints. In *Proceedings of the 17th ICDE*, 2001.

[14] A. Soulet and B. Crémilleux. Mining constraint-based patterns using automatic relaxation. *Intell. Data Anal.*, 13(1):109–133, Jan. 2009.

[15] J. Vreeken, M. van Leeuwen, and A. Siebes. Krimp: mining itemsets that compress. *Data Mining and Knowledge Discovery*, pages 1–46, 2011.

[16] C. Wang and S. Parthasarathy. Learning approximate mrfs from large transactional data. *Statistical Network Analysis: Models, Issues, and New Directions*, pages 182–185, 2007.

[17] J. Wang, J. Han, Y. Lu, and P. Tzvetkov. Tfp: An efficient algorithm for mining top-k frequent closed itemsets. *Knowledge and Data Engineering, IEEE Transactions on*, 2005.

[18] T. Washio and H. Motoda. State of the art of graph-based data mining. *ACM SIGKDD Explorations Newsletter*, 2003.

PARMA: A Parallel Randomized Algorithm for Approximate Association Rules Mining in MapReduce

Matteo Riondato, Justin A. DeBrabant, Rodrigo Fonseca, and Eli Upfal
Dept. of Computer Science, Brown University
Providence, RI, USA
{matteo, debrabant, rfonseca, eli}@cs.brown.edu

ABSTRACT

Frequent Itemsets and Association Rules Mining (FIM) is a key task in knowledge discovery from data. As the dataset grows, the cost of solving this task is dominated by the component that depends on the number of transactions in the dataset. We address this issue by proposing PARMA, a parallel algorithm for the MapReduce framework, which scales well with the size of the dataset (as number of transactions) while minimizing data replication and communication cost. PARMA cuts down the dataset-size-dependent part of the cost by using a random sampling approach to FIM. Each machine mines a small random sample of the dataset, of size independent from the dataset size. The results from each machine are then filtered and aggregated to produce a single output collection. The output will be a very close approximation of the collection of Frequent Itemsets (FI's) or Association Rules (AR's) with their frequencies and confidence levels. The quality of the output is probabilistically guaranteed by our analysis to be within the user-specified accuracy and error probability parameters. The sizes of the random samples are independent from the size of the dataset, as is the number of samples. They depend on the user-chosen accuracy and error probability parameters and on the parallel computational model. We implemented PARMA in Hadoop MapReduce and show experimentally that it runs faster than previously introduced FIM algorithms for the same platform, while 1) scaling almost linearly, and 2) offering even higher accuracy and confidence than what is guaranteed by the analysis.

Categories and Subject Descriptors

H.2.8 [**Database Management**]: Database Applications—*data mining*; H.3.4 [**Systems and Software**]: Distributed Systems

General Terms

Algorithms, Experimentation, Performance, Theory

Keywords

MapReduce, Frequent Itemsets, Association Rules, Sampling

1. INTRODUCTION

The discovery of (top-K) Frequent Itemsets and Association Rules (FIM) is a fundamental primitive in data mining and databases applications. The computational problem is defined in the general setting of a transactional dataset – a collection of transactions where each transaction is a set of items. With datasets increasing both in size and complexity, the computation for FIM faces scalability challenges in both space and time. Datasets have now reached the tens of terabytes scale and it is no longer reasonable to assume that such massive amounts of data can be easily processed by a single machine in a sequential fashion.

A typical exact algorithm scans the entire dataset, possibly multiple times, and stores intermediate counts of a large number of possible frequent itemsets candidates [2, 17]. The cost of these algorithms can be split in two independent components: the *scanning* cost and the *mining* cost. The scanning cost includes all operations that directly handle the transactions in the dataset, and scales with the *size* of the dataset, i.e., the number of such transactions. Examples include the scanning of the dataset to build the FP-Tree in FP-Growth [17] or to compute the actual frequencies of candidate frequent itemsets in APriori [1]. The mining cost refers to the operations in derived data structures and does not require access to the dataset. Examples include the operations performed on the FP-Tree once it has been generated, and the creation of candidate itemsets of length $i + 1$ at the end of phase i in APriori. This cost scales with the *complexity* of the dataset, i.e., the number of items, the number and distribution of frequent itemsets, and the underlying process that generated the transactions. It also depends on parameters given to the algorithm, such as the desired frequency threshold.

In this paper we are concerned with the scalability of FIM with respect to the size of the dataset, or the number of transactions. In many practical settings for FIM, the process generating the data changes very slowly or not at all, especially when compared to the data generation rate, therefore the number and frequency distribution of the frequent itemsets grows much slower than the size of the dataset. For example, the number of items available on the catalog of an e-commerce website grows much slower than the number of purchases by customers, each of which corresponds to a transaction. Therefore the scanning component grows faster than the mining one, and soon becomes dominant.

We introduce a randomized parallel algorithm for approximate frequent itemset mining, PARMA, that makes the scanning step of FIM embarassingly parallel, thus exhibiting near-linear speedup with the number of machines. PARMA combines random sampling and parallelization techniques in a novel fashion. It mines, in parallel, a set of small random samples and then filters and aggregates the collections of frequent itemsets or association rules obtained from each sample. Our work is orthogonal to other approaches, like PFP [18], which focuses on parallelizing the mining phase in order to decrease the corresponding component of the cost. Due to the use of random sampling, the output of PARMA is an approximation of the collection of FI's or AR's in the dataset, but leveraging on previous work [29], PARMA offers tight probabilistic guarantees on the quality of the approximated collections returned in output. In particular it guarantees that the output is an ε-approximation of the real collection with probability at least $1 - \delta$, where ε and δ are parameters specified by the user (see Section 3 for formal definitions). PARMA is designed on MapReduce [11], a novel parallel/distributed architecture that has raised significant interest in the research and industry communities. MapReduce is capable of handling very large datasets and efficiently executing parallel algorithms like PARMA.

To our knowledge PARMA is the first algorithm to exploit the combination of random sampling and parallelization for the task of Association Rules Mining. A number of previous works explored either parallel algorithms [4, 8, 12, 13, 22, 25, 30, 34] or random sampling [32, 35, 26, 28, 20, 29] for the FIM task, but the two approaches have been seen somewhat orthogonal until today. In PARMA, the disadvantages of either approach are evened out by the advantages of the other. In the spirit of *moving computation to the data* to minimize communication, we avoid data replication, and preserve the advantages of parallelization by using of multiple independent small random samples of the dataset which are mined in parallel and have only their results aggregated. Similarly, we are not subject to the inherent trade-off between the size of the random sample and the accuracy of the approximation that can be obtained from it, as PARMA would only have to mine more samples of the same size in parallel to get higher quality approximations.

Although PARMA is not the first algorithm to use MapReduce to solve the Association Rule Mining task, it differs from and enhances previous works [10, 14, 16, 18, 19, 33, 36] in two crucial aspects. First, it significantly reduces the data that is replicated and transmitted in the *shuffle* phase of MapReduce. Second, PARMA is not limited to the extraction of Frequent Itemsets but can also directly compute the collection of Association Rules in MapReduce. In previous works, association rules had to be created sequentially after the Frequent Itemsets had been computed in MapReduce.

We conducted an extensive experimental evaluation to test the relative performance, scalability and accuracy of PARMA across a wide range of parameters and datasets. Our results suggest that PARMA can significantly outperform exact mining solutions, has near-linear speedup, and, as data and nodes are scaled together, is able to achieve near constant runtimes. Also, our accuracy evaluation shows that PARMA consistently computes approximated collections of higher quality than what can be analytically guaranteed.

In this paper:

1. We present PARMA, the first randomized MapReduce algorithm for discovering approximate collections of frequent itemsets or association rules with near-linear speedup.
2. We provide analytical guarantees for the quality of the approximate results generated by the algorithm.
3. We demonstrate the effectiveness of PARMA on many datasets and compare the performance of our implementation to that of several exact FIM algorithms on MapReduce.

2. PREVIOUS WORK

The task of mining frequent itemsets is a fundamental primitive in computer science, with applications ranging from market basket analysis to network monitoring. The two most well known algorithms for extracting frequent itemsets from a dataset are APriori [2] and FP-growth [17].

The use of parallel and/or distributed algorithms for Association Rules Mining comes from the impossibility to handle very large datasets on a single machine. Early contributions in this area are presented in a survey by Zaki [34]. In recent years, the focus shifted to exploit architecture advantages as much as possible, such as shared memory [30], cluster architecture [4] or the massive parallelism of GPUs [13]. The main goal is to avoid communication between nodes as much as possible and minimize the amount of data that are moved across the network [8, 12, 22, 25].

The use of sampling to mine an approximation of the frequent itemsets and of association rules is orthogonal to the efforts for parallelizing frequent itemsets mining algorithm, but is driven by the same goal of making the mining of massive datasets possible. It was suggested in [23] almost as soon as the first efficient algorithms for Association Rules Mining appeared. Toivonen [32] presented the first algorithm to extract an approximation of the Frequent Itemsets using sampling. Many other works used different tools from probability theory to improve the quality of the approximations and/or reduce the size of sample. We refer the interested reader to [29] for a review of many contributions in this area.

The MapReduce [11] paradigm enjoys widespread success across both industry and academia. Research communities in many different fields uses this novel approach to distributed/parallel computation to develop algorithms to solve important problems in computer science [5, 6, 15, 21, 27]. Not only MapReduce can easily perform computation on very large datasets, but it is also extremely suited in executing embarassingly parallel algorithms which make a very limited use of communication. PARMA fits in this description so MapReduce is an appropriate choice for it.

A number of previous works [10, 14, 16, 18, 19, 33, 36] looked at adapting APriori and FP-growth to the MapReduce setting. Somewhat naively, some authors [10, 19, 33] suggest a distributed/parallel counting approach, i.e. to compute the support of every itemset in the dataset in a single MapReduce round. This algorithm necessarily incurs in a huge data replication, given that an exponential number of messages are sent to the reducers, as each transaction contains a number of itemsets that is exponential in its length. A different adaptation of APriori to MapReduce is presented in [16, Chap.4]: similarly to the original formulation of APriori, at each round i, the support for itemsets of length i is computed, and those that are deemed frequent are then used to generate candidate frequent itemsets of length $i + 1$, although outside of the MapReduce environment. Apart from this, the major downsides of such approach are that some data replication still occurs, slowing down the shuffling phase, and that the algorithm does not complete until the longest frequent itemset is found. Given that length is not known in advance, the running time of the algorithm can not be computed in advance. Also the entire dataset needs to be scanned at each round, which can be very expensive, even if it is possible to keep additional data structures to speed up this phase.

An adaptation of FP-Growth to MapRreduce called PFP is presented in [18]. First, a parallel/distributed counting approach is used to compute the frequent items, which are then randomly partitioned into groups. Then, in a single MapReduce round the transactions in the dataset are used to generate group-dependent transactions. Each group is assigned to a reducer and the corresponding group-dependent transactions are sent to this reducer which then builds the local FP-tree and the conditional FP-trees recursively, computing the frequent patterns. The group-dependent transactions are such that the local FP-trees and the conditional FP-trees built by different reducers are independent. This algorithm suffers from a data replication problem: the number of group-dependent transactions generated for each single transaction is potentially equal to the number of groups. This means that the dataset may be replicated up to a number of times equal to the number of groups, resulting in a huge amount of data to be sent to the reducers and therefore in a slower synchronization/communication (*shuffle*) phase, which is usually the most expensive in a MapReduce algorithm. Another practical downside of PFP is that the time needed to mine the dependent FP-tree is not uniform across the groups. An empirical solution to this load balancing problem is presented in [36], although with no guarantees and by computing the groups outside the MapReduce environment. An implementation of the PFP algorithm as presented in [18] is included in Apache Mahout [3].

The authors of [14] presents an high-level library to perform various machine learning and data mining tasks using MapReduce. They show how to implement the Frequent Itemset Mining task using their library. The approach is very similar to that in [18], and the same observations apply about the performances and downsides of this approach.

3. DEFINITIONS

A *dataset* $\mathcal{D}$ is a collection of *transactions*, where each transaction τ is a subset of a ground set (alphabet) $\mathcal{I}$. There can be multiple identical transactions in $\mathcal{D}$. Members of $\mathcal{I}$ are called *items* and members of $2^{\mathcal{I}}$ are called *itemsets*. Given an itemset $A \in 2^{\mathcal{I}}$, let $T_{\mathcal{D}}(A)$ denote the set of transactions in $\mathcal{D}$ that contain A. The *support* of A, $\sigma_{\mathcal{D}}(A) = |T_{\mathcal{D}}(A)|$, is the number of transaction in D that contains A, and the *frequency* of A, $f_{\mathcal{D}}(A) = \frac{|T_{\mathcal{D}}(A)|}{|\mathcal{D}|}$, is the fraction of transactions in $\mathcal{D}$ that contain A.

A task of major interest in this setting is finding the *Frequent Itemsets with respect to a minimum frequency threshold.*

Definition 1. Given a *minimum frequency threshold* θ, $0 < \theta \leq 1$, the *Frequent Itemsets mining task with respect to* θ is finding all itemsets with frequency $\geq \theta$, i.e., the set

$$\mathsf{FI}(\mathcal{D}, \mathcal{I}, \theta) = \{(A, f_{\mathcal{D}}(A)) \ : \ A \in 2^{\mathcal{I}} \text{ and } f_{\mathcal{D}}(A) \geq \theta\}.$$

For the top-K Frequent Itemsets definition we assume a fixed *canonical ordering* of the itemsets in $2^{\mathcal{I}}$ by decreasing frequency in $\mathcal{D}$, with ties broken arbitrarily. We label the itemsets $A_1, A_2, \ldots, A_m$ according to this ordering and denote with $f_{\mathcal{D}}^{(K)}$ the frequency $f_{\mathcal{D}}(A_K)$ of the K-th most frequent itemset A_K. For a given K, with $1 \leq K \leq m$, the set of top-K Frequent Itemsets (with their respective frequencies) is defined as

$$\mathsf{TOPK}(\mathcal{D}, \mathcal{I}, K) = \mathsf{FI}(\mathcal{D}, \mathcal{I}, f_{\mathcal{D}}^{(K)}). \tag{1}$$

One of the main uses of frequent itemsets is in the discovery of *association rules*.

Definition 2. An *association rule* W is an expression "$A \Rightarrow B$" where A and B are itemsets such that $A \cap B = \emptyset$. The *support* $\sigma_{\mathcal{D}}(W)$ (resp. frequency $f_{\mathcal{D}}(W)$) of the association rule W is the support (resp. frequency) of the itemset $A \cup B$. The *confidence* $c_{\mathcal{D}}(W)$ of W is the ratio $\frac{f_{\mathcal{D}}(A \cup B)}{f_{\mathcal{D}}(A)}$ of the frequency of $A \cup B$ to the frequency of A.

Given a minimum frequency threshold θ and a minimum confidence level γ, we define the set $\mathsf{AR}(\mathcal{D}, \mathcal{I}, \theta, \gamma)$ of triplets

$$(W, f_{\mathcal{D}}(W), c_{\mathcal{D}}(W))$$

s. t. W is an association rule with $f_{\mathcal{D}}(W) \geq \theta$ and $c_{\mathcal{D}}(W) \geq \gamma$.

In this work we are interested in computing well defined approximations of the above sets.

Definition 3. Given two parameters $\varepsilon_1, \varepsilon_2 \in (0, 1)$, an $(\varepsilon_1, \varepsilon_2)$-approximation of $\mathsf{FI}(\mathcal{D}, \mathcal{I}, \theta)$ is a set $\mathcal{C} = \{(A, f_A, \mathcal{K}_A) \ : \ A \in 2^{\mathcal{I}}, f_A \in \mathcal{K}_A \subseteq [0, 1]\}$ of triplets $(A, f_A, \mathcal{K}_A)$ where f_A approximates $f_{\mathcal{D}}(A)$ and $\mathcal{K}_A$ is an interval containing f_A and $f_{\mathcal{D}}(A)$. $\mathcal{C}$ is such that:

1. $\mathcal{C}$ contains all itemsets appearing in $\mathsf{FI}(\mathcal{D}, \mathcal{I}, \theta)$;
2. $\mathcal{C}$ contains no itemset A with frequency $f_{\mathcal{D}}(A) < \theta - \varepsilon_1$;
3. For every triplet $(A, f_A, \mathcal{K}_A) \in \mathcal{C}$, it holds
   (a) $|f_{\mathcal{D}}(A) - f_A| \leq \varepsilon_2$.
   (b) f_A and $f_{\mathcal{D}}(A)$ belong to $\mathcal{K}_A$.
   (c) $|\mathcal{K}_A| \leq 2\varepsilon_2$.

If $\varepsilon_1 = \varepsilon_2 = \varepsilon$ we refer to $\mathcal{C}$ as a ε-approximation of $\mathsf{FI}(\mathcal{D}, \mathcal{I}, \theta)$.

This definition extends easily to the case of top-K frequent itemsets mining using the equivalence from (1). An $(\varepsilon_1, \varepsilon_2)$-approximation to $\mathsf{FI}\left(\mathcal{D}, \mathcal{I}, f_{\mathcal{D}}^{(K)}\right)$ is an $(\varepsilon_1, \varepsilon_2)$-approximation to $\mathsf{TOPK}(\mathcal{D}, \mathcal{I}, K)$.

For association rules, we have the following definition.

Definition 4. Given two parameters $\varepsilon_1, \varepsilon_2 \in (0, 1)$ an $(\varepsilon_1, \varepsilon_2)$-approximation of $\mathsf{AR}(\mathcal{D}, \mathcal{I}, \theta, \gamma)$ is a set

$$\mathcal{C} = \{(W, f_W, \mathcal{K}_W, c_W, \mathcal{J}_W) \mid \text{AR } W, f_W \in \mathcal{K}_W, c_W \in \mathcal{J}_W\}$$

of tuples $(W, f_W, \mathcal{K}_W, c_W, \mathcal{J}_W)$ where f_W and c_W approximate $f_{\mathcal{D}}(W)$ and $c_{\mathcal{D}}(W)$ respectively and belong to $\mathcal{K}_W \subseteq [0, 1]$ and $\mathcal{J}_W \subseteq [0, 1]$ respectively. $\mathcal{C}$ is such that:

1. $\mathcal{C}$ contains all association rules appearing in $\mathsf{AR}(\mathcal{D}, \mathcal{I}, \theta, \gamma)$;
2. $\mathcal{C}$ contains no association rule W with frequency $f_{\mathcal{D}}(W) < \theta - \varepsilon_1$;
3. For every tuple $(W, f_W, \mathcal{K}_W, c_W, \mathcal{J}_W) \in \mathcal{C}$, it holds $|f_{\mathcal{D}}(W) - f_W| \leq \varepsilon_2$ and $|\mathcal{K}_W| \leq 2\varepsilon_2$.
4. $\mathcal{C}$ contains no association rule W with confidence $c_{\mathcal{D}}(W) < \gamma - \varepsilon_1$;
5. For every tuple $(W, f_W, \mathcal{K}_W, c_W, \mathcal{J}_W) \in \mathcal{C}$, it holds $|c_{\mathcal{D}}(W) - c_W| \leq \varepsilon_2$ and $|\mathcal{J}_W| \leq 2\varepsilon_2$.

If $\varepsilon_1 = \varepsilon_2 = \varepsilon$ we refer to $\mathcal{C}$ as an ε-approximation of $\mathsf{AR}(\mathcal{D}, \mathcal{I}, \theta, \gamma)$.

The following result from [29] is at the core of our algorithm for computing an ε-approximation to $\mathsf{FI}(\mathcal{D}, \mathcal{I}, \theta)$. A similar result also holds for $\mathsf{TOPK}(\mathcal{D}, \mathcal{I}, K)$ [29, Lemma 3].

LEMMA 1. *[29, Lemma 1] Let $\mathcal{D}$ be a dataset with transactions built on an alphabet $\mathcal{I}$, and let d be the maximum integer such that $\mathcal{D}$ contains at least d transactions of size at least d. Let $0 < \varepsilon, \delta, \theta < 1$. Let $\mathcal{S}$ be a random sample of $\mathcal{D}$ containing $|\mathcal{S}| = \frac{2}{\varepsilon^2}\left(d + \log\frac{1}{\delta}\right)$ transactions drawn uniformly and independently at random with replacement from those in $\mathcal{D}$, then with probability at least $1 - \delta$, the set $\mathsf{FI}(\mathcal{S}, \mathcal{I}, \theta - \frac{\varepsilon}{2})$ is a $(\varepsilon, \varepsilon/2)$-approximation of $\mathsf{FI}(\mathcal{D}, \mathcal{I}, \theta)$.*

For computing a ε-approximation to $\mathsf{AR}(\mathcal{D}, \mathcal{I}, \theta)$, we make use of the following Lemma.

LEMMA 2. *[29, Lemma 6] Let $\mathcal{D}$ be a dataset with transactions built on an alphabet $\mathcal{I}$, and let d be the maximum integer such that $\mathcal{D}$ contains at least d transactions of size at least d. Let $0 < \varepsilon, \delta, \theta, \gamma < 1$ and let $\varepsilon_{\text{rel}} = \frac{\varepsilon}{\max\{\theta, \gamma\}}$. Fix $c > 4 - 2\varepsilon_{\text{rel}}$, $\eta = \frac{\varepsilon_{\text{rel}}}{c}$, and $p = \frac{1-\eta}{1+\eta}\theta$. Let $\mathcal{S}$ be a random sample of $\mathcal{D}$ containing $\frac{1}{\eta^2 p}(d \log\frac{1}{p} + \log\frac{1}{\delta})$ transactions from $\mathcal{D}$ sampled independently and uniformly at random. Then $\mathsf{AR}(\mathcal{S}, \mathcal{I}, (1-\eta)\theta, \frac{1-\eta}{1+\eta}\gamma)$ is an $(\varepsilon, \varepsilon/2)$ approximation to $\mathsf{AR}(\mathcal{D}, \mathcal{I}, \theta, \gamma)$.*

3.1 MapReduce

MapReduce is a programming paradigm and an associated parallel and distributed implementation for developing and executing parallel algorithms to process massive datasets on clusters of commodity machines [11]. Algorithms are specified in MapReduce using two functions, **map** and **reduce**. The input is seen as a sequence of ordered key-value pairs (k, v). The **map** function takes as input one such $(key, value)$ pair at a time, and can produce a finite multiset of pairs $\{(k_1, v_1), (k_2, v_2), \cdots\}$. Let $\mathcal{U}$ be the multiset union of all the multisets produced by the **map** function when applied to all input pairs. We can partition $\mathcal{U}$ into sets $\mathcal{U}_{\bar{k}}$ indexed by a particular key $\bar{k}$. $\mathcal{U}_{\bar{k}}$ contains all and only the values v for which there are pairs $(\bar{k}, v)$ with key $\bar{k}$ produced by the function **map** ($\mathcal{U}_{\bar{k}}$ is a multiset, so a particular value v can appear multiple times in $\mathcal{U}_{\bar{k}}$). The **reduce** function takes as input a key $\bar{k}$ and the multiset $\mathcal{U}_{\bar{k}}$ and produce another set $\{(k_1, v_1), (k_2, v_2), \cdots\}$. The output of **reduce** can be used as input for another (different) **map** function to develop MapReduce algorithms that complete in multiple *rounds*. By definition, the **map** function can be executed in parallel for each input pair. In the same way, the computation of the output of **reduce** for a specific key k^* is independent from the computation for any other key $k' \neq k^*$, so multiple copies of the **reduce** function can be executed in parallel, one for each key k. We denote the machines executing the **map** function as *mappers* and those executing the **reduce** function as *reducers*. The latter will be indexed by the key k assigned to them, i.e., reducer r processes the multiset $\mathcal{U}_r$. The data produced by the mappers are split by key and sent to the reducers in the so-called *shuffle* step. Some implementations, including Hadoop and the one described by Google [11], use sorting in the shuffle step to perform the grouping of map outputs by key. The shuffle is transparent to the algorithm designer but, since it involves the transmission of (possibly very large amount of) data across the network, can be very expensive.

4. ALGORITHM

In this section we describe and analyze PARMA, our algorithm for extracting ε-approximations of $\mathsf{FI}(\mathcal{D}, \mathcal{I}, \theta)$, $\mathsf{TOPK}(\mathcal{D}, \mathcal{I}, \theta)$, and $\mathsf{AR}(\mathcal{D}, \mathcal{I}, \theta, \gamma)$ from samples of a dataset $\mathcal{D}$ with probability at least $1 - \delta$. In this section we present the variant for $\mathsf{FI}(\mathcal{D}, \mathcal{I}, \theta)$. The variants for the cases of $\mathsf{TOPK}(\mathcal{D}, \mathcal{I}, \theta)$ and $\mathsf{AR}(\mathcal{D}, \mathcal{I}, \theta, \gamma)$ can be easily derived from the one we present here. We outline them in Section 4.4. Detailed presentations for them will appear in the full version of the paper.

4.1 Design

We now present the algorithmic design framework on which we developed PARMA and some design decisions we made for speeding up the computation.

Model. When developing solutions for any computational problem, the algorithm designer must always be aware of the trade-off between the available computational resources and the performance (broadly defined) of the algorithm. In the parallel computation setting, the resources are usually modeled through the parameters p and m, representing respectively the number of available processors that can run in parallel and the amount of local memory available to a single processor. In our case we will express m in terms of the number of transactions that can be stored in the main memory of a single machine. When dealing with algorithms that use random samples of the input, the performances of the algorithm are usually measured through the parameters ε and δ. The former represents the desired accuracy of the results, i.e., the maximum tolerable error (defined according to some distance measure) in the solution computed by the algorithm using the random sample when compared to an exact solution of the computational problem. The parameter δ represents the maximum acceptable probability that the previously defined error in the solution computed by the algorithm is greater than ε. The measure we will use to evaluate the performances of PARMA in our analysis is based on the concept of ε-approximation introduced in Definition 3.

Trade-offs. We are presented with a trade-off between the parameters ε, δ, p, and m. To obtain a ε-approximation with probability at least $1 - \delta$, one must have a certain amount of computational resources, expressed by p and m. On the other hand, given p and m, it is possible to obtain ε-approximations with probability at least $1-\delta$ only for values of ε and δ larger than some limits. By fixing any three of the parameters, it is possible to find the best value for the fourth by solving an optimization problem. From Lemma 1 we know that there is a trade-off between ε, δ, and the size w of a random sample from which it is possible to extract a $(\varepsilon, \varepsilon/2)$-approximation to $\mathsf{FI}(\mathcal{D}, \mathcal{I}, \theta)$ with probability at least $1 - \delta$. If $w \leq m$, then we can store the sample in a single machine and compute the ε-approximation there using Lemma 1. For some combinations of values for ε and δ, though, we may have that $w > m$, i.e. the sample would be too large to fit into the main memory of a single processor, defeating one of the goals of using random sampling, that is to store the set of transactions to be mined in main memory in order to avoid expensive disk accesses. To address the issue of a single sample not fitting in memory, PARMA works on multiple samples, say N with $N \leq p$, each of size $w \leq m$ so that **1)** each sample fits in the main memory of a single processor and **2)** for each sample, it is possible to extract an $(\varepsilon, \varepsilon/2)$-approximation of $\mathsf{FI}(\mathcal{D}, \mathcal{I}, \theta)$ from it with probability at least $1 - \phi$, for some $\phi > \delta$. In the first stage, the samples are created and mined in parallel and the so-obtained collections of Frequent Itemset are then aggregated in a second stage to compute the final output. This approach is a perfect match for the MapReduce framework, given the limited number of synchronization and communication steps that are needed. Each stage is performed in a single MapReduce round. The computational and data workflow of PARMA is presented in Figure 1, which we describe in detail in the following paragraphs.

Computing N and w. From the above discussion it should be clear that, once p, m, ε and δ have been fixed, there is a trade-off between w and N. In the MapReduce setting, often the most expensive operation is the movement of data between the mappers and the reducers in the shuffle phase. In PARMA, the amount of data to be shuffled corresponds to the sum of the sizes of the samples, i.e., Nw, and to the amount of communication needed in the aggregation stage. This second quantity is dependent on the number of frequent itemsets in the dataset, and therefore PARMA has no control over it. PARMA tries to minimize the first quantity when computing N and w in order to achieve the maximum speed. It is still possible to minimize for other quantities (e.g. ε or δ if they have not been fixed), but we believe the most effective and natural in the MapReduce setting is the minimization of the communication. This intuition was verified in our experimental evaluation, where communication proved to be the dominant cost. We can formulate the problem of minimizing Nw as the following Mixed Integer Non Linear Programming (MINLP) problem:

- **Variables:** non-negative integer N, real $\phi \in (0, 1)$,
- **Objective:** minimize $2N/\varepsilon^2(d + \log(1/\phi))$.

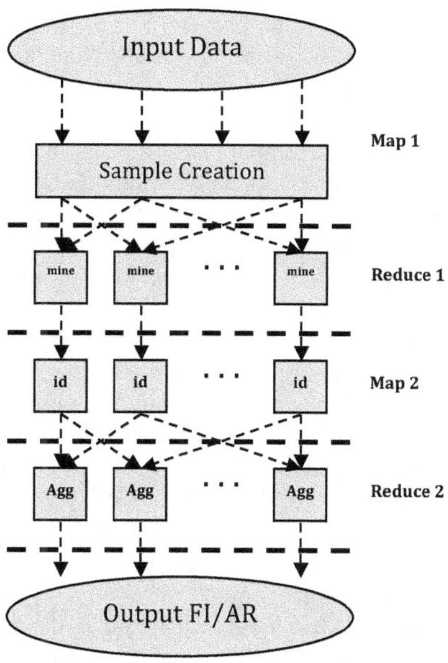

Figure 1: A system overview of PARMA. Ellipses represent data, squares represent computations on that data and arrows show the movement of data through the system.

- **Constraints:**

$$N \leq p \tag{2}$$

$$\phi \geq e^{-m\varepsilon^2/2+d} \tag{3}$$

$$N(1-\phi) - \sqrt{N(1-\phi)2\log(1/\delta)} \geq N/2+1 \tag{4}$$

Note that, because of our requirement **2)** on w, the sample size w is directly determined by ϕ through Lemma 1, so the trade-off is really between N and ϕ, while w does not appear in the above problem. Since ϕ is a probability we restrict its domain to the interval $(0, 1)$, but it must also be such that the single sample size w is at most m, as required by **1)** and expressed by Constraint (3). The limit to the number of samples N is expressed by Constraint (2). The last constraint (4) is a bit more technical and the need for it will be evident in the analysis of the algorithm. Intuitively, it expresses the fact that an itemset must appear in a sufficiently high fraction (at least 1/2, possibly more) of the collections obtained from the samples in the first stage in order to be included in the output collection. Due to the integrality constraint on N, this optimization problem is not convex, although when the constraint it is dropped the feasibility region is convex, and the objective function is convex. It is then relatively easy and fast to find an integer optimal solution to the problem using a global MINLP solver like BARON [31].

4.2 Description

In the following paragraphs we give a detailed description of PARMA. The reader is also referred to Figure 1 for a schematic representation of PARMA's data/computational workflow.

Stage 1: Sampling and Local Mining. Once ϕ, w and N have been computed, PARMA enters the first MapReduce round to create the N samples (phase Map 1 in Figure 1) and mine them (Reduce 1). We see the input of the algorithm as a sequence

$$(1, \tau_1), (2, \tau_2), \cdots, (|\mathcal{D}|, \tau_{|\mathcal{D}|}),$$

where the τ_i are transactions in $\mathcal{D}$. In the Map phase, the input of the **map** function is a pair (tid, τ), where tid is a natural from 1 to $|\mathcal{D}|$ and τ is a transaction in $\mathcal{D}$. The map function produces in output a pair $(i, (\ell_\tau^{(i)}, \tau))$ for each sample $\mathcal{S}_i$ containing τ. The value $\ell_\tau^{(i)}$ denotes the number of times τ appears in $\mathcal{S}_i$, $1 \leq i \leq N$. We use random sampling with replacement and ensure that all samples have size w, i.e., $\sum_{\tau \in \mathcal{D}} \ell_\tau^{(i)} = w$, $\forall i$. This is done by computing (serially) how many transactions each mapper must send to each sample. In the Reduce phase, there are N reducers, with associated key i, $1 \leq i \leq N$. The input to reducer i is $(i, \mathcal{S}_i)$, $1 \leq i \leq N$. Reducer i mines the set $\mathcal{S}_i$ of transactions it receives using an exact sequential mining algorithm like Apriori or FP-Growth and a lowered minimum frequency threshold $\theta' = \theta - \varepsilon/2$ to obtain $\mathcal{C}_i = \mathsf{FI}(\mathcal{S}_i, \mathcal{I}, \theta')$. For each itemset $A \in \mathcal{C}_i$ the Reduce function outputs a pair $(A, (f_{\mathcal{S}_i}(A), [f_{\mathcal{S}_i}(A) - \varepsilon/2, f_{\mathcal{S}_i}(A) + \varepsilon/2]))$.

Stage 2: Aggregation. In the second round of MapReduce, PARMA aggregates the result from the first stage to obtain a ε-approximation to $\mathsf{FI}(\mathcal{D}, \mathcal{I}, \theta)$ with probability at least $1-\delta$. The Map phase (Map 2 in Figure 1) is just the identity function, so for each pair

$$(A, (f_{\mathcal{S}_i}(A), [f_{\mathcal{S}_i}(A) - \varepsilon/2, f_{\mathcal{S}_i}(A) + \varepsilon/2])$$

in the input the same pair is produced in the output. In the Reduce phase (Reduce 2) there is a reducer for each itemset A that appears in at least one of the collections $\mathcal{C}_j$ (i.e., $\forall A$ such that there is a $\mathcal{C}_j$ containing a pair related to A). The reducer receives as input the itemset A and the set $\mathcal{F}_A$ of pairs

$$(f_{\mathcal{S}_i}(A), [f_{\mathcal{S}_i}(A) - \varepsilon/2, f_{\mathcal{S}_i}(A) + \varepsilon/2])$$

for the samples $\mathcal{S}_i$ such that $A \in \mathcal{C}_i$. Now let

$$R = N(1-\phi) - \sqrt{N(1-\phi)2\log(1/\delta)}. \tag{5}$$

The itemset A is declared *globally frequent* and will be present in the output if and only if $|\mathcal{F}_A| \geq R$. If this is the case, PARMA computes, during the Reduce phase of the second MapReduce round, the estimation $\tilde{f}(A)$ for the frequency $f_\mathcal{D}(A)$ of the itemset A in $\mathcal{D}$ and the confidence interval $\mathcal{K}_A$. The computation for $\tilde{f}(A)$ proceeds as follows. Let $[a_A, b_A]$ be the *shortest* interval such that there are at least $N - R + 1$ elements from $\mathcal{F}_A$ that belong to this interval. The estimation $\tilde{f}(A)$ for the frequency $f_\mathcal{D}(A)$ of the itemset A is the central point of this interval:

$$\tilde{f}(A) = a_A + \frac{b_A - a_A}{2}$$

The confidence interval $\mathcal{K}_A$ is defined as

$$\mathcal{K}_A = \left[a_A - \frac{\varepsilon}{2}, b_A + \frac{\varepsilon}{2}\right].$$

The output of the reducer assigned to the itemset A is

$$(A, (\tilde{f}(A), \mathcal{K}_A)).$$

The output of PARMA is the union of the outputs from all reducers.

4.3 Analysis

We have the following result:

LEMMA 3. *The output of the PARMA is an ε-approximation of $\mathsf{FI}(\mathcal{D}, \mathcal{I}, \theta)$ with probability at least $1-\delta$.*

PROOF. For each sample $\mathcal{S}_i$, $1 \leq i \leq N$ we define a random variable X_i that takes the value 1 if $\mathcal{C}_i = \mathsf{FI}(\mathcal{S}_i, \mathcal{I}, \theta')$ is a $(\varepsilon, \varepsilon/2)$-approximation of $\mathsf{FI}(\mathcal{D}, \mathcal{I}, \theta)$, $X_i = 0$ otherwise. Given our choices of w and θ', we can apply Lemma 1 and have that $\Pr(X_i = 1) \geq 1 - \phi$. Let $Y = \sum_{r=1}^{N} X_r$ and let Z be a random variable with binomial distribution with parameters N and $1 - \phi$. For any constant $Q < N(1 - \phi)$ we have

$$\Pr(Y \leq Q) \leq \Pr(Z \leq Q) \leq e^{-N(1-\phi)(1-\frac{Q}{N(1-\phi)})^2/2},$$

where the last inequality follows from an application of the Chernoff bound [24, Chap. 4]. We then have, for our choice of ϕ and N and for $Q = R$ (defined in Eq. (5)), that with probability at least $1 - \delta$, at least R of the collections $\mathcal{C}_i$ are $(\varepsilon, \varepsilon/2)$-approximations of $\mathsf{FI}(\mathcal{D}, \mathcal{I}, \theta)$. Denote this event as $\mathcal{G}$. For the rest of the proof we will assume that $\mathcal{G}$ indeed occurs.

Then $\forall A \in \mathsf{FI}(\mathcal{D}, \mathcal{I}, \theta)$, A belongs to at least R of the collections $\mathcal{C}_i$, therefore a triplet $(A, \tilde{f}(A), \mathcal{K}_A)$ will be in the output of the algorithm. This means that Property 1 from Def. 3 holds.

Consider now any itemset B such that $f_{\mathcal{D}}(B) < \theta - \varepsilon$. By definition of $(\varepsilon, \varepsilon/2)$-approximation we have that B can only appear in the collections $\mathcal{C}_i$ that are not $(\varepsilon, \varepsilon/2)$-approximations. Given that $\mathcal{G}$ occurs, then there are at most $N - R$ such collections. But from Constraint (4) and the definition of R in (5), we have that $N - R < R$, and therefore B will not be present in the output of PARMA, i.e. Property 2 from Def. 3 holds.

Let now C be any itemset in the output, and consider the interval $S_C = [a_C, b_C]$ as computed by PARMA. S_C contains at least $N - R + 1$ of the $f_{\mathcal{S}_i}(C)$, otherwise C would not be in the output. By our assumption on the event $\mathcal{G}$, we have that at least R of the $f_{\mathcal{S}_i}(C)$'s are such that $|f_{\mathcal{S}_i}(C) - f_{\mathcal{D}}(C)| \leq \varepsilon/2$. Then there is an index j such that $|f_{\mathcal{S}_j}(C) - f_{\mathcal{D}}(C)| \leq \varepsilon/2$ and such that $f_{\mathcal{S}_j}(C) \in S_C$. Given also that $f_{\mathcal{S}_j}(C) \geq a_C$, then $f_{\mathcal{D}}(C) \geq a_C - \varepsilon/2$, and analogously, given that $f_{\mathcal{S}_j}(C) \leq b_C$, then $f_{\mathcal{D}}(C) \leq b_C + \varepsilon/2$. This means that

$$f_{\mathcal{D}}(C) \in \left[a_C - \frac{\varepsilon}{2}, b_C + \frac{\varepsilon}{2}\right] = \mathcal{K}_C, \tag{6}$$

which, together with the fact that $\tilde{f}_C \in \mathcal{K}_C$ by construction, proves Property 3.b from Def. 3. We now give a bound to $|S_C| = b_C - a_C$. From our assumption on the event $\mathcal{G}$, there are (at least) R values $f_{\mathcal{S}_i}(C)$ such that $|f_{\mathcal{S}_i}(C) - f_{\mathcal{D}}(C)| \leq \varepsilon/2$, then the interval $[f_{\mathcal{D}}(C) - \varepsilon/2, f_{\mathcal{D}}(C) + \varepsilon/2]$ contains (at least) R values $f_{\mathcal{S}_i}(C)$. Its length ε is an upper bound to $|S_C|$. Then the length of the interval $\mathcal{K}_C = [a_C - \varepsilon/2, b_C + \varepsilon/2]$ is at most 2ε, as requested by Property 3.c from Def. 3. From this, from (6), and from the fact that $\tilde{f}(C)$ is the center of this interval we have $|\tilde{f}(C) - f_{\mathcal{D}}(C)| \leq \varepsilon$, i.e., Property 3.a from Def. 3 holds. □

4.4 Top-K Frequent Itemsets And Association Rules

The above algorithm can be easily adapted to computing, with probability at least $1 - \delta$, ε-approximations to $\mathsf{TOPK}(\mathcal{D}, \mathcal{I}, K)$ and to $\mathsf{AR}(\mathcal{D}, \mathcal{I}, \theta, \gamma)$. The main difference is in the formula to compute the sample size w (Lemma 1), and in the process to extract the local collections from the samples. The case of top-K is presented in [29] and is a minor modification of Lemma 1, while for the association rule case we can use Lemma 2. These are minimal changes to the version of PARMA presented here, and the modified algorithms guarantee the same levels of accuracy and confidence.

5. IMPLEMENTATION

The entire PARMA algorithm has been written as a Java library for Hadoop, the popular open source implementation of MapReduce. Because all experiments were done using Amazon Web Service (AWS) Elastic MapReduce, the version of Hadoop used was 0.20.205, the highest supported by AWS. The use of Java makes possible future integration with the Apache Mahout parallel machine learning library [3]. Mahout also includes an implementation of PFP [18] that we used for our evaluation of PARMA.

In PARMA, during the mining phase (i.e. during the reducer of stage 1), any frequent itemset or association rule mining algorithm can be used. We wanted to compare the performances of PARMA against PFP which only produces frequent itemsets, therefore we chose to use a frequent itemset mining algorithm instead of an association rule mining algorithm. Again, this choice was merely for ease of comparison with existing parallel frequent itemset mining algorithms as no such algorithms for association rule mining exist. While there are many frequent itemset mining algorithms available, we chose the FP-growth implementation provided by [7]. We chose FP-growth due to its relative performance superiority to other Frequent Itemsets mining algorithms. Additionally, since FP-growth is the algorithm that PFP has parallelized and uses internally, the choice of FP-growth for the mining phase in PARMA is appropriate for a more natural comparison.

We also compare PARMA against the naive distributed counting algorithm (DistCount) for computing frequent itemsets. In this approach, there is only a single MapReduce iteration. The map breaks a transaction τ into its powerset $\mathcal{P}(\tau)$ and emits key/value pairs in the form $(A, 1)$ where A is an itemset in $\mathcal{P}(t)$. The reducers simply count how many pairs they receive for each itemset A and output the itemsets with frequency above the minimum frequency threshold. This is similar to the canonical wordcount example for MapReduce. However, because the size of the powerset is exponential in the size of the original transaction (specifically $2^{|\tau|}$, where $|\tau|$ denotes the number of items in a given transaction), this algorithm incurs massive network costs, even when combiners are used. This is very similar to the algorithms presented in [10, 19, 33]. We have built our own implementation of DistCount in Java using the Hadoop API.

6. EXPERIMENTAL EVALUATION

We evaluate the performance of PARMA using Amazon's Elastic MapReduce platform. We used instances of type *m1.xlarge*, which contain roughly 17GB of memory and 6.5 EC2 compute units. For data, we created artificial dataset using the synthetic data generator from [9]. This implementation is based on the generator described in [2], which can be parameterized to generate a wide range of data. We used two distinct sets of parameters to generate the datasets: the first set, shown in Table 1, for the experiments comparing PARMA and the distributed counting algorithm (DistCount), and the second set, shown in Table 2, for the experiments comparing PARMA and PFP. The parameters were chosen to mimic real-world datasets on which PARMA would be run. For a full description of the relevant parameters, we refer the reader to [2]. The reason we needed two distinct datasets is that DistCount did not scale to the larger dataset sizes, as the amount of data it generates in the map phase grows exponentially with the length of the individual transactions in the dataset. We found that DistCount would run out of memory using datasets with longer transactions, and we had to generate datasets with both shorter and less transactions for its comparisons.

Because PARMA is an approximate algorithm, the choice of accuracy parameters ε and δ are important, as is θ, the minimum frequency at which itemsets were mined. In all of our experiments, $\varepsilon = 0.05$ and $\delta = 0.01$. This means that the collection of itemsets mined by PARMA will be a 0.05-approximation with probability 0.99. In practice, we show later that the results are much more accurate than what this. For all experiments other than the minimum

number of items	1000
average transaction length	5
average size of maximal potentially large itemsets	5
number of maximal potentially large itemsets	5
correlation among maximal potentially large itemsets	0.1
corruption of maximal potentially large itemsets	0.1

Table 1: Parameters used to generate the datasets for the runtime comparison between DistCount and PARMA in Figure 2.

number of items	10000
average transaction length	10
average size of maximal potentially large itemsets	5
number of maximal potentially large itemsets	20
correlation among maximal potentially large itemsets	0.1
corruption of maximal potentially large itemsets	0.1

Table 2: Parameters used to generate the datasets for the runtime comparison between PFP and PARMA in Figure 2.

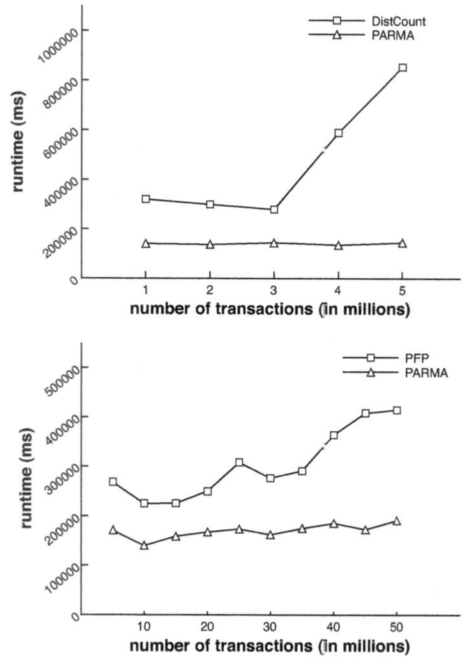

Figure 2: A runtime comparison of PARMA with DistCount (top) and PFP (bottom).

frequency performance comparison in Figure 4 and for the accuracy comparison in Figures 7 and 8, θ was kept constant at 0.1.

Due to space limitations, we do not report the results of the experiments to evaluate the performances of PARMA as the parameters of the optimization problem change.

6.1 Performance Analysis

For the performance analysis of PARMA, we analyze the relative performance against two exact FIM algorithms on MapReduce, *DistCount* and *PFP*, on a cluster of 8 nodes. We also provide a breakdown of the costs associated with each stage of PARMA.

Figure 2 (top) shows the comparison between PARMA and DistCount. For DistCount, longer itemsets affect runtime the most, as the number of key/value pairs generated from each transaction is exponential in the size of the transaction. This is not to say that more transactions does not affect runtime, just that the length of those transactions also has a significant impact. Because of this, it is possible to have datasets with fewer transactions but with more "long" transactions that take longer to mine. This effect is seen in the first three datasets (1-3 million). Of course, since these datasets were generated independently and with the same parameters, this was purely by chance. However, as the number of transactions continues to increase, the exponential growth in the number of intermediate key/value pairs is seen by the sharp increase in runtime. While we tried to test with a dataset with 6 million transaction, DistCount ran out of memory. The lack of ability to handle either long individual transactions or a large number of transactions in a dataset limits DistCount's real-world applicability.

For the performance comparison with PFP, 10 datasets were generated using parameter values from Table 2 and ranging in size from 10 to 50 million transactions. The results are shown in Figure 2 (bottom). For every dataset tested, PARMA was able to mine the dataset roughly 30-55% faster than PFP. The reason for the relative performance advantage of PARMA is twofold. The first (and primary) reason is that for larger datasets the size of the dataset that PARMA has sampled (and mined) is staying the same, whereas PFP is mining more and more transactions as the dataset grows. The second reason is that as the dataset grows, PFP is potentially duplicating more and more transactions as it assigns transactions to groups. A transaction that belongs to multiple groups is sent to multiple reducers, resulting in higher network costs.

The most important aspect of the comparison of PFP to PARMA is that the runtimes as data grows are clearly diverging due to the reasons discussed above. While 50 million transactions is very sizable, it is not hard to imagine real-world datasets with transactions on the order of billions. Indeed, many point-of-sale datasets would easily break this boundary. In these scenarios a randomized algorithm such as PARMA would show increasing performance advantages over exact algorithms such as any of the standard non-parallel algorithms or PFP, which must mine the entire dataset. At that scale, even transmitting that data over the network (several times in the case of PFP) would become prohibitive.

To understand the performance of PARMA it is important to analyze the runtimes at each of the various stages in the algorithm. To do this, we have implemented runtime timers at very fine granularities throughout our algorithm. The timers' values are written to Hadoop job logs for analysis. This breakdown allows us to not only analyze the overall runtime, but also the sections of the algorithm whose runtimes are affected by an increase in data size. In Figure 3, a breakdown of PARMA runtimes is shown for each of the six segments of the algorithm, which include a map, shuffle and reduce phase for each of the two stages. Due to space limitations, we only show the breakdown for a subset of the datasets we tested. We observed the same patterns for all datasets. This breakdown demonstrates several interesting aspects of PARMA. First, the cost of the mining local frequent itemsets (stage 1, reduce) is relatively constant. For many frequent itemset mining implementations, this cost will grow with the size of the input. This is not the case in PARMA, because local frequent itemset mining is being done on constant-sized sample of the input. Indeed another interesting observation, as expected, is that the only cost that increases as sample size increases is the cost of sampling (stage 1, map). This is because in order to be sampled the input data must be read, so larger input data means larger read times. In practice, this cost is minimal and grows linearly with the input, hence it will never be prohibitive,

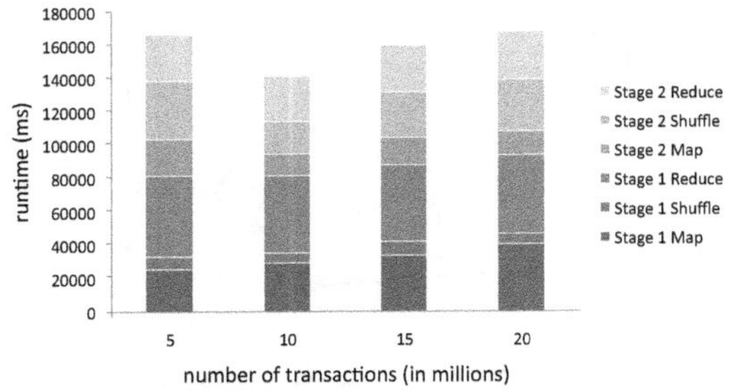

Figure 3: A comparison of runtimes of the map/reduce/shuffle phases of PARMA, as a function of number of transactions. Run on an 8 node Elastic MapReduce cluster.

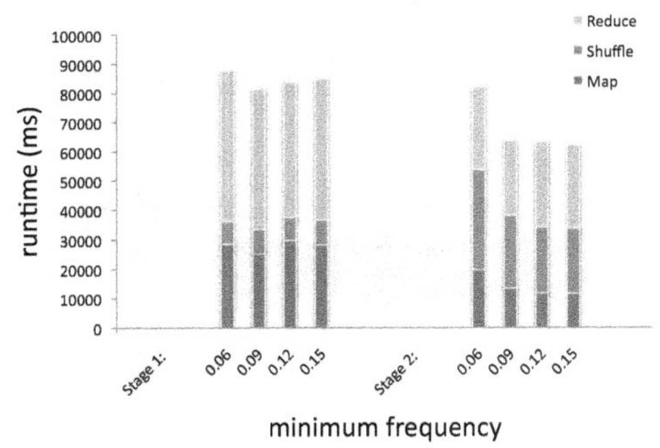

Figure 4: A comparison of runtimes of the map/reduce/shuffle phases of PARMA, as a function of minimum frequency. Clustered by stage. Run on an 8 node Elastic MapReduce cluster.

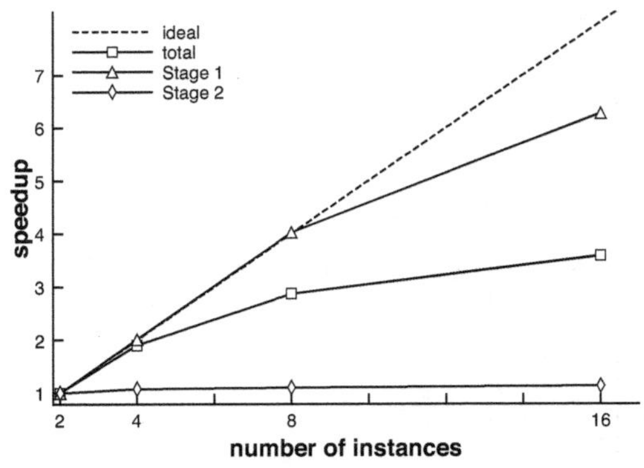

Figure 5: The speedup analysis of PARMA, broken down by stages.

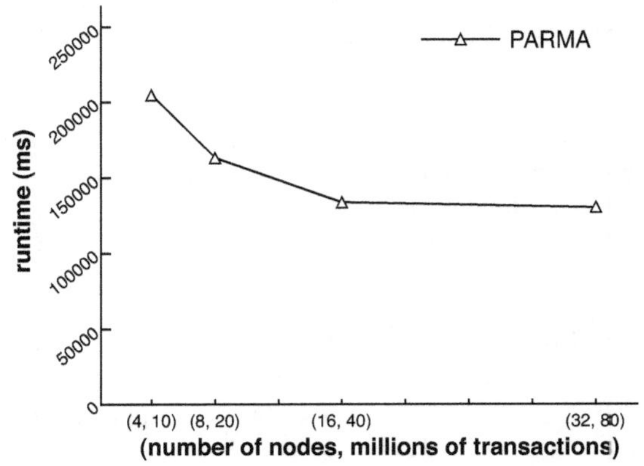

Figure 6: The scalability of PARMA as both data and cluster size are increased.

especially considering all other current algorithms must read the entire input data at least once, and in many cases multiple times.

There is one outlier in the graph, which is the dataset with 5 million transactions. Because each dataset was independently generated, it is possible for a dataset to have a larger number of frequent itemsets than other datasets, even if it has less transactions. This is the case with the 5 million transaction dataset, which takes longer to run mine for both PARMA and PFP due to the relatively greater number of frequent itemsets.

Figure 4 shows the breakdown of PARMA runtimes as the minimum frequency at which the data is mined at is changed. Data size was kept constant at 10 million transactions. Minimum frequency is used by the local frequent itemset mining algorithm to prune itemsets; itemsets below the minimum frequency are not considered frequent, nor is any superset since a superset must, by definition, contain the not frequent set and therefore cannot be frequent itself. Intuitively, a lower minimum frequency will mean more frequent itemsets are produced. Other than a runtime increase in the local frequent itemset mining phase (stage 1, reduce), the effects of this can be seen in the stage 2 shuffle phase as well, as there is more data to move across the network. Still, the added costs of mining with lower frequencies are relatively small.

6.2 Speedup and Scalability

To show the speedup of PARMA, we used a two-nodes cluster as the baseline. Because PARMA is intended to be a parallel algorithm, the choice of a two-nodes cluster was more appropriate than the standard single node baseline. For the dataset, we used a 10 million transaction database generated using the parameters in Table 2. The results are shown in Figure 5. The three lines on this graph represent the relative speedup of both stage 1 and stage 2 as well as the overall PARMA algorithm. The graph indicates that stage 1 is highly parallelizable and follows a near-ideal speedup for up to 8 nodes, after which a slight degradation of speedup occurs. There are two reasons for this slight degradation. In the map phase of stage 1, due to an implementation decision in Hadoop, the smallest unit of data that can be split is one HDFS block. As we continue to add more nodes to the cluster, we may have more available map slots than HDFS data blocks, resulting in some slots being unused. Theoretically, this could be fixed by allowing smaller granularity splitting in Hadoop. Another cause of the slightly sub-ideal speedup in stage 1 is from the reducer. Because the data in this experiment was held constant, the slight degradation in speedup as more than 8 nodes were added was a result of an inefficient oversplitting of transaction data. If each reducer in stage 1 is mining a very small subset of the transactions, the overhead of building the FP-tree begins to dominate the cost of mining the FP-tree. This is because the cost of mining the FP-tree is relatively fixed. Thus, we can "over-split" the data by forcing the reducer to build a large FP-tree only to mine a small set of transactions. For larger samples, the size of the cluster where speedup degradation begins to occur would also increase, meaning PARMA would continue to scale.

Also, as is clearly visible in the graph, the sub-ideal overall speedup is due largely to the poor speedup of stage 2. Stage 2 is bound almost entirely by the communication costs of transmitting the local frequent itemsets from stage 1 to the reducers that will do the aggregation. Because the amount of local frequent itemsets does not change as more nodes are added, the communication for this stage does not change. What does change is the number of itemsets each node must aggregate. During the reduce phase, each node is assigned a set of keys. All key/value pairs emitted from the map phase are sent to the reducer assigned their respective key. The reducer is in charge of aggregating the values and emitting one aggregate value per key assigned to it. As more reducers are added to the cluster, each reducer will have fewer keys assigned to it, and therefore must aggregate across fewer values, resulting in faster aggregation. The small but existent positive change in the line for stage 2 is a result of this slight speedup of the reduce phase.

Figure 6 depicts the scalability of PARMA as both the size of the dataset (i.e. number of transactions) and the number of nodes in the cluster are increased. The data and nodes are scaled proportionally so that the ratio of data to nodes remains constant across all experiments. This result shows that as nodes and data are increased proportionally, the total runtime actually begins to decrease for larger datasets. This is because as nodes are added to the cluster, the runtime of the Stage 1 reducer (FIM) is decreased while the relative costs of the Stage 1 mapper and Stage 2 remain the same. There is a leveling off of the runtime between the 40M and 80M datasets, which can be explained using Amdhal's law; because only portions of the algorithm are parallelizable, there is a theoretical maximum speedup that is possible. Still, the constant runtime as data is increased demonstrates PARMA's potential scalability to real-world cluster and dataset sizes.

6.3 Accuracy

The output of PARMA is a collection of frequent itemsets which approximates the collection one can obtain by mining the entire dataset. Although our analysis shows that PARMA offers solid guarantees in terms of accuracy of the output, we conducted an extensive evaluation to assess the actual performances of PARMA in practice, especially in relation to what can be analytically proved.

We compared the results obtained by PARMA with the exact collection of itemsets from the entire dataset, for different values of the parameters ε, δ, and θ, and for different datasets. A first important result is that in all the runs, the collection computed by PARMA was indeed a ε-approximation to the real one, i.e., all the properties from Definition 3 were satisfied. This fact suggests that the confidence in the result obtained by PARMA is actually greater than the level $1-\delta$ suggested by the analysis. This can be explained by considering that we had to use potentially loose theoretical bounds in the analysis to make it tractable.

Given that all real frequent itemsets were included in the output, we then focused on how many itemsets with real frequency in the interval $[\theta-\varepsilon,\theta)$ were included in the output. It is important to notice that these itemsets would be *acceptable* false positives, as Definition 3 does not forbid them to be present in the output. We stress again that the output of PARMA never contained *non-acceptable* false positives, i.e. itemsets with real frequency less than the minimum frequency threshold θ. The number of acceptable false positives included in the output of PARMA depends on the distribution of the real frequencies in the interval $[\theta-\varepsilon,\theta)$, so it should not be judged in absolute terms. In Table 3 we report, for various values of θ, the number of real frequent itemsets (i.e., with real frequency at least θ, the number of acceptable false positives (AFP) contained in the output of PARMA, and the number of itemsets with real frequency in the interval $[\theta-\varepsilon,\theta)$, i.e., the maximum number of acceptable false positives that may be contained in the output of PARMA (Max AFP). These numbers refers to a run of PARMA on (samples of) the 10M dataset, with $\varepsilon=0.05$ and $\delta=0.01$. It is evident that PARMA does a very good job in filtering out even acceptable false positives, especially at lower frequencies, when their number increases. This is thanks to the fact that an itemset is included in the output of PARMA if and only if it appears in the majority of the collections obtained in the first stage. Itemsets with real frequencies in $[\theta-\varepsilon,\theta)$ are not very likely to be contained in many of these collections.

θ	Real FI's	Output AFP's	Max AFP's
0.06	11016	11797	201636
0.09	2116	4216	10723
0.12	1367	335	1452
0.15	1053	299	415

Table 3: Acceptable False Positives in the output of PARMA

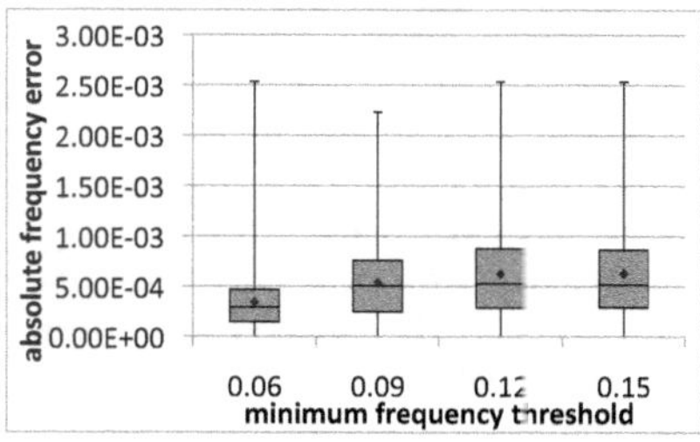

Figure 7: Error in frequency estimations as frequency varies.

We conducted an evaluation of the accuracy of two other components of the output of PARMA, namely the estimated frequencies for the itemsets in the output and the width of the confidence bounds for these estimations. In Figure 7 we show the distribution of the absolute error in the estimation, i.e. $|\tilde{f}(X)-f_{\mathcal{D}}(X)|$ for all itemsets X in the output of PARMA, as θ varies. The lower end of the "whisker" indicates the minimum error, the lower bound of the box corresponds to the first quartile, the segment across the box to the median, and the upper bound of the box to the third quartile. The top end of the whisker indicates the maximum error, and the central diamond shows the mean. This figure (and also Figure 8) shows the values for a run of PARMA on samples of the 10M dataset, with $\varepsilon=0.05$ and $\delta=0.01$. We can see that even the maximum values are one order of magnitude smaller than the threshold of 0.05 guaranteed by the analysis, and many of the errors are two or more orders of magnitude smaller. It is also possible to appreciate that the distribution of the error would be heavily concentrated in a small interval if the maximum error were not so high, effectively an outlier. The fact that the average and the median of the error, together with the entire "box" move down as the minimum frequency threshold decrease can be explained by the fact that at lower frequencies more itemsets are considered, and this makes the distribution less susceptible to outliers. Not only this is a sign of the high level of accuracy achieved by PARMA, but also of its being consistently accurate on a very large portion of the output.

Finally, in Figure 8 we show the distribution of the widths of the confidence intervals $\mathcal{K}(A)$ for the frequency estimations $\tilde{f}(A)$ of the itemsets A in the output of PARMA. Given that $\varepsilon=0.05$, the maximum allowed width was $2\varepsilon=0.1$. It is evident from the figures that PARMA returns much narrower intervals, of size almost ε. Moreover, the distribution of the width is very concentrated, as shown by the small height of the boxes, suggesting that PARMA is extremely consistent in giving very high quality confidence intervals for the estimations. We state again that in all runs of PARMA in our tests, all the confidence intervals contained the estimation

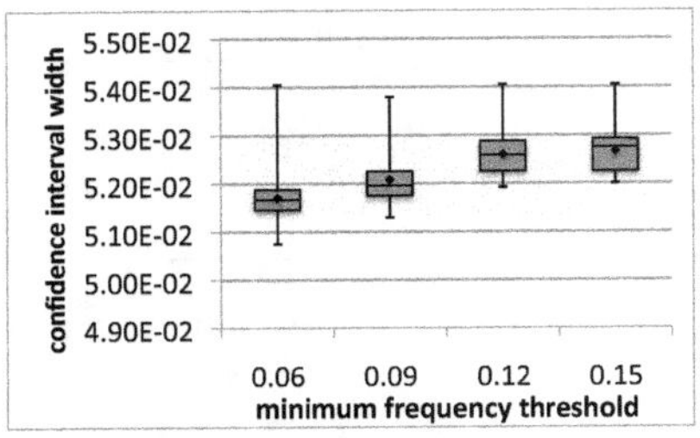

Figure 8: Width of the confidence intervals as frequency varies.

and the real frequency, as requested by Definition 3. As seen in the case of the estimation error, the distribution of the widths shifts down at lower thresholds θ. This is motivated by the higher number of itemsets in the output of PARMA at those frequencies. Their presence makes the distribution more robust to outliers. We can conclude that PARMA gives very narrow but extremely accurate confidence intervals across the entirety of its output.

This analysis of the accuracy of various aspects of PARMA's output shows that PARMA can be very useful in practice, and the confidence of the end user in the collections of itemsets and estimations given in its output can be even higher than what is guaranteed by the analysis.

7. CONCLUSIONS

In this paper, we have described PARMA, a parallel algorithm for mining quasi-optimal collections of frequent itemsets and association rules in MapReduce. We showed through theoretical analysis that PARMA offers provable guarantees on the quality of the output collections. Through experimentation on a wide range of datasets ranging in size from 5 million to 50 million transactions, we have demonstrated a 30-55% runtime improvement over PFP, the current state-of-the-art in exact parallel mining algorithms on MapReduce. Empirically we were able to verify the accuracy of the theoretical bounds, as well as show that in practice our results are orders of magnitude more accurate than is analytically guaranteed. Thus PARMA is an algorithm that can scale to arbitrary data sizes while simultaneously providing nearly perfect results.

8. ACKNOWLEDGMENTS

The work of Riondato, DeBrabant, and Upfal was supported in part by NSF award IIS-0905553.

9. REFERENCES

[1] R. Agrawal, T. Imieliński, and A. Swami. Mining association rules between sets of items in large databases. SIGMOD '93.

[2] R. Agrawal and R. Srikant. Fast algorithms for mining association rules in large databases. VLDB '94.

[3] Apache Mahout. `http://mahout.apache.org/`.

[4] G. Buehrer, S. Parthasarathy, S. Tatikonda, T. Kurc, and J. Saltz. Toward terabyte pattern mining: an architecture-conscious solution. PPoPP '07.

[5] F. Chierichetti, R. Kumar, and A. Tomkins. Max-cover in Map-Reduce. WWW '10.

[6] C.-T. Chu, S. K. Kim, Y.-A. Lin, Y. Yu, G. R. Bradski, A. Y. Ng, and K. Olukotun. Map-Reduce for machine learning on multicore. NIPS '06.

[7] F. Coenen. `http://www.cxc.liv.ac.uk/~frans/KDD/Software/FPgrowth/fpGrowth.html`

[8] S. Cong, J. Han, J. Hoeflinger, D. Padua. A sampling-based framework for parallel data mining. PPoPP '05.

[9] L. Cristofor. ARTool. `http://www.cs.umb.edu/~laur/ARtool/`, 2006.

[10] J.-D. Cryans, S. Ratté, and R. Champagne. Adaptation of APriori to MapReduce to build a warehouse of relations between named entities across the web. DBKDA '10.

[11] J. Dean and S. Ghemawat. MapReduce: Simplified data processing on large clusters. *CACM*, 51(1):107–113, 2008.

[12] M. El-Hajj and O. Zaiane. Parallel leap: large-scale maximal pattern mining in a distributed environment. ICPADS '06.

[13] W. Fang, K. K. Lau, M. Lu, X. Xiao, C. K. Lam, Y. Yang, B. He, Q. Luo, P. V. Sander, and K. Yang. Parallel data mining on graphics processors. Technical Report 07, The Hong Kong University of Science & Technology, 2008.

[14] A. Ghoting, P. Kambadur, E. Pednault, and R. Kannan. NIMBLE: a toolkit for the implementation of parallel data mining and machine learning algorithms on MapReduce. KDD '11.

[15] M. T. Goodrich, N. Sitchinava, and Q. Zhang. Sorting, searching, and simulation in the MapReduce framework. *CoRR*, abs/1101.1902, 2011.

[16] S. Hammoud. *MapReduce Network Enabled Algorithms for Classification Based on Association Rules*. PhD thesis, Brunel University, 2011.

[17] J. Han, J. Pei, and Y. Yin. Mining frequent patterns without candidate generation. *SIGMOD Rec.*, 29:1–12, May 2000.

[18] H. Li, Y. Wang, D. Zhang, M. Zhang, and E. Y. Chang. PFP: Parallel FP-Growth for query recommendation. RecSys '08.

[19] L. Li and M. Zhang. The strategy of mining association rule based on cloud computing. BCGIN '11.

[20] Y. Li and R. Gopalan. Effective sampling for mining association rules. AI '04.

[21] J. Lin and M. Schatz. Design patterns for efficient graph algorithms in MapReduce. MLG '10.

[22] L. Liu, E. Li, Y. Zhang, Z. Tang. Optimization of frequent itemset mining on multiple-core processor. VLDB '07.

[23] H. Mannila, H. Toivonen, and I. Verkamo. Efficient algorithms for discovering association rules. KDD '94.

[24] M. Mitzenmacher and E. Upfal. *Probability and computing*. Cambridge University Press, 2005.

[25] E. Ozkural, B. Ucar, and C. Aykanat. Parallel frequent item set mining with selective item replication. *IEEE Trans. on Paral. and Distrib. Sys.*, 22(10):1632–1640, 2011.

[26] S. Parthasarathy. Efficient progressive sampling for association rules. ICDM '02.

[27] A. Pietracaprina, G. Pucci, M. Riondato, F. Silvestri, and E. Upfal. Space-round tradeoffs for MapReduce computations. ICS' 12.

[28] A. Pietracaprina, M. Riondato, E. Upfal, and F. Vandin. Mining top-K frequent itemsets through progressive sampling. *Data Min. and Knowl. Disc*, 21:310–326, 2010.

[29] M. Riondato and E. Upfal. Efficient discovery of association rules and frequent itemsets through sampling with tight performance guarantees. *CoRR*, abs/1111.6937v3, 2012.

[30] J. Ruoming, Y. Ge, and G. Agrawal. Shared memory parallelization of data mining algorithms: techniques, programming interface, and performance. *IEEE Trans. on Knowl. and Data Engin.*, 17(1):71–89, 2005.

[31] N. V. Sahinidis and M. Tawarmalani. *BARON 9.0.4: Global Optimization of Mixed-Integer Nonlinear Programs,* User's Manual, 2010.

[32] H. Toivonen. Sampling large databases for association rules. VLDB '96.

[33] X. Y. Yang, Z. Liu, and Y. Fu. MapReduce as a programming model for association rules algorithm on Hadoop. ICIS '10.

[34] M. Zaki. Parallel and distributed association mining: a survey. *IEEE Concurrency*, 7(4):14 –25, 1999.

[35] M. Zaki, S. Parthasarathy, W. Li, and M. Ogihara. Evaluation of sampling for data mining of association rules. RIDE '97.

[36] L. Zhou, Z. Zhong, J. Chang, J. Li, J. Huang, and S. Feng. Balanced parallel FP-Growth with MapReduce. YC-ICT '10.

Interactive Pattern Mining on Hidden Data: A Sampling-based Solution *

Mansurul Bhuiyan, Snehasis Mukhopadhyay, and Mohammad Al Hasan
Dept. of Computer and Info. Science, Indiana University–Purdue University, Indianapolis, USA
mbhuiyan@iupui.edu, smukhopa@cs.iupui.edu, alhasan@cs.iupui.edu

ABSTRACT

Mining frequent patterns from a hidden dataset is an important task with various real-life applications. In this research, we propose a solution to this problem that is based on Markov Chain Monte Carlo (MCMC) sampling of frequent patterns. Instead of returning all the frequent patterns, the proposed paradigm returns a small set of randomly selected patterns so that the clandestinity of the dataset can be maintained. Our solution also allows interactive sampling, so that the sampled patterns can fulfill the user's requirement effectively. We show experimental results from several real life datasets to validate the capability and usefulness of our solution; in particular, we show examples that by using our proposed solution, an eCommerce marketplace can allow pattern mining on user session data without disclosing the data to the public; such a mining paradigm helps the sellers of the marketplace, which eventually boost the marketplace's own revenue.

Categories and Subject Descriptors

H [**Information Systems**]: Miscellaneous; I [**Computing Methodologies**]: Miscellaneous

Keywords

MCMC Sampling, Interactive Pattern Mining

1. INTRODUCTION

Frequent pattern mining plays a key role in exploratory data analysis. Over the last two decades, researchers invented various efficient algorithms for mining patterns of varying degrees of complexity–such as, sets [1, 16], sequences [30], trees [31] and graphs [21, 29]. All these algorithms assume that the entire dataset is available to the analyst before the mining task is commenced. This assumption holds if the data owner and the data analyst are the same entity; however, in real life, data may be owned by an enterprise and an analyst who mines the data in quest of interesting patterns may be an outsider who does not have full access on the data. The data owner, though interested in maintaining the confidentiality of the data, wants to help the analyst by providing her a curated set of frequent patterns that would benefit her the most. A real-life example is provided in the following paragraph.

User session data, which contains the collection of related query-set that a user executes in a session, is a valuable data source for an eCommerce marketplace; it helps the marketplace to build features such as query suggestion [18], query segmentation [24], and product recommendation [20]. To maintain the competitive advantage, the data manager of the marketplace keeps the user session data inaccessible. However, the marketplace also has incentives to make a summary of the user session data, say, a random sample of frequent itemsets of user queries available to its sellers so that the sellers are aware of the demand trends in the marketplace. Availability of frequent itemsets of user session queries also helps the sellers in choosing an informative title for their product to facilitate effective matching of seller's product with the buyer's query—eventually, boosting the marketplace's revenue. Since different sellers may be interested in different sets of queries, the key challenge for the marketplace in this task is to find a mechanism to assist a seller by providing frequent itemsets of queries that would benefit that specific seller the most—all without risking the leakage of significant part of the session data.

There exist quite a few works that perform data analytics over databases that are hidden behind a form-like query interface [11, 10, 12]. Similar to these works, we consider the task of mining frequent patterns from a hidden dataset; however, the similarity ends right there, as we adopt a different system setup, and a different methodology. In our setup, the owner of the hidden dataset allows a data analyst to obtain random samples of frequent patterns from the dataset. Thus, by returning a (small) random subset of frequent patterns, instead of returning all the frequent patterns, the data owner maintains the confidentiality of the data in the sense that using these samples the analyst can not reconstruct the entire dataset with high level of accuracy; Dinur et. al. [13] named such a dataset a private dataset. It is relevant to mention that though the exact reconstruction of a dataset from the list of frequent itemsets is $\mathcal{NP}$-complete, approximate reconstruction is possible when all the frequent itemsets and their supports are available [27].

Besides the above, the sampling mechanism in our mining

*This research is supported by an NSF CAREER Award (IIS-1149851)

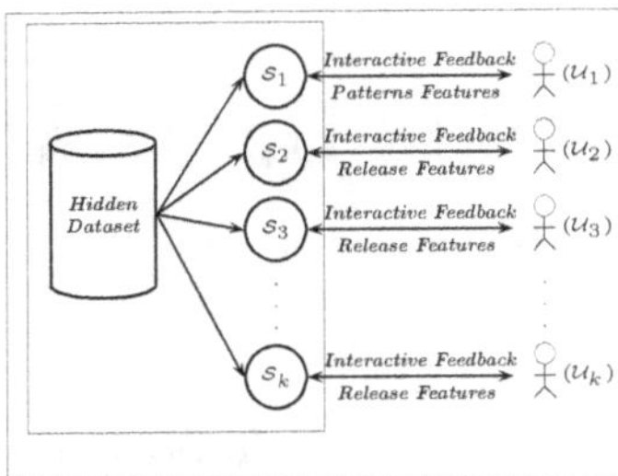

Figure 1: Sampling based Interactive Pattern Mining on a Hidden Dataset

system is interactive so that the analyst can obtain the most fruitful mining results. Given that the dataset is hidden, the analyst only has a vague idea about the dataset's content, so interactive mining is essential so that the sampling process can retrieve the patterns that best serve the analyst. Simply put, our system enables the analyst to provide feedbacks on the quality of the patterns that she receives; the sampling mechanism uses these feedbacks to bias the sampling towards the preferences of the analyst, so that the patterns obtained from subsequent samples are more useful to the analyst.

Even if the data is not hidden, the interactive sampling of frequent patterns is useful on its own merit. For example, in an interdisciplinary research, the domain data may not be hidden to the domain expert; however, she has little knowledge about the quality of the patterns that she obtains by mining those data. Effective discovery of useful patterns requires domain knowledge; on the other hand, effective incorporation of domain knowledge requires an interactive console. Existing pattern mining algorithms are not interactive; further, they generate an enormous list of frequent patterns, in which, a high degree of redundancy prevails. Such a tool is hardly helpful for a domain scientist. An interactive pattern mining approach that enables the domain scientist to sample a small set of relevant frequent patterns is a better alternative.

Figure 1 illustrates the framework that we devise to mine patterns from a hidden dataset. In this figure, we show a set of k analysts, $u_1, u_2, \ldots, u_k$, that are simultaneously accessing frequent patterns from a hidden dataset. For a specific user, u_i, a dedicated sampler, s_i is assigned to facilitate the interactive mining session. Based on u_i's feedback on the sampled patterns, s_i updates the sampling distribution so that the analyst u_i is served in the most fruitful way. It is easy to see that the overall framework is generic and is easily applicable for sampling itemsets, trees, sequences and graphs.

We summarize the contributions of this work as below:

• We propose an interactive pattern mining system that is based on sampling of frequent patterns. Instead of enumerating all the frequent patterns in the dataset, the above system uses a sampler for returning a small set of randomly selected frequent patterns to the analyst. Through an interactive console, it (the system) enables the analyst to provide feedbacks on the quality of the sampled patterns. Based on these feedbacks, the mining engine updates its sampling criteria so that in subsequent iterations it samples patterns that are of better quality.

• The above interactive pattern mining system enables mining of frequent patterns from hidden data. It is evident that the sampler only relies on user's feedback to drive the pattern selection process, so a user does not need access to the actual dataset on which the mining is being accomplished. Rather, the user exploits the interactive pattern mining system to obtain the desired patterns.

• Our sampling-based pattern mining paradigm also overcomes the *information overload* problem that is caused by the large number of frequent patterns in a traditional pattern mining task.

2. RELATED WORKS

We discuss the related works under three different categories.

2.1 Data Analytics over Hidden Databases

Data analytics over hidden databases is an active research direction; typically, these hidden databases are part of the deep Web that can be accessed only by a form-like query interface. Along this research direction, various tasks are considered, such as, crawl the hidden Web [25], obtain a random tuple from a hidden database [11, 12], retrieve top-k records by sampling [23], and estimate the size and other aggregates over a hidden database [10]. These works are related to our work in the sense that we consider frequent pattern mining, also over the hidden databases. However, we do not assume a form-like interface to access the database, rather we assume that the data owner provides a random sampler to interact with the database and the sampler is guided by the data analyst through interactive feedbacks.

2.2 Interactive Pattern Mining

Surprisingly, existing works on interactive pattern mining (IPM) are sparse [7, 5, 14]. One of the main techniques that the existing works follow is constraint-based mining, where a user can add additional constraints as an interactive input. The mining system considers these constraints to filter the output set to tailor it according to the user's requirements. Setting constraints is effective for some mining problems, but for many others, applying hard constraints may yield sub-optimal results. Also, designing constraints to guide mining is not easy, particularly while mining from a hidden dataset; an analyst first needs to explore some example patterns before she can think about the constraints that would work best for her specific applications. This can best be described as *"I don't know what I am looking for, but I would definitely know if I see it"*.

Few methods on interactive mining exist that are not constraint-guided—probably the most similar to our work is [28]. However, our method differs from it in various ways. First, the above method requires to have a complete set of frequent patterns up-front, whereas our method unifies the exploration and selection of the frequent patterns using MCMC based random walk—thus, for many datasets, our method may not explore all the frequent patterns. Second, our method uses binary feedback instead of rank order feedback that the above method adopts—the latter puts more burden on the user, and in case of a hidden dataset, users may have little information to rank the patterns properly.

In interactive patterns mining, a user decides whether a pattern is interesting or not. There also exist a few notable works [22, 3, 26], which mine a small set of interesting patterns by defining novel interestingness metrics for frequent patterns. The scope of these works is complementary to the work that we present in this paper.

2.3 Frequent Pattern Sampling

For mining frequent patterns from a hidden dataset, we use an MCMC based random walk on the frequent pattern space. In recent years, various other works also follow a similar approach—most notable among these are [4, 19, 17]. In [19], Hasan et. al. proposed a mining framework, that they called *output space sampling*, which can sample frequent patterns using a user-defined distribution. The sampling framework that we devise in this work is similar to the work in [19]; however in [19], the sampling distribution remains static throughout the mining session, whereas in our work, the sampling distribution keeps changing in response to the user's feedback. Also, in [19], the random walk is performed over the edge of the Partial Order Graph (POG) (defined formally in Section 4); our work deviates from this by performing random walk over a state-transition graph in which a random graph is overlaid on top of the POG graph—the above modification improves the convergence of an MCMC walk significantly.

3. PROBLEM STATEMENT

In this section, we formally define the problem of interactive pattern mining from hidden data. Given a hidden dataset [1] $\mathcal{D}$, and a user u, an interactive pattern mining system (IPM) returns a sequence of randomly selected frequent patterns $p_1, p_2, \ldots p_t$ from $\mathcal{D}$ to u; optionally u can send feedbacks $f_1, f_2, \ldots f_t$ to the IPM regarding the quality of the patterns; in response to the feedback, IPM iteratively updates its sampling distribution so that the randomly selected patterns that it returns to u in subsequent iterations align better with u's interest. In the following paragraphs, we will detail the followings: (1) how does the IPM system find a pattern? (2) how does the user u form a feedback on a pattern?, and (3) how does the feedback from u is incorporated in the mining process to obtain a better pattern in subsequent iterations?

Given that user u has no access to the dataset, and the data owner has no intention to share all the frequent patterns, traditional frequent pattern mining algorithms are of no use in this scenario. We also assume that the dataset is large; therefore the complete enumeration of all the frequent patterns may be infeasible. So, the IPM adopts the output space sampling (OSS)-like [19] paradigm to obtain a frequent pattern and share it with the user u. However, OSS does not provide an option for interactive pattern mining, it merely allows the user to mine from a user-defined sampling distribution. So, to accommodate an interactive mining setup, IPM adapts the sampling distribution using u's feedback, so that it respects u's interest progressively. If we assume that u has an underlying *interestingness function*, γ, that maps each frequent pattern to a non-negative real value (higher value stands for more interesting), the adaptation of sampling distribution by using the feedback translates to the inverse problem of learning the γ function.

An important question that is yet to be answered is what is the composition of u's feedback on a pattern. In this work, we consider a simple feedback mode, where the response of the user u on a pattern p is purely binary: *interesting* and *non-interesting*. One can always consider a more complex feedback mechanism, may be in the form of a profile vector,

[1] the words *dataset*, and *database* are used synonymously this this document

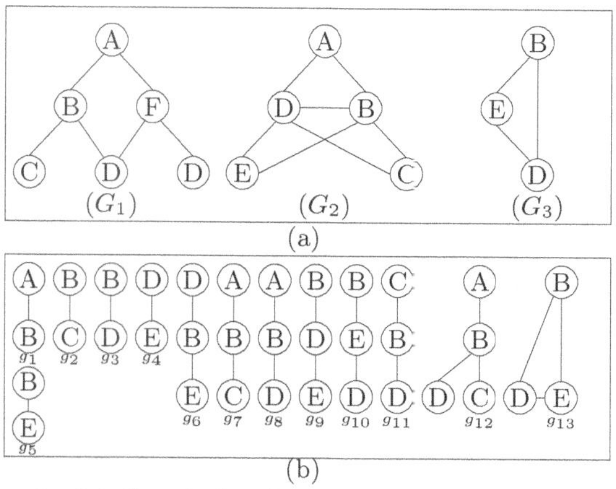

Figure 2: (a) Graph database with 3 graphs (b) Frequent subgraph of (a) with *minsup* = 2

in which the user u represents the pattern p as a composition of a set of sub-patterns and uses a probabilistic vector to define her interest in each of these parts; however, we do not explore this option in this work. Now, under the scope of a binary response, the set of frequent patterns can be divided into two groups: useful and non-useful, and it is left to the IPM to deduce the underlying discriminating function by which the user u is building her opinion.

We like to clarify that our problem formulation is generic and it considers the task of mining all kinds of patterns, such as, sets, sequences, trees or graphs. In most of our discussion in this paper, we will refer to the term "pattern" and will dictate the discussion considering a graph pattern, but with minor or almost no adjustment the discussion will fit for different kinds of patterns. In the experiment section, we will show results involving both itemset and graph patterns.

4. BACKGROUND

In this section, we define several key concepts that will be useful to understand our research work.

4.1 Frequent pattern Mining

Let, $\mathcal{G} = \{G_1, G_2, \ldots, G_n\}$ be a graph database, where each $G_i \in \mathcal{G}, \forall i = \{1 \ldots n\}$ represents a labeled, undirected and connected graph. $\mathbf{t}(g) = \{G_i : g \subseteq G_i \in \mathcal{G}\}, \forall i = \{1 \ldots n\}$, is the *support-set* of the graph g. This set contains all the graphs in $\mathcal{G}$ that has a subgraph isomorphic to g. The cardinality of the *support-set* is called the *support* of g. g is called frequent if $support \geq \pi^{\min}$, where $\pi^{\min}$ is predefined/user-specified *minimum support (minsup)* threshold. The set of frequent patterns are represented by $\mathcal{F}$. **example:** Figure 2(a) shows a database with 3 graphs (G_1, G_2 and G_3). With $\pi^{\min} = 2$, there are thirteen frequent subgraphs as shown in Figure 2(b).

4.2 Frequent Graph Partial Order

Based on the sub-graph relationship, the set of all frequent sub-graphs ($\mathcal{F}$) forms a partial order called *Subgraph partial order*. The lowest pattern in this partial order is the null ($\emptyset$) pattern. The partial order can be represented as a graph, called *partial order graph (POG)*. Every node in the POG corresponds to a distinct frequent graph pattern, i.e., each graph in POG is the canonical representative (with the minimal DFS code [29]) for all other graphs that are isomorphic to it. Every edge in POG represents a possible extension of a

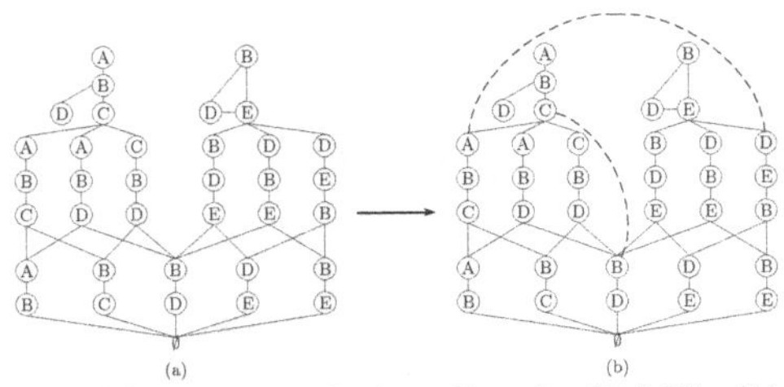

Figure 3: (a) Partial Order Graph (POG) (b) State-transition Graph

frequent pattern to a larger (by one edge) frequent pattern. Algorithms for enumerating all frequent subgraphs typically traverse the POG in either depth-first or breadth-first manner, starting from the lowest pattern. Figure 3(a) shows the frequent subgraph partial order for the graph mining task shown in Figure 2. It is easy to see that for the case of mining other patterns, such as, sets, sequences and trees, a similar POG can be built, using the subset, subsequence or subtree relationship, respectively.

4.3 Markov chains, Random walk, Metropolis-Hastings (MH) Algorithm

A **Markov chain** is the sequence of Markov process over the state space S. The state-transition event is guided by a matrix, T, called *transition probability matrix*. A Markov chain is said to reach a stationary distribution π, when the probability of being in any particular state is independent of the initial condition. Markov chain is reversible if it satisfies the *reversibility condition* $\pi(i)T(i,j) = \pi(j)T(j,i), \forall i,j \in S$. A Markov chain is *ergodic* if it has a stationary distribution. If the state space (S) of a Markov chain is the vertices of a POG and the state transition happens only between adjacent nodes in POG, then this Markov process simulates a random walk on the frequent pattern space ($\mathcal{F}$).

The main goal of the Metropolis-Hastings algorithm is to draw samples from some distribution $\pi(x)$, called the *target distribution*, where, $\pi(x) = f(x)/K$; here K is a normalizing constant which may not be known and difficult to compute. MH algorithm can be used together with a random walk to perform Markov Chain Monte Carlo (MCMC) sampling. For this, the MH algorithm draws a sequence of samples from the target distribution as follows:
i. It picks an initial state (say, x) satisfying $f(x) > 0$.
ii. From current state x, it samples a point y using a distribution $q(x,y)$, referred as *proposal distribution*.
iii. Then, it calculates the *acceptance probability*,

$$\alpha(x,y) = \min\left(\frac{\pi(y)q(y,x)}{\pi(x)q(x,y)}, 1\right) = \min\left(\frac{f(y)q(y,x)}{f(x)q(x,y)}, 1\right) \tag{1}$$

and accepts the proposal move to y with probability $\alpha(x,y)$. The process continues until the Markov chain reaches to a stationary distribution.

As shown in [19], a Metropolis-Hastings (MH) based MCMC algorithm can be used for sampling frequent pattern with a desired sampling distribution. In such a method, the set of frequent patterns ($\mathcal{F}$) is the state space of the random walk and the edges of POG define the possible state transitions. Importantly, the POG are generated locally as needed; for instance, when the random walk resides on a pattern x, the local neighborhood of the pattern x, which consists of all frequent super patterns (whose sizes are larger by one than the size of x) and all frequent sub-patterns (whose sizes are smaller by one than the size of x), is constructed. The random walk then jumps to one of its neighbors using the acceptance probability (Equation 1) of MH algorithm. MH requires to choose a proposal distribution (q), which can simply be the uniform distribution i.e., each of the neighbors of the pattern x in POG is equally likely to be chosen. If y is a neighbor of the pattern x, d_x and d_y are the degrees of the pattern x and y in POG, and γ is the target distribution, following the equation 1, the acceptance probability for choosing the proposal move is as below:

$$\alpha(x,y) = \mathbf{min}\left(\frac{\gamma(y)\cdot(1/d_y)}{\gamma(x)\cdot(1/d_x)}, 1\right) = \mathbf{min}\left(\frac{\gamma(y)d_x}{\gamma(x)d_y}, 1\right) \tag{2}$$

The following Lemma holds:

LEMMA 1. *The random walk on POG converges to a stationary distribution which is equal to the desired target distribution, γ.*
PROOF: *See [19]* ■

5. INTERACTIVE SAMPLING ALGORITHM

We also use MH as the underlying sampling algorithm to mine patterns from the hidden database, $\mathcal{D}$. Each sampler s_i in Figure 1 (b) runs an instance of MH sampling with the objective that MH's target sampling distribution (γ in Equation 2) matches with the desired sampling distribution of the user u_i. Achieving the above objective is challenging because the sampler has no knowledge of the desired sampling distribution. To overcome this difficulty, we sample patterns using MH with a default sampling distribution, and update the default distribution using each of the user feedbacks so that the effective distribution converges towards γ with the updates.

5.1 User's Scoring function

We represent the user's desired distribution as a scoring function, $f : \mathcal{F} \to \mathbb{R}_+ \cup 0$; f maps each pattern in $\mathcal{F}$ (frequent pattern-set) to a non-negative real number. From this scoring function, we can obtain user's desired distribution by $\frac{f(P)}{\sum_{q\in\mathcal{F}} f(q)}$, i.e., the probability of a pattern in the desired distribution is directly proportional to the $f(\cdot)$ (f-score) of that pattern [2].

For the sake of learning, we must impose bias on γ and assume that γ is taken from some family of functions [3]. For this, we use the similarity between interactive pattern mining (IPM) and the task of Query by Example in information retrieval (QEIR) [8]—*given a set of documents that a user has liked, retrieve other documents that he is likely to like*; for IPM, the set of patterns for which the user provides a positive feedback plays a role that is similar to the role of the given documents in a QEIR task. Typically, QEIR uses the vector space model of words and phrases to construct user's preference profile. Similarly, to model γ we also adopt a vector space model of unit-size patterns. For example, unit-size patterns for a graph are its edges; for an itemset, they are the items. In this vector space model, each unit-size pattern has a weight, expressed as b^i where $b \in (1, +\infty)$ and $|i| \in 0, 1, \ldots, |\mathcal{F}|$. The γ-score of a pattern is simply the

[2]In this paper, we will use the phrases *scoring function* and the corresponding *sampling distribution* synonymously.
[3]this argument is known as *No Free Lunch Theorem* in the machine learning domain

multiplication of these weights [4]. If P is a pattern of size k and P_j are the unit-size patterns that compose the pattern P, we have:

$$\gamma(P) = \prod_{j=1}^{k} \mathbf{w}[P_j], \ \forall P_j \in P \text{ and } |P| = k \qquad (3)$$

Note that, if two patterns x and y are structurally similar, they will have high overlap between their constituting unit-size patterns; hence, under the above assumption, they will have similar γ-score.

To assign a weight on each unit-size patterns, we assume that the set of frequent patterns are partitioned into two sets: *interesting* ($\mathcal{I}$) and *non-interesting* ($\mathcal{N}$); so, $\mathcal{F} = \mathcal{I} \cup \mathcal{N}$. Also, assume that $\mathcal{F}_1$ is the set of all unit-size frequent patterns. Now, consider a weight vector $\mathbf{w}$ of size $|\mathcal{F}_1|$; each entry $\mathbf{w}[\cdot]$, in this vector corresponds to one of the unit-size frequent patterns; for a unit-size pattern p, $\mathbf{w}[p]$ is equal to b^{u-v}, where $(u, v) \in [0, 1, \ldots, |\mathcal{F}|]$ are the number of interesting and non-interesting patterns (according to a user) in which p is embedded. In this way, if a unit-size pattern is part of x interesting (from the set $\mathcal{I}$) and y non-interesting (from the set $\mathcal{N}$) patterns, its weight will be b^{x-y}.

Example: In Figure 2 (b), if $\mathcal{I} = \{g_1, g_2, g_7, g_{12}\}$. Suppose $b = 2$, then, $\mathbf{w}[A\text{-}B] = 2^{3-1}$ as the unit-size pattern A-B is part of three (g_1, g_7, g_{12}) interesting and one (g_8) non-interesting patterns. On the other hand, $\mathbf{w}[B\text{-}D] = 2^{1-6}$, as this edge appears in 1 interesting and 6 non-interesting patterns. Also, $\gamma(g_7) = 2^4$, which we obtain by multiplying the weights of each of its edges (unit-size patterns). ■

5.2 User interaction Design

For interactive pattern mining, we assume that the γ belongs to the family of the functions described in Section 5.1. Since, γ is unknown to the sampler, the sampler (s_i) uses a proxy distribution (say β) as the effective target distribution, which the sampler updates with each of the feedbacks. If $\beta^0, \beta^1, \ldots, \beta^k$ are sequences of β's along with the updates, then hypothetically, $\mathbf{Lim}_{k\to\infty}\beta^k = \gamma$. Since, β requires to converge to γ, we ensures that each of the β^k distribution also belongs to the same family of distribution as of γ. Thus, the $\beta(\cdot)$ (β-score) of a pattern is computed as the multiplication of the weight of its constituting unit-size patterns, identically as it is computed for the γ-score (see Equation 3).

At initialization, all unit-size patterns have a weight of 1, and sampling using such a β (let's name it β^0) as the target distribution yields a random initial distribution. The sampler starts sampling from the initial distribution by using the MCMC based random walk; suppose, at some step of the walk, it (the sampler) picks a pattern P of length k for user's feedback. If the pattern P has already been used for feedback, the pattern is discarded and the process continues until another pattern is found for which the feedback has not been sought yet. Then, for the selected pattern, the user provides her feedback by indicating whether she likes the pattern P or not. If the feedback is positive, the sampler increases the weight of each of k length-one sub-patterns of P exponentially, i.e. it multiplies the current weight of those length-one sub-patterns by b. On the other hand, if the feedback is negative, the sampler decrease the weight of those length-one sub-patterns by dividing the current weight by b. This weight modification updates the existing sampling distribution β. The sampling step and the interaction step are repeated intermittently as the β function iteratively moves closer to the user's desired distribution γ. The above weight update also ensures that in all β^k, there exists a positive probability to visit any frequent pattern from any other frequent pattern; which maintains the ergodicity of the random walk.

[4] An additive γ function may also be considered, but we notice that such a function has slow convergence compared to multiplicative functions.

LEMMA 2. ***Lim***$_{t\to\infty}\beta^t = \gamma$.

PROOF: β^t is the updated sampling distribution after t iterations; in each of these iterations, exactly one pattern is sent for user's feedback; hence, total patterns for which feedback is sought is t.

Now, consider, any unit-size pattern p, and assume that it appears in $r(\leq t)$ patterns out of those t patterns. Now, let's partition the r patterns into two set, based on their feedback status, interesting or non-interesting. If the size of these sets are r_i and r_n, respectively, according to the weight update mechanism, in β^t the weight of the pattern p, $\mathbf{w}[p]$, is equal to $b^{r_i - r_n}$.

Now, in all sampling distribution, $\beta^k : 0 \leq k \leq \infty$, every interesting/non-interesting pattern in $\mathcal{I}$ and $\mathcal{N}$ has a non-zero probability to be visited; hence, as t goes to infinity, all the patterns in the set $\mathcal{I}$ and $\mathcal{N}$ will be sent to the user (at least once) for feedback; Also, for each pattern, we consider it's feedback exactly once. So, the weight of p in the limiting distribution β^∞ is exactly equal to b^{x-y}, where x and y are the count of interesting and non-interesting patterns of which p is part-of, which is identical to $\mathbf{w}[p]$ of γ. Hence, $\beta^\infty = \gamma$ ■.

Lemma 2 proves that the user interaction that we design works perfectly when the γ function is constructed as was shown in Equation 3. While this is a reasonable assumption about γ, in real life, an interestingness function can be different. Nevertheless, any interestingness function that a user uses should have some structure; alternatively, it should be non-random, where structural similarity between a pair of patterns should have strong influence on the possible γ-scores of these patterns. As a result, the above proxy distribution β should work reasonably well.

5.3 State-transition graph and convergence of MH-based Random Walk

In [19], the authors use partial order graph (POG) as the state-transition graph for sampling frequent patterns. However, by construction, POG is a multi-stage graph—the patterns that have the same size belong to the same stage, and a pattern in stage i have neighbors only from stage $i+1$ and stage $i-1$. Such a graph has a large diameter (at least, as large as the size of the largest frequent pattern), which causes slow mixing for any random walk on it (the graph). The slower the mixing, the worse the sampling quality. In particular, for our task, fast mixing is crucial—we update the effective distribution (β^t) frequently, so we desire that the random walk to mix well before the effective distribution β^t is updated. The mixing time of a random walk is characterized by the number of steps the walk takes to reach its stationary distribution. For a known target distribution, the mixing time can be estimated by computing the spectral gap [9] of the transition probability matrix P. In short, the higher the spectral gap, the faster the convergence.

To achieve fast mixing, we overlay a random graph on POG, by introducing random edges in the partial POG in a periodic manner with the exploration of a batch of new nodes of the POG. In Figure 3, we show two such random edges (shown as dotted line in the right figure), between patterns (*A-B-C*, *D-E-F*) and (*A-B-C-D*, *B-D*). Addition of these two edges reduces the diameter of the POG in Figure 3 by 40% (from 5 to 3). The reason for overlaying a random graph is due to the well known fact that a random graph exhibits rapidly mixing property—for instance, the mixing time of an MCMC random walk on a connected Erdos-Renyi random graph is $\Theta(\log^2 n)$ [2]. In all our experimental datasets, introducing random edges increases the spectral gap almost by 100%. Table 1 shows the improvement in the spectral gap for Mushroom, Chess and Connect datasets after setting the *randomedge_factor* (explain in Section 5.4) to 20%.

Dataset	spectral gap (μ)	
	POG + Random edge	POG
Mushroom	0.045	0.020
Chess	0.082	0.040
Connect	0.085	0.047

Table 1: Effect of random edges in POG on Spectral gap

Importantly, the addition of random edges maintains the ergodicity of the MCMC walk. This is due to the fact that the random edges are symmetric (allow transition along both the directions of the edge), and addition of these edges maintains the reversibility condition.

```
Interactive_Sampling
(D, minsup, miniter, feedback_count, b):
1. P = generate_any_frequent_pattern(D, minsup)
2. d_P = compute_degree(P)
3. π(P) = compute_β-value(P)
4. while (true)
5.    choose a neighbor, Q, uniformly from, all possible
      frequent super and sub patterns
6.    d_Q = compute_degree(Q)
7.    π(Q) = compute_β-value(Q)
8.    acceptance_probability = min ( π(Q)d_P / π(P)d_Q , 1)
9.    if uniform(0, 1) ≤ acceptance_probability
10.      P = Q
11.      iter = iter + 1
12.   if( #ofNodeInCurrentPOG / #ofNodeInOldPOG >= 3)
13.      insert_random_edge()
14.   if iter % miniter == 0 feedback_count >=0
15.      get_and_process_feedback(P, b)
16.   else
17.      goto line 5

compute_degree(D, P, minsup):
1. super_pat = all_frequent_super_pattern(P)
2. sub_pat = all_sub_pattern(P)
3. neighbor_list = super_pat ∪ sub_pat
4. save the neighbor list in POG data structure
5. return size(neighbor_list)

compute_β-value(P):
1. for each single length p in pattern P
2.    value = value * w[p]
3. return value

get_and_process_feedback(P, b):
1. if feedback is positive
2.    for each single length p in pattern P
3.       w[p] = w[p] * b
4. else
5.    for each single length p in pattern P
6.       w[p] = w[p] * 1/b
7. feedback_count = feedback_count − 1
```

Figure 4: Interactive Sampling Algorithm

5.4 Algorithm

For an incoming user, the IPM creates a new sampler instance which executes the subroutine *Interactive_Sampling* shown in this Figure 4. Besides the database, $\mathcal{D}$, the method also takes four more parameters: (1) a minimum support ($0 \leq \pi^{\min} \leq 1$) value, which defines whether a pattern is frequent or not; (2) a minimum number of walks (*miniter*) before the sampler returns a pattern to the user for feedback; (3) Total number of feedback (*feedback_count*) and (4) a value for the base (b) which is used to update weight of unit size pattern.

In Line 1 of Figure 4, the sampler starts with any arbitrary frequent pattern P; a unit-length frequent pattern suffices. Then, it computes all frequent super and sub-patterns of P (Line 2). The degree of P is the size of the union set of super and sub-patterns. Then it chooses a pattern (Q) from P's neighbors (Line 5) uniformly and computes the acceptance probability in Line 8. If the move is accepted, Q becomes the resident state; otherwise, the sampler chooses another neighbor identically and repeat the whole process. If the user abort the sampling, the infinite while loop breaks.

During the MCMC walk, if the condition in Line 12, i.e., the ratio of the number of nodes in the current POG and the same in the previously marked POG is greater than 3, the sampler inserts a set of random edges to the current POG. We use a variable called *randomedge_factor* to control the number of inserted random edges. The value of *randomedge_factor* is not that important as long as a small fraction of edges in the state-transition graph are from the random graph; for all our experiment, we keep this fraction equal to 0.20.

The condition on Line 14 checks whether the sampler should send the resident pattern (P) to the user for feedback. If condition succeeds, depending on the feedback's status, the sampler updates the weight of each of the unit-size sub-patterns of P, which forces a change in the target distribution (β).

The above pseudo-code is generic and can easily be adapted for sampling any kind of patterns, e.g. itemsets, trees, sequences or graphs.

Example: Assume a random walk on the POG in Figure 3(b). At some stage of this walk, the resident state of the random walk is the pattern $g7$ (see Figure 2). It has 4 neighbors ($d_{g7} = 4$), one super-pattern ($g12$), two sub-patterns ($g1$ and $g2$), and a random edge. Assume that the existing weights (chosen arbitrarily) of the unit-size patterns $g1, g2, g3, g4$, and $g5$ are $\langle 2, 1, 2, 1, 1\rangle$ in that order. So, the weight of the pattern $g7$ is 2. If the proposal distribution chooses the pattern $g12$, to compute acceptance probability, we first compute the followings: β-score($g12$) = 4, $d_{g12} = 4$; now the acceptance probability of the proposal move using equation 2 is: $\mathbf{min}\left(\frac{4*(1/4)}{2*(1/4)}, 1\right) = 1$. So, this move will always be accepted. If we send $g12$ to the user and the user likes it, the weight of pattern $g1, g2$, and $g3$ will be incremented by the multiple of b and the new weight vector for the unit-size patterns will be $\langle 2*b, b, 2*b, 1, 1\rangle$. ■

Choosing ***miniter*:** In our interactive pattern mining, the effective sampling distribution is β^t, which changes once a feedback on a pattern is received. So before returning a subsequent sample, the sampler needs to perform a few walk on the frequent pattern space—the parameter, *miniter*, decides the number of walks. Now, exactly how many walks the sampler should perform depends on how fast the random walk mixes, which we can compute from the spectral gap. However, this computation requires the knowledge of P, which the user is unaware of. On the other hand, the sampler can't pre-compute P as it requires the effective target distribution β^t, which is always changing based on user's feedback. Also it may be overkill to compute P for every possible β^t, so the best is to leave this as a parameter to the user who can choose a suitable value based on the feedback interval that suits best for her. In all of our experiments, we fix this interval to be 25, i.e., the sampler returns a pattern to the user after it makes 25 walks.

Choosing base (b): The base (b) has a large significance in regard to learning the user's desired distribution, γ. A large value of b sharply increases (or decreases) the weight of a unit-length pattern in response to a positive (or negative) feedback. If we consider the learning of γ as a multi-arm bandit problem, each unit-length pattern can be considered as an arm, and we are trying to find a weight for each arm, so that using this weight in equation 3, we can approximate the user's desired distribution, γ. Under this assumption, the parameter b is simply the exploration-exploitation trade-off parameter. Choosing high value of b imposes higher weights on unit-length patterns that are part of some of the interesting patterns that have already been explored; as a result, the sampler is biased to choose patterns that are composed of these items. However, this bias restricts the sampler to explore other yet-to-be-explored patterns that may be interesting, but are not composed of unit-length patterns that have already been explored. For this reason, a higher value for b increases the sampler's precision since sampler will traverse patterns that are composed of (already known) interesting unit-length patterns; however, this yields poor recall as many other interesting patterns may remain unexplored. It is hard to choose a good operation point on the precision-recall curve, because in a hidden dataset the user has no idea about the number of interesting patterns that exist in the hidden dataset—a value that is needed to compute the recall. We found that b in the range of $(1, 2]$ works well for most of the datasets. We use b=1.75 for all our experiments.

5.5 Implementation Details

The algorithm that we show in Figure 4 is generic, and is not tied to any specific kind of patterns. Underlying the sampling process, the method shown in this algorithm also solves the frequent pattern discovery problem, as the sampler only visits frequent patterns. The task of frequent pattern discovery is embedded in the **compute_degree** method that finds *frequent* super-patterns and sub-patterns of a resident pattern. In our work, the implementation of this part is identical to the Hasan et.al's work on output space sampling—for details, the reader can check the Section 6 of [19].

5.6 Mining Patterns from Hidden Datasets

To mine a pattern from a hidden dataset, a user interface is used through which the user provides her feedback. At the initiation of an interactive mining session with a user u_i, the interactive system creates a new sampler process (say, s_i) that runs in the host machine (that stores the dataset) for managing dedicated communication between u_i and s_i (see Figure 1(b)). The sampler executes the interactive mining algorithm that is shown in Figure 4; the parameters of this algorithm, such as *minsup* and *miniter* can be obtained from the user. Through the user interface, the sampler sends a pattern to the user, gathers her feedback and updates the sampling distribution, by executing the method in Line 15 of Figure 4. The infinite loop terminates once the connection is closed by the user. The above setup enables interactive pattern mining by considering a semi-honest model [15], where each party obeys the protocol.

Dataset	# of trans-actions	Avg. transac-tion size	$\tau^{\mathbf{min}}$	$\|\mathcal{F}\|$	$\|\mathcal{F}_1\|$
Chess	3196	37	2100	99262	29
Mushroom	8124	22	1200	53628	45
Connect	67557	43	58000	109664	24
eBay Query	10000	27	30	41130	3368
Mutagenicity-I	4336	17	195	3446	11
Mutagenicity-II	687	14	20	2935	13

Table 2: Dataset Statistics

6. EXPERIMENTS & RESULTS

We conduct several experiments to manifest the main purpose of interactive pattern sampling, which is to mine a set of interesting patterns by utilizing the binary feedback from the user. Our experiments show results both from graph and itemset mining.

6.1 Experiment setup

For our experiment, we require to define an interestingness function (γ) by which the user makes an opinion about a pattern. We mark $m\%$ randomly selected unit-size patterns among all the frequent (for a given *minsup*) unit-size patterns as interesting according to a user. With these $m\%$ patterns we build a set called I_p. We assume that the user is interested in patterns where the majority of the single length sub-patterns are from the set I_p; thus, the scoring function, γ for a pattern P is defined as, $\gamma(P) = \frac{\sum_{i=1}^{k} I(p_i)}{k} * 100$

Here, $p_1, p_2, \ldots, p_k$ are the unit-length sub-patterns of P, and I is an indicator random variable that defines whether a pattern p_i is from the set I_p or not. The γ-score of a pattern varies between 0 and 100, and the patterns that have γ-score more than 50 are interesting to the user, for which user provides a positive feedback; for the remaining patterns user provides a negative feedback. We set $m = 30\%$ in all of our experiments, unless specified otherwise.

6.2 Dataset

We show experimental results on six real-life datasets shown in Table 2. The first four among them are itemset datasets and the remaining two are graph datasets. We obtain Mushroom, chess and connect dataset from the UCI Machine Learning repository [5]. *eBay Query* is the remaining itemset dataset that we generate by scrapping queries from the *"Related Searches"* [6] feature of eBay. We build a query-graph where related queries are neighbors and populate the row of an itemset dataset by performing short random walks on this graph; in this way, the list of the queries that such a walk visits makes a transaction in the eBay Query dataset. Since related search suggestion is built by using user session

[5] `http://archive.ics.uci.edu/ml/`

[6] When a user search for an item in `www.ebay.com` with a query phrase, the search result page shows (at most) 10 keywords related to the original query.

data [18], this dataset is a metaphorical user session data, where a transaction can be regarded as the set of queries that a user executes in a user session. The remaining two datasets, Mutagenicity-I and Mutagenicity-II are chemical (graph) datasets that we obtained from the authors of [6].

Table 2 also shows some statistics of the datasets. The second and third column shows the number and average size of each transaction, the fifth column shows the number of frequent patterns, considering the minimum support value listed on the fourth column. The sixth column shows the total number of distinct unit-size frequent patterns.

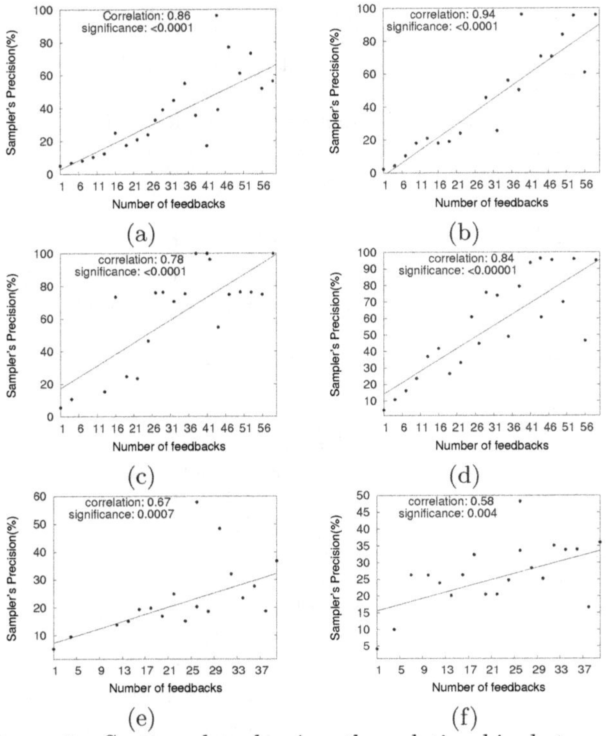

Figure 5: Scatter-plot showing the relationship between the sampler's precision and the number of feedbacks in (a) Mushroom (b) chess (c) eBay (d) connect (d) Muatgenicity-I and (f) Mutagenicity-II. A least-square fitted straight line with positive slope shows that for all the datasets the pair of variables are positively correlated

6.3 Analysis of sampler's performance

The objective of these set of experiments is to show the dependency of sampler's convergence with various parameters of the interactive sampling. We first show that with an increasing number of feedbacks, the sampler converges to a distribution, where the interesting patterns are more likely to be sampled. For this, we run the sampler for a large number of iterations and compute the percentage of iterations in which the sampler visits an interesting pattern; we call this percentage *samplers precision* (SP). We compute SP from many independent runs, each using a different value for the *feedback_count*. Then we find the correlation between the number of feedbacks and SP. Since the process is randomized, SP value for each *feedback_count* is also computed by averaging over 10 runs.

We show our results in Figure 5. As we can see, the number of feedback and the samplers precision are highly correlated—SP increases along with the feedback count. Also note that,the strength of correlation varies across various

base(b)	Avg sampler's precision(%)	Avg. recall (%)
1.5	43	70
1.75	56.7	61
2	61.7	43
2.5	96.5	9.6

Table 3: effects of parameter b on Mushroom dataset

datasets—specifically, the correlations are poor for graph datasets, and good for itemset datasets. This is expected, because in our scoring function (γ), we are treating a graph as if it is simply a multiset of labeled edges (unit-pattern)—this assumption ignores the neighborhood structure of a graph, which may degrade the sampling quality. Another important observation is that, it does not take many feedbacks for the sampler to achieve a fairly good correlation; in all the plots, the maximum number of feedback that we use is less than 60, which is a negligible fraction of the entire frequent pattern set—see the fifth column of Table 2 for a count of frequent patterns in each of the datasets. 60 is also a reasonable number considering the real-life scenario, where a human inspects the patterns and provides feedback on them.

To show the effect of b, the exploration-exploitation trade-off parameter, we run our sampling method for several b values and report average samplers precision and recall. Here the precision is as we defined earlier, and the recall is the fraction of interesting patterns that the sampler have explored out of all the interesting patterns. The result is shown in Table 3, where the precision and recall are averaged over 10 distinct runs; as we expect, an increment of b increases the samplers precision with a reduction in the recall value.

We also study, how the sampler's performance changes, as the fraction of interesting patterns in the frequent pattern set ($\mathcal{F}$) changes. For this, we vary the parameter m which defines what fraction of unit-size items are interesting to the user. For this experiment, we use the Mushroom dataset with a support value of 1200. The number of frequent patterns, i.e., $|\mathcal{F}| = 53628$ and the number of unit-size patterns ($\mathcal{F}_1$) is $= 45$. For $m = 10\%$, on average, 5 unit-size patterns from the set $\mathcal{F}_1$ will be chosen as interesting, and the number of interesting pattern is 56, on average. Samplers precision for this m value is 5.8%, i.e, out of 1000 sampled patterns, 58 patterns are interesting. This seems to be a low number, but considering the fact that a uniform sampler will pick one interesting pattern from every thousand samples ($56 * 1000/53628 \sim 1$), the interactive sampler is 58 times more efficient. For $m = 20\%, 30\%, 40\%$, and 50%, the average samplers precision is 26.5%, 56.7%, 63.2% and 74%, respectively. Sampler's precision increases with the increment of m, as there are more interesting patterns in the search space ($\mathcal{F}$). Results on other datasets are similar, which are not shown due to the page restriction.

6.4 Interactive vs Uniform Sampling

Does user interaction really help? If we let the sampler perform a uniform sampling, will that achieve as good result as an interactive sampling session? We somewhat answer the question in the last paragraph of the earlier subsection, here we answer it in more details. For this, we compare between interactive sampling and uniform sampling. Note that, for uniform sampling, every pattern in $\mathcal{F}$ has equal probability to be sampled; i.e., the γ-score is $\frac{1}{|\mathcal{F}|}$ for all the patterns. In our implementation of interactive sampling, we simply

Dataset	Sampler's Precision(%)	
	Uniform	Interactive
Mushroom	0.182	56.70
Chess	2.293	95.74
Connect	4.53	94.32
eBay Query	15.23	98.50
Mutagenicity-I	1.94	36.76
Mutagenicity-II	1.15	35.00

Table 4: Average sampler's accuracy measure of uniform and interactive sampling.

turned off the feedback and use the above γ to obtain a version of MCMC sampling that would obtain a uniform sampling. For interactive sampling, we fix the $feedback\_count$ to 60 for the itemset datasets i.e. Mushroom, chess, connect, eBay and 40 for the graph datasets i.e. Mutagenicity-I and II. Our comparison metric in this experiment is sampler's precision, which is defined in the description of the previous experiment. The result is shown in Table 4; for all the datasets the interactive sampling significantly improves the sampler's precision. Hasan et.al [19] propose the uniform sampling of frequent patterns as a mechanism of frequent pattern summarization; however the above experiment shows that while mining patterns from a hidden data, an interactive approach will provide more rewarding sampling experience.

6.5 Timing Analysis

In this experiment, we analyze the execution time of this algorithm for varying minimum support and dataset size [7]. We run our algorithm with Mutagenicity-II dataset with different minimum supports and different database size and compute average time interval between 20 consecutive positive feedbacks. Figure 6 shows that, as expected, the time between successive positive feedbacks increases almost linearly with an increase in the database size or a decrease in the support value; for an example, user's waiting time between successive positive feedback is 24 (480/20) seconds for 5% support, but it is just 3 seconds for 10% support. However, the reader should note that, majority of the time is spent in computing the state-transition graph for MH-based subgraph sampling, so for larger dataset, the sampler could pre-compute the state-transition graph (for typical support threshold) and save it for future use; in that case, the timing performance of the interactive sampling will improve substantially. We conduct an experiment with Mutagenicity-II dataset. Without pre-computation, the execution of 1 million iterations takes 1676 seconds, but the same job executes in only 230 seconds, if we pre-compute the state-transition graph.

6.6 Real-life utility of Interactive Mining: Results from eBay Datasets

In this experiment, the user imitates a seller at eBay marketplace, who is interested to find related queries in the smart-phone, tablet, and game console categories. To accomplish this, the seller performs an interactive pattern mining on the eBay query dataset by providing positive feedback on frequent patterns that are related to the above product categories; some of the frequent patterns that she samples

[7]This experiment is performed in a 2GHz dual-core machine with a 2 GB physical memory.

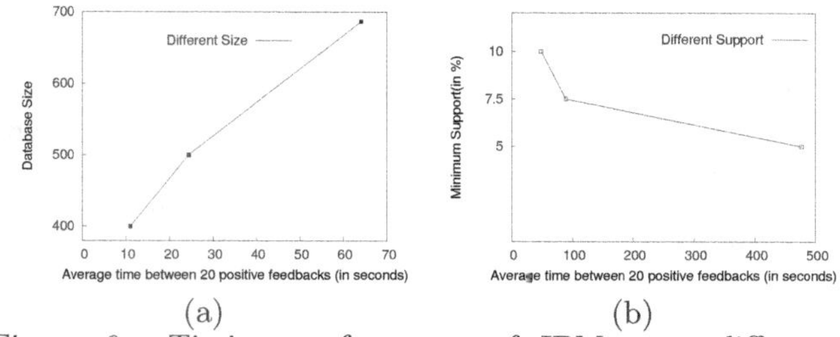

Figure 6: Timing performance of IPM w.r.t different database size and minimum support for Mutagenicity-II dataset

google tablet, android tablet, tablet pc 10
iphone 4, iphone 3gs unlocked
samsung galaxy s, samsung vibrant, samsung captivate

Table 5: Some frequent Patterns from eBay Query Dataset

from the hidden user session dataset is shown in Table 5. These patterns can educate her about the buyer demand trend at eBay marketplace; further, they could assist her in choosing a more rewarding title for her product, which would boost her chance to market it. At eBay, a seller's item in surfaced on the search result page if the title of the item contains *all* the words in a user's query [8]. If the seller wants to sell a `samsung galaxy s` smart-phone, the knowledge of the pattern in the third row of Table 5 would encourage her to add the words `vibrant` and `captivate` with the title phrase `samsung galaxy s`, so that her product would also surface against the queries like `samsung vibrant` and `samsung captivate`. Readers who are up-to-date on the latest smart-phone market may know that these two words are chosen by the US cell phone career T-mobile and AT&T to market the `samsung galaxy s` phone with their phone plans. Similarly, a title like, `google tablet android` would match with more user queries than those that would match with the title `google tablet`. In summary by educating a seller through interactive pattern mining on hidden user session dataset, the marketplace can increase sales transactions and eventually can boost their own revenue.

7. DISCUSSION AND CONCLUSION

This is a novel research problem and our work is just the beginning, so the opportunity of future work is abundant. For example, in this work we have considered a semi-honest model, whereas in real-life a malicious model may be needed. Specifically, an interesting follow-up research could be to understand how to safeguard the interactive mining system from a malicious user who intend to reconstruct the entire dataset by exploiting the sampling system; even more interesting is the scenario when a group of malicious users jointly attack the system to achieve a similar goal. Our work considers a binary feedback, an important future work is to consider a richer interaction model between the sampler and the user. One option is that the sampler returns a set of (random) patterns and the user provides a preference-based ranking of those patterns as her feedback. The sampler then updates the sampling distribution by utilizing this feedback.

Mining interesting patterns from a hidden dataset is an important research task; an effective solution to this task

[8]however, eBay allows 55 characters for the title, so experience sellers always optimize the title of their product

brings information to its end-user, thus democratize the information for its better usages. In this paper, we show examples from eCommerce domain, but such a solution will be useful in many application domains; for instance, in heath informatics research, private mining of patient health record located at a remote server will enable a large number of researchers to find interesting patterns involving diseases, and medicines.

To conclude, in this paper, we introduce a new research problem, i.e., mining frequent pattern from a hidden dataset through interactive pattern sampling. We formulate a solution to this problem by adopting interactive pattern sampling framework, where the effective sampling distribution is continuously updated by binary feedback from the user. We provide real-life examples to illustrate the usefulness of this research task and also show experimental results to validate the feasibility and effectiveness of our solution. Specifically, we show that the number of feedback that a user is required to provide is practical for a real-life scenario.

8. REFERENCES

[1] R. Agrawal and R. Srikant. Fast algorithms for mining association rules in large databases. In *Proc. of VLDB*, pages 487–499, 1994.

[2] I. Benjamini, G. Kozma, and W. N. The mixing time of the giant component of a random graph. 2006.

[3] T. D. Bie. Maximum entropy models and subjective interestingness: an application to tiles in binary databases. *Data Mining and Knowledge Discovery.*

[4] M. Boley and H. Grosskreutz. Approximating the number of frequent sets in dense data. *Knowledge and Information Systems*, 21:65–89, 2009.

[5] F. Bonchi, F. Giannotti, A. Mazzanti, and D. Pedreschi. Exante: Anticipated data reduction in constrained pattern mining. In *Proc. of the 4th PKDD*, pages 59–70, 2003.

[6] S. Bringmann, A. Zimmermann, L. Raedt, and S. Nijssen. Don't be afraid of simpler pattern. In *PKDD*, pages 55–66, 2004.

[7] C. Bucila, J. Gehrke, and D. K. andW. White. Dualminer: A dual-pruning algorithm for itemsets withconstraints. *Data Mining and Knowledge Discovery*, 2003.

[8] T. K. Chia, K. C. Sim, H. Li, and H. T. Ng. A lattice-based approach to query-by-example spoken document retrieval. In *Proc. of the 31st ACM SIGIR conference on Research and development in information retrieval*, pages 363–370, 2008.

[9] R. K. Chung. *Spectral Graph Theory.* Americal Mathematical Society, 1997.

[10] A. Dasgupta, X. Jin, B. Jewell, N. Zhang, and G. Das. Unbiased estimation of size and other aggregates over hidden web databases. In *Proceedings of the 2010 international conference on Management of data*, pages 855–866, 2010.

[11] A. Dasgupta, N. Zhang, and G. Das. Leveraging count information in sampling hidden databases. In *ICDE '09*, pages 329 –340, 2009.

[12] A. Dasgupta, N. Zhang, and G. Das. Turbo-charging hidden database samplers with overflowing queries and skew reduction. In *Proceedings of the 13th International Conference on Extending Database Technology*, pages 51–62, 2010.

[13] I. Dinur and K. Nissim. Revealing information while preserving privacy. In *Proc. of the twenty-second ACM SIGMOD-SIGACT-SIGART symposium on Principles of database systems*, pages 202–210, 2003.

[14] B. Goethals, S. Moens, and J. Vreeken. Mime: A framework for interactive visual pattern mining. In *ECML*, pages 757 –760, 2011.

[15] O. Goldreich. *Foundations of Cryptography Volume II Basic Applications.* Cambridge University Press, 2004.

[16] J. Han, J. Pei, Y. Yin, and R. Mao. Mining frequent patterns without candidate generation: A frequent-pattern tree approach. *Data Mining and Knowledge Discovery*, 8, Jan. 2004.

[17] M. Hasan and M. Zaki. Uniform sampling of k maximal patterns. In *SIAM Data Mining*, 2009.

[18] M. A. Hasan, N. Parikh, G. Singh, and N. Sundaresan. Query suggestion for e-commerce sites. In *Proc. of the fourth ACM international conference on Web search and data mining*, WSDM '11, pages 765–774, 2011.

[19] M. A. Hasan and M. J. Zaki. Output space sampling for graph patterns. In *Proc. International Conference on Very Large Data Bases (VLDB)*, pages 730–741, 2009.

[20] S. Jagabathula, N. Mishra, and S. Gollapudi. Shopping for products you don't know you need. In *Proc. of the fourth ACM international conference on Web search and data mining*, pages 705–714, 2011.

[21] M. Kuramochi and G. Karypis. Frequent subgraph discovery. In *In Proc. of ICDM'01.*

[22] M. Mampaey, N. Tatti, and J. Vreeken. Tell me what i need to know: succinctly summarizing data with itemsets. In *Proc. of the 17th ACM SIGKDD.*

[23] A. Marian, N. Bruno, and L. Gravano. Evaluating top-k queries over web-accessible databases. *ACM Trans. Database Syst.*, 29, 2004.

[24] N. Mishra, R. Saha Roy, N. Ganguly, S. Laxman, and M. Choudhury. Unsupervised query segmentation using only query logs. In *Proc. of the 20th international conference companion on WWW'11*, pages 91–92.

[25] S. Raghavan and H. Garcia-Molina. Crawling the hidden web. In *Proc. of the 27th VLDB*, pages 129–138, 2001.

[26] P. N. Tan, V. Kumar, and J. Srivastava. Selecting the right interestingness measure for association patterns. In *Proc.of SIGKDD*, pages 32–41, 2002.

[27] Y. Wang and X. Wu. Approximate inverse frequent itemset mining: Privacy, complexity, and approximation. In *Proc. of the 5th ICDM*, 2005.

[28] D. Xin, X. Shen, Q. Mei, and J. Han. Discovering interesting patterns through user's interactive feedback. In *Proc. of the 12th ACM SIGKDD*, 2006.

[29] X. Yan and J. Han. gspan: Graph-based substructure pattern mining. In *In proc. of ICDM*, 2002.

[30] M. Zaki. Spade: An efficient algorithm for mining frequent sequences. *Machine Learning, 42*, 2001.

[31] M. J. Zaki. Efficiently mining frequent trees in a forest: Algorithms and applications. In *IEEE Tans. on knowledge and data engineering, 17:8*, 2005.

An Analysis of Systematic Judging Errors in Information Retrieval

Gabriella Kazai[2] Nick Craswell[1] Emine Yilmaz[2] S.M.M. Tahaghoghi[1]

[1]Microsoft, Bellevue, WA, USA

[2]Microsoft Research, Cambridge, UK

{v-gabkaz,nickcr,eminey,stahagh}@microsoft.com

ABSTRACT

Test collections are powerful mechanisms for evaluation and optimization of information retrieval systems. There is reported evidence that experiment outcomes can be affected by changes in the judge population or in judging guidelines. We examine such effects in a web search setting, comparing the judgments of four groups of judges: NIST Web Track judges, untrained crowd workers and two groups of trained judges of a commercial search engine. Our goal is to identify systematic judging errors by comparing the labels contributed by the different groups. In particular, we focus on detecting systematic differences in judging depending on specific characteristics of the queries and URLs. For example, we ask whether a given population of judges, working under a given set of judging guidelines, are more likely to overrate Wikipedia pages than another group judging under the same instructions. Our approach is to identify judging errors with respect to a consensus set, a judged gold set and a set of user clicks. We further demonstrate how such biases can affect the training of retrieval systems.

Categories and Subject Descriptors

H.3.4 [**Information Storage and Retrieval**]: Systems and Software—*performance evaluation (efficiency and effectiveness)*

General Terms

Experimentation, Measurement, Performance

Keywords

Relevance labeling, assessor errors, crowdsourcing

1. INTRODUCTION

In information retrieval (IR), test collections, comprising documents, topics and human-generated relevance judgments, are typically used to evaluate and optimize the performance of IR systems [21]. To build a test collection that reflects real users, it is possible to select a corpus and a sample of queries that is representative of the real-world usage of some IR system, such as a Web search engine. The more difficult aspect is to design a relevance judging procedure that can lead to relevance labels that reflect real-world user satisfaction. Arguably, this requires maximizing the judges' understanding of the real users' information needs. For example, faced with the query *shania twain*, an assessor may reason that the user is looking for the Wikipedia page on the celebrity, while the real user need may have been to go the star's official site or to read the latest news or celebrity gossip, or vice versa.

Traditionally, relevance judging methods rely on a fixed group of expert judges, who are trained to interpret user queries as accurately as possible and label documents accordingly. However, the growing volume and diversity of the topics and documents to be judged is driving an increasing adoption of crowdsourcing methods, where relevance judgments are distributed over a large population of humans, a *crowd* [11]. Crowdsourcing platforms, such as Amazon's Mechanical Turk, allow thousands of crowd workers to be hired temporarily for micro-payments to complete small human intelligence tasks (HITs), such as labeling images or documents. Clearly, such a model is in stark contrast to the highly controlled methods that characterize the work of trained judges. For example, in a micro-task based crowdsourcing setup, worker training is usually minimal or non-existent. Furthermore, it is widely reported that labels provided by crowd workers can vary in quality, leading to noisy labels [9, 12, 1]. On the other hand, it may be argued that training procedures and judging guidelines may actually lead to biased judgments, e.g., consistent overrating of some document types, like Wikipedia pages. Untrained judges, as a group, are less likely to demonstrate such biases. Another potential benefit of crowdsourcing is the diversity of its workers that may better reflect that of real users in Web search.

Judging errors and their impact on the outcome of an evaluation experiment has been the subject of extensive study in the past, while the growing reliance on crowdsourcing prompted a renewed interest in the topic. For example, low levels of inter-assessor agreements are often reported both for trained judges and crowd workers [19, 1]. Furthermore, evaluation outcomes have been shown to be affected when using different judge populations [2, 14] or different judging guidelines [6].

In this paper, we study differences between four groups of relevance judges: NIST Web Track judges from 2009 and 2010, crowd workers, and two different groups of trained

CIKM'12, October 29–November 2, 2012, Maui, HI, USA.

judges of a commercial Web search engine. We characterize and compare the judge groups according to their inter-assessor agreement, their agreement with click-based gold sets and with label-based gold sets. Rather than overall judge agreement, much of our analysis focuses on characterizing differences with respect to three specific types of judgments: Judgments of Wikipedia pages, judgments where the query text matches the URL text, and judgments where the URL is the root page of a site (and thus likely a homepage). This allows us to study, for example, whether crowd judges or trained judges are more likely to overrate or underrate Wikipedia pages with respect to a given gold set. Future work might extend to many more than these three types, automatically identifying the most important types of judgment where judge groups differ, and then making measurable improvements in judging procedures. Our current scope is to develop analysis methods that could be used, for a given type of judgment, to identify systematic differences between judge groups. In addition, we study the impact that systematic errors can have on the training of a supervised ranker, demonstrating that systematic differences in labeling can lead to different learned rankers.

2. RELATED WORK

Relevance judgments are the core of most IR experiments. This has led to numerous studies of the judgments themselves and their impact on the evaluation experiments. For example, it is well known that human judgments are subjective, influenced by various situational, cognitive, perceptual and motivational biases [3, 16]. Indeed, a wide range of factors that can impact on the variability of relevance judgments have been identified in the literature [17], including, for example, document variables, judgment conditions and scales, and personal factors [7].

Despite the subjective nature of relevance and the judgment disagreements at the query-document level [19, 1], the study by Voorhees showed that the outcome of experiments, in terms of system orderings, was robust against changes in the group of assessors [19]. However, in her study, all assessors were from the same population, i.e., all judges were trained on the same task, using the same guidelines. In contrast, evaluation outcomes have been shown to be affected when using different judge populations [2, 14], different judging guidelines [6, 10], simulated noisier judgments [5] or even taking the earlier vs. the later judgments in cases of intra-judge inconsistency [18]. For example, the study by Bailey et al. [2] compared three groups of judges: Gold judges who were topic originators and domain experts, silver judges who were domain experts only, and bronze judges who were neither experts nor topic originators. They found that switching between judge types resulted in changes to the system ordering. A similar comparison of expert and non-expert judges in [15] showed that non-expert judges tended to give shallow, inaccurate ratings compared to experts. Non-experts also disagree on the underlying meaning of queries significantly more often than experts, and often appear to "give up" and fall back on surface features such as keyword matching.

Within a single judge population, there is some evidence that changing the judging guidelines can change the evaluation outcome. Voorhees [20], for example, instructed judges to label on more than a binary scale, by also identifying highly relevant documents and the best document for each query. The relative effectiveness of the evaluated runs then differed depending on how the different levels were used or collapsed in the evaluation, highlighting the effects of the instructions on the number of levels and their definitions. The judging instructions at the TREC Web Track have also changed over the years reflecting the varying usefulness of link evidence depending on the task [10], e.g., informational adhoc judgments vs. navigational homepage finding judgments. In this case, the different tasks had different judging instructions but also used different query sampling methods, so some combination of these factors led to the relative differences in the performance of systems with and without link evidence.

With no change in the judge population or in the instructions, the work by Scholer et al. [18] demonstrated that the conclusions of an evaluation experiment can change by simply using judgments made at different times by the same judge. Webber et al. [22] studied the impact of judging errors on estimates of recall, where assessment pool sampling is stratified based on the results of the systems participating in the evaluation. They showed that assessor error is in general a greater source of inaccuracy than sampling error.

Our research contributes to the above studies by investigating the impact that changes in the population of judges or changes in the judging guidelines can have on the quality of the resulting relevance labels. We study both trained judges and untrained crowd workers, working under the same or different instructions and compare their judgments for documents with different characteristics. We measure label quality in terms of agreement with consensus, a gold set of labels and user clicks. This holistic approach allows us to analyze which types of errors are more likely by the different judge groups, to characterize their disagreements and, in some cases, to identify systematic biases.

3. TYPES OF JUDGING ERRORS

For the purposes of this study a judging error is a disagreement with some reference data, for example a gold set. This section describes some sources of judging error, what we mean by systematic bias in judgment and the three examples of bias that we use in our experiments.

Due to its subjectivity, the assessment of relevance can be particularly challenging by a third party. To mitigate such issues, assessors at TREC are often involved in the creation of the test topics. In addition, they are subjected to training, judging procedures and guidelines, aiming to aid them in providing consistent judgments. Measured in terms of consistency, label quality is thus predicated on the judges accurately understanding and conscientiously following a common set of guidelines. In practice, however, this is difficult to achieve and judges often make mistakes. Based on the analysis of a large sample of judgments collected from trained judges of a commercial search engine, we list some of the most commonly observed reasons for judging errors:

Intent mismatch: Judges may not understand the intent of a real user. For example, the query *circuit breaker* could relate to the electrical device, or to a program of this name run by the Illinois Department on Aging. On a 5-point scale, the one that is rated higher by a judge may not be the one that users would prefer. Beyond the ambiguity of a query, intent considerations may include aspects whether the user may prefer a lay overview of a medical condition over specialist content; or the latest gossip about a celebrity over a peer-reviewed biography on Wikipedia.

Content quality: Aspects of quality such as the correctness or authoritativeness of a web page can be important for certain queries. For example, user-contributed song lyrics may contain errors; much online medical advice is questionable; and some sites simply copy or aggregate content from other sources. The challenge of assessing the quality of a page can be further exacerbated by a mismatch in the impression of quality made by the design of the page; "content farms" exploit this by framing often inane content on well-laid out pages with relevant keywords.

Judge biases: Judges may develop biases based on the training examples that they have seen, and then base their assessment on their own inferred rules. Judges may also have intrinsic biases and may rate too harshly or too generously, or keep their ratings within a narrow band of the rating scale.

The above is not intended as a comprehensive or dichotomous classification of judging errors. What is of interest to us is when judges make systematic errors in their judgments for any of the above reasons. For example, judges may consistently underrate navigational results in favor of results that better fit the informational interpretation of the query. We consider such consistent judging mistakes as examples of systematic error or bias, where an error means a disagreement with a given ground-truth, i.e., consensus or gold label. Moreover, we are not interested in the individual bias of a particular judge, but the systematic errors of a group of judges with common characteristics, e.g., trained judges working under a given set of instructions. In order to detect the presence of such systematic errors among a group of judges, we propose a method that compares across different groups of judges and judging conditions, i.e., trained vs. untrained judges, working under the same vs. different guidelines, measured against a diverse set of baselines, i.e., consensus, gold set labels and user clicks. To make our investigation feasible, we focus on three specific cases that may be prone to such judging errors. These are simple to calculate based on properties of the query-URL pairs, and have been observed as potentially interesting cases in a commercial search judging setting and/or at TREC [10, 13]:

Wikipedia bias: Can we see systematic errors in judges' treatment of Wikipedia pages? To answer this question we will compare labels by the different judge groups and guideline conditions across two subsets of the judged documents: Wikipedia (**WP**) vs. non-Wikipedia (**nWP**) pages. When the URL of the judged document contains the string "en.wikipedia.org", we classify it as a WP page and as an nWP page otherwise.

URL query bias: Can we find systematic errors in the judgment of documents whose URL contains the query words? Such cases may be indicative of a more navigational user intent, searching for a known site. Again, our approach is to split the judged corpus based on this document feature and compare the labels across the two subsets. When the query words appear in the URL (in the same sequence) then we tag the topic-document pair as **QiU** (short for "Query in URL") and with **nQiU** otherwise. For example, the query espn sports occurs in the URL `http://en.wikipedia.org/wiki/ESPN_Sports_Poll`, so this pair is tagged as QiU.

Homepage bias: Can we detect a systematically different judging of homepages in different judging conditions? Assuming that homepages are more likely to have root URLs that only contain domain information without a path, we split the corpus into root-URL (**RU**) and not-root-URL (**nRU**) subsets.

4. EXPERIMENT DESIGN

Our goal is to identify systematic judging errors by comparing the labels contributed by the different groups, working under the same or different judging guidelines. More specifically, we want to investigate if we can observe different types of systematic judging mistakes, e.g., a consistent overrating of homepages by one group of judges – as described in the previous section – in the different judging conditions.

In order to analyze the effects of a change in the guidelines, our case study is the ad hoc task of the TREC Web Track. In 2009, the track used three judging levels: Not Relevant (0), Relevant (1) and Highly Relevant (2). Non-English documents were to be judged non-relevant, and assessors were instructed that pages with misleading or malicious content should also be considered non-relevant. In 2010, in an effort to better support the assessment of queries with navigational intent, and to separate spam results from non-relevant, the Track adopted the following 5-level judging scale:

Nav (3) This page represents a homepage of an entity directly named by the query; the user may be searching for this specific page or site, e.g., `www.yahoo.com` for the query *yahoo*.

Key (2) This page or site is dedicated to the topic; authoritative and comprehensive, it is worthy of being a top result in a web search engine.

Rel (1) The content of this page provides useful information on the topic.

Non (0) The content of this page does not provide useful information on the topic.

Junk (-2) This page does not appear to be useful for any reasonable purpose; it may be spam or junk.

In order to study the effect of a changes in the judge population, we collect relevance labels from both trained and untrained judges. For our untrained judge group we recruit crowd workers – from the US only – through Clickworker, a labor market similar to Amazon's Mechanical Turk. To participate, workers are first qualified via a basic Web judging task, but receive no training. We will refer to these judges as "Crowd". For our trained judges, we recruited two groups of professional assessors, 10 in each group, employed and trained by a commercial search engine. One group is trained in Web search judging (we will call them "ProWeb") and thus would be aware of aspects of search engine usage, for example the importance of navigational results. The other group is trained for a different judging task, not for Web search ("ProNonWeb"). The NIST judges of the Web Track 2009/2010 campaigns comprise the fourth judge group.

In our analysis we identify judging errors with respect to a consensus based ground-truth set, a judged gold set and a set of user clicks, extracted from the query log of a commercial web search engine. In the following, we describe the different datasets we use for analysis in more detail.

4.1 Experiment Data

4.1.1 WT (Web Track) set

We designate the Web Track ad hoc task relevance judgments provided by the judges hired and trained by NIST as our **WT** (Web Track) set, with WT 2009 and WT 2010 identifying the labels collected for a given year of the track. This set consists of nearly 50k relevance labels for 100 topics[1], roughly 25k labels per year. In this set we only have a single label per topic-document pair. As discussed in the previous section, the labels in 2009 span a 3-level relevance scale, and a 5-level scale in 2010. We note that while the document corpus used in these two years of the track was the same, the sample of documents assessed by NIST judges may have been different, which could have given rise to collection bias. There may also have been differences in the query sampling procedure.

4.1.2 ST (Sampled TREC) set

In addition to the WT set, we collected relevance labels from both trained and untrained judges. We first took the 100 Web track 2009/2010 topics and using these as queries we scraped the top 10 search results from Google and Bing for each query. This gave us a total of 1,603 unique query-URL pairs over the 100 topics. We chose this method of re-sampling documents for the TREC topics, instead of re-labeling a sample of the WT set, in order to ensure up to date coverage of the topics and high overlap with the query-document pairs that appear in the query logs of the commercial search engine, which we aim to use in our analysis later on. To collect relevance labels for our sample of documents for the 100 Web track queries, we designed a simple judging interface that showed judges a query and a web search result (in an iframe) and asked judges to rate the search result's usefulness to the query using a five-point scale[2]:

Ideal (4) User seeing this result would think it ideal.
Very happy (3) User seeing this result would be very happy.
Happy (2) User seeing this result would be happy.
Somewhat happy (1) User would be somewhat happy.
Unhappy (0) User seeing this result would be unhappy as this is a useless result for the current search.

We collected relevance labels from our Crowd, ProWeb and ProNonWeb judge groups in separate experiments using the same judging interface. While we recruited 20 professional judges (10 ProWeb and 10 ProNonWeb), our Crowd judge group is made up of the 45 US workers who chose to work on our HITs on Clickworker (workers were pre-filtered by the platform). We gathered up to 3 labels per query-document pair, per judge group. We stopped at 2 labels in case of agreement, or collected a third label when the first two disagreed. We obtained a total of 12,879 relevance labels across the three judge groups. We designate the obtained labels set as our **ST** (Sampled TREC) label set.

[1]The actual total number of topics with NIST judgments is 98; topics 95 and 100 have no labels.

[2]Judges could skip a query-document pair (by selecting the "I can't tell" option). They could also research a query by viewing the top 10 results from Google and Bing.

4.1.3 HQ (Hard Queries) set

Finally, we collected relevance labels from trained Web judges and untrained crowd workers for a hand-picked set of 689 query-URL pairs, sampled from the commercial search engine's query log, that is representative of the types of judging errors we described in Section 3. This set has of a total of 74,530 labels, 72,463 of which was contributed by 193 professional Web judges (average 375 labels per judge or 105 labels per query-URL pair) and 2,067 labels by 18 crowd workers (115 labels per judge, 3 labels per query-URL pair). We will call this data our **HQ** (hard queries) set.

The relevance data and judge groups used in the experiments are summarized in Table 1.

Table 1: Datasets and judge groups

Set	Queries	Query-URLs	Labels	Judge groups
WT	98	48,501	48,917	NIST judges
ST	100	1,603	12,879	10 ProWeb; 10 ProNonWeb; 45 Crowd
HQ	665	689	74,530	193 ProWeb; 18 Crowd

4.1.4 Click data set

The click log data set contains raw click count information for sets of query-URL pairs from 18 months of user traffic for a commercial Web search engine, with a minimum threshold of at least 10 clicks. 1,583 of the 1,603 unique query-URLs in our ST dataset and 1,367 of the 48,501 query-URLs in the WT set have click information in the logs (1,231 in common across ST and WT). As the HQ set contains mostly tail queries, we have no corresponding click data.

4.2 Analysis Methodology

When collecting multiple ratings from judges, a consensus label may be derived, e.g., using simple majority vote or methods that take into account judge reliability [8]. However, it is not always feasible to rely on consensus; with a semi-skilled pool of judges, incorrect rating may be the rule rather than the exception. Hence, it is important that ratings provided by the judges be not only internally *consistent*, but also *correct*. One way to assess correctness is to sample the labels and evaluate each one against a known "gold" rating. The generation of gold sets is however expensive and it may not be practical to test each judge on all the gold data. Alternative gold sets may be derived from click evidence. For example, one can create pairs of URLs for a query with known click preference relations and then check if the judgments agree with the click preference.

In our analysis we use all of these methods, i.e., consensus and gold sets based on labels and clicks, in order to identify systematic errors in the judging behavior of the four different groups of assessors: NIST, ProWeb, ProNonWeb, and Crowd. We start with the consensus based analysis in the next section.

5. CONSENSUS ANALYSIS

5.1 Inter-assessor Agreement Analysis

In Table 2, we report values of Fleiss' kappa, a well-known technique that estimates the degree of consensus between n

judges by correcting for agreement by chance alone, calculated over the labels contributed by the different groups of judges in our ST set.

Table 2: Fleiss' kappa agreement levels per judge group and per feature for the ST set (p<0.001, Q=unique queries, QU=unique query-URL pairs)

SubSet	#Q	#QUs	Labels	Kappa
Crowd	100	1603	4442	**0.33**
WP	78	138	401	0.28
nWP	100	1465	4041	0.34
QiU	71	690	1917	0.32
nQiU	96	913	2525	0.34
RU	89	472	1281	0.35
nRU	99	1131	3161	0.33
ProWeb	100	1603	4047	**0.59**
WP	78	138	365	0.51
nWP	100	1465	3682	0.60
QiU	71	690	1721	0.63
nQiU	96	913	2326	0.56
RU	89	472	1195	0.54
nRU	99	1131	2852	0.61
ProNonWeb	100	1603	4390	**0.33**
WP	78	138	390	0.26
nWP	100	1465	4000	0.33
QiU	71	690	1891	0.33
nQiU	96	913	2499	0.33
RU	89	472	1304	0.27
nRU	99	1131	3086	0.35

It is easy to see that professional Web judges have a much higher level of within-group agreement than crowd workers (κ of 0.59 for ProWeb vs. 0.33 for Crowd). This is even more evident in the HQ set (not shown), where a ProWeb agreement level of $\kappa = 0.57$ is matched only by $\kappa = 0.16$ for the Crowd. Interestingly crowd workers do as well as professional judges who are not trained in Web search judging ($\kappa = 0.33$ for both groups). This can be taken as evidence in support of the need for judge training and calibration.

Although disagreement analysis is informative, it may well be that not all disagreements are bad. In some cases disagreements among judges may reflect the diverse opinions of real-world users. For example, for the query *gps*, we obtain an average σ of 0.68 among the judgments of the Crowd per judged URLs, compared with $\sigma = 0.14$ for ProWeb and $\sigma = 0.47$ for ProNonWeb. The URLs for this query include the Wikipedia page on GPS, the `www.gps.gov` and various shopping result pages. Similarly, for the query *kcs*, judges may rate the homepage of the Kansas City Southern Railway and the related Wikipedia page differently. Thus, the diversity of the judgments can reflect the diversity of the associated user needs.

With the aim to gain deeper insights into judging disagreements, we calculate agreement levels over subsets of the data set, divided based on one our analysis features, e.g., Wikipedia, query URL, homepage. We see that inter-assessor agreement is lower for Wikipedia pages across all judge groups (0.28, 0.51, 0.26 for Crowd, ProWeb, ProNonWeb, respectively), compared with nWP judgments (0.34, 0.6, 0.33, resp.). This suggests that Wikipedia pages are inherently more controversial and are harder to judge consistently.

Dividing the sets of relevance labels based on whether the query words occur in the URL, we observe different behavior by the different judge groups. ProNonWeb judges show the least influence of this property on their judgments ($\kappa = 0.33$ for both QiU and nQiU). Crowd judges agree slightly more in the nQiU subset (with 0.02 difference in κ). However, most strikingly, the ProWeb judges show much better agreement when the query does appear in the URL ($\kappa_{QiU} = 0.63$ while $\kappa_{nQiU} = 0.56$). The latter may be an indication of possible judging guideline bias for ProWeb judges, but it could equally signal a noise-reduction and calibration effect of the guidelines on the judges.

We also see inconsistent behavior between the judge groups on agreeing about the relevance of root vs. non-root URLs. Crowd workers agree slightly more in the RU subset (0.02 increase in κ over nRU), while both ProWeb and ProNonWeb judges have higher agreement levels on nRU (0.07-0.08 differences in κ). We found the same trends in the HQ set (not shown).

Based on the observations so far, we can conclude that judge training on a specific judging task does indeed increase assessors' judging consistency. Furthermore, we may argue that observed changes in judgment behavior across different datasets with different properties can signal healthy judging procedures, especially when the same changes are mirrored across different groups of judges. On the other hand, we also see that different groups of judges exhibit different behaviors on the same dataset. Can, in such cases, disagreement signal judging bias? Indeed, what is not clear from this agreement analysis is whether higher agreement actually reflects higher label quality. Can higher agreement simply be a result of skewed label distributions that are not necessarily correct? For example, a group of judges who are evaluated and paid based on their inter-assessor agreement may learn to optimize their judging by reducing the use of risky labels (e.g., adopting a middle of the road approach), thus skewing the distribution of labels. In the following, we aim to answer this question by comparing the judgments to gold labels.

5.2 Probability of a Label

Figure 1 shows the label probability distributions in the ST and HQ data sets for the different judge groups. We see very different label probability patterns across the groups. We observe evidence of judge calibration among the trained judges, whereby the top relevant grades are assigned very sparingly, while untrained judges tend to be more liberal. We see that professional judges are characterized by a skewed distribution, peeking at the middle grades (or below for ProNonWeb). Such a skew can mean that the 5 point scale is in essence reduced and can also boost agreement statistics. Crowd workers produce a more uniform distribution with a flatter bell shape on the ST set. Interestingly, crowd judgments show a top grade heavy distribution for the HQ set. This may be a result of the crowd's leniency and possible unawareness of a query's potentially diverse intents. For example, while trained judges may grade results that satisfy a less likely informational intent for a query lower than a navigational result, crowd workers may rate both types of results equally highly. This could be addressed by gathering labels using a HIT with multiple results per query.

Looking at Wikipedia vs. non-Wikipedia judgments, we can observe clear shifts in the label probability distributions for all three judge groups. Crowd judges show an in-

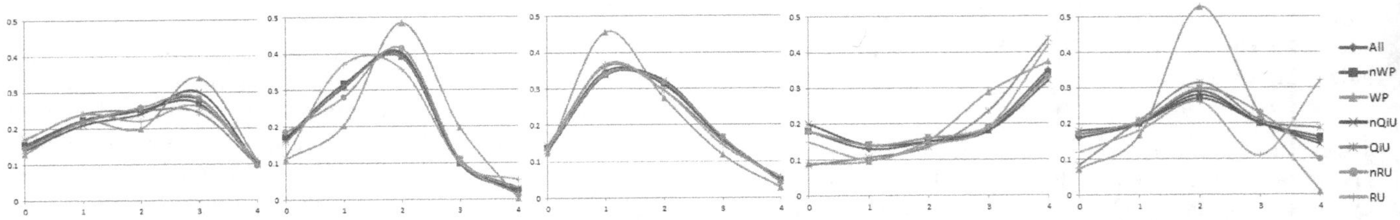

a) ST, Crowd b) ST, ProWeb c) ST, ProNonWeb d) HQ, Crowd e) HQ, ProWeb

Figure 1: Label probability distributions

creased probability level for grade 3 (shift from grade 2) for Wikipedia pages ($p(3) = 0.34$ for WP vs. 0.27 for nWP), while ProWeb judges have increased probability levels for both $p(2) = 0.48$ and $p(3) = 0.20$ for WP vs. $p(2) = 0.39$ and $p(3) = 0.10$ for nWP. Interestingly, ProNonWeb judges are more likely to assign lower grades to Wikipedia than to non-Wikipedia pages. These more skewed judging patterns for WP, combined with the observed lower inter-assessor agreement levels, suggest that the shift in judging patterns is not consistent across the individual judges and the documents. Unlike the judging patterns for the WP/nWP feature, no such clear patterns are observed for the QiU/nQiU feature across the judge groups. Ratings for homepages (RU) show some irregularities compared to the other patterns, especially on the HQ set. Paired t-tests over all feature pairs confirmed significant differences for WP/nWP judgments in both the ST and HQ sets and for all judges ($p_t < 0.001$, apart from ProNonWeb on ST with $p_t < 0.005$). On the ST set significant differences were found for QiU/nQiU judgments by the Crowd ($p_t < 0.001$) and ProNonWeb judges ($p_t < 0.05$), and for RU/nRU labels by ProWeb judges ($p_t < 0.001$). On the HQ set all feature pairs showed statistically significant judging patterns for both Crowd and ProWeb ($p_t < 0.001$).

So, thus far, we saw that trained judges are more reliable in terms of inter-assessor agreement, but that they show label probability distributions skewed toward the middle grades. The latter may be a result of the combined effects of a stricter interpretation of the value associated with high relevance grades (inherent or trained) as well as their intentional or unintentional optimization for agreement, a metric often used to evaluate judges. We also observed that Wikipedia pages receive spacial treatment by all groups, but lead to the lowest levels of inter-assessor agreement overall.

We conduct a similar analysis of the WT set, comparing NIST judgments from 2009 and 2010, but note that the observed differences in this case cannot be clearly attributed to changes in judging behavior due to the different query sets and pools in the two years. We find that NIST judges in 2009 were twice as likely to label a Wikipedia page as highly relevant than a non-Wikipedia page: $p(2) = 0.16$ for WP vs. 0.08 for nWP. In 2010, we observe mixed effects: the probability of a WP being labeled as Key (2) is 0.09 vs. 0.03 for nWP. However, the probability of a WP labeled as Rel (1) is only 0.13 compared with 0.16 for nWP. The probability of a WP result being irrelevant has also shifted in the two years. In 2009, it was more likely that a nWP result would be labeled irrelevant, while in 2010 this is reversed. Regarding the assessment of URLs where the query occurs in the URL, we find that NIST judges were more likely to label QiU documents as relevant than nQiU documents: $p(> 0) = 0.36$ and 0.24 for QiU, and 0.26 and 0.19 for nQiU, in 2009 and 2010, respectively. Paired t-tests confirmed significant differences between the means of two distributions for all feature pairs in both years and over the whole WT dataset, apart from RU/nRU in 2009 with $p_t = 0.4013$.

6. GOLD SET ANALYSIS

An alternative method of measuring label quality to inter-assessor agreement is via the use of gold judgments. We consider two types of gold data: 1) a set of labels provided by a group of highly trusted judges (super judges) and 2) a click-based gold set reflecting real Web users.

6.1 Click-based Pairwise Preferences

From our click data set, we first construct pairs of URLs per query and remove pairs where the difference in click counts is less than the median over the whole set (25 clicks for the WT set and 52 clicks for the ST set). For each URL pair, the relative click volume gives us a click preference relation. We then compare the click preference relations with the preferences derived from the collected relevance labels – by a given group of judges – for the respective query-URLs in each pairing. We consider label preferences that point in the same direction as the user click preferences to be correct, and label preferences that point in the opposite direction to be incorrect. We use an insensitive category when the click preference relation is not detected in the labels, i.e., the same label is assigned to both URLs. We repeat the same analysis using only the top two most-clicked URLs per query. Figure 2 shows the percentage of correct, incorrect and insensitive label vs. click preferences for the WT set (also broken down by year) and for the ST data set (broken down by judge group).

As we can see in Figure 2a), a high ratio of NIST label pairs do not distinguish between URLs with different volumes of clicks: 46% of the label preferences are insensitive. Comparing the two years, we can see a lot of improvement in 2010 over 2009 in the labels better reflecting real Web users: in 2010, 35% of the label preferences agree with click preferences, compared with only 29% in 2009. This demonstrates the impact of the change in guidelines from one year to the next, i.e., moving from a three point scale to a more sensitive five point scale. However, over the subset with the top two clicked URLs per query, see Figure 2b), we see that 2010 judgments have actually lower ratio of correct (down to 28% from 39% in 2009) and higher levels of insensitivity (39%, up from 24% in 2009). A detailed look at the differences reveals that most insensitivity errors occur for Key (2) and Non (0) labels, providing support for a finer grained relevance scale. Alternatively, it could also mean that judges are less able or willing to be more discriminative in their ratings for these types of query-document pairs.

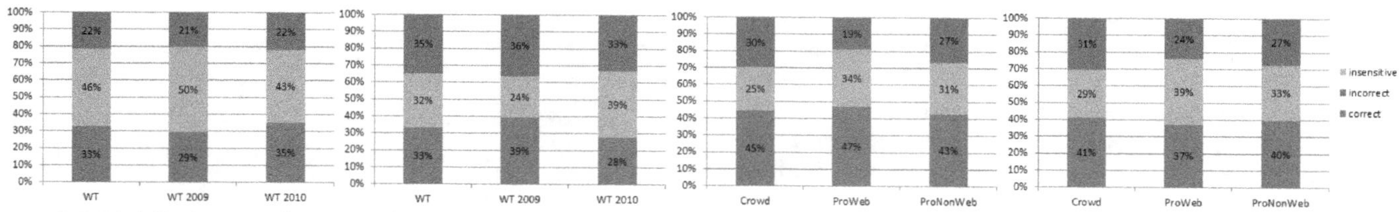

a) WT (all click data) b) WT (top 2 clicked) c) ST (all click data) d) ST (top 2 clicked)

Figure 2: Ratios of correct/incorrect/insensitive label preferences when compared to click preference relations for the different data sets and judge groups

Ratios of correct preferences per our feature set are summarized in Table 3 (over all click preferences). It is interesting to note that NIST assessors perform differently in relation to the different document features. For example, they show high agreement with click preferences in 2010 when one or both URLs are Wikipedia pages (WP1=40%, WP2=51%, compared with nWP=31%). Lowest agreements with clicks is found in 2009 when judging similar results, e.g., when both results were WP (17% correct), QiU (22%) or RU (15%). This suggests that the 3 point scale was not sufficient to differentiate between such results or that judges developed internal judging rules based on document types, leading to possible bias.

Table 3: Percentage of label preferences that agree with user click preferences for pairs of URLs per query-URL feature (WP1/WP2/nWP: one/both/none of the URL(s) in the pair is a Wikipedia page, etc.)

WT dataset	All	2009	2010
WP1/WP2/nWP	38/39/30	34/**17**/28	40/51/31
QiU1/QiU2/nQiU	35/30/36	35/**22**/34	36/34/38
RU1/RU2/nRU	35/20/34	32/**15**/32	37/29/35
ST dataset	Crowd	ProWeb	ProNonWeb
WP1/WP2/nWP	44/42/44	45/37/45	43/46/42
QiU1/QiU2/nQiU	42/44/45	45/45/46	42/40/44
RU1/RU2/nRU	44/45/43	47/50/43	42/41/42

Turning our attention to the ST dataset and the differences between the three groups of judges, we observe that the ProWeb judges have the highest agreement with click preferences (47%), see Figure 2c), i.e., they are the most successful at interpreting the real user needs. Interestingly, crowd workers perform better (45%) than the ProNonWeb judges (43%). On the other hand, we can also see that ProWeb judges show the highest insensitivity levels (34%), while crowd judges appear to be the most opinionated, resulting in 25% insensitive but also 30% incorrect preferences. Focusing only on the top two clicked URLs per query, we find that crowd workers are actually the best at agreeing with real users (41%), see Figure 2d). Similarly to NIST judges, we observe a high ratio of insensitivity for ProWeb judges (39%), which can signal the need for a finer grade scale or the judges' unwillingness to be more discriminative in their ratings. The latter is supported by the findings of skewed label probability distributions, favoring middle relevance grades (see Section 5.2).

Overall, for our cross-judge group experiments, we find so far that trained judges perform best both according to inter-assessor agreement levels and agreement with user clicks. At the same time, we also see emerging judging patterns that can indicate bias, as in the case of rating Wikipedia pages.

6.2 Ratings for Most Popular URLs

Next we focus our investigation on the most popular, in terms of clicks, URLs per query and calculate how likely it is that a given judge group rates the most clicked URL highly. We calculate two probabilities. The first one is the probability p_a of a judge assigning one of the two highest labels, e.g., Key (2) and Nav (3) in the WT set, to the URL that has the highest volume of clicks for the given query, where we limit to URLs with a minimum of 100 clicks for the WT set and over 1000 clicks for the ST set. Since for some queries, the most clicked URL may not actually be included in the judged set, it may not be reasonable to expect a high relevance grade. Thus, we calculate a second metric, p_r, which is the probability that a top clicked judged URL is labeled highest among the judged URLs for the query. Table 4 reports the obtained probability values.

On the WT data, we see that although judges in 2009 were less likely to rate popular URLs highly ($p_a = 0.24$) in absolute terms than in 2010 (0.48), they actually did better in labeling them relative to the less clicked URLs for the given query ($p_r = 0.68$ vs. 0.62). Broken down by WP/nWP, we find that the rating of highly clicked Wikipedia pages improved greatly in 2010 ($p_a = 0.53$ in 2010, up from 0.23; and $p_r = 0.75$, up from 0.71). Interestingly, the likelihood of rating a highly clicked nWP result highly in relative terms drops in 2010 to 0.53 from 0.67 in 2009. Thus, it seems that while NIST judges may have become better at rating popular Wikipedia pages in 2010, their accuracy in rating popular non-Wikipedia pages reduced.

On the ST data, we observe that both Crowd and ProWeb judges consistently label popular URLs highly. However, while crowd judges tend to give high grades in absolute terms to the most clicked URLs of a query ($p_a = 0.69$), they are less accurate in rating results relative to each other ($p_r = 0.59$). This is partly a result of crowd workers' leniency to assign high grades. ProWeb judges show a different tendency: they are more conservative in their ratings ($p_a = 0.61$), but their relative ratings correctly reward the popular URLs ($p_r = 0.77$). Judges trained in other tasks perform the worst against these measures. When broken down by WP/nWP, we see no differences in rating accuracy for crowd judges: $p_a \approx 0.70$ and $p_r \approx 0.60$ for both WP and nWP. ProWeb judges show a different behavior: they are more likely to assign top grades to highly clicked non-Wikipedia pages than for Wikipedia ($p_a = 0.66$ for nWP and 0.54 for WP). Despite this, they are more likely to assign the relative best label for a query to the highly clicked

WP results than to nWP results ($p_r = 0.82$ for WP and 0.75 for nWP). This suggests a slight tendency of ProWeb judges to underrate WP results compared to click evidence.

Table 4: Probability of a high grade relevance label (p_a) and (/) probability of relative highest grade label per query (p_r) being assigned to the highest clicked judged URL for the query

WT dataset	2009	2010	
All	0.24/0.68	0.48/0.62	
WP	0.23/0.71	0.53/0.75	
nWP	0.25/0.67	0.44/0.53	
ST dataset	Crowd	ProWeb	ProNonWeb
All	0.69/0.59	0.61/0.77	0.45/0.50
WP	0.70/0.60	0.54/0.82	0.38/0.51
nWP	0.68/0.59	0.66/0.75	0.50/0.50

6.3 Gold Label Set based Analysis

In this section we analyze the labels collected in our HQ set with respect to a gold label set contributed by highly trained Web (super) judges. Given a gold label, we calculate judging error as the distance between the relevance grades assigned by a judge and the gold label. Thus, for our five point scale, error can take a value in the range of [-4,4], where an error of -3 means that a judge underrated the given query-URL pair by 3 grades, e.g., labeling it as grade 1 when the gold label is grade 4. Figure 3 summarizes the error distributions per judge groups and features.

Overall, ProWeb judges are much more accurate while crowd workers are much more noisy against our gold set: crowd judges are less likely to have 0 error (only 31% on their labels are correct, compared with 73% for ProWeb). Crowd workers are also skewed towards overrating results: 25% of their labels fall in the +1 error category, compared with 10% for ProWeb judges.

Interestingly both judge groups show a tendency to overrate Wikipedia pages. For Crowd the label distribution peaks at +1 error for WP (37%). The probabilities to underrate, overrate or be correct are shown in Table 5. This confirms crowd workers' tendency to overrate, with especially high probabilities for WP, QiU and nRU results (p=0.68, 0.56 and 0.51, resp.). In contrast, ProWeb judges are more likely to underrate results overall. The only case where ProWeb judges are more likely to overrate is when the URL is a Wikipedia page (p(under)=0.05 and p(over)=0.14 for WP, compared with p(under)= 0.14 and p(over)=0.13 for nWP). This is interesting since as we saw earlier ProWeb judges tend to pick middle grade labels for WP results (Section 5.2), which then led to insensitivity compared to click evidence (Section 6.1), but show up as slight tendency to overrate according to the gold set. On the other hand, crowd workers are much more likely to grade leniently and overrate WP results according to the gold set, but achieve better agreement with click preferences. The different behaviors suggests possible guideline bias whereby ProWeb judges may learn to treat Wikipedia pages in a specific way, which, in this study, disagrees with the click evidence.

6.4 Regression analysis

Using the HQ gold set as target we fit a linear regression model over our query-URL feature set to determine which features have significant impact in the two judge groups.

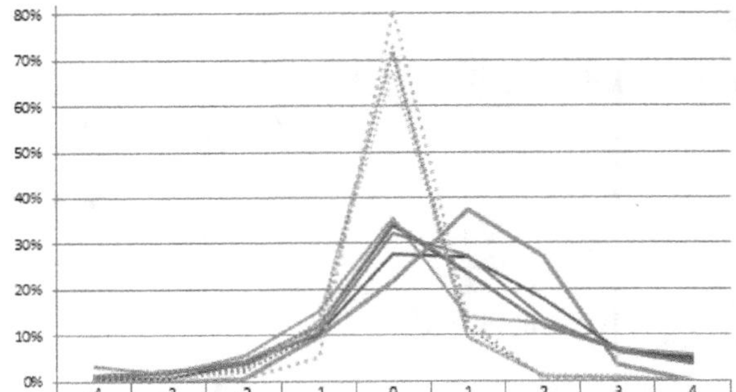

	-4	-3	-2	-1	0	1	2	3	4
Crowd nWP	1%	2%	4%	12%	34%	23%	12%	7%	4%
Crowd WP	0%	0%	1%	10%	22%	37%	27%	3%	0%
Crowd QiU	1%	1%	4%	10%	28%	27%	18%	6%	5%
Crowd nQiU	1%	2%	4%	12%	34%	24%	12%	7%	4%
Crowd RU	3%	2%	6%	15%	36%	14%	12%	7%	6%
Crowd nRU	1%	2%	4%	11%	32%	27%	14%	6%	4%
ProWeb nWP	1%	1%	3%	13%	71%	10%	1%	1%	0%
ProWeb WP	0%	0%	0%	5%	81%	13%	1%	0%	0%
ProWeb QiU	1%	1%	2%	10%	73%	12%	1%	1%	0%
ProWeb nQiU	1%	1%	3%	13%	72%	9%	1%	0%	0%
ProWeb RU	1%	2%	5%	11%	68%	10%	1%	1%	0%
ProWeb nRU	0%	1%	2%	13%	73%	10%	1%	0%	0%

Figure 3: Levels of judging error per query-document feature and judge group on the HQ set

Table 5: Probability to underrate, overrate or be correct when compared to gold label set per judge group and query-URL feature

Feature	p(under)	p(over)	p(correct)
	Crowd		
WP/nWP	0.10/0.20	**0.68**/0.47	0.22/0.34
QiU/nQiU	0.16/0.20	**0.56**/0.46	0.28/0.34
RU/nRU	0.26/0.17	0.39/**0.51**	0.36/0.32
	ProWeb		
WP/nWP	**0.05**/0.18	**0.14**/0.11	0.81/0.71
QiU/nQiU	0.14/0.17	0.13/0.11	0.72/0.68
RU/nRU	0.20/0.16	0.13/0.11	0.68/0.73

Table 6 shows that for ProWeb judges both WP/nWP and RU/nRU are significantly correlated to the gold label, although WP/nWP positively correlates while RU/nRU negatively. For Crowd, both QiU/nQiU and RU/nRU features have significant impact, QiU positively while RU negatively. Due to the bias in crowd workers to overrate Wikipedia pages, this feature is less predictive of the gold labels.

Looking at the predictive power of the various features for estimating the actual label that different judges would assign, we find that for both Crowd and ProWeb judges, the RU/nRU feature has the greatest impact(coefficient of 81 and 84, respectively), followed by WP/nWP (71 and 72) and finally QiU/nQiU (70 and 68), all significant.

Table 6: Regression coefficients per query-URL feature on the HQ set, * indicates $p_t < 0.001$**

Feature	Estimate	Std. Err.	p_t
	Crowd		
WP/nWP	-0.079	0.167	0.637
QiU/nQiU	0.253	0.108	0.019 *
RU/nRU	-0.306	0.114	***
	ProWeb		
WP/nWP	0.0124	0.017	***
QiU/nQiU	0.021	0.010	0.0467
RU/nRU	-0.184	0.010	***

7. IMPACT ON RANKER TRAINING

Even though judgments may be biased or noisy, they may not impact the training or evaluation of retrieval systems. To test whether judgments obtained from the different judges affect the training of ranking systems, we use the LambdaRank [4] learning to rank algorithm to train different rankers using judgments from all different judge groups and report the test set performance of each ranker when the judgments of the different judge groups are used to create the test set. We focus only on the WP/nWP feature here, which was found to be the most problematic to judge in the previous sections.

For our training experiments, we use five fold cross-validation, where the data is divided into five different parts. For each fold, three parts are used for training, and one part each for validation and testing. In Table 7, we report the average performance obtained over the five folds using NDCG at rank 10 as the test metric. Each row corresponds to training LambdaRank using judgments obtained from a given judge group. For each judge group, we train three different rankers using three different feature sets: (1) BM25, (2) WP, and (3) BM25 and WP. In the case of using just one feature such as BM25 or WP, our goal is to identify whether these features get a positive or negative weight during training. We use the ranker obtained using BM25 as the ranking feature as our baseline ranker and everything that is significantly different than this baseline is marked with a * (t-test, $p = 0.05$).

We see that rankers trained on the WP feature alone achieve a reasonable NDCG@10 performance for all training sets. If we focus on training and testing on judgments obtained from the NIST judges, it can be seen that the test set performance obtained using the WP feature alone is significantly better than test set performance obtained using BM25 (0.5518 vs. 0.5257). Using BM25 together with the WP feature in training does not result in much further improvement over when using the WP feature alone (0.5518 vs. 0.5564). This suggests that there is an extremely strong Wikipedia bias for NIST judges.

In the case of ProWeb judges, training on the WP feature alone obtains significantly worse performance than training on the BM25 feature (0.6623 vs. 0.7335). When the WP feature is used together with BM25, we see only small improvements over the baseline.

The effect of Wikipedia bias seems the weakest for crowd judges: using the WP feature alone results in worse performance than the baseline (though difference is not statistically significant). However, using the BM25 and WP features together does not seem to make much difference in the test set performance.

These results show that ranker training and evaluation can indeed be affected by the different judgment biases. For example, a Web Track run that ranks Wikipedia documents containing query terms at the top is likely to achieve good performance when evaluated on the NIST judgments.

When NDCG values across different datasets are compared, one can see that the range of NDCG scores obtained can vary highly depending on which judge group is used in the test set (higher NDCG values are obtained using the ProWeb judgments in the test set). On the other hand, when training on judgments obtained from different judge groups is compared, the test set values do not seem to differ much. So, the judges seem to be replaceable for the purposes of creating training data.

Table 7: NDCG10 results using different ground-truth sets by the different judge groups, * indicates significant with p<0.05

Training labels	BM25	WP/nWP	BM25+WP/nWP
NIST labels as test set			
NIST	0.5257	0.5518*	0.5564*
ProWeb	0.5257	0.5518*	0.5583*
Crowd	0.5257	0.5518*	0.6011*
ProWeb labels as test set			
NIST	0.7335	0.6623*	0.7409*
ProWeb	0.7335	0.6623*	0.7335
Crowd	0.7335	0.6623*	0.7409*
Crowd labels as test set			
NIST	0.6566	0.6369	0.6582
ProWeb	0.6566	0.6369	0.6566
Crowd	0.6566	0.6369	0.6583

8. CONCLUSIONS

Past studies have shown that changes in judging procedures can change the outcome of experiments. With an increasing use of crowdsourcing for IR relevance judging, it becomes even more important to consider judge quality. When judging procedures do affect outcomes, tools are needed not only to detect such differences, but to understand which procedure was correct, what systematic errors occurred, and how to make progress on improving procedures.

In this paper, we investigated several methods for comparing different populations of judges and their judgments. Agreement with consensus can be used, and broken down into sub-cases based on features of the query-document, like whether the document is from Wikipedia. However a greater agreement on Wikipedia documents could either indicate reduced noise or could mean for example that judges adopted a rule of thumb or used a smaller range of labels for Wikipedia pages. For this reason we introduced gold set analysis, using clicks and labels.

Using a click-based gold set, we can identify cases where real users of a system have a preference, and check the level of agreement with judges. If a test collection is seen as a user model, and if click preferences on average reflect the preferences of real users, then judgments that agree more often with click preferences give us a better user model. In our comparison of judgments with the top two clicked URLs, we found agreement most often from crowd workers. This result bears more investigation in future, whether the population of crowd judges are representative of the population of clicking users.

Using a labeled gold set, we can identify difficult cases where judges are likely to make mistakes, then take care to identify the label we would like to see from judges. We can measure the calibration and noisiness of judges with respect such a set. We can also repeat the breakdown by features. In our HQ gold set experiments we identified crowd judges as being more likely to overrate Wikipedia pages. If we trust our gold judgments, that the Crowd really have this systematic bias, then we can change the interface or instructions to try and correct for this

Our ranking experiments demonstrated that systematic differences in labeling can lead to differences in ranker training and evaluation. For a ranking system optimized against training data, this allows us to draw a connection between differences that exist in the relevance judging procedures and differences in the characteristics of the ranking seen by end users.

Overall this paper has demonstrated a number of approaches for analyzing relevance judgments, beyond just inter-judge agreement. We have analyzed multiple populations of judges and found different cases of systematic judging error. In the context of machine learned ranking, which is powerful enough to reproduce biased results if given biased training judgments, reducing systematic errors is particularly important. We have demonstrated empirically that different characteristics of training sets lead to different learned rankers.

Through methods such as those introduced in this paper, it may be possible to track the ability of judges to agree with real users, and follow to judging guidelines. This could lead to better training and measurement of real-world IR systems, but also IR research conducted with the confidence that the test collection models a real-world search task.

9. REFERENCES

[1] O. Alonso and R. Baeza-Yates. Design and implementation of relevance assessments using crowdsourcing. In *Proc. of the 33rd European Conference on Advances in Information Retrieval*, ECIR'11, pages 153–164. Springer-Verlag, 2011.

[2] P. Bailey, N. Craswell, I. Soboroff, P. Thomas, A. P. de Vries, and E. Yilmaz. Relevance assessment: are judges exchangeable and does it matter. In *Proc. of the 31st International ACM SIGIR Conference on Research and Development in Information Retrieval*, SIGIR '08, pages 667–674. ACM, 2008.

[3] P. Borlund. The concept of relevance in IR. *Journal of the American Society for Information Science and Technology*, 54(10):913–925, May 2003.

[4] C. J. C. Burges, R. Ragno, and Q. V. Le. Learning to rank with nonsmooth cost functions. In *NIPS*, pages 193–200. MIT Press, 2006.

[5] B. Carterette and I. Soboroff. The effect of assessor error on IR system evaluation. In *Proc. of the 33rd International ACM SIGIR Conference on Research and Development in Information Retrieval*, SIGIR '10, pages 539–546. ACM, 2010.

[6] C. L. Clarke, N. Craswell, I. Soboroff, and A. Ashkan. A comparative analysis of cascade measures for novelty and diversity. In *Proceedings of the fourth ACM international conference on Web search and data mining*, WSDM '11, pages 75–84. ACM, 2011.

[7] C. Cuadra and R. Katter. The relevance of relevance assessment. *Proc. of the American Documentation Institute*, page 95âĂŞ99.

[8] A. P. Dawid and A. M. Skene. Maximum likelihood estimation of observer error-rates using the em algorithm. *Journal of the Royal Statistical Society. Series C (Applied Statistics)*, pages 20–28.

[9] C. Grady and M. Lease. Crowdsourcing document relevance assessment with mechanical turk. In *Proc. of the NAACL HLT 2010 Workshop on Creating Speech and Language Data with Amazon's Mechanical Turk*, pages 172–179, 2010.

[10] D. Hawking and N. Craswell. The very large collection and web tracks. In E. Voorhees and D. Harman, editors, *TREC: Experiment and Evaluation in Information Retrieval*. MIT Press, 2005.

[11] J. Howe. *Crowdsourcing: Why the Power of the Crowd Is Driving the Future of Business*. Crown Publishing Group, New York, NY, USA, 1 edition, 2008.

[12] P. G. Ipeirotis, F. Provost, and J. Wang. Quality management on amazon mechanical turk. In *Proc. of the ACM SIGKDD Workshop on Human Computation*, HCOMP '10, pages 64–67. ACM, 2010.

[13] K. H. Jiyin He, Krisztian Balog and E. Meij. Heuristic ranking and diversification of web documents. In *TREC*, 2009.

[14] G. Kazai, J. Kamps, M. Koolen, and N. Milic-Frayling. Crowdsourcing for book search evaluation: impact of HIT design on comparative system ranking. In *Proc. of the 34th International ACM SIGIR Conference on Research and Development in Information Retrieval*, SIGIR '11, pages 205–214. ACM, 2011.

[15] K. A. Kinney, S. B. Huffman, and J. Zhai. How evaluator domain expertise affects search result relevance judgments. In *Proc. of the 17th ACM Conference on Information and Knowledge Management*, CIKM '08, pages 591–598. ACM, 2008.

[16] E. Pronin. Perception and misperception of bias in human judgment. *Trends in cognitive sciences*, 11(1):37–43, 2007.

[17] T. Saracevic. Relevance: A review of the literature and a framework for thinking on the notion in information science. part iii: Behavior and effects of relevance. *J. Am. Soc. Inf. Sci. Technol.*, 58(13):2126–2144, Nov. 2007.

[18] F. Scholer, A. Turpin, and M. Sanderson. Quantifying test collection quality based on the consistency of relevance judgements. In *Proc. of the 34th International ACM SIGIR Conference on Research and Development in Information Retrieval*, SIGIR '11, pages 1063–1072. ACM, 2011.

[19] E. M. Voorhees. Variations in relevance judgments and the measurement of retrieval effectiveness. In *Proc. of the 21st International ACM SIGIR Conference on Research and Development in Information Retrieval*, SIGIR '98, pages 315–323. ACM, 1998.

[20] E. M. Voorhees. Evaluation by highly relevant documents. In *Proc. of the 24th International ACM SIGIR Conference on Research and Development in Information Retrieval*, SIGIR '01, pages 74–82. ACM, 2001.

[21] E. M. Voorhees and D. K. Harman, editors. *TREC: Experimentation and Evaluation in Information Retrieval*. MIT Press, 2005.

[22] W. Webber, D. W. Oard, F. Scholer, and B. Hedin. Assessor error in stratified evaluation. In *Proc. of the 19th ACM International Conference on Information and Knowledge Management*, CIKM '10, pages 539–548. ACM, 2010.

On Caption Bias in Interleaving Experiments

Katja Hofmann*
ISLA, University of Amsterdam
k.hofmann@uva.nl

Fritz Behr
Microsoft
fritzb@microsoft.com

Filip Radlinski
Microsoft
filiprad@microsoft.com

ABSTRACT

Information retrieval evaluation most often involves manually assessing the relevance of particular query-document pairs. In cases where this is difficult (such as personalized search), interleaved comparison methods are becoming increasingly common. These methods compare pairs of ranking functions based on user clicks on search results, thus better reflecting true user preferences. However, by depending on clicks, there is a potential for bias. For example, users have been previously shown to be more likely to click on results with attractive titles and snippets. An interleaving evaluation where one ranker tends to generate results that attract more clicks (without being more relevant) may thus be biased.

We present an approach for detecting and compensating for this type of bias in interleaving evaluations. Introducing a new model of caption bias, we propose features that model bias based on (1) per-document effects, and (2) the (pairwise) relationships between a document and surrounding documents. We show that our model can effectively capture click behavior, with best results achieved by a model that combines both per-document and pairwise features. Applying this model to re-weight observed user clicks, we find a small overall effect on real interleaving comparisons, but also identify a case where initially detected preferences vanish after caption bias re-weighting is applied. Our results indicate that our model of caption bias is effective and can successfully identify interleaving experiments affected by caption bias.

Categories and Subject Descriptors

H.3 [**Information Storage and Retrieval**]: H.3.3 Information Search and Retrieval

Keywords: Interleaving, Implicit feedback, Evaluation

1. INTRODUCTION

Most information retrieval (IR) evaluation methods rely on manual relevance assessments of query-document pairs [26, 30]. When used to evaluate Web search retrieval functions, such an evaluation assumes that assessors can reliably infer users' information needs from very limited information (usually only the queries). Accurately making such inferences may be difficult for ambiguous queries, and even more so in settings where relevance can vary widely by user, such as personalized or localized search.

In settings where such relevance assessment is difficult, interleaved comparison methods are a promising alternative [4, 19]. These methods compare two retrieval functions (also called rankers) by presenting users with a list of results that combines documents returned by the two rankers, inferring preferences based on users' clicks. Because interleaving can be applied transparently to all results shown to users, and Web search engines can collect click data at low cost, interleaving offers a scalable way of performing evaluation that reflects true user needs and preferences.

A drawback of current interleaving methods is that they do not account for potential click bias introduced by effects of result presentation (in particular Web result captions), rather assuming that this bias affects all rankers equally.[1] Users' click behavior is known to be influenced by e.g., highlighting [32], as well as URL length, the occurrence of the query in result titles, and other aspects of result presentation [5]. Thus, rankers that rank results with these characteristics highly may attract more clicks than warranted by the quality of the ranking, thereby biasing interleaving outcomes.

This is the problem that we address in this paper: How are interleaving outcomes affected by differences in result presentation in practice? On the one hand, as previous work has assumed, caption bias may affect rankers equally. This would increase variance in evaluation but not introduce bias. On the other hand, typical ranker optimization changes may affect captions (for example, by favoring titles with more highlighting), thereby creating a systematic bias. When interleaving methods are applied to measure preferences between rankers, it is important to be able to identify both when bias may be occurring, and to be able to avoid this bias. Specifically, our contributions are:

1. We introduce a general probabilistic approach for modeling caption bias in user clicks.
2. We propose two types of features to instantiate this model based on (1) an assumption that caption bias independently affects clicks on each document, and (2) modeling interactions between caption effects on nearby documents.
3. We apply this approach to real interleaving experiments, finding that the method identifies caption bias when expected and produces de-biased interleaving outcomes.

*Most of this research was done while the author was at Microsoft.

[1] We use *click bias* to refer to any characteristic of a search result that systematically influences click behavior in such a way that a result receives more or fewer clicks than would be warranted by the item's content-based relevance to the query alone. We use *caption bias* to refer to forms of click bias related to the visual presentation of results on a search result page.

CIKM'12, October 29–November 2, 2012, Maui, HI, USA.

The results of our analysis have implications for how and in what cases interleaving methods can be applied in practice. In particular, our work contributes to better understanding IR evaluation using interleaving methods, and making them more reliable and robust. Further, to the best of our knowledge, this is the first work on compensating for caption bias in interleaving methods.

The remainder of this paper is organized as follows. We give an overview of related work in Section 2 and detail our approach in Section 3. Our experiments and results are presented in Section 4.

2. RELATED WORK

In this section we review related work on using click behavior for IR evaluation (§2.1), then consider interleaving in particular (§2.2). Finally, we review prior work on caption bias (§2.3).

2.1 Click Based Evaluation

User behavior as captured by clicks on Web search results is a rich source of information on user preferences. Clicks are part of the natural interaction between users and Web search engines, and in comparison to other types of feedback can be collected in large quantities at very low cost. Consequently, a large body of work has focused on using click behavior both to improve search result quality (e.g., [1, 2, 8, 19, 28]), and to infer information about users' satisfaction with the search results (e.g., [3, 21, 25]). An overview of a large variety of other types of implicit feedback, in addition to click behavior, was presented by Kelly and Teevan [22].

It has also long been apparent that click data is strongly biased, in particular by the position of documents in the presented result list (i.e., by position bias, cf., 2.3). For instance, top-ranked Web search results are clicked much more frequently than lower-ranked results, even in the absence of a strong difference in relevance (e.g., [20]). In the context of evaluation, it has also been found that clicks vary considerably between users and between search tasks [27]. This means that clicks cannot be interpreted as absolute judgments beyond certain narrow settings (e.g., [16]).

2.2 Interleaving Methods

A solution to the problem of position bias in particular is to interpret clicks as relative preferences, either between a pair of documents [19, 24] or a pair of retrieval functions [20, 25, 31]. For example, a higher-ranked document that was not clicked can be interpreted as likely less relevant than a lower-ranked document that was clicked by the user. This relative interpretation was found to be much more reliable than absolute interpretations [20].

Based on the relative comparison intuition, interleaving combines search results from two competing rankers and presents these to the user. The results are selected so that it is likely that a user who clicks on more relevant results will be interpreted as preferring the ranker that places more relevant ranks highly, while a randomly clicking user will be interpreted as preferring neither. For instance, given two rankings A and B produced by retrieval functions r_A and r_B for a given query, Team Draft interleaving [25] iteratively creates a combined list as follows: Toss a fair coin. If r_A wins the coin toss, its top result is selected as the first result in the combined list and then the first different result from B is selected as the second result in the combined list. Conversely, if r_B wins the coin toss, r_B selects first and then r_A. This toss-then-two-selections is repeated (each time finding the first result in each ranker that is different from all previously selected results) until sufficiently many results are in the combined list. When users are presented with the combined list, clicks are mapped back to the ranker that selected each clicked result. The ranker that selected the larger number of clicked results is deemed to "win" the comparison for this query.

Note that interleaving involves showing each user results returned by both retrieval functions, allowing the user's selection process to provide evidence as to which retrieval function, in expectation, returns relevant results more often. By doing this direct comparison, interleaving has been shown to be more sensitive than alternative approaches. Radlinski and Craswell [23] compared the reliability and sensitivity of Team Draft interleaving to judgement-based evaluation in a Web search setting, and Chapelle et al. [4] provide a detailed comparison and evaluation of several interleaving approaches. Alternative interleaving approaches have also been proposed [20], as well as alternative scoring approaches [15]. However, it has been shown that all these interleaving algorithms may potentially be affected by position bias in subtle cases [17, 25]. These biases are addressed by the Probabilistic Interleave approach, recently developed by Hofmann et al. [17]. Probabilistic Interleave has favorable theoretical properties, but has not yet been evaluated in a real search setting.

Probabilistic Interleave is based on a probabilistic formulation of Team Draft interleaving. First, rather than always allowing both rankers to select a document after a coin toss, only the ranker winning the coin toss selects the next document. Second, rather than always selecting the next-highest ranked document from the winning ranker, Probabilistic Interleave selects documents with frequency decaying in the position of the document. Finally, instead of a document being assigned to the ranker that selected each document shown to users, Probabilistic Interleave computes all possible coin toss sequences that could have generated the list of results shown to users, and computes the preference between rankers as an expectation across these possible coin toss sequences.

2.3 Click Behavior and Caption Bias

While clicks are becoming more popular as a source of preference indications on search results, a number of studies have found that click behavior is affected by bias. In this section we give a brief overview of the types of bias previously found to affect users' click behavior in Web search.

In the context of interleaved comparisons, position bias has been addressed. Position bias results from the layout of a search result page. Because users generally expect more relevant items to be listed at the top of a page, and because people are used to reading pages from top to bottom, top-ranked results are typically the most likely to be examined. This phenomenon was first confirmed in eye-tracking studies such as [11, 12]. Craswell et al. [6] developed models of user behavior to describe position bias, and described a cascade model to explain this effect. The model was refined in several follow-up studies, e.g., to account for multiple clicks on the same result page [14], and to account for differences in click behavior for different types of queries and search goals [13].

In addition to position bias, which reflects *where* on the page a result was displayed, click behavior is also affected by caption bias, caused by *how* the result was displayed. Clarke et al. [5] studied caption bias by comparing features and click behavior on pairs of search results. They found that results were more often clicked on when they had longer snippets, shorter URLs, more query terms matching the caption, matches of the whole query as a phrase, if the caption was more readable, or if it contained the term "official" or terms related to images. Yue et al. [32] compared click data on result documents that were sampled to minimize position bias using the Fair Pairs approach [24] to editorial judgments. They identified a bias towards captions that included more highlighted (bold) terms, i.e., items with more bold terms would be clicked more frequently than similar results with fewer bold terms.

Other factors affecting click behavior include the domain of the search result [18], whether or not search results are grouped (e.g., by intent) [9], page loading time [31], the amount of context shown in the snippet [29], and the relation between task and result caption [7]. In this work we focus on effects of visual factors that are most common in a Web search setting. However, our approach is generally applicable to other sources of click bias.

3. METHOD

Our method is based on the following idea: when assigning credit for clicks to rankers in an interleaving experiment, the credit can be re-weighted to reflect a likelihood of the user clicking on the result based on just caption bias. This is similar to the ideas presented in [4, 32], although here we focus on improving the fidelity rather than the sensitivity of interleaving experiments.

We will re-weight clicks by the inverse of their caption-based click probability. Results that are very likely to be clicked due simply to visual characteristics receive a low weight, while higher weights are assigned to results whose representation is less likely to attract clicks. Thus, clicks on relatively less "clickable" results are taken to provide a more reliable indication of relevance, while more "clickable" results are considered prone to attracting clicks unwarranted by their relevance and receive a lower weight. This principle is implemented in the following 3-step approach: (1) model the probability of a click as a combination of position, relevance and caption bias, (2) learn the weights of this model using observations of past user behavior, and then (3) factor out the caption bias component from interleaving evaluations to make clicks better reflect relevance. We now detail each of these three steps.

3.1 Modeling Caption Bias

The first step is to model caption bias. To obtain an interpretable model, we choose to model the probability of a click using a simple model of the form

$$P(C|X_r, X_p, X_c) = [1 + exp(-W_r X_r - W_p X_p - W_c X_c)]^{-1} \quad (1)$$

Here, $P(C|X_r, X_p, X_c)$ denotes the probability of a click on a result document, that is characterized by relevance features X_r, position features X_p, and caption features X_c. We train the parameters of this model, W_r, W_p, and W_c, using logistic regression. We note that while a model that takes into account non-linear combinations of bias features may produce somewhat more accurate results, this model is easy to interpret, less prone to overfitting than more complex models, and was found to perform well when validated on the task of predicting clicks (cf., Section 4.2).

Note that only caption features X_c are used when applying the model to compensate for caption bias (cf., Section 3.4). The remaining features are included during model training only, to remove effects of document relevance and position when training the components of weight vector W_c. In this way we obtain a model of a document's click likelihood given its presentation. The caption features used in this study are detailed in Section 3.2 below.

For model training, relevance and position features are formulated as follows: $X_r(q, d)$ models the relevance of a document d to a query q as a vector of five binary features. They represent standard 5-point relevance judgments that range from "not relevant" to "highly relevant". Our position features X_p follow the formulation in [32]. Specifically, we use six binary indicator features that indicate whether each document was presented at rank 1, 2, 3, 4 to 5, 6 to 9, or 10 and below.

In a preliminary study, we also considered two alternative approaches. First, we assessed document-wise models that do not take into account relevance information, but simply model caption bias using visual and position features. However, we found that models that do take relevance into account model click behavior more accurately. Second, we evaluated a pairwise model that predicted which of two documents was more likely to be clicked, based on features that captured visual differences between them (i.e., predicting $P(Click_A > Click_B)$ for two candidate documents A and B, similarly to Clarke et al. [5] and Yue et al. [32]). Here, we found the per-document formulation in Equation 1 to be much more effective in explaining click behavior, and therefore focus on this model in the rest of this work. Nevertheless, we found that pairwise features, that capture the relationship between the document for which clicks are predicted and its neighboring documents, can be combined with our per-document model to further improve performance (implemented as pairwise features, cf., Section 3.2).

3.2 Caption Bias Features

We use two types of visual features to model caption bias in X_c: per-document features and pairwise features. We now introduce each in turn. For all features, we assume a standard result page of a Web search engine. Results are displayed with title, URL, and a snippet that shows how each document relates to the user's query.

Per-Document Caption Features

Our per-document features are designed to capture characteristics of individual search result captions, and model aspects that may make them likely to attract (or discourage) user clicks. We started with the features investigated in Clarke et al [5], such as *short snippet*, *term matches in the title*, and *URL length*.

From the initial set of features, we restricted our features to those that we believed may capture visual characteristics relevant to our task, yet not likely to be strongly affected by document relevance. In an initial study we found a statistically significant effect of e.g., the number of query term matches with the document title, and the number of phrase matches with the snippet on click behavior. However, we were not confident that these effects were not strongly affected by the rankers used to collect our training data. E.g., a ranker may over- or under-emphasize the importance of matches in the document title, while the 5-point relevance judgments (cf., §3.1) used to remove major effects of relevance may not be sufficiently fine-grained to compensate for these ranker effects. To avoid contamination of our caption bias model with such ranker effects, we decided to remove features for which these were a concern.

We binarized all per-document features to avoid cases where the model would be dominated by individual unbounded values. For each "raw" feature (e.g., title length), we started with natural thresholds, such as the first and third quartile, the mean, and points identified by visual inspection of the feature's histogram. Next, binary features representing these bins were added to a model of document relevance and position, which was then trained using logistic regression. The thresholds were then manually tuned to maximize the model's fit to the training data (i.e., thresholds were increased and decreased and the model re-trained, until the magnitude of the residuals from the fitted model did not decrease further).

Finally, all constructed binary features were combined in one model, and features that did not have a significant effect on the models' prediction (measured using a χ^2 test, and $p < 0.001$) were removed from the model. In this step we reduced the number of features from 25 to the final set of 10 per-document features.

Our per-document features are presented in Table 1. The feature *deep links* refers to links to sub-sections of a website that are grouped under a main title result as illustrated in Figure 1. We included this feature because a strong relation with click behavior was found, and this type of presentation is common to most major

Feature	Description
Deep links	The result was presented with deep links
Short URL	The length of the displayed URL is 30 or less characters
URL slashes	The URL of the presented result contains more than 5 slashes
URL bold	The presented URL has more than 1 highlighted section
Short title	The presented title consisted of less than 3 words
Long title	The presented title consisted of more than 7 words
Title start	The title begins with an exact match of the query
Title bold	The title contained more than 2 highlighted sections
Short snippet	The displayed snippet was shorter than 40 characters
Long snippet	The displayed snippet was longer than 170 characters

Table 1: Per-document features for capturing visual characteristics of individual result captions.

Feature	Description
Δ URL length above / below	The difference between the length of the URL of the current document and of the document ranked immediately above it / immediately below it
Δ URL slashes above / below	The difference in the number of slashes in the URL
Δ URL bold above / below	The difference in the number of words highlighted in the URL
Δ title length above / below	The difference in title length (in characters or words)
Δ title bold above / below	The difference in the number of highlighted words or sections in the title
Δ snippet length above / below	The difference in the length of the snippet (in characters or words)
Δ snippet bold above / below	The difference in the number of highlighted words or sections in the snippet

Table 2: Pairwise visual features for capturing caption bias.

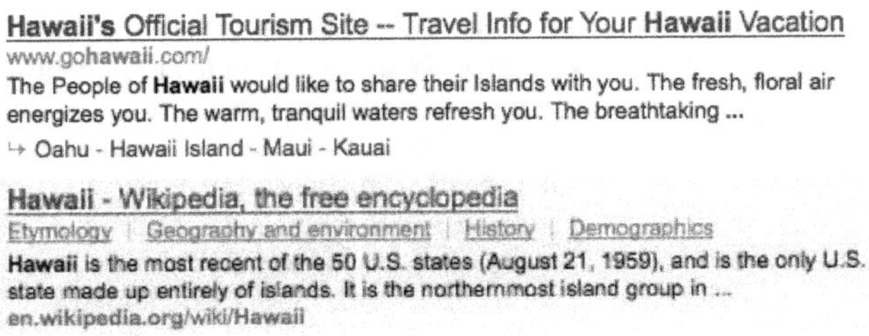

Figure 1: Example search results of two commercial Web search engines, with deep links included in addition to the title link.

Web search engines. The length-related features *short URL*, *short title*, *long title*, *short snippet*, and *long snippet* were converted to binary values as described above. For longer URLs, the number of slashes was found more informative than the number of characters. Similarly, for title length, the number of words was more informative than the number of characters. For snippet length, we note that the threshold for *short snippets* corresponds to roughly half a line of text, while the threshold for *long snippets* corresponds to a length where the text would flow onto a third line.

Here, we only list the final features and exclude features where no significant effect on click behavior was detected (e.g., highlighting in the snippet). In addition to those listed, we initially tested the following features proposed in earlier studies [5]: the number of query term matches with the title, snippet, and URL respectively, and the respective number of phrase matches. However, because our models were developed to specifically capture changes in click behavior due to visual characteristics, we removed these features that may be more strongly affected by document content.

Pairwise Caption Features

Our second set of features considers not individual documents, but pairs of documents. The intuition behind these features is that documents presented in response to a query attract clicks not only based on their own representations, but also depending on other, surrounding documents. For example, a somewhat attractive result may attract clicks when placed next to a poorly presented result, but may not get much attention when placed next to a result with a better presentation. Although we found per-document models to perform better individually, we hypothesized that click behavior could best be captured by a combination of characteristics of a document's own representation, and those of surrounding documents.

As for our per-document features, we avoided unbounded features to prevent individual features from dominating the model (this may happen when e.g., directly including the difference in URL length). We achieved this by encoding all pairwise features as ternary values (i.e., with possible values $(-1, 0, 1)$. Thus, e.g., the feature Δ *URL length above* would be -1 if the URL length of the current document is less than that of the document ranked immediately above it, 0 if there was no difference, and 1 if the URL was longer than that of the document ranked above it.

A complete list of the pairwise features investigated is provided in Table 2. The features Δ *title bold above / below (in words)* and Δ *snippet bold above / below (in words)* are designed to capture relationships between neighboring documents that are as close as possible to those explored in [32], so that effects found here can be compared to this earlier work. In addition, we include features that capture differences in highlighting of the URL, and consider the number of highlighted sections (e.g., phrases) in addition to that of individual words. Finally, we add features capturing the length differences of URL, title, and snippet. As for the document-wise features, we exclude features based on term matches, to focus on visual aspects of the search result captions.

3.3 Interleaving Methods

We apply our caption bias models to Team Draft [23, 25] and a variant of Probabilistic Interleave [17]. We describe both below, focusing on how each method aggregates clicks observed within a search result page to infer a comparison outcome, as this is the component that is affected by our caption re-weighting mechanism.

Our implementation of the Team Draft method follows [4]. As explained above, for each observed query an interleaved result list is generated and presented to the user (cf., Section 2.2). User clicks on result documents are observed and then mapped back to the ranker that contributed the corresponding documents. Then, given n observed samples (q, C_A, C_B), where $q \in Q$ is a query, and C_A and C_B are the sets of documents clicked that were contributed by ranker A and B respectively, our first scoring function for comparing ranked lists is defined as the mean of observed click differences:

$$\Delta_{TD} = \frac{1}{n}\sum_{i=1}^{n}(|C_{A_i}| - |C_{B_i}|). \qquad (2)$$

This scoring function is equivalent to the aggregation method called Δ_{click} in [4]. Note that in earlier work, click preferences were re-centered to let a value of 0.5 denote "no preference" (i.e., the rankers are inferred to perform equally well). Then, a win for ranker A is detected if the observed score is statistically significantly higher than 0.5. Here we follow the same convention, and report all scores centered around 0.5. Finally, we ignore clicks on documents above the first document for which the ranked lists produced by A and B differ, to reduce variance [4, 23].

Our implementation of Probabilistic Interleave is a variant of the method originally proposed in [17]. In particular, we use the same interleaving process as Team Draft (that is, we do not interleave probabilistically) to minimize effects on user experience. However, we compute comparison outcomes as if Probabilistic Interleave had been used. This results in comparisons that weight clicks by the magnitude of the difference in position between rankers. For example, a ranker would gain a small win (in terms of weighted click) for moving a document up by one rank, and a large win when the clicked document was moved up from a much lower rank.

Next, we define the scoring function for Probabilistic Interleave. In contrast to the Team Draft method, we now do not observe the number of clicks attributed to each ranker, but instead observe a vector C, that indicates which documents of the interleaved list were clicked. This is done so that click counts can be obtained for all possible combinations in which rankers could have contributed documents to the interleaved list. Individually, such a combination of contributing rankers is called an *assignment* $g \in G$. For example, an assignment could be $[A, B, B, A]$, denoting that, for a ranked list of length 4, the first and last documents were contributed by ranker A, and the remaining documents were contributed by B. Further, we use C_{A_g} to denote the number of clicks in C that would be obtained by ranker A when assuming assignment g.

We can then define a scoring function for Probabilistic Interleave that marginalizes over all possible assignments for n observed samples consisting each of a query q, an interleaved list l, and a click vector c, and weights the score for each assignment by its probability $P(g|l_i, q_i)$:

$$\Delta_{PI} = \frac{1}{n}\sum_{i=1}^{n}\sum_{g\in G}(|C_{A_g}| - |C_{B_g}|)P(g|l_i, q_i). \qquad (3)$$

As in [17], we compute this quantity using $P(G|L,Q) = P(L|G, Q)\ P(G|Q)/P(L|Q)$, where $P(G|Q) = P(G) = 1/|G|$, and $P(L|G,Q) = \prod_{r=1}^{|L|} P(L[r]|G[d], L[1, r-1], Q)$. Here, $P(L[r])$ is the probability of observing document $L[r]$ at rank r of an interleaved list L for query Q, given that it was contributed by the ranker specified in the assignment, i.e., $G[r]$; and documents $L[1, r-1]$ have already been placed in L. Finally, we define the probability of a document inversely proportional to its cubed rank, as in [17].

3.4 Re-weighting clicks

We now come to the key innovation of our approach, namely correcting the outcome of interleaving experiments for the effect of caption bias.

Specifically, for each click by a user, rather than summing up all clicks for each query giving equal weight to each click, we credit each ranker inversely proportionally to the estimated probability of a click based just on the caption shown:

$$\alpha = [exp(W_c \cdot X_c)]^{-1}, \qquad (4)$$

where X_c is the vector of all visual features of the document (i.e., rank and relevance are ignored), and W_c is the weight vector as obtained by the trained regression model. This weighting scheme is a direct application of regression models, where weights for each feature reflect the ratio of the click likelihood for a document given the feature value as opposed to a document without that feature.

For example, consider a result with a very short URL (i.e., *short URL* is true), and 3 highlighted sections in the displayed result title (*title bold*). Also, assume that the estimated weights for these features, obtained from the model, are 0.4 and 0.7. Then, the weight for this document is $\alpha = 1/exp(1.1) = 0.3329$. This low weight indicates that the result was much more likely to be clicked than other documents (as the weight is much lower than 1), hence should contribute little to the outcome of the interleaving experiment.

Given the caption bias weights predicted by our model, we adjust our scoring functions to apply re-weighting as follows.

$$\Delta_{W-TD} = \frac{1}{n}\sum_{i=1}^{n}\left(\sum_{c\in C_{A_i}} \alpha_c \cdot c - \sum_{c\in C_{B_i}} \alpha_c \cdot c\right). \qquad (5)$$

Thus, this weighted Team Draft scoring function applies the caption bias click weight to each observed click before aggregating over those clicks.

For Probabilistic Interleave, the scoring function becomes:

$$\Delta_{W-PI} = \frac{1}{n}\sum_{i=1}^{n}\sum_{g\in G}\left(\sum_{c\in C_{A_g}} \alpha_c \cdot c - \sum_{c\in C_{B_g}} \alpha_c \cdot c\right) P(g|l_i, q_i). \qquad (6)$$

Our method for modeling caption bias and applying the resulting model to obtain re-weighted interleaving scores is experimentally validated in the next section.

4. EXPERIMENTS AND RESULTS

In this section we detail our experimental setup and results in three parts. First, we focus on training caption bias models (4.1). Results of this step give insights into the features that were found to be useful for explaining click behavior and their relative importance. Second, we assess the quality of the trained models, by comparing their predictions to observed click behavior (4.2). Third, we show how our caption bias models can be applied to infer user preferences from clicks (4.3). Finally, we apply our best-performing caption-bias model to interleaving experiments and analyze its effect on experiment outcomes (4.4).

4.1 Modeling Caption Bias

In our first experiment we train several instantiations of our caption bias model as defined in Equation 1. Analyzing which visual features contribute to explaining click behavior, and what their relative importance is in each of the models, allows us to better understand the observed caption bias. In this experiment we consider the following instantiations of our model:

- **highlighting** - uses only pairwise highlighting features, similar to [32]
- **document-wise** - uses the per-document features in Table 1
- **pairwise** - uses only the pairwise features listed in Table 2
- **combined** - considers all visual features in Tables 1 and 2

All four models were trained on a sample of log data obtained from a large commercial Web search engine. The data is a random sample of queries and result pages collected on February 16, 2012. To account for the effect of relevance, the log data was intersected with a large set of previously collected relevance judgments (standard 5-point scale). This intersection resulted in approximately 420,000 (non-unique) query-URL pairs.

Note that, due to the intersection with relevance judgments, our training data set does not constitute a random sample. Rather, the use of previously collected judgments introduced bias in the data set, as more judgments were available for e.g., frequent queries, and for documents that were previously ranked highly by the search engine. However, this bias only affects our training data, and not the data sets used for evaluation and analysis.

The weights for our trained models are shown in Table 3. Recall that when we apply our model of caption features to re-weighting clicks, we only use the weights of the caption features to determine the relative change in click attractiveness, and ignore position and relevance features (cf., Eq. 4). Therefore, we only report and analyze the regression weights for these visual features.

For the *highlighting* model, we find a relatively weak effect for all included features. URL bolding has a positive effect (i.e., more bold increases the click likelihood of a result), but only when compared to the document ranked below. Increased highlighting in the title always increases click probabilities, and this effect is stronger than that of highlighting in the snippet (in agreement with [32]). For increased highlighting in the snippet, a small negative effect is detected, which may be caused by easily identifiable caption spam.

For the *document-wise* model we identify several features that have a strong correlation with click behavior. The highest regression weight is obtained for our deep links feature. This result matches our observation that results with deep links tend to attract more clicks (even on the title link), perhaps because they take up more space on the result page. For highlighting in the result title, a much stronger effect is observed than for the pairwise version of this feature. Finally, click probability is found to decrease for URLs with many slashes, and for short snippets, as expected.

Results for the *pairwise* model are similar, although the trained weights are larger in magnitude. For URL length, a negative impact is detected when the current result has a longer URL than the document above, however this effect is reversed when the URL is compared to the result below.

Finally, in our combined model we find that all per-document features found to be statistically significant previously again have a statistically significant impact, even when combined with pairwise features. However, significant effects are also found for additional pairwise features, suggesting that the click behavior observed in our training data can best be explained when document-wise and pairwise features are combined. The pairwise features that had a statistically significant effect when included in the combined model are Δ URL slashes below, Δ title length below, as well as all highlighting features for result title and snippet.

To summarize, the visual features that have the largest effect are for models that take per-document features into account. Less impact was identified for pairwise features, but a combined model best explains observed click behavior.

4.2 Evaluating Caption Bias Models

Above, we presented four models of caption bias given visual features. Here, we compare the performance of these models by applying the models to predict user clicks on a new data set.

The data for this experiment was again obtained from the commercial Web search engine, but was collected several days after the training data. We obtained three non-overlapping random samples (by user), from February 23 to 26, 2012. Each data set consists of queries, the presented search results, and the observed clicks. Below, we refer to these evaluation sets as A, B, and C.

The task on which we evaluate the trained models of caption bias is to predict whether a given document will be clicked or not, based on its visual characteristics and its position in the result list. As ground truth, we use the actually observed clicks.

We measure performance in terms of perplexity, a measure that is typically used to compare the quality of the predictions of a probabilistic model to observed outcomes, e.g., to evaluate click prediction methods [10]. It is formulated as $2^{-\sum_{i=1}^{N} \frac{1}{N} log_2 q(x_i)}$, where x_i are observed events (here, whether a document was clicked or not), $q(x_i)$ is the probability of an observed event predicted by our model, and N is the number of observations. Intuitively, perplexity captures the degree of "surprise" that remains after a predictive model is applied. When applying a perfect model that can accurately predict all observed events, no surprise remains, and perplexity is 1. A uniformly random model would obtain a perplexity of 2, indicating that the model would not provide any information as to whether or not a result document is clicked.

In addition to the four models discussed in the previous section, we add a **baseline** model, that does not take any visual features into account (but is trained using relevance and position features, and predicts click behavior using document position alone).

Our results are presented in Table 4. Surprisingly, we find that the least predictive model is not the baseline (without any visual features), but the highlighting model. It performs worse than the baseline in all cases, even though it better explained click behavior on the training data. This suggests that the highlighting model may be overfitting the training data. The pairwise model is little better than the baseline, suggesting that pairwise features alone may not be able to accurately represent users' click decisions. Better performance is achieved by our document-wise model. The best performance (lowest perplexity) over all data sets is obtained by our combined model. Apart from data set C, where the document-wise mode is not statistically different from the combined model, all other models on all other data sets perform significantly worse than our best-performing model. Our results suggest that a combined model of visual features, that takes both document-wise and pairwise features into account, may be most successful at modeling users' click decisions.

To better understand how well our combined model captures caption bias, we conduct a more detailed analysis of its performance on different segments of queries drawn from data set B. We analyze prediction performance by (1) query frequency, and (2) the type of the information need expressed by the query.

Table 5 shows the perplexity of the baseline and combined models, split by query frequency. We divide queries into three groups: *head*, which consists of the 20% most frequent queries, *body*, which consists of queries between the 20th and 80th frequency percentile, and *tail*, which consists of the 20% least frequent queries.

We find that on *head* queries, perplexity is best for both models, and that the performance of the combined model is lower than that of the baseline. The reason is that these very frequent queries are typically "easy", because many users search for the same things, usually with a clearly identifiable goal. For this type of query, users

		highlighting	document-wise	pairwise	combined
Per-document features	Deep links		1.041 (±0.021)		1.048 (±0.021)
	Short URL		0.470 (±0.022)		0.403 (±0.022)
	URL slashes		-0.425 (±0.116)		-0.493 (±0.117)
	URL bold		0.314 (±0.028)		0.271 (±0.027)
	Short title		0.387 (±0.021)		0.264 (±0.023)
	Long title		0.353 (±0.021)		0.461 (±0.021)
	Title start		0.352 (±0.017)		0.292 (±0.017)
	Title bold		0.845 (±0.036)		0.672 (±0.037)
	Short snippet		-0.534 (±0.129)		-0.716 (±0.128)
	Long snippet		0.192 (±0.048)		0.324 (±0.049)
Pairwise features	Δ URL slashes above			-0.184 (±0.020)	
	Δ URL slashes below			0.160 (±0.015)	0.109 (±0.015)
	Δ URL bold above				
	Δ URL bold below	0.104 (±0.028)			
	Δ title length above (in characters)				
	Δ title length below (in characters)			-0.237 (±0.010)	-0.270 (±0.011)
	Δ title bold above (in words)	0.267 (±0.024)		0.305 (±0.024)	0.248 (±0.023)
	Δ title bold below (in words)	0.191 (±0.018)		0.260 (±0.018)	0.172 (±0.018)
	Δ snippet length above (in characters)			-0.159 (±0.010)	
	Δ snippet length below (in characters)				
	Δ snippet bold above (in sections)	-0.042 (±0.009)		-0.127 (±0.017)	-0.088 (±0.016)
	Δ snippet bold below (in sections)	-0.063 (±0.007)		-0.062 (±0.012)	-0.049 (±0.012)

Table 3: Results (modeling caption bias): Visual features included in each trained model, with estimated regression weights and standard error of the weight estimates. Of the candidate features for each model, only those with a statistically significant effect on click predictions are included (with $p < 0.001$).

data set	baseline	highlighting	document-wise	pairwise	combined
A	1.664 *	1.675 *	1.578 *	1.650 *	**1.552**
B	1.627 *	1.640 *	1.540 *	1.627 *	**1.521**
C	1.646 *	1.656 *	1.565	1.633 *	**1.540**

Table 4: Results (evaluating caption bias models): Perplexity of all caption bias models when predicting clicks. The *combined* model performs best in all cases. Significant perplexity increases in comparison with the best model are indicated by '*' ($p = 0.01$).

Segment	baseline	combined
Head	**1.105** *	1.111
Body	1.400 *	**1.347**
Tail	2.057 *	**1.855**

Table 5: Perplexity of the baseline and combined models, split by query frequency segment. Best performance per segment is highlighted in bold. '*' indicates significant differences between the models ($p = 0.01$).

Segment	baseline	combined
Enhanced Navigational	**1.143** *	1.149
Navigational	1.357	**1.339**
Non-navigational	1.924 *	**1.744**

Table 6: Perplexity of the baseline and combined models, split by the type of information need. Best performance per type is highlighted in bold. '*' indicates significant differences between the models ($p = 0.01$).

are likely to recognize target result pages, e.g., by the URL. Thus caption bias is low for this type of query, as reflected in our results. For the less frequent *body* queries, perplexity is higher for both models. Here, the performance of the combined model is significantly better than that of the baseline model. The trend continues for the *tail* query segment.

Table 6 shows the results obtained when splitting queries by the type of information need. Here, we use two sources of information to categorize queries. First, we use information provided by the search engine used for data collection. For queries with one predominantly clicked result, this top result is given more space on the result page. Our log data provides information on which queries were treated with such "enhanced navigational" results, and we use queries marked as such as our first category. For the remaining queries, a simple click-entropy based classifier divides queries into navigational and non-navigational.

We observe a similar pattern to that obtained using query frequency. For *enhanced navigational* queries, perplexity is lowest, and the baseline model performs better than the combined model. As the *head* queries above, results for these queries are the least likely to suffer from caption bias. These queries have one main target result, and this result is easy to identify on the result page, so caption bias is expected to play a small role here. For both navigational and non-navigational queries perplexity is higher for both models, but the combined model performs significantly better in both cases. Again, the performance improvement of the combined over the baseline model is largest for non-navigational queries, where caption bias is expected to be strongest.

To summarize, we validated our models of caption bias on the task of predicting clicks on interleaved result lists. Our combined model, that includes both document-wise and pairwise features to model caption bias, performed best overall. We also found that our

Rank	Example interleaved result list for the query "today in two minutes"	Visual features	Ranker	Weight
1	www.clicker.com http://www.clicker.com/web/today-in-2-minutes/	URL bold, short title, short snippet, Δ URL slashes below $= -1$, Δ title length below $= -1$, Δ title bold below $= -1$, Δ snippet length below $= -1$, Δ snippet bold below $= -1$	B	1.003
2*	05-03-10: TODAYshow.com Launches "TODAY In 2 Minutes" - NBC ... http://www.msnbc.msn.com/id/37339479/ns/nbc_press/t/todayshowcom-launches-today-minutes/ TODAYshow.com Launches "TODAY In 2 Minutes" Viewers can jumpstart their day in two minutes with top stories from America's No. 1 morning program	URL slashes, URL bold, long title, title bold, Δ title bold above $= 1$, Δ snippet bold above $= 1$	A	0.343
3	TODAY Video Player http://today.msnbc.msn.com/id/26184891/ TODAY: ... future: Success! In the future you can now use Facebook to log into your account.	short title, title bold, Δ URL slashes below $= 1$, Δ title length below (in characters) $= -1$, Δ title bold below $= -1$, Δ snippet length below $= -1$, Δ snippet bold below $= -1$	B	0.517
4*	Latest News in 2 Minutes, Breaking News in Just Two Minutes | Top ... http://economictimes.indiatimes.com/et2minutes.cms Latest Breaking News on Economic Times: ET in 2 Minutes is your quick meal of news, if you are hungry for news but pressed for time. Get top stories, events snapshot ...	long title, title bold, Δ title bold above $= 1$, Δ snippet bold above $= 1$	A	0.274

Table 7: Example interleaving impression with visual features, contributing ranker, and click weight. The ranks of clicked results are marked with '*' and corresponding result titles are highlighted in purple.

model worked best on queries where caption bias is expected to affect clicks the most, namely infrequent, non-navigational queries.

4.3 Predicting User Preferences

In the previous subsections we presented our results for training and evaluating caption bias models, and found that our combined model best predicted observed click behavior. In this section we show how applying this model to re-weight clicks affects interleaving scores on individual results, and show how such a re-weighting can be used to predict user preferences.

To show how compensating for caption bias affects interleaved comparisons in detail, consider Table 7. For the query "today in two minutes", four search results are shown. The first has a visual representation that results in a weight of 1.003, which is close to the average (i.e., the result is about as likely to be clicked as a result for which all visual features are false / zero). Click probability increases e.g., due to the short title, and highlighting in the URL, but decreases due to the missing snippet and the lack of highlighting in the title. Overall, the result is relatively unlikely to be clicked based on attractiveness alone. In contrast, the lower-ranked results look more attractive, and consequently receive lower click weights. In this result list, the two results with the lowest weights (i.e., the most attractive visually) were clicked by the user. This suggests that click behavior may have been affected by caption bias.

We can now compare the outcomes that would be obtained in the above example when inferring a Team Draft outcome with and without applying our model of caption bias. We observe that both clicked results were contributed by ranker A, leading to a win of 2 clicks over B. When applying the caption bias model, the low click weights of the clicked results are taken into account, leading to a much smaller win of 0.617. This example shows how the caption bias model decreases the impact of clicks that may have been biased towards more attractive results.

As an additional proof-of-concept, we applied our caption-bias weighting scheme to a small sample of search result impressions for which two different URLs had been clicked by different users. When a model predicted a lower weight for one of the clicked URLs, this URL would be inferred to be more likely to be clicked due to its presentation, and the URL with the higher click weight would be inferred to be preferred due to its content. For this small data set, we asked human annotators to judge which of two landing

baseline	highlighting	document-wise	pairwise	combined
0 / 86 / 0	44 / 1 / 41	43 / 11 / 32	43 / 0 / 43	**47 / 0 / 39**

Table 8: Preference predictions by caption bias models. For each model we include the number of correct / no preference / incorrect predictions (the best result is marked in bold).

pages (for the two competing URLs) they would prefer for a given query.

Table 8 shows how often our model predictions agree with the human preference judgments. For the baseline model, no preferences can be inferred, as both URLs were clicked for the given query. Prediction quality of the pairwise model is the same as a random model would achieve, while accuracy for the document-wise and highlighting models are slightly higher. The best preference predictions are obtained by our combined model.

4.4 Interleaving Outcomes

In this section we address our central research question: *How are interleaving outcomes affected by differences in result presentation in practice?* To better understand this effect, we apply our caption bias model to interleaved comparisons conducted on live Web search traffic, and analyze how results are affected.

We conducted six interleaving experiments, selecting experiments that represented small changes in ranking quality that are typical of incremental ranker improvements at major Web search engines. We also selected pairs such that the competing rankers used methods for applying previously collected clickthrough data, and different weights to make the influence of clicks weaker or stronger. Selecting ranker pairs in this way increased our chances of detecting changes in interleaving outcomes due to caption bias. Below, we refer to the interleaving experiments as **E1**-**E6**.

The interleaving experiments were run on a sample of live traffic from the same Web search engine as used in the previous two sections. These experiments were run within three weeks of collecting the data sets for model training and evaluation, so that no major changes in click behavior are expected. Interleaved result lists were generated using the Team Draft method. After observing user clicks, four different scoring methods were applied to compute interleaved comparison outcomes as defined in Equations 2–3 (without compensating for caption bias) and 5–6 (with the com-

Experiment	Team Draft		Probabilistic Interleaving	
	Unweighted (Eq. 2)	Weighted (Eq. 5)	Unweighted (Eq. 3)	Weighted (Eq. 6)
E1	0.5033 *	0.5017 *	0.5018 *	0.5011 *
E2	0.5040 *	0.5020 *	0.5024 *	0.5016 *
E3	0.5017 *	0.5010 *	0.5008 *	0.5006 *
E4	0.5031 *	0.5005 *	0.5010 *	0.5000
E5	0.5018 *	0.5014 *	0.5008 *	0.5008 *
E6	0.4999	0.4998 *	0.5000	0.4999 *

Table 9: Results (interleaving outcomes): Interleaving scores before and after applying caption-bias models to six interleaved comparison experiments. '*' denotes that a statistically significant difference between the rankers was detected ($p < 0.01$).

bined caption bias model). Note that the final scores are re-centered and re-normalized to conform to scoring schemes used in previous work, as explained in Section 3.3.

Table 9 gives an overview of the interleaved comparison outcomes obtained with Team Draft and Probabilistic Interleave, before and after caption bias re-weighting. We can see that scores are generally close to 0.5. These scores reflect the incremental ranker changes typically tested at major Web search engines (e.g., changes that affect a small percentage of queries). Scores above 0.5 mean that the experimental ranker was found to perform better than the baseline ranker. We also find that, despite the relatively small changes in ranking, most experiments detect a statistically significant difference between the rankers.

We first compare the outcomes obtained under the two baseline methods, i.e., without re-weighting. Outcomes for all experiments agree in direction and in whether the difference is statistically significant. However, the magnitude of outcomes differs, with e.g., a relatively big difference for E4, and a relatively small difference for E1. The reason is that under the Team Draft method, individual comparison outcomes are binary, independently of the magnitude of the difference between rankers. Under Probabilistic Interleave, outcomes are weighted by the rank distance of clicked documents. E.g., if a click was observed on a document placed at ranks 3 and 4 by the competing rankers, the magnitude of the interleaving outcome would be much smaller than if one ranker had placed the document at rank 1 and the other at rank 10. Thus, for experiments where there is a large absolute difference between Team Draft and Probabilistic Interleave outcomes, a large portion of the differences detected under Team Draft is expected to be caused by relatively small differences between rankings (e.g., E4).

After applying re-weighting, we find that the detected interleaving gains are generally smaller than under the original scoring methods. This suggests that a portion of the observed clicks was on results with low weights (i.e., with high click probability). However, in most cases, experiments for which significant differences between rankers were detected before re-weighting, are still significantly different after re-weighting (E1, E2, E3, E5).

One example where comparison outcomes appear to be strongly affected by caption bias is ranker pair E4. For this pair, the original comparison using Team Draft results in a statistically significant gain for one of the rankers (0.5031, a relatively big difference in typical ranker evaluations). After re-weighting, a much smaller (but still significant) improvement of 0.5005 is observed, indicating that most of the gain observed under Team Draft may be due to caption bias. Comparing to the outcome obtained under the probabilistic method, we find that another portion of observed improvements is due to only small ranking changes. After our model of caption bias is applied to Probabilistic Interleave, no difference between rankers can be detected. This finding suggests that the initially detected improvement was due to small ranking changes and caption bias, and that there is no true improvement in ranker quality. After analyzing ranker pair E4 in more detail, we found that the competing ranker in this experiment relied particularly heavily on click data. Thus, this experiment is highly likely to be affected by caption bias.

For experiment E6, the comparison outcome changes from non-significant to significantly worse when caption bias re-weighting is applied. For this experiment, the original comparison would support the conclusion that the compared rankers are equivalent. However, the re-weighted outcome indicates that the experimental ranker was really significantly worse than the baseline ranker.

To summarize, our final evaluation applied our best-performing caption bias model to interleaving experiments conducted on search engine traffic. We found small effects of caption bias on all experiments. For an experiment that was particularly strongly affected by caption bias, an initially detected interleaving preference vanished after applying caption bias re-weighting to Probabilistic Interleave. Our results suggest that our approach to modeling and compensating for caption bias can successfully identify interleaving experiments where caption bias may lead to unreliable outcomes.

5. CONCLUSION

In this paper we addressed the problem of caption bias in interleaving experiments. Interleaving experiments compare rankers by generating result lists that combine results from two rankers in a way that minimizes position bias, and infer differences in ranking quality from observed user clicks on result documents. In such an evaluation setup, bias introduced by differences in result presentation may affect inferred comparison outcomes. In extreme cases, this could lead to inferring a preference for the wrong ranker.

We started our investigation of caption bias by introducing a set of models designed to model bias using features that capture visual characteristics of individual result documents, and pairwise features that capture relationships with neighboring documents. We evaluated these models by using them to predict clicks. We found that overall, per-document features were more successful in capturing click behavior than pairwise features. However, best results were achieved using a combined model, that uses both feature sets. We also found that a combined caption bias model was the most successful at predicting click behavior, especially when caption bias is expected to be strongest (such as non-navigational queries).

Finally, we applied our best model to six interleaving experiments conducted on a small portion of live search traffic of a major commercial web search engine. We found that compensating for caption bias led to small changes on experiment outcomes overall, although in one case the outcome for a ranker tuned to click-through data was nullified. These results indicate that the proposed approach can successfully model caption bias and identify interleaving outcomes that may be unreliable due to caption bias.

This work constitutes a first step towards understanding how caption bias affects interleaving experiments, and how such experiments can be made more reliable by compensating for it. One direction for future work is to consider more complex models of click behavior. Here, we preferred relatively simple logistic regression models because they are relatively resistant to over-fitting and because of their interpretability. However, modeling click behavior is an active research topic in itself [10]. Although most click models to date model user behavior on individual queries, extensions that model factors across queries have been proposed [34]. Particularly, models that separate perceived relevance from judged relevance, and models that take additional user aspects of user behavior into account [33] are promising in this context.

Acknowledgments

The authors would like to thank Sreekar Krishna, Nick Craswell, Tapas Kanungo, and Kuansan Wang for their valuable feedback and discussion throughout this project. This research was partially supported by the Netherlands Organisation for Scientific Research (NWO) under project nr 612.061.814.

References

[1] E. Agichtein, E. Brill, and S. Dumais. Improving web search ranking by incorporating user behavior information. In *SIGIR '06*, pages 19–26. ACM, 2006.

[2] J. Boyan, D. Freitag, and T. Joachims. A machine learning architecture for optimizing web search engines. In *AAAI Workshop on Internet Based Information Systems*, pages 1–8, 1996.

[3] B. Carterette and R. Jones. Evaluating search engines by modeling the relationship between relevance and clicks. In *NIPS'07*, 2007.

[4] O. Chapelle, T. Joachims, F. Radlinski, and Y. Yue. Large-scale validation and analysis of interleaved search evaluation. *ACM Trans. Inf. Syst.*, 30(1):6:1–6:41, 2012.

[5] C. L. A. Clarke, E. Agichtein, S. Dumais, and R. W. White. The influence of caption features on clickthrough patterns in web search. In *SIGIR '07*, pages 135–142, 2007.

[6] N. Craswell, O. Zoeter, M. Taylor, and B. Ramsey. An experimental comparison of click position-bias models. In *WSDM'08*, pages 87–94, 2008.

[7] E. Cutrell and Z. Guan. What are you looking for?: an eye-tracking study of information usage in web search. In *CHI'07*, pages 407–416, 2007.

[8] Z. Dou, R. Song, X. Yuan, and J. R. Wen. Are click-through data adequate for learning web search rankings? In *CIKM '08*, pages 73–82, 2008.

[9] S. Dumais and E. Cutrell. Optimizing search by showing results in context. In *CHI'01*, pages 277–284, 2001.

[10] G. E. Dupret and B. Piwowarski. A user browsing model to predict search engine click data from past observations. In *SIGIR '08*, pages 331–338, 2008.

[11] L. A. Granka, T. Joachims, and G. Gay. Eye-tracking analysis of user behavior in www search. In *SIGIR'04*, pages 478–479, 2004.

[12] Z. Guan and E. Cutrell. An eye tracking study of the effect of target rank on web search. In *CHI'07*, pages 417–420, 2007.

[13] F. Guo, L. Li, and C. Faloutsos. Tailoring click models to user goals. In *WSDM '09*, pages 88–92, 2009.

[14] F. Guo, C. Liu, and Y. M. Wang. Efficient multiple-click models in web search. In *WSDM '09*, pages 124–131, 2009.

[15] J. He, C. Zhai, and X. Li. Evaluation of methods for relative comparison of retrieval systems based on clickthroughs. In *CIKM'09*, pages 2029–2032, 2009.

[16] K. Hofmann, B. Huurnink, M. Bron, and M. de Rijke. Comparing click-through data to purchase decisions for retrieval evaluation. In *SIGIR '10*, pages 761–762, 2010.

[17] K. Hofmann, S. Whiteson, and M. de Rijke. A Probabilistic Method for Inferring Preferences from Clicks. In *CIKM'11*, pages 249–258, 2011.

[18] S. Ieong, N. Mishra, E. Sadikov, and L. Zhang. Domain bias in web search. In *WSDM '12*, pages 413–422. ACM, 2012.

[19] T. Joachims. Optimizing search engines using clickthrough data. In *KDD '02*, pages 133–142, 2002.

[20] T. Joachims, L. Granka, B. Pan, H. Hembrooke, F. Radlinski, and G. Gay. Evaluating the accuracy of implicit feedback from clicks and query reformulations in Web search. *ACM Trans. Inf. Syst.*, 25(2), 2007.

[21] J. Kamps, M. Koolen, and A. Trotman. Comparative analysis of clicks and judgments for ir evaluation. In *WSCD '09*, pages 80–87, 2009.

[22] D. Kelly and J. Teevan. Implicit feedback for inferring user preference: a bibliography. *SIGIR Forum*, 37(2):18–28, 2003.

[23] F. Radlinski and N. Craswell. Comparing the sensitivity of information retrieval metrics. In *SIGIR '10*, pages 667–674, 2010.

[24] F. Radlinski and T. Joachims. Minimally invasive randomization for collecting unbiased preferences from clickthrough logs. In *AAAI'06*, pages 1406–1412, 2006.

[25] F. Radlinski, M. Kurup, and T. Joachims. How does clickthrough data reflect retrieval quality? In *CIKM '08*, pages 43–52, 2008.

[26] M. Sanderson. Test collection based evaluation of information retrieval systems. *Foundations and Trends in Information Retrieval*, 4(4):247–375, 2010.

[27] F. Scholer, M. Shokouhi, B. Billerbeck, and A. Turpin. Using Clicks as Implicit Judgments: Expectations Versus Observations. In *ECIR'08*, pages 28–39, 2008.

[28] X. Shen, B. Tan, and C. Zhai. Context-sensitive information retrieval using implicit feedback. In *SIGIR '05*, SIGIR '05, pages 43–50, 2005.

[29] A. Tombros and M. Sanderson. Advantages of query biased summaries in information retrieval. In *SIGIR '98*, pages 2–10, 1998.

[30] E. M. Voorhees and D. K. Harman. *TREC: Experiment and Evaluation in Information Retrieval*. Digital Libraries and Electronic Publishing. MIT Press, 2005.

[31] K. Wang, T. Walker, and Z. Zheng. PSkip: estimating relevance ranking quality from web search clickthrough data. In *KDD '09*, pages 1355–1364, 2009.

[32] Y. Yue, R. Patel, and H. Roehrig. Beyond position bias: examining result attractiveness as a source of presentation bias in clickthrough data. In *WWW '10*, pages 1011–1018, 2010.

[33] F. Zhong, D. Wang, G. Wang, W. Chen, Y. Zhang, Z. Chen, and H. Wang. Incorporating post-click behaviors into a click model. In *SIGIR '10*, pages 355–362, 2010.

[34] Z. A. Zhu, W. Chen, T. Minka, C. Zhu, and Z. Chen. A novel click model and its applications to online advertising. In *WSDM '10*, pages 321–330, 2010.

Alternative Assessor Disagreement and Retrieval Depth

William Webber
College of Information Studies
University of Maryland
Maryland, USA
wew@umd.edu

Praveen Chandar, Ben Carterette
Department of Computer & Information Sciences
University of Delaware
Delaware, USA
{pcr,carteret}@cis.udel.edu

ABSTRACT

Assessors are well known to disagree frequently on the relevance of documents to a topic, but the factors leading to assessor disagreement are still poorly understood. In this paper, we examine the relationship between the rank at which a document is returned by a set of retrieval systems and the likelihood that a second assessor will disagree with the relevance assessment of the initial assessor, and find that there is a strong and consistent correlation between the two. We adopt a metarank method of summarizing a document's rank across multiple runs, and propose a logistic regression predictive model of second assessor disagreement given metarank and initially-assessed relevance. The consistency of the model parameters across different topics, assessor pairs, and collections is considered. The model gives comparatively accurate predictions of absolute system scores, but less consistent predictions of relative scores than a simpler rank-insensitive model. We demonstrate that the logistic regression model is robust to using sampled, rather than exhaustive, dual assessment. We demonstrate the use of the sampled predictive model to incorporate assessor disagreement into tests of statistical significance.

Categories and Subject Descriptors

H.3.4 [**Information Storage and Retrieval**]: Systems and software—*performance evaluation.*

Keywords

Retrieval experiment, evaluation, sampling

General Terms

Measurement, performance, experimentation

1. INTRODUCTION

When two humans are asked to assess the one document for relevance to a topic, they are surprisingly likely to disagree. One study finds that even expert assessors with similar backgrounds have only a 60% probability of agreeing that a document is relevant [Voorhees, 2000]. Not just the set of actually relevant documents, but the measured reliability of a document retrieval, can vary substantially depending upon which assessor is used; and in human-intensive document productions, the results of comparative evaluation can depend on whether you agree with the humans who developed the production, or the humans who assessed it [Oard et al., 2008].

While several studies observe assessor disagreement, and a few have investigated its impact upon evaluation, little work has been done on characterizing, modeling, and predicting disagreement. It is not known what share of disagreement is attributable to assessor inattention, what to differing relevance conceptions, and what to variable thresholds for detecting relevance. Identifying correlates of disagreement will help predict, adjust for, and correct assessor disagreement and its impact upon evaluation; and better determining the nature and causes of disagreement will enable preventative steps to be taken, and improve our understanding of the human perception of relevance.

In this paper, we examine a potential correlate of assessor disagreement, namely the ranks at which a document is retrieved by a set of retrieval systems. We summarize retrieval rank information across the run set using metarank scores, similar to the score aggregation methods used to metasearch. Working with the same TREC 4 and TREC 6 AdHoc datasets as Voorhees [2000], we then estimate the probability of second-assessor disagreement given metarank score, developing separate logistic models for documents assessed relevant and assessed irrelevant by an initial assessor. Making the model dependent upon the first assessor's assessment reflects the question facing the practicing evaluator after an initial assessment: which of these assessments should I have checked by a second assessor?

Our experiments find the relationship between metarank and assessor disagreement to be a strong one; a high metarank document assessed relevant by one assessor is almost twice as likely to be assessed irrelevant by a second assessor as a low metarank one, and the relationship is even stronger for documents assessed as irrelevant by a first assessor. The strength of the relationship, however, varies markedly between different topics, there are clearly other, topic-dependent factors at play in determining assessor disagreement, and a universal model has limited predictivity.

Models of disagreement by rank can be used to create artificial document assessment sets (or qrels), to simulate and explore the effects of assessor disagreement. Qrels simulated from per-topic rank-sensitive models give much more accurate estimates of absolute scores under alternate assessment than do rank-insensitive flip-rate models. Rank-sensitive simulated qrels, however, provide less stable relative evaluations and system rankings than flip-rate

CIKM'12, October 29–November 2, 2012, Maui, HI, USA.
Copyright 2012 ACM 978-1-4503-1156-4/12/10 ...$15.00.

qrels, at least for the metarank scoring method we use. Metarank score is evidently not independent of system, and (we hypothesize) the same reinforcement of like systems can be observed here as in other simulated relevance methods [Soboroff et al., 2001].

We demonstrate that rank-sensitive models based on sampled dual assessment produce absolute and relative score simulations almost as reliable as those of exhaustive dual assessment. Moreover, sampled rank-sensitive models are more reliable than sampled rank-insensitive ones even for relative evaluation. Thus, one can predict the effect of assessor disagreement with only a fraction of repeat assessment effort.

Traditional tests of the significance of a comparative retrieval evaluation consider only the topics as variable, holding documents, assessors, and other aspects of the experiment fixed. With reliable, sample-based models of assessor disagreement available, variability in the assessor dimension can be simulated at a fraction of the cost of exhaustive multiple assessment. We demonstrate the use of our rank-sensitive model to determine evaluation significance with tests in which assessors can vary.

The remainder of the paper is structured as follows. Related work is surveyed in Section 2, and our materials and methods in Section 3. Section 4 describes our experiments, and Section 5 summarizes our findings and sketches future work.

2. RELATED WORK

The high level of inter-assessor disagreement on relevance has been noted by a number of studies. Voorhees [2000] examines multiple assessments of the TREC 4 and TREC 6 AdHoc collections (the same datasets used here), finding overlap of between 0.42 and 0.49 on TREC 4. Roitblat et al. [2010] find even lower levels of inter-assessor agreement on an e-discovery production. Bailey et al. [2008] survey earlier studies with similar results.

Several studies have concluded that impact of assessor disagreement upon the comparative (rather than absolute) evaluation of automated retrieval systems is minor. Voorhees [2000] finds a mean Kendall's τ of 0.938 between system rankings produced by different assessors, suggesting a high degree of stability between assessment sets. Trotman and Jenkinson [2007] compare using multiple (non-overlapping) assessors per topic with a single assessor, and find a mean Spearman's rank correlation coefficient of 0.986. The effect upon relative assessment may be greater for runs created with a large amount of manual involvement, however, including through training classifiers; the correction of assessor errors led to large relative score changes in the interactive task of the TREC Legal Track [Oard et al., 2008].

The interactive task of the TREC Legal Track corrects assessor errors through participant appeals and adjudication by a topic authority [Oard et al., 2008]. Webber et al. [2010] propose instead that assessments be sampled for authoritative verification, and error rates estimated from these samples. Sheng et al. [2008] investigate using multiple overlapping assessors in annotation tasks.

Cuadra and Katter [1967] identify five factors influencing perceptions of relevance: document variables; topic statement variables; judgment conditions; judgment scales; and personal factors. Saracevic [2007] surveys of experiments on these factors. Webber et al. [2010] present a taxonomy of topical grounds for appeal from the appeal documents submitted by a TREC Legal Interactive participant. Re-analyzing appealed assessments from the Interactive task, Grossman and Cormack [2011] conclude that the great majority of assessor error is due to inarguable failure to follow the task's detailed relevance assessment guidelines; however, their sample is biased by that fact that participants only appealed assessments they felt to be inarguable errors. Webber et al. [2012] find that more detailed instructions do not lead to fewer assessor errors.

Orig	Alt 1		Alt 2		Total
	Rel	!Rel	Rel	!Rel	
Rel	4.2%	4.0%	5.1%	3.1%	8.2%
!Rel	4.8%	87.0%	7.5%	84.3%	91.8%
Total	9.0%	91.0%	12.6%	87.4%	

Table 1: Macro-averaged estimated proportional contingency tables between original and two alternatives assessors across the TREC 4 AdHoc topics. Agreement observed on sampled documents extrapolated to the rest of the pool.

Aslam et al. [2005] present a metasearch approach known as meta-AP in which documents are weighted by their implicit average precision scores in each ranking; we adopt meta-AP as a predictor of assessor disagreement in our models. Aslam and Montague [2001] and Lee [1997] describe simpler metasearch scoring methods, similar to our baseline predictors. As part of an evaluation score estimation method known as minimal test collection (MTC), Carterette [2007] explicitly builds a multi-level logistic model of probability of relevance based on retrieval rank and system reliability. The relative values of the estimated scores are a reliable estimate of full assessment, but the absolute estimated values are not, suggesting that absolute probabilities of document relevance are misestimated.

Soboroff et al. [2001] explore randomly assigning relevance assessments to documents, and find that the system ranking that results is moderately correlated with the human-assessed ranking. Carterette and Soboroff [2010] use variable flip rate probabilities to simulate "conservative" and "liberal" assessors, finding that "conservative" assessors maintain stable system rankings, while "liberal" assessors disrupt them.

Voorhees [1998] introduces the use of Kendall's τ as a measure of the stability of system ranking in the face of changes in the evaluation setup. Savoy [1997] proposes the use of Bootstrap significance tests in information retrieval evaluation. Bodoff and Li [2007] argue that choice of assessor should be included alongside choice of topics in assessing the generalizability of information retrieval evaluation results.

3. MATERIALS AND METHODS

This section describes our data sets and methods. For data (Section 3.1), we use the TREC 4 AdHoc collection, runsets, and qrels, including multiple assessments performed by TREC assessors; we also use the TREC 6 collection, with additional assessments performed by one of the track participants. We model assessor disagreement using logistic regression, with document rank as a predictor (Section 3.2). Our experiments randomly generate qrels following models built from the dataset, and investigate the stability of system evaluation using them (Section 3.3).

3.1 Materials

The TREC 4 AdHoc test collection consists of 49 topics. Documents for assessment were selected by depth-100 pooling. In addition to the 33 systems that ran on the full collection in the adhoc task, all of which were pooled, additional pooled documents were drawn from systems that ran on a subset of the collection, or ran in a different modality [Harman, 1995]. Only the 33 adhoc full-collection runs are included in this study. Initial assessment

Orig	Alt 1		Total
	Rel	!Rel	
Rel	2.4%	3.3%	5.7%
!Rel	2.1%	92.2%	94.3%
Total	4.5%	95.5%	

Table 2: Macro-averaged estimated proportional contingency tables between original and alternative (Waterloo) assessors across the TREC 6 AdHoc topics.

was performed by the author of the topic; we refer to this as the "original" assessor. Each topic was then re-assessed by two other TREC assessors, whom we refer to as the first and second alternative assessors. We follow Voorhees [2000] in dropping Topic 214, as the first alternative assessor found no documents relevant for it. If there were more than 200 relevant or irrelevant documents in the pool, then 200 were uniform randomly sampled for re-assessment [Voorhees, 2000]. The average number of reassessed relevant documents is 105, with 12 topics having 200 or more relevant documents; all topics have more than 200 irrelevant documents, with the average being 1,627. Though Voorhees [2000] does not describe a systematic difference in the allocation of assessors as first and second alternate assessors, the first assessor finds an average of 17.3 more document relevant than the second assessor (sd $= 51.2$). This difference is statistically significant ($p = 0.02$ in two-tailed, pair t test). The reason for this difference is not known; it may simply be non-randomness in assigning additional assessors (for instance, assessors who finished their initial assessments faster may have been more likely to be assigned as first than as second alternative assessors).

Table 1 gives macro-averaged proportional contingency tables between the original and the two alternative assessors for the TREC 4 AdHoc topics. We estimate agreement on the pool from agreement on the sample. In contrast, Voorhees [2000] calculates statistics on the sample only. Since a higher proportion of originally-relevant documents is sampled than of originally-irrelevant (a macro-average of 91.3% of the former, versus 13.6% of the latter), agreement on the sample tends strongly to overstate agreement on the pool. So, for instance, Voorhees [2000] quotes a (sample) positive overlap with the original assessor of 0.421 for the first and 0.494 for the second alternative assessor, whereas the estimated figures on the pool are 0.301 and 0.340, respectively. (The pool itself is a selective, non-random sample. Agreement on the full collection, had it been exhaustively assessed or randomly sampled from, would be different yet again, and probably lower still, since the number of originally-irrelevant documents would greatly increase.)

The TREC 6 AdHoc multiple-assessment dataset was created as part of a run production by the TREC participant team from the University of Waterloo [Cormack et al., 1997]. The run was produced by interactively developing queries, retrieved ranked results, and judging of top-ranked documents. The documents assessed as part of this process constitute the "alternative" assessments to the (subsequently formed) official assessments of the TREC assessors. The Waterloo assessors used a three-level relevance scale, with a middle grade of marginally relevant; following Voorhees [2000], we collapse the marginally relevant documents to not relevant.

Besides being performed by assessors with a different background and mode of operation from the official assessors, the TREC 6 alternative assessments differ from those from TREC 4 in that they are not a random sample. Rather, they are the documents returned

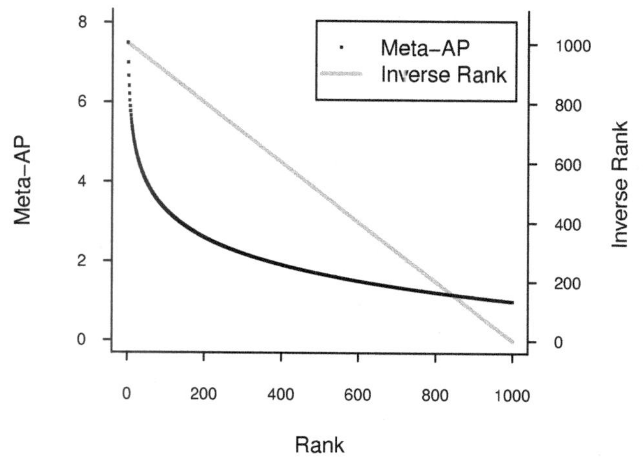

Figure 1: Metarank weights for Meta-AP and Inverse Rank weighting schemes, for a single document ranking.

at top ranks by a series of interactive queries. The non-randomness of the selection of the alternative assessments makes it impossible to extrapolate agreement measures to the full TREC pool, and may bias models built upon dual-assessed documents; the random sampling of the pool used in TREC 4, however, should ensure that the models have only sampling error, not systematic bias, though only for pooled documents. The proportional macro-averaged contingency table for the TREC 6 dataset is shown in Table 2. The macro-averaged overlap is 0.328.

3.2 Modeling assessor disagreement

We propose to model assessor disagreement as a function of document rank. This requires three components: a statistic for summarizing rank information (Section 3.2.1); a modeling method (Section 3.2.2); and a way of choosing which statistic provides the best fit for the data under the modeling method adopted (Section 3.2.3).

3.2.1 Metarank measures

A metarank measure summarizes the ranks at which a document is returned across a set of runs for a single topic. (Where metarank is used to form an aggregate ranking, the technique is referred to as metasearch.) Let N be the rank to which metarank measures are scored. We say that document returned in a run s at rank k has an inverse rank I in that run of $N - k$, or 0 if $k > N$. Two simple measures are then maximum and mean inverse rank, which can be compared to the metasearch methods CombMax [Lee, 1997] and Borda count [Aslam and Montague, 2001].

Aslam et al. [2005] propose a metarank measure based upon the weighting of the average precision (AP) metric. For AP evaluating to depth N, the implicit weight of a document at rank k is $1 + H_N - H_k$, where H_n is the n'th harmonic number, or 0 if $k > N$. The mean meta-AP score for a document is its average AP weight across the set of runs.

We take $N = 1{,}000$, the run depth in the ad-hoc tracks of TREC, as our metarank evaluation depth . The meta-AP score for rank 1 in evaluation to this depth is 7.5. The relationship between meta-AP and inverse rank as a function of rank is shown in Figure 1.

3.2.2 Logistic regression

We predict the probability that a document will be judged relevant by assessor B, based upon its metarank and the fact that assessor A has judged it either relevant or irrelevant: $p(B = 1|s, A = r)$, building separate models for $A = 1$ and $A = 0$. We apply a logistic regression to this problem:

$$p(B = 1|s, A = r) = \frac{e^{\beta_0 + \beta_1 s}}{1 + e^{\beta_0 + \beta_1 s}} \quad (1)$$

where the metarank score s is the predictor variable, and the probability p is the predicted value. The probability of disagreement is $p(B = 1)$ if $A = 1$, and $1 - p(B = 1)$ is $A = 0$. Logistic regression is preferable to linear regression since the latter produces "probabilities" outside of the range $[0, 1]$; logistic regression is more robust than smoothed average methods to sparse data, which can occur for topics that have very few relevant documents.

The fitted value β_0 in Equation 1 is the intercept, which gives the log-odds of relevance when the score is 0, while β_1 is the score coefficient, which gives the change or "slope" in log odds of relevance for every one point increase in metarank. The slope gives the strength of the relationship between metarank and probability of relevance, while the intercept shifts the regression curve up or down the score axis. An intercept of -1 means there is a $1 : e \approx 27\%$ chance of relevance when the score is 0. Conversely, a slope of 1 means than an increase of 1 in the score will take probabilities from $1 : 1 = 50\%$ to $e : 1 \approx 73\%$. If we regard the observed documents as a sample from a larger population, then the slope on the sample is predictive of the population, and this prediction can be checked for statistical significance. Where all documents receive the same alternative relevance assessment, no proper model can be constructed, though 0 or 1 probabilities can be assigned to all scores.

A model can be built for each topic individually, or else alternative assessments and metarank scores from the full collection can be pooled into a single model. The degree to which a per-collection or "universal" model is a good approximation for per-topic models depends upon the strength of per-topic factors in influencing disagreement. The closer the per-collection model is to the per-topic models, the more likely it is that a generalized model can be built that is able to predict assessor disagreement on new collections based only on metarank scores.

A simpler, rank-insensitive model of assessor disagreement is the flip rate model, which notes the proportion of originally-relevant documents that the alternative assessor assesses as irrelevant, and vice versa. Taking the original assessor as the objective standard, the flip rate is a pair of proportions, giving the false-positive and false-negative rates for the alternative assessor.

3.2.3 Model goodness-of-fit

There are various ways to measure the goodness-of-fit of a logistic regression. A simple measure, found by [Hosmer et al., 1997] nevertheless to be more powerful than many more complex ones, is the unweighted residual sum-of-squares (RSS):

$$\widehat{S} = \sum_{i=1}^{n} (y_i - \widehat{\pi}_i)^2 \, . \quad (2)$$

The sum across all n observations i; y_i is the actual value of observation i (here, whether document i is relevant or not), and $\widehat{\pi}_i$ is the estimated probability of relevance for an item with the predictor variables of item i (here, the metarank of document i). Instead of RSS itself, we report RMSE:

$$\text{RMSE} = \sqrt{\widehat{S}/n} \, . \quad (3)$$

The RMSE value is rank-equivalent to RSS for a single topic, but is more comparable between topics; moreover, being in the same units as the probability values themselves, it is indicative of the degree of deviation of estimated probability from actual (0, 1) relevance.

3.3 Experimental methods

Our experiments in Sections 4.3, 4.4, and 4.5, involve generating qrels that simulate the assessments of an alternative assessor, and then examining the stability of system scores and rankings. To do this, we build a model of assessor disagreement from the original assessments, the metarank predictor, and a set of observed alternative assessments. The simulated alternative qrels are generated by applying the predictive model to the original qrels. Each original assessment is plugged into the model with its metarank score to generate a probability of assessor disagreement. An independent uniform random number U in the range $[0, 1]$ is then generated. If U is less than the flip probability, then document relevance is flipped in the simulated qrels; otherwise, the original document relevance is maintained. The same process is used for the metarank and the flip-rate models, except the latter takes no account of document metarank, and also for per-topic and universal models.

In Section 4.4, we compare the stability of our models when based on exhaustive and on sampled dual assessment. For the sampled dual assessment, n originally-relevant and n originally-irrelevant documents (where $n = 20$ is used in our experiments) are sampled, and the metarank and flip-rate models are built using just the samples. Uniform random sampling is used for both the flip-rate and the metarank models.

For the system score stability experiments in Sections 4.3 and 4.4, we generate $s = 1{,}000$ simulated alternative qrel sets for each model, and calculate the MAP scores achieved by systems for each alternative qrel set. The means and the 2.5% and 97.5% percentiles of these MAP scores are reported. Absolute change in system score is calculated by root mean squared error (RMSE) between the observed and all of the simulated MAP scores. Relative stability is calculated using mean Kendall's τ between the system ranking under the observed alternative assessments and under the simulated qrels.

4. EXPERIMENTS

In this section we present a series of experiments on various aspects of the model and its use. We start with the choice of predictor (Section 4.1), then evaluate the fidelity of the model of disagreement (Section 4.2). We next use the model to simulate qrels for use in calculating MAP in TREC evaluation experiments (Section 4.3). We investigate the use of sampling dual assessments to fit better models (Section 4.4), and finally investigate the use of simulated qrels to estimate variance due to differences in assessor when testing significance (Section 4.5).

4.1 Choice of metarank measure

Section 3.2.1 described three alternative metarank measures: mean meta-AP; mean inverse rank; and maximum inverse rank. Figure 2 compares the goodness-of-fit of these these metarank measures, using RMSE of predicted and actual value (Section 3.2.3), and compares them with the simple, rank-insensitive flip-rate model. There is not a great apparent difference in RMSE scores, but meta-AP gives significantly ($p < 0.01$) better fit than both alternative metarank schemes on both conditions, except when compared to mean inverse rank on the given-irrelevant condition, where the difference is not significant. All three metarank models are significantly better fits than the flip rate model ($p < 0.001$). We select meta-AP as the metarank measure for the remaining experiments, and compare it with flip-rate in later sections.

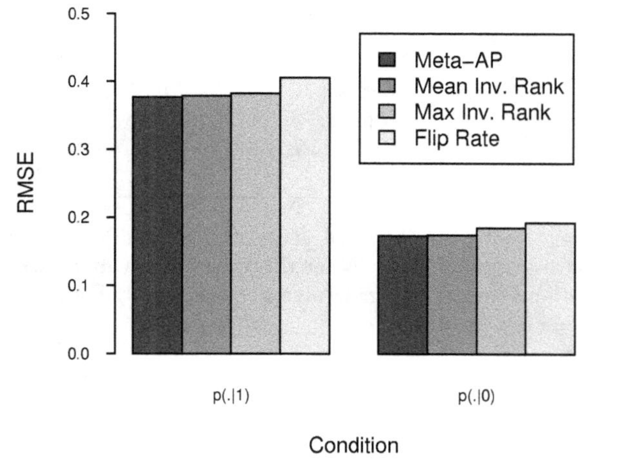

Figure 2: Goodness-of-fit in RMSE of models built from different metarank measures, for the given-relevant and given-irrelevant cases, on the TREC 4 AdHoc dataset, averaged across all 48 topics and both first and second alternative assessors. Lower values indicate better fit.

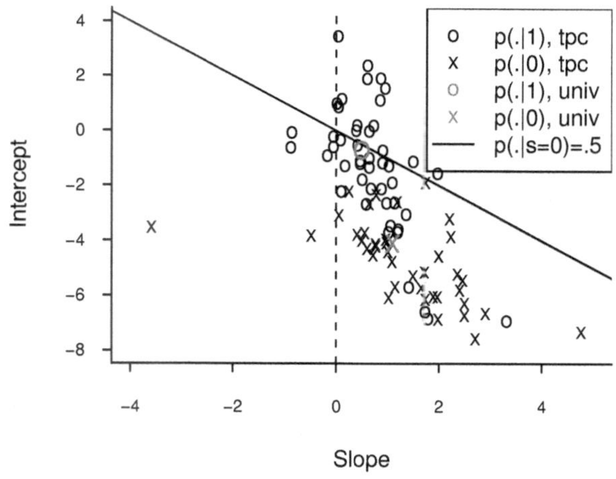

Figure 3: Per-topic and universal logistic regression coefficients for the first alternate assessor on the TREC 4 AdHoc dataset. The diagonal line shows the combination of intercept and slope for which the probability of alternative-assessor relevance at a meta-AP score of 0 is 50%.

Dataset	Condition	Positive		Improper	Negative	
		Sig	!Sig		!Sig	Sig
T4, alt1	$p(\cdot\|1)$	23	19	2	5	0
	$p(\cdot\|0)$	24	13	10	2	0
T4, alt2	$p(\cdot\|1)$	21	24	0	4	0
	$p(\cdot\|0)$	28	10	6	5	0
T6	$p(\cdot\|1)$	22	20	3	3	2
	$p(\cdot\|0)$	36	7	3	4	0
Total		154	93	24	23	2

Table 3: Number of per-topic models for TREC 4, both alternative assessors, and TREC 6 datasets, giving ($p < 0.05$) significantly and non-significantly positive, improper, and significantly and non-significantly negative slopes.

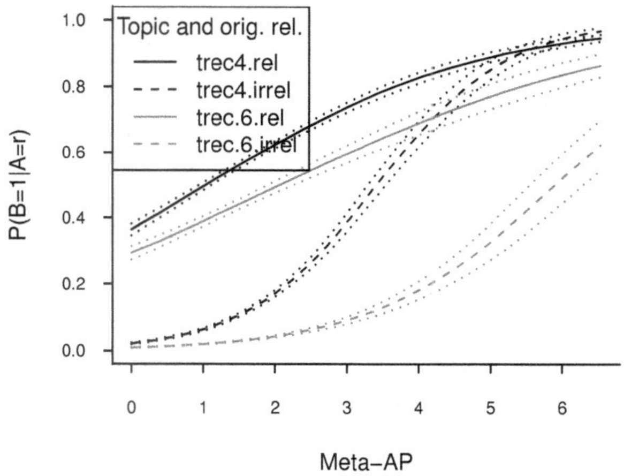

Figure 4: Universal logistic regression models for TREC 4 and TREC 6, with 95% error bounds. The TREC 4 model combines both alternative assessors.

4.2 Modeling rank and disagreement

The number of per-topic models giving slopes of different directions and significances across both datasets is tabulated in Table 3 (see Section 3.2.2 for the mean of these values). Over 80% of models show positive slopes (90% if improper models are ignored), and 60% of these are significant. None of the models for the randomly-sampled TREC 4 alternative assessments have a significantly negative slope, and only two of the determinately-sampled TREC 6 models have a significantly negative slope. In summary, there is a strong and consistent relationship between document rank and the probability that an alternative assessor will disagree with an original assessor's assessment.

The dispersion of slope and intercept coefficients for per-topic and universal models is shown in Figure 3, for the first alternative assessor of TREC 4. As a group, models for initial assessments of relevant have higher probability of alternative relevance (higher intercepts) than models for initial assessments of irrelevant, as one would expect. Parameters are highly variable in both slope and intercept between topics, however; the universal model for each condition, though centered amongst the per-topic models, does not well characterize the spread of the per-topic models. Metarank alone (at least as measured by meta-AP) fails to capture all of the variance in assessor disagreement, even for the one collection; other, topic or assessor-pair, features also have an impact.

The universal regression models for TREC 4 and TREC 6 are shown in Figure 4. We have included both the first and the second alternative assessors in the TREC 4 model. A marked difference between TREC 4 and TREC 6 can be observed, particularly for the given-irrelevant model; this is likely due to the different selection and assessment methods for the TREC 6 alternative assessments. For the TREC 4 universal model, we can see that a relevant assessment on a high-ranking document is almost certain to be confirmed by a second assessor, whereas a relevant judgment on a low-ranking document is as likely as not to be overturned. The relationship is even stronger for documents initially assessed as irrelevant:

the alternative assessor is very likely to agree with the initial assessment for low-ranked documents, but for the (rare) high-ranked documents initially assessed as relevant, the alternative assessor is very likely to disagree with the initial assessment.

Figure 5 gives regressions for three example topics. For Topic 215, the given-relevant model dominates the given-irrelevant one, and predicts over four times the probability of alternative-relevance for high metarank than for low metarank documents. For Topic 211, the given-irrelevant model has low intercept but high slope, meaning a sudden transition from strongly-irrelevant to strongly-relevant, based on a small number of alternative-relevant documents; smoothing would give a less sudden transition. For Topic 250, the given-positive model has a negative slope, assigning a lower probability of alternative relevance to higher ranked documents; the negative slope is based on a small number of alternatively-irrelevant observations, however, and is not significant.

4.3 Predicting system scores

A probabilistic model of a process can be tested by seeing how well a simulation based on the model reproduces the outcomes of the process; if the simulation performs well, it can then be used to predict process outcomes when the process itself is absent. The assessments in our datasets were made to form test collection qrels, used in calculating effectiveness metrics on system retrievals. If the qrels of an alternative assessor are used, then different effectiveness metric values will result. How well do probabilistic models based upon the observed assessor disagreement simulate the actual change in absolute and relative system scores?

We examine model accuracy in predicting system scores in Figure 6. Mean AP scores for each TREC 4 system are shown, for the official qrels and for the qrels produced by the first alternative assessor. Simulated qrels are generated using the method described in Section 3.3, and the range of scores induced on each system by the randomly generated qrels are shown. The models we consider are a rank-insensitive universal flip rate based on disagreements micro-averaged across all topics (Figure 6(a)); a separate flip-rate model built for each topic (Figure 6(b)); a universal logistic regression model based upon meta-AP scores, pooling assessments across all topics (Figure 6(c)); and a different logistic model for each topic (Figure 6(d)). We also show the per-topic logistic regression model on the second alternate assessors for TREC 4 (Figure 6(e)), and the single alternative assessor for TREC 6 (Figure 6(f)).

The metarank models (Figures 6(c) and (d)) achieve much more accurate absolute scores than the flip-rate models (Figures 6(a) and (b)), with the flip-rate models generating MAP scores that are half or less of the true MAP scores. There is little difference between the universal and per-topic flip-rate models. There is, however, a noticeable difference between the universal and per-topic rank-sensitive models, with the per-topic models generating more accurate simulations of alternative-assessor scores; the universal model, in contrast, tends systematically to underestimate MAP scores. This result is not surprising, given the variance in per-topic model coefficients (Figure 3).

For comparative scores, however, the accuracy of the metarank and flip-rate models is reversed. Although the flip-rate models grossly understate true MAP, they do so by similar amounts for each system, leading to a ranking that is relatively consistent with the original. In contrast, while the average change in absolute scores is much smaller for the metarank models, the scores of different systems change by different amounts and directions, leading to instability in relative ranking. These observations are summarized by the RMSE and τ scores reported in Table 4.

Model	Context	RMSE	$\bar{\tau}$
Flip-rate	Universal	0.102	0.911
	Per-topic	0.114	0.919
Meta-AP	Universal	0.035	0.851
	Per-topic	0.015	0.867
	TREC 4 alt2	0.015	0.857
	TREC 6	0.080	0.815

Table 4: Root mean squared error and Kendall's τ, averaged across simulations, between MAP scores from alternative-assessor and from model-generated qrels; summarizing the information in Figure 6.

The explanation for the better absolute but worse relative score stability of the metarank model, compared to the flip-rate model, is that while the metarank model is a much more accurate model of probability of disagreement, it is less independent of systems. Since the overwhelming majority of per-topic models have positive slopes (Table 3), documents with higher metaranks have more chance of remaining (if originally assessed relevant), or flipping to (if originally irrelevant), relevant. Systems that return more documents with higher metarank will have more positive score changes under the model than systems that return fewer such documents. Metarank, however, is an average of ranking position across different runs, so the more systems that return a document, the higher its metarank. This behavior is by design; but it does mean that documents returned by similar systems get higher metaranks, and hence the systems bigger boosts, than documents returned by dissimilar systems. We have returned to a common problem with these predictive models, that they favor conformist systems (say, automated methods using a standard document similarity measure) over non-conformist ones (say, hand-crafted manual runs). Down-weighting the vote of conformist systems, if possible, would likely lead to a more accurate model.

The metarank model applied to the second alternative assessor for TREC 4 (Figure 6(e)) gives similar results as for the first. Interestingly, although the absolute scores under the second assessor differ from those for the first, the relationships between the observed and the simulated scores for each system are similar. For instance, the simulated scores for `CLARTF` and `CLARTN` (seventh and eighth systems from the left) both fall below the observed alternative scores by a similar amount, even though the observed scores are higher for the second alternative assessor than for the first. This consistency in error reinforces the hypothesis that the errors are due to system-dependent mutual reinforcement, rather than assessor-dependent or purely random factors.

Finally, Figure 6(f) shows the per-topic metarank model applied to the alternative assessor for TREC 6. As described in Section 3.1, the dual assessments were not randomly sampled, but were made by one of the participants in the course of run development. Perhaps as a result of this, the MAP scores on the observed alternative assessments differ from the official ones more than for TREC 4. The simulated alternative assessments induce MAP scores that also depart further from the observed than for TREC 4. This may be a sign that the non-random selection of alternative assessments have biased the model.

4.4 Sampled models

Exhaustive dual assessment is expensive. An alternative is to perform second assessments on a sample of documents, and estimate a model of assessor disagreement on the sample. A flip-rate

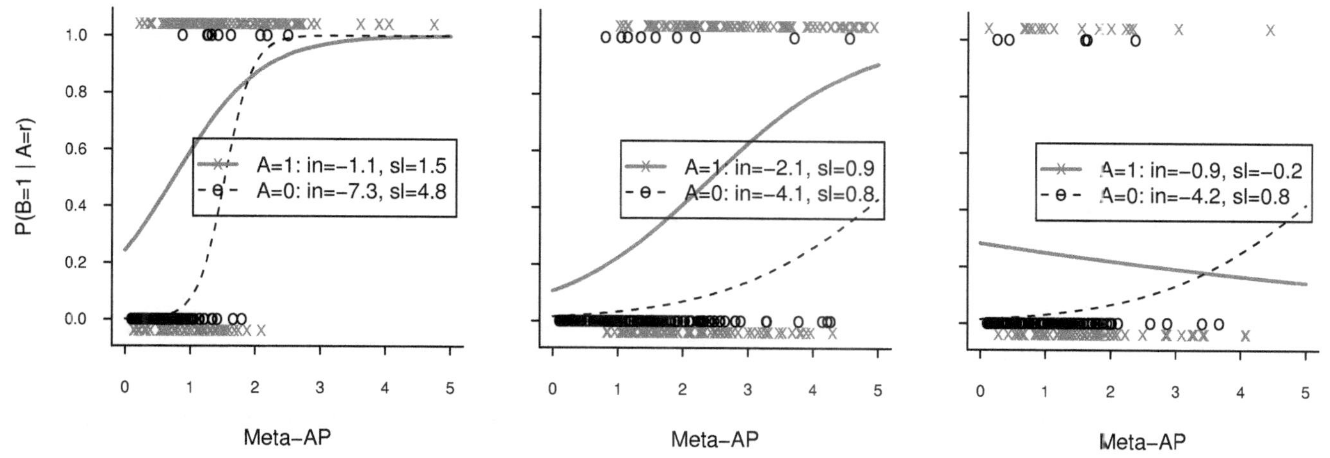

(a) Topic 211 (b) Topic 215 (c) Topic 250

Figure 5: Logistic regression models for example topics from TREC 4, first alternative assessor. Each figure shows alternative assessments of relevance (top) and irrelevance (bottom), for documents initially assessed as relevant (crosses) or irrelevant (circles). The logistic regression curves for the given-relevant (A=1) and given-irrelevant (A=0) conditions are shown, along with their intercept and slope.

Model	Sampling	RMSE	$\bar{\tau}$
Flip-rate	Uniform	0.162	0.779
Meta-AP	Uniform	0.018	0.867
	Even	0.018	0.848

Table 5: Sampled dual assessment: root mean squared error and Kendall's τ, averaged across simulations, between MAP scores from alternative-assessor and from model-generated qrels; summarizing the information in Figure 7.

model is estimated by observing the flip rate on the sample; a logistic metarank model by fitting the regression curve to the sampled documents. Which model is more robust to sampling?

Figure 7 compares the reliability of the flip-rate and metarank models for sampled dual assessment. Only per-topic models are examined. Twenty relevant and twenty irrelevant documents are sampled, making an average of 19% of the former and precisely 10% of the latter. The comparisons are summarized statistically in Table 5. (These results should be compared to the full dual assessment reported in Figure 6 and Table 4). As before, the metarank models produce much more accurate absolute score estimates than the rank-insensitive flip-rate models. Indeed, while the RMSE of the flip-rate model increases by 0.060 or 60% with sampling, while the metarank model RMSE is only 0.003 or 20% higher. Unlike for full dual-assessment, however, the ranking and relative scores of the metarank models for sampled assessment are more stable than for the flip-rate models. Flip rate τ falls from 0.919 to 0.779 with sampling, whereas metarank τ remains the same on 0.867.

The results in Figure 7 and Table 5 demonstrate that the metarank logistic models are highly robust to sampling: with only 10% to 20% of the pool dual-assessed, absolute and relative scores are almost as reliable as with full dual-assessment. Again, this demonstrates the accuracy of the model as a predictor of disagreement (the dependence between metarank score and system conformity aside). In contrast, the flip-rate model degrades badly with sampling, giving absolute scores as much as 80% below the correct values, and introducing sufficient noise that relative scores, and hence system ranking, become unreliable.

4.5 Effect of disagreement on significance

The purpose of significance testing is to determine whether a measured difference in the effectiveness of two retrieval algorithms is due to "chance". In practice, this almost always means determining the extent to which variance due to the topic sample overrides the difference in effectiveness. There are other sources of variance apart from the topic sample, however; variance due to disagreement between assessors is one potentially important source. If two systems are significantly different for a sample of topics but *not* significantly different once assessor disagreement is modeled, the strength of the conclusion is reduced.

To incorporate disagreement into a significance test, we use our simulated qrels in a bootstrap-style significance procedure. For each pair of systems in the TREC-4 set, we sample a set of qrels produced by one of the models described above. We compute the significance between the two systems for that qrels. We can then compare this to the significance between the same two systems for the original qrels. Over many trials, we obtain a sense of the variance in significance due to disagreement as modeled by the simulated assessors.

The above procedure only models variance due to assessors—it no longer models variance due to the topic sample because the topic sample is held fixed in every experiment. To model both sources of variance, when we select two systems to compare, we also obtain a bootstrap sample of 48 topics over which to compare them; since the 48 topics and the qrels will vary with each experiment, this will produce a bootstrap distribution that incorporates variance due to both topic and assessor.

We compare the results of significance tests using the original assessments using three measures: precision (the proportion of system pairs found significant using simulated assessments that are also significant with the original assessments), recall (the proportion of system pairs significant with the original assessments that are also significant with the simulated assessments), and accuracy (the agreement between original and simulated assessments on both

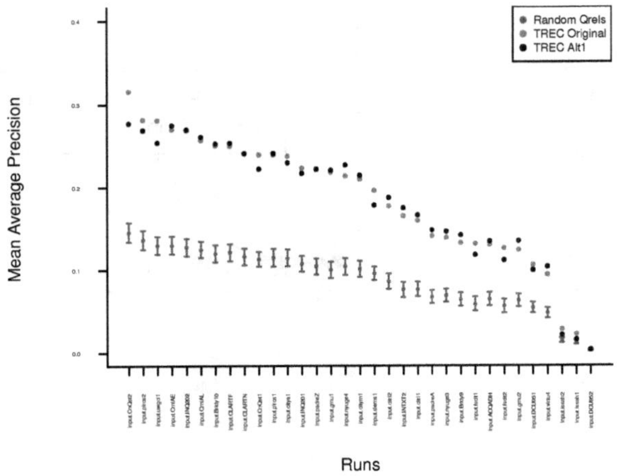

(a) FNR/FPR universal

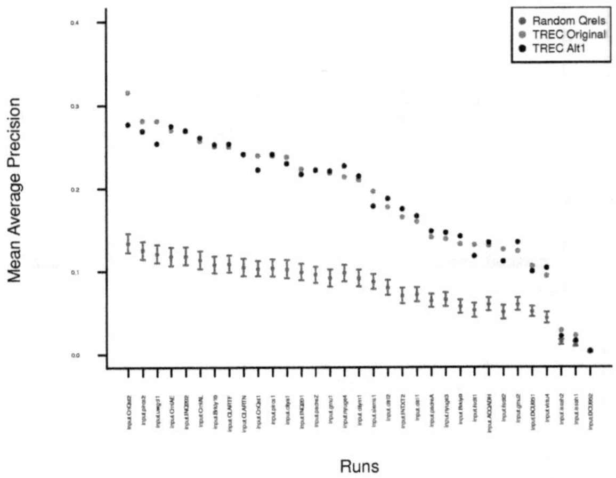

(b) FNR/FPR per-topic

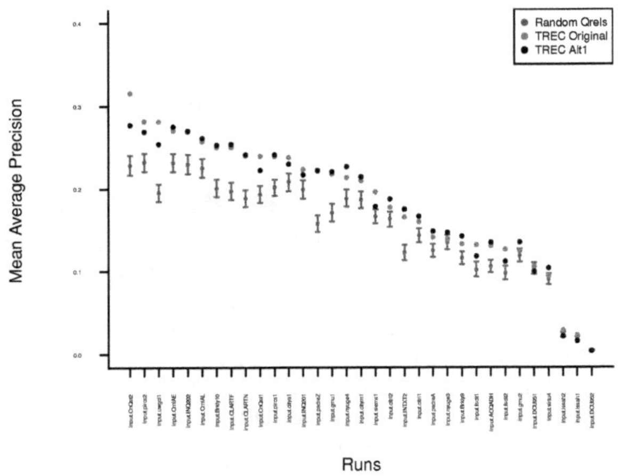

(c) Meta-AP universal

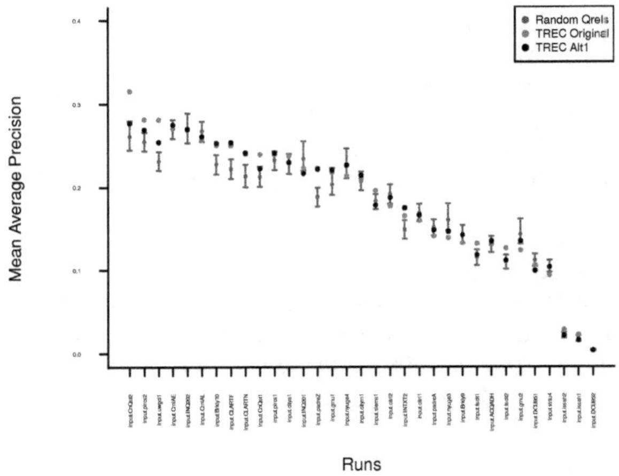

(d) Meta-AP per-topic

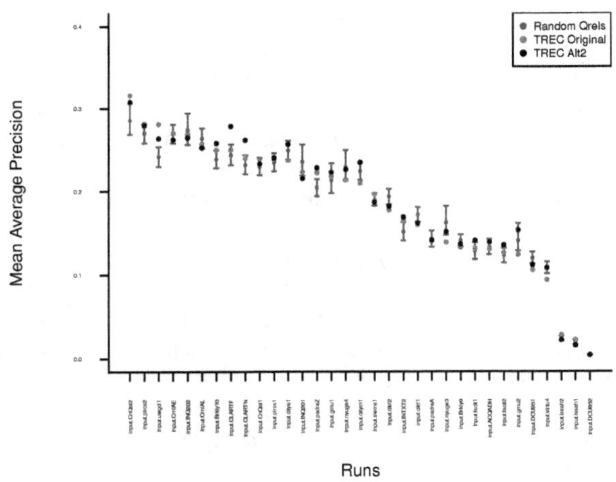

(e) Meta-AP per topic, second assessor

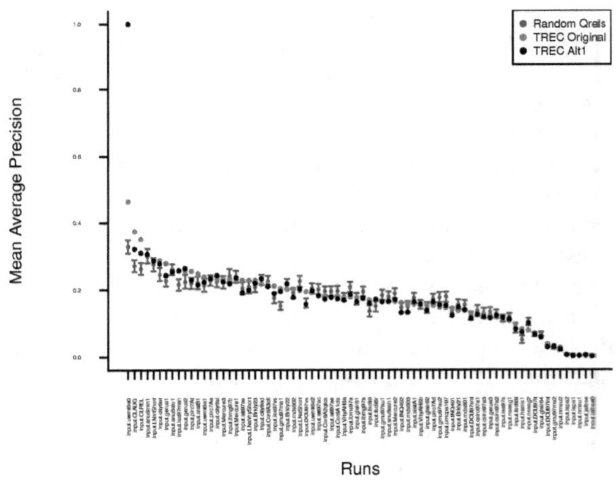

(f) Meta-AP per topic, TREC 6

Figure 6: System MAP scores under original and first alternative qrels, and 95% MAP score ranges under qrels randomly generated from original using different models of assessor disagreement. 1,000 **qrels were simulated for each model.**

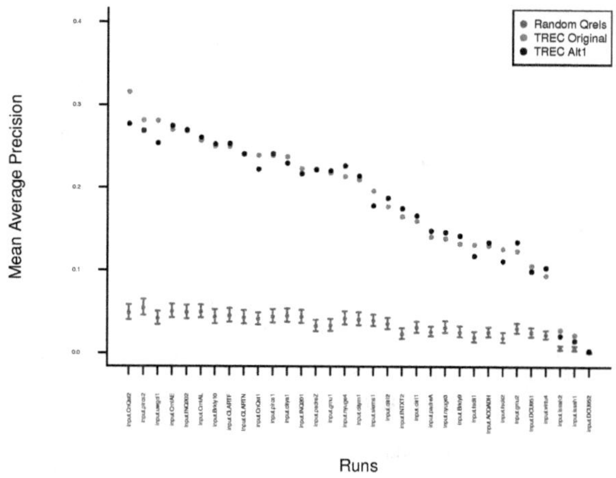

(a) Flip-rate

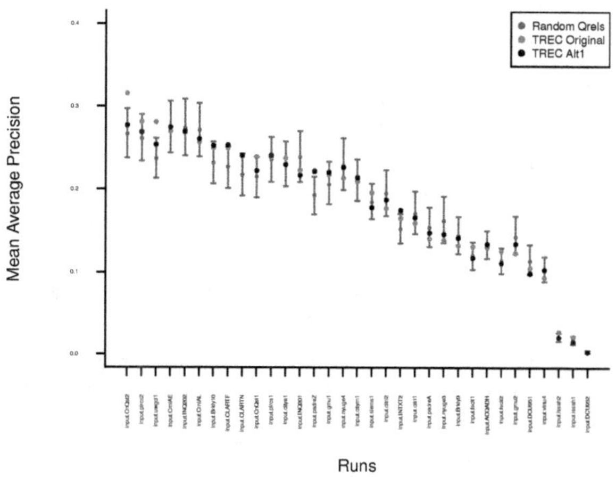

(b) Meta-AP

Figure 7: System MAP scores for random qrels generated from sampled dual-assessment. For each topic, twenty originally-relevant and twenty originally-irrelevant documents were sampled for re-assessment by the first alternative assessor.

significance and non-significance). Note that higher values of these measures indicate greater agreement with the original assessors, but they are not necessarily *better*. If the values were 1.0 across all three, it would suggest that variance due to assessors has no effect whatsoever on significance.

Table 6 summarizes results for four models of disagreement using both procedures. The first set of results, with variance due only to assessor disagreement, has very high recall but fairly low precision and accuracy. Using simulated assessments without varying the topic sample results in significance being found at a higher rate than it is when varying the topic sample without varying assessments. This suggests that variance due to assessments is generally lower than variance due to the topic sample. Within these results there is not a great deal of difference due to the choice of model for simulation.

In the second set of results, varying both assessments and topics, we see decreases in recall but increases in both precision and accuracy; all three are very close in value. Disagreements now tend to be "symmetric": a roughly equal number of pairs go from significant to non-significant as do the other direction. The flip-rate model has slightly higher numbers than the metarank model, suggesting it is more conservative in its modeling of assessor disagreement.

Test	Model	Context	Prec.	Rec.	Acc.
Assessor only	Flip-rate	Universal	0.794	0.995	0.813
		Per-topic	0.813	0.992	0.831
	Meta-AP	Universal	0.802	0.989	0.818
		Per-topic	0.802	0.992	0.820
Assessor + topic	Flip-rate	Universal	0.944	0.942	0.919
		Per-topic	0.943	0.928	0.909
	Meta-AP	Universal	0.880	0.934	0.862
		Per-topic	0.921	0.929	0.892

Table 6: Summary of comparisons between statistical significance with the original TREC-4 assessors and significance with simulated assessors.

The results are somewhat unexpected in that when incorporating more variance into an experiment, one would generally expect that fewer pairs would be found significant, i.e. that recall would decrease while precision would remain high. In our experiment, some pairs that had not been significantly different became significantly different with simulated assessments. One possible reason is bias introduced by the simulation. The models are imperfect, and may assign relevance in such a way that works in favor of certain systems that are less-favored by human assessors. Nevertheless, these results suggest that significance in IR is fairly robust to assessor disagreement.

5. CONCLUSIONS AND FUTURE WORK

In this paper, we have examined the relationship between the rank at which documents are returned and the probability that assessors will disagree about their relevance. Logistic regression has been deployed to test and model this relationship. The meta-AP metarank scoring method has been shown to be the best predictor of three metarank methods considered. We have found that there is a strong and consistent relationship between rank and probability of disagreement. An alternative assessor is much more likely to disagree with an original assessor's relevant judgment if a document has low rank and is returned by few systems. Conversely, a high-ranked document that the original assessor found irrelevant is more likely to produce disagreement from an alternative assessor than is a low-ranked one.

Models of assessor disagreement allow for the simulation of the phenomenon. We have found that rank-sensitive models produce more accurate predictions of absolute scores than rank-insensitive ones, but less accurate relative scores, suggesting a dependence between systems and metarank scores. However, metarank models based upon sample dual assessment are more reliable than rank-insensitive ones for both absolute and relative measures. Indeed, sampled metarank models are almost as reliable as exhaustively-assessed ones, at a fraction of the assessment cost. Finally, we have demonstrated the use of such sampled models in adding assessor variability to test the significance of retrieval evaluation results, finding that while the rate of significance overall does not change, around a tenth of system pairs switch from being significantly to non-significantly different, or vice versa.

We have observed that the dependence between systems and the meta-AP metarank measure produces simulated qrel sets that favor conformist systems. Finding a metarank score that avoids this bias, or developing a method that corrects for it if it occurs, is future work. For instance, metarank contributions from similar systems could be down-weighted. Also, the distribution of meta-AP scores is dependent on both assessment depth and the number of systems in the pool; it is desirable to find a metarank measure less dependent on these factors.

Finally, we observed in Figure 5 that models based even on exhaustive assessment can be sensitive to the assessment and metascore of a small number of documents, making them prone to anomalous behavior (inverse regression, for instance, or sudden transitions in probability, or again models that give zero probability to alternative relevance no matter what the metarank score). This sensitivity will be heightened for sample-based models, and higher still as sample size decreases. A multi-level Bayesian model would help alleviate this problem, by smoothing the logistic models for one topic based upon results on other topics.

Acknowledgments

Ellen Voorhees provided, and helped with the interpretation of, the TREC 4 and TREC 6 multiple-assessment data sets.

References

Javed Aslam and Mark Montague. Models for metasearch. In W. Bruce Croft, D. J. Harper, D. H. Kraft, and Justin Zobel, editors, *Proc. 24th Annual International ACM SIGIR Conference on Research and Development in Information Retrieval*, pages 276–284, New Orleans, Louisiana, USA, September 2001.

Javed Aslam, Virgiliu Pavlu, and Emine Yilmaz. Measure-based metasearch. In Gary Marchionini, Alistair Moffat, John Tait, R. Baeza-Yates, and N. Ziviani, editors, *Proc. 28th Annual International ACM SIGIR Conference on Research and Development in Information Retrieval*, pages 571–572, Salvador, Brazil, August 2005. doi: http://doi.acm.org/10.1145/1076034.1076133.

Peter Bailey, Nick Craswell, Ian Soboroff, Paul Thomas, A. de Vries, and Emine Yilmaz. Relevance assessment: are judges exchangeable and does it matter? In Sung-Hyon Myaeng, Douglas W. Oard, Fabrizio Sebastiani, Tat-Seng Chua, and Mun-Kew Leong, editors, *Proc. 31st Annual International ACM SIGIR Conference on Research and Development in Information Retrieval*, pages 667–674, Singapore, Singapore, July 2008.

D. Bodoff and P. Li. Test theory for assessing IR test collections. In Charles L. A. Clarke, Norbert Fuhr, Noriko Kando, W. Kraaij, and A. de Vries, editors, *Proc. 30th Annual International ACM SIGIR Conference on Research and Development in Information Retrieval*, pages 367–374, Amsterdam, the Netherlands, July 2007.

Ben Carterette. Robust test collections for retrieval evaluation. In Charles L. A. Clarke, Norbert Fuhr, Noriko Kando, W. Kraaij, and A. de Vries, editors, *Proc. 30th Annual International ACM SIGIR Conference on Research and Development in Information Retrieval*, pages 55–62, Amsterdam, the Netherlands, July 2007.

Ben Carterette and Ian Soboroff. The effect of assessor errors on IR system evaluation. In Hsin-Hsi Chen, Efthimis N. Efthimiadis, Jacques Savoy, Fabio Crestani, and Stephanie Marchand-Maillet, editors, *Proc. 33rd Annual International ACM SIGIR Conference on Research and Development in Information Retrieval*, pages 539–546, Geneva, Switzerland, July 2010.

Gordon V. Cormack, Charles L. A. Clarke, Christopher R. Palmer, and Samuel S. L. To. Passage-based refinement (MultiText experiments for TREC-6). In Ellen Voorhees and Donna Harman, editors, *Proc. 6th Text REtrieval Conference*, pages 303–320, Gaithersburg, Maryland, USA, November 1997. NIST Special Publication 500-240.

C. Cuadra and R. Katter. The relevance of relevance assessment. *Proc. American Documentation Institute*, 4:95–99, 1967.

Maura R. Grossman and Gordon V. Cormack. Inconsistent assessment of responsiveness in e-discovery: difference of opinion or human error? In *DESI IV: The ICAIL Workshop on Setting Standards for Searching Electronically Stored Information in Discovery Proceedings*, pages 1–11, Pittsburgh, PA, USA, June 2011.

Donna Harman. Overview of the fourth text REtrieval conference (TREC-4). In Donna Harman, editor, *Proc. 4th Text REtrieval Conference*, pages 1–23, Gaithersburg, Maryland, USA, November 1995. NIST Special Publication 500-236.

D. W. Hosmer, T. Hosmer, S. le Cessie, and S. Lemeshow. A comparison of goodness-of-fit tests for the logistic regression model. *Statistics in Medicine*, 16:965–980, 1997.

Joon Ho Lee. Analyses of multiple evidence combination. In Nicholas J. Belkin, A. Desai Narasimhalu, Peter Willett, and William Hersh, editors, *Proc. 20th Annual International ACM SIGIR Conference on Research and Development in Information Retrieval*, pages 267–276, Philadelphia, PA, USA, July 1997.

Douglas W. Oard, Bruce Hedin, Stephen Tomlinson, and Jason R. Baron. Overview of the TREC 2008 legal track. In Ellen Voorhees and Lori P. Buckland, editors, *Proc. 17th Text REtrieval Conference*, pages 3:1–45, Gaithersburg, Maryland, USA, November 2008. NIST Special Publication 500-277.

Herbert L. Roitblat, Anne Kershaw, and Patrick Oot. Document categorization in legal electronic discovery: computer classification vs. manual review. *Journal of the American Society for Information Science and Technology*, 61(1):70–80, 2010.

T. Saracevic. Relevance: A review of the literature and a framework for thinking on the notion in information science. Part III: Behavior and effects of relevance. *Journal of the American Society for Information Science and Technology*, 58(13):2126–2144, 2007.

Jacques Savoy. Statistical inference in retrieval effectiveness evaluation. *Information Processing & Management*, 33(4):495–512, 1997.

Victor S. Sheng, F. Provost, and Panagiotis G. Ipeirotis. Get another label? improving data quality and data mining using multiple, noisy labelers. In Ying Li, Bing Liu, and Sunita Sarawagi, editors, *Proc. 14th ACM SIGKDD International Conference on Knowledge Discovery and Data Mining*, pages 614–622, Las Vegas, Nevada, USA, August 2008.

Ian Soboroff, Charles Nicholas, and Patrick Cahan. Ranking retrieval systems without relevance judgments. In W. Bruce Croft, D. J. Harper, D. H. Kraft, and Justin Zobel, editors, *Proc. 24th Annual International ACM SIGIR Conference on Research and Development in Information Retrieval*, pages 66–73, New Orleans, Louisiana, USA, September 2001.

Andrew Trotman and Dylan Jenkinson. IR evaluation using multiple assessors per topic. In MingFang Wu, Andrew Turpin, and Amanda Spink, editors, *Proc. 12th Australasian Document Computing Symposium*, pages 9–16, Melbourne, December 2007.

Ellen Voorhees. Variations in relevance judgments and the measurement of retrieval effectiveness. In W. Bruce Croft, Alistair Moffat, C. J. van Rijsbergen, Ross Wilkinson, and Justin Zobel, editors, *Proc. 21st Annual International ACM SIGIR Conference on Research and Development in Information Retrieval*, pages 315–323, Melbourne, Australia, August 1998.

Ellen Voorhees. Variations in relevance judgments and the measurement of retrieval effectiveness. *Information Processing & Management*, 36(5): 697–716, September 2000.

William Webber, Douglas W. Oard, Falk Scholer, and Bruce Hedin. Assessor error in stratified evaluation. In *Proc. 19th ACM International Conference on Information and Knowledge Management*, pages 539–548, Toronto, Canada, October 2010.

William Webber, Bryan Toth, and Marjorie Desamito. Effect of written instructions on assessor agreement. In William Hersh, Jamie Callan, Yoelle Maarek, and Mark Sanderson, editors, *Proc. 35th Annual International ACM SIGIR Conference on Research and Development in Information Retrieval*, Portland, Oregon, USA, August 2012. to appear.

Incorporating Variability in User Behavior into Systems Based Evaluation

Ben Carterette[*], Evangelos Kanoulas[‡], Emine Yilmaz[†]
carteret@cis.udel.edu, ekanoulas@gmail.com, {eminey@microsoft.com, eyilmaz@ku.edu.tr}
[*] Department of Computer & Information Sciences, University of Delaware, Newark, DE
[‡] Information School, University of Sheffield, Sheffield, UK
[†] Microsoft Research, Cambridge, UK & Koc University, Istanbul, Turkey

ABSTRACT

Click logs present a wealth of evidence about how users interact with a search system. This evidence has been used for many things: learning rankings, personalizing, evaluating effectiveness, and more. But it is almost always distilled into point estimates of feature or parameter values, ignoring what may be the most salient feature of users—their variability. No two users interact with a system in exactly the same way, and even a single user may interact with results for the same query differently depending on information need, mood, time of day, and a host of other factors. We present a Bayesian approach to using logs to compute posterior distributions for probabilistic models of user interactions. Since they are distributions rather than point estimates, they naturally capture variability in the population. We show how to cluster posterior distributions to discover patterns of user interactions in logs, and discuss how to use the clusters to evaluate search engines according to a user model. Because the approach is Bayesian, our methods can be applied to very large logs (such as those possessed by Web search engines) as well as very small (such as those found in almost any other setting).

Categories and Subject Descriptors

H.3.4 [**Information Storage and Retrieval**]: Systems and Software—*Performance Evaluation*

Keywords

test collections, user logs, evaluation

1. INTRODUCTION

Every user approaches search in their own way. Some users only ever use web search engines like Google, and they trust these engines implicitly to give them the only result they need at rank one. Others use web search engines for more involved tasks, clicking through several links, reformulating queries, and using advanced features of the system. Still more use other search systems (such as those that index newswire, case law, or biomedical research) frequently; their approach in those systems is probably different from their approach on the web. And of course these groups do not begin to cover the whole space, not to mention the fact that a single user may have different approaches depending on their information need, mood, and a host of other unmeasurable factors.

Recently there has been interest in developing measures that explicitly model user interaction, notably *rank-biased precision* (RBP) [10], *expected reciprocal rank* (ERR) [3], *expected browser utility* (EBU) [16], and time-calibrated measures [14]. These measures use parameterized probabilistic models of actions users may take when browsing ranked results. But when the parameters are set to a single fixed value, these measures lose the ability to reflect variability in the user space. They essentially assume that however that single value is decided on, whether it be based on logs or based on pure rational thought, it reflects users as an aggregate. Like traditional measures, they may miss out on segments of the user population that experience search results in very different ways from the majority.

Fortunately, logs contain a lot of information about variability in how users are interacting with the system. With the right methods, we can take advantage of that variability to more precisely measure the effectiveness of the system to different segments of the user base. We present a Bayesian method for using logged user data to estimate probabilistic models of user interaction: starting with a prior distribution over users, we use a log to update it and produce a posterior distribution representing variability over the user space. We then show how we can use such distributions to evaluate systems, find separate clusters of behavior types for more targeted analysis, and analyzing the log to formulate hypotheses about how users interact with the engine.

One advantage of our approach is that it does not require huge logs, and thus can be used for search systems or tasks that have much smaller user bases than web search (which is the "traditional" domain for applications of mining user logs). This contrasts with other log-based approaches to evaluation and analysis such as bucket testing [7] and interleaving [11], which rely on large amounts of data to draw statistically-powerful conclusions.

This paper is organized as follows: in Section 2, we introduce the idea of forming a probability distribution based on

CIKM'12, October 29–November 2, 2012, Maui, HI, USA.

a structural user model and informed by user logs and show how to compute it. In Section 3, we illustrate the use of this idea to partition a log into smaller segments and analyze behavior within those segments. Section 4 takes this a step further, using clustering to automatically partition the log into segments that may not be obvious to people analyzing a log, and showing that some of the clusters that emerge are quite interesting. In Section 5 we provide evidence that evaluating system quality on the basis of the appropriate segments of user logs can offer new insights into the performance of retrieval systems. We conclude in Section 6 with some directions for future work.

2. BEHAVIOR MODELS AND PROFILES

There are many effectiveness evaluation measures represented in the information retrieval literature. Almost all of them can be seen as encoding a model of a user that interacts with ranked results by stepping down the ranking one-by-one, looking at each document, and deriving utility from those that are relevant. For example, precision at rank k could be seen as modeling a user that always goes to rank k (never beyond) and finds every relevant document to that rank. Average precision (AP) can be understood as modeling a user that browses the retrieved documents from top to bottom and is equally likely to stop at any relevant document. When the user stops at a particular relevant document d, average precision assumes that she has found every relevant document to the rank at which d is retrieved [12] (this may be an unrealistic user model, but it is a user model nevertheless). Discounted cumulative gain has a more explicit user model, using graded judgments to model relative differences in utility amongst relevant documents and a reciprocal-log discount to model waning interest on the part of the user in continuing down the ranking.

Recently there has been interest in describing user interactions with a parameterized *probabilistic* model. The first such example may be Cooper's Expected Search Length (ESL) [4], which can be described as the average number of documents a user must examine before observing all documents relevant to the query. But the probabilistic component in ESL is related more to a system's approach to breaking ties than to anything about a user's behavior. More recently, rank-biased precision (RBP) was the first measure to be based on an explicit probabilistic model of the user: it models a user who, at each rank, flips a biased coin to decide whether to continue to the next document. If the coin comes up tails, the user continues; otherwise, the user abandons the search. This results in the rank of abandonment k having a geometric distribution: $P(k) = (1-\theta)^{k-1}\theta$, where θ is the probability that the coin comes up heads. Then RBP is defined as a sum over ranks k:

$$RBP = \sum_{k=1}^{\infty} rel_k P(k) = \sum_{k=1}^{\infty} rel_k (1-\theta)^{k-1}\theta$$

Another way of understanding θ is as the user's impatience[1] for continuing down the ranked results. The higher θ is, the less patient the user is and the more likely they are to abandon the search early; likewise, the lower θ is, the more documents they are likely to see during their session.

2.1 The cascade model

RBP's model is very simple; there is much about user behavior that it does not model. The *cascade model* is a more complex model that has been shown to more accurately model behavior [5]. Like RBP, it assumes a user stepping down ranked results one by one. Unlike RBP, it does not assume that the probability of continuing is constant over the ranking. In the most general form of the model introduced by Craswell et al. [5], each URL can have its own probability of continuing; these probabilities (which we will call θ_d) could be based on features of the URL, the summary shown for it [16], prior distributions of dwell times [14], and even global features of the ranking or interface. Then the probability that a user stops at rank k is:

$$P(k|\theta) = \theta_{d_k} \prod_{i=1}^{k-1}(1-\theta_{d_i})$$

Using a fixed θ such that $\theta_d = \theta$ for all d produces RBP.

Chapelle et al.'s expected reciprocal rank (ERR) is an effectiveness measure based on the cascade model and graded judgments. It defines θ_d as a function of the relevance grade of d, so that the probability of a user continuing depends on the relevance of the document they are currently looking at [3]. Thus we can say $\theta_{d_g} = \theta_g$ for all documents d judged by a human assessor to have relevance grade g, thereby reducing the parameter space to $|\mathcal{G}|$, the number of grades. ERR is then defined as the expectation of reciprocal ranks:

$$ERR = \sum_{k=1}^{\infty} \frac{1}{k}\theta_{d_k} \prod_{i=1}^{k-1}(1-\theta_{d_i})$$

Chapelle et al. set $\theta_g = (2^g-1)/2^{g_{max}}$, with $g \in \{0, 1, ..., g_{max}\}$ [3]. This is a heuristic, though, and not based on direct empirical evidence pertaining to utility.

Rather than one parameter like RBP, ERR has as many parameters as there are grades in the evaluation. When there are five grades, there are five parameters ($\theta_0 < \theta_1 < \theta_2 < \theta_3 < \theta_4$) each representing the probability that a user stops after seeing a document of that grade. The highest grade in a five-grade system (usually called "perfect") has the highest probability of stopping, modeling a user that is very unlikely to look at anything else after seeing the perfect result. These can also be thought of as representing "patience", but they are now more specifically patience given a particular level of relevance.

Expected browser utility (EBU) [16] is another evaluation measure that is based on the cascade model. Similar to ERR, EBU also assumes that the probability of a user continuing after reaching a particular rank k depends on the relevance of the document at rank k, but adds even more complexity, including the probability that a user clicks on a link given the attractiveness of the snippet (summary) of the document at rank k. Further complexity is possible; the only limiting factors are computation time and the ability to estimate model parameters.

2.2 Computing models from logs

Since the parameters in a user model are meant to reflect user behavior, it makes sense to use logs of user behavior—query logs—to estimate them [17, 18, 16, 9]. Most work

[1]Or patience; we use the two terms interchangeably. If θ represents patience, $1-\theta$ represents lack thereof, and the model can always be reparameterized.

focuses on estimating point values of parameters. But point estimates fail to capture variability in the population. Consider RBP's patience parameter: some information needs will naturally require less patience than others, for example the query "google" versus "linux guide". Furthermore, some users will naturally have more patience than others for the same query; using a point estimate assumes that the model captures all users equally, i.e. each user has equal chances of being satisfied and stopping at the first rank of the results for all queries. We argue that it is more interesting to look at a *distribution* of a parameter and compute distributions of effectiveness evaluation measures over the distribution of the parameter rather than point estimates of evaluation measures.

In general, let θ be a vector of parameters. Let $P(action|\theta)$ be a model of user actions parameterized by θ. For the RBP model, we could define $action$ = stop at rank $k, k \in 1, 2, \ldots$ and $P(k|\theta) = (1-\theta)^{k-1}\theta$. Here θ is the probability that a user goes on to look at result $k+1$ given that they are currently looking at result k, and can be thought of as "impatience" just as we described above. Given no information about user patience, we may initially assume that all values of θ are equally likely, e.g. $\theta \sim Unif(0,1)$. Then we could compute a distribution of RBPs over the population of users by sampling a θ (which models a user) and then computing RBP with that θ.

2.2.1 Rank-biased precision

Of course, a uniform distribution does not come close to modeling the actual population of user patience. Fortunately we have a large source of data from which to glean information about user patience: a query log. Given a log L containing queries and clicks, we will want a posterior for θ conditional on the log:

$$P(\theta|L) \propto P(L|\theta)P(\theta)$$

Carterette et al. [2] showed how to compute $P(\theta|L)$ with a single pass over a log. First, for each individual search (unique query/user pair at a unique time) registered in the log, they count c (the number of clicked URLs) and r (the number of unclicked URLs before the last rank clicked); c is modeled as a function of r and θ using the negative binomial distribution. Using a beta prior for $P(\theta)$, which is conjugate to the negative binomial distribution, gives the following three equations to compute $P(\theta|L)$ in one pass:

$$P(\theta|L) = \sum_{r=0}^{\infty} P(r|L)P(\theta|r,L)$$

$$P(r|L) = \frac{M_r + 1}{\sum_{i=0}^{\infty} M_i + 1}$$

$$P(\theta|r,L) = Beta\left(\theta|\alpha + \sum_{i=1}^{M_r} C_i, \beta + rM_r\right)$$

Here M_r is the total number of searches with r unclicked URLs and the sum $\sum_{i=1}^{M_r} C_i$ is the total number of clicks for searches with r unclicked URLs. α and β are hyperparameters which we define to be 1. There is a special case when r and c are both 0: since there are no clicks from which to estimate patience, we also keep a flat prior that has probability of being sampled from equal to the proportion of searches for which r and c are both 0. The pseudocode in Algorithm 1 illustrates this.

Algorithm 1 Compute posterior distribution $P(\theta|L)$ for ERR with a single pass over a log L.

Require: A log L in which each line has a user/cookie ID, a query ID, URLs with relevance judgments, and the ranks clicked.
Ensure: A multivariate distribution $P(\theta|L)$.

```
for each line ℓ in L do
    c ← total number of clicks
    k_last ← rank of deepest click
    for each grade g with a URL in ℓ do
        if c = 0 then
            M_g[null] ← M_g[null] + 1
        end if
        k_g ← min rank of URL with grade g
        c_g ← number of clicks on documents with rank ≥ k_g
        if c_g > 0 then
            r ← k_last − c_g
            M_g[r] ← M_g[r] + 1
            C_g[r] ← C_g[r] + c_g
        end if
    end for
end for
for each grade g do
    for B trials do
        sample a value r from indexes of M_g according to
        frequency distribution
        if r = null then
            sample θ_g from Beta(1, 1)
        else
            sample θ_g from Beta(1 + C_g[r], 1 + r · M_g[r])
        end if
    end for
end for
```

To compute $P(\theta|L)$ with a single pass, we will assume that each line in the log has (at a minimum) a user or cookie ID, a query ID, and the ranks of clicked URLs. From that information we extract the deepest rank clicked k_{last}, the total number of clicks c, and then compute $r = k_{last} - c$. We increment M_r by one and increment C_r by c. When complete, we know the total number of queries with r no-clicks as well as the total number of clicks for those queries; this is what we need to compute $P(\theta|r,L)$. To do that, we repeatedly sample a value of r from the M_r distribution and use the corresponding M_r and C_r to compute parameters for a beta distribution from which we sample to generate θs.

2.2.2 Expected reciprocal rank

In ERR, the parameter θ represents the probability of a user continuing to browse conditional on seeing a document of a particular grade. We will need to estimate a distribution $P(\theta|L,g)$ for each grade g. As with our RBP distribution, we sum over r to obtain:

$$P(\theta|L,g) = \sum_{r=0}^{\infty} P(r|L,g)P(\theta|r,L,g)$$

We will understand the distribution $P(r|L,g)$ as the probability of observing a query with r unclicked documents given that there is a document of grade g in its results. $P(\theta|r,L,g)$ is the probability that the user will have patience to continue browsing *past* the document of grade g in those results.

We change the RBP algorithm outlined above to only

		ℓ_1			ℓ_2	
rank	g	URLs	click?	g	URLs	click?
1	4	URL_1	✓	1	URL_1	✓
2	0	URL_2		2	URL_2	
3	0	URL_3		1	URL_3	
4	0	URL_4		2	URL_4	✓
5	0	URL_5		1	URL_5	
6	1	URL_6		0	URL_6	
7	0	URL_7		2	URL_7	✓
8	0	URL_8		0	URL_8	✓
9	0	URL_9		0	URL_9	
10	0	URL_{10}		0	URL_{10}	✓

Table 1: Two example rankings of URLs with relevance judgments (given as a numeric grade g) and clicks (✓).

count clicks that occur on or below a document of a particular grade; Algorithm 1 gives complete pseudocode. The first 16 lines compute numbers from the log, storing counts of queries and total numbers of clicks for each r and each grade in the $M_g[]$ and $C_g[]$ arrays. The special case when $r = 0$ and $c = 0$ is held in a special place in M_g given a *null* index in this pseudocode. The last 10 lines actually perform the sampling.

As an example of how the algorithm works, suppose we have a log with two lines shown in Table 1 (as columns). The first, ℓ_1, has a "perfect" document at rank 1 and a "fair" document at rank 6. The user has clicked at rank 1, and that is the last registered click. There are no unclicked documents, so $r = 0$. $M_4[0]$, the number of lines with at least one "perfect" document in the ranking and no unclicked documents, is incremented by 1; $C_4[0]$, the total number of clicks for lines with at least one "perfect" document and no unclicked documents, is also incremented by 1. Since there were no clicks on or after the "fair" document, we simply assume the user never saw it, and thus do not take it into consideration; M_1 and C_1 are unchanged (as are M_2, C_2, M_3, and C_3).

The second line, ℓ_2, has three "fair" documents (at ranks 1, 3, and 5) and three "good" documents (at ranks 2, 4, and 7). The user has clicked on ranks 1, 4, 7, 8, and 10. For $g = 1$, there are 5 unclicked documents and 5 total clicks on or below the first rank with a "fair" document; $M_1[5]$ is incremented by 1, and $C_1[5]$ is incremented by 5. For $g = 2$, $k_g = 2$. Then, treating the document at rank 1 as unclicked, there are 6 unclicked documents and 4 total clicks, so $M_2[6]$ is incremented by 1 and $C_2[6]$ is incremented by 4. The click at rank 1 provides no evidence for whether a user will continue after rank 2, so treating the document at rank 1 as unclicked functions as a prior for the user having the patience to get to rank 2 in the first place (independently of the relevance judgments).

2.3 Fitting the models to data

To fit one of the models above, we need query log data. For RBP, we only require queries and ranks of clicks. For ERR we need query, ranks of clicks, and relevance judgments. The *amount* of query log data is somewhat incidental; we can compute a posterior whether the log is very large or very small.

We have accumulated a rather large amount of log data from different search engines. The AOL data is well-known;

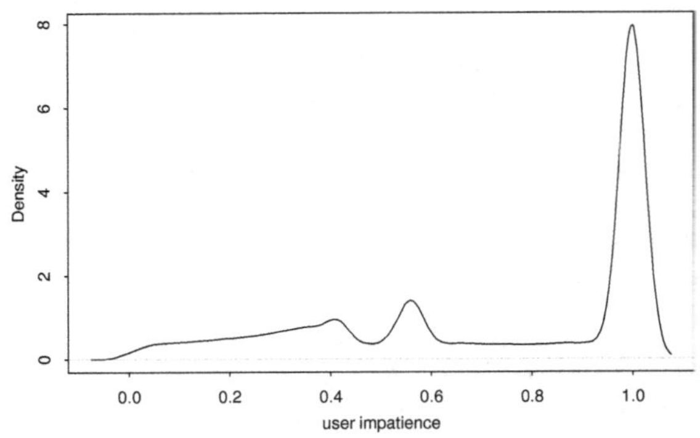

Figure 1: Posterior distribution for RBP's patience parameter θ computed from a web search engine log. Note that higher values of θ reflect *less* patience for browsing down a ranked list.

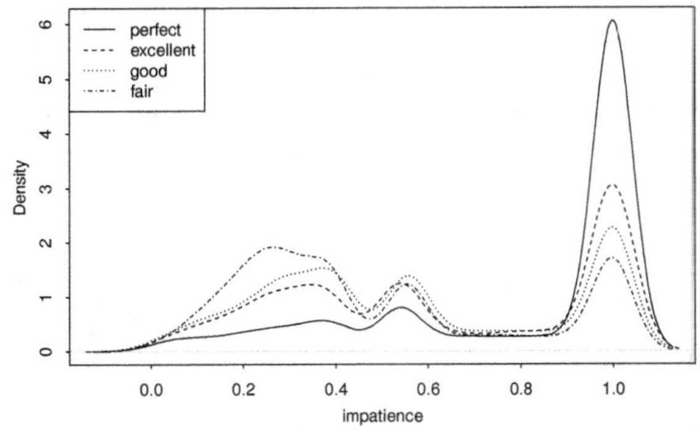

Figure 2: Posterior distributions for ERR's parameters $\theta_1..\theta_4$ computed from a web search engine log. Note that higher values of θ reflect greater likelihood of stopping after encountering a document of that grade.

it has queries, user IDs, and click ranks, but no relevance judgments. Yahoo! recently released log data under its Academic Relations Webscope program[2] consisting of anonymized query IDs, cookie IDs, click ranks, and graded relevance judgments (on a five-point scale). We have an additional proprietary log that is similar to the Yahoo! log but that also contains human judgments of query type. Most of the results we present are based on the Yahoo! log.

We have elected to define $\theta_0 \equiv 0$, i.e. we assume that a user will never abandon the search after seeing a "bad" URL (they will always continue to look at the next one). This is partly because ERR will not use judgments of nonrelevance otherwise, and partly because there are many missing judgments in our log data. These missing judgments likely affect the distribution of θ_0 more than any other parameter, since there are far fewer documents that have actually been judged "bad" versus "fair".

Figure 1 shows a posterior distribution for RBP's θ based on a web search engine log. Note the high peak at $\theta \approx 1$; this means that it is very common for users to only click on the top-ranked result. Figure 2 shows four posterior distribu-

[2]`http://webscope.sandbox.yahoo.com`

tions, one for each of ERR's parameters for four relevance grades. Note that the peak is present in all four, but its prominence decreases dramatically as relevance decreases, while the prominence of the hump to the left increases as relevance decreases. This supports the assumption of the cascade model that users are less likely to continue browsing after seeing more highly-relevant documents.

2.3.1 *Qualities of the distribution*

We note a few peculiar qualities of the distribution plots in Figures 1 and 2. First, there are clear peaks at certain points. Second, the peaks begin to disappear below 0.4, with the distribution becoming more smooth. Third, the distribution is quite flat in between the peaks above 0.4.

All three of these qualities are emergent from the Bayesian updating of the negative binomial model. The key parameters are c, the number of clicks, and r, the number of unclicked URLs. Consider an infinitely-long log in which every query has the same values of c and r. Using our approach, a posterior distribution of θ given this log will have all its mass at a single fixed value of θ. The negative binomial distribution is such that for most values of c and r, those θs occur below 0.4; thus if c and r were uniformly distributed through the log, the distribution would have most of its mass to the left. This is counteracted by the fact that low values of c and r are far more common—in particular, $c = 1$ and $r = 0$ or $r = 1$ (i.e. clicks at ranks 1 and 2)—and result in higher values of θ. For $c = 1, r = 0$ (a single click at rank 1) in an infinite log, θ will be 1; since this case is common in logs, there is a peak there. For $c = 1, r = 1$ (a single click at rank 2), it will be 0.5, and the peak near 0.5 is again explained by the commonness of that case. As c increases and r stays low (i.e. as users click more and more of the ranked URLs), values of θ increase towards 1, but these cases are rare in the logs, and therefore mostly subsumed by the flat prior. As r increases (and users click fewer of the ranked URLs), low values of θ become more frequent and less discriminant, and therefore the distribution is smoother in the lower range.

So while the distributions look somewhat strange, the peculiarities are explainable from the model and the nature of the log. Furthermore, a log that looks fundamentally different (by not having so many queries for which users abandon early, for instance) will have a different distribution. We shall see some examples below.

2.4 Evaluating using parameter distributions

Once we have a posterior distribution, we can form a marginal distribution for an evaluation measure reflecting effectiveness over the population. For each possible value of RBP for a topic, we compute the probability of getting that value if we were to sample θ from the posterior $P(\theta|L)$:

$$P(RBP = y) = \int P(RBP = y|\theta)P(\theta)d\theta \qquad (1)$$

where $P(RBP = y|\theta)$ is 1 if RBP computed with parameter θ is y and 0 otherwise. This looks a bit complicated but it is really quite simple; we can compute it by sampling θs from $P(\theta|L)$, computing RBP based on that θ, and over many trials forming the density $P(RBP)$. When we have many topics to evaluate, we just do this for each one, then average the RBPs for each value of θ. The marginal distribution is then over mean RBP.

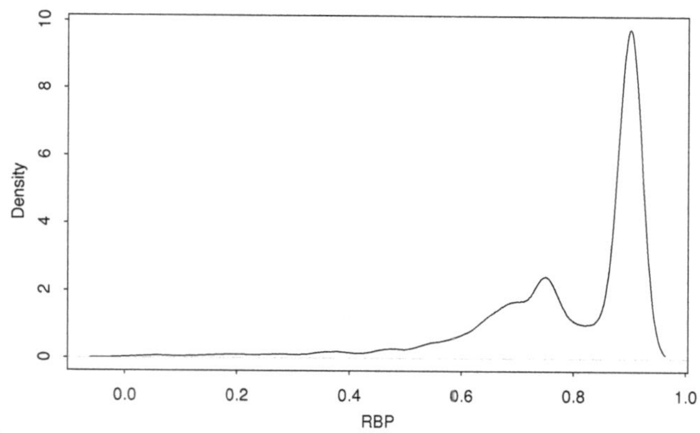

Figure 3: Distribution of mean RBP over the distribution of θ shown in Figure 1.

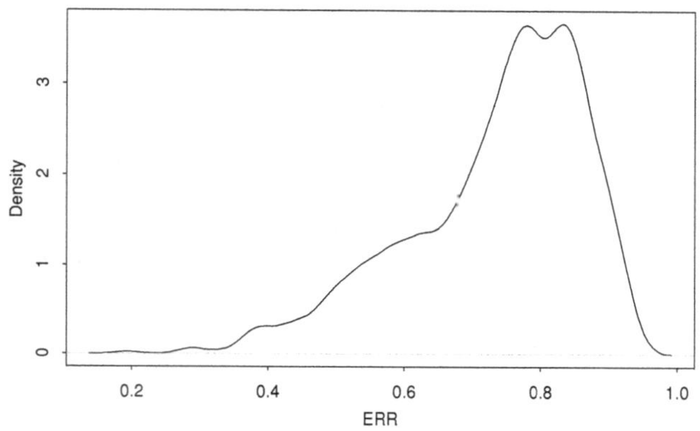

Figure 4: Distribution of mean ERR over the distribution of θs shown in Figure 2.

Similarly,

$$P(ERR = y) = \int \cdots \int P(ERR = y|\theta)P(\theta)d\theta_1 \cdots d\theta_{g_{max}} \qquad (2)$$

Since θ is a vector of $|\mathcal{G}|$ parameters, there is an integral over each parameter. Still, computing $P(ERR)$ is as simple as computing $P(RBP)$; we sample a vector of parameters θ from distributions such as those in Figure 2 and compute ERR with those parameters. Note that we are *not* integrating over θ_0. As discussed above, we fix $\theta_0 = 0$, since ERR does not make sense otherwise.

Figure 3 shows the distribution of mean RBP for one of our web search engines based on $P(\theta|L)$ computed from its log. Note the peak near RBP = 0.9; this reflects the fact that for most users only the first document is examined, and for many queries that is indeed good enough. Figure 4 shows the distribution of mean ERR for the same engine based on the distributions in Figure 2. ERR's more precise user model suggests that while this engine has a high ERR for most users, there may be some for which the user experience is substantially less positive.

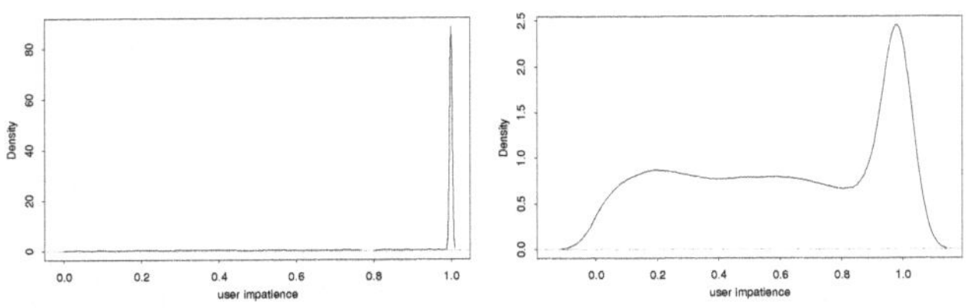

Figure 5: Left: posterior distribution for RBP's parameter θ for the query "google" in the AOL log. Right: the same for the query "weather".

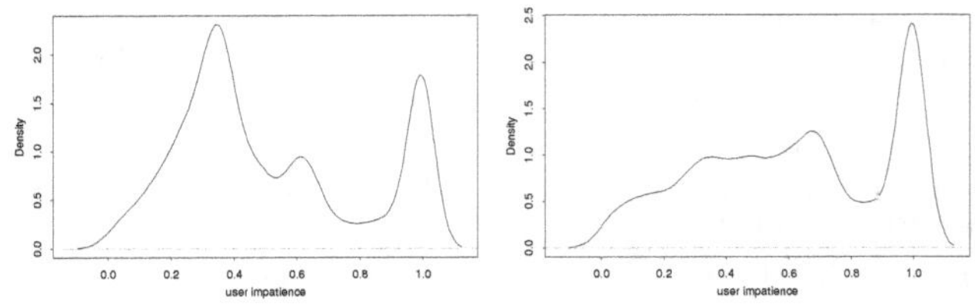

Figure 6: Posterior distributions for RBP's parameter θ for two users in the AOL log. Both users submitted more than 1,000 queries in the log.

3. DECOMPOSING USER PROFILES

Above we showed how to compute a distribution for an effectiveness measure parameter given a complete log. The log encompasses a great variety of different types of users, queries, and tasks or information needs. Instead of computing one distribution for the whole log, it may make sense to compute different distributions for different segments of the log, then evaluate separately using those distributions.

For instance, returning to the example of "google" and "linux guide", one would expect that for queries similar to "google", most users would interact with the search engine in a similar way, mainly clicking on the top returned result. Hence, we expect a narrow distribution of the parameter θ around high values. On the other hand, for queries similar to "linux guide" we expect users to demonstrate a high variability in their interaction with the returned results. It makes more sense for queries similar to "google" that the retrieval system to be evaluated against a narrow distribution of the parameters θ, while for queries similar to "linux guide" it be evaluated against a different and possibly high-variance distribution of the parameters θ. (Note that similarity will be defined more carefully in Section 4.)

In the limit, we could compute a distribution for a single user interacting with results for a single query; this would reflect the possibility that a user could interact with results differently depending on many factors that are not captured in the log, not known to researchers currently, or cannot be measured in any practical way.

3.1 Query profiles

We can take a log and partition it into multiple smaller logs, one for each unique query. We can then use these smaller logs (which we will call L_q) to inform a posterior distribution for θ, which we can denote as $P(\theta_q|L_q)$. Looking at a posterior distribution for a query tells us something about how users are interacting with the system for that particular query; comparing distributions between two queries tells us something about differences in user interactions for the two. We have done this for all of our logs, but the only one that has original query text is the AOL log, so in this section we focus on that. Note that since the AOL log has no relevance judgments, we can only look at the RBP parameter, not the ERR parameters.

Figure 5 shows the RBP distribution for the queries "google" and "weather" in the AOL query log. The former is clearly highly navigational: 75% of users who input the query clicked on rank 1 and stopped, and another 22% didn't click anything. The remaining 3% went deeper into the ranking, with about half of those looking at rank 3 and the other half going beyond rank 3.

The latter is more varied. It has some navigational qualities, as 74% of users that clicked something clicked on the top-ranked result. But only about 36% of users with this query clicked anything; 64% did not click any of the ranked results. This may suggest that the query is poorly-formed (some users may be looking for a site like `weather.com`, others may be looking for local weather). It may also suggest that there was a weather vertical in the interface (like there is in modern search engines) that gave the user everything they needed without requiring a click. Clearly using the same distribution of the parameter θ when evaluating a system over these two queries is not appropriate.

3.2 User profiles

Similarly, we can partition the log into multiple smaller logs, one for each unique user. We will call these L_u, and again we can use them to inform a behavioral profile for an individual user. Looking at these can tell us something about how individual users experience results (conditional on the queries they are submitting).

Again, the AOL log is the only one with user information that can be directly linked to queries. The other logs have dissociated user information from queries and so cannot be used for these illustrations.

Figure 6 shows the RBP parameter distributions for two different users in the AOL query log (both of whom have more than 1,000 queries in the log). These users are quite different; both are patient enough to have significant probability mass in the left part of the distribution, though both submit a significant number of queries for which they only click at rank 1. The right plot shows a user that clicks often enough that there is only a small dip at $\theta_u = 0.8$; as we discussed in Section 2.3.1, most of these distributions have a gap between $\theta_u \approx 1$ and $\theta_u \approx 0.5$ because few users click more times than they do not click (i.e. c is rarely greater than r except when $c = 1$ and $r = 0$). This particular user *does* have a tendency to click on many results, and that shows up in the shape of the distribution.

3.3 Task profiles

If we have some indication of user task, we can aggregate over user/queries that match that task. One example alluded to above is *informational* and *navigational*, a very common classification scheme for web queries. We have human navigational and informational judgments for one of our search engine logs; the posterior parameter distributions for the two classes are shown in Figure 7. The navigational class clearly shows a high peak near $\theta = 1$ with almost nothing below that. The informational class also has a peak near $\theta = 1$, but it is a smaller peak and there is still significant

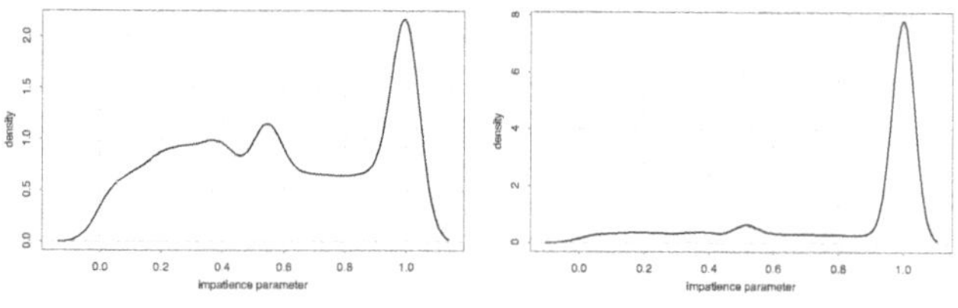

Figure 7: Profiles for informational and navigational classes.

density in the lower part of the domain. These reflect the expected behavior for these two query types.

An interesting question here is whether there are queries that have been assigned a particular task class but have particular instances for which user behavior reflects a different class. For example, "google" is almost certainly a navigational query, and indeed 76% of users with that query in the AOL log clicked only on rank 1. But there is a small group of users—about 3%—that click as far down as rank 5; for these, it might be argued that they have a more informational need that spurred that query. The remaining 21% did not click anything.

4. CLUSTERING PROFILES

Clustering query logs is useful for discovering patterns in the ways users are interacting with an engine. Most work on clustering within logs focuses on clustering queries, using similarities among clicked URLs [15, 1] or similarities in terms used in query refinements [13]. Such work could be applied to users as well, forming clusters based on similar query formulations [8].

Behavior profiles give us the ability to cluster the log according to a user model and the *variability* of interaction with the engine rather than anything about text or specific URLs. Text-based clustering cannot capture some of the most fundamental divisions that have been identified in logs, particularly informational versus navigational needs—there is not much in the way of term similarity to connect two randomly-chosen navigational queries, for instance, nor is there much that would allow a clustering algorithm to put two randomly-chosen informational queries together. By clustering on distributions, we use click position information, but we also take advantage of variability in click positions. Furthermore, we can cluster along any dimension of interest we can identify in the log (e.g., clustering per query, per user, per session, etc.).

Apart from revealing interesting behavior profiles, clustering can be helpful in evaluating retrieval systems. If we could collect clicks for every query in a test collection such as those produced by TREC, then we could infer a patience distribution for each query separately and evaluate retrieval systems using the appropriate parameter distribution. In systems-based experimentation, we do not have the ability to observe users interacting with the retrieval systems. If query clustering based on behavior profiles could provide a classification of queries with meaningful semantics (e.g. navigational vs informational queries, or precision-oriented vs recall-oriented queries), then human assessors could identify the class for each query in the collection and use a single parameter distribution for each such class.

4.1 Clustering algorithm

As mentioned above, we can form posterior distributions for a single instance of a query, all instances of a single unique query, any single search performed by a user, all searches performed by one user, or any other groups of queries or users. In this section we assume we have some number m of posterior distributions $P(\theta_m|L)$ and our goal is to cluster them.

In order to cluster the distributions, we use the clustering algorithm proposed by Kejzar et al. [6] for clustering discrete distributions. The proposed algorithm is based on a modification to the standard K-means (leaders) clustering algorithm. Instead of using the standard squared Euclidean distance as the distance metric, it uses the *relative error metric*, which its authors have shown to provide more informative results than the Euclidean distance.

Our distributions are (strictly speaking) continuous, not discrete, so to use this algorithm we must transform them to discrete distributions. We do this by sampling and binning: for each value of θ sampled from a posterior $P(\theta|L)$, we place it into one of eleven bins by rounding it to the nearest tenth. Therefore we are essentially clustering on 11 features, each of which represents the probability that a sampled θ would have (roughly) a particular value, or in other words, the probability that a sampled "user" would have a given degree of patience for browsing results. We tried other discretizations into more bins, but they did not produce substantially different clusters than what we show here.

Once the algorithm has placed each posterior distribution into a cluster C_i, we re-compute a posterior $P(\theta_{C_i}|L)$ for the cluster by aggregating log data. When the clustering is complete, we have K posterior distributions, each associated with one of our clusters.

4.2 Cluster-based exploration

We first computed posterior distributions $P(\theta_q|L)$ for every unique query in our proprietary log. We then formed increasing numbers of clusters of queries to look for patterns. Our first two clusters are shown in Figure 8. Note the similarity to the posterior distributions for the navigational and informational classes shown in Figure 7: our first cluster looks very much like the navigational class, and the second looks like the informational class only with less of a peak at $\theta_{C_2} \approx 1$.

For our proprietary log we have human labels of navigational/informational intent, and we compared the queries in each cluster to those judgments. The first cluster in Figure 8 consists of about 1600 queries, of which about 1200 (75%) have been labeled "navigational" by a human assessor. The second cluster consists of about 3900 queries, with 700 (18%) labeled "navigational". About 62% of all navigational queries fell into the first cluster, with the remaining 38% in the second. Thus, while the clusters seem similar to navigational and informational intents, they are also somewhat different. It is gratifying to see that the informational/navigational split is "real" (indeed seemingly the primary dimension along which queries are clustered), but also interesting that there are queries that have been labeled as one class but have behavioral patterns more like the other. It may be that instead of an informational/navigational split, the more salient description is "high-precision" versus "high-recall", with users issuing the former satisfied by one highly-relevant document (which may be a Wikipedia page for an

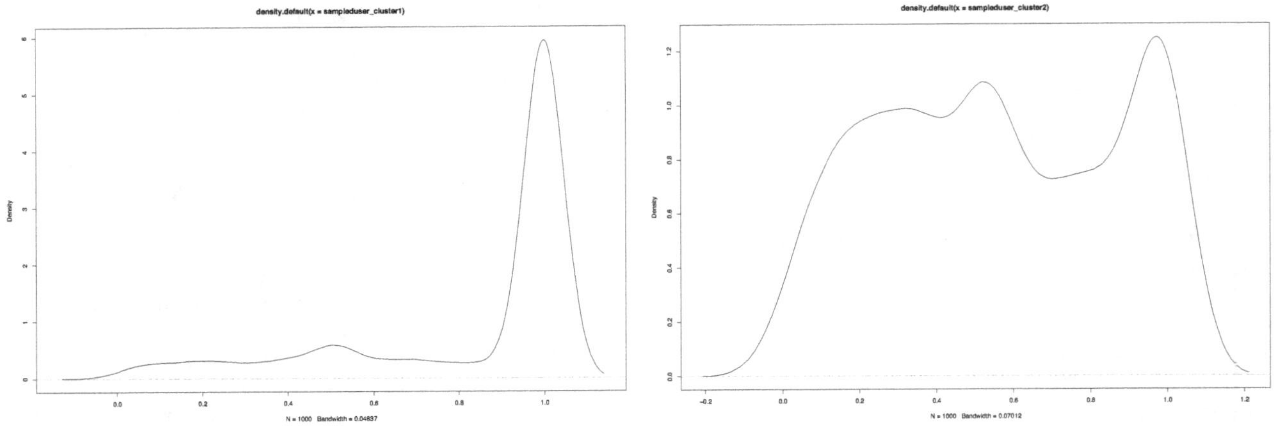

Figure 8: **Posterior distributions computed from click information for two clusters of queries. The left seems to be a "navigational" cluster and the right an "informational" cluster, but these labels are not perfectly correlated to the clusters.**

informational query) and users issuing the latter requiring more relevant documents and thus progressing deeper into the ranking.

We also tried forming three clusters from this data (not shown). In this case there are two clusters that are even more clearly navigational and informational (comprising 83% and 15% navigational queries respectively), with a third cluster that is somewhere in between (37% navigational). This third cluster seems to consist of lower-volume queries for which there is not much click evidence to move the prior, but it may still suggest that there are types of intents other than the two described above.

Figure 9 shows two clusters of queries for the Webscope log, this time with the distributions superimposed. These distributions look quite similar to those in Figure 8: one has a very high peak near 1 with little density elsewhere, while the other has a smaller peak at 1 that is only slightly higher than the other high points in the distribution. We do not have navigational/informational class labels for this data, but since we have relevance judgments we can look at the proportion of queries that have at least one "perfect" document that appear in each cluster (assuming that a query that has an associated document labeled as "perfect" is likely to have navigational intent). By that measure, the first cluster has 63% of the queries with at least one "perfect"; the other has about 37%.

Figure 10 shows four clusters of queries for the same log. The first two clusters look very similar to the two in Figure 9, and the next two look very flat, with only a slight rise in cluster C_4 near $\theta_{C_4} \approx 0.8$. Their flatness suggests that they are clusters of queries with low click volume; there does not seem to be information to update the prior. Looking at them closer shows that they have peaks and valleys much like others we have seen, and thus are capturing *something* about behavior, but at this scale those peaks and valleys are not visible. It turns out, however, that they are meaningful; we will see this in Section 5 below.

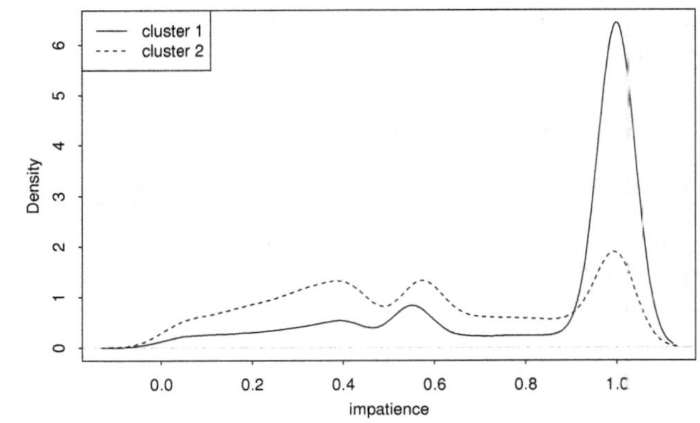

Figure 9: Posterior distributions computed from click information for two clusters of queries.

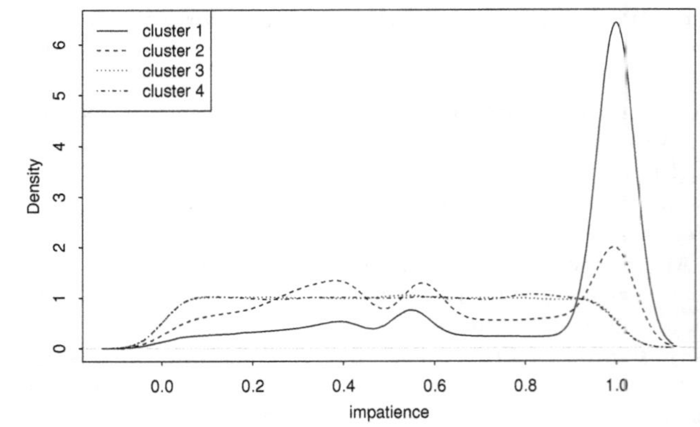

Figure 10: Posterior distributions computed from click information for four clusters of queries.

5. EVALUATION BASED ON CLUSTERS

The next question is whether the evaluation of a system differs depending on which data it has been evaluated against, and in particular whether the choice of cluster affects conclusions drawn from the evaluation. If we reach substantially different conclusions about a system depending on the cluster we evaluate against, it suggests that system evaluation should *not* be performed with the same uniform set of parameters, but instead should be adapted for the particular query, user, or task.

To perform these evaluations, we used the cluster distributions shown above in Eq. 1 and 2 to generate distributions for mean RBP and mean ERR; that is, we select a patience cluster, sample a value of θ (either a scalar or a vector value, depending on measure) from that cluster, evaluate all queries in the log using that value of θ in RBP or ERR, and then average the RBP/ERR values over queries. Over many such trials we obtain a marginal distribution for the measure over the parameter posterior distribution in each chosen cluster. Note that all of our clusters are based on the RBP parameter distributions; we formed posterior distributions for ERR parameters by computing them from the queries and clicks in each existing cluster based on RBP.

Figure 11 shows evaluation results given the two clusters in Figure 9. The left plot shows distributions for mean RBP: it is always quite high (above 0.8), but it also clearly tracks the differences between the two clusters. RBP calculated against the first cluster has a high peak near RBP $\approx$ 1, since most queries that fall into that cluster have a "perfect" document at rank 1 that is the only one that users click on. There are still enough queries in this cluster with clicks deeper in the ranking that some of the users it represents are more patient; these patient users find few relevant documents after the top-ranked one and therefore find the system has a lower RBP (the peak around 0.75). RBP calculated against the second cluster has a much smaller peak at RBP $\approx$ 1 and more mass lower in the distribution. For more patient users, the system represented by this log is significantly underperforming on average.

The right plot in Figure 11 shows distributions for mean ERR. They are clearly very different from each other. The distribution based on the first cluster evaluates the system highly on average, but has a great deal of variability, with values below 0.5 not uncommon. The peak around ERR$\approx$ 0.8 reflects the high probability of users abandoning after the first "perfect" document. The distribution based on the second cluster tends to evaluate the system much worse, with an expected ERR around 0.55. This strongly suggests that the data used to evaluate the engine is important, and different sources of data can lead to very different conclusions.

We also looked at evaluation against four patience clusters. Recall from Figure 10 that two of the clusters seemed quite flat, with little apparent different between them, suggesting that they may be artifactual rather than reflect some real difference in user behavior. But as Figure 12 shows, the evaluation results for the four clusters differ greatly. The first two clusters result in similar RBP distributions as those in Figure 11, suggesting that queries in the other two clusters are not important to defining the shape of the first two clusters (in some sense supporting the idea that those two clusters reflect something real about behavior). The two new clusters are similar, but one clearly has a higher peak at RBP$\approx$ 0.8, reflecting the very slight bump in the posterior distribution near $\theta_{C_4} \approx 0.8$ above θ_{C_3}. Furthermore, these two distributions are both very different from the other two.

Figure 12 also shows distributions for mean ERR. Again the first two are similar to those in Figure 11, and the two new distributions are both different from each other as well as different from the original two.

These results point to a very high variability in how users will perceive a system's effectiveness depending on both the query and the users themselves. There is therefore much potential for improving effectiveness.

6. CONCLUSIONS

We have presented a method for estimating a posterior distribution for parameters of a probabilistic user model from log data. In particular, we showed how to apply the method to the user models that the evaluation measures RBP and ERR are based on and compute posterior distributions for RBP's "patience" parameter and ERR's relevance grade-based parameters with a single pass over a log. Since our method is Bayesian (and thus involves updating a prior based on evidence), it can be used with very small amounts of log data as well as very large. We used it to form distributions for unique queries, unique users, and individual submissions of a query by a user. With these sorts of distributions, we can cluster instances in the log according to similarity in browsing behavior; by examining these clusters we found that evaluation results can depend heavily on the data used to estimate evaluation measure parameters.

As noted above, this reveals a great deal of opportunity for better understanding and improving effectiveness. Techniques could include using different retrieval algorithms for queries or personalizing the retrieval algorithm for users, in both cases depending on which patience cluster they fall into. Our results also support the idea that a simple evaluation by RBP or ERR using point estimates of parameters is not enough to understand system effectiveness; there is still too much variance in users that is not modeled by those parameter values.

We further intend to extend the models we have presented to more complex models of user behavior, such as those presented recently using summary quality [16] or user dwell time [14]. There has been much work on this in the information science and information retrieval literature, and we believe we have a novel contribution to the body of literature.

7. REFERENCES

[1] Doug Beeferman and Adam Berger. Agglomerative clustering of a search engine query log. In *Proceedings of the sixth ACM SIGKDD international conference on Knowledge discovery and data mining*, KDD '00, pages 407–416, 2000.

[2] Ben Carterette, Evangelos Kanoulas, and Emine Yilmaz. Simulating simple user behavior for system effectiveness evaluation. In *Proceedings of the 20th ACM international conference on Information and knowledge management*, CIKM '11, pages 611–620, New York, NY, USA, 2011. ACM.

[3] Olivier Chapelle, Donald Metzler, Ya Zhang, and Pierre Grinspan. Expceted reciprocal rank for graded relevance. In *Proceedings of CIKM*, 2009.

[4] William S. Cooper. On selecting a measure of retrieval effectiveness. Part I. *Readings in Information Retrieval*, pages 191–204, 1997.

[5] Nick Craswell, Onno Zoeter, Michael Taylor, and Bill Ramsey. An experimental comparison of click position-bias models. In *Proceedings of the international conference on Web search and web data mining*, WSDM '08, pages 87–94, New York, NY, USA, 2008. ACM.

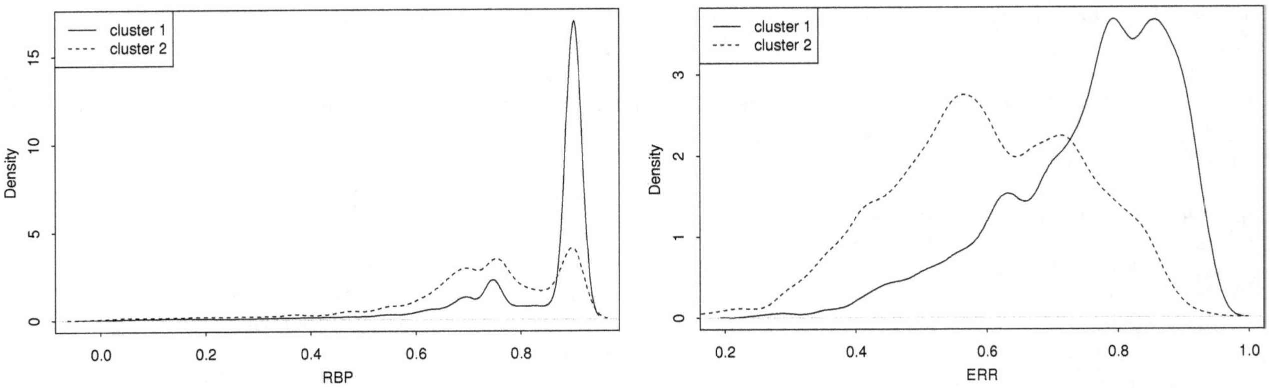

Figure 11: Left: distributions of mean RBP given the two cluster-based posterior distributions in Figure 9. Right: distributions of mean ERR given posterior distributions computed from queries in the clusters in Figure 9.

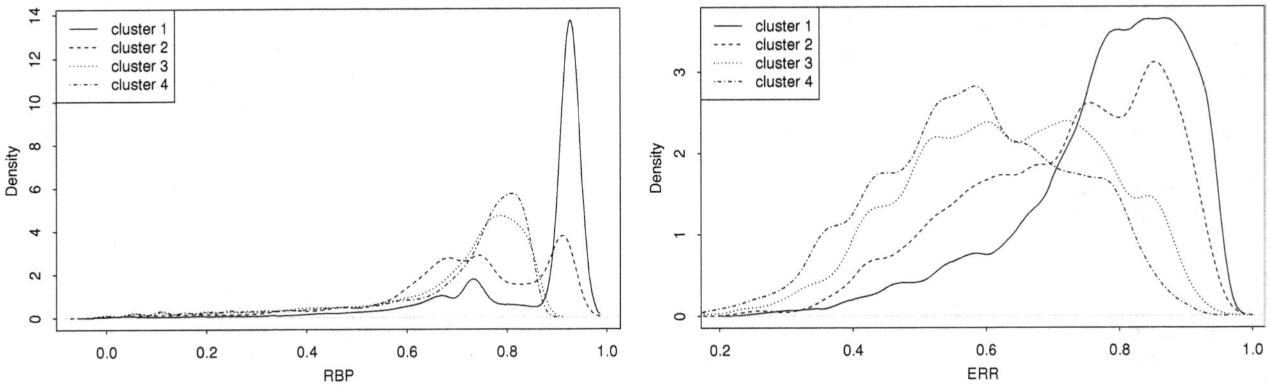

Figure 12: Left: distributions of mean RBP given the four cluster-based posterior distributions in Figure 10. Right: distributions of mean ERR given posterior distributions computed from queries in the clusters in Figure 10.

[6] Natasa Kejzar, Simona Korenjak-Cerne, and Vladimir Batagelj. Clustering of distributions: A case of patent citations. *Journal of Classification*, 28(2):156–183, 2011.

[7] Ron Kohavi, Thomas Crook, and Roger Longbotham. Online experimentation at microsoft, 2009.

[8] Lyes Limam, David Coquil, Harald Kosch, and Lionel Brunie. Extracting user interests from search query logs: A clustering approach. In *Proceedings of the 2010 Workshops on Database and Expert Systems Applications*, DEXA '10, pages 5–9, 2010.

[9] Yury Logachev, Lidia Grauer, and Pavel Serdyukov. Tuning parameters of the expected reciprocal rank. In Alain Mille, Fabien L. Gandon, Jacques Misselis, Michael Rabinovich, and Steffen Staab, editors, *WWW*, pages 571–572. ACM, 2012.

[10] Alistair Moffat and Justin Zobel. Rank-biased precision for measurement of retrieval effectiveness. *ACM Trans. Inf. Syst.*, 27(1):1–27, 2008.

[11] Filip Radlinski, Madhu Kurup, and Thorsten Joachims. How does clickthrough data reflect retrieval quality? In *Proceedings of the 17th ACM conference on Information and knowledge management*, CIKM '08, pages 43–52, New York, NY, USA, 2008. ACM.

[12] Stephen Robertson. A new interpretation of average precision. In *Proceedings of the 31st annual international ACM SIGIR conference on Research and development in information retrieval*, SIGIR '08, pages 689–690, New York, NY, USA, 2008. ACM.

[13] Eldar Sadikov, Jayant Madhavan, Lu Wang, and Alon Halevy. Clustering query refinements by user intent. In *WWW 2010*, pages 841–850. Stanford InfoLab, April 2010.

[14] Mark D. Smucker and Charles L. A. Clarke. Time-based calibration of effectiveness measures. In *Proceedings of SIGIR*, 2012.

[15] Ji-Rong Wen, Jian-Yun Nie, and Hong-Jiang Zhang. Query clustering using user logs. *ACM Trans. Inf. Syst.*, 20:59–81, January 2002.

[16] Emine Yilmaz, Milad Shokouhi, Nick Craswell, and Stephen Robertson. Expected browsing utility for web search evaluation. In *Proceedings of CIKM*, pages 1561–1564, 2010.

[17] Yuye Zhang, Laurence A. Park, and Alistair Moffat. Click-based evidence for decaying weight distributions in search effectiveness metrics. *Inf. Retr.*, 13:46–69, Feb 2010.

[18] Yuye Zhang, Laurence A. F. Park, and Alistair Moffat. Parameter sensitivity in rank-biased precision. In *Proceedings of ADCS*, 2008.

Constructing Test Collections by Inferring Document Relevance via Extracted Relevant Information

Shahzad Rajput Matthew Ekstrand-Abueg Virgil Pavlu Javed A. Aslam

College of Computer and Information Science, Northeastern University
{rajput, mattea, vip, jaa}@ccs.neu.edu

ABSTRACT

The goal of a typical information retrieval system is to satisfy a user's information need—e.g., by providing an answer or information "nugget"—while the actual search space of a typical information retrieval system consists of documents—i.e., collections of nuggets. In this paper, we characterize this relationship between nuggets and documents and discuss applications to system evaluation.

In particular, for the problem of test collection construction for IR system evaluation, we demonstrate a highly efficient algorithm for simultaneously obtaining both relevant *documents* and relevant *information*. Our technique exploits the mutually reinforcing relationship between relevant documents and relevant information, yielding document-based test collections whose efficiency and efficacy exceed those of typical Cranfield-style test collections, while also generating sets of highly relevant information.

Categories and Subject Descriptors: H.3.3 [Information Search and Retrieval]

General Terms: Performance measurement

Keywords: information retrieval, relevance assessment, evaluation, nuggets

1. INTRODUCTION

Retrieval systems are traditionally evaluated by (1) constructing a test collection of documents (the "corpus"), (2) constructing a test collection of queries (the "topics"), (3) judging the relevance of the documents to each query (the "relevance judgments", or qrel file), and (4) assessing the quality of the ranked lists of documents returned by each retrieval system for each topic using standard measures of performance such as precision-at-cutoff, nDCG, average precision, and so forth.

Much thought and research has been devoted to each of these steps in, for example, the annual text retrieval conference TREC [19]. While most of TREC tasks use *documents as units of relevance*, in recent papers [17, 15, 14, 28, 31] it has been shown that many evaluation tasks such as novelty, diversity, ambiguity, redundancy and entailment require a finer granularity. This can be obtained either directly by assessing fragments or *nuggets* of text [15, 28, 33], or indirectly by deciding if any two assessed documents are on the same "subtopic" [14]. Clearly the former is more powerful, but also far more expensive, as it requires that the assessors produce relevance grades for perhaps millions of nuggets extracted from relevant documents. To our knowledge, no previous work that uses some form of nuggets as the unit of relevance presents an efficient and reliable method to obtain such nuggets; such an efficient and reliable methodology is the subject of this paper.

In previous work [28], we demonstrated the power of a carefully constructed set of nuggets for building test collections. Briefly, for each query, a sample of documents is judged by an assessor, and from the judged relevant documents, the assessor extracts relevant nuggets of information in the form of sentences.[1] This set of relevant nuggets is then used to *infer* the relevance of all unjudged documents via a form of text matching: Those documents containing such known and extracted relevant information are (automatically) judged "relevant", while those not containing relevant information are judged "non-relevant". The resulting judged pool—containing both inferred and actual relevance assessments—is far more comprehensive than typical Cranfield-style pools, and the quality of such pools is demonstrated by the accuracy of both the inferred assessments and, in turn, their assessments of retrieval systems (both those that contributed to the pool and those that did not).

While nugget-based assessments clearly represent important progress over the typical Cranfield-style pooling technique, some aspects of the existing nuggets-based methodology are impractical, principally:

1. The manual extraction and processing of nuggets is time consuming.
2. The sample of documents to be judged is fixed and drawn in advance; i.e., it is a "batch" process that cannot adapt "on-line", given a partial set of judged documents and nuggets.

In this paper we present a methodology that solves these

[1]In our past experiments, approximately 200 documents per query were judged, yielding approximately 87 (relevant) nuggets extracted per query, on average. The limited number of relevant nuggets found was primarily due to the difficulty of manual nugget extraction, a problem we directly address in this work.

CIKM'12, October 29–November 2, 2012, Maui, HI, USA.

problems by adapting the well known principle of "Active Learning" [35, 7]: If the learning algorithm can intelligently *choose* the instances on which to train, then it can iteratively select the most useful data points, obtaining the same learning performance with only a small fraction of the training set.

To apply Active Learning to the assessment process, we first recognize that there is a natural *mutual relevance reinforcement* between nuggets and documents: good nuggets match relevant documents and relevant documents yield good nuggets. As such, we devise an interactive active learning process that (1) maintains sets of judged documents and candidate relevant nuggets, (2) uses the set of nuggets to select new documents for assessment, and (3) uses the set of judged documents to extract more candidate relevant nuggets. Such a framework shares commonalities with Reinforcement Learning [39] and the Expectation-Maximization (EM) algorithm [9].

Our main contribution is handling the *extraction* and *scoring* of candidate relevant nuggets completely automatically; neither require direct input from the assessor, thus minimizing the effort to 30% or less of the typical Cranfield-style judging effort. (Assessors provide *indirect* input on nuggets by judging documents.) Our nuggets-based qrel contains both *actual* and *inferred* relevance assessments, and it is comprehensive in the sense that any document can be automatically assessed for relevance given the set of relevant information extracted in the form of nuggets. The actual and inferred document relevance assessments together form our "nugget-based qrel", which can be used to accurately and efficiently evaluate IR systems using standard performance metrics. Furthermore, given that our qrel is comprehensive via inferred relevance assessments, we demonstrate that our nuggets-based evaluations are quite *reusable*, accurately evaluating even unseen (and unpooled) systems that retrieve large number of unique relevant documents. In effect, our methodology evaluates systems based on whether they accurately and comprehensively retrieve *relevant information* rather than merely whether they retrieve a limited and incomplete set of judged *relevant documents.*

Furthermore, though not explored in this work, the set of relevant nuggets may themselves be of independent interest as this set corresponds to the collected *relevant information* for a given topic. One can imagine, for instance, using such nuggets to evaluate topical summaries, to obtain clusters in information-space corresponding to natural subtopics, and so forth. These and other future directions are discussed in Section 6.

We begin by discussing related work in Section 1.1. Section 2 describes the technical details of our proposed nuggets-based methodology. Section 3 details experiments using three TREC datasets: Adhoc99, Web09 and Robust05. In Section 4, we provide an analysis of the quality of our automatically extracted candidate relevant nuggets. Section 5 gives a detailed analysis of those cases where our methodology succeeds and those where it does not (together with potential remedies), and we conclude with future work in Section 6.

1.1 Related Work

Judging documents for relevance cannot scale with modern collections. TREC, a U.S. government effort, coordinates professional assessors to judge up to 3,000 documents per query (ad hoc tracks). While this is a significant effort, it has been shown that there are large assessor disagreements, fatigue driven labeling mistakes [13], and a large number of relevant documents not even considered for assessment as the number of relevant documents can reach millions [28]. Several methods have been proposed to address the problem of scale [5, 12], and while they are efficient at sampling the document space, they are still dependent on the number of documents considered, which can grow into the billions. However, the actual amount of information/nuggets relevant to the query remains small.

Several specific evaluation needs, including diversity measurements, require relevance grades on a sub-document scale. These methods often rely on subtopic assessment by obtaining more than one judgment for each document [14]. Not only are these subtopics sometimes poorly imposed, but the assessment effort remains directly proportional to both number of subtopics and the number of documents.

Researchers have shown the benefits of nuggets [23], but have not provided an easy way to obtain them. Crowdsourcing [2] is faster and cheaper at assessing documents; however, it is not more scalable than TREC methods and is far less reliable [22]. Nuggets of a different nature are widely used in the evaluation of question answering systems [17, 42], where the quality of the system is determined by having humans assess if the output contains correct answers. [26, 27] propose a method to automatically evaluate the quality of a question answering system's output by matching it with manually extracted correct answers. However, their method is not likely to work when the output of the system is of the size of a document. Similarly, different forms of nuggets are also used in a limited context for novelty and diversity [15]. In the former case, the nuggets tend to be very short and specific answers to "who", "when", and "where" questions. In the latter case, nuggets were not used as the sole basis of evaluation and vast quantities of document judgments were still required. Others have proposed using sets of relevant and non-relevant keywords to assess arbitrary documents [3], though we believe that nuggets can capture more information than simple keywords. Another issue with this approach is the use of non-relevant keywords: In principle, a document can contain any amount of non-relevant information; it is relevant if and only if it contains at least one piece of relevant information. [30] uses nuggets to evaluate the quality of a system's response to a given query; however, the nugget extraction and the evaluations are performed entirely manually. Our previous work [28] tackles the problem in the general domain using manual nugget extraction as well.

The use of click-through data has also been proposed [29], but this is only applicable to the web and only for those queries and documents with sufficient "clicks." Evaluating IR systems without relevance assessments has also been the subject of research [36, 38, 32]; however, these methods tend to lack the capability of inferring the relevance of arbitrary documents outside the pool, limiting reusability.

Finally, Intensive Natural Language Processing has been used in recognizing textual entailment [8], which is a significant part of our problem too. While we are not employing sophisticated NLP methods in this paper, we believe that an improved matching can be obtained by embedding a minimum of NLP to detect synonyms and negations.

2. METHODOLOGY

The fundamental thesis of this paper is that finding relevant information immediately leads to relevant documents, which in turn lead to more relevant information. Additionally, marked non-relevant documents can determine non-relevant information; in particular, TREC assessment philosophy that a document is relevant if it contains any bit of relevant information fits our thesis well: any nuggets found in marked non-relevant documents *must be non-relevant*, up to reasonable assessor disagreement and label noise.

2.1 Concept

We are proposing a framework of mutual, iterative reinforcement between nuggets and documents, most similar to Active Learning [35, 7] mechanisms. As in Active Learning, the feedback (relevance assessment) is given *iteratively* only on the documents/data. Thus, for our IR setting, no effort is added to the current assessor practice.

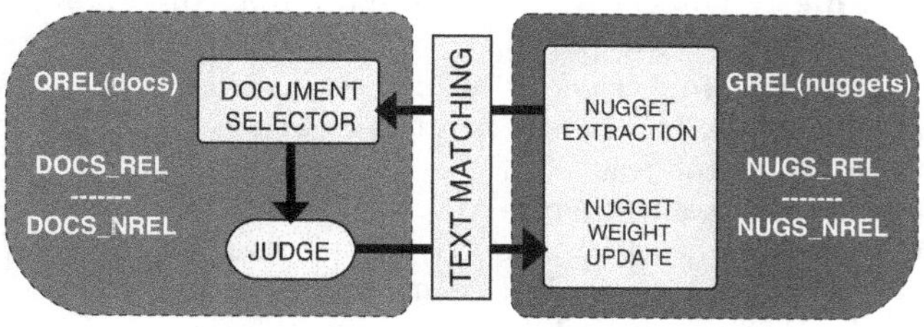

Figure 1: The overall design of assessment process: Iteratively, documents are selected and assessed, and nuggets are extracted and [re]weighted.

Figure 1 illustrates such framework, with the MATCHING being the reinforcing procedure from documents to nuggets and vice-versa:

- the iterative loop selects documents based on the current notion of relevance (as expressed by current set of nuggets G); documents are judged and put into the set of documents (docs QREL);
- for relevant documents, all nuggets are extracted and added to G
- all nugget weights/qualities are updated given the relevant and non-relevant documents judged so far and how well they match each nugget

This framework uses three components that can be designed somewhat independently. (1) The text MATCHING between nuggets and documents is both the syntactic problem of measuring whether the nugget and the document describe the same people, places, locations, dates, facts, actions, etc and the semantic, or textual entailment problem of reflecting the fact that the document entails (presents the semantical information found in) the nugget. (2) The document SELECTOR decides what documents to be judged next, given the current nuggets and their weights, matches, and possibly other contextual information like position of documents in retrieved lists, or the specifics of task, or the desired balance between exploration and exploitation. Finally, (3) the nugget EXTRACTION is responsible for deciding what nuggets to consider from judged-relevant documents, and also responsible in deciding how much each nugget currently matters (updating nugget weight).

A fourth component, not explored in this paper, is the JUDGE model. Here we assume the judge follows the traditional NIST assessor, simply labeling binary documents as relevant (contains something of some relevance) or non-relevant; a more sophisticated judge can review and modify the nuggets extracted, categorize documents, use graded relevance, annotate important keywords, or classify the query.

2.2 Implementation

We present our chosen implementations for SELECTION, EXTRACTION and MATCHING, noting that for each of these we settled on these methods after trying various ideas. While ours work well, each can be independently replaced by more suited techniques for specific tasks.

Text MATCHING. As presented in [28], the matching algorithm is based on a variant of *shingle matching*, which is often used in near-duplicate detection [10, 11]. A shingle is a sequence of k consecutive words in a piece of text. For example, after stopwording, the nugget `"John Kennedy was elected president in 1960"` has the following shingles for $k = 3$: (`John Kennedy elected`), (`Kennedy elected president`), and (`elected president 1960`).

Shingle score: For any nugget and each shingle of size k, let S be the minimum *span* of words in the document that contains all shingle words in any order. A shingle matches well if it is contained in a small span. We use the algorithm presented in [25] to find the shortest span of shingle words in a text document in linear time. We define the shingle matching as

$$shingleMatch = \lambda^{(S-k)/k}.$$

where λ is a fixed decay parameter. We found $\lambda = 0.95$ to be an effective value by trial and error. A shingle that matches "perfectly" will have a score of 1. Note that, in contrast to standard *shingle matching* used for duplicate detection, we do not require all shingle words to be present in the matching document in the same order or contiguously. Our method is inspired by near-duplicate detection, but is in fact quite different. High scores indicate a match of known relevant information, not necessarily of redundant or duplicate text. Furthermore, while a known nugget is required to be present in a document for a good match, the document often contains new/unknown relevant information as well.

Nugget matching: To obtain a matching score for nugget n against document d, we average the scores for each of nugget shingles:

$$\begin{aligned} nuggetmatch &= M(n,d) = \\ &= \frac{1}{\#shingles} \sum_{s \in shingles(n)} shingleMatch(s,d) \end{aligned}$$

While looking for a good but simple text matching strategy, we considered two bag-of-words possibilities: BM25 and Jaccard's Coefficient; both significantly underperformed the presented shingle technique (see 3.1). We speculate that more sophisticated NLP techniques can be used to improve the matching, possibly inspired from textual entailment [8].

Document SELECTION. At each iteration of the document - nugget loop, one or more documents are selected and immediately assessed by the judge. The selection has two parts: First, a ranking function ranks all candidate documents based on a score obtained by matching existing nuggets: at round r, G is the current set of nuggets $n \in G$, each with current quality weight q_n. Then the document score is a dot product of quality and matching

$$DocScore(d) = \sum_{n \in G} q_n * M(n, d)$$

Since some documents can equally match the nugget set (a zero match in the worst case), we add to the document score a retrieval value considering the positions of the documents in various retrieved lists (submitted IR systems in TREC case). Such methods have been developed before[6, 16, 12]; we use the method described in [6].

Second, a probabilistic procedure picks a number of documents from the ranking. We found that a good balance between exploitation and exploration can be achieved by sampling from a scaled geometric distribution

$$\alpha(K)p(1-p)^{r-1}$$

associated with the document ranks r (not scores), with the geometric base $p = 0.4$ found empirically.

Nugget EXTRACTION and Weighting. Nuggets are extracted *only from relevant documents* by a simple NLP script which looks for sentences; stemming and stopwording is performed on the nuggets to improve matching specificity. We treat the nuggets as *experts* and at each iteration we compute the *current nugget quality* q_n, an *importance weight* used by the document selector when computing document scores. These weights are only an indication of the current belief that a nugget is relevant: if matching documents are proven non-relevant, the weight becomes insignificant; a nugget only maintains a high weight across many iterations if it consistently matches relevant documents.

The weighting mechanism is adapted from experts combination/online learning, where the problem has been exhaustively studied. We use the "Hedge" algorithm[18], the internal engine of AdaBoost and Rankboost (but without boosting), which has been shown to have good theoretical properties [34] and fast implementations. A relevant document d increases the weight of the matching nugget n based on the matching score:

$$q_n^{new} = q_n^{old} / \beta_1^{M(n,d)}, normalized$$

while non-relevant document decreases the weight:

$$q_n^{new} = q_n^{old} * \beta_2^{M(n,d)}, normalized$$

Some nuggets are extracted very early in the loop, while others enter G very late; for consistency, the initial weight of each nugget is computed as if the nugget existed in G all along. The two beta values are found by trial and error and for our systems are set at $\beta_1 = 0.8$ and $\beta_2 = 0.5$. This hedge variant with β values associated with each feedback outcome (relevant, non-relevant) was first described in [4]. Other minor heuristics are used to prevent nugget weights from being extremely large. A particularly important feature of Hedge is its adaptability[18]: nugget quality is high as long the nugget brings in relevant documents; after that, it decreases if non-relevant documents match the nugget, or the nugget becomes irrelevant (irrespective of quality q_n) if no other documents match it.

3. EXPERIMENTS

In this section, we describe experiments to show the ability of our process to quickly form test collections by achieving a high recall with high precision. Additionally, we demonstrate how creating a set of nuggets with weights allows us to infer relevance of documents in systems not present during the initial judgments. Finally, we show justification for our choices of the components and how they can be used to improve other procedures. All of this is done using far less manual effort with little reduction in utility as compared to our previous work.

We evaluate the performance of our system against three datasets of varying complexity and document types: AdHoc99, Robust05, and Web09. The specifics of these datasets can be seen in Table 1.

Dataset	Collection	Queries	Docs Assessed	Relevant Docs
AdHoc99	Tipster disks	50	86,830	4,728
Robust05	AQUAINT	50	37,798	6,561
Web09	Clueweb09	50	40,642	10,313

Table 1: Queries and Documents per collection.

The Ad Hoc track 1999 [1] uses a collection of half a million clean text newswire articles. This is also referred to as the ad hoc track TREC 8. With an average of 1,736 documents assessed (depth-100 pool) for each of 50 queries, it is considered to have effectively complete relevance assessments. There were 129 IR systems submitted to this track.

The Robust track 2005 [41] is a more challenging dataset that uses one million clean text documents from the AQUAINT collection. It has an average of 756 documents assessed for each of 50 queries. The queries used in this track are known to be difficult. There were 75 IR systems submitted to this track.

The Web track 2009 [14] uses the ClueWeb09 collection of one billion web documents. With an average of 812 documents assessed (depth-10 pool) for each of 50 queries, it is considered to have incomplete relevance assessments. There were 120 IR systems submitted to this track. The web track possess additional challenges: (1) some of the documents are difficult to parse due to html complexities, (2) detecting spam on the web is a well known but not solved problem, and (3) transforming the web documents to clean text is a challenge; in particular, removing menus and ads from the documents is non-trivial.

Due to issues in basic sentence extraction, text was not extracted from all documents. For our methodology, this is equivalent to finding no nuggets in a document, and therefore using only the ranking score during document selection.

3.1 Recall

We analyze how quickly we obtain effectively complete document relevance assessments. We also compare our results against depth-pooling, the current standard for TREC collection generation, as well as relevance feedback and Support Vector Machines (SVM) ranking.

In this paper, we used SVMRank [24] for ranking unassessed documents. For Relevance Feedback [37], we used top 20 terms from labeled relevant documents to modify the query and rerun BM25. The process is repeated a number times.

Figure 2 shows that the Nugget-based Test Collections consistently require fewer documents to achieve all recall values as compared to depth-pooling, relevance feedback and support vector machines. For instance, obtaining 90% recall on AdHoc99 requires the Nugget-based method, depth-

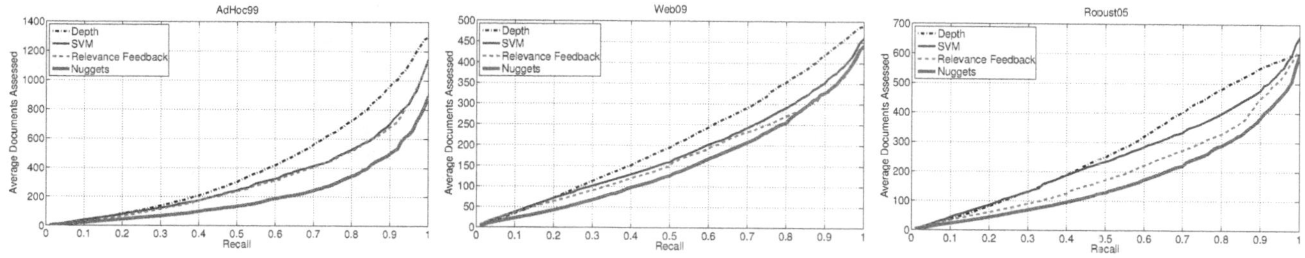

Figure 2: Recall vs. Average Document Assessed

	Recall				
	60%	70%	80%	90%	100%
AdHoc99					
Depth-pooling	417	561	724	962	1,302
Relevance Feedback	313	407	516	681	1,130
SVM	323	413	523	704	1,147
Nuggets	187	245	343	498	892
Web09					
Depth-pooling	248	291	352	418	487
Relevance Feedback	196	232	263	326	447
SVM	201	243	291	353	460
Nuggets	129	169	245	325	448
Robust05					
Depth-pooling	321	402	481	553	600
Relevance Feedback	222	274	328	447	614
SVM	284	334	398	477	657
Nuggets	183	231	287	378	594

Table 2: Number of documents assessed: The nuggets method requires less assessed documents than other methods to achieve the same recall.

	Average Documents Assessed					
Method	50	100	150	200	250	300
AdHoc99						
Shingles	0.3934	0.5351	0.6262	0.6898	0.7370	0.7785
BM25	0.3987	0.5077	0.5877	0.6553	0.7046	0.7470
Web09						
Shingles	0.1916	0.3142	0.4125	0.4973	0.5660	0.6179
BM25	0.1683	0.2646	0.3450	0.4089	0.4761	0.5406
Robust05						
Shingles	0.2849	0.4672	0.5834	0.6631	0.7349	0.7893
BM25	0.2402	0.4055	0.5191	0.6177	0.6795	0.7369

Table 3: Recall comparison when nuggets are matched with documents using Shingles vs BM25.

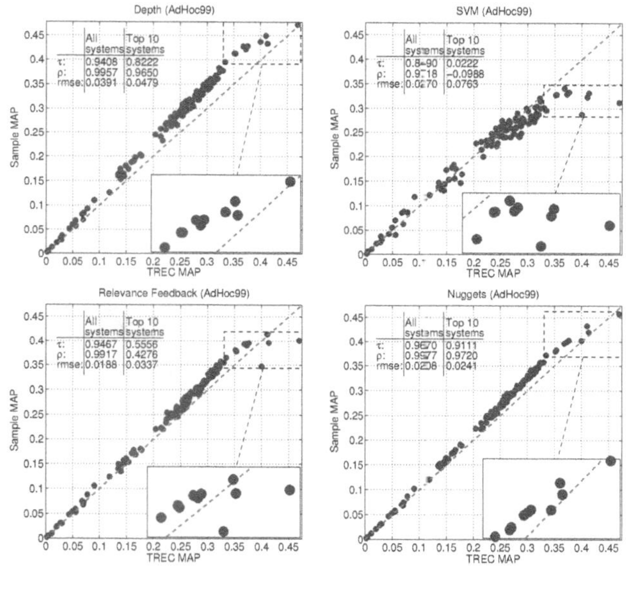

Figure 3: IR System evaluation performed by assessing 350 documents on AdHoc99.

pooling, relevance feedback and support vector machines to assess 498 documents, 962 document, 681 documents and 704 documents respectively. In this case, the Nugget-based method achieves an improvement of about 48% over depth-pooling, 27% over relevance feedback and 29% over support vector machines. Similarly, obtaining 100% recall on AdHoc99 requires the Nugget-based method, depth-pooling, relevance feedback and support vector machines to assess 892 documents, 1,302 document, 1,130 documents and 1,147 documents respectively. In this case, the Nugget-based method achieves an improvement of about 31% over depth-pooling, 21% over relevance feedback and 22% over support vector machines. See Table 2 for comparisons for various different recall points on AdHoc99, Web09 and Robust05.

Shingle-matching vs simple BM25. We evaluate to a small extent the validity of our choice of matching nuggets with documents, were we could have used a standard IR function like BM25. For this comparison, we match the nuggets with documents using BM25 instead of using shingle-matching, and all other components are kept constant. Table 3 provides recall comparisons. It is evident from this table that nuggets matching with documents using the shingle-based method obtains a significantly higher recall as compared to the recall obtained when using BM25.

3.2 IR System Evaluation

The Nugget-based method iteratively selects documents to be assessed, assesses the selected document, and extracts and [re]weights the nuggets.

The assessor may decide to stop at any point. The set of documents assessed together with the assessments forms the nugget-based qrel at that point. This qrel, also referred as the "Sample," can then be used to evaluate the systems.

We produce four separate qrels (each by assessing 350 documents for all queries) based on: depth-pooling, relevance feedback, support vector machines, and the Nugget-based method. Using these qrels, we evaluate all systems over all 50 queries separately for AdHoc99, Web09 and Robust05. The results for AdHoc99, Web09 and Robust05 are shown in Figures 3, 4 and 5 respectively, with each data point

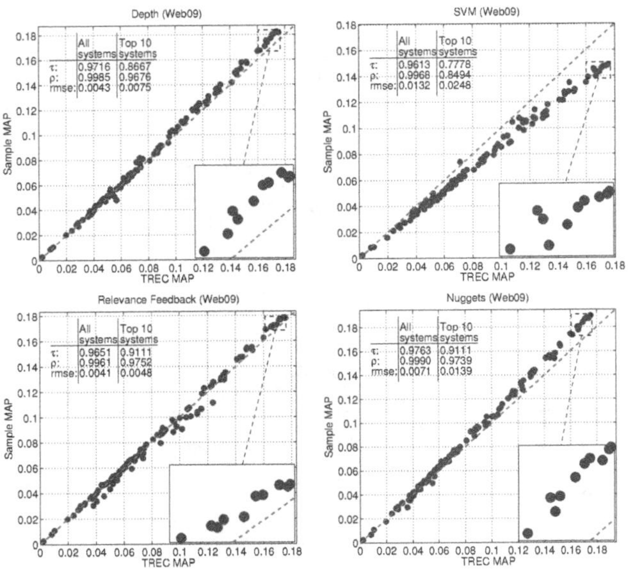

Figure 4: IR System evaluation performed by assessing 350 documents on Web09.

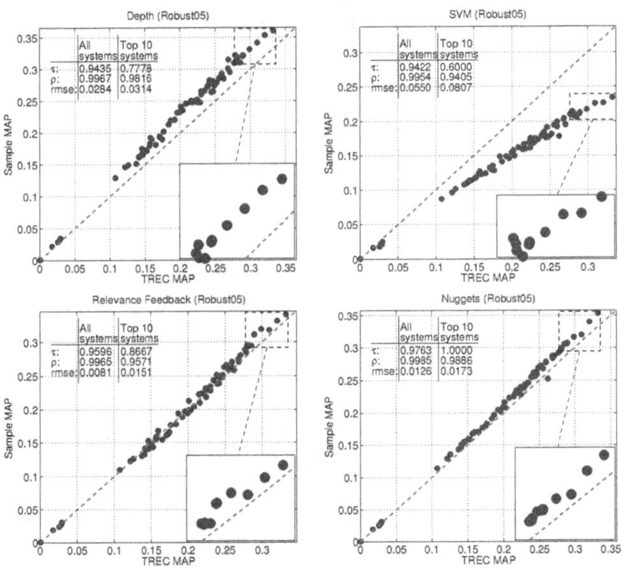

Figure 5: IR System evaluation performed by assessing 350 documents on Robust05.

representing an IR system. Perfect performance would correspond to all data points falling on the line $y = x$. Three different statistics are reported on the plot: Kendall's τ (a measurement of rank agreement), linear correlation coefficient ρ (the goodness of fit to a straight line, which implies rank correlation), and root mean squared error (the difference of estimated scores and true scores, which implies both linear and rank correlation). In most circumstances, evaluation accuracy matters most for the top systems; therefore, these statistics are separately reported both for all systems and the top 10 systems. The top 10 systems are also expanded in the plot for careful analysis. It is clear from these plots that IR system evaluation performed using the nuggets-based qrel is better that that of depth-pooling, relevance feedback and support vector machine-based qrels.

AdHoc99	Robust05	Web09
cirtrc82	indri05RdmmT	NeuRRWeb300
READWARE	rmit5t1025	THUIR09AbClu
Dm8Nbn	RIMam051050	THUIR09QeDiv
orcl99man	juruManTit	twJ48rsU
iit99ma1	indri05RdmeD	Sab9wtBfDiv
8manexT3D1N0	indri05RdmeT	ICTNETDivR3
kdd8qe01	sab05ror1	twCSodpRNB
GE8MTD2	sab05roa2	twCSrs9N
READWARE2	uic0501	udelFMWG
kuadhoc	RIMam051200	uwgym
932	738	672

Table 4: Systems removed for reusability experiments. Removed systems as a group bring the most unique relevant documents to the pool. AdHoc99, Robust05: pool depth is taken to be 100 documents; Web09: pool depth is taken to be 10 documents. Last row shows the total unique relevant documents removed.

Generally, the evaluations of the top 10 systems are significantly better with the nugget-based method.

3.3 Inference and Reusability

A test collection is reusable if it accurately assesses the performance of *unseen* systems, ones that did not contribute to its own construction. We can measure the reusability of a test collection by holding out a set of *seen* systems—eliminating their contribution to the test collection—and assessing the ability of the modified test collection to accurately assess both the held-out systems and the systems that yet remain.

We pick 10 systems greedily based on their high number of unique relevant documents (not retrieved by other systems). Systems removed from each dataset are listed in Table 4.

Documents Assessed	SVM	Relevance Feedback	Nuggets
AdHoc99			
100	0.3006	0.5322	0.5934
350	0.4298	0.7237	0.7448
600	0.5627	0.8057	0.8815
Web09			
100	0.4841	0.7186	0.6977
350	0.8557	0.9029	0.9036
600	0.9631	0.9184	0.9916
Robust05			
100	0.3452	0.6794	0.6614
350	0.6570	0.8462	0.8353
600	0.8576	0.8822	0.9695

Table 5: Document Relevance Inference performance (MAP), using 100, 350 and 600 assessed documents (training).

The results are shown in Figure 6. Note that we did not include the results for depth-pooling both because it is well known to suffer wildly from the exclusion of the systems with most unique relevant documents and, more importantly, it has no way to infer the relevance of the removed documents. Examining the plots, we can conclude that overall, Nugget-based test collections are more reusable than the other active learning-based approaches.

Next, we investigate the performance of the removed systems by comparing their inferred and true MAP values (the

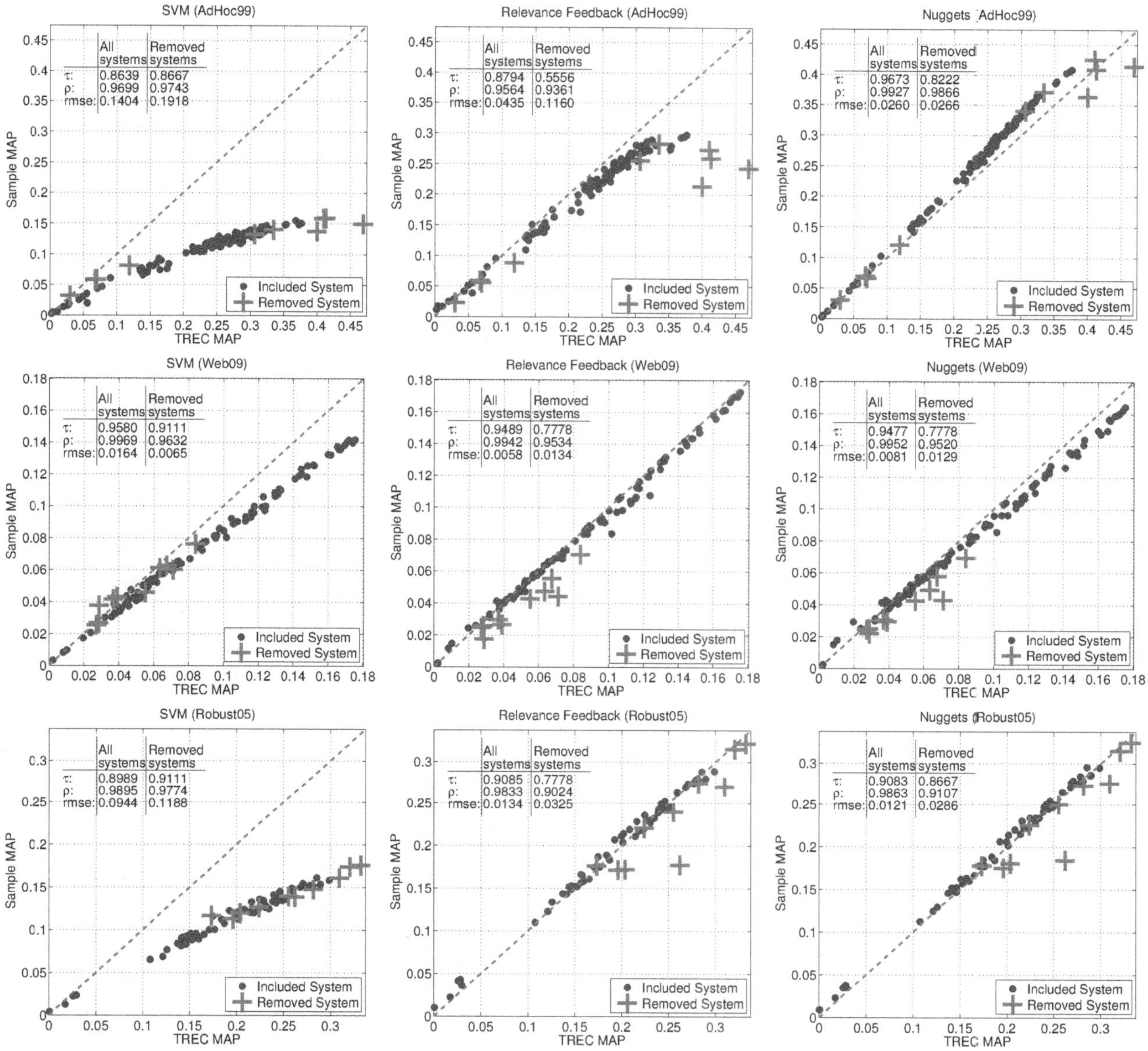

Figure 6: Resuability: IR System evaluation performed by assessing 350 documents. Top: AdHoc99; Middle: Web09; Bottom: Robust05; Left: SVM; Center: Relevance Feedback; Right: Nuggets. Red plus indicate systems removed from the dataset.

latter computed using TREC qrel). Table 6 shows the comparison when an average of about 350 documents are assessed per query. The estimated MAP values produced by the Nugget-based method are generally much close to their true MAP values than those of other methods.

We can also measure reusability by ranking all the documents by their inferred relevance scores such that the judged relevant documents are at the top of the list and those judged non-relevant are at the bottom and then computing the MAP of the list. Table 5 shows the result when 100, 350, and 600 documents are assessed per query on average; the relevance of the remaining documents are inferred and MAP value produced as described above.

4. NUGGETS QUALITY

The nuggets themselves have important practical use, but in order to rely on them, we must evaluate how well our system can separate relevant and nonrelevant nuggets. In order to measure this nugget quality, two notions are necessary at each round of the active learning process: (1) the ability to distinguish good vs bad nuggets–the Average Precision (AP) of ranked nuggets; and (2) the Recall of the nugget set "G"–the proportion of discovered nuggets which are relevant.

We conducted a large crowdsourced study to analyze these notions. First, a set of nuggets was sampled for each query, non-uniformly and without replacement, Table 7; an inclusion probability is stored for each sampled nugget such that the estimated quantities below are essentially unbiased. Each sampled nugget was then presented to 5 different assessors (Mechanical Turks), in batches consisting of 10 random nuggets and 5 random trap questions (nuggets with known relevance grades) for a single query. Binary relevance was

Removed System	True MAP	Estimated MAP		
		RF	SVM	Nuggets
AdHoc99				
READWARE2	0.4692	0.2432	0.1499	0.4142
orcl99man	0.4130	0.2595	0.1594	0.4089
iit99ma1	0.4103	0.2734	0.1586	0.4256
READWARE	0.4000	0.2138	0.1378	0.3636
8manexT3D1N0	0.3346	0.2830	0.1404	0.3712
GE8MTD2	0.3065	0.2557	0.1329	0.3399
kdd8qe01	0.1186	0.0885	0.0814	0.1208
kuadhoc	0.0698	0.0558	0.0588	0.0662
Dm8Nbn	0.0675	0.0593	0.0582	0.0696
cirtrc82	0.0301	0.0231	0.0320	0.0303
Web09				
udelFMWG	0.0840	0.0706	0.0762	0.0694
uwgym	0.0712	0.0443	0.0601	0.0429
THUIR09AbClu	0.0676	0.0554	0.0627	0.0577
ICTNETDivR3	0.0635	0.0474	0.0613	0.0493
Sab9wtBfDiv	0.0551	0.0427	0.0459	0.0425
THUIR09QeDiv	0.0389	0.0267	0.0431	0.0295
twCSodpRNB	0.0368	0.0298	0.0416	0.0306
NeuRRWeb300	0.0287	0.0175	0.0377	0.0220
twCSrs9N	0.0284	0.0259	0.0268	0.0249
twJ48rsU	0.0272	0.0247	0.0255	0.0245
Robust05				
indri05RdmmT	0.3323	0.3216	0.1764	0.3245
indri05RdmeT	0.3204	0.3153	0.1745	0.3148
uic0501	0.3095	0.2706	0.1615	0.2761
indri05RdmeD	0.2818	0.2742	0.1475	0.2734
sab05ror1	0.2621	0.1780	0.1382	0.1850
sab05roa2	0.2553	0.2395	0.1392	0.2502
rmit5t1025	0.2238	0.2203	0.1262	0.2250
RIMam051050	0.2035	0.1727	0.1193	0.1812
RIMam051200	0.1961	0.1721	0.1128	0.1759
juruManTit	0.1732	0.1769	0.1165	0.1785

Table 6: Reusability: Evaluation of removed IR systems based on qrel formed by assessing 350 documents for all queries and adding inferred relevant documents to the qrel.

collected for each nugget in the batch if the assessor successfully passed the trap questions. Finally, an EM-like procedure [20, 22] was run in order to obtain reliable probabilities of relevance for each nugget by estimating the worker quality and accounting for bias[2].

For the nugget set ("G"), the recall at each round can be obtained in an unbiased fashion using the Horvitz-Thompson estimator [40]. To measure the ability of a system to separate relevant and non-relevant nuggets, we used the following ranking algorithm, independent of the nuggets sampled for assessment, and estimated Avg Precision for the obtained ranked-list of nuggets using the statAP estimator [5] on Turk-assessed nuggets. Both the Recall and the AP are estimated with high confidence [5], but we believe there is at least 5-10% nugget assessment error made by the crowdsourcing, despite using 5 assessors per nugget and a sophisticated post-assessing procedure.

The nugget ranking algorithm is a dual to that of the algorithm for ranking documents for selection and assessment. Each nugget is scored by using it to rank all documents retrieved so far by the matching score with each document and

[2]This procedure is publicly available at [21]

	Total Nuggets	Sampled Nuggets	Sampled Relev Nuggets
Adhoc99	10986.54	256	57.4
Web09	13083.48	111.48	57.38
Robust05	5872.56	93.96	26.88

Table 7: Nuggets sampled and assessed by Mechanical Turks (Query average)

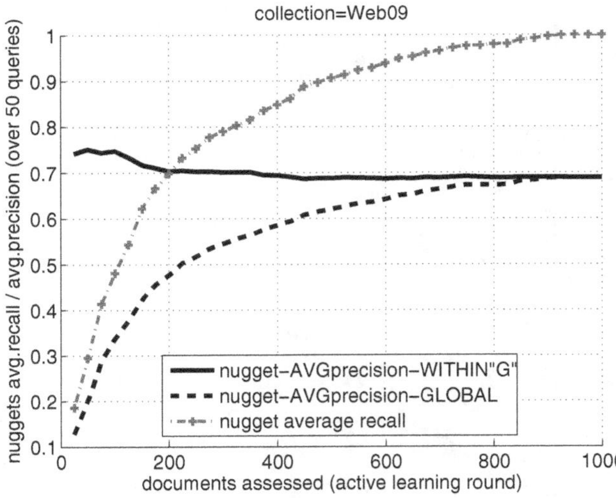

Figure 7: Nugget set Recall and Ranking Precision as a function of the documents assessed

then calculating the AP of the resulting ranked list. These scores form a ranked list of the relevance of all retrieved nuggets for a given query. We separate this into two lists: an AVGprecision-WITHIN"G", which uses the ranking of all nuggets seen so far, thus representing the ability to rank all nuggets at a given round; and an AVGprecision-GLOBAL, which includes all undiscovered and thus unranked nuggets, which represents information quality by round. These results are plotted in Figure 7 for the Web09 collection along with the average recall, the proportion of relevant nuggets which have been discovered, for that round. Note that after 300 documents are assessed, 80% of the relevant nuggets are discovered. The within-G AP is roughly constant at .7, which we believe to be an excellent value, essentially separating the relevant nuggets within the nugget set.

5. FAILURE ANALYSIS

To define the utility and limitations of our system, we analyze the conditions under which it fails to quickly achieve acceptable recall levels and the points at which documents are incorrectly selected. Due to the interconnected nature of the judgments, text extraction, and document selection, a case of an inappropriately selected document may be symptomatic of issues with one or more other documents. We therefore create a more detailed system to fully identify the sources of errors, allowing us to remedy many of the failures and to report on the limitations of the system and ideas for its further improvement.

To perform this analysis, we use heuristics to identify documents which are likely candidates for false positives and false negatives. We manually view these documents in the context of a query and system, which allows us to discern the source of the problem. We analyzed at least 5 docu-

Source of Error	Documents (%)
Assessor Disagreement	92 (33.70%)
Lack of Matching Nuggets	69 (25.27%)
Low Nugget Weights	121 (44.32%)
Extraneous Nugget Text	9 (3.30%)
Nugget Missing Keyword	7 (2.56%)
Bad Document Length Weighting	19 (6.96%)
Matching Well In Wrong Context	14 (5.12%)
Query Too General	2 (0.73%)
Incorrect Weighting	7 (2.56%)
Stopping Key Terms	2 (0.73%)
Matching Many Marginal Nuggets	27 (9.89%)

Table 8: Sources of Error for AdHoc99 DataSet.

ments per query for the AdHoc99 DataSet, totaling over 270 documents. Our findings are shown in Table 8 and described here. Note that some documents fit multiple categories, therefore the total percentage is greater than 100.

• Assessor disagreement: There are numerous cases in which a document can be considered either relevant or not, and in a number of cases we find documents with similar text in both classes.

• Lack of matching nuggets: The document did not sufficiently match nuggets, making our system unable to accurately classify it. Whether due to overly strict requirements for a match in our matching algorithm, overly general queries, or inability to match synonymous text, it was a pervasive issue in our sample. In many cases, it is also true that although the document contains relevant information, the keywords and ideas are scattered throughout the document, so no small section matches well with good nuggets.

• Low nugget weights: The weights of matching nuggets have been lowered, either due to their short length or by matching non-relevant documents, such that they do not help in selecting this document. This may occur even though the nugget appears relevant, due to the issues detailed below.

• Extraneous nugget text: By using only sentences as candidate nuggets, a nugget may contain non-relevant information in addition to the relevant portions. This non-relevant text may match documents in a different context, which are therefore non-relevant. One remedy would be to use nuggets of varying size, which is a source of our future work.

• Nugget missing keyword: The majority of a nugget may be relevant, but it is missing a keyword or phrase to separate it from non-relevant documents. This is especially an issue with pronouns.

• Bad Document Length Weighting: We attempted to use an inverse document length in the scoring function, but found it to be more harmful than beneficial in practice.

• Matching well in wrong context: As one might imagine, there are many documents which can discuss a similar subject, but may be lacking a specific entity or topic which would make it relevant to the query. However, the document may match a large portion of many good nuggets, and be incorrectly inferred as likely relevant.

• Query Too General: The matching function requires similar text between documents. With a general query, there may not be information concerning one document which matches well with information of any other document. For example, the AdHoc99 query "creativity" is a general concept with a wide variety of relevant documents. This could likely be improved with either more documents with which to match or a method for matching synonyms.

• Incorrect Weighting: Cases in which it was clear that noise in judgments caused good nuggets to be decreased in weight, or bad nuggets to increase in weight.

• Stopping Key Terms: The stopword list we use occasionally removes words which are key to a particular query, for example "Three" in the query "Three Gorges Project."

• Summing many marginal nuggets: A document can match many nuggets of small quality to a small degree, accumulating to a large nugget score.

In the cases of the small percentages, they tended to be harder issues to diagnose, but ones which may have contributed to other categories. Examples of this include the query being too general, which can cause difficulty in matching nuggets, and harmful stopping, which can prevent otherwise useful matches and lower match scores and nugget weights. Areas such as handling noise in labels and removing extraneous nugget text are planned for future study.

6. CONCLUSION

We have demonstrated a principled method of automatic nugget extraction while assessing documents, and its ability to improve the efficiency of creating test collections. Our method creates the collection qrel while minimizing the effort required by the document assessors. The nuggets based qrels were shown to produce very accurate system evaluations, but more important, shown to be reusable. This approach works on various types of documents from very different collections.

Nuggets have uses beyond IR system evaluation. They encode information relevance at a finer granularity level than documents do. As many researchers before us noted, they can be used for understanding specific behavior of users, query types, evaluate novelty/diversity/ambiguity, produce summaries, create clusters or natural subtopics, encode user cost of reading long documents.

A particular future work direction is improving the matching function by embedding NLP into our shingle-based method. We are already exploring use of look-up tables of synonyms; while better results can be obtained if we manually select the proper synonyms, we could not improve the current results using available ontologies like WordNet. Negations and coreference problems, which we believe responsible for major matching failures, requires more sophisticated NLP.

A simple way to improve matching and to filter documents is to emphasize certain keywords, related to query relevance information; we have tried this, but the only way to get such keywords is to require them from the assessor. A different assessor model is a possible direction for future research, but taking into consideration that there are quite a few things an assessor can do quickly (not time consuming): deciding different query aspects, look at nuggets with high weights and provide feedback, state keywords or synonyms etc.

Acknowledgment: This material is based upon work supported by the National Science Foundation under Grant No. IIS-1017903. Any opinions, findings and conclusions or recommendations expressed in this material are those of the author(s) and do not necessarily reflect the views of the National Science Foundation (NSF).

7. REFERENCES

[1] *The Eighth Text REtrieval Conference (TREC-8).* U.S. Government Printing Office, 2000.

[2] *33rd ACM SIGIR Workshop on Crowdsourcing for Search Evaluation*, Geneva, Switzerland, 2010.

[3] E. Amitay, D. Carmel, R. Lempel, and A. Soffer. Scaling IR-system evaluation using term relevance sets. SIGIR '04.

[4] J. Aslam. Improving algorithms for boosting. In N. Cesa-Bianchi and S. Goldman, editors, *Proceedings of the Thirteenth Annual Conference on Computational Learning Theory*, July 2000.

[5] J. A. Aslam and V. Pavlu. A practical sampling strategy for efficient retrieval evaluation, technical report.

[6] J. A. Aslam, V. Pavlu, and R. Savell. A unified model for metasearch and the efficient evaluation of retrieval systems via the hedge algorithm. SIGIR '03.

[7] Y. Baram, R. El-Yaniv, and K. Luz. Online choice of active learning algorithms. *J. Mach. Learn. Res.*, Volume 5, December 2004.

[8] L. Bentivogli, P. Clark, I. Dagan, H. T. Dang, and D. Giampiccolo. The sixth PASCAL recognizing textual entailment challenge. In *The Text Analysis Conference (TAC 2010)*, 2010.

[9] C. M. Bishop. *Pattern Recognition and Machine Learning (Information Science and Statistics).* 2006.

[10] A. Z. Broder. Identifying and filtering near-duplicate documents. COM '00, London, UK, 2000.

[11] A. Z. Broder, S. C. Glassman, M. S. Manasse, and G. Zweig. Syntactic clustering of the web. WWW'97.

[12] B. Carterette, J. Allan, and R. K. Sitaraman. Minimal test collections for retrieval evaluation. SIGIR'06.

[13] B. Carterette and I. Soboroff. The effect of assessor error on IR system evaluation. SIGIR '10.

[14] C. L. A. Clarke, N. Craswell, and I. Soboroff. Overview of the TREC 2009 web track, 2009.

[15] C. L. A. Clarke, M. Kolla, G. V. Cormack, O. Vechtomova, A. Ashkan, S. Büttcher, and I. MacKinnon. Novelty and diversity in information retrieval evaluation. SIGIR'08.

[16] G. V. Cormack, C. R. Palmer, and C. L. A. Clarke. Efficient construction of large test collections. SIGIR'98, pages 282–289, Aug. 1998.

[17] H. T. Dang, J. J. Lin, and D. Kelly. Overview of the TREC 2006 question answering track 99. In *TREC*, 2006.

[18] Y. Freund and R. E. Schapire. A decision-theoretic generalization of on-line learning and an application to boosting. COLT '95.

[19] D. Harman. Overview of the third text REtreival conference (TREC-3). In *Overview of the Third Text REtrieval Conference (TREC-3).* U.S. Government Printing Office, Apr. 1995.

[20] M. Hosseini, I. J. Cox, N. Milic-Frayling, G. Kazai, and V. Vinay. On aggregating labels from multiple crowd workers to infer relevance of documents. In *ECIR*, volume 7224 of *ECIR '12*, 2012.

[21] P. G. Ipeirotis. get-another-label: A set of tools for managing redundant answers collected from amazon. http://code.google.com/p/get-another-label/.

[22] P. G. Ipeirotis, F. Provost, and J. Wang. Quality management on amazon mechanical turk. HCOMP '10.

[23] K. Järvelin and J. Kekäläinen. Cumulated gain-based evaluation of IR techniques. *ACM Trans. Inf. Syst.*, Volume 20, 2002.

[24] T. Joachims. Training linear svms in linear time. KDD '06, pages 217–226, New York, NY, USA, 2006. ACM.

[25] S. Krenzel. Finding blurbs. Website. http://www.stevekrenzel.com/articles/blurbs.

[26] J. Lin and D. Demner-Fushman. Automatically evaluating answers to definition questions. HLT '05.

[27] J. Lin and D. Demner-Fushman. Will pyramids built of nuggets topple over? HLT'06.

[28] V. Pavlu, S. Rajput, P. B. Golbus, and J. A. Aslam. IR system evaluation using nugget-based test collections. WSDM '12.

[29] F. Radlinski, M. Kurup, and T. Joachims. How does clickthrough data reflect retrieval quality? CIKM '08.

[30] T. Sakai, M. P. Kato, and Y.-I. Song. Click the search button and be happy: evaluating direct and immediate information access. CIKM '11.

[31] T. Sakai, M. P. Kato, and Y.-I. Song. Overview of NTCIR-9 1CLICK. 2011.

[32] T. Sakai and C.-Y. Lin. Ranking Retrieval Systems without Relevance Assessments — Revisited. In *the 3rd International Workshop on Evaluating Information Access (EVIA) — NTCIR-8*, 2010.

[33] T. Sakai and R. Song. Evaluating diversified search results using per-intent graded relevance. SIGIR '11.

[34] R. E. Schapire, Y. Freund, P. Bartlett, and W. S. Lee. Boosting the Margin: A New Explanation for the Effectiveness of Voting Methods. *The Annals of Statistics*, 26(5), 1998.

[35] H. S. Seung, M. Opper, and H. Sompolinsky. Query by committee. COLT '92.

[36] I. Soboroff, C. Nicholas, and P. Cahan. Ranking retrieval systems without relevance judgments. SIGIR '01.

[37] A. Spink. Term relevance feedback and query expansion: relation to design. SIGIR '94.

[38] A. Spoerri. Using the structure of overlap between search results to rank retrieval systems without relevance judgments. *Inf. Process. Manage.*, 43, 2007.

[39] R. S. Sutton and A. G. Barto. *Reinforcement Learning: An Introduction (Adaptive Computation and Machine Learning).* The MIT Press, Mar. 1998.

[40] S. Thompson. *Sampling.* Wiley series in probability and mathematical statistics: Applied probability and statistics. 1992.

[41] E. M. Voorhees. Overview of the TREC 2005 robust retrieval track. TREC 2005.

[42] E. M. Voorhees. Question answering in TREC. CIKM '01.

Twevent: Segment-based Event Detection from Tweets

Chenliang Li, Aixin Sun, Anwitaman Datta
School of Computer Engineering, Nanyang Technological University, Singapore
{lich0020,axsun,anwitaman}@ntu.edu.sg

ABSTRACT

Event detection from tweets is an important task to understand the current events/topics attracting a large number of common users. However, the unique characteristics of tweets (*e.g.,* short and noisy content, diverse and fast changing topics, and large data volume) make event detection a challenging task. Most existing techniques proposed for well written documents (*e.g.,* news articles) cannot be directly adopted. In this paper, we propose a segment-based event detection system for tweets, called *Twevent*. *Twevent* first detects bursty tweet segments as event segments and then clusters the event segments into events considering both their frequency distribution and content similarity. More specifically, each tweet is split into non-overlapping segments (*i.e.,* phrases possibly refer to named entities or semantically meaningful information units). The bursty segments are identified within a fixed time window based on their frequency patterns, and each bursty segment is described by the set of tweets containing the segment published within that time window. The similarity between a pair of bursty segments is computed using their associated tweets. After clustering bursty segments into candidate events, Wikipedia is exploited to identify the realistic events and to derive the most newsworthy segments to describe the identified events. We evaluate *Twevent* and compare it with the state-of-the-art method using 4.3 million tweets published by Singapore-based users in June 2010. In our experiments, *Twevent* outperforms the state-of-the-art method by a large margin in terms of both precision and recall. More importantly, the events detected by *Twevent* can be easily interpreted with little background knowledge because of the newsworthy segments. We also show that *Twevent* is efficient and scalable, leading to a desirable solution for event detection from tweets.

Categories and Subject Descriptors

H.3.3 [**INFORMATION STORAGE AND RETRIEVAL**]: Information Search and Retrieval—*Clustering; Information filtering*

Keywords

Event detection, Twitter, Microblogging, Tweet segmentation

CIKM'12, October 29–November 2, 2012, Maui, HI, USA.

1. INTRODUCTION

Twitter, as a social networking service and microblogging service, has gained great success in recent years. Twitter users not only share and communicate with friends and family, but also to the general public. The unique gene of the latter enables Twitter users to access and contribute *"the latest stories, ideas, opinions, and news*[1]*"* about what many users find interesting. As a result, Twitter has become one of the top-10 most visited website on the Internet[2]. As of March 2012, there are more than 140 million active users with over 340 million tweets published a day[3].

1.1 Motivation

In Twitter, each user becomes an individual news media that not only absorbs/assembles information (such as breaking news), but also publishes/propagates opinions, sentiments, and stories of themselves [9, 20]. The message unit, called a *tweet*, is limited to maximum 140 characters in length. Such a concise unit enables information updates at extremely low-cost and in realtime, making Twitter a timely fresh information resource [3]. Consequently, the intensive interaction between users in realtime enables timely event detection by monitoring tweet updates and many prominent events are timely spotlighted by Twitter users. For example, a record number of tweet updates per second was set within a 30-sec period after the 2010 FIFA World Cup match between Japan and Cameroon on June 14, 2010. Three days later, the record was broken right after the Lakers' victory in the 2010 NBA Finals on June 17, 2010[4]. Other than sports related events, it has been reported that earthquake detection based on Twitter is faster than the detection based on traditional media [19]. Moreover, event detection from tweets would help us gain timely understanding of users' opinion/sentiment with respect to the detected events, making it possible for company/organization to take a fast response to any emerging crisis. Event detection from Twitter stream would also contribute to the study of mass communication by analyzing the types of events general users are mostly interested in [22] as well as the reactions by users at different geographical regions [15].

Event detection from Twitter stream is challenging for at least three reasons: short and noisy content, diverse and fast changing topics, and large data volume. The task of event detection has been intensively studied in the past mostly on formal texts, *e.g.,* news articles, blog posts, or academic papers [4–6, 8]. However, tweets are significantly different from well written texts because of the shortness and informal writing style. According to the principle of

[1] `https://twitter.com/about`

[2] `http://www.alexa.com/siteinfo/twitter.com`

[3] `http://blog.twitter.com/2012/03/twitter-turns-six.html`

[4] `http://bits.blogs.nytimes.com/2010/06/18/sports-fans-break-records-on-twitter/`

least effort [26], people are used to communicate information with the least context, especially in the situation where a short message with free style is allowed. This makes tweets contain a lot of misspellings and informal abbreviations [17]. Because of the noise and shortness, direct adoption of most existing approaches developed for formal texts (*e.g.,* clustering bursty features with co-occurrence measure [5, 6]) is doomed to fail on Twitter streams.

Tweets cover very diverse topics and about half of the tweets are not event-related according to a study by PearAnalytics [12]. They manually categorized 2, 000 tweets into six categories: news (3.6%), spam (3.75%), self-promotion (5.85%), pointless babble (40.55%), conversational (37.55%) and pass-along value (8.7%). The numbers indicate the percentage of the tweets in each category. Based on their analysis, about 50% (*i.e.,* spam, self-promotion, pointless babble) of tweets are not related to events. Similar observations are also made in our pilot study of the tweets data used in our experiments. However, a large number of features would be expected being bursty from tweets of *pointless babble* category. Obviously, none of these bursty features would help in detecting any event, but would mislead the event detection algorithm and also incur unnecessary computational cost. The situation would be further exaggerated with the fast changing topics in tweets. For example, many users would discuss about a football match during the match or within a few hours right after the match but not for a few days.

1.2 Overview of Twevent

To address the above challenges, we present *Twevent*, a novel segment-based event detection system for tweets. One novel feature of *Twevent* is to use the notion of *tweet segment* instead of unigram to detect and describe events. A tweet segment is one or more consecutive words (or phrase) in a tweet message. We observe that tweet segments contained in a large number of tweets are likely to be named entities (*e.g.,*Steve Jobs) or some semantically meaningful unit (*e.g.,*Argentina vs Nigeria). Therefore, a tweet segment often contains much more specific information than any of the unigrams contained in the segment. The use of tweet segment instead of unigrams therefore greatly reduces the noise in the event detection process and also makes the event detected much easier to be interpreted. For example, *Twevent* detected an event with the following five segments [south korea, greece, korea vs greece, korea won, korea] on 12 June 2010; the event is self-explanative. Another novel feature of *Twevent* is the utilization of external knowledge base in guiding the event detection process. In the following, we brief the main steps in *Twevent* for event detection from tweets.

Given tweets published in a Twitter stream, *Twevent* firstly segments each individual tweet into a sequence of consecutive phrases (*i.e.,* segments). Then bursty segments are identified by modeling the frequency of a segment as a Gaussian distribution based on predefined fixed time-window (*e.g.,* a day or an hour). To detect events attracting a larger number of users, we also utilize user frequency (or user support) of the tweet segments to identify the event-related bursty segments, called event segments. After that, we apply an efficient clustering algorithm to group event-related segments as candidate events, which requires only a single pass through each pair of event segments. To compute the similarity between a pair of event segments, we consider the frequency distribution and the content of the tweets containing each of the tweet segments published within the time-window. The result of event segment clustering is a set of candidate events detected in that time window. The knowledge encoded in Wikipedia is then harnessed to help us figure out the realistic events detected from the trivial ones and to derive the most representative segments for describing the realistic events. As the result, each event detected by *Twevent* is represented by a ranking list of segments including many named entities for easy interpretation.

Twevent holds several features to address the challenges of event detection from tweets. Tweet segmentation employed in *Twevent* identifies informative phrases which reduces noise in further processing. The use of user frequency in bursty event segment extraction makes *Twevent* robust to the negative impact of the tweets of *Spam* and *Self-Promotion*. The external knowledge base offers *Twevent* the ability to resist the adverse impact of diverse and dynamic topics of tweets, such as tweets of *Pointless Babble*, and derive interpretable event descriptions. Lastly, *Twevent* is efficient and scalable by utilizing only the frequency of segments for bursty segment extraction and non-iterative clustering algorithm.

We evaluated *Twevent* with more than 4.3 million tweets published by Singapore-based users over a one month period. In our experiments, *Twevent* achieves much better performance compared to the state-of-the-art method [21] in terms of both precision and recall. More specifically, *Twevent* achieves a precision of 86.1%, and a recall of 75 distinct events detected from the one-month data. Our experimental results also demonstrate the effectiveness of using tweet segments compared to the same detection process using unigrams. To illustrate that the events detected by *Twevent* often contain named entities or convey concise information, we list the most newsworthy segments detected by *Twevent* in Table 2 as part of the experimental results.

The rest of the paper is organized as follows. Section 2 surveys related work. Section 3 describes *Twevent* and its components in detail. Section 4 presents the experimental results. We conclude this paper in Section 5.

2. RELATED WORK

Event detection has a long history, which can be traced back to the Topic Detection and Tracking (TDT) project[5], which is to detect and track events from news stream. Two main approaches have been studied in the literature: *document-pivot* and *feature-pivot* approaches. The former aims to cluster documents related to the same events and then extract event-based features from the document clusters [1, 2, 23–25]. The latter aims to firstly identify the representative features of the hidden events from the stream, which are assumed to have bursty frequency patterns along time. Then events are detected by clustering these representative features [8]. Because the proposed *Twevent* is a feature-pivot method, in our literature survey, we therefore mainly focus on *feature-pivot* methods for event detection from formal texts.

2.1 Event Detection from Formal Texts

Kleinberg [8] proposed to detect events by analyzing frequency patterns along time. An infinite-state automation is used to model the changes of word frequency, and the state transitions are considered as events. Fung *et al.* [5] proposed to identify bursty features as representatives for the events hidden in text stream. The frequency of each feature (*i.e.,* unigram word) is modeled with a binomial distribution. The bursty feature extraction is then based on the perspective of statistics. The events are then detected by maximizing the co-occurrences among documents and the consistence of the frequency distributions for all bursty features within an event. The timestamp for an event is calculated based on the bursty periods of the bursty features related to that event. The authors further presented an event-based search framework in [4] to retrieve groups of documents such that the documents in each group are about the same event. In their result, the events are organized

[5] `http://projects.ldc.upenn.edu/TDT/`

in a time-based hierarchy. In this event-based framework, a set of related bursty features with similar frequency distributions are retrieved firstly. Then, documents related to the bursty features are extracted and clustered into a hierarchy of events. Instead of using frequency directly, He *et al.* [6] proposed to use *Discrete Fourier Transformation* (DFT) to extract bursty features. They build a signal for each feature using *document frequency - inverse document frequency* ($df \times idf$) scheme along time domain. Then, DFT transforms the signal in time domain to frequency domain, *i.e.*, a spike in frequency domain indicates a corresponding high frequency signal source. Similar to [5], they group bursty features into events by considering both features' co-occurrence and their distributions in time domain. To estimate the timestamp of the events, they model a $df \times idf$ signal with a Gaussian mixture.

Unlike formal texts that are formally written and published in moderate rate, tweets are short, informally written, and published at an enormous amount. Thus, bursty feature extraction solely based on statistics would result in a huge number of bursty features, particulary when unigram feature representation is used. Similarly, the application of DFT would be dread and prohibited. Further, co-occurrence measures used in [5,6] may not work well in the context of twitter due to sparsity.

2.2 Event Detection from Tweets

Recently, event detection on twitter stream becomes a hot research topic. Michael and Nick [11] presented a trend detection system over twitter stream. They firstly identify the bursty terms based on queueing theory. Then bursty terms are grouped into the events based on their co-occurrences. For a detected trend, PCA, SVD and entity extraction techniques are then applied to derive contextual information for the trend description. Petrović *et al.* [13] tracked events on twitter stream by applying locality sensitive hashing (LSH). LSH is applied to each tweet to measure the similarity to existing tweets. The tweets similar to each other are grouped as events. Swit and Tsuyoshi [14] proposed an approach for breaking news detection and tracking by clustering the similar tweets together. The approach only focuses on the tweets with a specific hashtag #breakingnews. The similarity between two tweets of breaking news is measured by using a variant of $tf \cdot idf$ scheme where the named entities detected by a Named Entity Recognizer (NER) are further boosted. Popescu *et al.* [16] proposed a method for entity-based event detection on twitter streams. A set of tweets containing the predefined target entity are processed and machine learning techniques are used to predict whether the tweets constitute an event regarding the entity. Very recently, Li *et al.* [18] proposed to detect crime and disaster related Events (CDE) from tweets. Conventional text mining techniques are applied to extract the meta information (*e.g.*, geo-location names, temporal phrase, and keywords) for event interpretation. To summarize, most existing approaches for detecting events from tweets are applicable to certain types of tweets (*e.g.*, having a specific hashtag, containing a predefined entity, or related to crime and disaster). The other solutions including [11] and [13] involve complicated processing and lead to heavy computational cost.

The most related work to ours, is the approach proposed by Weng and Lee, named *EDCoW* [21]. There are three steps in their approach. Firstly *wavelet transformation* and *auto correlation* are applied to measure the bursty energy of each word. The words with outstanding high energies are retained as event features. Then they measure the similarity between each pair of event features by using *cross correlation*. At last, modularity-based graph partitioning is used to detect the events, each of which contains a set of words with high *cross correlation*. However, several issues get in the way of the practical application for their approach. *Wavelet transformation* and *auto correlation* for each word of the twitter stream would require a huge amount of computation, making it not a scalable choice. Moreover, utilizing only *cross correlation* for similarity measure would lead to the resulted event consisting of several distinct events which happened at the same period by coincidence (*e.g.*, two football matches hold at the same time during FIFA 2010 World Cup). Thirdly, the detected events with unigram features are difficult for human interpretation. In *Twevent*, we segment each tweet into possible semantic phrases, making the detected events easy to interpret. During the detection process, we do not employ computational costly Wavelet transformation and auto correlation for tweet segments. Instead, only the tweet frequency and user frequency are needed for bursty tweet segment detection. To distinguish events that happened at the same period, *Twevent* computes content similarity for a pair of tweet segments. Each tweet segment is described by the content of the tweets containing the segment. Although pair-wise similarity computation is computational costly, it is only applied to a relatively small set of bursty tweet segments detected within one time window.

3. TWEVENT

In this section, we present a feature-pivot event detection framework. Illustrated in Figure 1, our framework consists of three main components: *tweet segmentation*, *event segment detection*, and *event segment clustering*. After receiving a tweet from a Tweet stream, tweet segmentation component splits the tweet into non-overlapping segments. A tweet segment can be either a unigram or multi-gram (*e.g.*,[mtv movie awards], [steve jobs]), and each segment may or may not represent a semantic unit. The resultant tweet segments obtained from a tweet, together with the content and timestamp of the tweet, are indexed in the segment index. The event segment detection component detects abnormal bursty segments by considering tweets frequency distribution and user frequency of the segments. The event segments about the same event are then grouped together to form the event by the event clustering component. In the rest of this section, we describe each component in detail following the order of their usage in our framework.

3.1 Tweet Segmentation

The notion of *tweet segment* was firstly proposed in our recent work [10] for named entity recognition, not related to event detection. In the following, we brief the techniques for tweet segmentation.

Given a tweet $d \in \mathcal{T}$, the problem of tweet segmentation is to split d into m non-overlapping and consecutive segments, $d = \langle s_1 s_2 ... s_m \rangle$, where a segment s_i is either a word (or unigram) or a phrase (or multi-gram). We formulate tweet segmentation problem as an optimization problem with the following objective function, where C is the function measures the *stickiness* of a segment or a tweet.

$$\arg\max_{s_1,\ldots,s_m} C(d) = \sum_{i=1}^{m} C(s_i), \qquad (1)$$

A high *stickiness* score of segment s indicates that further splitting segment s would break the correct word *collocation*. In other words, segment s cannot be further split at any internal position if it has a high stickiness score. We define *stickiness* function by using the generalized *Symmetric Conditional Probability* (SCP) for n-grams with $n \geq 2$, supported by statistical information derived from Microsoft Web N-Gram service[6] and Wikipedia.

[6]http://research.microsoft.com/en-us/collaboration/focus/cs/web-ngram.aspx

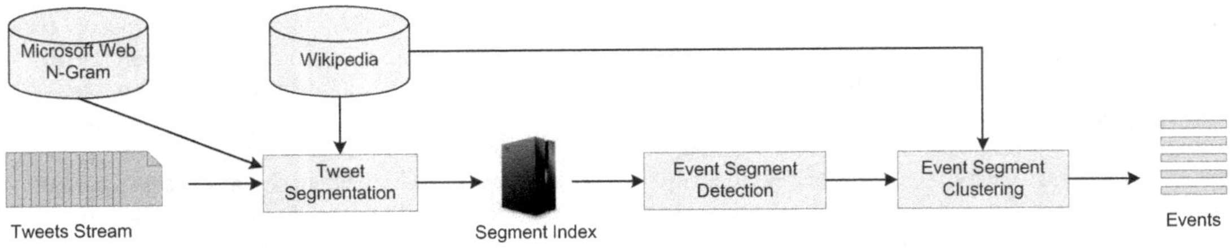

Figure 1: Segment-based Event Detection System Architecture

SCP is defined to measure the "cohesiveness" of a segment $s = \langle w_1 ... w_n \rangle$ $(n > 1)$ by considering all possible binary segmentations, as shown in the following equation, where $\Pr(\cdot)$ denotes the prior probability derived from Microsoft Web N-Gram service.

$$SCP(s) = \log \frac{\Pr(s)^2}{\frac{1}{n-1}\sum_{i=1}^{n-1} \Pr(w_1 ... w_i) \Pr(w_{i+1} ... w_n)} \quad (2)$$

In this equation, the logarithm value is taken to avoid underflow. Note that, $SCP(s) = 2 \log Pr(w)$ if segment s is of unit length (*i.e.*, $|s| = 1$ or $n = 1$).

Based on $SCP(s)$, we define the stickiness score of segment s by considering the high quality semantic resources in Wikipedia. That is, segments which frequently appear as anchor texts in Wikipedia are further favored. The *stickiness* function is then defined as:

$$C(s) = \mathcal{L}(s) \cdot e^{Q(s)} \cdot \mathcal{S}(SCP(s)) \quad (3)$$

$$\mathcal{L}(s) = \begin{cases} \frac{|s| - 1}{|s|}, \text{ for } |s| > 1 \\ 1, \text{ for } |s| = 1 \end{cases} \quad (4)$$

where $Q(s)$ is the probability that s appears as the anchor text in the Wikipedia articles that contain s, and $\mathcal{S}(\cdot)$ is the sigmoid function. The function $\mathcal{L}$ defined in Equation 4 is used to give moderate preference for longer segments. With this stickiness function, the tweet segmentation defined in Equation 1 can be finished efficiently in linear time with dynamic programming.

3.2 Event Segment Detection

One salient characteristic of emerging events in text streams is that there is a significant coverage of topics related to an event within a certain time period. Accordingly, given a collection of segments of the tweets published within a fixed time window, bursty segments in terms of frequency would be potentially related to some hot events talked and shared by Twitter users. However, considering the dynamic nature and the large volume of tweets published everyday, efficiently detecting bursty segments is non-trivial.

Let N_t denote the number of tweets published within time-window t from Twitter stream, $f_{s,t}$ be the number of tweets containing s published within t, *i.e.*, the tweet frequency of segment s in time-window t. The probability of observing frequency $f_{s,t}$ of segment s in t can be modeled by a binomial distribution [5].

$$P(f_{s,t}) = \binom{N_t}{f_{s,t}} p_s^{f_{s,t}} (1 - p_s)^{N_t - f_{s,t}} \quad (5)$$

where p_s is the expected probability of tweets that contain segment s in a random time window. Given that N_t is very large in the case of Twitter stream, it is reasonable to approximate $P(f_{s,t})$ with Gaussian distribution:

$$P(f_{s,t}) \sim \mathcal{N}(N_t p_s, N_t p_s (1 - p_s)). \quad (6)$$

Thus, given segment s, the expected number of tweets containing s would be $E[s|t] = N_t p_s$. The more the additional tweets containing s with respect to $E[s|t]$, the more bursty the segment is. On the other hand, segment s with frequency $f_{s,t} <= E[s|t]$ is considered as a non-bursty segment and will not be considered for further processing. Hence, we define bursty segment as follows.

Definition 1. **[Bursty Segment]** A segment s is a bursty segment in time window t if its tweet frequency $f_{s,t} > E[s|t]$.

Next we transfer the frequency of a bursty segment into range of $(0, 1]$ indicating its ***bursty probability***.

We consider a bursty segment s to be extremely bursty and assign $P_b(s, t) = 1$ if its tweet frequency $f_{s,t} \geq E[s|t] + 2\sigma[s|t]$, where $\sigma[s|t] = \sqrt{N_t p_s (1 - p_s)}$ is the standard deviation based on Equation 6. For a bursty segment whose tweet frequency $f_{s,t}$ falls within the range $(E[s|t], E[s|t] + 2\sigma[s|t])$, we use the following equation to compute its bursty probability.

$$P_b(s, t) = \mathcal{S}\left(10 \times \frac{f_{s,t} - (E[s|t] + \sigma[s|t])}{\sigma[s|t]}\right) \quad (7)$$

where $\mathcal{S}(\cdot)$ is the sigmoid function, and a constant 10 is introduced in the equation because the sigmoid function $\mathcal{S}(x)$ smooths reasonable well for x in the range of $[-10, 10]$.

With the above statistical method, we are able to detect the bursty segments and assign each a bursty probability. However, Twitter is significantly different from most text streams (*e.g.*, news stream and blog stream) that have been extensively studied in the literature for bursty feature/event detection, because of its informal writing style and topic diversity. Therefore, a large number of tweet segments would be detected to be bursty segments. A simple statistics in our study shows that the number of distinct bursty segments is about 75% of the number of distinct tweets in a randomly chosen time window. Among the bursty segments detected, many contain misspelling words and informal abbreviations. These noisy bursty segments would not only incur unnecessary computational cost but also hurt the event detection accuracy in the further processing. We therefore source for the wisdom of the crowds to filter the bursty segments.

Instead of solely relying on the tweet frequency of a segment, we believe that a bursty segment has a higher chance to be related to an event if there are more users post tweets containing the segment. Hence, we define ***user frequency*** $u_{s,t}$ of a segment s, which is the number of users who post tweets containing s during the time period t.

With the two factors, bursty probability and user frequency, the most simple approach to detect the event-relatedness of a bursty segment is to take the product of the two factors. However, this simple approach would make the top-ranked segments dominated by the ones used by most users, such as "i'm", "i'll", and "guys". To some extent, bursty segments with higher user frequencies are correlated with some events. However, considering the limited length of tweets, the bursty segments with higher user frequencies may not be semantically meaningful and are often ambiguous. For instance, "nigeria", "argentina" and "argentina vs nigeria" are all related to a single event: *a 2010 world cup match between nigeria and ar-*

gentian. However, the bursty segment "argentina vs nigeria" has a relatively much lower user frequency due to the principle of the least effort [26]. In contrast, comparing "argentina vs nigeria" with either "nigeria" or "argentina", the segment "argentina vs nigeria" would convey much more information about the event. Based on this observation, we assign each bursty segment s a weight $w_b(s,t)$ by using a logarithm function.

$$w_b(s,t) = P_b(s,t)\log(u_{s,t}) \quad (8)$$

The above weight scheme would keep the more bursty segments of the higher user frequency being ranked higher and the more bursty segments of the moderate user frequency being ranked relatively higher than the others.

By ranking the bursty segments by their weights $w_b(s,t)$, we then retain the top-K bursty segments as potential event-related segments (or simply event segments) for further processing. The value of K is non-trivial because a small K would result in a very low recall of events detected, and a large K may bring in more noise, leading to much higher computational cost as well as lower precision on the detected events. In practical, the optimal K value depends on the size of the time window, and requires some expertise knowledge (*e.g.*,, users from different regions may be interested in different topics [15]). In this work, we apply a heuristic strategy to filter out the bursty segments by setting K to $\sqrt{N_t}$.

Definition 2. **[Event Segment]** A bursty segment s is a potential event-related segment (or simply event segment) in time window t if it is ranked among top-K bursty segments by $w_b(s,t)$ in descending order, where $K = \sqrt{N_t}$.

3.3 Event Segment Clustering

Given a set of event segments detected from the previous step, we now cluster them into groups, each of which corresponds to a *possible* realistic event. Some event segments that cannot be clustered into groups are considered noise or non-event-related. These non-event-related segments are dropped from further processing.

3.3.1 Event Segment Similarity

Accordingly, we need to derive a similarity measure for each pair of event segments. Various similarity measures have been used in the past to cluster bursty features detected in formal texts, mainly based on co-occurrences of bursty features [5, 6]. However, similarity measure based on co-occurrence would not work well on tweets because they are much shorter in number of words compared to formal documents. Moreover, the topics in tweets are extremely dynamic and fast changing. Considering these two factors, we propose to measure similarity between two event segments by the content of their associated tweets and their temporal frequency patterns.

For each time window t, we further divide the time period evenly into M sub-time-window: $t = \langle t_1 ... t_M \rangle$. The tweet frequency of an event segment s in sub-window t_m is denoted by $f_t(s,m)$. Let $T_t(s,m)$ be the set of tweets that each contains segment s and is published within sub-window t_m. We define the similarity between a pair of segments s_a and s_b within time window t as follows:

$$sim_t(s_a,s_b) = \sum_{m=1}^{M} w_t(s_a,m)w_t(s_b,m)sim\left(T_t(s_a,m),T_t(s_b,m)\right) \quad (9)$$

where $sim(T_1,T_2)$ measures the similarity between two sets of tweets T_1 and T_2, and $w_t(s,m)$ weighs the importance of sub-window t_m to segment s. To compute $sim(T_1,T_2)$, we concatenate all tweets in T_1 (resp. T_2) to form a pseudo document, and use cosine similarity with $tf \cdot idf$ scheme. The importance of sub-window t_m to segment s is the normalized frequency distribution over M sub-windows:

$$w_t(s,m) = \frac{f_t(s,m)}{\sum_{m'=1}^{M} f_t(s,m')} \quad (10)$$

Equation 9 illustrates that two event segments are similar if they have both similar tweet content and consistent frequency patterns along the time sub-windows. Either dissimilar tweet content or inconsistent frequency patterns leads to low similarity. More specifically, dissimilar tweet content suggests that two event segments refer to two distinct events. Inconsistent frequency pattern may suggest that the two event segments refer to two similar events but happened at different time points (*e.g.*, two football matches at the same day).

To be shown in our experiments (Section 4.3) content similarity is necessary to distinguish segments of different events having very similar tweet frequency distributions. Note that, because of the specific information conveyed by tweet segment, we believe that the content similarity of using all tweets containing the tweet segment is more meaningful than that using unigram. For example, the tweets containing segment steve jobs will be very different from the tweets containing either steve or the tweets containing jobs only.

3.3.2 Clustering by k-Nearest Neighbor Graph

Given the similarity measure in Equation 9, clustering event segments into possible events become straightforward and many existing clustering algorithms can be directly applied. We apply an variant of Jarvis-Patrick algorithm [7] for event segment clustering.

Given a graph of objects with edges indicating the similarity between any two objects, Jarvis-Patrick clustering algorithm partitions the graph by measuring the number of common neighbors among the k-nearest neighbors of the two objects. The partitioning involves two parameters: k and ℓ. Two objects are put into the same cluster if: 1) they are in each others' k-nearest neighbors, and 2) they share at least ℓ common nearest neighbors among the k-nearest neighbors. Note that, Jarvis-Patrick requires a single scan of all pairs of objects for clustering, which offers great scalability for Twitter stream-based event detection.

Considering the unique properties of short length and informal writing style of tweets, two event segments referring to the same event may not share a large number of common k-nearest neighbors to each other. Nevertheless, an event segment referring to a realistic event would likely appear in another event segment's k-nearest neighbors, and vice versa, given that the two event segments referring to the same event. We therefore relax the clustering criterion by considering only the first requirement: *two event segments appearing in each others' k-nearest neighbors are put into the same cluster*. With this relaxation, given a complete graph of event segments, the clustering becomes to retain any edge between two event segments s_a and s_b if and only if they appear in each other's k-nearest neighbors. The resultant connected components are considered as ***candidate events***. If an event segment is in isolation and not grouped into any cluster, it is considered not event related and dropped from further processing. The clustering of event segments therefore requires only one parameter k and we set $k = 3$ in our experiments.

3.3.3 Candidate Event Filtering

Cambridge Dictionaries Online defines an *event* as "anything that happens, especially something important and unusual"[7]. However, we observe that many candidate events detected through clustering event segments are not realistic events. For instance, the

[7] http://dictionary.cambridge.org/dictionary/british/event?q=event

segments "friday night", "friday", "weekends", "trip" and "enjoy" are returned as a possible event by the above procedures at some Friday (*e.g.,* Jun 18, 2010 covered in our dataset). More detailed human investigation shows that the tweets of this candidate event are from people who were talking about the plan or schedule for the coming weekend. Apparently, this kind of events can not be considered as realistic events. This calls for a mechanism to evaluate the "important and unusual" aspect of a candidate event obtained from event segment clustering.

We observe that many events involve well-known entities (*e.g.,* person names, locations, festivals) and many of these entities are documented in Wikipedia. Recall that each segment is produced in Section 3.1 with the preference towards Wikipedia entities (see Equation 3). We therefore again utilize Wikipedia to approximately evaluate "important and unusual" aspect of a candidate event. More specifically, we define *newsworthiness* measures for event segment and candidate event respectively.

Definition 3. **[Segment Newsworthiness]** The newsworthiness $\mu(s)$ of a segment s is

$$\mu(s) = \max_{\ell \in s} e^{Q(\ell)} - 1$$

where ℓ is any sub-phrase of s, and $Q(\ell)$ is the prior probability that ℓ appears as anchor text in Wikipedia articles that contain ℓ.

The exponential function is used in the equation since it is an increasing function with an increasing first derivative in the range of [0, 1]. That is, a segment with a larger $Q(\ell)$ would gain a relatively higher *newsworthiness* value. Next, we define the *newsworthiness* of a candidate event as follows.

Definition 4. **[Event Newsworthiness]** The newsworthiness $\mu(e)$ of an event e containing a set of event segments $e_s = \{s\}$ is

$$\mu(e) = \frac{\sum_{s \in e_s} \mu(s)}{|e_s|} \cdot \frac{\sum_{g \in E_e} sim(g)}{|e_s|}$$

where E_e is a set of edges that are retained during applying Jarvis-Patrick clustering, and *sim(g)* is the similarity of edge g which is calculated by using Equation 9.

Observe that *newsworthiness* of a candidate event considers both the newsworthiness of its member event segments (*i.e.,* the first component) and the topology of the connected component formed by its member event segments (*i.e.,* the second component). The latter is equivalent to measure the density of the connected component in the clustering result. Therefore, a candidate event receives a high newsworthiness score if some phrases in its member segments are commonly used as anchor text in Wikipedia (indicating well known entities) and the member segments are well connected with strong cohesive topology.

We observe in our experiments, most top-ranked candidate events by newsworthiness are likely related to realistic events. On the other hand, noisy events likely have much lower *newsworthiness* scores. That is, the distribution of newsworthiness scores has a positive skewness. Let μ_x be the highest newsworthiness score among all candidate events detected in a given time-window. Based on the above observation, we consider a candidate event e to be a realistic event if the ratio between μ_x and $\mu(e)$ is smaller than a threshold τ, *i.e.,* $\frac{\mu_x}{\mu(e)} < \tau$, otherwise noise. Naturally, a lower threshold results in better precision of the detected events but poorer recall, and vice versa. We investigate the impact of τ empirically in Section 4.

After filtering away noisy events, we represent each detected event with its member event segments sorted by *newsworthiness* scores. The top-ranked segments are used to describe the event. In this work, the top-5 segments are used to describe the event.

3.4 Discussion

The efficiency of *Twevent* is a non-trivial factor from a practical perspective. Recall that *Twevent* contains three main components: tweet segmentation, event segment detection, and event segment clustering, shown in Figure 1. We next discuss the computational cost for each component.

The running time of tweet segmentation is linear to the length of a tweet (in number of the words). As segmentation of one tweet is independent of segmentation of other tweets, parallel computing techniques can be easily utilized in this component. More importantly, tweet segmentation can be considered as a part of preprocess because all segments are stored in an index for further processing.

Event segment detection only requires one scan of segments' tweet frequency and user frequency. The time complexity is linear to the number of segments in each time window.

Most computation time is consumed by calculating the similarity between two event segments, and event segment clustering. However, the pair-wised event segment similarity is computed for a relatively small set (*e.g.,* $K = \sqrt{N_i}$) of event segments where N_i is the number of tweets published within a time window. That is, the time complexity is $O(K^2)$. The Jarvis-Patrick clustering algorithm used for event segment clustering requires one scan of all pairs of event segments within a time window. Given the relative small number of detected events in each time window, the running time for the candidate event filtering is negligible.

We conducted our experiments on a workstation with a 2.40GHz Xeon quad-core CPU and 24GB of RAM. Without considering the time taken for tweet segmentation[8], *Twevent* takes about 18 seconds to detect events from average 143K tweets published in one day (*i.e.,* the time window).

4. EXPERIMENTS

In this section, we report our extensive experiments on evaluating *Twevent*. We show that *Twevent* outperforms the state-of-the-art approach with both better precision and recall. We show that newsworthy segments make the detected events much easier to be interpreted by users. Further, we evaluate the usefulness of the notion of tweet segment against unigram, the effect of the parameters in *Twevent*.

4.1 Dataset and Experimental Setting

Wikipedia Data. The Wikipedia data used in tweet segmentation (Section 3.1) and *newsworthiness* measure (Section 3.3.3) are based on the Wikipedia dump released on 30 Jan, 2010. It contains 3,246,821 articles and 266,625,017 hyperlinks. In total, there are 4,342,732 distinct entities appeared as anchor texts in the Wikipedia dump.

Twitter Stream. A collection of tweets published by Singapore-based users (based on the location specified in user profile) in June 2010 is used to simulate a Twitter stream. This dataset was built by Weng and Lee for evaluating the *EDCoW* event detection method in [21]. There are a total of 4,331,937 tweets published by 19,256 unique users in the dataset. A number of realistic events happened in the data collection period, such as FIFA World Cup 2010, WWDC 2010, and MTV Movie Awards 2010.

Figure 2(a) shows the average number of tweets published within each hour of a day. Most tweets are published within 6AM to 6PM, with relatively more tweets published in the afternoon.

Parameter Setting. There are several parameters that could affect

[8]In our experiments, the speed of tweet segmentation relies on Microsoft Web N-Gram Web service.

Table 1: Detection results of *Twevent*, *Twevent$_u$*, and *EDCoW*.

Method	No. events detected	Precision	Recall	DERate
EDCoW	21	76.2%	13	23.1%
Twevent	101	**86.1%**	75	**16.0%**
Twevent$_u$	146	75.3%	**78**	41.0%

the performance of *Twevent*. The size of the time-window t and the number of sub-time-windows M are the two basic parameters for *Twevent*. In our evaluation, we fix t to be a day and set $M = 12$. That is, each sub-time-window is 2 hours.

Recall that we retain only top $K = \sqrt{N_t}$ bursty segments as event segments, where N_t is the number of tweets published in the time window t; For Jarvis-Patrick clustering, we set $k = 3$ for the number of nearest neighbors in the graph; To distinguish realistic events from noise, we set threshold on the ratio of newsworthiness τ. In our experiments, we observe that parameter τ affects the event detection accuracy of *Twevent* more significantly than the other two parameters K and k. We therefore evaluate the impact of varying τ and fix $K = \sqrt{N_t}$ and $k = 3$ throughout our evaluation.

Evaluation Metric. The dataset does not come with ground truth labels on all realistic events within the data collection period. Because it is infeasible to manually label the over 4 million tweets in the dataset, we choose to manually evaluate the detected events returned by *Twevent*. We use *precision* and *recall* to evaluate the accuracy of the events detected.

We follow the definition of **Precision** used in [21], which is defined as the fraction of the detected events that are related to a realistic event. However, recall was not defined in [21] because of the lack of the ground truth labels in the dataset. In our paper, we choose to report **Recall** as *the number of distinct realistic events detected* from the dataset on daily basis. Note that, if two detected events are both related to the same realistic event within the same time window (*i.e.*, one day), then both are considered correct in terms of precision, but only *one* realistic event is considered in counting recall. Due to this reason, we also define *Duplicate Event Rate* (or simply **DERate**) to denote the percentage of events that have been duplicately detected among all realistic events detected.

4.2 Statistics on Tweet Segmentation

We first report statistics on the tweet segments returned by the tweet segmentation component. After removal of stop-words and words with non-English characters, there are 662,088 distinct words or unigrams retained in the data. Tweet segmentation is then applied to each tweet. A total of 1,275,809 distinct segments are obtained after segmentation.

Observe from Figure 2(b), the tweet frequency of a segment follows a power-law distribution. On average, each segment is contained in 19 tweets. In Figure 2(c), we report the distribution of unigram and multi-gram segments. The figure shows that about 50% of the segments are 2-grams; segments with more than 3 grams are very rare. We observe that 2-gram segments cover a large proportional of named entities, such as "lady gaga" and "justin bieber", or location name like "orchard road". Moreover, many 3-grams segments are very informative, like "mtv movie awards" and "penalty shoot out". More examples are given in Table 2.

4.3 Event Detection Results

We compare *Twevent* with two methods: *EDCoW* and *Twevent$_u$*. The latter is a variant of *Twevent* without using tweet segment but using unigram in the event detection process, with the same parameter settings as *Twevent* except the setting for threshold τ. In this set

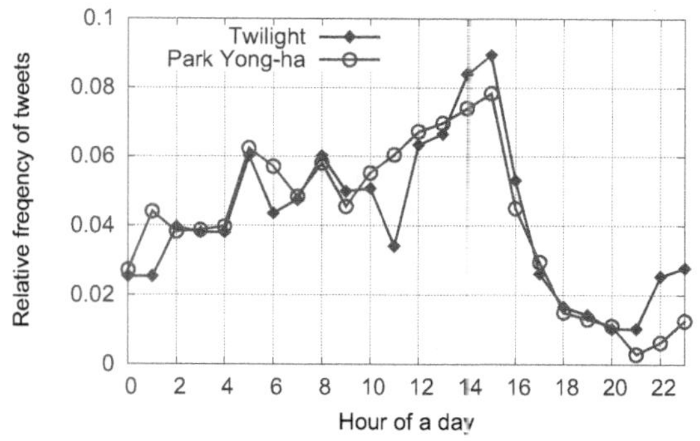

Figure 3: Comparison of frequency distributions for the two events: Twilight and Park Yong-ha

of experiments, we set $\tau = 4$ for *Twevent* and $\tau = 3$ for *Twevent$_u$*. The impact of varying τ will be reported in Section 4.4.

Recall that we measure the segment's newsworthiness using Definition 3. Based on this definition, a unigram is likely to have zero newsworthiness score. Thus, we change the newsworthiness definition for unigram to be $\mu(w) = e^{Q(w)}$ for a unigram w. The modified definition strongly favors informative unigrams, leading to better representations for the detected events. Next, we report the event detection accuracy of the three methods.

Event detection accuracy. Table 1 reports the number of events detected, the precision and recall, of the three methods respectively. The results of *EDCoW* are reproduced from [21][9]. Shown in the table, our proposed method *Twevent* yields the best precision of 86.1% which is significantly larger than the precisions achieved by *EDCoW* and *Twevent$_u$*. Observe that our method *Twevent* detects 101 events with a recall of 75 realistic events. On the same dataset, *EDCoW* detects 21 events in total with 13 realistic events. *Twevent$_u$* yields a slighter worse precision than *EDCoW* (75.3% vs 76.2%) but detects the largest number of realistic events. In terms of DERate, *Twevent* achieves the lowest rate despite that our method detects much more events than *EDCoW* (101 vs 21). On the other hand, we observe that *Twevent$_u$* delivers the worst DERate, more than double of *Twevent* (41% vs 16.0%). That is, the unigrams about the same event are clustered into two or more events. Because a tweet segment usually conveys very specific information, the tweets containing the tweet segment are all about the same topic (*e.g.*, the event). Two tweet segments about the same event are therefore have higher chance to be clustered together.

From the list of events detected, we observe that an event is redetected mainly because users discuss the event from different perspectives, or one event is a sub-event of another. We use the two events e_{22} and e_{20} detected on 12 Jun 2012 as an example for illustration. Listed in Table 2, e_{22}, detected with segments [usa, england, eng, vs], refers to the football match between England and USA in 2010 World Cup; e_{20} with [steven gerrard, captain, score, scored, gerrard] refers to the caption of England, Steve Gerrard, scored a goal in this match. Because both events refer to the same match, we count them as one realistic event in our recall.

Event interpretation. We argue that the notion of *tweet segment* not only benefits better precision in event detection, but also makes the detected events much easier to be interpreted. In above discussion, we show that person name [steven gerrard] is detected as an event segment in the result. We now give more examples by listing all the events detected by *Twevent* between June 07 to

[9]All events detected by *EDCoW* are reported in Table 1, Page 407 in [21].

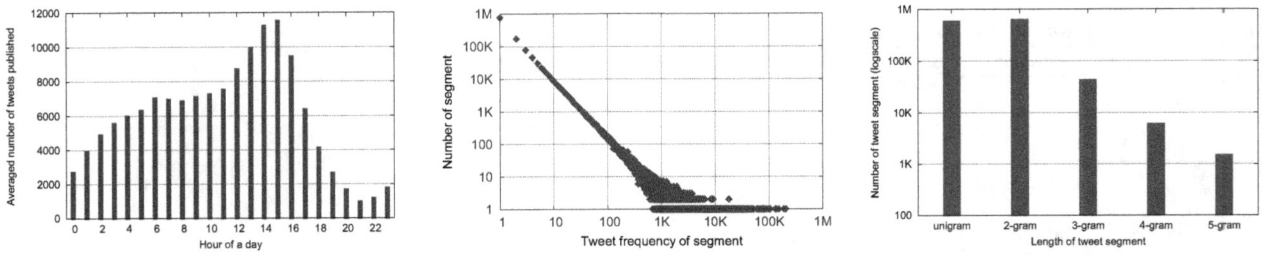

(a) Tweet volume against hour of day (b) Segment tweet frequency distribution (c) Segment length distribution

Figure 2: Statistics on tweets and tweet segments

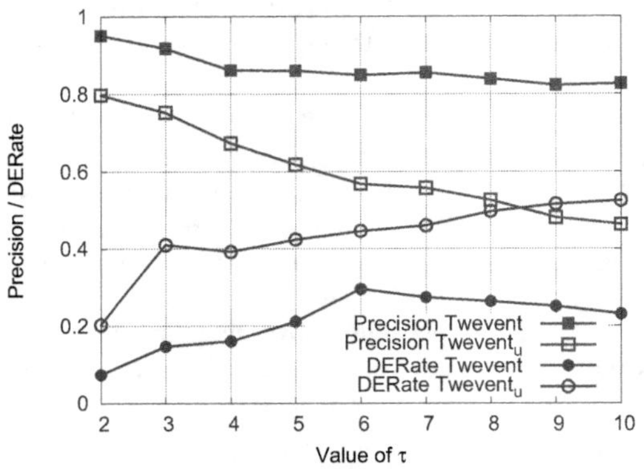

(a) Precision and DERate

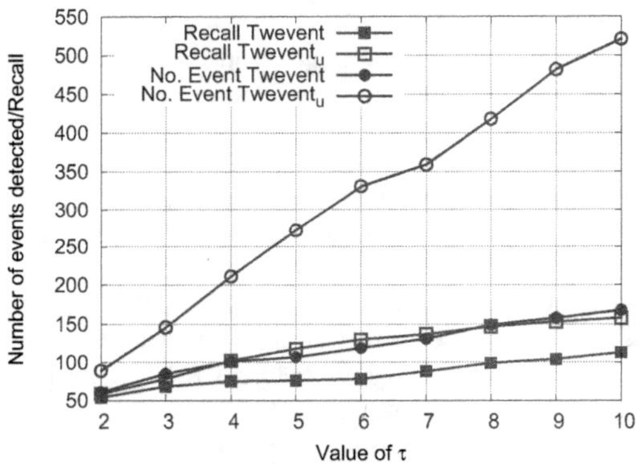

(b) Recall and number of detected event

Figure 4: *Twevent* and *Twevent$_u$* against different τ values

June 12, 2010[10]. This 6-day period is chosen because it covers a wide range of events that happened in June, 2010, including Apple WWDC 2010, MTV Movie Awards 2010, and FIFA World Cup 2010, among others.

From Table 2, we make two observations. First, many event segments are multi-gram segments such as various types of named entities [steve jobs], [mtv movie awards], [katy perry], and [karate kid], and segments conveying concrete information like [argentina vs nigeria] and [season finale]. These segments make the events much easier to be interpreted than some unigram keywords. For comparison, we also list the keywords of all the 8 events detected by *EDCoW*, reproduced from [21], and the keywords of all the 40 events detected by *Twevent$_u$* during the 6-day period in Tables 3

[10]Due to page list, we do not list all the 101 events detected by *Twevent* for the whole month of June 2010. The full list is available at `http://www.cais.ntu.edu.sg/~lichenliang/twevent/eventlist.txt`.

Table 3: Events detected by *EDCoW* in June 07 – June 12, 2010 (reproduced from [21], following their event id.)

Day	e_{ID}	Event keywords
7	e_7.	kobe, kristen
	e_8.	#iphone4, ios4, iphone
8	e_9.	reformat, hamilton
	e_{10}.	avocado, commence, ongoing
9	e_{11}.	#failwhale, twitter
10	e_{12}.	vuvuzela, soccer
11	e_{13}.	#svk, #svn
12	e_{14}.	#kor, greec, #gre

and 4, respectively. We can see that the keywords detected by *EDCoW* is relatively hard to interpret than the two methods *Twevent* and *Twevent$_u$*. Compare the latter two methods, we argue that *Twevent* detects more semantically meaningful keywords/phrases than *Twevent$_u$*. For instance, we use the first two events detected by both methods as example. Although both methods detect similar keywords for the WWDC 2010 event, [steve jobs, imovie, wwdc, iphone, wifi] is more easy to interpret than [wwdc, keynote, live, jobs, steve]. Similarly, *Twevent* detects [mtv movie awards, mtv, new moon, twilight, awards] while *Twevent$_u$* outputs [mtv, moon, twilight, movie, awards]; the phrase [mtv movie awards] makes the event much more easy to interpret. Second, the detected events by *Twevent* cover a wide range of events, such as Korea music bands, Apple WWDC 2010, MTV Movie Awards 2010, release of music videos and movies, and football matches of World Cup 2010. That is, *Twevent* does not favor certain types of events than others. Among the 22 events listed in Table 2, only 1 event has no corresponding real-life events leading to a precision of 95.5% in this 6-day period.

Case study. We use a case study to illustrate the importance of using content in event detection from tweets. Figure 3 plots the relative frequency of tweets published on June 30, 2010 related to two events. The first event with segments [harry potter, twilight, hours, trailer] is about the movie *The Twilight Saga: Eclipse*, which was released on June 30, 2010. The trailer of the Movie *Harry Potter and the Deathly Hallows Part 1* was shown before *The Twilight Saga: Eclipse*. The second event, with segments [park yong ha, rip, peace, hope, park] refers to the suicide case of Korean actor Park Yong-ha on June 30, 2010. Observe from Figure 3, the two events have very similar tweet frequency distribution over the 24 hours of the day. The tweet frequency of an event is defined as the relative frequency of the tweets published in an hour that contain any event segment of the event. We argue that it is hard to distinguish the two events without using content similarity between the event segments (see Section 3.3).

Table 2: List of the 22 events detected by *Twevent* during the period of June 07 to June 12, 2010.

Day	e_{ID}	[Event Segments]: Event Description
7	e_1.	**[steve jobs, imovie, wwdc, iphone, wifi]**: iPhone4 was released during WWDC 2010.
	e_2.	**[mtv movie awards, mtv, new moon, twilight, robe]**: The movie *The Twilight Saga: New Moon* was the biggest winner in MTV Movie Awards 2010; it took 4 out of 10 "Best" Awards.
	e_3.	**[yesung, yesung oppa, kyuhyun, oppa, kyu]**: Korean popular band Super Junior's showcase was held on June 6, 2010 at Singapore. Yesung Oppa and Kyuhyun Oppa are members of Super Junior.
8	e_4.	**[lady gaga, music video, gaga, mv, alejandro]**: The music video *Alejandro* by Lady GaGa was premiered officially on June 8, 2010.
	e_5.	**[ss501, indonesia, ariel, sama, trend]**: No clear corresponding real-life event.
	e_6.	**[singapore, iphone 4g, iphone 3gs, iphone, coming out]**: Related to event e_1. People started to talk about the release date of iPhone 4 in Singapore.
9	e_7.	**[lady gaga, youtube, youtube video, music video, gaga]**: Related to event e_4.
	e_8.	**[twitter, whale, stupid, capacity, over again]**: A number of users complained they could not use twitter due to over-capacity. A logo with whale is usually used to denote over-capacity.
	e_9.	**[ipad, iphone, apple, new]**: Related to event e_1.
	e_{10}.	**[watching glee, glee, season finale, season, channel]**: The season finale of the American TV series *Glee* was broadcasted on June 8, 2010.
10	e_{11}.	**[lady gaga, youtube, youtube video, music video, amber]**: Related to event e_7.
	e_{12}.	**[justin bieber, try, pa, took, each]**: Related to event e_{15}. The song *Never Say Never* by Justin Bieber serves as the theme song for the movie *The Karate Kid*, which was released on June 10, 2010 in Singapore.
	e_{13}.	**[yesung, tweeted]**: Super Junior's Yesung posted a photo about his pet turtles.
	e_{14}.	**[twitter, whale, stupid, capacity, over]**: Related to event e_8.
	e_{15}	**[karate kid, watch movie, movie]**: The movie *The Karate Kid* was released on June 10, 2010 in Singapore.
11	e_{16}.	**[uruguay vs france, uruguay, france, vs]**: A match between Uruguay and France in World Cup 2010.
	e_{17}.	**[south africa, vs mexico, mexico, goal, first goal]**: A match between South Africa and Mexico in World Cup 2010. And the first goal of the 2010 World Cup was scored in the match.
12	e_{18}.	**[arg, argentina, argentina vs nigeria, nigeria, messi]**: A match between Argentina and Nigeria in World Cup 2010.
	e_{19}.	**[south korea, greece, korea vs greece, korea won, korea]**: A match between South Korea and Greece in World Cup 2010.
	e_{20}.	**[steven gerrard, captain, gerrard, scores]**: Related to event e_{22}. The captain of England, Steve Gerrard scored a goal in the match.
	e_{21}.	**[ji sung, park, scored, jisung]**: Related to event e_{19}. Park Ji-Sung, the caption of South Korea, scored a goal against Greece.
	e_{22}.	**[usa, england, eng, vs]**: A match between England and USA in World Cup 2010.

4.4 Impact of τ in Twevent

While event segments are clustered into candidate events, the ratio threshold τ defines the boundary between the realistic events and the noisy events. We next analyze the effect of τ value on the performance of *Twevent* and *Twevent*$_u$.

Figure 4(a) plots the precision and DERate of the two methods when changing τ from 2 to 10. We make the two main observations. First, for both methods, precision degrades along the increase of τ as more events are considered as realistic events. Nevertheless, the rate of degradation for *Twevent* is much smaller than that of *Twevent*$_u$. Observe that *Twevent* maintains very good precision above 80% even when $\tau = 10$, which is better than the best precision achieved by *Twevent*$_u$ with all τ values. Second, increasing of τ leading to increase in DERate. Shown in Figure 4(a), the DERate of *Twevent* is about half of *Twevent*$_u$ for most τ values and stop increasing when $\tau > 6$. In summary, the use of tweet segmentation in event detection contribute to much higher precision and much lower duplicate event detection rate.

Figure 4(b) reports the number of events detected and the recall values along the change of τ values for the two methods. For both methods, increase τ leads to better recall. Observe that, although *Twevent*$_u$ always achieves better recall than *Twevent*, the differences between the recall values do not change much along the increase of τ. However, increment of τ leads to sharp increase of the number of events detected for *Twevent*$_u$. But due to the poorer precision along the increase of τ, the number of realistic events detected does not increase at the same pace as the number of detected events.

5. CONCLUSION

Twitter, as a new type of social media, has experienced an explosive growth in terms of both users and information volume in recent years. The characteristics of tweets propose severe challenges to many tasks including event detection. In this paper, we present a novel event detection system for Twitter stream, called *Twevent*, to tackle the adverse impacts of tweets: short and noisy content, diverse and dynamic topics, and large data volume. One of the key concept in *Twevent* is to use tweet segment instead of unigram for identifying the bursty features and then distinguishing the realistic events from the noisy ones. *Twevent* demonstrates outstanding performance in our experiments: effectiveness, informativeness, and efficiency. As a part of our future work, we will investigate the effectiveness of utilizing more features from tweets (*e.g.,* retweet rate and hashtags) in *Twevent*. Another important task is to investigate the effectiveness of *Twevent* when none of the segments of an event is covered by Wikipedia.

6. ACKNOWLEDGEMENT

This work was partially supported by MOE AcRF Tier-1 Grant RG13/10, Singapore. We thank Jianshu Weng from HP Labs Singapore for providing us the dataset used in [21].

Table 4: Events detected by *Twevent$_u$* in June 07 – June 12, 2010

Day	e_{ID}	Event keywords
7	e_1.	wwdc, keynote, live, jobs, steve
	e_2.	mtv, moon, twilight, movie, awards
	e_3.	yesung, ryeowook, oppa, hope, welcome
	e_4.	indonesia, blues, rain, weather, star
	e_5.	iphone, apple, video, available, os
	e_6.	singapore, asia, showcase, junior, tickets
	e_7.	check, website, gain, member, site
	e_8.	justin, both, pa, took, each
	e_9.	perry, katy
	e_{10}.	singtel, samsung, galaxy, cute, aniversary
	e_{11}.	tumblr, white, black, hair, model
8	e_{12}.	gaga, lady, mv, alejandro
	e_{13}.	singapore, iphone, apple, july, features
	e_{14}.	wwdc, keynote, jobs, steve
	e_{15}.	right, think, one, need, know
9	e_{16}.	twitter, whale, capacity, fail, over
	e_{17}.	fan, wish, pretty, follow
	e_{18}.	youtube, glee, season, video, finale
	e_{19}.	gaga, lady, mv, alejandro
	e_{20}.	rice, chicken, eat, food, lunch
	e_{21}.	mtv, asia, wednesday, awards
	e_{22}.	try, pa, took
	e_{23}.	home, out, going, i'm
10	e_{24}.	day, work, one, need, know
	e_{25}.	youtube, gaga, video, lady, liked
	e_{26}.	twitter, whale, stupid, capacity, fail
	e_{27}.	radio, station, heard, addicted
	e_{28}.	justin, try, pa, took
	e_{29}.	karate, movie, kid, watched
	e_{30}.	congrats, blue, jay, name, jaywalkers
	e_{31}.	boss, centre, thursday, suntec, fair
	e_{32}.	facebook, internet, camera, photo, photos
	e_{33}.	cup, world, opening
11	e_{34}.	mexico, africa, goal, scored, south
	e_{35}.	uruguay, france
12	e_{36}.	park, ji, sung, jisung
	e_{37}.	argentina, nigeria, usa, england, messi
	e_{38}.	captain, steve, gerrard, scores
	e_{39}.	greece, korea, koreans, han, min
	e_{40}.	goalkeeper, robe, green, ball, mistake

7. REFERENCES

[1] J. Allan, R. Papka, and V. Lavrenko. On-line new event detection and tracking. In *SIGIR*, pages 37–45, 1998.

[2] T. Brants, F. Chen, and A. Farahat. A system for new event detection. In *SIGIR*, pages 330–337, 2003.

[3] A. Dong, R. Zhang, P. Kolari, J. Bai, F. Diaz, Y. Chang, Z. Zheng, and H. Zha. Time is of the essence: improving recency ranking using twitter data. In *WWW*, pages 331–340, 2010.

[4] G. P. C. Fung, J. X. Yu, H. Liu, and P. S. Yu. Time-dependent event hierarchy construction. In *SIGKDD*, pages 300–309, 2007.

[5] G. P. C. Fung, J. X. Yu, P. S. Yu, and H. Lu. Parameter free bursty events detection in text streams. In *VLDB*, pages 181–192, 2005.

[6] Q. He, K. Chang, and E.-P. Lim. Analyzing feature trajectories for event detection. In *SIGIR*, pages 207–214, 2007.

[7] R. A. Jarvis and E. A. Patrick. Clustering using a similarity measure based on shared near neighbors. *IEEE Trans. Comput.*, 22(11):1025–1034, Nov. 1973.

[8] J. Kleinberg. Bursty and hierarchical structure in streams. In *SIGKDD*, pages 91–101, 2002.

[9] H. Kwak, C. Lee, H. Park, and S. Moon. What is twitter, a social network or a news media? In *WWW*, pages 591–600, 2010.

[10] C. Li, J. Weng, Q. He, Y. Yao, A. Datta, A. Sun, and B.-S. Lee. Twiner: Named entity recognition in targeted twitter stream. In *SIGIR*, 2012.

[11] M. Mathioudakis and N. Koudas. Twittermonitor: trend detection over the twitter stream. In *SIGMOD*, pages 1155–1158, 2010.

[12] PearAnalytics. Twitter study, August 2009. Available online `http://www.pearanalytics.com/blog/wp-content/uploads/2010/05/Twitter-Study-August-2009.pdf`.

[13] S. Petrović, M. Osborne, and V. Lavrenko. Streaming first story detection with application to twitter. In *HLT-NAACL*, pages 181–189, 2010.

[14] S. Phuvipadawat and T. Murata. Breaking news detection and tracking in twitter. In *WI-IAT*, pages 120–123, 2010.

[15] B. Poblete, R. Garcia, M. Mendoza, and A. Jaimes. Do all birds tweet the same?: characterizing twitter around the world. In *CIKM*, pages 1025–1030, 2011.

[16] A.-M. Popescu, M. Pennacchiotti, and D. Paranjpe. Extracting events and event descriptions from twitter. In *WWW*, pages 105–106, 2011.

[17] A. Ritter, S. Clark, Mausam, and O. Etzioni. Named entity recognition in tweets: An experimental study. In *EMNLP*, pages 1524–1534, 2011.

[18] L. Rui, L. Kin, K. Ravi, and C. Kevin. Tedas: a twitter based event detection and analysis system. In *ICDE*, pages 1273–1276, 2012.

[19] T. Sakaki, M. Okazaki, and Y. Matsuo. Earthquake shakes twitter users: real-time event detection by social sensors. In *WWW*, pages 851–860, 2010.

[20] J. Teevan, D. Ramage, and M. R. Morris. #twittersearch: a comparison of microblog search and web search. In *WSDM*, pages 35–44, 2011.

[21] J. Weng and B.-S. Lee. Event detection in twitter. In *ICWSM*, pages 401–408, 2011.

[22] S. Wu, J. M. Hofman, W. A. Mason, and D. J. Watts. Who says what to whom on twitter. In *WWW*, pages 705–714, 2011.

[23] Y. Yang, T. Ault, T. Pierce, and C. W. Lattimer. Improving text categorization methods for event tracking. In *SIGIR*, pages 65–72, 2000.

[24] Y. Yang, J. G. Carbonell, R. D. Brown, T. Pierce, B. T. Archibald, and X. Liu. Learning approaches for detecting and tracking news events. *IEEE Intelligent Systems*, 14(4):32–43, July 1999.

[25] Y. Yang, T. Pierce, and J. Carbonell. A study of retrospective and on-line event detection. In *SIGIR*, pages 28–36, 1998.

[26] G. K. Zipf. *Human Behavior and the Principle of Least Effort: An Introduction to Human Ecology*. Hafner Pub. Co, 1949.

Making Your Interests Follow You on Twitter

Marco Pennacchiotti
eBay Inc., San Jose, US
mpennacchiotti@ebay.com

Fabrizio Silvestri
ISTI - CNR, Pisa, Italy
f.silvestri@isti.cnr.it

Hossein Vahabi
ISTI - CNR, Pisa, Italy
IMT Lucca, Italy
hossein.vahabi@isti.cnr.it

Rossano Venturini
Dept. of Computer Science,
University of Pisa, Italy
rossano@di.unipi.it

ABSTRACT

In this paper we introduce the task of *tweet recommendation*, the problem of suggesting tweets that match a user's interests and likes. We propose an Information-Retrieval-like model that leverages the content of the user's tweets and those of her friends, and that effectively retrieves a set of tweets that is personalized and varied in nature. Our approach could be easily leveraged to build, for example, a Twitter or Facebook timeline that collects messages that are of interest for the user, but that are not posted by her friends. We compare to typical approaches used in similar tasks, reporting significant gains in terms of overall precision, up to about +20%, on both a corpus-based evaluation and real world user study.

Categories and Subject Descriptors

H.4 [**Information Systems Applications**]: Miscellaneous; H.3.4 [**INFORMATION STORAGE AND RETRIEVAL**]: Systems and Software—*User profiles and alert services*

General Terms

Algorithms

Keywords

Twitter recommendation, Information Filtering

1. INTRODUCTION

Social media is having an unprecedented success in terms of popularity in recent years. Twitter and Facebook, the two most popular social media hubs, occupy high positions in the top-10 of the most visited sites, rivaled only by big search engines and by Wikipedia[1]. In January 2012 Twitter has been visited 2.5 billion times, more than double than 6 months before[2]. In October 2011, Twitter revealed that 250 million tweets are posted every day, with a user base of about 300 million people.

With a rate of roughly 3,000 tweets per seconds, social media are today facing the same challenge of information overloading that the Web faced more than 10 years ago. More than that, we are today also facing the challenge of *information hiding*. By no means can a Twitter user possibly read all the messages s/he might consider important. Indeed, only a very small percentage of tweets spreads to a significant number of users [25]. It is quite likely that users miss lots of interesting tweets just because none of the people in their network retweet or mention them. Social search engines can help to solve the problem by providing a simple means to retrieve information. However, these engines cannot predict what the user may like and push interesting information for her. The solution is therefore a combination of social search and algorithms for personalizing, summarizing and recommending social content.

In this paper we focus on the latter task of social content recommendation. We propose two Information Retrieval inspired methods for recommending engaging tweets to a user, matching her interests and likes. The methods are based on the idea of building a user profile from her tweets and a weighted combination of those posted by her friends, and to match this profile on incoming tweets. Our extensive evaluation performed on both an in-house dataset and on real users, shows that our methods successfully recommend interesting tweets when compared to other approaches. Our system differs from most previous work on social recommendation, where the focus is predominantly on recommending web content using social signals, and on recommending new connections. Our primary objective here is to recommend the social content itself, i.e., tweets. Although the methods we use to approach the tweet recommendation problem are derived from information retrieval techniques, their application to our context requires, as we shall see in the rest of the paper, some adjustments and additions to make them work in social media settings.

The most direct practical application of our system is to provide a social media user with a new timeline[3] that contains messages that strongly match her interests, but that have not been posted by any of her friends. The benefits of

[1] `http://www.alexa.com/topsites`

[2] `http://www.quantcast.com/twitter.com`

[3] The user entry point in most social media hubs like Twitter and Facebook is the personal timeline, where the user is shown the recent messages posted by her friends.

CIKM'12, October 29–November 2, 2012, Maui, HI, USA.

having this additional timeline are twofold. Firstly, the user will not miss messages that are relevant to her, because our method will show them. Second, authors of recommended tweets may be considered relevant by the user who receives the recommendation. Our tweet recommendation system may therefore indirectly serve also as a mechanism to "*implicitly*" recommend accounts to follow.

Summing up, the original contributions of this paper are:

- We define two novel models for tweet recommendation: TWEETREC aims at recommending the most interesting tweets; INTERESTS-SPANNING TWEETREC aims at recommending a set of tweets, minimizing overlapping informative content. As a result, INTERESTS-SPANNING TWEETREC provides more diverse recommendations.
- The two proposed models define a measure of tweet *interestingness* for a user. We propose an effective measure to estimate interestingness by considering the content of tweets posted by the user herself, and also by her *most authoritative* friends. We prove the impact of the newly proposed measure by using both an automatic and user-study-based evaluation.

The paper is structured as follows. Section 2 presents an overview of the current state of the art in areas that are related to our work. Section 3 presents a formal definition of the problem, while Section 4 describes the proposed solutions. Experiments are presented in Section 5 along with a careful description of the datasets we are using and a definition of the metrics we evaluate. We conclude the paper in Section 6 with a final analysis and future work.

2. RELATED WORK

Research on recommender systems has been widely studied in the past decade (e.g., see [22, 4, 7, 21]). Recommenders have been applied to many different items including movies, videos, music, users, restaurants, news stories, journal articles, and much more (see [22] and references therein). To the best of our knowledge, tweet recommendation has not been yet explicitly defined. This task relates to four main areas of research: *tweet-based content recommendation*, *tweet ranking*, *tweet classification*, and *information spreading in social networks*.

Tweet-based content recommendation systems use Twitter for recommending other types of content. Among others, Abel *et al.* [1] propose a URL recommendation system for Twitter users. They build a linguistic model for the user, as the frequency weighted vector of the hashtags and entities that he/she mentions in his/her tweets. A similar vector is computed from the content of candidate URLs. The web pages that have the highest cosine similarity with the user are recommended [1]. Chen *et al.* present similar models for the same task, where the user profile is represented as the bag-of-word vector of all terms in the user's tweets (or his/her friends' tweets); and the URL model is built from the terms in the tweet that mention it [8]. Our work differs from the above two, in that we recommend tweets instead of URLs, which is a harder task since there is less linguistic material available. Yet, like them, we leverage the linguistic content of the user's tweets and of his/er friends' tweets.

Tweet ranking is the task of ranking tweets given an input query. Duan *et al.* [11] use user and social features to feed a RankSVM algorithm. They report good DGC results by using a variety of information, including user authority features and cosine similarity between the texts of the retrieved tweets. Similar ranking systems have been proposed at the TREC-2011 Microblog Track[4]. In general, typical models for web document ranking such as BM25 and text similarity, can be easily adapted to tweet ranking, showing good performance. Yet, microblogging specific features, such as social feedback and annotations (e.g., number of retweets and hashtags), the authority of the user posting the tweet, tweet length and freshness also play a key role. Tweets have also been used to improve document ranking: Dong *et al.* [10] show that integrating Twitter features (e.g., user and textual properties of the tweets mentioning the URLs) significantly improve state of the art web search algorithms, in ranking documents by relevance and freshness. The task presented in this paper differs from tweet ranking, in that our task is query independent and user centric. Instead of ranking tweets for a given query, we recommend tweets to a user according to his/her interests. There are however similarities between the two tasks, e.g., in both cases there is a specific user need to answer, and similar features can be used.

Short texts classification is a relatively new problem that is receiving more and more attention. Tweet classification is a specialization of this problem where text fragments propagate through social networks. The main issue for classification of microblog messages is their small size. The same issue holds also in different domains where fragments of text are small. Take for instance search snippets, forum messages and Instant Message service texts. The main issue is that messages are small in size, and therefore difficult to classify. Several studies have approached this problem from different angles. Banerjee *et al.* [3] exploit Wikipedia as an external source for improving the accuracy of clustering short texts by enriching their representation with features coming from Wikipedia pages related to terms appearing in the short text. Schonhofen [24] presents a similar approach exploiting Wikipedia as a taxonomy for topics showing significant improvements on clustering accuracy. Phan *et al.* [20] use topic models for building short and sparse text classifiers. They build a a Latent Dirichlet Allocation [5] topic model from this dataset, and then use it to classify short texts.

Information spreading in social networks is another important and well-studied problem in social networks. This research area is important as results can be immediately exploited in several ways, e.g., to spread a marketing campaign or to block spread diseases. One of the seminal papers dealing with this problem is that of Kempe *et al.* [16]. In the paper an approximation algorithm to find the most influential nodes in a network is devised. The algorithm is further refined by Leskovec *et al.* [18] and by Goyal *et al.* [14]. A similar problem, but with the opposite purpose, is defined by Budak *et al.* [6]. The goal of their algorithm is to block a "*bad*" advertisement campaign as soon as it is initiated. As in the case of Kempe *et al.* [16] authors formulate the problem as an optimization problem described by a sub-modular objective function. The standard greedy algorithm for this kind of functions [12] is used with the goal of identifying a subset of individuals that need to be convinced to adopt

[4]`sites.google.com/site/microblogtrack`

the competing (or "good") campaign so as to minimize the number of people that adopt the "bad" campaign at the end of both propagation processes.

3. PROBLEM DEFINITION

We give here a definition of the notation and the problems we shall study in the rest of the paper. Let $\mathcal{T}$ be a stream of tweets, each tweet $t_1, t_2, \ldots \in \mathcal{T}$ is indexed by the timestamp at which it arrives. For each user u, we assume to know the *interestingness* of a tweet $t \in \mathcal{T}$, denoted by $\mathcal{I}_u(t)$. Hereinafter, we consider a single user u and we omit the subscript u from $\mathcal{I}_u$ whenever the user can be inferred from the context.

We shall define two problems whose goal is to select a subset of tweets $S \subseteq \mathcal{T}$ to be recommended to a given user. The first problem aims at selecting $S \subseteq \mathcal{T}$ of size k, without considering the goodness of the set in its entirety. Namely, each tweet in S is selected independently from the already selected tweets. We refine the idea of tweet subset selection in the second problem, where the set of tweets $S \subseteq \mathcal{T}$ is further required to maximize the overall information conveyed to u. To the best of our knowledge both problems are novel and have never been proposed before in the context of social media systems such as Twitter.

We begin by introducing the first problem, namely the TweetRec problem, defined as follows.

PROBLEM 1 (TWEETREC). *Given a user u and a positive integer k, we aim at finding a set S of k tweets in $\mathcal{T}$ maximizing the overall "interestingness". More formally, we would like to find*

$$\max_{\substack{S \subseteq \mathcal{T} \\ |S|=k}} \sum_{t \in S} \mathcal{I}(t) \tag{1}$$

Essentially, we are looking for the set of k tweets S having the largest interestingness under the assumption that the tweets independently convey their interesting content. The nicest property of TWEETREC is that its solution is optimally discoverable in $O(|\mathcal{T}| \log k)$ time by the obvious greedy algorithm selecting the most interesting, (i.e., top-k) tweets. The drawback of this solution is that we are assuming independence of tweet content in the solution set. This, indeed, is far from being satisfactory for a user. Suppose, in fact, that all the tweets selected for being included in the set S are highly correlated to each other. This represents a feasible solution of TWEETREC but the user may be far from being satisfied. For instance, each of these two tweets "What's new in Linux 3.2? #linux" and "New features in Linux 3.2. #linux" may be highly interesting for a user but reporting both of them is useless.

The issue in TWEETREC is given by the fact that we are not considering interdependency among selected tweets. The objective function in TWEETREC assumes the independence of all the tweets and does not consider the *overall* interestingness of the identified set S in its entirety.

In order to overcome this limitation, we restate the tweet recommendation problem in an "idependency aware" setting, where shared (i.e., duplicated) information is avoided. Given $S \subseteq \mathcal{T}$, we want to maximize the *overall* interestingness $F(S)$ of the content of tweets $t \in S$ for the user u. Formally, $F(S) = \mathcal{I}\left(\bigsqcup_{t \in S} t\right)$. In this definition *overall* means that duplicate information across tweets is not going to increase the value of the objective function $F(S)$. We also define $\mathcal{I}\left(\bigsqcap_{t \in S} t\right)$ as the interestingness for user u in the *shared* informative content among all tweets in $t \in S$.

PROBLEM 2 (INTERESTS-SPANNING TWEETREC). *Given a user u, a positive integer k, and the stream of tweets $\mathcal{T}$, we aim at finding the k tweets t in $\mathcal{T}$ maximizing the overall interestingness. More formally, we would like to identify the set $\mathcal{T}$ such that*

$$\max_{\substack{S \subseteq \mathcal{T} \\ |S|=k}} \quad F(S) = \sum_{j=1}^{k} \left((-1)^{j+1} \sum_{\substack{I \subseteq S \\ |I|=j}} \mathcal{I}\left(\bigsqcap_{t \in I} t\right) \right) \tag{2}$$

The derivation of the equation in the objective function of INTERESTS-SPANNING TWEETREC is an instantiation of the Inclusion-Exclusion principle to the set $S \subseteq \mathcal{T}$ of tweets. As in TWEETREC, we are looking for the set of k tweets S having the largest overall interestingness for the user u. However, in this case we are taking into consideration all possible dependencies, i.e., shared content among the tweets in the set.

INTERESTS-SPANNING TWEETREC is NP-Hard as proven in the following Theorem.

THEOREM 1. *The* INTERESTS-SPANNING TWEETREC *problem is NP-hard.*

PROOF. The reduction is from Independent Set [13]. Assume we have a graph $G = (V, E)$ with $n = \mid V \mid$ and we want to compute the maximum independent set of G. The independent set can be computed by creating an appropriate instance of our problem. Vertexes in V are considered as tweets. Each vertex is assigned an interestingness equal to $\frac{1}{n}$. Any set S has an overall interestingness equal to $\frac{1}{n} \mid S \mid$ if and only if it does not exist a pair of vertexes in S connected by an edge in E. The interestingness is set to be smaller than $\frac{1}{n} \mid S \mid$, otherwise. To conclude the reduction we observe that, fixed k, the set S identified by a solution of INTERESTS-SPANNING TWEETREC has probability $\frac{k}{n}$ if and only if G has an independent set of size k. In this case, nodes in S are exactly the nodes of one of these independent sets. □

Despite being complex, the objective function of our problem has the property of being a non-negative *submodular* function, as stated in the following Theorem 2. This theorem requires that the function F is monotone (namely, any set S of tweets is at most as interesting as any of its subsets). Obviously, whether $\mathcal{I}$ is monotone depends on its particular instantiation (i.e., the real formula used to its estimation). The monotonicity is a natural assumption to make and, indeed, it holds in our estimation of $\mathcal{I}$ defined in Section 4.

THEOREM 2 (SUBMODULARITY OF $F(X)$). *Let k be a positive integer and let S be a set of k tweets. Then, the function*

$$F(S) = \sum_{j=1}^{k} \left((-1)^{j+1} \sum_{\substack{I \subseteq X \\ |I|=j}} \mathcal{I}\left(\bigsqcap_{t \in I} t\right) \right)$$

is submodular.

PROOF. We have to show, by the definition of submodularity, that given $A \subseteq B \subseteq \mathcal{T}$ and a tweet $c \in \mathcal{T}$, $F(\{c\} \cup A) - F(A) \geq F(\{c\} \cup B) - F(B)$.

The theorem is proven by observing that since $F(X) = \mathcal{I}\left(\bigsqcup_{t \in X} t\right)$ then $F(\{c\} \cup X) = \mathcal{I}(c) + \mathcal{I}\left(\bigsqcup_{t \in X} t\right) - \mathcal{I}\left(c \sqcap \bigsqcup_{t \in X} t\right)$.

Thus, $F(\{c\} \cup A) - F(A) = \mathcal{I}(c) - \mathcal{I}\left(c \sqcap \bigsqcup_{t \in A} t\right)$. Similarly, $F(\{c\} \cup B) - F(B) = \mathcal{I}(c) - \mathcal{I}\left(c \sqcap \bigsqcup_{t \in B} t\right)$.

The thesis easily follows by observing that $\mathcal{I}\left(c \sqcap \bigsqcup_{t \in A} t\right) \leq \mathcal{I}\left(c \sqcap \bigsqcup_{t \in B} t\right)$ since $A \subseteq B \subseteq \mathcal{T}$.

□

Given that our objective function is submodular, its maximization can be obtained by the greedy algorithm presented in [9, 19]. This algorithm incrementally builds the set S in k steps. At each step, the element that has the largest marginal gain is added. This simple algorithm guarantees to obtain a $(1 - 1/e)$ approximation. The following Theorem summarizes this very well-known result.

THEOREM 3 (SUBMODULARITY APPROXIMATION). *[9, 19] For a non-negative, monotone submodular function F, let S be a set of size k obtained by selecting elements one at a time, each time choosing an element that provides the largest marginal increase in the function value. Let $S^\star$ be a set that maximizes the value of F over all k-element sets. Then $F(S) \geq (1 - 1/e)F(S^\star)$.*

4. INTERESTINGNESS ESTIMATION

The TWEETREC and INTERESTS-SPANNING TWEETREC problem definitions give a good formalization for a tweet recommendation system. Yet, these formalizations assume that for any user u and tweet $t \in \mathcal{T}$, we know the score $\mathcal{I}(t)$ measuring the interestingness of the tweet t for the user u. In order to build a functioning recommendation system we therefore need an estimator of interestingness.

In this section, we present one example of an estimator based on a linguistic model. The main assumption is that the interests of a user u are implicitly expressed in his/her tweets. By comparing the linguistic content of the user's tweets and that of a generic tweet t, we can therefore estimate the interestingness $\mathcal{I}(t)$.

In details, we estimate the interestingness as a linear combination of two distinct similarity measures between the set of tweets of the user and a candidate tweet (or set of tweets). In these two measures, sets are compared either by using *item-wise* or *pair-wise* comparisons between their enclosed terms. Our estimation is detailed in Section 4.1.

A drawback of the above-mentioned measure is that it heavily relies on the (textual content of the) set of tweets produced by the user. Indeed, there exist (a class of) users, namely *passive users*, that post a small number of tweets in their lifetime, and adopt Twitter mostly for reading news published by other users. In Section 4.2, we show how to extend the set of tweets written by a passive user u with other carefully chosen tweets that have been posted by users that are highly authoritative.

4.1 Exploiting textual similarities

In this section, we show how to estimate $\mathcal{I}(t)$ by computing the similarity between the set of user's tweets T_u and any subset of tweets from $\mathcal{T}$.

First, given a generic set of tweets X, we define the *bag-of-words* $\mathsf{BT(X)} = \{\omega_1, \omega_2, ..., \omega_n\}$ as the set of distinct terms ω_i contained in at least a tweet $t \in X$. Similarly, we define the *bag-of-pairs* $\mathsf{BP(X)} = \{\rho_1, \rho_2, ..., \rho_n\}$ as the set of distinct *pairs* of terms ρ_i that co-occur (possibly not consecutively) in at least a tweet $t \in X$.

We define two score functions for terms and pairs with respect to a set of tweets X.

DEFINITION 1 (TERM SCORE). *Given a term ω and a set of tweets X, we define the score of ω given X as*

$$\mathsf{tscore}(\omega, X) = \mathsf{TF_T}(\omega, X) \cdot \mathsf{IDF_T}(\omega)$$

where $\mathsf{TF_T}(\omega, X)$ is the number of tweets in X containing term ω, $\mathsf{IDF_T}(\omega) = \log \frac{|\mathcal{T}|}{\mathsf{DF_T}(\omega)}$, and $\mathsf{DF_T}$ is the number of tweets in the stream $\mathcal{T}$ containing ω.

As we will show in the experimental section, the sum of the $\mathsf{tf} - \mathsf{idf}$ [23] of the terms used by the user is particularly useful for tweets. Indeed, apart from increasing the importance of co-occurrences of rare terms, it privileges longer tweets with respect to shorter ones.

Similarly to what we have just done we define a score function for *pairs* of terms.

DEFINITION 2 (PAIR SCORE). *Given a pair of terms ρ and a set of tweets X, we define the score of ρ given X as*

$$\mathsf{pscore}(\rho, X) = \mathsf{TF_P}(\rho) \cdot \mathsf{IDF_P}(\rho) \tag{3}$$

where TF is the number of tweets in X containing pair of terms ρ, $\mathsf{IDF_P} = \log \frac{|\mathcal{T}|}{\mathsf{DF_P}(\rho)}$, and $\mathsf{DF_P}(\rho)$ is the number of tweets in the stream $\mathcal{T}$ containing the pair of terms ρ.

The rationale behind the measure defined by Equation 3 is that since tweets are relatively small documents usually consisting of few sentences, there are good chances that two tweets having pairs of terms in common have higher correlation than tweets sharing only terms.

We observe that both scores implicitly consider the overlapping content between sets of tweets only once. This is an important aspect of the scoring functions that complies with the concept of overall interestingness discussed in the previous section.

Finally, by combining Definitions 1 and 2, we define a score that establishes the similarity of a set of tweets with respect to another.

DEFINITION 3 (SET SIMILARITY). *Given two sets of tweets X_1 and X_2, we define the similarity of X_1 with respect to X_2 as*

$$\begin{aligned}\mathsf{int}_\lambda(X_1, X_2) = \; & (1-\lambda) \cdot \textstyle\sum_{\omega \in \mathsf{BT}(X_1) \bigcap \mathsf{BT}(X_2)} \mathsf{tscore}(\omega, X_2) \\ & + \lambda \cdot \textstyle\sum_{\rho \in \mathsf{BP}(X_1) \bigcap \mathsf{BP}(X_2)} \mathsf{pscore}(\rho, X_2),\end{aligned}$$

where $\lambda \in [0, 1]$ is the linear combination coefficient.

Observe that the similarity is computed by considering only terms whenever λ is equal to 0. Conversely, the similarity is computed by considering only pairs of terms when λ is equal to 1. Note that it is possible to define a score for triples of terms or more, similar to what we have done for terms and term pairs. In that case the function int_λ is defined by a linear combination of different scores, using coefficients $\lambda_1, \lambda_2, \lambda_3, \ldots$ such that $\lambda_1 + \lambda_2 + \lambda_3 + \ldots = 1$.

Given the above definitions, we are now ready to estimate $\mathcal{I}(t)$. Given a user u and his set of tweets T_u, for any value $\lambda \in [0, 1]$ we estimate the interestingness of a set of tweets X for user u, by setting $\mathcal{I}_u(X) = \mathsf{int}_\lambda(X, T_u)$.

We can now solve the TWEETREC problem by selecting the k tweets in $\mathcal{T}$ having the largest values of int_λ with respect to T_u. Obviously, this considers the contribution of each tweet $t \in X$ to the overall interest of X for a user independently. In fact, the content of two tweets may overlap. When this overlap is non-negligible, the contribution of these two tweets to the overall interestingness of the pair is far from being the sum of the two independent contributions.

We can similarly solve the INTERESTS-SPANNING TWEETREC problem, directly applying Definition 3 to Equation 2 to address this issue. It is straightforward to prove that int_λ satisfies all the requisites of Theorem 2 and, thus, it is submodular.

4.2 Enhancing precision for passive users

The main assumption of our approach is that the number of tweets $|T_u|$ posted by a user is large enough to build a rich language model. Unfortunately a large portion of Twitter users are *passive*, i.e., they post only few or no tweets, as shown in Figure 1(a) and by other analytic studies (e.g., [15]). According to Twitter, as of September 2011, 40% of the users "sign in just to observe". Building a language model for such users is thus prohibitive.

We therefore enhance our approach by including in the user model the tweets posted by the user's friends. The intuition is that the user's interests are expressed not only in his own feed, but also in the feeds of the people he follows. Indeed, contrary to other social networks, social connections in Twitter are based more on shared interests than on real world friendships [2, 17].

A further important observation is that some friends are intuitively more relevant than others when building a user model. Friends that are more authoritative should be weighted more in the model, because they provide more contentful and relevant information. We model this intuition by integrating Definition 1 with the following new formulation of tscore:

$$\mathsf{tscore}(\omega, X) = \mathsf{IDF_T}(\omega) \cdot \sum_{x \in X} \mathsf{auth}(u_x) \cdot \mathsf{in}(\omega, x) \qquad (4)$$

where $\mathsf{in}(\omega, x)$ is 1 if the tweet x contains term ω, 0 otherwise; and $\mathsf{auth}(\mathsf{u_x})$ is the authoritativeness of the user that originally posted x, obtained as described next. Likewise, we also modify Definition 2 by considering pairs of terms instead of single terms.

As a side note, we experimented with another similar approach for solving the problem of passive user, where instead of considering authoritative users, we considered friends that the user often retweets, i.e., users that likely share her interests. This approach, obtained by replacing the $\mathsf{auth}(u_x)$ score in the above formula with a *retweet score*, showed no improvements over the authority approach, and has therefore not been included in the paper for lack of space.

4.3 User authority

A clear definition of user authority in Twitter is very difficult to draw and to model being often subjective and task dependent.

In our case, authoritative users are those that post relevant information that is engaging for other users. Authoritative users, often called *information sources*, are usually characterized by a high number of followers and a high ratio between followers and friends. Although other indicators of authority may serve in this context, e.g , number of retweets or PageRank scores, we prefer to keep the computation of the score as simple as possible, given the real-time high-load nature of our application[5].

For each user u in our corpus, we define the authority score $\mathsf{auth}(u) \in [0, 1]$ as a linear combination of two logistic functions[6]:

$$\mathsf{auth}(u) = A \cdot \frac{1}{1 + e^{-\frac{\mathsf{ffRatio}(u)}{\alpha}}} + (1 - A) \cdot \frac{1}{1 + e^{-\frac{\mathsf{foll}(u)}{\beta}}} \qquad (5)$$

where $\mathsf{ffRatio}(u) = \mathsf{foll}(u)/\mathsf{fri}(u)$. $\mathsf{foll}(u)$ and $\mathsf{fri}(u)$ are respectively the number of followers and friends of the user; $A \in [0, 1]$ is the linear parameter; α and β are logistic parameters. All the parameters have been set using a greedy search on a small manually ranked dataset of authoritative users. The resulting parameter values are as following: $A = 0.5$, $\alpha = 2$ and $\beta = 2000$.

5. EXPERIMENTS

This section shows the experiments we conducted in order to assess the effectiveness of our recommendation methods.

After describing the datasets in Section 5.1, we assess the effectiveness of the int_λ function as an estimator of the interestingness of a tweet for a user, and we provide a comparison against two well-known methods (Section 5.2). These comparisons are done by using both an automatic evaluation and a user study. After assessing the effectiveness of int_λ, we use it to find solutions for the TWEETREC and the INTERESTS-SPANNING TWEETREC problems. Eventually, in Section 5.3 we compare the solutions obtained by approaching these two problems, and we show that results produced by solving INTERESTS-SPANNING TWEETREC are of a higher quality.

5.1 Dataset

Our corpus consists of about 182,000 tweets posted between October 30 and November 4, 2011. The corpus was collected as follows. A large set of more than 14 million tweets was downloaded from Twitter using the Spritzer API, that provides access to a 1% random sample of all tweets. This set was then *pruned* to obtain our final corpus containing informative and non-junk English tweets on which we run our experiments. In details, the pruning process was as follows. First, we discarded all the tweets shorter than 30

[5]Despite other indicators, the number of followers and the number of friends are indeed directly available from the Twitter streaming API.

[6]Normalization omitted for clarity.

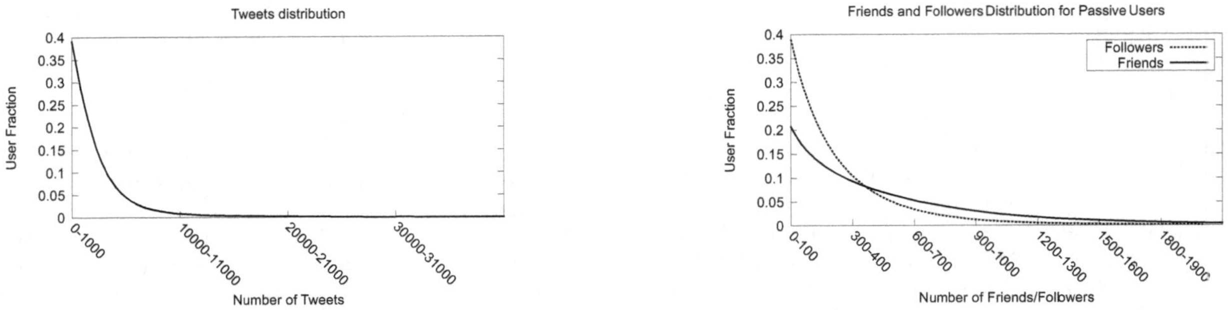

(a) Distribution of the number of tweets per user in our corpus. The y-axis indicates the fraction of users in the corpus that have a given number of tweets.

(b) Distribution of Friends and Followers for users with less than 200 tweets posted since they joined Twitter.

Figure 1: Statistical data on our Tweets Stream.

characters and having less than 8 tokens (i.e., terms, hashtags, and usernames). Then, we removed tweets containing less than 3 English nouns and more than 5 English stopwords. To do that, we performed part of speech tagging using the NLTK[7] toolkit. Finally, we discarded directed tweets (i.e., tweets starting with the @ symbol), that are usually personal in nature, and therefore not interesting for recommendation purposes.

Table 1 reports general statistics regarding our corpus. Figure 1(a) shows the distribution of the number of tweets per user. Each point on the x-axis corresponds to a bucket of 1,000 tweets. The corresponding y-axis value is the overall fraction of users that have posted that number of tweets. As expected the distribution follows a power-law. Almost 40% of users have posted less than $1,000$ tweets since they joined Twitter. This confirms the need for strategies capable of handling "*passive*" users, as described in Section 4.2. Figure 1(b) shows the distribution of the friends and followers in Twitter for "*passive*" users with less than 200 tweets posted since they joined Twitter. Values on the x-axis are buckets of 100 friends or followers. We observe that about 80% has more than 100 friends, while around 40% has less than 100 followers.

Number of tweets	$14,720,718$
Number of tweets after filtering	$182,054$
Number of hashtags	$43,026$
Number of distinct terms	$108,295$
Number of pairs with freq. ≥ 2	$262,081$

Table 1: Statistics regarding our tweet corpus.

5.2 Evaluating int_λ quality

In this section, we show the effectiveness of int_λ by comparing it to two baselines: Cosine and Hashtags. Comparisons are done both using an automatic evaluation and a user-study-based methodology.

5.2.1 Automatic Evaluation

We base this set of experiments on the assumption that a user is likely to find his own tweets more interesting than random tweets from other users. Building on this assumption we randomly select a set of 250 users from our corpus. For each one of these users u we use 90% of his tweets (we call it the set T_u) for building the user profile. The remaining 10% is mixed with all the tweets from other users in the corpus, forming the testing set.

Ideally, the correct recommendations for a given user correspond to tweets from the 10% of his own tweets. More formally, we divide the test set into a positive set $\mathcal{P}$, consisting of the 10% of the user's tweets, and a negative set $\mathcal{N}$ formed by all other tweets. We consider correct a tweet belonging to the positive set.

As evaluation metrics we use standard Information Retrieval measures. For each user we compute:

- P@k. *Precision at rank k* is the fraction of correct tweets in the top-k tweets ranked by the method.
- S@k. *Success at rank k* is the probability of finding at least a correct tweet on the top-k ranked ones.
- MRR. *Reciprocal Rank* is the inverse of the position of the first correct tweet in the ranking produced by the method.

To compute the final metrics' scores we take the average of the above measures across all the 250 users.

Optimizing λ. The aim of our first experiment is to identify the value of λ in int_λ that provides the best performance. Figure 2 reports results of int_λ in terms of P@k (a), S@k (b), and MRR (c), for different λ values.

Results show that adopting λ values close to 1, corresponding to give more importance to pscore, the model achieves better performance. Maximum P@k and S@k values, in fact, are obtained when $\lambda = 1$. In addition, in Figure 2(c) we observe that a value of $\lambda = 0.9$ corresponds to a significant MRR decrease, i.e., the rank of the best tweets in the positive set P significantly increases.

We can overall conclude that by setting $\lambda = 0.9$ the int_λ metric performs very well in terms of both precision and recall, and ranks interesting tweets high in the ranked list. Hereinafter, we therefore adopt the $\text{int}_{0.9}$ metric to estimate the interestingness of tweets for a user.

Comparing the different methods. We are now ready to compare $\text{int}_{0.9}$ against the following two baselines.

Cosine. A baseline model based on cosine similarity. For each tweet t in $\mathcal{T}$, interestingness is estimated as the cosine

[7] http://www.nltk.org/

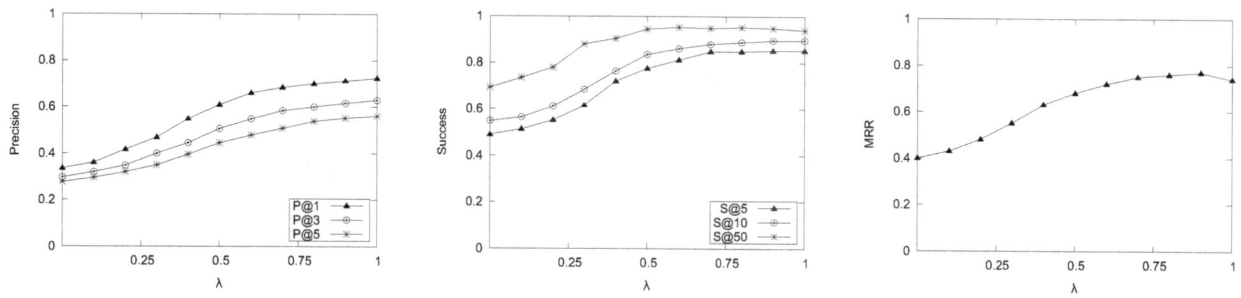

(a) P@k (b) S@k (c) MRR

Figure 2: P@k (a), S@k (b), and MRR (c) of int_λ by varying λ.

similarity between the term vectors of t and T_u, where each vector is obtained by using the classical information retrieval tf − idf [23] score.

Hashtags. A baseline similar to the above, where the vectors are not filled with terms, but with hashtags, similar to what proposed by Abel *et al.* [1]. The intuition is that hashtags explicitly summarize the topic(s) of a tweet (e.g., "`I am flying to #NY today! #travel`").

We also run experiments to compare our models with those generated by Latent Dirichlet Allocation (LDA) [5]. Surprisingly, despite being one at the state of the art model, the LDA method performs very poorly. An analysis of the topics discovered by LDA reveals that terms clustered in the same topic do not have a well defined semantic relation. For example one of the topics has as the top-most representative words "`art`, `box`, `winner`, `soul`, `alabama`, `adam`, `master`, `live`". We conclude that the hypothesis that LDA topics can be mapped to user's interests does not hold in our specific case. One possible explanation is that our dataset is probably not big enough to correctly estimate the model parameters. Another issue is that LDA may be very sensitive to the short nature of the tweets. While a whole set of user's tweets may suffice to infer the user's topics of interest, a single tweet is too short to be reliably assigned topics. We will not report results of LDA given its extremely poor performance. However, we acknowledge that a deeper investigation is necessary to better understand the reasons behind poor LDA performances. We defer this to an extended version of this paper.

	P@1	P@3	P@5	S@5	S@10	S@50	MRR
$\text{int}_{0.9}$	**0.71**	**0.62**	**0.55**	**0.85**	**0.90**	**0.95**	**0.77**
Cosine	0.30	0.25	0.23	0.39	0.46	0.68	0.48
Hashtags	0.32	0.28	0.24	0.52	0.59	0.71	0.50

Table 2: Comparison of $\text{int}_{0.9}$ with Cosine, and Hashtags.

Table 2 shows the comparative results among the tested methods. We observe that $\text{int}_{0.9}$ is the best performing method for all measures. In particular, for the P@1 metric, $\text{int}_{0.9}$ ranks a correct tweet in first position in 71% of the cases. Hashtags, which is the second best performing method, instead ranks a correct tweet in the first position in only 32% of cases.

$\text{int}_{0.9}$ is the most effective method also in terms of S@k, with a 0.85 accuracy in finding correct results in the top-5 ranked tweets. The good performance of $\text{int}_{0.9}$ is confirmed also for the MRR metric. Correct tweets are ranked higher on average by $\text{int}_{0.9}$ than the other two methods.

	P@1	P@3	P@5	S@5	S@10	S@50	MRR
$\text{int}_{0.9}$	**0.40**	**0.37**	**0.44**	**0.70**	**0.70**	**0.98**	**0.48**
Cosine	0.22	0.30	0.31	0.33	0.33	0.78	0.31
HashTags	0.20	0.20	0.12	0.29	0.30	0.35	0.28

Table 3: Comparison of $\text{int}_{0.9}$ with Cosine, and Hashtags on a subset of highly related users.

The high results for $\text{int}_{0.9}$ may have been obtained because of bias in the data, i.e., a user might use a very peculiar writing style that makes his tweets highly distinguishable. In order to remove this bias we manually selected 20 pairs of users having very similar interests. The selection was done by using the Twitter user recommender system. The evaluation for this experiment works as follows: for each pair of users we add all the tweets of the second user in the stream; the task consists to re-retrieving them by using the set of tweets of the first user as the user profile.

Table 3 shows the results of this experiment, with a comparison against Cosine, and Hashtags. Once again, it is confirmed that $\text{int}_{0.9}$ performs better than the baselines. This suggests that the bias induced by the user's writing style is very limited.

5.2.2 User Study Evaluation

In addition to the automatic evaluation just shown, we also test the effectiveness of $\text{int}_{0.9}$ by running a user study. We experiment with the following methods: Cosine[8], $\text{int}_{0.9}$, and $\text{int}_{0.9}$ enhanced with the authoritative friends strategy described in Section 4.2 (hereafter referred as $\text{int}_{0.9}$+auth).

The assessment is conducted by a group of 7 professional assessors that regularly post tweets (Active users, in our terminology), and a group of 5 professional assessors that are using Twitter mainly for reading tweets (Passive users).

For each assessor and each method, we generate the top-20 tweet suggestions. Each assessor is provided with a random combination of tweets selected by the different methods, and is asked to state his personal interest on each tweet, using the following scale:

[8]To reduce the load on human assessors we did not evaluate Hashtags since in the most conservative experiments in Table 3, they were performing worse than Cosine.

- **Excellent**: if the tweet is *"very interesting/very informative/very funny with respect to his/her interests"*;
- **Good**: if the tweet is *"interesting/informative/funny with respect to his/her interests"*;
- **Fair**: if the tweet is *"somehow interesting, but nothing bad if he/she would have skipped it"*;
- **Bad**: if the tweet is *"not interesting, and he/she would have preferred not to have it in his/her timeline"*.

All the experimented models were built using a maximum of 200 tweets from the assessor's Twitter stream. As evaluation metrics we use absolute Discounted Cumulative Gain (DCG), Precision computed over all assessed tweets of each method, and MRR.

Active users

	DCG	Precision	MRR
$\mathsf{int}_{0.9}$	23.29	**0.67**	0.57
$\mathsf{int}_{0.9}$+auth	**24.42**	**0.67**	**0.86**
Cosine	19.28	0.56	0.80

Passive users

	DCG	Precision	MRR
$\mathsf{int}_{0.9}$	25.50	0.67	0.75
$\mathsf{int}_{0.9}$+auth	**36.60**	**0.88**	**1.00**
Cosine	14.60	0.47	0.90

Active + Passive users

	DCG	Precision	MRR
$\mathsf{int}_{0.9}$	24.09	0.67	0.64
$\mathsf{int}_{0.9}$+auth	**29.50**	**0.76**	**0.92**
Cosine	17.33	0.52	0.84

Table 4: User study results for $\mathsf{int}_{0.9}$ and Cosine for Active and Passive users separately. We consider a tweet annotated as E, G, or F as useful.

Table 4 reports results for Active users, Passive users, and both classes combined. Table 5 reports more in detail the percentage of Excellent, Good, Fair and Bad judgments for each method. For Active users, both our methods outperform Cosine in DCG and Precision, consolidating the results obtained in the automatic evaluation. As expected, $\mathsf{int}_{0.9}$+auth is the best performing system. The addition of the authoritative friends' tweets thus proves to be principled, as well as the criterion we used to select authoritative users, described in Section 4.3. For Active users, $\mathsf{int}_{0.9}$ only reports 0.57 in MRR, i.e., the top recommended tweet is often not correct. A closer look at the errors shows that this happens when the user's model shares with a bad tweet a term pair with a high pscore (thus boosting $\mathsf{int}_{0.9}$), but the term pair is not representative of the user interests (e.g., '`have`'-'`today`'). This effect disappears in $\mathsf{int}_{0.9}$+auth, where the larger size of the tweet set smoothes the impact of idiosyncratic term pairs.

In general, we verified that the most common errors across all methods are recommendations of '*status update*' tweets, e.g., "`Almost home! God can't wait to get in my bed`" or "`None of my dog friends around here raw feed`". Even if these tweets may contain terms that define an interest (e.g., '`raw feed`' and '`dog`'), they are personal in nature and therefore not interesting. In future work we will explore heuristics to classify and discard status updates.

top-5 tweets	Excellent	Good	Fair	Bad
Cosine	15%	22%	26%	37%
$\mathsf{int}_{0.9}$	22%	16%	27%	35%
$\mathsf{int}_{0.9}$+auth	30%	33%	15%	22%
top-10 tweets	**Excellent**	**Good**	**Fair**	**Bad**
Cosine	10%	17%	27%	46%
$\mathsf{int}_{0.9}$	21%	21%	30%	28%
$\mathsf{int}_{0.9}$+auth	27%	28%	18%	27%
top-20 tweets	**Excellent**	**Good**	**Fair**	**Bad**
Cosine	8%	19%	27%	46%
$\mathsf{int}_{0.9}$	16%	21%	31%	32%
$\mathsf{int}_{0.9}$+auth	20%	25%	25%	30%

Table 5: Percentage of Excellent, Good, Fair and Bad judgments in the top-k tweets suggested to Passive and Active users.

	TweetRec	Equal	Interests-Spanning TweetRec
$\mathsf{int}_{0.9}$	18%	45%	37%
$\mathsf{int}_{0.9}$ + auth	8%	58%	34%

Table 6: Results of pairwise comparison of TweetRec and Interests-Spanning TweetRec, as judged by the assessors.

$\mathsf{int}_{0.9}$+auth stands out even more for Passive users than Active users. This proposes $\mathsf{int}_{0.9}$+auth as a promising robust solution for tweet recommendation, for Active users as well as Passive users. In both cases, it is important to leverage the tweets of the users' authoritative friends, that mostly post informative tweets.

The overall precision of our baseline Cosine is 0.52, which is relatively higher than expected w.r.t. our $\mathsf{int}_{0.9}$. We further investigate this issue by reporting in Table 5 the results of the user study for different scores. $\mathsf{int}_{0.9}$ is almost always 1.5 times better than Cosine in ranking Excellent results. The difference is even higher if we consider the effectiveness of the top-10 Excellent or Good results. As a matter of fact, we have that only 27% of Cosine are Excellent or Good w.r.t. 66% of $\mathsf{int}_{0.9}$+auth.

5.3 TweetRec vs. Interests-Spanning TweetRec

In this section, we compare the quality of the solutions of TweetRec versus Interests-Spanning TweetRec. As described in previous sections, a solution for the latter problem should recommend a more heterogeneous, and therefore interesting, set of tweets to the user. As in the previous section, we both conduct an automatic and a user-based assessment.

top-5 TWEETREC	top-5 INTERESTS-SPANNING TWEETREC
1. President Obama LinkedIn Town Hall About Jobs (VIDEO)...	1. President Obama LinkedIn Town Hall About Jobs (VIDEO)...
2. #WWLP President Obama has declared a state of emergency for Massachusetts	2. I've set my email filters so the President's messages go straight to my spam folder.
3. Let me state it bluntly and clearly, Obama sucks as president and is quite the amateur!	3. UN leader Ban Ki-moon arrived on Wednesday in Libya for a ...
4. I've set my email filters so the President's messages go straight to my spam folder.	4. Jerry Sandusky, faces charges of sex crimes ...
5. Do you have questions on Obama's plan to help Federal student ...	5. New issue will be in our office in about an hour! re-tweet ...

Table 7: An example of pairwise comparison, where the top-5 tweets from INTERESTS-SPANNING TWEETREC were preferred over TWEETREC. Tweets are shortened for lack of space.

Automatic Evaluation. Goal of the automatic evaluation is to assess if the INTERESTS-SPANNING TWEETREC solution successfully recommends a set of tweets that spans a larger set of user's interests, with respect to TWEETREC.

We proceed by randomly selecting 15 sets of 20 lists[9] each. The assumption is that each list represents a specific user interest. For each list we download 800 tweets. We then create 15 *virtual users* with 8,000 (= 20 × 400) tweets, one per each set, by selecting 400 tweets per list. We use the remaining 400 tweets per list to build a single virtual stream of tweets. The resulting dataset is a set of 15 virtual users spanning 20 different interests and having produced 8,000 tweets.

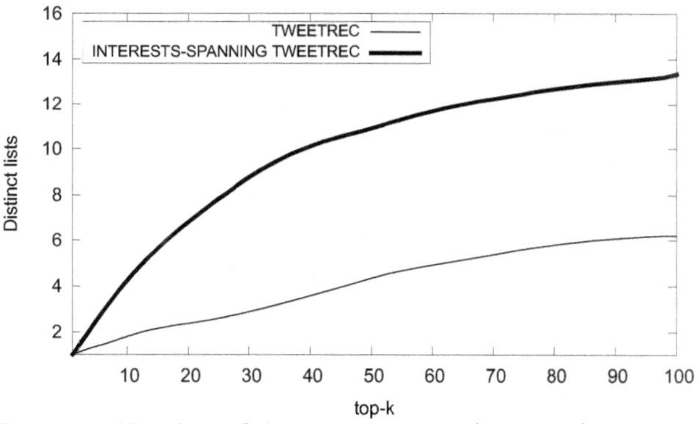

Figure 3: Number of distinct interests (i.e., lists) present in the top-k recommended tweets.

We now evaluate how many different lists (i.e., interests) are present in the top-k tweets recommended by our functions. Figure 3 shows the number of distinct lists in the top-k recommended tweets by using the solutions of TWEETREC and INTERESTS-SPANNING TWEETREC. Results show that, given a user, the set of tweets reported by solving INTERESTS-SPANNING TWEETREC spans multiple different interests, whereas the set returned by solving TWEETREC is more biased towards a very small set (usually one) of interests. This experimentally proves the value of solving INTERESTS-SPANNING TWEETREC.

User study Evaluation. We further investigate the difference between TWEETREC and INTERESTS-SPANNING TWEETREC, by evaluating which of the two solutions is preferred by real, i.e., human, users. We use the same group of assessors as in Section 5.2.2. For each assessor and for each method, we generate the set of top-5 recommended tweets. We then ask the assessors to perform a pairwise comparison of the top-5 sets from two different methods. We ask them to select the most interesting set or, alternatively, to indicate that the two sets are equally interesting.

Results are reported in Table 6, for two different configurations: $\mathsf{int}_{0.9}$ and $\mathsf{int}_{0.9} + \mathsf{auth}$. For both configurations, the top-5 recommended tweets are equally interesting in about half of the cases. If they are not, preference is mostly given to INTERESTS-SPANNING TWEETREC, because in most cases it selects a set of tweets that spans several user's interests.

For example in Table 7, the tweets selected by TWEETREC are mostly focused on Barack Obama while those selected by INTERESTS-SPANNING TWEETREC are about a variety of political topics.

[9]A *Twitter list* aggregates the tweets of users that share a common interest.

6. CONCLUSIONS AND FUTURE WORK

We presented different methods for recommending tweets to Twitter users. Results over a large experimental study show that our proposed solutions outperform existing baselines, and that selecting tweets that are about a variety of the user's interests, improves the user experience.

There is a large avenue for future work. First, we are interested in improving the precision of our methods by devising automatic strategies to filter out tweets that are uninteresting 'status updates'. We also plan to improve the selection power of INTERESTS-SPANNING TWEETREC by providing tweet deduping at higher levels of semantics (e.g., adopting Textual Entailment Recognition techniques).

Our recommendation system could work in several application scenarios, e.g., providing to users a more interesting timeline than the one currently available in Twitter. We plan to carry out simulation trials to test the computational cost of our methods when facing a real-time load of thousands of tweets per second.

7. ACKNOWLEDGMENTS

This research has been partially funded by the EU CIP PSP-BPN ASSETS Project, Grant Agreement no. 250527, and by the EU CIP-ICT PSP 2011.4.1 InGeoCloudS Project, Grant Agreement no. 297300. This work was completed before Marco Pennacchiotti joined eBay Inc..

References

[1] F. Abel, Q. Gao, G.-J. Houben, and K. Tao. Analyzing Temporal Dynamics in Twitter Profiles for Personalized Recommendations in the Social Web. In *Proceedings of ACM WebSci '11, 3rd International*

Conference on Web Science, Koblenz, Germany. ACM, June 2011.

[2] E. Bakshy, J. M. Hofman, W. A. Mason, and D. J. Watts. Everyone's an influencer: quantifying influence on Twitter. In *Proceedings of the fourth ACM international conference on Web search and data mining*, WSDM '11, pages 65–74, New York, NY, USA, 2011. ACM.

[3] S. Banerjee, K. Ramanathan, and A. Gupta. Clustering short texts using Wikipedia. In *Proceedings of the 30th annual international ACM SIGIR conference on Research and development in information retrieval*, SIGIR '07, pages 787–788, New York, NY, USA, 2007. ACM.

[4] N. J. Belkin and W. B. Croft. Information filtering and information retrieval: two sides of the same coin? *Commun. ACM*, 35:29–38, December 1992.

[5] D. M. Blei, A. Y. Ng, and M. I. Jordan. Latent Dirichlet Allocation. *J. Mach. Learn. Res.*, 3:993–1022, Mar. 2003.

[6] C. Budak, D. Agrawal, and A. El Abbadi. Limiting the spread of misinformation in social networks. In *Proceedings of the 20th international conference on World wide web*, WWW '11, pages 665–674, New York, NY, USA, 2011. ACM.

[7] R. Burke. Hybrid recommender systems: Survey and experiments. *User Modeling and User-Adapted Interaction*, 12(4):331–370, Nov. 2002.

[8] J. Chen, R. Nairn, L. Nelson, M. Bernstein, and E. Chi. Short and tweet: experiments on recommending content from information streams. In *Proceedings of the 28th international conference on Human factors in computing systems*, CHI '10, pages 1185–1194, New York, NY, USA, 2010. ACM.

[9] G. Cornuejols, M. L. Fisher, and G. L. Nemhauser. Location of bank accounts to optimize float: An analytic study of exact and approximate algorithms. *Management Science*, 23(8):789–810, 1977.

[10] A. Dong, R. Zhang, P. Kolari, J. Bai, F. Diaz, Y. Chang, Z. Zheng, and H. Zha. Time is of the essence: improving recency ranking using twitter data. In *Proceedings of the 19th international conference on World wide web*, WWW '10, pages 331–340, New York, NY, USA, 2010. ACM.

[11] Y. Duan, L. Jiang, T. Qin, M. Zhou, and H.-Y. Shum. An empirical study on learning to rank of tweets. In *Proceedings of the 23rd International Conference on Computational Linguistics*, COLING '10, pages 295–303, Stroudsburg, PA, USA, 2010. Association for Computational Linguistics.

[12] M. L. Fisher, G. L. Nemhauser, and L. A. Wolsey. An analysis of approximations for maximizing submodular set functions – II. In *Polyhedral Combinatorics*, volume 8 of *Mathematical Programming Studies*, pages 73–87. Springer Berlin Heidelberg, 1978. 10.1007/BFb0121195.

[13] M. R. Garey and D. S. Johnson. *Computers and Intractability: A Guide to the Theory of NP-Completeness.* W. H. Freeman & Co., New York, NY, USA, 1979.

[14] A. Goyal, W. Lu, and L. V. Lakshmanan. Celf++: optimizing the greedy algorithm for influence maximization in social networks. In *Proceedings of the 20th international conference companion on World wide web*, WWW '11, pages 47–48, New York, NY, USA, 2011. ACM.

[15] P. Judge. Barracuda labs, annual report, 2009.

[16] D. Kempe, J. Kleinberg, and E. Tardos. Maximizing the spread of influence through a social network. In *Proceedings of the ninth ACM SIGKDD international conference on Knowledge discovery and data mining*, KDD '03, pages 137–146, New York, NY, USA, 2003. ACM.

[17] H. Kwak, C. Lee, H. Park, and S. Moon. What is twitter, a social network or a news media? In *WWW '10: Proceedings of the 19th international conference on World wide web*, pages 591–600, New York, NY, USA, 2010. ACM.

[18] J. Leskovec, A. Krause, C. Guestrin, C. Faloutsos, J. VanBriesen, and N. Glance. Cost-effective outbreak detection in networks. In *Proceedings of the 13th ACM SIGKDD international conference on Knowledge discovery and data mining*, KDD '07, pages 420–429, New York, NY, USA, 2007. ACM.

[19] G. L. Nemhauser, L. A. Wolsey, and M. L. Fisher. An analysis of approximations for maximizing submodular set functions. *Mathematical Programming*, 14:265–294, 1978. 10.1007/BF01588971.

[20] X.-H. Phan, L.-M. Nguyen, and S. Horiguchi. Learning to classify short and sparse text & web with hidden topics from large-scale data collections. In *Proceeding of the 17th international conference on World Wide Web*, WWW '08, pages 91–100, New York, NY, USA, 2008. ACM.

[21] P. Resnick and H. R. Varian. Recommender systems. *Commun. ACM*, 40(3):56–58, Mar. 1997.

[22] F. Ricci, L. Rokach, B. Shapira, and P. B. Kantor. Recommender systems handbook. *Media*, 54(3):217–253, 2011.

[23] G. Salton, A. Wong, and C. S. Yang. A vector space model for automatic indexing. *Commun. ACM*, 18:613–620, November 1975.

[24] P. Schonhofen. Identifying Document Topics Using the Wikipedia Category Network. In *Proceedings of the 2006 IEEE/WIC/ACM International Conference on Web Intelligence*, WI '06, pages 456–462, Washington, DC, USA, 2006. IEEE Computer Society.

[25] S. Ye and S. F. Wu. Measuring message propagation and social influence on Twitter.com. In *Proceedings of the Second international conference on Social informatics*, SocInfo'10, pages 216–231, Berlin, Heidelberg, 2010. Springer-Verlag.

Generating Event Storylines from Microblogs

Chen Lin
Xiamen University
Shanghai Key Laboratory of Intelligent Information Processing
Xiamen, China
chenlin@xmu.edu.cn

Chun Lin
Xiamen University
Xiamen, China
chunlin@stu.xmu.edu.cn

Jingxuan Li
Florida International University
Miami, FL, U.S.A.
jli003@cs.fiu.edu

Dingding Wang
Florida International University
Miami, FL, U.S.A.
dwang003@cs.fiu.edu

Yang Chen
Duke University
Durham NC, U.S.A
ychen@cs.duke.edu

Tao Li
Florida International University
Miami, FL, U.S.A.
taoli@cs.fiu.edu

ABSTRACT

Microblogging service has emerged to be a dominant web medium for billions of individuals sharing and spreading instant news and information, therefore monitoring the event evolution on microblog sphere is crucial for providing both better user experience and deeper understanding on real-time events. In this paper we explore the problem of generating storylines from microblogs for user input queries. This problem is challenging due to the sparse, dynamic and social nature of microblogs. Given a query of an ongoing event, we propose to sketch the real-time storyline of the event by a two-level solution. We first propose a language model with dynamic pseudo relevance feedback to obtain relevant tweets, and then generate storylines via graph optimization. Comprehensive experiments on Twitter data sets demonstrate the effectiveness of the proposed methods in each level and the overall framework.

Categories and Subject Descriptors

H.2.8 [**Information Systems**]: Database applications—*Data mining*; H.3.3 [**Information Search and Retrieval**]: Information filtering

General Terms

Algorithms, Design, Experimentation

Keywords

Social media, microblog, language model, dynamic pseudo relevance feedback, storyline

1. INTRODUCTION

Microblogging service has rapidly increased its popularity in recent years. People are attracted to microblogging sites, such as Twitter, for instant first-hand reports on real-life events. In the meantime, instead of using web search engines, users are more willing to propose event queries on Twitter to obtain information about an ongoing event [33]. Systems that deliver realtime event notification on Twitter are also available [28].

It would be helpful for industry, academia, and end-users, if a skeleton of an event by request is automatically generated from the huge volume of tweets. We refer this problem as *Generating Event Storyline from Microblogs (GESM)*. For example, Figure 1 presents the storyline based on an event query of "Egypt Revolution". The vertical location of each frame indicates the time-stamp of the corresponding phase. The hierarchical structure depicts how major progress happens in adjacent phases. The branches partition simultaneously happened tweets into different semantic groups. Auto-generated storylines facilitates easy navigation in microblogoshpere and also supports a wide range of mining systems on collective intelligence.

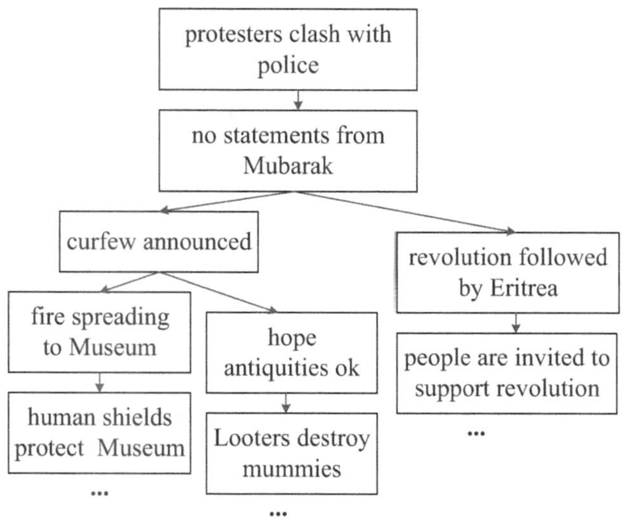

Figure 1: A sample storyline for event query "Egypt Revolution"

GESM is a challenging problem. There exist studies in generating storylines from news articles [21, 36, 13]. Also,

CIKM'12, October 29–November 2, 2012, Maui, HI, USA.

there are fruitful research efforts on the area of topic detection and tracking (TDT) [1]. However, differences between GESM and prior studies are remarkable. 1) All of previous studies are designed for a collection of well edited facts, e.g., news articles and high quality web pages, which lack effective mechanisms for handling extremely short noisy text streams such as microblogs. 2) To facilitate users information preferences, GESM requires user identified queries as inputs. Compared with TDT, GESM provides personalized service in massive microblog data. 3) Since GESM is tailored for user input queries, a two-level framework is necessary: at the low level, finding all relevant tweets through the time-line of the event by a retrieve model; and at the high level, summarizing relevant tweets and the latent structure to produce a storyline.

Challenges of microblog storyline generation arise from the following aspects. First of all, the dynamic and sparse nature of microblogs remains a large obstacle to improve performance of microblog retrieval system for event queries. Event queries usually only contain basic descriptive terms, e.g., the location of the event, the person involved, and the main theme, etc. Microblogs are streams of very short texts reporting recent brief updates. How to match the underlying event expressed by the vague event query to potential relevant tweets which possibly not contain any query terms is a severe problem. State-of-art IR models including a number of variants of pseudo relevance feedback have been proposed as attempts at this problem. However, they expand the original query based on frequencies, therefore temporal relevant keywords during certain periods may be misjudged if they are not significant in frequency throughout the timeline of event. As we shall see in later sections, this framework should be modified to better capture the dynamic of microblogs. Secondly, the social nature of tweets increases the difficulty of integrating semantic similarity with chronological order in generating a storyline. Information sharing in microblog sphere yields numerous duplicate tweets and direct and undirect re-tweets. Duplicate tweets and re-tweets are created after the right time point, and they will trigger confusion in partitioning the event time-line. Thus a naive method, which employs traditional text summarization strategy in each time segment, is not applicable.

In this work, we focus on resolving the above challenges. Major contributions of this work are: (1) A novel problem of generating event storylines from microblogs is proposed and a two-level solution to this problem is provided. (2) A *dynamic pseudo relevance feedback (DPRF)* language model is presented to retrieve relevant tweets given an event query. By making an assumption that the prior probability of pseudo relevance feedback is dependent on the burst periods of given event, DPRF expands the original query with representative keywords in active phases of the event. Thus the accuracy of retrieval is enhanced. (3) The problem of storyline generation on the retrieved microblogs is formulated as a graph-based optimization problem and is solved by approximation algorithms of minimum-weight dominating set and directed Steiner tree. The generated storylines ensure both temporal continuity and content coherence.

The rest of the paper is organized as follows. Section 2 introduces related work on information retrieval, multi-document summarization and microblog mining. Overview of the framework is presented in section 3. Language model based query expansion via dynamic pseudo relevance feedback is described in Section 4. Section 5 presents the framework for storyline generation. In Section 6, experimental results are analyzed and a user study is conducted. We conclude our work in Section 7.

2. RELATED WORK

Several research directions are related to our work, including microblog mining, information retrieval, and multi-document summarization.

2.1 Microblog Mining

The emergence of Twitter motivates recent research works on mining microblogs, including microblog search [8], identifying emerging topics on Twitter [23], and summarizing tweets in a certain period [32]. A few research works have been devoted to event detection [28, 29], but they focus on the detection of novel events without a global view.

To achieve a better performance, several research methods have been proposed to deal with the unique characteristics of microblogs, e.g. expanding tweets by hashtags [7], utilizing social relations for identifying influential tweets [10], incorporating sentiment categorization [3], promoting most recent tweet [9], employing transfer latent topic models for overcoming abbreviated texts [42], and expanding queries by recently frequently co-occurred terms [22].

The dynamic and social nature of microblogs is not fully explored by previous research efforts. By adding a temporal dimension in the event storyline generation system, our work sheds light on the understanding and mining of microblogosphere.

2.2 Language Model for IR

Pseudo relevance feedback (PRF) has been proved to be helpful in the IR community. The state-of-art PRF by language model approaches are surveyed in [41]. In addition, to reinforce model-based feedback, a classifier is adopted before query expansion to determine the "goodness" of expansion candidates in [4]. Adaptive query expansion is implemented in [38] to select query expansion candidates from different sources.

A few works study text stream retrieval. For example, time-based model in [19] assigns documents with prior associated with the "freshness" of documents. The temporal factor can be introduced into query expansion [9, 22]. But all of the above mentioned approaches favor only recent documents, therefore are not applicable to cover the lifespan of the whole event. In [11], a temporal profile is constructed for each query throughout its lifespan to categorize the query and predict query performance, however there is no mechanism to incorporate the temporal profile into query expansion.

Most PRF methods expand the original query in a static manner. On the contrary our method selects event specific expansion terms, which are temporally correlated with query terms in the pseudo relevant documents. Our empirical study shows that our DPRF method is superior than previous researches in the scenario of event query retrieval.

2.3 Text Summarization and TDT

Multi-document summarization conveys the main and most important meaning of several documents. One type of summarization systems select representative sentences, e.g. with significant frequency [40], or structural centroid in sentence graph [18, 13]. Another type is based on matrix decomposition [17, 35, 31]. Some prior researches focus on clustering query-induced results [37].

Unlike multi-document summarization, research in the area of topic detection and tracking (TDT) [1] aims to thread streams of texts. TDT includes five main tasks: story segmentation, topic tracking, topic detection, first story detection and link detection. Among the five tasks, topic tracking and link detection are similar to components of the GES problem addressed in this paper. Most researches in story segmentation and link detection are devoted to clustering and classifying similar texts, without considering the timestamps of articles, e.g. relevance model in [16] adopts symmetric similarity comparison. Others consider the influence among articles to be unidirectional and directly dependent, e.g. topic structure is identified in [25] by forgetting out-of-date statistics, the bursty structure is recognized in [12] by estimating state transition probability in an infinite state automation.

To conclude, although these methods have been successfully applied in several domains, they are not applicable to the event storyline generation problem. The quality of generated storyline is determined by the quality of summary in each phase, and the quality of phase segmentation, and previous summarization and TDT methods lack the ability to generate a complete and coherent storyline. On the contrary, our graph optimization based method has a built-in mechanism to simultaneously generate the summary for each virtual phase and naturally integrate the generated summaries to form the storyline.

2.4 Timeline and Storyline Construction

Not until recently, a limited number of studies devote to summarizing documents with time stamps, mostly news articles. For example, in [24], an HMM style model is presented to discover evolutionary theme patterns (term distributions). BlogScope [2] discovers hot trend and temporal keyword correlations. Similarly, a burstness-aware search framework is presented in [15]. A finite mixture model is presented in [25] for tracking dynamics of topic trends. ETS [36] returns the evolution skeleton along the timeline by extracting representative and discriminative sentences at each phase. In [39] representative sentences are chosen based on relevance, coverage, coherence and cross-date diversity. In [32] summarization consists of median tweets in each time segment. These timeline generation methods can hardly be applied to our storyline generation problem because the asynchronism of information propagation in the microblogosphere makes it difficult to partition the timeline of an event into different phases.

There also exists few studies on storyline generation. [21] proposes a storyline generation framework to identify events using self-organizing maps and to extract the main storyline by assigning weights to different events based on the similarity between the events and given topics. The system then generates storyline-based summaries using term weighting schemes, but does not take the temporal information into consideration. Very recently a pictorial storyline generation method has been proposed [34] that combines image and text analysis to obtain a storyline containing textual, pictorial, and structural information to provide a sketch of the topic evolution. This method first constructs a multi-view graph, in which each node is a picture and its text description. Then representative nodes are selected by finding a minimum dominant set on the graph. Finally, a Steiner tree approximation is employed to connect the dominating nodes to form a pictorial storyline. In this paper, we take the storyline generation procedures in [34]. However, our work differs from [34] as follows. Unlike the traditional text and image analysis, our work focuses on microblogs which have their unique characteristics. For example, the length of a microblog entry is limited, the content may be noisy, and tags and links appear frequently. These characteristics make storyline generation from microblogs very challenging. Dealing with the dynamic and sparse nature of microblogs is one of the most important contributions in this work.

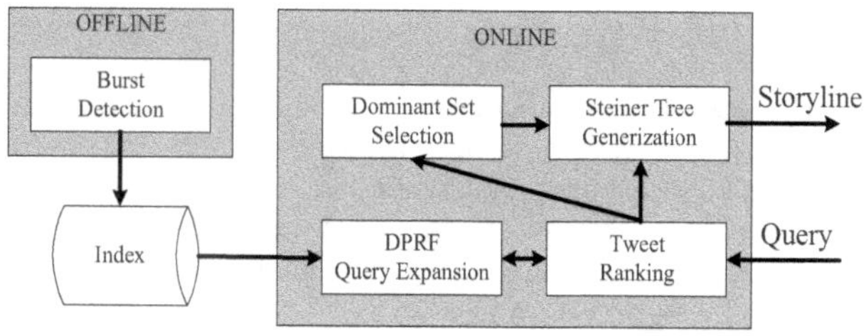

Figure 2: The System Architecture for Event Storyline Generation

3. THE FRAMEWORK OVERVIEW

Given an event query Q, which is a set of user defined keywords or phrases describing an ongoing event in real life, our goal is to mine the storyline from the relevant tweets. The generated storyline should be a graph structure, where each node is labeled by a summary of an individual phase of the event, and each edge represents causal relationship between two phases. Consequently, the proposed framework consists of two models for retrieving relevant tweets and generating storyline respectively. Figure 2 shows the framework of our proposed storyline generation system. In the off-line layer, each tweet is indexed, and the temporal information of each term is stored and pre-processed in the burst detection module. The retrieving module and storyline generation module are implemented in cascade online layers, details of which will be introduced in section 4 and 5.

4. THE RETRIEVAL MODEL

4.1 Preliminaries

In modern information retrieval, language model approaches estimate probability distribution θ_d over the vocabulary W for each document d in the corpus C. By modeling each query Q as θ_Q, relevant documents can be ranked according to query likelihood. However, the original query is usually short and vague, and can not fully cover the underlying information need. To enhance the query expressibility, query expansion is adopted to replace the original query Q by a new high quality query Q'. In a pseudo relevance manner, suppose the few top ranked documents $d+$ by the initial query Q builds a relevant model θ_F, we can set the new query to be a linear combination of original query Q and relevant model θ_F [41]:

$$p(w|\theta_{Q'}) = (1-\alpha)p(w|\theta_Q) + \alpha p(w|\theta_F), \quad (1)$$

where α controls the degree of coherence of the new query to pseudo relevance.

In this paper, we follow relevance model method to infer θ_F. The relevance model method approximates θ_F as the query model, and each pseudo relevant document is a sample from the query model. Therefore relevance model method defines term distribution in θ_F as the likelihood of generating terms from pseudo relevance:

$$p(w|\theta_F) \propto \sum_{d+\in F} p(d+)p(w|d+)p(Q|d+), \quad (2)$$

where $p(Q|d+) = \prod_{q\in Q} p(q|d+)$.

4.2 Dynamic Pseudo Relevance Feedback

In traditional pseudo relevance feedback (PRF), the prior $p(d+)$ is usually set to be uniform. However, this assumption doesn't hold in an instant broadcast medium like Twitter. Consider the event "Egypt Revolution" in Figure 1, there are several distinct phases (e.g. 2011-01-24 to 2011-01-26, 2011-02-01 to 2011-02-03) during which the event encounters major progress and discussion bursts out.

Intuitively, in the initial search results of an event query of "Egypt Revolution", a top tweet published on 2011-01-25 is more likely to be a truly relevant tweet than a tweet published on 2011-01-01 on a near position in the ranking list. Suppose that the event is detected to have K burst periods (detection detail is introduced in the next subsection), the prior distribution of relevant tweets should be centered around each burst period.

We first assume that the prior probability of relevant document $d+$ is dependent on the distance of t_{d+} to the centroid of burst periods, denoted as $\Phi = \{\phi_1 \cdots \phi_K\}$. We define the following three probability functions, each of which is controlled by scale parameter σ. As shown in Figure 3, these probability functions have various mechanisms to model the effective range of burst period, decay coefficient and skewness.

1. **Mixture Gaussian Distribution** assumes that the prior probability is normally distributed, with multiple peaks located at the centroid of each burst period:

$$p(d+) = \Sigma_{i=1}^{K} \frac{1}{K} \times \frac{\exp -\frac{(t_{d+}-\phi_i)^2}{2\sigma^2}}{\sqrt{2\sigma^2\pi}}, \quad (3)$$

where σ implies the effective range of each peak.

2. **Local Power Distribution** assumes that the prior probability is restricted to the neighborhood around the nearest burst period. This is the major difference from mixture Gaussian distribution, in which the information diffusion is cumulative from each burst period. Suppose that the probability decreases as the distance $r(d+, \phi_k)$ between $d+$ and the nearest centroid ϕ_k increases in a polynomial function $(1+r(d+,\phi_k))^{-\sigma}$, the effective range of each burst period is $\mathcal{R}$, a subset of $[\frac{\phi_k+\phi_{k-1}}{2}, \frac{\phi_k+\phi_{k+1}}{2}]$, which means that $p(d+) = 0$ outside $\mathcal{R}$. The distribution can be written as

$$p(d+) = \frac{1}{N} \times \frac{(1 + r(d+, \phi_k))^{-\sigma}}{C(\Phi)}, \quad (4)$$

where $C(\Phi)$ is a constant for ϕ_k to guarantee $\int p(d+) = 1$, It is a function of all boundaries R for burst periods. If we set the boundary to be in middle of every two adjacent period, then $C(\Phi) = (\sigma - 1)\Sigma_{k=1}K(2 - (1+\frac{\phi_k-\phi_{k-1}}{2})^{1-\sigma} - (1+\frac{\phi_{k+1}-\phi_k}{2})^{1-\sigma})$. Otherwise for fixed $\mathcal{R} = [\phi_k - R_1, \phi_k + R_2]$,$C(\Phi) = K(\sigma-1)(2-(1+R_1)^{1-\sigma} - (1+R_2)^{1-\sigma})$. $\sigma > 1$ is the scale parameter controlling the degree of probability decay.

3. **Skewed Linear Distribution** assumes that the prior probability is positive skew, with a longer tail after the burst period. It is difficult to derive a probability distribution with a defined peak. Therefore we use a linear density function to approximate the skewed disribution:

$$p(d+) \propto \sum_{k=1}^{K} C - r(d+, \phi_k), \quad (5)$$

where $r(d+, \phi_k)$ has different definition before and after the burst period.

$$r(d+, \phi_k) = \begin{cases} 0 & \text{if } \phi_k - R \leq t_{d+} \leq \phi_k + R \\ \sigma(t_{d+} - \phi_k - R) & \text{if } t_{d+} > \phi_k + R \\ C & \text{else} \end{cases} \quad (6)$$

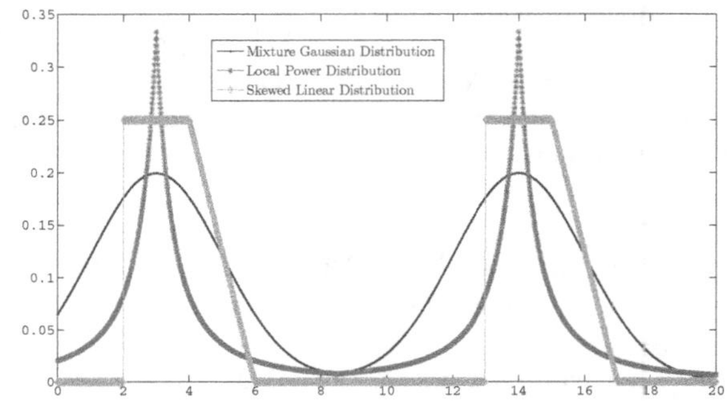

Figure 3: An illustration of prior probabilities of pseudo relevant tweets, with two burst periods centered at time points 3 and 14.

4.3 Burst Period Detection

Intuitively, at time point ϕ_k, each query term should 1) appear more frequently than usual 2) be continuously frequent around the time point. Following these intuitions, we propose to detect burst periods of the event by 1) for each query term, finding the time intervals with arbitrary length in which the query term appears constantly frequent; 2) picking the time points within these intervals with the largest sum of frequencies over all query terms.

We first borrow the definition of a term's "bursty score" from [15]. Suppose that w is a term, which occurs for $tf(w,T)$ times in any time interval T, then the bursty score of w is defined in Eq.(7):

$$B(w,T) = \frac{tf(w,T)}{\sum_{T'} tf(w,T')} - \frac{|T|}{|\sum_{T'}|}, \quad (7)$$

where $|T|$ is the length of the time interval, and $|\sum_{T'}|$ is the length of observation time, which is experimentally set to be time span of the whole corpus. The bursty score of a term is positive if it has above average observation frequency.

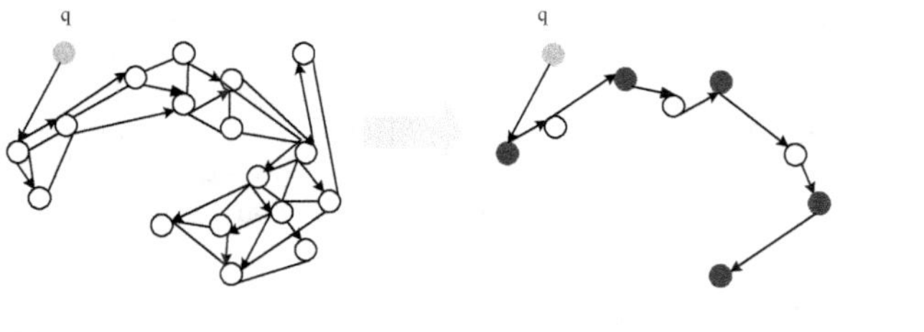

Figure 4: An illustration of the storyline generation

A linear time algorithm in [27] is proposed to find time interval $T_{w,j} =< st, et, LS, RS >$ with the maximal cumulative burst score $B(w, T_{w,j})$, where st is the starting time of $T_{w,j}$, et is the ending time of $T_{w,j}$, LS is the cumulative bursty score before $T_{w,j}$, RS is the cumulative bursty score after $T_{w,j}$.

Next, we present Eq.(8) to compute the score of any query term q at each time point:

$$H(q,t) = \begin{cases} \frac{B(q,T_j)}{|T_j|} & \text{if } \exists T_j, t \in T_j \\ 0 & \text{else} \end{cases}, \quad (8)$$

where $B(q, T_j)$ is the bursty score of q in maximal interval T_j which is super segment of t. Then we rank each time point by $\sum_{q\in Q} H(q,t)$ and choose the largest K time point ϕ_k.

5. STORYLINE GENERATION

As discussed in Section 1, to generate the storylines from relevant tweets, obstacles are duplicated tweets and indirect retweets. Intuitively, we can pick up a good tweet to represent similar or duplicated tweets. The representative tweets provide the basic outline for each phase. Then the representative tweets are connected appropriately to depict the evolving structure of the event. In order to eliminate noisy retweets, only texts published after a certain time can be considered as subsequent phases. Finally, there may be different ways of connecting these representative tweets, and an optimistic connection should be the one that connects them most smoothly.

The storyline generation follows the processes described in [34]. Thus, the storyline generation procedure consists of three parts. In the first part, a multi-view tweet graph is constructed, in which the semantic and temporal information among relevant tweets is stored. Next, representative tweets are extracted by finding a minimum dominant set on the tweet graph. Finally, a minimum steiner tree algorithm is employed to connect the representative tweets in each phase [30].

Given an event query Q and a collection of relevant tweets by the method described in Section 4, we can construct a multi-view tweet graph.

DEFINITION 1 (MULTI-VIEW TWEET GRAPH). *A multi-view graph $G = (V, W, E, A)$, where V is a set of vertices (nodes), W is the weights of V, E is a set of undirected edges, which represents the similarities between tweets, and A is a set of directed edges (arcs), which represents the time continuity of the tweets.*

Construction of such a graph is controlled by three non-negative real parameters α, τ_1, τ_2, $\tau_1 < \tau_2$. Each node in G represents a tweet. We use the cosine measure to calculate similarity between two tweets. To define E, we join the two nodes by an edge if and only if the text similarity between the two responding tweets is greater than α. To define A, we draw an arc from v_i to v_j if and only if $\tau_1 \le t_j - t_i \le \tau_2$, where t_i and t_j are their respective time stamps. We call $[\tau_1, \tau_2]$ the temporal window. Also, for each node v_i, its vertex weight, $w(v_i)$, is $1 - score(Q, v_i)$. In our method, we first find the dominating set on the undirected graph $G = (V, W, E)$ (i.e., without considering A in the multi-view graph), and then perform the steiner tree algorithm to connect the dominating set on the directed graph $G = (V, W, A)$ (i.e., without considering E in the multi-view graph) which takes the time continuity into consideration and leads to a coherent storyline.

A subset S of the vertex set of an undirected graph is a dominating set if for each vertex u, either u is in S or is adjacent to a vertex in S. The problem of finding a set of representative summaries can be viewed as the minimum-weight dominating set problem on the undirected graph (V, W, E).

DEFINITION 2 (MWDS). *The Minimum-Weight Dominating Set Problem (MWDS) is the problem of finding, given a vertex- weighted undirected graph G, from all dominating sets of $G = (V, W, E)$, the one whose total vertex weight is the smallest.*

We use the following straightforward greedy algorithm for obtaining an approximate solution (Algorithm 1). This algorithm views that the weight of a newly added vertex is evenly shared among its newly covered neighbors and selects the node that minimizes this share at each round of iteration. The approximation rate of this algorithm is $1 + \log(\Delta \| OPT \|)$, where Δ is the maximal degree of G and OPT is the optimal dominating set.

Algorithm 1: Greedy $MWDS$ Approximation

```
Input: G = (V, W, E)
Output: dominant set S
S ← ∅, T ← ∅;
while |S| < W&&S ≠ V do
    for v ∈ V − S do
        s(v) = ||{v'|(v', v) ∈ E} \ T| ;
        v* = arg min_v w(v)/s(v) ;
        S ← S ⋃{v*};
        T ← T ⋃{v''|(v'', v*) ∈ E};
    end
end
```

Once we select the most representative summary in each phase using the dominating set approximation, we need to generate a natural storyline capturing the temporal and structural information of the event-relevant tweets. To study this problem we use the concept of Steiner trees. Here a Steiner tree of a graph G with respect to a vertex subset S is the edge-induced sub-tree of G that contains all the vertices of S having the minimum total cost, where the cost is the total weight of the vertices.

DEFINITION 3 (STEINER TREE). *Given a directed graph $G = (V, W, A)$, a set S of vertices (terminals), and a root $q \in S$ from which every vertex of S is reachable in G, find the subtree G rooted at q containing S with the smallest total vertex weight.*

Algorithm 2: Steiner Tree Algorithm

```
Input: G = (V, W, A), S, q, k ≥ 1
Output: Steiner tree T rooted at q covering at least k
        vertices in S
T ← ∅;
while k > 0 do
    T_best ← ∅;
    cost(T_best) ← ∞;
    for v ∈ V, (v_0, v) ∈ A, 1 ≤ k' ≤ k do
        Tp ← A_{i-1}(k', v, S) ⋃ {(v_0, v};
        if cost(T_best) > cost(T') then
            T_best ← T';
        end
        T ← T ⋃ T_best;
        k ← k − ||S ⋂ V(T_best)||;
        S ← S \ V(T_best);
    end
end
```

We apply the Steiner tree approximation in [34] to generate the storyline. In this algorithm, the initial call of $A_i(k, q, S)$ with S set to the dominating set calculated by algorithm 2, q set to be event vertex assigned with the earliest time stamp, and k set to be the size of S. The algorithm takes a level parameter $i \geq 1$. $i = 1$ is the default case where the straightforward algorithm selects l vertices closest to root and returns the union of the shortest paths. The length of an arc $(u, v) \in A$ is the vertex weight of u. We will interpret the output tree as the storyline transition from the root to all the other dominating objects as illustrated in Figure 4. For a constant i, the algorithm is known to run in polynomial time and produce an $O(k^{1/i})$ approximation.

6. EXPERIMENTS

In the experiments, we evaluate the performance of the proposed framework. In particular, Section 6.2 presents the experiments on tweet retrieval, and Section 6.3 conducts the comparisons on storyline generation. We also conduct a user study to compare our system with different document understanding systems in Section 6.4.

6.1 Data Set

The data set is Tweets2011 corpus for TREC 2011 microblog track. The corpus is comprised of 2 weeks (23th January 2011 until 8th February) of sampled tweets from Twitter. Different types of tweets are presented, including replies and retweets. The corpus is multilingual, including English, Japanese and so on. More details of the collection are illustrated in Table 1.

Number of tweets	15137399
Number of English tweets	9318772
Number of retweets	1487299
Number of English retweets	1069006
Number of users	4670516
Median Tweet Length	8.66
Median English Tweet Length	10.76

Table 1: Statistics of Data set

In pre-processing, we do not remove stop-words. Instead, mentions (@somebody) are removed from the vocabulary. Non-English tweets containing less than one English word with more than 2 characters are filtered. Explicit re-tweets with HTTP code 302 are filtered. Empty tweets and forbidden tweets with HTTP code 403 and 404 are also filtered. Porter stemmer is adopted in indexing.

6.2 Tweet Retrieval

TREC 2011 microblog track provides 49 queries and relevance judgements for these queries. Each query is associated with an time stamp. Only tweets published before the time stamp are under consideration. After examination, we believe that each query is describing an ongoing real event. Therefore we use the TREC queries in this subsection. We use both highly relevant and relevant tweets annotated by TREC as the ground truth.

The dominant evaluation metric is the precision at top 30 tweets (P@30). However we also provide the mean average precision(MAP), the precision at top 100 tweets (P@100), and the R-precision (R-PREC) as supplementary measures.

6.2.1 Comparative Study

We conduct extensive comparative study to verify the enhancement of the proposed query expansion technology. The retrieve models used in the comparative study include: (1) Lucene Baseline: It searches the original query in Lucene[1]; (2) PL2: It is a language modeling baseline by Terrier [26], which scores each document as the divergence from randomness, with Poisson estimation for randomness, Laplace succession for first normalization, and Normalization 2 for term frequency normalization. The default parameter is set to 10.99; (3) KLJM: The document-query score is computed as the KL-divergence between the document language model to the query model. We adopt JM smoothing for unobserved tokens, $p_s(q|\theta_d) = \lambda p(q|d) + (1-\lambda)p(q|C)$, $\lambda = 0.5$; (4) RLM: The recency language modeling baseline in [9], which promotes most recent tweets by adding a document prior; (5) Rocchio: It is the pseudo relevance feedback (PRF) query expansion according to the Rocchio formula. The initial results are obtained by RLM. We test the performance of all PRF methods with different numbers of pseudo-relevant tweets (from 20 to 50) and different numbers of expansion terms (from 5 to 20). Due to the limit of space, we only report the best performance generated by 10 expansion terms from 30 pseudo-relevant tweets. (6) BO1: Pseudo relevance feedback by Terrier, using the scoring model PL2, query expansion model BO1; (7) KL: Pseudo relevance feedback by Terrier, using the scoring model JMKL, query expansion by maximizing the KL-divergence of pseudo relevance to the collection; (8) MG: Dynamic pseudo relevance feedback (DPRF) with mixture Gaussian distribution, with $\alpha = 0.5$,$n = 4$, most 4 burst periods, scale parameter $\sigma = 5$. Top 30 documents retrieved by RLM on the original query are selected as pseudo relevance feedback; (9) LP: Dynamic pseudo relevance feedback (DPRF) with local power distribution, with $n = 5$ burst periods, scale parameter $\sigma = 1$. We do not limit the effect range R. Other settings are the same as MG; (10) SL: Dynamic pseudo relevance feedback (DPRF) with skewed linear distribution, with $n = 2$ burst periods, scale parameter $\sigma = 7$. We set $R = 2$, by making the assumption that each burst period lasts for 4 days. Other settings are the same as MG and LP.

[1]http://lucene.apache.org/

From Table 2, we have the following observations. 1) Among the four baselines, recency language model performs best, which validates the importance of introducing a non-uniform document prior in microblog retrieval. Language modeling approaches outperform naive Lucene baseline. PL2 outperforms KLJM, because PL2 favors longer tweets, while longer tweets are usually of higher quality. 2) PRF can increase the system accuracy, compared with their original scoring functions. However, the significance of the increment depends on how well the baseline performs. 3) Dynamic pseudo relevance feedback method performs best in terms of P@30, MAP, and R-PREC, no matter which distribution is used in quantifying the pseudo relevance prior. It nearly boosts the P@30 performance of Lucene baseline for two times. It also outperforms the recency based method by nearly 20%, and the traditional PRF by nearly 40%. Significance tests show that all the DPRF methods outperforms the best comparative method RLM with a confidence level larger than 99% (denoted as ++ in Table 2), compared with the null hypothesis that DPRF is equivalent with RLM.

6.2.2 Parameter Tuning

In this subsection, we compare the P@30 performance of various parameters for the three strategies used in dynamic pseudo relevance feedback. The effects of the number of detected burst periods n and the scale parameter σ are shown in Figure 5. We have the following observations. 1) Generally, dynamic pseudo relevance feedback is not extremely sensitive to parameters. The worst P@30 performance is higher than 0.405, which is better than all the baselines and PRF models. 2) An event is unlikely to have very few burst periods. Therefore $n = 1$ and $n = 2$ usually perform worst. However, since the corpus only consists of tweets published within 17 days, large n does not perform good. Appropriate value is $n = 4$ or $n = 5$. 3) For a fixed n, the best scaling parameter is between $\sigma = 3$ and $\sigma = 5$ for mixture Gaussian distribution. The performance decreases when σ is too small or too large. Note that a burst period usually lasts no more than 3 days, therefore the scaling parameter is likely to fit in a burst period. 4) For local power distribution, the bigger σ is, the more accurate the expansion terms are. Note that big σ indicates smooth decay in local power distribution. Similarly, for skewed linear distribution, the smaller σ is, the higher performance can be achieved. Therefore it is safe to claim that the information propagation process in microblogosphere is a long process.

6.3 Summarization Capability

Note that after retrieving the relevant tweets, various document summarization methods can be adapted to form the storyline by extracting the most relevant tweets. In this section, we conduct experiments to compare the summarization performance of different approaches including our proposed one, aiming to show the advantages of using the Dominant Set and the Steiner Tree to generate the storyline from the summarization aspect.

The measurement used in this subsection is mainly based on Recall-Oriented Understudy for Gisting Evaluation (ROUGE) – an evaluation toolkit for document summarization [20] which automatically determines the quality of a summary by comparing it with the human generated summaries through counting the number of their overlapping textual units (e.g., n-gram, word sequences, and etc.). In particular, F-measure scores of ROUGE-2 and ROUGE-SU4 are presented for our experiments. 49 queries provided by TREC 2011 microblog track are used in the experiments. For each query, first, DPRF is utilized to retrieve the top 1,000 tweets, then 8 students are invited to manually generate the "storyline" (50 tweets are selected) from these 1,000 tweets as the ground truth.

6.3.1 Comparison on Different Summarization Approaches

We compare our method with several well-known and recent summarization approaches including:

1. Random: randomly selects the sentence as the summary;
2. MostRelevant: picks up the sentences which are most relevant with the topic as the summary;
3. Latent Semantic Analysis (LSA): identifies semantically important sentences by conducting latent semantic analysis;
4. K-means: performs K-means over the sentences, then treats centers of all sentence clusters as the summary;
5. Non-negative Matrix Factorization (NMF) [17]: performs NMF on the sentence-term matrix and selects the high ranked sentences.
6. Symmetric Non-negative Matrix Factorization (SNMF) [35]: calculates sentence-sentence similarities by sentence level semantic analysis, clusters the sentences via symmetric non-negative matrix factorization, and extracts the sentences based on the clustering result;
7. Spectral Clustering with Normalized Cuts (NCut) [31]: performs the Spectral Clustering using Normalized Cut to cluster the sentences, and then uses centers of clusters as the summary;
8. Query-sensitive Mutual Reinforcement Chain (Qs-MRC) [37]: extends the mutual reinforcement principle between sentence and term to document-sentence-term mutual reinforcement chain, and uses query-sensitive similarity to measure the affinity between the pair of texts;
9. Multi-Document Summarization using Submodularity (MSSF) [18]: a multi-document summarization framework based on Submodularity;
10. Dominant Set (DS only): Document summarization using the Dominant Set algorithm (i.e., Algorithm 1 in Section 5).

The comparison of our proposed method (DS+ST) with other summarization methods is presented in Table 3. It can be seen from the results that our proposed DS+ST outperforms all the other summarization methods. In addition to the comparison of DS+ST against the other summarization methods, we employ the standard t-test to determine whether the performance improvement of DS+ST over the others is statistically significant. The results show that the improvements of our DS+ST on both ROUGE2 and ROUGE-SU are significant.

Type	Model	P@30	P@100	MAP	R-PREC
Baseline	Lucene	0.2306	0.1582	0.1697	0.2257
	PL2	0.3054	0.2065	0.1697	0.2245
	KLJM	0.2986	0.1900	0.2299	0.2614
	RLM	0.3837	0.1151	0.1804	0.2297
PRF	Rocchio	0.3551	0.1065	0.1727	0.2182
	Bo1	0.3265	0.2259	0.2560	0.2961
	KL	0.3041	0.2102	0.2364	0.2781
DPRF	MG	0.4388(++)	0.1890(++)	0.2547(++)	0.3055(++)
	LP	0.4333(++)	0.1900(++)	**0.2588**(++)	**0.3206**(++)
	SL	**0.4401**(++)	0.1900(++)	0.2549(++)	0.3038(++)

Table 2: Average P@30, P@100, MAP and R-PREC value of various retrieval models and query expansion methods, ++ indicates the proposed DPRF methods significantly outperforms the best comparative methods with a confidence level greater than 99%

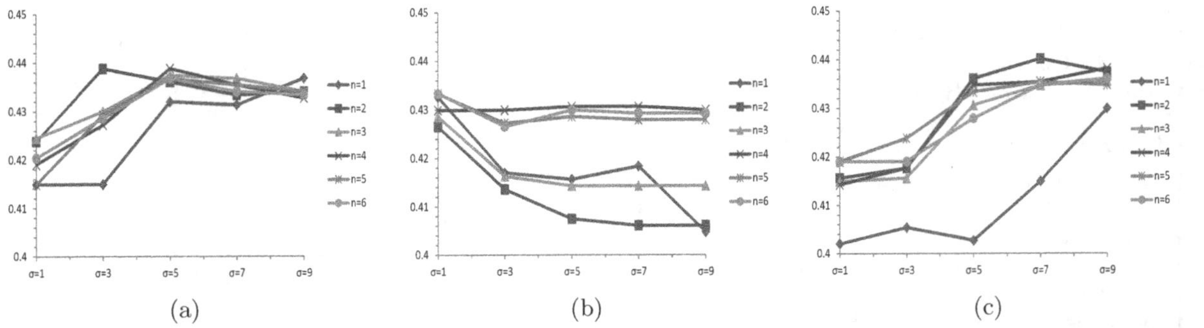

Figure 5: P@30 performance of various parameters for (a) Mixture Gaussian Distribution; (b) Local Power Distribution; (b) Skewed Linear Distribution

Methods	ROUGE2	ROUGE-SU
Random	0.0425	0.0903
MostRelevant	0.0526	0.1075
LSA	0.0403	0.0857
K-means	0.0489	0.1002
NMF	0.0534	0.1043
SNMF	0.0593	0.1203
NCut	0.0635	0.1156
Qs-MRC	0.0647	0.1255
MSSF	0.0639	0.1324
DS Only	0.0731	0.1280
DS+ST	0.0895(++)	0.1363(+)

Table 3: The comparison among different summarization methods. Notice that "DS" denotes "Dominant Set", and "ST" represents "Steiner Tree". "++" and "+" indicate that DS+ST significantly outperforms the best comparative methods with a confidence level greater than 99% and 95%, respectively.

The good results of our method benefit from the following two aspects. (1) The Dominant Set algorithm (i.e., Algorithm 1) used in our method can select tweets which are similar to both the given query and all the other tweets. Thus it is not only good at extracting the representative information from the given sentences to form a reasonable summary, but also providing an appropriate mechanism to select the "dominant" nodes to generate storylines. (2) The Steiner Tree algorithm (i.e., Algorithm 2) is capable of detecting the "outline" of all the given sentences from the dominant nodes. Thus comparing with the other traditional summarization methods, it is able to generate more natural and logical storylines/summaries.

As a result, by combining the Dominant Set algorithm and the Steiner Tree algorithm, our proposed method is suitable for generating the "storyline" from the messages delivered by microblog services.

6.3.2 *Parameter Tuning*

In addition to the above comparison with different methods, we further study the summarization results by tuning the parameters of the Dominant Set algorithm and the Steiner Tree algorithm.

First of all, we study the Dominant Set algorithm by varying the "similarity threshold". We vary the threshold for the similarity between each tweet and the given query from 0.5 to 0.9 with a step size of 0.1 (totally 5 steps).

Secondly, one may notice that a key step before performing the Steiner Tree algorithm is to pick up a ***root*** node. A good root node could start a good story from tweets. In general, a good root should satisfy two conditions: 1) it should start as early as possible in terms of the post date of the tweet; 2) it should be similar to the given query. Usually, we choose the earliest node within the Dominant set as the root. However, we also study how the "similarity to the given query" influences the final summarization results. In other words, the earliest node may not necessarily be the root, but a later node from which every node of the Dominant set is reachable in graph G can be the root as long as it is more similar to the given query. To choose the root, we vary the similarity to the given query from 0.5 to 0.9 by a step size of 0.1. The comparison results by tuning the parameters are shown in in Figure 6(a) and 6(b).

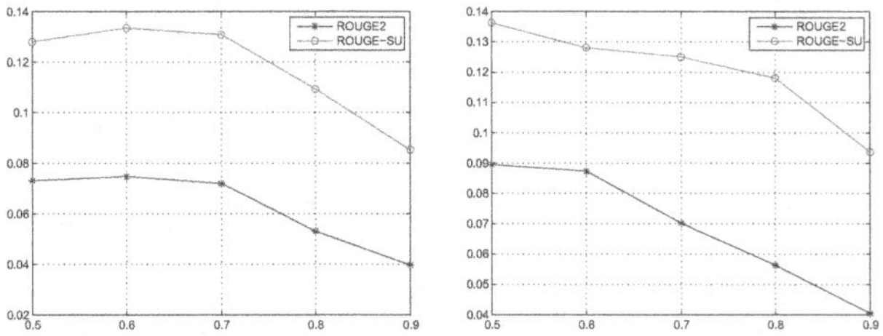

(a) (b)

Figure 6: (a) Similarity (between a node and the given query) threshold; (b) Similarity between Root and Query

We have two observations from Figure 6(a). (1) The selection of the similarity threshold does influence the summarization performance of the Dominant Set algorithm. An inappropriate similarity threshold may weaken the Dominant Set greatly. (2) It is hard to claim that a larger similarity threshold would result in a better performance. In fact, when the similarity threshold is greater than 0.6, the summarization performance decreases as the threshold increases. The intuitive explanation is that a large similarity threshold may induce the algorithm to omit some important tweets which are not similar enough to the given query.

The observation from Figure 6(b) is that as the similarity to the given query increases, the summarization performance on both ROUGE2 and ROUGE-SU keeps going down. By analyzing it, we find that a large similarity threshold could lead to a "late" root. For example, a "late" root may exactly match the query, however, it would start the story from the middle of the whole storyline. In such a case, the tweets before the storyline's middle point are omitted, thus the evolving structure of the storyline is not well maintained.

6.4 A User Study

Since storyline generation is a subjective process, to better evaluate the retrieved tweets and the generated storylines, we conduct a user survey. The subjects of the survey are 18 students at different levels and from various majors of a research university. In this survey, we randomly sample 10 queries and 500 English tweets. Each participant is asked to read these tweets and 3 queries, and compare the results of different systems in a random order from the following point of views: relevance, coverage, coherence, and overall satisfaction. A score of 1 to 5 needs to be assigned to each system according to the user's satisfaction of the results. A rank of 5 (or 1) indicates that the result of the system is the most (or least) satisfactory. We implement the following systems for comparison. (1) Top10-Recency: presents the top 10 retrieved tweets by the recency language model RLM on the original queries. (2) Top10-DPRF: presents the top 10 retrieved tweets using the DPRF query expansion. (3) RecencySum: performs document summarization based on the retrieved tweets using the recency language model. MSSF is used as the document summarization method since it obtains the best results in Section 6.3.1. (4) DPRFSum: performs MSSF based on the retrieved tweets using the DPRF query expansion. (5) RecencyTimeline: generates timeslines [39] based on the retrieved tweets using the recency language model. (6) DPRFTimeline: generates timelines based on the retrieved tweets using DPRF query expansion. (7) RecencyStoryline: generates storylines using the methods proposed in Section 5 based on the tweets retrieved by the recency language model. (8) DPRFStoryline: generates storylines based on the tweets retrieved by DPRF query expansion.

	Relevance	Coverage	Coherence	Overall
Top10-Recency	3.06	1.67	1.50	2.06
Top10-DPRF	3.39	1.83	1.56	2.28
RecencySum	2.94	2.33	2.39	2.72
RecencyTimeline	3.06	3.06	2.83	3.33
RecencyStoryline	3.06	3.78	4.00	3.78
DPRFSum	3.22	2.50	2.44	3.05
DPRFTimeline	3.33	3.33	3.06	3.83
DPRFStoryline	**3.39**	**4.17**	**4.28**	**4.12**

Table 4: Survey Results: User ratings on different systems based on their satisfaction

Table 4 shows the user rated scores for each system. From the results, we have observations as follows. (1) The performance of tweet retrieval is critical. The proposed DPRF query expansion approach outperforms the recency language method. (2) Although the listed top 10 query results are highly relevant to the query, there also exists high redundancy among the top-ranking query results, thus the coverage and coherence of the results are poor. (3) Summarization based results achieve higher overall satisfaction than the methods of listing top query results because it can help users better understand the tweets. (4) Users prefer structured results such as timelines and storylines than pure text summaries. (5) The proposed storyline generation methods outperform the timeline generation method because the structures contained in the storylines can assist users quickly grasp the event evolution.

7. CONCLUSION

Generating storylines from microblogs can shed insight into several fields, including event detection, short text mining, and text stream mining, etc. The proposed dynamic pseudo relevance feedback model is embedded in a sophisticated theoretical framework. Experiments show that it is robust to parameters. The heuristic strategy for finding minimum weighted Steiner tree on a dominant set of relevant tweets is efficient to produce summary and evolvement structure.

This is a pioneer work on generating storylines from social media. In the future, we will further improve the approaches in the following aspects. First, the density function in Section 4 attempts to model the event prior. However since the relevance set is usually small, the assumption may not be satisfied by the observation. Second, in our work, the number of burst periods is pre-fixed in the detection. Advanced burst period detection methods can be investigated and incorporated into our current framework. Last but not least, our current storyline generation is based on multi-view tweet graph and we plan to investigate new frameworks for generating concise and coherent storylines.

Acknowledgement

Chen Lin is partially supported by Shanghai Key Laboratory of Intelligent Information Processing under grant No. IIPL-2011-004, China Natural Science Foundation under grant No.61102136,61001013, the Natural Science Foundation of Fujian Province of China under grant No.2011J05158), the Fundamental Research Funds for the Central Universities under Grant No.2011121049. Jingxuan Li and Tao Li are partially supported by US NSF grants IIS-0546280, HRD-0833093, and CNS-1126619 and DHS grants 2009-ST-062-000016 and 2010-ST-062-000039.

8. REFERENCES

[1] J. Allan Introduction to Topic Detection and Tracking. In *Topic Detection and Tracking 2002(12)*, pages 1-16.

[2] N. Bansal and N. Koudas. Blogscope: a system for online analysis of high volume text streams. In *Proceedings of VLDB 2007*, pages 1410–1413.

[3] A. Bermingham and A. F. Smeaton. Classifying sentiment in microblogs: is brevity an advantage? In *Proceedings of CIKM 2010*, pages 1833–1836.

[4] G. Cao, J.-Y. Nie, J. Gao et al. and S. Robertson. Selecting good expansion terms for pseudo-relevance feedback. In *Proceedings of SIGIR 2008*, pages 243–250.

[5] C. Castillo, M. Mendoza, and B. Poblete. Information credibility on twitter. In *Proceedings of WWW 2011*, pages 675–684.

[6] C. Chen, F. Li, B. C. Ooi, et al. and S. Wu. Ti: an efficient indexing mechanism for real-time search on tweets. In *Proceedings of SIGMOD 2011*, pages 649–660.

[7] M. Efron. Hashtag retrieval in a microblogging environment. In *Proceedings of SIGIR 2010*, pages 787–788.

[8] M. Efron. Information search and retrieval in microblogs. *J. Am. Soc. Inf. Sci. Technol.*, 62:996–1008, June 2011.

[9] M. Efron and G. Golovchinsky. Estimation methods for ranking recent information. In *Proceedings of SIGIR 2011*, pages 495–504.

[10] J. Hannon, M. Bennett, and B. Smyth. Recommending twitter users to follow using content and collaborative filtering approaches. In *Proceedings of RecSys 2010*, pages 199–206.

[11] R. Jones and F. Diaz. Temporal profiles of queries. *ACM Trans. Inf. Syst.*, 25, July 2007.

[12] J. Kleinberg, Bursty and Hierarchical Structure in Streams In *Data Mining and Knowledge Discovery 2003(7)*, pages 373-397.

[13] R. Kumar, U. Mahadevan, and D. Sivakumar. A graph-theoretic approach to extract storylines from search results. In *Proceedings of SIGKDD 2004*, pages 216–225.

[14] H. Kwak, C. Lee, H. Park, and S. Moon. What is twitter, a social network or a news media? In *Proceedings of WWW 2010*, pages 591–600.

[15] T. Lappas, B. Arai, M. Platakis, D. Kotsakos, and D. Gunopulos. On burstiness-aware search for document sequences. In *Proceedings of SIGKDD 2009*, pages 477–486.

[16] V. Lavrenko, J. Allan, E. DeGuzman, D. LaFlamme, V. Pollard, and S. Thomas. Relevance models for topic detection and tracking In *Proceedings of HLT 2002*, pages 115–121.

[17] D. Lee and H. Seung. Algorithms for non-negative matrix factorization. *Advances in neural information processing systems*, 13, 2001.

[18] J. Li, L. Li, and T. Li. Mssf: a multi-document summarization framework based on submodularity. In *Proceedings of SIGIR 2011*, pages 1247–1248.

[19] X. Li and W. B. Croft. Time-based language models. In *Proceedings of CIKM 2003*, pages 469–475.

[20] C. Lin. Rouge: A package for automatic evaluation of summaries. In *Proceedings of the Workshop on Text Summarization Branches Out (WAS 2004)*, pages 25–26.

[21] F. ren Lin and C.-H. Liang. Storyline-based summarization for news topic retrospection. *Decision Support Systems*, 45(3):473 – 490, 2008.

[22] K. Massoudi, M. Tsagkias, M. de Rijke, and W. Weerkamp. Incorporating query expansion and quality indicators in searching microblog posts. In *Proceedings of ECIR 2011*, pages 362–367.

[23] M. Mathioudakis and N. Koudas. Twittermonitor: trend detection over the twitter stream. In *Proceedings of SIGMOD 2010*, pages 1155–1158.

[24] Q. Mei and C. Zhai. Discovering evolutionary theme patterns from text: an exploration of temporal text mining. In *Proceedings of SIGKDD 2005*, pages 198–207.

[25] S. Morinaga and K. Yamanishi. Tracking dynamics of topic trends using a finite mixture model. In *Proceedings of SIGKDD 2004*, pages 811–816.

[26] I. Ounis, G. Amati, V. Plachouras, B. He, C. Macdonald, and C. Lioma. Terrier: A High Performance and Scalable Information Retrieval Platform. In *Proceedings of ACM SIGIR-OSIR Workshop 2006*.

[27] W. Ruzzo and M. Tompa. A linear time algorithm for finding all maximal scoring subsequences. In *Proceedings of ISMB 1999*, pages 234–241.

[28] T. Sakaki, M. Okazaki, and Y. Matsuo. Earthquake shakes twitter users: real-time event detection by social sensors. In *Proceedings of WWW 2010*, pages 851–860.

[29] D. A. Shamma, L. Kennedy, and E. F. Churchill. Peaks and persistence: modeling the shape of microblog conversations. In *Proceedings of CSCW '11*, pages 355–358.

[30] C. Shen and T. Li. Multi-Document Summarization via the Minimum Dominating Set. In *Proceedings of the 23rd International Conference on Computational Linguistics (COLING 2010)*, 2010.

[31] J. Shi and J. Malik. Normalized cuts and image segmentation. *Pattern Analysis and Machine Intelligence, IEEE Transactions on*, 22(8):888–905, 2000.

[32] H. Takamura, H. Yokono, and M. Okumura. Summarizing a document stream. In *Proceedings of ECIR 2011*, pages 177–188.

[33] J. Teevan, D. Ramage, and M. R. Morris. #twittersearch: a comparison of microblog search and web search. In *Proceedings of WSDM 2011*, pages 35–44.

[34] D. Wang, T. Li, and M. Ogihara. Generating Pictorial Storylines via Minimum-Weight Connected Dominating Set Approximation in Multi-View Graphs. In *Proceddings of AAAI 2012*.

[35] D. Wang, T. Li, S. Zhu, and C. Ding. Multi-document summarization via sentence-level semantic analysis and symmetric matrix factorization. In *Proceedings of SIGIR 2008*, pages 307–314.

[36] D. Wang, L. Zheng, T. Li, and Y. Deng. Evolutionary document summarization for disaster management. In *Proceedings of SIGIR 2009*, pages 680–681.

[37] F. Wei, W. Li, Q. Lu, and Y. He. Query-sensitive mutual reinforcement chain and its application in query-oriented multi-document summarization. In *Proceedings of SIGIR 2008*, pages 283–290.

[38] Y. Xu, G. J. Jones, and B. Wang. Query dependent pseudo-relevance feedback based on wikipedia. In *Proceedings of SIGIR 2009*, pages 59–66.

[39] R. Yan, X. Wan, J. Otterbacher, L. Kong, X. Li, and Y. Zhang. Evolutionary timeline summarization: a balanced optimization framework via iterative substitution. In *Proceedings of SIGIR 2011*, pages 745–754.

[40] W. Yih, J. Goodman, L. Vanderwende, and H. Suzuki. Multi-document summarization by maximizing informative content-words. In *Proceedings of IJCAI*, 2007.

[41] C. Zhai. Statistical language models for information retrieval a critical review. *Foundations and Trends in Information Retrieval*, 2(3):137–213, 2008.

[42] D. Zhang, Y. Liu, R. D. Lawrence, and V. Chenthamarakshan. Transfer latent semantic learning: Microblog mining with less supervision. In *Proceedings of AAAI 2011*, pages 561–566.

Social Book Search: Comparing Topical Relevance Judgements and Book Suggestions for Evaluation

Marijn Koolen[1] Jaap Kamps[1,2] Gabriella Kazai[3]

[1] Archives and Information Studies, University of Amsterdam, The Netherlands
[2] ISLA, Informatics Institute, University of Amsterdam, The Netherlands
{marijn.koolen,kamps}@uva.nl
[3] Microsoft Research, Cambridge UK,
v-gabkaz@microsoft.com

ABSTRACT

The Web and social media give us access to a wealth of information, not only different in quantity but also in character—traditional descriptions from professionals are now supplemented with user generated content. This challenges modern search systems based on the classical model of topical relevance and ad hoc search: How does their effectiveness transfer to the changing nature of information and to the changing types of information needs and search tasks? We use the INEX 2011 Books and Social Search Track's collection of book descriptions from Amazon and social cataloguing site LibraryThing. We compare classical IR with social book search in the context of the LibraryThing discussion forums where members ask for book suggestions. Specifically, we compare book suggestions on the forum with Mechanical Turk judgements on topical relevance and recommendation, both the judgements directly and their resulting evaluation of retrieval systems. First, the book suggestions on the forum are a complete enough set of relevance judgements for system evaluation. Second, topical relevance judgements result in a different system ranking from evaluation based on the forum suggestions. Although it is an important aspect for social book search, topical relevance is not sufficient for evaluation. Third, professional metadata alone is often not enough to determine the topical relevance of a book. User reviews provide a better signal for topical relevance. Fourth, user-generated content is more effective for social book search than professional metadata. Based on our findings, we propose an experimental evaluation that better reflects the complexities of social book search.

Categories and Subject Descriptors: H.3.3 [**Information Storage and Retrieval**]: Information Search and Retrieval—*Search process)*

General Terms: Experimentation, Measurement, Performance

Keywords: Book search, User-generated content, Evaluation

1. INTRODUCTION

The web has made the landscape of search more complex. Traditional IR models were developed in a time when the information that was available was limited. Retrieval systems indexed titles, abstracts and keywords assigned by professional cataloguers for collections of officially published documents. On the web, there is much more information. Every aspect of human life is published on the web, which leads to different search tasks and different notions of relevance. Traditional IR was mainly based on the ad hoc search methodology of a user who wants information that is topically relevant to her information need [24]. Many state-of-the-art retrieval systems are still based on classical IR models and are evaluated using this ad hoc search methodology. Increasingly, research in areas such as web [10], blog [18] and realtime search [26] has focused on new search tasks in this changing environment.

In this paper we aim to study how search has changed by directly comparing classical IR and social search. Sites like Amazon and LibraryThing offer an opportunity to do this, as they provide traditional descriptions—titles, abstract and keywords of books—as well as user-generated content data in the form of user tags, reviews, ratings and discussions. To gain more insight in these changes, we compare classical IR with social book search in the context of the LibraryThing discussion forums, where members ask for book suggestions. We use a large collection of book descriptions from Amazon and LibraryThing, which contain both professional metadata and user-generated content, and compare book suggestions on the forum with Mechanical Turk judgements on topical relevance and recommendation for evaluation of retrieval systems. Amazon and LibraryThing are typical examples were users can add their own content about books, but like many similar sites, do not include user-generated content in the main search index. Any direct searching in the collection is done on professional metadata. One reason for users to ask for suggestions on discussion forums may be that they cannot search sites directly on the subjective content provided by other users, which indicates these suggestion are more than just topical relevance judgements.

Relevance in book search—as in many other scenarios—is a many-faceted concept. There may be dozens or hundreds of books that are topically relevant, but the user often wants to know which one or two to choose. This is where the information need goes beyond topical relevance: searchers also care about how interesting, well-written, recent, fun, educational or popular it is. Some of these facets are covered by professional metadata, such as subject headings for topical facets, and publication data for recency, size, binding and price. Affective aspects, such as how well-written and interesting a book is, is not covered by professional metadata, but can be covered by reviews. Social book search has elements of subject search as well as recommendation. We use the book requests and suggestions as a real world scenario of book search, and as examples of relevance judgements, with the aim to investigate how this search task differs from traditional ad hoc search. Can we em-

CIKM'12, October 29–November 2, 2012, Maui, HI, USA.

ulate these scenarios with known-item search or traditional ad hoc retrieval based on topical relevance? We use Amazon Mechanical Turk to obtain judgements about the topical relevance of books as well as about recommendation. Our main research question is:

- How does social book search compare to traditional search tasks?

For this study, we set up the Social Search for Best Books (SB) task as part of the INEX 2011 Books and Social Search Track.[1] One of the goals of this track is to build test collections for this and other book search tasks. The book requests from the forum are used as information needs and the book suggestions as relevance judgements. These are real information needs and human suggestions. With these suggestions we avoid problems with pooling bias [5]. We hope to find out whether the suggestions really are the best books on the topic or just a sample of a much larger set of books that are just as good. The latter case would mean the list of suggested books is incomplete. We compare these suggestions with judgements of topical relevance and recommendation, which we obtained through Amazon Mechanical Turk[2] (MTURK). Specifically, we address the following questions:

- Can we use book requests and suggestions from the LibraryThing forum as topics and relevance judgements for system evaluation?
- How is social book search related to known-item search, ad hoc search and recommendation?
- Do users prefer professional or user-generated content for judging topical relevance and for recommendation?

Professional metadata is evenly distributed—no single book is privileged. A book usually has only one classification number, and often no more than two or three subject headings. For user-generated content this is dramatically different. The amount of content added is related to how many users added content, which leads to a more skewed distribution. Popular books may have many more ratings, reviews and tags than less popular books. This leads to the following questions:

- How do standard IR models cope with user-generated content?
- How effective are professional and user-generated content for book suggestion?

The rest of this paper is organized as follows. We first discuss related work in Section 2. Next, we describe the search task and scenario in detail in Section 3, and then describe the document collection, information needs and the Mechanical Turk experiment in Section 4. We discuss the system-centered evaluation in Section 5, and the user-centered evaluation in Section 6. Finally, we draw conclusions in Section 7.

2. RELATED WORK

In this section, we discuss related work on novel search tasks, classical information retrieval based on controlled vocabularies, and crowdsourcing in IR.

2.1 Search Tasks

At TREC, many of the evaluations still focus on the ad hoc search methodology where the aim is to find information that is topically relevant. Other evaluations have addressed that change in search task caused by a change in the information environment. There is information on the web of any level of subjectivity and quality. Research areas such as web search [10] and blog search [18] have identified search tasks very different from traditional subject search in catalogues, where other aspects of relevance play a role. For web search aspects of popularity and authority [19] and diversity [6] are important, for blog and twitter search, aspects of subjectivity [18] and credibility [26] play a role. [22] interviewed 194 book readers about their reading experiences and book selections. She found that readers welcome recommendations from known and "trusted" sources to reduce the number of candidates for selection and like to know what other readers have chosen. Reading a book is a substantial investment of time and energy, so searchers use a variety of clues to choose one or a few books from among a much longer list. This is supported by [21], who identified 46 factors that influenced children's assessment of relevance when selecting books along dimensions such as content, accessibility, engagement and familiarity.

2.2 Controlled Vocabularies and Retrieval

The Cranfield tests for evaluating information retrieval systems [7] showed that indexing based on natural language terms from documents was at least as effective for retrieval as formal indexing schemes with controlled languages. However, controlled vocabularies still hold the potential to improve completeness and accuracy of search results by providing consistent and rigorous index terms and ways to deal with synonymy and homonymy [14, 23]. One of the problems with traditional metadata based on controlled vocabularies and classification schemes is that it is difficult for both indexers and searchers to use properly. On top of that, searchers and indexers might use different terms because they have different perspectives. Buckland [4] describes the differences between vocabularies of authors, cataloguers, searchers, queries as well as the vocabulary of syndetic structure. With all these vocabularies used in a single process, there is the possibility of mismatch. Users of library catalogues use keyword search, which often does not match the appropriate subject headings [2, p.7]. People use the principle of least effort in information seeking behavior: they prefer information that is easy to find, even if they know it is of poor quality, over high quality information that is harder to find. [2, p.4] One of the interesting aspects of user-generated metadata in this respect is that it has a smaller gap with the vocabulary of searchers [17].

Tags have also been compared to subject headings for book descriptions with the growing popularity of sites like Delicious, Flickr, and LibraryThing. Tags can be seen as personal descriptors for organizing information. Golder and Huberman [8] distinguish between tags based on their organizing functions. What (or who) it is about, what it is, who owns it, refining categories, qualities or characteristics, self reference and task organizing. Lu et al. [16] compared LibraryThing tags and LCSH. They find that social tags can improve accessibility to library collections. Yi and Chan [28] explored the possibility of mapping user tags from folksonomies to Library of Congress subject headings (LCSH). They find that with word matching, they can link two-thirds of all tags to LC subject headings. In subsequent work [27], they use semantic similarity between tags and subject headings to automatically apply subject headings to tagged resources.

Peters et al. [20] look at the retrieval effectiveness of tags taking into account the tag frequency. They found that the tags with the highest frequency are the most effective. Kazai and Milic-Frayling [12] incorporate social approval votes based on external resources for searching in a large digitized book corpus. They evaluate their model with a set of queries from a book search transaction log and traditional topical relevance judgements by paid assessors. Their

[1] `https://inex.mmci.uni-saarland.de/tracks/books/`
[2] `http://www.mturk.com`

results show that social approval votes can improve a BM25F baseline that indexes both full-text and MARC records.

2.3 Crowdsourcing Relevance Judgements

There is a lot of recent research on using crowdsourcing for relevance assessment [1, 9]. To make sure the quality of judgements is sufficient, numerous quality-control measures have been proposed [11, 13, 15]. A minimal approval rate (how many of the previous tasks have been approved by the task owner), trap questions ("check this box if you did NOT read the instructions"), captcha's and flow-dependent questions (the next question depends on the answer to the previous question) are all effective quality-control mechanisms. Crowdsourced relevance judgements have been effectively used at INEX to evaluate book page retrieval tasks [13].

3. SOCIAL SEARCH FOR BEST BOOKS

In this section we detail the Social Search for Best Books (SB) task as run at INEX 2011, and the used collection.

3.1 Social Book Search Task

The goal of the SB task is to evaluate the relative value of controlled book metadata versus user-generated or social metadata for retrieving the most relevant books for search requests on online book discussion forums. Controlled metadata, such as the Library of Congress Classification and Subject Headings, is rigorously curated by experts in librarianship. On the other hand, user-generated content lacks vocabulary control by design. However, such metadata is contributed directly by the users and may better reflect the terminology of everyday searchers. Both types of metadata seem to have advantages and disadvantages. With this task we want to investigate the nature of book search in an environment where book descriptions are a mixture of both types of metadata, with the aim to develop systems that can deal with more complex information needs and data sources.

The scenario is that of a user turning to Amazon Books and LibraryThing to search for books they want to read, buy or add to their personal catalogue. Both services host large collaborative book catalogues that may be used to locate books of interest. On LibraryThing, users can catalogue the books they read, manually index them by assigning tags, and write reviews for others to read. Users can also post messages on a discussion forum asking for help in finding new, fun, interesting, or relevant books to read. The forums allow users to tap into the collective bibliographic knowledge of hundreds of thousands of book enthusiasts. On Amazon, users can read and write book reviews and browse to similar books based on links such as "customers who bought this book also bought... ". Neither service includes reviews or tags in the search index. Users have to browse through individual book descriptions to be able to search through the user-generated content.

The SB task assumes a user issues a request to a retrieval system, which returns a (ranked) list of book records as its result. The request can be a list of keywords, a natural language statement. We assume the user inspects the results list starting from the top and works her way down until she has either satisfied her information need or gives up. The retrieval system is expected to order results by relevance to the user's information need. User requests can be complex mixtures of topical aspects ("I want a book about X"), genre aspects (fiction/non-fiction, poetry, reference), style aspects (objective/subjective, engaging, easy-to-read, funny), and other aspects such as comprehensiveness, recency, etc. The user context, i.e., their background knowledge and familiarity with specific books, adds further complexity. They might have found a number of books already, read some of them and discarded other options, and want to know what else is available. This aspect of user context was left out of the SB task in the first year but will be included in future years. Participants of the SB task are provided with a set of book search requests from the LibraryThing discussion forums and are asked to submit the ranked lists of results returned by their retrieval systems. We assume one of the reasons why readers turn to the discussion forums is that they can ask such complex questions that are hard to address with current search engines.

Table 1: Statistics on the Amazon/LibraryThing collection

type	*min*	*max*	*median*	*mean*	*std. dev.*
Professional					
Dewey	0	1	1	0.61	0.49
Subject	0	29	1	0.66	0.72
BrowseNode	0	213	18	19.84	10.21
User-generated					
Tag	0	50	5	11.45	14.55
Rating/Review	0	100	0	5.05	14.98
Automatic					
Similar product	0	15	1	2.37	2.40

3.2 Professional and User Generated Book Information

To study social book search, we need a large collection of book records that contains professional metadata and user generated content, for a set of books that is representative of what readers are searching for. We use the INEX Amazon/LibraryThing corpus [3].

The collection consists of 2.8 million book records from Amazon, extended with social metadata from LibraryThing, marked up in XML.[3] This set contains books that are available through Amazon. These records contain title information as well as a Dewey Decimal Classification (DDC) code and category and subject information supplied by Amazon. Each book is identified by its ISBN. Since different editions of the same work have different ISBNs, there can be multiple records for a single intellectual work. Each book record is an XML file with fields like <isbn>, <title>, <author>, <publisher>, <dimensions>, <numberofpage> and <publicationdate>. Curated metadata comes in the form of a Dewey Decimal Classification in the <dewey> field, Amazon subject headings are stored in the <subject> field, and Amazon category labels can be found in the <browseNode> fields. The social metadata from Amazon and LibraryThing is stored in the <tag>, <rating>, and <review> fields. The reviews and tags were limited to the first 50 reviews and 100 tags respectively during crawling.

How many of the book records have curated metadata? In the Amazon/LibraryThing data, there is a DDC code for 61% of the collection and 57% has at least one subject heading. The classification codes and subject headings together cover 78% of the collection. There is also a large hierarchical structure of categories called *browseNodes*, which is the category structure used by Amazon. All but 296 books in the collection have at least one browseNode category. Most records have a Dewey code and a subject heading (Table 1), but some have no Dewey code or subject heading. Records never have more than one Dewey code (to determine the location of the physical book on the shelves), but can have multiple subject headings. The low standard deviation of the subject headings indicates that the vast majority of records have zero, one or two

[3] See `https://inex.mmci.uni-saarland.de/data/nd-agreements.jsp` for information on how to get access to this collection.

headings. The BrowseNode distribution is more dispersed, with a median (mean) of 18 (19.84) BrowseNode categories, but a minimum of 0 and a maximum 213. The median number of subject headings per book is 1. For the next edition of this task at INEX we extend the collection with records from the British Library and the Library of Congress, which may have more headings per book.

How many of the book records have user-generated metadata? Just over 82% of the collection has at least one LibraryThing tag, but less than half (47%) has at least one rating and review. The median (mean) number of tags per record is 5 (11.45) and the median (mean) number of ratings and reviews is 0 (5.05). The distribution of the amount of UGC is thus much more skewed than the distribution of the amount of professional metadata. This is due to a popularity effect. Multiple users can add content to a book description, and more popular books will receive more tags and reviews than less popular books. This is an important difference between professional and user-generated content. UGC not only lacks vocabulary control, but also introduces an imbalance in the exhaustivity and redundancy of book descriptions. The impact of this imbalance is discussed in Sections 5 and 6.

4. SOCIAL BOOK RECOMMENDATIONS

In this section we describe the book recommendation requests at the LibraryThing (LT) forums, and the Mechanical Turk experiment we ran to obtain relevance judgements.

4.1 Topics and Recommendations

LibraryThing users discuss their books in forums dedicated to certain topics. Many of the topic threads are started with a request from a member for interesting, fun new books to read. They describe what they are looking for, give examples of what they like and do not like, indicate which books they already know and ask other members for recommendations. Other members often reply with links to works catalogued on LT, which have direct links to the corresponding records on Amazon. These requests for recommendations are natural expressions of information needs for a large collection of online book records, and the book suggestions are human recommendations from members interested in the same topic. Each topic consists of a title, group name, thread, narrative and so-called 'touchstones'.

Title of the topic, a short description of what the topic is about.

Group name identifying the discussion group where the topic was posted.

Narrative describing the topic, it is the first message in the thread explaining what the topic creator is looking for.

Thread containing the messages posted by members of the discussion group in response to the initial request.

Touchstones listing the books suggested by members, usually identified by the LT work ID. Members can use a Wiki-type syntax around the title of a work to have LT automatically identify it as a book title and link it to the a dedicated LT page on that book. When LT misidentifies a book, members can and often do correct the link.

We distributed the topics, which included the Title, Group name and Narrative to participants of the INEX 2011 Book Track, who could use any combination of these fields for retrieval. We note that the title and narrative of a topic may be different from what the user would submit as queries to a book search system such as Amazon, LT, or a traditional library catalogue. However, as the message is addressed to other members, we consider this a natural expression of the information need. As an example, consider a topic titled *Help: WWII pacific subs* from a user in the *Second World War History* discussion group, with the following narrative:

> *Can anyone recommend a good strategic level study of us sub campaign in pacific? All I seem to scare up is exploits of individual subs. I have ordered clay blairs big study but I would like something from this decade if it exists.*

The topic of the request is the US submarines in the Pacific in World War 2. The user has already found some books on US submarines, but no 'strategic level studies'. The user already knows about and ordered a relevant book by Clay Blair, but is looking for something more recent and something 'good'. The latter qualification is of course subjective. Does the user mean comprehensive or accurate, easy to read or engaging, or all of these? The thread has eight replies in which five books are recommended and automatically identified in the Touchstone list, including the one mentioned above by Clay Blair.

We note that the requester may consider only few or even none of the suggestions by the forum members as interesting or useful. However, we argue that these suggestions are valuable judgements that are likely to be relevant to the information need, because they are suggested by the very members of the discussion group who share the same interest and suggest books on the topic that they have read or know about.

We use these suggested books as initial relevance judgements for evaluation. Some of these suggestions link to a different book from the one intended, and suggested books may not always be what the topic creator asked for, but merely be mentioned as a negative example or for some other reason. From this it is clear that the collected list of suggested books can contain false positives and is probably incomplete as not all relevant books will be suggested (false negatives), so may not be appropriate for reliable evaluation. The suggestions as relevance judgements avoid the problem of pooling bias [5]. Although the judgements were pooled by a number of LT members, these LT members are not evaluated.

We crawled over 18,000 topics from the forums, with over 11,000 topics having at least one suggested book. We filtered these using regular expressions such as "I'm looking for" and "can you recommend" and a number of others to locate topics that have actual book requests. This resulted in 1,800 topics, from which we manually selected all topics that really contain a request for book suggestions, reducing the set to 945 topics. The other topics contained requests ranging from information from non-book sources, tips on how to do something or places to go to related to their topic. We use the titles of the topic threads as natural succinct expressions of the information need. Many of these 945 titles do not reflect the actual information needs, which would make them unsuitable as queries. We ran all 945 titles as queries on a full-text index of our collection (see Section 5.2 for indexing details) and kept only those topics for which at least 50% of the books suggested by the forum members were retrieved, leaving us with 211 topics from 122 discussion groups. We note that this introduces a bias towards topics for which the full-text index gets high recall. However, we think that the other topics would introduce noise in the evaluation and creating our own queries for them would reduce the realistic nature of the topic set. The 211 topics form the official topic set for the Social Search for Best Books task in the INEX 2011 Book Track. For the Mechanical Turk experiment we focus on a subset of 24 topics.

We manually classified topics as requesting fiction or non-fiction books, or both, as there are some topics where the creator requested both fiction and non-fiction books. In total, there 79 fiction topics (37%), 122 non-fiction topics (58%) and 10 mixed topics (5%). For our selection of 24 topics, we selected 12 fiction and 12 non-fiction topics. Arguably, fiction-related needs are less concerned with the topic of a book than non-fiction needs, and more with genre, style and affective aspects like interestingness and familiarity. For such needs it seems more clear that the traditional IR approach of gathering topical relevance judgements is the wrong task model.

4.2 MTurk Judgements

We want to compare the LT forum suggestions against traditional judgements of topical relevance, as well as against recommendation judgements. We set up an experiment on Amazon Mechanical Turk to obtain judgements on document pools based on top-k pooling.

The SB task had 4 participating teams who together submitted 22 runs. From the 211 topics in the total set, we manually selected 24 topics with a short and clear request for which to obtain relevance judgement from MTURK. The books to be judged are based on top 10 pools of all 22 official runs. In cases where the top 10 pools contained fewer than 100 books, we increased the pool depth to the smallest rank k at which the pool contained at least 100 books.

We designed a HIT (Human Intelligence Task) to ask Mechanical Turk workers to judge the relevance of 10 books for a given book request. Apart from a question on topical relevance, we also asked whether they would recommend a book to the requester and which part of the metadata—curated or user-generated—was more useful for determining the topical relevance and for recommendation. At the beginning of the HIT we asked how familiar they are with the topic and afterwards how difficult the HIT was, which they could answer with a 5-point Likert scale.

As on Amazon, we show only the 3 most helpful reviews. Each review has a total number of votes T and a number of helpful votes H with $H \leq T$. On Amazon, the most helpful review seems to be determined by the number of helpful votes and the ratio of helpful to total votes. We use $ln(H+1)*(\frac{H}{T})^n$ to score helpfulness, where n controls the relative weight of the ratio $\frac{H}{T}$. With $n = 3$ we found the resulting ranking of reviews to closely resemble the ranking of the top 3 reviews for books on Amazon. For popular books with many reviews and votes, we expect the votes to filter out bad reviews and review spam (fraudulent reviews written to promote or damage a book, author or publisher). For more obscure books with few or no votes, helpfulness has little impact and fake reviews may be selected. It is not clear how many fake reviews there are, how to identify them, nor what their impact is. We therefore do not address this issue in this paper.

We asked the following questions per book:

Q1. Is this book useful for the topic of the request?
Workers could pick one of the following answers

- Very useful (perfectly on-topic).
- Useful (related but not completely the right topic).
- Not useful (not the right topic)
- Not enough information to determine.

Q2. Which type of information is more useful to answer Q1?
Workers see a 5-point Likert scale, with *Official description* on the left side and *User-generated description* on the right side.

Q3. Would you recommend this book?
Workers could pick one of the following answers:

- Yes, this is a great book on the requested topic.
- Yes, it's not exactly on the right topic, but it's a great book.
- Yes, it's not on the requested topic. but it's great for someone interested in the topic of the book.
- No, there are much better books on the same topic.
- I don't know, there is not enough information to make a good recommendation (skip Q4).

Q4. Which type of information is more useful to answer Q3?
Again, workers could choose on a five-point scale between *Official description* and *User-generated description*.

Q5. Please type the most useful tag (in your opinion) from the LibraryThing tags in the User-generated description, with a text box and next to it a check box with the text *(or tick here if there are no tags for this book.)*

In addition, workers could give optional comments in a comment box per book. We included some quality assurance and control measure to deter spammers and sloppy workers, and approved new assignments once a day over a period of 6 days.

LT agreement Each HIT contained at least one book that was recommended on the LT forums. Workers doing multiple HITs can easily be checked on agreement with LT forum members. For workers who do only one or two HITs, agreement cannot be reliably determined and is not used for approval. Once workers did 3 or more HITs, we rejected a HIT if it made their LT agreement level drop below 60%.

Relevance contradiction A worker first saying a book is related, then saying it is on-topic is inconsistent, but is not contradicting her- or himself. We consider the answers to Q1 and Q3 to be contradicting when a worker answers *on-topic* for Q1, then *unrelated* for Q3 or the other way around. Also, when a worker answers *not enough information* for Q1, then either *on-topic*, *related* or *unrelated* for Q3

Type contradiction A metadata type contradiction is made when a worker answer that the UGC is more useful than the professional metadata when there is no UGC.

Tag occurs Finally, we asked workers to type in the most useful tag from the UGC (or tick the adjacent box when the UGC contains no tags). The LibraryThing tags were placed at the bottom of the UGC description, so this question forced workers to at least scroll down to the bottom of the description and check if there are tags.

Qualification Based on previous MTurk experiments, we used two worker qualifications. Workers had to have an approval rate of 95% with at least 50 approved HITs—i.e. only workers whose previous work on MTurk was of high quality—and we only accepted workers registered in the US.

We created a total of 272 distinct HITs. With 3 workers per HIT we ended up with 816 assignments. Only 7 assignments were rejected, either because workers skipped the last few books in the HIT (4 cases) or because their agreement was too low (3 cases).

In total, there were 133 different workers, of which 90 did only one HIT, 13 did two HITs and 30 workers did three or more. The distribution of HITs per worker is highly skewed, with more than half of the 816 HITs done by only 7 workers. This power-law-like distribution is typical of crowdsourcing experiments [1, 13]. Averaged over workers the LT agreement is 0.52. Low agreement was found for workers who did only one HIT, where there is only one data point to compute agreement, which is not enough to reliably compute agreement or reject a HIT. Workers who did at least 3 HITs (covering 86% of all HITs) have a median (mean) LT agreement of 0.67 (0.65). Averaged over assignments the agreement is

0.84, which shows that the few workers who did many HITs scored very high on agreement.

There are only 18 Relevance contradictions, spread over 15 approved HITs. From these, we discarded the books with contradicting judgements. No Type contradictions were made. In the answer categories of both the topical relevance and recommendation questions, we used the same levels of topical relevance (*perfectly on-topic, related, unrelated*). If workers choose the same level of topical relevance for both Q1 and Q3, or *not recommended* or *not enough information* for Q3, their answers are consistent, which was the case for 95% of the assignments. Time to complete a single HIT ranged between 3 and 111 minutes with an average of 13 minutes and 9 seconds. These numbers suggest workers performed most HITs conscientiously. Per Worker, an average of 68% of the tags they filled in for Q5 exactly matched a tag in the book description (median 70%). When there was no matching tag, this was mostly because workers combined two separate tags or made misspellings.

Most workers are not very familiar with the search topics for which they have to judge books. On a scale from 0 (totally unfamiliar) to 4 (very familiar), the median (mean) familiarity is 1 (1.5). For 3 topics the median familiarity is 0, for 12 topics it is 1, for 8 topics it is 2 and for 1 topic it is 3. Although workers are not very familiar with the topic of request, they indicate the work is not difficult. On a scale from 0 (very easy) to 4 (Very difficult), for 21 topics the median difficulty is 1 (fairly easy) and for 3 topics the median difficulty is 2 (medium difficulty). For only 9 assignments (1%) workers thought the HIT was very difficult, for 86 assignments (11%) they chose 3 (fairly difficult). We discuss the results of the MTurk experiment in the user-centered analysis in Section 6.

5. SYSTEM-CENTERED ANALYSIS

In this section we focus on system-centred evaluation. We want to know whether the forum suggestions are similar to any of the three known tasks—known-item search, ad hoc search, and recommendation—and whether the suggestions are complete and reliable enough for evaluation. First, we look at the official submissions of the Social Search for Best Books task, and compare the system rankings of the different sets of judgements. Second, we use additional runs we created ourselves to compare different index fields for professional metadata and user-generated content.

5.1 Comparing System Rankings

If we want know whether two sets of relevance judgements can be used to evaluate the same retrieval task, we can compare the system rankings they produce. If the sets of judgements model the same task, they should give the same answer when asked to choose which of two systems is the better one. We compare the system rankings of the 22 officially submitted runs based on the topical relevance judgements from MTurk and on the LT forum suggestions. We use Kendall's Tau and Tau$_{AP}$ [29]. The latter puts more weight on ranking the top scoring systems similarly than on ranking the lower scoring systems similarly.

The set of relevance judgements based on the suggestions for the 211 forum topics is denoted as LT-211, the subset of 24 topics selected for MTurk, but still using the forum suggestions as relevance judgements is denoted as LT-24 and with the Amazon MTurk topical relevance judgements as AMT-24-Rel. The system rank correlations are shown in Table 2. Recall that the subset of 24 topics is not randomly selected. The LT-24 subset still leads to a similar system ranking as the LT-211 set. The forum suggestions seem robust against non-random selection. The system ranking based on the AMT-24-Rel judgements is very different from those of the forum suggestions. The difference between τ and τ_{AP} is bigger between the AMT-24-Rel judgements and the two LT sets, showing that mainly disagree on the top systems.

Table 2: Kendall's τ and τ_{AP} system ranking correlations on nDCG@10 between the three sets of judgements (τ/τ_{AP})

	LT-24	AMT-24-Rel
LT-211	0.90/0.83	0.39/0.20
LT-24	–	0.36/0.19

Why do these sets produce such different system rankings? The AMT-24-Rel judgements are based on the top 10 results of all the official submissions, so the nDCG@10 scores do not suffer from incomplete judgements. The LT forum suggestions are not based on pools, but are provided by a small number of forum members who may have limited knowledge of all the relevant books. It could be that their suggestions are highly incomplete, and that many of the top 10 results of the official runs are just as relevant.

To get a better idea of the completeness of the forum suggestions we zoom in on the best scoring runs (the top one being a Language Model run that uses all user-generated content and pseudo-relevance feedback). The best system has a Mean Reciprocal Rank (MRR) of 0.481 and a Precision at rank 10 (P@10). of 0.207. There are several systems from different participants that get lower but similar scores. Considering that most topics have a small number of suggestions (the median number of suggested books is 7), these are remarkably high scores, and indicate the system is performing well. In a collection of millions of books, this retrieval system picks out several of the small number of books suggested by forum members. This indicates that the suggestions by forum members are not an arbitrary sample of a much larger set of books that are relevant to the topic, but are a relatively complete set in and of themselves. If the suggestions were only a small sample from a set of equally relevant books (say 7 out of 100, thus highly incomplete), the chances of a retrieval system consistently (for 211 topics) ranking at least one of those 7 at rank 2 or 3 are very small. The suggestions form a set of books that stand out. With top-k pooling the above argument cannot be made, since the small number of judgements is biased towards the evaluated systems. But this is not a pooling effect, since the suggestions are independent of the submitted runs. With a P@10 of 0.207, the best performing system ranks 2 of the suggested books, out of a collection of 2.8 million, in the top 10, on average over 211 topics, lending further support that the suggestions are relatively complete.

5.2 Effectiveness of Metadata Fields

For indexing we use Indri,[4] Language Model (without belief operators), with Krovetz stemming, stopword removal and default smoothing (Dirichlet, μ=2,500). The titles of the forum topics are used as queries. In our base index, each xml element is indexed in a separate field, to allow search on individual fields. For the LibraryThing tags we create two versions of the index. One where we index distinct tags only once (Tag Set) and one where we use the tag frequency (how many users tagged a book with the same tag) as the term frequency (Tag Bag). That is, if 20 users applied tag t to book b, the Tag Set index will have a term frequency of 1 for (b, t) and the Tag Bag index will have a term frequency of 20 for (b, t).

The book records have unique ISBNs, but some records are different editions of the same *intellectual work*. Having multiple versions of the same work in the ranking is redundant for the user, so we ignore any other version after the first version found in the rank-

[4]URL: `http://lemurproject.org/indri/`

Table 3: Known-item and forum suggestion evaluation of runs over different index fields

	Known-item			Forum suggestions		
Field	MRR	R@10	R@1000	MRR	R@10	R@1000
Title	0.414	0.540	**0.820**	0.118	0.048	0.350
BrowseNode	0.004	0.000	0.240	0.083	0.028	0.261
Dewey	0.000	0.000	0.000	0.002	0.000	0.022
Subject	0.010	0.020	0.020	0.012	0.002	0.009
Review	**0.480**	**0.680**	0.800	**0.382**	**0.227**	**0.680**
Tag (set)	0.118	0.220	0.540	0.213	0.125	0.616
Tag (bag)	0.227	0.400	0.560	0.342	0.178	0.602

ing. To identify multiple manifestations of the same work, we use the mappings provided by LibraryThing.[5] With these mappings, we replace the ISBNs in the result lists and in the judgements with LibraryThing work IDs. With duplicate IDs in the ranking we keep only the highest ranked result with that ID.

5.2.1 *Known-item versus Forum Suggestions*

It is possible that the small set of suggestions are ranked high because book suggestion is very similar to known-item search. To check this possibility, we created a set of 50 known-item topics. We pooled all the suggested books for all 211 topics and randomly selected 50 books, to make sure the known-item topics target books from the same distribution.

There is a popularity effect that can explain why reviews and tag frequency work well. There is a plausible overlap between the people who buy, tag and review, e.g., *historical fiction* books and the people who suggest books in the *historical fiction* groups. Their suggestions are probably based on the books they have read, which are the books that they made popular. Is our finding a trivial one then? Not at all. They could suggest very different books from the ones that every historical fiction fan reads, or could be a non-representative sample of historical fiction readers.

The Known-item evaluation results of the individual metadata fields are shown in Table 3. The Title field is very effective. The controlled subject access fields are not at all effective, which is not surprising since they serve a different purpose. The tags are more effective than the controlled subject access points, but less than the title. The reviews are the most effective field, even outperforming the title field. Named access points in the formal metadata are effective for known-item search, but user-generated content without any formal and controlled metadata can be just as effective.

The competitiveness of the Title field for known-item topics is in stark contrast with its low scores for the forum suggestions. Book suggestion on the LT forum seems different from known-item search. Next, we compare the book suggestions with traditional topical relevance judgements.

5.2.2 *MTurk evaluation results*

The performance of systems on the topical relevance judgements (AMT-Rel) is shown in columns 2–4 in Table 4, on the recommendation judgements (AMT-Rec) in columns 5–7 and on the topical relevance + recommendation (AMT-Rel&Rec) in columns 8–10. The results for the forum suggestions (LT-Sug) are in columns 11–13. Generally, systems perform better on AMT-Rec than on AMT-Rel, and AMT-Rel&Rec and worst on LT-Sug. The suggestions seem harder to retrieve than books that are topically relevant.

[5] http://www.librarything.com/feeds/thingISBN.xml.gz

The exception is that the Review field is more effective for AMT-Rel&Rec than for topical relevance alone, apart form nDCG@10. Reviews become more effective when there is a recommendation element involved. The Title field is the most effective of the non-UGC fields. It achieves better precision and recall than the BrowseNode, Dewey and Subject fields across all sets of judgements. The Dewey and Subject fields are the least effective fields. The Review field is more effective than the Tag field. The bag of tags is more efficient than the set of tags for precision, but less effective for recall. The review and tag fields have similar R@1000 for all four sets of judgements. This last observation merits further discussion. The title field is reasonably effective for the AMT judgements, which are based on judgement pools from the 22 official submissions, which used much more than just the title field. The Title field scores between 0.601 for R@1000 (recall at rank 1,000) for topical relevance, but 0.35 for the forum suggestions. Note that for all runs and sets of judgements, the queries are the same. Even though book titles alone provide little information about books, with Title field the majority of the judged topically relevant books can be found in the top 1,000, but only a third of the suggestions. There is something about suggestions that goes beyond topical relevance, which the UGC fields are better able to capture. Furthermore, the retrieval system is a standard language model, which was developed to capture topical relevance. Apparently these models can also deal with other aspects of relevance.

The official submissions all used UGC, creating a bias in the judgement pools. The runs based on professional metadata have a larger fraction of non-judged results in the top ranks than the runs based on UGC. The performance of the Title field on the AMT judgements may be an underestimation. This cannot be the case for the LT forum suggestions, as they have no pool bias.

It also suggests the workers find the reviews more useful for topical relevance and recommendation than any other part of the book descriptions. Note that the LT forum members may not have seen any of the Amazon reviews before they made suggestions, whereas the workers were explicitly pointed at them, which could at least partly explain the higher scores for the AMT judgements.

We also looked at the difference between fiction-related requests and requests for non-fiction books. There are no meaningful differences between the two topic types. All runs score slightly better on the fiction topics, by the same degree, which is probably due to the fact that fiction topics have more suggested books than non-fiction topics. The different types of metadata have the same utility for forum suggestions of fiction and non-fiction topics.

It may not seem surprising that the longer descriptions of the reviews are more effective than the shorter descriptions of the other metadata fields. What is surprising however, is how ineffective book search systems are if they ignore reviews. Even though there are many short, vague and unhelpful reviews, there seems to be enough useful content to substantially improve retrieval. This is different from general web search, where low quality and spam documents need to be dealt with.

6. USER-CENTERED ANALYSIS

In this section we compare the MTURK judgements with the book suggestions from a user perspective, extending the analysis of system effectiveness above. The workers answered questions on which part of the metadata is more useful to determine topical relevance and which part to determine whether to recommend a book. On top of that, we can also look at the relation between the amount of user-generated content that is available and the particular answer given. As mentioned before, the amount of user-generated content is more skewed than the amount of professional metadata.

Table 4: MTurk and LT Forum evaluation of runs over different index fields

Field	AMT-Rel			AMT-Rec			AMT-Rel&Rec			LT-Sug		
	nDCG10	MAP	R@1000	nDCG10	MAP	R@1000	nDCG10	MAP	R@1000	nDCG10	MAP	R@1000
Title (field)	0.212	0.105	0.601	0.260	0.107	0.545	0.172	0.088	0.591	0.055	0.040	0.350
BrowseNode	0.096	0.052	0.322	0.142	0.056	0.321	0.083	0.046	0.328	0.043	0.031	0.261
Dewey	0.000	0.000	0.009	0.003	0.000	0.007	0.000	0.000	0.005	0.001	0.001	0.022
Subject	0.016	0.002	0.008	0.021	0.002	0.010	0.016	0.003	0.009	0.003	0.002	0.009
Review	**0.579**	**0.309**	0.720	**0.786**	**0.389**	**0.756**	**0.542**	**0.333**	**0.783**	**0.251**	**0.174**	**0.680**
Tag (set)	0.337	0.173	**0.744**	0.422	0.199	0.711	0.288	0.158	0.754	0.125	0.097	0.616
Tag (bag)	0.368	0.182	0.694	0.435	0.197	0.665	0.320	0.176	0.718	0.216	0.154	0.602

Table 5: Impact of presence of reviews and tags on judgements

	Reviews		Tags	
	0 rev.	≥1 rev.	0 tags	≥10 tags
Top. Rel. (Q1)				
Not enough info.	0.37	0.01	0.09	0.09
Relevant	0.30	0.54	0.49	0.48
Recommend. (Q3)				
Not enough info.	0.53	0.01	0.14	0.12
Rel. + Rec.	0.22	0.51	0.46	0.45

6.1 Overlap between LT and MTurk

What is the overlap between the books suggested by forum members and the books judged by workers? Recall that we added at least one forum suggestion to each HIT. Of the 8,260 answers, 1,516 are for books that were suggested on the forums. Workers labelled 47% of all books as topically relevant (23% as related to the topic of request). In contrast, they labelled 66% of the suggested books as topically relevant (a further 18% at least related). Topical relevance is an important aspect for suggestions. For the recommendation question, 43% of all books are labelled as relevant and recommended (15% as related and recommended), and 62% of suggested books (13% related and recommended). If we consider only the recommendation aspect, 69% of all books and 80% of suggested books are recommended. Books suggested on the forum are more often recommended than other topically relevant books.

6.2 Relevance, Recommendation and UGC

How do forum suggestions compare with MTURK labels in terms of the amount of UGC? Recall that workers could indicate the description does not have enough information to answer questions Q1 (topical relevance) and Q3 (recommendation). Is this answer related to the number of reviews and tags in a description? We see in Table 5 the fraction of books for which workers did not have enough information split over the descriptions with no reviews (column 2), at least one review (column 3), no tags (column 4) and at least 10 distinct tags (column 5). First, without reviews, workers indicate they do not have enough information to determine whether a book is topically relevant in 37% of the cases, and label the book as relevant in 30% of the cases. When there is at least one review, in only 1% of the cases do workers have too little information to determine topical relevance, but in 54% of the cases they label the book as relevant. Reviews contain important information for topical relevance. The presence of tags seems to have no effect. With no tags, workers have too little information to determine topical relevance in 9% of the cases and label a book as relevant in 49% of the cases, and with at least 10 tags this is 9% and 48% respectively. The percentages are the same for books with at least 40 or 50 tags.

We see a similar pattern for the recommendation question (Q3). When there is no review, workers find it difficult to make a recommendation–not enough information in 53% of the cases, and only in 22% of the cases do they recommend a book. With at least one review, there is not enough information in only 1% of the cases, and a book is recommended in 51% of the cases. As with topical relevance, the presence and number of tags has little impact on recommendation. Without tags there is not enough information for recommendation in 14% of the cases and 46% of the books are recommended. With at least 10 tags, there is not enough information for 12% of the books and 45% is recommended.

In summary, the presence of reviews is important for both topical relevance and recommendation, while the presence and quantity of tags plays almost no role. It seems they do not provide user with additional value on top of the professional metadata, even though tags are more effective for retrieval in terms of topical relevance and recommendation (see Table 4). As with the system-centered analysis, we split the data over fiction and non-fiction topics but observed no difference. Workers seem to use the same metadata for requests for fiction books and requests for non-fiction books.

Some workers provided comments to explain their judgements. The following comments for the topic on recent books about US submarines in the pacific illustrate how user-generated content affects judgements:

- **Not enough information**:
  "Couldn't do much with no information but a title.",
  "I have a title that states submarines but that isn't enough.",
- **Related**:
  "This is fiction, and I think the person was asking for reference."
  "I'd be worried about recommending this one. It was described by users as being rather subjective."
- **Relevant, not recommended**:
  "Again, no description on the book, but going by the title, this might also work for the requester.",
- **Relevant + recommended**:
  "The user-generated review was so enthusiastic, I would recommend it just based on that. A memoir is still fiction-y but could be useful."
  "Looks good, and from 2001. So far, this would be my main recommendation choice."

The first comments indicate how professional metadata is often not specific enough. A novel on submarines in the pacific is considered not relevant because it is fiction. One worker does not recommend a book about submarines because it is "rather subjective" while another recommends a memoir because the review is so enthusiastic. These comments reveal the complexity of relevance in book search.

Table 6: Impact of the presence of reviews on metadata preference

	Q2. Relevance			Q4. Recommendation		
	all	0 rev.	≥1 rev.	all	0 rev.	≥1 rev.
Prof.	0.29	0.51	0.20	0.16	0.33	0.10
Equal	0.27	0.40	0.21	0.18	0.22	0.17
UGC	0.43	0.06	0.57	0.53	0.08	0.71
Skip	0.02	0.02	0.02	0.12	0.37	0.03

We assume most workers have not read any or only a few of the books they judge. Without having read the book, professional metadata and tags are not sufficient to determine whether a book is relevant or to make a recommendation. When there are reviews, workers almost always have enough information to determine relevance and make a recommendation. However, workers seem to use only one review, which may be an efficiency aspect. They get paid a fixed amount per HIT, so they can earn more per time unit by reading fewer reviews per book. They have no incentive to read more reviews, because to them the recommendation has little value.

Do users consider UGC as more of the same content or as content of a different nature? Tags seem to provide information of a similar nature to professional metadata. Reviews on the other hand radically affect the judgement of workers. Although workers seem to use only one review, the presence of reviews makes it easy for workers to make a recommendation and also helps in determining the topical relevance of books.

6.3 Utility of Metadata Types

To determine the relevance of books, do users prefer professional metadata, or UGC, or are they equally happy with either? If they prefer UGC, is this because it provides more metadata than the curated metadata? Or because it provides a different kind of metadata? Tags are similar in nature to subject headings [25, 28], while ratings and reviews are more opinionated and evaluative.

The distribution of preferences for metadata types is given in Table 6. In column 2 we see the fraction of all answers for each type for topical relevance. The professional metadata is considered more useful to judge the topical relevance of books in 29% of the cases, equally useful to UGC in 27% of the cases and less useful in 43% of the cases. The UGC is on average more useful than the professional metadata. For recommendation (column 5), UGC is considered more useful in the majority of cases (53%), while in only 16% of the cases the professional metadata is considered more useful. For recommendation, the number of cases where the question is skipped is given is much higher (12%) than for topical relevance (2%), which is mainly when workers indicated the book description does not provide enough data to make a recommendation, in which case they were asked to skip Q4.

How is the preference for professional metadata or UGC related to presence of reviews? The relation between the presence of at least one review and the utility of metadata types for topical relevance is shown in Table 6, in columns 3 and 4. The difference between no reviews and at least one review is big. With no reviews, most workers find professional metadata more useful for topical relevance, but 40% of workers find the two types of metadata equally useful. Only 6% find UGC more useful. With at least one review, this completely changes. The majority of workers finds UGC more useful and only 20% find professional metadata more useful. We found that further reviews do no affect the distribution, which suggests again that workers only use one review, even when multiple reviews are available.

For recommendation (columns 6 and 7 in Table 6), we see a similar pattern in the relation between the number of reviews and the utility of metadata types. With no reviews, the utility of UGC is low, but for recommendation, the lack of reviews makes it harder to answer the question; in more than a third of the cases (37%), workers skipped the question. This is strongly related to the answer given to Q3 (*Would you recommend this book?*). In 88% of the cases where the question is skipped, workers indicated at Q3 that there was not enough information to make a recommendation. When there is not enough information for recommendation, the question which type of metadata is more useful is hard to answer sensibly. This gives further evidence of workers filling in the questions seriously. When there is at least one review, the number of skipped questions drops to 3% and for 71% of the cases workers found the UGC more useful. Not surprisingly, UGC is even more important for recommendation than for determining topical relevance.

7. CONCLUSIONS

In this paper we ventured into unknown territory by studying the domain of book search that has rich descriptions in terms of traditional metadata descriptions—structured fields written by professionals—now complemented by a wealth of user generated descriptions—uncontrolled tags and reviews from the public at large. We also focused on the actual types of requests and recommendations that users post in real life based on the social recommendations of the forums. Relevance in book search—as in many other scenarios—is a many-faceted concept. Searchers do not only care about topical relevance (sometimes not at all), but also about how interesting, well-written, recent, fun, educational or popular it is.

We expected the forum suggestions, based on the collective knowledge of those answering the request, to cover only a small sample of the potentially relevant books. If this were the case, systems would perform poorly when evaluated on these suggestions, due to large numbers of retrieved and potentially relevant but unjudged documents. High precision is hard to achieve for a system that did not contribute to the pool of judged documents, if the judged relevant documents are highly incomplete. A system could still get a high precision for a single topic by accident. However, over 211 topics, a high precision is improbable. Yet, a standard IR model using an index based on user-generated content scores high on MRR and nDCG@10, even with a small number of suggested books in a collection of millions of book records. Hence, we observe that the forum suggestions are complete enough to be used as evaluation. The system ranking over all 211 topics correlates strongly with that of a non-random subset of 24 topics. This approach to test collection building based on forum requests and suggestions models a realistic, modern search task, that seems robust against topic selection and avoids pooling bias.

Next, we wanted to know how social book search is related to standard tasks like known-item search, ad hoc search on topical relevance, and topical recommendation. The system rankings of official submissions on the forum suggestions have a low correlation with those based on topical relevance judgements. Experiment with our own indexes also indicate suggestion is different. Book titles and professional metadata are both effective for known-item search, book titles give decent recall on topical relevance tasks, but neither is effective for the forum suggestions. However, part of the poor performance on the MTURK judgements may be due to a pooling bias. In contrast, user-generated content is much more effective for all tasks, including book suggestion. The LT forum suggestions seem different in nature than known-item topics and the MTURK judgements on topical relevance and recommendation.

Standard language models seem to deal well with the skewed distribution of user-generated content across book descriptions. The low effectiveness of professional metadata may also be partly due to a lack of useful term frequency information within a book description. However, the short book titles perform much better on topical relevance than on forum suggestions, indicating this is mainly a problem for aspects of relevance other than topicality. Although we have not explored all possible ways to exploit professional metadata, the user-centred evaluation corroborates our finding that user-generated content is more effective than professional metadata and covers more than topical relevance.

Even though most online book search systems ignore user-generated content, our experiments show that this content can improve traditional ad hoc retrieval effectiveness and is essential for book suggestions.

In the final part of our investigation we looked at how MTURK workers valued professional and user-generated content. The amount of tags has little impact on how useful they are for workers, and may perform similar functions to professional metadata. Workers on MTURK find reviews more useful than professional metadata and user tags, both for topical relevance and recommendation. For recommendation it seems obvious that ratings and opinionated reviews are more useful than objective tags and subject headings. For topical relevance, it may be that reviews contain more detail to determine how a book bears on the information need behind a book request on the LT forums.

How is social book search related to traditional search tasks? Topical relevance is a necessary condition of book suggestion, but not a sufficient one. Not all topically relevant books are suggested or recommended, indicating that other (more subjective) aspects also play a role. These other aspects are better captured by user-generated content than by professional metadata: reviews are more useful for the book suggestions on the forums. In future work we will incorporate profiles and personal catalogue data from forum members which may help capturing the affective aspects of book search relevance. Our results highlight the relative importance of professional metadata and user-generated content, both for traditional known-item and ad hoc search as well as for book suggestions.

Acknowledgments

This research was supported by the Netherlands Organization for Scientific Research (NWO projects # 612.066.513, 639.072.601, and 640.005.001) and by the European Community's Seventh Framework Program (FP7 2007/2013, Grant Agreement 270404).

REFERENCES

[1] O. Alonso and R. A. Baeza-Yates. Design and Implementation of Relevance Assessments Using Crowdsourcing. In *ECIR 2011*, volume 6611 of *LNCS*, pages 153–164. Springer, 2011.

[2] M. J. Bates. Task Force Recommendation 2.3 Research and Design Review: Improving user access to library catalog and portal information. In *Library of Congress Bicentennial Conference on Bibliographic Control for the New Millennium*, 2003.

[3] T. Beckers, N. Fuhr, N. Pharo, R. Nordlie, and K. N. Fachry. Overview and Results of the INEX 2009 Interactive Track. In *ECDL*, volume 6273 of *LNCS*, pages 409–412. Springer, 2010.

[4] M. Buckland. Vocabulary as a Central Concept in Library and Information Science. In *Digital Libraries: Interdisciplinary Concepts, Challenges, and Opportunities. CoLIS3*, 1999.

[5] C. Buckley, D. Dimmick, I. Soboroff, and E. Voorhees. Bias and the limits of pooling for large collections. *Inf. Retr.*, 10(6):491–508, 2007.

[6] C. L. Clarke, M. Kolla, G. V. Cormack, O. Vechtomova, A. Ashkan, S. Büttcher, and I. MacKinnon. Novelty and diversity in information retrieval evaluation. In *SIGIR '08: Proceedings of the 31st annual international ACM SIGIR conference on Research and development in information retrieval*, pages 659–666, 2008. ACM.

[7] C. W. Cleverdon. The Cranfield tests on index language devices. *Aslib*, 19:173–192, 1967.

[8] S. A. Golder and B. A. Huberman. Usage patterns of collaborative tagging systems. *Journal of Information Science*, 32(2):198–208, 2006.

[9] C. Grady and M. Lease. Crowdsourcing document relevance assessment with mechanical turk. In *CSLDAMT '10*, pages 172–179, 2010.

[10] D. Hawking and N. Craswell. Very large scale retrieval and web search. In *TREC: Experiment and Evaluation in Information Retrieval*, chapter 9. MIT Press, 2005.

[11] G. Kazai. In Search of Quality in Crowdsourcing for Search Engine Evaluation. In *ECIR 2011*, volume 6611 of *LNCS*, pages 165–176. Springer, 2011.

[12] G. Kazai and N. Milic-Frayling. Effects of Social Approval Votes on Search Performance. *Information Technology: New Generations, Third International Conference on*, 0:1554–1559, 2009.

[13] G. Kazai, J. Kamps, M. Koolen, and N. Milic-Frayling. Crowdsourcing for Book Search Evaluation: Impact of HIT Design on Comparative System Ranking. In *SIGIR*. ACM Press, New York NY, 2011.

[14] F. W. Lancaster. *Vocabulary control for information retrieval*. Information Resources Press, Arlington VA, second edition, 1986.

[15] J. Le, A. Edmonds, V. Hester, and L. Biewald. Ensuring quality in crowdsourced search relevance evaluation: The effects of training question distribution. In *SIGIR 2010 Workshop on Crowdsourcing for Search Evaluation*, pages 21–26, 2010.

[16] C. Lu, P. Jung-ran, and X. Hu. User tags versus expert-assigned subject terms: A comparison of LibraryThing tags and Library of Congress Subject Headings. *Journal of Information Science*, 36(6): 763–779, 2010.

[17] A. Mathes. Folksonomies - Cooperative Classification and Communication Through Shared Metadata, December 2004.

[18] I. Ounis, C. Macdonald, M. de Rijke, G. Mishne, and I. Soboroff. Overview of the TREC 2006 Blog Track. In *TREC*, volume Special Publication 500-272. NIST, 2006.

[19] L. Page, S. Brin, R. Motwani, and T. Winograd. The PageRank Citation Ranking: Bringing Order to the Web. Technical report, Stanford Digital Library Technologies Project, 1998.

[20] I. Peters, L. Schumann, J. Terliesner, and W. G. Stock. Retrieval Effectiveness of Tagging Systems. In *Proceedings of the 74rd ASIS&T Annual Meeting*, volume 48, 2011.

[21] K. Reuter. Assessing aesthetic relevance: Children's book selection in a digital library. *JASIST*, 58(12):1745–1763, 2007.

[22] C. S. Ross. Finding without seeking: the information encounter in the context of reading for pleasure. *Information Processing & Management*, 35(6):783 – 799, 1999.

[23] E. Svenonius. Unanswered questions in the design of controlled vocabularies. *JASIS*, 37(5):331–340, 1986.

[24] E. M. Voorhees. The Philosophy of Information Retrieval Evaluation. In *CLEF '01*, pages 355–370, 2002. Springer-Verlag.

[25] J. Voss. Tagging, folksonomy & co - renaissance of manual indexing? *CoRR*, abs/cs/0701072, 2007.

[26] W. Weerkamp and M. de Rijke. Credibility improves topical blog post retrieval. In *Proceedings of ACL-08: HLT*, pages 923–931, June 2008. Association for Computational Linguistics.

[27] K. Yi. A semantic similarity approach to predicting Library of Congress Subject Headings for social tags. *JASIST*, 61(8): 1658–1672, 2010.

[28] K. Yi and L. M. Chan. Linking folksonomy to Library of Congress Subject Headings: an exploratory study. *Journal of Documentation*, 65(6):872–900, 2009.

[29] E. Yilmaz, J. A. Aslam, and S. Robertson. A new rank correlation coefficient for information retrieval. In *SIGIR*, pages 587–594. ACM, 2008.

Content-Based Crowd Retrieval on the Real-Time Web

Krishna Y. Kamath
Texas A&M University
College Station, TX 77843
kykamath@cs.tamu.edu

James Caverlee
Texas A&M University
College Station, TX 77843
caverlee@cse.tamu.edu

ABSTRACT

In this paper, we propose and evaluate a novel content-driven crowd discovery algorithm that can efficiently identify newly-formed communities of users from the real-time web. Short-lived crowds reflect the real-time interests of their constituents and provide a foundation for user-focused web monitoring. Three of the salient features of the algorithm are its: (i) prefix-tree based locality-sensitive hashing approach for discovering crowds from high-volume rapidly-evolving social media; (ii) efficient user profile updating for incorporating new user activities and fading older ones; and (iii) key dimension identification, so that crowd detection can be focused on the most active portions of the real-time web. Through extensive experimental study, we find significantly more efficient crowd discovery as compared to both a k-means clustering-based approach and a MapReduce-based implementation, while maintaining high-quality crowds as compared to an offline approach. Additionally, we find that expert crowds tend to be "stickier" and last longer in comparison to crowds of typical users.

Categories and Subject Descriptors

H.3.4 [**Information Storage and Retrieval**]: Systems and Software—*Information networks*

General Terms

Algorithms, Experimentation

Keywords

clustering, social media, community detection, real-time web

1. INTRODUCTION

The real-time web has grown at an astonishing rate in the past several years. As one example, Twitter has rapidly grown from handling 5,000 tweets per day in 2007 to 50 million tweets per day in 2010 to 140 million per tweets per day in 2011. During the recent run-up and immediate aftermath of President Obama's announcement about Osama Bin Laden, Twitter boasted a peak of 5,000 tweets per second (corresponding to 432 million tweets per day) and a sustained average rate of 3,000 tweets per second over several hours (corresponding to 259 million tweets per day).[1] At an order of magnitude higher, Facebook reported in 2009 that it was handling around 1 billion chat messages per day,[2] and there is widespread evidence of massive growth in web-based commenting systems (like on Reddit, Digg, and NYTimes) and other real-time "social awareness streams".

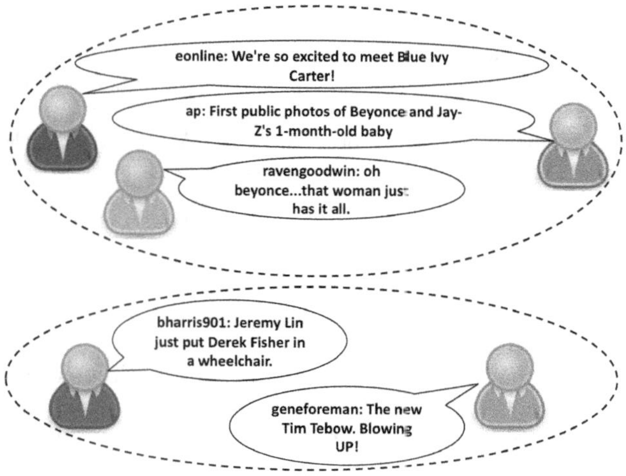

Figure 1: Examples of content based crowds.

While long-lived communities have been one of the key organizing principles of the Web, the real-time web supports the near instantaneous formation of ad-hoc communities linked by the real-time interests of their constituents. These "crowds" range from groups of loosely-connected Twitter users responding to a live presidential address, to users sharing pictures about a chemical fire at a nearby refinery, to flash mobs congregating at particular locations (and revealing this location via services like Foursquare), and so on. For example, Figure 1 shows example of two content based crowds, one discussing the public release of Jay-Z and Beyonce's baby pictures with 3 users (eonline, ap, ravengoodwin), and another crowd about NY Knicks vs LA Lakers basket ball game with 2 users (bharris901, geneforeman).

[1]http://blog.twitter.com/2011/03/numbers.html

[2]http://www.facebook.com/note.php?note_id=91351698919

CIKM'12, October 29–November 2, 2012, Maui, HI, USA.

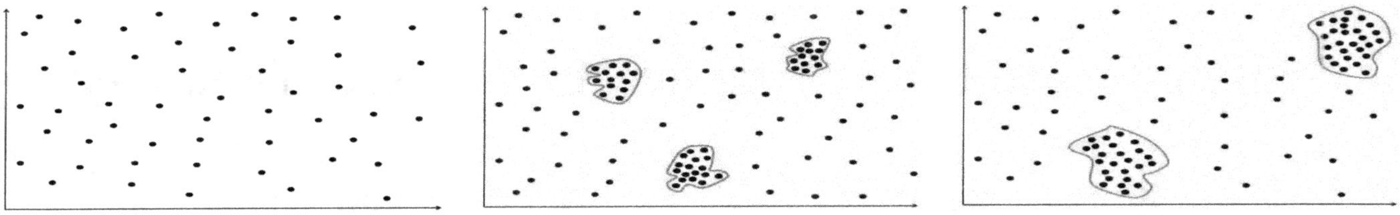

(a) t_n (b) t_{n+1} (c) t_{n+2}

Figure 2: Example of user vectors in 2-dimensional space showing the evolution of users during three time intervals. Crowds are shown using a red boundary.

In contrast to traditional long-lived communities, these crowds are dynamically formed and potentially short-lived, often with only implicit signals of their formation within the massive scale of the real-time web. While much research has focused on community mining from large-scale systems [10, 21, 25, 26], of event detection on the Web and in social media [7, 8, 17, 24], and topic detection and tracking over streaming news items [3, 4, 12], there is a great opportunity to explore the near real-time extraction of crowds in the critical moments of their initial formation. Efficiently identifying these crowds of related users as they form and as they evolve can benefit many domains including epidemiological and disease control experts searching for evidence of new outbreaks and the reaction of the public to new vaccines, municipalities interested in responding to local events (like the recent Vancouver riots), finance experts monitoring stock price jumps or crashes, political scientists tracking chatter about presidential debates, as well as average users interested in local crowds (what restaurants are hot?) and crowds associated with particular topics (e.g., sports, movies).

In this paper we formalize the problem of crowd discovery over rapidly evolving social media and provide solutions for efficiently identifying crowds. Although we focus on text-based social media streams popularized by Twitter and related services, the discussion and techniques are designed for generic application to other temporally ordered social media resources. Concretely, this paper makes the following contributions:

- We present an efficient algorithm for identifying clusters of related users (*crowds*) from the real-time web using a prefix-tree based locality hashing approach.
- We describe an efficient method for updating user profiles in rapidly evolving social media as users post new messages.
- We show how to focus crowd detection via key dimension identification, so that crowd detection can be focused on the most active portions of the real-time web and so resources are not wasted.
- We evaluate the performance of the proposed crowd discovery algorithm over two Twitter datasets and we find the proposed approach is significantly faster than alternative approaches while maintaining high crowd quality.

2. RELATED WORK

In addition to the works cited in the introduction, there have been many efforts aimed at detecting cluster structure in text-based collections [19, 9, 5]. But, these approaches, however, are typically not designed for high-volume incrementally updated domains as on the real-time web. Alternatively, there is a large body of stream-oriented clustering work for finding correlations in streaming data. For example, StatStream [28] clusters evolving time series data using the Discrete Fourier Transform. Both [3] and [11] explore two-stage approaches for finding clusters in low dimensional data (unlike the case of text clustering, which typically is very high-dimensional due to the number of tokens observed). Clustering over text streams has been studied in [2, 18, 14]. These efforts have focused on the clustering of independent text elements (e.g., new messages), whereas our focus is on finding groups of related users by their sequences of related posts to the real-time web.

The solution approach in this paper relies on locality-sensitive hashing (LSH) for finding nearest-neighbors as a primitive for crowd detection. Nearest-neighbor and approximate nearest-neighbor search in a high-dimensional vector space is a difficult problem that Indyk and Motwani [15, 13] approach through the use of a family of randomized hash functions that generate similar vector signatures if the vectors are closer to each other in the high-dimensional space. In [6], Charikar constructed the LSH function for cosine similarity, which supports fast similarity between two high-dimensional vectors by reducing them to bit-arrays of much smaller dimensions. This result has been used in several problems, including efficient noun clustering [23, 20, 22]. In previous work, we studied crowd detection based on user communication, without regard for the content of the messages as we do here [16].

3. CROWD DISCOVERY: OVERVIEW AND SOLUTION APPROACH

Let $U = \{u_1, u_2, \ldots, u_i \ldots\}$ be a (potentially) unbounded set of users posting messages to a real-time web stream such as Twitter or Facebook. Each user may contribute an arbitrary number of messages, where the messages are ordered in a non-decreasing fashion using the time-stamp values of the messages. We say that a crowd $C = \{u_i, u_2 \ldots u_i\}$, at a given time, is defined as a subset of users that are close to each other at that time, where closeness is measured using a similarity function $sim(u_i, u_j)$. For example Figure 2, shows a simple scenario where users are mapped into a 2-dimensional space (say, by using TF-IDF weights of the words in the messages). In the initial figure at time t_n, users are sparsely distributed in the space and there are no clear crowds. As users generate more messages, we see in the following two intervals the formation of several tight clusters of users ("crowds"). Intuitively, these crowds correspond to collections of users who are posting messages about similar topics (e.g., the Super Bowl on one day and Presidential elections the next day).

Given a user similarity measure $sim(\vec{u_i}, \vec{u_k})$ and a user similarity threshold ϵ, we formulate crowd detection as an operation that preserves the following two properties:

Property 1: Every user in a crowd has at least one other user in the same crowd, such that the similarity between them is at least ϵ. That is, $\forall\ u_i \in C\ \ \exists\ u_k : u_k \in C, u_i \neq u_k\ and\ sim(\vec{u_i}, \vec{u_k}) \geq \epsilon$

Property 2: Every user in a crowd has no other user outside the crowd, such that the similarity between them is at least ϵ. $\forall\ u_i \in C\ \neg\exists\ u_k : u_k \in S \setminus C\ and\ sim(\vec{u_i}, \vec{u_k}) \geq \epsilon$

These two properties ensure that (i) all users within a crowd are more similar to users within the crowd than outside of the crowd; and that (ii) there does not exist any user outside of a crowd who is similar to users within a crowd.

By viewing crowd detection in this way, we can avoid memory-intensive approaches that require maintaining the overall cluster structure (which may be unreasonable for high-volume text); instead, we can formulate the crowd detection problem using nearest-neighbor search as a primitive, as illustrated in Algorithm 1. That is, for every new message posted to the real-time web, we determine the user nearest to the user posting the new message. If the similarity between the user posting the new message and the nearest user is at least ϵ, we add the user to the crowd to which this nearest user belongs, if he is not already in it. If the similarity does not exceed ϵ, we create a new crowd for the given user. K_t is the set of all current crowds at time t. While such an approach may allow long chains of users (where the first user in a crowd is quite distant from the last user), it has the compelling advantage of efficiency.

Algorithm 1 Crowd Discovery

```
for (u, d, t) ∈ I do
    Determine the user nearest to u, u_n, and the crowd
    u_n belongs to C_n.
    if sim(u, u_n) ≥ ε then
        if u is not in crowd C_n then
            Add u to C_n
        end if
    else
        Create a new crowd C with a single user u and
        add it to K_t.
    end if
end for
```

Towards efficiently discovering crowds from the real-time web, we make note of the following three challenges:

- **Efficient User Profile Updating**: Compared to traditional document clustering, in which documents themselves are static and the goal is to find clusters of related documents, crowd discovery seeks to find clusters of similar users in which users are constantly changing (by posting new messages, changing areas of interest, and so on). Hence, the first challenge is to develop an appropriate representation for users that reflects their current interests accurately and can be easily updated every time they generate a new message.

- **Efficient Crowd Assignment**: The second challenge is to determine an efficient method to determine nearest neighbor for crowd assignment. To find nearest neighbors there are several possible methods (including linear search) and several space partitioning data structures (e.g., k-d trees). However, due to the scale of real-time web updates, such methods may incur a high overhead. Hence, we propose a prefix-tree based locality sensitive hashing method that supports $O(1)$ lookup of a user's nearest neighbor, leading to efficient crowd assignment.

- **Identifying Key Dimensions**: Even with a reasonable method for updating user profiles and assigning users to crowds, the real-time web is constantly growing due to the insertion of new phrases, hashtags, and other artifacts of user-contributed content. Figure 3 shows the number of unique tokens encountered over two 10-day Twitter samples (described more fully in Section 4.1), leading to a linear growth in the dimensions for representing users. Hence, the third challenge is to develop a method to identify important dimensions, so that crowd detection can be focused on the most active portions of the real-time web and so resources are not wasted.

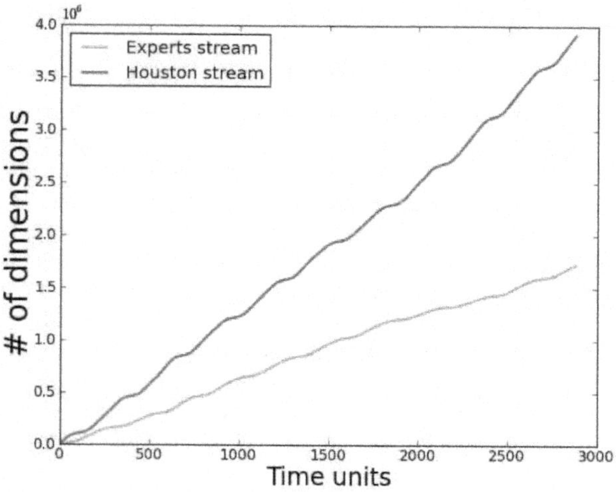

Figure 3: Linear growth of dimensions

In the following, we approach each of these three challenges in turn, before turning to an experimental evaluation.

3.1 Efficient User Profile Updating

In this section, we first develop a vector representation for users that decays temporally, so that users are assigned to crowds that reflect their current interests and then we show

how to efficiently update these user profiles as new messages are generated.

3.1.1 Vector Representation with Fading Memories

Adopting a vector space model for users, let $\vec{u_i}$ be the vector representation for user u_i, where the elements of the vector correspond to tokens parsed from u_i's messages. There are many domain-dependent choices for parsing messages, including language-dependent parsers, entity extraction, stemming, and so forth; for simplicity, we adopt a simple unigram parser that treats all strings separated by whitespace as valid tokens. Since the number of unique tokens corresponding to dimensions are not known in advance, we represent each user profile vector using an infinite co-ordinate space F^∞ [1]. Under this model, a user u_i at time t is represented as:

$$\vec{u_i}^t = (V_{i1}^t, V_{i2}^t, \ldots, V_{im}^t, \ldots)$$

where the User Vector Dimension (UVD) value V_{im}^t, is the value for u_i in the mth dimension at time t. Let x_{im}^t be the number of times u_i generates m at time t, and $X_{im}^{t_l} = \{x_{im}^1, x_{im}^2 \ldots x_{im}^{t_l}\}$ be the set all occurrences of m generated by u_i until t_l, then $V_{im}^{t_l}$ is defined as:

$$V_{im}^{t_l} = \sum_{x_{im}^t \in X_{im}^{t_l}} \mathcal{F}(x_{im}, t, t_l) = \sum_{x_{im}^t \in X_{im}^{t_l}} x_{im}^t \quad (1)$$

where $\mathcal{F}$ is a function of x_{im}, t and t_l and is called the UVD function.

In this way, a user is represented as the sum of his entire message history. However, since crowds are designed to reflect users with a similar current interest, such an approach may favor crowds of users who are similar in the long-term. For example, we may identify crowds of students, of entertainers, and of politicians, but miss cross-cutting crowds that are drawn together by their current situation (e.g., emergency-oriented crowds reacting to a local earthquake). An alternate approach is to construct user profile vectors using the latest messages only. While such an approach has the advantage of being memory-less (and so, old messages may be dropped with no penalty), grouping users based only on their most recent messages may result in high crowd fluctuation since crowd assignments may vary with each new message.

To balance these two extremes, we propose to adopt a representation that fades user vectors such that recently used dimensions have higher values and older dimensions have lower values. To decay user vectors, we design another UVD function $\mathcal{D}$, which decreases the score of inactive dimensions and increases the score of active dimensions in user vectors. The function $\mathcal{D}$, re-calculates scores for $x_{im}^{t_o}$ at time t_n, as shown:

$$\mathcal{D}(x_{im}, t_o, t_n) = \lambda_u^{t_n - t_o} x_{im}^{t_o} \quad (2)$$

where $\lambda_u \in [0,1]$ is a constant know as the *user dimension score decay rate.* Hence, we can re-write $V_{im}^{t_l}$ as:

$$V_{im}^{t_l} = \sum_{x_{im}^t \in X_{im}^{t_l}} \mathcal{D}(x_{im}, t, t_l) = \sum_{x_{im}^t \in X_{im}^{t_l}} \lambda_u^{t_l - t} x_{im}^t \quad (3)$$

Note that when $\lambda_u = 1$, the value of $V_{im}^{t_l}$ is same as that calculated using $\mathcal{F}$ as the UVD function.

3.1.2 Efficient Updates

To calculate $V_{im}^{t_l}$ using (3), we have to maintain the entire set $X_{im}^{t_l}$. In the context of the real-time web, this can be inefficient since it requires maintaining $X_{im}^{t_l}$ for all users and all dimensions and since the calculation of $V_{im}^{t_l}$ would be $O(|X_{im}^{t_l}|)$. To solve this problem we prove a proposition that will help us calculate the value of $V_{im}^{t_l}$ efficiently in $O(1)$ time without requiring us to maintain the set $X_{im}^{t_l}$.

PROPOSITION 3.1. *If t_{n-k} is the latest time when u_i generated a message with dimension m until t_n, then the value of the dimension at time t_n, is given by:*

$$V_{im}^{t_n} = \lambda_u^{(t_n - t_{n-k})} V_{im}^{t_{n-k}} + x_{im}^{t_n}$$

where, $V_{im}^{t_{n-k}}$ and $V_{im}^{t_n}$ are the values of dimension m for u_i at time t_{n-k} and t_n respectively.

PROOF. Let $X_{im}^{t_{n-k}}$ be the set all occurrences of dimension m in the messages generated by u_i up to time t_{n-k}. Then, using (3) we get:

$$V_{im}^{t_{n-k}} = \sum_{x_{im}^t \in X_{im}^{t_{n-k}}} \lambda_u^{t_{n-k} - t} x_{im}^t \quad (4)$$

Using (2), $\forall x_{im}^t \in X_{im}^{t_{n-k}}$ we can write:

$$\mathcal{D}(x_{im}, t, t_n) = \lambda_u^{t_n - t} x_{im}^t = \lambda_u^{(t_n - t_{n-k}) + (t_{n-k} - t)} x_{im}^t \quad (5)$$

$$\mathcal{D}(x_{im}, t, t_n) = \lambda_u^{(t_n - t_{n-k})} \lambda_u^{(t_{n-k} - t)} x_{im}^t \quad (6)$$

where t is the time-stamp of every occurrence of m in messages generated by u_i.

Using (3) again, we write,

$$\begin{aligned} V_{im}^{t_n} &= \sum_{x_{im}^t \in X_{im}^{t_n}} \mathcal{D}(x_{im}, t, t_n) \\ &= \sum_{x_{im}^t \in X_{im}^{t_{n-k}}} \mathcal{D}(x_{im}, t, t_n) + \sum_{n'=n-k+1}^{n} \mathcal{D}(x_{im}, t_{n'}, t_n) \end{aligned}$$

Using (4) and (6) we can now write

$$V_{im}^{t_n} = \lambda_u^{(t_n - t_{n-k})} V_{im}^{t_{n-k}} + \sum_{n'=n-k+1}^{n} \mathcal{D}(x_{im}, t_{n'}, t_n)$$

Since u_i did not generate any messages with dimension m after t_{n-k} until t_n, $\forall\, n' \in [n-k+1 \,..\, n-1]$, we have:

$$\mathcal{D}(x_{im}, t_{n'}, t_n) = \lambda_u^{t_n - t_{n'}} x_{im}^{t_{n'}} = \lambda_u^{t_n - t_{n'}}.0 = 0$$

Hence,

$$V_{im}^{t_n} = \lambda_u^{(t_n - t_{n-k})} V_{im}^{t_{n-k}} + \mathcal{D}(x_{im}, t_n, t_n)$$

$$V_{im}^{t_n} = \lambda_u^{(t_n - t_{n-k})} V_{im}^{t_{n-k}} + x_{im}^{t_n}$$

Note that, by definition $x_{im}^{t_n} \neq 0$ if u_i generates a message with m, else it is 0. This proves the proposition. □

In brief, we have described an approach to represent users in high-dimensional vector space that reflects their current interests and we have shown how to update this user profile efficiently upon the arrival of each new user message.

3.2 Efficient Crowd Assignment

Given the user profile developed in the previous section, we now turn to the challenge of assigning users to crowds as outlined in Algorithm 1. This is the core step in crowd detection and is, in essence, a nearest-neighbor problem. To find nearest neighbors there are several possible methods. The simplest algorithm to determine nearest neighbor is through linear $O(n)$ search, which is not efficient due to the large number of users on the real-time web. Alternatively, we can use efficient space-partitioning methods like k-d trees, which have a complexity of $O(\log n)$. Here, we propose a specialized variation of the randomized approach to discover nearest neighbors by using locality sensitive hashing (LSH). In this specialized version, we use an additional prefix tree data structure to support $O(1)$ lookup of a user's nearest neighbor, at a cost of requiring $O(n)$ to look up the user's next nearest neighbor. But by constructing crowd detection as a requiring only user's single nearest neighbor (recall the two properties at the beginning of this section), we can support efficient crowd detection over the real-time web.

3.2.1 Similarity using Locality-Sensitive Hashing

We first describe a function to calculate the similarity between two vectors using LSH and then describe how we can use this similarity function to determine nearest neighbors efficiently using a prefix tree. Since users are represented as vectors, we can use a metric like cosine similarity to determine the nearest neighbor. But, as described in [15], determining nearest neighbors using cosine similarity is inefficient in high dimensions. Hence, we calculate the approximate cosine distance between two vectors using the approach proposed by Charikar [6].

In [6], the author proposed using LSH functions generated using random hyperplanes to calculate approximate cosine distance. Consider a set of vectors in the collection R^m. Let $\vec{r}$ be a m-dimensional random vector, such that each dimension in it is drawn from a 1-dimensional gaussian distribution with mean 0 and variance 1. Then the hashing function $h_{\vec{r}}$ corresponding to $\vec{r}$ is:

$$h_{\vec{r}}(\vec{v}) = \begin{cases} 1 & \text{if } \vec{r}.\vec{v} \geq 0 \\ 0 & \text{Otherwise} \end{cases}$$

Now, if we have a set $R = \{\vec{r_1}, \vec{r_2} \dots r_{|\vec{R}|}\}$ of such m-dimensional random vectors, then for a vector $\vec{v}$, we can generate its signature $\bar{v} = (h_{\vec{r_1}}(\vec{v}), h_{\vec{r_2}}(\vec{v}), \dots h_{r_{|\vec{R}|}}(\vec{v}))$. Given two user vectors $\vec{u_i}$ and $\vec{u_j}$, the approximate cosine similarity between them is given as:

$$sim(\vec{u_i}, \vec{u_j}) = cos(\theta(\vec{u_i}, \vec{u_j})) = cos((1 - Pr[\bar{u}_i = \bar{u}_j])\ \pi) \tag{7}$$

So, the closer the signatures, the greater is the cosine similarity, and the more dissimilar the signatures, the lesser is their cosine similarity. This equation measures approximate cosine distance, and accuracy of this approximation can be improved by using a longer signature, i.e, a larger R.

3.2.2 Nearest Neighbor using Prefix Tree

We now describe the procedure to find the nearest user u_n for a user u, from whom we can determine the nearest crowd C_n. We determine u_n using a set of permutation functions $P = \{\pi_1, \pi_2, \dots, \pi_{|P|}\}$, where each permutation function is of the form:

$$\pi(x) = (ax + b) mod\ p$$

where, p is a prime number and a, b are chosen randomly.

Let $\mathcal{P}$ be a collection of $|P|$ prefix trees, where every prefix tree corresponds to a permutation function $\pi \in P$. Now, to add a vector $\vec{v}$ to $\mathcal{P}$, first its signature $\bar{v}$ is determined, and then the signature is inserted into every prefix tree in $\mathcal{P}$ after permuting it using the corresponding permutation function. So for a given vector, $|P|$ permutations of its signature are stored in $\mathcal{P}$. Every time we observe a new user vector it is added to $\mathcal{P}$. Similarly, every time we modify a user vector, we remove its old signature from all the prefix trees in $\mathcal{P}$ and add the new one.

To determine the crowd nearest to $\vec{u}$ in $\mathcal{P}$, we first calculate its signature $\bar{u}$. Then for every prefix tree in $\mathcal{P}$, we permute this signature using the corresponding permutation function and find the nearest signature in the prefix tree, by iterating through the tree one level at a time starting from the root. After doing this step we end up with $|P|$ signatures, of which the crowd corresponding to the signature with smallest hamming distance is picked as the nearest neighbor of $\vec{u}$. As a result, we see that using a prefix tree in combination with LSH, we can design an efficient algorithm to assign users to crowds.

3.3 Identifying Key Dimensions

The final challenge is a consideration of the purpose of the crowd monitoring application in the selection of the key dimensions for representing user vectors. For example, if the crowd detection system is intended for topic-focused crowd detection (e.g., identify all "earthquake" related crowds, find all crowds related to "politics"), then the user vectors could be weighted toward these key dimensions (e.g., as in a scheme for weighting the dimensions corresponding to the tokens "obama", "debate", "republican" as more important dimensions than non-politics dimensions). Potential solutions include pre-seeding the crowd detection system with expert-labeled keywords or in identifying high value terms by their *inverse document frequency (IDF)*, which weights key terms by their relative rarity across all documents.

In this paper, we propose to select as key dimensions those that reflect the general consensus of the real-time web. That is, we seek to identify tokens that are globally popular at a particular time for biasing the crowd detection toward these tokens. In this way, crowds are defined both by users who have posted similar messages recently (as described in the previous section) and by reflecting topics of great importance to the overall system.

Concretely, our goal is to select from all dimensions the most m significant dimensions. As the real-time web evolves the list of top-m dimensions can then be updated frequently to remove old dimensions and add new ones. Hence, we require a metric to score the dimensions observed so far. To score the dimensions observed in the stream, we use an approach similar to the one used in scoring dimension score for a user vector in Section 3.1.

Let y_d^t be the number of times a dimension d appeared in the stream at time t. Then the score for $y_d^{t_o}$ at time t_n,

Algorithm 2 Crowd Discovery

Create R: Create the set $R = \{\vec{r_1}, \vec{r_1} \ldots \vec{r_{|R|}}\}$ of random Gaussian vectors such that $|R| << m$.

Initialize $\mathcal{P}$: Create the set of permutation functions $P = \{\pi_1, \pi_2, \ldots, \pi_{|P|}\}$, where each permutation function is defined using a prime number p and values a, b chosen randomly. Initialize $\mathcal{P}$ as a collection of $|P|$ prefix trees and assign a unique permutation function from P to every prefix tree in $\mathcal{P}$.

for $(u, d, t) \in I$ **do**

    Update $\vec{u}$: Update the user vector $\vec{u}$ using (d, t) as described in Section 3.1. Generate new signature for $\vec{u}$ and add or replace it in $\mathcal{P}$.

    Generate $\bar{u}$: Generate the $|R|$-bit signature for $\vec{u}$, $\bar{u}$ using R.

    Step 1: Determine u_n **and** C_n: Get the user nearest to u, u_n and the crowd u_n belongs to $C_n \in K_t$.

    if $sim(\vec{u}, \vec{u_n}) \geq \epsilon$ **then**

        if u is not in crowd C_n **then**

            Step 2: Add u **to** C_n: Add u to crowd C_n.

        end if

    else

        Step 3: Create C: Create a new crowd C with a single user u and add it to K_t.

    end if

end for

$t_n \geq t_o$, is given by a function $\mathcal{E}$, defined as:

$$\mathcal{E}(y_d, t_o, t_n) = \lambda_d^{t_n - t_o} y_d^{t_o} \tag{8}$$

where $\lambda_d \in [0, 1]$ is a constant know as the *dimension score decay rate.*

Since a dimension can be observed several times in a stream, the score for a dimension d at time t, W_d^t, is calculated as shown in Proposition 3.2

PROPOSITION 3.2. *If t_{n-k} is the latest time when dimension d was observed on the stream until t_n, then the dimension score for the dimension at time t_n, is given by:*

$$W_d^{t_n} = \lambda_d^{(t_n - t_{n-k})} W_d^{t_{n-k}} + y_d^{t_n}$$

where, $W_d^{t_{n-k}}$ and $W_d^{t_n}$ are the dimension scores at time t_{n-k} and t_n respectively.

PROOF. The proof for this is similar to the proof of Proposition 3.1. □

Hence, we can identify dimensions that reflect the consensus of the current activity of the real-time web, so that crowd detection can be focused on the most active portions of the real-time web and so resources are not wasted.

3.4 Putting it All Together

Taken together, the high-level crowd discovery algorithm described in Algorithm 1 and the three methods developed – efficient user profile updating, efficient crowd assignment, and identifying key dimensions – give us the crowd discovery algorithm in Algorithm 2.

4. EXPERIMENTS

In this section, we report a series of experiments to study crowd discovery. We evaluate the running time performance of the proposed crowd discovery algorithm with other algorithms for crowd discovery. We define metrics to measure quality of crowds discovered and using these metrics we evaluate the quality of crowds discovered by several crowd discovery algorithms. We study the factors impacting the performance of the proposed algorithm, and finally we analyze the properties of crowds discovered over two Twitter datasets.

4.1 Dataset

To simulate a Twitter stream, we selected a set of Twitter users and crawled their tweets using Twitter API. The users in this set are labeled using 4 classes – technology, entertainment, politics and sports. To collect this labeled dataset we used the snowball sampling approach. This approach is as follows:

- First, for every class we selected a set of 5 Twitter users, called seed users, that belong to this class and 5 key words that describe the class. For example, for the class sports, a seed user was "espn" and a keyword was "sports".
- We then used Twitter API to select all Twitter lists that contain a seed user, such that the list's name contains a class specific key word. For example if "sports_news" and "news" are Twitter lists that contain "espn", then we select "sports_news" but not "news", since the former has the keyword "sports" in its name.
- We then extracted a set of new users from the lists selected in previous step and crawled their lists like before.

Following these steps resulted in a "snowball" or chain of crawling actions, which we stopped once we observed sufficient users. At the end of this crawl, we were left with a set of users, lists they belong to, with lists labeled with the class they belong to. Using this information, for each domain we selected around 1,200 top users and used their tweets to simulate a labelled Twitter stream, resulting in about 1.6 million tweets for 30 days. A similar approach for sampling class specific Twitter data is described in [27]. In addition to this dataset (which we shall call the Experts dataset), we collected a location-based dataset of users tweeting from the Houston region who were selected through random sampling. A 30-day sampling of this stream had about about 15 million tweets from about 107 thousand users. We use the Experts dataset for all of our experiments, except for the experiments in Section 4.7.

4.2 Setup

We compare the crowd discovery algorithm (*CDA*) proposed in this paper with four alternatives: k-means clustering (*k-means*), a Map-Reduce implementation of k-means clustering (*MR k-means*), a deterministic batched version of the CDA approach (*Iterative-CDA*) – in which we iterate through all the pairs of user vectors to find the best crowds possible, and a Map-Reduce implementation of Iterative-CDA (*MR-CDA*).

For user vector processing, we set the following parameters: number of dimensions $m = 199,999$, user dimension score decay rate $\lambda_u = 0.75$ and dimension score decay rate $\lambda_d = 0.75$. For efficeint crowd assignment, we set signature length $|R| = 23$, number of permutation functions $|P| = 13$ and $\epsilon = 0.005$.

In initial experiments, we varied the choice of k for k-means, finding in many cases that k-means identified many singleton crowds. For the experiments reported here, we set the number of clusters as $k = 0.95\times$number of items to cluster.

4.3 Running Time Analysis

To evaluate the running time performance of the proposed approach, we perform two experiments: (i) we use tweet sets of varying sizes as input to all the algorithms and determine the time taken by them to discover crowds; (ii) we measure the tweet processing rate of the algorithms. For these experiments we use a 30 day sample of Experts stream.

Running Time with Clustering Algorithms: The plot in Figure 4(a), shows the running times for the two k-means clustering algorithms and CDA to discover crowds on data collection of varying sizes. The running times graph is a log-log graph, hence there are orders of magnitude difference between the running times of the algorithms. We see that the time required to discover crowds using the proposed algorithm is significantly lesser than that required by the clustering algorithms. As the size of the message collection increases, both the clustering algorithms become slower. This behavior is expected in case of iterative k-means, because of the extra iterations required by the algorithm, but was not expected in the Map-Reduce version. Generally, the Map-Reduced running time increases at a much slower rate, but is still lesser than that of the iterative version. We believe the worsening performance is because of the large value of k. Larger k results is passing of greater number of centroids to a map job which slows down the algorithm. Hence, either of these algorithms are not efficient to discover crowds.

Running Time with CDA Algorithms: We now run similar experiments with the other crowd discovery algorithms. As in the case of the clustering algorithms, we see that CDA, in Figure 4(b), performs much better than the batched CDA algorithms. The Iterative-CDA performs the worst while the MR-CDA performs better after about 10^4 messages. The bad performance of MR-CDA on initial message sets can be attributed the time spent by the MR cluster in setting up the job and passing messages between various workers.

Message Processing Rate with CDA Algorithms: To compare the rate at which the algorithms process messages as they arrive, we note the number of messages that the algorithms have processed at equally spaced time intervals. This comparison is shown in Figure 4(c). As expected, we observe that the number of messages processed by the proposed algorithm is more than that for the other CDA algorithms. This result supports the result we observed with running time Figure 4(b). Similar results were observed for k-means clustering as well but are omitted due to the space constraint.

4.4 Crowds Quality Analysis

We now evaluate the quality of crowds discovered using the proposed crowd discovery approach. We know the class to which users in our Twitter stream belong, hence, to evaluate crowd quality we can compare the crowds discovered to this "ground truth". While we do not expect all users belonging to a particular class (e.g., "sports") to form a single large crowd, we do expect that crowds that form will tend to be composed of users belonging to these classes. We use the same 30 day sample of the stream that we used in Section 4.3. Like before, the experiments are run with the same value for parameter m. We next describe evaluation metrics that we use to measure quality of crowds and then present performance of CDA against k-means clustering algorithms and deterministic CDAs.

Quality metrics: Consider the set of crowds $K = \{C_1, C_2, \ldots, C_n\}$ for users in set U and a set of classes $\Omega = \{\omega_1, \omega_2, \ldots, \omega_w\}$ to which users in U belong. To measure the quality of crowds generated using crowd discovery algorithms we use the following metrics.

Purity: To compute purity, we assign crowd to the domain which is most frequent in it, and then the accuracy of this assignment is measured by calculating the ratio of correctly assigned users.

$$purity(K, \Omega) = \frac{1}{|U|} \sum_{n} \max_{w} |C_i \cap \omega_j|$$

NMI: Purity gives a good understanding of quality. But, it is susceptible because high purity can be achieved when there are large number of crowds, which we expect in crowd discovery problem. Hence, to deal with this issue, we use a secondary information theory based quality metric called Normalized Mutual Information (NMI). It is defined as:

$$NMI(K, \Omega) = \frac{I(K, \Omega)}{[H(K), H(\Omega)]/2}$$

$$I(K, \Omega) = \sum_{n} \sum_{w} \frac{|C_n \cap \omega_w|}{|U|} \log \frac{|U||C_n \cap \omega_w|}{|C_n||\omega_w|}$$

$$H(K) = -\sum_{n} \frac{|C_n|}{|U|} \log \frac{|C_n|}{|U|}$$

where, $I(K, \Omega)$ is mutual information and H entropy.

Comparison with Clustering Algorithms: The comparison between quality of crowds discovered using the Iterative k-means and that discovered using CDA is shown Figure 5(a). We see that despite the significant improvements in running time, the crowds discovered by the CDA are still of high quality. We also notice, for all the metrics, the quality of crowds generated using CDA is better than the quality of crowds generated using a clustering algorithm. The relatively poor performance of the clustering algorithm can be attributed to the difficulties in estimating the number of clusters k.

Comparison with CDA Algorithms: The comparison between quality of crowds discovered using the Iterative-CDA and that discovered using CDA is shown in Figure 5(a). We see that crowds discovered by Iterative-CDA are always better than that discovered using CDA. The lower values for

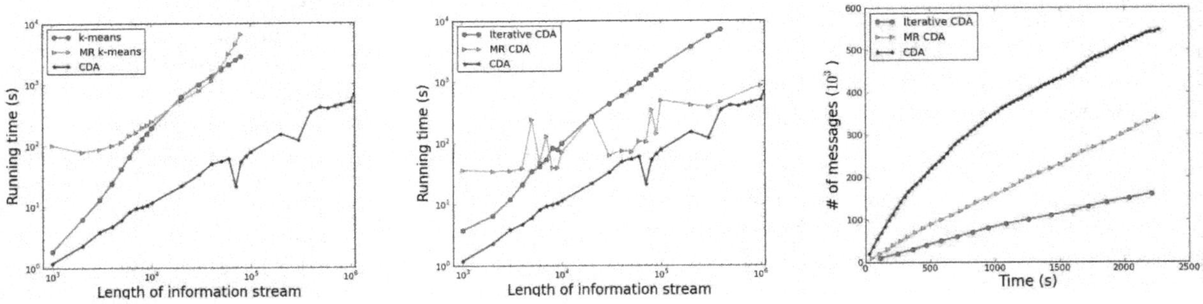

(a) Comparison with k-means (b) Comparison with CDA (c) Message processing rate comparison of CDAs

Figure 4: Comparing the efficiency of crowd discovery (CDA) versus alternatives

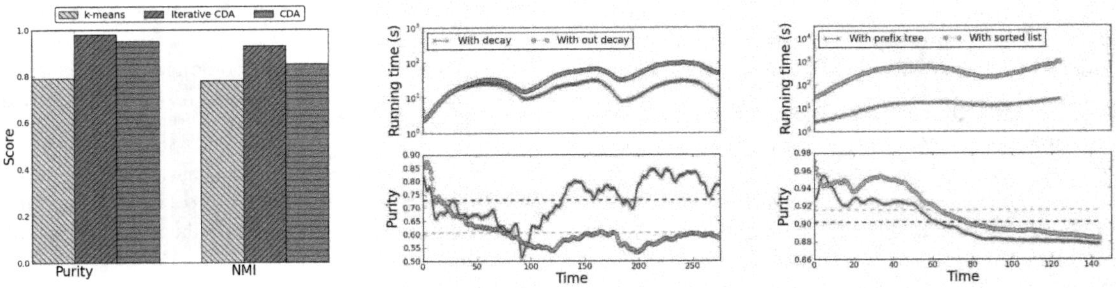

(a) Quality of crowd discovery (b) User vector representation (c) Crowd assig. with prefix trees.

Figure 5: Crowd algorithm analysis

these metrics is expected in case of CDA, as it is a randomized and an approximate algorithm whereas Iterative-CDA is an deterministic algorithm.

4.5 Impact of User Vector Representation

In Section 3.1, we described the method to exponentially decay user vectors to help us discover temporally relevant crowds. We evaluate the effectiveness of this approach by analyzing the performance of CDA when the user vectors are exponentially decayed and when they are not. To evaluate the performance of the algorithm without decay, we set $\lambda_u = 1.0$. The difference in quality of the crowds generated by the algorithm using these two approaches is shown in Figure 5(b).

The top plot of Figure 5(b), shows the running time of the algorithms for this experiment. We observe that, thought the running times for the algorithms is almost the same initially, the difference between them increases with time. This is because, as time increases, the algorithm that decays user vector and uses techniques to score dimensions, has the ability to remove dimensions when they become stale. This feature is not possible when the algorithm is run without decay.

As shown in the bottom plot of Figure 5(b), the quality of crowds discovered using exponential decay is much better than the crowds discovered without decay. When user vectors are not decayed, old dimensions are not removed from it, resulting in crowds being discovered which contain users from different domains. This results in lower quality crowds.

4.6 Impact of Prefix Trees

We next analyze the impact of using prefix trees on efficient crowd assignment. An alternative approach described in [23] suggests representing $\mathcal{P}$ as a collection of sorted lists of signatures rather than prefix trees. Such a structure is robust in the sense that signatures are sorted and hence nearest neighbor can be found faster than linear search, but has the downside that determining the nearest neighbor and adding a new vector takes $O(\log n)$ time, considering $|P|$ is constant. To characterize the impact of the prefix-tree based locality-sensitive hashing approach, we run CDA both with prefix trees and with sorted lists. The results are shown in Figure 5(c).

The top plot shows the running time and the bottom plot shows the quality of crowds discovered. We see that by using prefix trees, we can discover crowds at speeds several times the speed using sorted lists. As mentioned before, the improved speed efficiency is because of the constant time required to retrieve crowds in case of prefix tree instead of $O(\log n)$ as in case of sorted lists.

The quality of crowds generated varies initially when the number of crowds in the prefix tree is small because of randomization involved in determining the nearest neighbor. This variance is overcome as the number of crowds in the prefix tree increases and the mean quality of crowds discovered remains almost the same. After sometime, once we have observed sufficient crowds, we observe that the crowds quality is almost same while using both prefix tree and sorted lists.

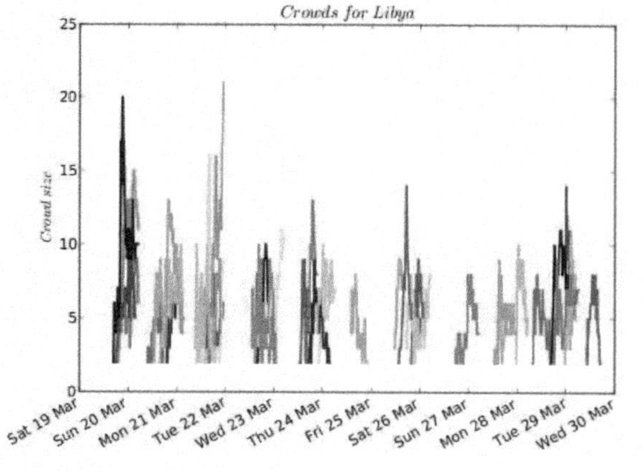

Figure 6: Example of crowds related to Libya

4.7 Comparing Crowds

Finally, we explore the impact of the kind of users on crowd formation. We compare the crowd size distribution, followed by the lifespan distribution of the crowds. Then we plot these two properties towards understanding crowding behaviors in these two datasets.

The distribution of crowd sizes is shown in Figure 7(a). We see that the Houston dataset tends to have larger crowds in comparison to the Experts dataset. These larger crowds may be attributed to the fact that the Houston dataset has relatively more users in comparison to the Experts dataset, and hence more users talking about a particular event resulting in the formation of larger crowds. To understand these dynamics better, we show the lifespan of these crowds in Figure 7(b). The lifespan distribution shows that expert crowds, despite being smaller, are mostly longer lasting than the larger crowds discovered in Houston. Based on further analysis, we find that the experts stream is more *sticky* – that is, crowds in the experts stream added new users over time and decayed more slowly.

We attribute this finding to the crowd formation properties of the Experts dataset, whereby crowds are initiated by users who are popular within a particular domain and hence tend to tweet similar things more often. This shared interests among users forms crowds that discuss chains of events resulting in longer lifespans. While users in the Houston dataset, which is made up of users with relatively varied interests, form crowds that last only as long as the event they are discussing is popular. Continuing this avenue of investigation, we plot crowd size versus life span in Figure 7(c). If the crowds in the Experts dataset are really sticky, as we expect, this should be observed across all the crowds of different sizes, i.e, only larger crowds should not have contributed in making the life span distribution in Figure 7(b) appear the way it does. We observe that irrespective of crowd size, expert crowds always seem to have a higher lifespan than Houston crowds. This clearly shows the way users in expert crowds are tweeting and the content of their tweets is making them stick together longer than Houston crowds. In addition to this observation, we also see that the stickiness of the crowds increases with crowd size. This is observed both for the experts and Houston crowds.

We also find that events that last for a long time have more number of crowds that are spread across the event's duration. An example of such a long term event is the revolution in Libya, and crowds related to this appear throughout the experiment duration following a daily pattern based on users activity, as shown in Figure 6.

5. CONCLUSION

We have seen how the proposed content-driven crowd discovery algorithm can efficiently identify newly-formed communities of users from the real-time web. The approach leverages optimizations to locality-sensitive hashing via prefix trees, incorporates efficient user profile updating, and identifies key dimensions for supporting crowd detection. In our continuing work we are interested to understand the dynamics if crowds formation and their evolution. We are also interested in analyzing the impact geography and culture has on crowd formations.

6. ACKNOWLEDGMENTS

This work was supported in part by NSF grant IIS-1149383, DARPA grant N66001-10-1-4044 and a Google Research Award. Any opinions, findings and conclusions or recommendations expressed in this material are the author(s) and do not necessarily reflect those of the sponsors.

7. REFERENCES

[1] Infinite coordinate space. wikipedia: Examples of vector spaces, 2011.

[2] C. C. Aggarwal. A framework for clustering massive text and categorical data streams. In *In: Proc. SIAM conference on Data Mining*, pages 477–481, 2006.

[3] C. C. Aggarwal, J. Han, J. Wang, and P. S. Yu. A framework for clustering evolving data streams. In *Proceedings of the 29th international conference on Very large data bases - Volume 29*, VLDB '2003, pages 81–92. VLDB Endowment, 2003.

[4] J. Allan. *Introduction to topic detection and tracking*, pages 1–16. Kluwer Academic Publishers, Norwell, MA, USA, 2002.

[5] D. M. Blei, A. Y. Ng, and M. I. Jordan. Latent dirichlet allocation. *J. Mach. Learn. Res.*, 3:993–1022, March 2003.

[6] M. S. Charikar. Similarity estimation techniques from rounding algorithms. In *Proceedings of the thiry-fourth annual ACM symposium on Theory of computing*, STOC '02, pages 380–388, New York, NY, USA, 2002. ACM.

[7] S. Chen, H. Wang, S. Zhou, and P. S. Yu. Stop chasing trends: Discovering high order models in evolving data. In *ICDE '08: Proceedings of the 2008 IEEE 24th International Conference on Data Engineering*, pages 923–932, Washington, DC, USA, 2008. IEEE Computer Society.

[8] H. Choi and H. Varian. Predicting the present with google trends. Technical report, Google, 2009.

[9] D. R. Cutting, D. R. Karger, J. O. Pedersen, and J. W. Tukey. Scatter/gather: a cluster-based approach

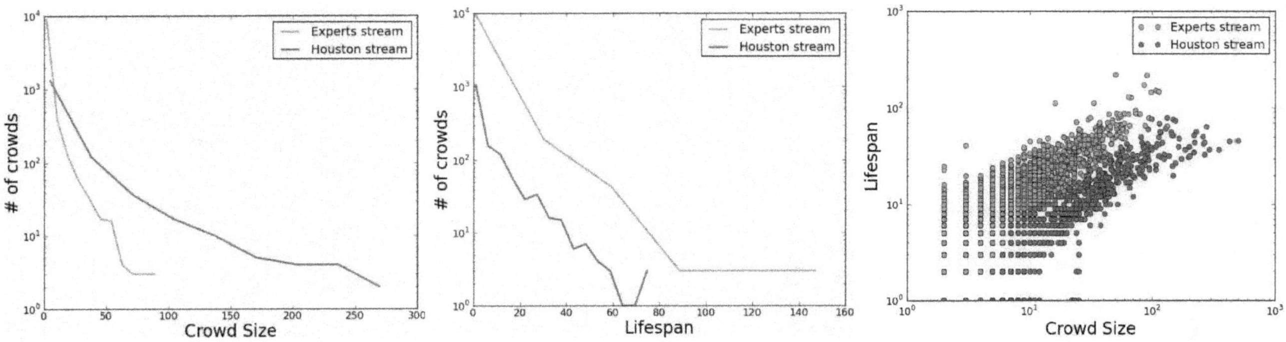

(a) Crowd size distribution (b) Lifespan distribution (c) Crowd size Vs Lifespan

Figure 7: Comparing crowds discovered across the two datasets

to browsing large document collections. In *Proceedings of the 15th ACM SIGIR*, SIGIR '92, pages 318–329, New York, NY, USA, 1992. ACM.

[10] I. Dhillon, Y. Guan, and B. Kulis. A fast kernel-based multilevel algorithm for graph clustering. In *KDD '05*, pages 629–634, New York, NY, USA, 2005. ACM.

[11] W. Fan, Y. Koyanagi, K. Asakura, and T. Watanabe. Clustering over evolving data streams based on online recent-biased approximation. chapter Knowledge Acquisition: Approaches, Algorithms and Applications, pages 12–26. Springer-Verlag, Berlin, Heidelberg, 2009.

[12] M. Franz, T. Ward, J. S. McCarley, and W.-J. Zhu. Unsupervised and supervised clustering for topic tracking. In *Proceedings of the 24th annual international ACM SIGIR conference on Research and development in information retrieval*, SIGIR '01, pages 310–317, New York, NY, USA, 2001. ACM.

[13] A. Gionis, P. Indyk, and R. Motwani. Similarity search in high dimensions via hashing. In *Proceedings of the 25th International Conference on Very Large Data Bases*, VLDB '99, pages 518–529, San Francisco, CA, USA, 1999. Morgan Kaufmann Publishers Inc.

[14] L. Gong, J. Zeng, and S. Zhang. Text stream clustering algorithm based on adaptive feature selection. *Expert Syst. Appl.*, 38:1393–1399, March 2011.

[15] P. Indyk and R. Motwani. Approximate nearest neighbors: towards removing the curse of dimensionality. In *Proceedings of the thirtieth annual ACM symposium on Theory of computing*, STOC '98, pages 604–613, New York, NY, USA, 1998. ACM.

[16] K. Y. Kamath and J. Caverlee. Transient crowd discovery on the real-time social web. In *Proceedings of the fourth ACM international conference on Web search and data mining*, WSDM '11, pages 585–594, New York, NY, USA, 2011. ACM.

[17] C. X. Lin, B. Zhao, Q. Mei, and J. Han. PET: A statistical model for popular events tracking in social communities. In *Proceedings of the 16th ACM SIGKDD international conference on Knowledge discovery and data mining (KDD)*, pages 929–938, New York, NY, USA, 2010. ACM.

[18] Y.-B. Liu, J.-R. Cai, J. Yin, and A. W.-C. Fu. Clustering text data streams. *Journal of Computer Science and Technology*, 23(1):112–128, 2008.

[19] C. D. Manning, P. Raghavan, and H. Schtze. *Introduction to Information Retrieval*. Cambridge University Press, New York, NY, USA, 2008.

[20] F. Moerchen, K. Brinker, and C. Neubauer. Any-time clustering of high frequency news streams. 2007.

[21] M. E. J. Newman. Fast algorithm for detecting community structure in networks, September 2003.

[22] S. Petrović, M. Osborne, and V. Lavrenko. Streaming first story detection with application to twitter. In *Human Language Technologies: The 2010 Annual Conference of the North American Chapter of the Association for Computational Linguistics*, HLT '10, pages 181–189, Stroudsburg, PA, USA, 2010. Association for Computational Linguistics.

[23] D. Ravichandran, P. Pantel, and E. Hovy. Randomized algorithms and nlp: using locality sensitive hash function for high speed noun clustering. In *Proceedings of the 43rd Annual Meeting on Association for Computational Linguistics*, ACL '05, pages 622–629, Stroudsburg, PA, USA, 2005. Association for Computational Linguistics.

[24] T. Sakaki, M. Okazaki, and Y. Matsuo. Earthquake shakes twitter users: real-time event detection by social sensors. In *WWW '10*, pages 851–860, New York, NY, USA, 2010. ACM.

[25] L. Tang and H. Liu. *Community Detection and Mining in Social Media*. Morgan and Claypool, 2010.

[26] X. Wang, L. Tang, H. Gao, and H. Liu. Discovering overlapping groups in social media. In *Proceedings of the 2010 IEEE International Conference on Data Mining (ICDM)*, pages 569–578, Washington, DC, USA, 2010. IEEE Computer Society.

[27] S. Wu, J. M. Hofman, D. J. Watts, and W. A. Mason. Who says what to whom on twitter. *WWW 2011*, 2011.

[28] Y. Zhu and D. Shasha. Statstream: statistical monitoring of thousands of data streams in real time. In *Proceedings of the 28th international conference on Very Large Data Bases*, VLDB '02, pages 358–369. VLDB Endowment, 2002.

Graph Classification: A Diversified Discriminative Feature Selection Approach

Yuanyuan Zhu, Jeffrey Xu Yu, Hong Cheng, Lu Qin
The Chinese University of Hong Kong, Hong Kong, China
{yyzhu,yu,hcheng,lqin}@se.cuhk.edu.hk

ABSTRACT

A graph models complex structural relationships among objects, and has been prevalently used in a wide range of applications. Building an automated graph classification model becomes very important for predicting unknown graphs or understanding complex structures between different classes. The graph classification framework being widely used consists of two steps, namely, feature selection and classification. The key issue is how to select important subgraph features from a graph database with a large number of graphs including positive graphs and negative graphs. Given the features selected, a generic classification approach can be used to build a classification model. In this paper, we focus on feature selection. We identify two main issues with the most widely used feature selection approach which is based on a discriminative score to select frequent subgraph features, and introduce a new diversified discriminative score to select features that have a higher diversity. We analyze the properties of the newly proposed diversified discriminative score, and conducted extensive performance studies to demonstrate that such a diversified discriminative score makes positive/negative graphs separable and leads to a higher classification accuracy.

Categories and Subject Descriptors

H.2.8 [**Database management**]: Database applications—*Data mining*; I.5.2 [**Pattern Recognition**]: Design Methodology —*Feature evaluation and selection*

Keywords

Graph Classification, Feature Selection, Diversity

1. INTRODUCTION

A graph models complex structural relationships among objects, and has been prevalently used in a wide range of applications, such as chemical compound structures in chemistry, attributed graphs in image processing, food chains in ecology, electrical circuits in electricity, protein interaction networks in biology, etc. With the increasing popularity of graph databases that contain a large number of graphs in various applications, building an automated classification model emerges as one important problem for predicting the unknown graphs or understanding complex structures between different classes. For example, with a chemical compound dataset, chemists want to be able to predict which chemical compounds are active and which are inactive.

The graph classification framework being widely used is first to select a set of features by mining frequent subgraphs from the graph database that consists of positive graphs and negative graphs, and then to employ a generic classification model using the set of features selected. Such an approach has been shown achieving promising classification accuracy [5], and the key issue is how to select features. In order to achieve a higher classification accuracy, discriminative based approaches have been extensively studied that select a set of discriminative frequent features [20, 16]. The discriminative frequent features mined are the features that are frequent in the positive graph set but are infrequent in the negative graph set.

LEAP [20] is one of the first work that studies how to directly mine discriminative subgraph features instead of finding the discriminative features from the frequent features mined. Some recent work study how to speed up the process of mining discriminative subgraph features such as graphSig [16], COM [11], and GAIA [12]. graphSig [16] provides an efficient solution for mining discriminative subgraph features with extremely low frequencies. First, graphSig converts graphs into feature vectors by performing a random walk with restarts on every vertex. Second, graphSig divides graphs into small groups such that graphs in the same group have similar vectors. Third, graphSig mines frequent subgraphs in each group with high frequency thresholds, because high similarity among vectors in the same group indicates that the corresponding graphs in the group share highly frequent subgraphs. COM [11] takes into account the co-occurrences of subgraph features. Co-occurrences of small subgraph features are able to approximate large features and thereby significantly reduce the mining time for large features. Both graphSig and COM are much faster than LEAP. For accuracy in classifying chemical compounds, COM has a comparable classification accuracy to that of LEAP, and GraphSig produces a higher accuracy than LEAP. GAIA [12] proposes an evolutionary computation method to mine discriminative subgraph features for graph classification using a randomized searching strategy. The randomized search strategy simulates biological evolution to select discriminative subgraph features. GAIA is the up-to-date approach in graph classification.

All the existing works select discriminative subgraph features by a discriminative score such as G-test [20], Fisher score [4] and log ratio score [11, 12]. We classify them as a single feature discriminative score, because they assign a score to a feature by only considering its own occurrences in the positive/negative sets. A-

CIKM'12, October 29–November 2, 2012, Maui, HI, USA.

mong them, the log ratio score shows better classification accuracy as reported in [11, 12].

However, the question to be asked is whether there exists a better score with which a better set of features can be selected and a graph classification model can be built with an even higher accuracy. The reason to ask such a question is that there does not exist a ground truth. First, for graph classification over a large graph database with positive/negative graphs, the number of frequent subgraph features is huge. It is known to be impractical to explore all the possible subsets of frequent subgraph features for classification. Second, it is still an open problem to identify the true optimal feature selection, because the connection between the features selected and the accuracy of the graph classification is unknown yet. Therefore, discriminative score is important, but it may not be sufficient to select features that make the positive and negative graphs separable. We identify two issues with the single feature discriminative score. (Issue-1) The discriminative features selected can be highly overlapped. They may not lead to a good classification accuracy, because one of them is redundant in a sense that they appear frequently together and share a large part between them. (Issue-2) Some important features may be missed out, because there exists a restriction on the number of discriminative features to be selected and selecting highly overlapped discriminative features may squeeze out important features which are less discriminative and barely overlapped with other features. Although feature selection is a well studied problem in the literature for conventional classification tasks on high-dimensional data [4, 15, 6], such methods have limited power for graph datasets. The underlying reasons are: each feature is treated equivalently, and the relevance and redundancy is evaluated by their distributions over binary vectors. However, in a graph database, features have more complicated relationship with each other in terms of the topological structures and the locations. In addition, a pattern has an exponential number of subgraphs, which makes the patterns not uniformly distributed. This leads to a huge redundancy and complex overlapping of patterns.

To address these two issues, in this paper, we study a new score, called a diversified discriminative score. The main idea is to explore the additional value of the diversity together with the discriminativity. By diversity, we explore how to reduce the overlapping between two features that share a large part, based on an edge-cover. In addition, to further enhance diversity, we explore how to reduce the overlapping between a feature and a set of features. We do this because a feature f to be selected may not have a large overlapping with any specific feature already selected, but it can be overlapped with the set of features already selected, i.e., many features in the set are partially overlapped with feature f, and the feature set end up to be overlapped with the major part of feature f. In other words, such a feature f may not add additional value to make positive/negative graphs separable. The main contributions of this paper are summarized below. In addition to the new diversified discriminative score, we also analyze the properties of our newly proposed diversified discriminative score from many viewpoints. We propose algorithms to select such features, and conduct extensive experimental studies. We show that the features selected by the diversified discriminative score outperform the up-to-date graph classification approach GAIA [12].

The rest of the paper is organized as follows. Section 2 gives the problem statement. In Section 3, we discuss two main issues with the existing discriminative scores, and propose a new diversified and discriminative score. In Section 4, we discuss the discriminative power of our new diversified and discriminative score by investigating the statistic information of the new score in comparison with the existing discriminative scores. We give our algorithms in Section 5. We further develop an ensemble method to select features and build classification model in Section 6. Our experimental results are shown in Section 7. We discuss the related work in Section 8, and conclude this paper in Section 9.

$\mathcal{D}$	f_1	f_2	f_3	f_4	f_5	Class Label
P_1	1	0	0	1	0	+
P_2	1	1	1	0	1	+
P_3	1	1	1	0	1	+
P_4	0	1	0	1	1	+
P_5	0	0	1	1	1	+
P_6	0	0	1	1	1	+
N_1	1	0	0	1	0	-
N_2	0	1	0	1	0	-
N_3	0	0	0	0	0	-
N_4	0	0	0	0	1	-
N_5	0	0	1	0	1	-
N_6	0	0	1	0	1	-

Table 1: The Feature Containment

2. PROBLEM STATEMENT

Given a set of labels Σ, we model a graph as $g = (V, E, l)$ where V is the set of vertices, $E \subseteq V \times V$ is the set of edges, and l is a labeling function on vertices and edges, where the label of a vertex $u \in V$ is specified by $l(u)$ and the label of an edge (u, v) is specified by $l(u, v)$. We use $V(g)$ and $E(g)$ to denote the set of vertices and the set of edges of a graph g, respectively, and use $|V(g)|$ and $|E(g)|$ to denote the numbers of vertices and edges in g.

Definition 2.1: Subgraph Isomorphism. Given two graphs $g' = (V', E', l')$ and $g = (V, E, l)$, g' is *subgraph isomorphic* to g, if there exists an injective function $\varphi : V' \to V$ such that (1) for $\forall u, v \in V'$ and $u \neq v$, $\varphi(u) \neq \varphi(v)$, (2) for $\forall v \in V'$, $\varphi(v) \in V$ and $l'(v) = l(\varphi(v))$, and (3) for $\forall(u, v) \in E'$, $(\varphi(u), \varphi(v)) \in E$ and $l(u, v) = l'(\varphi(u), \varphi(v))$. □

A graph g' is a subgraph of another graph g, denoted as $g' \subseteq g$, if g' is *subgraph isomorphic* to g. Here, g is a supergraph of g', denoted as $g \supseteq g'$, if g' is a subgraph of g.

Problem Statement: Let $\mathcal{D} = \{g_1, g_2, \cdots, g_n\}$ be a graph database of size $|\mathcal{D}|$ that consists of many graphs g_i, for $1 \leq i \leq |\mathcal{D}|$. Among the graphs in $\mathcal{D}$, there are a set of positive graphs, denoted as $\mathcal{D}^+$ ($\subseteq \mathcal{D}$), and a set of negative graphs, denoted as $\mathcal{D}^-$ ($\subseteq \mathcal{D}$), where $\mathcal{D}^+ \cap \mathcal{D}^- = \emptyset$. The feature selection problem is to select a set of features $\mathcal{F}_s$ with which a model $\mathcal{M}$ can be built for classifying unseen graphs with a high classification accuracy.

Following the existing works, we select frequent subgraphs (pattern) from $\mathcal{D}$ as features. Given $\mathcal{D}$, the frequency of a feature f is given as

$$freq(f) = \frac{|sup(f, \mathcal{D})|}{|\mathcal{D}|}$$

where $sup(f, \mathcal{D}) = \{g_i \mid g_i \in \mathcal{D}, f \subseteq g_i\}$ is the support set of f. The support of the subgraph f in $\mathcal{D}$ is $|sup(f, \mathcal{D})|$. A subgraph f is called a frequent subgraph if $freq(f) \geq \tau$, where τ ($0 \leq \tau \leq 1$) is a user specified minimum support threshold. For simplicity, we use $sup(f)$ as an alternative notation for $sup(f, \mathcal{D})$ in the following discussions.

Example 2.1: Fig. 1 shows a graph database $\mathcal{D} = \mathcal{D}^+ \cup \mathcal{D}^-$. Here, $\mathcal{D}^+ = \{P_1, P_2, P_3, P_4, P_5, P_6\}$ is a set of positive graphs, and $\mathcal{D}^- = \{N_1, N_2, N_3, N_4, N_5, N_6\}$ is a set of negative graphs. From this graph database, a frequent subgraph set can be mined which might contain a large number of subgraphs. Suppose we select a subset $\mathcal{F}_s = \{f_1, f_2, f_3, f_4, f_5\}$ as the features as shown

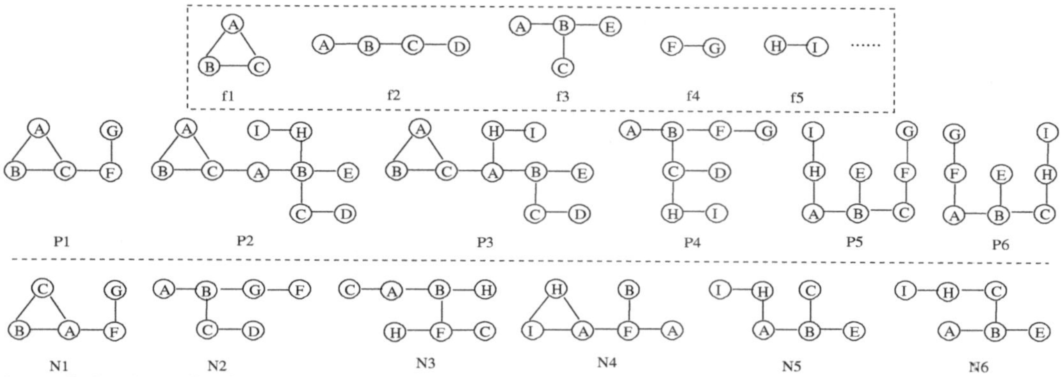

Figure 1: A graph database $\mathcal{D}$ with 6 positive graphs P_i ($1 \le i \le 6$) and 6 negative graphs N_j ($1 \le j \le 6$), and pattern set $\mathcal{F}_s$

in Fig. 1. Table 1 shows whether a feature $f \in \mathcal{F}_s$ is a subgraph of P_i ($1 \le i \le 6$) or N_j ($1 \le j \le 6$). The corresponding value is 1 if it is, otherwise 0. Then a generic classification model can be built for the graph database based on Table 1. If we choose another different subset $\mathcal{F}'_s$ as the feature set, the graph database will be mapped to a different vector space which might lead to building a quite different classifier. In other words, the quality of the classifier in terms of the accuracy for a graph database heavily depends on the feature set $\mathcal{F}_s$. □

3. DISCRIMINATIVE SCORE

Frequent features mined from the graph database $\mathcal{D}$ are widely used in graph classification. As observed in many existing works, it does not necessarily mean that all frequent features are equally important for building a good classification model, because some of them may occur frequently in both $\mathcal{D}^+$ and $\mathcal{D}^-$. Such frequent features are not discriminative and consequently do not lead to a good classification model. To address this issue, people explore to use the discriminative frequent features that appear in $\mathcal{D}^+$ frequently but appear in $\mathcal{D}^-$ infrequently. Several statistic measures are proposed to evaluate the discriminative power of a feature, such as G-test [20], Fisher score [4] and log ratio score [11, 12]. We call them as a single feature discriminative score, because they assign a score to a feature by merely considering its own occurrences in the positive/negative graph sets.

3.1 The Single Feature Discriminative Score

In this work, we focus on the log ratio score which has recently been widely used due to the better classification accuracy as reported in [11, 12].

Given a graph database $\mathcal{D}$ with a set of positive graphs, $\mathcal{D}^+$, and a set of negative graphs, $\mathcal{D}^-$. The positive and negative frequencies of a subgraph feature f, denoted as $r^+(f)$ and $r^-(f)$, are defined as follows.

$$\begin{cases} r^+(f) = \dfrac{|sup(f, \mathcal{D}^+)|}{|\mathcal{D}^+|} \\ r^-(f) = \dfrac{|sup(f, \mathcal{D}^-)|}{|\mathcal{D}^-|} \end{cases}$$

The discriminative score of feature f by the log ratio is defined below.

$$score(f) = \log \frac{r^+(f)}{r^-(f)} \quad (1)$$

It considers the log ratio of the positive and negative frequencies. To avoid using a zero denominator, when calculating the negative frequencies, it adds a virtual negative graph that contains any subgraph features.

Given the log ratio as a discriminative score, a commonly used approach is to select the feature that has the largest discriminative score from the unselected features iteratively. For example, the works in [11, 12] consider to extend a subgraph to generate its supergraphs only based on its discriminative score or the score increment. However, there are two main issues with the existing feature selection approaches.

- **Issue-1: Highly Overlapped Features**. The discriminative features selected can be possibly highly overlapped. In other words, two discriminative features, f_i and f_j, may share a large common part. They may not lead to a good classification accuracy, because one of them is redundant in a sense that they appear frequently together in graphs in $\mathcal{D}$, as guided by the definition of log ratio.
- **Issue-2: Missing Important Features**. Some important features may be missed out. The number of discriminative features selected for building a classifier is often restricted due to efficiency and effectiveness considerations. As discussed in Issue-1, the highly overlapped discriminative features may squeeze out the important features which are less discriminative and barely overlapped with other features due to the limited feature number.

3.2 A New Diversified Discriminative Score

Considering these two issues, in this section, we give a new diversified discriminative score. First, we introduce the concept of embedding.

Definition 3.1: Embedding. Given two graphs f and g. Suppose $f \subseteq g$ by a subgraph isomorphic injection function φ. The subset of vertices of $V(g)$, $V(g)_\varphi = \{\varphi(u) | u \in V(f)\}$, is a vertex embedding of f in g. In a similar way, the subset of edges of $E(g)$, $E(g)_\varphi = \{(\varphi(v), \varphi(u)) | (v, u) \in E(f)\}$ is an edge embedding of f in g. □

With edge embedding, we consider a feature f from the viewpoint of coverage. A feature f covers certain edges in g when there is an edge embedding of f in g. With such coverage, we further explore how many edges a feature f can cover in graph database $\mathcal{D}$, which is the union of edges covered by f in all graphs in $\mathcal{D}$.

Definition 3.2: Feature Edge-Cover. Given a graph database $\mathcal{D} = \{g_1, g_2, \cdots, g_n\}$ and a feature f, a graph $g_i \in \mathcal{D}$ is covered by f if there is an edge embedding of f in g_i, and $e \in E(g_i)$ is covered by f if $e \in E(g_i)_\varphi$. We denote the set of edges in g covered by feature f as $E_c(f, g)$. The feature edge-cover of f is the set of edges that are covered by f in all graphs in $\mathcal{D}$, denoted as $C_e(f) = \cup_{g_i \in sup(f)} E_c(f, g_i)$. The edge-cover score of f is the number of edges covered by f, denoted as $S_c(f) = \sum_{g_i \in sup(f)} |E_c(f, g_i)|$. We use $S_c(f)$ and $|C_e(f)|$ alternatively in the following discussion since $S_c(f) = |C_e(f)|$. □

A main idea behind the feature edge-cover of f is that it considers the embedding locations in every graph g_i in $\mathcal{D}$. Such implicit locations assist us to select diversified features in a sense that they are not overlapped with the features selected already, as we will discuss in the following. For the purpose of addressing the diversity as an answer to the two issues, we introduce an edge-cover probability. The edge-cover probability of a feature f regarding to the entire edge set in $\mathcal{D}$ is defined in Eq. (2).

$$p_c(f) = \frac{|C_e(f)|}{\sum_{g_i \in \mathcal{D}} |E(g_i)|} \tag{2}$$

Consider the diversity from the viewpoint of independence. If the graph features are independent of each other, the conditional probability of a feature with respect to another graph feature will be the same prior edge-cover probability of itself. In other words, given two features f_1 and f_2, they are independent if $p_c(f_2|f_1) = p_c(f_2)$. It indicates that two features can not be considered as diversified in terms of independence, if their edge-covers are largely overlapped. Therefore, the decision for selecting a feature f_2 with a feature f_1 already selected depends on the probability $p_c(f_2|f_1)$. Based on this consideration, we define a conditional edge-cover probability of feature f_2 with respect to another feature f_1 as follows.

$$p_c(f_2|f_1) = \frac{|C_e(f_1 \cap f_2)|}{|C_e(f_1)|} \tag{3}$$

where $C_e(f_1 \cap f_2) = C_e(f_1) \cap C_e(f_1)$. The joint edge-cover probability of f_1 and f_2 can be derived in the following.

$$\begin{aligned} p_c(f_1 \cap f_2) &= p_c(f_2|f_1) \cdot p_c(f_1) \\ &= \frac{|C_e(f_1 \cap f_2)|}{|C_e(f_1)|} \cdot \frac{|C_e(f_1)|}{\sum_{g_i \in D} |E(g_i)|} \\ &= \frac{|C_e(f_1 \cap f_2)|}{\sum_{g_i \in D} |E(g_i)|} \end{aligned} \tag{4}$$

Note that the value of $p_c(f_1 \cap f_2)$ is bounded by [0,1] and is also a symmetric measure, which means that $p_c(f_1 \cap f_2) = p_c(f_1|f_2) \cdot p_c(f_2)$ also holds. Based on Eq. (4), the union edge-cover probability of feature f_1 and f_2 can be derived as follows.

$$p_c(f_1 \cup f_2) = p_c(f_1) + p_c(f_2) - p_c(f_1 \cap f_2) \tag{5}$$

We extend the union edge-cover probability from two features to m features where $m > 2$. Let $\mathcal{F} = \{f_1, \cdots, f_m\}$ be a set of features, and let $\mathcal{F}_i = \{f_1, \cdots, f_i\}$ be a subset of $\mathcal{F}$ for $i = 1, \ldots, m$. The edge-cover probability of feature set $\mathcal{F}_m$ can be derived as follows.

$$\begin{aligned} p_c(\mathcal{F}_m) &= p_c(\bigcup_{i=1}^{m} f_i) \\ &= p_c(f_m) + p_c(\mathcal{F}_{m-1}) - p_c(f_m \cap \mathcal{F}_{m-1}) \end{aligned} \tag{6}$$

Thus, the diversity of f_m to be selected with respect to a set of features selected, $\mathcal{F}_{m-1}$, can be derived below.

$$\begin{aligned} p_d(f_m) &= p_c(\mathcal{F}_m) - p_c(\mathcal{F}_{m-1}) = p_c(f_m) - p_c(f_m \cap \mathcal{F}_{m-1}) \\ &= \frac{|C_e(f_m) - C_e(f_m \cap \mathcal{F}_{m-1})|}{\sum_{g_i \in \mathcal{D}} |E(g_i)|} \\ &= \frac{|C_e(f_m) - \bigcup_{j=1}^{m-1} C_e(f_m \cap f_j)|}{\sum_{g_i \in \mathcal{D}} |E(g_i)|} \\ &= \frac{\sum_{g_i \in sup(f_m)} |E_c(f_m, g_i)|}{\sum_{g_i \in \mathcal{D}} |E(g_i)|} \\ &- \frac{\sum_{g_i \in sup(f_m)} |\bigcup_{j=1}^{m-1} (E_c(f_m, g_i) \cap E_c(f_j, g_i))|}{\sum_{g_i \in \mathcal{D}} |E(g_i)|} \end{aligned} \tag{7}$$

Equipped with the diversity of f_m, we define a new diversified discriminative score for a new feature, f_m, to be selected with a feature set $\mathcal{F}_{m-1}$ that has been selected already. Here, let $p_d^+(f_m)$ be the diversity of f_m for the set of positive graphs ($\mathcal{D}^+$), and let $p_d^-(f_m)$ be the diversity of f_m for the set of negative graphs ($\mathcal{D}^-$). The diversified discriminative score of feature f_m is defined as follows.

$$score_d(f_m) = \log \frac{p_d^+(f_m)}{p_d^-(f_m)} \tag{8}$$

Our proposed diversified discriminative score measures the feature overlapping by evaluating their embeddings in graphs. If most of the embeddings of a new feature f_m have already been covered by the feature subset $\mathcal{F}_{m-1}$, the diversified discriminative score of f_m will be very low, thus f_m will not be selected, even though the log ratio score of f_m can be large. The diversified discriminative score measure can better address the two issues, namely, Issue-1 and Issue-2.

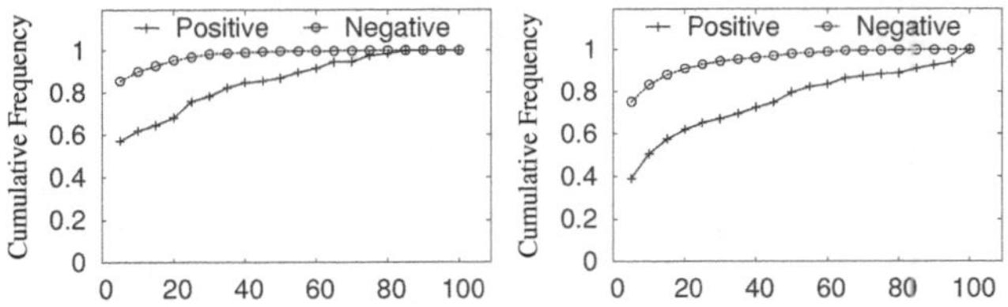

(a) # of Features (Logratio) (b) # of Features (D&D)

Figure 2: Cumulative Frequency of Features

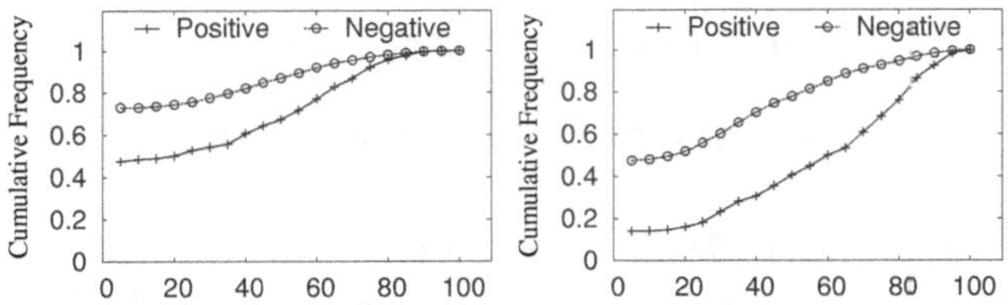

(a) # of Embeddings (Logratio) (b) # of Embeddings (D&D)

Figure 3: Cumulative Frequency of Embeddings

4. PROPERTY STATISTICS OF DISCRIMINATIVE SCORE

In this section, we discuss the discriminative power of our new diversified discriminative score by investigating the statistic information of our new score in comparison with the single feature discriminative score, log ratio, using a real chemical compound dataset containing 400 positive graphs and 1600 negative graphs. We compare two feature sets, each containing 100 features selected by two methods: Logratio and D&D. Logratio is a method that selects frequent features with the maximum single feature discriminative score defined by log ratio (Eq. (1)) iteratively. D&D is our proposed method that selects frequent features using the diversified discriminative score (Eq. (8)). We reemphasize the point that the diversified discriminative score controls the feature diversity by reducing the feature overlapping between features. We will discuss D&D in detail in Section 5. Below, we show how the two feature sets exhibit different properties in separating positive graphs from negative graphs.

Cumulative Frequencies: For each feature set selected by either Logratio or D&D, we count the number of features contained by each graph in the set of positive/negative graphs, and compute a cumulative frequency. The cumulative frequency for a number i is the percentage of positive (or negative) graphs that have no more than i features. We plot the cumulative frequencies in Fig. 2(a) and Fig. 2(b), for i to be taken from 1 to 100.

For Logratio, as shown in Fig. 2(a), we can see that the positive cumulative frequencies and the negative cumulative frequencies,

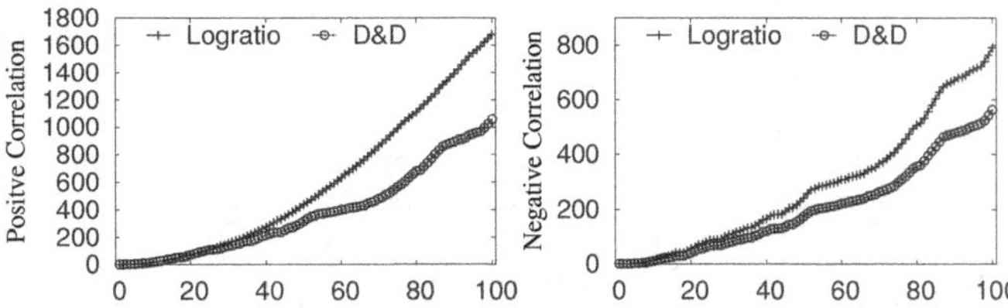

(a) # of Features in $\mathcal{D}^+$ (b) # of Features in $\mathcal{D}^-$

Figure 4: Correlation of Features

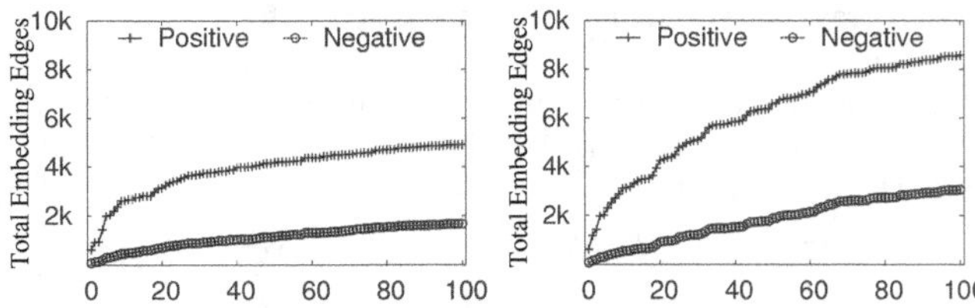

(a) # of Features (Logratio) (b) # of Features (D&D)

Figure 5: Total Embedding Edges Statistic

based on the positive graphs and the negative graphs respectively, are very close. This means that the feature occurrences in the positive and negative graphs are very similar, thus the features selected by the log ratio can not help too much to distinguish the positive graphs from the negative graphs. Therefore, there is a limit to build a classification model with high accuracy using the single feature discriminative score. On the other hand, for D&D, as shown in Fig. 2(b), the gap between the positive cumulative frequencies and the negative cumulative frequencies is larger. This means that the selected feature set makes the positives and negatives more separable. In addition, Fig. 3(a) and Fig. 3(b) show the cumulative frequencies of positive graphs and negative graphs containing the feature embeddings from the two selected feature sets. We can observe similar trends on the two feature sets. And the gap between the cumulative frequencies of positive graphs ($\mathcal{D}^+$) and negative graphs ($\mathcal{D}^-$) becomes larger with the new diversified discriminative score as shown in Fig. 3(b).

Correlation: The correlation between two features is an important indicator which can be evaluated by comparing their support sets [20]. A widely used measure is Jaccard Coefficient [4], which is defined as follows.

$$corr(f_1, f_2) = \frac{|sup(f_1) \cap sup(f_2)|}{|sup(f_1)| + |sup(f_2)| - |sup(f_1) \cap sup(f_2)|}$$

where $corr(f_1, f_2) \in [0, 1]$. Over a set of 100 features, the sum of pairwise correlations score is a number in the range of [0,10000]. Fig. 4 shows the sum of correlation scores between features when the number of features increases. Our new diversified discriminative score by D&D can reduce about 1/3 correlation score than that by Logratio, which means the features selected by Logratio are more redundant.

Total Embedding Edges: We count the total embedding edges for a feature set, which is the union of the feature edge-covers of all features in the feature set. Fig. 5(a) and Fig. 5(b) show the total embedding edges by the two feature sets selected by Logratio and D&D respectively. We can see that the gap between positive graphs and negative graphs with D&D in Fig. 5(b) is larger than that with Logratio in Fig. 5(a). Thus, the feature set selected by D&D can cover many edges in positive graphs and few edges in negative graphs and make positive and negative graphs more separable.

Diversified Discriminative Power: Fig. 6 shows the diversified discriminative score of the i_{th} feature being selected. Fig. 6(b)

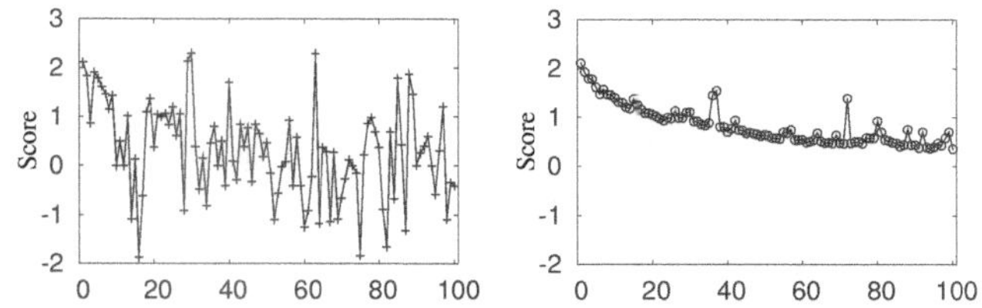

(a) i_{th} Feature (Logratio) (b) i_{th} Feature (D&D)

Figure 6: Feature Diversified Discriminative Score

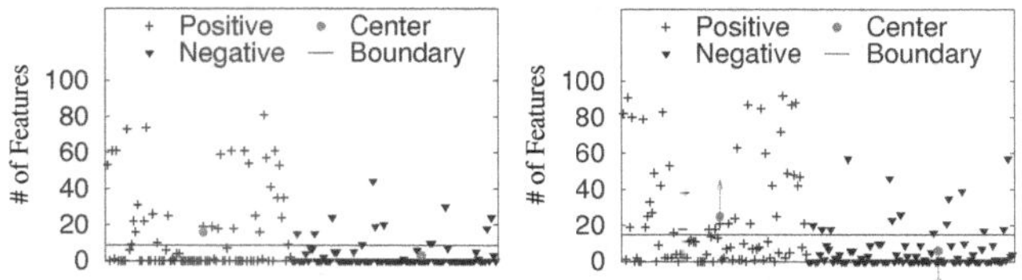

(a) # of Features Distributions (Logratio) (b) # of Features Distributions (D&D)

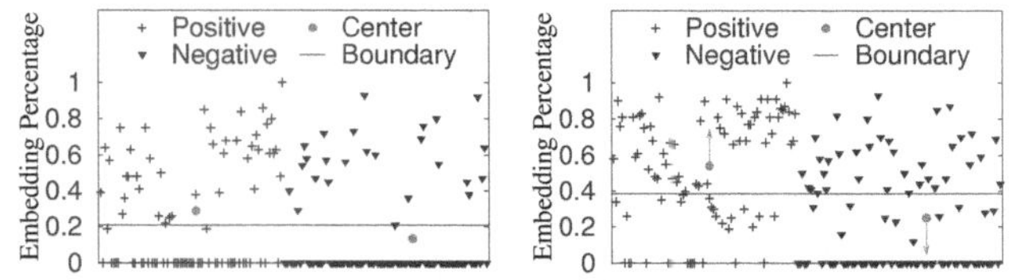

(c) Embedding Percentage Distributions (Logratio) (d) Embedding Percentage Distributions (D&D)

Figure 7: Statistic of Graphs

shows that D&D has steadily high diversified discriminative scores for the selected features. We also show the diversified discriminative scores for the features selected by Logratio in Fig. 6(a). As can be seen from Fig. 6(a), it has low and unstable diversified discriminative scores for the selected features, due to the large overlap between the selected features.

The Distributions: With the 100 features selected by Logratio or D&D, we show the feature distribution and embedding distribution on a graph dataset with 200 representative graphs (100 positive graphs and 100 negative graphs) among 2,000 graphs being tested. Fig. 7(a) and Fig. 7(b) show the number of features contained by each positive graph and negative graph, given the 100 feature sets selected by Logratio and D&D, respectively. The boundary line represents the average number of features contained by the 200 sample graphs. The two center points represent the average number of features in positive graph set and negative graph set respectively, where the positive center is above the boundary and the negative center is below the boundary. The positive and negative graphs in Fig. 7(b) spread farther apart based on the feature containment information, which indicates that our new diversified discriminative score selects a feature set which makes positive and negative graphs more separable. Similarly, Fig. 7(c) and Fig. 7(d) show that the embedding percentage in each positive graph and negative graphs. The embedding percentage for a graph is the ratio of the number of embedding edges in the graph to the number of graph edges. These two figures have a similar trend as shown in Fig. 7(a) and Fig. 7(b).

Based on the statistic information given above, it is clear that our proposed diversified discriminative score can help select more discriminative features with little overlap, thus make the positive and negative graphs more separable. With such a score, we are in a much better position to address the two issues, namely, Issue-1 and Issue-2.

Algorithm 1 D&D $(\mathcal{D}, \mathcal{F}, k)$

Input: A graph database $\mathcal{D} = (\mathcal{D}^+, \mathcal{D}^-)$, a set of frequent features $\mathcal{F}$, and the number of features k
Output: A selected feature set $\mathcal{F}_s$

1: $f \leftarrow \text{argmax}_{f\in\mathcal{F}} score(f)$;
2: $\mathcal{F}_s \leftarrow \{f\}$;
3: **while** $|\mathcal{F}_s| \leq k$ **do**
4: $\quad f \leftarrow \text{argmax}_{f\in\mathcal{F}\setminus\mathcal{F}_s} score_d(f)$;
5: $\quad \mathcal{F}_s \leftarrow \mathcal{F}_s \cup \{f\}$;
6: **return** $\mathcal{F}_s$;

Algorithm 2 D&D-Fast$(\mathcal{D}, \mathcal{F}, k)$

Input: A graph database $\mathcal{D} = (\mathcal{D}^+, \mathcal{D}^-)$, a set of frequent features $\mathcal{F}$, and the number of features k
Output: A selected feature set $\mathcal{F}_s$

1: $\mathcal{F}_s \leftarrow \emptyset$;
2: $\mathcal{H} \leftarrow$ max-heap initialized to be $\emptyset$;
3: **for all** $f \in \mathcal{F}$ **do**
4: $\quad \mathcal{H}.push(f, score(f))$;
5: **while** $|\mathcal{F}_s| \leq k$ **do**
6: $\quad h \leftarrow \mathcal{H}.pop()$;
7: $\quad \mathcal{F}_s \leftarrow \mathcal{F}_s \cup \{f'\}$; {$f'$ is obtained from h.}
8: $\quad$ update $(\mathcal{H}, \mathcal{F}, \mathcal{F}_s, f')$;
9: **return** $\mathcal{F}_s$;

10: **Procedure** update $(\mathcal{H}, \mathcal{F}, \mathcal{F}_s, f')$
11: **for all** $f \in \mathcal{F} \setminus \mathcal{F}_s$ **do**
12: $\quad C_e^-(f) \leftarrow C_e^-(f) - C_e^-(f) \cap C_e^-(f')$;
13: $\quad$ compute $\overline{score}_d(f)$;
14: $\quad$ **if** $\overline{score}_d(f) > head(\mathcal{H}).score_d()$ **then**
15: $\quad\quad C_e^+(f) \leftarrow C_e^+(f) - C_e^+(f) \cap C_e^+(f')$;
16: $\quad\quad$ compute $score_d(f)$;
17: $\quad\quad \mathcal{H}.update((f, score_d(f)))$;
18: $\quad$ **else**
19: $\quad\quad \mathcal{H}.update((f, \overline{score}_d(f)))$;

5. THE ALGORITHMS

In this section, we show the algorithm, named D&D, to select features based on the diversified discriminative score. The D&D algorithm is given in Algorithm 1. There are three inputs: a graph database $\mathcal{D}$ which contains a set of positive graphs $\mathcal{D}^+$ and a set of negative graphs $\mathcal{D}^-$, a set of frequent features (subgraphs) mined from the graph database $\mathcal{D}$ using [21], and a number k which indicates how many diversified discriminative features to be selected from $\mathcal{F}$. In the D&D algorithm, first, it selects the feature f with the largest log ratio score using $score(f)$ (Eq. (1)). This feature f has the highest discriminative power by itself. Then, in a while loop, it iteratively picks up a new feature f with the largest diversified discriminative score $score_d(f)$ (Eq. (8)). This process repeats until k features are selected.

To compute $score_d(f)$, it needs to compute $p_d(f)$ (Eq. (7)) first which involves a feature edge-cover intersection operation, as we describe below. This operation takes two feature edge-covers, $C_e(f)$ and $C_e(f')$, as input and produces their intersections $C_e(f\cap f')$. In this operation, we need first find the graphs that contained by both $sup(f)$ and $sup(f')$ and then compute the intersection of edge embeddings of f and f' for each of these graphs. Thus, the complexity of feature edge-cover intersection operation is $O(|s|_{max}\cdot |f|_{max})$, where $|s|_{max}$ is the maximum support size and $|f|_{max}$ is the maximum feature size.

In Algorithm 1, we need to compute $score_d(f)$ for each feature $f \in \mathcal{F} \setminus \mathcal{F}_s$ to select a feature with the maximum score value in line 4. To compute $score_d(f)$, we need to compute the intersection of $C_e(f)$ and $C_e(f')$ for each $f' \in \mathcal{F}_s$ and the union them. Hence, to select a feature with the maximum diversified discriminative score from $\mathcal{F}\setminus\mathcal{F}_s$, it needs $|\mathcal{F}_s|\cdot|\mathcal{F}\setminus\mathcal{F}_s|$ feature edge-cover intersection operations. To find the set of k features, the whole algorithm ends up with $O(k^2\cdot|\mathcal{F}|)$ feature edge-covers operations, where k is the number of features to be selected.

To reduce the time complexity, we design a faster algorithm which only needs $O(k\cdot|\mathcal{F}|)$ feature edge-cover intersection operations. The algorithm, named D&D-Fast, is shown in Algorithm 2. For each candidate feature f_j, we can record its two edge-cover scores. One is the positive edge-cover score, $|C_e^+(f_j)|$, based on the positive graph set $\mathcal{D}^+$, and the other is the negative edge-cover score, $|C_e^-(f_j)|$, based on the negative graph set $\mathcal{D}^-$. We update these scores in every iteration. Let these scores for a feature f_j at the i_{th} iteration be $|C_e^+(f_j)_i|$ and $|C_e^-(f_j)_i|$. Suppose at the i_{th} iteration, a feature f' with the maximum diversified discriminative score is selected. Then for each feature $f_j \in \mathcal{F}\setminus(\mathcal{F}_s\cup\{f'\})$, we update $C_e^+(f_j)_i$ and $C_e^-(f_j)_i$ as follows.

$$\begin{aligned} C_e^+(f_j)_i &= C_e^+(f_j)_{i-1} - C_e^+(f_j)_{i-1}\cap C_e^+(f') \\ C_e^-(f_j)_i &= C_e^-(f_j)_{i-1} - C_e^-(f_j)_{i-1}\cap C_e^-(f') \end{aligned} \tag{9}$$

By updating the edge-cover score for each feature $f_j \in \mathcal{F}\setminus(\mathcal{F}_s\cup\{f'\})$ immediately after the selection of a new feature f', we avoid computing the intersection of $C_e(f)$ and $C_e(f')$ for each $f' \in \mathcal{F}_s$ from scratch, and only need $O(k\cdot|\mathcal{F}|)$ feature edge-cover intersection operations.

In addition, we can further speed up the feature edge-cover intersection operation by an early stop bound of $score_d(f_j)$. We use a max-heap $\mathcal{H}$ to maintain the current $score_d(f_j)$ for each $f_j \in \mathcal{F}\setminus\mathcal{F}_s$ which is sorted according to the value of $score_d(f_j)$. Each entry in the heap is with the form $e = (pID, score_d(f_j))$, where pID is the feature ID and $score_d(f_j)$ is the score to be sorted in the heap. Note that we do not need to update $score_d(f_j)$ for all $f_j \in \mathcal{F}\setminus\mathcal{F}_s$. We can derive an upper bound of $score_d(f_j)$ as follows.

$$\begin{aligned} score_d(f_j)_i &= \log\frac{p_d^+(f_j)_i}{p_d^-(f_j)_i} \\ &= \log\frac{|C_e^+(f_j)_{i-1} - C_e^+(f_j)_{i-1}\cap C_e^+(f')|}{|C_e^-(f_j)_{i-1} - C_e^-(f_j)_{i-1}\cap C_e^-(f')|} \\ &\leq \log\frac{|C_e^+(f_j)_{i-1}|}{|C_e^-(f_j)_{i-1} - C_e^-(f_j)_{i-1}\cap C_e^-(f')|} \\ &= \overline{score}_d(f_j)_i \end{aligned} \tag{10}$$

where $\overline{score}_d(f_j)_i$ is an upper bound of $score_d(f_j)_i$. In Algorithm 2, before updating $C_e^+(f)$ for each f in the i_{th} iteration (line 15), we first update the edge-cover score $C_e^-(f)$ (line 12) and compute the upper bound $\overline{score}_d(f)$ (line 13). If $\overline{score}_d(f)$ is larger than maximum score in the heap, we will updating $C_e^+(f)$ and compute $score_d(f)$. Otherwise, we will skip updating $C_e^+(f)$ and record i. If in the i'_{th} iteration ($i < i' < k$), $\overline{score}_d(f)$ is no longer larger than the maximum score in the heap, we will update $C_e^+(f)$ by considering the i_{th} to i'_{th} features in $\mathcal{F}_s$. By this upper bound, we can skip $C_e^+(f)$ computation for many $f \in \mathcal{F}\setminus\mathcal{F}_s$, which can speed up the feature edge-cover intersection operation. The updated procedure is shown in Algorithm 2 (line 10-19).

6. ENSEMBLE D&D

We discuss a new ensemble approach. In the D&D method, we select a subset of diversified and discriminative features $\mathcal{F}_s$ from a given feature set. The selected features will complementarily enhance each other to build a good classifier. Since different feature set $\mathcal{F}_s$ might lead to different classifiers. One feature set might lead to a classifier which can correctly classify part of of training graphs, while a different feature set might lead to another classifier which can correctly classify a different part of training graphs. Hence, after building one classifier for feature subset $\mathcal{F}_s$, we adopt an iterative procedure to focus on graphs that are incorrectly predicted by previous classifiers to improve the performance.

The whole ensemble process of is a boosting like method. We utilize the weight of graph to guide the features selection process. We iteratively build a set of base classifiers from the training data and perform classification by taking a weighted vote on the predictions made by each base classifier. The voting weight of a base classifier C_i depends on its accuracy. As in [11, 12], we use the normalized accuracy which is defined as follows.

$$\begin{aligned} Sensitivity &= \frac{\#\ of\ true\ positives}{\#\ of\ positives} \\ Specificity &= \frac{\#\ of\ true\ negatives}{\#\ of\ negatives} \\ Normalized\ accuracy &= \frac{Sensitivity + Specificity}{2} \end{aligned} \quad (11)$$

The voting weight and the weights of training graphs are defined and updated based on AdaBoost. Suppose the accuracy for classifier C_i is a_i, its voting weight is defined as $b_i = \frac{1}{2}\ln(\frac{a_i}{1-a_i})$. Suppose the weight of each graph is initially set to 1. Then in iteration i, the weight of each graph g_j is updated as follows

$$w_j^{i+1} = \frac{w_j^i}{Z_i} \times \begin{cases} \exp^{-b_i} & \text{if } g_j \text{ is correctly classified} \\ \exp^{b_i} & \text{if } g_j \text{ is misclassified} \end{cases} \quad (12)$$

where Z_i is the normalization factor used to ensure that $\sum_{g_j \in \mathcal{D}} w_j^{i+1} = |\mathcal{D}|$. The weight update formula given in Eq. (12) increases the weights of incorrectly classified graphs and decreases the weights of those classified correctly.

After updating the weights of graphs in the iteration i, we use such weights to guide our feature selection process in the next iteration $i+1$. In doing so, we extend the edge-cover score defined in Definition 3.2 to a weighted edge-cover score as follows.

$$S_c'(f) = \sum_{g_i \in sup(f)} w_i \times |E_c(f, g_i)| \quad (13)$$

Accordingly, the diversity of feature f_m defined in Eq. (7) can be update as follows.

$$p_d'(f_m) = \frac{\sum_{g_i \in sup(f_m)} w_i \times |E_c(f_m, g_i)|}{\sum_{g_i \in \mathcal{D}} |E(g_i)|} - \frac{\sum_{g_i \in sup(f_m)} w_i \times |\bigcup_{j=1}^{m-1}(E_c(f_m, g_i) \cap E_c(f_j, g_i))|}{\sum_{g_i \in \mathcal{D}} |E(g_i)|} \quad (14)$$

Finally , we update the diversified discriminative score in Eq. (8) as follows.

$$score_d'(f_m) = \log \frac{p_d'^{+}(f_m)}{p_d'^{-}(f_m)} \quad (15)$$

Based on Eq. (15), if a pattern f_m covers a lot of misclassified positive graphs, $score_d'(f_m)$ will increase, so f_m will have a higher chance to be selected. If a pattern f_m covers a lot of misclassified negative graphs, $score_d'(f_m)$ will decrease and f_m will have less chance to be selected. By assigning a weight to a graph, we can choose the patterns that are in the misclassified positive graphs, and discard the patterns that frequently occur in the misclassified negative graphs in the next iteration to improve accuracy.

7. PERFORMANCE STUDIES

In this section, we evaluate our algorithms from three aspects. First, we evaluate our D&D and ensemble D&D feature selection criteria. We compare D&D with two feature selection strategies: maximum single feature discriminative score selection and conventional feature selection strategy on high-dimensional data which considers the relevance and redundancy of features. We denote the former as Logratio, and for the latter, we use the latest work MMRFS [4] as a representative of the recent existing works [4, 6, 15]. Second, we compare our method with three alternative graph classification approaches: GAIA [12], COM [11], and graphSig [16]. Third, we test the performance of the algorithms on the pattern set mined by GAIA. We implemented our algorithms, Logratio, and MMRFS using C++ and obtained the GAIA implementation from the authors which also includes the implementation of COM and graphSig. For our algorithm implementations, we use LIBSVM [2] as the classification model. As widely used in previous work [12, 11, 16, 20], the classification accuracy is evaluated with 5-fold cross validation and the normalized accuracy defined in Eq. (11) is computed for each classifier. All tests were conducted on a PC with 2.66GHz CPU and 3.43GB memory running Windows XP.

Table 2: List of Selected Bioassays

ID	Assay ID	Tumor description	Total number of actives	Total number of inactives
1	83	Breast	2287	25510
2	123	Leukemia	3123	36741
3	1	Non-Small Cell Lung	2047	38410
4	109	Ovarian	2072	38551
5	330	Leukemia	2194	38799
6	41	Prostate	1568	25967
7	47	Central Nerv Sys	2018	38350
8	145	Renal	1948	38157
9	81	Colon	2401	38236
10	33	Melanoma	1642	38456
11	167	Yeast anticancer	9467	69998

Table 3: List of Selected SCOP Families

ID	SCOP ID	Family name	Number of selected proteins
1	46463	Globins	51
2	47617	Glutathione S-transferase (GST)	36
3	48623	Vertebrate phospholipase A2	29
4	48942	C1 set domains	38
5	50514	Eukaryotic proteases	44
6	51012	alpha-Amylases, C-terminal beta-sheet domain	26
7	51487	beta-glycanases	32
8	51751	Tyrosine-dependent oxidoreductases	65
9	51800	Glyceraldehyde-3-phosphate dehydrogenase-like	34
10	52541	Nucleotide and nucleoside kinases	27
11	52592	G proteins	33
12	53851	Phosphate binding protein-like	32
13	56251	Proteasome subunits	35
14	56437	C-type lectin domains	38
15	88634	Picornaviridae-like VP	39
16	88854	Protein kinases, catalytic subunit	41

We evaluate the algorithms on two real datasets: chemical compound datasets and protein datasets, which are also used in [20, 11, 12].

Chemical datasets: Chemical compound datasets are available at PubChem (`http://pubchem.ncbi.nlm.nih.gov`). In PubChem, each dataset belongs to a certain type of cancer screen with the outcome active or inactive. There are 11 graph datasets classified by their biological activities and the detailed description is provided in Table 2. These are all the bioassays used in [20] and [12]. Each compound can be either active or inactive in a bioas-

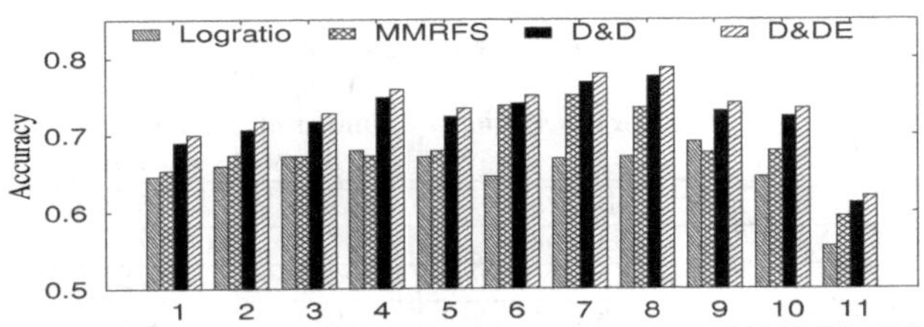

Figure 8: Accuracy Comparison for Logratio, MMRFS, D&D **and** D&DE **(Balanced Chemical Datasets)**

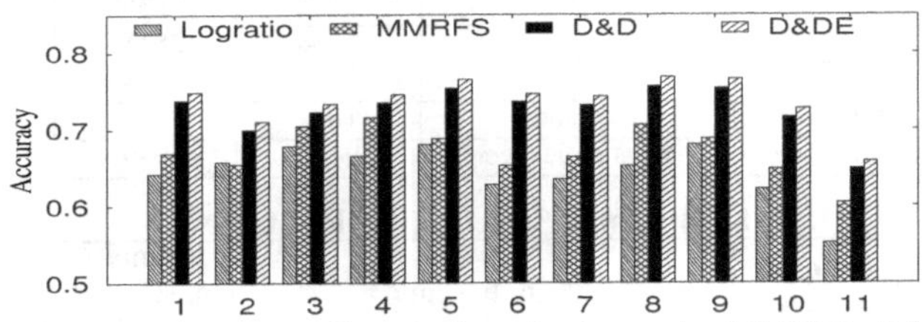

Figure 9: Accuracy Comparison for Logratio, MMRFS, D&D **and** D&DE **(Unbalanced Chemical Datasets)**

say. As in [12], we randomly select 400 active compounds as the positive set and 400 inactive compounds as the negative set as a balanced dataset for each bioassay. We also randomly select 400 active compounds and 1,600 negative compounds as an unbalanced dataset. The graph representation of compounds is straightforward. We remove hydrogen atoms, represent each atom by a node labeled with the atom type and each chemical bond by an edge labeled with the bond type. On average, each compound graph has about 25 nodes and 27 edges.

Protein datasets: The protein datasets consist of protein structures from Protein Data Bank (`http://www.rcsb.org/pdb/`) classified by SCOP (`http://scop.mrc-lmb.cam.ac.uk/scop/`). We use 16 protein datasets generated from all the large SCOP families with more than 25 members (listed in Table 3). In each dataset, protein structures in a selected family are taken as the positive set. Unless otherwise specified, we randomly select 256 other proteins (i.e., not members of the 16 families) as a common negative set used by all protein datasets. For each family, the selected proteins (as the positive graphs) and the 256 negative graphs form a dataset which is unbalanced. We also create a balanced dataset for each family by selecting the same number of negative graphs from the 256 proteins as the number of positive ones in that family. To generate a protein graph, each graph node denotes an amino acid, whose location is represented by the location of its alpha carbon. There is an edge between two nodes if the distance between the two alpha carbons is less than 11.5 angstroms. Nodes are labeled with their amino acid type and edges are labeled with the distances between the alpha carbons. On average, each protein graph has 250 nodes and 2,700 edges.

7.1 D&D Performance Analysis

In this subsection, we study the performance of our method D&D by comparing it with two feature selection strategies: Logratio and MMRFS. Logratio incrementally selects frequent features with maximal single feature discriminative score. MMRFS iteratively selects features with the maximum marginal relevance. To investigate our ensemble strategy, we also compare the performance of a single D&D and ensemble D&D of our method, denoted as D&D and D&DE respectively. Unless other specified, for all algorithms, we select the features from a given feature set mined by gSpan [21] with a minimum support 10%. Since our method is independent of the mining method, we only report the time of feature selection

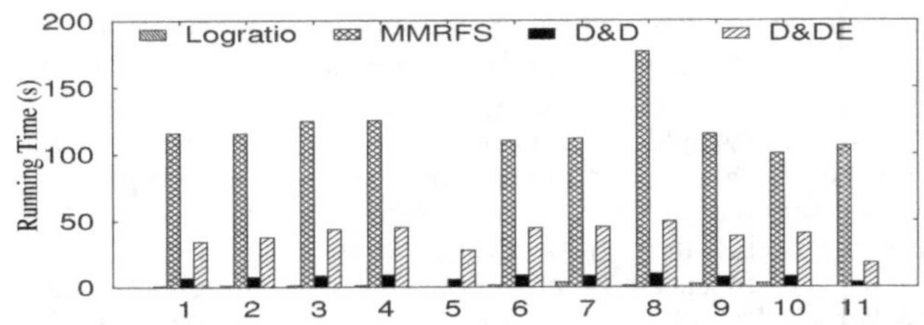

Figure 10: Runtime Comparison for Logratio, MMRFS, D&D **and** D&DE **(Unbalanced Chemical Datasets)**

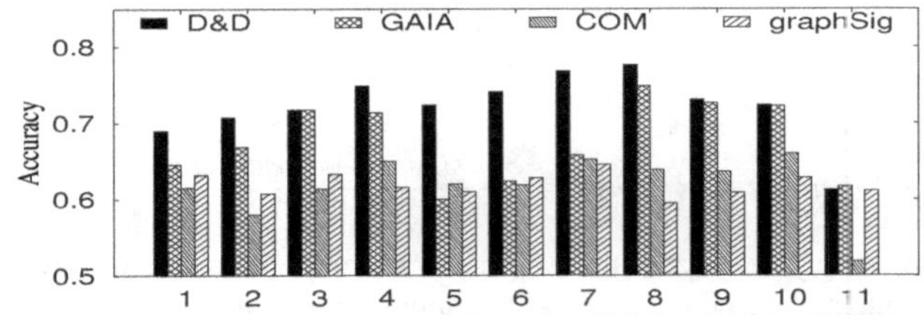

Figure 11: Accuracy Comparison for D&D, **GAIA, COM and graphSig (Balanced Chemical Datasets)**

and classification. In this subsection, we only evaluate algorithms on chemical datasets since graphs in protein datasets are very large and gSpan can not mine frequent patterns within reasonable time.

Fig. 8 shows the classification accuracy by different methods on balanced chemical datasets. Our method D&D outperforms Logratio and MMRFS on the total 11 chemical datasets. Logratio performs worst among all the methods. This shows that the single feature discriminative score in feature selection is not sufficient. MMRFS performs better than Logratio, which proves taking redundancy into consideration in feature selection is necessary. MMRFS is outperformed by D&D due to its limitation on capturing the graph structure. D&DE can get better accuracy than D&D. Fig. 9 shows the classification accuracy by different methods on unbalanced chemical datasets, which has a similar trend as Fig. 8.

The time cost for these algorithms have a similar trend on balanced datasets and unbalanced datasets. Due to the lack of space, we only show the time for unbalanced datasets since they are larger than balanced datasets and usually need more time. Fig. 10 shows running time for different methods on unbalanced chemical datasets. Logratio is the fastest because it only needs to sort the single feature discriminative score for each pattern. MMRFS is the most costly since each time it needs to scan all the rest of features to select the one with the maximum marginal score, and in each marginal score computation, it needs to compute the redundancy between the new feature with the already selected $k-1$ features. Our D&D method with the best performance on accuracy is efficient, based on our proposed gradual update strategy and the early stop bound based pruning.

7.2 Comparison with Existing Algorithms

In this section, we compare our method D&D with GAIA, COM and graphSig on chemical datasets. For these three algorithms, we use the parameters that deliver the best results as suggested in [12, 11, 16]. We will report the evaluation results on protein datasets in next subsection.

Fig. 11 shows the classification accuracy by different methods on the 11 balanced chemical datasets. Our method wins on 10 out of the 11 datasets. This clearly demonstrates the effectiveness of our graph features, when the feature overlap is considered based on our proposed diversified discriminative score. With this score measure, more important features with little overlap will be picked.

Fig. 12 shows the classification accuracy by different classification methods on the 11 unbalanced chemical datasets. As in

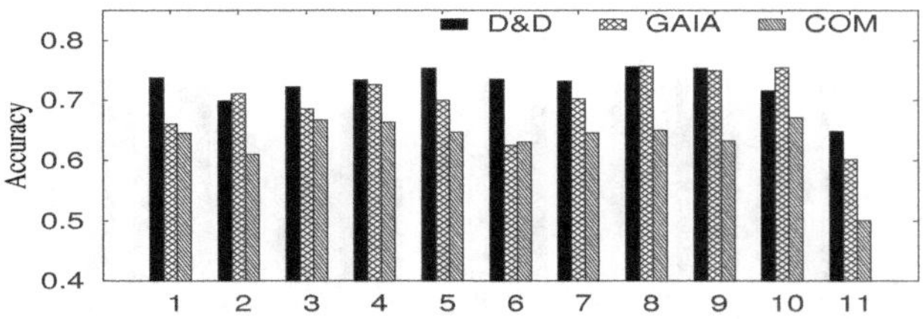

Figure 12: Accuracy Comparison for D&D, GAIA and COM (Unbalanced Chemical Datasets)

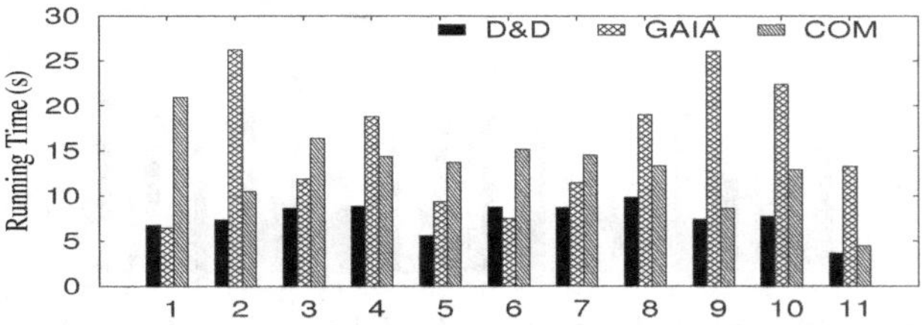

Figure 13: Runtime Comparison for D&D, GAIA and COM (Unbalanced Chemical Datasets)

[12], we did not compare with graphSig since it can not handle unbalanced datasets. Our method wins on 9 out of the 11 datasets and GAIA wins on the other 2. This result again demonstrates the superiority of our diversified discriminative score. Fig. 13 shows running time by different methods on the 11 unbalanced chemical datasets. On most of the datasets, our method is the most efficient, based on our proposed gradual update strategy and the early stop bound based pruning

7.3 Performance on Patterns Mined by GAIA

Our D&D feature selection method is independent of the frequent pattern mining process, because D&D can perform on any given feature set $\mathcal{F}$. We validate the power of D&D feature selection method on a given frequent pattern set mined by gSpan, which usually contains a large number of features. In this subsection, we investigate the performance of D&D on any given incomplete frequent pattern set with a small number of features. We take the pattern set mined by GAIA as the given pattern set, and perform D&D to see whether it can improve the performance of classification. We compare D&D and GAIA on both chemical datasets and protein datasets.

Fig. 14 shows the classification accuracy for D&D and GAIA on balanced chemical datasets. Our method obtains higher accuracy on total 11 chemical datasets, which validates the effectiveness of our D&D criteria on even small and incomplete pattern set. We notice that the improvement is not as significant as on the frequent pattern set compared to Logratio. The underlying reasons are: the patterns mined by GAIA are not complete, and some important patterns miss, which limit the classification accuracy of D&D.

Fig. 15 shows the performance for D&D and GAIA on the unbalanced chemical datasets. D&D improves the accuracy on 10 out of 11 datasets. Fig. 16 shows the running time by D&D and GAIA on 11 unbalanced chemical datasets. The time of D&D includes GAIA's mining time, D&D's feature selection time and the classification time. The result shows that we can improve the classification accuracy with a small overhead on feature selection by D&D.

Fig. 17 shows the classification accuracy for D&D and GAIA on the balanced protein datasets. Our method gets better accuracy on 15 out of 16 datasets. The improvement is more significant compared to that on chemical datasets.

Fig. 18 shows the performance for D&D and GAIA on the unbalanced protein datasets. D&D wins on 14 out of 16 datasets. Fig. 19 shows the running time for D&D and GAIA on the unbalanced protein datasets. Again, the time of D&D includes GAIA's mining time, D&D's feature selection time and the classification time. D&D only adds a small overhead on GAIA for feature selection, but improves the classification accuracy substantially.

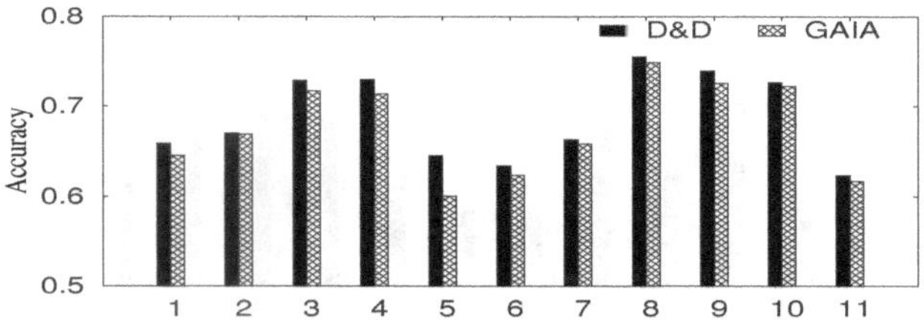

Figure 14: Accuracy Comparison for D&D and GAIA (Balanced Chemical Datasets)

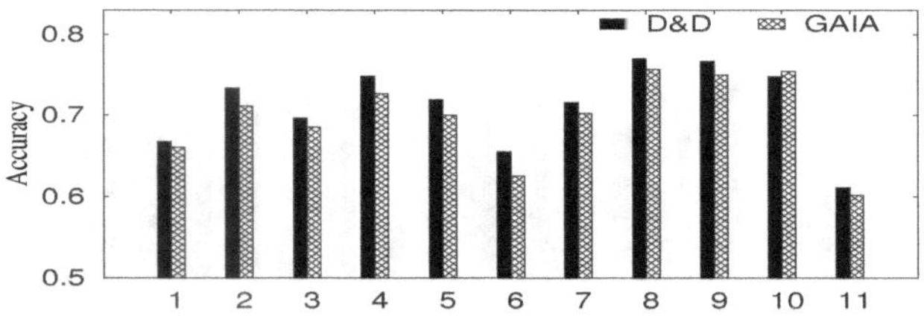

Figure 15: Accuracy Comparison for D&D and GAIA (Unbalanced Chemical Datasets)

8. RELATED WORK

In the literature, there have been a number of studies on discovering or selecting different kinds of patterns to build a graph classification model. One traditional way is to mine frequent patterns first, then select interesting features, and finally build a classification model [4] [5] [1]. Recently people have proposed mining algorithms that directly mine the most discriminative features efficiently [20, 17, 18, 16, 11, 12]. Yan et al. [20] proposed an efficient algorithm, called LEAP, for mining the most discriminative subgraph. The algorithm focuses on searching dissimilar subgraphs using structural leap search and achieves significant speedup over the widely used branch-and-bound approach. [17] proposed an iterative subgraph mining method based on partial least squares regression (PLS), combined with a weighted pattern mining algorithm. [18] proposed a feature selection approach on frequent subgraphs, called CORK, that optimizes a submodular quality criterion and integrates the criterion into gSpan for subgraph mining. Ranu and Singh [16] proposed GraphSig, a scalable method to mine significant (measured by p-value) subgraphs based on a feature vector representation of graphs. The first step in the mining process is to convert each graph into a set of feature vectors where each vector represents a region within the graph. Prior probabilities of features are computed empirically to evaluate statistical significance of patterns in the feature space. Then frequent subgraph mining techniques can be used to mine significant patterns in a scalable manner. [11] designs a new classification method based on pattern co-occurrence to derive graph classification rules. [12] proposes a subgraph mining method, GAIA, which employs a novel subgraph encoding approach to support an arbitrary subgraph pattern exploration order and explores the subgraph pattern space using evolutionary computation. In this manner, GAIA is able to find discriminative subgraph patterns much faster than other algorithms. Most of the above methods do not rigorously measure the feature overlap. Different from the above studies, [24] proposes to use graph metrics, such as non-tree density, degree distribution, diameter, global clustering coefficient, etc., as features for graph classification.

Graph pattern mining has been widely studied and can be catego-

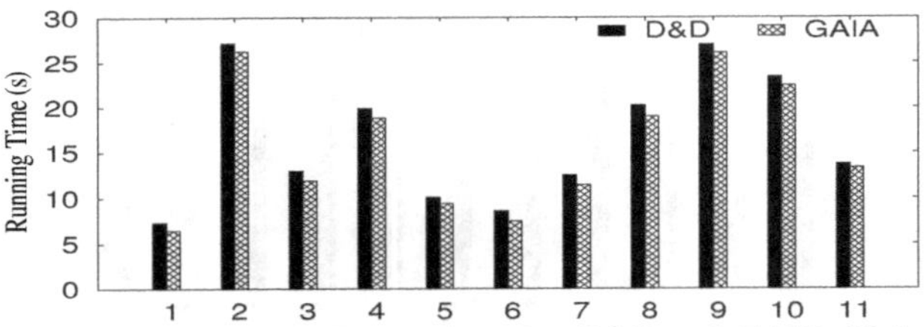

Figure 16: Runtime Comparison for D&D and GAIA (Unbalanced Chemical Datasets)

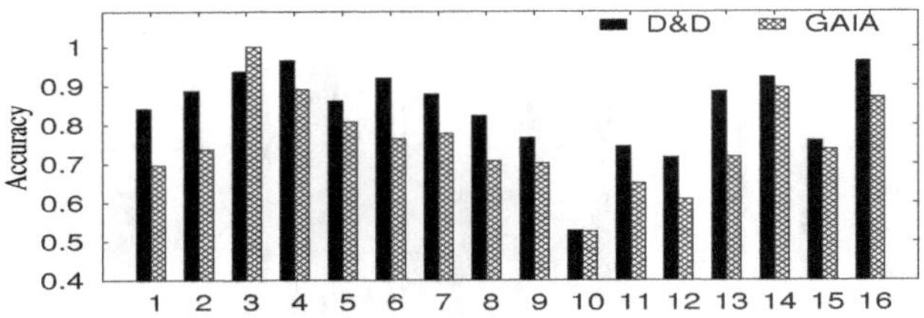

Figure 17: Accuracy Comparison for D&D and GAIA (Balanced Protein Datasets)

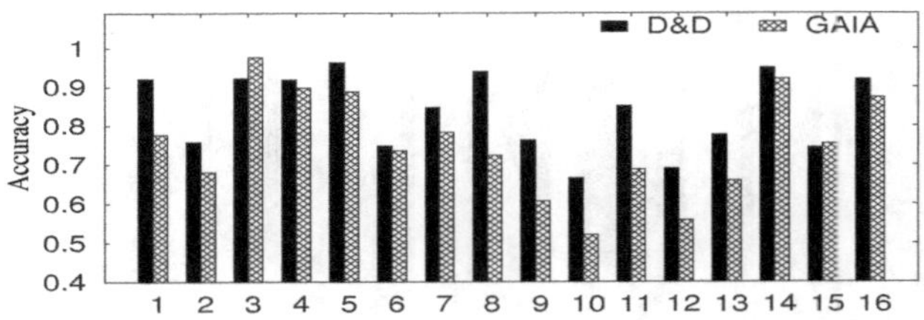

Figure 18: Accuracy Comparison for D&D and GAIA (Unbalanced Protein Datasets)

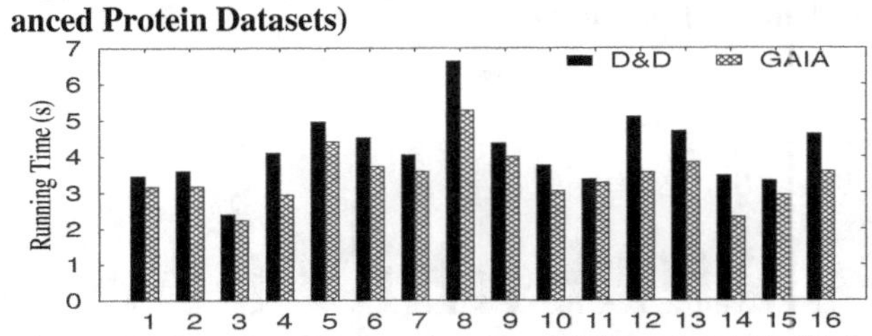

Figure 19: Runtime Comparison for D&D and GAIA (Unbalanced Protein Datasets)

rized in three types: exact graph mining such as gSpan [21], FFSM [9], Gaston [14] and FSG [13] ; approximate graph mining such as SUMMARIZE-MINE [3], TFP [7], Monkey [23] and sampling method [8]. Other methods include maximal pattern mining [10] and closed pattern mining [22].

Feature selection is a critical step for building accurate classification model [19, 6, 15, 4]. In conventional classification tasks on high-dimensonal data, feature selection is a well studied problem in the literature, which aims to select highly relevant and less redundant features, such as CMIM [6], mRmR [15], and MMRFS [4]. However, such feature selection methods have limit power when they are directly applied to graph database. This is because these methods treat each feature as an independent unit and evaluate their relationship only by their distributions over binary vectors. While in graph database, features have complicated relationships in terms of the topological structures and the locations. Moreover, a pattern has an exponential number of subgraphs, and the patterns are not uniformly distributed. This leads to a huge redundancy and complex overlapping of patterns.

9. CONCLUSION

In this paper we study graph classification by designing a diversified discriminative feature selection approach. Our proposed score can reduce the overlap between selected features by considering the embedding overlaps in the graphs. We analyze the properties of our score measure and show that the selected features make the positive and negative graphs more separable. Experimental results show that we can achieve a higher classification accuracy compared with the state-of-the-art graph classification methods with our proposed diversified discriminative feature selection method.

Acknowledgments The work was supported by grants of the Research Grants Council of the Hong Kong SAR, China No. 419109, 411310, 411211 and 418512.

10. REFERENCES

[1] D. Bandyopadhyay, J. Huan, J. Liu, J. Prins, J. Snoeyink, W. Wang, and A. Tropsha. Structure-based function inference using protein family-specific fingerprints. *Protein Science*, 15(6):1537–1543, 2006.

[2] C.-C. Chang and C.-J. Lin. Libsvm: A library for support vector machines, 2001. software available at http://www.csie.ntu.edu.tw/ cjlin/libsvm.

[3] C. Chen, C. X. Lin, M. Fredrikson, M. Christodorescu, X. Yan, and J. Han. Mining graph patterns efficiently via randomized summaries. *PVLDB*, 2(1):742–753, 2009.

[4] H. Cheng, X. Yan, J. Han, and C.-W. Hsu. Discriminative frequent pattern analysis for effective classification. In *ICDE*, pages 716–725, 2007.

[5] M. Deshpande, M. Kuramochi, N. Wale, and G. Karypis. Frequent substructure-based approaches for classifying chemical compounds. *TKDE*, 17(8):1036–1050, 2005.

[6] F. Fleuret. Fast binary feature selection with conditional mutual information. *JMLR*, 5:1531–1555, 2004.

[7] J. Han, J. Wang, Y. Lu, and P. Tzvetkov. Mining top-k frequent closed patterns without minimum support. In *ICDM*, pages 211–218, 2002.

[8] M. A. Hasan and M. J. Zaki. Output space sampling for graph patterns. *PVLDB*, 2(1):730–741, 2009.

[9] J. Huan, W. Wang, and J. Prins. Efficient mining of frequent subgraphs in the presence of isomorphism. In *ICDM*, pages 549–552, 2003.

[10] J. Huan, W. Wang, J. Prins, and J. Yang. Spin: mining maximal frequent subgraphs from graph databases. In *KDD*, pages 581–586, 2004.

[11] N. Jin, C. Young, and W. Wang. Graph classification based on pattern co-occurrence. In *CIKM*, pages 573–582, 2009.

[12] N. Jin, C. Young, and W. Wang. Gaia: graph classification using evolutionary computation. In *SIGMOD*, pages 879–890, 2010.

[13] M. Kuramochi and G. Karypis. Frequent subgraph discovery. In *ICDM*, pages 313–320, 2001.

[14] S. Nijssen and J. N. Kok. A quickstart in frequent structure mining can make a difference. In *KDD*, pages 647–652, 2004.

[15] H. Peng, F. Long, and C. H. Q. Ding. Feature selection based on mutual information: Criteria of max-dependency, max-relevance, and min-redundancy. *TPAMI*, 27(8):1226–1238, 2005.

[16] S. Ranu and A. K. Singh. Graphsig: A scalable approach to mining significant subgraphs in large graph databases. In *ICDE*, pages 844–855, 2009.

[17] H. Saigo, N. Krämer, and K. Tsuda. Partial least squares regression for graph mining. In *KDD*, pages 578–586, 2008.

[18] M. Thoma, H. Cheng, A. Gretton, J. Han, H. Kriegel, A. Smola, L. Song, P. Yu, X. Yan, and K. Borgwardt. Near-optimal supervised feature selection among frequent subgraphs. In *SDM*, 2009.

[19] J. Weston, S. Mukherjee, O. Chapelle, M. Pontil, T. Poggio, and V. Vapnik. Feature selection for svms. *NIPS*, pages 668–674, 2001.

[20] X. Yan, H. Cheng, J. Han, and P. S. Yu. Mining significant graph patterns by leap search. In *SIGMOD*, pages 433–444, 2008.

[21] X. Yan and J. Han. gspan: Graph-based substructure pattern mining. In *ICDM*, pages 721–724, 2002.

[22] X. Yan and J. Han. Closegraph: mining closed frequent graph patterns. In *KDD*, pages 286–295, 2003.

[23] S. Zhang, J. Yang, and V. Cheedella. Monkey: Approximate graph mining based on spanning trees. In *ICDE*, pages 1247–1249, 2007.

[24] L. Zhu, W. K. Ng, and S. Han. Classifying graphs using theoretical metrics: A study of feasibility. In *DASFAA*, 2011.

Multi-Scale Link Prediction

Donghyuk Shin
Dept. of Computer Science
University of Texas at Austin
Austin, TX 78712-1188, USA
dshin@cs.utexas.edu

Si Si
Dept. of Computer Science
University of Texas at Austin
Austin, TX 78712-1188, USA
ssi@cs.utexas.edu

Inderjit S. Dhillon
Dept. of Computer Science
University of Texas at Austin
Austin, TX 78712-1188, USA
inderjit@cs.utexas.edu

ABSTRACT

The automated analysis of social networks has become an important problem due to the proliferation of social networks, such as LiveJournal, Flickr and Facebook. The scale of these social networks is massive and continues to grow rapidly. An important problem in social network analysis is proximity estimation that infers the closeness of different users. Link prediction, in turn, is an important application of proximity estimation. However, many methods for computing proximity measures have high computational complexity and are thus prohibitive for large-scale link prediction problems. One way to address this problem is to estimate proximity measures via low-rank approximation. However, a single low-rank approximation may not be sufficient to represent the behavior of the entire network. In this paper, we propose Multi-Scale Link Prediction (MSLP), a framework for link prediction, which can handle massive networks. The basic idea of MSLP is to construct low-rank approximations of the network at *multiple scales* in an efficient manner. To achieve this, we propose a fast tree-structured approximation algorithm. Based on this approach, MSLP combines predictions at multiple scales to make robust and accurate predictions. Experimental results on real-life datasets with more than a million nodes show the superior performance and scalability of our method.

Categories and Subject Descriptors

H.2.8 [**Database Management**]: Database Application—*Data mining*; J.4 [**Computer Applications**]: Social and Behavioral Sciences—*Sociology*

General Terms

Algorithms, Experimentation

Keywords

Low Rank Approximation, Hierarchical Clustering, Link Prediction, Social Network Analysis

CIKM'12, October 29–November 2, 2012, Maui, HI, USA.

1. INTRODUCTION

Social network analysis has become essential due to the proliferation of social networks, such as LiveJournal, MySpace, Flickr and Facebook. The scale of these social networks is massive and continues to grow rapidly. For example, Facebook now has more than 900 million active users with over 700,000 new users joining everyday. This has significantly changed the way people interact and share information with others and has led to unprecedented research opportunities.

An important problem for social network analysis is proximity estimation that infers the "closeness" of different users. Proximity measures quantify the interaction between users based on the structural properties of a graph, such as the number of common friends. An important application of proximity estimation in social networks is link prediction, which is a key problem in social network analysis [15, 23]. Using proximity estimation for link prediction is based on the assumption that a pair of users with a high proximity score indicates they are close in terms of social relatedness and hence this pair of users will have a good chance to become friends in the future.

Simple proximity measures, such as neighborhood-based measures, e.g., Adamic-Adar score [1] and common neighbors [18], can be computed efficiently. However, they describe a very localized view of interaction. There are more comprehensive proximity measures that capture a broader perspective of social relationships by considering all paths between users. These path based methods, such as Katz [12] or rooted PageRank [15], are often more effective. Nonetheless, they are also well known for their high computational complexity and memory usage, which limits their applicability to massive graphs with more than a million users.

To solve this problem, a great deal of work has been done on scalable proximity estimation [4, 22]. One basic idea is to perform dimensionality reduction on the original graph and then compute the proximity based on its low-rank approximation. Recently, clustered low rank approximation (CLRA) has been proposed which develops a fast and memory efficient method [20, 23].

However, a single low-rank approximation may not be sufficient to represent the whole network. Furthermore, the approach in [20] only uses a single clustering structure making it sensitive to a particular clustering and biased against links that happen to be between clusters. More notably, a recent study has shown that large social networks tend to lack large well-defined clusters which suggests that a single clustering structure can be problematic [14].

To address the above problems, we propose a multi-scale approximation of the graph to obtain multiple granular views of the network in order to perform link prediction in a scalable and accurate manner. This is achieved by taking a hierarchical clustering approach and generating low-rank approximations at each level in the hierarchy. Although we use a single hierarchical representation of the graph, we do not require it to be the optimal structure. The main purpose of using hierarchical clustering is not to detect the underlying community structure of the graph, but to use it as a tool for efficient multi-scale approximation. In the experimental section, we show that under clustering structures of varying quality, our proposed algorithm can still achieve better results compared to other link prediction algorithms (for example, in the `Epinions` network [19] which was also used in [14]).

Specifically, in this paper we propose a robust, flexible, and scalable framework for link prediction on social networks that we call, *multi-scale link prediction* (MSLP). MSLP exploits different scales of low-rank approximation of social networks by combining information from multiple levels in the hierarchy in an efficient manner. Higher levels in the hierarchy present a more global view, while lower levels focus on more localized information. MSLP works by first performing hierarchical clustering on the graph by utilizing a fast graph clustering algorithm, and then performing multi-scale approximation based on the produced hierarchy. Since different levels have different approximation, each level will give different approximated proximity scores. MSLP combines approximated proximity scores from each level and makes the final prediction based on the combined scores. As a result, MSLP captures both local and global information of the network.

We list the benefits of our framework as follows:

- MSLP makes predictions based on information from multiple scales and thus can make more accurate and robust predictions.
- MSLP is fast and memory-efficient as it uses a simple and fast tree-structured subspace approximation method, which speeds up the computation of our multi-scale approximation while re-using memory across different levels. As a result, it can be applied to social networks with millions of users.
- MSLP is flexible in two aspects: (1) it can be used with any other reasonably good clustering algorithm to generate a multi-scale view of the graph as it does not depend on a particular hierarchical structure, (2) as a dimensionality reduction method, it is not tied down to a particular proximity measure, e.g., Katz and CN, and others can be used.

The rest of the paper is organized as follows. In Section 2, we survey some related work on link prediction. Next, some background material is introduced in Section 3. In Section 4, we propose our proposed MSLP algorithm. Experimental results on real-world large-scale social networks are presented in Section 5. Finally, we present our conclusions in Section 6.

2. RELATED WORK

Link prediction refers to the problem of inferring new interactions among members in a network. The first systematic treatment of the problem appeared in [15], where a variety of proximity measures, such as Common Neighbors [18] and the Katz measure [12] were used as effective methods for link prediction. In addition to unsupervised approaches, there is also rising interest in supervised approaches for link prediction [3, 10, 16]. In supervised link prediction, node and/or edge features are extracted from the network and link prediction is treated as a classification problem. However, engineering good features and handling the class imbalance problem are still challenging tasks. Recently, link prediction has been shown to benefit from exploring additional information external to the network, such as node or edge attributes [11, 21]. However, these approaches require additional information, which may be difficult to obtain due to privacy and security issues.

Many popular proximity measures that are used for link prediction have high computational complexity and do not scale well to large-scale networks. A great deal of recent work has been devoted to speed up the computation. For example, [24] truncates the series expansion of Katz and only considers paths of limited length. In [8, 15, 22], dimensionality reduction methods, such as the eigen-decomposition, are used to construct low-rank approximations of a graph, which are then used to compute approximated proximity measures. The more recent work in [4] applies the Lanczos/Stieltjes procedure to iteratively compute upper and lower bounds of a single Katz value and shows that these eventually converge to the real Katz value.

Efficient proximity estimation is essential for scalable link prediction. However, one should be able to make accurate and robust predictions with the estimated measures. For example, [22] explores the low-rank approximation of social networks to speed up large-scale link prediction. Another way to improve the link prediction performance is to explore the community structure of a network. For example, LinkBoost [6] explores the community structure by a novel degree dependent cost function and shows that minimization of the associated risk can lead to more links predicted within communities than between communities. However, considering a single community structure may not lead to robust predictions, because even detecting the 'best' community structure itself is still an open question.

Very little work has been done using hierarchical structures for link prediction. One exception is the method proposed by [5], which works by sampling a number of competitive hierarchical random graphs from a large pool of such graphs. Each sampled graph is associated with a probability indicating the strength of community structure over the original network. The probability of a link appearing between any two nodes is averaged over the corresponding connecting probability on the sampled graphs. However, to predict potential links, this algorithm needs to enumerate and average over almost all possible hierarchical partitions of a given network and thus is very costly to compute even for small networks. Compared with [5], our algorithm is much more efficient in terms of speed and thus can be scaled up to large-scale link prediction problems with millions of users.

3. BACKGROUND

Assume we are given a graph $G = (\mathcal{V}, \mathcal{E})$, where $\mathcal{V} = \{1, \cdots, n\}$ is the set of vertices representing the users in a social network and $\mathcal{E} = \{e_{ij} | i, j \in \mathcal{V}\}$ is the set of weighted edges quantifying the connection between user i and user j. Let $A = [a_{ij}]$ be the corresponding $n \times n$ adjacency matrix of G such that $a_{ij} = e_{ij}$, if there is an edge between i and j and

0 otherwise. For simplicity, we assume G is an undirected graph, i.e., A is symmetric.

As shown in [15], proximity measures can be computed from A. Many of these measures can be represented as a matrix function $f(A)$, where the (i,j)-th element represents the value of a proximity measure between user i and user j [9]. One popular measure is the number of common neighbors, which can be captured by $f_{cn}(A) = A^2$, describing a very localized view of interactions between vertices by considering only paths of length 2. A more extensive measure is the popular Katz measure [12]. Such path-based proximity measures often achieve better accuracy at the cost of higher computational complexity. The Katz measure is defined as follows

$$f_{kz}(A) = \sum_{k=1}^{\infty} \beta^k A^k = (I - \beta A)^{-1} - I,$$

where I is the identity matrix and $\beta \leq 1/\|A\|_2$ is a damping parameter. As we can see, the Katz measure takes $O(n^3)$ time, which is computationally infeasible for large-scale networks with millions of nodes.

Here, dimensionality reduction methods, such as the singular value decomposition (SVD), play an important role. These methods are particularly useful, since it suffices to have a reasonably good estimation of a given proximity measure for most applications. Furthermore, low-rank approximation of the adjacency matrix serves as a useful conceptual and computational tool for the graph.

Assume that we are given a rank-r approximation of the $n \times n$ matrix A as follows

$$A \approx \tilde{A} = USU^T,$$

where U is an $n \times r$ orthonormal matrix (i.e. $U^T U = I_r$ is an identity matrix), and S is an $r \times r$ matrix. Using this low-rank approximation $\tilde{A}$, the CN measure can be approximated as $f_{cn}(A) \approx US^2U^T$. Similarly, the Katz measure is approximated by

$$\begin{aligned} f_{kz}(A) &\approx \sum_{k=1}^{\infty} \beta^k \tilde{A}^k = \sum_{k=1}^{\infty} \beta^k (USU^T)^k \\ &= U(\sum_{k=1}^{\infty} \beta^k S^k)U^T = U((I - \beta S)^{-1} - I)U^T. \end{aligned}$$

In general, $f(A) \approx Uf(S)U^T$, which requires less computational resources as the matrix function is only evaluated on the much smaller S matrix.

However, computing the low-rank approximation of a massive graph via SVD or other popular dimensionality reduction methods can still be a computational bottleneck. Recently, the technique of clustered low rank approximation (CLRA) was proposed in [20] as a scalable and accurate low-rank approximation method. The basic idea of CLRA is to preserve important structural information by clustering the graph G into c disjoint clusters. Then it computes a low-rank approximation of each cluster, which is finally extended to approximate the entire graph.

Assume that the graph has been clustered into c clusters and the vertices are ordered as follows

$$A = \begin{bmatrix} A_{11} & \cdots & A_{1c} \\ \vdots & \ddots & \vdots \\ A_{c1} & \cdots & A_{cc} \end{bmatrix},$$

where the diagonal blocks A_{ii}, $i = 1, \ldots, c$, correspond to the local adjacency matrix of each cluster i. For every cluster, the best rank-r approximation is computed as $A_{ii} \approx U_i \Lambda_i U_i^T$, where Λ_i is a diagonal matrix with the r largest eigenvalues of A_{ii}, and U_i is an orthonormal matrix with the corresponding eigenvectors. Finally, CLRA aligns the low-rank approximation of each cluster together to obtain the clustered low-rank approximation of the entire adjacency matrix A. Mathematically,

$$A \approx \begin{bmatrix} U_1 & \ldots & 0 \\ \vdots & \ddots & \vdots \\ 0 & \ldots & U_c \end{bmatrix} \begin{bmatrix} S_{11} & \ldots & S_{1c} \\ \vdots & \ddots & \vdots \\ S_{c1} & \ldots & S_{cc} \end{bmatrix} \begin{bmatrix} U_1 & \ldots & 0 \\ \vdots & \ddots & \vdots \\ 0 & \ldots & U_c \end{bmatrix}^T,$$

where $S_{ij} = U_i^T A_{ij} U_j$, for $i, j = 1, \ldots, c$, which is the optimal S in the least squares sense. Note that the block-diagonal matrix $U = \text{diag}(U_1, \ldots, U_c)$ is also orthonormal and $S_{ii} = \Lambda_i$ are diagonal. It is shown in [20] that CLRA achieves accurate approximations while being efficient in both computational speed and memory usage. However, the drawback of CLRA is that it only uses one clustering structure, whereas it has been shown that many large social networks lack such structure [14]. In this paper, we overcome this limitation by taking a multi-scale approach.

Based on the estimated proximity measures, we can perform link prediction on social networks. Link prediction deals with networks that evolve over time Specifically, given a snapshot of a network at time t_1, the task is to predict links that would form at a future time step t_2. A high proximity score between two users captures the high correlation between them and thus a high chance to form a new link in the future.

4. PROPOSED ALGORITHM

In this section we present our *multi-scale link prediction* (MSLP) framework for social networks. Our method mainly consists of three phases: hierarchical clustering, subspace approximation and multi-scale prediction. Specifically, we first construct a hierarchy tree with a fast top-down hierarchical clustering approach. Then, a multi-scale low-rank approximation to the original graph is computed when traversing the hierarchy in a bottom-up fashion. An important technical contribution of our paper is a fast tree-structured approximation algorithm that enables us to compute the subspace of a parent cluster quickly by using subspaces of its child clusters. This allows us to compute each level's low-rank approximation efficiently. Finally, we combine proximity measures, which are computed using the multi-scale low-rank approximation of the graph, and make our final predictions.

4.1 Hierarchical Clustering

The first step of our method is to hierarchically cluster or partition a given graph. The purpose of this is to efficiently generate a multi-scale approximation of the graph using the constructed hierarchical structure. This, in turn, makes predictions more accurate and robust as we combine predictions at each level of the hierarchy in the final step.

Generally, there are two main approaches for hierarchical clustering: agglomerative (or bottom-up) approach and divisive (or top-down) approach. The agglomerative approach initially treats each vertex as one cluster and continually merges pairs of clusters as it moves up the hierarchy. The

Table 1: Percentage of within-cluster edges using Graclus. Numbers in brackets represent random clustering. It can be seen that Graclus is quite effective in finding good clustering structure. (these networks contain about 2 million nodes – details are given in Table 3.)

Hierarchy	Flickr	LiveJournal	MySpace
Level 1	96.2 (68.1)	99.3 (60.1)	98.6 (61.6)
Level 2	95.1 (61.7)	98.8 (51.7)	88.0 (35.2)
Level 3	88.1 (54.3)	85.0 (28.6)	69.5 (18.0)
Level 4	85.2 (51.4)	79.4 (15.2)	64.3 (13.0)
Level 5	66.7 (27.2)	70.0 (9.4)	56.3 (8.4)

divisive approach takes the opposite direction, that is, all vertices are placed in a single cluster and recursively partitioned into smaller clusters. Due to the large scale of the problem and the availability of efficient clustering software, such as Graclus [7], we employ the divisive approach in our work.

Given a graph $G = (\mathcal{V}, \mathcal{E})$, our goal is to construct a level ℓ hierarchy, so as to generate a multi-scale view of the graph. We form c nodes (clusters) at the first level of the hierarchy by clustering $\mathcal{V}$ into c disjoint sets $\mathcal{V}_1^{(1)}, \mathcal{V}_2^{(1)}, \ldots, \mathcal{V}_c^{(1)}$, where the superscript denotes the level of the hierarchy. Then, we proceed to the second level of the hierarchy tree by further clustering each node in the first level $\mathcal{V}_i^{(1)}$, $i = 1, \ldots, c$, and generate c child nodes from each of them as $\mathcal{V}_{i1}^{(2)}, \mathcal{V}_{i2}^{(2)}, \ldots, \mathcal{V}_{ic}^{(2)}$, such that $\mathcal{V}_i^{(1)} = \bigcup_{j=1}^{c} \mathcal{V}_{ij}^{(2)}$. As a consequence, we will have c^2 nodes on the second level of the hierarchy. This process repeats until the desired number of levels ℓ is reached. Many classic clustering methods can be used as a base clustering method. In this paper, we use the Graclus algorithm [7] to cluster each node because of its ability to scale up to very large graphs. However, our algorithm can utilize any other graph clustering method.

The hierarchy of A at level p, after sorting the vertices, can be written as

$$A = \begin{bmatrix} A_{11}^{(p)} & \ldots & A_{1\hat{c}}^{(p)} \\ \vdots & \ddots & \vdots \\ A_{\hat{c}1}^{(p)} & \ldots & A_{\hat{c}\hat{c}}^{(p)} \end{bmatrix},$$

where $\hat{c} = c^p$ is the number of nodes in level p and each diagonal block $A_{ii}^{(p)}$, $i = 1, \ldots, \hat{c}$, is an $m_i \times m_i$ matrix that can be viewed as a local adjacency matrix of cluster i at level p. The off-diagonal $m_i \times m_j$ blocks, $A_{ij}^{(p)}$, where $i \neq j$, contains the set of edges between clusters i and j.

As it is desirable to capture most of the links within clusters, we compare with random clustering in terms of the percentage of within-cluster links on three large-scale social networks in Table 1. For each level of the hierarchy tree, the within-cluster links are those that connect two vertices in the same cluster. As shown in Table 1, the percentage of within-cluster edges of random clustering is much smaller than the hierarchical clustering scheme used in this paper, and the gap becomes much larger when going down the hierarchy. Even at the deepest level, the clustering scheme we use can still capture more than half of the edges compared with less than 10% in the `LiveJournal` and `MySpace` graphs when using random clustering.

As a final remark, we note that the hierarchical clustering

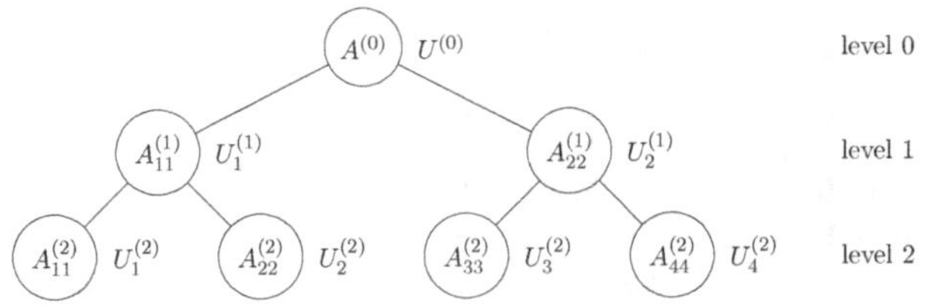

Figure 1: Hierarchical structure example.

scheme is also very fast. Clustering the three networks of Table 1 into 5 levels with 2 clusters at each level can be completed in just 5 minutes on a 8-core 3.40GHz machine. In the next section, we show how to use the hierarchy structure to efficiently construct a multi-scale approximation of large-scale graphs.

4.2 Subspace Approximation

After constructing the hierarchy for a given graph, we can compute low-rank approximations of A at each level of the hierarchy to obtain a multi-scale approximation. Specifically, we employ CLRA to obtain the approximation. Figure 1 gives an example of a simple three level hierarchy to better illustrate our method. By applying CLRA on each of the 3 levels in the example, we have 3 clustered low-rank approximations of A as follows

- Level 0:

$$A \approx \tilde{A}^{(0)} = U^{(0)} S^{(0)} U^{(0)^T},$$

- Level 1:

$$A \approx \tilde{A}^{(1)} = \begin{bmatrix} U_1^{(1)} & 0 \\ 0 & U_2^{(1)} \end{bmatrix} \begin{bmatrix} S_{11}^{(1)} & S_{12}^{(1)} \\ S_{21}^{(1)} & S_{22}^{(1)} \end{bmatrix} \begin{bmatrix} U_1^{(1)} & 0 \\ 0 & U_2^{(1)} \end{bmatrix}^T,$$

- Level 2:

$$A \approx \tilde{A}^{(2)} = U^{(2)} S^{(2)} U^{(2)^T}$$
$$= \begin{bmatrix} U_1^{(2)} \ldots & 0 \\ \vdots \ \ddots & \vdots \\ 0 & \ldots U_4^{(2)} \end{bmatrix} \begin{bmatrix} S_{11}^{(2)} \ldots S_{14}^{(2)} \\ \vdots \ \ddots \ \vdots \\ S_{41}^{(2)} \ldots S_{44}^{(2)} \end{bmatrix} \begin{bmatrix} U_1^{(2)} \ldots & 0 \\ \vdots \ \ddots & \vdots \\ 0 & \ldots U_4^{(2)} \end{bmatrix}^T,$$

where the columns of $U_i^{(p)}$ are the set of orthonormal basis vectors forming the subspace for cluster i at level p and $S_{ij}^{(p)} = U_i^{(p)^T} A_{ij}^{(p)} U_j^{(p)}$, $1 \leq i, j \leq 2^p$. Level 0 can be viewed as a special case of CLRA, where the entire graph is treated as a single cluster, which yields a global view of the entire matrix A. Lower levels in the hierarchy will preserve more local information within each cluster. Thus, each level of approximation concentrates on different levels of granularity, resulting in a multi-scale approximation of A.

An important issue here is how to compute each level's approximation of A efficiently. A straightforward solution would be use standard dimensionality reduction methods,

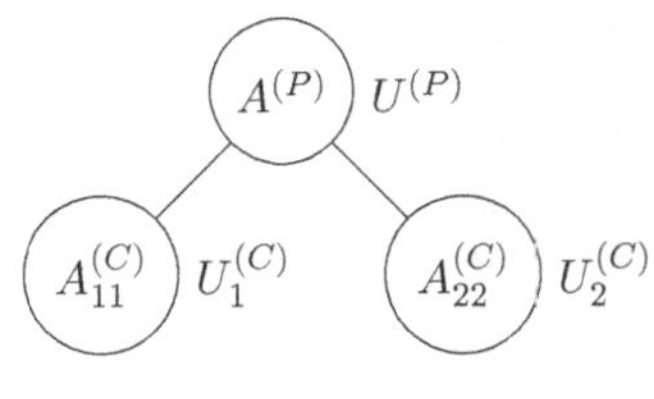

Figure 2: Approximating parent cluster's subspace.

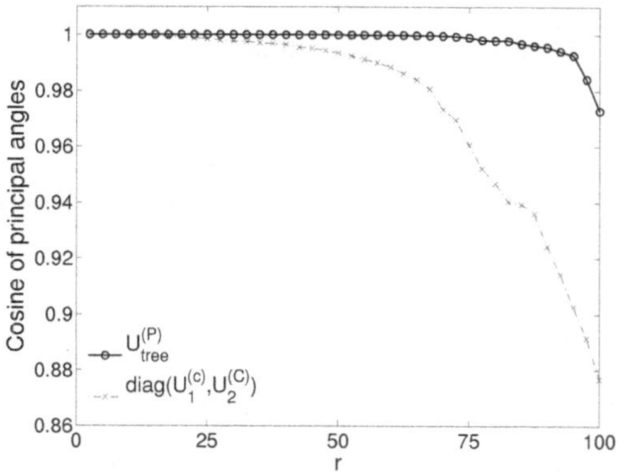

Figure 3: Principal angles between parent cluster's subspace and two other subspaces: child cluster's subspace diag($U_1^{(C)}, U_2^{(C)}$) and parent cluster's subspace $U_{tree}^{(P)}$ computed using Algorithm 1.

such as SVD. This can be computed efficiently for clusters at the deepest level of the hierarchy tree, since the size of each cluster is relatively small. However, the computational cost becomes prohibitive as the size of the cluster increases, which is the case for upper levels in the hierarchy tree. We propose a more scalable and effective method to address this issue. For clarity and brevity, we focus on a local view of the hierarchy as shown in Figure 2, where $A^{(P)}$ is a parent cluster and $A_{11}^{(C)}$ and $A_{22}^{(C)}$ are its two child clusters.

A key observation we make is that the subspaces between any two adjacent levels in the hierarchy tree should be close to each other. That is, $U^{(P)}$ should be close to diag($U_1^{(C)}, U_2^{(C)}$). This is because many of the links that are in $A^{(P)}$ should be captured by its child clusters $A_{11}^{(C)}$ and $A_{22}^{(C)}$. Consequently, if we are given diag($U_1^{(C)}, U_2^{(C)}$), one should be able to compute $U^{(P)}$ faster than computing it from scratch. Thus, we propose an algorithm that uses the child cluster's subspace to compute the parent cluster's subspace.

Our proposed method, *tree-structured approximation of subspace*, is listed in Algorithm 1. The main idea is to construct a matrix $Y = A^{(P)}\Omega$ that covers as much of the range space of $A^{(P)}$ as possible. This can be done efficiently using $\Omega = \text{diag}(U_1^{(C)}, U_2^{(C)}, \ldots, U_c^{(C)})$. Note that both $A^{(P)}$ and Ω are sparse. Then, an orthonormal matrix Q is computed from Y as a basis for the range of Y (e.g. using the QR-decomposition). Finally, Q is further used to compute $U^{(P)}$ via the eigen-decomposition of the matrix $B = Q^TAQ$. This last step is also fast since B is a small $cr \times cr$ matrix, where r is the rank of the approximation of each child node.

The subspace approximation scheme in Algorithm 1 is more efficient than the truncated eigen-decomposition (EIG), since the latter needs to be computed from scratch and is time consuming when dealing with large-scale matrices. We note that $Y = (AA^T)A\Omega$ can be used for higher accuracy, though we did not find any significant improvement in the results.

Figure 3 shows principal angles between the parent cluster's subspace $U_{eig}^{(P)}$ computed via eigen-decomposition and the child cluster's subspace diag($U_1^{(C)}, U_2^{(C)}$) for the `Flickr` dataset. The cosine of principal angles are close to 1, supporting our observation that the subspaces of two adjacent

---

Algorithm 1: Tree-structured approximation of dominant subspace of parent cluster from child clusters

Input: $n \times n$ adjacency matrix of parent cluster $A = A^{(P)}$, child cluster's subspaces $U_1^{(C)}, \ldots, U_c^{(C)}$, target rank r.
Output: dominant subspace for parent cluster $A^{(P)}$, i.e. $U^{(P)}$.

$\Omega \leftarrow \text{diag}(U_1^{(C)}, U_2^{(C)}, \ldots, U_c^{(C)})$.
Compute $n \times cr$ matrix $Y = A\Omega$.
Compute Q as an orthonormal basis for the range of Y.
Compute $B = Q^TAQ$. // $A \approx Q(Q^TAQ)Q^T$
Compute rank-r eigen-decomposition of $B \approx V\Lambda V^T$.
Compute $U^{(P)} = QV$.

Algorithm 2: Multi-Scale Link Prediction (MSLP)

Input: adjacency matrix A, number of levels ℓ, number of clusters c at each node, target rank r, weights $w_0, w_1, \ldots, w_\ell$.
Output: top-k predictions.

```
/* Hierarchical clustering */
```
$A_{11}^{(0)} \leftarrow A$.
for $i = 0$ **to** ℓ **do**
  for $j = 1$ **to** c^i **do**
    Cluster $A_{jj}^{(i)}$ into c clusters. `// e.g. Graclus`
  end
end
```
/* Subspace approximation */
// approximation for deepest level.
```
Compute $U^{(\ell)}$, $S^{(\ell)}$ using CLRA.
```
// approximation for intermediate levels.
```
for $i = \ell - 1$ **to** 0 **do**
  Compute $U^{(i)}$ using Algorithm 1.
  $S^{(i)} = U^{(i)T}AU^{(i)}$.
end
```
/* Multi-scale prediction */
```
for $i = \ell$ **to** 0 **do**
  $K_i = f(A^{(i)}) = U^{(i)}f(S^{(i)})U^{(i)T}$ `// e.g. Katz`
end
$P = w_0K_0 + w_1K_1 + \ldots + w_\ell K_\ell$.
return top-k predictions according to P.

---

levels are close to each other. We also show principal angles between $U_{eig}^{(P)}$ and the parent cluster's subspace $U_{tree}^{(P)}$ computed using Algorithm 1. We see that these subspaces are even closer to each other, showing that our algorithm can accurately approximate the parent cluster's subspace.

4.3 Multi-Scale Link Prediction

As mentioned in Section 2, many proximity measures for link prediction $f(A)$ are expensive to compute on large-scale networks because of their high complexity. One solution is to approximate A by a low-rank approximation $\tilde{A}$ and then compute approximated proximity measures with $f(\tilde{A})$ to make predictions. This stems from the idea that most of the action in A can be captured by a few latent factors, which can be extracted with low-rank approximations of A.

It has been shown that CLRA provides an accurate and scalable low-rank approximation, and can be used for effi-

Table 2: Computational time (in minutes) for subspace approximation by MSLP (Algorithm 1) and EIG on three large-scale social networks.

Network		LiveJournal	Flickr	MySpace
EIG		157.10	146.28	211.29
MSLP	Level 0	30.74	29.98	38.27
	Level 1	20.18	21.95	35.86
	Level 2	18.93	17.25	29.17
	Level 3	14.01	15.33	26.36
	Level 4	13.74	15.79	26.36
	Level 5	121.26	132.93	188.26
MSLP Total		218.88	233.33	344.02

cient proximity estimation [23]. However, CLRA just uses one clustering structure making it sensitive to a particular clustering and biased against links that appear between clusters. Our proposed method alleviates such problem with a multi-scale approach.

The main idea is that, under a hierarchical clustering, all links will eventually belong to at least one cluster. That is, even if we miss a between-cluster link at a certain level, it still has a good chance of getting corrected by upper levels as it will eventually become a within-cluster link. Moreover, links that lie within clusters at multiple levels, such as from the deepest level, get emphasized multiple times. Those links will have the propensity of being included in the final prediction, which aligns with the intuition that links are more likely to form within tight clusters.

Once the multi-scale low-rank approximation of A is obtained, we now perform multi-scale link prediction. From each low-rank approximation of the hierarchy, $\tilde{A}^{(i)}$, $i = 0, 1, \ldots, \ell$, the approximated proximity measure can be computed with $f(\tilde{A}^{(i)})$. This gives a total of $\ell + 1$ proximity measures for each link, which are combined to make final predictions. Formally, our multi-scale predictions are given by

$$g(w_0 f(\tilde{A}^{(0)}) + w_1 f(\tilde{A}^{(1)}) + \ldots + w_\ell f(\tilde{A}^{(\ell)})),$$

where w_i's are the weights for different levels and $g(\cdot)$ is the predictor, e.g. top-k scoring links. For simplicity, we use the same weight for all levels in this work, i.e. $w_i = 1/(\ell + 1)$.

The entire flow of our proposed method, Multi-Scale Link Prediction (MSLP), is listed in Algorithm 2. Next, we analyze the computation time and memory usage of MSLP.

Computation time: As mentioned earlier, the hierarchical clustering is fast and linear in the number of edges in the network and can be finished in a few hundred seconds on networks with 2 million nodes. Computing the approximated proximity scores as a final step for a given user is simply a matrix multiplication of low-rank matrices and time complexity is $O(\ell nr^2)$. In general, we set the number of clusters c and the rank in each cluster r to be fairly small. Among the three phases of MSLP, the subspace approximation phase is the dominant part of the computation time. In Table 2, we compare the CPU time for subspace approximation by Algorithm 1 and EIG on three large-scale social networks with about 2 million users. We can see in Table 2 that for each intermediate level from 4 to 0, the subspace approximation in MSLP is up to 10 times faster than that of EIG, demonstrating the effectiveness of Algorithm 1. Furthermore, since we operate on each cluster independently, MSLP can be easily parallelized to gain greater speedups.

Memory usage: For a rank-r approximation, EIG needs to store r eigenvectors and eigenvalues which takes $O(nr + r)$ memory. Compared with EIG, CLRA is memory efficient as it only takes $O(nr + c^{2\ell}r^2)$ memory for a larger rank-$c^\ell r$ approximation [20]. MSLP basically has the same memory usage as CLRA. While MSLP achieves a multi-scale approximation, it is not necessary to store the subspaces for all levels simultaneously. We can reuse the memory allocated for the child cluster's subspace to store the parent cluster's subspace using Algorithm 1.

5. EXPERIMENTAL EVALUATION

In this section we present experimental results that evaluate both accuracy and scalability of our method, Multi-Scale Link Prediction (MSLP), for link prediction. First we present a detailed analysis of our method using the Karate club network as a case study. This will give a better understanding of our algorithm and illustrate where it succeeds. Next we provide results under different parameter settings on a large social network. Lastly, we compare MSLP to other popular methods on massive real-world social networks with millions of users and demonstrate its superior performance.

5.1 Case study: Karate club

We first start our performance analysis on a well-known small social network, Zachary's Karate club network [25]. The Karate club network represents a friendship network among 34 members of the club with 78 links. The clustering structure of the Karate club network is a standard example for testing clustering algorithms. We adopt the clustering results from [2], where the clustering is found via modularity optimization. Figure 4 shows the hierarchy of the Karate club network. The first level has 2 clusters (circle and triangle) with 68 within-cluster links and the second level has 4 clusters (red, yellow, green and blue) with 50 within-cluster links.

As the Karate club network is a small network, we apply the *leave-one-out* method to compare different methods. We first remove a single link from the network, treat the held out edge as 0 in A, and perform link prediction on the resulting network. For each leave-one-out experiment, we compute the rank of the removed link based on its proximity measure. If the rank of the removed link appears in the top-k list, we count it as a *hit*. The number of top-k hits is the number of hits out of all leave-one-out experiments.

We compare MSLP to four other methods: RandCluster, common neighbors (CN), Katz and CLRA. In RandCluster, we randomly partition the graph into 4 clusters and compute the Katz measure using CLRA with these clusters. Figure 5 shows the number of top-k hits for each method. Clearly, our method significantly outperforms other methods by achieving a much higher number of hits. This implies that MSLP makes more accurate predictions by considering the hierarchical structure of the network. RandCluster performs the worst, while CLRA has comparable performance with Katz indicating that the network's property can be captured by a few latent factors.

For a better illustration of the advantage of our method, we annotate Figure 4 with the results of top-3 hits. The solid blue links correspond to hits made by MSLP and the dashed red links are hits made by both CLRA and MSLP, i.e. the set of links successfully predicted by CLRA is a subset of that of MSLP. We can see that all hits made by

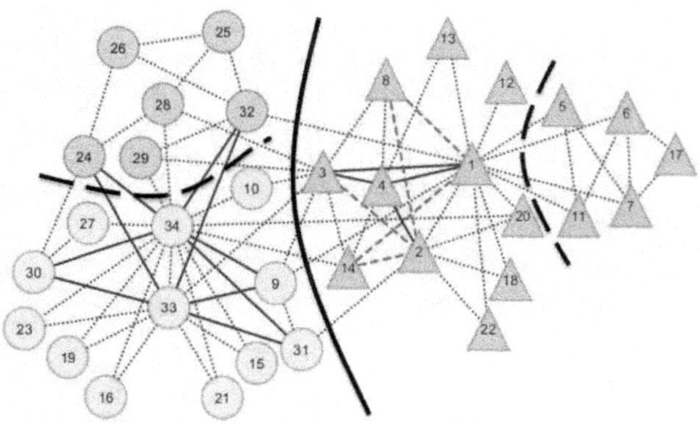

Figure 4: Hierarchy of the Karate club network with 2 levels, two clusters on the first level and four clusters on the second level.

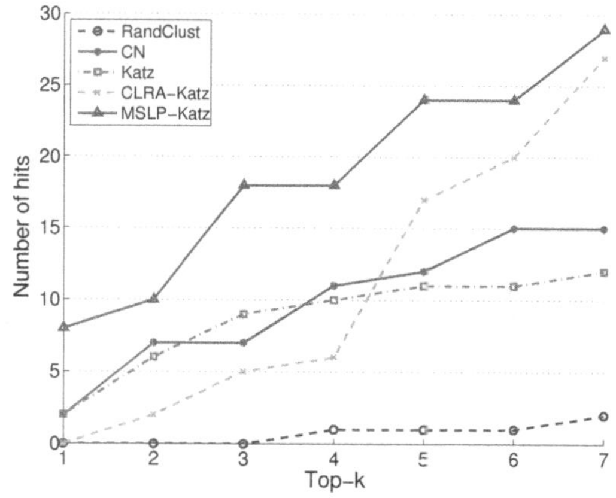

Figure 5: Number of top-k hits for different methods on the Karate club network.

CLRA are within-cluster links (green cluster), showing that CLRA favors within-cluster links. In contrast, MSLP can predict not only more within-cluster links, but also links between clusters (red and yellow). The ability to correctly predict both within and between-cluster links is one of the main advantages of our multi-scale approach.

5.2 Experiments on Large Datasets

In this section we present the results of link prediction on large real-world datasets. We start by examining how the parameters of MSLP affect performance. Particularly, we investigate how different hierarchical clustering structures impact the performance of MSLP. For this, we use a large real-world network: `Epinions`, which is an online social network from Epinions.com with 32,223 users and 684,026 links [19].

Next we use three real-world massive online social networks with millions of nodes: `Flickr` [17], `LiveJournal` and `MySpace` [22], and compare MSLP to other methods. These datasets have timestamps associated with them and we summarize each snapshot in Table 3. The adjacency matrix at the first timestamp, A_{t_1}, is used to compute proximity measures, and the adjacency matrix at the next timestamp, A_{t_2}, is used for testing and evaluation. Since these networks are very large, we randomly select 5,000 users and evaluate on these users. Performance measures are averaged over 30 iterations of such sampling.

As pointed out in [13], most of all newly formed links in social networks close a path of length two and form a triangle, i.e., appear in a user's 2-hop neighborhood. All three datasets show that this is the case for at least 90% of test links in the second timestamp. For similar reasons as in [3], we focus on predicting links to users that are within its 2-hop neighborhood.

Table 3: Summary of networks with timestamps.

Network	Date	# of nodes	# of links
`Flickr`	5/6/2007	1,994,422	42,890,114
	5/17/2007	1,994,422	43,681,874
`LiveJournal`	3/4/2009	1,757,326	84,366,676
	4/3/2009	1,757,326	85,666,494
`MySpace`	1/11/2009	2,086,141	90,918,158
	2/14/2009	2,086,141	91,587,516

5.2.1 Evaluation methodology

We evaluate the accuracy of different methods by computing the *true positive rate* (TPR) and the *false positive rate* (FPR), defined by

$$\text{TPR} = \frac{\text{\# of correctly predicted links}}{\text{\# of actual links}},$$

$$\text{FPR} = \frac{\text{\# of incorrectly predicted links}}{\text{\# of non-friend pairs}},$$

for all links in a sampled test set. Our evaluation is based on *receiver operating characteristic* (ROC) curve and its *area under the ROC curve* (AUC) that present achievable TPR with respect to FPR. Predicting links with proximity measures involves some thresholding on the measures to produce top-k predictions. The ROC curves captures the full spectrum of prediction performance by varying the decision threshold.

However, in a practical sense, a user is recommended only a small number of top-k predictions and the hope is that most of them are correct. Thus, we focus on the region of low FPR by plotting FPR along the x-axis in log-scale, since it reflects the quality of these top-k links. In the same spirit, we also use the *Precision at Top-k*, i.e., the number of correct predictions out of top-k recommendations, as our evaluation metric.

Other methods for comparison: We have carefully chosen a variety of proximity measures to compare with: Preferential Attachment (PA), Adamic-Adar score (AA), Random Walk with Restarts (RWR), common neighbors (CN) and Katz [15]. The actual values of Katz quickly becomes difficult to compute as scale increases due to its high computational cost. Therefore, we employ the Lanczos method [4] for its speed and good approximation of the real Katz values. We also consider a supervised machine learning method (LR) [3, 10]. For the latter, we extracted five network-based features: paths of lengths 3, 4 and 5, CN, and AA. Using these features, a logistic regression model is trained over a sampled set of positive and negative links from 10,000 users as in [3].

5.2.2 Varying parameters

Next we evaluate on different parameter settings by varying the three main parameters of MSLP: number of levels in the hierarchy ℓ, number of clusters at each node in the

Table 4: Varying rank of approximation on Epinions dataset. MSLP consistently outperforms EIG and CLRA for different ranks in terms of AUC and precision at top-20.

r	EIG-Katz		CLRA-Katz		MSLP-Katz	
	AUC	Prec	AUC	Prec	AUC	Prec
10	0.8247	4.52	0.8075	5.07	0.8533	5.42
20	0.8303	4.91	0.7928	4.93	**0.8550**	**5.62**
50	0.8168	5.09	0.7527	4.31	0.8287	5.54
100	0.7903	4.98	0.7037	3.72	0.7985	5.21
200	0.7605	4.62	0.6539	3.11	0.7663	4.77

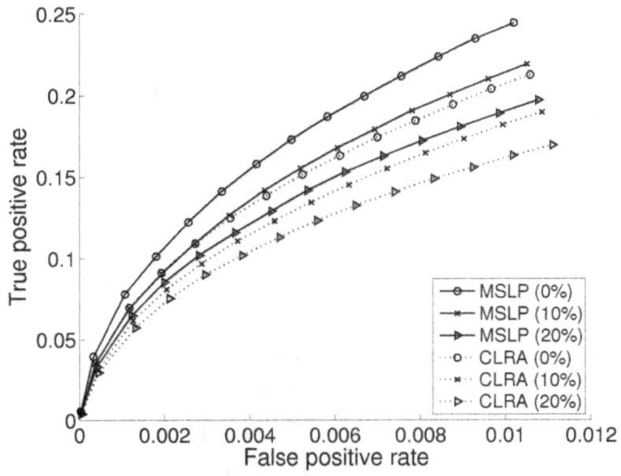

Figure 6: Robustness results for MSLP and CLRA on Epinions dataset. Numbers in brackets are the % of vertices shuffled.

hierarchy c, and rank r. We fix $\ell = 3$, $c = 2$, and $r = 20$ while changing one parameter at a time and measure AUC and precision at top-20. The Epinions network does not have time information, thus we randomly sample a number of links and treat them as test links in A_{t_2}. The sampling is performed such that about 90% of test links appear in a user's 2-hop neighborhood.

We compare the performance of our method to two other low-rank approximation methods: eigen-decomposition (EIG), clustered low rank approximation at the deepest level in the hierarchy tree (CLRA).

Rank: Table 4 shows performance of the three low-rank approximation methods with different ranks. MSLP consistently performs better in terms of both AUC and Precision at Top-20 than the other two methods. The accuracy of CLRA deteriorates as the rank increases. This implies that the low-rank approximation of each cluster starts to accumulate noise at larger ranks. It is shown that low-rank approximation methods tend to perform best at an intermediate rank [15], which is also the case here with $r = 20$.

Hierarchical clustering structure: Next we experiment with various hierarchical clustering structures. Table 5 shows how the performance changes as the hierarchical clustering structure changes. For a complete comparison, results of other methods are also given in Table 5(c). The second column in Tables 5(a) and 5(b) represents the percentage of within-cluster edges. It is clear that as the number of clusters at the bottom level increases the percentage decreases. While the accuracy of CLRA degrades as the percentage decreases, MSLP is still able to perform better than other methods in all cases with the only exception of Table 5(a) at $c = 5$. The results clearly show that MSLP is robust to different hierarchical structures.

Furthermore, to see that MSLP is robust to cluster structures, we randomly perturb clusters at the deepest level of the hierarchy by moving vertices from their original cluster to another random cluster. Figure 6 shows the result of moving 0%, 10% and 20% of vertices. Even with 10% of vertices shuffled, MSLP still outperforms CLRA with no shuffling. It is clear that, while CLRA's performance decreases rapidly, MSLP still performs well in low FPR regions.

Table 5: Varying hierarchical clustering structure by changing (a) the number of clusters per node at each level and (b) the number of levels on Epinions dataset. Results show that MSLP is not only more robust than CLRA to different clustering structures, but also outperforms other methods in most cases. Percentage is the percentage of within-cluster edges (Numbers in brackets represent percentage of within-cluster edges of random clustering).

(a) Changing the number of clusters per node at each level.

c	Percentage	CLRA-Katz		MSLP-Katz	
		AUC	Prec	AUC	Prec
2	53.41 (13.42)	0.7928	4.93	**0.8550**	**5.62**
3	41.91 (6.41)	0.7649	4.32	0.8520	5.48
4	37.33 (5.47)	0.7426	3.80	0.8463	5.27
5	34.03 (3.12)	0.7293	3.74	0.8276	4.80

(b) Changing the number of levels.

ℓ	Percentage	CLRA-Katz		MSLP-Katz	
		AUC	Prec	AUC	Prec
2	67.54 (26.51)	0.7970	5.02	0.8459	5.33
3	53.31 (13.42)	0.7928	4.93	**0.8550**	**5.62**
4	47.77 (8.59)	0.7825	4.60	0.8508	5.55
5	43.54 (5.39)	0.7633	4.15	0.8498	5.37

(c) Results of other methods.

Method	AUC	Prec
PA(Preferential Attachment)	0.7717	2.09
AA(Adamic-Adar)	0.8378	5.16
RWR(Random Walk /w Restarts)	0.8468	2.68
LR(Logistic Regression)	0.8227	4.60
CN(Common Neighbors)	0.8163	4.78
Katz(Katz)	0.8352	4.77

5.2.3 Results on Large-scale social networks

In this section, we present results on real-world networks with millions of nodes presented in Table 3. We construct a hierarchical structure with $\ell = 5$ and $c = 2$ for all three networks, and use $r = 100$ for EIG, CLRA and MSLP. We set $\beta = 0.0005$ for the Katz measure, which yields the best results.

Tables 6 and 7 give AUC and precision at top-100 results for the various methods, respectively. MSLP-Katz gives a significant improvement over the Katz measure and outperforms all other methods. Specifically, it gains a relative improvement of up to 4% in AUC and 15% in precision over the next best performing method. We emphasize the superior

Table 6: AUC results for Flickr, LiveJournal and MySpace datasets.

Method	Flickr	LiveJournal	MySpace
PA	0.6981	0.6075	0.8325
AA	0.8758	0.7709	0.8767
RWR	0.7872	0.7113	0.8357
LR	0.7115	0.7055	0.7487
CN	0.8649	0.7630	0.8801
EIG-CN	0.8583	0.7317	0.8732
CLRA-CN	0.8506	0.7390	0.8587
MSLP-CN	0.8621	0.7538	0.8743
Katz	0.8429	0.7651	0.8492
EIG-Katz	0.8887	0.7547	0.8638
CLRA-Katz	0.8611	0.7531	0.8646
MSLP-Katz	**0.8924**	**0.7890**	**0.8850**

Table 7: Precision at top-100 results for Flickr, LiveJournal and MySpace datasets.

Method	Flickr	LiveJournal	MySpace
PA	1.02	1.32	4.57
AA	7.29	5.93	7.44
RWR	5.49	3.46	1.30
LR	2.54	2.23	4.95
CN	7.08	5.94	7.18
EIG-CN	6.88	5.34	6.99
CLRA-CN	6.91	5.21	6.88
MSLP-CN	7.03	5.59	7.05
Katz	7.17	5.86	6.18
EIG-Katz	11.26	5.62	7.55
CLRA-Katz	12.13	6.11	7.64
MSLP-Katz	**13.34**	**6.72**	**8.38**

performance in terms of precision at top-100 of MSLP-Katz as shown in Table 7. This is a very appealing aspect of MSLP as it reflects the quality of top recommendations. In contrast, MSLP-CN remains comparable to CN, but performs better than EIG and CLRA. Surprisingly, the supervised method LR does not perform well, which is consistent with results found in [3]. Note that we only use network-based features and no additional features for training. However, engineering for more features is a difficult task and constructing good features itself can be computationally expensive.

Figure 7 gives ROC curves focused on the low FPR region for the three large-scale networks. We note that only one representative method from methods that have similar performance is plotted for the sake of clarity. We observe that MSLP-Katz performs the best in all three datasets with significant improvements over Katz. For a given TPR, MSLP reduces FPR by 10% on average and at most 20% compared to others in all datasets. For completeness, we present the full range of the ROC curve for LiveJournal in Figure 8. Note that much of the performance boost comes from the left side of the curve, which corresponds to the area of interest. That is, MSLP achieves good prediction quality for the highest predicted scores.

While dimensionality reduction methods, such as EIG and CLRA, tend to perform well in all three datasets, they are limited to a single low-rank representation of the network. Furthermore, CLRA has the largest drop in relative per-

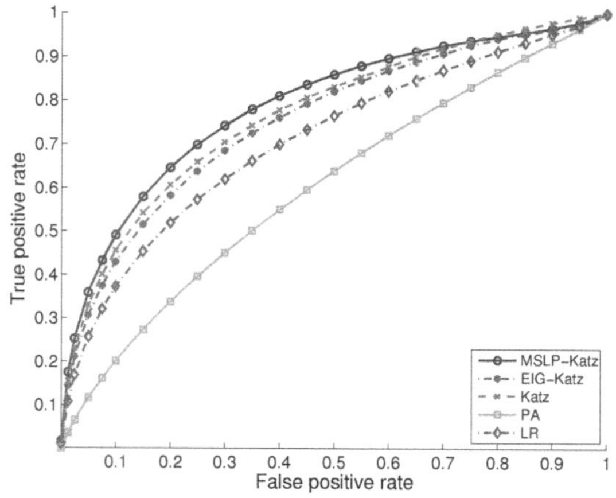

Figure 8: Full ROC curve for LiveJournal.

formance in terms of precision compared to MSLP in the MySpace dataset, where only 56% of the edges are within clusters, whereas MSLP achieves the best result. Overall, the superior performance of MSLP illustrates the effectiveness of our multi-scale approach.

We note that the majority of time is taken by computing CLRA at the deepest level and thereafter low-rank approximations of upper levels can be obtained efficiently due to Algorithm 1. However, CLRA can be easily parallelized as computing the subspace of each cluster is independent to other clusters. Thus, MSLP can achieve much more speedup by using a parallel implementation and serve as a highly scalable method for link prediction.

6. CONCLUSIONS

In this paper, we have presented a general framework for multi-scale link prediction by combining predictions from multiple scales using hierarchical clustering. A novel tree-structured approximation method is proposed to achieve fast and scalable multi-scale approximations. Extensive experimental results on large real-world datasets have been presented to demonstrate the effectiveness of our method. This significantly widens the accessibility of state-of-the-art proximity measures for large-scale applications.

For future work, we plan to investigate methods to learn the weights for various levels of the hierarchy, since some levels may have better predictions and deserve larger weights in the final prediction. In this work, we use a balanced hierarchical structure mainly for its simplicity in combining predictions. However, a more realistic setting would be to use an unbalanced hierarchical clustering structure. The issue here is how to combine predictions from different levels as some links may not receive predictions at certain levels. We also plan to develop a parallelized version of MSLP as each level of the hierarchy can be easily parallelized.

7. ACKNOWLEDGMENTS

This research was supported by NSF grants CCF-1117055 and CCF-0916309.

8. REFERENCES

[1] L. A. Adamic and E. Adar. Friends and neighbors on the web. *Social Networks*, 25(3):211–230, 2003.

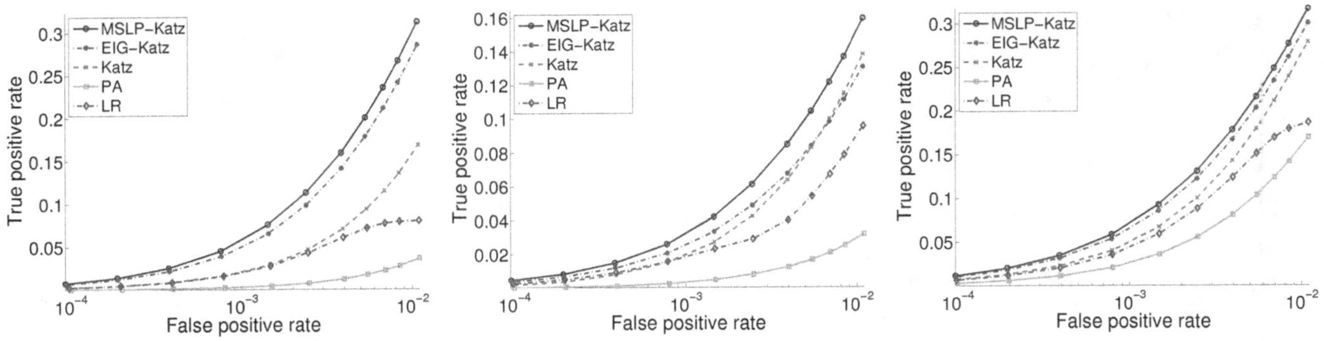

(a) Flickr (b) LiveJournal (c) MySpace

Figure 7: ROC curve on low FPR region of different methods for `Flickr`, `LiveJournal` and `MySpace` datasets. MSLP performs the best on all three datasets.

[2] G. Agarwal and D. Kempe. Modularity-maximizing graph communities via mathematical programming. *European Physical Journal B*, 66(3):409–418, 2008.

[3] L. Backstrom and J. Leskovec. Supervised random walks: predicting and recommending links in social networks. In *WSDM*, pages 635–644, 2011.

[4] F. Bonchi, P. Esfandiar, D. F. Gleich, C. Greif, and L. V. S. Lakshmanan. Fast matrix computations for pair-wise and column-wise commute times and Katz scores. *Internet Mathematics*, 8(1-2):73–112, 2012.

[5] A. Clauset, C. Moore, and M. E. J. Newman. Hierarchical structure and the prediction of missing links in networks. *Nature*, 453(7191):98–101, 2008.

[6] P. M. Comar, P.-N. Tan, and A. K. Jain. LinkBoost: A novel cost-sensitive boosting framework for community-level network link prediction. In *ICDM*, pages 131–140, 2011.

[7] I. S. Dhillon, Y. Guan, and B. Kulis. Weighted graph cuts without eigenvectors: a multilevel approach. *IEEE Trans. on Pattern Anal. Mach. Intell.*, 29(11):1944–1957, 2007.

[8] D. M. Dunlavy, T. G. Kolda, and E. Acar. Temporal link prediction using matrix and tensor factorizations. *ACM Trans. Knowl. Discov. Data*, 5(2):10:1–10:27, 2011.

[9] E. Estrada and D. J. Higham. Network properties revealed through matrix functions. *SIAM Rev.*, 52(4):696–714, 2010.

[10] M. A. Hasan, V. Chaoji, S. Salem, and M. Zaki. Link prediction using supervised learning. In *Proc. of SDM 06 workshop on Link Analysis, Counterterrorim and Security*, pages 556–559, 2006.

[11] W. H. Hsu, J. Lancaster, M. S. R. Paradesi, and T. Weninger. Structural link analysis from user profiles and friends networks: a feature construction approach. In *Int. Conf. on Weblogs and Social Media*, pages 75–80, 2007.

[12] L. Katz. A new status index derived from sociometric analysis. *Psychometrika*, 18(1):39–43, 1953.

[13] J. Leskovec, L. Backstrom, R. Kumar, and A. Tomkins. Microscopic evolution of social networks. In *KDD*, pages 462–470, 2008.

[14] J. Leskovec, K. J. Lang, A. Dasgupta, and M. W. Mahoney. Community structure in large letworks: natural cluster sizes and the absence of large well-defined clusters. *Internet Mathematics*, 6(1):29–123, 2009.

[15] D. Liben-Nowell and J. Kleinberg. The link prediction problem for social networks. In *CIKM*, pages 556–559, 2003.

[16] R. N. Lichtenwalter, J. T. Lussier, and N. V. Chawla. New perspectives and methods in link prediction. In *KDD*, pages 243–252, 2010.

[17] A. Mislove, H. S. Koppula, K. P. Gummadi, P. Druschel, and B. Bhattacharjee. Growth of the Flickr social network. In *Proc. of the First Workshop on Online Social Networks*, pages 25–30, 2008.

[18] M. E. J. Newman. Clustering and preferential attachment in growing networks. *Phys. Rev. E*, 64(025102), 2001.

[19] M. Richardson, R. Agrawal, and P. Domingos. Trust management for the semantic web. In *ISWC*, pages 351–368, 2003.

[20] B. Savas and I. S. Dhillon. Clustered low rank approximation of graphs in information science applications. In *SDM*, pages 164–175, 2011.

[21] S. Scellato, A. Noulas, and C. Mascolo. Exploiting place features in link prediction on location-based social networks. In *KDD*, pages 1046–1054, 2011.

[22] H. H. Song, T. W. Cho, V. Dave, Y. Zhang, and L. Qiu. Scalable proximity estimation and link prediction in online social networks. In *9th ACM SIGCOMM Conf. on Internet Measurement*, pages 322–335, 2009.

[23] H. H. Song, B. Savas, T. W. Cho, V. Dave, Z. Lu, I. S. Dhillon, Y. Zhang, and L. Qiu. Clustered embedding of massive social networks. In *Proc. of 12th ACM SIGMETRICS*, pages 331–342, 2012.

[24] C. Wang, V. Satuluri, and S. Parthasarathy. Local probabilistic models for link prediction. In *ICDM*, pages 322–331, 2007.

[25] W. W. Zachary. An information flow model for conflict and fission in small groups. *Journal of Anthropological Research*, 33:452–473, 1977.

An Analysis of How Ensembles of Collective Classifiers Improve Predictions in Graphs

Hoda Eldardiry
Palo Alto Research Center
Palo Alto, CA, USA
hoda.eldardiry@parc.com

Jennifer Neville
Purdue University
West Lafayette, IN, USA
neville@cs.purdue.edu

ABSTRACT

We present a theoretical analysis framework that shows how ensembles of collective classifiers can improve predictions for graph data. We show how collective ensemble classification reduces errors due to variance in learning and more interestingly inference. We present an empirical framework that includes various ensemble techniques for classifying relational data using collective inference. The methods span single- and multiple-graph network approaches, and are tested on both synthetic and real world classification tasks. Our experimental results, supported by our theoretical justifications, confirm that ensemble algorithms that explicitly focus on both learning and inference processes and aim at reducing errors associated with both, are the best performers.

Categories and Subject Descriptors

I.2 [**Computing Methodologies**]: Artificial Intelligence

Keywords

Collective classification, Ensemble learning

1. INTRODUCTION

Ensemble methods have been widely studied as a means of reducing classification error by combining multiple models for prediction. Much of the earlier work on ensemble techniques has focused on i.i.d. domains (where objects are independent and identically distributed, and models use exact inference techniques). While there has been some recent investigation of ensembles for relational domains [5, 10, 17], these previous works have a number of limitations in that: (1) there is no theoretical analysis to show the mechanism by which ensembles reduce model error in relational domains, (2) they focus on the reduction of only one type of error (due to either learning or inference), and (3) they make an assumption about the datasets having multiple relations.

In this work, we formulate a theoretical framework to compare the errors made by different relational ensembles and show the reason why some methods do better than others. Moreover, we present a relational ensemble framework that combines a relational ensemble learning approach with a relational ensemble inference approach. We use the first method for learning the ensemble, while focusing on reducing error due to variance in learning. We use the second method for applying the ensemble for inference, while focuses on reducing error due to variance in inference. We show how the unique combination of these methods offers the largest classification accuracy improvement, compared to various other approaches on both synthetic and real-world datasets. Furthermore, our ensemble model is applicable in domains that do not necessarily have multiple relational graphs, thereby overcoming that limitation of existing relational ensembles. In fact, our framework is applicable in both single-graph and multi-graph settings.

Traditional design choices for i.i.d. ensembles include methods for input data treatment (see Figure 1.a) and methods for aggregating the output of the models (see Figure 1.d). The goal of the data treatment method is to ensure variety among the learned models. For example, bagging approaches (e.g., [3]) use resampling to generate multiple bootstraps to learn the models from, and aggregate predictions from multiple models, while boosting approaches (e.g., [2, 18, 21]) construct the models in a coupled fashion so that their weighted vote gives a good fit to the data.

In relational domains, different design choices must be considered. First, the treatment of input data must consider the relational data characteristics. For example, some approaches [5, 17] use the multple link types available in the network to subset the data to learn the component models of a relational ensemble. Another technique [1] instead uses a feature subset approach which samples from the node features, and applies this approach in a relational setting. Second, relational or collective inference models can be used as the base component models of the ensemble, because they have been shown to improve predictions for relational data. Fire example, some recent work [13] proposed using boosting for learning relational dependency networks to reduce the bias component of error. Third, work on relational ensembles that considered collective classification for the base models [5] also proposed a new approach to aggregating predictions across the models during collective inference to reduce variance in inference. Finally, aggregation of the models' predictions has been used in both i.i.d. ensembles as well as relational ensembles to reduce the variance in learning.

The goal of this work is to analyze the different error components of relational ensembles theoretically to show the

CIKM'12, October 29–November 2, 2012, Maui, HI, USA.

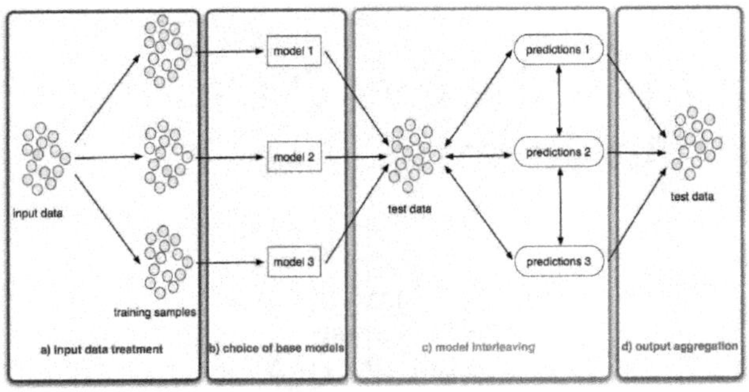

Figure 1: Ensemble classification design dimensions.

mechanisms by which different approaches reduce classification error. In i.i.d. domains, ensemble learning methods have been shown to reduce classification error by reducing variance (e.g., bagging [3]) or reducing bias (e.g., boosting [21]). However, since previous analysis has focused on i.i.d. data, the models are assumed to use exact inference techniques that have no associated error—thus the only error is attributed to the learning process. On the other hand, collective inference models applied to relational data have been shown to have additional sources of error due to the inference process [14]. We use a bias/variance decomposition for our analysis, and extend it for the ensemble setting, to consider not just a single model, but an ensemble of collective inference models. Specifically, we reason about two classes of ensemble models: (1) a relational ensemble model that runs the base classifiers independently for inference and aggregates the final predictions, and (2) an across-model approach, which runs the component models simultaneously for collective inference and aggregates intermediate predictions across the models during inference. Throughout this paper, we refer to the first model as the relational ensemble model, and we refer to the second model as the interleaved model. The goal of our theoretical analysis is to decompose the errors associated with each ensemble and show how the different ensemble approaches can reduce the error of a single model. Specifically, we show that an interleaved ensemble produces the greatest error reduction due to its ability to reduce learning and inference error without an increase in bias. To our knowledge, this is the first analytical investigation of error for relational ensembles.

Based on our analysis, we note that aggregating the base models' predictions at the end of inference reduces error due to variance in learning, while interleaving the models' predictions during collective inference reduces error due to inference. We also note that the aggregation process reduces the variance in learning in proportion to the amount of true variance approximated by the learned models. This has led us to consider learning the ensemble in a way that can better approximate the true variance in relational data, to maximize the reduction in learning variance, and combine this technique with the inference interleaving proposed earlier to additionally reduce inference variance. Specifically, we use a relational resampling approach to capture the increased variance in relational data, allowing the ensembles to reduce more of the variance due to learning. We combine it with interleaved inference, which allows the ensembles to reduce more of the variance due to inference. In contrast to our proposed ensemble method, previous methods have focused on reducing errors due to variance in learning [17], or due to variance in inference [5], but not both simultaneously. Furthermore, this combination allows our ensemble approach to be applicable for all kind of graphs regardless of the amount of infromation available. Our model is applicable to networks with single or multiple link types. Since we now propose to learn the ensembles from bootstrap samples from a single training graph, while the interleaved method was proposed to learn the models from different link graphs. We empirically compare our proposed ensemble approach to several baselines using synthetic and real-world classification tasks and demonstrate its superior performance.

The main contributions of this work are:

- Formalization of an error analysis framework for relational ensemble models.
- Theoretical analysis to show the error reduction offered by alternative relational ensembles.
- A novel ensemble method for relational domains that can reduce both learning and inference errors, which is applicable for both networks with only a single relation as well as networks with multiple relations.
- Empirical evaluation on real and synthetic data, which shows significant performance gains for our proposed method compared to alternative ensembles.

2. PROBLEM DEFINITION

Collective classification.

We describe the general relational learning and collective classification problem as follows. Given a fully-labeled training set composed of a graph $G_{tr} = (V_{tr}, E_{tr})$ with nodes V_{tr} and edges E_{tr}, observed features X_{tr}, and observed class labels Y_{tr}, a model f defining a joint probability distribution over the labels of V_{tr}, conditioned on the observed attributes and graph structure in G_{tr} is learned. Given a partially-labelled test set composed of a graph $G_{te} = (V_{te}, E_{te})$ with nodes V_{te} and edges E_{te}, observed features X_{te}, and partially-observed class labels $\tilde{Y}_{te} \subset Y_{te}$, the model f is applied for collective inference to output a set of marginal probability distributions P (i.e., predictions) for each unlabeled node in V_{te}. We assume the G_{tr} used for learning is different from the G_{te} used for collective inference.

Relational ensembles.

We describe the general relational ensemble classification problem as follows. The input consists of a fully-labeled training set graph $G_{tr} = (V_{tr}, E_{tr})$ with nodes V_{tr} and edges E_{tr}, observed features X_{tr}, and observed class labels Y_{tr}. From the input G_{tr}, the algorithm generates a set of m sample graphs $\{G_{tr_1}, ..G_{tr_m}\}$, which we refer to as *pseudosamples.* Then, using a relational learner, a set of models $F = \{f_1, ..f_m\}$ is learned from $\{G_{tr_1}, ..G_{tr_m}\}$, one model from each pseudosample graph. During prediction, each model $f_i \in F$ is applied for collective inference to G_{te} to output a set of marginal probability distributions P_i (i.e., predictions) for each unlabeled node in V_{te}. Finally, the predictions $P_1, .., P_m$ from the m models are aggregated and the final predictions P are generated for nodes in G_{te}.

3. THEORETICAL ANALYSIS

In this section we use bias/variance analysis to explore the differences between single collective models and the various relational ensembles. Specifically, we focus on squared loss as a measure of classification performance and show the error reduction offered by the different types of ensembles. The analytical results shows how the simple relational ensemble improves performance over the single collective classifier, as well as how the interleaved ensemble improves performance over the simple relational ensemble. To the best of our knowledge, this is the first analytical exploration of classification error for relational ensembles.

3.1 Framework

We formalize the collective classification task in order to describe the setting we use for this analysis. Let $\mathcal{D}$ be a population of attributed graphs G. Each sample $D := [G=(V,E), X_V, Y_V]$ is drawn from $\mathcal{D}$, where V is the set of instances in D, E is the set of links, and $|V| = g$.

Let $f := P(\mathbf{Y}_g|\mathbf{X}_g, G)$ represent a model of the joint distribution over class labels Y of instances in a graph G, given attributes of the instances $\mathbf{X}$. Let $D_L \in \mathcal{D}$ be a training graph. Let $D_I \in \mathcal{D}$ be a partially labeled test graph where $\mathcal{T} \in V_I$ is the set of labeled instances in G_I. Let $\mathbf{Y}_\mathcal{T}$ be the set of known labels available to the inference process. For this analysis, we assume that D_L and D_I are drawn independently from $\mathcal{D}$ and that $D_I \neq D_L$.

The goal is to learn f from the training set D_L and apply it to the test set D_I to collectively predict class labels for each unlabeled instance $i \in V_{I/\mathcal{T}}$:

$$y_f^i := f(i, D_I, \mathcal{T}) = P(Y^i{=}t^i|\mathbf{Y}_\mathcal{T}, \mathbf{X}, G_I) \quad (1)$$

Since relational models that use collective inference have an additional source of error due to the inference process, we need to isolate the errors due to learning from the errors due to inference. To achieve this, we also consider the performance of an *exact inference* model, which does not use collective inference and simply makes a prediction for i conditioned on the set of Bayes-optimal values for all instances except i. Below, we use $\dot{\mathbf{Y}}_{V_{I/i}}$ to refer to the Bayes-optimal prediction for all instances in the dataset D_I except i.

3.1.1 Model definitions

We consider four models in our analysis: a single collective inference model (f_s), a simple relational ensemble model (f_e), an interleaved collective inference model (f_c), and the "true" model (f_*). We define each of these models below.

True model: We define f_* as the "true" model for the population $\mathcal{D}$, where P_* is the "true" joint distribution, which can be estimated as the expected model f_s that will be learned over samples drawn from the population $\mathcal{D}$:

$$f_* = P_*(\mathbf{Y}_g|\mathbf{X}_g, G) = E[f_s] = \sum_{D_L \in \mathcal{D}} f_s * p(D_L) \quad (2)$$

Single model: Let f_s be a single collective inference model learned from a sample $D_L \in \mathcal{D}$, which estimates P_s. The model f_s is then used to make predictions for each unlabeled instance i in a partially labeled dataset $< D_I, \mathcal{T} >$:

$$\begin{aligned} y_{f_s}^i &:= f_s(i, D_I, \mathcal{T}) \\ &= P_s(Y^i{=}t^i|\mathbf{Y}_\mathcal{T}, \mathbf{X}, G_I) \end{aligned} \quad (3)$$

Simple relational ensemble model (RE): Let $F = \{f_{s_1}, .., f_{s_m}\}$ be a set of m collective inference models learned from $\{D_{L_1}, .., D_{L_m}\}$ generated from D_L. Each f_s gives a different estimate of the true joint distribution P_*. For a description of how $\{D_{L_1}, .., D_{L_m}\}$ are generated from a single given D_L, please see section 3.2.4.

Let f_e be a simple relational ensemble model that aggregates predictions from $F = \{f_{s_1}, .., f_{s_m}\}$, where each $f_s \in F$ runs n Gibbs iterations independently for inference. A prediction $y_{f_e}^i$ for an instance i is then calculated by averaging the final predictions for i from all m models $F = \{f_{s_1}, .., f_{s_m}\}$. Each base model makes its predictions as described for the single model above.

$$\begin{aligned} y_{f_e}^i &:= \frac{1}{m}\sum_{k=1}^{m} f_k(i, D_I, \mathcal{T}) \\ &= \frac{1}{m}\sum_{k=1}^{m} P_k(Y^i{=}t^i|\mathbf{Y}_\mathcal{T}, \mathbf{X}, G_I) \end{aligned} \quad (4)$$

Interleaved ensemble model (CEC): As described above, let $F = \{f_{s_1}, .., f_{s_m}\}$ be a set of m collective inference models learned from $\{D_{L_1}, .., D_{L_m}\}$ generated from D_L. Then let f_c be an interleaved model that aggregates predictions from the m collective inference base models in F, at each Gibbs iteration $j \in \{1..n\}$. At each iteration j, predictions made by all the base models are aggregated and used to make a prediction for each model $k \in \{1..m\}$. These predictions are for $V_{I/\mathcal{T}}$. For the instances in $\mathcal{T}$, we use the true labels. The final prediction for an instance i is estimated from the average of the component models' predictions at the last inference iteration n. This defines the interleaved model $f_c = \check{f}_{k,n}$.

$$\begin{aligned} \check{y}_{k,j}^i &= \frac{1}{m}\sum_{k'=1}^{m} f_{k',j}(i, D_I, \mathcal{T}) \\ &= \frac{1}{m}\sum_{k'=1}^{m} P_{k'}(Y^i{=}t^i|\mathbf{Y}_\mathcal{T}, \hat{Y}_{V_{I/\{\mathcal{T}+i\}},j}, \mathbf{X}, G_I) \\ y_{f_c}^i &= \check{y}_{k,n}^i \end{aligned} \quad (5)$$

3.1.2 Error decomposition

We decompose error of collective classification models into bias, variance and noise components based on the work of Neville and Jensen [14]. Here we consider squared loss as a measure of classification performance. The loss L for model f on instance i is defined as the expected squared loss for prediction y_f^i given i's true label of t^i:

$$\text{Loss: } L_f^i = E\left[(t^i - y_f^i)^2\right] \quad (6)$$

Here E refers to the total expectation, which is taken over training sets ($D \in \mathcal{D}$) used to learn the model f and subsets of true labels $\mathcal{T}$ available for inference. For ease of reading, when it is clear from context, we drop the superscript i and the subscript f.

Note that in conventional settings, the expectation E would refer to aspects of *learning* and represent the effect of training sets on models/predictions. However, in collective inference settings the relational inference process introduces another source of error [14]. Thus, to reason about the performance of different relational ensembles, we need to make a distinction between the expectation over *learning* and the expectation over *inference* and the expectation over both. We define these expectations below.

To analyze performance differences, loss can be decomposed into bias, variance, and noise components, and compared across models. For squared loss, the decomposition is additive: $L = V + B + N$. We show the decomposition and define each component below.

$$\begin{aligned}
&E[L]\\
&= E[(t-y)^2]\\
&= E[t^2 - 2ty + y^2]\\
&= E[y^2] - 2E[t]E[y] + E[t^2]\\
&= E[y^2] - 2E[t]E[y] + E[t^2] + E[y]^2 - E[y]^2\\
&= V + E[y]^2 - 2E[t]E[y] + E[t^2]\\
&= V + E[y]^2 - 2E[t]E[y] + E[t^2] + E[t]^2 - E[t]^2\\
&= V + (E[t] - E[y])^2 - E[t]^2 + E[t^2]\\
&= V + B + E[t^2] - E[t]^2\\
&= V + B + N
\end{aligned}$$

Variance: Here variance, $V = E\left[(E[y] - y)^2\right]$, is the average loss incurred by all predictions y, relative to the mean prediction $E[y]$.

Bias: Here bias, $B = (E[t] - E[y])^2$, is the loss incurred by the mean prediction, relative to the Bayes-optimal value for instance i: $E[t]$ (the expected value of the true label).

Noise: Here noise, $N = E\left[(t - E[t])^2\right]$, is the loss incurred due to noise in the labels of the data, which is independent of the learning algorithm.

3.1.3 Expectations

We define the three types of expectations that will be used in the proofs—expectations over *learning*, *inference*, and *both*. Note that these expectations are defined for the predictions that will be made by the single model f_s for a test data set D_I.

Expected learning prediction: This is the expectation over *learning*, where the prediction for an instance i is estimated using *exact inference* based on the set of Bayes-optimal predictions for the rest of the graph, $\tilde{\mathbf{Y}}_{V_{I/i}}$:

$$\begin{aligned}
E_L[y^i_{f_s}|D_I] &= \sum_{D_L \in \mathcal{D}} P_s(Y^i = t_i|\tilde{\mathbf{Y}}_{V_{I/i}}, \mathbf{X}, G_I) * p(D_L)\\
&= P_*(Y^i = t_i|\tilde{\mathbf{Y}}_{V_{I/i}}, \mathbf{X}, G_I) \qquad (7)
\end{aligned}$$

Expected inference prediction: This is the expectation over *inference*, where the prediction for an instance i is estimated using the model $f_s^{D_L}$ learned from a single training set D_L:

$$\begin{aligned}
E_I[y^i_{f_s}|D_I, f_s^{D_L}] &= \sum_{\mathcal{T}} P_s(Y^i = t_i|\mathbf{Y}_{\mathcal{T}}, \mathbf{X}, G_I) * p(\mathbf{Y}_{\mathcal{T}})\\
&= P_s(Y^i = t_i|\mathbf{X}, G_I) \qquad (8)
\end{aligned}$$

Expected total prediction: This is the *total* expectation over learning and inference, where the prediction for an instance i reflects the prediction that would be made from the true distribution:

$$\begin{aligned}
E_T[y^i_{f_s}|D_I] &= E_{LI}[y^i_{f_s}|D_I]\\
&= \sum_{\mathcal{T}} p(\mathbf{Y}_{\mathcal{T}}) \sum_{D_L \in \mathcal{D}} P_s(Y^i = t_i|\mathbf{Y}_{\mathcal{T}}, \mathbf{X}, G_I) * p(D_L)\\
&= P_*(Y^i = t_i|\mathbf{X}, G_I) \qquad (9)
\end{aligned}$$

3.2 Analysis

Given the framework described above, we compare the performance of the ensemble models to the single model and show how the ensembles reduce total loss. Specifically, we decompose the error of the single collective inference model f_s, the simple relational ensemble model f_e, and the interleaved ensemble model f_c. Our analysis shows that the interleaved ensemble results in the greatest reduction in error, through its reduction of *both* learning and inference variance.

We refer to y_s as an arbitrary prediction from a single collective inference model f_s, y_e as an arbitrary prediction from a simple relational ensemble f_e, and y_c as an arbitrary prediction from an interleaved ensemble model f_e. The proofs below make use of the following assumptions.

Noise equivalence: We note that the noise component of error is dependent upon the data set, and is independent of the classification algorithm. Therefore:

$$N_s = N_e = N_c \qquad (10)$$

Dataset independence: The data graph samples $\{D_{L_s}\}_{s=1..m}$ used for learning the m models and D_I used for inference are drawn independently from the population of graphs $\mathcal{D}$. When the datasets are independent, the total expectation can be computed from the learning and inference expectations as follows:

$$E_T[.] = E_I[E_L[.]] \qquad (11)$$

Predictions from simple relational ensemble: In the simple relational ensemble f_e, when the number of base models m approaches ∞, the ensemble prediction $y^i_{f_e}$ approaches the expected prediction of the single model f_s, when the expectation is over *learning* (i.e., $E_L[y^i_s]$). But since the predictions from f_e are conditioned on a single labeling $\mathcal{T}$, the ensemble prediction does not approach the *total* expected prediction of the single model (i.e., it does not reflect the variation over inference).

$$\lim_{m\to\infty} y_e = E_L[y_s] = P_*(Y^i = t^i|\tilde{\mathbf{Y}}_{V_{I/i}}, \mathbf{X}, G_I) \qquad (12)$$

Predictions from interleaved relational ensemble: In the interleaved relational ensemble f_c, when both the number of base models m and the number of inference iterations n approach ∞, the interleaved prediction $y^i_{f_c}$ approaches the expected prediction of the single model f_s, where the expectation is over *both* learning and inference (i.e., $E_T[y^i_s]$). This is because the interleaving process, which conditions on $\hat{Y}_{D_{I/\{\mathcal{T}+i\}},j}$ at each inference iteration j, simulates draws from alternative labelings $\mathcal{T}$ over the course of inference.

$$\lim_{m,n\to\infty} y_c = E_T[y_s] = P_*(Y^i = t^i|\mathbf{X}, G_I) \qquad (13)$$

3.2.1 Variance reduction

When squared loss is decomposed, the variance component is $V_T = E_T\left[(E_T[y]-y)^2\right]$. Here we consider the expected *total* error, over both learning and inference. We now show that a simple relational ensemble reduces the variance of a single model, and an interleaved ensemble reduces the variance of a simple relational ensemble.

Theorem 1: Let f_s be a single collective inference model with variance V_s, f_e be a simple relational ensemble with variance V_e, and f_c be an interleaved ensemble model with variance V_c. Then $V_s \geq V_e \geq V_c$.

$$1.1 \quad V_s - V_e \geq 0$$
$$1.2 \quad V_e - V_c \geq 0$$

Proof of Theorem 1.1

$$\begin{aligned}
&V_s - V_e\\
&= E_T\left[(E_T[y_s]-y_s)^2\right] - E_T\left[(E_T[y_e]-y_e)^2\right]\\
&= E_T[E_T[y_s]^2 - 2y_sE_T[y_s] + y_s^2] - E_T[E_T[y_e]^2 - 2y_eE_T[y_e] + y_e^2]\\
&= E_T[y_s]^2 - 2E_T[y_s]^2 + E_T[y_s^2] - E_T[y_e]^2 + 2E_T[y_e]^2 - E_T[y_e^2]\\
&= -E_T[y_s]^2 + E_T[y_s^2] + E_T[y_e]^2 - E_T[y_e^2]\\
&= -E_T[y_s]^2 + E_T[y_s^2] + E_T\left[E_L[y_s]\right]^2 - E_T\left[E_L[y_s]^2\right] && \textbf{(by 12)}\\
&= -E_I[E_L[y_s]]^2 + E_T[y_s^2] + E_I[E_L[y_s]]^2 - E_T\left[E_L[y_s]^2\right] && \textbf{(by 11)}\\
&= E_T[y_s^2] - E_T\left[E_L[y_s]^2\right]\\
&= E_I\left[E_L[y_s^2]\right] - E_I\left[E_L[y_s]^2\right] && \textbf{(by 11)}\\
&= E_I\left[E_L[y_s^2] - E_L[y_s]^2\right]\\
&\geq 0 && (E_L[y_s^2] - E_L[y_s]^2 \geq 0 \textbf{ by Jensen's Inequality})
\end{aligned}$$

□

Proof of Theorem 1.2

$$\begin{aligned}
&V_e - V_c\\
&= E_T\left[(E_T[y_e]-y_e)^2\right] - E_T\left[(E_T[y_c]-y_c)^2\right]\\
&= E_T[E_T[y_e]^2 - 2y_eE_T[y_e] + y_e^2] - E_T[E_T[y_c]^2 - 2y_cE_T[y_c] + y_c^2]\\
&= E_T[y_e]^2 - 2E_T[y_e]^2 + E_T[y_e^2] - E_T[y_c]^2 + 2E_T[y_c]^2 - E_T[y_c^2]\\
&= -E_T[y_e]^2 + E_T[y_e^2] + E_T[y_c]^2 - E_T[y_c^2]\\
&= -E_T\left[E_L[y_s]\right]^2 + E_T\left[E_L[y_s]^2\right] + E_T[y_c]^2 - E_T[y_c^2] && \textbf{(by 12)}\\
&= -E_T\left[E_L[y_s]\right]^2 + E_T\left[E_L[y_s]^2\right] + E_T\left[E_T[y_s]\right]^2\\
&\quad - E_T\left[E_T[y_s]^2\right] && \textbf{(by 13)}\\
&= -E_T\left[E_L[y_s]\right]^2 + E_T\left[E_L[y_s]^2\right] + E_T[y_s]^2 - E_T[y_s]^2\\
&= -E_I\left[E_L[y_s]\right]^2 + E_I\left[E_L[y_s]^2\right] && \textbf{(by 11)}\\
&= E_I\left[E_L[y_s]^2\right] - E_I\left[E_L[y_s]\right]^2\\
&\geq 0 && \textbf{(by Jensen's Inequality)}
\end{aligned}$$

□

Single collective models f_s have two sources of variance in their predictions—variance due to learning the models from different training graphs, and variance due to applying the model for inference given different labeled subsets of the test graph. Simple relational ensembles f_e average models predictions from different learned models and reduce the variance due to learning. Thus, $V_s \geq V_e$.

Similar to simple relational ensembles, interleaved ensembles f_c reduce the variance due to learning. Moreover, interleaving predictions across the base models during each collective inference iteration simulates draws from alternative labeled subsets of the inference graph, and prevents any of the base models from converging to extreme state. This allows an additional reduction of the inference variance. Thus, $V_c \geq V_e$.

3.2.2 Bias reduction

When squared loss is decomposed, the bias component is $B_T = (E_T[t] - E_T[y])^2$. Again we consider the expected *total* error, over both learning and inference. We now show that the two relational ensembles have the same bias as the single model. Since bias depends on how well the models can approximate the true model, it is not corrected by the relational or interleaved ensemble.

Theorem 2: Let f_s be a single collective inference model with bias B_s, f_e be a simple relational ensemble with bias B_e, and f_c be an interleaved ensemble model with bias B_c. Then $B_s = B_e = B_c$

$$2.1 \quad B_s - B_e = 0$$
$$2.2 \quad B_e - B_c = 0$$

Proof of Theorem 2.1

$$\begin{aligned}
&B_s - B_e\\
&= (E_T[t] - E_T[y_s])^2 - (E_T[t] - E_T[y_e])^2\\
&= (E_T[t] - E_T[y_s])^2 - (E_T[t] - E_T\left[E_L[y_s]\right])^2 && \textbf{(by 12)}\\
&= (E_T[t] - E_T[y_s])^2 - (E_T[t] - E_T[y_e])^2\\
&= 0
\end{aligned}$$

□

Proof of Theorem 2.2

$$\begin{aligned}
&B_e - B_c\\
&= (E_T[t] - E_T[y_s])^2 - (E_T[t] - E_T[y_c])^2\\
&= (E_T[t] - E_T\left[E_L[y_s]\right])^2 - (E_T[t] - E_T\left[E_T[y_s]\right])^2 && \textbf{(by 12, 13)}\\
&= (E_T[t] - E_T[y_s])^2 - (E_T[t] - E_T[y_s])^2\\
&= 0
\end{aligned}$$

□

3.2.3 Loss reduction

Now, given the reduction in variance and equivalent bias, we can analyze the reduction in error that the ensembles offer. Recall that we define total loss as the expected error over learning and inference $L = E_T[(t^i - y_f^i)^2]$ and this decomposes additively into variance, bias and noise components: $L = V + B + N$. We now show that a simple relational ensemble reduces the loss of a single model, and an interleaved ensemble reduces the loss of a simple relational ensemble.

Corollary 1: Let f_s be a single collective inference model with loss L_s, f_e be a simple relational ensemble with loss L_e, and f_c be an interleaved ensemble model with loss L_c. Then $L_s \geq L_e \geq L_c$

$$1.1 \quad L_s - L_e \geq 0$$
$$1.2 \quad L_e - L_c \geq 0$$

Proof of Corollary 1.1

$$\begin{aligned}
&L_s - L_e \\
&=(V_s + B_s + N_s) - (V_e + B_e + N_e) \\
&=(V_s + B_s + N_s) - (V_e + B_s + N_s) && \textbf{(by 10, Thm 2)} \\
&=V_s - V_e \\
&\geq 0 && \textbf{(by Thm 1.1)}
\end{aligned}$$

□

Proof of Corollary 1.2

$$\begin{aligned}
&L_e - L_c \\
&=(V_e + B_e + N_e) - (V_c + B_c + N_c) \\
&=(V_e + B_s + N_s) - (V_c + B_s + N_s) && \textbf{(by 10, Thm 2)} \\
&=V_e - V_c \\
&\geq 0 && \textbf{(by Thm 1.2)}
\end{aligned}$$

□

Following the results of Theorems 1 and 2, and according to the definition of noise, it is straightforward to make the above conclusion about reduction in error. A simple relational ensemble model will reduce the error of a single collective inference model by reducing the learning variance, and an interleaved ensemble will reduce the error even further by reducing *both* learning variance *and* inference variance.

3.2.4 Ensemble learning

The analysis presented above applies regardless of what approach is used for learning the base models in f_e or f_c. In particular, it shows that the final prediction aggregation reduces learning variance while interleaved model aggregation during inference additionally reduces inference variance. While previous relational ensembles learn the models in F from pseudosamples formed from different link graphs or random subsets of features, we focus here on resampling to generate multiple pseudosamples from the single input training graph. The benefit of using resampling is that it is applicable to all kind of graphs regardless of the amount of information available (e.g., number of features or number of link types).

The error analysis applies to ensembles constructed from either relational subgraph resampling (RSR) or the traditionally used IID resampling, where instances are sampled independently with replacement. When the number of pseudosamples m approaches ∞, the bootstrap samples approximate the true population distribution $\mathcal{D}$ and the models in F approximate P_*. This indicates that for the ensemble model f_e, assumption 12 holds regardless of the learning approach. In other words, the ensemble prediction $y^i_{f_e}$ approaches the expected prediction of the single model f_s over *learning* (i.e., $E_L[y^i_s]$) for both resampling methods:

$$\lim_{m\to\infty} y_e^{RSR} = \lim_{m\to\infty} y_e^{IID} = E_L[y_s] \tag{14}$$

However, y_e^{RSR} converges faster than y_e^{IID}—because RSR pseudosamples more accurately reflect the correlations in relational data. Thus, given a finite ensemble size m, predictions made by models learned from RSR pseudosamples will capture and reduce more learning variance (because RSR more accurately captures the increased variance in network data). The same argument applies to f_c. Thus assumption 13 holds regardless of the resampling approach, but in finite ensemble sizes, RSR pseudosamples will capture and reduce more variance.

Our analysis illustrates the errors due to different phases of an ensemble algorithm. This understanding points to an additional way of reducing error due to variance in learning. In particular, the better the set of training samples can approximate the true population variance, the more reduction in learning variance the final model aggregation can achieve. We note that using relational subgraph resampling (RSR) can more accurately capture the increased variance in relational data, specifically using a small number of bootstrap samples. Following this observation, we propose to use RSR to enable the final predictions aggregation to reduce more learning variance. We combine the use of RSR with the interleaved inference aggregation (CEC) to additionally reduce inference variance. We outline the algorithmic details in the next section.

4. RELATIONAL ENSEMBLE FRAMEWORK

We propose an ensemble model that uses relational subgraph resampling (RSR) for generating the bootstrap pseudosamples to learn the ensembles from, and collective ensemble classification (CEC) for inference. RSR was originally proposed for accurate estimation of variance for network data [6]. We utilize RSR to accurately capture the learning variance during ensemble construction. This enables our ensemble method to reduce more variance in learning than traditional independent resampling approaches. In addition, using CEC in our method facilitates the reduction of inference error. In contrast, the majority of existing ensembles focus on reducing learning error alone. Using these two approaches allows a combined reduction of learning and inference variance, and extends the utility of CEC to single network settings. Note that, CEC was developed for domains with multiple types of relations (e.g., a network with email, phone, and SMS links)—and the method requires multiple link types to learn a model from each typed subnetwork. However, using RSR for learning enables a generalization of the method to domains that do not necessarily have multiple link graphs. The psuedosamples we use for learning are networks sampled with replacement from a *single* training graph (regardless of the link types in the graph).

Given a training dataset, our algorithm uses RSR to generate m bootstrap pseudosamples to learn an ensemble of m models. The models are applied for collective inference on a single test set using CEC, which iteratively interleaves the inferences across the m models. After inference is done, the predictions output by each base model are aggregated for each node independently as in traditional ensembles.

4.1 Ensemble learning

Our ensemble learning approach using bootstrap sampling is outlined in Algorithm 1, showing how an ensemble of size m models is constructed. A pseudosample $G_{ps} = (V_{ps}, E_{ps})$ is generated by resampling from G_{tr} (line 3) and a model F is learned from G_{ps} (line 4). F is a joint probability distribution over the labels of V_{ps}, conditioned on the observed attributes and graph structure in G_{ps}. The ensemble set of m learned models is returned (line 6). Note that the two main components needed for an implementation of the algorithm are: a resampling algorithm (step 3) and a relational learning algorithm (step 4). We describe each below.

Algorithm 1 Ensemble Learning: EL($G_{tr} = (V_{tr}, E_{tr}), m$)

$Ensemble \leftarrow \emptyset$
for $j := 1$ **to** m **do**
  $G_{ps_j} = Resample(G_{tr})$
  $F_j = LearnModel(G_{ps_j})$
  $Ensemble = Ensemble \cup \{F_j\}$
return $Ensemble$

Resampling.

RSR is an approach for resampling relational data to accurately capture the increased variance due to linkage and autocorrelation. RSR samples *subgraphs* with replacement instead of the typical independent sampling technique that samples *instances* (i.e., nodes) with replacement. When instances are resampled independently at random the resulting pseudosamples *underestimate* the amount of variance if the data exhibits network autocorrelation.

The RSR procedure is outlined in Algorithm 2. Given a sample relational data graph $G = (V, E)$, it returns a pseudosample data graph $G_{PS} = (V_{PS}, E_{PS})$. A set of $N_S = \lceil \frac{|V|}{b} \rceil$ subgraphs of size b are sampled from G. Each of N_S subgraphs is sampled using a breadth-first search from a randomly selected seed nodes. As a node v_s is added to the sampled subgraph node set V_s, v_s's neighbors are added to a list Q, from which the next node v_s is taken. This continues until the subgraph size b is reached.

Algorithm 2 Relational Subgraph Resampling (RSR)

RSR($G = (V, E), b$)
$V_{PS} \leftarrow \emptyset$; $E_{PS} \leftarrow \emptyset$
for $s := 1$ **to** $\lceil \frac{|V|}{b} \rceil$ **do**
  $V_S \leftarrow \emptyset$; $E_S \leftarrow \emptyset$; $Q \leftarrow \emptyset$
  v_s = randomly select node from V
  $V_S \leftarrow V_S \cup v_s$
  push neighbors of v_s onto Q
  while $(|V_S| < b) \wedge (|Q| > 0)$ **do**
    v_s = pop Q
    $V_S \leftarrow V_S \cup v_s$
    push neighbors of v_s onto Q
  $E_S = \{e_{ij} \in E \;\; s.t. \;\; v_i, v_j \in V_S\}$; $V_{PS} \leftarrow V_{PS} + V_S$; $E_{PS} \leftarrow E_{PS} + E_S$
return $G_{PS} = (V_{PS}, E_{PS})$

Note that the sampling is with replacement from the graph, so a node may appear in multiple subgraphs, one subgraph, or none. The pseudosample node set (V_{PS}) consists of all the nodes selected in the subgraphs (suitably relabeled so multiple copies of the same original node are distinguishable for the learning algorithm). The pseudosample edge set (E_{PS}) consists of all the edges within the selected subgraphs.

The key idea behind sampling subgraphs is that when autocorrelation is high (i.e., neighbors are correlated), the effective sample size is going to be closer to the number of "groups" of correlated instances than the number of nodes in the network. To account for this, RSR attempts to sample these "groups" instead of single instances, thus it more accurately approximates the effective sample size of the data. Moreover, sampling subgraphs preserves the local relational dependencies among instances in the subgraph so the relational model is better able to utilize the interrelated attribute dependencies to improve classification. In the traditional independent sampling technique, a node in the pseudosample will not necessarily have its neighbors from the original sample, and therefore the model will be less capable of exploiting the link structure. We compare to a method that uses independent sampling as a baseline. It is described in more detail the experimental section.

Relational learning.

We learn relational dependency network (RDN) [16] models as the component collective classification models. Since RDNs are selective models based on decision trees, they exhibit the instability that typically works well in bagged ensembles. RDNs use pseudolikelihood estimation to efficiently learn a full joint probability distribution over the labels of the data graph, and are typically applied with Gibbs sampling for collective inference. Note that the full joint distribution over the test data need not be estimated for accurate inference and it is sufficient to accurately estimate the per instance conditional likelihoods, which is easy to do with Gibbs sampling (i.e., has been shown to converge within 500-2000 Gibbs iterations [16]).

4.2 Ensemble inference

For inference, we use collective ensemble classification (CEC). However, instead of learning the ensemble from multiple link graphs as previously proposed [5], we learn the ensemble from bootstrap pseudosamples constructed using RSR as described above. This has an additional advantage of being applicable in single-graph network settings. The CEC procedure is included in Algorithm 3 for completeness. CEC uses *across-models* collective classification for inference, which propagates predictions across the component models during collective inference.

Given a test network G with partially labeled nodes V, and m base models $F_1, F_2, \ldots, F_k$ learned as described in section 4.1, the models are applied simultaneously to collectively predict the values of unknown labels (lines 5-11). First, the labels are randomly initialized (lines 1-4). Next, at each collective inference iteration, the model F_i is used to infer a label for each node v conditioned on the current labels of the neighbors of v (line 8). This corresponds to a typical collective inference iteration. Then instead of using the prediction from F_i directly for the next round, it is averaged with the inferences for v made by each other model F_j s.t. $j \neq i$ (line 9). This interleaves inferences across the component models and pushes the variance reduction gains into the collective inference process itself. At the end, the predictions are calculated for each model based on the stored prediction values from each collective inference iteration (lines 12-13). Finally, model outputs are averaged to produce the final predictions (lines 15-16).

Note that the manner in which CEC uses inferences from other models (for the same node) provides more information to the inference process that is not available if the collective inference processes are run independently on each base model. Since each collective inference process can experience error due to variance from approximate inference, the ensemble averaging during inference can reduce these errors before they propagate throughout the network. This results in significant reduction of inference variance, which is achieved solely by CEC.

CEC assumes a collective classification model as the base component of the ensemble, we use RDNs, but any collec-

Algorithm 3 Collective Ensemble Classification (CEC)

CEC($F_1, F_2, \ldots, F_m$, $G=(V,E), X, \tilde{Y}$, $F_m = P(Y_i|G,X,Y)$)

for all i in 1 to m **do**
  $\hat{Y}^i = \tilde{Y}; \mathbf{Y^i_T} = \emptyset$
  for all $v_j \in V$ $s.t.$ $y_j \notin \tilde{Y}$ **do**
    Randomly initialize $\hat{y}^i_j$; $\hat{Y}^i = \hat{Y}^i \cup \hat{y}^i_j$
repeat
  for all $i = 1$ to m **do**
    for all $v_j \in V$ $s.t.$ $y_j \notin \tilde{Y}$ **do**
      $\hat{y}^{i_{new}}_j = F^i : P^i(Y_j|\mathbf{X}_{i.j}, \mathbf{X}_{\mathbf{i.R}}, \mathbf{\hat{Y}^i_R})$ *where* $\mathbf{R} = \{v_k : e_{jk} \in E_i\}$
      $\hat{y}^{i_{agg}}_j = \frac{1}{m}\sum_{j=1}^{m} \hat{y}^{i_{new}}_j$
      $\hat{Y}^i = \hat{Y}^i - \{\hat{y}^i_j\} + \{\hat{y}^{i_{agg}}_j\}$; $\mathbf{Y^i_T} = \mathbf{Y^i_T} \cup \hat{y}^{i_{agg}}_j$
until *terminating_condition*
for all $i = 1$ to m **do**
  Compute $\mathbf{P^i} = \{P^i_j : y_j \notin \tilde{Y}\}$ using $\mathbf{Y^i_T}$
$P = \emptyset$
for all $v_j \in V$ **do**
  $p_j = \frac{1}{m}\sum_{i=1}^{m} p^i_j$; $P = P \cup \{p_j\}$
return P

tive classification model can be used instead. However, our analysis shows that the approach will work particularly well for models that exhibit learning and/or inference variance.

4.3 Experimental evaluation

We refer to our proposed ensemble as RSR-CEC. We evaluate the ensemble method on both synthetic and real world datasets, and the results show that combining RSR with CEC significantly outperforms using either approach alone.

4.3.1 Baseline approaches

We use a number of baseline methods to compare the proposed model to alternative approaches while controlling for model representation.

SM.

A *single model* baseline is used to evaluate the improvement achieved by each ensemble approach. Here, a collective classification model is learned from the original training sample and applied once on the given test set. Note that all the ensembles we discuss below, including the proposed model, generate the bootstrap pseudosamples from this original training sample, and use the same collective classification algorithm as the base component model.

IID-RE.

This model uses IID resampling for generating the training pseudosamples and learns a relational model for each base classifier. IID resampling works by sampling instances independently at random from the network, with replacement. A link in the original sample will only appear in the pseudosample if both nodes it connects were selected. A simple *relational ensemble* (RE) approach is then used for inference, where each base model is applied independently for collective inference to produce a set of probability estimates for nodes predictions. Then for each node, the base models' predictions are averaged to get the node's final prediction. We compare to this approach to evaluate the combined improvement achieved by using RSR for resampling and CEC for inference over a method that does not use either approach. The goal is to show the total variance reduction offered by RSR and CEC.

RSR-RE.

This baseline uses RSR for constructing the ensemble and RE for inference. Comparing the performance of our proposed model to this approach allows us to evaluate the improvement achieved by CEC for inference, while controlling for the resampling method (RSR) used by our proposed approach.

IID-CEC.

This baseline uses IID resampling for ensemble construction, and CEC for inference. Comparing the performance of our proposed model to this approach allows us to evaluate the improvement achieved by RSR for sampling, while controlling for the inference method (CEC) used by our proposed approach.

4.3.2 Datasets

We evaluate the methods on synthetic and real world network data. Synthetic datasets are generated with a latent group model [15]. They are homogeneous (i.e., with a single object type) data graphs with autocorrelation due to an underlying (hidden) group structure. Each object has a boolean class label C (that is determined by the type of group to which it belongs), and three attributes. The class label C has an autocorrelation level of 0.75. We independently constructed five training and test pairs of such datasets, each consisting of 500 objects.

The Facebook dataset used in this work is a sample of Purdue University Facebook network. We construct a friendship graph from the links between friends. Each user has a boolean class label which indicates whether their political view is 'Conservative'. In addition, we considered nine node features which record user profile information. We use 4 sampled networks of users (based on membership in various Purdue subnetworks): [Purdue Alum'07, Purdue'08, Purdue'09, Purdue'10] with node sizes of: [921, 827, 1268, 1384] respectively. Then we construct 4 different training and test pairs by testing on one subnetwork and training on two subnetworks from the previous and preceding class networks. For example we learn the model from Purdue Alum'07 and Purdue'09, and apply the model on Purdue'08.

4.3.3 Methodology

The RSR algorithm uses a subgraph size $b = 50$ and $b = 10$ for the synthetic and Facebook experiment, respectively. The methods described are learned and evaluated using RDNs as the base collective classification model, using $450 - 500$ Gibbs iterations for collective inference. We use the following setting to compare the various approaches.

For each experiment, the proportion of the test set that is labeled before inference is specified, and for each trial a random set of nodes is chosen to label. The random labeling process is repeated 10 times. The area under the ROC (AUC) is measured to assess the prediction accuracy of each model. The 10 trials are repeated for 4 training and test pairs, and the averages of the $10 \times 4 = 40$ AUC measurements from each approach are reported. Note that, all methods are run on the same random labeling of the

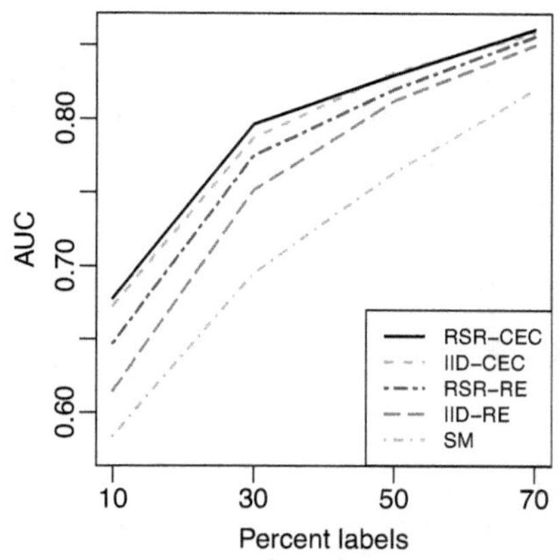

Figure 2: Synthetic experiments show significant accuracy improvement of RSR-CEC at various proportions of available true labels in the test graph.

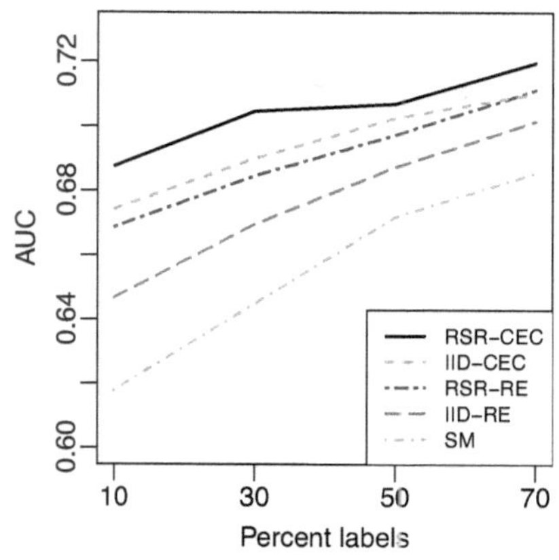

Figure 3: Facebook experiments show significant accuracy improvement of RSR-CEC at various proportions of available true labels in the test graph.

test set. From each training test set and for each sampling approach, we construct 5 bootstrap pseudosamples and learn the ensemble models (i.e., $m = 5$). This is repeated for 4 different labeling proportions (l) in each experiment. $l = \{10\%, 30\%, 50\%, 70\%\}$ denotes the x-axis in the figures, while the y-axis plots the AUC values.

4.3.4 Results

Figures 2 and 3 show the results of the synthetic and Facebook experiments, respectively. The main finding is that our proposed RSR-CEC approach has significantly higher classification accuracy than all the baseline comparison methods at all percent labelings, and across both the synthetic and Facebook experiments. We measured significance using paired t-tests and all significance reported here correspond to $p < 0.0001$ unless stated otherwise. The superior performance of RSR-CEC can be explained by the combined benefit of learning and inference variance reduction.

In addition, the accuracy of the single model baseline is significantly less than *all* the ensemble models, at all percent labelings for both experiments. Moreover, IID-CEC significantly outperforms IID-RE at all percent labelings for both experiments. This is because CEC reduces inference variance while RE only reduces learning variance. RE applies the models independently for inference which does not reduce inference variance–since prediction aggregation happens after inference, possibly after inference variance has propagated through the graph. Furthermore, RSR-RE significantly outperforms IID-RE at all percent labelings for both experiments, with $p < 0.01$ and $p < 0.03$ for the 50% and 70% synthetic experiments. This is because RSR captures more variance in the data than IID resampling. Therefore, RE can reduce more learning variance when used with RSR. Finally, IID-CEC significantly outperforms RSR-RE at $\{10\%, 30\%, 50\%\}$ for the synthetic experiment. This shows that CEC can reduce both learning and inference variance, even when combined with IID resampling.

We also ran an experiment to test the effect of increasing the number of models on performance of ensembles learned using different resampling approaches, the results shown in Figure 4 show that while controlling for the inference approach, ensembles learned using IID bootstraps perform closer to those learned from RSR bootstraps, as the number of base models increase. This confirms our theoretical finding.

To summarize the empirical findings:

- Ensembles using RSR outperform ensembles using IID resampling, since RSR reduces more learning variance than IID resampling.
- Ensembles using CEC outperform ensembles using RE, since CEC reduces inference variance which is not reduced by RE.
- Combining RSR with CEC results in significant gains in accuracy, since the combination reduces the largest amount of variance (due to learning and inference).
- Ensembles using IID resampling and RSR resampling converge as more base models are used.

5. RELATED WORK

There are two main lines of research related to the analysis we present here. Error analysis for ensemble classifiers and collective classification models, and work on relational methods that reduce bias or variance. For error analysis, earlier work has used conventional bias/variance analysis to evaluate model performance [4, 8, 9, 11]. However, the focus has been on single models and on errors in learning.

For error analysis of ensembles, Breiman [3] has shown theoretically that bagging reduces total classification error by reducing the error due to variance. However, the work is based on the assumption that the data is i.i.d. and therefore the models run exact inference. Consequently, Breiman's work has focused on theoretical analysis for this type of

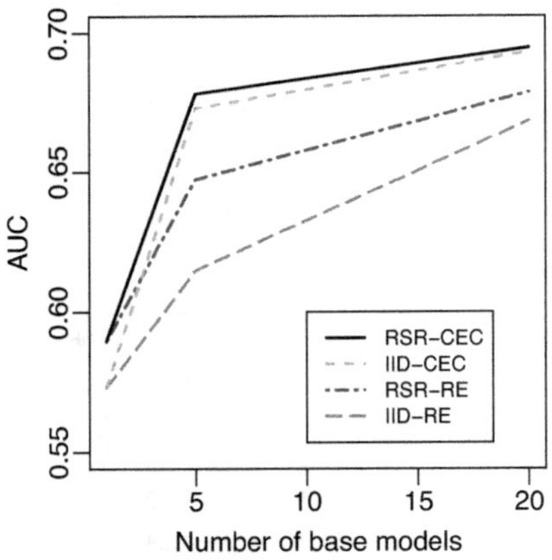

Figure 4: Synthetic experiments show accuracy covergence using IID resampling and RSR resampling as the number of base models increases.

models where the error is only associated with the learning process. Other work has presented an analytical framework to quantify the improvements in classification results due to combining or integrating the outputs of several classifiers [19]. Their work is based on analysis of decision boundaries and is applied on linearly combined neural classifiers.

For error analysis of collective classification models, Neville and Jensen [14] have shown that collective classification introduces an additional source of error due to variation in the inference process. While other work has presented another type of error decomposition for collective classification [20], by studying the propagation error in collective inference with maximum pseudolikelihood estimation.

Some work [5, 6] has extended ensembles to improve classification accuracy for relational domains. Including a method for constructing ensembles while accounting for the increased variance of network data [6], a method for ensemble classification on multi-source networks [5], and an ensemble method for reducing variance in the inference process for collective classification [5]. Other recent work [7] has showed that stacking [12] improves collective classification by reducing inference bias. This work compares to our model as it evaluated model performance in single source relational datasets. However, it is interesting to note that stacking reduces inference bias, while our method reduces inference variance.

6. CONCLUSION

We presented theoretical analysis that shows that an interleaved ensemble model reduces total loss over a simple relational ensemble model which reduces total loss over a single model (corollary 1). We showed that this is achieved by the reduction of variance (theorem 1), not bias (theorem 2). We proposed an ensemble model that significantly improves classification accuracy of network data by reducing errors due to variance in both learning and inference. We evaluated our ensemble model using both synthetic and real-world classification tasks and empirically showed its superior performance to alternative approaches.

7. ACKNOWLEDGMENTS

This research is supported by NSF under grant number(s) IIS-1149789 and CCF-0939370. The U.S. Government is authorized to reproduce and distribute reprints for governmental purposes notwithstanding any copyright notation hereon.

8. REFERENCES

[1] A. V. Assche, C. Vens, H. Blockeel, and S. Dzeroski. A random forest approach to relational learning. In *ICML'04 Workshop on SRL and its Connections.*

[2] R. S. Y. F. P. Bartlett and W. Lee. Boosting the margin: A new explanation for the effectiveness of voting methods. In *ICML'97.*

[3] L. Breiman. Bagging predictors. *MLJ'96.*

[4] P. Domingos. A unified bias-variance decomposition for zero-one and squared loss. In *AAAI'00.*

[5] H. Eldardiry and J. Neville. Across-model collective ensemble classification. In *AAAI'11.*

[6] H. Eldardiry and J. Neville. A resampling technique for relational data graphs. In *SNA-SIGKDD'08.*

[7] A. Fast and D. Jensen. Why stacked models perform effective collective classification. In *ICDM'08.*

[8] J. Friedman. On bias, variance, 0/1-loss, and the curse-of-dimensionality. *DMKD'97.*

[9] S. Geman, E. Bienenstock, and R. Doursat. Neural networks and the bias/variance dilemma. *NC'92.*

[10] A. HeB and N.Kushmerick. Iterative ensemble classification for relational data: a case study of semantic web services. In *ECML'04.*

[11] G. James. Variance and bias for general loss functions. *MLJ'03.*

[12] Z. Kou and W. W. Cohen. Stacked graphical models for effecient inference for markov random fields. In *SDM'07.*

[13] S. Natarajan, T.Khot, K. Kersting, B. Gutmann, and J. Shavlik. Gradient-based boosting for statistical relational learning: The relational dependecy network case. *MLJ'12.*

[14] J. Neville and D. Jensen. A bias/variance decomposition for models using collective inference. *MLJ'08.*

[15] J. Neville and D. Jensen. Leveraging relational autocorrelation with latent group models. In *ICDM'05.*

[16] J. Neville and D. Jensen. Relational dependency networks. *JMLR'07.*

[17] C. Preisach and L. Schmidt-Thieme. Ensembles of relational classifiers. *KIS'08.*

[18] J. Quinlan. Bagging, boosting and c4.5. In *AAAI'96.*

[19] K. Tumer and J. Ghosh. Analysis of decision boundaries in linearly combined neural classifiers. *Pattern Recognition'96.*

[20] R. Xiang and J. Neville. Understanding propagation error and its effect on collective classification. In *ICDM'11.*

[21] Y.Freund and R.E.Schapire. Experiments with a new boosting algorithm. In *ICML'96.*

Density Index and Proximity Search in Large Graphs

Nan Li
Computer Science
UC Santa Barbara
Santa Barbara, CA 93106
nanli@cs.ucsb.edu

Xifeng Yan
Computer Science
UC Santa Barbara
Santa Barbara, CA 93106
xyan@cs.ucsb.edu

Zhen Wen
Social Network Analytics
IBM Research
Hawthorne, NY 10532
zhenwen@us.ibm.com

Arijit Khan
Computer Science
UC Santa Barbara
Santa Barbara, CA 93106
arijitkhan@cs.ucsb.edu

ABSTRACT

Given a large real-world graph where vertices are associated with labels, how do we quickly find interesting vertex sets according to a given query? In this paper, we study *label-based proximity search* in large graphs, which finds the top-k query-covering vertex sets with the smallest diameters. Each set has to cover all the labels in a query. Existing greedy algorithms only return approximate answers, and do not scale well to large graphs. We propose a novel framework, called gDensity, which uses density index and likelihood ranking to find vertex sets in an efficient and accurate manner. Promising vertices are ordered and examined according to their likelihood to produce answers, and the likelihood calculation is greatly facilitated by density indexing. Techniques such as progressive search and partial indexing are further proposed. Experiments on real-world graphs show the efficiency and scalability of gDensity.

Categories and Subject Descriptors

G.2.2 [**Discrete Mathematics**]: Graph Theory—*graph algorithms*

Keywords

Graph mining, Proximity search, Indexing

1. INTRODUCTION

Graphs and networks can model various types of interactions in a myriad of applications [12, 15, 18]. They are used to encode complex relationships such as chemical bonds, entity relations, social interactions, and so on. In contemporary graphs, vertices and edges are often associated with attributes. While searching the graphs, what is interesting is not only the connectivity, but also the attributes, such as labels and weights. Figure 1 shows a graph where vertices contain numerical labels. Consider a succinct yet fundamental graph query formula: given a set of labels, find vertex sets covering these labels and rank the sets by their connectivity. Viable connectivity measures include diameter, edge density, and minimum spanning tree. In Figure 1, if we want to find vertex sets that cover labels $\{1, 2, 3\}$, and the diameter of a vertex set is its longest pairwise shortest-path, we can return S_3, S_1 and S_2 in ascending order of diameters.

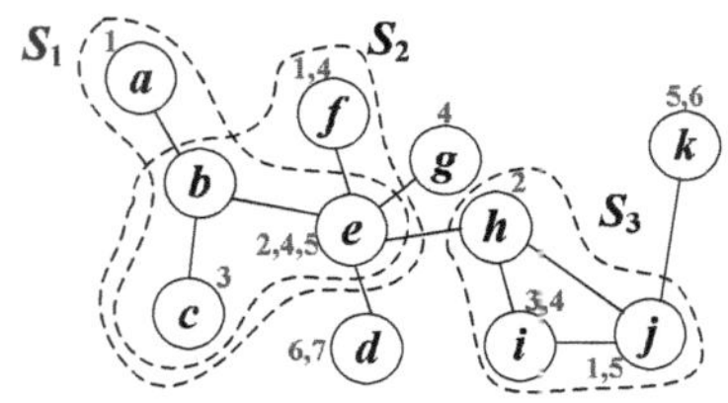

Figure 1: Label-Based Proximity Search

Applications of such a setting abound. The vertex labels can represent movies recommended by a user, functions carried by a gene, skills owned by a professional, and so on. Such queries help solve various interesting problems in real-world graphs: (1) in a protein network where vertices are proteins and labels are their annotations, *find a set of closely-connected proteins with certain annotations*; (2) in a collaboration network where vertices are experts and labels are their skills, *find a well-connected expert team with required skills* [18]; (3) in an intrusion network where vertices are computers and labels are intrusions they initiate, *find a set of intrusions that happen closely together*. The list of applications continues: finding a group of close friends with certain hobbies, finding a set of related movies covering certain genres, finding a group of well-connected customers interested in certain products, and many others.

We study *label-based graph proximity search*, to find the top-k vertex sets with the smallest diameters, for a query containing distinct labels. Each set covers all the labels in the query. The advantages of using diameter as a measure are shown in [16]. *Graph proximity query* is a general and simple way to query graphs. Lappas et al. [18] studied a similar problem called DIAMETER-TF for expert team formation and adopted a greedy algorithm, `RarestFirst`, to return a 2-approximate answer (the returned set has a di-

CIKM'12, October 29–November 2, 2012, Maui, HI, USA.

ameter no greater than two times of the optimal diameter). DIAMETER-TF is NP-hard [18]. In this paper, we propose a scalable solution to find top-k answers efficiently in large graphs, for queries with moderate sizes. Our goals are: (1) finding the *exact* top-k answers, not approximate answers; (2) designing a novel graph index for fast query processing.

Other similar studies include [16] and [8]. Kargar and An [16] studied finding the top-k r-cliques with smallest weights, where an r-clique is a set of vertices covering all the input keywords and the distance between each two is constrained. Two algorithms are proposed: branch and bound and polynomial delay. The former is an exact algorithm, but it is slow and does not rank the answers; the latter ranks the answers, but is a 2-approximation. Gajewar and Sarma [8] studied the team formation problem with subgraph density as the objective to maximize and focused on approximation algorithms. The problem definition is different in our paper and we aim for exact and fast solutions.

A naive approach is to enumerate all query-covering vertex sets, linearly scan them and return the top-k with the smallest diameters. This is costly for large graphs. It is desirable to have a mechanism to identify the most *promising* graph regions, or local neighborhoods, and examine them first. If a neighborhood covers the query labels, and meanwhile has high edge density, it tends to contain vertex sets with small diameters that cover the query. We propose a framework, called gDensity, to address the proximity search problem using this principle. Empirical studies on real-world graphs show that gDensity improves the query performance over competing methods.

Our contributions. (1) We introduce density index in graphs and the workflow to answer graph proximity queries using such index. (2) We demonstrate that if the neighborhoods are sorted and examined according to the likelihood, the search time can be reduced. (3) We propose partial indexing techniques to significantly reduce index size and index construction time, with negligible loss in query performance. (4) Empirical studies on real-world graphs show that gDensity is effective and scalable.

2. PRELIMINARIES

For a vertex-attributed graph $G = (V, E, \mathbb{L})$, each vertex is attached with a set of labels from $\mathbb{L} = \{\alpha_1, \dots, \alpha_l\}$. $L(u)$ denotes the label set of vertex u. For the ease of presentation, we focus on un-directed and un-weighted graphs. However, the proposed framework can be extended to directed and weighted graphs as well.

DEFINITION 1 (COVER). *Given a vertex-attributed graph $G = (V, E, \mathbb{L})$, a vertex set $S \subseteq V$, and a query $Q \subseteq \mathbb{L}$, S "covers" Q if $Q \subseteq \bigcup_{u \in S} L(u)$. S is also called a query covering vertex set. S is a minimal cover if S covers Q and no subset of S covers Q.*

DEFINITION 2 (DIAMETER). *Given a graph $G = (V, E)$ and a vertex set $S \subseteq V$, the diameter of S is the maximum of the pairwise shortest distances of all vertex pairs in S, i.e., $\max_{u,v \in S}\{dist(u, v)\}$, where $dist(u, v)$ is the shortest-path distance between u and v in G.*

The diameter of a vertex set S, denoted by `diameter(S)`, is different from the diameter of a subgraph induced by S, since the shortest path between two vertices in S might not completely lie in the subgraph induced by S.

PROBLEM 1 (GRAPH PROXIMITY SEARCH). *Given a vertex attributed graph $G = (V, E, \mathbb{L})$ and a query Q containing q labels ($|Q| = q$), label-based graph proximity search finds the top-k vertex sets $\{S_1, S_2, \dots, S_k\}$ with the smallest diameters. Each set S_i is a minimal cover of Q.*

In many applications, it might not be useful to generate sets with large diameters, especially for graphs exhibiting the small-world property. One might apply a constraint such that `diameter(`S_i`)` does not exceed a threshold.

`RarestFirst` is a greedy algorithm proposed by [18] that approximates the top-1 answer. First, `RarestFirst` finds the rarest label in query Q that is contained by the smallest number of vertices in G. Secondly, for each vertex v with the rarest label, it finds its nearest neighbors that contain the remaining labels in Q. Let R_v denote the maximum distance between v and these neighbors. Finally, it returns the vertex with the smallest R_v, and its nearest neighbors containing the other labels in Q, as an approximate top set. `RarestFirst` yields a 2-approximation in terms of diameter, i.e., the diameter of the top set found by `RarestFirst` is no greater than two times that of the real top set.

`RarestFirst` can be very fast if all pairwise shortest distances are pre-indexed. This is costly for large graphs. gDensity does not have such prerequisite. Besides, the goal of gDensity is finding the *real* top-k answers (not approximate answers). gDensity works well for queries with small-diameter answers, which are common in practice. For small graphs where all pairwise shortest distances can be pre-indexed, or for some difficult graphs where optimal solutions are hard to derive, `RarestFirst` could be a better option. In Section 8, we implement a modified top-k version of `RarestFirst` using the proposed progressive search technique, whose query performance is compared with gDensity.

2.1 Cost Analysis and Observations

The naive solution in Section 1 scales poorly to large graphs because: (1) It entails calculating all-pairs shortest distances. It takes $O(|V|^3)$ time using the Floyd-Warshall algorithm and $O(|V||E|)$ using the Johnson's algorithm. (2) It examines all query-covering sets without knowing their likelihood to be a top-k set. The time complexity is $O(|V|^q)$, with q being the size of the query.

An alternative approach is to examine the local neighborhoods of promising vertices, and find high-quality top-k candidates quickly. The search cost is the number of vertices examined times the average time to examine each vertex. It is important to prune unpromising vertices. A possible pruning strategy is: let d^* be the maximum diameter of the current top-k candidates. d^* decreases when new query covers are found to update the top-k list. d^* can be used to prune vertices which do not locally contain covers with diameter $< d^*$. gDensity instantiates such idea using nearest label pruning and progressive search, to quickly prune vertices which are unable to produce qualified covers. The key is to find vertices whose neighborhoods are likely to produce covers with small diameters, so that the diameter of the discovered top-k candidates can be quickly reduced.

DEFINITION 3 (d-NEIGHBORHOOD). *Given a graph $G = (V, E, \mathbb{L})$ and a vertex u in G, the d-neighborhood of u, $N_d(u)$, denotes the set of vertices in G whose shortest distance to u is no more than d, i.e., $\{v | dist(u, v) \le d\}$.*

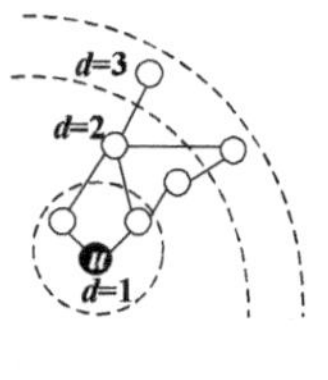

Figure 2: d-Neighborhood Example

Intuitively, the d-neighborhood of u, $N_d(u)$, can be regarded as a sphere of radius d centered at u. Figure 2 shows an example of the 1-neighborhood, 2-neighborhood and 3-neighborhood of vertex u. For each vertex u in G, we have to determine if its d-neighborhood is likely to generate vertex sets with small diameters to cover the query. The key question is: how do we estimate such likelihood?

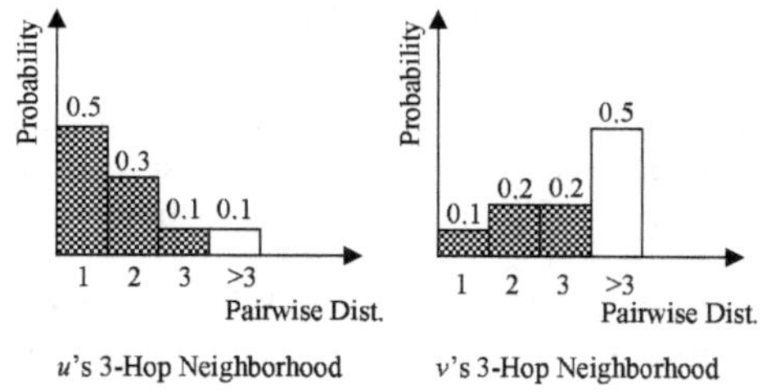

Figure 3: Pairwise Distance Distribution Example

We propose density index to solve the likelihood estimation problem. Figure 3 shows the intuition behind density index. Assume there are two regions, i.e., the 3-neighborhoods of vertices u and v. The distributions of pairwise shortest distances in both regions are plotted in Figure 3. The horizontal axis is the pairwise distance, which are 1, 2, 3 and greater than 3. The vertical axis shows the percentage of vertex pairs with those distances. Given a query Q, if both regions exhibit similar label distribution, which one has a higher chance to contain a query cover with smaller diameter? Very likely u's ! This is because there is a much higher percentage of vertex pairs in u's neighborhood that have smaller pairwise distances. Density index is built on this intuition. For each vertex, the pairwise distance distribution in its local neighborhood is indexed offline, which will later be used to estimate its likelihood online. Section 4 describes our indexing techniques in depth.

3. PROXIMITY SEARCH FRAMEWORK

gDensity consists of the following components.

Density Index Construction: We create a histogram-like profile for each vertex depicting the distribution of the pairwise shortest distances in its d-neighborhood, for $1 \leq d \leq d_I$. d_I is a user specified threshold.

Seed Vertex Selection: Instead of examining the entire vertex set V, we only examine the neighborhoods of the vertices containing the least frequent label in the query Q. These vertices are called *seed vertices*. Since a qualified vertex set must contain at least one seed vertex, we can solely focus on searching the neighborhoods of seed vertices.

Likelihood Ranking: Seed vertices are examined according to their likelihood to produce qualified vertex sets in their local neighborhoods. Vertices with the highest likelihoods are examined first.

Progressive Search: We maintain a buffer, $\mathbf{B}_k$, of the top minimal query covers discovered so far. A sequential examination finds qualified vertex sets with diameters $1, 2, \ldots$, until the top-k buffer is full (contains k answers). This mechanism enables early termination of the search. Once the top-k buffer is full, the algorithm stops, because all of undiscovered vertex sets will have diameter at least as large as the maximum diameter in the top-k buffer.

Nearest Label Pruning: Let d be the current diameter used in progressive search. Once d is determined, gDensity traverses seed vertices to find query covers with diameter exactly as d. The value of d increases from 1 and is used to prune seed vertices that are unable to generate qualified covers. Such seeds have their nearest neighbor with any query label further than d.

gDensity Algorithm. Algorithm 1 shows the overall work flow of gDensity. In the following sections, we elaborate the details regarding the above components.

Algorithm 1: gDensity Framework

Input: Graph G, indexing radius d_I, query Q, k
Output: The top-k vertex sets with the smallest diameters

```
Indexing G from 1 to d_I;
α1 ← the least frequent label in Q;
Seed vertices V_α1 ← the vertices with label α1;
Top-k buffer B_k ← ∅, d ← 1;
while true do
    Compute the likelihood for all the seed vertices;
    Rank the seeds decreasingly using the likelihood;
    for each seed vertex in the ranked list do
        if it is not pruned by the nearest label rule then
            Check its d-neighborhood for minimal query
            covers with diameter d;
            Update B_k with discovered minimal covers;
            if B_k is full then
                return B_k;
    d++;
```

4. INDEXING AND LIKELIHOOD RANK

In order to estimate the likelihood online fast, we propose density indexing to pre-compute indices that reflect local edge connectivity. How to utilize the density index to facilitate likelihood estimation is discussed in Section 4.2.

4.1 Density Index

Density indexing records the pairwise shortest distance distribution of a local neighborhood. In order to maintain a succinct index structure, the density index is solely based on topology. For each vertex u, we first grow its d-neighborhood, $N_d(u)$, using breadth-first search. The pairwise shortest distances for all vertex pairs in $N_d(u)$ are then calculated. Some pairwise distances might be greater than d (at most $2d$). Density index records the histogram of the discrete distance distribution, i.e., the percentage of pairs whose distance is h, for $1 \leq h \leq 2d$, as shown in Figure 3. Density index only needs to record the distribution, not all-pairs shortest distances. Section 6 will discuss how to derive density index approximately.

Let I be an indicator function and $P(h|N_d(u))$ be the percentage of vertex pairs with distance h. We have

$$P(h|N_d(u)) = \frac{\sum_{v_i,v_j \in N_d(u)} I(dist(v_i,v_j) = h)}{\sum_{v_i,v_j \in N_d(u)} I(1)}. \quad (1)$$

Users can reduce the histogram size by combining the percentage of pairs whose distance is greater than a certain threshold $\hat{h}$, as in Eq. (2). Usually $\hat{h} = d$.

$$P(> \hat{h}|N_d(u)) = \frac{\sum_{v_i,v_j \in N_d(u)} I(dist(v_i,v_j) > \hat{h})}{\sum_{v_i,v_j \in N_d(u)} I(1)}. \quad (2)$$

Since the distribution can change with respect to the radius of the neighborhood, we build the histograms for varying d-neighborhoods of each vertex, with $1 \le d \le d_I$, where d_I is a user-specified indexing locality threshold. Figure 2 shows the neighborhoods of vertex u with different radii. For each radius d, we build a histogram similar to Figure 3. Intuitively, if $N_d(u)$ contains a higher percentage of vertex pairs with small pairwise distances and it also covers Q, $N_d(u)$ should be given a higher priority during search. This intuition leads to the development of likelihood ranking.

Supplementary indices are also used to facilitate likelihood ranking and nearest label pruning (Section 5.2). (1) For each label α_i in G, global label distribution index records the number of vertices in G that contain label α_i. (2) Inspired by the indexing scheme proposed by He et al. [12], gDensity further indexes, for each vertex in G, its closest distance to each label within its d-neighborhood.

Since density index has histogram structure as in Figure 3, the space cost of density index is$\Sigma_{d=1}^{d=d_I} O(|V|d) = O(|V|d_I^2)$. For index time, suppose the average vertex degree in G is b, then for each vertex u, the expected size of its d-neighborhood is $O(b^d)$. If we use all pairwise distances within $d \in [1, d_I]$ to build the density index, the total time complexity will be $O(|V|b^{2d_I})$. The index time might be huge even for small d_I. This motivates us to design partial indexing (Section 6), which greatly reduces index time and size, while maintaining satisfying index quality.

4.2 Likelihood Ranking

Given a query $Q = \{\alpha_1, \alpha_2, \ldots, \alpha_q\}$, let $\alpha_1 \in Q$ be the label contained by the smallest number of vertices in G. α_1 is called the *rarest* or *least frequent* label in Q. Let $V_{\alpha_1} = \{v_1, v_2, \ldots, v_m\}$ be the vertex set in G containing label α_1. These vertices are referred to as the *seed vertices*. Algorithm 1 shows that the d-neighborhoods of all seed vertices will be examined according to their likelihood to produce minimal query covers with diameter exactly as d, while d is gradually relaxed. For each seed vertex $v_i (i = \{1, \ldots, m\})$, its likelihood depends on the pairwise distance distribution of its d-neighborhood, $N_d(v_i)$. The likelihood reflects how densely the neighborhood is connected and can be computed from the density index.

4.2.1 Likelihood Computation

DEFINITION 4 (DISTANCE PROBABILITY). *Randomly selecting a pair of vertices in $N_d(v_i)$, let $p(v_i, d)$ denote the probability for this pair's distance to be no greater than d. $p(v_i, d)$ can be obtained from the density index, $P(h|N_d(v_i))$,*

$$p(v_i, d) = \sum_{h=1}^{d} P(h|N_d(v_i)). \quad (3)$$

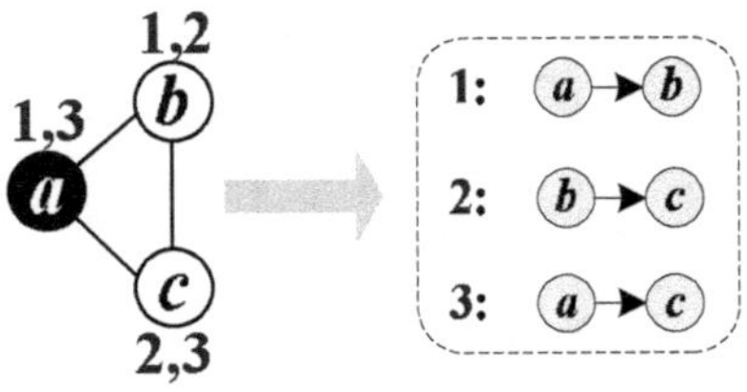

Figure 4: Minimal Cover Example

DEFINITION 5 (LIKELIHOOD). *Randomly selecting a vertex set with q vertices in $N_d(v_i)$, let $\ell(v_i, d)$ denote the probability for this set's diameter to be no greater than d. With density index (Eq. (1)), $\ell(v_i, d)$ can be estimated as*

$$\ell(v_i, d) \sim p(v_i, d)^{q(q-1)/2}$$
$$\sim (\sum_{h=1}^{d} P(h|N_d(v_i)))^{q(q-1)/2} \quad (4)$$

If the diameter of a vertex set is no greater than d, all the vertex pairs within this set must be at most d distance away from each other. If we assume independency of pairwise distances among vertex pairs, Eq. (4) can be obtained, given that the vertex set has size q. Certainly, it is an estimation, since pairwise distances should follow some constraints, such as triangle inequality in metric graphs. For a given query Q of size q, gDensity uses $\ell(v_i, d)$ as the likelihood to rank all the seed vertices. Apparently, seed vertices whose local neighborhoods exhibit dense edge connectivity tend to be ranked with higher priority. With the presence of density index, likelihood can be easily computed as in Eq. (4).

For all the seed vertices in V_{α_1}, we sort them in descending order of $\ell(v_i, d)$ and find minimal query covers with diameter d individually. For each seed vertex under examination, we first perform (unordered) cartesian product across query label support lists to get candidate query covers, and then select minimal covers from those covers. Such approach assures that all possible minimal query covers will be found from each seed vertex's d-neighborhood.

4.2.2 Cartesian Product and Query Covers

For each seed vertex v_i with label α_1, we generate a support vertex list for each label in the query $Q = \{\alpha_1, \alpha_2, \ldots, \alpha_q\}$ in v_i's d-neighborhood. Let n_j be the size of the support list for α_j. Let $\pi_d(v_i)$ denote the total number of possible query covers generated by performing a cartesian product across all label support lists, where each cover is an unordered vertex set consisting of one vertex from each support list.

$$\pi_d(v_i) = \prod_{j=1}^{q} n_j. \quad (5)$$

Not all such covers are minimal. In Figure 4, if $Q = \{1, 2, 3\}$, three support lists are generated in a's 1-neighborhood. For example, label 1 has two vertices in its list, a and b. One of the covers across the lists is $\{a, b, c\}$, which is not minimal. From $\{a, b, c\}$, we shall generate 3 minimal covers, $\{a, b\}$, $\{b, c\}$ and $\{a, c\}$. For each seed vertex, gDensity scans all candidate covers and generates those minimal ones to update the top-k list. Note that generating minimal covers from the supporting lists is an NP-hard problem itself. Here we find the minimal covers in a brute-force manner. It

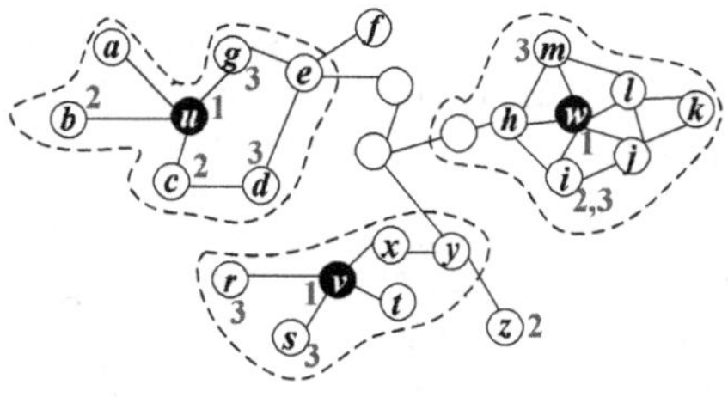

Figure 5: Pruning and Progressive Search Example

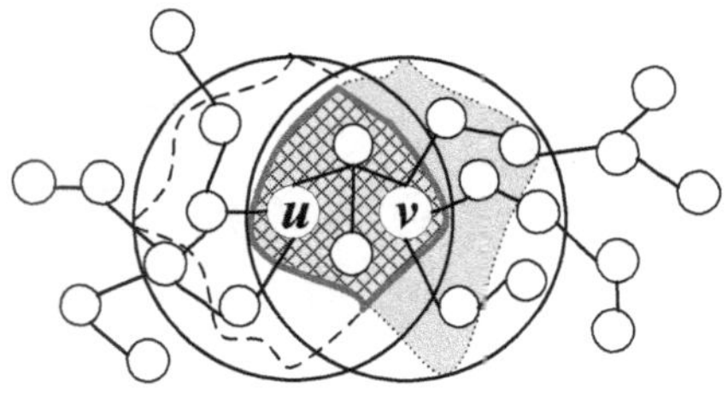

Figure 6: Partial Materialization Example

is a relatively a time-consuming process. However, with progressive search, which will be described later, we only need to do this locally in a confined neighborhood. Experiment results will show that gDensity still achieves good empirical performance on large graphs.

5. PROGRESSIVE SEARCH AND PRUNING

Progressive search enables search to terminate once there are k answers found. Nearest label pruning is used together with progressive search to prune unpromising seed vertices.

5.1 Progressive Search

The search cost increases exponentially when d increases. Instead of testing a large value of d first, we propose to check neighborhoods with gradually relaxed radii. A top-k buffer, $\mathbf{B}_k$, is maintained to store the top vertex sets with the smallest diameters found so far. We progressively examine the neighborhoods with $d = 1$, $d = 2$, and so on, until $\mathbf{B}_k$ is full. Such mechanism allows the search to terminate early. For example, if k answers are found while checking the 1-hop neighborhoods of all seed vertices, the process can be terminated without checking neighborhoods with $d \geq 2$. In Figure 5, suppose the query is $Q = \{1, 2, 3\}$, and we have three seed vertices $\{u, v, w\}$. Starting with $d = 1$, we explore the 1-hop neighborhoods of all three, looking for covers with diameter 1, which gives us $\langle\{w, i\}, 1\rangle$. Here, $\langle\{w, i\}, 1\rangle$ means the diameter of $\{w, i\}$ is 1. Moving onto $d = 2$, we explore the 2-hop neighborhoods of all the three vertices (in dashed lines), seeking covers with diameter 2, which gives us $\{\langle\{u, c, d\}, 2\rangle, \langle\{u, c, g\}, 2\rangle, \langle\{u, b, g\}, 2\rangle\}$. If $k = 4$, search process can terminate here.

5.2 Nearest Label Pruning

We further propose a pruning strategy called nearest label pruning. Used together with progressive search, it is able to prune unfavorable seeds from checking. Suppose the current diameter used in progressive search is d. For each seed vertex v_i, we calculate its shortest distance to each label in Q within its d-neighborhood, $N_d(v_i)$. If there is a label $\alpha \in Q$ such that the shortest distance between a vertex with α and v_i is greater than d, we skip checking v_i and its neighborhood, since $N_d(v_i)$ is not able to generate a query cover with diameter $\leq d$. Furthermore, v_i and the edges emanating from it can be removed. For example in Figure 5, if $Q = \{1, 2, 3\}$ and at certain point $d = 2$. Four query covers have been inserted into $\mathbf{B}_k$ together with their diameters, which are $\{\langle\{w, i\}, 1\rangle, \langle\{u, c, d\}, 2\rangle, \langle\{u, c, g\}, 2\rangle, \langle\{u, b, g\}, 2\rangle\}$. We no longer need to check the neighborhood of vertex v. This is because the shortest distance between v and label 2 is 3, which is greater than the current diameter constraint $d = 2$.

6. PARTIAL INDEXING

Building the complete density index for large graphs can be expensive. We propose partial indexing to build an approximate index using partial neighborhood information.

6.1 Partial Materialization

Using random sampling, *partial materialization* allows density index to be built approximately by accessing only a portion of the local neighborhoods. For each vertex u to index: (1) only a subset of vertices in u's d-neighborhood are used to form an approximate neighborhood; (2) only a percentage of vertex pairs are sampled from such approximate neighborhood to construct the partial density index. More specifically, the following steps are performed.

(a) Given a vertex u and an indexing distance d, a subset of vertices are randomly sampled from $N_d(u)$. An approximate d-neighborhood, $\tilde{N}_d(u)$, consists of those sampled vertices and their distances to u.

(b) Randomly pick a vertex v from $\tilde{N}_d(u)$.

(c) Get the intersection of $\tilde{N}_d(u)$ and $\tilde{N}_d(v)$, $\chi_d(u, v)$. For a random vertex x in $\chi_d(u, v)$, sample the pair (x, v) and record their distance as in $\tilde{N}_d(v)$.

(d) For a random vertex x in $\tilde{N}_d(u)$ but not in $\chi_d(u, v)$, sample the pair (x, v) and record their distance as $> d$.

(e) Repeat Steps (b) to (d) until a certain percentage, p, of vertex pairs are sampled from $N_d(u)$.

(f) Draw the pairwise distance distribution using sampled pairs to approximate the real density distribution in $N_d(u)$.

Figure 6 (better viewed in color) shows an example. The solid circles centered at vertices u and v are their actual 2-neighborhoods. The white free-shaped region surrounding u is its approximate 2-neighborhood, $\tilde{N}_2(u)$; similarly, the gray free-shaped region surrounding v is $\tilde{N}_2(v)$. The region with grid pattern circumscribed by a solid red line is the intersection of both approximate neighborhoods, $\chi_2(u, v)$. Each sampled vertex x from u's approximate 2-neighborhood forms a pair with v, (x, v). If x is in the intersection, $\chi_2(u, v)$, the pair (x, v) is sampled with a pairwise distance recorded as in $\tilde{N}_d(v)$; otherwise it is sampled with a pairwise distance recorded as $> d$. A localized version of Metropolis-Hastings random walk (MHRW) sampling [6, 9] is used to sample vertices from $N_d(u)$ (Step (a)).

6.2 Representative Vertices

Partial materialization reduces the indexing cost for an individual vertex. To further reduce the indexing cost, we can reduce the number of vertices to be indexed. The intuition is: if two vertices u and v have similar local topological

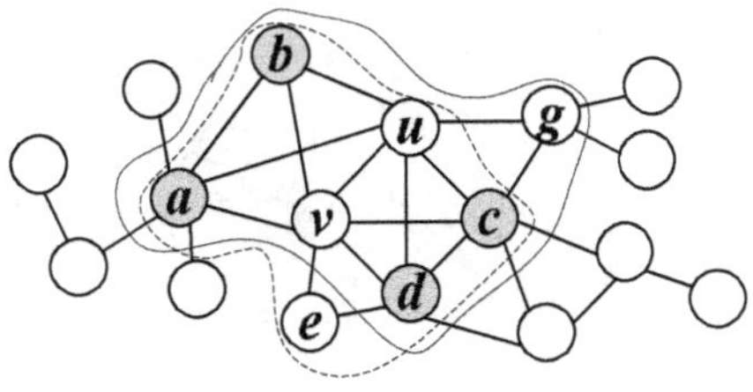

Figure 7: Representative Vertex Example

structure, there is no need to build the density index for u and v separately, given that the distance distributions in the neighborhoods of u and v are similar. For example, in Figure 7, the 1-hop neighborhoods of vertices u and v overlap each other to a great extent. The common adjacent neighbors of u and v in Figure 7 are $\{a, b, c, d\}$, which is 66.7% of u and v's 1-neighborhoods. Can we build the density index of v with the aid of the density index of u?

A simple strategy employed in gDensity is to use the density of u to *represent* that of v (or vice versa), if the percentage of common 1-hop neighbors of u and v exceeds a certain threshold in both u and v's neighborhoods. Let σ denote such threshold. In this case, vertex u is considered as the *representative vertex* of v. We only index those vertices which are representatives of some others, and use their density index to represent others'. Such strategy quickly cuts down the number of vertices to index, thus reduces the index time and index size. As experimented in Section 8, $\sigma \geq 30\%$ would suffice to produce effective partial index, which still yields good online query processing performance.

7. OPTIMALITY OF GDENSITY

THEOREM 1 (OPTIMALITY OF gDensity). *For a query, gDensity finds the optimal top-k answers. Partial indexing and likelihood ranking affect the speed of query processing, but not the optimality of the results.*

PROOF SKETCH. Since seed vertices contain the least frequent label in the query, all query covers contain at least one seed vertex. Confining the search to the neighborhoods of seed vertices does not leave out any answers. Progressive search assures that the diameters of unexamined vertex sets will be no less than the maximum diameter in the top-k buffer. Therefore the final top-k answers returned will have the smallest diameters. Indexing and likelihood ranking identify "promising" seed vertices and guide the algorithm to discover the top-k answers *faster*. If more promising seeds are ranked higher, the top-k buffer will be filled up faster. It is possible for a seed vertex, whose neighborhood contains good answers, to be ranked lower than other less promising seeds. However, this would only affect the *speed* of filling up the top-k buffer. It would not change the fact that the top-k buffer contains the top-k smallest diameters. Partial indexing further reduces the indexing cost by indexing only partial information. It approximates the *indexing* phase, and will not affect the optimality of the *query* phase. Therefore gDensity always returns the optimal answers. □

The likelihood computed in Eq. (4) for ranking seed vertices assumes independence among distances between vertices, which might not be valid for some seeds due to possible skewed distribution. However, as long as it is valid for some seed vertices, the top-k buffer can be quickly updated with answers discovered surrounding those seeds, thus speeding up the search. The goal of likelihood ranking is to locate promising regions containing many potential answers and fill up the top-k buffer quickly. Section 8.2.3 empirically confirms the effectiveness of likelihood ranking.

We reiterate that partial indexing only affects the estimated density and likelihood ranking. Only the speed of the top-k search will be affected by partial indexing. Partial indexing will not impair the optimality of gDensity in terms of returning the top-k answers with the smallest diameters.

8. EXPERIMENTS

The empirical evaluation contains: (1) comparison between gDensity and the modified `RarestFirst`; (2) evaluation of partial indexing; (3) scalability test of gDensity. All experiments are run on a machine that has a 2.5GHz Intel Xeon processor (only one core is used), 32G RAM, and runs 64-bit Fedora 8 with LEDA 6.0 [22].

8.1 Data Sets

DBLP Data. DBLP is a collaboration network in computer science. Each vertex is an author and each edge is a collaborative relation. We consider the keywords in the paper titles of an author as vertex labels. The DBLP graph used contains 387,547 vertices and 1,443,873 edges.

Intrusion Data. In this graph, each vertex is a computer and each edge is an attack. A vertex has a set of labels, which are intrusion alerts initiated by this computer. There are 1035 distinct alerts. Intrusion alerts are logged periodically. We use one daily data set (*IntruDaily*) with 5,689 vertices and 6,505 edges, and one annual data set (*IntruAnn*) with 486,415 vertices and 1,666,184 edges.

WebGraph Data. Web graph (`http://webgraph.dsi.unimi.it/`) is a collection of UK web sites. Each vertex is a web page and each edge is a link. A routine is provided to attach the graph with random integer labels following Zipf distribution [20]. Five subgraphs are used, whose vertex numbers are 2M, 4M, 6M, 8M and 10M, and whose edge numbers are 9M, 16M, 23M, 29M and 34M. The 2M graph is a subgraph of the 4M graph, and so on.

50 queries are generated for each graph used. Query time is averaged over all the queries. Table 1 shows some query examples. Indexing is conducted up to 3 hops for all the graphs. If not otherwise specified, partial indexing is the default indexing. The vertex pair sampling percentage is 40% and the 1-hop neighborhood similarity threshold in representative vertex selection is $\sigma = 30\%$.

8.2 gDensity vs. Baselines

8.2.1 Baselines

We discovered in our experiments that the original `RarestFirst` method does not scale well to large graphs. Thus we add a constraint D on the diameters of the top-k vertex sets in `RarestFirst`, limiting the search to each seed's D-neighborhood. We further use progressive search to speed up `RarestFirst`. Algorithm 2 outlines the customized top-k `RarestFirst`. Another baseline method is a variant of gDensity, called "gDensity w/o LR", which removes likelihood ranking from gDensity. All of the other components are still kept in gDensity w/o LR. gDensity w/o LR examines the seed vertices in a random order. The goal is to inspect the

Table 1: Query Examples

DBLP Graph			
ID	Query	ID	Query
1	"Ranking", "Databases", "Storage"	4	"Intelligence", "TCP/IP", "Protocols"
2	"Bayesian", "Web-graphs", "Information"	5	"Complexity", "Ranking", "Router", "Generics"
3	"Mining", "Graph", "Stream"	6	"Image", "Allocation", "Statistical", "Multi-core"

Intrusion Graph	
ID	Query
1	"HTTP_Fields_With_Binary", "HTTP_IIS_Unicode_Encoding", "MSRPC_RemoteActivate_Bo"
2	"FTP_Mget_DotDot", "HTTP_OracleApp_demo_info", "HTTP_WebLogic_FileSourceRead"
3	"Content_Compound_File_Bad_Extension", "HTTP_URL_Name_Very_Long", "HTTP_URL_Repeated_Dot"
4	"SMB_Startup_File_Access", "pcAnywhere_Probe", "HTTP_Viewsrc_fileread", "Failed_login-unknown_error"
5	"HTTP_Passwd_Txt", "DNS_Windows_SMTP_Overflow", "OSPF_Link_State_Update_Multicast", "POP_User"

Algorithm 2: `RarestFirst` With Progressive Search

Input: Graph G, Query Q, diameter constraint D, k
Output: Top-k vertex sets with smallest diameters
$\alpha_1 \leftarrow$ the least frequent label in Q;
while *the top-k buffer is not full* **do**
  for *d from 1 to D* **do**
    for *each vertex v with α_1* **do**
      $N_d(v) \leftarrow v$'s d-neighborhood;
      $S \leftarrow \{v$ and v's nearest neighbors in $N_d(v)$ that contain other labels in $Q\}$;
      Extract minimal covers from S;
      for *each minimal cover* **do**
        If it is not yet in the top-k buffer, and its diameter $\leq D$, insert it into the buffer according to its diameter;
        if *the top-k buffer is full* **then**
          return top-k buffer;

actual effect of likelihood ranking. Both methods are used for comparative study against gDensity.

8.2.2 Evaluation Methods

The comparison is done on two measures, query time (in seconds) and answer miss ratio (in percentage). `RarestFirst` could miss some real top-k answers since it is an approximate solution. Miss ratio is the percentage of real top-k answers `RarestFirst` fails to discover. For example, if the real top-5 all have diameter 2 and if 2 of the top-5 answers returned by `RarestFirst` have diameter greater than 2, the miss ratio is $2/5 = 40\%$. gDensity and gDensity w/o LR are able to find all real top-k answers.

We also examine the impact of label distribution. There is an interesting tradeoff here. If labels are densely distributed (the average number of vertices containing each label is high), each neighborhood might potentially contain many answers and the algorithm stops early; if the labels are sparsely distributed, the seed vertex list is shorter and the candidate set for each seed is smaller. We thus design a group of experiments where we synthetically regenerate labels for graphs *DBLP*, *IntruAnn* and *WebGraph* 10M, under certain label ratios. The ratio is measured as $|L|/|V|$, where $|L|$ is the total number of distinct labels in G. Each vertex is randomly assigned one of those synthetic labels.

8.2.3 Query Time Comparison

Figure 8 shows the query time comparison of gDensity, gDensity w/o LR and the modified `RarestFirst`. The left-most column shows how the average query time changes with k. The advantage of gDensity over the modified `RarestFirst` is apparent. The effectiveness of likelihood ranking is evident on *DBLP* and *IntruAnn*, where gDensity greatly outperforms gDensity w/o LR. Likelihood ranking does not work as well on *WebGraph* 10M. It is possible that *WebGraph* 10M does not contain many patterns or dense regions, rendering it difficult to rank seed vertices effectively.

The remaining columns depict how the average query time changes with the synthetic label ratio, $|L|/|V|$. The tradeoff between dense (small label ratio) and sparse (large label ratio) label distribution clearly shows on *DBLP*, where the gDensity query time first goes up and then goes down. It goes up because as label distribution becomes sparse, more seeds and larger values of d need to be examined to find the top-k, since each region contains less answers. It then goes down because the seed vertex list gets shorter and the set of candidate covers to check for each seed gets smaller. `RarestFirst` sometimes outperforms gDensity because the diameter constraint lets `RarestFirst` finish without finding all the optimal top-k sets. In the next section, we will show the percentage of answers missed by `RarestFirst`.

8.2.4 Query Optimality Comparison

Query optimality is measured by the answer miss ratio. gDensity discovers the real top-k answers, thus the miss ratio of gDensity and gDensity w/o LR will be 0. Figure 10 shows how the miss ratio of `RarestFirst` changes with k. Miss ratio gradually increases with k. In the worst case, `RarestFirst` misses 52.8% of the real top-k answers. On average, the miss ratio is around 30%. Clearly, compared to gDensity, `RarestFirst` suffers from the drawback of possibly leaving out the optimal answers.

We also observe how miss ratio changes with the synthetic label ratio, $|L|/|V|$, in Figure 9. `RarestFirst` again is disadvantageous in terms of top-k optimality. The average miss ratios are 46.6%, 23.6% and 35.1% for synthetically labeled *DBLP*, *IntruAnn* and *WebGraph* 10M, respectively.

8.3 Partial Indexing Evaluation

Partial indexing reduces cost by indexing a subset of vertices using their approximate neighborhoods. We refer to the alternative, indexing all vertices using their exact neighborhoods, as "all indexing". The query performances of both indexing techniques are compared. Three thresholds of representative vertex selection are used for partial indexing: $\sigma = \{10\%, 30\%, 50\%\}$. Since all indexing is very time-consuming for large graphs, we can only afford to conduct the comparison on a small graph, *IntruDaily*.

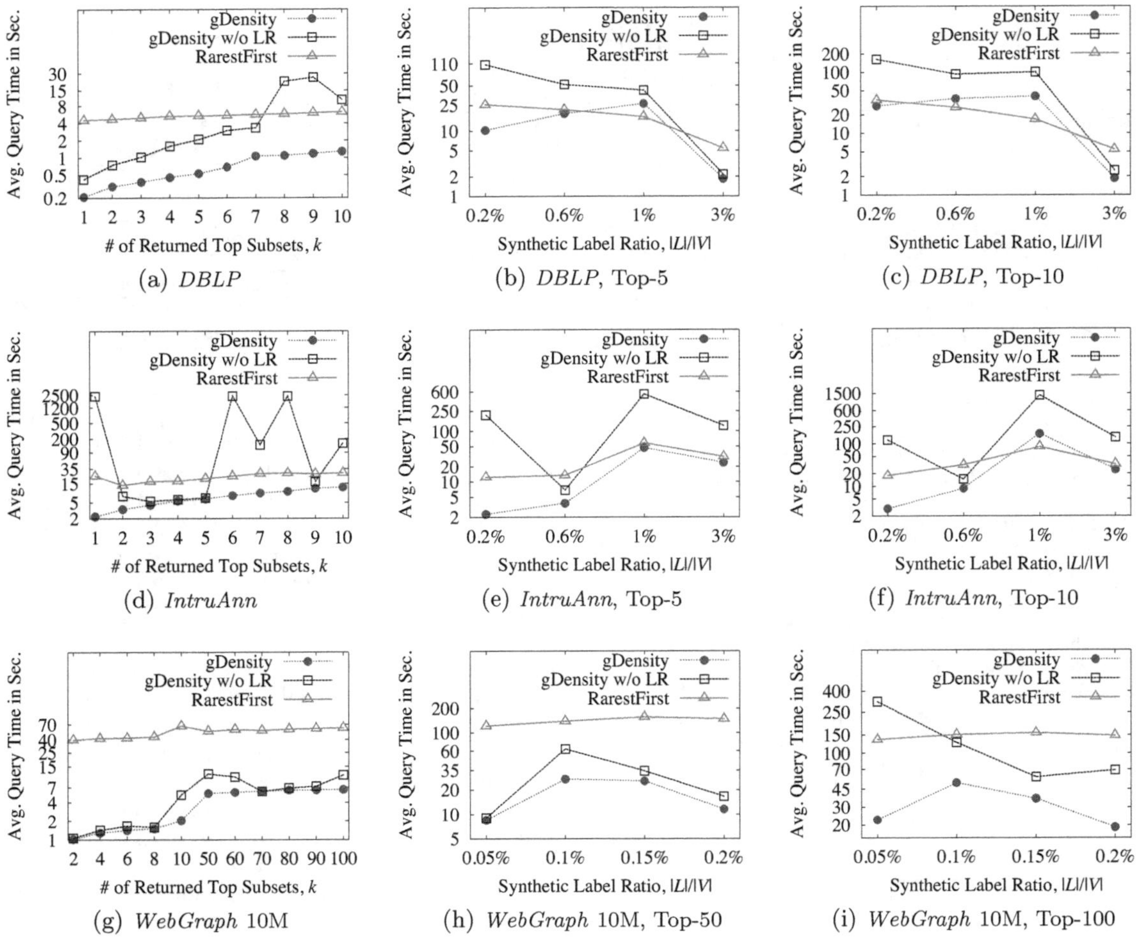

(a) *DBLP* (b) *DBLP*, Top-5 (c) *DBLP*, Top-10

(d) *IntruAnn* (e) *IntruAnn*, Top-5 (f) *IntruAnn*, Top-10

(g) *WebGraph* 10M (h) *WebGraph* 10M, Top-50 (i) *WebGraph* 10M, Top-100

Figure 8: gDensity vs. Baseline Methods, Query Time

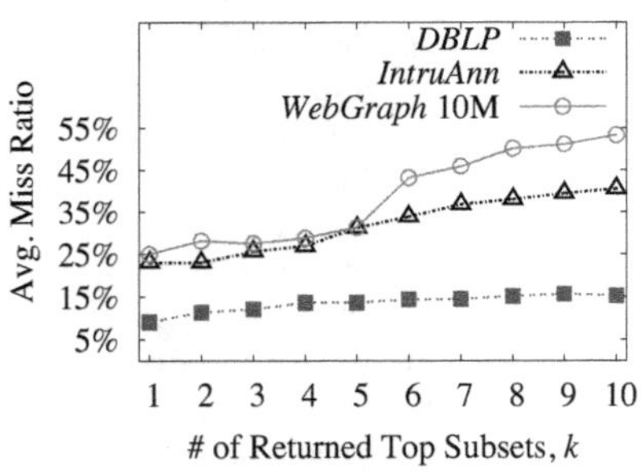

Figure 10: RarestFirst Miss Ratios vs. k

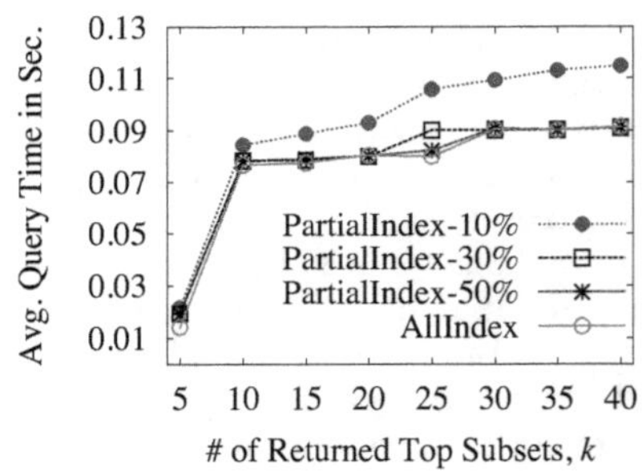

Figure 11: gDensity Partial vs. All Index: Query Time

As shown in Figure 11, the additional online query time partial indexing induces over all indexing is almost negligible, especially when $\sigma \geq 30\%$. The moderate performance margin between $\sigma = 10\%$ and $\sigma \geq 30\%$ might be attributed to the fact that there are not that many vertex pairs whose neighborhood similarity falls between 10% and 30%.

Table 2 shows the indexing time (seconds) and index size (MB) comparison. Partial indexing effectively reduces indexing cost. The indexing cost increases with the representative vertex threshold, because a higher threshold means a larger number of representative vertices to index.

8.4 gDensity Scalability Test

We conduct experiments on web graphs of increasing size to show the scalability of gDensity. Table 3 shows how the index time and size change when the graph increases from 2M to 10M vertices. Overall, the index time is satisfying and reasonable. The largest graph only takes 3.9 hours to index. The index size is no more than 30% of the graph size. Most importantly, the index time and size are approximately linear to the size of the graph. Therefore, partial indexing exhibits satisfying scalability over large graphs.

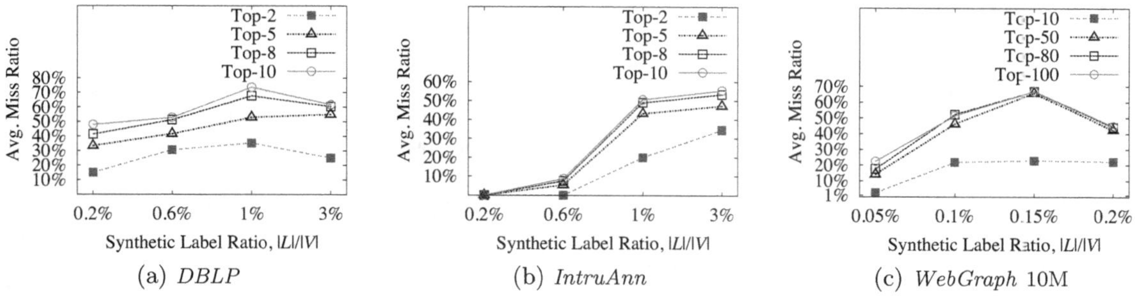

Figure 9: RarestFirst Miss Ratios vs. Synthetic Label Ratio

Table 2: Partial vs. All Index: Time & Size

Indexing Scheme	Time (Seconds)	Size (MB)
Partial Indexing, $\sigma = 10\%$	6.959	0.013
Partial Indexing, $\sigma = 30\%$	7.337	0.016
Partial Indexing, $\sigma = 50\%$	7.452	0.019
All Indexing	533.243	0.312

Table 3: gDensity Scalability Test: Index Time & Size

Vertex #	2M	4M	6M	8M	10M
Index Time (Hours)	0.92	1.65	2.53	3.23	3.85
Graph Size (MB)	234	390	528	678	786
Index Size (MB)	72	123	174	222	259

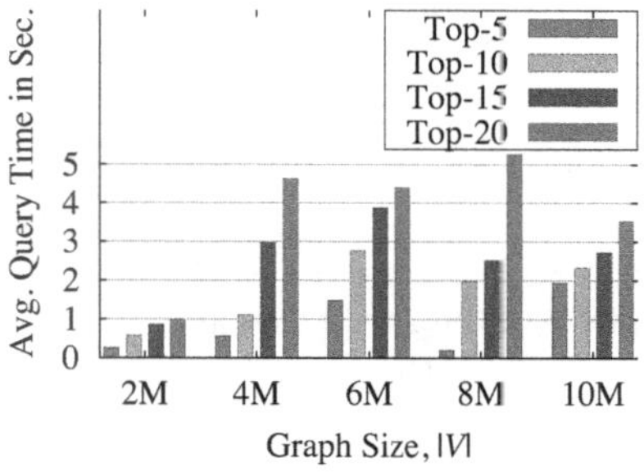

Figure 12: gDensity Scalability Test: Query Time

Figure 12 shows how query time changes when the graph size increases from 2M to 10M vertices, for various k values. We can see that the query time gradually increases and is still satisfying even for very large graphs. The query time is contingent on a number of factors such as the graph structure, the graph size, the label distribution, the query, k, and so on. Since the queries are randomly generated on each of the web graphs, it is possible for a smaller graph to encounter a more difficult query that entails longer processing time. Even for the same query, it is possible for it to be processed faster in a larger graph, since more answers might be found at an early stage. If we compare the runtime of top-5 for *WebGraph* 2M, top-10 for *WebGraph* 4M, top-15 for *WebGraph* 6M, and top-20 for *WebGraph* 8M (i.e., the value of k increases with the graph size), it is observed that the runtime increases linearly. Overall, gDensity is scalable with respect to the graph size.

9. RELATED WORK

Proximity Search. Typical proximity search in social networks includes link prediction [24], expert team formation [2, 8, 18, 26, 27]. The latter finds a team of experts with required skills. Existing methods include generic algorithms [26], simulated annealing [2], and so on. [18] adopts a 2-approximation algorithm to find a team of experts with the smallest diameter, where all-pairs shortest distances need to be pre-computed and no index structure is used to expedite the search. [8] presents approximation algorithms to find teams with the highest edge density. Proximity search is also studied in Euclidean space [1, 11], such as finding the smallest circle enclosing k points. Since the diameter of such a circle is not equal to the maximum pairwise distance between the k points, even with mapping methods such as ISOMAP [25], the techniques for the k-enclosing circle problem can not be directly applied here. The points here also do not contain label information.

Motif Finding in Graphs. Label-based graph proximity search is also related to the graph motif problem, introduced by [17] in the bioinformatics field. [7] further investigates three variants of the initial problem. A key difference is that diameter is not used to rank the discovered motifs.

Ranked Keyword Search in Graphs. Ranked keyword search in graphs [3, 12, 15] has focused on answers structured as rooted-trees. An answer is ranked mainly by the aggregate distances from the leaves to the root [12]. The distance among leaves is not considered. gDensity ranks an answer by its entire diameter. Finding subgraphs instead of trees is also studied in [16, 19]. Finding r-cliques that cover all the keywords is proposed in [16], which only finds answers with 2-approximation. [19] finds r-radius Steiner graphs that cover all the keywords.. [10] uses personalized PageRank vectors to find answers in the vicinity of vertices matching the query keywords in entity-relation graphs. [13] proposes XKeyword for efficient keyword proximity search in large XML graph databases. gDensity differs since it does not require a schema on the graphs. gDensity focuses on the diameter of a vertex set. and ensures optimality.

Top-k Query Processing. Top-k query processing is also studied for RDBMS [4, 10, 23] and middleware [5, 14, 21]. Supporting top-k queries in SQL is proposed in [4]. In middleware, top-k query is abstracted as getting objects with the top-k aggregate ranks from multiple data sources. Our work is different since gDensity answers top-k queries on a single source with graph data. Existing techniques for RDBMS and middleware are no longer applicable.

10. CONCLUSIONS

In this paper, we study the label-based graph proximity search problem, which finds the top-k query-covering vertex sets with the smallest diameters. The proposed gDensity framework introduces likelihood ranking of seed vertices to speed up the search. Fast pruning and early stopping are enabled by nearest label pruning and progressive search. Density indexing is proposed for fast likelihood estimation. Partial indexing is further proposed to reduce indexing cost. Empirical studies show the efficiency and scalability of gDensity. Our future works include: (1) extending gDensity to weighted and directed graphs; and (3) extending gDensity to handle other objective functions besides diameter.

11. ACKNOWLEDGMENTS

This research was sponsored in part by the U.S. National Science Foundation under grant IIS-0905084 and the Army Research Laboratory under Cooperative Agreement Number W911NF-09-2-0053 (NS-CTA). The views and conclusions in this document are those of the authors and should not be interpreted as representing the official policies, either expressed or implied, of the Army Research Laboratory or the U.S. Government. The U.S. Government is authorized to reproduce and distribute reprints for Government purposes notwithstanding any copyright notation here on.

12. REFERENCES

[1] A. Aggarwal, H. Imai, N. Katoh, and S. Suri. Finding k points with minimum diameter and related problems. *J. Algorithms*, 12(1):38–56, 1991.

[2] A. Baykasoglu, T. Dereli, and S. Das. Project team selection using fuzzy optimization approach. *Cybern. Syst.*, 38(2):155–185, 2007.

[3] G. Bhalotia, A. Hulgeri, C. Nakhe, S. Chakrabarti, and S. Sudarshan. Keyword searching and browsing in databases using BANKS. In *ICDE*, pages 431–440, 2002.

[4] M. Carey and D. Kossmann. On saying "enough already!" in SQL. In *SIGMOD*, pages 219–230, 1997.

[5] K. Chang and S. Hwang. Minimal probing: supporting expensive predicates for top-k queries. In *SIGMOD*, pages 346–357, 2002.

[6] S. Chib and E. Greenberg. Understanding the Metropolis-Hastings algorithm. *The American Statistician*, 49(4):327–335, Nov. 1995.

[7] R. Dondi, G. Fertin, and S. Vialette. Finding approximate and constrained motifs in graphs. In *CPM*, pages 388–401, 2011.

[8] A. Gajewar and A. D. Sarma. Multi-skill collaborative teams based on densest subgraphs. In *SDM*, pages 165–176, 2012.

[9] M. Gjoka, M. Kurant, C. T. Butts, and A. Markopoulou. Walking in facebook: a case study of unbiased sampling of OSNs. In *INFOCOM*, pages 2498–2506, Piscataway, NJ, USA, 2010. IEEE Press.

[10] M. Gupta, A. Pathak, and S. Chakrabarti. Fast algorithms for top-k personalized PageRank queries. In *WWW*, pages 1225–1226, 2008.

[11] S. Har-Peled and S. Mazumdar. Fast algorithms for computing the smallest k-enclosing circle. *Algorithmica*, 41(3):147–157, 2005.

[12] H. He, H. Wang, J. Yang, and P. Yu. BLINKS: ranked keyword searches on graphs. In *SIGMOD*, pages 305–316, 2007.

[13] V. Hristidis, Y. Papakonstantinou, and A. Balmin. Keyword proximity search on XML graphs. In *ICDE*, pages 367–378, 2003.

[14] I. Ilyas, G. Beskales, and M. Soliman. A survey of top-k query processing techniques in relational database systems. *ACM Comput. Surv.*, 40(4):1–58, 2008.

[15] V. Kacholia, S. Pandit, S. Chakrabarti, S. Sudarshan, R. Desai, and H. Karambelkar. Bidirectional expansion for keyword search on graph databases. In *VLDB*, pages 505–516, 2005.

[16] M. Kargar and A. An. Keyword search in graphs: Finding r-cliques. *PVLDB*, 4(10):681–692, 2011.

[17] V. Lacroix, C. G. Fernandes, and M.-F. Sagot. Motif search in graphs: Application to metabolic networks. *IEEE/ACM Trans. Comput. Biol. Bioinformatics*, 3(4):360–368, Oct. 2006.

[18] T. Lappas, K. Liu, and E. Terzi. Finding a team of experts in social networks. In *KDD*, pages 467–476, 2009.

[19] G. Li, B. C. Ooi, J. Feng, J. Wang, and L. Zhou. Ease: an effective 3-in-1 keyword search method for unstructured, semi-structured and structured data. In *SIGMOD*, pages 903–914, 2008.

[20] W. Li. Random texts exhibit Zipf's-law-like word frequency distribution. *IEEE Transactions on Information Theory*, 38(6):1842–, 1992.

[21] A. Marian, N. Bruno, and L. Gravano. Evaluating top-k queries over web-accessible databases. *ACM Trans. Database Syst.*, 29(2):319–362, 2004.

[22] K. Mehlhorn and S. Näher. *LEDA: a platform for combinatorial and geometric computing.* Cambridge University Press, 1999.

[23] L. Qin, J. X. Yu, L. Chang, and Y. Tao. Querying communities in relational databases. In *ICDE*, pages 724–735, 2009.

[24] P. Sarkar, A. W. Moore, and A. Prakash. Fast incremental proximity search in large graphs. In *ICML*, pages 896–903, 2008.

[25] J. Tenenbaum, V. Silva, and J. Langford. A global geometric framework for nonlinear dimensionality reduction. *Science*, (5500):2319–2323.

[26] H. Wi, S. Oh, J. Mun, and M. Jung. A team formation model based on knowledge and collaboration. *Expert Syst. Appl.*, 36(5):9121–9134, 2009.

[27] A. Zzkarian and A. Kusiak. Forming teams: an analytical approach. *IIE Transactions*, 31(1):85–97, 1999.

Gelling, and Melting, Large Graphs by Edge Manipulation

Hanghang Tong
IBM T.J. Watson Research
Hawthorne, NY, USA
htong@us.ibm.com

B. Aditya Prakash
Virginia Tech.
Blacksburg, VA, USA
badityaprakash@gmail.com

Tina Eliassi-Rad
Rutgers University
Piscataway, NJ, USA
eliassi@cs.rutgers.edu

Michalis Faloutsos
Univ. of California Riverside
Riverside, CA, USA
michalis@cs.ucr.edu

Christos Faloutsos
Carnegie Mellon University
Pittsburgh, PA, USA
christos@cs.cmu.edu

ABSTRACT

Controlling the dissemination of an entity (e.g., meme, virus, etc) on a large graph is an interesting problem in many disciplines. Examples include epidemiology, computer security, marketing, etc. So far, previous studies have mostly focused on removing or inoculating *nodes* to achieve the desired outcome.

We shift the problem to the level of edges and ask: which edges should we add or delete in order to speed-up or contain a dissemination? First, we propose effective and scalable algorithms to solve these dissemination problems. Second, we conduct a theoretical study of the two problems and our methods, including the *hardness* of the problem, the *accuracy* and *complexity* of our methods, and the *equivalence* between the different strategies and problems. Third and lastly, we conduct experiments on real topologies of varying sizes to demonstrate the effectiveness and scalability of our approaches.

Categories and Subject Descriptors

H.2.8 [**Database Management**]: Database Applications – Data Mining

General Terms

Algorithm, experimentation

Keywords

edge manipulation, immunization, scalability, graph mining

1. INTRODUCTION

Managing the dissemination of an entity (e.g., meme, virus, etc) on a large graph is a challenging problem with applications in various settings and disciplines. In its generality, the propagating entity can be many different things, such as a meme, a virus, an idea, a new product, etc. The propagation is affected by the topology and the properties of the entity: its 'virality', its speed, its 'stickiness' or the duration of the infection of a node. Our focus here is the *topology*, since we assume that we cannot alter the properties of the propagating entity.

The problem we address is how we can affect the propagation by modifying the *edges* of the graph. In fact, we address two different problems. First, in the ***NetMelt* problem**, we want to contain the dissemination by removing a given number of edges. For example, we can consider the distribution of malware over a social network. Deleting user accounts may not be desirable, but deleting edges ('unfriending' people) may be more acceptable. More specifically, we want to delete a set of k edges from the graph to minimize the infected population. Second, in the ***NetGel* problem**, we want to enable the dissemination by adding a given number of edges. Specifically, we want to add a set of k new edges into the graph to maximize the population that adopt the information. For example, we could extend the social network scenario using the recent 'arab spring' which often used Facebook and Twitter for coordinating events: we may want to maximize the spread of a potential piece of information. Note that an additional, key requirement for both problems is computational efficiency: the solution should scale to large graphs.

Both problems are challenging for slightly different reasons. For the *NetMelt* problem, most of the existing methods operate on the *node-level*, e.g., deleting a subset of the nodes from the graph to minimize the infected population from a propagating virus. In the above social spam example, this means that we might have to shutdown some legitimate user accounts. Can we avoid this by operating on a finer granularity, that is, only deleting a few edges between users to slow down the social spam spreading? For the *NetGel* problem, things are even more challenging because of its high intrinsic time complexity. Let n be the number of the nodes in the graph. There are almost n^2 non-existing edges since many real graphs are very sparse. In other words, even if we only want to add one single new edge into the graph, the solution space is $O(n^2)$. This complexity 'explodes' if we aim to add multiple new edges collectively, where the solution space becomes *exponential*. To date, there does not exist *any* scalable solution for the *NetGel* problem.

The overarching contribution of this paper is the formulation and theoretical study of the dissemination management via edge manip-

CIKM'12, October 29–November 2, 2012, Maui, HI, USA.

ulation: how to place a set of edges[1] to achieve the desired outcome. The main contributions of the paper can be summarized as follows:

- *Algorithms.* We propose effective and scalable algorithms to optimize the leading eigenvalue, the key graph parameter that controls the information dissemination processes for both *NetMelt* and *NetGel*, respectively;
- *Proofs and Analysis.* We show the *accuracy* and the *complexity* of our methods; the *hardness* of the problem, and *equivalence* between the different strategies;
- *Experimental Evaluations.* Our evaluations on real large graphs show that our methods are both effective and scalable (see Fig. 1 as an example).

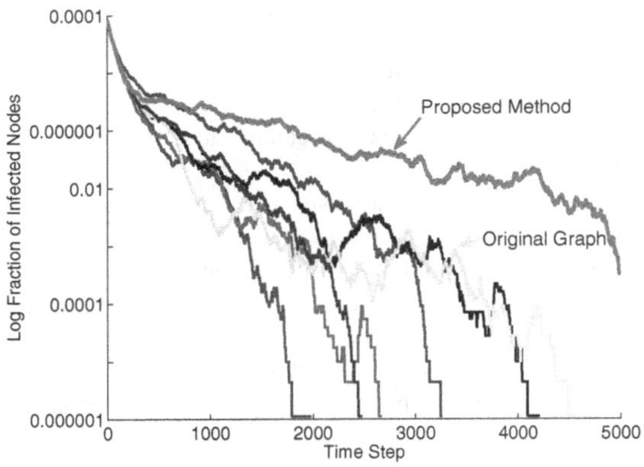

Figure 1: Comparison of maximizing the outcome of the information dissemination process. Larger is better. The proposed method (red) leads to the largest number of 'infected' nodes (e.g., having more people in the social networks to adopt a piece of good idea, etc). Notice that all the alternative methods are mixed with the result on the original graph (yellow), which means that they fail to affect the outcome of the dissemination process. See Section 6 for detailed experimental setting.

The rest of the paper is organized as follows. We introduce notation and formally define the *NetGel* and *NetMelt* problems in Section 2. We present and analyze the proposed algorithms in Section 3 and Section 4, respectively. We provide experimental evaluations in Section 5. We review the related work in Section 6 and conclude in Section 7.

2. PROBLEM DEFINITIONS

Table 1 lists the main symbols used throughout the paper. We consider directed, irreducible unipartite graphs. For ease of presentation, we discuss the unweighted graph scenario although the algorithms we propose can be naturally generalized to the weighted case. We represent a graph by its adjacency matrix. Following the standard notation, we use bold upper-case for matrices (e.g., $\mathbf{A}$), bold lower-case for vectors (e.g., $\mathbf{a}$), and calligraphic fonts for sets (e.g., $\mathcal{I}$). We denote the transpose with a prime (i.e., $\mathbf{A}'$ is the transpose of $\mathbf{A}$). Also, we represent the elements in a matrix using a convention similar to Matlab, e.g., $\mathbf{A}(i,j)$ is the element at

[1]In this paper, we use the terms 'link' and 'edge' interchangeably.

Table 1: Symbols

Symbol	Definition and Description
$\mathbf{A}, \mathbf{B}, \ldots$	matrices (bold upper case)
$\mathbf{A}(i,j)$	the element at the ith row and the jth column of $\mathbf{A}$
$\mathbf{A}(i,:)$	the ith row of matrix $\mathbf{A}$
$\mathbf{A}(:,j)$	the jth column of matrix $\mathbf{A}$
$\mathbf{A}'$	transpose of matrix $\mathbf{A}$
$\mathbf{a}, \mathbf{b}, \ldots$	vectors
$\mathcal{I}, \mathcal{J}, \ldots$	sets (calligraphic)
λ	the largest (in module) eigenvalue of $\mathbf{A}$
$\mathbf{u}, \mathbf{v}$	the $n \times 1$ left eigenvector and right eigenvector associated with λ.
n	the number of the nodes in the graph
m	the number of the edges in the graph
k	the budget (i.e., the number of deleted or added edges)

the ith row and j^{th} column of the matrix $\mathbf{A}$, and $\mathbf{A}(:,j)$ is the jth column of $\mathbf{A}$, etc.

When we discuss the relationship between the two different strategies (node deletion vs. edge deletion) for the *NetMelt* problem, it is helpful to introduce the concept of line graph, where the nodes represent the edges in the original graph. Formally, each edge in the original graph $\mathbf{A}$ becomes a node in the line graph $L(\mathbf{A})$; and there is an edge from one node to the other in the line graph if the target of the former edge is the same as the source of the latter edge in the original graph $\mathbf{A}$. It is formally defined as follows:

DEFINITION 1 (**LINE GRAPH**). *Given a directed graph $\mathbf{A}$, its directed line graph $L(\mathbf{A})$ is a graph such that each node of $L(\mathbf{A})$ represents an edge of $\mathbf{A}$, and there is an edge from a node e_1 to e_2 in $L(\mathbf{A})$ iff for the corresponding edges $\langle i_1, j_1\rangle$ and $\langle i_2, j_2\rangle$ in $\mathbf{A}$, $j_1 = i_2$.*

With the notation of the line graph $L(\mathbf{A})$, we have two equivalent ways to represent an edge. Let e_x ($e_x = 1, \ldots, m$) be the index of the nodes (i.e., the edges in $\mathbf{A}$) in the line graph. We can also represent the edge e_x by the pair of its source and target nodes in the original graph $\mathbf{A}$: $\langle i_x, j_x\rangle$, i.e., the edge e_x starts with the node i_x and ends at node j_x.

In order to design an effective strategy to optimize the graph structure to affect the outcome of an information dissemination process, we need to answer the following three questions. (1) *(Key graph parameters/metrics)* What are key graph metrics/parameters that determine/control the dissemination process? (2) *(Graph operations)* What types of graph operations (e.g., deleting nodes/edges, adding edges, etc) are we allowed to change the graph structure? (3) *(Affecting algorithms)* For a given graph operation, how can we design effective, scalable algorithms to optimize the corresponding key graph parameters?

For information dissemination on real graphs, a major finding [41, 33] is that, for a large family of dissemination processes, the largest (in module) eigenvalue λ of the adjacency matrix $\mathbf{A}$ or an appropriately defined system matrix is the *only* graph parameter that determines the tipping point of the dissemination process, i.e., whether or not the dissemination will become an epidemic (see Section 6 for a review of related work). In principle, this gives a clear guidance on the algorithmic side, that is, *an ideal, optimal strategy to affect the outcome of the information dissemination process should* *change the graph structure so that the leading eigenvalue λ is minimized or maximized.*

Based on this observation, now we can transform the original problem of affecting the dissemination process to the **eigenvalue optimization problem**, that is,

(1) minimize the leading eigenvalue λ for *NetMelt*;

(2) maximize the leading eigenvalue λ for *NetGel*.

In this paper, we focus on operating on the *edge-level* to design affecting algorithms. With the above notation, our problems can be formally defined as the following two sub-problems:

PROBLEM 1. ***NetMelt* (Edge Deletion)**

Given: *A large $n \times n$ graph $\mathbf{A}$ and an integer (budget) k;*

Output: *A set of k edges from $\mathbf{A}$ whose deletion from $\mathbf{A}$ creates the largest decrease of the leading eigenvalue of $\mathbf{A}$.*

PROBLEM 2. ***NetGel* (Edge Addition)**

Given: *A large $n \times n$ graph $\mathbf{A}$ and an integer (budget) k;*

Find: *A set of k non-edges of $\mathbf{A}$ whose addition to $\mathbf{A}$ creates the largest increase of the leading eigenvalue of $\mathbf{A}$.*

As we will show soon, both problems are combinatorial.

3. PROPOSED ALGORITHM FOR *NetMelt*

In this section, we address the *NetMelt* problem (Prob. 1), that is, to delete k edges from the original graph $\mathbf{A}$ so that its leading eigenvalue λ will decrease as much as possible. We first study the relationship between two different strategies (edge deletion vs. node deletion), and then present our algorithm, followed by the analysis of its effectiveness as well as efficiency.

3.1 Edge Deletion vs. Node Deletion

Roughly speaking, in the *NetMelt* Problem (Edge Deletion), we want to find a set of k 'important' edges from the graph $\mathbf{A}$ to delete. With the notation of the line graph $L(\mathbf{A})$, intuitively, such 'important' edges in $\mathbf{A}$ might become 'important' nodes in the line graph $L(\mathbf{A})$. In this section, we briefly present the relationship between these two strategies (node deletion vs. edge deletion).

Our main result is summarized in Lemma 1, which says that the eigenvalues of the original graph $\mathbf{A}$ are also the eigenvalues of its line graph $L(\mathbf{A})$.

LEMMA 1. **Line Graph Spectrum.** *Let λ be an eigenvalue of the graph $\mathbf{A}$. Then λ is also the eigenvalue of the line graph $L(\mathbf{A})$.*

PROOF. Omitted for brevity. □

By Lemma 1, it seems that edge deletion (Prob. 1) can be transformed to the node deletion problem on the line graph – that is, select a subset of k nodes from the line graph $L(\mathbf{A})$ whose deletion creates the largest decrease in terms of the leading eigenvalue of $L(\mathbf{A})$. However, by the following lemma, the node deletion problem itself is still a challenging task.

LEMMA 2. **Hardness of Node Deletion.** *It is NP-Complete to find a set of k nodes from a graph $\mathbf{A}$, whose deletion will create the largest decrease of the largest eigenvalue of the graph $\mathbf{A}$.*

PROOF. The proof can be done by the reduction from the independent node set problem, which is known to be NP-Complete [17]. The detailed proof is omitted for brevity. □

That said, we seek an effective algorithm that directly solves the *NetMelt* problem next.

3.2 Proposed K-EDGEDELETION Algorithm

The key to solving Prob. 1 (*NetMelt*) is to quantify the impact of deleting a set of edges in terms of the leading eigenvalue λ. The naive way is to recompute the leading eigenvalue λ after deleting the corresponding set of edges - the smaller the new eigenvalue, the better the subset of the edges. But it is computationally infeasible for large graphs since it takes $O(m)$ time for each of the $\binom{m}{k}$ possible sets, as in general, the impact for a given set of the edges (in terms of decreasing the leading eigenvalue λ) is *not* equal to the summation of the impact of deleting each individual edge.

Let $\mathbf{u}$ and $\mathbf{v}$ be the leading left eigenvector and right eigenvector of the graph $\mathbf{A}$, respectively. Intuitively, the left eigen-score $\mathbf{u}(i)$ and the right eigen-score $\mathbf{v}(j)$ $(i, j = 1, ..., n)$ provide some importance measure for the corresponding nodes i and j. The core idea of the proposed K-EDGEDELETION algorithm is to quantify the impact of each edge by the corresponding left and right eigenscores *independently* (step 9) . Our upcoming analysis in the next subsection shows that this strategy (1) leads to a good approximation of the actual impact wrt decreasing the leading eigenvalue; and (2) naturally de-couples the dependence among the different edges. As a result, we can avoid the combinatorial enumeration in Prob. 1 by picking the top-*k* edges with the highest individual impact scores (step 9).

Note that steps 2-7 in Alg. 1 are to ensure that all the eigenscores (i.e., $\mathbf{u}(i), \mathbf{v}(j)(i, j = 1, ..., n)$) are non-negative. According to the Perron-Frobenius theorem [10], such eigenvectors $\mathbf{u}$ and $\mathbf{v}$ always exist.

Algorithm 1 K-EDGEDELETION

Input: the adjacency matrix $\mathbf{A}$ and the budget k

Output: k edges

1: compute the leading eigenvalue λ of $\mathbf{A}$; let $\mathbf{u}$ and $\mathbf{v}$ be the corresponding left and right eigenvectors, respectively;
2: **if** $\min_{i=1,...,n}\mathbf{u}(i) < 0$ **then**
3: assign $\mathbf{u} \leftarrow -\mathbf{u}$
4: **end if**
5: **if** $\min_{i=1,...,n}\mathbf{v}(i) < 0$ **then**
6: assign $\mathbf{v} \leftarrow -\mathbf{v}$
7: **end if**
8: **for** each edge $e_x : (i_x, j_x)$ $e_x = 1, ..., m; i_x, j_x = 1, ..., n$ **do**
9: score$(e_x) = \mathbf{u}(i_x)\mathbf{v}(j_x)$;
10: **end for**
11: return top-*k* edges with the highest score(e_x)

3.3 Proofs and Analysis

Here, we analyze the accuracy and the efficiency of the proposed K-EDGEDELETION algorithm.

The accuracy of the proposed K-EDGEDELETION is summarized in Lemma 3. According to Lemma 3, the first-order matrix perturbation theory, together with the fact that many real graphs have large eigen-gap, provides a good approximation to the impact of a set of edges in terms of decreasing the leading eigenvalue. What is more important, with such an approximation, the impact of the different edges are now de-coupled from each other. Therefore, we can avoid the combinatorial enumeration of Prob. 1 by simply returning the top-*k* edges with the highest individual impact scores (step 9 in Alg. 1).

Notice that by Lemma 3, there is an $O(k)$ gap between the approximate and the actual impact of a set of edges in terms of decreasing the leading eigenvalue. Our experimental evaluations show that the correlation between the approximate and the actual impact is very high (See Section 6 for details), indicating that it indeed provides a good approximation for the actual decrease of the leading eigenvalue.

LEMMA 3. *Let $\hat{\lambda}$ be the (exact) first eigenvalue of $\hat{\mathbf{A}}$, where $\hat{\mathbf{A}}$ is the perturbed version of $\mathbf{A}$ by removing all of its edges indexed by the set $\mathcal{S}$. Let $\delta = \lambda - \lambda_2$ be the eigen-gap of the matrix $\mathbf{A}$ where λ_2 is the second eigenvalue of $\mathbf{A}$, and $c = 1/(\mathbf{u}'\mathbf{v})$. If λ is the simple first eigenvalue of $\mathbf{A}$, and $\delta \geq 2\sqrt{k}$, then $\lambda - \hat{\lambda} = c\sum_{e_x \in \mathcal{S}} \mathbf{u}(i_x)\mathbf{v}(j_x) + O(k)$.*

PROOF. Let $\lambda_i (i = 1, ..., n)$ be the ordered eigenvalues of $\mathbf{A}$ (i.e., $|\lambda| = |\lambda_1| \geq |\lambda_2| ... \geq |\lambda_n|$). Let $\tilde{\lambda}_i (i = 1, ..., n)$ be the corresponding eigenvalues of $\hat{\mathbf{A}}$. Notice that we omitted the subscripts for the leading eigenvalues (i.e., $\lambda_1 = \lambda$, and $\tilde{\lambda}_1 = \hat{\lambda}$).

Let $\hat{\mathbf{A}} = \mathbf{A} + \mathbf{E}$. We have $\|\mathbf{E}\|_{Fro} = \sqrt{k}$.

According to the first-order matrix perturbation theory (p.183 [38]), we have

$$\begin{aligned} \tilde{\lambda}_1 &= \lambda_1 + \frac{\mathbf{u}'\mathbf{E}\mathbf{v}}{\mathbf{u}'\mathbf{v}} + \mathrm{O}(\|E\|^2) \\ &= \lambda_1 - c\sum_{e_x \in \mathcal{S}} \mathbf{u}(i_x)\mathbf{v}(j_x) + O(k) \qquad (1) \end{aligned}$$

Next, we will show that $\tilde{\lambda}_1$ is indeed the leading eigenvalue of $\hat{\mathbf{A}}$. To this end, again by the matrix perturbation theory (p.203 [38]), we have

$$\begin{aligned} \tilde{\lambda}_1 &\geq \lambda_1 - \|\mathbf{E}\|_2 \geq \lambda_1 - \|\mathbf{E}\|_{Fro} \geq \lambda_1 - \sqrt{k} \\ \tilde{\lambda}_i &\leq \lambda_i + \|\mathbf{E}\|_2 \leq \lambda_i + \|\mathbf{E}\|_{Fro} \leq \lambda_i + \sqrt{k} (i \geq 2) \quad (2) \end{aligned}$$

Since $\delta = \lambda_1 - \lambda_2 \geq 2\sqrt{k}$, we have $\tilde{\lambda}_1 \geq \tilde{\lambda}_i (i = 2, ..., n)$. In other words, we have that $\tilde{\lambda}_1 = \hat{\lambda}$ is the leading eigenvalue of $\hat{\mathbf{A}}$. Therefore,

$$\lambda - \hat{\lambda} = c\sum_{e_x \in \mathcal{S}} \mathbf{u}(i_x)\mathbf{v}(j_x) + O(k) \qquad (3)$$

which completes the proof. □

The efficiency of the proposed K-EDGEDELETION is summarized in the following lemma, which says that with a fixed budget k, K-EDGEDELETION is *linear* wrt the size of the graph for both time and space cost.

LEMMA 4. **Efficiency of K-EDGEDELETION.** *The time cost of Alg. 1 is $O(mk + n)$. The space cost of Alg. 1 is $O(n + m + k)$.*

PROOF. Using the power method, step 1 takes $O(m)$ time. Steps 2-7 take $O(n)$ time. Steps 8-10 take $O(m)$ time. Step 11 takes $O(mk)$ time. Therefore, the overall time complexity of Alg. 1 is $O(mk + n)$, which completes the proof of the time cost.

We need $O(m)$ to store the original graph $\mathbf{A}$. It takes $O(n)$ and $O(1)$ to store the eigenvectors and eigenvalue, respectively. We need additional $O(m)$ to store the scores (Step 9) for all the edges. Finally, it takes $O(k)$ for the selected k edges. Therefore, the overall space complexity of Alg. 1 is $O(m + n + k)$, which completes the proof of the space cost. □

4. PROPOSED ALGORITHM FOR *NetGel*

In this Section, we address the *NetGel* problem (Prob. 2), where we want to *add* a set of new links into the graph $\mathbf{A}$ so that its leading eigenvalue λ will increase as much as possible. We first present the proposed K-EDGEADDITION algorithm, and then analyze its accuracy as well as efficiency.

4.1 Proposed K-EDGEADDITION Algorithm

Let $\mathcal{T}$ be a set of non-existing edges in $\mathbf{A}$, that is, for each $e_x : \langle i_x, j_x \rangle \in \mathcal{T}$, we have $\mathbf{A}(i_x, j_x) = 0$. Let $\hat{\lambda}$ be the leading eigenvalue of the new adjacency matrix $\hat{\mathbf{A}}$ by introducing the new edges indexed by the set $\mathcal{T}$. By the similar procedure as in the proof of Lemma 3, we can show that the impact of the new set of edges $\mathcal{T}$ in terms of increasing the leading eigenvalue $\hat{\lambda} - \lambda$ can be approximated as

$$\hat{\lambda} - \lambda \approx \sum_{e_x \in \mathcal{T}} \mathbf{u}(i_x)\mathbf{v}(j_x) \qquad (4)$$

Therefore, it seems that we could use a similar procedure as K-EDGEDELETION to solve the *NetGel* problem (referred to as '*Naive-Add*'): for each non-existing edge $e_x : \langle i_x, j_x \rangle$, calculate its score as score$(e_x) = \mathbf{u}(i_x)\mathbf{v}(j_x)$; and pick top-*k* non-existing edges with the highest scores.

However, many real graphs are very sparse, i.e., $m << n^2$. Therefore, we have $O(n^2 - m) \approx O(n^2)$ possible non-existing edges. In other words, *Naive-Add* requires *quasi-quadratic* time wrt the number of the nodes (n) in the graph, which does not scale to large graphs.

To address this issue, we propose an efficient algorithm, which is summarized in Alg 2. The core idea of K-EDGEADDITION is to prune a large portion of the non-existing edge pairs based on their left and right eigen-scores. As in Alg. 1, we take the same procedure to make sure that the left and right eigenvectors $(\mathbf{u}, \mathbf{v})$ are non-negative. We omit these steps in Alg 2 for brevity.

Algorithm 2 K-EDGEADDITION

Input: the adjacency matrix $\mathbf{A}$ and the budget k
Output: k non-existing edges

```
1: compute the left (u) and right (v) eigenvectors of A that correspond to the leading eigenvalue (u, v ≥ 0);
2: calculate the maximum in-degree (d_in) and out-degree (d_out) of A, respectively;
3: find the subset of k + d_in nodes with the highest left eigen-scores u_i. Index them by I;
4: find the subset of k + d_out nodes with the highest right eigen-scores v_j. Index them by J;
5: for each edge e_x : <i_x, j_x> i_x ∈ I, j_x ∈ J, A(i_x, i_j) = 0 do
6:     score(e_x) = u(i_x)v(j_x). Index them by P;
7: end for
8: return top-k non-existing edges with the highest scores among P.
```

4.2 Proofs and Analysis

Here, we analyze the accuracy and efficiency of the proposed K-EDGEADDITION.

The accuracy of the proposed K-EDGEADDITION is summarized in Lemma 5, which says that K-EDGEADDITION selects the same set of edges as *Naive-Add*.

LEMMA 5. **Effectiveness of K-EDGEADDITION.** *Alg. 2 outputs the same set of non-existing edges as* Naive-Add.

PROOF. Omitted for brevity. □

The efficiency of the proposed K-EDGEADDITION is summarized in the following lemma.

LEMMA 6. **Efficiency of K-EDGEADDITION.** *The time cost of Alg. 2 is $O(m + nt + kt^2)$. The space cost of Alg. 2 is $O(n + m + t^2)$, where $t = max(k, d_{in}, d_{out})$.*

PROOF: Using the power method, step 1 takes $O(m)$ time. Step 2 takes $O(m+n)$ time. Steps 3-4 take $O(n(d_{in}+k))$ and $O(n(d_{out}+k))$ time respectively, both of which can be written as $O(nt)$. Steps 5-7 take $O((k+d_{in})(k+d_{out})) = O(t^2)$ time. Step 8 takes $O((k+d_{in})(k+d_{out})k) = O(kt^2)$. Therefore, the overall time cost is $O(m+nt+kt^2)$, which completes the proof of the time complexity.

We need $O(m)$ to store the original graph $\mathbf{A}$. It takes $O(n)$ to store the eigenvectors $\mathbf{u}$ and $\mathbf{v}$. Step 2 takes additional $O(n+1)$ space. Steps 3-4 take $O(d_{in}+k)$ and $O(d_{out}+k)$ space respectively, both of which can be simplified as $O(t)$. Steps 5-7 take at most $O((k+d_{in})(k+d_{out})) = O(t^2)$ space. Step 9 takes $O(k)$ space. Therefore, the overall space cost (by omitting the smaller terms) is $O(m+nt+kt^2)$, which completes the proof of the space complexity. □

5. EXPERIMENTAL EVALUATIONS

In this section, we provide empirical evaluations for the proposed K-EDGEDELETION and K-EDGEADDITION algorithms. Our evaluations mainly focus on (1) the effectiveness and (2) the efficiency of the proposed algorithms.

5.1 Experimental Setup

Data sets. We used a popular set of real graphs for our experiments - the Oregon AS (Autonomous System) router graphs, which are AS-level connectivity networks inferred from Oregon route-views[2]. These were collected once a week, for 9 consecutive weeks. Table 2 summarizes the nine graphs we used in our evaluations.

Evaluation criteria. As mentioned before, the leading eigenvalue λ of the graph is the only graph parameter that determines the epidemic threshold for a large family of information dissemination processes. Therefore, we report the change of the leading eigenvalue for the effectiveness comparison - for both *NetMelt* and *NetGel* problems. A larger change of the leading eigenvalue is better, which suggests that we can affect the outcome of the dissemination process more. In addition, we also run virus propagation simulations to compare how different methods affect the actual outcome of the propagation. For the computational cost and scalability, we report the wall-clock time.

Machine configurations. All the experiments ran on the same machine with four 2.4GHz AMD CPUs and 48GB memory, running Linux (2.6 kernel).

5.2 Effectiveness of K-EDGEDELETION

Approximation Quality. For both K-EDGEDELETION and K-EDGEADDITION, we want to approximate the actual change of the leading eigenvalue by the first order matrix perturbation theory. This is the *only* place we introduce the approximation. By Lemma 3, it says that the quality of such an approximation depends on both the budget k as well as the eigengap of the original graph, with an $O(k)$ gap. Here, let us experimentally evaluate how good this approximation is on real graphs. We compute the linear correlation coefficient between the actual and approximate leading eigenvalue after we randomly remove k ($k = 10, 50, 100, 500, 1000$) edges. The results are shown in table 3. It can be seen that the approximation is very good - in all the cases, the linear correlation coefficient is greater than 0.92, and often it is very close to 1.

The Impact of Decreasing the Leading Eigenvalue. Here, we evaluate the effectiveness of the proposed K-EDGEDELETION in terms of decreasing the leading eigenvalue λ of the graph. Lemma 1 suggests that the 'important' edges on the original graph $\mathbf{A}$ might become 'important' nodes on the line graph $L(\mathbf{A})$. We follow this intuition to design the following comparative strategies: (1) randomly select k edges from the original graph $\mathbf{A}$ (referred to as 'Rand'); (2) select k edges with the highest degrees in the line graph $L(\mathbf{A})$ (referred to as 'Line-Deg'); (3) select k edges with the highest eigen-scores in the line graph $L(\mathbf{A})$ (referred to as 'Line-Eig'); and (4) select k edges with the highest PageRank scores in the line graph $L(\mathbf{A})$ (referred to as 'Line-Page'). For 'Rand', we run the experiments 100 times and report the average result. For 'Line-Deg', we have two variants by using out-degree or in-degree. In our evaluation, we found that these two variants give the similar results. Therefore, we only report the results by out-degree. For the same reason, we only report the results by the right eigen-scores for 'Line-Eigs'. For 'Line-Page', there is an additional parameter of the teleport probability. We run the experiments with the different teleport probabilities and report the best results.

For brevity, we only present the results on *Oregon-A*, *Oregon-B* and *Oregon-C* since the results on the rest six graphs are similar. From Fig. 2, it can be seen that our K-EDGEDELETION always leads to the biggest decrease in terms of the leading eigenvalue. For example, on *Oregon-C* graph, the proposed K-EDGEDELETION decreases the leading eigenvalue by *3.8* with the budget $k = 50$, which is almost double of the second best method (e.g., *2.0* by 'Line-Deg'). Therefore, we expect that K-EDGEDELETION would affect the outcome of the dissemination processes better than the alternative choices, e.g., having less number of infected nodes in the graph, etc. We validate this next.

Affecting Virus Propagation. Next, we evaluate the effectiveness of the proposed K-EDGEDELETION in terms of minimizing the outcome of the information dissemination processes. To this end, we simulate the virus propagation for the SIS model (susceptible-infective-susceptible) on the graph [41]. For each method, we delete $k = 200$ edges from the original graph. Let $s = \lambda b/d$ be the normalized virus strength (bigger s means stronger virus), where b and d are the infection rate and death rate, respectively. The results are presented in Fig. 3, which is averaged over 1,000 runs. It can be seen that the proposed K-EDGEDELETION is always the best - its curve is always the lowest which means that we always, as desired, have the least number of infected nodes in the graph with this strategy. In Fig. 3, 'Original' (the yellow curve) means that we simulate the virus propagation on the *original* graph without deleting any edges. Notice that when the virus becomes stronger (Fig. 3(b)), all the curves except the proposed method mix with 'Original', which means that they all fail to affect the virus propagation in this case. In contrast, our proposed method (the red curve) can still significantly reduce the number of infected nodes.

Node Deletion vs. Edge Deletion. Finally, in some applications, e.g., to stop malware propagation on the computer networks, both node deletion (e.g., shutting down some machines) and edge deletion (e.g., blocking some links between machines) are feasible. In this case, we want to know which strategy (node deletion or edge deletion) is more effective in affecting the outcome of such propagation process. To this end, we use an effective node immunization algorithm [39] to delete $\tilde{k} = 1, 10$ nodes respectively (referred to as 'Node-Del'). For each $\tilde{k}$, we then use our proposed K-EDGEDELETION to delete the same amount of edges from the original graph (referred to as 'Edge-Del'). We compare the decrease of the leading eigenvalues of the two methods. The results are summarized in Fig. 4. It can be seen that 'Edge-Del' always leads to a bigger decrease of the leading eigenvalue - which suggests that by operating on the edge level, we can design a more

[2] http://topology.eecs.umich.edu/data.html

Dataset	n	m
Oregon-A	633	2,172
Oregon-B	1,503	5,620
Oregon-C	2,504	9,446
Oregon-D	2,854	9,864
Oregon-E	3,995	15,420
Oregon-F	5,296	20,194
Oregon-G	7,352	31,330
Oregon-H	10,860	46,818
Oregon-I	13,947	61,168

Table 2: Dataset summary.

Dataset	$k = 10$	$k = 50$	$k = 100$	$k = 500$	$k = 1000$
Oregon-A	0.999	0.997	0.995	0.973	0.924
Oregon-B	0.999	0.999	0.998	0.993	0.988
Oregon-C	1.000	0.999	0.999	0.996	0.991
Oregon-D	0.999	0.999	0.999	0.994	0.988
Oregon-E	1.000	0.999	0.999	0.998	0.995
Oregon-F	1.000	0.999	0.999	0.998	0.997
Oregon-G	1.000	0.999	0.999	0.999	0.998
Oregon-H	1.000	1.000	0.999	0.999	0.999
Oregon-I	1.000	1.000	0.999	0.999	0.999

Table 3: Evaluations on the approx. quality. Larger is better.

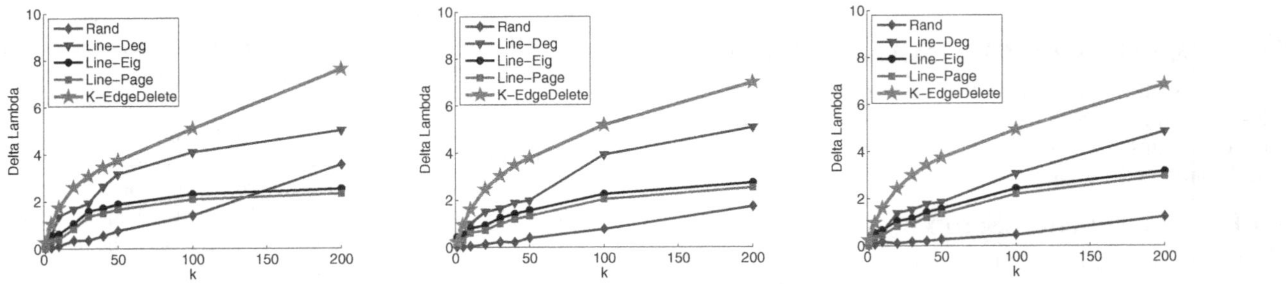

(a) *Oregon-A* (b) *Oregon-B* (c) *Oregon-C*

Figure 2: The decrease of the leading eigenvalue vs. the budget k. Larger is better. The proposed K-EDGEDELETION always leads to the biggest decrease of the leading eigenvalue.

effective algorithm with the same budget to affect the outcome of the information dissemination process. The results are consistent with the intuition - not all the edges adjacent to the 'important' nodes, which the node immunization algorithm aims to delete, are also 'important' (e.g., many edges adjacent to an 'important' node might link to/from some degree-1 nodes). In other words, edge deletion enables us to optimize the underlying graph structure on a finer granularity by picking each individual edge one by one.

5.3 Effectiveness of K-EDGEADDITION

To our best knowledge, there are no existing methods to add k new links into an existing graph in order to increase its leading eigenvalue. Let $\bar{\mathbf{A}}$ be the complementary graph of $\mathbf{A}$, which has the same node set as $\mathbf{A}$, and $\bar{\mathbf{A}}(i,j) = 1$ iff $\mathbf{A}(i,j) = 0$. With the notation of the complementary graph, we use the following intuition to design the comparative methods: to select k 'important' edges from the *complementary graph* $\bar{\mathbf{A}}$ and add them into the original graph $\mathbf{A}$. More specifically, we compare the proposed K-EDGEADDITION with the following strategies: (1) randomly select k edges (referred to as 'Rand'); (2) select k edges with the highest out-degrees in the line graph of the complementary graph $\bar{\mathbf{A}}$ (referred to as 'CompDeg'); (3) select k edges with the highest right eigen-scores in the line graph of the complementary graph $\bar{\mathbf{A}}$ (referred to as 'CompEigs'); (4) select k edges with the highest PageRank scores in the line graph of the complementary graph $\bar{\mathbf{A}}$ (referred to as 'CompPage'); and (5) select k edges by running K-EDGEDELETION in the complementary graph $\bar{\mathbf{A}}$ (referred to as 'CompDelete'). Again, for 'Rand', we run the experiments 100 times and report the average result. We only report the results of 'CompDeg' by out-degree and those of 'CompEig' by right eigen-scores, respectively, since the other variants give the similar performance. For 'CompPage', we run the experiments with the different teleport probabilities and report the best results.

The Impact of Increasing the Leading Eigenvalue. We first evaluate the effectiveness of the proposed K-EDGEADDITION in terms of *increasing* the leading eigenvalue of the graph. For brevity, we only present the results on *Oregon-A*, *Oregon-B* and *Oregon-C* since the results on the rest of the graphs are similar. From Fig. 5, it can be seen that the proposed K-EDGEADDITION always leads to the biggest increase in terms of the leading eigenvalue of the graph. Notice that for all the comparative methods, they behave like 'Rand' (blue curve), especially when the budget k is small.

Affecting Virus Propagation. We also evaluated the effectiveness of the proposed K-EDGEADDITION in terms of *maximizing* the outcome of the information dissemination process. To this end, again, we simulate the virus propagation for the SIS model on the graph. For each method, we add $k = 200$ new edges into the graph. Again, let $s = \lambda b/d$ be the normalized virus strength, with bigger s being stronger virus. Here, our goal is to *increase* the number of 'infected' nodes (e.g., having more people in the social networks to adopt a piece of good idea, etc) by introducing a set of new links into the graph. The result is presented in Fig. 6, which is averaged over 1,000 runs. It can be seen that the proposed K-EDGEADDITION is always the best - its curve is always the highest which means that we always have the largest number of 'infected' nodes in the graph with this strategy. Notice that when the strength of the virus is weak (Fig. 6(a)), all the curves except the proposed method mix with or are very close to 'Original' (yellow curve), which means that they have little impact to boost the outcome of the propagation in this case. In contrast, our proposed method (the red curve) can still significantly increase the number of 'infected' nodes. Therefore, we conclude that our proposed K-

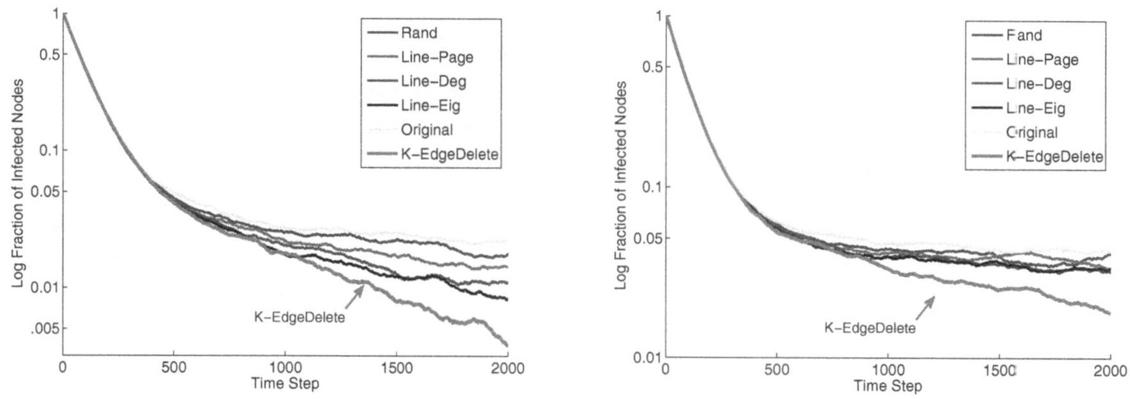

(a) $s = 2.8$ (b) $s = 4.3$

Figure 3: Comparison of minimizing the outcome of the virus propagation. Fraction of infected nodes vs. time stamp. Lower is better. The proposed K-EDGEDELETION always leads to the least number of infected nodes. Notice that y-axis is in the logarithmic scale.

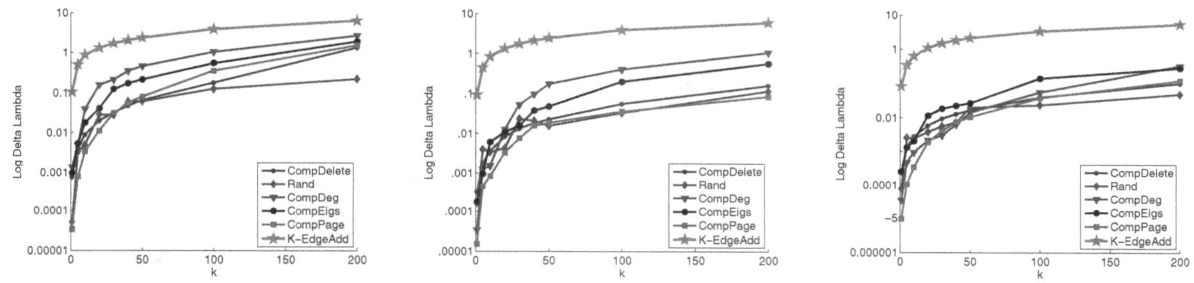

(a) *Oregon-A* (b) *Oregon-B* (c) *Oregon-C*

Figure 5: The increase of the leading eigenvalue vs. the budget k. Larger is better. The proposed K-EDGEADDITION always leads to the largest increase of the leading eigenvalue. Notice that y-axis is in the logarithmic scale.

EDGEADDITION is much more effective to guild the outcome of the dissemination process.

5.4 Scalability

We use the subsets of the largest data set *Oregon-I* to evaluate the scalability of the proposed algorithms. The results are presented in Fig. 7. We can see that the proposed K-EDGEDELETION and K-EDGEADDITION scale almost near-linearly wrt m, which means that they are suitable for large graphs. Notice that for both cases, we also observe a slight super-linear trend. This is due to the following two reasons: (1) for both K-EDGEDELETION and K-EDGEADDITION, we use the power method to compute the leading eigenvalue and the corresponding eigenvectors. When m increases, the actually iteration number in the power method also tends to increase; (2) for K-EDGEADDITION when m increases, the maximum degree ($\max(d_{in}, d_{out})$) also increases even though we fix the number of the nodes (n).

6. RELATED WORK

In this section, we review the related work, which can be categorized into three parts: information dissemination, affecting algorithms and node/edge importance measure.

Information Dissemination. Many research works in virus propagation have been devoted to studying the so-called epidemic threshold, that is, to determine the condition under which an epidemic will break out. While earlier works [13] focus on some specific types of graph structure (e.g., random graphs, power-law graphs, etc), Wang et al. [41] and its follow-up paper by Ganesh et al. [8] found that, for the flu-like SIS model, the epidemic threshold for any *arbitrary, real* graph is determined by the leading eigenvalue of the adjacency matrix of the graph. Prakash et. al. [33] further discovered that the leading eigenvalue (and a model-dependent constant) is the only parameter that determines the epidemic threshold for *all* virus propagation models (more than 25 models, including H.I.V.) in the standard literature. In this work, we aim to take one step further, i.e., how to optimize (minimize or maximize) the leading eigenvalue of the graph by deleting or adding a set of links.

There are also many research interest in studying other types of information dissemination processes on large graphs, including (a) information cascades [1, 9], (b) blog propagations [24, 11, 21, 35], and (c) viral marketing and product penetration [18, 23].

Affecting Algorithms. Hayashi et al. [12] derived the extinction conditions under random and targeted immunization for the SHIR model (Susceptible, Hidden, Infectious, Recovered). Tong et

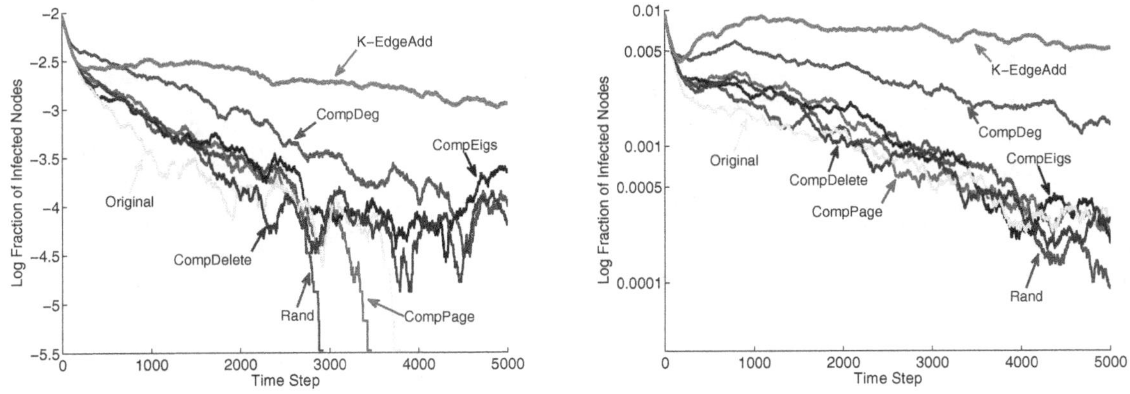

(a) $s = 1.1$ (b) $s = 1.3$

Figure 6: Comparison of maximizing the outcome of virus propagation. Fraction of 'infected' nodes vs. time stamp. Larger is better. The proposed K-EDGEADDITION always leads to the largest number of 'infected' nodes. Notice that y-axis is in the logarithmic scale.

al. [39] proposed an effective node immunization strategy for the SIS model by approximately minimizing the leading eigenvalue. Briesemeister et al. [3] studied the defending policy in power-law graphs. Prakash et. al. [34, 40] proposed effective algorithms to perform node immunization on time-varying graphs. Other algorithms to affect the outcome of the information dissemination include the influence maximization [18, 6, 5], finding effectors in social networks [22], etc. Notice that all these works focus on operating on the node level (i.e., delete or inoculate a set of 'best' nodes) to affect the outcome of the dissemination. In contrast, we study the equally important, but much less studied affecting algorithms by operating on the edge level.

There exist some *empirical evaluations* on edge removal strategies for slightly different purposes, such as, slowing down the influenza spreading [26], minimizing the average infection probability [36], evaluating and comparing the attack vulnerability [14], etc. The closest related work to our K-EDGEDELETION algorithm is [2], which proposed a convex optimization based approach to approximately minimize the leading eigenvalue of the graph. However, the method is based on semi-definite programming and does not scale to large graphs. Moreover, for all these methods, it remains unclear if they can be generalized to address the even more challenging *NetGel* problem, where we want to *add* new edges to promote the information dissemination.

Measuring the Importance of Nodes and Edges. In the literature, there are a lot of node importance measurements, including betweenness centrality, both the one based on the shortest path [7] and the one based on random walks [29, 16] PageRank [30], HITS [19], and coreness score [28]. Our work is also related to the so-called k-vital edges problem, which aims to delete a set of links from the graphs to increase the shortest path length [25] or the weight of the minimum spanning tree of the remaining graph [37]. K-vital edge problem itself is known to be NP-Hard. Other remotely related work includes graph augmentation [31, 4], graph sparsification [20], network inhibition [32] and network-interdiction [42, 15]. Both network inhibition and network interdiction are NP-Hard.

7. CONCLUSION

In this paper, we study the problem of how to optimize the link structure to affect the outcome of information dissemination processes. The main contributions of the paper are:

- *Algorithms.* We observe that for a large family of information dissimilation processes, the problem boils down to the eigenvalue optimization problem. We propose an effective, scalable algorithm to optimize such a key graph parameter (i.e., the leading eigenvalue) that controls the information dissemination process, for both *NetMelt* and *NetGel*, respectively;

- *Proofs and Analysis.* We show the *accuracy* (Lemma 3 and Lemma 5) and the *complexity* of our methods (Lemma 4 and Lemma 6); the *hardness* of the problem (Lemma 2), and the *equivalence* between the different strategies (Lemma 1, Lemma 7 and Lemma 8);

- *Experimental Evaluations.* Our evaluations on real large graphs show that (a) compared with alternative choices to optimize the link structure, our methods are much more effective to affect the outcome of the dissemination process; (b) compared with the node deletion strategy, our K-EDGEDELETION offers a more effective way by operating on the edge level; and (c) both K-EDGEDELETION and K-EDGEADDITION scale to large graphs.

8. ACKNOWLEDGEMENT

This material is based upon work supported by the Army Research Laboratory under Cooperative Agreement No. W911NF-09-2-0053, the U.S. Defense Advanced Research Projects Agency (DARPA) under Agreement Number W911NF-12-C-0028, and the National Science Foundation under Grant No. IIS-1017415. The content of the information in this document does not necessarily reflect the position or the policy of the Government, and no official endorsement should be inferred. The U.S. Government is authorized to reproduce and distribute reprints for Government purposes notwithstanding any copyright notation here on.

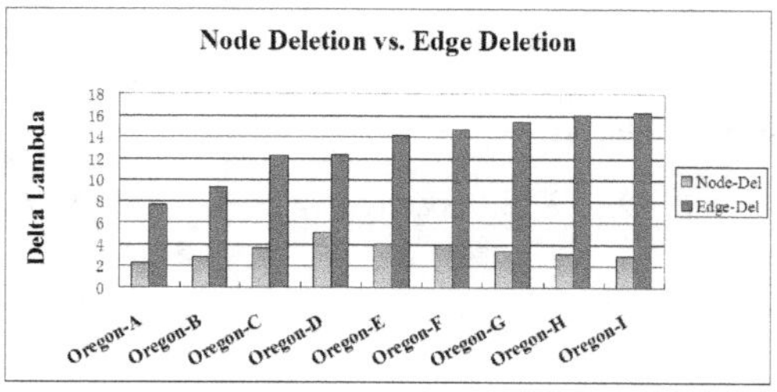

(a) $\tilde{k} = 1$

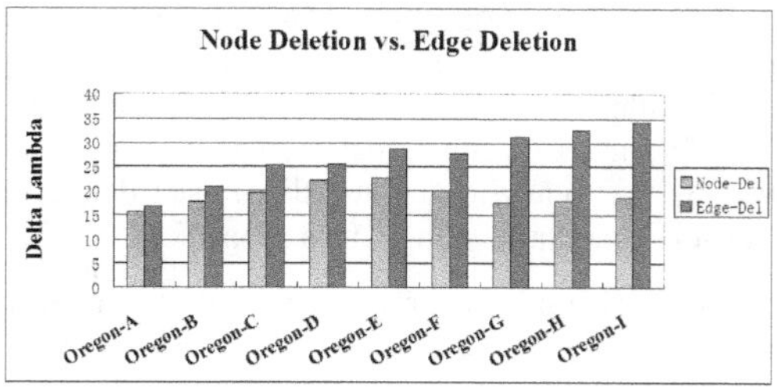

(b) $\tilde{k} = 10$

Figure 4: Comparison between node deletion vs. edge deletion. Larger is better. With the same amount of edges deleted, our proposed K-EDGEDELETION (red) leads to a bigger decrease in terms of the leading eigenvalue.

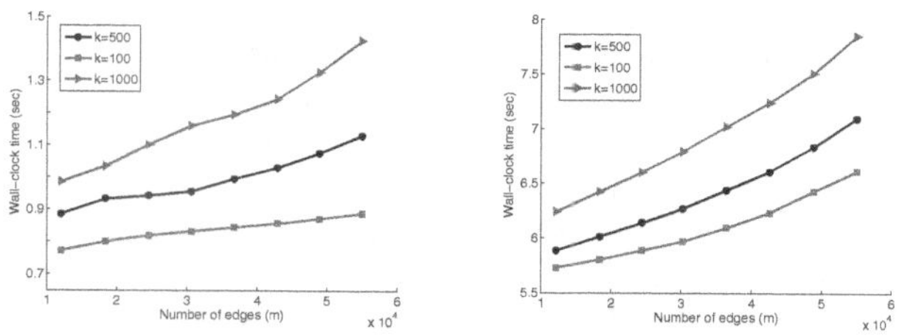

(a) K-EDGEDELETION (b) K-EDGEADDITION

Figure 7: Scalability of proposed algorithms. Both K-EDGEDELETION and K-EDGEADDITION scale near-linearly wrt the size of the graph.

9. REFERENCES

[1] S. Bikhchandani, D. Hirshleifer, and I. Welch. A theory of fads, fashion, custom, and cultural change in informational cascades. *Journal of Political Economy*, 100(5):992–1026, October 1992.

[2] A. N. Bishop and I. Shames. Link operations for slowing the spread of disease in complex networks. *EPL*, 95(1), 2011.

[3] L. Briesemeister, P. Lincoln, and P. Porras. Epidemic profiles and defense of scale-free networks. *WORM 2003*, Oct. 27 2003.

[4] V. Chaoji, S. Ranu, R. Rastogi, and R. Bhatt. Recommendations to boost content spread in social networks. In *WWW*, pages 529–538, 2012.

[5] W. Chen, C. Wang, and Y. Wang. Scalable influence maximization for prevalent viral marketing in large-scale social networks. In *KDD*, pages 1029–1038, 2010.

[6] S. Datta, A. Majumder, and N. Shrivastava. Viral marketing for multiple products. In *ICDM*, pages 118–127, 2010.

[7] L. C. Freeman. A set of measures of centrality based on betweenness. *Sociometry*, pages 35–41, 1977.

[8] A. Ganesh, E. Massouli, and D. Towsley. The effect of network topology on the spread of epidemics. In *INFOCOM*, 2005.

[9] J. Goldenberg, B. Libai, and E. Muller. Talk of the network: A complex systems look at the underlying process of word-of-mouth. *Marketing Letters*, 2001.

[10] G. H. Golub and C. F. V. Loan. *Matrix Computations*. The Johns Hopkins University Press, 1996.

[11] D. Gruhl, R. Guha, D. Liben-Nowell, and A. Tomkins. Information diffusion through blogspace. In *WWW '04*, 2004.

[12] Y. Hayashi, M. Minoura, and J. Matsukubo. Recoverable prevalence in growing scale-free networks and the effective immunization. *arXiv:cond-mat/0305549 v2*, Aug. 6 2003.

[13] H. W. Hethcote. The mathematics of infectious diseases. *SIAM Review*, 42:599–653, 2000.

[14] P. Holme, B. J. Kim, C. N. Yoon, and S. K. Han. Attack vulnerability of complex networks. *Phys. Rev. E*, 2002.

[15] E. Israeli and R. K. Wood. Shortest-path network interdiction. *Networks*, 40(2):97–111, 2002.

[16] U. Kang, S. Papadimitriou, J. Sun, and H. Tong. Centralities in large networks: Algorithms and observations. In *SDM*, pages 119–130, 2011.

[17] R. M. Karp. *Reducibility Among Combinatorial Problems*. New York, 1972.

[18] D. Kempe, J. Kleinberg, and E. Tardos. Maximizing the spread of influence through a social network. In *KDD*, 2003.

[19] J. M. Kleinberg. Authoritative sources in a hyperlinked environment. In *ACM-SIAM Symposium on Discrete Algorithms*, 1998.

[20] A. Kolla, Y. Makarychev, A. Saberi, and S.-H. Teng. Subgraph sparsification and nearly optimal ultrasparsifiers. In *STOC*, pages 57–66, 2010.

[21] R. Kumar, J. Novak, P. Raghavan, and A. Tomkins. On the bursty evolution of blogspace. In *WWW*, 2003.

[22] T. Lappas, E. Terzi, D. Gunopulos, and H. Mannila. Finding effectors in social networks. In *KDD*, pages 1059–1068, 2010.

[23] J. Leskovec, L. A. Adamic, and B. A. Huberman. The dynamics of viral marketing. In *EC*, pages 228–237, New York, NY, USA, 2006. ACM Press.

[24] J. Leskovec, M. McGlohon, C. Faloutsos, N. Glance, and M. Hurst. Cascading behavior in large blog graphs: Patterns and a model. In *Society of Applied and Industrial Mathematics: Data Mining (SDM07)*, 2007.

[25] W. Liang, X. Shen, and Q. Hu. Finding the most vital edge for graph minimization problems on meshes and hypercubes. *International Journal of Parallel and Distributed Systems and Networks*, 2000.

[26] J. Marcelino and M. Kaiser. Reducing influenza spreading over the airline network. *PLoS*, 2009.

[27] A. Milanese, J. Sun, and T. Nishikawa. Approximating spectral impact of structural perturbations in large networks. *Phys. Rev. E*, 81, 2010.

[28] J. Moody and D. R. White. Social cohesion and embeddedness: A hierarchical conception of social groups. *American Sociological Review*, pages 1–25, 2003.

[29] M. Newman. A measure of betweenness centrality based on random walks. *Social Networks*, 27:39–54, 2005.

[30] L. Page, S. Brin, R. Motwani, and T. Winograd. The PageRank citation ranking: Bringing order to the web. Technical report, Stanford Digital Library Technologies Project, 1998. Paper SIDL-WP-1999-0120 (version of 11/11/1999).

[31] M. Papagelis, F. Bonchi, and A. Gionis. Suggesting ghost edges for a smaller world. In *CIKM*, pages 2305–2308, 2011.

[32] C. A. Phillips. The network inhibition problem. In *STOC*, pages 776–785, 1993.

[33] B. A. Prakash, D. Chakrabarti, M. Faloutsos, N. Valler, and C. Faloutsos. Threshold conditions for arbitrary cascade models on arbitrary networks. In *ICDM*, 2011.

[34] B. A. Prakash, H. Tong, N. Valler, M. Faloutsos, and C. Faloutsos. Virus propagation on time-varying networks: Theory and immunization algorithms. In *ECML/PKDD (3)*, pages 99–114, 2010.

[35] M. Richardson and P. Domingos. Mining knowledge-sharing sites for viral marketing. *SIGKDD*, 2002.

[36] C. M. Schneider, T. Mihaljev, S. Havlin, and H. J. Herrmann. Restraining epidemics by improving immunization strategies. *CoRR*, abs/1102.1929, 2011.

[37] H. Shen. Finding the k most vital edges with respect to minimum spanning tree. *Acta Informatica*, 36:405–424, 1995.

[38] G. W. Stewart and J.-G. Sun. *Matrix Perturbation Theory*. Academic Press, 1990.

[39] H. Tong, B. A. Prakash, C. E. Tsourakakis, T. Eliassi-Rad, C. Faloutsos, and D. H. Chau. On the vulnerability of large graphs. In *ICDM*, pages 1091–1096, 2010.

[40] N. Valler, B. A. Prakash, H. Tong, M. Faloutsos, and C. Faloutsos. Epidemic spread in mobile ad hoc networks: Determining the tipping point. In *Networking (1)*, pages 266–280, 2011.

[41] Y. Wang, D. Chakrabarti, C. Wang, and C. Faloutsos. Epidemic spreading in real networks: An eigenvalue viewpoint. *SRDS*, 2003.

[42] R. K. Wood. Network interdiction problem. *Mathematical and Computer Modeling*, 17(2):1–18, 1993.

APPENDIX

Higher-Order *NetMelt*. From Lemma 3, it can be seen that the only place we introduce the approximation in Alg. 1 is to approximate the actual decrease of the leading eigenvalue by the first-order matrix perturbation theory. The readers might wonder if we can further improve the quality by using higher-order matrix perturbation theory, while maintaining the linear scalability of the algorithm.

We explored second-order matrix perturbation theory to approximate the actual decrease of the leading eigenvalue, and found that (1) it generates very similar results as the proposed K-EDGEDELETION algorithm and (2) it requires 5-10x more wall-clock time. The reason might be that for the *NetMelt* problem, the first-order perturbation already gives a very good approximation. Therefore, in practice, we recommend K-EDGEDELETION for simplicity.

Nonetheless, the new algorithm based on the second-order perturbation exhibits some interesting theoretic properties. It also helps understand the relationship between edge deletion and node deletion on the algorithmic level. We present it here for the completeness.

Let $c = \frac{1}{\mathbf{u}'\mathbf{v}}$, with second-order matrix perturbation, we can approximate[3] the impact of deleting a set of edges $\mathcal{S}$ in terms of the leading eigenvalue as:

$$\lambda - \hat{\lambda} \simeq \text{Impact}(\mathcal{S}) = c\Big(\sum_{e_x \in \mathcal{S}} \mathbf{u}(i_x)\mathbf{v}(j_x) - \frac{1}{2\lambda} \sum_{e_x \in \mathcal{S}, e_y \in \mathcal{S}, j_x = i_y} \mathbf{u}(i_x)\mathbf{v}(j_y)\Big) \quad (5)$$

Compared with the first-order perturbation (eq. (3)), we have an additional penalized term in eq. (5): $\mathbf{u}(i_x)\mathbf{v}(j_y)$ for any two adjacent edges e_x and e_y. The intuition is to encourage the edges in the set $\mathcal{S}$ to be far away (not adjacent) from each other.

By eq. (5), the impact of different edges in the set $\mathcal{S}$ is no longer independent with each other. At the first glance, this might complicate the algorithm since now we need to optimize at the set level, that is, to find a set of edges that *collectively* maximize eq. (5). However, by the following lemma, the impact defined in eq. (5) exhibits some nice diminishing return properties.

LEMMA 7. **Second-Order Approximation Properties.** *The Impact($\mathcal{S}$) defined in eq. (5) has the following properties:*

(1) Impact(Φ) $= 0$, where Φ is an empty set;

(2) Impact($\mathcal{S}$) is monotonically non-decreasing wrt the set $\mathcal{S}$;

(3) Impact($\mathcal{S}$) is sub-modular wrt the set $\mathcal{S}$.

PROOF. Omitted for brevity. □

Thanks to such diminishing return properties, it naturally leads to the following greedy algorithm (K-EDGEDELETION++) to find a *near-optimal* subset of edges to delete from the original graph $\mathbf{A}$. And it can be shown that the overall time complexity of K-EDGEDELETION++ remains linear wrt the size of the graph.

Algorithm 3 K-EDGEDELETION++

Input: the adjacency matrix $\mathbf{A}$ and the budget k

Output: k edges indexed by set $\mathcal{S}$

compute the first eigen-value λ of $\mathbf{A}$; compute the corresponding left and right eigenvectors $\mathbf{u}$ and $\mathbf{v}$ ($\mathbf{u}, \mathbf{v} \geq 0$), respectively;
initialize the set $\mathcal{S}$ to be empty;
score(e_x) $= \mathbf{u}(i_x)\mathbf{v}(j_x)$ ($e_x : \langle i_x, j_x \rangle$, $e_x = 1, ..., m$);
for $k_0 = 1, ..., k$ **do**
  find $e_0 = \text{argmax}_{e_x, e_x \notin \mathcal{S}} \text{score}(e_x)$;
  add the new edge $e_0 : \langle i_0, j_0 \rangle$ into $\mathcal{S}$;
  for each edge $e_y : \langle i_y, j_y \rangle$ s.t. $j_y = i_0$ **do**
    score(e_y) $\leftarrow$ score(e_y) $- 1/(2\lambda)\mathbf{u}(i_y)\mathbf{v}(j_0)$;
  end for
  for each edge $e_y : \langle i_y, j_y \rangle$ s.t. $i_y = j_0$ **do**
    score(e_y) $\leftarrow$ score(e_y) $- 1/(2\lambda)\mathbf{u}(i_0)\mathbf{v}(j_y)$;
  end for
end for

An interesting property of Alg. 3 is that it builds the equivalence between edge deletion and node deletion on the algorithmic level:

LEMMA 8. **Equivalence of Alg. 3 to Node Immunization.** *Let $\mathcal{S}$ be the set of edges by running Alg. 3 on graph $\mathbf{A}$; $\mathcal{T}$ be the set of edges by running the node immunization algorithm [39] on the line graph $L(\mathbf{A})$; and $|\mathcal{S}| = |\mathcal{T}|$. We have $\mathcal{S} = \mathcal{T}$.*

PROOF. Omitted for brevity. □

[3] This formulas is similar as the one in [27]

One Seed to Find Them All: Mining Opinion Features via Association

Zhen Hai, Kuiyu Chang, Gao Cong
School of Computer Engineering, Nanyang Technological University
50 Nanyang Avenue, Singapore 639798
{haiz0001, askychang, gaocong}@ntu.edu.sg

ABSTRACT

Feature-based opinion analysis has attracted extensive attention recently. Identifying features associated with opinions expressed in reviews is essential for fine-grained opinion mining. One approach is to exploit the dependency relations that occur naturally between features and opinion words, and among features (or opinion words) themselves. In this paper, we propose a generalized approach to opinion feature extraction by incorporating robust statistical association analysis in a bootstrapping framework. The new approach starts with a small set of feature seeds, on which it iteratively enlarges by mining feature-opinion, feature-feature, and opinion-opinion dependency relations. Two association model types, namely likelihood ratio tests (LRT) and latent semantic analysis (LSA), are proposed for computing the pair-wise associations between terms (features or opinions). We accordingly propose two robust bootstrapping approaches, LRTBOOT and LSABOOT, both of which need just a handful of initial feature seeds to bootstrap opinion feature extraction. We benchmarked LRTBOOT and LSABOOT against existing approaches on a large number of real-life reviews crawled from the cellphone and hotel domains. Experimental results using varying number of feature seeds show that the proposed association-based bootstrapping approach significantly outperforms the competitors. In fact, one seed feature is all that is needed for LRTBOOT to significantly outperform the other methods. This seed feature can simply be the domain feature, e.g., "cellphone" or "hotel". The consequence of our discovery is far reaching: starting with just one feature seed, typically just the domain concept word, LRTBOOT can automatically extract a large set of high-quality opinion features from the corpus without any supervision or labeled features. This means that the automatic creation of a set of domain features is no longer a pipe dream!

CIKM'12, October 29–November 2, 2012, Maui, HI, USA.

Categories and Subject Descriptors

H.3.3 [**Information Search and Retrieval**]: Information Filtering; I.2.7 [**Artificial Intelligence**]: Natural Language Processing—*Text Analysis*

General Terms

Algorithms, Experimentation

Keywords

opinion mining, sentiment analysis, aspect, feature, seed, bootstrapping, association

1. INTRODUCTION

Opinion mining, also known as sentiment analysis, is the computational study of subjectivity, i.e., the sentiments and opinions expressed in online review texts. Opinions expressed in reviews can be analyzed at different resolutions [6, 17, 24, 8, 25]. Document-level opinion mining identifies the overall opinion expressed in a review document, but often fails to associate specific opinions with different aspects of the commented subject (or entity). This problem also happens, though to a lesser extent, in sentence-level opinion mining, as shown in Example 1.1:

EXAMPLE 1.1. *"The exterior is very beautiful, also not expensive, though the battery is not durable, I still unequivocally recommend this cellphone!"*

Example 1.1 on a whole expresses a positive opinion on the cellphone, but contains conflicting opinions associated with different aspects of the cellphone. The opinion orientations for the "cellphone" itself and its "exterior" are positive, but the opinion polarity for the aspect of "battery" is negative. Generally such fine-grained opinions may very well tip the balance in purchase decisions. Consumers are usually not satisfied with just the overall opinion rating of a product, but are eager to find out why it receives the rating, that is, which positive or negative features contribute to the overall rating of the product. It is thus important to extract the specific opinionated aspects and associate them with the corresponding opinions.

An *opinion feature*, or *feature* in short, is defined as the object or aspect on which users have expressed their opinions. A feature is called an *explicit feature*, if it is explicitly mentioned in a sentence, typically as a noun or noun phrase. If it is not expressed explicitly but is implied, the feature is called an *implicit feature*. Example 1.1 contains three explicit opinion features and one implicit feature. The explicit features, i.e., "exterior", "battery", and "cellphone" are associated with opinion words, "beautiful", "durable", and "recommend", respectively. The implicit feature "price" does not appear explicitly, but is implied in the opinion word "expensive". In this paper, we focus on identifying explicit opinion features from reviews.

Existing approaches to feature extraction can be classified roughly into supervised and unsupervised learning categories. Supervised learning approaches tend to yield relatively accurate results in a given domain, e.g., cellphone reviews, provided that a large set of annotated training data is available. However, the models must be retrained when applied to different domains such as hotel reviews [11, 14, 10]. Moreover, high-quality annotated training review data are hard to come by, which can be tedious and expensive to collect.

In contrast, unsupervised learning approaches have no such limitations, given the ready availability of unlabeled review data online. *Natural language processing* (NLP) methods attempt to recognize features by manually defining extraction rules or templates based on syntactic parsing [21, 19]. Though giving good domain independence, NLP methods do not work well with the informal writing styles used in online reviews, which often contain overly concise or grammatically incorrect sentences. One other problem associated with NLP methods is the limited coverage of the manually compiled syntactic rules.

Unsupervised corpus statistical approaches aim to extract opinion features by capturing their distributional characteristics from the corpus [26, 8, 18]. As a result, they are somewhat resistant to the colloquial nature of online reviews, provided that a suitably large corpus is used. However, the lack of ground-truth knowledge, such as annotated feature terms (i.e., seeds), frequently leads to incoherent and imprecise results. The results quickly deteriorate with every additional iteration, as the error accumulates, as in the case of blind leading the blind. In addition, unsupervised topic modeling approaches tend to discover coarse-grained and generic opinion topics or aspects, which are just clusters of related opinion features instead of the specific opinionated features themselves [7, 1, 22].

It is observed that co-occurrence dependency relations exist naturally between opinion words and features, even among features (opinion words) themselves. For example, an opinion word "expensive" is often used to modify the feature "price" in cellphone reviews. Such statistical associative relations between pair-wise terms (features or opinions) can be exploited to bootstrap opinion features based on a labeled set of feature seeds.

In this paper, we therefore propose a generalized bootstrapping framework to identify opinion features by employing term-to-term corpus statistics association analysis. The bootstrapping approach starts from a small manually prespecified list of feature seeds, which it then iteratively enlarges by mining pair-wise feature-opinion, feature-feature, and opinion-opinion associative relations between terms (features or opinion words) in the corpus. Two association model types are introduced in the bootstrapping framework, namely *likelihood ratio tests* (LRT) [4] and *latent semantic analysis* (LSA) [3], which we termed LRTBOOT and LSABOOT, respectively.

The proposed association-based bootstrapping framework has two advantages: (1) The statistical association analysis is more robust in mining dependency relations between pair-wise terms (features and opinion words), compared to syntactic parsing, and works especially well on real-life online text reviews; (2) The bootstrapping strategy achieves surprisingly good performance with only one word in the seed set. This single seed could simply be the domain concept term, e.g., "cellphone" for cellphone reviews and "hotel" for hotel reviews. Experiments conducted on real-life review domains demonstrate the effectiveness of our approach.

The remainder of this paper is structured as follows: In Section 2, we discuss related work. In Section 3, we describe the proposed corpus statistics association based bootstrapping approach to opinion feature extraction. We evaluate our association-based bootstrapping approach in Section 4 and conclude the paper with a brief discussion in Section 5.

2. RELATED WORK

In feature-based opinion mining, identifying a feature associated with an opinion is essential for fine-grained analysis of online reviews. Feature extraction is an ongoing research problem, with the vast majority of existing work done in the product review domain.

By formulating opinion mining as a joint structural tagging problem, supervised learning models including Hidden Markov Models and Conditional Random Fields have been used to tag features or aspects of commented entities [11, 14]. Supervised models may be carefully tuned to perform well on a given domain, but need extensive retraining when applied to a different domain, unless transfer learning is adopted [16].

Syntactic relationships between features and opinions can be naturally used to locate opinion features in an unsupervised manner. A syntactic parsing based *double propagation* (DP) approach was proposed to address the extraction of features as well as opinion words [19, 20]. DP recognizes the dependency relations between pair-wise terms (features and opinions) by manually defining eight syntactic rules. It then extracts features and opinion words iteratively using the extracted known features and opinions via the recognized syntactic relations. Independently, a similar method was proposed to extract opinionated features by defining a set of dependent syntactic rules between features and opinions in [21]. In addition, a semantic role labeling based approach was introduced to recognize opinion features by analyzing their semantic roles and local context in sentences of online news media texts [13].

Topic modeling approaches, such as *latent Dirichlet allocation* (LDA), which is a generative three-way (term-topic-document) probabilistic model [1], have been used to solve aspect-based opinion mining (or sentiment analysis) problems. The approaches actually tend to identify coarse-grained topics or aspects that correspond to distinguishing properties of the commented entities, which may not necessarily be opinionated product features, but rather user-defined clusters of specific opinion features [7, 1, 22, 15, 28]. For example, "where" could be a valid LDA topic-word associated with cellphone reviews, since users like to discuss about phone vendors, but it is not a product feature per se. In addition, the approach usually assumes that each review sentence contains exactly one topic [12], which is often violated in real-life online reviews.

An unsupervised corpus statistics approach was proposed to extract product features by using association rule mining [9]. The approach mines frequent itemsets as potential features, i.e., frequent nouns with high sentence frequencies (i.e., support). Pruning is necessary to remove many irrelevant features. The limitations of this approach lie in: (1) Frequent but invalid features are extracted incorrectly, and (2) rare but valid features may be missed out.

Our work aims to extract opinion features, which is related to the aforementioned existing work, but differs in three aspects. First, we use corpus statistics term-to-term associations to bootstrap feature terms, which performs better than simple syntactic parsing, especially on colloquial or informal review data. Second, in contrast with typical unsupervised statistics models, a manually pre-defined list of feature seeds is used. Third, the seed features are used not to train a model but as references for the iterative extraction process. In a way, our proposed statistical association based bootstrapping approach can be viewed as a semi-supervised approach. In the extreme case of using a single domain concept word (e.g., "cellphone" for cellphone review domain) as the sole seed feature, our approach even borders on the unsupervised.

3. OPINION FEATURE EXTRACTION

3.1 Overview

When users express their comments on a feature, a certain cluster of opinion words will be frequently used. For example, the feature term "price" is often associated with a cluster of opinion words like "expensive", "cheap", etc. Quite similarly, an opinion word usually covers a certain group of feature terms that are semantically related to each other. Semantic dependency relations thus exist naturally between opinion words and features in real-world reviews. In some instances, co-occurrence associations also exist among features (opinion words) themselves, since a user could express his or her opinions on several different product features in a single review. e.g., "screen" and "battery".

Such co-occurrence associative patterns between features and opinion words, as well as among features (or opinion words) themselves, can be measured and quantified. We therefore propose to exploit the distributional characteristics of opinion features in review corpus, with the goal of identifying them.

We define three types of term-to-term associations, i.e., *feature-opinion* (FO or OF), *feature-feature* (FF), and *opinion-opinion* (OO) to capture the aforementioned co-occurrence dependency relations in our opinion feature extraction task. Moreover, if opinion feature extraction uses only FO association, it could miss out a lot of related feature as well as opinion words. For example, given a known opinion word "expensive", we can extract a set of feature terms semantically related to "price" via the FO association analysis. However, we would miss out some valid co-occurring opinion words like "high" if we do not consider OO associations, which in return limits the feature extraction performance. Likewise, from the extracted known features like "price", we may only recognize semantically related opinion terms like "expensive" or "cheap" using the FO association. In this case, we would miss out valid features like "screen" that tend to co-occur with the features unless we consider FF associations. Thus in practice we need to consider FF and OO associations in addition to the FO association. This is a fact that is frequently overlooked in features identification analysis, since most existing research tends to focus on only the FO relationship.

We observed that candidate features strongly associated with invalid features (or opinions) tend to be non-features, while candidates strongly associated with valid features (opinions) are most likely true opinion features. Paraphrasing the age-old adage, "features of a feather flock together". In other words, without any ground truth in the form of known seed features, pair-wise term association based approaches may lead to too many frivolous features. Therefore, to extract opinion features reliably, we must start out with a manually crafted set of seed features, which is also known as the initial ground truth seed set. We then iteratively enlarge this feature set by adding newly identified candidate features that are statistically and strongly associated with a known member in the set.

The feature set is thus like an exclusive invitation-only finals club, where a new member (feature) is inducted into the club if and only if he or she is well-known (strongly associated) to any existing member (feature in the feature set). The initial club founders (seed features) thus play an essential role; They must "know" the most important future members (features) of the club, who would bring in yet more members (features).

Given a review corpus, our proposed approach initially extracts a set of candidate features and a set of candidate opinion words. It identifies two new sets of features and opinions that have strong FF and FO associations with the known set of features (a pre-defined list of feature seeds for the first step, and extracted known features thereafter), respectively. Based on the extracted known opinion set, the approach then identifies two sets of opinions and features via OO and FO association analysis, respectively. The feature identification process is performed iteratively until a suitable stopping criterion is met. Upon termination, we can finally bootstrap a validated set of opinion features (as well as an opinion word set).

We will describe our term-to-term association based bootstrapping algorithm in detail below.

3.2 Association-based Bootstrapping

Given a review corpus $\mathcal{C}$, we first need to generate two candidate sets of features and opinions, from which valid features as well as opinions are bootstrapped via corpus statistics association.

Opinion features typically occur as nouns (noun phrases), and tend to be the subject or object of a sentence. Simply selecting nouns or nouns phrases as feature candidates gives good coverage (recall), but comes at the expense of letting in too many noisy candidates, which may negatively impact the subsequent feature extraction process.

Using dependency parsing, we attempt to accurately generate a candidate feature set $\mathcal{CF}$ ($\mathcal{CF}=\{cf_1, \ldots, cf_i, \ldots, cf_M\}$, M: set size), which comprises only nouns (noun phrases) with "SBV" (subject-verb), "VOB" (verb-object), or "POB" (preposition-object) dependency relations in the corpus $\mathcal{C}$. According to experimental results, our candidate feature extraction yields respectable recall rates of 83.8% and 75.22% on the cellphone and hotel domains, respectively. Next we use all adjectives and verbs in the review corpus $\mathcal{C}$ to form a candidate opinion word set $\mathcal{CO}$ ($\mathcal{CO}$=$\{co_1, \ldots, co_j, \ldots, co_N\}$, N: set size).

Matrix	Entry	Association Type
M_{FO}	$A(cf_i, co_j)$	*feature-opinion* (FO)
M_{FF}	$A(cf_{i_1}, cf_{i_2})$	*feature-feature* (FF)
M_{OO}	$A(co_{j_1}, co_{j_2})$	*opinion-opinion* (OO)

Table 1: Association matrices for bootstrapping opinion feature extraction.

We then compute a pair-wise term association matrix for each of the three aforementioned types of associative relations based on the set of candidate features as well as the candidate set of opinion words. As shown in Table 1, M_{FO}, M_{FF}, and M_{OO} represent *feature-opinion* (FO or OF), *feature-feature* (FF), and *opinion-opinion* (OO) association matrices, respectively. Let A denote the generalized corpus statistics association model used to compute the pair-wise term association. Accordingly, the $A(cf_i, co_j)$ ($cf_i \in \mathcal{CF}$, $co_j \in \mathcal{CO}$), $A(cf_{i_1}, cf_{i_2})$ (cf_{i_1}, $cf_{i_2} \in \mathcal{CF}$), and $A(co_{j_1}, co_{j_2})$ (co_{j_1}, $co_{j_2} \in \mathcal{CO}$) are FO, FF, and OO association scores estimated using the association model A on the given review data $\mathcal{C}$.

Taking the *feature-opinion* association matrix M_{FO} for instance, to calculate the pair-wise term association entry $A(cf_i, co_j)$ of the matrix, we first need to obtain the corpus occurrence statistics related to candidate feature cf_i and candidate opinion co_j. We then estimate the association score between the candidates cf_i and co_j based on their corpus statistics by applying the association model A. We compute two other association matrices M_{FF} and M_{OO} in a similar manner.

Our generalized corpus statistics association based bootstrapping approach, ABOOT in short, is summarized in Algorithm 1. Some variables in the algorithm are defined as follows:

1. $\mathcal{S}$: a manually annotated feature seed set that is used to supervise the bootstrapping of feature extraction.
2. $\mathcal{F}$: a feature set that keeps track of the extracted features, initially $\mathcal{F} = \mathcal{S}$.
3. $\mathcal{O}$: opinion word set that tracks the extracted opinion words.
4. $A(t_1, t_2)$: an association score estimated via an association model A for terms t_1 and t_2.
5. *foth*, *ffth*, and *ooth*: three thresholds for the FO (or OF), FF, and OO associations, respectively.

In Algorithm 1, We first extract two candidate sets of features and opinions in line 1 and line 2, respectively. The known feature set $\mathcal{F}$ is initialized with the annotated set of feature seeds in line 3. From line 6 to line 19, we bootstrap new features as well as opinion words, which have strong associations with the known or extracted features in the set $\mathcal{F}$. We then bootstrap more opinion words and features based on the extracted known opinion set $\mathcal{O}$ from line 20 to line 33. In line 34 of the algorithm, we update both known feature and opinion sets $\mathcal{F}$ and $\mathcal{S}$ with the extracted features and opinion words. The bootstrapping process is performed repeatedly from line 5, and will be terminated until no new opinion features are identified, as shown in line 35. Finally, a validated set of opinion features can be bootstrapped from the given review corpus $\mathcal{C}$.

Algorithm 1 Corpus statistics association based bootstrapping algorithm.

Require: Review corpus $\mathcal{C}$, a labeled feature seed set $\mathcal{S}$
Ensure: A validated set of opinion features

```
1: CF ← Extract a candidate feature set from corpus C;
2: CO ← Extract a candidate opinion set from corpus C;
3: F←S;
4: O←∅;
5: repeat
6:   for each known feature f in F do
7:     for each candidate feature cf in CF do
8:       if (A(f,cf) ≥ ffth) AND (cf ∉ F) then
9:         Identify candidate cf as a feature;
10:        Remove candidate cf from set CF;
11:      end if
12:    end for
13:    for each candidate opinion word co in CO do
14:      if (A(f,co) ≥ foth) AND (co ∉ O) then
15:        Identify candidate co as an opinion word;
16:        Remove candidate co from set CO;
17:      end if
18:    end for
19:  end for
20:  for each known opinion word o in O do
21:    for each candidate opinion word co in CO do
22:      if (A(o,co) ≥ ooth) AND (co ∉ O) then
23:        Identify candidate co as an opinion word;
24:        Remove candidate co from set CO;
25:      end if
26:    end for
27:    for each candidate feature cf in CF do
28:      if (A(o,cf) ≥ foth) AND (cf ∉ F) then
29:        Identify candidate cf as a feature;
30:        Remove candidate cf from set CF;
31:      end if
32:    end for
33:  end for
34:  Update F and O with identified features and opinions;
35: until No new opinion features are identified
36: return An identified opinion feature set F
```

We illustrate Algorithm 1 using a straightforward example in Figure 1. Given a sample review corpus $\mathcal{C}$ (which contains 4 reviews only), We first extract two candidate feature and opinion sets $\mathcal{CF}$ and $\mathcal{CO}$ from the corpus $\mathcal{C}$. We then compute a table of pair-wise term association scores by employing an associative model A based on the two candidate sets, as shown at the lower portion of the figure. Note that the association matrix (matrices) shown in the shaded grey area of the table corresponds to FO associative relation, and the matrices shown at the top left and bottom right of the table correspond to FF and OO association relations, respectively. Given a pre-specified threshold *thd* =2.0 (which is used for FO, FF, and OO associations), by applying the ABOOT algorithm, we finally bootstrapped an extended feature set $\mathcal{F}$ as well as an opinion set $\mathcal{O}$, based on a manually annotated feature seed set $\mathcal{S}$ (which contains a noun feature "screen" only), as shown at the upper right portion of the figure.

Reviews:

1. The screen is really big, but the price is too expensive!
2. The price is expensive, students don't buy it usually.
3. The screen is beautiful, but the price is not!
4. The screen is big and beautiful!

CF={screen, price, student}
CO={big, expensive, buy, beautiful}

S={screen}
thd=2.0
F={screen, price}
O={big, beautiful, expensive}

A	screen	price	student	big	expensive	buy	beautiful
screen		2.5	0.5	3.0	1.5	0.5	3.0
price	2.5		1.0	1.5	3.0	1.5	1.5
student	0.5	1.0		0.5	0.5	1.0	0.5
big	3.0	1.5	0.5		2.0	0.5	2.0
expensive	1.5	3.0	0.5	2.0		1.0	2.0
buy	0.5	1.5	1.0	0.5	1.0		0.5
beautiful	3.0	1.5	0.5	2.0	2.0	0.5	

Figure 1: A working example for the ABOOT algorithm.

3.3 Association Models for Bootstrapping

As shown in Algorithm 1, the proposed generalized strategy for opinion feature extraction is called ABOOT (Association-based Bootstrapping). Different pair-wise term association measures can lead to different instance approaches.

There are two schools of thoughts on estimating pair-wise dependency relations: one is the tests for statistical significance, the other is the association measure. On the tests for statistical significance front, we choose the likelihood ratio tests model to estimate the pair-wise association for feature bootstrapping, which we call LRTBOOT (Likelihood Ratio Tests based Bootstrapping). For the association measure, we use latent semantic analysis as well as cosine similarity, which we call LSABOOT (Latent Semantic Analysis based Bootstrapping). Other types of association models can be evaluated as part of future work.

3.3.1 Likelihood Ratio Tests for Bootstrapping

We first describe the *likelihood ratio tests* (LRT) [4] association model. The LRT is well known for not relying critically on the assumption of normality, instead, it uses the asymptotic assumption of the generalized likelihood ratio. In practice, the use of likelihood ratios tends to result in significant improvements in text-analysis performance, even with relatively small amount of data [4].

LRT computes a contingency table of two term T_i and T_j, derived from corpus statistics, as given in Table 2, where $k_1(T_i, T_j)$ is the number of documents (reviews) containing both terms T_i and T_j; $k_2(T_i, \bar{T}_j)$ is the number of documents containing term T_i but not T_j; $k_3(\bar{T}_i, T_j)$ is the number of documents containing term T_j but not T_i; $k_4(\bar{T}_i, \bar{T}_j)$ is the number of documents containing neither T_i nor T_j. Note that our purpose here is to measure how greatly pair-wise terms are associated with each other given the corpus statistics, rather than performing an actual statistics test.

Corpus statistics	T_j	$\bar{T}_j$
T_i	$k_1(T_i, T_j)$	$k_2(T_i, \bar{T}_j)$
$\bar{T}_i$	$k_3(\bar{T}_i, T_j)$	$k_4(\bar{T}_i, \bar{T}_j)$

Table 2: Contingency table derived from corpus statistics.

Based on the corpus statistics shown in Table 2, the *likelihood ratio tests* (LRT) [4] model captures the statistical association between terms T_i and T_j by employing the following function:

$$
\begin{aligned}
-2log\lambda = 2[logL(p_1, k_1, n_1) + logL(p_2, k_2, n_2) \\
-logL(p, k_1, n_1) - logL(p, k_2, n_2)]
\end{aligned}
\quad (1)
$$

where,
$L(p, k, n) = p^k(1-p)^{n-k}$; $n_1 = k_1 + k_3$; $n_2 = k_2 + k_4$;
$p_1 = k_1/n_1$; $p_2 = k_2/n_2$; $p = (k_1 + k_2)/(n_1 + n_2)$;

The higher the quantity $-2log\lambda$, the greater the statistical association between term T_i and term T_j. We abbreviate this LRT based bootstrapping as LRTBOOT.

3.3.2 Latent Semantic Analysis for Bootstrapping

Generally, given a term-by-document matrix representing a collection of documents, *latent semantic analysis* (LSA) [3] applies *singular value decomposition* (SVD) to the matrix to statistically estimate the latent dimensions (or factors) and term-term associations of the collection.

In particular, we first build a term by document matrix X, given a corpus of review documents. By applying SVD, the term-by-document matrix is then decomposed into a product of three matrices:

$$X = LVR'$$

where L and R are the left and right singular matrices, and V is a diagonal matrix of *singular values*.

Let r be the rank of the raw matrix X. We select a value $k \ll r$. Let V_k denote the diagonal matrix generated by choosing the top k singular values from the matrix V, and let L_k and R_k be matrices generated by selecting the corresponding columns from the matrices L and R, respectively. We thus obtain a reduced matrix X_k by multiplying the three new matrices:

$$X_k = L_k V_k R'_k$$

The matrix X_k is the best low rank (k) approximation to the raw matrix X, which minimizes the *Frobenius norm* [5] or reconstruction error in the form:

$$\parallel E \parallel_F = \sqrt{\sum_{t=1}^{T} \sum_{d=1}^{D} |e_{td}|^2}$$

where $E = X$ - X_k, e_{td}: element of matrix E, T: term set size, and D: corpus size.

In the new latent space, we measure pair-wise term associations via cosine similarity of the corresponding row vectors of the "smoothed" matrix X_k. The LSA model is one type of the generalized association model A used to compute the FF, FO, and OO term associations in Algorithm 1. We abbreviate this approach as LSABOOT.

4. EXPERIMENTS

We evaluate our new corpus statistics association based bootstrapping approach using a large number of real-life Chinese reviews on two different domains of cellphone and hotel. Note that the proposed approach is language independent and can be easily extended to different language based feature extraction applications.

4.1 Review Data

The cellphone review corpus comprises 7800 real-world reviews (or 12,564 sentences) collected from a major Chinese product website [1]. The hotel review corpus contains 4900 reviews (or 18,239 sentences) crawled from a famous Chinese travel portal [2]. All review documents in the two corpora were parsed using a Chinese language analysis tool named *Language Technology Platform* (LTP) [2].

To create a golden standard for the evaluation of feature extraction, 508 reviews were randomly selected from the cellphone review corpus and two annotators independently labeled opinion features. An annotated opinion feature is confirmed valid if it is marked by both annotators. If only one annotator marked an opinion feature, a third person made the final judgement. We obtained a total of 995 opinion features for the cellphone reviews. Similarly, we annotated 1013 opinion features from 206 randomly selected hotel reviews. The Kappa coefficients, a quantitative measure of inter-annotator agreement, are 0.66 and 0.62 on the cellphone and hotel reviews, respectively. Generally, a Kappa value in the range of 0.6-0.8 denotes substantial agreement [23].

4.2 Precision versus Recall

We first evaluate the feature extraction performance of the proposed LRTBOOT and LSABOOT against two state-of-art competitors, DPHITS and DP, and a BASELINE method.

The BASELINE approach simply evaluates precision and recall for the features in the seed feature set $\mathcal{S}$. DP (*double propagation*) extracts opinion features by using syntactic relations identified via manually defined dependency rules [19, 20]. Though giving good domain-independency, DP cannot effectively parse online real-world reviews, which are mostly informal and frequently contain grammatically incorrect sentences. As a result the defined syntactic rules have very limited coverage in real-world application. Notwithstanding, it is difficult to come up with a comprehensive set of dependency relations between features and opinions to cover all real-life cases. DPHITS uses *hyperlink-induced topic search* algorithm (HITS) to validate potential features recognized by DP plus two additional syntactic patterns of "part-whole" and "no" [27].

To be fair, the evaluation results for all methods used the same set of 10 seed features and the same review data partition. The choice of 10 seed features seems reasonable, as most people can easily come up with 10 features for a review domain.

4.2.1 Cellphone Reviews

In Table 3, we first list the best F-measure performance for the proposed association-based bootstrapping methods, LRTBOOT and LSABOOT, as well as three comparison methods, DPHITS, DP, and BASELINE, using 10 feature seeds on cellphone reviews. LRTBOOT achieved the best F-measure of 73.25%, which is 9.96%, 13.32%, and 22.66% better than that of DPHITS, DP, and BASELINE, respectively. LSABOOT had F-measure of 71.07%, which is 7.78%, 11.14%, and 20.48% better than DPHITS, DP, and BASELINE. The maximum recall for LSABOOT is 81.11%.

[1] product.tech.163.com

[2] www.lvping.com/hotels

Method	Precision	Recall	F-measure
LRTBOOT	68.00%	79.40%	**73.25%**
LSABOOT	63.25%	**81.11%**	71.07%
DPHITS	71.00%	57.08%	63.29%
DP	70.42%	52.16%	59.93%
BASELINE	**95.80%**	34.37%	50.59%

Table 3: Best feature extraction F-measure on cellphone reviews.

BASELINE has the largest precision of 95.80% but gives the lowest recall of 34.37%. This is expected since it selects only the top 10 seeds as the identified features. Dependency parsing rule based methods like DP tend to perform badly on real-life review corpus that contains large amounts of informal language or grammatically incorrect content. By employing the *hyperlink-induced topic search* (HITS) algorithm to filter potential features extracted by DP, in addition to engaging two new syntactic dependency patterns, DPHITS improves the feature extraction performance compared to DP. However, it still performed worse than LRTBOOT and LSABOOT.

We then plot precision versus recall curves at various parameter settings for LRTBOOT and LSABOOT, as well as the three competing methods, as shown in Figure 2. Note that the precision-recall curve for DPHITS terminated early at recall levels less than 60%. For DP and BASELINE, only one precision-recall point is obtained each, as indicated by the "diamond" and "circle", respectively.

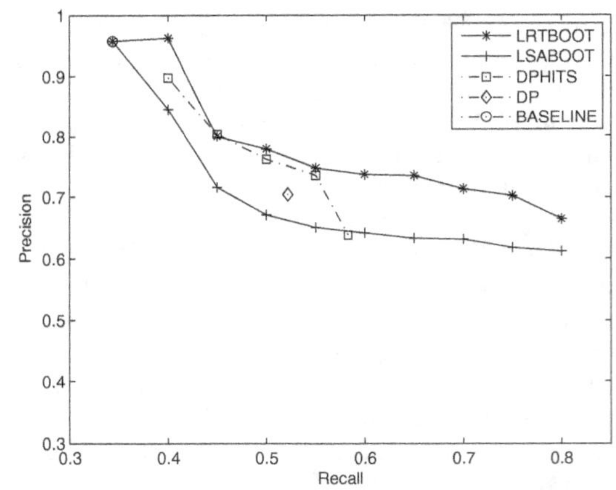

Figure 2: Cellphone Feature extraction performance.

From Figure 2, we see that the LRTBOOT curve lies well above those of DPHITS, DP, and BASELINE. Though starting out at a similar precision as LRTBOOT (as well as BASELINE) at the recall rate of approximately 35%, LSABOOT performed worse than LRTBOOT at increasing recall levels. At low recall levels, nearly all the methods perform well, achieving high precision.

Note that BASELINE achieved very high precision of 95.80% at its only precision-recall pair indicated by the "circle", which also happens to coincide with that of LRTBOOT and LSABOOT. DP attained a 70.42% precision at its unique recall of about 50%, which is 7.39% worse than LRTBOOT, but 3.25% better than LSABOOT. Across the recall levels from 40% to 60%, the mean precision of DPHITS is 76.72%

which is 3.75% lower than LRTBOOT, but 6.16% better than LSABOOT. This is not a serious problem considering that both the proposed LSABOOT and LRTBOOT can achieve much better coverage (higher recall) compared to other methods which stops at recall levels of less than 60%. In practice, a high recall and precision is more desirable.

Though giving good precision, BASELINE leads to bad coverage in the form of the low 35% recall. DP (the point indicated by a "diamond") has relatively better coverage/recall due to its eight manually crafted syntactic rules compared to BASELINE, but still performed worse than LRTBOOT and LSABOOT. This is expected due to the mismatch between DP rules and informal language used in online reviews. DPHITS is only marginally better than DP due to its use of HITS algorithm as well as two additional syntactic patterns. However, its coverage is still limited to at most 58.29% recall, with a corresponding 63.88% precision.

Based on the experiment results, LSABOOT did not achieve respectable precision values, though it outperformed the 3 other competitors in terms of having the highest recall rates of up to 81.11%. Thanks to the high recall rates, LSABOOT was able to achieve the overall second best F-measure of 71.07%, which is 7.78% better than the next competitor, DPHITS. LRTBOOT is the overall winner in terms of robustness and absolute F-measure. It was the de facto precision leader at all levels of recalls, and was able to achieve a recall of about 80%, at which its best F-measure of 73.25% was also achieved.

4.2.2 *Hotel Reviews*

The best results in F-measure for the two proposed approaches, LRTBOOT and LSABOOT, as well as the 3 benchmark methods of DPHITS, DP, and BASELINE, on hotel reviews are shown in Table 4.

Method	Precision	Recall	F-measure
LRTBOOT	57.43%	67.13%	**61.90%**
LSABOOT	45.34%	**69.60%**	54.91%
DPHITS	62.03%	52.42%	56.82%
DP	55.69%	50.74%	53.10%
BASELINE	**92.67%**	31.19%	46.68%

Table 4: Best feature extraction F-measure on hotel reviews.

Even though having the largest precision of 92.67%, BASELINE obtained the worst recall of 31.19%. LRTBOOT again obtained the best F-measure of 61.90%, which is 5.08%, 8.80%, and 15.22% better than that of DPHITS, DP, and BASELINE, respectively, LSABOOT achieved its best F-measure of 54.91% (at 69.60% recall level), which is 1.81% and 8.23% better than that of DP and BASELINE respectively, but 1.91% worse than DPHITS. However, LSABOOT still achieved the overall best recall of 69.60%.

Figure 3 plots the precision-recall performance curves for all methods, LRTBOOT, LSABOOT, DPHITS, DP, and BASELINE, on hotel reviews. Similarly to the cellphone results, LRTBOOT lies far above that of competitors for all recall levels, while LSABOOT is way inferior to LRTBOOT. At about 30% recall, the BASELINE precision is 92.67%, which is the same as that of both LRTBOOT and LSABOOT. DP achieved a 55.69% precision at its unique precision-recall point of approximately 50% recall. This is 15.13% lower than LRTBOOT, but 8.51% better than

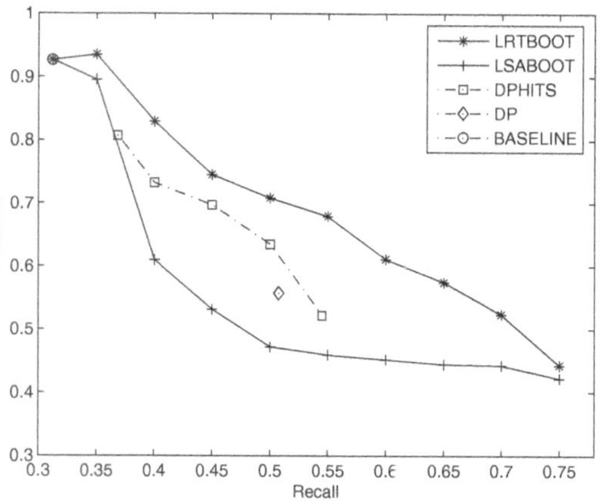

Figure 3: Hotel Feature extraction performance.

LSABOOT. Spanning the recall levels from 35% to 55%, the mean precision of DPHITS is around 67.87%, which is 10.08% worse than that of LRTBOOT, but 8.52% better than the mean LSABOOT precision.

Different from cellphone reviews, hotel reviews contain a large number of complex and noisy sentences, including a large number of irrelevant personal anecdotes or stories. This basically makes the exploration of latent (high-level) factors or structures of review data by LSA more challenging, and thus leads to relatively poor feature extraction performance of LSABOOT.

Based on the experimental results obtained on the cellphone and hotel review domains, we therefore conclude that the proposed statistical association based bootstrapping approach, especially LRTBOOT, gives significant performance improvement for opinion feature extraction, compared to the dependency parsing rule based methods of DP and DPHITS, as well as a dictionary (seed set) based BASELINE. Given a suitably large review corpus, statistical association analysis based bootstrapping method like LRTBOOT can more robustly discover the co-occurrence dependency relationships between pair-wise terms (features and opinions), and thus better discriminate valid features from the invalid ones, especially on real-life raw reviews that typically contain grammatically incorrect sentences or informal language.

4.3 Performance versus Seed Size

We then study the effect of seed set size on feature extraction for both LRTBOOT and LSABOOT, as well as DPHITS, DP, and BASELINE on cellphone and hotel reviews, respectively. To collect seed features, we simply rank all feature candidates by descending document frequency for each review domain. We manually selected up to the top 50 truthful features as seeds.

4.3.1 *Cellphone Reviews*

Figure 4 plots the feature extraction performance in F-measure versus top K seeds (50 seeds max) for LRTBOOT, LSABOOT, and the three benchmark methods on cellphone reviews. Clearly, both LRTBOOT and LSABOOT outperformed the competitors for all seed sizes from 1 to 50. In particular, the mean F-measure of LRTBOOT across all observations is 73.62%, which is 10.35%, 14.07%, and 21.13% better than that of DPHITS, DP, and BASELINE, respectively. The mean F-measure of LSABOOT is 71.02%, which is 7.75%, 11.47%, and 18.53% better than that of DPHITS, DP, and BASELINE, respectively.

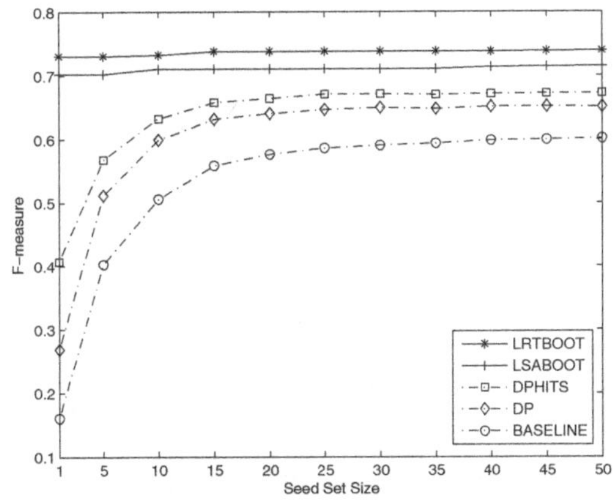

Figure 4: F-measure versus seed size for cellphone reviews.

Furthermore, when increasing seeds from 1 to 50, the F-measure for LRTBOOT remained almost constant, i.e., it does not depend critically on the seed set size. Remarkably, LRTBOOT achieved excellent performance with only one seed word, i.e., the domain concept term "cellphone"! A similar situation can also be observed for LSABOOT for cellphone reviews. This is because both LRTBOOT and LSABOOT bootstrap opinion features by relying on corpus statistics association analysis. In other words, given suitable association thresholds, the candidates that have relatively strong associations with the domain concept word (top 1 seed) or extracted known features (opinions) can be identified after several bootstrapping iterations. Therefore, we can always bootstrap a great many features via robust statistical association analysis based on a properly-sized seed set of 20 seeds or less. Moreover, a seed set size of one will also work as well as a seed size of 20!

The performance for DPHITS, DP, and BASELINE increases significantly over the lower spectrum of seed sizes, and begin to level-off at around 15 seeds. Clearly, seed set size has a big effect on the performance of DPHITS, DP, and BASELINE for feature extraction. This agrees well with the observation that dependency parsing based methods tend to suffer from the feature extraction coverage problem for their manually defined syntactic rules. On the other hand, their performance curves are in line with expectation, since the number of product features is finite, that is, when users comment on products, the feature vocabulary they use will converge [8]. Additionally, our feature seeds were hand-picked from the topmost frequent nouns (noun phrases). Thus we see a miniature version of Zipf's and Heap's Law at work here. Therefore, in order to achieve a decent performance for DPHITS, DP, and BASELINE, a relatively large seed set is needed in practice. In contrast, just one domain word suffices for our proposed LRTBOOT or LSABOOT.

4.3.2 Hotel Reviews

We evaluate the performance of LRTBOOT and LSABOOT versus seed size on the domain of hotel reviews. Figure 5 plots the F-measure performance for LRTBOOT and LSABOOT, as well as DPHITS, DP, and BASELINE.

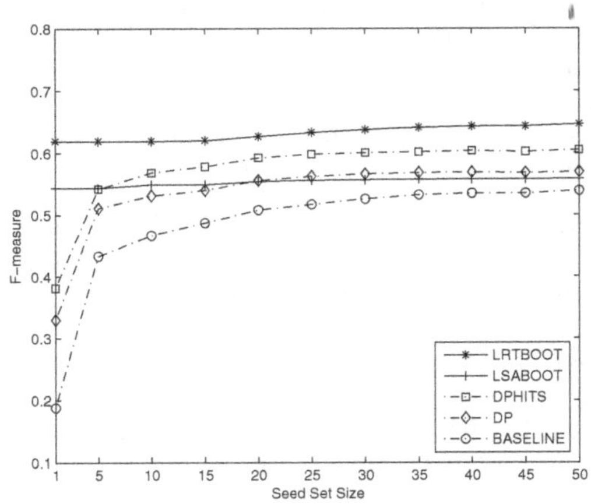

Figure 5: F-measure versus seed size for hotel reviews.

LRTBOOT still gives superior performance, and this time round LRTBOOT enjoys a slight visible improvement from 15 to 50 seed words. Again the LRTBOOT curve lies well above that of DPHITS, DP, and BASELINE for all seed sizes. The average F-measure of LRTBOOT across all observations is 63.15%, which is 6.14%, 9.81%, and 15.28% better than that of DPHITS, DP, and BASELINE, respectively. Compared to the BASELINE, LSABOOT showed better performance for all seed sizes, however it still underperformed LRTBOOT. LSABOOT outperformed DPHITS for 5 or less seeds, but did worse when seed size increased from 5 to 50. Similarly, compared to DP, though LSABOOT achieved better performance with less than 20 seeds, its curve lied under that of DP for seed sizes 20 to 50. The average F-measure of LSABOOT across all seed sizes is 55.27%, which is 1.93% and 7.40% better than DP and BASELINE, but 1.74% lower than that of DPHITS.

Moreover, the performance curves of both LRTBOOT and LSABOOT still exhibit little variation across all seed numbers on the hotel reviews. The results again validated our observation on the cellphone reviews. We hence conclude that seed set size has no large performance influence on our proposed bootstrapping approach. In fact we can again select just the domain concept word to apply LRTBOOT as well as LSABOOT to real-life reviews and achieve great feature extraction results with no supervision at all.

4.4 Association Thresholds

The choice of thresholds for FO, FF, and OO associations is very important for our proposed method to work in practice. In this section, we give evaluations on the performance (in F-measure) versus the thresholds, in an attempt to shine some light on this issue.

Figure 6 plots the LRTBOOT feature extraction performance versus FO association threshold, while keeping both FF and OO thresholds at 21.0 and 12.0 on the cellphone reviews, and 21.0 and 43.0 on the hotel reviews, respectively (note that FF and OO association thresholds are obtained experimentally). Similarly, we can also plot the performance versus FF or OO association threshold on the two domains.

In Figure 6, The performance of LRTBOOT initially in-

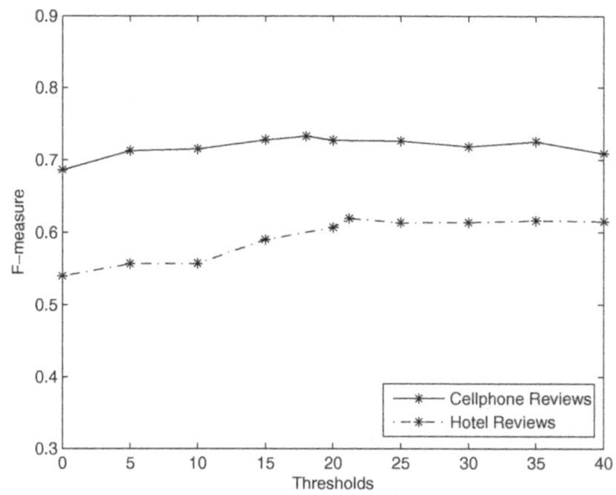

Figure 6: LRTBOOT F-measure vs FO association threshold on cellphone and hotel domains.

creased with the FO threshold, achieving the best F-measure of 73.25% and 61.90% at the FO thresholds of 18.0 and 21.0 on the cellphone and hotel reviews, respectively, and declined slightly thereafter. This is expected as a higher FO threshold will weed out the insignificant or noisy associations, which gives higher-quality features, However, increasing it beyond a certain point will kill some legitimate associations as well.

As shown in Figure 7, similar trends are observed in the performance curves of F-measure versus FO thresholds for LSABOOT, with both FF and OO thresholds at 0.54 and 0.60 on the cellphone, and 0.51 and 0.55 on the hotel domains. The LSABOOT curve grows gradually with the FO threshold, and subsequently achieved the best F-measure of 71.07% and 54.91% at the thresholds of 0.53 and 0.52 on the cellphone and hotel reviews, respectively. If we raise the threshold further, the curves will be further degraded.

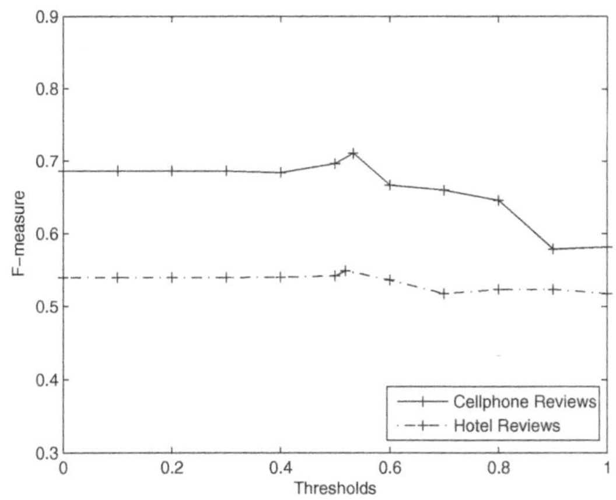

Figure 7: LSABOOT feature extraction F-measure vs. FO association threshold on cellphone and hotel reviews.

Association thresholds for our proposed statistical association based bootstrapping approach must be set. We currently use a standard grid-search procedure to find suitable threshold values that produce good opinion feature extraction performance. For instance, the FO threshold scores for both LRTBOOT and LSABOOT, in our case, can be selected near 20.0 and 0.5, respectively. In practice, suitable thresholds can be determined experimentally via cross-validation on a labeled dataset, which renders our approach a semi-supervised one.

5. CONCLUSIONS

In this paper, we propose a generalized corpus statistics association based bootstrapping approach for opinion feature extraction. Starting from a small manually labeled set of feature seeds, LRTBOOT as well as LSABOOT can bootstrap a large number of valid features by mining pairwise term associations via an effective statistical association model. Experimental results using varying numbers of seeds on the cellphone and hotel review domains demonstrate improvements of the proposed association-based approaches of LRTBOOT and LSABOOT over two state-of-art methods and one baseline method. In fact, LRTBOOT, as well as LSABOOT, achieved quite good performance with only one seed word, which is simply the domain concept word. This makes our proposed statistical association based bootstrapping approach, especially LRTBOOT, powerful and effective for practical opinion feature extraction in opinion mining and sentiment analysis.

Several weaknesses still exist:

(1) As a corpus statistics approach, the proposed approach is less successful in dealing with infrequent feature extraction. For instance, the infrequent feature "FM" (a slang for radio in cellphone reviews) is missed out. Basically, it is not a serious problem, since the number of infrequent features, compared to the number of frequent features, is minor. Moreover, frequent features are basically more important than infrequent ones [8].

(2) Our new approach does not currently extract non-noun opinion features, e.g., design, decorate.

(3) Our approach is at the mercy of errors in the POS-tagging and syntactic parsing for candidate feature extraction.

For future work, we will employ more advanced techniques like fine-grained topical modeling to jointly identify opinion features, including non-noun features, infrequent features, and implicit features as well. We also plan to further test the extracted opinion features in a real opinion mining system by giving every product a feature-specific sentiment summary.

Acknowledgements

This research was supported in part by Singapore Ministry of Education's Academic Research Fund Tier 2 grant ARC 9/12 (MOE2011-T2-2-056).

6. REFERENCES

[1] D. M. Blei, A. Y. Ng, and M. I. Jordan. Latent dirichlet allocation. *Journal of Machine Learning Research*, 3:993–1022, 2003.

[2] W. Che, Z. Li, and T. Liu. Ltp: a chinese language technology platform. In *Proceedings of the 23rd International Conference on Computational Linguistics*, pages 13–16, 2010.

[3] S. Deerwester, S. T. Dumais, and R. Harshman. Indexing by latent semantic analysis. *Journal of the American Society for Information Science and Technology*, 41:391–407, 1990.

[4] T. Dunning. Accurate methods for the statistics of surprise and coincidence. *Computational Linguistics*, 19(1):61–74, 1993.

[5] G. Golub and C. Van Loan. Matrix computations. *The Johns Hopkins University Press*, 3rd edition, 1996.

[6] V. Hatzivassiloglou and J. M. Wiebe. Effects of adjective orientation and gradability on sentence subjectivity. In *Proceedings of the 18th conference on Computational linguistics - Volume 1*, pages 299–305, 2000.

[7] T. Hofmann. Unsupervised learning by probabilistic latent semantic analysis. *Machine Learning Journal*, 42:177–196, 2001.

[8] M. Hu and B. Liu. Mining and summarizing customer reviews. In *Proceedings of the 10th ACM SIGKDD international conference on Knowledge Discovery and Data Mining*, pages 342–351, 2004.

[9] M. Hu and B. Liu. Mining opinion features in customer reviews. In *Proceedings of the 19th national conference on Artificial Intelligence*, pages 755–760, 2004.

[10] N. Jakob and I. Gurevych. Extracting opinion targets in a single- and cross-domain setting with conditional random fields. In *Proceedings of the 2010 Conference on Empirical Methods in Natural Language Processing*, pages 1035–1045, 2010.

[11] W. Jin and H. H. Ho. A novel lexicalized hmm-based learning framework for web opinion mining. In *Proceedings of the 26th Annual International Conference on Machine Learning*, pages 465–472, 2009.

[12] Y. Jo and A. H. Oh. Aspect and sentiment unification model for online review analysis. In *Proceedings of the 4th ACM international conference on Web Search and Data Mining*, pages 815–824, 2011.

[13] S.-M. Kim and E. Hovy. Extracting opinions, opinion holders, and topics expressed in online news media text. In *Proceedings of the Workshop on Sentiment and Subjectivity in Text*, pages 1–8, 2006.

[14] F. Li, C. Han, M. Huang, X. Zhu, Y.-J. Xia, S. Zhang, and H. Yu. Structure-aware review mining and summarization. In *Proceedings of the 23rd International Conference on Computational Linguistics*, pages 653–661, 2010.

[15] C. Lin and Y. He. Joint sentiment/topic model for sentiment analysis. In *Proceeding of the 18th ACM conference on Information and Knowledge Management*, pages 375–384, 2009.

[16] S. J. Pan and Q. Yang. A survey on transfer learning. *IEEE Transactions on Knowledge and Data Engineering*, 22(10):1345–1359, 2010.

[17] B. Pang, L. Lee, and S. Vaithyanathan. Thumbs up? sentiment classification using machine learning techniques. In *Proceedings of the 2002 conference on Empirical Methods in Natural Language Processing*, pages 79–86, 2002.

[18] A. Popescu and O. Etzioni. Extracting product features and opinions from reviews. In *Proceedings of Human Language Technology Conference and Conference on Empirical Methods in Natural Language Processing (HLT/EMNLP)*, pages 339–346, 2005.

[19] G. Qiu, B. Liu, J. Bu, and C. Chen. Expanding domain sentiment lexicon through double propagation. In *Proceedings of the 21st international jont conference on Artificial Intelligence*, pages 1199–1204, 2009.

[20] G. Qiu, B. Liu, J. Bu, and C. Chen. Opinion word expansion and target extraction through double propagation. *Computational Linguistics*, 37:9–27, 2011.

[21] G. Qiu, C. Wang, J. Bu, K. Liu, and C. Chen. Incorporate the syntactic knowledge in opinion mining in user-generated content. In *Proceedings of the NLPIX'08 Workshop*, 2008.

[22] I. Titov and R. McDonald. Modeling online reviews with multi-grain topic models. In *Proceeding of the 17th international conference on World Wide Web*, pages 111–120, 2008.

[23] A. J. Viera and J. M. Garrett. Understanding interobserver agreement: the kappa statistic. *Family Medicine*, 37(5):360–363, 2005.

[24] J. Wiebe, T. Wilson, R. Bruce, M. Bell, and M. Martin. Learning subjective language. *Computational Linguistics*, 30(3):277–308, 2004.

[25] T. Wilson, J. Wiebe, and P. Hoffmann. Recognizing contextual polarity in phrase-level sentiment analysis. In *Proceedings of the conference on Human Language Technology and Empirical Methods in Natural Language Processing*, pages 347–354, 2005.

[26] J. Yi, T. Nasukawa, R. Bunescu, and W. Niblack. Sentiment analyzer: Extracting sentiments about a given topic using natural language processing techniques. In *Proceedings of the 3rd IEEE International Conference on Data Mining*, pages 427, 2003.

[27] L. Zhang, B. Liu, S. H. Lim, and E. O'Brien-Strain. Extracting and ranking product features in opinion documents. In *Proceedings of the 23rd International Conference on Computational Linguistics: Posters*, pages 1462–1470, 2010.

[28] W. X. Zhao, J. Jiang, H. Yan, and X. Li. Jointly modeling aspects and opinions with a maxent-lda hybrid. In *Proceedings of the 2010 Conference on Empirical Methods in Natural Language Processing*, pages 56–65, 2010.

Topic-Driven Reader Comments Summarization*

Zongyang Ma, Aixin Sun, Quan Yuan, Gao Cong
School of Computer Engineering, Nanyang Technological University, Singapore 639798
{zma4, qyuan1}@e.ntu.edu.sg, {axsun, gaocong}@ntu.edu.sg

ABSTRACT

Readers of a news article often read its comments contributed by other readers. By reading comments, readers obtain not only complementary information about this news article but also the opinions from other readers. However, the existing ranking mechanisms for comments (*e.g.*, by recency or by user rating) fail to offer an overall picture of topics discussed in comments. In this paper, we first propose to study **To**pic-driven **R**eader **C**omments **S**ummarization (TORCS) problem. We observe that many news articles from a news stream are related to each other; so are their comments. Hence, news articles and their associated comments provide context information for user commenting. To implicitly capture the context information, we propose two topic models to address the TORCS problem, namely, Master-Slave Topic Model (MSTM) and Extended Master-Slave Topic Model (EXTM). Both models treat a news article as a master document and each of its comments as a slave document. MSTM model constrains that the topics discussed in comments have to be derived from the commenting news article. On the other hand, EXTM model allows generating words of comments using both the topics derived from the commenting news article, and the topics derived from all comments themselves. Both models are used to group comments into topic clusters. We then use two ranking mechanisms Maximal Marginal Relevance (MMR) and Rating & Length (RL) to select a few most representative comments from each comment cluster. To evaluate the two models, we conducted experiments on 1005 Yahoo! News articles with more than one million comments. Our experimental results show that EXTM significantly outperforms MSTM by perplexity. Through a user study, we also confirm that the comment summary generated by EXTM achieves better intra-cluster topic cohesion and inter-cluster topic diversity.

Categories and Subject Descriptors

H.3.1 [**INFORMATION STORAGE AND RETRIEVAL**]: Content Analysis and Indexing—*Abstracting methods*

*This work was partially supported by MINDEF-NTU-DIRP/2010/03 and MOE AcRF Tier-1 Grant RG13/10, Singapore.

CIKM'12, October 29–November 2, 2012, Maui, HI, USA.

Keywords

Comments Summarization, Topic Model, Master-Slave Document

1. INTRODUCTION

The popularity of Web 2.0 platforms and applications prompts users' engagement in expressing and sharing their opinions online by commenting. Not only commenting through social platforms, users are allowed to comment on news articles on most news websites. For instance, Yahoo! News allows users to comment on its news articles, to rate comments, as well as to reply other readers' comments. Through reading others' comments, a reader may get additional information about an event reported in a news article, including the background, the other related events, and opinions of other readers. It has been reported that such commenting mechanism enables news sites to extend their user volume as well as to increase advertising revenue [33].

Due to the large readership, a popular news article may easily accumulate thousands of comments within a short time period. For instance, on average, there are 1059 comments per article among the most-commented articles collected from Yahoo! News in our study. It is time-consuming for users to read all comments of an article and they may feel disincentivized to read unorganized comments. Currently, comments can be ranked in a number of ways to ease users' reading overload. Taking Yahoo! News as an example, comments can be ranked by recency, popularity (*e.g.*, based on user ratings) and the number of replies a comment receiving. None of the mentioned ranking mechanisms offers readers an overview of all topics discussed among commenters. In particular, the user-rating based ranking suffers from the *rich get richer* effect. Consequently comments about one dominating topic may occupy all top-ranked positions while comments on other topics are ranked much lower. Nevertheless, to the best of our knowledge, *there is no service or existing research work on summarizing comments of an article to offer an easy overview of all topics discussed in the comments.*

In this paper, we take the first step to study the problem of **To**pic-driven **R**eader **C**omments **S**ummarization (TORCS). We aim to identify the latent topics among all comments of an article and subsequently select a small number of most salient comments to give a concise representation of all comments according to the identified topics. TORCS benefits users by offering an alternative way of quickly ascertaining overall topics of thousands of comments of an article in addition to the existing comments ranking mechanisms. Moreover, TORCS enables a user to selectively read comments on one specific topic chosen by her from all latent topics identified. We argue that TORCS not only benefits Web users, but more importantly offers great value to mobile users. Due to the relatively limited screen size, mobile users do not have the luxury of reading a large number of comments without scrolling. Grouping comments by latent topics and selecting the most salient comments under each topic bring a more organized way of reading comments through mobile devices.

One key challenge in TORCS is to group comments by their latent topics. Considering a comment is usually a piece of short text[1], at first glance, techniques on short text clustering and classification (*e.g.*, search snippets clustering [29, 31] and classification [9]) can be directly applied. However, these techniques do not consider the *news-comment*, *comment-comment*, and *news-news* relationships. First, as defined in Merriam-Webster dictionary, a comment is "a note explaining, illustrating, or criticizing the meaning of a writing" or "an observation or remark expressing an opinion or attitude". In news commenting, a comment is always associated with a news article. For this reason, we also call the news article *master document* and its comments *slave documents*. Second, for a given news article, we observe that a subset of its comments may discuss the topics mentioned in the news article, but usually not all of its comments. For instance, a news article talking about tax policy in US may have comments on tax policy, comments on health care reform, or gossip of persons mentioned in the article. That is, comments may extend the discussion with topics related to the news article or even more general topics completely irrelevant to the news article. Third, in a news stream, many news articles are on similar topics (or even the same event). For example, many news articles are about the ongoing US presidential election.

To identify the latent topics in comments with consideration of the relationships between comments and news articles, we propose two topic models, namely, ***Master-Slave Topic Model*** (MSTM) and ***Extended Master-Slave Topic Model*** (EXTM). The former assumes that all the topics discussed in comments are derived from the corresponding news articles. The latter is based on our observation that comments may discuss the topics derived from news articles as well as the extended topics not directly derived from news articles. In both models, we assume that each comment has exactly one topic due to the short length of most comments. Such simple topic assignment makes the comment clustering efficient. A cluster is formed by simply grouping comments with the same topic. After clustering process, we select representative comments using two methods, namely, Maximal Marginal Relevance (MMR) and Rating & Length (RL). The former is widely used in document summarization to select comments based on topical relevance while avoiding redundancy; the latter considers the user rating and the length of comment for representative comments selection. Users get more comprehensive understanding of the comments by giving topical and distinctive comments than representing summary merely using keywords. In our evaluation, we observe that the proposed topic-driven approach avoids redundancy problem faced by the word-based clustering approach to some extent. Our main contributions are summarized as follows:

- To the best of our knowledge, we are the first to define and study the problem of *Topic-Driven Reader Comments Summarization* (TORCS), which aims to summarize comments into topic clusters with respect to their associated news articles. Different from existing works on short text clustering, comment clustering is guided by the context information of their associated news articles.
- We present two topic models, MSTM and EXTM, to integrate the generative process of news articles and that of comments in a unified way. Both models are based on the observation that topics of news articles have significant effect on topics of comments, and a single comment usually is specific to one topic. EXTM further considers topics that are generated from comments themselves which are not strongly related to news articles, simulating the generative process of news-comments document in a more natural manner.
- We conducted experiments on 1005 most-commented Yahoo! news articles with more than one million comments. We first evaluated MSTM and EXTM by perplexity, a standard metric to evaluate topic models, and show that EXTM significantly outperforms MSTM. We then conducted user study to evaluate summaries generated by 6 methods. These 6 methods involve 3 comment clustering techniques (MSTM, EXTM, and CLUTO as a non-topic-model approach) and 2 comment ranking schemes (MMR and RL). Our user study shows that EXTM-MMR yields the best intra-cluster topic cohesion and inter-cluster topic diversity among the summaries generated by all methods.

[1] More than 60% of comments in our data collection has fewer than 10 words each.

The rest of the paper is organized as follows. Section 2 surveys the existing studies on comments and recent advances in topic models. In Section 3, we define the TORCS problem, detail the two models proposed, and describe the two comment ranking schemes. The evaluation of MSTM and EXTM using perperlexity is reported in Section 4, followed by the user study in Section 5. Finally, Section 6 concludes this paper.

2. RELATED WORK

We begin with a brief overview of the research works conducted on comments. We then review the related topic models, and lastly we discuss the differences between TORCS and short text clustering.

Being the most prevalent type of user-generated content, comments have gained much interest from the research community. Depending on the type of resources/objects being commented, the research works can be broadly categorized into two groups: study of comments on non-textual resources (*e.g.*, photo, video), and study of comments on textual-resources (*e.g.*, news article, blog post, and product description).

Comments on non-textual resources. For non-textual objects like photos and videos, content-based search solely relying on low-level features (*e.g.*, color, texture, and shape) remains challenging [16]. Comments therefore become valuable resource to describe these non-textual resources to improve searching. It is reported that comment-based approach outperforms visual content-based approach for aesthetic photo search [30], and video search accuracy is improved by 15% by incorporating comments [38]. In [34], the authors presented a detailed analysis of YouTube video comments and aimed to reveal the relationship between the content and the ratings of comments.

Most similar to our work is on clustering YouTube comments by using topic model reported in [20]. In their study, for each YouTube video, a topic model is trained on all its comments. The comments are clustered by their topic assignment. Within each cluster, a small set of comments is selected using PageRank-style algorithm on the comment graph. In this graph, a link between two comments exists if the recently published comment contains at least m words from the earlier comment (where m is a predefined number). Our approach is significantly different. We consider not only the topic distribution in comments but also the topic distribution in news articles, and the latter would guide the overall discussion in comments. More specifically, we train our topic models using both the set of news articles and all of their comments to take care of the news-news, news-comment, and comment-comment relationships.

Moreover, we use different approaches to select comments from a cluster, based on the comment's topical representativeness as well as the user rating.

Comments on textual resources. The study of the comments on product review mainly focuses on sentiment analysis and product feature/aspect identification from comments [11, 18, 37]. The way of summarizing product comments is therefore significantly different from ours. On the other hand, blog posts share large similarity with news articles. Our work is therefore more related to the study of comments on blog posts and news articles. Mishne and Glance conducted a large-scale analysis of blog comments and showed that comments help in improving blog search recall and facilitate better ranking of blog search results [26]. More related to our work, Hu *et al.* proposed to summarize blog post by incorporating information from its associated comments [14]. The main idea is to rank comments by their importance considering three types of relations (*i.e.,* mention, quotation, and topic) among them. The blog post is summarized by extracting the sentences containing the keywords identified from the important comments as well as the content of the blog post. The comments, however, are not summarized.

Comments on news articles have been studied from different aspects, including spam detection [19], discussion structure extraction [32], comment volume prediction [36], comment rating prediction [21], comment-based news recommendation [33] and comment ranking [10]. The collaborative-filtering approach in [33] for personalized news recommendation considers ratings as well as features derived from social networks. For comment ranking, Dalal *et al.* proposed a unified ranking framework for multi-objective comment ranking [10]; the comments can be ranked by ratings, commenter reputation, or recency. To the best of our knowledge, there is no existing work on summarizing comments of news articles.

Topic Model. Latent Dirichlet Allocation (LDA) was first proposed in [5], which provides an unsupervised way to discover latent topics in text collection. The promising performance of LDA inspires various extensions. In the following, we name a few. Correlated Topic Model [4] captures relations of topics based on a more natural assumption that topics are not independent and gives a better fit of the data. Dynamic Topic Model [3] incorporates time feature into LDA, aiming to analyze topics evolution. Author-Topic Model [28] utilizes authorship information to simultaneously model author interest and document topic. Multi-grain Topic Model [35] extracts ratable aspects of objects from online reviews. In [25], the authors formulated Topic Model with network structure regularization to discover topical community. Several topic-sentiment models have also been proposed [18, 22]. This type of models generates topics as well as sentiment using review collection.

Most germane to this work are the correspondence LDA (corrLDA) model [2, 6] and the topic-perspective model [23], both proposed for analyzing social tag annotation (*e.g.,* tags annotated to documents in social bookmark systems like `delicious.com`). The corrLDA model assumes that tag topics are generated due to word topics of the annotated document; hence the model captures strong relations between document topics and its corresponding tag topics. The topic-perspective model, on the other hand, relaxes this rigid assumption. The authors argued that tags could also be generated from user perspective (*e.g.,* tags like happy, delicious, and so on reflect perspective of users themselves). This model therefore incorporates a switch, which controls tag generation from document topic or user perspective. Each user has a user perspective distribution to describe her preference and interest.

However, both models cannot be applied directly to comments

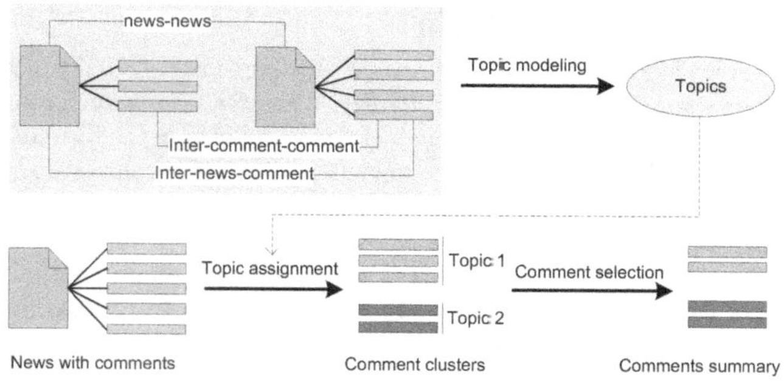

Figure 1: Topic-driven reader comments summarization

because of the significant differences between tags and comments. First, the primary motivations for tagging are organizational and social [24]. Hence, a tag is usually assigned to a set of documents related to the keyword defined by the user (*i.e.,* the tag itself). Naturally, each tag leads to multiple topics derived from its set of annotated documents. A comment, on the other hand, is an expression from a user to one particular article without organizational motivation. We observe that most comments are short and specific to one point (or one topic). Moreover, the social motivation for commenting is much weak compared to tagging evidenced by a large number of comments from anonymous users. Many users prefer to voice out through commenting without releasing their identity.

Our proposed MSTM model is similar to CorrLDA but with the constraint that words from a single comment share the same topic derived from the news article (*i.e.,* the master document). The same constraint is imposed to the proposed EXTM model. However, different from MSTM, EXTM allows a comment to have topic derived from not only the news article but also other comments in the collection by using a switch. The switch in our model is at document-level not at tag-level as in topic-perspective model. Another major difference between EXTM and topic-perspective model is that in EXTM we do not model user information due to the aforementioned reason.

Short Text Clustering. Most studies on short text clustering focus on clustering search result snippets. A detailed survey is given in [8]. One key research issue is the similarity measure between two short texts due to the word sparsity. The state-of-the-art approach is to enrich short text representation by using external knowledge bases like WordNet and Wikipedia [9, 15, 27]. In [9], a Topic Model-based approach is proposed to derive multiple granularity latent topics to enrich short text representation. A graph-based approach for short text clustering is reported in [31]. Each snippet is represented as a graph of topics and the clusters are realized by graph-cut. On the other hand, a transfer learning approach is proposed in [17] to cluster tweets (short text with limited 140 characters in Twitter) by utilizing topically related long texts as the auxiliary data. In these studies, short texts (*e.g.,* search snippets) are independent from each other. In our problem setting, a comment is associated with a master document (*i.e.,* news article). Moreover, the topic distribution among the comments of a news article is largely affected by the topics discussed in the article.

3. TORCS PROBLEM AND MODELS

In this section, we first describe the TORCS problem and then present two generative models that extend LDA. The models integrate both generative process of news article content and generative process of comment content.

3.1 TORCS Problem

Given a news article and its associated comments received from a news stream, the task of ***Topic-driven Reader Comment Summarization*** is to generate a summary of comments in the form of comment clusters, where (i) comments in each cluster are on one major topic, and (ii) each comment cluster is represented by a few salient comments.

Note that, different from most existing document summarization tasks where a summary is usually a set of sentences extracted or generated from the given document(s), our comment summary is a subset of comments because a comment is usually very short (see Figure 3). Consequently, the two major challenges in addressing the TORCS problem are (i) identifying the topics discussed among comments, and (ii) identifying the most representative comments from each topical comment cluster.

In our problem setting, a comment exists only if it is associated with a news article. Therefore, in our discussion, we also refer to a news article as a *master document* and its associated comments *slave documents*. Further, a master document and its associated slave documents can be considered as "a unified document with star structure[2]", shown in Figure 1.

Recall that the first challenge is to identify the topics discussed among the comments of a given news article. The most straightforward approach is to cluster them based on content similarity (*e.g.,* cosine similarity over word features of the comments). However, this simple approach largely ignores the context information of the comments (*e.g.,* related news or comments). Considering all news articles received from a news stream, many news articles are related to each other (*e.g.,* reporting the same event, or events about the same personal and so on); so are their comments. In fact, grouping news articles about the same event or topic is one of the major research issue in topic detection and tracking (TDT) [1]. Between news articles and comments, we observe at least three kinds of relationships: *news-news*, *comment-comment*, and *news-comment* relationship, illustrated in the top left corner of Figure 1.

News-news: Two news articles are related if they report the same event (*e.g.,* USA presidential election); a series of news articles are often published to trace the status of an event. News articles may also refer to recently published articles if reporting similar type of events (*e.g.,* traffic accidents, natural disaster).

Comment-comment: There are two types of comment-comment relationships: *intra-comment-comment* relationship to relate the comments of the same news article (*e.g.,* reply or on similar topics), and *inter-comment-comment* relationship to relate comments of different news articles. That is, readers may extend the discussion in comments to refer to the event(s) reported in multiple news articles including the current article she is commenting on. In other words, such a comment can be applied to any of the news articles reporting the event. For example, a reader may give her comment to support a candidate/party in the election. Such comments are strongly related to each other but not closely related to any one particular news article.

News-comment: Similarly, there are two types of news-comment relationships:*intra-news-comment* relationship to relate the comments of its associated news article, and *inter-news-comment* relationship to relate the comments of one news article to another news article. That is, a user may comment the current news article based on the information reported in another news article.

[2]Note that, in this paper we do not consider the reply relationship. It is a part of our future work to incorporate reply relationship in our models.

Based on the three types of relationships, we argue that in order to accurately identify the topics discussed among the comments associated with a news article, one has to consider the context information (*e.g.,* the related news articles/comments). In this paper, we propose two topic models to identify the topics from recently published (*e.g.,* within the past two weeks) news and comments. Given a news article, whose comments are to be summarized, we first assign a topic to each of its comments and then group the comments by the assigned topics to form topic clusters. From each topic cluster, the most representative comments are then identified to form the comment summary. These two steps are illustrated in the lower part of Figure 1.

In the following, we present the two topic models, Master-Slave Topic Model (MSTM) and Extended Master-Slave Topic Model (EXTM). The former implicitly models the news-news, intra-news-comment, intra-comment-comment relationships. EXTM extends MSTM by modeling the remaining two types of relationships: inter-news-comment and inter-comment-comment. The graphical representation of the two models are shown in Figure 2 and the notations are summarized in Table 1.

3.2 Master-Slave Topic Model (MSTM)

We aim to discover latent topics in slave documents (comments) with respect to their associated master documents (news articles). In a generative model, the generation of slave document relies on its associated master document, such as the generative process in corrLDA [6].

Similar to corrLDA, our proposed Master-Slave Topic Model assumes that all topics of the slave documents are directly derived from topic distribution of master document. That is, the generative process of the slave documents solely depends on the generative process of master document. However, due to the different vocabularies used in news articles and comments, different words for news articles and comments respectively could be generated for the same topic. We therefore name the same topic ***master topic*** and ***slave topic*** when we refer to the topic in the generative process of master and slave documents respectively.

A major difference between MSTM and corrLDA is that MSTM imposes a constraint that each slave document has exactly one slave topic. Recall that most comments are very short. Plotted in Figure 3(c), among one million comments in our dataset, more than 60% of comments each has fewer than 10 words and more than 80% of comments each has fewer than 16 words. Probably because of the length, we observe that most comments are specific to one point. We therefore constrain that each slave document has exactly one slave topic.

The graphical representation of MSTM is shown in Figure 2(a) and the generative process is summarized in Procedure 1. In MSTM, each master document has multiple master topics, and the generative process of the master document is same as in LDA (Lines 4-6 in Procedure 1). MSTM generates the unique topic of each slave document based on uniform word topic distribution of its associated master document, and then generates all words of slave document given the unique slave topic (Lines 7-9).

The exact inference is intractable. We therefore utilize Gibbs Sampling (an approximate approach) to inference the latent variables. Similar to the Collapsed Gibbs Sampling algorithm presented in [12], we construct a Markov chain on latent topics. At each transaction step, a topic of word from master document or a topic of slave document is generated with respect to its conditional probability.

The topic of word from master document is drawn from the following conditional probability, which is the same as LDA.

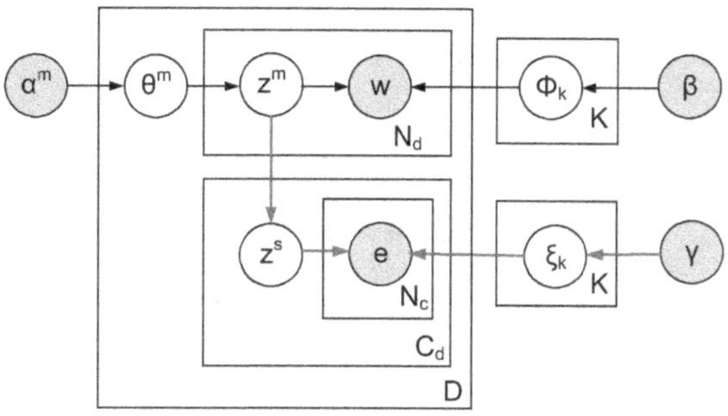

(a) MSTM

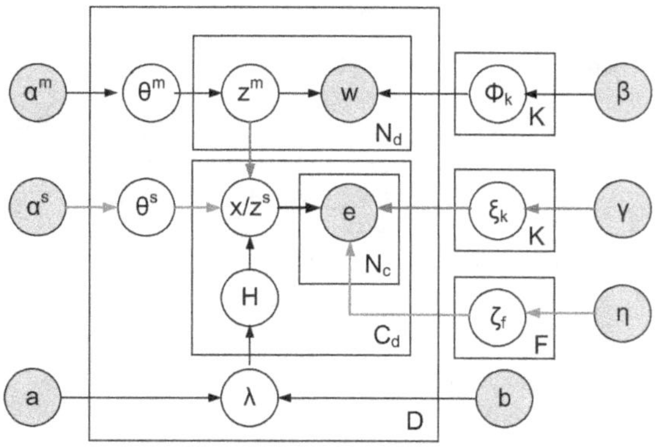

(b) EXTM

Figure 2: MSTM and EXTM. The red line illustrates slave topics are derived from news articles; the green line illustrates the extended topics are derived from comments.

$$P(z_i^m = k | w_i = v, \mathbf{z}_{\neg i}^m, \alpha^m, \beta) \propto \frac{Q_{kd,\neg i}^{KD} + \alpha^m}{\sum_{k'} Q_{k'd,\neg i}^{KD} + K\alpha^m} \times \frac{Q_{vk,\neg i}^{VK} + \beta}{\sum_{v'} Q_{v'k,\neg i}^{VK} + V\beta}$$

The topic of slave document is drawn from conditional probability:

$$P(z_c^s = k | \mathbf{z}_{\neg c}^m, \mathbf{e}_{\neg c}, \gamma) \propto \frac{Q_{kd}^{KD}}{\sum_{k'} Q_{k'd}^{KD}} \times \frac{\prod_{e_j \in E_c^d, e_j = u_j} \prod_{g=0}^{N_{dc}^{e_j}-1} (Q_{u_j k,\neg c}^{UK} + \gamma + g)}{\prod_{y=0}^{N_{dc}-1} (\sum_{u'} Q_{u'k,\neg c}^{UK} + U\gamma + y)}$$

3.3 Extended Master-Slave Topic Model (EXTM)

Extended Master-Slave Topic Model aims to simulate the generative process of both master document and slave document in a more natural way. MSTM follows a rigid constraint that all topics of slave documents have to be derived from the topic distribution of their master documents. EXTM relaxes this rigid constraint and allows some slave documents to have topics irrelevant to their master documents. We call this type of topic ***extended topic***. As discussed earlier, a reader is not constrained by the topic presented in the news article when commenting. She may provide some additional information (*e.g.,* background information about a news article) which is not covered in the news article. Extended topics are introduced in the EXTM model to take care of such topics.

The graphical representation of EXTM is shown in Figure 2(b) and the generative process is summarized in Procedure 2. In EXTM, the generative process of master document is same as that in MSTM (Lines 5-7 in Procedure 2). Similar to MSTM, each slave document has one unique topic. However, the topic can be either derived from topic distribution of its associated master document, or from extended topic distribution of all comments. We use a switch H to decide whether the topic is a slave topic or an extended topic (Line

Table 1: Notations for MSTM and EXTM

D, C	Number of master documents, of slave documents
N_d, N_c	Number of words in master document d, in slave document c
V, U	Vocabulary size of master documents, of slave documents
w, e	Word in master document, in slave document
E_c^d	Set of words in slave document c of master document d
N_{dc}^e	Number of times word e occurs in slave document c of master document d
K	Number of master topics
F	Number of extended topics
z^m, z^s, x	Master topic, slave topic, and extended topic
θ^m, θ^s	Multinomial distribution over master topics, over extended topics
α^m, α^s	Dirichlet prior vector for θ^m, and θ^s
ϕ_k, ξ_k, ζ_f	Multinomial distribution over words of master document for master topics, over words of slave document for slave topics, over words of slave document for extended topics
β, γ, η	Dirichlet prior vector for ϕ_k, ξ_k, and ζ_f
H	Switch to decide whether the topic is a slave topic or an extended topic
λ, a, b	Probability of topic of slave document being slave topic, and beta prior for λ
$Q_{kd,\neg i}^{KD}$	Number of times master topic k is assigned to master document d, excluding the current word w_i
$Q_{vk,\neg i}^{VK}$	Number of times word v of master document is generated from master topic k, excluding the current word w_i
$Q_{uk,\neg c}^{UK}$	Number of times word u of slave document is generated from slave topic k, excluding all words in slave document c
$Q_{uf,\neg c}^{UF}$	Number of times word u of slave document is generated from extended topic f, excluding all words in slave document c
$Q_{H=1,\neg c}^{CD}$	Number of times H is 1 in document d, excluding the current slave document c
$Q_{H=0,\neg c}^{CD}$	Number of times H is 0 in document d, excluding the current slave document c
$Q_{fd,\neg c}^{FD}$	Number of times extended topic f is assigned to slave documents of master document d, excluding the current slave document c

10 and 13). If H equals 1, words of slave document are drawn from the slave topic sampled from uniform word topic distribution of its associated master document (Lines 11 and 12); if H equals 0, words of slave document are drawn from the extended topic sampled from extended topic distribution θ^s (Lines 14 and 15).

Similar to that in MSTM, we utilize Gibbs Sampling to inference the latent variables of EXTM. Because the sampling topic of words from master document is the same as MSTM, we only present sampling topic of slave document. Reported in Table 2, the topic of slave document is drawn from conditional probability $P(H = 1, z_c^s = k | \mathbf{z}_{\neg c}^m, \mathbf{e}_{\neg c}, \gamma, a, b)$ when $H = 1$, and drawn from probability $P(H = 0, x_c = f | \mathbf{x}_{\neg c}, \mathbf{e}_{\neg c}, \alpha^s, \eta, a, b)$ when $H = 0$.

3.4 Salient Comments Selection

Because of the assumption that each comment has exactly one topic, topic clustering becomes straightforward by grouping the comments of the same topic together. The importance of each comment cluster is evaluated by the number of comments contained in the cluster. The next major task is to select a few most salient comments from each cluster for a concise representation of each comment cluster. Considering each comment is analogous to a sentence because of its short length, most sentence ranking/selection techniques studied in document summarization can be directly applied. We evaluate two comment selection techniques, namely, Maximal Marginal Relevance (MMR) and Rating & Length (RL).

Maximal Marginal Relevance. MMR [7] is a commonly used technique in document summarization to select topically relevant sentences while avoiding redundancy. Given a cluster of comments

Table 2: Conditional probability of topic of slave document in EXTM

$$P(H=1, z_c^s = k|\mathbf{z}_{\neg c}^m, \mathbf{e}_{\neg c}, \gamma, a, b) \propto \frac{Q_{H=1,\neg c}^{CD} + a}{Q_{H=1,\neg c}^{CD} + Q_{H=0,\neg c}^{CD} + a + b} \times \frac{Q_{kd}^{KD}}{\sum_{k'} Q_{k'd}^{KD}} \times \frac{\prod_{e_j \in E_c^d, e_j = u_j} \prod_{g=0}^{N_{dc}^{e_j}-1} (Q_{u_j k,\neg c}^{UK} + \gamma + g)}{\prod_{y=0}^{N_{dc}-1} (\sum_{u'} Q_{u'k,\neg c}^{UK} + U\gamma + y)}$$

$$P(H=0, x_c = f|\mathbf{x}_{\neg c}, \mathbf{e}_{\neg c}, \alpha^s, \eta, a, b) \propto \frac{Q_{H=0,\neg c}^{CD} + b}{Q_{H=1,\neg c}^{CD} + Q_{H=0,\neg c}^{CD} + a + b} \times \frac{Q_{fd,\neg c}^{FD} + \alpha^s}{\sum_{f'} Q_{f'd,\neg c}^{FD} + F\alpha^s} \times \frac{\prod_{e_j \in E_c^d, e_j = u_j} \prod_{g=0}^{N_{dc}^{e_j}-1} (Q_{u_j f,\neg c}^{UF} + \eta + g)}{\prod_{y=0}^{N_{dc}-1} (\sum_{u'} Q_{u'f,\neg c}^{UF} + U\eta + y)}$$

Procedure 1: Generative process of MSTM

For each of the D master documents d, draw $\theta_d^m \sim Dirichlet(\alpha^m)$;
For each of the K master topics k, draw $\phi_k \sim Dirichlet(\beta)$;
For each of the K slave topics k, draw $\xi_k \sim Dirichlet(\gamma)$;
for *each word w_i in master document d* **do**
    Choose a master topic $z_i^m \sim Multinomial(\theta_d^m)$;
    Generate a word $w_i \sim Multinomial(\phi_{z_i^m})$;
for *each slave document c of master document d* **do**
    Choose a slave topic $z_c^s \sim Uniform(z_{w_1}^m, ..., z_{w_{N_d}}^m)$;
    Generate all words in $c \sim Multinomial(\xi_{z_c^s})$;

Procedure 2: Generative process of EXTM

For each of the D master documents d, draw $\theta_d^m \sim Dirichlet(\alpha^m)$ and draw $\theta_d^s \sim Dirichlet(\alpha^s)$;
For each of the K master topics k, draw $\phi_k \sim Dirichlet(\beta)$;
For each of the K slave topics k, draw $\xi_k \sim Dirichlet(\gamma)$;
For each of the F extended topics f, draw $\zeta_f \sim Dirichlet(\eta)$;
for *each word w_i in master document d* **do**
    Choose a master topic $z_i^m \sim Multinomial(\theta_d^m)$;
    Generate a word $w_i \sim Multinomial(\phi_{z_i^m})$;
for *each master document d, draw $\lambda_d \sim Beta(a, b)$* **do**
    For each slave document c, draw a switch $H \sim Binomial(\lambda_d)$;
    if $H = 1$ **then**
        Choose a slave topic $z_c^s \sim Uniform(z_{w_1}^m, ..., z_{w_{N_d}}^m)$;
        Generate all words in $c \sim Multinomial(\xi_{z_c^s})$;
    else /* $H = 0$ */
        Choose an extended topic $x_c \sim Multinomial(\theta_d^s)$;
        Generate all words in $c \sim Multinomial(\zeta_{x_c})$;

to be summarized, we compute its centroid feature vector, denoted by c_m, to be the query vector whose relevance is computed for each of the member comments in the cluster using MMR. Let C_s be the set of comments selected so far, the score of a candidate comment c to be selected is computed using the following equation. In our experiments, we use cosine similarity to define $sim(\cdot,\cdot)$ and set $\delta = 0.8$.

$$Score(c) = \delta \times sim(c, c_m) - (1 - \delta) \times max_{c' \in C_s}(sim(c, c'))$$

Because of the short length, we do not use $TF \times IDF$ based word weighting scheme to define the comment feature vectors. Instead, words in comments are weighed based on the topic distribution generated from ξ_k or ζ_f (recall that in topic modeling, each topic is a probability distribution over words).

Rating & Length. Instead of solely relying on content of comments, with RL, we utilize the ratings from readers in comment selection. Rating has always been considered important features in comments [10, 13]. In Yahoo! News website, readers evaluate others' comments by clicking "like" or "dislike" button. The more likes or dislikes a comment receives, the more attention it gains from the readers. We sum the likes and dislikes a comment receiving to be its rating score. In addition, we also consider the length of the comments in number of words. It has been reported that comment length as a feature can be utilized to improve prediction accuracy of ranking comments [13]. We normalize the rating scores $Rating(\cdot)$ and length scores $Length(\cdot)$ in $[0, 1]$ using min-max normalization, and then rank comments by the linear combination of the two scores, where σ is a factor to balance rating score and length score. In our experiments, we set $\sigma = 0.6$ to give more weights to the rating score.

$$Score(c) = \sigma \times Rating(c) + (1 - \sigma) \times Length(c)$$

4. EXPERIMENTS

To evaluate the proposed solution for TORCS problem, we conducted experiments using the most-commented news articles and their comments from Yahoo! News. We conducted two sets of evaluations, to evaluate the proposed MSTM and EXTM models and to evaluate the resultant summaries, respectively. In the following, we detail the dataset and report the evaluation of the two topic models using perplexity. The resultant summaries are evaluated through a user study in Section 5.

4.1 Data Set

To obtain news articles with reasonable number of comments, we crawled the top-100 most-commented news articles from Yahoo! News[3] on daily basis, from 29 Apr 2012 to 11 May 2012. After duplicate removal, our dataset has 1005 unique news articles. The preprocessing of the news articles and comments includes word stemming, removal of stopwords, removal of words appeared fewer than 3 times in the collection.

The number of comments per article is plotted in Figure 3(a). On average, each news article has 1059 comments with the minimum and maximum number of comments per article being 65 and 18,758 respectively. The total number of comments in our dataset is 1,064,655, slightly above 1 million. Plotted in Figures 3(b) and 3(c), most comments are short with fewer than 10 words. Nevertheless, the vocabulary size of comments is 66,064 while the vocabulary size of news articles is 21,533, about one-third that of comments. That is, comments often extend topics of news articles and bring additional words to the vocabulary.

[3]http://news.yahoo.com/all-sections--most-commented/most-popular/1.html

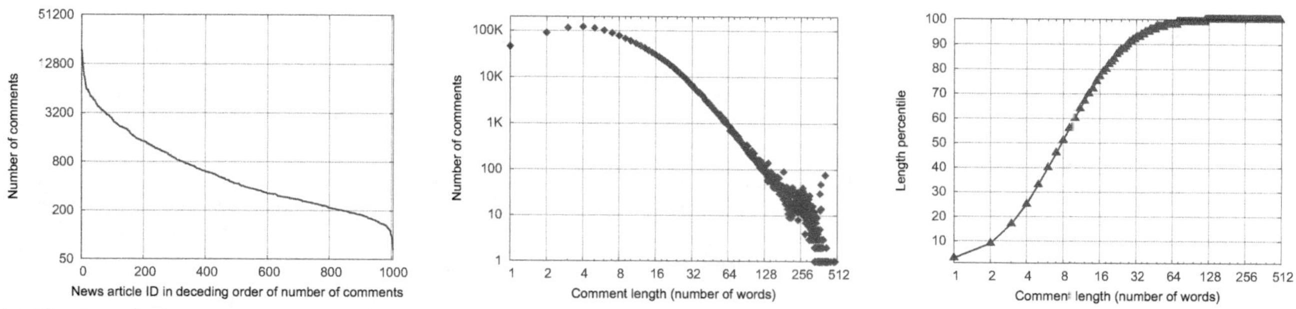

(a) Number of comments per news article (b) Comment length distribution (c) Comment length percentile

Figure 3: Comments per news article and comment length distribution

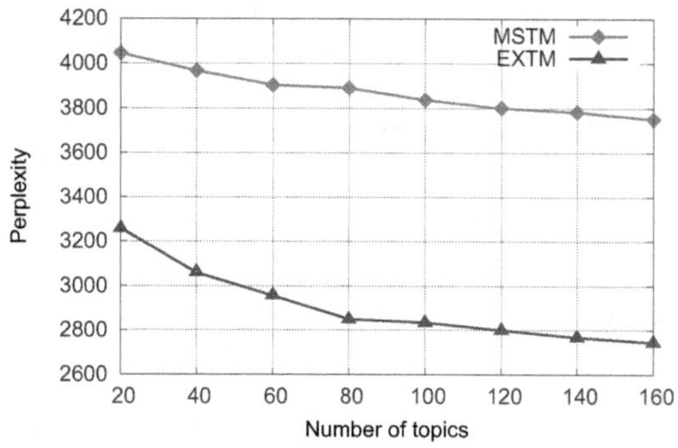

Figure 4: MSTM and EXTM with different number of topics. In MSTM, the number of topics equals the number of slave topics; in EXTM, number of topics is the sum of number of slave topics and extended topics.

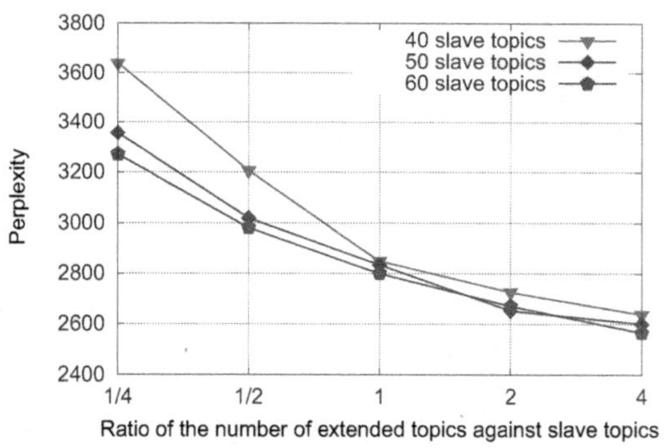

Figure 5: EXTM with different number of extended topics.

4.2 Evaluation

Because both master and slave documents in our dataset are not manually labeled, we adopt a type of density estimation – perplexity [5], which is the standard metric for evaluating topic models. It measures model ability of generalizing unseen data; lower perplexity indicates larger likelihood and better model performance. Perplexity is defined in the equation below where D_{test} indicates the set of test documents (*i.e.*, the held-out set not used in training the model), and $p(E_c^d)$ indicates the probabilities of words in slave document c of master document d.

$$Perpleixty(D_{test}) = exp\{-\frac{\sum_{d=1}^{D_{test}} \sum_{c=1}^{C_d} \log p(E_c^d)}{\sum_{d=1}^{D_{test}} \sum_{c=1}^{C_d} N_{dc}}\}$$

In many cases, topic model is sensitive to the choices of hyper-parameters. However, in our experiments, through extensive evaluations, we observe that both our MSTM and EXTM models are not very sensitive to the hyper-parameters. In our following evaluation, we fix their settings: $\alpha^m = 0.1$, $\alpha^s = 0.1$, $\beta = 0.01$, $\gamma = 0.01$, $\eta = 0.01$, $a = 0.5$ and $b = 0.5$. We calculate the perplexity of the two models using 10% held-out test set (100 documents) and the results reported are averaged over 3 runs

In general, the larger the number of topics defined, the better the generative performance for topic model. We therefore compared MSTM and EXTM by setting the same number of the topics for both models. More specifically, the number of slave topics in MSTM was the sum of the number of slave topics and number of extended topics in EXTM. Note that, in EXTM, we also set the number of slave topics same as the number of extended topics. Plotted in Figure 4, EXTM outperforms MSTM for all numbers of topics evaluated from 20 to 160. Observe that the differences in perplexities of the two models grow along the increment of number of topics. This result suggests that in EXTM, allowing words in comments to be generated from not only slave topics but also extended topics enhances the model generalization ability and guides the words of the same topic to cluster together with higher probability.

In the next set of evaluation, we evaluated the effect of setting different number of slave topics and extended topics. We fixed the number of slave topics to be 40, 50 and 60 respectively, then set the number of extended topics to be 1/4 to 4 times of slave topics. The perplexity result is plotted in Figure 5. Observe that by doubling the number of extended topics for a fixed number of slave topics (*e.g.*, 40), the perplexity drops significantly and the slope of dropping is larger when the number of extended topics is small. Differences in perplexities between curves for any two fixed number of slave topics become smaller with increasing number of extended topics. This is because there exists an inherent number of extended topics in the dataset, and setting a larger number does not benefit the model performance much.

4.3 Topic Discovery

We now present example topics discovered by EXTM. The example topics presented are generated by setting both the number of master/slave topics and number of extended topics to be 50. Due to page limit, we randomly select 8 master topics from the 50 topics derived from news articles and list their top words in the order of corresponding probabilities ($p(w|z^m)$) in Table 3 (see the second column). Observe that EXTM discovers comprehensive and distinctive master topics: Topic 10 is about presidential campaign in US; Topic 23 refers to Obama's speech on the death of Bin Laden;

Table 3: Example topical keywords for master topics and their corresponding slave topics and extended topics.

ID	Master Topic	Slave Topic	Extended Topic
0	police protest people day immigrate illegal officer report building arrest occupy law sheriff court movement	people protest occupy ows job police time movement day america street riot idiot try property	illegal law america country mexico people joe obama border immigrate sheriff enforce government job immigrant
8	job time people month add april report hire times twitter launch suggest company plan look	job america people pay union country rich class money republican worker china business middle corporation	job unemployment obama people rate look month million economy america drop unemployed create count report
9	zimmerman martin death florida prosecutor police jones charged riot website king black people murder march university	people death kill murder martin guy zimmerman life prison police justice trial crime law america	black white people sharpton zimmerman race racist riot media martin trayvon violence jackson hate kill america racial
10	romney obama campaign republican president mitt candidate presidential former politics primary voter gop democratic nominee	obama romney bush america president job republican mitt vote country policy people economy gop tax war debt money	romney obama mccain mitt palin vote president endorse pick republican running sarah guy gop john
23	afghanistan laden bin pakistan obama attack kill america president war osama release raid house death	obama bin laden bush president kill osama credit seal romney america killing terrorist war republican	obama bin bush laden america president war afghanistan troops kill iraq osama people country romney
25	church smith million god mormon fox company scout international kimmel rupert catholic belief dinner faith religion religious	god jesus sin bible christ people lord love christian homosexual believe obama gods gay life	people god religion muslim christian believe bible islam world jesus church america religious mormon hate
27	cut rate tax billion spend debt vote student percent economy loan increase million budget business	tax pay cut rich job income obama romney rate class people bush money america spend	money tax pay spend people obama government cut america dollar country debt war military billion
48	police found car told time inside officer death die investigate hit injury gun son vehicle	shot fire story bullet gun hole wife kill family shoot warning attack happen die husband	road car people driver driving kid bear happen family accident time stupid sunbathe child drive

Table 4: Least relevant extended topics derived from comments

ID	Extended topic keywords
20	animal wild cheetah people attack pet cat pictures taking tame human stupid try maul play
11	ticket trash threw judge money lottery woman store winner found lady throw winning claim sign
15	family god bless parent little prayer heart avery love life sad story time hope pray
4	kid school parent bully child girl people children little time grade sexual teacher suspend home
6	girl scout boys play women team priest school bishop little people bar rape boy own
47	eat shrimp food kfc people chicken china baby asia chip time tiger fast america fry
24	yahoo story article comment news read people post time report reading articles picture video headline
13	movie bond character avenge love movies people film animal inmate craig james watch prison time

Topic 27 is on tax policy and Topic 48 focuses on car accident. All these master topics are related to hot events during the crawling period. This result suggests that EXTM can mine semantically meaningful and distinctive master topics from news articles.

To illustrate the relationship between the master topics, slave topics, and extended topics. Columns 3 and 4 in Table 3 report the most relevant[4] slave topic and extended topic for the 8 selected master topics. Comparing master topics and their corresponding slave topics and extended topics, we observe that EXTM model captures strong relationships between the three types of topics. Consider master topics and slave topics first. The table shows that master topics and their corresponding slave topics share a large number of common keywords. For instance, both master and slave topics for Topic 10 are about presidential campaign; that for Topic 23 are about the death of Bin Laden. Recall that the size of slave document vocabulary is three times of the size of master document vocabulary. This result suggests the generative process of slave documents is under control of that of master documents to a large extent. Now we consider the extended topics. Recall that extended topics can be considered as extensions of master topics from another perspectives. Take Topic 9 as an example, both master and slave topics are closely related to the event itself[5] while the extended topic captures the discussion on alleged race issues (*e.g.*, black, white, race, racist, and racial). Similarly, the extended topic associated with Topic 8 concentrates more on unemployment when talking about job issue.

To further illustrate that some extended topics are not specific to any particular news article, in Table 4, we list the 8 extended topics which are least relevant to master topics. Observe that most these 8 topics are casual discussions and not specific to some events happened during the crawling period. In particular, Topic 24 is about Yahoo! News in general (*e.g.*, the selection of its news articles and the quality of services); Topic 15 is more on reader sentiment on news stories.

5. USER STUDY

In this section, we report our user study on the evaluation of the summaries generated by the proposed methods. Document sum-

[4]The topic relevance is determined by cosine similarity over the word-feature-vector based on the multinomial distributions of the words for topics.

[5]http://en.wikipedia.org/wiki/Shooting_of_Trayvon_Martin

marization is commonly evaluated against a ground truth summary (*e.g.*, a human generated summary or a set of manually-labeled sentences). In our setting, however, generating such ground-truth labeling becomes extremely difficult because of the large number of comments to each news article (*i.e.*, on average 1059 comments per news article). Moreover, *topic* is not predefined making it even harder to manually label the comments. We therefore choose to evaluate the summaries generated by the different methods for a subset of news articles.

Methods. By applying 3 clustering methods CLUTO, MSTM and EXTM and 2 ranking methods RL and MMR, we evaluated 6 methods in total.

We evaluated CLUTO[6] as an alternative method without using topic modeling. The bisecting clustering algorithm (with default parameter settings) provided by CLUTO was used to cluster comments of a news article due to its high efficiency and promising performance. The number of clusters was set to 50. Note that bisecting clustering was applied independently on slave documents of each master document. We use CLUTO-MMR and CLUTO-RL to denote the comment summaries selected by MMR and RL respectively, based on the clusters generated by CLUTO. Note that we used $TF \times IDF$ based word weighting scheme to define the comment feature vectors in CLUTO-MMR due to the lack of word topic weights.

For the two topic models MSTM and EXTM, the comments are clustered based on the topics discovered by the corresponding model. The number of topics for MSTM was set to 100. Correspondingly, we set the number of slave topics to be 50 and the number of extended topics to be 50 for EXTM. Similarly, we use postfixes -MMR and -RL to distinguish the MMR and RL comment selection method.

Evaluation Setting and Criteria. We randomly selected 50 articles from the 1005 news articles for user evaluation. To make the manual evaluation feasible, we fixed the number of comments selected in a comment summary to be 15 for any given article. More specifically, given all comments of a news article, a summarization method first selects the top-3 largest clusters (by number of comments) to represent the 3 major topics discovered from the comments. From each cluster, 5 most representative comments are selected to represent that topic. In short, a comment summary for a news article contains exactly 15 comments covering 3 major topics, by any of the 6 methods. To evaluate the 6 methods, a volunteer therefore needs to read $50 \times 15 \times 6 = 4500$ comments in total.

For each comment summary generated by a method, a volunteer gives a rating from 1 (lowest) to 5 (highest) to each of the following three criteria used in our evaluation.

- *Topic cohesion*: To what extent the 5 comments in each comment cluster are topically cohesive.
- *Topic diversity*: To what extent the 3 topic clusters cover 3 different topics.
- *News relatedness*: To what extent the 3 topic clusters are related to the content of the news article.

Evaluation Results. The ratings from three volunteers (undergraduate students in computer science major) are averaged by the method producing the comment summary, reported in Figure 6. In addition to each of the three criteria, we also report the average rating across the three criteria in the last column of the bar chart. We make three observations.

[6] http://glaros.dtc.umn.edu/gkhome/views/cluto

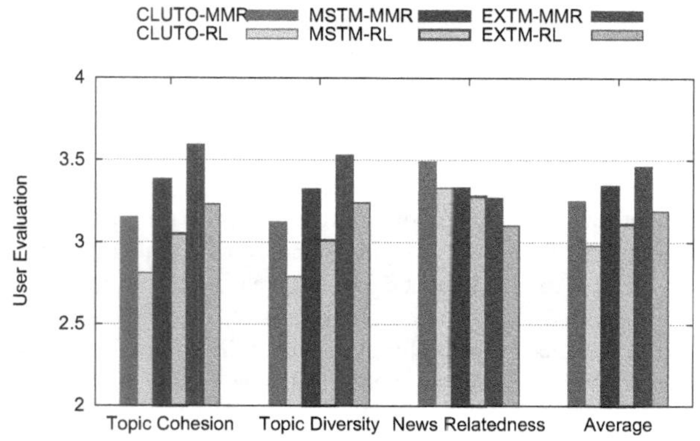

Figure 6: User Evaluation

First, across all three clustering methods, MMR ranking outperforms RL ranking. A possible reason is that RL suffers from rating sparsity and its resultant ranking by length is biased to long (and maybe even redundant) comments, which hurts topic cohesion and topic diversity. Conversely, MMR tries to select comments that are closest to the centroid of a comment cluster but with different word distributions (due to its redundancy control). In particular, EXTM-MMR yields the best topic cohesion rating of 3.59 and the best topic diversity rating of 3.52. It outperforms CLUTO-MMR by 14% on topic cohesion and by 13% on topic diversity, respectively.

Second, we observe that comparing with traditional clustering approach CLUTO, topic model based methods are more likely to generate clusters with better intra-cohesive and inter-diverse topics. However, CLUTO based methods yield the best news relatedness. This is because that CLUTO is independently applied on the comments of every news article. The clustering is therefore not affected by any additional (or contextual) information provided in other news articles/comments. Both MSTM and EXTM based methods capture such contextual information by definition. Nevertheless, such contextual information may not be known to our volunteers due to the random selection of the news articles for evaluation; hence the news relatedness of topic model based methods are rated lower.

Third, between MSTM and EXTM, EXTM-based methods outperform MSTM-based methods on topic cohesion and topic diversity, but are slightly poorer on news relatedness. The latter is probably because EXTM discovers extended topics discussed among comments only, but not in news articles. Considering all evaluation criteria of equally importance (*i.e.*, the average of the three), EXTM-MMR is the best performing method among the 6 methods evaluated.

6. CONCLUSION

In this paper, we first define the topic-driven reader comments summarization problem. The main objective of the research is to present to users a summary of comments covering the major topics discussed among the readers. After analyzing the important relationships between news and comments, we propose two generative models, namely, Master-Slave Topic Model and Extended Master-Slave Topic Model respectively, to implicitly model these relationships. Both models treat news article as master document and comment slave document and assume each slave document has exactly one topic. While MSTM constrains that the topic of a slave document has to be derived from its master document, EXTM allows the topic of a slave document derived from all slave documents. Evaluated using perplexity, in our experiments EXTM significantly outperforms MSTM for grouping comments with the same topics. To generate the comment summary, we utilize two comment ranking schemes MMR and RL to select the most representative comments from each comment cluster. Our user study shows that EXTM-MMR outperforms the other 5 methods by topic-cohesion and topic-diversity measures.

Both our proposed models ignore the reply relationship among comments which provides rich structure information about comments. In our future work, we plan to incorporate reply relationship in our models to take advantage of the rich structural information in comments. We also observe that the topics discovered might be affected by some extremely long comments. To improve our model for better handling long comments is also part of our future work.

7. REFERENCES

[1] J. Allan, editor. *Topic detection and tracking*. Kluwer Academic Publishers, 2002.

[2] D. M. Blei and M. I. Jordan. Modeling annotated data. In *SIGIR*, pages 127–134, 2003.

[3] D. M. Blei and J. D. Lafferty. Dynamic topic models. In *ICML*, 2006.

[4] D. M. Blei and J. D. Lafferty. A correlated topic model of science. *AAS*, 1(1):17–35, 2007.

[5] D. M. Blei, A. Y. Ng, and M. I. Jordan. Latent dirichlet allocation. *J. Mach. Learn. Res.*, 3:993–1022, 2003.

[6] M. Bundschus, S. Yu, V. Tresp, A. Rettinger, M. Dejori, and H.-P. Kriegel. Hierarchical bayesian models for collaborative tagging systems. In *ICDM*, pages 728–733, 2009.

[7] J. Carbonell and J. Goldstein. The use of MMR, diversity-based reranking for reordering documents and producing summaries. In *SIGIR*, pages 335–336, 1998.

[8] C. Carpineto, S. Osiński, G. Romano, and D. Weiss. A survey of web clustering engines. *ACM Comput. Surv.*, 41(3):17:1–17:38, 2009.

[9] M. Chen, X. Jin, and D. Shen. Short text classification improved by learning multi-granularity topics. In *IJCAI*, pages 1776–1781, 2011.

[10] O. Dalal, S. H. Sengemedu, and S. Sanyal. Multi-objective ranking of comments on web. In *WWW*, pages 419–428, 2012.

[11] K. Dave, S. Lawrence, and D. M. Pennock. Mining the peanut gallery: opinion extraction and semantic classification of product reviews. In *WWW*, pages 519–528, 2003.

[12] T. L. Griffiths and M. Steyvers. Finding scientific topics. *PNAS*, 101(suppl. 1):5228–5235, 2004.

[13] C.-F. Hsu, E. Khabiri, and J. Caverlee. Ranking comments on the social web. In *Proc. Int'l Conf. on Computational Science and Engineering (Vol. 04)*, pages 90–97, 2009.

[14] M. Hu, A. Sun, and E.-P. Lim. Comments-oriented document summarization: understanding documents with readers' feedback. In *SIGIR*, pages 291–298, 2008.

[15] X. Hu, N. Sun, C. Zhang, and T.-S. Chua. Exploiting internal and external semantics for the clustering of short texts using world knowledge. In *CIKM*, pages 919–928. ACM, 2009.

[16] R. Jain and P. Sinha. Content without context is meaningless. In *ACM Multimedia*, pages 1259–1268, 2010.

[17] O. Jin, N. N. Liu, K. Zhao, Y. Yu, and Q. Yang. Transferring topical knowledge from auxiliary long texts for short text clustering. In *CIKM*, pages 775–784, 2011.

[18] Y. Jo and A. H. Oh. Aspect and sentiment unification model for online review analysis. In *WSDM*, pages 815–824, 2011.

[19] R. Kant, S. H. Sengamedu, and K. S. Kumar. Comment spam detection by sequence mining. In *WSDM*, pages 183–192, 2012.

[20] E. Khabiri, J. Caverlee, and C.-F. Hsu. Summarizing user-contributed comments. In *ICWSM*, 2011.

[21] E. Khabiri, C.-F. Hsu, and J. Caverlee. Analyzing and predicting community preference of socially generated metadata: A case study on comments in the digg community. In *ICWSM*, 2009.

[22] C. Lin and Y. He. Joint sentiment/topic model for sentiment analysis. In *CIKM*, pages 375–384, 2009.

[23] C. Lu, X. Hu, X. Chen, J.-R. Park, T. He, and Z. Li. The topic-perspective model for social tagging systems. In *KDD*, pages 683–692, 2010.

[24] C. Marlow, M. Naaman, D. Boyd, and M. Davis. Ht06, tagging paper, taxonomy, flickr, academic article, to read. In *ACM HyperText'06*, pages 31–40, 2006.

[25] Q. Mei, D. Cai, D. Zhang, and C. Zhai. Topic modeling with network regularization. In *WWW*, pages 101–110, 2008.

[26] G. Mishne and N. Glance. Leave a reply: An analysis of weblog comments. In *In Third annual workshop on the Weblogging ecosystem*, 2006.

[27] X. H. Phan, M. L. Nguyen, and S. Horiguchi. Learning to classify short and sparse text & web with hidden topics from large-scale data collections. In *WWW*, pages 91–100. ACM, 2008.

[28] M. Rosen-Zvi, T. Griffiths, M. Steyvers, and P. Smyth. The author-topic model for authors and documents. In *UAI*, pages 487–494. AUAI Press, 2004.

[29] M. Sahami and T. D. Heilman. A web-based kernel function for measuring the similarity of short text snippets. In *WWW*, pages 377–386, 2006.

[30] J. San Pedro, T. Yeh, and N. Oliver. Leveraging user comments for aesthetic aware image search reranking. In *WWW*, pages 439–448, 2012.

[31] U. Scaiella, P. Ferragina, A. Marino, and M. Ciaramita. Topical clustering of search results. In *WSDM*, pages 223–232, 2012.

[32] A. Schuth, M. Marx, and M. de Rijke. Extracting the discussion structure in comments on news-articles. In *WIDM*, pages 97–104, 2007.

[33] E. Shmueli, A. Kagian, Y. Koren, and R. Lempel. Care to comment?: recommendations for commenting on news stories. In *WWW*, pages 429–438, 2012.

[34] S. Siersdorfer, S. Chelaru, W. Nejdl, and J. San Pedro. How useful are your comments?: analyzing and predicting youtube comments and comment ratings. In *WWW*, pages 891–900, 2010.

[35] I. Titov and R. McDonald. Modeling online reviews with multi-grain topic models. In *WWW*, pages 111–120, 2008.

[36] M. Tsagkias, W. Weerkamp, and M. de Rijke. Predicting the volume of comments on online news stories. In *CIKM*, pages 1765–1768, 2009.

[37] H. Wang, Y. Lu, and C. Zhai. Latent aspect rating analysis on review text data: a rating regression approach. In *KDD*, pages 783–792, 2010.

[38] W. G. Yee, A. Yates, S. Liu, and O. Frieder. Are web user comments useful for search. In *Workshop on Large-Scale Distributed Systems for Information Retrieval (LSDS-IR) at SIGIR'09*, pages 63–70, 2009.

Visualizing Timelines: Evolutionary Summarization via Iterative Reinforcement between Text and Image Streams

Rui Yan [‡,†]
[†]Dept. of Computer Science and Information Engineering
National Taiwan University
Taipei 10617, Taiwan
r.yan@pku.edu.cn

Xiaojun Wan
Institute of Computer Science and Technology
Peking University
Beijing 100871, P. R. China
wanxiaojun@pku.edu.cn

Mirella Lapata
Institute for Language, Cognition and Computation
University of Edinburgh
Edinburgh EH8 9AB, UK
mlap@inf.ed.ac.uk

Wayne Xin Zhao
[‡]Dept. of Computer Science and Technology
Peking University
Beijing 100871, P. R. China
zhaoxin@net.pku.edu.cn

Pu-Jen Cheng
Dept. of Computer Science and Information Engineering
National Taiwan University
Taipei 10617, Taiwan
pjcheng@csie.ntu.edu.tw

Xiaoming Li [♮,‡]
[♮]State Key Lab of Virtual Reality Tech. and Systems
Beihang University
Beijing 100083, P. R. China
lxm@pku.edu.cn

ABSTRACT

We present a novel graph-based framework for timeline summarization, the task of creating different summaries for different timestamps but for the same topic. Our work extends timeline summarization to a multimodal setting and creates timelines that are both textual and visual. Our approach exploits the fact that news documents are often accompanied by pictures and the two share some common content. Our model optimizes local summary creation and global timeline generation jointly following an iterative approach based on mutual reinforcement and co-ranking. In our algorithm, individual summaries are generated by taking into account the mutual dependencies between sentences and images, and are iteratively refined by considering how they contribute to the global timeline and its coherence. Experiments on real-world datasets show that the timelines produced by our model outperform several competitive baselines both in terms of ROUGE and when assessed by human evaluators.

Categories and Subject Descriptors

H.3.1 [**Information Storage and Retrieval**]: Content Analysis and Indexing—*Abstracting methods*; I.4.9 [**Image Processing and Computer Vision**]: Application

General Terms

Algorithms, Experimentation, Performance

Keywords

Evolutionary summarization, iterative reinforcement, visual timeline, text-to-image translation

CIKM'12, October 29–November 2, 2012, Maui, HI, USA.

1. INTRODUCTION

With the rapidly growing amounts of information now being available over the Internet, it is becoming increasingly important to develop improved computer-based methods for document access, filtering, and content extraction. Document summarization is one of the oldest applications of information gathering. A summary can be loosely defined as a text that is derived from one or more original texts, conveys the most important information in them, and is substantially shorter in length.

Of the many types of summaries that have been identified over the years (see [20] and [16] for comprehensive overviews), perhaps the most important distinctions concern whether the summary is being created over a *single* or *multiple* documents, whether it is an *extract* (portions of the original text appear in the summary verbatim) or an *abstract* (the extracted content is reformulated in novel terms), and whether it is *indicative* (it merely provides an indication of the subject matter of the input text) or *informative* (it is a shortened version of the content of the original one).

In this paper we address a relatively new summarization task, namely *timeline summarization*. The idea behind timeline summarization is to capture how a news topic evolves over time. Timelines consist of several component summaries that are linked to different timestamps. Each component summary provides a *local view* on the news story for a specific point in time, whereas the timeline provides a *global view* on the development of the story across time. Timeline summarization is related to but different from update summarization [25]. Update summaries focus on what is new relative to a previous body of information, whereas timelines involve not a single but several steps of updates. Both tasks produce multi-document, typically extractive, summaries for a set of articles on the same topic.

Our work extends timeline summarization to a multimodal setting. Most online news articles contain images whose role is to complement or emphasize what is described in the text. An example is shown in Table 1; the article describes a devastating earthquake in Japan and the picture accentuates the extent of damage it caused. We argue that incorporating visual information into timelines is desirable for several reasons. Firstly, images will supplement the textual summaries by providing additional information. Secondly, visual timelines can be seen as an extreme form of summarizing the content of very large document collections. Users need not read the textual summaries; instead, they can only look at the images to get an impression of how a story developed over time. Thirdly, by exploiting the natural dependence between articles and their images during modeling, it is possible to improve the output of the textual summaries as the images provide cues about important content.

Our approach exploits the fact that news documents are often accompanied by pictures and the two share some common content. Our summarization model formalizes the following intuitions. Component summaries must capture *local* importance in relation to specific timestamps (e.g., corresponding to specific dates). They consist of two heterogeneous streams, i.e., images and text which are correlated and thematically matched. Component summaries must combine to create a *globally* coherent timeline across timestamps. Our model optimizes local summary creation and global timeline generation jointly following an iterative approach based on mutual reinforcement and co-ranking (see Figure 1 for an illustration). Our algorithm operates over sentences and images whose dependencies are captured in a heterogeneous network consisting of three types of graphs. One graph represents how individual sentences (and analogously images) relate to each other, a bipartite graph represents how sentences relate to images, and a third graph captures global dependencies between local sentences (and images) and the timeline created at each time step. The main idea behind co-ranking is that there is a mutually reinforcing relationship between sentences and images which influences their ranking and whether they should be included in the timeline or not.

An important component of the framework sketched above is to be able to express and quantify the meaning shared between images and the documents that contain them. With the help of image annotation techniques [6, 7, 8], we create a translation model that bridges the gap between textual and visual information. We preprocess images so that they resemble word-like units and define a probabilistic model that translates a visual word into a textual word and vice versa.

Experiments on real-world datasets show that the timelines generated by our model outperform several competitive baselines both in terms of ROUGE and when assessed by humans. Interestingly, our results also indicate that the model selects images and sentences that are thematically related and that the visual information helps create better textual summaries in addition to improving the timelines altogether. The remainder of this paper is structured as follows. In Section 2 we present an overview of previous work and then move on to formalize our summarization model (Section 3). We describe our experimental setup in Section 4 and present our results in Section 5. Section 6 concludes the paper.

2. RELATED WORK

Most work to date focuses on extractive summarization. The idea is to create a summary automatically simply by identifying and subsequently concatenating the most important sentences in a document. The approach is robust (it can be easily ported to different languages and domains) and produces grammatical output. One of the most popular extractive methods that have been proposed for multi-document summarization is centroid-based. It operates on a document collection with a common subject. A cluster centroid is built representing the most important words from the whole collection. The centroid is then used to determine which sentences from the individual documents are most representative of the collection. MEAD [19] is a publicly available implementation of this approach. NeATS [11] adds topic signatures and term clustering to sentence selection. Both MEAD and NeATS use MMR [9] to remove redundancy. Information based on themes in documents has been also used for sentence selection [22, 26].

A massive earthquake has hit off north-east of Japan today, triggering a tsunami that has caused extensive damage. Japan's TV

showed cars, ships and even buildings being swept away in the Fukushima prefecture, after the 8.9 magnitude earthquake.

Officials said a wave as high as 6 m (20 ft) could strike the coast. The quake struck about 250 miles (400km) from Tokyo at a depth of 20 miles, shaking buildings in the capital for several minutes.

Table 1: An excerpt of a news report from the BBC website and its accompanying image.

More recently, graph-based methods have been proposed to rank sentences based on "votes" or "recommendations" between them. TextRank [17] and LexPageRank [5] use algorithms similar to PageRank and HITS to compute sentence importance. These methods first construct a graph representing the relationships between sentences and then evaluate their importance or salience based on the topology of the graph. Wan et al. [23, 22] present an improved graph-ranking algorithm which differentiates *intra-* and *inter-*document linkage between sentences [24] and incorporates topic cluster information in manifold-ranking.

A few methods have been developed specifically for timeline summarization For example, Swan et al. [21] construct timelines by extracting clusters of noun phrases and named entities. Later they build a system to provide timelines which consist of one sentence per date, based on their usefulness and novelty. Chieu et al. [3] present a system that extracts events (i.e., sentences) relevant to a query from a collection of documents and places such events along a timeline. Events are considered important if they are widely cited in many documents for a period of time. Yan et al. [27, 28] improve timeline summarization by modeling the evolutionary nature of news articles. Specifically, they model correlations among component summaries using inter-date and intra-date sentence dependencies.

To the best of our knowledge, the use of visual information in timeline summarization is unexplored in previous work. We propose a novel framework for this task which is based on iterative reinforcement: text-to-image correlations and local-to-global dependencies are taken into account simultaneously in order to create component summaries which are locally informative and globally coherent.

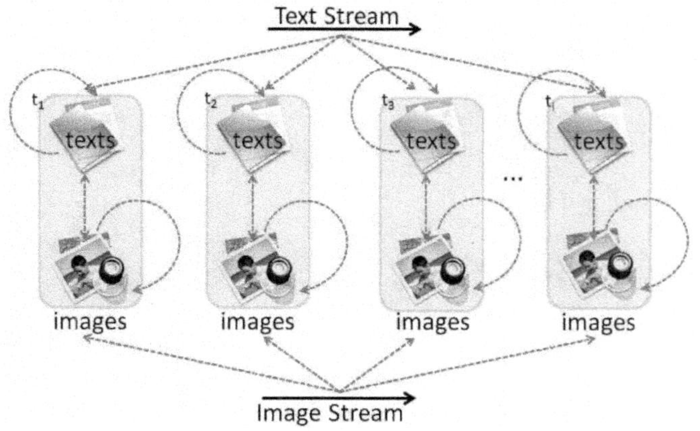

Figure 1: Iterative reinforcement for VTS. Shaded areas denote texts and images published on the same date; arrows between them indicate mutual reinforcement.

3. PROBLEM FORMULATION

The input to our visual timeline summarizer consists of a document collection C relating to a specific news subject (e.g., an earthquake or a disease). C is partitioned into sentences S and images M, i.e., $C{=}\{S, M\}$. Each sentence $s \in S$ and each image $m \in M$ is associated with a timestamp, i.e., the published date of the source document where the sentence and image appeared. The sentence collection S is further partitioned into $S{=}\{S_1, S_2, \ldots, S_{|T|}\}$, according to timestamps $T{=}\{t_1, t_2, \ldots, t_{|T|}\}$. Analogously, the image collection M is partitioned into $M{=}\{M_1, M_2, \ldots, M_{|T|}\}$. Let $C_i{=}\{S_i, M_i\}$ denote the collection consisting of sentence set S_i and image set M_i published on the same date t_i.[1] The output of our system is a series of individual but correlated component summaries $I{=}\{I_1, I_2, \ldots, I_{|T|}\}$. Each component $I_i{=}\{I_{s_i}, I_{m_i}\}$ on t_i is a subset of C_i, ($I_i \subseteq C_i$) with I_{s_i} being extracted from S_i ($I_{s_i} \subseteq S_i$) and I_{m_i} from M_i ($I_{m_i} \subseteq M_i$), respectively.

We conceptualize VTS in terms of three components, namely sentence selection, image selection, and sentence-to-image matching. Rather than optimizing each component in isolation, we introduce a global framework that performs the optimization task jointly, and thus exploits inter- and intra-component dependencies. For example, ranking individual sentences depends on image selection, and the selection of images should also relate to the sentence ranking.

We propose an iterative reinforcement framework for *co-ranking* sentences and images. The framework is illustrated in Figure 1 and formalized in Section 3.1. As can be seen, sentences and images (and their ranking) are coupled together and dependent on each other.

3.1 Iterative Reinforcement Framework

The mutual reinforcement chain shown in Figure 1 captures the following intuitions behind the VTS problem. A *local sentence* is important if (1) it associates to other important local sentences; (2) it associates to important *local images*; and (3) associates to other important sentences selected for neighboring timestamps (we refer to these as *global neighbors* of sentences). Analogously, a *local image* is important if (1) it associates to other important local images; (2) it associates to important *local sentences*; and (3) associates to important images selected for neighboring timestamps (called *global neighbors* of images).

[1] We use day-based timestamps [1, 3, 28, 27].

For each timestamp $t{\in}T$ we aim to find the most important or salient local sentences I_{s_t} and the most important local images I_{m_t}, so that they semantically related. Selected sentences should explain the images and selected images ought to depict some of the sentences' content. We derive the ranking of local sentences and local images *iteratively* from the mutual reinforcement chain across different timestamps. To simplify notation, we remove the subscript t from all local component choices when there is no ambiguity. We use two vectors $\mathbf{s}{=}[\pi(s_i)]_{1\times|\mathbf{s}|}$ and $\mathbf{m}{=}[\pi(m_i)]_{1\times|\mathbf{m}|}$ to denote the saliency scores $\pi(.)$ of local sentences and local images from timestamp t. We use vectors $\mathbf{u}{=}[\phi(s_i)]_{1\times|I_s|}$ and $\mathbf{v}{=}[\phi(m_i)]_{1\times|I_m|}$ to denote the candidate sentences and images in each iteration; the discrimination function $\phi(.)$ records the saliency scores of candidate sentences (and images) that are *selected* for timelines (see Equation (4)).

We use an adjacency matrix $[\hat{U}]_{|\mathbf{s}|\times|\mathbf{s}|}$ to represent the *homogeneous affinity* between local sentences, and matrix $[\bar{U}]_{|\mathbf{m}|\times|\mathbf{m}|}$ to describe the affinity between local images.

$$\mathbf{s} \propto \hat{U}^T\mathbf{s}, \qquad \mathbf{m} \propto \bar{U}^T\mathbf{m} \tag{1}$$

We use adjacency matrix $[\hat{W}]_{|\mathbf{s}|\times|\mathbf{m}|}$ to capture the local *heterogeneous affinity* between sentences and images; analogously matrix $[\bar{W}]_{|\mathbf{m}|\times|\mathbf{s}|}$ represents the heterogeneous affinity between images and sentences.

$$\mathbf{s} \propto \hat{W}^T\mathbf{m}, \qquad \mathbf{m} \propto \bar{W}^T\mathbf{s} \tag{2}$$

We use two matrices to represent neighboring sentences and images that are globally salient. Let $[\hat{N}]_{|\mathbf{s}|\times|I_s|}$ denote global neighboring sentences and $[\bar{N}]_{|\mathbf{m}|\times|I_m|}$ global neighboring images.

$$\mathbf{s} \propto \hat{N}^T\mathbf{u}, \qquad \mathbf{m} \propto \bar{N}^T\mathbf{v} \tag{3}$$

Elements $u_i{=}\phi(s_i)$ and $v_j{=}\phi(m_i)$ indicate saliency scores retained in vectors **u**, **v**; this is the case for sentences or images that are selected as summary candidates:

$$u_i = \begin{cases} \pi(s_i) & \text{if } s_i \in I_s \\ 0 & \text{otherwise} \end{cases}, \quad v_j = \begin{cases} \pi(m_j) & \text{if } m_j \in I_m \\ 0 & \text{otherwise} \end{cases} \tag{4}$$

We are now ready to formulate our iterative procedure for text-to-image co-ranking. The following two steps are used to select sentences and their corresponding images until convergence. We initialize the algorithm by setting the the saliency scores for all sentences and images to 1:

Step 1: compute the saliency scores of local sentences, and then normalize using ℓ-1 norm.

$$\begin{aligned} \mathbf{s}^{(n+1,k)} &= \alpha\hat{U}^T\mathbf{s}^{(n,k)} + \beta\hat{W}^T\mathbf{m}^{(n,k)} + \gamma\hat{N}^T\mathbf{u}^{(0,k-1)} \\ \mathbf{s}^{(n,k)} &= \mathbf{s}^{(n,k)}/||\mathbf{s}^{(n,k)}||_1 \end{aligned} \tag{5}$$

Step 2: compute the saliency scores of local images, and then normalize in ℓ-1 norm.

$$\begin{aligned} \mathbf{m}^{(n+1,k)} &= \alpha\bar{U}^T\mathbf{m}^{(n,k)} + \beta\bar{W}^T\mathbf{s}^{(n,k)} + \gamma\bar{N}^T\mathbf{v}^{(0,k-1)} \\ \mathbf{m}^{(n,k)} &= \mathbf{m}^{(n,k)}/||\mathbf{m}^{(n,k)}||_1 \end{aligned} \tag{6}$$

Parameters α, β and γ specify the relative contributions to the final saliency scores from 1) the affinity between homogeneous local sentences (and analogously images), 2) the affinity between heterogeneous local sentences and images, and 3) the affinity from homogeneous global salient nodes. For simplicity, we let $\alpha{+}\beta{+}\gamma{=}1$. In

Algorithm 1 Local Text-Image Reinforced Co-Ranking

1: **procedure** L-CoRank($\mathbf{u}$,$\mathbf{v}$)
2: calculate $\hat{U}, \bar{U}, \hat{W}, \bar{W}, \hat{N}, \bar{N}$
3: n←0, initialize $\mathbf{s}$, $\mathbf{m}$
4: **repeat**
5: $\mathbf{s}' \leftarrow \mathbf{s}$, $\mathbf{m}' \leftarrow \mathbf{m}$
6: $\mathbf{s} \leftarrow \alpha\hat{U}^T\mathbf{s}' + \beta\hat{W}^T\mathbf{m}' + \gamma\hat{N}^T\mathbf{u}$
7: $\mathbf{m} \leftarrow \alpha\bar{U}^T\mathbf{m}' + \beta\bar{W}^T\mathbf{s}' + \gamma\bar{N}^T\mathbf{v}$
8: $\mathbf{s} \leftarrow \mathbf{s}/||\mathbf{s}||$, $\mathbf{m} \leftarrow \mathbf{m}/||\mathbf{m}||$
9:

$$\nabla_L \leftarrow \max\begin{pmatrix}||\mathbf{s}-\mathbf{s}'||\\ ||\mathbf{m}-\mathbf{m}'||\end{pmatrix}$$

10: n← n+1
11: **until** $\nabla_L < \epsilon$
12: choose top ranked sentences/images by $\mathbf{s}$ and $\mathbf{m}$
13: *// update the saliency scores of local sentences/images*
14: $\mathbf{u}' \leftarrow$ UPDATE($\mathbf{u}$)
15: $\mathbf{v}' \leftarrow$ UPDATE($\mathbf{v}$)
16: **return** $\mathbf{u}'$,$\mathbf{v}'$
17: **end procedure**
18:
19: **function** UPDATE($\mathbf{x}$)
20: **for all** $x_i \in \mathbf{x}$ **do**
21: **if** $x_i \in I$ **then**
22: *// highly-ranked ones are chosen as candidates*
23: $x_i \leftarrow x_i$
24: **else**
25: $x_i \leftarrow 0$
26: **end if**
27: **end for**
28: **end function**

Algorithm 2 Visual Timeline Summarization

1: k←0, initialize $\mathbf{u}$, $\mathbf{v}$
2: **repeat**
3: $\mathbf{u}' \leftarrow \mathbf{u}$, $\mathbf{v}' \leftarrow \mathbf{v}$
4: **for** $t \leftarrow 1$ to |T| **do**
5: ($\mathbf{u}$, $\mathbf{v}$) ← L-CoRank($\mathbf{u}'$,$\mathbf{v}'$)
6: **end for**
7: $\mathbf{u} \leftarrow \mathbf{u}/||\mathbf{u}||$, $\mathbf{v} \leftarrow \mathbf{v}/||\mathbf{v}||$
8:

$$\nabla_G \leftarrow \max\begin{pmatrix}||\mathbf{u}-\mathbf{u}'||\\ ||\mathbf{v}-\mathbf{v}'||\end{pmatrix}$$

9: k← k+1
10: **until** $\nabla_G < \epsilon$
11: OUTPUT($\mathbf{u}$,$\mathbf{v}$) *// output non-zero elements as summaries*
12:
13: **function** OUTPUT($\mathbf{x}$)
14: **for all** $x_i \in \mathbf{x}$ **do**
15: **if** x_i >0 **then**
16: select x_i into timeline
17: **end if**
18: **end for**
19: **end function**

order to guarantee the convergence of the iterative form, we must force the transition matrix to be stochastic and irreducible. To this end, we must make the **s** and **m** *column stochastic* [10]. We therefore normalize **s** and **m** after each iteration in Equations (5) and (6).

When all component summaries are generated, **u** and **v** are updated and the algorithm returns to Step 1 and the same procedure is repeated until convergence. Note that n and k are different iteration indicators. n controls the iteration towards convergence among local sentences/images (see Algorithm 1). k controls the iteration towards global convergence at the timeline level, shown in Algorithm 2. Empirically, the algorithm converges when the difference between the scores computed at two successive iterations for any sentences/images falls below a small threshold ϵ (set to 0.001 in this study).

The framework just described critically explores the relationship between elements within the same modality and across modalities. In order to capture which images correspond to which summaries and vice versa we need some means of translating between visual and textual information. In the following, we explain how we model text-to-image correspondences and then move on to describe the estimation of our affinity matrices.

3.2 Text-to-Image Translation

Texts and images represent distinct modalities. Images live in a continuous feature space, whereas words are discrete. We follow previous work [6, 2, 4] in converting the visual features from a continuous onto a discrete space, thereby rendering image features more like word units. In order to do this, we use the Scale Invariant Feature Transform (SIFT) algorithm [13]. The general idea behind the algorithm is to identify local image regions using a difference-of-Gaussians point detector. Importantly, this detector is, to some extent, invariant to to small shifts in position, changes in illumination, noise, and viewpoint and can be used to perform reliable matching between different views of an object or scene. Each detected region is represented with a SIFT descriptor which is a histogram of edge directions at different locations. We further quantize the SIFT descriptors using the K-means clustering algorithm to obtain a discrete set of visual words which form our visual vocabulary. Each entry in this vocabulary stands for a group of image regions which are similar in content or appearance and assumed to originate from similar objects. Formally, each image is expressed in a bag-of-visual-words format vector, $[w_{v_1}, w_{v_2}, ..., w_{v_L}]$.

Both visual and textual modalities are represented as a bag-of-units, i.e., a vector of textual or visual terms. Given this representation, we can then define a translation model between the two modalities under the assumption that they express related concepts. Our model defines the probability of translating a textual word into a visual word and vice versa. We learn image-to-text correspondences from training data consisting of documents and the images embedded in them. In this work, we make use of news articles which are often accompanied with images illustrating events, objects or people mentioned in the text.

Let images m denote a set of visual words m={w_v}, and texts s denote words w. Let Ψ={m, s} denote a training pair consisting of a document and its corresponding image. The translation model can be estimated by maximizing the likelihood of images given their surrounding texts:

$$w_v^* = \operatorname*{argmax}_{w_v} \prod_{\{m,s\}\in\Psi} \Pr(m|s,w) \tag{7}$$

Although we could use EM to estimate Equation (7), we approximate it heuristically with a simpler form which is considerably more efficient to compute [14]:

Gaussian kernel

$$\Gamma(\Delta t) = \exp[\frac{-\Delta t^2}{2\sigma^2}]$$

Triangle kernel

$$\Gamma(\Delta t) = \begin{cases} 1 - \frac{\Delta t}{\sigma} & \text{if } \Delta t \leq \sigma \\ 0 & \text{otherwise} \end{cases}$$

Window kernel

$$\Gamma(\Delta t) = \begin{cases} 1 & \text{if } \Delta t \leq \sigma \\ 0 & \text{otherwise} \end{cases}$$

Circle kernel

$$\Gamma(\Delta t) = \begin{cases} \sqrt{1 - (\frac{\Delta t}{\sigma})^2} & \text{if } \Delta t \leq \sigma \\ 0 & \text{otherwise} \end{cases}$$

Cosine (Hamming) kernel

$$\Gamma(\Delta t) = \begin{cases} \frac{1}{2}[1 + \cos(\frac{\Delta t \cdot \pi}{\sigma})] & \text{if } \Delta t \leq \sigma \\ 0 & \text{otherwise} \end{cases}$$

Table 2: Kernel functions for temporal biased projection.

$$\begin{aligned} w_v^* &\approx \underset{w_v}{\text{argmax}} \Pr(w_v|w) \\ &\approx \underset{w_v}{\text{argmax}} \frac{\#(w_v, w)}{\#w} \end{aligned} \tag{8}$$

where $\#(w_v, w)$ is the number of times w_v and w co-occur in Ψ, and $\#w$ is the total number of times w occurs in the training set.

The model in Equation (8) allows us to translate a visual word into a textual word, which we denote as $w_v = f(w)$. Analogously, we use $w = f^{-1}(w_v)$ to denote the translation of a textual word into a visual word. We can also translate an image m containing a set of visual words into a set of textual words ($f^{-1}(m)$) as well as a sentence into visual words ($f(s)$).

3.3 Affinity Matrices

In this section we explain how our affinity matrices are calculated. Recall from Section 3.1 that our co-ranking framework makes use of a local homogeneous affinity matrix ($\hat{U}, \bar{U}$), a local heterogeneous affinity matrix ($\hat{W}, \bar{W}$), and a global homogeneous affinity matrix ($\hat{N}, \bar{N}$).

3.3.1 Homogeneous Affinity Matrix

The local sentence collection can be modeled as a weighted undirected graph. Nodes in the graph represent sentences, edges represent intra-sentential relatedness, and their weights are computed via cosine similarity. The adjacency matrix U describes such a graph with each entry corresponding to the weight of an edge. Analogously, we calculate the cosine similarity between images represented by visual words. The adjacency matrix for sentences $U^s = [U^s_{ij}]_{|\vec{s}|\times|\vec{s}|}$ and images $U^m = [U^m_{ij}]_{|\vec{m}|\times|\vec{m}|}$ are defined as follows:

$$U^s_{ij} = \frac{\mathbf{s_i} \cdot \mathbf{s_j}}{||\mathbf{s_i}||||\mathbf{s_j}||}, \qquad U^m_{ij} = \frac{\mathbf{m_i} \cdot \mathbf{m_j}}{||\mathbf{m_i}||||\mathbf{m_j}||} \tag{9}$$

where $\mathbf{s}$ and $\mathbf{m}$ represent vectors of textual and visual words, respectively. Vector components are set to their *tf.idf* values [18]. *tf* is the term frequency (visual or textual) and *idf* is the inverse

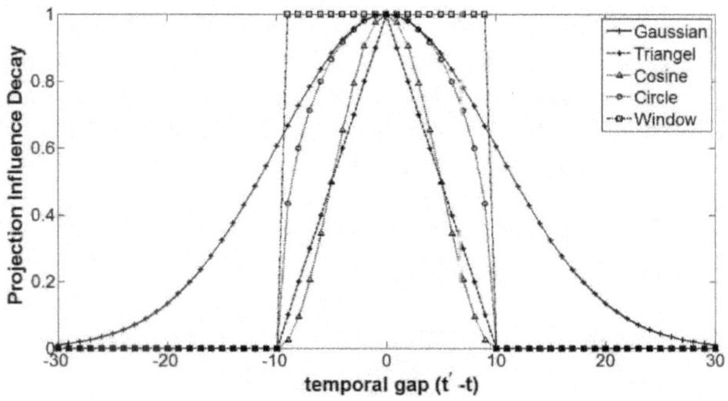

Figure 2: Proximity-based kernel functions, where σ=10.

sentence frequency in the case of textual words and inverse image frequency in the case of visual words.

Both matrices are normalized to make the sum of each row equal to 1, i.e., U^s is normalized into $\hat{U}$ and U^m into $\bar{U}$:

$$U_{ij} = \begin{cases} \frac{U_{ij}}{\sum_j U_{ij}}, & \text{if} \sum_j U_{ij} \neq 0 \\ 0, & \text{otherwise} \end{cases} \tag{10}$$

3.3.2 Heterogeneous Affinity Matrix

We capture the dependencies between sentences S and and images $M{=}\{m \in M\}$, in a bipartite graph. Graph edges are weighted according to semantic relatedness:

$$W_{ij} = \frac{1}{2}\left(\frac{\mathbf{s_i} \cdot f^{-1}(\mathbf{m_j})}{||\mathbf{s_i}||||f^{-1}(\mathbf{m_j})||} + \frac{\mathbf{m_j} \cdot f(\mathbf{s_i})}{||\mathbf{m_j}||||f(\mathbf{s_i})||} \right) \tag{11}$$

To ensure that images and texts contribute equally to the definition of the matrix, we take the average similarity of the bidirectional translation; again we calculate similarity using the cosine measure. Vector components representing sentences and images are set to their *tf.idf* values as mentioned above. W is normalized to $\hat{W}$ to make the sum of each row equal to 1. In addition, we normalize the transpose of W, i.e., W^T, to $\bar{W}$ to make the sum of each row in W^T equal to 1.

3.3.3 Neighboring Affinity Matrix

We represent the relationship between local sentences (or images) and the summary candidates $\vec{u}$ (or $\vec{v}$) as a weighted graph:

$$\begin{aligned} N^s_{ij} &= \frac{\mathbf{s_i} \cdot \mathbf{u_j}}{||\mathbf{s_i}||||\mathbf{u_j}||} \cdot \Gamma(|t(\mathbf{s_i}) - t(\mathbf{u_j})|), \\ N^m_{ij} &= \frac{\mathbf{m_i} \cdot \mathbf{v_j}}{||\mathbf{m_i}||||\mathbf{v_j}||} \cdot \Gamma(|t(\mathbf{m_i}) - t(\mathbf{v_j})|) \end{aligned} \tag{12}$$

Function $t(.)$ denotes the timestamp of the sentence or image. The adjacency matrix N^s describes the affinity between local sentences and candidate timeline sentences. Each entry of the matrix corresponds to the linkage weight and is normalized to $\hat{N}$ so that the sum of each row equals 1. Similarly, the image matrix N^m is normalized to $\bar{N}$.

Function $\Gamma(\Delta t)$ is a temporal decay function denoting the time distance between two component summaries. Intuitively, component summaries with a temporal gap will have less influence on each other [28, 27]. Following [15], we experiment with five representative kernel functions expressing temporal bias: Gaussian, Triangle, Cosine, Circle, and Window. The functions are defined in Table 2 and illustrated in Figure 2. Different kernels lead to different projections. For instance, the Window kernel treats neighboring component summaries equally within a certain scope while the Gaussian kernel models a gradient decaying relationship.

All kernels are parameterized by σ which controls the spread of the kernel curve, i.e., it restricts the projection scope of each sentence and image. In general, the optimal setting for σ may vary across datasets. For example, some news subjects may evolve quickly and require a small value of σ, whereas others may evolve slowly and require a higher σ value.

4. EXPERIMENTAL SETUP

4.1 Datasets

Our experiments used the data provided in [28], a collection of articles gathered from British (e.g., BBC), American (e.g., CNN, ABC, Reuters), and Chinese (e.g., Xinhua) news sources. We created four datasets, each covering a different news topic (i.e., science, disasters, accidents, and politics). Table 3 provides basic statistics for each dataset. Aside from documents and images, the datasets are accompanied with timeline summaries (text-based, or image-based, or both) written by professional editors. We treat these as gold standard and use them for the system evaluation.

News Subjects	#Doc	#Sent	#Img	#T	#RT
Influenza A	2557	115026	952	331	11
BP Oil Spill	1468	63021	337	135	9
Haiti Quake	247	12073	175	83	5
Obama Presidency	2160	79761	813	349	16

Table 3: Datasets used in our experiments (#Doc: number of documents, #Sent: number of sentences, #Img: number of images, #T: number of timestamps, #RT: number of reference timelines).

4.2 Model Training

In order to train our model and estimate the affinity matrices from Section 3.3, we decomposed news articles into sentences. We also removed stop-words and performed stemming. We trained a translation model based on pairs of images and their surrounding text found in our datasets. Each pair comes from the same web document. We generate a component summary for each timestamp according to a user specified *compression rate*. All component summaries constitute the global timeline.

Source documents bear temporal tags, i.e., the time of their publication. Sentences inherit temporal tags from their documents, as well as images. The sentence and image collections S and M are further partitioned according to their timestamps (e.g., $S = S_1 \cup S_2 \cup \cdots \cup S_{|T|}$). As mentioned previously, I_{s_i} is generated from sub-collection S_i, and I_{m_i} from M_i. The sizes of component summaries are not necessarily equal. Users specify the overall compression rate ϕ, and we extract more content (either texts or images) for important dates and less for other dates. The importance of dates is measured by their *burstiness* with probable significant occurrences [3]. The compression rate on t_i is set as $\phi_{s_i} = \frac{|S_i|}{|S|}\phi$ for sentences and $\phi_{m_i} = \frac{|M_i|}{|M|}\phi$ for images.

4.3 System Comparison

We compared our approach against a wide range of well-known summarization methods. All comparison systems were subject to the same preprocessing procedures as our own algorithm, including the image-to-text translation model. As these methods have not been developed with images in mind, we selected images by translating them into pseudo-sentences which we then subsequently ranked. However, note that none of the comparison systems take the mutual dependence of images and sentences into account. Instead, they select sentences and images in parallel.

Our first baseline selects sentences or images randomly for each document collection (Random). Our second method uses MEAD algorithm [19] to extract sentences and images according to centroid value and positional value (Centroid). The third baseline applies the graph-based summarization model proposed by Wan et al. [22]. It first constructs a sentence (or image) connectivity graph based on cosine similarity and then selects important sentences or images based on eigenvector centrality (GBS). We also compared our method against the evolutionary timeline summarization algorithm proposed by Yan et al. [28] which is the state of the art but ignores the image stream (ETS).

4.4 Evaluation

We evaluated the summaries produced by our system and the baselines automatically using the ROUGE evaluation metric [12]. ROUGE counts the number of overlapping units such as N-grams, word sequences, and word pairs between a candidate summary and reference summaries. There are several variants of ROUGE, all aiming at measuring similarity between system and reference summaries. We formally describe ROUGE-N below, one of the most widely used variants. We first define ROUGE-N-R and ROUGE-N-P, two N-gram metrics based on recall and precision, respectively.

$$\text{ROUGE-N-R} = \frac{\sum\limits_{\text{I}\in\text{GT}}\sum\limits_{\text{N-gram}\in\text{I}} \text{Count}_{\text{match}}(\text{N-gram})}{\sum\limits_{\text{I}\in\text{GT}}\sum\limits_{\text{N-gram}\in\text{I}} \text{Count (N-gram)}} \tag{13}$$

$$\text{ROUGE-N-P} = \frac{\sum\limits_{\text{I}\in\text{CT}}\sum\limits_{\text{N-gram}\in\text{I}} \text{Count}_{\text{match}}(\text{N-gram})}{\sum\limits_{\text{I}\in\text{CT}}\sum\limits_{\text{N-gram}\in\text{I}} \text{Count (N-gram)}} \tag{14}$$

Here N is the length of the N-gram and N-gram∈GT denotes the N-grams in the reference timeline GT, while N-gram∈CT denotes the N-grams in the system timeline CT. $\text{Count}_{\text{match}}$(N-gram) is the maximum number of N-grams in the candidate summary and in the set of reference summaries. $\text{Count}_{\text{(N-gram)}}$ is the number of N-grams in the reference summaries or system summary. Rouge-N is the harmonic mean of ROUGE-N-R and ROUGE-N-P:

$$\text{ROUGE-N} = \frac{2 \times \text{ROUGE-N-P} \times \text{ROUGE-N-R}}{\text{ROUGE-N-P} + \text{ROUGE-N-R}} \tag{15}$$

We evaluated our textual summaries using all variants provided by the ROUGE package (version 1.55) and obtained similar results across the board. For the sake of brevity we only report ROUGE-1, ROUGE-2, and the weighted longest common subsequence ROUGE-W (with W set to 1.2). We evaluated our visual summaries in a similar fashion. Recall that we represent images as a bag of visual words. We can therefore use ROUGE to measure the visual word overlap between the images selected by our system and those found in the reference summaries. Since visual words do not have sequential dependencies, we only report ROUGE-1.

Finally, as the timeline consists of a series of individual summaries I which are not equally significant, we compute ROUGE-N scores for timelines as the weighted average ROUGE-N of all summaries:

$$\text{ROUGE-N(I)} = \frac{1}{|\text{I}|}\frac{\sum\limits_{I_i\in I}\phi_i \cdot \text{ROUGE-N}(\text{I}_\text{i})}{\sum\limits_{I_i\in I}\sum\limits_{I_k\in I}\phi_k \cdot \text{ROUGE-N}(\text{I}_\text{k})} \tag{16}$$

System	R_s-1	R_s-2	R_s-W	R_m-1	A(s,m)	H(s,m)
Random	0.317	0.039	0.081	0.126	0.079	0.784
Centroid	0.331	0.050	0.114	0.267	0.223	1.25
GBS	0.364	0.062	0.130	0.283	0.259	1.512
ETS	0.396	0.085	**0.139**	0.297	0.285	2.016
VTS	**0.402**	**0.087**	0.138	**0.320**	**0.376**	**3.380**
INFLUENZA A (ROI* category: Science)						

System	R_s-1	R_s-2	R_s-W	R_m-1	A(s,m)	H(s,m)
Random	0.266	0.043	0.093	0.114	0.139	0.806
Centroid	0.362	0.060	0.129	0.256	0.175	1.651
GBS	0.380	0.106	0.137	0.237	0.198	1.871
ETS	0.481	0.123	0.160	0.316	0.259	2.509
VTS	**0.488**	**0.128**	**0.163**	**0.339**	**0.387**	**3.595**
HAITI EARTHQUAKE (ROI* category: Disasters)						

System	R_s-1	R_s-2	R_s-W	R_m-1	A(s,m)	H(s,m)
Random	0.262	0.041	0.096	0.317	0.157	0.512
Centroid	0.369	0.062	0.128	0.317	0.196	1.482
GBS	0.389	0.084	0.139	0.317	0.217	1.782
ETS	0.483	0.119	0.163	0.369	0.298	2.248
VTS	**0.486**	**0.121**	**0.168**	**0.394**	**0.402**	**3.630**
BP OIL (ROI* category: Accidents)						

System	R_s-1	R_s-2	R_s-W	R_m-1	A(s,m)	H(s,m)
Random	0.254	0.039	0.084	0.085	0.039	0.206
Centroid	0.325	0.053	0.111	0.117	0.099	1.089
GBS	0.359	0.061	0.129	0.128	0.124	0.091
ETS	0.388	0.083	0.134	**0.233**	0.179	1.780
VTS	**0.393**	**0.103**	**0.138**	0.228	**0.339**	**3.085**
OBAMA PRESIDENCY (ROI* category: Politics)						

Table 4: System comparison on four datasets (Influenza A, BP Oil Spill, Haiti Quake, and Presidency).

We set the weight ϕ_i to the compression rate for a sentence component summary or an image component summary.

We also assessed the semantic fit between the selected images and sentences directly. We used Equation (11) to measure the correlation between images and texts, under the assumption that higher values indicate higher similarity between sentences and images, and should thus correspond to better timelines.

We also obtained human judgements for the same task. We asked 15 participants to read the output summaries based on texts and images and rate how well the two correlate. Participants used a 5-point rating scale and were advised to use high numbers in cases where texts and images were a good match and low numbers otherwise (0-terrible, 1-bad, 2-normal, 3-good, 4-excellent).

Components	R_s-1	R_s-2	R_s-W	R_m-1	A(s,m)
LOA	**0.373**	**0.079**	**0.134**	**0.268**	0.244
LEA	0.335	0.078	0.133	0.252	**0.399**
GHA	0.334	0.078	**0.134**	0.241	0.201
−LOA	**0.309**	**0.077**	**0.132**	**0.241**	0.365
−LEA	0.381	0.080	0.143	0.254	**0.244**
−GHA	0.428	0.100	0.151	0.343	0.400
VTS	0.442	0.109	0.152	0.321	0.376

Table 5: Performance of individual components and component combinations for the VTS system.

5. RESULTS

5.1 System Performance

Our results are summarized in Table 4. We report results on each dataset using the following cross-validation scheme: we train parameters on one news set and examine the performance on the others. After 4 training-testing iterations, we take the average performance on all sets. We report results on textual summaries using ROUGE-1 (denoted as R_s-1 in the table), ROUGE-2 (denoted as R_s-2) and ROUGE-W (denoted as R_s-W). We use ROUGE-1 to evaluate the similarity between reference visual summaries and system summaries (denoted as R_m-1). We also show results using an automatic measure of the semantic fit between textual and visual summaries (denoted as A(s,m)) and the human judgments (denoted as H(s,m)).

As can be seen from Table 4 the VTS approach outperforms the comparison systems on almost all datasets, and evaluation measures. The random baseline (Random) performs worst across the board. This is not entirely surprising as it does not take into account the importance of texts or images. The centroid-based system (Centroid) performs better than Random as it tries to identify important sentences and images by taking into account positional information as well as content overlap. The GBS system outperforms the Centroid method in terms of ROUGE and the correlation evaluation introduced in Section 4.4. This is due to the fact that the PageRank-based framework ranks sentences (and images) using eigenvector centrality which implicitly accounts for information subsumption among all sentences or images. ETS produces better timelines than more traditional methods since it has explicit mechanisms for capturing how information evolves over time. A major difference between ETS and VTS is that the former does not take the correlation between images and text into account. Visual and textual timelines are generated independently and as result the fit between the two is not perfect. Taking into account the dependency between the two modalities, improves textual and visual summarization across the board and also produces thematically coherent timelines with the textual and visual components being properly matched. Notice that VTS outperforms all comparison methods on A(s,m) and H(s,m) scores by a large margin on all datasets.

The results in Table 4 have been produced with optimal parameter values. We explore the influence of different parameters in the following sections. Examples of system output are given in Tables 6 and 7 using a compression rate of 5%. Our implementation allows users to have access to the source documents by clicking on the extracted sentences that make up the output summary.

5.2 Component Analysis

We next examine the relative contribution of the individual components of our algorithm. Specifically, we assess the algorithm's performance using only one of the three affinity matrices: Local Homogeneous Affinity (LOA), Local Heterogeneous Affinity (LEA) and Global Homogeneous Affinity (GHA). We also perform ablation studies where one component is removed at a time. Table 5 shows the performance of the individual components (upper half) and the results of our ablation studies (lower half; we use the symbol '−' to indicate which component has been removed). For comparison, we also show the performance of our VTS system. Scores in the table are averages across all four datasets. We use boldface to indicate which components incur remarkable performance changes.

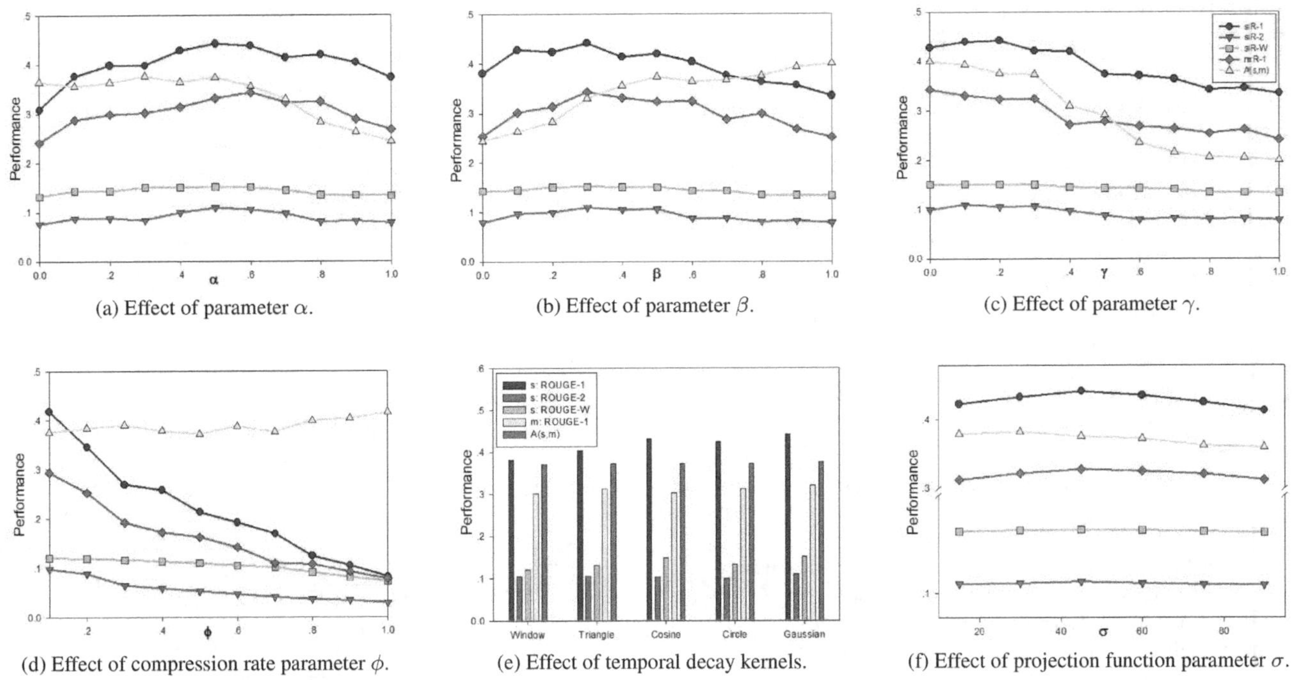

(a) Effect of parameter α.

(b) Effect of parameter β.

(c) Effect of parameter γ.

(d) Effect of compression rate parameter ϕ.

(e) Effect of temporal decay kernels.

(f) Effect of projection function parameter σ.

Figure 3: Parameter effect on system performance using R_s-1, R_s-2, R_s-W, R_m-1 and A(s,m).

As can be seen, LOA has the highest effect on system performance when the latter is measured in terms of ROUGE. LEA on the other hand is important for achieving a good semantic fit between visual and textual summaries. This component, on its own, achieves the highest A(s,m) score. Its removal from the VTS system results in the lowest A(s,m) score.

5.3 Parameter Settings

Recall that our co-ranking framework is parameterized with respect to the relative influence of three different affinities. Parameters α, β, and γ (see equations (5) and (6)) control the contribution of the local homogeneous, local heterogeneous, and global homogeneous affinities. We performed a series of experiments to determine the optimal parameter values for our VTS framework. We varied one parameter at a time, keeping all other parameters fixed as illustrated in Figure 3. Our results indicate that the local homogeneous affinity (parameter α) has the greatest effect on system performance. High values of the γ parameter (global homogeneous affinity) have a negative influence on performance as do very low or very high values of the β parameter (local heterogeneous affinity). Optimal parameter values were set to α=0.6, β=0.3, and γ=0.1.

We also experimented with the effect of the compression rate ϕ. Note that typically ϕ is regulated by users. For example, users who want to read more content, might favor a larger ϕ. We varied ϕ from 0.1 to 1 with a step of 0.1. Generally, the ROUGE lines are down-sloping (see Figure 3d) as our ground truth timelines are small compared to the large source collection our system has access to. Interestingly, the correlation line (see A(s,m) in Figure 3d) is more stable, indicating the intrinsic dependence between texts and images within the news documents.

Finally, an important parameter in timeline summarization is σ which controls the influence of the temporal projection for sentences/images from different dates and thus influences the weights of the neighboring affinity. Changes in σ values do not incur large differences in performance (see Figure 3f). This is partly due to the small value of γ=0.1. We experimented with $\sigma \in [20, 80]$ and empirically set the parameter to σ=35. Given this value, we next examined the effect of different projections. Generally, the Gaussian kernel is the best performing projection and the window kernel the worst performing one. We attribute this to the fact that the Gaussian kernel provides the best smoothing effect without imposing any arbitrary cutoffs.

6. CONCLUSIONS

In this paper we introduced visual timeline summarization, a novel summarization task that creates visual and textual timeline summaries for news topics. We proposed a framework that ranks images and sentences jointly whilst taking into account how a sentence (or an image) associates to other sentences (or images), how sentences and images related to each other, and how the two relate to the overall textual and visual summaries being created. Our model explores the relationship between elements within the same modality and across modalities. We proposed an algorithm that selects images and sentences through mutual reinforcement: it uses the global timeline summary to iteratively refine the local component summaries.

Experimental results on four datasets show that our system outperforms previously proposed competitive baselines. Analysis of the components of our system and its parameters indicates that the semantic fit between images and sentences is important for VTS (β=0.3) as well as taking auxiliary global information into account (γ=0.1). The local homogeneous affinity would perform best in isolation and its absence would lead to the most significant performance drop.

Currently our model treats sentences and images equally without using any prior information with respect to how important they are. In the future, we plan to use prior knowledge to select seed sentences and images. Such knowledge can be based on the positional information of sentences in the document, their timestamps and so on. This way we can ensure better local optima and faster convergence.

7. ACKNOWLEDGMENTS

We thank the anonymous reviewers for their valuable feedback. This work was partially supported by NSFC Grant No.60933004 and HGJ Grant No. 2011ZX01042-001-001; Xiaojun Wan was supported by NSFC Grant No. 61170166, Beijing Nova Program (2008B03) and the National High Technology Research and Development Program of China (2012AA011101). Rui Yan was supported by the MediaTek Fellowship.

8. REFERENCES

[1] J. Allan, R. Gupta, and V. Khandelwal. Temporal summaries of new topics. In *Proceedings of the 24th Annual International ACM SIGIR Conference on Research and Development in Information Retrieval*, pages 10–18, 2001.

[2] K. Barnard, P. Duygulu, D. Forsyth, N. de Freitas, D. M. Blei, and M. I. Jordan. Matching words and pictures. *Journal of Machine Learning Research*, 3:1107–1135, Mar. 2003.

[3] H. L. Chieu and Y. K. Lee. Query based event extraction along a timeline. In *Proceedings of the 27th Annual International ACM SIGIR Conference on Research and Development in Information Retrieval*, pages 425–432, 2004.

[4] P. Duygulu, K. Barnard, J. De Freitas, and D. Forsyth. Object recognition as machine translation: Learning a lexicon for a fixed image vocabulary. In *Proceedings of 7th European Conference on Computer Vision*, pages 349–354, 2002.

[5] G. Erkan and D. Radev. Lexpagerank: Prestige in multi-document text summarization. In *Proceedings of the Conference on Empirical Methods in Natural Language Processing*, 2004.

[6] Y. Feng and M. Lapata. Automatic image annotation using auxiliary text information. In *Proceedings of the 46th Annual Meeting on Association for Computational Linguistics with the Human Lauguage Technology Conference*, pages 272–280, 2008.

[7] Y. Feng and M. Lapata. How many words is a picture worth? automatic caption generation for news images. In *Proceedings of the 48th Annual Meeting on Association for Computational Linguistics*, pages 1239–1249, 2010.

[8] Y. Feng and M. Lapata. Topic models for image annotation and text illustration. In *Human Language Technologies: The 2010 Annual Conference of the North American Chapter of the Association for Computational Linguistics*, pages 831–839, 2010.

[9] J. Goldstein, M. Kantrowitz, V. Mittal, and J. Carbonell. Summarizing text documents: sentence selection and evaluation metrics. In *Proceedings of the 22nd Annual International ACM SIGIR Conference on Research and Development in Information Retrieval*, pages 121–128, 1999.

[10] A. Langville and C. Meyer. Deeper inside pagerank. *Internet Mathematics*, 1(3):335–380, 2004.

[11] C.-Y. Lin and E. Hovy. From single to multi-document summarization: a prototype system and its evaluation. In *Proceedings of the 40th Annual Meeting on Association for Computational Linguistics*, pages 457–464, 2002.

[12] C.-Y. Lin and E. Hovy. Automatic evaluation of summaries using n-gram co-occurrence statistics. In *Proceedings of North American Chapter of the Association for Computational Linguistics on Human Language Technology*, pages 71–78, 2003.

[13] D. Lowe. Object recognition from local scale-invariant features. In *Proceedings of 7th IEEE International Conference on Computer Vision*, pages 1150–1157, 1999.

[14] Y. Lu, J. He, D. Shan, and H. Yan. Recommending citations with translation model. In *Proceedings of the 20th ACM International Conference on Information and Knowledge Management*, pages 2017–2020, 2011.

[15] Y. Lv and C. Zhai. Positional language models for information retrieval. In *Proceedings of the 32nd Annual International ACM SIGIR Conference on Research and development in information retrieval*, pages 299–306, 2009.

[16] I. Mani. *Automatic Summarization*. John Benjamins Pub Co, 2001.

[17] R. Mihalcea and P. Tarau. A language independent algorithm for single and multiple document summarization. In *Proceedings of the International Joint Conference on Natural Language Processing*, 2005.

[18] J. Neto, A. Santos, C. Kaestner, D. Santos, et al. Document clustering and text summarization. 2000.

[19] D. Radev, H. Jing, M. Stys, and D. Tam. Centroid-based summarization of multiple documents. *Information Processing & Management*, 40(6):919–938, 2004.

[20] K. Sparck Jones. Automatic summarizing: Factors and directions. In I. Mani and M. T. Maybury, editors, *Advances in Automatic Text Summarization*, pages 1–33. MIT Press, Cambridge, 1999.

[21] R. Swan and J. Allan. Automatic generation of overview timelines. In *Proceedings of the 23rd Annual International ACM SIGIR Conference on Research and development in information retrieval*, pages 49–56, 2000.

[22] X. Wan and J. Yang. Multi-document summarization using cluster-based link analysis. In *Proceedings of the 31st Annual International ACM SIGIR Conference on Research and Development in Information Retrieval*, pages 299–306, 2008.

[23] X. Wan, J. Yang, and J. Xiao. Manifold-ranking based topic-focused multi-document summarization. In *Proceedings of the 18th International Joint Conference on Artificial Intelligence*, pages 2903–2908, 2007.

[24] X. Wan, J. Yang, and J. Xiao. Single document summarization with document expansion. In *Proceedings of the 21st Conference on Artificial Intelligence*, pages 931–936, 2007.

[25] D. Wang and T. Li. Document update summarization using incremental hierarchical clustering. In *Proceedings of the 19th ACM International Conference on Information and Knowledge Management*, pages 279–288, 2010.

[26] D. Wang, T. Li, S. Zhu, and C. Ding. Multi-document summarization via sentence-level semantic analysis and symmetric matrix factorization. In *Proceedings of the 31st Annual International ACM SIGIR Conference on Research and Development in Information Retrieval*, pages 307–314, 2008.

[27] R. Yan, L. Kong, C. Huang, X. Wan, X. Li, and Y. Zhang. Timeline generation through evolutionary trans-temporal summarization. In *Proceedings of the Conference on Empirical Methods in Natural Language Processing*, pages 433–443, 2011.

[28] R. Yan, X. Wan, J. Otterbacher, L. Kong, X. Li, and Y. Zhang. Evolutionary timeline summarization: a balanced optimization framework via iterative substitution. In *Proceedings of the 34th International SIGIR Conference on Research and Development in Information Retrieval*, pages 745–754, 2011.

April 23, 2009

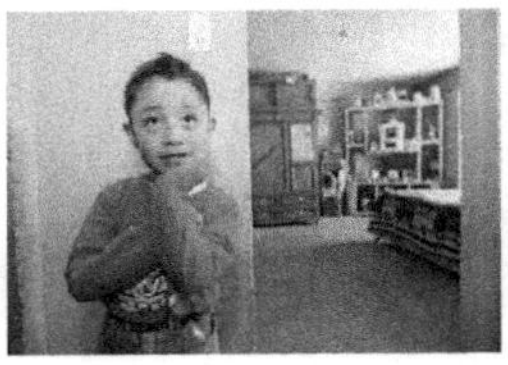

s_1: Edgar Hernandez, known as the "patient zero" to have contracted the swine flu, lives in the southern Mexican town of La Gloria.
s_2: The WHO makes its first report about the so-called Swine Influenza (A) H1N1.

April 25, 2009

s_1: The government hands out masks at Mexico City: the outbreak of swine flu is making people cautious.
s_2: The World Health Organization has declared a global flu pandemic after holding an emergency meeting.
s_3: U.S. emergency departments step up efforts to control the virus should...
s_4: The Mexican Director-General declares Swine Influenza (A) H1N1 a public health emergency.

April 27, 2009

s_1: The World Health Organization raises the pandemic alert one level to phase 4, which is two steps short of declaring a full-blown pandemic.
s_2: Mexico city shut down schools, museums, libraries and state-run theaters across the overcrowded capital.
s_3: Massachusetts public health officials yesterday mobilized against a possible swine flu outbreak as the alert level is raised.
s_4: European Union's health commissioner warns Europeans to avoid nonessential travel to Mexico and the United States.
s_5: The number of confirmed flu infection cases in the U.S. climbs to 20 in five states.

April 29, 2009

s_1: The World Health Organization (WHO) declares A/H1N1 flu pandemic, raises alert level to highest.
s_2: The CDC said that the number of laboratory-confirmed cases of H1N1 virus infection had climbed to 91 people in 10 states.
s_3: Staff members check the temperature of passengers with the help of machines at Hong Kong International Airport in Hong Kong, south China.

October 2, 2009

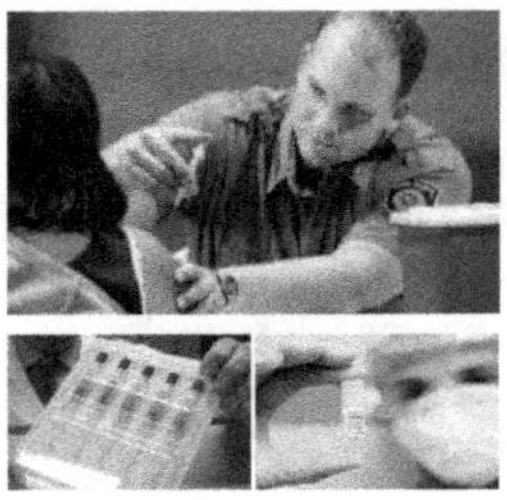

s_1: The US announces implementation of a massive campaign to vaccinate millions of Americans against swine flu, with the first 600,000 doses to be distributed in coming days.
s_2: Five doses of swine flu vaccine, part of the first shipment of vaccine sent to Methodist Hospital in Omaha.
s_3: Made H1N1 vaccine is expected to go into mass production soon.

October 5, 2009

s_1: WHO said pharmaceutical firms can produce only 3 billion doses of H1N1 vaccines a year, covering less than half of the global population.
s_2: The U.S. Centers for Disease Control and Prevention says the worst could be yet to come, so Americans need to prepare for a large outbreak this fall and winter.

Table 6: Visual timeline generated by our model on Influenza A.

April 20, 2009

s_1: Explosion and fire on the BP-licensed Transocean drilling rig Deepwater Horizon in the Gulf of Mexico.
s_2: An explosion on the rig on April 20, 2010, killed 11 people working on the rig and injured 16 others.
s_3: The rig was drilling in about 5,000ft (1,525m) of water, pushing the boundaries of deepwater drilling technology.

April 22, 2009

s_1: The Deepwater Horizon sinks to the bottom of the Gulf after burning for 36 hours, raising concerns of a catastrophic...
s_2: A bird covered in oil from the BP Deepwater Horizon spill struggles to climb on to a boom in Gulf of Mexico.
s_3: Search-and-rescue operations by the US National Response Team begin.

April 23, 2010

s_1: The rig is found upside down about a quarter-mile from the blowout preventer.
s_2: Underwater robots and equipment swarm the blowout preventer, bottom left, as oil rises at the spill site.
s_3: Deepwater Horizon clean-up workers fight to prevent disaster.
s_4: The Coast Guard increases its oil spill estimate to 5,000 barrels a day, or 210,000 gallons - five times more than what was originally believed.

April 26, 2010

s_1: BP's shares fall 2% amid fears that the cost of cleanup and legal claims will hit the company hard.
s_2: BP CEO reckons the $100 million cost of drilling a well to divert the flow from a leaking oil well in the Gulf of Mexico is the biggest hit.

Table 7: Visual timeline generated by our model on BP Oil.

Fast Multi-task Learning for Query Spelling Correction

Xu Sun
Dept. of Statistical Science
Cornell University
Ithaca, NY 14853
xusun@cornell.edu

Anshumali Shrivastava
Dept. of Computer Science
Cornell University
Ithaca, NY 14853
anshu@cs.cornell.edu

Ping Li
Dept. of Statistical Science
Cornell University
Ithaca, NY 14853
pingli@cornell.edu

ABSTRACT

In this paper, we explore the use of a novel online multi-task learning framework for the task of search query spelling correction. In our procedure, correction candidates are initially generated by a ranker-based system and then re-ranked by our multi-task learning algorithm. With the proposed multi-task learning method, we are able to effectively transfer information from different and highly biased training datasets, for improving spelling correction on all datasets. Our experiments are conducted on three query spelling correction datasets including the well-known TREC benchmark dataset. The experimental results demonstrate that our proposed method considerably outperforms the existing baseline systems in terms of accuracy. Importantly, the proposed method is about one order of magnitude faster than baseline systems in terms of training speed. Compared to the commonly used online learning methods which typically require more than (e.g.,) 60 training passes, our proposed method is able to closely reach the empirical optimum in about 5 passes.

Categories and Subject Descriptors

H.3.3 [**Information Storage and Retrieval**]: Information Search and Retrieval—*Query Alteration*

General Terms

Algorithms, Performance, Experimentation

Keywords

Query Spelling Correction, Multi-task Learning

1. INTRODUCTION

Search queries present a particular challenge for traditional spelling correction methods, for at least three reasons [3]. Firstly, spelling errors are more common in search queries than in regular written texts. For example, [12] showed that roughly 10-15% of queries contain misspelled terms. Secondly, most search queries consist of only a few key words rather than grammatical sentences, making a grammar-based approach inappropriate. Most importantly, many queries contain search terms, such as proper nouns and names, which are not well established in the language. For example, Chen *et al.* [10] reported that 16.5% of valid search terms do not occur in their spelling lexicon, which contains more than 200,000 entries.

Due to the practical importance, query spelling correction has received much attention and a variety of datasets have been developed (from different domains). As discussed in [17], queries in one specific dataset can be very biased from another dataset, and combining such biased datasets for query spelling correction is difficult. In fact, in this paper, we will also demonstrate an empirical phenomenon that simply merging biased datasets for training a unified speller may not bring improvement at all.

The difficulty in effectively combining biased datasets for spelling correction lies in at least three aspects: (i) their error-patterns can be high biased; (ii) their distributions of misspelled queries can be quite different; (iii) their domains can be quite different (hence, a domain adaptation problem exists). Thus, a natural question arises: *how can we effectively integrate such highly biased datasets for improving query spelling correction?* To the best of our knowledge, there are still no satisfactory solutions in the literature.

Our goal in this paper is to solve this well-known difficult problem with high accuracy as well as high efficiency. The training speed can be crucial because industrial query spelling correction tasks may have to deal with very large-scale training data (e.g., click-through query spelling logs which contain more than millions of entries, see [34]). Our proposed multi-task learning framework for query spelling correction is capable of adaptively integrating highly biased training datasets via automatically learning the task-relationships (data-similarities). This allows us to "softly" merge biased datasets for learning a unified speller.

In our procedure, the fist step is to generate a large number of spelling correction candidates using a candidate generation module. Then the top candidates are accurately identified through our novel multi-task learning algorithm. Encouragingly, with the ability to effectively transfer information among those biased training datasets, our proposed method is capable of improving spelling correction accuracies on *all* related datasets. The prior standard practice for combining different datasets is to simply merge them and feed them to a single-task learner. Compared to this

CIKM'12, October 29–November 2, 2012, Maui, HI, USA.

baseline, our experimental results will demonstrate that our new approach will result in significantly better performance.

Our **major contributions** can be summarized as follows:

- To the best of our knowledge, this is the first study of multi-task learning for query spelling correction. The proposed method outperforms the state-of-the-art results on the TREC dataset.
- Our novel *adaptive* multi-task learning framework can effectively utilize *2nd-order gradient information*.
- Our method is of fast convergence speed. It is able to approach close to the empirical optimum in only a few (e.g., ≤ 5) passes. This is about one order of magnitude faster than traditional training (e.g., batch or online) methods. Fast training speed is crucial for large-scale query spelling correction tasks (e.g., [34]).

The rest of this paper is structured as follows. Section 2 describes the architecture of our spelling correction system. Section 3 presents the proposed multi-task learning framework for query spelling correction. Section 4 presents the extensive experiments on query spelling correction. Section 5 reviews related work, and Section 6 concludes the paper.

2. SYSTEM ARCHITECTURE

2.1 Candidates Generation

We first describe our procedure for generating correction candidates. Following Ganjisaffar *et al.* [17], we implement three candidate generators in our system to produce about 2,000 candidates (on average) for each query. Initially, a character-based candidate generator is adopted for producing all possible candidates within an edit distance 1. It considers replacing each character with all possible characters in the alphabet, transposing each pair of adjacent characters, deleting each character, inserting all possible characters after each character, and so on.

The AOL query logs showed that 16% of the query corrections are different from the original query only in adding/removing spaces [17]. For example, "ebayauction" is a query which should be corrected to "ebay auction". As a more complicated example, the long query "broccoliandcheesebake" actually indicates "broccoli and cheese bake". In order to handle this class of queries, we implement the word segmentation algorithm based on the Microsoft word breaker[1], with some minor modifications. For each possible segmentation of the character sequence, we use a language model to compute the probability of the segmentation. The most probable segmentation candidates are then added to the candidate list.

Neither of the above two candidate generators is able to produce candidates which have more than 1 edit distance from the original query (in spite of adding or removing multiple spaces). For example, for the query "washton university", we might want to have "washington university" as a candidate, which however can not be produced by the above two candidate generators. To ease this problem, we perform a fuzzy search process based on a lexicon containing most frequent words, to quickly find known unigrams with a small edit distance to unigrams and bigrams located in the original query. For the lexicon containing frequent-word, we use the top 100K words based on their frequency on the web. With the three candidate generators, we can generate 2,000 candidates (on average) for each query.

[1] `http://web-ngram.research.microsoft.com`

2.2 Naive Ranking

An important factor in selecting and ranking the correction candidates is the prior probability of a correction phrase. It represents our prior belief about how likely a query will be chosen by the user without seeing any input from the user. In this work we make use of the Web n-gram service provided by Microsoft. Web n-gram model intends to model the n-gram probability of English phrases with the parameters estimated from the entire Web data. It also differentiates the data sources to build different language models from the title, anchor text and body of Web pages, as well as the queries from query log. To build our spelling system, we make use of the tri-gram language model. Note that, even though the Web n-gram model contains a large amount of entries, it may still suffer from data sparseness in higher-order language models.

2.3 Re-Ranking

Re-ranking of top search results has shown to improve the quality of rankings in query spelling correction [17, 28]. Since the main focus of spelling correction is on the top ranked list of candidates, we add a re-ranker on top of the naive ranker. This step significantly improved the results of the naive ranker, and the cost is tractable. This is because re-ranking only needs to deal with top-k candidates, and k is typically small (in our case, following [28], we set $k = 40$). Hence, the re-ranker is solving a much easier problem, compared to the original naive ranker which needs to consider about 2,000 candidates for each query.

We use a conditional log-linear method, the *Maximum Entropy* model, for re-ranking. The maximum entropy model produces a probability distribution over multiple classes and have the advantage of handling large numbers of overlapping features. Assuming a feature function that maps a pair of observation sequence $\boldsymbol{x}$ and a classification label y to a feature vector $\boldsymbol{f}$, the probability of y conditioned on the observation sequence $\boldsymbol{x}$ is modeled as follows [23]:

$$P(y|\boldsymbol{x}, \boldsymbol{w}) = \frac{\exp\left[\boldsymbol{w}^\top \boldsymbol{f}(y, \boldsymbol{x})\right]}{\sum_{\forall y'} \exp\left[\boldsymbol{w}^\top \boldsymbol{f}(y', \boldsymbol{x})\right]}, \tag{1}$$

where $\boldsymbol{w}$ is a weight vector. Given a training set consisting of n labeled samples, $(\boldsymbol{x}_i, y_i)$, for $i = 1 \ldots n$, weights are gained via maximizing the objective function,

$$\mathcal{L}(\boldsymbol{w}) = \sum_{i=1}^{n} \log P(y_i|\boldsymbol{x}_i, \boldsymbol{w}) - R(\boldsymbol{w}). \tag{2}$$

The first term of this equation represents a conditional log-likelihood of the training data. The second term is a regularizer for reducing overfitting. We employe an L_2 prior. In what follows, we denote the conditional log-likelihood of each sample, $\log P(y_i|\boldsymbol{x}_i, \boldsymbol{w})$, as $\ell(i, \boldsymbol{w})$. Then, we have

$$\mathcal{L}(\boldsymbol{w}) = \sum_{i=1}^{n} \ell(i, \boldsymbol{w}) - \frac{||\boldsymbol{w}||^2}{2\sigma^2}. \tag{3}$$

Since the evaluation is based on expected F-score, probability information is required in computing expected F-score.

The original conditional probability produced by maximum entropy models is not proper for computing expected F-score, because the sum of conditional probabilities of top-k candidates are not 1. To deal with this problem, we re-compute the probability of a candidate as follows:

$$P'(y) = \exp[cP(y)] / \sum_{k'=1,\ldots,k} \exp[cP(y_{k'})],$$

where c is a scalar to control the density of the distribution. Since essentially c has a similar function like the σ in regularization, to avoid introducing new hyper-parameters, we simply set c based on σ.

2.4 Re-Ranking Features

In the re-ranking phase we add features which are extracted from top-k query-candidate pairs. In addition, other than the features which based on transformations between query-candidate pairs, we also design features which consider the top candidates of the query (i.e., comparisons with other candidates in the top-k list). In this way, the features can include valuable information that may help in the ranking process.

We have about 30 feature templates for each query-candidate pair. These features include: error model features (e.g., edit distance), candidate language model features, query language model features, surface features capturing differences of the query and the candidate, frequency of the query and the candidate, the rank of the candidate in the naive ranking phase, and so on. Although we have used language model scores for naive ranking for producing top candidates, we keep using Web-scale n-gram language model features for re-ranking the top candidates, and we find such Web-scale n-gram language model features are still quite useful in the re-ranking phase.

In the Web-scale n-gram language model features, the log of n-gram language model probabilities of an original query and its candidate corrections are used for re-ranking. In addition, the average, max, min, and standard deviation of the language model probabilities of the top-k candidates are employed as features.

2.5 Online Learning

There are two major approaches for training a log-linear model: batch training and online training. Batch training methods include, for example, steepest gradient descent, conjugate gradient descent (CG), and limited-memory BFGS (LBFGS) [30]. In such training methods, gradients are computed by using all training instances. Typically, the training process is quite slow in practice.

To speed up the training process, online algorithms have become increasingly popular. A representative online learning method is the stochastic gradient descent (SGD) [7]. The SGD uses a small randomly-drawn subset of the training samples to approximate the gradient of the objective function, which allows one to update the model weights much more frequently, and consequently, to speed up the convergence. Suppose $\hat{\mathcal{S}}$ is a randomly drawn subset of the full training set $\mathcal{S}$, the stochastic objective function is then given by

$$\mathcal{L}_{stoch}(\boldsymbol{w}, \hat{\mathcal{S}}) = \sum_{i \in \mathcal{S}} \ell(i, \boldsymbol{w}) - \frac{|\hat{\mathcal{S}}|}{|\mathcal{S}|} \frac{||\boldsymbol{w}||^2}{2\sigma^2}.$$

The extreme case is a batch size of 1, and it gives the maximum frequency of updates, which we adopt in this work. In this case, $|\hat{\mathcal{S}}| = 1$ and $|\mathcal{S}| = n$ (suppose the full training set contains n samples). In this case, we have

$$\mathcal{L}_{stoch}(\boldsymbol{w}, \hat{\mathcal{S}}) = \ell(i, \boldsymbol{w}) - \frac{1}{n} \frac{||\boldsymbol{w}||^2}{2\sigma^2}, \quad (4)$$

where $\hat{\mathcal{S}} = \{i\}$. Model weights are updated like this:

$$\boldsymbol{w}_{k+1} = \boldsymbol{w}_k + \gamma_k \nabla_{\boldsymbol{w}_k} \mathcal{L}_{stoch}(\boldsymbol{w}, \hat{\mathcal{S}}), \quad (5)$$

where k is the update counter, γ_k is the learning rate.

3. OUR PROPOSAL

In this section, we introduce our adaptive (and online) *m*ulti-*t*ask *l*earning framework (MTL below). For every positive integer q, we define $\mathcal{N}_q = \{1, \ldots, q\}$. Let T be the number of tasks which we want to simultaneously learn. For each task $t \in \mathcal{N}_T$, there are n data examples $\{(\boldsymbol{x}_{t,i}, \boldsymbol{y}_{t,i}) : i \in \mathcal{N}_n\}$ available. In practice, the number of examples per task may vary but we keep it constant for simplicity of notation. We use $\boldsymbol{D}$ to denote the $n \times T$ matrix whose t-th column is given by the vector $\boldsymbol{d}_t$ of data examples.

3.1 Adaptive Multi-Task Learning Model

Our goal is to learn the weight vectors $\boldsymbol{w}_1, \ldots, \boldsymbol{w}_T$ from the data $\boldsymbol{D}$. For simplicity of notation, we assume that each of the weight vectors is of the same size f (this is also the feature dimension), and corresponds to the same ordering of features. We use $\boldsymbol{W}$ to denote the $f \times T$ matrix whose t-th column is given by the vector $\boldsymbol{w}_t$. We learn $\boldsymbol{W}$ by maximizing the objective function,

$$\text{Obj}(\boldsymbol{W}, \boldsymbol{D}) \triangleq \text{Likelihood}(\boldsymbol{W}, \boldsymbol{D}) - R(\boldsymbol{W}), \quad (6)$$

where Likelihood$(\boldsymbol{W}, \boldsymbol{D})$ is the accumulative likelihood over all interactive tasks, namely,

$$\text{Likelihood}(\boldsymbol{W}, \boldsymbol{D}) = \sum_{t \in \mathcal{N}_T} \mathcal{L}(\boldsymbol{w}_t, \boldsymbol{D}), \quad (7)$$

and $\mathcal{L}(\boldsymbol{w}_t, \boldsymbol{D})$ is defined as follows:

$$\mathcal{L}(\boldsymbol{w}_t, \boldsymbol{D}) \triangleq \sum_{t' \in \mathcal{N}_T} \left[\alpha_{t,t'} \mathcal{L}(\boldsymbol{w}_t, \boldsymbol{d}_{t'})\right]. \quad (8)$$

$\alpha_{t,t'}$ is a real-valued *task-similarity*, with $\alpha_{t,t'} = \alpha_{t',t}$ (symmetric). Intuitively, a task-similarity $\alpha_{t,t'}$ measures the *similarity of patterns* between the t-th task and the t'-th task. $\mathcal{L}(\boldsymbol{w}_t, \boldsymbol{d}_{t'})$ is defined as follows:

$$\begin{aligned} \mathcal{L}(\boldsymbol{w}_t, \boldsymbol{d}_{t'}) &\triangleq \sum_{i \in \mathcal{N}_n} \log P(\boldsymbol{y}_{t',i} | \boldsymbol{x}_{t',i}, \boldsymbol{w}_t) \\ &= \sum_{i \in \mathcal{N}_n} \ell_{t'}(i, \boldsymbol{w}_t), \end{aligned} \quad (9)$$

where $P(\cdot)$ is a prescribed probability function. We can flexibly use any prescribed probability function. This makes our MTL method a flexible and general framework for no matter structured or non-structured classification tasks. In this paper, we will adopt the maximum entropy probability function (Eq. 1), which works well for spelling correction.

Finally, $R(\boldsymbol{W})$ is a regularization term for dealing with overfitting. In this paper, we simply use L_2 regularization:

$$R(\boldsymbol{W}) = \sum_{t \in \mathcal{N}_T} \frac{||\boldsymbol{w}_t||^2}{2\sigma_t^2}. \quad (10)$$

MTL with *fixed* task-similarities (**MTL-F**)

Input: Initialize $\boldsymbol{W}^{(0)}$; given $\boldsymbol{D}, \boldsymbol{A}^*, \beta$; $k \leftarrow 0$
for $t \leftarrow 1$ to T
. Initialize $\boldsymbol{\eta}^{(0)}$
. **Repeat** until convergence
. . $\boldsymbol{g}_t \leftarrow -\frac{1}{n}\nabla_{\boldsymbol{w}_t}\frac{||\boldsymbol{w}_t||^2}{2\sigma_t^2}$
. . **for** $t' \leftarrow 1$ to T
. . . Draw $i \in \mathcal{N}_n$ at random
. . . $\boldsymbol{g}_t \leftarrow \boldsymbol{g}_t + \boldsymbol{A}^*_{t,t'}\nabla_{\boldsymbol{w}_t}\ell_{t'}(i, \boldsymbol{w}_t)$
. . $\boldsymbol{w}_t^{(k+1)} \leftarrow \boldsymbol{w}_t^{(k)} + \boldsymbol{\eta}^{(k)} \cdot \boldsymbol{g}_t$
. . **if** $k+1 \bmod 2 = 0$
. . . $\boldsymbol{v}_i \leftarrow \frac{\boldsymbol{w}_t^{(k+1)}(i) - \boldsymbol{w}_t^{(k)}(i)}{\boldsymbol{w}_t^{(k)}(i) - \boldsymbol{w}_t^{(k-1)}(i)}$
. . . Lower-bounds $\boldsymbol{v}_i$ with β
. . . $\boldsymbol{\eta}^{(k+1)} \leftarrow \boldsymbol{v} \cdot \boldsymbol{\eta}^{(k)}$
. . else
. . . $\boldsymbol{\eta}^{(k+1)} \leftarrow \boldsymbol{\eta}^{(k)}$
. . $k \leftarrow k+1$
Output: $\forall t$, $\boldsymbol{w}_t^{(k)}$ converges to $\boldsymbol{w}_t^*$: $\boldsymbol{W}^{(k)}$ converges.

MTL with *unknown* task-similarities (**MTL**)

Input: Initialize $\boldsymbol{W}^{(0)}, \boldsymbol{A}^{(0)}$; given $\boldsymbol{D}$; $k \leftarrow 0$
Repeat until convergence
. $\boldsymbol{W}^{(k+1)} \leftarrow$ MTL-F$(\boldsymbol{W}^{(k)}, \boldsymbol{A}^{(k)}, \boldsymbol{D})$
. **for** $t \leftarrow 1$ to T
. . **for** $t' \leftarrow 1$ to T
. . . Update $\boldsymbol{A}_{t,t'}^{(k+1)}$ with Eq.20/21
. $k \leftarrow k+1$
Output: $\boldsymbol{A}^{(k)}$ converges to $\hat{\boldsymbol{A}}$; $\boldsymbol{W}^{(k)}$ converges to $\hat{\boldsymbol{W}}$.

Figure 1: MTL algorithms (using batch size of 1). The derivation of $\frac{1}{n}$ before the regularization term was explained in Eq. 4. Lower-bounding $\boldsymbol{v}_i$ with β is for stability consideration in the online setting.

To summarize, the overall objective function is as follows:

$$\text{Obj}(\boldsymbol{W}, \boldsymbol{D}) = \sum_{t,t' \in \mathcal{N}_T}\Big[\alpha_{t,t'}\sum_{i\in\mathcal{N}_n}\ell_{t'}(i, \boldsymbol{w}_t)\Big] - \sum_{t\in\mathcal{N}_T}\frac{||\boldsymbol{w}_t||^2}{2\sigma_t^2}.$$

To simplify denotations, we introduce a $T \times T$ matrix $\boldsymbol{A}$, such that $\boldsymbol{A}_{t,t'} \triangleq \alpha_{t,t'}$. We also introduce a $T \times T$ functional matrix $\boldsymbol{\Phi}$, such that $\boldsymbol{\Phi}_{t,t'} \triangleq \mathcal{L}(\boldsymbol{w}_t, \boldsymbol{d}_{t'})$. Then, the objective function can be compactly expressed as follows:

$$\text{Obj}(\boldsymbol{W}, \boldsymbol{D}) = \text{tr}(\boldsymbol{A}\boldsymbol{\Phi}^\top) - \sum_{t\in\mathcal{N}_T}\frac{||\boldsymbol{w}_t||^2}{2\sigma_t^2}, \tag{11}$$

In the following content, we will first discuss a simple case that the task-similarity matrix $\boldsymbol{A}$ is fixed. After that, we will focus on the case that $\boldsymbol{A}$ is unknown, because the task-relationships are unknown among the three query spelling correction tasks that we will focus on.

3.2 MTL with Fixed Task-Similarities

Although the task-similarities are unknown for query spelling correction, we will present a learning algorithm that iteratively reduce the problem to a case of fixed task-similarities. Hence, it is important to discuss the case of fixed task-similarities. With fixed task-similarities, the optimization problem is as follows:

$$\boldsymbol{W}^* = \underset{\boldsymbol{W}}{\text{argmax}}\left[\text{tr}(\boldsymbol{A}^*\boldsymbol{\Phi}^\top) - \sum_{t\in\mathcal{N}_T}\frac{||\boldsymbol{w}_t||^2}{2\sigma_t^2}\right]. \tag{12}$$

It is clear to see that we can independently optimize $\boldsymbol{w}_t$ and $\boldsymbol{w}_{t'}$ $(t \neq t')$ given fixed task-similarities. Hence, we can independently optimize each column of $\boldsymbol{W}$ and derive $\boldsymbol{W}^*$:

$$\boldsymbol{w}_t^* = \underset{\boldsymbol{w}_t}{\text{argmax}}\, \psi(\boldsymbol{w}_t, \boldsymbol{D}), \tag{13}$$

where $\psi(\boldsymbol{w}_t, \boldsymbol{D})$ has the form as follows:

$$\psi(\boldsymbol{w}_t, \boldsymbol{D}) = \sum_{t'\in\mathcal{N}_T}\Big[\alpha^*_{t,t'}\mathcal{L}(\boldsymbol{w}_t, \boldsymbol{d}_{t'})\Big] - \frac{||\boldsymbol{w}_t||^2}{2\sigma_t^2}. \tag{14}$$

3.2.1 2nd-Order Gradient Information

For high convergence speed, an important issue of MTL-F is to effectively and efficiently approximate the Hessian matrix. Following the work of [20] on single-task learning, we present a simple yet effective method to approximate the eigenvalues of the Jacobian matrix of a fixed point iterative mapping. In MTL-F, the update formula is as follows:

$$\boldsymbol{w}_t^{(k+1)} = \boldsymbol{w}_t^{(k)} + \boldsymbol{\eta}_t \cdot \boldsymbol{g}_t, \tag{15}$$

The update term $\boldsymbol{g}_t$ is derived by weighted sampling over different tasks. The weighted sampling is based on fixed task-similarities, $\boldsymbol{A}^*$. $\boldsymbol{g}_t$ has a form as follows:

$$\boldsymbol{g}_t = \sum_{t'\in\mathcal{N}_T}\Big[\alpha^*_{t,t'}\nabla_{\boldsymbol{w}_t}\ell_{t'}(i_{t'}, \boldsymbol{w}_t)\Big] - \frac{1}{n}\nabla_{\boldsymbol{w}_t}\frac{||\boldsymbol{w}_t||^2}{2\sigma_t^2}, \tag{16}$$

where $\alpha^*_{t,t'} = \boldsymbol{A}^*_{t,t'}$ and $i_{t'}$ indexes a random sample selected from $\boldsymbol{d}_{t'}$. Then, the expectation (over distribution of data) of the update term is as follows:

$$\begin{aligned}\text{E}(\boldsymbol{g}_t) &= \sum_{t'\in\mathcal{N}_T}\left\{\alpha^*_{t,t'}\left[\frac{1}{n}\nabla_{\boldsymbol{w}_t}\mathcal{L}(\boldsymbol{w}_t, \boldsymbol{d}_{t'})\right]\right\} - \frac{1}{n}\nabla_{\boldsymbol{w}_t}\frac{||\boldsymbol{w}_t||^2}{2\sigma_t^2}\\ &= \frac{1}{n}\left\{\sum_{t'\in\mathcal{N}_T}\Big[\alpha^*_{t,t'}\nabla_{\boldsymbol{w}_t}\mathcal{L}(\boldsymbol{w}_t, \boldsymbol{d}_{t'})\Big] - \nabla_{\boldsymbol{w}_t}\frac{||\boldsymbol{w}_t||^2}{2\sigma_t^2}\right\}\\ &= \frac{1}{n}\nabla_{\boldsymbol{w}_t}\psi(\boldsymbol{w}_t, \boldsymbol{D}).\end{aligned}$$

In addition, $\boldsymbol{\eta}_t \in \mathbb{R}^f_+$ is a positive vector-valued step size and $\cdot$ denotes component-wise (Hadamard) product of two vectors. As presented in [6], the optimal step size is the one that asymptotically approaches to $\boldsymbol{H}_t^{-1}$, the inverse Hessian matrix of $\psi(\boldsymbol{w}_t, \boldsymbol{D})$ in our setting. To avoid actually evaluating $\boldsymbol{H}_t^{-1}$, we can approximate $\boldsymbol{H}_t^{-1}$ with its eigenvalues. Following [20], we consider an update iterate as a fixed-point iterative mapping (though a stochastic one) $\mathcal{M}$. Taking partial derivative of $\mathcal{M}$ with respect to $\boldsymbol{w}_t$, we have

$$\boldsymbol{J}_t = \mathcal{M}' = \boldsymbol{I} - diag(\boldsymbol{\eta}_t)\boldsymbol{H}_t. \tag{17}$$

By exploiting this linear relation between Jacobian and Hessian, we can obtain approximate eigenvalues of inverse Hessian using eigenvalues of Jacobian:

$$eigen_i(\boldsymbol{H}_t^{-1}) = \frac{\boldsymbol{\eta}_t(i)}{1 - eigen_i(\boldsymbol{J}_t)}. \tag{18}$$

In addition, $eigen_i(\boldsymbol{J}_t)$ can be asymptotically approximated:

$$eigen_i(\boldsymbol{J}_t) \approx \lambda_i \triangleq \frac{\boldsymbol{w}_t^{(k+1)}(i) - \boldsymbol{w}_t^{(k)}(i)}{\boldsymbol{w}_t^{(k)}(i) - \boldsymbol{w}_t^{(k-1)}(i)}. \tag{19}$$

When k is sufficiently large, λ_i will be sufficiently close to $eigen_i(\boldsymbol{J}_t)$. Therefore, we can asymptotically approximate the inverse of the Hessian matrix via efficient estimation of the Jacobian matrix of fixed-point mapping.

In multi-task setting, this optimization problem is a cost-sensitive optimization problem. To summarize our discussion, we present the *2nd-order gradient based MTL algorithm with fixed task-similarities* (*MTL-F* below) in Figure 1 (upper). As we can see, the algorithm iteratively approximates the eigenvalues of the inverse Hessian matrix via Eq. 19. This approximation is based on data points that are cost-sensitively sampled from multiple tasks. Then, it updates the vector-valued step size based on the inverse Hessian information, and the multi-task model weights are updated accordingly. This iterative process continues until convergence.

3.3 MTL with Unknown Task-Similarities

For our query spelling correction tasks, the task-similarities are unknown. To solve this problem, we present an algorithm to learn the task-similarities and model weights in an alternating optimization manner. Our alternating learning algorithm with unknown task-similarities, called *MTL*, is presented in Figure 1 (bottom).

In the MTL learning, the MTL-F algorithm is employed as a subroutine. In the beginning of the MTL, model weights $\boldsymbol{W}$ and task-similarities $\boldsymbol{A}$ are initialized. $\boldsymbol{W}$ is then optimized to $\hat{\boldsymbol{W}}$ by using the MTL-F algorithm, based on the fixed $\boldsymbol{A}$. Then, in an alternative way, $\boldsymbol{A}$ is updated based on the optimized weights $\hat{\boldsymbol{W}}$. After that, $\boldsymbol{W}$ are optimized based on updated (and fixed) task-similarities. This iterative process continues until empirical convergence of $\boldsymbol{A}$ and $\boldsymbol{W}$.

In updating task-similarities $\boldsymbol{A}$ based on $\boldsymbol{W}$, a natural idea is to estimate a task-similarity $\alpha_{t,t'}$ based on the similarity between weight vectors, $\boldsymbol{w}_t$ and $\boldsymbol{w}_{t'}$. It is unclear which similarity measure best fits the tasks of query spelling correction. To study this, we propose two candidate similarity measures for query spelling correction:

Polynomial kernel (Poly): We can use (normalized) polynomial kernel to estimate similarities:

$$\alpha_{t,t'} \triangleq \frac{1}{C}\frac{\langle \boldsymbol{w}_t, \boldsymbol{w}_{t'}\rangle^d}{||\boldsymbol{w}_t||^d \cdot ||\boldsymbol{w}_{t'}||^d}, \tag{20}$$

where $\langle \boldsymbol{w}_t, \boldsymbol{w}_{t'}\rangle$ means inner product between the two vectors; d is the degree of the polynomial kernel; $||\boldsymbol{w}_t||^d \cdot ||\boldsymbol{w}_{t'}||^d$ is the normalizer. C is a real-valued constant for tuning the magnitude of task-similarities. Intuitively, a big value of C will result in "weak multi-tasking" and a small value of C will make "strong multi-tasking". For example, when $d = 1$, the normalized kernel has exactly the form $\frac{1}{C}\cos\theta$, where θ is the angle between $\boldsymbol{w}_t$ and $\boldsymbol{w}_{t'}$ in the Euclidean space.

Correlation (Cor): Since the *covariance* of task weight vectors is a natural way to estimate inter-task interactions, we consider using covariance information for estimating task-similarities. However, we find directly using a covariance matrix (to estimate task-similarities) faces the problem of stability in our online setting. Hence, we use the correlation matrix via normalizing the covariance matrix.

$$\alpha_{t,t'} \triangleq \frac{1}{C}cor(\boldsymbol{w}_t, \boldsymbol{w}_{t'}) = \frac{1}{C}\frac{cov(\boldsymbol{w}_t, \boldsymbol{w}_{t'})}{std(\boldsymbol{w}_t)std(\boldsymbol{w}_{t'})}, \tag{21}$$

Table 1: Statistics of the three spelling correction datasets, and the top-1 accuracy of naive ranking (without re-ranking). *#Candidates* is the number of correction candidates generated for re-ranking.

Data	#Queries	#Candidates	Top-1 Acc. of NR (%)
JDB	1.2×10^4	4.8×10^5	45.7
MSN	5.0×10^3	2.0×10^5	35.5
TREC	6.0×10^3	2.4×10^5	31.0

where $cov(\boldsymbol{w}_t, \boldsymbol{w}_{t'})$ is the covariance between $\boldsymbol{w}_t$ and $\boldsymbol{w}_{t'}$. $std(\cdot)$ is *standard deviation*.

3.4 Accelerated MTL Learning

The MTL learning algorithm can be further accelerated. The naive 2MTL learning algorithm waits for the convergence of the model weights $\boldsymbol{W}$ (in the MTL-F step) before updating the task-similarities $\boldsymbol{A}$. In practice, we can update task-similarities $\boldsymbol{A}$ before the convergence of the model weights $\boldsymbol{W}$.

For example, we can update task-similarities $\boldsymbol{A}$ after running the MTL-F step over a small number of training passes. We will adopt this accelerated version of the MTL learning for experiments so that the task-similarities will not be repeatedly updated. In the experiment section, we will compare the accelerated MTL method with a variety of strong baseline methods.

4. EXPERIMENTS ON TARGET DATA

We will test the proposed method on three query spelling correction tasks. We will study the MTL method with different similarity measures for spelling correction, and compare them against a number of strong baselines, including traditional batch and online learning methods. The results have been averaged over 5 runs for random permutations of the training data order, and standard deviations are given.

4.1 Datasets

Since the **TREC** dataset (released by Microsoft Speller Challenge 2011) is a new and well-known benchmark dataset for query spelling correction, we will use this dataset for experiments. The TREC dataset is based on the publicly available TREC queries (2008 Million Query Track). This dataset contains 5,892 queries and corrections annotated by the Speller Challenge organizers. There could be more than one plausible corrections for a query. In this dataset only 5.3% of queries are judged as misspelled. We use the same split of the training and testing data.

To improve the performance of query spelling correction, we use two auxiliary datasets for performing multi-task learning. One auxiliary dataset is the **JDB** dataset [17] collected from the publicly available AOL query sets, with a total of 12,000 samples, and 2,000 of them (16.7%) are different from the original query. The second auxiliary dataset is collected from **MSN** queries, and for each query there is at most only one correction. In this dataset, about 11% of queries are judged as misspelled. Also, we evenly split the two auxiliary datasets into training and testing data. We show the statistics of the three datasets in Table 1. In the table, we also show the top-1 accuracy (accuracy of the top-1 candidate) of naive ranking using language models (without

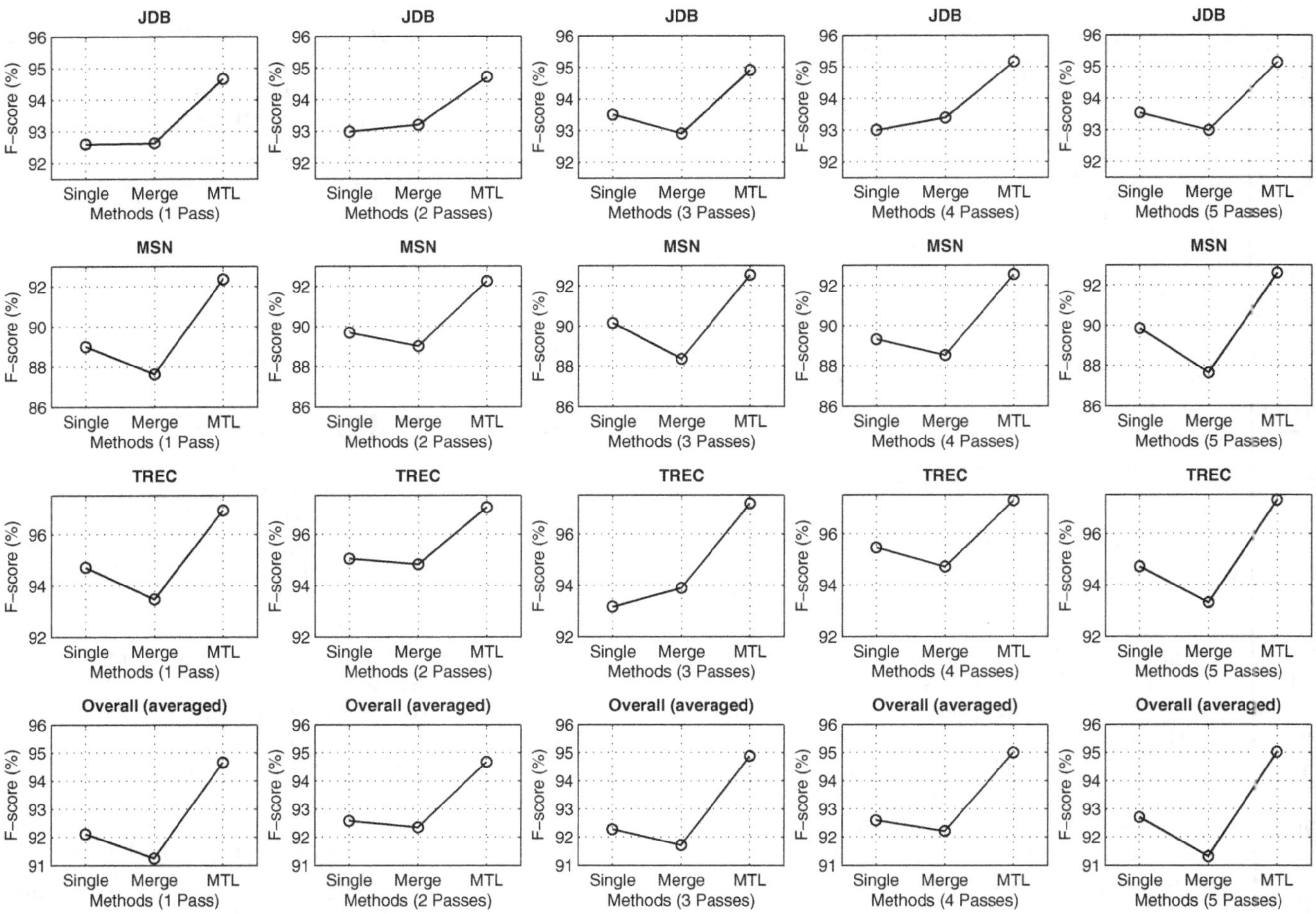

Figure 2: F-scores of different methods in 5 passes. *Single* and *Merge* are based on SGD training.

re-ranking). As we can see, the naive ranking has low accuracies. This reflects the importance of the re-ranking.

The two auxiliary datasets are biased from the TREC dataset in three aspects. First, the queries in those datasets are from three different domains: TREC, AOL, and MSN domains. Second, the distribution of misspelled queries are very different: 5.3% in TREC dataset, 16.7% in JDB dataset, and 11% in MSN dataset. Finally, the number of correct spelling suggestions are different: For the MSN dataset, for each query there is only one correction. On the other hand, for the TREC and JDB datasets, for each query there can be multiple corrections. Hence, it is expected to be a big challenge to integrate those three highly biased datasets for improving spelling correction.

4.2 Settings

Four baselines are adopted to make a comparison with the proposed multi-task learning method, including the limited-memory BFGS batch training method [30] with *single-task setting* (LBFGS-Single), the limited-memory BFGS batch training method with *merged setting* (LBFGS-Merge), the stochastic gradient descent method with single-task setting (SGD-Single), and the SGD method with merged setting (SGD-Merge). For the *single-task setting*, it uses only the task's data to train the re-ranker of the speller (i.e., no data from other spelling correction tasks). For the *merged setting*, it merges all of the training datasets of different tasks to train a unified re-ranker for the speller.

For the multi-task learning method, its hyper-parameters of similarity kernels are tuned in preliminary experiments, and we find using $d = 1$ worked well. In practice, we break the symmetric setting of C (in similarity kernels) and set different values of C for different tasks. We set $\beta = 0.99$ for the proposed MTL method, following the prior work on single-task learning [20]. The proposed method and the four baseline methods use exactly the same features, which is presented before. For the LBFGS method, we use the OWLQN software. The hyper-parameters of LBFGS were left unchanged from the default settings of the OWLQN software.

4.3 Results

We use the expected F1 score as the evaluation metric. This is the same evaluation metrics as the Speller Challenge 2011[2]. Following the previous work of [28], top 40 corrections are used as the default setting. Using this setting, we can compare our results with the results of [28].

The performance comparisons from 1-pass to 5-pass settings are highlighted in Figure 2. In this figure, the *MTL* represents MTL-Poly; *Single* represents the *SGD-Single* baseline. Similarly, *Merge* represents *SGD-Merge*. We can

[2]`http://web-ngram.research.microsoft.com/spellerchallenge/Rules.aspx`

Table 2: **Results (expected F1-score, standard deviation, and training time) of MTL and baselines in 5 passes. *MTL-Poly* and *MTL-Cor* represent the MTL method with polynomial kernel and correlation kernel, respectively. The standard deviations have been derived over 5 runs for random permutations of the training data order.**

Method (#passes)	JDB F1 (%)	MSN F1 (%)	TREC F1 (%)	Overall F1 (%)	Overall Time (sec)
LBFGS-Single (1) (batch)	19.3	15.8	10.8	15.3 (±0.0)	6.0
LBFGS-Single (5) (batch)	93.6	91.1	77.7	87.4 (±0.0)	36.4
LBFGS-Merge (1) (batch)	19.5	15.7	10.7	15.3 (±0.0)	5.5
LBFGS-Merge (5) (batch)	93.5	90.9	96.4	93.6 (±0.0)	35.5
SGD-Single (1) (online)	92.5	88.9	94.7	92.1 (±0.4)	22.3
SGD-Single (5) (online)	93.5	89.8	94.7	92.7 (±0.5)	111.3
SGD-Merge (1) (online)	92.6	87.6	93.4	91.2 (±1.1)	24.2
SGD-Merge (5) (online)	92.9	87.6	93.3	91.3 (±1.6)	116.4
MTL-Poly (1) (new)	94.6	92.3	96.9	94.6 (±0.1)	23.1
MTL-Poly (5) (new)	95.1	92.6	97.2	95.0 (±0.1)	226.7
MTL-Cor (1) (new)	94.7	92.1	96.9	94.6 (±0.1)	22.1
MTL-Cor (5) (new)	95.2	92.6	97.3	95.0 (±0.1)	226.7

Table 3: Results of different methods on their convergence.

Method (#passes)	JDB F1 (%)	MSN F1 (%)	TREC F1 (%)	Overall F1 (%)	Overall Time (sec)
LBFGS-Single (200) (batch)	95.0	92.3	97.0	94.8	1479.1
LBFGS-Merge (200) (batch)	95.0	91.9	97.2	94.7	1360.9
SGD-Single (60) (online)	95.1	92.2	96.9	94.7	1370.9
SGD-Merge (60) (online)	95.0	91.8	97.2	94.7	1393.4
MTL-Poly (30) (new)	95.3	92.5	97.3	95.1	1463.3
MTL-Cor (30) (new)	95.3	92.5	97.3	95.1	1468.1

see that the proposed method MTL achieves much better F-score than all of the baseline methods on the 1-pass setting. In a similar way, MTL outperforms all of the baselines on the 2-pass, 3-pass, 4-pass, and 5-pass settings, and most of the differences are statistically significant.

In general, we find SGD-Merge does not have considerable advantage over the SGD-Single method. This indicates that it is difficult to combine such highly biased datasets for spelling correction, and a simple merge of such biased datasets does not give considerable improvement.

The experimental results in 5 passes are summarized in Table 2 with more details, including the results of batch training, the training time of different methods, and the comparisons between different similarity kernels. In addition, the results of different methods on their convergence state are shown in Table 3.

As we can see, the batch training (LBFGS) has weak performance in 5 passes, compared with SGD and MTL online training methods. The two similarity kernels (polynomial one and correlation one) have very similar performance on the MTL setting. Comparing the 5-pass results of MTL with the baseline results on their convergence, we find the MTL (with 5 passes) outperforms the SGD with 60 passes and LBFGS with 200 passes. In addition, the MTL with 5 passes is quite close to its empirical optimum on convergence. Compared with no matter the online or batch baselines, the MTL method is about one-order magnitude faster in terms of the empirical convergence speed.

In addition, we summarize all F-score curves by changing the number of passes, so that we can check the training process. The curves are shown in Figure 3. We also show the F-score curves based on training time. As we can see, the MTL method can achieve better performance than baselines, with fewer training passes and fewer training time.

5. RELATED WORK

5.1 Spelling Correction

Spelling correction for regular written text is a long standing research topic. Previous researches can be roughly grouped into two categories: correcting non-word errors and real-word errors. In non-word error spelling correction, any word that is not found in a pre-compiled lexicon is considered to be misspelled. Then, a list of lexical words that are similar to the misspelled word are proposed as candidate spelling corrections.

Most traditional systems use a manually tuned similarity function (e.g., edit distance function) to rank the candidates, as reviewed by [11, 22]. During the last two decades, statistical error models learned on training data (i.e., query-correction pairs) have become increasingly popular, and have proven more effective [21, 37].

Real-word spelling correction is also referred to as context sensitive spelling correction (CSSC). Real-word spelling correction tries to detect incorrect usages of a valid word based on its context. A common strategy in CSSC is as follows. First, a pre-defined confusion set is used to generate candidate corrections, then a scoring model, such as a tri-gram language model or naive Bayes classifier, is used to rank the candidates according to their context (e.g., [19, 29]).

When designed to handle regular written text, both CSSC and non-word error speller systems rely on a pre-defined vocabulary (i.e., either a lexicon or a confusion set). However, in query spelling correction, it is impossible to compile such a vocabulary, and the boundary between the non-word

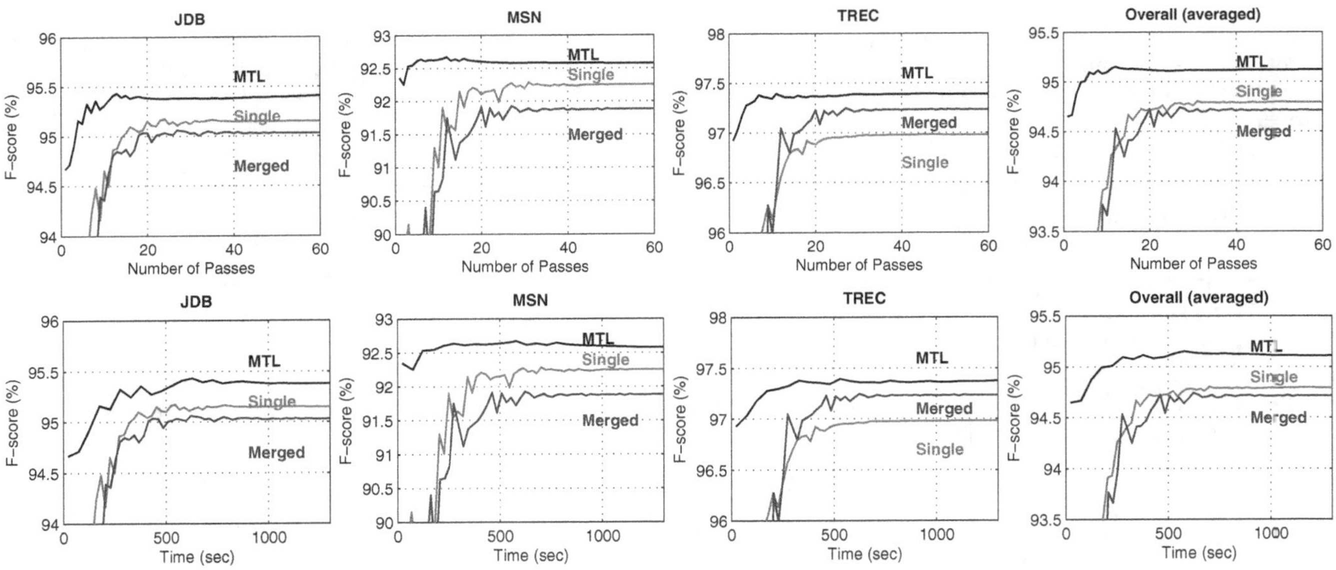

Figure 3: F-score curves of different methods. Upper panels are based on training passes. Bottom panels are based on training time (seconds). *Single* and *Merge* are based on SGD training.

and real-word errors is quite vague. Therefore, recent research on query spelling correction has focused on exploiting noisy Web data and query logs to infer knowledge about misspellings and word usage in search queries.

Cucerzan and Brill [12] discuss in detail the challenges of query spelling correction, and suggest the use of query logs. Ahmad and Kondrak [3] propose a method of estimating an error model from query logs using the EM algorithm. Li et al. [25] extend the error model by capturing word-level similarities learned from query logs. Chen *et al.* [10] suggest using web search results to improve spelling correction. Whitelaw *et al.* [39] present a query speller system in which both the error model and the language model are trained using Web data. Research in this direction also includes more recent work on utilizing large web corpora and query logs [10, 17, 28], employing large-scale n-gram models [17, 28], training phrase-based error model from clickthrough data [34, 18], and so on. Other related work includes [38, 15, 32, 36].

5.2 Multi-task Learning

Multi-task learning has been the focus of much interest in machine learning societies over the last decade. Traditional multi-task learning methods include: sharing hidden nodes in neural networks [8]; feature augmentation among interactive tasks [13]; producing a common prior in hierarchical Bayesian models [42, 43]; sharing parameters or common structures on the learning or predictor space [24, 4]; multi-task feature selection [41]; and matrix regularization based methods [5, 40], among others.

Recent development of multi-task learning is online multi-task learning, started from [14]. [14] assumes the tasks are related by a global loss function and the goal is to reduce the overall loss via online algorithm. With a similar but somewhat different motivation, [1] and [2] studied alternate formulations of online multi-task learning under traditional expert advice models. This is a formulation to exploit low dimensional common representations [16, 31]. Online multi-task learning is also considered via reducing mistake bounds [9], and via perceptron-based online multi-task learning [33].

One of our target is adaptive online multi-task learning. Our adaptive (online) multi-task learning methods not only learn model weights, but also learn task relationships simultaneously from data [35]. More importantly, the proposed method can effectively estimate 2nd-order information, so that we can achieve very fast convergence of the multi-task learning. Finally, our proposal is a general framework which allows *non-structured* and *structured* classification.

6. CONCLUSIONS AND FUTURE WORK

In this paper, we proposed an adaptive (and online) multi-task learning method to integrate highly biased datasets for query spelling correction. We performed experiments on three different query spelling correction datasets, including the well-known TREC benchmark dataset. Experimental results demonstrated that the proposed method considerably outperformed the existing baseline systems in terms of accuracy.

Importantly, the proposed method was about one-order magnitude faster than baseline systems in terms of training speed. In contrast to the baseline methods which require more than 60 passes in training, the proposed method can approach very close to the empirical optimum in five passes. Since query spelling correction can have very large-scale training data in industrial applications (e.g., query spelling logs which contain more than millions of entries, see [34]), the proposed method's ability to approach empirical optimum in 1-pass or a few passes will be of critical importance in such large-scale applications.

The proposed multi-task learning method is a general technique, and it can be easily applied to other classification tasks. As future work, we plan to apply this method to other large-scale web search and data mining tasks. Also, we will explore the possibility of integrating online learning with modern hashing algorithms [26, 27] to solve extremely large-scale problems.

7. ACKNOWLEDGMENTS

This work is partially supported by NSF (DMS-0808864, SES-1131848), ONR (YIP-N000140910911), and DARPA (FA-8650-11-1-7149). Xu Sun was a Postdoctoral Associate supported by ONR and NSF. Anshumali Shrivastava is a Ph.D. student supported by ONR and NSF. The authors thank Yanen Li for helpful discussions.

8. REFERENCES

[1] ABERNETHY, J., BARTLETT, P., AND RAKHLIN, A. Multitask learning with expert advice. In *COLT'07* (2007), vol. 4539 of *Lecture Notes in Computer Science*, Springer, pp. 484–498.

[2] AGARWAL, A., RAKHLIN, A., AND BARTLETT, P. Matrix regularization techniques for online multitask learning. Tech. Rep. UCB/EECS-2008-138, University of California, Berkeley, Oct 2008.

[3] AHMAD, F., AND KONDRAK, G. Learning a spelling error model from search query logs. In *HLT-EMNLP'05* (October 2005), pp. 955–962.

[4] ANDO, R. K., AND ZHANG, T. A framework for learning predictive structures from multiple tasks and unlabeled data. *Journal of Machine Learning Research 6* (2005), 1817–1853.

[5] ARGYRIOU, A., MICCHELLI, C. A., PONTIL, M., AND YING, Y. A spectral regularization framework for multi-task structure learning. In *Proceedings of NIPS'07* (2007), MIT Press.

[6] BENVENISTE, A., METIVIER, M., AND PRIOURET, P. Adaptive algorithms and stochastic approximations. *Berlin: Springer* (1990).

[7] BOTTOU, L. Online algorithms and stochastic approximations. *Online Learning and Neural Networks. Saad, David. Cambridge University Press* (1998).

[8] CARUANA, R. Multitask learning. *Machine Learning 28*, 1 (1997), 41–75.

[9] CAVALLANTI, G., CESA-BIANCHI, N., AND GENTILE, C. Linear algorithms for online multitask classification. In *COLT'08* (2008), Omnipress, pp. 251–262.

[10] CHEN, Q., LI, M., AND ZHOU, M. Improving query spelling correction using web search results. In *EMNLP-CoNLL'07* (Prague, Czech Republic, June 2007), pp. 181–189.

[11] CHURCH, K. W., AND GALE, W. A. Probability scoring for spelling correction. *Statistics and Computing volumn 1* (1991), 93–103.

[12] CUCERZAN, S., AND BRILL, E. Spelling correction as an iterative process that exploits the collective knowledge of web users. In *EMNLP'04* (Barcelona, Spain, July 2004), pp. 293–300.

[13] DAUMÉ III, H. Frustratingly easy domain adaptation. In *ACL'07* (Prague, Czech Republic, June 2007), pp. 256–263.

[14] DEKEL, O., LONG, P. M., AND SINGER, Y. Online multitask learning. In *COLT'06* (2006), vol. 4005 of *Lecture Notes in Computer Science*, Springer, pp. 453–467.

[15] DUAN, H., AND HSU, B.-J. P. Online spelling correction for query completion. In *WWW'11* (2011), ACM, pp. 117–126.

[16] EVGENIOU, T., MICCHELLI, C. A , AND PONTIL, M. Learning multiple tasks with kernel methods. *Journal of Machine Learning Research 6* (2005), 615–637.

[17] GANJISAFFAR, Y., ZILIO, A., JAVANMARDI, S., CETINDIL, I., SIKKA, M., KATUMALLA, S. P., KHATIB-ASTANEH, N., LI, C., AND LOPES, C. qSpell: Spelling correction of web search queries using ranking models and iterative correction. In *Spelling Alteration for Web Search Workshop* (July 2011).

[18] GAO, J., LI, X., MICOL, D., QUIRK, C., AND SUN, X. A large scale ranker-based system for search query spelling correction. In *COLING'10* (2010), pp. 358–366.

[19] GOLDING, A. R., AND ROTH, D. Applying winnow to context-sensitive spelling correction. In *ICML'96* (1996), Morgan Kaufmann, pp. 182–190.

[20] HSU, C.-N., HUANG, H.-S., CHANG, Y.-M., AND LEE, Y.-J. Periodic step-size adaptation in second-order gradient descent for single-pass on-line structured learning. *Machine Learning 77*, 2-3 (2009), 195–224.

[21] KERNIGHAN, M. D., CHURCH, K. W., AND GALE, W. A. A spelling correction program based on a noisy channel model. In *COLING'90* (1990), pp. 205–210.

[22] KUKICH, K. Techniques for automatically correcting words in text. *ACM Comput. Surv. 24*, 4 (1992), 377–439.

[23] LAFFERTY, J., MCCALLUM, A., AND PEREIRA, F. Conditional random fields: Probabilistic models for segmenting and labeling sequence data. In *ICML'01* (2001), pp. 282–289.

[24] LAWRENCE, N. D., AND PLATT, J. C. Learning to learn with the informative vector machine. In *ICML'04* (2004), vol. 69, ACM.

[25] LI, M., ZHU, M., ZHANG, Y., AND ZHOU, M. Exploring distributional similarity based models for query spelling correction. In *COLING-ACL'06* (Sydney, Australia, July 2006), pp. 1025–1032.

[26] LI, P. AND KONIG, A.C. Theory and Applications of b-bit Minwise Hashing. *Communications of the ACM 54* (2011), 101–109.

[27] LI, P., SHRIVASTAVA, A., MOORE, J., AND KONIG, A.C. Hashing Algorithms for Large-Scale Learning. In *NIPS'11* (Granada, Spain, December 2011).

[28] LI, Y., DUAN, H., AND ZHAI, C. Cloudspeller: Spelling correction for search queries by using a unified hidden markov model with web-scale resources. In *Spelling Alteration for Web Search Workshop* (July 2011).

[29] MANGU, L., AND BRILL, E. Automatic rule acquisition for spelling correction. In *ICML'97* (Nashville, TN, 1997), Morgan Kaufmann, pp. 187–194.

[30] NOCEDAL, J., AND WRIGHT, S. J. Numerical optimization. *Springer* (1999).

[31] RAI, P., AND III, H. D. Infinite predictor subspace models for multitask learning. *Journal of Machine Learning Research - Proceedings Track 9* (2010), 613–620.

[32] REYNAERT, M. Character confusion versus focus word-based correction of spelling and ocr variants in corpora. *IJDAR 14*, 2 (2011), 173–187.

[33] SAHA, A., RAI, P., DAUMÉ III, H., AND VENKATASUBRAMANIAN, S. Online learning of multiple tasks and their relationships. In *AISTATS'10* (Ft. Lauderdale, Florida, 2011).

[34] SUN, X., GAO, J., MICOL, D., AND QUIRK, C. Learning phrase-based spelling error models from clickthrough data. In *ACL'10* (Uppsala, Sweden, July 2010), pp. 266–274.

[35] SUN, X., KASHIMA, H., TOMIOKA, R., UEDA, N., AND LI, P. A new multi-task learning method for personalized activity recognition. In *ICDM'11* (2011), IEEE.

[36] SUN, X., SHRIVASTAVA, A., AND LI, P. Query spelling correction using multi-task learning. In *WWW (Companion Volume)* (2012), A. Mille, F. L. Gandon, J. Misselis, M. Rabinovich, and S. Staab, Eds., ACM, pp. 613–614.

[37] TOUTANOVA, K., AND MOORE, R. Pronunciation modeling for improved spelling correction. In *ACL'02* (Philadelphia, USA, 2002), pp. 144–151.

[38] WANG, Z., XU, G., LI, H., AND ZHANG, M. A fast and accurate method for approximate string search. In *ACL'11* (2011), pp. 52–61.

[39] WHITELAW, C., HUTCHINSON, B., CHUNG, G., AND ELLIS, G. Using the web for language independent spellchecking and autocorrection. In *EMNLP'09* (2009), pp. 890–899.

[40] XUE, Y., DUNSON, D., AND CARIN, L. The matrix stick-breaking process for flexible multi-task learning. In *ICML'07* (Corvalis, Oregon, 2007), ACM, pp. 1063–1070.

[41] YANG, H., KING, I., AND LYU, M. R. Online learning for multi-task feature selection. In *CIKM'10* (2010), ACM, pp. 1693–1696.

[42] YU, K., TRESP, V., AND SCHWAIGHOFER, A. Learning gaussian processes from multiple tasks. In *ICML'05* (2005), vol. 119, ACM, pp. 1012–1019.

[43] ZHANG, J., GHAHRAMANI, Z., AND YANG, Y. Learning multiple related tasks using latent independent component analysis. In *NIPS'05* (2005).

Cross-Argument Inference for Implicit Discourse Relation Recognition

Yu Hong Xiaopei Zhou Tingting Che Jianmin Yao Guodong Zhou Qiaoming Zhu
Key Laboratory of Natural Language Processing of Jiangsu Province
School of Computer Since and Technology, Soochow University,
No.1 Shizi Street, Suzhou City, Jiangsu Province, China (zip code: 215006)
+86-18604601106
tianxianer@gmail.com

ABSTRACT

Motivated by the critical importance of connectives in recognizing discourse relations, we present an unsupervised cross-argument inference mechanism to implicit discourse relation recognition. The basic idea is to infer the implicit discourse relation of an argument pair from a large number of comparable argument pairs, which are automatically retrieved from the web in an unsupervised way. In this way, the inference proceeds from explicit relations to implicit ones via connective as bridge. This kind of pair-to-pair inference is based on the assumption that two argument pairs with high content similarity (i.e. comparable argument pairs) should have similar discourse relationship. Evaluation on PDTB proves the effectiveness of our inference mechanism in implicit relation recognition to the four level-1 relations. It also shows that our mechanism significantly outperforms other alternatives.

Categories and Subject Descriptors

I.2.7 [**Computing Methodologies**]: Artifical Intelligence – *Natual Language Processing (Discourse).*

General Terms

Algorithms, Measurement, Experimentation, Languages.

Keywords

Implicit discourse relation, pair-to-pair inference.

1. INTRODUCTION

The task of discourse relation recognition is to automatically predict the internal structure and logical relationship between adjacent text spans (clauses, sentences or paragraphs), such as the ones explored in our paper, Comparison, Contingency (also called Causal), Temporal and Expansion, as annotated in the Penn Discourse Tree Bank [1]. Thereafter in this paper, we limit the discourse corpus and the discourse relations to PDTB and these four relationships respectively, otherwise specified.

Corresponding Author: Guodong Zhou

CIKM'12, October 29–November 2, 2012, Maui, HI, USA.

In PDTB, a discourse relation can be either explicit or implicit. While an explicit relation is signaled directly by the use of an overt discourse connective (also called cue word) in original texts, e.g. "because", an implicit relation can only be inferred by readers according to the context of the utterance and general world knowledge, in the case that original texts don't offer the overt connective. Following two texts illustrate examples for both cases, where connective "*so*" in example (2) is missing from the text and can be only inferred by readers:

(1) He worked all night **because** the submission deadline is coming. (*Explicit relation*)

(2) He worked all night yesterday, **[Implicit=so]** slept all day today. (*Implicit relation*)

While it is easy to recognize explicit discourse relations, e.g. Pitler and Raghupathy (2008)[2] achieved the performance of more than 90% in accuracy, recognizing implicit discourse relations is very challenging, e.g. the state-of-the-art system, as described in Wang and Su (2010)[3] only received the performance of about 40% in accuracy. It is also surprising to notice that the Expansion relationship occupies more than 50% of implicit relations. That is, simply choosing the majority relationship would significantly outperform Wang and Su's system[3] by more than 10% in accuracy. The supervising low performance in current implicit relation recognition systems may be due to three major issues: the missing of connectives, the failure of finding effective linguistic features and the data sparseness problem.

For the first issue, the importance of connectives is obvious and in most cases, the discourse relationship can be determined correctly by the occurrence of a connective, as confirmed in Pitler and Raghupathy (2008) [2].

For the second issue, so far there are no previous studies on systematically exploring why implicit relations don't need the cue words (i.e. connectives). Our observation suggests that implicit relations often occur in parallelism, antithesis, polite formula, rhetorical question, idiom and dialogism, indicating the habitually default cue of well-known and acknowledged discourse relations, or that of relations in casual conversations.

This makes it quite difficult to recognize implicit discourse relations by using the existing linguistic features. Example (3) shows the difficulty to use syntactic features to recognize implicit relations in parallelism due to the failure for syntactic parse trees to reflect the rhetorical structure of parallelism, while example (4) shows the difficulty of predicate word-pair features in dialogism

& rhetorical question: What can the keyword pair "*go-Go*" do for the discourse analysis?

(3) Current college students study 24 hours a day, **[Implicit=and]** 7 days a week, **[Implicit=but]** two weeks a year. (*Parallelism*)

(4) You wanna go? **[Implicit=then]** Go now. (*Dialogism & Rhetorical question*)

Motivated by the critical importance of connectives in recognizing explicit discourse relations, this paper proposes a cross-argument inference mechanism to overcome the three major issues in recognizing implicit relations. Here, an argument (abbr., Arg) denotes a text span by the definition of PDTB. The basic idea is to infer the implicit discourse relation of an argument pair from a large number of comparable argument pairs, which are automatically retrieved from the web in an unsupervised way. This kind of pair-to-pair inference is based on the assumption that two argument pairs with high content similarity (i.e. comparable argument pairs) should have similar discourse relationship. In this way, the inference proceeds from explicit relations to implicit ones via connective as bridges. Example (5) shows two argument pairs meeting the requirements of the cross-argument inference:

(5) Arg1: Bush beats McCain,
Arg2: **and** wins the election.
(*Explicit relation*)

Arg1: Obama beats McCain,
Arg2: **[Implicit=and]** winning the election.
(*Implicit relation*)

Obviously, above three major issues can be well addressed by our cross-argument inference mechanism, i.e. through employing connective as bridge to achieve the inference from explicit relations to implicit relations, avoiding the intricate linguistic or rhetorical analysis via direct discourse relation mapping between comparable argument pairs and data sparseness via retrieving comparable argument pairs from the large-scale web data.

The rest of the paper is organized as follows. Section 2 overviews related work. Section 3 introduces PDTB. Section 4 describes our cross-argument inference mechanism for implicit discourse relation recognition. Section 5 shows the experiments and discussion. Finally, we conclude our work in Section 6.

2. RELATED WORK

Similar to explicit relation recognition, all the existing studies on implicit recognition adopt a supervised learning framework with focus on exploring various kinds of linguistic features.

Pitler and Louis (2009) [4] explored several linguistically informed features, including polarity tag, Levin verb class, length of verb phrase, modality, context, and lexical features. They worked with Penn Discourse Treebank [1], the largest available annotated corpora of discourse relations, showing performance increases over a random classification baseline.

Lin and Kan (2009)[5] inherited this theme and expended the contextual features by using the dependency patterns and the possible correlations between pairs of discourse relations. Their classifier considered the context of the two arguments, as well as the arguments' internal constituent and dependency parses, showing an accuracy of 40.2% on PDTB.

Wang and Su (2010) [3] focused on syntactic knowledge via a tree kernel based approach. They achieved the performance of 40.0% in accuracy on PDTB, slightly outperforming a flat-syntactic-path based approach.

Using the RST corpus (Carlson and Marcu, 2001)[6], which contains 385 Wall Street Journal articles annotated according to the Rhetorical Structure Theory (Mann and Thompson, 1988) [7], Soricut and Marcu (2003)[8] exploited the fact that many of the useful features in explicit discourse relation recognition, syntax in particular, would not be applicable to the analysis of implicit relations that occur intersententially. While their earlier work (Marcu and Echihabi, 2002) [9] showed that the co-occurrence probability of word pairs that extracted from two text spans respectively is useful for detecting implicit discourse relation. Saito and Yamamoto (2006) [10] extended this theme, to show improvements by phrasal patterns extracted from text span pairs. These imply the feasibility of statistical methods in implicit discourse relation recognition.

Meanwhile, Wellner and Pustejovsky (2006) [11] showed that the features of discourse connectives and the distance between the two text spans have the most impact to both explicit and implicit discourse relation analysis. Their experiments on GraphBank (Wolf and Gibson, 2005) [12] achieved 81% accuracy in relation sense disambiguation. However, their system may not work well for implicit relations alone, as the two features only apply to explicit relations: implicit relations don't have discourse connectives and the two text spans of an implicit relation are usually adjacent to each other. Besides, the GraphBank annotations don't differentiate between implicit relations and explicit ones, so it is difficult to verify success for the implicit relations.

Nevertheless, Zhou and Xu (2010)[13] adopted a bigram language model to predict implicit discourse connectives between arguments, which improved their supervised binary classification (either positive or negative relation) on almost four 1-level implicit discourse relations. Besides, they built an unsupervised classification, which mapped each predicted connective to its most frequent relation sense in training data and used the sense to directly appoint the implicit discourse relation. However, this approach only achieved improvements for Contingency and Temporal relations with accuracies of 70.79% and 70.51% respectively, although it can reach more than 97% accuracy for every relation independently when using gold-truth implicit connectives. This shows the shortcoming of connective prediction.

3. PENN DISCOURSE TREE BANK

For our experiments, we use the Penn Discourse Treebank [1], the largest resource of annotated discourse relations. The annotation covers the same one million word Wall Street Journal corpus used for the Penn Treebank [14].

The PDTB adopts the connective-argument view of discourse relations, where a discourse connective (e.g., *because*) is treated as a trigger that takes two text spans as its arguments. The argument that the discourse connective structurally attaches to is called Arg2, and the other argument is called Arg1. Example (6) shows two arguments triggered by the connective "*because*".

(6) **Arg1**: He is very tired,
Arg2: **Because** he played football all morning.

(Contingency-wsj_*ID*)

The PDTB is the first corpus to systematically identify and distinguish explicit and implicit discourse relations, allowing us to concentrate solely on the implicit relations. By definition, an explicit relation is triggered by the presence of a discourse connective which occurs overtly in the text. The discourse connective can essentially be viewed as a discourse-level predicate which takes two clausal arguments. Example 6 shows an explicit Contingency relation triggered by the discourse connective "*because*", where the last line shows the relation type and the file (*ID* indicates file number) in the PDTB from which the example is drawn. The corpus recognizes 100 such explicit connectives and contains annotations for 19,458 explicit relations.

Implicit relation is inferred by the reader but not marked by an overt discourse connective in the text. In this case, for a pair of adjacent spans, the annotator was asked to provide a connective that best captured the inferred relation. Example (7) shows an implicit relation, where the annotator inferred a Contingency relation and inserted an implicit connective "*so*" (i.e., the original text does not include "*so*"). There are a total of 16,584 implicit relations annotated in the corpus.

(7) **Arg1**: You look tired.
Arg2: **[Implicit=So]** Better to have a rest.

(Contingency-wsj_*ID*)

In addition to discourse relations and their arguments, the PDTB also provides the senses of each relation (Miltsakaki and Livio, 2008). The tagset of senses is organized hierarchically into three levels. The top level consists of four major relation classes: Temporal, Contingency, Comparison, and Expansion. For each class, a second level of types is defined to provide finer semantic distinctions. A third level of subtypes is defined for only some types to specify the semantic contribution of each argument. In this paper, we focus on implicit relation recognition to the Level 1 classes, as until recently, the classes could be predicted with only 40.2% in accuracy at best (Lin and Kan, 2009) [5].

4. CROSS-ARGUMENT INFERENCE

In this section, we firstly give the framework of our cross-argument inference method, and then approach the issues of comparable argument pair mining, relation sense disambiguation and pseudo-cue filtering. The first is to detect the comparable argument pairs to form the basis of the inference; the second is to disambiguate the relation senses of explicit connectives in the mapping process (e.g. discrimination between Contingency and Temporal senses of the connective "since"); the third is to shield the inference from the misleading cues caused by the unbalanced distribution of discourse relations (averagely 42.45% Expansion relations but only 12.89% Temporal in PDTB).

The cross-argument inference framework predicts the implicit relation for a given relational argument pair with four basic steps (see Table 1). To perform the pair-to-pair inference from explicit relations to implicit ones, the first step only focuses on mining the comparable argument pairs, which have explicit connectives. On the basis, the second and third steps attempt to select the optimal comparable argument pairs to explore the most possible connective (cue word) for the inferred argument pair. The last step implements the relation mapping with the help of the normally well-defined correspondence between relation senses and connectives (e.g. the connective "because" signals the "Expansion" sense with 100% probability in PDTB).

Table 1: The cross-argument inference framework

Target: **Arg1** [implicit=?] **Arg2**
Task: Predict the implicit **relation**
Inference Procedure
Step 1: Mine the candidate comparable argument pairs for the target from Web; Step 2: Calculate the similarity between the target and each candidate in content, and rank the candidates based on the similarity; Step 3: Select top N' candidates in the ranked list as the comparable argument pairs, and insert the most frequently occurring connective in the comparable pairs into the slot [implicit=?]; Step 4: Map the connective to a relation sense by which to signal the implicit relation of the target.

The proposal that comparable argument pairs can be successfully mined is ensured by the existence of a massive amount of reproduced and adapted texts in different information medium. Actually, once texts represent the same knowledge, even if the texts are created independently, they can still form the comparable resources because inevitably involving the same components of the knowledge as well as their inherent relations, e.g. every *attack* instance involves the element of *hurt* or even *death*. Example (8) shows two instances of the knowledge "*Attack*", which form the comparable resources by the same components "*attack*", "*hurt*", "*death*" and their Contingency and Expansion relations.

(8) **Instance 1**: Our soldier *attacked* the terrorists, **caused** 3 *dead*, **and** 1 *injured*.
Instance 2: The terrorists *attacked* our base, 1 *dead*, 3 *injured*.

(*cause*: Contingency; *and*: Expansion)

Perfect relation mapping can only be ensured by the one-to-one (viz., unambiguous) correspondence between connectives and relation senses. However, despite few, there exist exceptive connectives often signaling multiple relation senses, e.g. the connective *since* has Contingency and Temporal as its senses with almost equal probability in PDTB (Pitler and Raghupathy, 2008) [2]. In this case, the relation mapping should be supplemented by relation sense disambiguation (see section 4.3). And according to ambiguity identification for connectives, the cross-argument inference framework decides whether to perform one-to-one relation mapping or mapping with relation sense disambiguation.

Our inference method regards the most frequently occurring connectives in comparable argument pairs as cues to signal the inferred implicit relations. However, the frequency statistics will be unavoidably confused by the unbalanced distribution of discourse relations. Table 2 shows the distribution between the four main relation classes and their type of realization (implicit or explicit) in PDTB. It can be found that the Expansion relations are distributed predominantly in both explicit and implicit, having the largest number of discourse instances connected by such relation. On the contrary, the Temporal relations are always distributed sparsely, particularly in implicit with only 5.73% occurrence. Thus, if this is the natural distribution in overall linguistic resources, our frequency based connective selection will bring in the connectives of more widely distributed relations, to make noises (pseudo-cues) in recognizing sparse relations. Therefore, the connective selection should be supplemented by an additional treatment of pseudo-cue filtering.

Table 2: Discourse relation distribution in explicit/implicit classes in the PDTB

Class	Explicit (%)	Implicit (%)
Comparison	5590 (28.73%)	2505 (15.10%)
Contingency	3741 (19.23%)	4261 (25.69%)
Temporal	3696 (18.99%)	950 (5.73%)
Expansion	**6431 (33.05%)**	**8868 (53.47%)**
	Total = 19,458	Total = 16,584

4.1 Mining Comparable Argument Pairs

In this paper, we propose a web-driven comparable argument pair mining method for the unsupervised cross-argument inference. It includes two basic steps: the first is to use information retrieval with a regular expression constrained query to roughly search possible comparable argument pairs (candidates); and the second is to select the most similar candidates with the tested argument pairs in content to generate the final comparable corpus.

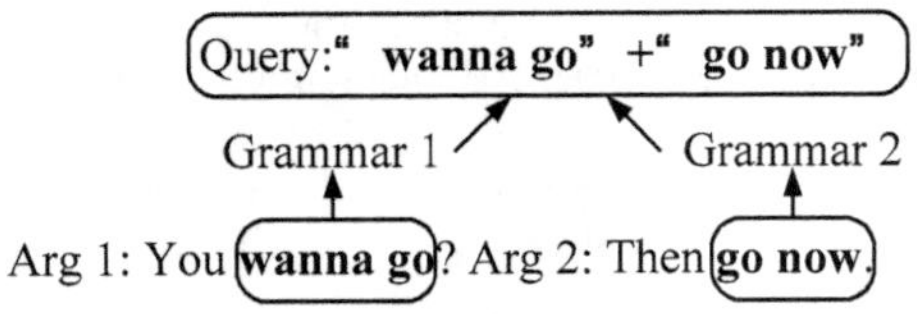

Figure 1. Example of query structure

We perform the information retrieval on the search engine Google. The query is generated by the use of two grammars extracted from the tested argument pair: one grammar (*PreGram*) from the prepositive argument, and another (*PosGram*) from the postpositive. And the query follows the regular expression "*PreGram*"+"*PosGram*", within which the double quotes and the plus sign are both necessary parts, as shown in Figure 1. A query expressed as "X"+"Y" in Google can ensure that all search results (especially snapshots) contain X and Y simultaneously but in different spans.

For each tested argument pair, we use all possible combinations of its "*PreGram*" and "*PosGram*" to generate queries, and use snapshots of top N (N=500) search results as resources for extracting candidate comparable argument pairs. We select the snapshots but not full texts as the resources because the former provide closers comparable pairs in short texts (averagely 3 to 4 spans), helping to obtain adjacent comparable pairs efficiently. And obviously the adjacent pairs have more useful relations for our inference than estranged pairs.

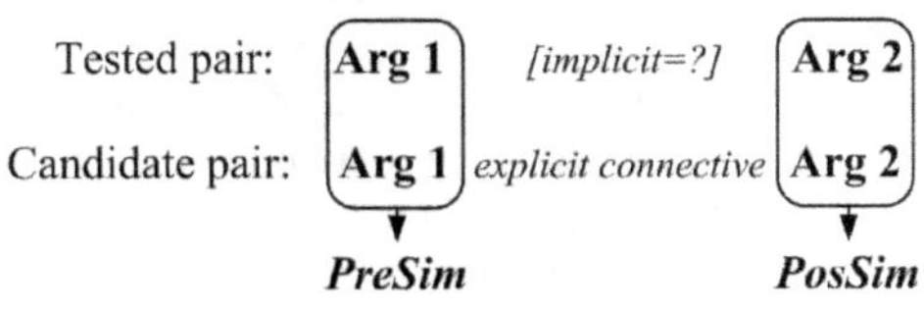

Figure 2. Calculation of *PreSim* and *PosSim*

To support Explicit-to-Implicit inference, we only select the adjacent pairs which have explicit connectives to generate the candidate comparable corpora. Besides, if a query can't contribute more than n (n=5) eligible comparable pairs (viz. adjacent pairs with an explicit connective) in top N search results, we ignore the query along with its comparable pairs. This is because the sparse eligible pairs imply invalidity of the query in exploring discourse relations, and thus the pairs may occur randomly and very possibly become noises in the candidate comparable corpora.

On the basis, we measure the comparable similarity in content between the candidates and the tested argument pair, and select the N' (N'=20) most similar candidates as the final comparable corpora. In the measurement, the similarity of prepositive arguments (*PreSim*) and that of postpositive (*PosSim*) are calculated respectively (see Figure 2), and the whole similarity is the sum of *PreSim* and *PosSim*, divided by the exponentially smoothed absolute value of their difference:

$$Sim = \frac{PreSim + PosSim}{2 \cdot e^{|PreSim - PosSim|}} \qquad (1)$$

where, the exponential function is to ensure nonzero denominator, and the number 2 normalizes the whole similarity. We calculate the similarity like this is to ensure unbiased contributions of *PreSim* and *PosSim* to comparable detection. The bias is measured by the difference between *PreSim* and *PosSim* (viz. |PreSim-PosSim| in the denominator). Thus a good comparable pair should have high similarities *PreSim* and *PosSim* simultaneously with the tested pair. We calculate the *PreSim* and *PosSim* using VSM-based Cosine metric, and use bi-gram as the grammars in query generation and argument representation. Besides, the values of n (n=5), N (N=500) and N' (N'=20) are fine-tuned on all explicit arguments of PDTB v2.0 with a sub-system of predicating connectives.

4.2 Relation Sense Disambiguation

In our inference method, the relation sense mapping can be confused by ambiguous senses of some connectives. In this paper, we propose a local rigorous connective based relation sense disambiguation method.

The sense disambiguation uses unambiguous connectives in comparable corpora (local rigorous connectives) to infer the senses of ambiguous connectives in three basic steps: given an ambiguous connective, the first is to cluster comparable argument pairs; the second is to measure the divergence between local rigorous connectives and the ambiguous connective in the clusters; and the third detects the close rigorous connectives and use their most frequently occurring sense as the sense of the ambiguous connective. Therefore, the disambiguation actually performs a sense inference among similar comparable pairs in content.

We cluster the comparable corpora using the agglomerative hierarchical clustering algorithm (Davidson and Ravi, 2005) [15], by which to generate the cluster tree with the comparable pairs as leaf nodes, where each node is represented by its connective. On the basis, we calculate the divergence by the path length between leaf nodes. We statistically model the close rigorous connective based sense inference as:

$$P(s) = \frac{P_s}{log(div_s)} \qquad (2)$$

where, $P(s)$ is the probability of sense s acting as the sense of the ambiguous connective in the comparable corpora, P_s is the prior probability of s, $\overline{div_s}$ denotes the average divergence between the ambiguous connective and rigorous connectives of sense s in the cluster tree, and the logarithmic function smoothes the sharp difference of divergences.

The sense inference model tends to recommend senses of closer rigorous connectives when the prior probability P_s closes to 0.5. Such probability (P_s=0.5) means corresponding relation senses are the most ambiguous, e.g. the 52.17% probability of sense Contingency of connective "*since*" in Table 3. On the contrary, when P_s is much high (indicating unambiguous), e.g. the 95.99% probability of Contingency of "*moreover*" in Table 3, the model normally can't influence the predominant senses of connectives with the help of logarithmic function. Therefore, it can facilitate sense ascertainment of very ambiguous connectives in the meanwhile avoid confusing senses of approximate rigorous connectives.

Table 3: Percentage of occurrences of connective in its predominant sense (prior probability)

Comparison: <u>*while* (66.07%)</u>, *But* (97.19%), *yet* (97.03%), *still* (98.42%), *however* (99.59%), *although* (99.70%), *though* (100.00%)
Expansion: *in fact* (92.68), *indeed* (95.19%), *and* (96.83%), *or* (96.94%), *instead* (97.32%), *unless* (98.95%), *also* (99.94%), *for example* (100.00%), *in addition* (100.00%), *moreover* (100.00%), *for instance* (100.00%), *separately* (100.00%)
Contingency: <u>*since* (52.17%)</u>, *if* (95.99%), *because* (100.00%), *so* (100.00%), *thus* (100.00%), *as a result* (100.00%)
Temporal: <u>*meanwhile* (48.70)</u>, <u>*as* (70.26%)</u>, <u>*when* (80.18%)</u>, <u>*until* (87.04%)</u>, *then* (93.24%), *once* (95.24%), *later* (98.90%), *after* (99.65), *before* (100.00%)

More directly, we define connectives with more than 90% prior probability of occurrence in their predominant senses as the rigorous connectives, and those less than the probability as ambiguous ones. The sense disambiguation only proceeds when meeting the defined ambiguous connectives. We show all explicit connectives that appear more than 50 times in the PDTB, as well as the prior probability in their predominant senses (see Table 3). It can be found only a few connectives (e.g. while, since, meanwhile, etc) need to be disambiguated, and thus most connectives can be used as rigorous connectives to support the sense inference. In our Explicit-to-Implicit relation inference, only explicit connectives are used in sense mapping. So we divide explicit connectives of PDTB into rigorous (82 in total 102 explicit connectives) and ambiguous (the rest 20) to perform disambiguation.

4.3 Filtering Pseudo-Cues

As discussed in section 4.1, the unbalanced distribution of discourse relations will make our frequency based connective selection easily bring in the connectives of more widely distributed relations, resulting in noisy connectives (pseudo-cues) in sense mapping for sparsely distributed relations. For example, the word "*and*" is an Expansion connective the most frequently occurring in most linguistic resources. However, the spans, which are connected by the connective "*and*", don't always have Expansion relation (See Example 9). In this case, the connective "*and*", as a noise, brings in a pseudo-cue for the discourse relation prediction.

(9) They read lots of books, **and <u>later</u>** made a plan.
(Original connective: *and* - Expansion)
(Latent connective: *later* - Temporal)

By analyzing the connectives in comparable corpora for section 23 of PDTB v2, we found that most pseudo-cues are the connectives which indeed don't trigger discourse relations. Example (9) shows a Temporal relation but has an Expansion connective, where the real trigger should be the word "*later*" but not the connective "*and*".

Actually, this is very common because connectives also have the function of expressing mood (i.e. modal particle), e.g. coherence, pause, emphasis, etc. And, in these cases, discourse relations are normally triggered by other latent connectives, e.g. "*later*" in Example (9). However, although there are many latent connectives, most of them are never publicly released, especially in PDTB.

The latent connectives can be divided into two classes as follows:

- **Connective Triggers (CTs)**: They are the connectives (e.g. "*later*" in Example 9) which trigger discourse relations but don't connect argument pairs. They normally co-occur with pseudo-cues (e.g. "*and*" in Example 9) (Note: Pseudo-cues are the connectives which connect argument pairs but don't trigger discourse relations)
- **Functional Triggers (FTs)**: They aren't connectives but have the function of triggering discourse relations (e.g. "*lead to*" triggers Contingency relations). (Note: FTs haven't publicly released so far). Table 4 shows several FTs that frequently occur in PDTB corpus (The whole FTs are listed in the section of our experiments).

Table 4: Examples of Functional Trigger

Contingency: *cause, make, lead to, result in, bring about*
Expansion: *restatement, to illustrate, including, coupled with*
Comparison: *compared with, similar to*
Temporal: *last year, recently, sometimes, immediately, suddenly*

In this paper, the comparable argument pairs, which involve both an original connective and a latent connective (either connective trigger or functional trigger), are regarded as the samples whose discourse relations are at risk of being misled by pseudo-cues. To reduce the negative influence of the samples in Slot Prediction [implicit=?] (see Step 3 in Table 1) and Relation Sense Mapping (see Step 4 in Table 1), we adopt four methods of pseudo-cue filtering:

- **Rough Filtering**: directly filter out the samples from the set of comparable argument pairs. Hereafter, the samples will not be used to predict the connective of the slot [implicit=?], perform sense mapping, disambiguate relation sense and any part of cross-argument inference.
- **Agent Filtering**: ignore the original connectives of the samples, and use the latent connectives as agents to perform the inference. E.g. in example (9), the latent connective "*later*" is actually used to predict the slot [implicit=?] but not the original connective "*and*".

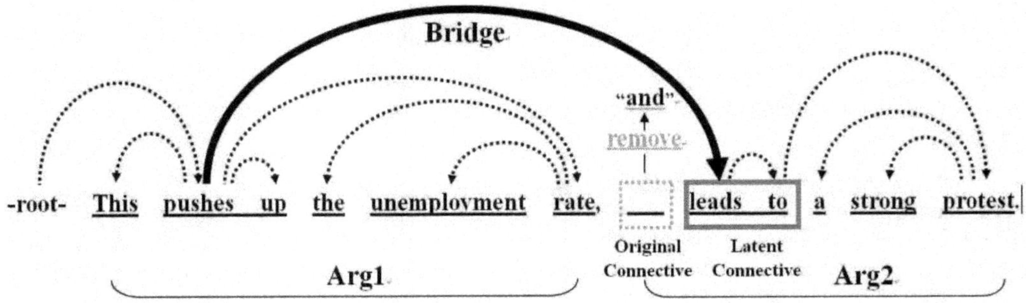

Figure 3. An example of Sneak Filtering for Functional Trigger ("*and*"-Expansion; "*lead to*"-Contingency)

- **Sneak Filtering (for FTs)**: remove original connectives from the samples, and then parse the samples (Stanford dependency parser[1] is used). In a dependency tree, if a FT has the bridge connecting Arg1 and Arg2, it will be regarded as the true connective and used to predict the slot [implicit=?], else the original connective will be used insusceptibly. See the example of sneak filtering in Figure 3, where after removing the original connective "*and*", the only bridge (dependency arc connect two Args) points to the FT "*lead to*", which will be used as the true inference cue (Note: when two Args have no FT or have but triggering a clause but not the bridge between the Args, the sneak filtering is unavailable).

- **Sneak Filtering (for CTs)**: remove original connectives from the samples, and then parse the samples. In a dependency tree, if a CT has a direct dependency arc with the word which bridges two text spans, it will be regarded as the true connective, else the original connective will be used insusceptibly. See the example of sneak filtering in Figure 4, where after removing the original connective "*and*", the only bridge points to the word "*go*", and the CT "*later*" has a direct dependency arc with it, according to which, sneak filtering regards the CT as the true inference cue.

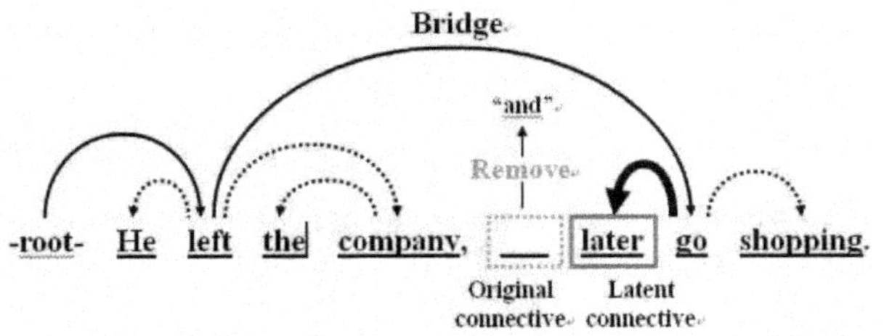

Figure 4. An example of Sneak Filtering for Connective Trigger ("*and*"-Expansion; "*later*"-Contingency)

Sneak filtering aims to determine whether a latent connective can bridge two arguments instead of an original connective when the two connectives occur in the same sentence. If yes, the latent connective will be used as the true inference cue in our discourse relation recognition scheme. This is under the hypothesis that if a content word (Functional Trigger) or a connective which depends on the content word (Connective Trigger) has reflected the semantic or logistical relation between text spans, the original connective will not trigger the main discourse relation or even just a modal particle.

1 http://nlp.stanford.edu:8080/parser/index.jsp

In comparison, the Rough Filtering avoids using the comparable argument pairs, which have ambiguous relations, to infer implicit discourse relations. The Agent Filtering utterly biases toward applying discourse relations of latent connectives to the inference. But the Sneak Filtering exposes the possible pseudo-cues and selectively replaces those using latent connectives (including FTs and CTs) before the inference.

5. EXPERIMENTATION

5.1 Experimental Settings

We experiment on the four top-level discourse relations Temporal (abbr., *Tem.*), Contingency (*Con.*), Expansion (*Exp.*) and Comparison (*Com.*) of PDTB v2 corpus. We use implicit instances in sections 23-24 for testing. However, unlike previous work, which uses instances in the rest of sections for training, we don't need training corpus for our unsupervised inference. The parameters *n* (5), *N* (500) and *N'* (20) are fine-tuned from the optimization process of comparable corpora mining on all explicit instances. Table 5 shows the distribution of test instances in the top-level relations.

Table 5: Distributions of instances (argument pairs)

Relation	*Exp.*	*Con.*	*Com.*	*Tem.*
Instance	606	338	208	40
	(50.80%)	(28.40%)	(17.40%)	(3.40%)

We implement four cross-argument inference systems to respectively test comparable pair mining, sense disambiguation and pseudo-cue filtering:

- **System 1**: Perform the inference using candidate comparable corpora retrieved from Google;

- **System 2**: Optimize the comparable corpora of System1 using comparable similarity measurement (see equation (1));

- **System 3**: Optimize the sense mapping of System 2 by using local rigorous connective based relation sense disambiguation;

- **System 4**: Improve System 3 by using the best pseudo-cue filtering method (Sneak Filtering). We will exclusively compare the performances of the filtering methods in Section 5.3.

Besides, we reproduced and tested Zhou et al (2010)'s method[13] on the same corpus (viz., sections 23-24 of PDTB v2) which use a language model to mine consistent expression patterns, by which to predict connectives and further implicit relations. It is a good statistical method to compare with our inference method. And we also reported the performance of Wang et al (2010)'s method [3], which improves the syntactic-feature based discourse relation classification with the tree kernel. We compared it with our method (both being tested on sections 23-24) to verify the feasibility of statistical modeling in discourse relation analysis. The performance is evaluated as:

$$Accuracy = \frac{TruePositive + TrueNegative}{All} \quad (3)$$

This metric is specially used to evaluate individual relation recognition, where an instance is inferred to be a target relation (*positive*) or not (*negative*). When evaluating the accuracy for all relations (*four-way*), the *TrueNegative* always equals to 0, to generate a whole accuracy (i.e. percentage of correctly inferred instances).

Table 6: Accuracy of our systems

	System1	System2	System3	System4
Exp. vs. Other.	43.04%	57.95%	58.09%	55.98%
Con. vs. Other.	45.53%	68.15%	69.72%	**72.51%**
Com. vs. Other.	69.25%	81.12%	82.39%	**85.16%.**
Tem. vs. Other.	88.29%	95.30%	96.13%	**96.86%**
Four-way	38.03%	52.85%	54.61%	**57.55%**

5.2 Main Results

We firstly inspect the performance of our systems on recognizing an individual relation. Table 6 lists the accuracy for each of the target relations. The worst performance of system 1 illustrates our web-driven approach with comparable corpora mining initially offers rough resources for comparable relation detection. System 2 optimizes the initial corpora through effective comparable similarity measurement, achieving substantial improvements on overall target relations (22.62% at best). System 3 further slightly improves System 2 (1.57% at best). System 4 achieves the optimal four-way performance and considerable improvements on Contingency and Comparison (2.79% at best), but shows a little worse on Expansion than System 3.

Table 7: Number of correctly inferred instances

	System2	System3	System4	Total
Exp.	346	346(↑0)	319(↓27)	606
Con.	151	162(↑11)	195(↑33)	338
Com.	113	122(↑9)	151(↑29)	208
Tem.	20	21(↑1)	21(↑0)	40

We analyze the results of our systems for each of the target relations, to explore the nature of the performance of System 3 and System 4. Table 7 lists the number of correctly inferred instances by System 3, which only offers 21 new correct inferences in total 1192 test samples. This might suggest that our sense disambiguation doesn't work very well. But actually only 138 test samples have ambiguous connectives and 104 have been correctly inferred before System 3 (by System 2), so our disambiguation method has a recall of 61.76% (21/34) in the rest 34 ambiguous relations.

Besides, Table 7 shows System 4 loses 27 Expansion instances, resulting in the reduction in accuracy on the relation. On the contrary, System 4 brings in more correct inferences for Contingency and Comparison. This sharp contrast illustrates our pseudo-cue filtering tends to detect the pseudo-cues derived from Expansion connectives, and thus shield the inference on Contingency and Comparison from noisy connectives of Expansion, but simultaneously filter some other originally correct Expansion connectives. This, to some extent, is unavoidable because Expansion connectives distribute so widely that their risk of being filtered wrongly is increased. Table 8 shows the major connectives filtered as pseudo-cues, which are mostly Expansion connectives.

Table 8: Connectives filtered as pseudo-cue (*num*)

Expansion: *and* (1,891), *or* (698), *instead* (155), *nor* (96), *indeed* (59), *in fact* (34), *also* (29)
Comparison: *but* (304), *yet* (56), *while* (19)
Temporal: *once* (86), *later* (62), *then* (5[illegible])

Table 9: The whole latent connectives occurred in PDTB (including Connective Triggers and Functional Triggers)

Contingency	**The 3 most frequent in PDTB: "cause", "make", "lead to".** *due to, plainly, in that case, arouse, evoke, induce, provoke, generate, bring about, contribute to, result from, result in, set off, stem from, be attributed to, arise from, thanks to, in order to, such that, in this way, cause, make, lead to.* **(Sequence number: Con1-Con23).**
Expansion	**The 4 most frequent in PDTB: "restatement", "such as", "even", "including".** *a case in point, as an illustration, as an example, just as, just like, namely, to illustrate, to demonstrate, chiefly, markedly, particularly, for one thing, in this case, along with, equally, apart from, similar to, coupled with, aside from, barring, excluding, outside of, by the way, incidentally, above all, as a matter of fact, most important, obviously, to be sure, undoubtedly, actually, emphasis, no doubt, in summary, to conclude, to sum up, conclude, as a rule, as usual, for the most part, ordinarily, usually, by and large, in any case, in any event, on the whole, in the long run, on balance, in my opinion, restatement, such as, even, including.* **(Sequence number: Exp1-Exp53).**
Comparison	**The 5 most frequent in PDTB: "than", "like", "compared with", "despite", "similar to".** *similar to, compared with, unlike, after all, same, in spite of, except for, in comparison, different from, worst of all, alike, together with, admittedly, than, like, compared with, despite.* **(Sequence number: Com1-Com21).**
Temporal	**The 4 most frequent in PDTB: "last year", "recently", "sometimes", "immediately".** *suddenly, the moment, for now, at first, in time, after that, all of a sudden, in the first place, till, after a while, for the time being, at that moment, the next week, in an hour, the next step, in a few days, at present, from now on, last year, recently, sometimes, immediately.* **(Sequence number: Tem1-Tem22).**

5.3 Filtering Performance Comparison

To support the pseudo-cue filtering, we manually collected 165 Functional Triggers (FTs) which are all content words (verbs, adjectives, adverbs) or their corresponding phrases. After expanding the triggers according to the hyponymy of WordNet [16], we finally obtained 396 FTs, including 98 Contingency, 179 Expansion, 51 Comparison and 68 Temporal. We regard the FTs as the key latent connectives. Besides, we expanded the 101 connectives of PDTB by adding 18 new connectives (e.g. "*than*"), which all are conjunctions or prepositions and their combinations. When the connectives co-occur in the same sentences, the connectives, which don't connect text spans, will be automatically regarded as latent Connective Triggers (viz., CTs, see Section 4.3). There are totally 186 FTs and 15 new connectives occurring in PDTB. Table 9 lists 119 of them which occur more than 5 times.

We inspected the distributions of Functional Triggers (FTs) respectively in implicit and explicit relations (see Figure 5), by which to validate the feasibility of using the FTs as the cues of our relation inference. Figure 5 shows the FTs more frequently occur in implicit relations than in explicit relations, especially the most frequent FTs give extremely obvious differences. It to some extent illustrates that when there aren't explicit connectives, the FTs can instead express the discourse relations.

However, there are few implicit argument pairs having FTs (51% cases in PDTB corpus), especially the FTs which indeed connect the argument pairs are sparse (only 31% cases in the sections 23-24 of PDTB v2). Thus it is hard to directly use FTs to predict implicit relations (by sense mapping in Table 9). An alternative way is to use the distributions of FTs in a large scale of comparable argument pairs (mined from Web data) to statistically predict the most possible FT and perform sense mapping. However, the cases that FTs solely occur in the argument pairs are fewer than the cases that FTs co-occurred with explicit connectives. This may derived from that people normally avoid the informal usage of FTs in directly connecting text spans. All in all, the following reasons motivate us to use FTs to filter pseudo explicit connectives (viz., pseudo-cues) but not solely use it to perform relation prediction:

- FTs has the function to express discourse relations;
- FTs normally co-occurred with explicit connectives but sparsely solely occur;

We performed the pseudo-cue filtering methods (see Section 4.3) and use them respectively to improve the system 3 (viz., our cross-argument inference system after optimizing comparable corpora and sense mapping). The performances are shown in Table 10. Within the table, the baseline 1 detects the target

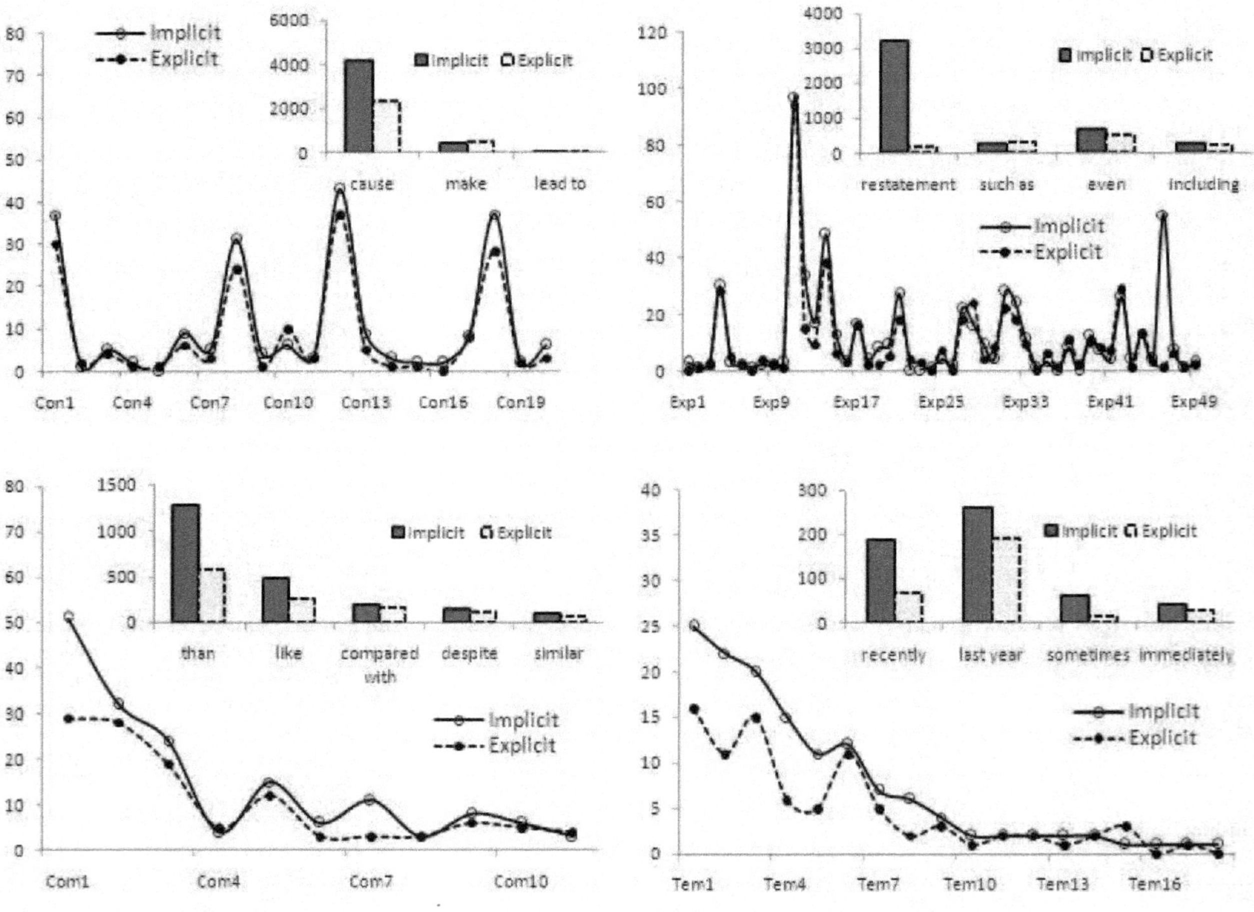

Figure 5. The distributions of Functional Triggers (FTs) in implicit and explicit relations (The vertical axis indicates the occurrence frequency of FTs, the horizontal axis indicates the sequence number of FTs which have been mentioned in Table 9)

implicit argument pairs (in the sections 23-24 of PDTB v2) which involve FTs and uses the FTs to directly predict relations (by using the sense mapping in Table 9), and other targets maintain the original output of System3. And the baseline 2 detects the comparable argument pairs (in the mined comparable corpora) which involve FTs and uses the FTs to directly predict relations. For System 3, the Rough filtering removes all comparable pairs which involves both original connectives and latent connectives (including CTs and FTs). The Agent filtering uses the latent connectives to replace the original connectives. Sneak filtering selectively performs the replacement according to the dependencies of the latent connectives (see Section 4.3).

Table 10: Filtering Comparison (The performance of System 3 is 54.61% on Four-way)

Method	Accuracy
System 3+ **Filtering Baseline 1**	28.50% ↓
System 3+ **Filtering Baseline 2**	29.25% ↓
System 3+**Rough**	52.62% ↓
System 3+**Agent**	49.34% ↓
System 3+ **Sneak (CTs)**	**55.21% ↑**
System 3+ **Sneak (FTs)**	**56.92% ↑**
System 3+ **Sneak (CTs + FTs)**	**57.55% ↑**

It can be found that the three methods of Sneak Filtering all improve the performance of System 3, especially the Sneak which considers both FTs and CTs. And after analyzing the experimental data, we found the sneaks should bring in more improvements if the dependency parser is more precise.

In contrast, the Agent filtering and the Rough filtering reduce the performance of System 3, especially to directly replace original connectives by latent connectives in Agent filtering brings in much more performance drawback. So compared with discarding some uncertainty, to unlimitedly replace original connectives is at the risk of bringing in more noises. The baseline 1 and 2 show the worst performances. But in fact the baseline 1 should achieve an approximately 31% accuracy because the percentage of the FTs, which connect the argument pairs, is about 31%. This implies some incorrect relation sense mapping or ambiguous senses of our FTs. Besides, we find the baseline 1 can be improved if we further expand the set of latent connectives, e.g. adding the combination of synonyms (e.g. "...*beauty*...*pretty*..." - Expansion) and that of antonyms (e.g. "...*love*...*hate*..." - Comparison).

Therefore, to improve pseudo-cue identification and filtering, it is necessary to deal with the following issues:

- To further expand the set of latent connectives;
- To disambiguate multiple senses of latent connectives;
- To improve the precision of dependency parser.

5.4 Inference Performance Comparison

We compare our best system with that of Wang et al's Tree kernel method[3] and Zhou et al's language model based unsupervised method[13]. Besides, we use the majority relation class (see Table 4) as the baseline, where all instances are classified as Expansion, yielding an accuracy of 50.80%. Table 11 lists the accuracy for all relations (four-way). Our method (System 4) shows the best performance, better than Wang et al's and Zhou et al's respectively by 17.55% and 16.20% respectively, although only better than the baseline by 6.75% in accuracy.

Table 11: Overall results for tested methods

Method	Accuracy
Tree Kernel (Wang et al's)	40.00%
Language Model (Zhou et al's)	41.35%
Our best (System3 + Sneak (FTs+CTs))	57.55%
Baseline	50.80%
Human 1	**61.29%**
Human 2	**59.78%**

Although we use our best system (System 4) to compare with Wang et al's and Zhou et al's, actually our system 2 (i.e. the system only use comparable corpora) has had great superiority than their work (more than 11.5% accuracy). So, compared to our sense disambiguation and pseudo-cue filtering, our web-driven comparable corpora mining provides the main improvement. Actually, our System 2 is partially the same with Zhou et al's work: both predict connectives and perform Explicit-to-Implicit inference. However, Zhou et al's work only use a Tri-gram language model to search consistent expression patterns in small-scale local dataset (PDTB), which results in strict limitation for pattern mining. Especially the patterns (more like phrase pairs) cannot effectively reflect the comparable relation among argument pairs, hardly to support connective predication. By contrast, our web-driven method can obtain abundant candidate comparable resources from large-scale web data, and further our comparable similarity algorithm can simultaneously ensure the similarity in both text spans (respectively in preposition and postposition) of argument pair. Thus our method improves the capacity of comparable corpora mining by performing from-loose-to-tight similarity measurement.

In spite of that, Zhou et al's work, as well as ours, shows better performance than Wang et al's work. This illustrates the feasibility of a statistical model in implicit relation recognition. Especially, with the help of relatively easy relation sense mapping, the cross-argument inference mechanism avoids complicated linguistic analysis, reducing the probability of being misled by mistakes of intermediate steps. Besides, because of the high accuracy (more than 90%, Pitler and Raghupathy, 2008) [2] of explicit relation classification, the Explicit-to-Implicit inference can be jointly used with the explicit classification to generate automatic processing chain of connective identification, sense mapping and relation inference.

However, our best performance is still low with only 6.75% improvement than the baseline. And Wang et al's and Zhou et al's work (Table 11 shows its best performance reported in ACL 2010) are even much worse than the baseline. This reflects implicit relation discourse recognition is very difficult (even for human). Table 11 shows the capacity of human being (two second year postgraduates working on discourse relation recognition) in recognizing the relations, which achieves only 61.29% at best. It is because implicit relation inherently involves subjectivity and ambiguity, e.g. instance (10) shows two possible relations when using different connectives *so* (Contingency) and *but* (Comparison):

(10) He worked all night yesterday, [Implicit= **so** or **but**] slept all day today. (Both Contingency and Comparison are reasonable)

6. CONCLUSION

We have presented the first study on using unsupervised method to recognize implicit discourse relation, as well as the statistical method of relation sense disambiguation. Unlike prior work, our method bypasses the complicated linguistic analysis, and performs Explicit-to-Implicit relation mapping by well using comparable corpora in large-scale web data. Results on PDTB show a significant improvement.

Our analysis revealed several difficulties in current implicit relation recognition: 1) rhetorical structure is important feature for implicit relation analysis, but the rhetoric analysis itself is a hard work so far; 2) discourse relation recognition involves subjectivity and ambiguity, see instance (10), so it shouldn't proceed without the support of context analysis, however, to search the most relative context will bring in another relation analysis; 3) modal connectives (e.i. connectives act as modal particle) normally make pseudo-cues for implicit relation inference, e.g. "I *love* you, *and* [modal particle] I *hate* you too" should be Comparison relation (by "*love*" and "*hate*") but not Expansion signaled by the modal connective "*and*", therefore, to filter modal connectives and instead use latent relation connectives (e.g. *love* & *hate*) to signal relations is very necessary.

In future work, we focus on the automatic method of modal particle identification with the help of sentiment analysis, and on the basis to deeply explore the latent connective mining and application in discourse relation recognition.

7. ACKNOWLEDGMENTS

This research is supported by the National Natural Science Foundation of China (No. 60970056, 60970057, 61003152, 90920004), the Special fund project of the Ministry of Education Doctoral Program (2009321110006, 20103201110021), the Natural Science Foundation of Jiangsu Province (No. BK2011282), the Major Project of College Natural Science Foundation of Jiangsu Province (No. 11KIJ520003) and the Natural Science Foundation of Jiangsu Province, Suzhou City (SYG201030).

8. REFERENCES

[1] Prasad, R., Dinesh, N., Lee, A., Miltsakaki, E., Robaldo, L., Joshi, A., and Webber, B. 2008. The Penn Discourse TreeBank 2.0. In Proceedings of the 6th International Conference on Language Resources and Evaluation (LREC 2008), Marrakesh, Morroco.

[2] Pitler, E., Raghupathy, M., Mehta, H., Nenkova, A., Lee, A., and Joshi, A. 2008. Easily identifiable discourse relations. In Proceedings of the 22nd International Conference on Computational Linguistics (COLING 2008), Posters, Manchester, UK, 87–90.

[3] Wang, W. T., Su, J., and Tan, C. L. 2010. Kernel Based Discourse Relation Recognition with Temporal. In Proceedings of the 48th Annual Meeting of the Association for Computational Linguistics, 11-16 July, Uppsala, Sweden, 710-719.

[4] Pitler, E., Louis, A., and Nenkova, A. 2009. Automatic sense prediction for implicit discourse relations in text. In Proceedings of the Joint Conference of the 47th Annual Meeting of the Association for Computational Linguistics and the 4th International Joint Conference on NLP of the Asian Federation (ACL-IJCNLP 2009), August, Singapore, 683-691.

[5] Lin, Z. H., Kan, M. Y., and Tou, N. G. H. 2009. Recognizing Implicit Discourse Relations in the Penn Discourse Treebank. In Proceedings of the 2009 Conference on Empirical Methods in Natural Language Processing (EMNLP 2009), Singapore, 343-351.

[6] Carlson, L., Marcu, D., and Okurowski, M. E. 2001. Building a discourse-tagged corpus in the framework of rhetorical structure theory. In Proceedings of the Second SIGdial Workshop on Discourse and Dialogue (SIGDIAL2001), 1-2 September, Aalborg, Denmark, 1–10.

[7] Mann, W. C., and Thompson, S. A. 1988. Rhetorical structure theory: Towards a functional theory of text organization. Text, 8(3), 243-281.

[8] Soricut, R., and Marcu, D. 2003. Sentence Level Discourse Parsing Using Syntactic and Lexical Information. In Proceedings of the 2003 Conference of the North America Chapter of the Association for Computational Linguistics on Human Language Technology (NAACL 2003), 27 May - 1 June, Edmonton, Canada, 149-156.

[9] Marcu, D., and Echihabi, A. 2002. An unsupervised approach to recognizing discourse relations. In Proceedings of the 40th Annual Meeting of the Association for Computational Linguistics (ACL 2002), Morristown, NJ, USA, 368–375.

[10] Saito, M., Yamamoto, K., and Sekine, S. 2006. Using phrasal patterns to identify discourse relations. In Proceedings of the Human Language Technology Conference of the North American Chapter of the Association for Computational Linguistics (HLT-NAACL 2006), June, New York, USA, 133-136.

[11] Wellner, B., Pustejovsky, J., Havasi, C., Rumshisky, A., and Sauri, R. 2006. Classification of discourse coherence relations: An exploratory study using multiple knowledge sources. In Proceedings of the 7th SIGdial Workshop on Discourse and Dialogue, July, Sydney, Australia.

[12] Wolf, F., and Gibson, E. 2005. Representing discourse coherence: a corpus-based analysis. In Proceedings of the 20th International Conference on Computational Linguistics (COLING 2004), Morristown, NJ, USA, 134–140.

[13] Zhou, Z. M., Xu, Y., Niu, Z. Y., Lan, M., Su, J., and Tan, C. L. 2010. Predicting Discourse Connectives for Implicit Discourse Relation Recognition. In Proceedings of the 23th International Conference on Computational Linguistics (COLING 2010), Poster, August, Beijing, China, 1507-1514.

[14] Eleni, M., Robaldo, L., Lee, A., and Joshi, A. 2008. Sense annotation in the penn discourse treebank. Computational Linguistics and Intelligent Text Processing, Lecture Notes in Computer Science, 4919:275-286.

[15] Davidson, I., and Ravi, S. S. 2005. Agglomerative Hierarchical Clustering with Constraints: Theoretical and Empirical Results. In Proceedings of 9th European Conference on Principles and Practice of Knowledge Discovery in Databases (PKDD), Porto, Portugal, 59-70.

[16] Budanitsky, A., and Hirst, G. 2001. Semantic Distance in WordNet: An experimental, application-oriented evaluation of five neasures. In Proceedings of (NAACL-2000) Workshop on WordNet and Other Lexical Resources, June, Pittsburgh, PA, UAS, 29-34.

Interpreting Keyword Queries over Web Knowledge Bases

Jeffrey Pound Alexander K. Hudek Ihab F. Ilyas[†] Grant Weddell
David R. Cheriton School of Computer Science
University of Waterloo, Waterloo, Canada
[†]Qatar Computing Research Institute (QCRI)
{jpound,akhudek,gweddell}@cs.uwaterloo.ca, [†]ikaldas@qf.org.qa

ABSTRACT

Many keyword queries issued to Web search engines target information about real world entities, and interpreting these queries over Web knowledge bases can often enable the search system to provide exact answers to queries. Equally important is the problem of detecting when the reference knowledge base is not capable of answering the keyword query, due to lack of domain coverage.

In this work we present an approach to computing structured representations of keyword queries over a reference knowledge base. We mine frequent query structures from a Web query log and map these structures into a reference knowledge base. Our approach exploits coarse linguistic structure in keyword queries, and combines it with rich structured query representations of information needs.

Categories and Subject Descriptors

H.3.3 [**Information Systems**]: Information Search and Retrieval—*Query formulation, Retrieval models*

1. INTRODUCTION

As the amount of structured data on the Web continues to grow, the ability to exploit this data for keyword search becomes increasingly important. Efforts such as DBpedia[1], Freebase[2], and Linked Data[3] have produced large heterogeneous *knowledge bases* that encode great amounts of information about many real world entities. Web search queries seeking information about these entities could be better served by interpreting the query over a knowledge base in order to provide an exact answer to the query, or to enhance document retrieval by understanding the entities described by the query.

For example, consider a user searching for *"songs by jimi hendrix."* While a text search may retrieve relevant documents to the query terms, it leaves the user with the task of scouring textual results in search of the information they are seeking. This user's query could be better served by returning a list of particular songs by the musician Jimi Hendrix (precise answers to the query), possibly along with information about each song (e.g., structured facts from a knowledge base or documents resulting from a text search for the particular song). Similarly, the keyword query *"author of moby dick"* could be better answered if a search system understood that "moby dick" describes a particular book, "author of" describes a relationship, and the *query intent* is to find the unspecified entity that has an "author of" relationship to "moby dick."

We refer to the process of interpreting keyword queries over a knowledge base as *semantic query understanding.* This problem has the following characteristics that pose difficult technical challenges.

- **Ambiguity** Keyword queries tend to be short, ambiguous, and underspecified. For a given keyword query there may be multiple possible ways to interpret the underlying query intent. Semantic query understanding systems need to accurately interpret entity-based keyword queries when the underlying reference knowledge base contains the relevant information.
- **Representation & Coverage** Not all keyword queries have an entity focus (so called, *entity-based keyword queries*). A query such as *"corporate tax laws buyout"* may intentionally be seeking documents that mention the given query terms, and an attempt to represent the query in terms of knowledge base entities may produce an incorrect interpretation and harm the quality of results. Similarly, some entity-based queries may seek information that does not exist in a given reference knowledge base. A high accuracy semantic query understanding system will answer queries only when the query intent can be represented and evaluated over the reference knowledge base.
- **Scale** Web knowledge bases tend to be very large and heterogenous, meaning approaches cannot be engineered to exploit domain specific regularities or depend on small fixed schemas with complete data. Semantic query understanding techniques must scale to large heterogeneous Web knowledge bases.

1.1 Motivation

Query understanding is a broad phrase used to describe many techniques applied to keyword queries in order to

[1]http://dbpedia.org
[2]http://www.freebase.com
[3]http://linkeddata.org

CIKM'12, October 29–November 2, 2012, Maui, HI, USA.
Copyright 2012 ACM 978-1-4503-1156-4/12/10 ...$15.00.

Figure 1: Overview of the query understanding process.

represent the underlying information need in a way that a search system can exploit. Some popular approaches include topic classification, in which the topic of a query is determined using a statistical classifier. Topic classification aids a search system by giving it context, or by allowing the system to select the appropriate data source to search. For example, the query

$$\text{"songs by jimi hendrix"} \quad (1)$$

may be classified as a music query. However query classification does not give any insight into precisely what the query is looking for within the domain of music.

Another query understanding approach that has received recent attention from researchers is term annotation. Term annotation labels individual query terms with annotations that describe the role these terms play with respect to an underlying information system. Following our example query, the terms *"jimi hendrix"* may be annotated as a *name*, and the term *"songs"* annotated as an entity *type*. While query annotations can aid a search system in understanding the meaning of individual terms, the annotations do not describe the underlying structure of the query as a single coherent query interpretation. Continuing the example, we want to model the latent query structure that expresses the query intention as finding entities of type *song* that are created by an entity named *"jimi hendrix."* (as opposed to finding, for example, information about the person named *"jimi hendrix"* who is known to have written songs, or a song named *"jimi hendrix"*).

The goal of *semantic query understanding* is to compute a formal interpretation of an ambiguous information need. Figure 1 shows our proposed semantic query understanding process for a variation of our running example information need. Our example keyword query can be structurally understood as finding all *entities* of a *type* described as "songs," that have a "by" *relationship* to an entity described as "jimi hendrix". This is given as the following conjunctive query.

$$q(x)\text{:-}\exists y.\texttt{SONG}(x) \wedge createdBy(x,y) \wedge y = \texttt{Jimi\_Hendrix} \quad (2)$$

Where the predicates `SONG` and *createdBy*, and the entity `Jimi_Hendrix` are part of a Web knowledge base. The difficulty in mapping a keyword query to a formal interpretation lies in the inherent ambiguity in keyword queries, and the many possible mappings query terms can have over very large reference data collections. For example, the term *"hendrix"* matches 68 data items in our data set, and the term *"songs"* matches 4,219 items, and the term *"by"* matches 7,179 items (see Section 5 for details on the data set used for our experiments). This yields a space of over two billion possible conjunctive queries constructed by mapping each query term to a syntactically similar predicate. This does not count the possibility of additional predicates existing in the underlying conjunctive query that are not explicitly represented by a term in the keyword query. There is also great variation in how queries are expressed; many Web queries are very short and underspecified. For example, the query *"hendrix songs"* shown in Figure 1 shares the same logical structure as example query 1, even though the *createdBy* relation is not explicitly represented by any query terms. It is the job of the query understanding system to infer the existence of such latent relations.

In this work we propose a method for interpreting keyword queries over Web knowledge bases. We use an annotated Web search query log as training data to learn a mapping between keyword queries and their underlying semantic structures. Because of the very high cost in creating training data, we design an approach that maps high level representations of keyword queries to schema-level representations of structured queries, greatly reducing the amount of training data needed to accurately learn these mappings. Our approach integrates state-of-the-art techniques in natural language processing with top-k search over structured data and knowledge base query processing, bridging the gap between language models for statistical representations of keyword queries and database formalisms for structured representations of information needs.

1.2 Contributions

In this work, we make the following contributions.

- We propose a novel method for interpreting keyword queries over Web knowledge bases that computes probable semantic structures based on a statistical model learned from real user queries, and maps them into a knowledge base.
- We show an encoding of the semantic annotation problem as a parameter estimation problem for a conditional random field, and propose a method of structuring annotated queries that uses a high level representation of both keyword queries and the target knowledge base query structure. This high level representation allows us to learn a mapping from *semantic summaries* of keyword queries to *structured query templates* by exploiting the redundancy of the summaries and templates shared by different queries in a query log.
- We present the results of an analysis of a real Web search log, giving insight into the types of entity-based queries asked by real users. Our analysis shows the importance of addressing entity-based queries due to the large number of these queries issued by users. The analysis also establishes relationships between linguistic structure and semantic structure, and gives insight into the types of structures that repeatedly occur in keyword queries.

We demonstrate the viability of our proposed approach with an experimental evaluation of both the effectiveness and efficiency of a prototype implementation of the system.

1.3 Outline

The remainder of the paper is organized as follows. Section 2 gives an overview of the keyword query understanding problem, outlines the basis of our formalism for modeling query intentions, and gives an overview of our approach to semantic query understanding. The details of our approach are presented in Section 3. Section 4 describes the results of our analysis of a Web query log. In Section 5 we empirically evaluate our proposal. We review relevant work in Section 6 and conclude in Section 7.

2. DATA AND PROBLEM DEFINITIONS

2.1 Representing Knowledge and Queries

We adopt a formal model of knowledge representation as a collection of assertions based on the OWL2 EL Profile[4] extended with unary *entity* sets (allowing an entity to represent a class containing only itself), and with attributes that map to values in a concrete domain such as strings, numbers, or dates.

Definition 1. **(Concept)** A *concept* C is defined by the following grammar, where A is an entity type (a.k.a, entity class), R is a relation, R^- is the inverse of relation R, e is an entity, f is an attribute, k is a constant, and $\sqcap$ denotes concept conjunction (intersection)

$$C \ ::= \ A \mid \exists R(C) \mid \exists R^-(C) \mid C_1 \sqcap C_2 \mid f = k \mid \{e\}.$$

Definition 2. **(Knowledge base)** Facts about entities are represented as assertions. An *assertion* has one of the following forms:

$$A(e) \ \mid \ R(e_1, e_2) \ \mid \ f(e, k)$$

This first construct asserts that an entity e has type A, for example: `GUITARIST(Jimi_Hendrix)`. The second construct asserts that a relation R holds between two entities, for example: *createdBy*(`Foxy_Lady`, `Jimi_Hendrix`). This also implies the inverse *createdBy*$^-$(`Jimi_Hendrix`, `Foxy_Lady`). The last construct asserts that an entity has a particular value for a given attribute. This is a special case of a relation assertion, where the entity relates to a value. For example, *dateOfBirth*(`Jimi_Hendrix`, 1942-11-27). The assertion *subClassOf*(A_1, A_2) is used to encode transitive class hierarchies among types.

A *knowledge base* $\mathcal{K}$ is represented as a set of assertions. We write $\mathcal{K} \models C$ to denote that concept C is consistent with $\mathcal{K}$ and $\mathcal{K} \models C(e)$ to denote that the knowledge base $\mathcal{K}$ entails that entity e can be inferred to be an instance of C.

We will ultimately use concepts in the given KB formalism to represent query intentions using the following definition of a search query over a knowledge base.

Definition 3. **(Concept Search Query)** A *concept search query* is given by a concept C expressed using Definition 1. The answer to the query C over a given knowledge base $\mathcal{K}$ is the set of entities inferred to be instances of C

$$answer(C, \mathcal{K}) = \{e \mid \mathcal{K} \models C(e)\}.$$

Our example query from Equation 2 can be modeled as the following: `SONG` $\sqcap\ \exists$*createdBy*({`Jimi_Hendrix`}).

2.2 The Query Understanding Problem

We can abstract a concept search query C as a conjunctive query λ^C consisting of u unary predicates and b binary predicates with a single distinguished variable. (This equivalence is straightforward, and can be seen in the relationship between assertions and concept expressions defined in Section 2.1.) Let $\mathcal{K}_\mathcal{P}$ denote the set of predicates occurring in a knowledge base $\mathcal{K}$, and $\lambda^C_\mathcal{P}$ denote the set of predicates (unary and binary) occurring in a conjunctive query λ^C. Let $\mathcal{L}(P)$ denote the set of textual labels that can be used to describe a predicate P. The space of possible queries λ^C for a given keyword query $Q = \langle q_1 q_2 \ldots q_n \rangle$ is given by the following expression.

$$\lambda^C(x) \ = \ \bigwedge_{i=1}^{u} P_i(x_j) \wedge \bigwedge_{i=1}^{b} P_i(x_j, x_k) \text{ s.t.} \tag{3}$$

$$\forall P \in \lambda^C_P, P \in \mathcal{K}_P \tag{4}$$

$$\forall q \in Q, \exists P \in \lambda^C_P . q \in \mathcal{L}(P) \tag{5}$$

$$\mathcal{K} \models C \tag{6}$$

Equation 3 defines a space of all possible conjunctive queries with u unary predicates and b binary predicates. Equation 4 constrains all predicates to be part of the given knowledge base, ensuring the query is safe. Equation 5 ensures coverage of all query terms and Equation 6 ensures that the query is consistent with the knowledge base. Ideally we expect that $\mathcal{L}(P)$ contains all possible representations of P, including synonyms and linguistic variations of terms (e.g., lemmatized forms). In practice, we approximate this by relaxing the constraint $q \in \mathcal{L}(P)$ to allow fuzzy and partial string matching.

The *query understanding problem* is to find the most probable concept search query C, subject to the constraints in Equation 3, for a given keyword query Q:

$$C = \text{argmax}_{C'} \ \Pr(C'|Q) \tag{7}$$

such that C represents the intention of Q with respect to a knowledge base $\mathcal{K}$. In the rest of this paper, we propose methods for estimating the quantity in Equation 7 by learning from a Web query log.

2.3 Solution Overview

Estimating the distribution in Equation 7 directly would require a large amount of labeled training examples. The space of possible keyword queries mapping to possible KB queries is very large, and estimating such a mapping directly is not feasible when training data is limited. Because of the manual effort required in creating labeled training data, we need to design an approach that can maximize the utility of a small collection of training examples.

Our semantic query understanding approach is summarized as a sequence of four steps, as illustrated in Figure 1.

1. **Keyword Query Annotation** Queries are first annotated with the semantic constructs from a knowledge representation language (i.e., entity, type, attribute, value, relation). We use part-of-speech tags as features that suggest probable semantic constructs for each query term. The mapping from part-of-speech tags to semantic constructs is learned from an annotated query log.
2. **Keyword Query Structuring** Annotated queries are structured by computing the most probable structured query templates given the annotations as a semantic summary of the query contents. This relationship between annotations and query structures is

[4]http://www.w3.org/TR/owl-profiles/#OWL_2_EL

learned from an annotated query log. Learning a mapping directly from keywords to structured queries would require large amounts of training examples. By learning the mapping from semantic summaries to query templates, we take advantage of the redundancy in the training data caused by many queries sharing the same summaries and templates.

3. **Knowledge Base Mapping** Semantically annotated keyword queries can be combined with a structured query template to form a structured representation of the keyword query known as a *structured keyword query*. We extend an existing approach [18] to map structured keyword queries into concept search queries.
4. **Knowledge Base Query Evaluation** Concept search queries are then executed over the knowledge base to find entities and values described by the query. This process performs query-time inference, exploiting the semantics encoded in the knowledge base to compute query answers using a custom knowledge base engine (discussion of the knowledge base engine is beyond the scope of this paper, however any database system that can implement the semantics defined in Section 2.1 could be substituted).

The main focus of this paper is on the first two steps, we build on existing methods to address the final two steps. Note that at steps 1 and 2 of the process, we are not yet concerned with how query terms map to particular knowledge base items as would be done in traditional keyword search over graphs. Inferring probable structures of the query terms first will allow us to constrain the possible mappings into the knowledge base. This can improve performance by fixing the structure of possible mappings into the knowledge base, and improve effectiveness by only allowing structures that have a high probability of being representative of query intentions. Inferring query structures also gives us the ability to know precisely what piece of information is being requested, much like a projection in structured query languages.

3. STRUCTURING KEYWORD QUERIES

As a first step to modeling the semantics of a keyword query, we map keyword sequences to structures representing their intents, known as *structured keyword queries*, addressing steps 1 and 2 of Figure 1. A structured keyword query describes a query in two ways: it breaks it into *segments* that represent particular semantic constructs, and it describes how these constructs relate to each other. In order to form structured keyword queries from a given keyword query, we will have to address these two problems.

3.1 Query Segmentation & Annotation

We define a keyword query Q to be a sequence of query terms $Q = q_1, q_2, \ldots, q_n$ over a vocabulary $\mathcal{V}$. A semantically annotated keyword query assigns *semantic constructs* from a schema language to sequences of keyword query terms.

Definition 4. **(Semantically Annotated Query)** Given a vocabulary $\mathcal{V}$, a keyword query Q and the knowledge representation language defined in Definition 1, a *semantically annotated keyword query AQ* (or simply *annotated query* when clear from context) is a sequence of keyword phrase-semantic construct pairs

$$AQ = \langle q_1 q_2 \ldots q_i \rangle{:}a_1 \ \langle q_{i+1} \ldots q_j \rangle{:}a_2 \ldots \langle q_{j+1} \ldots q_n \rangle{:}a_n$$

where each $q_i \in \mathcal{V}$ and each $a_i \in \{ent, type, rel, attr, val\}$.

A semantically annotated version of our example query is given by the following.

"songs":type *"by"*:rel *"jimi hendrix"*:ent

An algorithm that annotates keyword queries with semantic constructs must solve both the *segmentation problem* (the problem of determining the boundaries that separate multi-term phrases) and the annotation problem. We want to compute the probability of an annotated query given a keyword query, $\Pr(AQ|Q)$.

Research has shown that part-of-speech (POS) tagging can be accurately performed over keyword queries [2]. Our approach to annotating queries exploits query terms, their POS tags, and sequential relationships between terms and tags to concurrently infer a segmentation and semantic annotation of a part-of-speech annotated keyword query. To do this, we use a conditional random field (CRF) [12], a state-of-the-art machine learning method for labeling sequence data. As a baseline method for comparison, we also try a technique that directly classifies terms independently with semantic constructs. We then segment the query by joining any adjacent terms sharing the same semantic construct.

Baseline term classification Our baseline term classification aims to exploit the relationship between part-of-speech tags and semantic constructs by using a term's part-of-speech as a proxy for the term. Intuitively, there is a relationship between semantic constructs (e.g., entities, relations) and the parts-of-speech used in describing instances of those constructs. For example, entities are generally expressed using proper nouns like "Jimi Hendrix" or "New York." Relations are often described by prepositions, such as "in" or "by." The mapping between parts-of-speech and semantic constructs however, is not always so clear. Relations can sometimes be described by parts-of-speech other than prepositions (e.g., the noun "birthplace"); nouns can often describe many different semantic constructs, such as types, relations, and attributes; and perhaps the most challenging side of using part-of-speech tags to infer semantic constructs is that many entities, types, and relations are made up of multi-word phrases that can contain many different parts-of-speech (e.g., the relation "has won prize," or the type "Chancellors of Germany").

We model an annotated query log as set of triples $L = \{\langle Q, \pi, \sigma \rangle\}_i$ where Q is a keyword query, π is a function mapping query terms to POS tags, and σ is a function mapping query terms to semantic constructs. To classify terms via their part of speech tags, we use the standard naïve Bayes classification method. We perform naïve Bayes classification by directly estimating the joint probability distribution of POS tags and their semantic constructs from the query log. The conditional probability of a particular semantic construct C given a POS tag P is then the frequency of that query term's POS tag, P, mapping to C, versus the frequency of P mapping to *any* semantic construct, $\Pr(\mathrm{C}|\mathrm{P}) = \Pr(\mathrm{C},\mathrm{P})/\Pr(\mathrm{P})$ which is estimated from the query log by the following frequencies.

$$\Pr(\mathrm{C}|\mathrm{P}) = \frac{|\{\langle Q, \pi, \sigma \rangle \in L \ s.t. \exists q \in Q, \pi(q) = \mathrm{P}, \sigma(q) = \mathrm{C}\}|}{|\{\langle Q, \pi, \sigma \rangle \in L \ s.t. \exists q \in Q, \pi(q) = \mathrm{P}\}|}$$

With a distribution over semantic constructs given the part-of-speech of a query term, we can estimate the probability of assignments of semantic constructs to individual part-of-speech tagged query terms for a whole query. Assuming independence of query terms for tractability, this yields the following equation.

$$\Pr(AQ|Q) = \Pi_{q:C \in AQ} \Pr(C|\ \pi(q))$$

CRF feature design A CRF is an undirected probabilistic graphical model that models sequential data. Given a trained model and an input sequence, a CRF enables the computation of the most probable, or k most probable labelings according to the model. Specifically, a labeling is an assignment of state labels $y_1, \ldots, y_n$, to an input sequence $x_1, \ldots, x_n$, where each y_i corresponds to a state in the model and each x_i corresponds to a feature vector.

We base our CRF model on the design for noun-phrase detection proposed by Sha and Pereira [21] since our problem shares similarities. For input position x_i corresponding to query term q_i, we define a feature vector containing the following features: all query terms and POS tags in a size five window around position x_i; all query term bigrams in a size three window; all POS tag bigrams in a size five window; and all POS tag trigrams in a size five window. We include the actual query terms as features to allow important repetitive terms to be captured (e.g., "in" describing a relation such as *"restaurants in barcelona"*), but discard any generated feature that appears only once to avoid overfitting the particular terms in the training data.

We deviate from the model of Sha and Pereira in label design. The labels must encode both the semantic constructs we want to annotate as well as the boundaries between multi-term semantic constructs. We create two output labels for every semantic construct in our chosen knowledge representation language: a "begin" (B) and a "continue" (C) label. This is the minimal encoding that allows us to identify segmentation boundaries as well as semantic constructs. To generate training data, we label each multi-term phrase in the training data with the begin and continue labels corresponding the phrase's semantic construct. For example, the correct labeling of our running example is the following.

"songs":type-B *"by"*:rel-B *"jimi"*:ent-B *"hendrix"*:ent-C

Here, the query term *"hendrix"* is annotated as a continuation of the entity starting with *"jimi"*, yielding the following annotated query.

"songs":type *"by"*:rel *"jimi hendrix"*:ent

Unlike our baseline term classification approach, the CRF model can distinguish between multiple instances of the same semantic construct occurring in succession. We train our model using the Broyden-Fletche-Goldfarb-Shanno (BFGS) algorithm, a type of hill climbing approach for solving non-linear optimization problems. To avoid overfitting we use L2 regularization. The probability $\Pr(AQ|Q)$ is then given directly by the CRF model.

3.2 Structuring Annotated Queries

An annotated query reveals part of the latent structure of an entity-based keyword query by indicating the semantic role represented by various parts of the query. However query annotation alone does not describe how these various recognized semantic constructs interact to model the underlying query intention. In our running example query, we know (after annotation) that the query contains a type, a relation, and an entity. However there is still ambiguity in what the query is seeking. Is it ultimately describing entities of the given type that are related to the given entity? Or is it seeking information about the given entity within the context of the given type?

To illustrate the ambiguity in query structure, consider the following two queries: *"john smith dentist"* and *"new york restaurants"*. Both queries contain an entity followed by a type. The first query seeks information about the given entity (*"john smith"*), with a type (*"dentist"*) given as context to disambiguate among possible interpretations of the entity. Whereas the second query is seeking instances of the given type (*"restaurants"*), within the context of the given entity (*"new york"*).

To model high level query structure, we follow the logical connectives from the knowledge representation language.

Definition 5. **(Structured Query Template)** A *structured query template* T is a schema-level description of a concept search query, expressed in the following grammar

$$T \quad ::= \quad node \ \mid \ edge(T) \ \mid \ T_1 \sqcap T_2$$

where $node \in \{ent, type, val\}$ and $edge \in \{rel, attr\}$.

A structured query template describes the overall graph structure of the query as well as the node and edge types of the query predicates. For example, the structured query template for our example query is $type \sqcap rel(ent)$.

We want to estimate the probability of a query template given a semantically annotated keyword query, $\Pr(T|AQ)$. We assume access to an annotated query log containing both semantically annotated queries and their structured query templates, $L = \{(AQ_i, T_i)\}$.

Our structuring approach directly estimates the probability of a structured template given an annotated query by aggregating over all queries in the training log that share the same high-level summary of semantic annotations.

Definition 6. **(Semantic Summary)** Given an annotated query $AQ = \langle q_1{:}a_1, q_2{:}a_2, \ldots, q_n{:}a_n \rangle$, a *semantic summary* is an ordered list of semantic constructs occurring in AQ, and is given by the function $S : AQ \rightarrow C^n$ s.t. $S(AQ) = \langle a_1, a_2, \ldots, a_n \rangle$

For example, $S($*"songs"*:type *"by"*:rel *"jimi hendrix"*:ent$) = \langle type, rel, ent \rangle$.

We directly estimate $\Pr(T|AQ)$ from labeled training examples in our query log from the definition of conditional probabilities, using the semantic summary as a high level representation of the annotated query.

$$\Pr(T|AQ) = \frac{|\{\langle AQ', T' \rangle \in L \ s.t. T = T', S(AQ) = S(AQ')\}|}{|\{\langle AQ', T' \rangle \in L \ s.t. S(AQ) = S(AQ')\}|}$$

The probability of a query template given an annotated query is estimated by the proportion of queries with the same semantic summary that are structured using that template, versus the total number of queries with the same semantic summary and *any* structuring.

3.3 From Structures to KB Interpretations

Combing an annotated query with a structured query template yields a structured version of the keyword query. Combining the annotated running example query with its template gives the following query *"songs"*$\sqcap$ *"by"*(*"jimi hendrix"*) by swapping the annotated constructs into their respective positions in the template. We allow relations and attributes

POS	Ex.	Query	Token	Sem	Freq.
Proper noun	waterloo	77.1%	28.7%	ent	99.1%
				type	0.9%
Noun	musician	42.6%	15.9%	type	49.5%
				ent	42.7%
				attr	6.8%
				rel	0.9%
Plural noun	songs	13.6%	5.1%	type	68.0%
				ent	20.0%
				attr	8.0%
				rel	4.0%
Adjective	big	11.6%	4.3%	ent	60.0%
				type	40.0%
Preposition	in	7.8%	2.9%	rel	55.6%
				ent	44.4%
Number	2008	6.6%	2.5%	ent	53.8%
				val	46.2%
URI	yahoo.ca	5.0%	1.9%	ent	100%
Verb	run	4.7%	1.7%	ent	100%
Determiner	the	3.1%	1.2%	ent	100%
Gerund	winning	2.7%	1.0%	rel	66.7%
				type	33.3%

Figure 2: The ten most frequently occurring part-of-speech tags among entity-based queries, with the distribution of how frequently that tag mapped to various semantic constructs.

to be unmapped (e.g., see Figure 1), however we do not consider mappings in which entities or types are unmapped.

This type of expression is called a *structured keyword query*, and methods to map these expressions into Web knowledge bases have been developed [18]. The method proposed in [18] first generates a list of possible KB items for each keyword phrase in the query. These items are sorted by syntactic similarity, forming ordered input lists. The inputs are then processed using a variation of a top-k threshold algorithm.

In this work we extend the the method proposed in [18] in order to support the class of query structures discovered in our query log analysis. Our variation of structured keyword queries is given by the following grammar.

$$SKQ \ ::= \ k \ | \ k(SKQ) \ | \ *(SKQ) \ | \ SKQ_1 \sqcap SKQ_2$$

Where k is a sequence of keywords and $\sqcap$ denotes conjunction. This grammar follows the knowledge representation language defined in Section 2.1. We extend the original structured keyword query framework by adding the construct $*(SKQ)$ which allows nested queries with unknown relations. For this construct we must consider all possible relations in the knowledge base. We accomplish this by modifying the top-k algorithm used in [18] to dynamically add all relations that have non-zero knowledge base support to any KB item in adjacent input lists. We also add support to the underlying KB formalism to account for inverse relations and an explicit model of attributes.

Given a structured keyword query SKQ, the KB mapping system will return the most probable (or the top-k most probable) concept search query $C = \text{argmax}_{C'} \Pr(C'|SKQ)$. The probability of a structured keyword query (represented as a semantically annotated query and a query template $SKQ = \langle AQ, T \rangle$) is given by $\Pr(SKQ|Q) = \Pr(T|AQ) \cdot \Pr(AQ|Q)$. We can compute the first term using the tech-

Template	Frequency
ent	44.9%
$type \sqcap rel(ent)$	12.8%
$ent_0 \sqcap rel(ent_1)$	7.7%
$ent \sqcap type$	5.8%
$type$	5.8%
$attr(ent)$	3.8%
$ent_1 \sqcap rel(ent_0)$	3.2%
$rel(ent)$	1.9%
$ent_0 \sqcap rel(ent_1, rel(ent_2))$	1.3%
$type_1 \sqcap rel(type_0)$	1.3%

Figure 3: The ten most frequently occurring templates among entity-based queries.

niques discussed in Section 3.1 and the second term using the method presented in Section 3.2. Our overall goal is to approximate the probability distribution given in Equation 7. Given a keyword query Q, the concept search query C representing the intent of Q is estimated as:

$$C = \text{argmax}_{C'} \ \Pr(C'|SKQ) \cdot \Pr(SKQ|Q) \qquad (8)$$

for some structured keyword query SKQ. Our produced concept search queries satisfy the problem definition in Equation 3. The queries are safe since all predicates are retrieved from the KB, they cover all query terms by only considering complete mappings into the KB, and they are guaranteed consistent as we evaluate resulting concept search queries and only include those that are non-empty.

4. ANALYSIS OF A WEB QUERY LOG

We analyzed a sample of keyword queries available from the Yahoo WebScope program [25]. We inspected queries keeping only those that have a *semantic construct* as the primary query intention, following the classification proposed in [19]. We annotated 258 queries with the part-of-speech tags and semantic constructs. We did not consider misspelled, non-English, or other queries that were not clearly understandable. Among the annotated queries, 156 queries had some semantic construct as their primary intention (*entity-based queries*). That is approximately 60% of queries having a semantic construct as the primary intent of the query. This is consistent with the analysis done in [19] which was performed over a different Web query log and reported 58% of queries having a semantic construct as the primary intent.

Our part-of-speech tag set is based on the analysis in [2], which is a reduced tag set designed for annotating Web queries. Figure 2 shows the distribution of part-of-speech tags over query tokens as well as the percentage of entity-based queries that contain that part-of-speech. The figure also illustrates the distribution of terms with the given part-of-speech over semantic constructs. This distribution captures the relationship between part-of-speech tags and semantic constructs, which plays a key role in our annotation methods described in Section 3.1. Not surprisingly, there is a very strong correlation between proper nouns and entities. Interestingly, plural nouns are a strong indicator of a term representing a *type*, while regular nouns are split between denoting *type* and *entity* labels.

From the 156 entity-based queries, we also annotated the structured query template underlying our interpretation of the intent of the query. In the cases where there were multiple possible structurings, we annotated all of them and count them as individual queries when computing the frequencies for the equations described in Section 3.

Figure 3 shows the ten most frequent structured query templates in our training query log, along with the percentage of queries exhibiting that structure (over all entity-based queries). Many queries tend to repeat the same structures.

5. EXPERIMENTAL EVALUATION

5.1 System Implementations

We implemented all of the techniques described in Section 3. We use CRF++[5] to learn the CRF models and use the tool for mapping structured keyword queries into a KB described in [18] with the modifications described in Section 3.3. We consider the top-10 structures (unless otherwise specified) and union the results of the best KB mapping for each structure. For unary queries (not having multiple terms to perform disambiguation) we employ a heuristic requiring 0.95 syntactic similarity for an interpretation to qualify.

We create two system configurations, the first using the naïve Bayes (NB) term classifier for query annotation and the second using the CRF approach (CRF). Both systems use the direct approach (Drct) to structuring (Section 3.2) and the same KB mapping tool described in Section 3.3 to map the computed structured keyword queries into the knowledge base and evaluate the resulting concept search queries. We omit structures containing more than one unknown relation to avoid the exponential blow-up caused by matching over all possible pairs of relations. We have found this does not have a significant impact on the quality of results. We implement a simple POS-tagger that builds on the Brown and Wall Street Journal POS tagged lexicon. Our tagger assigns the most frequent POS tag for each known word (suitably mapped to our reduced tag set as described in Section 4), and assigns proper noun to unseen tokens (the most frequent tag in our query log). We find this to be sufficiently accurate for our purposes. Building and evaluating a more sophisticated POS tagger is an orthogonal problem beyond the scope of this paper.

For comparison, we also implement two alternative ways of mapping keyword queries into knowledge base entities. The first method implements traditional keyword search over graphs, with a number of heuristics taken from the literature. The process of keyword search over graphs is to find all nodes and edges that match query terms, then search among these *seed* matches to see if they can be connected. A result graph is a subgraph of the data graph that spans all query terms. This can be viewed as an instance of the Steiner tree problem. Our implementation uses a breadth-first search approach to finding Steiner trees. We use the same Lucene index and graph database used by the KB mapping tool. Seed nodes are processed in order of syntactic similarity to the query term they match. The graph search will generate a given parameter number of results and return the k highest scoring. The parameter is set to 10,000 in the effectiveness experiments and is set to 10 in the performance experiments. Scoring is based on the same syntactic scoring (3-gram distance) used by the KB mapping tool, normalized by the answer graph size to promote more compact answers.

The heuristics used in our graph search implementation include traversal of outgoing edges only, incoming edges only, bi-directional edge traversal [10], search depth limiting as recommended in [24] (we use a depth of three), and a last heuristic that forces *type* nodes to be leaves in answer graphs. Note that this system returns subgraphs of the knowledge base, and cannot precisely interpret queries in order to find *specific answers*. In our evaluation, we give this system the benefit of considering any answer graph as correct if it contains the answer anywhere in the graph.

The second comparison approach builds a text representation of each node in the knowledge base, then performs traditional keyword search over the text representations. We use Lucene to create an index over all labels in a one hop radius around each node (including edge labels).

5.2 Data and Workload

We use YAGO [22] as our knowledge base, a high quality fact collection with a rich type hierarchy over entities and a part of the Linked Data Web. Our training data is the Yahoo query log described in Section 4. To evaluate our approaches, we use both queries from the query log and a hand-crafted workload designed with specific properties we wish to evaluate. The query workload consists of 96 queries, half of which have an underlying query intention that *can* be modeled with the data in YAGO, and half taken from the Yahoo log that describe data *not* occurring in YAGO. The half that have YAGO answers, called *positive queries*, are created to exhibit the 12 most frequent structures found in our analysis, accounting for over 90% of all entity-based queries. We create four examples of each of these structures. The second half are entity-based queries taken from the Yahoo log for which we have manually verified that no interpretation exists in YAGO. We refer to these queries as *negative queries*.

The gold standard result for positive queries is defined by manually constructing a structured query over YAGO, and the correct answer for negative queries is defined as the empty set. This query workload explicitly exercises both of the problems of interpreting queries when possible, and recognizing when an interpretation is not possible. We manually create the queries to ensure all structures are represented, and to control for KB coverage. Finding examples of queries with all of the desired structures in a Web query log, such that they also have intentions existing in YAGO would require a huge manual effort, and possibly a larger query sample. Existing benchmarks also do not capture all of the structures we want to evaluate while controlling for KB coverage. The positive queries from the workload are available online[6].

5.3 Effectiveness Results

To evaluate effectiveness we conducted a direct evaluation of the query annotations, an evaluation of the computed KB interpretations, and an end-to-end evaluation of the full system in finding exact answers to keyword queries.

Precision is defined as the fraction of returned results that are correct. Recall is defined as the fraction of all possible correct results that get returned. MRR measures the (reciprocal) average rank where the (first) correct answer occurs. Given a set of queries $\mathcal{Q}$ and a function $rank(i)$ that returns the rank of the first correct answer for query i, MRR is given by the following.

[5]http://crfpp.sourceforge.net/

[6]http://cs.uwaterloo.ca/~jpound/cikm2012/workload.txt

System	Avg. Query Recall k=1	k=5	k=10	Avg. Token Recall k=1	k=5	k=10
CRF	0.461	0.703	0.832	0.626	0.797	0.923
NB	0.432	0.500	0.547	0.616	0.711	0.736

Figure 4: Average number of queries with the correctly annotated query occurring in the top-k annotations (query recall), and average number of correctly annotated tokens for the best annotation occurring in the top-k (token recall).

$$\text{MRR}(\mathcal{Q}) = \frac{1}{|\mathcal{Q}|}\sum_{i}^{|\mathcal{Q}|} \frac{1}{rank(i)}$$

For all measures, we count a value of 0 if a system does not return any result for a positive query or if any result is returned for a negative query.

5.3.1 Annotation Accuracy

Figure 4 shows the results of both the NB and CRF annotation approaches. Results are averages using 10-fold cross validation over the 156 entity-based queries from the Yahoo query log. We measure average query recall, the frequency in which the top-k annotations of a query generates the correct complete annotation. The figure also shows average token recall for the best annotation in a query's top-k annotations. This is the fraction of query terms annotated correctly for the best annotation produced for each query. This is relevant because our structuring and KB mapping tools are tolerant to errors, meaning an incorrect segmentation or annotation can still produce a correct concept search query. While both approaches perform similarly at k=1, the superiority of the CRF approach is clear as we consider the top-5 to top-10 annotations.

5.3.2 Query Interpretation

There are four possible outcomes when interpreting a query. The first is that the query is interpreted over the KB, and the interpretation is correct (true positive); the second is that the query is interpreted but the interpretation is incorrect (false positive); the third is that the query does not get interpreted though an interpretation does exist in the data (false negative); and the last is that the query does not get interpreted because no interpretation exists in the data (true negative). Figure 5 shows the confusion matrices for these outcomes for both the CRF and NB approaches when considering the top-10 structures over the workload outlined in Section 5.2. The figure shows that the CRF approach is superior with respect to both types of error, and exhibits a higher overall true positive rate (correct interpretations) than the NB approach. Overall the CRF-based approach produces a correct interpretation or recognizes an uninterpretable query almost 93% of the time. We found the CRF's ranked list of query interpretations to have an MRR of 0.698 on the positive query set. This means that the correct interpretation is found generally in the first or second position on average. The NB approach had an MRR of 0.589, also slightly better than the second position on average.

5.3.3 Keyword Query Answering

We used the workload outlined in Section 5.2 to evaluate the ability of the proposed approaches to interpret and answer keyword queries. Figure 6 shows the results of each of the systems, as well the best run for each measure by *any* of the graph search system's configurations. The superior CRF-based annotator paired with the the semantic summary-based structuring approach has the best performance across all metrics. While the NB approach is comparable, the improved annotation accuracy of the CRF approach yields better results. The graph search approach achieves reasonable recall and MRR, meaning it can find many correct answers and return good answers at decent ranks, however the answer set also becomes polluted with many non-relevant results hurting precision. The approach has no capacity to determine which results are proper answers and which are coincidental keyword matches. Also, the graph search is given the advantage of not having to find the precise answer to queries (any answer graph containing the query answer is considered correct). Not surprisingly, the text graph approach has very low precision as it is designed to find resources related to the query terms and does not attempt to interpret queries in order to find exact answers. Precision is never higher than 0.1 for any value of k. While the unbounded text graph approach achieves 97% recall on the positive query set, it has no means of detecting the negative queries and answers each incorrectly, bringing down the average considerably.

CRF.Drct	f (Incorrect)	t (Correct)	Total +/−
+ (Interp)	3 (3.1%)	45 (46.9%)	48 (50%)
− (No Interp)	4 (4.2%)	44 (45.8%)	48 (50%)
Total f/t	7 (7.3%)	89 (92.7%)	

NB.Drct	f (Incorrect)	t (Correct)	Total +/−
+ (Interp)	3 (3.1%)	36 (37.5%)	39 (40.6%)
− (No Interp)	12 (12.5%)	45 (46.9%)	57 (59.4%)
Total f/t	15 (15.6%)	81 (84.4%)	

Figure 5: Confusion matrices for the query interpretation task. Raw counts and percentages are shown for the true/false positive/negatives, as well as the marginals. The 96 query workload contains 48 positive queries and 48 negative queries.

System	Prec.	Recall	MRR
CRF.Drct	0.789	0.819	0.825
NB.Drct	0.722	0.784	0.768
graph search	0.516	0.682	0.644
text graph, $k = 10$	0.034	0.178	0.118
text graph, k unbounded	0.000	0.486	0.125

Figure 6: Average Precision, MRR, and Recall over the combined positive/negative query workload.

5.4 Efficiency Results

Precision and recall can be traded off for run-time performance by varying the number of candidate structures. Figure 7 shows the effect of varying the number of structures considered from 1 to 10 for the CRF.Drct approach. As the data points move from left to right, the total number of structures is increasing. This gives an increase in precision and recall as we explore more of the search space to find the correct query interpretation, but at the expense of greater

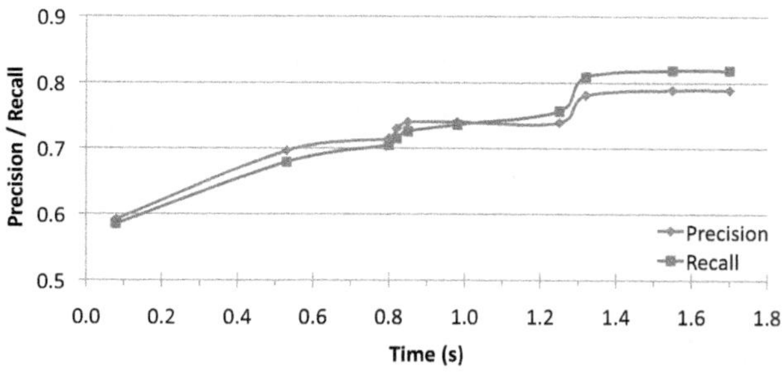

Figure 7: Average precision and recall vs. average run time for varying number of KB interpretations.

run times. Occasionally an incorrect interpretation is found causing a dip in precision. It is important to note that the lower precision configurations of our system are most often due to queries *not being answered*, as opposed to being answered incorrectly. The highest precision (0.789) is obtained for a configuration that takes 1.5 seconds per query on average. An average precision of approximately 0.74 can be achieved in sub-second query processing time.

Figure 8 shows a breakdown of the average run-time for each component of the system when considering the top-10 structures. The actual annotation and structuring time accounts for only a small percent of the total run time, with the majority of time spent mapping candidate structures into the knowledge base. The graph search approach ($k = 10$) took around 67 seconds on average, often hitting an imposed two minute timeout. This is often due to the graph search attempting to walk the entire search space if it is unable to find k results. The text graph approach is very efficient at $k = 10$, but at the cost of effectiveness.

6. RELATED WORK

Tran et al. [24] have explored mapping keyword queries into conjunctive queries by matching terms against knowledge base items and searching for connections among the matches. This approach is similar to our graph search approach used in the evaluation, though their top-k algorithm may explore less of the total search space than our BFS approach. Zhou et al. have also proposed a similar data driven approach [26]. These techniques are in contrast to our query-log driven approach which elicits structures from the information needs of real users. Lei et al. use manually defined templates to map query terms into formal structured queries over a knowledge base, and employ heuristics to reduce the search space when the query contains more than two terms [13]. Fagin et al. [5] use user specified grammars and vocabularies to annotate query terms with type and attribute labels. Our proposed approach could possibly be used to learn these types of grammars from a query log.

Many recent works have also looked at annotating individual terms in a keyword query with various levels of semantic meaning, such as part-of-speech tags [2], and attribute labels from a relational schema [20]. These works do not address how terms relate to form single coherent expressions of the underlying query intent. Manshadi and Li have also proposed query interpretation using pre-defined grammars. They also annotate terms that specify operations such as "SortOrder" [17]. Li proposed a method of determining the *intent head* of a query, the part of the query that represents what the user is looking for (e.g., "songs" in our example

System	Struct	Map	Exec	Total
CRF.Drct	0.002s	1.23s	0.32s	1.55s
NB.Drct	0.001s	0.94s	0.29s	1.24s
graph search	-	-	-	67.27s
text graph, $k = 10$	-	-	-	0.33s
text graph, k unbounded	-	-	-	17.33s

Figure 8: Avg. time for annotation and structuring (Struct), KB mapping (Map) and execution (Exec).

query) [14]. Our approach implicitly identifies the intent head of the query by the root of the concept search query.

Agarwal et al., mined query templates from a query log [1]. Templates would generalize terms that match KB items, for example *"jobs in #location"*. These templates were used to find relevant websites based on clicks. Cheng et al. allowed user queries to specify a similar template, which explicitly specifies the intended return type [4]. Our template mining is similar in nature that of Agarwal, though our templates fully specify semantic structure and not just types occurring in keyword queries. Also, we do not rely on input query terms exactly matching a set of known types, but instead match against syntactically similar types and resolve ambiguity from the query context. Our Web knowledge base setting also yields over 250,000 possible types.

Search over relational data can be viewed as a form of semantic query understanding. Query terms are mapped into structured data producing structured queries that can be used to retrieve data that contains the queried terms. There is a long line of research for search over structured data, starting with the DISCOVER [8] and BANKS systems [9] that aim to efficiently find tuples that span all query terms, as well as extensions that aim to integrate IR style ranking [7] or augment the graph traversal algorithm [10]. The heuristics used in our graph search approach are based on this line of research. Tata et. al, extend keyword search over structured data to include aggregates and top-1 queries [23]. Queries are translated to SQL with the allowance of various aggregation keywords such as *num* or *avg*.

Blanco et al. have used relevance based retrieval to search for nodes in large knowledge bases [3]. This approach however does not attempt to interpret the semantics of queries, and thus does not necessarily provide exact answers.

Semantic parsing of natural language questions shares a similar high level goal with semantic query understanding. Both tasks are to construct a logical representation of a query. Semantic parsing aims to parse natural language queries to lambda calculus expressions of the intention (see for example [15]). Semantic parsing approaches depend on fully specified domain-relevant questions, as opposed to short underspecified keyword queries. Also, these approaches are applied to small controlled domains with relatively small homogeneous knowledge bases, as opposed to the massive heterogeneous knowledge bases found on the Web.

Exploiting Web knowledge bases for question answering (QA) has also been explored. Fernandez et al. propose the PowerAqua system [6, 16] that integrates a front-end QA system on a semantic search back-end to answer questions over Linked Data knowledge bases. Katz et al. have built the OMNIBASE+START system that answers questions using a knowledge base extracted from the Web [11]. While QA has a similar high level goal to our task, QA approaches generally depend on either having properly formatted questions that can be parsed to take advantage of the grammatical structure, or they depend on having the relatively large amount of text (as compared to keyword queries) from the question in order to match against answer candidates.

7. CONCLUSIONS AND FUTURE WORK

We have shown how keyword queries can be interpreted over large scale heterogeneous Web knowledge bases by learning semantic structures from an annotated query log.

Future directions include exploring refinements on the granularity of semantic annotations. For example, distinguishing locations from other types of entities could provide additional structuring hints, since locations often appear as context information in keyword queries. We are also interested in applying these techniques to other data sets and search verticals such as product and medical knowledge bases.

8. REFERENCES

[1] G. Agarwal, G. Kabra, and K. C. Chang. Towards rich query interpretation: walking back and forth for mining query templates. In *Proc. 19th intl. conference on World wide web*, pages 1–10. ACM, 2010.

[2] C. Barr, R. Jones, and M. Regelson. The linguistic structure of english web-search queries. In *Proc. Conference on Empirical Methods in Natural Language Processing*, EMNLP '08, pages 1021–1030. ACL, 2008.

[3] R. Blanco, P. Mika, and S. Vigna. Effective and efficient entity search in rdf data. In *The Semantic Web - ISWC 2011*, volume 7031 of *Lecture Notes in Computer Science*, pages 83–97, 2011.

[4] T. Cheng, X. Yan, and K. C. Chang. EntityRank: searching entities directly and holistically. In *VLDB*, pages 387–398, 2007.

[5] R. Fagin, B. Kimelfeld, Y. Li, S. Raghavan, and S. Vaithyanathan. Understanding queries in a search database system. In *Proc. twenty-ninth ACM symposium on Principles of database systems*, PODS '10, pages 273–284. ACM, 2010.

[6] M. Fernandez, V. Lopez, M. Sabou, V. Uren, D. Vallet, E. Motta, and P. Castells. Semantic search meets the web. In *Semantic Computing, 2008 IEEE intl. conference on*, pages 253 –260, Aug. 2008.

[7] V. Hristidis, L. Gravano, and Y. Papakonstantinou. Efficient IR-style keyword search over relational databases. In *Proc. 29th intl. conference on Very large data bases*, pages 850–861. VLDB Endowment, 2003.

[8] V. Hristidis and Y. Papakonstantinou. Discover: keyword search in relational databases. In *Proc. 28th intl. conference on Very Large Data Bases*, VLDB '02, pages 670–681. VLDB Endowment, 2002.

[9] A. Hulgeri and C. Nakhe. Keyword searching and browsing in databases using BANKS. In *Proc. 18th intl. conference on Data Engineering*, ICDE '02. IEEE Computer Society, 2002.

[10] V. Kacholia, S. Pandit, S. Chakrabarti, S. Sudarshan, R. Desai, and H. Karambelkar. Bidirectional expansion for keyword search on graph databases. In *Proc. 31st intl. conference on Very large data bases*, VLDB '05, pages 505–516, 2005.

[11] B. Katz, S. Felshin, D. Yuret, A. Ibrahim, J. J. Lin, G. Marton, A. J. McFarland, and B. Temelkuran. Omnibase: Uniform access to heterogeneous data for question answering. In *NLDB*, pages 230–234, 2002.

[12] J. D. Lafferty, A. McCallum, and F. C. N. Pereira. Conditional random fields: Probabilistic models for segmenting and labeling sequence data. In *Proc. Eighteenth intl. conference on Machine Learning*, ICML '01, pages 282–289, 2001.

[13] Y. Lei, V. S. Uren, and E. Motta. SemSearch: a search engine for the semantic web. In *EKAW*, pages 238–245, 2006.

[14] X. Li. Understanding the semantic structure of noun phrase queries. In *Proc. 48th Association for Computational Linguistics*, ACL '10, pages 1337–1345. ACL, 2010.

[15] P. Liang, M. I. Jordan, and D. Klein. Learning Dependency-Based compositional semantics. In *ACL*, pages 590–599, 2011.

[16] V. Lopez, M. Fernndez, E. Motta, and N. Stieler. PowerAqua: supporting users in querying and exploring the semantic web content. *Semantic Web Journal*, 2011.

[17] M. Manshadi and X. Li. Semantic tagging of web search queries. In *Proc. Joint Conference of the 47th ACL and the 4th Intl. Joint Conference on Natural Language Processing*, pages 861–869. ACL, 2009.

[18] J. Pound, I. F. Ilyas, and G. Weddell. Expressive and flexible access to web-extracted data: a keyword-based structured query language. In *Proc. 2010 intl. conference on Management of data*, SIGMOD '10, pages 423–434. ACM, 2010.

[19] J. Pound, P. Mika, and H. Zaragoza. Ad-hoc object retrieval in the web of data. In *Proc. 19th intl. conference on World wide web*, WWW '10, pages 771–780. ACM, 2010.

[20] N. Sarkas, S. Paparizos, and P. Tsaparas. Structured annotations of web queries. In *Proc. 2010 intl. conference on Management of data*, SIGMOD '10, pages 771–782. ACM, 2010.

[21] F. Sha and F. Pereira. Shallow parsing with conditional random fields. In *Proc. 2003 Conference of the North American Association for Computational Linguistics*, NAACL '03, pages 134–141, 2003.

[22] F. M. Suchanek, G. Kasneci, and G. Weikum. Yago: A core of semantic knowledge - unifying WordNet and wikipedia. In *16th Intl. World Wide Web Conference (WWW 2007)*, pages 697–706, 2007.

[23] S. Tata and G. M. Lohman. SQAK: doing more with keywords. In *Proc. 2008 ACM SIGMOD intl. conference on Management of data*, SIGMOD '08, pages 889–902. ACM, 2008.

[24] T. Tran, H. Wang, S. Rudolph, and P. Cimiano. Top-k exploration of query candidates for efficient keyword search on graph-shaped (rdf) data. In *Data Engineering, 2009. ICDE'09. IEEE 25th intl. conference on*, pages 405–416, 2009.

[25] Yahoo! Academic Relations. http://webscope.sandbox.yahoo.com/catalog.php - L13 - Yahoo! Search Query Tiny Sample.

[26] Q. Zhou, C. Wang, M. Xiong, H. Wang, and Y. Yu. SPARK: adapting keyword query to semantic search. In *The Semantic Web*, volume 4825 of *Lecture Notes in Computer Science*, pages 694–707. Springer Berlin / Heidelberg, 2007. 10.1007/978-3-540-76298-0_50.

RDF Pattern Matching using Sortable Views

Zhihong Chong
Southeast University
SiPaiLou #2, Nanjing, China, 210096
chongzhihong@seu.edu.cn

He Chen
Southeast University
SiPaiLou #2, Nanjing, China, 210096
hchen.seu@gmail.com

Zhenjie Zhang
Advanced Digital Sciences Center
Illinois at Singapore Pte. Ltd., Singapore
zhenjie@adsc.com.sg

Hu Shu
Southeast University
SiPaiLou #2, Nanjing, China, 210096
hshu.seu@gmail.com

Guilin Qi
Southeast University
SiPaiLou #2, Nanjing, China, 210096
qiguiling@seu.edu.cn

Aoying Zhou
East China Normal University
3663 Zhongshan Rd (North), Shanghai, China, 200062
ayzhou@sei.ecnu.edu.cn

ABSTRACT

In the last few years, RDF is becoming the dominating data model used in *semantic web* for knowledge representation and inference. In this paper, we revisit the problem of pattern matching query in RDF model, which is usually expensive in efficiency due to the huge cost on join operations. To alleviate the efficiency pain, view materialization techniques are usually deployed to accelerate the query processing. However, given an arbitrary view, it remains difficult to identify how to reuse the view for a particular query, because of the NP-hardness behind the algorithm matching patterns and views. To fully exploit the benefit of the materialized views, we propose a new paradigm to enhance the effectiveness of the materialized view. Instead of choosing materialized views in arbitrary form, our paradigm aims to select the views *only if* they are *sortable*. The property of *sortability* raises huge gains on the pattern-view matching, bringing down the cost to linear complexity in terms of the pattern size. On the other side, the costs on identifying sortable views and searching over the views using inverted index are affordable. Moreover, sortable views generally improve the overall performance of pattern matching, by means of a cost model used to optimize the query rewriting on the most appropriate views. Finally, we demonstrate extensive experimental results to verify the superiority of our proposal on both efficiency and effectiveness.

Categories and Subject Descriptors: H.2.4 [Database Management]: Query processing

Keywords: RDF Query, RDF Indexing, sortable view.

1. INTRODUCTION

In the last few years, RDF is becoming the dominating data model used in *semantic web* for knowledge representation and inference [3, 11], because of its advantages on describing heterogeneous and unstructured data. Table 1 is an example of RDF graph G, representing relationships among a group of persons. The records in the table, for example, show that 1) *Alice* marries *Bob*; 2) *Alice* is *Chris*'s mother; 3) *Chris* coauthored with *Bob* and *Frank*, etc. The evaluation of RDF queries usually resorts to the pattern matching methods in the standard SPARQL language[3]. In Figure 1, we present an example pattern V_1, by which the user is able to find father-son pairs coauthoring on the same papers. As shown in figure, a variable begins with prefix ? and a labeled edge represents a triple pattern.

CIKM'12, October 29–November 2, 2012, Maui, HI, USA.

subject	predicate	object
Alice	*Marry*	*Bob*
Alice	*isMother*	*Chris*
Chris	*coAuthor*	*Bob*
Chris	*coAuther*	*Frank*
Alice	*isMother*	*David*
...	...	...

Table 1: An Example RDF Data Graph

In Table 2, we list all valid results to query V_1, in which the row with $?x = Alice$, $?y = Bob$ and $?z = Chris$ implies that Bob is father of $Chris$ and they have coauthored before. This simple example illustrates the advantages of RDF on flexible data representation and powerful knowledge inference. However, answering such queries typically involves a long chain of join operations. The cost of *join proliferation* becomes an efficiency bottleneck[20].

Materialization techniques are usually deployed on RDF models to alleviate the difficulty of pattern matching. Assume that another query Q_1 shown in Figure 1 is submitted. Although it looks very different from V_1, one can easily verify the existence of a mapping, i.e., $\phi_1 = \{?x \mapsto ?a, ?y \mapsto ?c, ?z \mapsto ?b\}$, to transform V_1 to Q_1', which is a sub-query/subgraph of Q_1.

The mapping above, known as *containment mapping* [17], implies that the results of V_1 in Table 2 could be recycled to find all matchings to Q_1', by renaming $?x$, $?y$ and $?z$ with $?a$, $?c$ and $?b$, respectively. Therefore, the RDF engine is capable of deriving the complete answer to Q_1 by joining the results of Q_1' and $Q_1 - Q_1'$. This evaluation procedure only involves a single join operation, which is much more efficient than the query processing scheme answering the query completely from scratch.

Despite of the huge performance gain using materialization ap-

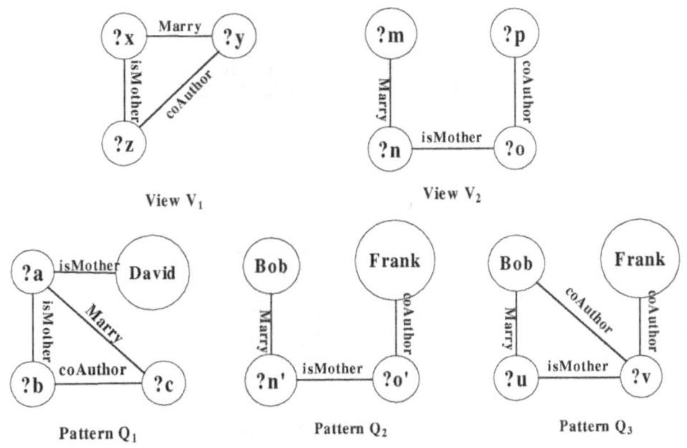

Figure 1: Running Example

V_1	?x	?y	?z
Instance $[V_1]$	*Alice*	*Bob*	*Chris*
	...	...	...

Table 2: Materialize View $[V_1]_G$ for V_1

proaches [17, 15], there remain technical challenges in query rewriting with respect to the materialized views. Given a pattern query for matching and an existing materialized view, it is generally NP-hard to find the containment mapping between the query and the view [17], due to the equivalence between the matching problem and subgraph isomorphism problem [23, 21]. This means the complexity of finding a containment mapping is exponential to the number of variables and references in the worst case, unless P=NP. In this paper, we explore on a new direction to fully utilize the advantage of materialized views without the overhead on containment mapping identification. Specifically, instead of selecting arbitrary views for materialization, our approach aims to select the views *only if* they are *sortable*, namely there is a unique order on the nodes in the pattern graph of the views.

Sortable views are generally attractive on a couple of different aspects. Firstly, given a sortable materialized view, there exists a linear algorithm to recover the containment mapping between the view and the query pattern, even when the query pattern is not *sortable*. This property enables fast verification on the reusability of the materialized views on *any* pattern query matching. Secondly, the construction/selection of sortable views does not incur significant costs. From a conventional RDF view, a simple topological ordering on the graph nodes is sufficient for a reconstruction following the requirements on sortability. Thirdly, traditional inverted index structure seamlessly supports fast retrieval on potential sortable views, when a large pool of candidate views are available to pattern matching queries. We show that a particular view is subject to certain containment mapping to part of the query, only when every edge in the sortable view has a unique matching to the query edge, after careful query expansion. Last but not least, the sortable view technique leads to a simple optimization model, which facilitates the system to find the combination of views with minimal expected cost on query processing. All these features make our sortable views as an enticing enhancement on top of the existing materialized view methods in RDF engines. We hereby summarize the main contributions of the paper as follows.

1. We revisit the problem of answering queries using views in the context of RDF model and raise the problem of simplifying pattern rewriting via reasonably restricting view selection.
2. We identify a special class of views, called sortable views, for restricting view selection, which potentially provides huge gain in pattern rewriting.
3. We present efficient index for query rewriting and optimization model to prune redundant views.
4. We implement a prototype system using the view selection method based on sortable views, which could be seamlessly integrated with traditional relational databases.

The remainder of the paper is organized as follows. Section 2 reviews existing studies on RDF query processing and graph matching. Section 3 introduces the problem definitions and preliminaries. Section 4 presents sortable views and analyzes its properties. Section 5 proposes the pattern rewriting techniques and discuss how to support the rewriting with inverted index. Section 6 covers the experimental results and finally Section 7 concludes this paper.

2. RELATED WORK

The problem of join proliferation in RDF query has received considerable attention [20, 9]. The current practices mainly resort to speeding up operations by either index [1, 14, 20] or optimization techniques [20, 22]. In this paper, we aims to reduce join operations using views. Our work differs from flat storage schema [9] for this purpose in that it does not demand a prior defined storage schema and therefore is more flexible.

The problem of reformulating queries using views for query optimization or database design dates back to equivalent conjunctive queries in relational data model [17, 5], and were expanded to encompass recursive queries [13] or even queries with aggregation functions [10] and later revisited in semi-structural data model with regular path queries [16]. In addition to theoretical interests on complexity [2], minimization [8] of reformulation of queries and other constraints [19] in the presence of materialized views, practical and scalable solutions to exploiting views are intensively studied, including [6]. In this paper, we focus on the view exploitation [17] and particularly answer which views are usable for a given RDF pattern, covering view selection in view design and rewriting for view exploitation [6].

While addressed in relational [5] and XML models [16], it yet raises additional complexity for controlling join proliferation [20, 3, 11] in RDF query evaluation. On one hand, views defined by patterns in RDF model syntactically resemble those defined by conjunctive queries in relational model. On the other hand, data in RDF model are grouped together in one table other than distributed over several flat tables in relational model. This seemly minor difference introduces additional difficulties. Different table names involved in relational conjunctive queries help reduce the number of candidate containment mappings, because containment mapping must relate the same table names from view and query, respectively. In a similar way, tree-structured XML pattern helps reduce the difficulty of XML rewriting [16], compared with graph-structured patterns in RDF model.

Our solution to RDF pattern rewriting using views is different from the recent work about RDF views [15, 12, 4], targeted at simplifying pattern rewriting. The view selection defined in [15] is thoroughly different from our sortable view selection, optimizing a candidate view set for given queries. Thus, our work is orthogonal to the view selection in [15]. Although, the works in [12, 4] touche on which views to be possibly involved in query optimization, our work clearly departs from them, dedicated to simplifying pattern rewriting via sortable view selection; [12] studies shortcuts especially for RDF path queries while [4] focusing on cost model for view selection. Therefore, our work can be considered as a generalization of shortcuts in [12] and a different effort from [4].

Serialization for matching also appears in other work [21], targeted at reducing the space of candidate matchings. However, our solution technique identifies itself in that it produces a mapping rather than reducing searching space; an order is defined to sort triple patterns in view and serialize those in query. This sorting and serialization produces a containment mapping which is a kind of matching.

3. PROBLEM DEFINITIONS AND PRELIMINARIES

3.1 Pattern Matching

We use $\mathbb{D}_u$ and $\mathbb{D}_v$ to denote the disjoint domains of URI references (simply references) and variables respectively. Let $\mathbb{D} = \mathbb{D}_u \cup \mathbb{D}_v$. Note that blank nodes are not considered as explained in [3]. Triple space is $\mathbb{T} = \mathbb{D}_u \times \mathbb{D}_u \times \mathbb{D}_u$ and Triple pattern space is $\mathbb{P} = \mathbb{D} \times \mathbb{D} \times \mathbb{D}$. Given a triple pattern q, $q[1]$ denotes the subject of q. Similarly, $q[2]$ and $q[3]$ stand for the predicate and object, respectively.

Data graph G is a set of triples in $\mathbb{T}$, i.e. $G \subseteq \mathbb{T}$. Query pattern Q (simply pattern) is a set of triple patterns, i.e. $Q = \{q_1, q_2, \ldots, q_n\}$, where $q_i \in \mathbb{P}$ for $1 \leq i \leq n$. They are used to represent the conjunctive semantics of triple patterns. For a pattern Q, $\text{var}(Q)$, $\text{uri}(Q)$ denote the sets of variables and references in Q, respectively. Let $\text{dom}(Q) = \text{var}(Q) \cup \text{uri}(Q)$.

A matching μ on pattern Q with respect to data graph G is defined as $\mu : \text{var}(Q) \rightarrow \mathbb{D}_u$, transforming a pattern Q to a graph $\mu(Q)$ by replacing every variable $?x \in \text{var}(Q)$ with the corresponding reference $\mu(?x)$. Let $[Q]_G$ denote the set of all matchings of Q on data graph G, i.e. $[Q]_G = \{\mu | \mu(Q) \subseteq G\}$. The subscription of G can be omitted if the context is clear. Recall the example of V_1, one matching $\mu = \{?x \mapsto Alice, ?y \mapsto Bob, ?z \mapsto Chris\}$ is stored in Table 2. Essentially, $\mu(V_1)$ transforms pattern V_1 to a sub-graph.

3.2 Pattern Rewriting

View $[V]$ is the materialized matchings for pattern V. Pattern V is also called the definition of view $[V]$. Therefore, we interchangeably use a view and its definition without ambiguity. The containment mapping is the core component of answering queries using views [17], which concerns which views to be used and how to use them. We give a formal definition below, in the context of pattern matching for RDF query [3, 11].

DEFINITION 1. ***Containment Mapping***
Containment mapping ϕ is a partial injective mapping $\phi : \mathbb{D}_v \rightarrow \mathbb{D}$ with domain $\text{dom}(\phi)$ and range $\text{ran}(\phi)$.

Recall our previous example for V_1 and Q_1 in Figure 1. Containment mapping $\phi_1 = \{?x \mapsto ?a, ?y \mapsto ?c, ?z \mapsto ?b\}$ maps V_1 to Q_1', i.e., $\phi(V_1) = Q_1'$. To be precise, for triple pattern q, $\phi(q)$ is obtained by replacing $x \in \text{dom}(q) \cap \text{dom}(\phi)$ with y according to $x \mapsto y$. Hence, $\phi(Q) = \{\phi(q) | q \in Q\}$. For empty mapping ϕ, we define $\phi(q) = q$.

DEFINITION 2. ***Containment***
Pattern V contains Q, denoted by $V \sqsupseteq Q$, if there is a containment mapping ϕ such that $\phi(V) \subseteq Q$.

For example, $V_1 \sqsupseteq Q_1$ under containment mapping ϕ_1 in the previous example.

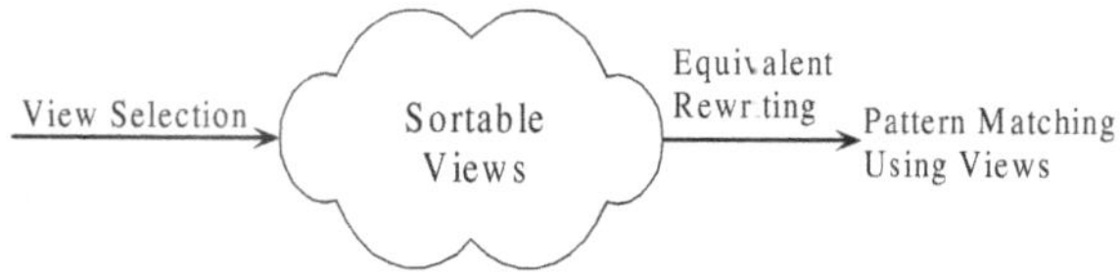

Figure 2: Framework

A view base Γ is a set of views, i.e., $\Gamma = \{V_1, V_2, \cdots, V_n\}$. The problem of pattern rewriting against it is defined as follows.

DEFINITION 3. ***Pattern Rewriting***
Given pattern Q against view base Γ, pattern rewriting is to rewrite Q into a set $\Gamma(Q)$ of patterns, i.e., $\Gamma(Q) = \{\phi_i(V_i) | V_i \in \Gamma, V_i \sqsupseteq Q\}$. Its matchings $[\Gamma(Q)]$ is defined as $[\Gamma(Q)] = \cdots \bowtie [\phi_i(V_i)] \bowtie \cdots$, where $\phi_i(V_i) \in \Gamma(Q)$.

It worths noting that $[\phi_i(V_i)]$ is considered as a table for storing matchings as shown in Table 2. Therefore, two tables $[\phi_i(V_i)]$ and $[\phi_j(V_j)]$ can be joined with relational operator $\bowtie$ on common variables(or common attributes).

Let $\Gamma = \{V_1, V_2\}$ in Figure 1, $\Gamma(Q_3) = \{\phi_{3_1}(V_1), \phi_{3_2}(V_2)\}$ since one can verify $V_1 \sqsupseteq Q_3$ and $V_2 \sqsupseteq Q_3$ under some containment mappings ϕ_{3_1} and ϕ_{3_2}, respectively.

3.3 Pattern Matching via Pattern Rewriting

In this par of the section, we discuss how to employ pattern rewriting to complete pattern matching using view V. In particular, $V \sqsupseteq \phi(V)$ under containment mapping ϕ. Let $\phi = \phi^v \cup \phi^u$, where ϕ^v maps variables to variables and ϕ^u to references.These two parts are used to determine relational renaming operator ρ_{ϕ^v} and selection operator σ_{ϕ^u}, respectively. Here, for $?x \mapsto ?y$ in ϕ^v, the renaming operator renames $?x$ with $?y$. In the similar way, for $?x \mapsto y$ in ϕ^u, select operator works with the selection of $?x = y$.

LEMMA 1. *Given two patterns V and Q with the same length, if $V \sqsupseteq Q$ under the containment mapping ϕ, we have,*

$$[Q] = [\phi(V)] = \pi_{\text{var}(\phi(V))}(\rho_{\phi^v}(\sigma_{\phi^u}([V]))).$$

For example, the containment mapping $\phi_2 = \{?m \mapsto Bob, ?p \mapsto Frank, ?n \mapsto ?n', ?o \mapsto ?o'\}$ between V_2 and Q_2 in Figure 1 consists of two parts. The first part $\phi_2^v = \{?n \mapsto ?n', ?o \mapsto ?o'\}$ maps variables to variables and the second part $\phi_2^u = \{?m \mapsto Bob, ?p \mapsto Frank\}$ maps variables to references. To obtain $[Q_2]$, we could apply selection operator $\sigma_{?m=Bob,?p=Frank}$ with respect to ϕ^u on materialized view $[V_2]$, and renaming one $\rho_{?n \mapsto ?n',?o \mapsto ?o'}$ with respect to ϕ^v. Finally, by applying projection operator $\pi_{?n',?o'}$, we get

$$[Q_2] = \pi_{?n',?o'}(\rho_{?n \mapsto ?n',?o \mapsto ?o'}(\sigma_{?m=Bob,?p=Frank}([V_2]))).$$

Lemma 1 illustrates how to evaluate via pattern rewriting $\Gamma(Q)$. For each $\phi_i(V_i) \in \Gamma(Q)$, it can be obtained via view V_i by using basic relational operators. Let $Q - \Gamma(Q) = Q - \bigcup_{\phi_i(V_i) \in \Gamma} \phi_i(V_i)$. We summarize how pattern rewriting is used to solve pattern matching in Theorem 1.

THEOREM 1. *Given pattern Q against view base Γ, $[Q] = [\Gamma(Q)] \bowtie [Q - \Gamma(Q)]$.*

We use Figure 2 to illustrate the main idea behind Theorem 1. Generally speaking, the rewriting consists of two steps, namely view selection and equivalent pattern rewriting [17]. In view selection, instead of using existing cost model [25], we consider view selection on behalf of rewriting. In particular, we select sortable views for materialization, because of its attractive advantages for query rewriting.

4. SORTABLE VIEW

Theorem 1 states the efficacy of pattern rewriting defined in Definition 3. The key problem involved in this theorem is how to find containment mapping ϕ_i between view V_i and Q such that $[\phi_i(V_i)]$ is evaluated in terms of Lemma 1. Consequently, $[\Gamma(Q)]$ is obtained using views. To achieve this goal, an order, called *containment order*, is introduced. The order is used to sort views and serialize patterns. The sorting and serialization greatly simplifies the searching for containment mapping.

4.1 Containment Order

The intuition behind containment order is that it preserves the equivalence between tripe patterns v and $\phi(v)$ under any containment mapping ϕ. Therefore, this order can be used as a necessary condition for containment verification because each triple pattern in view must be mapped to its equivalent patterns in query. We find lexical order suffices this goal.

DEFINITION 4. ***Containment Order on*** $\mathbb{D}$
$(\preceq, \mathbb{D})$: *$\forall x, y \in \mathbb{D}_u$, $x \prec y$, iff x precedes y in terms of lexical order. In other case, $\forall x, y \in \mathbb{D}_u \cup \mathbb{D}_v$, they are equivalent, denoted by $x \simeq y$. Further, $x \preceq y$ if $x \prec y$ or $x \simeq y$.*

Essentially, if $x \simeq y$, there is a containment mapping ϕ such that $\phi(x) = y$ or $\phi(y) = x$. The defined *containment order* is naturally extended to triple pattern space $\mathbb{P}$.

DEFINITION 5. ***Containment Order on*** $\mathbb{P}$
$(\preceq, \mathbb{P})$: *A triple pattern q_1 is ordered before triple pattern q_2, if $q_1[i] \prec q_2[i]$ for $q_1[j] \simeq q_2[j]$ and $1 \leq j < i$. We say q_1 and q_2 are equally ranked, denoted by $q_1 \simeq q_2$, if $q_1[i] \simeq q_2[i]$ for $i = 1, 2, 3$.*

The following lemma demonstrates the equivalence between triple patterns v and $\phi(v)$ for any containment mapping ϕ.

LEMMA 2. *If pattern V contains pattern Q under containment mapping ϕ, for any $v \in V$, $v \simeq \phi(v) \in Q$.*

PROOF. Because $V \sqsupseteq Q$ under containment mapping ϕ, for any $v \in V$, there is a triple pattern $q \in Q$ such that $\phi(v) = q$. Moreover, the triple pattern q is obtained by replacing variables appearing in v with variables or references according to ϕ. Therefore, for $l = 1, 2, 3$, $v[l] \simeq q[l]$ according to the definition of containment order where a variable is ranked equal with anything. The lemma is proved. □

4.2 Sortable View

While containment order connects v with $\phi(v)$ under any containment mapping ϕ, it is not sufficient to derive containment relationship. In particular, the order relationship between tripe patterns v_i and v_j at the view side cannot carry over to those $\phi(v_i)$ and $\phi(v_j)$ at the query pattern side even if $\phi(V) = Q$, i.e., if $v_i \prec v_j$ and $v \simeq \phi(v)$ for any triple pattern v, it can not be obtained that $\phi(v_i) \prec \phi(v_j)$. If not, the order can be used to sort triple patterns in view and query pattern, respectively. The containment mapping must relate the triple patterns at the same positions. Nevertheless, it can be proved that the sortable view can make the order relationship extendable from the view to the query. Theorem 2 claims the containment order can be used to filter out unpromising searching of containment mapping.

DEFINITION 6. ***Sortable View***
View $V = \{v_1, \cdots, v_l\}$ is called sortable if there exist an order such that $v_j \prec v_k$ for any $j < k$.

Given sortable view V, its triple patterns can be sorted increasingly in terms of containment order. Hence, let $V[i]$ be the ith triple pattern in its sorting. Given general pattern Q, its triple patterns can be arbitrarily serialized into an array and let $Q[i]$ be the triple pattern at the ith position under this serialization. However, among various serializations of Q, one is special, called V-serialization against sortable view V.

DEFINITION 7. V***-Serialization***
If the serialization of Q satisfies $Q[i] \simeq V[i]$ for $i = 1..|V|$, this serialization is called V-serialization of Q.

THEOREM 2. *Given pattern Q against sortable view V, $V \sqsupseteq Q$ if and only if there is a containment mapping ϕ such that $\phi(V[i]) = Q[i]$ for V-serialization of Q.*

REMARK 1. *View V_2 is sortable and $V_2 \sqsupseteq Q_2$. However, Q_2 is not sortable. There are two different orders available for Q_2, as is shown below.*

$(Frank, coAuthor, ?o') \prec (?n', isMother, ?o') \prec (Bob, Marry, ?n')$

or

$(?n', isMother, ?o') \prec (Bob, Marry, ?n') \prec (Frank, coAuthor, ?o')$

While Q_2 is not sortable, its V_2-serialization is determined in the following.

$V_2[1]$	$V_2[2]$	$V_2[3]$
$(?p, coAuthor, ?o)$	$(?n, isMother, ?o)$	$(?m, Marry, ?n)$
$Q_2[1]$	$Q_2[2]$	$Q_2[3]$
$(Frank, coAuthor, ?o')$	$(?n', isMother, ?o')$	$(Bob, Marry, ?n')$

By Theorem 2, if a containment mapping ϕ exists, then $\phi(V_2[1]) = Q_2[1]$, $\phi(V_2[2]) = Q_2[2]$ and $\phi(V_2[3]) = Q_2[3]$.

REMARK 2. *Given pattern Q against sortable view V, its V-serialization can be efficiently obtained if it exists. Each triple pattern $q \in Q$ is put into the ith position of $Q[i]$ if $q \simeq V[i]$.*

Before giving the proof of Theorem 2, two basic lemmas are first proved which are extensions from Lemma 2 in the case of sortable views. Lemma 3 states that there is no more than one triple pattern in Q which is equivalent with $V[i]$. Lemma 4 further shows that containment mapping must relate equivalent triple patterns. These two lemmas together establish the foundation of Theorem 2 on the contribution of the equivalence relationship between $Q[i]$ and $V[i]$ to the containment mapping.

REMARK 3. *Based on Lemma 3 and 4, Theorem 2 claims that view containment can be reduced to comparison of triple patterns with respect to containment order.*

To simply the presentation, let $P(V, q)$ be the set of equivalent triple patterns of q, i.e., $P(V, q) = \{v \in V | v \simeq q\}$.

LEMMA 3. *Given sortable view V and pattern Q with the same length, if $V \sqsupseteq Q$ then for any $q \in Q$, $|P(V, q)| = 1$*

PROOF. Since $V \sqsupseteq Q$, there is a containment mapping ϕ such that $\forall q \in Q$, $\exists v \in V$, $\phi(v) = q$. By Lemma 2, $v \simeq q$, so $v \in P(V, q)$. If $|P(V, q)| > 1$, there is another triple pattern, say v', in V such that $v' \simeq q$. Since V is a sorted pattern, without loss of generality, we assume $v \prec v'$. Since $v \prec v'$, there exists l such that both $v[l]$ and $v'[l]$ are references and $v[l] \prec v'[l]$. However, we know that $v \simeq q$ and $v' \simeq q$, so $q[l]$ is a variable. This is a contradiction since a containment mapping has $\mathsf{var}(V)$ as its domain and $\mathsf{dom}(Q)$ as its range. The lemma is proved. □

LEMMA 4. *Given sortable view V and pattern Q with the same length, $V \sqsupseteq Q$ if and only if there is a containment mapping ϕ such that for any $q \in Q$, $\phi(P(V,q)) = \{q\}$.*

PROOF. *IF* part: If there is a containment mapping ϕ such that $\phi(P(V,q)) = \{q\}$, we have $|P(V,q)| = 1$ since V is a sorted pattern. Furthermore, if there is another triple pattern $q' \in Q$ such that $P(V,q') = P(V,q)$, then $\phi(P(V,q')) = \phi(P(V,q)) = \{q\}$. However, we have $\phi(P(V,q')) = \{q'\}$, this is a contradiction. Therefore, for each $v \in V$, we cannot find q and q' in Q such that $\phi(v) = q$ and $\phi(v) = q'$. Since $|V| = |Q|$, we must have ϕ is a bijection from V to Q. Therefore, we have $\bigcup_{q \in Q} P(V,q) = V$, this infers that $\phi(V) = Q$. That is, $V \sqsupseteq Q$.

ONLY IF part: Based on Lemma 2, if $\phi(v) = q$, then $v \in P(V,q)$. Based on our previously proved Lemma 3, $P(V,q) = \{v\}$ and therefore $\phi(P(V,q)) = \phi(\{v\}) = \{q\}$. □

Proof of Theorem 2. The if part is immediately obtained. Only if part: Since $V \sqsupseteq Q$, Q is V-serializable, i.e., $V[i] \simeq Q[i]$. At the same time, there is a containment mapping ϕ from V to Q. Due to Lemma 2, $\phi(V[i]) \simeq V[i]$. Combined with Lemma 4, we have $\phi(V[i]) = Q[i]$. □

4.3 Containment Searching Algorithm

Theorem 2 immediately results in Algorithm 1 for view containment. It receives pattern Q against sortable patterns V with the same length and returns the containment mapping ϕ if $V \sqsupseteq Q$, otherwise an empty mapping. After sorting the view V and serializing pattern Q, for each i, contain builds the containment mapping mapping ϕ_i from $V[i]$ to $Q[i]$ such that $\phi_i(V[i]) = Q[i]$. Finally, if $\phi = \bigcup \phi_i$ is a containment mapping then $\phi(V) = Q$, otherwise, $\phi = \emptyset$.

An example is given for building mapping ϕ_i. Let $V[i] = (?x$, isMother, $?z)$ and $Q[i] = (?a$, isMother, *Bob*$)$, we have $\phi_i = \{?x \mapsto ?a, ?z \mapsto Bob\}$ such that $\phi_i(V[i]) = Q[i]$.

Algorithm 1 contain(V, Q)

```
{ V is sortable and |V| = |Q| }
1: initiate containment mapping φ with empty;
2: if there is no V-serialization of Q then
3:     return ∅;
4: end if
5: for i = 1 to |V| do
6:     build mapping φ_i such that φ_i(V[i]) = Q[i];
7:     φ = φ ∪ φ_i;
8:     if φ is not a mapping then
9:         return ∅;
10:    end if
11: end for
12: return φ;
```

The testing in line 8 keeps ϕ is a mapping, i.e., there are no conflicts of mapping a variable to different images or different variables to an image.

When $|Q| > |V|$, the verification of whether $V \sqsupseteq Q$ involves iterative calls of contain(V, Q') for each $Q' \subset Q$ with the length of $|V|$. This naive iteration is time prohibitive. In Algorithm 2, we present contain$^+(V,Q)$, removing the pre-condition of $|Q| = |V|$. Although the algorithm still takes exponential time in the worst case, the number of candidate $Q' \subseteq Q$ is greatly reduced by exploiting the containment order. In the following, we use an example to illustrate its efficiency.

For patterns $V_3 = \{v_1 = (?x$, Marry, $?y)$, $v_2 = (?x$, isMother, $?z)\}$ and $Q_4 = \{q_1 = (?c$, Marry, Bob$)$, $q_2 = (?c$, isMother, $?d)$, $q_3 = (?d$, isBrother, $?e)\}$. In the similar way to the previous example, $P(V_1, q_1) = \{v_1\}$, $P(V_1, q_2) = \{v_2\}$, but $P(V_1, q_3) = \emptyset$, which implies that there is no triple pattern in V_1 which can be mapped to q_3. Therefore, q_3 is excluded from candidates and the only possible candidate is $Q'_4 = \{q_1, q_2\}$. It is only necessary to invoke contain(V_1, Q'_4) once for further verification.

Algorithm contain$^+(V,Q)$ consists of two phases. At the first phase, it computes $P(Q,V) = \bigcup_{v \in V} P(Q,v)$. It is immediately verified that $P(Q,V) \subseteq Q$ and $V \sqsupseteq Q$ if and only if $V \sqsupseteq P(Q,V)$.

At the second phase, it builds a partition on $P(Q,V)$. With respect to sortable view V, two triple patterns q and q' are conflict, denoted as $q \oslash q'$, if and only if $P(V,q) = P(V,q')$. By applying the equivalent relation $\oslash$ on $P(Q,V)$ and a partition of $P(Q,V)$ is obtained, i.e., $P(Q,V) = \bigcup_{k=1..|V|} Q_k$, where Q_k is an equivalence class. By retrieving one triple pattern from each Q_k, a query pattern Q' is composed, i.e., $Q' = \{q_k \in Q_k | k = 1..|V|\}$. It is obvious that no conflict triple patterns exist in Q'. Let Ω be the collect of all such composed patterns Q' and input it to contain for further verification. The details are presented in Algorithm 2.

Algorithm 2 contain$^+$(V, Q)

```
{ V is sortable and |Q| > |V| }
if |P(Q,V)| ≥ |V| then
    partition P(Q,V) in terms of equivalence relation ⊘;
else
    return ∅;
end if
for each composed pattern Q' do
    if contain(V, Q') ≠ ∅ then
        output Q' and φ; /*φ returned by contain()*/;
    end if
end for
```

4.4 Sortable View Selection

In this part of the section, we discuss the feasibility of sortable views in RDF model. To be precise, the question is on the existence of an efficient algorithm to construct sortable views. We are also interested in finding certain approach to transform/rebuild unsortable views to sortable ones. Positive answers are provided in the following for both of the questions above.

Given pattern Q, a directed graph order(Q), called *ordered graph* of Q, can be constructed, where order(Q) $=< V_Q, E_Q >$. Let $V_Q = Q$ and a directed edge (q_i, q_j) from q_i to q_j is included in E_Q if and only if $q_i \prec q_j$. Therefore, there is a topological sort for order(Q) if it is acyclic.

THEOREM 3. *Pattern V is sortable if and only if there is a unique topological sort of order(V).*

PROOF. If part: If the topological sort of order(V) does not exist, then order(V) must be cyclic, i.e., there is a cyclic path, $v_1 \prec \cdots \prec v_1$, implying V is not sortable based on Definition 6. Hence, if a given V can be sorted, there is a topological sort of order(V).

Only if part: We first prove the fact that if there are more than one topological sort of order(V), there are at least two triple patterns with no edges between them. To obtain the topological sort, we repeat retrieving and deleting the node with indegree 0 on the current order(V) step by step. If there are two topological sorts, there must be a step where there are two triple patterns whose indegrees are both zero, meaning we have two choices of retrieval and deletion. Further, there are no edges between them. Hence there are two triple patterns in V without $\prec$ or $\succ$ relation, meaning V

Algorithm 3 $\text{rewrite}(Q, \Gamma)$

```
for each V_i ∈ Γ do
    if P(V_i, Q) = V_i and contain⁺(V_i, Q) then
        insert φ_i(V_i) into Γ(Q);
    end if
end for
output Γ(Q);
```

can not be sorted. Finally, the unique topological sort $v_1 \prec v_2 \cdots$ of order(V) determines the increasing sorting of triple patterns in pattern V. $\square$

Clearly, Theorem 3 provides a way of testing whether a view is sortable. Given view V, construct order(V) and do topological sort on order(V). During the topological sort, if there are two nodes with indegree zero, V is not sortable, otherwise, V is sortable.

On the other hand, Theorem 3 provides an efficient way of generating sortable views. In a similar way, for view V, do topological sort on order(V). At each step of this sort, if there is one node with indegree zero, delete the node and put it into V', otherwise, delete one of them. Finally, V' is sortable.

REMARK 4. *If there is a triple pattern in V' which does not share variables with other triple patterns, it is isolated and should be deleted from V' further.*

In practice, given view V, generate sortable view V' from V in the above way. Repeat it on $V - V'$ for another sortable view V''. Finally, a view is partitioned into the union of sortable views. Thereafter, query are evaluated step by step via RDF query engine, say RDF-3x [20]. At each step, a sortable view is evaluated. Finally, join all these results together to finish the input query. During this procedure, it can be decided whether to materialize the sortable view.

5. REWRITING AND OPTIMIZATION

While previous section focuses on the property of sortable view for containment mapping search and feasibility. In this section, we first provide the basic complete query rewriting algorithm using sortable views. We then present an inverted index structure for fast retrieval of candidate views in the evaluation of particular pattern query Q. We also discuss how to optimize the selection of view from large candidate pool, to remove redundant views for expected evaluation cost minimization.

Consider our running example in Figure 1, where $\Gamma = \{V_1, V_2\}$, $V_1 \sqsupseteq Q_1$ but $V_2 \not\sqsupseteq Q_1$ as we have shown. It is desirable not to invoke $\text{contain}^+(V_2, Q_1)$ for further verification. The following lemma provides a necessary requirement to filter out unpromising views. Recall that $P(V, Q) = \bigcup_{q \in Q} P(V, q)$.

LEMMA 5. *If $V \sqsupseteq Q$, then $P(V, Q) = V$.*

PROOF. It is clear $V \supseteq P(V, Q)$. We show $P(V, Q) \supseteq V$. For any $v \in V$, there exists $q \in Q$ such that $\phi(v) = q$. By Lemma 2, $v \in P(V, Q)$. Hence $P(V, Q) \supseteq V$. $\square$

Based on Lemma 5, we present a complete algorithm $\text{rewrite}(Q, \Gamma))$ for pattern rewriting (See Algorithm 3). Specifically, the algorithm retrieves those promising patterns V_i in view base such that $P(V_i, Q) = V_i$ and then invoke $\text{contain}^+(V_i, Q)$ for further verification.

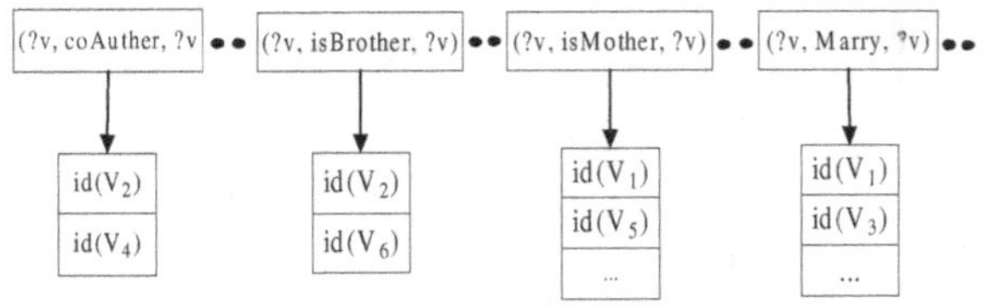

Figure 3: Example of inverted list index.

5.1 Inverted Index Structure

To support the retrieval of promising views, we build inverted lists and put all triple patterns in Γ into $\mathcal{V}$, i.e., $\mathcal{V} = \{(v, \text{id}(V_i)) | V_i \in \Gamma, v \in V_i\}$, where $\text{id}(V_i)$ is the identification of V_i. Given $q \in Q$, let $P(\mathcal{V}, q) = \{(v, \text{id}(V_i)) | q \simeq v, (v, \text{id}(V_i)) \in \mathcal{V}\}$ and $P(\mathcal{V}, Q) = \bigcup_{q \in Q} P(\mathcal{V}, q)$. Finally, grouping $(v, \text{id}(V_i))$ by $\text{id}(V_i)$ component in $P(\mathcal{V}, Q)$, we can retrieve complete patterns V_i for further verification.

Unfortunately, the containment order is not desirable to compute $P(\mathcal{V}, q)$ since $\simeq$ is not a transitive relation. For example, $q_1 \simeq q$ and $q_2 \simeq q$ but no $\simeq$ between q_1 and q_2, meaning triple patterns ranked equal with q may not be grouped together. To tackle this problem, we define a total order, called *index order* for fast retrieval.

DEFINITION 8. ***Index Order on $\mathbb{D}$***
Index order $(\preceq^i, \mathbb{D})$: 1) $\forall x, y \in \mathbb{D}_u$, $x \prec^i y$ iff x precedes y in terms of lexical order. 2) $\forall x \in \mathbb{D}_u, y \in \mathbb{D}_v$, $x \prec^i y$. 3) two variables $?x, ?y \in \mathbb{D}_v$ are ranked equal, denoted by $?x \simeq^i ?y$.

DEFINITION 9. ***Index Order on $\mathbb{P}$***
$(\preceq^i, \mathbb{P})$: A triple pattern $q_1 = (s_1, p_1, o_1)$ is ordered before triple pattern $q_2 = (s_2, p_2, o_2)$, if 1) $s_1 \prec^i s_2$, or 2) $s_1 \simeq^i s_2$ and $p_1 \prec^i p_2$, or 3) $s_1 \simeq^i s_2$, $p_1 \simeq^i p_2$ and $o_1 \prec^i o_2$. We say q_1 and q_2 are equally ranked, denoted by $q_1 \simeq^i q_2$, if $s_1 \simeq^i s_2$, $p_1 \simeq^i p_2$ and $o_1 \simeq^i o_2$.

LEMMA 6. *Index order $\preceq^i$ on $\mathbb{P}$ is a total order. Specifically, $\simeq^i$ is an equivalence relation on $\mathbb{P}$.*

PROOF. We only show the transitivity of $\preceq^i$, i.e., if $q_1 \preceq^i q_2$ and $q_2 \preceq^i q_3$, then $q_1 \preceq^i q_3$. Since $q_1 \preceq^i q_2$, $\exists l$, $q_1[l] \preceq^i q_2[l]$ for $l = 1, 2, 3$. Similarly, $\exists l'$, $q_2[l'] \preceq^i q_3[l']$ for $l' = 1, 2, 3$. W.l.o.g, we assume $l \leq l'$, we have $q_1[i] \simeq^i q_2[i] \simeq^i q_3[i]$ for $i < l$ while $q_1[l] \prec q_2[l] \simeq^i q_3[l]$. Hence, $q_1[l] \prec q_3[l]$ and therefore, $q_1 \preceq^i q_3$. Similarly, we can prove that $\simeq^i$ is an equivalent relation. $\square$

Given an index order, the inverted list index is constructed by grouping the triple patterns with equivalence relationship under index order $\simeq^i$. Each inverted list keeps a list of the identifications $\text{id}(V_i)$ of patterns V_i in Γ, such that V_i contains a triple pattern in this equivalence class. In Figure 3, we present an example of the inverted lists. Based on the definition, each of $\text{id}(V_1)$ and $\text{id}(V_2)$ is stored in two inverted lists for the two triple patterns in it. Note that all variables are replaced with a common variable symbol $?v$ in the index, since all variables are regarded as equal in the index order $\simeq^i$.

While the index order delivers complete equivalence classes in the triple space $\mathbb{P}$, this order does not directly guarantee the correctness when retrieving candidate patterns for a query Q, since $\simeq$ is different from $\simeq^i$. To retrieve a complete candidate set for $P(V_i, Q)$, it is important and necessary to fill the semantics gap between $\simeq$ and $\simeq^i$, i.e., by expanding the triples in the query Q before the candidate retrieval.

Generally speaking, the expansion is done by 1) replacing all variables with the unique variable symbol $?v$, and 2) generating

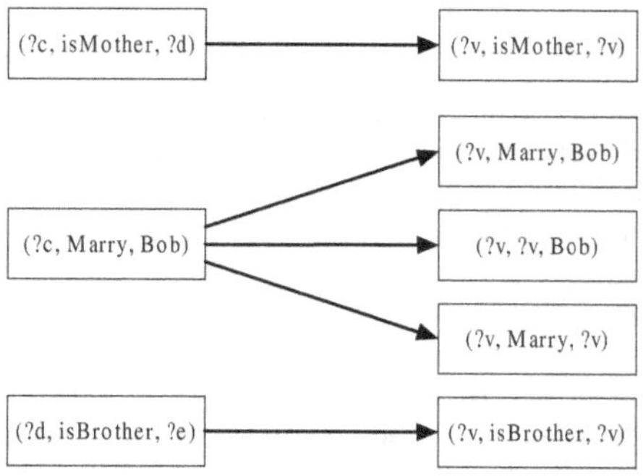

Figure 4: Example of query expansion on Q_2.

new triple patterns by generalizing references to variables, when there are more than one reference in the triple pattern. For triple pattern $q_2 = (?c, \text{Marry}, \text{Bob})$, for example in Figure 4, there are two references, Marry and Bob. Therefore, we expands on both references, substituting each reference with the common variable $?v$. This leads to three triple patterns to query on the inverted list index. The expansion operation is important, because it ensures that there is no promising patterns lost in the candidate retrieval. For triple pattern q, let $\mathsf{exp}(q)$ be the set of all expanded triple patterns via the above expansion process. Let $q_i \sqsupseteq q_j$ denote $\{q_i\} \sqsupseteq \{q_j\}$. The relation between $\simeq$ and $\simeq^i$ is summarized as follows.

LEMMA 7. *Given two triple patterns $q_i \sqsupseteq q_j$, $q_i \simeq q_j$ if and only if $\exists q \in \mathsf{exp}(q_j)$, $q \simeq^i q_i$.*

PROOF. We first give the following two observations, which are immediately verified based on the related definitions. First, given two triple patterns $q_1 \simeq^i q_2$, if triple pattern $q \simeq q_1$, then $q \simeq q_2$. Second, for $q' \in \mathsf{exp}(q)$, $q' \simeq q$.

If part: Since $q \in \mathsf{exp}(q_j)$, $q_i \simeq q$ based on the second observation. Further, because $q \simeq^i q_j$, we have $q_i \simeq q_j$ based on the first observation.

Only if part: Since $\{q_i\} \sqsupseteq \{q_j\}$ and $q_i \simeq q_j$, we can obtain the containment mapping ϕ such that $\phi(q_i) = q_j$. Hence, $\phi^-(q_j) \simeq^i q_i$, where ϕ^- is the inverse mapping of ϕ. It is clear $\phi^-(q_j) \in \mathsf{exp}(q_i)$. This finishes the proof. □

Since every triple pattern has at most two variables, there are at most three triple patterns after the expansion, the expanded triple patterns do not introduce heavy additional workloads. For each expanded triple pattern, the system quickly marks the equivalent inverted lists w.r.t $\simeq^i$. Finally, the algorithm counts the number $\#\mathsf{id}(V_i)$ of $\mathsf{id}(V_i)$ appearing in the marked lists. Note that the appearance of an identification in a list is counted once. For $\#\mathsf{id}(V_i)$, we have the following theorem.

THEOREM 4. *Given sortable view in base Γ, for any V_i in Γ, $P(V_i, Q) = V_i$ if and only if $\#\mathsf{id}(V_i) = |V_i|$.*

PROOF. Note that identification $\mathsf{id}(V_i)$ for pattern V_i can appear at most once in any list because any pattern in the view base is kept sortable. If part: since $\#\mathsf{id}(V_i) = |V_i|$, each list containing $\mathsf{id}(V_i)$ is visited, meaning $p(V_i, Q) = V_i$. Only if part: since $P(V_i, Q) = V_i$, for each $q \in Q$, all inverted lists whose entries are ranked equal to q in terms of $\simeq^i$ are marked. Remember $\#\mathsf{id}(V_i)$ is the number of appearances of $\mathsf{id}(V_i)$ in the marked lists. Since each $\mathsf{id}(V_i)$ can appear at most once in any list, $\#\mathsf{id}(V_i) = |V_i|$. □

The details of pattern rewriting method with index are summarized in Algorithm $\mathsf{rewrite}^+(Q, \Gamma)$ (see Algorithm 4). The algorithm receives pattern Q and the set Γ of views and returns the

Algorithm 4 rewrite$^+(Q, \Gamma)$

1: **for** each $q \in Q$ **do**
2: expand q;
3: mark the entry equal to one of the expansions;
4: **end for**
5: count $\#\mathsf{id}(V_i)$ among the marked lists;
6: **for** each $\#\mathsf{id}(V_i) = |V_i|$ **do**
7: invoke $\mathsf{contain}^+(V_i, Q)$ for further verification;
8: insert $\phi_i(V_i)$ into $\Gamma(Q)$ if $V_i \sqsupseteq Q$;
9: **end for**

rewriting $\Gamma(Q)$ of Q. It consists of two phases. At the first phase, it finds all promising patterns in the view base based on Theorem 4 (line 6). At the second phase, for each promising pattern, it invokes $\mathsf{contain}^+(V_i, Q)$ to do further verification

REMARK 5. *The process of marking inverted lists can be improved by applying a B^+-tree index structure on the entries of the inverted lists due to the total order $\preceq^i$.*

5.2 Expected Cost Optimization

Theorem 1 states a possible way of exploiting views to evaluate pattern matching. However, the evaluation of $\Gamma(Q)$ defined in Definition 3 possibly uses redundant views. To be precise, it is possible that $\phi_k(V_k) \subseteq \phi_i(V_i) \cup \phi_j(V_j)$ or $\phi_k(V_k) \supseteq \phi_i(V_i) \cup \phi_j(V_j)$. The term $[\phi_k(V_k)]$ in the former case or $[\phi_i(V_i)] \bowtie [\phi_j(V_j)]$ in the latter case can be deleted from the expression of $[\Gamma(Q)]$ in Definition 3 without compromising the correctness of Theorem 1. Such views are called redundant views in pattern rewriting. Formally, if there is view base $\Gamma' \subset \Gamma$ such that $[\Gamma'(Q)] = [\Gamma(Q)]$ for any graph G, The views in $\Gamma - \Gamma'$ are called redundant views.

Redundant views are pruned from pattern rewriting such that the cost of pattern rewriting is minimized. To be precise, each view V_i is associated with a cost $c(V_i)$ which indicates the cost of obtaining $[\phi_i(V_i)]$ from $[V_i]$. The cost $c(\Gamma(Q))$ of pattern rewriting $\Gamma(Q)$ is the sum of $c(V_i)$ for $\phi_i(V_i) \in \Gamma(Q)$. That is,

$$c(\Gamma(Q)) = \sum_{\phi_i(V_i) \in \Gamma(Q)} c(V_i)$$

Therefore, it becomes an optimization problem to find $\Gamma' \subseteq \Gamma$ such that the cost of $c(\Gamma'(Q))$ is minimized under the constraint of $[\Gamma'(Q)] = [\Gamma(Q)]$.

DEFINITION 10. ***Optimum Pattern Rewriting***
The pattern rewriting $\Gamma'(Q)$ is optimum if its cost $c(\Gamma'(Q))$ is minimized under the constraints of $\Gamma' \subseteq \Gamma$ and $[\Gamma'(Q)] = [\Gamma(Q)]$ for any RDF graph.

The optimization problem we consider here can be reduced to set cover problem [18]: $\bigcup_{\phi_i(V_i) \in \Gamma(Q)} \phi_i(V_i)$ acts as the universe set and $\Gamma(Q)$ as the collect of sets to cover the universe set such that the union of the them includes it with the minimized cost. It worths noting that when $c(V_i) = 1$, this reduction can output the minimized number of views for pattern rewriting.

REMARK 6. *When put $Q - \Gamma'(Q)$ into Γ for any $\Gamma' \subset \Gamma$, the optimum pattern rewriting may ignore a view V_i in its rewriting even if $V_i \sqsupseteq Q$. That is, some views are not always useful when the cost of using them exceeds the cost of ignoring them.*

para.	description	default
$\mathcal{L}$	average length of patterns	10
$\mathcal{V}$	average number of variables	5
M	mode of triple generation	D
V	mode of variable generation	D

Table 3: Parameter settings in experiments

6. EMPIRICAL EVALUATION

Based on Theorem 1, we implement a view aware evaluation engine,sSeg, which segments a query into parts. Some parts can be answered by materialized views. The final answer is obtained by joining answers to these parts. In particular, it first rewrites pattern Q into $\Gamma(Q)$ via rewrite(Q, Γ) and then evaluate Q via Theorem 1. For comparison, we use Rdf-3x [20], a RISC-style engine for RDF queries as the baseline, as well as our backend RDF query engine for obtaining $[Q - \Gamma(Q)]$ component in Theorem 1.

For testing the efficiency of rewrite(Q, Γ), we also implement another view aware evaluation engine, gSeg. It is a little different from sSeg by employing graph containment searching [7] for pattern rewriting, reducing containment mapping to subgraph isomorphism.

We tested all the approaches on the data sets used in [20]. Since most of the data sets display similar results, we only report our experimental results on *Yago* data set in this paper. The Yago data set contains 40,114,899 distinct triples and 33,951,636 distinct strings, consuming 3.1 GB as (factorized) triple dump. Rdf-3x [20] needs 2.7 GB for all indexes and the string dictionary. All the programs, for both sSeg and gSeg, are compiled with GCC 4.3 in Ubuntu 10.04 LTS. The codes of Rdf-3x [20] are obtained from open source. All the experiments were run on a server with Intel(R) Core(TM)2 CPU 4300@1.80GHz and 2G main memory.

Pattern Generation. We used random walk on Yago data set to generate query patterns. First of all, an edge exists between two triples, if they share at least one common reference, on subject, predict or object. For a particular triple p, the set $N(p)$ contains all its neighboring triples. Given a subgraph (a set of triples) $P \subseteq G$, the neighborhood of P is defined as $N(P) = \bigcup_{p \in P} N(p)$. The degree of a triple p is $|N(p)|$. The frequency of a reference is the number of triples in the data set which contain the reference.

There are several parameters controlling the generation of the query patterns, including *average pattern length* $\mathcal{L}$, *variable number* $\mathcal{V}$, *triple mode* M and *variable mode* V. While the first two parameters are straightforward, the last two parameters are much more complicated, which are closely related to the generation mechanism. Every pattern Q_i was generated through some random walk on the data graph. Before the generation, the generator randomly selected the number of triple patterns in Q_i, following the uniform distribution on $[0.5L, 1.5L]$. After the selection of the triple number n, a two-phase generation scheme was invoked. In the first phrase, the generator randomly picked up a triple from the data as the seed, i.e $Q_i = \{t_1\}$. It then continued adding neighbors to the current triples in Q_i, until there are exactly n triples in Q_i. For neighbor set $N(Q_i)$, there are different strategies on the selection of next triple. If M =U, all the neighbors were chosen uniformly. If triple mode M =F (M =D resp.), a triple in $p = N(Q_i)$ was selected with probability proportional to the appearance frequency of p (the degree of p, i.e. $N(p)$, resp.). In the second phase, some of the references were selected and replaced by the variables. Similar to the first phase, the variable mode V has three options, including U, F and D, which follows uniform selection, frequency-based selection and degree-based selection respectively.

View Selection. We first generated 10,000 patterns and then applied algorithms for frequent pattern discovery [24] to mine frequent patterns frequently included in query patterns. The mined frequent patterns were inserted into view base Γ_g and their answers were materialized in relational tables. To run sSeg, we keep all views in view base Γ_s sortable. We deleted the minimum number of triple patterns from a non-sortable pattern such that the left triple patterns form a sortable one (reference Theorem 3).Views with one triple pattern are deleted from Γ_s. If there is a triple pattern which shares no common variables with others in a view, this view is also deleted from Γ_s. In this way, view base Γ_g was transformed to Γ_s.

To reduce the effect of randomness, all of our experiments were run on 100 different queries. The average of these results are reported in this section. To test the impact of the correlation between the query patterns and patterns in view base, we also controlled the coverage $C_{\Gamma_g}(Q)$ of Γ_g, i.e. $C_{\Gamma_g}(Q) = |Q_{\Gamma_g}|/|Q|$. In the same way, $C_{\Gamma_s}(Q) = |Q_{\Gamma_s}|/|Q|$.

Query Efficiency. Figure 5 shows the query processing time when varying the cardinality of the database size from 10×10^6 to 40×10^6. In particular, the tests conducted on two query workloads generated with two different parameter settings. The results are presented in Figure 5(a) and 5(b), respectively. On both query workloads, the average query processing time of all methods increase exponentially with the expansion of the triple database. It can be observed that the overall query efficiency of gSeg is significantly worse than the standard RDF data engine Rdf-3x. On the other hand, sSeg presents competitive performance against Rdf-3x. When the number of triples reaches 40×10^6, the average processing time of sSeg is faster than Rdf-3x by 25%, on both of the workloads. This validates the effectiveness of sSeg especially for large data set.

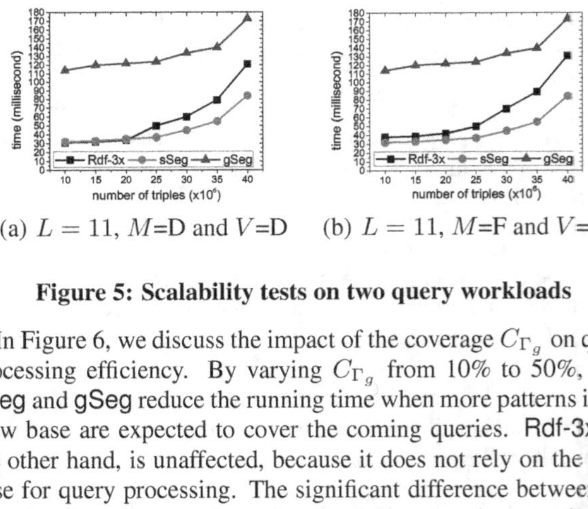

(a) $L = 11$, M=D and V=D (b) $L = 11$, M=F and V=F

Figure 5: Scalability tests on two query workloads

In Figure 6, we discuss the impact of the coverage C_{Γ_g} on query processing efficiency. By varying C_{Γ_g} from 10% to 50%, both sSeg and gSeg reduce the running time when more patterns in the view base are expected to cover the coming queries. Rdf-3x, on the other hand, is unaffected, because it does not rely on the view base for query processing. The significant difference between the two view-based approaches arises from the expensive containment decision employed in gSeg. Again, the overhead for sSeg looks ignorable.

In Figure 7, we discuss the relationship between answer cardinality and query processing efficiency. Specifically, we generate 10 groups of random queries and record the number of matches on the triple patterns from the graph database G. Intuitively, the query processing takes more CPU time when there are more matchings with the queries. However, we did observe some exceptions in some of the experiments, as is shown in the figure. In particular, both gSeg and Rdf-3x show large variances on the computation time. For example, gSeg and Rdf-3x take more than 2.2 seconds when there are 4120 matchings. Our solution sSeg, on the other hand, shows more stable performance. sSeg finishes the

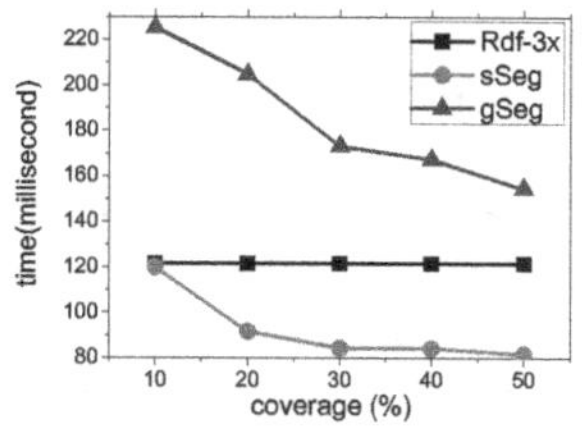

Figure 6: Coverage vs. time

whole computation within 1 second, even when there are more than 15,000 matchings.

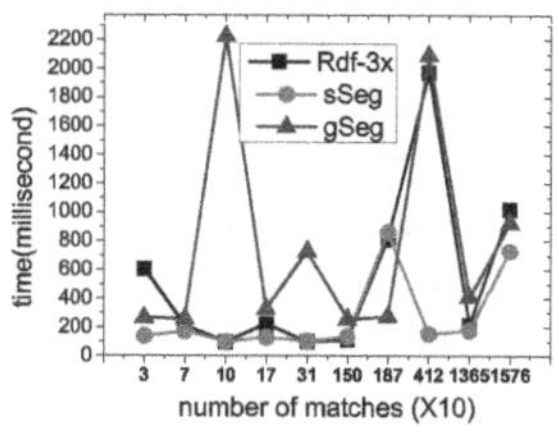

Figure 7: Number of matches vs. time

In Figure 8, we evaluate the influence of the query length, i.e. the average number of the triple patterns in the queries. The results in the figure show that sSeg is more scalable than the other two, in terms of the query length. The CPU time of gSeg increases sharply when the length is lifted from 11 to 13, while the computation time of sSeg remains within linear increase. The abrupt increase of computation cost of gSeg roots in its exponential complexity.

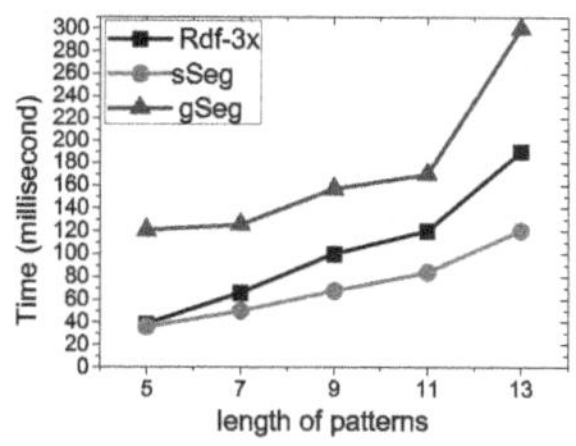

Figure 8: Query length vs. time

Finally, in Figure 9, we compare the methods when the number of variables in the queries expanded from 3 to 11. The number of variables is increased by replacing some of the same variables in triple patterns with different variables. For example, the variable $?x$ appears n times and some of them are replaced with new ones. The time cost increases as the number of unique variables increases in all methods. We also observe that the number of matchings increases with the increasing number of unique variables since more variables lead to less joins between triple patterns and therefore more matchings.

In our experiment, we find Rdf-3x can lead to machine crash when it evaluates some query patterns of more than 9 triple patterns. When the machine crashes, we delete the query pattern it is evaluating and continue with the remaining queries. The effect of the failure is not recorded.

Summary. Except for the length of query patterns, the number of matchings, as well as the intermediate partial matchings, makes

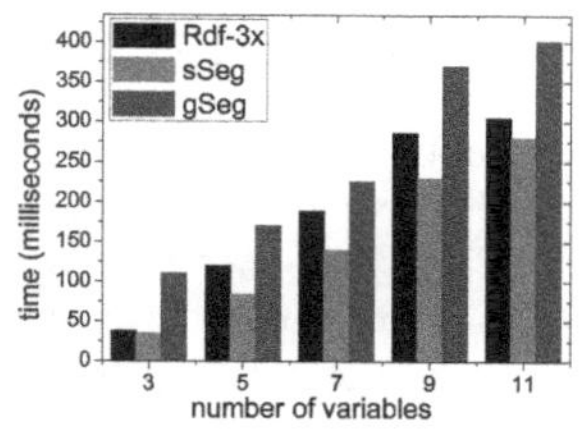

Figure 9: Number of variables vs. time

a significant impact on query efficiency. View-based approaches, especially sSeg, exhibit a good scalability in terms of the size of database, as well as pattern length.

Pattern Rewriting. In this part, we focus on the evaluation of pattern rewriting involved in sSeg and gSeg with respect to the average length of patterns/views and the size of view base. We report the results on CPU time. We also report the relation between Γ_g and Γ_s to verify the reasonableness of sortable views.

In Table 4, we report the impact of average length $\mathcal{L}$ of patterns in view base Γ_g . A set of 100 patterns with 10 triple patters each was generated as query patterns Q. When $\mathcal{L}$ on Γ_g was varied from 3 to 9, the difference between $\mathcal{L}$ on Γ_g and Γ_s was ignorable. This means the restriction of sortable views was applicable. It is more interesting that view base with short patterns can improve the coverage as shown in C_{Γ_s} column. As expected, the time cost for gSeg is much higher than sSeg because the length of $Q - \Gamma(Q)$ is increased as keeping $C_{\Gamma_g} = 30\%$. sSeg shows stable time cost with minor increase. The fluctuation is due to the structure updates of view base when the average length $\mathcal{L}$ of view base is enlarged. Despite of the fluctuation, our serialization method is a clear winner.

$\mathcal{L}$ on Γ_g	$\mathcal{L}$ on Γ_s	C_{Γ_s}	sSeg	gSeg
3	3	30%	1.1	110.6
5	4	33%	2.1	121
7	6	37%	3.4	204
9	7.5	41%	3.6	417

Table 4: Average length L of patterns in Γ_g vs. Time of pattern segmentation (milliseconds, $C_{\Gamma_g} = 30\%$)

In Table 5, we report the impact of the average length of query patterns on a given view base with default $\mathcal{L}$. The coverage fluctuates around the default coverage 30% in both methods. The minor advantage of sSeg stems from the short average length of patterns in view base Γ_s. However, with respect to time efficiency, sSeg is a clear winner again with enlarged advantages in the case of long query patterns.

L	C_{Γ_g}	C_{Γ_s}	sSeg	gSeg
9	30%	32%	1.1	110.6
11	33%	34%	2.1	121
13	31%	31%	3.4	204
15	32%	37%	3.6	417

Table 5: Average length L of query patterns vs. Time cost of pattern segmentation (milliseconds, $C_{\Gamma_g} = 30\%$) for patterns with average length 9

In Table 6, we list the average time of pattern rewriting of both sSeg and gSeg, on view bases with different cardinalities. The results in the table shows that our sSeg method is faster than gSeg by almost two orders of magnitude. The efficiency comparisons verify our statement on the superiority of our serialization-based pattern rewriting in terms of efficiency. With the expansion of view base, the pattern rewriting time of both sSeg and gSeg increase. The exponential increase of time cost in gSeg is observable while the minor increase in sSeg. This phenomenon verifies the exponential time cost of sub graph isomorphism decision underlying gSeg. The efficiency advantage of sSeg stems from the restriction of sortable views.

$R_g = \|\Gamma_g\|$	sSeg	gSeg
1,000	1.1	172.6
2,000	2.7	335.1
3,000	3.4	456.2
4,000	3.6	603.5
5,000	4.3	800.0

Table 6: Impact of $|\Gamma_g|$ on time cost (milliseconds)

Effectiveness of Enhancement. To test the effectiveness of some enhancements in algorithm contain$^+(V, Q)$, we implemented a comparison version contain$^-(V, Q)$, where we naively enumerated all sub set Q' of Q such that $|Q'| = |V|$. Then, for each Q', we invoked contain(V, Q') for further verification.

We fixed the length of pattern V with 4 and slide the length of Q from 4, 6, 8 to 10. The time cost ratio of contain$^-(V, Q)$ to contain$^+(V, Q)$ is listed in Figure 10. The ratio exhibits an exponential increase with increasing length of pattern, verifying the effectiveness of our enhancements embedded in contain$^+(V, Q)$. In particular, the advantage of contain$^+(V, Q)$ comes from the serialization-enabled reduce of search space.

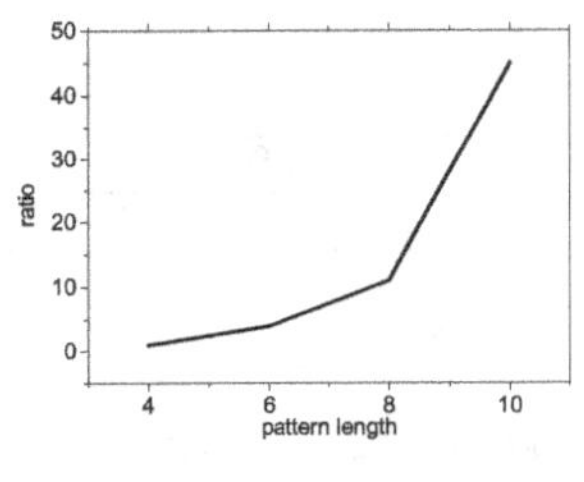

Figure 10: Time Cost Ratio of contain$^-$ to contain$^+$

7. CONCLUSION AND FUTURE WORK

In this work, we put the ends of answering queries using views together, exploiting sortable view selection at one end on behalf of pattern rewriting at the other end. A compact index for pattern rewriting and optimization for pruning redundant views are further considered. The integration of our pattern rewriting and existing optimizers will be detailed in our future work.

8. ACKNOWLEDGMENTS

Chong, Chen, Shu and Qi are supported by the National Natural Science Foundation of China under grant No. 60973023. Zhang is partly supported by Singapore A*STAR's Human Sixth Sense Project (HSSP) in Advanced Digital Sciences Center (ADSC).

9. REFERENCES

[1] D. J. Abadi, A. Marcus, S. R. Madden, and K. Hollenbach. Sw-store: a vertically partitioned dbms for semantic web data management. *The VLDB Journal*, 18(2), 2009.

[2] S. Abiteboul and O. M. Duschka. Complexity of answering queries using materialized views. In *Proc. of PODS '98.*

[3] M. Arenas, C. Gutierrez, and J. Pérez. Foundations of rdf databases. 2009.

[4] R. Castillo and U. Leser. Selecting materialized views for rdf data. In *Proc. of ICWE'10*, 2010.

[5] A. K. Chandra and P. M. Merlin. Optimal implementation of conjunctive queries in relational data bases. In *Proc. of STOC '77.*

[6] S. Chaudhuri, R. Krishnamurthy, S. Potamianos, and K. Shim. Optimizing queries with materialized views. In *Proc. of ICDE '95.*

[7] C. Chen, X. Yan, P. S. Yu, J. Han, D.-Q. Zhang, and X. Gu. Towards graph containment search and indexing. In *Proc. of VLDB '07.*

[8] D. Chen and C.-Y. Chan. Minimization of tree pattern queries with constraints. In *Proc. of SIGMOD'08.*

[9] E. I. Chong, S. Das, G. Eadon, and J. Srinivasan. An efficient sql-based rdf querying scheme. In *Proc. of VLDB '05.*

[10] S. Cohen, W. Nutt, and Y. Sagiv. Rewriting queries with arbitrary aggregation functions using views. *ACM Trans. Database Syst.*, 31(2), 2006.

[11] F. T. L. De Virgilio, Roberto; Giunchiglia. *Semantic Web Information Management.* Springer Heildelberg Dordrecht London New York, 2010.

[12] V. Dritsou, P. Constantopoulos, A. Deligiannakis, and Y. Kotidis. Optimizing query shortcuts in rdf databases. In *Proc. of ESWC'11*, 2011.

[13] O. M. Duschka and M. R. Genesereth. Answering recursive queries using views. In *Proc. of PODS '97.*

[14] G. H. Fletcher and P. W. Beck. Scalable indexing of rdf graphs for efficient join processing. In *Proc. of CIKM '09.*

[15] F. Goasdoué, K. Karanasos, J. Leblay, and I. Manolescu. View selection in semantic web databases. *PVLDB*, 5(2), 2011.

[16] P. Godfrey, J. Gryz, A. Hoppe, W. Ma, and C. Zuzarte. Query rewrites with views for xml in db2. In *Proc. of ICDE '09.*

[17] A. Y. Halevy. Answering queries using views: A survey. *The VLDB Journal*, 10(4), 2001.

[18] E. t. Jon Kleinberg. *Algorithm design.* Person Education, Inc., 2006.

[19] C. Li. Computing complete answers to queries in the presence of limited access patterns. *The VLDB Journal*, 12(3), 2003.

[20] T. Neumann and G. Weikum. The rdf-3x engine for scalable management of rdf data. *The VLDB Journal*, 19(1), 2010.

[21] H. Shang, Y. Zhang, X. Lin, and J. X. Yu. Taming verification hardness: an efficient algorithm for testing subgraph isomorphism. *Proc. VLDB Endow.*, 1(1), 2008.

[22] M. Stocker, A. Seaborne, A. Bernstein, C. Kiefer, and D. Reynolds. Sparql basic graph pattern optimization using selectivity estimation. In *Proc. of WWW '08.*

[23] J. R. Ullmann. An algorithm for subgraph isomorphism. *J. ACM*, 23(1), 1976.

[24] J. X. Yu, Z. Chong, H. Lu, and A. Zhou. False positive or false negative: Mining frequent itemsets from high speed transactional data streams. In *VLDB'04*, 2004.

[25] J. X. Yu, X. Yao, C.-H. Choi, and G. Gou. Materialized view selection as constrained evolutionary optimization. *Systems, Man, and Cybernetics, Part C: Applications and Reviews, IEEE Transactions on*, 2003.

Efficient Algorithms for Generalized Subgraph Query Processing

Wenqing Lin, Xiaokui Xiao, James Cheng, Sourav S. Bhowmick
School of Computer Engineering, Nanyang Technological University, Singapore
{wlin1, xkxiao, assourav}@ntu.edu.sg, j.cheng@acm.org

ABSTRACT

We study a new type of graph queries, which injectively maps its edges to paths of the graphs in a given database, where the length of each path is constrained by a given threshold specified by the weight of the corresponding matching edge. We give important applications of the new graph query and identify new challenges of processing such a query. Then, we devise the cost model of the branch-and-bound algorithm framework for processing the graph query, and propose an efficient algorithm to minimize the cost overhead. We also develop three indexing techniques to efficiently answer the queries online. Finally, we verify the efficiency of our proposed indexes with extensive experiments on large real and synthetic datasets.

Categories and Subject Descriptors

H.2.4 [**Database Management**]: System—*Query processing*

Keywords

Graph Databases, Graph Matching Algorithm, Graph Indexing, Graph Querying

1. INTRODUCTION

Graph is a powerful data model that can naturally represent various entities and their relationships. Graph data is ubiquitous today and being able to query such graph data is beneficial to many applications. For example, in bio-informatics and chemical informatics, graphs can model compounds and proteins, and graph queries can be used for screening, drug design, motif discovery in protein structures, and protein interaction analysis. In computer vision, graphs represent organization of entities in images and graph queries can be used to identify objects and scenes. In heterogeneous web-based data sources and e-commerce sites, graphs model schemas and graph matching can be applied to solve problems of schema matching and integration. There are also many other applications, such as program flows, software and data engineering, taxonomies, etc., where data is modeled as graphs and it is essential to search and query the graph data.

Existing research focuses on mainly two types of graph datasets, one consisting of a single large graph (e.g., an online social network or the entire citation graph in a certain domain) and the other consisting of a large set of small or medium-sized graphs. We focus on the later, which are also very popular in real life (e.g., most of the examples we listed earlier belong to this type).

To query a graph database, $\mathcal{G}$, that consists of many small graphs, there are three types of queries commonly studied in the literature. Let q be a query graph. The first one is *subgraph query* [4, 9, 13, 15, 18, 21, 23], which finds the subset of graphs $\mathcal{A}$ of $\mathcal{G}$ such that q is a *subgraph* of any graph in $\mathcal{A}$. The second one is *supergraph query* [2, 3, 14, 22], which finds the subset of graphs $\mathcal{A}$ of $\mathcal{G}$ such that q is a *supergraph* of any graph in $\mathcal{A}$. The third one is *similarity query* [12, 19, 20, 24], which finds the subset of graphs $\mathcal{A}$ of $\mathcal{G}$ such that q is a *similar graph* of any graph in $\mathcal{A}$ according to a given similarity measure.

The three types of queries are useful in different applications. However, both subgraph queries and supergraph queries are too rigid and therefore similarity queries are proposed as an alternative. Existing similarity queries are mostly measured by the edit distance [20, 24] or maximum common subgraph [12, 19], which is reasonable for some applications but often fails to capture meaningful patterns or targets in applications where critical objects or entities may have to be matched or they may be within a distance from each other that is beyond the specified similarity distance (i.e., the similarity threshold). We show such an application, where both exact queries and similarity queries are not applicable, by the following example.

EXAMPLE 1. *Consider a drug design system, which supports the inventive process of finding new medications based on the knowledge of the biological target. Figure 1 shows some compounds in the database, i.e., g_1, g_2, and g_3. A compound can be naturally modeled as a graph, where atoms are vertices, the chemical name of the atom is the label of the correspond vertex, and the chemical bonds between any two atoms are modeled as edges in the graph. Among many drug design methods, the pharmacophore model is the most popular one whose goal is to find the substructures that are closely matched to the objective. ALADDIN [17] is a computer program for the design and recognition of compounds that meet geometric, steric, and sub-structural criteria. AL-*

CIKM'12, October 29–November 2, 2012, Maui, HI, USA.
Copyright 2012 ACM 978-1-4503-1156-4/12/10 ...$15.00.

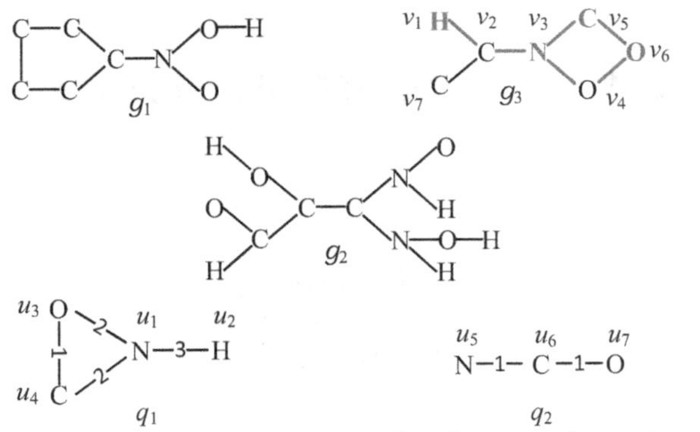

Figure 1: A drug database, $\mathcal{G} = \{g_1, g_2, g_3\}$, and two query graphs, q_1 and q_2

Table 1: A graph query in ALADDIN language

POINT `N` ; POINT `H` ; POINT `O` ; POINT `C` ;
DISTANCE (1, 2) 1 3 ; DISTANCE (1, 3) 1 2 ;
DISTANCE (1, 4) 1 2 ; DISTANCE (3, 4) 1 1 ;

ADDIN also uses a precise geometric description language to define the properties of a designed molecule.

The query shown in Table 1 is written in the ALADDIN language, which is to find a graph pattern where

1. *there are four atoms:* `N`, `H`, `O`, *and* `C`, *whose positions are at* 1, 2, 3, *and* 4, *respectively;*
2. *the distance between* `N` *and* `H` *is 1 to 3, and similarly 1 to 2 between* `N` *and* `O`, *1 to 2 between* `N` *and* `C`, *and exactly 1 between* `O` *and* `C`.

Since the distance between all pairs of atoms can be estimated [11], the distance can be further modeled as the number of bonds that connect the atoms. Thus, the query in Table 1 can be converted to a graph query which finds all graphs in the database such that

1. *there exist four vertices u_1 to u_4 in the graph whose labels are* `N`, `H`, `O`, *and* `C`, *respectively;*
2. *let $P = \langle u_i, \ldots, u_j \rangle$ be a path that connects u_i and u_j and $|P|$ be the length of the path:*

   there exist paths $P_1 = \langle u_1, \ldots, u_2 \rangle$, $P_2 = \langle u_1, \ldots, u_3 \rangle$, $P_3 = \langle u_1, \ldots, u_4 \rangle$, and $P_4 = \langle u_3, \ldots, u_4 \rangle$, respectively, where $1 \leq |P_1| \leq 3$, $1 \leq |P_2| \leq 2$, $1 \leq |P_3| \leq 2$, and $|P_4| = 1$.

Such a query can be naturally represented as the query graph[1] q_1 shown in Figure 1, and the answer to this query is $\{g_3\}$. In such a query, subgraph query cannot be applied, while similarity query is also not suitable when the matching paths are long.

In this paper, we study this new type of graph queries as described in Example 1, which will be formally defined in Section 2. But intuitively, the new query is a generalization of the subgraph query, which generalizes exact edge matching to path matching constrained by a path length; that is, instead of matching each edge as in a subgraph query, we find a path with two matching end vertices for each edge in the query graph, where the length of the matching path must be within the specified edge weight. Thus, the new query has a much stronger expressive power than a subgraph query.

[1]We assume that path length cannot be negative.

Such a query is also useful in many other applications. For example, in querying user online traversal graphs, one may be only interested in whether users have visited certain important sites within a certain number of clicks, while an exact or a quality similar matching may not exist. In searching pictures in an image database, it is often rare to find an exact or even similar matching due to the huge amount of irrelevant information in the background (note that similarity measure by edit distance or maximum common subgraph often counts all such irrelevant information in the matching); in this case, we can specify a few features to be focused in the matching while relaxing the links between the features by some reasonable edge weight.

Processing the new query, however, is significantly more challenging. For both subgraph and supergraph query processing, it involves subgraph isomorphism which is NP-hard. The relaxation in the new query from exact edge matching to approximate path matching essentially further explodes the already exponential search space. Existing pruning techniques cannot be directly applied or they are simply not adequate, since our generalized query graph is different from the indexed features. Therefore, this paper proposes new effective pruning techniques and efficient data structures to solve this challenging problem.

Our contributions. The contributions of this paper are four-fold. First, we propose the problem of generalized subgraph query processing, which is useful in applications where subgraph queries are too restrictive to apply while similarity queries may return low quality answers due to large edit distance arisen from abundant irrelevant information. Second, we devise a fast algorithm for generalized subgraph matching, which is a significantly more complicated matching problem than subgraph isomorphism. Third, we develop three indexes for the efficient processing of generalized subgraph queries, namely, a *distance-based* index, a *frequent-pattern-based* index, and a *star-structure-based* index. We discuss in details the strengths and limitations of the indexes. Fourth, we verify the efficiency of our matching algorithm (for candidate verification) and our indexes (for filtering) using both real and synthetic datasets.

Paper Organization. Section 2 gives the notations and formally defines the problem. Section 3 presents the generalized subgraph matching algorithm. Section 4 discusses in details the three indexes. Section 5 reports the experimental results. Section 6 discusses the related work and Section 7 concludes the paper.

2. PROBLEM STATEMENT

Let $\mathcal{G}$ be a database that contains a set of simple and labeled graphs. We denote each graph $g \in \mathcal{G}$ as a triplet $g = (V_g, E_g, l_g)$, where V_g and E_g are the sets of vertices and edges in g, respectively, and l_g is a labelling function that maps each vertex in g to a label in a finite alphabet. For ease of exposition, we assume that all edges in g are undirected; our results can be easily extended for directed graphs.

For any vertices u and v in a graph $g \in \mathcal{G}$, we define the *distance* between u and v, denoted as $dist_g(u, v)$, as the number edges in the shortest path between u and v. For instance, in the graph g_3 in Figure 1, we have $dist_{g_3}(v_1, v_3) = 2$, since the shortest path between v_1 and v_3 contains two edges (v_1, v_2) and (v_2, v_3).

We aim to support *generalized subgraph queries* on $\mathcal{G}$. In particular, a *generalized subgraph* q is a simple, undirected, and labelled graph where each edge carries a positive integer weight. We denote q as a quadruple (V_q, E_q, l_q, t), where V and E are the sets of vertices and edges in q, respectively, l_q is the labelling function for q, and t is a function that maps each edge in q to its weight. We say that a graph $g \in \mathcal{G}$ *matches* q, if there exists an injective function f from V_q to V_g, such that for any edge (u, v) in q, (i) the labels of u and $f(u)$ are the same, (ii) the labels of v and $f(v)$ are the same, and (iii) the distance between $f(u)$ and $f(v)$ in g is no more than the weight of (u, v).

For example, in Figure 1, the graph g_3 matches the generalized subgraph q_1. To explain this, let us consider an injective function f that maps u_1 to v_3, u_2 to v_1, u_3 to v_6, and u_4 to v_5. For the edge (u_1, u_2) in q_1, we have $f(u_1) = v_3$ and $f(u_2) = v_1$, and the distance $dist_{g_3}$ between v_3 and v_1 in g_3 equals 2, which is no more than the weight associated with (u_1, u_2). The cases for the other edges in q_1 can be verified in a similar manner.

Given a generalized subgraph q, a generalized subgraph query on $\mathcal{G}$ returns the graphs in $\mathcal{G}$ that match q. For convenience, we refer to q as the *query graph*, and the graphs in $\mathcal{G}$ as the *data graphs*. In addition, we say that a data graph g *contains* q (denoted by $q \subseteq g$), if g matches q.

3. GENERALIZED SUBGRAPH MATCHING ALGORITHM

To enable generalized subgraph queries on $\mathcal{G}$, we need to first address a crucial problem: *How do we decide whether a data graph $g \in \mathcal{G}$ matches the query graph q?* We refer to this problem as the *generalized subgraph matching* problem. It is not hard to see that this problem is NP-hard; in particular, when the weights of all edges in q equal 1, testing whether a data graph g matches q is equivalent to the *subgraph isomorphism* problem, which has been shown to be NP-complete [5].

Given that generalized subgraph matching is theoretically intractable, we resort to heuristics and propose a solution that provides practical efficiency. The core of our solution is a cost-based matching approach that significantly extends and improves the existing heuristic algorithms [13, 16] for the subgraph isomorphism problem. In what follows, we will first introduce the existing methods for subgraph isomorphism (in Section 3.1), and then present the details of our solution (in Section 3.2).

3.1 Existing Algorithms for Subgraph Isomorphism

The classic solution for the subgraph isomorphism is Ullmann's algorithm [16], which matches the vertices in the query graph q to the vertices in the data graph g in an iterative manner. Specifically, in each iteration, the algorithm selects an unmatched vertex u in q, maps it to an unmatched vertex in g with the same label, and then checks whether the mapping is *feasible*, i.e., whether any two matched vertices in q that induce an edge in q are mapped to two vertices in g that induce an edge in g. If the mapping is feasible, the algorithm will enter the next iteration to match the remaining vertices in q. Otherwise, the algorithm will try matching u to another unmatched vertex in g. If there is no vertex that u can be matched to, the algorithm backtracks to the last matched vertex u' in q, re-maps u' to an unmatched vertex in g, and then re-starts the current iteration.

For example, in Figure 1, given the query graph q_2 and the data graph g_3, Ullmann's algorithm may first map u_5 to v_3, and then map u_6 to v_5. In that case, u_5 and u_6 induce an edge in q_2, while v_3 and v_5 also induce an edge in g_3, i.e., the matching is feasible. Assume that, in the next iteration, the algorithm maps u_7 to v_4. Then, u_6 and u_7 induce an edge in q_2, but the vertices that they are mapped to (i.e., v_5 and v_4) do not induce any edge in g_3. As a consequence, the mapping is infeasible, and hence, the algorithm would proceed to re-map u_7 to another unmatched vertex in g_3.

Intuitively, the efficiency of Ullmann's algorithm depends on the order in which the vertices in q are matched. For instance, assume that q contains only two vertices u_1 and u_2, such that u_1 has the same label with only one vertex v_1 in the data graph g, whereas u_2 has the same label with almost all vertices in g. If we invoke Ullmann's algorithm and map u_1 to v_1 in the first iteration, then in the remaining iterations, we only need to examine whether u_2 can be mapped to a vertex adjacent to v_1. In contrast, if the first iteration maps u_2 (instead of u_1) to some vertex v in g, then in the remaining iterations, we not only need to try mapping u_1 to the neighbors of v, but also need to consider other possible mappings that match u_2 to other vertices in g, i.e., the search space of the algorithm becomes significantly larger.

Despite the importance of vertex mapping order, it is not taken into account in Ullmann's algorithm. This motivates a more advanced method called *QuickSI* [13], which improves over Ullmann's algorithm by heuristically choosing a mapping order that is likely to reduce computation cost. Specifically, QuickSI decides the vertex mapping order based on two sets of statistics pre-computed from the graph database $\mathcal{G}$. First, for any vertex u that can possibly appear in a query graph, QuickSI pre-computes its *frequency* in $\mathcal{G}$, i.e., the average number of vertices in each data graph (in $\mathcal{G}$) that have the same label with u. Second, for any edge e that may appear in a query graph, QuickSI also pre-computes its frequency in $\mathcal{G}$, i.e., the average number of edges in each data graph that have endpoints with labels matching those of the endpoints of e. With these statistics, for any given query graph q, QuickSI first generates a spanning tree of q, such that vertices and edges closer to the root of tree tend to have lower frequencies in $\mathcal{G}$. After that, QuickSI generates an ordering of the vertices in q following a traversal of the spanning tree that recursively visits the branch with the least frequent edge. The resulting vertex order is then used whenever QuickSI compares a data graph g with q. Intuitively, this vertex order improves efficiency, as it tends to ensure that the search space of the matching algorithm would be reduced significantly after each iteration.

3.2 A Cost-based Approach for Generalized Subgraph Isomorphism

Both Ullmann's algorithm and QuickSI can be extended for generalized subgraph isomorphism, with a modified feasibility check in each iteration. Specifically, each time after we map a vertex u in the query graph q to a vertex v in the data graph g, we would decide whether the mapping is feasible by examining every edge e in q that is induced by u and any vertex u' in q that has been matched. Let v' be the vertex in g that u' is mapped to. If for each e, the distance $dist_g(v, v')$ between v and v' is no more than the weight $w(e)$ of e, then the mapping is feasible, and we would proceed to the next iteration. Otherwise, we would re-map u to other unmatched vertex in g; if there does not exist any feasible mapping for u, we would backtrack to the last matched vertex in q and re-map it (as with the case of subgraph isomorphism).

The aforementioned extensions of Ullmann's algorithm and QuickSI, however, leave much room for improvements. In particular, Ullmann's algorithm does not exploit the order of vertex mapping for efficiency; QuickSI heuristically tunes the vertex mapping order, but its tuning method is rather ah hoc and is without a formal model that justifies mapping a vertex ahead of any other. To remedy this, we propose a novel algorithm for generalized subgraph isomorphism that incorporates a cost model for selecting a preferable order of vertex mapping. In the following, we will first present the rationale behind our method, and then provide the details about our cost model and algorithm.

Assume that the query graph q and the data graph g contain m and n vertices, respectively. Totally, there exist $P(n,m) = n!/(n-m)!$ different ways to map the vertices in q to distinct vertices in g, and these $P(n,m)$ possible matchings constitute the search space for the generalized subgraph isomorphism algorithm. ($P(m,n)$ denotes the number of m-permutations of n.) To efficiently decide whether g matches q, it is essential that the algorithm should traverse the search space in a judicious order that enables it to pinpoint a solution (if any) as quickly as possible. This motivates us to match vertices in q in an order based on how likely they can reduce the search space that we need to explore. Note that we use the same node mapping order for all data graphs (as in QuickSI), so as to avoid the overhead of re-computing the node order for each data graph.

Specifically, to pick the first vertex in q to be matched, we would inspect each edge e in q, and examine the *frequency of* e (denoted as $c(e)$) in the data graphs in $\mathcal{G}$. The frequency of (u', u^*) in q is defined as the average number of vertex pairs (v', v^*) in each data graph in $\mathcal{G}$, such that (i) the labels of u' and v' are the same, (ii) the labels of u^* and v^* are the same, and (iii) the distance between v' and v^* is no more than the weight of (u', u^*). (To facilitate this step of the algorithm, we pre-compute the frequency of any edge that may appear in the query graph.)

For each e, we intuitively estimate that it can be matched to $c(e)$ vertex pairs in the data graph. Given this estimation, if a vertex u is an endpoint of e and we choose to match u first, then the search space size induced by mapping u can be estimated as $c(e) \cdot P(\bar{n}-1, m-1)$, where $\bar{n}$ denotes the average number of vertices in the data graphs. The rationale here is that u is expected to be mapped to around $c(e)$ vertices in a data graph, and the other unmatched $m-1$ vertices in q are expected to be matched to around $\bar{n}-1$ vertices in g in $P(\bar{n}-1, m-1)$ different ways; therefore, the number of possible matchings that remain to explored can be estimated as $c(e) \cdot P(\bar{n}-1, m-1)$. Accordingly, we pick a vertex u incident to the edge e with the smallest $c(e)$, and set u as the first vertex to be matched. The term $P(\bar{n}-1, m-1)$ is ignored since its value is the same for all vertices in q. (This helps us avoid the pathological case when $\bar{n} < m$, in which case $P(\bar{n}-1, m-1)$ is undefined.) Given that the edge e with the smallest $c(e)$ has two endpoints, we choose the endpoint u with the smaller frequency $c(u)$.

The order of the remaining vertices is decided in a similar manner. Assume that we have picked a set S of k vertices and we are about to choose the next vertex to be matched. Let u' be any vertex that has not be selected. If u' is not connected to any vertex in S by an edge in q, then we estimate the search space size induced by mapping u' as

$$\min_{\text{any edge } e \text{ adjacent to } u'} c(e) \cdot N(S) \cdot P(\bar{n}-k-1, m-k-1), \quad (1)$$

where $N(S)$ denotes the number of ways to match the first k vertices, and $P(\bar{n}-k-1, m-k-1)$ is the number of ways to match the remaining $m-k-1$ vertices except u'. As will be shown shortly, we do not need to compute the values of $N(S)$ and $P(\bar{n}-k-1, m-k-1)$.

On the other hand, if u' has some edges that are incident to the vertices in S, then our estimation of the search space size would take those edges into account. Let E be the set of edges in q that connect u' to the vertices in S. For each e in E that connects u' to a vertex u^*, we examine the frequency of u^* (denoted as $c(u^*)$) in $\mathcal{G}$, as well as the frequency of e (denoted as $c(e)$). Given $c(u^*)$ and $c(e)$, we intuitively estimate that the vertex u^* is connected to around $c(e)/c(u^*)$ vertices that have the same label with u'. Therefore, the search space size induced by mapping u' is estimated as

$$c(e)/c(u^*) \cdot N(S) \cdot P(\bar{n}-k-1, m-k-1), \quad (2)$$

where $\sum_{u \in S} c(u)$ and $P(\bar{n}-k-1, m-k-1)$ are as explained in Equation 1. We refer to $c(e)/c(u^*)$ as the *matching rate of* u' *implied by* e, and we denote it as $r(u', e)$.

Observe that each edge $e \in E$ may imply a different matching rate of u', leading to different estimations of the search space size. We combine all estimations by taking the smallest one, i.e., the size of the search space is estimated as

$$\min_{e \in E} r(u', e) \cdot N(S) \cdot P(\bar{n}-k-1, m-k-1). \quad (3)$$

For convenience, we let $r(u') = \min_{e \in E} r(u', e)$ if u' is connected to the vertices in S by at least one edge in the data graph, otherwise we let $r(u')$ be the minimum frequency of an edge in q that is adjacent to u'. Given Equations 1 and 4, we choose the next vertex u' to be matched as the one that minimizes the estimated search space size, i.e.,

$$u' = \arg\min_{u} \{r(u)\}. \quad (4)$$

Note that Equation 4 does not involve the terms $N(S)$ and $P(\bar{n}-k-1, m-k-1)$ (which appear in both Equations 1 and 4). This is because their values are the same for all possible u', and hence, they have no effect on the selection of u'.

In summary, our algorithm optimizes the vertex matching order by a qualitative prediction of how each vertex may help reduce the search space size. As will be shown in Section 5, our experimental results demonstrate the superiority of our algorithm over both Ullmann's algorithm and QuickSI on both standard and generalized subgraph isomorphism tests.

4. INDEXING TECHNIQUES

Although in Section 3 we proposed a reasonably fast algorithm for generalized subgraph matching, it is still impractical to answer a query by sequentially scanning the input database and matching the query graph with each data graph, especially if the database is large. We apply the *filtering*-and-*verification* strategy to reduce the matching cost, that is, we first filter out as many unmatching data graphs as possible and then verify the remaining candidate data graphs by matching them with the query graph one by one. To do this, it is important to design an effective indexing technique to filter out the unmatching data graphs.

In this section, we propose three indexing techniques: **D-Index**, **FP-Index** and **S-Index**. First, in Section 4.1 we present D-Index, which can be easily constructed but its pruning power is relatively weak. Then, we propose FP-Index in Section 4.2, which has an expensive construction cost but is partially verification-free. Lastly, in Section 4.3 we propose S-Index, which explores the star structures to achieve effective pruning as well as a low construction cost.

4.1 Distance Index

We first present D-index, which is constructed based on the distance among pairs of vertices in each data graph. Given a data graph $g = (V_g, E_g, l_g) \in \mathcal{G}$, we obtain the *distance set* ($\mathcal{DS}$) of all triplets of every two vertices consisting of their ordered labels and the correspond distance in g as follows.

$$\mathcal{DS}(g) = \{(l_g(u), l_g(v), dist_g(u,v)) : u, v \in V_g, l_g(u) \leq l_g(v)\}$$

A distance triplet $(l_1, l_2, d) \in \mathcal{DS}(g)$ is subsumed by another distance triplet $(l_1, l_2, d') \in \mathcal{DS}(g)$ if $d > d'$. We say that a subset $\mathcal{DS}_{min}(g) \subseteq \mathcal{DS}(g)$ is minimal if each distance triplet in $\mathcal{DS}_{min}(g)$ is not subsumed by any other distance triplet, that is, for each $(l_1, l_2, d) \in \mathcal{DS}_{min}(g)$, there does not exist $(l_1, l_2, d') \in \mathcal{DS}_{min}(g)$ such that $d' < d$.

EXAMPLE 2. *Assume that vertex labels are ordered lexicographically, i.e.,* O<N<H<C. *Consider the data graph g_3 in Figure 1, the distance set of g_3 is $DS(g_3)$ = {(C,C,1), (C,C,2), (C,C,3), (H,C,1), (H,C,2), (H,C,3), (N,C,1), (N,C,2), (O,C,1), (O,C,2), (O,C,3), (O,C,4), (N,H,2), (O,H,3), (O,H,4), (O,N,1), (O,N,2), (O,O,1)}, and $\mathcal{DS}_{min}(g_3)$ = {(C,C,1), (H,C,1), (N,C,1), (O,C,1), (N,H,2), (O,H,3), (O,N,1), (O,O,1)}. Note that $|\mathcal{DS}(g_3)| = 18$ while $|DS_{min}(g_3)| = 8$.*

The minimal set of distinct distance triplets in the database is then given by

$$\mathcal{DS} = \cup_{g \in \mathcal{G}} \mathcal{DS}_{min}(g).$$

For each distance triplet $(l_1, l_2, d) \in \mathcal{DS}$, the set of data graphs that contain (l_1, l_2, d) is given by

$$\mathcal{A}(l_1, l_2, d) = \{g : (l_1, l_2, d) \in \mathcal{DS}_{min}(g)\}.$$

The *Distance Index (D-index)* is constructed on $\mathcal{DS}$ and $\mathcal{A}(l_1, l_2, d)$ for each $(l_1, l_2, d) \in \mathcal{DS}$, which is to be detailed as follows.

4.1.1 Index Construction

The structure of D-index consists of the following parts:

- A B+-tree index, called the *Label Pair Index (LPI)*, stores all pairs of labels of the triplets in $\mathcal{DS}$.
- A sorted list of distance values for each label pair $(l_1, l_2) \in LPI$, denoted by $LPI(l_1, l_2).DV$, that is, $LPI(l_1, l_2).DV = \{d : (l_1, l_2, d) \in \mathcal{DS}\}$.
- Each distance value $d \in LPI(l_1, l_2).DV$ for any $(l_1, l_2) \in LPI$ is associated with a set of data graphs $\mathcal{A}(l_1, l_2, d)$, we further denote it as $LPI(l_1, l_2).DV(d) = \mathcal{A}(l_1, l_2, d)$.

Algorithm 1: BUILD-DINDEX($\mathcal{G}$)

input : the graph database, $\mathcal{G}$
output: the D-index, LPI

1 **for** $g \in \mathcal{G}$ **do**
2   Compute $\mathcal{DS}_{min}(g)$;
3   **for** $(l_1, l_2, d) \in \mathcal{DS}_{min}(g)$ **do**
4         $LPI \leftarrow (l_1, l_2)$;
5         $LPI(l_1, l_2).DV \leftarrow d$;
6         $LPI(l_1, l_2).DV(d) \leftarrow g$;
7 **return** LPI

Algorithm 2: QUERY-DINDEX($q, LPI, \mathcal{G}$)

input : the query graph, $q = (V_q, E_q, l_q, t)$
D-Index, LPI
the graph database, $\mathcal{G}$
output: the candidate set of q, $\mathcal{C}(q)$

1 $\mathcal{C}(q) \leftarrow \mathcal{G}$;
2 **for** $(l_1, l_2, d) \in \mathcal{DS}_{min}(q)$ **do**
3     $\mathcal{C}(l_1, l_2, d) \leftarrow \emptyset$;
4   **for** $k \in LPI(l_1, l_2).DV$ *and* $k \leq d$ **do**
5         $\mathcal{C}(l_1, l_2, d) \leftarrow \mathcal{C}(l_1, l_2, d) \cup LPI(l_1, l_2).DV(k)$;
6     $\mathcal{C}(q) \leftarrow \mathcal{C}(q) \cap \mathcal{C}(l_1, l_2, d)$;
7 **return** $\mathcal{C}(q)$

The algorithm for D-index construction, BUILD-DINDEX, is shown in Algorithm 1. For each data graph $g \in \mathcal{G}$, we first compute its minimal distance set $\mathcal{DS}_{min}(g)$ (Line 2). Then, for each distance triplet $(l_1, l_2, d) \in \mathcal{DS}_{min}(g)$, we assign (l_1, l_2) to LPI and put the distance value d to the sorted list $LPI(l_1, l_2).DV$ (Line 4-5). Finally, g is included in $LPI(l_1, l_2).DV(d)$ (Line 6).

4.1.2 Query Processing

Given a query graph $q = (V_q, E_q, l_q, t)$, we first obtain its minimal distance set $\mathcal{DS}_{min}(q)$ by all pairs shortest path algorithm. For each distance triplet $(l_1, l_2, d) \in \mathcal{DS}_{min}(q)$, the correspond candidate set $\mathcal{C}(l_1, l_2, d)$ can be obtained by merging all the graph sets associated with $LPI(l_1, l_2).DV(k)$ for $1 \leq k \leq d$. The final candidate set $\mathcal{C}(q)$ for verification is the intersection of all the candidate sets of each distance triplet $(l_1, l_2, d) \in \mathcal{DS}_{min}(q)$, that is

$$\mathcal{C}(q) = \cap_{(l_1, l_2, d) \in \mathcal{DS}_{min}(q)} \mathcal{C}(l_1, l_2, d).$$

As shown in Algorithm 2, processing the query graph q by D-index obtains the candidate set for each distance triplet $(l_1, l_2, d) \in \mathcal{DS}_{min}(q)$ (Lines 3-5), and then intersects them to output the candidate set of q (Line 6).

LEMMA 1. *Given a query graph $q = (V_q, E_q, l_q, t)$, its answer set $\mathcal{A}(q)$ is a subset of* BUILD-DINDEX($q, LPI, \mathcal{G}$).

PROOF. Consider a data graph $g = (V_g, E_g, l_g) \in \mathcal{G}$ that matches q. For each edge $(v, u) \in E_q$, we can map it to a path $P = \langle f(v), \ldots, f(u) \rangle$ such that $|P| \leq t(v, u)$. Without the loss of generality, we assume that $l_g(f(v)) \leq l_g(f(u))$. Consider the distance triplet $(l_g(f(v)), l_g(f(u)), d) \in \mathcal{DS}_{min}(g)$, we have $d \leq |P|$, that is $d \leq t(v, u)$, which completes the proof. □

4.1.3 Complexity Analysis

Assume that α is the average number of vertices and β is the average number of edges for the graphs in $\mathcal{G}$, the space complexity of D-index is $O(\alpha^2|\mathcal{G}|)$. Since the construction time for each $\mathcal{DS}_{min}(g)$ is $O(\alpha\beta)$ by starting a BFS from each vertex in g, the time complexity of constructing D-index is $O(\alpha\beta|\mathcal{G}|)$.

The generation of minimal distance set of query graph q can be done in $O(|V_q|^3)$ time. For each distance triplet in $\mathcal{DS}_{min}(q)$, the response time of D-index is $O(\log(md))$ where m is the number of distinct labels in $\mathcal{G}$ and d is the largest distance. Thus, the index response time for the graph pattern is $O(|V_q|^3 + k^2\log(md))$, where k is the number of distinct labels in q. Note that, in practice, both $|V_q|$ and k are very small.

4.2 Frequent Pattern Index

The shortcoming of D-index is that it loses the structural information of data graphs. As a result, the filtering is not effective enough, leading to a lot of unmatched candidate graphs. Although there are graph indexing approaches that retain structural information of data graphs [4,9,15,18,23], they cannot be directly applied to answer generalized subgraph queries.

In order to employ structural information for answering generalized subgraph queries, we propose the concept of *frequent generalized subgraph* (*FGG*) patterns and apply FGGs to design a structural index called *Frequent Pattern Index* (*FP-index*). The challenges, however, are 1) how to efficiently mine the FGGs, 2) how to apply and index FGGs for filtering. We address the two challenges as follows.

The first challenge can be addressed by the pattern-growth approach [1]. The difference is that in an FGG, edges are weighted. To obtain weighted edges for FGGs, we grow the frequent patterns from weighted edges. We initialize the set of weighted edges by taking the set of distinct distance triplets $\mathcal{E} = \cup_{g\in\mathcal{G}}\mathcal{DS}(g)$ introduced in Section 4.1, where each distance triplet $(l_1, l_2, d) \in \mathcal{E}$ is considered as an edge (l_1, l_2) with weight d, while $|\mathcal{C}(l_1, l_2, d)|$ is the frequency of the edge.

A subgraph pattern f is frequent if its frequency is greater than a pre-defined threshold σ. Since the number of FGGs can be too large and indexing a large number of FGGs will increase the index size and hence the search time, we apply a maximum pattern size threshold, γ, and a maximum edge weight threshold, ρ, to obtain only FGGs with size at most γ and any edge weight at most ρ. In our experiments, we set these thresholds as the best possible values such that the FGGs can fit in the machine memory.

4.2.1 Index Construction

The FP-index consists of two parts: *frequent pattern graph index* (*FPG-index*) and *edge index* (*E-index*). FPG-index stores the FGGs in a B+-tree, with the key as an FGG and the data value as the set of data graphs containing the FGG. To answer queries that may contain infrequent edges, we also construct E-index that builds a B+-tree on the set of infrequent edges and frequent large-weight edges whose weights are larger than ρ, with the key as an edge and the data value as the set of data graphs containing the edge.

4.2.2 Query Processing

Given a query graph q, we process the query with FP-index as follows:

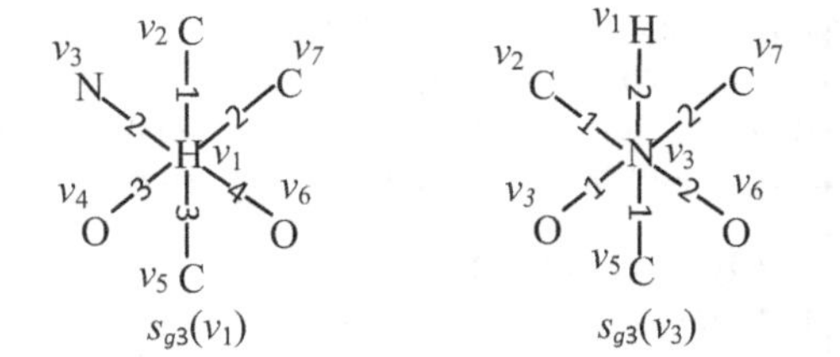

Figure 2: Two star structures: $s_{g_3}(v_1)$ and $s_{g_3}(v_3)$

- Case 1: q is an FGG indexed by FPG-index. In this case, we obtain q's answer set from the index directly without verification.
- Case 2: q is not an FGG indexed by FPG-index. If q contains infrequent edges, then the candidate set of q is relatively small (at most $\sigma|\mathcal{G}|$), which can be retrieved from E-index. Otherwise, we reduce the weight of some edges in q to obtain an FGG q', then we have a partial answer, $\mathcal{A}(q')$, of q, without verification. And then, we obtain the rest of the answer, i.e., $\mathcal{A}(q) \setminus \mathcal{A}(q')$, as follows. We decompose q into several FGGs in FPG-index and frequent large-weight edges in E-index, as $f_1, f_2, \ldots, f_k$, and compute the candidate set by intersecting the answer sets of these frequent patterns: $\cap_{1\leq i\leq k}\mathcal{A}(f_i)$.

4.2.3 Complexity Analysis

Similar to other structural graph indexes such as FG-index [4], the construction cost of FP-index is dominated by the cost of mining FGGs and the index size is dominated by the overall size of FGGs. Likewise, the query processing complexity also heavily depends on the number of FGGs indexed as well as the value of $\sigma|\mathcal{G}|$. However, the complexity of mining FGGs, as well as the size and number of FGGs, may vary significantly from database to database and we are not aware of any formal analysis for these factors in the literature.

4.3 Star Index

Since the number of FGGs can be large, FP-index can only be used to process queries of small size efficiently. Moreover, mining FGGs may also be too expensive. Thus, we propose another index, called *Star Index* (*S-index*), which uses only star structures (instead of subgraph structures) to reduce both the index construction and storage overhead, while still capturing much of the structural information for effective filtering in query processing.

For a vertex v in a data graph $g = (V_g, E_g, l_g) \in \mathcal{G}$, we define the *star structure* of v as $s_g(v) = (V_g, E_g^v, l_g, w)$, where (1) v is the center of the star structure; (2) E_g^v consists of the edges from v to other vertices in V_g, that is $E_g^v = \{v\} \times (V_g \setminus \{v\})$; (3) w is a function that assigns the distance $dist_g(v, u)$ to each edge $(v, u) \in E_g^v$, i.e., $w(v, u) = dist_g(v, u)$. For example, Figure 2 shows the star structures of v_1 and v_3 of the graph g_3 in Figure 1.

We group the weights of the edges in a star structure by the label of the non-center end vertex. Let $L = \{l_g(u) : u \in V_g \setminus \{v\}\}$. We obtain a *multiset* of weights (called *weight multiset*) for each label as follows

$$\mathcal{W}_g(v, l) = \{w(u, v) : l_g(u) = l, l \in L, \text{ and } u \in V_g \setminus \{v\}\}.$$

The weight values in the weight multiset are sorted in ascending order. Table 2 lists all the weight multisets for

Table 2: Weight multisets of g_3

Vertex v	$l_{g_3}(v)$	N	C	O	H
v_1	H	2	1,2,3	3,4	
v_2	C	1	1,2	2,3	1
v_3	N		1,1,2	1,2	2
v_4	O	1	2,2,3	1	3
v_5	C	1	2,3	1,2	3
v_6	O	2	1,3,4	1	4
v_7	C	2	1,3	3,4	2

Table 3: Compressed weight multisets of g_3

Label	N	C	O	H
N		1,1,2	1,2	2
C	1	1,2	1,2	1
O	1	1,2,3	1	3
H	2	1,2,3	3,4	

each label and each star structure of g_3. For example, for the star structure $s_{g_3}(v_1)$, $\mathcal{W}_{g_3}(v_1, \mathtt{C}) = \{1, 2, 3\}$, $\mathcal{W}_{g_3}(v_1, \mathtt{O}) = \{3, 4\}$, and $\mathcal{W}_{g_3}(v_1, \mathtt{N}) = \{2\}$.

Given two weight multisets $\mathcal{W}_1 = \{w_1, \ldots, w_k\}$ and $\mathcal{W}_2 = \{w'_1, \ldots, w'_t\}$, where $k \leq t$. We define the merge of $\mathcal{W}_1$ and $\mathcal{W}_2$ as follows.

$$\mathcal{W}_1 \cap \mathcal{W}_2 = \{\min(w_1, w'_1), \ldots, \min(w_k, w'_k), w'_{k+1}, \ldots, w'_t\}.$$

For some vertices in a graph, they may share the same label. So, we further compress the weight multisets as follows.

$$\mathcal{W}_g(l_1, l_2) = \cap_{l_g(v)=l_1, v \in V_g} \mathcal{W}_g(v, l_2).$$

Table 3 lists the compressed weight multisets. For example, v_2 and v_5 share the same label C, so $\mathcal{W}_{g_3}(v_2, \mathtt{H}) = \{1\}$ and $\mathcal{W}_{g_3}(v_5, \mathtt{H}) = \{3\}$ are merged into one $\mathcal{W}_{g_3}(\mathtt{C}, \mathtt{H}) = \{\min(1, 3)\} = \{1\}$.

The set of distinct compressed weight multisets of each label pair (l_1, l_2) in the database $\mathcal{G}$ can be obtained as follows.

$$\mathcal{W}(l_1, l_2) = \cup_{g \in \mathcal{G}} \mathcal{W}_g(l_1, l_2).$$

For each compressed weight multiset $w \in \mathcal{W}(l_1, l_2)$, the set of data graphs whose corresponding compressed weight multiset is w is defined as follows.

$$\mathcal{A}(w) = \{g : \mathcal{W}_g(l_1, l_2) = w \text{ and } g \in \mathcal{G}\}.$$

4.3.1 Index Structure

S-index is constructed based on $\mathcal{W}(l_1, l_2)$ for each distinct label pair (l_1, l_2) and $\mathcal{A}(w)$ for each $w \in \mathcal{W}(l_1, l_2)$. The index structure of S-index consists of the following parts:

- A B+-tree on the set of distinct label pairs with each pair (l_1, l_2) as the key and $\mathcal{W}(l_1, l_2)$ as the data value. We name this B+-tree as SI.
- A nested B+-tree on the set of distinct compressed weight multisets $\mathcal{W}(l_1, l_2)$ for each pair (l_1, l_2), where each compressed weight multiset $w \in \mathcal{W}(l_1, l_2)$ is the key and $\mathcal{A}(w)$ is the data value. We name this nested B+-tree as $SI(l_1, l_2)$.

Algorithm 3 outlines the construction of S-index. For each data graph $g \in \mathcal{G}$, for each distinct label pair (l_1, l_2) in g, we obtain the compressed weight multiset $\mathcal{W}_g(l_1, l_2)$, and store it in the record with the key (l_1, l_2) in SI. Then, we access the record with the key $\mathcal{W}_g(l_1, l_2)$ in the nested B+-tree $SI(l_1, l_2)$ and add g to the corresponding record.

Algorithm 3: BUILD-SINDEX($\mathcal{G}$)

input : the graph database, $\mathcal{G}$
output: the S-index, SI

```
for g ∈ 𝒢 do
    Let L(g) = {(l_g(u), l_g(v)) : u, v ∈ V_g and u ≠ v} ;
    for (l1, l2) ∈ L(g) do
        Compute w = 𝒲_g(l1, l2) ;
        Add w to the record in SI with key (l1, l2) ;
        Add g to the record in SI(l1, l2) with key w ;
return SI
```

Algorithm 4: QUERY-SINDEX($q, SI, \mathcal{G}$)

input : the query graph, $q = (V_q, E_q, l_q, t)$
S-Index, SI
the graph database $\mathcal{G}$
output: the candidate set of q, $\mathcal{C}(q)$

```
𝒞(q) ← 𝒢 ;
Let L(q) = {(l_g(u), l_g(v)) : u, v ∈ V_g and u ≠ v} ;
for (l1, l2) ∈ L(q) do
    Compute 𝒲_q(l1, l2) ;
    𝒞(l1, l2) ← ∅ ;
    for w ∈ SI(l1, l2) and w ≤ 𝒲_q(l1, l2) do
        𝒞(l1, l2) ← 𝒞(l1, l2) ∪ 𝒜(w) ;
    𝒞(q) ← 𝒞(q) ∩ 𝒞(l1, l2) ;
return 𝒞(q)
```

4.3.2 Query Processing

We now discuss query processing by S-index. Given two compressed weight multisets $\mathcal{W}_1 = \{w_1, \ldots, w_k\}$ and $\mathcal{W}_2 = \{w'_1, \ldots, w'_t\}$, we say that $\mathcal{W}_1 \leq \mathcal{W}_2$ if and only if 1) $k \geq t$, and 2) $w_r \leq w'_r$ for $1 \leq r \leq t$.

LEMMA 2. *Let $s_g(u)$ and $s_q(v)$ be two star structures, such that u and v are vertices in graphs $g = (V_g, E_g, l_g)$ and $q = (V_q, E_q, l_q, t)$, respectively. If $s_g(u)$ matches $s_q(v)$, then we have $\mathcal{W}_g(l_1, l_2) \leq \mathcal{W}_q(l_1, l_2)$ for all distinct label pairs (l_1, l_2) of q.*

PROOF. Consider a label pair (l_1, l_2) of q, l_1 is the label of the center vertex of a star structure of q and l_2 is the label of a non-center vertex. Since g matches q, the number of vertices in V_g with label l_2 is no smaller than the number of vertices in V_q with the same label. Therefore, we have $|\mathcal{W}_g(l_1, l_2)| \geq |\mathcal{W}_q(l_1, l_2)|$. Moreover, for each vertex $v' \in V_q$ of label l_2, there exists a vertex $u' \in V_g$ such that u' maps to v' and $dist_g(u, u') \leq dist_q(v, v')$. Thus, the proof is complete. □

According to Lemma 2, we process a query by S-index as shown in Algorithm 4. For each distinct label pair (l_1, l_2) of q, we merge all the candidate sets associated with (l_1, l_2) that are smaller than $\mathcal{W}_q(l_1, l_2)$, which gives $\mathcal{C}(l_1, l_2)$. The candidate set of q is then obtained by intersecting $\mathcal{C}(l_1, l_2)$ for all distinct pairs (l_1, l_2) of q.

4.3.3 Complexity Analysis

Let m be the average number of distinct labels in a data graph. Thus, the number of distinct label pairs is $O(m^2)$, and the number of compressed weight multisets in

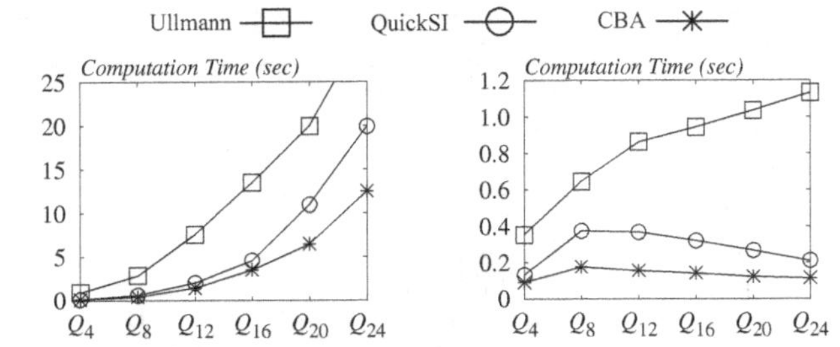

(a) Average Edge Weight = 1.5 (b) Average Edge Weight = 1

Figure 3: Efficiency of Generalized Subgraph Isomorphism Algorithms

the database $\mathcal{G}$ is $O(m^2|\mathcal{G}|)$. Assume that the average number of vertices in a data graph is α, then the average size of a compressed weight multiset is α/m. Thus, the space complexity of S-index is $O(\alpha m|\mathcal{G}|)$.

Assume that the number of distinct labels in a query graph q is t. The index response time is the summation of the time for searching the compressed weight multisets of q, thus the running time complexity is $O(t^2 \log(m^2|\mathcal{G}|))$. Note that, in real life queries, the number of distinct labels is often small.

5. EXPERIMENTAL RESULTS

This section experimentally evaluates our indices and algorithms for generalized subgraph matching. Section 5.1 describes the experimental settings. Section 5.2 evaluates our algorithms for the generalized subgraph isomorphism problem, and Section 5.3 tunes the parameters for the proposed FP-Index. After that, Sections 5.4 and 5.5 demonstrate the efficiency of our indexing methods on real and synthetic datasets, respectively.

5.1 Experimental Settings

Datasets. We use two benchmark datasets commonly adopted in the literature [8, 18]. Both datasets contain graphs that represent chemical molecules. The first one is the AIDS Antiviral Screen Dataset [18], which consists of 10,000 graphs. The second dataset is referred to as PubChem [18], and it contains 100,000 graphs. We use PubChem.mK to denote a sample set of PubChem with m thousands of graphs. In addition, we use synthetic datasets produced from GraphGen[2], a public available synthetic graph generator.

Query sets. For the AIDS dataset, we adopt the query sets from [18], but we ignore the label on each edge and add a weight on the edge (since we target at query graphs where the edges are unlabelled and weighted). For the other datasets, we generate the query sets by first extracting generalized subgraphs from the graphs in the datasets, such that the number of data graphs matching each extracted generalized subgraph is at most 10% of the total number of data graphs. In other words, we avoid generating generalized subgraph matching queries that would return excessive numbers of results.

All of our experiments are conducted on a machine with a Intel Xeon 2.4GHz CPU with 48GB RAM.

5.2 Generalized Subgraph Isomorphism

Our first set of experiments compares three algorithms for generalized subgraph isomorphism: our cost-based approach (denoted as CBA), as well as the extensions of Ullmann's algorithm and QuickSI. Figure 3 illustrates the average running time required by each algorithm to match each query graphs in query set Q_i to all data graphs in the AIDS dataset. In particular, each query set Q_i contains 1000 query graphs, and each query graph in Q_i contains i vertices. Figure 3a shows the results when the edges in the query graph have average weight 1.5. Observe that CBA considerably outperforms the extension of QuickSI, which in turn is superior than the extension of Ullman's algorithm. Figure 3b shows the results when the average edge weight in the query graph equals 1, i.e., when the generalized subgraph isomorphism problem degenerates to the standard subgraph isomorphism problem. Even in this degenerated case, CBA still consistently outperforms QuickSI and Ullmann's algorithm. This demonstrates the superiority of our cost-based method for optimizing vertex matching order. We have conducted a similar set of experiments on the PubChem datasets, and we found that the results are qualitative similar; we omit those results for the interests of space.

[2]http://www.cse.ust.hk/graphgen/

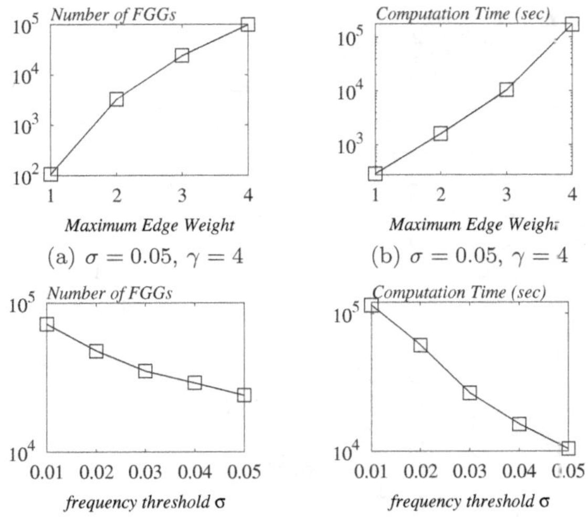

(a) $\sigma = 0.05$, $\gamma = 4$ (b) $\sigma = 0.05$, $\gamma = 4$ (c) $\rho = 3$, $\gamma = 4$ (d) $\rho = 3$, $\gamma = 4$

Figure 4: Space and Pre-computation Costs of the FP-index

5.3 Tuning the FP-index

The second set of our experiments evaluation the space and pre-computation costs of the FP-index (presented in Section 4.2) on a set of 40 thousands data graphs sampled from the PubChem dataset. Figure 4a illustrates the number of Frequent Generalized subGraphs (FGG) that need to be stored in the FP-index, varying the maximum edge weight ρ in the graph patterns from 1 to 4, with the frequency threshold set to $\sigma = 0.05$ and the maximum number of vertices in the FGGs set to $\gamma = 4$. Note that the number of FGGs increases exponentially with maximum edge weight ρ. Figure 4b shows the time required to mine the FGGs, which also exhibits an exponential growth with the increase of ρ. These results indicate that maximum edge weight adopted in the construction in the FP-index have to be carefully selected and has to be reasonably small.

Figures 4c and 4d illustrate the number of FGGs and pre-computation time required by FP-index, respectively, varying the frequency threshold σ from 0.01 to 0.05, with the maximum edge weight set to $\rho = 3$ and the maximum number of vertices in the FGGs set to $\gamma = 4$. Observe that

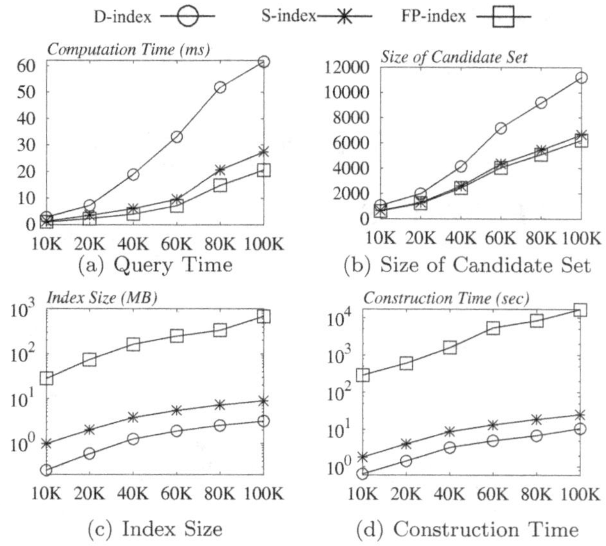

(a) Query Time (b) Size of Candidate Set

(c) Index Size (d) Construction Time

Figure 5: Index Performance v.s. Dataset Size

both the number of FGGs and the pre-computation time decreases exponentially when the frequency threshold σ increases. Hence, we may use a large σ to reduce the space and pre-computation cost of the FP-index. One may be tempted to set σ to be even larger than 0.05, which, however, may significantly reduce the effectiveness of FP-index, as an excessively large σ would make it difficult for FP-index to answer a query without invoking the verification process.

Based on the results in Figure 4, we set $\rho = 3$, $\sigma = 0.05$, and $\gamma = 4$ for the FP-index in all following experiments.

5.4 Performance of Indices

Our next set of experiments compares the performance of the three proposed indices (i.e., D-index, S-index, and FP-index) in terms of query processing performance, space overhead, and construction time. For these experiments, we use sample sets of PubChem dataset with sizes varying from 10K to 100K. We do not use the AIDS dataset as it contains only a small number of data graphs.

Figure 5a illustrates average query processing time of each index for a query set with 1000 graphs, such that on average each graph has 5 vertices and 7 edges, and the average edge weight equals 2.5. Both the S-index and the FP-index significantly outperforms the D-index, and the FP-index is slightly better than the S-index. This is consistent with the results in Figure 5b, which shows the average size of the candidate set induced by each index during query processing. As shown in Figures 5c and 5d, however, the space and construction overheads of FP-index are significantly higher than those of the S-index, which in turn are higher than those of the D-index.

Figure 6a shows the average query time of each index for query sets V_iE_j on the dataset with 40K data graphs, such that each query set V_iE_j contains 1000 query graphs, each of which has i vertices and j edges, and the average weight of the edges equals 2.5. The FP-index achieves the smallest query time when the numbers of vertices and edges in the query graphs are small, but it is outperformed by the S-index on large query graphs. In addition, the D-index is consistently slower than both the FP-index and the S-index.

Figure 6b illustrates the average query time of each index for query set V_5E_7, with the average edge weight varying

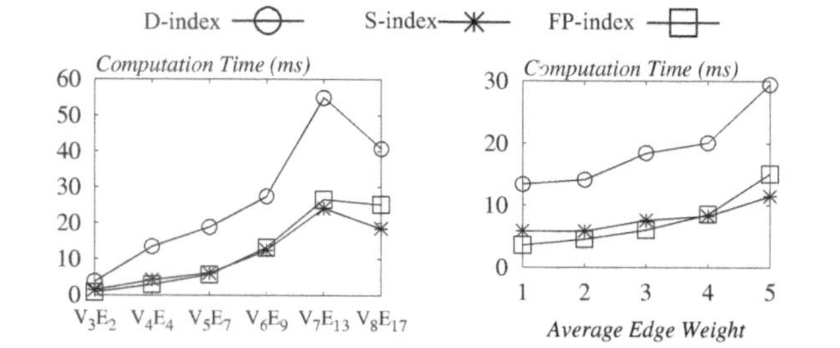

(a) Varying Query Graph Size (b) Varying Max. Edge Weight

Figure 6: Index Performance v.s. Parameters of the Query Graphs

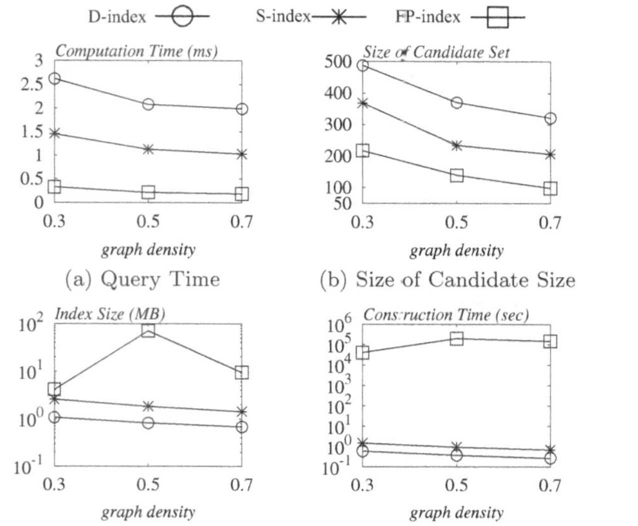

(a) Query Time (b) Size of Candidate Size

(c) Index Size (d) Construction Time

Figure 7: Index Performance v.s. Graph Density

from 1 to 5. The FP-index performs the best when the average edge weight is no more than 3, which is the maximum edge weight handled in its preprocessing step. When the average edge weight is larger than 3, however, the performance of the FP-index degrades, and the S-index becomes the most efficient one.

5.5 Performance on Synthetic Dataset

The experiments use synthetic datasets to evaluate the performance of our indices with respect to a parameter that has not been investigated in the previous experiments, i.e., the densities of the data graphs. In particular, the density of a data graph with n vertices and m edges equals $m/\binom{n}{2}$. We generate synthetic graphs with densities varying from 0.3 to 0.7, and we use them to construct datasets, such that each dataset contains 10K data graphs, each of which has 30 edges and a fixed density. The query graphs for each dataset is constructed in a manner similar to previous experiments, such that each query graph on average has 5 vertices, 7 edges, with an average edge weight 2.5.

Figure 7 illustrates the performance of each index as a function of the data graph density. As with our previous experiments, the FP-index achieves the best query performance, but it incurs the highest space and pre-computation overheads. The D-index requires the smallest space and preprocessing time, but its query time is the largest. The S-index consistently lands on the middle ground between the FP-index and the D-index.

Summary. Our experiments show that the FP-index offers superior query performance at the cost of space and pre-computation time. Therefore, it is suitable for the applications where (i) efficient query processing is crucial, and (ii) space and pre-computation overheads are not a major concern. In contrast, the D-index entails relatively high query cost, but it incurs minimal space and preprocessing overhead. This renders it preferable in the scenarios with stringent requirements on space consumption or pre-computation time. Finally, the S-index's space and pre-computation costs are only slightly higher than that of the D-index, but its query efficiency is almost comparable to that of FP-index. Hence, it offers user a choice to strike a good balance between query processing and space (preprocessing) overheads.

6. RELATED WORK

There are some existing studies of graph matching problem by allowing edges to map to paths for graphs [6,7,10,25]. However, their queries are too rigid by fixing the length of all the mapping paths [25], or too relax by allowing node similarity matching [7]. Besides, all these works are tailored to query a single large graph making them unsuitable for querying a large set of small or medium-sized graphs.

On the other hand, various types of graph query processing on a large set of small or medium-sized graphs have been studied in the literature in recent years and we restrict our discussion on the closely related ones, namely subgraph query processing [4, 9, 13, 15, 18, 21, 23], supergraph query processing [2, 3, 14, 22], and similarity graph query processing [12, 19, 20, 24]. All these works proposed some indexing techniques to filter out as many unmatching data graphs as possible. Although many different types of graph indexing techniques have been proposed, none of them is similar to our indexes except FG-index [4], which is similar to FP-index. However, the only similarity lies on the use of frequent patterns to avoid verification and the use of infrequent edges to reduce the candidate set size, while the index structure of FP-index (which builds on B+-trees) is totally different from that of FG-index (which is an unbalanced tree built on the clusters of frequent patterns). Apart from that, both D-index and S-index are entirely different from all existing indexes. In addition, our work is the first to propose indexes for processing generalized subgraph queries.

7. CONCLUSIONS

We studied a new type of graph queries, generalized subgraph queries. We proposed a succinct and effective cost model to minimize the cost of generalized subgraph isomorphism. We also developed three indexes that can effectively filter out unmatching data graphs, which significantly reduces the total query response time. We evaluated our algorithms with experiments on both real datasets and synthetic datasets. The results show that our matching algorithm is efficient in candidate verification as it considerably outperforms the direct extension of existing graph matching algorithms, while our indexes are also effective in filtering. Thus, the results verify that our method is efficient in query processing (in both filtering and candidate verification). Although some of the indexes have weaknesses, we show how the weaknesses are addressed by another index; in particular, our results show that S-index achieves both a low index construction cost and a short query response time.

8. ACKNOWLEDGMENTS

Xiaokui Xiao was supported by Nanyang Technological University under SUG Grant M58020016 and AcRF Tier 1 Grant RG 35/09, and by the A*STAR SERG Grants 1021580074. James Cheng was supported in part by the A*STAR TSRP Grants 1021580034 and 1121720013.

9. REFERENCES

[1] C. C. Aggarwal and H. Wang, editors. *Managing and Mining Graph Data*, volume 40 of *Advances in Database Systems*. Springer, 2010.

[2] C. Chen, X. Yan, P. S. Yu, J. Han, D.-Q. Zhang, and X. Gu. Towards graph containment search and indexing. In *VLDB*, pages 926–937, 2007.

[3] J. Cheng, Y. Ke, A. W.-C. Fu, and J. X. Yu. Fast graph query processing with a low-cost index. *VLDB J.*, 20(4):521–539, 2011.

[4] J. Cheng, Y. Ke, W. Ng, and A. Lu. Fg-index: towards verification-free query processing on graph databases. In *SIGMOD*, pages 857–872, 2007.

[5] S. A. Cook. The complexity of theorem-proving procedures. In *STOC*, pages 151–158, 1971.

[6] W. Fan, J. Li, S. Ma, N. Tang, and Y. Wu. Adding regular expressions to graph reachability and pattern queries. In *ICDE*, pages 39–50, 2011.

[7] W. Fan, J. Li, S. Ma, H. Wang, and Y. Wu. Graph homomorphism revisited for graph matching. *PVLDB*, 3(1):1161–1172, 2010.

[8] W.-S. Han, J. Lee, M.-D. Pham, and J. X. Yu. igraph: A framework for comparisons of disk-based graph indexing techniques. *PVLDB*, 3(1):449–459, 2010.

[9] H. He and A. K. Singh. Closure-tree: An index structure for graph queries. In *ICDE*, page 38, 2006.

[10] W. Jin and J. Yang. A flexible graph pattern matching framework via indexing. In *SSDBM*, pages 293–311, 2011.

[11] C. L. S. John W. Moore and P. C. Jurs. *Chemistry: The Molecular Science*, volume 2. Brooks Cole, 2007.

[12] H. Shang, X. Lin, Y. Zhang, J. X. Yu, and W. Wang. Connected substructure similarity search. In *SIGMOD*, pages 903–914, 2010.

[13] H. Shang, Y. Zhang, X. Lin, and J. X. Yu. Taming verification hardness: An efficient algorithm for testing subgraph isomorphism. *In VLDB*, 2008.

[14] H. Shang, K. Zhu, X. Lin, Y. Zhang, and R. Ichise. Similarity search on supergraph containment. In *ICDE*, pages 637–648, 2010.

[15] D. Shasha, J. T.-L. Wang, and R. Giugno. Algorithmics and applications of tree and graph searching. In *PODS*, pages 39–52, 2002.

[16] J. R. Ullmann. An algorithm for subgraph isomorphism. *J. ACM*, 23(1):31–42, 1976.

[17] J. H. Van Drie, D. Weininger, and Y. C. Martin. Aladdin: An integrated tool for computer-assisted molecular design and pharmacophore recognition from geometric, steric, and substructure searching of three-dimensional molecular structures. *Journal of Computer-Aided Molecular Design*, 3:225–251, 1989.

[18] X. Yan, P. S. Yu, and J. Han. Graph indexing: A frequent structure-based approach. In *SIGMOD*, pages 335–346, 2004.

[19] X. Yan, P. S. Yu, and J. Han. Substructure similarity search in graph databases. In *SIGMOD*, pages 766–777, 2005.

[20] Z. Zeng, A. K. H. Tung, J. Wang, J. Feng, and L. Zhou. Comparing stars: On approximating graph edit distance. *PVLDB*, 2(1):25–36, 2009.

[21] S. Zhang, M. Hu, and J. Yang. Treepi: A novel graph indexing method. In *ICDE*, pages 966–975, 2007.

[22] S. Zhang, J. Li, H. Gao, and Z. Zou. A novel approach for efficient supergraph query processing on graph databases. In *EDBT*, pages 204–215, 2009.

[23] P. Zhao, J. X. Yu, and P. S. Yu. Graph indexing: Tree + delta >= graph. In *VLDB*, pages 938–949, 2007.

[24] X. Zhao, C. Xiao, X. Lin, and W. Wang. Efficient graph similarity joins with edit distance constraints. In *ICDE*, pages 834–845, 2012.

[25] L. Zou, L. Chen, and M. T. Özsu. Distancejoin: Pattern match query in a large graph database. *PVLDB*, 2(1):886–897, 2009.

G-SPARQL: A Hybrid Engine for Querying Large Attributed Graphs

Sherif Sakr*
National ICT Australia
UNSW, Sydney, Australia
ssakr@cse.unsw.edu.eu

Sameh Elnikety
Microsoft Research
Redmond, WA, USA
samehe@microsoft.com

Yuxiong He
Microsoft Research
Redmond, WA, USA
yuxhe@microsoft.com

ABSTRACT

We propose a SPARQL-like language, *G-SPARQL*, for querying attributed graphs. The language expresses types of queries which of large interest for applications which model their data as large graphs such as: pattern matching, reachability and shortest path queries. Each query can combine both of structural predicates and value-based predicates (on the attributes of the graph nodes and edges). We describe an algebraic compilation mechanism for our proposed query language which is extended from the relational algebra and based on the basic construct of building SPARQL queries, *the Triple Pattern.* We describe a hybrid Memory/Disk representation of large attributed graphs where only the topology of the graph is maintained in memory while the data of the graph is stored in a relational database. The execution engine of our proposed query language splits parts of the query plan to be pushed inside the relational database while the execution of other parts of the query plan are processed using memory-based algorithms, as necessary. Experimental results on real datasets demonstrate the efficiency and the scalability of our approach and show that our approach outperforms native graph databases by several factors.

Categories and Subject Descriptors

E.1 [**Data Structures**]: Graphs and networks

Keywords

Graphs, Graph Queries, SPARQL

1. INTRODUCTION

Recently, graph query processing has attracted a lot of attention from the database research community due to the increasing popularity of modeling the data as large graphs in various application domains such as social networks, bibliographical networks and knowledge bases. In many real applications of these domains, both the graph topological structure in addition to the properties of the vertices and edges are important. For example, in a social network, a vertex which represents a *person* object can be described with a property that represents the *age* of a person while the topological structure could represent different types of relationships (directed edges) with a group of people. Each of these relations can be described by a *start date* property. Each vertex is associated with a basic descriptive attribute that represents its *label* while each edge has a *label* that describes the type of relationship between the connected vertices. Figure 1 shows a snippet of an example large graph where a vertex represents an entity instance (e.g., *author, paper, conferences*) and an edge represents a structural relationship (e.g., *co-author, affiliated, published*). In addition, there are attributes (e.g., *age, keyword, location*) that describe the different graph vertices while other attributes (e.g., *order, title, month*) describe the graph edges.

In general, there are three common types of queries which of large interest for applications with large graphs: 1) *Pattern match query* that tries to find the existence(s) of a pattern graph (e.g., path, star, subgraph) in the large graph [21, 6]. 2) *Reachability query* that verifies if there exists a path between any two vertices in the large graph [4, 8]. 3) *Shortest path query* which returns the shortest distance (in terms of number of edges) between any two vertices in the large graph [1, 18]. In practice, a user may need to pose a query on the large graph that can involve more than one of the common graph query types. The problem studied in this paper is to query a graph associated with attributes for its vertices and edges (called as *attributed graph*) based on both structural and attribute conditions. Unfortunately, this problem did not receive much attention in the literature and there is no solid foundation for building query engines that can support a combination of different types of queries over large graphs. In particular, examples of motivating queries to our work include:

1) Find the names of two authors, `X` and `Y`, where `X` and `Y` are connected by a path of any length (number of edges), the author `X` is affiliated at `UNSW`, the author `Y` is affiliated at `Microsoft` and each of the authors has published a paper in `VLDB'12`. *This query involves pattern matching and reachability expressions.*

2) Find the names of two authors, `X` and `Y`, where `X` and `Y` are connected by a path of any length, the author `X` is affiliated at `UNSW`, the author `Y` is affiliated at `Microsoft`, each of the authors has published a paper in `VLDB'12` as a `first` author and each of the authors has an `age` which is more than 35. *This query involves pattern matching expression with conditions on the attributes of graph nodes and edges in addition to reachability expression.*

3) Find the names of two authors, `X` and `Y`, and the connecting path(s) between them where `X` and `Y` are connected by a path with a length which is less than 3 edges, the author `X` is affiliated

---

*This work has been done while the author was visiting Microsoft Research Laboratories, Redmond, USA

CIKM'12, October 29–November 2, 2012, Maui, HI, USA.

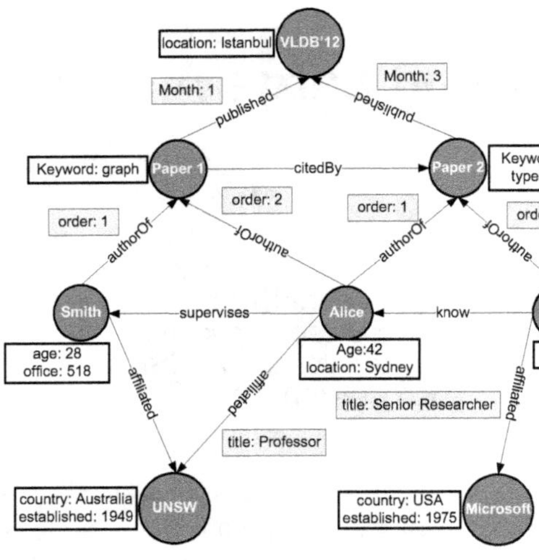

Figure 1: An example attributed graph.

at `UNSW`, the author `Y` is affiliated at `Microsoft` and each of the authors has published a paper in `VLDB'12` as a `first` author. *This query involves pattern matching expression in addition to a reachability expression which is constrained by a path filtering condition. The query returns the information of the connecting paths(s) as part of the results.*

In this paper, we present an approach for querying large attributed graphs which relies on a hybrid main memory/disk-based relational representation of the graph database and devising efficient algebraic-based query processing mechanisms for different types of graph queries. In our approach, the incoming queries are compiled into algebraic plans where parts of the query plans are pushed down and executed inside the relational database layer while the rest of the query plan is processed using memory-based algorithms. In principle, the main reason behind our decision for relying on a relational database at the physical storage layer is to leverage the decades' worth of research in the database systems community. Some optimizations developed during this period include the careful layout of data on disk, indexing, sorting, buffer management and query optimization. By combining the memory representation of the graph topology and memory-based graph algorithms with the storage layer of the RDBMS, we are able to gain the best features of both worlds. Our goal is to optimize the performance of query processing while minimizing the memory consumption and achieving the scalability goals. In particular, our main contributions can be summarized as follows:

1) We propose a SPARQL-like language, called *G-SPARQL*, for querying attributed graphs. The language enables combining the expression of different types of graph queries into one request. We show that the language is sufficiently expressive to describe different types of interesting queries (Section 3).

2) We present an efficient hybrid Memory/Disk representation of large attributed graphs where only the *topology* of the graph is maintained in memory while the *data* of the graph is stored and processed using relational database (Section 4).

3) We describe an execution engine for our proposed query language which applies a split query evaluation mechanism where the execution of parts of the query plan is pushed inside the relational database while the execution of other parts is processed using memory-based algorithms, as necessary, for optimizing the query performance (Section 5).

4) We conduct extensive experiments with real datasets that demonstrate the efficiency of our approach (Section 6).

2. RELATED WORK AND LIMITATIONS OF EXISTING APPROACHES

Several techniques have been proposed in the literature for querying large graphs. However, in practice, the existing techniques turn to be inadequate, in many cases, for querying large attributed graphs due to the following limitations:

a) Most of the existing graph querying techniques follow the approach of building an index for storing information about the main features of the graph database. The structure and content of this index is usually optimized for accelerating the evaluation of *only one* of the common types of the graph queries but usually they cannot be used for accelerating the evaluation of other types of queries. For example, different subgraph query processing techniques exploit different types of graph features for building their indices (e.g., path [21], tree [20], subgraph [19]) while proposed techniques for handling reachability queries use different indexing mechanisms such as the 2-hop cover [4] and 3-hop cover [8]. In practice, answering user requests that can involve more than one of the common graph query types would require maintaining different type of indices which would be very expensive in terms of memory consumption. In addition, given the increasing sizes of the graph database, the efficiency of such indexing techniques will break down after a certain limit is reached.

b) The existing graph querying methods that have been presented in the literature mainly focus on querying the topological structure of the graphs [15, 19, 21] and very few of them have considered the use of attributed graphs [17, 5]. In practice, it is more common that the querying requirements for the applications of large graph databases (e.g., social networks or bibliographical networks) would involve querying the graph data (attributes of nodes/edges) in addition to the graph topology. Answering queries that involve predicates on the attributes of the graphs (vertices or edges) in addition to the topological structure is more challenging as it requires extra memory consumption for building indices over the graph attributes in addition to the structural indices in order to accelerate the query evaluation process. Furthermore, it makes the query evaluation and optimization process more complex (e.g., evaluation and join orders).

c) Several techniques have been proposed for querying RDF graphs [12, 7]. However, these approaches cannot be reused for querying general attributed graphs due to the differences in the data model and the specifications of the query requirements. For example, in the RDF data model, graph edges *cannot* be described by attributes. The initial specifications of SPARQL [14] did not provide any facility for expressing *path queries* or *reachability* expressions. In addition, some query types that are of common interest in the general domain of large graph such as *shortest path* queries might not be of direct interest in the scope of RDF/SPARQL domain and is thus, so far, not been considered.

d) Recently, some native graph database systems have been introduced (e.g., Neo4j[1], HypergraphDB[2]). These sys-

[1]http://neo4j.org/

[2]http://www.kobrix.com/hgdb.jsp

tems are mainly designed to provide efficient graph traversal functions[3]. However, these systems lack the support of *declarative* query interfaces and do not apply any query optimization strategies. In particular, they are language-specific and have their own APIs and low-level interfaces. Therefore, the efficiency of any graph query evaluation is *programmer-dependent*. Thus, it can turn to be quite inefficient in many cases especially when the programmer has no or little knowledge about the characteristics of the underlying graph.

In the following sections, we present our approach for querying large attributed graphs which aims to address the above mentioned challenges.

3. THE G-SPARQL QUERY LANGUAGE

The SPARQL query language is the official W3C standard for querying and extracting information from RDF graphs [14]. It is based on a powerful *graph matching* facility that allows the binding of variables to components in the input RDF graph. In principle, the RDF data model represents a special kind of the general model of attributed graph which represents our main focus in this paper. In particular, the main differences between the two kind of models (RDF and attributed graph) can be specified as follows:

a) In the RDF data model, graph edges are used for representing the structural relationships (graph topology) between the graph entities (connecting two vertices) in addition to representing the *graph data* by connecting the graph entities to the information of their attribute values (connecting a vertex with a literal value). Such uniform treatment leads to a significant increase in the size of the graph topology as the graph data is considered as a part of the topology and not as a separate part. The situation is different in the attributed graph model where the graph data (attributes of graph nodes/edges) are represented differently from the structural information of the graph.

b) In attributed graphs, edges are treated as first class citizens where any edge (similar to any vertex) can be described by an arbitrary set of attributes. That is not the case of the RDF model where there is no support for edges to be described by any attribute information (only vertices).

We introduce *G-SPARQL* as a SPARQL-like query language that employs the basic graph matching facilities of the SPARQL language. However, the language introduces new constructs that handle the above mentioned differences in the data model in addition to compensating the lack of some querying requirements that are not supported by the standard specification of the SPARQL language. In particular, our language aims to fulfill the following set of large graph querying requirements:

1) The language supports querying structural graph patterns where filtering conditions can be specified on the attributes of the graph vertices and/or edges which are participating in the defined patterns as well.

2) The language supports various forms for querying graph paths (sequence of edges) of possibly unknown lengths that connect the graph vertices. In particular, the language enables the expression of reachability queries and shortest path queries between the graph vertices where filtering conditions can be applied on the queried path patterns (e.g., constraints on the path length).

[3]A traversal refers to visiting the graph vertices sequentially by following the graph edges in some algorithmic fashion (e.g., depth-first or breadth-first)

```
        <Query> =  SELECT <VarList>
                   WHERE{ <Triple>+
                   [FILTER (<Predicate>)]*
                   [FILTERPATH (<PathPredicate>)]* }
      <VarList> =  {?var | <PathVar>}
      <PathVar> =  ??var | ?*var
       <Triple> =  <Term> (<Term> | <Edge> | <Path> ) <Term>
         <Term> =  literal | ?var
         <Edge> =  literal | literal+ | @literal | ?var(literal)
         <Path> =  <PathVar> | <PathVar>(literal)
    <Predicate> =  BooleanFunction
<PathPredicate> =  Length(<PathVar>, Predicate) |
                   AtLeastNode(<PathVar>, number, Predicate) |
                   AtMostNode(<PathVar>, number, Predicate) |
                   ALLNodes(<PathVar>, Predicate) |
                   AtLeastEdge(<PathVar>, number, Predicate) |
                   AtMostEdge(<PathVar>, number, Predicate) |
                   AllEdges(<PathVar>, Predicate)
```

Figure 2: *G-SPARQL* grammar.

Figure 2 shows the grammar of the *G-SPARQL* language whereas non-terminal `Query`, defining a *G-SPARQL* query, is the start symbol of this grammar. More details about the syntax and semantics of the *G-SPARQL* language are discussed in the following subsections.

3.1 Querying Attributes of Nodes and Edges

According to the standard specifications of the language, each SPARQL query defines a graph pattern P that is matched against an RDF graph G where each variable in the query graph pattern P is replaced by matching elements of G such that the resulting graphs are contained in G (pattern matching). The basic construct of building these graph patterns is the so-called a *Triple Pattern* [13]. A Triple Pattern represents an RDF triple `(subject, predicate, object)` where *subject* represents an entity (vertex) in the graph and *predicate* represents a relationship (edge) to an *object* in the graph. This object in the triple pattern can represent another entity (vertex) in the graph or a *literal* value. Each part of this triple pattern can represent either a constant value or a variable `(?var)`. Hence, a set of triple patterns concatenated by `AND (.)` represents the query graph pattern. The following example shows a simple SPARQL query that finds all persons who are affiliated at UNSW and are at least of 42 years old.

```
SELECT   ?X
 WHERE   {?X affiliatedAt UNSW. ?X age ?age.
         FILTER (?age >= 42).}
```

In our context, we need to differentiate between the representation of two types of query predicates. a) *Structural predicates*: specify conditions on the structural *relationship* between graph vertices. The *subject*, and *object* of the triple pattern refer to vertices and the *predicate* to an edge. b) *Value-based predicates*: specifies a condition on the value of an *attribute* of a graph element. The *subject* is either a vertex (or an edge as we explain below), the *predicate* is the attribute name, and the *object* is the attribute value.

Therefore, the *G-SPARQL* syntax uses the symbol (@) at the *predicate* part of the query triple patterns that represent value-based predicates and differentiate them from the standard structural predicates. To illustrate, let us consider the following example of two query triple patterns:

```
T1 --> ?Person affiliatedBy UNSW
       T2 --> ?Person @age 42.
```

where $T1$ represents a structural predicate specifying that the graph vertices represented by the variable `?Person` are connected by an `affiliatedBy` edge to a vertex with the label UNSW. In contrast, $T2$ represents a value-based predicate that specifies the condition of having the vertices represented by the variable ?Person described by an age attribute storing the value 42.

Unlike the RDF data model, the model of attributed graphs enables describing each graph edge with an arbitrary set of attributes. Therefore, our query language enables representing two types of *value-based* predicates: 1) *Vertex predicates* which enables specifying conditions on the attributes of the graph vertices. 2) *Edge Predicates* which enables specifying conditions on the attributes of graph edges. In particular, we rely on the standard query triple pattern to represent both types of predicates. However, we use the round brackets () for the *subject* part of the query triple pattern to differentiate edge predicates. In these predicates, the subject parts refers to graph edges and not for graph vertices. Let us consider the following example of query triple patterns:

```
T3 --> ?Person ?E(affiliatedBy) UNSW
T4 --> ?E @Role "Professor"
T5 --> ?Person @officeNumber 518
```

where $T3$ represents a structural predicate that specifies the condition that the vertices represented by the variable ?Person is connected to a vertex with the label UNSW with an affiliatedBy relationship. $T4$ represents an *edge predicate* that determines that the *Role* attribute of the affiliatedBy relationship (where the edge representing the relationship is bound to the variable E) should store the value $Professor$. $T5$ represents a *vertex predicate* that specifies the condition that $Person$ is described by an officeNumber attribute that stores the value 518.

3.2 Querying Path Patterns

G-SPARQL supports expressing paths of arbitrary length and querying path patterns in two main ways. First, using explicit relationships, in compatible with the recent recommendation of the SPARQL 1.1 language[4], as described in the following triple patterns.

```
T5 --> ?Person knows+ John.
T6 --> ?Person knows+ ?X.
```

where $T5$ represents a structural predicate that describes a reachability test verifying that the vertices assigned to ?Person are connected to a vertex with label John by any path of knows edges. On the other hand, $T6$ assigns to the variable X all vertices that can be reached from the vertices that are represented by the variable ?Person through any path of knows edges. The symbol (+) indicates that the path can be of any length where each edge in the path needs to represent the relationship knows.

Second, *G-SPARQL* allows path variables in the *predicate* position of a triple pattern. In particular, it supports the following options for binding path variables in the path patterns.

```
T7 --> subject ??P object.
T8 --> subject ?*P object.
T9 --> subject ??P(predicate) object.
T10 --> subject ?*P(predicate) object.
```

where $T7$ binds the path variable P to the connecting paths between the two vertices of the subject and object. The symbol (??) indicates that the matching paths between the subject and object can be of any arbitrary length. In $T8$, the symbol (?*) indicates that the variable P will be matched with the *shortest* path between the two vertices of subject and object. $T9$ ensures that each edge in the

[4]http://www.w3.org/TR/sparql11-query/

Node Label

ID	Value
1	John
2	Paper 2
3	Alice
4	Microsoft
5	VLDB'12
6	Paper 1
7	UNSW
8	Smith

age

ID	Value
1	45
3	42
8	28

office

ID	Value
8	518

location

ID	Value
3	Sydney
5	Istanbul

keyword

ID	Value
2	XML
6	graph

type

ID	Value
2	Demo

established

ID	Value
4	1975
7	1949

country

ID	Value
4	USA
7	Australia

authorOf

eID	sID	dID
1	1	2
5	3	2
6	3	6
11	8	6

affiliated

eID	sID	dID
3	1	4
8	3	7
12	8	7

published

eID	sID	dID
4	2	5
10	6	5

citedBy

eID	sID	dID
9	6	2

order

ID	Value
1	2
5	1
6	2
11	1

know

eID	sID	dID
2	1	3

supervise

eID	sID	dID
7	3	8

title

ID	Value
3	Senior Researcher
8	Professor

month

ID	Value
4	3
10	1

Figure 3: Relational Representation of Attributed Graph.

matching paths represents the specified relationship predicate. Similarly, $T10$ ensures that each edge in the matched shortest path represents the relationship predicate.

In general, any two vertices can be connected with multiple paths. Therefore, *G-SPARQL* enables expressing filtering conditions that can specify *boolean* predicates on the nodes and the edges of the matching paths which are bound to the path variable. In particular, *G-SPARQL* supports the following filtering conditions over the matched paths.

a) Length(PV, P): verifies that the length (number of edges) of each matching path which is bound to the variable PV satisfies the predicate P and filters out those paths which do not satisfy the predicate P. For example, the following path filtering condition FilterPath (Length(??X, < 4)) ensures that the length of each path which is assigned to the path variable (X) is less than 4 edges.

b) At[Least|Most][Node|Edge](PV, N, P): verifies if at least (most) N number of nodes (edges) on each path which is bound to the variable PV satisfies the predicate P and filters out those paths which do not satisfy the predicate P.

c) All[Nodes|Edges](PV, P): ensures that every node (edge) of each path which is bound to the variable PV satisfies the predicate P.

4. HYBRID GRAPH REPRESENTATION

Relational database systems are efficient in executing queries that benefit from indexing (e.g., B-tree) and query optimization techniques (e.g., selectivity estimation and join ordering). Relational systems are, however, inefficient in evaluating queries that require looping or recursive access to a large number of records by executing multiple expensive join operations which may yield a large intermediate result. Therefore, we rely on algorithms that execute on main memory data structures to answer graph queries that require extensive traversal operations on the graph topology. In particular, we use a hybrid representation for attributed graphs where the entire graph information (topology + data) is stored in a relational database, and only the graph topology information needs to be loaded to the main memory.

There are multiple approaches to store an attributed graph in a relational database. We adopt the fully decomposed storage model (DSM) [3] which is agnostic to the graph schema and therefore can be applied to any attributed graph. In addition, it permits efficient attribute retrieval during query processing. Figure 3 illustrates an example of our relational representation for the attributed graph in Figure 1. In particular, we start by assigning identifiers (IDs) to each vertex and edge in the graph. Vertex attributes are stored in M two-column tables, where M is the number of *unique* attributes of the graph vertices. Similarly, edge attributes

Operator	Description	Relational
$\texttt{NgetAttVal}_{id,(attName):id,value}$	returns the values of an attribute for a set of nodes.	Yes
$\texttt{EgetAttVal}_{id,(attName):id,value}$	returns the values of an attribute for a set of edges.	Yes
$\texttt{getEdgeNodes}_{sID,[(eLabel)]:sID,eID,dID}$	returns adjacent nodes, optionally through a specific relation, for a set of graph nodes.	Yes
$\texttt{strucPred}_{sID,(eLabel),(dNLabel):sID,[eID]}$	returns a set of vertices that are adjacent to other vertices with a specific relationship and optionally returns the connecting edges.	Yes
$\texttt{edgeJoin}_{sID,dID,[(eLabel)]:sID,dID,[eID]}$	returns pairs of vertices that are connected with an edge, optionally of a specified relationship, and optionally returns the connecting edges.	Yes
$\texttt{pathJoin}_{sID,dID,[(eLabel)]:sID,dID,[pID,pRel]}$	returns pairs of vertices which are connected by a sequence of edges of any length, optionally with a specified relationship, and optionally returns connecting paths.	No
$\texttt{sPathJoin}_{sID,dID,[(eLabel)]:sID,dID,pID,pRel}$	returns pairs of vertices which are connected by a sequence of edges of any length, optionally with a specified relationship, and returns the *shortest* connecting path.	No
$\texttt{filterPath}_{pID,pRel,(cond):pID,pRel}$	returns paths that satisfy a condition.	No

Table 1: *G-SPARQL* algebraic operators.

are stored in N two-column tables where N is the number of *unique* attributes of the graph edges. The first column (ID) of a two-column attribute table stores the identifiers of those vertices/edges that are described by the associated attribute, and the second column ($Value$) stores the literal values for those attributes. For example, the vertex with label *Alice* is assigned ($ID = 3$) in table *nodeLabel* and the age attribute is stored in table *age* in row (3, 42). Each table is sorted as clustered index on the ID column in order to enable a fast merge join when multiple attributes of the same vertex/edge are retrieved. In addition, a secondary index on the $Value$ column is created for each table to reduce access costs for value-based predicates on the attributes.

The graph edges are stored in P three-column tables, where P is the number of *unique* relationships that exist between the graph vertices. These P three-column tables capture the graph *topology*. Each of these tables groups the information of all graph edges that represent a particular relationship. Each edge is described by (1) the edge identifier (eID), (2) the identifier of the source vertex (sID), and (3) the identifier of the destination vertex (dID).

In our hybrid graph representation, we rely on a native pointer-based data structure for representing the graph topology information in main memory. In particular, this memory representation of the graph topology encodes the information of the P relationship tables that store the *structural* information of the graph edges. In principle, this information is needed for executing the index-free and memory-based algorithms that involve heavy traversal operations on the graph topology and for recursive algorithms. Example algorithms include Dijkstra's algorithm to obtain the shortest path between two vertices or performing a breath-first search (BFS) to answer reachability queries [2]. Therefore, our hybrid representation achieves a clear reduction in main memory data structures as we show in Table 2 in Section 6.

5. QUERY EXECUTION ENGINE

This section presents the query compilation and optimization process that effectively translates a *G-SPARQL* query into a physical execution plan on our hybrid graph representation. In general, one of the key effective query optimization techniques for any query language is the availability of a powerful algebraic compilation and rewriting framework of logical query plans. In our approach, we rely on a dialect of *tuple algebra* for compiling *G-SPARQL* queries. In particular, our algebra considers *tuples* as the basic unit of information where each algebraic operator manipulates collections of tuples [11, 10]. Hence, we can leverage the

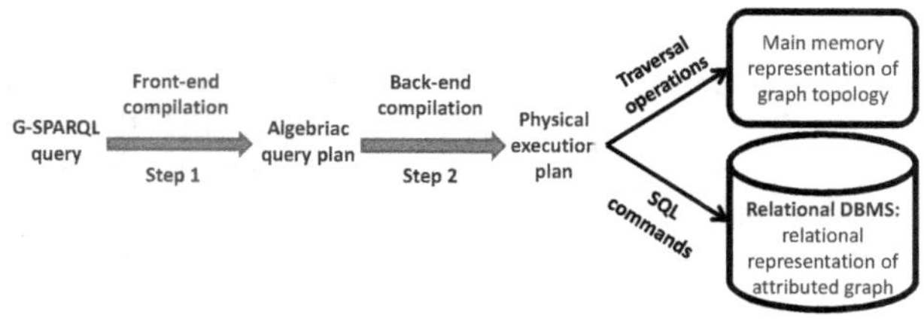

Figure 4: Execution Steps of a *G-SPARQL* query.

well-established relational query planning and optimization techniques in several venues before further translating our query plans (or parts of them) into SQL queries. However, our logical algebra extends the set of traditional relational algebraic operators (e.g., selection, projection, join) with a set of logical operators that are capable of expressing complex *G-SPARQL* operations that can not be matched with the semantics of the traditional relational operators.

As shown in Figure 4, the compilation process consists of two main steps : (1) *Front-end compilation* which translates the input *G-SPARQL* query into an algebraic query plan expressed using the intermediate language. (2) *Back-end compilation* which translates the algebraic query plan to the physical execution plan on the hybrid engine. We first present the algebraic operators which are used in describing our algebraic query plans, and then we describe the steps of the query compilation process.

5.1 Algebraic Operators

In general, the design of our logical operators are independent of any specific disk or memory representation of the attributed graph. In addition, they are independent of the underlying query evaluation engine. The descriptions of our algebraic operators are listed in Table 1. For example, the `NgetAttVal` is a unary operator which is used for retrieving the values of a specific attribute for a set of graph nodes. The operator receives a set of tuples where the column (id) of the input relation identifies the graph nodes and the name of the attribute to be accessed ($attName$). The schema of the output tuples extends the schema of the input tuples with the ($value$) column that represent the values of the accessed attribute. Similarly, the `EgetAttVal` operator retrieves the values of a specific attribute for a set of graph edges. The traditional relational `Selection` operator (σ_p) is used for representing value-based predicates over the values of the attributes of graph nodes or edges. It selects only those tuples of an input relation for which a value-based predicate (p) over a specific column holds. Hence, it represents the right match for reflecting the expressivity of the SPARQL `FILTER` expressions. Based on the attributed graph of Figure 1 and its relational representation in Figure 3, Figure 5(a) illustrates an example for the behavior of the `EgetAttVal` operator where it retrieves the values of the `title` attribute for an input relation with the (id) of two graph edges. The schema of the output relation extends the schema of the input relation with an attribute that stores the value of the accessed attribute.

The `getEdgeNodes` is a unary operator which is used for retrieving a set of adjacent nodes. The operator receives a set of tuples where the column (id) of the input relation identifies the graph nodes and *optionally* a specified relation for accessing the adjacent nodes ($eLabel$). The schema of the output tuples extends the schema of the input tuples with the two columns that represent the identifiers of the connecting edges (eID) and the adjacent nodes (dID). If the operator receives the ($eLabel$) parameter then it filters out the nodes that do not have adjacent nodes connected with the specified relationship. The `strucPred` is another unary operator which is used for filtering a set of nodes based on a specified structural predicate. It receives a set of tuples where the column (sID) of the input relation identifies the graph nodes and a structural predicate which is described by the label of the connecting relation ($eLabel$) and the label for the adjacent node that should be accessed through this relation ($dNLabel$). Figure 5(b) illustrates an example of the `strucPred` operator where it applies a structural predicate which filters out the graph vertices that are not connected to an adjacent vertex with the label `Smith` through the `know` relationship and projects the information of the connecting edges that represent the structural predicate.

The `edgeJoin` is a binary join operator which receives two relations (S and D) where the two columns (sID) and (dID) identify the graph nodes of S and D, respectively. The operator checks for each pair of nodes whether it is connected with any graph edge, filters out the not connected pairs and returns the tuples of the connected pairs as a result. The output of the operator is a single relation where the schema of the output tuples concatenates the columns of (S and D). The operator can receive an optional parameter which imposes a condition on the connecting edge between each pair of nodes to be representing a specified relationship label ($eLabel$). Figure 5(c) illustrates another example of the `edgeJoin` operator where it receives two sets of graph vertices - (`"John"`,`"Alice"`,`"Smith"`) and (`"Microsoft"`) - and returns pairs of graph vertices that are connected through an `affiliated` relationship. Moreover, the `edgeJoin` operator can optionally project the information of the connecting edge(s) where it extends the schema of the output relation by an additional column (eID) that represents the identifiers of the connecting edges between each pair of nodes.

The `pathJoin` operator is another binary join operator which receives two relations (S and D) where the two columns (sID) and (dID) identify the graph nodes of S and D, respectively. The operator checks for each pair of nodes whether it is connected by a sequence of edges (of any length), filters out the not connected pairs and returns the tuples of the connected pairs as a result. The operator can receive an optional parameter which imposes a condition on the edges of each connecting path between each pair of nodes to be representing a specified relationship ($eLabel$). Moreover, the

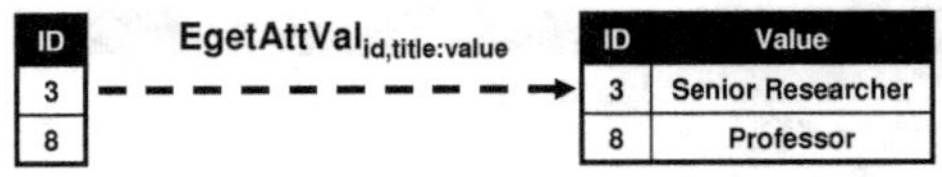

(a) `EgetAttVal` operator: returns the *title* attribute.

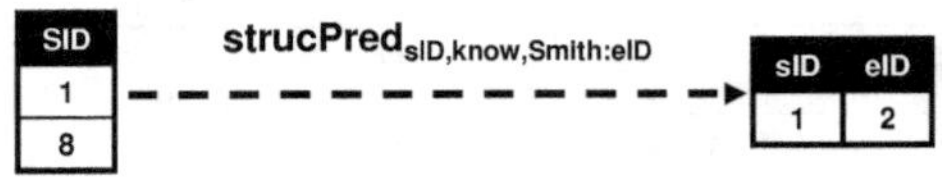

(b) `strucPred` operator: returns vertices having *know* edge to vertex *Smith*.

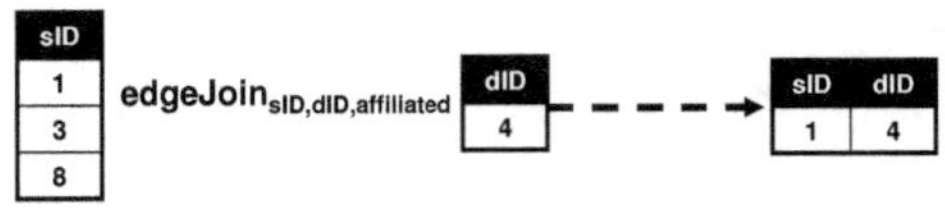

(c) `edgeJoin` operator: returns vertex pairs connected by *affiliated* edge.

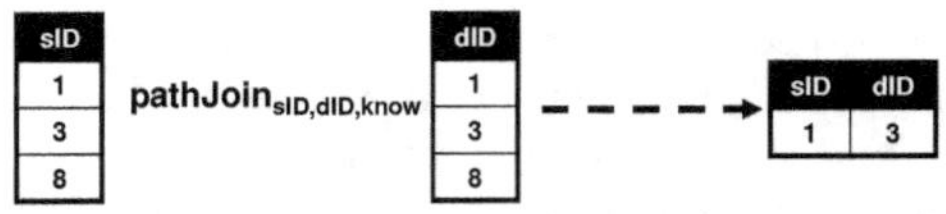

(d) `pathJoin` operator: returns vertex pairs connected by path of *know* edges.

Figure 5: Examples of the *G-SPARQL* Operators.

`pathJoin` operator can optionally project the information of the connecting path(s) as follows:

1) It extends the schema of the input relation by an additional column (pID) that represents an assigned identifier for each connecting edge between each pair of nodes. It should be noted that each pair of nodes can be connected with multiple paths. Therefore, each input pair of nodes can have multiple representing tuples that describes the information of the bound paths.

2) It returns another output relation ($pRel$) which describes the information of the resulting paths where each path is described by a sequence of tuples that represent the nodes and edges constituting the path in an orderly manner. The value of a path variable in the query output is represented by a serialization of the ($Label$) information of its associated tuples in this relation according to their ascending ($order$).

Figure 5(d) illustrates an example of the `pathJoin` operator where it receives two sets of graph vertices, (`"John"`, `"Alice"`, `"Smith"`) and (`"John"`, `"Alice"`, `"Smith"`), returns pairs of graph vertices that are connected through a sequence of any length of `know` relationships and projects the information of the resulting connecting paths. The `sPathJoin` operator works in the same way as the `pathJoin` operator with only one difference being that it returns a *single* path that represents the *shortest* connection between each pair of nodes (if exist a connection). The `filterPath` is a binary operator which receives two relations (R and $pRel$) where the column (pID) of the relation (R) represents the path identifiers that have their associated description information represented by the relation ($pRel$). The operator returns the relation (R) where the tuples which have paths (pID) with information ($pRel$) that do not fulfill the condition ($cond$) are filtered out. The ($cond$) parameter represents one of the path filtering conditions which was previously described in Section 3.2. For more examples of the behavior of our algebraic operators, we refer to our technical report [16].

$$\texttt{NgetAttVal}_{nodeID,(attName):value} \Rightarrow \pi_{R.*,attName.value}(R \bowtie_{R.nodeID=attName.ID} attName)$$
$$\texttt{EgetAttVal}_{edgeID,(attName):value} \Rightarrow \pi_{R.*,attName.value}(R \bowtie_{R.edgeID=attName.ID} attName)$$
$$\texttt{getEdgeNodes}_{sID,(eLabel):eID,dID} \Rightarrow \pi_{R.*,eLabel.eID,eLabel.dID}(R \bowtie_{R.sID=eLabel.sID} eLabel)$$
$$\texttt{strucPred}_{sID,(eL),(dNL):eID} \Rightarrow \pi_{R.*,eL.eID}(\sigma_{nodeLabel.Value=dNL}((R \bowtie_{R.sID=eL.SID} eL) \bowtie_{eL.dID=nodeLabel.ID} nodeLabel))$$
$$\texttt{edgeJoin}_{R.sID,S.dID:eID} \Rightarrow \pi_{R.*,S.*,allEdges.eID}((R \bowtie_{R.sID=allEdges.SID} allEdges) \bowtie_{allEdges.dID=S.dID} S)$$
$$\texttt{edgeJoin}_{R.sID,S.dID,(eLabel):eID} \Rightarrow \pi_{R.*,S.*,eLabel.eID}((R \bowtie_{R.sID=eLabel.SID} eLabel) \bowtie_{eLabel.dID=S.dID} S)$$

Figure 6: Relational Representation of *G-SPARQL* Algebraic Operators.

As shown in Table 1, not all of our algebraic operators can be represented by the standard relational operators. Based on our relational representation of the attributed graphs, Figure 6 depicts the mappings for those operators that can be translated into a pattern of standard relational operators. Since the semantics of the operators **getEdgeNodes** and **edgeJoin** can be not restricted by a specified relationship (*eLabel*), compiling these operators using the standard relational operators requires joining the input relation(s) with each of the *relation* tables, separately, and then union all the results. To simplify, we have created a materialized view (**allEdges**) that represents such union of all *relation* tables. For the SQL translation templates of our algebraic operators, we refer to our technical report [16].

$$\frac{\texttt{Map(?var)} \in \texttt{R} \qquad \texttt{Col(?var)} \equiv \texttt{ID}}{\texttt{(?var, @attName, ?var2)} \Rightarrow \begin{array}{l}\texttt{NgetAttVal}_{ID,(attName):value}\texttt{(R)}\\ \texttt{Col(?var2)} \equiv \texttt{value}\end{array}} \quad (\text{OpMap-1})$$

$$\frac{\texttt{Map(?var)} \in \texttt{R} \qquad \texttt{Col(?var)} \equiv \texttt{sID}}{\texttt{(?var, eLabel, dNLabel)} \Rightarrow \texttt{strucPred}_{sID,(eLabel),(dNLabel)}\texttt{(R)}} \quad (\text{OpMap-2})$$

$$\frac{\begin{array}{c}\texttt{(?E, predicate, object)} \in \texttt{Triple(q)}\\ \texttt{Map(?var)} \in \texttt{R} \qquad \texttt{Col(?var)} \equiv \texttt{sID}\\ \texttt{Map(?var2)} \in \texttt{S} \qquad \texttt{Col(?var2)} \equiv \texttt{dID}\end{array}}{\texttt{(?var, ?E(eLabel), ?var2)} \Rightarrow \begin{array}{l}\texttt{(R) edgeJoin}_{sID,dID,(eLabel):eID}\texttt{ (S)}\\ \texttt{Col(?E)} \equiv \texttt{eID}\end{array}} \quad (\text{OpMap-3})$$

$$\frac{\begin{array}{c}\texttt{Map(?var)} \in \texttt{R} \qquad \texttt{Col(?var)} \equiv \texttt{sID}\\ \texttt{Map(?var2)} \in \texttt{S} \qquad \texttt{Col(?var2)} \equiv \texttt{dID}\end{array}}{\texttt{(?var, ??P, ?var2)} \Rightarrow \texttt{(R) pathJoin}_{sID,dID}\texttt{ (S)}} \quad (\text{OpMap-4})$$

Figure 7: Example of *G-SPARQL* Operator Mapping Rules.

5.2 Query Compilation

Front-end Compilation. In this step of our compilation process, we start by assigning for each query triple pattern, a mapping onto algebraic operators. Figures 7 illustrates examples of the inference rules for mapping the *G-SPARQL* query triple patterns into our algebraic operators. (the full list of the inference rules are available in our technical report [16]). A sample interpretation of the inference rule OpMap-1 is that it maps a query triple pattern (`?var, @attName, ?var2`) of query q into the algebraic operator ($\texttt{NgetAttVal}_{ID,(attName):value}$) where the variable `?var2` is bound to the column `value` (`Col(?var2)` $\equiv$ `value`) of the output relation from applying the **NgetAttVal** operator *given that* the mapping of the variable `?var` (`Map(?var)`) is bound to the column `ID` as a part of the input relation `R`. Figure 8 illustrates an example algebraic compilation for the following *G-SPARQL* query:

```
SELECT  ?L1 ?L2
WHERE   {?X @label ?L1.  ?Y @label ?L2.
         ?X @age ?age1.  ?Y @age ?age2.
         ?X affiliated UNSW. ?X livesIn Sydney.
         ?Y ?E(affiliated) Microsoft.  ?E @title "Researcher".
         ?X ??P ?Y.
         FILTER(?age1 >= 40).  FILTER(?age2 >= 40)}
```

During this compilation step, a set of query rewriting rules is applied in order to optimize the execution time of the query evaluation. In addition, this compilation step uses three main heuristics to reorder the query triple patterns according to their *restrictiveness* (the more restrictive pattern has higher precedence) in order to optimize the join order for the generated SQL statments based on the following rules. Let `t1, t2` $\in$ `Triple(q)` be two triple patterns of query `q`.

1) `t1` is defined as less restrictive than `t2` (`t1` $\gg$ `t2`) if `t1` contains more number of path variables (`??` or `?*`) than `t2`.

2) `t1` is defined as more restrictive than `t2` (`t1` $\ll$ `t2`) if `t1` contains less number of variables than `t2`.

3) `t1` is defined as more restrictive than `t2` (`t1` $\ll$ `t2`) if `t1` has the same number of variables than `t2` and the number of filter expressions over the variables of `t1` is more than the number of filter expressions over the variables of `t2`.

Back-end Compilation. The second compilation step is specific to our hybrid memory/disk representation of attributed graphs where we start by mapping the operators of the plan to their relational representation, when applicable (Figure 6), then we start optimizing the algebraic plans using a set of rules. These rules includes the traditional rules for relational algebraic optimization (e.g., pushing the selection operators down the plan) in addition to some rules that are specific to the context of our algebraic plans. In particular, the main strategy of our rules is to push the non-standard algebraic operators (with memory-based processing) above all the standard relational operators (that can be pushed inside the relational engine) in order to delay their execution (which is the most expensive due to its recursive nature) to be performed after executing all data access and *filtering* operations that are represented by the standard relational operators. At the execution level, the basic strategy of our query processing mechanism is to push those parts of query processing that can be performed independently into the underlying RDBMS by issuing SQL statements [9]. In particular, our execution split mechanism makes use of the following two main heuristics:

1) Relational databases are very efficient for executing queries that represent structural predicates or value-based predicates on the graph attributes (vertices or edges) due to its powerful indexing mechanisms and its sophisticated query optimizers. In addition, relational databases are very efficient on finding the most efficient physical execution plan including considering different possible variants such as different join implementations and different join orderings.

2) Relational databases are inefficient for executing queries with operators of a recursive nature (e.g., path patterns). Main memory algorithms are much faster for evaluating such types of operators which require heavy traversal operations over the graph topology.

As shown in Figure 8, our algebraic plans come in a DAG shape. Therefore, we perform the translation of these plans into SQL queries by traversing the algebraic plan in a bottom-up fashion (starting from the leaves and then climb the different paths back to the root) using a set of defined pattern-based translation rules [9]. This climbing process for each path stops if it hits one of the operators that does not have

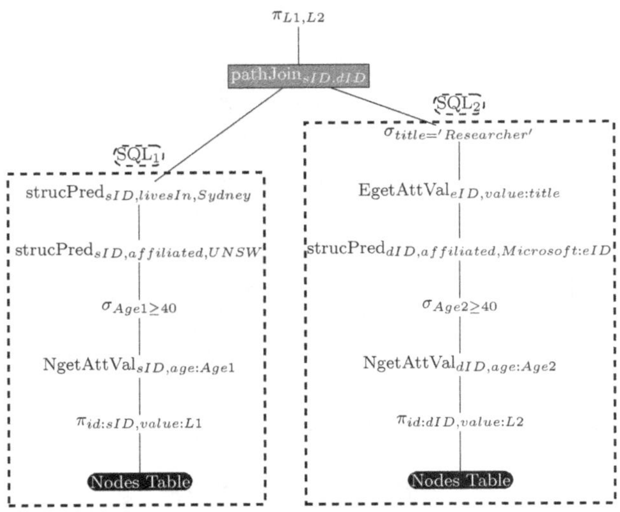

Figure 8: Front-end compilation of a G-SPARQL query into an algebraic plan.

a standard relational representation for its semantics or if it reaches the root. Each generated SQL query is tempting to simply then rely on the underlying relational backends for the physical optimization and processing. For example, in Figure 8, all operators can be translated into standard relational operators except of the `pathJoin` operator (filled with gray color). In this example, as indicated by dashed rectangles in the figure, two SQL queries are generated (SQL_1 and SQL_2) where the results of these queries are then passed for further memory-based processing using the `pathJoin` operator and the following operators in the plan.

The main implementation of our query evaluation engine relies on index-free main memory algorithms for evaluating reachability and shortest path operators [2]. However, our algebraic compilation approach remains agnostic to the physical execution of its logical operator and can make use of any available indexing information for accelerating the query evaluation process of the different types of queries taking into consideration the trade-off of building and maintaining their indices in addition to their main memory consumption.

6. EXPERIMENTAL EVALUATION

Implementation: We implemented a native pointer-based memory representation of the graph topology in addition to the Dijkstra and BFS algorithms using C++. We used IBM DB2 RDBMS for storage, indexing and performing all SQL queries. In order to measure the relative effectiveness of our query split execution mechanism, we compared the performance results of our approach with the performance of the native graph database system, Neo4j (version 1.5 GA). Neo4j is an open source project which is recognized as one of the foremost graph database systems. According to the Neo4j website, "*Neo4j is a disk-based, native storage manager completely optimized for storing graph structures for maximum performance and scalability*". It has an API that is easy to use and provides powerful traversal framework that can implement all queries which can be expressed by *G-SPARQL*. Neo4j uses Apache Lucene for indexing the graph attributes. We conducted our experiments on a PC with 3.2 GHz Intel Xeon processors, 8 GB of main memory storage and 500 GB of SCSI secondary storage. It should be noted

	Vertices	Edges	Attribute Values	Topology Information
Small	126,137	297,960	610,302	9%
Medium	242,074	761,558	1,687,465	11%
Large	825,433	3,680,156	7,336,899	12%

Table 2: Characteristics of real datasets.

that because of the expressiveness of our language, we were unable to consider either the traditional RDF query processors [12, 7] (they do not support path patterns, reachability or shortest path queries) or traditional structural graph indexing and querying techniques [4, 8, 20, 19, 21] (each of them supports only one specific type of graph queries and do not consider querying the attributes of the graph vertices or edges) as options for our performance comparison.

Dataset: We used the ACM digital library dataset (which includes the information of all ACM publications till September 2011) to construct the attributed graph. The graph vertices represent 8 different types of entities (e.g., *author*, *article*, *conference*), 12 different types of relationships between the graph entities (e.g., *authorOf*, *citedBy*, *partOfIsuue*), and a total of 76 unique attributes, of which 62 attributes are describing the graph vertices and 14 attributes are describing the graph edges. In our experiments, we used 3 scaling sizes of graph subsets (small, medium and large) in order to test the scalability of our approach. Table 2 lists the characteristics of the three sets. For more experiments on synthetic graphs, we refer to our technical report [16].

Query Workload: Our query workload consists of 12 query templates (Figure 9) where we used random literal values to generate different query instances. The queries are designed to cover the different types of the triple patterns that are supported by *G-SPARQL*. We refer to our technical report [16] for detailed descriptions and the algebraic plans of our query templates. As we have previously described, the efficiency of execution for any graph query using Neo4j is programmer-dependent and each query template can have different ways of implementations using Neo4j APIs. In our experiments, for each query template, we created two associated Neo4j implementations. The first implementation is an optimized version that considers a pre-known knowledge about the result size of each query step (triple pattern) while the second version is a non-optimized one that does not consider this knowledge. Each query template is instantiated 20 times where the data values are generated randomly.

Query Evaluation Times: The average query evaluation times for the 20 instances of each of the 12 query templates are shown in Figure 10 for the small (Figure 10(a)), medium (Figure 10(b)) and large (Figure 10(c)) graphs. As has been well recognized in conventional query processing, a good query plan is a crucial factor in improving the query performance by orders of magnitude. The results of the experiments show that our approach is on average 3 times faster than the Neo4j non-optimized implementations of the query workload on the small subset, 4 times faster on the medium subset and 5 times faster on the large subset of the experimental graph. In particular, our approach outperforms the Neo4j non-optimized implementations in each of the defined query templates. The results of the experiments also show that the average query evaluation times of our approach is 17% faster than the Neo4j optimized implementations on the small subset, 22% faster on the medium subset and 28% faster on the large experimental graph. The

Q1	`SELECT ?Name1 ?Name2 WHERE {?X @name ?Name1. ?Y @name ?Name2. ?X @prolific "High". ?Y @prolific "High". ?X @affilation "%affiliation1%". ?Y @affilation "%affiliation2%". ?X ?E(co-author) ?Y. ?E @noPapers ?NO. FILTER (?NO >= 2).}`
Q2	`SELECT ?Name1 ?Name2 WHERE {?X @name ?Name1. ?Y @name ?Name2. ?X @prolific "High". ?Y @prolific "High". ?X @affilation "%affiliation1%". ?Y @affilation "%affiliation2%". ?X co-author+ ?Y.}`
Q3	`SELECT ?Name1 ?Name2 ??P WHERE {?X @name ?Name1. ?Y @name ?Name2. ?X @prolific "High". ?Y @prolific "High". ?X @affilation "%affiliation1%". ?Y @affilation "%affiliation2%". ?X ??P(co-author) ?Y.}`
Q4	`SELECT ?Name1 ?Name2 ?*P WHERE {X @name ?Name1. Y @name ?Name2. ?X @prolific "High". ?Y @prolific "High". X @affilation "%affiliation1%". Y @affilation "%affiliation2%". ?X ?*P(co-author) ?Y.}`
Q5	`SELECT ?Name1 ?Name2 ??P WHERE {X @name ?Name1. Y @name ?Name2. ?X @prolific "High". ?Y @prolific "High". X @affilation "%affiliation1%". Y @affilation "%affiliation2%". ?X ??P ?Y.}`
Q6	`SELECT ?Name1 ?Name2 ??P WHERE {?X @name ?Name1. ?Y @name ?Name2. ?X @prolific "High". ?Y @prolific "High". ?X @affilation "%affiliation1%". ?Y @affilation "%affiliation2%". ?X ??P(co-author) ?Y. FilterPath(Length(??P, <= 3)).}`
Q7	`SELECT ?Name1 ?Name2 ??P WHERE {?X @name ?Name1. ?Y @name ?Name2. ?X @prolific "High". ?Y @prolific "High". ?X @affilation "%affiliation1%". ?Y @affilation "%affiliation2%". ?X ??P(co-author) ?Y. FilterPath(AllNodes(??P, @prolific "High")).}`
Q8	`SELECT ?Name ?Title ?Year WHERE {?X @name ?Name. ?X @prolific "High". ?X ?E(authorOf) ?Paper. ?E @seqNo 1. ?Paper @title ?Title. ?Paper @keyword "%keyword%". ?Paper partOf ?Issue. ?Issue @year ?Year. ?Issue issueOf ?Journal. ?Journal @code "%code%".}`
Q9	`SELECT ?Title ?Name1 ?Name2 ?Name3 WHERE {?P @title Title. ?P @keyword "%keyword%". ?P citedBy ?P1. ?P citedBy ?P2. ?P citedBy ?P3. Au1 authorOf ?P1. ?Au2 authorOf ?P2. ?Au3 authorOf ?P3. ?AU1 @prolific "High". ?AU2 @prolific "High". ?AU3 @prolific "High". ?Au1 @name ?Name1. ?Au2 @name ?Name2. ?Au3 @name ?Name3.}`
Q10	`SELECT ?T1 ?T2 WHERE {?X @name ="%name%". ?X authorOf ?Paper1. ?Paper1 @Title ?T1. ?Paper2 @Title ?T2. ?Paper1 @Keyword "%keyword%". ?Paper2 @Keyword "%keyword%". ?Paper1 ??P(citedBy) ?Paper2. FilterPath(Length(??P, <= 2)).}`
Q11	`SELECT ?T1 ?T2 WHERE {?X @name ="%name%". ?X authorOf ?Paper1. ?Paper1 @Title ?T1. ?Paper2 @Title ?T2. ?Paper1 @Keyword "%keyword%". ?Paper2 @Keyword "%keyword%". ?Paper1 ??P(citedBy) ?Paper2. FilterPath(Length(??P, <= 4)). FilterPath(AllEdges(??P, @source "Ext")).}`
Q12	`SELECT ?Name WHERE {?X @name ?Name. ?Y @name "%name1%". ?Z @name "%name2%". ?X ??E1(co-author) ?Y. ?X ??E2(co-author) ?Z. FilterPath(Length(??E1, <= 2)). FilterPath(Length(??E2, <= 2)). FilterPath(AllEdges(??E1, @noPapers >2)).}`

Figure 9: Query templates of our experimental workload.

Neo4j optimized implementations outperforms our approach in 2 of the 12 query templates (Q11 and Q12) while our approach performs better in the rest of the queries.

In general, the well-known maturity of the indexing and built-in optimization techniques of physical query evaluation (e.g., join algorithms) provided by the underlying RDBMs play the main role of outperforming Neo4j optimized implementations. For example, the performance of relational partitioned B-tree indices outperforms the performance of the indexing service of Neo4j that uses Lucene which is more optimized for full-text indexing rather than traditional data retrieval queries. To better understand the reasons for the differences in performance between our approach and optimized Neo4j implementations, we look at the performance differences for each query. Q1, Q8 and Q9 are pattern matching queries that involve structural predicates in addition to value-based predicates on the attributes of the graph nodes and edges. In our approach, the whole executions of these queries can be pushed inside the underlying RDBMS. Relational engine has shown to be more efficient than Neo4j as a native graph engine in performing such pattern matching queries that purely relies on the efficiency of the underlying physical execution properties of the engine, mainly physical indices and join algorithms, and do not involve any recursive operations. The scalability feature of the relational database engine is also shown by the increasing percentage of improvement for these queries over Neo4j with the increasing size of the underlying graph size. For example, for Q8, the relational execution is 3.3 times faster than the optimized Neo4j execution for the small subset of the experimental graph graph while it is 4.2 times faster on the large subset of the experimental graph.

Q2, Q3, Q4, Q5, Q6 and Q7 are queries that involve recursive join operations between two filtered set of vertices. In particular, all of these queries are seeking for two sets of authors where each set is filtered based on the `prolific` and `affiliation` attributes. Q2 verifies for each pair of vertices (one from each filtered set) whether they are connected by a sequence of edges of any length where all edges of the connecting path represent the `co-author` relationship. Assuming the numbers of vertices in the first and second sets are equal to M and N respectively, then the number of verification operations (represented by the `pathJoin` operator) equals $M * N$. Q3 is similar to Q2 but it returns additional information about the connecting paths between each pair of vertices ($\texttt{pathJoin}_{sID,dID,co-author:eID}$). That is why Q3 is slightly more expensive than Q2. Q4 is again similar to Q3. However, it only returns the information of the *shortest path* between each pair of vertices ($\texttt{sPathJoin}_{sID,dID,co-author:eID}$). Evaluating the *shortest path* over the graph topology is also slightly more expensive than the general reachability verification (Q2 and Q3). Q5 represents a more expensive variant of Q2 that generalizes the reachability verification test for each pair of vertices so that they can be connected by a sequence of edges of any length where each edge in the connecting path can represent any relationship ($\texttt{pathJoin}_{sID,dID:eID}$). Q6 and Q7 extend Q3 by adding filtering conditions on the connecting paths between each pair of vertices (the `filterPath` operator). In particular, Q6 filters out the paths with more than 3 edges. Q7 verifies that the `author` vertices for each of the resulting paths between each pair of vertices are highly `prolific`. Our hybrid approach outperforms the optimized Neo4j implementations for all of these queries by splitting the execution of the query plans between the underlying relational engine and the available topology information in the main memory. In particular, it leverages the efficiency of the relational engine for retrieving each set of vertices, utilizes memory topology information for fast execution of the required traversal operations and avoids loading unnecessary information that are not involved in evaluated queries.

In our approach, the execution of the path filtering condi-

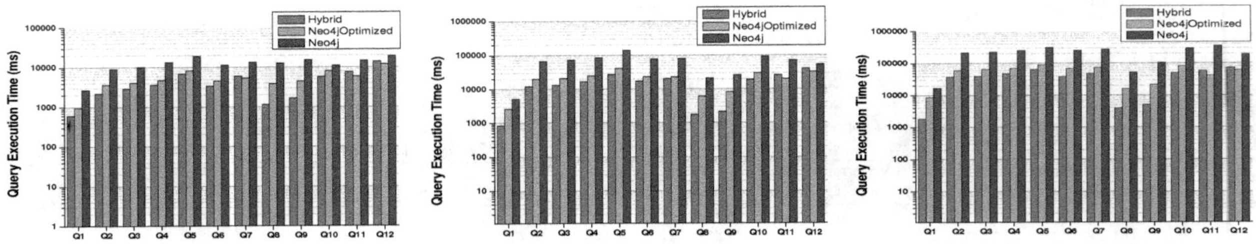

(a) Small Graph Size (b) Medium Graph Size (c) Large Graph Size

Figure 10: Average query evaluation times of real datasets.

tion of Q7 is an expensive operation as it can only be applied in a post-processing step after determining all the connecting paths between each pair of vertices. This post-processing step needs to issue an SQL statement that retrieves the values of the `prolific` attributes for all nodes of the connecting paths as they are not available in the topology information which are loaded onto the main memory and then filters out all paths that contains any node that does not satisfy the filtering condition over the retrieved attribute values. On the contrary, the post-processing execution of the path filtering condition of Q6 (based on path length) is rather cheap as it does not need to retrieve any data from the underlying database during the memory-based processing.

Q10 and Q11 are another two queries that involve recursive join operations between two filtered set of vertices. In particular, Q10 is seeking for two sets of papers where both sets are filtered based on the same value-based predicate on the `keyword` attribute and one of the sets is further filtered to only those papers that are authored by a specific author. Q10 verifies for each pair of vertices whether they are connected by a path with a length that is less than or equal to 4 edges where all edges represent the `citedBy` relationship. Q11 extends Q10 by further filtering the connecting paths to only those paths where all of their edges are described as `external` on their `source` attribute. While our approach is faster on evaluating Q10, Neo4j is faster for evaluating Q11. The main reason behind this is the expensive cost of retrieving the `external` attribute of the edges of the connecting paths for further filtering them. Optimized Neo4j implementation outperforms our approach in Q12 as well where it needs to ensure that all edges of the connecting paths are described by `noPapers` greater than 2. One approach to overcome this limitation in our approach is to load onto the main memory, the frequently used attributes in path filtering conditions in addition to the graph topology. For example, for our query workload by loading the edge attributes `source` and `noPapers`, the performance of our approach for queries Q11 and Q12 is improved by an average of 31% and thus we can outperform the Neo4j optimized implementation. Obviously, there is a trade-off between the memory consumption and the performance that can be gained on evaluating the path filtering conditions by loading more attributes of the graph nodes/edges. However, determining which attributes should be loaded onto the memory would require pre-known knowledge about the characteristics of the query workloads.

7. CONCLUSIONS

We presented *G-SPARQL*, a novel language for querying large attributed graphs. The language supports querying structural graph patterns where filtering conditions can be specified on the attributes of the graph vertices/edges. In addition, it supports various forms for querying and conditionally filtering path patterns. We presented an efficient hybrid Memory/Disk graph representation where only the topology of the graph is maintained in memory while the data of the graph are stored in a relational database. We developed an algebraic compilation technique for our execution engine with a split of execution mechanism for the generated query plans. Experimental studies on real graphs validated the efficiency and scalability of our approach.

8. REFERENCES

[1] J. Cheng and J. Yu. On-line exact shortest distance query processing. In *EDBT*, 2009.

[2] T. Cormen, R. Rivest, C. Leiserson, and C. Stein. *Introduction to Algorithms*. The MIT Press, third edition, 2009.

[3] D. Abadi et al. Scalable Semantic Web Data Management Using Vertical Partitioning. In *VLDB*, 2007.

[4] E. Cohen et al. Reachability and Distance Queries via 2-Hop Labels. *SIAM J. Comput.*, 32(5), 2003.

[5] H. Tong et al. Fast best-effort pattern matching in large attributed graphs. In *KDD*, 2007.

[6] L. Zou et al. Answering pattern match queries in large graph databases via graph embedding. *VLDB J.*, 32(5), 2011.

[7] L. Zou et al. gStore: Answering SPARQL Queries via Subgraph Matching. *PVLDB*, 4(8), 2011.

[8] R. Jin et al. 3-HOP: a high-compression indexing scheme for reachability query. In *SIGMOD*, 2009.

[9] T. Grust, M. Mayr, J. Rittinger, S. Sakr, and J. Teubner. A SQL: 1999 code generator for the pathfinder XQuery compiler. In *SIGMOD*, 2007.

[10] T. Grust, M. Mayr, J. Rittinger, and T. Schreiber. FERRY: database-supported program execution. In *SIGMOD*, 2009.

[11] T. Grust, S. Sakr, and J. Teubner. XQuery on SQL Hosts. In *VLDB*, 2004.

[12] T. Neumann and G. Weikum. RDF-3X: a RISC-style engine for RDF. *PVLDB*, 1(1), 2008.

[13] J. Pérez, M. Arenas, and C. Gutierrez. Semantics and complexity of SPARQL. *TODS*, 34(3), 2009.

[14] E. Prud'hommeaux and A. Seaborne. SPARQL Query Language for RDF, W3C Recommendation.

[15] S. Sakr. GraphREL: A Decomposition-Based and Selectivity-Aware Relational Framework for Processing Sub-graph Queries. In *DASFAA*, 2009.

[16] S. Sakr, S. Elnikety, and Y. He. G-SPARQL: A Hybrid Query Engine for Querying Large Attributed Graphs. Technical Report MSR-TR-2011-138, Microsoft Research. http://research.microsoft.com/apps/pubs/?id=157417.

[17] M. Sarwat, S. Elnikety, Y. He, and G. Kliot. Horton: Online Query Execution Engine For Large Distributed Graphs . In *ICDE*, 2011.

[18] F. Wei. TEDI: efficient shortest path query answering on graphs. In *SIGMOD*, 2010.

[19] X. Yan, P. Yu, and J. Han. Graph indexing: a frequent structure-based approach. In *SIGMOD*, 2004.

[20] S. Zhang, M. Hu, and J. Yang. TreePi: A Novel Graph Indexing Method. In *ICDE*, 2007.

[21] P. Zhao and J. Han. On Graph Query Optimization in Large Networks. *PVLDB*, 3(1), 2010.

A Graph-Based Approach for Ontology Population with Named Entities

Wei Shen[1], Jianyong Wang[1], Ping Luo[2], Min Wang[2]
[1]Department of Computer Science and Technology, Tsinghua University, Beijing, China
[2]HP Labs China, Beijing, China
[1]chen-wei09@mails.tsinghua.edu.cn, jianyong@tsinghua.edu.cn
[2]{ping.luo, min.wang6}@hp.com

ABSTRACT

Automatically populating ontology with named entities extracted from the unstructured text has become a key issue for Semantic Web and knowledge management techniques. This issue naturally consists of two subtasks: (1) for the entity mention whose mapping entity does not exist in the ontology, attach it to the right category in the ontology (i.e., fine-grained named entity classification), and (2) for the entity mention whose mapping entity is contained in the ontology, link it with its mapping real world entity in the ontology (i.e., entity linking). Previous studies only focus on one of the two subtasks and cannot solve this task of populating ontology with named entities integrally. This paper proposes APOLLO, a grAph-based aPproach for pOpuLating ontoLOgy with named entities. APOLLO leverages the rich semantic knowledge embedded in the Wikipedia to resolve this task via random walks on graphs. Meanwhile, APOLLO can be directly applied to either of the two subtasks with minimal revision. We have conducted a thorough experimental study to evaluate the performance of APOLLO. The experimental results show that APOLLO achieves significant accuracy improvement for the task of ontology population with named entities, and outperforms the baseline methods for both subtasks.

Categories and Subject Descriptors

H.3.3 [**Information Systems**]: Information Storage and Retrieval—*Information Search and Retrieval*

General Terms

Algorithms, Experimentation

Keywords

Ontology population, Named entity classification, Entity linking, Label propagation

CIKM'12, October 29–November 2, 2012, Maui, HI, USA.

1. INTRODUCTION

The trend to advance the traditional keyword-based search to the semantic entity-based search has attracted a lot of attention in recent years. A critical step to achieve this goal is to construct a comprehensive machine-understanding ontology about the world's entities, their semantic categories and their mutual relationships. Despite there exist some ontologies such as WordNet [11] which are constructed manually, they have limited coverage in various regions. Furthermore, as world evolves, new facts come into existence and are digitally expressed on the Web. Therefore, populating and enriching the existing ontology with the newly extracted facts become more and more important. Manually populating ontology requires substantial human effort and is usually time consuming. This has motivated the research on the automatic ontology population techniques.

The development of the information extraction techniques makes the automatic ontology population techniques possible. Recently, information extraction from large document collections has received a lot of attention, and a variety of information extraction problems have been considered such as named entity recognition [17, 10], named entity classification [12, 21] and relation extraction [3, 25]. Integrating the newly extracted knowledge derived from the information extraction systems with the existing ontology requires to deal with the task of populating ontology with named entities.

Ontology population with named entities is the task to locate the right place of the detected named entity in the ontology. Given a named entity mention detected from the unstructured text, if the mapping entity of the entity mention is not contained in the ontology, we should find the right category node to which the entity mention should be attached in the ontology, which is known as the task of fine-grained named entity classification. Otherwise, if the mapping entity of the entity mention exists in the ontology, the aim of this task is to link this detected entity mention with its corresponding real world entity in the ontology, which is known as the entity linking task. For example, we assume that the ontology contains the entity of NBA player named "Michael Jordan", and there is only one entity named "Michael Jordan" in the ontology. In the text "Professor Michael Jordan has a talk on machine learning.", the mapping entity of the entity mention "Michael Jordan" is the Berkeley professor whose name is also "Michael Jordan". Since the ontology does not contain such an entity, we should perform the fine-grained named entity classification task and obtain the category (i.e., *Professor*) to which the mapping entity of this entity mention belongs. Then we create a new node for this entity mention "Michael Jordan" and attach this node to the category node *Professor* in the ontology. While for the entity mention appearing in the text "Michael Jordan wins NBA champion.", we should map this mention of "Michael Jordan" to the entity of NBA player existing in the ontology, which is called the entity linking task.

Ontology population with named entities has received much attention recently, and several solutions to this task have been proposed in research [15, 14, 28, 6, 8, 7]. However, these state-of-the-art systems only focus on one of the two subtasks (i.e., fine-grained named entity classification and entity linking). It calls for a unified framework to resolve the task of populating ontology with named entities integrally.

The ontology-based fine-grained named entity classification problem has been addressed by many researchers [15, 14, 28, 6, 13]. These systems classify the named entities detected from the text into a large number of categories specified by an ontology or a multi-level taxonomy. In most of these studies, they suppose that the entity disambiguation/linking process has been completed, and all identified entity mentions have been mapped to their unique representations. Besides, some of them consider that the entity mentions identified in the data set are not ambiguous, and thus ignore the ambiguity problem of the named entity. However, in realistic scenario, the mention form of the named entity is highly ambiguous. For example, the entity mention of "Michael Jordan" can refer to the famous basketball player, the computer science professor or some other persons. Henceforth, in APOLLO, we do not ignore the ambiguity problem of the named entity, and resolve the task of populating ontology with named entities integrally.

The solutions proposed in [4, 7, 8, 24] address the entity linking task, and they all aim to link the textual mention form of the named entity with the corresponding real world entity in the existing ontology. If the matching entity of certain entity mention does not exist in the ontology, they just return NIL (denoting an unlinkable entity mention) for this mention form, and cannot attach this unlinkable entity mention to the right category in the ontology.

In this paper, we propose APOLLO, a graph-based weakly supervised framework to resolve the task of automatic ontology population with named entities integrally. Meanwhile, our proposed framework APOLLO can be directly applied to either of the two subtasks with minimal revision. APOLLO is based on the assumption that if the contexts where two named entities appear are semantically similar, they are likely to belong to the same category, which is the extension of the distributional hypothesis [16]. The only training data for APOLLO is an initial ontology, in which there are a list of labeled named entities whose categories are known to us beforehand. Therefore, APOLLO is weakly supervised and needs minimal human involvements. Given each entity mention/named entity and its associated document context, we firstly recognize all the Wikipedia concepts appearing in this context, and we consider the set of these detected Wikipedia concepts as the *semantic signature* of this entity mention/named entity. Then we construct a graph consisting of the nodes coming from all the entity mentions which need to be populated into the ontology, the named entities contained in the ontology, and the Wikipedia concepts existing in their corresponding *semantic signatures*. We weight the edges between the Wikipedia concept nodes in the graph, by leveraging the rich semantic knowledge embedded in the link structure of the Wikipedia articles. The nodes of the named entities contained in the ontology are annotated with their category labels, and other unlabeled entity mention nodes are required to be classified. Subsequently, the Adsorption label propagation algorithm [2] is applied to this constructed graph to produce a probability distribution over categories for each unlabeled entity mention node, based on the rich graph structure. Finally, for each entity mention, we have to validate whether there exists a named entity in the ontology we could link this entity mention with. Otherwise, we attach this entity mention to the category that has the largest distribution. It is noted that a very preliminary two-page version of this paper [22] has been published in WWW'12. In this paper, we make further enhancements, and give a complete and in-depth description of our proposed APOLLO framework.

To summarize, we make the following contributions.

- We propose APOLLO, a novel graph-based unified framework which leverages the rich semantic information derived from Wikipedia to deal with the task of ontology population with named entities integrally. Previous studies only focus on one of the two subtasks. Moreover, APOLLO can be directly applied to either of the two subtasks with minimal revision.
- APOLLO is a weakly supervised framework that requires minimal human involvements. Moreover, APOLLO is open-domain as it is independent of the underlying ontology.
- To validate the effectiveness of APOLLO, we conducted a thorough experimental study, and the experimental results demonstrate that APOLLO achieves a significant improvement in accuracy for the task of ontology population with named entities.
- We extensively evaluated the performance of APOLLO over both subtasks, and the experimental results show that APOLLO outperforms the baseline methods for both subtasks.

The remainder of this paper is organized as follows. Section 2 formulates the problem and presents the APOLLO framework. Next, the three modules of APOLLO (i.e., Graph Creation, Label Propagation and Linking Validation) are respectively introduced in Section 3, Section 4 and Section 5. Section 6 presents our experiments and Section 7 discusses the related work. We conclude this paper in Section 8.

2. ONTOLOGY POPULATION WITH NAMED ENTITIES

In this section, we will study the problem of automatically populating ontology with named entities extracted from the large text corpus. For this purpose, we will firstly give some notations and formulate the problem of ontology population with named entities in Section 2.1. Subsequently, the overall framework of APOLLO will be introduced in Section 2.2.

2.1 Notations and Problem Formulation

The only input of our framework APOLLO is a collection of documents and an initial ontology. Let D be the collection of the input documents and Ω be the initial ontology.

Let ζ be the set of all entity mentions recognized from the document set D, and each entity mention $s \in \zeta$ needs to be populated into the ontology Ω. Suppose that there are a list of labeled named entities whose categories are known within the initial ontology Ω. Let N_Ω denote the set of all named entities contained in the ontology Ω, and C_Ω be the set of all categories in the taxonomy of Ω.

Entity mention and mapping entity: An entity mention $s \in \zeta$ is a token sequence in the text document which refers to some named entity. Let n_s denote the corresponding real world named entity the entity mention s refers to. We should differentiate between the entity itself and its various entity mentions. In reality, an entity may have multiple entity mentions. For example, the entity *Hewlett-Packard* has its abbreviation "HP". On the contrary, one entity mention may also refer to several different real world entities. For instance, the entity mention of "Michael Jordan" can refer to the famous basketball player, the computer science professor or some other persons. Henceforth, the mapping entity n_s of the entity mention s depends on the context where the entity mention s occurs.

Document context: We define the document context η_s of the entity mention $s \in \zeta$ as a window of words around the occurrence of the entity mention s. Assume that the entity mention s of length $|s|$ words appears in a document d at position p. The size-k document context η_s of entity mention s with respect to d is the window $w_{p-k}, \ldots, w_{p-1}, w_{p+|s|}, \ldots, w_{p+|s|+k-1}$ of words around the occurrence of s (w_i represents the word at position i). For instance, the entity mention of "Michael Jordan" occurs in a document containing such a sentence, "In the NBA Final of 1991, Michael Jordan shot 12 free throws." When the size k is set to 5, the size-k document context η_s is "the NBA Final of 1991 shot 12 free throws". On the other hand, for each named entity $n \in N_\Omega$, we define the document context η_n of the named entity n as the description context for n in the ontology. As both the entity mention $s \in \zeta$ and the named entity $n \in N_\Omega$ have document contexts, we use η to denote the document context corresponding to an entity mention or a named entity.

Semantic signature: To capture the semantic information existing in the document context η, we recognize all the Wikipedia concepts γ appearing in η, and consider the set of these detected Wikipedia concepts as the *semantic signature* δ. Here, Wikipedia concept means the concept which has its corresponding descriptive article in Wikipedia, and each Wikipedia concept is represented by the title of its Wikipedia article. For the general textual document, we utilize the open source toolkit Wikipedia-Miner[1] to detect the Wikipedia concepts appearing in the context. The Wikipedia-Miner toolkit takes the general unstructured text as input and uses the machine learning approach to detect the Wikipedia concepts in the input document [20]. For the document context in the example mentioned above, this Wikipedia-Miner toolkit returns two Wikipedia concepts, i.e., *NBA Final* and *Free throw*. Therefore, it can be seen that these detected Wikipedia concepts are highly semantically related to the NBA player *Michael Jordan*, and we can leverage this semantic information contained in this *semantic signature* to populate this entity mention "Michael Jordan" into the ontology Ω effectively. As we know, the document from the Wikipedia has its special layout to organize its content, i.e., *Wiki markup*[2]. The references to other Wikipedia concepts in the Wikipedia document are within pairs of double square brackets. Henceforth, for a Wikipedia document, we can identify the Wikipedia concepts appearing in it directly and accurately by leveraging the characteristic of *Wiki markup*.

Now we can formulate the problem of ontology population with named entities.

Ontology population with named entities: *Given a collection of documents D, an initial ontology Ω and a set of entity mentions ζ detected from D, the task of ontology population with named entities is to locate the right place for each entity mention $s \in \zeta$ in the ontology Ω. For each $s \in \zeta$, if the mapping entity $n_s \notin N_\Omega$, the entity mention s has to be attached to the proper category $c_s \in C_\Omega$; If the mapping entity $n_s \in N_\Omega$, the goal of this task is to return this mapping entity n_s.*

2.2 The APOLLO framework

Based on the problem definition, we propose a framework called APOLLO, to address the task of ontology population with named entities using three modules as follows:

- **Graph Creation**
  To represent all the available information about the relationships between the entity mentions ζ and the named entities N_Ω in a unified way, this module constructs a graph G consisting of the nodes which come from all the entity mentions ζ, the named entities N_Ω and the Wikipedia concepts in their *semantic signatures* δ. Meanwhile, this module embeds the rich semantic information derived from the link structure of the Wikipedia articles into the graph, in the form of weighting the edges between these Wikipedia concept nodes.

- **Label Propagation**
  In this module, we assign each entity mention $s \in \zeta$ to the proper category $c_s \in C_\Omega$ via graph label propagation. Each named entity node $n \in N_\Omega$ is annotated with its corresponding category label in the graph G, and other unlabeled entity mention nodes $s \in \zeta$ are required to be classified. We then present the Adsorption label propagation algorithm [2], which is applied to the graph G to ultimately produce the predicted category $c_s \in C_\Omega$ for each unlabeled entity mention node $s \in \zeta$, based on the rich graph structure.

- **Linking Validation**
  If the mapping entity n_s of the entity mention $s \in \zeta$ exists in the ontology Ω, we have to link this entity mention s with its mapping entity n_s, i.e., the entity linking task. Otherwise, we return c_s as the category for entity mention s. Henceforth, we add this module to validate whether its mapping entity $n_s \in N_\Omega$.

In the following sections, we will introduce those three modules in details.

3. GRAPH CREATION

To represent all the available information in a unified form, we need a representation capable of encoding efficiently all the complicated relationships between the entity

[1]http://wikipedia-miner.cms.waikato.ac.nz/

[2]http://en.wikipedia.org/wiki/Wiki_markup

mentions ζ and the named entities N_Ω. To achieve this goal, we select the graph as the representation, since the graph can encode different types of objects (i.e., entity mentions, named entities and Wikipedia concepts) as the nodes in the graph, and represent various relationships between these objects as the edges between these nodes. Furthermore, the graph makes the potential label propagation paths explicit, and the label information can be propagated along these connecting paths from the labeled named entity nodes to the unlabeled entity mention nodes. For example, if the *semantic signatures* of the entity mention "Michael Jordan" and the named entity *Yao Ming* both contain the Wikipedia concept *NBA Final*, then this can be treated as an evidence that this entity mention "Michael Jordan" may have the same category as the named entity *Yao Ming*. Henceforth, the path connecting the two nodes (i.e., "Michael Jordan" and *Yao Ming*) via the Wikipedia concept node (i.e., *NBA Final*) may help to forward the label information of the labeled named entity node *Yao Ming* to the unlabeled entity mention node "Michael Jordan".

Specifically, we construct a single graph $G = (V, E, W)$ to represent all the information available for this task, where V denotes the set of nodes, E is the set of edges and $W : E \rightarrow \mathbf{R}$ is the weight function which gives positive weight for each edge in E. It is noted that we define the graph G as an undirected graph. The node set V consists of the nodes which come from all the entity mentions ζ, the named entities N_Ω and the Wikipedia concepts in their *semantic signatures* δ. Specifically, for each entity mention $s \in \zeta$, we pair it with each Wikipedia concept $\gamma \in \delta_s$ where δ_s denotes the *semantic signature* of s, to create the triple (s, γ, w), and the weight w could be $1/dist(s, \gamma)$ where $dist(s, \gamma)$ is the distance between the positions of s and γ in the context. In the experiment, we set this weight w to 1.0 for the purpose of simplicity. For each triple (s, γ, w), s and γ are added to V and the edge (s, γ) is added to E, with $W(s, \gamma) = w$. And for each named entity $n \in N_\Omega$, we also pair it with each Wikipedia concept $\gamma \in \delta_n$ where δ_n denotes the *semantic signature* of n, to create the triple (n, γ, w), where the weight w could be the degree of importance for γ in the description context of entity n. The degree of importance for γ could be calculated as its average semantic relatedness to all other Wikipedia concepts in δ_n. However, we set this weight w to 1.0 in the experiment for simplicity as well. For each triple (n, γ, w), n and γ are added to V and the edge (n, γ) is added to E, with $W(n, \gamma) = w$. After the triple (s, γ, w) for each entity mention $s \in \zeta$ and the triple (n, γ, w) for each named entity $n \in N_\Omega$ are all added into the graph G, two nodes of the entity mention or the named entity in the graph G are just connected via the Wikipedia concept nodes which co-occur in both of their *semantic signatures*. Therefore, we define the current status of the graph G as G_{co}, denoting that this graph just contains the co-occurrence information between the entity mentions or named entities and the Wikipedia concepts in their *semantic signatures*.

To forward the label information over the graph more effectively, the semantically related Wikipedia concept nodes should be connected by some edges to enrich the information propagation paths. For instance, if the *semantic signature* of the entity mention "Michael Jordan" contains the Wikipedia concept *Free throw*, and the *semantic signature* of the named entity *Yao Ming* contains the Wikipedia concept *Technical foul*, this entity mention "Michael Jordan" is

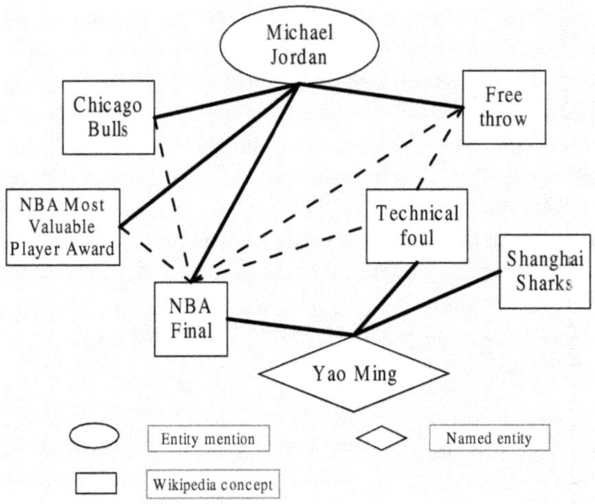

Figure 1: An example of the created graph

expected to have the same category as the named entity *Yao Ming*, since the two Wikipedia concepts are highly semantically related. Thus, we incorporate the semantic relatedness between the Wikipedia concepts into the graph.

Since the link structure of the Wikipedia articles expresses the rich semantic relations, two Wikipedia concepts are considered to be semantically related if there are many Wikipedia concepts that link to both. In order to measure the strength of the semantic relatedness, we adopt the Wikipedia Link-based Measure (WLM) described in [19] to calculate the semantic relatedness between Wikipedia concepts. The WLM modeled from the Normalized Google Distance [5] is based on the Wikipedia's hyperlink structure. Given two Wikipedia concepts u_1 and u_2, we define the semantic relatedness between them as follows:

$$SR(u_1, u_2) = 1 - \frac{log(max(|U_1|, |U_2|)) - log(|U_1 \bigcap U_2|)}{log(|WP|) - log(min(|U_1|, |U_2|))} \quad (1)$$

where U_1 and U_2 are the sets of Wikipedia concepts that link to u_1 and u_2 respectively, and WP is the set of all concepts in Wikipedia. This definition gives higher value to more related concept pair and the value of $SR(u_1, u_2)$ is varied from 0.0 to 1.0. For each pair of Wikipedia concept nodes (γ_1, γ_2) in the graph, if the semantic relatedness $SR(\gamma_1, \gamma_2)$ is greater than some threshold τ, we add an edge (γ_1, γ_2) to E, with $W(\gamma_1, \gamma_2) = SR(\gamma_1, \gamma_2)$.

Figure 1 shows an example of the created graph, in which there are one entity mention node (i.e., "Michael Jordan") and one named entity node (i.e., *Yao Ming*). We assume that the *semantic signature* of the entity mention "Michael Jordan" has four Wikipedia concepts (i.e., *NBA Most Valuable Player Award*, *NBA Final*, *Chicago Bulls* and *Free throw*), while the *semantic signature* of the named entity *Yao Ming* has three Wikipedia concepts (i.e, *NBA Final*, *Technical foul* and *Shanghai Sharks*). In Figure 1, we add a real line between each entity mention/named entity node and each Wikipedia concept node in its *semantic signature*. From Figure 1, we can see that the Wikipedia concept node *NBA Final* is connected with both the entity mention node "Michael Jordan" and the named entity node *Yao Ming*. The dash lines added between the semantically related Wikipedia concept nodes in Figure 1 make the paths connecting the entity mention node "Michael Jordan" and the named entity node *Yao Ming* more abundant, which also demonstrate that the entity mention "Michael Jordan" is likely to have the same category as the named entity *Yao Ming*.

It is noted that in our framework, the semantic relatedness can be computed by other methods such as the type hierarchy based similarity and distributional context similarity introduced in [23] or combination of them, which gives flexibility to APOLLO in an efficient and simple way.

4. LABEL PROPAGATION

The aim of this section is to assign each entity mention $s \in \zeta$ to the proper category $c_s \in C_\Omega$. Firstly, we annotate each named entity node $n \in N_\Omega$ with its corresponding category label in the graph G. In this paper, the named entity category is used as the label for the node, and we assume that each named entity just belongs to one category for the purpose of simplicity. The remaining question is how to propagate the category labels present on the labeled named entity nodes to the unlabeled entity mention nodes in the graph. To solve this problem, we apply the Adsorption label propagation algorithm introduced in [2] to the graph G, to produce the predicted category $c_s \in C_\Omega$ for each unlabeled entity mention node $s \in \zeta$ based on the rich graph structure. Furthermore, the Adsorption algorithm supports incremental updates and can be easily parallelized, which are important for large scale ontology population task. The Adsorption algorithm works on the graph G, and ultimately produces for each unlabeled entity mention node $s \in \zeta$ a label distribution L_s, representing which category labels are appropriate for the unlabeled entity mention s. Our framework APOLLO assumes that named entities that occur in semantically similar contexts belong to the same category. Specifically, we consider that named entities that co-occur with semantically related Wikipedia concepts may have the same category. Therefore, the label propagation algorithm is to forward the category label between the related named entity nodes and entity mention nodes.

The Adsorption algorithm has three different but equivalent interpretations, whose details are introduced in [2]. However, in this paper, we use two interpretations to classify the unlabeled entity mention into the proper category.

Adsorption via Averaging: In this view of the algorithm, the labels are propagated from one node to all its neighbors. Thus each node in the graph has two roles, forwarding labels and collecting labels, and each node keeps track of the history of all labels it receives. For the sake of presentation, we preprocess the original graph G to generate the augmented graph $G' = (V', E', W')$ in the way that, for each labeled named entity node $n \in N_\Omega$, we create a "shadow" node $\tilde{n}$ which has just one neighbor n in G', with an edge $(\tilde{n}, n)$ connecting them with $W'(\tilde{n}, n) = 1$. Let $\tilde{N_\Omega}$ denote the set of "shadow" nodes, $\tilde{N_\Omega} = \{\tilde{n} | n \in N_\Omega\}$, $\tilde{N_\Omega} \subset V'$. Thus, $V' = V \bigcup \tilde{N_\Omega}$, $E' = E \bigcup \{(\tilde{n}, n) | n \in N_\Omega\}$ and $W'(\tilde{n}, n) = 1$ for $n \in N_\Omega$, $W'(v_1, v_2) = W(v_1, v_2)$ for $v_1, v_2 \in V$. Meanwhile, we give the label distribution L_n of each $n \in N_\Omega$ to its "shadow" node $\tilde{n}$ in G', and leave n in graph G' with no label distribution. We define ϕ as the label which represents lack of information about the actual labels. Then, at the beginning of the algorithm, we define the initial label distribution I_v for all $v \in V'$. Specifically, for each "shadow" node $\tilde{n} \in \tilde{N_\Omega}$, $I_{\tilde{n}} = L_n$, and for all other nodes $v \in V', v \notin \tilde{N_\Omega}$, $I_v = L^\phi$ where L^ϕ represents that we have no information about the label distribution of the node v. Subsequently, the algorithm proceeds as follows: for each node $v \in V'$, we compute the label distribution as the weighted average of the label distributions of all its neighbors, i.e., $L_v = \sum_u W'(u, v) L_u$.

Adsorption via Random Walks: This view takes random walks over the edge-reversed version of the graph G' to find the label distribution for each node, which has been proved to be equivalent with the Averaging view, as described in [2]. As the graph G' is undirected, its edge-reversed version of G' is the same as itself. Therefore, to estimate the label distribution L_v for each node $v \in V'$, we perform a random walk on graph G' starting from node v. When the random walk reaches a node t, there are three choices: (a) continue the random walk to the neighbors of t; (b) abandon the random walk; (c) stop the random walk and inject the initial label distribution I_t. We assume the probabilities of these three events are $P_c(t)$, $P_a(t)$ and $P_i(t)$ respectively. Finally, L_v is set to be the expectation of all labels injected from random walks starting from node v.

Algorithm 1 *Adsorption Algorithm*

Input: $G' = (V', E', W')$, $\{I_v | v \in V'\}$.
Output: $\{L_v | v \in V'\}$.

1: **for all** $v \in V'$ **do**
2: $L_v = I_v$
3: **end for**
4: **repeat**
5: **for all** $v \in V'$ **do**
6: $M_v = \Sigma_u W'(u, v) L_u$
7: **end for**
8: Normalize M_v to have unit M_1 norm
9: **for all** $v \in V'$ **do**
10: $L_v = P_c(v) * M_v + P_i(v) * I_v + P_a(v) * L^\phi$
11: **end for**
12: **until** convergence

We combine these two interpretations of the Adsorption algorithm to generate the label distribution L_v for each node $v \in V'$ with Algorithm 1 like [27]. Algorithm 1 firstly initializes the label distributions for all nodes in the graph (line 1-line 3). Then, for each node $v \in V'$, the algorithm iteratively computes the weighted average of the label distributions of all its neighbors (line 5-line 7), and normalizes the computed label distribution M_v to have unit norm (line 8). Next, we use the random walk probabilities to estimate the new label distribution L_v for each node $v \in V'$ (line 9-line 11). Until convergence, each node $v \in V'$ carries a label distribution and outputs L_v as the final results. Convergence occurs if the label distributions of all nodes do not change in a round. However, in practice, we run the algorithm for a fixed number of iterations alternatively. In Algorithm 1, via using the variable M_v in line 10, we compute the label distribution for node v in the ith iteration entirely based on its neighbors' label distributions from the $(i-1)^{th}$ iteration. Therefore, Algorithm 1 has the memoryless property and can be easily parallelized, which is beneficial for large scale ontology population task.

To set the random walk probabilities, we used the following heuristics from [27]. Let $c_v = \frac{log\beta}{log(\beta + exp(H(v)))}$, where $H(v) = -\Sigma_u p_{uv} * log(p_{uv})$ with $p_{uv} = \frac{W'(u,v)}{\sum_{u'} W'(u',v)}$. There-

Table 1: A part of the dictionary DT

K (Surface form)	$K.value$ (Mapping entity)
Yao Ming	*Yao Ming*
Microsoft Corporation	*Microsoft*
Michael Jordan	*Michael Jordan* *Michael I. Jordan* *Michael Jordan (mycologist)* *Michael Jordan (footballer)* ...
Kobe Bryant	*Kobe Bryant*

fore, if node v has many neighbors, c_v is low. In the experiment, we set $\beta = 2$. If node $v \in N_\Omega$, we set $i_v = (1 - c_v) * \sqrt{H(v)}$; otherwise, $i_v = 0$. Then let $z_v = max(c_v + i_v, 1)$. Lastly, we computed the random walk probabilities for each node $v \in V'$ as follows:

$$P_c(v) = c_v/z_v \tag{2}$$

$$P_i(v) = i_v/z_v \tag{3}$$

$$P_a(v) = 1 - P_c(v) - P_i(v) \tag{4}$$

According to Formula 2, we can see that for the high-degree node, the continue probability $P_c(v)$ is low. Thus we can decrease the probability of the random walk running into the unrelated regions in the graph, and make the random walk stay relatively close to its source node.

5. LINKING VALIDATION

For each entity mention $s \in \zeta$, we obtain the label distribution L_s over the categories C_Ω in the Label Propagation module. We consider the category which has the largest distribution in L_s as the predicted category c_s for the entity mention s. According to the task definition of ontology population with named entities, if the mapping entity n_s of the entity mention s exists in the ontology Ω, we have to link this entity mention s with its mapping entity n_s. Henceforth, we add this module to validate whether its mapping entity $n_s \in N_\Omega$.

As stated in Section 2.1, one entity mention may refer to several different real world entities. Thus, given an entity mention s, we firstly retrieve the set of entities that may be referred by this entity mention s, and we denote this set of entities as the candidate entity set CN_s for s. Intuitively, the candidate entities in CN_s should have the name of the entity mention of s. To solve this problem, we need to build a dictionary DT that contains vast amount of information about various mention forms of the named entities, like name variations, abbreviations, confusable names, spelling variations, nicknames, etc. In our paper, the dictionary DT is a <key, value> mapping, where the column of the key K is a list of entity mentions and the column of the mapping value $K.value$ is the set of named entities which are referred by the key K. We construct the dictionary DT by leveraging the following four structures of Wikipedia: **Entity page**, **Redirect page**, **Disambiguation page** and **Hyperlink in Wikipedia article**. The detailed construction method is introduced in [24, 23]. A part of the dictionary DT is shown in Table 1.

For each entity mention $s \in \zeta$, we look up the dictionary DT and search for s in the column of the key K. If a hit is found, i.e., $s \in K$, we add the set of the mapping entities $s.value$ to the candidate entity set CN_s. Suppose that any two entities belonging to the same category do not have the same name. For example, there is only one entity named "Michael Jordan" belonging to the category of NBA basketball player. Therefore, if two entity instances having the same name belong to the same category, we can predict that these two entity instances are the instances of the same entity. Thus, if there exists some entity $n \in CN_s$ whose category is also c_s, the same category as the predicted category for the entity mention s, then we can predict that this entity n is the mapping entity n_s of the entity mention s, and we should link this entity mention s with this entity n; otherwise, we can predict that the mapping entity of the entity mention s does not exist in the ontology Ω, that is to say, $n_s \notin N_\Omega$.

6. EXPERIMENTS

To evaluate the effectiveness of APOLLO, we conducted a thorough experimental study in this section. Firstly, we tested APOLLO over both of the two subtasks, i.e., fine-grained named entity classification task (described in Section 6.1) and the entity linking task (introduced in Section 6.2), respectively. Subsequently, we demonstrate the experimental results of APOLLO for the task of ontology population with named entities in Section 6.3.

6.1 Fine-grained named entity classification task

6.1.1 Experimental setting

To the best of our knowledge, there is no publicly available data set for the fine-grained named entity classification task, and the page for accessing the data set provided in [9] is also unavailable. Thus, we constructed the data set for the fine-grained named entity classification task, from the May 2011 version of Wikipedia and YAGO(1)[3] of version 2009-w10-5. To generate the training and test data, we chose 20 categories which are the subclasses of the *person* category from YAGO. Since the numbers of the instances belonging to different categories vary much, we randomly selected at most 200 instances for each selected category by querying the YAGO ontology, and the created data set DS_{NEC} consists of 3304 distinct instances belonging to the 20 categories in total. Since person names are more ambiguous and the categories of person entities are more diverse, the person name classification is much more challenging. Moreover, the experiments of previous methods [12, 28, 15, 14, 13] are all carried out with person names for the fine-grained named entity classification task.

We compared our framework APOLLO with the classification based approach proposed in [13], which significantly outperforms the single-context rule-based extractor similar to several state-of-the-art techniques for the task of fine-grained named entity classification [13]. We refer to this baseline method as *Ganti-KDD*. The approach *Ganti-KDD* considers two types of features, which are text n-gram feature and the list-membership feature. Since these features are all extracted from the **multi-context**, the union of all contexts across multiple documents within which the entity occurs, they assume that each entity identified in the corpus has been converted to its *canonical* representation. However, in the real application, the general documents corpus cannot satisfy this assumption.

[3]http://www.mpi-inf.mpg.de/yago-naga/yago/

Table 2: Experimental results over the DS_{NEC} data set

Approach \ ρ	0.5		0.6		0.7		0.8		0.9	
	MRR	Accu.	MRR	Accu.	MRR	Accu.	MRR	Accu.	MRR	Accu.
Ganti-KDD	-	0.7036	-	0.6989	-	0.7337	-	0.7247	-	0.7112
APOLLO$_{CO}$	0.7771	0.6915	0.7901	0.7049	0.8135	0.7409	0.7914	0.7201	0.8412	0.7750
APOLLO$_{SR}$	**0.8059**	**0.7223**	**0.8184**	**0.7366**	**0.8399**	**0.7703**	**0.8225**	**0.7489**	**0.8535**	**0.7903**

According to the original experimental setting in [13], we used the support vector machine model, *libsvm*[4], as the underlying classifier. To generate the multi-context features, we employed 3.5 million Wikipedia pages as the document corpus, where each entity in the *Wikitext* has been converted to its *canonical* representation, and this characteristic of the Wikipedia document corpus satisfies the assumption of *Ganti-KDD*. To compute the n-gram features, we extracted all n-grams in the size-4 *document context* for each occurrence of an entity, using the presence/absence of the 10K most frequent n-grams among them as features [13]. For the list-membership features, we used the entire document an entity occurs in as the aggregate context of this entity, using a 10% sample of the entities in the training data for each category as the list corpus [13].

To evaluate the performance of APOLLO over the fine-grained named entity classification task, we just eliminated the Linking Validation module in APOLLO, and let the Label Propagation module output the final label distribution for each test entity. To generate the *semantic signature* for each entity in DS_{NEC}, we used its corresponding entire entity page in Wikipedia as the document context. In the experiment, we set the edge weight between a named entity and each Wikipedia concept in its *semantic signature* to 1.0 for the purpose of simplicity. In this experiment, the threshold τ is experimentally set to 0.34, which yields the best performance. The created graph G_{co} contains 82,833 nodes and 155,450 edges, and after we added edges between the semantically related Wikipedia concept nodes into the graph, the final graph G consists of about 2.5 million edges. We refer to the results of our framework APOLLO applied to the graph G_{co} as APOLLO$_{CO}$, and denote the results of APOLLO applied to G as APOLLO$_{SR}$. In the Label Propagation module, the number of iterations for the Adsorption algorithm was set to 10.

6.1.2 Experimental results

In this subsection, we present the evaluation results of APOLLO for the fine-grained named entity classification task. As the output of our framework is a label distribution, we computed the Mean Reciprocal Rank (MRR) of the test entity with respect to the gold standard target category. In addition, since the baseline method *Ganti-KDD* employs the SVM model which produces the predicted category for each test entity, we used the usual metric of *Accuracy* (Accu.) on the classification results to evaluate the performance of *Ganti-KDD*. Meanwhile, to give a fair comparison, the accuracy of the predicted category which has the largest distribution in the label distribution of each test entity is also computed for APOLLO. To demonstrate the performance of these approaches with different numbers of training entities, we made the parameter ρ denote the proportion of the training entities in the data set DS_{NEC}. To split the data set DS_{NEC} into the training and test data set with respect to ρ, for each selected category in DS_{NEC}, we randomly selected the corresponding number of entities belonging to this category as the training entities, and the remaining entities are regarded as the test entities.

Table 2 shows the experimental results of these approaches over the DS_{NEC} data set under the different settings of the parameter ρ, varying from 0.5 to 0.9. From the results, we can see that the baseline method *Ganti-KDD* and the approach APOLLO$_{CO}$ have the similar accuracy when ρ is set from 0.5 to 0.8. But when ρ equals to 0.9, the accuracy achieved by APOLLO$_{CO}$ is much higher than what can be achieved by *Ganti-KDD*. However, it is noticed that the features of the baseline method *Ganti-KDD* are all extracted from the **multi-context**, the union of all contexts across multiple documents within which the entity occurs, while the approach APOLLO$_{CO}$ only leverages the co-occurrence information of the Wikipedia concepts in the *semantic signature* extracted from the **single context**. When the features of the baseline method *Ganti-KDD* are extracted from the **single context**, the accuracy achieved by *Ganti-KDD* decreases greatly, which will be confirmed in Section 6.3.2. By leveraging the semantic knowledge embedded in Wikipedia, the approach APOLLO$_{SR}$ significantly outperforms the baseline method *Ganti-KDD* in terms of accuracy and the approach APOLLO$_{CO}$ in terms of both MRR and accuracy. Overall, the experimental results indicate that the Wikipedia concepts extracted from the document context and the semantic relations between them are quite useful for the task of fine-grained named entity classification.

The detailed results for each category of these three approaches are shown in Table 3 when the training entity proportion ρ equals to 0.8. It can be seen from the results in Table 3 that some of these categories are relatively easy to distinguish (e.g., Presidents of the United States and Chinese emperors), while some categories (e.g., American socialists and American revolutionaries) are very difficult to be classified accurately. In Table 3, for each row (category), the best accuracy is in bold, and the results show that APOLLO$_{SR}$ obtains the highest accuracy for 12 categories, while the approaches *Ganti-KDD* and APOLLO$_{CO}$ get the highest accuracy for 7 and 8 categories respectively.

6.2 Entity linking task

6.2.1 Experimental setting

Entity linking is initiated as a task in the track of Knowledge Base Population (KBP) at the Text Analysis Conference (TAC). The data set for TAC-KBP track in 2009[5] is available for us, so we used it as the test data set for APOLLO over the entity linking task. According to the problem formulation of ontology population with named en-

[4]http://www.csie.ntu.edu.tw/~cjlin/libsvm/

[5]http://apl.jhu.edu/~paulmac/kbp.html

Table 3: Accuracy for each category over the DS_{NEC} data set ($\rho = 0.8$)

Category	*Ganti-KDD*	APOLLO$_{CO}$	APOLLO$_{SR}$
American chief executives	0.5263	0.4211	**0.5789**
American entrepreneurs	**0.625**	0.4474	0.5405
Presidents of the United States	**1.0**	**1.0**	**1.0**
American singers	0.7027	0.7027	**0.7179**
American film actors	0.8837	0.9070	**0.9268**
American basketball coaches	**0.9**	**0.9**	0.875
American labor leaders	0.6842	0.7949	**0.8421**
England international footballers	0.9	**0.975**	0.95
Harvard Law School alumni	0.45	0.7	**0.825**
American computer scientists	0.7027	0.825	**0.9268**
Olympic athletes of the United States	0.725	0.7	**0.85**
English poets	0.775	0.825	**0.85**
American philosophers	0.8780	**0.9512**	0.875
American academics	**0.7045**	0.2439	0.2381
American socialists	**0.3333**	0.3125	0.2353
American revolutionaries	0.125	**0.25**	**0.25**
English Formula One drivers	**0.9231**	**0.9231**	**0.9231**
American diplomats	**0.6579**	0.5385	0.5385
American television journalists	0.8	**0.85**	0.8
Chinese emperors	0.7143	**1.0**	**1.0**

tities, our entity linking subtask focuses on the entity mention whose mapping entity exists in the ontology, which is called the linkable entity mention. In this TAC-KBP data set, there are total 1675 linkable entity mentions, which require to be linked with the ontology.

To perform the entity linking task, APOLLO firstly produces the candidate entity set CN_s for each entity mention s using the dictionary DT introduced in Section 5. To generate the *semantic signature* for each entity mention in the TAC-KBP data set, we used the entire document where the entity mention occurs as the document context. Next, for each entity mention s, APOLLO creates a graph consisting of the nodes coming from the entity mention s itself, the Wikiepdia concepts in its *semantic signature* δ_s and the candidate entities in CN_s. In the experiment, we also set the edge weight between the entity mention s and each Wikipedia concept in δ_s to 1.0. Since all candidate entities in CN_s are Wikipedia concepts, so we computed the semantic relatedness between each candidate entity in CN_s and each Wikipedia concept in δ_s according to Formula 1. If the semantic relatedness is greater than the threshold τ, APOLLO creates an edge between them and weights the edge using the relatedness measure. In this experiment, the threshold τ is experimentally set to 0.086, which yields the best performance. Next, APOLLO annotates each candidate entity node in the graph with a unique label, and after running the Adsorption algorithm, the candidate entity whose corresponding label has the largest distribution in L_s is regarded as the mapping entity for the entity mention s. In addition, due to many spelling errors existing in the set of entity mentions, we also tried to correct them using the query spelling correction supplied by Google.

6.2.2 Experimental results

To evaluate the performance of APOLLO over the TAC-KBP data set, we adopted the evaluation measure *Accuracy*, which is used in most work about entity linking. The accuracy is calculated as the number of correctly linked entity mentions divided by the total number of all entity mentions. The experimental results of APOLLO over the TAC-KBP data set are shown in Table 4. The results of the top 4 systems which perform best over the set of linkable entity mentions in TAC-KBP track of 2009 [18] are also shown in Table 4, for the purpose of comparison. Besides the accuracy, we also show the number of correctly linked entity mentions. The results in Table 4 show that APOLLO outperforms the best systems in TAC-KBP track of 2009, which demonstrates the effectiveness of APOLLO over the entity linking task.

Table 4: Experimental results over the TAC-KBP data set compared with top 4 ranked systems in TAC-KBP track of 2009

System	Accuracy	# of correctly linked
Rank 1	0.7725	1294
Rank 2	0.7654	1282
Rank 3	0.7588	1271
Rank 4	0.7063	1183
APOLLO	**0.7845**	**1314**

6.3 Ontology population with named entities task

6.3.1 Experimental setting

To evaluate the performance of APOLLO over the task of ontology population with named entities, the test data set should contain both unlinkable entity mention that requires to be attached to the proper category, and linkable entity mention that should be linked with the entity existing in the ontology. We denote the DS_{NEC} data set used in Section 6.1.1 when the parameter ρ equals to 0.8 as $DS_{NEC\rho=0.8}$, which consists of 2643 training entities and 661 test entities. In the following experiments, we regard the training entities in the $DS_{NEC\rho=0.8}$ data set as the set of named entities contained in the ontology. In addition, besides the test entity mentions in $DS_{NEC\rho=0.8}$ which are all unlinkable, we added some new test entity mentions which can be linked with the named entities existing in the ontology. To make the newly added test entity mentions linkable, we randomly sampled 20% of the named entities for each category existing in the ontology, and regarded the names of these sampled entities as the set of newly added test entity mentions. For each newly added test entity mention, we obtained its document context via querying its name with Google. The top ranked page which is not from Wikipedia is regarded as its candidate document context, because the corresponding Wikipedia page has been regarded as the document context for its corresponding mapping entity in the ontology. Then we verified whether the entity described in the candidate document context is the same as the corresponding mapping entity by human judgments. If so, we added this test entity mention and its candidate document context to the test data set; Otherwise, we removed it. Finally, we obtained the data set for the ontology population task (which we refer to DS_{OP}), in which the set of named entities contained in the ontology is the same as the training data set of $DS_{NEC\rho=0.8}$, and the test data set consists of 661 unlinkable test entity mentions from the original test data set of $DS_{NEC\rho=0.8}$ and the newly added 372 linkable test entity mentions.

We added the Linking Validation module of APOLLO to the baseline method *Ganti-KDD* introduced in Section 6.1.1

to create the baseline method $BASELINE_{OP}$ for the ontology population task. The features for the named entities existing in the original $DS_{NEC\rho=0.8}$ data set are extracted from the multi-context in the same way as in Section 6.1.1. Whereas for the newly added linkable test entity mention whose document context is not *Wikitext*, we are only able to extract the features existing in this single context, rather than across multiple documents, since we cannot obtain the *canonical* representation of the entity mention. It is fairly common for one of the mention forms of an entity in a document to be a long and typical mention form of that entity (e.g., "Michael Jordan"), while the other mention forms of the same entity are shorter mention forms (e.g., "Jordan"). To generate richer features for each linkable test entity mention for the $BASELINE_{OP}$ method, we used a simple in-document coreference resolution method which is to map shorter mention forms to the long and typical entity mention form in the same document.

We applied APOLLO to the DS_{OP} data set to evaluate the performance of APOLLO for the task of ontology population with named entities. We used the same setting for APOLLO as described in Section 6.1.1. The final graph G contains 99,609 nodes and about 3.1 million edges.

6.3.2 Experimental results

To evaluate the performance of APOLLO and $BASELINE_{OP}$ over the DS_{OP} data set, we also adopted the evaluation measure *Accuracy* (Accu.), which is used in both of the two subtasks. For the unlinkable test entity mention, if it is attached to the gold standard category, it is regarded as correct. And for the linkable test entity mention, if it is linked with the correct entity, we consider it as correct. The overall accuracy is calculated as the number of all correctly assigned entity mentions divided by the total number of the entity mentions.

The experimental results of APOLLO and $BASELINE_{OP}$ over the DS_{OP} data set are shown in Table 5. We show the accuracy and the number of correctly assigned entity mentions for both APOLLO and $BASELINE_{OP}$, according to the different types of the test entity mentions (i.e., all, unlinkable and linkable). From the results in Table 5 we can see that APOLLO achieves significantly higher accuracy compared with the baseline method $BASELINE_{OP}$ in all aspects. For the set of linkable test entity mentions, the accuracy achieved by $BASELINE_{OP}$ (23.66%) is much lower than the accuracy achieved by APOLLO (81.72%) which leverages the rich semantic information derived from Wikipedia. Furthermore, from the experimental results shown in Table 5 and Table 2, we can see that for the same set of the unlinkable test entity mentions, APOLLO obtains higher accuracy (75.34%) over the DS_{OP} data set in comparison with the accuracy (74.89%) achieved over the $DS_{NEC\rho=0.8}$ data set. The main reason is that via adding some linkable test entity mentions and the Wikipedia concepts existing in their *semantic signatures*, the graph created from the DS_{OP} data set is more beneficial for the process of label propagation. Therefore, it can be seen that APOLLO can obtain better performance over the richer graph structure, which demonstrates the scalability of APOLLO.

7. RELATED WORK AND DISCUSSION

The classic named entity classification task is confined to classify named entities into coarse-grained categories, such as person, location and organization. It has been investigated for several years by means of supervised approaches, which require a large number of manually tagged texts as the training data. As ontology generally contains hundreds of entity categories, supervised methods are not directly applicable for ontology-based fine-grained named entity classification, because the amount of the training data they need is too large, and the process of manually creating such annotated data requires too much human effort. Recently, many weakly supervised systems have emerged to address the task of fine-grained named entity classification [6, 28, 15, 14, 13].

Table 5: Experimental results over the DS_{OP} data set

	APOLLO		$BASELINE_{OP}$	
	Accu.	#	Accu.	#
All	**0.7764**	**802**	0.5489	567
Unlinkable	**0.7534**	**498**	0.7247	479
Linkable	**0.8172**	**304**	0.2366	88

Cimiano and Völker [6] addressed the fine-grained classification of named entities based on the Harris' distributional hypothesis as well as the vector space model. This method assigns a named entity to the contextually most similar concept from the ontology. The empirical results show that the pseudo-syntactic dependencies are an interesting alternative to the word window-based approaches.

Tanev and Magnini [28] proposed a weakly supervised approach to automatically populating a part of their ontology with named entities from text. For each category in the ontology, the algorithm learns a feature vector exploiting the lexico-syntactic information extracted from the contexts where the entities belonging to this category occur. They assumed that the named entities in the test data set are not ambiguous and they did not consider the problem of entity ambiguity. However, this assumption does not remain true in the real data sets.

Giuliano and Gliozzo [15] presented an instance-based learning algorithm for fine-grained named entity classification against the People ontology, an excerpt of the WordNet ontology. This proposed approach is based on a lexical substitution technique, and the plausibility of the generated sentence is estimated using the Web data. In a similar setting, Giuliano [14] proposed a kernel-based method that implicitly maps entities, represented by aggregating all contexts in which they occur, into a latent semantic space derived from Wikipedia. However, in both of these two approaches, to collect sufficient contextual information for each named entity, these systems query the search engine with the name of the entity, and consider all snippets retrieved by the search engine referring to the same entity. Therefore, they ignored the problem of ambiguity of proper names.

The approach presented in [13] is the baseline method introduced in Section 6.1.1. The experimental results in [13] show that this method significantly outperforms the single-context rule-based extractor similar to several state-of-the-art techniques for the task of fine-grained named entity classification. In this study, the authors assumed that each entity identified in the corpus has been converted to its *canonical* representation. However, in the real application, the general documents corpus cannot satisfy this assumption.

As more and more knowledge bases like DBpedia [1] and YAGO [26] are available publicly, the entity linking task has attracted great interests of many researchers starting from Bunescu and Pasca [4], who used the bag of words model to measure the cosine similarity between the context of the entity mention and the text of the Wikipedia article. Cucerzan [7] proposed a solution which is the first system to recognize the global document-level topical coherence of the entities. The system addresses the entity linking problem through a process of maximizing the agreement between the context of the entity mention and the contextual information extracted from the Wikipedia, as well as the agreement among the categories associated with the candidate entities. The learning based solution in [8] focuses on the classification framework to resolve entity linking. It develops a comprehensive feature set based on the entity mention, the contextual document and the knowledge base entry, and then uses a SVM ranker to score each candidate entity. Our previous work [24] proposed LINDEN to deal with the entity linking task. LINDEN is a novel framework to link named entities in text with a knowledge base unifying Wikipedia and WordNet, by leveraging the rich semantic knowledge embedded in the Wikipedia and the taxonomy of the knowledge base. Overall, the essential step of the entity linking task is to define a similarity measure between the text around the entity mention and the document associated with the entity.

8. CONCLUSION

In this paper, we have studied the problem of ontology population with named entities. We propose APOLLO, a novel unified framework to resolve the task of automatic ontology population with named entities integrally via random walks on graphs. APOLLO is a weakly supervised framework and can be easily parallelized. To evaluate the effectiveness of APOLLO, a thorough experimental study was conducted, and the experimental results demonstrate that APOLLO achieves significantly higher accuracy for the ontology population task compared with the baseline method, by leveraging the rich semantic knowledge embedded in the Wikipedia. Furthermore, we extensively evaluated the performance of APOLLO over both subtasks, and the experimental results show that APOLLO outperforms the baseline methods for both subtasks.

9. ACKNOWLEDGMENTS

This work was supported in part by National Natural Science Foundation of China under Grant No. 60833003, National Basic Research Program of China (973 Program) under Grant No. 2011CB302206, and an HP Labs Innovation Research Program award.

10. REFERENCES

[1] S. Auer, C. Bizer, G. Kobilarov, J. Lehmann, and Z. Ives. Dbpedia: A nucleus for a web of open data. In *ISWC'07*, pages 11–15.

[2] S. Baluja, R. Seth, D. Sivakumar, Y. Jing, J. Yagnik, S. Kumar, D. Ravich, and R. M. Aly. Video suggestion and discovery for youtube: Taking random walks through the view graph. In *WWW'08*, pages 895–904.

[3] M. Banko, M. J. Cafarella, S. Soderl, M. Broadhead, and O. Etzioni. Open information extraction from the web. In *IJCAI'07*, pages 2670–2676.

[4] R. Bunescu and M. Pasca. Using encyclopedic knowledge for named entity disambiguation. In *EACL'06*, pages 9–16.

[5] R. L. Cilibrasi and P. M. B. Vitanyi. The google similarity distance. *IEEE Trans. on Knowl. and Data Eng.*, 19:370–383, March 2007.

[6] P. Cimiano and J. Völker. Towards Large-Scale, Open-Domain and Ontology-Based Named Entity Classification. In *RANLP'05*, pages 166–172.

[7] S. Cucerzan. Large-scale named entity disambiguation based on wikipedia data. In *EMNLP and CoNLL*, pages 708–716, 2007.

[8] M. Dredze, P. McNamee, D. Rao, A. Gerber, and T. Finin. Entity disambiguation for knowledge base population. In *COLING'10*, pages 277–285.

[9] A. Ekbal, E. Sourjikova, A. Frank, and S. P. Ponzetto. Assessing the challenge of fine-grained named entity recognition and classification. In *Proceedings of the 2010 Named Entities Workshop*, pages 93–101, 2010.

[10] O. Etzioni, M. Cafarella, D. Downey, A.-M. Popescu, T. Shaked, S. Soderland, D. S. Weld, and A. Yates. Unsupervised named-entity extraction from the web: an experimental study. *Artif. Intell.*, 165:91–134, 2005.

[11] C. Fellbaum, editor. *WordNet: An Electronic Lexical Database.* MIT Press, Cambridge, MA, 1998.

[12] M. Fleischman and E. Hovy. Fine grained classification of named entities. In *COLING'02*, pages 1–7.

[13] V. Ganti, A. C. König, and R. Vernica. Entity categorization over large document collections. In *SIGKDD'08*, pages 274–282.

[14] C. Giuliano. Fine-grained classification of named entities exploiting latent semantic kernels. In *CoNLL'09*, pages 201–209.

[15] C. Giuliano and A. Gliozzo. Instance-based ontology population exploiting named-entity substitution. In *COLING'08*, pages 265–272.

[16] Z. Harris. Distributional structure. *Word*, 10(23):146–162, 1954.

[17] A. McCallum and W. Li. Early results for named entity recognition with conditional random fields, feature induction and web-enhanced lexicons. In *CONLL'03*, pages 188–191.

[18] P. McNamee, H. Simpson, and H. T. Dang. Overview of the tac 2009 knowledge base population track. In *Text Analysis Conference (TAC 2009).*

[19] D. Milne and I. H. Witten. An effective, low-cost measure of semantic relatedness obtained from Wikipedia links. In *WIKIAI'08.*

[20] D. Milne and I. H. Witten. Learning to link with wikipedia. In *CIKM'08*, pages 509–518.

[21] D. Nadeau and S. Sekine. A Survey of Named Entity Recognition and Classification. *Journal of Linguisticae Investigationes*, 30(1):1–20, 2007.

[22] W. Shen, J. Wang, P. Luo, and M. Wang. Apollo: a general framework for populating ontology with named entities via random walks on graphs. In *WWW'12*, pages 595–596.

[23] W. Shen, J. Wang, P. Luo, and M. Wang. Liege: Link entities in web lists with knowledge base. In *SIGKDD'12*, pages 1424–1432.

[24] W. Shen, J. Wang, P. Luo, and M. Wang. Linden: linking named entities with knowledge base via semantic knowledge. In *WWW'12*, pages 449–458.

[25] W. Shen, J. Wang, P. Luo, M. Wang, and C. Yao. Reactor: a framework for semantic relation extraction and tagging over enterprise data. In *WWW'11*, pages 121–122.

[26] F. M. Suchanek, G. Kasneci, and G. Weikum. Yago: A core of semantic knowledge unifying wordnet and wikipedia. In *WWW'07*, pages 697–706.

[27] P. P. Talukdar, J. Reisinger, M. Paşca, D. Ravichandran, R. Bhagat, and F. Pereira. Weakly-supervised acquisition of labeled class instances using graph random walks. In *EMNLP'08*, pages 582–590.

[28] H. Tanev and B. Magnini. Weakly supervised approaches for ontology population. In *Proceeding of the 2008 conference on Ontology Learning and Population: Bridging the Gap between Text and Knowledge*, pages 129–143.

Decomposition-by-Normalization (DBN): Leveraging Approximate Functional Dependencies for Efficient Tensor Decomposition*

Mijung Kim
Arizona State University
Tempe, AZ 85287, USA
mijung.kim.1@asu.edu

K. Selçuk Candan
Arizona State University
Tempe, AZ 85287, USA
candan@asu.edu

ABSTRACT

For many multi-dimensional data applications, tensor operations as well as relational operations need to be supported throughout the data lifecycle. Although tensor decomposition is shown to be effective for multi-dimensional data analysis, the cost of tensor decomposition is often very high. We propose a novel `decomposition-by-normalization` scheme that first normalizes the given relation into smaller tensors based on the functional dependencies of the relation and then performs the decomposition using these smaller tensors. The decomposition and recombination steps of the `decomposition-by-normalization` scheme fit naturally in settings with multiple cores. This leads to a highly efficient, effective, and parallelized `decomposition-by-normalization` algorithm for both dense and sparse tensors. Experiments confirm the efficiency and effectiveness of the proposed `decomposition-by-normalization` scheme compared to the conventional nonnegative CP decomposition approach.

Categories and Subject Descriptors

H.2.4 [**Database Management**]: Systems—*Query processing, Relational databases*; H.3.3 [**Information Storage and Retrieval**]: Information Search and Retrieval—*Clustering*

General Terms

Algorithms, Experimentation

Keywords

Tensor Decomposition, Tensor-based Relational Data Model

*This work is supported by the NSF Grant #1043583 - 'MiNC: NSDL Middleware for Network- and Context-aware Recommendations' and the NSF Grant #1116394 'RanKloud: Data Partitioning and Resource Allocation Strategies for Scalable Multimedia and Social Media Analysis'

1. INTRODUCTION

For many multi-dimensional data applications, tensor operations as well as relational operations need to be supported throughout the data lifecycle (from collection to analysis). Tensors are high-dimensional arrays. Due to the convenience they provide when representing relationships among different types of entities, tensor representation has been increasingly used for relational data in various fields from scientific data management to social network data analysis. Tensor based representations have proven to be useful for multi-aspect data analysis and tensor decomposition has been an important tool to capture high-order structures in multi-dimensional data [2, 11, 12, 17, 20, 23].

Although tensor decomposition is shown to be effective for multi-dimensional data analysis, the cost of tensor decomposition is often very high, especially in dense tensor representations where the cost increases exponentially with the number of modes of the tensor. While decomposition cost increases more slowly (linearly with the number of nonzero entries in the tensor) for sparse tensors. the operation can still be very expensive for large data sets In fact, in many data intensive systems, data is commonly high-dimensional and large-scale and, consequently, of all the operations that need to be supported to manage the data, tensor decompositions tend to be the costliest ones. Recent attempts to parellelize tensor decomposition [2, 17, 23] face difficulties, including large synchronization and data exchange overheads.

1.1 Contribution of this Paper: Decomposition-by-Normalization (DBN)

Our goal is to tackle the high computational cost of tensor decomposition process. Since, especially for dense data sets, the number of modes of the tensor data is one of the main factors contributing to the cost of tensor operations, we focus on how we reduce the dimensionality and the size of the input tensor. In particular, we argue that if

- a high-dimensional data set (i.e., a tensor with large number of modes) can be normalized (i.e., vertically partitioned) into lower-dimensional data sets (i.e., tensors with smaller number of modes) and
- each vertical partition (sub-tensor) is decomposed independently,

then the resulting partial decompositions can be efficiently combined to obtain the decomposition of the original data set (tensor). We refer to this as the `decomposition-by-normalization` (DBN) scheme.

workclass	education	ID	occupation	income
Self-emp-not-inc	Masters	1	Exec-managerial	>50K
Never-worked	Bachelors	2	-	<=50K
Private	Some-college	3	Sales	>50K
...	...	...	...	...

workclass	education	ID
Self-emp-not-inc	Masters	1
Never-worked	Bachelors	2
Private	Some-college	3
...	...	...

ID	occupation	income
1	Exec-managerial	>50K
2	-	<=50K
3	Sales	>50K
...	...	...

(a) Normalization

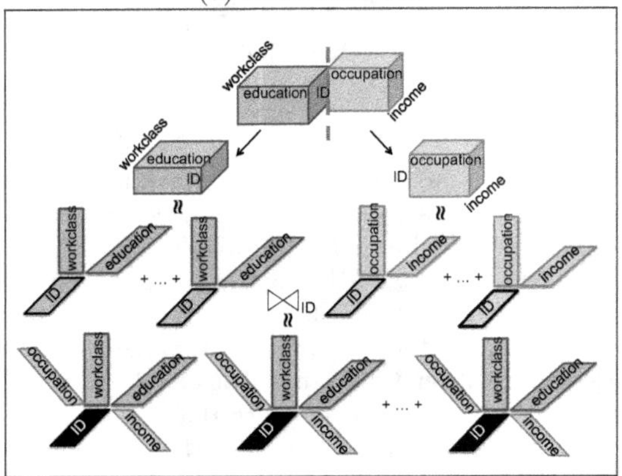

(b) `decomposition-by-normalization` (DBN) process

Figure 1: (a) Normalization of a relation $\mathcal{R}$(`workclass, education, ID, occupation, income`) into two relations $\mathcal{R}_1$(`workclass, education, ID`) and $\mathcal{R}_2$(`ID, occupation, income`) based on the key (`ID`); (b) `decomposition-by-normalization`: normalization of $\mathcal{R}$ into $\mathcal{R}_1$ and $\mathcal{R}_2$ and rank-r_1 CP decomposition of $\mathcal{R}_1$ and rank-r_2 CP decomposition of $\mathcal{R}_2$ that are combined on the ID mode into rank-r CP decomposition of $\mathcal{R}$.

EXAMPLE 1.1. *Consider the 5-attribute relation, $\mathcal{R}$(**`workclass, education, ID, occupation, income`**), in Figure 1(a) and assume that we want to decompose the corresponding tensor for multi-dimensional analysis.*

*Since high-dimensional tensor decomposition is expensive, we argue that a better processing scheme would involve first normalizing this relation into the smaller tensors (based on the functional dependencies of the relation) and then performing the decompositions of these smaller tensors. These normalized tensors are lower-dimensional than the original input tensor, therefore these decompositions are likely to be much less expensive than the decomposition of the original input tensor. Figure 1(a) illustrates an example normalization which divides the 5-attribute relations into two smaller relations with 3 attributes, $\mathcal{R}_1$(**`workclass, education, ID`**) and $\mathcal{R}_2$(**`ID, occupation, income`**) respectively.*

Figure 1(b) illustrates the proposed DBN scheme: Once the two partitions are decomposed, we combine the resulting core and factor matrices to obtain the decomposition of the original tensor corresponding to the relation $\mathcal{R}$.

In the above example, if the relation $\mathcal{R}$ is *dense*, we expect that decompositions of relations $\mathcal{R}_1$ and $\mathcal{R}_2$ will be much faster than that of the relation $\mathcal{R}$ and the gain will more than compensate for the normalization cost of the initial step and the combination cost of the last step of DBN.

If the relation $\mathcal{R}$ is *sparse*, on the other hand, the decomposition cost is not only determined by the number of modes, but also the number of nonzero entries in the tensor. As a result, unless the partitioning provides smaller number of tuples for both relations, DBN may not provide sufficient savings to compensate the normalization and combination overheads. However, as we will experimentally verify in Section 6, the decomposition and recombination steps of the DBN scheme fit naturally in multiple cores. This leads to a highly efficient, effective, and parallelized DBN strategy under both dense and sparse tensors.

In general, a relation can be vertically partitioned into two in many ways: we need to first select a join attribute and then, we need to decide which attributes to include in which vertical partition. The join attribute (`ID` in the above example) around which we partition the data is important for two different reasons. First of all, we need to ensure that the join attribute is selected in such a way that the normalization (i.e., the vertical partitioning) process does not lead to spurious tuples. Secondly, the join attribute need to partition the data in such a way that the later step in which decompositions of the individual partitions are combined into an overall decomposition does not introduce errors.

Task 1.1. One way to prevent the normalization process from introducing spurious data is to select an attribute which *functionally determines* the attributes that will be moved to the second partition. *This requires an efficient method to determine functional dependencies in the data.* This is difficult because the total number of functional dependencies in the data can be exponential.

Task 1.2. A second difficulty is that many data sets may not have perfect functional dependencies to leverage for normalization. *In that case, we need to identify and rely on approximate functional dependencies in the data.* In this paper, we argue that we can rely on pairwise approximate functional dependencies that are incomplete, yet very efficient to compute.

Task 1.3. Once the approximate functional dependencies are identified, *we need to partition the data into two partitions in such a way that will lead to least amount of errors during later stages.* In this paper, we argue that partitioning the attributes in a way that minimizes *inter-partition* functional dependencies and maximizes *intra-partition* dependencies will lead to least amount of errors in recombination step. After data is vertically partitioned and individual partitions are decomposed, the individual decompositions need to be recombined to obtain the decomposition of the original relation. This process needs to be done in a way that is efficient and parallelizable.

1.2 Organization of the Paper

The organization of the paper is as follows:

- We first provide the relevant background and discuss the related works in Section 2.
- We next provide an overview of the proposed DBN scheme in Section 3.
- We then focus on selecting the best partitions for the normalization step of DBN (Section 4).
- In Section 5, we present rank-pruning strategies to further reduce the cost of DBN.
- Next, we experimentally evaluate DBN in Section 6 in both stand-alone and parallel configurations. We focus on the accuracy and the running time of the alternative algorithms. Experimental results provide evidence that while being significantly faster, DBN can approximate well the fitness of the conventional tensor decomposition with respect to the original tensor.

We conclude the paper in Section 7.

2. BACKGROUND AND RELATED WORK

Tensor Decomposition. The two most popular tensor decompositions are the Tucker [21] and the CANDECOMP/PARAFAC [7, 4] decompositions. The Tucker decomposition generalizes singular value matrix decomposition (SVD) to higher-dimensional matrices. CANDECOMP [4] and PARAFAC [7] decompositions (together known as the CP decomposition) take a different approach and decompose the input tensor into a sum of component rank-one tensors. More specifically, the CP Decomposition of $\mathcal{P}$ is a weighted sum of rank-one tensors as the following (an alternative way to view the decomposition is in the form of a diagonal tensor and a set of factor matrices of the input tensor):

$$\mathcal{P}_{I_1 \times I_2 \times \cdots \times I_N} \sim \sum_{k=1}^{r} \lambda_k \circ U_k^{(1)} \circ U_k^{(2)} \circ \cdots \circ U_k^{(N)}.$$

where λ is a vector of size r and each $U^{(n)}$ is a matrix of size $I_n \times r$, for $n = 1, \cdots, N$.

Many of the algorithms for decomposing tensors are based on an iterative process that approximates the best solution until a convergence condition is reached. The *alternating least squares* (ALS) method is relatively old and has been successfully applied to the problem of tensor decomposition [4, 7]. ALS estimates, at each iteration, one factor matrix, maintaining other matrices fixed; this process is repeated for each factor matrix associated to the dimensions of the input tensor.

Nonnegative Tensor Decomposition (NTF). Note that these decompositions can be interpreted probabilistically, if additional constraints (nonnegativity and summation to 1) are imposed. In the case of the CP decomposition, for example, each nonzero element in the core and the values of entries of the factor matrices can be thought of as a cluster and the conditional probabilities of the entries given clusters, respectively. The N-way Toolbox for MATLAB [1] provides both CP and Tucker decomposition with nonnegativity constraints.

Scalable Tensor Decomposition. Tensor decomposition is a costly process. In dense tensor representation where the cost increases exponentially with the number of modes of the tensor. While decomposition cost increases more slowly (linearly with the number of nonzero entries in the tensor) for sparse tensors, the operation can still be very expensive for large data sets due to the high computational cost and memory requirement to build up the approximate tensor [17]. A modified ALS algorithm proposed in [17] computes Hadamard products instead of Khatri-Rao products for efficient PARAFAC for large-scale tensors. Kolda *et al.* [11] developed a greedy PARAFAC algorithm for large-scale, sparse tensors in MATLAB.

The ALS in Tucker decompositions involves SVD which is the most computationally challenging part [20]. To address this, randomized sampling is used in [20]. MET decomposition proposed in [12] addresses intermediate blowup problem in Tucker decomposition.

Parallel Tensor Decomposition. Phan and Cichocki [17] proposed a modified ALS PARAFAC algorithm called grid PARAFAC for large scale tensor data. The grid PARAFAC divides a large tensor into sub-tensors that can be factorized using any available PARAFAC algorithm in a parallel manner and iteratively combined into the final decomposition. The grid PARAFAC can be converted to grid NTF by enforcing nonnegativity.

Zhang *et al.* [23] parallelized NTF for mining global climate data in such a way that the original 3-mode tensor is divided into three semi-NMF sub-problems based on ALS approach and these matrices are distributed to independent processors to facilitate parallelization. Antikainen *et al.* [2] presented an algorithm for NTF that is specialized for Compute Uniform Device Architecture (CUDA) framework that provides a parallel running environment.

Note that since these block-based parallel algorithms are based on an ALS approach where one variable can be optimized given that the other variables are fixed, the communication cost among each block is not avoidable. In the parallelized DBN strategy, on the other hand, each block is completely separable and run independently.

Functional Dependency (FD). A functional dependency (FD) is a constraint between two sets of attributes X and Y in a relation denoted by $X \rightarrow Y$, which specifies that the values of the X component of a tuple uniquely determine the values of the Y component.

The discovery of FDs in a data set is a challenging problem since the complexity increases exponentially in the number of attributes [15]. Many algorithms for FD and approximate FD discovery exist [8, 13, 15, 22]. TANE proposed in [8] used the definition of approximate FDs based on the minimum fraction of tuples that should be removed from the relation to hold the exact FDs.

The computation of FDs in TANE and Dep-Miner [13] is based on levelwise search [16]. Dep-Miner finds the minimal FD cover of a hypergraph using a levelwise search. Similarly, FastFD [22] finds the minimal cover, however, differently from Dep-Miner, it uses a depth-first search to address the problem in the levelwise search that the cost increases exponentially in the number of attributes. The main factor in the cost of FastFD is the input size. FastFD works well when the number of attributes is large. TANE takes linear time with respect to the size of the input whereas FastFD takes more than linear time of the input size.

CORDS [9] generalized FDs to determine statistical dependencies, which is referred to as soft FD. In a soft FD, a value of an attribute determines a value of another attribute with high probability. CORDS only discovers pairwise correlations reducing a great amount of complexity that nevertheless can remove most of correlation-induced selectivity error. In this paper, we also leverage pairwise FDs to measure dependency *between* partitions (interFD) and *within* a partition (intraFD).

3. DECOMPOSITION-BY-NORMALIZATION (DBN)

As we discussed earlier, our goal in this paper is to tackle the high computational cost of decomposition process. Since, especially for dense data sets, the number of modes of the tensor data is one of the main factors contributing to the cost of tensor operations, we focus on how we reduce the dimensionality and the size of the input tensor. In particular, we argue that a large relation can be vertically partitioned into multiple relations relying on the approximate functional dependencies in the data, and the decompositions of these relations can be combined to obtain the overall decomposition. Without loss of generality, in this paper, we consider

2-way partitioning of the input data. The process can easily be generalized for multiple partitions.

In this section, we provide an overview of this DBN process. We first introduce the relevant notations and provide background on key concepts.

3.1 Background and Key Concepts

Without loss of generality, we assume that relations are represented in the form of *occurrence tensors*.

3.1.1 Tensor Representation of Relational Data

Let $A_1, \ldots, A_n$ be a set of attributes in the schema of a relation, R, and $D_1, \ldots, D_n$ be the attribute domains. Let the relation instance $\mathcal{R}$ be a finite multi-set of tuples, where each tuple $t \in D_1 \times \ldots \times D_n$.

DEFINITION 3.1 (OCCURRENCE TENSOR). *An* occurrence tensor $\mathfrak{R}_o$ *corresponding to the relation instance* $\mathcal{R}$ *is an n-mode tensor, where each attribute* $A_1, \ldots, A_n$ *is represented by a mode. For the* i^{th} *mode, which corresponds to* A_i*, let* $D'_i \subseteq D_i$ *be the (finite) subset of the elements such that*

$$\forall v \in D'_i\ \exists t \in \mathcal{R}\ s.t.\ t.A_i = v$$

and let $idx(v)$ *denote the rank of* v *among the values in* D'_i *relative to an (arbitrary) total order,* $<_i$*, defined over the elements of the domain,* D_i*. The cells of the* occurrence tensor $\mathfrak{R}_o$ *are such that*

$$\mathfrak{R}_o[u_1, \ldots, u_n] = 1 \leftrightarrow \exists t \in \mathcal{R}\ s.t. \forall_{1 \leq j \leq n}\ idx(t.A_j) = u_j$$

and 0 *otherwise. Intuitively, each cell indicates whether the corresponding tuple exists in the multi-set corresponding to the relation or not.*

3.1.2 Normalization (Vertical Partitoning) and Functional Dependencies

First introduced by Codd [5], the normalization process of the relational model evaluates relations based on the underlying functional dependencies of the data and vertically partitions a large relation into smaller relations (with lesser number of attributes) to minimize redundancy and insertion, deletion, and update anomalies.

Functional Dependency (FD). The functional dependency, between two sets of attributes $\mathcal{X}$ and $\mathcal{Y}$, in a relational model is defined as the following.

DEFINITION 3.2 (FUNCTIONAL DEPENDENCY). *A functional dependency (FD), denoted by* $\mathcal{X} \rightarrow \mathcal{Y}$*, holds for relation instance* $\mathcal{R}$*, if and only if for any two tuples* t_1 *and* t_2 *in* $\mathcal{R}$ *that have* $t_1[\mathcal{X}] = t_2[\mathcal{X}]$*,* $t_1[\mathcal{Y}] = t_2[\mathcal{Y}]$ *also holds.*

The key idea of the normalization process is that if $\mathcal{A} = \{A_1, \ldots, A_n\}$ is a set of attributes in the schema of a relation, R, and $\mathcal{X}, \mathcal{Y} \subseteq \mathcal{A}$ are two subsets of attributes such that $\mathcal{X} \rightarrow \mathcal{Y}$, then the relation instance $\mathcal{R}$ can be vertically partitioned into two relation instances $\mathcal{R}_1$, with attributes $\mathcal{A} \setminus \mathcal{Y}$, and $\mathcal{R}_2$, with attributes $\mathcal{X} \cup \mathcal{Y}$, such that $\mathcal{R} = \mathcal{R}_1 \bowtie \mathcal{R}_2$; in other words the set of attributes $\mathcal{X}$ serves as a foreign key and joining vertical partitions $\mathcal{R}_1$ and $\mathcal{R}_2$ on $\mathcal{X}$ gives back the relation instance $\mathcal{R}$ without any missing or spurious tuples. Note that, while for some data sets, FDs are known at the database design time, for many data sets they need to be discovered by analyzing the available data sets.

Approximate FD. As described above, the search for exact FDs is a costly process. Moreover, in many data sets, attributes may not have perfect FDs due to exceptions and outliers in the data. In such cases, we may search for approximate FDs instead of exact FDs.

DEFINITION 3.3 (APPROXIMATE FD). *An approximate FD (aFD), denoted by* $\mathcal{X} \overset{\sigma}{\rightarrow} \mathcal{Y}$ *holds for relation instance* $\mathcal{R}$*, if and only if*

- *there is a subset* $\mathcal{R}' \subseteq \mathcal{R}$*, such that* $|\mathcal{R}'| = \sigma \times |\mathcal{R}|$ *and, for any two tuples* t_1 *and* t_2 *in* $\mathcal{R}'$ *that have* $t_1[\mathcal{X}] = t_2[\mathcal{X}]$*,* $t_1[\mathcal{Y}] = t_2[\mathcal{Y}]$ *also holds; and*
- *there is no subset* $\mathcal{R}'' \subseteq \mathcal{R}$*, such that* $|\mathcal{R}''| > \sigma \times |\mathcal{R}|$ *where the condition holds.*

We refer to the value of σ *as the support of the aFD* $\mathcal{X} \overset{\sigma}{\rightarrow} \mathcal{Y}$.

As described above, the concept of relational normalization (vertical partitioning) relies on the relational join operation. Since in this paper we represent relations as occurrence tensors, we also need to define a corresponding *tensor join* operation that operates in the domain of tensors.

3.1.3 Tensor Join

Let $\mathfrak{P}$ and $\mathfrak{Q}$ be two tensors, representing relation instances $\mathcal{P}$ and $\mathcal{Q}$, with attribute sets, $A^P = \{A^P_1, \ldots, A^P_n\}$ and $A^Q = \{A^Q_1, \ldots, A^Q_m\}$, respectively. In the rest of this section, we denote the index of each cell of $\mathfrak{P}$ as $(i_1, i_2, ..., i_n)$; similarly, the index of each cell of $\mathfrak{Q}$ is denoted as $(j_1, j_2, ..., j_m)$. The cell indexed as $(i_1, \ldots, i_n)$ of $\mathfrak{P}$ is denoted by $\mathfrak{P}[i_1, \ldots, i_n]$ and the cell indexed as $(j_1, \ldots, j_m)$ of $\mathfrak{Q}$ is denoted by $\mathfrak{Q}[j_1, \ldots, j_m]$.

DEFINITION 3.4 (JOIN ($\bowtie$)). *In relational algebra, given two relations* $\mathcal{P}$ *and* $\mathcal{Q}$*, and a condition* φ*, the* join *operation is defined as a cartesian product of the input relations followed by the selection operation. Therefore, given two relational tensors* $\mathfrak{P}$ *and* $\mathfrak{Q}$*, and a condition* φ*, we can define their join as*

$$\mathfrak{P} \bowtie_\varphi \mathfrak{Q} \overset{def}{=} \sigma_\varphi(\mathfrak{P} \times \mathfrak{Q}).$$

Given two relations $\mathcal{P}$ *and* $\mathcal{Q}$*, with attribute sets,* $A^P = \{A^P_1, \ldots, A^P_n\}$ *and* $A^Q = \{A^Q_1, \ldots, A^Q_m\}$*, and a set of attributes* $A \subseteq A^P$ *and* $A \subseteq A^Q$*, the* equi-join *operation,* $\bowtie_{=,A}$*, is defined as the join operation, with the condition that matching attributes in the two relations will have the same values, followed by a projection operation that eliminates one instance of* A *from the resulting relation.*

3.2 Overview of the Decomposition-By-Normalization (DBN) Process

The pseudo-code of the DBN algorithm is shown in Figure 2. In this subsection, we provide an overview of the steps of the algorithm. Then, in the following sections, we study in detail the key steps of the process.

In its first step, DBN evaluates the pairwise FDs among the attributes of the input relation. For this purpose, we employ and extend TANE [8], an efficient algorithm for the discovery of FDs. Our modification of the TANE algorithm returns a set of (approximate) FDs between the attribute pairs and, for each candidate dependency, $A_i \rightarrow A_j$, it provides the corresponding support, $\sigma_{i,j}$.

The next steps involves selecting the attribute, X, that will serve as the foreign key and partitioning the input relation $\mathcal{R}$ into $\mathcal{R}_1$ and $\mathcal{R}_2$ around X. Note that if the selected

DBN algorithm (input: a relation $\mathcal{R}$)

Evaluate pFD (pairwise FDs between all pairs of attributes of $\mathcal{R}$)
Select the attribute A_k with the highest $\sum_{k \neq j} \sigma_{k,j}$ such that $\sigma_{k,j} \geq \tau_{support}$ as the vertical partitioning (and join) attribute X (Desiderata 1 and 2)
if $\mathcal{R}$ is a sparse tensor **then**
  if X (approximately) determines all attributes of $\mathcal{R}$ **then**
    findInterFDPartition(pFD,false) (see Figure 3)
  else
    Move X and all attributes determined by X to $\mathcal{R}_1$; move X and remaining attributes to $\mathcal{R}_2$ (Desideratum 4 and 5).
  end if
else {i.e., $\mathcal{R}$ is a dense tensor}
  if X (approximately) determines all attributes of $\mathcal{R}$ **then**
    findInterFDPartition(pFD,true)
  else
    Move X and attributes determined by X to $\mathcal{R}_1$; move X and remaining attributes to $\mathcal{R}_2$ – these moves are constrained such that the number of attributes of $\mathcal{R}_1$ and $\mathcal{R}_2$ are similar (Desideratum 3 and 5)
  end if
end if
Partition $\mathcal{R}$ into $\mathcal{R}_1$ and $\mathcal{R}_2$.
If the selected X does not perfectly determine the attributes of $\mathcal{R}_1$ then remove sufficient number of outlier tuples from $\mathcal{R}$ to enforce the FDs between X and the attributes of $\mathcal{R}_1$
Create occurrence tensors of $\mathcal{R}_1$ and $\mathcal{R}_2$
Decompose the tensors corresponding to $\mathcal{R}_1$ and $\mathcal{R}_2$, join the decompositions to obtain candidate combined decompositions, and select the one that is likely to provide the best fit to $\mathcal{R}$

Figure 2: Pseudo-code of DBN (see Section 4)

findInterFDPartition (input: pFD, balanced)

Create a complete pairwise FD graph, where the nodes are attributes and edge weights are the support values of pFD.
if balanced == false **then**
  Run minimum average cut on the pairwise FD graph to find a maximally independent partitioning (Desideratum 5)
else {i.e., balanced == true}
  Run minimum average cut on the pairwise FD graph to find a balanced, maximally independent partitioning (Desideratum 3 and 5)
end if

Figure 3: Pseudo-code of interFD-based partition algorithm; this is detailed in Section 4.3

join attribute X does not perfectly determine the attributes of $\mathcal{R}_1$, then to prevent introduction of spurious tuples, we will need to remove sufficient number of outlier tuples from $\mathcal{R}$ to enforce the FDs between the attribute, X, and the attributes selected to be moved to $\mathcal{R}_1$.

Desideratum 1: Therefore, to prevent over-thinning of the relation $\mathcal{R}$, the considered approximate FDs need to have high support; i.e., $\sigma_{i,j} \geq \tau_{support}$, for a sufficiently large support lower-bound, $\tau_{support}$.

We next consider various criteria for vertical partitioning of the input relation:

- First of all, as we discussed earlier, when we vertically partition the relation $\mathcal{R}$ with attributes $\mathcal{A} = \{A_1, \ldots, A_n\}$ into $\mathcal{R}_1$ and $\mathcal{R}_2$, one of the attributes X of $\mathcal{R}_2$ should serve as a foreign key into $\mathcal{R}_1$ to ensure that joining vertical partitions $\mathcal{R}_1$ and $\mathcal{R}_2$ on X gives back $\mathcal{R}$ without any missing or spurious tuples.

  Desideratum 2: If $\mathcal{A}_1$ is the set of attributes of vertical partition $\mathcal{R}_1$ and $\mathcal{A}_2$ is the set of attributes of vertical partition $\mathcal{R}_2$, then there must be an attribute $X \in \mathcal{A}_2$, such that for each attribute $Y \in \mathcal{A}_1$, $X \xrightarrow{\sigma} Y$, for $\sigma \geq \tau_{support}$.

- Since for dense tensors, the complexity of the decomposition process is exponential in the number of modes [11], we would prefer that the number of attributes in each partition should be balanced.

  Desideratum 3: For dense tensors, the vertical partitioning should be such that the number of attributes of $\mathcal{R}_1$ and $\mathcal{R}_2$ are similar.

- For sparse tensors the number of modes impact the decomposition cost only linearly. In fact, in this case, the major contributor to the decomposition cost is the number of nonzero entries in the tensor [11].

  Desideratum 4: Therefore, for sparse tensors, the vertical partitioning should be such that the total number of tuples of $\mathcal{R}_1$ and $\mathcal{R}_2$ are minimized.

- Any information encoded with the FDs crossing relations $\mathcal{R}_1$ and $\mathcal{R}_2$ is risked to be lost when $\mathcal{R}_1$ and $\mathcal{R}_2$ are individually decomposed in the final step of the DBN algorithm. This leads to our final desideratum:

  Desideratum 5: The vertical partitioning should be such that the support for the inter-partition FDs (except for the FDs involving the join attribute X) are minimized.

We elaborate on these desiderata and their implications on the vertical partitioning of $\mathcal{R}$ into $\mathcal{R}_1$ and $\mathcal{R}_2$ in Section 4.

Once $\mathcal{R}_1$ and $\mathcal{R}_2$ are obtained, the final steps of the DBN process include decomposition of the tensors corresponding to $\mathcal{R}_1$ and $\mathcal{R}_2$, joining of the decompositions to obtain candidate combined decompositions, and selecting the one that is likely to provide the best fit to $\mathcal{R}$. For these, we rely on the `join-by-decomposition` scheme proposed in [10]: in order to construct a rank-r decomposition of a joined tensor, `join-by-decomposition` first finds all rank-r_1 and rank-r_2 decompositions of the two input tensors, such that $r_1 \times r_2 = r$. The rank-r_1 and rank-r_2 decompositions of the input decompositions are then combined along the given factor matrix, which corresponds to the join attribute in the equi-join operation. Finally the algorithm finds the $r_1 \times r_2$ pair which provides the least approximation error, given all possible factorizations, $r_1 \times r_2$ of r. Note that `join-by-decomposition` involves creation of multiple alternative join pairs (corresponding to different $r_1 \times r_2$ factorizations of r), which are independently evaluated for accuracy and the one that is predicted to provide the best accuracy is used for obtaining the final result. This provides a natural way to parallelize the entire operation by associating each pair of rank decompositions (and the computation of the corresponding pair selection measure) to a different processor core. In Section 6, we also evaluate the applicability of such parallelizations in the context of the DBN operation.

4. VERTICAL PARTITIONING STRATEGIES

Based on the desiderata discussed in Section 3.2, here we discuss the vertical partitioning strategies for sparse and dense tensors. For each situation, we consider the cases: (Case 1) the join attribute (approximately) determines a subset of attributes and (Case 2) it determines all attributes of the input relation.

4.1 Sparse Tensors

For the first case (i.e., the join attribute X (approximately) determines a subset of the attributes of $\mathcal{R}$), we create a partition $\mathcal{R}_1$ with all the attributes determined with a support higher than the threshold ($\tau_{support}$) by the join attribute. This helps us satisfy Desiderata 1 and 2. The second partition, $\mathcal{R}_2$ consists of the join attribute X and all the remaining attributes. Since inter-partition FDs of the form $X \rightarrow *$ are all less than $\tau_{support}$, this also reflects Desideratum 5.

Note that by construction, the size of $\mathcal{R}_2$ is equal to the number of tuples in $\mathcal{R}$ independent of which attributes are included in it. The size of $\mathcal{R}_1$, on the other hand, can be minimized (to satisfy Desideratum 4) down to the number of unique values of X by eliminating all the duplicate tuples.

For the second case, where the join attribute X determines all attributes of $\mathcal{R}$, we apply the interFD-based vertical partitioning strategy detailed later in Section 4.3.

4.2 Dense Tensors

For the first case, similarly to sparse tensors, we create partitions, $\mathcal{R}_1$ and $\mathcal{R}_2$, by considering the FDs of the form $X \rightarrow *$, where X is the join attribute. Differently from the sparse tensors, in this case we also consider Desideratum 3, which prefers balanced partitions:

- When there are fewer attributes with support higher than $\tau_{support}$, we move the attributes with the highest support from $\mathcal{R}_2$ to $\mathcal{R}_1$ to promote balance. This is equivalent to relaxing the support threshold.
- When there are more attributes with support higher than $\tau_{support}$, we move the attributes with the lowest support from $\mathcal{R}_1$ to $\mathcal{R}_2$ to promote balance. This is equivalent to tightening the support threshold.

For the second case, as in the sparse tensors, we apply the interFD-based vertical partitioning strategy detailed later in Section 4.3. The major difference is that in this case, we also promote balance.

4.3 Vertical Partitioning Based on Supports of Attribute Pair Dependencies

Desideratum 5 implies that the vertical partitioning strategy should minimize inter-partition FDs. As discussed earlier, this helps minimize the likelihood of error when the individual partitions are decomposed and the resulting decompositions are combined to obtain the overall decomposition. Kim and Candan [10] have shown that, given a join operation, $\mathcal{R} = \mathcal{R}_1 \bowtie_A \mathcal{R}_2$, it is possible to obtain a rank-r decomposition of $\mathcal{R}$ by combining rank-r_1 and rank-r_2 decompositions of $\mathcal{R}_1$ and $\mathcal{R}_2$, as long as $r = r_1 \times r_2$ and that rank r_1 and r_2 decompositions of the input tensors lead to clusters that are independent relative to the join attribute, A. Authors have also argued theoretically and experimentally that the accuracy of the decomposition is especially high if the other attributes of the two relations $\mathcal{R}_1$ and $\mathcal{R}_2$ are independent from each other. Relying on this observation (which we also validate in Section 6), DBN tries to partition the input relational tensor $\mathcal{R}$ in such a way that the resulting partitions, $\mathcal{R}_1$ and $\mathcal{R}_2$, are as independent from each other as possible.

Remember that the support of an approximate FD is defined as the percentage of tuples in the data set for which the FD holds. Thus, in order to quantify the dependence of pairwise attributes, we rely on the supports of pairwise FDs. Since we have two possible FDs ($X \rightarrow Y$ and $Y \rightarrow X$) for each pair of attributes, we use the average of the two as the overall support of the pair of attributes X and Y. Given these pairwise supports we approximate the overall dependency between two partitions $\mathcal{R}_1$ and $\mathcal{R}_2$ using the average support of the pairwise FDs (excluding the pairwise FDs involving the join attribute) crossing the two partitions. We refer to this as *interFD* and the partitioning based on interFD as the interFD-based partitioning strategy.

We formulate this interFD-based partitioning problem as a graph partitioning problem: Let the pairwise FD graph, $G_{pfd}(V, E)$, be a complete, weighted, and undirected graph, where each vertex $v \in V$ represents an attribute and the weights of the edge between nodes v_i and v_j is the average support of the approximate FDs $v_i \rightarrow v_j$ and $v_j \rightarrow v_i$. The problem is then to locate a cut on G_{pfd} with the minimum *average* weight.

This graph partitioning problem is similar to the minimum cut problem [19], with some key differences. The major difference is that we do not seek a cut with minimum *total* weight, but a cut with minimum *average* weight. Also, depending on whether we are operating on dense or sparse networks, we may or may not seek to impose a balance criterion on the partitions: for sparse tensors, the cost of tensor decomposition increases linearly with the number of modes and since the total number of modes of the two partitions is constant, we do not need to seek balance.

In DBN, we use a modified version of the minimum cut algorithm proposed in [19] to seek minimum average cuts. Given an undirected graph $G_{pfd}(V, E)$, for each vertex $v \in V$, the algorithm finds a vertex with the *minimum average cut* that separates it from the rest of the graph and creates a subset of vertices V' where the vertex is merged with its neighbor vertex, connected to the rest of the graph with the least average weight; the edges from these two vertices are replaced by a new edge weighted by the *average* of the weights of the original edges. The process is repeated while $V' \neq V$. The minimum of the minimum average cuts at each step of the algorithm is returned as the overall minimum average cut. When balance of the number of attributes is needed, the minimum is selected among the steps that lead to similar number of attributes. The complexity of this minimum average cut algorithm is $O(|V||E| + |V|^2 log|V|)$. Figure 4 shows an example of the process.

5. RANK PRUNING BASED ON INTRA-PARTITION DEPENDENCIES

Given a partitioning of $\mathcal{R}$ into of $\mathcal{R}_1$ and $\mathcal{R}_2$, to obtain a rank-r decomposition of $\mathcal{R}$, we need to consider rank-r_1 and rank-r_2 decompositions of $\mathcal{R}_1$ and $\mathcal{R}_2$, such that $r = r_1 \times r_2$ and pick the $\langle r_1, r_2 \rangle$ pair which is likely to minimize recombination errors.

We note, however, that we can rely on the supports of the dependencies that make up the partitions $\mathcal{R}_1$ and $\mathcal{R}_2$ to prune $\langle r_1, r_2 \rangle$ pairs which are not likely to give good fits. In particular, we observe that the higher the overall dependency between the attributes that make up a partition, the more likely the data in the partition can be described with a smaller number of clusters. Since the number of clusters of a data set is related to the rank of the decomposition, this leads to the observation that

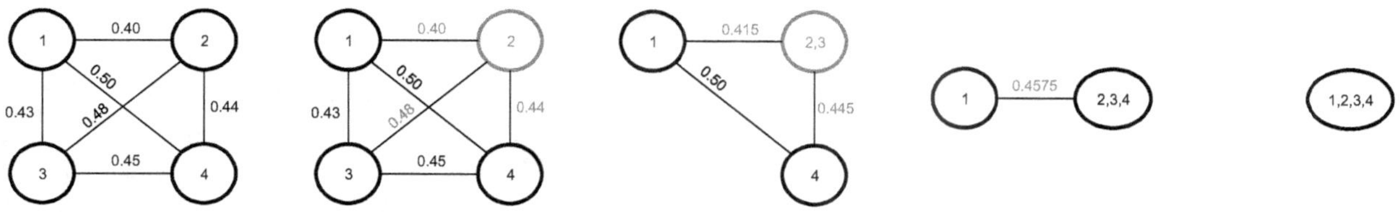

(a) $G_{pfd}(V,E)$ (b) Step 1 (c) Step 2 (d) Step 3 (e) Step 4

Figure 4: Minimum average cut algorithm for (a) $G_{pfd}(V,E)$. (b) Step 1: a cut between {2} and {1,3,4} is the minimum average cut (0.44). (c) Step 2: vertex 2 is merged with vertex 3 which has the minimum average weight to the rest of the vertices and a cut between {2,3} and {1,4} is the minimum average cut (0.43). (d) Step 3: vertices 2 and 3 are merged with vertex 4 and a cut between {1} and {2,3,4} is the minimum average cut (0.4575). (e) Step 4: the process ends since the subset of vertices is equal to V. The minimum of the minimum average cuts at each step is (c) {2,3} and {1,4}.

	Data set	Size
D1	Adult	$118 \times 90 \times 20263 \times 5 \times 2$
D2		$7 \times 20263 \times 5 \times 6 \times 16$
D3		$72 \times 20263 \times 90 \times 2 \times 2$
D4		$20263 \times 14 \times 2 \times 6 \times 94$
D5		$20263 \times 5 \times 2 \times 90 \times 72$
D6	Breast Cancer Wisconsin [14]	$645 \times 10 \times 11 \times 2 \times 10$
D7		$10 \times 645 \times 9 \times 10 \times 10$
D8		$10 \times 10 \times 11 \times 10 \times 645$
D9		$2 \times 10 \times 10 \times 10 \times 645$
D10		$10 \times 10 \times 645 \times 9 \times 10$
D11	IPUMS Census Database [18]	$3890 \times 4 \times 13 \times 3 \times 3$
D12		$545 \times 3 \times 17 \times 3 \times 2$
D13		$11 \times 3 \times 4 \times 5 \times 3$
D14	Mushroom	$10 \times 3 \times 5 \times 2 \times 7$
D15	Dermatology	$62 \times 5 \times 5 \times 5 \times 3$

Table 1: Relational tensor data sets with 5 attributes

Data set	Attributes	Join attr. (X)	Support of X	exec. time for FDs
D1	$\{A_{11}, A_{12}, A_3, A_9, A_{10}\}$	A_3	97%	0.024s
D2	$\{A_2, A_3, A_9, A_8, A_4\}$	A_3	80%	0.022s
D3	$\{A_1, A_3, A_{12}, A_{15}, A_{10}\}$	A_3	80%	0.025s
D4	$\{A_3, A_7, A_{15}, A_8, A_{13}\}$	A_3	75%	0.023s
D5	$\{A_3, A_9, A_{15}, A_{12}, A_1\}$	A_3	80%	0.023s
D6	$\{A_1, A_4, A_7, A_{11}, A_6\}$	A_1	96%	0.004s
D7	$\{A_4, A_1, A_{10}, A_8, A_9\}$	A_1	96%	0.003s
D8	$\{A_6, A_5, A_7, A_8, A_1\}$	A_1	96%	0.002s
D9	$\{A_{11}, A_9, A_6, A_3, A_1\}$	A_1	98%	0.003s
D10	$\{A_5, A_4, A_1, A_{10}, A_8\}$	A_1	96%	0.003s
D11	$\{A_8, A_{17}, A_{19}, A_3, A_2\}$	A_8	99%	0.007s
D12	$\{A_{53}, A_2, A_{21}, A_3, A_4\}$	A_{53}	98%	0.006s
D13	$\{A_{13}, A_{48}, A_{17}, A_{14}, A_2\}$	A_{13}	98%	0.005s
D14	$\{A_4, A_9, A_{18}, A_{17}, A_2\}$	A_2	88%	0.004s
D15	$\{A_{34}, A_{24}, A_{33}, A_{25}, A_{11}\}$	A_{34}	80%	0.002s

Table 2: Different attribute sets, join attributes (X), supports of X (the lowest of all the supports of $X \to *$), and execution times for FDs discovery for D1-D15 where A_n is the nth attribute of each data set

the higher the overall dependency between the attributes in a partition, the smaller should be the decomposition rank of that partition.

Thus, given $\mathcal{R}_1$ and $\mathcal{R}_2$, we need to consider only those rank pairs $\langle r_1, r_2 \rangle$, where if the average intra-partition FD support for $\mathcal{R}_1$ is larger than the support for $\mathcal{R}_2$, then $r_1 < r_2$ and vice versa. We refer to this as the *intraFD* criterion for rank pruning. Similarly to interFD, given the supports of FDs, we define intraFD as the average support of the pairwise FDs (excluding the pairwise FDs involving the join attribute) within each partition.

In the next section, we evaluate the effect of the interFD-based partitioning and intraFD-based rank pruning strategy of DBN for both dense and sparse tensor decomposition in terms of the efficiency and the accuracy.

6. EXPERIMENTAL EVALUATION

Here, we present experimental results assessing the efficiency and effectiveness of the proposed DBN scheme relative to the conventional implementation of the tensor decomposition in both stand-alone and parallelized versions. We used various data sets from UCI Machine Learning Repository [6].

6.1 Partitioning Cases

We consider two partitioning cases discussed in Section 4:

Case 1. Firstly, we evaluate DBN for the case where the join attribute X determines only a subset of the attributes of the relation $\mathcal{R}$. In this case, as long as one partition $\mathcal{R}_1$ has X and the determined attributes of X, the number of nonzero entries of $\mathcal{R}_1$ is less than or equal to that of $\mathcal{R}$ and the number of nonzero entries of the other partition $\mathcal{R}_2$ is same as that of $\mathcal{R}$. For dense tensor decomposition, we make the number of attributes of $\mathcal{R}_1$ and $\mathcal{R}_2$ similar.

For this case, we used a 5-mode relational tensor of dimensions $118 \times 90 \times 20263 \times 5 \times 2$ of the Adult data set (D1). We ran TANE [8] to find FDs on this data set. TANE identified almost exact FDs $A_3 \to A_9$ and $A_3 \to A_{10}$ (with 99% and 98% confidence respectively) where A_n is the nth attribute. Now we take A_3 as the join attribute and remove unmatched tuples (1.72%) for these two FDs to get the exact FDs. Next the tensor is normalized into two 3-mode tensors $\mathcal{R}_1$ $\{A_3, A_9, A_{10}\}$ and $\mathcal{R}_2$ $\{A_3, A_{11}, A_{12}\}$. We then create relational tensors corresponding to different table sizes by randomly selecting entries from the data.

Case 2. Secondly, we evaluate DBN in the case where the join attribute X determines all attributes of the relation $\mathcal{R}$. In this case, all partitioning cases generate as many tuple (nonzero entries) as the relation $\mathcal{R}$ and thus, it is not possible to select a configuration which better minimizes the total number of nonzero entries than the rest. In this case, for each pairwise FD support above a support threshold, $\tau_{support} = 75\%$, we take an attribute with the highest total pairwise FD support among all attributes of the input relation as the join attribute. For these experiments, we took 15 different data sets (D1-D15) with different sizes and different attribute sets (see Table 1) and we experimented all partitioning cases with the same number of tuples for $\mathcal{R}$, $\mathcal{R}_1$, and $\mathcal{R}_2$ for each data set.

All tensors were encoded as occurrence tensors (see Definition 3.1), where each entry is set to 1 or 0, indicating whether the corresponding tuple exists or not. Therefore, we report the number of nonzero entries. We also report the tensor size for the dense tensor decomposition since the decomposition cost of dense tensor decomposition depends on the size of dense tensors.

We experimented with rank-12 decompositions. DBN uses 6 combinations (1×12, 2×6, 3×4, 4×3, 6×2, and 12×1) for rank-12 decomposition for each relation in Table 1.

6.2 Implementation

Discovery of FDs. We employed TANE [8] and made an extension to detect approximate FDs for all pairs of attributes for pairwise FDs and remove all unmatched tuples to get the exact FDs for the normalization process based on the supports of the approximate FDs.

The supports of the approximate FDs for each attribute set of different relational data sets are shown in Table 2. The table also shows the execution times to discover FDs for each data set. The modified TANE algorithm is efficient when the number of attributes is small (5 attributes in these experiments). The overall cost increases linearly in the size of the input [8]. Since the execution times for finding approximate FDs are negligible compared to the tensor decomposition time, we focus on the decomposition times.

Tensor Decomposition. We experimented with alternative algorithms for both nonnegative CP tensor decomposition on the original tensors (NNCP) and DBN. Table 3 shows the various algorithms we use in our experiments.

The first decomposition algorithm we considered is the N-way PARAFAC algorithm with nonnegativity constraint (we call this N-way PARAFAC in the rest of the paper) which is available in the N-way Toolbox for MATLAB [1]. We refer to DBN and NNCP using N-way PARAFAC implementation as DBN-NWAY and NNCP-NWAY respectively.

Since MATLAB's N-way PARAFAC implementation uses a dense tensor (multi-dimensional array) representation, it is too costly to be practical, especially for sparse tensors. Another PARAFAC implementation, the CP-ALS algorithm [3], on the other hand, can run with both sparse and dense tensors. In the sparse tensor model, the cost increases linearly as the number of nonzero entries of the tensor increases. The CP-ALS, however, does not support nonnegative constraints. Therefore, we implemented a variant of the single grid NTF [17] using CP-ALS as the base PARAFAC algorithm. We refer to DBN and NNCP based on CP-ALS as DBN-CP and NNCP-CP respectively.

For the parallel version of the NNCP, we implemented the grid NTF algorithm [17] with two different partition strategies (2 and 6 grid cells along the join mode) using N-way PARAFAC and CP-ALS as the base PARAFAC algorithms. Each grid is run with the base PARAFAC algorithm separately in parallel and results are iteratively combined into the final decomposition based on an ALS-like approach. We refer to the grid NTF algorithm for the parallel NNCP using N-way PARAFAC with 2 and 6 grid cells as NNCP-NWAY-GRID2, and NNCP-NWAY-GRID6 respectively. Similarly, we refer to CP-ALS based implementations as NNCP-CP-GRID2 and NNCP-CP-GRID6.

For the parallel version of DBN, we implemented pairwise parallel DBN-NWAY and DBN-CP, referred to as pp-DBN-NWAY and pp-DBN-CP, respectively.

Finally, for DBN with a subset of pairs, DBN with 2 and 3 pairs selected based on the intraFD-based rank pruning strategy are referred to as DBN2 and DBN3 respectively. For all alternative DBN strategies can be DBN2 or DBN3

Algorithm	Description
DBN-NWAY	DBN using N-way PARAFAC
DBN-CP	DBN using single grid NTF (CP-ALS)
NNCP-NWAY	NNCP using N-way PARAFAC
NNCP-CP	NNCP using single grid NTF (CP-ALS)
pp-DBN-NWAY	pairwise parallel DBN-NWAY
NNCP-NWAY-GRID2	NNCP using grid NTF with 2 grid cells (N-way PARAFAC)
NNCP-NWAY-GRID6	NNCP using grid NTF with 6 grid cells (N-way PARAFAC)
pp-DBN-CP	pairwise parallel DBN-CP
NNCP-CP-GRID2	NNCP-CP with 2 grid cells
NNCP-CP-GRID6	NNCP-CP with 6 grid cells
DBN2	intraFD-based DBN with 2 pairs
DBN3	intraFD-based DBN with 3 pairs

Table 3: Algorithms. Note that the decomposition algorithms in parentheses are the base PARAFAC algorithm for the grid NTF.

according to the number of pairs selected (e.g., DBN2-CP for DBN-CP with 2 pairs selected).

We ran our experiments on an 6 cores Intel(R) Xeon(R) CPU X5355 @ 2.66GHz with 24GB of RAM. We used MATLAB Version 7.11.0.584 (R2010b) 64-bit (glnxa64) for the general implementation and MATLAB Parallel Computing Toolbox for the parallel implementation of DBN and NNCP.

6.2.1 Accuracy

We use the following *fit* function to measure tensor decomposition accuracy: The fit measure is defined as

$$\text{fit}(\mathfrak{X}, \hat{\mathfrak{X}}) = 1 - \frac{\|\mathfrak{X}, \hat{\mathfrak{X}}\|}{\|\mathfrak{X}\|}, \quad (1)$$

where $\|\mathfrak{X}\|$ is the Frobenius norm of a tensor $\mathfrak{X}$. The fit is a normalized measure of how accurate a tensor decomposition of $\mathfrak{X}$, $\hat{\mathfrak{X}}$ with respect to a tensor $\mathfrak{X}$.

$\|\hat{\mathfrak{X}}\|$ is also used as an approximate fit measure of $\mathfrak{X}$ to substitute for fit computation for large data sets. The intuition behind this measure is as follows: For any $\mathcal{W}$ it can be shown that $\|\mathcal{W} - \hat{\mathcal{W}}\| \geq \|\mathcal{W}\| - \|\hat{\mathcal{W}}\|$. Therefore, as long as $\|\mathcal{W}\| \geq \|\hat{\mathcal{W}}\|$ holds, we can minimize the term $\|\mathcal{W} - \hat{\mathcal{W}}\|$ by maximizing $\|\hat{\mathcal{W}}\|$.

Our evaluation criteria also include *fit ratio* which indicates how accurate one strategy compared with the other strategy in terms of *fit* to the input tensor. For example, the fit_ratio of DBN to NNCP is defined as

$$\text{fit\_ratio} = \frac{\text{fit}(\mathfrak{X}, \hat{\mathfrak{X}}_{dbn})}{\text{fit}(\mathfrak{X}, \hat{\mathfrak{X}}_{nncp})} \quad (2)$$

where $\mathfrak{X}$ is the input tensor, $\hat{\mathfrak{X}}_{nncp}$ is the tensor obtained by re-composing the NNCP tensor, and $\hat{\mathfrak{X}}_{dbn}$ is the tensor obtained by re-composing the DBN tensor.

6.3 Results

6.3.1 Execution time

As discussed in Section 6.1, we evaluate the execution times of DBN vs. the conventional nonnegative CP (NNCP) algorithms (Table 3) for two partitioning cases: in the first case, the join attribute X determines only a subset of the attributes of the relation $\mathcal{R}$; that is, $\text{nnz}(\mathcal{R}_1) \leq \text{nnz}(\mathcal{R})$ and $\text{nnz}(\mathcal{R}_2) = \text{nnz}(\mathcal{R})$ where $\text{nnz}(\mathcal{X})$ denotes the number of nonzero entries of $\mathcal{X}$. In the second case, the join attribute X

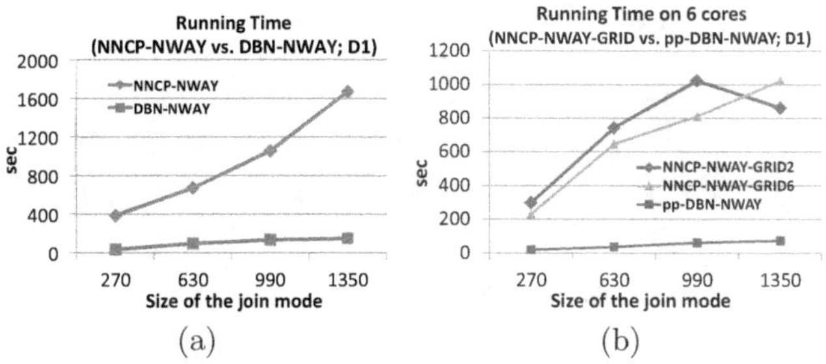

Figure 5: Average running times of (a) NNCP-NWAY vs. DBN-NWAY and (b) NNCP-NWAY-GRID vs. pp-DBN-NWAY on 6 cores for Adult data set (D1)

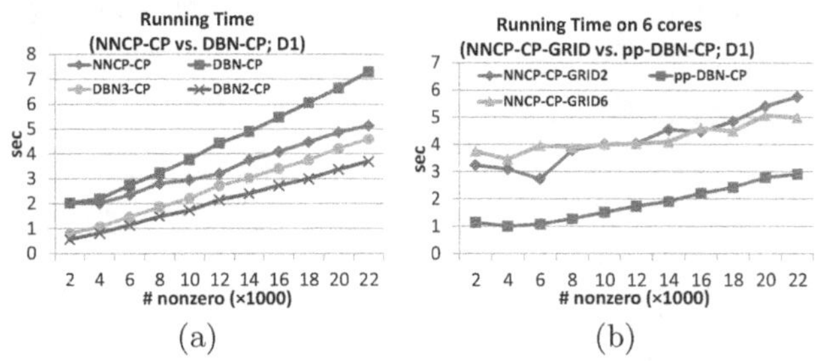

Figure 6: Average running times of (a) NNCP-CP vs. DBN-CP with different pair selections and (b) NNCP-CP-GRID vs. pp-DBN-CP on 6 cores for Adult data set (D1)

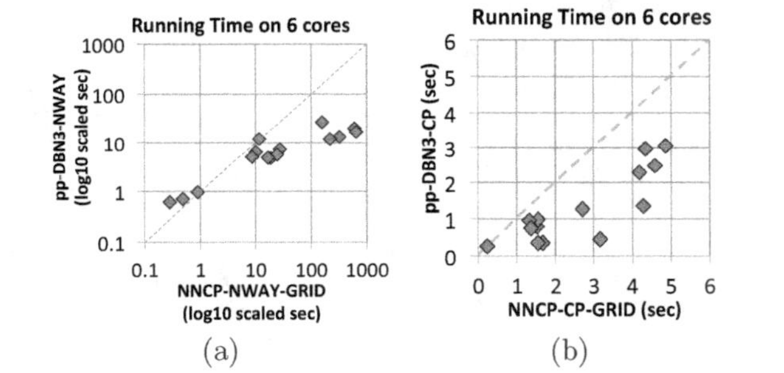

Figure 7: Average running times of (a) NNCP-NWAY-GRID (avg of GRID2 and GRID6) vs. pp-DBN3-NWAY and (b) NNCP-CP-GRID vs. pp-DBN3-CP on 6 cores for D1-D15. In both cases, most of data points are located under the diagonal, which indicates that DBN outperforms NNCP

determines all attributes of the relation $\mathcal{R}$; that is nnz($\mathcal{R}_1$) = nnz($\mathcal{R}_2$) = nnz($\mathcal{R}$).

Case 1: X does not determine all attributes of $\mathcal{R}$.

First we present the execution times for dense tensor decomposition. As seen in Figure 5, for NNCP-NWAY, as the tensor size increases, the execution time increases fast. DBN-NWAY, running on smaller number of modes than NNCP, saves significant amount of time.

Figure 5 (b) shows the running time of NNCP-NWAY-GRID2 and NNCP-NWAY-GRID6 vs. pp-DBN-NWAY on 6 cores. Comparing the execution times in the figure against the single core execution times in Figure 5 (a) shows that the DBN-NWAY benefits more from parallelization. Since the grid NTF divides a larger tensor into smaller sub-tensors but with the same number of modes as the original tensor, parallelization does not save as much as in pp-DBN-NWAY where a larger tensor is divided into sub-tensors with a smaller number of modes.

Figure 6 presents results for sparse tensor decompositions, NNCP-CP vs. DBN-CP with different pair selections on single-core and NNCP-CP-GRID vs. pp-DBN-CP on 6 cores. Since we select a foreign key for normalizing the input relation, one of the normalized relations in DBN-CP has the same number of nonzero entries as that of the original relation. As a result, when using a single core, the sparse tensor DBN time (which is determined by the number of tuples) exceeds the time required to decompose the original relation. As discussed in Section 5, we address this using the intraFD-based rank pruning strategy. Figure 6 (a) shows that we achieve the better performance by choosing 2 pairs or 3 pairs in DBN based on intraFD.

Furthermore, as shown in Figure 6 (b), when using multiple cores, the proposed pp-DBN-CP achieves greater execution time savings and, therefore, significantly outperforms parallelized versions of NNCP. As seen in the figure, pp-DBN-CP has the lowest execution time. The grid based parallelization of NNCP does not improve the running time much, since the underlying ALS-based combining approach involves significant communication overheads.

Case 2: X determines all attributes of $\mathcal{R}$.

Since in this case, selection of a configuration is especially difficult, we also consider intraFD-based rank pruning strategy that can maximize the performance of DBN. We experiment NNCP-NWAY-GRID (avg. of NNCP-NWAY-GRID2 and NNCP-NWAY-GRID6) vs. pp-DBN3-NWAY for dense tensor decomposition and NNCP-CP-GRID (avg. of NNCP-CP-GRID2 and NNCP-CP-GRID6) vs. pp-DBN3-CP for sparse tensor decomposition for D1-D15 on 6 cores. We use the average of all different partitioning cases for each data set. As shown in Figure 7, in most cases of both experiments, DBN outperforms NNCP, especially for dense tensor decomposition. In few cases, the running times are too small to make a significant difference between NNCP and DBN.

6.3.2 *Result Accuracy*

We compare the accuracy of DBN against standard NNCP. Note that we include results for DBN-CP and NNCP-CP (results for DBN-NWAY and NNCP-NWAY are similar). We measured the fit ratios for all different partitioning cases of D1-D15 (Table 1). Note that fit computation requires a lot of memory (the computation is not feasible for some larger datasets). Thus, for large datasets with the size of the join mode bigger than 1,000, we created subsets of each tensor by sampling random 1,000 entries from the join mode and compute fit for NNCP-CP and DBN-CP.

As shown in Figure 8 (a), for an overwhelming majority of the experimented data sets, fit ratio falls in the range between 0.8 and 1 indicating that the proposed DBN scheme is, in addition to being efficient, also highly effective.

6.3.3 *InterFD-based Partitioning*

As discussed in Section 4.3, the proposed DBN strategy first identifies alternative normalized partitions of the relational tensor and then selects the most promising pair of partitions to compute the final decomposition. More specifically, the algorithm picks the most independent partitions according to the interFD.

In these experiments, we use 15 different configurations in Table 1. In order to quantify the benefits of the interFD-based partitioning strategy, we measure the ratio of the difference between the approximate fits of interFD-based partitions and the minimum approximate fits against the difference between the maximum and minimum approximate fits among all partitioning alternatives of each data set.

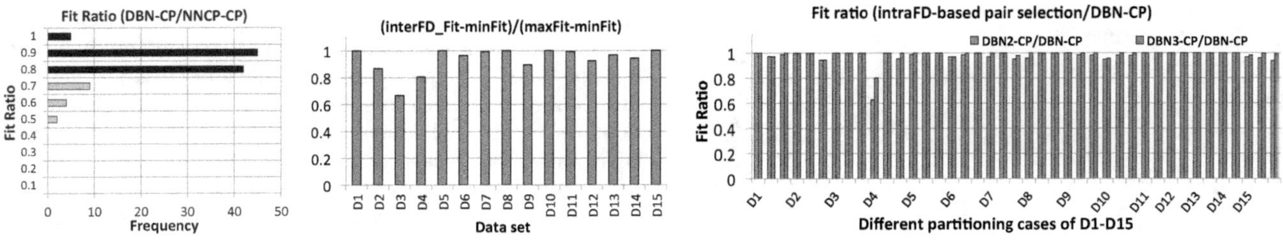

(a) (b) (c)

Figure 8: (a) Frequencies of fit ratios DBN-CP/NNCP-CP for all partitioning cases (108 cases) of D1-D15 (Table 1), (b) ratios of the difference between the approximate fits of interFD-based partitions and the minimum approximate fits against the difference between the maximum and minimum approximate fits among different partitioning cases of each data set, D1-D15, and (c) approximate fit ratio of DBN-CP with 2 and 3 pairs to DBN-CP with original 6 pairs for the partitioning cases (41 cases) of D1-D15 where each partition has more than 2 attributes

Results shown in Figure 8 (b) indicates that the interFD-based partitioning strategy results in fits very close to the optimal partitioning strategy. The few cases where the interFD-based strategy provides only 70 – 80% of the optimal attribute partitioning is largely due to the pairwise nature of interFD. This tends to miss multi-attribute dependencies of the form $AB \to C$ with high support, e.g., in D3, we miss $A_1A_3 \to A_{15}$ whose support is 94%.

6.3.4 IntraFD-based Rank Pruning

We compare the approximate fit of DBN-CP with 2 and 3 pairs selected based on the intraFD-based rank pruning strategy against that of DBN-CP using the original 6 pairs. Note that we use only the cases (41 cases) where each subtensor has more than 2 attributes (only the join attribute and a determined attribute) for each data set since the intraFD does not include pairwise FDs involving the join attribute. As shown in Figure 8 (c), the intraFD-based rank pruning strategy of DBN-CP has a good accuracy. The approximate fit ratios in the most of cases of DBN3-CP are close to 1; in other words, one of the 3 pairs in DBN3-CP gives the best approximate fit. Note that the data set D4 (with partitions $\{A_3, A_7, A_{15}\}$ and $\{A_3, A_8, A_{13}\}$) gives the worst approximate fit for both DBN2-CP and DBN3-CP, with fit ratios 0.63 and 0.80 respectively. This is because, the intraFD strategy with only pairwise dependencies may on occasion fail to take into account critical dependencies, such as $A_3A_7 \to A_{15}$ with 92% support.

7. CONCLUSIONS

Lifecycle of most data includes various operations, from capture, integration, projection, to data decomposition and analysis. To address the high cost of tensor decompsition, which is highest among these operations, we proposed a highly efficient, effective, and parallelized DBN strategy for approximately evaluating decompositions by normalizing a large relation into the smaller tensors based on the FDs of the relation and then performing the decompositions of these smaller tensors. We also proposed interFD-based partitioning and intraFD-based rank pruning strategies for DBN based on pairwise FDs across the normalized partitions and within each normalized partition, respectively.

Experimental results confirmed the efficiency and effectiveness of the proposed DBN scheme, and its interFD and intraFD based optimization strategies, compared to the conventional NNCP approach.

8. REFERENCES

[1] C. A. Andersson and R. Bro. The N-way Toolbox for MATLAB. Chemometr. Intell. Lab., 52(1):1-4, 2000.

[2] J. Antikainen *et al.* Nonnegative Tensor Factorization Accelerated Using GPGPU. In TPDS, 22(7):1135-1141, 2011. National Laboratories, 2006.

[3] B. W. Bader and T. G. Kolda. MATLAB Tensor Toolbox Ver. 2.2, 2007.

[4] J. D. Carroll and J. J. Chang. Analysis of individual differences in multidimensional scaling via an N-way generalization of 'Eckart-Young' decomposition. Psychometrika, 35:283-319, 1970.

[5] E. F. Codd. Further normalization of the data base relational model. In Rustin, 1972.

[6] A. Frank and A. Asuncion. UCI Machine Learning Repository. Irvine, CA: U. of California, School of ICS, 2010.

[7] R. A. Harshman. Foundations of the PARAFAC procedure: Models and conditions for an "explanatory" multi-modal factor analysis. UCLA working papers in phonetics, 1970.

[8] Y. Huhtala *et al.* TANE: An efficient algorithm for discovering functional and approximate dependencies. Comput. J., 42 (2):100-111, 1999.

[9] I. F. Ilyas *et al.* CORDS: Automatic discovery of correlations and soft functional dependencies. In SIGMOD, 647-658, 2004.

[10] M. Kim and K. S. Candan. Approximate tensor decomposition within a tensor-relational algebraic framework. In CIKM, 2011.

[11] T. G. Kolda *et al.* Higher-order web link analysis using multilinear algebra. In ICDM, 2005.

[12] T. G. Kolda and J. Sun. Scalable tensor decompositions for multi-aspect data mining. In ICDM, 363-372, 2008.

[13] S. Lopes *et al.* Efficient discovery of functional dependencies and armstrong relations. In EDBT, 2000.

[14] O. L. Mangasarian and W. H. Wolberg. Cancer diagnosis via linear programming. SIAM News, 23(5):1-18, 1990.

[15] H. Mannila and K. Räihä. On the complexity of inferring functional dependencies. Discrete Appl. Math., 40:237-243, 1992.

[16] H. Mannila and H. Toivonen. Levelwise search and borders of theories in knowledge discovery. Data Min. Knowl. Discov., 1(3):259-289, 1997.

[17] A. H. Phan and A. Cichocki. PARAFAC algorithms for large-scale problems. Neurocomputing, 74(11):1970-1984, 2011.

[18] S. Ruggles and M. Sobek. Integrated Public Use Microdata Series: Version 2.0 Minneapolis: Historical Census Projects, U. of Minnesota, 1997.

[19] M. Stoer and F. Wagner. A simple min-cut algorithm. J. ACM, 44 (4):585-59, 1997.

[20] C. E. Tsourakakis. Mach: Fast randomized tensor decompositions. In SDM, 2010.

[21] L. R. Tucker. Some mathematical notes on three-mode factor analysis. Psychometrika, 31, 1966.

[22] C. M. Wyss *et al.* FastFDs: A heuristic-driven, depth-first algorithm for mining functional dependencies from relation instances. In DaWak, 2001.

[23] Q. Zhang *et al.* A parallel nonnegative tensor factorization algorithm for mining global climate data. ICCS, 2009.

A Filter-based Protocol for Continuous Queries over Imprecise Location Data

Yifan Jin† Reynold Cheng† Ben Kao† Kam-Yiu Lam‡ Yinuo Zhang§*

†University of Hong Kong ‡City University of Hong Kong §University of Southern California

†{yfjin, ckcheng, kao}@cs.hku.hk ‡cskylam@cityu.edu.hk §yinuozha@usc.edu

ABSTRACT

In typical location-based services (LBS), moving objects (e.g., GPS-enabled mobile phones) report their locations through a wireless network. An LBS server can use the location information to answer various types of *continuous queries*. Due to hardware limitations, location data reported by the moving objects are often uncertain. In this paper, we study efficient methods for the execution of *Continuous Possible Nearest Neighbor Query* (CPoNNQ) that accesses imprecise location data. A CPoNNQ is a standing query (which is active during a period of time) such that, at any time point, all moving objects that have non-zero probabilities of being the nearest neighbor of a given query point are reported. To handle the continuous nature of a CPoNNQ, a simple solution is to require moving objects to continuously report their locations to the LBS server, which evaluates the query at every time step. To save communication bandwidth and mobile devices' batteries, we develop two *filter-based protocols* for CPoNNQ evaluation. Our protocols install "filter bounds" on moving objects, which suppress unnecessary location reporting and communication between the server and the moving objects. Through extensive experiments, we show that our protocols can effectively reduce communication costs while maintaining a high query quality.

Categories and Subject Descriptors

H.2.8 [**Database Management**]: Database Applications

General Terms

Algorithms, Performance

Keywords

continuous queries, uncertain database, communication cost

*Work done in the University of Hong Kong

CIKM'12, October 29–November 2, 2012, Maui, HI, USA.

1. INTRODUCTION

With the advances in mobile computing devices and mobile communication technologies, various location-based services (LBS), such as navigation and map-based services, have emerged. Fig. 1(a) shows a simple location-based system in which a location server maintains a database that continuously registers the most updated locations of a set of moving objects. The location of the moving objects can be acquired by positioning devices, e.g., *Global Positioning System* (GPS). Once the location of an object is captured, it is reported as a location update to the location server through a wireless network. The location information collected at the server can support different spatial queries, for instance, "Tell me whether one of my friends is in the same building as me".

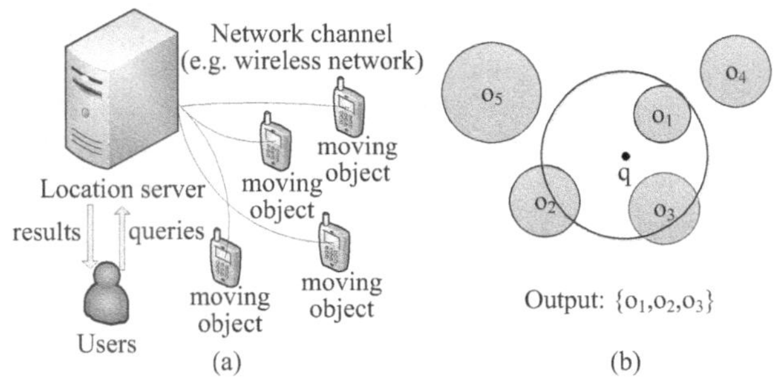

Figure 1: (a) A simple location-based system. (b) An example of *CPoNNQ*.

Due to the imprecision of location sensing devices, location values captured by the moving objects are only approximation at best [1, 2, 3, 4]. The actual locations of objects are therefore uncertain. Various studies have been conducted on how to improve the quality of queries' answers given that object locations are uncertain. The most prominent approach is to impose an uncertainty model on objects' locations and evaluate queries based on this model [2, 5, 6, 7]. A typical uncertainty model defines an *uncertainty region* for each object, which is a closed region that confines the possible location of that object. For example, in Fig. 1(b), the location uncertainty of objects is modeled using circular uncertainty regions.

One of the most studied spatial queries is the nearest neighbor query (NNQ). Given a query point q, the NNQ on q returns the object that is the closest to q in space. With location uncertainty, the answer to an NNQ is uncertain as well. An approach is to evaluate the possibility of each object being the NNQ's answer. Efficient methods have previously been put forward to solve this problem [2, 3, 6, 8]. We note that existing solutions to the NNQ problem assume that a snapshot of the objects' locations (and their uncertainty models) is given. The answer returned, therefore, is good only for a particular time instant. In many cases, however, we are interested in answering an NNQ *continuously* over an extensive period of time. For example, one might want to be continuously informed about which battalion is the closest to a military base while the troops are in motion. In this case, the NNQ is a standing query that is evaluated continuously.

We remark that existing methods for answering NNQ are inadequate in handling continuous NNQ. This is because a snapshot of the moving objects' locations have to be reported at every single time step. This imposes big demands on the communication bandwidth and battery power on the mobile devices, as well as on the computation overhead on the location server. To solve this problem, we consider two ideas: (1) Objects that have a zero chance of being the answer of an NNQ could be *muted* (i.e., they do not have to report their locations by each time step and their locations need not be considered by the location server in computing NNQ answers). (2) Location updates that do not change the NNQ answer need not be sent. Note that these two ideas help reducing the number of location updates (messages) sent from the moving objects as well as reducing the number of objects that have to be processed in determining the nearest neighbor. Continuous NNQ can therefore be answered more efficiently.

To realize the two ideas, we study the evaluation of *Continuous Possible Nearest Neighbor Query* (or *CPoNNQ*). Given a query point q, the *CPoNNQ* on q returns all moving objects that have non-zero probabilities of being the closest neighbors of q. As an example, in Fig 1(b), we see that the location of object o_4 is always farther away from q than that of object o_1. Therefore object o_4 is not a possible nearest neighbor of q. The same can be said for object o_5. The answer set of executing *CPoNNQ* on q is therefore $\{o_1, o_2, o_3\}$. Solving *CPoNNQ* realizes the first of the above two ideas. In particular, objects that are not in the answer set of a given *CPoNNQ* need not be handled and their location updates can be safely ignored.

We realize the second idea by studying message-efficient methods for executing *CPoNNQ*. Specifically, we propose *filter-based* protocols to avoid *redundant* location-update messages. A filter-based protocol installs *filter bounds* on each object. Essentially, a filter bound is a simple distance constraint that can be easily verified by the moving object. As long as an object satisfies its filter bounds, its location updates can be suppressed because the protocol ensures that those updates do not affect the query answer. We propose two filter-based protocols. For the first one, the *basic filter protocol* (BFP), we focus on designing effective filter bounds whose violations precisely capture the moments at which the *CPoNNQ* answer could be changed. When such violations occur, moving objects are probed for their most updated locations and new revised filters are installed in them. For the second protocol, the *optimized filter protocol* (OFP), we focus on identifying objects whose locations need not be reported and filter bounds that need not be updated even when filter violations occur. OFP can therefore save even more communication bandwidth and battery power compared with BFP.

The rest of paper is organized as follows. Section 2 presents the related work. We introduce the system model and define the *CPoNNQ* in Section 3. The Basic Filter Protocol (BFP) and the Optimized Filter Protocol (OFP) are presented in Sections 4 and 5, respectively. We give our experimental results evaluating the performances of BFP and OFP in Section 6. In Section 7 we conclude the paper with a brief discussion on the future work.

2. RELATED WORK

Filter bound algorithms. To support continuous query evaluation in LBS and sensor networks, location and sensor data are constantly acquired from the external environments. Due to the limited battery power of the sensing devices (e.g., mobile phones and temperature sensors), as well as network bandwidth, it is crucial to maintain a low communication cost during query evaluation. Recently, the concept of *filter bounds* have been proposed, which controls when a sensor should report its value. In [9, 10, 11], the authors proposed filter bound protocols for nearest neighbor queries. The authors in [12, 13, 14] developed filter bound protocols for range and top-k queries. The work in [10] studied the use of filter bounds in a peer-to-peer environment. However, all these work do not consider the important issue of *data uncertainty*, which can lead to incorrect results if it is not managed carefully. So far, few filter bound algorithms have considered data uncertainty. The authors in [7, 15] studied filter bound algorithms for continuous range queries on uncertain data. These protocols treat the user query range as a filter bound, and send it to the sensors involved. It is not clear how this protocol can be used to handle a *CPoNNQ*, since the query range is not defined in a *CPoNNQ*. In this paper, we explain how to design filter bounds for supporting this query, which, to our best knowledge, has not been studied before.

Nearest neighbor queries for uncertain data. In [2, 3, 16], the problem of efficiently evaluating a nearest-neighbor query on uncertain data was studied. They assume a *snapshot* query model; that is, the query is evaluated only once. A *CPoNNQ* stays in the system for an extensive amount of time, during which query answers need to be constantly refreshed. In [6], the authors studied the evaluation of a continuous NNQ. That paper focuses on how to incrementally recompute a query answer, after a new data value is received. However, it does not control when a sensor should report its value, and therefore cannot reduce communication costs. In this paper, we examine the use of filter bound protocols, with the goal of reducing communication and energy costs. Since the server receives less updates from sensors, the computation cost between the server and the sensors, as demonstrated in our experiments, can also be reduced.

3. PROBLEM DEFINITION AND THE BASELINE PROTOCOL

We now describe the architecture of an LBS system, and formally define *CPoNNQ* (Section 3.1). In Section 3.2, we describe a simple protocol for maintaining the answer of a *CPoNNQ*. Table 1 lists the symbols used in the paper.

Table 1: Description of symbols

Symbol	Description
q	The query point of a *CPoNNQ*
k	The number of moving objects
o_i	A moving object
$n_i(t)$	The distance from q to the closest point on o_i's uncertainty region at timestamp t
$f_i(t)$	The distance from q to the farthest point on o_i's uncertainty region at timestamp t
t_u	The time at which the most recent filter bounds are set by the location server.
t'_u	The time at which filter bounds were set just before t_u
$[l(n_i(t)), u(n_i(t))]$	A filter bound on $n_i(t)$ at timestamp t.
$[l(f_i(t)), u(f_i(t))]$	A filter bound on $f_i(t)$ at timestamp t.
$o_{\sigma(t)}$	The min-max object at timestamp t
$M(t)$	The set of objects with non-zero probabilities to be the NN of q, excluding $o_{\sigma(t)}$, at timestamp t
$F(t)$	The set of objects that cannot be NN of q at timestamp t
$A(t)$	The answer of *CPoNNQ* at timestamp t, i.e., $M(t) \cup \{o_{\sigma(t)}\}$

3.1 System Architecture

Fig. 2 depicts an LBS system. It consists of three parties: users, a location server, and a number (k) of moving objects maintained in the database (DB). We assume that each moving object is equipped with a positioning device, which captures the location of the object periodically with a periodicity of once every *dt* seconds. Different objects could have different periodicities (*dt*). In our simplest protocol (called *baseline* in Section 3.2), the location of a moving object is sent to the server as a location update message immediately after it is generated. Once the server receives an update message (from any object), it registers the update in the uncertain database together with the timestamp at which the update is generated. We can consider time being marked by a sequence of such timestamps $< t_0, t_1, ..., >$. In this paper, we define a timestamp to be a time instant at which an update is generated by an object. Between two consecutive timestamps, no location updates are made and the answer to a *CPoNNQ* is considered unchanged. We assume that the uncertainty region of a moving object is represented by a circular region similar to the one shown in Fig. 1(b) and the server can deduce the uncertainty region of an object based on the received location value.

A user submits a *CPoNNQ* to the location server, which processes the query via a Query Manager. This module accesses the uncertain database, and computes the answer based on the latest locations of the objects and their uncertainty regions. We now formally define a *CPoNNQ* below:

Definition 1. Given a query point q, a time interval $[t_s, t_e]$, a **Continuous Possible Nearest Neighbor Query** (or **CPoNNQ** in short) returns an answer set $A(t)$ for each timestamp $t \in [t_s, t_e]$ such that all and only those objects with non-zero probabilities of being the nearest neighbor of q at timestamp t are in $A(t)$.

As we have mentioned in Section 1, we aim to achieve savings in communication bandwidth by applying the filter-based protocols. In Fig. 2, the server employs a Filter Manager, which determines the filters to be sent to and installed

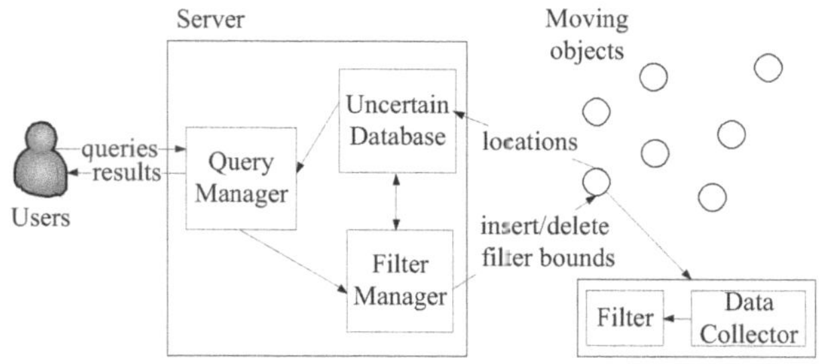

Figure 2: System architecture

at the moving objects. These filters are computed based on the standing *CPoNNQ* and the objects' locations. Once a *CPoNNQ* terminates (i.e., whose end time t_e is passed), the Filter Manger removes the filters that are associated with the query from the objects. The details of the Filter Manager will be covered in Sections 4 and 5.

3.2 The Baseline Protocol

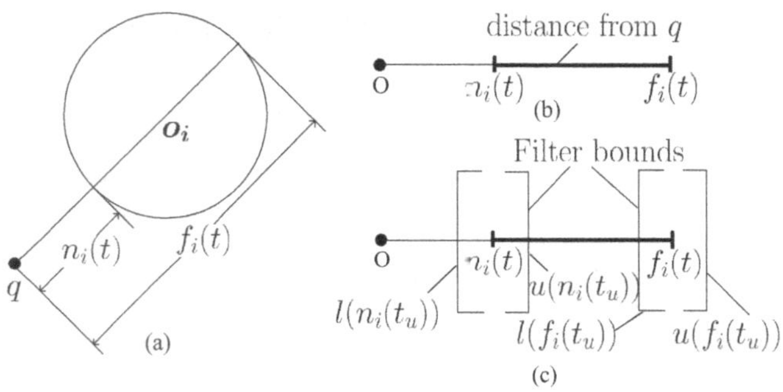

Figure 3: (a)Illustrating $n_i(t)$ and $f_i(t)$. (b) Distance of o_i from q. (c) Filter bounds for $n_i(t)$ and $f_i(t)$.

We now discuss a *baseline* protocol for processing *CPoNNQ*. A *CPoNNQ* with an interval $[t_s, t_e]$ submitted to the server becomes *active* at t_s. At t_s, the server broadcasts a message to all objects to acquire their most updated locations and activates their periodic location updates. The server then computes the answer set $A(t_s)$ by executing the procedure ComputePoNNQ (Algorithm 1. We will elaborate on this procedure shortly.) After that, each moving object o_i reports its location to the server once every dt_i seconds, where dt_i is the periodicity of o_i. Whenever a location update arrives at the server, ComputePoNNQ is executed again to refresh the answer. If the answer differs from the one of the previous timestamp, the revised answer will be reported to the user. At the end time of the query, t_e, if there are no more standing *CPoNNQ*s, the server instructs the moving objects to turn off location update messages.

At a given timestamp t, the procedure ComputePoNNQ first computes $n_i(t)$ and $f_i(t)$, which are the distances from q to the nearest point and the farthest point of each object o_i's uncertainty region, respectively. Fig. 3(a) illustrates these quantities. Then, the object with the smallest $f_i(t)$ is identified as the *min-max object*. Let $\sigma(t)$ be the index of this object and so $f_{\sigma(t)}(t) = \min_{i=1}^{k}\{f_i(t)\}$ is the min-max distance. It is easy to observe that for any object o_j, o_j is in

$A(t)$ if and only if $n_j(t) \leq f_{\sigma(t)}(t)$. All objects that satisfy the inequality are thus collected into the answer set $A(t)$.

```
A(t) ← ∅;
∀1 ≤ i ≤ k, compute n_i(t) and f_i(t) ;
σ(t) ← 1 ;
for i ← 2 to k do
    if f_i(t) < f_σ(t)(t) then
        σ(t) ← i;
Add o_σ(t) to answer set A(t);
for each object o_i do
    if n_i(t) ≤ f_σ(t)(t) then
        Add o_i to answer set A(t);
Return A(t);
```

Algorithm 1: ComputePoNNQ(timestamp t)

Although *baseline* maintains a correct answer set for *CPoNNQ*, it is very expensive because each object has to report its updated locations at every timestamp. To reduce the communication cost for sending location updates, we next propose two filter-based protocols, namely BFP and OFP.

4. BASIC FILTER PROTOCOL (BFP)

With the Basic Filter Protocol (BFP), at either the start time of a query or when a location update is received at the server, the server computes filter bounds that are sent and installed at each moving object. At any timestamp t, let t_u ($t_u \leq t$) be *the most recent* timestamp at which filter bounds are made. For each object o_i, recall that $n_i(t)$ and $f_i(t)$ are the nearest and the farthest distances of the query point q from the uncertainty region of o_i (see Figure 3). The filter bounds installed by the server on object o_i at timestamp t_u are two intervals: $[l(n_i(t_u)), u(n_i(t_u))$and $[l(f_i(t_u)), u(f_i(t_u))$[1], which constrain the values of $n_i(t)$ and $f_i(t)$, respectively[2] (see Figure 3(c)). As object o_i moves, its location and hence its uncertainty region change. However, as long as $n_i(t)$ and $f_i(t)$ are within the intervals defined by their filter bounds, any location updates generated by o_i are suppressed. This gives us the following filtering rule:

> **Filtering Rule:** When object o_i generates an update at timestamp t, if $n_i(t) \in [l(n_i(t_u)), u(n_i(t_u))$ and $f_i(t) \in [l(f_i(t_u)), u(f_i(t_u))$, then the update is not sent.

By suppressing update messages, our filter-based protocols save communication bandwidth. The key to the protocols is how to set the filters correctly so that the answer set to a *CPoNNQ* remains correct despite missing updates. In the rest of this section, we will first describe BFP by assuming that filters are correctly set. Then, in Section 4.1, we show how filters are derived and prove their correctness.

BFP is shown in Algorithm 2. It consists of an initialization phase, a maintenance phase, and a cleanup phase.

[1]To simplify our correctness proof, each interval is closed on the left and open on the right.

[2]The parameter t_u shown in the intervals indicates that the filter bounds were set at t_u, which is the timestamp of the most recent update. Since there are no location updates between two consecutive timestamps, the filter bounds set at t_u remain valid and are in effect at t, the current time instant.

The initialization phase is similar to that of the Baseline Protocol (Section 3.2). At the start time, t_s, of a *CPoNNQ*, the server broadcasts a message to all the objects to acquire their locations and computes the answer set $A(t_s)$. Then, the server derives the filter bounds for all the objects and sends the bounds to them. After that, the server switches to the maintenance phase. During the maintenance phase, when an update arrives (because a filter bound is violated by an object), the server probes all the objects to acquire their locations and recomputes the answer set. It revises the filter bounds and sends the bounds to the objects. At the end time of the query, the server enters the cleanup phase. It instructs objects to remove their filter bounds that are associated with the query.

```
Initialization:
Broadcast to all objects to acquire their most updated
  locations;
A(t_s) ← ComputePoNNQ(t_s);
for each object o_i do
    Compute filters [l(n_i(t_s)), u(n_i(t_s))) and
      [l(f_i(t_s)), u(f_i(t_s))) ;
    Send filters to o_i;
t_u ← t_s;
Maintenance:
Upon receiving an update at timestamp t, trigger:
A(t) ← ComputePoNNQ(t);
for each object o_i do
    Compute filters [l(n_i(t)), u(n_i(t))) and
      [l(f_i(t)), u(f_i(t))) ;
    Send filters to o_i;
t_u ← t;
Cleanup:
Broadcast to all objects to remove filters associated with
  the query;
```

Algorithm 2: BFP

4.1 Setting Filters

In Section 3.2, at timestamp t, we define $o_{\sigma(t)}$ to be *the min-max object* at t, i.e., $f_{\sigma(t)}(t)$ is the smallest among those of all objects. We have argued that for any object o_j, $o_j \in A(t)$ iff $n_j(t) \leq f_{\sigma(t)}(t)$. The object $o_{\sigma(t)}$, the objects that satisfy the above inequality, and the objects that do not satisfy the inequality thus form three groups of objects. We denote them as $o_{\sigma(t)}$, $M(t)$, and $F(t)$, respectively. Our protocol BFP defines three sets of filter bounds, one for each group.

Definition 2. $o_{\sigma(t)}$, $M(t)$ **and** $F(t)$
At any timestamp t, the min-max object $o_{\sigma(t)}$ is the one such that $f_{\sigma(t)}(t) = \min\{f_i(t) \mid o_i \in DB\}$.[3] Then, the set $M(t) = \{o_j \in DB - \{o_{\sigma(t)}\} | n_j(t) \leq f_{\sigma(t)}(t)\}$, and the set $F(t) = \{o_i \in DB - \{o_{\sigma(t)}\} | n_i(t) > f_{\sigma(t)}(t)\}$.

Let t_u be the timestamp at which the most recent update was received at the server. By our definition, $o_{\sigma(t_u)}$ is the min-max object at timestamp t_u. Its min-max distance $f_{\sigma(t_u)}(t_u)$ determines the sets $M(t_u)$ and $F(t_u)$, and together, they define the answer set $A(t_u)$ at timestamp t_u. We note that the three groups of objects $o_{\sigma(t)}$, $M(t)$ and $F(t)$ are defined based on the three conditions mentioned in Definition 2. Specifically, they are:

[3]If there are more than one such objects, we randomly pick one as $o_{\sigma(t)}$.

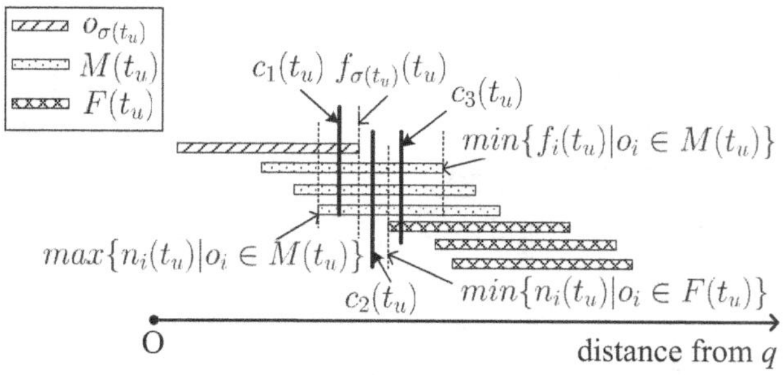

Figure 4: Illustration of three cutoff values at t_u.

(1) σ-condition: The object $o_{\sigma(t)}$ has to satisfy $f_{\sigma(t)}(t) = \min\{f_i(t) \mid o_i \in DB\}$.
(2) M-condition: All objects $o_j \in M(t)$ have to satisfy $n_j(t) \le f_{\sigma(t)}(t)$.
(3) F-condition: All objects $o_i \in F(t)$ have to satisfy $n_i(t) > f_{\sigma(t)}(t)$.

Now, at any timestamp $t > t_u$, if we can guarantee that the three conditions hold when we substitute $\sigma(t) = \sigma(t_u)$, $M(t) = M(t_u)$, and $F(t) = F(t_u)$, then we have $A(t) = A(t_u)$. That is, the answer set remains unchanged.

To ensure that the conditions hold, BFP determines three demarcations. The purpose of these demarcations is to detect any potential violations of the three conditions. As an example, we can set a demarcation at a cutoff value c such that at any timestamp $t > t_u$, the min-max object at timestamp t_u, i.e., $o_{\sigma(t_u)}$, submits an update message only if $f_{\sigma(t_u)}(t) < c$ and any object $o_j \in M(t_u)$ submits an update message only if $n_j(t) \ge c$. Then, if no messages are received from them, we know that $n_j(t) < c \le f_{\sigma(t_u)}(t)$ for all objects $o_j \in M(t_u)$. If we can further show that $\sigma(t) = \sigma(t_u)$, then $f_{\sigma(t_u)}(t) = f_{\sigma(t)}(t)$, and hence $n_j(t) < f_{\sigma(t)}(t)$ for all objects $o_j \in M(t_u)$. As a result, the M-condition stays valid if we substitute $M(t)$ by $M(t_u)$.

BFP uses three *cutoff values*, $c_1(t_u)$, $c_2(t_u)$, and $c_3(t_u)$ to detect the violations of the M-condition, the F-condition, and the σ-condition, respectively. Specifically, $c_1(t_u)$ is some value between $\max\{n_i(t_u)|o_i \in M(t_u)\}$ and $f_{\sigma(t_u)}(t_u)$, i.e.,

$$c_1(t_u) = (1-\alpha)\cdot\max\{n_i(t_u)|o_i \in M(t_u)\}+\alpha\cdot f_{\sigma(t_u)}(t_u) \quad (1)$$

The exact value of $c_1(t_u)$ is controlled by α, which is a real value between 0 and 1. Here we assume that $\alpha = 0.5$, i.e., $c_1(t_u)$ is in the middle of $\max\{n_i(t_u)|o_i \in M(t_u)\}$ and $f_{\sigma(t_u)}(t_u)$. We also tested different values of α in our experiments. The cutoff values $c_2(t_u)$ and $c_3(t_u)$ are similarly defined:

$$c_2(t_u) = (1-\alpha)\cdot f_{\sigma(t_u)}(t_u)+\alpha\cdot\min\{n_i(t_u)|o_i \in F(t_u)\} \quad (2)$$

$$c_3(t_u) = (1-\alpha)\cdot f_{\sigma(t_u)}(t_u)+\alpha\cdot\min\{f_i(t_u)|o_i \in M(t_u)\} \quad (3)$$

Fig. 4 illustrates $c_1(t_u)$, $c_2(t_u)$, and $c_3(t_u)$. We define the filter bounds of each object based on these values, as shown in Table 2. For example, for $o_{\sigma(t_u)}$, the bounds of $f_{\sigma(t_u)}(t)$ is $[c_1(t_u), \min\{c_2(t_u), c_3(t_u)\})$; for $o_j \in M(t_u)$, the bounds of $n_j(t)$ is $[0, c_1(t_u))$. So, if no filter bounds are violated, we have, $\forall o_j \in M(t_u), n_j(t) < c_1(t_u) \le f_{\sigma(t_u)}(t)$. From our previous discussion, this is exactly what we wanted to achieve with the demarcation c. Note that it is easy to verify that the intervals shown in Table 2 are well-defined. For example, we can show that $c_1(t_u) \le \min\{c_2(t_u), c_3(t_u)\}$.

Table 2: Filter bounds for $o_{\sigma(t_u)}$, $M(t_u)$ and $F(t_u)$ at timestamp t

Type	$l(n_i(t))$	$u(n_i(t))$	$l(f_i(t))$	$u(f_i(t))$
$o_{\sigma(t_u)}$	0	$f_i(t)$	$c_1(t_u)$	$\min\{c_2(t_u), c_3(t_u)\}$ [4].
$M(t_u)$	0	$c_1(t_u)$	$c_3(t_u)$	$+\infty$
$F(t_u)$	$c_2(t_u)$	$f_i(t)$	$n_i(t)$	$+\infty$

Hence the interval constraint for $f_{\sigma(t_u)}(t)$ is a valid interval. We now prove the correctness of BFP.

LEMMA 1. *Let t_u be the most recent timestamp at which filter bounds of objects are set. For any timestamp $t > t_u$, if no filter violations have occurred since t_u, $A(t) = A(t_u)$.*

Proof: Following our discussion, it suffices to show that the three conditions, namely, σ-condition, M-condition, and F-condition all hold if we substitute $\sigma(t)$ by $\sigma(t_u)$, $M(t)$ by $M(t_u)$, and $F(t)$ by $F(t_u)$.

σ-condition: If we substitute $\sigma(t)$ by $\sigma(t_u)$, the σ-condition becomes $f_{\sigma(t_u)}(t) = \min\{f_i(t)|o_i \in DB\}$, i.e., $o_{\sigma(t_u)}$ remains the min-max object at timestamp t. Since no filter violations have occurred, from Table 2, we know that
(1) $f_{\sigma(t_u)}(t) < \min\{c_2(t_u), c_3(t_u)\}$[5],
(2) $\forall o_j \in M(t_u), f_j(t) \ge c_3(t_u)$, and
(3) $\forall o_i \in F(t_u), f_i(t) > n_i(t) \ge c_2(t_u)$.
Hence, $f_{\sigma(t_u)}(t) < f_j(t)$, $\forall o_j \in (M(t_u) \cup F(t_u)) = DB - \{o_{\sigma(t_u)}\}$. The σ-condition thus follows.

M-condition: We have already shown that the M-condition holds if $\sigma(t) = \sigma(t_u)$. With the proof that the σ-condition holds, the M-condition follows.

F-condition: With the three substitutions, the F-condition reads: $\forall o_i \in F(t_u), n_i(t) > f_{\sigma(t_u)}(t)$. Again, with no filter violations, according to Table 2, we have (1) $f_{\sigma(t_u)}(t) < \min\{c_2(t_u), c_3(t_u)\}$ and (2) $\forall o_i \in F(t_u), n_i(t) \ge c_2(t_u)$. Hence, the F-condition follows.

In summary, if no filter violations have occurred since t_u, then at any timestamp $t > t_u$, $A(t) = A(t_u)$. Thus, BFP correctly maintains the answer set at timestamp t.

COROLLARY 1. *Given a* CPoNNQ *with start time t_s and end time t_e, BFP correctly maintains the answer set of the query at any timestamp $t \in [t_s, t_e]$.*

Proof: Let there be m and only m filter violations within the interval $(t_s, t_e]$, which occur at timestamps t_{u_1}, t_{u_2}, ... t_{u_m}. Let us use t_{u_0} to denote t_s, and $t_{u_{m+1}}$ to denote t_e. At any timestamp t_{u_i} $(0 \le i \le m)$, the server broadcasts to all the objects to acquire their locations. Hence the answer sets at those timestamps are correctly computed. For any other timestamps t, such that $t_{u_i} < t < t_{u_{i+1}}$ for some $0 \le i \le m$, protocol BFP returns $A(t_{u_i})$ as the answer. From Lemma 1, we know that $A(t) = A(t_{u_i})$. Hence BFP maintains correct answer sets at all timestamp $t \in [t_s, t_e]$.

5. OPTIMIZED FILTER PROTOCOL(OFP)

The main drawback of BFP is that whenever an update is received from an object, a large maintenance cost is involved:

[4]If the cardinality of $M(t_u)$ is zero, there is no $c_1(t_u)$ and $c_3(t_u)$ exist, here $u(f_i(t))$ is $c_2(t_u)$.

[5]Recall that the filter bound intervals are closed on the left and open on the right.

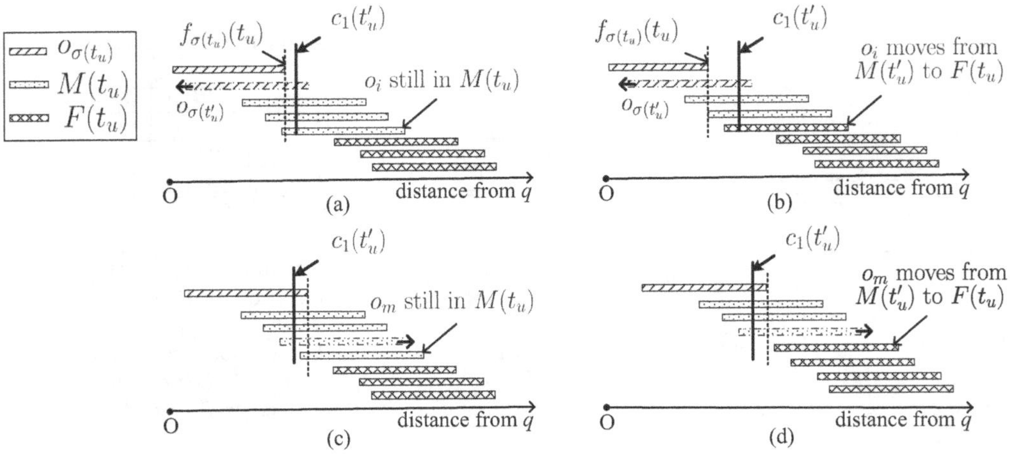

Figure 5: (a)e_σ case 1: no object in $M(t'_u)$ is assigned to $F(t_u)$. (b) e_σ case 2: some object $o_i \in M(t'_u)$ is assigned to $F(t_u)$. (c)e_M case 1: no object in $M(t'_u)$ is assigned to $F(t_u)$. (d)e_M case 2: $o_m \in M(t'_u)$ is assigned to $F(t_u)$.

the server has to request for the locations of all objects, recompute their filter bounds, and send these bounds to the objects. This is not always necessary. We now show how the maintenance overhead for two types of updates in BFP can be reduced. In this improved solution, *Optimized Filter Protocol (OFP)*, updates other than those related to o_σ and M are handled in the same way as in BFP. In Sections 5.1 and 5.2, we explain how to efficiently handle updates related to object o_σ and M, respectively.

5.1 Handling Updates of o_σ

We again let t_u be the timestamp at which the most recent filter bounds are set by the server. Let t'_u be the timestamp at which filter bounds were set just before t_u. We define the *update event*, called e_σ, for object $o_{\sigma(t'_u)}$, which occurs at timestamp t_u:

> **Event** e_σ: At timestamp t_u, the filter bound condition, $f_{\sigma(t'_u)}(t_u) \geq l(f_{\sigma(t'_u)}(t_u))$, is violated.

When e_σ occurs, $o_{\sigma(t'_u)}$ sends its location to the server. Instead of undergoing the costly maintenance phase of BFP, the server executes Algorithm 3. The algorithm has two goals: (1) it produces the correct answer set $A(t_u)$ (Steps 1-8), and (2) assigns filters correctly to the objects (Steps 9-20), which is proved by the following two lemmas.

LEMMA 2. *Steps 1-8 of Algorithm 3 correctly derive the query answer (i.e., $A(t_u)$) at timestamp t_u.*

Proof: We first claim that $\sigma(t'_u) = \sigma(t_u)$. Observe that:
(1) $o_{\sigma(t'_u)}$ is the min-max object from time $t \in [t'_u, t_u)$,
(2) $f_{\sigma(t'_u)}(t_u) < f_{\sigma(t'_u)}(t'_u)$ (since e_σ occurs), and
(3) No filter violations have occurred at any timestamp $t \in [t'_u, t_u)$.

Hence, $o_{\sigma(t'_u)}$ is the min-max object at timestamp t_u, and Step 3 correctly assigns $\sigma(t'_u)$ to $\sigma(t_u)$.

We next show that $M(t_u)$ and $F(t_u)$ can be correctly obtained. Step 2 fetches the latest values of $M(t'_u)$ and $o_{\sigma(t'_u)}$. Step 3 copies the information obtained at timestamp t'_u to the sets defined at timestamp t_u. In Steps 4-8, we check whether it is possible for some object $o_i \in M(t'_u)$ to be moved to $F(t_u)$. This is illustrated in Fig. 5(b), where after $o_{\sigma(t'_u)}$ (dotted-line rectangle) has moved to the left at t_u, $f_{\sigma(t'_u)}(t_u)$ is smaller than $n_i(t_u)$ of some object o_i. Hence, this o_i becomes a member of $F(t_u)$, as handled by Steps 6-7. Notice that all objects in $F(t'_u)$ remain in $F(t_u)$, since (1) for all $o_i \in F(t'_u), n_i(t_u) \geq c_2(t'_u)$; and (2) $c_2(t'_u) > c_1(t'_u) > f_{\sigma(t'_u)}(t_u)$. Thus, $n_i(t_u) > f_{\sigma(t'_u)}(t_u)$. Hence, Steps 1-8 correctly derives $A(t_u)$.

In Step 8, the variable *m2f* indicates whether an object o_i, originally in $M(t'_u)$, now belongs to $F(t_u)$. It is used to compute filter bounds, as discussed next.

1 *m2f* $\leftarrow$ false;
2 Broadcast to $o_i \in (M(t'_u) \cup o_{\sigma(t'_u)})$ to acquire their newest locations;
3 $\sigma(t_u) \leftarrow \sigma(t'_u)$; $M(t_u) \leftarrow M(t'_u)$; $F(t_u) \leftarrow F(t'_u)$; $A(t_u) \leftarrow A(t'_u)$;
4 **for** *each object o_i in $M(t_u)$* **do**
5   **if** $n_i(t_u) > f_{\sigma(t_u)}(t_u)$ **then**
6   Move o_i from $M(t_u)$ to $F(t_u)$;
7   Delete o_i from $A(t_u)$;
8   *m2f* $\leftarrow$ true;
9 Obtain $c_1(t_u)$ and $c_3(t_u)$ using Equations 1 and 3;
10 **if** *m2f* $=$ *true* **then**
11     $c_2(t_u) \leftarrow (1-\alpha) \cdot f_{\sigma(t_u)}(t_u) + \alpha \cdot \min\{n_i(t_u) | o_i \in (M(t'_u) - M(t_u))\}$;
12 **else**
13     $c_2(t_u) \leftarrow c_2(t'_u)$;
14 **for** *each object o_i in $o_{\sigma(t_u)}$ or $M(t_u)$* **do**
15   Compute filters $[l(n_i(t_u)), u(n_i(t_u)))$ and $[l(f_i(t_u)), u(f_i(t_u)))$;
16   Send filters to o_i;
17 **if** *m2f* $=$ *true* **then**
18   **for** *each object o_i in $F(t_u)$* **do**
19   Compute filters $[l(n_i(t_u)), u(n_i(t_u)))$ and $[l(f_i(t_u)), u(f_i(t_u)))$;
20   Send filters to o_i;

Algorithm 3: OFP: maintenance for e_σ at t_u

LEMMA 3. *Let t_u be the most recent timestamp at which filter bounds of objects are set by Steps 9-20 of Algorithm 3. For any timestamp $t > t_u$, if no filter violations have occurred since t_u, then $A(t) = A(t_u)$.*

Proof: We now prove that σ-condition, M-condition, and F-condition all hold if we substitute $\sigma(t)$ by $\sigma(t_u)$, $M(t)$ by $M(t_u)$, and $F(t)$ by $F(t_u)$.

σ-condition: Lemma 2 shows that we correctly obtain $\sigma(t_u)$ and $M(t_u)$. In Step 3, we get their latest values. Hence, $c_1(t_u)$ and $c_3(t_u)$ can be set in the same way as BFP (Step 9). However, we cannot use Equation 2 to set $c_2(t_u)$, since the values of objects in $F(t_u)$ are *not* acquired by the algorithm. Our solution is to assign another value to $c_2(t_u)$, by considering two scenarios:

• $M(t_u) = M(t'_u)$. This is illustrated in Fig. 5(a), where after $o_{\sigma(t'_u)}$ (dotted rectangle) has moved to the left at timestamp t_u, $f_{\sigma(t'_u)}(t_u)$ is larger than all the $n_i(t_u)$ values for all $o_i \in M(t'_u)$. Hence, $M(t_u) = M(t'_u)$, and $F(t_u) = F(t'_u)$. Step 13 assigns $c_2(t'_u)$ to $c_2(t_u)$. This is correct, because:
(1) $f_{\sigma(t'_u)}(t_u) = f_{\sigma(t_u)}(t_u)$ ($\because \sigma(t_u) = \sigma(t'_u)$ as shown in Lemma 2),
(2) $f_{\sigma(t'_u)}(t_u) < c_2(t'_u)$ ($\because$ no filter violation for the upper bound of $f_{\sigma(t'_u)}(t_u)$), and
(3) $\min\{n_i(t_u)|o_i \in F(t_u)\} \geq c_2(t'_u)$ ($\because$ no filter violation for $F(t'_u)$, and $F(t'_u) = F(t_u)$).
We can thus see that:

$$c_2(t'_u) \in (f_{\sigma(t_u)}(t_u), \min\{n_i(t_u)|o_i \in F(t_u)\}] \quad (4)$$

Observe that $c_2(t'_u)$ is within the same range $(f_{\sigma(t_u)}(t_u), \min\{n_i(t_u)|o_i \in F(t_u)\}]$ of $c_2(t_u)$ (Equation 2). We thus replace $c_2(t_u)$ by $c_2(t'_u)$ in Table 2, and use arguments similar to those of Lemma 1 to show that the σ-condition holds.

• $M(t_u) \subset M(t'_u)$. There exists object o_i, where $o_i \in M(t'_u)$ but $o_i \in F(t_u)$. This is shown in Fig. 5(b). In Step 11, $c_2(t_u)$ is assigned the value of

$$\begin{aligned} c_2(t_u) \leftarrow & (1-\alpha)\cdot f_{\sigma(t_u)}(t_u) + \\ & \alpha \cdot \min\{n_i(t_u)|o_i \in (M(t'_u) - M(t_u))\} \end{aligned} \quad (5)$$

Observe that:
(1) $F(t_u) = F(t'_u) \cup (M(t'_u) - M(t_u))$,
(2) $\min\{n_i(t_u)|o_i \in (M(t'_u) - M(t_u))\} < c_1(t'_u)$ ($\because$ no violation in $M(t'_u)$),
(3) $\min\{n_i(t_u)|o_i \in F(t'_u)\} \geq c_2(t'_u)$ ($\because$ no violation in $F(t'_u)$).

Since $c_2(t'_u) > c_1(t'_u)$, we have $\min\{n_i(t_u)|o_i \in F(t_u)\} = \min\{n_i(t_u)|o_i \in (M(t'_u) - M(t_u))\}$. If we substitute this to Equation 2, we obtain Equation 5. Following the proof of Lemma 1, we see that the σ-condition holds.

M-condition: Step 2 of Algorithm 3 acquire the newest values of $o_{\sigma(t'_u)}$ and $M(t'_u)$. Step 9 uses these results to compute $c_1(t_u)$ and $c_3(t_u)$. Since these two values are used to compute the bound of $M(t_u)$ in Table 2, we can use the same argument of Lemma 1 to show that the M-condition holds.

F-condition: We have argued that the new value of $c_2(t_u)$, set in Steps 10-13, leads to the satisfaction of the σ-condition. We can use a similar argument to show that the F-condition holds. The details are skipped due to space limitation. Notice that when *m2f* is false, the old values of $c_2(t'_u)$ are used as $c_2(t_u)$. According to Table 2, $F(t_u)$ only depends on $c_2(t_u)$, with is equal to $c_2(t'_u)$. Hence, there is *no need* to send the filters to $F(t_u)$ (Steps 14-16). When *m2f* is true, the filter bounds computed based on $c_2(t_u)$ obtained in Step 11 are sent to all objects in $F(t_u)$ (Steps 17-20).

The advantage of Algorithm 3 is that it does not require the updated location of $F(t'_u)$. In case *m2f* is false, $F(t'_u) = F(t_u)$, no filter bounds are sent to $F(t_u)$. If the size of $F(t_u)$ is large, this can save a significant amount of communication cost.

```
1  m2f ← false;
2  Broadcast to o_i ∈ (M(t'_u) ∪ o_σ(t'_u)) to acquire their
   newest locations;
3  σ(t_u) ← σ(t'_u); M(t_u) ← M(t'_u); F(t_u) ← F(t'_u);
   A(t_u) ← A(t'_u);
4  if n_m(t_u) > f_σ(t_u)(t_u) then
5      Move o_m from M(t'_u) to F(t_u);
6      Delete o_m from A(t_u);
7      m2f ← true;
8  Obtain c_1(t_u) and c_3(t_u) using Equations 1 and 3;
9  if m2f = true and n_m(t_u) < c_2(t'_u) then
10     c_2(t_u) ← (1 − α) · f_σ(t_u)(t_u) + α · n_m(t_u);
11 else
12     c_2(t_u) ← c_2(t'_u) ;
13 for each object o_i in o_σ(t_u) or M(t_u) do
14     Compute filters [l(n_i(t)), u(n_i(t))) and
       [l(f_i(t)), u(f_i(t))) ;
15     Send filters to o_i;
16 if m2f = true then
17     if n_m(t_u) < c_2(t'_u) then
18         for each object o_i in F(t_u) do
19             Compute filters [l(n_i(t_u)), u(n_i(t_u))) and
               [l(f_i(t_u)), u(f_i(t_u))) ;
20             Send filters to o_i;
21     else
22         Compute filters [l(n_m(t_u)), u(n_m(t_u))) and
           [l(f_m(t_u)), u(f_m(t_u)));
23         Send filters to o_m;
```

Algorithm 4: OFP: maintenance for e_M at t_u

5.2 Handling Updates of Objects in M

Another update event, related to the set M, also allows communication cost savings. Let o_m be an object in $M(t_u)$. We now define the update event, called e_M, for any object o_m, as follows:

> **Event** e_M: At timestamp t_u, the filter bound condition, $n_m(t_u) < u(n_m(t_u))$, is violated.

When this event occurs, o_m sends its updated location value to the server. Two scenarios occur:

• $M(t_u) = M(t'_u)$, as illustrated in Fig. 5(c).

• $M(t_u) \subset M(t'_u)$, as shown in Fig. 5(d).

Notice that the cases described here are exactly the same as the ones for event e_σ. Specifically, in Fig. 5(a) and Fig. 5(c), no object in $M(t'_u)$ move to $F(t_u)$, whereas in Fig. 5(b) and Fig. 5(d), one or more objects change their type from $M(t'_u)$ to $F(t_u)$. Moreover, the upper bound $u(n_m(t_u))$ mentioned in e_M is $c_1(t'_u)$, which is the same as the lower bound $l(f_{\sigma(t'_u)}(t_u))$ described in e_σ. Hence, the solution we developed for handling e_M, Algorithm 4, is a slightly changed version of Algorithm 3. The main benefit of this algorithm is that if *m2f* is false, the update and filter bound assignment effort for $F(t_u)$ is saved. Otherwise, if $n_m(t_u) < c_2(t'_u)$, we update $c_2(t_u)$ and send the new filters to $F(t_u)$ (Steps 17-20). The detailed proof of this algorithm, which is similar to that of Algorithm 3, is skipped here due to space limitation.

To summarize, OFP is an enhanced version of BFP. In particular, the filter violation events e_σ and e_M are handled by Algorithms 3 and 4 respectively. To manage other kinds of filter violation, OFP borrows the event handling method of BFP. Next, we discuss the experimental results of our protocols.

6. PERFORMANCE EVALUATION

We now report the results obtained from the performance studies on the three protocols: the Baseline, the Basic Filter Protocol (BFP), and the Optimized Filter Protocol (OFP). In Section 6.1, we describe the experimental setup. We present the experimental results in Section 6.2.

6.1 Experimental Setup

We use VanetMobiSim [17], an open-source vehicular traffic generator, to simulate the movement of objects. This simulator can handle multi-lane roads, speed limits for different road categories, and traffic lights. We use the environment data provided by the TIGER data source [18], where the map used is a 10km × 10km region clipped from Washington DC. The simulation time (logical) is 300 seconds. In our experiments, an object's motion is based on the *Intelligent Driver Model with Lane Changing* model [19], which regulates an object's speed based on the movement of neighboring objects. The speed range of an object provided by this simulator is between 8.33 and 13.89m/s. We assume that every object is equipped with a GPS device, which can be used to obtain the current location of the object. The GPS device captures the location of the object once every second (i.e., periodicity $dt = 1$). The number of objects simulated is $1k$ by default, producing a total of $300k$ location values. The error of a location value is represented by a circle, with a radius of 10m. This number is based on the result of GPS error analysis provided by [20]. According to [21], the amount of energy required for sending (receiving) a message of each object is 77.4mJ (25.2mJ).

For each CPoNNQ, its query point is randomly generated within the map. Unless stated otherwise, each query has a lifetime of 300 seconds. In the latter part of the experiments, we will also explain the details of simulating multiple concurrent queries. We compare the performance of the three protocols studied here (i.e., baseline, BFP, and OFP) in terms of their communication and energy costs for executing a CPoNNQ. For communication costs, we measure their number of *uplink* and *downlink* messages. An uplink message is used by an object to send a location update to the server, while a downlink message is used by the server to send filter information to an object. We present the total number of these messages per second. We also analyze the rate of energy consumed by the objects for sending and receiving messages. Each data point presented in the figures is obtained by averaging over the results for 100 queries.

The simulation program is developed in Java, and the experiments are performed by using a PC, with a configuration of Intel E8300 2.83GHz CPU and 2048MB of main memory. Table 3 summarizes the parameters and their values used.

6.2 Experimental Results

1. Scalability. Fig. 6(a) illustrates the communication costs against the database size. For the baseline protocol, the number of messages increases linearly, because the larger the number of objects, the more uplink messages will be generated (Fig. 6(b)). Notice that BFP performs better than baseline: it saves about 56% of the number of messages created by baseline. This is because the filters installed to objects by BFP effectively reduces the number of uplink messages. As we can see from Fig. 6(b), when the number of objects, k, is 1,000, baseline generates 1,000 uplink messages per second, while BFP produces 117 of them, which is 88.3% less. The price of this improvement is the use of more downlink messages (Fig. 6(c)). While baseline does not produce any downlink messages, BFP needs 117 of them at $k = 1,000$. However, since the number of uplink messages saved by BFP (883) is much higher than that of the downlink messages it generates (117), the total number of messages required by BFP is still less than that of baseline.

Table 3: Parameters used in the experiments (default values are marked with asterisks)

Parameter	Values
Number of Objects	$500, 1k^{\star}, 1.5k, 2k, 4k, 6k, 8k, 10k$
Uncertainty Region Size (m)	$0, 10^{\star}, 50, 100, \ldots, 300$
α	$0.1, 0.2, \ldots, 0.5^{\star}, \ldots, 0.9$
Number of Queries	$50, 100^{\star}, 150, 200$
Query lifetime	300 seconds

Fig. 6(a) shows that OFP outperforms BFP. On average, OFP requires 22% less messages than BFP. This is because OFP uses better routines to handle events e_σ and e_M, which reduce the number of uplink messages required (Fig. 6(b)). Since fewer uplink messages are received by the server, it also has less chance to generate downlink messages. Hence, the number of downlink messages required by OFP is less than that of BFP (Fig. 6(c)). At $k = 1,000$, the number of downlink messages drops from 117 (for BFP) to 96 (for OFP). Consequently, OFP needs fewer messages than BFP.

We also study the energy consumption costs of the protocols. As we can see from Fig. 6(d) that the overall trend of energy consumption is similar to that of the communication costs in Fig. 6(a). They can be explained by the reasons stated above. Notice that there is an importance difference between these two figures. Particularly, BFP addresses an improvement of 71% over baseline in terms of energy consumption cost, which is *larger* than the savings in communication costs (56%). This is because the amount of energy required for sending an uplink message is about 3 times that of the downlink messages. Hence, the amount of energy saved by BFP, relative to baseline, is higher than the relative amount of communication costs it saves. We can make a similar observation about OFP. While OFP requires 22% less messages than BFP, it consumes 24% energy less than BFP.

2. Effect of Uncertainty Region Size. In the second set of experiments, we examine the effect of uncertainty region size on the performance of the protocols. Here we use the radius of the uncertainty region to denote its size. Notice that if the radius equals zero, it means that all locations of objects are exact. As shown in Fig. 7(a), the total number of messages remains unchanged for baseline; for BFP and OFP, the communication cost increases with the radius. To understand why, first observe that when the size of an uncertainty region increases, the value of $f_{\sigma(t)}(t)$ at timestamp t increases accordingly. Hence, more objects may become a member of the answer set (i.e., $M(t)$), and satisfy the M-condition at the time filters are installed at them. Secondly, with a larger uncertainty region, an object previously not in an an-

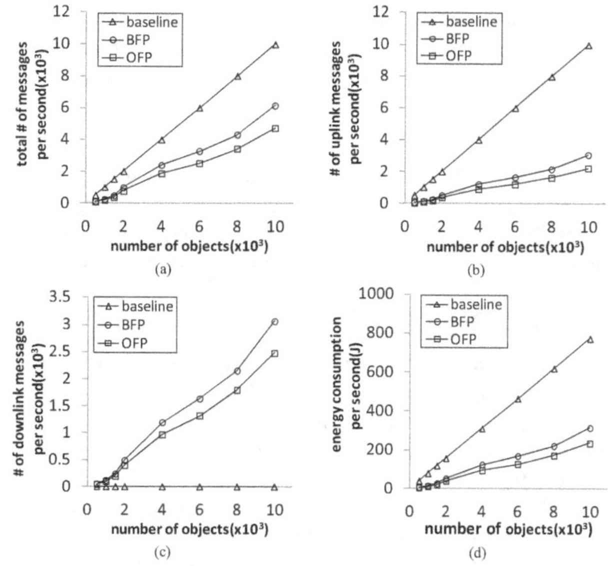

Figure 6: Effect of scalability: (a) Total # of messages; (b) # of uplink messages; (c) # of downlink messages; and (d) Energy consumption.

swer set can become a member of $M(t)$ more easily. Since the size of $M(t)$ is larger, the chance that the M-condition is later violated by any of the objects in $M(t)$ also increases. Finally, with a larger $M(t)$, the chance that any of these objects becomes o_σ later also rises. When this occurs, filters need to be regenerated for both BFP and OFP, thereby increasing their costs. Nevertheless, over a wide range of uncertainty region sizes, both protocols are still much better than baseline. When the radius is 300, for instance, BFP saves about 35% of messages required by baseline. In general, OFP performs better than BFP; when the radius is 300, it saves about 34% of BFP's communication cost. Fig. 7(b) illustrates the energy consumption costs of the three protocols. The performance is similar to Fig. 7(a), and the trend can be explained by using the same reason we just discussed.

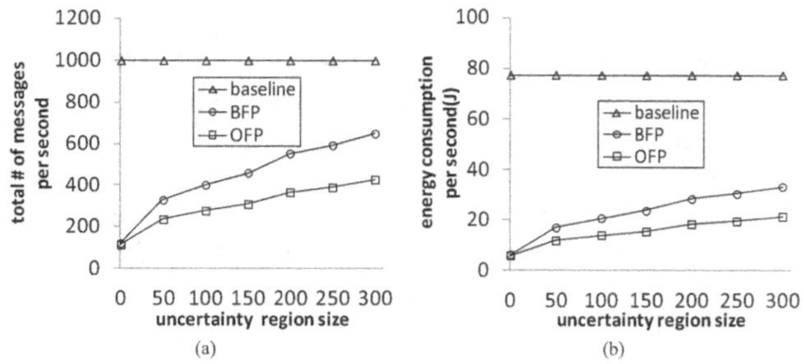

Figure 7: Effect of uncertainty region size: (a) Total # of messages; and (b) Energy consumption.

3. Effect of α. Recall that the parameter α, defined in Section 4, is used to determine the cutoff values (i.e., $c_1(t)$, $c_2(t)$, and $c_3(t)$). Fig. 8(a) shows how the communication cost of BFP is affected by this value. We can see that the number of messages is the minimum at around $\alpha = 0.6$, and is the highest when α is very small (0.1) or large (0.9). To understand why, recall from Table 2 that the three cutoff

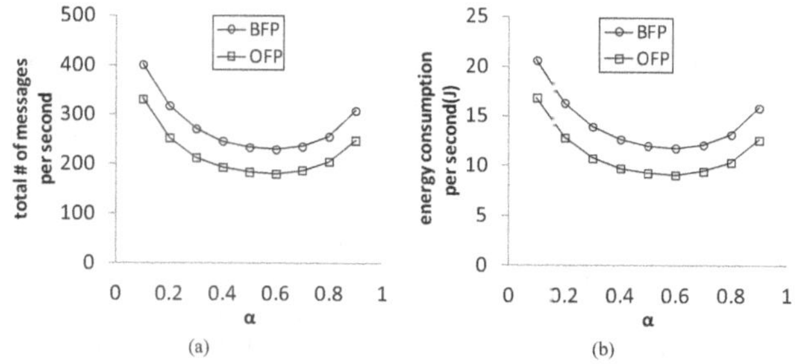

Figure 8: Effect of α: (a) Total # of messages; and (b) Energy consumption.

values determine the filter bounds used in BFP. When α increases, the three cutoff values, as well as the lower bounds of the filters, increase. When objects move towards the query point q, these filter bounds are violated more easily. For example, at timestamp t_u, for object $o_{\sigma(t_u)}$, the lower bound of $f_{\sigma(t_u)}(t)$ is $c_1(t_u)$. When α increases, so is $c_1(t_u)$. If $o_{\sigma(t_u)}$ moves towards q, $f_{\sigma(t_u)}(t)$ decreases, and so it can violate the lower bound more easily. When α approaches 1, even a slight decrease of $f_{\sigma(t_u)}(t)$ can cause a filter violation event. We can similarly argue that moving α closer to 0 decreases the upper bounds of filters, thereby increasing the chance of filter violation. If a filter violation occurs, a large maintenance cost can incur: collecting positions from objects, and sending filters to them, in Steps 10-13 of Algorithm 2. Hence, the performance of BFP suffers from the use of extremely small or large values of α.

In these experiments, we use $\alpha = 0.5$, which is just 1% worse than the optimal case ($\alpha = 0.6$). Moreover, observe that over a wide range of α (0.3 to 0.7) the performance of BFP is relatively stable. A similar observation can be made for OFP (Fig. 8(a)), as well as energy consumption costs (Fig. 8(b)). Without any knowledge about the movement patterns of objects (e.g., whether they tend to move towards or away from q), $\alpha = 0.5$ is a reasonable choice.

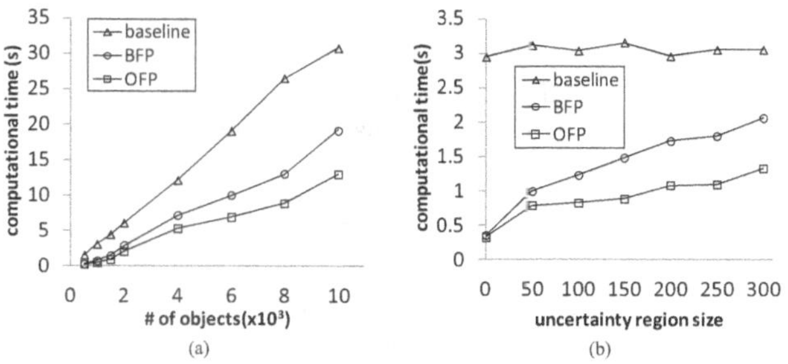

Figure 9: Computational Time vs. (a) # of objects; and (b) Uncertainty region size

4. Computational Time Analysis. Next, we measure the computational time required by the server for supporting the protocols studied here. Fig. 9(a) shows that this quantity increases with the database size, for all the protocols. To understand why, notice that the server needs to (1) retrieve the objects' locations and compute the initial query results; and (2) recompute query results and filter information upon receiving uplink messages from the objects of interest. When the number of objects increases, the burden of handling activities (1) and (2) becomes heavier. Observe that BFP requires less time than baseline. For example, when $k = 10,000$, BFP requires 38% less computational time than baseline. This is because the filters employed in BFP significantly reduces the number of update messages to be sent to the server (c.f. Fig. 6). Hence, the computational effort required to handle (2) for BFP is also less than baseline. The computational time of OFP is smaller than that of BFP. For instance, when $k = 10,000$, OFP requires 32% less time than BFP. This is because in OFP, when events e_σ and e_M occur, the server does not need to handle the locations of objects in $F(t_u)$.

Fig. 9(b) shows the effect of the uncertainty region size. As explained before, a larger uncertainty region triggers more updates, and therefore the effort of handling activity (2) increases. Again, OFP is the winner here.

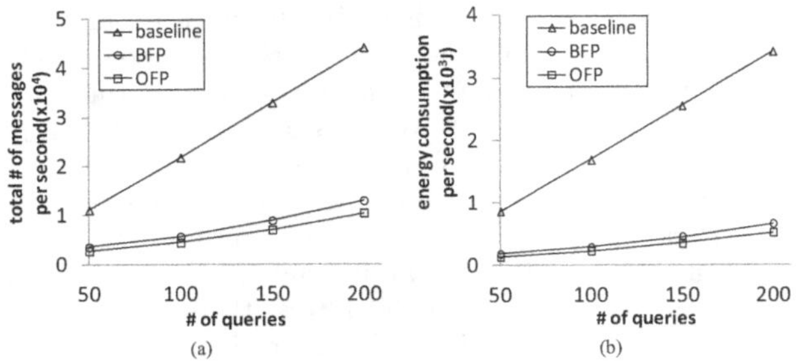

Figure 10: Results on multiple queries: (a) Total # of messages; and (b) Energy consumption.

5. Multiple Queries. In the final set of experiments, we examine the performance of our protocols in handling *multiple* queries, which are submitted to the system at different times. The simulation period spans a total of 1800 seconds. The starting time of each query is randomly distributed during the simulation period, and the lifetime of each query follows a uniform distribution in $[180, 600]$ seconds. To handle simultaneous query requests, we need to make some slight adjustments to our protocols. Specifically, the server has to maintain the filter information for every query; for each object, the filters for each query are stored. After a query has finished its execution, the server and the objects delete their filter information about this query. In these experiments, we assume that the object is capable of storing the filter information of all queries.

Figs. 10(a) and (b) show the performance result under this setting. On average, BFP saves 71% of messages and 81% of energy required by the baseline. Compared with BFP, OFP saves 21% of messages, and 22% of energy. Hence, under the multiple-user environment, OFP still performs the best.

7. CONCLUSIONS

Uncertainty management is an important issue in location-based services. In this paper, we study the communication cost of evaluating a CPoNNQ. We examine two *filter-based protocols*, namely BFP and OFP, where filter bounds are used to control when objects should report their updates. The OFP, which is an enhanced version of BFP, demonstrates superior performance in both communication and energy consumption costs. In this paper, we study how to improve the system's performance in handling events e_σ and e_M. Our next step is to consider other events (e.g., when an object changes from type F to M). We will also extend our approaches to support other complex queries in an LBS, such as k-nearest neighbor queries and skyline queries.

Acknowledgments

Reynold Cheng, Yifan Jin, and Yinuo Zhang were supported by the Research Grants Council of Hong Kong (GRF Projects 711110, 711309E, 513508). We would like to thank the anonymous reviewers for their insightful comments.

8. REFERENCES

[1] D. Pfoser and S. Jensen. Capturing the uncertainty of moving-object representations. In *SSD 1999.*

[2] R. Cheng et al. Probabilistic verifiers: Evaluating constrained nearest-neighbor queries over uncertain data. In *ICDE 2008.*

[3] H. Kriegel et al. Probabilistic nearest-neighbor query on uncertain objects. In *DASFAA 2007.*

[4] R. Cheng, D. Kalashnikov, and S. Prabhakar. Querying imprecise data in moving object environments. *TKDE 2004.*

[5] R. Cheng et al. Evaluating probability threshold k-nearest-neighbor queries over uncertain data. In *EDBT 2009.*

[6] J. Chen et al. Scalable processing of snapshot and continuous nearest-neighbor queries over one-dimensional uncertain data. *VLDBJ 2009.*

[7] Y. Zhang, R. Cheng, and J. Chen. Evaluating continuous probabilistic queries over imprecise sensor data. In *DASFAA 2010.*

[8] Y. Tao, D. Papadias, and Q. Shen. Continuous nearest neighbor search. In *VLDB 2002.*

[9] J. Zhu et al. A probabilistic filter protocol for continuous nearest-neighbor query. In *YC-ICT 2009.*

[10] C. Chow, M. Mokbel, and H. Leong. On efficient and scalable support of continuous queries in mobile peer-to-peer environments. *Mobile Computing 2011.*

[11] K. Mouratidis et al. A threshold-based algorithm for continuous monitoring of k nearest neighbors. *TKDE 2005.*

[12] R. Cheng et al. Adaptive stream filters for entity-based queries with non-value tolerance. In *VLDB 2005.*

[13] R. Cheng et al. Filtering data streams for entity-based continuous queries. *TKDE 2010.*

[14] C. Olston et al. Adaptive filters for continuous queries over distributed data streams. In *SIGMOD 2003.*

[15] J. Chen et al. A probabilistic filter protocol for continuous queries. In *QuaCon 2009.*

[16] G. Trajcevski et al. Continuous probabilistic nearest-neighbor queries for uncertain trajectories. In *EDBT 2009.*

[17] J. Härri et al. Vanetmobisim: generating realistic mobility patterns for vanets. In *VANET 2006.*

[18] `http://www.census.gov/geo/www/tiger/shp.html`.

[19] M. Fiore et al. Vehicular mobility simulation for vanets. In *ANSS 2007.*

[20] Bradford W. and James J. Spilker. GPS error analysis. In *Global Positioning System: Theory and Applications 1996.*

[21] *MPR-Mote Processor Radio Board User's Manual.*

Leveraging Read Rates of Passive RFID Tags for Real-Time Indoor Location Tracking

Da Yan, Zhou Zhao and Wilfred Ng
The Hong Kong University of Science and Technology
Clear Water Bay, Kowloon, Hong Kong
{yanda, zhaozhou, wilfred}@cse.ust.hk

ABSTRACT

RFID (radio frequency identification) technology has been widely used for object tracking in many real-life applications, such as inventory monitoring and product flow tracking. These applications usually rely on passive RFID technologies rather than active ones, since passive RFID tags are more attractive than active ones in many aspects, such as lower tag cost and simpler maintenance.

RFID technology is also important for indoor location tracking systems that require high degree of accuracy. However, most existing systems estimate object locations by using active RFID tags, which usually incur localization error of more than one meter. Although recent studies begin to investigate the application of passive tags for indoor location tracking, these methods are far from deployable and research of this application is still in its infancy.

In this paper, we propose a new indoor location tracking system, named PassTrack, which relies on the read rates of passive RFID tags for location estimation. PassTrack is designed to tolerate noise arising from external environmental factors, by probabilistically modeling the relationship between tag read rate and tag-reader distance, and updating the model parameters based on the current readings of reference tags.

Besides tolerance of noise, PassTrack is also outstanding in terms of localization accuracy and efficiency. Several new approaches for location inference are supported by PassTrack, and the best one incurs an average error of around 30 cm, and is able to carry out over 7500 location estimations per second on an ordinary machine. Furthermore, as a result of using passive RFID tags, PassTrack also enjoys the many other benefits of passive RFID tags mentioned before. We have conducted extensive experiments on both real and synthetic datasets, which demonstrate that our PassTrack system outperforms the previous localization approaches in localization accuracy, tracking efficiency and space applicability.

Categories and Subject Descriptors

H.2.4 [**Database Management**]: Systems

Keywords

Passive, RFID, tag, read rate, localization

CIKM'12, October 29–November 2, 2012, Maui, HI, USA.

1. INTRODUCTION

A variety of methods have been proposed for the purpose of object location tracking, such as those based on GPS, ultrasound, infrared and RFID [10]. While GPS-based localization systems are widely utilized for outdoor environments, the GPS technology has poor performance for indoor applications, due to its requirement of line-of-sight signal reception from the satellites. For indoor location tracking, RFID-based localization technologies have become popular due to the simplicity of attaching tags to target objects, as well as their better tolerance to errors.

There has been over a decade of research on RFID localization, most of which make use of active tags [1, 9, 14] due to their long read range of up to 100 meters. Recently, passive RFID tags are advocated in several studies [3, 6, 10] for location estimation, since they are more attractive than active ones in the following aspects:

- **Lower cost.** The cost of a passive tag is significantly lower than that of an active tag, and therefore passive tags are suitable for those applications where tracking tags are used in a one-off manner. (e.g. inventory monitoring and product flow tracking).
- **Easier maintenance.** Active tags are battery-powered and thus have limited lifetime. For a system using a large set of active tags, the long term maintenance process (e.g. battery replacement) can be complex and costly.
- **Smaller error.** Localization systems that are based on active tags usually incur meters of error [1], which is too large for some indoor applications (e.g. resident monitoring in an elderly house).

Despite the above benefits, most existing research and applications on passive RFID tags simply focus on determining the general existence or non-existence information within the range of RFID detection [2, 3, 5, 6, 8], and research on location estimation using passive tags is still in its infancy.

However, high-accuracy object location estimation is desired for many applications, such as tracking equipment and personnel in hospitals, and providing location-specific information in supermarkets, museums and libraries. For example, the PlaceLab Couple 1 Dataset[1] records the RFID tagging data about a one month stay of a couple in the PlaceLab. In this application, the activities "using a computer" and "sleeping deeply" of a subject cannot be differentiated by an active-tag-based localization system, if the bed is only one meter away from the computer desk. Other applications

[1] `http://architecture.mit.edu/house_n/data/PlaceLab/PLCouple1.htm`

include using the estimated trajectory data for trajectory mining using existing algorithms [15, 16, 17, 18] which can tolerate a certain degree of inaccuracy.

In this paper, we propose a passive RFID system for real-time indoor location tracking, named PassTrack, which translates streams of raw RFID readings into estimated object trajectories with high efficiency. This is important for many database applications involving RFID data.

Our main contributions are summarized as follows:

- Novelty: We are the first to model the relationship between tag read rate and tag-reader distance by a sigmoid curve, while earlier studies use over-simplistic models such as piecewise constant functions [3]. This reader detection model is integrated into a sound probabilistic inference model that enables efficient location inference.
- Noise Tolerance: PassTrack learns the reader detection models online, and is thus able to dynamically adapt the detection model to the changing environment.
- Localization accuracy: We propose several new algorithms for indoor location tracking based on the read rates of passive RFID tags. Our system estimates the location of a constantly moving object (or a static object) with an average error of around 30cm (or below 20cm), which is several times smaller than that of the LANDMARC system [1] that uses active tags.
- Tracking efficiency: Our most accurate algorithm (and thus the slowest due to its heavier computational overhead) is able to perform over 7500 location estimations per second on an ordinary computer, which is still orders of magnitude faster than the sampling-based method of [3].
- Space applicability: We demonstrate that our approach can estimate object locations in a much larger area than that reported in the state-of-the-art work of [10].

The rest of the paper is organized as follows: Section 2 introduces the components of the PassTrack system, including the adaptive reader detection model and the likelihood-based location inference model. The former is further described in Section 3, and the latter is explained in detail in Section 4. In Section 5, we report extensive experiments which verify that our approach is superior to the existing methods in both localization accuracy and efficiency. Finally, we review the related work in Section 6, and conclude the paper in Section 7.

2. PASSTRACK SYSTEM

The setting of our tracking system is outlined as follows: We use n RFID readers/antennae $\{R_1, R_2, \ldots, R_n\}$, m passive reference tags $\{T_1, T_2, \ldots, T_m\}$, and u passive tracking tags $\{O_1, O_2, \ldots, O_u\}$ to track u objects. The key to our approach is to decouple the *reader detection model* from the location inference process:

- For each reader/antenna R_i, its detection model is "learned" from the current read rate of the reference tags dynamically, where the read rates are determined from the readings.
- Using the learned reader detection models, for each tracking tag O_i, we find its most likely location based on the observed read rate of O_i from each reader.

This decoupling strategy is important for PassTrack. While external factors such as changes in temperature and humidity, and the number of objects nearby may influence the detection performance of a reader, our approach is able to dynamically adapt the detection model to the changing environment, due to the online learning of the reader detection models. We elaborate on these parts in the following two sections.

3. READER DETECTION MODEL

3.1 Reader Detection Model Learning

The location inference model of PassTrack relies on the *reader detection model*, which estimates the distance of a tag to an RFID antenna, by the readings of that tag received by the antenna. RSSI (received signal strength indicator), which is widely adopted in the active-tag-based systems [1, 9, 11, 12, 14], is usually not available for passive tags [10]. Therefore, we leverage the read rate information for distance estimation.

The read rate of a tag by an antenna is usually estimated by the tag response count in a fixed number of interrogation cycles sent from the antenna. For example, if an antenna detects the response from a tag in 3 out of a series of 10 interrogation cycles, the read rate is estimated to be 0.3.

We formally define the reader detection model as follows:

DEFINITION 1 (READER DETECTION MODEL). *The reader detection model of a reader/antenna R is a function $p(\ell)$ such that, given the Euclidean distance $\ell = ||T, R||$ between a tag T and the reader R, returns the expected read rate of T by R.*

Both [2] and [3] observed that the read rate of a passive tag remains high (close to 1) when the tag is within a certain distance δ_{major} from the reader, and then decreases almost linearly with the increment of the distance until the read rate reaches 0, where the corresponding distance is δ_{minor}. The former range (0 to δ_{major}) is termed the *major detection region*, while the latter (δ_{major} to δ_{minor}) is termed the *minor detection region*.

The shape of the "read rate vs. distance" curve is like an upside-down curve of the logistic function $f(\ell) = \frac{1}{1+e^{-\ell}}$, where ℓ is the distance between the tag and the antenna. Therefore, we choose the function $p(\ell) = \frac{1}{1+e^{a\ell+b}}$ $(a > 0, b < 0)$ to fit the reader detection model, where a can be adapted to control how sharp the read rate decreases in the *minor detection region*, and b can be adapted to control the range of the *major detection region*.

Now, we formulate our reader detection model for reader R_i as follows:

$$p_i = \frac{1}{1 + e^{a_i \ell_i + b_i}} \ (a_i > 0, b_i < 0). \qquad (1)$$

where p_i is the tracking/reference tag read rate at R_i, and ℓ_i represents the distance from the tracking/reference tag at location $\vec{l} = (x, y)$, to reader R_i at location (x_i, y_i), and is given by:

$$\ell_i = \sqrt{(x - x_i)^2 + (y - y_i)^2}. \qquad (2)$$

For each reader R_i, there are two parameters (a_i and b_i) that can be determined dynamically. This allows for the adaption of the model to a changing environment. We next explain how to estimate the current model parameters a_i and b_i, based on the read rates of the reference tags.

Let p_{ij} denote the current read rate of each reference tag T_j estimated by reader R_i. Furthermore, since the locations of the readers and the reference tags are fixed, we can easily get the distance $\ell_{ij} = ||R_i, T_j||$ between R_i and T_j. As a result, during each time step, we

(a) Experimental Setting on the Ground (b) Experimental Setting on the Shelf

Figure 1: Experimental Setting for Reader Detection Model

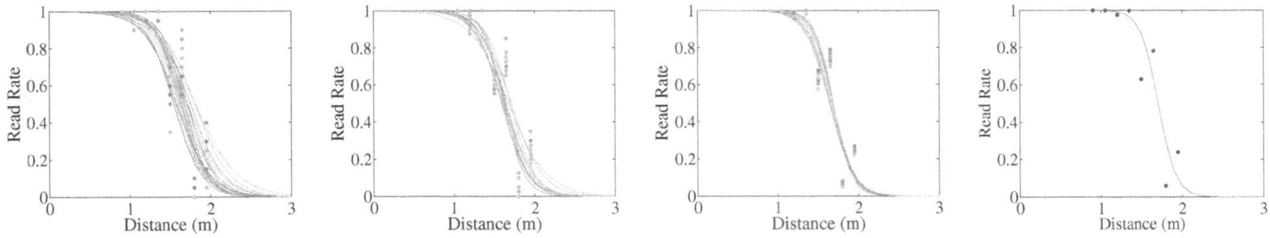

(a) 10 cycles (b) 20 cycles (c) 100 cycles (d) Average

Figure 2: Read Rate vs. Tag Distance for the Ground-Level Setting

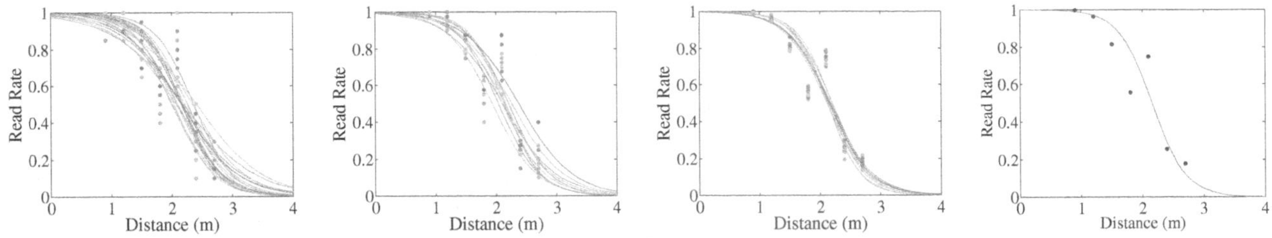

(a) 10 cycles (b) 20 cycles (c) 100 cycles (d) Average

Figure 3: Read Rate vs. Tag Distance for the Waist-Level Setting

have access to a set of pairs $\{(p_{i1}, \ell_{i1}), (p_{i2}, \ell_{i2}), \ldots, (p_{im}, \ell_{im})\}$ for each reader R_i.

Equation (1) implies that $\ln(\frac{1}{p_i} - 1) = a_i\ell_i + b_i$. Thus we can employ the least square method to estimate a_i and b_i, using the transformed set of pairs $\{(\ln(\frac{1}{p_{i1}} - 1),\ \ell_{i1}),\ (\ln(\frac{1}{p_{i2}} - 1),\ \ell_{i2}),\ \ldots,\ (\ln(\frac{1}{p_{im}} - 1),\ \ell_{im})\}$.

Our approach is cost-effective, since we can afford to distribute many cheap passive tags in the whole tracking region to enable the learning of an accurate model. Note that very far (or close) reference tags with read rate 0 (or 1) should be discarded, since Equation (1) does not allow $p = 0$ (or $p = 1$).

Our reader detection model is more accurate than the 3-state model in [3] which simply assumes a fixed constant read rate value among the *minor detection region*. More importantly, our model is adaptive to the environment and thus gives rise to more accurate location estimation.

3.2 Effect in Real Experimental Setting

We evaluated our reader detection model in the real indoor environments shown in Figures 1(a) and (b). In our experiments, 3 to 4 passive reference tags are placed in each of the four orthogonal directions around an antenna, with different distances to the antenna.

Figure 1(a) simulates the case where the readers/antennea and the reference tags are deployed on the ground, and each moving object sticks a tag at the bottom. For example, if the tracking objects are people, the tracking tags can be stick on the side of their shoes. To avoid the directional effect of the tags, each person can stick two tags of the same ID on both sides of their shoes. The reference tags are put at distances 1.05m, 1.35m, 1.65m and 1.95m from the antenna in two directions, and at distances 0.9m, 1.2m, 1.5m and 1.8m from the antenna in the other two directions. The tag positions are interleaved on the two pairs of directions, so as to provide more (*distance, read rate*) pairs for model fitting.

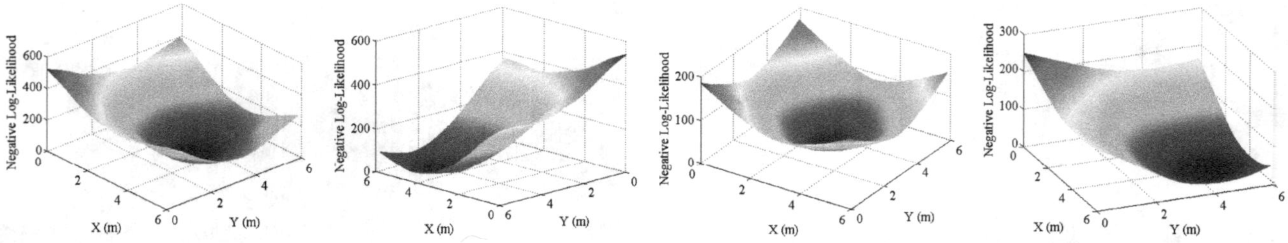

(a) Gound_level, Center (b) Gound_level, Border (c) Waist_level, Center (d) Waist_level, Border

Figure 4: Negative Log-Likelihood vs. Object Locations

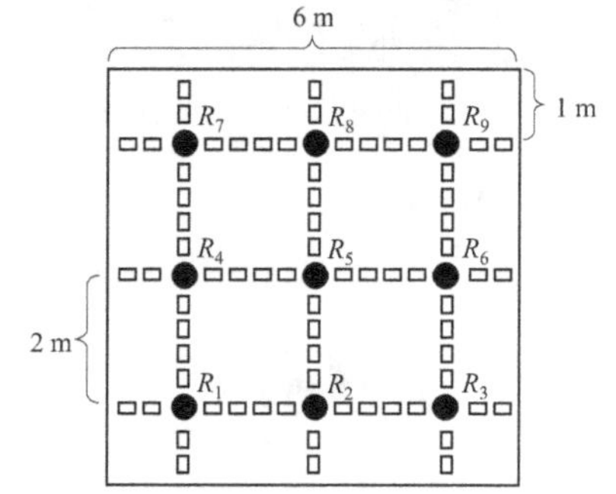

Figure 5: Tracking Area for Experimental Study

Figure 1(b) simulates the case where the readers/antennea and the reference tags are deployed 1m above the ground, e.g. stuck on the side of desks or walls. We make a shelf to build this setting. The shelf is made of styrofoam to minimize its impact on RFID detection. In this scenario, tracking tags can be stuck around the waists of people. The reference tags are put at distances 0.9m, 1.5m, 2.1m and 2.7m from the antenna in two directions, and at distances 1.2m, 1.8m and 2.4m from the antenna in the other two directions.

We use the Intermec IF61 smart reader which supports connection with 4 antennae, and connect it to an FCC-4 tuned dipole antenna produced by A.H. Systems. The antenna is omni-directional, which conforms to the models in the previous studies such as [3]. As for the passive tags, we use UHF Gen2 DogBone RFID tags from UPM Raflatac. We set the response timeout parameter so that it takes about 1 second to accomplish 5 interrogation cycles.

We measure the read rates based on 10 interrogation cycles for 20 times, 20 cycles for 15 times, and 100 cycles for 10 times. Figures 2 and 3 present the "read rate vs. distance" relations for the two experimental settings. For example, Figure 2(a) shows the tag read rates (points) and the learned curves for all the 20 runs based on 10 cycles in the ground-level setting. Figures 2(b)–(c) and 3(a)–(c) are similarly obtained. In Figures 2(d) and 3(d), the blue points are the average read rates of the 10 runs based on 100 cycles, and the red curves are obtained by least squares on these points.

It is obvious that the slopes of the curves in Figure 3 are gentler than those in Figure 2, which implies that read rate decays more slowly with distance in the waist-level setting, possibly due to less interference of the ground. Clearly, the read rate measurements based on 100 interrogation cycles are the most stable ones, and therefore, we determine the parameters a and b based on readings from the latest 100 cycles (around 20s). By fitting $p(\ell) = \frac{1}{1+e^{a\ell+b}}$ we have $a = 9.4831$ and $b = -16.2015$ in Figure 2(d), and $a = 3.6423$ and $b = -7.8597$ in Figure 3(d).

4. LOCATION INFERENCE MODEL

In this section, we describe our approach of estimating object locations using the dynamic reader detection model.

Consider the event that during the latest N interrogation cycles, the object with a tracking tag O responds to reader R_i for k_i times. This happens with probability $\binom{N}{k_i} p_i^{k_i}(1-p_i)^{N-k_i}$. If we assume that each reader detects the tag of each object independently, which is also assumed in other work such as [3], then the probability that O responds k_i times to reader R_i $(i = 1, 2, \cdots, n)$ is given by

$$L = \prod_{i=1}^{n} \binom{N}{k_i} p_i^{k_i}(1-p_i)^{N-k_i} \triangleq C \prod_{i=1}^{n} p_i^{k_i}(1-p_i)^{N-k_i}, \quad (3)$$

where $C = \prod_{i=1}^{n} \binom{N}{k_i}$ is a constant.

Our aim is to find the value of O's location $\vec{l} = (x, y)$ that maximizes the likelihood L, which is equivalent to minimizing the corresponding negative log-likelihood $\mathcal{L} = -\ln(L/C)$ (without considering the constant $C > 0$):

$$\mathcal{L} = -\sum_{i=1}^{n} [k_i \ln p_i + (N - k_i)\ln(1-p_i)] \triangleq -\sum_{i=1}^{n} \mathcal{L}_i. \quad (4)$$

Figure 5 shows a tracking area of 6 m × 6 m = 36 m^2, where the 9 black circles represent readers/antennae, and the small rectangles represent reference tags. This setting will be used to evaluate the performance of PassTrack in Section 5.

Note that PassTrack actually allows for much more flexible deployment that caters to the actual building structures, as long as (1) for each antenna, there exist sufficient reference tags with different distances to it, and (2) for most of the indoor locations, a tracking tag there can be detected by at least 3 to 4 nearby antennae.

The first requirement ensures that there are sufficient learning samples for estimating the reader detection model parameters. The second requirement is called *detection range overlap*. Besides improving localization accuracy, it also allows the system to work even if some reader/antenna gets disconnected.

Refer to the tracking setting in Figure 5 again. We now denote the vector of response count information by $\vec{k} = \{k_1, k_2, \ldots, k_9\}$, where k_i denotes the response count obtained by reader R_i. Figure 4(a) demonstrates the values of the negative log-likelihood $\mathcal{L}$ at various locations when the actual location of the object to track is close to the center of the tracking area ($\vec{k} = \{0, 0, 0, 0, 0, 4, 0, 3, 5\}$), and Figure 4(b) is when the actual location is close to the border ($\vec{k} = \{0, 0, 0, 0, 5, 5, 0, 5, 0\}$). Both Figures 4(a) and 4(b) are for the ground-level setting. Figures 4(c) ($\vec{k} = \{0, 0, 0, 0, 2, 5, 0, 5, 5\}$) and 4(d) ($\vec{k} = \{0, 2, 0, 3, 5, 5, 1, 3, 0\}$) are for the waist-level setting, and are plotted in a similar manner. For Figures 4(a)–(d), the read rate estimation is based on 5 cycles (which takes around 1s).

We now study how to use the likelihood model of Equation (4) for efficient location inference. One approach is to impose a grid structure on the tracking area, and to evaluate the negative log-likelihood $\mathcal{L}$ using Equation (4) at each location on the grid. The location of the object to track is estimated as the location on the grid with the minimum value of $\mathcal{L}$. However, the granularity of the grid structure influences the accuracy of the estimation, and evaluation on a too fine-grained grid structure is time-consuming.

Another approach to find the location that minimize $\mathcal{L}$ is to use Newton's method [7], which is well-known for function optimization. Newton's method enables faster convergence than gradient descent, since it is based on the second-order Taylor approximation of the target function. As shown in Figures 4(a)–(d), $\mathcal{L}$ is almost convex, which is appropriate for applying Newton's method. Since $\mathcal{L}$ is not strictly convex, the choice of the initial location to start Newton's method is very important for avoiding being stuck at those non-convex locations, and we choose it to be the result location of the grid-based method described above, so as to make it close to the global minimum. In this case, a coarse-grained grid structure is adequate, and we adopt an 8×8 grid for the tracking area in Figure 5. Algorithm 1 shows the details of our Newton's method, which is adapted from [7].

Algorithm 1 Object Location Inference by Newton's Method

1: **given** tolerance $\epsilon > 0$
2: Compute the starting point (x_0, y_0) using grid search
3: $\vec{l} \leftarrow (x_0, y_0)$
4: **repeat**
5: Compute $\nabla\mathcal{L}(\vec{l})$
6: Compute $\nabla^2\mathcal{L}(\vec{l})$
7: Compute the Newton step: $\Delta\vec{l} \leftarrow -(\nabla^2\mathcal{L}(\vec{l}))^{-1}\nabla\mathcal{L}(\vec{l})$
8: Compute decrement: $\lambda^2 \leftarrow \nabla\mathcal{L}(\vec{l})^T(\nabla^2\mathcal{L}(\vec{l}))^{-1}\nabla\mathcal{L}(\vec{l})$
9: **quit** if $\lambda^2/2 \le \epsilon$
10: Choose step size t by backtracking line search
11: $l \leftarrow \vec{l} + t\Delta\vec{l}$
12: **end repeat**

Line 10 of Algorithm 1 uses the backtracking line search algorithm shown in Algorithm 2. The default parameters we use for backtracking line search are $\alpha = 0.2$, $\beta = 0.6$ and $\epsilon = 10^{-6}$.

Algorithm 2 Backtracking Line Search

1: **given** a descent direction $\Delta\vec{l}$ at $\vec{l}$,
constants $\alpha \in (0, 0.5)$, $\beta \in (0, 1)$
2: $t \leftarrow 1$
3: **while** $\mathcal{L}(\vec{l} + t\Delta\vec{l}) > \mathcal{L}(\vec{l}) + \alpha t(\nabla\mathcal{L}(\vec{l}))^T\Delta\vec{l}$ **do**
4: $t \leftarrow \beta t$
5: **end while**

In our experiments, we find that Algorithm 1 always terminates within 10 iterations. However, we still set an upperbound of 100 iterations for Algorithm 1. Another special case we handle is when the inferred location leaves the tracking area. In this case, the algorithm immediately returns the location estimation of the previous iteration. A third possible scenario is when an object is not detected by any reader/antenna within the current time window, in which case we use the old location estimation as the current one. We never encounter such a scenario in our experiments, although it is possible for the RFID readers/antennea to miss readings when there are too many tags in their detection ranges. We do not include the above details in the pseudo-code in Algorithm 1 for better readability.

Note that Algorithm 1 requires the computation of the gradient (see Line 5) and Hessian matrix (see Line 6) of $\mathcal{L}$. Fortunately, they have elegant forms that can be evaluated efficiently, as is formalized by Theorem 1 below.

THEOREM 1. *Given the negative log-likelihood function $\mathcal{L}$ (Equation (4)), its gradient $\nabla\mathcal{L}(\vec{l})$ and Hessian matrix $\nabla^2\mathcal{L}(\vec{l})$ are given by:*

$$\nabla\mathcal{L} = \begin{bmatrix} \frac{\partial\mathcal{L}}{\partial x} \\ \frac{\partial\mathcal{L}}{\partial y} \end{bmatrix} = \sum_{i=1}^{n} B_i \begin{bmatrix} \Delta x_i/\ell_i \\ \Delta y_i/\ell_i \end{bmatrix}, \tag{5}$$

$$\begin{aligned} \nabla^2\mathcal{L} &= \begin{bmatrix} \frac{\partial^2\mathcal{L}}{\partial x^2} & \frac{\partial^2\mathcal{L}}{\partial x\partial y} \\ \frac{\partial^2\mathcal{L}}{\partial y\partial x} & \frac{\partial^2\mathcal{L}}{\partial y^2} \end{bmatrix} \\ &= \sum_{i=1}^{n}\left(\frac{A_i}{\ell_i^2}\begin{bmatrix} \Delta x_i^2 & \Delta x_i\Delta y_i \\ \Delta x_i\Delta y_i & \Delta y_i^2 \end{bmatrix}\right. \\ &\quad \left. + \frac{B_i}{\ell_i^3}\begin{bmatrix} \Delta y_i^2 & -\Delta x_i\Delta y_i \\ -\Delta x_i\Delta y_i & \Delta x_i^2 \end{bmatrix}\right), \end{aligned} \tag{6}$$

where

$$\Delta x_i = x - x_i\,, \tag{7}$$

$$\Delta y_i = y - y_i\,, \tag{8}$$

$$A_i = a_i^2 N p_i(1 - p_i)\,, \tag{9}$$

$$B_i = a_i(k_i - Np_i)\,. \tag{10}$$

PROOF. Since x and y are symmetric, we only need to compute $\frac{\partial\mathcal{L}}{\partial x}$, $\frac{\partial^2\mathcal{L}}{\partial x^2}$ and $\frac{\partial^2\mathcal{L}}{\partial x\partial y}$. Note that $\mathcal{L}$ is a function of p_i (Equation (4)), which is in turn a function of l_i (Equation (1)), which is further a function of x and y (Equation (2)). For ease of presentation, we define the following notation:

$$\delta_i = \Delta y_i/\Delta x_i\,. \tag{11}$$

We will use the following property in the computation, which can be easily verified:

LEMMA 1. *The derivative of $p(\ell) = \frac{1}{1-e^{a\ell+b}}$ $(a > 0, b < 0)$ is $p'(\ell) = p(\ell)\cdot(p(\ell) - 1)$.*

By taking the partial derivative of $\mathcal{L}$ with respect to x, we have

$$\begin{aligned} \frac{\partial\mathcal{L}}{\partial x} &= -\sum_{i=1}^{n}\left[\frac{\partial\mathcal{L}_i}{\partial p_i}\cdot\frac{\partial p_i}{\partial(a\cdot\ell_i + b)}\cdot\frac{\partial(a\cdot\ell_i + b)}{\partial x}\right] \\ &= -\sum_{i=1}^{n}\left[\left(\frac{k_i}{p_i} + \frac{N - k_i}{p_i - 1}\right)\cdot p_i(p_i - 1)\right. \\ &\quad \left.\cdot\frac{a_i(x - x_i)}{\sqrt{(x - x_i)^2 + (y - y_i)^2}}\right] \\ &= -\sum_{i=1}^{n}\left[(Np_i - k_i)\cdot\frac{a_i(x - x_i)}{\sqrt{(x - x_i)^2 + (y - y_i)^2}}\right] \\ &= \sum_{i=1}^{n}\frac{a_i(k_i - Np_i)}{\sqrt{1 + \delta_i^2}} \\ &= \sum_{i=1}^{n} a_i(k_i - Np_i)\frac{\Delta x_i}{\ell_i}\,. \end{aligned} \tag{12}$$

Next, we compute the second derivatives:

$$\begin{aligned}
\frac{\partial^2 \mathcal{L}}{\partial x^2} &= \frac{\partial}{\partial x}\left[\sum_{i=1}^{n} \frac{a_i(k_i - Np_i)}{\sqrt{1+\delta_i^2}}\right] \\
&= \sum_{i=1}^{n}\left[\frac{1}{\sqrt{1+\delta_i^2}} \cdot \frac{\partial}{\partial x}(a_i(k_i - Np_i))\right. \\
&\quad \left. + a_i(k_i - Np_i) \cdot \frac{\partial}{\partial x}\left(\frac{1}{\sqrt{1+\delta_i^2}}\right)\right] \\
&= \sum_{i=1}^{n}\left[\frac{-a_i N}{\sqrt{1+\delta_i^2}} \cdot \frac{\partial p_i}{\partial x}\right. \\
&\quad \left. - a_i(k_i - Np_i) \cdot \left(\delta_i (1+\delta_i^2)^{-\frac{3}{2}}\right) \cdot \frac{\partial \delta_i}{\partial x}\right] \\
&= \sum_{i=1}^{n}\left[\frac{-a_i N}{\sqrt{1+\delta_i^2}} \cdot \frac{a_i p_i (p_i - 1)}{\sqrt{1+\delta_i^2}} - a_i(k_i - Np_i)\right. \\
&\quad \left. \cdot \left(\frac{\Delta y_i}{\Delta x_i}\left(\frac{\Delta x_i^2 + \Delta y_i^2}{\Delta x_i^2}\right)^{-\frac{3}{2}}\right) \cdot \left(-\frac{\Delta y_i}{\Delta x_i^2}\right)\right] \\
&= \sum_{i=1}^{n}\left[\frac{a_i^2 N p_i (1-p_i)}{1+\delta_i^2} + a_i(k_i - Np_i)\frac{\Delta y_i^2}{\ell_i^3}\right] \\
&= \sum_{i=1}^{n}\left[a_i^2 N p_i (1-p_i)\frac{\Delta x_i^2}{\ell_i^2} + a_i(k_i - Np_i)\frac{\Delta y_i^2}{\ell_i^3}\right].
\end{aligned}$$

$$\begin{aligned}
\frac{\partial^2 \mathcal{L}}{\partial x \partial y} &= \frac{\partial}{\partial y}\left[\sum_{i=1}^{n} \frac{a_i(k_i - Np_i)}{\sqrt{1+\delta_i^2}}\right] \\
&= \sum_{i=1}^{n}\left[\frac{1}{\sqrt{1+\delta_i^2}} \cdot \frac{\partial}{\partial y}(a_i(k_i - Np_i))\right. \\
&\quad \left. + a_i(k_i - Np_i) \cdot \frac{\partial}{\partial y}\left(\frac{1}{\sqrt{1+\delta_i^2}}\right)\right] \\
&= \sum_{i=1}^{n}\left[\frac{-a_i N}{\sqrt{1+\delta_i^2}} \cdot \frac{\partial p_i}{\partial y}\right. \\
&\quad \left. - a_i(k_i - Np_i) \cdot \left(\delta_i (1+\delta_i^2)^{-\frac{3}{2}}\right) \cdot \frac{\partial \delta_i}{\partial y}\right] \\
&= \sum_{i=1}^{n}\left[\frac{-a_i N}{\sqrt{1+\delta_i^2}} \cdot \frac{a_i p_i (p_i - 1)}{\sqrt{1+\delta_i'^2}} - a_i(k_i - Np_i)\right. \\
&\quad \left. \cdot \left(\frac{\Delta y_i}{\Delta x_i}\left(\frac{\Delta x_i^2 + \Delta y_i^2}{\Delta x_i^2}\right)^{-\frac{3}{2}}\right) \cdot \frac{1}{\Delta x_i}\right] \\
&= \sum_{i=1}^{n}\left[a_i^2 N p_i (1-p_i)\frac{\Delta x_i \Delta y_i}{\ell_i^2}\right. \\
&\quad \left. - a_i(k_i - Np_i)\frac{\Delta x_i \Delta y_i}{\ell_i^3}\right].
\end{aligned}$$

□

To compare with the likelihood-based method described above, we also incorporate a baseline algorithm based on the idea of nearest neighbors (NN), which are popular with the active-tag-based RFID localization systems (see Section 6). The location of an object O is estimated as $(x, y) = \sum_{i=1}^{n} w_i(x_i, y_i)$, where the weight w_j of reader R_j is empirically set to be $w_j = \frac{k_j}{\sum_{i=1}^{n} k_i}$ or $w_j = \frac{k_j^2}{\sum_{i=1}^{n} k_i^2}$, to give higher weight to a reader that detects O with a higher read rate. Our extensive experiments described in Section 5 have shown that the naive NN-based approach incurs several times more error than our Newton's-method-based approach, which verifies that, our Newton's-method-based approach best brings out the information contained in read rates.

As there are only 5 interrogation cycles in each second, if we estimate the location of an object for each second solely using the read rates that are measured based on these 5 cycles, we cannot obtain read rate values of high precision. Therefore, we use a sliding window of multiple cycles to measure the read rates. While a larger window usually improves the precision of read rate measurements for static objects, this is not the case for moving objects due to the outdated readings in the window. We will study the relationship between window size and localization accuracy in Section 5.5.

5. EXPERIMENTS

In this section, we evaluate the performance of PassTrack in the 6m×6m tracking area shown in Figure 5, which is equipped with 9 antennae. To save our research time, we simply use synthetic data instead of real data for the experiments. In order to run experiments in a wide variety of settings, we built a data generator that simulates the multi-antennae scenario according to the real-world study on one-antenna described in Section 3.2.

Data Generator. In each time step (which is 1s), our data generator first generates the locations of the moving objects to track, and then, the readings of each reader are generated according to its reader detection model: in each of the 5 cycles, the tag of a moving object is detected by the reader with the probability p computed from Equation (1).

To avoid generating too idealized readings, we design our data generator to also be able to generate noisy readings that better simulate the real-world scenarios. In the ideal case, the response count value conforms to the binomial distribution with standard deviation $\sqrt{Np(1-p)}$. Our data generator generates noisy readings by adding or subtracting (with equal probability) the original response count by $\tilde{\beta}\sqrt{Np(1-p)}$, where the random variable $\tilde{\beta} \sim$ *Uniform*$[0, \beta]$, and β is a user-specified parameter that controls the noise level. If the resulting response count is below 0 (or above N), it is set to 0 (or N).

We use $[w_\ell, w_u]$ to configure the sliding window to include the previous w_ℓ time steps and the succeeding w_u time steps besides the current one. For example, $[0, 0]$ denotes that the window contains only the 5 cycles in the current second, while $[-1, 1]$ denotes that the window contains the cycles from the previous second to the next second ($N = 15$).

Unless otherwise stated, we fix the reader model parameters a_i and b_i during data generation and location inference. We set $a_i = 9.4831$ and $b_i = -16.2015$ ($a_i = 3.6423$ and $b_i = -7.8597$) for the experiments in the ground-level (waist-level) setting.

In the sequel, we denote our grid-based localization method as *Grid*, our Newton's method that uses *Grid* for initialization as *Newton*, our two nearest-neighbor-based methods as *NN* (where $w_j = k_j / \sum_{i=1}^{n} k_i$) and *NN2* (where $w_j = k_j^2 / \sum_{i=1}^{n} k_i^2$). We assume the speed of a moving object to be 1m/s to simulate walking speed.

All the experiments are run on a Lenovo IBM ThinkPad X201i laptop with a 2.53Hz Intel Core i3 GPU and 2GB memory.

5.1 Localization Accuracy for Moving Objects

To visualize the effectiveness of our localization approach in scenarios where objects are always moving, we generate the data that correspond to an object moving in circular and Z-shaped trajecto-

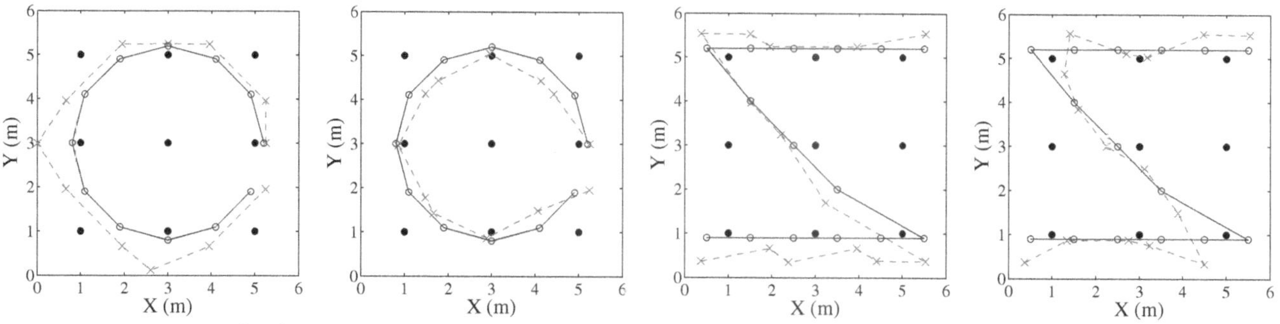

(a) Circle, Window = $[0, 0]$ (b) Circle, Window = $[-1, 1]$ (c) Z-Curve, Window = $[0, 0]$ (d) Z-Curve, Window = $[-1, 1]$

Figure 6: Real and Inferred Trajectories in the Waist-Level Setting

ries, and invoke *Newton* to estimate its location at each time step. The experiments are done in the waist-level setting and the results are shown in Figure 6. In Figures 6(a)–(d), the blue points (connected by the solid lines) are the true locations (trajectories) of the object, and the red points (connected by the dotted lines) are the inferred locations (trajectories). The estimated trajectory in Figure 6(b) has a smaller radius than the true circular trajectory, because the window contains the readings from the previous and the next second. For the experiments in Figures 6(a)–(d), *Newton* is able to recover the original trajectory of an object with reasonable accuracy: the average error never exceeds 30cm.

5.2 Localization Accuracy for Static Objects

A larger sliding window usually improves the precision of read rate measurements for static objects, which in turn tends to increase the accuracy of object location estimation. In this subsection, we study the relationship between window size and localization quality for static objects. We randomly generate the locations for 5 static objects, and run our localization algorithms on the data for 3000 time steps in both the ground-level setting and the waist-level setting, with different window sizes. We adopt the window configuration $[-w, w]$, where the parameter w controls the size of the window (which is $2w + 1$).

For each of the 15,000 (5×3000) location estimations, we compute its error distance as the Euclidean distance between the estimated location and the true location. One measurement of localization accuracy that we use is the average of these 15,000 error distances. Another measurement is the cumulative percentile of error distance which is also adopted in [1].

Figure 7(a) shows the average error distance of our localization algorithms with different window sizes, where the suffix "_slf" (or "_gnd") means that the corresponding algorithm works at the waist-level (or ground-level) setting. We can see that *Newton* incurs the least localization error and thus achieves the best accuracy. The average errors of all the algorithms decrease with the increment of window size, and when $w = 5$, *Newton_slf* is already around 10cm and *Newton_gnd* is already around 17cm. In this case, the window size is $2w + 1 = 11$, and as there are 5 cycles in each time step, only 55 interrogation cycles are used to estimate the read rates. This result is much better than the work of [10], which uses 100 cycles to estimate the read rates and still incurs an average error of 19cm.

Since the reader detection range is longer at the waist-level setting than at the ground-level one, an object tends to be detected by more readers. As a result, at the waist-level setting, *Newton* can use more information for location estimation and therefore incurs less error than if it works at ground-level, as illustrated in Figure 7(a). However, this is not the case for the NN-based algorithms: the

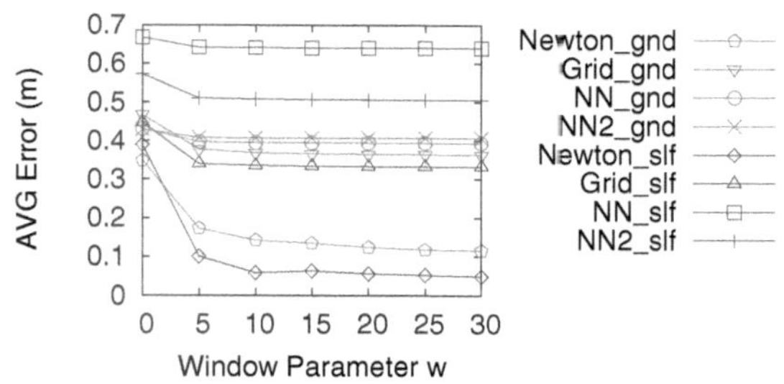

(a) Window Size vs. AVG Error

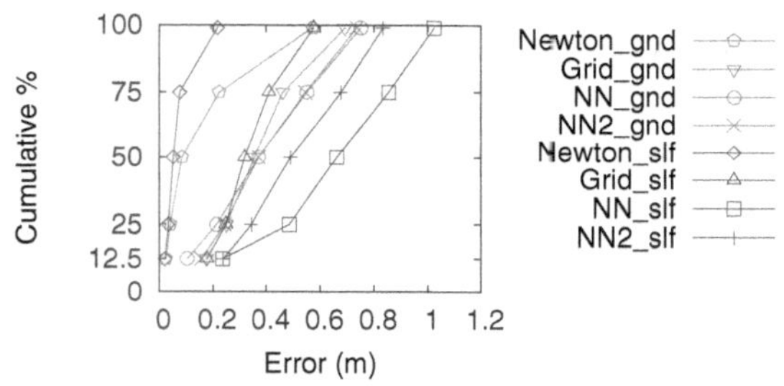

(b) Cumulative Percentile of Error When $w = 10$

Figure 7: Effect of Window Size for Static Object Localization

waist-level versions are shown to be worse than the ground-level ones in Figure 7(a). This is because the NN-based heuristics lack the support of a formal underlying inference model.

Figure 7(b) shows the cumulative percentile of error distance for our localization algorithms when $w = 10$, from which we have the similar observations that *Newton* incurs the least error and the waist-level version works better than the ground-level one. From Figure 7(b), we can see that *Newton* can estimate the location of an object within 22cm error with 75% probability.

5.3 Effect of Object Moving Frequency

We studied the performance of our localization algorithms for constantly moving objects in Section 5.1 and for static objects in Section 5.2. However, a more practical scenario is when objects frequently change their locations, and stop for some time between two consecutive movements. For example, in inventory monitoring, the goods are not likely to change their locations all the time, although they may be moved to different shelves from time to time. The application of resident monitoring also requires to recognize activities such as "reading paper" (e.g. on sofa) and "using a computer" (e.g. on a desk), which involve the stay at a specific location for a while.

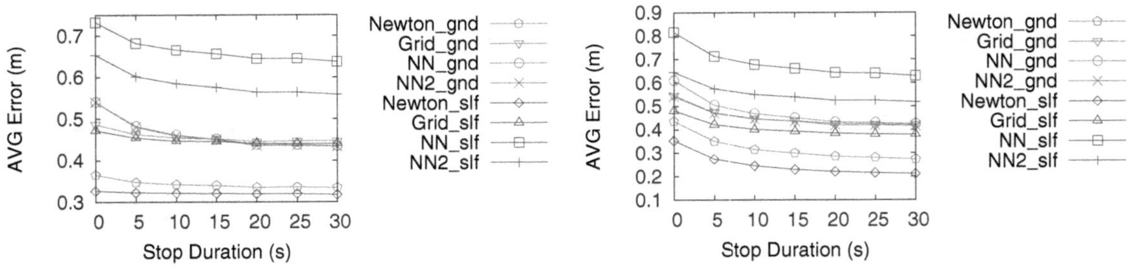

(a) Window = $[0, 0]$ (b) Window = $[-1, 1]$

Figure 8: Effect of Object Moving Frequency on Localization Accuracy

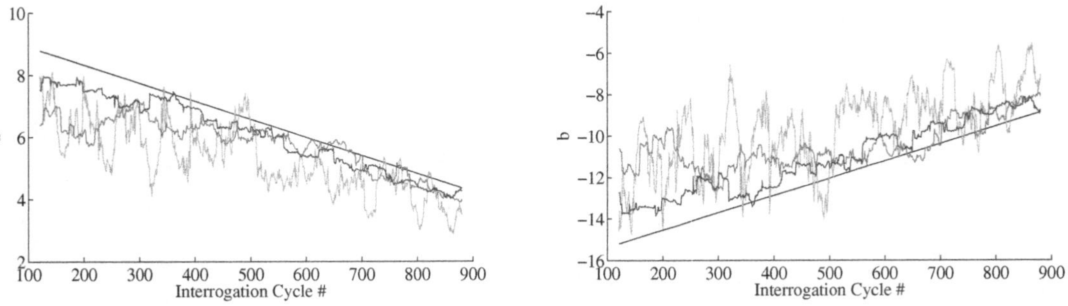

Figure 9: Learned v.s. True Model Parameters

To study the effect of object moving frequency on localization accuracy, we generate the trajectories of 5 objects that interleave between staying and moving for 3000 time steps. We parameterize our data generator with stop duration T, so that each object moves for k steps (turns around if it reaches the wall), where $k \in \{1, 2, 3, 4, 5\}$ is randomly picked, then stops for T time steps, and then repeats the above process until 3000 time steps are reached.

Figure 8(a) (or Figure 8(b)) shows the average error distance of our localization algorithms with window $[0, 0]$ (or $[-1, 1]$) for various stop durations. While both Figures 8(a) and (b) verify the intuition that all the algorithms incur less error for longer stop duration (and thus less frequent movements), the *Newton* algorithms have more dramatic drop in error with the increment of stop duration in Figure 8(b). This is because more interrogation cycles are used for read rate estimation when window $[-1, 1]$ is adopted, which leads to more accurate read rate estimation, and thus more accurate localization. Both figures confirm that *Newton* incurs the least error and the waist-level version works better than the ground-level one.

5.4 Results of Model Parameter Learning

In Section 3.2, we studied the quality of the reader detection models learned using read rate estimations of reference tags based on 10, 20 and 100 interrogation cycles, and showed that estimating read rates based on 100 cycles gives the most stable model.

In this subsection, we further study the effect of window size for reference tag read rate estimation on localization accuracy. While a larger window size gives more accurate read rate estimations of the reference tags, the model learned from these read rate estimations may not be close to the true reader detection model. This is because the true reader detection model changes with time, and the large window contains responses to early interrogation cycles. In fact, there is a delay between the learned model and the true one, and the larger the window size, the longer the delay.

To study the effect of window size on the difference between the learned model and the true one, we randomly generate the locations

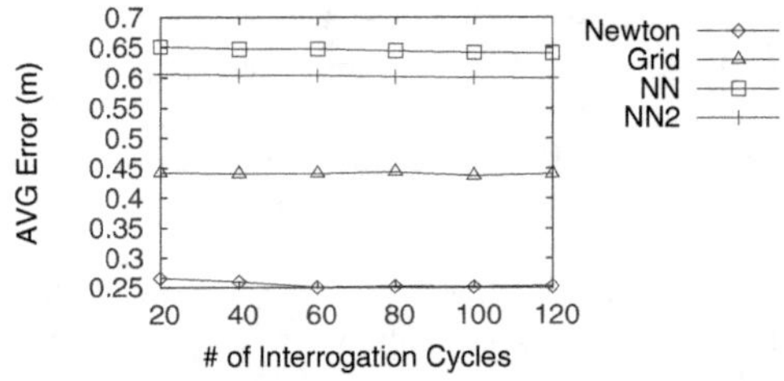

Figure 10: Window Size vs. Localization Accuracy

for 5 static objects, and run our localization algorithms on the data for 200 time steps (1000 cycles). We simulate the change of true reader detection model, by changing the model parameters a and b linearly from the ground-level parameters (at the beginning of the 1000 cycles) to the waist-level parameters (at the end of the 1000 cycles). Note that this is a more abrupt model change than what is likely to happen in a real world scenario. Then, we learn the reader detection model from read rate estimations of reference tags based on 20, 40, 60, 80, 100 and 120 interrogation cycles.

Figures 9(a) and (b) show both the true model parameters and the learned model parameters in the 200 time steps, where the black lines correspond to the true model parameters, and the green, red and blue curves correspond to the model parameters learned from read rate estimations based on 20, 60 and 120 interrogation cycles, respectively. In Figures 9(a) and (b), the learned model parameters present an obvious delay from the true parameters (i.e. the learned parameter curves are approximately the true parameter curves shifted towards the left), and the larger the number of interrogation cycles, the longer the delay (note that the colors of the curves from left to right are green, red, blue and black in order). Besides, model parameters learned from read rate estimations based on small windows such as the 20-cycle one (the green curve) are very unstable.

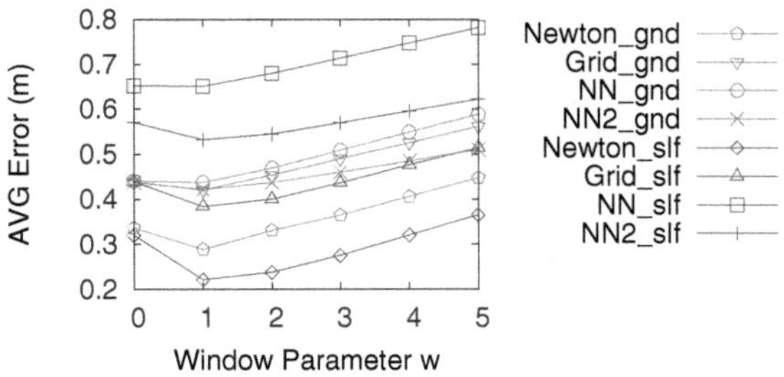

(a) Stop Duration = 20

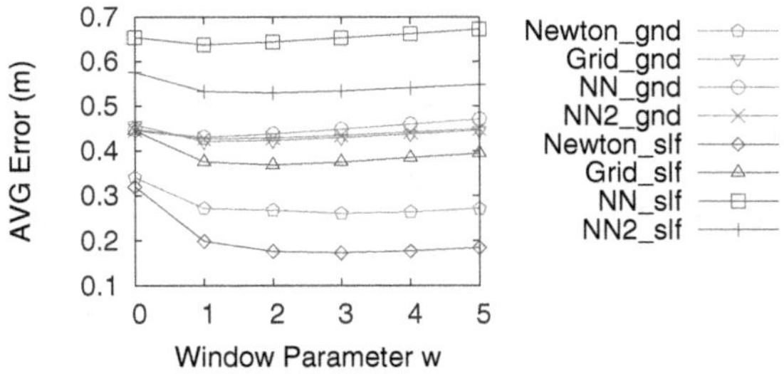

(b) Stop Duration = 80

Figure 11: Effect of Window Size on Localization Accuracy

Figure 10 shows the average error distance of our localization algorithms with different window size for reference tag read rate estimation, where we use window $[-1, 1]$ for tracking tag read rate estimation. We can see that the 60-cycle window leads to the least localization error (around 25cm) for *Newton*. In the real scenario, the model change is not likely to be as abrupt as our experimental setting, and larger window size such as 100 cycles is likely to be a better choice.

5.5 Effect of Window Size for Moving Objects

In Section 5.2, we have seen that a larger window increases the accuracy of location estimation for static objects. However, larger window size may not always imply higher localization accuracy for moving objects. On the one hand, a larger window contains more interrogation cycles, which give rise to read rate measurements of higher precision. On the other hand, the outdated readings in a larger window have a negative impact on the localization accuracy, since the tracking object is assumed to be at a fixed location throughout the time in the window.

Therefore, with the increment of window size, one can expect that the localization error drops when the window size is small, and then rises as the window size further increases. The optimal window size depends on the average moving frequency of the tracking objects, and needs to be tuned according to the application. For example, while window $[-1, 1]$ is better than window $[0, 0]$ for tracking constantly moving objects as shown in Section 5.1, the reverse is true for the experiments on static objects in Section 5.2.

To study the relationship between optimal window size and object moving frequency, we generate the trajectories of 5 objects for 3000 time steps with different stop durations T. Part of the results are shown in Figure 11. Figure 11(a) shows the average error distance of our localization algorithms when $T = 20$, where we can see that the optimal window parameter is $w = 1$. In Figure 11(b) which corresponds to $T = 80$, we can see that the optimal window parameter is $w = 3$. To sum up, the optimal window size is larger for objects that move less frequently.

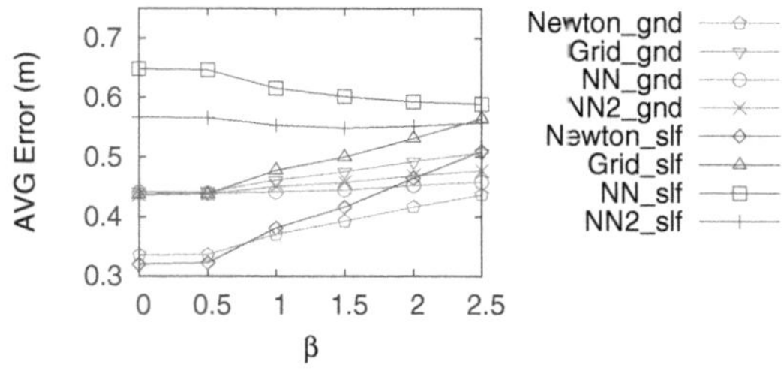

(a) Window = $[0, 0]$

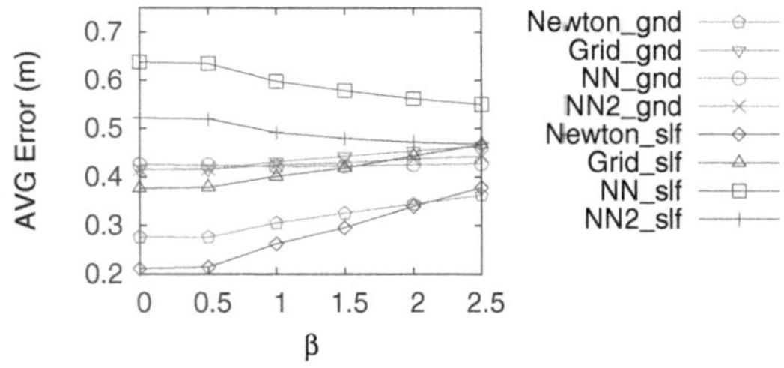

(b) Window = $[-1, 1]$

Figure 12: Effect of External Interference

5.6 Tolerance to External Interferences

So far, we have been assuming that the response count of a tag to a reader within N interrogation cycles strictly follows the binomial distribution. In this set of experiments, we study the tolerance of our algorithm to external interference by varying the parameter β of our data generator, which is described at the beginning of this section. We set the maximum value of β to be 2.5 so that the read count can be biased by at most 2.5 times its standard deviation, which is a very significant deviation.

Figure 12(a) (or Figure 12(b)) shows the average error distance of our localization algorithms with window $[0, 0]$ (or $[-1, 1]$) for various noise levels, where we can see that the error of *Newton_slf* increases more dramatically than and finally exceeds that of *Newton_gnd*, and therefore *Newton_gnd* is more tolerant to external interference than *Newton_slf*. From the figures we can see that our localization algorithms, including *Newton*, all have good tolerance to external interference, and *Newton* still incurs the least error in noisy environments.

5.7 Scalability

To test the scalability of our localization algorithms, we generate the trajectories of 20 constantly moving objects for varying time steps t, and run our algorithm on these data with window set to $[-1, 1]$. The execution times of all the algorithms increase linearly with the total number of location estimations (which is $20t$).

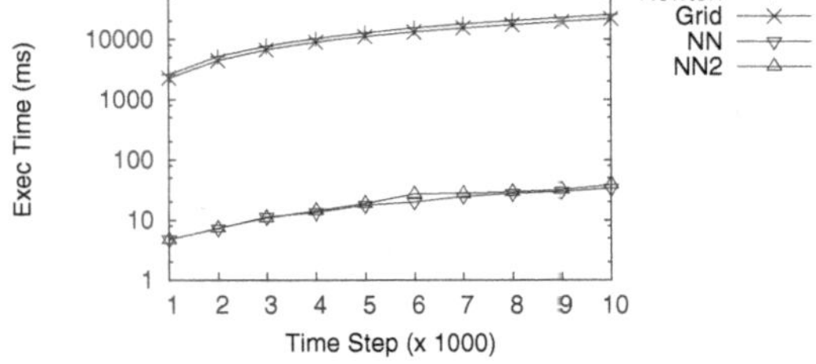

Figure 13: Scalability Results

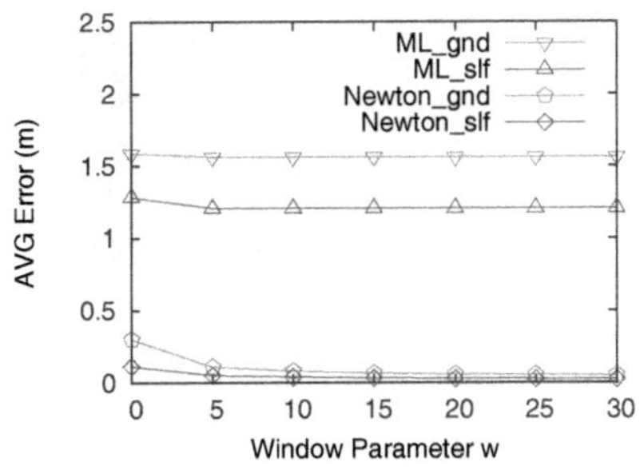

Figure 14: *Newton* vs. *Multilateralization* (*ML*)

Figure 13 shows the results of our scalability test, where the NN algorithms take only around 0.1% of the time consumed by *Newton* on the same number of location estimations, and *Grid* takes around 85% of the time consumed by *Newton*. For $t = 10{,}000$, the 200,000 ($= 20t$) location estimations are accomplished by *Newton* in less than 26s. Therefore, over 7500 location estimations can be done for each second by an ordinary computer, which is sufficient for supporting large scale real-time location tracking applications.

5.8 Comparison with Multilateration

In this subsection, we compare our best algorithm, i.e. *Newton*, with the best algorithm, i.e. *Multilateralization* (*ML*), in the pioneering work of [10] that uses passive tags for indoor localization.

We randomly generate the locations for 4 static objects, and run both localization algorithms on the data for 3000 time steps in both the ground-level setting and the waist-level setting, with different window sizes. Figure 14 shows the results of comparison, where we can see that the average error of *ML* is over 1m. In fact, *ML* is not as accurate as the nearest neighbor based methods, let alone *Newton*. The low accuracy of *ML* is caused by the small number (3 to 4) of readers that can detect an tracking object, since *ML* is effective only when many readers can detect an object. However, for passive tags with low detection range, this implies a dense deployment of readers/antennea, which is too costly to be carried out.

6. RELATED WORK

Most existing localization systems are based on the active RFID technology[1, 9, 11, 12, 14]. The nearest neighbor based algorithms are adopted by RADAR [9] and LANDMARC [1] for location inference, where the location of the target is estimated by properly averaging the locations of the reference points whose received signal strength distribution is similar to that of the target. Other more advanced models based on the signal propagation characteristics include those proposed in [11, 12, 13, 14], such as multilateration and Bayesian graphical modeling.

Passive RFID technology has been studied for data cleaning purpose [2, 3, 5, 6, 8]. However, very few work is done to track objects using passive tags, except the pioneering work of [10], which is still primitive in that its experiments are conducted in a very small area of 1.83m×1.83m.

7. CONCLUSION

Motivated by many advantages of passive RFID tags such as low tag cost and convenience of maintenance, we explore the techniques of using passive tags for indoor RFID localization. Our localization system, PassTrack, learns for each reader an adaptive reader detection model that has good tolerance to external interference. Several algorithms are supported by PassTrack for location inference based on read rates of passive RFID tags, and the best one, *Newton*, incurs an average localization error of around 30 cm, and is able to carry out over 7500 location estimations per second on an ordinary machine. The excellent tracking accuracy and efficiency of PassTrack enables it to support large-scale real-time indoor localization applications.

8. ACKNOWLEDGEMENTS

This work is partially supported by HKUST RFID Center under grant numbers ITP/022/02LP and SSRI08RGC, and GRF under grant number HKUST 617610.

9. REFERENCES

[1] L. M. Ni, Y. Liu, Y. C. Lau and A. P. Patil. "LANDMARC: Indoor Location Sensing Using Active RFID". In *Wireless Networks*, 2004.

[2] S. R. Jeffery, M. Garofalakis and M. J. Franklin. "Adaptive Cleaning for RFID Data Streams". In *VLDB*, 2006.

[3] H. Chen, W. Ku, H. Wang and M. Sun. "Leveraging Spatio-Temporal Redundancy for RFID Data Cleansing". In *SIGMOD*, 2010.

[4] S. Han, J. Kim, C.-H. Park, H.-C. Yoon and J. Heo. "Optimal Detection Range of RFID Tag for RFID-Based Positioning System Using the k-NN Algorithm". In *Sensors*, 2009.

[5] M. Kodialam and T. Nandagopal. "Fast and Reliable Estimation Schemes in RFID Systems". In *Mobicom*, 2006.

[6] T. Tran, C. Sutton, R. Cocci, Y. Nie, Y. Diao and P. Shenoy. "Probabilistic Inference over RFID Streams in Mobile Environments". In *ICDE*, 2009.

[7] S. Boyd and L. Vandenberghe. "Convex Optimization". *Cambridge University Press*. http://www.stanford.edu/~boyd/cvxbook/bv_cvxbook.pdf

[8] L. W. F. Chaves, E. Buchmann and K. Böhm. "TagMark: Reliable Estimations of RFID Tags for Business Processes". In *KDD*, 2008.

[9] P. Bahl and V. N. Padmanabhan. "RADAR: An In-Building RF-based User Location and Tracking System". In *INFOCOM*, 2000.

[10] J. Zhou and J. Shi. "RFID Localization Algorithms and Applications — A Review". In *Journal of Intelligent Manufacturing*, Vol. 20, No. 6, pp. 695–707, 2009.

[11] A. Savvides, C. Han and M. B. Srivastava. "Dynamic Fine-Grained Localization in Ad-Hoc Networks of Sensors". In *MOBICOM*, 2001.

[12] D. Madigan, E. Einahrawy, R. P. Martin, W. Ju, P. Krishnan and A. S. Krishnakumar. "Bayesian Indoor Positioning Systems". In *INFOCOM*, 2005.

[13] T. Roos, P. Myllymäki and H. Tirri. "A Statistical Modeling Approach to Location Estimation". In *IEEE Trans. Mob. Comput.* (TMC)1(1):59–69 (2002).

[14] R. Öktem and E. Aydin. "An RFID Based Indoor Tracking Method for Navigating Visually Impaired People". In *Turk J Elec Eng & Comp Sci*, Vol. 18, No. 2, 2010.

[15] A. Monreale, F. Pinelli, R. Trasarti and F. Giannotti. "WhereNext: A Location Predictor on Trajectory Pattern Mining". In *KDD*, 2009.

[16] F. Giannotti, M. Nanni, F. Pinelli and D. Pedreschi. "Trajectory Pattern Mining". In *KDD*, 2009.

[17] J. Lee, J. Han and K. Whang. "Trajectory Clustering: A Partition-and-Group Framework". In *SIGMOD*, 2007.

[18] J. Lee, J. Han and X. Li. "Trajectory Outlier Detection: A Partition-and-Detect Framework". In *ICDE*, 2008.

Location-Aware Instant Search

Ruicheng Zhong[†], Ju Fan[†], Guoliang Li[†], Kian-Lee Tan[‡], Lizhu Zhou[†]
[†]Department of Computer Science and Technology, Tsinghua National Laboratory for Information Science and Technology (TNList), Tsinghua University, Beijing, China
[‡]Department of Computer Science, School of Computing, National University of Singapore, Singapore
zrc1101001@gmail.com; fan-j07@mails.thu.edu.cn;
{liguoliang,dcszlz}@tsinghua.edu.cn; tankl@comp.nus.edu.sg

ABSTRACT

Location-Based Services (LBS) have been widely accepted by mobile users recently. Existing LBS-based systems require users to type in complete keywords. However for mobile users it is rather difficult to type in complete keywords on mobile devices. To alleviate this problem, in this paper we study the location-aware instant search problem, which returns users location-aware answers as users type in queries letter by letter. The main challenge is to achieve high interactive speed. To address this challenge, in this paper we propose a novel index structure, prefix-region tree (called PR-Tree), to efficiently support location-aware instant search. PR-Tree is a tree-based index structure which seamlessly integrates the textual description and spatial information to index the spatial data. Using the PR-Tree, we develop efficient algorithms to support single prefix queries and multi-keyword queries. Experiments show that our method achieves high performance and significantly outperforms state-of-the-art methods.

Categories and Subject Descriptors

H.2.8 [**Database Applications**]: Spatial databases

General Terms

Algorithms, Design, Experimentation, Performance

Keywords

Type-ahead search, Keywords search, Spatial databases

1. INTRODUCTION

Location-Based Services (LBS) have become more and more popular and attracted significant attention from both academic and industrial communities recently. Many LBS based systems, such as AT&T Location Information Services[1], have been deployed to provide users with location-aware experiences, and they are widely accepted by millions of mobile users, thanks to the modern mobile devices.

[1]http://www.wireless.att.com/lbs/

CIKM'12, October 29–November 2, 2012, Maui, HI, USA.

Most of the existing studies adopt a *spatial keyword search* based method to help users retrieve location-aware answers [7, 5]. Given a set of objects with spatial information and textual description (e.g., points-of-interest (POIs)) and a user query with location and keywords, spatial keyword search finds top-k relevant objects by considering the distance and textual relevance between the query and objects. For example, if a user wants to find a gas station nearby, she can issue a keyword query "`gas station`" to a LBS system, which returns the relevant gas stations by considering the user's location and keywords.

Traditional spatial keyword search method requires users to type in *complete* keywords for finding location-aware answers. However for mobile users, typing a complete keyword is tedious and also susceptible to errors. To alleviate this problem, instance search (also known as type-ahead search or search-as-you-type) [1, 17, 16, 3, 15, 14, 18] is proposed to provide users with new search experiences, which returns relevant answers as users type in queries letter by letter. Recently many systems, e.g., Google, have been deployed to support instant search.

It is very natural to extend instant search to support spatial keyword search. To this end, in this paper we study the location-aware instant search problem. In our method, as a user types in queries letter by letter, the system returns the location-aware answers on-the-fly, and provides the user with instant replies. Figure 1 provides an example of location-aware instant search over 13 POIs. At every keystroke a user types in our system, the system takes her current input string as a query and returns the relevant location-aware answers instantly. For instance, as shown in Figure 1(b), when the user types in a partial query "`park s`", the nearest objects containing complete keyword "`park`" and the prefix "`s`", i.e., o_9 and o_8, are returned. Obviously this new search method can help users to find desired answers in a more friendly way than the traditional methods.

ID	*Name*	*Location*
1	*Stadium*	*(41.754, -76.779)*
2	*Palace Street*	*(42.434, -75.975)*
3	*Pavement*	*(42.265, -75.582)*
4	*Stephan Park*	*(42.187, -75.818)*
5	*Shipyard*	*(42.188, -73.983)*
6	*Stock*	*(41.735, -74.221)*
7	*Parliament*	*(41.623, -74.819)*
8	*Studio Park*	*(41.834, -75.126)*
9	*Skydive Park*	*(41.508, -75.809)*
10	*Police*	*(40.799, -74.378)*
11	*Spring*	*(40.684, -76.312)*
12	*Post*	*(40.457, -73.462)*
13	*Station*	*(42.761, -75.674)*

(a) Data Sample.

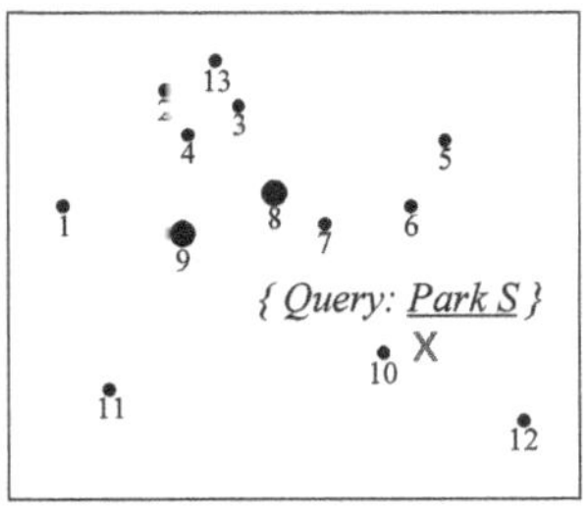

(b) Search Scenario.

Figure 1: An example for location-aware instant search on query "`park s`" and located at "×".

It is rather challenging to support location-aware instant search due to the requirement of a high interactive speed. Existing studies [13, 21] devise hybrid index structures to address this challenge. However, [13] has very limited filtering power for short or frequent query prefixes. [21] cannot support multi-keyword queries and it also consumes a large amount of memory. Moreover, both of them cannot perform well for large data sets since they fail to fully utilize the textual and spatial pruning simultaneously.

To address these limitations, in this paper, we propose a novel index structure, prefix-region tree (called PR-Tree), to efficiently support location-aware instant search. PR-Tree is a tree-based index structure. Different from traditional indices, PR-Tree considers both textual partitioning and spatial partitioning simultaneously to build the index. Thus it can achieve great improvement of efficiency for location-aware instant search.

Our contributions are summarized as follows.

- We propose a novel data structure, called PR-Tree. It seamlessly integrates the spatial information and textual description to index the spatial data.
- Using our PR-Tree index structure, we develop effective algorithms to efficiently answer single prefix queries and multi-keyword queries.
- We have conducted thorough experiments and the experimental results show that our method achieves high performance and significantly outperforms state-of-the-art methods.

The rest of this paper is organized as follows. We formulate the problem of location-aware instant search and discuss related work in Section 2. We introduce our proposed index structure PR-Tree in Section 3. We develop efficient search algorithms in Section 4. In Section 5, we discuss how to support sophisticated ranking functions in PR-Tree. Experiments are provided in Section 6. Finally, we conclude the paper in Section 7.

2. PRELIMINARIES

In this section, we first formalize the problem of location-aware instant search in Section 2.1, and review related work in Section 2.2.

2.1 Problem Definition

Data Model. Our work considers a set of objects, $\mathcal{O} = \{o_1, o_2, \ldots, o_{|\mathcal{O}|}\}$ in a spatial database. Each object $o \in \mathcal{O}$ consists of spatial information $o.l$ and textual information $o.W$, denoted by $o = (l, W)$. Specifically, the spatial information $o.l$ represents a location in the two-dimensional geographic space, and the textual information $o.W$ is a set of distinct words, denoted by $o.W = \{w_1, w_2, \ldots w_{|o.W|}\}$. For example, Figure 1 shows 13 objects, each of which has a location and a set of words, e.g., $o_2 = (l_2, \{\texttt{palace}, \texttt{street}\})$.

Query Model. Our paper focuses on supporting location-aware instant query q that consists of a location $q.l$, a set of *complete* keywords $q.W = \{w_1, w_2, \ldots, w_{|q.W|}\}$ that a user has typed, a prefix $q.p$ that the user is typing in and an integer k, denoted by $q = (l, W, p, k)$. Given a set of objects $\mathcal{O}$, the answer of q, denoted by $\mathcal{R}$, is the k *nearest* objects sorted by their distances to query location $q.l$, where each object o satisfies

(1) object o contains all complete keywords in the query, i.e., $o.W \supseteq q.W$, and
(2) o has at least one word with $q.p$ as its prefix, i.e., $\exists w \in o.W, p \preceq w$, where $p \preceq w$ denotes that p is a prefix of w.

We assume that $\forall w_i, w_j \in q.W$ that $w_i(w_j)$ is not a prefix of $w_j(w_i)$. Let $\texttt{dist}(q, o)$ represent the distance between query location $q.l$ and object location $o.l$. In this paper, we use Euclidean distance as the distance measurement.

Problem Formulation. Based on these notations, we formulate the location-aware instant search problem.

DEFINITION 1 (LOCATION-AWARE INSTANT SEARCH). *Consider a set of objects $\mathcal{O} = \{o_1, o_2, \ldots, o_{|\mathcal{O}|}\}$ and a location-aware instant query $q = (l, W, p, k)$. It returns the top-k objects $\mathcal{R} \subseteq \mathcal{O}$ such that each object $o \in \mathcal{R}$ satisfies $o.W \supseteq q.W$ and $\exists w \in o.W, p \preceq w$, sorted by their distances to the query location.*

To make it consistent with existing work [13, 21], we only use the distance to rank the answers. We will discuss how to support other complex ranking functions in Section 5.

2.2 Related Work

Location-Aware Instant Search: Existing studies devised different index structures [13, 21] to support location-aware instant search.

Ji et al. [13] proposed an R-tree based method called Filtering-Effective Hybrid Indexing (FEH). The method first builds an R-tree on top of locations of all objects. Then, in each R-tree node, it adds textual filters with possible prefixes contained by the objects in this node. Given a query, it traverses the R-tree from the root to the leaves using the best-first-search strategy [10]. Whenever a tree node is reached, it first employs the filter to decide whether to insert its child nodes or objects into a priority queue. The search stops when the first k answers have been found. However, the FEH algorithm is very expensive for short and frequent prefixes, since the number of the potential candidate objects is extremely large, and the filters have poor pruning power.

Materialized Trie (MT) is a trie based method [21]. First, it builds a trie structure on top of words of all objects. Each leaf node has an inverted list to record those objects which contain the corresponding word. To incorporate spatial pruning power into the trie structure, spatial information is added in each trie node. For a trie node with a prefix p, it divides the whole query space into R regions and maintains an upper-bound score for each region to indicate that a query with prefix p will reach the maximal score in this region. However it is rather expensive to materialize the information for all trie nodes. Thus it proposes to select M nodes for materialization. The main problem for MT is that it will consume a large amount of memory. To achieve high performance, it needs to divide the space into a large number of smaller regions, thus incurs significant of space utilization. Another limitation of MT is that it cannot support multi-keyword queries, which is common in many applications.

Spatial Keyword Search: Spatial keyword search has been widely studied in the database community [24, 4, 9, 7, 5, 23, 22, 20, 19, 6, 11]. Given a set of points-of-interest (POIs) and a query with keywords and location, the spatial keyword search aims to find the relevant POIs by considering both spatial proximity and textual relevance. [24, 9, 4]

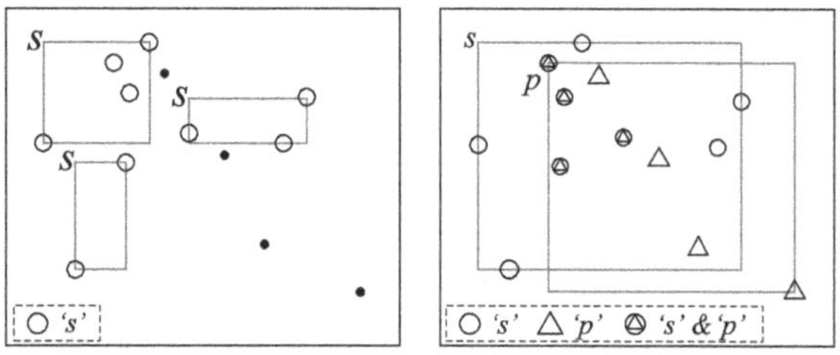

(a) Spatial partition for the same prefix "s".
(b) Textual partition for a specific region.

Figure 2: Spatio-textual partition.

solved the range query problem by the use of R-tree. Felipe et al. [7] integrated signature files into R-tree. Cong et al. [5] proposed the IR-tree by combining the inverted files and R-tree. Yao et al. [23] studied how to support approximate string matching. Wu et al. [22] studied spatial keyword search for moving objects and Lu et al. [20] tracked reverse spatial and textual k nearest neighbor search.

Traditional spatial keyword search method requires users to type in *complete* keywords to find location-aware answers. In this paper, we study a more user-friendly search method, location-aware instant search. The method returns relevant POIs on-the-fly when users type in keywords letter by letter, which helps users find information with less typing efforts.

3. PREFIX-REGION TREE

In this section, we introduce a novel index structure, called prefix-region tree, to support efficient location-aware instant search. We first introduce our basic idea in Section 3.1 and give an overview of the prefix-region tree in Section 3.2. Then, we respectively discuss the tree construction and update in Section 3.3 and Section 3.4. Finally we discuss some issues on PR-Tree in Section 3.5.

3.1 Basic Idea

We can extend existing textual index structures (e.g., trie) or spatial index structures (e.g., R-Tree) to support location-aware instant search. Using a trie index based on the textual information of objects, we can adopt a *text-only* strategy to obtain the top-k answers as follows. Given a query q, we first retrieve the objects which satisfy the textual constraints, i.e., such $o \in \mathcal{O}$ that $o.W \supseteq q.W$ and $\exists w \in o.W, q.p \preceq w$, and then sort them in ascending order by their distances to $q.l$ to get the top-k answers. Obviously, this method is inefficient since it never considers the spatial pruning, and may involve a huge number of objects which are not the top-k answers.

On the other hand, using an R-tree index based on the spatial information of objects, we can employ a *spatial-only* strategy. Specifically, we can adopt the best-first traversal method [10] to iteratively find the nearest objects. Then, we examine whether the objects satisfy the textual constraints mentioned above. However, this method fails to consider the textual pruning since the traversal over the R-tree ignores the words of the underlying objects.

To address these problems, we aim to build a more effective index structure which integrates both the textual and spatial information seamlessly. To achieve this goal, we have the following observations.

(1) Given a specific prefix p, the objects with p may scatter in different areas. Based on the spatial distribution, we can partition the objects into several regions to facilitate effective spatial pruning. Figure 2(a) shows objects containing prefix "s" (represented by circles), which can be partitioned into three regions. Using these regions, we can estimate objects' distance bounds to the query location, and utilize spatial pruning to efficiently obtain top-k answers.

(2) Given a specific region r, the objects in r may contain different prefixes but it is hard to distinguish them by spatial information only. Thus, we can partition the objects based on the prefixes, in order to facilitate effective textual pruning. Figure 2(b) provides some objects in a region. We can partition the objects based on different prefixes they contain, e.g., "s" and "p", and efficiently prune the objects dissatisfying the textual constraints.

If we partition the objects by simultaneously using the textual and spatial information, we can fully utilize the spatial textual pruning at query time. However it is non-trivial to devise an index structure that seamlessly combines textual and spatial partitions. To address this challenge, we propose the prefix-region tree in the following sections.

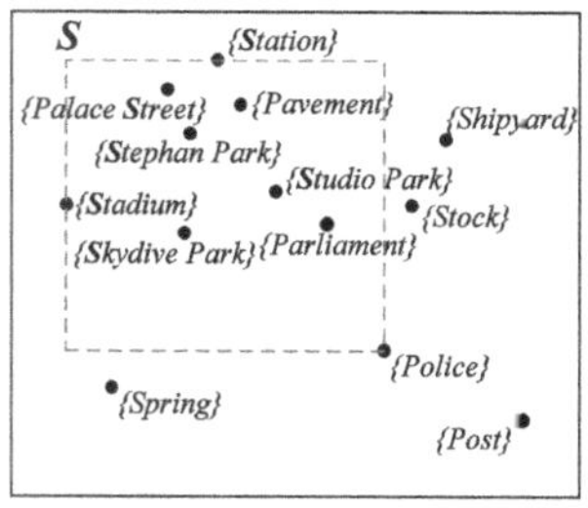

Figure 3: Prefix region.

3.2 Prefix-Region Tree

For ease of presentation, we first introduce an important concept, called *prefix region*. Intuitively, a prefix region consists of a prefix for textual partition and a region for spatial partition. Formally, the prefix region is defined as follows.

DEFINITION 2 (PREFIX REGION). *Let p denote a prefix and r denote an* MBR *(Minimum Bounding Rectangle). A prefix region is defined as a combination of prefix p and region r, denoted by $f = \langle p, r \rangle$.*

Given a prefix region f, we use $\mathcal{O}_f$ to represent the objects satisfying f, that is, each object $o \in \mathcal{O}_f$ has prefix $f.p$ and its location $o.l$ is within region $f.r$. Take Figure 3 as an example. Consider a prefix region $f = \langle \text{"s"}, r \rangle$ and a set of objects $\mathcal{O} = \{o_1, o_2, o_3, o_4, o_7, o_8, o_9, o_{10}, o_{13}\}$. We have $\mathcal{O}_f = \{o_1, o_2, o_4, o_8, o_9, o_{13}\}$ since all objects in $\mathcal{O}_f$ have prefix "s" and their locations are within r, as illustrated by the dashed-line rectangle labelled with prefix "s" in Figure 3. In addition, we define that a prefix region f_1 is *subsumed* by another prefix-region f_2, if and only if 1) $f_2.p$ is a prefix of $f_1.p$, denoted by $f_2.p \preceq f_1.p$, and 2) $f_2.r$ encloses $f_1.r$, denoted by $f_1.r \subseteq f_2.r$.

Then, we define the prefix-region tree (or PR-Tree for short) as follows. PR-Tree organizes all objects in $\mathcal{O}$ in a hierarchical manner, where each node is a prefix region[2]. In the PR-Tree, each non-leaf node subsumes all its child nodes. Each leaf node, say $f_l = \langle p_l, r_l \rangle$ is associated with an object list, denoted by `ObjectList`, which contains the objects with prefix p_l located within region r_l. In particular, the root is $f_{root} = \langle \emptyset, r_{all} \rangle$, where r_{all} represents the MBR of all objects in $\mathcal{O}$. Obviously, in a PR-Tree, the region sizes of nodes in lower levels are smaller than those in higher levels.

[2]For ease of presentation, we use "prefix region" and PR-Tree node interchangeably.

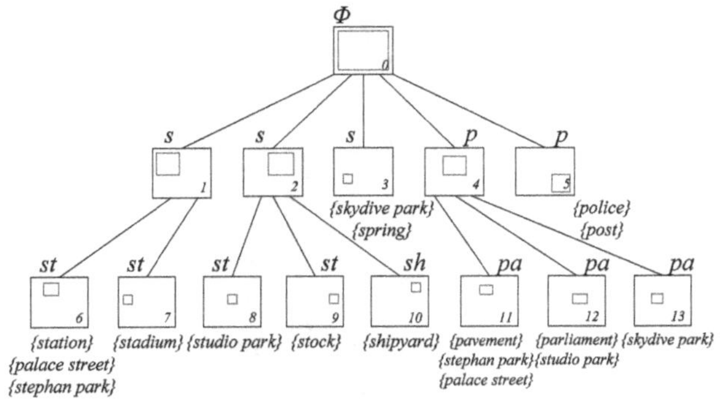

Figure 4: A PR-tree.

In order to avoid large tree depths, we introduce a parameter M to allow at most M objects contained in every leaf. Figure 4 provides an example of a PR-Tree. The string on the top-left of the node box denotes the prefix $f.p$, and the inner frame denotes the region $f.r$.

3.3 Tree Construction

We construct a PR-Tree in a top-down manner. We first initialize the root node $f_{root} = \langle \emptyset, r_{all} \rangle$ with object set $\mathcal{O}$. Then, we split $\mathcal{O}$ into subsets to generate child nodes. Similarly, we recursively split the generated nodes until the number of objects in each leaf node is not greater than M. Obviously, the essential task is how to split a node f. To this end, we consider both textual and spatial partitioning.

Textual partitioning groups the objects $\mathcal{O}_f$ of node f based on the textual information. Specifically, consider a set of words W_f with prefix $f.p$ contained by the objects in $\mathcal{O}_f$. Based on W_f, we can construct a radix trie[3] where each path from the root to a node corresponds to a prefix. Using the radix trie, we can define `Next`($f.p$) as the child nodes of $f.p$ in the trie. For example, given a set of keywords W_f ={`pavement, palace, park, parliament, police, post`}, we have `Next`("p") ={`pa, po`} and `Next`("pa")= {`pavement, palace, par`}. Based on prefixes in `Next`($f.p$), we can partition objects $\mathcal{O}_f$ into subsets for generating child nodes in the PR-Tree. Figure 5(a) provides an example of textual partitioning. The root node "$\emptyset$" is partitioned into two child nodes respectively with prefixes "s" and "p" in `Next`($\emptyset$). Then, node with prefix "p" is further partitioned into two child nodes respectively having "pa" and "po".

Spatial partitioning groups objects $\mathcal{O}_f$ of node f based on the spatial information. Specifically, we partition region $f.r$ into subregions, each of which contains subsets of $\mathcal{O}_f$. In this paper, we consider one of the most fundamental strategies, i.e., to partition one region into four non-overlapped subregions by splitting at a central point horizontally and vertically. We omit discussing other partitioning methods in this paper due to the space limitation.

More formally, we partition region $f.r$ into four regions, r^{ll} (lower left), r^{ul} (upper left), r^{lr} (lower right) and r^{ur} (upper right), and respectively represent the object sets in the regions as $\mathcal{O}_f^{ll}$, $\mathcal{O}_f^{ul}$, $\mathcal{O}_f^{lr}$ and $\mathcal{O}_f^{ur}$. A straightforward method is to simply partition r into four regions of the same size, which is used in a quad-tree [8]. However, this method may result in skew distribution of objects, that is, some regions may contain more objects than the others. To make the partitioning as even as possible, i.e., each subset contains nearly the same number of objects, we select the *centroid* as the center for spatial splitting. As shown in Figure 5(b), the objects are partitioned into four sub-regions. Note that the partition strategies may produce less than four sub-regions, since some regions contain no object.

[3]A radix trie is a space-optimized trie structure where each node with only one child is merged with its child.

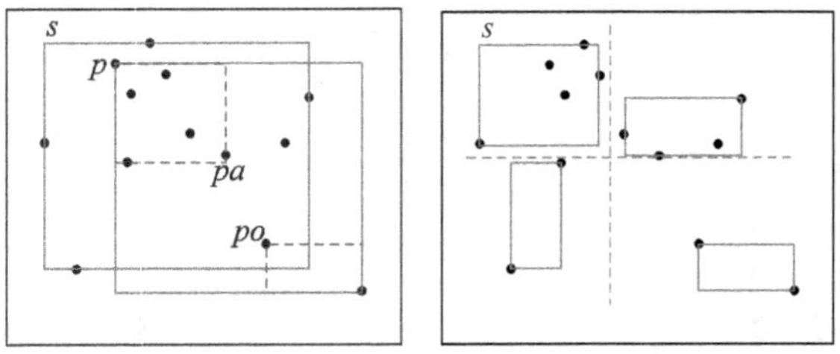

(a) Textual Partition. (b) Spatial Partition.

Figure 5: Textual partition and spatial partition.

Based on the textual and spatial partitioning, we present the algorithm for constructing a PR-Tree, as shown in Algorithm 1. The algorithm first initializes a root node $f_{root} = \langle \emptyset, r_{all} \rangle$, and puts the root with its corresponding objects $\mathcal{O}$ into a stack. Then, the algorithm iteratively employs the following textual and spatial partitioning operations on each node f, which is illustrated in Figure 6.

1) The algorithm employs textual partitioning to obtain several *intermediate* nodes, i.e. $\langle p_1, r_{p_1} \rangle, \langle p_2, r_{p_2} \rangle, \dots, \langle p_k, r_{p_k} \rangle$, where $p_i \in$ `Next`($f.p$).

2) For each intermediate node $\langle p_i, r_{p_i} \rangle$, the algorithm employs spatial partitioning to further generate four nodes, $\langle p_i, r^{ll}_{\mathcal{O}_{p_i}} \rangle$, $\langle p_i, r^{ul}_{\mathcal{O}_{p_i}} \rangle$, $\langle p_i, r^{lr}_{\mathcal{O}_{p_i}} \rangle$ and $\langle p_i, r^{ur}_{\mathcal{O}_{p_i}} \rangle$. These nodes are then assigned to be the children for the node $\langle p, r_{\mathcal{O}} \rangle$.

This above node-splitting procedure stops when every leaf node contains no more than M objects.

Algorithm 1: ConstructPRTree ($\mathcal{O}$, M)

```
Input: O: An object set; M: a parameter
Output: T: A constructed PR-Tree
begin
    Initialize a PR-Tree T.root ← ⟨∅,r_O⟩ ;
    Initialize a stack, Stack ← ∅ ;
    Stack.Push(⟨ T.root, O ⟩ ) ;
    while Stack not empty do
        ⟨ n, O_n ⟩ ← Stack.Pop() ;
        if |O_n| ≤ M then
            n.ObjectList ← O_n ;
        else
            C_t ← TextPartition (n.p, O_n) ;
            foreach c ∈ C_t do
                C_ts ← SpatialPartition (c) ;
                n' ← CreateTreeNode ( C_ts ) ;
                Stack.Push( ⟨n', C_ts⟩ ) ;
end
```

3.4 Tree Update

In this section, we discuss the update operations, i.e., insertion and deletion of the PR-Tree.

3.4.1 Insertion

We discuss an algorithm to insert an object $o = \langle l, W \rangle$ into a PR-Tree. The basic idea is to traverse the PR-Tree and select an appropriate node for insertion. Specifically, for every word w_i in $o.W$, the algorithm traverses the PR-Tree from the root. For a visited node f, the algorithm identifies

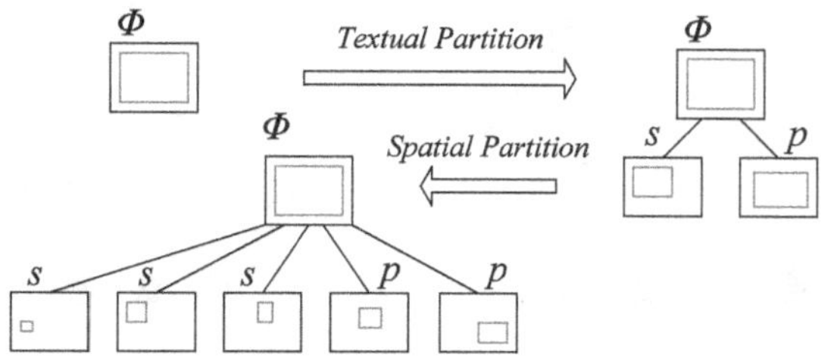

Figure 6: PR-tree construction.

the nearest child node f_c that $f_c.p \preceq w_i$ with respect to $o.l$. After selecting the child node f_c, the algorithm updates f_c as follows. If $o.l$ is not contained within region $f_c.r$, the algorithm enlarges region $f_c.r$ to a region containing $o.l$. We can recursively apply the above procedure until reaching a leaf node f_l. If f_l contains less than M objects, we simply insert o into f_l's object list. Otherwise, we employ the textual and spatial partitioning in Section 3.3 to further split f_l, and insert o into a new leaf node.

The time complexity scales to the height of the PR-Tree tree. Formally, it takes $\mathcal{O}(\log N)$ to finish an insertion operation, where N is the number of objects.

3.4.2 Deletion

We propose a bottom-up algorithm for deleting an object from a PR-Tree. When deleting an object o, the algorithm first finds all the leaf nodes which containing o, and removes it from the object list in the leaf nodes. Then, it updates the intermediate nodes of the PR-Tree in a bottom-up way. The basic idea is to examine whether the MBRs of intermediate nodes are affected by the object deletion. Specifically, if $o.l$ is located at the border of the MBR of a given intermediate node, the MBR needs to be re-calculated based on the MBRs of its child nodes. The algorithm terminates when reaching the root of the PR-Tree.

Note that, according to our tree construction, a node must have at least two child nodes. Therefore, if a node f is empty after deletion, we examine the number of its child nodes for the parent node of f. If f is an only child, we merge the node f to its parent node.

Then we analyse the time complexity. Since a deletion operation needs to examine $|o.W|$ paths from leaves to root, the time complexity is bounded to $O(|o.W| \log N)$.

3.5 Discussion on PR-Tree

In this section, we discuss three issues on PR-Tree. The first is on the balancing issue, the second is on the space complexity and the third is on the storage alternatives.

3.5.1 Balancing Issue

PR-Tree is not a balanced tree, since the textual partitioning cannot guarantee that each child node contains the same number of objects[4]. However, it does not affect the searching efficiency on the PR-Tree due to the following reasons.

1) The height of our PR-Tree is not very large since the fanout of each intermediate node is large. Let Σ denote the alphabet generating all words. The fanout of each intermediate node is at most $|\Sigma| \times 4$, which is usually large. We constructed PR-Trees on two real datasets in our experiments, and the heights were respectively 6.35 and 5.29.

2) There are no rather long branches due to our spatial partitioning strategies. Since we choose centroid as the center for spatial partitioning, the descendant nodes would contain roughly the same number of objects, leading to the maximum length of branches scaling to $\log N$. For example, in our experiments, the maximum branch lengths of the PR-Trees on the two datasets were respectively 12 and 14.

Therefore, although the PR-Tree is not balanced, the time of traversing different branches would differ insignificantly.

3.5.2 Space Complexity

In this section, we analyse the space complexity of the PR-Tree. Recall that the partitioning process of a node terminates when it contains at most M objects. Therefore, we can prove that the upper bound of the total number of leaf nodes in a PR-tree is within $[\frac{\sum |o_i.W|}{M}, \sum |o_i.W|]$, as shown in Lemma 1.

LEMMA 1. *The bound for the total number of leaf nodes in a PR-tree is* $[\frac{\sum |o_i.W|}{M}, \sum |o_i.W|]$

PROOF. We first prove that any object will appear in at most $|o.W|$ leaf nodes of the PR-tree. According to the building process, the regions for the nodes with the same prefix will never be overlapped. Each word of the objects in $\mathcal{O}$ will finally be included in one leaf node, and hence an object o is contained in at most $|o.W|$ leaf nodes. Thus the upper bound is $\sum |o_i.W|$.

On the other hand, each leaf node contains M objects, thus the lower bound is $\frac{\sum |o_i.W|}{M}$. □

Based on Lemma 1, the indexing size is scalable to the volume of the data set, i.e., $\sum |o.W|$.

3.5.3 Storage Alternatives

In this paper, we only consider maintaining the PR-Tree in memory. Nevertheless, PR-Tree is feasible to be disk-based. Since each non-leaf node only needs to store a few number of attributes, i.e., prefix, MBR and child list, and each leaf node needs to store the `ObjectList`, the information on one node is possible to be stored in one page of disk. However, in this paper, we mainly focus on devising the PR-Tree in memory and demonstrate its supreme efficiency, while taking the disk-based alternative as future work.

4. SEARCH ALGORITHMS

In this section, we first propose an algorithm for single-prefix queries in Section 4.1, and then extend the algorithm to support multi-keyword queries in Section 4.2.

4.1 Algorithm for Single-Prefix Queries

We first consider a single prefix query q with empty complete-keyword set, i.e., $q.W = \emptyset$. Given the query, we employ the effective best-first traversal algorithm (BFT) [10], to efficiently retrieve the top-k answers using the PR-Tree. The BFT algorithm uses a priority queue for maintaining the nodes and objects in the PR-Tree that need to be visited. For each node f in the queue, we compute the minimum distance between query location $q.l$ and the corresponding MBR $f.r$, denoted by MIND($q.l, f.r$). For each object o in the queue, we compute its distance to $q.l$, i.e., `dist`(q, o). Then, we sort the elements in the queue in ascending order by their minimum distances.

Due to the space limitation, we omit the details for BFT and only show an example of Algorithm 2 in this section.

[4] It is similar to a radix-tree since we employ `Next()` function.

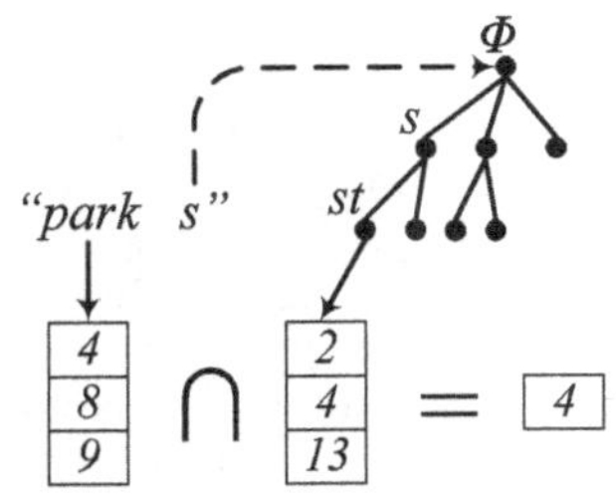

Figure 7: Multi-keyword query processing.

Example 1. *Consider the objects in Figure 1 and the PR-Tree in Figure 4. For a query $q = \{(40.5, -74.0), \emptyset,$ 'p', $2\}$, we compute top-2 answers as follows.*

Step 1: *Enqueue root node with $\langle\emptyset,0\rangle$.*

Queue: | $\langle\emptyset,0\rangle$ |

Step 2: *Dequeue the top element $\langle\emptyset,0\rangle$, expand its child nodes containing prefix 'p', calculate their minimal distances to q.l and enqueue them.*

Queue: | $\langle p,0\rangle$ | $\langle p,1.19\rangle$ |

Step 3: *Dequeue the $\langle p,0\rangle$, expand all objects containing prefix 'p', and enqueue them.*

Queue: | $\langle o_{10},0.38\rangle$ | $\langle o_{12},0.54\rangle$ | $\langle p,1.19\rangle$ |

Step 4: *Dequeue $\langle o_{10},0.38\rangle$. Since it is an object, we directly put it into the result list. So does $\langle o_{12},0.54\rangle$. Now, top-2 answers have been retrieved. Algorithm terminates.*

Algorithm 2: kNNQuery (p, l, k, T)

```
Input: p : Prefix; l: Location; k: Number; T: PR-Tree
Output: R: The top-k result list
begin
    Initialize a priority queue Q ← ∅ ;
    Q.Enqueue(⟨ T.root, 0⟩) ;
    while R.Size() < k & Q not empty do
        n ← Q.Dequeue() ;
        if n is an object then Insert n into R ;
        else if n is a leaf node then
            foreach Object o contains prefix p do
                Q.Enqueue(⟨ o, dist(l, o.l)⟩);
        else if n is an intermediate node then
            foreach Child node c ∈ of n do
                if c.p ⪯ p or p ⪯ c.p then
                    Q.Enqueue(⟨ c, MIND(l, c.r)⟩) ;
end
```

4.2 Algorithm for Multi-Keyword Queries

In this section, we extend our algorithm to support queries with multiple keywords, i.e., $q.W \neq \emptyset$. We first introduce an intersection-based method and then propose a cost-based method to improve the performance.

4.2.1 An Intersection-based Method

To support multi-keyword queries by PR-Tree, a straightforward method is to simply extend the algorithm for single-prefix queries. Specifically, consider a query $q = (l, W, p, k)$ where $q.W \neq \emptyset$. Each time when a dequeued element is a leaf node, we can only enqueue the objects which contain all keywords in $q.W$. To efficiently examine whether an object contains all keywords in $q.W$, we pre-compute and maintain a global inverted list that maps each word to the objects containing such word, denoted by $\mathcal{I}(w)$. Thus, we can efficiently obtain the promising objects containing the $q.W$ by computing the intersection of $\mathcal{I}(w_i)$.

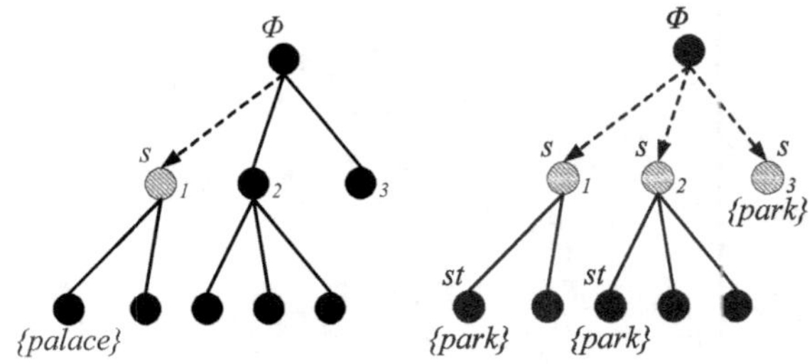

(a) Rare word "palace". (b) Frequent word "park".

Figure 8: Two circumstances for occurrence list.

Figure 7 provides an example to illustrate the method. Consider a query with $W = \{\texttt{park}\}$ and prefix "*s*". We first obtain the object list using inverted list $\mathcal{I}(\texttt{park})$, i.e., $\{o_4, o_8, o_9\}$. Then, we examine each object contained in a leaf node, say "*st*", and only enqueue the objects contained in $\mathcal{I}(\texttt{park})$, i.e., o_4.

Next, we analyse the time complexity of the above method. Since the size of `ObjectList` in a leaf is strictly less than or equal to M, and the size of the $\mathcal{I}(w)$ is maximally equal to the size of the data N, thus the time complexity for intersection on one node is $\mathcal{O}(M \log N \cdot |W|)$.

However, in the worst case, we have to examine all the leaf nodes, which leads to low performance. Thus, according to Lemma 1, the overall time complexity is $\mathcal{O}(NM \log N \cdot |W|)$. Obviously, this method visits many *unnecessary* leaf nodes which do not contain all keywords in $q.W$. For example, given query "`palace s`", for the prefix "`s`", there may be many leaf nodes that need to be visited. However, the number of leaf nodes containing word "`palace`" is rather small (See Figure 8(a)). We can see that the expanding child nodes labelled with '2', '3' is useless for producing the answers.

4.2.2 A Cost-based Method

To avoid unnecessary traversal, we must include additional textual information for early termination. Inspired by our observation in Figure 8(a), for any keyword w on node n, we can explicitly use a child list to indicate that only the children of n in the list will contain the keyword w. We call such a list an *occurrence list*, denoted by $\texttt{OL}(n, w)$. Thus, when traversing to such a node n, we only need to expand $\cap\, \texttt{OL}(n, w_i), w_i \in q.W$ into the priority queue to prune the unpromising descendants.

Obviously, if we store occurrence lists for all possible keywords on every tree node, the pruning power will be fully utilized. However, it will result in high memory cost, since the space requirement for storage will be $N \cdot |Vocabulary|$ in a worst case. In fact, sometimes occurrence list may have no effect on the performance. It happens when a keyword is frequent in the spatial database, and thus many leaf nodes may contain such word. Figure 8(b) shows this case. The keyword "park" appears in the sub-tree of every child of the root node, and thus it is useless to store occurrence list for "`park`" on the root node.

Therefore, we need to judiciously select keywords and nodes for storing occurrence lists. To this end, we first consider the *cost* of storing $\texttt{OL}(n, w)$ as its length.

Definition 3 (Cost).

$$Cost(\texttt{OL}(n, w)) = Length(\texttt{OL}(n, w))$$

Each $\texttt{OL}(n, w)$ will benefit query processing by ignoring those child nodes of n which do not contain keyword w. Therefore, the benefit can be described in two parts: (1)

the overhead saved on priority queue operations, e.g. enqueue or dequeue, and (2) the overhead saved on leaf nodes intersection. Let $\texttt{CL}(n)$ denote the original children list for node n. Let $\texttt{PQO}(n')$ denote the overhead on priority queue operations for all nodes rooted at n' and $\texttt{LNO}(n')$ denote the overhead on intersection for all leaf nodes in sub-tree of n', we define the benefit of $\texttt{OL}(n, w)$ as:

DEFINITION 4 (BENEFIT).

$$Benefit(\texttt{OL}(n,w)) = \Sigma_{\{n'|n'\in\texttt{CL}(n)\wedge n'\notin\texttt{OL}(n,w)\}}(\texttt{PQO}(n') + \texttt{LNO}(n')),$$

where $p(w)$ is the probability for word w being queried.

Conventionally, $\texttt{PQO}(n')$ is equal to the number of tree nodes under n', and $\texttt{PQO}(n')$ is estimated by the number of objects under n'.

Finally, for a given amount of memory budget $\mathcal{B}$, we want to maximize the overall benefit for different selected keywords and nodes. The formal problem is stated as follows.

DEFINITION 5. (MEMORY-CONSTRAINED KEYWORDS NODES SELECTION OPTIMIZATION) *Given the budget $\mathcal{B}$, the keyword set $\mathcal{K}$ and the node set $\mathcal{N}$, we want to find a collection of* keyword-node *pairs, that achieve maximum benefits within the budget $\mathcal{B}$.*

$$(n^*, w^*) \leftarrow \underset{\forall(n,w)\in\mathcal{K}\times\mathcal{N}}{\text{argmax}} \quad Benefit(\texttt{OL}(n,w))$$

$$s.t. \sum Cost(\texttt{OL}(n,w)) \leq \mathcal{B}\ .$$

We now prove this problem is NP-Complete.

THEOREM 1. *Memory-Constrained Keywords and Nodes Selection Optimization is NP-Complete.*

PROOF. The problem can be reduced from the 0-1 Knapsack Problem. Since the budget $\mathcal{B}$ is equivalent to the knapsack's volume, $Cost(\texttt{OL}(n,w))$ is the size of the items and $Benefit(\texttt{OL}(n,w))$ can be looked as item's value. Thus, proof is done. □

We propose a greedy heuristic algorithm to solve this problem. We sort all the (n,w) by $\frac{Benefit(\texttt{OL}(n,w))}{Cost(\texttt{OL}(n,w))}$ in descending order, then choose the current best (n,w) so long as the budget is not exhausted. Previous study [12] showed that the approximate ratio for greedy algorithm is 2. Note that, the $Cost(\texttt{OL}(n,w)$ is far smaller than the budget $\mathcal{B}$, thus the results would not be bad. Example 2 shows a scenario for multi-keyword search on a materialized PR-Tree.

EXAMPLE 2. *Consider a multi-keyword query "*`palace s`*" at location (40.5,-74.0).*
Step 1: *We start to push the ⟨∅,0⟩ into the queue:*
Queue: ⟨∅,0⟩
Step 2: *⟨∅,0⟩ is dequeued, and we check child nodes ⟨s,1.84⟩, ⟨s,1.22⟩ and ⟨s,1.38⟩. Since only the node ⟨s,1.84⟩ has been materialized with keyword "*`palace`*", we discard the other two unpromising nodes and only enqueue node ⟨s,1.84⟩.*
Queue: ⟨s,1.84⟩
Step 3: *The objects list for node ⟨s,1.84⟩ is {2,4,13}, and we intersect it with the global inverted list for keywords "*`palace`*" {2}. Finally only object o_2 has been enqueued;*
Queue: ⟨o_2,2.76⟩
Thus, we get the answers for query "`palace s`*" on the materialized PR-Tree.*

5. EXTENSION ON RANKING FUNCTIONS

Existing studies on keyword search in spatial database [5] can support more sophisticated ranking functions, which consider not only the spatial proximity but also textual relevancy between queries and objects. Here we discuss how to use our PR-Tree to support such ranking functions.

Given a query q and an object o, a general ranking function D_{st} to compute their similarity can be defined as

$$D_{st}(q,o) \quad = \quad \alpha(1 - \frac{\texttt{dist}(q,o)}{maxD_s}) + (1-\alpha)\frac{\texttt{rel}(q,o)}{maxD_t},$$

where $maxD_s$ is the maximum distance on space, $maxD_t$ is the maximum distance on text, and $\texttt{rel}(q,o)$ is the tf*idf based textual relevance between q and o.

$$\texttt{rel}(q,o) = \sum_{s\in q.W} tf(s,o) * idf(s,\mathcal{O}),$$

where $tf(w,o)$ is the term frequency of term w in object o and $idf(w,\mathcal{O})$ is the inverse document frequency of term w in the object set $\mathcal{O}$.

Next we discuss how to use the PR-Tree to support the new ranking function. We add a list of ⟨*keyword*, *weight*⟩ pairs on each node of the PR-Tree, which indicates that for all objects in the sub-tree of this node the maximum tf*idf for *keyword* is *weight*. Formally speaking, on a tree node f and for a specific keyword w, the *weight* is calculated by:

$$weight(w,f) = \max_{o\in\texttt{SubTreeObj}(f)} tf(w,f) * idf(w,\mathcal{O}).$$

where $\texttt{SubTreeObj}(f)$ denotes all the objects in the sub-tree of node f.

At query time, we can compute the textual relevancy by $\sum_{w\in q.W} weight(w,f)$, then aggregate the spatial distance to obtain the ranking score $D_{st}(q,f)$. This overall value can be used as the maximum boundary value for a given query q at node f on the PR-Tree, facilitating effective pruning.

Similarly, our PR-Tree is also capable of supporting the ranking function in [21].

6. EXPERIMENT

In this section, we report the experimental results. We implemented two baseline algorithms, FEH [13] and MT [21], as mentioned in Section 2.2. For FEH, we used R*-tree [2] as reported in the paper. We compared our PR-Tree based method (denoted by PRT) with the two baseline methods.

6.1 Experiment Setup

We used two real datasets in our experiments.

1) OPENSTREET**:** We extracted 2 million POIs for day-life in USA, such as government buildings, parking lots, schools, etc., from the OpenStreet open-source spatial database[5].

2) BUSINESS**:** We obtained 5 million POIs for business in USA, such as cafe, company, restaurant, etc., from a popular directory website, Factual[6].

Table 6.1 provides some statistics of the two data sets, such as number of objects, data size, etc.

All baseline indices and our PR-Tree were memory-resident. The parameters of the baseline algorithms were set as the default values in the original papers. All the algorithms were implemented in C++, and all the experiments were

[5]http://planet.openstreetmap.org
[6]http://www.factual.com

Table 1: Statistics of the two datasets.

Dataset	OPENSTREET	BUSINESS
Number of objects	2,003,608	5,073,369
Original Data Size	183M	1,461M
# of distinct words	97,342	565,510
Avg. # of words per object	3.23	5.45

conducted on an 2.66MHz Intel Xeon processor and 24GB RAM, running on Ubuntu 11.04.

6.2 Comparison for Single-Prefix Queries

We evaluated the query performance for single prefix queries. Since the MT algorithm could not support word segmentation on text, we conducted the following two experiments. We first compared our method PRT with FEH under the word-segmentation setting, and then compared PRT with MT by taking the whole text of each object as a single string.

6.2.1 *PRT vs. FEH*

We randomly chose 1000 words from the vocabulary, and generated three prefixes from one selected word. For example, consider a selected word "`park`". We generated three prefixes, i.e., "`p`", "`pa`" and "`par`" for query evaluation. Compared with long prefixes, the short prefixes were much better for evaluating the query performance, since users always start from scratch when typing to search.

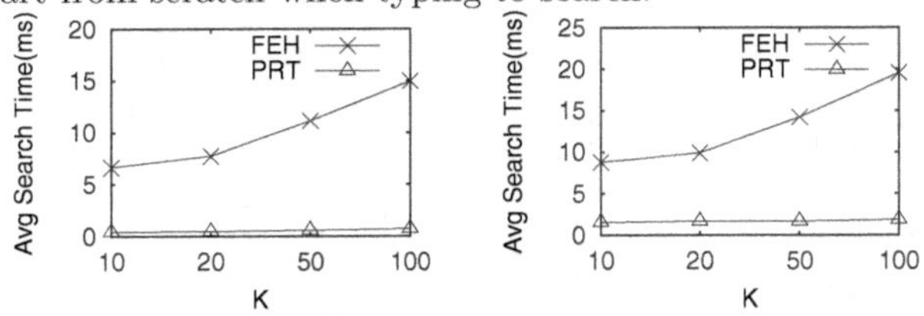

(a) OPENSTREET dataset. (b) BUSINESS dataset.

Figure 9: PRT vs. FEH for single-prefix queries with different k (prefix lengths are within $[1, 3]$).

Figure 9 shows the experimental results on the two datasets with different k. We can see that our algorithm outperformed the FEH algorithm in both datasets. On the OPENSTREET dataset, our PRT algorithm is about 15 times faster than FEH. On the BUSINESS dataset, PRT was about 5 times faster than FEH. The improvement of the performance was mainly attributed to our novel index structure, since PR-Tree can utilize both textual and spatial pruning simultaneously. Using the PR-Tree, we can efficiently find the promising objects which not only contain the query prefix, but also are near our query location. In contrast, FEH only utilizes a pure spatial index and does not consider textual pruning.

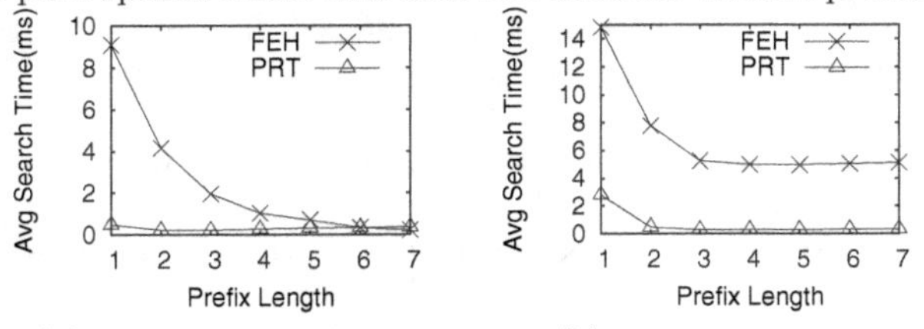

(a) OPENSTREET dataset. (b) BUSINESS dataset.

Figure 10: PRT vs. FEH for single-prefix queries with different prefix lengths ($k = 20$).

We also conducted an experiment to evaluate the performance on different prefix lengths between PRT and FEH. Given 1,000 selected words mentioned above, we generated all possible prefixes for each word. Figure 10 provides the results for $k = 20$. Though there were lots of candidates for shorter prefixes, they could still be distinguished by different nodes on PR-Tree that represent different regions. Thus, PRT achieved better performance than FEH.

6.2.2 *PRT vs. MT*

To compare PRT and MT, we took the text of each POI as a single string without word-segmentation. Similar to previous experiments, we generated 1000 prefixes whose length were within $[1, 3]$. Figure 11 provides the experimental results on both datasets for different k values.

We can see that the PRT algorithm was much more efficient than the MT algorithm. The poor performance of MT was due to its trie-based index structure, which failed to utilize effective spatial pruning.

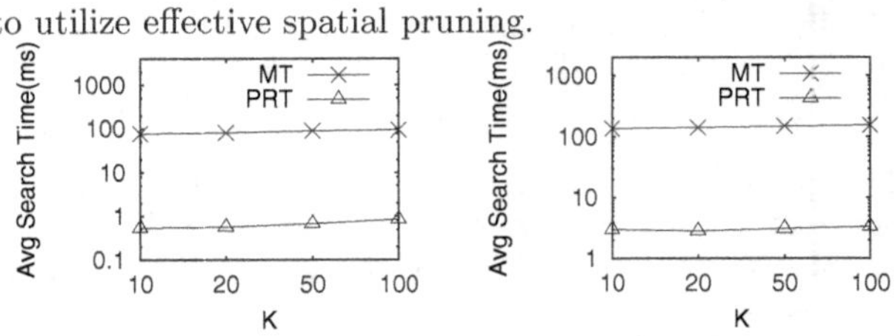

(a) OPENSTREET dataset. (b) BUSINESS dataset.

Figure 11: PRT vs. MT for single-prefix queries with different k (prefix lengths are within $[1, 3]$).

6.2.3 *Index Sizes*

We then examined the space complexity of different indices. Table 2 provides the memory usage on two data sets. As shown, PRT consumed less memory, compared with FEH and MT. To achieve better performance, FEH maintained two filters on each R-Tree node for a huge amount of prefixes, and MT materialized a lot of tree nodes with a small granularity of regions. Compared with these algorithms, our method only maintained a PR-Tree, which scaled to the size of original data as proved in Section 3.5.2.

Table 2: Index size for three algorithms (MB).

	Data Size	PRT	FEH	MT
OPENSTREET	183	122	223	231
BUSINESS	1,461	487	1,328	2,344

6.3 Comparison for Multi-Keyword Queries

6.3.1 *Tuning of Materialization Size*

We examined the query performance of our cost based algorithm (Section 4.2) by varying memory budget $\mathcal{B}$, to investigate the impact of materialization size on the performance. On each data set, we randomly selected 1000 objects and randomly chose 3 keywords from $o.W$ in each selected objects as a query. Then, we took the first two keywords as complete words, and generated a random length of prefix from the last keyword. For example, given an object with text "`Washington State Driving School`", one possible keyword query generated from it was "`Driving Washington Sc`".

Figure 12 provides the experimental results for multi-keyword queries on the OPENSTREET dataset. We can see that different materialization sizes had great impact on query performance. Specifically, we can see that the average query time

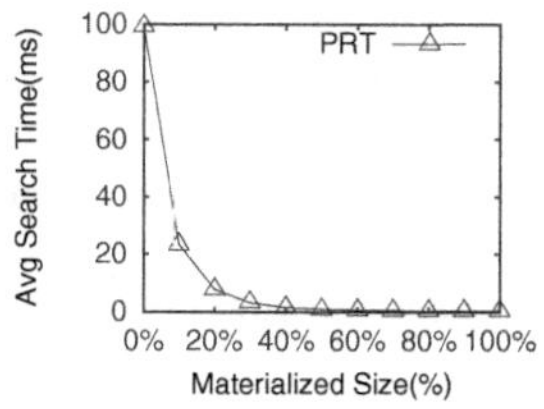

Figure 12: Performance with different budgets.

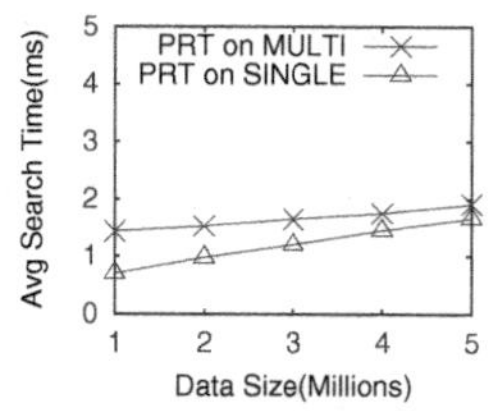

Figure 13: Time Scalability.

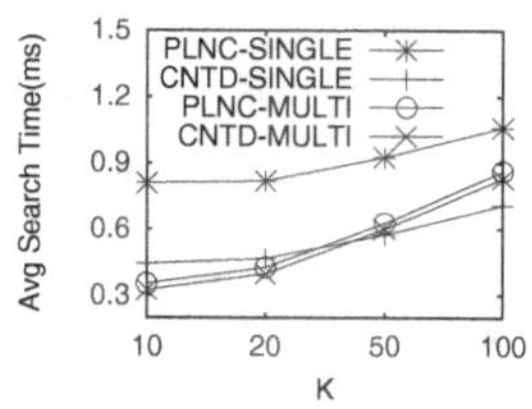

Figure 14: On two spatial partition strategies

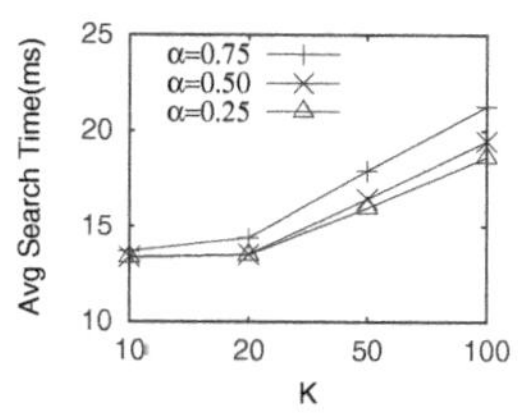

Figure 15: On tf*idf ranking function.

varies dramatically when $\mathcal{B}$ is 0% to 60% of the original data size. When $\mathcal{B}$ is larger, the difference is not significant. Based on this observation, we could judiciously select a proper memory budget in practice, in order to balance the space and time. In the remainder of our experiments, we set the budget percentage as 70%.

6.3.2 *Efficiency on Multi-Keyword Search*

We evaluated performance for multi-keywords queries for our intersection-based method (denoted by PRT-I), cost-based method (denoted by PRT-C) and the baseline FEH algorithm. All the settings were the same as those in Section 6.3.1

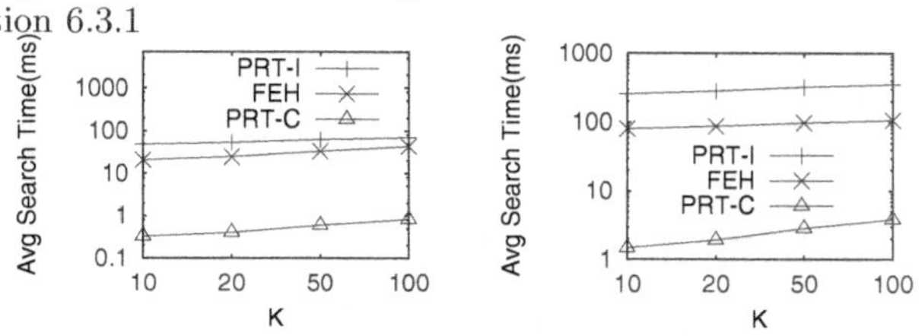

(a) OpenStreet dataset. (b) On Business dataset.

Figure 16: PRT vs. FEH for multi-keyword queries with different k (2 complete keyword and 1 prefix).

Figure 16 provides the experimental results on the two datasets for different k values. We can see that our PRT-C algorithm was approximately 100 times faster than the FEH algorithm for both data set. This significant improvement results from the fact that PR-Tree has guaranteed that the visited leaf nodes satisfy the constraints on query prefix $q.p$, thus it would not bring any unnecessary work of traversal. On the other hand, FEH might traverse many unpromising leaf nodes which could not produce any top-k answer. Moreover, the PRT-I algorithm achieved poor performance. This is because that PRT-I did not utilize the occurrence list and a lot of unnecessary nodes might be visited at query time.

In addition, we compare the algorithms by varying different numbers of complete keywords. Figure 17 provides the experimental results. As PRT-C was always better than PRT-I, in the figure we only show the results of PRT-C and FEH. We can see that the time of PRT increases sub-linearly with the increase of complete keyword numbers. This shows that our cost-based method of materialization achieves good performance on multi-keywords queries.

6.4 On Spatial Partitioning Strategies

We evaluated the query performance on two spatial partitioning settings, i.e., planar center or centroid as the quad-split point, which mentioned in Section 3.3. We first built two different PR-Trees, then applied single prefix and multi-keyword queries to make comparisons. All the query settings were the same as those in Sections 6.2 and 6.3.

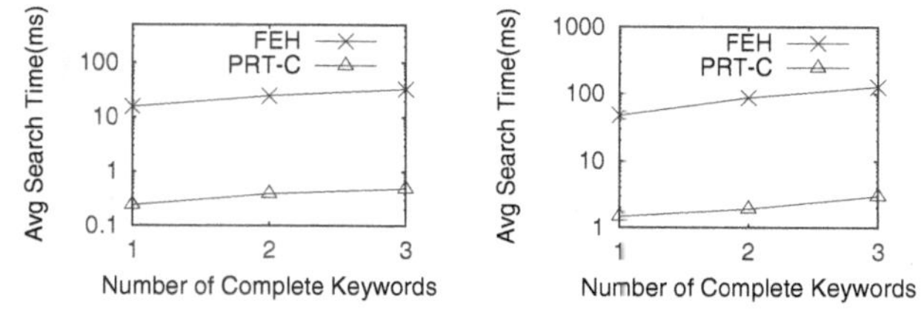

(a) OpenStreet dataset. (b) Business dataset.

Figure 17: PRT vs. FEH for multi-keyword queries with different keyword numbers.

Figure 14 shows the results, where "PLNC" denotes the "planar center" and "CTND" denotes the "centroid". We can see that, by using centroid as the splitting point, we could achieve about 40% speed improvement for single prefix query compared to planar center. This is because using the centroid will result in a more even partitioning of objects on space. However, for multi-keyword queries, the improvement is not significant. The reason is that utilization of occurrence list results in early terminations, and thus long branches have little effect on the query time.

6.5 Scalability

We examined the scalability of our best algorithm on the Business dataset, since it contains POIs in the whole region of USA. We used the same experimental settings as we applied in Sections 6.2 and 6.3.

6.5.1 *Time Scalability*

We first evaluated the time scalability for single-prefix and multi-keyword queries with different sizes of the original data. Figures 13 shows the experimental results. We can see that the query time for both queries increased sub-linearly when the data size increased from 1 to 5 millions. From the results we can see that our PRT algorithm could support location-aware instant search on large datasets.

6.5.2 *Space Scalability*

We evaluated the space scalability of PRT. Figure 18(a) provides the experimental results for single-prefix queries. We can see that with the increase of data sizes, both the size of the PR-Tree and the inverted lists in the leaf nodes increased sub-linearly, which was consistent with the analysis on space complexity mentioned in Section 3.5.2. To further improve the storage utility, we can store the inverted list in disk, and only maintain the PR-Tree in memory.

Figure 18(b) provides the experimental results for multi-keyword queries, where the global keyword inverted index and keyword occurrence materialization were included. We can see that the size of the global keyword inverted index consumed little memory, and the total materialization size was adjusted linearly to the size of the data. Thus the indexing memory of our PR-tree also scaled to the data size.

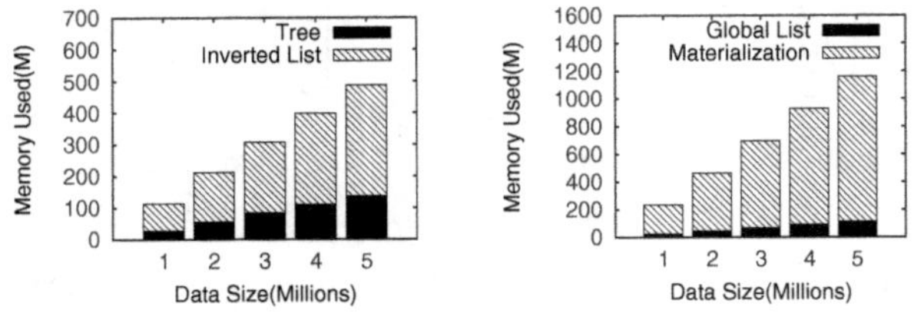

(a) Single-prefix queries. (b) Multi-keyword queries.

Figure 18: Space Scalability.

6.6 Evaluation on Construction and Updates

In this section, we evaluated the performance of PR-Tree operations, i.e., construction, insertion, deletion, on the two datasets. We first conducted 1000 insertion and deletion operations for testing. Figure 3 shows that the PR-Tree can be efficiently maintained.

Table 3: Performance of tree operations.

Operation	OPENSTREET	BUSINESS
Construction	147 s	1066 s
Materialization	432 s	6559 s
Insertion per Object	0.480 ms	2.940 ms
Deletion per Object	0.093 ms	0.290 ms

We also conducted the throughput experiments on PRT. We generated a series of operations, i.e., 10% insertions, 10% deletions and 80% random queries. Figure 19 shows the high throughput of our PRT algorithm.

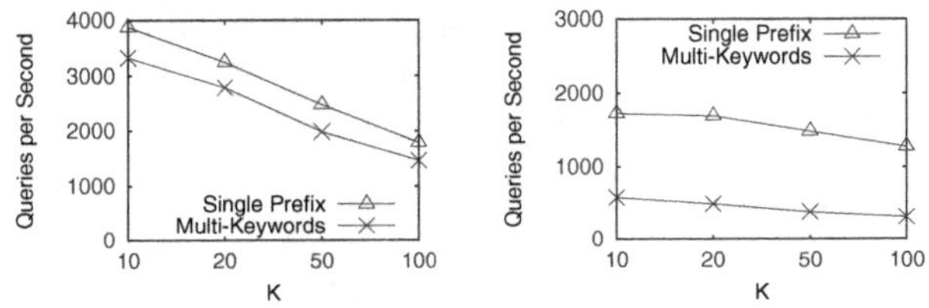

(a) OPENSTREET dataset. (b) BUSINESS dataset.

Figure 19: Evaluation on throughput (10% insertions, 10% deletions, 80% top-k queries).

6.7 Evaluating Ranking Functions

We evaluated the efficiency of the *tf*idf* based ranking function mentioned in Section 5. We generated 1000 queries, each of which only contained complete words(the length varied from 1 to 3).

Figure 15 provides the experimental results on the OPENSTREET dataset with different k values. We can see that with the increase of parameter α, the average query time decreased. This is because for large parameter α, the impact of spatial filtering became insignificant. The experimental results showed that although we focus on prefix search, the PR-Tree can still support the *tf*idf* ranking function.

7. CONCLUSIONS

In this paper, we have studied the problem of location-aware instant search. We proposed a novel indexing structure PR-Tree to support location-aware instant search. We used prefix-regions to partition the spatial data by considering the spatial information and textual description simultaneously. We discussed how to construct and update the PR-Tree. Using the PR-Tree, we devised effective algorithms to support single prefix queries and multi-keyword queries. We proposed a best-first traversal based algorithm to answer single prefix queries. We developed an intersection-based algorithm and a cost-based algorithm to answer multi-keyword queries. We have implemented our techniques and experimental results show that our method achieved high performance and outperformed state-of-the-art approaches.

8. ACKNOWLEDGEMENT

This work was partly supported by the National Natural Science Foundation of China under Grant No. 61003004, the National Grand Fundamental Research 973 Program of China under Grant No. 2011CB302206, a project of Tsinghua University under Grant No. 20111081073, and the "NExT Research Center" funded by MDA, Singapore, under the Grant No. WBS:R-252-300-001-490.

9. REFERENCES

[1] H. Bast and I. Weber. Type less, find more: fast autocompletion search with a succinct index. In *SIGIR*, pages 364–371, 2006.

[2] N. Beckmann, H.-P. Kriegel, R. Schneider, and B. Seeger. The r*-tree: An efficient and robust access method for points and rectangles. In *SIGMOD Conference*, pages 322–331, 1990.

[3] S. Chaudhuri and R. Kaushik. Extending autocompletion to tolerate errors. In *SIGMOD Conference*, pages 707–718, 2009.

[4] Y.-Y. Chen, T. Suel, and A. Markowetz. Efficient query processing in geographic web search engines. In *SIGMOD Conference*, pages 277–288, 2006.

[5] G. Cong, C. S. Jensen, and D. Wu. Efficient retrieval of the top-k most relevant spatial web objects. *PVLDB*, 2009.

[6] J. Fan, G. Li, L. Zhou, S. Chen, and J. Hu. Seal: Spatio-textual similarity search. *PVLDB*, 5(9):824–835, 2012.

[7] I. D. Felipe, V. Hristidis, and N. Rishe. Keyword search on spatial databases. In *ICDE*, 2008.

[8] R. A. Finkel and J. L. Bentley. Quad trees: A data structure for retrieval on composite keys. *Acta Inf.*, 4:1–9, 1974.

[9] R. Hariharan, B. Hore, C. Li, and S. Mehrotra. Processing spatial-keyword (SK) queries in geographic information retrieval (GIR) systems. In *SSDBM*, 2007.

[10] G. R. Hjaltason and H. Samet. Ranking in spatial databases. In *SSD*, pages 83–95, 1995.

[11] W. Huang, G. Li, K.-L. Tan, and J. Feng. Efficient safe-region construction for moving top-k spatial keyword queries. In *CIKM*, 2012.

[12] O. H. Ibarra and C. E. Kim. Fast approximation algorithms for the knapsack and sum of subset problems. *J. ACM*, 22(4):463–468, 1975.

[13] S. Ji and C. Li. Location-based instant search. In *SSDBM*, pages 17–36, 2011.

[14] S. Ji, G. Li, C. Li, and J. Feng. Efficient interactive fuzzy keyword search. In *WWW*, pages 371–380, 2009.

[15] G. Li, J. Feng, and C. Li. Supporting search-as-you-type using sql in databases. *IEEE TKDE*, 2011.

[16] G. Li, S. Ji, C. Li, and J. Feng. Efficient type-ahead search on relational data: a tastier approach. In *SIGMOD Conference*, pages 695–706, 2009.

[17] G. Li, S. Ji, C. Li, and J. Feng. Efficient fuzzy full-text type-ahead search. *VLDB J.*, 20(4):617–640, 2011.

[18] G. Li, J. Wang, C. Li, and J. Feng. Supporting efficient top-k queries in fuzzy type-ahead search. In *SIGIR*, 2012.

[19] G. Li, J. Xu, and J. Feng. Desks: Direction-aware spatial keyword search. In *ICDE*, 2012.

[20] J. Lu, Y. Lu, and G. Cong. Reverse spatial and textual k nearest neighbor search. In *SIGMOD Conference*, pages 349–360, 2011.

[21] S. B. Roy and K. Chakrabarti. Location-aware type ahead search on spatial databases: semantics and efficiency. In *SIGMOD Conference*, pages 361–372, 2011.

[22] D. Wu, M. L. Yiu, C. S. Jensen, and G. Cong. Efficient continuously moving top-k spatial keyword query processing. In *ICDE*, pages 541–552, 2011.

[23] B. Yao, F. Li, M. Hadjieleftheriou, and K. Hou. Approximate string search in spatial databases. In *ICDE*, 2010.

[24] Y. Zhou, X. Xie, C. Wang, Y. Gong, and W.-Y. Ma. Hybrid index structures for location-based web search. In *CIKM*, 2005.

Indexing Uncertain Spatio-Temporal Data

Tobias Emrich[1], Hans-Peter Kriegel[1], Nikos Mamoulis[2],
Matthias Renz[1], Andreas Züfle[1]
[1]Institute for Informatics, Ludwig-Maximilians-Universität-München
[2]Department of Computer Science, University of Hong Kong
{emrich, kriegel, renz, zuefle}@dbs.ifi.lmu.de, nikos@cs.hku.hk

ABSTRACT

The advances in sensing and telecommunication technologies allow the collection and management of vast amounts of spatio-temporal data combining location and time information. Due to physical and resource limitations of data collection devices (e.g., RFID readers, GPS receivers and other sensors) data are typically collected only at discrete points of time. In-between these discrete time instances, the positions of tracked moving objects are uncertain. In this work, we propose novel approximation techniques in order to probabilistically bound the uncertain movement of objects; these techniques allow for efficient and effective filtering during query evaluation using an hierarchical index structure. To the best of our knowledge, this is the first approach that supports query evaluation on very large uncertain spatio-temporal databases, adhering to possible worlds semantics. We experimentally show that it accelerates the existing, scan-based approach by orders of magnitude.

Categories and Subject Descriptors

H.3.3 [**INFORMATION STORAGE AND RETRIEVAL**]: Information Search and Retrieval

Keywords

Uncertain Spatio-Temporal Data, Uncertain Trajectory, Indexing

1. INTRODUCTION

Efficient management of large collections of spatio-temporal data pertaining to mobile entities whose locations change over time is paramount in a large variety of application domains: military applications, structural and environmental monitoring, disaster/rescue management and remediation, Geographic Information Systems (GIS), Location-Based Services (LBS). The technological enabling factors for such applications are advances in sensing and communication/networking, along with the miniaturizations of the computing devices and development of embedded systems. In almost every application domain, the location data at different (discrete) time-instants is obtained via some positioning devices, like GPS-enabled mobile devices, RFID or road-side sensors. In addition, to reduce the communication cost, improve the bandwidth utilization, and cope with storage constraints, often the recorded object trajectories undergo simplification, eliminating some recorded values. Having object trajectories sampled only at discrete time-instants and/or simplified, renders the movement in-between samples *uncertain* and query evaluation challenging.

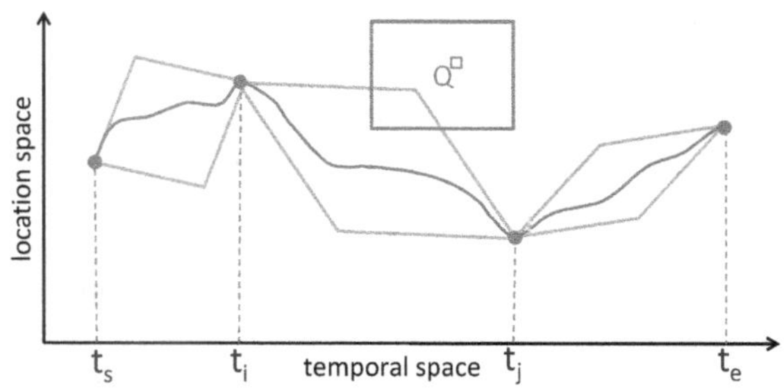

Figure 1: Spatio-Temporal Data.

Consider an object o, moving in a one-dimensional space, as illustrated in Figure 1. Having complete information about this trajectory enables answering a query asking whether the object intersects a spatio-temporal window Q. However, this task becomes difficult if only a few positions (at times $\{t_s, t_i, t_j, t_e\}$ in the example) of the exact trajectory are recorded. A simple interpolation approach, which connects temporally consecutive observations by line segments and assumes a movement with constant direction and speed between these points, is unacceptable for applications where probabilistic analysis of the uncertain movement is required. When taking uncertainty under consideration, the main challenge is that the space of possible $(location, time)$ positions between two observations can grow very large. More importantly, the number of possible trajectories between two observed locations explodes.

A common method to approximate possible locations between two observations is the beads (or necklace) model ([11, 22]). This model is based on some constraints about the motion of an object. In particular, assuming a maximum speed in each direction of each dimension, the possible locations that an object can visit between two exact observations is bounded. Recent work [8] follows the pragmatic assumption that the uncertain movement of an object between consecutive observations can be described by a Markov-Chain model, which captures the time dependencies between consecutive locations. [8] shows how the space of possible worlds (i.e., trajectories between consecutive observations) can be efficiently analyzed by multiplying Markov-Chain transition matrices and that probabilistic query evaluation can be facilitated by integrating pruning mechanisms into the Markov Chain matrices. All these are sufficient for the case where there are few queried objects, following similar movements; however, if there is a large number of objects in the database, with different movements, evaluating a probabilistic spatio-temporal query directly against each object individually (i.e., a scan-based approach) would be very expensive.

CIKM'12, October 29–November 2, 2012, Maui, HI, USA.

In this paper, we propose an indexing framework to efficiently cope with large spatio-temporal data bases. Our work also assumes that the movement of each object follows a Markov-Chain model (described in Section 2). The objective of our index (described in Section 4) is to minimize the number of objects for which exact probabilistic evaluation has to be performed. To achieve this goal, in Section 3, we propose a number of *uncertain spatio-temporal (UST) object approximations*, which are stored in the index and a set of corresponding pruning methods, which use the approximations to efficiently eliminate objects that may not qualify a given probabilistic query. Section 5 presents an extensive experimental evaluation, which demonstrates the effectiveness of our indexing approach. Related work is discussed in Section 6. Finally, Section 7 concludes the paper.

2. PRELIMINARIES

This section formally defines the type of spatio-temporal data that we index, the stochastic model that we use for uncertain trajectories derived from the data, and the query types that we handle.

Data: We consider a discrete time and space domain, i.e., the common assumption of many existing works (e.g. [18, 1, 10, 8]), where $\mathcal{S} = \{s_1, ...s_{|\mathcal{S}|}\} \subseteq \mathbb{R}^D$ is a finite set of possible locations, which we call *states*, in a D-dimensional space and $\mathcal{T} = \mathbb{N}_0^+$ is the time domain. Given this spatio-temporal domain, the (certain) movement of an object o corresponds to a *trajectory* represented as function $o : \mathcal{T} \rightarrow \mathcal{S}$ of time defining the location $o(t) \in \mathcal{S}$ of o at a certain point of time $t \in \mathcal{T}$. We consider incomplete (and/or imprecise) spatio-temporal data, where the motion of an object is not recorded by a crisp trajectory. Instead, we are only given a set $o.T_{obs}$ of $(location, time)$ observations for each object o. At any time $t \notin o.T_{obs}$, the position of o is uncertain, i.e., a random variable. In many applications, a stochastic model can be built and used to infer knowledge about this uncertainty.

Uncertain Data Model: We refer to the *spatio-temporal approximation* of a trajectory of an object o in a time interval spanned by two consecutive observations of o at t_i and t_j as a *bead* or *diamond* $\diamond(o, t_i, t_j)$. The diamond can be computed by considering the maximum and minimum (singed) velocities of the object in each dimension [25]. The whole approximation of the trajectory based on a set T_{obs} of observations (i.e., a chain of beads) is referred to as a *necklace*. For example, the movement of the object in Figure 1 is bounded by a chain of diamonds.

Existing studies on modeling uncertain trajectories ([23, 25, 24, 26, 15]) naively consider all possible trajectories bounded by a necklace equi-probable. However, given two consecutive observations $o(t_i)$ and $o(t_j)$ of object o, there are time dependencies between consecutive locations between $o(t_i)$ and $o(t_j)$, which render some locations in the corresponding diamond (e.g., those near the line segment that connects $o(t_i)$ and $o(t_j)$) more probable to be visited by o than others (e.g., those near the boundary of the diamond). Therefore, these models possibly yield incorrect inferences resulting in incorrect answers to probabilistic queries. To overcome this problem, in our proposal each uncertain spatio-temporal (UST) object $o \in \mathcal{D}$ is associated with an *uncertain object trajectory*, which is represented by a stochastic process. The stochastic process assigns to each $t \in T$ exactly one random variable; random variables at consecutive time moments can be mutually dependent. This dependency is vital in most applications, where the locations of an object at two close points of time are highly correlated. Thus, the uncertain trajectory $o(t)$ of object o comprises a set of (crisp) trajectories, each assigned with a probability indicating its likelihood to be the true trajectory of o. Thereby, each trajectory with a non-zero probability is called a *possible world* of o. Assuming that objects are mutually independent, our semantics comply with the classic possible worlds model [6]. If $t \in o.T_{obs}$ (i.e., the exact location of o at time t has been observed), then $o(t)$ corresponds to a (trivial) random variable having one possible location (i.e., state) with probability 1.

The main challenge in answering a probabilistic spatio-temporal query is to correctly consider the possible worlds semantics in the model. In other words, the query results should comply with the possible worlds model. Naively, this can be done by evaluating the query predicate on each possible world, and summing up the probabilities of possible worlds satisfying the query predicate. In general, the number of possible worlds to be considered is $O(|S|^T)$; exhaustively examining all of them requires exponential time, even for finite time and space domains. Clearly, any naive approach that enumerates all possible worlds, is not feasible.

In this work, we model the uncertain movement of an object within a diamond, using a first-order Markov-chain model. This approach models the movement between successive points in time, based on background knowledge (e.g., physical laws) and has proven capable of effectively capturing the behavior of real objects in practice. For instance, [1] and [10] show how Markov-models can effectively capture the movement of vehicles on road networks for prediction purpose. In [18], it is shown that Markov-models can also be used to model the indoor movement of people, as tracked in RFID applications.

DEFINITION 1. *A stochastic process $o(t), t \in \mathcal{T}$, is called a Markov-Chain if and only if*

$$\forall t \in \mathbb{N}_0 \forall s_j, s_i, s_{t-1}, ...s_0 \in S :$$

$$P(o(t+1) = s_j | o(t) = s_i, o(t-1) = s_{t-1}, ..., o(0) = s_0) =$$

$$P(o(t+1) = s_j | o(t) = s_i),$$

where the conditional probability

$$o.P_{i,j}(t) := P(o(t+1) = s_j | o(t) = s_i)$$

is the (single-step) *transition probability* of object o from state s_i to state s_j at time t. The matrix $o.M(t) := (o.P_{i,j})_{i,j}$ is called *transition matrix*. Let $o.P(t) = (p_1, \ldots, p_{|S})$ be the distribution vector of an object o at time t, where p_i corresponds to the probability that o is located at state s_i at time t. The distribution vector $o.P(t+1)$ can be inferred from $o.P(t)$ as follows:

$$o.P(t+1) = o.P(t) \cdot o.M(t)$$

Queries: Within the scope of this paper, we focus on selection queries specified by the following parameters: (i) a spatial window $S^\square \subseteq \mathcal{S}$, (ii) a contiguous time window $T^\square \subseteq \mathcal{T}$, and (iii) a probability threshold τ. In the remainder, we use $\mathcal{Q}^\square = \mathcal{S}^\square \times \mathcal{T}^\square$ to denote the search space of a query. The most intuitive definition of a probabilistic spatio-temporal query is given below:

DEFINITION 2. *[Probabilistic Spatio-Temporal τ Exists Query] Given a query window $\mathcal{S}^\square$ in space and a query window $\mathcal{T}^\square$ in time, a* probabilistic τ spatio-temporal exists query *(PST$\tau\exists$Q), retrieves all objects $o \in \mathcal{D}$ such that $P(\exists t \in \mathcal{T}^\square : o(t) \in \mathcal{S}^\square) \geq \tau$; i.e., the trajectory of o intersects the query window $\mathcal{Q}^\square$ with probability at least τ.*

For example, consider the trajectory of Figure 1 and assume that we only know for certain its observed locations at $\{t_s, t_i, t_j, t_e\}$; a PST$\tau\exists$Q query defined by rectangle $\mathcal{Q}^\square$ would return the depicted trajectory, only if the probability that the trajectory intersects $\mathcal{S}^\square$ at any time within $\mathcal{T}^\square$ exceeds τ. Another query type is the Probabilistic Spatio-Temporal $\mathcal{T}$ ForAll Query ([8]), denoted as (PST$\mathcal{T}\forall$Q), which requires an object to remain in the spatial window $\mathcal{S}^{\square}$ for the whole time window $\mathcal{T}^{\square}$. Due to space constraints, we will not discuss this query in this work, but note that our techniques proposed for PST$\mathcal{T}\exists$Q queries can easily be adapted.

By modeling the movement within a diamond using a Markov-chain model, the true probability that an object o satisfies a PST$\mathcal{T}\exists$ query, can be computed in PTIME [8], exploiting that the matrix M is generally sparse (only a few states are directly connected to a single state). Still, query evaluation remains too expensive over a large spatio-temporal database, where we have to compute the qualification probabilities of all objects. In view of this, we define a set of approximations of uncertain object trajectories enabling spatio-temporal and probabilistic filtering in Section 3. We then show in Secion 4 how we can organize these approximations in an index in order to perform efficient query evaluation.

3. APPROXIMATING UST-OBJECTS

In this section, we introduce (conservative) spatio-temporal as well as probabilistic (conservative) spatio-temporal (UST-) object approximations, which serve as building blocks for our proposed index, to be presented in Section 4.

3.1 Spatio-Temporal Approximation

To bound the possible locations of an object o between two subsequent observations $(o(t_i), o(t_j))$, we need to determine all state-time pairs $(s,t) \in S \times T, t_i \leq t \leq t_j$ such that o has a non-zero probability of being at state s at time t. This is done by considering all possible paths between state $o(t_i)$ at time t_i and state $o(t_j)$ at time t_j. An example of a small set of such paths is depicted in Figure 2(a). Here, we can see a set of five possible trajectories of an object o, i.e., all possible $(state, time)$ pairs of o in the time interval $[t_i, t_j]$. In practice, the number of possible paths becomes very large. Nonetheless, we can efficiently compute the set of possible $(state, time)$ pairs using the Markov-chain model: The set of state-time pairs S_i reachable from $o(t_i)$ can be computed by performing $t_j - t_i$ transitions using the Markov chain $o.M(t)$ of o, starting from state $o(t_i)$ and memorizing all reachable $(state, time)$ pairs. Similarly, we can compute S_j as all state-time pairs $(s,t) \in \mathcal{S} \times \mathcal{T}, t_i \leq t \leq t_j$ such that o can reach state $o(t_j)$ at time t_j by starting from state s at time t. S_j can be computed in a similar fashion, starting from state $o(t_j)$ and using the transposed Markov chain $o.M(t)^T$. The intersection $S_{i,j} = S_i \cap S_j$ yields all state-time pairs which are consistent with both observations. Let us note that in practice, it is more efficient to compute S_i and S_j in a parallel fashion, to reduce the explored space. When the computation of S_i and S_j meet at some time $t_i \leq t \leq t_j$, we can prune any states which are not reachable by both $s(t_i)$ at time t_i and $s(t_j)$ at time t_j. However, the number $|S_{i,j}|$ of possible state-time pairs in $S_{i,j}$ can grow very large, so it is impractical for our index structure (proposed in Section 4) to store all $S_{i,j}$ for each $o \in DB$ in our index structure. Thus, we propose to conservatively approximate $S_{i,j}$. The issue is to determine an appropriate approximation of $S_{i,j}$ which tightly covers $S_{i,j}$, while keeping the representation as simple as possible. The basic idea is to build the approximation by means of both object observations $o(t_i)$ and $o(t_j)$ with the corresponding velocity of propagation in each dimension. To do so, we first compute for the set of state-time pairs S_i to derive the maximum and minimum possible velocity in the time interval $[t_i, t_j]$:

$$v_d^{\leqq} := max_{(s,t)\in S_i}(\frac{s[d] - o(t_i)[d]}{t - t_i})$$

$$v_d^{\leqslant} := min_{(s,t)\in S_i}(\frac{s[d] - o(t_i)[d]}{t - t_i})$$

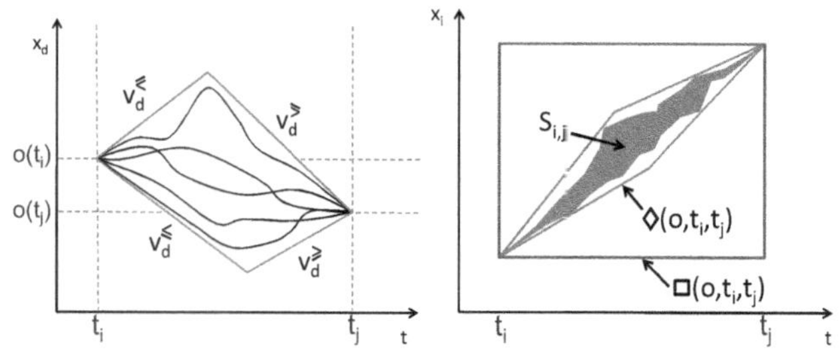

(a) Approximating trajectories (b) Diamond vs MBR

Figure 2: Spatio-Temporal Approximation.

where $s[d]$ $(o(t_i)[d])$ denotes the projection of state s $(o(t_i))$ to the d-th dimension. By definition, we can guarantee that for any $t_i \leq t \leq t_j$ it holds that

$$o(t)[d] \leq o(t_i)[d] + (t - t_i) \cdot v_d^{\leqq} \text{ and}$$

$$o(t)[d] \geq o(t_i)[d] + (t - t_i) \cdot v_d^{\leqslant}$$

Furthermore, we bound the velocity of propagation at which o can have reached state $o(s_j)$ at time t_j from each location in the state-space S_j:

$$v_d^{\geqq} := max_{(s,t)\in S_j}(\frac{o(t_j)[d] - s[d]}{t_j - t})$$

$$v_d^{\geqslant} := min_{(s,t)\in S_j}(\frac{o(t_j)[d] - s[d]}{t_j - t})$$

Again, we can bound the position of o in dimension $1 \leq d \leq D$ at time $t_i \leq t \leq t_j$ as follows:

$$o(t)[d] \leq o(t_j)[d] - (t_j - t) \cdot v_d^{\geqslant}, \text{ and}$$

$$o(t)[d] \geq o(t_j)[d] - (t_j - t) \cdot v_d^{\geqq}$$

In summary, using the positions $o(t_i)$ at time t_i and $o(t_j)$ at time t_j, and using velocities $v_d^{\leqq}, v_d^{\leqslant}, v_d^{\geqq}, v_d^{\geqslant}$, we can bound the random variable of the position $o(t)$ of o at time $t_i \leq t \leq t_j$ by the interval

$$o(t)[d] \in I_d(t) := [max(o(t_i)[d]+(t-t_i)\cdot v_d^{\leqslant}, o(t_j)[d]-(t_j-t)\cdot v_d^{\geqq})),$$

$$min(o(t_i)[d] + (t - t_i) \cdot v_d^{\leqq}, o(t_j)[d] - (t_j - t) \cdot v_d^{\geqslant})] \quad (1)$$

Deriving these intervals for each dimension, yields an axis-parallel rectangle, approximating all possible positions of o at time t. In the following, we will call this time dependent spatial approximation of $o(t)$ in the time interval $[t_i, t_j]$ between two observations $o(t_i)$ and $o(t_j)$ a spatio-temporal *diamond*, denoted as $\diamond(o, t_i, t_j)$. A nice geometric property of this approximation is that computing the intersection with the query window at each time t is very fast. Another advantage is that existing spatial access methods (e.g., R-trees) can be easily used to efficiently organize these approximations. To store the approximation, we only need to store the $4 \cdot D$ real values $v_d^{\leqq}, v_d^{\leqslant}, v_d^{\geqq}, v_d^{\geqslant}, 1 \leq d \leq D$. A diamond is reminiscent to a time-parameterized rectangle, used to model the worst-case MBR for a set of moving objects in [19]; however, the way of deriving velocities is different in our case. As an example, Figure 2(a) shows for one dimension $d \in D$, positions $o(t_i)$ at time t_i and $o(t_j)$ at time t_j. The diamond formed by the velocity bounds $v_d^{\leqq}, v_d^{\leqslant}, v_d^{\geqq}$ and $v_d^{\geqslant}$ conservatively approximates the possible $(location, time)$ pairs. Note that it is possible to use a minimal bounding rectangle $\square(o, t_i, t_j)$ instead of the diamond $\diamond(o, t_i, t_j)$ to conservatively approximate the $(location, time)$ space $S_{i,j}$. In cases, however, where the movement of an object in one dimension is biased

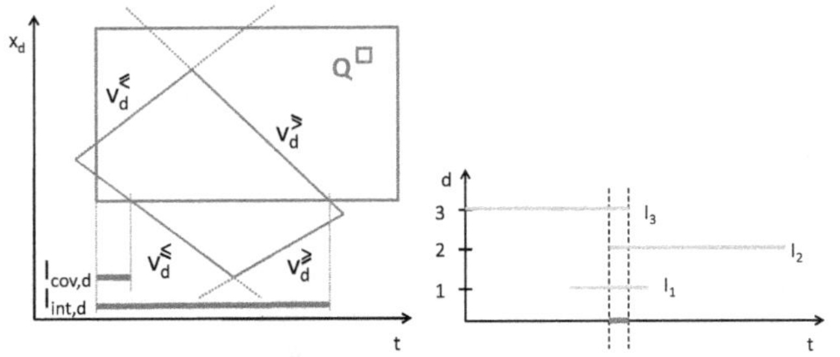

(a) query intersection (b) dimension-wise intersections

Figure 3: Intersection between query and diamond

in one direction, a rectangle may yield a very bad approximation (see Figure 2(b) for an example). Our index employs both approximations $\Box(o, t_i, t_j)$ and $\diamond(o, t_i, t_j)$ for spatio-temporal pruning; $\Box(o, t_i, t_j)$ is used for high-level indexing and filtering, while $\diamond(o, t_i, t_j)$ is used as a second-level filter.

3.2 Spatio-Temporal Filter

Based on the spatio-temporal approximation of an uncertain object as described in the previous section, it is possible to perform filtering during query processing.

If none of the diamonds assigned to an object $o \in \mathcal{D}$ intersects the query window, then o is safely pruned. In turn, if a diamond of o is inside the query window $\mathcal{S}^\Box$ in space, i.e. fully covered by $\mathcal{S}^\Box$, at any point of time $t \in \mathcal{T}^\Box$, then o is a *true hit* and, thus, o can be immediately reported as result of the query. In order to employ the above spatio-temporal pruning conditions, for a diamond $\diamond(o, t_i, t_j)$ of an object o we need to determine the points of time when it intersect the query window $\mathcal{S}^\Box$ in space, as well as the points of time when $\diamond(o, t_i, t_j)$ is fully covered by $\mathcal{S}^\Box$. For this purpose, it is helpful to focus on the spatial domain $\mathcal{S}$ and interpret a diamond as well as the query as a time-parameterized (moving) rectangle. By doing so, we can adapt the techniques proposed in [19]: In general, a rectangle R_1 intersects (covers) another rectangle R_2, if and only if R_1 intersects (covers) R_2 in each dimension. Thus, for each spatial dimension d ($d \in \{1, \ldots D\}$), we compute the points of time when the extents of the rectangles intersect in that dimension and the points of time when the extents of the diamond rectangle are fully covered by the query rectangle $\mathcal{S}^\Box$.

For a single dimension d, with Equation 1 the query window given by $\mathcal{Q}^\Box_d$ intersects the diamond given by $o(t_i)[d]$, $o(t_j)[d]$, $v_d^\leqslant$, $v_d^{\leqslant}$, $v_d^\geqslant$ and $v_d^\geqslant$ within the points of time

$$I_{int,d} := \{t \in (\mathcal{T}^\Box \cap [t_i, t_j] | I_d(t) \cap \mathcal{S}^\Box_d\}.$$

Similarly, $\mathcal{Q}^\Box_d$ fully covers the diamond within the points of time

$$I_{cov,d} := \{t \in \mathcal{T}^\Box \cap [t_i, t_j] | I_d(t) \subseteq \mathcal{S}^\Box_d\}.$$

An example is illustrated in Figure 3(a). To compute both sets $I_{int,d}$ and $I_{cov,d}$, we intersect the margins of the diamond with the query window resulting in a set of time intervals, which subsequently have to be intersected accordingly in order to derive $I_{int,d}$ and $I_{cov,d}$. Now, let us consider the overall intersection time interval $I_{int} = \bigcap_{d=1}^{D} I_{int,d}$ (e.g., see Figure 3(b)) and the overall points of covering time $I_{cov} = \bigcap_{d=1}^{D} I_{cov,d}$.

If, for an object $o \in \mathcal{D}$, there is no diamond yielding a non-empty set I_{int}, o can be safely pruned. If any diamond of o yields a non-empty set I_{cov}, o can be reported as result.

In summary, the spatio-temporal filter can be used to identify uncertain object trajectories having a probability of 100% or 0% intersecting (remaining in) the query region $\mathcal{Q}^\Box$. Still, the probability threshold τ of the query is not considered by this filter. In addition, the object approximation may cover a lot of dead space if there exist outlier state-time pairs which determine one or more of the velocities, despite having a very low probability. In the following, we show how to exclude such unlikely outliers in order to shrink the approximation, while maintaining probabilistic guarantees that employ the probability threshold τ.

3.3 Probabilistic UST-Object Approximation

We now propose a tighter approximation, based on the intuition that the set of possible paths within a diamond is generally not uniformly distributed: paths that are close to the direct connection between the observed locations often are more likely than extreme paths along the edges of the diamond. Therefore, given a query with threshold τ, we can take advantage of a tighter approximation, which bounds all paths with cumulative probabilities τ to perform more effective pruning.

Based on this idea, we exploit the Markov-chain model in order to compute new diamonds, which are spatio-temporal subregions, called subdiamonds, of the (full) diamond $\diamond(o, t_i, t_j)$, as depicted in Figure 4(a). For each such subdiamond, we will then show how to compute the cumulative probability of all possible trajectories of o passing only through this subdiamond. Let us focus on restricting the diamond at one direction of one dimension; we choose one dimension $d \in D$, and one direction $dir \in \{\wedge, \vee\}$. Direction $\wedge$ ($\vee$) corresponds to the two diamond sides $v_d^\leqslant$ and $v_d^\geqslant$ ($v_d^\leqslant$ and $v_d^\geqslant$). To obtain the subdiamond, we scale the corresponding sides by a factor $\lambda \in [0, 1]$ relative to the average velocity $v_d^{avg} = \frac{o(t_j)[d] - o(t_i)[d]}{t_j - t_i}$. We obtain the adjusted velocity values for direction $\wedge$ as follows:

$$v^{\leqslant\lambda}_{d} = ((v_d^\leqslant - v_d^{avg}) \cdot \lambda) + v_d^{avg}$$

$$= v_d^\leqslant \cdot \lambda + v_d^{avg} \cdot (1 - \lambda)$$

and

$$v^{\geqslant\lambda}_{d} = ((v_d^\geqslant - v_d^{avg}) \cdot \lambda) + v_d^{avg}$$

$$= v_d^\geqslant \cdot \lambda + v_d^{avg} \cdot (1 - \lambda)$$

The adjusted velocity values for direction $\vee$ can be computed analogously. Thus, for a given diamond $\diamond(o, t_i, t_j)$, dimension $d \in D$, direction $dir \in \{\wedge, \vee\}$ and scalar $\lambda \in [0, 1]$, we obtain a smaller diamond $\diamond(o, t_i, t_j, d, dir, \lambda)$, derived from $\diamond(o, t_i, t_j)$ by scaling direction dir in dimension d by a factor of λ. Figure 4(b) illustrates some subdiamonds for one dimension, the $\wedge$ direction and for various values of λ.

To use such subdiamonds for probabilistic pruning, we first need to compute the probability $P(inside(o, \diamond(o, t_i, t_j, d, dir, \lambda)))$ that object o will remain within $\diamond(o, t_i, t_j, d, dir, \lambda)$ for the whole time interval $[t_i, t_j]$, in a correct and efficient way. The main challenge for correctness, is to cope with temporal dependencies, i.e. the fact that the random variables $o(t_i)$ and $o(t_i + \delta t)$ are highly correlated. Thus, we cannot simply treat all random variables $o(t)$ as mutually independent and aggregate their individual distributions. To illustrate this issue, consider Figure 4(a), where one subdiamond is depicted. Assume that each of the five possible trajectories has a probability of 0.2. We can see that three trajectories are completely contained in the subdiamond, so that the probability $P(inside(o, \diamond(o, t_i, t_j, d, dir, \lambda)))$ that o fully remains in the subdiamond $\diamond(o, t_i, t_j, d, dir, \lambda)$ is 60%. However, multiplying for all time instants $t \in [t_i, t_j]$ the individual probabilities that o is located in $\diamond(o, t_i, t_j, d, dir, \lambda)$ at time t produces an arbitrarily small and incorrect result, as time dependencies are ignored. Further-

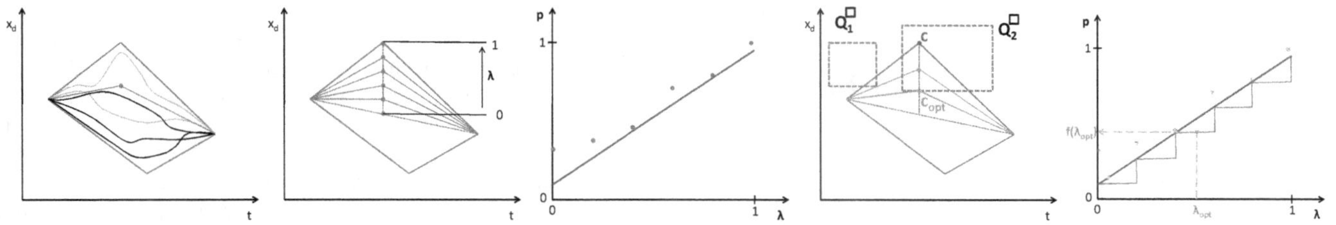

(a) A sub-diamond (b) Possible sub-diamonds (c) linear optimization (d) Computing λ_{opt} (e) conservative approx.

Figure 4: Probabilistic Diamonds

more, due to the generally exponential number of possible trajectories, $P(inside(o, \diamond(o, t_i, t_j, d, dir, \lambda)))$ is too expensive to compute by iterating over all possible trajectories. Instead, we compute this probability efficiently and correctly, as follows.

To compute the probability of possible trajectories between $o(t_i)$ at t_i and $o(t_j)$ at t_j that are completely contained in $\diamond(o, t_i, t_j, d, dir, \lambda)$, an intuitive approach is to start at $o(t_i)$ at time t_i and perform $t_j - t_i$ transitions using the Markov-chain $o.M(t)$. After each transition, we identify states that are outside $\diamond(o, t_i, t_j, d, dir, \lambda)$. Any possible trajectory which reaches such a state is flagged. Upon reaching t_j, we only need to consider possible trajectories in state $o(t_j)$, since all other worlds have become impossible due to the observation of o at t_j. The fraction of un-flagged worlds at state $o(t_j)$ at time t_j yields the probability that o does not completely remain in $\diamond(o, t_i, t_j, d, dir, \lambda)$.

To formalize the above approach, we first rewrite the probability $P(inside(o, \diamond)|o(t_i), o(t_j)))$ that the trajectory of o remains in the subdiamond $\diamond$,[1] given the observations $o(t_i)$, $o(t_j)$ at times $t_i, t_j \in o.T_{obs}$, using the definition of conditional probability:

$$P(inside(o, \diamond)|o(t_i), o(t_j)) = \frac{P(o(t_j)|inside(o, \diamond), o(t_i))}{P(o_{t_j}|o_{t_i})},$$

where $P(o(t_j)|inside(o, \diamond), o(t_i))$ denotes the probability that o reaches the state $o(t_j)$ observed by observation $o(t_j)$, given that o, starting at $o(t_i)$ at time t_i remains inside $\diamond$. $P(o(t_j)|o(t_i))$ denotes the probability that state $o(t_j)$ at time t_j is reached, given that o starts at $o(t_i)$ at time t_i, regardless whether o remains in $\diamond$.

3.4 Finding the optimal Probabilistic Diamond

In the previous section, we described, how to compute the probability of a probabilistic diamond $\diamond(o, t_i, t_j, d, dir, \lambda)$ from a diamond $\diamond(o, t_i, t_j)$, dimension d, direction dir, and scaling factor λ. In this section we will show how to find, for a given query window $\mathcal{Q}^\square$ and a given query predicate the subdiamond with the highest pruning power. Let us focus on PST$\tau\exists$ queries first. That is, our aim is to find a value for d, dir and λ, such that the resulting subdiamond $\diamond(o, t_i, t_j, d, dir, \lambda)$ does not intersect $\mathcal{Q}^\square$, and at the same time it has a high probability $P(inside(o, \diamond))$. This probability can be used to prune o as we will show later. Formally, we want to efficiently determine

$$argmax_{d \in D, dir \in \{\vee, \wedge\}, \lambda \in [0,1]}[P(inside(o, \diamond(o, t_i, t_j, d, dir, \lambda))]$$

constrained to $\mathcal{Q}^\square \cap \diamond(o, t_i, t_j, d, dir, \lambda) = \emptyset$.

For a single dimension d, and the *north* direction, a possible situation is depicted in Figure 4(d). Here, the projection $\diamond_d(o, t_i, t_j)$ of the full diamond $\diamond(o, t_i, t_j)$ to the d-th dimension and the projections $\mathcal{Q}_1^\square[d]$ and $\mathcal{Q}_2^\square[d]$ of two query windows $\mathcal{Q}_1^\square$ and $\mathcal{Q}_2^\square$ are depicted. The aim is to find the largest values λ_{opt} of λ, such that the corresponding probabilistic diamond $\diamond(o, t_i, t_j, d, \wedge, \lambda_{opt}^{\exists})$ which we call optimal subdiamond, does not intersect $\mathcal{Q}_1^\square$ ($\mathcal{Q}_2^\square$). To solve this problem, we distinguish between the following cases.

Case 1: the direct line between observations $(o(t_i), t_i)$ and $(o(t_j), t_j)$ in dimension d intersects $\mathcal{Q}^\square[d]$. In this case, there cannot exist any $\lambda \in [0, 1]$ such that $\mathcal{Q}^\square \cap \diamond(o, t_i, t_j, d, dir, \lambda) = \emptyset$. Therefore, our problem has no solution in dimension d, and d is ignored.

Case 2: the direct line between $(o(t_i), t_i)$ and $(o(t_j), t_j)$ does not intersect $\mathcal{Q}^\square[d]$, and we assume without loss of generality that $\mathcal{Q}^\square[d]$ is located above this line.[2] In addition, in this case, the time value of the north corner c of $\diamond_d(o, t_i, t_j)$ is located in the interval $\mathcal{T}^\square$ (e.g., see $\mathcal{Q}_2^\square$ in Figure 4(d)).[3] In this case, the edge $v_{opt}^{\leqslant}$ of the optimal subdiamond $\diamond(o, t_i, t_j, d, dim, \lambda_{opt}^{\exists})$ is given by $(o(t_i), t_i)$ and (s, t) where s corresponds to the lower bound of $\mathcal{S}^\square[d]$ and t equals to the time component of c.

Case 3: $\mathcal{Q}^\square$ is above the direct line between $(o(t_i), t_i)$ and $(o(t_j), t_j)$ (as in Case 2), but the time value of the north corner c of $\diamond_d(o, t_i, t_j)$ is not located in the time interval $\mathcal{T}^\square$ (e.g. $\mathcal{Q}_1^\square$ of Figure 4(d)). In this case, the optimal subdiamond must touch a corner of $\mathcal{Q}^\square[d]$ due to convexity of both $\mathcal{Q}^\square[d]$ and any diamond. If $\mathcal{Q}^\square[d]$ is located to the left of c (the right direction is handled symmetrically), then the edge $v_{opt}^{\leqslant}$ of the optimal subdiamond is given by the line between $(o(t_i), t_i)$ and the lower right corner of $\mathcal{Q}^\square[d]$ (e.g., see Figure 4(d)).

The optimal value $\lambda_{opt}^{\exists}$ for cases 2 and 3 equals the quotient $\frac{v_{opt}^{\leqslant} - v_{avg}}{v^{\leqslant} - v_{avg}}$, i.e., the fraction of the maximum velocity of the optimal subdiamond and the maximum velocity of the full diamond, both normalized by the average velocity $v_{avg} = \frac{s(t_j)[d] - s(t_i)[d]}{t_j - t_i}$. After identifying the value for $\lambda_{opt}^{\exists}$, for a dimension d and a direction dir, we can compute the probability of the corresponding subdiamond $\diamond(o, t_i, t_j, d, dir, \lambda_{opt}^{\exists})$. Since we can guarantee, that any path in this subdiamond does not intersect the query window, we can obtain a lower bound

$$P_{LB}(never(o, t_i, t_j, \mathcal{Q}^\square)) = P(inside(o, \diamond(o, t_i, t_j, d, dir, \lambda_{opt}^{\exists}))) \quad (2)$$

of the event that o never intersects the query window in the time interval $[t_i, t_j]$. This directly yields an upper bound

$$P_{UB}(sometimes(o, t_i, t_j, \mathcal{Q}^\square)) =$$

$$1 - P(inside(o, \diamond(o, t_i, t_j, d, dir, \lambda_{opt}^{\exists}))) \quad (3)$$

of the probability that the reverse event that o intersects the query

[1] Since the context is clear, we simply use $\diamond$ to denote $\diamond(o, t_i, t_j, d, dir, \lambda)$.

[2] If $\mathcal{Q}^\square[d]$ is below the line, we consider direction $dir = \vee$ symmetrically.

[3] Corner c is given by the intersection of lines $(o(t_i), t_i) + v^{\leqslant}$ and $(o(t_j), t_j) + v^{\geqslant}$.

window at least once in $[t_i, t_j]$. This bound can be used for probabilistic pruning for PST$\mathcal{T}\exists$ queries, as we will see in Section 3.6.

3.5 Approximating Probabilistic Diamonds

The main goal of our index structure, proposed in Section 4, is to avoid expensive probability computations for subdiamonds. Since the query window is not known in advance, $2D$ computations (i.e., one for each dimension and direction) have to performed in order to identify the optimal subdiamond for a given query and candidate object o. To avoid these computations at run-time, we propose to precompute, for each diamond $\diamond(o, t_i, t_j)$ in $\mathcal{D}$, probabilistic subdiamonds for each dimension and direction and for a set Λ of λ-values. This yields a catalogue of probability values, i.e. a probability for each $\diamond(o, t_i, t_j, d, dir, \lambda), d \in D, dir \in \{\vee, \wedge\}, \lambda \in \Lambda$.

Given a query window, the optimal value λ_{opt} computed in Section 3.4 may not be in Λ. Thus, we need to conservatively approximate the probability of probabilistic diamonds $\diamond(o, t_i, t_j, d, dir, \lambda)$ for which $\lambda \notin \Lambda$. We propose to use a conservative linear approximation of $P(inside(o, \diamond(o, t_i, t_j, d, dir, \lambda)))$ which increases monotonically with λ, using the precomputed probability values. For example, Figure 4(c), shows the $(\lambda, probability)$-space, for six values $\Lambda = \{0, 0.2, 0.4, 0.6, 0.8, 1\}$. The corresponding precomputed pairs $(\lambda, P(inside(o, \diamond(o, t_i, t_j, d, dir, \lambda))))$ are depicted. Our goal is to find a function $f(\lambda)$ that minimizes the error with respect to $P(inside(o, \diamond(o, t_i, t_j, d, dir, \lambda))$, while ensuring that $\forall \lambda \in [0, 1] : f(\lambda) \leq P(inside(o, \diamond(o, t_i, t_j, d, dir, \lambda))$. The latter constraint is required to maintain the conservativeness property of the approximation, which will be required for pruning. We model this as a linear programming problem: find a linear function $l(\lambda) = a \cdot \lambda + b$ that minimizes the aggregate error with respect to the sample points, under the constraint that the approximation line does not exceed any of the sample values (e.g., the line in Figure 4(c)). That is, we compute:

$$argmin_{a,b}(\sum_{\lambda \in \Lambda} P(\lambda) - (a + b \cdot \lambda))$$

$$\text{subject to: } \forall \lambda \in \Lambda : P(\lambda) \geq a + b \cdot \lambda$$

We use the simplex algorithm to solve fast this optimization problem. In summary, a probabilistic spatio-temporal object o is approximated by a set of $|o.T_{obs}| - 1$ diamonds, one for each subsequent time points $t_i, t_j \in o.T_{obs}$. Each diamond approximation contains its spatio-temporal diamond $\diamond(o, t_i, t_j)$, consisting of four real values $v^{\lessdot}, v^{\leqslant}, v^{\gtrdot}, v^{\geqslant}$, and a set of $2 \cdot D$ linear approximation functions $f_{d,dir}(\lambda)$, one for each dimension $d \in D$ and each direction $dir \in \{\vee, \wedge\}$. Next, we will show how to use these object approximations for efficient query processing over uncertain spatio-temporal data.

3.6 Probabilistic Filter

For each dimension $d \in D$ and direction $dir \in \{\vee, \wedge\}$, we now have a linear function to approximate all $(\lambda, P(o, t_i, t_j, d, dim, \lambda))$. However, using this line directly, may violate the conservativeness property, since the true function may have any monotonic increasing form, and thus, for a value λ_Q located in between two values λ_1 and λ_2 ($\lambda_1, \lambda_2 \in \Lambda, \lambda_1 < \lambda_Q < \lambda_2$) the probability is bounded by $P(\lambda_1) \leq P(\lambda_Q) \leq P(\lambda_2)$. To avoid this problem, we can exploit that the catalogue Λ is the same for all diamonds, dimensions and directions. Thus, we chose the function $f(\lambda) = l(\lfloor \lambda \rfloor)$, where $\lfloor \lambda \rfloor$ denotes the largest element of Λ such that $\lfloor \lambda \rfloor \leq \lambda$. In our running example, the function $f(\lambda)$ is depicted in Figure 4(e). In this example, assume that we have computed an optimal value λ_{opt} in the previous steps. The corresponding conservative approximation $f(\lambda_{opt})$ is shown.

Now, we show how these probability bounds can be used to bound the probability that an object (i.e. its corresponding chain of diamonds) satisfies the query predicate. This is done by probing each uncertain trajectory approximation (each necklace) on the query region $\mathcal{Q}^\square$. Obviously, we only have to take into account diamonds intersecting the query time range $\mathcal{T}^\square$. In turn, when probing an uncertain trajectory approximation $\diamond(o, t_i, t_j)$ on the query range $\mathcal{Q}^\square$, we only have to take the time range $[t_i, t_j]$ into account; i.e., if the time range $\mathcal{T}^\square$ of the query spans beyond $[t_i, t_j]$, we truncate $\mathcal{T}^\square$ accordingly. Consequently, in the case where more than one diamonds of an object intersect $\mathcal{T}^\square$, we can split $\mathcal{Q}^\square$ at the time dimension and separately probe the object diamonds on the corresponding query parts. The resulting probabilities obtained for individual diamonds can be treated as independent.

LEMMA 1. *Let $\diamond(o, t_i, t_j)$, $\diamond(o, t_j, t_k)$ be two successive diamonds of object o and $\diamond_1 := \diamond(o, t_i, t_j, d_1, dir_1, \lambda_1)$, $\diamond_2 := \diamond(o, t_j, t_k, d_2, dir_2, \lambda_2)$ be probabilistic subdiamonds, associated with respective probabilities $P(\diamond_1)$ and $P(\diamond_2)$ that o intersects these subdiamonds. Then, the probability $P(\diamond_1 \wedge \diamond_2)$ that o intersects both subdiamonds, is given by*

$$P(inside(o, \diamond_1) \wedge inside(o, \diamond_2)) =$$

$$P(inside(o, \diamond_1)) \cdot P(inside(o, \diamond_2))$$

PROOF. We first rewrite $P(inside(o, \diamond_1) \wedge inside(o, \diamond_2))$ using conditional probabilities.

$$P(inside(o, \diamond_1) \wedge inside(o, \diamond_2)) =$$

$$P(inside(o, \diamond_1)) \cdot P(inside(o, \diamond_2) | inside(o, \diamond_1))$$

Furthermore, we exploit the knowledge that object o is at the observed location $o(t_j)$ at time t_j

$$P(inside(o, \diamond_1) \wedge inside(o, \diamond_2)) =$$

$$P(inside(o, \diamond_1)) \cdot P(inside(o, \diamond_2) | inside(o, \diamond_1) \wedge o(t_j))$$

Based on the Markov model assumption, we know that, given the position at t_j, the behavior of o in the time interval $[t_j, t_k]$ is independent of any position at times $t < t_j$. Thus, we obtain:

$$P(\diamond_1 \wedge \diamond_2) = P(\diamond_1) \cdot P(\diamond_2 | o(t_j))$$

Finally, the lemma is proved based on the fact that the position $o(t_j)$ has been observed, and thus, is not a random variable. □

Lemma 1 shows that the random events of two successive probabilistic diamonds of the same object are conditionally independent, given the observation in between them. This observation allows us to compute the probability $P^\exists(o)$ that the whole chain of diamonds of o intersects a query window $\mathcal{Q}^\square$. Let $\{t_i, t_j\} \subseteq_{seq} o.T_{obs}$ be the set of pairs of subsequent observations in $o.T_{obs}$. Then,

$$P^\exists(o) = P(\bigvee_{\{t_i, t_j\} \subseteq_{seq} o.T_{obs}} sometimes(o, t_i, t_j, \mathcal{Q}^\square))$$

That is, o satisfies a PST$\mathcal{T}\exists$ query, if and only if at least one diamond of o intersects $\mathcal{Q}^\square$ at least once. Rewriting yields

$$P^\exists(o) = 1 - P(\bigwedge_{\{t_i, t_j\} \subseteq_{seq} o.T_{obs}} never(o, t_i, t_j, \mathcal{Q}^\square).$$

Exploiting Lemma 1 yields

$$P^\exists(o) = 1 - \prod_{\{t_i, t_j\} \subseteq_{seq} o.T_{obs}} P(never(o, t_i, t_j, \mathcal{Q}^\square))$$

Using our probability bounds derived in Section 3.4, we obtain

$$P^{\exists}(o) \leq 1 - \prod_{\{t_i,t_j\} \subseteq_{seq} o.T_{obs}} P_{LB}(never(o, t_i, t_j, \mathcal{Q}^{\square}))$$

which can be used to prune o, if

$$1 - \prod_{\{t_i,t_j\} \subseteq_{seq} o.T_{obs}} P_{LB}(never(o, t_i, t_j, \mathcal{Q}^{\square})) < \tau \quad (4)$$

If Equation 4 cannot be applied for pruning, we propose to iteratively refine single diamonds of o. Thus, the exact probability $P(sometimes(o, t_i, t_j, \mathcal{Q}^{\square}))$ is computed using the technique proposed in [8]. This exact probability of a single diamond can then be used to re-apply the pruning criterion of Equation 4 , by using the true probability as lower bound. When all diamonds of o have been refined, Equation 4 yields the exact probability $P^{\exists}(o)$.

4. THE UST-TREE

In the previous section, we showed that we can precompute a set of approximations for each object, which can be progressively used to prune an object during query evaluation. In this section, we introduce the UST-tree, which is an R-tree-based hierarchical index structure, designed to organize the object approximations and efficiently prune objects that may not possibly qualify the query; for the remaining objects the query is directly verified based on their Markov models, as described in [8] *(refinement step)*. Section 4.1 describes the structure of the UST-tree and Section 4.2 presents a generic query processing algorithm for answering $PST\tau\exists$ queries.

4.1 Architecture

The UST-tree index is a hierarchical disk-based index. The basic structure is illustrated in Figure 5. An entry on the leaf level corresponds to an approximation of an object o represented by a quadruple $(\square(o, t_i, t_j), \diamond(o, t_i, t_j), \{f_{d,dir} : d \in D, dir \in \{\vee, \wedge\}\}, oid)$, containing (i) the MBR approximation $\square(o, t_i, t_j)$ (cf. Section 3.1), (ii) the diamond approximation $\diamond(o, t_i, t_j)$ (cf. Section 3.1), (iii) a set $\{f_{d,dir} : d \in D, dir \in \{\vee, \wedge\}\}$ of $2 \cdot D$ linear approximation functions for the precomputed probabilistic diamonds of o (cf. Section 3.5), and (iv) a pointer *oid* to the exact uncertain spatio-temporal object description (raw object data). Intermediate node entries of the UST-tree have exactly the same structure as in an R-tree; i.e., each entry contains a pointer referencing its child node and the MBR of all MBR approximations stored in pointed subtree. Note that the necklace of each object is decomposed into diamonds, which are stored independently in the leaf nodes of the tree. Since the directory structure of the UST-tree is identical to that of the R-tree, the UST-tree uses the same methods as the R*-tree [2] to handle updates.

4.2 Query Evaluation

Given a spatio-temporal query window $\mathcal{Q}^{\square}$, the UST-tree is hierarchically traversed starting from the root, recursively visiting entries whose MBRs intersect $\mathcal{Q}^{\square}$; i.e., the subtree of an intermediate entry e is pruned if $e.mbr \cap \mathcal{Q}^{\square} = \emptyset$. For each leaf node entry e, we progressively use the spatio-temporal and probabilistic diamond approximations stored in e to filter the corresponding object.

In the spatio-temporal filter step, we first use $\square(o, t_i, t_j)$ (ST-MBR Filter) using simple rectangle intersection tests. If this filter fails, we proceed using $\diamond(o, t_i, t_j)$ (ST-Diamond filter) by performing intersection tests against $\mathcal{Q}^{\square}$ as described in Section 3.2. Note that sometimes multiple leaf entries associated with an object are required to prune an object or confirm whether it is a *true hit*. Therefore, candidates are stored in a list until all their diamond approximations have been evaluated.

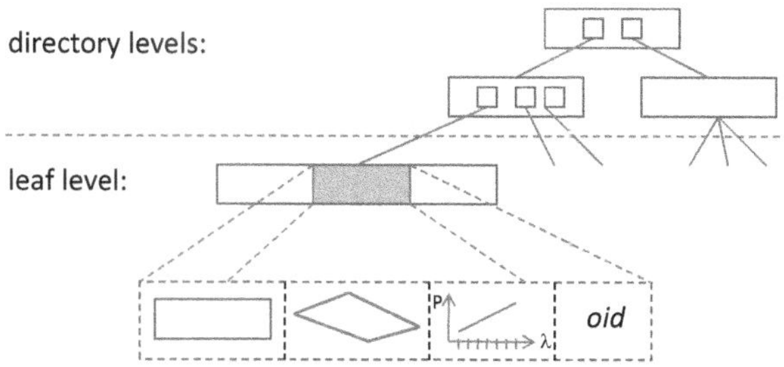

Figure 5: The UST-tree.

Finally, for the remaining candidates we exploit the probabilistic filter (Probabilistic Diamond Filter) as described in Section 3.6. Thereby, we use the linear approximation functions $\{f_{d,dir} : d \in D, dir \in \{\vee, \wedge\}\}$ stored in the leaf-node entry in order to derive an upper bound of the qualification probability $P(\exists t \in (\mathcal{T}^{\square} \cap [t_i, t_j]) : o(t) \in \mathcal{S}^{\square})$ or $P(\forall t \in (\mathcal{T}^{\square} \cap [t_i, t_j]) : o(t) \in \mathcal{S}^{\square})$ (depending on the query predicate). For each object o which is not pruned (or reported as true hit), we accumulate in a list $L(o)$ all upper bounds of its qualification probabilities from the leaf entries that index the diamonds of o. After collecting all candidate objects, the qualification probabilities stored in the list $L(o)$ for each candidate o are aggregated in order to derive the upper bound of the overall qualification probability $P(\exists t \in \mathcal{T}^{\square} : o(t) \in \mathcal{S}^{\square})$ for o, as described in Section 3.6. If this probability falls below τ we can skip o, otherwise we have to refine o by accessing the exact object data referenced by *oid*.

5. EXPERIMENTAL EVALUATION

In order to evaluate the proposed techniques we used data derived from a real application and several synthetic data sets.

Real Data. As a basis for the real world data served the trajectory data set containing one-week trajectories of 10,357 taxis in Beijing from [27]. This heterogeneous dataset contains trajectories having different samples rates, ranging from one sample every fives seconds to one sample every 10 minutes. The average time between localization updates (observations) is 177 seconds. The average distance between two observations is 623 m. We applied the techniques from [4] to obtain both a set of possible states (mostly corresponding crossroads) and a transition matrix reflecting the possible movements of the taxis. We only included data of taxis where the time between two GPS signals (observations) is no more than two minutes to train the Markov chain. The resulting data set consists of 3008 states and 11699 possible transitions between theses states.

Synthetic Data. In order to demonstrate the behavior of the proposed techniques depending on the underlying data we also generated a set of synthetic data sets with different characteristics. For the possible states, we generated n points uniformly distributed in the $[0, 1]^2$ space. Each point was then connected to the points which have an Euclidean distance smaller than ϵ. Those connections correspond to the possible movements of an object in the space and we randomly assigned probabilities to each connection such that the sum of all outgoing edges sums up to 1. These values are the entries for the corresponding transition matrix. As a default for this dataset we generated 1000 objects each with 100 observations (= 99.000 probabilistic diamonds) and the parameters were set to $n = 10000$, $\epsilon = 0.02$ and the catalogue size $|\Lambda| = 10$.

Observations. Additionally to the positions of the states and the transition matrix, we further need observations from each object in order to build a database. The observations were constructed

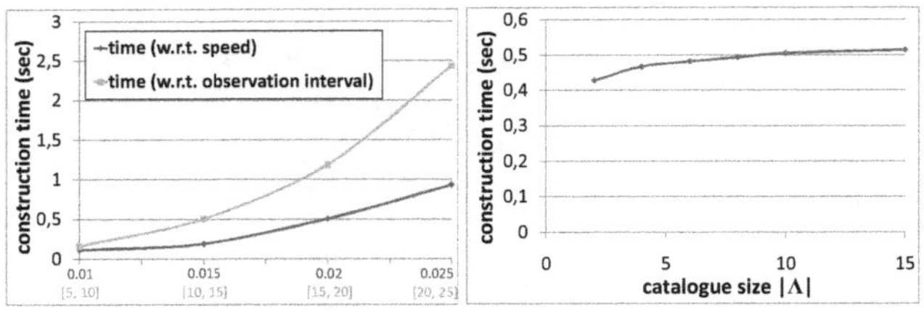

(a) diamond parameter (b) catalogue size

Figure 6: diamond construction

by a directed random walk through the underlying graph (states = vertices and non-zero transitions = edges). At some time steps we memorize the current position of the object and take these time-state-tuples as an observation of the object. The time steps between two successive observations was randomly chosen from the interval [10,15] if not stated otherwise. For the observations of the real dataset we used the GPS data of taxis, where the time between two signals is between 2 and 20 minutes.

All experiments were run on a Quad Intel Xeon server running Windows Server 2008 with 16 GB RAM and 3.0 GHz. The UST-tree was implemented in Java. For all operations involving matrix operations (e.g., the refinement step of queries) we used MATLAB for efficient processing. All query performance evaluation results are averaged over 1000 queries. The spatial extent of the query windows in each dimension was set to 0.1 and the duration of the queries was set to 10 time steps by default. Unless otherwise stated, we experimented with PST$\tau\exists$ queries, with $\tau = 0.5$. The page size of the tree was set to 4 KB. Our experiments assess the construction cost of the UST-tree structure and its performance on query evaluation. For experiments regarding the effectivity of the Markov-chain model, and an evaluation of its capability to capture the real world in various applications, we refer to previous work, e.g., [1, 4, 10, 18], where Markov Chains were proved successful in modeling spatio-temporal data.

5.1 UST-tree Construction

The first experiment investigates the cost of index construction. In particular, we evaluate the cost for generating the spatio-temporal and probabilistic diamond approximations used to build the entries of the leaf level; this is the bottleneck of constructing and updating the tree, since restructuring operations always take at most 1ms. On the other hand, constructing the probabilistic diamonds is typically 2-3 orders of magnitude costlier, as illustrated in Figure 6(a). Still, this cost is reasonable, since the construction of a probabilistic diamond is comparable to the construction of $2 \cdot D \cdot |\Lambda|$ subdiamonds, which in turn corresponds to one refinement step (considering the subdiamond as a query window). Construction times pay off, when the query load on the database is reasonable. Figure 6(a) illustrates the construction time as a function of the speed of the objects (upper x-axis values) and the number of time steps between successive observations (lower x-axis values). From a theoretical point of view, both parameters linearly increase the number of reachable states, i.e., the density of the sparse vectors representing the uncertain position of an object at one point of time. The results reflect the theoretical considerations showing a quadratic runtime behavior with respect to both parameters. In a streaming scenario with several updates/insertions per second and large probabilistic diamonds (due to high speed of objects or large intervals between observations), the construction of probabilistic diamonds can be performed in parallel and is therefore still feasible. Figure 6(b) shows the construction cost as a function of parameter $|\Lambda|$ (which determines the number of subdiamonds). Theoretically this parameter should have a linear impact on the construction time. However our implementation exploits the monotonicity of the uncertain trajectories regarding probabilistic subdiamonds; a trajectory which is not included in the probability of a subdiamond, is also excluded from larger subdiamonds in the same dimension and direction. This explains the sublinear runtime w.r.t. $|\Lambda|$.

5.2 Query Performance

In the first set of query performance experiments, we compare the cost of using UST-tree with two competitors on synthetic data (see Figure 7). *Scan+* is a scan based query processing implementation, i.e., without employing any index [8]. For each pair of two successive observations of an object, refinement is performed immediately, i.e., there is no filter cost. We enhanced the implementation of *Scan+* by prepending a simple temporal filter, which only considers observation pairs which temporally overlap the query window. The *R*-Tree* competitor approximates all possible locations (i.e. state-time pairs) between two successive observations of an object using only $\Box(o, t_i, t_j)$. These MBRs are then indexed using a conventional R*-Tree [2]. In Figure 7(a), we show the average CPU cost per query (I/O cost is not the bottleneck in this problem), for the three competitors. The cost are split into filter and refinement costs. Although the R*-Tree has lower filter cost, the overall query performance of the UST-tree is around 3 times better than that of the R*-Tree (note the logarithmic scale). This is attributed to the effectiveness of the different filter steps used by the UST-tree; the overhead of the UST-tree filter is negligible compared to the savings in refinement cost.

Figure 7(b) shows the cost and the effectiveness of the individual filter steps of the filter-refinement pipeline used by the UST-tree. The bars show the overall runtime (query time) of each filter and the numbers on top of the bars show the effectiveness of the filter in terms of remaining (observation pair) candidates after the corresponding filter has been applied. We clearly see that the spatio-temporal filters reduce the number of candidates and, thus, the number of required refinements, drastically. We can also observe that the probabilistic filter can reduce the number of refinements by 30% after applying the sequence of spatio-temporal filters. Comparing the cost of the probabilistic filter (which is comparable to that of the spatio-temporal filter) to the cost of candidate refinement, we can observe that the cost required to perform the probabilistic filter can be neglected. This experiment shows that each of the filters incorporated in the UST-tree indeed pays off in terms of CPU cost.

Although I/O cost is not the bottleneck under our setting, the I/O costs of *R*-Tree* and the UST-tree are illustrated in Figure 7(c) for completeness. Filter cost here means all costs which occur during the traversal of the corresponding index structure, i.e., access to intermediate and leaf nodes. Refinement cost includes the number of page accesses to refine the observation pairs that pass the filter step, assuming one I/O per such pair. Note, that the cost of a refinement can be much higher than one page access (e.g. if the Markov Chain, which can become very large does not fit in one disk page) under different settings. The UST-tree has higher filtering cost, since the representation of the probabilistic diamonds requires more space and the tree is larger than the R*-Tree, which only stores MBR approximations but incurs much higher I/O cost for refinements.

The above experiments unveil that the most costly operation is the refinement of spatio-temporal diamonds; thus, we now take a closer look at the effectiveness of the three different methods on pruning spatio-temporal diamonds. The next experiments measure the number of spatio-temporal diamonds which have to be refined at the refinement step; these results can be directly translated to runtime differences of the different approaches.

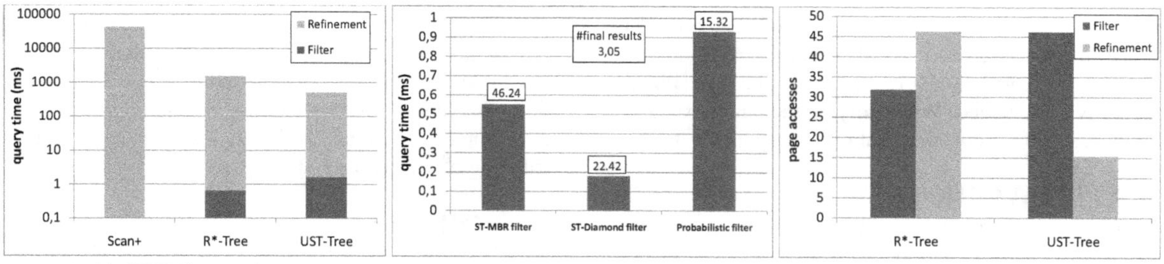

(a) CPU Comparison (b) CPU Time of Filter (c) Page Accesses

Figure 7: Overall Performance (Synthetic Data Set)

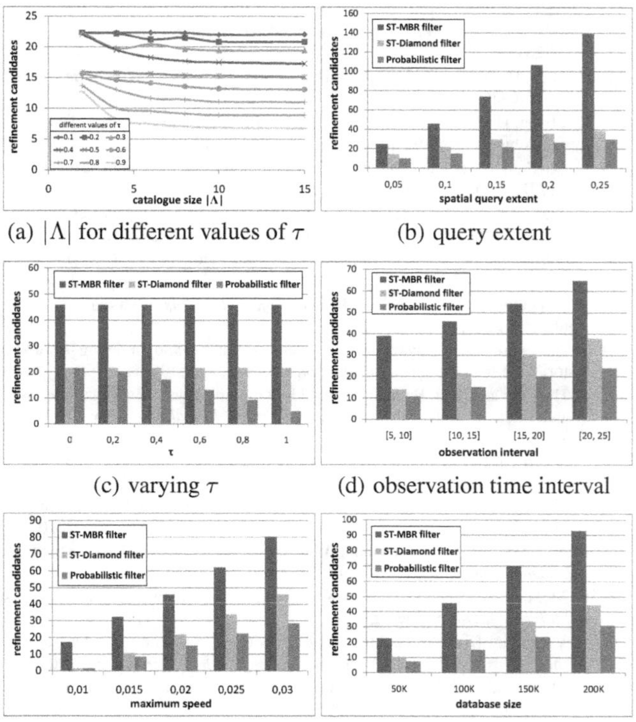

(a) $|\Lambda|$ for different values of τ (b) query extent

(c) varying τ (d) observation time interval

(e) varying maximum speed (f) database size

Figure 8: Experiments on Synthetic Data

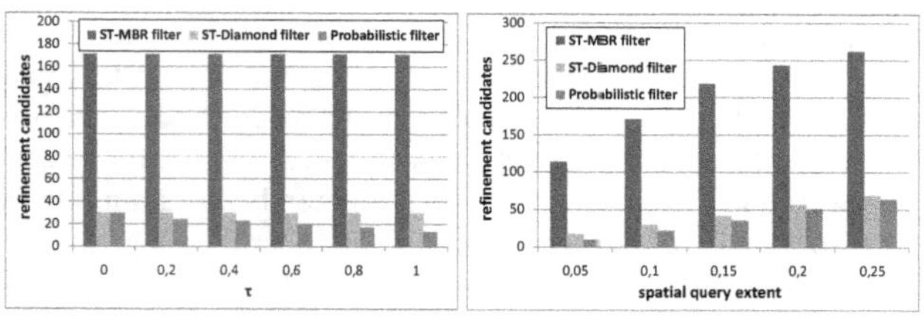

(a) varying τ (b) query extent

Figure 9: Experiments on Real Data ($\forall$)

Size of the Catalogue $|\Lambda|$. An important tuning parameter for the index is the size of the catalogue which is used for building the probabilistic diamond approximations. In Figure 8(a), it can be observed that the filter effectiveness converges at around $|\Lambda| = 10$ (default value for the experiments). Depending on the query parameter τ, a too small catalogue yields up to twice as much candidates which have to be refined. Note that the number of refinement candidates does not decrease monotonically in $|\Lambda|$. In general a larger catalogue results in a linear function with a larger approximation error. However, the step-function for the conservative approximation becomes smoother which results in a smaller approximation error. Because of these two contrary effects a larger catalogue does not always result in higher filter effectiveness.

Query Parameters. The characteristics of the query have different implications on the index performance. Increasing the spatial extent of the query obviously yields more candidates since more diamonds in the database are affected (cf. Figure 8(b)). The spatio-temporal filter utilizing the diamond approximations becomes more effective in comparison to the ST-MBR-Filter. The percentage of the diamonds which can be pruned using the probabilistic filter remains rather constant (at around 30%) in comparison to the spatio-temporal filter. Another query parameter is the temporal extent of the query. Increasing the length of the query time window $\mathcal{T}^{\square}$ increases the number of refinement candidates. The results are very similar to the results when increasing the spatial extent of the query; we do not include the comparison plot due to space limitations.

Changing the value of τ obviously only affects the probabilistic filter (cf. Figure 8(c)). The higher τ is set, the more candidates can be pruned by the probabilistic filter. From a value of around 20%, the candidates which have to be refined decrease linearly with τ.

Influencing Variables of ST Diamonds. The size of the spatio-temporal diamonds is generally affected by two parameters. One is the time interval between successive observations, since a larger interval increases the space that can be reached by the moving object between the two observations. For this experiment, the number of time steps between successive observations in the data set was chosen randomly from the intervals on the x-axis in Figure 8(d). The second parameter is the speed of the object and has a similar effect. The speed corresponds to the parameter ϵ, which reflects the maximum distance of points which can be reached by an object within one time step (cf. Figure 8(e)). Since larger spatio-temporal diamonds usually result in more objects which intersect the query window, the number of candidates to be refined increase when increasing these two parameters. Interestingly, the effectiveness of the ST-Diamond Filter decreases over the ST-MBR-Filter, whereas the pruning effectiveness of the Probabilistic Filter increases. This shows, that the probabilistic filter copes better with more uncertainty in the data than the other two filters.

Database Size. We evaluated the scalability of the UST-tree by increasing the amount of observations (cf. Figure 8(f)). The number of results increases linearly with the database size. The experiment also shows that the number of refined candidates increase linearly.

Real Data. The experiments on the real world data, show similar behavior as those on the synthetic data. Due to space limitations, we only show excerpts from the evaluation. Figure 9(a) illustrates the results for PST$\tau\forall$ queries when varying the value of τ. It is notable that the ST-Diamond Filter seems to even perform better (compared to the ST-MBR-Filter) on the real dataset. The reason for this is that the real dataset has much more inherent irregularity (regarding the locations and the movement of obejcts). This favors the ST-Diamond filter over the MBR approximation (since diamonds are more skewed as in Figure 2(b)). The probabilistic filter is apparently not affected. When varying the query extent (cf Figure 9(b)) the results resemble the results on the synthetic dataset.

6. RELATED WORK

The problem of managing, mining and querying spatio-temporal data has received continuous attention over the past decades (for a comprehensive coverage, see [9]). Specifically for efficient query processing a vast amount of indexing structures for different purposes and data characteristics has been developed (an overview and a classification can be found in [14] and [16]). From this body of work, our approach is mostly related to spatio-temporal data indexing for predictive querying, for example indexes like [19, 12] and approaches like [20]. Still, these papers neither consider probabilistic query evaluation nor model the data with stochastic processes.

However, in scenarios where data is inherently uncertain, such as in sensor databases, answering traditional queries using expected values is inadequate, since the results could be incorrect [3]. One of the first works that deal with uncertainty in trajectories is [17]. This work reviews the sources of error which yield to uncertain trajectories and proposes a filter refinement approach for simple query types. The prevalent approach is to bound the possible positions of an object at each point of time by simple a spatial structure resulting in a spatio-temporal approximation. Examples include static ellipses [25, 24, 23], dynamic MBRs (Minimum Bounding Rectangles) [15] and dynamic ellipses [22, 13] yielding skewed cylinders, diamonds and beads, respectively. To answer queries most of the existing works restrict the possible queries. Often no specific assumption is made about the probability density function (pdf) of the object positions over time ([17, 25, 24, 23, 22, 28, 7]). Thus quantifiers such as "always", "sometimes", "definitely" and "possibly" are used to indicate whether an object intersects a given spatio-temporal query window. These types of queries can be answered by only considering the spatio-temporal approximations. As a consequence, these approaches do not compute probabilities for objects to qualify the queries. A possibility for returning probabilistic results is to restrict the temporal window of the query, such that queries refer to exactly one point in time (cf. [5, 28]). All the aforementioned approaches avoid modeling and considering the time dependencies between successive object locations (see Section 2). These dependencies were first considered in [8], where a Markov Chain model is used, and [18], where certain event detection is the main focus (this work does not handle window queries).

Our work is also inspired by methods for indexing uncertain spatial data. The U-Tree [20, 21] and its extension [29] bound each spatial uncertain object with an MBR and additionally associate it with a set of "probabilistically constrained regions" (PCR). These PCRs can be used for probabilistic pruning during query processing. For efficiency reasons the set of PCRs are conservatively approximated by a linear function over the parameters of the PCRs.

7. CONCLUSIONS

In this work, we proposed the UST-tree which is an index structure for uncertain spatio-temporal data. The UST-tree adopts and incorporates state-of-the art techniques from several fields of research in order to cope with the complexity of the data. We showed how the most common query types (spatio-temporal $\exists$- and $\forall$-window queries) can be efficiently processed using probabilistic bounds which are computed during index construction. To the best of our knowledge, this is the first approach that supports query evaluation on very large uncertain spatio-temporal databases, adhering to possible worlds semantics. Outside the scope of this work is the consideration of an object's location before its first and after its last observation. In both cases, the resulting diamond approximation would be unbounded. An approach to solve this problem is to define a maximum time horizon for which diamond approximations are computed. Beyond this horizon, we can use the stationary distribution of the model M to infer the location of an object.

8. REFERENCES

[1] D. Ashbrook and T. Starner. Using gps to learn significant locations and predict movement across multiple users. *Personal Ubiquitous Comput.*, 7:275–286, 2003.

[2] N. Beckmann, H.-P. Kriegel, R. Schneider, and B. Seeger. The R*-Tree: An efficient and robust access method for points and rectangles. In *Proc. SIGMOD*, pages 322–331, 1990.

[3] G. Beskales, M. A. Soliman, and I. F. Ilyas. Efficient search for the top-k probable nearest neighbors in uncertain databases. *Proc. VLDB Endow.*, 1(1):326–339, 2008.

[4] Z. Chen, H. T. Shen, and X. Zhou. Discovering popular routes from trajectories. In *Proc. ICDE*, pages 900–911, 2011.

[5] R. Cheng, D. V. Kalashnikov, and S. Prabhakar. Querying imprecise data in moving object environments. *TKDE*, 16(9):1112–1127, 2004.

[6] N. Dalvi and D. Suciu. Efficient query evaluation on probabilistic databases. *The VLDB Journal*, 16(4):523–544, 2007.

[7] Z. Ding. Utr-tree: An index structure for the full uncertain trajectories of network-constrained moving objects. In *MDM*, pages 33–40, 2008.

[8] T. Emrich, H.-P. Kriegel, N. Mamoulis, M. Renz, and A. Züfle. Querying uncertain spatio-temporal data. In *Proc. ICDE*, 2012.

[9] R. H. Güting and M. Schneider. *Moving Objects Databases*. Morgan Kaufmann, 2005.

[10] R. Hariharan and K. Toyama. Project lachesis: parsing and modeling location histories. In *In Geographic Information Science*, pages 106–124, 2004.

[11] K. Hornsby and M. J. Egenhofer. Modeling moving objects over multiple granularities. *Annals of Mathematics and Artificial Intelligence*, 36:177–194, 2002.

[12] C. S. Jensen, D. Lin, and B. C. Ooi. Query and update efficient b+-tree based indexing of moving objects. In *Proc. VLDB*, pages 768–779, 2004.

[13] B. Kuijpers and W. Othman. Trajectory databases: Data models, uncertainty and complete query languages. *J. Comput. Syst. Sci.*, 76(7):538–560, 2010.

[14] M. F. Mokbel, T. M. Ghanem, and W. G. Aref. Spatio-temporal access methods. *IEEE Data Eng. Bull.*, 26(2):40–49, 2003.

[15] H. Mokhtar and J. Su. Universal trajectory queries for moving object databases. In *Mobile Data Management*, 2004.

[16] L.-V. Nguyen-Dinh, W. G. Aref, and M. F. Mokbel. Spatio-temporal access methods: Part 2 (2003 - 2010). *IEEE Data Eng. Bull.*, 33(2):46–55, 2010.

[17] D. Pfoser and C. S. Jensen. Capturing the uncertainty of moving-object representations. In *Proc. SSD*, 1999.

[18] C. Ré, J. Letchner, M. Balazinksa, and D. Suciu. Event queries on correlated probabilistic streams. In *Proc. SIGMOD*, pages 715–728, New York, NY, USA, 2008. ACM.

[19] S. Saltenis, C. S. Jensen, S. T. Leutenegger, and M. A. Lopez. Indexing the positions of continuously moving objects. In *Proc. SIGMOD*, pages 331–342, 2000.

[20] Y. Tao, R. Cheng, X. Xiao, W. K. Ngai, B. Kao, and S. Prabhakar. Indexing multi-dimensional uncertain data with arbitrary probability density functions. In *Proc. VLDB*, pages 922–933, 2005.

[21] Y. Tao, X. Xiao, and R. Cheng. Range search on multidimensional uncertain data. *ACM TODS*, 32(3):15, 2007.

[22] G. Trajcevski, A. N. Choudhary, O. Wolfson, L. Ye, and G. Li. Uncertain range queries for necklaces. In *Mobile Data Management*, pages 199–208, 2010.

[23] G. Trajcevski, R. Tamassia, H. Ding, P. Scheuermann, and I. F. Cruz. Continuous probabilistic nearest-neighbor queries for uncertain trajectories. In *Proc. EDBT*, pages 874–885, 2009.

[24] G. Trajcevski, O. Wolfson, K. Hinrichs, and S. Chamberlain. Managing uncertainty in moving objects databases. *ACM Trans. Database Syst.*, 29(3):463–507, 2004.

[25] G. Trajcevski, O. Wolfson, F. Zhang, and S. Chamberlain. The geometry of uncertainty in moving objects databases. In *Proc. EDBT*, pages 233–250, 2002.

[26] M.-Y. Yeh, K.-L. Wu, P. S. Yu, and M. Chen. PROUD: a probabilistic approach to processing similarity queries over uncertain data streams. In *Proc. EDBT*, pages 684–695, 2009.

[27] J. Yuan, Y. Zheng, X. Xie, and G. Sun. Driving with knowledge from the physical world. In *Proc. KDD*, pages 316–324, 2011.

[28] M. Zhang, S. Chen, C. S. Jensen, B. C. Ooi, and Z. Zhang. Effectively indexing uncertain moving objects for predictive queries. *PVLDB*, 2(1):1198–1209, 2009.

[29] Y. Zhang, X. Lin, W. Zhang, J. Wang, and Q. Lin. Effectively indexing the uncertain space. *IEEE TKDE*, 22(9):1247–1261, 2010.

Local Anomaly Descriptor: A Robust Unsupervised Algorithm for Anomaly Detection based on Diffusion Space

Hao Huang, Hong Qin
Department of Computer Science,
Stony Brook University
{haohuang,qin}@cs.stonybrook.edu

Shinjae Yoo, Dantong Yu
Computational Science Center,
Brookhaven National Laboratory
{sjyoo,dtyu}@bnl.gov

ABSTRACT

Current popular anomaly detection algorithms are capable of detecting global anomalies but oftentimes fail to distinguish local anomalies from normal instances. This paper aims to improve unsupervised anomaly detection via the exploration of physics-based diffusion space. Building upon the embedding manifold derived from diffusion maps, we devise Local Anomaly Descriptor (LAD) whose originality results from faithfully preserving intrinsic and informative density-relevant neighborhood information. This robust and effective algorithm is designed with a weighted umbrella Laplacian operator to bridge global and local properties. To further enhance the efficacy of our proposed algorithm, we explore the utility of anisotropic Gaussian kernel (AGK) which can offer better manifold-aware affinity information. Comprehensive experiments on both synthetic and UCI real datasets verify that our LAD outperforms existing anomaly detection algorithms.

Categories and Subject Descriptors

H.2.8 [**Database Management**]: Database Applications—*Data Mining*; I.5.1 [**Pattern Recognition**]: Models—*Unsupervised Anomaly Detection*

Keywords

Anomaly detection, diffusion space, LAD

1. INTRODUCTION

Anomaly detection or outlier detection is of great significance to many applications [40] [28]. Its primary goal is similar to that of a classification problem except that it further distinguishes normal instances from a small portion of new or abnormal instances (anomalies) [5] [19] [20]. In many applications, anomalies are sparse and quite diverse, learning with the known anomalies [9] [38] [3] may not be necessarily useful in detecting the unknown ones in unseen data [34]. On the other hand, labeling known datasets can be extremely time-consuming for real-life applications and sometimes even unpractical to detect new types of rare events. Therefore, the key challenge of anomaly detection still lies in its robust ability to quantitatively and unsupervisedly characterize the intrinsic and informative density distribution around every instance.

Our proposed unsupervised method in this paper, called Local Anomaly Descriptor (LAD), computes a measurement of anomalousness based on physics-based diffusion theory, which is more **informative** and **intrinsic** compared with the existing algorithms ([4] [25] [19] [36] [1] etc.). First of all, our algorithm projects origin instances onto a diffusion space. In the diffusion space, distance between anomalies and normal instances will be magnified, which makes the density of anomalies even less and therefore more salient compared with those in the original space. However, the perfect diffusion maps are usually unreachable. Oftentimes anomalies are hard to be totally distinguished from the normal instances that are not too far away. To better set anomalies apart from the nearby normal instances, we innovatively apply a weighted Laplace umbrella operator on the projected diffusion space, called Local Anomaly Descriptor (LAD). With the novel LAD which bridges the gap between global and local properties, we can not only obtain intrinsic local density information, but also take the quantity of similar instances into consideration. Therefore the representation is more reliable than original attribute distribution, and more informative since it covers a sufficiently large neighborhood for each instance. Furthermore, LAD provides reasonably stable performance as the scaling parameters vary (the neighborhood size k and Gaussian scaling parameter σ).

In this paper, we employ heat kernel to build the diffusion maps, which offers a statistical description on random walks. However, the pivotal techniques of our algorithm are fundamentally different from the current existing data mining research based on heat kernel theory [15] or other similar diffusion methods [6] [30] [29]. Our proposed LAD has distinctive uniqueness on balancing local and global properties, and its advantage on both performance and robustness on real world datasets for anomaly detection.

1.1 Related Work

According to the most classical definition by Hawkins [12], an anomaly is "an observation which deviates so much from the other observations as to arouse suspicion that it was generated by a different mechanism". However, it is far from trivial to define the quantitative scope of "other observations". As Figure 1(a) illustrates, global anomalies (in yellow) are those with global minimum neighborhood density, and

CIKM'12, October 29–November 2, 2012, Maui, HI, USA.
Copyright 2012 ACM 978-1-4503-1156-4/12/10 ...$15.00.

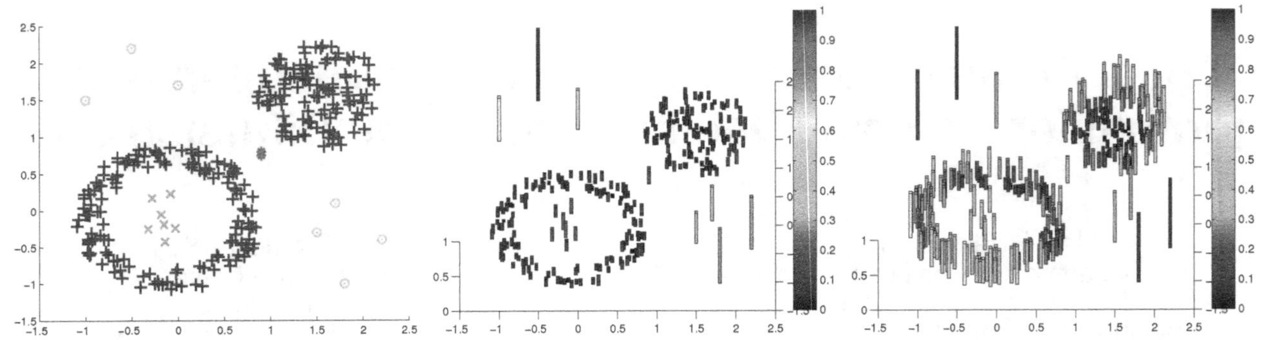

(a) Synthetic Dataset Example (b) LOF Score ($k = 10$) (c) IForest Score ($nt = 100$, $\rho = 4000$)

Figure 1: 1(a) Synthetic dataset with normal instances (blue), global anomalies (yellow), and local anomalies (red and green); 1(b) LOF score with $k = 10$; 1(c) IForest score. The anomalousness are visualized as height bar over all the instances. We can see that both LOF and IForest fail to totally distinguish local anomalies from normal instances.

distinct with respect to (almost) the entire dataset. While local anomalies (in red and green) are those with local minimum neighborhood density, and distinct with respect to instances in their local neighborhood. Profoundly speaking, local anomalies can be thought of as a generalization of global anomalies, as global anomalies will typically also be local anomalies, but not vice versa [7].

In implementation, kNN-based algorithms such as LOF [4] and LDOF [39] define anomaly if its distance (usually in Euclidean space) to its k-th nearest neighbor (kNN) is large relative to the distances of its neighbors to their own k-th nearest-neighbors. Recent research [7] extended LOF to high-dimensional dataset by using random projection. Two major drawbacks of these approaches are: (1) they tend to miss local anomalies (Figure 1(b)) since it is not peculiar that kNN distances of local anomalies are similar to their normal instance neighbors'; (2) it is of extreme importance to determine the value of k, because k can not be too small to avoid statistical error. In other words, we need to ensure that for each instance, especially those forming micro-cluster of anomalies, it does intend to use a neighborhood size which is large enough to include more normal instances than anomalies. However, too large k will lead to miss some genuine anomalies. In Section 6.2 we will show that LOF is statistically vulnerable by analyzing the sensitivity of k.

Instead of detecting anomalies based on average neighborhood distance, recent approaches such as IForest [19] [20] and Mass [36] are to separate the anomalies from normal instances with their unique attribute distribution. A representative anomaly definition [19] in the aforementioned papers states that anomalies should have "attribute-values that are very different from those of normal instances", and at the same time are "minority consisting of fewer instances". Therefore these approaches have the capacity to handle anomalies with different attribute distribution compared with normal instances [18]. Nonetheless, these approaches may fail to detect some local anomalies when their attributes have similar distribution with some normal instances'. From Figure 1(c) we can see that, even though IForest did a good job on global anomaly detection, it fails to distinguish local anomalies (green and red instances in Figure 1(a)) from the "boundary" instances in the normal instance clusters (blue instances in Figure 1(a)). The reason is that, these anomaly detectors partition instances mainly based on observable attributes, or more precisely, the attribute distribution in original data space. Therefore it will fail miserably when the anomaly distribution becomes far less discriminative by sharing similar attribute range/distribution pattern with parts of the normal instances. In Figure 2 we can see that some anomalies have overlapped distribution on the first four eigenvectors with normal instances in Ionosphere dataset (a popularly used dataset for anomaly detection [19] [13] [23]). Such overlapping also appears at nonclassical multidimensional scaling as well. So, this problem indeed exists in some real world datasets.

A few techniques [1] tried to find an approximation of the data using a combination of attributes that capture the bulk of the variability in the data, and then detect anomalies on the projected space. This kind of approaches adopted by spectral techniques is to determine manifold subspaces in which the anomalous instances can be easily identified [5]. However, the existing algorithms are based on techniques such as isometric feature mapping (ISM) and locally linear embeddings (LLE) [1] which are highly sensitive to density-varying data distribution [16] [37].

1.2 Motivation

Motivated by the aforementioned problems, we re-define anomaly as follows:

Definition: Anomalies are those instances with (1) **local minimum neighborhood density** and (2) **small quantity** compared with normal instances.

To capture anomalies under such definition, we consider the heat equation in diffusion theory, which has intrinsic relationship with manifold reconstruction and built-in robustness of scaling parameters [15]. The reason why we resort to manifold space is that normal instances usually lie on some low dimensional manifold structures in high density regions, moreover, the anomalies deviate from the normal instances which makes them even more discriminative. Diffusion distance is based on Markov matrix which is a stochastic matrix representing random walks on graph [22], it can consider up to t steps out of all the possible paths bridging any two instances, which makes it more robust than Euclidean and geodesic distance [6] [16] [37]. However, different from the

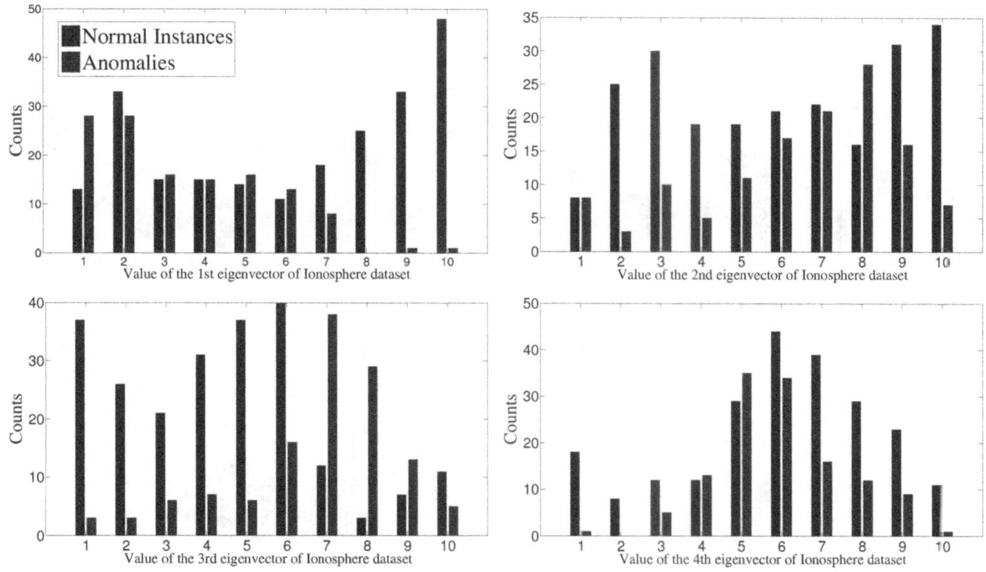

Figure 2: Histogram of anomaly (red) and normal instance (blue) on the first four eigenvectors (*) of Ionosphere dataset (a popular benchmark dataset for anomaly detection [19] [13] [23]). Some anomalies have overlapped distribution with parts of normal instances and therefore it is nontrivial to separate them only by simple attribute distribution. *Since the dataset is high-dimensional, dimension reduction is required to provide a concise illustration. Although eigenvectors do not necessarily show full distribution of the original data, it tends to show certain patterns of partial dimensions in the original space.

current diffusion-related research with the goal of clustering [30] [29] [15], diffusion mapping for anomaly detection has crucial requirement for connecting similar instances and at the same time avoiding excessive-connection. To our best knowledge, this diffusion-based utility on anomaly detection has never been explored yet.

In this paper, we propose Local Anomaly Descriptor (LAD) which offers a natural mechanism to express intrinsic neighborhood density information through heat diffusion process. To offer a solution to the inherent problem from the perspective of heat diffusion, LAD provides a meaningful trade-off between local and global manifold awareness by applying a weighted Laplacian umbrella operator. Experiments show that LAD is immediately useful for a wide variety of anomaly detection applications.

1.3 Contribution

This paper articulates a novel unsupervised anomaly detection algorithm which is intrinsic, informative, and robust to scaling parameters with the following contributions:

(1) We quantitatively characterize local density information based on heat diffusion theory (Section 2) and anisotropic Gaussian kernel (Section 3). This method is both intrinsic and informative in that, it has a more locally adaptive scope of manifold-aware neighborhood and therefore can very well satisfy the first property of the above definition in Section 1.2 more insightfully and intrinsically compared with the existing algorithms.

(2) In order to take the amount of similar instances into account (the second property of the above definition in Section 1.2) which can better separate local anomalies from normal instances, we explore the use of weighted umbrella Laplacian operator (Section 4) which can bridge the gap between local and global information.

(3) We systematically evaluate the proposed algorithm with several closely-related baseline algorithms on a number of benchmark datasets (Section 6). Our algorithm shows not only better average performance but also more stable results than the other popular algorithms. Moreover, our algorithm affords robustness for parameter selections (neighborhood size and Gaussian scaling parameters).

2. HEAT KERNEL SIGNATURE BASED ON DIFFUSION SPACE

Our proposed work is strongly inspired by heat diffusion theory [14] in that it can provide information intimately related to local density. Heat theory can be interpreted as the transition density function of Brownian motion [33], which is the most fundamental continuous time Markov process. Laplace operator is intimately related to heat diffusion, connecting geometry of a manifold with the properties of the heat flow. Using the discrete Laplace operator, the heat equation can be simplified, and generalized to matrix operation over spaces with an arbitrary number of dimensions. In practice the heat equation is often associated with random walk graph Laplacian [6], L_{rw}. Random walk is a stochastic process which randomly jumps from vertex to vertex. Heat equation therefore can be defined by

$$\frac{\partial H_t}{\partial t} = -L_{rw} H_t, \tag{1}$$

where $H_t = e^{-tL_{rw}}$ is the heat kernel on Riemannian manifold $\mathcal{M}$ and t is the time scaling parameter [11]. For $L_{rw} = \psi' \lambda \psi$ (ψ and λ are the eigenvectors and eigenvalues of L_{rw}

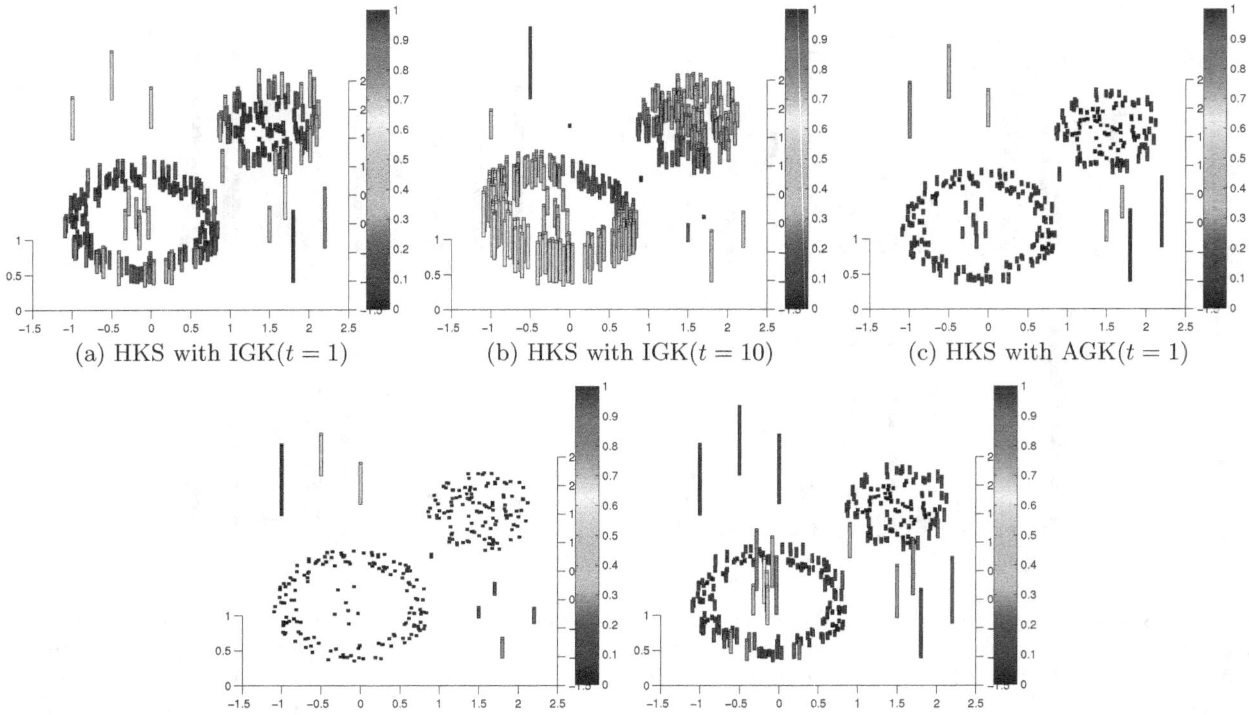

(a) HKS with IGK($t = 1$) (b) HKS with IGK($t = 10$) (c) HKS with AGK($t = 1$)

(d) HKS with AGK($t = 10$) (e) LAD ($t = 1$ and $k = 10$)

Figure 3: HKS score with IGK (Isotropic Gaussian Kernel) and AGK and LAD score of the synthetic dataset in Figure 1(a). We can see that LAD is the most sensitive to both global and local anomalies.

), the heat kernel can be re-formulated as follows:

$$H_t(i,j) = \sum_{p=1}^{N} [e^{-\lambda_p t} \psi_p(i) \psi_p(j)], \quad (2)$$

where $H_t(i,j)$ represents the amount of heat being transferred from i to j in time t given a unit heat source at i. The scaling parameter t in heat kernel is used to control the transitive connectivity: small t makes the loosely-connected graph into slightly stronger connection within t connections, while large t makes the graph tend to be more strongly-connected.

In 2009, Sun et.al [33] proposed a concise form given by the heat kernel from one instance to itself

$$HKS_t(i) = H_t(i,i) = \sum_{p=1}^{N} [e^{-\lambda_p t} \psi_p^2(i)], \quad (3)$$

which is called Heat Kernel Signature (HKS). The physical meaning of HKS is the amount of heat each instance keeps within itself in time t. **The property of heat diffusion process states that heat tends to diffuse slower at instances with more sparse neighborhood and faster at instances with denser neighborhood. Therefore HKS can intuitively depict the local density of each instance (the first property in our anomaly definition).** Besides, HKS also has the following properties which make it a very lucrative candidate for local density measurement: 1) it is intrinsic to the local manifold structure; 2) it is informative since it contains density information about the whole neighborhood in t scale; and 3) the probabilistic interpretation of heat diffusion can well support the stableness of HKS against small perturbation in the neighborhood.

However, Heat equation is assumed to build on the underlying manifold. But in most applications, the underlying manifold is unknown. In practice, HKS is usually built on isotropic Gaussian kernel (IGK) on observed space. Although graph Laplacian normalizations [6] based on simple IGK on observed space can recover manifold structure to certain extent, non-uniformly sampled instances tend to show unpreserved density distribution on the reconstructed manifold. HKS on IGK will fail to reveal local density faithfully in such reconstructions. Figure 3(a) and 3(b) shows the performance of HKS on anomaly detection with $t = 1$ and $t = 10$ based on simple IGK and random walk graph Laplacian normalization. When $t = 10$ (Figure 3(b)) the heat is extremely easy to dissipate, which blends both local and a few global anomalies into normal instances. Meanwhile many marginal instances of the two normal instance clusters stand out due to the fact that the HKS on IGK fails to show manifold-aware properties. When $t = 1$ (Figure 3(a)), although the short period of heat dissipation has salient effect on global anomalies, HKS on IGK still fails to distinguish local anomalies from normal instances on the boundary area of normal clusters. Therefore an alternative way is indispensable to build better manifold-aware affinity matrix. One of the most preferable candidates is anisotropic Gaussian kernel (AGK) [31] [32].

3. ANISOTROPIC GAUSSIAN KERNEL

In this section we integrate anisotropic Gaussian kernel (AGK) [31] into HKS to achieve better manifold reconstruction. In Figure 4 we can see the 70 nearest neighbors of red instance when using IGK (Figure 4(a)) and AGK (Figure 4(b)), which shows that the intra-manifold distances are much shorter than the inter-manifold by using AGK. To further support this idea, in Figure 3(c) and 3(d) we show that anomaly detection can directly benefit from the use of AGK. In Figure 3(d) with $t = 10$, the global anomalies are highlighted even though the local anomalies are latent (compared with Figure 3(b)). This is because if the manifold is well reconstructed, global anomalies should be separated far away from normal instances even with large t scale. Furthermore, in the small scope of $t = 1$ (Figure 3(c)), both local and global anomalies can be detected, which illustrates that with the support from AGK, HKS is capable of revealing the density information of the intrinsic manifold structure.

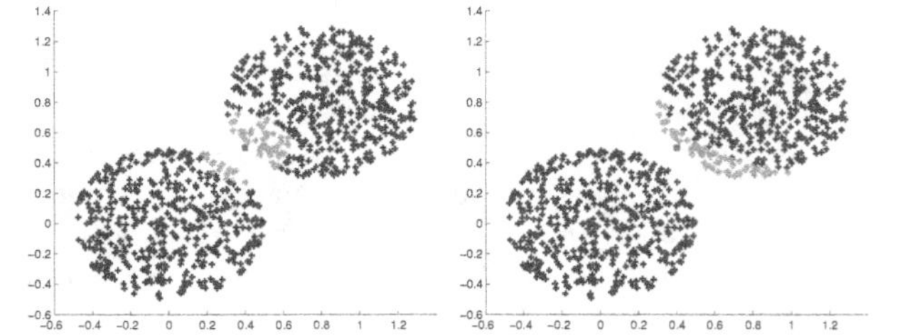

(a) (b)

Figure 4: 70 nearest neighbors (in green) of red instance on IGK (a) and AGK (b), which shows that AGK has better manifold-aware property than IGK.

In the rest of this section we briefly introduce AGK on the observed space Y that approximates the isotropic Gaussian kernel on the underlying manifold X. The idea is to approximate the Euclidean distance between instances $x^{(j)}$ in the manifold space X using covariance matrix $C = JJ^T$ where J is the Jacobian matrix [31] and the instances $y_j = f(x_j)$ in the observable space Y. Let x, ϵ be two instances in the manifold space X and $y = f(x)$, $\eta = f(\epsilon)$ be their mapping to the observable space Y. Let $g : Y \to X$ be the inverse mapping of $f : X \to Y$, that is, $g(f(x)) = x$ and $f(g(y)) = y$, $\forall x \in X$, $\forall y \in Y$. Expanding the functions $x = g(y)$ in a Taylor series at the instance y gives

$$\begin{aligned}\epsilon_i &= x_i + \Sigma_j g_{i(j)}(y)(\eta_j - y_j)\\ &+ \frac{1}{2}\Sigma_{kl} g_{i(kl)}(y)(\eta_k - y_k)(\eta_l - y_l) + O(\| \eta - y \|^3).\end{aligned} \quad (4)$$

where $g_{i(j)} = \frac{\partial g_i}{\partial y_j}$. Therefore,

$$\begin{aligned}\|\epsilon - x \|^2 &= \Sigma_{ijk} g_{i(j)}(y) g_{i(k)}(y)(\eta_j - y_j)(\eta_k - y_k)\\ &+ \frac{1}{2}\Sigma_{ijkl} g_{i(j)}(y) g_{i(kl)}(y)(\eta_j - y_j)(\eta_k - y_k)(\eta_l - y_l) \quad (5)\\ &+ O(\| \eta - y \|^4).\end{aligned}$$

A similar expansion can be built at instance η and the average of these two equations can be produced as

$$\begin{aligned}&\| \epsilon - x \|^2 =\\ &\frac{1}{2}(\eta - y)^T[(JJ^T)^{-1}(y) + (JJ^T)^{-1}(\eta)](\eta - y) \quad (6)\\ &+ O(\| \eta - y \|^4),\end{aligned}$$

given that the Jacobian of the inverse g is the inverse of the Jacobian J (a detailed description of calculation can be referred to [31]). So we can construct the anisotropic Gaussian kernel

$$AGK(y_i, y_j) = e^{\{-\frac{\|J^{-1}(y_i)(y_i - y_j)\|^2 + \|J^{-1}(y_j)(y_j - y_i)\|^2}{\sigma^2}\}}, \quad (7)$$

where $i, j = 1, ..., N$.

AGK has the desired attributes that it is separable, and its first (nontrivial) eigenfunctions are monotonic functions of the independent parameters [32]. It also has been proved that the eigenvectors of AGK reveal the independent components [31]. HKS, built on such approximation, can better capture the manifold structure of data as shown in Figure 3(c) and 3(d), which is difficult or even impossible to achieve by using IGK or other similar techniques.

4. LOCAL ANOMALY DESCRIPTOR

Although HKS on AGK has the capability to offer desirable local density information, it is of importance to select the right time scaling parameter t, which provides a trade-off between the effects of local and global information. However, it is hard to get the "best of both worlds" with single setting for this parameter. Even with better manifold reconstruction, if t is large the heat is still easy to dissipate regardless of normal instances or local anomalies, although not for global anomalies, which is shown in Figure 3(d). This is because with large t scale, the distance between local anomalies and the normal instances around them would still be close. So local anomalies cannot retain their heat. On the other hand, if t is small, the heat diffusion runs for only a short period of time, and the resulting anomalousness are usefully local, but almost carry the same value for instances with similar density inside a very restrained neighborhood, which is the major reason why it sometimes assimilates local anomalies into some normal instances. In Figure 3(c) we can see HKS assigns similar scores to the local anomalies and some of the boundary normal instances. Intuitively speaking, HKS on AGK still fails to take the amount of similar instances into account with off-the-sweet-spot t setting.

In order to handle the above problem, we propose to use the umbrella operator [35] [8] to consider the quantity of similar instances in neighborhood by bridging the gap between global and local properties. The main motivation for using this operator is to compute the average difference between a point (x_i) and its k neighbors ($nb(i, k)$).

$$\Delta x_i = \sum_{x_j \in nb(x_i, k)} W_{i,j}(x_j - x_i), \quad (8)$$

where $W_{i,j}$ is the weight between x_i and x_j. If we use $AGK(i, j)$ for $W_{i,j}$, then we may define the Local Anomaly Descriptor (LAD) for a point i as follows:

$$LAD(i) = HKS_t(i) - \frac{1}{k}\Sigma_{j \in nb(i,k)} HKS_t(j) \cdot AGK(i, j). \quad (9)$$

The geometric meaning of LAD is illustrated in Figure 5 where we measure the difference between a single $HKS_t(i)$ and its neighborhood's average $HKS_t(j)$ value. Note that the heat kernel signature value is always positive and it means the degree of global anomaly level and thus $LAD(i)$ indicate the level of both global and local properties.

If an instance is globally anomalous, its HKS would be already high enough to discriminate itself to the other instances. While it is locally anomalous, its HKS is likely to be similar to some normal instances' with similarly sparse

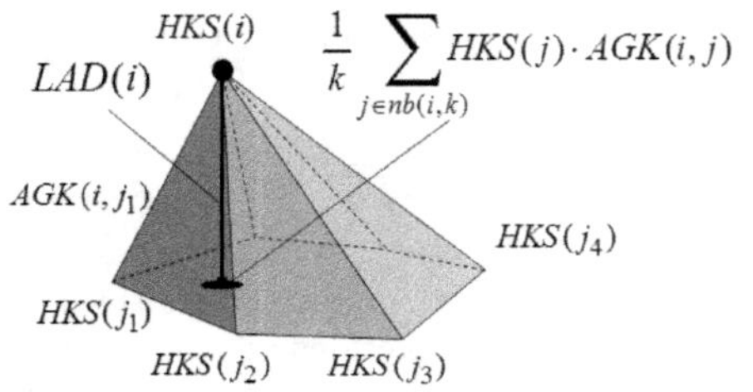

Figure 5: Illustration of Local Anomaly Descriptor which calculates weighted average of neighbor differences. It is one of the ways taking into consideration the neighborhood structures [35].

neighborhood. However, the amount of similar instances, if it is taken into account, can serve to recognize the local anomalies from normal instances. Since local anomaly only has a small amount of neighbors with close HKS, but normal instances, on the other hand, have more such neighbors. **LAD has a very lucrative property in considering the amount of similar instances (the second property in our anomaly definition): with similar intra-cluster density, AGK tends to assign larger affinity value to two instances inside a larger manifold/cluster, and less value to those inside a smaller manifold/cluster, and much less value to those not inside the same manifold/cluster [31].** So even though k is not large enough to include the whole appropriate neighborhood, LAD can still capture the information related to the amount of similar instances.

The benefits of LAD in comparison with HKS can be seen in Figure 3(e), which shows the LAD score of synthetic dataset (Figure 1(a)). Note that HKS with AGK possesses good global properties for long enough time ($t = 10$ in Figure 3(d)) and good local properties for small time ($t = 1$ in Figure 3(c)), but not both. Nevertheless, Figure 3(e) shows that our proposed LAD has a penetrating awareness on both global and local anomalies primarily because of the power of our proposed umbrella operator.

We now justify the LAD utility by briefly documenting its theoretic connections with a few existing methods, which also lays a solid foundation for LAD's attractive properties in practical use.

Biharmonic Operator. HKS itself is directly derived from the Laplace operator and its eigen-decomposition, so that HKS is intrinsically a second-order property relevant to the Laplace's equation. The aforementioned derivation of LAD can be intuitively related to the biharmonic process, because the Laplace operator is essentially applied twice (to compute both HKS and its umbrella operator of HKS). It provides a good balance in the sense that it decays slowly in small cluster around the source instance and fast enough to be structurally inherent in dense areas. This specific "balancing" is intimately derived from the biharmonic equation with properties such as local support, global informative, and shape-aware [17].

Signal Processing. LAD also has strong connection to signal processing . In lowpass filtering, the divergence of a sample from its average neighborhood is the easiest way to pinpoint those inconsistent instances if the desired signal has significant high frequency content. As in traditional signal processing [35], it is possible for LAD to quantify the frequency response by computing an adjoining sum of the Laplacian operator in its immediate vicinity. As a result, this enables LAD to distinguish between normal instances and inconsistent instances (anomalies) with greater precision.

kNN-based Approaches. kNN-based methods [4] [7] [39] approach local density for each instance using its neighborhood information. Like LAD, they require scaling parameters to capture a reasonably large neighborhood, and the density information is based on this prescribed local region. However, kNN-based methods has strictly local context in that they simply fix the neighborhood size with k. In contrast, LAD employs locally adaptive neighborhood size directly benefited from the physics-inspired properties of heat diffusion. Moreover, Euclidean distance in kNN-based methods is a pair-wise local quantity, while heat kernel used in LAD considers all the possible paths between two instances within time t, therefore LAD is more stable than kNN-based methods.

Attribute-based Approaches. Attribute-based methods [19] [20] [36] try to compute local density by adding up a sequence of values from an attribute-based function [36], equivalent to a kernel density function such as heat kernel. The global instance distribution is based on each attribute and how deviated each instance is from the other instances in that specific attribute, which indeed is more informative than kNN-based approaches. However, the strong emphasis on attribute distribution along its dimension is also a "double-sided sword": on the one hand it is much faster without any distance calculation, on the other hand, such distribution based on attributes still fails to consider local anomalies.

Diffusion-based Clustering. Some recent research [30] [29] [15] proposed the unified probabilistic clustering approach based on diffusion map. By integrating all time scales of kernel function into one single term, this kind of techniques completely removes the time scaling parameter of diffusion dissipation, therefore it has the built-in robustness to data perturbation and scaling parameter modification [15]. However, as a side-effect, this process of "integration" assimilates local anomalous instances into normal instance clusters since the excessive-diffusion tends to connect everything together. LAD, in sharp contrast, is built upon kernel function with small time scale and weighted umbrella operator instead of integrating all scales together. Therefore it avoids the above-mentioned excessive-connection problem.

5. ALGORITHMIC FRAMEWORK

After investigating some attractive properties of LAD, it now sets a stage for us to introduce a novel anomaly detection algorithm, which is sensitive to both global and local anomalies. Let X be a matrix of size $n \times m$, where n is the number of instances and m the number of dimensions, our framework is detailed in Algorithm 1. This algorithm undergoes a kind of data warping process by using AGK (Step 1) and Laplacian Random Walk normalization (Step 2). Then we perform the eigen-decomposition (Step 3) and construct HKS for each instance (Step 4). Equation 9 is used as the last step to compute Local Anomaly Descriptor for the final measurement of anomalousness.

In Step 4, we adopt the notation in [10] by normalizing the time scale $t \leftarrow t/(2\lambda_1)$ to achieve scale invariance. Henceforth, with little abuse of notation, heat diffusion time in

Algorithm 1: LocalAnomalyDescriptor(X, σ, t, k)

Input: Input data $X \in R^{n \times m}$; σ the Gaussian scaling parameter; t the time scaling parameter; k the neighborhood size

Output: LAD score for each instance

1 Construct anisotropic Gaussian kernel W using Equation 7 and σ;
2 Construct Laplacian random walk normalization on W ;
3 Compute generalized eigenvectors $\psi(i)$ and corresponding eigenvalues λ_i, $i = 1, 2, ..., n$. ;
4 Construct Heat Kernel Signature in time scale t using Equation 3 ;
5 Compute Local Anomaly Descriptor using Equation 9 with Heat Kernel Signature and anisotropic Gaussian kernel in the k neighborhood for each instance ;

our paper will actually denote $t/(2\lambda_i)$, where λ_i is the first non-trivial eigenvalue.

Regarding computational complexity, eigen-decomposition (Step 3) is the most time-consuming step, which will dominate our computation. There are many iterative methods to conduct eigenvalue decomposition, but in general finding the eigenvalues reduces to matrix multiplication by computing a symbolic determinant, which gives a running time of $O(n^3 + n^2 log^2 n)$ [24]. An alternative way of estimating the heat kernel $K_t = e^{-1 L_{rw}} D^{-1}$ is to use a partial sum of infinite series with

$$e^{-tL_{rw}} = \Sigma_{i=0}^{\infty} \frac{(-tL_{rw})^i}{i!}. \qquad (10)$$

This method would be especially attractive for small values of t, since only a few terms would be needed to obtain an accurate estimation of $e^{-tL_{rw}}$ [2].

6. EXPERIMENTAL ANALYSIS

6.1 Experimental Setup

Dataset. To demonstrate the performance of our proposed method, we evaluate our algorithm on nine UCI benchmark datasets including three medical datasets (WDBC, Pima, and Arrhythmia), three biological datasets (Ecoli, Yeast, and Abalone), and three physics datasets (Glass, Ionosphere, and Magic), whose statistics are summarized in Table 1. All these data have been popularly used in anomaly detection research (related references for each dataset are listed in Table 1). Anomalies in some of the datasets (WDBC, Pima, Arrhythmia, etc.), although carrying a large number of instances, have scattered and sparse distribution (Figure 6). Therefore the anomalies in these datasets should be treated as a combination of many small anomalous clusters instead of one or a few normal clusters with high density [7] [23], which has nothing inconsistent with our definition about anomaly in Section 1.2. Such diverse combination of data is intended for our comprehensive studies. In the data preprocessing step, all nominal (including binary) attributes or attributes with missing value are removed.

Baselines. We choose six states of the art competitors in three categories to show the outstanding performance of our proposed LAD. For kNN-based algorithms, we choose Local Outlier Detection (LOF) [4] and Local Correlation Integral (LOCI) [25]. Specially, LOCI provides an automatic,

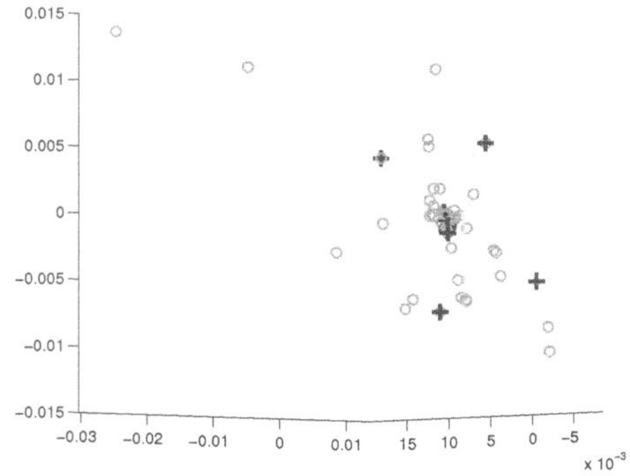

Figure 6: Anomalous instances in green (37.3%) are more scattered and sparse than normal instances in blue (62.7%) in WDBC dataset (shown with the first three eigenvectors). Therefore these anomalies, although have a large amount of instances, should be treated as many small abnormal clusters.

data-dictated cut-off to determine whether an instance is an anomaly based on probabilistic reasoning. For attribute-based methods, we include IForest [19] and Mass [36]. For manifold-based methods, we refer readers to two different manifold-based techniques in [1] including locally linear embeddings (LLE), and isometric feature mapping (ISM), followed by LOF to obtain anomalousness measurement.

Evaluation Metrics. Since we have the ground truth of labels for each data, we compare our anomaly detection results with labels. Due to space limitation, AUC (Area under Receiver Operating Characteristics Curve) is used as the only listed evaluation metric in this paper because it is commonly used to evaluate anomaly detectors and it is cut-off independent. Detailed definition of AUC can be referred to [21]. In our paper we also show that our LAD has the most robust and stable performance for all the datasets by using macro paired t-tests [41] against each competitor respectively. Note that a score of macro paired t-tests (p-value) should be no more than 0.05 to be considered statistically significant.

Parameters. Our proposed algorithm has three scaling parameters, namely Gaussian kernel scaling parameter σ, time scaling parameter t, and the size of neighborhood k. We set $t = 1$ which makes our proposed LAD capable of depicting local minimum density. As the default setting for most of the other algorithms, we fix $\sigma = 1$ and $k = 10$ for the experiments in Table 2 and 3. But the LAD robustness to the change of these two parameters will be shown in Figure 7. For LOF we try $k = 10, 25, 50$ for all the datasets. Since in practice, single setting of k for LOF may introduce statistical errors [25]. As for LOCI, we set $k = 10$ and $k = 50$ due to its instinctive stability on k which comes from a multi-granularity deviation factor [25]. Radius coefficient is set as $\alpha = 0.5$ in LOCI, which is the same to their paper [25]. As for IForest, even though in their paper [19] Liu et al. claimed that a small sub-sampling size ρ provides high AUC and a further increase of ρ is not necessary, in practice when ρ increases, anomalies in-between data groups will become more detectable by IForest [18]. To conduct safe and fair comparison, we set $\rho = 4000$ and the number of trees $nt = 100$ since they are the recommended settings in the authors' technical report [18]. Similarly, in Mass we

Table 1: Statistics of our evaluation datasets.

	Dataset	# Instance	# Attribute	% Anomalies(classes)	References
1	WDBC	569	29	37.3% (malignant)	[39] [23]
2	Pima	768	8	34.9% (positives)	[19] [23]
3	Arrhythmia	452	279	45.0% (abnormal)	[7] [19] [23]
4	Ecoli	336	7	2.7% (omL,imL and imS)	[13] [23]
5	Yeast	1484	8	3.7% (vac, pox and erl)	[23] [27]
6	Abalone	4177	7	8.0% ($age < 5$ or > 15)	[23] [26]
7	Glass	214	9	4.2% (tableware)	[13] [23]
8	Ionosphere	351	34	35.9% (bad)	[19] [13] [23]
9	Magic	19020	10	35.2% (hadron)	[23]

Table 2: Comparison of LAD and other four popular methods (with different k for LOF and LOCI) on nine datasets using AUC metrics. The bold-faced numbers indicate the best method on a particular dataset; the numbers in parentheses indicate the ranks of our LAD. Average is the average of performance across all the datasets respectively. A $*$ indicates a p-value of 5% or lower and $**$ indicates a p-value of 1% or lower in the statistical significance test for performance comparison w.r.t. LAD.

Dataset	LOF(k=10)	LOF(k=25)	LOF(k=50)	LOCI(k=10)	LOCI(k=50)	Mass	IForest	LAD
WDBC	0.5874	0.6192	0.7784	0.7573	0.8119	0.7974	0.7760	**0.8864** (1)
Pima	0.4847	0.5270	0.6003	0.5946	0.6089	0.5812	0.6630	**0.6936** (1)
Arrhythmia	0.7419	0.7547	0.7482	0.7482	0.7483	0.6363	0.7456	**0.7558** (1)
Ecoli	0.8260	0.8614	0.8454	0.8641	0.8549	0.7699	**0.8754**	0.8692 (2)
Yeast	0.4159	**0.6253**	0.5986	0.6076	0.6035	0.5712	0.6159	0.6183 (2)
Abalone	0.5724	0.6056	0.6525	0.6932	0.7058	0.6923	**0.7466**	0.7398 (2)
Glass	0.7474	0.7008	0.7528	0.7480	0.7593	**0.8922**	0.6933	0.8612 (2)
Ionosphere	0.9064	0.8709	0.7982	0.8512	0.7923	0.8269	0.8467	**0.9240** (1)
Magic	0.6420	0.6804	0.6970	0.5672	0.6825	0.6984	0.7506	**0.7516** (1)
Average	0.6582^{**}	0.6939^{**}	0.7190^{**}	0.7146^{**}	0.7297^{**}	0.7184^{**}	0.7459^{*}	**0.7889** (1)

set the number of mass estimation $ne = 100$ and the sub-sampling size as $\#instance$ of dataset. On the other hand, IForest and Mass are based on random sub-sampling which makes their performance very unstable. In an attempt to get more stable results, for each dataset we run 30 times for both IForest and Mass and use the average AUC in the final comparison. For LLE and ISM, we conduct experiments on size of neighborhood $k = 10$, 50 and 100 with the best number of dimensions d in $[2, 30]$ respectively, in order to compare their performance and robustness in k.

6.2 Algorithm Performance Comparison

In this section we evaluate our proposed LAD and the other six anomaly detection algorithms. Table 2 documents the anomaly detection comparison result (in AUC and p-value) of LAD and other four popular algorithms: LOF, LOCI, Mass, and IForest. While the manifold-based methods comparison including LLE and ISM (all followed by LOF), and our proposed LAD are also listed in Table 3.

In Table 2 LAD shows the best average performance (0.7889) across all the datasets. For each dataset LAD has the best or very close to the best performance. Specifically, LAD is the top-ranked one for all the three medical datasets and has almost unbeatable performance for the three physics datasets. Although LAD ranks the second among all the methods on the three biological datasets. The AUC score are actually very close to the best one (no more than 0.008 difference in AUC). As for Glass dataset the AUC score of our LAD (0.8612) is still comparable to the best one (0.8922) by Mass, meanwhile beats the third best (LOCI with $k = 50$) for more than 13%. IForest shows the second best (0.7459) average performance of real datasets, which supports the argument that it is able to take both global and local contexts into consideration [18]. This is different from kNN-based methods (LOF and LOCI) which only concern with instance-wise local context. Compared with LOF, LOCI performs robustly when k varies. It ranks the third (0.7297) when $k = 50$ and fifth (0.7146) when $k = 10$. This moderately stable performance comes from the built-in concept of a multi-granularity deviation factor. LOF, although has the third best score (0.7190) when $k = 50$, shows seriously unstable performance as k changes, which can be explained as follows: LOF is based on a direct normalization of anomaly scores for a very limited neighborhood. Although Mass (0.7184) only keeps the fourth record, it has the fastest computation speed compared with the other competitors, especially LAD.

Table 3 shows performance of three different manifold-based algorithms. Generally, LAD evidently outperforms the other methods with average AUC 0.7889. In terms of stability, although LLE has similar average score with $k = 10$, 50 and 100, it shows fluctuation for some datasets especially Ecoli, Glass and Ionosphere. Part of the reason comes from that LLE assumes the data manifold is sufficiently smooth and densely sampled that it is locally approximately linear, while this is not the true story for many real world datasets. Similarly, ISM's AUC score varies as k changes in several datasets (Ecoli, Yeast, Glass etc.). It is because ISM is highly vulnerable to the local data perturbation since the embedding given by the ISM tends to recovers the geodesic distances between points on the man-

Table 3: Comparison of LAD and other two manifold-based methods (with different k) on nine datasets using AUC metrics. The bold-faced numbers indicate the best method on a particular dataset; the numbers in parentheses indicate the ranks of our LAD. Average is the average of performance across all the datasets respectively. A $**$ indicates a p-value of 1% or lower in the statistical significance test w.r.t. LAD.

Dataset	LLE(k=10)	LLE(k=50)	LLE(k=100)	ISM(k=10)	ISM(k=50)	ISM(k=100)	LAD
WDBC	0.7572	0.7561	0.8517	0.5903	0.6359	0.6942	**0.8864** (1)
Pima	0.5183	0.5815	0.6270	0.5234	0.5925	0.5546	**0.6936** (1)
Arrhythmia	0.5564	0.6174	0.6234	0.5694	0.5878	0.6184	**0.7558** (1)
Ecoli	**0.9205**	0.8709	0.5739	0.6259	0.7934	0.8406	0.8692 (3)
Yeast	0.5994	0.6289	**0.6464**	0.4924	0.5802	0.5965	0.6183 (3)
Abalone	0.5764	0.6054	0.6039	0.5520	0.6637	0.6513	**0.7398** (1)
Glass	0.8385	0.6797	0.7100	0.5453	0.6607	0.7957	**0.8612** (1)
Ionosphere	0.6125	0.4526	0.4731	0.4444	0.4188	0.4837	**0.9240** (1)
Magic	0.5638	0.6152	0.6010	0.5742	0.5981	0.6328	**0.7516** (1)
Average	0.6603^{**}	0.6453^{**}	0.6344^{**}	0.5464^{**}	0.6146^{**}	0.6520^{**}	**0.7889** (1)

ifold, which is very locally sensitive compared with random walk [16] [37].

To systematically manifest the robustness of our proposed LAD on different neighborhood size k and Gaussian scaling parameter σ, we test our algorithm respectively on a series of k and σ on seven small datasets: WDBC, Pima, Arrhythmia, Ecoli, Yeast, Glass, and Ionosphere due to limited space, and also with the reason that in theory, datasets with smaller number of instances are more sensitive to the change of k and σ. Therefore these seven datasets are the more effective choices to show whether our LAD is robust to these two parameters. For k our test range is in $[10, 100]$. As for σ, the test range is in $[0.1, 8]$, with 0.05 as step size between 0.1 to 1 and 0.5 as step size between 1 to 8. From Figure 7(a) we can see that our new LAD algorithm has more stable performance than LOF, LLE and ISM on different k (shown in Table 2 and Table 3). Similarly, Figure 7(b) shows that our proposed LAD retains certain level of robustness as σ changes. The stability of LAD has an inherent relationship with diffusion maps and random walk.

As for the macro paired t-tests across all the datasets, compared with LOF, LOCI, Mass, LLE and ISM respectively, LAD has extremely small p-value (less than 1%). Compared with IForest, LAD has p-value less than 5%. This, once again, proves that our LAD has the most stable average performance. Overall, LAD outperforms the selected kNN-based, attribute-based and manifold-based algorithms in that it is more intrinsic, informative, and manifold-aware.

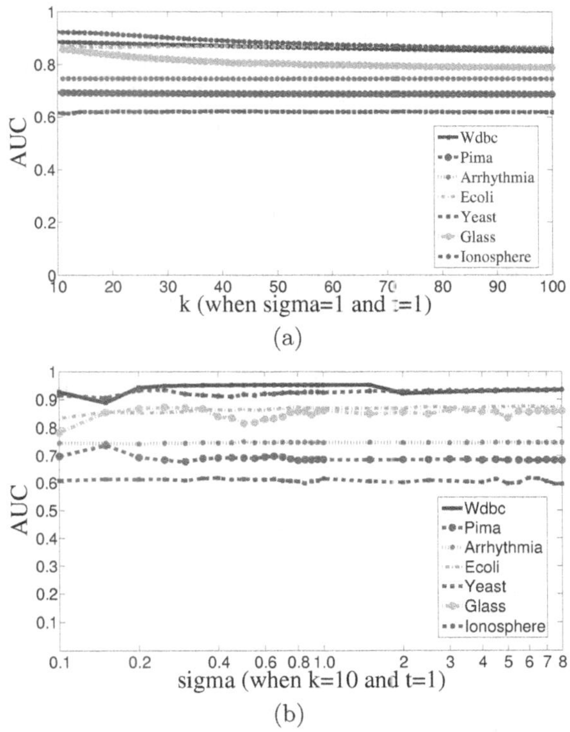

Figure 7: LAD robustness on different k and σ.

7. CONCLUSION

This paper has documented an original unsupervised anomaly detection algorithm, called Local Anomaly Descriptor (LAD), which is based on the physics-inspired diffusion space and weighted umbrella operator. Compared with the existing algorithms, our proposed LAD has demonstrated many important properties such as intrinsic, informative to local density, and stable to small parameter perturbation. Together with its more manifold-aware property for the goal of anomaly detection, we expect it to be useful for any type of data distribution. Nonetheless, much more extensive experiments are still required to validate this conjecture, which is part of our near-future research. Another direction is to investigate the possible connection with global structure and pattern mining such as clustering and feature classification.

8. ACKNOWLEDGEMENTS

We gratefully thank all the anonymous reviewers for constructive suggestions toward paper improvement. This research is supported in part by NSF grants IIS-0949467, IIS-1047715, and IIS-1049448. It is also supported by United States Department of Energy, Grant No. DE-SC0003361, funded through the American Recovery and Reinvestment Act of 2009. In addition, this project is also supported in part by DOE Systems Biology Knowledgebase (DE-AC02-98CH10886).

9. REFERENCES

[1] A. Agovic, A. Banerjee, A. R. Ganguly, and V. Protopopescu. Anomaly detection in transportation corridors using manifold embedding. *the 1st*

International Workshop on Knowledge Discovery from Sensor Data, 2007.

[2] R. Badeau, B. David, and G. Richard. Fast approximated power iteration subspace tracking. *IEEE Signal Processing*, pages 2931–2941, 2005.

[3] G. Blanchard, G. Lee, and C. Scott. Semi-supervised novelty detection. *JMLR*, 11:2973–3009, 2010.

[4] M. M. Breunig, H. P. Kriegel, R. T. Ng, and J. Sander. Lof: identifying density-based local outliers. *ACM SIGMOD*, pages 93–104, 2000.

[5] V. Chandola, A. Banerjee, and V. Kumar. Anomaly detection: a survey. *ACM Computing Surveys*, 2009.

[6] R. R. Coifman and S. Lafon. Diffusion maps. *Applied and Computational Harmonic Analysis*, 21(1):5–30, 2006.

[7] T. de Vires, S. Chawla, and M. Houle. Finding local anomalies in very highdimensional space. *IEEE ICDM*, pages 128–137, 2010.

[8] M. Desbrun, M. Meyer, P. Schrder, and A. Barr. Implicit fairing of arbitrary meshes using diffusion and curvature flow. *ACM SIGGRAPH*.

[9] J. Gao, H. Cheng, and P. N. Tan. Semi-supervised outlier detection. *ACM SAC*, pages 635–636, 2006.

[10] F. Goes, S. Goldenstein, and L. Velho. A hierarchical segmentation of articulated bodies. *Symposium on Geometry*, 2008.

[11] A. Grigoryan. Estimates of heat kernels on riemannian manifolds. *ICMS*, pages 140–225, 1999.

[12] D. Hawkins. *Identification of outliers*. Chapman and Hall, London, 1980.

[13] K. Hempstalk, E. Frank, and I. H. Witten. One-class classification by combining density and class probability estimation. *European Conference on Machine Learning and Knowledge Discovery in Databases*, 2008.

[14] E. Hsu. Stochastic analysis on manifolds. *Graduate Studies in Mathematics*, 2002.

[15] H. Huang, S. Yoo, H. Qin, and D. Yu. A robust clustering algorithm based on aggregated heat kernel mapping. *IEEE ICDM*, pages 270–279, 2011.

[16] S. Lafon, Y. Keller, and R. R. Coifman. Data fusion and multi-cue data matching by diffusion maps. *IEEE TPAMI*, 28(11):1784–1797, 2006.

[17] Y. Lipman, R. Rustamov, and T. Funkhouser. Biharmonic distance. *ACM Transactions on Graphics*, 2010.

[18] F. T. Liu and K. M. Ting. Can isolation-based anomaly detectors handle arbitrary multi-modal patterns in data? *Technical Report*, 2010.

[19] F. T. Liu, K. M. Ting, and Z. H. Zhou. Isolation forest. *IEEE ICDM*, pages 413–422, 2008.

[20] F. T. Liu, K. M. Ting, and Z. H. Zhou. Isolation-based anomaly detection. *ACM TKDD*, 2011.

[21] C. Marzban. A comment on the roc curve and the area under it as performance measures. *Technical Report*, 2004.

[22] M. Meila and J. Shi. A random walks view of spectral segmentation. *the 8th International Workshop on Artificial Intelligence and Statistics*, 2001.

[23] K. Noto, C. E. Brodley, and D. Slonim. Anomaly detection using an ensemble of feature models. *IEEE ICDM*, 2010.

[24] V. Y. Pan and Z. Q. Chen. The complexity of the matrix eigenproblem. *ACM STOC*, pages 507–516, 1999.

[25] S. Papadimitriou, H. Kitagawa, P. B. Gibbons, and C. Faloutsos. Loci: Fast outlier detection using the local correlation integral. *IEEE ICDE*.

[26] D. Pelleg and A. W. Moore. Active learning for anomaly and rare-category detection. *NIPS'05*, pages 1073–1080, 2005.

[27] C. Plant, C. Bohm, B. Tilg, and C. Baumgartner. Enhancing instance-based classification with local density: a new algorithm for classifying unbalanced biomedical data. *Bioinformatics, Oxford Journals*, pages 981–988, 2010.

[28] B. Pogorelc and M. Gams. Discovery of gait anomalies from motion sensor data. *IEEE ICTAI*, pages 331–336, 2010.

[29] H. Qiu and E. R. Hancock. Clustering and embedding using commute times. *IEEE TPAMI*, 29(11):1873–1890, 2007.

[30] J. W. Richards, P. E. Freeman, A. B. Lee, and C. M. Schafer. Accurate parameter estimation for star formation history in galaxies using sdss spectra. *MNRAS*, pages 1044–1057, 2009.

[31] A. Singer and R. R. Coifman. Non-linear independent component analysis with diffusion maps. *Applied and Computational Harmonic Analysis*, 25(2):226–239, 2008.

[32] A. Singer and R. R. Coifman. Anisotropic diffusion on sub-manifolds with application to earth structure classification. *Technical Report*, 2011.

[33] J. Sun, M. Ovsjanikov, and L. Guibas. A concise and provably informative multi-scale signature based on heat diffusion. *SGP*, 2009.

[34] Z. Syed and I. Rubinfeld. Unsupervised risk stratification in clinical datasets: Identifying patients at risk of rare outcomes. *ICML*, pages 1023–1030, 2010.

[35] G. Taubin. A signal processing approach to fair surface design. *ACM SIGGRAPH*, 1995.

[36] K. M. Ting, G. T. Zhou, F. T. Liu, and J. S. Tan. Mass estimation and its applications. *ACM KDD*, 2010.

[37] L. van der Maaten, E. Postma, and J. van der Herik. Dimensionality reduction: A comparative review. *Technical report*, 2009.

[38] M. Wu and J. Ye. A small sphere and large margin approach for novelty detection using training data with outliers. *IEEE TPAMI*, 31(11):2088–2092, 2009.

[39] K. Zhang, M. Hutter, and H. Jin. A new local distance-based outlier detection approach for scattered real-world data. *Advances in Knowledge Discovery and Data Mining*, pages 813–822, 2009.

[40] X. Zhu, X. Wu, and C. Zhang. Vague one-class learning for data streams. *IEEE ICDM*, pages 657–666, 2009.

[41] D. W. Zimmerman. A note on interpretation of the paired-samples t test. *Journal of Educational and Behavioral Statistics*, 22(3):349–360, 1997.

Fast and Reliable Anomaly Detection in Categorical Data

Leman Akoglu
CMU, SCS
5000 Forbes Ave
Pittsburgh PA 15213
lakoglu@cs.cmu.edu

Hanghang Tong
IBM T. J. Watson
19 Skyline Drive
Hawthorne, NY 10532
htong@us.ibm.com

Jilles Vreeken
University of Antwerp
Middelheimlaan 1
B2020 Antwerp, Belgium
jilles.vreeken@ua.ac.be

Christos Faloutsos
CMU, SCS
5000 Forbes Ave
Pittsburgh PA 15213
christos@cs.cmu.edu

ABSTRACT

Spotting anomalies in large multi-dimensional databases is a crucial task with many applications in finance, health care, security, etc. We introduce COMPREX, a new approach for identifying anomalies using pattern-based compression. Informally, our method finds a collection of dictionaries that describe the *norm* of a database succinctly, and subsequently flags those points dissimilar to the norm—with high compression cost—as anomalies.

Our approach exhibits four key features: 1) it is *parameter-free*; it builds dictionaries directly from data, and requires no user-specified parameters such as distance functions or density and similarity thresholds, 2) it is *general*; we show it works for a broad range of complex databases, including graph, image and relational databases that may contain both categorical and numerical features, 3) it is *scalable*; its running time grows linearly with respect to both database size as well as number of dimensions, and 4) it is *effective*; experiments on a broad range of datasets show large improvements in both compression, as well as precision in anomaly detection, outperforming its state-of-the-art competitors.

Categories and Subject Descriptors

H.2.8 [**Database Applications**]: Data mining; E.4 [**Coding and Information Theory**]: Data compaction and compression

Keywords

anomaly detection, categorical data, data encoding

1. INTRODUCTION

Detecting anomalies and irregularities in data is an important task, and numerous applications exist where anomaly detection is vital, e.g. detecting network intrusion, credit card fraud, insurance claim fraud, and so on. In addition to revealing suspicious behavior, anomaly detection is useful for spotting rare events such as rare diseases in medicine, in addition to data cleaning and filtering. Finding anomalies, however, is a difficult task, in particular for complex multi-dimensional databases.

In this work, we address the problem of anomaly detection in multi-dimensional categorical databases using pattern-based compression. Compression-based techniques have been explored mostly in communications theory, for reduced transmission cost and increased throughput and in databases, for reduced storage cost and increased query performance. Here, we improve over recent work that identified compression as a natural tool for spotting anomalies [22]. Simply put, we define the *norm* by the patterns that compress the data well. Then, any data point that can not be compressed well is said not to comply with the norm, and thus is *abnormal*.

The heart of our method, COMPREX, is to use a set of dictionaries to encode a database. We exploit correlations between the features in the database, grouping those with high information gain, and build dictionaries (also look-up tables or code tables [25]) for each group of strongly interacting features. Informally, these dictionaries capture the data distribution in terms of patterns; the more often a pattern occurs, the shorter its encoded length. The goal is to find the optimal set of dictionaries that yield the minimal lossless compression, and then spot tuples with long encoded lengths.

Dictionary based compression has been shown to be highly effective for anomaly detection in [22], which employs the KRIMP itemset-based compressor introduced by [21]. Besides high performance, it allows for characterization: one can easily inspect how tuples are encoded, and hence why one is deemed an anomaly. In this paper we show that our COMPREX can *do better*, yielding *both* better compression (and relatedly, higher detection accuracy) *as well as* lower running time.

The intuition behind our method achieving better compression is that it uses *multiple* code tables to describe the data, whereas KRIMP builds a *single* code table. As such, our method can better exploit correlations between *groups* of features, as by doing away with uncorrelated features it can locally assign codes more effectively. Moreover, we build code tables directly from data in a bottom-up fashion, instead of filtering very large collections of pre-mined candidate patterns, which becomes exponentially costly with increasing database dimension, i.e. number of features.

Furthermore, by not requiring the user to provide a collection of candidate itemsets, nor a minimal support threshold, COMPREX is parameter free in both theory and practice. We employ the Minimum Description Length principle to automatically decide the number of feature groups, which features to group, what patterns to include in the code tables, as well as to point out anomalies. In contrast, most existing anomaly detection methods have several parameters, such as the choice of a similarity function, density or distance thresholds, number of nearest neighbors, etc.

In a nutshell, we improve over the state of the art by encoding data using multiple code tables, instead of one—allowing us to better grasp strongly interacting features. Moreover, we build our models directly from data—avoiding the expensive step of mining and filtering large collections of candidate patterns.

CIKM'12, October 29–November 2, 2012, Maui, HI, USA.

Experiments show the resulting models obtain high performance in anomaly detection, improving greatly over the state of the art for categorical data. We further show COMPREX is very generally applicable; after discretization it matches the state of the art for numerical data, and correctly identifies anomalies both in translated large graphs and image data.

2. PRELIMINARIES AND BACKGROUND

In this section, we give the preliminaries and notation, and introduce basic concepts used throughout the paper.

2.1 Preliminaries

In this paper we consider categorical databases. A database D is a bag of n tuples over a set of m categorical features $\mathcal{F} = \{f_1, \ldots, f_m\}$. Each feature $f \in \mathcal{F}$ has a domain $dom(f)$ of possible values $\{v_1, v_2, \ldots\}$. The number of values $v \in dom(f)$ is the *arity* of f, i.e. $arity(f) = |dom(f)| \in \mathbb{N}$.

The domains are distinct between features. That is, $dom(f_i) \cap dom(f_j) = \emptyset, \forall i \neq j$. The domain of a feature set $F \subseteq \mathcal{F}$ is the Cartesian product of the domains of the individual features $f \in F$, i.e., $dom(F) = \prod_{f \in F} dom(f)$.

A database D is simply a collection of n tuples, where each tuple t is a vector of length m containing a value for each feature in $\mathcal{F}$. As such, D can also be regarded as a n-by-m matrix, where the possible values in a column i are determined by $dom(f_i)$.

An *item* is a feature-value pair $(f = v)$, with $f \subseteq \mathcal{F}$, and $v \in dom(f)$. A itemset is then a pair $(F = v)$, for a set of features $F \subseteq \mathcal{F}$, and $v \in dom(F)$ is a vector of length $|F|$. We typically refer to an itemset as a *pattern*.

A tuple t is said to contain a pattern $(F = v)$, denoted as $p(F = v) \subseteq t$ (or $p \subseteq t$ for short), if for all features $f \in F$, $t_f = v_f$ holds. The support of a pattern $(F = v)$ is the number of tuples in D that contain it: $supp(F = v) = |\{t \in D \mid (F = v) \subseteq t\}|$. Its frequency is then $freq(F = v) = supp(F = v)/|D|$.

Finally, the entropy of a feature set F is defined as

$$H(F) = - \sum_{v \in dom(F)} freq(F = v) \log freq(F = v) \ .$$

All logarithms are to base 2, and by convention, $0 \log 0 = 0$.

2.2 The MDL principle

The Minimum Description Length (MDL) principle [20] is a practical version of Kolmogorov Complexity [16], and can be regarded as model selection based on lossless compression.

Given a set of models $\mathcal{M}$, MDL identifies the best model $M \in \mathcal{M}$ as the one that minimizes

$$L(M) + L(D \mid M) \ ,$$

in which $L(M)$ is the length in bits of the description of the model M, and $L(D \mid M)$ is the length of the description of the data encoded by M. That is, the MDL-optimal model for a database D encodes D most succinctly among all possible models; it provides the best possible lossless compression.

MDL provides us a systematic approach for selecting the model that best balances the complexity of the model and its fit to the data. While models that are overly complex may provide an arbitrarily good fit to the data and thus have low $L(D \mid M)$, they overfit the data, and are penalized with a relatively high $L(M)$. Overly simple models, on the other hand, have very low $L(M)$, but as they fail to identify important structure in D, their corresponding $L(D \mid M)$ tends to be relatively high. As such, the MDL-optimal model provides the best balance between model complexity and goodness of fit.

2.3 Dictionary based compression

To use MDL, we need to define what a model is, how to encode the data with such a model, and how to encode a model.

2.3.1 Data encoding

As models, we will use code tables. A code table is a simple two column table. The first column contains *patterns*, which are ordered descending (1) first by length and (2) second by support. The second column contains the code words $code(p)$ corresponding to each pattern p. An illustrative database with 6 tuples and an example code table for the database is illustrated in Table 1.

Table 1: An illustrative database D and an example code table CT for a set of three features, F={f_1, f_2, f_3}.

Data	*Code Table*			
$f_1 f_2 f_3$	$p(F = v)$	$code(p)$	$usage(p)$	$L(code(p))$
a b x	a b x	0	4	1 bit
a b x	a c	10	2	2 bits
a b x	x	110	1	3 bits
a b x	y	111	1	3 bits
a c x				
a c y				

The code words in the second column of a code table CT are not important: their lengths are. The length of a code word for a pattern depends on the database we want to compress. Intuitively, the more often a pattern occurs in the database, the shorter its code should be. The *usage* of a pattern $p \in CT$ is the number of tuples $t \in D$ which contain p in their *cover*, i.e. have the code of p in their encoding.

The encoding of a tuple t, given a CT, works as follows: the patterns in the first column are scanned in their predefined order to find the first pattern p for which $p \subseteq t$. p is then said to be *used* in the *cover* of t , and the corresponding code word for p in the second column becomes part of the encoding of t. If $t \setminus p \neq \emptyset$, the encoding continues with $t \setminus p$ until t is completely covered, which yields a unique set of patterns that form the *cover* of t.

Given the usages of the patterns in a CT, we can compute the lengths of the code words for the optimal prefix code [20]. Shannon entropy gives the length for the optimal prefix code for p:

$$L(code(p) \mid CT) = -\log \left(\frac{usage(p)}{\sum_{p' \in CT} usage(p')} \right).$$

The number of bits to encode a tuple t is simply the sum of the code lengths of the patterns in its cover, that is,

$$L(t \mid CT) = \sum_{p \in cover(t)} L(code(p) \mid CT).$$

The total length in bits of the encoded database is then the sum of the lengths of the encoded data tuples,

$$L(D \mid CT) = \sum_{t \in D} L(t \mid CT).$$

2.3.2 Model encoding

To find the MDL-optimal compressor, we also need to determine the encoded size of the model, the code table in our case. Clearly, the size of the second column in a given code table CT that contains the prefix code words $code(p)$ is trivial; it is simply the sum of their lengths. For the size of the first column, we need to consider all the singleton items $\mathcal{I}$ contained in the patterns, i.e., $\mathcal{I} = \bigcup_{f \in \mathcal{F}} dom(f)$.

For encoding the patterns in the left hand column we again use an optimal prefix code. We first compute the frequency of their appearance in the first column, and then by Shannon entropy calculate the optimal length of these codes. Specifically, the encoding of the first column in a code table requires $cH(P)$ bits, where c is the total count of singleton items in the patterns $p \in CT$, $H(.)$ denotes the Shannon entropy function, and P is a multinomial random variable with the probability $p_i = \frac{r_i}{c}$ in which r_i is the number of occurrences of singleton item $i \in \mathcal{I}$ in the first column (for the actual items, one could add an ASCII table providing the matching from the prefix codes to the original names. Since all such tables are over $\mathcal{I}$, this only adds an additive constant to the total cost). All in all,

$$L(CT) = \sum_{p \in CT} L(code(p) \mid CT) + \sum_{i \in \mathcal{I}} -r_i \log(p_i).$$

3. PROPOSED METHOD

3.1 Compression with Set of Tables: Theory

In the previous section, we showed how to encode a database D using a *single* code table CT. In fact, this is the approach introduced in [21] to compress transaction databases, employing frequent itemset mining to generate the candidate patterns for the code table. Here, we do not regard transaction data, but regular relational data, where tuples are data points in a multi-dimensional categorical feature space. In this space, some groups of features may be highly correlated; and hence may be compressed well together.

As a result we can *improve* by using multiple code tables—as we can then exploit correlations, and build a separate, probably smaller CT for each highly correlated group of features instead of a single, large CT for all, possibly uncorrelated features. As such, using *multiple*, that is a *set* of code tables, and mining these efficiently (bypassing the costly frequent itemset mining), are two of the main contributions of our work.

Next, we formally introduce the concept of feature partitioning, and give our problem statement.

DEFINITION 1. *A feature partitioning $\mathcal{P} = \{F_1, \ldots, F_k\}$ of a set of features $\mathcal{F}$ is a grouping of $\mathcal{F}$, for which (1) each partition contains one or more features: $\forall F_i \in \mathcal{P} : F_i \neq \emptyset$, (2) all partitions are pairwise disjoint: $\forall i \neq j : F_i \cap F_j = \emptyset$, and (3) every feature belongs to a partition: $\bigcup F_i = \mathcal{F}$.*

FORMAL PROBLEM STATEMENT 1. *Given a set of n data tuples in D over a set of m features in $\mathcal{F}$, find a partitioning $\mathcal{P}$: $\{F_1, F_2, \ldots, F_k\}$ of $\mathcal{F}$ and a set of associated code tables $\mathcal{CT}$: $\{CT_{F_1}, CT_{F_2}, \ldots, CT_{F_k}\}$, such that the total compression cost in bits given below is minimized.*

$$L(\mathcal{P}, \mathcal{CT}, D) = L(\mathcal{P}) + \sum_{F \in \mathcal{P}} L(\pi_F(D) | CT_F) + \sum_{F \in \mathcal{P}} L(CT_F) ,$$

in which $\pi_{F_i}(D)$ is the projection of D on feature subspace F_i.

Note that the number of features m and the number of tuples n are fixed over all models we consider for a D, and hence are a constant additive that we can safely ignore.

3.1.1 Partition encoding

The first term of $L(\mathcal{P}, \mathcal{CT}, D)$ denotes the length of encoding the partitioning, which consists of two parts; encoding (a) the number of partitions and (b) the features per partition.

(a) Encoding the number of partitions: First, we need to encode k, the number of partitions and code tables. For this, we use the MDL-optimal encoding of an integer [12]. The cost for encoding an integer value k is $L^0(k) = \log^\star(k) + \log(c)$, with $c = \sum 2^{-\log(n)} \approx 2.865064$,, and $\log^\star(k) = \log(k) + \log\log(k) + \cdots$ sums over all positive terms. Note that as $\log(c)$ is constant for all models, we ignore it.

(b) Encoding the features per partition: Then, for each feature we have to describe to which partition it belongs. This we do using $m \log(k)$ bits.

In summary, $L(\mathcal{P}) = \log^\star(k) + m\log(k)$.

3.1.2 Data encoding

The second term of $L(\mathcal{P}, \mathcal{CT}, D)$ denotes the cost of encoding the data with the given set of code tables. To do so, each tuple is partitioned according to $\mathcal{P}$, and encoded using the optimal codes in the corresponding code tables following the procedure in §2.3.1.

3.1.3 Model encoding

The last term of $L(\mathcal{P}, \mathcal{CT}, D)$ denotes the model cost, that is the total length of encoding the code tables. Each code table is encoded following the procedure described in §2.3.2.

We note that the number of feature groups k is not a parameter of our method but rather is determined by MDL. In particular, MDL ensures that we will not have two separate code tables for a pair of highly correlated feature groups as it would yield lower data cost to encode them together. On the other hand, combining feature groups may yield larger code tables, that is higher model cost, which may not compensate for the savings from the data cost. In other words, we group features for which the total encoding cost $L(\mathcal{P}, \mathcal{CT}, D)$ is reduced. Basically, we employ MDL to both guide us in finding which features to group, as well as in deciding how many groups we should have.

Also note that compression is a type of statistical method, however, instead of having to choose a prior distribution appropriate for the data (normal, chi-square, etc.) we use a rich model class (code tables) to induce the distribution from the data.

3.2 Mining Set of Code Tables: Algorithm

Having defined the cost function as $L(\mathcal{P}, \mathcal{CT}, D)$, we need an algorithm to search for the best set of code tables $\mathcal{CT}$ for the optimal vertical partitioning $\mathcal{P}$ of the data such that the total encoded size $L(\mathcal{P}, \mathcal{CT}, D)$ is minimized.

The search space for finding the best code table for a given set of features, yet alone for finding the optimal partitioning of features, however, is quite large. Finding the optimal code table for a set of $|F_i|$ features involves finding all the possible patterns with different value combinations up to length $|F_i|$ and choosing a subset of those patterns that would yield the minimum total cost on the database induced on F_i. Furthermore, the number of possible partitioning of a set of m features is the well-known Bell number B_m.

While the search space is prohibitively large, it neither has a structure nor exhibits monotonicity properties which could help us in pruning. As a result, we resort to heuristics. Our approach builds the set of code tables in a greedy bottom-up, iterative fashion. We give the pseudo-code as Algorithm 1, and explain it in more detail in the following.

COMPREX starts with a partitioning $\mathcal{P}$ in which each feature belongs to its own group (1), and separate, elementary code tables CT_i for each feature f_i associated with the feature sets (2).

DEFINITION 2. *An elementary code table CT encodes a database D induced on a single feature $f \in \mathcal{F}$. The patterns $p \in CT$ consist of all length-1 unique items $v_1, \ldots, v_{arity(f)}$ in $dom(f)$. Finally, $usage(p \in CT) = freq(f = v)$.*

Typically, some features of the data will be more strongly correlated than others, e.g., the age of a car and its fuel efficiency, or the weather temperature and flu outbreaks. In such cases, it will be worthwhile to represent features for which the correlation is 'high enough' together within one CT, as we can then exploit correlation to save bits.

More formally, we know from Information Theory that given two (sets of) random variables (in our case feature groups) F_i and F_j, the average number of bits we can save when compressing F_i and F_j together instead of separately, is known as their Information Gain. That is,

$$IG(F_i, F_j) = H(F_i) + H(F_j) - H(F_i, F_j) \geq 0,$$

In fact, the IG of two (sets of) variables is always non-negative (zero when the variables are independent from each other), which implies that the data cost would be the smallest if all the features were represented by a single CT. On the other hand, our objective function also includes the compression cost of the CTs.

Clearly, having one large CT over many (possibly uncorrelated) features will typically require more bits in model cost than it saves in data cost. Therefore, we can use IG to point out good merge candidates, subsequently employing MDL to decide if the total cost is reduced, and hence, whether to approve the merge or not.

The first step then is to compute the IG matrix for all pairs of the current feature sets, which is a non-negative and symmetric matrix (3). Let $|F_i|$ denote the cardinality, i.e. the number of features in the feature set F_i. We sort the pairs of feature sets in decreasing order of IG-per-feature, i.e. normalized by their total cardinality, and start *outer* iterations to go over these pairs as the candidate CTs to be merged, say CT_i and CT_j (5). The starting cost $cost_{init}$ is set to the total cost with the initial set of CTs (6). The construction of the new $CT_{i|j}$ then works as follows: we put all the existing patterns $p_{i,1}, \ldots, p_{i,n_i}$ and $p_{j,1}, \ldots, p_{j,n_j}$ from both CTs into the new CT (7). Following the convention, they are sorted first by length (from longer to shorter) and second by usage (from higher to lower) (8). Candidate partitioning $\hat{\mathcal{P}}$ is built by dropping feature sets F_i and F_j from $\mathcal{P}$ and including the concatenated set $F_{i|j}$ (9). Similarly, we build a temporary code table set $\hat{\mathcal{CT}}$ by dropping the candidate tables CT_i and CT_j and adding the new $\hat{CT}_{i|j}$ (10).

Next, we find all the unique rows of the database induced on $F_{i|j}$ (11). These patterns of length ($|F_i|$+$|F_j|$) are sorted in decreasing order of their occurrence in the database and constitute the candidates to be inserted into the new CT. Let $p_{i|j,1}, \ldots, p_{i|j,n_{i|j}}$ denote these patterns of the combined feature set $F_{i|j}$ in their sorted order of frequency. In our *inner* iterations (12), we insert these one-by-one (13), update (i.e. decrease) the usages of the existing overlapping patterns (14), remove those patterns whose usage drops to zero (15), recompute the code word lengths with updated usages (16) and compute the total cost after each insertion. If total cost is reduced, we store the candidate partitioning $\hat{\mathcal{P}}$ and associated set of code tables $\hat{\mathcal{CT}}$ (18), otherwise we continue insertions (from 12) with the next candidate patterns for possible future cost reduction.

In the outer iterations, if total cost is reduced the IG between the new feature set $F_{i|j}$ and the rest are computed (22). Otherwise the merge is rejected and the candidates $\hat{\mathcal{P}}$ and $\hat{\mathcal{CT}}$ are discarded (24). Next the algorithm continues to search for future merges, and the search terminates when there are no more pairs of feature sets that can be merged for reduced cost. The resulting set of feature sets and their corresponding set of code tables constitute our solution.

Note that the data from which we induce code tables may include outliers. As by MDL we only allow patterns in our code tables that help compression, we are not prone to include spurious patterns. See [22] for a more complete discussion.

Algorithm 1 COMPREX

Input: Database D with n tuples and m (categorical) features

Output: A heuristic solution to Problem Statement 1: a feature partitioning $\mathcal{P} : \{F_1, \ldots, F_k\}$, associated set of code tables $\mathcal{CT} : \{CT_1, \ldots, CT_k\}$, and total encoded size $L(\mathcal{P}, \mathcal{CT}, D)$

1: $\mathcal{P} \leftarrow \{F_1, \ldots, F_m\}$, $F_i = \{f_i\}, 1 \leq i \leq m$
2: $\mathcal{CT} \leftarrow \{CT_1, \ldots, CT_m\}$, where each CT_i is elementary
3: Compute IG between $\forall (F_i, F_j) \in \mathcal{P}, i > j$
4: **repeat**
5:   **for** each $(F_i, F_j) \in \mathcal{P}$ in decreasing normalized IG **do**
6:     Compute $cost_{init} \leftarrow L(\mathcal{P}, \mathcal{CT}, D)$
7:     Put patterns $p \in CT_i$ and $p \in CT_j$ into a new $\hat{CT}_{i|j}$
8:     Sort $p \in \hat{CT}_{i|j}$, (1) by length and (2) by usage
9:     $\hat{\mathcal{P}} \leftarrow \mathcal{P} \backslash (F_i \cup F_j) \cup F_{i|j}$
10:     $\hat{\mathcal{CT}} \leftarrow \mathcal{CT} \backslash (CT_i \cup CT_j) \cup \hat{CT}_{i|j}$
11:     Find unique rows (candidate patterns) $p_{i|j}$ in $D_{F_{i|j}}$
12:     **for** each unique row $p_{i|j,x}$ in decreasing frequency **do**
13:       Insert $p_{i|j,x}$ to new $\hat{CT}_{i|j}$
14:       Decrease usages of overlapping patterns $p \in \hat{CT}_{i|j}$ and $p \in cover(p_{i|j,x})$ by $freq(p_{i|j,x})$
15:       Remove patterns $p \in \hat{CT}_{i|j}$ with $usage(p)$=0
16:       Recompute $L(code(p \in \hat{CT}_{i|j}))$ with new $usages$
17:       **if** $L(\hat{\mathcal{P}}, \hat{\mathcal{CT}}, D) < L(\mathcal{P}, \mathcal{CT}, D)$ **then**
18:         $\mathcal{P} \leftarrow \hat{\mathcal{P}}$ and $\mathcal{CT} \leftarrow \hat{\mathcal{CT}}$
19:       **end if**
20:     **end for**
21:     **if** $L(\mathcal{P}, \mathcal{CT}, D) < cost_{init}$ **then**
22:       Compute IG between $F_{i|j}$ and $\forall F_x \in \mathcal{P}, F_x \neq F_{i|j}$
23:     **else**
24:       Discard $\hat{\mathcal{P}}$ and $\hat{\mathcal{CT}}$
25:     **end if**
26:   **end for**
27: **until** convergence, i.e. no more merges

3.3 Computational Speedup and Complexity

In Algorithm 1, computationally most demanding steps are (1) finding all the unique rows in the database under a particular feature subspace when two feature sets are to be merged (11) and (2) after each insertion of a new pattern to the code table, finding the existing overlapping patterns the usages of which to be decreased (14).

With a naive implementation, step (1) is performed on the fly scanning the entire database once and possibly using many linear scans and comparisons over the unique rows found so far in the process. Furthermore, step (2) requires a linear scan over the current patterns in the new code table $\hat{CT}_{i|j}$ for each new insertion. The total computational complexity of these linear searches depends on the database, however, with the outer and inner iteration levels (Lines 5 and 12, respectively), those may become computationally infeasible for very large databases.

We improve with a simple design choice. Instead of an integer vector of $usage$ per pattern in CT, we have a sparse matrix C for patterns versus data points, the binary entries c_{ji} indicating whether data tuple i contains pattern j in its $cover$. Note that the row sum of the C matrix gives the $usage$s of the patterns. In such a setting, step (1) (mining for candidate patterns) works as follows: Let F_i and F_j denote the feature sets to be merged. Let C_i denote the $n_i \times n$ patterns versus data tuples matrix for code table CT_i and similarly C_j denote the $n_j \times n$ matrix for CT_j, in which n_i and n_j respectively denote the number of patterns each table has. We obtain the usages for the new candidate patterns (merged unique rows) under the merged feature subspace $F_{i|j}$ by multiplying C_i and C_j^T into a $n_i \times n_j$ matrix U, which takes $\mathcal{O}(n_i n n_j)$.

Next, we sort the merged patterns in decreasing order by their usage $U_{x,y}$ and insert them to $\hat{CT}_{i|j}$ one-by-one. Note that we exploit the existing patterns in the code tables to be merged, rather than finding all the unique rows of the database. This way, we quickly identify good frequent candidates and consider only $n_i n_j$ of them. Since $n_i, n_j \ll n$, we practically reduce the number of inner iterations (12) to a constant.

From here, step (2) (insertions) works as follows: Let $U_{x,y}$ denote the highest usage associated with the merged pattern $p_i(x)|p_j(y)$. The insertion of $p_i(x)|p_j(y)$ into the code table simply means the addition of a new row to the $C_{i|j}$ matrix ($C_{i|j}$ is obtained by concatenating the rows of C_i and C_j and reordering its rows (1) by length and (2) by usage of the patterns it initially contains). The new row is then the dot product (i.e. logical AND) of row x in C_i and the row y in C_j (data tuples which contain *both* $p_i(x)$ and $p_j(y)$ in their cover). Moreover, we decrease the usages of the merged patterns $p_i(x)$ and $p_j(y)$ by subtracting the new row from both of their corresponding rows. All these updates are $\mathcal{O}(n)$.

All in all, the inner loop (starting in 12) goes over $n_i n_j$ ($\approx$constant) number of candidate patterns and each insertion takes $\mathcal{O}(n)$. Therefore, the inner loop takes $\mathcal{O}(n)$.

Next, we consider the outer loop (starting in 5), which tries to merge pairs of code tables. In the worst case we get $\mathcal{O}(m^2)$ trials when all merges are discarded. As a result the worst case complexity of COMPREX becomes $\mathcal{O}(m^2 n)$. In practice, however, many features are correlated and we obtain a merge at almost every step, yielding about linear complexity in both data size and dimension.

3.4 COMPREX at Work: Anomaly Detection

Compression based techniques are naturally suited for anomaly and rare instance detection. Next we describe how we exploit our dictionary based compression framework for this task.

In a given code table, the patterns with short code words, that is those that have high usage, represent the patterns in the data that can effectively compress the majority of the data points. In other words, they capture the trends summarizing the *norm* in the data. On the other hand, the patterns with longer code words are rarely used and thus encode the sparse regions in the data. Consequently, the data tuples in a database can be scored by their encoding cost for anomalousness.

More formally, given a set of code tables $CT_1, \ldots, CT_k$ found by COMPREX, each data tuple $t \in D$ can be encoded by one or more code words from each $CT_i, i = \{1, \ldots, k\}$. The corresponding patterns constitute the *cover* of t as discussed in §2.3.1. The encoding cost of t is then considered as its *anomalousness* score; the higher the compression cost, the more likely it is "to arouse suspicion that it was generated by a different mechanism" [13].

$$\begin{aligned} \textit{score(t)} &= L(t|CT) = \sum_{F \in \mathcal{P}} L(\pi_F(t)|CT_F) \\ &= \sum_{F \in \mathcal{P}} \sum_{p \in cover(\pi_F(t))} L(code(p)|CT_F) \end{aligned}$$

Having computed the compression costs, one can sort them and report the top k data points with the highest scores as possible anomalies. An alternative way [22] is to determine a decision threshold θ and flag those points with a compression cost greater than θ as anomalies. One can use the Cantelli's Inequality [11] which provides a well-founded way to determine a good value for the threshold θ for a given confidence level, that is, an upper bound for the false positive rate. For generality, in our experiments we show the accuracy at all decision thresholds.

4. EMPIRICAL STUDY

In our study, we explored the general applicability of COMPREX by considering rich data. We experimented with many (publicly available) datasets[1] from diverse domains, as shown in Tables 2 and 3. Other datasets we used include graph and satellite image datasets, which we will discuss in §4.2.3 and §4.2.4, respectively. The source code of COMPREX is available for research purposes[2].

We evaluated our method with respect to four criteria: (1) compression cost in bits, (2) running time, (3) detection accuracy, and (4) scalability. We also compared our results with two state of the art methods, KRIMP [25] and LOF [4] (note that KRIMP was shown [22] to outperform single-class classification methods, like NNDD and SVDD, for the anomaly detection task; therefore for reasons of space we only compare to the winner). KRIMP is also a compression based anomaly detection method, but uses a single code table to encode a dataset. It performs the costly frequent itemset mining as a pre-processing step to generate candidate patterns for the code table. LOF is a density-based outlier detection method that computes the local-outlier-factor of data points with respect to their nearest neighbors. Neither LOF nor KRIMP are parameter-free, they respectively require the minimum support threshold and the number of neighbors to be considered. COMPREX, in contrast, automatically determines the number of necessary code tables, as well as which patterns to include, and as such has no parameters.

4.1 Compression cost and Running time

One goal of our study is to develop a fast method that would model the *norm* of the data and hence give low compression cost in bits. In this section, we use both COMPREX and KRIMP for compressing our datasets and show the total cost in bits and the corresponding running times in Figure 1 (a) and (b), respectively. Note that the results for our largest datasets Enron, Connect-4, and Covertype are given with broken y-axes with values in millions for cost and thousands for time.

We note that COMPREX achieves very nice compression rates, outperforming KRIMP for all of the datasets, and providing up to 96% savings in bits (47% on average).

With respect to running time, we notice that for most of the (smaller) datasets, our running time is only slightly higher than that of KRIMP but still remains under 15 seconds. Even though for small datasets the run time of KRIMP is negligible, for datasets especially with large number of features, its running time increases significantly. The computationally most demanding part of KRIMP is the frequent itemset mining, making it less feasible for large and high dimensional categorical datasets. For example, for the Connect-4 dataset with 42 features and the Chess (king,rook vs. king,pawn) datasets with 36 features, KRIMP cannot finish within reasonable time due to very large candidate sets.

To alleviate this problem, KRIMP accepts a *minsup* parameter, which is the minimum number of occurrences of an itemset in the database to be considered as frequent. The higher the *minsup* is set, the fewer the extracted itemsets are. However, high *minsup* comes with a trade-off; the higher the *minsup*, the smaller the number of candidates, the smaller the search space and the worse the final code table approximates the optimal code table. In contrast,

[1] http://archive.ics.uci.edu/ml/datasets.html
[2] http://dl.dropbox.com/u/17337370/CompreX_12_tbox.tar.gz

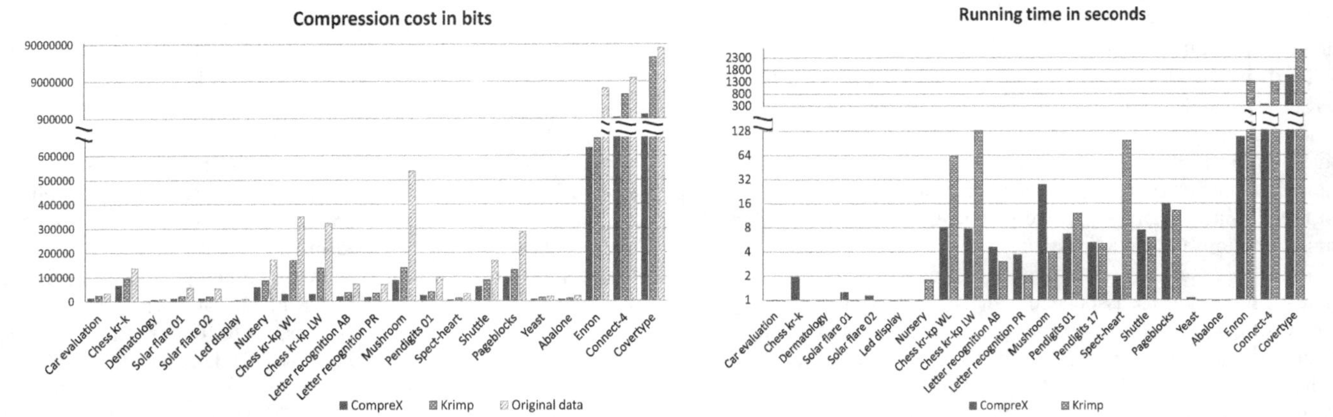

Figure 1: (left) Compression cost (in bits) when encoded by COMPREX vs. KRIMP. (right) Run time (in seconds) of COMPREX vs. KRIMP. For large datasets, extremely many frequent itemsets negatively affect the runtime for KRIMP.

our method does not require any sorts of parameters and frequent itemset mining.

In our experiments, we find *closed* frequent itemsets with *minsup* set to 5000 and 500 for the Connect-4 and Chess (kr-kp) datasets, respectively. Even then, the running time of our method remains lower than that of KRIMP (see Fig. 1). On the other hand, the time required for frequent itemset mining also depends on the dataset characteristics. For example, we observe in Figure 1 that the running time of KRIMP on the (larger) Mushroom dataset is much smaller than that on the (smaller) Spect-heart dataset, with both having the same number of (22) features.

For our largest datasets (in terms of size and number of features) in Figure 1, notice that the running time of KRIMP is quite large (about 20 mins) for Enron and Connect-4, and (45 mins) for Covertype. Moreover, its compression cost is still higher than that our method provides. Therefore, we conclude that our method becomes more advantageous especially for large datasets.

4.2 Detection accuracy

Besides achieving high compression rate, we would also (if not more) want our method to be effective in spotting anomalies. In this section, we experiment with various types of data including relational, graph and image databases.

For measuring detection performance, we use two-class datasets. The number of data points from one class is significantly smaller than that from the other class. We call these classes as minority and the majority classes, respectively. The data points from the minority class are considered to be the "anomalies". The underlying assumption is that different classes have different distributions –some classes may be more similar than others, just like with real anomaly(-classes). Examples to the classes include poisonous vs. edible in Mushroom data, unaccountable vs. very good in Car data, and win vs. loss in Connect-4 data.

As a measure of accuracy, we use *average precision*; the average of the precision values obtained across recall levels. We plot the detection precision, that is the ratio of the number of true positives to the total number of predicted positives, against the recall (=detection rate), that is the fraction of total true anomalies that are detected. A point on the plot is obtained by setting a threshold compression cost—any record with a cost larger than that threshold is flagged as an anomaly. The corresponding precision and recall are then calculated. By varying the threshold, we obtain the curve for the entire range of recalls. The *average precision* then approximates the area under the precision-recall curve.

4.2.1 COMPREX *on categorical data*

Figure 2 shows the precision-recall plots of COMPREX and KRIMP on several of our categorical datasets. Here, a higher curve denotes better performance, since it corresponds to a higher precision for a given recall. The average precision values are also given in Table 2, for all the categorical datasets. Notice that for most datasets COMPREX achieves higher accuracy than KRIMP. This is obvious especially for the Car, Chess, Led and Nursery datasets. We notice that the performance of the methods also depends on the detection task. For example, both methods perform well on the Mushroom dataset, for which the poisonous ones exhibit quite different features than the edible ones. However, the accuracies of both methods drop for the Connect-4 dataset for which the detection task, i.e. which player is going to win the game given the 8-ply positions, is much harder.

Table 2: Average precision (normalized area under precision-recall curve) for categoric datasets, comparing COMPREX and KRIMP. Further, we give dataset size, number of features and partitions, $minsup$ for KRIMP (star denotes *closed* itemsets).

Dataset	$\|D\|$	$\|\mathcal{F}\|$	$\|\mathcal{P}\|$	$min\ sup$	Cp'X	Kr'p
Car evaluation	1275	6	6	1	**0.99**	0.06
Chess (k)	4580	6	4	1	**0.67**	0.01
Dermatology	132	12	12	1	**0.45**	0.37
Solar flare 0–1	1312	10	6	1	**0.19**	0.15
Solar flare 0–2	1211	10	6	1	**0.11**	0.10
Led display	370	7	7	1	**0.99**	0.31
Nursery	4648	8	6	1	**1.00**	0.52
Chess (kp) W-L	1689	36	18	500*	**0.14**	0.06
Chess (kp) L-W	1547	36	18	500*	**0.03**	**0.03**
Letter rec. A–B	809	16	11	1*	0.17	**0.18**
Letter rec. P–R	823	16	11	1*	**0.57**	0.34
Mushroom	4258	22	5	1*	**1.00**	0.93
Digit rec. 0–1	1163	16	12	10	**0.75**	0.63
Digit rec. 1–7	1163	16	9	20	**0.51**	0.34
Spect–heart	267	22	16	1*	**0.12**	**0.12**
Connect–4	44k	42	11	5k*	**0.02**	0.01
Covertype	286k	44	6	280k*	**0.46**	0.27
				average	**0.48**	0.26

4.2.2 COMPREX *on numerical data*

While COMPREX is designed to work with categorical datasets, it can also be used to detect anomalies in datasets with numerical features. For that, we first convert the continuous numerical

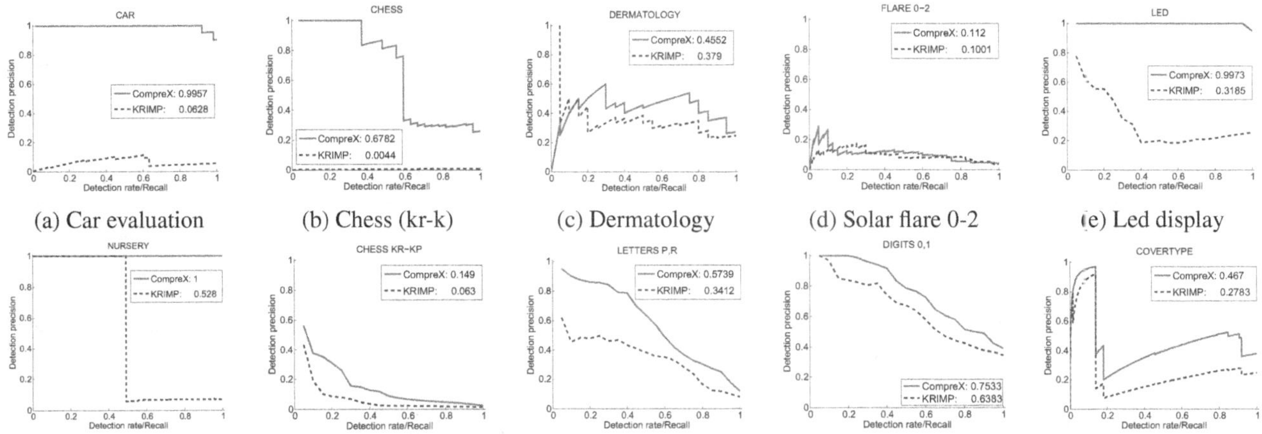

(a) Car evaluation (b) Chess (kr-k) (c) Dermatology (d) Solar flare 0-2 (e) Led display

(f) Nursery (g) Chess (kr-kp) (h) Letters P-R (i) Digits 0-1 (j) Covertype

Figure 2: Performance of COMPREX vs KRIMP on two-class categorical datasets. Given are precision vs. recall for various thresholds to flag tuples as anomalous. Note that COMPREX outperforms KRIMP for most detection tasks.

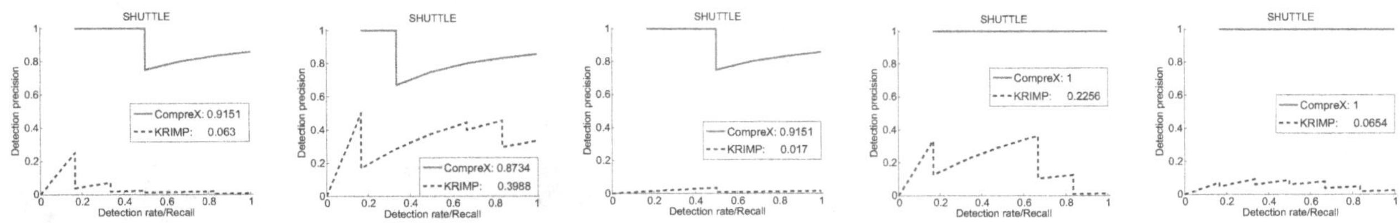

(a) LOG-bins (b) 5-LINbins (c) 10-LINbins (d) 3-SAXbins (e) p0.01-MDLbins

Figure 3: Performance of COMPREX vs KRIMP on the two-class numerical transaction dataset Shuttle. Notice that COMPREX outperforms KRIMP consistently for various discretization methods used.

features to discretized nominal features. There exist various techniques to this end. In our study, we consider several: linear, logarithmic, SAX [17], and MDL-based [14] binning. Linear binning involves dividing the value range of each feature into equal sized intervals. Logarithmic binning first sorts the feature values and assigns the lower b-fraction to the first bin, the next b-fraction of the rest to the second bin, and so on, until all the values are assigned to a bin. SAX has proved to be an effective symbolic representation, especially for time series data. MDL-based binning estimates variable-width histograms with optimal bin count automatically, for a given data precision.

We experiment with these various discretization methods under various parameter settings. In Figure 3, we show the accuracy of COMPREX versus KRIMP on the Shuttle dataset, using logarithmic binning with b=0.5, linear binning with 5 and 10 bins, SAX with 3 bins, and MDL-based binning with precision 0.01. Results are similar for many other settings and for the rest of the numerical datasets, which we omit for brevity. Notice that regardless of the discretization used, COMPREX performs consistently better than its competitor KRIMP.

To this end, we also compare our method with LOF on several numerical datasets. LOF is a widely used outlier detection method based on local density estimation. While it is quite powerful when applied to numeric data, it cannot be directly applied to categorical datasets. In this comparison, both methods require the careful choice of a parameter; number of nearest neighbors k for LOF, and a binning method and its corresponding parameter for COMPREX.

In Figure 4, we show the accuracy of LOF versus COMPREX with their best parameter choices on our numerical two-class datasets.

Table 3: Average precision for the numerical datasets, comparing COMPREX, KRIMP and LOF. Further, dataset size, number of features and partitions, $minsup$ used for KRIMP.

Dataset	$\|D\|$	$\|\mathcal{F}\|$	$\|\mathcal{P}\|$	$min\ sup$	Cp'X	Kr'p	LOF
Shuttle	3416	9	5	1	**1.00**	0.22	0.83
Pageblocks	4941	10	6	1	**0.46**	0.37	0.23
Yeast	468	8	8	1	**0.49**	0.17	0.48
Abalone	703	7	3	1	**0.42**	0.15	0.24
				average	**0.59**	0.23	0.45

Table 3 gives the corresponding average precision scores for all three methods. Notice that COMPREX achieves comparable or better performance than LOF, even though it operates on discretized data which loses some information due to this process, and thus is not as optimized as LOF for numeric data. This shows that COMPREX can also be applied to datasets with numerical or with a hybrid of both categorical and numerical features.

4.2.3 COMPREX *on graph data*

Given data points and their features in numerical or categorical space, our method can also be applied to other complex data, including graphs. To this end, we study the Enron graph[3], in which nodes represent individuals and the edges represent email interactions. In our setting the nodes correspond to the data points, and the features to the ego-net features we extract from each node. The

[3] http://www.cs.cmu.edu/~enron/

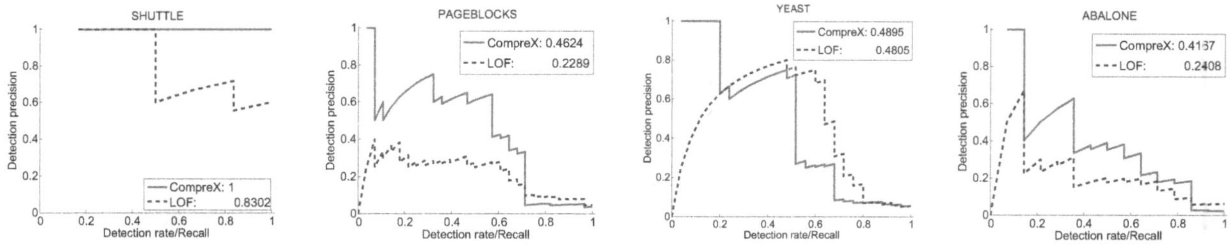

(a) Shuttle (b) Page blocks (c) Yeast (d) Abalone

Figure 4: Performance of LOF vs COMPREX with the best choice of parameters on the numerical transaction datasets. Notice that COMPREX achieves comparable or better performance than LOF even after discretization.

ego-net of a node (ego) is defined as the subgraph of the node, its neighbors, and all the links between them. We extract 14 numerical ego-net features, such as the number of edges, total weight, ego-net degree (number of edges connecting the ego-net to the rest of the graph), in- and out-degree, etc. We refer the reader to [2] for more on ego-net features. Features are discretized into 10 linear bins.

In Table 4, we show the top 5 email addresses with the highest compression cost found by COMPREX. The dataset does not contain any ground truth anomalies, therefore we provide anecdotal evidence for the discovered "anomalies". Our first observation is the significantly high compression cost of the listed points—103 to 107 bits given a global average of 6.72 bits (median is 4.27). This is due to the rare and high number of patterns used in their cover. Notice that each of them are covered with 7 patterns compared to a global average of 2.05 (median is 2). Moreover, the usages of the cover patterns is quite small—thus longer code words and high total compress-cost. Further inspection justifies our results: for example, 'sally.beck' (employee chief operating officer) contains the highest number of (31k) edges in its ego-net and the highest ego-net degree (of 85k), implying that she is highly connected to the rest of the graph as opposed to many other nodes in the graph.

Table 4: Top-5 anomalies for Enron, with one regular-joe example. Given are, email address, compression cost, size of cover, and average usages of the cover patterns; high usages correspond to short codes. Average cost is 6.72 bits, average number of covering patterns is 2.05.

name@enron.com	*cost (bits)*	$\|cover\|$	*avg usage±std of cover patterns*
sally.beck	107.28	7	3.7 ± 5.4
jeff.dasovich	107.11	7	3.4 ± 3.9
outlook.team	106.70	7	4.8 ± 6.3
david.forster	105.11	7	4.1 ± 5.2
kenneth.lay	103.24	7	5.8 ± 7.5
⋮	⋮	⋮	⋮
robert.badeer	1.53	2	52k ± 4.3k

4.2.4 COMPREX *on image data*

Next, for our image datasets[4] for which class labels also do not exist, we provide an anecdotal and visual study. The image datasets are the satellite images of four major cities from around the world as shown in Figure 5. Each image is split into 25x25 rectangle tiles, for which we extracted 15 numerical features, and subsequently discretized into 10 linear bins. The first three features denote the mean RGB values for each tile and the rest denote Gabor features.

[4] `http://geoeye.com/CorpSite/gallery/`

In Figure 5, top tiles with high compression cost are highlighted in red. We observe that COMPREX effectively spots interesting and rare regions. For example, the districts of Roman Catholic Church in Vatican and the Washington Memorial in Washington D.C. that distinctively stand out in the images are captured in top anomalies. In Forbidden city, COMPREX spots the three lakes (Beihai, Zhonghai, Nanhai), the Jingshan Park on its right, as well as the Tiananmen Square on the south. Finally, in London COMPREX marks the part of Thames river, the Buckingham Palace as well as several rare plain fields in the city.

(a) Holy see, Vatican

(b) Washington D.C., USA

(c) Forbidden city, Beijing

(d) London, UK

Figure 5: "Anomalous" tiles—with high compression cost—on the image datasets are highlighted with red borders (figures best viewed in color). Notice that COMPREX successfully spots qualitatively distinct regions that stand out in the images.

4.3 Scalability

KRIMP falling short on large datasets arises the question of scalability, which is maybe even more important than the issue of speed. Therefore, in Figure 6, we also show the running time of both methods for growing dataset and feature sizes on Enron and Connect-4.

We observe that the running time of KRIMP grows significantly with the increasing size in both cases. The difference is evident especially for growing feature size. This is due to frequent itemset mining scaling exponentially with respect to number of features.

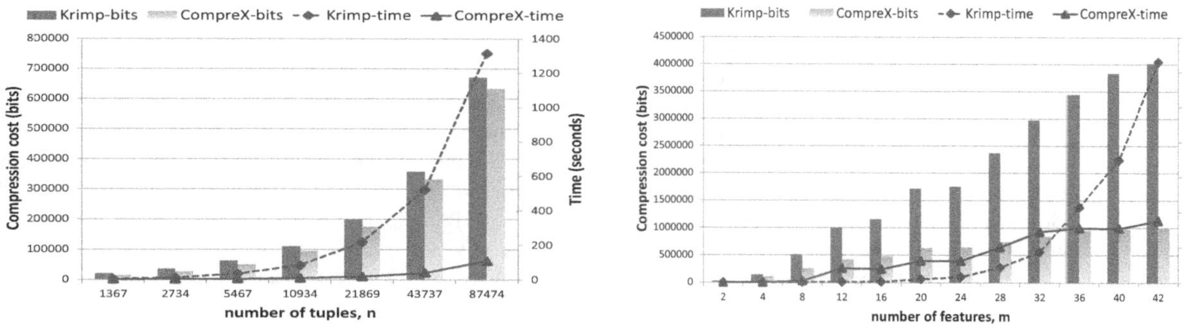

(a) time vs. data size

(b) time vs. feature size

Figure 6: Scalability of COMPREX and KRIMP with increasing dataset and feature size. (a) Enron with large n, (b) Connect-4 with large m. Notice that COMPREX achieves better scalability for large databases, following a linear trend in growth.

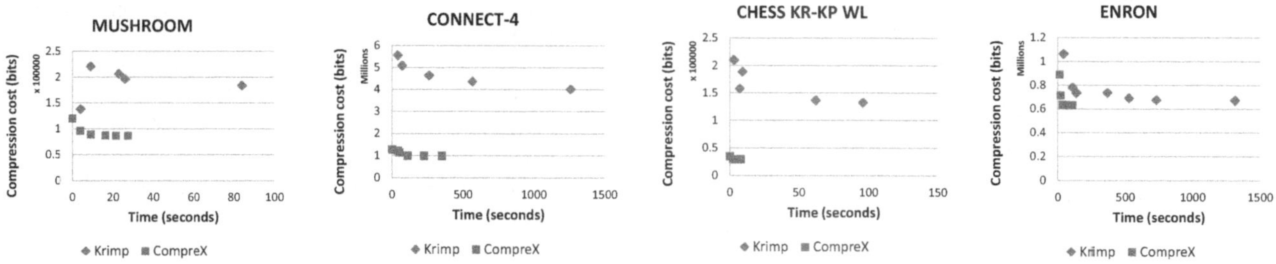

Figure 7: Scatter plots of compression cost versus running time of COMPREX and KRIMP. Notice that COMPREX achieves lower cost at any given time, which KRIMP cannot catch up with even when let to run for longer.

On the other hand, the increase in running time for our method follows a linear trend indicating that COMPREX scales better with increasing database size and dimension.

Another advantage of our method is that it can work as an *any-time* algorithm. Since it is a bottom-up approach which seeks for lower total cost over iterations via more merges, the compression procedure can be stopped at any point given the availability of time. The same goal can be achieved for KRIMP by tuning the *minsup* parameter; the higher the minsup, the lower the running time.

To compare the methods, we show the compression costs achieved at various durations in Figure 7. Notice that for any given run-time duration, COMPREX achieves lower compression cost than its competitor. Moreover, even KRIMP is allowed to run for longer, it still cannot reach as low of a cost as COMPREX can in much less time.

5. RELATED WORK

Our contributions are two-fold: finding descriptive pattern sets, and anomaly detection in categoric data.

5.1 Data Description

COMPREX builds upon the KRIMP algorithm by Siebes et al. [21, 25], and likewise employs the MDL principle [12] to define the best set of patterns as those that compress the data best. KRIMP heuristically approximates the optimum by considering a collection of itemsets in a fixed order, greedily selecting itemsets that contribute to better compression. The code tables KRIMP discovers have been shown to characterize data distributions very well, providing competitive performance on a variety of tasks [22, 25].

Unlike KRIMP, COMPREX can detect and exploit independent groups of attributes by using *sets of* code tables. Whereas KRIMP requires the user to provide a set of candidate itemsets (or a minimal support threshold to mine these), COMPREX is parameter-free in both theory and practice. Furthermore, as the expensive mining and sorting steps are avoided, COMPREX can be used as an any-time algorithm. However, while KRIMP is defined for transaction data in general, we restrict ourselves to categorical data.

The PACK algorithm [24] also follows a bottom-up MDL approach, using a decision tree per attribute to encode binary data 0/1 symmetrically. By translating these trees into downward-closed families of itemsets, patterns can be extracted. Although good compression results are obtained, by the downward-closed requirement typically large groups of itemsets are returned, hindering usability.

Further examples of pattern set mining methods that describe data include Tiling [9], Noisy Tiling [15], and Boolean matrix factorization [19]. As these do not define a score for individual rows, it is not trivial to apply them for anomaly detection.

Attribute clustering [18] is related in that it can be regarded as a crude form of COMPREX. With the goal of only providing a high-level summarization of the data, instead of a detailed characterization, the authors employ MDL to find the optimal grouping of binary attributes. These groups are described using crude code tables, consisting of all attribute-value combinations in the data; unlike in our setting where code tables can consist of itemsets of different lengths, providing better characterization of the local structure. Unlike COMPREX, it can only describe shown attribute-value combinations, and not trivially generalize, nor can it meaningfully capture structure local within the regarded attribute group.

Recently, [23] proposed the SLIM algorithm for mining a *single* code table directly from binary data. The code tables are shown to perform on par with KRIMP for classification and anomaly detection. Here, we consider multiple code tables, obtaining much better anomaly detection results than KRIMP. Moreover, by focusing on categorical data, COMPREX can search more efficiently, returning its code tables in only a fraction of the times reported in [23].

5.2 Anomaly Detection

Identifying outliers in multi-dimensional real-valued data has been studied extensively. Examples of proposals to this end include [1, 3, 4, 7, 10]. These typically exploit the (continuous) ordered domains of the attributes to define meaningful distance functions between tuples, which cannot be straightforwardly applied on nominal (categorical) data. Furthermore, most of these methods require several parameters to be specified by the user. For example, [4] and [10] take the number of nearest neighbors k to be compared to as input. They also require a distance metric for finding the k-nns of the data points, which often suffers from the curse of dimensionality in high dimensions. Lastly, these methods do not build a model, and thus cannot provide anomaly *characterization*. Model-based approaches like COMPREX, on the other hand, capture the *norm* of the data and can pindown the deviations from it, providing better interpretability for the claimed anomalies.

While most work on outlier detection has focused on numerical datasets, there also exist some work on anomaly detection for discrete data. [6] surveys methods for finding the anomalous sequences in a given set of sequences. The main disadvantage of the methods therein (kernel-,window-based, etc.) is that their performance is highly reliant on the choice of their parameters (similarity measure, window size, etc.). Proposals for anomaly detection in categorical data include [5, 8, 26] and recently [22]. [5] learns a structure and the parameters of a Bayesian network, and uses the log-likelihood values as the anomalousness score of each record. [8, 26] address the problem of finding anomaly *patterns*. They build a Bayes net that represents the baseline distribution, and then score the rules with unusual proportions compared to the baseline. They restrict their method to work with only one and two component rules due to high computation required. COMPREX is most related to [22], which employs KRIMP [21] as its compressor for anomaly detection. The key differences are that KRIMP finds a *single* code table, performs costly frequent itemset mining for candidate generation, and requires a minimum support parameter.

6. CONCLUSIONS

The contributions of this work are two-fold: (1) we achieve fast characterization of data by mining subspace code-tables, i.e. patterns sets, and (2) we apply our descriptive patterns to reliable anomaly detection in categorical data.

We introduce a novel, *parameter-free* method, COMPREX, that builds a data compression model using multiple dictionaries for encoding, and reports the data points with high encoding cost as anomalous. Our method proves *effective* for both tasks: It provides higher compression rates at lower run times especially for large datasets, and it is capable of spotting rare instances effectively, with detection accuracy often higher than its state-of-the-art competitors. Experiments on diverse datasets show that COMPREX successfully *generalizes* to a broad range of datasets including image, graph, and relational databases with both categorical and numerical features. Finally our method is *scalable*, with running time growing linearly with increasing database size and dimension.

Future work can generalize our method to time-evolving data for detecting anomalies over time, where the challenge is to efficiently update the code tables to effectively capture the trending patterns.

Acknowledgement

Research was sponsored by NSF under Grant No. IIS1017415, ARL under Coop. Agreement No. W911NF-09-2-0053, and ADAMS program sponsored by DARPA under Agreements No. W911NF-11-C-0200 and W911NF-11-C-0088. Jilles Vreeken is supported by a Post-Doctoral Fellowship of the Research Foundation – Flanders (FWO).

7. REFERENCES

[1] C. C. Aggarwal and P. S. Yu. Outlier detection for high dimensional data. In *SIGMOD*, 2001.

[2] L. Akoglu, M. McGlohon, and C. Faloutsos. Oddball: Spotting anomalies in weighted graphs. In *PAKDD*, 2010.

[3] A. Arning, R. Agrawal, and P. Raghavan. A linear method for deviation detection in large databases. In *KDD*, 1996.

[4] M. M. Breunig, H. Kriegel, R. T. Ng, and J. Sander. LOF: Identifying density-based local outliers. In *SIGMOD*, 2000.

[5] A. Bronstein, J. Das, M. Duro, R. Friedrich, G. Kleyner, M. Mueller, S. Singhal, and I. Cohen. Using bayes-nets for detecting anomalies in Internet services. In *INM*, 2001.

[6] V. Chandola, A. Banerjee, and V. Kumar. Anomaly detection for discrete sequences: A survey. *IEEE Trans. Knowl. Data Eng.*, 24(5):823–839, 2012.

[7] A. Chaudhary, A. S. Szalay, and A. W. Moore. Very fast outlier detection in large multidimensional data sets. In *DMKD*, 2002.

[8] K. Das and J. G. Schneider. Detecting anomalous records in categorical datasets. In *KDD*, 2007.

[9] F. Geerts, B. Goethals, and T. Mielikäinen. Tiling databases. In *DS*, pages 278–289, 2004.

[10] A. Ghoting, S. Parthasarathy, and M. E. Otey. Fast mining of distance-based outliers in high-dimensional datasets. *Data Min. Knowl. Discov.*, 16(3):349–364, 2008.

[11] G. Grimmett and D. Stirzaker. *Probability and Random Processes*. Oxford University Press, 2001.

[12] P. Grünwald. *The Minimum Description Length Principle*. MIT Press, 2007.

[13] D. Hawkins. *Identification of outliers*. Chapman and Hall, 1980.

[14] P. Kontkanen and P. Myllymäki. MDL histogram density estimation. In *AISTAT*, 2007.

[15] K.-N. Kontonasios and T. De Bie. An information-theoretic approach to finding noisy tiles in binary databases. In *SDM*, 2010.

[16] M. Li and P. Vitányi. *An Introduction to Kolmogorov Complexity and its Applications*. Springer, 1993.

[17] J. Lin, E. J. Keogh, S. Lonardi, and B. Y. Chiu. A symbolic representation of time series, with implications for streaming algorithms. In *DMKD*, pages 2–11, 2003.

[18] M. Mampaey and J. Vreeken. Summarising categorical data by clustering attributes. *Data Min. Knowl. Disc.*, 2012.

[19] P. Miettinen, T. Mielikäinen, A. Gionis, G. Das, and H. Mannila. The discrete basis problem. *IEEE TKDE*, 20(10):1348–1362, 2008.

[20] J. Rissanen. Modeling by shortest data description. *Automatica*, 14(1):465–471, 1978.

[21] A. Siebes, J. Vreeken, and M. van Leeuwen. Item sets that compress. In *SDM*, pages 393–404. SIAM, 2006.

[22] K. Smets and J. Vreeken. The odd one out: Identifying and characterising anomalies. In *SDM*, pages x–y. SIAM, 2011.

[23] K. Smets and J. Vreeken. SLIM: Directly mining descriptive patterns. In *SDM*, pages 1–12. SIAM, 2012.

[24] N. Tatti and J. Vreeken. Finding good itemsets by packing data. In *ICDM*, pages 588–597, 2008.

[25] J. Vreeken, M. van Leeuwen, and A. Siebes. KRIMP: Mining itemsets that compress. *DAMI*, 23(1):169–214, 2011.

[26] W.-K. Wong, A. W. Moore, G. F. Cooper, and M. M Wagner. Bayesian network anomaly pattern detection for disease outbreaks. In *ICML*, 2003.

TALMUD – Transfer Learning for Multiple Domains

Orly Moreno, Bracha Shapira, Lior Rokach, Guy Shani
Department of Information Systems Engineering
Ben-Gurion University of the Negev
P.O.B. 653, Beer-Sheva, 84105. Israel
Deutsche Telekom Laboratories at Ben-Gurion University
Beer-Sheva, Israel
{orlymore, bshapira, liorrk, shanigu}@bgu.ac.il

ABSTRACT

Most collaborative Recommender Systems (RS) operate in a single domain (such as movies, books, etc.) and are capable of providing recommendations based on historical usage data which is collected in the specific domain only. Cross-domain recommenders address the sparsity problem by using Machine Learning (ML) techniques to transfer knowledge from a dense domain into a sparse target domain. In this paper we propose a transfer learning technique that extracts knowledge from multiple domains containing rich data (e.g., movies and music) and generates recommendations for a sparse target domain (e.g., games). Our method learns the relatedness between the different source domains and the target domain, without requiring overlapping users between domains. The model integrates the appropriate amount of knowledge from each domain in order to enrich the target domain data. Experiments with several datasets reveal that, using multiple sources and the relatedness between domains improves accuracy of results.

Categories and Subject Descriptors

H.3.3 [**Information Storage and Retrieval**]: Information search and Retrieval – *information filtering;* H.2.8 [**Database Management**]: Database Applications – *data mining.*

General Terms

Algorithms, Experimentation

Keywords

Recommender Systems, Transfer Learning, Cross Domains, Collaborative Filtering

1. INTRODUCTION

The overwhelming amount of information existing nowadays raises the need for intelligent systems that will provide personalized recommendations and services. Usually, recommender systems (RS) provide recommendations or rating predictions for a single domain (such as movies, books, etc). In this domain the RS provides recommendations based on historical usage data that was collected only in the specific domain.

In many cases, in particular when the system is new, the data sparsity problem arises, and prevents the system from generating accurate recommendations. This problem is especially critical when using collaborative filtering (CF) algorithms whose accuracy relies on the availability of observed ratings from a sufficient number of users. If two users do not share a sufficiently large set of rated items, then the user-to-user similarity computation is not reliable and cannot support accurate rating predictions [5].

Over the web there exists a considerable number of publicly available user-item rating datasets from multiple sources. One can leverage this abundance of available data for boosting the performance of a specific recommender system of interest, by reducing the sparsity of its dataset. Unfortunately, one rarely possesses datasets which contain the exact same items, and even more rarely the exact same users. Clearly some domains are more closely related to the target domain then others. For example, books are more closely related to movies than to electronic gadgets. Thus, sophisticated methods are required to leverage data collected on one domain to be useful for another domain. These methods are often known as cross-domain recommenders in the recommendation system literature.

Cross-domain techniques typically originate in the machine learning literature and most specifically from Transfer Learning (TL). Transfer learning is a set of methods for extracting knowledge from one task or domain to be used in another task or a different domain [16]. Recently, transfer learning techniques were proposed for recommender systems applications in order to improve predictions in sparse target domains by reusing related domains data [14, 15, 20]. For example, Li et al. [14] suggested transferring user-item rating patterns from a dense source rating matrix in a single domain, to a sparse rating matrix in a related target domain. However, these previous methods assume that all domains are equally related and can positively contribute to the target system.

When transferring knowledge from one domain to another, we might transfer destructive information or data which is not consistent with the target domain. For example, if the domains are rarely related, or the users in the domains behave differently (they tend to be more critical in one domain and more favorable in another), using user behavior data from one domain for the other would have a negative effect on the model. This phenomenon is known as Negative Transfer [16] and may result in decreasing the target model accuracy.

In light of the above discussion and following Li et al. [14] we propose a novel approach which we call TALMUD (Transfer Learning for Multiple Domains) to alleviate the sparsity problem. Our method enables to predict missing values in the target domain by extracting knowledge from multiple source domains and transferring it to a single sparse target domain. We do not assume

CIKM'12, October 29 - November 2, 2012, Maui, HI, USA.

an identical level of relatedness between the domains. Rather, the algorithm automatically learns the degree of relatedness according to the rating patterns correspondence between the domains. Thus, it determines the amount of knowledge to be transferred from each source domain according to its relatedness to the target domain and its sparseness. This is done without assuming that there are shared users or items between the source and target domains.

The rest of this paper is organized as follows. We survey several studies which applied cross domain techniques for recommender systems in Section 2. In Section 3 we present our method. Section 4 reports preliminary experimental results based on several recommendation datasets. Section 5 presents an improved version of the algorithm and experimental results. Concluding remarks and future work are discussed in Section 6.

2. BACKGROUND

In this section we survey recommender systems, collaborative filtering, and the data sparsity problem. Next, we discuss the transfer learning approach to enhance machine learning datasets. Finally, we discuss in depth previous attempts of using transfer learning in recommender systems.

2.1 Recommender Systems

Recommender systems provide either recommended items, or rating predictions, in many commercial applications nowadays. For example, in NetFlix[1], the popular online video rental service, a user can view the predicted ratings for movies she has not yet seen. This can help the user in making intelligent choices when deciding which movie to rent.

Perhaps the most widely used approach for computing rating prediction is collaborative filtering (CF), where user or item (e.g. movie) correlation is based on previously observed user-item ratings. In CF, the dataset used for prediction can be modeled as a user-item rating matrix, where each row represents a user and each column represents an item, and each cell represents a user-item rating. Clearly, as users seldom rate more than a few items in many domains, this matrix is expected to be very sparse. The accuracy of the rating prediction, however, is often improved as the matrix becomes denser. This is known as the sparsity problem in CF.

There are many available CF algorithms, such as direct user-user correlation [2], singular value decomposition (SVD) [12], clustering [9], and many more.

2.2 Transfer Learning

Transfer learning (TL) aims at extracting knowledge that was learned for one task in a domain and use it for a target task in a different domain [16]. In the field of Machine Learning we usually train a model based on data that is available for the problem that we are interested in (training data). This model is used for predicting the behavior in the examined domain (using the testing data). For example, in recommender systems this model can help us predict whether the user will like the movie or not.

As stated in [16] many machine learning methods are based on the hypothesis that the training and the testing datasets have common features and distribution. In contrast to those techniques, transfer learning allows the domains, tasks and distribution of the training and testing to differ. Thus, when having insufficient data in the domain of interest, we can exploit data from mature applications (domains) which already have enough data. We can transfer the knowledge that is consistent with the target domain in order to train a model for it. For the text mining field transfer learning might be used when labeled documents exist only for mature domains and are not available for other domains. For example, Dai et al. [4] utilized labeled documents from one domain in order to classify unlabeled documents of a different domain with different distribution, using co-clustering as a bridge between the source and target domain. Xue et al. [19] had also coped with the problem of unavailable labeled data for classifying text in a new domain. They built a topic-bridge PLSA model that uses the common topics between the domains in order to classify the new domain's documents.

Another important characteristic of TL is that it does not necessarily require content overlap between the different domains. Regarding the recommender systems application, TL does not require that the source and target domain will share users or items, as it aims at finding common consumption patterns which exist in related domains by recognizing latent behavior groups [14]. Let us consider for example the Music and Games domains. Although these domains do not seem to be strongly connected, we can still find the same latent groups of users in both domains. For example, there might be a group of consumers that always purchase the new and trendy items, another group which likes to consume low cost products, and other users that mainly like childish items.

Transferring knowledge between domains is a very challenging task because it cannot be guaranteed that the knowledge of one domain is useful for another domain. The success of transfer learning depends on a variety of factors, e.g. how correlated the domains are (for example, it is possible that movies and books are more correlated than movies and jokes), the data characteristics (sparsity level, rating scale etc.) and whether the domains share resources like items or users.

Henceforth, we refer to the system or domain for which the recommendations are required as the ***target domain*** and the domain from which data is extracted as the ***source domain***.

2.3 Recommender Systems Cross-Domain Techniques

In recommender systems, the transfer learning problem is often known as cross-domain recommendation [13]. Several studies have been conducted on applying cross domain techniques, and transfer learning in particular.

Perhaps the simplest approach to cross-domain recommendations is by importing relevant data from a different domain and aggregating the data with the original target data. This aggregation is simple when the domains share information on the same users. Berkovsky et al. [1] refer to this problem as cross domain mediation and introduce several techniques for importing relevant data. For example, it is possible to merge the rating matrices such that the items of the remote domain are added as additional features. Then, executing any CF algorithm on the combined matrix allows the system to leverage rating behavior similarity in one domain to predict ratings in the other domain.

Possibly the most relevant work is by Li et al [14]. They suggested that when insufficient data in the target domain prevents us from training an accurate recommendation model, it is possible to borrow useful knowledge from a different domain and

[1] www.Netflix.com

use its data to train the model. Li et al. [14] introduced the idea that rating matrices of different domains may share similar user-item rating patterns. Thus, they learn a user-item rating matrix of the source domain which is referred to as a "codebook", and transfer the rating patterns to the target domain in order to fill in the target domain missing values.

Their algorithm consists of two steps. First, a rating pattern (codebook) of the dense domain is created, which summarizes the original rating data. Second, the codebook is expanded in order to learn the missing values in the target domain.

The codebook consists of k users clusters, and l item clusters and is constructed by simultaneously clustering the users (rows) and items (columns) of the source rating matrix, using the orthogonal non-negative matrix tri-factorization (ONMTF) clustering algorithm [7]. This method is equivalent to the two-way K-means clustering algorithm. As a result of the above process the codebook indicates the rating that a user who belongs to a specific user cluster will give to an item that belongs to a specific item cluster.

The second step of the algorithm is based on the assumption that there is a set of users/items in the target matrix that behaves like the i-th user/item cluster pattern in the source domain. Thus, the model maps target users and items to the corresponding source clusters. Those mappings are denoted by the matrices U_{tgt} and V_{tgt} respectively. Each row in U_{tgt} and V_{tgt} indicates a target user (for U_{tgt}) or item (for V_{tgt}) while each column indicates the source domain user's cluster or item's cluster respectively. U_{tgt} and V_{tgt} consist of binary values where "1" indicates a membership of a user (from U_{tgt}) or an item (from V_{tgt}) to a cluster from the source domain. Li et al. [14] assume (and we follow their assumption), that each user and item belongs only to one user's and item's cluster. Thus, only one value of "1" can be assigned to each row. For example, Figure 1 shows that user u_1 from the target domain, which is denoted as X_{tgt} , belongs to users cluster k_1 in the source domain, whereas item v_1 belongs to items cluster L_2 in the source domain. Thus, according to the source domain codebook, the missing rating of user u_1 to item v_1 is 1.

After the cluster memberships U_{tgt} and V_{tgt} are constructed, the target matrix can be filled using:

$$\tilde{X}_{tgt} = W \circ X_{tgt} + [1 - W] \circ [U_{tgt} B V_{tgt}^T]$$

The matrix W is a binary matrix where $W_{ij} = 1$ if $X_{tgt_{ij}} \neq 0$ (this entry is rated), otherwise $W_{ij} = 0$. The notation of $\circ$ denotes the entry-wise product. The target rating matrix reconstruction is demonstrated in Figure 2. The examples in Figure 1 and Figure 2 are adopted from Li et al. [14]. Experimental results have shown that additional information from a related domain can be gained and improve recommendations in the target domain. However, they do not measure the relatedness between the domains. Moreover, this method enables to utilize knowledge from one source domain only.

Li et al. [15] extended this method to integrate several sparse domains. In this work they assume that multiple sources share a single latent pattern. They discover this pattern and then learn the probabilities of each user and item to belong to this shared latent structure. In many cases, however, sources do not necessarily share such a latent pattern, a problem that we address here. Moreover, our work differs in the problem it aims to solve. While our approach searches for the optimal solution that will most accurately enrich the target domain, Li et al. [15] aim to simultaneously enrich several domains, and there is no source-target distinction. Their proposed model equally takes into consideration the limitation and needs of all the domains and therefore does not guarantee that the solution is the most optimal one for a single domain. In Transfer learning, this is called the multi task problem [16] and is generally treated differently. For completeness we will compare our suggested method with the method proposed in [15].

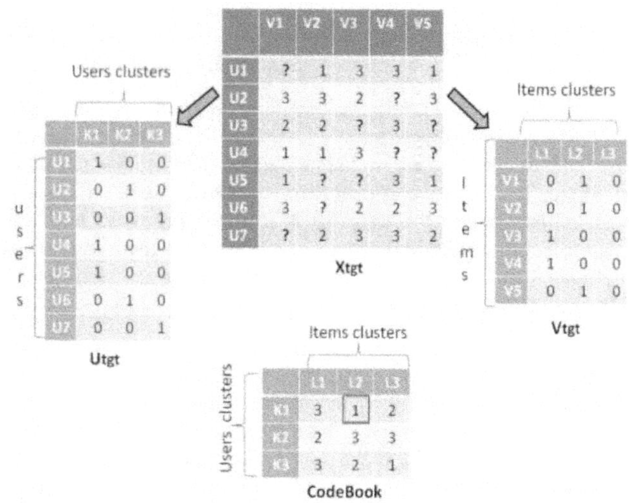

Figure 1. Decomposition of the target matrix (X_{tgt}) into user membership matrix (U_{tgt})and item membership matrix (V_{tgt})according to the source domain clusters

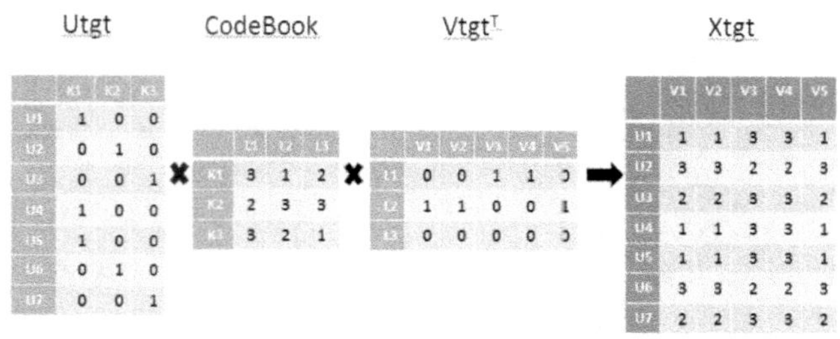

Figure 2. The reconstruction of the target rating matrix X_{tgt}

2.4 Other Related Works

Pan et al. [17] address two limitations of previous studies. First, they transform knowledge from domains which have heterogeneous forms of user feedback. For example, one domain has ratings records while another domain records user's events on the system. Second, they do not assume that the knowledge on both the users and the items can be learned from the same domain. They suggest that the user dimension can be learned from one domain that has information on the same users, while the items dimension can be learned from another domain that shares items with the target domain. However, their proposed method can only be applied in cases where the first source domain and the target domain share the same users, and that the second source domain and the target domain share the same items. In many real-world applications such shared data does not exist.

Cao et al. [3] refer to the recommendation problem as a Link-Prediction problem. Link prediction is defined by Getoor et al. [8] as a problem that predicts the existence of a link between two entities. In recommender systems we wish to predict a possible link between a user and an item. This paper handles data sparsity and the cold start problem, where a new user or a new item are added to the system and we do not have enough data which is relevant to them. The proposed method aims to improve the performances of all recommendation tasks, by exploring the correlation between link prediction tasks in multiple heterogeneous domains and transfer the shared knowledge among similar tasks. In order to find the different correlations between the domains, they use a task similarity kernel while assuming that the users in the different domains overlap. In our proposed approach this is not a mandatory requirement.

Zhang et al. [20] address the sparsity problem by considering collaborative filtering recommendation tasks of multiple sparse domains together as one problem. This method models the rating prediction problem using probabilistic matrix factorization. The correlation between the domains is learned and exploited in the model. However, similarly to Li et al. [15], this method refers to the multi task problem [16] and simultaneously enriches several domains.

To conclude, all the studies discussed above demonstrate the effectiveness of applying cross domain techniques to alleviate the sparsity problem comparing to other methods which mine only single domain data. However, the majority of these papers assume that the source and target domains are related but do not suggest methods to calculate or estimate this relatedness.

The studies that do measure the correlation between the domains assume that the domains share resources like items and users although this restriction is unrealistic when one wishes to leverage publicly available datasets to augment a specific recommender system. Moreover, the studies that deal with using multiple domains do not define a target domain which is sparse, but build a model from all the domains in order to enrich all of them simultaneously. The proposed approach measures the relatedness between domains, without assuming overlapping users or items, while allowing the use of multiple sources domains.

3. TALMUD

We now discuss our new method which we call TALMUD (Transfer Learning for Multiple Domains), that allows us to automatically learn the relatedness of multiple data sources, and transfer knowledge from all these sources into a single target domain.

Our method extends the algorithm proposed by Li et al. [14], for transferring data from a single domain, allowing for transferring data from multiple source domains with varying levels of relevance. We use N user-item source matrices, each represented as an $r_n \times m_n$ rating matrix, and denoted X_{src_n} for source matrix $n \in \{1 \dots N\}$. The target matrix is a sparse $p \times q$ rating matrix, denoted X_{tgt}. The codebook B_n encodes the user-item clusters in X_{src_n}. B_n is a $k_n \times l_n$ matrix where k_n and l_n are user defined parameters that define the cluster dimensions. Each codebook represents the transferred knowledge from its corresponding source domain.

The proposed method linearly integrates the rating patterns of all source domains into one model in order to enable prediction of the target matrix missing values. The main challenge is in defining the integration of knowledge from the different sources, and the amount of knowledge that needs to be transferred from each source domain. We hence define three sets of decision variables $\{U_{tgt_n}, V_{tgt_n}, \alpha_n\}$ for each source domain n. Equation 1 formulates the optimization problem that finds the best users' and items' cluster memberships and the relatedness coefficients. Thus, the error of the prediction in the target domain is minimized. Henceforth, U_{tgt_n} and V_{tgt_n} are denoted U_n and V_n for each source domain n.

$$\min_{\substack{U_n \in \{0,1\}^{p \times k_n} \\ V_n \in \{0,1\}^{q \times l_n} \\ \alpha_n \in R\ \forall n \in N}} \left\| \left[X_{tgt} - \sum_{n=1}^{N} \alpha_n \left(U_n B_n V_n^{\,T} \right) \right] \circ W \right\|_F^2 \tag{1}$$

$$S.T.\, U_n 1 = 1, V_n\, 1 = 1$$

The first set of variables refers to the users' cluster memberships U_n for each source n. U_n is a $p \times k_n$ matrix. The second set refers to the items' cluster memberships V_n for each source n. V_n is a $q \times l_n$ matrix. U_n and V_n are binary matrices, where "1" indicates a membership of user or item to a cluster respectively. Following Li et al. [14], we use the notation $\circ$ for entry-wise product and the notation $U_n 1 = 1, V_n\, 1 = 1$ to ensure that each user or item will be assigned to one cluster only. The observed ratings of the target domain are reflected in the binary Matrix W where $W_{ij} = 1$ if $X_{tgt_{ij}} \neq 0$ (i.e. this entry is rated), else $W_{ij} = 0$. Using this matrix we ensure that the error is calculated based only on the observed ratings

We find the target's users and items clusters by examining the different combinations of users/items clusters in all source domains and choosing the combination that best predicts the target ratings. This process is further described in Algorithm 1. Since we utilize knowledge form multiple source domains, we believe that the interaction between the sources affects the relatedness of the user to the cluster in each source domain. Thus the cluster memberships should be based on the user's global behavior rather than on her behavior in a single domain.

For example, let us assume that we have only a single movie source domain and respectively only one codebook B_1, where user u_1 fits best to cluster k_1 according to the learned model. When we take into account an additional music source domain, and more knowledge is available, the best cluster memberships for the same user u_1 based on data from all domains simultaneously, might become cluster k_2 of the movie codebook B_1.

Based on this intuition, we learn for each source domain n its correspondent matrices U_n and V_n based on all source domains simultaneously, rather than learning each domain separately and combining the models. This process results in multiple codebooks.

The third set of variables is α_n where $\alpha_n \in R\ \forall n \in N$. α_n denotes the relatedness coefficient between source domain n and the target domain. We aim to find the optimal α_n values such that the MSE is minimized, while U_n and V_n are fixed. The error function denoted as E is defined in Equation 2. In practice, minimizing E is equivalent to minimizing the MSE.

$$E = \left\| \left[X_{tgt} - \textstyle\sum_{n=1}^{N} \alpha_n \left(U_n B_n V_n^{\,T} \right) \right] \circ W \right\|_F^2 \tag{2}$$

For simplicity, henceforth we denote $(U_n\, B_n\, V_n^T) \circ W$ as T_n and $X_{tgt} \circ W$ as X. Note that $[U_n B_n V_n^{\,T}] \in R^{p \times q}$.

Equation 2 can be rewritten as follows:

$$E = \sum_{i=1}^{p} \sum_{j=1}^{q} \left([X_{ij} - \sum_{n=1}^{N} \alpha_n [T_n]_{ij}] \right)^2 \quad (3)$$

Thus, the optimization formulation is defined as

$$\vec{\alpha} = argmin_{\vec{\alpha}}[E] \quad (4)$$

In order to solve equation 4, we calculate the gradient of $\vec{\alpha}$ and set it equal to zero as shown in equation 5.

$$\frac{\partial E}{\partial \alpha_{n^*}} = -2 \sum_{i,j} \left(X_{ij} - \sum_{n=1}^{N} \alpha_n [T_n]_{ij} \right) [T_{n^*}]_{ij} = - \sum_{i,j} X_{ij} [T_{n^*}]_{ij} + \sum_{n=1}^{N} \sum_{i,j} \alpha_n [T_n]_{ij} [T_{n^*}]_{ij} = 0 \quad (5)$$

And rearranging gives:

$$\sum_{n=1}^{N} \sum_{i,j} \alpha_n [T_n]_{ij} [T_{n^*}]_{ij} = \sum_{i,j} X_{ij} [T_{n^*}]_{ij} \quad (6)$$

Thus we obtain the following set of linear equations:

$$\begin{pmatrix} \sum_{i,j}[T_1]_{ij}^2 & \cdots & \sum_{i,j}[T_1]_{ij}[T_N]_{ij} \\ \sum_{i,j}[T_2]_{ij}[T_1]_{ij} & \cdots & \vdots \\ \vdots & \ddots & \vdots \\ \sum_{i,j}[T_N]_{ij}[T_1]_{ij} & \cdots & \sum_{i,j}[T_N]_{ij}^2 \end{pmatrix} \begin{pmatrix} \alpha_1 \\ \alpha_2 \\ \vdots \\ \alpha_N \end{pmatrix} = \begin{pmatrix} \sum_{i,j} X_{ij}[T_1]_{ij} \\ \sum_{i,j} X_{ij}[T_2]_{ij} \\ \vdots \\ \sum_{i,j} X_{ij}[T_N]_{ij} \end{pmatrix} \quad (7)$$

Finally, the optimal α_n values can be obtained by solving (7):

$$\begin{pmatrix} \alpha_1 \\ \alpha_2 \\ \vdots \\ \alpha_N \end{pmatrix} = \begin{pmatrix} \sum_{i,j}[T_1]_{ij}^2 & \cdots & \sum_{i,j}[T_1]_{ij}[T_N]_{ij} \\ \sum_{i,j}[T_2]_{ij}[T_1]_{ij} & \cdots & \vdots \\ \vdots & \ddots & \vdots \\ \sum_{i,j}[T_N]_{ij}[T_1]_{ij} & \cdots & \sum_{i,j}[T_N]_{ij}^2 \end{pmatrix}^{-1} \begin{pmatrix} \sum_{i,j} X_{ij}[T_1]_{ij} \\ \sum_{i,j} X_{ij}[T_2]_{ij} \\ \vdots \\ \sum_{i,j} X_{ij}[T_N]_{ij} \end{pmatrix} \quad (8)$$

We learn the decision variables $\{ U_n, V_n, \alpha_n \}$ until converging to the local minimum.

After solving the optimization problem in equation (1) we can construct from each source domain a full matrix with the same dimensions as the target matrix using $U_n B_n V_n^T$. As shown in equation 9, a linear combination between those matrices, weighted by the set of α_n, will establish the full target matrix. We denote the full rating matrix as $\tilde{X}_{tgt}$.

$$\tilde{X}_{tgt} = W \circ X_{tgt} + [1 - W] \circ [\sum_{n=1}^{N} \alpha_n (U_n B_n V^T{}_n)] \quad (9)$$

3.1 Algorithm

The proposed cross-domain recommendation algorithm consists of the following stages. On the first stage the algorithm learns the rating patterns of each source domain separately. It constructs a codebook B_n from each source domain X_{src_n} as described by Li et al. [14]. On the next stage, the optimization problem defined above (shown in Algorithm 1) is solved by learning the target cluster memberships U_n and V_n and the relatedness coefficients α_n $\{\forall n \in N\}$. The optimization problem is solved iteratively; Each iteration t consists of three steps. On each step we solve one of the three variable set types $\{U_n, V_n, \alpha_n\}$ while fixing the other two [10]. First, we initialize the three sets of variables (lines 1-9). Then, to solve U_n (lines 11-14) we create possible rating rows for each user by expanding the codebooks, based on the item clusters V_n that were discovered at the former iteration. Then, we find the best linear combination of the target user's clusters, using the α values that minimize the error of the observed target ratings. In line 12 we examine the different existing combinations of user's clusters in all source domains and choose the combination that decreases the differences between the observed ratings and the ratings that are predicted using the model. We evaluate these differences using a quadratic loss function. We adopt Li et al. [14] notation to denote the weighted l_2 norm $\|X\|_{W_{i*}}^2 = [X^T diag(W_{i*}) X]$, where $[\cdot]_{i*}$ denotes the i-th row in a matrix and $[\cdot]_{*i}$ denotes the i-th column. We use an auxiliary vector $\vec{j}$ (line 12) to maintain the best user's clusters indexes from each domain. Then we calculate $U_n^{(t)}$ (line 13) for each source domain and use it to create optional rating columns to the target item. Similarly, we find the item's clusters correspondence and calculate $V_n^{(t)}$ (lines 15-18). Then, we learn the relatedness coefficient α_n (line 19), by minimizing the error based on the observed target ratings as shown in equation 4.

Algorithm 1 Optimization Problem Solution

Input: Target rating matrix X_{tgt}, source domains Codebooks B_n, number of sources N.

Output: the filled-in target rating matrix $\tilde{X}_{tgt}$

1. for $n \leftarrow 1, \ldots N$ do
2. for $i \leftarrow 1, \ldots, q$ do
3. Randomly select $\hat{j}$ from $\{1, \ldots, l_n\}$
4. $[V_n{}^{(0)}]_{i\hat{j}} \leftarrow 1; [V_n{}^{(0)}]_{i\hat{j}} \leftarrow 0$ for $j \in \{1, \ldots, l_n\}/\hat{j}$
5. end for
6. end for
7. for $n \leftarrow 1, \ldots, N$ do
8. $\alpha_n^{(0)} \leftarrow \frac{1}{N}$
9. end for
10. for $t \leftarrow 1, \ldots, T$ do
11. for $i \leftarrow 1, \ldots, p$ do
12. $\vec{j} = argmin_{\vec{j}} \left\| [X_{tgt}]_{i*} - \sum_{n=1}^{N} \alpha_n^{(t-1)} \left[B_n [V_n{}^{(t-1)}]^T \right]_{j*} \right\|_{W_{i*}}^2$
13. $[U_n^{(t)}]_{i,\vec{j}[n]} \leftarrow 1; [U_{tgt}^{(t)}]_{i,j} \leftarrow 0$ for $j \in \{1, \ldots, k_n\}/\vec{j}[n]$
14. end for
15. for $i \leftarrow 1, \ldots, q$ do
16. $\vec{j} = argmin_{\vec{j}} \left\| [X_{tgt}]_{*i} - \sum_{n=1}^{N} \alpha_n^{(t-1)} [U_n{}^{(t)} B_n]_{*j} \right\|_{W_{*i}}^2$
17. $[V_n^{(t)}]_{i,\vec{j}[n]} \leftarrow 1; [V_n{}^{(t)}]_{ij} \leftarrow 0$ for $j \in \{1, \ldots, l_n\}/\vec{j}[n]$
18. end for
19. $\vec{\alpha}^{(t)} = \min_{\alpha_n} \left\| \left[X_{tgt} - \sum_{n=1}^{N} \alpha_n^{(t)} \left(U_n B_n V_n{}^T \right) \right] \circ W \right\|_F^2$
20. end for
21. $\tilde{X}_{tgt} = W \circ X_{tgt} + [1 - W] \circ [\sum_{n=1}^{N} \alpha_n (U_n B_n V_n^T)]$

This iterative process stops with convergence to the local minimum (or after performing t iterations). Finally, we fill the target rating matrix using equation 9. The knowledge required for filling the rating matrix X_{tgt} is drawn from each source domain according to the degree of relatedness α_n.

4. PRELIMINARY RESULTS

We now present some preliminary experiments that show the strength of TALMUD, but also expose some problems. Then, we propose how these problems can be reduced.

4.1 Datasets

For our experiments we used two benchmark datasets in the RS community - Netfilx and Jester[2]. Additionally we used two proprietary datasets obtained from Deutsche Telecom

[2] http://goldberg.berkely.edu/jester-data/

Laboratories. Following is a summarization of the main data set characteristics.

- We used a subset of Netflix –A movies ratings dataset with a rating scale of 1 to 5. We extracted 110 users, 110 items and 12,100 rating records to ensure no sparsity (the matrix is full of ratings) for using it as source matrix in the experiments.
- Jester is a jokes rating dataset (scale -10 to 10). We used a subset with no sparsity that contains 500 users, 100 items and a total of 50,000 rating records. In order to achieve consistent rating scale of 1-5 ratings, we uniformly normalized the rating scale from 1 to 5.
- The Music Loads[3] and Games Loads[4] datasets consist of recorded user's events on products in the system (e.g., a user buys an item, a user clicks on an item, etc). Since the matrices are very sparse (99.99%), the most dense matrices that we managed to extract are of ~97% sparsity. We randomly selected 632 users that have events on at least 10 different items, and 817 music items with at least 5 events of different users. We performed the same process on the Games Loads dataset resulting with 632 users and 1264 items. As a preparation of the data for the preliminary evaluation we transformed the data from events to ratings. We use an exponential scale to score the events in order to emphasis the difference between the events. E.g. the most meaningful user event, buying an item, gets the highest score. Moreover, we considered the number of events that a user performed on the same item. That is, if a user plays a song a couple of times it may indicate that the user really likes the item compared to another song that he plays only once. The process is demonstrated in Table 1 and Table 2. Table 1 shows score categories. For example, a score of 2 is assigned when the user either clicks on an item or clicks to recommend the item. Table 2 demonstrates the aggregation of scores in a case that a user has multiple events on the same item. This is done by multiplying the score of the event by the number of times it occurred. In order to make sure that the rating scale is identical for all the users, we performed individual normalization for each user, so that the rating is between1-5.

4.2 Experimental Settings

The goal of the proposed method is to learn the missing values in a target matrix using multiple domains. Thus, we compare the accuracy results of our method TALMUD (Transfer Learning for Multiple Domains) to Li et al. [14] method, CBT, which learns only from one source domain.

We conducted two experiments. In the first experiment we use the Games loads dataset as target domain while the other domains were used as source domains. In the second experiment the Music loads dataset was used as target domain. The target domain was divided into training and testing datasets. The training data consisted of 80% of the ratings while the testing data consisted of the remaining 20%. Since the Loads datasets events have time stamps we used the most recent 20% of the events for testing.

Both TALMUD and CBT were executed with three different combinations of source domains for building the model. Each combination of two source domains was examined (e.g. on the first experiment the combinations were: movies and jokes, music and jokes, music and movies). Using this setting we are able to

[3] http://www.musicload.de/

[4] http://www.gamesload.de/

Table 1. Music Loads and Games Loads events scores

Score 2	Score 4	Score 8	Score 16
User clicks item	User adds to watch list	User plays item	User buys item
User clicks recommend ed item	User tags item	User streams item	User buys recommended item
	User comments item	User adds to shopping cart	
	Users adds to play list		

Table 2. An example of calculating the score of user u to item v based on his events regarding the item

Event	Score	Number of events	Sum score
User clicks item	2	5	10
User plays item	8	3	24
User buys item	16	1	16
Total score	-	-	50

create multiple scenarios to compare the two approaches. The codebook dimensions, k and l , were set according to the intuition suggested by Li et al. [15] that the clusters model should be compact enough to avoid over-fitting, but expressive enough to capture significant behavior patterns. We set k and l to 20 for all source domains similarly to Li et al. [15].

In addition, we compared our method with a trivial linear combination of multiple source domains. That is, we built a model on each source domain separately using the CBT algorithm and aggregated the models by extracting an equal amount of knowledge from each source domain. This method was applied with the same domain combinations as TALMUD. We used Mean Absolute Error as the evaluation metric (MAE). $MAE = \frac{\sum_{i=1}^{T}|P_i-R_i|}{T}$ where P_i is the predicted rating and R_i is the actual rating. Smaller MAE values indicate higher accuracy.

4.3 Experimental Results

The experiment results are reported in Table 3 and Table 4. Table 3 shows the results of the first experiment, where games is the target domain, while Table 4 shows the results of the second experiment where music is used as the target domain. In each section of the tables we present a scenario in which only two specific source domains are available. In each scenario we examine the effectiveness of using just one of the sources or the combination of the two sources. We tested the results for significance using a paired sign test. For each scenario, an asterisk (*) indicates that the method was significantly outperformed by TALMUD, whereas a plus ($^+$) sign indicates that the method significantly outperformed TALMUD.

Examining the results in Table 3, we can see that when Jokes and Music are the available sources, using more than one source domain improves the prediction accuracy. The same trend is observed in the second scenario. These results reinforce our assumption that the use of multiple source domains can improve the accuracy of the prediction.

Table 3. MAE on Games Loads using jokes movies and music as source domains

CBT		TALMUD		Simple Linear Combination	
Jokes	Music	Jokes + Music		Jokes + Music	
		α=2.520	α=-1.331	α=0.5	α=0.5
0.914*	0.883*	**0.5644**		0.9092*	
Jokes	Movies	Jokes + Movies		Jokes + Movies	
		α=0.511	α=0.681	α=0.5	α=0.5
0.914*	0.533*	**0.4867**		0.9366*	
Music	Movies	Music + Movies		Music + Movies	
		α=-1.120	α=2.030	α=0.5	α=0.5
0.883*	**0.533**	0.6144		0.9068*	

Table 4. MAE on Music Loads using jokes, movies and games as source domains

CBT		TALMUD		Simple Linear Combination	
Jokes	Games	Jokes + Games		Jokes + Games	
		α=3.568	α=-1.606	α=0.5	α=0.5
0.907*	1.098*	**0.7957**		0.7960	
Jokes	Movies	Jokes + Movies		Jokes + Movies	
		α=0.419	α=0.660	α=0.5	α=0.5
0.907*	**0.7484**	0.7614		0.8358*	
Games	Movies	Games + Movies		Games + Movies	
		α=-0.489	α=1.631	α=0.5	α=0.5
1.098*	0.7484^{+}	0.8208		**0.6743**$^{+}$	

In some cases, the optimal relatedness coefficient for a source domain changes when we use this source together with different additional source domains. For example, in Table 3, when using jokes and movies as sources, the relatedness coefficient of jokes is significantly smaller compared to the use of jokes with music. It should be noted that the relatedness coefficient are learned for specific datasets of domains, but they do not represent a general relatedness level between the domains. The relatedness may be affected by various factors such as the data sparsness level, the interaction between the source domains, etc. Thus, the relatedness coefficient should be learned specifically for each problem at hand. In future work we intend to investigate the factors that the relatedness coefficient is influenced by. The meaning of a nonzero coefficient value, positive or negative, is that the source domain contributes to the model and balances the predicted error. A zero coefficient means that it is better not to use the source because it would have a negative impact on the model.

In the third scenario, when using music and movies as sources, the algorithm sets nonzero α_i values to both source domains, which means that the learner uses both sources, but it performs worse than a learner which uses a single source only. This is an example of the Negative Transfer phenomenon which the algorithm fails to recognize due to the well-known over fitting problem in machine learning [6]. As we add more source domains to the problem, the model becomes more complex and therefore

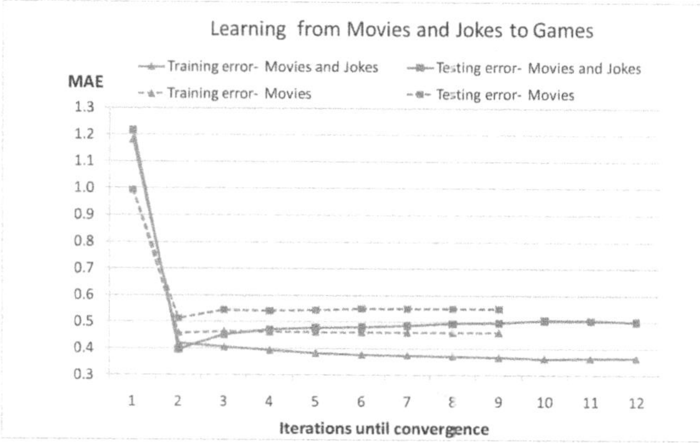

Figure 3. The learning process from a single domain (Movies) and multiple domains (Movies and Jokes)

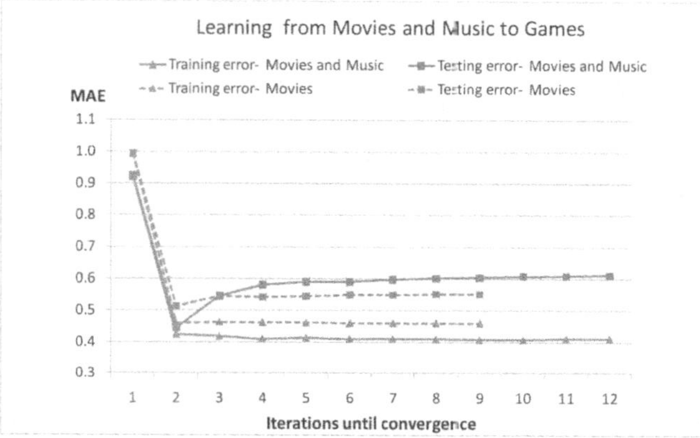

Figure 4. The learning process from a single domain (Movies) and multiple domains (Movies and Music)

adapts itself better to the training data. Thus, when building the model on the training data, it seems better to use multiple sources in order to improve prediction. But, when examining the results on the testing data, it is preferable to consider only one source domain. The same problem can be observed in Table 4. In the first scenario, when only games and jokes are the available datasets, the use of both source domains improves accuracy. But for the second and third scenarios using only one source domain outperformed the use of multiple source domains.

The over fitting phenomenon is demonstrated using Figure 3 and Figure 4. In both figures, we compare the MAE results of the learning process from a single source domain (movies) and the results of learning from multiple domains (movies and jokes in Figure 3, and movies and music in Figure 4). At the end of each iteration we compute the MAE value that is achieved on the training data and on the testing data. We present for the learning process only the first iterations since the exact same trend continuous until convergence.

In Figure 3, observing the training curves, we see that the model that uses the two source domains achieves a smaller error on the training data, compared to the model that learns from one source domain only. This is also the case when examining the models on the testing data. The curve that describes multiple domains transfer learning is always below the curve that describes the single domain transfer learning, which means that the error is consistently smaller.

In Figure 4, however, a different trend is observed. While the use of multiple source domains is superior when measuring the MAE of training data, the accuracy on the testing data shows opposite results. That is, on the training data, the model that uses two sources is superior, while on the testing data, the model that uses a single source performs better.

The complexity of the model that uses two source domains leads to an over fitting of the model to the training data and degrades the accuracy of the resulting model on the testing data. We next propose an improved algorithm that mitigates the problem of over fitting and prevents negative transfer.

When comparing TALMUD to the simple linear combination for predicting games ratings (Table 3), it can be seen that TALMUD is significantly superior in all examined scenarios.

For predicting music (Table 4), TALMUD is superior in two scenarios out of three. When using games and movies to predict music, a smaller error is achieved while using a simple linear combination due to the over fitting problem. In the other scenarios TALMUD outperformed the simple linear combination significantly. This clearly demonstrates the value of learning the relatedness coefficients in most cases.

5. HEURISTIC DOMAIN ORDERING

In order to deal with the over fitting problem, we suggest an improvement to our algorithm. We propose a heuristic method that considers the trade- off between the knowledge that is gained by using multiple source domains and the over fitting problem that arises when the model complexity increases due to the additional source.

The method consists of two stages. First, it heuristically ranks the available sources from the most correlated to the target domain to the least correlated. Then, sources are added by decreasing heuristic correlation estimate until an over fitting problem is detected.

For computing the heuristic correlation estimate, the algorithm constructs a codebook for each domain using the method proposed by Ding et al. [7]. We then permute the rows and columns, and calculate the distance between each source matrix and the target matrix. The distance is computed by applying the codebook transfer phase of the CBT algorithm from the source domain codebook to the target domain codebook. Thus, the similarity between the domains' clusters (codebooks) is computed. The underlying heuristic assumption is hence that the source cluster that is most similar to the target cluster (has the smallest distance) is also most correlated to it.

After computing the heuristic estimates, the algorithm builds a model only from the most correlated source domain. Then, it tries to add more sources in decreasing heuristic estimate order. We use a wrapper method [11] in order to examine if using N source domains is better than using $N + 1$ source domains. We build the model with only 80% of the training data and examine the error on the remaining 20% of the training data (often called the validation set). We then compare the error achieved by each model and decide whether to stop or not.

At the end of this process we identify the source domains that can be used for building the complete model without over fitting. Then, we use the entire training data to build the final complete model that will be used to predict ratings.

5.1 Experimental Results

We ran the improved algorithm with four domains, namely: games, music, movies and jokes as described above. In two separate runs we use games and music as target domains and the other three domains as optional sources from which the algorithm chooses the related sources that it is worth learning from. Here we also compare our results to results obtained by running the RMGM method [15] that aims to fill missing values in all sparse domains. For RMGM we use the same cluster level settings ($l = 20, k = 20$), and we examine the results obtained for the defined target domains.

Table 5 and Table 6 present the results of building a model for the games target domain while Table 7 and Table 8 present the results of building a model for the music target domain. Table 5 shows the MAE observed on the training data that are used to build the model, while Table 6 presents the results obtained from using the final model. The first row in Table 5 shows the similarity computation results between each of the codebook source domains and the codebook target domain. As can be seen in the table, Movies is the most correlated domain (has the smallest distance) to the target and Music is the least correlated, given our heuristic estimate. The rest of Table 5 (Rows 2, 3, 4) presents the decisions that the algorithm made at each step based on the computed MAE, where each row corresponds to an iteration of the algorithm. As explained above, on this stage the algorithm uses only the training data. The model is built using 80% of the training data and the error is computed using the validation set, which is the remaining 20% of the training data.

On the first step, the algorithm computes the MAE from learning only from Movies (the most correlated domain) using the CBT method [14]. Then, the algorithm adds the next correlated source domain, Jokes, and performs TALMUD for multiple source domains (row 3). The use of two source domains is preferable and obtains more accurate results (MAE=0.4864) than using one source domain. Therefore, the algorithm continues to add another source domain, Music, to the model (row 4). As can be observed in rows 3 and 4, the use of two source domains outperformed the use of three source domains. Thus, the algorithm selects only two source domains, Movies and Jokes, for the complete model construction.

Finally, the algorithm uses the complete training data to train the model using Movies and Jokes and computes the final MAE on the testing data. The final model is presented in Table 6. The results in Table 5 are consistent with results from Table 3. The most accurate predictions were achieved using the Movies and Jokes source domains. Given the three source domains we were able to reach this result without examining all possible combinations (e.g., movies and music, jokes & music, or each of the domains separately). The improved algorithm built the most accurate model given the three source domains.

On the games domain, however, the error on the validation set increases after adding the second source domain. As Table 7 shows, our algorithm indicates that if we start with Movies, and then add the Jokes source, then the MAE increase. Thus, it is better to use only a single source in this case – the movies domain. This is consistent with the results in Table 4, where the movies domain alone was superior to TALMUD.

Table 9 presents the results of comparing TALMUD to the RMGM method. Table 9 shows that TALMUD outperforms RMGM significantly for both target domains.

TALMUD heuristically chooses the source domain to learn from and does not necessarily use all the available related domains while RMGM builds the model from all source domains. Moreover, TALMUD aims to optimize predictions with regards to a single target domain while RMGM optimizes for all domains simultaneously.

Table 5. A demonstration of the algorithm performances of choosing the source domains when Games Loads is the target domain

	Method	Source domains			MAE on validation data
		Movies	Jokes	Music	
1	Heuristic correlation	0.0198	0.5286	0.6100	-
2	CBT	α=1	-	-	0.5338
3	TALMUD	α=0.67	α=0.50	-	**0.4864**
4	TALMUD	α=2.78	α=2.99	α=-4.76	0.6859

Table 6. Final model results for Games Loads

	Source domains		MAE on testing data
	Jokes	Movies	
TALMUD	α=0.511	α=0.681	**0.4867**

Table 7. A demonstration of the algorithm performances of choosing the source domains when Music Loads is the target domain

	Method	Source domains			MAE on validation data
		Movies	Jokes	Games	
1	Heuristic correlation	0.026	0.045	0.678	-
2	CBT	α=1	-	-	**0.7810**
3	TALMUD	α=0.693	α=0.373	-	0.7835

Table 8. Final model results for Music Loads

	Source domains	MAE on testing data
	Movies	
CBT	α=1	**0.7484**

Table 9. A comparison between the MAE results using TALMUD and RMGM

Target domain	TALMUD	RMGM
Games loads	**0.4867**	0.5458*
Music loads	**0.7484**	0.7806*

6. CONCLUSION AND FUTURE WORK

In this paper we presented TALMUD, a new multi-domain transfer learning method aimed at addressing the sparsity problem in recommender systems. The proposed method augments the codebook-based knowledge transfer (CBT) method which extracts knowledge from only one source domain to transfer knowledge from multiple source domains. Our method takes into consideration the possible interaction between the source domains, as well as the different degrees of relatedness between the sources and the target domain. It learns this relatedness and linearly integrates the rating patterns of all source domains into one model in order to enable prediction of the target matrix missing values. Although the complexity of building the model is high, it is a preprocessing stage that is performed offline that does not affect the recommendation time (and therefore should not pose a problem in practice). We address an applicative problem in which there is no guarantee of overlapping users or items between the domains, as is common in real-world scenarios. Our results show that using multiple source domains leads to more accurate predictions of the missing ratings. Thus, our method is useful for collaborative filtering applications. We further demonstrate that learning from multiple sources can lead to an over-fitting problem. We address this issue by heuristically choosing the best sources to learn from. The experimental results in the last section demonstrate the improvement in the accuracy gained by heuristically choosing the source domains according to their relatedness to the target domain.

In future work we intend to extend this research in the following directions:

An analytical proof of convergence. In this paper we assume Algorithm 1 convergence based on empirical evidence of our experiments. We demonstrate the convergence process in Figure 1 and Figure 2. We next intend to provide an analytical proof that Algorithm 1 monotonically decreases the objective function that is described in equation 1.

Evaluating the effect of data features. We further intend to examine the influence of different data features on the algorithm's performance. This will be done by extending the number of source domains as well as using larger datasets with different degrees of density.

Parameters calibration. The codebook dimensions, k and l, directly influence the quality of knowledge that is learned from the source domains. The number of the clusters should not be too small since it may cause a loss of knowledge, but using too many clusters can lead to over-fitting and is also computationally intensive. Thus, we intend to examine this tradeoff and formulate a rule of thumb that will help to determine the size of the codebooks.

Handling over fitting. We would like to further investigate the use of methods that may overcome the over fitting problem and compare them to our proposed solution.

Handling binary data. Prediction accuracy is the most discussed property in the recommendation system literature [18]. However, in industry most data is composed of binary preference or event data since users do not cooperate in providing explicit ratings. We would like to extend our method to support binary data.

7. REFERENCES

[1] S. Berkovsky, T. Kuflik, and F. Ricci. Cross-domain mediation in collaborative filtering. *User Modeling 2007*, pages 355-359, 2007.

[2] J. Breese, D. Heckerman, C. Kadie, et al. Empirical analysis of predictive algorithms for collaborative filtering. In *Proceedings of the 14th conference on Uncertainty in Artificial Intelligence*, pages 43-52, 1998.

[3] B. Cao, N. Liu, and Q. Yang. Transfer learning for collective link prediction in multiple heterogeneous domains. In *Proceedings of the 27th International Conference on Machine Learning, Haifa, Israel*. Citeseer, 2010.

[4] W. Dai, G. Xue, Q. Yang, and Y. Yu. Co-clustering based classification for out-of-domain documents. In *Proceedings of the 13th ACM SIGKDD international conference on Knowledge discovery and data mining*, pages 210-219. ACM, 2007.

[5] C. Desrosiers and G. Karypis. A comprehensive survey of neighborhood-based recommendation methods. *Recommender Systems Handbook*, pages 107-144, 2011.

[6] T. Dietterich. Overfitting and undercomputing in machine learning. *ACM Computing Surveys*, 27(3):326-327, 1995.

[7] C. Ding, T. Li, W. Peng, and H. Park. Orthogonal nonnegative matrix t-factorizations for clustering. In *Proceedings of the 12th ACM SIGKDD international conference on Knowledge discovery and data mining*, pages 126-135. ACM, 2006.

[8] L. Getoor and C. Diehl. Link mining: a survey. *ACM SIGKDD Explorations Newsletter*, 7(2):3-12, 2005.

[9] T. Hofmann and J. Puzicha. Latent class models for collaborative filtering. In *International Joint Conference on Artificial Intelligence*, volume 16, pages 688-693. LAWRENCE ERLBAUM ASSOCIATES LTD, 1999.

[10] H. Kiers. Setting up alternating least squares and iterative majorization algorithms for solving various matrix optimization problems. *Computational statistics & data analysis*, 41(1):157-170, 2002.

[11] R. Kohavi and D. Sommerfield. Feature subset selection using the wrapper method: Overfitting and dynamic search space topology. In *Proceedings of the First International Conference on Knowledge Discovery and Data Mining*, pages 192 U-197, 1995.

[12] Y. Koren and R. Bell. Advances in collaborative filtering. *Recommender Systems Handbook*, pages 145-186, 2011.

[13] B. Li. Cross-domain collaborative filtering: A brief survey. In *2011 23rd IEEE International Conference on Tools with Artificial Intelligence*, pages 1085-1086. IEEE, 2011.

[14] B. Li, Q. Yang, and X. Xue. Can movies and books collaborate? cross-domain collaborative filtering for sparsity reduction. In *Proceedings of the 21st international jont conference on Artificial intelligence*, pages 2052-2057. Morgan Kaufmann Publishers Inc., 2009.

[15] B. Li, Q. Yang, and X. Xue. Transfer learning for collaborative filtering via a rating-matrix generative model. In *Proceedings of the 26th Annual International Conference on Machine Learning*, pages 617-624. ACM, 2009.

[16] S. Pan and Q. Yang. A survey on transfer learning. *Knowledge and Data Engineering, IEEE Transactions on*, 22(10):1345-1359, 2010.

[17] W. Pan, E. Xiang, N. Liu, and Q. Yang. Transfer learning in collaborative filtering for sparsity reduction. In *Proceedings of the 24rd AAAI Conference on Artificial Intelligence*, 2010.

[18] G. Shani and A. Gunawardana. Evaluating recommendation systems. *Recommender Systems Handbook*, pages 257-297, 2011.

[19] G. Xue, W. Dai, Q. Yang, and Y. Yu. Topic-bridged plsa for cross-domain text classification. In *Proceedings of the 31st annual international ACM SIGIR conference on Research and development in information retrieval*, pages 627-634. ACM, 2008.

[20] Y. Zhang, B. Cao, and D. Yeung. Multi-domain collaborative filtering. *In Proceedings of the 26th Conference on Uncertainty in Artificial Intelligence (UAI), Catalina Island, California, USA*, 2010.

Utilizing Common Substructures to Speedup Tensor Factorization for Mining Dynamic Graphs

Wei Liu, Jeffrey Chan, James Bailey, Christopher Leckie, and Ramamohanarao Kotagiri
Dept of Computing and Information Systems, The University of Melbourne, Australia
{wei.liu, jeffrey.chan, baileyj, caleckie, kotagiri}@unimelb.edu.au

ABSTRACT

In large and complex graphs of social, chemical/biological, or other relations, frequent substructures are commonly shared by different graphs or by graphs evolving through different time periods. Tensors are natural representations of these complex time-evolving graph data. A factorization of a tensor provides a high-quality low-rank compact basis for each dimension of the tensor, which facilitates the interpretation of frequent substructures of the original graphs. However, the high computational cost of tensor factorization makes it infeasible for conventional tensor factorization methods to handle large graphs that evolve frequently with time.

To address this problem, in this paper we propose a novel iterative tensor factorization (ITF) method whose time complexity is linear in the cardinalities of all dimensions of a tensor. This low time complexity means that when using tensors to represent dynamic graphs, the computational cost of ITF is linear in the size (number of edges/vertices) of graphs and is also linear in the number of time periods over which the graph evolves. More importantly, an error estimation of ITF suggests that its factorization correctness is comparable to that of the standard factorization method. We empirically evaluate our method on publication networks and chemical compound graphs, and demonstrate that ITF is an order of magnitude faster than the conventional method and at the same time preserves factorization quality. To the best of our knowledge, this research is the first work that uses important frequent substructures to speed up tensor factorizations for mining dynamic graphs.

Categories and Subject Descriptors

H.2.8 [**Database Applications**]: Data mining

General Terms

Algorithms

Keywords

Tensor factorization; dynamic graphs; scalability.

1. INTRODUCTION

Widely used statistical data mining methods that detect dynamic patterns are usually based on matrix operations, such as SVD [7] and PCA [14], which can only deal with two "dimensions" of the original data (by the "row dimension" and the "column dimension" of matrices). When data sets are multi-dimensional such as dynamic time-evolving networks, tensor-based methods can more effectively and naturally represent all dimensions of the data. However, similar to performing SVD on matrices, the use of tensors raises the problem of tensor factorizations, from which it is possible to identify the principle low-rank factors of a tensor (i.e., the linear combinations of original dimensions that contribute the most to the overall variance of the tensor). These low-rank factors are important since the new feature space formed by these factors preserves the main variance of the original tensor.

To successfully perform tensor factorization on dynamic graphs, a major challenge that needs to be addressed is how to handle scalability. Scalability is an issue not only because tensors are composed of multiple dimensions, but also because the cardinality of each dimension in itself can be very large. For example, if we use a 3-mode tensor, $authors \times journalNames \times publicationTime$, to represent a dynamic publication network, each of the three dimensions can have thousands or more unique values. For another example, when one uses a tensor to represent a collection of chemical compounds (e.g., $atoms \times bonds \times compounds$) where each compound is a graph of atoms [11], the cardinality of the third dimension of this tensor is usually in the tens of thousands. Moreover, with new bioassays constantly being tested over time, the number of compounds that need to be incorporated into the tensor will tend continue to grow larger. This phenomenon makes the computational cost of the standard tensor factorization extremely expensive and infeasible for analyzing time-varying graphs/networks[1].

Given the scalability challenge, a good tensor factorization method should be able to *(1)* factorize large tensors efficiently using much less time than standard methods, while at the same time *(2)* obtain low-rank factors that preserve the main variance of the tensors. To achieve this goal, in this

[1]Due to the generic nature of the iterative tensor factorization technique we propose, we use the two terms "network" and "graph" interchangeably.

paper we propose to reduce the time complexity of tensor factorization by updating the factor matrices in an iterative manner. The rationale behind this design is based on the observation that, in many practical domains, the most important substructures of graphs are commonly shared by all graphs, or by graphs evolving in different time periods. In other words, it is usually not the important substructures, but the actual combinations of these substructures, which are changing with time or changing across different graphs. If one has discovered the most important substructures of a set of graphs at an earlier time, then in many domains the graphs at a later time can generally be well explained by those earlier substructures using an efficient updating procedure. From the perspective of tensor factorization on graphs, if we have found low-rank factors of a subset of a tensor, then after we iteratively update these factors at a very low cost, the rest of the tensor data can also be well represented by the updated factors. The notion of an important substructure is essentially a column vector from a low-rank factor matrix, which comprises a linear combination of the original features (e.g., edges). Note that we do not assume the structural changes of the graphs are smooth – even if the graphs change frequently, the later graphs can still be explained by the earlier factor matrices as long as the later graphs are comprised of important substructures (i.e., rather than being comprised of noisy or random substructures).

In the preceding chemical compound example, although there are a huge number of compounds that can be encoded into a tensor, most of these compounds share many common substructures, such as aromatic rings, hydroxyls and amines. The major difference among chemical compounds, in terms of preserving the main variance of the data, is in what formulations of those substructures comprise each compound. There might be some special substructures that only exist in a few specific compounds, but we note that such substructures would contribute very little in representing the main variance of a data set, and thus would have little influence in the decomposed factor matrices. Similarly for publication networks, the publication patterns of an author at different times would vary in the concrete combinations of journals or conferences in which the author has published. For example, we expect authors in the number theory domain to continue to publish in number theory journals, rather than change their focus to marketing or finance journals. To this end, the combination of number theory journals are the common important factors that can be discovered early on from a subset of a tensor.

Based on these observations, in this paper we propose a novel factorization strategy that first factorizes a subset of a tensor, and then iteratively refines its factor matrices by efficient and effective updating operations on the remaining data in the tensor. Moreover, we generalize the iterative factorization process from one mode to all modes of a tensor, which further reduces its overall time complexity. In summary, the major contributions of this paper are as follows:

1. We propose an iterative tensor factorization method (`ITF`), which significantly reduces the time complexity of standard tensor factorization.

2. We derive an analytical error estimation of the iterative approximation made by `ITF`, and demonstrate that `ITF` can theoretically preserve as much variance as a standard method, when important substructures are frequently shared among different graphs.

3. We apply the general `ITF` algorithm to practical problems of discovering emerging publication trends and classifying chemical compounds, both of which demonstrate that `ITF` is capable of significantly reducing computation time while solving the two practical problems with high accuracy in comparison to the standard factorization method.

The rest of the paper is structured as follows. We review related literature in Section 2. Section 3 defines the tensor factorization problem, and introduces our `ITF` algorithm with an error estimation. We explain how tensor decomposition can be applied to dynamic graph mining in Section 4. Details of the dataset we use and the empirical evaluations are reported in Section 5. We conclude in Section 6 with directions for future work.

2. LITERATURE REVIEW

In this section, we review existing methods that are closely related to this research. A detailed survey on tensor factorization methods can be found in [9].

Many factorization methods have been proposed for tensor analysis based broadly on two approaches: Tucker decomposition [19] and canonical polyadic decomposition (aka PARAFAC/CANDECOMP decomposition) [3], both of which can be considered as higher-order generalizations of matrix SVD and PCA. Kroonenberg *et al.* [12] proposed to use the method of alternating least squares (ALS) in solving Tucker decomposition for three-way arrays, which was then extended and popularized by Kapteyn *et al.* [8] for n-way arrays. Sun *et al.* [16,17] have proposed methods for incremental tensor analysis, which are aimed at solving the decomposition problem when there is a stream of many tensors: in [16] they used sliding windows to track the changes of covariance matrices, based on which their algorithms made decisions on whether to update the projection matrices; and in [17] they introduced the notion of a "forgetting factor" which is added onto older covariance matrices. This forgetting factor controlled the amount of information that could be considered in future updates. However, these methods did not avoid the extremely expensive computational costs of diagonalization/eigen-decomposition on any mode of a tensor, which severely limits the efficiency of their methods. Moreover, they did not provide any analysis of the error estimation of their methods. Kolda *et al.* [10] designed algorithms to improve memory efficiency for sparse tensors, but when tensors are not highly sparse their method requires much more CPU time than normal decompositions. Recently, Schifanella *et al.* [15] proposed to use metadata, which is a priori background knowledge in addition to the original data, to design a domain hierarchy by which they reduce the time of tensor decomposition. However, this method cannot address more general scenarios where such metadata is not available for the original data.

The major difference between our proposed iterative method and the above existing methods is that the method proposed in this paper avoids the full decomposition / diagonalization on the covariance matrix in all modes of a tensor, which is the main cause of the high computational complexities of tensor factorization. Furthermore, we provide an error estimation of our method, which illustrates its suitability for

Table 1: Notation used in this paper

Notation	Definition and Description
a	lowercase normal font represents scalar values
$\mathbf{a}$	boldface lowercase represents vectors
$\mathbf{U}$	boldface uppercase represents matrices
$\mathbf{U}_{i,j}$	the scalar at the $\{i, j\}$ position of $\mathbf{U}$
$\mathcal{X}, \mathcal{Y}, \mathcal{S}$	calligraphic font represents tensors
$\mathcal{X}_{i,j,k,...}$	the scalar at the $\{i, j, k, ...\}$ position of $\mathcal{X}$
$\mathbf{U}^i$	the projection factor matrix on the ith dimension of $\mathcal{X}$
$\mathbb{U}$	the set of projection matrices $\mathbf{U}^i$ on all dimensions i; we also use $\mathbf{U}^d\|_{d=i}^{j}$ to define the range of i in $\mathbb{U}$
n_i	the cardinality of the ith dimension of the original tensor $\mathcal{X} \in \mathbb{R}^{n_1 \times n_2 \times ... \times n_M}$
r_i	the desired rank of the ith dimension of the original tensor $\mathcal{X}$, which is also the cardinality of the ith dimension of the core tensor $\mathcal{Y}$
$\times_d$	the tensor mode product of a tensor and a matrix on the tensor's dth dimension

mining graph data. A detailed analytical presentation of the proposed method is provided in the next section.

3. TENSOR DECOMPOSITION

The dimensionality of a tensor is also called the tensor's *modes*. For example, matrices are tensors of 2 modes. Table 1 lists the notation we use in the rest of the paper. We denote scalars by letters in lowercase normal font, e.g., a; vectors (tensors of 1 mode) by boldface lowercase letters, e.g., $\mathbf{a}$; matrices (tensors of 2 modes) by boldface uppercase letters, e.g., $\mathbf{U}$; and tensors with 3 or more modes by letters of calligraphic font, e.g., $\mathcal{X}$. A tensor can be represented in general by a multi-dimensional array in $\mathbb{R}^{n_1 \times n_2 \times ... \times n_M}$, where n_i $(1 \le i \le M)$ is the cardinality of the ith mode, and M is the total number of modes. Now we give the following essential definitions to introduce the overall tensor factorization problem.

DEFINITION 1. (**Tensor mode product**): The product of the dth mode of a tensor $\mathcal{X} \in \mathbb{R}^{n_1 \times n_2 \times ... \times n_M}$ and a matrix $\mathbf{U} \in \mathbb{R}^{n_d \times r}$, denoted by $\mathcal{X} \times_d \mathbf{U}$, is a new tensor of size $\mathbb{R}^{n_1 \times ... \times n_{d-1} \times r \times n_{d+1} \times ... \times n_M}$ defined element-wise as:

$$(\mathcal{X} \times_d U)_{i_1,...,i_{d-1},r,i_{d+1},...,i_M} = \sum_{i_d=1}^{n_d} \mathcal{X}_{i_1,i_2,...,i_M} U_{i_d,r}.$$

DEFINITION 2. (**Tensor mode unfolding**): The unfolding (i.e., matricization) on the dth mode of a tensor $\mathcal{X} \in \mathbb{R}^{n_1 \times n_2 \times ... \times n_M}$, denoted by unfold$(\mathcal{X}, d)$, leads to a matrix $\mathbf{X} \in \mathbb{R}^{n_d \times \prod_{i \neq d} n_i}$ by keeping the index d fixed and varying the other indices of $\mathcal{X}$.

Tucker Factorization

The overall problem we aim to solve in this paper is to efficiently factorize a tensor in the manner of Tucker factorization [19], which approximates a large tensor by using a small core tensor by changes of basis:

DEFINITION 3. (**Tucker tensor factorization**): Given a M-mode tensor $\mathcal{X} \in \mathbb{R}^{n_1 \times n_2 \times ... \times n_M}$ and desired low ranks on each mode $r_1, r_2, ..., r_M$, factorize $\mathcal{X}$ into a core tensor $\mathcal{Y} \in \mathbb{R}^{r_1 \times r_2 \times ... \times r_M}$ and M projection matrices $\mathbf{U}^d \in \mathbb{R}^{n_d \times r_d} (1 \le d \le M)$, such that the factorization error $\|\mathcal{X} - \mathcal{Y} \times_1 \mathbf{U}^1 \times_2 \mathbf{U}^2 .... \times_M \mathbf{U}^M\|$ is minimized.

Algorithm 1 HOSVD$(\mathcal{X}, r_1, r_2, ..., r_M)$: the standard method for higher-order singular value decomposition.

Input: the original tensor $\mathcal{X}$, and the desired ranks on each mode r_1, r_2, ..., r_M.
Output: a core tensor $\mathcal{Y}$, and projection factor matrices $\mathbf{U}^d (1 \le d \le M)$.

1: **for** d = 1,2,...,M **do**
2: $\quad \mathbf{X}_d \leftarrow$ unfold$(\mathcal{X}, d)$ by Definition 2;
3: $\quad$ Compute the covariance matrix of the dth mode unfolded matrix $\mathbf{C}_d = \mathbf{X}_d \mathbf{X}_d^T$;
4: $\quad \mathbf{U}^d \leftarrow$ the first r_d eigenvectors of $\mathbf{C}_d$;
5: **end for**
6: $\mathcal{Y} \leftarrow \mathcal{X} \times_1 (\mathbf{U}^1)^T \times_2 (\mathbf{U}^2)^T ... \times_M (\mathbf{U}^M)^T$;
7: **return** $\mathcal{Y}$ and $\mathbf{U}^d (1 \le d \le M)$.

Algorithm 2 Tucker$(\epsilon, \mathcal{X}, r_1, r_2, ..., r_M)$: the standard alternating least square method for Tucker tensor decomposition.

Input: convergence threshold ϵ, original tensor $\mathcal{X}$, and the desired ranks $r_1, r_2, ..., r_M$.
Output: core tensor $\mathcal{Y}$, and the projection matrices $\mathbf{U}^d (1 \le d \le M)$.

Initialize $\mathbf{U}^d (1 \le d \le M)$ by HOSVD$(\mathcal{X}, r_1, r_2, ..., r_M)$;
repeat
$\quad$ **for** d = 1, 2, ..., M **do**
$\quad\quad \mathcal{X}' \leftarrow \mathcal{X} \times_i (\mathbf{U}^i|_{i=1\&i\neq d}^{M})^T$;
$\quad\quad \mathbf{X}'_d \leftarrow$ unfold$(\mathcal{X}', d)$;
$\quad\quad$ Covariance matrix of current mode $\mathbf{C}'_d \leftarrow \mathbf{X}'_d \mathbf{X}'^T_d$;
$\quad\quad \mathbf{U}^d \leftarrow$ the first r_d eigenvectors of $\mathbf{C}'_d$;
$\quad$ **end for**
$\quad \mathcal{Y} \leftarrow \mathcal{X} \times_d (\mathbf{U}^d|_{d=1}^{M})^T$.
until the increase of $\|\mathcal{Y}\|$ is less than ϵ.
return $\mathcal{Y}$ and $\mathbf{U}^d (1 \le d \le M)$.

In other words, the Tucker tensor factorization is equivalent to solving the following minimization problem:

$$\min f(\mathcal{Y}, \mathbf{U}^d) = \min \|\mathcal{X} - \mathcal{Y} \times_1 \mathbf{U}^1 .... \times_M \mathbf{U}^M\| \quad (1)$$

where $1 \le d \le M$. The core tensor $\mathcal{Y}$ is an approximation of the original tensor $\mathcal{X}$ by changing its basis through projecting all original data into $\mathbf{U}^d$ on each dimension. The function $f(\mathcal{Y}, \mathbf{U}^d)$ can be minimized to zero if $r_d = n_d$ for all modes d. How to solve Equation 1 scalably and effectively is the main challenge we address in this paper. We start from introducing the standard method of solving Equation 1 in the next subsection.

3.1 Standard Method for Tensor Decomposition

Higher-order singular value decomposition (HOSVD) [4] forms the basis of many tensor decomposition methods developed recently [5, 18]. Details of the HOSVD method are shown in Algorithm 1.

In line 2 of Algorithm 1, the matrix $\mathbf{X}_d$ obtained from unfolding on the dth mode of $\mathcal{X}$ is of size $n_d \times \prod_{i \neq d} n_i$, and hence the formulation of the covariance matrices has com-

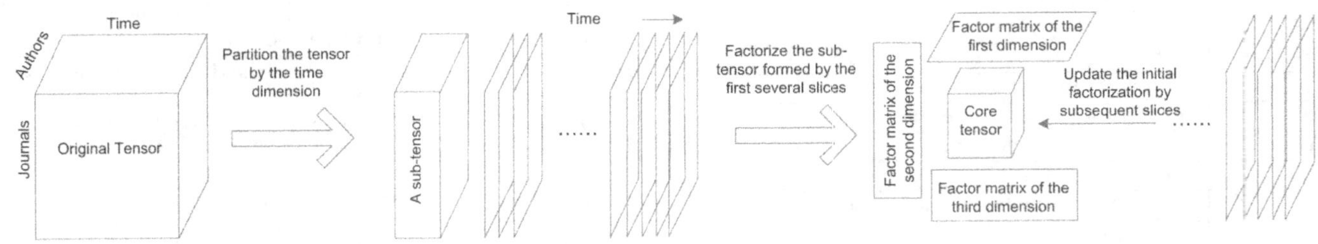

Figure 1: Graphical representation of the main process of the one-mode ITF algorithm. For illustrative purposes, we use the notion of two dimensional "slices" to represent the partitions of the original tensor. However we note that the ITF algorithm is designed to deal with partitions of any number of dimensions.

plexity $O(n_d^2 \prod_{i \neq d} n_i)$. The covariance matrix $\mathbf{C}$ obtained in line 3 is of size $n_d \times n_d$, which means the time complexity for computing the eigenvectors of $\mathbf{C}$ in line 4 is $O(n_d^3)$ [2]. Therefore the overall time complexity for Algorithm 1 is $O(\sum_{d=1}^{M} n_d^3 + \sum_{d=1}^{M} n_d^2 \prod_{i \neq d} n_i)$, which is in cubic time for each mode.

In the standard Tucker tensor factorization, it is common to use alternating least squares (ALS) (shown in Algorithm 2) to repeat the singular vector projection process until the variance of the core tensor $\mathcal{Y}$ stops increasing. Because the size of the projected matrix $\mathbf{X}'_d$ formed in line 5 of Algorithm 2 is of size $n_d \times \prod_{i \neq d} r_i$, the complexity of the covariance matrix formulation in line 6 is $O(n_d^2 \prod_{i \neq d} r_i)$. The body of the *for loop* of the Tucker method is very similar to HOSVD, which makes it easy to show that the overall time complexity of the Tucker method is $O(C(\sum_{d=1}^{M} n_d^3 + \sum_{d=1}^{M} n_d^2 \prod_{i \neq d} r_i))$, where the first term is for the eigen-decomposition and the second is for computing the covariance matrices (the factor C is the number of iterations needed for convergence, which can be non-trivial). The complexity of the standard Tucker method is also in cubic time to each mode of a tensor, which is very expensive.

3.2 ITF Method for One-mode Iterative Factorization

In this subsection, we explain how we solve the factorization problem iteratively in one mode. The solution to the problem in Equation 1 has the following property:

$$\mathcal{X} \approx \mathcal{Y} \times_1 \mathbf{U}^1 .... \times_M \mathbf{U}^M \tag{2}$$

For brevity, we use $\mathbb{U}$ to denote the product of projection factor matrices $\mathbf{U}^d|_{d=1}^{M}$, and use $\mathcal{Y}\mathbb{U}$ to denote the product of the core tensor $\mathcal{Y}$ with all projection matrices. Then Equation 2 can be rewritten as $\mathcal{X} \approx \mathcal{Y}\mathbb{U}$. From the orthogonality of $\mathbb{U}$ we know that $\mathcal{Y} = \mathcal{Y}\mathbb{U}\mathbb{U}^T \approx \mathcal{X}\mathbb{U}^T$, which means $\mathcal{Y}$ is $\mathcal{X}$ projected on the subspace formed by $\mathbb{U}$. Similarly we have

$$\mathcal{X} \approx \mathcal{Y}\mathbb{U} \approx (\mathcal{X}\mathbb{U}^T)\mathbb{U} \approx \mathcal{X}\mathbb{U}^T\mathbb{U}. \tag{3}$$

Now we derive our one-mode ITF method which refines the core tensor and projection matrices iteratively in one mode. As illustrated in Figure 1, we first factorize a small sub-tensor $\mathcal{S}$ from the original tensor $\mathcal{X}$, and then update the obtained factorization by gradually taking into account the remaining data of $\mathcal{X}$. Counting from the zero index on the dth mode of $\mathcal{X}$, we extract a sub-tensor whose dth mode is the same size as the desired core tensor and whose other modes are the same sizes as those of $\mathcal{X}$, so we have a sub-tensor $\mathcal{S} \in \mathbb{R}^{n_1 \times n_2 \times ... n_{d-1} \times r_d \times n_{d+1} ... \times n_M}$.

Without loss of generality, we assume it is the *1st* mode of $\mathcal{X}$ where a sub-tensor $\mathcal{S}$ is extracted, so $\mathcal{S} \in \mathbb{R}^{r_1 \times n_2 ... \times n_M}$. We denote the formulation of $\mathcal{S}$ by $\mathcal{S} \equiv \mathcal{X}_{1:r_1}$ where we use the subscripts to represent the size of $\mathcal{S}$ on the *1st* mode and omit the fixed sizes n_d $(2 \leq d \leq M)$ on other modes. By partitioning the first mode of $\mathcal{X}$ and extracting the sub-tensor, the original tensor can be represented as:

$$\mathcal{X} = \{\mathcal{X}_{1:r_1}, \mathcal{X}_{r_1+1}, \mathcal{X}_{r_1+2}, ..., \mathcal{X}_{n_1}\},$$

where the size of $\mathcal{X}_{r_1+i}$ $(1 \leq i \leq n_1 - r_1)$ is $1 \times n_2 \times n_3 ... \times n_M$, which we call a *slice* of $\mathcal{X}$.

Suppose we have obtained the factorization of the sub-tensor: $\mathcal{S} \equiv \mathcal{X}_{1:r_1} \approx \tilde{\mathcal{Y}} \times_1 \tilde{\mathbf{U}}^1 \times_2 \tilde{\mathbf{U}}^2 ... \times_M \tilde{\mathbf{U}}^M$, where $\tilde{\mathcal{Y}}$ is of the same size as the desired core tensor, $\tilde{\mathbf{U}}^1$ is of size $r_1 \times r_1$, and $\tilde{\mathbf{U}}^i|_{i=2}^{M}$ is of size $n_i \times r_i$. Then from Equation 3 we know $\mathcal{X}_{1:r_1} \approx \mathcal{X}_{1:r_1}\tilde{\mathbb{U}}^T\tilde{\mathbb{U}}$, where $\tilde{\mathbb{U}}$ denotes $\tilde{\mathbf{U}}^i|_{i=1}^{M}$. Since the next *slice* after $\mathcal{X}_{1:r_1}$ (e.g., $\mathcal{X}_{r_1+1}$) was not included in the decomposition of $\mathcal{S}$, it is possible that this next *slice* cannot be recovered from the projection in the subspace formed by $\tilde{\mathbb{U}}$. So we introduce the notion of "*departure*", denoted by Δ, with which the projection recovery in Equation 3 can hold true for $\mathcal{X}_{r_1+1}$:

$$\mathcal{X}_{r_1+1} = \mathcal{X}_{r_1+1}\tilde{\mathbb{U}}^T\tilde{\mathbb{U}} + \Delta. \tag{4}$$

We now explain the rationale of using the departure Δ from a graph mining perspective. By using a tensor to represent dynamic graphs, the columns of $\tilde{\mathbb{U}}$ (i.e., the singular vectors) are necessarily the major substructures (linear combinations of original features) of previous graphs. The information contained in Δ denotes new formulations of substructures from the current graph that cannot be represented by previously discovered substructures in $\tilde{\mathbb{U}}$. Intuitively, when important representative substructures are shared among current and previous graphs, the value of Δ would always be small.

After factorizing the sub-tensor, we form a new tensor $\{\tilde{\mathcal{Y}}, \mathcal{X}_{r_1+1}\tilde{\mathbb{U}}^T + \Delta\tilde{\mathbb{U}}^T\}$, where the second term of this new tensor comprises the component of $\mathcal{X}_{r_1+1}$ that can be represented in the subspace formed by $\tilde{\mathbb{U}}$, and also the "*departure*" of $\mathcal{X}_{r_1+1}$ (i.e., Δ) that cannot be recovered from the subspace projection. We factorize this new tensor into

$$\{\tilde{\mathcal{Y}}, \mathcal{X}_{r_1+1}\tilde{\mathbb{U}}^T + \Delta\tilde{\mathbb{U}}^T\} = \mathcal{Y}' \times_1 \mathbf{U}^{1'} \times_2 \mathbf{U}^{2'} ... \times_M \mathbf{U}^{M'} \tag{5}$$

where $\mathbf{U}^{1'}$ is of size $(r_1 + 1) \times r_1$ and $\mathbf{U}^{i'}|_{i=2}^{M}$ are all of size $r_i \times r_i$. Then the new updated projection matrices for $\{\mathcal{X}_{1:r_1}, \mathcal{X}_{r_1+1}\}$ are $\mathbb{U}'\tilde{\mathbb{U}}$, where $\mathbb{U}'$ denotes the set of projection matrices $\mathbf{U}^{i'}|_{i=1}^{M}$.

Algorithm 3 `ITF_OneMode`($\mathcal{X}, r_1, r_2, ..., r_M, l$): iteratively decomposing one mode of a tensor by using the *1st* mode as an illustration.

Input: original tensor $\mathcal{X}$, the desired ranks r_1, r_2, ..., r_M, and a mode index l on which the tensor is to iteratively decomposed (we use l=1 as an example to explain this algorithm in the paper's texts).
Output: core tensor $\mathcal{Y}$, and the set of all projection matrices $\mathbb{U}$.

1: Form a sub-tensor $\mathcal{X}_{1:r_l}$ from the first r_1 slices of $\mathcal{X}$;
2: $\{\tilde{\mathcal{Y}}, \tilde{\mathbb{U}}\} \leftarrow$ `HOSVD`($\mathcal{X}_{1:r_l}, r_1, r_2, ..., r_M$);
3: $\mathcal{Y}_{old} \leftarrow \tilde{\mathcal{Y}}$;
4: $\mathbb{U}_{old} \leftarrow \tilde{\mathbb{U}}$;
5: **for** i=1, 2, ..., $n_1 - r_1$ **do**
6:    Obtain the "departure" $\Delta \leftarrow \mathcal{X}_{r_1+i}\mathbb{U}^T\mathbb{U} - \mathcal{X}_{r_1+i}$;
7:    Form a tensor $\mathcal{X}_{new} \leftarrow \{\mathcal{X}_{1:r_l}, \mathcal{X}_{r_1+i}\mathbb{U}_{old} + \Delta\mathbb{U}_{old}\}$
8:    $\{\mathcal{Y}_{new}, \mathbb{U}_{new}\} \leftarrow$ `HOSVD`($\mathcal{X}_{new}, r_1, r_2, ..., r_M$);
9:    $\mathbb{U} = \mathbb{U}_{new}\mathbb{U}_{old}$;
10: **end for**
11: $\mathcal{Y} \leftarrow \mathcal{X}\mathbb{U}^T$;
12: **return** $\mathcal{Y}$ and $\mathbb{U}$.

We then take $\{\mathcal{X}_{1:r_1}, \mathcal{X}_{r_1+1}\}$ as a new sub-tensor that replaces $\mathcal{S}$, and treat $\mathcal{X}_{r_1+2}$ as the new *next slice* from the original $\mathcal{X}$. This iterative process is repeated until we reach the final *slice* of $\mathcal{X}$ (i.e., $\mathcal{X}_{n_1}$). We call such an iterative updating procedure the one-mode `ITF` method.

The complete procedure of `ITF_OneMode` is presented in Algorithm 3, where lines 2 and 8 reuse HOSVD as a subroutine. Line 1 has the time complexity of $O(r_1^3 + \sum_{d=2}^{M} n_d^3 + r_1^2 \prod_{i\neq 1} n_i + \sum_{d=2}^{M} n_d^2 \prod_{i\neq d} n_i)$, line 8 has the complexity of $O((r_1+1)^3 + \sum_{d=2}^{M} r_d^3 + (r_1+1)^2 \prod_{i\neq 1} r_i + \sum_{d=2}^{M} r_d^2 \prod_{i\neq d} r_i)$, so the overall time complexity of `ITF_OneMode` is $O(r_1^3 + \sum_{d=2}^{M} n_d^3 + r_1^2 \prod_{i\neq 1} n_i + \sum_{d=2}^{M} n_d^2 \prod_{i\neq d} n_i + (n_1 - r_1)\big[(r_1+1)^3 + \sum_{d=2}^{M} r_d^3 + (r_1+1)^2 \prod_{i\neq 1} r_i + \sum_{d=2}^{M} r_d^2 \prod_{i\neq d} r_i\big])$, where among the five terms the first four terms are for decomposing the first sub-tensor, and the last term is for updating all successive $n_1 - r_1$ slices of the original tensor. Note that n_1 only appears as a linear coefficient in the complexity expression, and that is why it is possible to design a graph mining technique based on `ITF` that is linear in the size of the graphs. Moreover, as we explain in the next subsection, this computational complexity can be further significantly reduced by applying `ITF` onto all modes of a tensor.

Compared to the complexity of standard decomposition methods, the reduced complexity of `ITF_OneMode` arises from computations on the magnitude of r_1 rather than n_1 in both the covariance matrices formulation and their eigen-decompositions. We note that the standard Tucker method becomes a special case of `ITF_OneMode` when $r_1 = n_1$.

3.3 ITF Method for All-mode Factorization

By applying the above iterative updating process to all modes of a tensor, we obtain the final `ITF` method shown in Algorithm 4. Starting from the first mode (line 2 to 4), this algorithm constructs and factorizes a sub-tensor extracted from all modes of the original tensor (line 21) before proceeding to the iterative refinement of factor matrices. We use a recursion to formulate sub-tensors, so that after one mode completes its updating procedure, the algorithm recursively returns the decomposition of that mode to other modes, until it reaches the last mode. This makes Algorithm

Algorithm 4 `ITF`($\mathcal{X}, r_1, r_2, ..., r_M, l$): a recursive algorithm for iteratively decomposing all modes of a tensor.

Input: original tensor $\mathcal{X}$, the desired ranks r_1, r_2, ..., r_M, and a mode index l (for recursion purposes).
Output: core tensor $\mathcal{Y}$, and the set of all projection matrices $\mathbb{U}$.

1: // l is uninitialized in the beginning of the algorithm.
2: **if** mode index l is uninitialized **then**
3:    Initialize $l \leftarrow 1$;
4: **end if**
5: **if** l has not reached the last mode of $\mathcal{X}$ **then**
6:    // A recursion for applying `ITF` to all modes.
7:    $l \leftarrow l + 1$;
8:    $\{\tilde{\mathcal{Y}}, \tilde{\mathbb{U}}\} \leftarrow$ `ITF`($\mathcal{X}, r_1, r_2, ..., r_M, l$);
9:    $\mathcal{Y}_{old} \leftarrow \tilde{\mathcal{Y}}$;
10:    $\mathbb{U}_{old} \leftarrow \tilde{\mathbb{U}}$;
11:    // Iteratively update factor matrices on the lth mode
12:    **for** i=1, 2, ..., $n_l - r_l$ **do**
13:       Obtain the "departure" $\Delta \leftarrow \mathcal{X}_{r_l+i} - \mathcal{X}_{r_l+i}\mathbb{U}^T\mathbb{U}$;
14:       Form a tensor $\mathcal{X}_{new} \leftarrow \{\mathcal{X}_{1:r_l}, \mathcal{X}_{r_l+i}\mathbb{U}_{old} + \Delta\mathbb{U}_{old}\}$
15:       $\{\mathcal{Y}_{new}, \mathbb{U}_{new}\} \leftarrow$ `HOSVD`($\mathcal{X}_{new}, r_1, r_2, ..., r_M$);
16:       $\mathbb{U} = \mathbb{U}_{new}\mathbb{U}_{old}$;
17:    **end for**
18:    $\mathcal{Y} \leftarrow \mathcal{X}\mathbb{U}^T$;
19: **else**
20:    // Factorize a sub-tensor extracted from all modes
21:    $\{\tilde{\mathcal{Y}}, \tilde{\mathbb{U}}\} \leftarrow$ `HOSVD`($\mathcal{X}_{1:r_1,1:r_2,1:r_3,...,1:r_l}, r_1, r_2, ..., r_M$);
22:    $\mathcal{Y}_{old} \leftarrow \tilde{\mathcal{Y}}$;
23:    $\mathbb{U}_{old} \leftarrow \tilde{\mathbb{U}}$;
24:    // Iteratively update factor matrices on the last mode
25:    **for** i=1, 2, ..., $n_l - r_l$ **do**
26:       Obtain the "departure" $\Delta \leftarrow \mathcal{X}_{r_l+i} - \mathcal{X}_{r_l+i}\mathbb{U}^T\mathbb{U}$;
27:       $\mathcal{X}_{new} \leftarrow \{\mathcal{X}_{1:r_1,1:r_2,1:r_3,...,1:r_l}, \mathcal{X}_{r_l+i}\mathbb{U}_{old} + \Delta\mathbb{U}_{old}\}$
28:       $\{\mathcal{Y}_{new}, \mathbb{U}_{new}\} \leftarrow$ `HOSVD`($\mathcal{X}_{new}, r_1, r_2, ..., r_M$);
29:       $\mathbb{U} = \mathbb{U}_{new}\mathbb{U}_{old}$;
30:    **end for**
31:    $\mathcal{Y} \leftarrow \mathcal{X}\mathbb{U}^T$;
32: **end if**
33: **return** $\mathcal{Y}$ and $\mathbb{U}$.

4 different to Algorithm 3 in that any tensor being factorized in Algorithm 4 is of size $r_1 \times r_2 \times r_3 \times ... \times r_M$, in contrast to that of $r_1 \times n_2 \times n_3 \times ... \times n_M$ in Algorithm 3.

For Algorithm 4, the complexity of line 21 (for decomposing the first sub-tensor) is $O(\sum_{d=1}^{M} r_d^3 + \sum_{d=1}^{M} r_d^2 \prod_{i\neq d} r_i)$, and those of line 15 and line 28 on mode i (for decomposing a new sub-tensor containing a successive slice) are $O((r_i+1)^3 + \sum_{d\neq i} r_d^3 + (r_i+1)^2 \prod_{d\neq i} r_d + \sum_{d\neq i} r_d^2 \prod_{i\neq d} r_i)$. On each mode i, there exist $n_i - r_i$ slices to be updated, so the overall complexity of Algorithm 4 is $O(\sum_{d=1}^{M} r_d^3 + \sum_{d=1}^{M} r_d^2 \prod_{i\neq d} r_i + \sum_{i=1}^{M} (n_i - r_i)\big[(r_i+1)^3 + \sum_{d\neq i} r_d^3 + (r_i+1)^2 \prod_{d\neq i} r_d + \sum_{d\neq i} r_d^2 \prod_{i\neq d} r_i\big])$. This complexity expression explains that using *one* slice to update the decomposition is cheaper than using *multiple* slices at a time. It also shows that the complexity of `ITF` is *linear in all modes* of a tensor, with all $n_i (1 \leq d \leq M)$ being linear coefficients only. We can observe that the reduction in time complexity of `ITF` compared to that of the standard Tucker method results from the avoidance of computations on the magnitude of n_i, but on r_i, for all modes.

Similar to the standard method, we apply the ALS method to `ITF` by replacing line 1 and line 7 of Algorithm 2 with our iterative decompositions. We omit the details of ALS for ITF due to page limits.

3.4 Error Estimation of ITF

Our ITF method uses the notion of departure ("Δ") in the tensor approximations. By deriving the following theorem, we show that in ITF the update of slice $\mathcal{X}_{r_1+1}$ on the factorization of sub-tensor $\mathcal{X}_{1:r_1}$ is an effective approximation of a standard direct decomposition on $\{\mathcal{X}_{1:r_1}, \mathcal{X}_{r_1+1}\}$.

THEOREM 1. *Given the factorization of all previously observed slices $\mathcal{X}_{1:r_1+1} = \tilde{\mathcal{Y}}\tilde{\mathbb{U}}$ and a new data slice $\mathcal{X}_{r_1+1}$, denote the information loss of projecting $\mathcal{X}_{r_1+1}$ onto $\tilde{\mathbb{U}}$ by $\Delta = \mathcal{X}_{r_1+1} - \mathcal{X}_{r_1+1}\tilde{\mathbb{U}}^T\tilde{\mathbb{U}}$, then the approximation error of using ITF compared to using the standard method is no higher than $||\Delta - \Delta\tilde{\mathbb{U}}^T\tilde{\mathbb{U}}||_F$, where $||\cdot||_F$ represents the Frobenius norm.*

PROOF. From Equation 5 we have:

$$\{\mathcal{Y}, \mathcal{X}_{r_1+1}\tilde{\mathbb{U}}^T + \Delta\tilde{\mathbb{U}}^T\} = \mathcal{Y}'\mathbb{U}'.$$

By multiplying both sides of the above equation by $\tilde{\mathbb{U}}$, we obtain:

$$\begin{aligned} & \{\mathcal{Y},\ \mathcal{X}_{r_1+1}\tilde{\mathbb{U}}^T + \Delta\tilde{\mathbb{U}}^T\}\tilde{\mathbb{U}} &=& (\mathcal{Y}'\mathbb{U}')\tilde{\mathbb{U}} \\ \Rightarrow & \{\mathcal{Y}\tilde{\mathbb{U}},\ \mathcal{X}_{r_1+1}\tilde{\mathbb{U}}^T\tilde{\mathbb{U}} + \Delta\tilde{\mathbb{U}}^T\tilde{\mathbb{U}}\} &=& (\mathcal{Y}'\mathbb{U}')\tilde{\mathbb{U}} \\ \Rightarrow & \{\mathcal{X}_{1:r_1},\ \mathcal{X}_{r_1+1}\tilde{\mathbb{U}}^T\tilde{\mathbb{U}} + \Delta\tilde{\mathbb{U}}^T\tilde{\mathbb{U}}\} &=& (\mathcal{Y}'\mathbb{U}')\tilde{\mathbb{U}} \\ \Rightarrow & \{\mathcal{X}_{1:r_1},\ \mathcal{X}_{r_1+1} - \Delta + \Delta\tilde{\mathbb{U}}^T\tilde{\mathbb{U}}\} &=& (\mathcal{Y}'\mathbb{U}')\tilde{\mathbb{U}} \end{aligned} \tag{6}$$

The tensor $\{\mathcal{X}_{1:r_1},\ \mathcal{X}_{r_1+1} - \Delta + \Delta\tilde{\mathbb{U}}^T\tilde{\mathbb{U}}\}$ is in the size of $(r_1+1)\times n_2\times n_3\times ...\times n_M$ and the slice $\{\mathcal{X}_{r_1+1} - \Delta + \Delta\tilde{\mathbb{U}}^T\tilde{\mathbb{U}}\}$ is in $n_2 \times n_3 \times ... \times n_M$.

By contrast, a direct decomposition on the new tensor $\{\mathcal{X}_{1:r_1}, \mathcal{X}_{r_1+1}\}$ is

$$\{\mathcal{X}_{1:r_1}, \mathcal{X}_{r_1+1}\} = \hat{\mathcal{Y}}\hat{\mathbb{U}}. \tag{7}$$

Then by incorporating the definition of the Frobenius norm[2], the approximation error of using ITF compared to using the standard method is

$$\begin{aligned} & ||\ \hat{\mathcal{Y}}\hat{\mathbb{U}} - (\mathcal{Y}'\mathbb{U}')\tilde{\mathbb{U}}\ ||_F \\ =\ & ||\ \{\mathcal{X}_{1:r_1}, \mathcal{X}_{r_1+1}\} - \{\mathcal{Y},\ \mathcal{X}_{r_1+1}\tilde{\mathbb{U}}^T + \Delta\tilde{\mathbb{U}}^T\}\tilde{\mathbb{U}}\ ||_F \\ =\ & ||\ \{\mathcal{X}_{1:r_1}, \mathcal{X}_{r_1+1}\} - \{\mathcal{Y}\tilde{\mathbb{U}},\ \mathcal{X}_{r_1+1}\tilde{\mathbb{U}}^T\tilde{\mathbb{U}} + \Delta\tilde{\mathbb{U}}^T\tilde{\mathbb{U}}\}\ ||_F \\ =\ & ||\ \{\mathcal{X}_{1:r_1}, \mathcal{X}_{r_1+1}\} - \{\mathcal{X}_{1:r_1},\ \mathcal{X}_{r_1+1} + (\Delta\tilde{\mathbb{U}}^T\tilde{\mathbb{U}} - \Delta)\}\ ||_F \\ =\ & \sqrt{\sum_{i=1}^{\min\{r_1+1,n_2,n_3,\ldots,n_M\}} \sigma_i} \\ \leq\ & \sqrt{\sum_{i=1}^{\min\{n_2,n_3,\ldots,n_M\}} \sigma'_i} \\ =\ & ||\Delta - \Delta\tilde{\mathbb{U}}^T\tilde{\mathbb{U}}||_F \end{aligned}$$

where σ and σ' denote the singular values of tensor $\{\mathcal{X}_{1:r_1}, \mathcal{X}_{r_1+1}\} - \{\mathcal{X}_{1:r_1},\ \mathcal{X}_{r_1+1} + (\Delta\tilde{\mathbb{U}}^T\tilde{\mathbb{U}} - \Delta)\}$ and $\{\Delta - \Delta\tilde{\mathbb{U}}^T\}$ respectively. □

[2]Given a tensor $\mathcal{A}$ and its smallest cardinality $min^{\mathcal{A}}$, the Frobenius norm can be derived as $||\mathcal{A}||_F = \sqrt{tr(\mathcal{A}\mathcal{A}^*)} = \sqrt{\sum_{i=1}^{min^{\mathcal{A}}} \sigma_i^{\mathcal{A}}}$, where $tr()$ is the trace function, $\sigma_i^{\mathcal{A}}$ are $\mathcal{A}$'s singular values, and $\mathcal{A}^*$ is the conjugate transpose of $\mathcal{A}$.

This theorem demonstrates that, compared to the standard method, the approximation error of ITF in the worst case is upper bounded by a linear expression of the departure Δ and the projection matrices $\tilde{\mathbb{U}}$, where the columns of $\tilde{\mathbb{U}}$ indicate previously discovered major frequent substructures. This result can be used to estimate the effects of the iterative updating operations on graph mining. As discussed in Section 3.2, when important frequent substructures are commonly shared across different graphs, the value of the departure Δ would typically be small, which suggests low factorization errors of ITF. This expectation is further confirmed by the empirical results in Section 5.

4. APPLYING ITF TO GRAPH MINING

In the previous section we introduced different ways of decomposing tensors. Now we explain how we use these tensor decomposition methods to *(1)* weight emerging edges (word pairs) in publication networks, and *(2)* classify graphs.

4.1 Weighting Emerging Edges

By using the example of publication networks, we define an edge in a graph as a pair of key words extracted from paper titles. We treat the mode of word pairs in a tensor as a feature of the network, and use tensor factorization to perform feature selection (i.e., dimensionality reduction) on this mode. Given the original data tensor $\mathcal{X}$, both the standard Tucker factorization (Algorithm 2) and our ITF method (Algorithm 4) produce two outputs, the core tensor $\mathcal{Y}$, and the projection matrices $\mathbf{U}^d$ $(1 \leq d \leq M)$. Moreover, the matrices in all dimensions of $\mathcal{Y}$ are arranged in decreasing order of the magnitudes of their variances (i.e., the ordered singular values for the case of matrix decomposition), which is an indication of the significance of the corresponding column vector in $\mathbf{U}^d$. In this regard, to analyze the original tensor $\mathcal{X}$, we only need to keep a small number of column vectors in each projection matrix $\mathbf{U}^d$, the variances of whose corresponding matrices in $\mathcal{Y}$ can preserve the major variances of $\mathcal{X}$. Thus, suppose word pairs are in the first mode of the tensors, in order to reduce the number of features in the word pair mode (assume it is the first mode of $\mathcal{X}$), we only have to look at the r_1 columns contained in $\mathbf{U}^1$. The r_1 columns of $\mathbf{U}^1$ are linear combinations of the original features, so if we take the Frobenius norm of each of the n_1 rows of $\mathbf{U}^1$, these norms can be used as indications of the significance (weights) of the original n_1 features. To this end, all original n_1 word pairs have the obtained weights associated with them. These weights suggest the significance of word pairs in each time period, which we use to weight emerging research topics.

4.2 Classifying Graphs

We apply ITF to classification problems by utilizing the new data points that lie in the new low-dimension feature space formed by factor matrices. Given a set of graphs, each of which is associated with a class, the task is to predict the class of a new graph. For many type of graphs, one can generalize their adjacency matrices and extend them to a tensor of 5 modes: *vertices* × *vertices* × *verticesLabels* × *edgeLabels(or weights)* × *observations(graph instances)*. One can think of the 5-mode tensors as standard *features* × *observations* data sheets where the *features* are represented by 4-mode tensors. Suppose it is the first vertex dimension on which we want to obtain low-dimension new features, then the new feature spaces are defined by the columns of factor matrix $\mathbf{U}^1$. Given the original data points $D_{original}$, we obtain new data points D_{new} which lie in the new spaces by projecting the original data onto the first factor matrix: $D_{new} = D_{original}\mathbf{U}_1$. When D_{new} is of multi-mode, we unfold D_{new} (c.f. Definition 2) on its instance dimension so that it can be learned by standard classifiers. These new data points D_{new} produced by ITF are what we use in the classification process in comparison with data points produced by the standard Tucker method.

5. EXPERIMENTS AND ANALYSIS

The objectives of our experiments are to *(1)* evaluate the computation time costs and preservation of variances of the ITF algorithms for different settings of the desired ranks, and to *(2)* test the practical usefulness of the variance preserved by ITF in terms of weighting emerging edges and classifying graphs. We implement[3] ITF by using the Matlab Tensor Toolbox [1]. We use the DBLP bibliography [13] to obtain the publication networks, and use chemical compound data to perform graph classification. The convergence threshold ϵ of ALS (c.f. Algorithm 2) is set to 10^{-4} for both the standard Tucker and the ITF method. Experiments are conducted on a PC with a 3.0GHz CPU and 4GB memory.

5.1 Weighting Publication Networks

From the DBLP repository, we select journals and conferences whose full book/proceeding titles contain the phrases "data mining" or "knowledge discovery" over a 20 year period from 1991 to 2010. Four properties (i.e., dimensions) are extracted: *(i)* pairs of words that appeared in paper titles; *(ii)* (co-)authors; *(iii)* booktitles (names of journals and conferences/workshops proceedings); *(iv)* time of publication. To avoid using trivial features, we only include word pairs that appeared at least 5 times and authors who have at least 5 publication records in DBLP through the 20 years. After removing stop words, we obtain 11917 word pairs (with 1897 unique words), 6399 authors and 171 booktitles, which form 20 tensors (one for each year) in the space of $\mathbb{R}^{11917\times 6399\times 171}$. For tracking the changes of patterns over time, we calculate the difference of all consecutive two years of tensors and use the resulting "difference tensors" as the input of the decomposition algorithms.

In the settings of the following experiments, we evaluate ITF on the first dimension (i.e., word pairs) of the tensors, and set the desired number of singular vectors of other dimensions (r_2 and r_3) consistently to 50. We note that the focus of this paper is not to determine the best number of singular vectors in approximating the original tensors, but to investigate the improvements of ITF over the standard Tucker method on a consistent number of singular vectors. Hence we do not evaluate the effects of different r_2 and r_3 values, but study the performance of different factorization methods using constant values of r_2 and r_3.

5.1.1 Factorizing Tensors

Comparisons between the Tucker method and ITF method in factorizing the 20 years of tensors are shown in Figure 2. Figure 2(a) demonstrates that compared to the standard Tucker method, ITF uses significantly less time to factorize the same tensor on the same number of desired singular vectors. This advantage of ITF is more apparent when r_1 is small – for example when $r_1 = 10$, ITF is able to finish the decomposition process in less than 50 minutes for all the 20 years. By contrast, the standard method whose time complexity is independent of the value of r_1 takes a much longer time to finish (e.g., about 10 times longer than ITF). More-

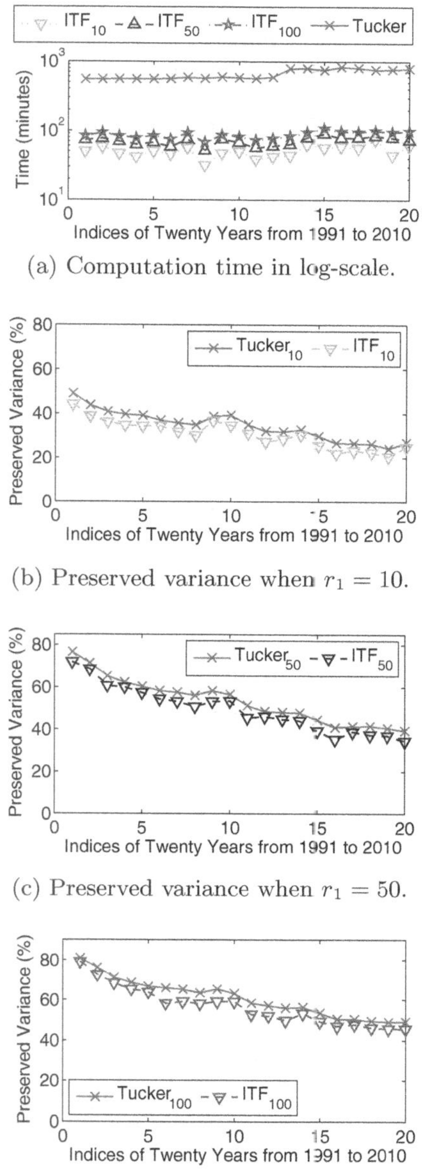

(a) Computation time in log-scale.

(b) Preserved variance when $r_1 = 10$.

(c) Preserved variance when $r_1 = 50$.

(d) Preserved variance when $r_1 = 100$.

Figure 2: Comparisons between Tucker and ITF on computation time and preserved variance when factorizing tensors of DBLP data. We can observe that ITF is able to preserve almost the same amount of variance compared to the standard method while using significantly less computation time. The notations $\text{Tucker}_{\{10,50,100\}}$ and $\text{ITF}_{\{10,50,100\}}$ in the sub-figures' legends represent the standard method and the ITF method for $r_1 = \{10, 50, 100\}$. Note that the time complexity of standard method is a function of n_1 (besides other dimensions) and is independent of r_1.

[3]We provide our implementation of ITF at `http://people.eng.unimelb.edu.au/liuw/ITF.html`.

Table 2: Comparisons of ITF and Tucker on paper weight assignments. The weight of a paper is the sum of the weights of word pairs that can be matched with the paper's title, where word pairs are the edges of emerging subgraphs weighted by the ITF or the Tucker method. In this table, columns 2 to 5 show examples of paper weight formulations, while in the last column the p-values are obtained from paired t-tests of two groups of weights on 50 papers in each year: one group contains weights assigned by ITF, and the other group contains weights assigned by the Tucker method.

Year	Paper title examples	Matched edges (word pairs of paper titles) from subgraphs weighted by ITF	ITF weights	Tucker weights	t-tests from top 50 papers
1996	A density-based algorithm for discovering clusters in large spatial databases with noise.	algorithm&density (0.5571), cluster&database (0.6496), large&spatial (0.9252), algorithm&database (0.1757), algorithm&noise (0.6544), density&spatial (0.7119), algorithm&spatial (0.1785), algorithm&cluster (0.2078)	3.9664	3.9015	0.7365
1997	New algorithms for fast discovery of association rules.	algorithm&discovery (0.974), algorithm&association (0.97), fast&rule (0.7516), algorithm&rule (0.9681), fast&discovery (0.1134)	3.7771	3.6983	0.8744
1998	An efficient approach to clustering in large multimedia databases with noise.	clustering&noise (0.8097), clustering&database (0.2281), efficient&multimedia (0.1027), clustering&large (0.1495), efficient&large (0.7172), clustering&time (0.1464), efficient&time (0.1713), clustering&database (0.9997), large&time (0.1282), approach&large (0.0937), large&multimedia (0.9548)	4.5013	4.3550	0.6893
1999	Fast and effective text mining using linear-time document clustering.	fast&linear (0.1022), effective&time (0.6865), effective&text (0.7618), mining&text (0.0545), document&time (0.7505), fast&mining (0.4674), clustering&document (0.7231), fast&text (0.7005)	4.2465	4.4001	0.8541
2000	FreeSpan: frequent pattern-projected sequential pattern mining.	mining&pattern (0.9605), mining&project (1.0), mining&sequential (0.7944), frequent&sequential (0.6906), frequent&pattern (0.746)	4.1915	4.0825	0.7976
2001	Co-clustering documents and words using bipartite spectral graph partitioning.	graph&partition (0.6302), clustering&word (0.8961), clustering&graph (0.6363), bipartite&graph (0.978)	3.1407	3.2672	0.9368
2002	Privacy preserving association rule mining in vertically partitioned data.	data&rule (0.6316), association&rule (0.9663), data&mining (0.4072), privacy&rule (0.6591), privacy&vertically (0.5433), preserving&vertically (0.6749)	3.8824	4.1041	0.5831
2003	Mining distance-based outliers in near linear time with randomization and a simple pruning rule.	mining&pruning (0.834), distance&outlier (0.8845), mining&outlier (0.775), base&rule (1.0), mining&rule (0.4337)	3.9273	3.7618	0.6498
2004	Systematic data selection to mine concept-drifting data streams.	data&selection (0.4054), data&mine (0.5996), data&stream (0.9991), concept&drift (0.8912), concept&stream (0.1294), selection&system (0.9889)	4.0256	4.1218	0.8519
2005	Discovering evolutionary theme patterns from text: an exploration of temporal text mining.	discovering&temporal (0.352), discovering&mining (0.5347), mining&text (0.7071), discovering&pattern (0.7155), pattern&text (0.5704), pattern&temporal (0.746), evolutionary&mining (0.7072)	4.3329	4.5085	0.7176

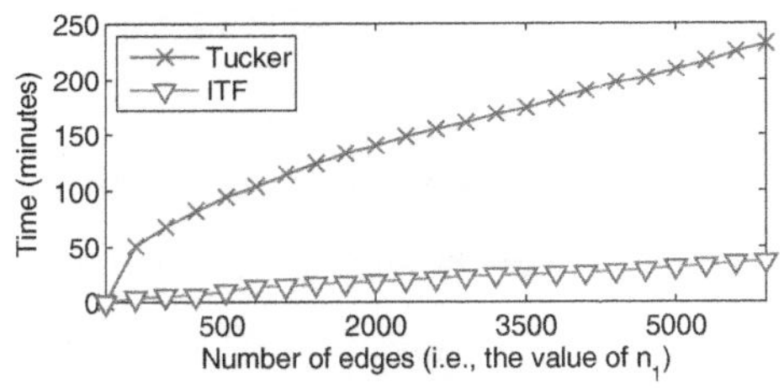

Figure 3: Computation time of the standard Tucker method and the ITF method on a controlled number of graph edges when r_1 is fixed at 100.

over, the variances preserved by ITF are highly comparable to the standard decomposition method. The values shown in Figures 2(b), 2(c) and 2(d) illustrate that the core tensors obtained from ITF can represent almost as much variance as those obtained from the standard method.

We are also interested in the computation time of the standard and ITF methods when the size of the tensor grows. This scenario is closely related to the dynamic graph mining problem in an online setting, since the number of edges (e.g., word pairs) in practical networks and graphs are usually very likely to increase with time. We control the number of word pairs in the original graphs (which is also the cardinality of the first dimension of the original tensor), and vary it from 500 to more than 5000. The computation time needed in the decompositions by the standard Tucker method and the ITF method is shown in Figure 3. The trends in the figure demonstrate that the computational cost of ITF is not only linear to the value of n_1 but also much lower than that of the standard decomposition method. Moreover, it also can be observed that the larger the size of the graph (i.e., the value of n_1), the larger the difference between the computation time needed for ITF and for the standard Tucker method.

5.1.2 Weighting Emerging Topics

In Section 4 we explained how the outputs of tensor factorization can be applied in weighting the original word pairs, and in this experiment we use that theory to evaluate the correctness of ITF against the Tucker method. After we decomposed twenty years of tensors, from each year we obtained a list of weights for the original word pairs. To discard trivial word pairs, we only consider those whose weights are higher than the threshold 0.0001 (note that the column vectors in the projection matrices are *unit vectors*, which means the weight of a word pair is typically between 0 and 1). After deleting those word pairs that do not pass this threshold, we obtain subgraphs of the original graphs. To find how popular a research topic is, we weight paper titles by using the edges of these subgraphs. We calculate the sum of the weights of the word pairs that a paper title contains as the weight of that paper title. Thus, paper titles that have higher weights are the ones whose words occupy more variance in the original tensor.

To test whether the weights of paper titles assigned by ITF are similar to those from the standard Tucker method, in each year we select 50 papers that are the highest weighted by ITF, and compare them with the weights produced by the Tucker method. Since the weights suggest the variance in their corresponding tensors, we conduct these comparisons to check whether the weights found by ITF agree with those found by the Tucker method on the same set of word pairs. We apply paired t-tests on the two groups of weights, one from ITF and the other from the Tucker method, under the null hypothesis that the weights are not significantly different between the two groups. The last column[4] of Table 2 shows the p-values returned from the t-tests, which are mostly very large. This does not reject the null hypothesis, suggesting that ITF and Tucker assign insignificantly different weights to the same set of word pairs. This result validates the correctness of the factorization produced by ITF, in that the main variance of key word pairs preserved by ITF is as good as that preserved by the computationally expensive Tucker method.

5.2 Classifying Chemical Compounds

In this experiment, we compare the IFT and the Tucker method on graph classification problems, where we classify the points that are projected into the row-rank feature spaces defined by the factor matrices. We use chemical compound data sets from anti-cancer bioassays[5], where each compound is treated as a graph of atoms. The task is to predict whether a compound is positive or negative in anti-cancer activities. Although there are limited types of atoms and bonds in the data, the total number of compounds is very large (Table 3).

Table 3: Statistics of chemical compound data sets. "pos%" represents the proportion of compounds that are positive.

Index	#graphs	pos%	Description
1	27784	8.2	Breast Cancer
2	40700	5.9	Colon Cancer
3	40152	7.8	Leukemia
4	40460	5.1	Lung Cancer
5	40209	4.1	Melanoma
6	40691	5.1	Ovarian Cancer
7	27585	5.7	Prostate Cancer
8	40164	4.9	Renal Cancer

5.2.1 *Factorizing Tensors*

Similar to the graph formulations discussed in Section 4.2, for each chemical compound data set we construct a tensor of 5 modes, where the types of atoms in a compound are converted to labels of vertices, and the lengths of bonds between atoms are treated as weights of edges. Figure 4 shows comparisons of the ITF and the Tucker method in their factorization time and preserved variance of each data set. It is easy to observe that ITF factorizes each data set by using much less time than the Tucker method, while preserving

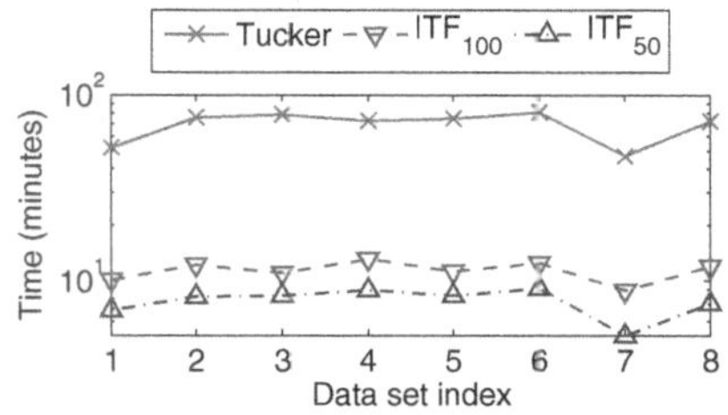

(a) Log-scale computation time.

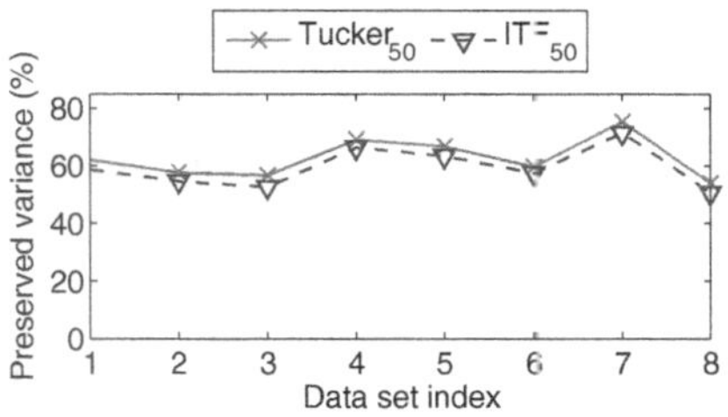

(b) Preserved variance when $r_1 = 50$.

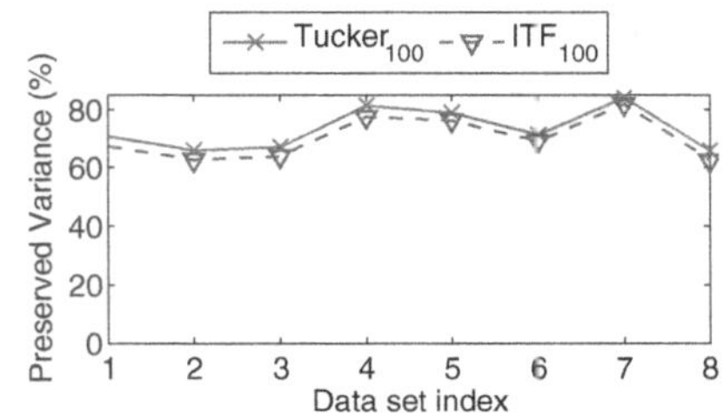

(c) Preserved variance when $r_1 = 100$.

Figure 4: Comparisons between the Tucker and the ITF methods on factoring tensors of chemical compound data sets.

similar amounts of variance. Such results indicate that ITF is able to capture the most important substructures that are shared across different compounds.

5.2.2 *Classification on Compounds*

In addition to the evaluation of preserved variances, we test the correctness of the factor matrices produced by ITF by examining the new data points that lie in the new spaces defined by the factor matrices. A linear logistic regression is used to learn and classify these data points by 5-fold cross validation with 10 repeated runs. The results of classification on different factorization methods is reported in Table 4. Note that due to the class imbalance, we use the area under the ROC curve (AUC) as the evaluation metric, which is more appropriate than using overall accuracy as the metric.

While there are various ways to compare classifiers across multiple data sets, we adopt the strategy proposed in [6] which evaluates classifiers by performing Friedman tests. We compare the ITF and the Tucker methods on the same ranks ($r_1 = 50$ and $r_1 = 100$), where p-values that are lower than 0.05 reject the hypothesis with 95% confidence that the classifiers in the comparison are not statistically different. As we can see from the high p-values in the bottom of table Table 4, the data points projected onto subspaces formed by ITF are *insignificantly* different to those by the

[4]Due to space limit, in this table we only present comparisons in nine years time from 1996 to 2005.

[5]`http://pubchem.ncbi.nlm.nih.gov`

Table 4: Comparisons of ITF and Tucker on classifying the data points located in their corresponding subspaces, using linear logistic regression. "*F. test*" represents the Friedman significance test.

Data	AUC from logistic regression			
	$Tucker_{50}$	ITF_{50}	$Tucker_{100}$	ITF_{100}
Breast	.583±.09	.593±.08	.740±.05	.722±.05
Colon	.670±.06	.678±.04	.754±.06	.713±.02
Leukemia	.602±.04	.607±.06	.699±.07	.683±.04
Lung	.608±.05	.645±.06	.652±.03	.633±.05
Melanoma	.687±.06	.703±.05	.693±.06	.710±.04
Ovarian	.699±.04	.711±.04	.740±.04	.731±.02
Prostate	.641±.04	.635±.03	.686±.04	.689±.05
Renal	.568±.02	.589±.04	.661±.06	.653±.08
F. test	0.2573		0.5236	

Tucker method from the perspective of distinguishing class labels. This suggests that the factor matrices generated by ITF capture as much intrinsic variance as those by the Tucker method in both class labels, and that the new features (e.g., columns of a factor matrix) from ITF are competent representatives of the row-rank basis of the compound data sets. Moreover, the setting of cross validation also indicates that ITF is insensitive to the orderings of graphs.

6. CONCLUSIONS AND FUTURE WORK

The main focus of this paper is on scalably factorizing tensors that represent dynamic graphs. A good tensor factorization method should be able to decompose tensors in a computationally cheap manner and also be able to preserve the main variance of the data. We have shown that the proposed ITF method is able to significantly reduce computation time compared to the standard factorization method, while the variance preserved by ITF is comparably effective. The superiority of ITF arises from the fact that important substructures are usually shared among different graphs, or graphs across different time periods. We have applied ITF to the weighting of emerging research topics in dynamic publication networks/graphs, and have shown that the time complexity of ITF is linear in the size of the networks or graphs, which makes ITF feasible to be applied in an online setting. We have also applied ITF to graph classification problems using chemical compound data sets, showing that ITF is not only a significant speed up of the Tucker method but also captures the intrinsic variance of the original data with respect to different class labels. Moreover, the results from cross validations on graph classification experiments demonstrate that the iterative algorithm ITF is insensitive to the orderings of graphs.

The advantage of ITF is not limited to Tucker decomposition. Other tensor factorization methods such as canonical polyadic decomposition and non-negative tensor factorization can also benefit from the iterative procedure of ITF. These are the future research directions of ITF we are planning to investigate.

Acknowledgements

This research was supported under Australian Research Council's Discovery Projects funding scheme (DP110102621).

7. REFERENCES

[1] B. Bader and T. Kolda. Efficient Matlab computations with sparse and factored tensors. *SIAM Journal on Scientific Computing*, 30(1):205–231, 2007.

[2] J. Bunch and J. Hopcroft. Triangular factorization and inversion by fast matrix multiplication. *Mathematics of Computation*, pages 231–236, 1974.

[3] J. Carroll and J. Chang. Analysis of individual differences in multidimensional scaling via an n-way generalization of "Eckart-Young" decomposition. *Psychometrika*, 35(3):283–319, 1970.

[4] L. De Lathauwer, B. De Moor, and J. Vandewalle. A multilinear singular value decomposition. *SIAM Journal on Matrix Analysis and Applications*, 21(4):1253–1278, 2000.

[5] L. De Lathauwer and D. Nion. Decompositions of a higher-order tensor in block terms. *SIAM J. Matrix Analysis and Applications*, 30(3):1067–1083, 2008.

[6] J. Demšar. Statistical comparisons of classifiers over multiple data sets. *Journal of Machine Learning Research*, 7:1–30, 2006.

[7] G. Golub and C. Van Loan. *Matrix computations*, volume 3. Johns Hopkins Univ Pr, 1996.

[8] A. Kapteyn, H. Neudecker, and T. Wansbeek. An approach to n-mode components analysis. *Psychometrika*, 51(2):269–275, 1986.

[9] T. Kolda and B. Bader. Tensor decompositions and applications. *SIAM review*, 51(3):455, 2009.

[10] T. Kolda and J. Sun. Scalable tensor decompositions for multi-aspect data mining. In *Proc of ICDM*, pages 363–372, 2008.

[11] X. Kong and P. Yu. Semi-supervised feature selection for graph classification. In *Proc of KDD*, pages 793–802, 2010.

[12] P. Kroonenberg and J. De Leeuw. Principal component analysis of three-mode data by means of alternating least squares algorithms. *Psychometrika*, 45(1):69–97, 1980.

[13] M. Ley. The DBLP computer science bibliography: evolution, research issues, perspectives. In *String Processing and Information Retrieval*, pages 481–486. Springer, 2002.

[14] K. Ravi Kanth, D. Agrawal, and A. Singh. Dimensionality reduction for similarity searching in dynamic databases. *ACM SIGMOD Record*, 27(2):166–176, 1998.

[15] C. Schifanella, K. Candan, and M. Sapino. Fast metadata-driven multiresolution tensor decomposition. In *Proc of CIKM*, pages 1275–1284, 2011.

[16] J. Sun, S. Papadimitriou, and P. Yu. Window-based tensor analysis on high-dimensional and multi-aspect streams. In *Proc of ICDM*, pages 1076–1080, 2006.

[17] J. Sun, D. Tao, and C. Faloutsos. Beyond streams and graphs: dynamic tensor analysis. In *Proc of KDD*, pages 374–383, 2006.

[18] J. Sun, D. Tao, S. Papadimitriou, P. Yu, and C. Faloutsos. Incremental tensor analysis: theory and applications. *ACM Transactions on Knowledge Discovery from Data*, 2(3):11, 2008.

[19] L. Tucker. Some mathematical notes on three-mode factor analysis. *Psychometrika*, 31(3):279–311, 1966.

Predicting Emerging Social Conventions in Online Social Networks

Farshad Kooti
MPI-SWS
farshad@mpi-sws.org

Winter A. Mason
Stevens Institute of Technology
m@winteram.com

Krishna P. Gummadi
MPI-SWS
gummadi@mpi-sws.org

Meeyoung Cha
KAIST
meeyoungcha@kaist.edu

ABSTRACT

The way in which social conventions emerge in communities has been of interest to social scientists for decades. Here we report on the emergence of a particular social convention on Twitter—the way to indicate a tweet is being reposted and attributing the content to its source. Despite being invented at different times and having different adoption rates, only two variations became widely adopted. In this paper we describe this process in detail, highlighting the factors that come into play in deciding which variation individuals will adopt. Our classification analysis demonstrates that the date of adoption and the number of exposures are particularly important in the adoption process, while personal features (such as the number of followers and join date) and the number of adopter friends have less discriminative power in predicting adoptions. We discuss implications of these findings in the design of future Web applications and services.

Categories and Subject Descriptors

J.4 [**Computer Applications**]: Social and Behavioral Sciences; H.2.8 [**Database Applications**]: Database Management—*data mining*

Keywords

Social Conventions, Microblog, Prediction

1. INTRODUCTION

The importance of social norms in a society can hardly be understated. They can affect our most basic perceptions [2] and are the basis of massive social movements [34]. They guide everyday behaviors of the general public [1] as well as those of the most extreme members of a society [43]. As a consequence of their importance, social norms have been the topic of a multitude of studies in anthropology [5], sociology [24], and psychology [17,41].

Social norms may begin as social conventions, i.e., simple habits of social interaction. Over time, some social conventions become more strongly associated with the group identity and some even become so central that failure to obey the social convention results in censure—at which point they have transitioned from a social convention to a social norm. This transformation can serve multiple purposes; it reinforces the system that acts as a guide in social interactions [21,33], enhances group identity and feelings of belongingness [36], and facilitates group performance on tasks by establishing standardized roles [30].

The factors influencing an individual's decision to conform to a social norm have been studied extensively in psychology [17]. In some cases, the individual is adopting a norm because they believe doing so leads to more accurate and useful judgments; that is, because they believe it is practically useful to adopt the norm [20] and their peers are providing "social proof" [16]. For instance, one may believe that the reason everyone owns an iPod is because they are objectively better than the alternative portable music players. In these cases, factors like unanimity [2], the publicness of the action [20], the authority or personal importance of the source(s) [9], and the size of the relevant group [9,26] all affect the probability that an individual will adopt a social norm.

In other cases, the motivation to adopt a social norm has more to do with a desire to build and maintain relationships with group members. In this case, the decision to adopt a norm has less to do with the correctness of the normative behavior but instead more with "fitting in." As before, the publicness of the action [28] is important, as is the extent to which the individual identifies with the group that embodies the norm. Similarly, the extent to which the norm is enforced by other members of the group [32] is important in the decision to adopt it. There are also individual differences that affect the likelihood of adopting a social norm, such as one's need for social approval [47].

However, nearly all of these conclusions are based on the assumption that a social norm is firmly established in the group before individuals are in a situation in which they could be influenced by the norm. While the factors that lead an individual to conform to a social norm of a group are well-studied, the factors that come into play when an individual decides to adopt a *social convention* are not as well understood. In this case, the decision to adopt a particular convention has an impact on whether that convention comes to be widely adopted. This in turn could affect the likelihood it will ever become associated with group identity or become proscriptively normative.

Social conventions can be established in many different ways. They may be created and enforced by institutions, such as the International System of Units for units of measurements. Many times, however, there is no established institutional code or even an in-

CIKM'12, October 29–November 2, 2012, Maui, HI, USA.

stitution, in which case a convention *evolves*, arising from interpersonal interaction and spreading from person to person within a community [33].

In this research, we observe the emergence of a social convention that evolves over time and document the characteristics of the convention, the environment, and the dynamics of competing variations of the convention. Specifically we focus on the Twitter online community and the convention used to indicate that one is reposting a tweet to one's followers while attributing the content to the source—an act commonly known as "retweeting" [10]. We study seven variations of this convention: RT, via, Retweeting, Retweet, HT, R/T, and the recycle icon. Utilizing a near-complete collection of tweets, we track the birth and spread of each of these retweeting variations over the first 3.5 years of Twitter's existence.

There are several unique advantages in studying the retweeting convention. To begin with, the convention is specific to Twitter, therefore is unlikely to be imported from existing conventions in the way other conventions have been, such as greetings in other online communities [7]. This also means that before the convention was established, a user was most likely to encounter it through his or her contacts on Twitter. Consequently, another advantage of studying retweeting is that one's contacts on Twitter are explicit, so we can observe how a convention spreads from one user to another. A third advantage is that the convention is not usable outside of Twitter, so nearly all uses of the convention will have been on Twitter, limiting potential exposures outside the environment.

Because we have nearly all of the tweets, this means that we also have nearly all of the uses of the convention. In other words, by studying this particular convention we can explore not just the micro-level processes of adoption or the macro-level outcomes but actually explore how one led to the other. Among many findings, some of our key results are as follows:

1. The final reach of the retweeting variations does not seem to be strongly related to either the amount of time each variation had to grow or the rate at which it initially grew.

2. Nearly all adopters had been exposed to the convention through their friends on Twitter, suggesting that social relations play an important role in the adoption process.

3. When users adopted multiple variations, they were loyal to certain variations over others. The longer variations such as Retweeting had higher probabilities of being abandoned.

4. RT and via were the most popular in almost all geographical regions, indicating that a common retweeting practice was adopted independent of cultural and linguistic borders.

5. The decision to adopt a particular variation has more to do with the global popularity of the variation rather than its popularity in the local neighborhood or personal preference.

6. The number of exposures had more discriminative power than the number of adopter friends in predicting adoptions, suggesting that volume may be more important than independent sources—contrary to other social diffusion models.

We built a classifier that predicts which variation individuals would have adopted at a given time—*micro-level prediction*. Despite much effort, it was increasingly clear from our analysis that the micro-level processes of convention adoption could not be easily predicted. Before adopting a variation, most users (96.71%) had been exposed to it at least once, but this was not sufficient to predict the adoption. Considering a wide range of features, our classifier could achieve an accuracy of on average 22% improvement against the baseline (i.e, predicting 61% of cases correctly) and up to 65% improvement for less popular variations (i.e., predicting 82.3% of cases correctly). After ensuring stronger definitions of social ties (i.e., mentioning links) and adoptions (i.e., usage of at least 3 or 5 times), the overall prediction accuracy improved by an additional 10%.

The uncertainty in the outcome of which variation will be adopted at the micro-level perhaps may be intrinsic to the process of convention spreading. Similar to the uncertainty introduced by social feedback mechanisms [39], the choice of adoption may be inherently difficult to predict reliably or accurately. This is especially likely given that a similar uncertainty is observed at the macro-level; what was once the dominant variation (e.g., via, Retweeting) was no longer the most popular after a few months.

This paper is one of the first to analyze the underlying process in the establishment of a social convention with a massive data set. We believe our research, although preliminary, opens the door to new methods for studying social conventions. In the future, we hope to replicate this study over a much longer period of time (e.g., 10 years) to examine how social conventions turn into social norms.

The remainder of this paper is organized as follows. In Section 2, we review literature on social norms, social conventions, and social influence. In Section 3, we describe the Twitter data set and our methodology to extract variations of the convention. Section 4 presents the analysis of possible features that could be used to determine the adoption process of the convention and Section 5 presents the results of the prediction analysis based on these features. In Section 6, we discuss further implications of our work and we conclude in Section 7.

2. RELATED WORK

One of the first studies that observed the effect of norms on human behavior was Sherif's study on the *phi* effect [41]. In his study, peoples' estimates of how much a dim light moved in a dark room not only stabilized when participants were organized in pairs or teams, but also converged to each other's estimates. The influence of other people's judgments affected the participants' judgments of simple perceptual phenomena. This effect was more dramatically demonstrated by Asch [2], who asked participants to decide which of three lines was the shortest. One line was clearly shorter, but when a set of confederates all chose a longer line, participants conformed to the group's decision and gave an incorrect response in 37% of cases.

Since these studies established the powerful effects social norms can have, others have sought to identify the features that influence the decision to adopt a social norm. Cialdini and Trost [17] review a large body of work and highlight a few of the factors that have been identified as most important. One of the main motivations they cite is merely the accurate interpretation of the world; when many peers adopt a particular behavior, it is a signal that the behavior is optimal in some way [20]. For instance, Stanley Milgram and colleagues found that a large number of people were induced to stare at blank space simply by having others engage in the same behavior [31]. The other main motivation Cialdini and Trost identify is the need to belong [6]. When this social affiliation need is activated, the perceived *injunctive* norm—what one's peers approve or disapprove of—becomes more important than the *descriptive* norms—what one's peers actually do. These injunctive norms can be powerful; one study found it to be the second largest predictor of whether one would engage in extradyadic sex [12].

For both kinds of motivations, certain factors can influence the likelihood of adopting the norm. The perceived relative proportion [9] and absolute number [26, 28] of one's peers who have adopted the norm are positively related to the likelihood of adoption. The greater the perceived similarity between one's self and the perceived group, the more likely one is to adopt the norm [22]. Similarly, the more one values the group [9,25,32], the more likely one will be to adopt the norm. However, most or all of these factors in the decision to adopt a social norm assume that the norm is firmly established in the group. There has been much less work on how people respond when social conventions are just emerging.

There have been laboratory studies on how conventions arise, most of which frame the emergence of a social convention as a solution to a coordination problem. One of the first to explicitly investigate how people solve coordination problems focused on linguistic conventions for reference. In [46], participants were asked to develop short-hand verbal code for referring to images that allowed them to communicate more efficiently and therefore complete tasks with the images more quickly. As a result of the need to coordinate efficiently, the participants developed linguistic or pseudo-linguistic conventions. Such an experiment in a controlled environment allows the examination of the exact steps involved in the process of creating a social convention.

A more popular approach to study the emergence of social conventions has been to create mathematical or computational models that embody a theory, in order to demonstrate how a specific mechanism could lead to the emergence of social conventions [3, 11]. In many of these models, the decision of agents to adopt a norm or a convention is assumed in the model [44] or proves beneficial to the agents because of the reward structure that is implicit in the model [27,42]. Even models that factor in social network structures in the emergence of a social norm do not focus on the individual's decision to adopt the corresponding social convention [19,40].

It seems plausible that when social conventions emerge, the individual's decision to adopt a particular variation of a convention may not be simply the economically rational outcome of a coordination problem, but instead may be influenced by other factors such as the number or proportion of one's peers who are using that particular variation and the desire to affiliate with the group that is using the variation. Moreover, since peer influence is clearly a factor in the decision to adopt an established norm and in the resolution of coordination problems, it is probable that the process may resemble other forms of social diffusion.

In one of the seminal works on social diffusion, Christakis and Fowler find evidence for the spread of obesity [15] and cooperative behavior [23] through social networks (but see [18]). In [13], Centola studies the spread of behavior in an online social network experiment with almost 1500 users. The study shows that individual adoption is much more likely when participants received social reinforcement from multiple neighbors in the social network. Even more importantly, Bakshy and colleagues [4] conducted an experiment on Facebook to demonstrate the role of social networks in information diffusion. They randomly assigned users to be exposed to a link shared by a friend or to have the link hidden and found that users who were exposed to peer influence are 7 times more likely to share a piece of information than those who never saw the link.

These studies strongly suggest that peer influence is critical in the spread of information and normative behavior [15]. In this work, we seek to find the factors that influence an individual's decision to adopt one variation of a social convention over another. The factors we consider include the behavior of one's peers, as well as the number and proportion of one's peers who have adopted it. By identifying which factors play a key role, we hope to gain a deeper understanding of the micro-level process underlying the emergence of a social convention.

3. METHODOLOGY

This paper focuses on the retweeting convention in Twitter, which is used for indicating when a message is reposted while attributing the source. In this section, we describe the Twitter dataset and its high-level characteristics. We also present the methods we employed to identify the retweeting convention and briefly introduce the seven retweeting variations that we analyze in this paper.

3.1 Dataset

We obtained the Twitter data set from [14], which comprises the following three types of information: profiles of 54 million users, 1.9 billion directed follow links among these users, and 1.7 billion public tweets posted by the collected users. The oldest tweet in the data set is from March 2006, when the Twitter service was publicly launched. The follow link information is a snapshot taken at the time of data collection in September 2009, while the user and tweet information is near-complete because user IDs were sequentially queried from all possible ranges (0–80 million) at the time of data collection. Therefore, this data set provides a unique opportunity to study the birth and progress of new collective behaviors in Twitter.

The Twitter network exhibits topological features that distinguish it from other online social networks. First, although the distributions for both in- and out-degree are heavy-tailed similar to other networks, certain Twitter users have extremely large in-degrees (i.e., the number of followers), at a scale that is unprecedented. The maximum in-degree is on the order of millions (as opposed to tens of thousands in other social networks). This is because Twitter users include celebrity and mainstream media accounts like Oprah Winfrey and BBC. Second, the social links are directional and only 23.8% of the links are reciprocal. In contrast, in other social networks social links are bidirectional by design or the majority are reciprocal. These differences should be taken into account when trying to apply the results of convention propagation described in this paper to a broader context.

3.2 The Retweeting Convention

Several different variations of the retweeting convention emerged during the first few years of Twitter [29]. They arose organically and became widely adopted by many individuals and third-party applications, until and even after Twitter rolled out the official, built-in "retweet" button in November 2009. The retweeting convention typically had a syntax of "token @username repeated-text" [10]. We searched for this syntax in the tweet data set to find all potential variations of this convention. Among them, we study the four most frequently used variations ("RT", "via", "Retweet", and "Retweeting") and three lesser used ones ("HT", "R/T", and recycle icon[1], shown below).

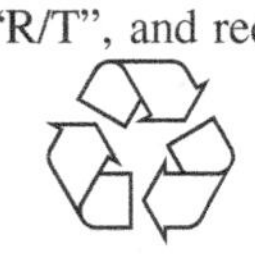

RT is short for "retweet" and HT stands for "heard through" or "hat tip."

We say a user *adopted* a given retweeting variation if the user has employed the variation at least once. Table 1 shows the number of adopters and tweets according to this definition. The two most popular variations, RT and via, reach 1.8 million and 750 thousand adopters respectively, yet the rest reach a far fewer number of adopters. In total, 2 million or 3.7% of all Twitter users adopted the retweeting convention and an impressive 59 million or 3.5% of all tweets ever posted used any variation of this convention.

[1]Can be used by copying and pasting the symbol from Unicode symbol map.

convention	# of adopters	# of usages	First usage
RT	1,836,852	53,221,529	2008-01
via	751,547	5,367,304	2007-03
Retweeting	50,400	296,608	2008-01
Retweet	36,601	110,616	2007-11
HT	8,346	22,657	2007-10
R/T	5,300	28,658	2008-06
recycle icon	3,305	18,255	2008-09
Total	2,059,350	59,065,627	-

Table 1: The number of adopters and tweets per convention

The table also shows the date when the seven variations first appeared. The birth of the retweeting convention establishes that there is a need on Twitter to indicate a message is passed on from another source and to attribute the message to the source. The first variation ever used was via in the following context,

> @JasonCalacanis (via @kosso) - new Nokia N-Series phones will do Flash, Video and YouTube

which indicates that the original tweet message came from another user (@kosso). This tweet was posted in March of 2007, only twelve months from the launch of Twitter and only 4 months after the first "@username" reference appeared in Twitter.

For most variations, their invention seems to arise naturally from the need to replicate a message. Nearly nine months after via was invented, we see the the very first usage of RT:

> RT @BreakingNewsOn: "LV Fire Department: No major injuries and the fire on the Monte Carlo west wing contained east wing nearly contained."

The tweet had exactly 140 characters, the length limit set by Twitter. This finding suggests that the invention of RT was a result of a previous variation being adapted to the constraints of the social environment.

The recycle icon, on the other hand, seems to have been created for the purpose of improving the existing variations, as it appeared explicitly in the discussion of which variation should be used on Twitter. The recycle icon variation was in fact the last one to be invented, in 2008 September. More details about the emergence process are described in [29]

4. THE RETWEETING CONVENTION

The seven variations, although started at various points in time with different contexts, were invented to act as a convention indicating retweeting and once introduced in Twitter were subsequently adopted by other users who were exposed to them. In this work, we ask *are there any features in the Twitter data set that would allow one to predict which variation would have been adopted by whom and when?* As we demonstrate shortly, the final reach of these variations does not seem to be strongly related either to the amount of time each variation had to grow or the rate at which it grew. Therefore, we sought to investigate the user-level traits and the social network characteristics that determine the adoption process.

The longitudinal tweet data set allows us to track how each of the variations was adopted. Figure 1 shows the time series of week-to-week usages over the first 3.5 years of Twitter's existence. Via started early with a slow growth pattern relative to the other variations, but ended with the second highest number of adopters. In contrast, RT started late but soon became a leading variation. The recycle icon, HT, and R/T continued to add new users, but their popularity seems to have nearly stabilized. Retweet and Retweeting once grew as fast or faster than any other variations, but never approached the reach of RT. In fact, they began losing popularity in late 2008, as the number of usages declined.

With respect to predicting the future popularity of a social convention, we focus on one specific problem, which we call the **Convention Prediction Problem** and define as follows: Suppose we are given a social network with records of users and times of adoptions, but information about which variation was adopted by user u at time t is hidden. How reliably can we infer which variation v the user chose to adopt?

The prediction problem takes into account a wide range of features including personal preference (e.g., in-degree and geo-location of adopters) as well as social correlation due to homophily and influence (e.g., the frequency and degree of exposures from friends). We chose these features because they correspond to potential causes identified in the research on adopting existing social norms [17] and the diffusion of other social phenomena [4]. In the remainder of this section, we consider the effect of some of the key features in the emergence of the retweeting convention. Then in Section 5, we describe our solution to the prediction problem, considering the combined effect of all features.

4.1 Personal Features

One way to distinguish the small group of users who adopted one of the variations of the retweeting convention from the typical Twitter user is a simple count of one's followers and followings. Adopters had higher in-degree than the average Twitter user. In fact, as can be seen in Figure 2, adopters have an order of magnitude more followers than the typical user. The figure also shows that RT and via were adopted by less popular users than the other variations. We hence consider *in-degree and out-degree of adopters* as one of the predictive features.

An in-depth examination revealed that in-degree distributions of the first 500 adopters were not particularly different from one variation to another [29]. This finding may suggest that when a variation becomes extremely popular, it starts to be adopted by users beyond the circle of highly-connected core users and reach more peripheral users—a finding that is in tune with the famous "diffusion of innovations" theory [37]. In contrast, adopters of the less popular variations may have never broken out of the core group of Twitter users who pay attention to the new trends and technologies of the service.

We also examined whether a user's geographical location affects her decision to adopt a variation. It is possible that the conventions differed from location to location because of language or cultural differences. In order to infer the geo-location of adopters, we em-

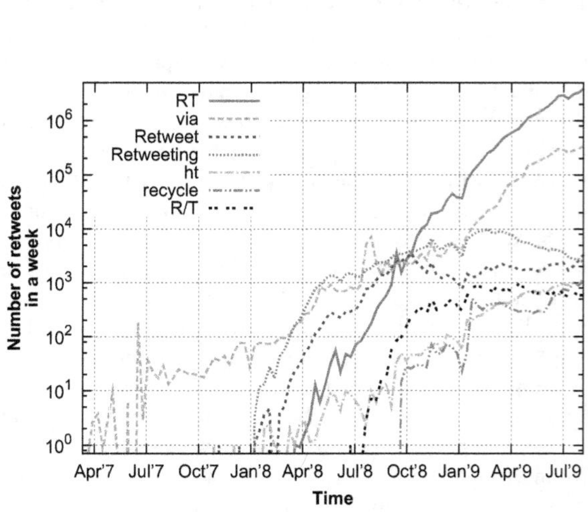

Figure 1: Number of usages of different variations over time

Country	Total adopters	RT	via	Retweeting	Others
US	1,239,708	0.668	0.285	0.021	0.025
UK	137,848	0.664	0.295	0.022	0.019
Brazil	112,465	0.746	0.234	0.014	0.006
Canada	89,803	0.656	0.298	0.023	0.023
Germany	48,575	0.632	0.316	0.033	0.019
Australia	46,438	0.659	0.294	0.023	0.023
Japan	28,859	0.731	0.234	0.005	0.030
Iran	27,330	0.622	0.315	0.024	0.038
France	18,934	0.600	0.341	0.042	0.018
India	17,449	0.623	0.320	0.033	0.024

Table 2: The fraction of different variations in top 10 countries

ployed two fields from user profiles: the location field and the time zone field. The location field is a free-text string entered by users, while the time zone field is a drop-down menu in Twitter. To resolve the free-text string in the location field, we used both the Yahoo! Map and the Bing Map APIs (Application Programming Interfaces) and obtained the country-level information for each user. The time zone field has a location name appended with the Unix Time offset, with which we can resolve the country individual users belong to. We annotated users with the geo-location information only when at least two of the three inference results matched. In this manner, we were able to retrieve the geo-location for 75.5% of all adopters.

Investigating the distribution of variations across geography, we found that geo-location had little impact in the spread of popular variations like RT and via. However, geo-location showed some variability for less popular variations like HT and recycle icon. Table 2 shows the top 10 countries based on the total number of adopters and the distribution of variations within that country. In all ten countries (and in most other countries not listed in the table), RT was the leading variation, followed by via. For the remaining variations, however, the ordering was not consistent. For instance, users in France and Germany preferred the recycle icon to Retweet, while users in Iran and Australia preferred HT much more than in other countries. In order to capture the effect of geo-location, we consider *the country of the adopters* as a predictive feature.

4.2 Social Features

One of the key factors that is essential in convention adoption is *exposures*. These are so crucial because of informational influence [20]; that is, users are made aware of the variation by their peers and as a consequence adopt the variation. This is especially true when conventions are first being established, because there is a utility simply in coordinating on the same variation [33]. Of course, it is likely that some users independently invented the same variation or learned about the variations through some external source. However, because retweeting is specific to Twitter, there is a high chance that adopters of this convention were exposed to the variation through their social contacts in Twitter. We call these users *internal adopters*.

Table 3 shows the percentage of internal adopters. It should be noted that these percentages are likely an overestimate, as the graph of social contacts is based on a snapshot at the end of the data set in mid 2009, and connections in online social networks are much more likely to be added than deleted. Nonetheless, the proportion of adopters whom we assume learned about the convention internally is so high (96.71%) that it is unlikely the amount we overestimate the internal adoptions would be so substantial as to affect our conclusions. The three most popular variations (i.e., RT, via, and Retweeting) have the highest fraction of internal adopters. The overall high rate of internal adopters indicate that exposure is a key factor in the spread of a convention. From this observation, we later consider *frequency of exposure to a particular variation* and *the number of adopter friends* as prediction features.

The effect of exposure sometimes became stronger with repetition. Figure 3 shows a plot of the fraction of users who adopted a given variation after k of her friends adopted the same variation, as a function of k. RT and via show a two-phase pattern: a ramp-up to a peak followed by a decline, where the peak values are at k=20 and k=11, respectively. This observation indicates that the more a user is exposed to the variation up to these points, the more likely she will adopt it. The three lesser popular variations (i.e., HT, R/T, and recycling icon) do not have a ramp-up period and their peaks are at k=1. This means that for these variations repeated exposures were less effective than the first exposure.

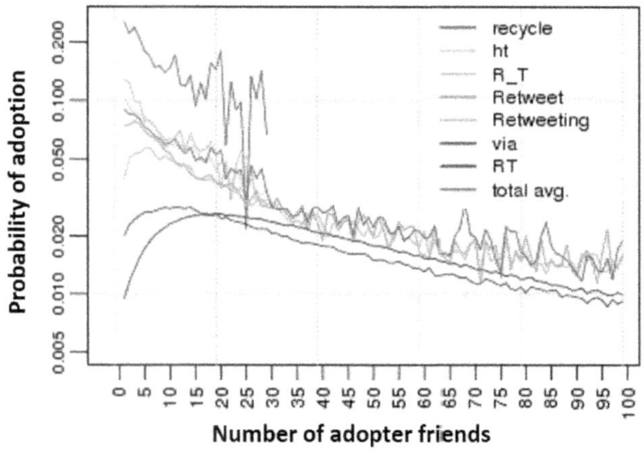

Figure 3: Exposure curve for seven variations

Convention	Internal adopters
RT	97.93%
via	94.36%
Retweeting	95.56%
Retweet	89.17%
HT	89.32%
R/T	88.98%
recycle icon	81.97%
Total	96.71%

Table 3: Percentage of internal adopters for each variation

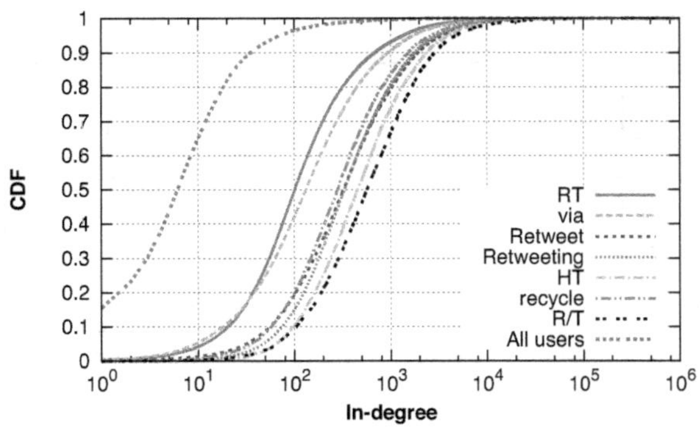

Figure 2: Comparison of in-degree of users

Convention	Switch-out	Switch-in
RT	23.30%	18.66%
via	18.13%	13.85%
Retweeting	73.61%	0.84%
Retweet	67.61%	0.67%
HT	30.94%	0.28%
R/T	57.81%	0.15%
recycle icon	35.67%	0.11%

Table 4: Loyalty of the convention adopters

Despite the fact that social exposure significantly increases the chance of adoption, it does not necessarily mean that the prediction problem is easy. The reason is two-fold. First, most adopters are exposed to not just one but multiple variations before adopting any of them. In fact, a mere 2.49% of the adopters were exposed to exactly one variation. Second, people do not always choose to use the variation that they are most frequently exposed to. Of those who adopted RT, 80.40% had been exposed to RT the most frequently. However, for the other variations, only 6.17%–30.39% of adopters had been exposed to that variation more than any other variation.

Amazingly, despite the fact that nearly every adopter was exposed to more than one variation, a great majority of the users (72.68%) only adopted a single variation. Most others (24.47%) switched from one variation to another once or used two different variations back and forth. Only a small fraction of users (2.85%) adopted three or more variations. In order to understand why users adopt multiple variations, we analyzed how frequently users switch between different variations.

We approach this by treating adoption of convention as a Markov process, in which we model the usage of each variation as individual states and switching from one variation to another as a transition between states. These individual decisions to switch from one variation to another on aggregate also reflect the proportion of the population moving from one variation to another. Let the transition probability from state i to state j be P_{ij} and let V denote the set of all variations. Then, we may calculate the probability of *switching-in* and *switching-out* of a particular variation i as $\sum_{j \in V} P_{ji}$ and $\sum_{j \in V} P_{ij}$, respectively. The former represents the attractiveness of the variation, while the latter represents the loyalty of an adopter upon employing the variation.

Table 4 shows the two transition probabilities. RT and via have relatively low switch-out probabilities; once a user employs these variations, he will likely continue to use it further. Retweeting and Retweet have high switch-out probabilities; once a user employs these variations, he is likely to switch to another variation in the future. This is potentially because Retweeting and Retweet are attractive at first because of their straightforward meaning, but are costly for subsequent usages because of their long length, given the 140 character limit. In terms of the switch-in probability, HT and recycle icon have the highest attractiveness upon exposure.

4.3 Global Features

We can also examine the switch-in and switch-out probabilities at different points in time. Figure 4 shows how the switch-out probability changes for each variation when we divide the data set into four different time windows. During the first phase until October 2008—a year and a half after the first usage of the retweeting convention—there is not much difference in the switch-out probabilities across the seven variations. Until this time, the concept of retweeting was still settling within the Twitter community and there was no agreement as to which variation should be used.

However, by the end of the second phase in February 2009, RT became much more popular than the other variations, with hundreds of thousands of uses compared to only thousands for the other variations. After this time period, the switch-out probability for redundant variations of RT such as Retweeting, Retweet, and R/T show a sharp increase. This trend reflects the collective action that users who previously adopted these variations quickly switched to a new variation (i.e., RT). Other variations also exhibit changes in the switch-out probability over time, albeit at a marginal level.

This collective switch out action can be observed clearly in the state diagram of the Markov model in Figure 5, which shows the normalized switch out probability from each state so that the sum of probabilities outgoing from each state adds up to one. A transition in the model indicates what fraction of adopters of a given variation ever switched out to another variation. A self-loop represents the fraction of adopters who used exactly one variation. Self-loops are more evident for popular variations than the less popular ones. When switch out happens, we find that RT and via are the most popular destinations. In particular, adopters of HT and recycle icon preferred to switch out to via, while adopters of all other variations preferred RT over via.

The time-varying switch-out probability implies that the choice of which variation to adopt is no longer a local decision but a global one, where individuals are affected by the phase of the entire convention spreading process. What seems to play a role here is the global popularity of each variation. In order to incorporate this finding, we later consider *the date of adoption* as a feature of the convention prediction problem.

5. CONVENTION PREDICTION PROBLEM IN TWITTER

In this section, we use features about a user's characteristics and behavior on Twitter (*personal*), the behavior of those they follow on Twitter (*social*), and the date of adoption (*global*) to predict the behavior of individuals who adopted the retweeting convention in Twitter. By examining how well we can predict an individual's decision to use one variation over another, we aim to understand which features play a key role in the adoption.

5.1 Features and Classifiers

The quality of any prediction algorithm depends on the choice of features. Based on the observations from the previous section, we considered the following features from the three categories described above: (1) *personal* features including the join date, geolocation, in-degree, out-degree, the number of tweets, and the number of URLs; (2) *social* features including the number of exposures to each variation and the number of friends who exposed the user to each variation; and (3) *global* features like the date of adoption. We

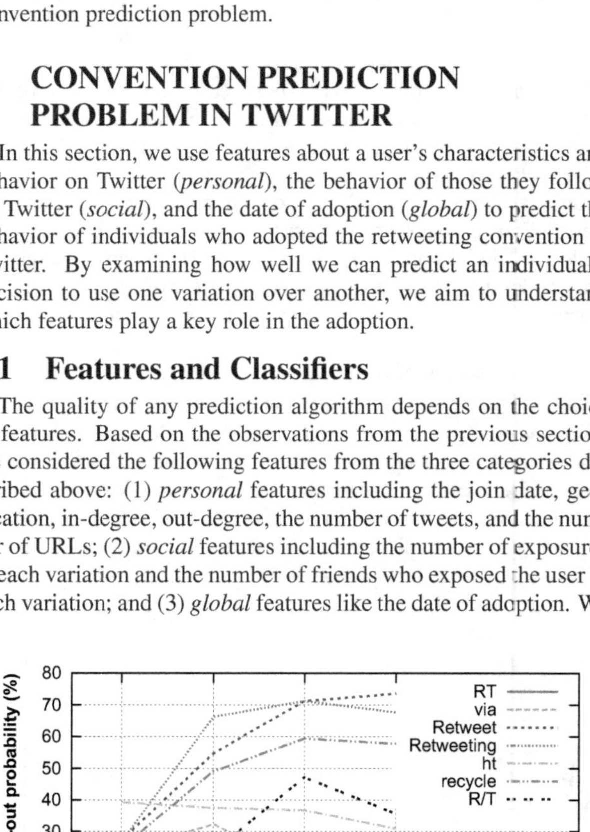

Figure 4: Switch out probability over time

Sample data entry	625, Germany, 321, 167, 252, 57, 54, 22, 5, 12, 1, 0, 4, 30, 18, 4, 6, 1, 0, 4, 665, RT

Table 5: An example of the data sample given to the classifier

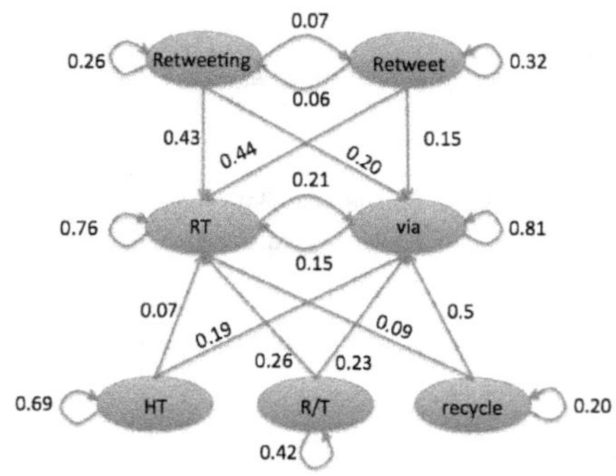

Figure 5: Transition probabilities between different variations (Probabilities below 0.05 are not drawn for visual clarity.)

consider the date of adoption because it correlates with the global popularity of the adopted variation.

Table 5 shows a sample data point. This sample represents a single adoption instance of an individual with different features at the time of adoption separated by comma in the order we introduced the features in the previous paragraph. The first number (i.e., 625) shows the join date of the adopter, in terms of number of days after Twitter was started. The next number indicates the location of the adopter, Germany in this case. The third and fourth numbers are the in-degree (321) and out-degree of the adopter (167), respectively. The numbers of posted tweets (252) and URLs (57) are the next two fields. The next seven fields are the total number of exposures to the seven different variations, which means the adopter was exposed 54 times to RT, 22 times to via, 5 times to Retweeting, and so on. Similarly, the next seven numbers show the number of adopter friends: 30 RT-adopter friends, 18 via-adopter friends, and so on. The last number represents the date of adoption in terms of number of days after Twitter was launched, 665 in this case, which is 40 days after the user joined Twitter. The final field shows the target variation of adoption (RT) that we want to predict.

In order to determine the discriminative power of each one of the 21 features, we computed the chi-square (χ^2) value and the information gain. Table 6 shows the order of all features based on the χ^2 value, where a larger value indicates a higher discriminative power. The order of the features were very similar when ranked by information gain (i.e., the Kullback-Leibler divergence), and in both cases the top three features span all three categories: global (date of adoption), social (the number of exposures to RT), and personal (the number of posted URLs).

Analysis of the discriminative power of the 21 features brings two key insights. First, the fact that the global feature (i.e., date of adoption) had the most predictive power suggests that the decision at the microscopic level—individuals deciding which variation to adopt—has more to do with the global popularity of the variations than its local popularity or a user's personal traits. Second, for each of the seven variations, the number of exposures had more predictive power than the number of adopter friends of that variation. This difference is important because most existing models of diffusion and adoption, such as the independent cascade model or the linear threshold model, are based on the distinct number of adopting friends rather than the sheer volume of exposures.

Rank	Feature	Type	χ^2 value
1	date of adoption	Global	300,666
2	# of exposures to RT	Social	106,627
3	# of posted URLs	Personal	80,728
4	# of exposures to via	Social	64,160
5	join date of the adopter	Personal	48,071
6	# of posted tweets	Personal	44,523
7	# of RT-adopter friends	Social	44,079
8	# of exposures to Retweeting	Social	43,100
9	# of exposures to HT	Social	42,807
10	# of exposures to Retweet	Social	36,604
11	# of exposures to recycle	Social	32,889
12	in-degree of the adopter	Personal	30,762
13	# of HT-adopter friends	Social	24,338
14	out-degree of the adopter	Personal	24,338
15	# of exposures to R/T	Social	23,370
16	# of Retweeting-adopter friends	Social	8,141
17	# of Retweet-adopter friends	Social	7,507
18	country of the adopter	Personal	4,476
19	# of via-adopter friends	Social	4,429
20	# of R/T-adopter friends	Social	203
21	# of recycle-adopter friends	Social	67

Table 6: Predictive features and their discriminative power

5.2 Classification Results

To test the combined effect of the 21 features described in Table 6, we built a classifier that predicts which variation a user adopts given the time of adoption. Predicting which of multiple variations a user will adopt (i.e., multi-class classification) is hard in this case because the classes are unbalanced. In total, 68.2% of all adoptions were RT, which means that a classifier that always predicts that a user will adopt RT will achieve at least that level of accuracy. In contrast, all other variations had much fewer adopters, for instance, recycle icon was only adopted by 0.2% of users. This means a classifier can achieve an accuracy of 99.8% for recycle icon by always predicting that the user did *not* adopt recycle icon, which is a very difficult baseline to improve upon.

For prediction, we used several classifiers in the WEKA machine learning toolkit [45] including SVM, Bayesian models, boosting, and decision trees. In particular, we used a popular ensemble classification technique, *bagging*, to achieve very high classification accuracy. Bagging aggregates the decision from a number of classifiers such that the accuracy is always at least as good as, and typically better than, the best classifier in the ensemble. In order to promote model variance, bagging trains each model in the ensemble using a randomly-drawn subset of the training set and then makes a prediction by taking an equally-weighted vote across all classifiers in the ensemble.

We tried many different combinations and subsets of the features and found that excluding 8 features (e.g., the number of adopter friends for each variation and the geo-location of the adopter) produced the best result. Table 7 shows the results of the multi-class prediction by using a random half of the data samples for training and the other half for testing. We correctly predicted 72.6% of the instances. Compared to the baseline of 70.4%, which is also shown in the table, this is a marginal improvement (<2.2%).

Variation	Baseline	Accuracy	Precision	Recall	AUC
RT	0.682	0.712	0.728	0.920	0.681
via	0.720	0.726	0.521	0.237	0.666
Retweeting	0.981	0.980	0.431	0.177	0.905
Retweet	0.986	0.985	0.343	0.084	0.801
HT	0.996	0.997	0.505	0.039	0.849
R/T	0.998	0.998	0.190	0.001	0.815
recycle icon	0.998	0.999	0.359	0.009	0.823
Weighted average	0.704	0.726	0.657	0.698	0.683

Table 7: Result of multi-class prediction for each variation

Variation	Accuracy	Precision	Recall	AUC
RT	0.613	0.607	0.631	0.662
via	0.607	0.606	0.601	0.650
Retweeting	0.591	0.589	0.618	0.641
Retweet	0.569	0.566	0.566	0.604
HT	0.823	0.828	0.815	0.896
R/T	0.773	0.770	0.772	0.838
recycle icon	0.815	0.831	0.802	0.898
Weighted average	0.610	0.607	0.615	0.657

Table 8: Result of predicting variations separately

As mentioned earlier, the classes are unbalanced and this makes it hard to see how much each feature helps to predict an adoption. To investigate whether the features were at all useful for predicting which variation a user would adopt, we selected all of the cases where a target variation and another variation were adopted on the same date. In this way, we ensured a balanced set of adoptions and controlled for the shifting popularity that we observed in the multi-class prediction problem. After selecting these cases, we performed the analysis with the same tool, method, and features (other than the date of adoption).

Table 8 shows the results of predicting variations separately. The classifier could achieve the accuracy of on average 22.0% improvement over the baseline, which is now 0.50 for all seven variations. The classifier could more accurately predict the adoptions for variations with fewer total adopters. In the case of HT, 82.3instances were correctly predicted, a 65This difference could be explained by the fact that adopters of these variations are in general more active and popular than the adopters of popular variations (Figure 2).

In order to understand the extent to which classification results are sensitive to any assumptions made, we repeated the prediction analysis with two stronger definitions of a social tie. Therefore, a user was not considered an adopter unless she had used a given variation at least three or five times. In addition, we considered the network structure based on user interactions rather than a simple follow link. In building the social network, we define user A to be linked to user B if and only if user A explicitly mentioned user B's name using "@username" in her tweets at least twice, following the definition of a "friend" in [8]. Directing a post to someone is called a *mention* in Twitter. Compared to a typical follow link, a "mention" link represents a stronger social relationship.

Figure 6 shows the prediction results under these different assumptions about a social link as well as the results for the standard definition of adoption and links as shown in Table 8. The accuracy when enforcing the 3-use threshold is better for the top five variations, but slightly worse for the bottom two variations. This is because having a stronger definition of adoption lead to fewer samples, and this meant the less popular variations had less data

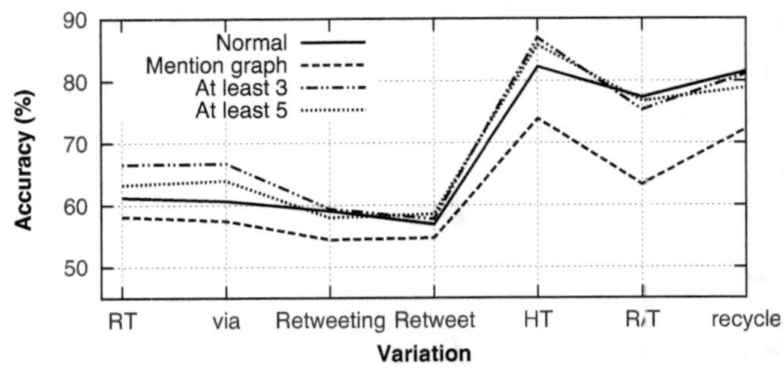

Figure 6: Prediction accuracy under different assumptions

for training. The overall prediction accuracy improved by an additional 5.4% compared to the previous prediction. Continuing to enforce a stronger definition (i.e., the 5-use threshold), however, did not continue to increase accuracy for the popular variations.

The prediction results for limiting the diffusion over the mention links as opposed to regular follow links are worse than the original prediction for all seven retweeting variations. This suggests that enforcing a stronger definition of social relationship does not necessarily improve the prediction power. This only resulted in cases where we could not explain the adoption process through social network. What seems more important is the exposure to the social convention itself, rather than the information source in the spread of retweeting convention in Twitter.

6. IMPLICATIONS

Our analysis suggests that the most important feature in predicting the user-level adoption was the global trend, as opposed to social or personal features. This is surprising, as one would expect that for this domain—where the convention is only useful within Twitter and is most likely to be learned about from one's peers on Twitter—the importance of local features would be greater.

There are, however, a number of possible reasons why the global trend would outweigh personal features. One could be that the Twitter culture was changing in ways over time that we did not measure or were unobservable. For instance, a different kinds of people could have joined Twitter, where the first group of people preferred via and later people preferred RT. Or it could be that independent of the new users, the culture within Twitter or even outside of Twitter was changing in some way that led users to prefer one variation over another (e.g., an increase in the sharing of breaking news and URLs). If this is true, it raises questions about how these changes in the culture are affecting the Twitter population *en masse* if it is not evident in the interactions between individuals.

We could also reasonably assume that some users prefer to adopt the more globally popular convention as opposed to the more locally popular one. Users can get the global view in different ways; for example popular users and celebrities who are followed by many users could represent the global view. Users can also be exposed to a set of random tweets shown in the front page of Twitter or from the search results.

It is worth pointing out that just because a global feature proved to be the strongest predictor, it does not mean that the most popular variation at the moment will necessarily receive strictly more adopters. Twitter was not a "winner-take-all" market. In fact, the dominant variant was no longer the most popular after a few months; the top ranked variation was initially via for nearly a year, then switched back and forth between Retweeting and via for half a year until RT became the dominant one in late 2008 (Figure 1). This means that there may be a process of constant re-evaluation within the Twitter community, through which the rank of the variations could change.

A second key results is that the number of exposures had more discriminative power than the number of adopter friends. This is interesting because other work has suggested that the number of distinct adopter friends is crucial for predicting one's adoption [28]. However, we saw that the number of adopter friends was less important than the volume of repeated exposures. With respect to the effect of repeated exposures in adoptions, Romero and colleagues found a similar positive effect in the spread of political hashtags in Twitter [38]. They describe this as "complex contagion" and explain that when a particular behavior is controversial or contentious, people may need more exposure to it from others before adopting it themselves. In the case of the retweeting convention, people may also need to be exposed to this new practice multiple times before they start to adopt it. This seems especially likely, since in the development of a social convention, as framed in the coordination problem [42], users require even more "social proof" before deciding to adopt the convention.

7. CONCLUSION

How do social conventions emerge and settle in human societies? In this paper, we presented one of the first studies using large-scale empirical data to study the emergence of a social convention. The convention we study is not based on simulations or experiments in a controlled environment as in most existing work, but is an actual practice that was adopted by more than 2 million people in the popular social network Twitter. The retweeting convention we studied is specific to Twitter, hence serves as a relatively clean case study in which we have records of nearly all usages and exposures of the convention.

Given the need to establish a convention for retweeting, a number of variations of the convention emerged organically in Twitter. As we saw in the tweets of the early adopters, users actively engaged in the discussion of which variation should be used. Throughout the course of the first few years, different variations competed to reign as a leading practice and in this process certain variations (e.g., longer ones) showed to be more easily abandoned than others. When it comes to individual's decision to adopt a variation, a number of factors such as social exposures and the date of adoption played an important role. However, predicting the adoption process at a user level turned out to be challenging.

There are several exciting directions to pursue. Since the features we considered only represent simple personal traits such as the node degree and geo-location, we believe more nuanced features about the adopters (e.g., socio-economic factors) would have the potential to improve the prediction. For instance, Pennacchiotti and Popescu demonstrated that users' political affiliation, ethnicity, and affinity for a particular business can be inferred in Twitter [35], and these features may be useful for determining which retweeting variation a user will adopt. Furthermore, it is possible that by leveraging the features we studied as well as other potential features, one may be able to extrapolate to the macroscopic problem of predicting which variation would come to be the most popular based on early usages.

Acknowledgements

Meeyoung Cha was supported by Basic Science Research Program through the National Research Foundation, Korea (2011-0012988).

8. REFERENCES

[1] I. Ajzen and M. Fishbein. The prediction of behavior from attitudinal and normative variables. *Journal of Experimental Social Psychology*, 6:466–487, 1970.

[2] S. E. Asch. Opinions and Social Pressure. *Scientific American*, 193:31–35, 1955.

[3] R. Axelrod. An Evolutionary Approach to Norms. *American Political Science Review*, 1986.

[4] E. Bakshy, I. Rosenn, C. Marlow, and L. Adamic. The Role of Social Networks in Information Diffusion. In *proc. of the International World Wide Web Conference*, 2012.

[5] F. Barth. *Process and Form in Social Life*. Routledge & Kegan Paul, 1981.

[6] R. Baumeister and M. Leary. The Need to Belong: Desire for Interpersonal Attachments as a Fundamental Human Motivation. *Psychological Bulletin*, 1995.

[7] B. Becker and G. Mark. Social conventions in collaborative virtual environments. In *proc. of the International Conference on Collaborative Virtual Environments*, 1998.

[8] D. M. R. Bernardo A. Huberman and F. Wu. Social networks that matter: Twitter under the microscope. *First Monday*, 14(1), Jan. 2009.

[9] Bibb Latané and S. Wolf. The social impact of majorities and minorities. *Psychological Review*, 88:438–453, 1981.

[10] d. boyd, S. Golder, and G. Lotan. Tweet, Tweet, Retweet: Conversational Aspects of Retweeting on Twitter. In *proc. of the Hawaii International Conference on System Sciences*, 2010.

[11] R. Boyd and P. J. Richerson. Why does culture increase human adaptability? *Ethology and Sociobiology*, 16:125–143, 1995.

[12] B. P. Buunk and A. B. Bakker. Extradyadic sex: The role of descriptive and injunctive norms. *Journal of Sex Research*, 32(4):313–318, Jan. 1995.

[13] D. Centola. The Spread of Behavior in an Online Social Network Experiment. *Science*, 329(5996):1194–1197, Sept. 2010.

[14] M. Cha, H. Haddadi, F. Benevenuto, and K. Gummadi. Measuring User Influence in Twitter: The Million Follower Fallacy. In *proc. of the International AAAI Conference on Weblogs and Social Media*, 2010.

[15] N. Christakis and J. H. Fowler. The Spread of Obesity in a Large Social Network over 32 Years. *New England Journal of Medicine*, 2007.

[16] R. B. Cialdini. *Influence: Science and practice*. HarperCollins, 3 edition, 1993.

[17] R. B. Cialdini and M. R. Trost. Social Influence: Social norms, conformity, and compliance. In D. T. Gilbert, S. T. Fiske, and L. Gardner, editors, *The Handbook of Social Psychology*, pages 151–192. McGraw-Hill, New York, 1998.

[18] E. Cohen-Cole and J. M. Fletcher. Is obesity contagious? Social networks vs. environmental factors in the obesity epidemic. *Journal of Health Economics*, 27:1382–1387, 2008.

[19] J. Delgado. Emergence of social conventions in complex networks. *Artificial Intelligence*, 141(1-2):171–185, 2002.

[20] M. Deutsch and H. B. Gerard. A study of normative and informative social influences upon individual judgment. *Journal of Abnormal Psychology*, 51:629–636, 1955.

[21] D. C. Feldman. The development and enforcement of group norms. *The Academy of Management Review*, 9(1):47–53, 1984.

[22] L. Festinger. A theory of social comparison processes. *Human Relations*, 7(2):117–140, 1954.

[23] J. H. Fowler and N. A. Christakis. Cooperative behavior cascades in human social networks. *Proceedings of the National Academy of Sciences*, 107(12):5334–5338, Mar. 2010.

[24] N. E. Friedkin. Norm Formation in Social Influence Networks. *Social Networks*, 23:167–189, 2001.

[25] H. B. Gerard. The Anchorage of Opinions in Face-to-Face Groups. *Human Relations*, 7(3):313–325, Aug. 1954.

[26] H. B. Gerard, R. A. Wilhelmy, and E. S. Conolley. Conformity and group size. *Journal of Personality and Social Psychology*, 8:79–82, 1968.

[27] S. Goyal and M. C. W. Janssen. Non-Exclusive Conventions and Social Coordination. *Journal of Economic Theory*, 77(1):34–57, 1997.

[28] C. A. Insko, R. H. Smith, M. D. Alicke, J. Wade, and S. Taylor. Conformity and group size: The concern with being right and the concern with being liked. *Personality and Social Psychology Bulletin*, 11:41–50, 1985.

[29] F. Kooti, H. Yang, M. Cha, K. Gummadi, and W. A. Mason. The emergence of conventions in online social networks. In *proc. of the International AAAI Conference on Weblogs and Social Media*, 2012.

[30] J. Levine and R. L. Moreland. Progress in Small Group Research. *Annual Reviews in Psychology*, 41:585–634, 1990.

[31] S. Milgram, L. Bickman, and L. Berkowitz. Note on the drawing power of crowds of different size. *Journal of Personality and Social Psychology*, 13(2):79–82, 1969.

[32] T. M. Newcomb. *Personality and social change*. Dryden, 1943.

[33] K.-D. Opp. How do norms emerge? An outline of a theory. *Mind & Society*, 3(2):101–128, 2001.

[34] E. Ostrom. Collective Action and the Evolution of Social Norms. *The Journal of Economic Perspectives*, 14:137–158, 2000.

[35] M. Pennacchiotti and A.-M. Popescu. Democrats, Republicans and Starbucks Afficionados: User Classification in Twitter. In *proc. of the ACM SIGKDD Conference on Knowledge Discovery and Data Mining*, 2011.

[36] A. Riley and P. J. Burke. Identities and Self-Verification in the Small Group. *Social Psychology Quarterly*, 58(2):61–73, 1995.

[37] E. M. Rogers. *Diffusion of Innovations*. Free Press, 1983.

[38] D. M. Romero, B. Meeder, and J. Kleinberg. Differences in the Mechanics of Information Diffusion Across Topics: Idioms, Political Hashtags, and Complex Contagion on Twitter. In *proc. of the International World Wide Web Conference*, 2011.

[39] M. Salganik, P. S. Dodds, and D. J. Watts. Experimental Study of Inequality and Unpredictability in an Artificial Cultural Market. *Science*, 311:854–856, 2006.

[40] B. Savarimuthu, S. Cranefield, and M. Purvis. Role Model Based Mechanism for Norm Emergence in Artificial Agent Societies. In *proc. of the AAMAS '07 Workshop on Coordination, Organization, Institutions and Norms in Agent Systems*, 2007.

[41] M. Sherif. *The psychology of social norms*. Harper, 1936.

[42] Y. Shoham and M. Tennenholtz. On the emergence of social conventions: modeling, analysis, and simulations. *Artificial Intelligence*, 94(1-2):139–166, 1997.

[43] D. M. Taylor and W. Louis. Terrorism and the quest for identity. In F. M. Moghaddam and A. J. Marsella, editors, *Understanding terrorism: Psychosocial roots, consequences, and interventions*, volume 343, pages 169–185. American Psychological Association, 2004.

[44] A. Walker and M. Wooldridge. Understanding the emergence of conventions in multi-agent systems. In *proc. of the International Conference on Multi-Agent Systems*, 1995.

[45] WEKA website. http://www.cs.waikato.ac.nz/ml/weka.

[46] D. Wilkes-Gibbs and H. Clark. Coordinating beliefs in conversation. *Journal of Memory and Language*, 31(2):183–194, 1992.

[47] M. P. Zanna and J. M. Olson. Individual differences in attitudinal relations. In M. P. Zanna, E. T. Higgins, and C. P. Herman, editors, *Consistency in social behavior: The Ontario Symposium*, volume 2, pages 75–103. Erlbaum, 1982.

Collective Intelligence in the Online Social Network of Yahoo!Answers and Its Implications

Ze Li, Haiying Shen, Joseph Edward Grant
Department of Electrical and Computer Engineering, Clemson University
Clemson, SC, 29631, USA
{zel, shenh, jegrant}@clemson.edu

ABSTRACT

Question and Answer (Q&A) websites such as Yahoo!Answers provide a platform where users can post questions and receive answers. These systems take advantage of the collective intelligence of users to find information. In this paper, we analyze the online social network (OSN) in Yahoo!Answers. Based on a large amount of our collected data, we studied the OSN's structural properties, which reveals strikingly distinct properties such as low link symmetry and weak correlation between indegree and outdegree. After studying the knowledge base and behaviors of the users, we find that a small number of top contributors answer most of the questions in the system. Also, each top contributor focuses on only a few knowledge categories. In addition, the knowledge categories of the users are highly clustered. We also study the knowledge base in a user's social network, which reveals that the members in a user's social network share only a few knowledge categories. Based on the findings, we provide guidance in the design of spammer detection algorithms and distributed Q&A systems. We also propose a friendship-knowledge oriented Q&A framework that synergically combines current OSN-based Q&A and web Q&A. We believe that the results presented in this paper are crucial in understanding the collective intelligence in the web Q&A OSNs and lay a cornerstone for the evolution of next-generation Q&A systems.

Categories and Subject Descriptors

H.3.4 [**Systems and Software**]: Question-answering (fact retrieval) systems

General Terms

Measurement, Performance

Keywords

Collective intelligence, On-line social networks, Knowledge networks

CIKM'12, October 29–November 2, 2012, Maui, HI, USA.

1. INTRODUCTION

Web search engine (e.g., Google and Bing) enables us to search information by keywords on the Internet. Recently, web search engines are improved by combining with social networks [1–5], enabling social friends to collaborate with each other to determine the relevance of the returned results to their queries. Users use web annotations or bookmarks to indicate the search results they are interested in, which helps their common-interest friends to quickly identify results useful to themselves.

However, picking up useful information from the overwhelming returned results still remains a challenge. Users sometimes prefer to directly receive the answers rather than going through a long tedious searching process. In addition, although the search engine based information retrieval performs very well in answering factual queries for information already existing in databases, it is not suitable for non-factual or context-aware queries, which are more subjective, relative and multi-dimensional in context, especially for information not existing in databases (e.g., suggestions, recommendations and advices). This remains as a formidable challenge facing current search engines without big breakthroughs in machine learning and natural language processing techniques.

Actually, people are the most "intelligent machines" that are capable of parsing, interpreting and answering questions, provided they are familiar with the questions. Each person has knowledge from his careers, education, life, experience, interests and so on, which forms his *knowledge base*. By collecting the intelligence of people to find information, Question and Answer (Q&A) websites such as Yahoo!Answers [6] (YA) and Ask.com [7] have naturally emerged as an alternative way for Q&A. These websites provide a platform where users can post questions and receive answers. If user A wants to frequently visit/track all questions and answers of user B, A adds B to its contact list by building a link to B. Then, A becomes B's fan. Thus, a knowledge-oriented online social network (OSN) with unidirectional links between nodes is formed in the Q&A system. YA classifies knowledge into 26 *general knowledge categories (KCs)* (e.g., Sports, Health). Each general knowledge categories has a number of *detailed KCs* (e.g., Golf, Tennis). Users with many points are recognized as *top contributors*, whose profiles indicate the general and details KCs they are knowledgeable in.

Although Q&A websites are becoming increasingly popular and can provide high quality answers [8], they have some shortcomings in satisfying users' needs. First, the latency for receiving a satisfying answer is high with the average equals

2:52:30 (hh:mm:ss) even when the number of the registered users is very large (290,000) [9]. This is because most users log in the Q&A website only when they have questions to ask. Even if some users may intend to answer others' questions, since all questions in one topic appear together in one forum, it is difficult for a user to identify the questions he can answer. Second, as Q&A websites are normally open to all anonymous users in Internet, spam is a difficult problem.

In recent years, OSN-based Q&A systems [8, 10–14] have been developed. Facebook launched a Q&A application in July, 2010. In an OSN-based Q&A system, users post and answer questions through the OSN in order to take advantage of the collective intelligence of their friends. Specifically, a centralized server identifies possible answers from the questioner's friends in his social network, and forwards the question directly to them. Expertise location systems [15–18] that search experts in specified fields share similarity with OSN-based Q&A in answerer location. Research [12] shows that the answerers in the OSN are willing to and able to provide more tailored and personalized answers to the questioners since they know a great deal about the backgrounds and preference of the questioners. However, the characteristics of the knowledge of the friends in a user's social network may affect the qualify of the answers for the user's questions. Factual questions such as "what is the time complexity of the X algorithm" need the answers from experts in the computing theory field, which may not be offered by the OSN-based Q&A systems.

By synergistically integrating the web Q&A system and OSN-based Q&A system, both systems' shortcomings can be overcome. To achieve this, it is important to understand the nature and impact of collective intelligence in the OSNs of both systems. However, no previous work has been devoted to studying the OSN in the Q&A websites, though previous research investigated the OSN-based Q&A systems. In this paper, we analyze the OSN in YA, a popular online Q&A website. For this effort, we have collected Q&A trace data during three months, and a large amount of personal data and their associated relationship in YA. The main contribution of this paper is an extensive trace-driven analysis of OSN structure, user behavior, user knowledge base and their relationships. Our analysis yields very interesting results and the highlights of our work are summarized as follows:

- Examination on the structural properties of the YA OSN shows that though it shares a common property with other previously studied OSNs in that the node indegree and outdegree exhibit power-law distribution, it has strikingly distinct properties: (1) It has low link symmetry; (2) It exhibits weak correlation between indegree and outdegree; (3) Users tend to connect to other users with different degrees from their own; (4) Users exhibit an extremely low clustering coefficient.
- Investigation on the knowledge base and behaviors of users in YA reveals that (1) A small portion of the users (i.e., 10%) contribute to the most of the high quality answers; (2) The 12 most popular general KCs account for 80% of all general KCs in the system; (3) The top contributors steadily contribute high-quality answers. Many top contributors focus on one general KC, and 56.5% of them have multiple general KCs, but all of the them have multiple detailed KCs; (4) There exists positive linear correlation between the number of fans and points of a user but no correlation between the number of contacts and points of a user; (5) The KCs of the users are highly clustered.
- Analysis on the relationship of knowledge base and OSN structure shows that (1) The size of the knowledge base within a user's one-hop OSN neighbors is small, and increases, though not significantly, within two-hop OSN neighbors; (2) Reciprocity (i.e., bidirectional connected) users share more common KCs than one-way connected users, who share more KCs than disconnected users.
- We finally discuss the implications of our findings on the design of spammer detection algorithms in Q&A systems and a distributed Q&A system that integrates both web Q&A system and OSN-based Q&A system.

# of nodes in the social network	119175
# of links in the contact network	1,786,036
# of links in the fan network	1,265,305
Ave. # of contacts per user in the contact network	14.98
Ave. # of fans per user in the fan network	10.61
Ave. # of general KCs in a user's contact network	2.1
Ave. # of detailed KCs in a user's contact network	4.2
Ave. # of general KCs in a user's fan network	2.2
Ave. # of detailed KCs in a user's fan network	4.2

Table 1: High level statistic of the crawled YA social network.

Our analysis provides critical insights regarding the different properties of the YA OSN and other friendship and/or knowledge oriented OSNs. The analytical results provide cornerstone for the performance improvement on current Q&A systems and the evolution of next-generation Q&A systems.

2. BACKGROUND AND MEASUREMENT METHODOLOGY

YA, as a knowledge market, was launched by Yahoo! on July 5, 2005. It has an OSN with unidirectional links between nodes. The nodes in a user's contact list are called *outdegree nodes*, which form *the node's contact network*, and the nodes in a node's fan list are called *indegree nodes*, which form *the node's fan network*. Thus, YA OSN incorporates two directional networks: *contact network* and *fan network*. The former includes all nodes and their outdegree nodes and the latter includes all nodes and their indegree nodes.

We wrote a crawler using Python. The crawler started from the first 4000 top contributors and inserted these users into an initially empty queue. It fetched the first user from the queue, recorded his profile information (i.e., total number of earned points, answers, best answers and questions), retrieved and inserted his public visible contacts and fans to the queue, and finally removed this user from the queue. This process repeated until the queue became empty. Crawling was started on Aug. 17 and ended on Oct. 19, 2011. As the crawled OSN data is seeded at 4000 different users with various KCs, it can well represent an actual knowledge-oriented OSN. In addition, for each user, we recorded its profile information for the activities during every week from Aug. 17 to Oct. 19 2011. In our trace data, about 8% of the users are top contributors. Table 1 shows the high level statistics of the crawled YA OSN.

3. ANALYSIS OF OSN STRUCTURE

In this section, we study the structural characteristics of the YA OSN. We also are interested in answering a ques-

Social network website	Reciprocity rate
Facebook [19]	100%
Flickr [20]	68%
Yahoo!360 [21]	84%
Digg [22]	39.4%
Yahoo!Answers	30.7%
Twitter [23]	22.1%

Table 2: Reciprocity rate of different OSN.

tion: does it show similar structural characteristics as other OSNs?

3.1 Reciprocity

In an OSN, the pairwise bidirectional relationship between two nodes is called *reciprocity*. We define the *reciprocity rate* of an OSN as the number of reciprocity links over all links of all users. Table 2 shows the reciprocity rate of YA and a number of other OSNs from other studies [19–23]. We see that the reciprocity rate of YA is 30.7%. It is similar to the reciprocate rate (39.4%) of the content rating website Digg. Twitter also has a low reciprocity rate of 22.1%. In contrast, Facebook, Flickr and Yahoo!360 have high reciprocity rates, and they are 100%, 68% and 84%, respectively. In these OSNs, a large part of the users connect with each other by their real social ties (i.e., friendship) in their daily lives. Therefore, most links in these OSNs are bidirectional and their reciprocity rate is high. On the contrary, Digg, YA, Twitter are mainly information/knowledge sharing websites, in which people are mainly connected according to their interests. Therefore, most links in these websites are unidirectional and their reciprocity rate is low. Twitter generates the lowest reciprocity rate. This is because Twitter currently is treated as a social media by large companies and celebrities to publish information [23]. YA has the second lowest reciprocity rate. Our crawled dataset also shows that 16.7% of the users only have fans but no contacts. This implies that users prefer to connect to users who are knowledgable in certain categories, and knowledgable users can attract more fans.

3.2 Power-law Node Degree

One striking property of the general OSNs is that their node degree follows a power-law distribution. That is, the majority of nodes have small degree while a few nodes have significantly higher degree. The power-law distribution is caused by the *preferential attach process*, in which the probability of a user A connecting to a user B is proportional to the number of B's existing connections.

Figure 1 shows the indegree and outdegree complementary cumulative distribution functions (CCDF). The figures show that the indegree and outdegree conform to a distribution that is close to a power-law distribution. In other words, the *preferential attach process* also occurs in the YA knowledge sharing system. We also see that there is a sharp drop at Figure 1(a) at around x=200. In 2007, YA launched a new policy that each user can have maximum 200 contacts. As a result, only few old registered users have more than 200 contacts, and the size of most users' contact lists is close to 200, which produces the sharp decrease.

We ranked the users based on their number of earned points. Specifically, we sorted the users based on their number of points in a descending order and assigned a rank to each node sequentially; rank 1 was assigned to the top node.

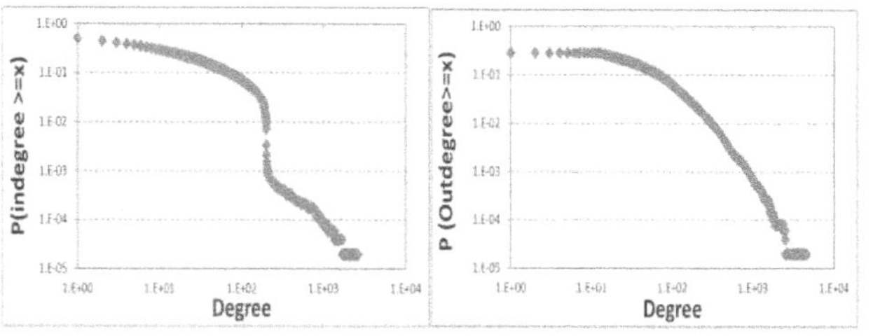

(a) Outdegree (contacts) (b) Indegree (Fans)

Figure 1: Log-log plot of indegree and outdegree CCDF.

We then plotted the number of points a node has versus its rank in Figure 2. We see that the number of points of users also conforms to a power-law distribution. This implies that a small amount of users are very active in answering questions and the rest are not active. Also, some of these nodes may give high-quality answers so that they can earn more points quickly. This phenomenon explains the power-law distribution of node indegree, that is, users are likely to connect to the users that are active and knowledgable in their interested categories. We will show the detail of the reason in Section 4.4.

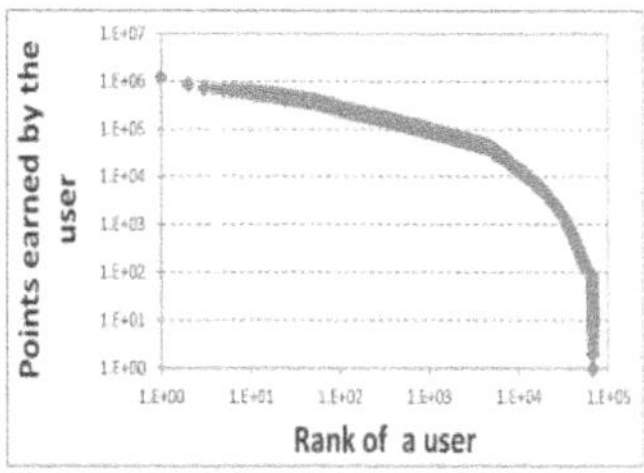

Figure 2: Distribution of points.

The power-law distribution of node degree is also caused by the popularity of the KCs, which affects the number of people involved in a KC. Users tend to connect to other users in popular KCs. Also, the users that are active in non-popular topics may not attract as much attention and has fewer fans. We will further investigate how the active answerers and category popularity affect the node degree in Section 4.

3.3 Correlation between Indegree and Outdegree

In general OSNs such as YouTube, Flickr, Digg and LiveJournal, the nodes with high outdegree tend to have high indegree. Specifically, the top 1% of nodes ordered by outdegree have a more than 58% overlap with the top 1% of nodes ranked by indegree [24]. To study the correlation between indegree and outdegree, we ranked nodes by indegree and outdegree, respectively, and generated two rank lists. We use L_{in} and L_{out} to denote the top x% of nodes in the ranked indegree list and ranked outdegree list, respectively. We define the *overlap* of L_{in} and L_{out} as $\frac{L_i \cap L_j}{L_i \cup L_j}$. Figure 3(a) shows the overlap between the top x% of nodes in the two ranked lists. We see the top 1% of nodes ordered by outdegree have a 29% overlap with the top 1% of nodes ranked by indegree. YA's overlap is much less than that of general OSNs. This means that some high-indegree nodes do not have high outdegree while some high-outdegree nodes do not have high indegree. In general OSNs, nodes connect to each other mainly for interaction and very socially active nodes should have both high indegree and outdegree. In YA, instead of aggressively making friends, the main purpose for user A to connect user B is to learn from user B in his interested KCs. Therefore, active and knowledgable nodes would have high indegree since many nodes connect to them and they may not connect to many nodes. Similarly, nodes who

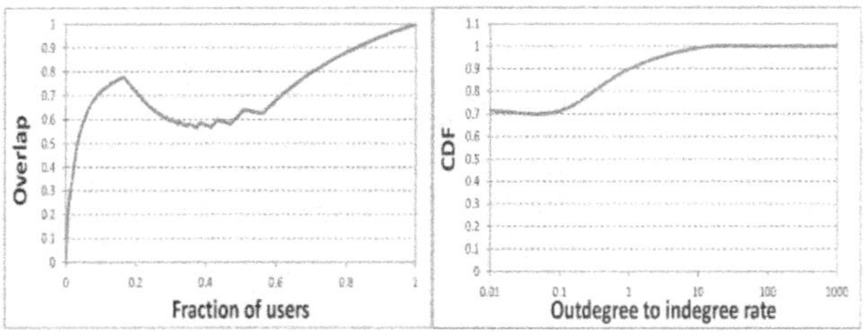

(a) Overlap between outdegree nodes and indegree nodes (b) Outdegree-to-indegree ratio

Figure 3: Correlation between indegree and outdegree.

eager to learn would have high outdegree by connecting to many other nodes and they would not be connected by many nodes if they are not active in answering. The nodes in the 29% overlap are both eager to learn and are learned by many nodes. They may mutually establish relationships in order to exchange knowledge.

We further explore the indegree and outdegree of individual users in YA. Figure 3(b) shows the cumulative distribution function (CDF) of outdegree-to-indegree ratio of users in YA. The CDF in YA differs from those of YouTube, LiveJournal, Digg, and Flickr [22] in two ways. First, in YA, 71% of the nodes have an outdegree-to-indegree ratio lower than 1%, while that of the other four websites is less than 56%. The main reason is that in YA, the number of contacts a user has is limited to 200, and the number of fans of a user is not limited. In the general OSNs, the number of either indegree or outdegree of a node is not limited. Second, in YA, about 9.12% of nodes have an indegree within 20% of their outdegree, which is similar to the rate of 14.56% in Digg, while the percentage for the other three friendship-oriented OSNs is more than 50%. In addition to the 200 contact limit in YA, this is also because in friendship-oriented OSNs, users tend to aggressively make friends with others, while in the YA knowledge-oriented OSN, users selectively choose active and knowledgable users in their interested fields as contacts. We also see that YA has less than 10% of nodes whose outdegree-to-indegree ratio is around 1. Thus, it has much weaker correlation between indegree and outdegree than the other three OSNs. This can be explained by a much lower level of link symmetry in YA.

3.4 Link Degree Correlation

In the general OSNs (e.g., Flickr, LiveJournal and Orkut), high degree nodes tend to connect to other high degree nodes [24]. It implies that highly social nodes tend to connect with each other. We are interested to see whether this phenomenon also exists in YA. If so, it means knowledgable users tend to share knowledge between each other.

To answer this question, we examined how often nodes of different degrees connect to each other represented by *joint degree distribution*, which can be approximated by the degree correlation function K_{nn}. The K_{nn} of outdegree d is measured as the average indegree of all nodes connected to nodes with d outdegree [24]. An increasing K_{nn} implies a tendency of higher-degree nodes to connect to other high degree nodes while a decreasing K_{nn} indicates the opposite trend. Figure 4(a) depicts K_{nn} for YA associated with its trend line, from which we see that as a user's outdegree increases to around 200, the K_{nn} exhibits a sharp decrease. Also, when the outdegree is lower than 200, the K_{nn} remains significantly higher than outdegree constantly. The watershed of 200 is caused by the outdegree limit of 200 in YA. Then, we can conclude that YA exhibits different behaviors from the general OSNs where K_{nn} increases as outdegree increases. This is caused by the celebrity-driven nature in YA, i.e., there are a few extremely active and knowledgable users to whom many inactive users link to. We can also see that some nodes have indegree much lower than their outdegree, which means that some inactive users connect to many other nodes but rarely linked by other nodes. These results are consistent with those in Figures 1 and Figure 2.

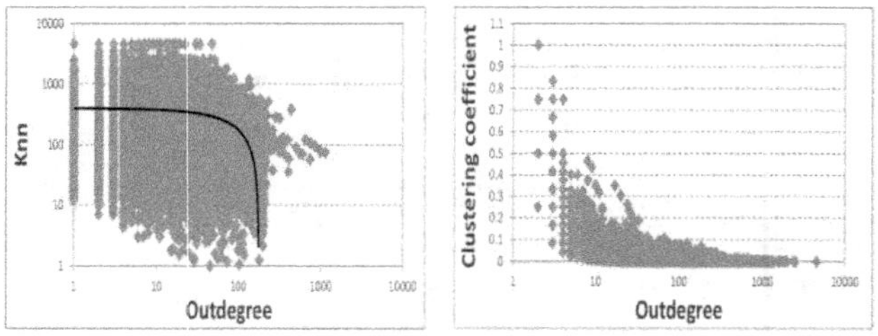

(a) Degree correlation function (b) Average clustering coefficient

Figure 4: Link degree correlation and clustering coefficient.

3.5 Clustering Coefficient

We then explore the connection density of the neighborhood of a node, which is quantified by the *clustering coefficient*. The clustering coefficient of a node with N neighbors is defined as the ratio of the number of directed links existing between the node's N neighbors and the number of possible directed links that could exist between these neighbors ($N(N-1)$). The average of individual nodes' clustering coefficients is 0.029 in YA. This value is much lower than those of YouTube, Orkut, Flickr, LiveJournal and Digg that range from 0.136 to 0.330 [22]. In the friendship-oriented OSNs such as Facebook and Flickr, users tend to be introduced to other users via mutual contacts, increasing the probability that two contacts of a single user are also contacts to each other. Other OSNs such as YouTube, Orkut, LiveJournal and Digg are oriented by both friendship and knowledge, and they should have lower clustering coefficient than the pure friendship-oriented OSNs. YA is a pure knowledge-oriented OSN, and a user adds contacts only when he finds the contacts are knowledgable in the fields he is interested in.

Figure 4(b) shows the clustering coefficient of each node with respect to its outdegree. Nodes of low outdegree have higher clustering coefficients, indicating significant clustering among low-outdegree nodes. High-outdegree nodes, on the other hand, show much lower clustering coefficients due to their large number of diverse contacts. We conjecture that the contacts of low-outdegree nodes are most likely in a limited number of KCs. Since users in the same KC tend to connect to each other, low-outdegree nodes have high clustering coefficient. In contrast, the contacts of high-outdegree nodes are likely to belong to many KCs. As users in different knowledge community are less likely to connect with each other, their clustering coefficients are small.

3.6 Summary

The YA OSN shares similar power-law structural property with other studied OSNs (Section 3.2). That is, a few power-law indegree nodes are active and knowledgable answerers that own many fans, and a few power-law outdegree nodes create many contacts and are active in learning others'

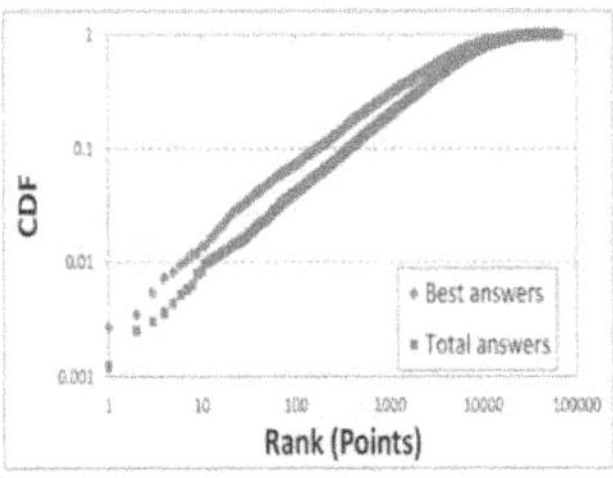

Figure 5: The CDF of the best answers and all answers.

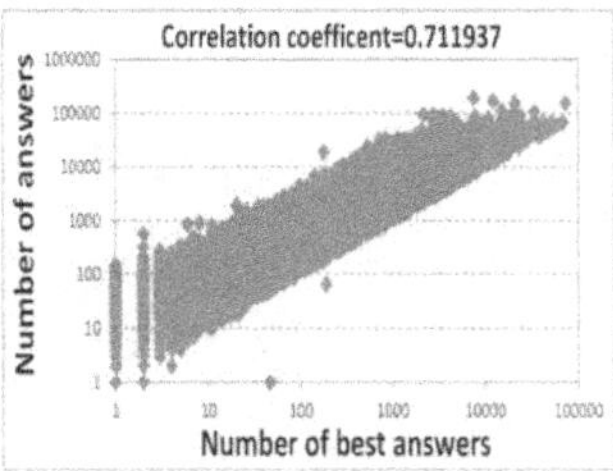

Figure 6: The correlation between best answers and all answers.

knowledge. However, YA OSN has the following strikingly different properties from other general OSNs:

(1) YA shows a much lower level of link reciprocity, which means that the connection between two nodes tend to be unidirectional from an active learner to an active answerer. Since a fan-contact link means the fan's trust on the contact, the trust transitivity property along the links can be exploited to identify reputed sources and detect spammers in the Q&A system (Section 3.1).

(2) YA exhibits weaker correlation between indegree and outdegree. Nodes with high outdegree do not necessarily have high indegree, and nodes with high indegree do not necessarily have high outdegree. This means active knowledgable answerers are not necessarily active learner, and active learners are not necessarily active answerers (Section 3.3).

(3) YA does not have a tendency of higher-degree nodes to connect to other high degree nodes. Instead, nodes with a high indegree are connected by nodes with various outdegree due to celebrity-driven nature, in which many nodes tend to connect to a small number of active and knowledgable nodes (Section 3.4).

(4) The users in YA exhibit an extremely low clustering coefficient comparing to other friendship-oriented major OSNs due to its tendency of unidirectional connections to active and knowledgable answerers (Section 3.5).

4. ANALYSIS OF KNOWLEDGE DISTRIBUTION AND USER BEHAVIOR

As the Q&A OSN is knowledge-oriented, it is very important to examine the user knowledge distribution and associated user behaviors.

4.1 User Behavior

Figure 5 shows the CDFs of the best answers and all answers versus user rank based on the number of points. We see both CDFs follow a power-law distribution. 80% of the best answers are provided by 7628 users who are ranked in the top 10% of all users. Similarly, 80% of the answers are provided by 15739 users who are ranked in the 19% of all users. We also notice that all of the top contributors are within the top 10% users, which means that the best answers are from them. Therefore, in YA, a small portion of the users (i.e., 10%) contribute to most of the high-quality answers.

Figure 6 shows the number of all answers versus the number of best answers of each user. We calculated the Pearson correlation coefficient between these two numbers of all users, which is around 0.712. We can see that there is a positive linear relationship between the number of answers

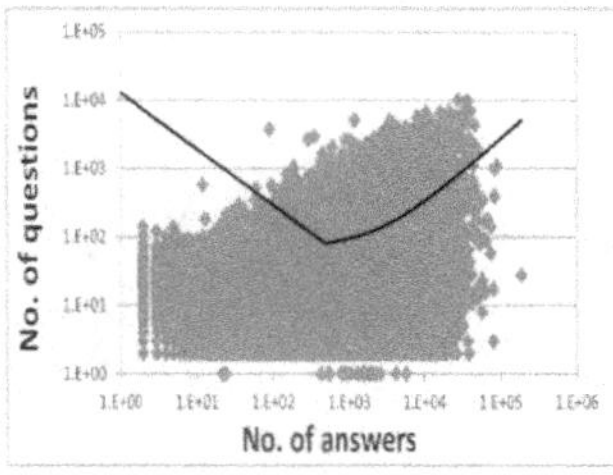

Figure 7: Correlation between # of questions and answers.

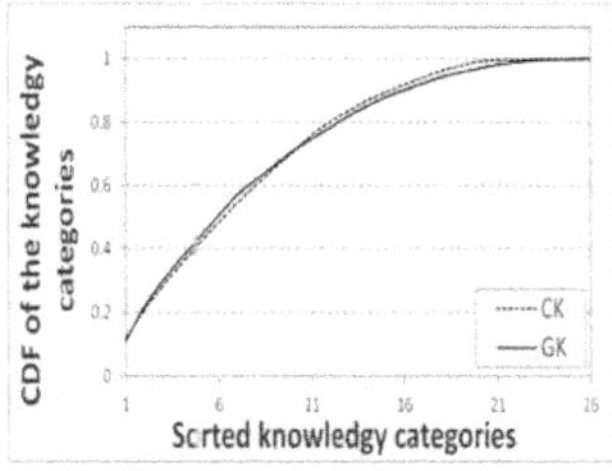

Figure 8: CDF of KCs.

and the number of best answers and the correlation coefficient is very high. This is because as the number of answers provided by a user increases, the number of the best answers also increases.

Figure 7 shows the correlation between the number of questions and the number of answers from each user with the log-log scale. We also plot the trend line for the data based on linear regression. From the trend line, we see that users with a small number of answers have a large number of questions. However, as the number of answers increases, the number of questions decreases linearly and then increases linearly at the point of x=1000. We use the ratio of the number questions to the number of answers r_{qa} to reflect the querying and answering activities of the users. $r_{qa} > 1$ means a user's asked questions are more than his answered questions. Our data shows the average r_{qa} is 0.437, the variance is 5.61. 23.1% of the users have $r_{qa} < 0.01$, which are the selfless nodes that answer much more questions than the questions they ask. 13.6% of the users have $r_{qa} > 100$, which are likely to be free-riders that ask many questions while answer only a few questions. All top contributors are in the 23.1% of the selfless nodes. It is also very interesting to see that in the top 1409 users who answer more than 10,000 question, 110 (7%) of them did not ask any questions. We conjuncture that YA hires experts to answer others' questions in order to improve the quality of Q/A service.

4.2 Distribution of Knowledge Categories

We study the knowledge base of users by examining the KCs of the top contributors and normal users. Since the system does not specify the KCs in the profiles of normal users, we study their KCs through the questions in all the system's general KCs. This is reasonable because as Figure 5 shows, most of the normal users in the Q&A system are knowledge consumers, and they either provide low qualify answers or provide only a few answers. We call the KCs appearing in the top contributors' profiles *contributor's knowledge (CK)*. We notice that the KCs in CK include all *general knowledge (GK)* in the system.

We ranked the KCs in CK based on the appearance frequency of each KC in CK, and ranked those in GK based on the number of questions posted in each KC in GK. Figure 8 plots the CDF of the category rank in CK and GK, respectively. The figure shows that 80% of all questions are in the top 12 KCs in GK, and 80% of all contributors' KCs are also in the top 12 KCs in CK. This result means that users in the system are interested in the top 12 KCs in GK, and the active and knowledgable answerers also answer questions focused on the top 12 KCs in CK.

Each KC i has a pair of CK value and GK value, denoted by (v_{c_i}, v_{g_i}). A KC's CK value is defined as the percent

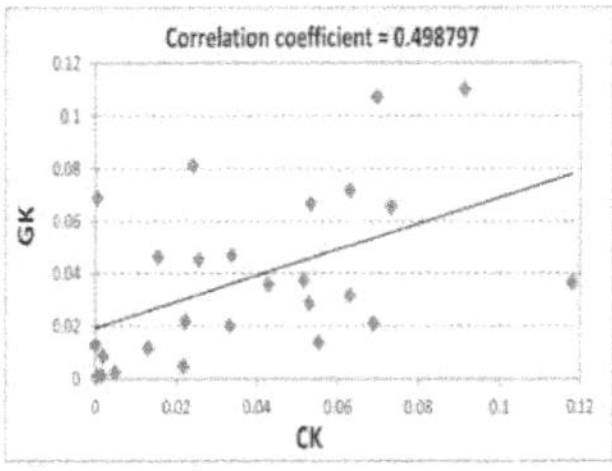

Figure 9: Distribution of KCs.

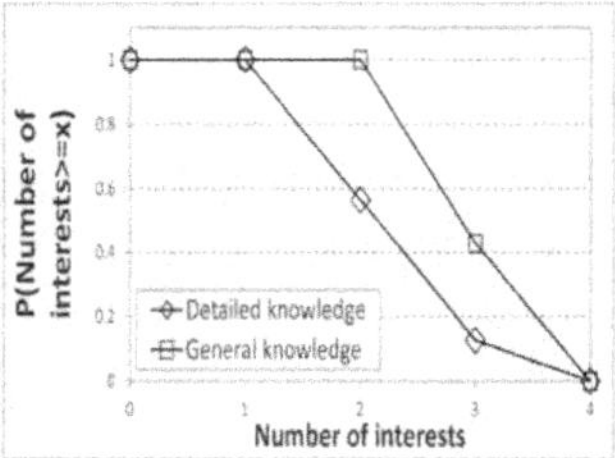

Figure 10: CCDF of KCs.

of its appearance frequency in the sum of the appearance frequencies of all categories in CK, and its GK value is the percent of its number of questions in the total number of questions. Our measurement shows that the Pearson correlation coefficient between the two values of all KCs equals 0.4988, which shows a strong correlation between CK and GK. Each point in Figure 9 shows (v_{c_i}, v_{g_i}) of each knowledgable category $i \in [1, 26]$. We see that the KC that has a large CK value tends to have a large GK value. The KCs that are popular in top contributors are also popular in general knowledge of all users, because the KCs in which top contributors frequently answer questions are also the KCs, in which users frequently ask questions.

4.3 Behavior and Knowledge Base of Top Contributors

Section 3.2 shows that the node indegree exhibits a power-law distribution. The behavior of high-indegree users may greatly affect the attractiveness of the application as these users contribute significantly more than normal users. We like to study these users' behaviors including answering frequency and earning points, which also indicate the effort needed to attract application users. We quantified the number of answers submitted and points earned by the 4000 top contributors that have the highest indegree from Aug. 17th to Oct. 19th, 2011. Table 3 and Table 4 show the maximum, average and minimum numbers of the answers submitted and points earned by these users during each week during the time period. We see that the average number of submitted answers (around 40) and earned points (around 300) during each week remain nearly constant. Also, a few users are very active in answering questions, the largest number of questions answered per week is over 1100. In addition, because the users that provide more best answers earn more points, the quality of the answers from some users is also very high. The maximum number of earned points in the week of maximum 1524 submitted questions is 16742. The highest points earned by a user is 19975 in a week with 1405 maximum submitted questions.

Given the KCs of users, we are very interested in how knowledge and expertise are spread across different domains. Figure 10 shows the CCDFs of the general KCs and the detailed KCs of the top contributors. We see all of the top contributors have 2 or more detailed KCs. Only 56.5% of the top contributors have 2 or more general KCs. The result shows that many top contributors like to answer questions within one general KC, in which they may participate in answering questions in at least two detailed categories.

4.4 Relationship Between Degree and Rank

Figure 11 and Figure 12 show the number of each user's contacts and fans versus his rank based on the number of points, respectively. Figure 11 shows that in the contact network, there are no correlations between the number of a user's contacts and his points. This result implies that how active a user is in learning is not determined by how active he is in answering questions. Also, most users have less than 200 contacts, and some outliers have more than 200 contacts. This is because YA constrains the number of the contacts of each user within 200 since 2007. We found that the outliers' account creation times are all in 2007, while all other users' account creation times are after 2007. From Figure 12, we see a user with higher rank is likely to have larger number of fans. This is because active and knowledgable nodes having many points are more likely to attract fans. This is one of the most important reason for the power-law distribution of user indegree.

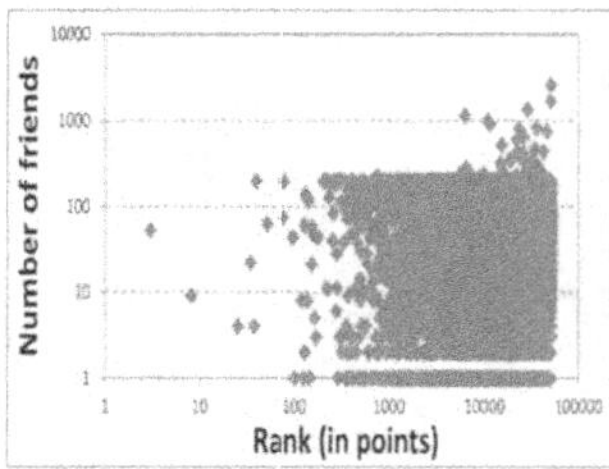

Figure 11: Number of contacts vs. rank.

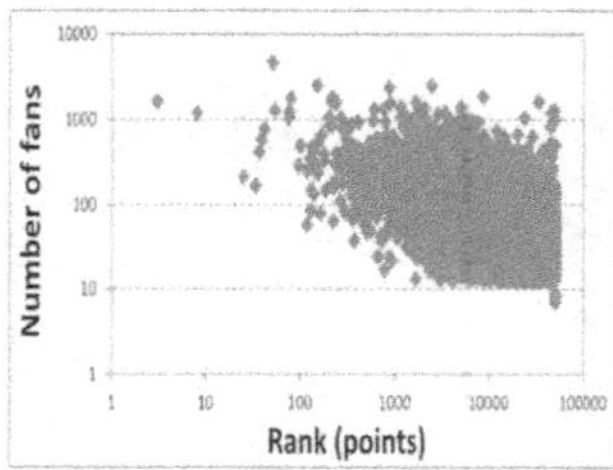

Figure 12: Number of fans vs. rank.

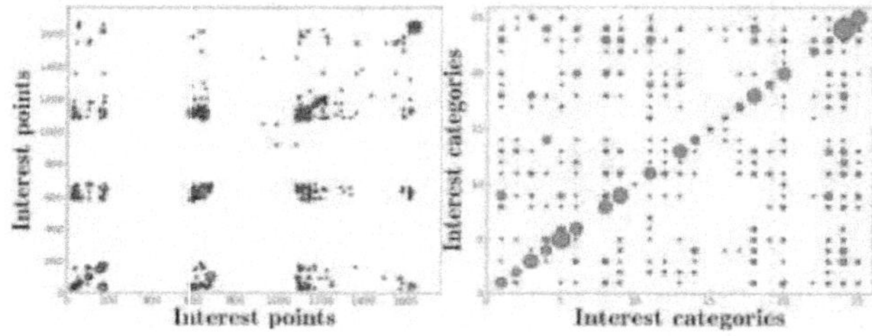

(a) Detailed KCs (b) General KCs

Figure 13: Correlation between detailed KCs and between general KCs.

4.5 Relationship Between Knowledge Categories

We assigned a numerical ID to each detailed KC so that the detailed KCs in the same general KC have close numerical IDs. We use matrix A[x][y] to represent the coexistence of two detailed KCs with ID x and ID y in one top contributor. Figure 13(a) shows the relationship between detailed KCs represented by the points of A[x][y]. We see that the detailed KCs are highly clustered. The KCs with IDs in [0,200], [600,700], [1000, 1200] are very likely to coexist with each other. However, KCs with IDs in [200, 600], [700, 1000], [1200, 1500] are seldom interested by top contributors because there KCs have extremely low popularity. Using the same way, we plot Figure 13(b) to show the relationship of the general KCs, which are assigned with ID from 1 to 26. We see that the top contributors are likely to have knowledge within the same category. It is also very likely for other kinds of category combinations to exist in a top contributor's specialized field.

4.6 Summary

(1) In YA, a small portion (10%) of the users (i.e., top contributors) contribute to most of the high quality answers. There is a strong correlation between best answers and all answers for a user with correlation coefficient equals

Period	Aug.17-Aug.22	Aug.23-Aug.30	Aug.31-Sep.08	Sep.09-Sep.14	Sep.15-Sep.21	Sep.22-Sep.29	Sep.30-Otc.06	Otc.07-Otc.13	Oct.13-Otc.19
Max	1367	1105	1306	1410	1500	1405	1235	1445	1524
Ave.	28.4	43.7	52.0	41.25	40	36.9	38.7	49.2	51.2
Min	0	0	0	0	0	0	0	0	0

Table 3: The number of answers submitted by top contributors during each week.

Period	Aug.17-Aug.22	Aug.23-Aug.30	Aug.31-Sep.08	Sep.09-Sep.14	Sep.15-Sep.21,	Sep.22-Sep.29	Sep.30-Otc.06	Otc.07-Otc.13	Oct.13-Otc.19
Max	8449	15808	13875	14435	15401	19975	14532	15643	16742
Ave.	302.8	302.1	301.3	274.1	300.0	322.4	321.2	314.4	309.7
Min	0	0	0	0	0	0	0	0	0

Table 4: The number of points earned by top contributors during each week.

0.712. At least 13.6% of the users are very likely to be free-riders (Section 4.1).

(2) In both contributor's knowledge and general knowledge, the top 12 KCs account for 80% of all knowledge. Meanwhile, there is a strong correlation between CK and GK with correlation coefficient equals 0.4988, which means the distribution of KCs in top contributors' profiles can represent the distribution of KCs of questions of all users (Section 4.2).

(3) The top contributors steadily and selflessly contribute knowledge to the system. 56.5% of the top contributors have multiple general KCs, and all of the top contributors have multiple detailed KCs (Section 4.3).

(4) There is no correlation between the number of contacts and the number of points of a user, but there is a positive linear relationship between the number of fans and the number of points of a user (Section 4.4).

(5) The KCs of the users are highly clustered, and users are likely to have knowledge within the same general KC. Different kinds of general category combinations are still likely to exist in a top contributor's specialized field (Section 4.5).

5. ANALYSIS OF KNOWLEDGE BASE IN A USER'S SOCIAL NETWORK

Users interested in the same KC tend to connect to each other as contacts and fans to facilitate knowledge sharing. In this section, we are interested in answering two questions: "how many different KCs exist within a certain hops of a user's contact network and fan network?" and "how shared KCs affect the link establishment between users?"

5.1 Relationship between Knowledge Base and Social Network Scope

We are interested in answering a question: "how many KCs are there in a user's contacts or fans?" We define the size of the general (or detailed) knowledge base of a user within x hops in his contact (or fan) network as the size of the union of all general (or detailed) KCs of the contacts (or fans) within x hops in his contact (or fan) network. Figure 14(a) shows the CDF of the size of the general knowledge base of users within i ($1 \leq i \leq 3$) hops in their contact networks. We see that 80% of the users have a knowledge base with size <2 within 1 hop, and have a knowledge base with size <3 within 2 hops in their contact networks. The knowledge size distribution within 3 hops is approximately the same as that within 2 hops. Figure 14(b) shows the CDF of the size of the general knowledge base of users within i ($1 \leq i \leq 3$) hops in their fan networks. The distribution of the knowledge base in fan networks exhibits the same pattern as that in contact networks. Although a few users can have a knowledge base with size up to 21, 80% of the users have a knowledge size <3 within 1 hop, and have a knowledge size < 4 within 2 hops. Figures 15(a) and (b) show the CDF of the size of the detailed knowledge base of users within i ($1 \leq i \leq 3$) hops in their contact networks and fan networks, respectively. The results exhibit the same pattern as in Figure 14.

The small knowledge base size is caused by the reason that users are clustered at KCs. As YA OSN is knowledge-oriented, users with the same knowledge interest are likely to connect to each other. Also, as some of the KCs are highly correlated as shown in Figure 13, some users tend to share multiple KC interests. The knowledge base size for 3-hop scope is not significantly increased for both general KCs and detailed KCs. This is because the knowledge-oriented clusters are likely to be disconnected to each other and the 3-hop neighbors are still likely to be within the same knowledge cluster.

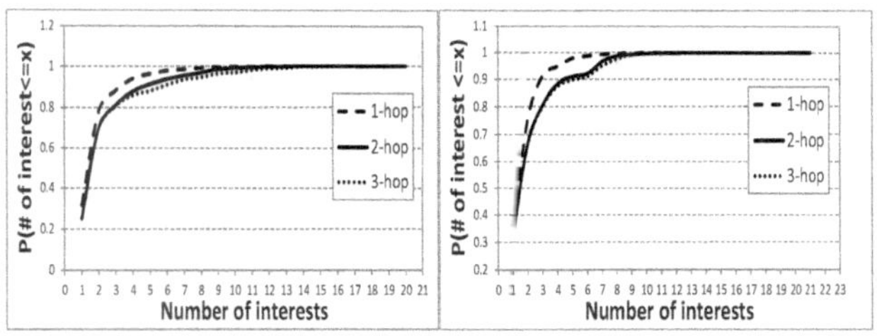

(a) Contact network (b) Fan network

Figure 14: Number of general KCs in the neighbors.

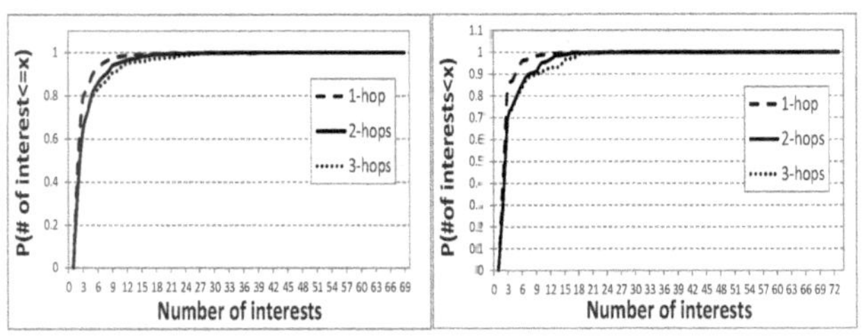

(a) Contact network (b) Fan network

Figure 15: Number of detailed KCs in the neighbors.

5.2 Homophily

Homophily is a tendency that "a contact between similar people occurs at a higher rate than among dissimilar people" [24]. In this section, we examine the pattern of homophily among users in the YA system by investigating the common KCs between each top contributor with his one-way connected contacts and fans, reciprocally connected users, and users without any relationship. Figure 16(a) shows the CDF of the number of common general KCs for users with one-way relationship, reciprocal relationship and no rela-

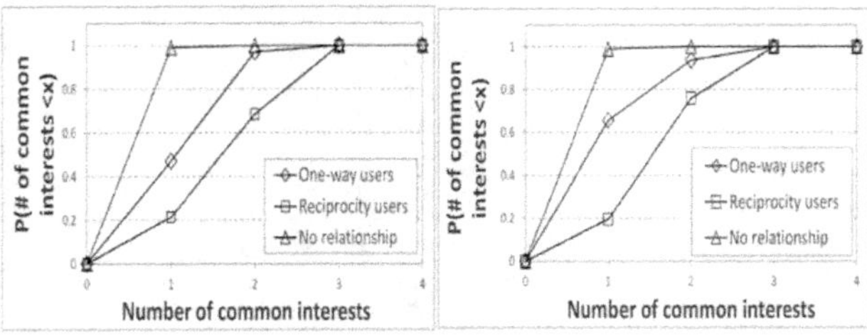

(a) General KCs. (b) Detailed KCs.

Figure 16: Common KC interests between users.

tionship, respectively. We see 80% of the reciprocity users share more than 2 common KCs; 80% of the one-way users share more than 1 and less than 2 KCs; 80% of the users without relationship share less than 1 KC. Figure 16(b) shows the CDF of the number of common detailed KCs for users with one-way relationship, reciprocal relationship and no relationship, respectively. We can also see that the distribution of detailed KCs for different users is similar to that of the general KCs. That is, no matter for detailed KC or general KC, reciprocity users share more interests than users with one-way relationship, which share more interests than users without relationship.

5.3 Summary

(1) Users in the social networks of the YA are clustered and centered by KCs. Some of the KC clusters are likely to be disjointed. (Section 5.1).

(2) Reciprocity users share more common KCs than one-way users, who share more common KCs than users without relationship (Section 5.2).

6. FURTHER DISCUSSIONS

In this section, we discuss some implications of our findings. While our findings are applicable to many different purposes and applications, we concentrate on spammer detection and distributed Q&A system design.

6.1 Implications to Spammer Detection in Q&A Systems

In YA, every registered users can post answers. Spammers might post commercial spam to earn attentions for their products.

Our study on YA presents two implications in the spammer detection algorithm design.

Best answer percent. Summary 4.6 shows that there is a linear relationship between the number of best answers and the number of all answers of a user with correlation coefficient equals 0.712. A spammer tends to post many answers but few of which would be selected as best answers. Therefore, by monitoring the ratio of the two numbers of a user, we can quickly identify the users with high ratios as suspicious spammers. Although the spammers can collude to rate their own answers as best answers, as the best answers are highlighted in the Q&A forum with high visibility to many other users, the false best answers can be easily identified using the abuse report policy.

Trust transitivity-based reputation. Summary 3.6 indicates that YA shows a very low level of link symmetry. Also, nodes with high indegree do not necessarily have high outdegree. i.e., user A connects to B only when user A trusts B's knowledge. Based on this property, we can evaluate node reputation based on the rationale that the users with many best answers should have a high reputation value and the users in the contact lists of high-reputed nodes should also be trustable and have high reputations. Similarly, in the HITS [25] and PageRank [26] algorithms, a webpage that is linked to by many webpages with high PageRank receives a high rank itself. Leveraging these algorithms, we can calculate the reputation value of users in order to detect the spammers:

$$R(u_i) = \frac{1-d}{N} + d \cdot \sum_{u_j \in S(u_i)} \frac{R(u_j)}{N(u_j)}, \quad (1)$$

where $R(u_i)$ denotes the reputation value of user u_i, d is a weight parameter, $S(u_i)$ denotes the set the users in u_i's fan network, and $N(u_j)$ denotes the outdegree of user u_j.

We use *Pagerank* to denote the above reputation calculation method, and use *Percentage* to denote the method that directly uses the percent of a user's best answers in his all answers as his reputation. We then ranked the user in the descending order of user reputation. Figure 17 shows the distribution of scaled reputation ([0,1]) of the users in *Pagerank* and *Percentage*. We see that *Pagerank* can more accurately reflect the reputations of users. Users with high best question percentage have high *Pagerank* reputation values and vice versa. However, *Percentage* results in approximately the same reputation values regardless of their best question percentages. The result indicates the effectiveness of *Pagerank* in reflecting node reputations.

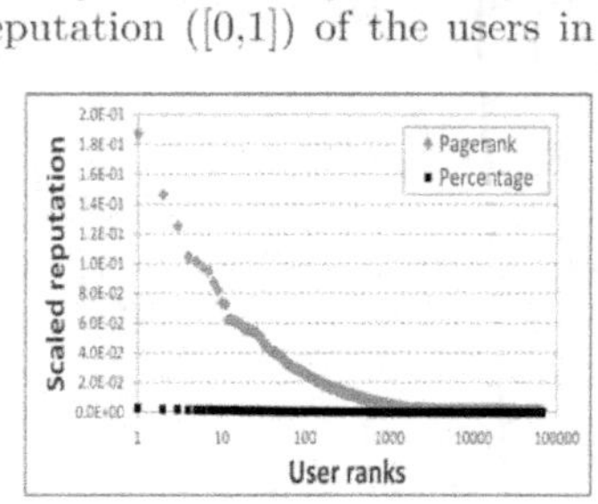

Figure 17: Reputation distribution of users.

6.2 Implications to Distributed Q&A Systems

Distributed Q&A systems [12–14, 27] identify the possible answerers in a questioner's social network in a centralized server and directly forward questions to the possible answerers. Google spent 50 million dollars to buy the Aardvark distributed Q&A system [14] on February 11, 2010. However, Google announced it would discontinue the Aardvark service in September 2011. Though we do not know the reasons, but our findings from YA can help enhance the performance of distributed Q&A systems, including Aardvark.

Embrace load imbalance. In order to balance the load between experts, the distributed Q&A systems [12–14, 27] use load balancing algorithm to evenly distribute the traffic among different experts. However, the assumption that every expert is willing to answer questions does not hold true. Summary 4.6 indicates that most users in the Q&A system are not actively in answering questions or are not be able to provide satisfying answers, while a small number of nodes (10%) are very willing to answer questions and able to offer satisfying answers. Therefore, rather than aiming to achieve load balance, forwarding more questions to those selfless answerers should be more effective in performance enhancement. Meanwhile, effective incentives such as reputation system or service pricing system are needed to encourage users to participate in question answering.

Bridge disjoint clusters. Summary 5.3 indicates that in the knowledge-oriented OSNs, some of the social network clusters centered on KCs are likely to be disjointed. Therefore, a user may not receive the answers for his questions in the distributed Q&A system because his connected users have small knowledge base and they cannot reach other parts of the social network. Therefore, we need to create bridges between social network clusters to prevent the isolation of some users' social networks.

Hierarchical searching. Summary 4.6 indicates that users tend to have knowledge within the same general KC, and have several detailed KCs. To facilitate answerer search, users can be first indexed by their specialized general KC and then by detailed KC. To search an answerer, we can first identify the general knowledge cluster, and then use detailed KC to identify the experts.

Global index for unpopular topics. Summary 4.6 shows that the number of KCs interested or specialized by users conforms to the power-law distribution. If the Q&A activity is conducted in a distributed manner in YA, since a user prefers to connect to experts, it should be easy to find the experts to answer questions in popular KCs, but may take a long time to identify answerers in unpopular KCs. Therefore, we can use a global index (e.g., distributed hash table) for fast expert identification in unpopular topics.

In the framework, users invite their friends and knowledgable and active answerers to connect to. Such a hybrid friendship-knowledge oriented framework can leverage the advantage of the friendship-oriented OSNs that can provide trustable and personalized answers and knowledge-oriented OSNs that guarantee a small delay for answerer identification for both factual and non-factual questions. Bridges are added to isolated users' social networks to form a connected network. Thus, questions can be uninterruptedly forwarded along the connected friends to find answerers in a distributed manner. During the forwarding process, the probability that a user is identified as answerer should be determined by the user's both willingness and ability to answer the question based on his historical answering activity in the KC of the question. In addition, the experts in unpopular topics form a DHT structure for easy identification.

7. RELATED WORK

Online social networks. The rising popularity of OSN services has spurred a larger amount of research on OSNs. Most researches studied network structure and growth patterns. Backstrom *et al.* [28] investigated the evolution of network structure and group membership in MySpace and LiveJournal and showed that homophily can be used to improve predictive models of group membership. Zhu [22] measured and analyzed an online content voting network, Digg. He studied the structural properties of Digg OSN and the impact of OSN on user digging activities, and investigated the issues of content promotion and content filtering. Kwak *et al.* [23] studied the OSN structures in Twitter. Viswanath *et al.* [29] studied the network structure of Facebook, with an emphasis on the evolution of activity between users. Mislove *et al.* [24] analyzed the structures of multiple OSNs: Flickr, YouTube, LiveJournal and Orkut, and found they share some similar features. For example, the indegree of user nodes tends to match the outdegree, networks contain a densely connected core of high degree nodes.

Yahoo!Answers (YA). A number of the researches have been conducted on YA on other aspects. Adamic *et al.* [30] studied the content characteristics of the answers, based on which, they try to predict whether a particular answer will be chosen as the best answer. Su *et al.* [31] studied the quality of human reviewed data on the Internet using the answer ratings in YA. By using content analysis and human coding, Kim *et al.* [32] studied the selection criteria for best answers in YA. Cao *et al.* [33] proposed a category-based framework for search in YA. The framework uses language models to exploit categories of questions for improving answer search. Liu *et al.* [34] presented a general prediction model with a variety of content, structure, and community-focused features to predict whether a question author will be satisfied with the answers submitted by the community participants. As far as we know, our work is the first to study the structure, user behavior, user knowledge in the YA OSN from the perspective of knowledge sharing oriented OSN.

Knowledge sharing. Knowledge sharing has been studied for a long time. Initially, it was largely studied within organizational settings (e.g., Davenport [35]). The Internet gave rise to OSNs that aim at facilitating collaboration between people by providing an environment for mutual sharing and interaction (e.g., Wikipedia). Expert location systems [15–18] have been proposed to facilitate users to identify the experts of interests. Numerous online Q&A systems also have emerged in the Internet [6, 7], in which the anonymous users post and respond to others' questions. However, the latency in receiving a satisfying answer to a question is high. Some works studied Q&A behaviors in OSNs. Morris and Teevan [10, 11] studied how people use status messages in an OSN to ask questions. Similar to the status message, Hsieh *et al.* [8] proposed a market-based Q&A service called MiMir, in which all questions are broadcasted to all users in the system. However, by using status messages, only direct friends of a user can see the questions. Also, the broadcasting generates high overhead. White and Richardson [12, 13] developed a synchronous Q&A system called IM-an-Expert, which automatically identifies experts via information retrieval techniques and facilitates real-time dialog via instant messaging without broadcasting. However, IM-an-Expert focuses on the direct friends of a user. Meanwhile, the synchronous communication may face challenges with interruption costs and the availability of knowledge at the question time. Aardvark [14] tries to automatically route the question from a user to the most appropriate person in the Aardvark community. Yang *et al.* [27] proposed a social network-based system for supporting interactive collaboration in knowledge sharing over a peer-to-peer network. They found that applying social network-based collaboration support to knowledge sharing helps people find relevant content and knowledgable collaborators.

8. CONCLUSIONS

Regarding YA as a knowledge-oriented OSN, we have investigated the collective intelligence in the YA OSN in terms of OSN structure, user behavior and knowledge, and the knowledge base in a user's social network. Our study on the OSN structure shows that compared to other major OSNs, the YA OSN has some very distinct features. It has low level link symmetry, exhibits weak correlation between indegree and outdegree, and nodes tend to connect to nodes with different degree from their own. By studying the knowledge base and behaviors of users, we find that 10% of the users contribute to 80% of the best answers and 70% of the all answers. The first 12 most popular KCs include 80% of the questions among all questions. The top contributors steadily and selflessly contribute knowledge to the system. The KCs of the users are highly clustered since users are likely to have knowledge within the same general KC. By studying the knowledge base in a user's social network, we find that the knowledge base of a user's social network is small because common-interest users are likely to be clustered. Also, a strong pattern of homophily is observed. We have outlined how these observed properties can be leveraged for spammer detection and distributed Q&A system design. In the future, we will further study the knowledge base of the non-top contributors and investigate the relationship between their knowledge base and behaviors.

Acknowledgements

This research was supported in part by U.S. NSF grants OCI-1064230, CNS-1049947, CNS-1156875, CNS-0917056 and CNS-1057530, CNS-1025652, CNS-0938189, CSR-2008826, CSR-2008827, Microsoft Research Faculty Fellowship 8300751, and U.S. Department of Energy's Oak Ridge National Laboratory including the Extreme Scale Systems Center located at ORNL and DoD 4000111689.

9. REFERENCES

[1] B. M. Evans and E. H. Chi. An elaborated model of social search. *IPM*, 2009.

[2] E. Amitay, D. Carmel, N. Har'El, Ofek-Koifman, and et al. Social search and discovery using a unified approach. In *Proc. of HT*, 2009.

[3] D. Carmel, N. Zwerdling, I. Guy, S. Ofek-Koifman, and et al. Personalized social search based on the user's social network. In *Proc. of CIKM*, 2009.

[4] S. Kolay and A. Dasdan. The value of socially tagged urls for a search engine. In *Proc. of WWW*, 2009.

[5] S. Bao, G. Xue, X. Wu, Y. Yu, B. Fei, and Z. Su. Optimizing web search using social annotations. In *Proc. of WWW*, 2007.

[6] Yahoo!Answer. http://answers.yahoo.com.

[7] Ask. http://www.ask.com.

[8] F. M. Harper, D. Raban, S. Rafaeli, and J. A. Konstan. Predictors of answer quality in online q&a sites. In *Proc. of SIGCHI*, 2008.

[9] G. Hsieh and S. Counts. mimir: A market-based real-time question and answer service. In *Proc. of SIGCHI*, 2009.

[10] M. R. Morris, J. Teevan, and K. Panovich. What do people ask their social networks, and why?: a survey study of status message Q&A behavior. In *Proc. of CHI*, 2010.

[11] J. Teevan, M. R. Morris, and K. Panovich. Factors affecting response quantity, quality, and speed for questions asked via social network status messages. In *Proc. of AAAI*, 2011.

[12] R. W. White, M. Richardson, and Y. Liu. Effects of community size and contact rate in synchronous social Q&A. In *Proc. of SIGCHI*, 2011.

[13] M. Richardson and R. W. White. Supporting synchronous social q&a throughout the question lifecycle. In *Proc. of WWW*, 2011.

[14] D. Horowitz and S. D. Kamvar. The anatomy of a large-scale social search engine. In *Proc. of WWW*, 2010.

[15] H. H. Chen, L. Gou, X. Zhang, and C. L. Giles. Collabseer: A search engine for collaboration discovery. In *Proc. of JCDL*, 2011.

[16] C. Y. Lin, N. Cao, S. X. Liu, S. Papadimitriou, J. Sun, and X. Yan. Smallblue: Social network analysis for expertise search and collective intelligence. In *Proc. of ICDE*, 2009.

[17] H. Kautz, B. Selman, and M. Shah. Referral web: combining social networks and collaborative filtering. *Communications of the ACM*, 1997.

[18] D. W. McDonald and M. S. Ackerman. Expertise recommender: a flexible recommendation system and architecture. In *Proc. of CSCW*, 2000.

[19] Facebook. http://www.facebook.com.

[20] A. Mislove M. Cha and K. P. Gummadi. A measurement-driven analysis of information propagation in the flickr social network. In *Proc. of WWW*, 2010.

[21] R. Kumar, J. Novak, and et al. Structure and evolution of online social networks. In *Proc. of KDD*, 2009.

[22] Y. Zhu. Measurement and analysis of an online content voting network: a case study of Digg. In *Proc. of WWW*, 2010.

[23] H. Kwak, C. Lee, H. Park, and S. Moon. What is twitter, a social network or a news media? In *Proc. of WWW*, 2010.

[24] A. Mislove, M. Marcon, K. P. Gummadi, P. Druschel, and B. Bhattacharjee. Measurement and analysis of online social networks. In *Proc. of IMC*, 2007.

[25] J. M. Kleinberg. Authoritative sources in a hyperlinked environment. *Journal of ACM*, 1999.

[26] L. Page, S. Brin, R. Motwani, and T. Winograd. The pagerank citation ranking: bringing order to the web. Technical report, Stanford Digital Library Technologies Project, 1998.

[27] S. J. H. Yang and I. Y. L. Chen. A social network-based system for supporting interactive collaboration in knowledge sharing over peer-to-peer network. *IJHCS*, 2008.

[28] L. Backstrom, D. Huttenlocher, and et al. Group formation in large social networks: membership, growth, and evolution. In *Proc. of SIGKDD*, 2006.

[29] B. Viswanath, A. Mislove, M. Cha, and K. P. Gummadi. On the evolution of user interaction in facebook. In *Proc. of WOSN*, 2009.

[30] L. A. Adamic, J. Zhang, E. Bakshy, and M. S. Ackerman. Knowledge sharing and yahoo!answers: everyone knows something. In *Proc. of WWW*, 2008.

[31] Q. Su, D. Pavlov, J. Chow, and W. Baker. Internet-scale collection of human-reviewed data. In *Proc. of WWW*, 2007.

[32] S. Kim, J. S. Oh, and S. Oh. Best-answer selection criteria in a social q&a site from the user-oriented relevance perspective. In *Proc. of ASIST*, 2007.

[33] X. Cao, G. Cong, B. Cui, C. S. Jensen, and C. Zhang. The use of categorization information in language models for question retrieval. In *Proc. of CIKM*, 2009.

[34] Y. Liu, J. Bian, and E. Agichtein. Predicting information seeker satisfaction in community question answering. In *Proc. of SIGIR*, 2008.

[35] T. Davenport and L. Prusak. Working knowledge: how organizations manage what they know. *Harvard Business School Press*, 1998.

From Face-to-Face Gathering To Social Structure

Chunyan Wang
Dept. of Applied Physics
Stanford University
California, USA
chunyan@stanford.edu

Mao Ye
Social Computing Group
HP Labs
California, USA
mxy177@cse.psu.edu

Wang-chien Lee
Dept. of Computer Science and Engineering
The Pennsylvania State University
Pennsylvania, USA
wlee@cse.psu.edu

ABSTRACT

The rapid development of on-line social networking sites has dramatically changed the way people live and communicate. One particularly interesting phenomena came along with this development is the prominent role of various on-line networking portals played in scheduling and organizing off-line group events and activities. In this paper, we focus on studying the face-to-face(f2f) group formed through, or facilitated by, on-line portals. We first show the distinct characteristics of such f2f groups by analyzing datasets collected from Whrrl and Meetup. Next, we propose a dynamic model for group gathering based on the process of friend invitation to interpret how a f2f group is formed on-line. The results of our model are confirmed by empirical observations. Finally, we demonstrate that using such group information can effectively improve the accuracies of social tie inference and friend recommendation.

Categories and Subject Descriptors

J.4 [**Computer Applications**]: Social and Behavior Sciences; G.3 [**Mathematics of Computing**]: Probability and Statistics

General Terms

Human Factors,Theory, Measurement

Keywords

group-gathering, social networks, social tie inference

1. INTRODUCTION

The process by which people come together, attract new members, and form groups has long been regarded as a crucial research issue due to its potential impacts on opinion formation, viral marketing and decision making [1, 2, 3, 4]. In the Web, characterization of various on-line groups has also attracted a lot of research interests recently. Existing works on on-line groups mostly focus on studying "cyber groups" (e.g., on-line communities [5, 6], social media websites [7, 8] and forums [9]), where group members interact with each other and thus do not need to present themselves at a "physical location". One special kind of groups largely unexplored thus far is the ones that are formed through on-line portals but taking place off-line at a real physical location. In fact, recent growth of social networking sites such as Meetup[1], Whrrl[2] and Facebook[3] have greatly facilitated people to schedule and organize such off-line group activities, from celebration parties, social networking banquet, to even larger events, such as demonstrations. Before, during and after the physical activities, users may share information such as location and group members through these social websites, which results in an unprecedented opportunities for researchers to better understand the behavior of group user at geographical locations.

Different from on-line "cyber groups" and individual activities in location based social networks (LBSN) [10, 11, 12, 13, 14, 15], the f2f group (group-gathering) in this study is constrained not only by spatial and temporal factors, but also social factors like influences from each other in the group. It would thus be interesting to better understand the user behaviors in these aspects and to answer the following research questions: (i) What are the differences between group activities compared with individual ones in the LBSN? (ii) What is the social structure within such a group? (iii) How is the group for face-to-face gathering formed through on-line portals? (iv) What kind of information can we extract from studying the characteristics of group-gatherings? In this paper, we focus on addressing these problems through investigating the "group check-in" dataset form Whrrl and the "group invitation" data form Meetup. The contributions of our study can be summarized in three complementary dimensions:

- **Characterization of the f2f groups.** We demonstrate the basic characteristics of group-gathering discovered from analysis of real datasets. Interestingly, we find that group-gathering activities exhibit striking differences compared with individual activities, both in spatial and temporal aspects. By further examining the social structures within groups, we find that many people joining the same group do not actually know

CIKM'12, October 29–November 2, 2012, Maui, HI, USA.

[1]http://meetup.com
[2]http://whrrl.com
[3]http://facebook.com

each other beforehand. The probability of friendship is inversely related with the size of the group.

- **Modeling of the f2f group formation process.** We propose a model to capture the dynamic process of f2f group formation based on an on-line friend invitation process. Based on our model, the size distribution of groups is expected to follow a power law distribution, which is verified by empirical observations. The model also reproduces the exponential duration of invitation process, and the inverse relationship between group size and the probability of friends.

- **Applications of the f2f group formation model.** We demonstrate that information exhibited in group-gathering activities has an implication regarding both the social closeness and geographical proximity features. We apply group information into the problem of social tie inference and friend recommendation. Through extensive experiments on real datasets, we show that such group information can significantly improve existing methods for social tie inference and friend recommendation.

The rest of the paper is organized in the following way. Section 2 introduces the observed characteristics of group-gathering. Section 3 introduces our model for group formation based on on-line friend invitation. Section 4 applies the group-gathering information to the problem of social tie inference and friend recommendation. Section 5 reviews the related work. Section 6 concludes the paper with discussions and future work.

2. CHARACTERISTICS OF GROUP

In this section, we focus on exploring interesting characteristics of group-gathering, by utilizing the check-in records in an LBSN site, Whrrl, as well as an on-line social networking portal for scheduling off-line events, Meetup. From the Whrrl dataset, we are able to compare differences between individual check-ins and group ones from the temporal, spatial and social aspects. The Meetup dataset also helps us to observe and confirm group-gathering patterns. We also present an analysis of social structures within the group at the end of this section.

2.1 Data

Whrrl is a popular LBSN that allows users to explore, rate and share points-of-interest. It also allows users to declare friendship among socially connected users and visits through check-ins at a physical place. Users could check in by using a mobile application on a GPS-equipped smart phone. Types of places include restaurant, hotel, bookstore and so on. A distinctive feature of this dataset is that a user could check-in by herself or with a group of other people, which is referred as *group check-in.* Users of the site are identified by unique user-ids. In our study, we crawl a friendship network consisting of 24,002 users and 145,228 social ties and collect the check-in records of these users' activities from January 2009 to January 2011. The undirected graph has an average degree of 12.101 and an average shortest-path length 4.718, which is a typical small-world social network. We crawled all the 357,393 check-in records over 120,726 different places associated with these users in the observation period. For each check-in record, we have information such as the exact location (i.e., longitude and latitude), time of check-in and the users involved (i.e., there may be more than one user-id for group check-ins).

Another dataset included in our study is from Meetup, an on-line social networking portal for scheduling off-line meetings. We collect over 11,423 scheduled group events taking place in Boston, Cupertino, Las Angeles, New York, Orlando and San Francisco. For each of these group activities, we keep records of the scheduled time, location, the number of people responding to attend, and also the time of their responses to the invitation. Different from Whrrl, the friendship structure on Meetup is not explicitly available, which is typical for many on-line and off-line communities.

2.2 Temporal and Spatial Characteristics

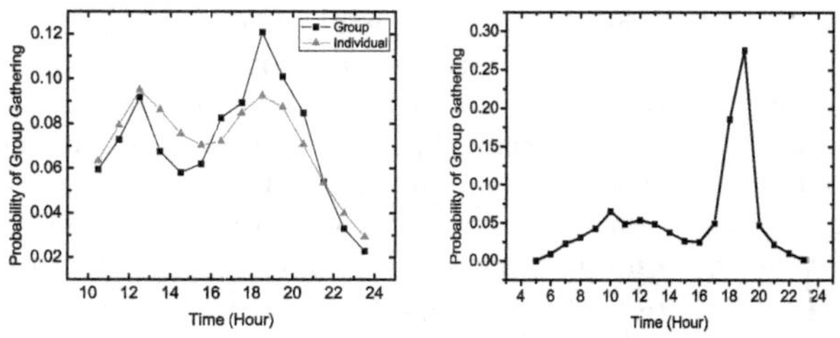

(a) Whrrl (b) Meetup

Figure 1: Density plot of group-gathering and individual activities at different hours of the day in (a) Whrrl and (b)Meetup.

We start by investigating the temporal and spatial characteristics of group-gathering. As mentioned before, one interesting feature of the group in our study is that it requires its members to appear at a specific time and a real location. Natural questions to ask regarding such groups are their temporal and spatial patterns. For example, what is the peak hour for group activities? How far group members would travel from their center of movement to join the group? Are they willingly to travel more or less for group activities compared with an individual one? To answer these questions, we divide our check-in dataset from Whrrl into two categories: individual check-in records and group check-in records. To study the temporal pattern of group-gathering, we make a density plot of an individual check-in and a group check-in at any given hour in the day, as shown in Figure 1. In this figure, we use black squares to denote group activities, and red triangles to denote individual ones. It could be observed from Figure 1(a) that there exists two peaks in the noon (around 13:00pm) and evening (around 19:00pm) for activities. More interestingly, the evening peak for group activities is higher than that of individual check-ins. This bias in evening hours for group activities is further confirmed by the time pattern of group activities in Meetup dataset as shown in Figure 1(b). One possible explanation is that the scheduled time for group events is constrained by all the members in the group. While it is more likely for all the members to be available in the evening than in the noon, a constraint is weaker for individual activities.

Another interesting observation about group-gathering is its spatial patterns. Particularly, we are interested in look-

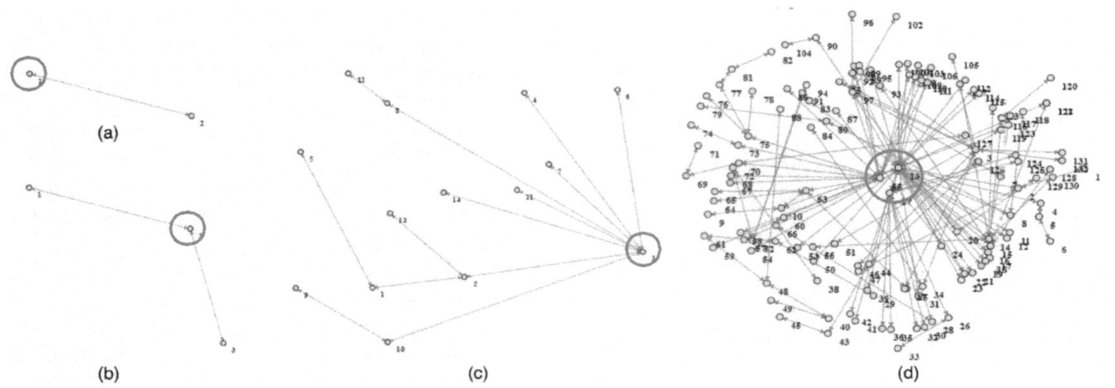

Figure 3: Four examples of social network structures within group-gathering events with different group sizes with (a) 2, (b) 3, (c) 14, (d) 135 from Whrrl. Red circles in the plot symbolifies the hubs in the social graph.

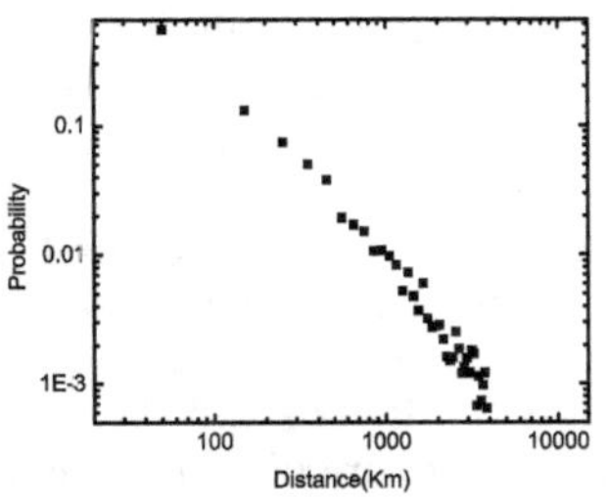

(a) Individual Activity

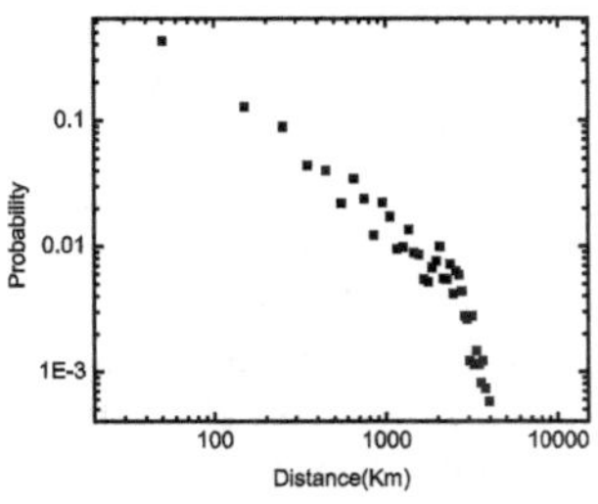

(b) group-gathering

Figure 2: Density plot of the distance travelled from center of movement for (a) individuals and (b) groups.

ing at the geographical distances from the user's home location to places of check-ins. Here, center of all check-ins belonging to a certain user is used as an approximation of the user's home location [14]. For each check-in, we calculate its geographical distance from the center of movement. In Figure 2, the probability of distance traveled from home for individual activities (Figure 2(a)) and group events (Figure 2(b)) is plotted in a log-log scale. The linear relationship suggests a power-law distribution of the mobility pattern for individual movements. Using the maximum likelihood estimation (MLE), the exponent of power-law distribution has a value of -1.593. This result is consistent with prior works related to the levy flight of human mobility [16, 17, 10, 14, 18]. More importantly, for group-gathering events, a sharp drop in probability is noticeable when the distance from home reaches the spatial bound. The distribution of distance from home distinctly deviates from that of individuals with a shorter tail. This observation suggests a spatial bound from home location for people to join group events. One possible explanation for this observation is that people with a high degree of spatial proximity are more likely to form a group-gathering event. Due to the spatial bound coming from other group members, people are less freedom than they were alone. We will further discuss the interplay between group-gathering and spatial proximity in Section 4. For now, we focus on describing characteristics of group-gathering itself.

2.3 Social Characteristics

Thus far, we have examined the temporal and spatial characteristics of group-gathering. We found that group-gathering has special characteristics constrained both temporally and spatially, which characteristics distinct such f2f group from other on-line groups. Given a group or community, another aspect of interests is the social structure within the formed group. Next, we turn our attention to the social aspects of group-gathering both in microscopic and macroscopic scale. Figure 3 shows the detailed structure of friendship network graphs of four sampled group-gathering activities of different group sizes, ranging from (a) 2, (b) 3, (c) 14 to (d) 135 in Whrrl. What is different from our expectations is that not all the people attending the same activity know each other (declare friendship on-line) before they join the group. In fact, for large groups, as in Figure 3(d), most of the individuals joining the group do not have links with each other. One interesting phenomenon for group-gathering is the existence of hubs (marked by red circle) observed from the social graph. We define such hubs as the user in the group who has a social tie out-degree significantly larger than the average of other nodes in the group. In Figure 3(a), either of the two users can be the hub. The existence of such hubs itself could be related to the inequality in social status of groups. Here, we explain this observation by the following formation process of group-gathering: when one or a few persons want to initiate a group activity, the process starts by them asking their friends to join the event. As the group grows, the initiators of the event would thus know more people than others. In this way, the social graph would most likely have initiators well connected as hubs surrounded by individuals later invited.

From the perspective of macroscopic properties, we find that the probability of friendship scales inversely with the number of people joining the group. The red line in Figure 4 plots a sharp drop in probability of friendship within the group as the group size increasing. This drop suggests that the connectivity within a group becomes weaker for larger group activities compared with smaller ones. Nevertheless, even for very large groups, the probability of friendship re-

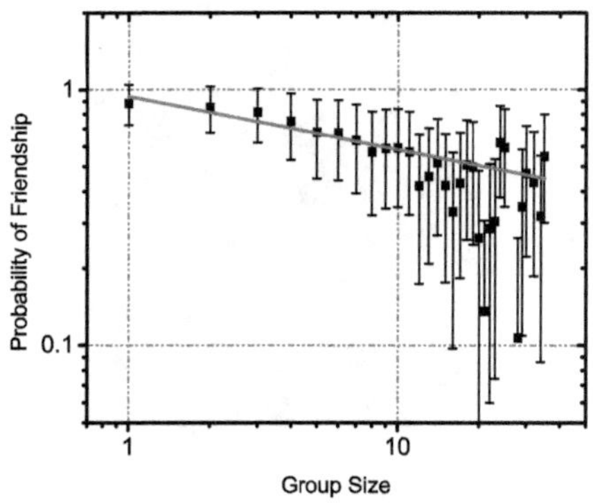

Figure 4: Probability of friendship within the aggregated group is inversely related to the group size.

mains over 0.20, which is much higher than 2.42×10^{-5}, the measured probability for two random nodes of being friends in the network. This fact suggests that even though people attending a group-gathering do not necessarily know each other, joining a group together itself is a strong indicator of friendship. We further study the strength of a social tie between two persons as a function of number of times the two persons joined group together in Figure 5. We use the number of common friends divided by the total number of friends of a pair of users as a measurement of tie strength. As can be seen from Figure 5, without much surprise, the social tie strength increases as the number of times people joined the same group and saturates around 4. On one hand, the observation suggests the important role of group activity in the process of friendship formation. On the other hand, the fact that a very small number of co-group can lead to orders-of-magnitude greater probabilities of friendship suggests the need for a deeper understanding of the underlying group formation mechanism and also further explorations of its potential application, as will be described in the following sections.

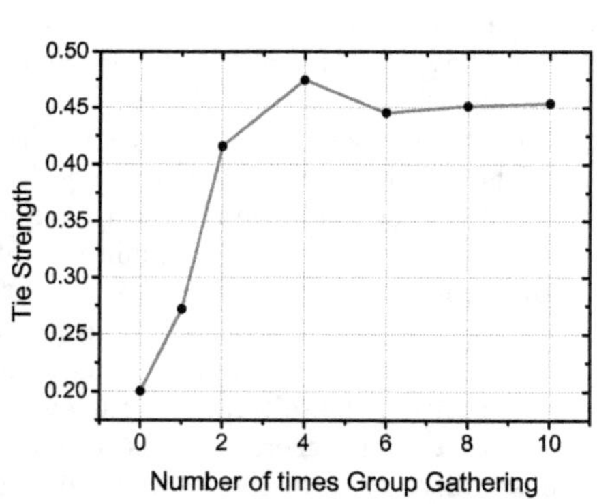

Figure 5: Social tie strength as a function of number of times group-gathering.

3. MODEL FOR F2F GROUP

In the last section, we describe our observations about the distinct characteristics of group-gathering from different aspects. From the observations, especially the social structure aspect, we find interesting properties such as the existence of hubs, the inverse scaling relationship between probability of friendship and group size. One would naturally ask how this kind of off-line groups is formed through on-line portals. A simple dynamic model that could capture the key structures of the group and also reproduce the observed properties in this case can help us to better understand the formation of group-gathering. Thus, we aim to capture the group formation process by proposing a model based on online invitation process. In the following, we demonstrate that the properties of group-gathering we described are robust, in that they can arise even on very simple assumptions of group formation. Our model capture these basic effects, and also yields a power-law scaling of group size distribution, which is generally recognized as one of the basic properties for group behavior [19, 20].

We begin by assuming that for each group event, there is one or a few initiators of the group, e.g., the first person who starts an event by asking his friends to join at time 0. At any point of time t, users in the existing group would attempt to invite one more friend to join the group. For simplicity, we also assume that the person receiving invitation has a fixed probability α to join. We use N to denote the total number of users in the network, $k(t)$ to denote the number of people in the group at time t, K to denote the final size of the group. We simplify the problem by considering the case that each user has the same number of friends and the same probability to accept invitation. If there are $k(t)$ individuals already in the group, the increment of group size at the time t should be $\alpha k(t)$. We have

$$\frac{\partial k(t)}{\partial t} = \alpha k(t). \tag{1}$$

Given that when $t = 0$, $k(0)$ is equal to 1, we have $k(t) = e^{\alpha t}$ and $K = e^{\alpha T}$, in which T is the duration of the invitation process. Thus we have

$$\Pr(K < l) = \Pr(T < \frac{\ln l}{\alpha}). \tag{2}$$

If there is a probability λ for the group to cease the inviting new users at each time step, it naturally follows that the distribution of T should be a geometric distribution with

$$\Pr(T = m) = (1 - \lambda)^{m-1}\lambda. \tag{3}$$

When m is large and λ is small, the distribution could be approximated by its continuous counter part, the exponential distribution. So in our continuous model, the distribution of T has a cumulative form of

$$\Pr(T < m) = 1 - e^{-\lambda m}. \tag{4}$$

Next, by combining Eq. (4) and Eq. (2), we have

$$\Pr(K < l) = 1 - e^{-\frac{\lambda}{\alpha}\ln l} = 1 - l^{-\frac{\lambda}{\alpha}}. \tag{5}$$

Since $\Pr(K = l) = \frac{\partial \Pr(K<l)}{\partial l}$, by taking the differentiation we obtain that

$$\Pr(K = l) \sim l^{-\frac{\lambda}{\alpha}-1}, \tag{6}$$

which is a power law distribution for group size. We will later show that this property is consistent with empirical observations.

For now, noting that to arrive at the power law scaling of group size distribution, one fundamental assumption is the exponential distribution of invitation duration, which point needs to be verified empirically. To this end, we measure the distribution of invitation duration. For an approximation of the duration, in our dataset, we record the time when the event was first set up by the initiator and the time when the last person responses to the event. We use the time interval in between as the invitation duration. We find that the distribution could be well approximated by an exponential distribution as shown in the semi-log plot in Figure 6. The exponential fit of red line in the figure yields $\lambda = 731.73$. The exponential distribution is repeated for similar but different definitions of invitation duration.

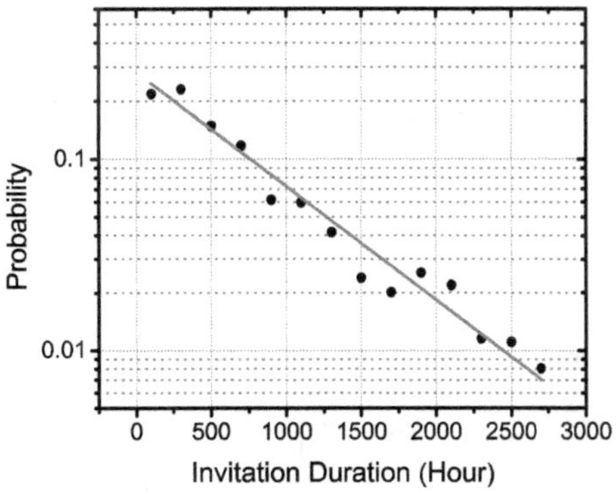

Figure 6: Distribution of invitation duration in semi-log scale. The red straight line in the figure suggests an exponential distribution of the duration.

As an extension of our model, we derive the inverse relationship between group size and the probability of friendship as shown in Figure 4. To arrive at the probability of friendship, we need to know the expected number of total existing links in the K size group, which equals to $\frac{K\langle m\rangle}{2}$, where $\langle m\rangle$ is the expected number of links from a user. According to our model, the number of users in the group that are invited by a specific user s is proportional to the duration that s stays in the propagation process. For simplicity, here we consider the case of a sparse graph, in which the probability of s has a link with users other than the ones invited by him or invite him goes to zero. Thus if we use d_s to denote the duration between the time point that person s joins the group and the time point T that the process ends, then $m_s \sim d_s$. And we have $d_s = T - t_s$, in which t_s is the time point that user s joins the group. For a random selected user in the group, based on Eq. (1), we have

$$\Pr(t_s < l) = \frac{e^{\alpha l}}{e^{\alpha T}}. \quad (7)$$

By taking the derivative on the cumulative distribution,

$$\Pr(t_s = l) = \frac{\alpha e^{\alpha l}}{e^{\alpha T}}. \quad (8)$$

This yields the distribution of arrival time of different users. Since we are interested in the expected number of links from a random selected user in the group, we take the average of d over s

$$\langle d\rangle_s = \int_0^T (T-l)\frac{\alpha e^{\alpha l}}{e^{\alpha T}}dl = \frac{1}{\alpha} - \frac{1}{\alpha}e^{-\alpha T} - Te^{-\alpha T}. \quad (9)$$

Taking the asymptotic form when T is large,

$$\langle d\rangle_s = \int_0^T (T-l)\frac{\alpha e^{\alpha l}}{e^{\alpha T}}dl \sim \frac{1}{\alpha}. \quad (10)$$

Thus the total number of edges $\frac{\langle m\rangle K}{2}$ would be proportional to $\langle d\rangle K \sim \frac{K}{\alpha}$, with a constant multiplier. And since there are $\frac{1}{2}K(K-1)$ potential edges in the group, the probability of two persons being friends in a K size group should scale as

$$\Pr(F) \sim (K-1)^{-1}. \quad (11)$$

The probability of friendship within a formed group is thus inversely related to the size of the group. Despite of the discrepancies in fitted exponents and predictions, the model qualitatively explains the inverse scaling between friendship and group size described in Figure 4.

(a) Whrrl.com

(b) Meetup.com

Figure 7: People attend group-gathering activities for different purposes, e.g., to hang out for recreation, to attend a meeting, or to march for a protest. Word clouds for the purposes of group-gathering activities.

From the above derivations, we see that the model captures key characteristics of the on-line invitation process and also the inverse scaling relationship described in Section 2. One direct implication of the model is the power law distribution of group size, which is suppose to be irrelevant with the purposes of the group, due to the fact that groups with different purposes share the same underlying formation mechanisms. Here, for a verification of our model, we analyze the purposes of group-gatherings and their impact on group size. The word cloud in Figure 7 shows the most frequent types of group-gathering purposes in Whrrl and Meetup datasets. It could be seen that, the most frequently visited places of the two sites are not identically the same.

We measure size distributions of groups in Whrrl and Meetup. Figure 8 (a)-(d) show the group size distribution from Whrrl dataset. Figure 8(a) is the size distribution of all groups in the dataset. A linear fit of the data in log-log scale has R-square value of 0.946. The power law exponents of group size are estimated to be 3.13 from MLE. For the size distribution of groups belonging to different categories, they share similar exponent values. Here, we use tags associated with the group check-in record to identify the categories of

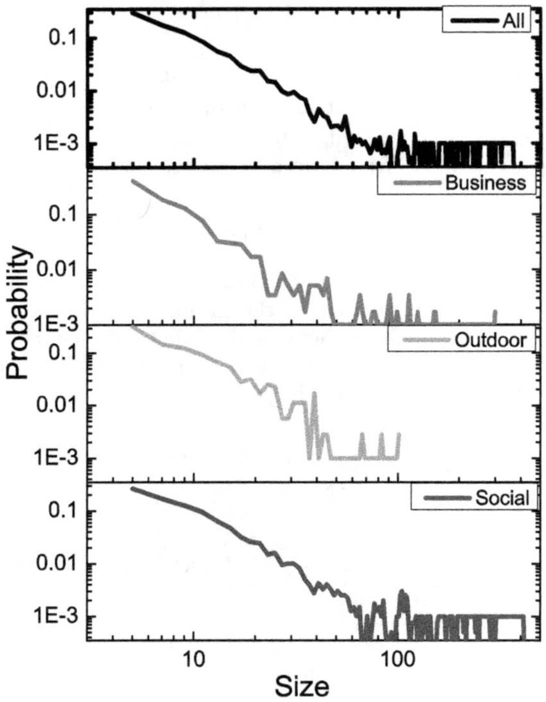

Figure 8: Distribution of group size for different categories of activity types. (a) all groups on Whrrl and (b)-(d) size distribution of certain types of group. The distribution of group size in different types are all governed by the same type of distribution.

the group [21, 22]. As can be observed from Figure 8(b)-(d) the size distribution is universal for all types of activities, even though the estimated exponent value may vary. Similarly, for an analysis on the Meetup dataset, we also obtain the exact same scaling relationship, which is consistent with our model. Due to the limitation of space, we omit figures for the group size distribution of Meetup.

4. APPLICATIONS

Our investigations of f2f group so far have been focused on studying and explaining the phenomena. From these investigations, we demonstrated that group gathering contains rich information that could be applied to solve key problems in social network analysis. In this section, we demonstrate two applications that leverage out the knowledge discovered from group-gathering. The first one is the *social tie inference* problem, where friendship structure is not explicitly declared such as in criminal networks [23] and people need to infer the social structure of the network [24]. The second application is for *friend recommendation*, where people use existing social or non-social information to recommend a list of users for given user to make friends with.

4.1 Group-Gathering Information

Inspired by prior works [24, 23, 18], we first look at the interplay of various similarity features, including group-gathering, spatial and social features on the network scale. From now on, we use GG to denote the number of times that two persons join group-gathering event together. We explore the connections of GG to a series of similarity features including social proximity and geographic proximity measures, by calculating the Pearson correlation coefficients. For network proximity in the social graph, we select three representative quantities, which have been proven to be reasonably good indicators of social closeness. In the following, we let V denotes the set of users and E denotes the set of edges.

- **Common friends (C).** The number of friends that nodes u and v have in common.
$$C(u,v) = |\Gamma(u) \cap \Gamma(v)|, \tag{12}$$
where $\Gamma(x) = y|y \in V(x,y) \in E$ is the set of friends of x.

- **Weighted common friends (aa) [25].** A weighted common friends based on their degrees
$$aa(u,v) = \sum\nolimits_{w \in \Gamma(u) \cap \Gamma(v)} \frac{1}{\log|\Gamma(w)|}. \tag{13}$$

- **Jaccard's coefficient (jc).** Defined as the number of the inter-section of the friends of two nodes divided by the size of union
$$jc(u,v) = \frac{|\Gamma(u) \cap \Gamma(v)|}{|\Gamma(u) \cup \Gamma(v)|}. \tag{14}$$

To measure the geographic or spatial closeness [23, 18] of two users, we use the following indicators.

- **Distance.** We use the great circle distance of any two users' home coordinates as a measure of geographic distance between them.

- **Number of times of Co-location.** In our observation period, the number of times that two users u and v visit the same geographic grid (0.1°) at the same time frame (one day). Note that two users co-located may to attend their separate activities. For instance, two users may both work at two companies close to one another, i.e., they are co-located, but they may never meet each other or join group activities together.

- **Spatial cosine similarity (Scos).** The cosine similarity of two users' trajectories, capturing how similar their visiting frequencies to places are, i.e., the angle between the two vectors of number of visits at each location for user u and v.

The two categories of closeness indicators listed above together with GG are all measurements of similarity. The correlation of each pair of the indicators is as shown in Table 1. In the table, social closeness features have a strong correlation with each other, and mobility closeness features are also well correlated with each other. More importantly, the GG indicator has a strong correlation with both of the two types of indicators. GG has a stronger correlation with social closeness indicators than geographic similarity measurements do, and vice versa. This stronger correlation suggests that GG indicator is a combination of information from both geographic, movement, and social closeness. It would thus be of great interests to apply GG into similarity based predictions and recommendations.

	GG	Co-location	Distance	Scos	Common friend	aa	jc
GG	1	0.7275	-0.08072	0.2411	0.7118	0.7403	0.6904
Co-location	0.7275	1	-0.09209	0.1912	0.6399	0.6318	0.5966
Distance	-0.08072	-0.09209	1	-0.09765	-0.1302	-0.1176	-0.138
Scos	0.2411	0.1912	-0.09765	1	0.2767	0.2625	0.3117
Common friend	0.7118	0.6399	-0.1302	0.2767	1	0.9862	0.9326
aa	0.7403	0.6318	-0.1176	0.2625	0.9862	1	0.9164
jc	0.6904	0.5966	-0.138	0.3117	0.9326	0.9164	1

Table 1: Pearson Correlation of different indicators of mobile closeness(Co-location and distance) and social closeness(Scos, common friend, aa and jc). group-gathering(GG) has a strong correlation with both of the two types of indicators.

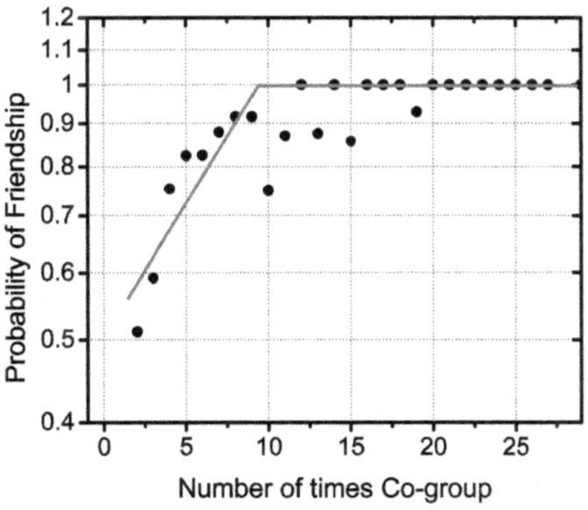

Figure 9: Probability of friendship as a function of the number of times group-gathering together, with probability in log scale.

4.2 Social Tie Inference

In this section, we employ the group-gathering information to infer social ties. Given that two persons have appeared on the same group-gathering event, how likely are they to be friends of each other? Social link declared explicitly on Whrrl is used as proximity of the ground truth of friendship. Figure 9 demonstrates empirical observations from the Whrrl dataset. For each pair of two users, we count the number of times they attended group-gathering events together in a period of one year. From Figure 9, we find that the probability of friendship grows exponentially fast with the number of times that the two users join group-gathering.

To interpret the above observations and develop a framework for social tie inference from group-gathering, we provide a probabilistic model based on the frameworks of prior studies [26, 23, 18]. From the model derived in last section, each pair of users has a probability $\Pr(F) = \frac{M}{N-1}$ to be friends. Let us use C_l to denote the fact that two persons have a total number of l times attending the same group-gathering, i.e. group check-in together in this case, during a period of L days. We assume that each pair of friends has a probability of p_1 to attend a group event, and each pair of non-friends has a probability of p_2 to attend a group event on any given day. Based on our invitation model, one significant conclusion is that p_2 is non-zero, since there's always a chance that a pair of persons not knowing each other are both invited to the event by others. For simplification, we also assume that the network structure does not evolve within the L days of observation period. Whether a pair of user goes out together each day is independent event. So the number of times they co-group follows a binomial distribution.

$$\Pr(C_l|F) = \frac{L!}{l!(L-l)!}p_1^l(1-p_1)^{L-l}. \quad (15)$$

Similarly, for a pair of non-friends,

$$\Pr(C_l|\overline{F}) = \frac{L!}{l!(L-l)!}p_2^l(1-p_2)^{L-l}. \quad (16)$$

From Bayes' Law, we have

$$\Pr(F|C_l) = \frac{\Pr(C_l|F)\Pr(F)}{\Pr(C_l)}. \quad (17)$$

We could thus derive the probability of $\Pr(F|C_l)$ if we know $\Pr(C_l)$. Notice that

$$\Pr(C_l) = \Pr(C_l|F)\Pr(F) + \Pr(C_l|\overline{F})\Pr(\overline{F}), \quad (18)$$

take this back to $\Pr(F|C_l)$,

$$\Pr(F|C_l) = \frac{\frac{M}{N-1}\frac{L!}{l!(L-l)!}p_1^l(1-p_1)^{L-l}}{\frac{M}{N-1}\frac{L!}{l!(L-l)!}p_1^l(1-p_1)^{L-l} + \frac{N-1-M}{N-1}\frac{L!}{l!(L-l)!}p_2^l(1-p_2)^{L-l}}$$
$$= \frac{Mp_1^l(1-p_1)^{L-l}}{Mp_1^l(1-p_1)^{L-l} + (N-1-M)p_2^l(1-p_2)^{L-l}}. \quad (19)$$

Given that $M \ll N$, the above equation could be approximated as

$$\Pr(F|C_l) \approx \frac{M}{N}\left(\frac{1-p_1}{1-p_2}\right)^L\left[\frac{p_1(1-p_2)}{p_2(1-p_1)}\right]^l$$
$$= \frac{M}{N}\left(\frac{1-p_1}{1-p_2}\right)^L e^{l\ln\left[\frac{p_1(1-p_2)}{p_2(1-p_1)}\right]}. \quad (20)$$

This result explains the fact that the probability for two persons to be friends increases exponentially with the number of times joining group activities together observed in Figure 9, and provides us a framework to infer social ties based on group-gathering.

Next, we compare social tie inference from group-gathering with two baseline models from prior work that performs reasonably well. The first baseline model predicts friendship based on geographical distance between two persons [26]. The second one infers social ties based on geographic coincidences [23]. For each pair of users in the network, we use their center of movement to measure the distance between

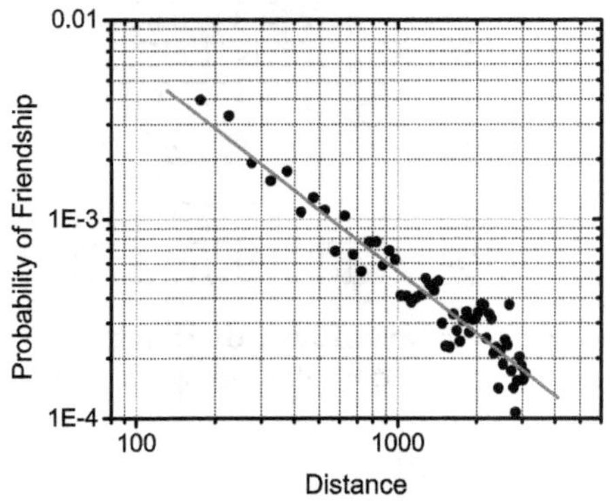

Figure 10: Probability of friendship as a function of the distance between two users, in log-log scale.

them and to obtain the probability of friendship by averaging all pairs of users within a given distance range. We use the number of times that two users both located within the same geographical grid (s) [26] on the same day in the one year observation period as the number of times of co-location. The probability of friendship as a function of the above two indicators is shown in Figure 10 and Figure 11. In Figure 10, the red line shows the distribution of power law with an exponent of -1.03. For the first method based on geographical distance, the best achievable probability is smaller than 0.01 for any distance over 100 km. In Figure 11, the number of times of co-location has to be greater than or equal to 100, in order to reach the saturation region of high probability in friendship. Compared to the baseline models, group-gathering method has advantages in its potential high accuracy prediction using very limited amount of information.

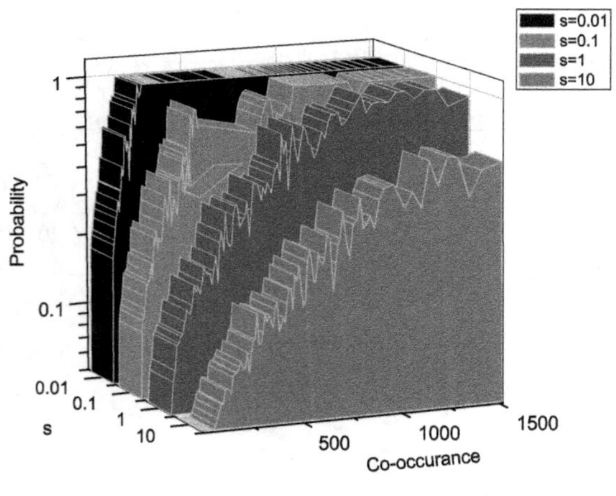

Figure 11: Probability of friendship as a function of co-location under different cell sizes, s, in a semi-log scale.

To test the performance of our framework based on group-gathering for social tie inference, we use data from Whrrl to train an SVM for prediction of the social tie. We compare the prediction accuracy of group-gathering with three baseline features, including distance, number of times of co-location and spatial cosine similarity (Scos) [26, 23, 18]. In our experiments we select a strongly connected component of over 2,000 users as a subset, hide different percentage (mark-off rate) of pairs for training, and use the rest for testing. Figure 12 shows the prediction accuracy as a function of mark-off rate. Interestingly, we can observe that the group-gathering feature outperforms other baseline features both in precision and recall. The experiments suggest that group-gathering information could improve the predictions accuracy in social tie inference problem.

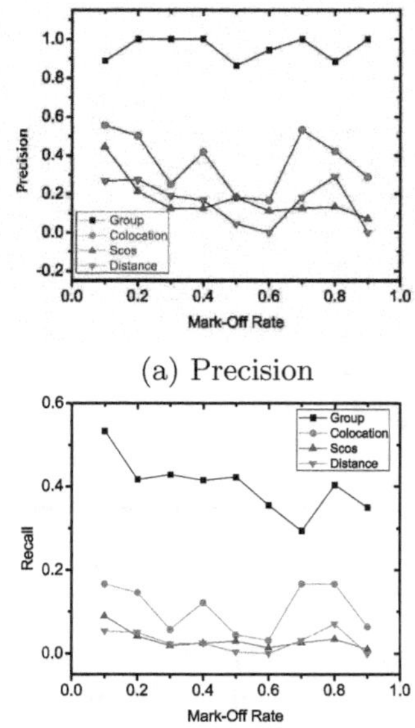

(a) Precision

(b) Recall

Figure 12: Social tie inference accuracy as a function of mark-off rate. In the graph, the *GG* feature outperforms other base-line features in terms of both precision and recall.

4.3 Friend Recommendation

Next, we exploit the group-gathering information in the friend recommendation problem. Besides the simple strategy of suggesting friends-of-friends [27], several type of information, such as co-tagging and co-location records, that are related to pairs of users, have been explored to facilitate friend recommendation in [18, 27, 28]. To study the effectiveness of adding group-gathering information in friend recommendation, we perform a series of experiments in comparing the precision and recall of prediction results. Here, we use SP to denote a combination of spatial features including distance, co-location and $Scos$. We use SO to denote a combination of social features including common friend count, aa and jc in Section 3. In our experiments, we hide the same percentage of pairs for each person for testing and use the rest as training. By ordering the probability of these hidden pairs predicted by trained model from SVM, we conclude a recommended friendship if the pair's probability is among the N highest of all hidden pairs. We compare the precision and recall of the recommended friendship using different features. As shown in Figure 13, the GG feature alone outperforms the combination of SP features. More importantly,

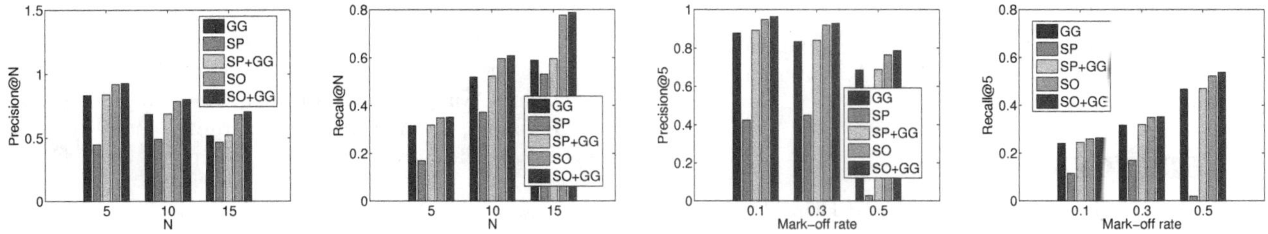

(a) Precision@N (b) Recall@N (c) Precision@5 (d) Recall@5

Figure 13: (a) Precision as a function of N. (b) Recall as a function of N. The figures suggest a performance improvement by adding GG in friend recommendation. (c)-(d)Precision and recall as a function of mark-off rate. By adding GG in friend recommendation, the performance improves.

by combining GG with SO and SP, the prediction results are improved. This finding suggests a promising application of GG for friend recommendation.

5. RELATED WORK

In this section, we discuss some of the relevant studies categorized in three sub-areas.

5.1 On-line Group and LBSN

Research related to on-line groups and location based social networks are the two fields most related to our work. Both of the two attract great recent research interest for their novelty impacts and potential applications. As discussed in the introduction section however, most existing works on on-line groups focus on studying "cyber groups"[5, 6, 7, 8, 9]), where group members interact with each other in cyberspace and thus do not constrained geographically. This fact differentiates the special kind of group in our study from others. Here in our study, social networking websites are serving as subsidiaries in helping organize or form the group, rather than a venue or platform for communications. And also, from the perspective of research related to LBSN [10, 11, 12, 13, 14, 15], fruitful results have been obtained by applying individual check-in record in various prediction tasks such as place-of-interest recommendation and link prediction. Yet, few documented research has linked to the check-in record of a group. Thus exploring group behavior under the context of LBSN should be of interests for researchers from both of the two fields.

5.2 Social Tie Inference

Knowing patterns of relationship in a social network is very useful with various applications such as to investigate collaborations among criminals and to exploit social relationships for e-commerce promotion [29]. However, in various organizations, neighborhoods, on-line communities and social service websites, friendship structure is not explicitly declared. Existing works on social tie inference primarily use criteria such as self-report [30], communication [31, 24, 32], similarities of opinion [25] and spatial-temporal co-occurrence [29, 26, 23]. Particularly for the last criteria, recent works bring the interplay between human mobility and friendship into consideration [14, 18, 33].

5.3 Friend Recommendation

Recommending people in social networks is an important task for many recommender systems. Many prior work proposed to recommend potential friends to users or predict future links in a social network [18, 22, 27, 28, 34, 13]. Besides of the simple strategy of suggesting friends-of-friends [27], content-based approaches were proposed to match the content of user profiles and determine user similarities for recommendation in [27, 28, 34]. Furthermore, multiple types of information, such as co-tagging, co-commenting records and co-location records, that are related to pairs of users, have been explored to facilitate friend recommendation in [18, 27, 28]. In this paper, we aim to exploit group-gathering information to improve the friend recommendation performance. To our best knowledge, this type of information has not been explored before; while we consider this type information have strong indication about potential friendship, i.e., people join the same group-gathering activities usually have overlapped social circles and spatial closeness. It would thus be extremely interesting to study the effectiveness of group-gathering information applied into friend recommendation problem.

6. CONCLUSION AND FUTURE WORK

In this paper, we study the phenomena of (off-line) face-to-face group that are organized through on-line social portals, by using datasets collected from Whrrl and Meetup. First, based on the analytical study, we find that group-gathering activities exhibit striking differences compared with individual activities both in temporal and spatial aspects. We also analyze the social structure properties with-in such a group. Next, to understand the formation process of group-gathering, we propose a dynamic model based on the concept of on-line friend invitation process. The proposed model well reproduces the empirical observations. Finally, we discuss how to apply group-gathering information into problems of social tie inference and friend recommendation. Right now, our model incorporates only the social aspect of group gathering characteristics, potential refinements of the model may take into consideration the spatial and temporal constraints, and also the impact of microscopic differences between different users. In closing, we point out that although the focus in this paper has been on face-to-face groups that are formed through social networking websites, the framework of our model may be applicable to other types of groups and communities. The issue here raised in the paper - off-line user behavior facilitated or changed by on-line networking - is fundamentally important and therefore will provide ample opportunities for further future work.

7. ACKNOWLEDGMENTS

C. W. would like to thank HP Labs for financial support. C. W. and M. Y. would like to thank B. A. Huberman for fruitful discussions in this work.

8. REFERENCES

[1] Stefan Wuchty, Benjamin F. Jones, and Brian Uzzi. The increasing dominance of teams in production of knowledge. *Science*, 316(5827):1036–1039, 2007.

[2] Roger Guimera, Brian Uzzi, Jarrett Spiro, and Luis A. Nunes Amaral. Team assembly mechanisms determine collaboration network structure and team performance. *Science*, 308(5722):697–702, 2005.

[3] G. Palla, A. Barabasi, and T. Vicsek. Quantifying social group evolution. *Nature*, 446:664–667, 2007.

[4] Lars Backstrom, Dan Huttenlocher, Jon Kleinberg, and Xiangyang Lan. Group formation in large social networks: membership, growth, and evolution. In *KDD*, pages 44–54. ACM Press, 2006.

[5] N.F Johnson, Chen Xu, Zhenyuan Zhao, Nicolas Ducheneaut, Nicholas Yee, George Tita, and P.M. Hui. Human group formation in on-line guilds and off-line gangs driven by a common team dynamic. *Phys. Rev. E*, 79:066117, 2009.

[6] Lei Tang, Huan Liu, Jianping Zhang, and Zohreh Nazeri. Community evolution in dynamic multi-mode networks. In *KDD*, pages 677–685, 2008.

[7] Munmun De Choudhury. Modeling and predicting group activity over time in on-line social media. In *Hypertext*, pages 349–350, 2009.

[8] Daniel M. Romero, Wojciech Galuba, Sitaram Asur, and Bernardo A. Huberman. Influence and passivity in social media. In *WWW*, pages 113–114, 2011.

[9] Xiaolin Shi, Jun Zhu, Rui Cai, and Lei Zhang. User grouping behavior in on-line forums. In *KDD*, pages 777–786, 2009.

[10] Nan Li and Guanling Chen. Analysis of a location-based social network. In *CSE*, pages 263–270, 2009.

[11] Vincent Wenchen Zheng, Yu Zheng, Xing Xie, and Qiang Yang. Collaborative location and activity recommendations with gps history data. In *WWW*, pages 1029–1038, 2010.

[12] Mao Ye, Dong Shou, Wang-Chien Lee, Peifeng Yin, and Krzysztof Janowicz. On the semantic annotation of places in location-based social networks. In *KDD*, pages 520–528, 2011.

[13] Salvatore Scellato, Anastasios Noulas, and Cecilia Mascolo. Exploiting place features in link prediction on location-based social networks. In *KDD*, pages 1046–1054, 2011.

[14] Eunjoon Cho, Seth A. Myers, and Jure Leskovec. Friendship and mobility: user movement in location-based social networks. In *KDD*, pages 1082–1090, 2011.

[15] Huiji Gao, Jiliang Tang, and Huan Liu. Exploring social-historical ties on location-based social networks. In *ICWSM*, 2012.

[16] M.C. Gonzales, C.A. Hidalgo, and A.L. Barabasi. Understanding individual human mobility patterns. *Nature*, 453(7196):779–782, 2008.

[17] Bin Jiang, Junjun Yin, and Sijian Zhao. Characterizing the human mobility pattern in a large street network. *Phys. Rev. E*, 80:021136, Aug 2009.

[18] Dashun Wang, Dino Pedreschi, Chaoming Song, Fosca Giannotti, and A.L. Barabasi. Human mobility, social ties, and link prediction. In *KDD*, pages 1100–1108, 2011.

[19] E. Bonabeau, L. Dagorn, and P. Freon. Scaling in animal group-size distributions. *PNAS*, 96:4472–4477, 1999.

[20] D.J.T. Sumpter. Collective animal behavior. In *Princeton University Press*, 2010.

[21] Denis Helic, Markus Strohmaier, Christoph Trattner, Markus Muhr, and Kristina Lerman. Pragmatic evaluation of folksonomies. In *WWW*, pages 417–426, 2011.

[22] Rossano Schifanella, Alain Barrat, Ciro Cattuto, Benjamin Markines, and Filippo Menczer. Folks in folksonomies: social link prediction from shared metadata. In *WSDM*, pages 271–280, 2010.

[23] David J. Crandall, Lars Backstrom, Dan Cosley, Siddharth Suri, Daniel Huttenlocher, and Jon Kleinberg. Inferring social ties from geographic coincidences. *PNAS*, 107(52):22436–22441, 2010.

[24] Nathan Eagle, Alex (Sandy) Pentland, and David Lazer. Inferring friendship network structure by using mobile phone data. *PNAS*, 106(36):15274–15278, 2009.

[25] Lada A. Adamic and Eytan Adar. Friends and neighbors on the web. *Social Networks*, 25:211–230, 2001.

[26] David Liben-Nowell, Jasmine Novak, Ravi Kumar, Prabhakar Raghavan, and Andrew Tomkins. Geographic routing in social networks. *PNAS*, 102(33):11623–11628, 2005.

[27] Jilin Chen, Werner Geyer, Casey Dugan, Michael J. Muller, and Ido Guy. Make new friends, but keep the old: recommending people on social networking sites. In *CHI*, pages 201–210, 2009.

[28] Ido Guy, Inbal Ronen, and Eric Wilcox. Do you know?: recommending people to invite into your social network. In *IUI*, pages 77–86, 2009.

[29] Hady Lauw, Ee-Peng Lim, HweeHwa Pang, and Teck-Tim Tan. Social network discovery by mining spatio-temporal events. *Computational and Mathematical Organization Theory*, 11:97–118, 2005.

[30] S. Wasserman and K. Faust. Social network analysis: Methods and applications. In *Cambridge University*, 1994.

[31] Munmun De Choudhury, Winter A. Mason, Jake M. Hofman, and Duncan J. Watts. Inferring relevant social networks from interpersonal communication. In *WWW*, pages 301–310, 2010.

[32] Honglei Zhuang Wenbin Tang and Jie Tang. Learning to infer social ties in large networks. In *ECML/PKDD*, pages 381–397, 2011.

[33] G. Mangesh and E. R. Tina. Measuring tie strength in implicit social networks. *Arxiv*, 2011.

[34] Daniele Quercia and Licia Capra. Friendsensing: recommending friends using mobile phones. In *RecSys*, pages 273–276, 2009.

Delineating Social Network Data Anonymization via Random Edge Perturbation

Mingqiang Xue
I[2]R, Singapore
xuem@i2r.a-star.edu.sg

Panagiotis Karras
Rutgers University, USA
karras@business.rutgers.edu

Chedy Raïssi
INRIA Nancy, France
chedy.raissi@inria.fr

Panos Kalnis
KAUST, Saudi Arabia
panos.kalnis@kaust.edu.sa

Hung Keng Pung
NUS, Singapore
dcsphk@nus.edu.sg

ABSTRACT

Social network data analysis raises concerns about the privacy of related entities or individuals. To address this issue, organizations can publish data after simply replacing the identities of individuals with pseudonyms, leaving the overall structure of the social network unchanged. However, it has been shown that attacks based on structural identification (e.g., a *walk-based attack*) enable an adversary to re-identify selected individuals in an anonymized network. In this paper we explore the capacity of techniques based on *random edge perturbation* to thwart such attacks. We theoretically establish that *any* kind of structural identification attack can effectively be prevented using random edge perturbation and show that, surprisingly, important properties of the whole network, as well as of subgraphs thereof, can be accurately calculated and hence data analysis tasks performed on the perturbed data, given that the legitimate data recipient knows the perturbation probability as well. Yet we also examine ways to enhance the *walk-based attack*, proposing a variant we call *probabilistic attack*. Nevertheless, we demonstrate that such probabilistic attacks can *also* be prevented under sufficient perturbation. Eventually, we conduct a thorough theoretical study of the probability of success of *any* structural attack as a function of the perturbation probability. Our analysis provides a powerful tool for delineating the identification risk of perturbed social network data; our extensive experiments with synthetic and real datasets confirm our expectations.

Categories and Subject Descriptors

H.2.7 [**Database Management**]: Database Administration—*Security, integrity, and protection*; H.2.8 [**Database Management**]: Database applications—*Data mining*; K.4.1 [**Computers and Society**]: Public Policy Issues—*Privacy*

Keywords

privacy, social network, random perturbation, graph utility

CIKM'12, October 29–November 2, 2012, Maui, HI, USA.

1. INTRODUCTION

Today *data owners* (e.g., private corporations, public organizations) can store large volumes of digital human interactions. Examples include interactions among groups of players in an online game, for file-sharing in P2P networks, and among individuals in online social networks. In most cases, the network at hand can be represented by a graph $G = (V, E)$, where vertices stand for individuals and edges for interactions or relations. Data owners wish to publish such graphs, e.g. for social studies and marketing.

Nevertheless, publication should not reveal sensitive personal information contained in the network. A *naïve graph anonymization* approach is to remove identifying attributes such as names, e-mails or IP addresses, and still publish the network in a way that allows all kind of analysis of its graph properties.

Unfortunately, this naïve anonymization approach does not guarantee privacy protection. As Hay et al. [8] discerned, the structural characteristics of the published graph, combined with background knowledge, can expose individuals. For instance, assume an adversary has access to graph G_n in Figure 1(b), the naïvely anonymized version of the graph in Figure 1(a) and and knows that Suzanne has 3 friends, none of whom has more than 2 friends. With this knowledge, the adversary can identify Suzanne as node 3.

Backstrom et al. [1] have shown that a practical way for an adversary to gain structural knowledge is to embed a known subgraph (e.g., register dummy users in an online social network and link them to victims). Figure 1(c) shows our example graph including an embedded subgraph (nodes $\{11, 12, 13, 14, 15\}$). Malicious nodes were connected to Suzanne and Robert (e.g., by tricking them to respond to a bogus friendship invitation). An adversary capable to locate the inserted subgraph efficiently can also identify Suzanne and Robert and hence infer other attributes of theirs.

Let $G_A = (V_A, E_A)$ be the inserted subgraph and $k = |V_A|$ the number of vertices in G_A. Typically, it suffices for k to be in the order of $\sqrt{\log |G_o|}$, as the number of possible k-node subgraphs, hence the probability that the inserted subgraph is unique, grows exponentially with k^2. Locating G_A is an intractable problem [7], hence impractical for large graphs. Therefore, [1] only considers subgraphs having a *connected backbone* (i.e., a Hamiltonian path of their k nodes), and describes an efficient *walk-based attack*: an adversary can locate G_A by searching for k-node paths having the same *degree sequence* as G_A (e.g., the subgraph of nodes $\{11 \ldots 15\}$ in Figure 1(c) has degree sequence $[2, 5, 3, 4, 2]$).

In this paper, we study the effectiveness of random edge perturbation as a tool for preventing structural identification in an anony-

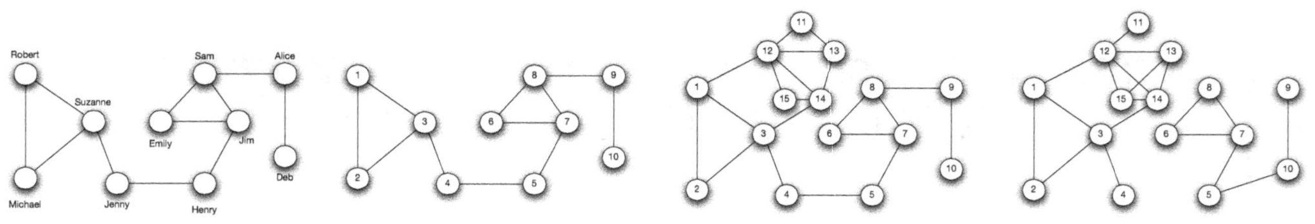

(a) Original graph G_o. (b) naïvely anonymized G_n. (c) G_n with malicious nodes. (d) Perturbed graph G_p.

Figure 1: Example of a social network graph

mized graph. We assume that the original graph G_o is first transformed to G_n by naïve anonymization, and then G_n is altered to G_p by random edge perturbation with perturbation probability μ. Figure 1(d) shows a perturbed graph G_p, in which edges $(4, 5)$, $(8, 9)$ and $(11, 13)$ in G_n have been removed, whereas edges $(13, 15)$ and $(5, 10)$ have been added. Fittingly, the degree sequence of G_A cannot be found in G_p; therefore the *walk-based attack* fails.

Remarkably, Ying and Wu [12] reject random edge perturbation as a method for privacy preservation on the grounds that it obfuscates important graph characteristics; Bonchi and Tassa arrive at a similar, albeit more positive result [2]. We inspect such claims by showing that estimation algorithms can accurately *recover* important graph properties (e.g., density, degree distribution, transitivity, modularity, etc) from the perturbed graph, not only for the complete original graph, but more crucially, even for subgraphs thereof - for which publishing such measures directly to the end-user would not be a solution. We apply this methodology on several graph metrics used in graph analysis [5]. Our estimation algorithms are not applicable only on the presented metrics; in addition, we introduce a generic framework for estimating a class of utility metrics.

Nevertheless, we are wary that an adversary can employ a methodology similar to ours so as to launch sophisticated attacks. We demonstrate this potential by generalizing the *walk-based attack* of [1] to a *probabilistic walk-based attack*, which examines multiple possible degree sequences, each with its own probability of appearance. We show that, while being more computationally intensive than the deterministic variant, our probabilistic attack is practicable in perturbed graphs with higher success probability. Furthermore, we generalize our study to take into account *any* possible structural attack, even by extremely powerful adversaries having the computational power to enumerate all possible subgraphs of size k inside G_n. Our analysis delineates the probability of success in that case, for subgraph size k and perturbation probability μ.

To summarize, our contributions are outlined as follows: We show how important graph properties can be accurately **recovered** from a perturbed graph, *even though this perturbed graph does not* look *like the original.* We introduce a novel **probabilistic attack**, more powerful than the one [1]. We compute the probability of success of *any* structural attack, offering a yardstick for **assessing the privacy risk** entailed by the publication of perturbed graph data.

2. RELATED WORK

The idea that privacy can be preserved after randomization while data characteristics can be partially recovered, which we espouse, was debuted in the context of association rule mining [6, 11].

Backstrom et al. [1] were the first to present an attack demonstrating that naïve anonymization is insufficient to ensure privacy in graph data. They emphasize the differences between *active* attacks, where the adversary adds nodes and edges before publication, and *passive* attacks, where they do not, and propose the *walk-based* and *cut-based* attacks; the extent to which random edge perturbation can protect from this family of active attacks was not examined in [1]. Hay et al. [9] proposed a privacy protection technique based on random edge insertions and deletions, similar to the random edge perturbation that we study. However, the efficiency and utility preservation of their scheme were not studied. In [8], Hay et al. formalize two adversary knowledge models based on subgraph queries and hub fingerprints, and propose an approach using structure aggregation and sampling to protect from such attacks; however this method does not preserve the complete graph structure. Ying and Wu [12] assert that random edge perturbation significantly degrades a graph's utility; this assertion is true if utility metrics are measured on the perturbed graph; however [12] does not attempt to recover graph properties by estimation algorithms.

Zhou and Pei [13] use edge addition (along with generalization of node labels) in order to ensure that, for every node in the graph, there exist at least $k-1$ other nodes that share isomorphic neighborhoods. Similarly, Liu and Terzi [10] bring a graph in a form such that, for each node, there exist at least $k-1$ other nodes having the same degree, while Cormode et al. [4] study the anonymization problem for bipartite graphs and propose the notion of *safe groupings*. Zou et al. [14] propose the model of k-automorphism, which guarantees that the anonymized graph consists of k structurally indistinguishable subgraphs; Cheng et al. [3] expand on this concept with k-isomorphism, in which a graph is published in the form of k identical disjoint subgraphs. Unfortunately, such *syntactic* anonymization methods can severely alter the nature of the published network so as to conform to the privacy guarantee they provide. For example, by k-isomorphism, a connected graph is converted to an assortment of k identical disjoint graphs; thus, the published graph is *not* an anonymized version of the *whole* original, but only of $\frac{1}{k}$ thereof. Besides, the computational complexity of these syntactic schemes renders them inapplicable on very large graphs.

Recently, Bonchi et al [2] used an entropy-based privacy metric to evaluate several graph anonymization techniques; they conclude that techniques based on random perturbation are comparable to syntactic methods. Our work builds upon these findings by inspecting the potential to estimate a graph's original properties and the viability of structural attacks after random perturbation.

3. UTILITY MEASURE ESTIMATION

Let $G_o = (V, E)$ be an undirected graph representing the original social network and let $N = |V|$. Without loss of generality, we assume that V is ordered and $V[i]$ refers to the ith node in the set. Naïve anonymization replaces all labels in G_o with random pseudonyms. The resulting graph is denoted by G_n, where new labels are given by $L(V[i], G_n)$, $i \in [1, N]$. As G_n and G_o contain the same set of nodes and edges, $G_n = (V, E)$.

Random edge perturbation yields a perturbed graph $G_p = (V, E_p)$ from a naïvely anonymized graph G_n by adding or removing edges. Let $\mu \in [0, \frac{1}{2})$ be a user-defined *perturbation probability*, known to the legitimate data recipient, and $(V[i], V[j])$ denote the edge between nodes $V[i]$ and $V[j]$. For every pair of nodes $V[i], V[j] \in V$ it holds that:

$$\Pr\left((V[i], V[j]) \notin E_p \mid (V[i], V[j]) \in E\right) = \mu$$
$$\Pr\left((V[i], V[j]) \in E_p \mid (V[i], V[j]) \notin E\right) = \mu$$

We assume that the adversary knows a subgraph $G_A = (V_A, E_A)$ in the original graph G_o. G_A contains k ordered nodes, with labels $L(V_A[i], G_A)$ known to the adversary; the latter aims to identify G_A in G_p, i.e., an ordered set Y of k nodes in G_p, such that $L(Y[i], G_o) = L(V_A[i], G_A)$, for $1 \leq i \leq k$. We are interested to quantify the probability that the adversary will succeed.

Before we study the adversary's success probability, we study the effect of perturbation on different graph utility metrics. No single metric for measuring a graph's utility exists, as organizations may use a graph for different purposes. Still, there are a few widely accepted metrics [5]. We study four popular metrics: density, degree distribution, transitivity, and modularity. While past research has asserted that such metrics rapidly degrade with random edge perturbation [12], we outline how, even when the metrics measured on the perturbed graph vary greatly from those of the original, we can still accurately *estimate* their original values.

3.1 Density Estimation

The density metric for a general graph is the ratio of the number of edges in the graph over the number of possible edges. It describes the average level of connectivity between nodes. Formally, the density value is defined as follows:

$$density = \frac{2|E|}{|V|(|V|-1)} \tag{1}$$

The density metric is widely used in social network data analysis. Admittedly, due to perturbation, the number of edges in the perturbed graph will differ from that in the original graph. However, we can use the known perturbation probability to estimate the original density. Since the density value depends on the graph size and the number of edges, when the graph size is known, we only need to estimate the original number of edges. Let $h = |E|$ be the (unknown) number of edges in G_o, and $h_p = |E_p|$ the observed number of edges in the perturbed graph G_p. We can estimate the value of h via the maximum-likelihood estimator $\hat{h}$, defined as:

$$\hat{h} = \arg\max_h(\Pr(h_p|h)) \tag{2}$$

where $\Pr(h_p|h)$ is the probability of observing h_p edges in the perturbed graph when the original graph has h edges. Intuitively, the estimator $\hat{h}$ is the number of edges in the original graph that is most likely to result in h_p edges in the perturbed graph.

To estimate $\hat{h}$, we need to find a value h that maximizes $\Pr(h_p|h)$. Alternatively, we can find the value of $\hat{h}$ by deriving an equation with the following rationale: since each edge removal and addition during perturbation can be viewed as an independent Bernoulli trial, the value of h that maximizes $\Pr(h_p|h)$ is the one that renders the *expected* number of edges in the perturbed graph equal to h_p. Given that each existing edge survives with probability $(1-\mu)$ and each non-existing one is created with probability μ, the equality in consideration is expressed as follows:

$$h_p = \hat{h} \cdot (1-\mu) + \left(M - \hat{h}\right) \cdot \mu \tag{3}$$

where $M = \frac{N(N-1)}{2}$ is the number of possible edges in the graph. The quantity on the right-hand side of the equation is the expected number of edges in G_p when the number of edges in G_o is $\hat{h}$. Solving Equation 3 for $\hat{h}$, we get:

$$\hat{h} = \frac{h_p - M \cdot \mu}{1 - 2\mu} \tag{4}$$

3.2 Degree Distribution Estimation

The *degree* is a cardinal feature of a node. In social networks, degrees describe the number of friends a person has. In many real-world networks, degrees exhibit a power-law distribution.

Our estimation for degree distribution is similar to that for density estimation, as a node's original degree can be estimated via its degree in the perturbed graph. While there may be a high error in the estimation for an individual node, the total degree distribution can still be accurately estimated. We first focus on estimating the original degree of a single node. Let d_p be a node's observed degree in G_p, and $\hat{d}_o$ our estimator of its degree in G_o, respectively. As in our density estimation solution, we can estimate $\hat{d}_o$ by setting d_p to be equal to the *expected* degree of the node at hand in G_p when its original degree is $\hat{d}_o$. Therefore it is:

$$d_p = \hat{d}_o \cdot (1-\mu) + (N - 1 - \hat{d}_o) \cdot \mu \tag{5}$$

Solving the latter for $\hat{d}_o$, we get:

$$\hat{d}_o = \frac{d_p - (N-1) \cdot \mu}{(1-2\mu)} \tag{6}$$

Let $\hat{d}_o[i]$ be the estimator of the ith node's degree. Then $[\hat{d}_o[1], \hat{d}_o[2], \ldots, \hat{d}_o[N]]$ forms an estimation of the degree sequence of all nodes in G_o, whence we derive an estimate of the distribution.

3.3 Transitivity Estimation

Transitivity measures the incidence of order-3 loops in a graph. In a social network, if v_1 is connected to both v_2 and v_3, then there is a relatively high probability that v_2 and v_3 are also connected (i.e., *a friend's friend is a friend*). Most social networks present high transitivity. Formally, a network's transitivity $\mathcal{T}$ is defined as:

$$\mathcal{T} = \frac{3N_\Delta}{N_3} \tag{7}$$

In the above formula, N_Δ is the number of *triangles* in the network, and N_3 is the number of *connected triplets*, i.e., subgraphs of exactly 3 connected nodes (albeit not necessary triangular).

To compute a graph's transitivity, we have to count the number of triangles and the number of connected triplets therein. Such structures may be destroyed post-perturbation, yet we can still count the number of different triplet structures in G_p, and thereby estimate the number of triangles and connected triplets in G_o.

Given any triplet of nodes in G_o, the possible edge connections therein fall into the following four patterns:

- *Pattern 1*: They form a *triangle* (i.e., a triplet of *three edges*). We denote the number of triangles in G_o as T_o and their *observed* number in G_p as T_p.
- *Pattern 2*: They form a *connected triplet* with *two edges*. Let X_o (X_p) be the original (observed) number of connected triplets in G_o (G_p).
- *Pattern 3*: They form a disconnected triplet with only *one edge*. Again, let I_o (I_p) be the original (observed) numbers of this pattern in G_o (G_p).

		T_p	X_p			I_p			D_p
T_o		$(1-\mu)^3$	$(1-\mu)^2\mu$	$(1-\mu)^2\mu$	$(1-\mu)^2\mu$	$(1-\mu)\mu^2$	$(1-\mu)\mu^2$	$(1-\mu)\mu^2$	μ^3
X_o		$(1-\mu)^2\mu$	$(1-\mu)^3$	$(1-\mu)\mu^2$	$(1-\mu)\mu^2$	μ^3	$(1-\mu)^2\mu$	$(1-\mu)^2\mu$	$(1-\mu)\mu^2$
I_o		$(1-\mu)\mu^2$	$(1-\mu)^2\mu$	μ^3	$(1-\mu)^2\mu$	$(1-\mu)\mu^2$	$(1-\mu)\mu^2$	$(1-\mu)^3$	$(1-\mu)^2\mu$
D_o		μ^3	$(1-\mu)\mu^2$	$(1-\mu)\mu^2$	$(1-\mu)\mu^2$	$(1-\mu)^2\mu$	$(1-\mu)^2\mu$	$(1-\mu)^2\mu$	$(1-\mu)^3$

Figure 2: Converting a pattern in G_o to another

- *Pattern 4*: They are completely disconnected with *no edges.* Similarly, we denote the original (observed) numbers of this pattern in G_o (G_p) as D_o (D_p).

Given a triplet pattern in G_o, we can calculate the probability that it will be transformed into one of the three other patterns in G_p. For instance, a triangle in G_o can become a triplet of either *Pattern 2*, *Pattern 3* or *Pattern 4*, or remain unchanged. Figure 2 depicts the calculations of the probabilities that a pattern in G_o is converted to another pattern in G_p. We emphasize that these calculations are obtained under the simplistic assumption that each triplet conversion is independent of others. This assumption serves our objective of deriving an estimation, which is ultimately tested in our experiments. Thus, for example, the probability that a triangle in G_o remains unchanged in G_p is $(1-\mu)^3$; the probability that a triangle becomes a triplet of *Pattern 2* (for which three possible cases as shown in Figure 2) is $3(1-\mu)^2\mu$. Given the counts of triplets in different patterns (T_p, X_p, I_p and D_p) in G_p, and the pattern convertion probabilities in Figure 2, we can devise a system of linear equations with four unknown estimator variables $\hat{T_o}$, $\hat{X_o}$, $\hat{I_o}$ and $\hat{D_o}$, as we did for density and degree distribution estimation. Solving this system of equations, we get:

$$\begin{aligned}\hat{T_o} = &\tfrac{1}{(2\mu-1)^3}(D_p\mu^3 - I_p\mu^2 + I_p\mu^3 - T_p \\ &+3\mu T_p - 3\mu^2 T_p + \mu^3 T_p + \mu X_p \\ &-2\mu^2 X_p + \mu^3 X_p)\end{aligned} \tag{8}$$

$$\begin{aligned}\hat{X_o} = &\tfrac{1}{(2\mu-1)^3}(2I_p\mu - 3D_p\mu^2 - 4I_p\mu^2 \\ &+3D_p\mu^3 + 3I_p\mu^3 + 3\mu T_p - 6\mu^2 T_p + 3\mu^3 T_p \\ &-X_p + 3\mu X_p - 5\mu^2 X_p + 3\mu^3 X_p)\end{aligned} \tag{9}$$

Then, given the maximum-likelihood estimators of triangles $\hat{T_o}$ and connected triplets $\hat{X_o}$, we estimate the transitivity of G_o as:

$$\hat{\mathcal{T}} = \frac{3\hat{T_o}}{\hat{X_o}} \tag{10}$$

3.4 Modularity Estimation

Social networks exhibit community structures. A characteristic of such a community is that intra-community links are more than inter-community links. The modularity is a metric measuring whether a partition of graph exhibits community properties. To compute modularity, the network is partitioned into a fixed number of communities. A symmetric matrix A is formed such that the elements $A[i,i]$ (i.e., the diagonal of matrix A) are the fractions of links between the nodes in the same community i. The other elements $A[i,j]$ are the fractions of links between communities i and j. The network's modularity is defined as:

$$\mathcal{M} = \sum_i \left[A[i,i] - \left(\sum_j A[i,j]\right)^2\right] \tag{11}$$

The modularity value depends on the entries in matrix A. To estimate modularity, we first create an estimator $\hat{A}$ for A. To do so, we use an auxiliary symmetric matrix, B, in which $B[i,i]$ is the number of edges within community i and $B[i,j]$ the number of edges between community i and community j. B_p and $\hat{B}$ refer to the matrix in the perturbed graph and the estimator for B, respectively. Once $\hat{B}$ is computed, $\hat{A}$ can be derived from $\hat{B}$ by dividing each entry by the estimated total number of edges. Since the entries in B are counts of edges between nodes, we can apply similar technique as in density estimation to estimate $\hat{B}$. B_p is directly computed by counting the edges within and between partitions in the perturbed graph. The relation between $\hat{B}[i,i]$ and $B_p[i,i]$ is:

$$\hat{B}[i,i] = \frac{2B_p[i,i] - (z_i^2 + z_i)\cdot\mu}{2-4\mu} \tag{12}$$

In the above equation z_i is the number of nodes in partition i. Assuming the number of nodes in community i (j) is z_i (z_j), the relation between $\hat{B}[i,j]$ and $B_p[i,j]$ is:

$$\hat{B}[i,j] = \frac{B_p[i,j] - z_i\cdot z_j\cdot\mu}{1-\mu} \tag{13}$$

Each entry in $\hat{A}$ is then computed by dividing the corresponding entry in $\hat{B}$ by the estimated number of edges in the network.

3.5 A Generic Estimation Framework

While it is impossible to provide an exhaustive enumeration of estimation methods for every possible graph utility metric, in this section we provide a generic framework for the estimation a particular class of such metrics.

A common characteristic of the above four metrics is that the utility value relies on the counts of certain substructures (a subgraph) in the graph. For example, the density value relies on the count of disconnected pairs of nodes and the count of connected pairs of nodes. Similarly, the transitivity value relies on the count of connected triplets and the count of triangles in the graph. Generally, the class of the utility metrics whose values rely on the counts of substructures can be estimated using a generic framework. The generic framework for estimation is described as follows.

Let $\mathcal{S}$ be a set of s_{max} substructures relevant to a particular utility metric, where $\mathcal{S}_i$ refers to the ith substructure. For example, in transitivity estimation, $s_{max} = 2$, and the two substructures are triangles and connected triplets. $\mathcal{S}_i.c$ refers to the count of the ith substructure in the original graph. Therefore, the utility value is a function of the counts of different structures in $\mathcal{S}$, i.e. $f(\mathcal{S}_1.c, \mathcal{S}_2.c, \ldots, \mathcal{S}_{s_{max}}.c)$. To estimate the utility value, we need to estimate the value of $\mathcal{S}_i.c$ for all substructures in $\mathcal{S}$. Let $\mathcal{S}_i.s$ be the number of nodes in the ith substructure. For transitivity estimation, the number of nodes in the two substructures (triangles and triplets) are both 3. In the perturbed graph, we count the number of all substructures involving $\mathcal{S}_1.s, \mathcal{S}_2.s, \ldots, \mathcal{S}_{s_{max}}.s$ nodes. The count of all the substructures in the perturbed graph is denoted as $p_1, p_2, \ldots, p_{t_{max}}$. For transitivity estimation, they are the counts of the four patterns involving three nodes. The $\hat{\mathcal{S}}_i.c\ \forall i$, are maximum likelihood estimations for the parameters $\mathcal{S}_i.c$, and can be derived by solving the following maximization problem:

$$\hat{\mathcal{S}}_1.c, \hat{\mathcal{S}}_2.c, \ldots, \hat{\mathcal{S}}_{s_{max}}.c = \underset{\mathcal{S}_i.c\ \forall i}{\arg\max}(\Pr(p_1, p_2, \ldots, p_{t_{max}} | \mathcal{S}_i.c\ \forall i))$$

Given the estimation $\hat{\mathcal{S}}_i.c\ \forall i$, we can compute the estimated utility value using function f. Note that the counting of all substructures is only feasible for substructures involving a small number of nodes. For example, in density, we count substructures involving two nodes, and in transitivity substructures involving three nodes only. For utility metrics involving substructures of a larger number of nodes, we can use sampling (defining an upper limit for counting or execution time) to estimate their values.

While not all utility metrics can be effectively recovered, there exists an ineffective algorithm (impractical due to the computation cost) that follows standard procedures to estimate all the metrics. The algorithm is described as follows: Let $\mathcal{G}$ denote the set of all possible graphs on N number of nodes. For each possible graph $\mathcal{G}[i]$, there is a probability that $\mathcal{G}[i] = G_o$, which can be computed based on $\mathcal{G}[i]$, G_p and μ, and denoted by $\Pr(\mathcal{G}[i] = G_o|G_p)$. Consider a particular metric Z, we can measure its value $val_i(Z)$ on each $\mathcal{G}[i]$. Lastly, the sum of $val_i(Z)\cdot\Pr(\mathcal{G}[i] = G_o|G_p), \forall i$ forms an estimation to the metric Z in the original graph. Although theoretically sound, this algorithm is impracticable as it requires the enumeration of all possible graphs on N nodes. A more efficient recovery of specific other metrics is left as an open problem.

The quality of our estimations is also a concern. To assess that quality, we can compute the standard error of the mean, $StErr$. For example, from Equation 4, we estimate the variance of $\hat{h}$ as:

$$\sigma^2(\hat{h}) = \frac{\sigma^2(h_p)}{(1-2\mu)^2} \tag{14}$$

Let $R = 1$ ($R = 0$) denote the event there exists (does not exist) an edge between a particular pair of nodes. Therefore, $\Pr(R = 1) = \frac{h}{M}\cdot(1-\mu) + (1-\frac{h}{M})\cdot\mu$, and $\Pr(R = 0) = \frac{h}{M}\cdot\mu + (1-\frac{h}{M})\cdot(1-\mu)$. Therefore, $\sigma^2(h_p) = M\cdot\Pr(R = 1)\cdot\Pr(R = 0)$. Substituting in Equation 14, we get:

$$\sigma(\hat{h}) = \sqrt{M\cdot\left[\frac{1}{16\cdot(\frac{1}{2}-\mu)^2} - \left(\frac{h}{M}-\frac{1}{2}\right)^2\right]} \tag{15}$$

4. ATTACKING THE PERTURBED GRAPH

As we argued, by carefully designing estimation algorithms, many of the original graph properties can be accurately estimated. Nevertheless, the same potential can also be exploited by an adversary to launch more sophisticated attacks.

4.1 Principles of the Probabilistic Attack

The *probabilistic attack* starts out from the observation that an adversary can confidently estimate a degree interval (i.e., range) for each embedded malicious node. Using an approach similar to that of the *walk-based attack* [1], the adversary can efficiently enumerate a list of candidate *degree sequences* that will include, with high probability, the one that represents the embedded subgraph G_A. In most cases, the adversary can arrive at a single *degree sequence* that represents with high probability the subgraph embedded in G_o. This disposition is enabled by the fact that candidate degree sequences are *filtered* out in our attack methodology using two tests: the *interval degree check* and the *error-tolerant edge check*. These tests work differently from those of the *walk-based attack* [1].

	$k = 10$	$k = 20$	$k = 30$
$\mu = 0.0001$	0.9991	0.9981	0.9971
$\mu = 0.001$	0.9910	0.9812	0.9714
$\mu = 0.01$	0.9135	0.8262	0.7472

Table 1: Probability that k-path in G_A is preserved

We face a few challenges in demonstrating the feasibility of the attack: first, the prediction of degree ranges should be correct with high probability. Second, the length of the predicted interval for an adversary's node should be as small as possible, as a large interval may result in a large number of nodes passing the *degree check*, causing a severe penalty to the attack's time complexity. Last, in order for our attack to succeed, the perturbation may alter the attacker's subgraph but must not have destroyed the k-path (i.e., path of k nodes) therein. In Table 1 we show the probability that this k-path is preserved (i.e., all its edges are preserved after perturbation) for several combinations of different μ and k, computed as $(1-\mu)^{k-1}$ under perturbation probability μ. As this probability is quite high, the adversary can reasonably assume that the embedded subgraph's k-path is preserved in G_p after perturbation.

4.2 Predicting the Degree Interval

Let d_o be the degree of a malicious node in G_o and d_p the degree of the same node after perturbation. In the following, we first compute $\Pr(d_p|d_o)$, i.e., the probability that, given that the node's original node degree is d_o, its degree after perturbation is d_p.

Let r be the number of neighbors *eventually* removed from the set of d_o's neighbors in G_o, and a the number of new neighbors added, due to perturbation. Without loss of generality, suppose that the d_p neighbors of the malicious node at hand are generated in two steps: first, r neighbors are disconnected and the number of remaining neighbors is $d_o - r$; then, $a = d_p - (d_o - r)$ nodes are connected and become neighbors, so the total number of neighbors is $d_o - r + a = d_p$. Then the following three inequalities hold:

$$r \geq 0, \quad d_o - r \geq 0, \quad d_p - (d_o - r) \geq 0 \tag{16}$$

It follows that r is in the range of $[\max\{0, d_o - d_p\}, d_o]$. The r neighbors can be removed in $\binom{d_o}{r}$ ways, and new neighbors added in $\binom{N-d_o-1}{d_p-d_o+r}$ ways. Hence, $\Pr(d_p|d_o)$ is equal to:

$$\sum_r \binom{d_o}{r}\binom{N-d_o-1}{d_p-d_o+r}\cdot(1-\mu)^{N-1-(d_p-d_o+2r)}\mu^{d_p-d_o+2r}$$

Thus, an adversary can efficiently compute $\Pr(d_p|d_o)$. The possible values of d_p after perturbation ranges from 1 to $N-1$. Yet the distribution of these values is not uniform. For each embedded node, the adversary can select a small subset of d_p values and build an interval $\mathcal{I}$ representing the range of possible degrees for that node. We check inclusion in this interval as our *degree check*.

The removal and addition of neighbors of an embedded node can be viewed as two *independent Binomial processes*. The expected values for r and a are $\mathrm{E}[r] = d_o\cdot\mu$ and $\mathrm{E}[a] = (N - d_o - 1)\cdot\mu$, respectively. $\Pr(d_p|d_o)$ is maximized for $r = \mathrm{E}[r]$ and $a = \mathrm{E}[a]$ (hence $d_p = \mathrm{E}[d_p]$). Then the chosen interval $\mathcal{I}$ for the embedded node at hand is centered at $d_p = \mathrm{E}[d_p]$, with w other values to its left and right, where w is a small non-negative integer. Eventually, the predicted degree interval for a selected malicious node in G_p is $\mathcal{I} = [\mathrm{E}[d_p] - w, \mathrm{E}[d_p] + w]$. Let $\Pr(d_p \in \mathcal{I})$ be the probability that the embedded node's degree is in $\mathcal{I}$ after perturbation. An effective attack is possible if the adversary can find a fine-tuned value of w such that $\Pr(d_p \in \mathcal{I})$ is sufficiently large and yet the width of $\mathcal{I}$ is small. Let $\mathcal{I}_{V_A[i]}$ be the degree interval for embedded node $V_A[i]$, and $\mathcal{D}_p$ be the degree sequence of the embedded graph G_A in G_p. Then the probability that *all* embedded nodes' degrees fall into their respective intervals is $\prod_{i=1}^{k} \Pr(\mathcal{D}_p[i] \in \mathcal{I}_{V_A[i]})$. This calculation is made under the assumption that the events of different embedded nodes' degrees falling into their respective intervals are independent of each other, which helps us derive our estimate.

Table 2 shows the values of $\Pr(d_p \in \mathcal{I})$ for selected values of μ and w with $k = 12$. We observe that, when the number of nodes in the network is $10,000$, the perturbation probability is 0.001 and $w = 4$, then the probability that a *single* embedded node falls into the interval $\mathcal{I}$ is close to 1. Moreover, the probability that *all* the embedded nodes' degrees fall into their respective intervals after perturbation is also close to 1 in the same configuration. We conclude that, with this configuration, the attacker is almost sure that all embedded nodes will pass the *interval degree check*.

μ	w	$\Pr(d_p \in \mathcal{I})$	$\prod_{i=1}^{k} \Pr(\mathcal{D}_p[i] \in \mathcal{I}_{V_A[i]})$
$\mu = 0.001$	0	0.3670	5.9643×10^{-6}
$\mu = 0.001$	2	0.9814	0.7983
$\mu = 0.001$	4	0.9994	0.9931
$\mu = 0.01$	0	0.1246	1.3935×10^{-11}
$\mu = 0.01$	4	0.8488	0.1399
$\mu = 0.01$	8	0.9927	0.9158

Table 2: $\Pr(d_p \in \mathcal{I})$ **with** $N = 10,000$ **and** $d_o = 50$

For example, in the graph in Figure 1(c), the adversary's *degree sequence* is $[2, 5, 3, 4, 2]$. Yet in the perturbed graph G_p the degree of the node labeled 11 has become 1. Then, if a *walk-based attack* is launched, this node will not be detected. Still, with a *probabilistic attack*, the adversary is able to estimate the degree interval for each embedded node. For example (after integer rounding) the estimated degree intervals can be $[\ [1,2], [4,5], [3,4], [3,4], [2,3]\ ]$. In this scenario node 11 can still be accepted by the adversary as a candidate embedded node, allowing for a successful attack.

Algorithm 1: The *probabilistic attack*

```
Data: G_p, G_A, μ, w as chosen, m = 0, k-path;
Result: A k-path containing identifiers of nodes in V_A;
1 while k-path not found and w_max, m_max unreached do
2     T=new Tree(); level = 0;
3     foreach V[i] in G_p do
4         localSearch(V[i], level, T.root());
5     if w < w_max then
6         w++;
7     else if m < m_max then
8         m++;
```

Function localSearch(*curnode, level, parent*)

```
1 if level = k then
2     return;
3 if curnode passes Interval Degree and ET-Edge checks then
4     T.add(curnode, parent);
5     foreach neighbor nb of curnode do
6         localSearch(nb, level++, curnode);
```

4.3 Attack Algorithm

Algorithm 1 describes our *probabilistic attack*. $\mathcal{T}$ is the tree of all candidate subgraphs, w is the width parameter for the degree intervals used in the *interval degree check* (chosen by the adversary as discussed) and m is the maximum number of errors that we allow in the employed *error-tolerant edge check*. The main block of the algorithm is a loop that continues until a k-path is found in $\mathcal{T}$ by the *localSearch* function (shown below), or both w and m reach their predefined maximum thresholds w_{max} and m_{max}.

Our probabilistic attack algorithm follows the pattern of a walk-based attack [1], with the key difference being on the two tests it performs (Line 3 in *localSearch*). To pass the *interval degree check*, a node's degree should fall in the predicted degree interval $V_A[level]$. To pass the *error-tolerant edge check*, the number of errors in *edge checks* accumulated in the path from this node to the root should not be larger than m. At each iteration of the main loop, if a k-path is not found, we relax the searching condition by either increasing w or m. However, using large w and m enlarges search space. The maximum w and m values that can be used depend on the attacker's computational resources.

4.4 Building Edges to Target the Victims

In order to compromise the victims' privacy, the adversary has to correctly identify the victims. However, due to perturbation, the links between the victim and the adversary's nodes may have changed which raises new challenges for identifying the victims. We propose a method that minimizes the impact of perturbation and establishes robust links against perturbation. Let the set of nodes that represent the victims in the network be $V_T = \{\tau_1, \tau_2, \dots \tau_q\}$. $S_{\tau_i} \subset V_A$ is the set of maliciously embedded nodes that are linked to victim τ_i, $1 \le i \le q$. Our approach is as follows: we define two parameters ρ_1 and ρ_2, where ρ_1 defines the minimum size of S_{τ_i}, and ρ_2 defines the minimum number of different members between the two sets S_{τ_i} and S_{τ_j}, for $i \neq j$. Formally:

$$\begin{cases} |S_{\tau_i}| \ge \rho_1 & \forall i \in [1, q] \\ |S_{\tau_i} \backslash S_{\tau_j}| \ge \rho_2 & \forall i, j \in [1, q] \text{ and } i \neq j \end{cases} \tag{17}$$

Moreover, we require that none of the adversary's nodes share common neighbors other than the nodes in V_T and V_A. To prove the robustness of the links between the victims and the adversary's nodes, we show analytically that the probabilities of the three events that affect the identification of the victims are negligible.

Claim 1: *The probability that S_{τ_i} for any τ_i changes due to perturbation tends to be 0 when $\mu \to 0$.*

PROOF. S_{τ_i} is preserved for any τ_i if the edge relations between this τ_i and all the adversary's nodes are preserved (i.e, $(1-\mu)^k$). Therefore, the probability that S_{τ_i} changes is $1 - (1-\mu)^k$. When $\mu \to 0$, $1 - (1-\mu)^k \to 0$. □

Claim 2: *The probability that there is a node v outside sets V_A and V_T such that E_v, the set of edges between v and the nodes from V_A, is equal to S_{τ_i} for the victim τ_i, decreases fast with the increase of ρ_1.*

PROOF. Let us consider a particular node v which already has an edge with a node in S_{τ_i}. The probability that it forms new edges with all other nodes in S_{τ_i} but not with the nodes in $V_A - S_{\tau_i}$ is at most $\mu^{\rho_1 - 1} \cdot (1-\mu)^{k-\rho_1+1}$. Moreover, the total number of such possible nodes v in the network is $N - k - q$. Therefore, $(N-k-q) \cdot \mu^{\rho_1-1} \cdot (1-\mu)^{k-\rho_1+1}$ is the probability for the event in this claim. When $\mu = \frac{c}{N}$, this probability at most $\frac{c^{\rho_1-1}}{N^{\rho_1-1}}$ (by taking $N-k-q$ as N and $(1-\mu)^{k-\rho_1+1}$ as 1), which decreases fast with the increase of ρ_1. □

Claim 3: *The probability that the set S_{τ_i} of malicious nodes connected to victim τ_i becomes the same as the set S_{τ_j} of malicious nodes connected to victim τ_j after perturbation decreases fast with the increase of ρ_2.*

PROOF. Let the number of non-common elements in S_{τ_i} and S_{τ_j} be x_{ij}. Similarly to the derivation of equation 27, S_{τ_i} is converted to S_{τ_j} by perturbation if and only if an x_{ij} number of edge additions and deletions occurs. Therefore, after perturbation, $\Pr(S_{\tau_i} = S_{\tau_j}) = (1-\mu)^{k-x_{ij}} \cdot \mu^{x_{ij}}$. Since $\rho_2 \leq x_{ij}$, $\Pr(S_{\tau_i} = S_{\tau_j}) \leq \mu^{\rho_2}$, which decreases fast with the increase of ρ_2. □

A trivial algorithm that builds our robust links operates as follows: for each victim τ_i, repetitively select a subset of nodes in V_A at random, until a subset that satisfies both ρ_1 and ρ_2 requirements is found; then link τ_i to all the nodes in this subset of V_A.

4.5 Preventing the Probabilistic Attack

The adversary can successfully identify his subgraph based on the assumption that the k-path is not broken. However, the publisher can increase the perturbation probability so that, with high probability, the k-path is broken and therefore the *probabilistic attack* is infeasible. Let ε, the secure parameter, be the maximum probability that the k-path is preserved. Therefore,

$$(1-\mu)^{k-1} \leq \varepsilon \tag{18}$$

The following inequality gives the minimum μ to be used so as to prevent the *probabilistic attack* with probability no less than $1-\varepsilon$:

$$\mu \geq 1 - \sqrt[k-1]{\varepsilon} \tag{19}$$

5. GENERIC STRUCTURAL ATTACK

We now provide a generic analysis of a structural attack's probability of success. We assume that any structural attack can be translated into an instance of the graph isomorphism problem and show that an adversary who can enumerate all permutations of k nodes in G_p, will also be able, with high probability, to detect the embedded nodes under a random perturbation scheme for low μ.

Let Y_i be the ith permutation of k nodes in the network. We assume an extreme case where the adversary has infinite computational power and is able to enumerate all permutations of k nodes in the network: $\mathcal{Y} = \{Y_i : 1 \leq i \leq P_k^N\}$ where $P_k^N = \frac{N!}{(N-k)!}$ is the total number of permutations. The adversary will then choose a particular permutation $Y \in \mathcal{Y}$ as a candidate for V_A and will assume that $Y[i]$ is $V_A[i]$. However, the adversary faces the following two challenges when choosing Y: first, the perturbation may have changed the embedded graph G_A in such a way that G_A cannot be detected in G_p. Second, even if the adversary succeeds in locating a permutation Y that matches subgraph G_A in appearance, there is still a probability that Y is not the actual V_A, but only a look-alike.

We define λ_Y as the probability that the chosen Y is V_A, given G_p. For the sake of conciseness, we use E_A^Y to denote the set of edges among the nodes in Y, after perturbation, in the event that this set has been created by perturbing the set E_A, i.e., in the event that $Y = V_A$. Then $\lambda_Y = \Pr(E_A^Y | E_p)$.

Let E_p^Y be the set of edges among the nodes in Y in the perturbed graph E_p. Then the following theorem holds:

THEOREM 5.1. *For a perturbed graph G_p of size N with a perturbation value μ, the probability that an adversary detects the embedded subgraph G_A, for a permutation of k nodes Y, is:*

$$\lambda_Y = \frac{\Pr(E_p^Y | E_A^Y)}{\sum_{i=1}^{P_k^N} \Pr(E_p^{Y_i} | E_A^{Y_i})} \tag{20}$$

PROOF. First, we rewrite the expression using Bayes' theorem,

$$\Pr(E_A^Y | E_p) = \frac{\Pr(E_p | E_A^Y) \cdot \Pr(E_A^Y)}{\sum_{i=1}^{P_k^N} \Pr(E_p | E_A^{Y_i}) \cdot \Pr(E_A^{Y_i})} \tag{21}$$

In the above equation, $\Pr(E_A^{Y_i})$ is the prior probability of Y being the attacker's nodes, which is the same for all i. Therefore:

$$\Pr(E_A^Y | E_p) = \frac{\Pr(E_p | E_A^Y)}{\sum_{i=1}^{P_k^N} \Pr(E_p | E_A^{Y_i})} \tag{22}$$

We first focus on the numerator $\Pr(E_p | E_A^Y)$ in Equation 22. We split the set of edges in the perturbed graph into two sets: E_p^Y, the edges between the nodes in Y, only and $\overline{E_p^Y}$, the other edges in E_p. By definition, $\overline{E_p^Y} = E_p - E_p^Y$. E_p^Y and $\overline{E_p^Y}$ are independent, hence:

$$\Pr(E_p) = \Pr(E_p^Y) \cdot \Pr(\overline{E_p^Y}) \tag{23}$$

Inserting the conditional variable E_A^Y to Equation 23, we get:

$$\Pr(E_p | E_A^Y) = \Pr(E_p^Y | E_A^Y) \cdot \Pr(\overline{E_p^Y} | E_A^Y) \tag{24}$$

Since $\overline{E_p^Y}$ and E_A^Y are independent, $\Pr(\overline{E_p^Y} | E_A^Y) = \Pr(\overline{E_p^Y}) = \frac{\Pr(E_p)}{\Pr(E_p^Y)}$ (by Equation 23). Then Equation 24 becomes:

$$\Pr(E_p | E_A^Y) = \Pr(E_p^Y | E_A^Y) \frac{\Pr(E_p)}{\Pr(E_p^Y)} \tag{25}$$

Combining Equations 22 and 25, and using $E_p^{Y_i}$ for E_p^Y, we get:

$$\Pr(E_A^Y | E_p) = \frac{\Pr(E_p^Y | E_A^Y)}{\sum_{i=1}^{P_k^N} \Pr(E_p^{Y_i} | E_A^{Y_i})} \tag{26}$$

□

The intuition behind the derived equation for λ_Y is the following: the numerator $\Pr(E_p^Y | E_A^Y)$ is the likelihood of the particular chosen permutation Y to be V_A. The denominator is the sum of the likelihoods of each permutation Y_i in the network being V_A. The ratio describes the probability of success of the particular selection Y being V_A. Thus, the value of λ_Y depends on the value of $\Pr(E_p^Y | E_A^Y)$ and the sum of $\Pr(E_p^{Y_i} | E_A^{Y_i})$ for all i. In effect, the computation of the exact λ_Y would require the enumeration of all permutation of k nodes in the graph. In the following, we study the conditional probability $\Pr(E_p^Y | E_A^Y)$ for a particular Y.

Given that Y is the set of embedded nodes and E_A^Y is the set of edges among the nodes in Y before perturbation, $\Pr(E_p^Y | E_A^Y)$ is the probability that the set of edges among the nodes in Y becomes E_p^Y after perturbation. With this fact in mind, the derivation of $\Pr(E_p^Y | E_A^Y)$ becomes easy: let m be the number of *non-common* edges in E_p^Y and E_A^Y. The minimum value of m is 0, achieved when E_A^Y and E_p^Y are identical, and its maximum value is $M = \frac{k^2-k}{2}$, obtained when E_A^Y and E_p^Y are totally foreign to each other. Since each edge removal or addition occurs with probability μ, the probability that E_A^Y is converted to E_p^Y is:

$$\Pr(E_p^Y | E_A^Y) = \mu^m \cdot (1-\mu)^{M-m} \tag{27}$$

5.1 Estimation of λ_Y

From a (computationally powerful) adversary's point of view, Equation (20) can be used to compute λ_Y for each $Y = Y_i$. The attacker will then assume that the set Y that gives the maximal value of λ_Y is the embedded subgraph V_A in G_p. In particular, given that the denominator is constant for a given E_A and G_p, the

μ	ℓ	$\hat{\lambda}_Y$ when $m = \ell$	$\Pr(m \leq \ell)$
0.0001	0	1	0.9955
0.0001	5	1	1
0.0001	10	1	1
0.001	0	1	0.9559
0.001	5	1	1
0.001	10	0.0031	1

Table 3: λ_Y with $k = 10$, $M = 45$, $N = 10,000$

adversary will simply opt for the set Y that maximizes the numerator in Equation (20). The best-case scenario for an adversary is that $m = 0$ (i.e., E_p^Y and E_A^Y are identical). Otherwise, an adversary will choose the Y that gives the most similar subgraph to G_A.

In the following we provide a simple method for estimating the value of λ_Y. For any permutation of k nodes Y_i, let $m_{Y_i} = |E_A^{Y_i} \cup E_p^{Y_i} - E_A^{Y_i} \cap E_p^{Y_i}|$. We consider $E_p^{Y_i}$ as a random subset chosen from all possible edges among the nodes of Y_i. Then the expected value of m_{Y_i} is $\frac{M}{2}$ and the expected value of $\Pr(E_p^{Y_i}|E_A^{Y_i})$ is $\mu^{\frac{M}{2}} \cdot (1-\mu)^{\frac{M}{2}}$. Then our simple estimate of λ_Y is:

$$\hat{\lambda}_Y = \min\left\{1, \frac{1}{P_k^N}\left(\frac{1-\mu}{\mu}\right)^{\frac{M}{2}-m}\right\} \tag{28}$$

Thus, our estimate of λ_Y depends on μ and m. Table 3 lists different λ_Y estimates with respect to different μ and m combinations in a network of $10,000$ nodes with 10 malicious nodes. Intuitively, m can be seen as the number of altered edges from E_A^Y to E_p^Y. We note that, unless both μ and m are high, $\hat{\lambda}_Y$ approaches 1.

We observe that $\hat{\lambda}_Y$ tends to be large only when m is small. If the lowest value of m is kept large (e.g., greater than 10, as in the last row of Table 3), then $\hat{\lambda}_Y$ is kept low. In effect, to assess the potential for a successful attack, we study the distribution of m under random edge perturbation. This perturbation can be seen as a binomial process that adds and deletes edges with probability μ. Then the probability distribution of m is:

$$\Pr(m \leq \ell) = \sum_{m=0}^{\ell} \binom{M}{m} (1-\mu)^{M-m}\mu^m \tag{29}$$

The last column of Table 3 shows instances of the probability distribution for m with the values of k and μ fixed. We observe that $\Pr(m = 0)$ equals 0.9955 and 0.9559 for $\mu = 0.0001$ and $\mu = 0.001$. This result shows that m tends to be rather small with high probability. Thus, we conclude that $\hat{\lambda}_Y$ tends to be large for such perturbation probabilities. This is good news for an adversary who has the computational powers to enumerate all subgraphs and choose the one most similar to the embedded one.

6. EXPERIMENTAL EVALUATION

We now present our experimental evaluation. First, we investigate the probability of success of the *probabilistic attack* under different values of μ, and measure its execution time. Next, we investigate the effect of perturbation on the graph properties.

All experiments ran on a 2.33GHz CPU, Windows-XP machine with 3.25GB RAM. We employ two real datasets: The Enron dataset[1] is the graph of email exchange among employees of Enron, having 4,644 accounts. Each account corresponds to a node and two accounts are linked if they have exchanged emails in both directions. The DBLP dataset[2] is a random subset of 20,000 authors from the DBLP bibliography. Each author corresponds to a node and two authors are linked if they are coauthors in at least one paper. The Wiki dataset[3] is a network Wikipedia encyclopedia writers around the world. It consists of 7,115 nodes and 103,689 edges.

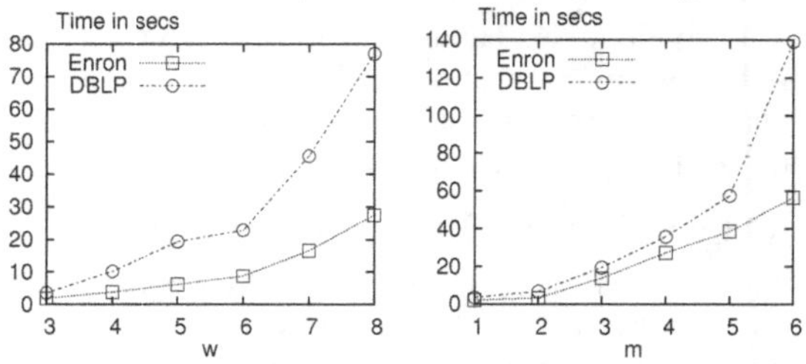

(a) Time vs. w (prob.) (b) Time vs. m (prob.)

Figure 3: Efficiency of the probabilistic attack

6.1 Assessing the Probabilistic Attack

In our first experiment, we assess the probability of success of our *probabilistic attack* as opposed to that of the classical *walk-based attack* [1]. We first test the *walk-based attack* on the Enron and DBLP data, measuring its success rate in trials of 200 separate attack runs, as a function of the perturbation probability μ. An attack run is considered to be successful, if the adversaries can detect the sequence of embedded nodes and re-identify at least one victim node. In [1], the suggested number of malicious nodes k is $\Theta(\log(N))$ and the number of victim nodes is $q = O(\log^2(N))$. Following this suggestion, we vary k at values 20, 25, 30 for both graphs, with number of victims 100, 157 and 225, respectively.

Figures 4a,e show our results, which provide a glimpse of the probability that an adversary successfully identifies the embedded nodes in perturbed DBLP and Enron data using a walk-based attack. When μ is 0, all attacks are 100% successful. Still, already for rather small values of μ (10^{-7} to 10^{-6}), the success rate drops drastically to very low values. In addition, the success rate is lower for larger k under the same perturbation value μ; that is because, with larger k, the node degree sequence of the malicious nodes is more likely to be changed or the backbone to be broken, making the attack more likely to fail. In effect, the walk-based attack can be effectively prevented through random edge perturbation, with minimal impact on the graph's structure (as μ is negligible).

On the other hand, Figures 4b-d,f-h show the success rate of the *probabilistic attack* on the same DBLP and Enron data, again in trials of 200 runs each. We show results for several values of the interval-width parameter w. As the search space of the attack algorithm grows with w, the success rate also rises with it. For $\mu \simeq 10^{-4}$, the probabilistic attack succeeds in almost 100% of the cases, in stark contrast to the walk-based one. Still, as μ grows further, the observed success rate swiftly drops for all values of w. As with the walk-based attack, the success rate falls as k grows.

Figures 3a,b show the execution time of our attack as a function of interval-width w and error-tolerance m, with $\mu = 10^{-3}$. The number of malicious nodes is $k = 4\log(N)$ and the number of victims $q = \log^2(N)$. The algorithm's search space grows with both w and m (Section 4.2), hence the execution time also ascends with them, yet remains lower than 3 minutes, rendering the attack rather feasible on reasonably-sized real-world data sets.

An adversary who successfully identifies the embedded subgraph inside the perturbed graph may yet not locate the target victims, as the edges between the embedded nodes and the victims may have been removed. Table 4 shows the measured percentage of victims that can be identified in a successful attack. The number of malicious nodes and the victims remain at $k = 4\log(N)$ and at

[1] http://www.cs.cmu.edu/~enron

[2] http://dblp.uni-trier.de/xml/

[3] http://snap.stanford.edu/data/wiki-Vote.html

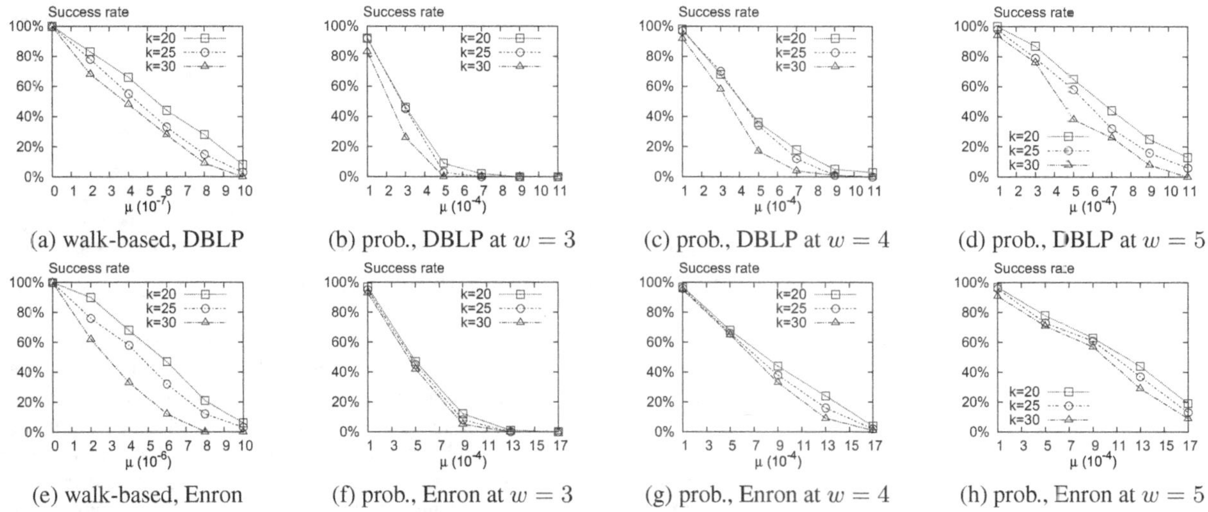

(a) walk-based, DBLP (b) prob., DBLP at $w = 3$ (c) prob., DBLP at $w = 4$ (d) prob., DBLP at $w = 5$

(e) walk-based, Enron (f) prob., Enron at $w = 3$ (g) prob., Enron at $w = 4$ (h) prob., Enron at $w = 5$

Figure 4: Evaluation of Probabilistic Attack

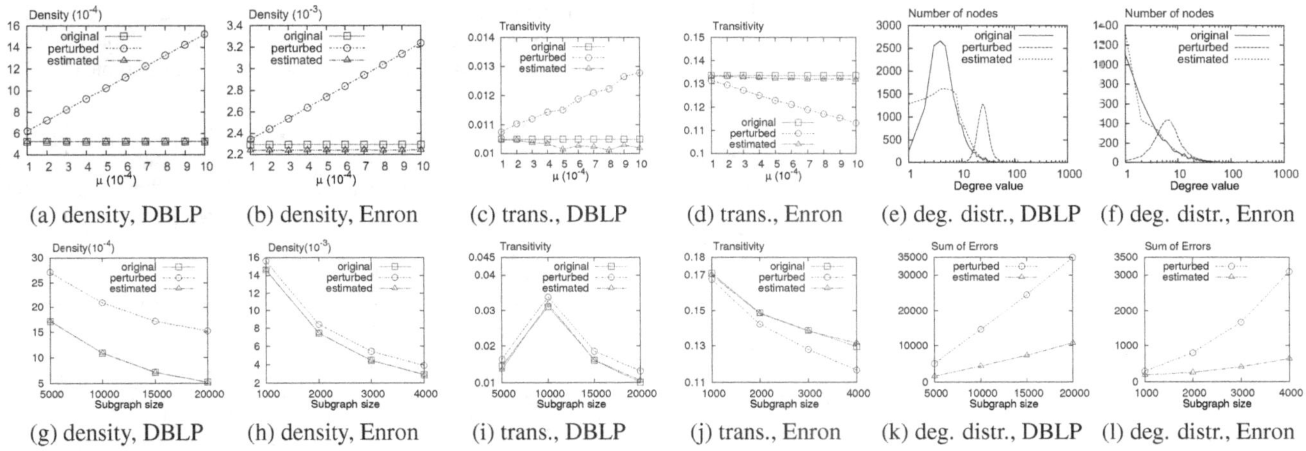

(a) density, DBLP (b) density, Enron (c) trans., DBLP (d) trans., Enron (e) deg. distr., DBLP (f) deg. distr., Enron

(g) density, DBLP (h) density, Enron (i) trans., DBLP (j) trans., Enron (k) deg. distr., DBLP (l) deg. distr., Enron

Figure 5: Evaluation of utility preservation

$q = \log^2(N)$. As the table shows, more than 91% of victims are identified when the attack succeeds.

μ	Enron	DBLP
1×10^{-4}	95.2%	98.3%
2×10^{-4}	93.6%	98.3%
3×10^{-4}	92.7%	96.7%
4×10^{-4}	91.9%	94.2%

Table 4: Percentage of affected victims

The error-tolerance m also affects an attack's probability of success. Table 5 shows an instance of this effect: in a trial of 100 attacks with $m = 0$ on the Enron graph perturbed with $\mu = 0.04$, there are 53 successes, 35 failures due to false predicted interval, and 6 due to broken path or edge check failures. Still, when we relax the requirement for passing the edge check test, we can increase the number of successes to 58 and 59.

Events	m=0	m=1	m=2
Success	53	58	59
False prediction	35	35	35
Broken path	6	6	6
Edge check fail	6	1	0

Table 5: Effect of m

To sum up, the probabilistic attack is more effective than the walk-based one *and* feasible in terms of runtime. Still, *both* can be prevented under random perturbation with sufficiently large μ.

6.2 Assessing Utility Preservation

We use the perturbed data derived in previous experiments to evaluate the extent to which graph properties are preserved. Figures 5a-f show the density, transitivity and degree distribution for perturbed DBLP and Enron data. Each figure shows the original, perturbed, and estimated values. Density and transitivity values vary with the perturbation probability μ, while the degree distribution is given as a single snapshot for $\mu = 10^{-3}$. We observe that, while graph properties deviate significantly from the originals as μ grows, our derived *estimates* are resilient to perturbation and approximate the original values well. Significantly, our estimation algorithms provide accurate approximations even under perturbation probabilities that render probabilistic attacks unviable.

Furthermore, we illustrate the benefit of our method in terms of measuring the properties of *subgraphs* of the original graph. This application of our technique offers an undeniable benefit, as publishing the graph cannot be substituted by directly publishing the measures of interest. We measure the same six structural properties over subgraphs of different sizes extracted from the original DBLP and Enron graphs, and average our results over 10 different randomly extracted subgraphs. Figures 5g-l show our results as a function of subgraph size, with $\mu = 0.001$. For density and transi-

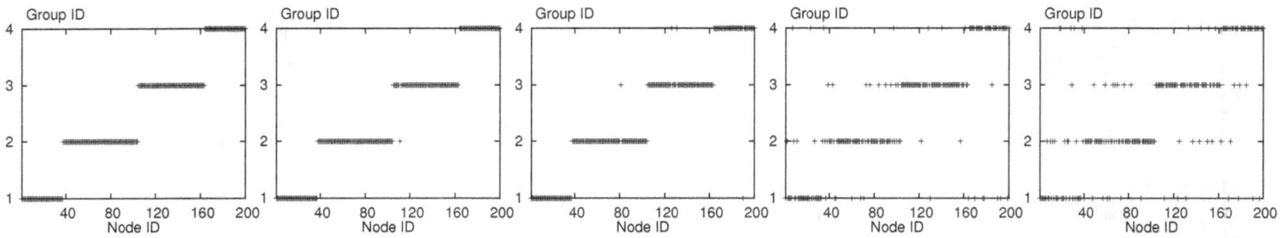

(a) Original (b) $\mu = 0.001$ (c) $\mu = 0.01$ (d) $\mu = 0.05$ (e) $\mu = 0.1$

Figure 6: Classification of nodes under perturbation

tivity, we show again the original, perturbed, and estimated values, for each subgraph size. For degree distribution, we now present the sum of absolute errors between the perturbed/estimate and original distribution values for each degree. Our results reconfirm our findings even with subgraphs extracted from the parent graphs.

Overall, our results corroborate our claim that a published graph allows accurate estimations of graph properties not only for the whole graph, but also for subgraphs thereof, where publishing the measures directly to end-users would not be a satisfactory solution.

6.3 Distance-based Classification

We now attempt to perform a specific data mining task, distance-based node classification, over perturbed data.

Social networks often possess hubs, i.e., nodes with very high degree. A particular person's connectivity pattern to the hubs indicates that person's interests. For example, in a social election, a person's voting pattern may indicate its political views. Thus, node classification based on such patterns is useful. We consider a classification of nodes based on the distance between their hub connectivity pattern (HCP) and some target patterns (TPs). Given a set of hubs, a node's HCP is the subset of hubs that this node has connectivity to. Each TP_i is a subset of the hubs defined by the analyst. Given a set of k hubs, HCP and TP_i are k-dimensional binary vectors. The distance between HPC and a particular TP_i is the edit distance between the two vectors. For each TP_i, a group of nodes G_i is formed by assigning group membership to the nodes that have closest distances to TP_i than to all other $\text{TP}_j (i \neq j)$. We aim to classify each node to the right group.

We use the Wiki graph. Hubs are chosen as the nodes that have top-10 degrees in the graph (ranging from 482 to 1,053). We extract a subset of 200 nodes for classification, each having at least 4 connections to the hubs. For instance, the 10-dimensional binary data (0 0 1 0 1 0 0 1 1 0) represent the HCP for a node that has connectivity to the 3rd, 5th, 8th and 9th hubs. We define four target patterns, TP_1 =(0 0 0 0 0 0 0 0 0 0), TP_2 =(0 1 0 1 0 1 0 1 0 1), TP_3 =(1 1 1 1 1 1 1 1 1 1) and TP_4 =(1 0 1 0 1 0 1 0 1 0), hence 4 classes of nodes. We assign IDs to the nodes so that nodes that are classified into the same group have consecutive IDs. Figure 6(a) visualizes the original classification. Figures 6(b,c,d,e) show the classification obtained from the perturbed graph with increasing μ. Remarkably, the classification is faithful even with $\mu = 0.01$, with which both *walk-based attack* and *probabilistic attack* fail (see Figure 4). Classification error becomes apparent with larger μ as Figures 6(d,e) show, while most nodes are still correctly classified.

7. CONCLUSIONS

In this paper we have delineated the effectiveness of random edge perturbation as a tool for privacy-preserving publication of graph data in the face of structural attacks. We have shown that sophisticated attacks based on probabilistic heuristics are feasible when the perturbation probability is sufficiently low, but can be thwarted as that probability grows. Moreover, we conducted an in-depth theoretical study of the probability of success for *any* structural attack. Our analysis offers a yardstick for assessing the privacy risk entailed by the publication of perturbed graph data. On the other hand, we developed methods that accurately estimate the properties of the original graph from the perturbed data. A thorough experimental study validates our analysis and explores the tradeoff between privacy and utility. Last, we have effectively demonstrated that data mining tasks such as distance-based node classification can be successfully performed even under random edge perturbation probabilities with which structural attacks typically fail.

8. ACKNOWLEDGEMENTS

We thank Dr. Yufei Tao for sharing insights on this topic, and Dr. Ee-Chien Chang and Dr. Hai Feng Yu for their constructive feedback. Mingqiang Xue is supported by I^2R grant.

9. REFERENCES

[1] L. Backstrom, C. Dwork, and J. M. Kleinberg. Wherefore art thou r3579x?: anonymized social networks, hidden patterns, and structural steganography. In *WWW*, 2007.

[2] F. Bonchi, A. Gionis, and T. Tassa. Identity obfuscation in graphs through the information theoretic lens. In *ICDE*, 2011.

[3] J. Cheng, A. W.-C. Fu, and J. Liu. k-isomorphism: privacy preserving network publication against structural attacks. In *SIGMOD*, 2010.

[4] G. Cormode, D. Srivastava, T. Yu, and Q. Zhang. Anonymizing bipartite graph data using safe groupings. In *VLDB*, 2008.

[5] L. da F. Costa, F. A. Rodrigues, G. Travieso, and P. R. V. Boas. Characterization of complex networks: A survey of measurements. *Adv. Phys.*, 2007.

[6] A. Evfimievski, R. Srikant, R. Agrawal, and J. Gehrke. Privacy preserving mining of association rules. In *KDD*, 2002.

[7] M. R. Garey and D. S. Johnson. *Computers and Intractability: A Guide to the Theory of NP-Completeness*. Freeman, 1979.

[8] M. Hay, G. Miklau, D. Jensen, D. Towsley, and P. Weis. Resisting structural re-identification in anonymized social networks. *PVLDB*, 1(1):102–114, 2008.

[9] M. Hay, G. Miklau, D. Jesen, P. Weis, and S. Srivastava. Anonymizing social networks. *Technical Report 07-19*, 2007.

[10] K. Liu and E. Terzi. Towards identity anonymization on graphs. In *SIGMOD*, 2008.

[11] S. J. Rizvi and J. R. Haritsa. Maintaining data privacy in association rule mining. In *VLDB*, 2002.

[12] X. Ying and X. Wu. Randomizing social networks: a spectrum preserving approach. In *SIAM SDM*, 2008.

[13] B. Zhou and J. Pei. Preserving privacy in social networks against neighborhood attacks. In *ICDE*, 2008.

[14] L. Zou, L. Chen, and M. T. Özsu. k-automorphism: A general framework for privacy preserving network publication. In *VLDB*, 2009.

Multiview Hierarchical Bayesian Regression Model and Application to Online Advertising

Tianbing Xu
Computer Science
University of California, Irvine
txu@ics.uci.edu

Ruofei Zhang, Zhen Guo
Advertising Sciences, Yahoo! Labs
Santa Clara, CA
{rzhang,zguo}@yahoo-inc.com

ABSTRACT

With the development of Web applications, large scale data are popular; and they are not only getting richer, but also ubiquitously interconnected with users and other objects in various ways, which brings about multi-view data with implicit structure. In this paper, we propose a novel hierarchical Bayesian mixture regression model, which discovers and then exploits the relationships among multiple views of the data to perform various machine learning tasks. A stochastic EM inference and learning algorithm is derived; and a parallell implementation in Hadoop MapReduce [9] paradigm is developed to scale up the learning. We apply the developed model and algorithm on click-through-rate (CTR) prediction and campaign targeting recommendation in online advertising to measure its effectiveness. The experiments on both synthetic data and large scale ads serving data from a real world online advertising exchange demonstrate the superior CTR prediction accuracy of our method compared to existing state-of-the-art methods. The results also show that our model can recommend high performance targeting features for online advertising campaigns.

Categories and Subject Descriptors

I.2.6 [**Artificial Intelligence**]: Learning; G.3 [**Probability and Statistics**]:

General Terms

Algorithms

Keywords

Hierarchical Bayesian Regression, Online Advertising

1. INTRODUCTION

Many kinds of data, such as web pages, academic papers, and online videos, have the characteristic of multi-views. For example, papers can be described by their textual content in one view. On the other hand, each paper can also be described by its author(s) and institution(s), which is another view. Similarly, online videos can be described by their content-based features, such as visual features in one view (denoted as *content view*), as well as their metadata(e.g. categories, publishers, tags etc) in another view (*meta view*). In most existing work, the attributes from the additional views are either ignored or are appended as additional features for data, which fails to discover and exploit the implicit structures among objects across multiple views. The implicit structure, when discovered with fidelity, can be very useful for different objectives in data mining tasks, such as classification or regression. Thus, it is important to develop models which can holistically leverage the different views in the data, such as content view and meta view, to boost classification or regression performance.

In this paper, we propose a novel hierarchical Bayesian mixture regression (HBMR) model to discover and exploit the interactions of multi-views of the data. The motivating application for our work is user response prediction and targeting recommendation in online advertising. In display advertising, display ad instances are shown to users on web pages in different formats such as image, flash, and video. Each display ad instance is called a creative and it belongs to one advertising campaign. Each campaign is associated with a list of targeting attributes from different aspects such as users, publishers etc., which specifies the targeted audience/webpage this campaign is intended to be shown to. For example, one campaign can target users of (gender:male, age: 20-26, location: Chicago, IL, behavior: consumer electronics fan) and target the creative venues to (publisher: tech.yahoo.com OR publisher: techcrunch.com). The number of possible targeting attribute combinations for each campaign is huge, and it is a challenging task to determine the optimal targeting in terms of advertiser desired performance metrics. Each creative impression is a high dimensional sample which contains the information from the user, the publisher, and the creative itself, as well as whether there is a user action (e.g., click) on the impression. In our context setting of creative impression data, these content features belong to content view, while the campaign related meta information is regarded as meta view.

By showing the creatives to users, advertisers aim to either promote brand awareness among users (brand advertising) or receive desirable responses from users (performance advertising), such as clicks on the advertisements (ads). In performance advertising, advertisers strive to optimize their campaign's performance metrics such as the effective cost per click (eCPC), which in turn relates to maximizing the

CIKM'12, October 29–November 2, 2012, Maui, HI, USA.

user response rate on the creatives as measured by click through rate (CTR). In this application, we have two objectives by applying the developed HBMR model on the ads serve data: 1) CTR prediction for a given campaign. 2) targeting attributes recommendation for campaigns to maximize their CTR.

For all the creative impressions, there are shared clustering patterns for the co-occurrence of targeting attribute features (e.g. geological regions, publishers, user segments) across all the advertising campaigns. We propose to learn those patterns by modeling both content view and meta view within the Bayesian framework. The intuition is that different creative impressions are generated from clustering patterns according to content view. The ads click is a rare event and CTR is regarded as a logistic regression signal from interactions of feature clusters (in content view) and campaign structures (meta view). The regressors for CTR are shared with different feature clusters and campaigns. Based on the clustering pattern discovered in content view, we obtain a cluster-specific regressors CTR prediction. In the mean time, from meta view of the data, campaign-specific regressors under each cluster are modeled explicitly to capture the relationship between campaign and the cluster patterns since impressions belonging to campaigns share different cluster patterns. Specifically, the contribution of this paper is four-fold:

1. The proposed multiview HBMR model is novel in the sense that it is a combination of generative and discriminative models in hierarchical Bayesian settings. It can learn the cluster patterns in content view as well as explore the implicit hierarchical structures with which meta view and content view features are coupled. Moreover, HRBM model is not only able to do regression/prediction, but also able to reveal important features for feature selection.

2. We develop a stochastic (Monte Carlo) EM based inference and learning algorithm for HBMR model to sample cluster states by applying Gibbs Sampling and MAP estimate of the regressors. To make the inference and learning algorithm scalable to real world data size, we develop a parallelized and distributed implementation in Map-Reduce [9, 5] framework on Hadoop.

3. The experiments of applying the model and the algorithm on CTR prediction and campaign targeting recommendation in online advertising, on both synthetic data and large scale ads serving data from a real world online advertising exchange, demonstrate the superior CTR prediction accuracy of our method compared to existing state-of-the-art methods. The results also show that the learned model can generate high performance targeting features for advertising campaign recommendation.

The rest of the paper is organized as follows. After discussion of the related work in Section 2, we introduce the HBMR model in Section 3. The derived stochastic EM based inference and learning algorithm is presented in Section 4. In Section 5 the developed Map-Reduce implementation of the learning algorithm is described. The experimental results for CTR prediction and campaign targeting recommendation in online advertising, as well as the discussion on convergence and efficiency of the Map-Reduce implementation, are discussed in Section 6. Finally, we conclude the paper with future work in Section 7.

2. RELATED WORK

Multi-view learning is originally introduced in [3], where Blum et al. propose a co-training method in bootstrap style by incrementally labeling unlabeled samples with high confidence by weak classifiers trained from different views of data. Conditional independence or weak dependence among multi-views given labels would be essential for better performance. Yu et al. [22] propose a Bayesian undirected graphical model for semi-supervised multi-view learning. Motivated by the insights from graphical model, a novel co-training kernel is developed for Gaussian process classifiers by using side information. However, the different views considered in their work are assumed to be flat structured and consensus potential is able to be logically decoupled, which are not valid in most real world data set. The content and meta views in our problem are coupled in more complicate way and are correlated with implicit hierarchical structure within each view. As it is challenging to ensemble content and meta views, our motivation is to capture the implicit structures among and within multi-views for modeling to achieve better classification or regression performance. Another difference is that our proposed model is not motivated for semi-supervised learning, instead it tries to exploit the prediction and recommendation of our tasks with labeled training samples more naturally and effectively.

For CTR prediction in online advertising system, there are a number of existing work. Chakrabarti et al. [4] proposes regularized logistic regression model with words from pages and ads augmenting ad-page relevance for contextual advertising. Richardson et al. [17] presents a logistic regression using features of ads, terms, and advertisers to predict CTR for new ads without history. Graepel et al. [12] describes a Bayesian CTR prediction algorithm based on probit regression model that maps features to probabilities. An approximated parallel inference is derived for large scale CTR prediction. However, clustering patterns and structures of certain features in the data are not explicitly modeled in their previous work. We will show that discovering and exploiting those patterns will improve CTR prediction. In addition, in our CTR prediction problem the advertiser campaign hierarchy is explicitly introduced in our model, which is not addressed in previous work.

The HBMR model is very general. It can be reduced into Dirichlet Process mixtures of generalized linear models [14] if there is only one object in meta view with one level of regressors and use generalized linear regression instead of logistic regression in our model. And it would reduce into Dirichlet Process multinomial logistic models [19] if we have only one object in meta view and binomial logistic response specified in the model. We note that HBMR model can find its applications in many problems with multi view data, CTR prediction and campaign targe ting recommendation presented in this paper are application instances. For different problems, specific distributions may be assumed but same HBMR model structure can be applied. One example is to predict whether a user likes particular articles in blogs or news. Here user meta data (demographic, interest etc) are the meta view, and each of his/her reply post and blogs or news (bag of words) are the content view. Users share

Figure 1: Graphical Representation for Hierarchical Bayesian Mixture Regression Model

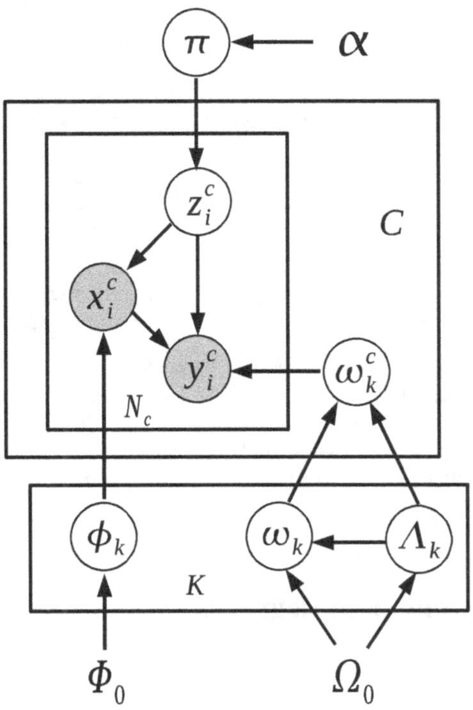

different topics (clusters) of bag of words features in corpus and a specific user's preference for a specific blogs or news is treated as regression response based on the user and topic specific regressors. In this setting, HBMR model fits very well and can be applied to the problem successfully.

3. HIERARCHICAL BAYESIAN MIXTURE REGRESSION MODEL (HBMR)

We use the online advertising problem as an instance to illustrate the formulation of multi-view hierarchical Bayesian mixture regression model. The content view in this problem contains feature vector x_i^c and response (click) y_i^c for each impression under campaign c; the meta view contains campaign identity. Here, meta view and content view are coupled together. Impression sample x_i^c of content view is generated from mixture model under possible clustering patterns; meta view also has influence on the clustering patterns (e.g., different campaigns have different prior CTR). Therefore, a random regressor ω_k^c is introduced to connect the response y_i^c in content view and campaign identity in meta view. For general content and meta view problems, the similar model can be applied that random variables are created to model the relationships between features in different views with appropriate distribution assumption made under specific problem formulation.

Figure 1 shows the graphical representation of the HBMR model. In the figure, each creative impression from a specific campaign is a high dimensional binary feature vector x_i^c. Each component of x_i^c denotes whether a user or publisher attribute (e.g., user age falls to bin 15-20, geological location=Washington DC, web site=tech.yahoo.com) is true or false. The feature vector is very sparse. This sample is generated from an underlying distribution F with cluster-specific parameter ϕ_k. A prior is put on this parameter from a base distribution G. We denote Φ_0 as the hyper-parameter for G. Distributions F and G depend on the specific problem and we can choose conjugate distributions for the purpose of easy computation. For data with numerical features such as the synthetic data used in our experiments, F is modeled as Gaussian distribution, thus parameters ϕ_k include mean and precision matrix. Accordingly G is modeled as Gaussian-Wishart distribution, and $\Phi_0 = \{\mu_0, \Sigma_0\}$ are its hyper-parameters. For multiview data with discrete features, such as the creative impression data in our problem or bag of words data in blog/news recommendation, F will be multinomial distribution, and G is Dirichlet distribution. $\Phi_0 = \{\beta_0\}$ is the hyper-parameter for Dirichlet distribution as $\boldsymbol{\phi} = \{\phi_k\}$ and $\phi_k \sim G(\beta_0)$.

For infinite (arbitrary) number of clusters, we may put the Dirichlet Process prior and construct an infinite mixture model for creative impression samples. The mixture proportions $\boldsymbol{\pi} \sim GEM(\alpha)$ is constructed from the stick breaking process [18],

$$\boldsymbol{\pi} = (\pi_k)_{k=1}^{\infty} \quad \pi_k = \pi_k{}' \prod_{l=1}^{k-1}(1 - \pi_l{}') \quad \pi_k{}' \sim \beta(1, \alpha)$$

Then we sample the cluster indicator z_i^c for impression i of campaign c, x_i^c from a multinomial $z_i^c \sim Mult(\boldsymbol{\pi})$. Once we know which cluster impression x_i^c is from, we have $x_i^c \sim F(\phi_{z_i^c})$. The click y_i^c is a response of the feature sample x_i^c. We adopt logistic regression to model their interactions in HBMR, but other regression model can also be used. One important observation is that click behavior also depends on latent clusters of features (e.g., user regions, publisher websites) which capture the intrinsic factors, as well as advertising campaign which describe the creative information. Based on this motivation, we develop a hierarchical structure for the regressors under different cluster and in different campaigns to explicitly model the interactions among those variables. Specifically, random variable ω_k is introduced to be the cluster-specific regressor for cluster k, and Λ_k is the corresponding precision matrix. Again, the Gaussian-Wishart prior is placed on them. Then the campaign specific regressor ω_k^c is a Gaussian sample with mean from the corresponding cluster specific regressor ω_k and precision matrix Λ_k

$$\omega_k^c \sim \mathcal{N}(\omega_k, (\Lambda_k)^{-1})$$

and conjugate prior is

$$\Lambda_k \sim \mathcal{W}(\nu_k, W_k) \quad \omega_k \sim \mathcal{N}(\mu_k, (\kappa_k \Lambda_k)^{-1})$$

Here, Λ_k is the Wishart distribution with ν_k degrees of freedom and $d \times d$ matrix W_k,

$$\mathcal{W}(\Lambda_k | \nu_k, W_k) \propto \det(\Lambda_k)^{\frac{\mu_k - d - 1}{2}} \exp\{-\frac{1}{2} Tr(W_k^{-1} \Lambda_k)\}$$

$\Omega_0 = \{\Omega_{k0} : \Omega_{k0} = \{\nu_k, \kappa_k, \mu_k, W_k\}\}$ is the hyper-parameters for the prior Gaussian-Wishart distribution of Ω_K; $\Omega_K = \{\Omega_k : \Omega_k = \{\omega_k, \Lambda_k\}\}$ is the means and precision matrices for all the cluster regressors; $\Omega_C = \{\Omega_c : \Omega_c = \{\omega_k^c\}_k\}$ is the set of campaign regressors under all clusters.

As logistic regression of y_i^c implies, CTR of an impression i in campaign c is the sigmoid function of impression features and campaign specific regressor learned from feature clusters:

$$ctr_i^c = p(y_i^c = 1|x_i^c, z_i^c) = \sigma(< x_i^c, \omega_{z_i^c}^c >) \tag{1}$$

where $\sigma(x) = 1/(1 + exp(-x))$ and $<>$ is inner product.

Finally, the click (or not) signal y_i^c is a Bernoulli sample from its CTR ctr_i^c.

$$y_i^c \sim bernoulli(ctr_i^c)$$

For each campaign c, the joint distribution of impressions $\{x_i^c\}$, clicks $\{y_i^c\}$ and hidden cluster indicator $\{z_i^c\}$ under parameters is derived by integrating out π,

$$p(\{x_i^c\}, \{y_i^c\}, \{z_i^c\}|\phi, \Omega_c, \alpha) = \prod_{i\in c} p(x_i^c|z_i^c, \phi)p(y_i^c|x_i^c, z_i^c, \Omega_c)p(z_i^c|\alpha) \tag{2}$$

For all the campaigns, the joint distribution of impressions X, clicks Y, and hidden cluster indicators Z under hyper-parameters can be calculated as,

$$p(X, Y, Z|\Omega_0, \Phi_0, \alpha) = \prod_c \{p(\{x_i^c\}, \{y_i^c\}, \{z_i^c\}|\phi, \Omega_c, \alpha)\}$$

$$\prod_k \{p(\phi_k|\Phi_0)p(\omega_k, \Lambda_k|\Omega_0)\} \prod_c \prod_k \{p(\omega_k^c|\omega_k, \Lambda_k)\} \tag{3}$$

4. INFERENCE AND LEARNING

In generative components of HBMR model, we need to sample the cluster state z_i^c for each impression i belonging to campaign c, and cluster-specific regression coefficients ω_k. In addition, regression coefficients ω_k^c for each cluster k in each campaign c need to be decided as well. We derive a stochastic Expectation-Maximization based inference and learning algorithm for our model. Following subsections describe the algorithm in detail.

4.1 Cluster States Z

To get cluster states for all impressions in all campaigns, we utilize Gibbs Sampling method. Gibbs Sampling is used to get the posterior states by cycling through the latent variables, sampling each from posterior distribution conditioned on other variables.

$$p(z_i^c = k|Z_{-(i,c)}, X_{-(i,c)}, Y_{-(i,c)}, x_i^c, y_i^c, \Phi_0, \Omega_C, \alpha) \propto$$
$$p(z_i^c = k|Z_{-(i,c)}, \alpha)p(x_i^c|z_i^c = k, X_{-(i,c)})p(y_i^c|x_i^c, \omega_k^c, z_i^c = k) \tag{4}$$

here, $X_{-(i,c)}$ is the data set with all impressions in all campaigns excluding the current impression x_i^c; $Y_{-(i,c)}$ is defined similarly for response variable y_i^c.

The conditional distribution for latent cluster variable z_i^c is from Chinese Restaurant Process [1]:

$$p(z_i^c = k|Z_{-(i,c)}, \alpha) = \begin{cases} \frac{n_k^c}{n_c-1+\alpha} & k \leq K \\ \frac{\alpha}{n_c-1+\alpha} & k = K+1 \end{cases}$$

where $n_k^c = \sum_{j\in c} 1(z_j^c = k)$ is the count of impressions in campaign c assigned to cluster k, and $n_c = \sum_{j\in c} 1(x_j^c)$ is the count of impressions in campaign c.

As distribution F and G are conjugate, we are able to integrate out cluster component parameters ϕ to get the predictive likelihood for x_i^c under cluster k.

$$p(x_i^c|z_i^c = k, X_{-(i,c)}) = \frac{p(x_i^c, X_{-(i,c)}|z_i^c = k)}{p(X_{-(i,c)}|z_i^c = k)}$$
$$= \frac{\int p(x_i^c|\phi_k) \prod_{z_j^c=k, j\neq i} p(x_j^c|\phi_k)p(\phi_k|\Phi_0)d\phi_k}{\int \prod_{z_j^c=k, j\neq i} p(x_j^c|\phi_k)p(\phi_k|\Phi_0)d\phi_k}$$

The integration has analytical solutions by conjugacy of prior and posterior. For Multinomial Dirichlet conjugacy, we have

$$p(x_i^c|z_i^c = k, X_{-(i,c)}) = \frac{B(\beta_k^* + x_i^c)}{B(\beta_k^*)}$$

And $B(\beta_k^*) = \frac{\prod_j \Gamma(\beta_{k,j}^*)}{\Gamma(\sum_j \beta_{k,j}^*)}$ is the normalizing constant for Dirichlet distribution, $\beta_k^* = \sum_{z_j^c=k} x_j^c + \beta_0$ is the updated parameter for posterior Dirichlet distribution. For unrepresented cluster $k = K+1$, $\beta_k = \beta_0$ as we have no observations for it. In experiments, we set $\beta_0 = 0.1 \times \mathbf{1}(d, 1)$ and d is the dimension of impression feature vectors.

The click y_i^c is simply Bernoulli distributed from logistic signal:

$$p(y_i^c|x_i^c, \omega_k^c, z_i^c = k) = \sigma(< x_i^c, \omega_k^c >)^{y_i^c}(1 - \sigma(< x_i^c, \omega_k^c >))^{1-y_i^c}$$

4.2 Campaign Regressors Ω_C

The posterior distribution for regressor ω_k^c of cluster k in campaign c is,

$$p(\omega_k^c|\{x_i^c\}, \{y_i^c\}, \{z_i^c\}, \omega_k, \Lambda_k) = p(\omega_k^c|\omega_k, \Lambda_k) \prod_{i\in c} p(y_i^c|x_i^c, \omega_k^c, z_i^c = k) \tag{5}$$

The posterior is the product of Gaussian and logistic function. We can Laplace approximate [2] it as a Gaussian with mean the MAP (maximum posterior) estimate of ω_k^c and precision matrix the second derivatives of the negative log likelihood

$$\omega_k^c \sim \mathcal{N}(\omega_k^c(MAP), (A_k^c)^{-1})$$
$$A_k^c = -\nabla\nabla \log p(\omega_k^c|\{x_i^c\}, \{y_i^c\}, \{z_i^c\}, \omega_k, \Lambda_k)$$

As in our CTR prediction problem, we have millions of samples and the variance would be reasonably small, thus the approximated Gaussian would be peaked. Thus in our experiment implementation we calculate ω_k^c from MAP estimation instead of sampling ω_k^c from $\mathcal{N}(\omega_k^c(MAP), (A_k^c)^{-1})$.

Maximizing Eq. 5 w.r.t ω_k^c to obtain MAP estimate is equivalent to $L2$ regularized logistic regression, we use iterative reweighed least squares (IRLS) method [13] to solve it. Newton-Raphson [8] method is adopted in the algorithm

$$\omega_k^c(new) = \omega_k^c(old) - (H_k^c)^{-1}\nabla E_k^c \tag{6}$$

where H_k^c is the Hessian matrix and E_k^c is the gradient for all samples of cluster k in campaign c.

$$\nabla E_k^c = \Lambda_k(\omega_k^c - \omega_k) + \sum_{z_i^c=k} (\delta_i^c - y_i^c)x_i^c$$
$$H_k^c = \Lambda_k + \sum_{z_i^c=k} \delta_i^c(1 - \delta_i^c)x_i^c x_i^{c\prime}$$

where $\delta_i^c = \delta(< x_i^c, \omega_k^c >)$ and $\delta(x) = 1/(1 + \exp(-x))$.

4.3 Cluster-Specific Regressors

In the model cluster-specific regressors $\{\omega_k\}$ and precision matrices $\{\Lambda_k\}$ are parameters for campaign regressors Ω_C. The prior for parameters $\Omega_K = \{\Omega_k : \Omega_k = \{\omega_k, \Lambda_k\}\}$ is from Gaussian-Wishart distribution,

$$p(\Omega_k|\Omega_{k0}) = \mathcal{N}(\omega_k|\mu_k, (\kappa_k\Lambda_k)^{-1})\mathcal{W}(\Lambda_k|\nu_k, W_k)$$

Once we have Gaussian "observations" Ω_C, we can obtain posterior Gaussian-Wishart as

$$p(\Omega_k|\Omega_{k0}, \Omega_C) = \mathcal{N}(\omega_k|\mu_k^*, (\kappa_k^*\Lambda_k^*)^{-1})\mathcal{W}(\Lambda_k|\nu_k^*, W_k^*) \quad (7)$$

The updated hyper-parameters Ω_0 can be derived using the method from [10] as follows,

$$\mu_k^* = \frac{\kappa_k^*\mu_k + C\bar{\omega}_k}{\kappa_k^* + C} \quad \kappa_k^* = \kappa_k + C \quad \nu_k^* = \nu_k + C$$

$$[W_k^*]^{-1} = [W_k]^{-1} + C\bar{S}_k + \frac{\kappa_k C}{\kappa_k + C}(\mu_k - \bar{\omega}_k)(\mu_k - \bar{\omega}_k)'$$

$$\bar{\omega}_k = \frac{1}{C}\sum_c \omega_k^c \quad \bar{S}_k = \frac{1}{C}\sum_c \omega_k^c\omega_k^{c\prime}$$

In our experiments, we set all $\mu_k = \mathbf{0}$, $\nu_k = d$, $\kappa_k = 1$, and $W_k = \boldsymbol{I}$.

Based on posterior Gaussian-Wishart distribution, we sample ω_k and Λ_k which are used in the *MAP* estimation of ω_k^c.

4.4 Stochastic EM (Expectation-Maximization) Algorithm

The inference and learning for Z, Ω_C and Ω_K in HBMR model is developed in a stochastic EM [16] (Monte Carlo EM [20])framework. Specifically, in E-Step we sample cluster states Z by Gibbs Sampling. In M-Step, we estimate the *MAP* of campaign regressors Ω_C based on the current states Z and cluster-specific regressors and precision matrices Ω_K. After that, cluster-specific regressors $\{\omega_k\}$ and precision matrices $\{\Lambda_k\}$ are sampled from updated posterior distribution of Gaussian-Wishart. An important hyper-parameter needed to be learned is the concentration parameter α for Dirichlet Process [7]. We adopt the method from Escobar and West [6]; they proposed a gamma prior and derived an auxiliary variable update for α. This estimation is used in synthetic data; in real online advertising data, we just fix $\alpha = \frac{0.1}{K}$ as we truncate Dirichlet Process.

Algorithm 1 Map-Reduce implementation of inference and learning for HBMR

for each stochastic EM iteration
loop
JobE, do Gibbs Sampling for posterior states Z of $P(Z|\Omega_C, X, Y)$
JobM, do *MAP* estimation of regressors Ω_C from $P(\Omega_C|X, Y, \Omega_K, Z)$
Update posterior hyper-parameters and sample Ω_K from $P(\Omega_K|\Omega_C, \Omega_0)$.
end loop

5. MAP-REDUCE IMPLEMENTATION

With millions or even billions of creative impressions and clicks generated every day in online advertising exchange, it's important to make the inference and learning algorithm for HBRM be able to scale up to real world data set size. To achieve this objective, we want to parallelize the algorithm so it can leverage distributed computing platform such as Hadoop Map-Reduce [9] for large scale data modeling.

Map-Reduce is a software development framework for developing applications which need processing of vast amounts of data in-parallel on large clusters of commodity hardware in a reliable, fault-tolerant manner. In the framework each Hadoop job has two interfaces, Mapper and Reducer, which are needed to be implemented for the desired logical functions. In the Hadoop job, the input dataset is split into independent chunks. Each chunk is processed by a Mapper task in parallel. The Mapper filters input key and value into output key and value. Then values are shuffled, combined and sorted to feed into the specific Reducer task according to the output key. In each Reducer, it processes a list of values with the same key and emits new key and value pairs line by line. Multiple Reducers on different key indexed data can be run simultaneously on different nodes.

In our Map-Reduce implementation, We construct two Hadoop jobs for each EM iteration in the algorithm, JobE for E-Step and JobM for M-Step. The algorithm architecture is shown in Algorithm 1.

JobE is mainly responsible for Gibbs Sampling of the cluster states. In the mapper of JobE, all the data including impressions and clicks (each impression represented as a *line* with a key *lineID*) are loaded and randomly split into reasonable number of data partitions with *randkey* as index.

<lineID, line> -> Mapper -> <randkey, line>

Then, all the lines with the same *randkey* are aggregated into a list during shuffle (or combiner) stage. In the Reducer, Gibbs Sampling is carried on for each of the individual partition fed together with model parameters. The reducer emits each *line* with the new output key as combination of cluster ID k and campaign ID c.

<randkey, list<line> > -> Reducer -> <(k,c), line >

This idea is similar to ADLDA [15]. The dependency between different impressions and clicks in different partitions are weak. As each partition has sufficient number of samples this approximated Gibbs Sampling would be quite accurate.

In JobM, *MAP* of campaign regressors ω_k^c is estimated by iterations of Newton-Raphson [8]. In more detail, impressions and clicks along with their computed cluster states from the output of JobE are loaded and filtered by identity mapper

<(k,c), line> -> Mapper -> <(k,c), line >

All samples (lines) with the same key (cluster and campaign IDs) would be aggregated together into a list of lines in shuffle (or combiner) stage. In each Reducer, Newton-Raphson is adopted to calculate *MAP* estimation based on all the corresponding samples (impressions and clicks) indexed by the same key.

<(k,c), list<line> > -> Reducer -> <(k,c), (ω_k^c, n_k^c) *>*

After JobM, we update the hyper-parameters Ω_0 based on Ω_C from all the Reducers of JobM. Then regressor parameters Ω_K are sampled from Gaussian-Wishart posterior distribution with updated hyper-parameters. A schematic view of the logical functions of Mapper and Reducer of JobE and JobM is shown by Algorithm 2.

As we have large scale samples of impressions and clicks in the data, IO operations (data loading, replication, and saving) would be very expensive. By far, Hadoop Map-Reduce framework is not efficient to work with iterative machine learning algorithms such as our stochastic EM because each iteration of computations in the algorithm needs to access all the data samples. If in JobE and JobM, we only take one iteartion to do computations (Gibbs Sampling or Newton method), the states of samples would mix poorly; the parameters would be poorly estimated and the outer loop of JobE and JobM would be very long. Consequently, the IO overhead across Hadoop jobs takes a large portion of overall running time in comparison with the computational expense needed by Gibbs Sampling and Newton-Raphson. To alleviate the expensive IO overhead, we run many iterations of Gibbs Sampling and Newton-Raphson in each iteration of JobE and JobM. With more iterations of computations within each pass of Stochastic EM Algorithm 2, two benefits are obtained: 1) the IO expense becomes relative smaller compared to the computational expense, and 2) we have more mixed cluster states and accurate parameters estimated.

One technical detail worth pointing out is that we use Distributed-Cache mechanism in Hadoop to store and pass model parameters between multiple jobs. Distributed-Cache is a facility in Hadoop to cache files (text, archives, jars and so on) needed by applications. In JobE, we load old regressors Ω_C from Distributed-Cache passed from previous JobM, and in JobM we save Ω_C into Distributed-Cache for further use. Other parameters such as Ω_0 and statistics n_k^c, n_c are similarly stored and passed through Distributed-Cache.

A challenging problem in the implementation on Hadoop is how to parallel Gibbs Sampling with arbitrary varying number of clusters. There are related works for parallelizing Gibbs Sampling for unstructured Graphical Models ([21, 11]); however, it is still difficult to handle the suitations when the number of variables are changing over time. For example, samples are split into different computing nodes and the Gibbs Sampling are running on each node. If old clusters are churning and new clusters are emerging on different nodes, we will no longer be able to track the exact correspondence of clusters between different computing nodes. Thus, for simplicity, we fix the number of clusters; although fully parallel Gibbs Sampling for varying number of variables in Graphical Models would be more accurate and need further investigation. This approximated truncation of Dirichlet Process in the implementation is simple yet effective.

Algorithm 2 Mapper and Reducer in JobE and JobM

JobE Mapper
for each sample, generate a rand key.
JobE Reducer
for all samples indexed by the same rand key, do Gibbs Sampling(Eq. 4) to get the cluster ID; and generate the output key combined with campaign ID for each sample.
JobM Mapper
Identity Mapper, pass outputs of JobE to inputs of JobM.
JobM Reducer
for samples indexed by cluster and campaign ID, do MAP (Eq. 6) estimation of parameters ω_k^c and get statistics n_k^c.

6. EXPERIMENTAL RESULTS

HBMR is a general probabilistic model to incorporate the multi-view asepcts of data. We investigate two important applications: CTR prediction and targeting attributes recommendation in the online advertising.

6.1 CTR Prediction

Click-through rate (CTR) is the click probability when ads are shown to users, and it measures the ads performance from users experience. Since HBMR directly models the click behavior, CTR can be computed from the learned model. The whole dataset are randomly splitted into training data $D_{train} = \{x_i^c, y_i^c\}_{train}$ and test data D_{test}. Given the model learned from the training data, CTR prediction for testing data item x_i^c is,

$$p(y_i^c = 1|x_i^c, D_{train}, \Omega_C) = \frac{p(y_i^c = 1, x_i^c|D_{train}, \Omega_C)}{\sum_{y_i^c \in \{0,1\}} p(y_i^c, x_i^c|D_{train}, \Omega_C)} \quad (8)$$

$$p(y_i^c, x_i^c|D_{train}, \Omega_C) = \sum_k p(z_i^c = k|D_{train}) p(x_i^c|z_i^c = k, D_{train}) p(y_i^c|x_i^c, z_i^c = k, \Omega_C)$$

$$\approx \sum_k \frac{n_k^c}{n_c} \frac{B(\beta_k^* + x_i^c)}{B(\beta_k^*)} \delta_i^c \quad (9)$$

where ω_k^c (in Ω_C) is the regression coefficients for campaign c in cluster k, n_k^c and n_c are the number of samples in different campaigns and clusters, and β_k^* is the posterior estimation of hyper-parameter for cluster k.

Note that one posterior sample of parameters (Ω_C, $\{\beta_k^*\}$) and statistics is used in Eq. (8) . To reduce the prediction variance, we might get several posterior samples of parameters and statistics after burn in of stochastic EM to calculate CTR prediction for test data.

6.2 Targeting Attributes Recommendation

Based on the count statistics inferred and parameters learned from training data, we are able to find suitable feature bits for each campaign x^c by optimizing objective function such as CTR in Eq. (8).

$$x^c = argmax_{x^c \in \{0,1\}^d} p(y^c = 1|x^c, D_{train}, \Omega_k) \quad (10)$$

The solution to Eq. (10) has specific feature bits turned on and we then rank these bits according to their weighted average of coefficient weights $\hat{\omega^c} = \sum_k \frac{n_k^c}{n_c} \omega_k^c$.

Based on the weight vector $\hat{\omega^c}$, the important targeting attributes with high weight can be recommended to advertisers such that advertisers are able to adjust the targeting profile accordingly. The improvement of ads performance (e.g., CTR) is expected with the adjusted targeting profile. On the other hand, it is necessary to evaluate the quality of the recommendation beforehand such that advertisers have better understanding of benefits that the adjusted targeting profile will bring.

If we exclude the impressions with one specific targeting attribute (e.g. gender female), we calculate CTR based on the corresponding data subset (e.g. without considering gender female). This CTR measures the importance of the specific targeting attribute (e.g. gender male) and is denoted as tCTR. If tCTR for specific targeting attribute is higher than the overall CTR from the overall data set, intuitively

Figure 2: CTR predictions comparison on Synthetic Data Set

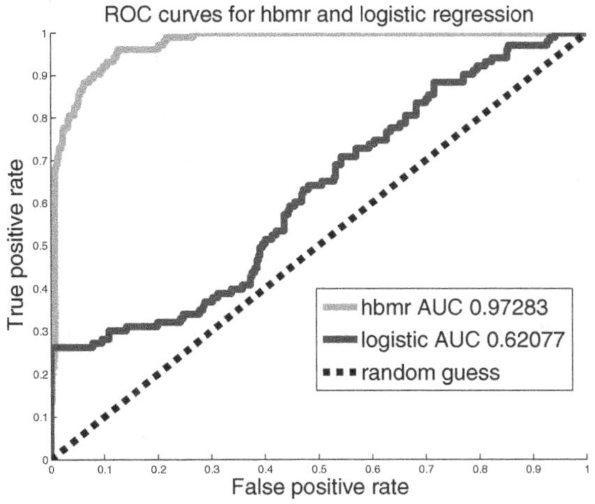

this targeting attribute is important and it should be recommended. Based on the learned model, the targeting attributes are ranked in descending order of weight, and the percentage of targeting attributes with higher tCTR than the overall CTR in the top positions (e.g., top 200) are calculated as ptCTR.

The metric ptCTR measures the consistency between the weight vector $\hat{\omega^c}$ and tCTR. However, ptCTR cannot measure how good the ranking of the targeting attributes with high tCTR. Inspired by normalized discounted cumulative gain (nDCG) in information retrieval, we propose the $nDCG_{ctr}$ metric defined as follows.

$$DCG_{ctr} = \sum_{i=1}^{p} \frac{2^{tCTR_i} - 1}{log_2(1+i)}, \quad nDCG_{ctr} = \frac{DCG_{ctr}}{IDCG_{ctr}}$$

where i denotes the position of targeting attributes in the descending order of learned weights and IDCG is the DCG score for perfect ranking where the order of tCTR is exactly the same as the order of learned weight in the HBMR model. $nDCG_{ctr}$ provides more reliable and accurate measurement for the consistency between the weight vector $\hat{\omega^c}$ and tCTR than ptCTR.

6.3 Experimental Evaluations

6.3.1 CTR Prediction on Synthetic Dataset

We generated 1000 data items (feature samples and responses), where each feature sample is from the mixture of two-dimensional gaussian distributions and each response is generated from logistic regression based on the corresponding feature sample and cluster-specific coefficient weights. As this is a relative small data set, our learning and inference algorithms are able to handle complex Dirichlet Process Prior and run with arbitrary number of clusterings. In the experiment, the number of campaign is set to be 1 since there is no concept of campaign in this simple data set. Thus, our HBMR model reduces to Dirichlet Process Mixture of Generalized linear model with L2 regularized logistic regression.

Figure 2 shows the CTR prediction performance comparison between our HBMR model and logistic regression using Eq. (8). HBMR achieves noticeable better prediction with AUC 0.97283 because the synthetic data has obvious clustering patterns with different underlying gaussian distributions and cluster-specific coefficient weights.

6.3.2 Exmperiments on RightMedia Ads Exchange

We apply our method to the world's largest performance ads exchange system, RightMedia, and conduct evaluation with real online event log data and advertising campaigns. In RightMedia's daily ads serving, the information of both publisher and user are logged. Users are anonymized to hide personal identifiable information. Those information are our features for model fitting. We sampled ads impressions from RightMedia's ads serving logs for the experiment. The data set has about 25 million impressions and clicks from 13 campaigns with more than 2GB storage. Each impression is a high dimensional sparse sample.

We pick region ID and publisher ID features as our targeting attributes; the original sample dimensionality is about 4000; each dimension is a binary feature bit. In order to speed up learning and inference while still preserving sufficient important feature bits; we plot the frequency histogram of these two attributes and pick about 300 region IDs and 500 publisher IDs to reduce the dimensionality. As there is the power law distribution of region IDs and publisher IDs; for top 300 regions and 500 publishers, we preserve about more than 96% and 98% samples.

Figure 3 illustrates the CTR prediction performance comparison between HBMR with number of clusters 10 and 50 and logistic regression on real media data set. Since there is no "campaign" conception in logistic regression, we run each logistic regression for all the impressions and clicks for each campaign. HBMR has better prediction with AUC 0.92699 for $K = 10$ and 0.9107 for $K = 50$ while AUC is 0.89609 for logistic regression. Here, the number of clusters is sensitive to performance of our HBMR. In our impression features, there are clustering patterns such as clustering of regional areas and publisher sites, therefore, the regression is able to take advantage of related impressions from different campaigns to aid the CTR prediction. Another contribution for the better prediction comes from the additional co-occurrence patterns of region and publisher features, which could be considered as extra nonlinear features. However, the performance gain in figure 3 is much lower than the simulation data in figure 2. The possible reason might be our parallel Gibbs Sampling is simply fixed the number of clusters and the number is not accurate enough. Another reason may be related to the semantic meaningful features we picked. Currently, we only consider the regions and publisheres; it is possible there are more significant semantic features such as user segments, creative IDs, channel IDs and so on. However, with introcutions of more higher dimensional features, feature selection and regularization would be needed in our models. Therefore, more further work need to carry on to verify our models and produce better prediction and recommedation performance.

We compare the performance on targeting recommendation between HBMR and logistic regression reported the results in Table 1. The larger values of $nDCG_{ctr}$ and ptCTR indicates that our model HBMR is more consistent with tCTR.

Table 2 lists the top targeting attributes in the publisher targeting for one campaign from the advertiser Netflix and corresponding regressor weights learned by HBMR. By run-

Figure 3: CTR predictions comparison on real Data set

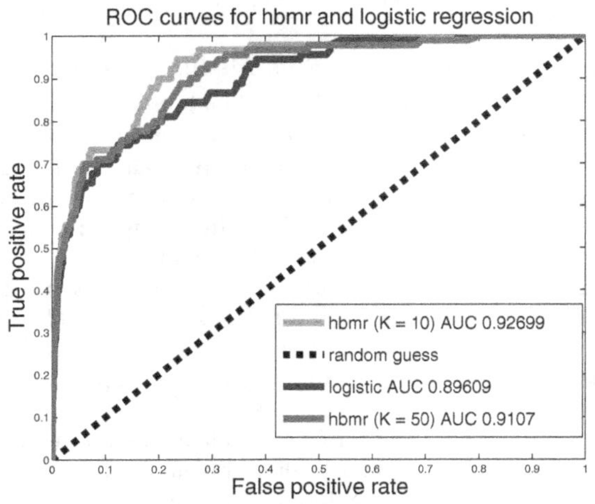

Table 1: Performance comparisons on targeting recommendation

Metrics	HBMR	logistic regression
ptCTR	0.94	0.89
$nDCG_{ctr}$	0.37	0.33

ning this campaign on various publisher sites, the advertiser Netflix promotes its online video service to interested users. The properties of specific publisher site reflects interests of users to some extent and thus significantly affects the campaigns' performance on the publisher site. As shown in the table, most of the top publishers are in the area of entertainment, and are closely related to this online video service campaign from Netflix. Therefore, the users on these publishers should have explicit or implicit interest on the online video service and the good performance of this campaign is expected. In fact, we submit these targeting recommendations to the advertisers who own those campaigns and they found those topics of publisher sites are related to their advertising products. After they take the recommended targeting, the CTR on their creatives are increased in a large margin.

Convergence Analysis

For each EM iteration, we have two MapReduce Jobs; one for E-Step Gibbs Sampling and another for M-Step parameter estimation. We use 30 iterations for Gibbs Sampling in E-Step; and 20 iterations for Newton-Raphson iterations in M-Step.

To study the convergence of Gibbs Sampling and Newton-Raphson method, the experiment results are plotted in Figures 4 and 5. In each node, 30 iterations Gibbs Sampling is enough for mixing; and as Newton-Raphson is quadratic rate of convergence, 20 iteration is enough. Within each EM pass, we have enough iterations to mix the cluster states and estimate the accurate parameters; only several dozens EM passes are needed for the inference and learning over the entire data at all nodes in our experiments. There is a trade-off between number of iterations within Gibbs Sampling and Newton-Raphson of each Job and the number of

Table 2: Top attributes for campaign from Netflix

Targeting Attributes	regressor weight
Movies	4.76
Mail	2.80
Pager	1.96
Entertainment	0.49
Games	0.44
Espanol	0.26
Real Estate	0.18
Health	0.09
Shopping	0.08

Figure 4: log likelihood within E-Step

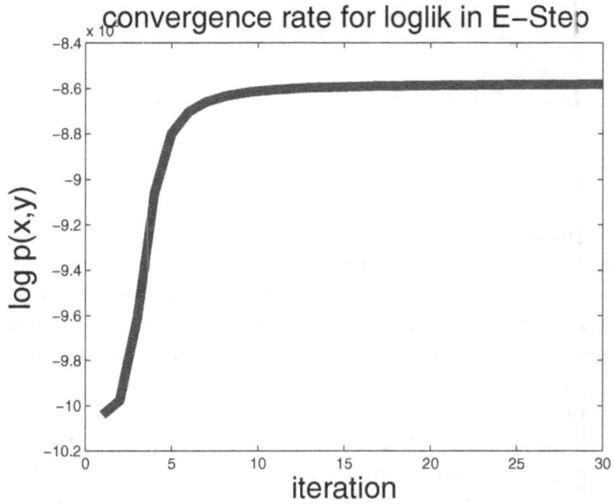

EM Job passes. If we have few iterations of Gibbs Sampling and Newton-Raphson; the states would mix poorly, while we need longer passes of EM Jobs in order to converge to the stationary for Gibbs Sampling and Newton-Raphson. As each Job is quite expensive to load and save so many samples; while the running time for computations (e.g. Gibbs Sampling and Newton-Raphson) would become relative light. Therefore, it would take longer times than our proposed algorithm.

Scalability Analysis

Table 3 reports computation time on two different data sets with about 25 millions and 1 million impressions, respectively. There are 518 targeting attributes and the number of clusters K is fixed at 10. We fixed 30 iterations within each E-Step and 20 iterations within each M-Step with early termination if the norm of difference of two weight vectors in consecutive iterations is less than threshold 0.0001. The fourth and fifth columns are number of mappers and reducers in JobE (E-Step) and JobM (M-Step). The computation cost of E-Step's Gibbs Sampling mainly depends on the number of clusters and number of impressions. MapReduce is able to put the same scale of samples to each node and consequently the running time would be at the same scale with more mappers and reducers for larger data set. The computational complexity for M-Step mainly depends on inverse of 518 × 518 Hessian matrix and number of samples used to calculate gradient and Hessian matrix. The resulting running times for M-Step of two data sets are at the same scale. Thus, for the billions of impressions or even larger data sets, we are able to scale our inference and learning

Figure 5: NewtonRaphson within M-Step

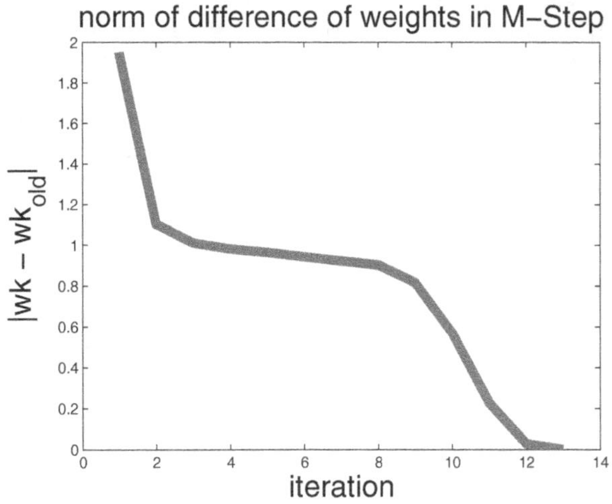

Table 3: Scalability in MapReduce implementation

Data Set	E-Step	M-Step	JE M/R	JM M/R
25M impressions	6'11"	4'14"	5/100	100/20
1M impressions	5'2"	1'8"	2/5	5/5

as long as we have enough number of mappers and reducers. Another important issue needed to be carefully handled is the IO expense (such as loading, passing and saving huge data), which would become relative large compared to computational expense such as Gibbs Sampling and Newton method. The running time would increase with the increasing scale of data set.

7. CONCLUSION AND FURTHER WORK

In this paper, we have proposed Hierarchical Bayesian Mixture Regression model to do CTR prediction and targeting attribute recommendation for online advertising. This multi-view hierarchical Bayesian model is the combination of generative and discriminative model with "campaign-impression" structure; and the graphical model structure is general for a class of similar problems with content and meta views. Compared to logistic regression for each campaign, our model is able to take advantage of side information such as extra co-occurrence features and related samples from different campaigns to do better prediction. We derive stochastic EM to do inference and learning for our model. Our stochastic EM is scalable to tens of millions of impressions in Hadoop MapReduce framework and achieves promising results against logistic regression.

For the further work, we need to scale our model into billions or even larger number of samples. Our model is feature extensible from content view; further investigation need to carry on to test on more different attributes such as user segments, creative IDs, channel IDs, user gender, age and so on. One limitation is the parallel approximation of the Gibbs Sampling with fixed number of clusters. This is still an open question in parallel inference.

8. REFERENCES

[1] D. Aldous. Exchangeability and related topics. *Ecole de Probabilites de Saint-Flour*, (XIII):1–198, 1983.

[2] C. M. Bishop. *Pattern Recognition and Machine Learning*. Springer, 2007.

[3] A. Blum and T. Mitchell. Combining labeled and unlabeled data with co-training. In *International Conference on Machine Learning(ICML)*, pages 92–100. Morgan Kaufmann Publishers, 1998.

[4] D. Chakrabarti, D. Agarwal, and V. Josifovski. Contextual advertising by combining relevance with click feedback. In *In Proceedings of the 16th international conference on World Wide Web*, pages 417–426. ACM Press, 2008.

[5] J. Dean and S. Ghemawat. Mapreduce: Simplified data processing on large clusters. In *USENIX Symposium on Operating Systems Design and Implementation (OSDI)*, pages 137–150, 2004.

[6] M. D. Escobar and M. West. Bayesian density estimation and inference using mixtures. *Journal of the American Statistical Association*, 90:577–588, 1994.

[7] T. S. Ferguson. A bayesian analysis of some nonparametric problems. *The Annals of Statistics*, 1(2):209–230, 1973.

[8] R. Fletcher. *Practical methods of optimization*. John Wiley & Sons, New York, 1987.

[9] A. Foundation. Hadoop mapreduce. `http://hadoop.apache.org/mapreduce/`.

[10] A. Gelman, J. B. Carlin, H. S. Stern, and D. B. Rubin. *Bayesian Data Analysis*. Chapman & Hall/CRC, 2003.

[11] J. Gonzalez, Y. Low, A. Gretton, and C. Guestrin. Parallel gibbs sampling: From colored fields to thin junction trees. In *In Artificial Intelligence and Statistics (AISTATS)*, May 2011.

[12] T. Graepel, J. Q. Candela, T. Borchert, and R. Herbrich. Web-scale bayesian click-through rate prediction for sponsored search advertising in Microsoft's bing search engine. In *The International Conference on Machine Learning (ICML)*, pages 13–20, 2010.

[13] P. J. Green. Iteratively reweighted least squares for maximum likelihood estimation, and some robust and resistant alternatives. *Journal of the Royal Statistical Society. Series B (Methodological)*, 46(2):–, 1984.

[14] L. A. Hannah, D. M. Blei, and W. B. Powell. Dirichlet process mixtures of generalized linear models. In *Proceedings of the 13th International Conference on Artificial Intelligence and Statistics (AISTATS)*, pages –, 2010.

[15] D. Newman, A. Asuncion, P. Smyth, and M. Welling. Distributed inference for latent dirichlet allocation. In *Neural Information Processing Systems (NIPS)*, 2007.

[16] S. F. Nielsen. The stochastic em algorithm: Estimation and asymptotic results. *Bernoulli*, 6(3):457–489, 2000.

[17] M. Richardson, E. Dominowska, and R. Ragno. Predicting clicks: estimating the click-through rate for new ads. In *In Proceedings of the 16th international conference on World Wide Web*, pages 521–530. ACM Press, 2007.

[18] J. Sethuraman. A constructive definition of Dirichlet priors. *Statistica Sinica*, 4:639–650, 1994.

[19] B. Shahbaba and R. M. Neal. Nonlinear models using dirichlet process mixtures. *Journal of Machine Learning Research*, 10:1829–1850, 2009.

[20] G. C. G. Wei and M. A. Tanner. A monte carlo implementation of the em algorithm and the poor man's data augmentation algorithms. *Journal of the American Statistical Association*, 85(411):699–704, 1990.

[21] T. Xu and A. Ihler. Multicore gibbs sampling in dense, unstructured graphs. In *In Artificial Intelligence and Statistics (AISTATS)*, May 2011.

[22] S. Yu, B. Krishnapuram, R. Rosales, H. Steck, and R. B. Rao. Bayesian co-training. In *Neural Information Processing Systems (NIPS)*, 2007.

Visual Appearance of Display Ads and Its Effect on Click Through Rate

Javad Azimi* ◇, Ruofei Zhang†, Yang Zhou†
Vidhya Navalpakkam‡, Jianchang Mao†, Xiaoli Fern◇
◇Oregon State University
†Yahoo! Labs, Silicon Valley
‡Google
{azimi,xfern}@eecs.oregonstate.edu
{rzhang,yangzhou,jmao}@yahoo-inc.com
vidhyan@google.com

ABSTRACT

One of the most important categories of online advertising is *display* advertising which provides publishers with significant revenue. Similar to other categories, the main goal in display advertising is to maximize user response rate for advertising campaigns, such as click through rates (CTR) or conversion rates. Previous studies have tried to optimize these parameters using objectives such as behavioral targeting. However, there is no published work so far to address the effect of the visual appearance of ads (creatives) on user response rate via a systematic data-driven approach. In this paper, we quantitatively study the relationship between the visual appearance and performance of creatives using large scale data in the world's largest display ads exchange system, RightMedia. We designed a set of 43 visual features, some of which are novel and others are inspired by related work. We extracted these features from real creatives served on RightMedia. We also designed and conducted a series of experiments to evaluate the effectiveness of visual features for CTR prediction, ranking and performance classification. Based on the evaluation results, we selected a subset of features that have the highest impact on CTR. We believe that the findings presented in this paper will be very useful for the online advertising industry in designing high-performance creatives. It also provides the research community with the first ever data set, initial insights into visual appearance's effect on user response propensity, and evaluation benchmarks for further study.

Categories and Subject Descriptors

I.4.7 [**Computing Methodologies**]: Image Processing and Computer Vision—*Feature Measurements*

Keywords

Online Advertising, Visual Features, Creative Recommendation

*This work was done while the first author was an Intern at Yahoo! Labs.
‡ This work was done while she was working at Yahoo! Labs.

CIKM'12, October 29–November 2, 2012, Maui, HI, USA.

1. INTRODUCTION

The Internet revolution has transformed how people experience information, media and advertising. Web advertising, although nonexisting twenty years ago, has become a vital component of the modern Internet, where advertisements are delivered from advertisers to users through different online channels. Recent trends have shown that an increasingly large share of advertisers' budgets are devoted to the online world, and online advertising spending has greatly outpaced some of the traditional advertising media, such as radio and magazine. Display advertising is one type of online advertising which, together with search advertising, contributes the majority of the revenue for many large Internet companies. In display advertising, display ad instances are shown to the user on webpages in different formats such as image, flash, and video. Each display ad instance is called a creative. By showing the creatives, advertisers aim to either promote brand awareness among users (brand advertising) or receive desirable responses from users (performance advertising), such as the action of purchasing, clicking or signing up for a promotion list from the advertiser's website. In performance advertising, the advertiser strives to optimize their ad's performance metrics such as the effective cost per click (eCPC) or effective cost per action (eCPA), which in turn relates to maximizing the user response rate on the creatives as measured by click through rates (CTR) or conversion rates (CVR). There are several factors that greatly influence the user response rate of display advertising campaigns: 1) the position of the ads on the webpage; 2) the relevancy of the ads to the online users, which is generally captured by the targeting profiles of the advertising campaigns; 3) the relevancy of the ads to the webpage content and 4) the quality and visual appearance of the creatives.

The problem of predicting the user response rate for online ads, especially CTR, has been studied by several researchers in the last few years. One major research focus has been in predicting clicks by studying the relationship between CTR and the aforementioned ad factors (and their combinations). For example in [2], the authors considered the ad's relevancy to the content of the webpage in predicting CTR. They show that improving the ad's content relevancy is more efficient than considering the content of ads by themselves [26]. Although it is generally believed that visually appealing ads can perform better in attracting online users, as a result of which advertisers always care about the creative designs, there is no, to the best of our knowledge, published work so far to quantitatively study the effect of visual appearance of creatives on campaign performance in online display advertising. This motivates us to investigate the correlation between the visual features of the creative and CTR, regardless of other ad factors, and to predict creative performance based on its visual appearance alone.

Our proposed approach consists of two main steps, 1) feature extraction and 2) correlation investigation. We first extract some informative visual features from the creatives. We introduce 43 visual features classified into three categories, 1) *global features* which characterize the overall properties of a given creative, 2) *local features* representing the properties of specific parts within a given creative and 3) *advanced features* which are a group of features developed based on more complicated algorithms such as the number of faces and number of characters in a creative. We then develop three regression approaches to predict the CTR based on these features. The study is conducted using real creatives and their performance data from the world's largest display ads exchange system, RightMedia. Based on the weights of developed features, we further select a subset of features that have high impact on the creative's CTR. The benefit of this work is three-fold. First, our findings on the visual features and their relationship to CTR can provide useful recommendations to designers on what features to consider while designing creatives, and/or can help in automated creative generation. Second, the visual features and the regression methods developed here can be used in addition to the traditionally investigated ad factors (such as ad relevancy, position etc.) for improving CTR prediction in online ads selection. Third, it provides the research community with the first ever data set, initial insights into the effect of visual appearance on user response propensity, and evaluation benchmarks for further study.

The paper is organized as follows. Section 2 introduces the related work. We introduce the visual features in Section 3. The regression and feature selection results for CTR prediction are presented in Section 4, followed by our conclusion in Section 5.

2. BACKGROUND AND RELATED WORK

The relationship between various print ad characteristics and measures of advertising effectiveness has been studied by advertising researchers for almost a century. A wide variety of characteristics have been investigated. These characteristics are roughly in two categories: mechanical and content-based. The mechanical characteristics include ad size, number of colors, proportional of illustrations to copy, the absence of borders, and type size. The content factors include message appeal like status, quality, fear and fantasy, attention-getting techniques like free offers, presence of women, and psycholinguistic variables like product or personal reference in headline, interrogative or imperative headline, visual rhetorics, among others. See [21] for summaries.

Even though the online advertising has taken a large market share of the advertising industry, and the whole industry is steadily and continuously shifting to the online domain, study on the effectiveness of the counterpart of print ads online, generally called display ads, is limited. We list the studies of several factors below.

Some existing studies try to investigate the effect of several different factors on the performance of display advertising campaigns. These factors include targeting and obtrusiveness [9], advertisement size (large vs. small) and ad exposure format (intrusive vs. voluntary) [4], cognitive impact from ad size and animation [19], emotional appeal and incentive offering in the ads [8], repetition of varied execution vs. single execution [31].

To the best of our knowledge, we are not aware of any study on the relationship between the visual appearance and the performance of creatives in online display ads. We try to tackle this problem by first defining a set of visual features and then evaluating their effects on ad performance, specifically CTR in our experiments, from the actively served ad campaigns on the world's largest ad exchange system, RightMedia. Below, we present some previous computational studies on image properties which provide us inspiration in designing our visual features.

There are several studies that try to investigate a specific property of images (photos or paintings) using computational approaches. Such properties include quality and aesthetic in photos [20, 16, 30, 7] or in paintings [18], saliency [15], composition [10, 25], color harmony [5] and memorability [13].

Initial work on image quality evaluation concentrated on evaluating and reconstructing low graded, compressed or degraded images by simple noise model [6, 1]. However, in most of the beauty evaluation work, including this paper, we assume that high quality images are available and we are interested in evaluating the visual aesthetic of images based on visual features.

Recently some researchers tried to evaluate the beauty of an image based on its visual features. In [16] the authors aim to classify the pictures into professional and snapshot photos using some basic features including spatial distribution of edges, color distribution and hue count, etc. In [7] the authors introduced a regression based approach for rating photos based on their beauty, using features such as average pixel density, colorfulness, saturation hue, and the rule of thirds. In addition to these studies, in [20] the author proposed an approach to classifying images into high and low quality. The main idea comes from the fact that a professional photographer makes the background blurry and the subject distinguishable in the image. By separating the blurry part of the image from the subject, they design a set of well-motivated features from both the subject and the whole image such as the clarity contrast of the subject, lighting, simplicity, color harmony and composition geometry. They show that the combination of these features can provide a promising performance. All of the above work tries to extract visual features from photos. Recently Li et al. [18] tried to extract some features from paintings to evaluate their beauty and classify them into high and low quality. They introduced a set of global and local features, 40 in total, to capture the painting properties such as the brightness contrast between segments, the brightness contrast across the whole image and the average saturation for the largest segment of the image.

Computational approaches have also been used to investigate other visual properties of an image. In [13] the authors studied what properties of images make them more memorable. They found that statistical properties of an image such as mean hue, mean saturation, intensity mean, intensity variance, intensity skewness and number of objects do not have any non-trivial correlation with memorability in their generated data set. However, they found that if they label the objects and scenes in the images, they can find a non-trivial and interesting correlation between images and their memorability. For example, their results show that the attendance of human being, close up objects and human scale objects in an image improve its memorability more than natural scene. This result is not possible to be applied to our work since it requires large amounts of supervision to tag different parts of the images. However, we evaluate the impact of the number of human faces in an image in our work.

Color harmonization is another approach for making an image more appealing. In [5] the authors proposed to harmonize the colors in a given image using harmonization templates from [32, 29], which include 8 different harmonized color templates. We also used color harmony models to evaluate the hue distribution of an image in our experiments.

In summary, existing work in related areas has focused primarily on properties of an image, photo or painting. In contrast, we examine creatives in online display ads, which contain both graphical features and text. In addition, some of the existing approaches require significant amount of supervision in their feature extraction step, which is not possible in large scale applications where we need to learn from large data sets with minimum amount of supervision. Finally, we would also like to extract a set of features that are visually understandable and can be practically controlled to guide the human designers or automatic creative generators (like in smart ads) to produce high-performance creatives. These objectives make our problem novel and interesting for the online advertising industry.

3. FEATURE EXTRACTION

In this section we introduce a set of 43 different visual features. We categorize the developed features into three different sets, 1) global features, 2) local features and 3) advanced features. A complete list of the features can be found in Table 3. Below we describe the detailed definition of the proposed features in each category.

In the following sections we use I to indicate an image and use $|I|$ to indicate the size of the image measured by the number of pixels. We use variable x to denote an arbitrary pixel when we do not care about its location in the image. Otherwise we use (i, j) to denote the pixel in the i-th row and j-th column in the image.

3.1 Global Features

Global features are a set of features which represent the overall properties of the whole image. We describe the details of 19 different global features in this section.

3.1.1 Gray Level Features

We describe 3 features extracted from the gray level histogram of the image, namely the gray level contrast f_1, number of dominant gray level bins f_2, and the standard deviation of the gray level values among all pixels f_3.

The gray level contrast is the width of the middle 95% mass in the gray level histogram [16]. From the original gray level histogram, we prune the extreme 2.5% from the 0 side and 2.5% from the 255 side. Gray level contrast feature f_1 is calculated as the width of the remaining histogram.

We count the number of dominant bins in the gray level histogram as our second feature. Suppose the set $G = \{g_0, g_1, \cdots, g_{255}\}$ indicates the set of 256 bins in the gray level histogram such that g_i is the number of pixel in i-th bins. We define the number of dominant gray level bins as $f_2 = \sum_{k=0}^{255} \mathbf{1}(g_k \geq c_1 \max_i g_i)$, where $\mathbf{1}(\cdot)$ is the indicator function and c_1 is a threshold value which is set to be 0.01 in this paper. [1]

The last gray level feature, f_3, is defined as the standard deviation of gray level values of all pixels in the image. It is used to capture the variance of the gray level distribution.

3.1.2 Color Distribution

To avoid distraction from objects in the background, professional photographers tend to keep the background simple. In [20], the authors use the color distribution of the background to measure this simplicity. We use a similar approach to measure the simplicity of color distribution in the image. For a given image, we quantize each RGB channel into 8 values, creating a histogram $H_{rgb} = \{h_0, h_1, \cdots, h_{511}\}$ of 512 bins, where h_i indicates the number of pixels in i-th bin. We define feature f_4 to indicate the number of dominant colors as $f_4 = \sum_{k=0}^{512} \mathbf{1}(h_k \geq c_2 \max_i h_i)$

[1]This parameter, and similar ones in the rest of the paper, is set inspired by related works such as [20].

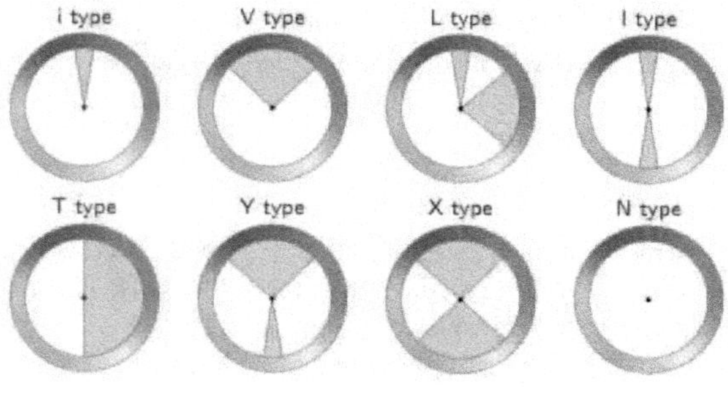

Figure 1: Color harmony models

where $c_2 = 0.01$ is the threshold parameter. We also calculate the size of the dominant bin relative to the image size as $f_5 = \frac{\max_i h_i}{|I|}$. This feature indicates the extent to which one of 512 colors is dominant in the image.

By replacing the RGB color map with HSV (Hue, Saturation, Value) color map and using the above methods in calculating features f_4 and f_5, we obtain two other features f_6 and f_7.

3.1.3 Model-Based Color Harmony

The concept of color harmony in this paper is based on 8 different harmonic color distributions (illustrated in Figure 1) that are based on the hue of the HSV color wheel [14, 32]. These distributions are called *i, V, L, I, T, Y, X, N*. Note that each distribution can be rotated by $0 \leq \alpha \leq 360$ degrees. The specific size of color harmony distributions are set as follows: the large sectors of types V, Y and X are 26% of the disk (93.6°); the small sectors of types i, L, I and Y are 5% of the disk (18°); the largest sector of type L is 22% of the disk (79.2%); the sector of type T is 50% of the disk (180°). The angle between the centers of the two sectors is 180° for I, X, Y, and 90° for L.

Let us define the set of 8 distributions as $\mathcal{D} = \{d^1, d^2, \cdots, d^8\}$. We say $\phi(d^i_\alpha, x)$ indicates the hue of the closest point in the i-th distribution to x after α degree rotation, where x is any arbitrary pixel in the image. We compute the distance between the hue distribution of our image I and the distribution $d^i \in \mathcal{D}$ as:

$$\gamma(I, d^i) = \arg\min_{\alpha} \frac{1}{|I|} \sum_{x \in I} \| \, hue(x) - \phi(d^i_\alpha, x) \, \| \cdot sat(x), \quad (1)$$

where $hue(x)$ and $sat(x)$ indicate the hue and saturation at pixel x, and $\| \cdot \|$ denotes the arc-length distance. We are interested in the best fitting model d^* which has the least $\gamma(\cdot)$ value, $d^* = \arg\min_{d^i} \gamma(I, d^i)$. We define feature $f_8 = \gamma(I, d^*)$. Intuitively, it tells us how different is the hue distribution of image I from the best fitting model of color harmony.

Some models are superset of other models in Figure 1 concluding that the $\gamma(\cdot)$ value of some smaller models are higher than some larger models given any image I, e.g. $\gamma(I, d_i) \geq \gamma(I, d_V) \geq \gamma(I, d_T)$. Therefore, if an image hue distribution fits into some small models, type i, V, L, I, it fits into larger models as well. This can emphasize the color harmony property of the images which can fit into a few models rather than just one model. We consider this property as one potential positive property of the image. To quantify this property, we introduce a new feature, f_9, which indicates the average color harmony deviation from the best two fitted models given an image I. In general, in addition to the deviation from the best fitted model illustrated by feature f_8, we consider the deviation from the second best fitted model as well, and the average of these two deviations is returned as f_9 Clearly, for the images fitting into small color harmony models, we will have f_8 and f_9

very close to each other. However, for the images which fit into the largest model, we will have f_9 considerably larger than f_8. We believe these two numerical features can represent the color harmony property of an image appropriately.

3.1.4 Color Coherence

We extract a set of features based on the color coherence of pixels resulting in connected coherent components [24]. A connected coherent component in an image is defined as:

- A set of pixels that fall into the same bin in the histogram.
- For any two pixels p_i and p_j in a connected coherent component $P = \{p_1, p_2, \cdots, p_m\}$ of m pixels, there is a path of sequential pixels, $p_i, p_{i+1}, \cdots, p_j$. Two sequential pixels in a path must be one of the 8 neighborhoods of each other.
- The size of the connected coherent component is larger than a predefined threshold c_4. In our experiment we set $c_4 = 0.01|I|$.

We denote the set of connected coherent components and their color index as $\mathcal{P} = \{(P_1, h_1), (P_2, h_2), \cdots (P_n, h_n)\}$, where P_i is the set of pixels in the i-th component, and h_i is its corresponding color in the HSV color histogram with 512 bins. We use $|P_i|$ to denote the number of pixels in P_i. We extract the following features based on the above definition:

- $f_{10} = n$, which indicates the number of connected coherent components in the image.
- $f_{11} = \frac{\max_i |P_i|}{|I|}$, which indicates the size of the largest component relative to the whole image.
- $f_{12} = \frac{\max\limits_{j, j \neq \arg\max\limits_i |P_i|} |P_j|}{|I|}$, representing the size of the second largest connected coherent component relative to the whole image.
- $f_{13} = \text{rank}(h_i), i = \arg\max_j |P_j|$, indicating the rank of the bin, considering the bin size in descending order, associated with the largest connected coherent component in the image. For example, the value of this feature is 1 if the bin associated with the largest coherent component, $\arg\max_j |P_j|$, is the largest bin in the color histogram as well; $\max_i |h_i|$ where h_i is the size of the $i - th$ bin in the color histogram. This feature indicates how the colors are disperse in the image. We expect to have value $f_{13} = 1$ if the colors in the images are not very randomly distributed. It means the pixel with the same colors are mostly connected together.
- $f_{14} = \text{rank}(h_i), i = \arg\max_{j, j \neq \arg\max_k |P_k|} |P_j|$, similar to f_{13}, it shows the bin rank, considering the bin size in descending order, of the second largest connected coherent component in the image.

3.1.5 Hue Distribution

In this section we introduce three features based on the hue in HSV color space. We quantize hues in an image in a similar way as in [18] by eliminating the pixels with saturation and value less than 0.2. This will eliminate all the pixels with white or black colors. Then we calculate the hue histogram of remaining pixels with 20 different bins, $18°$ for each bin, which results in $\mathcal{H}_{hue} = \{h_1, h_2, \cdots, h_{20}\}$ where h_i indicates the set of pixels in i-th bin. We then extract the following features:

- $f_{15} = \sum_{i=1}^{20} \mathbf{1}(|h_i| \geq c_5|I|)$ where $c_5 = 0.01$ in our experiments. This feature indicates the number of dominant hues in an image.
- $f_{16} = \max_{i,j} \| \, |h_i| - |h_j| \, \|$ where $|h_i| \geq c_5|I|$, and $\| \cdot \|$ is the arc length. This feature indicates the largest contrast between two dominant hues in the image.
- $f_{17} = \text{std}(\Phi)$ where $\Phi = \{\cup_{i \in I} \, \| \, h_i(i) - 0 \, \|\}$ and $\| \, . \, \|$ is the arc length value. This feature indicates the standard deviation of all pixel's hues distance from the origin 0. It simply can determine how much the hue colors in an images has been distributed from each other.

3.1.6 Lightness Features

We use the lightness L in the HSL color space to calculate feature f_{18} and f_{19}. In the HSL color space, L value is small when the color is white and is large when the color is black. The L value in HSL color space can be calculated as follows:

$$L(x) = \frac{\max(r(x), g(x), b(x)) + \min(r(x), g(x), b(x))}{2}, \quad (2)$$

where $r(x), g(x), b(x)$ denotes the R, G, B values of pixel x in RGB color space. We calculate two lightness features as:

- $f_{18} = \frac{1}{|I|} \sum_{x \in I} L(x)$, the average lightness of pixels in the image.
- $f_{19} = \text{std}(L(\cdot))$, the standard deviation of lightness of all pixels in the image.

3.2 Local Features

Local features represent a set of features extracted from specific parts of the image rather than the whole image. We apply the normalized cut segmentation method [27] to partition the image into 5 smaller segments. Let $\mathcal{S} = \{S_1, S_2, \cdots, S_5\}$ indicate the set of 5 different segments where S_i is the set of pixels in segment i. Note that a segment is considered as noise and is dropped if it is smaller than 5% of the image. We develop the following features based on the segmentation result.

3.2.1 Segment Size

Two features are extracted from segment size as follows:

- $f_{20} = \frac{\max_i |S_i|}{|I|}$, indicating the size of the largest segment relative to the whole image.
- $f_{21} = \frac{1}{|I|} \max_{i,j} ||S_i| - |S_j||$, indicating the contrast among the segmentation sizes of the image.

3.2.2 Segment Hues

Similar to section 3.1.5, we generate the hue histogram of each segment. We define the set of hue histograms of all 5 segments as $\mathcal{H}^s_{hue} = \{h_{1,1}, h_{1,2}, \cdots, h_{1,20}, h_{2,1}, \cdots, h_{5,20}\}$ where $h_{i,j}$ indicates the set of pixels that fall in the j-th bin of i-th segment. Then we extract five features to capture different hue properties. Below we describe the formal definition of developed features:

- $f_{22} = \sum_{j=1}^{20} \mathbf{1}(|h_{i,j}| \geq c_6|I|)$ where $i = \arg\max_i S_i$ and $c_6 = 0.01$. This feature denotes the number of image-wide dominant hues in the largest segment. In general, we would like to have most of the image hues in the largest segment.
- $f_{23} = \sum_{j=1}^{20} \mathbf{1}(|h_{i,j}| \geq c_6|S_i|)$ where $i = \arg\max_i S_i$. This feature denotes the number of segment-wide dominant hues in the largest segment.

- $f_{24} = \max_i q_i$ where $q_i = \sum_{j=1}^{20} \mathbf{1}(|h_{i,j} \geq c_6|S_i|)$ is the number of dominant hues in $i-th$ segment. This feature essentially denotes the largest number of dominant hues in one segment. We would like to have the same value as f_{23} for this feature illustrating that the largest segment has the largest number of dominant colors.

- $f_{25} = \max_{i,j} |q_i - q_j|$. This feature denotes the contrast of the number of dominant hues among the segments. We usually do not like to have lots of different hues in one segment and a few hues in another segment in an image. We expect to have unappealing images with large value for f_{25}.

- $f_{26} = \max_{j,k} \|h_{i,j} - h_{i,k}\|$ where $|h_{i,j}|, |h_{i,k}| \geq c_6|S_i|$, $i = \arg\max_i |S_i|$ and $\|\cdot\|$ is the arc length distance. This feature captures the contrast of number of pixels among the hue bins in the largest segment. In general, we expect to have an appealing image with one bin dominating the largest segment in addition to a few more small bins. This makes the contrast value very large.

- $f_{27} = \text{std}(T(\cdot))$ where $T(i) = \max_{j,k}, |h_{i,j}|, |h_{i,k}| \geq c_6|S_i|$. This feature returns the standard deviation of contrast among the segments. If we have different hue contrasts among different segments, this feature will achieve a significant value.

3.2.3 *Segment Color Harmony*

Two features are extracted based on the largest segment color harmony. Feature f_{28} is the minimum deviation from the best fitted color harmony model for the largest segment, and feature f_{29} is the average deviation of the best two fitted color harmony models for the largest segment. The details of color harmony models have been introduced in section 3.1.3.

3.2.4 *Segment Lightness*

Three segment lightness features are extracted using similar method as in section 3.1.6:

- f_{30}: average lightness in the largest segment.
- f_{31}: standard deviation of average lightness among the segments.
- f_{32}: contrast of average lightness among the segments.

3.3 Advanced features

In this section we develop a set of features based on more complicated algorithms. Most of the advanced features are based on the saliency map of the image which determines the visually salient areas in the image that are more likely to be noticed by the humans. We also extract two additional features related to the number of characters and number of faces in an image. Below we describe the details of these features.

3.3.1 *Saliency Features*

Saliency computation is a well known phenomenon in human vision where attention tends to be drawn to interesting parts of an image that appear visually different from the rest of the image (e.g., a red coke can in a green background appears salient and is immediately noticed, while the same coke can in an orange-reddish background is not salient and less likely to be noticed). We compute saliency according to the algorithm described in [12]. Figure 2 shows the saliency output of the algorithm presented in [12] for a sample creative. The areas with higher lightness in the saliency map indicate more salient part of the image.

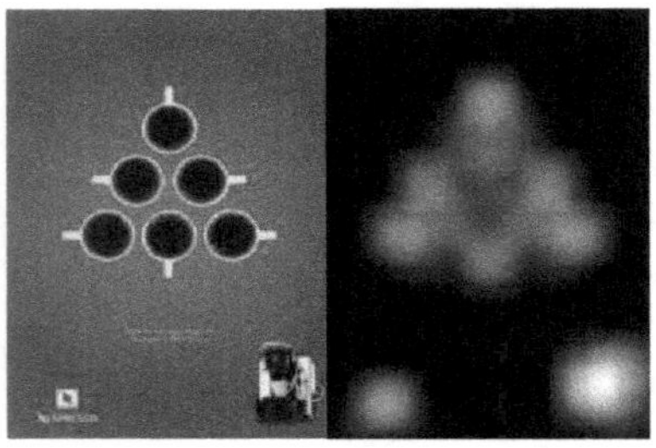

Figure 2: The saliency map of an image. Left: original image. Right: saliency map.

The saliency algorithm returns a matrix τ (also referred to as saliency map) where $\tau(i,j)$ represents the saliency value of pixel (i,j). We also extract a binary image based on the saliency map, by setting a threshold α to the saliency map where the pixels with saliency value larger than α are set to 1 and the rest of the pixels are set to 0. Similar to [12], the parameter α is set as $\alpha = 3\bar{\tau}$ where $\bar{\tau} = 1/n \sum_{i,j} \tau(i,j)$ is the average saliency value in the image. After this binarization, we have some connected components with value 1. These components indicate saliency areas, and the other parts of the image are considered as background. Then we extract the following features based on the saliency results, saliency map and binary saliency map.

- f_{33}: background size. Salient objects usually appear in the foreground and not in the background. Therefore we return the size of the background as a function of image size which is calculated as: $f_{33} = \frac{\sum_{i,j} \mathbf{1}(\tau(i,j)<\alpha)}{|I|}$.

- f_{34}: number of connected components in the binary map.

- f_{35}: size of the largest components in the binary saliency map relative to the whole image.

- f_{36}: average saliency value of the largest component in the binary saliency map.

- f_{37}: number of connected components in the image background. In some images, the saliency areas can divide the background into several disconnected segments. Usually it is not desirable to have multiple background components.

- f_{38}: size of the largest connected component in the background relative to the whole image. If the number of connected components in the background is equal to one, then this feature has the same value as f_{33}.

- f_{39}: distance between connected components. Let the set $C = \{c_1, c_2, \cdots, c_n\}$, $c_i = (x_i, y_i)$ indicates the set of n different points such that each c_i indicates a pixel corresponding to the center of mass of the i-th saliency area. To make the rest of the computation scale independent from the image size, we update the properties of each point c_i as $s_i = (x_i/I_x, y_i/I_y)$ such that I_x and I_y are the horizontal and vertical size of the image. Then we build up a complete weighted graph given the set C such that the weight $w_{i,j}$ between two vertices c_i, c_j is calculated as $w_{i,j} = \|s_i - s_j\|_2$. Then we return the summation of all edge weights as the distance between connected components.

Figure 3: The four interested points based on rule of third.

- f_{40}: distance from the rule of third points. Professional photographers usually locate their main object in one of the four interest points based on the rule of third. The four interest points in rule of third is the intersection of two vertical and two horizontal lines dividing the image into 9 equal segments. Figure 3 shows the four interested points based on rule of third. This is an important feature in photo beauty evaluation [18], motivating us to investigate its effect in creative performance. We define this feature as the minimum distance from the center of mass of the largest saliency area to one of the four interest points based on rule of third.

- f_{41}: distance from the center of image. This feature is the distance of saliency components to the center of image which is the most focused part of an image. The overall distance from the centers of all connected components to the center of image is returned as feature f_{41}. Note that for both features f_{40} and f_{41}, we normalize the position of each pixel similar as feature f_{39}.

3.3.2 Number of Characters

We consider the number of characters in an image as feature f_{42}. We tried a number of OCR toolbox and one of them provides us with appropriate results considering the number of characters in ads[23]. Note that we are interested in the number of characters in the image regardless of its meaning. To evaluate the accuracy of the OCR toolbox, we counted the true number of characters in 100 random images and compared it to the returned number of characters from the OCR toolbox. We found strong linear correlation of 0.80, suggesting that our toolbox is reasonably accurate in evaluating the number of characters in images. Note that extracting the exact text from ad creatives is challenging as they often appear in different fonts, sizes and orientations.

3.3.3 Number of Faces

The last feature, f_{43}, captures the effect of the human face appearance on creative performance. In [13] the authors concluded that the human appearance in an image could make the image more memorable. This motivates us to test whether face appearance affects creative performance. We count the number of faces in an image using an available toolbox [17]. Our toolbox is reasonably accurate and has a correlation more than 0.9 with the true number of faces in images in our experiments with a sample size of 100.

4. EXPERIMENTAL RESULTS

In this section we present the algorithms and experiments we designed to evaluate the relationship between visual features and the performance of creatives in online display advertising.

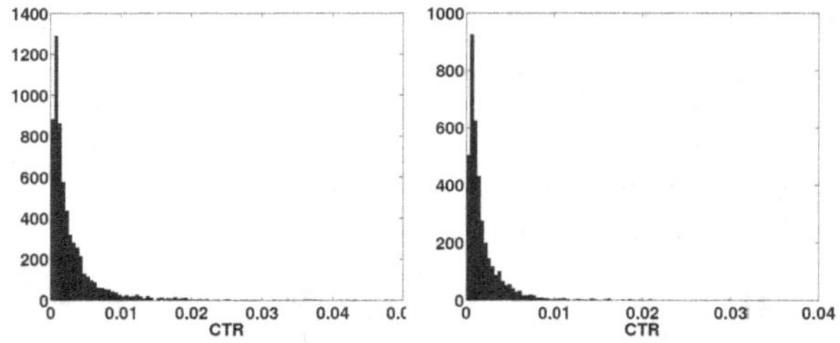

(a) Data set ID2 (b) Data set ID6

Figure 4: The CTR distribution of two data sets.

4.1 Data Set

We extracted creatives of advertising campaigns from the world's largest online advertising exchange system, RightMedia. We filtered out animated creatives because our features are designed for static images. We also calculated the average CTR of these creatives from online serving history log during a two-month period.

As discussed in Section 1, the performance of creatives is determined by many factors. One important factor is the ad position in the webpage. Generally the available position of a creative on a webpage is determined by the creative's size. To remove the impact on performance introduced by ad position (and size), we create two different data sets, each of which consists of creatives with the same size. The first data set, ID2, consists of 6272 creatives with size 250×300 pixels, and the second data set, ID6, includes 3888 images with 90×730 pixels. All of the creatives have a minimum of $100K$ impressions guaranteeing that their CTRs have converged to their true values. We believe this large number of impression (minimum of $100K$) can also guarantee that the calculated CTRs are not biased toward other effective factors such as user behavior or webpage content. The CTR distribution of each data set is shown in Figure 4.

To evaluate the effect of proposed features in each creative category, We further created two sub-categories from data set ID2: "dating" with 927 images and "traveling" with 599 images. Since there are not many images in these two categories, we consider the images with a minimum of $20k$ and $10k$ impressions for "dating" and "traveling" respectively.

4.2 Learning Methods

The main goal of this work is to study the relationship between the performance of creatives and their visual features. In the first step we try to predict CTR from visual features using regression methods. We used three different regression algorithms to predict CTR, 1) Linear Regression (LR), 2) Support Vector Regression with RBF kernel(SVR), and 3) Constrained Lasso (C-Lasso) which is a modification to Lasso [28].

We used LIBSVM [3] to implement the SVR and performed cross validation to determine the parameters of the model. We describe our constrained Lasso optimization approach as follows. Suppose we have a set of n creatives at disposal and the visual features of these creatives are represented as a matrix $A \in \mathbb{R}^{d\times n}$ such that $A = (\mathbf{a}_1, \mathbf{a}_2, \cdots, \mathbf{a}_n)$ where $\mathbf{a}_k \in \mathbb{R}^d$ is a column vector representing the d dimensional visual features of creative k. In our experiment $d = 43$. The CTR values of the n creatives are represented as a vector $\mathbf{y} = (y_1, \cdots, y_n)^\top \in \mathbb{R}^n$ where each y_k is the CTR of the k-th creative. We bound the CTR of each creative by $y_{min} \leq y_i \leq y_{\max}$ where y_{min} and y_{max} can be obtained from online serving history log. To predict CTR of the creatives, we try to solve the following optimization problem:

$$\begin{aligned} \min_{w} \quad & \|A^\top \mathbf{w} - \mathbf{y}\|_F^2 + \lambda\|\mathbf{w}\|_1 \\ s.t. \quad & y_{min} \le A^\top \mathbf{w} \le y_{max} \end{aligned} \tag{3}$$

where $\|\cdot\|_F^2$ is Frobinius-2 norm and $\|\cdot\|_1$ is ℓ_1 norm, also called lasso. We call the above optimization problem as constrained Lasso (C-Lasso) and we used [11] to find the solution of this optimization problem. Note that the proposed C-Lasso approach performs better than Lasso in our application.

4.3 Evaluation

In this section we present different evaluation methods to analyze the efficacy of the developed visual features in predicting the performance of creatives.

4.3.1 CTR Prediction

To evaluate the CTR prediction accuracy of the algorithms, we run each algorithm for 200 independent runs where in each run 80% of each data set is selected randomly for training and 20% for testing. The accuracy evaluation results are reported over the prediction of the test data. Mean Squared Error (MSE) is used to measure the prediction accuracy for each algorithm as follows:

$$MSE = \frac{1}{n}\sum_{k=1}^{n} |y_k - \hat{y}_k|^2 \tag{4}$$

where n is the number of test samples, y_k is the true CTR of the k-th creative calculated from history log, and $\hat{y}_k$ is the predicted CTR. To meaningfully interpret the MSE value, we introduce two baseline approaches, *Random* and *Constant Mean*(CM) policy.

Table 1: The prediction accuracy of each method against *Random* policy.

Data set	CM	LR	C-Lasso	SVR
ID2	$1.71 \pm .012$	$2.28 \pm .015$	$2.22 \pm .011$	$\mathbf{3.27} \pm .010$
ID6	$1.75 \pm .010$	$2.27 \pm .012$	$2.14 \pm .011$	$\mathbf{2.77} \pm .011$
ID2-Dating	$1.79 \pm .054$	$2.65 \pm .070$	$2.58 \pm .013$	$\mathbf{2.79} \pm .020$
ID2-Travel	$1.68 \pm .045$	$2.13 \pm .065$	$2.03 \pm .023$	$\mathbf{2.26} \pm .021$

The *Random* policy simply samples from the CTR distribution of the training data to predict the CTR of each testing creative, while the CM policy assigns a constant value, c_m, to all ads where c_m is the mean CTR of the training data. Table 1 shows the average results over 200 independent runs for each algorithm. Each entry is the MSE value of the random policy divided by MSE value of each algorithm with its variance via different runs. Results show that we can perform up to 3.27 times better than *Random* policy with small variance in predicting the CTR from visual features only. All learners perform consistently better than baseline CM as well. This result demonstrates the non-trivial impact of visual appearance of the creative on its advertising performance.

4.3.2 CTR Ranking

We introduce a ranking criterion to investigate the ability of using visual features to rank the creatives by their CTRs. Given a test set of creatives, suppose $c_1^-, c_2^-, \cdots, c_k^-$ represent the k images with the lowest CTR values and $c_1^+, c_2^+, \cdots, c_k^+$ represent the k images with the highest CTR. Therefore we have k^2 pairs (c_i^-, c_j^+) such that $ctr(c_i^-) \le ctr(c_j^+)$ for $i, j \in \{1, \cdots, k\}$. We wish to know whether our prediction of CTR using visual features preserves the ranking of pairs (c_i^-, c_j^+). To test this, we change the value of k as a function of test data size. We then measure the percentage of match between the predicted ranking of creatives, and the truly observed ranking in the test data. The results over 200 independent runs are shown in figure 5 for different data sets. The $x-$axis indicates the value of δ such that $k = \delta n$ for $\delta = 0.02, 0.04, 0.06, \cdots, 0.50$ where n is the number of creatives in the data set, and $y-$axis represents the percentage of correctly ranked pairs.

Results show that SVR consistently outperforms other learners. As we increase the size of k, the percentage of correctly ranked predictions decreases for all learning algorithms. This is as expected, since differentiating the images of creatives which have CTRs close to the mean of the CTR distribution, using visual features only, is very difficult even for a human. Interestingly, the results show that by just using visual features, we can preserve more than 90% of the ranking for data set ID2 (for $\delta = 0.1$). This number remains high at 75% when we consider all top-half images against low-half images for all data sets ($\delta = 0.5$). This is an encouraging result that demonstrates the utility of visual features in predicting the ranking of CTR.

4.3.3 CTR Classification

Previous studies in beauty evaluation [7, 16, 18] mostly try to classify the images into high and low quality category rather than assigning scores to their beauty based on visual features. Similarly, we evaluate the performance of classifying the creatives into high (**+1**) and low (**-1**) CTR category using visual features only. We use support vector machine with RBF kernel as our classifier. Similar to the previous section, we randomly separate 80% of data as training and use the rest as testing data. Then, we train our classifier on creatives that belong to the top and bottom 30% in CTR. In fact, we are disregarding 40% of data that are close to the training data CTR mean, μ_t, to reduce the noise for the classifier. Similar to the ranking experiments, we filter our test set by focusing on the k creatives with highest CTR values (labeled as positive) and the k creatives with the lowest CTR values (labeled as negative), where $k = \delta n$ is varied by changing δ. We obtain the classification accuracy by comparing the predicted classes to the true classes obtained from real CTR values. Figure 6 demonstrates the average classification accuracy over 200 independent runs where each run uses randomly selected training and testing data. The x-axis indicates the value of δ and y-axis represents the classification accuracy for each data set given a fixed value of δ. As seen in the figure, using visual features yields a classification accuracy of 70% when $\delta = 0.5$. Together with the previous results on predicting and ranking CTR, these results show the efficacy of using visual features of creatives in predicting CTR.

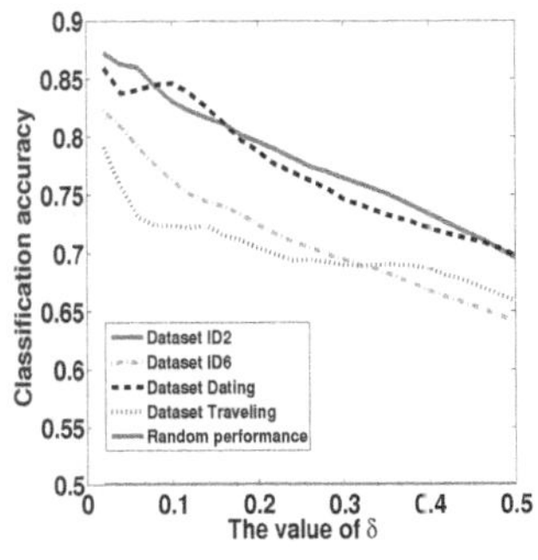

Figure 6: The classification accuracy for each data set.

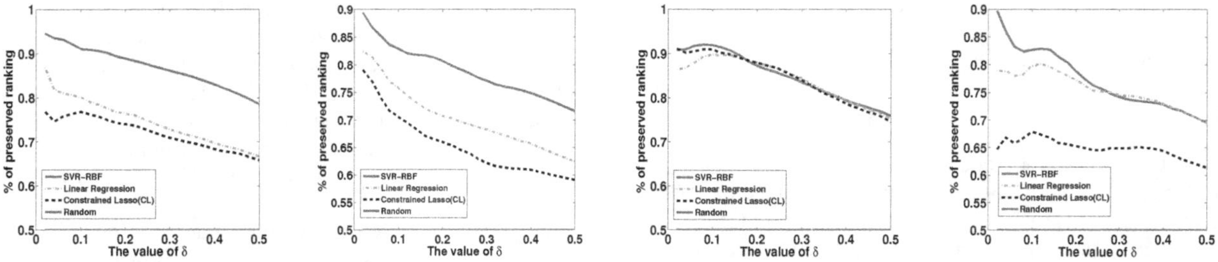

ID2 ID6 ID2-Dating ID2-Traveling, IMP$\geq 10k$

Figure 5: The amount of preserved ranking for each method.

4.4 Feature Selection

The above analysis shows that visual features are useful in predicting the performance of creatives in online advertising. A natural question is to identify the visual features that have strong impact on ad performance. Such information could be very useful in many areas. For example, human graphic designers may use this information to guide their design of high-performance creatives. Smart ads system may use this information to dynamically generate creatives that are more appealing to online users. Ad exchange system may use this information to determine which creative will win in the auction marketplace for each advertising opportunity. In this section we conduct a series of experiments to select such important visual features.

We first calculate the Linear Correlation (LC) and Mutual Information (MI) between all features and CTR in each data set. Mutual information can provide us with the information of non-linear correlation between features. Note that, to calculate the mutual information between any pair of features (X, Y), we discretized each feature and CTR values into 50 equal intervals.The results are shown in table 3. The top 5 features in each data set with highest absolute values are highlighted in bold. The table shows that there is no feature with high linear correlation or mutual information except f_{12} in data set ID6. Thus we use Forward Feature Selection (FFS) to select the top k features.

Before running FFS, we first cluster the features based on the Normalized Mutual Information (NMI) of all feature pairs. We discretize each feature into 50 equal intervals, and calculate NMI as follows:

$$NMI(X;Y) = \frac{I(X;Y)}{\sqrt{H(X)H(Y)}}, \quad (5)$$

where $H(X)$ is the entropy of random variable X. Then we cluster the features using the average linkage algorithm [22]. Two clusters are merged into one if their average NMI is at least 0.2. This results in 20 clusters for data set ID2 and 21 clusters for data set ID6. The resulting clusters are shown in Table 3. In the table, S_i represents a set of features in cluster i. We now apply a simple change to the FFS algorithm to select the top k clusters rather than features. After selecting a feature by FFS, all the correlated features that belong to the same cluster are removed from the next steps of FFS. The selected top $k = 10$ clusters are shown in table 2. Note that clustering the features in the above manner helps select different features (or feature sets) that are less correlated with each other. For example, all color harmony features are in the same cluster S_4. Therefore by selecting one of the features from this cluster, we indicate the importance of color harmony in CTR, and by removing the highly correlated features at each step in FFS, we can guarantee to select a set of features which are less correlated with each other. Below we investigate some of the selected clusters that are common to both data sets.

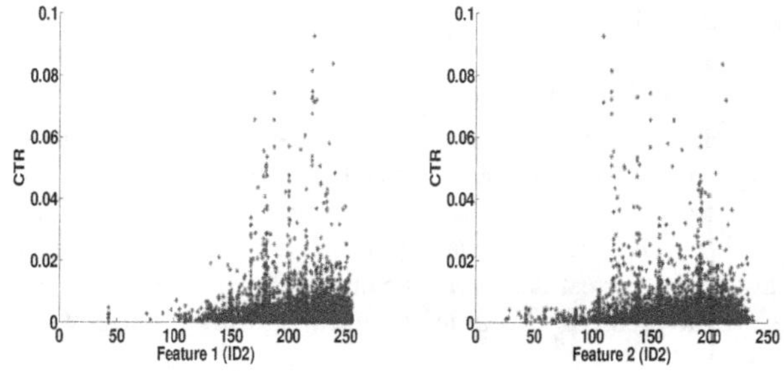

Figure 7: The scatter plot of f_1 and f_2 against CTR.

Table 2: The top 10 selected clusters by FFS.

Data Set	Selected Clusters
ID2	$S_5, S_1, S_{19}, S_{17}, S_{13}, S_{18}, S_{20}, S_{10}, S_{11}, S_9$
ID6	$S_1, S_2, S_{20}, S_5, S_{17}, S_{14}, S_9, S_{13}, S_4, S_{18}$

Table 2 shows that S_1 is the best feature set (or cluster) for data set ID6 and the second best set for data set ID2 which illustrates the importance of set S_1. S_1 consists of the gray level features f_1 and f_2 of the image. The scatter plot of both features in data set ID2 is shown in Figure7 (the scatter plot in data set ID6 is similar). Figure 7 shows that for creatives with small value in both features, high CTR value is unlikely, and creatives with high CTR values should have high values in these two features. This is consistent with the intuition that creatives with higher contrast should perform better. Note that having high values in these two features does not guarantee a high CTR value.

S_5 is the best feature set for data set ID2 and the fourth for ID6. It only includes f_{10} which is the number of connected coherent components. The scatter plot of f_{10} in both data sets are shown in figure 8. The scatter plot shows that creatives with more than 15 connected coherent components in data set ID6 and more than 20 in data set ID2 are unlikely to achieve a CTR higher than 0.01. In other words, this suggests that cluttered creatives containing many objects tend to have lower CTR.

The number of characters, S_{19} in data set ID2 and S_{20} in data set ID6, is interestingly the third important feature set in both data sets. Figure 9 shows the scatter plot of the number of characters in both data sets. It can be seen that the creatives with higher number of characters are unlikely to achieve high CTR values in both data sets, once again suggesting that textual clutter is undesirable.

The next selected categories is S_{17} which is the 4-th selected

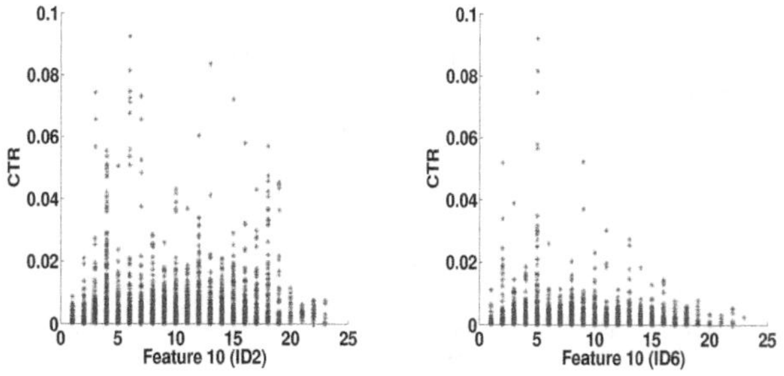

Figure 8: The scatter plot of f_{10}.

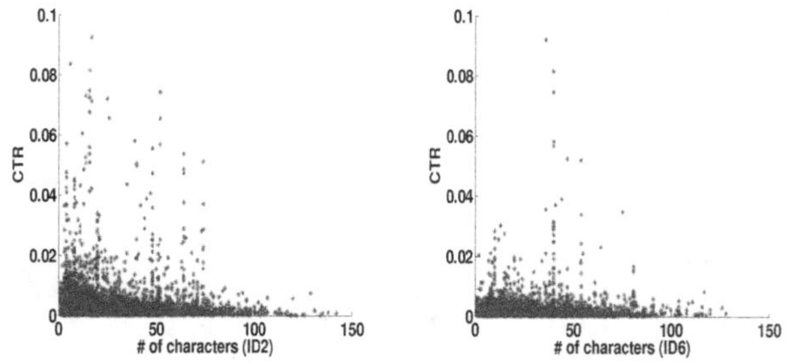

ID2 ID6

Figure 9: The scatter plot of number of characters.

category in ID2 and the 5-th in ID6. S_{17} represents the number of connected components in saliency binary map, distance between salient components, distance of saliency areas from the center of image and rule of third closest point. This indicates the importance of saliency features as well as considering professional photography rules such as the rule of third in designing ads. Intuitively, a small number of salient components, closer to the center of the creative, and consistent with the rule of third are desirable features in a creative. Finally, S_{13}, which contains features describing the number of hues and the contrast of hues in the largest segment of the image, is the 5-th important common category considering both data sets. Note that the scatter plot of the last 2 selected categories have been omitted due to space limit. In summary, our top 5 selected categories include the features from all proposed feature categories, global, local and advanced features, indicating the importance of each of them in predicting the creatives CTR.

5. CONCLUSION

In this paper we investigated the relationship between the user response rate and the visual appearance of creatives in online display advertising. To the best of our knowledge, this is the first work in this area. We designed 43 visual features for our experiments. We extracted the features from large scale data produced by the world's largest ad exchange system. We tested the utility of visual features in CTR prediction, ranking and classification. The experimental results demonstrate that our proposed framework is able to outperform baseline consistently, indicating the efficacy of visual features in predicting CTR. We also performed feature selection to select the top visual feature categories that have strongest importance for increasing CTR. The findings from this work will be useful for ads selection and developing visually appealing creatives with higher user response propensity in online display advertising.

6. REFERENCES

[1] A. C. Bovik, L. K. Cormack, J. K. Aggarwal, C. Bajaj, G. D. Veciana, J. Ghosh, H. R. Sheikh, H. R. Sheikh, and B. Sc. No-reference quality assessment using natural scene statistics: Jpeg2000. *JPEG2000*, 2005.

[2] D. Chakrabarti, D. Agarwal, and V. Josifovski. Contextual advertising by combining relevance with click feedback. In *WWW*, pages 417–426, 2008.

[3] C.-C. Chang and C.-J. Lin. LIBSVM: A library for support vector machines. *ACM Transactions on Intelligent Systems and Technology*, pages 1–27:, 2011.

[4] P. Chatterjee. Are unclicked ads wasted? enduring effects of banner and pop-up ad exposures on brand memory and attitudes. *Journal of Electronic Commerce Research*, pages 51–61, 2008.

[5] D. Cohen-Or, O. Sorkine, R. Gal, T. Leyvand, and Y.-Q. Xu. Color harmonization. In *ACM Transactions on Graphics*, pages 624–630.

[6] N. Damera-venkata, S. Member, T. D. Kite, W. S. Geisler, B. L. Evans, S. Member, and A. C. Bovik. Image quality assessment based on a degradation model. *IEEE Trans. Image Processing*, pages 636–650, 2000.

[7] R. Datta, D. Joshi, J. Li, and J. Z. Wang. Studying aesthetics in photographic images using a computational approach. In *ECCV*, pages 7–13, 2006.

[8] N. Donthu, R. Lohtia, T. Osmonbekov, and T. Xie. Emotional appeal and incentive offering in banner advertisements. *Journal of Interactive Advertising*, pages 30–37, 2004.

[9] A. Goldfarb and C. Tucker. Online display advertising: Targeting and obtrusiveness. *Marketing Science*, 2010.

[10] B. Gooch, E. Reinhard, C. Moulding, and P. Shirley. Artistic composition for image creation. In *Proceedings of the 12th Eurographics Workshop on Rendering Techniques*, pages 83–88, 2001.

[11] M. Grant and S. Boyd. CVX: Matlab software for disciplined convex programming, version 1.21, 2011.

[12] X. Hou and L. Zhang. Saliency detection: A spectral residual approach. *IEEE Computer Society Conference on Computer Vision and Pattern Recognition*, pages 1–8, 2007.

[13] P. Isola, J. Xiao, A. Torralba, and A. Oliva. What makes an image memorable? In *IEEE Conference on Computer Vision and Pattern Recognition*, pages 145–152, 2011.

[14] J. Itten. *The Art of Color*. 1960.

[15] L. Itti, C. Koch, and E. Niebur. A model of saliency-based visual attention for rapid scene analysis. *IEEE Transactions on Pattern Analysis and Machine Intelligence*, pages 1254–1259, 1998.

[16] Y. Ke, X. Tang, and F. Jing. The design of high-level features for photo quality assessment. In *CVPR*, pages 419–426, 2006.

[17] S. Krishna. Open cv viola-jones face detection, 2008.

[18] C. Li and T. Chen. Aesthetic visual quality assessment of paintings. *IEEE Journal of Selected Topics in Signal Processing*, pages 236–252, 2009.

[19] H. Li and J. L. Bukovac. Cognitive impact of banner ad characteristics: An experimental study. *Journalism and Mass Communication Quarterly*, pages 341–53, 1999.

[20] Y. Luo and X. Tang. Photo and video quality evaluation: Focusing on the subject. In *ECCV*, pages 386–399, 2008.

[21] E. McQuarrie and D. Mick. Visual rhetoric in advertising:

Table 3: Complete list of visual features.

Feature	Short Description	LC ID2	MI ID2	LC ID6	MI ID6	C-ID2	C-ID26
f_1	gray level contrast	-0.048	0.063	-0.102	0.098	S_1	S_1
f_2	number of dominant bins in gray level histogram	-0.107	0.071	**-0.137**	**0.112**	S_1	S_1
f_3	standard deviation of gray level images	-0.063	0.061	-0.016	0.082	S_2	S_2
f_4	number of dominant bins in RGB histogram	-0.083	0.067	-0.074	0.078	S_3	S_3
f_5	size of the dominant bin in RGB histogram	0.078	**0.093**	0.064	**0.104**	S_3	S_3
f_6	number of dominant bins in HSV histogram	-0.083	0.073	-0.078	0.092	S_3	S_3
f_7	size of the dominant bin in HSV histogram	0.119	**0.096**	0.085	0.094	S_3	S_3
f_8	deviation from the best color harmony model	-0.062	0.039	-0.040	0.052	S_4	S_4
f_9	average deviation from the best two color harmony models	-0.069	0.047	-0.046	0.063	S_4	S_4
f_{10}	number of connected coherent components	0.094	0.062	-0.004	0.064	S_5	S_5
f_{11}	size of the largest connected coherent component	0.102	**0.090**	0.069	0.099	S_3	S_3
f_{12}	size of the second largest connected coherent component	0.085	0.068	**0.315**	**0.122**	S_6	S_6
f_{13}	color size rank of the largest connected coherent component	-0.002	0.010	-0.012	0.014	S_7	S_7
f_{14}	color size rank of the second largest connected coherent component	-0.046	0.020	-0.039	0.022	S_8	S_8
f_{15}	number of dominant hues	-0.102	0.036	-0.119	0.045	S_9	S_9
f_{16}	contrast of dominant hues	-0.015	0.027	-0.015	0.046	S_9	S_9
f_{17}	standard deviation of hues	0.010	**0.084**	-0.039	**0.102**	S_{10}	S_{10}
f_{18}	average lightness	0.031	0.072	0.035	0.099	S_{11}	S_{11}
f_{19}	standard deviation of lightness	-0.065	0.063	-0.086	0.084	S_2	S_2
f_{20}	size of the Largest Segments (LS)	-0.052	0.058	-0.080	0.081	S_{12}	S_{12}
f_{21}	segments size contrast	-0.044	0.054	-0.122	0.092	S_{12}	S_{12}
f_{22}	number of image dominant hues in the LS	-0.104	0.044	-0.068	0.029	S_{13}	S_{13}
f_{23}	number of dominant hues in the LS	-0.102	0.032	-0.080	0.036	S_{13}	S_{13}
f_{24}	largest number of dominant hues in one segment	-0.079	0.031	**-0.125**	0.045	S_{14}	S_{14}
f_{25}	contrast of hues number among segments	-0.006	0.027	-0.098	0.033	S_{14}	S_{14}
f_{26}	contrast of hues in the LS	-0.120	0.032	-0.085	0.036	S_{13}	S_{13}
f_{27}	standard deviation of hues contrast among segments	-0.056	0.072	-0.073	0.098	S_{10}	S_{10}
f_{28}	deviation from the best color harmony model for LS	-0.047	0.030	-0.034	0.042	S_4	S_4
f_{29}	average deviation from the best two color harmony models for LS	-0.055	0.037	-0.049	0.053	S_4	S_4
f_{30}	average lightness in LS	0.027	0.075	0.065	0.096	S_{11}	S_{11}
f_{31}	standard deviation of average lightness among the segments	0.080	0.076	-0.049	0.091	S_{15}	S_{15}
f_{32}	contrast of average lightness among the segments	0.075	0.067	-0.027	0.081	S_{15}	S_{15}
f_{33}	background size in Saliency Map (SM)	**-0.165**	0.082	**-0.175**	**0.106**	S_{16}	S_{16}
f_{34}	number of connected components in SM	-0.111	0.029	-0.062	0.088	S_{17}	S_{17}
f_{35}	size of the largest connected components in SM	**0.132**	0.075	0.036	0.073	S_{16}	S_{18}
f_{36}	average saliency weight of largest connected component	**0.165**	0.075	0.071	0.080	S_{16}	S_{18}
f_{37}	number of connected components in image background SM	-0.012	0.015	-0.035	0.038	S_{18}	S_{19}
f_{38}	size of the largest connected component of background in SM	**-0.163**	**0.091**	**-0.145**	0.052	S_{16}	S_{16}
f_{39}	distance between connected components in SM	0.117	0.056	-0.027	0.072	S_{17}	S_{17}
f_{40}	distance from rule of third points in SM	**0.126**	0.063	0.010	0.086	S_{17}	S_{17}
f_{41}	distance from center of image in SM	0.091	0.065	0.011	0.087	S_{17}	S_{17}
f_{42}	number of characters (OCR)	-0.082	0.057	-0.017	0.071	S_{19}	S_{20}
f_{43}	number of faces in the image	-0.035	0.008	-0.024	0.011	S_{20}	S_{21}

text-interpretive, experimental, and reader-response analyses. *Journal of consumer research*, pages 37–54, 1999.

[22] F. Murtagh. A survey of recent advances in hierarchical clustering algorithms. *The Computer Journal*, pages 354–359, 1983.

[23] D. Orlando. Optical character recognition, 2007.

[24] G. Pass, R. Zabih, and J. Miller. Comparing images using color coherence vectors. In *Fourth ACM international conference on Multimedia*, pages 65–73, 1996.

[25] L. L. Renjie, C. Lior, W. D. Cohen-or, L. Liu, R. Chen, L. Wolf, and D. Cohen-or. Optimizing photo composition. In *Computer Graphics Forum*, pages 469–478, 2010.

[26] M. Richardson. Predicting clicks: Estimating the click-through rate for new ads. In *WWW*, pages 521–530, 2007.

[27] J. Shi and J. Malik. Normalized cuts and image segmentation. *IEEE Trans. Pattern Analysis and Machine Intelligence*, pages 888–905, 2000.

[28] R. Tibshirani. Regression shrinkage and selection via the lasso. *Journal of the Royal Statistical Society*, pages 267–288, 1996.

[29] M. Tokumaru, N. Muranaka, and S. Imanishi. Color design support system considering color harmony. In *Fuzzy Systems, 2002*, pages 378–383, 2002.

[30] H. Tong, M. Li, H. jiang Zhang, J. He, and C. Zhang. Classification of digital photos taken by photographers or home users. In *Proceedings of Pacific Rim Conference on Multimedia*, pages 198–205, 2004.

[31] I. Yaveroglu and N. Donthu. Advertising repetition and placement issues in on-line environments. *Journal of Advertising*, pages 31–44, 2008.

[32] Y.Mastuda. Color design. In *Asakura Shoten*, 1995.

The Wisdom of Advertisers: Mining Subgoals via Query Clustering

Takehiro Yamamoto[†‡♭*]
tyamamot@dl.kuis.kyoto-u.ac.jp

Tetsuya Sakai[†]
tetsuyasakai@acm.org

Mayu Iwata[†♯*]
iwata.mayu@ist.osaka-u.ac.jp

Chen Yu[†]
yu.chen@microsoft.com

Ji-Rong Wen[†]
jrwen@microsoft.com

Katsumi Tanaka[‡]
tanaka@dl.kuis.kyoto-u.ac.jp

†Microsoft Research Asia, China ‡Kyoto University, Japan ♭JST CREST, Japan ♯Osaka University, Japan

ABSTRACT

This paper tackles the problem of mining subgoals of a given search goal from data. For example, when a searcher wants to travel to London, she may need to accomplish several subtasks such as "book flights," "book a hotel," "find good restaurants" and "decide which sightseeing spots to visit." As another example, if a searcher wants to lose weight, there may exist several alternative solutions such as "do physical exercise," "take diet pills," and "control calorie intake." In this paper, we refer to such subtasks or solutions as subgoals, and propose to utilize sponsored search data for finding subgoals of a given query by means of query clustering. Advertisements (ads) reflect advertisers' tremendous efforts in trying to match a given query with implicit user needs. Moreover, ads are usually associated with a particular action or transaction. We therefore hypothesized that they are useful for subgoal mining. To our knowledge, our work is the first to use sponsored search data for this purpose. Our experimental results show that sponsored search data is a good resource for obtaining related queries and for identifying subgoals via query clustering. In particular, our method that combines ad impressions from sponsored search data and query co-occurrences from session data outperforms a state-of-the-art query clustering method that relies on document clicks rather than ad impressions in terms of purity, NMI, Rand Index, F_1-measure and subgoal recall.

Categories and Subject Descriptors

H.3.3 [**Information Storage and Retrieval**]: Information Search and Retrieval

General Terms

Algorithms, Experimentation

Keywords

User Intent, Sponsored Search, Query Clustering

*This research was conducted while the first and third authors were interns at Microsoft Research Asia.

CIKM'12, October 29–November 2, 2012, Maui, HI, USA.

1. INTRODUCTION

The information needs of a web search engine user are sometimes complex, and may span multiple queries or even multiple search sessions [21, 31]. When the user wants to travel to London, she may need to accomplish several subtasks such as "book flights," "book a hotel," "find good restaurants" and "decide which sightseeing spots to visit," and issue multiple queries accordingly, possibly over a length of time. As another example, for a user who wants to lose weight, there may exist several alternative solutions such as "do physical exercise," "take diet pills," and "control calorie intake." The user may not even be aware that these different solutions exist, so she will probably have to issue several queries to find out about them. In this paper, we refer to such subtasks or solutions as *subgoals*. Our precise definitions are as follows:

- A *search goal* is an *action* that the searcher wants to achieve, often represented by a verb plus possibly a noun phrase.
- A search goal x is a *subgoal* of another search goal y if achieving x helps the searcher to also achieve y either wholly or partially.

Note that while a subgoal "book flights" alone can only partially satisfy a search goal "travel (to) London," a subgoal "do physical exercise" may wholly satisfy "lose weight."

In this paper, we tackle the problem of automatically mining subgoals of a given search goal from data. To this end, we propose to utilize *sponsored search data* for finding subgoals of a given query by means of query clustering. Advertisements (ads) reflect advertisers' tremendous efforts in trying to match a given query with implicit user needs. Moreover, ads are usually associated with a particular action or transaction. We therefore hypothesized that they are useful for subgoal mining. To our knowledge, our work is the first to use sponsored search data for this purpose.

We further hypothesize that queries that represent a common subgoal are associated with similar ads, and employ a state-of-the-art query clustering algorithm [28] in order to mine subgoals

Table 1: Example search goals and their subgoals mined by our proposed method.

	search goal: **lose weight**
1.	fitness, gyms, health clubs, workout, ...
2.	alli, diet pills, best weight loss pills, hcg drops, ...
3.	diabetic recipes, diet recipes, healthy recipes, ...
4.	denise austin, jillian michaels, kathy smith
5.	high protein foods, protein, protein foods
6.	calorie counter
⋮	
	search goal: **relieve stress**
1.	cheap lexapro, generic lexapro, lexapro side effects, wellbutrin xl, wellbutrin xl 150 mg, ...
2.	baseball stress balls, stress ball, stress relief toy, stress toys
3.	body massage, massage therapist, massage therapy, stress factory, ...
4.	exercise heal, gaiam, holden, qigong
5.	anxiety medications, herbs anxiety
6.	zen garden
⋮	
	search goal: **travel London**
1.	cheap hotel london, london airport hotels, london hotel deals, london hotels, london luxury hotels, ...
2.	airfare london, airline tickets london, cheap airfare london, flights london, ...
3.	london 2012, london summer olympics, 2012 olympic games, 2012 olympics tickets, ...
4.	car rental london, london car rental
5.	london travel card, oyster card london
⋮	

from queries in the sponsored search data. Given a query that represents a search goal, our method first collects its related queries from sponsored search data, and then clusters them based on ad impressions as well as within-session query co-occurrences. Table 1 shows a few examples of goal-subgoal relationships mined using our proposed method. It can be observed that for the search goal "lose weight," query clusters that represent subgoals such as "do physical exercise," "take diet pills" and "control calorie intake" are obtained. Also, for the search goal "relieve stress," we can observe that query clusters that represent possible alternative solutions such as "take medicine," "buy stress relief toys" and "have a massage" are obtained. This hierarchy of search goals have many possible applications, including:

- Given a query, present the user with its possible subgoals, for example, as query suggestions;
- Given a query (e.g. "lose weight pills"), present the user with alternatives (e.g. "healthy diet recipes"), by identifying their common grand goal (e.g. "lose weight");
- Evaluating web search engines from the viewpoint of total user satisfaction, by means of goal-based evaluation as opposed to query-based evaluation as exemplified by nDCG [20]. Note that even though there are attempts at session-based IR evaluation [23], queries that represent subgoals of a search goal may span multiple sessions and users in general.

Figure 1 shows some example ads of a commercial search engine. In sponsored search, advertisers bid on various *bid phrases* so that their ads will be displayed in response to certain queries as

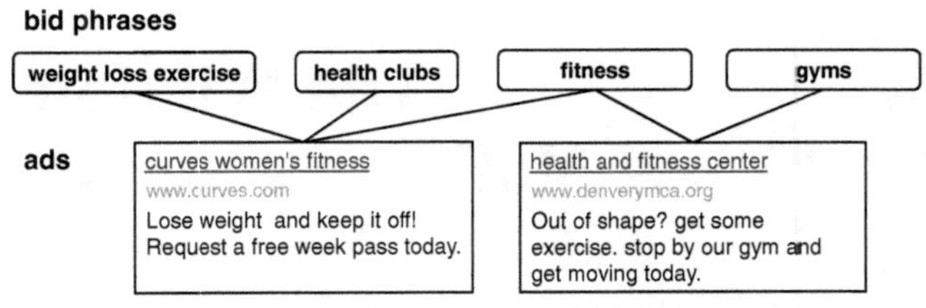

Figure 1: Example of ads and their bid phrases.

shown in the figure. Today's major commercial search engines have this kind of mechanism. According to our preliminary study with 10,000 head queries obtained over one recent week from a popular search engine, 68.3% of them had some ads displayed.

Our experimental results show that sponsored search data is a good resource for obtaining related queries and for identifying subgoals via query clustering. In particular, combining ad impressions with within-session query co-occurrence information outperforms a state-of-the-art query clustering method that uses document clicks rather than ad impressions, in terms of *purity, NMI, Rand Index,* F_1*-measure* and *subgoal recall* (See Section 4.4).

The rest of this paper is organized as follows. Section 2 discusses previous work related to our study. Section 3 describes our approach to mining subgoals using sponsored search data. Section 4 describes our experimental setup and Section 5 discusses the results. Finally, Section 6 concludes this paper.

2. RELATED WORK

2.1 Sponsored Search

Sponsored search has recently been an area of active research. The main research topics of this area have been the improvement of ads retrieval performance [6, 16, 27] and clickthrough rate (CTR) estimation for the retrieved ads [14, 32]. For example, Broder *et al.* [6] proposed a technique that leverages related organic (i.e. non-sponsored) search results as the source of query expansion to overcome the problem of low precision and recall of ads retrieval.

Some researchers have analyzed user behaviors in the context of sponsored search [7, 10, 17, 19]. In Jansen's experiments with e-commerce queries [17], the participants' relevance ratings for organic search results and those for ads were practically the same. Moreover, according to a CTR analysis by Danescu-Niculescu-Mizil *et al.* [10], users prefer ads that are dissimilar to organic results for navigational queries, and those that are similar to organic results for informational queries. The findings shown in both literature support the fact that ads play an important role in satisfying the users' information need along with organic search results.

2.2 Query Clustering

Next, we discuss prior art in query clustering, as our approach applies query clustering to sponsored search data in order to mine subgoals.

Query clustering is useful for understanding the underlying user intents and for improving query suggestions, and thus many query clustering techniques have been proposed. Most of existing work have relied on statistics derived from query session and clickthrough data: within-session query co-occurrences [13, 4, 29], similarity of clicked documents [2, 3, 30] and their combination [8, 28]. In this paper, we apply the query clustering algorithm proposed by Sadikov *et al.* [28] to sponsored search data, as it has been shown to achieve state-of-the-art performances through a large-scale user study. The main objective of this study is to show the usefulness of sponsored search data as a resource for mining subgoals: effective query clustering methods other than that by Sadikov *et al.* are also applicable to this problem.

We hypothesized that using the session data alone is not sufficient for the purpose of mining subgoals, because queries issued for a single search goal may span multiple sessions over a length of time and even span multiple users. Note that sessions are defined based on 10-30 minutes of inactivity in many studies, and also that a single session may contain queries for several different search goals.

In contrast to session and clickthrough data, sponsored search data may have the following advantages for the purpose of subgoal mining: (a) we may be able to mine goal-subgoal relationships across sessions and across users; (b) since ads reflect the advertisers' tremendous effort in trying to match queries with the underlying user intents, we can leverage high-quality query-ad relationships that go beyond surface-level matching; (c) as ads are designed to make the user perform an action or transaction, they may directly reflect goals and subgoals.

2.3 Query Intent Categorization

Categorizing queries into predefined classes is an alternative to the aforementioned bottom-up clustering approaches for the purpose of understanding user intents. Many researchers [18, 22, 24] have tackled the problem of categorizing queries into *navigational*, *informational* and *transactional* [5]. Moreover, in the context of sponsored search, Dai *et al.* classified queries into *commercial* (e.g. buy or sell something) and *non-commercial* [9]. Guo and Agichtein [15] further refined the commercial category into *research* and *purchase*. However, these top-down approaches are not appropriate for our purpose, as we need to mine a variety of *unknown* subgoals for a given search goal.

2.4 Search Missions and Goals

The work that is most closely related to our present study is that by Jones and Klinkner [21], who introduced the concepts of *search mission* and *search goal*. According to their definitions, a search goal is an atomic information need represented by one or more queries, while a search mission is a set of related information needs represented by one or more search goals. Although our goal-subgoal relationships are also defined hierarchically just like their mission-goal relationships, ours are different from theirs: while their aim is to analyze individual search tasks of a searcher and thus their mission-goal relationships represent the hierarchical needs for the searcher, our aim is to mine more general hierarchical needs of searchers, rather than limiting ourselves to a session of a single searcher. In addition, although they proposed a model to automatically determine whether a given pair of queries in the same session shares the same search mission or goal, the candidate query pairs are a given. In contrast, given a query, our approach mines its subgoals from related queries in the sponsored search data.

More recently, Aiello *et al.* have proposed a clustering algorithm that clusters search missions into underlying *topics* [1]. Their aim is to find broad topical user profiles of search engine users from query logs, rather than finding mission-goal relationships. For example, they aim at finding the general *travel* intent from related missions such as "Find information on travel to London."

3. SUBGOAL MINING METHOD

3.1 Overview

In response to a query, commercial search engines often present sponsored search results in addition to organic search results. This happens when the query matches with the advertisers' bid phrases,

Table 2: Structure of sponsored search data in this study.

query	ad	impression
fitness	ad1	2,300
fitness	ad2	530
health clubs	ad1	1,880

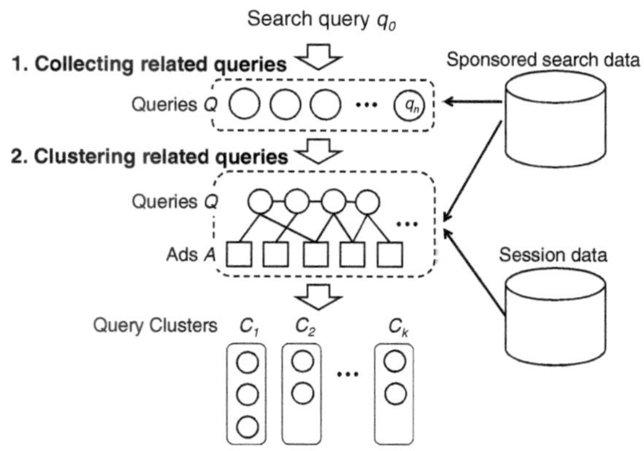

Figure 2: Overview of our method.

and the associated ads are ranked according to their bids and estimated CTR [10]. The contents of each ad, devised by the advertisers, are typically like the ones shown in Figure 1. The sponsored search data used in our work leverages the above mechanism: some examples are shown in Table 2. Each data record is a triple, consisting of the query issued by a search engine user, the ad, and its impression count, which represents the number of times the ad was displayed in response to the query.

Figure 2 shows the overview of our subgoal mining method. In this paper, we refer to the query that is input to our method as *search query*, to distinguish it from its related queries that are to be clustered by our method. Given the search query q_0, our first step is to collect a set of related queries $Q = \{q_1, \ldots, q_n\}$ for a given n by utilizing the ad contents of the aforementioned sponsored search data. Then, our second step outputs a set of query clusters $\mathcal{C} = \{C_1, \ldots, C_k\}$ for a given k. This step uses both sponsored search data and session data and applies the clustering algorithm by Sadikov *et al.* [28].

Sections 3.2 and 3.3 describe the above two steps in detail.

3.2 Collecting Queries

Given the search query q_0 and the required number of related queries n, we first collect a set of related queries $Q = \{q_1, \ldots, q_n\}$ using the ad contents of the sponsored search data, as described below.

Let $\mathcal{A}$ be the entire set of ads archived in the sponsored search data, and let $\mathcal{A}_{q_0} (\subseteq \mathcal{A})$ be the set of all ads whose ad contents contain q_0. For example, note that the ad on the left in Figure 1 contains "lose weight" which could be a search query. For each query q in the sponsored search data such that $w_{\text{imp}}(q, a) > 0$ for some $a \in \mathcal{A}_{q_0}$, where $w_{\text{imp}}(q, a)$ denotes the impression count (See Table 2), we compute its total impression across the relevant ads: $\sum_{a \in \mathcal{A}_{q_0}} w_{\text{imp}}(q, a)$. Then, we sort the queries by the total impression and take the top n. That is, we obtain n queries related to q_0, whose associated ads have high impressions.

3.3 Clustering Queries

Having thus obtained the set of related queries Q, we cluster the queries into k clusters, using the algorithm proposed by Sadikov *et al.* [28]. The original purpose of their clustering algorithm was to identify intents that are common across different query strings, and it relied on two assumptions: (1) If two queries share the same intent, they are associated with the same clicked documents; and (2) If two queries share the same intent, they co-occur within the same session. For the purpose of mining subgoals from sponsored search data, we adapt the above assumptions as follows:

- If two queries represent the same subgoal intent, they are associated with the same ads.
- If two queries represent the same subgoal intent, they co-occur within the same session.

Thus, our departures from the original method by Sadikov *et al.* are: (a) We construct a *query-ad* graph instead of a *query-document* graph; and (b) We use *ad impressions* for computing the query-ad transition probability instead of *document clicks*. Below, we provide more details of the clustering algorithm.

Query-Ad Graph.

Given the set of related queries Q for a search query, we construct a query-ad graph as follows. First, we obtain all ads from the sponsored search data that match a query from Q: let the set of these ads be A. Then we construct a query-ad graph $G = (V, E)$, where $V = Q \cup A$ denotes the set of nodes in G, and E denotes the set of edges in G. In G, the edge between any two queries exists iff they co-occur in the same session; and the edge between any query-ad pair exists iff there is an impression record for that pair in the sponsored search data.

Transition Probability Matrix.

Once we have constructed the query-ad graph G, we prepare a transition matrix $\mathbf{P}$, which represents the transition probabilities among the nodes in G. $\mathbf{P}$ contains three types of transition probabilities: query-to-query, query-to-ad, and ad-to-ad. Figure 3 shows the transition model. As this figure shows, the model contains a parameter called ϵ, which determines the probability of transition from a query node to ad nodes.

query-to-query transition: This probability is determined based on the probability that a pair of queries co-occurs in the same session. The transition probability from query q_i to query q_j is defined as:

$$p(q_j|q_i) = (1-\epsilon)\,\frac{w_{\text{cooc}}(q_i, q_j)}{\sum_{q' \in R(q_i)} w_{\text{cooc}}(q_i, q')},$$

where $w_{\text{cooc}}(q_i, q_j)$ denotes the number of sessions that q_i and q_j co-occurred, and $R(q_i)$ is the set of all queries that co-occurred with q_i within the same session. In practice, there are transitions from q_i to queries that are outside the set of related queries Q. We therefore introduce a special node f in G to collectively represent such queries, and we define the transition probability from q_i to f as follows:

$$p(f|q_i) = (1-\epsilon)\,\frac{\sum_{q' \in (R(q_i)-Q)} w_{\text{cooc}}(q_i, q')}{\sum_{q' \in R(q_i)} w_{\text{cooc}}(q_i, q')}.$$

That is, all transitions from each query q_i to queries outside Q are aggregated to node f. The node f has only the self-transition $p(f|f)$ with probability 1.

query-to-ad transition: This probability is defined as:

$$p(a_j|q_i) = \epsilon\,\frac{w_{\text{imp}}(q_i, a_j)}{\sum_{a' \in A} w_{\text{imp}}(q_i, a')}.$$

ad-to-ad transition: We define $p(a_j|a_i)$ to be 0 if $i \neq j$ and 1 if $i = j$.

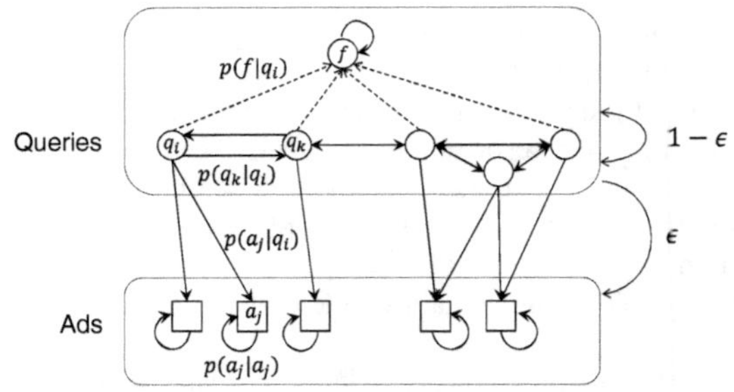

Figure 3: Example transitions on a query-ad graph. A random walk is applied on it for clustering queries.

Table 3: Data statistics.

(a) sponsored search data	
# of unique queries	25,394,581
# of unique ads	25,796,013
# of unique query-ad pairs	142,915,236
(b) clickthrough data	
# of unique queries	86,988,237
# of unique URLs	91,309,344
# of unique query-URL pairs	182,624,954
(c) session data	
# of queries	460,396,996
# of unique queries	142,253,653
# of sessions	214,396,433

Random Walk.

After preparing the transition probability matrix $\mathbf{P}$, we perform a random walk on the query-ad graph G. Let $\mathbf{P}^l$ be the transition probability matrix after an l-step random walk. The row in $\mathbf{P}^l$ for q_i can be interpreted as visit probabilities over the nodes in G after an l-step random walk that started at q_i.

As we can see from Figure 3, there is no ad-to-query transition, and there are only self-transitions among ads. Hence, for each q_i, the visit probabilities over Q approach zero while those over A converge as we iterate the random walk process. As Sadikov *et al.* notes, 3-5 iterations are enough in practice [28]. The transition probability matrix obtained after the convergence is referred to as $\mathbf{P}'$.

Query Clustering.

Finally, we cluster queries in Q using the transition probabilities from $\mathbf{P}'$. For each query $q_i \in Q$, its query vector is represented by a transition probability vector:

$$\mathbf{q}_i = [p'(a_1|q_i), \ldots, p'(a_j|q_i), \ldots, p'(a_{|A|}|q_i)],$$

where $p'(a_j|q_i)$ denotes the transition probability from q_i to a_j in $\mathbf{P}'$, which can be interpreted as the probability that ad a_j would be displayed to the searcher who starts with query q_i. When two query vectors $\mathbf{q}_i$ and $\mathbf{q}_j$ are similar, this implies that similar ads are likely to be displayed in response to two different queries.

Following Sadikov *et al.* [28], we use a complete-linkage clustering method with cosine similarity of the above query vectors to obtain a set of k query clusters $\mathcal{C} = \{C_1, \ldots, C_k\}$.

4. EXPERIMENTAL SETUP

4.1 Logs

In our experiments, we used three types of logs, namely, sponsored search data, clickthrough data and session data. As was shown in Table 2, a sponsored search data record is a query-ad-impression triplet. Similarly, a clickthrough data record is a triplet composed of a query, clicked document and its click count. The latter is used for our implementation of the document-click-based

Table 4: Inter-assessor agreement on the number of annotated subgoals among the assessors (A1, A2, A3).

	A2 #0	#1	#2	Total
A1 #0	574	10	100	684
A1 #1	5	4	4	13
A1 #2	105	3	87	195
Total	684	17	191	892

	A3 #0	#1	#2	Total
A1 #0	613	6	65	684
A1 #1	10	0	3	13
A1 #2	83	1	111	195
Total	706	7	179	892

	A3 #0	#1	#2	Total
A2 #0	585	6	93	684
A2 #1	10	0	7	17
A2 #2	111	1	79	191
Total	706	7	179	892

method of Sadikov *et al.* [28], which we use as a baseline in our experiments. As for session data, each record is a triplet composed of a session ID, a query and a timestamp, and a session is defined based on a 30-minute inactivity. All of these logs were sampled from a popular search engine and span exactly the same period from November 2011.

The raw sponsored search data contained some query-ad pairs for which queries and bid phrases were not *exact matches* (e.g. "health" vs. "health clubs"), thus we filtered out such pairs. This is because the query-ad pairs obtained through non-exact matches depend on the particular ads retrieval algorithm of the search engine, and we wanted to obtain results that are search engine independent. The statistics of the data thus obtained are shown in Table 3.

4.2 Proposed and Baseline Methods

To examine the effectiveness of our method that relies on sponsored search data, we implemented the following four methods.

(a) AdImp: This method clusters queries to mine subgoals as we described in Section 3. Given a search query, it obtains related queries from the sponsored search data, and then clusters them by combining ad impressions from the sponsored search data and query co-occurrences from the session data.

(b) AdImp (no cooc): This is the same as AdImp, except that query-to-query transitions derived from the session data are not used for clustering. That is, only query-to-ad transitions derived from the sponsored search data are utilized.

(c) DocClick: This is our implementation of the query clustering algorithm proposed by Sadikov *et al.* [28], which we treat as a baseline. Thus, given a search query, it obtains related queries from the session data, and then clusters them by combining document clicks from the clickthrough data and query co-occurrences from the session data. While Sadikov *et al.* originally obtained n most frequent queries that *follow* q_0 within the same session, we obtained n most frequent queries that *follow or is followed by* q_0 within the same session, as the order of issuing queries is not important for our purpose.

(d) DocClick (no cooc): This is the same as DocClick, except that query-to-query transitions derived from the session data are not used for clustering. That is, only query-to-document transitions derived from the clickthrough data are utilized.

Following Sadikov *et al.*, we set the number of related queries to $n = 80$ and the transition probability from query to ad or document to $\epsilon = 0.6$. Also, to construct the query-ad (or query-document) graph G for a given search query, we used only the top 15 most frequently displayed ads (or clicked documents) for each related query.

4.3 Test Collection Construction

In order to evaluate the effectiveness of our subgoal mining methods based on query clustering, we created our own test collections as described below.

4.3.1 Selecting Search Queries

Our first step was to select search queries that are to be used as input to our subgoal mining method. Thus, the input queries needed to be reasonably complex and to represent a search goal that may be associated with multiple subgoals. To select such input queries, we chose five domains (Business, Health, Recreation, Society and Sports) from the taxonomy used in the search engine, and extracted queries with high impressions from each domain[1]. From the high impression queries, we selected queries that contains at least one verb, or a noun that is *derivationally related* to a verb according to WordNet[2]. This is because we want to handle queries such as "weight loss" as well as explicitly verb-oriented queries like "lose weight." We thus obtained 892 candidate queries.

Three assessors independently annotated the above candidates to select input queries that are appropriate for subgoal mining. For each query, each assessor first judged whether it represents a search goal (i.e. a particular action that needs to be accomplished) either explicitly or implicitly; if it was judged as a search goal query, she wrote down up to two example subgoals in a *verb plus noun phrase* format (e.g. "do physical exercise" for a candidate query "lose weight").

Through the annotation task, 59 queries (6.6%) were annotated with two subgoals by all three assessors, and 349 queries (39.1%) were annotated with two subgoals by at least one assessor. Table 4 shows the inter-assessor agreement statistics on the number of annotated subgoals, where "#<number>" means the number of subgoals annotated by each assessor. The Fleiss' kappa [12] for this data set is 0.343, which is a moderate agreement. This is not altogether surprising, because given the same search queries, some people can think of good subgoals (i.e. subtasks or solutions), while others cannot. We are tackling the problem of subgoal mining precisely because we want to help the user by presenting possible subgoals that she may not be aware of.

From the annotated queries, we first selected those that were annotated with at least three unique subgoals, regardless of which assessor contributed them. Then, to increase the number of queries, we added some annotated queries for which at least one assessor identified two subgoals. Finally, we removed some queries from the set in order to avoid including very similar search goals. Through this selection process, we obtained a total of 125 search queries for our test collections, 25 queries for each of the five domains. Table 5 shows some example search queries. Note that although we selected these queries from the sponsored search data, these are also part of the session data, as these data sets were obtained from the same period.

4.3.2 Constructing Ground Truth Subgoals

In our present study, we view the problem of subgoal mining as a query clustering task. Thus, given a set of queries that are related to the search query, the problem is to cluster them appropriately, so that each query cluster represents an appropriate subgoal of the original search query. In order to evaluate this task, we need to build some ground truth data. We thus hired the same three assessors to *manually* cluster related queries and construct ground truth subgoals.

[1]Donato *et al.* reported that information needs in domains such as travel, health and education tend to be complex [11].

[2]WordNet, http://wordnet.princeton.edu/

Table 6: Statistics of each test collection. The mean and standard deviation are shown in the format of "<Mean>(<SD>)."

	Collection A			Collection B-1			Collection B-2		
	Both	Ads Only	Session Only	Both	Ads Only	Session Only	Both	Ads Only	Session Only
#search queries	98	–	–	23	–	–	23	–	–
#subgoals per query	9.65(2.80)	8.69(2.58)	7.77(2.49)	9.04(3.93)	7.30(3.37)	5.83(2.48)	9.87(2.29)	8.39(2.39)	7.48(2.26)
#Not Relevant per query	40.11(17.49)	6.59(7.18)	33.80(13.78)	75.30(17.10)	23.04(13.01)	52.91(11.22)	50.91(16.93)	9.13(6.92)	41.91(12.26)
#Not Subgoal per query	13.15(9.86)	7.89(7.57)	6.55(5.46)	30.74(16.55)	22.00(12.18)	12.43(8.80)	31.30(10.71)	22.13(8.48)	12.26(5.98)
Related query overlap per query	0.054(0.041)	–	–	0.059(0.042)	–	–	0.059(0.042)	–	–
Subgoal overlap per query	0.71(0.15)	–	–	0.51(0.24)	–	–	0.62(0.17)	–	–

Table 5: Example search queries in test collections.

Domain	Search query		
Business	car insurance project management	dept relief resume writing	lawn care
Health	back pain relief teeth whitening	eye care quit smoking	lose weight
Recreation	disney cruise vegas shows	fly fishing whale watching	hiking
Society	iq test us immigration	learn spanish wedding	sat prep
Sports	bodybuilding skateboarding	kayaking workout routines	hockey equipment

For each search query, we prepared a set of related queries by pooling the related queries obtained by AdImp and DocClick. Recall that the related queries of AdImp come from the sponsored search data, while those of DocClick come from the session data. As we want to compare the two approaches fairly, we included the related queries from both sides in order to manually identify possible subgoals.

We developed a simple GUI tool to facilitate the manual query clustering process, so that assessors could form clusters by dragging and dropping queries on the screen. Because not all of the pooled related queries represent a subgoal of the given search query, we prepared two special clusters called *Not Relevant* and *Not Subgoal*: the former was for queries that were topically non-relevant to the search goals, and the latter was for queries that are topically relevant but do not represent a subgoal. For example, for search query "lose weight," a related query "lose weight fast" should be put into the *Not Subgoal* cluster, as the latter is a specialization of the original query and does not represent a subgoal.

Using the GUI tool, the assessors manually clustered the displayed queries, and were also asked to provide a *subgoal label* in a "verb plus noun phrase" format. They were told that the target number of clusters was around 10, but were allowed to form fewer or more clusters if necessary. The tool also had a feature for assisting the assessor if she was unfamiliar with the related queries being displayed: by a right click on a related query, a web search result was shown to the user in a separate browser window.

Manual clustering is a tedious process: each assessor typically spent 30-60 minutes to complete the ground truth construction for one search query. In order to save the assessment cost while trying to maintain a reliable experimental environment, one assessor was assigned to 100 search queries, and the other two assessors were assigned to independently handle the remaining 25 search queries. Thus, we obtained two separate search query sets: the first one is relatively large but its ground truth data is constructed by only one assessor; the second one is relatively small but it has two sets of ground truth data.

4.3.3 Test Collection Statistics

As we mentioned above, we formed two separate sets of queries, one containing 100 and the other containing 25, and assigned one assessor to the former and two assessors to the latter. As a result of manual clustering, we found that two search queries from each query set did not contain enough relevant related queries, and therefore removed them. Thus, we obtained three subgoal mining test collections in the end: "Collection A" containing 98 search queries, as well as "Collection B-1" and "Collection B-2" sharing the same 23 search queries but annotated independently by two assessors. Using these three different test collections enables us to focus on general trends of the experimental outcome.

Table 6 shows the statistics of each test collection. The "Both" columns show statistics on the pooled related queries; "Ads Only" columns show statistics on the queries obtained from the sponsored search data (by the AdImp method); and "Session Only" columns shows those on the queries obtained from the session data (by the DocClick method). The "Related query overlap per query" shows the average of the Jaccard coefficient between the two sets of queries obtained from the sponsored search data and the session data. The "Subgoal overlap per query" shows the Jaccard coefficient between two subgoal sets that contain the queries obtained from the sponsored search data and those that contain the queries from the session data. In total, we obtained 1,375 ground truth subgoals (i.e. clusters) with 20,880 clustered related queries.

The "#Not Relevant" row of Table 6 indicates that many queries from the session data (obtained by the DocClick method) were classified as Not Relevant, i.e., off-topic. This suggests that sponsored search data may be a better resource than session data for obtaining topically related queries. On the other hand, the "#Not Subgoals" row shows that both sponsored search data and session data yield some related queries that are topically relevant but do not represent a subtopic of the input search query: recall the aforementioned "lose weight fast" example. In addition, through the analysis of "#Not Subgoals" queries obtained from the sponsored search data, we found some queries may be interpreted as *supergoals* of the given search query. For example, for the search query "kickboxing," related queries "lose weight" and "self defense" were obtained, due to the advertisers' effort in promoting kick-boxing lessons. That is, it is the *search query* "kickboxing" that can be interpreted as a subgoal of "lose weight" or "self defense."

The "Related query overlap per query" row shows that the overlap between the queries obtained based on the ad impressions in the sponsored search data and those obtained based on query co-occurrences in the session data is small. In contrast, the "Subgoal overlap per query" row shows that the overlap of identified subgoals between these two data sources is dramatically higher. This suggests that we may be able to obtain *searchers'* intents (often explicitly represented in session data) by leveraging the *advertisers'* efforts embedded in sponsored search data, even though the two data sources contain seemingly different queries.

As Collections B-1 and B-2 share the same input query set, we can measure inter-assessor agreement for the manually constructed ground truth clusters. For this, we compute the well-known F_1-measure, which measures how any given pair of items to be clustered is correctly grouped. Let TP denote the set of query pairs

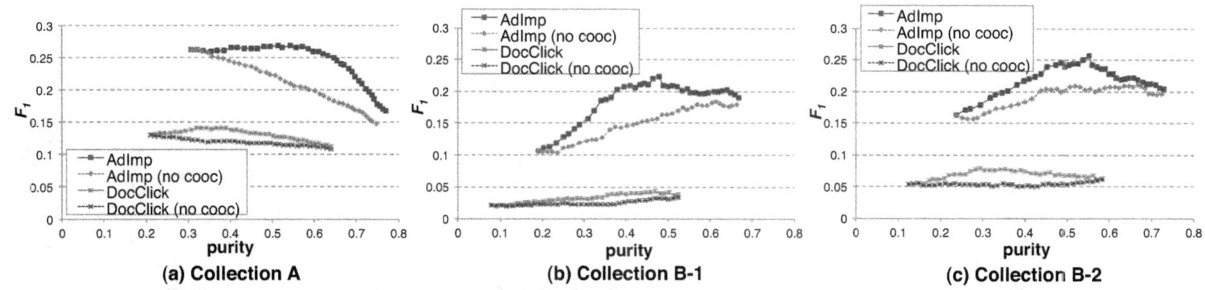

Figure 4: F_1 / purity graphs for the four methods, produced by varying the number of clusters k from 1 to 40.

from the same ground truth cluster that were correctly grouped together, FN denote the set for those that were incorrectly separated, and FP denote the set of query pairs from two different ground truth clusters but were incorrectly grouped together. Then $F_1 = \frac{2\text{PR}}{\text{P+R}}$ where $\text{P} = \frac{|\text{TP}|}{|\text{TP}|+|\text{FP}|}$ and $\text{R} = \frac{|\text{TP}|}{|\text{TP}|+|\text{FN}|}$. When the subgoals from B-1 are treated as the ground truth, the F_1 of the subgoals from B-2 is 0.55. Conversely, when the subgoals from B-2 are treated as the ground truth, the F_1 of the subgoals from B-1 is 0.69. Thus the assessor agreement between B-1 and B-2 is reasonably high.

4.4 Evaluation Metrics

In addition to F_1, we also computed purity, Normalized Mutual Information (NMI) and Rand Index (RI) [25] to evaluate the quality of query clusters that represent subgoals. Purity, which we use as our primary metric along with F_1, measures the homogeneity of each cluster. Given n queries, a set of k clusters $\mathcal{C} = \{C_1, \ldots, C_k\}$ obtained by clustering the queries, and a set of l ground truth clusters that represent subgoals $\mathcal{S} = \{S_1, \ldots S_l\}$, purity is given by: $\frac{1}{n}\sum_{C_i \in \mathcal{C}} |C_i \cap S^{(C_i)}|$, where $S^{(C_i)} = \underset{S_j \in \mathcal{S}}{\text{argmax}}\, |C_i \cap S_j|$, i.e. the "dominant" subgoal in C_i.

By definition, high purity can easily be achieved by choosing a high k (if every cluster contains exactly one query, then the purity is 1), while high F_1 can be achieved if k is close to the number of ground truth clusters. We thus plot F_1 against purity by varying k, to explore methods that achieve overall high accuracy *and* high within-cluster homogeneity.

In addition to the above well-known metrics, we also compute *subgoal recall* of a given cluster set $\mathcal{C}$ as: $\frac{|\cup_{C_i \in \mathcal{C}} S^{(C_i)}|}{|\mathcal{S}|}$.

In contrast to purity, this metric can penalize the case where multiple clusters correspond to the same dominant subgoal.

5. EXPERIMENTAL RESULTS

5.1 Results with All Related Queries

Figure 4 shows the F_1 / purity graphs for AdImp, AdImp (no cooc), DocClick and DocClick (no cooc), obtained by varying the number of clusters k from 1 to 40. Here, all of the related queries that were pooled (See Table 6) were included for evaluation. As for the Not Relevant and Not Subgoal queries in the ground truth data, each of them were treated as an independent cluster on its own when computing the metrics, as we are not interested in making the system form clusters out of these queries. From the figure, it can be observed that AdImp and AdImp (no cooc) achieve higher purity and F_1 compared to DocClick and DocClick (no cooc) for all three test collections. While our method uses an existing query clustering algorithm, it is clear from the results that our novel use of the ads data for the purpose of subgoal mining is highly effective. Moreover, it can be observed that utilizing the query co-occurrences from the session data for clustering is effective in both AdImp and DocClick.

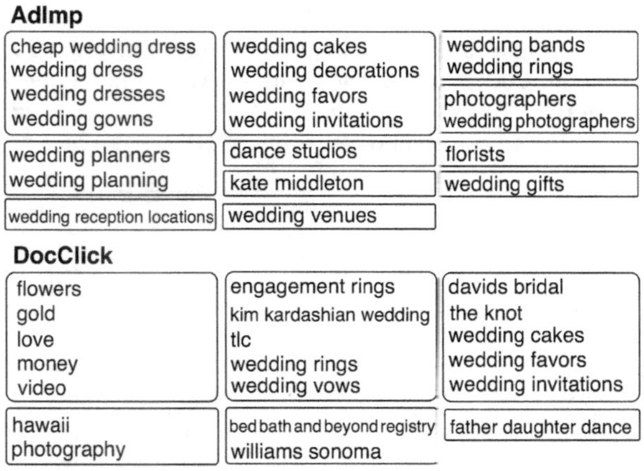

Figure 5: Query clusters produced by AdImp and DocClick, for the top 20 related queries of the search query "wedding."

As an example, Figure 5 contrasts some clusters obtained by AdImp and those obtained by DocClick for the search query "wedding." For each method, 80 related queries were clustered with the target number of clusters $k = 20$: only the top 20 high impression queries for AdImp and top 20 high co-occurrence queries for DocClick are shown in the figure. First, it can be observed that DocClick tends to produce more queries that (arguably) do not directly represent subgoals ("gold," "money." etc.) when compared to AdImp. Second, the clusters obtained by DocClick appear somewhat less homogeneous: for example, "kim kardashian wedding" ("kim kardashian" is the name of a celebrity) and "wedding ring" are in the same cluster. This happened because the query "kim kardashian wedding" shared the news article about her wedding with the query "wedding rings" in the clickthrough data. The query clusters for AdImp look somewhat more organized, thanks to the impressions of ads from various wedding services.

5.2 Results with Relevant Related Queries

While the results in Figure 4 appear to suggest that AdImp is much more effective than DocClick, it should be noted that there are at least two factors that may have contributed to the difference. The first is the quality of the related queries to be clustered: recall that while AdImp obtains related queries from the sponsored search data, DocClick (i.e. method by Sadikov *et al.*) obtains related queries from the session data, and the latter contains a lot of Not Relevant queries, as we have shown in Table 6. The second is the evidence we use for clustering: AdImp uses the ad impressions from the sponsored search data (with query co-occurrences from the session data), while DocClick uses the document clicks from the clickthrough data. Figure 4 does not show which of these factors are contributing by how much.

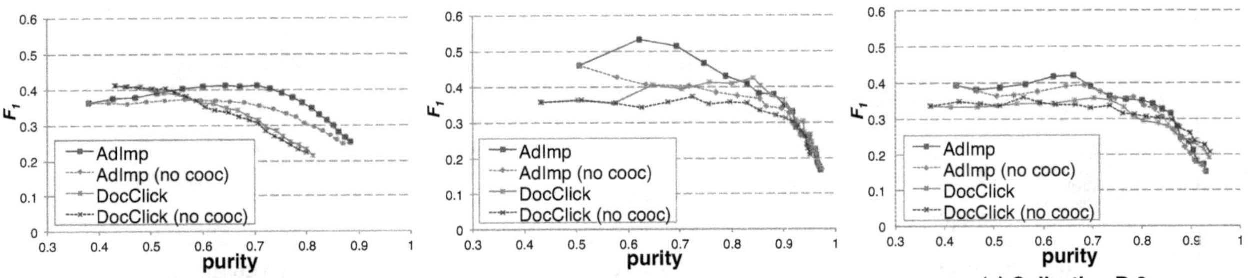

(a) Collection A (b) Collection B-1 (c) Collection B-2

Figure 6: F_1 / purity graphs for the four methods with relevant queries, produced by varying the number of clusters k from 1 to 20.

Table 7: Comparison of methods with different numbers of clusters k on Collection A, when only relevant related queries are clustered. Results that improved significantly (paired t-test) from DocClick are marked with "*" ($p < 0.05$) and "" ($p < 0.01$).**

		AdImp	AdImp (no cooc)	DocClick	DocClick (no cooc)
$k=5$	purity	**0.560***	0.526	0.524	0.528
	NMI	**0.408****	0.341**	0.257	0.257
	RI	**0.598****	0.526**	0.452	0.433
	F_1	0.401	0.367	0.389	**0.402**
	subgoal recall	**0.381****	0.369*	0.336	0.339
$k=10$	purity	**0.729****	0.681*	0.645	0.623
	NMI	**0.577****	0.518**	0.422	0.390
	RI	**0.750****	0.696**	0.601	0.550
	F_1	**0.402****	0.361	0.348	0.340
	subgoal recall	**0.569***	0.546	0.515	0.515

To separate the above two factors, Figure 6 shows the F_1 / purity graphs for the four methods *when only relevant related queries are clustered*, for k between 1 and 20. For each search query, let rel_{ad} and rel_{session} be the number of *relevant queries* (i.e. queries classified as neither Not Relevant nor Not Subgoal) obtained from the sponsored search data and the session data, respectively. We take $\min(rel_{\text{ad}}, rel_{\text{session}})$ relevant queries from both data sets, so that the contribution to the pool is equal in size for every search query. It can be observed that, even if we remove the effect of noise in the related queries to be clustered, AdImp generally achieves both high F_1 and high purity values.

Table 7 shows several metrics in the same "relevant queries only" setting for Collection A, when the number of required clusters k is 5 and 10. Significance differences with DocClick according to the paired t-test are indicated by asterisks, and the highest metric value among the four methods are indicated in bold. It can be observed, for example, that AdImp is significantly more effective than DocClick in terms of all metrics (purity, NMI, RI, F_1 and subgoal recall) when we require 10 clusters. Although not shown in this paper due to lack of space, the results for the other two test collections are generally similar.

These results suggest that the clustering step of AdImp, which relies on ad impressions, has advantages over that of DocClick, which relies on document clicks.

5.3 Results with Queries from the Same Source

The previous experiments showed that AdImp significantly outperforms DocClick, even if we remove the effect of noise in the related queries obtained from DocClick. Recall that while DocClick obtains related queries from the session data and then clusters them primarily based on document clicks from the clickthrough data, AdImp obtains related queries from the sponsored search data and then clusters them primarily based on ad impressions *from the same sponsored search data*. Thus, it is possible that the reason why AdImp works so well is that *queries from sponsored search data can be clustered accurately by leveraging the ad impressions from the same data*. In order to verify this hypothesis, we conducted two additional experiments: the first clustered only relevant queries that were obtained from the sponsored search data; the second clustered only relevant queries that were obtained from the session data.

Figure 7 shows the F_1 / purity graphs for these two additional experiments on Collection A, for k between 1 and 20. First, Figure 7(a) shows that, for clustering related queries obtained from the sponsored search data, AdImp is clearly more effective than DocClick. Moreover, as the difference between AdImp and AdImp (no cooc) and that between DocClick and DocClick (no cooc) show, using the query co-occurrences from the session data at the clustering stage helps. On the other hand, Figure 7(b) shows that, AdImp is *less* effective than DocClick for clustering related queries obtained from the session data. This does not contradict with the above hypothesis (queries from sponsored search data can be clustered accurately by leveraging the ad impressions from the same data). The main reason why AdImp is less effective for queries from the session data is probably due to low coverage of sponsored search data: some queries have few or no associated ads. However, from the Figure 7 (b), while DocClick does not seem to benefit much from the use of query co-occurrences (compare with DocClick (no cooc)), the same statistics boost the performance of AdImp. This implies that session data can compensate for the low coverage of sponsored search data.

5.4 Ad Impressions vs. Ad Clicks

As we explained in Section 3.3, we calculated the query-to-ad transition probability based on *ad impressions*. One alternative way of calculating it is the use of *ad clicks*, which means the number of times ads were clicked by the search engine users. To compare the effect of ad impressions with ad clicks, we implemented two additional methods, namely, "AdClick" and "AdClick (no cooc)," both of which cluster the related queries as AdClick and AdClick (no cooc) do, except that both methods use the top 15 most *clicked ads* for constructing a query-ad graph, and calculate query-to-ad transition probability based on the number of times the ads were clicked. Figure 8 shows the results of these four methods, by varying the number of clusters k from 1 to 20 in the same "relevant query" setting in Section 5.2 for Collection A. From the figure, we can see that AdImp consistently outperforms AdClick, and AdImp (no cooc) also outperforms AdClick (no cooc) in terms of purity and F_1. This result is probably due to the sparseness of ad clicks. It is well known that CTR of ads are much less than those of documents (i.e. organic search results). Thus, it is hard to obtain reliable number of clicks for clustering related queries from the sponsored search data. Note, however, that even AdClick generally achieves both higher F_1 and purity than DocClick shown in Figure 6(a).

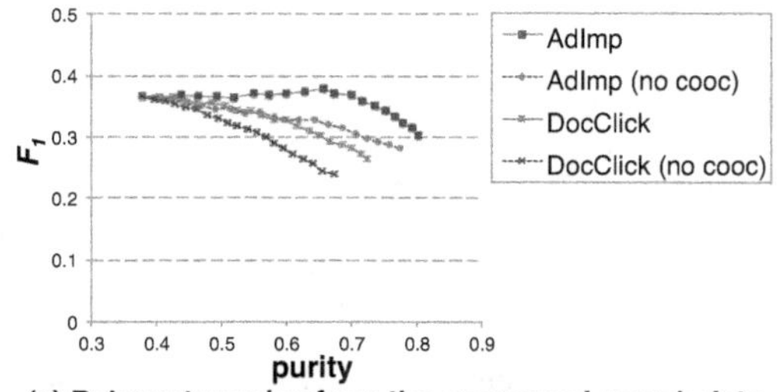

(a) Relevant queries from the sponsored search data

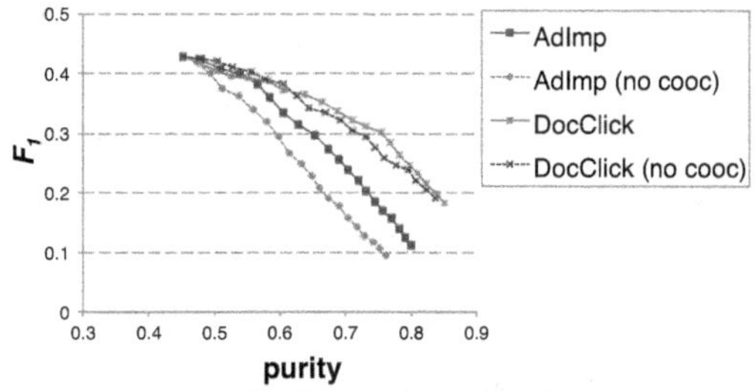

(b) Relevant queries from the session data

Figure 7: Comparison of ad impressions and document clicks under the same set of relevant queries on Collection A, for k between 1 and 20.

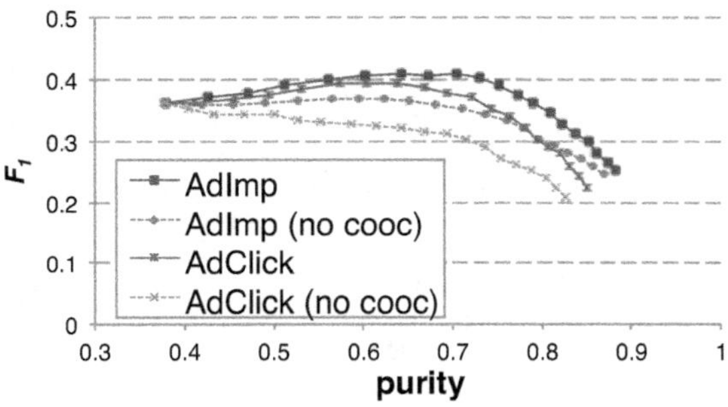

Figure 8: Comparison with ad impressions and clicks. The results were produced by AdImp on Collection A, for k between 1 and 20, when only relevant related queries are clustered.

5.5 Discussion

Our experiments showed that while AdImp generally outperforms DocClick, it is less effective for clustering related queries from the session data (See Section 5.3). As we discussed with Table 6, while the overlap of subgoals between queries from the sponsored search data and those from the session data is high, there are also subgoals that were obtained from only one of the data sources. On average across our three collections, 1.16 and 2.18 subgoals per search query were obtained from pure session data and from pure sponsored search data, respectively. In this subsection, we discuss some actual subgoals for these different cases.

Table 8 provides some examples from our three test collections. Table 8(a) shows subgoals that were formed only from the session data queries. As queries such as "causes of back pain" and "moving to do list" did not trigger any ads, the subgoals **learn about cause** and **make a TODO list** could not be obtained from the sponsored search data. Even if we increase the amount of sponsored search data, it is unlikely that our method will identify such subgoals as they are not strongly related to advertisement.

Table 8(b) shows a few example search queries for which both sponsored search data and session data were successful. Thus, both ad impressions and document clicks can successfully group queries like "moving truck" and "truck rental" together.

Table 8: Example of subgoals obtained: Each subgoal is a cluster of related queries with a manually assigned subgoal label.

(a) Subgoals that only contain queries from the session data.

Collection	B-2
search query	**back pain relief**
subgoal label	**learn about cause**
related queries	back pain causes, causes of back pain
Collection	B-1
search query	**moving**
subgoal label	**make a TODO list**
related queries	moving to do list, moving list of things to do, moving checklist, moving advice, ...

(b) Subgoals that contain queries obtained from both data sources.

Collection	B-1
search query	**learn spanish**
subgoal label	**build Spanish vocabulary**
related queries	learn spanish words, spanish dictionary, spanish verbs, spanish vocabrary, ...
Collection	B-2
search query	**moving**
subgoal label	**rent a truck**
related queries	moving truck, ryder, truck rental, ...

(c) Subgoals that only contain queries from the sponsored search data.

Collection	A
search query	**relieve stress**
subgoal label	**visit a zen garden**
related queries	zen garden
Collection	A
search query	**quit smoking**
subgoal label	**have acupuncture treatment**
related queries	acupuncture, acupuncture quit smoking, acupuncture stop smoking

Finally, Table 8(c) shows a few subgoals that were obtained only from the sponsored search data. Note that a search engine user who is looking for ways to "relieve stress" or to "quit smoking" may not even be aware that solutions such as **visit a zen garden** or **have acupuncture treatment** exist. Thus, it is the "wisdom of advertisers" that helps our method to *propose* such solutions to the searcher. It would be very difficult to find these "unexpected" solutions in the session data: if the searchers are unaware of these solutions, they are highly unlikely to issue queries about them.

6. CONCLUSIONS

In this study, we defined the problem of mining subgoals of a given search goal from data by means of query clustering, and proposed to utilize sponsored search data for this purpose. Our method (AdImp) first obtains related queries from the sponsored search data, and then clusters them based on ad impressions from the same data as well as query co-occurrences from session data. This was compared with a similar state-of-the-art method [28] (DocClick) that first obtains related queries from the session data, and then clusters them based on document clicks from clickthrough data as well as query co-occurrences from session data. Our experimental results using three in-house test collections showed that (1) related queries obtained from sponsored search data are more relevant than those obtained from session data; and (2) AdImp significantly outperforms DocClick in terms of purity, NMI, Rand Index, F_1 and subgoal recall.

There are several limitations to the present study. First, this study did not address the problem of generating a label for each query cluster (e.g. [26]). While our current representation of a subgoal is in the form of a cluster of several queries, it would be useful for the searcher if we could also provide an explicit label for each subgoal. We plan to tackle this problem by leveraging the ad contents: for example, the phrase "get some exercise" shown in Figure 1 is probably a good candidate as a subgoal label given the query "lose weight." Next, although we mentioned in Section 1 that around 68% of our head queries had some ads displayed with the organic search results, the applicability of our method is probably much lower than this number suggests. As we described in Section 4.3.1, only 39.1% of our candidate verb-oriented queries were annotated with multiple subgoals by at least one assessor. On a similar note, Jones and Klinkner [21], who defined the hierarchy of search missions and goals (See Section 2.4), also reported that only 20% of user queries from their Yahoo! query log were associated with hierarchically organized needs. Moreover, our method does not work if the query is not included in the sponsored search data, which is generally smaller compared to clickthrough and session data (See Table 3). However, although the fraction of queries that our method can handle may not be large, we argue that these queries represent a very important query segment, for which current search engines require breakthroughs.

As future work, we would like to refine our subgoal mining algorithm. As this study focused on verifying the usefulness of sponsored search data as a resource, we applied an existing query clustering algorithm. Thus, we did not have any explicit mechanisms, for example, for classifying subgoals of a given search query, *supergoals* of the query and queries that share the same goal with the query. Moreover, as we mentioned in Section 1, while some types of subgoal wholly accomplish the original search goal (e.g. "do physical exercise" may be a good solution to "lose weight"), others only partially accomplish the original search goal (e.g. "book flights" may be one step towards accomplishing the "travel London" search goal, but other subtasks such as "book a hotel" are also required). Furthermore, there may be temporal dependencies among these subtasks/subgoals: some subgoals need to be satisfied before others. Mining these different *types* of subgoal would be useful for improving search effectiveness and experience.

7. REFERENCES

[1] L. M. Aiello, D. Donato, U. Ozertem, and F. Menczer. Behavior-driven clustering of queries into topics. In *Proc. of CIKM*, pages 1373–1382, 2011.

[2] R. Baeza-Yates, C. Hurtado, and M. Mendoza. Query recommendation using query logs in search engines. In *Current Trends in Database Technology-EDBT 2004 Workshops*, pages 588–596, 2004.

[3] D. Beeferman and A. Berger. Agglomerative clustering of a search engine query log. In *Proc. of KDD*, pages 407–416, 2000.

[4] P. Boldi, F. Bonchi, C. Castillo, D. Donato, A. Gionis, and S. Vigna. The query-flow graph: model and applications. In *Proc. of CIKM*, pages 609–618, 2008.

[5] A. Broder. A taxonomy of web search. *ACM SIGIR Forum*, 36(2):3–10, 2002.

[6] A. Broder, P. Ciccolo, M. Fontoura, E. Gabrilovich, V. Josifovski, and L. Riedel. Search advertising using web relevance feedback. In *Proc. of CIKM*, pages 1013–1022, 2008.

[7] G. Buscher, S. T. Dumais, and E. Cutrell. The good, the bad, and the random: an eye-tracking study of ad quality in web search. In *Proc. of SIGIR*, pages 42–49, 2010.

[8] H. Cao, D. Jiang, J. Pei, Q. He, Z. Liao, E. Chen, and H. Li. Context-aware query suggestion by mining click-through and session data. In *Proc. of KDD*, pages 875–883, 2008.

[9] H. K. Dai, L. Zhao, Z. Nie, J.-R. Wen, L. Wang, and Y. Li. Detecting online commercial intention (OCI). In *Proc. of WWW*, pages 829–837, 2006.

[10] C. Danescu-Niculescu-Mizil, A. Z. Broder, E. Gabrilovich, V. Josifovski, and B. Pang. Competing for users' attention: on the interplay between organic and sponsored search results. In *Proc. of WWW*, pages 291–300, 2010.

[11] D. Donato, F. Bonchi, T. Chi, and Y. Maarek. Do you want to take notes?: identifying research missions in Yahoo! search pad. In *Proc. of WWW*, pages 321–330, 2010.

[12] J. Fleiss and J. Cohen. The equivalence of weighted kappa and the intraclass correlation coefficient as measures of reliability. *Educational and Psychological Measurement*, 1973.

[13] B. M. Fonseca, P. Golgher, B. Pôssas, B. Ribeiro-Neto, and N. Ziviani. Concept-based interactive query expansion. In *Proc. of CIKM*, pages 696–703, 2005.

[14] T. Graepel, J. Candela, T. Borchert, and R. Herbrich. Web-scale bayesian click-through rate prediction for sponsored search advertising in Microsoft's Bing search engine. In *Proc. of ICML*, pages 13–20, 2010.

[15] Q. Guo and E. Agichtein. Ready to buy or just browsing?: detecting web searcher goals from interaction data. In *Proc. of SIGIR*, pages 130–137, 2010.

[16] D. Hillard, S. Schroedl, E. Manavoglu, H. Raghavan, and C. Leggetter. Improving ad relevance in sponsored search. In *Proc. of WSDM*, pages 361–370, 2010.

[17] B. J. Jansen. The comparative effectiveness of sponsored and nonsponsored links for web e-commerce queries. *ACM Transactions on the Web*, 1(3), 2007.

[18] B. J. Jansen, D. Booth, and A. Spink. Determining the informational, navigational, and transactional intent of web queries. *Information Processing & Management*, 44(3):1251–1266, 2008.

[19] B. J. Jansen and M. Resnick. Examining searcher perceptions of and interactions with sponsored results. In *Workshop on Sponsored Search Auctions*, 2005.

[20] K. Järvelin and J. Kekäläinen. Cumulated gain-based evaluation of IR techniques. *ACM Transactions on Information Systems*, 20(4):422–446, 2002.

[21] R. Jones and K. L. Klinkner. Beyond the session timeout: automatic hierarchical segmentation of search topics in query logs. In *Proc. of CIKM*, pages 699–708, 2008.

[22] I. Kang and G. Kim. Query type classification for web document retrieval. In *Proc. of SIGIR*, pages 64–71, 2006.

[23] E. Kanoulas, B. Carterette, P. D. Clough, and M. Sanderson. Evaluating multi-query sessions. In *Proc. of SIGIR*, pages 1053–1062, 2011.

[24] Y. Liu, X. Ni, J.-T. Sun, and Z. Chen. Unsupervised transactional query classification based on webpage form understanding. In *Proc. of CIKM*, pages 57–66, 2011.

[25] C. D. Manning, P. Raghavan, and H. Schütze. *Introduction to Information Retrieval*. Cambridge University Press, 2008.

[26] M. P. Kato, T. Sakai, and K. Tanaka. Structured query suggestion for specialization and parallel movement: effect on search behaviors. In *Proc. of WWW*, pages 389–398, 2012.

[27] F. Radlinski, A. Broder, P. Ciccolo, E. Gabrilovich, V. Josifovski, and L. Riedel. Optimizing relevance and revenue in ad search: a query substitution approach. In *Proc. of SIGIR*, pages 403–410, 2008.

[28] E. Sadikov, J. Madhavan, L. Wang, and A. Halevy. Clustering query refinements by user intent. In *Proc. of WWW*, pages 841–850, 2010.

[29] X. Wang, D. Chakrabarti, and K. Punera. Mining broad latent query aspects from search sessions. In *Proc. of KDD*, pages 867–876, 2009.

[30] J.-R. Wen, J.-Y. Nie, and H.-J. Zhang. Clustering user queries of a search engine. In *Proc. of WWW*, pages 162–168, 2001.

[31] R. White and R. Roth. Exploratory search: Beyond the query-response paradigm. *Synthesis Lectures on Information Concepts, Retrieval, and Services*, 1(1):1–98, 2009.

[32] W. Xu, E. Manavoglu, and E. Cantu-Paz. Temporal click model for sponsored search. In *Proc. of SIGIR*, pages 106–113, 2010.

Sequential Selection of Correlated Ads by POMDPs

Shuai Yuan, Jun Wang
Department of Computer Science, University College London
{s.yuan, j.wang}@cs.ucl.ac.uk

ABSTRACT

Online advertising has become a key source of revenue for both web search engines and online publishers. For them, the ability of allocating *right* ads to *right* webpages is critical because any mismatched ads would not only harm web users' satisfactions but also lower the ad income. In this paper, we study how online publishers could optimally select ads to maximize their ad incomes over time. The conventional offline, content-based matching between webpages and ads is a fine start but cannot solve the problem completely because good matching does not necessarily lead to good payoff. Moreover, with the limited display impressions, we need to balance the need of selecting ads to learn true ad payoffs (exploration) with that of allocating ads to generate high immediate payoffs based on the current belief (exploitation). In this paper, we address the problem by employing Partially observable Markov decision processes (POMDPs) and discuss how to utilize the correlation of ads to improve the efficiency of the exploration and increase ad incomes in a long run. Our mathematical derivation shows that the belief states of correlated ads can be naturally updated using a formula similar to collaborative filtering. To test our model, a real world ad dataset from a major search engine is collected and categorized. Experimenting over the data, we provide an analyse of the effect of the underlying parameters, and demonstrate that our algorithms significantly outperform other strong baselines.

Categories and Subject Descriptors

I.2.6 [**Computing Methodologies**]: Artificial Intelligence—*Learning*; I.2.8 [**Computing Methodologies**]: Artificial Intelligence—*Problem Solving, Control Methods, and Search*

General Terms

Algorithms, Design, Performance

Keywords

computational advertising, revenue optimisation, correlation, POMDPs, value iteration

CIKM'12, October 29–November 2, 2012, Maui, HI, USA.

1. INTRODUCTION

Online advertising has received blooming development in recent years. The volume of the industry has grown from $8.1 billion in 2000 to $26 billion in 2010 with a new record every year [1]. Online advertising is vitally important for both web search engines and online content providers and publishers because it provides them with major sources of revenue. For example, Google search engine was serving 7.2 billion page views per day in 2011 [9] and its revenue is mainly driven by advertising products like AdWords, DoubleClick, and AdMob. Similarly, online content providers such as Yahoo! and news agencies such as New York Times increasingly choose advertising as the smarter alternative to conventional subscription based services.

Online publishers can make profit by selling *impressions* (an instance of an ad being seen on users' monitors). A fundamental problem faced by publishers is that given limited display impressions and ad slots, how to maximize their ad incomes over time. It is a complex problem because in practice publishers usually need to make decisions considering various aspects. First, they have to decide whether to deal private contracts with advertisers or agencies directly, or to participate in public ad networks or exchanges to reach more demands. In [14] a queuing system was proposed to find the optimal policy of selecting advertisers to make private contracts, whereas in [6, 20], the focus is on pricing ads properly in either of the two settings. Second, the payment scheme is different and the publishers need to choose between pay-per-view, pay-per-click, and possibly other models. A balance can be established in a static setting as reported in [21, 13, 19]. Lastly and most importantly, a decision has to be made on which page [8, 33] and which users [31, 28] these ads should be matched with, probably in a real-time fashion using text summaries [3]. Traditionally the matching is done by ad networks and advertisers are allowed to choose which keywords they intend to bid. Now publishers are getting more involved and can actively switch in real-time between different pricing schemes and different networks in order to increase their ad incomes, as demonstrated in the Google DFP Small Business system [15] and some ad exchanges like AdBrite (`http://www.adbrite.com/`).

This essentially allows online publishers to integrate the above decisions all together in a more general framework to optimize their ad revenue. Yet, the following challenges remain unsolved because of its dynamic settings: First, the prior analysis of the matching between content and ads provides a fine start but a good payoff is not necessarily guaranteed by a good matching and need to be verified over time.

With the limited display impressions, we also need to balance the need of selecting ads and their pricing schemes to learn the true payoffs (exploration) with that of allocating ads to generate high immediate payoffs based on the current belief (exploitation). Second, online publishers have more opportunities to explore from different ad networks and pricing schemes provided ads are correlated. A key question is how to make use of the correlations embedded in the data to improve the efficiency of the exploration and increase the ad incomes in a long run. In this paper, we study the above two issues and formulate the sequential ad selection problem by applying Partially observable Markov decision processes (POMDPs). To provide a basic understanding of publisher revenue problem when dealing with multiple ads or ad sources, we do not distinguish between various trade mechanisms and pricing models, but instead consider them essentially the same and focus on their payoffs. Moreover, to make our study focused, we formulate our problem by considering the correlation of ads, while bearing in mind that the same principle and result can be applied to the correlation of webpages and users. Our mathematical derivation shows that the belief states of correlated ads can be naturally updated using a formula similar to collaborative filtering. We examine the model on a carefully collected dataset, and the results show that our models, particularly with the new belief updates, outperform other strong baselines.

The remainder of the paper is organized as follows: in Section 2 we provide a discussion about related work and in Section 3 we present the proposed model and its approximate solutions. The experiments are given in Section 4 and conclusions are presented in Section 5.

2. RELATED WORK

Previous research on publisher revenue optimization has been mainly focused on display ads and their (private) contracts. Traditionally the research question is limited to how to choose advertisers to make (private) contracts with, as elaborated in [12, 14, 26]. In [14] the authors used a queueing system to accommodate advertisers and added constraint that advertisers are impatient and would leave if their ads cannot be displayed right way. A dynamic programming solution was provided in [26] by combining the available ad inventories and dynamically delivery of promised advertising contract to the viewers. Although our model also optimizes publisher revenue over time, the settings are different: we focus on contextual advertising, where ads can be specified using keywords or categories, and study how the matching between webpages and ads can be established w.r.t. payoffs over time. We introduce a simple yet general dynamical payoff model that helps to address the inventory management problem while taking into account the correlation of ads.

An interesting variation of ad inventory management problem is to find the optimal pricing models. The pay-per-view and pay-per-click models were discussed in [17]. In [21], the study concluded that a combination of pay-per-view and per-per-click pricing models may be the most optimal for an advertiser who has to choose between them. The same choice problem has later been studied in [13] and the author concluded that the optimal choice for a price taking publisher is either pay-per-view or per-per-click but not a combination of those two pricing models. Recently similar conclusion was reported in [19], in which the competition between two models was discussed but limited to a static setting: a single period of planning horizon. Similarly in [14] the authors assumed that the publisher could choose ad networks to utilize remnant impressions after fulfilling contracts. Our goal is similar to those papers since we are also targeted to find optimal ad sources. However, our model is focused on real-time impression-based setting; we also utilize the correlation of ads to accelerate the discovery process, and provide an analyse of the optimization problem over time. For instance, different from [13] we do not make any assumption on market elasticity; neither do we constraint the publisher to a contract-first setup [14].

Another aspect of publisher revenue optimization is ad scheduling with the constraint of geometrical features of website, uncertainty of advertisers and available ad inventory (impressions) [18, 26, 30]. If the publisher fails to deliver promised impressions a good-will penalty would be incurred. In [30] the ad scheduling problem was modelled in video games and a dynamic algorithm was developed. When considering pricing models, e.g. pay-per-click, publishers need to understand the webpage content and user preferences to achieve a better scheduling. Because now displaying ads may not earn the publisher anything if ads are not relevant or users are not interested therefore no clicks. Traditionally optimizing matching between webpages and ads belongs to the field of contextual advertising research [8, 24]. In [8] a system utilizing both semantic and syntactic features was proposed to address the problem. Similarly the correlation of user-ad (behaviour targeting) has also been studied previously in [32, 11], focusing on improving advertising effectiveness by modelling attitude and feedback from users. Our study can be consider as a dynamical extension of the above works. The contextual matching can be used as a prior belief in our model and it can be updated and verified using our update formulas sequentially.

In terms of techniques, our work is closely related to multi-arm bandit with dependent arms discussed in [23] as we also face a multi-period selection problem with an exploration and exploitation dilemma. In [23] the dependencies of candidates are modelled by clustering them first; after that, a multi-arm bandit algorithm runs twice: first selects a cluster and then a candidate in that cluster. Our paper is different in that we directly model the dependencies using a covariance matrix. The impact of correlation is well formulated and illustrated by rigorously deriving the belief updates once other correlated ads have been selected. Specifically, the problem is formulated by applying Partially Observable Markov Decision Processes (POMDPs) with discrete action (selection of ads), continuous observations (payoffs), and continuous hidden states (performance of ads). Our model is a special case of continuous POMDPs [10, 29], where two-stage Gaussian generative processes and no transit of hidden states are considered during the planning horizon. To provide an optimal ad selection, similar with [29, 27], we follow the Monte Carlo sampling approach to deal with continuous observations and to approximate a Dynamic Programming solution in the finite planning horizon. As a complement of the approximation approach, we also extend an Upper Confidence Bound algorithm [4] by integrating it with our belief update method.

3. THE PROPOSED MODEL

3.1 The Sequential Payoff Model

In this section we formulate the sequential ad selection problem for a publisher-side system. Suppose there is an online publisher who wants to put ads on their hosting webpages to generate profits. The ads could be obtained from various sources either by making contracts with advertisers directly, by registering with ad networks, or by employing a supply-side-platform [15]. We now formally introduce the sequential payoff model to describe how the publisher revenue is earned from ads. Suppose there are N ads from various ad networks or exchanges available for the publisher. For each display impression, the publisher needs to decide which ad should be selected. Without loss of generality, we consider to make our selection decisions every M impressions and denote the decision times as $t \in [1, ..., T]$. To stay focused, we consider the impression has only one ad slot, while bearing in mind that the scenario of multiple ad slots per impression can be addressed by incorporating user click-through models (for pay-per-click ads) to remove rank bias [25] or consider them from different impressions (for pay-per-view ads).

For each time step $t \in [1, ..., T]$, we define

$$\Psi(t) = \begin{bmatrix} s(1), & x(1) \\ \dots, & \dots \\ s(t-1), & x(t-1) \end{bmatrix} \quad (1)$$

as the available information up to time t, where $s(t) \in N$ denotes the decision, i.e. the index of ad selected for the time step t. We use the random variable $X(t)$ to denote the payoff gained at time step t and $x(t)$ its realization.

Let π be an arbitrary choosing policy according to the information obtained so far. We define

$$s(t) \equiv \pi(\Psi(t)) \quad (2)$$

To simplify our notation, we use them exchangeably in the rest of the paper. The cumulative payoff over time T with certain policy π is

$$R_\pi(T) \equiv M \sum_{t=1}^{T} X_{s(t)}(t) \quad (3)$$

Our goal is to choose an optimal policy to maximize $R_\pi(T)$. However, we do not observe any future $x_{s(t)}(t)$ (where $t \geq t'$) before making a decision about $s(t)$ (at $t = t'$). For a given webpage, we assume two generative processes to generate the payoffs as shown in Figure 1. First, we consider the matching between ads and the webpage and denote the true but unknown payoffs of ads over a webpage as $\boldsymbol{\mu}$, a N-dimension vector. This vector is generated from a multivariate Gaussian distribution governed by mean vector $\boldsymbol{\theta}$ and covariance matrix $\boldsymbol{\Sigma}$ as the following

$$\boldsymbol{\mu} \sim \mathcal{N}(\boldsymbol{\theta}, \boldsymbol{\Sigma}) \quad (4)$$

where $\boldsymbol{\theta}$ and $\boldsymbol{\Sigma}$ are the parameters of the model and can be estimated beforehand from data. Meanwhile, considering the fact that the payoffs are affected by either the visiting users, some unexpected factors, or the uncertainty that has not been well modelled from the Gaussian, the observed payoffs are generated from the true payoffs by

$$\boldsymbol{X} \sim \mathcal{N}(\boldsymbol{\mu}, \sigma_0^2 \cdot \boldsymbol{I}) \quad (5)$$

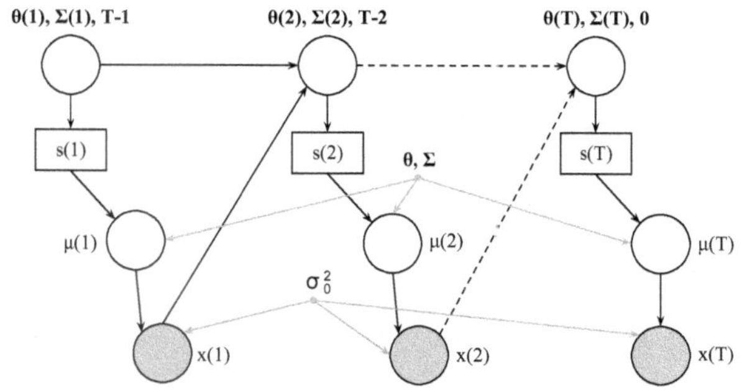

Figure 1: The payoff model illustrated by an influence diagram representation with generative processes of a finite horizon POMDP. In this diagram the non-filled circular nodes represent variables including belief states; the shaded nodes represent rewards as well as observations of the system; the black point nodes represent non-random values; and the non-filled square rectangular nodes represent actions. The dotted lines indicate indirect dependency and intermediate nodes are not drawn. Note that $s(\cdot)$ also depends on σ_0^2 but lines are not drawn for simplicity.

where $\boldsymbol{X}$ is a N-dimension observed payoff vector and $\boldsymbol{I}$ is the identity matrix. A simple variance σ_0^2 is used to model the noise. Note that our treatment of the uncertainty from the underlying users is basic that we use a universal constant to describe the possible noise. We will show in our experiments that the noise factor, although simple, plays an important role in controlling the sensitivity of our model. For a more advanced treatment about user modelling, we refer to [28]. Given the two-stage process, the objective of the publisher is to find the optimal policy which maximizes the expectation of the overall ad income through the period, i.e.

$$\begin{aligned} \pi^* &= \arg\max_\pi \mathbb{E}\left[R_\pi(T)\right] \\ &= \arg\max_\pi \mathbb{E}\left[\sum_{t=1}^{T} X_{s(t)}(t)\right] \\ &= \arg\max_\pi \sum_{t=1}^{T} \mathbb{E}\left[X_{s(t)}(t)\right] \\ &= \arg\max_\pi \sum_{t=1}^{T} \int_x x_{s(t)}(t) p(x_{s(t)}(t)|\Psi(t))dx \\ &= \arg\max_\pi \sum_{t=1}^{T} \theta_{s(t)}(t) \end{aligned} \quad (6)$$

where we drop M from Equation 3 because the decision is independent of it. Note that $\theta_{s(t)}(t)$ is the shorthand for $\hat{\mu}_{s(t)}|\Psi(t)$, denoting the estimated expectation of $\mu_{s(t)}$ at time step t giving all available information $\Psi(t)$. It presents our belief at time t. Our formulation is in fact a special case of continuous POMDPs [10, 29], where $\boldsymbol{\mu}$ is the hidden state and $\boldsymbol{X}$ is the observation over time and our belief about $\boldsymbol{\mu}$ would be sequentially updated using a posterior probability. Our next task is to provide the estimation $\theta_{s(t)}(t)$ at each time step t after an ad has been selected and its payoff has been observed. We are particularly interested in the update for correlated ads, which will be discussed in the next section.

3.2 Belief Updates

At each time step the publisher makes a decision, observes the payoff, then updates expected payoffs of all ads. In order to calculate the expected payoffs the publisher needs to calculate the value of $\boldsymbol{\theta}(t+1)$ and $\boldsymbol{\Sigma}(t+1)$ according to observation $x_{s(t)}(t)$ and previous belief. In this section we derive the update equation using Bayesian inference. Let us first look at the brief update of the same ads. Suppose the publisher has two ad candidates. The 1st ad was selected at time step t and received a payoff of $x_1(t)$. With Bayes' theorem and marginalizing μ_1 out, we obtain the p.d.f. of X_1 conditioned on the new observation $x_1(t)$ and previous available information $\Psi(t)$:

$$\begin{aligned} &p\left(x_1|x_1(t),\Psi(t)\right) \\ &= \int p\left(x_1|x_1(t),\Psi(t),\mu_1\right) p\left(\mu_1|x_1(t),\Psi(t)\right) d\mu, \end{aligned} \tag{7}$$

where we know

$$\begin{aligned} p(\mu_1|x_1(t),\Psi(t)) &\propto p(x_1(t)|\mu_1,\Psi(t))p(\mu_1|\Psi(t)) \\ &\propto \exp\left\{-\left(x_1(t)-\mu_1\right)^2-\left(\mu_1-\theta_1(t)\right)^2\right\} \end{aligned} \tag{8}$$

and by inspecting the exponent part, we can find the posterior distribution of μ_1 as

$$\begin{aligned} \mu_1|x_1(t) &\sim \mathcal{N}\left(\theta_1(t+1),\sigma_1^2(t+1)\right) \\ \theta_1(t+1) &= \frac{\sigma_1^2(t)x_1(t)+\sigma_0^2\theta_1(t)}{\sigma_1^2(t)+\sigma_0^2} \\ \sigma_1^2(t+1) &= \frac{\sigma_1^2(t)\sigma_0^2}{\sigma_1^2(t)+\sigma_0^2} \end{aligned} \tag{9}$$

where similarly we write $\sigma_i^2(t)$ as the shorthand for $\sigma_i^2|\Psi(t)$.

Substituting the posterior of μ_1 into Equation 7 gives the expected payoff of the selected ad as

$$X_1|x_1(t),\Psi(t) \sim \mathcal{N}\left(\theta_1(t+1),\sigma_0^2+\sigma_1^2(t+1)\right) \tag{10}$$

where recall that we assume the prior noise σ_0^2 is known.

3.2.1 *Correlated Ads*

In a real world situation the payoffs of ads are correlated. Similar products, using similar creative, or targeting similar potential customers will generate similar payoffs. By considering the correlation of ads the publisher could find a more efficient way of identifying best candidates because not only the beliefs of the selected ads themselves can be updated using Equation 10, but so do the other correlated ads. Again with Bayes' theorem and marginalizing μ_1 out, we obtain the p.d.f. of X_2 conditioned on the observation $x_1(t)$ and previous available information $\Psi(t)$

$$\begin{aligned} &p\left(x_2|x_1(t),\Psi(t)\right) \\ &= \int p\left(x_2|\mu_2,x_1(t),\Psi(t)\right) p(\mu_2|x_1(t),\Psi(t))d\mu_2 \end{aligned} \tag{11}$$

where

$$\begin{aligned} &p(\mu_2|x_1(t),\Psi(t)) \\ &\propto p(x_1(t)|\mu_2,\Psi(t))p(\mu_2|\Psi(t)) \\ &= p(\mu_2|\Psi(t))\int p(x_1(t)|\mu_1,\Psi(t))p(\mu_1|\mu_2,\Psi(t))d\mu_1 \end{aligned} \tag{12}$$

With the covariance known, we have the conditional distribution of μ_1 on μ_2 as

$$\begin{aligned} \mu_1|\mu_2 &\sim \mathcal{N}(\theta_1|\mu_2,\sigma_1^2|\mu_2) \\ \theta_1|\mu_2 &= \theta_1+\frac{\sigma_{1,2}}{\sigma_2^2}(\mu_2-\theta_2) \\ \sigma_1^2|\mu_2 &= \sigma_1^2-\frac{\sigma_{1,2}^2}{\sigma_2^2} \end{aligned} \tag{13}$$

where $\sigma_{1,2}$ is the covariance of $\{\mu_1,\mu_2\}$. Substituting them into Equation 12 gives

$$\begin{aligned} \mu_2|x_1(t) &\sim \mathcal{N}(\theta_2(t+1),\sigma_2^2(t+1)) \\ \theta_2(t+1) &= \theta_2(t)+\sigma_{1,2}\frac{x_1(t)-\theta_1(t)}{\sigma_1^2(t)+\sigma_0^2} \\ \sigma_2^2(t+1) &= \sigma_2^2(t)-\frac{\sigma_{1,2}^2}{\sigma_1^2(t)+\sigma_0^2} \end{aligned} \tag{14}$$

Similarly substituting the posterior of μ_2 from Equation 14 to Equation 11 we obtain the expected payoff of the non-selected ad as

$$X_2|x_1(t),\Psi(t) \sim \mathcal{N}\left(\theta_2(t+1),\sigma_0^2+\sigma_2^2(t+1)\right) \tag{15}$$

Note the correctness of the equation can be verified by setting the 1st and 2nd ads equal – if we have $\theta_1=\theta_2$ and $\sigma_1^2=\sigma_2^2=\sigma_{1,2}$, then Equation 14 becomes exactly Equation 9. Therefore we take Equation 14 as the unified equation covering both self and correlated updates. The objective function in Equation 6 is now completed with the belief update formulas (constraints), all of which are now summarized together as the following

$$\pi^* = \arg\max_{\pi} \sum_{t=1}^{T} \theta_{s(t)}(t) \tag{16}$$

subject to

$$\theta_{s(t+1)}(t+1) = \theta_{s(t+1)}(t)+\sigma_{s(t),s(t+1)}\frac{x_{s(t)}(t)-\theta_{s(t)}(t)}{\sigma_{s(t)}^2(t)+\sigma_0^2} \tag{17}$$

$$\sigma_{s(t+1)}^2(t+1) = \sigma_{s(t+1)}^2(t)-\frac{\sigma_{s(t),s(t+1)}^2}{\sigma_{s(t)}^2(t)+\sigma_0^2} \tag{18}$$

It is worth noticing that the update in Equation 17 is closely related to the "word of mouth" heuristic adopted in collaborative filtering [7, 16]. In the collaborative filtering approaches, particularly, the user-based ones, the rating of a target user is estimated by looking at other similar users; The more similar a user is, the more contribution he or she would have to the prediction. Using the heuristic, the final rating prediction is a weighted average across all similar users [16] and the similarity is usually measured by cosine similarity or Pearson's correlation coefficient and user means are used to remove the bias of mean ratings among users [7]. In this paper, using a simple Gaussian model, we naturally derive a collaborative update mechanism across correlated ads. The major difference is that the update is in a sequential way. As seen in Equation 17, the similarity measure here is the correlation normalized by the variance, and $\theta_{s(t+1)}(t)$ and $\theta_{s(t)}(t)$ are used to remove the bias from the mean payoffs between different ads. Moreover, Equation 18 naturally provides the confidence of the predictions.

Optimizing Equation 16 leads to the exploration and exploitation dilemma. The publisher would like to earn more by selecting the best known $\theta_{s(t)}(t)$ so far. But some ads with higher variances might potentially have higher payoffs and are also required to be selected in order to gather the feedback. Not selecting the local best may result in a loss of the immediate reward, but the loss, however, could be compensated if any better alternatives can be found in later stages. Besides, we can see from the model that the changing dataset problem is dealt with naturally: the new coming ads could be simply assigned high variances to encourage the exploration on them.

3.3 Exact Solution

3.3.1 Value Iteration

Our revenue optimization problem in Equation 16 could be solved exactly following a value iteration approach using Dynamic Programming [5]. Recall we use $\boldsymbol{\theta}$ and $\boldsymbol{\Sigma}$ to denote the belief of N ads true payoffs before $t=1$. Let $V^*(\boldsymbol{\theta}, \boldsymbol{\Sigma}, T)$ denote the max possible revenue the publisher could gain in T time steps. We have the following statement and the Bellman equation [5].

LEMMA 1. *For any given priori $\boldsymbol{\theta}$ and $\boldsymbol{\Sigma}$, there exists an optimal policy π^* to the problem in Equation 16, and $V^*(\boldsymbol{\theta}, \boldsymbol{\Sigma}, T)$ is achievable. More over $V^*(\boldsymbol{\theta}, \boldsymbol{\Sigma}, T)$ satisfy the following condition*

$$\begin{aligned} & V^*(\boldsymbol{\theta}, \boldsymbol{\Sigma}, T) \\ & = \max_{s(1)\in N} \mathbb{E}\left[X_{s(t)}(1) + V^*\left(\boldsymbol{\theta}|X_{s(t)}(1), \boldsymbol{\Sigma}|X_{s(t)}(1), T-1\right)\right] \end{aligned} \tag{19}$$

By solving this equation recursively we find the optimal policy. If $T=1$, we write the optimal revenue as

$$\begin{aligned} V^*(\boldsymbol{\theta}, \boldsymbol{\Sigma}, 1) &= \max_{s(1)\in N} \mathbb{E}\left[X_{s(1)}(1)\right] \\ &= \max_{s(1)\in N} \theta_{s(1)}(1) \end{aligned} \tag{20}$$

which indicates that the publisher should simply choose the ad with highest expected payoff. This choice is straightforward because no more time steps exist, thus no need of exploration.

For $T=2$ the optimal revenue is written as

$$\begin{aligned} & V^*(\boldsymbol{\theta}, \boldsymbol{\Sigma}, 2) \\ & = \max_{s(1)\in N} \mathbb{E}\left[X_{s(1)}(1) + V^*\left(\boldsymbol{\theta}|X_{s(t)}(1), \boldsymbol{\Sigma}|X_{s(t)}(1), 1\right)\right] \\ & = \max_{s(1)\in N} \int p(x_{s(1)})\left(x_{s(1)} + U^*(\boldsymbol{\theta}|x_{s(t)}(1), \boldsymbol{\Sigma}|x_{s(t)}(1), 1)\right) dx_{s(1)} \\ & = \max_{s(1)\in N} \int p(x_{s(1)})\left(x_{s(1)} + \max_{s(2)\in N}\left(\theta_{s(2)}(2)\right)\right) dx_{s(1)} \\ & = \max_{s(1)\in N}\left(\theta_{s(1)}(1) + \int \max_{s(2)\in N} p(x_{s(1)})\theta_{s(2)}(2) dx_{s(1)}\right) \end{aligned} \tag{21}$$

The difficulty lies in the last integral as it depends on the max operator. Using Chasles relation, it could be expanded to several regional integrals according to the random vector $\boldsymbol{\theta}(2)$. For instance, if the publisher has to choose from only two ads, and by solving $\theta_1(2) > \theta_2(2)$ the following answer is obtained

$$\theta_1(2) > \theta_2(2) \text{ when } x_i(1) > k \tag{22}$$

which indicates the publisher should choose the 1st ad when the observation from the 1st time step is bigger than some value k. Then the last integral of Equation 21 could be broken into two regional integrals with exact solution

$$\begin{aligned} V^*(\boldsymbol{\theta}, \boldsymbol{\Sigma}, 2) = \max_{i\in 1,2}\Big(\theta_1(1) + \int_{-\infty}^{k} p(x_i)\theta_2(2) dx_i \\ + \int_{k}^{+\infty} p(x_i)\theta_1(2) dx_i\Big) \end{aligned} \tag{23}$$

The above equation could be easily extended to N ads cases provided the solution of N inequalities for vector $\boldsymbol{\theta}$, where the only variable considered as unknown is the observation from the last time step. For simplicity we define that a region is *dominated* by some ad when the ad should be selected if the observation falls in the region. This is similar with [27] where the value function is expressed as a linear combination of α-functions. Formally we denote the region dominated by i-th ad at time step t as $[m_{i,t}, n_{i,t}]$. For a general case of N ads, Equation 21 is written as

$$V^*(\boldsymbol{\theta}, \boldsymbol{\Sigma}, 2) = \max_{s(1)\in N}\left(\theta_{s(1)}(1) + \sum_{s(2)}^{N} \int_{m_{s(2),2}}^{n_{s(2),2}} p(x_i)\theta_{s(2)}(2) dx_i\right) \tag{24}$$

where the regional integral could be solved as

$$\int_m^n x p(x) dx = -\sigma^2\Big(p(n) - p(m)\Big) + \mu\Big(\phi(n) - \phi(m)\Big) \tag{25}$$

where $\phi(x)$ is the c.d.f. for the Gaussian random variable X. Note that for some ads at some time steps, their dominant regions could be empty, simply indicating the ads would never be selected under such circumstances.

3.3.2 A Toy Example

We give an example to demonstrate the sequential selection mechanism with embedded correlated belief update. Assume a publisher have 2 ads to select from. The Gaussian noise from users is given by

$$\sigma_0^2 = 0.1$$

Random state $\boldsymbol{\mu}$ is defined by a bivariate Gaussian, i.e.

$$\boldsymbol{\mu} \sim \mathcal{N}(\boldsymbol{\theta}, \boldsymbol{\sigma})$$

where

$$\boldsymbol{\theta} = \begin{bmatrix} 1 \\ 0.95 \end{bmatrix} \quad \boldsymbol{\Sigma} = \begin{bmatrix} 10 & 0.2 \\ 0.2 & 50 \end{bmatrix}$$

Considering only one time step gives the expected revenue

$$\begin{aligned} V^*(\boldsymbol{\theta}, \boldsymbol{\Sigma}, 1) &= \max_{s(1)\in N} \mathbb{E}[X_{s(1)}(1)] \\ &= \max(1, 0.95) \\ &= 1 \quad \text{with } s(1) = 1 \end{aligned}$$

Now consider $T=2$. Suppose the 1st ad at the 1st time step is selected, which yields the following update for time step 2

$$\begin{aligned} & \text{when } s(1) = 1: \\ & \theta_1(2) = 1 - \frac{10 \times (1 - x_1(1))}{0.1 + 10} \\ & \theta_2(2) = 0.95 - \frac{0.2 \times (1 - x_1(1))}{0.1 + 10} \end{aligned}$$

which gives

$$\theta_1(2) > \theta_2(2) \text{ when } x_1(1) > 0.95$$

Thus, the optimal reward for $t = 2$ when choosing $s(1) = 1$ could be derived as

$$\begin{aligned} &V^*_{s(1)=1}(\boldsymbol{\theta}, \boldsymbol{\Sigma}, 2) \\ =&1 + \int_{0.95}^{+\infty} p(x_1)\theta_1(2)dx_1 + \int_{-\infty}^{0.95} p(x_1)\theta_2(2)dx_1 \\ =&3.1993 \end{aligned}$$

A small defect is that variable x stands for the payoff observed from the 1st time step and it cannot be smaller than zero. However, due to the Gaussian assumption, when calculating V^*, we integrate x over the Real space and sometime result in a negative expected reward. But such policy would vanish in later comparisons due to its low value and has little effect on our decision process.

Similarly selecting the 2nd ad at the 1st time step yields the following update for step 2

$$\begin{aligned} &\text{when } s(1) = 2: \\ &\theta_1(2) = 1 - \frac{0.2 \times (0.95 - x_2(1))}{0.1 + 50} \\ &\theta_2(2) = 0.95 - \frac{50 \times (0.95 - x_2(1))}{0.1 + 50} \end{aligned}$$

which gives

$$\theta_1(2) > \theta_2(2) \text{ when } x_2(1) < 1.00$$

Thus we have

$$\begin{aligned} &V^*_{i=2}(\boldsymbol{\theta}, \boldsymbol{\Sigma}, 2) \\ =&0.95 + \int_{-\infty}^{1} p(x_2)\theta_1(2)dx_2 + \int_{1}^{+\infty} p(x_2)\theta_2(2)dx_2 \\ =&4.7291 \end{aligned}$$

Finally the maximum expected payoff over two time steps is

$$V^*(\boldsymbol{\theta}, \boldsymbol{\Sigma}, 2) = \max(3.1993, 4.7291) = 4.7291$$

and the corresponding optimal policy is

$$\pi^* = \{s(1) = 2, s(2) = 1 \text{ if } x_1(1) < 1, s(2) = 2 \text{ otherwise}\}$$

From the result, we can see that the optimal policy is different from a myopic one, which tries to maximize the immediate reward only. Following the myopic policy the publisher would choose $s(1) = 1$ and receive a smaller payoff. One of the reasons of selecting the 2nd is because it has a higher variance (taking into account the correlations as well). We will show in the experiments that such high variance is ordinary in real world data.

3.4 Approximate Solution

In order to understand approximations we write the objection function as a combination of immediate reward estimation and exploration function, which utilizes the available information up to the decision time step, denoted by $\xi(\Psi(t), i)$ for the i-th candidate. The decision criteria is to maximize some the objective value function $V_{s(t)}(\Psi(t))$, i.e.

$$\begin{aligned} s(t) &= \arg\max_{s(t)\in N} V_{s(t)}(\Psi(t)) \\ &= \arg\max_{i\in N} (\bar{x}_i + \xi(\Psi(t), i)) \end{aligned} \tag{26}$$

Algorithm 1 The VI-COR algorithm using value iteration with Monte Carlo sampling.

```
function VALUEFUNC(θ, Σ, t)
    array V ← 0                                  ▷ Expected reward vector.
    loop i ← 1 to N
        V[i] ← θ_i(t)                            ▷ Expected immediate reward.
        if t < T then
            for all s in SAMPLE(θ, Σ) do
                [θ', Σ'] ← UPDATEBELIEF(θ, Σ, s, i)
                        ▷ New belief after selecting i and observing s.
                                                 ▷ Equations 17 and 18.
                V[i] ← V[i] + (1/M_0) VALUEFUNCTION(θ', Σ', t + 1)
            end for
        end if
    end loop
    return [MAX(V), MAXINDEX(V)]
end function
```

Algorithm 2 The UCB1-NORMAL-COR algorithm using multi-armed bandit with correlated update.

```
function PLAN(θ, Σ, Ψ(t))
    array V ← 0
    loop i ← 1 to N
        if t_i < ⌈8 log t⌉ then
            return i
        end if
    end loop
    [θ', Σ'] ← UPDATEBELIEF(θ, Σ, Ψ(t))
                    ▷ New belief of all ads with all available information.
                                                 ▷ Equations 17 and 18.
    loop i ← 1 to N
        V[i] ← θ'_i + sqrt(16 · (q_i − t_i θ'_i^2)/(t_i − 1) · (t − 1)/t_i)
                                                 ▷ Expected reward.
    end loop
    return [MAX(V), MAXINDEX(V)]
end function
```

For example, the exploration function in Equation 19 is

$$\xi = \int p(x_{s(1)})V^*\left(\boldsymbol{\theta}|x_{s(t)}(1), \boldsymbol{\Sigma}|x_{s(t)}(1), T-1\right)dx \tag{27}$$

of which the computation is expensive due to recursive calling and integral. In this section we present two approximate methods.

3.4.1 Value Iteration with Monte Carlo Sampling

For $T \geq 3$ the solution for N inequalities cannot be obtained easily. Instead we use Monte Carlo sampling to deal with the integral and avoid solving the inequalities. The exploration function is written as

$$\xi_{\text{VI-COR}} = \frac{1}{M_0}\sum_{x\in\mathbb{S}} p(x)V^*\left(\boldsymbol{\theta}|x, \boldsymbol{\Sigma}|x, T-1\right)dx \tag{28}$$

where $\mathbb{S}$ is the sample set and M_0 is the normalizing factor from sampling. The algorithm for a general $T \geq 3$ case is represented in Algorithm 1. We refer to this algorithm as VI-COR in our experiments.

3.4.2 The UCB1-Normal-COR *Algorithm*

The multi-armed bandit is a popular approach dealing with exploration-exploitation dilemma in sequential optimization problems [4]. Similar to the problem discussed above, in the multi-armed bandit scenario a player must decide which arm to play at each time step to maximize the cumulative reward over the entire planning horizon.

Most multi-armed bandit algorithms reduce the computational cost by approximating the exploration function. In this paper we base on the deterministic policy UCB1-NORMAL [4] and improve its performance by adding the correlated update. The original algorithm assumes the Gaussian distribution of the reward, independence between arms, and underlying mean and variance for reward distribution are unknown but fixed. The exploration function of UCB1-NORMAL is written as

$$\xi_{\text{UCB1-NORMAL}} = \sqrt{16 \cdot \frac{q_i - t_i \theta_i^2(t)}{t_i - 1} \cdot \frac{t-1}{t_i}} \tag{29}$$

where q_i is the sum of squared reward obtained from i-th arm, and t_i the times i-th has been played so far. We extend the algorithm for our problem by adding the correlated updates. The exploration function would remain the same form, but $\boldsymbol{\theta}(t)$ at each time step is updated according to Equations 17 and 18, instead of only updating the selected candidate. The algorithm, referred to as UCB1-NORMAL-COR in our experiments, is represented in Algorithm 2.

4. EMPIRICAL EXPERIMENTS

4.1 Dataset

We collected our test data set from Google AdWords service [2]. We consider the scenario that advertisers deploy campaigns through an advertiser (demand) side platform, whereas online publishers retrieve ads and earn revenue from a related publisher side platform. Generally, online publishers share the ad revenues with their chosen ad networks or exchanges with a fixed percentage. For instance, with Google AdSense online publishers gain 68% of advertisers' spending, where the ratio has not changed since 2003 [22]. Thus, it is reasonable for us to consider online publishers' ad revenue to be proportional to the corresponding revenue of Google AdWords and also the corresponding cost of the advertisers.

The test data was collected from 12/2011 to 5/2012[1]. The Google AdWords Traffic Estimation service provides real-time data to help advertisers to adjust budgets and select appropriate keywords. When given a keyword, budget, and various targets, the service will return a list of fields on a daily basis including clicks, global and local impressions, average position, average cost-per-click, and total cost. In addition, we also separated the US and UK markets using the geographical targeting option of the service. We have collected keywords across the Google Sponsored Search and Display Networks and do not make a distinction between the types of ads and their specific payment schemes. This allows online publishers to fully concentrate upon the revenue optimisation task. During the collection period 521 different keywords from various categories were collected and 310 have non-zero mean payoffs. As shown in Table 1, we manually categorized the keywords into 8 categories to reflect that fact that it is not necessary for online publishers to try out all the available ads; instead they should specify their target categories (based on hosting webpages content) and make optimal decisions within the targeted categories. In our experiments, ads associated with the collected keywords were considered as candidates and decision making was on a daily basis.

[1]The dataset is publicly available at `http://www.computational-advertising.org`.

Category	Count	Category	Count
Education	34	Person & organization	29
Shopping	86	(Personal) finance	51
Product & service	20	Information	52
Medical	25	Uncategorised	13

Table 1: Categorisation of the collected 310 keywords with non-zero mean payoffs.

4.2 Baselines and Experiment Setup

The baselines used in our experiment are:

- RANDOM policy, which selects candidates randomly (uniform);
- MYOPIC policy, which selects candidates based on immediate reward estimated so far;
- UCB1 policy, which assumes independent between candidates and is model-free of reward distribution [4]; and
- UCB1-NORMAL policy, which assumes independent between candidates and the reward following Gaussian distribution;

And our algorithms are:

- VI-COR policy, which uses value iteration with Monte Carlo sampling (Algorithm 1); and
- UCB1-NORMAL-COR policy, which consider the dependencies between candidates (Algorithm 2).

For each candidate we have about 150 daily payoff data points (some candidates have less due to later start of collection). For each category (except *Uncategorised*) we select candidates with close mean payoffs to form a dataset, emphasizing the challenge of planning with matching candidates. In order to test the statistical significance of algorithms performance, we divide daily payoff time series into 8 chunks for each dataset (with overlap). For each chunk, we use 20% as the training set to get the prior belief of ad performances, i.e. $\boldsymbol{\theta}(0)$ and $\boldsymbol{\Sigma}(0)$. Then we go over the remaining 80% with each algorithm reporting the cumulative reward at each time step. Besides, we report the averaged results with Wilcoxon signed-rank test for the significance of the best algorithm outperformed the second best within each dataset.

4.3 Results and Discussions

We compared our two algorithms with the baselines over the 10 selected datasets. In order to compare performances across categories we normalize the cumulative revenues against the GOLDEN solution (always picking up the best ads) to give a better representation due to the different scales of means from different categories. The results are summarized in Table 2 and are compared in Figure 2. We can see that, within the 10 different datasets, the proposed VI-COR algorithm performed the best for 8/10 with 5/8 significantly better. The UCB1-NORMAL-COR algorithm performed the best for 1/10 and was significantly better in that trail. With the "Shopping-1" dataset, the UCB1 algorithm performed the best, but the VI-COR had the comparable performance and the difference was not significant.

In Figure 2 we give daily performance comparison on "Education" and "People & Organization" datasets where algo-

Datasets	MYOPIC	RANDOM	UCB1	UCB1-NORMAL	VI-COR	UCB1-NORMAL-COR
Education	21.9	23.0	30.9	30.9	**41.2***	27.6
Finance-1	38.5	27.8	40.9	26.4	**44.5**	27.4
Finance-2	22.1	16.5	30.6	22.8	**38.0***	22.9
Information	14.1	12.9	27.8	15.9	**29.4**	15.9
People & Organization	41.6	30.4	50.5	31.4	**72.9***	63.3
Shopping-1	17.4	10.6	**42.3**	16.1	40.2	16.4
Shopping-2	29.9	14.5	34.3	75.3	52.9	**79.2***
Shopping-3	9.7	4.3	21.9	18.3	**27.3**	19.4
Product & Service	24.7	26.0	47.2	57.1	**67.9***	59.9
Medical	30.5	19.6	52.7	32.2	**58.0***	33.5

Table 2: The overall performance comparison. The cumulative payoffs are averaged on 8 chunks then normalized w.r.t. the GOLDEN policy for a better representation. In each row the one with highest cumulative payoff is in bold and with * if the difference with the second best is significant.

	eminem	justin bieber	michael jackson	selena gomez	wayne rooney
eminem	1.00	-0.43	-0.58	-0.50	-0.73
justin bieber		1.00	0.80	0.74	0.70
michael jackson			1.00	0.97	0.71
selena gomez				1.00	0.63
wayne rooney					1.00

Table 3: The sample correlation matrix for "People & Organization" category. The high correlations made the UCB1 and UCB1-Normal inefficient.

rithm were run on entire payoff data series. We cannot represent all 10 figures due to the space limit; the performances were however consistent across all datasets. We discuss our findings in the following subsections.

4.3.1 The Importance of Exploration

Firstly we study the importance of exploration. Figure 2 compares the daily accumulated revenues over time. As illustrated in Figure 2(a), in the beginning (between day-0 and day-10) the MYOPIC policy achieved excellent result and its cumulative payoff was the best until day-65. This is explained by the fact that there is no exploration involved in this policy and it exploits the current belief directly. However our algorithms with exploration quick outperformed it in the late stage as more profitable ads have been discovered from the exploration from the early stage. In the end, the MYOPIC policy failed to win due to no exploration in the beginning, and later stuck to suboptimal ads. It is similar in Figure 2(b) where the MYOPIC policy outperformed others between day-25 and day-35, but was caught up and passed very soon. These conclude that the exploration is valuable and important in the ad selection task. Note that we only show categories "Education" and "People & Organization" only, while the algorithms behaviours were consistent across all datasets.

4.3.2 The Effect of Correlation

Recall we consider the Gaussian noise constant for all webpages and users. The consequence is that X_1 and X_2 are conditional independent when we know μ_1 and μ_2. We can further derive the relationship between covariances of $X1$ and X_2 and that of μ_1 and μ_2 as,

$$\begin{aligned}\mathrm{cov}[X_1, X_2] &= \mathbb{E}\big[\mathrm{cov}[X_1, X_2|\mu_1, \mu_2]\big] \\ &\quad + \mathrm{cov}\,\big[\mathbb{E}[X_1|\mu_1, \mu_2], \mathbb{E}[X_2|\mu_1, \mu_2]\big] \\ &= \mathrm{cov}[\mu_1, \mu_2] \end{aligned} \tag{30}$$

which enables publishers to use either of correlations within the model. In experiments we used $\mathrm{cov}[X_1, X_2]$.

Like most multi-bandit machine approaches, the UCB1 algorithm assumes independence between candidates. Therefore when candidates have relatively low correlations, e.g. in the "Shopping-1" dataset, the algorithm would perform well. This was confirmed by the observation that the UCB1-NORMAL-COR algorithm reported only 0.3% improvement over UCB1-NORMAL in that dataset. But in the situation where the correlation of ads are high such as the "People & Organization" category (a sample correlation matrix is shown in Table 3), our algorithms utilizing the correlation during planning showed better results. For instance the VI-COR algorithm showed 22.4% improvement over the UCB1 and the UCB1-NORMAL-COR showed 31.9% improvement over the UCB1-NORMAL in the "People & Organization" dataset. In Figure 2(b) it was clear that UCB1-NORMAL-COR discovered the better options much quicker than the UCB1-NORMAL did. The same conclusion is obtained by comparing the VI-COR with the MYOPIC solution. From Figure 3, we can see a significant improvement by utilizing correlation of ads. The maximum improvement was obtained with "Product & Service" (43.3%) and on average it was 22.2% across all experiments.

4.3.3 The Impact of the Noise Factor σ_0^2

The introduction of the noise factor σ_0^2 is essential to the success of our model. On one hand, it helps capture the uncertainty which is unforeseeable and has not been properly modelled by the underlying $\boldsymbol{\theta}$ and $\boldsymbol{\Sigma}$ as we discussed be-

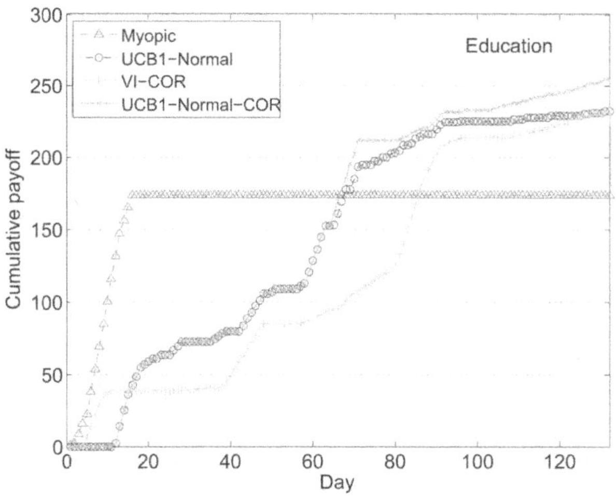

(a) "Education" category, 9 candidates.

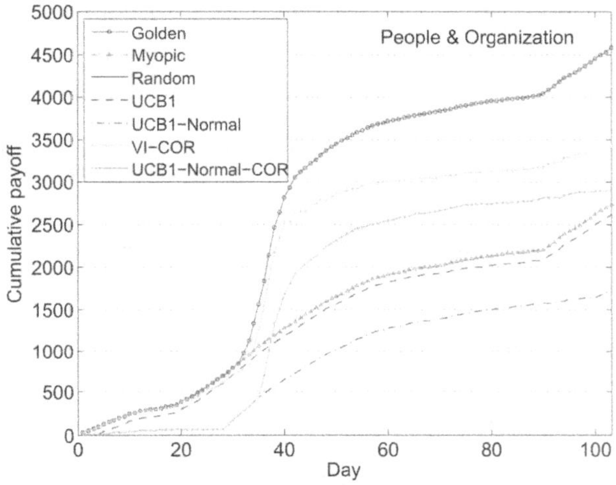

(b) "People & organization" category, 5 candidates.

Figure 2: Comparison on accumulated payoffs.

fore. The assumption about the Gaussian distribution may not be true in practice. This can be seen from Figure 4(a) and Figure 4(b). The noise factor provides us with a certain flexibility of tuning our algorithms towards the specific situations. In our experiments, we obtained the noise factor by tuning using training datasets.

On the other hand, the noise factor is also a control of the sensitivity of the algorithms towards the unexpected daily payoff fluctuation. From Equations 17 and 18 we see that the noise factor is in the denominator and a high noise factor leads to a steady policy while a low one leads to a highly responsive (sensitive) policy. A smaller value, for example $\sigma_0^2 = 0.01$, would make the algorithm switch probably too much, whereas a larger value would not be able to capture the fluctuation of the data. We found from the data that sometimes strong and short bursts may happen and be led by unexpected commercial activities. For instance, in the beginning of May, 2012 the Sumsang Galaxy S III and Nokia 808 PureView were presented for pre-ordering or purchasing, and both claimed to be the 'best' on the market. The competition of commercial campaigns caused the daily payoff of "best phones" became very high between 15/04/2012 and 05/05/2012 (Figure 4(b)). In order to response to such a short and strong abnormal activity a small noise factor is required. From Figure 4(c) we see that with $\sigma_0^2 \leq 40$ the VI-COR algorithm was able to identify and switch to "best phones" when the burst happened; but with $\sigma_0^2 \geq 60$ the algorithm was not able to switch, resulting in a loss of payoff.

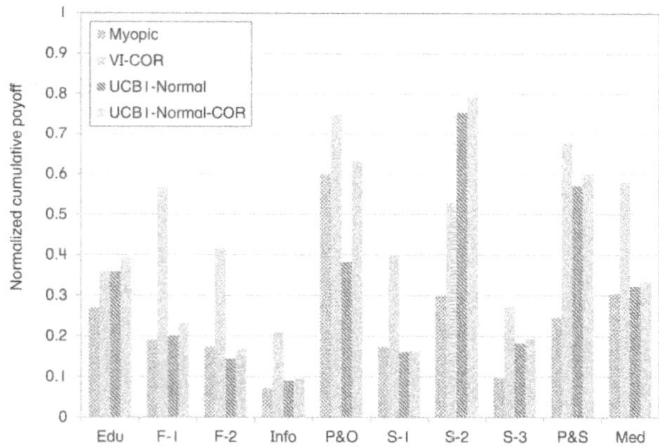

Figure 3: Comparison on accumulated payoffs on the 10 datasets. VI-COR always performed better than MYOPIC and UCB1-NORMAL-COR always performed better than UCB1-NORMAL across all datasets.

It is worth noticing that, as illustrated in Figure 4(c), the setting of the noise factor is algorithm-dependent as well. By contrast, the UCB1-NORMAL-COR approach requires a large noise value to deal with the burst – the best cumulative payoff was obtained at $\sigma_0^2 = 40$, and as the value of the noise factor decreased the performance dropped greatly. The different behaviour of two algorithms is due to the different structures of the exploration function. As shown in Equation 29, the exploration function of the UCB1-NORMAL-COR contains the squared expectation of the payoffs in the past, indicating that the candidate with a history of low payoffs would not be favoured especially with a sudden burst. Using a high noise value would increase the chance of selecting and exploring such candidates.

5. CONCLUSIONS

In this paper, we have presented a model of optimally selecting ads in an online setting. Based on POMDPs, we formulated the belief updates by taking the correlation of ads into account. We mathematically showed that the belief update across ads is similar to the "word of month" principle employed in collaborative filtering. Making use of the belief update, two approximate methods were proposed: one was derived from the Value Iteration and Sampling approach, whereas the other was based on the Upper Confidence Bound solution. In empirical experiments we compared our algorithms with various baselines using a collected real world dataset and showed that the Bayesian inference with correlations made the exploration more efficient and significantly improved the revenue optimization.

In the future, we intend to extend the basic model by considering the correlations between webpages as well to further improve the exploration. A further study is also needed in order to incorporate the user click-through model and remove rank bias on the same webpage [25].

6. REFERENCES

[1] The first half '11 internet advertising report. http://goo.gl/NRZ4S, 2011.

[2] ADWORDS, G. Google adwords traffic estimator. http://goo.gl/TYd0Q, 2012.

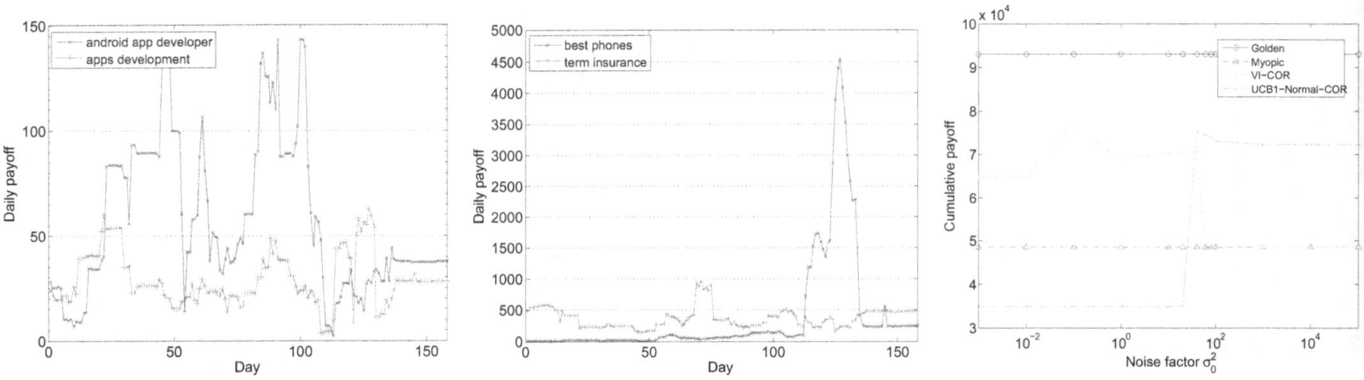

(a) cov = 0.60 (b) cov = −0.73 (c)

Figure 4: (a) The daily payoffs of two mobile development related ad candidates. (b) The daily payoff of two candidates with a sudden change. (c) The impact of the noise factor σ_0^2 for the situation in (b).

[3] ANAGNOSTOPOULOS, A., BRODER, A., GABRILOVICH, E., JOSIFOVSKI, V., AND RIEDEL, L. Just-in-time contextual advertising. In *Proceedings of the ACM-CIKM 07'*.

[4] AUER, P., CESA-BIANCHI, N., AND FISCHER, P. Finite-time analysis of the multiarmed bandit problem. *Machine learning 47*, 2 (2002), 235–256.

[5] BERTSEKAS, D. P. *Dynamic Programming and Optimal Control.* Athena Scientific, 1995.

[6] BHARADWAJ, V., MA, W., SCHWARZ, M., SHANMUGASUNDARAM, J., VEE, E., XIE, J., AND YANG, J. Pricing guaranteed contracts in online display advertising. In *Proceedings of the ACM-CIKM 10'*.

[7] BREESE, J. S., HECKERMAN, D., AND KADIE, C. Empirical analysis of predictive algorithms for collaborative filtering. In *Proceedings of the 14th conference on Uncertainty in artificial intelligence* (1998), UAI'98, pp. 43–52.

[8] BRODER, A., FONTOURA, M., JOSIFOVSKI, V., AND RIEDEL, L. A semantic approach to contextual advertising. In *Proceedings of the ACM-SIGIR 07'*.

[9] BULLAS, J. 50 amazing facts and figures about google. `http://goo.gl/EfrLS`, 2011.

[10] CASSANDRA, A. A survey of POMDP applications. In *Working Notes of AAAI 1998 Fall Symposium on Planning with Partially Observable Markov Decision Processes.*

[11] CHAKRABARTI, D., AGARWAL, D., AND JOSIFOVSKI, V. Contextual advertising by combining relevance with click feedback. In *Proceedings of the WWW 08'*.

[12] CHICKERING, D., AND HECKERMAN, D. Targeted advertising on the web with inventory management. *Interfaces* (2003), 71–77.

[13] FJELL, K. Online advertising: Pay-per-view versus pay-per-click a comment. *Journal of Revenue & Pricing Management 2*, 3 (2009), 200–206.

[14] FRIDGEIRSDOTTIR, K., AND ASADOLAHI, S. Revenue management for online advertising: Impatient advertisers. Tech. rep., Working paper, London Business School, 2007.

[15] GOOGLE WHITE PAPER. Profiting from non-guaranteed advertising: The value of dynamic allocation and auction pricing for online publishers, 2012.

[16] HERLOCKER, J. L., KONSTAN, J. A., BORCHERS, A., AND RIEDL, J. An algorithmic framework for performing collaborative filtering. In *Proceedings of the ACM-SIGIR '99.*

[17] HU, Y., SHIN, J., AND TANG, Z. Pricing of online advertising: Cost-per-click-through vs. cost-per-action. In *System Sciences (HICSS), 2010 43rd Hawaii International Conference on.*

[18] KUMAR, S., JACOB, V., AND SRISKANDARAJAH, C. Scheduling advertisements on a web page to maximize revenue. *European Journal of Operational Research 173*, 3 (2006), 1067–1089.

[19] KWON, C. Single period balancing of pay-per-click and pay-per-view online display advertisements. *Journal of Revenue & Pricing Management 10*, 3 (2011), 261–270.

[20] LI, Y., AND JHANG-LI, J. Pricing display ads and contextual ads: Competition, acquisition, and investment. *Electronic Commerce Research and Applications 8*, 1 (2009), 16–27.

[21] MANGANI, A. Online advertising: Pay-per-view versus pay-per-click. *Journal of Revenue & Pricing Management 2*, 4 (2004), 295–302.

[22] MOHAN, N. The adsense revenue share. `http://goo.gl/yP4Ln`, 2010.

[23] PANDEY, S., CHAKRABARTI, D., AND AGARWAL, D. Multi-armed bandit problems with dependent arms. In *Proceedings of the ICML 07'*.

[24] RIBEIRO-NETO, B., CRISTO, M., GOLGHER, P., AND SILVA DE MOURA, E. Impedance coupling in content-targeted advertising. In *Proceedings of the ACM-SIGIR 05'*.

[25] RICHARDSON, M., DOMINOWSKA, E., AND RAGNO, R. Predicting clicks: estimating the click-through rate for new ads. In *Proceedings of the WWW '07.*

[26] ROELS, G., AND FRIDGEIRSDOTTIR, K. Dynamic revenue management for online display advertising. *Journal of Revenue & Pricing Management 8*, 5 (2009), 452–466.

[27] SPAAN, M., AND VLASSIS, N. Perseus: Randomized point-based value iteration for POMDPs. *Journal of artificial intelligence research 24*, 1 (2005), 195–220.

[28] TANG, J., LIU, N., YAN, J., SHEN, Y., GUO, S., GAO, B., YAN, S., AND ZHANG, M. Learning to rank audience for behavioral targeting in display ads. In *Proceedings of the ACM-CIKM 11'*.

[29] THRUN, S. Monte carlo POMDPs. *Advances in neural information processing systems 12* (2000), 1064–1070.

[30] TURNER, J., SCHELLER-WOLF, A., AND TAYUR, S. Scheduling of dynamic in-game advertising. *Operations research 59*, 1 (2011), 1–16.

[31] TYLER, S., PANDEY, S., GABRILOVICH, E., AND JOSIFOVSKI, V. Retrieval models for audience selection in display advertising. In *Proceedings of the ACM-CIKM 11'*.

[32] WANG, C., ZHANG, P., CHOI, R., AND EREDITA, M. Understanding consumers attitude toward advertising. In *The 8th Americas conference on information systems.*

[33] WU, Z., XU, G., PAN, R., ZHANG, Y., HU, Z., AND LU, J. Leveraging wikipedia concept and category information to enhance contextual advertising. In *Proceedings of the ACM-CIKM 11'*.

Diversity in Blog Feed Retrieval

Mostafa Keikha*, Fabio Crestani*, W. Bruce Croft‡
* University of Lugano, Lugano, Switzerland
‡ CIIR, University of Massachusetts Amherst, Amherst, MA
mostafa.keikha@usi.ch, fabio.crestani@usi.ch
croft@cs.umass.edu

ABSTRACT

Blog distillation (blog feed retrieval) is a task in blog retrieval where the goal is to rank blogs according to their recurrent relevance to a query topic. One of the main properties of blog feed retrieval is that the unit of retrieval is a collection of documents as opposed to a single document as in other IR tasks. This collection retrieval nature of blog distillation introduces new challenges and requires new investigations specific to this problem.

Researchers have addressed this problem by considering a wide range of evidence and information resources. However, previous work has not studied the effect of on-topic diversity of blog posts in blog relevance. By on-topic diversity of blog posts we mean that those posts that are about the query topic need to have high diversity and cover different subtopics of the query.

In this study, we investigate three types of on-topic diversity and their effect on retrieval performance: topical diversity, temporal diversity and hybrid diversity. Our experiments over different blog collections and different baseline methods show that on-topic diversity can improve the performance of the retrieval system. Among the three types of diversity, hybrid diversity, that considers both topical and temporal diversities, achieves the best performance.

Categories and Subject Descriptors

H.3.3 [**Information Storage and Retrieval**]: Information Search and Retrieval

Keywords

Blog Retrieval, Diversity, Novelty

1. INTRODUCTION

Amongst all the information resources, the web is becoming the main source for providing new and useful information to users. Everyday, people receive up-to-date information via web-based services such as news web sites, social networks or blogs. User generated content like blogs, plays an important role in this phenomenon. Millions of people write about their experiences and express their opinions in blogs providing a rich source of information.

Considering this huge amount of user-generated data and its specific properties, designing new retrieval methods is necessary to facilitate addressing the different types of information needs that blog users may have. Studies show that one of the main categories of blog-related queries is about finding blogs that deal with a specific topic of interest [12]. These queries, which are called concept queries, are the focus of a blog distillation system [9]. The blog distillation task (also known as blog feed retrieval)[1] is concerned with ranking blogs according to their recurring central interest to the topic of a user's query. In other words, our aim is to discover relevant blogs for each topic[2] that a user can add to his reader and refer to in the future [10].

A relevant blog is expected to regularly publish posts about the topic. When it comes to blog relevance estimation, the usual emphasis is on the number of topic-related posts that a blog publishes. Nevertheless, the amount of new information that each of these posts add to the blog is another influential factor. If a blog publishes repetitive information with low novelty, it would be less interesting for the user to follow. In our diversity-based methods, we leverage this property and penalize those blogs that have low diversity in their posts related to the topic.

There are different scenarios where considering the diversity might help the retrieval performance. Table 1 shows some real examples of blogs that were affected by one of our diversity-based methods. The examples are part of our experiments on two selected topics of TREC09 and are compared to the best performing baseline method. We can see that by penalizing those blogs that have low diversity, we can filter out non-relevant blogs such as spam blogs or blogs that publish similar posts multiple times. On the other hand, it can help us to retrieve those relevant blogs that have high diversity among their posts even though they might have low initial score for the query.

In this paper, we discuss how to add a measure of diversity to the existing blog retrieval methods and study the effect on retrieval performance. Our main aim is to answer the following questions::

CIKM'12, October 29–November 2, 2012, Maui, HI, USA.

[1] We use words "feed" and "blog" interchangeably
[2] We use words "topic" and "query" interchangeably

Table 1: Examples where measuring diversity improves blog retrieval

Topic ID: 1107 Topic title: Mountain Climbing Topic description: Looking for blogs about equipment, clubs and good paths for climbing mountains as a beginner
Example 1 Feed no: BLOG08-feed-1167752 Blog URL: http://hockeycrew.livejournal.com Blog title: "I Smile Because I'm Confused" Explanation: This is a non-relevant blog that is retrieved by the best baseline method. The blog has multiple posts about Saturday hikes of the blogger. Those posts are written time to time with very general vocabulary and description that makes them very similar. Its rank in the baseline method: 10 Its rank after applying diversity: above 100 (not retrieved)
Example 2 Feed no: BLOG08-feed-1218342 Blog URL: http://playwintersports.blogspot.com Blog title: "INFORMATION ABOUT DIFFERENT TYPES OF WINTER SPORTS AND WHERE TO FIND EQUIPMENT" Explanation: This is another retrieved non-relevant blog that has four posts about *"Mount McKinley"* with identical content. Those posts are probably published mistakenly and considering all of them for scoring the blog gives a high score to the blog. Its rank in the baseline method: 61 Its rank after applying diversity: above 100 (not retrieved)
Example 3 Feed no: BLOG08-feed-070681 Blog URL: http://himadventures.blogspot.com Blog title: "Trekking, Camping, Climbing And Traveling In Himalayas" Explanation: This is a relevant blog that belongs to a professional climber who describes their trips to Himalayas. He describes the climbs and conditions of the mountains in very detail. The detailed description and in-depth vocabulary usage makes its posts very long with low scores in response to the query. Beside, these properties makes the posts less similar to each other while each one adds new information to the blog with respect to the query. Its rank in the baseline method: above 100 (not retrieved) Its rank after applying diversity: 81
Topic ID: 1122 Topic title: Skiing Topic description: looking for blogs with information and advice on skiing, ski resorts and ski organizations.
Example 4 Feed no: BLOG08-feed-616929 Blog URL: http://justjetskis.blogspot.com Blog title: "JUST SKI RESOURCES" Explanation: This is a spam blog advertising "jet ski". Most of the posts in the blog are advertisement for jet ski equipment with almost identical content. Its rank in the baseline method: 1 Its rank after applying diversity: above 100 (not retrieved)

- How important is the diversity of blog posts to blog relevance?
- What types of diversity can we define over blog posts?
- How can we capture the diversity of blog posts and integrate it into a blog feed retrieval method?
- For what type of queries can we expect diversity-based methods to be more effective?

The rest of the paper is organized as follows. In section 2 we review state of the art methods of blog retrieval. Section 3 describes the methods that rely on post level evidence aggregation for calculating blog relevance. Those methods are the baselines for our experiments and our diversity methods are developed based on them. Section 4 explains our proposed diversity-based methods. Experimental results over different data sets are discussed in section 5. Finally, we conclude the paper and describe future work in section 6.

2. RELATED WORK

Research in blog distillation started mostly after 2007, when the TREC organizers proposed the task as part of the blog track. Researchers have employed different approaches from related areas such as ad-hoc search, expert search, and resource selection in distributed information retrieval.

The simplest models use ad-hoc search methods for finding blog relevant to a specific topic. They treat each blog as one long document created by concatenating all of its posts [3, 4, 13]. These methods ignore any specific property of blogs and usually use standard IR techniques to rank blogs. Despite their simplicity, these methods perform fairly well in blog retrieval.

Some other approaches have been applied to blog retrieval based on expert search methods. Expert search is a task in the TREC Enterprise Track where systems are asked to rank candidate experts with respect to their predicted expertise about a query, using documentary evidence of the expertise found in the collection [14]. Based on the similarity between blog distillation and expert search, some researchers have adapted expert retrieval methods for blog retrieval [1, 9]. In these models, each post in a blog is seen as evidence of blog interest in the query topic. Balog *et al.* adapt two language modeling approaches of expert finding and show their effectiveness in blog distillation [1]. MacDonald *et al.* use data fusion models to combine post-based evidence to compute a final relevance score of the blog [9].

Other researchers have employed resource selection methods from distributed information retrieval for blog retrieval. In distributed information retrieval, the cost of searching all servers for each query is considered prohibitively expensive, so server selection algorithms are used [5]. Queries are then routed only to servers that are likely to have many relevant documents for the query. Elsas *et al.* deal with blog distillation as a resource selection problem [4]. They model each blog as a collection of posts and use a language modeling approach to select the best collection. Similar work is described by Seo *et al.*, which they call Pseudo Cluster Selection [13].

None of the previous work paid attention to the diversity of blog posts in their retrieval methods. Previously, the cohesiveness of a blog was assumed to be a positive sign of blog relevance [4, 13, 9, 6]. However, diversity, as a negatively correlated measure to cohesiveness, has never been studied. In the following, we consider the diversity of blog posts, its effect on the retrieval systems, and its relation with the cohesiveness of the blog.

3. AGGREGATION-BASED BLOG RETRIEVAL METHODS

In general, most of the blog distillation methods can be seen as an aggregation of the post-level relevance evidence to calculate the blog-level relevance score. The following are the main existing aggregation methods that we use as baselines in our experiments:

- *CombSum*: Summation of the post-level relevance scores is one of the simplest aggregation methods that can be applied in blog retrieval [9]:

$$score_{\text{CombSum}}(b_i, q) = \sum_{j=1}^{|b_i \cap R(q)|} score(p_{ji}, q)$$

  where b_i is a blog feed and q is the given query. Here $R(q)$ denotes the set of initially retrieved posts for query q and the intersection $b_i \cap R(q)$ denotes only those retrieved posts that belong to blog b_i. p_{ji} shows the j-th retrieved post from blog i and $score(p_{ji}, q)$ denotes the relevance score assigned to the post p_{ji} with respect to the query. MacDonald and Ounis use the exponential of the scores in the aggregation [9]. However our experiments show that with the language model scores the exponential function does not have any effect on the retrieval performance and thus we use the original scores.

- *PCS*: In the Pseudo Cluster Selection (PCS) method, Seo and Croft use the geometric mean of the top k retrieved posts of a blog as its score [13]:

$$score_{\text{PCS}}(b_i, q) = (\prod_{j=1}^{k} score(p_{ji}, q))^{\frac{1}{k}}$$

  here p_{ji} is the j-th top retrieved post from blog b_i. In this method, if the blog has more than k posts retrieved for the query, the rest of the posts are ignored. However, if the blog has m posts where $m < k$, we need to find a way to give a non-zero score to the $(k - m)$ missing operands. In the original PCS method, they use the minimum score among all the retrieved posts as the score of the missing posts. We use a slightly different choice and smooth the score of posts with the collection likelihood for the query:

$$score(p, q) = (1 - \gamma)score_{ini}(p, q) + \gamma score(C, q) \quad (1)$$

  where C is the collection. Since in all our experiments we use the language model query likelihood as the score, we can rewrite the smoothing as follows:

$$\begin{aligned} score(p, q) = P(q|p) &= (1 - \gamma)P_{init}(q|p) + \gamma P(q|C) \\ &= (1 - \gamma)P_{ini}(q|p) + \gamma \prod_{w \in q} P(w|C)^{P(w|q)} \end{aligned}$$

  where $P(w|C)$ is the probability of a query term in the collection, $P(w|q)$ is the probability of the term in the query, and $P_{ini}(q|p)$ is the query likelihood of the post. Using the smoothed scores, we do not need to use the minimum score of posts for blogs with less than k posts. We simply assume that the missing posts have initial score of zero and use their smoothed score. This can be seen as an equivalent of the Jelinek-Mercer smoothing of language model, however we mainly use it to give score to posts that have not been observed. Employing the smoothed scores, PCS performs better compared to the original method. Also this variation simplifies the calculation in our diversity-based method which we describe later.

- *SDM*: Small Document Model (SDM) is one of the best-performing and best-justified methods for blog feed retrieval [4]. Following the Language Modeling approach to IR, blogs are ranked according to their likelihood given the query:

$$P(b_i|q) = \frac{P(b_i)P(q|b_i)}{P(q)} \stackrel{rank}{=} \underbrace{P(b_i)}_{\substack{\text{Blog} \\ \text{Prior}}} \underbrace{P(q|b_i)}_{\substack{\text{Query} \\ \text{Likelihood}}}$$

  Blog prior, $P(b_i)$ can be set to a logarithmic function of the number of posts in the blog, so as to favor longer blogs, since they are more likely to contain useful information [4]. The query likelihood for a blog is calculated by summing the query likelihoods for each post in the blog scaled according to the probability (centrality) of the post within the blog:

$$P(q|b_i) = \sum_{j=1}^{|b_i \cap R(q)|} P(q|p_{ji})P(p_{ji}|b_i) \quad (2)$$

  Here p_{ji} is a post in the blog b_i, and $P(q|p_{ji})$ is the query likelihood for each post which is computed over query terms using Dirichlet smoothing [16]. Our experiments show that uniform estimations of $P(p_{ji}|b_i)$ over posts of each blog performs better and is easier to calculate than the original centrality score of the posts proposed by Elsas *et al.* [4]. Thus the final relevance score of a blog is calculated as follows:

$$score_{\text{SDM}}(q, b_i) = \frac{log(N_{b_i})}{N_{b_i}} \sum_{j=1}^{|b_i \cap R(q)|} P(q|p_{ji}) \quad (3)$$

where N_b is the number of posts in the blog b. We assume that the query likelihood of those posts that are not retrieved in $R(q)$ is equal to zero and thus we do not consider them in the summation. Similar estimations are used by Balog *et al.* [1].

All the mentioned methods have one parameter as the size of $R(q)$ which we call n. This parameter defines the size of the initially retrieved set of posts for the query that will be inputs of the aggregation methods. The value of n is learnt using a training set which will be described in more detail later. The PCS method has two more parameters that are assigned as follows:

- k: number of the top posts from each blog used in the calculations. Without any further tuning, we set this parameter to 5 in our experiments which is proved to be an optimal choice in the original work [13].
- Smoothing parameter γ: we set this parameter in all the experiments to 0.01 which was found to be an optimal choice for both baseline and respective diversity-based methods.

4. DIVERSITY IN BLOG RETRIEVAL

The relation between posts in each blog can give us useful information about the blog. Previous studies considered cohesiveness as a way to capture how posts in the blog are similar to the blog in general [4, 13, 9]. In these studies, a blog with higher cohesiveness and thus less diversity is considered a better blog to retrieve. Elsas *et al.* define the centrality of a post as its similarity to the blog as a whole. They assume that if the retrieved posts from a blog have high centrality, that blog is a better candidate for retrieval [4]. Seo and Croft penalize those blogs that have high diversity among their posts [13]. Defining the goal of blog retrieval system to retrieve topic-centric blogs, they assume that blogs with high diversity are not topic-centric and thus should be penalized. MacDonald and Ounis define similar measures to retrieve blogs with focused interests [9]. They also consider temporal distribution of posts to retrieve blogs with recurring interests.

In contrast to previous work where all the posts of the blog are used for estimations, we focus only on those posts that are about the query topic. While diversity of a blog as a whole might be negative evidence for blog relevance, we assume that on-topic diversity is an asset. In other words, we assume that a relevant blog should have a high coverage over sub-topics and thus should have a high diversity among posts that it publishes about the topic.

We define three types of diversity over the posts and investigate their effectiveness on performance of a blog retrieval system:

- Topical Diversity
- Temporal Diversity
- Hybrid Diversity

In the following we discuss each of the methods in more detail.

4.1 Topical Diversity of Blog Posts

First we study topical diversity among the posts of each blog. Blog distillation queries tend to be more general than normal web queries and thus have a wider range of sub-topics [4]. We assume that posts that are retrieved from each blog for the query should have high diversity in order to cover different sub-topics. We want to investigate how this on-topic diversity of posts can affect the relevance of a blog to the query.

In order to test if the diversity of blog posts is an important factor in the relevance of blogs, we carry out preliminary experiments on the Blog08 collection. In these experiments, we assume that higher similarity of blog posts indicates less diversity among them. This assumption is consistent with previous work on diversification [2].

For each query, we first retrieve the top n posts using a traditional retrieval method. Then for each blog that has more than one post in the retrieved set, we calculate the average similarity between its retrieved posts, which we call *On-topic Intra-feed Similarity* (OIS):

$$OIS(b_i, q) = \frac{\sum_{j=1}^{|b_i \cap R(q)|} \sum_{l=j+1}^{|b_i \cap R(q)|} sim(p_{ji}, p_{li})}{\binom{|b_i \cap R(q)|}{2}} \quad (4)$$

The higher the *OIS* value, the less diverse is the feed with respect to the query. We use cosine similarity as the similarity measure between two posts.

Figure 1 shows the distribution of *OIS* for relevant and non-relevant blogs. It can be seen that non-relevant blogs are more likely to have high *OIS* values. The mean of *OIS* for relevant blogs is `0.43` compared to `0.50` for non-relevant blogs. Based on the Welch two sample t-test, the difference between the mean values is statistically significant with a p-values equal to `2.6e-16`. This shows the possibility of using the diversity of posts for discriminating between relevant and non-relevant blogs and consequently having a better retrieval system.

In figure 1, we use the top 2000 posts for each topic. Similar behavior has been observed for a smaller number of posts. However, it is possible that with an increasing number of retrieved posts, we retrieve more posts for each blog and we end up with less diverse relevant blogs or more diverse non-relevant blogs. In order to test this possibility, we run the same analysis with the top 15000 posts for each query. Figure 2 shows the outcome of this experiment. The mean of *OIS* values for relevant blogs is `0.34` compared to `0.42` for non-relevant blogs. The difference between the mean values is statistically significant with the p-value less than `2.2e-16`.

As we can see, the *OIS* values decrease with increasing numbers of posts. However, the difference between relevant and non-relevant blogs still exists. This is quite surprising, since we expect that by retrieving more posts, we increase the chance that non-relevant blogs will have a more diverse set of retrieved posts.

The per-topic analysis in figure 3 shows the difference more clearly. This figure shows the average of *OIS* values

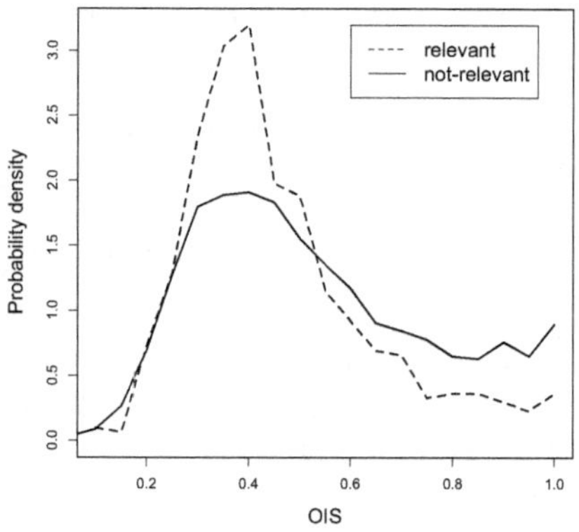

Figure 1: Distribution of On-topic Intra-feed Similarity(*OIS*) using top 2000 retrieved posts.

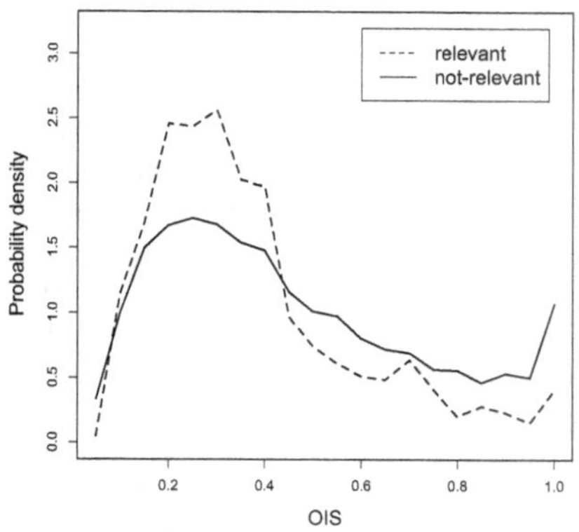

Figure 2: Distribution of On-topic Intra-feed Similarity(*OIS*) using top 15000 retrieved posts..

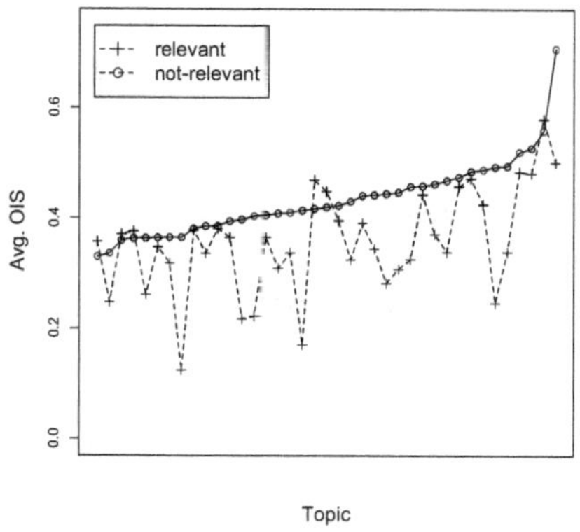

Figure 3: Average *OIS* values for each topic using top 15000 retrieved posts.

for relevant and non-relevant blogs for each query topic. For clarity, topics are sorted by the average *OIS* of their non-relevant feeds. As can be seen for most topics, non-relevant feeds have higher similarity among their posts compared to the relevant ones.

To capture the diversity of blog posts, we adapt a variation of Maximal Marginal Relevance (MMR) [2]. The goal of MMR is to maximize diversity of retrieved set of documents. It selects documents that are more similar to the query and less similar to already retrieved documents:

$$MMR \stackrel{def}{=} Arg\ max_{d_i \in R \setminus S} \left[\lambda sim(d_i, q) - (1-\lambda)\ max_{d_j \in S}\ sim(d_i, d_j)\right]$$

where R is an initial set of documents and S is the set of already retrieved documents.

Similar to the MMR method, our diversity detection method exploits the fact that similar documents are less diverse, thus it penalizes posts that are similar to other posts in the blog. In other words, only information of a post that does not appear in other blog posts can contribute to blog relevance:

$$score_{div-topical}(p_i, q) = score_{ini}(p_i, q)(1 - \lambda\ max_{p_j \in S}\ sim_{topical}(p_i, p_j)) \quad (5)$$

where $score_{ini}(p_i, q)$ is the initial score of post p_i for the query q. S is the set of posts that belong to the same blog and have higher scores than p_i. This method assumes that $sim(p_i, p_j)$ is in $[0, 1]$ and thus it decreases the post score based on its similarity to other posts. The parameter λ controls the importance of the post novelty in its score, which can vary for different similarity methods or different queries. $sim_{topical}$ captures the content similarity between the two posts and can be replaced by any similarity measure. We use *cosine* similarity, since it always has a value in $[0, 1]$ and does not need an extra normalization step:

$$sim_{topical}(p_i, p_j) = \frac{\sum_w tf(w, p_i) \times tf(w, p_j)}{\sqrt{\sum_w tf(w, p_i)^2 \times \sum_w tf(w, p_j)^2}} \quad (6)$$

where $tf(w, p)$ is the term frequency of the term w in the post p. When there is no similarity between a post and other blog posts that have higher score, the maximum of similarities will be zero. In this case, the diversity score of the post will be the same as its initial score and therefore all the relevance evidence of the post can contribute to the blog relevance score. In contrast, if there is another post very similar to the current post, then the cosine similarity will be close to one. As a result, depending on the value of λ, the diversity score of the post can be close to zero. Therefore, the blog will not gain any relevance from that post even if the post has high query likelihood.

After obtaining new scores for posts, any existing aggregation method can be used to aggregate the new scores and calculate the score of blogs. Applying the diversity-based scores introduces a new parameter λ that needs to be estimated.

4.2 Temporal Diversity of Blog Posts

In addition to the content of blog posts, temporal information is another important source of information that can be used by the retrieval system [8, 9]. Analogous to topical diversity, we can assume that a relevant blog should have a high temporal diversity among its published posts for the query. In other words, we expect that blog posts have high coverage over the temporal space and not be concentrated on specific time windows.

We employ a similar approach to the topical diversity where we penalize the posts that have high temporal similarity to other posts. To this end, we define a temporal similarity function between two posts as an un-normalized Gaussian function:

$$sim_{temporal}(p_i, p_j) = e^{-\frac{(t_i - t_j)^2}{2\sigma^2}} \quad (7)$$

where t_i is the time-stamp of p_i given in days. We can see that the temporal similarity has a value between zero and one. If the two posts are published in the same day their similarity will be one and the similarity will decrease when the temporal distance increases. Finally, we penalize post scores based on their temporal similarity:

$$score_{div-temporal}(p_i, q) = score_{ini}(p_i, q)(1 - \lambda\ max_{p_j \in S}\ sim_{temporal}(p_i, p_j)) \quad (8)$$

Using this method, if the post is published around the

same date as some other posts, it will contribute less to the blog relevance than a post which is published at a distant time. In other words, this captures the property of whether the blog posts are published all over the temporal space or if they are mostly published in some specific small time windows.

The temporal similarity function adds a new parameter σ to the model which is the standard deviation of the Gaussian function.

4.3 Hybrid Diversity

Finally, we can consider hybrid measure of diversity that takes both topical and temporal diversities into account. Two possible cases in which temporal and topical diversities can complement each other can be described as follows:

- Retrieve a relevant blog that writes about similar subtopics but in different time windows. This might be a subtopic that is discussed periodically over time. For example any seasonal query that repeats over time can have such a property. In this case the topical diversity would be low and the temporal diversity would be high. Thus a combination of the two diversities can better handle the situation than considering only topical diversity which would over-penalize the blog.
- Retrieve a relevant blog that writes about different subtopics in the same time window. A blog can heavily discuss the topic in some time periods and if the published posts are about different sub topics, they might be valuable for the blog relevance. In this case, we would have low temporal diversity and high topical diversity and may need a combination of the two measures for better representation.

To consider these cases in our method, we define an hybrid similarity function as follows:

$$sim_{hybrid}(p_i, p_j) = sim_{topical}(p_i, p_j) \ . \ sim_{temporal}(p_i, p_j)$$

where $sim_{topical}$ and $sim_{temporal}$ are calculated using formula 6 and formula 7 respectively. Similar to topical and temporal diversity scores in formulas 5 and 8, we penalize those posts that have high hybrid similarity with other posts.

We can see that in this method, we mainly penalize those posts that are published around the same date as other posts and also have very similar content to them. Thus, in any of the two mentioned scenarios where one of the similarities is high and the other one is low, the post will not be highly penalized and can still contribute to the blog relevance.

5. EXPERIMENTAL RESULTS

We conduct our experiments over four years worth of TREC blog track data from the blog distillation task, including TREC'07, TREC'08, TREC'09 and TREC'10 data sets. The TREC'07 and TREC'08 data sets include 45 and 50 queries respectively and use the Blog06 collection. The TREC'09 and TREC'10 data sets use Blog08, a new collection of blogs, and have 39 and 46 queries respectively. We use only the title of the topics as the queries.

The Blogs06 collection is a crawl of about one hundred thousand blogs over an 11-week period [10], and includes blog posts (permalinks), feed, and homepage for each blog. Blog08 is a collection of about one million blogs crawled over a year with the same structure as the Blog06 collection [11]. In our experiments we only use the permalinks component of the collection, which consist of approximately 3.2 million documents for Blog06 and about 28.4 million documents for Blog08.

We use the Terrier Information Retrieval system[3] to index the collection with the default stemming and stop-words removal. In all the methods, the language modeling approach using the Dirichlet smoothing has been used to score the posts and retrieve top posts for each query. Without further tuning, the Dirichlet smoothing parameter is set to 5000 [16].

We use the three blog retrieval methods discussed in section 2 as our baseline methods. We apply each of these methods on the language model scores and also on the three diversified scores calculated by our proposed methods.

Since TREC'07 and TREC'08 query sets share the same collection, we use one to tune the parameters for the other. We do the same for the TREC'09 and TREC'10 query sets that share the Blog08 collection. By fixing the parameters k and σ in the PCS method and the Dirichlet smoothing parameter across all the methods, the remaining parameters to be tuned are the following:

- The number of the top retrieved posts, n, that are initially retrieved for each query. The examined values for this parameter are 500, 1000, 2000, 4000, 8000 and 15000.
- The diversity parameter, λ, in each of the diversity methods. We tested different values for this parameter as follows: 0.01, 0.05, 0.1, 0.2, ..., 0.9, 0.95 and 0.99.
- The standard deviation of the gaussian function, σ, in the temporal and hybrid diversity methods. For the Blog06 collection we tried the values 3, 5, 7, 15, 30, 45, 60, 90. Since the Blog08 collection has a wider time span, we also tried the values 120, 250 and 370 for the TREC'09 and TREC'10 experiments.

Tables 2, 3, 4 and 5 show the performance evaluation of the methods over TREC'07, TREC'08, TREC'09 and TREC'10 respectively. The first three rows in each table represent the performance of baseline methods. The second three rows show the performance of the corresponding methods based on the topical diversity scores. The third three rows show the performance of the methods using the temporal diversity scores followed by the last rows that show the performance of the hybrid diversity scores.

Statistical significance tests are performed using the paired T-test at 0.05 level of significance. The symbol $\dagger$ indicates that a diversity method has a statistically significant improvement over its corresponding baseline. The symbols $\triangle$ and $\blacktriangle$ show that the hybrid diversity method has a statistically significant improvement over the temporal diversity and topical diversity methods respectively. The bold values in each column indicate the best performance for the corresponding evaluation measure.

As we can see in the tables, diversity-based methods generally improve their corresponding baseline methods. In most cases, these improvements are at a statistically significant level. The temporal diversity methods are not as effective as their topical diversity counterpart. However, when combined together, the resulting hybrid diversity methods

[3]http://ir.dcs.gla.ac.uk/terrier/

Table 2: Evaluation results for the implemented models over TREC'07 data set.

Model	MAP	P@10	Bpref
CombSum	0.2259	0.3844	0.2721
PCS	0.2695	0.4378	0.3115
SDM	0.2867	0.4444	0.3439
CombSum-topical	0.2506 ↑	0.4244 ↑	0.2859 ↑
PCS-topical	0.2901 ↑	0.4422	0.3184 ↑
SDM-topical	0.3168 ↑	0.4756 ↑	**0.3667** ↑
CombSum-temporal	0.2612 ↑	0.4267	0.2840 ↑
PCS-temporal	0.2844 ↑	0.4911 ↑	0.3134
SDM-temporal	0.3023 ↑	0.4756 ↑	0.3539
CombSum-hybrid	0.2466 ↑	0.4333 ↑	0.2866 ↑△
PCS-hybrid	0.2961 ↑△	0.4622	0.3197 ↑△
SDM-hybrid	**0.3191** ↑△	**0.5156** ↑△ ▲	0.3622 ↑△

Table 3: Evaluation results for the implemented models over TREC'08 data set.

Model	MAP	P@10	Bpref
CombSum	0.1719	0.3000	0.2380
PCS	0.2016	0.3400	0.2709
SDM	0.2096	0.3740	0.2699
CombSum-topical	0.1847	0.3340	0.2446
PCS-topical	0.2086	0.3460	0.2640
SDM-topical	0.2284 ↑	0.3820	0.2729
CombSum-temporal	0.1852 ↑	0.3380 ↑	0.2430
PCS-temporal	0.2073	0.3660 ↑	0.2540
SDM-temporal	0.2289 ↑	0.3800	0.2769
CombSum-hybrid	0.1918 ↑ ▲	0.3460 ↑	0.2422
PCS-hybrid	0.2179 ↑△	0.3500	0.2661
SDM-hybrid	**0.2329** ↑	**0.3840**	**0.2777**

Table 4: Evaluation results for the implemented models over TREC'09 data set.

Model	MAP	P@10	Bpref
CombSum	0.1889	0.3154	0.2148
PCS	0.2093	0.3103	0.2279
SDM	0.2636	0.3821	0.2858
CombSum-topical	0.2180 ↑	0.3282	0.2297 ↑
PCS-topical	0.2196 ↑	0.3282	0.2374 ↑
SDM-topical	0.2888 ↑	**0.4333** ↑	0.3091 ↑
CombSum-temporal	0.2087 ↑	0.3051	0.2187
PCS-temporal	0.2082	0.3103	0.2250
SDM-temporal	0.2759	0.3846	0.2909
CombSum-hybrid	0.2176 ↑△	0.3282 △	0.2334 ↑△
PCS-hybrid	0.2224 ↑△	0.3462 ↑△	0.2387 ↑△
SDM-hybrid	**0.2961** ↑△ ▲	0.4308 ↑△	**0.3125** ↑△

Table 5: Evaluation results for the implemented models over TREC'10 data set.

Model	MAP	P@10	Bpref
CombSum	0.1631	0.2696	0.1631
PCS	0.1758	0.2870	0.1771
SDM	0.2273	0.3022	0.2273
CombSum-topical	0.1856 ↑	0.2435	0.1856 ↑
PCS-topical	0.1843	0.2913	0.1843
SDM-topical	0.2420 ↑	0.3435 ↑	0.2559 ↑
CombSum-temporal	0.1623	0.2196	0.1623
PCS-temporal	0.1759	0.2500	0.1759
SDM-temporal	0.2151	0.2891	0.2231
CombSum-hybrid	0.1738 △	0.2239	0.1831 ↑△
PCS-hybrid	0.1842	0.3000 ↑	0.1842
SDM-hybrid	**0.2571** ↑△ ▲	**0.3500** ↑△	**0.2649** ↑△

usually produce the best results. In some cases, combining temporal diversity with topical diversity results in a statistically significant improvement over each one of them.

An interesting observation is that the *SDM* method, as the strongest baseline, benefits the most from the diversification. As a result, the *SDM-hybrid* method significantly outperforms the *SDM* method in most of the collections and evaluation metrics.

We previously mentioned that spam blogs are one category of non-relevant blogs that would be filtered using diversity-based methods. It is interesting to see what portion of blogs that are affected by diversity methods are in fact spam blogs. To this end, we manually checked non-relevant blogs that were initially retrieved by *SDM* and were removed from the ranked list after applying hybrid diversity measure. We chose ten random queries from the TREC'09 query set and compared their ranked lists before and after considering diversity. Among 106 non-relevant blogs that were removed from the ranked list, 27 of them (25%) were spam blogs and the rest were non-spam. This shows that considering diversity does not just filter out spam blogs, but also removes other non-relevant blogs from the ranked list. On the other hand, our examination shows that the method promotes relevant blogs in the ranking. For the examined queries, there were 30 new relevant blogs retrieved after applying diversity and only 6 relevant blogs were removed from the ranked list.

In order to test the robustness of proposed approaches, we analyze the sensitivity of their retrieval performance to the parameters. We analyze the results over the TREC'09 query set, as an example of a large collection, and the TREC'07 query set, as an example of a small collection. For simplicity, we only consider the *SDM* method and the corresponding diversity-based methods in this analysis. To study each of the parameters, we fix the other parameters with values that are learnt from the training set in the previous experiments.

Figures 4 and 7 show the effect of n, the number of initially retrieved posts, on the performance of retrieval systems. The diversity-based methods outperform the baselines at all the values of n. This confirms our analysis in section 4 that the difference between on-topic diversity of relevant blogs and non-relevant blogs does not change by increasing n. We can see that by increasing the number of posts, the performance increases and the difference of performances for values higher than 5000 are insignificant.

Figures 5 and 8 show the effect of λ when we fix the values of n and σ. We can see that the performance of the hybrid and topical diversity methods generally increase by increasing λ. In both collections, the best performance of these methods is achieved when λ has a value close to one. This shows that the maximum penalty for those blogs that publish repetitive information produces the best results. On the other hand, temporal diversity is less robust and the performance decreases for λ values higher than 0.5.

Finally, figures 6 and 9 show the effect of σ on the perfor-

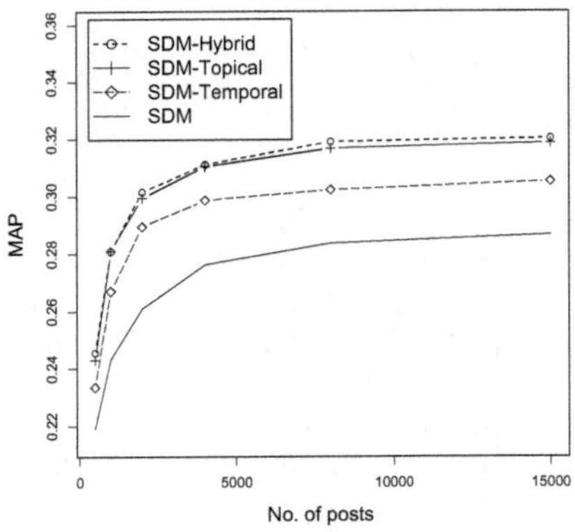

Figure 4: Effect of the number of the top retrieved posts in the performance over TREC'07 data set

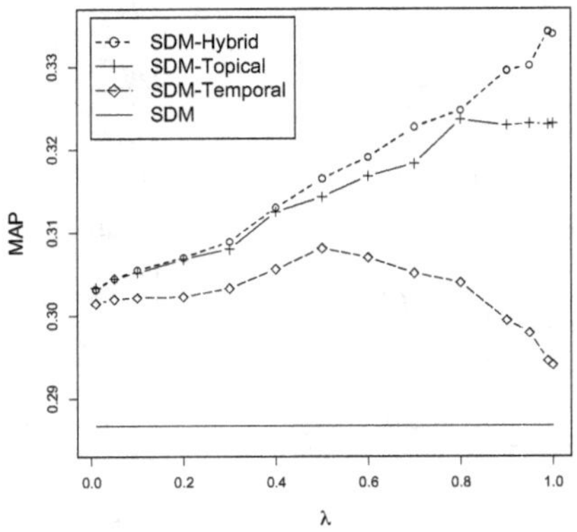

Figure 5: Effect of the diversity parameter λ in the performance over TREC'07 data set

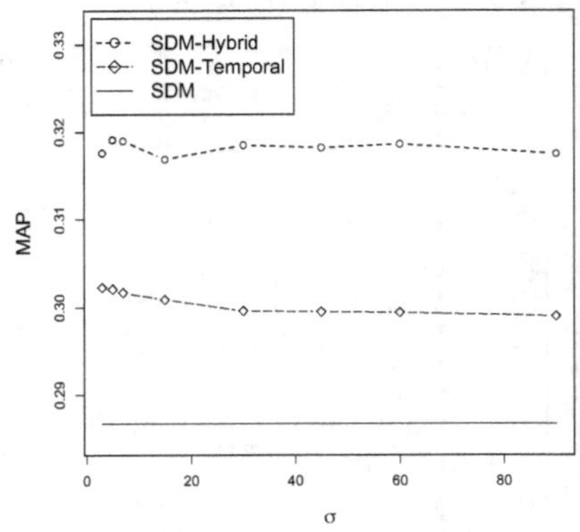

Figure 6: Effect of the parameter σ in the performance over TREC'07 data set

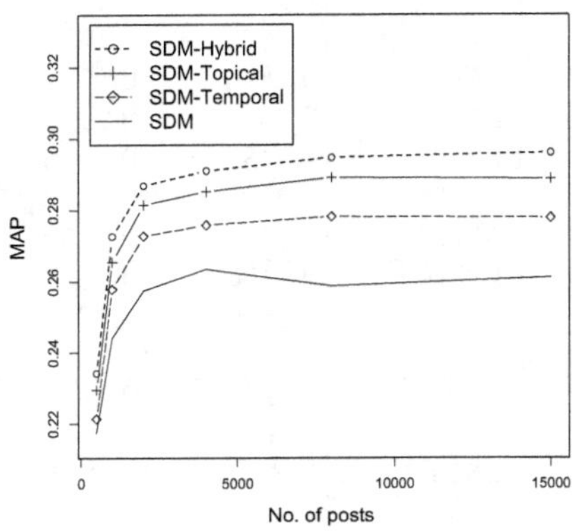

Figure 7: Effect of the number of the top retrieved posts in the performance over TREC'09 data set

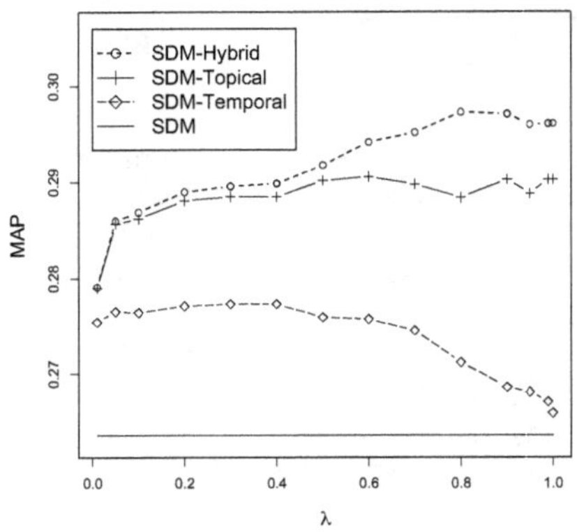

Figure 8: Effect of the diversity parameter λ in the performance over TREC'09 data set

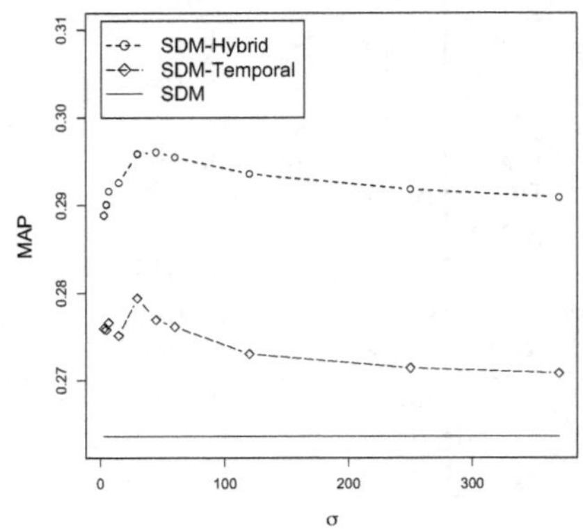

Figure 9: Effect of the parameter σ in the performance over TREC'09 data set

mance of temporal and hybrid diversity methods. It can be seen that σ is less influential on the performance and it has little negative effect when its value increases. It is interesting to see the relation between the size of the collection and the best value of σ. While for the TREC'07 collection the best performance is achieved when σ is around 5, this value for the TREC'09 collection is around 40.

5.1 Diversity vs. Cohesiveness of a blog

So far, we showed that blog post diversity is a discriminative feature in blog retrieval that can improve retrieval performance. In this section, we investigate a comparison between blog post diversity and the previously proposed blog cohesiveness measures. The cohesiveness of a blog is assumed to show whether the blog focuses on a specific topic or not. While it is a reasonable assumption, the proposed methods in previous work did not show any positive effect on retrieval effectiveness:

- MacDonald and Ounis suggest that high cohesiveness of a blog shows that most of the blog posts are about similar topics and thus we should give higher score to that blog. Adding their cohesiveness measure to the weighting model not only did not improve their results but also decreased the results in some cases [9].
- Seo and Croft define a penalty factor based on a clarity score [13]. They assume that a blog that covers many different topics has a language model similar to that of the collection and thus should be penalized. They add the clarity-based penalty to two weighting models and in both cases it decreased the performance of the system.
- Elsas *et al.* propose a centrality measure for each post to calculate $P(p_{ji}|b_i)$ in equation 2 [4]. The centrality captures how similar the post is to the blog as a whole. The assumption is that if the blog is cohesive, then the centrality of the posts is high and thus the overall score of the blog should be higher. Our experiments show that replacing the centrality measure with a simple uniform distribution over blog posts improves the retrieval performance [4].

[4]For clarity of the paper we do not report this comparison here.

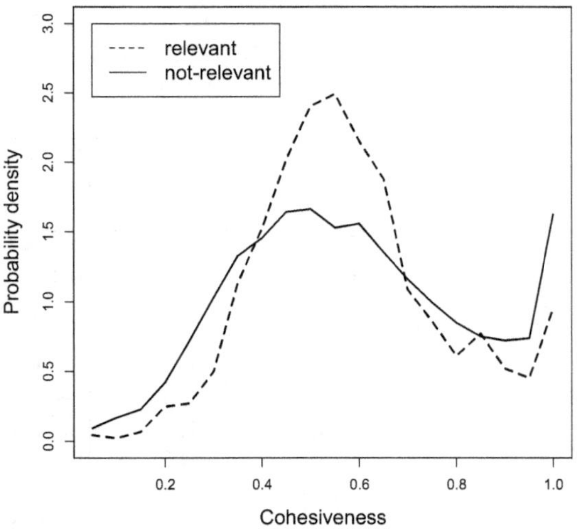

Figure 10: Cohesiveness distribution of relevant and non-relevant blogs

All these works assumed cohesiveness to be a positive feature of blog relevance and did not investigate if this is a valid assumption or not. In order to verify the validity of this assumption, we use the following cohesiveness measure to compare the relevant and non-relevant blogs:

$$cohesiveness(b_i, q) = \frac{\sum_{j=1}^{|b_i \cap R(q)|} sim(p_{ji}, VD(b_i))}{|b_i \cap R(q)|}$$

where $VD(b_i)$ is a virtual document created by concatenating all the posts of b_i. We use the cosine similarity measure for calculating $sim(p_{ji}, b_i)$, as the similarity between a post and a blog. This measure of cohesiveness compares the initially retrieved posts of a blog to the blog as a whole. In other words, it captures the cohesiveness of the blog with respect to the topic. It is similar to those measures used in other works mentioned earlier [9, 4].

Figure 10 shows the distribution of cohesiveness values for relevant and non-relevant blogs in TREC'09 data set. The value of n, the size of $R(q)$, is set to 15000 for this analysis. The mean value of cohesiveness for relevant blogs is 0.56 and for non-relevant blogs, it is 0.55. The difference between the mean values is not statistically significant and the p-value of the Welch t-test is 0.66. This shows that the cohesiveness is not a strong discriminative feature and explains why adding cohesiveness did not improve the performance of the retrieval systems in the previous works.

It is interesting to verify if cohesiveness is correlated with *IOS*, as defined in equation 4. If a blog has high cohesiveness, it is not surprising that it would also have high similarity among its posts and thus high *IOS* value. However if the top posts of a blog are very similar (high *IOS*), one can not directly conclude that the blog has high cohesiveness. In order to examine such a correlation we calculate the Pearson correlation between the cohesiveness and the *OIS* values. The correlation is statistically significant with a value of 0.83. The high correlation shows that blogs with high *OIS* are very likely to also have high cohesiveness.

5.2 Diversity in Facet Detection

In 2009, a more complex and refined version of the blog distillation task was introduced in TREC, named "Faceted Blog Distillation" [11]. The new task, which was first introduced by Hearst *et al.* [7], aims to consider not only the blog relevance to the topic but also the "quality aspects" (facets) of the blog. For each query, a specific facet is determined and only blogs that satisfy that facet are considered to be relevant. In this section, we discuss the effect of diversity on the performance of the system for different facets. Different facets can be seen as different categories of blogs that users might search for. It is important to be able to decide for what type of information needs we can use diversity to get the maximum overall performance.

We use the introduced facets in the TREC'09 and TREC'10 data collections which include Opinionated vs. Factual, Personal vs. Company and In-depth vs. Shallow facets [11]. Tables 6 and 7 compare the performance of the diversity method with the baseline method for each facet. Without further tuning, we use the same parameter values as the previous section.

The statistically significant improvements are shown by $\uparrow$. Since each facet has very few queries, the statistical significance tests will be very sensitive and do not always show a difference. Thus we report also the percentage of improvement over the baseline method. The maximum improvement for each measure is shown in bold.

As we can see, diversity improves the performance of the system for almost all of the facets and evaluation measures. This shows that the effectiveness of diversity is not restricted to specific categories of topics. As a result, one can expect to have improvements by applying diversity for any type of information needs in blog search.

It is interesting to notice the improvement of P@10 for the in-depth queries which is the maximum among all the facets. For the in-depth queries, a relevant blog is expected to have in-depth thoughts and analyses about the topic [11]. As we previously saw in example 3 in table 1, one of the scenarios where diversity is effective is in retrieving blogs with such an in-depth property. The obtained improvements for in-depth queries confirm our previous observation. The results shows that a diversity-based method retrieves in-depth blogs at the top ranks and significantly improves the P@10 measure.

6. CONCLUSION AND FUTURE WORK

In this paper, we studied the effect of employing different diversity measures on blog retrieval. We showed that diversity is an important feature that can help in distinguishing relevant blogs from non-relevant ones. We introduced three types of diversity and investigated their effect on the performance of the retrieval systems. Our experiments on standard blog retrieval collections showed improvements over different baseline methods.

We further showed that the common assumption of cohesiveness is not an indicative feature of blog relevance and that is in fact the reason that there is no improvement observed in the previous work.

Finally, we investigated the effect of diversity on different types of queries and showed that diversity can be beneficial to all query types.

Table 6: Effect of diversity on different facets over TREC'09 data set.

Facet	Model	MAP	P@10	Bpref
Opinionated	SDM	0.1153	0.1615	0.0998
	SDM-hybrid	0.1236	0.1923	0.1132
(13 queries)		(+7%)	(+19%)	(+13%)
Factual	SDM	0.1749	0.1692	0.1570
	SDM-hybrid	0.1788	0.1538	0.1661
(13 queries)		(+2%)	(-9%)	(+5%)
Personal	SDM	0.1840	0.2000	0.1384
	SDM-hybrid	0.2201	0.2375	0.1756
(8 queries)		(+19%) ↑	(+18%)	(**+26%**) ↑
Official	SDM	0.1876	0.1750	0.1537
	SDM-hybrid	0.2319	0.1750	0.1819
(8 queries)		(**+23%**)	(0.0%)	(+18%)
Indepth	SDM	0.2723	0.2222	0.2624
	SDM-hybrid	0.2872	0.2667	0.2526
(18 queries)		(+5%)	(**20%**) ↑	(-3%)
Shallow	SDM	0.1348	0.0889	0.1118
	SDM-hybrid	0.1540	0.1056	0.1378
(18 queries)		(+14%) ↑	(+18%)	(+23%)

Table 7: Effect of diversity on different facets ove TREC'09 data set.

Facet	Model	MAP	P@10	Bpref
Opinionated	SDM	0.1061	0.1800	0.1257
	SDM-hybrid	0.1260	0.2000	0.1369
(15 queries)		(+18%) ↑	(+11%)	(+8%)
Factual	SDM	0.1028	0.1000	0.0820
	SDM-hybrid	0.1190	0.1067	0.0985
(15 queries)		(+15%)	(+6%)	(**+20%**)
Personal	SDM	0.1290	0.1533	0.1095
	SDM-hybrid	0.1426	0.1467	0.1060
(15 queries)		(+10%)	(-4%)	(-3%)
Official	SDM	0.2057	0.1267	0.1697
	SDM-hybrid	0.2274	0.1400	0.1928
(15 queries)		(+10%)	(+10%)	(+13%)
Indepth	SDM	0.2396	0.1250	0.2079
	SDM-hybrid	0.2953	0.1625	0.2430
(16 queries)		(**+23%**) ↑	(**+30%**) ↑	(+16%)
Shallow	SDM	0.0833	0.1250	0.0818
	SDM-hybrid	0.1003	0.1313	0.0838
(16 queries)		(+20%)	(+5%)	(+2%)

One possible extension for future work is to apply the proposed approach to similar problems. It would be interesting to see if the diversity assumption holds for collection selection in distributed IR, expert search or user search in microblogs.

We are also interested in a more general framework for considering blog diversity that can be used in any existing blog retrieval method. So far, we have only applied diversity measures to the methods that are an aggregation of post-level scores. However, there are some methods that do not just aggregate post-level scores, such as the Blogger Model method [1] or two stage retrieval model [15]. It would be interesting to develop a framework to adapt diversity measures for those methods as well.

7. ACKNOWLEDGMENTS

This work was supported partly by the Center for Intelligent Information Retrieval and partly by the Swiss National Science Foundation. Any opinions, findings and conclusions or recommendations expressed in this material are those of the authors and do not necessarily reflect those of the sponsors.

We thank Jangwon Seo for his collaboration and comments while he was in CIIR. We also like to thank Armita Kaboli for her helpful discussions and comments.

8. REFERENCES

[1] K. Balog, M. de Rijke, and W. Weerkamp. Bloggers as experts: feed distillation using expert retrieval models. In *Proceedings of SIGIR'08*, 2008.

[2] J. Carbonell and J. Goldstein. The use of mmr, diversity-based reranking for reordering documents and producing summaries. In *Proceedings of SIGIR'98*, pages 335–336, 1998.

[3] M. Efron, D. Turnbull, and C. Ovalle. University of Texas School of Information at TREC 2007. In *Proceedings of TREC'07*, 2007.

[4] J. L. Elsas, J. Arguello, J. Callan, and J. G. Carbonell. Retrieval and feedback models for blog feed search. In *Proceedings of SIGIR'08*, pages 347–354, 2008.

[5] D. Hawking and P. Thomas. Server selection methods in hybrid portal search. In *Proceedings of SIGIR'05*, pages 75–82, 2005.

[6] J. He, W. Weerkamp, M. Larson, and M. de Rijke. An effective coherence measure to determine topical consistency in user-generated content. *IJDAR*, 12(3):185–203, 2009.

[7] M. A. Hearst, M. Hurst, and S. T. Dumais. What should blog search look like? In *Proceedings of the 2008 ACM workshop on Search in social media*, pages 95–98, 2008.

[8] M. Keikha, S. Gerani, and F. Crestani. Temper: A temporal relevance feedback method. In *Proceedings of ECIR'11*, pages 436–447, 2011.

[9] C. Macdonald and I. Ounis. Key blog distillation: ranking aggregates. In *Proceeding of CIKM'08*, pages 1043–1052, 2008.

[10] C. Macdonald, I. Ounis, and I. Soboroff. Overview of the TREC 2007 Blog Track. In *Proceedings of TREC'07*, 2007.

[11] C. Macdonald, I. Ounis, and I. Soboroff. Overview of the TREC-2009 Blog Track. In *Proceedings of TREC'09*, 2009.

[12] G. Mishne and M. de Rijke. A study of blog search. In *Proceedings of ECIR'06*, pages 289–301, 2006.

[13] J. Seo and W. B. Croft. Blog site search using resource selection. In *Proceedings of CIKM'08*, pages 1053–1062, 2008.

[14] I. Soboroff, A. de Vries, and N. Craswell. Overview of the TREC 2006 Enterprise Track. In *Proceedings of TREC'06*, 2006.

[15] W. Weerkamp, K. Balog, and M. de Rijke. Blog feed search with a post index. *Information Retrieval*, 14(5):515–545, 2011.

[16] C. Zhai and J. Lafferty. A study of smoothing methods for language models applied to information retrieval. *ACM Transactions on Information Systems*, 22(2):179–214, 2004.

Efficient Retrieval of Recommendations in a Matrix Factorization Framework

Noam Koenigstein
School of Electrical Engineering
Tel Aviv University

Parikshit Ram
Computational Science & Engineering
Georgia Institute of Technology

Yuval Shavitt
School of Electrical Engineering
Tel Aviv University

ABSTRACT

Low-rank Matrix Factorization (MF) methods provide one of the simplest and most effective approaches to collaborative filtering. This paper is the first to investigate the problem of efficient retrieval of recommendations in a MF framework. We reduce the retrieval in a MF model to an *apparently* simple task of finding the maximum dot-product for the user vector over the set of item vectors. However, to the best of our knowledge the problem of efficiently finding the maximum dot-product in the general case has never been studied. To this end, we propose two techniques for efficient search – (i) We index the item vectors in a binary spatial-partitioning metric tree and use a simple branch-and-bound algorithm with a novel bounding scheme to efficiently obtain exact solutions. (ii) We use spherical clustering to index the users on the basis of their preferences and pre-compute recommendations only for the representative user of each cluster to obtain extremely efficient approximate solutions. We obtain a theoretical error bound which determines the quality of any approximate result and use it to control the approximation. Both these simple techniques are fairly independent of each other and hence are easily combined to further improve recommendation retrieval efficiency. We evaluate our algorithms on real-world collaborative-filtering datasets, demonstrating more than $\times 7$ speedup (with respect to the naive linear search) for the exact solution and over $\times 250$ speedup for approximate solutions by combining both techniques.

Categories and Subject Descriptors

H.4 [**Information Systems Applications**]: Miscellaneous

General Terms

Algorithms

Keywords

inner-product, fast retrieval, collaborative filtering

CIKM'12, October 29–November 2, 2012, Maui, HI, USA.

1. INTRODUCTION

Recommender systems based on Matrix Factorization (MF) models have repeatedly demonstrated better accuracy than other methods such as nearest neighbor models and restricted Boltzmann machines [1, 8]. However, large scale MF models for real world recommender systems (e.g., [5, 12, 7]) run into a difficulty rarely discussed in the academic literature – the computational cost of finding the top-rated items for every user in the system once the model has been trained.

In MF models, the predicted rating of a user for an item boils down to a dot-product between two vectors representing the user and the item (we will discuss this explicitly in section 2). Constructing the entire *#USERS* $\times$ *#ITEMS* preference matrix (or even just for the top-rated items for every user) requires heavy computational (and space) resources. For example, the recently published Yahoo! Music dataset [8] has 1,000,990 users and 624,961 music items. Generating the optimal recommendations in this dataset requires over 6×10^{12} dot-products using a naive algorithm. A 50-dimensional model required 134 hours (over 5 days) to find optimal recommendations for all the users[1]. In terms of storage, saving the whole preference matrix requires over 5TB of disk-space. Moreover, this dataset of 10^6 users is just a small sample of the actual Yahoo! Music dataset and the problem worsens with larger numbers.

The problem of finding the maximum dot-product for a given query p (in this case, a user) over a set of points S (in this case, the items) is to find the point $q \in S$ such that:

$$p^\top q = \max_{q_i \in S} p^\top q_i. \quad (1)$$

Surprisingly, we did not find any technique to efficiently solve this problem; a linear search over the set of points appears to be the state-of-the-art! Moreover, the number of queries in our application is very high (possibly higher than the number of points). The focus of our paper is *to develop algorithms to solve* (1) *for multiple queries more efficiently than the linear-search algorithm.* Our contributions are:

- A simple branch-and-bound algorithm on a tree index with a novel bound to solve the exact problem.
- An approximate scheme that pre-computes solutions for certain representative queries and uses these solutions for the new queries. This makes the retrieval process extremely efficient. The representative queries are obtained by clustering the available queries.
- A theoretical error bound which determines the quality of the approximate results for a new query and is used to control the approximation by adaptively rejecting overly

[1]Using an Intel Xeon (E7320) CPU running at 2.13GHz.

(theoretically) inaccurate solutions and recomputing exact solutions for the query.

Parallelization.

The computational cost of recommendation retrieval can be mitigated by parallelization. One possible way of parallelizing involves dividing the users across cores/machines – each worker can compute the recommendations for a single user (or a small set of users). However, this is wasteful in resources and requires complex setups. Moreover, this form of parallelization does not mitigate the high latency of computing recommendations for a single user. Map-reduce parallelization can reduce the single user latency. However, a single map-reduce can at best take $O(\sqrt{\#ITEMS})$ time for the retrieval task of a single user.

Our proposed techniques are orthogonal to parallelization, and can be parallelized to improve the scalability. The branch-and-bound algorithm reduces single query latency (and can have $O(\log(\#ITEMS))$ retrieval time). Our approximate scheme reduces the number of users by only choosing a small set of representative users.

Efficient Retrieval Algorithms.

The problem of efficient Retrieval of Recommendations (RoR) in collaborative filtering has been previously studied. Large-scale recommender systems use techniques like min-hash clustering of users, probabilistic latent semantic indexing, and co-visitation counts to achieve fair scalability [5]. A more recent method based on multidimensional scaling embeds both the users and items in a common Euclidean space [11], reducing the retrieval task to the problem of k-nearest-neighbor search. The plethora of algorithms for nearest-neighbor search can then be used for efficient RoR. While these methods show significant improvements in retrieval times, they deviate from the more accurate MF framework. *Our proposed methods are the first efficient retrieval algorithms in the MF framework.*

This paper.

In section 2, we introduce the MF framework and reduce the task of RoR to a relatively simpler task of finding the best-matched items with respect to the dot-product of their representative vectors with the vector representing the user. Section 3 contrasts this dot-product based best matching problem to existing best matching problems in literature. In section 4, we index the items as a Metric tree and then propose a novel branch-and-bound algorithm to efficiently obtain the exact top predicted preferences for a single user. To obtain further scalability, section 5 presents an approximated method by clustering users with "similar tastes". The efficiency is obtained by pre-computing the top recommendations for the representative users (the cluster centers). We also present the theoretical worst-case error bound used to control the approximation. For further improvement, we combine both techniques and evaluate our proposed methods in section 6 on prominent collaborative filtering datasets.

Notation.

We reserve special indexing letters for distinguishing users from items: for users u and v, and for items i and j. A rating r_{ui} indicates the rating given by user u to item i. We denote by $\theta_{x,y}$ the angle between the vectors x and y at the origin. Finally, we denote the l_2-norm of a vector x as $\|x\|$.

2. MATRIX FACTORIZATION

In MF models, each user u is associated with a user-traits vector $p_u \in \mathbb{R}^D$, and each item i with an item-traits vector $q_i \in \mathbb{R}^D$. Predicted ratings are obtained using the rule:

$$\hat{r}_{ui} = \mu + b_i + b_u + p_u^\top q_i, \tag{2}$$

where μ is the overall mean rating value and b_i and b_u are scalers that represent the item and user biases respectively.

A user bias models a user's tendency to rate on a higher or lower scale than the average rater, while the item bias captures the extent of the item popularity. The user's trait vector p_u represents the user's preferences or "taste". Similarly, the item's traits vector represent the item's latent characteristics. The dot-product $p_u^\top q_i$ is the personalization component which captures user's u affinity to item i.

A significant strength of MF models is their natural ability to easily incorporate additional information. For example, temporal dynamics and taxonomy components can be easily incorporated into the MF model [6]. In such models the prediction equation takes a more complex form. Without loss of generality, we will only discuss the basic model (equation 2). However, the more complex models have more parameters which are usually additive. Hence, the proposed reduction can be easily extended and applied to these model as well. In fact, we use one such complex MF model (described in [6]) for evaluating our proposed methods.

Training.

There are various techniques for training MF models. Generally a cost function is defined on the prediction error (e.g., RMSE) and optimization is followed by Stochastic Gradient Descent or an Alternating Least Squares algorithm. The reader is referred to [13] for more details on those learning techniques. The training produces estimates of the MF model parameters (the trait vectors and the biases). Given these parameters, we will demonstrate that the user's preference for any item can be reduced to a simple dot-product.

2.1 Reduction of RoR

RoR in a trained MF model involves finding the set of K items for a user u with maximum predicted ratings. Equation 2 implies that for a given user u, ordering the items is independent of μ and the user's bias b_u. Thus, we can ignore these parameters without affecting the preferred ordering of the items and obtain an effective rating:

$$\tilde{r}_{ui} = b_i + p_u^\top q_i. \tag{3}$$

It is important to note that this is only applicable during the RoR phase (after the training). Ignoring these components during the training will inevitably result in poor accuracy.

By appending the item bias to the item vector, the effective rating (equation 3) reduces to a simple dot-product:

$$\tilde{r}_{ui} = \tilde{p}_u^\top \tilde{q}_i = \|\tilde{p}_u\| \; \|\tilde{q}_i\| \cos\left(\theta_{\tilde{p}_u,\tilde{q}_i}\right), \tag{4}$$

where $\tilde{p}_u = [p_u^\top \; 1]^\top$, $\tilde{q}_i = [q_i^\top \; b_i]^\top$ and $\theta_{\tilde{p}_u,\tilde{q}_i}$ is the angle between $\tilde{p}_u$ and $\tilde{q}_i$ at the origin.

Equation 4 implies that for a given user $\tilde{p}_u$, the items ordering is independent of the norm $\|\tilde{p}_u\|$ and only depends on the user vector through the angle $\theta_{\tilde{p}_u,\tilde{q}_i}$. Hence, without loss of generality, we normalize the user vector to a unit vector $\bar{p}_u = \tilde{p}_u / \|\tilde{p}_u\|$ to further simplify equation 4 to:

$$\bar{r}_{ui} = \bar{p}_u^\top \tilde{q}_i = \|\tilde{q}_i\| \cos\left(\theta_{\bar{p}_u,\tilde{q}_i}\right). \tag{5}$$

Note that while we normalize the concatenated user vectors, the concatenated item vectors can not be normalized without

Figure 1: The most popular musical tracks and genres in the Yahoo! Music dataset are embedded into a 2-dimensional. The open cone suggests the region of highly preferred items for the user (her logo is at the center of the cone). Note how the learned embedding separates Rock and similar items from Hip-Hop and similar items. The low dimensionality (which is required for a visualization), causes a small number of items to be wrongly folded near less related items (e.g., Bob Marley).

loss of accuracy. If the item vectors were normalized, the RoR problem would have been reduced to the well studied nearest neighbor search (as explained in section 3). However, such a normalization will introduce a distortion on the balance between the original item trait vector and the item bias which constitute the concatenated vector $\tilde{q}_i$. This would evidently result in an incorrect solution.

Denoting the concatenated user and item vectors as p_u and q_i respectively, and the effective rating for the task of retrieval as r_{ui}, RoR reduces to the following task: Given a user query p_u, we want to find an item $q_i \in S$ such that:

$$p_u^\top q_i = \max_{q \in S} p_u^\top q \tag{6}$$

Hence the RoR task is equivalent to the problem of finding the best-match for a query in a set of points with respect to the dot-product (described in equation 1). A very simplistic visualization of this task is depicted in Figure 1. For the given user, the best recommendations (in this case songs) lie within the open cone around the user vector (maximizing the $\cos(\theta_{p_u,q_i})$ term) and are as far as possible from the origin (maximizing the $\|q_i\|$ term).

3. ALGORITHMS FOR FINDING BEST-MATCHES

Efficiently finding the best match using the dot-product (equation 6) appears to be very similar to much existing work in the literature. Finding the best match with respect to the Euclidean (or more generally L_p) distance is the widely studied problem of nearest-neighbor search in metric spaces [4]. The nearest-neighbor search problem (in metric space) can be solved approximately with the popular *Locality-sensitive hashing* (LSH) method [9]. LSH has been extended to other forms of similarity functions (as opposed to the distance as a dissimilarity function) like the cosine similarity [3]. In this section, we show that the problem stated in equation 6 is different from these existing problems.

Nearest-neighbor Search in Metric Space.

The problem of finding the nearest-neighbor in this setting is to find a point $q_i \in S$ for a query p_u such that:

$$\begin{aligned} q_i &= \arg\min_{q \in S} \|p_u - q\|^2 = \arg\max_{q \in S} \left(p_u^\top q - \|q\|^2/2\right) \\ &\neq \arg\max_{q \in S} p_u^\top q \text{ (unless } \|q\|^2 = const \ \ \forall\, q \in S). \end{aligned}$$

If all the points in S are normalized to the same length, then the problem of finding the best match with respect to the dot-product is equivalent to the problem of nearest-neighbor search in any metric space. However, without this restriction, the two problems can yield very different answers.

Cosine similarity.

Finding the best match with respect to the cosine similarity is to find a point $q_i \in S$ for a query p_u such that

$$\begin{aligned} q_i &= \arg\max_{q \in S} p_u^\top q/(\|p_u\|\,\|q\|) = \arg\max_{q \in S} p_u^\top q/\|q\| \\ &\neq \arg\max_{q \in S} p_u^\top q \text{ (unless } \|q\| = const \ \ \forall\, q \in S). \end{aligned}$$

As in the previous case, the best match with cosine similarity is the best match with dot-products if all the points in the set S are normalized to the same length. Under general conditions, the best matches with these two similarity functions can be very different.

Locality-sensitive Hashing.

LSH involves constructing hashing functions h which satisfy the following for any pair of points $q, p \in \mathbb{R}^D$:

$$\Pr[h(q) = h(p)] = \mathrm{sim}(q, p), \tag{7}$$

where $\mathrm{sim}(q,p) \in [0,1]$ is the similarity function of interest. For our situation, we can scale our dataset such that $\forall\, q \in S, \|q\| \leq 1$ and assume that the data is in the first quadrant (such as in non-negative matrix factorization models [19]). In that case, $\mathrm{sim}(q,p) = q^\top p \in [0,1]$ is our similarity function of interest.

For any similarity function to admit a locality sensitive hash function family (as defined in equation 7), the distance function $\mathbf{d}(q,p) = 1 - \mathrm{sim}(q,p)$ must satisfy the triangle inequality (Lemma 1 in [3]). However, the distance function $\mathbf{d}(q,p) = 1 - q^\top p$ does not satisfy the triangle inequality. Hence LSH cannot be applied to the dot-product similarity function even in restricted domains (the first quadrant).

3.1 Why is finding the maximum dot-products harder?

Unlike the distance functions in metric space, dot-products do not induce any form of triangle inequality (even under some assumptions as mentioned in the previous section). Moreover, this lack of any induced triangle inequality causes the similarity function induced by the dot-products to have no admissible family of locality sensitive hashing functions. Any modification to the similarity function to conform to widely used similarity functions (like Euclidean distance or Cosine-similarity) will create inaccurate results.

Moreover, dot-products lack the basic property of *coincidence* – the self similarity is highest. For example, the Euclidean distance of a point to itself is 0; the cosine-similarity of a point to itself is 1. The dot-product of a point q to itself is $\|q\|^2$. There can possibly be many other points v_i $(i = 1, 2, \ldots)$ in the set such that $q^\top v_i > \|q\|^2$.

Without any assumptions, this problem of obtaining the best match with respect to the dot-product is inherently harder than the previously addressed similar problems. This is possibly the reason why there is no existing work for this problem without any restrictions on the domain.

4. FAST EXACT RETRIEVAL USING METRIC TREES

In this section, we describe metric trees and develop a novel bound to use with a simple branch-and-bound algorithm to provide the first method to efficiently obtain the exact best-matches with respect to the dot-products.

4.1 Metric Trees

Metric trees [16] are binary space-partitioning trees that are widely used for the task of indexing datasets in Euclidean spaces. The space is partitioned into overlapping hyper-spheres (balls) containing the points (figure 2). We use a simple metric tree construction heuristic that tries to approximately pick a pair of pivot points farthest apart from each other [15][2], and splits the data by assigning points to their closest pivot. The tree T is built hierarchically and each node in the tree is defined by the mean of the data in that node (T.center) and the radius of the ball around the mean enclosing the points in the node (T.radius). The tree has leaves of size at most N_0. The splitting and the recursive tree construction algorithm is presented in Algorithms 1 & 2.

The tree is space efficient since every node only stores the indices of the item vectors instead of the item vectors themselves. Hence the matrix for the items is never duplicated. Another implementation optimization is that the vectors in the items' matrix are sorted in place (during the tree construction) such that all the items in the same node are arranged serially in the matrix. This avoids random memory access while accessing all the items in the same leaf node.

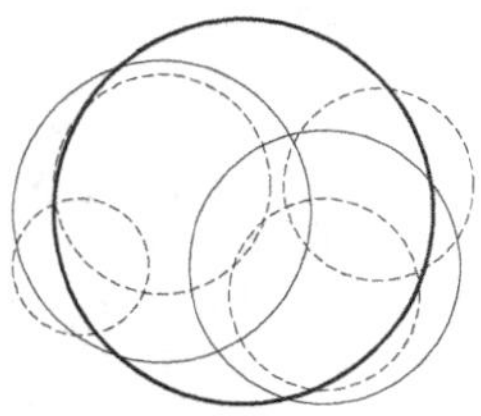

Figure 2: Metric-trees – note that while all the points in a child node lie also inside the parent ball, the child ball itself does not necessarily lie within the parent ball.

4.2 Branch-and-bound algorithm

Metric trees are used for efficient nearest neighbor search and are fairly scalable in moderately high dimensions [15,

[2]The intuition behind this heuristic is that these 2 points farthest from each other might lie in the principal direction (the direction of the principal eigenvector of the data).

Algorithm 1 MakeMetricTreeSplit(Data S)

```
Pick a random point x ∈ S
A ← arg max_{x'∈S} ||x − x'||
B ← arg max_{x'∈S} ||A − x'||
w ← (B − A)
b ← −1/2 (||B||^2 − ||A||^2)
return (w, b)
```

Algorithm 2 MakeMetricTree(Set of items S)

```
Input – Set S
Output – Tree Q
Q.S ← S
Q.center ← mean(S)
Q.radius ← max_{q_i∈S} ||T.center − q_i||
if |S| ≤ N_0 then
  // Leaf node
  return Q
else
  // else split the set
  (w, b) ← MakeMetricTreeSplit(S)
  S_l ← {q_i ∈ S: w^T q_i + b ≤ 0}
  S_r ← S \ S_l
  Q.left ← MakeMetricTree(S_l)
  Q.right ← MakeMetricTree(S_r)
  return Q
end if
```

Figure 3: Metric-tree Construction: The object $Q.S$ denotes the set of items in the node Q, Q.center denotes the Euclidean mean of the items in the node Q and Q.radius denotes the minimum radius of the ball centered around Q.center enclosing all the items in the node Q.

14]. The search employs a depth-first branch-and-bound algorithm. A nearest-neighbor query is answered by traversing the tree in a depth-first manner– going down the node closer to the query first and bounding the minimum possible distance to items in other branches with the triangle-inequality. If this branch is farther away than the current neighbor candidate, the branch is removed from computation.

Since the triangle inequality does not hold for the dot-product, we present a novel analytical upper bound for the maximum possible dot-product of a user vectors with points (in this case, items) in a ball. We then employ a similar branch-and-bound algorithm for the purposes of searching for the K-highest dot-products (as opposed to the minimum pairwise distance in K-nearest-neighbor search).

4.2.1 Bounding with a ball

Let $B^r_{q_c}$ be the ball of items centered around q_c with radius r. Suppose that q^* is the best possible recommendation in the ball $B^r_{q_c}$ for the user represented by the vector p_u, and r^* be the Euclidean distance between the ball center q_c and the best possible recommendation q^* (by definition, $r^* \leq r$). Let θ be the angle between the vector $\vec{q_c}$ and the vector $\vec{q_c q^*}$, θ_{p_u,q_c} and θ_{q^*,q_c} be the angles between the vector $\vec{q_c}$ and vectors $\vec{p_u}$ and $\vec{q^*}$ respectively (see figure 4). The distance of q^* from q_c is $r^* \sin\theta$ and the length of the projection of q^* onto q_c is $\|q_c\| + r^* \cos\theta$. Therefore we have:

$$\|q^*\| = \sqrt{(\|q_c\| + r^* \cos\theta)^2 + (r^* \sin\theta)^2}, \quad (8)$$

$$\cos\theta_{q^*,q_c} = \frac{\|q_c\| + r^* \cos\theta}{\|q^*\|}, \sin\theta_{q^*,q_c} = \frac{r^* \sin\theta}{\|q^*\|}. \quad (9)$$

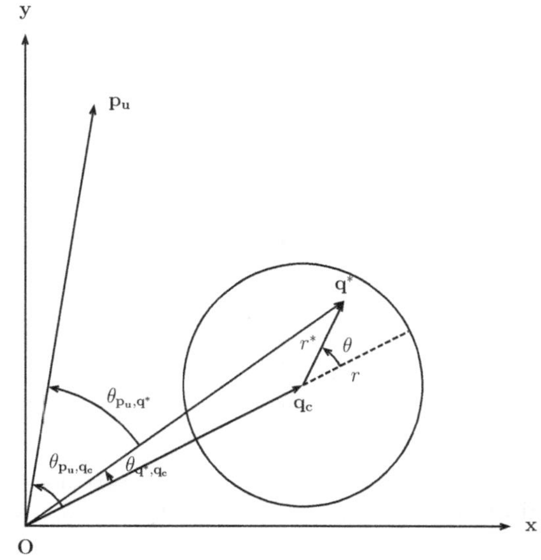

Figure 4: Bounding with a ball

Let θ_{p_u,q^*} be the angle between the vectors $\vec{p_u}$ and $\vec{q^*}$. This gives the following inequality regarding the angle between the user and the best possible recommendation (we assume that the angles lie in the range of $[-\pi, +\pi]$ instead of the usual $[0, 2\pi]$) :

$$|\theta_{p_u,q^*}| \geq |\theta_{p_u,q_c} - \theta_{q^*,q_c}|,$$

which implies

$$\cos\theta_{p_u,q^*} \leq \cos(\theta_{p_u,q_c} - \theta_{q^*,q_c}), \tag{10}$$

since $\cos(\cdot)$ is monotonically decreasing in the range $[0, \pi]$. Using this equality we obtain the following bound for the highest possible affinity between the user and any item within that ball:

$$\begin{aligned}\max_{q_i \in B^r_{q_c}} p_u^\top q_i &= p_u^\top q^* \text{(by assumption)} \\ &= \|p_u\| \ \|q^*\| \cos\theta_{p_u,q^*} \\ &\leq \|p_u\| \ \|q^*\| \cos(\theta_{p_u,q_c} - \theta_{q^*,q_c}),\end{aligned}$$

where the last inequality follows from equation 10. Substituting equations 8 & 9 in the above inequality, we have

$$\begin{aligned}\max_{q_i \in B^r_{q_c}} p_u^\top q_i &\leq \|p_u\| (\cos\theta_{p_u,q_c}(\|q_c\| + r^* \cos\theta) \\ &\quad + \sin\theta_{p_u,q_c}(r^* \sin\theta)) \\ &\leq \|p_u\| \max_\theta (\cos\theta_{p_u,q_c}(\|q_c\| + r^* \cos\theta) \\ &\quad + \sin\theta_{p_u,q_c}(r^* \sin\theta)) \\ &= \|p_u\| (\cos\theta_{p_u,q_c}(\|q_c\| + r^* \cos\theta_{p_u,q_c}) \\ &\quad + \sin\theta_{p_u,q_c}(r^* \sin\theta_{p_u,q_c})) \\ &\leq \|p_u\| (\cos\theta_{p_u,q_c}(\|q_c\| + r\cos\theta_{p_u,q_c}) \\ &\quad + \sin\theta_{p_u,q_c}(r \sin\theta_{p_u,q_c})) \\ &\quad \text{(since } r^* \leq r).\end{aligned}$$

The second inequality comes from the definition of maximum, and the next equality comes from maximizing over θ giving us the optimal value for $\theta = \theta_{p_u,q_c}$. Simplifying the final inequality gives us the following upper bound:

$$\max_{q_i \in B^r_{q_c}} p_u^\top q_i \leq p_u^\top q_c + r\,\|p_u\|\,. \tag{11}$$

Algorithm 3 SearchMetricTree(User p_u, Item Tree Node Q)

```
if p_u.ub < p_u^T Q.center + Q.radius · ||p_u|| then
  // This node has potential
  if isLeaf(Q) then
    for each q_i ∈ Q.S do
      if p_u^T q_i > p_u.ub then
        q' ← arg min_{q ∈ p_u.candidates} p_u^T q
        p_u.candidates ← {p_u.candidates \ {q'}} ∪ {q_i}
        p_u.ub ← min_{q ∈ p_u.candidates} p_u^T q
      end if
    end for
  else
    // best depth first traversal
    I_l ← p_u^T Q.left.center; I_r ← p_u^T Q.right.center;
    if I_l ≤ I_r then
      SearchMetricTree(p_u, Q.right);
      SearchMetricTree(p_u, Q.left);
    else
      SearchMetricTree(p_u, Q.left);
      SearchMetricTree(p_u, Q.right);
    end if
  end if
end if
// Else the node is pruned from computation
return;
```

Algorithm 4 FindExactRecommendations(User p_u, Item Tree Node Q)

```
p_u.ub ← 0;
p_u.candidates ← ∅;
SearchMetricTree(p_u, Q);
return p_u.candidates;
```

Figure 5: Metric-tree Search: The object p_u.candidates contains the set of current best K candidate items and p_u.ub denotes the lowest affinity between the user and its current best candidates.

4.2.2 The Algorithm

Using this upper bound (11) for the maximum possible dot-product, we present the depth-first branch-and-bound algorithm to search for the K-highest dot-products in Algorithm 3. The algorithm begins at the root of the tree of items. At each subsequent step, the algorithm is at a tree node. Using the bound in equation 11, the algorithm checks if the best possible item in this node is any better than the current best candidates for the user. If the check fails, this branch of the tree is not explored any more. Otherwise, the algorithm recursively traverses the tree, exploring the branch with the better potential candidates in a depth-first manner. If the node is a leaf, the algorithm just finds the best candidates within the leaf with the simple naive search. This algorithm ensures that the exact solution (i.e., the best candidates) is returned by the end of the algorithm.

Theoretical Runtime Bounds.

We do not have any runtime guarantees for the algorithm presented in this section. However, we can conjecture possible runtime bounds. If the metric-tree constructed with Algorithm 2 has a depth of $O(\log|Q|)$ (where Q is the set of items), then the runtime bound for the construction of the tree is $O(D|Q|\log|Q|)$ (since you only require $O(D|Q|)$

operations at each level of the tree and D is the dimensionality of the data). During the tree-search algorithm (Alg. 4), let us assume that the user visits L leaves. If L is much smaller and in fact independent of the number of items $|Q|$, we can say that the runtime bound for the search process for a single user is $O(DL\log|Q|)$. However, if L depends on $|Q|$ as well, then the best possible runtime bound is $O(D|Q|)$.

Since algorithm 2 does not enforce that the splits be balanced, it is quite possible that the depth of the tree might end up being $O(|Q|)$, in which case, the worst case runtime for the search process is $O(D|Q|)$. However, in practice, the tree depths have been seen to be way less than $O(|Q|)$.

5. FAST APPROXIMATE RETRIEVAL BY CLUSTERING USERS

The efficiency of the exact algorithm can be limited, and some applications may require even faster retrieval while allowing for some suboptimal recommendations. To this end, we propose a scheme to cluster the users into *cones* of similar "taste", pre-compute the recommendations for the cone centers (representative user tastes), and use these recommendations as approximate recommendations for incoming users with tastes similar to some existing user cluster.

Equation 5 specifies that the user preferences depend only on the angle (direction) of the corresponding user vectors. The smoothness of the cosine function implies that two users with vectors in similar directions will have very similar preferences. Hence, we partition the space into cones that aggregate users with similar taste. Let P_c be a set of cone centers where each $p_c \in P_c$ is a unit vector. The direction of p_c is the taste of the cone which can be used to pre-compute recommendations for the users in that cone.

For a new user query p_u, its best cone p_c^* is:

$$p_c^* \leftarrow \arg\max_{p_c \in P_c} p_u^\top p_c$$

After finding p_c^* we retrieve the pre-computed recommendations of p_c^* as the approximated recommendations for p_u. Figure 6 depicts a user's vector p_u and its best cone's vector p_c^*. If Δ, the angle between p_u and p_c^*, is small enough, then the approximated recommendations will be close to the optimal recommendations. The speedup is achieved since the number of cones is much smaller than the number of users or items, thus finding p_c^* is significantly easier than computing the exact recommendations for each user .

The approximation is controlled by using an upper bound on the relative approximation error in terms of Δ (this is presented in section 5.1). This bound evaluates the quality of the approximation. By defining a threshold T_r on the maximum acceptable error, we adaptively accept the pre-calculated approximate results when the error is below the threshold, or compute the exact results otherwise. The details of the approximate RoR algorithm are given in figure 7. The threshold T_r introduces a tradeoff between speedup and accuracy where maximal speedup is achieved when $T_r = \infty$.

Choosing cones.

In general, one would like to choose a set of user clusters (cones) which appropriately fits the distribution of possible queries. This can be efficiently achieved by spherical clustering of the user vectors. Spherical clustering defines groups of users with similar preferences or taste. Unit vectors in the direction of the clusters' centers define the cone centers.

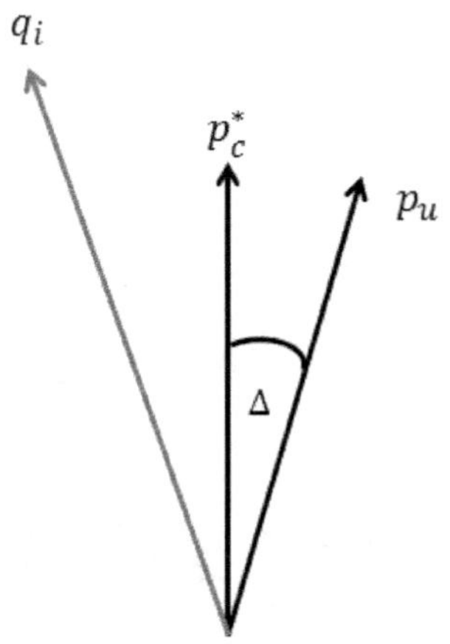

Figure 6: Here p_u is the user's vector, p_c^* is the cone's central direction, q_i is the item's vector and Δ is the angle between p_u^* and p_c.

Algorithm 5 PrepareCones(Users P, Items S)

```
Input – Set P, S
Output – User Cones P_c, Tree Q
P_c = ChooseCones(P);
Q = MakeMetricTree(S);
for all p_c ∈ P_c do
  p_c.candidates = FindExactRecommendations(p_c, Q);
end for
```

Algorithm 6 FindApproxRecommendations(User p_u, User Cones P_c, Threshold T_r, Item Tree Q)

```
p_c^* ← arg max_{p_c ∈ P_c} p_u^T p_c;
ErrorBound = ComputeErrorBound(p_c^*, p_u);
if ErrorBound ≤ T_r then
  return p_c^*.candidates;
else
  return FindExactRecommendations(p_u, Q);
end if
```

Figure 7: Approximate RoR: The subroutine *ChooseCones* chooses a set of cones that fits the set of user vectors P in the dataset. Then, the optimal recommendations are computed for each cone's center using the metric tree of section 4.
In *FindApproxRecommendations*, the subroutine *ComputeErrorBound* computes the error bound according to equation 14. The approximated recommendations are used for every query with an error bound below the error threshold T_r, otherwise exact recommendations are computed.

We chose spherical clustering because of its computational efficiency. Furthermore, the clustering already assigns the user vectors into cones and there is no need to search for the best matching cone for the existing users.

A requirement for a good clustering is that $\Delta < \frac{\pi}{2}$. Otherwise the dot-product between the user and an item in the direction of the cone's center can be negative, which implies that the user does not like the items that fit the cone's vector. Note that clustering assumes the presence of groups of users common tastes. This is a very natural assumption in every collaborative filtering algorithm.

5.1 Relative Error Bound

In this subsection we present a theoretical error bound on the relative approximation error for any user. This is used by the adaptive algorithm to control the approximation error.

The vector q_i in figure 6 depicts an item's vector that was chosen as an optimal recommendation based on the cluster's center p_c^*. Intuitively, as Δ decreases, the approximation error should decrease as well. We define the approximation error $err = exp - real$ as the difference between the expected rating based on the cluster $exp = q_i^\top p_c^*$ and the real dot-product with the user's trait vector $real = q_i^\top p_u$. The relative error is then:

$$\frac{err}{exp} = \frac{exp - real}{exp} = 1 - \frac{real}{exp} \tag{12}$$

We assume here that for every cone $exp > 0$; otherwise it means that there are no fitting recommendation for that cone, which is very unlikely and we never encountered this[3].

Since we want the worst-case bound, we ignore the case where $real > exp$ since this situation means that the affinity between p_u and q_i is better than expected. Hence, assuming that $real < exp$, we have the following:

$$\frac{real}{exp} = \frac{\|q_i\| \cos\left(\theta_{p_u,q_i}\right)}{\|q_i\| \cos\left(\theta_{p_c^*,q_i}\right)} \geq \frac{\cos\left(\theta_{p_c^*,q_i} + \Delta\right)}{\cos\left(\theta_{p_c^*,q_i}\right)} \tag{13}$$

The inequality follows from the fact that $\theta_{p_c^*,q_i} \leq \frac{\pi}{2}$ (because $exp \geq 0$) and $\Delta \leq \frac{\pi}{2}$ (a requirement of the clustering). Since $\cos(\cdot)$ is monotonically decreasing in the range $[0, \pi]$, we get $\cos\left(\theta_{p_u,q_i}\right) \geq \cos\left(\theta_{p_c^*,q_i} + \Delta\right)$. Substituting (13) into (12) we get the following upper bound on the relative error:

$$\frac{err}{exp} \leq 1 - \frac{\cos\left(\theta_{p_c^*,q_i} + \Delta\right)}{\cos\left(\theta_{p_c^*,q_i}\right)} \tag{14}$$

Note that this bound is a tight bound. Namely, when $\Delta \to 0$ we get $err \to 0$.

6. EXPERIMENTS

We begin this section by presenting the datasets and the evaluation metric used. Then we present the results of the exact RoR algorithm (section 4). In the following subsection, we present the performance of the approximate RoR method (section 5), demonstrating its efficiency-error trade-off. Finally, as a thought experiment, we also present the inaccuracies introduced by using existing best-match algorithms (nearest-neighbor search in Euclidean space and best-match with respect to cosine similarity) for the task of RoR.

Datasets.

We used the following publicly available datasets:

1. MovieLens – It consists of 1,000,206 ratings of 3,952 movies by 6,040 users. Ratings are integers in the range 1-5, and the dataset is 95.81% sparse.

2. Netflix [2] – It consists of 100,480,507 ratings of 17,770 movies by 480,189 users. The ratings in Netflix are on a scale of 1-5 as well, and the dataset is 98.82% sparse.

3. Yahoo! Music [8] – This dataset is the largest of the three consisting of 252,800,275 ratings of 624,961 music items by 1,000,990 users. The ratings are on a scale of 0-100 and the dataset is 99.96% sparse.

Currently the Yahoo! Music dataset is the largest publicly available collaborative filtering dataset. Both our algorithms perform best on this dataset. In fact, in most of our evaluations the results seems to improve with the size of the dataset. This is expected as overhead times become negligible when the number of queries (users) increase. All the above datasets were in fact sampled from real datasets which were possibly much larger. It is therefore likely that the results presented in this paper will further improve when the proposed algorithms are implemented in real world systems.

For the MovieLens and Netflix datasets, we built and trained a basic MF model (equation 2) using stochastic gradient descent minimization of the mean squared error. For the Yahoo! Music dataset, we used the model presented in [6] that incorporates music taxonomy and temporal effects. All models have 50-dimensional vectors to represent the user and item traits. The root mean squared errors of these three models were 0.839 in MovieLens, 0.899 in Netflix, and 22.592 in Yahoo! Music.

We quantify the improvement of an algorithm A over another (baseline) algorithm A_0 by the following term:

$$\text{Speedup}_{A_0}(A) = \frac{\text{Time taken by Algorithm } A_0}{\text{Time taken by Algorithm } A}. \tag{15}$$

Since there are no efficient search algorithms for maximum dot-products, our baseline is a naive algorithm that searches over all items to find the best recommendations for every user. We denote by T_{naive} the time taken by the naive algorithm. It is obvious that

$$T_{naive} = \Theta(\#USERS \times \#ITEMS \times D),$$

where D is the dimensionality of the vector (here $D = 50$).

As expected, the naive algorithm is extremely time consuming. For example, the baseline execution time for retrieving optimal recommendations for the Yahoo! Music dataset is 135.1 hours[4] (over 5 days). The mean latency for a single user query is 0.482 seconds. Using our proposed combined method (figure 7), we achieve up to $\times 258.08$ speedup, which is equivalent to just 31.4 minutes for the entire computation or an average single user latency of 1.87 milliseconds. It is important to note that while the overall computation time can also be reduced by means of parallelization, the latency for a single user might be harder to improve upon.

Implementation Details.

We used the *Cluto* clustering toolkit [10] for spherical clustering of the user vectors. We used 500, 1000, and 2000 clusters (cones) for the MovieLens, Netflix and Yahoo! Music respectively, because these values showed a good balance between performance and speedup. In Alg. 2, we used $N_0 = 2$ in all our experiments. In general, these parameters can be optimized using a cross-validation process.

6.1 Exact RoR

The time taken by the exact algorithm of Section 4 can be broken up into two parts as follows

$$T_{exact} = T_{tree\ building} + T_{tree\ search},$$

where $T_{tree\ building}$ is the time taken by Alg. 2 to build the tree on the set of item vectors, and $T_{tree\ search}$ is the total time taken by all the users to find their respective best

[3]Even if $exp < 0$ it is still possible to bound the error by following a very similar process to the one shown here.

[4]Using an Intel Xeon (E7320) CPU running at 2.13GHz

Dataset	$K = 1$	$K = 5$	$K = 10$	$K = 50$
MovieLens	3.01	1.82	1.73	1.21
Netflix	2.87	2.39	1.95	1.31
Yahoo! Music	7.26	5.25	4.7	3.01

Table 1: Speedups of Alg. 3 over naive search for different number of top recommendations (K).

recommendations using Alg. 3. The speedup is therefore:

$$\text{Speedup}_{naive}(exact) = \frac{T_{naive}}{T_{exact}}. \quad (16)$$

We present the speedups obtained for different numbers of top recommendations in Table 1. The results indicate that the exact algorithm can be up to ×7 faster than the naive algorithm. Another advantage of this method is its space efficiency – only the tree (which consists solely of pointers) has to be stored. The complete ($\#USERS \times \#ITEMS$) user-preference matrix does not have to be stored and the recommendations for a user can be obtained when required.

An important thing to note is that the tree-building task is extremely time efficient – for example, for the Yahoo! Music dataset, the time taken to build the metric-tree on the set of items (of size 624961×50) was less than 16 seconds (the time required to load the whole data into memory took more than 40 seconds!). The tree-building process is a one-time cost which is amortized by the more expensive tree-search process. Moreover, new items can be easily added to this metric-tree index[5]. Nevertheless, we include the tree-building times in our computation for completeness.

It is important to note that the search time increases with K (the number of top recommendations returned). This is because the bound for the best recommendations for the user (p_u.ub in Alg. 3) becomes smaller with increasing K (Line 8 in Alg. 3). This increases the number of nodes that have potential (Line 1 in Alg. 3), hence also increasing the number of leaves finally visited.

However, some applications may require more than just the top 50 items. In that case, the tree-based exact search does not provide any significant improvement over the naive algorithm. Therefore, we present further improvements in computational performance in the next subsection with the proposed approximate algorithm.

6.2 Approximate RoR

The time taken by the approximate algorithm of Section 5 can be broken up into four parts as follows:

$$T_{approx} = T_{clustering} + T_{tree\ building} + T_{search\ cones} + T_{search\ queries},$$

where $T_{clustering}$ is the time taken by the clustering algorithm, $T_{tree\ building}$ is the metric-tree-construction time, $T_{search\ cones}$ is the search time for optimal recommendations for all the cones and $T_{search\ queries}$ is the time taken to compute exact recommendations for queries that are above the threshold. The speedup of the approximate algorithm is:

$$\text{Speedup}_{naive}(approx) = \frac{T_{naive}}{T_{approx}}. \quad (17)$$

We define two terms to quantify the quality of the top K recommendations retrieved by the approximated method. The first quantity (*Precision*) denotes how similar the approximate recommendations are to the actual top K recommendations (which are retrieved by the naive approach):

$$Precision(K) \triangleq \text{mean}_u \left\{ \frac{|L_{rec}(u) \cap L_{opt}(u)|}{K} \right\}, \quad (18)$$

where $L_{rec}(u)$ and $L_{opt}(u)$ are the lists of the top K approximate and the top K optimal recommendations for the user u, respectively. Our evaluation metrics only care about the items at the top of the approximated and optimal lists ($L_{rec}(u)$ and $L_{opt}(u)$). In that case there is no real meaning to compute *Recall* because its natural definition would be identical to the *Precision*.

In addition, we define a secondary metric (*MedianRank*) which denotes the preference of the approximated recommendations with respect to the rest of the items:

$$MedianRank(K) \triangleq \text{median}\left\{\cup_u Rank(L_{rec}(u))\right\}, \quad (19)$$

where the function $Rank(L(u))$ returns a list of the optimal ranks for the items in $L(u)$ for user u (for example, $Rank(L_{opt}(u)) = \{1, 2, \ldots, K-1, K\}$).

A high value for *Precision* implies that the approximate recommendations are very similar to the optimal recommendations, and a low value of *MedianRank* implies that the approximate recommendations are highly preferred by the users. In many practical applications, it is very likely to have a low value for *Precision* as well as for *MedianRank*. This implies that the items recommended by the approximate algorithm are generally different from the optimal items for the users, but the items recommended are still very highly preferred by the users.

MovieLens

Threshold	0.25	0.5	0.75	∞
K=1	x2.49	x7.26	x9.02	x9.25
K=5	x1.6	x5.68	x7.66	x7.94
K=10	x1.52	x5.5	x7.49	x7.78
K=50	x0.89	x3.82	x7.73	x6.04

Netflix

Threshold	0.25	0.5	0.75	∞
K=1	x2.69	x5.65	x12.61	x17.29
K=5	x2.48	x5.3	x12.27	x17.26
K=10	x1.93	x4.29	x11.15	x17.18
K=50	x1.19	x2.81	x8.89	x16.97
K=500	x1.04	x2.5	x8.28	x16.89

Yahoo! Music

Threshold	0.25	0.5	0.75	∞
K=1	x10.49	x19.7	x150.87	x258.08
K=5	x7.67	x14.54	x128.46	x251.27
K=10	x6.88	x13.08	x120.77	x248.46
K=50	x4.45	x8.53	x91.78	x234.6
K=500	x1.49	x2.89	x39.1	x178.54

Table 2: Speedups of Alg. 6 over the naive algorithm for different values of K and the error threshold.

The speedups of the approximate algorithm for different values of the error bound threshold are summarized in Table 2. The results indicate that the approximate RoR method can be up to ×258 faster than the naive approach. The approximation quality for different levels of speedup is depicted in figures 8 & 9.

Figure 8 shows the tradeoff between precision and speedup achieved by using different values of the error bound threshold. When the threshold is high, the approximated result is less likely to be rejected. In this case, the precision is lower, speedup is higher, and performance is better for higher values of K. The latter is a result of the fact that precision

[5]Efficient item insertion is inherent to tree data structures.

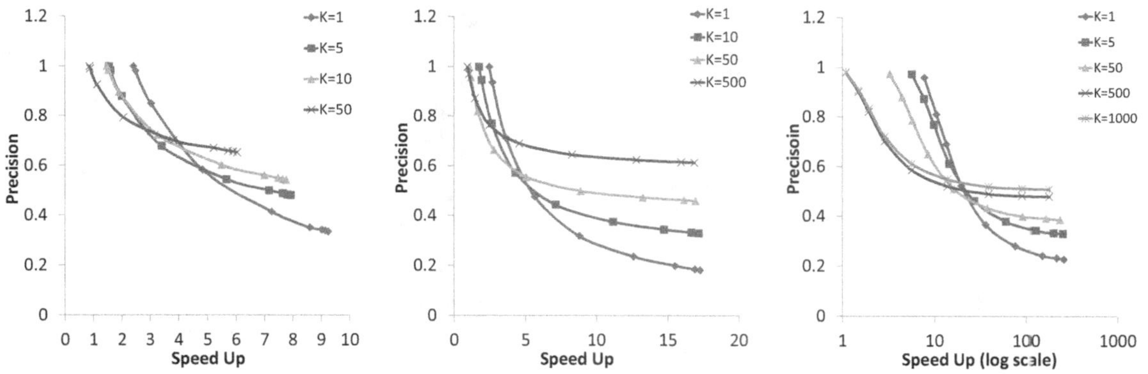

(a) MovieLens (b) Netflix (c) Yahoo! Music

Figure 8: Precision(K) of L_{rec} vs. speedup of the approximate algorithm. The error bound threshold defines a tradeoff between high precision to high speedup. We used higher values of K for datasets with more items.

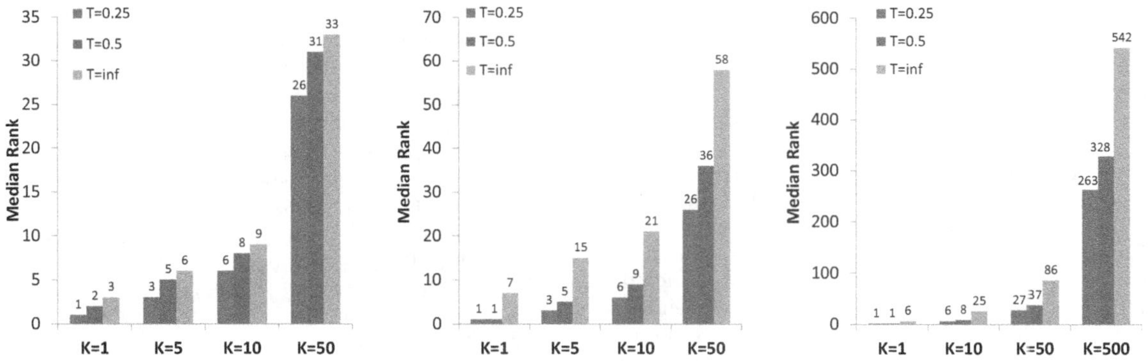

(a) MovieLens (b) Netflix (c) Yahoo! Music

Figure 9: *MedianRank*(K) of the adaptive algorithm for different values of the error bound threshold. Speedup values can be retrieved from table 2.

in a finite set is easier to achieve as K is higher. When the threshold is low, the approximated result is more likely to be rejected. In this case, the precision is higher, speedup is lower, and performance is better when K is lower. The latter is a result of the fact that we are more likely to fall back to using the metric tree and the fact that the tree performs worse on higher values of K (as explained earlier).

Figure 9 presents the *MedianRank* for different values of K and different values of the error bound threshold. Speedup values can be retrieved from table 2. We see that even when *Precison* values are low (e.g., when $T_r = \infty$) the *MedianRank* values are also relatively low, which indicate that the approximated recommendations are still highly preferred by the users.

6.3 Existing Best-Match Algorithms

Dataset	$K=1$	$K=5$	$K=10$	$K=50$	$K=100$
MovieLens	0.4	0.54	0.59	0.72	0.77
Netflix	0.19	0.24	0.28	0.35	0.39
Y! Music	0.055	0.08	0.08	0.112	0.133

Table 3: Precision of the top (K) best matches with respect to the l_2 distance

In this subsection we find the top recommendations for a user with respect to the Euclidean (l_2) distance and with respect to the cosine similarity. The first returns the K items closest to the user (in terms of the l_2 distance), and the second returns the K items making the smallest angles with

Dataset	$K=1$	$K=5$	$K=10$	$K=50$	$K=100$
MovieLens	0.05	0.12	0.16	0.35	0.46
Netflix	0.14	0.24	0.31	0.48	0.56
Y! Music	0.004	0.01	0.014	0.033	0.047

Table 4: Precision of the top (K) best matches with respect to the cosine similarity

the user at the origin (hence returning best matches with respect to the cosine similarity). The reason for this experiment is to demonstrate that existing nearest-neighbor search algorithms (like LSH) cannot be applied directly to the task of RoR in the *existing MF framework* without introducing high levels of error.

Tables 3 & 4 report the precision of the exact best-matches obtained with respect to Euclidean distance and cosine similarity respectively. As expected from our discussion in section 3, the precision of these results are very low (especially on the larger Yahoo! Music dataset). Contrasting these numbers to the precision of the approximate solutions obtained from Alg. 6 (figure 8), we see that our approximate algorithm performs as accurately (if not better) with significant amount of speedup. For example, for the Yahoo! Music data set with $K = 50$, the best-matches with l_2 distance and cosine similarity have a precision of 0.112 and 0.033 respectively. In contrast, our proposed algorithm shows a speedup of about $\times 200$ while achieving a precision level of around 0.4 (figure 8(c)).

It is important to note that these returned recommendations in both cases (l_2 distance and cosine-similarity) are the *exact best-matches with respect to their corresponding sense of similarity.* If the exact results are so inaccurate (in terms of recommendation quality), it is hard to expect good results once approximate techniques for these best-match problems like LSH is used. This indicates that any form of modification done to the RoR task in MF framework (equation 1 and hence equation 6) to fit into existing best-matching problems can introduce a high level of inaccuracies.

7. CONCLUSIONS

In this paper we address the problem of efficient retrieval of recommendations (RoR) within the MF framework. This problem is inherent in a myriad of online services and requires added attention with the current influx of users (and items) on the internet. The RoR task in MF frameworks can be formulated as finding best matches with respect to the dot-product similarity measure. However, there are no known solutions to this problem. We thus present an exact and an approximate novel algorithms to improve the scalability of this task. Efficient algorithms to find the maximum dot-product can possibly have impacts beyond the realm of collaborative filtering.

The exact method uses an existing indexing scheme to index the set of items, and the branch-and-bound algorithm with a novel bounding scheme to provide significant speedup (over $\times 7$ faster) over the naive algorithm, while having minimal space requirements. It can be easily adapted to include new items (or new users) into the system. However, being an exact algorithm, it shows limited improvement in computational performance. Hence we relax the problem of RoR and present an approximate algorithm based on the novel idea of grouping the users using spherical-cones. The method subsequently stores the best recommendations of each of the cone centers as the approximate best recommendations for all the users within that cluster. This method shows much better scalability (up to $\times 258$ speedup) with the trade-off of deviating from the otimal list of recommendations. However, we demonstrate that even when precision is low, the approximated items are still highly preferred by the users.

MF based models have demonstrated impressive performance in terms of scalability at training time as well as predictive accuracy. However, less accurate algorithms are often used in large scale web-services. This may be attributed to the computational bottleneck of retrieval of the recommendations. Long latency times are unacceptable in online services, and pre-computing recommendations to all the users is expensive in terms of computational time as well as storage. The methods presented in this paper alleviate this last obstacle, making the MF framework more approachable to large scale recommender-systems. This paper also gives the system's architects a choice of an exact algorithm with significant but limited scalability or an approximate algorithm with a favorable trade-off between quality and scalability.

The problem of fast RoR discussed in this paper inspired the solution to the general problem of fast maximum inner-product search [17]. Possible extensions of this work will be to develop approximate algorithms with user-specified bounded approximation. For example, the system can approximate the retrieval task to obtain any K-recommendations from among the best τ-recommendations where $K < \tau$ (similar to the approximation of the nearest-neighbor search problem in [18]).

8. REFERENCES

[1] R. M. Bell and Y. Koren. Lessons from the netflix prize challenge. *SIGKDD Explor. Newsl.*, 2007.

[2] J. Bennett and S. Lanning. The netflix prize. In *Proc. KDD Cup and Workshop*, 2007.

[3] M. S. Charikar. Similarity estimation techniques from rounding algorithms. In *Proceedings of the thiry-fourth annual ACM symposium on Theory of computing*, 2002.

[4] K. Clarkson. Nearest-neighbor searching and metric space dimensions. *Nearest-Neighbor Methods for Learning and Vision: Theory and Practice*, 2006.

[5] A. S. Das, M. Datar, A. Garg, and S. Rajaram. Google news personalization: scalable online collaborative filtering. In *Proceedings of the 16th international conference on World Wide Web*, 2007.

[6] G. Dror, N. Koenigstein, and Y. Koren. Yahoo! music recommendations: Modeling music ratings with temporal dynamics and item taxonomy. In *Proc. 5th ACM Conference on Recommender Systems*, 2011.

[7] G. Dror, N. Koenigstein, and Y. Koren. Web scale media recommendation systems. *Proceedings of the IEEE*, pages 1–15, 2012.

[8] G. Dror, N. Koenigstein, Y. Koren, and M. Weimer. The yahoo! music dataset and kdd-cup'11. *Journal Of Machine Learning Research*, 17:1–12, 2011.

[9] P. Indyk and R. Motwani. Approximate Nearest Neighbors: Towards Removing the Curse of Dimensionality. In *STOC*, 1998.

[10] G. Karypis. CLUTO a clustering toolkit. Technical report, Dept. of Computer Science, University of Minnesota, 2002.

[11] M. Khoshneshin and W. N. Street. Collaborative filtering via euclidean embedding. In *Proceedings of the fourth ACM conference on Recommender systems*, 2010.

[12] N. Koenigstein, N. Nice, U. Paquet, and N. Schleyen. The xbox recommender system. In *Proc. 6th ACM Conference on Recommender Systems*, 2012.

[13] Y. Koren, R. M. Bell, and C. Volinsky. Matrix factorization techniques for recommender systems. *IEEE Computer*, 2009.

[14] T. Liu, A. W. Moore, A. G. Gray, and K. Yang. An Investigation of Practical Approximate Nearest Neighbor Algorithms. In *Advances in Neural Information Processing Systems 17*, 2005.

[15] S. M. Omohundro. Five Balltree Construction Algorithms. Technical report, International Computer Science Institute, December 1989.

[16] F. P. Preparata and M. I. Shamos. *Computational Geometry: An Introduction*. Springer, 1985.

[17] P. Ram and A. Gray. Maximum inner-product search using cone trees. In *SIGKDD International Conference on Knowledge Discovery and Data Mining*. ACM, 2012.

[18] P. Ram, D. Lee, H. Ouyang, and A. G. Gray. Rank-approximate nearest neighbor search: Retaining meaning and speed in high dimensions. In *Advances in Neural Information Processing Systems 22*. 2009.

[19] S. Zhang, W. Wang, J. Ford, and F. Makedon. Learning from incomplete ratings using non-negative matrix factorization. In *Proceedings of the Sixth SIAM International Conference on Data Mining*, 2006.

KORE: Keyphrase Overlap Relatedness for Entity Disambiguation

Johannes Hoffart
Max Planck Institute for Informatics
jhoffart@mpi-inf.mpg.de

Stephan Seufert
Max Planck Institute for Informatics
sseufert@mpi-inf.mpg.de

Dat Ba Nguyen
Max Planck Institute for Informatics
datnb@mpi-inf.mpg.de

Martin Theobald
Max Planck Institute for Informatics
mtb@mpi-inf.mpg.de

Gerhard Weikum
Max Planck Institute for Informatics
weikum@mpi-inf.mpg.de

ABSTRACT

Measuring the semantic relatedness between two entities is the basis for numerous tasks in IR, NLP, and Web-based knowledge extraction. This paper focuses on disambiguating names in a Web or text document by jointly mapping all names onto semantically related entities registered in a knowledge base. To this end, we have developed a novel notion of semantic relatedness between two entities represented as sets of weighted (multi-word) keyphrases, with consideration of partially overlapping phrases. This measure improves the quality of prior link-based models, and also eliminates the need for (usually Wikipedia-centric) explicit interlinkage between entities. Thus, our method is more versatile and can cope with long-tail and newly emerging entities that have few or no links associated with them. For efficiency, we have developed approximation techniques based on min-hash sketches and locality-sensitive hashing. Our experiments on semantic relatedness and on named entity disambiguation demonstrate the superiority of our method compared to state-of-the-art baselines.

Categories and Subject Descriptors

H.3.1 [**Information Storage and Retrieval**]: Content Analysis and Indexing

Keywords

Semantic Relatedness, Entity Relatedness, Entity Disambiguation, Locality-Sensitive Hashing

1. INTRODUCTION

1.1 Motivation

Semantic relatedness measures between entities like people, places, songs, companies, etc. are a fundamental asset for many applications dealing with natural language processing (NLP), text mining, or Web analytics [4]. Its usefulness has been shown in a wide variety of tasks: named entity disambiguation [23, 19, 16], general word sense disambiguation [31, 24, 26], query expansion for information retrieval [18, 25], Web-based information extraction [1], knowledge base population [9, 30], and more.

In this paper, we focus on semantic relatedness of entities and its role in named entity disambiguation (NED). Consider the terms "Cash" and "Jackson" as an example. When trying to measure the relatedness between these surface forms, we face high ambiguity and would assess them as weakly related only. Most possible meanings of "Cash" and "Jackson", such as movies entitled "Cash" and people or cities named "Jackson", have nothing in common. At the entity level, however, once we identify the surface form "Cash" with the singer *Johnny Cash* and "Jackson" with a song he performed, *Jackson (song)*, the relatedness measure should be very high. Wikipedia and derived knowledge bases like DBpedia, YAGO, or Freebase provide us with millions of uniquely identifiable entities, and this enables computing relatedness measures at the entity level instead of ambiguous words or phrases. Conversely, entity relatedness is key for disambiguating names that occur in surface text. In our example, the entity names in a sentence like "The audience got wild when Cash performed Jackson." can be correctly disambiguated because only the singer-song combination, out of thousands of other pairs of entities named "Cash" and "Jackson", yields a semantically coherent interpretation.

State-of-the-art measures for entity relatedness that perform well in NED and other tasks are based on the extensive link structure of Wikipedia. Most notably, the *Milne-Witten measure* considers the overlap of the incoming links to two entity articles as a notion of their relatedness [22]. This is a great asset for the 3 million entities known to Wikipedia, but it is a limitation for other entities that do not (yet) have a Wikipedia page. For example, in the sentence "The audience was haunted when Cave performed Hallelujah.", the correct meaning of "Hallelujah" is neither the Händel chorus nor the Leonard Cohen composition, but a totally different song by the Australian singer Nick Cave. That song has a Web page in the music portal last.fm but there is no Wikipedia article for the song. Link-based relatedness has no chance to capture the tight connection between Nick Cave and his song. This limitation already applies to the long tail of not so prominent Wikipedia entities whose articles have only few incoming links. In these cases, the Milne-Witten measure does not properly capture the semantic relatedness between entities.

CIKM'12, October 29–November 2, 2012, Maui, HI, USA.

Our goal in this paper is to overcome this limitation of Wikipedia-link-based relatedness measures for named entities.

1.2 Our Approach

A relatedness measure for link-poor and out-of-Wikipedia entities needs to tap into information that is more widely available and can be gathered with reasonable effort. In this paper, we use entity-specific *keyphrases* to this end [21, 5]. Keyphrases can be mined from any text describing an entity: people not popular enough for Wikipedia have personal homepages, small companies have websites, singers and songs are discussed in online communities like last.fm or YouTube, and so on. For our difficult example, the last.fm page on Nick Cave's song contains keyphrases like "No More Shall We Part", "Australian singer", "Warren Ellis", "eerie cello", "Nick Cave and the Bad Seeds", etc. These exhibit significant overlap with phrases contained in the Wikipedia article about Nick Cave (or, alternatively, his Web page), thus giving cues for the high relatedness. We propose a new notion of entity relatedness, coined KORE, based on the overlap of two sets of keyphrases.

While the idea for this approach may seem obvious, it entails a number of technical difficulties, addressed in this paper:

Keyphrases and Weights: Multi-word keyphrases are more informative than single-token keywords and thus preferrable for characterizing entities. On the other hand, this makes it less clear which word sequences should be considered as salient keyphrases, and how we could associate them with weights that can be computed in an effective and efficient manner. If we simply used keywords, we could use precomputed *idf*-style weights; the generalization to keyphrases is not obvious.

Partial Matches: When comparing the keyphrases of two entities, the chance of finding exact matches drops with the length of multi-word phrases. For example, we may not find the phrases "Australian singer" and "Nick Cave and the Bad Seeds", associated with the song Hallelujah, in this exact form in the keyphrase-set of Nick Cave, where we may instead have "Australian male singer" and "Cave's Bad Seeds". Therefore, a viable notion of keyphrase-based overlap measure must consider partial matches between phrases as well.

Efficient Computation: In NED, we are interested in the relatedness of all entity pairs in the candidate space. For n potentially relevant entities, a straightforward approach would require $\binom{n}{2}$ computations. If we consider a short news article with say 10 mentions of ambiguous entity names, each of which has 10 possible meanings, we obtain 100 candidate entities and would need to compute the relatedness for 5000 pairs. This is too expensive for most online applications, and totally infeasible for longer input texts or mentions with higher degrees of ambiguity.

1.3 Contribution

Our approach addresses the above challenges in the following way. We extract particular kinds of noun phrases from entity-specific pages, and compute weights for both entire phrases and their constituent words. We use MI (mutual information) for phrases, contrasting the entity page with the entire Wikipedia corpus (or the Web), and idf (inverse document frequency) for single words, based on the Wikipedia corpus. We define the KORE measure in a two-stage manner, thus allowing for partial matches between keyphrases: 1) two keyphrases are paired up if there is a partial match of at least one word, with word-level weights influencing the matching score; 2) a weighted Jaccard coefficient captures the overlap between the keyphrase-sets of two entities, where the scores of the partially matching keyphrase pairs are aggregated and the phrase-level weights are considered. Finally, to solve the efficiency challenge, we use a two-level approximation technique: keyphrases, as sequences of words, are approximated by min-hash sketches, and these sketches are organized by locality-sensitive hashing (LSH). This way, for a given input set of entity pairs, we compute their relatedness only if their keyphrase representations are mapped to at least one common LSH bucket.

The novel contributions made in this paper are as follows:

- KORE improves the quality of assessing entity relatedness, compared to state-of-the-art link-based methods, while reducing the dependence on Wikipedia linkage and tapping into out-of-Wikipedia entities.
- KORE is integrated into a joint-inference NED method, outperforming the best prior methods on mentions of long-tail entities.
- KORE can be efficiently computed and avoids the quadratic complexity of all-pairs comparisons in NED-like tasks, by a judiciously devised two-stage hashing technique.
- Our improvements in the quality of semantic relatedness and NED accuracy are demonstrated by systematic experiments with different corpora. Run-time measurements show the efficiency gains of our approximation techniques.

2. RELATED WORK

2.1 Semantic Relatedness of Words

The classical approaches for quantifying the relatedness of words (common nouns, verbs, etc.) make use of the WordNet thesaurus, by measuring the token overlap of the glosses describing the concepts (Lesk) or by means of paths in the concept taxonomy or other lexical relations (Resnik, Wu & Palmer). Budanitsky and Hirst [4] give an overview of all these measures.

More recently, Gabrilovich and Markovitch [12] and Radinsky et al. [28] have exploited Wikipedia (and Zesch et al. Wiktionary [33]) to compute word relatedness. These methods represent words by vectors of the concepts they are used to describe, i. e. a word is represented by all the articles it occurs in. Then they use vector-space measures (e.g., cosine similarity) for relatedness. A powerful variant of this approach, proposed by Hassan and Mihalcea [14], is to represent words as vectors of co-occurring Wikipedia entities. However, the method crucially depends on the availability of a rich link structure like that of Wikipedia.

2.2 Semantic Relatedness of Entities

Work on semantic relatedness between entities (people, places, songs, companies, products, etc.) has started with the advent of large knowledge bases, largely derived from Wikipedia. This created huge opportunities for specifically dealing with named entities (as opposed to general words). The emerging need for lifting Web search and advertising to the entity level created a mega-application as well.

Ponzetto and Strube [27] applied previously WordNet-based measures to Wikipedia, showing that some work better on the larger though less rigorous collection of entities and classes. Milne and Witten [22] used the link structure in Wikipedia to model entity relatedness. Links within Wikipedia refer to canonical entities; thus, the source-target pairs of links can be used as the basis for a relatedness measure. Building on the co-occurrence-based information-theoretic model of [20, 6], the *Milne-Witten relatedness* measure, MW for short, for two entities e and f with sets of incoming Wikipedia links I_e and I_f, respectively, is defined as (where N is the total number of articles in Wikipedia):

$$\mathrm{MW}(e,f) = 1 - \frac{\log(\max\{|I_e|,|I_f|\}) - \log(|I_e \cap I_f|)}{\log(N) - \log(\min\{|I_e|,|I_f|\})}. \quad (1)$$

So far, the MW measure has achieved the best results on quantifying entity relatedness.

2.3 Named Entity Disambiguation (NED)

NED is the task of mapping surface names of entities (people, places, etc.) in text documents onto canonicalized entities registered in a knowledge base like DBPedia [2], Freebase.com, or YAGO [32], this way disambiguating the entity mentions. Classical approaches were based on comparing the *text similarity* of the context that surrounds a mention against textual descriptions of candidate entities. This can be cast into IR-style bag-of-words or language-model comparisons, using words, bigrams, noun phrases, and other linguistic features. The mentions in a given text are processed one at a time.

Cucerzan [8] was the first to recognize the potential of *joint inference* by mapping all named entities in a text simultaneously, aiming to enforce coherence among the chosen entities as expressed by their pair-wise semantic relatedness. Milne & Witten [23], Kulkarni et al. [19], Dredze et al. [9], Ferragina & Scaiella [10], and Hoffart et al. [16] extended and improved this line of methodology, using combinatorial or statistical-learning algorithms for joint inference. The best performing of these NED algorithms utilize the link-based MW measure as defined in Equation (1). None of the methods can robustly cope with long-tail entities that have only few or no Wikipedia links.

NED is a specific case of the more general task of word sense disambiguation (WSD) where all words in a text should be mapped onto canonicalized denotations: entities for proper nouns (i.e., names) and WordNet senses (so-called synsets) for common nouns and other words or phrases. This task can benefit from semantic relatedness as well. However, we do not consider general WSD in this paper. Navigli [24] surveys state-of-the-art WSD methods. Another task related to but different from NED is cross-document coreference resolution (e.g., [30]). Here, mentions are grouped into equivalence classes, but there is no explicit mapping onto entities in a knowledge base.

3. COMPUTING ENTITY RELATEDNESS

3.1 Definitions

All measures of semantic relatedness between entities described in this section are based on (multi-word) key*phrases* and their constituting (single-word) key*words*. When we do not need to distinguish between (multi-word) key*phrases* and (single-word) key*words* we speak of key*terms*.

Example. The keyphrase English rock guitarist is represented by the set of keywords {English, rock, guitarist}.

We gathered keyterms from the Wikipedia pages of each entity: *link anchors* of both internal and external links, *titles of citations*, and *names of categories*. The choice of Wikipedia is merely for convenience; keyterms can also be mined from other textual descriptions of entities, such as homepages of singers or scientists, or pages about songs in online communities. In these cases, we can use similar heuristics like focusing on link anchors, headings, etc., or alternatively extract all noun phrases. The latter will pick up noise, but our weighting scheme, described next, will keep the noise level low.

All keyterms are weighed by a combination of Inverse Document Frequency (idf), which is global and entity-independent, and Mutual Information (MI), which depends on the co-occurrence of the keyterms with entities.

Idf weights capture a global notion of how important a keyterm is. The weights are computed using the standard formula, $\log_2 \frac{N}{df}$, where N is the size of the collection (in this case the total number of entities in the knowledge base) and df is the number of entities that have the phrase among their keyphrases (for keyphrase idf) or have at least one keyphrase that contains the keyword (for keyword idf).

MI weights capture the notion of how important a keyterm is with respect to a given entity. It is based on the relative entropy between the events of an entity-keyterm pair occurring individually or jointly. For its computation, we define the superdocument of an entity to be the union of its keyphrases with the keyphrases of all entities linking to it. The joint occurrence of a keyterm and an entity is the occurrence of the keyterm in the superdocument. We use this definition in a normalized variant of MI, which is computed as follows:

$$\mu(E,T) = 2 \cdot \frac{H(E) + H(T) - H(E,T)}{H(E) + H(T)}, \quad (2)$$

where $H(E)$ and $H(T)$ are the marginal entropies of the entity and term, respectively, and $H(E,T)$ is the joint entropy. We compute the μ weights for all entity-keyphrase and entity-keyword pairs. Note that all weights are with respect to the keyphrase space, not the original texts they were mined from.

3.2 Keyterm Cosine Relatedness

If no links are available upon which the entity relatedness can be computed, a baseline method is as follows. We compare two entities (e,f) represented by keyterm sets $T(e)$ and $T(f)$ by casting the keyterms into a weighted vector. This works for both **keyphrases** and **keywords**. If the terms are phrasal in nature, they can either be treated as a single unit in the vector or tokenized before constructing the vector. In our experiments, the vectors are filled with the MI weights of the keyterms. The relatedness between these vectors can be calculated using cosine similarity. Let (e,f) denote a pair of entities with keyterm vectors V_e and V_f, respectively. The keyterm relatedness is:

$$\mathrm{ktr}(e,f) = \frac{V_e \cdot V_f}{\|V_e\|\,\|V_f\|} \quad (3)$$

If keywords are derived from keyphrases by tokenization, their weights should take the phrase weights into account.

We simply multiply the weights of the words with the average weight of the phrases from which the words are taken.

3.3 Keyphrase Overlap Relatedness

Concepts are often represented as phrases (at least in the English language, but to a large extent also in other languages); so relatedness measures should consider multi-word keyphrases instead of single keywords only. However, when entities are represented by keyphrases, it is crucial to consider partial matches rather than focusing solely on exact-match comparisons. For example, "English rock guitarist" should be more similar to "English guitarist" than to "German President". To solve this issue, the relatedness measure needs to match keyphrases based on overlap and needs to take into account both keyphrase and keyword weights.

Let (e, f) denote a pair of entities with keyphrase sets $P_e = \{p_1, p_2, \ldots\}$ and $P_f = \{q_1, q_2, \ldots\}$, respectively. A phrase is identified with the set of constituent terms $p_i := \{w_1, w_2, \ldots\}$. We associate with every keyword w a weight $\gamma_e(w)$ with respect to the entity e.

In the following, let $(p, q) \in P_e \times P_f$ denote a pair of phrases. This allows us to introduce a measure of *phrase overlap* (PO) for the pair (p, q), where its constituent words are weighted with respect to the entities (e, f), given by the weighted Jaccard similarity of the keywords:

$$\mathrm{PO}(p,q) = \frac{\sum_{w \in p \cap q} \min\{\gamma_e(w), \gamma_f(w)\}}{\sum_{w \in p \cup q} \max\{\gamma_e(w), \gamma_f(w)\}} \quad (4)$$

We use PO to measure the *keyphrase overlap relatedness* (KORE) of a pair of entities (e, f) based on the sets of their associated phrases P_e and P_f. The measure captures the spirit of weighted Jaccard similarity while at the same time allowing keyphrases to contribute to the measure based on their overlap with *all* keyphrases of the other entity. Keyphrases are weighted with respect to the entities; recall that these weights φ_e are different from the keyword weights γ_e. We define the keyphrase overlap relatedness measure:

$$\mathrm{KORE}(e,f) = \frac{\sum_{p \in P_e, q \in P_f} \mathrm{PO}(p,q)^2 \cdot \min\{\varphi_e(p), \varphi_f(q)\}}{\sum_{p \in P_e} \varphi_e(p) + \sum_{q \in P_f} \varphi_f(q)} \quad (5)$$

The factor $\mathrm{PO}(p, q)$ is squared to penalize phrases which do not fully overlap. Our experiments have shown that using MI weights for keyphrases (φ_e) and IDF weights for keywords (γ_e) works best. The numerator re-weights the phrase overlap PO with the lesser weight of the two phrases that match. The denominator sums up all the keyphrase weights of each entity to normalize the numerator. Notice that we do not normalize by maximum possible intersection, which would be the sum over the full cartesian product $\sum_{p \in P_e, q \in P_f} \max\{\varphi_e(p), \varphi_f(q)\}$. Using this for normalization would unduly penalize popular entities with a larger keyphrase set, as the Cartesian product grows much faster than the intersection.

4. EFFICIENT COMPUTATION

4.1 Need for Speed

Computing similarities between a set of n objects is an important step in many applications, not only in entity disambiguation, but also in clustering or coreference resolution (record linkage). The KORE measure is relevant for all these tasks, assuming that the input data is a keyphrase set and partial matching improves the quality of the similarity measure.

The naive approach is to compute all $\binom{n}{2}$ pairwise similarities. This quickly becomes a bottleneck for large n. Even if the task is parallelizable, overcoming the $O(n^2)$ complexity is necessary to achieve good scalability, especially for interactive tasks such as on-the-fly NED (e.g., for news streams) or high-throughput tasks such as NED on an entire corpus (e.g., one day's social-media postings).

Precomputing the similarities is prohibitive with regard to both space and time. Today's knowledge bases contain millions of entities. The quadratic space and time complexity would lead to more than 10^{12} pairs. Even if we merely needed a single byte to store a pair's relatedness value, we would consume Terabytes of storage, and potentially much more. This is not practically viable. So the goal is to avoid the quadratic effect and devise appropriate pre-processing that facilitates fact relatedness computations on the fly. To this end, we have developed hash-based approximation techniques, using min-hash sketches [3] and the method of locality-sensitive hashing (LSH), invented by Indyk et al. [17, 13]. LSH has been used in numerous applications, including clustering in the context of NLP tasks (e.g., [29]). To the best of our knowledge, no prior work has considered such hashing techniques for entity relatedness and NED tasks.

4.2 Two-Stage Hashing

Entities are represented as sets of (weighted) keyphrases, which in turn are represented as sets of (weighted) keywords. Thus, keyphrases should not be compared atomically. "President of the United States" should be more similar to "United States President" than to "German President".

If we want to use LSH to speed up the computation, partial matches among phrases must be taken into consideration. As a solution, we propose the following two-stage hashing scheme:

1. Bucketize all highly similar keyphrases. Entities are then represented as a set of identifiers of such keyphrase buckets without losing the notion of partial phrase matches.

2. Group entities together that have sufficiently high overlap in terms of keyphrase bucket identifiers. The exact pairwise relatedness score can then be computed within a single entity-group, reducing the complexity of $O(n^2)$ to linear in the number of entities if the hashing techniques achieve near-uniform distribution of keyphrases (step 1) and entities (step 2). In principle, skewed distributions could still incur bottlenecks; however, our experiments with millions of entities did not exhibit such adverse effects in practice.

In the following, we explain the two steps in more detail. Figure 1 gives a pictorial overview of our technique.

4.2.1 *Grouping Highly Similar Keyphrases*

The goal of this step is to group keyphrases that are near duplicates in the sense that their Jaccard similarity is very high. As a compact representation of the words in a keyphrase, we first compute min-hash sketches for each phrase.

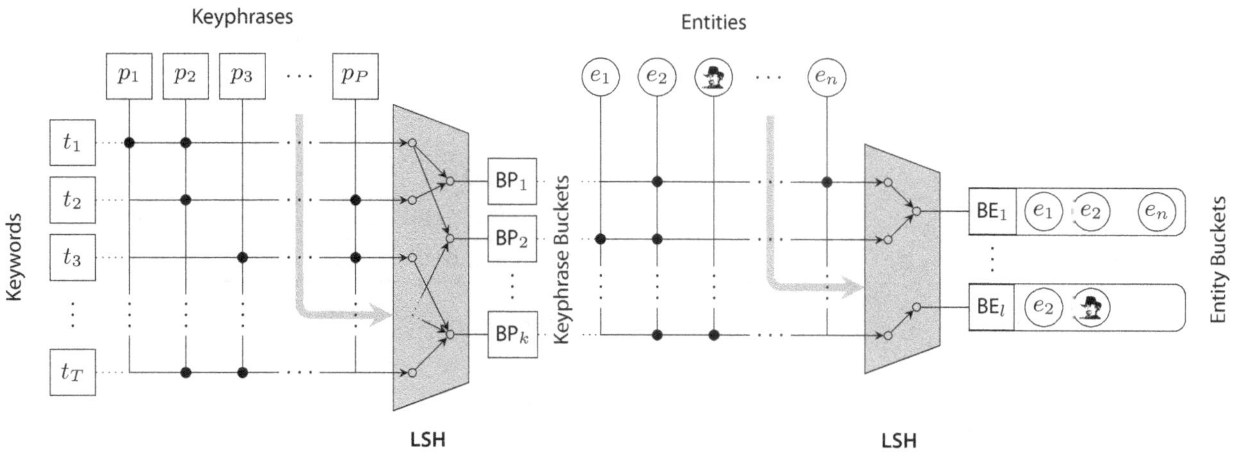

Figure 1: Overview of the two-stage hashing technique

This form of sketches allows us to approximate (as an unbiased estimator) the Jaccard similarity between sets (of words, in our case). To avoid the pair-wise comparison of all keyphrases, we apply LSH on the min-hash sketches of the phrases.

In detail, we first represent a keyphrase by a set of words and assign each word a globally unique id. For each keyphrase (the average length in our knowledge base is 2.5 words) we sample 4 times by min-hashing, thus representing each keyphrase by a vector of length 4. For LSH, we divide the vectors in two bands of length two, and combine the two ids in each band by summing up their ids, losing the order among them. Each keyphrase is finally represented by the two bucket ids (one per band) it was hashed to, combining near duplicate keyphrases. Note that we do not perform this stage-one hashing to reduce the dimensionality of the keyphrase space, but to capture the notion of partial overlapping keyphrases in KORE and to improve the second stage of grouping entities.

4.2.2 Grouping Related Entities

While the first stage above is precomputed for all entities and their keyphrases (with linear complexity), the second stage, described now, is executed at task run-time with a set of entities as input – for NED these are all candidate entities in a document. The algorithm first retrieves the sets of min-hash sketches for all input entities, pre-computed from the phrase-bucket ids output by the previous stage. These ids are now the input to a second stage of LSH. Algorithmically, this is fairly analogous to the first-stage technique, but the inputs are different from the first stage.

The exact KORE measure between two input entities is computed only if they share at least one hash bucket. Otherwise, we assume the entity relatedness is sufficiently low to consider the entities as unrelated. For the 3 million entities in our knowledge base we can fit the sketches for $\text{KORE}_{\text{LSH-G}}$ into main memory, merely requiring about 2 GBytes.

For $\text{KORE}_{\text{LSH-G}}$, a reasonably fast approximation of KORE which has nearly the same quality as KORE, we partition the sketched phrase-bucket id vectors into 200 bands of size 1. For $\text{KORE}_{\text{LSH-F}}$, a really fast approximation of KORE which degrades the approximation quality a bit, we use 1,000 bands of size 2, again combining the sketched ids by summing them up before hashing. $\text{KORE}_{\text{LSH-G}}$ is geared towards high recall so that the actual computation is executed between all somewhat related entities, but filters out noise. The speed-up is not so high, but the quality is close to exact KORE. Sometimes, quality is even improved as noisy candidates are removed. $\text{KORE}_{\text{LSH-F}}$ is geared towards higher precision with bands of size two, allowing LSH to prune even more entity pairs, speeding up the subsequent computation of the semantic relatedness due to fewer comparisons.

As we create the LSH hashtables dynamically during runtime for a given input set of entities, using more bands of larger size means that we need longer min-hash sketches – for $\text{KORE}_{\text{LSH-F}}$ a total of 2,000 per entity. This increases the time for constructing the hashtables. However, in our experiments the time difference in creating the candidate pairs using LSH for $\text{KORE}_{\text{LSH-G}}$ and $\text{KORE}_{\text{LSH-F}}$ is low; so the overall runtime is improved, especially for large sets of entities.

5. EXPERIMENTS ON RANKING RELATED ENTITIES

5.1 Dataset

Existing datasets to evaluate semantic relatedness quantify the relatedness between surface forms of words, not between entities registered in a knowledge base, which makes these datasets unsuitable for our task. We have created a new dataset to evaluate the quality of different measures for the relatedness between entities. A conceivable way to create such data would try to determine numeric scores for the degrees of relatedness (e.g., [11]). However, for most tasks a good ranking among the candidates is important; numeric scores are rarely needed. Moreover, semantic relatedness is difficult to judge by humans in an absolute manner. For these reasons, we settled for relative ranking judgments and use a crowdsourcing platform (Crowdflower) to average out the subjectivity of such judgments.

We selected a set of 20 entities from YAGO2 [15] from 4 different domains: IT companies, Hollywood celebrities, video games, and television series. For each of the 20 seed entities we selected 20 candidates from the set of entities linked to by the seed's Wikipedia article. Using entities from Wikipedia articles allows us to capture the candidates in the context which relates them to their seed entity. We tried to

Domain	KWCS	KPCS	MW	KORE	$\text{KORE}_{\text{LSH-G}}$	$\text{KORE}_{\text{LSH-F}}$
IT Companies	0.660	0.759	0.721	0.764	0.586	0.208
Hollywood Celebrities	0.722	0.715	0.667	0.646	0.647	0.522
Television Series	0.577	0.599	0.628	0.519	0.538	0.426
Video Games	0.604	0.760	0.431	0.780	0.722	0.499
Chuck Norris	0.481	0.498	0.571	0.585	0.585	0.653
Average (11 entities with $\leq$ 500 links)	**0.597**	**0.637**	**0.513**	**0.640**	**0.625**	**0.496**
Average (all 21 entities)	**0.633**	**0.698**	**0.610**	**0.673**	**0.621**	**0.425**

Table 1: Spearman correlation of relatedness measures with human ranking

Seed	Related Entity (Rank)
Apple Inc.	Steve Jobs (1), Steve Wozniak (2) ... NeXT (10), Safari (web browser) (11) ... Ford Motor Company (20)
Johnny Depp	Pirates of the Caribbean (1), Jack Sparrow (2) ... Into the Great Wide Open (10) ... Mad Love (20)
GTA IV	Niko Bellic (1), Liberty City (2) ... New York (10), Bosnian War (11) ... Mothers Against Drunk Driving (20)
The Sopranos	Tony Soprano (1), David Chase (2) ... Golden Globe Award (10), The Kinks (11) ... Big Love (20)
Chuck Norris	Chuck Norris facts (1), Aaron Norris (2), ... Northrop Corporation (10) ... Priscilla Presley (20)

Table 2: Example seed entities and gold-standard ranks of related entities

select the candidates in such a way that their semantic relatedness to the seed entity should be clearly distinguishable among each other, and included highly related as well as only remotely related entities in the set of candidates.

Example. For the entity *Chuck Norris* we have *United States Air Force* and *Chun Kuk Do* as candidates, described by the following context: "After serving in the *United States Air Force*, he began his rise to fame as a martial artist and has since founded his own school, *Chun Kuk Do*". This contextual information is given to the human judges, together with links to the Wikipedia articles for more detailed information. The crowdsourcing worker is then asked to rank *United States Air Force* versus *Chun Kuk Do* in terms of their relatedness to *Chuck Norris*. This included a "They are about the same" option.

The gold-standard ranking of the 20 candidate entities per seed is created as follows:

- All possible comparisons of the 20 candidates with respect to their seed are created (190 in total).
- 10 of the 190 comparison pairs are created as gold standard by the authors. The gold standard is used to compute the confidence in the human judges and to exclude them if they get too many wrong.
- For of the remaining 180 comparison pairs, 5 distinct judges are asked which of the given two entities is more related to the seed entity.
- All comparisons are aggregated by Crowdflower into a single confidence that one entity is more (or equally) related to the seed.
- The 20 candidate entities are then ranked by these confidence values as described by Coppersmith et al. [7], which has shown that the number of times an entity wins and the weights of the wins gives a good ranking.

The final output is a set of 20 ranked lists consisting of 20 entities each, against which we compare the rankings generated by the semantic relatedness measures. For the previous example, *Chun Kuk Do* was ranked 5 and *United States Air Force* 10, reflecting the stronger relatedness of a person to a school of martial arts initiated by him than to an organization he worked for. More examples of entity pairs with their crowdsourcing-derived ranks are given in Table 2.

All seed entities were chosen to be among the most popular individuals in their respective domain (*Apple* as IT company, *Johnny Depp* as Hollywood celebrity, *Grand Theft Auto IV* (GTA IV) as video game, and *The Sopranos* as television series). We also added *Chuck Norris* consisting only of *Chuck Norris* (a singleton set). The dataset, which contains a total of 441 entities (20 candidates for 21 seeds), is available at *http://www.mpi-inf.mpg.de/yago-naga/aida*.

5.2 Experimental Results

Experimental results for this dataset are given in Table 1. The numbers are the Spearman correlation between the gold-standard ranking and the automatically generated rankings by the relatedness measures.

The MW measure is by Milne and Witten (Equation (1)). KWCS is cosine similarity between the IDF-weighted keyword vectors derived from the (MI-weighted) keyphrases, KPCS is the cosine similarity on MI-weighted keyphrase vectors. KORE is the keyphrase overlap relatedness, with two configurations of LSH approximations. All measures are detailed in Section 3.

We see that all the measures using keyphrases – and do not depend on links – work better than the link-based MW, with KPCS performing best. The difference becomes even more obvious when we average the Spearman correlation not over all entities but only over those with less than 500 incoming links in Wikipedia (relatively "link-poor" entities) – here KORE works best. The small size of the dataset did not allow meaningful significance tests, though. We emphasize the point that even without links, the keyphrase-based measures perform at least as good as the MW measure. So we no longer depend on the rich Wikipedia link structure without losing quality, and we are well geared for dealing with truly long-tail entities that have very few or no links at all.

6. EXPERIMENTS ON NAMED ENTITY DISAMBIGUATION

For the NED experiments with different relatedness measures, we modified the AIDA framework [16] to incorporate the KORE measure. Figure 2 illustrates how AIDA represents the mentions in a text document and their entity candidates as a graph.

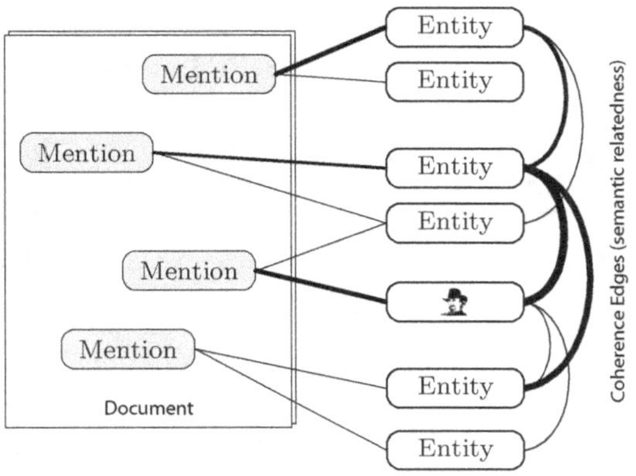

Figure 2: Disambiguation graph

Mention-entity edges have weights that combine a popularity-based prior (for a name denoting a specific entity) and the contextual similarity between a text window around the mention and a set of keyphrases for the candidate entity. Entity-entity edges have weights based on semantic relatedness measures. AIDA uses Milne and Witten's measure of semantic relatedness MW (Equation (1)). This method has outperformed all other coherence-aware alternatives in the experiments of [16]. AIDA does not consider keyphrases for entity-entity coherence.

6.1 Datasets

We conducted experiments on three datasets:

CoNLL-YAGO. The CoNLL-YAGO data set which is originally used in [16]. It is based on the CoNLL 2003 dataset, which consists of 1,393 newswire articles with an average article length of 216 words. In each article, all mentions are annotated and mapped to the correct entity in YAGO2. All numbers are from runs on the original 231 withheld test documents.

KORE50. We hand-crafted 50 difficult test sentences from five domains: celebrities, music, business, sports, and politics. The sentences were formulated according to a set of criteria:

- Short context: on average, only 14 words per sentence.
- High density of entity mentions: 148 mentions in 50 sentences, nearly 3 per sentence on average and a ratio of 20%. The mention-to-word ratio in CoNLL-YAGO is 12%.
- Highly ambiguous mentions: 631 candidate entities per mention, on average. In contrast, CoNLL-YAGO has only 27.
- Sentences contain long-tail entities with very few incoming links.

Examples are persons referred to by their first name only instead of last name or full name, or football clubs and players that are not well known outside their own home states. It is available at *http://www.mpi-inf.mpg.de/yago-naga/aida/*.

WP. This dataset is a prepared slice of Wikipedia with similar characteristics as KORE50. It contains all articles in categories ending with "heavy metal musical groups". Each article is split into sentences, and only sentences containing at least 3 named entities as link-anchor texts are kept. The link targets of these mentions provides us with ground-truth mappings. As a stress test, to make disambiguation more difficult, we replaced all occurrences of person names with the family name only (e.g. "Johnny Cash" replaced by "Cash"). In the same vein, we disabled the popularity-based prior for name-entity pairs for this dataset in all methods under comparison. We gathered 2,019 sentences this way, with an average length of 52 words. (The automatic sentence boundary detection did not always work properly, so some output segments were longer than expected). Each sentence has an average of 5 mentions with 64 candidates.

6.2 Experimental Results

We measured NED accuracy as the fraction of mentions that were correctly disambiguated, ignoring all mentions that do not have a candidate entity at all, following the evaluation methodology of [16]. The results are shown in Table 3: micro-averaged numbers aggregate over all mentions, macro-averaged numbers aggregate over all documents of a dataset. We also broke down the per-mention results by the number of Wikipedia inlinks of the mention's true entity. Link-averaged numbers are the macro-average over the groups of mentions with the same number of inlinks.

Overall, the KORE-based NED performed about as well as the original AIDA method, which uses the MW measure based on the rich link structure of Wikipedia. MW performs better on the CoNLL-YAGO dataset, KORE performs better on the KORE50 and WP datasets. A paired t-test shows that there is no significant difference between MW and KORE on CoNLL-YAGO or KORE50 for macro-average accuracy; however, KORE is significantly better on the WP dataset (p-value < 0.01 in a paired t-test). With link-averaged accuracy, KORE and KORE_{LS+G} also perform significantly better than MW on KORE50 (p-value < 0.01). On the WP dataset, Table 3 additionally gives the average accuracy for mentions whose true entities have few links, to emphasize the accuracy of KORE for long-tail entities.

Figure 3 shows a detailed comparison of MW and the KORE variations (using LSH) on the KORE50 dataset. The accuracy at each point x on the x-axis is the average accuracy of all entities with up to x links. As expected, KORE works a lot better for really link-poor entities, because it builds on keyphrases instead of links. With more links, the performance of KORE is still significantly better, but the difference between KORE and MW becomes smaller.

Performing well on link-poor entities is really important considering the fact that entities with ≤ 500 incoming links make up more than 90% of Wikipedia.

6.3 Efficiency

To evaluate the efficiency, we compared the running time of AIDA with the link-based MW measure against AIDA with the KORE measure, both in its exact form and with the LSH approximation for speed-up. We tested on the full CoNLL-YAGO collection consisting of 1,393 newswire articles (216 words on average) with a total of 27,820 mentions

Dataset	Evaluation	KWCS	KPCS	MW	KORE	$\text{KORE}_{\text{LSH-G}}$	$\text{KORE}_{\text{LSH-F}}$
CoNLL-YAGO	Micro Avg.	79.53%	82.18%	**82.31%**	80.71%	81.76%	81.18%
	Macro Avg.	79.07%	81.91%	**82.00%**	80.59%	81.22%	80.08%
	Link Avg.	79.28%	**82.31%**	81.34%	80.21%	81.80%	80.80%
WP	Micro Avg.	83.29%	85.30%	84.73%	**85.36%**	84.68%	84.50%
	Macro Avg.	82.50%	**84.59%***	83.86%	84.56%*	83.84%	83.61%
	Link Avg.	77.90%	80.49%	**82.45%**	80.12%	80.64%	80.36%
	Link Avg. $\leq$ 500 links	84.80%	86.80%	85.59%	**87.15%**	86.43%	86.29%
	Link Avg. $\leq$ 50 links	83.39%	85.19%*	83.87%	**85.52%***	84.56%	84.90%*
	Link Avg. $\leq$ 5 links	80.89%	81.10%	80.89%	**82.40%***	81.75%	81.38%
KORE50	Micro Avg.	55.56%	55.56%	57.64%	63.89%	**64.58%**	53.19%
	Macro Avg.	55.17%	54.70%	56.00%	62.17%	**62.60%**	52.07%
	Link Avg.	62.11%	61.79%	63.21%	70.75%*	**71.70%***	58.58%

Table 3: Disambiguation accuracy (best method per row is in boldface; statistically significant improvements over MW are marked with an asterisk)

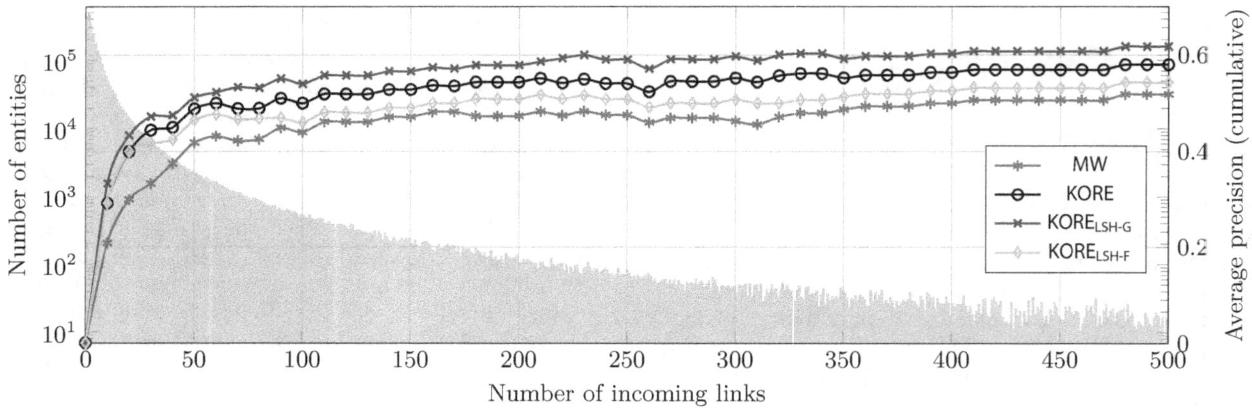

Figure 3: Accuracy of relatedness measures on entities with fewer than 500 incoming links on the KORE50 dataset

(we exclude mentions with no gold standard entity). On average, there are 25 mentions of named entities per article, and 73 entity candidates per mention. AIDA computes coherence weights only between candidate entities that are candidates for at least two different mentions. If they share only one mention, they are mutually exclusive candidates anyway. Thus, the number of comparisons (and the run-time) is still in the order of n^2, but it does not increase monotonically with the number of candidate entities for a document. Figure 4 shows the documents on the x-axis and the measured run-times for computing the NED on a document on the y-axis. The documents on the x axis are sorted in ascending order by the respective number of candidate entities ("largest" documents are thus rightmost).

We observe that the exact version of KORE is already much faster than MW. This is because MW is based on links, and some popular entities have a large number of incoming links (sometimes above 100,000, e.g., for places). In such cases, the intersection of bitvectors that AIDA uses to represent inlinks is very time-consuming. The number of keyphrases of popular entities does not nearly grow at the same rate, as it is bounded by the length of the document describing the entity. In contrast, incoming links can grow independently of the document size.

Table 4 gives detailed figures for the average run-time, its standard deviation, and the 90%-quantile of the run-time distribution (over the documents), and the same measures also for the number of entity-pair relatedness comparisons. KORE and MW perform the same number of comparisons, but the run-times differ significantly. The accelerated variants of KORE reduce the number of comparisons by a large margin and reduce the run-time further. In particular, the $\text{KORE}_{\text{LSH-F}}$ variant reduces the number of comparisons and the average run-time by an order of magnitude. For the 90%-quantile, which is relevant for being fast on the hardest cases, $\text{KORE}_{\text{LSH-F}}$ gains almost a factor of 20.

7. CONCLUSIONS

The keyphrase overlap relatedness measure KORE provides a high-quality notion of semantic relatedness of entities. In our experiments, KORE consistently performed at least as good as the best state-of-the-art methods, and often significantly better. Most importantly, KORE eliminates the reliance on explicit linkage between entities, and is thus geared for dealing with long-tail entities with few or no links. The approximate computation by the two-stage hashing method speeds up KORE and makes it suitable for online tasks that require interactive responses. These techniques also boost the throughput of KORE computations when applied in batch mode, e.g., for annotating an entire corpus (news, blogs, etc.) with NED mappings. Our future work will consider ap-

Method	Comparisons			Running time (s)		
	mean	stddev	0.9-quantile	mean	stddev	0.9-quantile
MW	898,253	3,578,524	1,594,226	5.335	27.357	9.738
KORE	898,253	3,578,524	1,594,226	1.884	6.592	3.519
KORE$_{LSH-G}$	315,302	1,306,293	548,561	1.285	3.925	2.308
KORE$_{LSH-F}$	60,580	301,712	87,240	0.413	1.557	0.586

Table 4: Results of timing experiments

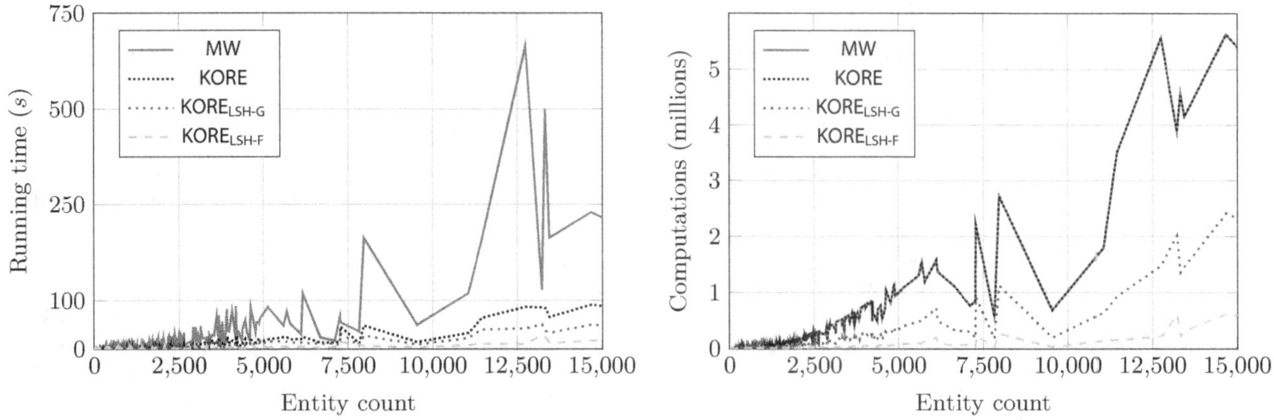

(a) Running time

(b) Number of computations

Figure 4: Efficiency on CoNLL-YAGO

plications of these techniques in the growing space of Linked Open Data and for social media on the Web.

8. ACKNOWLEDGMENTS

We would like to thank Edwin Lewis-Kelham for his help with the WP dataset, and also Mohamed Amir Yosef and Marc Spaniol for their contributions to the KORE50 dataset.

9. REFERENCES

[1] E. Alfonseca, M. Pasca, and E. Robledo-Arnuncio. Acquisition of Instance Attributes via Labeled and Related Instances. In *Proceeding of the 33rd International ACM SIGIR Conference on Research and Development in Information Retrieval, SIGIR 2010, Geneva, Switzerland*, pages 58–65, 2010.

[2] S. Auer, C. Bizer, G. Kobilarov, J. Lehmann, R. Cyganiak, and Z. Ives. DBpedia: A Nucleus for a Web of Open Data. In *Proceedings of the 6th International Semantic Web and 2nd Asian Semantic Web Conference, ISWC 2007/ASWC2007, Busan, South Korea*, pages 722–735, 2007.

[3] A. Z. Broder, M. Charikar, A. M. Frieze, and M. Mitzenmacher. Min-Wise Independent Permutations. In *Proceedings of the 30th Annual ACM Symposium on the Theory of Computing, STOC 1998, Dallas, Texas, USA*, pages 327–336, 1998.

[4] A. Budanitsky and G. Hirst. Evaluating WordNet-based Measures of Lexical Semantic Relatedness. *Computational Linguistics*, 32(1), 2006.

[5] K. Chakrabarti, S. Chaudhuri, T. Cheng, and D. Xin. EntityTagger: Automatically Tagging Entities with Descriptive Phrases. In *Proceedings of the 20th International Conference Companion on World Wide Web, WWW 2011, Hyderabad, India*, pages 19–20, 2011.

[6] R. L. Cilibrasi and P. M. Vitanyi. The Google Similarity Distance. *IEEE Transactions on Knowledge and Data Engineering*, 19:370–383, 2007.

[7] D. Coppersmith, L. K. Fleischer, and A. Rurda. Ordering by Weighted Number of Wins Gives a Good Ranking for Weighted Tournaments. *Transactions on Algorithms*, 6(3), 2010.

[8] S. Cucerzan. Large-Scale Named Entity Disambiguation Based on Wikipedia Data. In *Proceedings of the 2007 Joint Conference on Empirical Methods in Natural Language Processing and Computational Natural Language Learning, EMNLP-CoNLL 2007, Prague, Cech Republic*, pages 708–716, 2007.

[9] M. Dredze, P. McNamee, D. Rao, A. Gerber, and T. Finin. Entity Disambiguation for Knowledge Base Population. In *Proceedings of the 23rd International Conference on Computational Linguistics, COLING 2010, Beijing, China*, pages 277–285, 2010.

[10] P. Ferragina and U. Scaiella. TAGME: On-The-Fly Annotation of Short Text Fragments (by Wikipedia Entities). In *Proceedings of the 19th ACM Conference on Information and Knowledge Management, CIKM 2010, Toronto, Ontario, Canada*, pages 1625–1628, 2010.

[11] L. Finkelstein, E. Gabrilovich, Y. Matias, E. Rivlin, Z. Solan, G. Wolfman, and E. Ruppin. Placing Search

in Context: The Concept Revisited. *ACM Transactions on Information Systems*, 20(1):116–131, 2002.

[12] E. Gabrilovich and S. Markovitch. Computing Semantic Relatedness using Wikipedia-based Explicit Semantic Analysis. In *Proceedings of The 20th International Joint Conference for Artificial Intelligence, IJCAI 2007, Hyderabad, India*, pages 1606–1611, 2007.

[13] A. Gionis, P. Indyk, and R. Motwani. Similarity Search in High Dimensions via Hashing. In *Proceedings of 25th International Conference on Very Large Data Bases, VLDB 1999, Edinburgh, Scotland*, pages 518–529, Sept. 1999.

[14] S. Hassan and R. Mihalcea. Semantic Relatedness Using Salient Semantic Analysis. In *Proceedings of the 25th AAAI Conference on Artificial Intelligence, AAAI 2011, San Francisco, California, United States*, pages 884–889, 2011.

[15] J. Hoffart, F. M. Suchanek, K. Berberich, and G. Weikum. YAGO2: A Spatially and Temporally Enhanced Knowledge Base from Wikipedia. *Artificial Intelligence*, 2012.

[16] J. Hoffart, M. A. Yosef, I. Bordino, H. Fürstenau, M. Pinkal, M. Spaniol, B. Taneva, S. Thater, and G. Weikum. Robust Disambiguation of Named Entities in Text. In *Conference on Empirical Methods in Natural Language Processing, EMNLP 2011, Edinburgh, Scotland, 2011*, pages 782–792, 2011.

[17] P. Indyk and R. Motwani. Approximate Nearest Neighbors: Towards Removing the Curse of Dimensionality. In *Proceedings of the 30th Annual ACM Symposium on the Theory of Computing, STOC 1998, Dallas, Texas, United States*, pages 604–613, 1998.

[18] A. Kotov and C. Zhai. Tapping into Knowledge Base for Concept Feedback: Leveraging ConceptNet to Improve Search Results for Difficult Queries. In *Proceedings of the 5th ACM International Conference on Web Search and Data Mining, WSDM 2012, Seattle, Washington, United States*, pages 403–412, 2012.

[19] S. Kulkarni, A. Singh, G. Ramakrishnan, and S. Chakrabarti. Collective Annotation of Wikipedia Entities in Web Text. In *Proceedings of the 15th ACM SIGKDD International Conference on Knowledge Discovery and Data Mining, KDD 2009, Paris, France*, pages 457–466, 2009.

[20] M. Li, X. Chen, X. Li, B. Ma, and P. M. B. Vitányi. The Similarity Metric. *IEEE Transactions on Information Theory*, 50(12):3250–3264, 2004.

[21] R. Mihalcea and P. Tarau. TextRank: Bringing Order into Texts. In *Proceedings of the Conference on Empirical Methods in Natural Language Processing, EMNLP 2004, Barcelona, Spain*, pages 404–411, 2004.

[22] D. Milne and I. H. Witten. An Effective, Low-Cost Measure of Semantic Relatedness Obtained from Wikipedia Links. In *Proceedings of the AAAI 2008 Workshop on Wikipedia and Artificial Intelligence, WIKIAI 2008, Chicago, Illinois, United States*, 2008.

[23] D. Milne and I. H. Witten. Learning to Link with Wikipedia. In *Proceedings of the 17th ACM Conference on Information and Knowledge Mining, CIKM 2008, Napa Valley, United States*, pages 509–518, 2008.

[24] R. Navigli. Word Sense Disambiguation: A survey. *ACM Comput. Surv.*, 41(2), 2009.

[25] P. Pantel and A. Fuxman. Jigs and Lures: Associating Web Queries with Structured Entities. In *Proceedings of the 49th Annual Meeting of the Association for Computational Linguistics: Human Language Technologies, ACL 2011, Portland, Oregon, United States*, pages 83–92, 2011.

[26] S. P. Ponzetto and R. Navigli. Knowledge-Rich Word Sense Disambiguation Rivaling Supervised Systems. In *Proceedings of the 48th Annual Meeting of the Association for Computational Linguistics, ACL 2010, Uppsala, Sweden*, pages 1522–1531, 2010.

[27] S. P. Ponzetto and M. Strube. Knowledge Derived from Wikipedia for Computing Semantic Relatedness. *Journal of Artificial Intelligence Research*, 30(1):181–212, 2007.

[28] K. Radinsky, E. Agichtein, E. Gabrilovich, and S. Markovitch. A Word at a Time: Computing Word Relatedness using Temporal Semantic Analysis. In *Proceedings of the 20th International Conference on World Wide Web, WWW 2011, Hyderabad, India*, pages 337–346, 2011.

[29] D. Ravichandran, P. Pantel, and E. Hovy. Randomized Algorithms and NLP: Using Locality Sensitive Hash Functions for High Speed Noun Clustering. In *Proceedings of the 43rd Annual Meeting on Association for Computational Linguistics, ACL 2005, Ann Arbor, United States*, 2005.

[30] S. Singh, A. Subramanya, F. C. N. Pereira, and A. McCallum. Large-Scale Cross-Document Coreference Using Distributed Inference and Hierarchical Models. In *Proceedings of the 49th Annual Meeting of the Association for Computational Linguistics: Human Language Technologies, ACL 2011, Portland, Oregon, United States*, pages 793–803, 2011.

[31] R. Sinha and R. Mihalcea. Unsupervised Graph-based Word Sense Disambiguation Using Measures of Word Semantic Similarity. In *Proceedings of the 1st IEEE International Conference on Semantic Computing, ICSC 2007, Irvine, California, United States*, pages 363–369, 2007.

[32] F. M. Suchanek, G. Kasneci, and G. Weikum. YAGO: A Core of Semantic Knowledge. In *Proceedings of the 16th International Conference on World Wide Web, WWW 2007, Banff, Canada*, pages 697–706, 2007.

[33] T. Zesch, C. Müller, and I. Gurevych. Using Wiktionary for Computing Semantic Relatedness. In *Proceedings of the 23rd AAAI Conference on Artificial Intelligence, AAAI 2008, Chicago, Illinois, United States*, pages 861–867, 2008.

Shard Ranking and Cutoff Estimation for Topically Partitioned Collections

Anagha Kulkarni* Almer S. Tigelaar‡ Djoerd Hiemstra‡ Jamie Callan*

*Language Technologies Institute, School of Computer Science, Carnegie Mellon University
5000 Forbes Avenue,Pittsburgh, PA, USA 15213

‡Database Group, University of Twente, P.O. Box 217, 7500 AE, Enschede, The Netherlands

{anaghak,callan}@cs.cmu.edu {a.s.tigelaar,hiemstra}@cs.utwente.nl

ABSTRACT

Large document collections can be partitioned into *topical shards* to facilitate distributed search [19]. In a low-resource search environment only a few of the shards can be searched in parallel. Such a search environment faces two intertwined challenges. First, determining *which* shards to consult for a given query: *shard ranking*. Second, *how many* shards to consult from the ranking: *cutoff estimation*. In this paper we present a family of three algorithms that address both of these problems. As a basis we employ a commonly used data structure, the *central sample index* (CSI) [29], to represent the shard contents. Running a query against the CSI yields a *flat* document ranking that each of our algorithms transforms into a tree structure. A bottom up traversal of the tree is used to infer a ranking of shards and also to estimate a stopping point in this ranking that yields cost-effective selective distributed search. As compared to a state-of-the-art shard ranking approach the proposed algorithms provide substantially higher search efficiency while providing comparable search effectiveness.

Categories and Subject Descriptors

H.3 [**INFORMATION STORAGE AND RETRIEVAL**]: Information Search and Retrieval

Keywords

distributed information retrieval, selective search

1. INTRODUCTION

Distributed Information Retrieval (DIR) systems operate by partitioning the document collection into a number of smaller collections (*shards*) which are then searched in parallel [7, 8, 23, 24, 26]. This search strategy has become the de-facto standard in large-scale information retrieval environments [3, 4, 5, 27]. When operationalized on a large computing cluster, distributed search provides excellent gains in query response time [5, 12]. However, in a resource constrained environment where the parallelization opportunities are limited, processing a query against a large document collection is often inefficient. Kulkarni and Callan [19] proposed a solution that is based on dividing the collection into topically clustered partitions: *topical shards*. They demonstrate that such an organization of the collection ensures that the majority of the relevant documents for a given query are concentrated in a small number of shards[1], as opposed to being uniformly distributed across all shards. The skew in the distribution of relevant documents allows the search to be restricted to a few shards without incurring loss in search effectiveness. In this work we study two research problems that arise when selectively searching a partitioned collection: *which* shards to select and *how many* shards to select, specifically in the context of topical shards and low-resource environments.

A shard selection algorithm is responsible for identifying the partitions that should be consulted for a given query. The goal is to maximize the search accuracy by identifying the most *relevant shards* for the query and to simultaneously minimize the cost by searching as few shards as possible. A rich line of work exists for the problem of relevant shard identification and ranking [2, 10, 15, 16, 29, 32]. However, the task of estimating the *minimum number of shards* that should be searched for a given query has not received much attention. Most previous work resorts to using fixed cutoff values on the shard ranking that are query-agnostic [10, 25, 28, 29] or use other query independent criteria, such as, the load on the system to determine the number of shards that would process the query [26].

We show that a fixed rank cutoff either over or underestimates the minimum number of shards for many queries. This either wastes computational resources or returns sub par search results. Neither of these are acceptable choices for most search environments, but it is especially critical for search providers with limited computing resources to use a search strategy that is both efficient and effective.

In this paper we propose a solution that addresses both of the above problems, shard ranking and rank cutoff estimation, simultaneously in order to support cost-effective search. The task of estimating the minimal shard rank for a query is inherently dependent on the predicted ranking of the shards for the query. Solving these problems together

CIKM'12, October 29–November 2, 2012, Maui, HI, USA.

[1]For each query this could be a different set of shards.

allows for modeling the intrinsic dynamics between the two components.

All the algorithms studied in this paper assume the availability of a *central sample index* (CSI). This is an inverted index of a small sample of randomly selected documents from each shard. Running a query (q) against this index yields a ranking of the sample documents ($\mathbf{D}^q_{CSI}$). Since each document is associated with a specific shard, a shard ranking can be derived from this. The approach of inferring a shard ranking from $\mathbf{D}^q_{CSI}$ is a well established methodology that has been used in many other algorithms [28, 29, 32]. However, contrary to existing approaches, we derive a tree structure from this *flat* document ranking, using three different approaches: lexical hierarchical clustering, rank inferring, and connected rank inferring. We traverse through this tree to produce a final shard ranking and a minimal cutoff for a given query.

Often the sample used to create the CSI and thus the shard ranking is a very small portion of the complete collection. As such, the shard ranking algorithm is offered only a limited and incomplete view of the collection contents. Short queries can make the task of shard ranking further challenging. The intuition behind overlaying a hierarchy on the CSI document ranking is to capture the relations between the retrieved documents, in terms of their lexical similarities or shard memberships, with the goal of gleaning additional information for shard ranking and rank cutoff estimation.

The details about how we operationalize this intuition are given in Sections 3 through 5. Before that we position our work with respect to the existing work in the following section. The experimental details are shared in Sections 6 and 7. The results and our interpretations of the results are discussed in Section 8. Our conclusions from this investigation are shared in Section 9.

2. RELATED WORK

It has been well established that the problem of *ranking collections of documents* is inherently different from that of *ranking documents* and that it deserves its own solutions. As a result a rich line of research exists for the resource ranking problem which we review in this section. However, the problem of determining the shard cutoff has not received much attention. To the best of our knowledge the cutoff estimator by Thomas and Shokouhi [32] is the only investigation of this problem that is query-specific. In the context of Web search Puppin et al. [26] propose an approach for rank cutoff estimation that makes the number of contacted shards dependent on the current system load.

Several of the early works in shard ranking modeled this task after the well-studied problem of document ranking. The CORI [10] algorithm proposed an adaptation of the INQUERY [9] document ranking algorithm that viewed each shard as one *large document.* Xu and Croft [34] constructed language models (LMs) from the large documents and computed the Kullback-Leibler divergence between the shard LMs and the query LM to rank the shards. GlOSS [15] used term statistics, like the document frequency, in order to estimate the number of relevant documents in each shard for the query. These approaches are examples of a large family of shard ranking techniques that use content statistics of the shards to estimate their relevance for a query.

The other source of information, widely used by many shard ranking algorithms, is the *central sample index* (CSI) data structure. The CSI is created by pooling a sample of documents (S_R) from each shard (R). The ReDDE [29] algorithm runs the user query against the CSI and assumes that the top n retrieved documents are relevant. If n_R is the number of documents in n that are mapped to shard R then a score for each R is computed as $\theta_R = n_R * w_R$, where the shard weight w_R is the ratio of size of the shard ($|R|$) and the size of its sample ($|S_R|$). The shard scores θ_R are then normalized to obtain a valid probability distribution used to rank the shards. CSI creation is query-independent, and is thus performed only once. The CRCS [28] algorithm uses the rank information of the top 50 CSI documents to scale the membership function such that documents at higher ranks contribute more towards resource scores than those at lower ranks. CRCS also scales the accumulated resource scores by their sizes.

SUSHI [32] uses the scores and adjusted ranks of the top 50 CSI documents to fit curves for each resource represented in these documents. Three types of curves, linear, logarithmic, and exponential are tried. The curve with best fit is used to interpolate scores for the top m ranks for each resource. The interpolated points from each resource are merged into a single ranking and scores are aggregated to compute a relevance score for the resources. The number of unique resources present in the top R documents in this ranking is the predicted rank cutoff for the P@R metric. Empirical evaluatation using standard federated search datasets demonstrate that SUSHI predicts lower rank cutoffs on average as compared to a query-agnostic fixed cutoff of 10 and its precision at rank 10 is comparable to that of the baseline approach for many of the datasets.

The following three approaches cannot be categorized into either of the above families. Arguello et al. [2] took a classification based approach that uses CORI and CSI based ranking as classifier features. For each resource a binary classifier is learned that estimates the relevance probability. Document contents, query category and click-through logs are also used to define classifier features. The confidence score assigned for a prediction by each of the classifier is used to rank the shards. The fixed rank cutoffs of 1–5 are evaluated and the results demonstrate that the non-content features together with the conventionally used content features yield a robust ranking approach.

The usefulness of a query's topical category for the task of shard ranking was also noted by Ipeirotis and Gravano [16]. In fact, their approach organizes the shards into a topical hierarchy which is created using samples of shard contents. This hierarchy is static and query independent. The hierarchical shard selection is performed by evaluating the query against all of the shards at a particular level in the hierarchy using one of the *flat* shard ranking algorithms like CORI. The top scored shard at this level is then selected to be searched and the sub-tree rooted at that node is further explored. The experimental results show that this hierarchical shard ranking approach enables higher average precision as compared to the flat shard ranking technique.

Puppin et al. [25] use query logs to organize collections and to perform shard selection. They construct a contingency matrix from the queries observed in the query log and the documents returned for each of them. Co-clustering of this matrix provides *document clusters* and *query clusters.* The former are the partitions of the collection and the latter are used for shard selection. The experimental results show that a collection of about 6 million documents is partitioned into 18 shards using the proposed approach. One of the shards contains 52% of the collection documents which could not be clustered using the proposed technique. The results show that the proposed approach supports higher precision at early ranks (5, 10 and 20) than CORI.

In the context of geographically partitioned multi-site Web search Cambazoglu et al. [11] present an approach for query forwarding that uses training queries to infer the upper bounds on document scores for a given query at each of the non-local indexes. These bounds are then used to predict if a non-local index would contribute any document to the top k results for the query which in turn determines if the query is forwarded to that non-local index.

Peer-to-peer information retrieval is another line of related research where the task is to find a subset of peers that a query should be forwarded to. However, there is commonly either no central mediator or a light one that only suggests appropriate peers for a given query, but does not participate in the actual retrieval process. Each peer could be said to hold an index shard.

In networks where each peer holds a local index and is connected to a limited number of neighboring peers, the query is typically flooded: the querying peer sends it to its neighbors, and those neighbors send it to theirs, et cetera [1]. Since this does not scale, the forwarding has to be bounded, there is a fixed search horizon that results in a variable cutoff. Whilst this works well for popular queries with prolific results, it fares poorly for long tail queries. Query routing is complicated further by the fact that peers are not naturally topically clustered [31]. Hence, clustering peers by content [14, 20] is a possible solution as it has been shown to make query processing more efficient [6].

A topical cluster of cooperative peers is similar to a topical shard. However, no mechanism exists to dynamically determine the number of peer clusters to contact for a given query in this set-up, for example: Bawa et al. [6] proposed a heuristic cutoff equal to a quarter of the number of topical clusters. Furthermore, clustering mechanism may fail to discover the structure of the document distribution and may not work well for unpopular topics. Klampanos et al. [17] proposed replicating popular documents and using relevance feedback to dynamically alter cluster centroids.

3. TOPICAL SHARDS: RANKING AND CUTOFF ESTIMATION

When large document collections are divided into multiple smaller shards the resulting search environment offers several advantages, such as, distributed and parallel computing, higher fault tolerance, and easier load balancing. Randomly partitioning the collection into shards and then searching all of them in parallel is a well-established search strategy. However, Kulkarni and Callan [19] reason that if the collection is instead divided into topically focused shards, only a few of them need to be searched for each query[2]. They show that this substantially reduces the query processing cost while maintaining search accuracy. Although topical partitions may not support even load-balancing, their lower total search cost makes them an appropriate solution for low-resource search environments that must support large collections.

The topically homogeneous partitions have certain unique properties that can be exploited at query time. The distribution of relevant documents across shards is highly skewed for the majority of queries when shards are topically organized [19][3]. Secondly, many shard ranking algorithms, including ours, rely on a small subset of documents sampled from each shard to sufficiently represent its contents. This objective is harder to achieve when the shards are created using random partitioning. Sampling from topically focused shards is less likely to result in under or over-sampling errors, which in turn improves shard ranking effectiveness.

Motivated by these observations we propose three algorithms that address both shard ranking and cutoff estimation for topically sharded search environments. Later we also test the adaptability of the proposed algorithms by evaluating them on datasets that were not partitioned using the approach proposed by Kulkarni and Callan.

4. Sampling-based Hierarchical Relevance Estimation (SHiRE)

We propose a family of three shard ranking algorithms that share two characteristics: their use of a central sample index (CSI), and their approach to shard ranking that creates a hierarchy from the CSI documents retrieved for the query. What distinguishes these algorithms is the function they use to transform the *flat* CSI document ranking for a query into a tree structure.

In this work we construct the CSI from a small sample of randomly selected documents from each shard. We choose to use the CSI to represent the shard contents for two main reasons. Firstly, it is a time-tested approach that has been demonstrated to be highly effective by several previous studies [2, 29, 32]. Secondly, the CSI typically has a small memory footprint leading to an efficient shard ranking process. Also, note that the CSI creation happens during an offline phase that is not repeated for each query.

Each of the SHiRE algorithms starts with scoring the query against the CSI to obtain a ranking of the sampled documents ($\mathbf{D}^q_{CSI}$). The information contained in this ranking, such as, the rank of each document, the retrieval scores, and the shards represented by each of the retrieved sample documents, is used by each of the algorithms in a unique way to construct a query-specific hierarchy where the retrieved documents are at the leaf nodes. Note that the set of documents organized into a hierarchy for each query is quite small ($\mathbf{D}^q_{CSI} \ll CSI \lll C$, where C is the complete collection). The constructed hierarchy is traversed bottom-up starting at the leaf node that represents the top ranked CSI document for the query, until the root node is reached. Each step up reveals new leaf documents which 'vote' for the shards they represent. However, the votes are exponentially decayed at each level in this traversal. A document d revealed at step U in the traversal contributes a vote toward its parent shard as follows:

$$Vote(d) = V_d * B^{-U} \quad (1)$$

where V_d is either the document score assigned by the retrieval model or is a unit weight, and B is the base of the

[2]Verticals and groups of peers with similar content can also be regarded as instances of topical shards.

[3]For random partitioning the distribution of relevant documents across shards would be close to uniform.

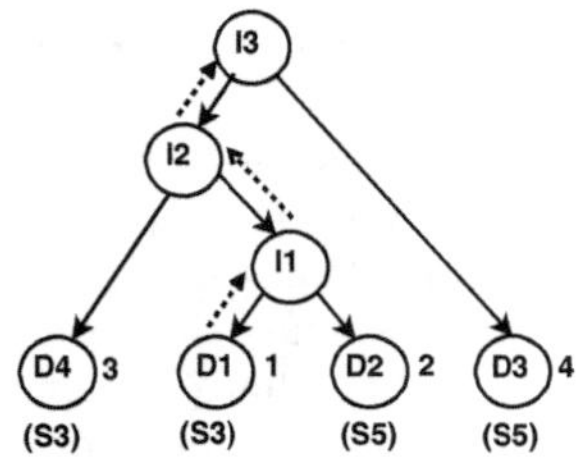

Figure 1: Lexical SHiRE. CSI ranking: $D1, D2, D3, D4$. Dashed arrows represent the path followed by the bottom-up traversal starting at $D1$. Numbers besides the leaf nodes specify the order of revelation of the documents. Parent shards specified in the brackets.

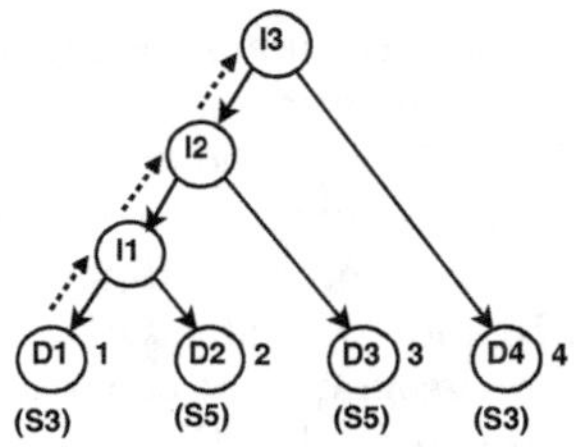

Figure 2: Rank SHiRE. CSI ranking: $D1, D2, D3, D4$. Dashed arrows represent the path followed by the bottom-up traversal starting at $D1$. Numbers besides the leaf nodes specify the order of revelation of the documents. Parent shards specified in the brackets.

exponential function. The resulting votes are accumulated for each of the shards and are interpreted as their estimated relevance scores which are then used to obtain a ranking of the shards for the query.

By anchoring the tree traversal at the top ranked CSI document these algorithms assert that the shard represented by the first document in the CSI ranking is likely to be the most relevant shard for the query. The process of dampening the votes at each step models the intuition that longer path lengths from the anchor node implies less similarity with it which further implies lower likelihood of relevance to the query (*cluster hypothesis* [33]). If a tree is very shallow, few shards would accumulate a zero relevance score, whereas a very deep tree will result in many shards with zero scores.

4.1 Lexical SHiRE (Lex-S)

The *Lex-S* algorithm organizes the CSI documents retrieved for a query into a hierarchy based on their lexical similarities. Such a hierarchy provides equal voting rights to all documents that are similar (attached to the same node in the tree) irrespective of their CSI ranking.

As a first step the Lex-S algorithm represents each of the CSI documents retrieved for the query as a vector of tf-idf weights for the unique terms. The Manhattan distance metric is used to compute pairwise lexical similarities between the document vectors and Ward's method for agglomerative clustering constructs the hierarchy (complexity: $O(n^3)$ where n is the number of CSI documents retrieved for the query, ranging between between 1700–2000 documents in this work). Such a hierarchy for a toy example consisting of four CSI documents retrieved for a query is shown in Figure 1. Dn represents the document at rank n in the CSI results.

The ranking of shards is derived by traversing up this tree, starting from the leaf node for the first document in the CSI ranking ($D1$). For the toy example in Figure 1 the next step would reach the internal node $I1$ and thus reveal the document $D2$. $D4$ would be observed next and $D3$ would be found the last. If V_{D1} is the vote that $D1$ ascribes to its parent shard then $D1$ will contribute: $V_{D1} * B^{-U}$, where U=1 is the number of steps traversed up the hierarchy, and B is the base of the exponential decay function. Similarly, $D2$, $D4$ and $D3$ will contribute: $V_{D4} * B^{-2}$, $V_{D3} * B^{-3}$, and, $V_{D4} * B^{-4}$ respectively, to their parent shards. The shard $S3$ will accumulate votes from documents $D4$ and $D1$, and shard $S5$ will accumulate votes from documents $D2$ and $D3$. The resulting score would be used to rank shards $S3$ and $S5$.

4.2 Rank SHiRE (Rank-S)

The *Rank-S* algorithm uses the rank information of the documents retrieved from CSI for the query to construct the hierarchy. We use a left-branching binary tree to encode the rank information since it provides a convenient structure that retains the CSI ranking during bottom-up traversal. It also facilitates a tree traversal based shard rank inference, which is a common characteristic of this family of algorithms. As shown in the tree representation of the toy example (Figure 2) the first CSI document is at the deepest node in this left-branching binary tree and the height of this tree is one less than the number of documents retrieved from the CSI for the query.

The procedure for inferring a shard ranking from this tree is similar to that used by Lex-S except for a *regularization* enforced on the vote assigned by the single top ranked CSI document. If the shard represented by the top ranked CSI document does not earn any other votes from the subsequent documents at the top m ranks then the vote of the top document is ignored. Recall that by anchoring the traversal at the top ranked document we allow it to assign the biggest vote. The regularization puts a check on the ability of the top ranked document to vote by requiring evidence of support from the subsequent ranks. If the shard represented by the top ranked document is also represented by at least 10% of the ranks in the top 30 CSI documents for the query then its vote is accumulated. We chose these values for the two parameters based on preliminary experiments. A more thorough study of the effects of these parameters is needed.

The simplicity of this algorithm makes it the most efficient algorithm of this family. This approach is most similar in spirit to the CRCS(e) ranking method [28]. However, other CSI based shard ranking methods, like ReDDE, can also be easily transformed to work with a left-branching binary tree of CSI documents where the votes are not decayed during the bottom-up traversal. As such, the computational complexity of Rank-S is very similar to that of ReDDE.

4.3 Connected SHiRE (Conn-S)

The *Conn-S* algorithm uses the *connections* between the retrieved CSI documents, specifically their shard membership, to guide the construction of the hierarchy. The top ranked CSI document is the deepest node in the hierarchy. The next document in the CSI ranking is either attached at the same level as the previous node, or it prompts creation of another level depending upon whether it belongs to the same shard as the previous document. As per the cluster hypothesis, for topical shards, documents from the same

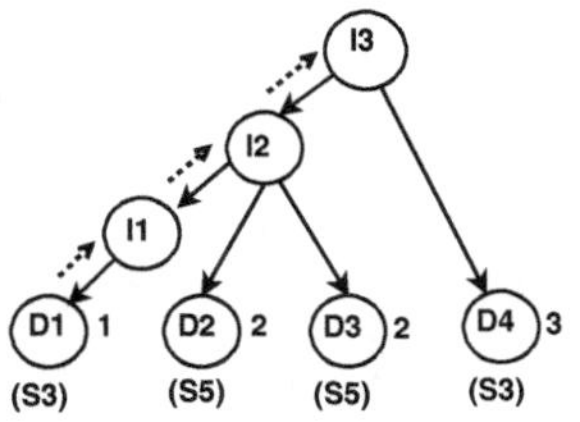

Figure 3: Connected SHiRE. CSI ranking: $D1, D2, D3, D4$. Dashed arrows represent the path followed by the bottom-up traversal starting at $D1$. Numbers besides the leaf nodes specify the order of revelation of the documents. Parent shards specified in the brackets.

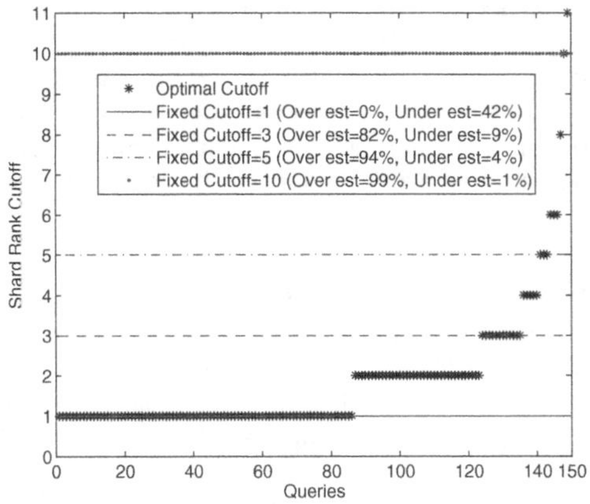

Figure 4: Minimal versus fixed shard rank cutoffs for ReDDE. Dataset: Gov2. Metric: P@10.

shard are likely to be relevant to the same information need. Placing such documents at the same internal node provides them equal voting rights.

In the toy example (Figure 3) document $D1$ belongs to a different shard as $D2$, which is why a new internal node is created as $D2$ is observed. In contrast, $D2$ and $D3$ belong to the same shard, and thus $D3$ attaches to the same node as $D2$. Finally, $D4$ leads to a creation of another internal node because it belongs to a different shard ($S3$) than $D3$ ($S5$). This continues until every document in the CSI ranking is processed. A CSI ranking that does not place any pair of documents from the same shard in consecutive ranks results in a left-branching binary tree using this method. A shard ranking is estimated from the resulting hierarchy using the same approach as that used by Lex-S: bottom-up traversal with exponential decays at each level.

5. SHARD RANK CUTOFF ESTIMATION

Once a ranking of shards is obtained for the query using one of the SHiRE algorithms, the next step is estimating the *minimal rank cutoff* in this ranking. A minimal rank cutoff is the smallest rank in a given shard ranking that provides search accuracy on par with exhaustive search. Notice that the minimal cutoff is specific to a shard ranking. Two different shard rankings for the same query could have different minimal cutoff values. The cutoff also depends on the evaluation metric under consideration.

Figure 4 plots the minimal rank cutoffs for 150 evaluation queries used with one of the datasets in this paper. The

Table 1: Datasets

Dataset (#Shards)	Size (GB)	#Doc (K)	#Voc (M)	Avg Doc Len
CW09-CatB (100)	1500	50220	96	918
Gov2 (50)	400	25205	39	918
TREC123-BySrc (100)	3.2	1078	0.9	420
TREC4-Kmeans (100)	2.0	567	0.6	480

Table 2: Query Sets

Dataset (#Queries)	Qry Set	Avg Qry Len	Avg #Rel Docs / Qry	Num Rel Grades
CW09-CatB (98)	0910:1-100	2.1	80 (± 49)	5
Gov2 (149)	701-850	3.1	179 (± 149)	3
TREC123-BySrc (50)	51-100	3.4	546 (± 375)	2
TREC4-Kmeans (50)	201-250	9.1	130 (± 115)	2

minimal rank cutoffs were computed for precision at rank 10 metric (P@10). The straight lines represent the commonly used query-agnostic fixed rank cutoffs. This figure illustrates that the minimal shard rank cutoffs (represented by asterisks) exhibit high variability across queries. A fixed cutoff leads to an under or overestimation error for many queries. A small fixed value, such as 1, would lead to a poor search accuracy for 42% of the queries in this example, while a larger fixed value of 10, would lead to an unwarranted increase in the search cost for 99% of the queries.

The SHiRE algorithms facilitate estimation of a query-specific minimal cutoff. Recall that the bottom-up traversal is accompanied by exponential decay of votes for each of the algorithms. This has the effect of driving the votes to zero as the traversal progresses which in turn drives the relevance scores, which are simply the accumulated votes, to zero for shards that are represented only higher up in the tree. Our hypothesis is that in the resulting shard ranking the point at which a shard's estimated relevance score converges to zero is often close to the minimal cutoff for the query. We use this rank cutoff estimator for each of the three SHiRE algorithms and interpret a shard's relevance score of 0.0001 as having converged to zero.

6. DATASETS

For a thorough evaluation of our algorithms we employ four datasets that provide a range of sizes and characteristics. The first two datasets described below (CW09-CatB and Gov2) are the main datasets that we use throughout the evaluation section. We use the other two datasets (TREC4-Kmeans and TREC123-BySrc) as supplementary datasets for their historic value and to test the adaptability of our approaches to different partitioning environments.

The two main datasets were partitioned into topical shards using a sample-based clustering technique proposed by Kulkarni and Callan [19]. This technique learns the *shard definitions* from a small randomly sampled subset of the collection. The remaining documents are then projected onto the topical spaces using the learned definitions.

The CW09-CatB dataset is a subset of the ClueWeb09 dataset. It consists of the first 50 million English Web pages of ClueWeb09. We divided this dataset into 100 topical shards obtaining an average shard size of 0.5 million, as specified by Kulkarni and Callan [19]. The Gov2 TREC corpus [13] consists of 25 million documents from the US government domains, such as .gov and .us, and also from certain government related websites. This dataset was partitioned into 50 shards using the above topical shard creation technique.

Although they are now considered small and outdated, TREC4-Kmeans and TREC123-BySrc are two of the most widely used datasets in distributed information retrieval research. TREC4-Kmeans was created by clustering the documents from the Text Research Collection, Volumes 2 and 3[4] into 100 clusters [34]. TREC123-BySrc dataset was created by dividing the Text Research Collection, Volumes 1, 2 and 3, into 100 partitions based on the source of the documents.

The summary statistics of these datasets are given in Table 1. The evaluation queries that were used with these datasets are summarized in Table 2. For CW09-CatB there are two queries and for Gov2 there is one query for which there are no relevant search results. These were not included conforming to the official TREC evaluations. Note that the CW09-CatB and Gov2 queries were judged on a 5-point and 3-point relevance scales, respectively, while the older datasets provide only binary relevance judgments.

7. EXPERIMENTAL SETUP

For efficient and convenient access to the document collections, each dataset was converted to an Indri[5] index. The documents were pre-processed before indexing to remove stopwords and reduce morphological variants using the Krovetz stemmer [18].

A central sample index (CSI) was created for each dataset using simple random sampling. From each shard 4% of the documents were sampled for the CSI. The choice of the sample size was guided by preliminary experiments that were performed to estimate the size of a small but effective sample. For each dataset the same CSI was used by all the shard ranking methods. Global statistics were assumed to be available to all the shards. As a result, the scores of the documents retrieved from different shards are comparable and the merging of documents is straightforward. A language modeling and inference network based retrieval model, Indri [21], was used for all the document retrieval tasks. The full-dependence model query representation [22], that encodes term co-occurrence information, was used for all the experiments.

For the comparative analysis of the different shard ranking approaches we use the following standard evaluation metrics: precision at rank 10, rank 30 (P@{10,30}), normalized discounted cumulative gain at rank 10 (ndcg@10), and the mean-average-precision (MAP) metric to measure the average search accuracy over all the queries. In order to compare the search efficiency enabled by each of the approaches we define a *cost* metric. The total amount of work required to process a query against a collection is typically proportional to the number of documents that *match* the query[6]. The volume of index data transferred and processed for a query (the dominant cost) as well as the computational cost of the query, both, are functions of the number of matched documents. We define the cost metric as follows:

$$cost = \frac{\sum_{q=1}^{|Q|} \sum_{t=1}^{T_q} |D_{S_t}|}{|Q|} \tag{2}$$

where Q is the set of evaluation queries, T_q is the number of top shards searched for the query q, and D_{S_t} is the set of matched documents in shard S at rank t in the predicted shard ranking for query q. Note that T_q would be a fixed value for each query in case of ReDDE. For the SHiRE algorithms T_q would be a query-specific value provided by the rank cutoff estimator.

The choice of this cost metric is especially well-suited for low-resource search environments, where the operational requirements place an upper bound on the amount of work permitted per query. Similar cost metrics have been used in other research by Moffat et al. [23] and Strohman et al. [30]. Most real-world search systems use query optimization techniques to improve query processing efficiency. The actual average search cost would typically be lower than the one computed above.

8. RESULTS AND DISCUSSION

Tables 3 and 4 report the search accuracy and cost results for the Gov2 and CW09-CatB datasets. The SHiRE algorithms with dynamic shard rank cutoff estimation are compared with two previously proposed shard rankers: ReDDE and SUSHI. Several different parameterizations were tested and the setting that provided the best trade-off in terms of search accuracy and processing cost was chosen for each algorithm. For ReDDE the parameter under consideration is the fixed shard rank cutoff (T) and for the SHiRE algorithms it is the base for the exponential decay function (B). The chosen values for these parameters are provided in the first column of the tables. The sensitivity of SHiRE algorithms to different parameterizations is analyzed later in Section 8.1. The differences in the search accuracies of ReDDE and the proposed approaches were tested for statistical significance using the paired T-test and were found to be not significant ($p < 0.01$). The last column in both tables compares each algorithm's query processing efficiency with that of ReDDE.

We observe that all the three SHiRE algorithms support a more efficient search than ReDDE. The average number of documents processed per query is smaller for the SHiRE algorithms while the search effectiveness is on par with that of ReDDE. The Rank-S algorithm cuts the search cost by 27% for Gov2 and by nearly half for CW09-CatB. The savings in cost offered by Lex-S and Conn-S are bigger for the larger collection. This is a desirable property for low-resource search environments. Providing cost-effective search, even when working with large collections, is one of the challenges in such search environments.

The shard rank cutoff estimator used by SUSHI optimizes its prediction for a particular precision metric (Section 2). The P@10 and P@30 values reported for SUSHI are thus from separate runs and the remaining values are an average over those two runs. For the Gov2 dataset SUSHI is as efficient as the Lex-S algorithm. However, the corresponding search accuracy for SUSHI is substantially lower than ReDDE. For the CW09-CatB dataset, although the search accuracy results for SUSHI are comparable to other

[4]http://trec.nist.gov/data/docs_eng.html

[5]http://www.lemurproject.org/indri/

[6]Every document that contains at least one of the query terms is considered as a matched document for the query.

Table 3: **Search accuracy and cost results for Gov2. Exhaustive search performance: P@10=0.58, P@30=0.52, MAP=0.32, ndcg@10=0.49, Cost=3.62M ▼ denotes significantly worse value than that with ReDDE** ($p < 0.01$).

	P@10	P@30	MAP	ndcg@10	Cost (million)	$Cost_{MtdX} - Cost_{ReDDE}$
ReDDE (T=3)	0.57	0.51	0.29	0.48	0.83	-
SUSHI	▼0.51	▼0.41	▼0.23	▼0.41	0.77	-7%
Lex-S (B=10)	0.56	0.49	0.27	0.46	0.78	-7%
Rank-S (B=10)	0.58	0.52	0.29	0.48	0.61	-27%
Conn-S (B=10)	0.58	0.52	0.31	0.48	0.81	-2%

Table 4: Search accuracy and cost results for CW09-CatB. Exhaustive search performance: P@10=0.27, P@30=0.26, MAP=0.18, ndcg@10=0.21, Cost=5.37M.

	P@10	P@30	MAP	ndcg@10	Cost (million)	$Cost_{MtdX} - Cost_{ReDDE}$
ReDDE (T=3)	0.29	0.28	0.17	0.21	0.47	-
SUSHI	0.29	0.26	0.16	0.21	0.54	15%
Lex-S (B=50)	0.29	0.26	0.15	0.22	0.39	-17%
Rank-S (B=50)	0.30	0.26	0.16	0.21	0.25	-47%
Conn-S (B=50)	0.28	0.26	0.16	0.20	0.31	-34%

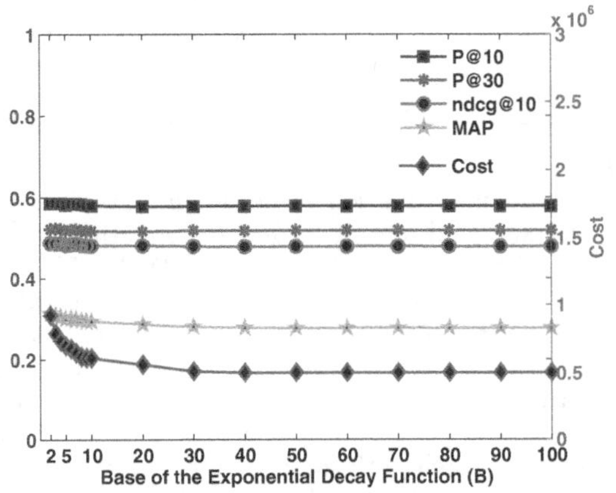

Figure 5: Sensitivity of Rank-S algorithm to parameter B. Dataset: Gov2

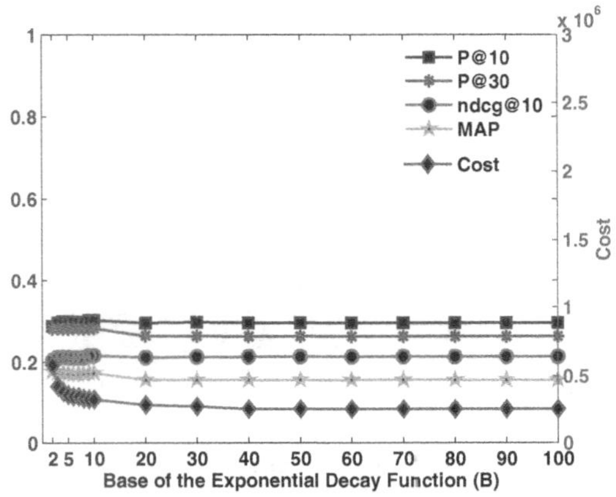

Figure 6: Sensitivity of Rank-S algorithm to parameter B. Dataset: CW09-CatB.

approaches the corresponding cost is much higher than all the other approaches. Overall SUSHI struggles to provide a cost-effective search setup and as such is a weaker baseline than ReDDE. In the remainder of the paper we compare the SHiRE algorithms only with the ReDDE algorithm.

We also note that almost all the shard rankers support efficient search that is just as effective as the exhaustive search. This is especially true for precision at early ranks. For both datasets, recall that the shards were created by partitioning the collection's documents into topical shards (Section 6). We see that all the ranking approaches benefit from the characteristic property of topical shards: a skewed distribution of relevant documents across shards (Section 3). These result trends are in agreement with observations made by Kulkarni and Callan [19].

Notice that even for ndcg@10, a metric that is sensitive to both the position and the relevance level of the documents in the results list, nearly all of the rankers are able to provide comparable values to those with exhaustive search. This is especially remarkable for the CW09-CatB dataset which offers 5 levels of graded relevance.

When comparing the SHiRE algorithms to each other we see that the Rank-S approach provides the largest reduction in cost for both datasets. The computational complexity of the Lex-S algorithm is much higher than the other two SHiRE algorithms. The transformation of the CSI results into a hierarchy requires agglomerative clustering of the results in case of Lex-S, whereas this transformation is trivial for Rank-S and Conn-S. Based on the above observations we recommend the SHiRE algorithms (especially Rank-S) over ReDDE for topically partitioned collections.

8.1 Sensitivity of SHiRE algorithms to parameter B

We experimented with a range of base values (B) for the exponential decay function (Equation 1) in order to analyze its influence on the performance of the SHiRE algorithms. Figures 5 and 6 present the results for the Rank-S algorithm with both datasets. The results for each of the precision metrics are fairly stable over a range of B values. We see more variation in the values for the cost metric. A small base value allows for more search budget (in terms of shard rank cutoff). As a result, the corresponding search cost increases as the base value decreases.

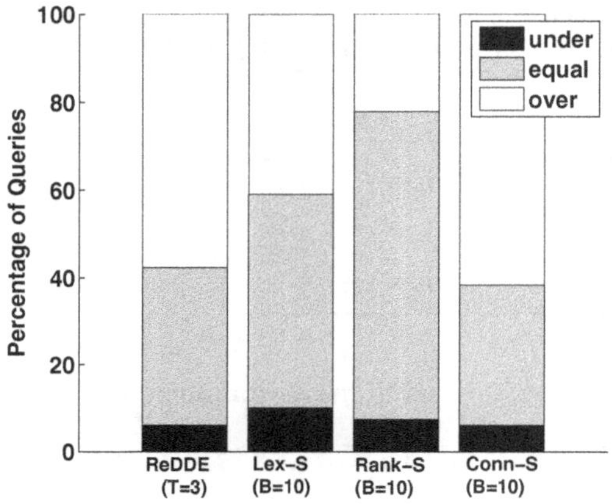

Figure 7: Shard rank cutoff estimation errors. Dataset: Gov2. Metric: P@10.

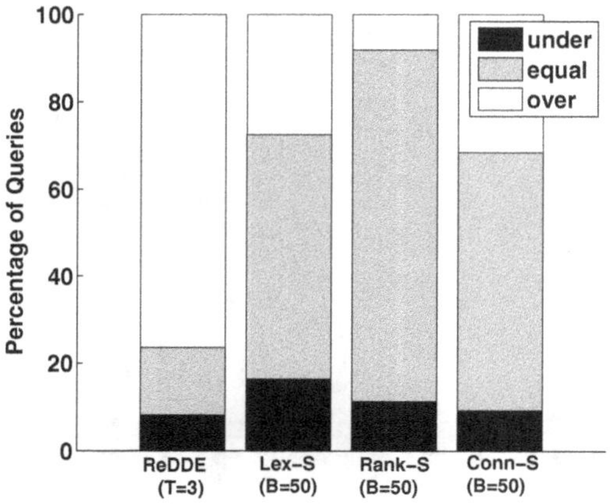

Figure 8: Shard rank cutoff estimation errors. Dataset: CW09-CatB. Metric: P@10.

We see similar trends for the Conn-S and Lex-S algorithms. However, for the latter the cost is much higher for smaller base values. Often the hierarchy learned from the CSI results of a query for the Lex-S algorithm is more flat than it is for the Rank-S and Conn-S algorithms. As a result, the votes accumulated at each level in the tree, decay at a much slower rate for the Lex-S algorithm. This results in a higher shard rank cutoff estimates and ultimately to higher search costs. Overall, these results demonstrate that the SHiRE algorithms are not highly sensitive to the parameter B and that we see consistent trends that are intuitive.

8.2 Shard Rank Cutoff Estimation

In this section we analyze the effectiveness of the SHiRE algorithms at predicting the minimal shard rank cutoff. We categorize the cutoff estimates into: under, equal and over estimates, based on comparison with the minimal rank cutoff. The equal category has a tolerance of ±1. An estimate that is off by +1 or -1 from the minimal value would be counted as an accurate estimate for this analysis. Recall that the minimal cutoff value for a query is specific to a metric. In these results the metric is P@10. We see similar trends for the other metrics.

Figures 7 and 8 plot the distribution of the estimation errors for the Gov2 and CW09-CatB datasets, respectively.

Table 5: Confusion matrix for shard rank cutoff estimation for Rank-S (B=10). Dataset: Gov2. Metric: P@10. Queries: 149. Cutoff averages: optimal=1.8 (±1.9), predicted=2.3 (±1.0).

		Predicted					
		1	2	3	4	5	>5
Optimal	1	34	37	26	5	2	0
	2	0	7	12	0	0	0
	3	0	4	5	2	0	0
	4	0	2	1	3	0	0
	5	1	1	0	0	0	0
	>5	1	2	3	1	0	0

Table 6: Confusion matrix for shard rank cutoff estimation for Rank-S (B=50). Dataset: CW09-CatB. Metric: P@10. Queries: 98. Cutoff averages: optimal=3.1 (±9.3), predicted=1.8 (±0.6).

		Predicted					
		1	2	3	4	5	>5
Optimal	1	28	44	8	0	0	0
	2	0	2	1	0	0	0
	3	2	4	0	0	0	0
	4	0	3	0	0	0	0
	5	0	1	0	0	0	0
	>5	0	5	0	0	0	0

We see that the over estimation errors are more frequent than the under estimation errors for nearly all the predictors. A fixed rank cutoff leads to over-estimation for the majority of the queries in case of ReDDE. This explains the large search costs associated with this search algorithm. All of the SHiRE algorithms lead to fewer prediction errors than ReDDE. However, Rank-S is most successful at predicting the minimal cutoff values (accuracy 71% and 81%, respectively for Gov2 and CW09-CatB) which explains its cost-effective search performance in Tables 3 and 4.

The above analysis provides a high-level validation of the minimal cutoff estimator's efficacy. For a more thorough understanding we study the *magnitude* of the cutoff prediction errors for the Rank-S algorithm. The confusion matrices in Tables 5 and 6 present these values for the Gov2 and CW09-CatB datasets, respectively. We see that the distribution of minimal rank cutoffs is highly skewed toward low cutoff values, specifically 1, for both datasets. This is mainly caused by the topical partitioning of the collection.

If we tolerate an estimation error of magnitude ±1 then the Rank-S estimator is accurate for 71% of the queries for the Gov2 dataset and for 81% of the queries for CW09-CatB. For ReDDE with a fixed cutoff (T) of 3 these numbers are 36% and 15% for Gov2 and CW09-CatB, respectively. The query-specific cutoff estimates by Rank-S are at least twice as accurate as the query-agnostic fixed cutoff.

Tables 5 and 6 show that for many queries the magnitude of the estimation error is not large for either datasets. However, for Gov2 we see a higher rate of over-estimation errors (22%), especially for the minimal cutoff of 1, than for CW09-CatB (8%). On the other hand, under-estimation errors occur for a larger percentage of queries (11%) for CW09-CatB than for Gov2 (7%). The prediction accuracy is especially low for the higher values of minimal cutoffs. Also, the magnitude of these errors is relatively higher. These errors primarily stem from the bias of the Rank-S algorithm

Table 7: Search accuracy and cost results for TREC123-BySrc. For ReDDE the top 25 shards (T) were searched for each query. For SHiRE algorithms the exponential base value of 3 (B) was used. Exhaustive search performance: P@10=0.48, P@30=0.47, MAP=0.21, Cost=0.15M, ▼ denotes significantly worse precision than ReDDE ($p < 0.01$)

	P@10	P@30	MAP	Cost (million)	$\text{Cost}_{MtdX} - \text{Cost}_{ReDDE}$ (%)
ReDDE	0.48	0.46	0.14	0.06	-
Lex-S	0.52	0.46	0.13	0.05	-24%
Rank-S	0.46	▼0.40	▼0.07	0.02	-73%
Conn-S	0.50	0.42	▼0.08	0.02	-71%

Table 8: Search accuracy and cost results for TREC4-Kmeans. For ReDDE the top 20 shards (T) were searched for each query. For SHiRE algorithms the exponential base value of 3 (B) was used. Exhaustive search performance: P@10=0.46, P@30=0.35, MAP=0.21, Cost=0.19M.

	P@10	P@30	MAP	Cost (million)	$\text{Cost}_{MtdX} - \text{Cost}_{ReDDE}$ (%)
ReDDE	0.45	0.34	0.19	0.09	-
Lex-S	0.45	0.33	0.15	0.05	-46%
Rank-S	0.40	0.32	0.16	0.02	-80%
Conn-S	0.41	0.33	0.16	0.02	-77%

toward smaller cutoff predictions, especially when parameterized with higher B values.

Overall, this query-specific rank cutoff estimator takes a step in the right direction and offers substantial improvements over the query-agnostic fixed cutoff approach. However, the above analysis also reveals the areas in which the estimator could be improved.

8.3 Additional Datasets

In this section we test the adaptability of the proposed shard rankers. We experiment with datasets that have not been topically partitioned using the technique proposed by Kulkarni and Callan [19]. We use the TREC123-BySrc and TREC4-Kmeans datasets described in Section 6. These datasets differ from those used in the previous sections on several dimensions, such as: size, average number of relevant documents per query, and topical shard homogeneity. The results for both datasets are given in Tables 7 and 8. As with the first two datasets, the differences in precision values of ReDDE and the SHiRE algorithms were tested for significance using the paired T-test ($p < 0.01$).

The prominent deviation from the trends seen until now is the low performance of the Rank-S algorithm. Although it provides substantial savings in search cost for both datasets, the corresponding search effectiveness is not comparable to the baseline performance. Instead, the Lex-S algorithm supports a more cost-effective partial search for these datasets. This trend reveals one of the weaknesses of Rank-S: its strong bias for predicting small rank cutoffs. At the same time it brings to light the strength of the Lex-S algorithm: its ability to support a more varied cutoff prediction range.

From these analysis we can conclude that the family of SHiRE algorithms together provide a search approach that has reasonable adaptability and is cost-effective for different search needs.

9. CONCLUSIONS

We presented three SHiRE shard ranking algorithms: Lex-S, Rank-S and Conn-S, that transform a flat CSI document ranking into a tree structure in order to encode additional information about the documents and the shards. The constructed hierarchy is also employed for estimating a query-specific minimal shard rank cutoff. The presented algorithms are one of the few approaches to dynamically predict query-specific shard rank cutoffs. The joint formulation of the two inter-dependent problems of shard ranking and cutoff estimation is an additional contribution of this work.

We tested the proposed algorithms on two large datasets that were both partitioned into topical shards. The search accuracy of the SHiRE algorithms is on par with a strong baseline and also with exhaustive search, while the search cost is substantially lower than both. The Rank-S algorithm is the most efficient search method for large topically partitioned collections. It reduced the search cost by a quarter for one of the datasets and by nearly a half for the larger dataset. Rank-S also supports query-specific minimal cutoff estimation that is at least twice as accurate as the best fixed cutoff value for topical shards.

Experiments with two supplementary datasets demonstrated that the conservative nature of the Rank-S cutoff estimator that enables very efficient search can be a detriment for smaller and topically less focused collections. However, Lex-S provides an attractive solution that is efficient and yet effective as compared to the baseline. Overall, the family of SHiRE algorithms offers cost-effective solutions for different search requirements.

10. ACKNOWLEDGMENTS

This work was in part supported by the National Science Foundation (NSF) grant IIS-0916553 and by the Netherlands Organisation for Scientific Research (NWO) under project 639.022.809. Any opinions, findings, conclusions and recommendations expressed in this paper are the authors' and do not necessarily reflect those of the sponsors.

11. REFERENCES

[1] K. Aberer and M. Hauswirth. An overview on peer-to-peer information systems. In *Proceedings of the Workshop on Distributed Data and Structures*, 2002.

[2] J. Arguello, J. Callan, and F. Diaz. Classification based resource selection. In *Proceeding of the ACM Conference on Information and Knowledge Management*, pages 1277–1286, 2009.

[3] R. Baeza-Yates, C. Castillo, F. Junqueira, V. Plachouras, and F. Silvestri. Challenges on distributed Web retrieval. In *The International Conference on Data Engineering*, pages 6–20, 2007.

[4] R. Baeza-Yates, V. Murdock, and C. Hauff. Efficiency trade-offs in two-tier Web search systems. In *Proceedings of the ACM SIGIR Conference on Research and Development in Information Retrieval*, pages 163–170, Boston, MA, USA, 2009.

[5] L. A. Barroso, J. Dean, and U. Hölzle. Web search for a planet: The Google cluster architecture. *IEEE Micro*, 23(2):22–28, 2003.

[6] M. Bawa, G. S. Manku, and P. Raghavan. SETS: Search enhanced by topic segmentation. In *Proceedings of the ACM SIGIR Conference on Research and Development in Information Retrieval*, pages 306–313, July 2003.

[7] B. Cahoon, K. S. McKinley, and Z. Lu. Evaluating the performance of distributed architectures for information retrieval using a variety of workloads. *ACM Trans. Inf. Syst.*, 18(1):1–43, Jan. 2000.

[8] J. Callan. Distributed information retrieval. In *Advances in Information Retrieval*, pages 127–150. Kluwer Academic Publishers, 2000.

[9] J. Callan, W. B. Croft, and S. M. Harding. The INQUERY retrieval system. In *Proceedings of the International Conference on Database and Expert Systems Applications*, pages 78–83, 1992.

[10] J. P. Callan, Z. Lu, and W. B. Croft. Searching distributed collections with inference networks. In *Proceedings of the ACM SIGIR Conference on Research and Development in Information Retrieval*, pages 21–28, NY, USA, 1995.

[11] B. B. Cambazoglu, E. Varol, E. Kayaaslan, C. Aykanat, and R. Baeza-Yates. Query forwarding in geographically distributed search engines. In *Proceedings of the ACM SIGIR conference on Research and development in information retrieval*, pages 90–97, NY, USA, 2010.

[12] A. Chowdhury and G. Pass. Operational requirements for scalable search systems. In *Proceedings of the ACM Conference on Information and Knowledge Management*, pages 435–442, USA, 2003.

[13] C. Clarke, N. Craswell, and I. Soboroff. Overview of the TREC 2004 Terabyte track. In *Proceedings of the 2004 Text Retrieval Conference*, 2004.

[14] A. Crespo and H. Garcia-Molina. Semantic overlay networks for P2P systems. In *Proceedings of the Agents and Peer-to-Peer Computing*, pages 1–13, Heidelberg, DE, July 2004. Springer.

[15] L. Gravano, H. García-Molina, and A. Tomasic. GlOSS: Text-source discovery over the internet. *ACM Transactions on Database Systems*, 24:229–264, 1999.

[16] P. G. Ipeirotis and L. Gravano. Distributed search over the hidden Web: Hierarchical database sampling and selection. In *Proceedings of Conference on Very Large Data Bases*, pages 394–405, 2002.

[17] I. Klampanos and J. M. Jose. An evaluation of a cluster-based architecture for peer-to-peer information retrieval. In *Proceedings of Database and Expert Systems Applications*, pages 380–391, Sept. 2007.

[18] R. Krovetz. Viewing morphology as an inference process. In *Proceedings of the ACM SIGIR Conference on Research and Development in Information Retrieval*, pages 191–202, NY, USA, 1993.

[19] A. Kulkarni and J. Callan. Document allocation policies for selective searching of distributed indexes. In *Proceedings of the ACM Conference on Information and Knowledge Management*, pages 449–458, 2010.

[20] J. Lu and J. Callan. Content-based peer-to-peer network overlay for full-text federated search. In *Proceedings of RIAO, Conference Adaptivity, Personalization and Fusion of Heterogeneous Information*, 2007.

[21] D. Metzler and W. B. Croft. Combining the language model and inference network approaches to retrieval. *Information Processing and Management*, 40(5):735–750, 2004.

[22] D. Metzler and W. B. Croft. A markov random field model for term dependencies. In *Proceedings of the ACM SIGIR Conference on Research and Development in Information Retrieval*, pages 472–479, NY, USA, 2005.

[23] A. Moffat, W. Webber, J. Zobel, and R. Baeza-Yates. A pipelined architecture for distributed text query evaluation. *Information Retrieval*, 10(3):205–231, 2007.

[24] S. Orlando, R. Perego, and F. Silvestri. Design of a parallel and distributed web search engine. In *Proceedings of Parallel Computing Conference*, pages 197–204. College Press, 2001.

[25] D. Puppin, F. Silvestri, and D. Laforenza. Query-driven document partitioning and collection selection. In *Proceedings of the Conference on Scalable Information Systems*, page 34, NY, USA, 2006.

[26] D. Puppin, F. Silvestri, R. Perego, and R. Baeza-Yates. Tuning the capacity of search engines: Load-driven routing and incremental caching to reduce and balance the load. *ACM Transactions on Information Systems*, 28(2):5:1–5:36, June 2010.

[27] K. M. Risvik, Y. Aasheim, and M. Lidal. Multi-tier architecture for Web search engines. *Web Congress, Latin American*, 0:132, 2003.

[28] M. Shokouhi. Central-rank-based collection selection in uncooperative distributed information retrieval. In *The European Conference on Information Retrieval*, Rome, Italy, 2007.

[29] L. Si and J. Callan. Relevant document distribution estimation method for resource selection. In *Proceedings of the ACM SIGIR Conference on Research and Development in Information Retrieval*, pages 298–305, NY, USA, 2003.

[30] T. Strohman, H. Turtle, and W. B. Croft. Optimization strategies for complex queries. In *Proceedings of the ACM SIGIR Conference on Research and Development in Information Retrieval*, pages 219–225, NY, USA, 2005.

[31] T. Suel, C. Mathur, J.-w. Wu, J. Zhang, A. Delis, M. Kharrazi, X. Long, and K. Shanmugasundaram. ODISSEA: A peer-to-peer architecture for scalable Web search and information retrieval. In *Proceedings of the Workshop on the Web and Databases*, pages 67–72, June 2003.

[32] P. Thomas and M. Shokouhi. SUSHI: Scoring scaled samples for server selection. In *Proceedings of the ACM SIGIR Conference on Research and Development in Information Retrieval*, pages 419–426, NY, USA, 2009.

[33] C. J. van Rijsbergen. *Information Retrieval.* Butterworths, 1979.

[34] J. Xu and W. B. Croft. Cluster-based language models for distributed retrieval. In *Proceedings of the ACM SIGIR Conference on Research and Development in Information Retrieval*, pages 254–261, NY, USA, 1999.

Daily-Deal Selection for Revenue Maximization

Theodoros Lappas
Boston University
tlappas@cs.bu.edu

Evimaria Terzi
Boston University
evimaria@cs.bu.edu

ABSTRACT

Daily-Deal Sites (DDS) like Groupon, LivingSocial, Amazon's Goldbox, and many more, have become particularly popular over the last three years, providing discounted offers to customers for restaurants, ticketed events, services etc. In this paper, we study the following problem: among a set of candidate deals, which are the ones that a DDS should feature as daily-deals in order to maximize its revenue? Our first contribution lies in providing two combinatorial formulations of this problem. Both formulations take into account factors like the diversification of daily deals and the limited consuming capacity of the userbase. We prove that our problems are NP-hard and devise pseudopolynomial – time approximation algorithms for their solution. We also propose a set of heuristics, and demonstrate their efficiency in our experiments. In the context of deal selection and scheduling, we acknowledge the importance of the ability to estimate the *expected revenue* of a candidate deal. We explore the nature of this task in the context of real data, and propose a framework for revenue-estimation. We demonstrate the effectiveness of our entire methodology in an experimental evaluation on a large dataset of daily-deals from Groupon.

Categories and Subject Descriptors

K.4.4 [**Computers and Society**]: Electronic Commerce; H.2.8 [**Database Management**]: Database applications—*Data mining*

Keywords

daily deals, revenue maximization, deal selection, e-commerce

1. INTRODUCTION

Daily Deal Sites (DDS), like Groupon[1], LivingSocial[2], and Amazon's Goldbox[3] are among the latest Internet sensations, recommending group deals to users on a daily basis. The deals offered by DDSs are typically geographically localized and include discounted prices to restaurants, cafes, event tickets, spa services etc. Groupon is a characteristic example of a DDS. Since its introduction in 2008, it has been one of the fastest-growing Internet-sales businesses in history. Groupon has since gone public, with its Initial Public Offering (IPO) valuing the company at almost 13 billion dollars.

The business model of DDSs: Every day, a DDS features a small number of *daily deals.* Each deal provides a discounted rate (usually a 40-60% discount) to some item or service. These deals are usually geographically localized, corresponding to services or products that are available to residents of a particular city or a bounded geographic area. For example, deals often correspond to discounted rates to a local restaurant or beauty salon. Every day, the registered DDS users receive an email that notifies them of the available daily deals in their area. Once a user decides to buy the discounted item, he logs in the DDS and expresses his interest in participating in the deal. If a sufficiently large number of users has expressed such interest by the end of a pre-specified period of availability (usually one or two days), the deal gets *materialized.* Then, the users who expressed interest get charged the pre-specified amount and are given a *coupon*, which they can subsequently use in return for the advertised service. In our work, we refer to the number of coupons sold per deal as the *size* of the deal. The *revenue* of the deal is then equal to its size multiplied by the price of the coupon. The DDS typically retains a percentage of the revenue of every deal. For example, for Groupon, a 50% [14] commision is applied on every deal.

Existing work on DDSs: The new e-commerce model adopted by DDSs has motivated a significant body of relevant work. Economists have tried to analyze the factors that affect the generated revenue [1], as well as the effect of daily deals on the merchants that provide the discounted services [11, 12]. More recently, data-mining researchers have been intrigued by the daily-deal phenomenon and conducted large-scale data-analytic studies on datasets from DDSs [5, 4, 21]. These studies focus on discovering (*i*) the effect of different factors on the revenue and size of daily deals [4], (*ii*) the effect of daily deals on customers' reviews [5] and (*iii*) the impact of the users' social network on the propagation of daily deals [21].

Our contribution: Although the above studies provide useful insights on some aspects of the daily-deal paradigm, the algorithmic problems that arise in this domain have not yet

[1]`www.groupon.com`
[2]`www.livingsocial.com`
[3]`http://www.amazon.com/gp/goldbox`

CIKM'12, October 29–November 2, 2012, Maui, HI, USA.

been tackled. In fact, despite the immense popularity of DDSs, there has been little research on modeling and solving the relevant computational problems in a principled and efficient manner. Our work is the first to formalize these problems and present appropriate algorithmic techniques for revenue-maximization. Specifically, the contributions of this paper are the following:

- Our work is the first to formalize the following problem: given a set of deals from local businesses, which of them should the DDS select, in order to maximize its expected revenue? In addition to revenue maximization, our formulation takes into account relevant factors with significant impact, such as the *diversity*[18, 15] of the selected set and the limited consuming *capacity* (size) of the market [7].
- From the computational point of view, we study two variants of the above problem, which we refer to as the DEAL SELECTION and the DEAL SCHEDULING problems. The first problem handles the selection of a set of deals for singly day, while the second one models a long-term scheduling strategy for multiple days. In a detailed analysis, we discuss the intricacies of the two problems and prove that they are both NP-hard.
- Considering the large amounts of data that need to be considered by a deal-selection algorithm, we identify the need for efficiency and scalability. Motivated by this, we present a pseudopolynomial optimal algorithm for the DEAL SELECTION problem, and a pseudopolynomial 2-approximation algorithm for the DEAL SCHEDULING problem. We also consider even more efficient heuristics for both problems, and use experiments on real data to demonstrate their competitiveness.
- In order for a deal-selection mechanism to be effective, it requires the ability to estimate the popularity and expected revenue of a deal. We develop a machine-learning methodology that estimates user-interest in a particular deal, by considering a number of contributing factors. These include, among others, the domain, location, and reputation of the participating merchant, the coupon price, and the discount percentage. Our framework performs well on real data and motivates interesting observations on the factors that affect the success of a deal.

Note that our algorithms for the DEAL SELECTION and DEAL SCHEDULING problems can also be applied *retrospectively* on a set of deals that have already been featured. The size and revenue of each deal are then already known. In this setting, our methods for deal-selection can be used to a-posteriori evaluate the strategies of deal allocation. While this is an interesting application, the ability to estimate the interest of users allows us to utilize our framework for *proactive* deal selection and scheduling. We consider this latter setting as the main application of our work.

Roadmap: The rest of the paper is organized as follows: in Section 2 we present the DEAL SELECTION and the DEAL SCHEDULING problems. In Section 4 we discuss our methodology for estimating user-interest in a daily deal. We discuss our experimental results in Section 5 and summarize related work in Section 6. We conclude the paper in Section 7.

2. DEAL SELECTION

In our setting, we focus on the operation of a DDS within a particular geographic area. Within each area, we assume that there are m possible *markets* $\mathcal{M} = \{M_1, \ldots, M_m\}$. Each market corresponds to a particular *type* of business, e.g., restaurants, beauty & spa, coffee shops etc. That is, all the businesses in a particular market serve the same needs for the users. Each market M_i consists of a set of n_i *businesses*. We assume the current mode of operation of DDSs, where each daily deal is about a single business.

Every business b, when featured as the vendor of a daily deal, has an *(expected) revenue*, denoted by $R(b)$. Typically, the revenue of a deal is computed by multiplying the price of the coupon with the (estimated) number of sold coupons (recall that the DDS keeps a constant percentage of this amount for every deal). We adopt this definition in our experiments. Alternatively, one could opt for a different instantiation of revenue (e.g. the number of new users that register to the DDS because of this deal). In addition, the DDS may choose to incorporate its marketing strategy to the revenue function. For example, this can be done by adopting a function that favors deals in emergent and promising markets, or deals from high-quality businesses that can help the public image of the DDS. In any case, our methodology is compatible with *any* definition of the revenue function.

A basic assumption in our framework is that it considers the financial, as well as the time-based resources of the registered DDS users. That is, users cannot spend an infinite amount of money, neither do they have the time to accept the services from a very large number of businesses within a limited time interval. Given the population of users (e.g., the registered users of a DDS), we use C to represent the population's *(consuming) capacity*. As with revenue, the capacity of the population can be quantified in different ways [4]. These include the total number of coupons the users are willing to buy, the total number of hours they can spend on recreational activities, and the total amount of dollars they can spend on coupons. In our experiments, we measure C using the total number of coupons the users are willing to buy within a fixed time interval. Capacity can be estimated in a number of different ways by the DDS. These include studying past coupon sales in area and considering the area's population, demographics and income levels. The estimation of capacity is an interesting problem that we plan to study in future work. In this paper, we assume that C is provided as part of the input, and explore its effect on revenue maximization in our experiments. Once a deal from a business b is materialized, it consumes a portion of C. We refer to this portion as the deal's *(expected) size* and denote it by $S(b)$.

The goal of the DDS is to select a set of deals that maximize each revenue within a pre-specified period of time (e.g., a day, a week or a month), given the limited consuming capacity of the user-base. In addition, our framework consider the additional constraint of *diversity* [18, 15]. This constraint enforces the diversification of the set of featured deals, ensuring that it includes different types of markets. In addition to providing users with more options, showing a diverse set also makes the set of deals appealing to a wider range of users. Further, the diversity constraint can be used to limit the number of deals from a specific market, based on estimates on

[4] `http://www.marketingprofs.com/Tutorials/marketsize1.asp`

the demand of the user-base for such deals. We capture this intuition by imposing an upper bound on the total number of deals that can be selected per market. That is, we impose that at most K_i deals with businesses from market M_i can be selected. Taking into consideration the capacity and diversity constraints, we formalize the problem as follows:

PROBLEM 1 (DEAL SELECTION). *Assume a population with capacity C and m markets $\mathcal{M} = \{M_1, \ldots, M_m\}$, where each market M_i includes of a set deals from different businesses. Then, given the expected revenue and size for each deal, select a set of deals $\mathcal{D}$ such that the total revenue*

$$\text{TOTALR}(\mathcal{D}) = \sum_{b \in \mathcal{D}} R(b)$$

is maximized and for every $i = 1, \ldots, m$

$$|\mathcal{D} \cap M_i| \leq K_i \text{ [diversity constraints]},$$

and

$$\sum_{b \in \mathcal{D}} S(b) \leq C \text{ [capacity constraint]}.$$

The above problem definition assumes that the K_i's and the value of C are given as part of the input. The effect of these parameters in the obtained results are demonstrated in the experimental section.

From the computational point of view, the DEAL SELECTION problem is NP-hard. This is due to the fact that DEAL SELECTION is a generalization of KNAPSACK, which is NP-hard [10]. More specifically, for $m = 1$ and $K_1 = n_1$, the problem is identical to KNAPSACK. In other words, our problem without the diversity constraints becomes identical to the KNAPSACK problem. The way the diversity constraints affect the algorithmic solution to the DEAL SELECTION problem is explored further in the next section.

2.1 An optimal algorithm for the DEAL SELECTION problem

In this section, we present an optimal algorithm for the DEAL SELECTION problem. Since our Problem 1 is a a generalization of the KNAPSACK problem [10], known techniques for the latter are not applicable. Therefore, we present a new algorithm, based on *nested dynamic-programming*, that is appropriate for our formulation. We refer to this algorithm as `DP-DP`.

In order to present the `DP-DP` algorithm we first need to define the *global revenue* and *market revenue* functions. The *global revenue* function, $\text{GR}(i, c)$, represents the maximum benefit of the optimal solution considering businesses from markets M_1 through M_i, and a population capacity equal to c. Using this definition, the optimal solution to the DEAL SELECTION problem corresponds to the value $\text{GR}(m, C)$.

Within a particular market M_i, we define the *market revenue* $\text{MR}_i(\ell, c, k)$ to be the maximum revenue that the DDS can earn from businesses in market M_i, given that (a) it can feature up to k out of the the first ℓ businesses of M_i, and (b) the total size of the selected businesses is no more than c. For a fixed capacity c, the optimal revenue that the DDS can have from market M_i is then $\text{MR}_i(n_i, c, K_i)$. Note that, although this definition assumes an order of the businesses within M_i, this order can be arbitrary.

Using the notation above, the optimal value of the optimization function TOTALR() (Problem 1) is equal to the value of $\text{GR}(m, C)$. Next, we show that the computation of $\text{GR}(m, C)$ can be done optimally using the following dynamic-programming recursion:

$$\text{GR}(m, C) = \max_{c=0,\ldots,C} \left\{ \text{GR}(m-1, C-c) + \text{MR}_m(n_m, c, K_m) \right\}. \tag{1}$$

Observe that the second term in the above recursion, (i.e., $\text{MR}_m(n_m, c, K_m)$ is the optimal revenue from market M_m given that only K_m businesses can be selected from M_m and the capacity allocated to this market can be at most c.

In order to compute the value of $\text{MR}_m(n_m, c, K_m)$, we need to invoke another dynamic-programming computation; in this case the recursion requires the evaluation of a 3-dimensional table. Next, we show the recursion for evaluating this table for market M_i. Observe that the same recursion can be used for every $i \in \{1, \ldots, m\}$. If for every market M_i we assume that the businesses within M_i are arranged in some random order $b_1, \ldots, b_{n_i}$, then we can evaluate $\text{MR}_i(n_i, c, K_i)$ using the following recursion:

$$\begin{aligned} \text{MR}_i(n_i, c, K_i) = & \\ \max & \left\{ \text{MR}_i(n_i - 1, c, K_i), \right. \\ & \left. \text{MR}_i(n_i - 1, c - S(b_{n_i}), k_i - 1) + R(b_{n_i}) \right\}. \end{aligned} \tag{2}$$

This recursion can be evaluated using dynamic programming. Observe that the running time for evaluating Recursion (2) is $O(n_i C K_i)$. One such evaluation needs to be done for each one of the m markets. However, since every business belongs to only one market, these computations can be done separately (and in parallel) for every market. Given that the values $\text{MR}_i(n_i, c, K_i)$ are precomputed, evaluating Recursion (1) requires $O(mC^2)$ time. Therefore, the running time of the `DP-DP` algorithm depends on C, which is not necessarily polynomial in the size of the input, making the overall running time of `DP-DP` to be pseudopolynomial.

Evaluating the dynamic-programming recursion expressed in Equation (1) requires another dynamic-programming computation, i.e., the one expressed by Recursion 2. For that reason, we say that `DP-DP` is a *nested dynamic-programming* algorithm. For `DP-DP`, we can state the following:

LEMMA 1. *The* `DP-DP` *algorithm solves the* DEAL SELECTION *problem optimally.*

If each market M_i is viewed as a super-item with revenue given by the function $\text{MR}_i()$, then Recursion (1) is a standard KNAPSACK-type recursion that computes the optimal global revenue $\text{GR}(m, C)$. In turn, the optimality of the market-revenue values can be argued through Recursion (2). In this recursion, the optimal values for every $\text{MR}_i(n_i, C, K_i)$ are computed. Given optimal market revenues, the global revenue computed by Recursion 1 is also optimal.

2.2 Efficient heuristics for the DEAL SELECTION problem

Although solving the DEAL SELECTION problem is an offline computation for the DDSs, the computational complexity of `DP-DP` could make it inefficient for very large datasets. In this section, we present some alternative heuristic algorithms for the DEAL SELECTION problem. As we show in our experiments, this algorithms achieve high-revenue solutions, while having a clear advantage over DP-DP in terms of computational cost.

The Fast-DP algorithm: The Fast-DP algorithm is based on the same principles as DP-DP. However, Fast-DP sacrifices optimality for efficiency. Recall that the inefficiency of DP-DP is due to the fact that the dynamic-programming tables GR and MR_i for $i = 1 \dots m$ have a single dimension of size C. When the value of C is very large, then DP-DP becomes rather inefficient. We overcome this computational problem by splitting the value of C into intervals (buckets) of size c. This way, the dimensionality of the dynamic-programming tables GR and MR_i for $i = 1 \dots m$ reduces to $m \times C/c$ and $n_i \times K_i \times C/c$ respectively. Therefore, instead of computing the global and the market revenue functions for all possible number of coupons, we only compute their values for increments of size c. We refer to this version of the DP-DP algorithm as Fast-DP(c); we parameterize it with the value of the increment c. In our experiments, we consider two values of c, namely $c = 10$ and $c = 100$. Other than that, Fast-DP is also a nested dynamic-programming algorithm that evaluates Equations (1) and (2) in a manner identical to that of DP-DP. The only difference is that Fast-DP operates on dynamic-programming tables that keep less information and have smaller size.

Observe that creating buckets of size c does not decrease the worst-case running time of Fast-DP, which remains equal to that of DP-DP. However, our experiments illustrate that, in practice, the Fast-DP algorithm is considerably faster than DP-DP, while achieving near-optimal revenue.

The Sort algorithm: The Sort algorithm is a heuristic approach that ignores the categorization of businesses into markets. The algorithm first sorts all the available businesses in decreasing order of the *sorting criterion*. Then, it traverses the set of businesses in this order and adds into the solution a deal with every business that satisfies the diversity and capacity constraints. Given that the sorting criterion can be computed for every business in constant time, the running time of the Sort algorithm is $O(n \log n)$. In our case we sort the businesses using the benefit-to-size ratio (BSR). Given business b, the benefit-to-size ratio of b is $\text{BSR}(b) = R(b)/S(b)$.

3. DEAL SCHEDULING

In this section, we explore the scenario where the DDS wants to schedule multiple sets of deals to be presented at different time intervals (e.g. days), instead of selecting a single set.

PROBLEM 2 (DEAL SCHEDULING)). *Assume a sequence of time intervals $T = \{t_1, \dots, t_k\}$. and a population that has the same capacity C at every interval. Additionally, assume m markets $\mathcal{M} = \{M_1, \dots, M_m\}$, where each market M_i consists of n_i deals from different businesses. Then, given the expected revenue and size for every deal, select the set of deals $\mathcal{D}_t$ to feature at every interval, such that every deal is featured only once and the following value is maximized (i.e. the total revenue of the DDS):*

$$\text{TOTALR}(\mathcal{D}_1, \dots, \mathcal{D}_t) = \sum_{t \in T} \sum_{b \in \mathcal{D}_t} R(b)$$

under the following constraints:

for every $t \in T$ and $i = 1, \dots, m$

$$|M_i \cap \mathcal{D}_t| \leq K_i \text{ [diversity constraint]}$$

for every $t \in \{1, \dots, T\}$

$$\sum_{b \in \mathcal{D}_t} S(b) \leq C \text{ [capacity constraint]}.$$

Observe that, in the definition of Problem 2, we have assumed that the revenue and the size of every deal are fixed across time intervals. A similar assumption was made for the population capacity, which remains the same across intervals. Although we make these assumptions for clarity of presentation, our algorithmic results carry over for the case where these parameters are different for each time interval.

The DEAL SCHEDULING problem is a generalization of the DEAL SELECTION problem and, therefore, it is also NP-hard. In fact, one can observe that the DEAL SCHEDULING problem is a generalized version of the MULTIPLE KNAPSACK problem [8]; for $m = 1$, the DEAL SCHEDULING problem is identical to the MULTIPLE KNAPSACK problem.

3.1 An algorithm for DEAL SCHEDULING

We solve the DEAL SCHEDULING problem using a greedy algorithm that works as follows. Let $\mathcal{M}^{(t)}$ be the set of deals that have not been selected up to time t. Then, the algorithm solves the DEAL SELECTION problem using $\mathcal{M}^{(t)}$ as input. Any of the the DP-DP, Fast-DP or Sort algorithms can be used for solving this problem. Let $\mathcal{D}_t$ be the set of deals selected by this step. Then, we get $\mathcal{M}^{(t+1)} = \mathcal{M}^{(t)} \setminus \mathcal{D}_t$, which is used as input to the DEAL SELECTION problem that needs to be solved for interval $(t+1)$. We refer to this algorithm as the **GreedySchedule** algorithm. Depending on the algorithm we use for solving the DEAL SELECTION problem at every interval t, we get a different version of the **GreedySchedule**. We denote the different versions as **GreedySchedule**(A) for $A = \{$DP-DP, Fast-DP, Sort $\}$. Clearly, the running time of the **GreedySchedule** algorithm is T times the running time of the algorithm that is used for solving the DEAL SELECTION problem, where T is the number of time intervals for which a different set of deals needs to be selected.

By applying the results of Cohen *et al.* [9] to our problem, we get the following result.

LEMMA 2. *The* **GreedySchedule***(DP-DP) algorithm is a 2-approximation algorithm for the* DEAL SCHEDULING *problem.*

Although we omit the complete proof, we simply state here that the results of Cohen *et al.*, translated to our setting, state that the **GreedySchedule**(A) algorithm is an $(1 + \alpha)$ approximation for the the DEAL SCHEDULING problem. The factor α in this statement corresponds to the approximation factor achieved by algorithm A, which is used to solve the DEAL SELECTION problem. When A is DP-DP, then $\alpha = 1$, since DP-DP is optimal for the DEAL SELECTION problem. Therefore, **GreedySchedule**(DP-DP) is a 2-approximation algorithm for the DEAL SCHEDULING problem.

4. ESTIMATING DEAL SIZE

Our framework for DEAL SELECTION and DEAL SCHEDULING assumes that we can estimate the expected size and revenue for every deal. The size of the deal is taken to be equal to the number of coupons that it is estimated to sell. The revenue can then be computed as the size multiplied by the price of the coupon. Since the price of the coupon is set by the merchant and is provided as input, we focus our efforts to estimating the size of the deal.

A naive way of predicting the size of a deal is by observing the sequence of past daily deals and then using the average observed size as an estimator. Obviously, this method disregards the impact of a number of factors that can greatly affect the number of coupons that a deal sells. Identifying these factors and measuring their effect on the size of the deal is a very challenging task. First, we describe the factors that we consider in our work, and discuss how they can be learned from real data. We then incorporate these factors into a machine-learning framework that predicts the size of a given deal. Given a candidate deal, we consider the following factors that can affect its outcome:

Deal location: Each deal is usually available in a particular city or area. It is likely that people in different cities have different tendencies and preferences with respect to different types of offers. Therefore, we consider the location of the merchant (or service) as a factor that influences the size of the deal. Information about a deal's location is usually made available on the DDS's website and is thus easy to retrieve.

Business reputation: DDSs serve as mediators between the users and the merchants. As in every e-commerce model, the reputation of the merchant can greatly affect the number of interested customers. For example, an offer for a restaurant with poor reputation is less likely to be popular.

For some types of merchants (e.g. restaurants), reputation can be quantified using the reviews that have been submitted by users. For example, one can adopt the average star rating or some other review-based quality measure to estimate the reputation of a restaurant. However, for other merchants, reviews may be unavailable or extremely rare. To address this, we quantify the reputation of a business by tapping into an additional resource: the popularity of the merchant's *website*. A number of portals exists that are dedicated to website-evaluation. Arguably, the most well-known among these portals is Alexa (`www.alexa.com`). For each website, Alexa reports two interesting popularity measures: the *global traffic rank* and the website's *reputation*. The former is based on the amount of traffic observed for the site. The latter quantifies popularity by counting the number of incoming hyperlinks to the site. Our intuition is that the reputation of a merchant's website is a reflection of the merchant's overall reputation and popularity. For example, a coupon for a well known, high-profile spa center is more attractive than one from a recently opened competitor. Such phenomena are bound to be captured by considering the popularity of the respective websites. In our experiments, we consider both user reviews and website-evaluation measures as factors that affect the size of a candidate deal.

Business type: The type of the offered product or service (e.g., spa, restaurant, ticketed event etc) is also expected to play a critical role with regards to the deal's selling potential. Although users can identify the type of a deal very easily, the automated extraction of a deal's type by crawling the DDS's website is not a trivial task. The challenge lies in the fact that deals are typically organized on the DDS's website by city, and the type is not always explicitly stated. For the user viewing the deal's page on the website, the type is made clear by pictures and textual information such as the title and the accompanying text. However, in order to automatically deduce the type of a deal, we need a method that can parse the deal's accompanying text and decide the type of the featured business. For this purpose, we use Latent Dirichlet Allocation (LDA) [3]. LDA is a well-known technique used to learn the topic distribution of each document in a given corpus, as well as the term distribution of each distinct topic. In our context, the text that accompanies each deal serves as a single document. We can then group deals based on the assigned topic distribution. One can think that different topics correspond to different markets. More details of this process are given in the experiments section.

Price: Intuitively, a lower-cost deal is expected to sell more than an expensive one. After all, cheap deals are attractive to a wider range of customers. The price of a deal is easy to retrieve, since it is always made available by the DDS.

Discount: The key for the DDSs' success is that they offer products and services at a rate lower than their standard market-price. The size of the discount is thus another factor to be considered, in addition to the price. For example, even though the price of a deal may be high, the deal can still be attractive if it applies a significant discount to the standard market-price. The original value and the offered discount are available in virtually every daily-deal website. **Seasonality:**

Another feature we extract from our data is the time of the year when the offer is made available. For example, it may be the case that people are more likely to opt for solarium treatments before or during the summer months.

Tipping point: The tipping point of a deal is the minimum number of users that need to express interest, in order for the deal to be materialized. This captures the fact that merchants are willing to offer their services at the discounted price only if the DDS guarantees to them a significantly large number of customers. Daily deals featuring established merchants will attract larger number of users and can thus tolerate larger tipping points. Hence, we consider the tipping point as a factor that could correlate with the size of the deal.

Using the above factors as dimensions, we represent every candidate deal as a point in the respective multidimensional space. We can then define the problem of estimating the number of coupons as a regression or classification problem, where the goal is to use the training data to build a model that can then estimate the size of a deal. Our own estimation mechanism is based on regression. Our experiments with different regression mechanisms revealed that the SVM-based regression model suggested by Shevade *et al.* [20] gave the best results. We evaluate our methodology on real datasets in Section 5.4 of the experiments, and present interesting findings that provide valuable insight on the estimation task.

5. EXPERIMENTS

In this section, we describe the experimental evaluation that we performed to verify the efficacy of our methodology. The section is organized as follows: first, we describe the dataset that we use in our experiments. Then, we present the evaluation of our algorithms for solving the DEAL SELECTION and the DEAL SCHEDULING problems. Our evaluation focuses both on the quality of the obtained solutions (as expressed by the objective function, i.e., the total revenue) and on the running time of the algorithms. Finally, we conclude this section with an evaluation of our machine-learning framework for estimating the size of daily deals.

5.1 Data

In order to evaluate our methodology, we collected a set of $n = 100,000$ materialized and closed (i.e., past) deals offered by Groupon. These are deals that started within the last six months, coming from all divisions (i.e., cities) in which Groupon features daily deals. For each deal, we extracted the following set of attributes: the date, the city of the merchant featured in the deal, the name of the merchant, the price of the offered coupon, the discount from the original value, the number of coupons sold, the descriptive text accompanying the deal, and the merchant's website. For every merchant that was featured in a deal, we also quantified the merchant's reputation in the following two ways. First, using the URL of the merchant's website, we probed Alexa (`www.alexa.com` to retrieve the website's *Rank* and *Reputation* scores. The first score quantifies the reputation of the website using as indication the observed traffic. The second score quantifies the website's reputation based on the number of sites that point to the merchant's website. In addition to using Alexa's scores, we quantify the reputation of a merchant based on user reviews. Given the name of the merchant appearing in the deal, we probe the popular review-hosting site Yelp (`www.yelp.com`) and we retrieve the set of reviews for this merchant that are available at Yelp. We do this either by directly querying Yelp for the merchant's name or by following the link to Yelp that is often in Groupon's page for the deal.

Further, we identify the market that each deal belongs to (i.e. its type). This refers to the type of service that the deal is offering (e.g. restaurants, spas, gym memberships etc.). Unfortunately, the type of each deal is not explicitly mentioned by the DDS. However, since we believe that this is an important feature that will allow us to predict the deal's performance, we learn the type of using the descriptive text of the deal as shown on the DDS website. As we have already described in Section 4, we do this by applying LDA to the dataset of collected deals. We learn a model consisting of 50 topics. The number 50 was chosen after experimentation with different numbers. An inspection of the term distribution of the learned topics showed that this number led to cohesive topics that represent real-life concepts. Therefore, our dataset has $m = 50$ distinct markets and each business belongs to one of these markets (or types). Each deal is assigned to the market corresponding to the topic with the highest probability in the deal's topic distribution.

5.2 Evaluating the algorithms for the DEAL SELECTION problem

In this section, we explore the behavior of the `DP-DP`, `Fast-DP` and `Sort` algorithms for the different values of the parameters of the DEAL SELECTION problem. For each experiment we report the value of the objective function (TOTALR) that was achieved by every algorithm, as well as the running time for every approach. For all our experiments, we use two instantiations of the `Fast-DP` algorithm, namely `Fast-DP`(10) and `Fast-DP`(100). In the first instantiation, we consider coupon increments of size 10, while in the second we consider increments of size 100. For these experiments we use the dataset we collected from Groupon and we described in Section 5.1. Recall that this dataset consists of $n = 100,000$ deals and $m = 50$ different markets.

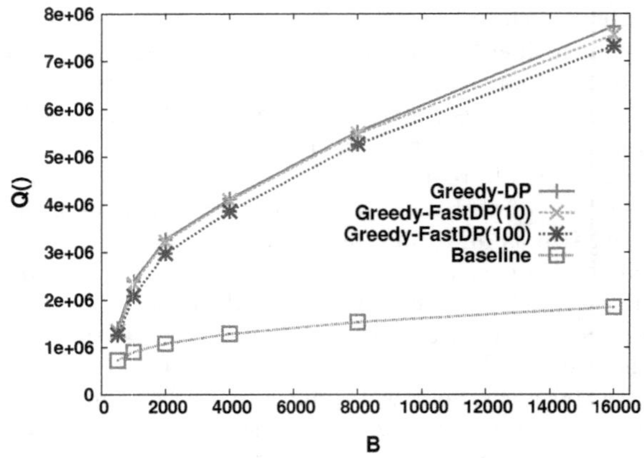

(a) Total revenue (TOTALR).

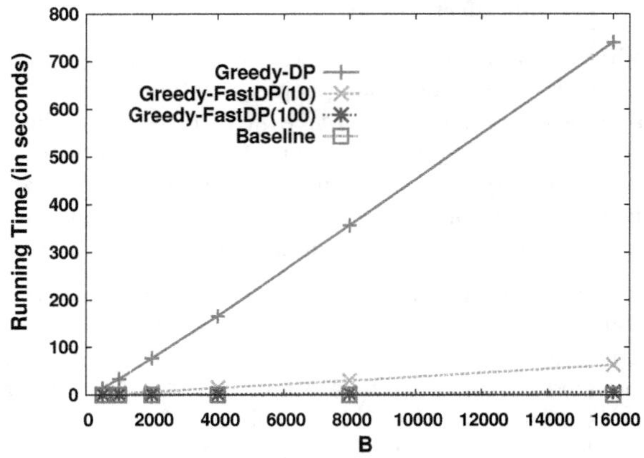

(b) Running time in seconds.

Figure 1: Total Revenue (Figure 1(a)) and Running Time (Figure 1(b)) of `DP-DP`, `Fast-DP`(10), `Fast-DP`(100) and `Sort` algorithms, as a function of the consuming capacity C of the population: $C \in \{500, 1000, 2000, 4000, 8000\}$. For all markets $i \in \{1, \ldots, 50\}$, $K_i = K = 50$.

5.2.1 Exploring the effect of the capacity constraint

First, we report the value of the total revenue (TOTALR) and the running times of the `DP-DP`, `Fast-DP` and `Sort` algorithms as a function of the population's consuming capacity C. For this, we experiment with values of $C \in \{500, 1000, 2000, 4000, 8000\}$. We also set the value K_i for all 50 markets to be equal to 3; i.e., $K_i = K = 3$. The total revenue of the solutions found by the different algorithms are shown in Figure 1(a). The corresponding running times for each one of the algorithms is shown in Figure 1(b).

As can be seen from Figure 1(a), all the versions of the nested dynamic-programming algorithms (i.e., `DP-DP`, `Fast-DP`(10) and `Fast-DP`(100)) clearly outperform `Sort`. That is, these algorithms report sets of deals that have significantly higher revenue. It is worth observing that `Fast-DP`(10) is extremely competitive, achieving almost-optimal values for all values of C. In addition, while the gap in revenue between `Fast-DP`(100) and the optimal `DP-DP` algorithm is larger than the gap between `Fast-DP`(10) and `DP-DP`, the revenue achieved by Fast-DP(100) is still competitive, and consistently outmatches Sort.

The results on the revenue of the obtained solutions should be seen together with the actual running times of these algorithms. These are shown in Figure 1(b). The observed running times demonstrate that although DP-DP is feasible to use in real data, it is still significantly slower than the rest of the algorithms. As expected, the Sort algorithm is the fastest, yet its results are the worse in terms of revenue. Noteworthy is the performance of Fast-DP(10) and Fast-DP(100); both algorithms achieve very low running times. This observation, combined with the near-optimal solutions reported by these algorithms, indicates that Fast-DP is an effective algorithmic solution to the DEAL SELECTION problem, providing a balance of efficiency and quality. This observation is consolidated by the experiments that follow.

5.2.2 *Exploring the effect of the diversity constraints*

In this experiment, we explore the effect of the diversity constraints on the performance of the different algorithms. For this we consider that the same upper bound on the number of same-market deals is imposed for all 50 markets. That is for every market i we assume that $K_i = K$. Given this, we report the total revenue achieved by the different algorithms (Figure 2(a)) and the corresponding running times (Figure 2(b)) as a function of $K \in \{1, 2, 3, 4, 5\}$. For this experiment, the value of C is set to 5000. The findings of this experiment are similar to the ones we reported in the previous section. As anticipated, larger values of K allow for more flexibility, and thus lead to higher revenues. As can be seen from Figure 2(a), the algorithms that are based on the nested dynamic-programing principle utilize this increased flexibility; all three of them clearly outperform Sort for all values of K. Again, Fast-DP(10) achieves near-optimal revenue values, overcoming Sort and even Fast-DP(100) – which is still extremely competitive.

The running times reported in Figure 2(b) verify our previous observation that Fast-DP(10) can combine near-optimal results with low computational times. This makes Fast-DP ideal to use in real settings, where the number of deals is large.

5.2.3 *Scalability experiment*

In this section, we evaluate the scalability of the algorithms for DEAL SELECTION, as a function of the number of candidate deals n. For this experiment, we fix $C = 5000$ and for each market i we use the same value of $K_i = K = 3$. Given the original dataset consisting of $N = 100,000$ deals, we create four more datasets by randomly sampling $N/16$, $N/8$, $N/4$ and $N/2$ deals from the whole collection. Then, we run DP-DP, Fast-DP(10), Fast-DP(100) and Sort on each one of the five datasets. In Figures 3(a) and 3(b) we show the total revenue and the running times of these algorithms as a function of the number of deals in the input. The results shown in Figures 3(a) and 3(b) consolidate the findings of the previous experiments, and are a testament to the scalability and effectiveness of the Fast-DP algorithm. Both variants of this approach follow the optimal DP-DP very closely in terms of the achieved revenue. This fact becomes more impressive as one considers the small running time of these two algorithms, demonstrated in Figure 3(b). In fact, Fast-DP algorithms are able to solve the DEAL SELECTION problem for even the largest of our datasets within few seconds. In

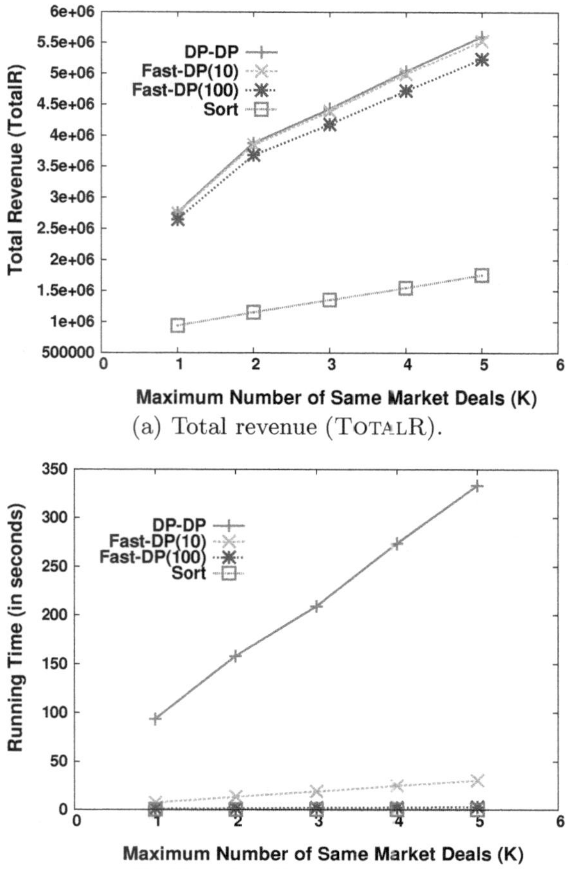

(a) Total revenue (TOTALR).

(b) Running time in seconds.

Figure 2: Total Revenue (Figure 2(a)) and Running Time (Figure 2(b)) of DP-DP, Fast-DP(10), Fast-DP(100) and Sort algorithms, as a function of the number of the upper bound K on the number of same-type deals: $K \in \{1, 2, 3, 4, 5\}$; $C = 5000$.

our experiments, the running time of these two algorithms is comparable to the running time of Sort. However, the latter fails to find solutions of satisfactory revenue. Finally, as anticipated, the optimal DP-DP algorithm fails in terms of scalability, as its computational time rises fast with the size of the input.

Combining the above scalability results with the findings we reported in the previous experiments, it becomes clear that Fast-DP is by far the most attractive algorithm for the DEAL SELECTION problem, since it consistently offers a combination of near-optimal solutions at a low computational cost.

5.3 Evaluating the algorithms for the DEAL SCHEDULING problem

Here, we study the performance of the GreedySchedule algorithm for the DEAL SCHEDULING problem. As we have already discussed, GreedySchedule is parameterized on the algorithm A, that it invokes for solving the DEAL SELECTION problem for every interval. For solving the DEAL SELECTION problem we use the four algorithms we experimented with in the previous section. That is, $A \in$ { DP-DP, Fast-DP(10), Fast-DP(100), Sort }. We experiment with the

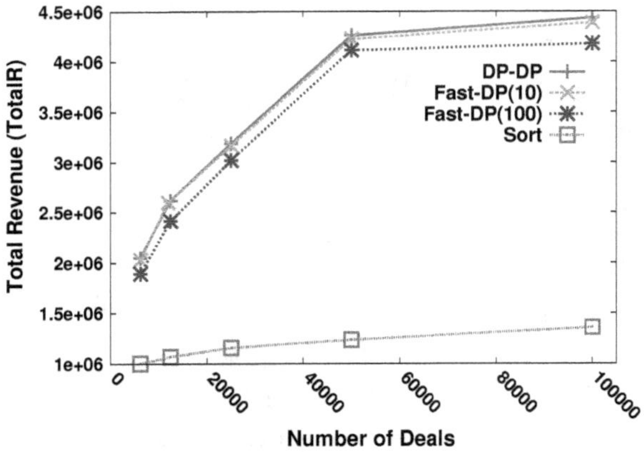

(a) Total revenue (TOTALR).

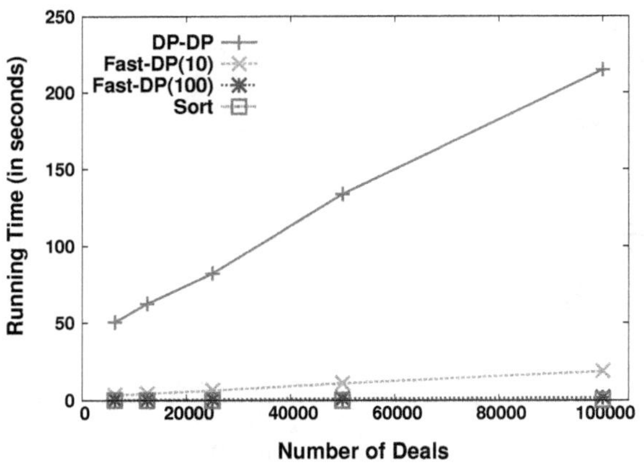

(b) Running time in seconds.

Figure 3: Total Revenue (Figure 3(a)) and Running Time (Figure 3(b)) of `DP-DP`, `Fast-DP`(10), `Fast-DP`(100) and `Sort` algorithms, as a function of the number of deals n in the input: $n \in \{N/16, N/8, N/4, N/2, N\}$ with $N = 100,000$. For all experiments, $C = 5000$ and $K_i = K = 3$ for all $i \in \{1, \ldots, 50\}$.

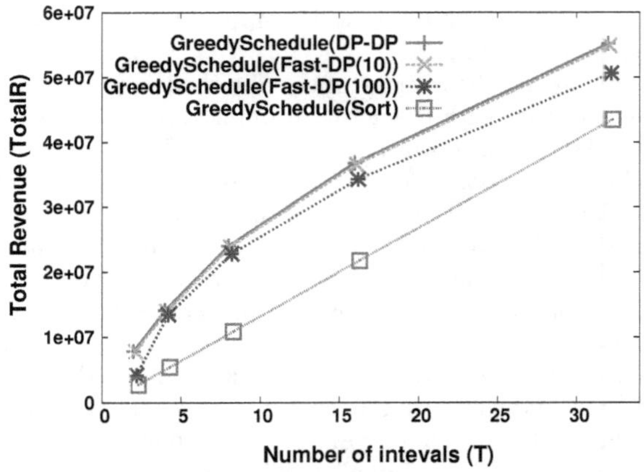

(a) Total revenue (TOTALR).

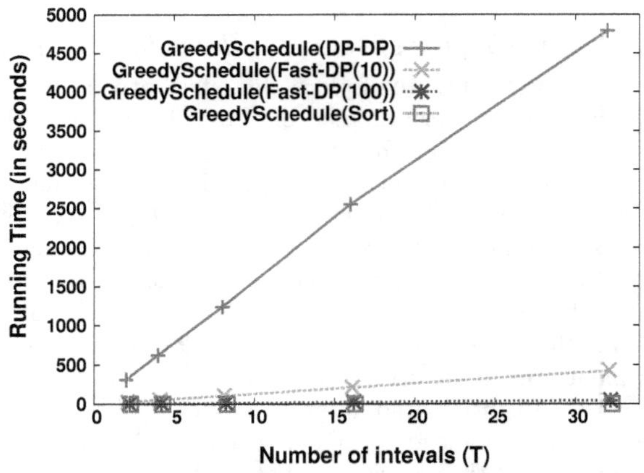

(b) Running time in seconds.

Figure 4: Total Revenue (Figure 4(a)) and Running Time (Figure 4(b)) of the `GreedySchedule`(A) algorithm, where $A \in \{$ `DP-DP`, `Fast-DP`(10), `Fast-DP`(100), `Sort`$\}$, as a function of the number of intervals T. For every interval T, $C = 5000$ and $K_i = K = 3$ for all $i \in \{1, \ldots, 50\}$.

dataset we described in Section 5.1, which consists of a set of 100,000 candidate deals and 50 markets. We report results for $T \in \{2, 4, 8, 16, 32\}$. Following the setup and findings of the previous experiments, we set the maximum number of same-market deals to be the same across markets (i.e., ($K_i = K = 3$ for all $i \in \{1, \ldots, 50\}$). We also assume that, for each interval, the population's capacity is the same and equal to $C = 5000$. The results for revenue and computational time achieved by `GreedySchedule`(A) are shown in Figures 4(a) and 4(b), respectively.

Clearly, the performance of `GreedySchedule`(A) is correlated with the performance of the algorithm that it uses for the DEAL SELECTION problem (algorithm A). Specifically, when either version of `Fast-DP` is used, `GreedySchedule`(A) achieves both low computational cost and high-revenue solutions. The revenue achieved by `GreedySchedule(Fast-DP`(10)) is almost identical to that achieved by `GreedySchedule` (`DP-DP`). In fact, even `GreedySchedule(Fast-DP`(100)) achieves near optimal solutions. On the other hand, while the revenue of `GreedySchedule(Sort)` increases with the number of intervals, its results are far from optimal.

5.4 Deal-size estimation

In this section, we evaluate our methodology for estimating the size of deals, i.e., the number of coupons they are expected to sell. For this experiment, we use the dataset described in Section 5.1. As discussed in Section 4, we consider a rich set of features for each deal. Given these features, we estimate deal-size by using the SVM-based regression method proposed by Shevade *at al.* [20]. We measure the accuracy of our framework using two standard measures: the *correlation coefficient* (CC) and the *mean absolute error* (MAE). For a given set of deals, CC is the value of the Pearson correlation coefficient between the actual and the predicted sizes for these deals. Similarly, the MAE is the average absolute difference between the actual and the predicted sizes. We use the absolute (rather than the relative) error for the evaluation of the accuracy because our algorithms for the DEAL SELECTION and the DEAL SCHEDULING problems take the actual size of the deals as input. Therefore, our goal is to measure the error that our predictor introduces in the input given to the corresponding algorithms for the two problems.

Market-based grouping of deals: A careful inspection of our data reveals that, although the 50 markets discovered by

LDA correspond to real-life concepts, many of these markets are really sparse, i.e., the have a small number of businesses in them. Further inspection of the term distribution of the original 50 markets reveals that they can be further clustered into larger *marketgroups* that correspond to more general markets. For example, the following 8 of the 50 markets can be classified under a more general food-related marketgroup: *Indian cuisine, pizza, Japanese cuisine, Mediterranean cuisine, Spanish cuisine, restaurants, chocolate & sweets, organic & healthy food.* Another identified marketgroup is "personal care", consisting of the topics *tanning, hair & beauty, skin & face treatment, massage.* Intuitively, we expect deals that belong in the same marketgroup to follow similar trends with respect to their appeal to the population. Given these observations, we use the Kullback-Liebler distance to cluster the initial 50 markets into 12 marketgroups (based on their term distributions). In this way, each original deal is associated with one marketgroup, namely the marketgroup that contains the original market of the deal. Alternatively, one could use a clustering method such as hierarchical LDA [2].

Given the 12 marketgroups, our regression mechanism builds a different regression model for each marketgroup. Note that the grouping of markets into marketgroups serves two purposes: first, by merging the original markets it increases the density of our data. Second, it provides a way of predicting the size of businesses that belong to smaller or nascent markets that are strongly correlated with denser markets.

The CC and MAE obtained for the deals within each of the discovered marketgroups are shown in the 2nd and 3rd columns of Table 1, respectively. One can observe that the CC values are more than 0.5 for most markets. The observed MAE is also a relatively small number when compared to the actual size of the deals, which is in the order of thousands of coupons.

Location-based grouping of deals: While the results obtained using this regression mechanism are promising, they remain far from perfect, especially for specific markets. Motivated by this, we enhance our methodology by applying a location-based partitioning of the deals.

Our experiments indicate that the city where the deal takes place (i.e., the deal's location) is an extremely influential feature in the context of size estimation. This is indeed a reasonable and easily interpretable finding: customers from a particular city share common preferences and requirements (e.g motivated by geography or local trends), which may be different from the preferences of people from other areas.

Taking this finding into consideration, we use the city of every deal to further partition the set of deals into groups that share the same marketgroup *and* the same city. In this case, for every (marketgroup,city) combination we have a different regression model. The results for this are shown are shown in the 2nd and 3rd columns of Table 1, respectively. These are the average values of the CC and the MAE of the models used for every city for all the deals that belong in the same marketgroup. As can be seen from the table, the results are clearly better than those reported without the location-based grouping step. This is true both for the CC (which now exhibits higher values) and the MAE (which exhibits lower values). Observe that, in many of the cases, CC values are near-perfect (very close to 1). In addition, the observed MAE values are consistently low, indicating that the predicted values were close to the actual size of the deals. Again, one should consider the MAE values as indicative of how much error the regression model introduces to the input of the DEAL SELECTION and DEAL SCHEDULING problems. Observe, that the largest error is no more than 185 coupons for deals that actually sell thousands.

6. RELATED WORK

Most of the published work on DDSs focuses on data-analytic studies and economic models that try to explain several phenomena in the domain of daily-deals. However, to the best of our knowledge, our work is the first to exploit data-analytic findings in order to solve a combinatorial problem that arises in this context.

Recent work by Byers *et al.* [4] has extensively analyzed the characteristics of daily-deals and the predictability of the success of a particular deal. Another relevant line or work [5, 19, 6, 17] has focused on the propagation of daily deals in social networks, as well as the effect that deals have on the customer reviews written for different businesses after their corresponding deal materializes. The data-analysis performed by Byers *et al.* provides a comprehensive view of the daily-deals domain and the social and business effects associated with it. In another relevant paper, Ye *et al.* [21] analyze data from daily-deal sites to study the propagation of daily deals within a social network. We consider our own work complementary to these efforts. Our focus is to analyze daily-deal datasets, and use our findings to create selection and scheduling algorithms for revenue maximization.

Models for evaluating the benefits and the drawbacks of Groupon from the point of view of the merchant have been considered by Edelman *et al.* [12]. Along the same lines, Dholokia [11] performed an empirical study on the experience of businesses that used Groupon. Finally, models that allow for merchants to analyze the business model of Groupon and identify the optimal ways to participate in DDSs has been studied by Arabshasi [1]. Although related, these papers are complementary to ours since they focus on analyzing and modeling the experience of the merchant, while our focus is to maximize the benefit of the DDS.

Kauffman and Wang [16] studied group-buying paradigms that can be considered as alternatives to DDSs. The focus of that work was to empirically analyze behavioral patterns customer data from `MobShop.com`. Finally, Grabchak et al. [13] explore a variant of the stochastic knapsack problem for online Ad campaigns. Their relevance to our work is limited to the fact that they consider a model similar to Groupon's mass-deal setting, in which a deal is activated only if a minimum number of users opt for it. Nonetheless, their application setting, problem formulation and algorithmic contribution are radically different from ours.

7. CONCLUSIONS

In this paper, we studied the problem of selecting daily deals in order to maximize the expected revenue of the DDS. We provided two combinatorial formulations for this problem and proposed algorithms for their solution. Both formulations take into account natural constraints, such as the limited consuming ability of the population and the diversification of deals across different markets. Our algorithms combine greedy and dynamic-programming techniques and have provable approximation bounds. We also discussed efficient variants of these algorithms that perform extremely well in practice. In order to utilize our deal-selection frame-

Table 1: Regression results per marketgroup: Correlation Coefficient (CC) and Mean Absolute Error (MAE)

	(Without location-based grouping)		(With location-based grouping)	
Marketgroup	**CC**	**MAE**	**CC**	**MAE**
Food	0.26	385.08	0.67	185.07
Personal Care	0.44	248.14	0.76	65.14
Art & Photography	0.54	105.84	0.84	25.91
Fashion & Apparel	0.6073	159.9062	0.72	50.38
Children/Parenthood	0.504	234.96	0.81	42.76
Fitness	0.57	118.015	0.81	43.65
Cars	0.52	207.50	0.91	37.25
Cinema/Theater	0.4717	173.95	0.7	19.51
Medical	0.5952	51.19	0.95	3.56
Hunting & Fishing	0.6653	175.61	0.96	31.72
Bed and Breakfast	0.52	170.92	0.96	46.91
Bowling	0.65	92.34	0.97	11.13

work, the DDS needs to have an estimate of how popular a deal about a particular business (or service) is going to be. We showed that predicting the popularity of a daily deal is feasible, given a set of different characteristics of the deal. Our experimental results demonstrated the efficacy of our algorithms for deal selection and scheduling, and the accuracy of our predictor for the success of a deal. Our work opens up a lot of directions for further research. For example, in the future, we plan to explore how correlations between businesses or markets, as well as external parameters (e.g., news stories, political and economic events), can help DDSs towards even more effective choices.

8. REFERENCES

[1] A. Arabshahi. Undressing groupon: An analysis of the groupon business model. 2010. Available at: `http://www.ahmadalia.com`.

[2] D. M. Blei, T. L. Griffiths, M. I. Jordan, and J. B. Tenenbaum. Hierarchical topic models and the nested chinese restaurant process. In *NIPS*, 2003.

[3] D. M. Blei, A. Y. Ng, and M. I. Jordan. Latent dirichlet allocation. *J. Mach. Learn. Res.*, 3:993–1022, 2003.

[4] J. W. Byers, M. Mitzenmacher, M. Potamias, and G. Zervas. A month in the life of groupon. *CoRR*, 2011.

[5] J. W. Byers, M. Mitzenmacher, and G. Zervas. Daily deals: Prediction, social diffusion, and reputational ramifications. *CoRR*, 2011.

[6] J. W. Byers, M. Mitzenmacher, and G. Zervas. The groupon effect on yelp ratings: A root cause analysis. *CoRR*, abs/1202.2369, 2012.

[7] J. R. Campbell and H. A. Hopenhayn. Market size matters. Working Paper 9113, National Bureau of Economic Research, August 2002.

[8] C. Chekuri and S. Khanna. A polynomial time approximation scheme for the multiple knapsack problem. *SIAM J. Comput.*, 35(3):713–728, 2005.

[9] R. Cohen, L. Katzir, and D. Raz. An efficient approximation for the generalized assignment problem. *Inf. Process. Lett.*, 100(4):162–166, 2006.

[10] T. H. Cormen, C. E. Leiserson, R. L. Rivest, and C. Stein. *Introduction to Algorithms.* MIT Press and McGraw-Hill, 1990.

[11] U. M. Dholakia. How effective are groupon promotions for businesses. 2010. Available at: `http://www.ruf.rice.edu/~dholakia`.

[12] B. Edelman, S. Jae, and S. Kominers. To groupon or not to groupon: The profitability of deep discounts. 2010. Available at: `http://www.scottkom.com/research.html`.

[13] M. Grabchak, N. Bhamidipati, R. Bhatt, and D. Garg. Adaptive policies for selecting groupon style chunked reward ads in a stochastic knapsack framework. WWW '11.

[14] Groupon, inc. s-1 filing. filed with the u.s. securities and exchange commission, 2011.

[15] A. I. Strategies for diversification. *Management Sci*, 35(5):113–124, 1957.

[16] R. J. Kauffman and B. Wang. New buyers' arrival under dynamic pricing market microstructure: The case of group-buying discounts on the internet. *J. Mange. Inf. Syst*, 18(2):157–188, 2001.

[17] V. Kumar and B. Rajan. Social coupons as a marketing strategy: a multifaceted perspective. *Journal of the Academy of Marketing Science*, 40:120–136, 2012. 10.1007/s11747-011-0283-0.

[18] C. A. Montgomery. Product-market diversification and market power. *Academy of Management Journal*, 28(4):789–798, 1985.

[19] M. Potamias. The warm-start bias of yelp ratings. *CoRR*, abs/1202.5713, 2012.

[20] S. K. Shevade, S. S. Keerthi, C. Bhattacharyya, and K. R. K. Murthy. Improvements to the smo algorithm for svm regression. *IEEE Transactions on Neural Networks*, 11(5):1188–1193, 2000.

[21] M. Ye, C. Wang, C. Aperjis, B. A. Huberman, and T. Sandholm. Collective attention and the dynamics of group deals. *CoRR*, 2011.

Enabling Direct Interest-Aware Audience Selection

Ariel Fuxman
Microsoft Research
Mountain View, CA
arielf@microsoft.com

Anitha Kannan
Microsoft Research
Mountain View, CA
ankannan@microsoft.com

Zhenhui Li*
University of Illinois
Urbana-Champaign, Illinois
zli28@uiuc.edu

Panayiotis Tsaparas†
University of Ioannina
Ioannina, Greece
tsap@cs.uoi.gr

ABSTRACT

Advertisers typically have a fairly accurate idea of the interests of their target audience. However, today's online advertising systems are unable to leverage this information. The reasons are two-fold. First, there is no agreed upon vocabulary of interests for advertisers and advertising systems to communicate. More importantly, advertising systems lack a mechanism for mapping users to the interest vocabulary.

In this paper, we tackle both problems. We present a system for direct interest-aware audience selection. This system takes the query histories of search engine users as input, extracts their interests, and describes them with interpretable labels. The labels are not drawn from a predefined taxonomy, but rather dynamically generated from the query histories, and are thus easy for the advertisers to interpret and use. In addition, the system enables seamless addition of interest labels provided by the advertiser.

The proposed system runs at scale on millions of users and hundreds of millions of queries. Our experimental evaluation shows that our approach leads to a significant increase of over 50% in the probability that a user will click on an ad related to a given interest.

Categories and Subject Descriptors

H.3.3 [**Information Storage and Retrieval**]: Information Search and Retrieval—*Clustering*; H.2.8 [**Database Management**]: Database Applications—*Data mining*

General Terms

Algorithms, Experimentation

Keywords

Online Targeted Advertising, Query-Log Clustering

*Work done while the author was an intern at Microsoft Research.

†Work done while the author was at Microsoft Research.

CIKM'12, October 29–November 2, 2012, Maui, HI, USA.

1. INTRODUCTION

In online advertising, advertisers want to target a specific audience that is more likely to engage with their campaign. Typically, advertisers are capable of describing this audience fairly accurately. However, in today's online advertising systems, they do not have the option to *explicitly* specify the characteristics of the users that they wish to target, except for broad demographic information. Instead, they bid on query terms, which act as a proxy for the user interests. But queries can be misleading when taken out of context. For example, if a user queries for "helmets", it is not obvious if she is looking for bike helmets or motorcycle helmets. Ads for both will appear, since this is a term related to both bike and motorcycle helmet companies. If we knew that the user who posed the query has a long-term interest in biking, then it would become clear that the query is more likely to be about bike helmets. The techniques that we present in this paper allow the bike helmet advertiser to *directly* specify that she prefers users who are interested in biking and the advertising system to identify the users who are interested in biking. Thus, a match between users and advertisers with intersecting interests can be easily made. We call this capability *direct interest-aware audience selection.*

Enabling advertisers to directly specify user interests is extremely powerful. For instance, part of the appeal of advertising on social media sites such as Facebook is the ability for advertisers to directly select their audience based on their expressed interests, as well as their "likes" and friends[1]. An expensive restaurant can select users who have specified interest in "Food and Wine", while a company that sells outdoors equipment can advertise to users who have declared interest in "Camping". This option is not available when advertising on search engines. The aforementioned restaurant would have to guess the terms with which a user will express their interest, and bid on these terms. In the case of "Food and Wine", this translates to a large set of terms related to restaurants, fine dining, wine selection, entertainment arrangements, etc. This places a huge burden on the advertisers to come up with the right terms, and they still run the risk of triggering incorrectly, or missing an important term.

Unlike social media users, search engine users do not explicitly state their interests and preferences. However, they give abundant *implicit* information about their interests

[1]See https://www.facebook.com/business#!/business/ads/.

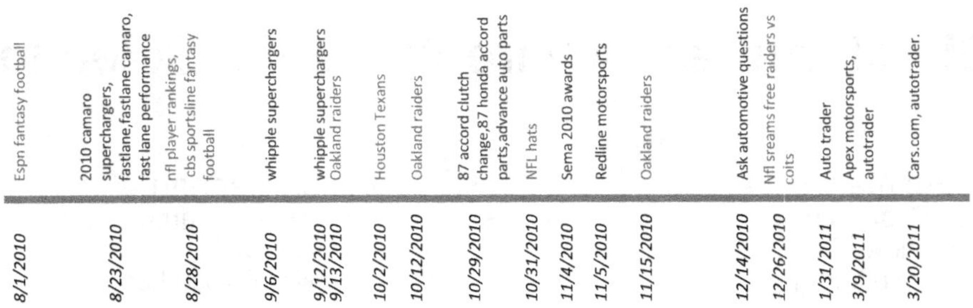

(a) A portion of the user history corresponding to queries for *only* two of the identified clusters, "football" and "cars". The clusters spread over a long period of time. Queries of the clusters are semantically related but do not necessarily share terms. For instance, the "football" cluster has queries "oakland raiders" and "houston texans" with no overlapping terms. Similarly, the "cars" cluster has queries including "Sema 2010 awards" and "redline motorsports". For best visualization, please see this figure in color.

Interest	Confidence
Cars	0.99
Football	0.88
Jobs	0.87
Music	0.66

(b) Top 4 inferred interests for the user.

Figure 1: Example of inference of user interests

furniture	travel	movies	basketball	games	fishing	coupons	wedding
airlines	dining	diet	food	recipes	hotels	cars	games
cruises	baby	chiropractic	music	health	lyrics	baking	commodities
brewers	divorce	timeshare	cycling	arthritis	roofing	orthopedic	flu

Table 1: A subset of interest labels identified using our approach

through their actions, and more specifically their queries. Users query about anything and everything that is on their mind. Compiling the long-term (*e.g.*, year-long) query history of a user reveals a variety of interests: ephemeral interests that correspond to short-term tasks such as buying a new washing machine; routine interests that correspond to queries that enable everyday tasks such as reading a newspaper or checking email; activities that correspond to long-term interests of the user such as diet, sports, gaming, and health care.

In this paper, we consider the problem of extracting user interests from query histories for enabling *direct* interest-aware audience selection. Given a collection of multiple user histories, we will produce a set of *interest labels*, and train a model that assigns interest labels to users. The labels are not drawn from a predefined taxonomy, but rather dynamically generated from the query histories, and thus easy for the advertisers to interpret and use for targeting specific users. A direct interest-aware audience selection capability is important for both sponsored search and display advertising. In the former, the targeted user interests would be provided by the advertisers alongside the usual bid terms; in the latter the interests would be specified together with demographic and other behavioral targeting information.

We contrast our approach to other audience selection approaches, where users may be associated to interests, but these interests cannot be directly used by the advertisers. For example in the work of Ahmed et al. [1] interests are represented by topics produced by a topic model, and used for ad click prediction. Advertisers do not have the option to directly specify the interests they want to target. Furthermore, the produced interests are not easily interpretable, and thus they cannot be used for direct targeting.

In a nutshell, our approach is as follows: First, we cluster the query history of each individual user in order to identify groups of queries that are about the same interest. For the clustering, we use a measure of semantic similarity between terms that we obtain by exploiting temporal relationships between queries. Figure 1(a) shows an illustrative example of two clusters obtained using our approach from a user history in our data set. Notice, for instance, the queries "oakland raiders" and "houston texans" being clustered together but having no terms in common.

Given the clustering of the query history, we extract a short description for each cluster consisting of the most popular query terms present in the cluster. Then, we generate the interest labels by finding terms that occur frequently across multiple user histories, and selecting a subset of these terms as our interest vocabulary. Table 1 lists some of the terms that our approach extracted as part of the interest vocabulary. We can see that the interests are represented using commonly used vocabulary found in search queries. In order to map the clusters into this vocabulary, we train a classifier using massive amounts of *automatically* created training data constructed from the queries in the labeled clusters. The classifier can then be applied to new users to map them to the set of interest labels. For the same user shown in Figure 1(a), Figure 1(b) shows the top four interests inferred by our approach.

Our contributions include the following:

- We address the problem of direct interest-aware audience selection. Our approach distinguishes itself from previous work on learning interests [1] by the fact that users are assigned a concise set of interpretable interest labels, empowering the advertisers to directly target users using these labels.

- At the core of our approach is a component for clustering queries within a user history that are thematically related. Our clustering algorithm uses a novel similarity measure, which makes use of the semantic relationships between terms defined by the temporal co-occurrence of queries across multiple user histories. Thus, our clustering approach exploits both the local (within a single user history) and global (across user histories) relationships between queries for deriving query clusters.
- We implement our approach on a distributed data storage and processing system. Our system runs at scale for millions of users and hundreds of millions of queries. We perform a thorough experimental evaluation that shows that our approach leads to a significant increase of over 50% in the probability that a user will click on an ad related to a given interest. The evaluation was performed at a large scale, on 150,000 users using 2 months of ad data and user histories consisting of 16 months of query activity.

We note that although in this work we consider the problem of audience selection, our work can also be applied to other tasks, such as personalization of search user experience. In this case, the user interests could be used to provide context for a query, and tailor the search engine response to the needs of the specific user.

The rest of the paper is structured as follows. In Section 2, we present related work. In Section 3, we provide an overview of our approach. In Section 4, we present the details of the modeling phase of our approach. In Section 5, we present experimental results. Finally, in Section 6, we make concluding remarks and give directions for future work.

2. RELATED WORK

Computational advertising is an emerging research field that considers the application of computational and algorithmic techniques to online advertising. We refer the reader to the course notes of *Introduction to Computational Advertising*[2] for a thorough review of the field. Behavioral targeting, the use of prior user history for improving the effectiveness of an online campaign, is a prominent research topic within this field and has received considerable attention [1, 5, 9, 14, 21, 22]. Pandey et at. [14], Chen et al. [5], and Yan et al. [22] model the user as a bag of events, such as clicks to pages or queries. Jaworska et al. [9] represent users as a vector of categories, by mapping their web page visits to a predefined taxonomy. A machine-learning model is then trained in order to predict whether a user will click on an ad. Tyler et al. [21] model the problem of audience selection as an information retrieval problem, where there is a repository of users, and some users that are known to respond well to a campaign are used as queries over the repository. Users are modeled again as a bag of events, queries, and web page clicks. Recent work [12, 17, 2] has also considered the use of social network information (friendships, email communication) for improving behavioral targeting. The scalability of the behavioral targeting problem has been addressed either with Map-Reduce implementations [5, 14] or sampling [1].

The closest work to our approach is the recent work by Ahmed et al. [1]. They consider the problem of behavioral targeting in display advertising, and use a generative topic model to define interests over histories of multiple users. Then, they use the interests of users who have clicked on an ad as features in a classifier that predicts whether a user will click on the ad. Their technique assumes the existence of previous ad click activity for the given ad. Furthermore, their interest topics are not directly used by the advertisers. In contrast, we associate users to a concise set of interpretable labels and empower the advertisers to directly specify such interest labels together with their ads.

Query logs are instrumental in the improvement of search engines, and they have been under intense analysis in the past few years. There is a voluminous literature on different aspects of query-log analysis. One important problem is that of breaking up a query history into sessions [7, 10, 11, 13, 16, 18], dealing with the fact that temporal coherence does not necessarily imply thematic coherence. This is a challenging task, since different tasks tend to be interleaved or span long periods of time. Temporal correlation between queries over large number of sessions has been exploited to define semantic correlations between queries [3, 8, 20] for tasks like reformulations or query suggestions. One key differentiation of our work is that we use temporal correlations between queries to define similarity between *terms*, and then we utilize this similarity to cluster queries. In contrast, previous works define relationships directly between queries. Related to our approach is the work by Richardson [19] that discovers long-term relationships between terms in query histories.

3. OVERVIEW OF OUR APPROACH

In this paper, we address the problem of identifying user interests from search query histories, and describing them using a concise vocabulary. Given a user u and their query history Q_u, we want to assign user u a set of labels L_u, drawn from a larger vocabulary $\mathcal{L}$ of possible interests. The choice of the vocabulary $\mathcal{L}$ is of paramount importance in enabling the advertisers to select the appropriate audience for their campaign. We propose a methodology for generating the interest vocabulary $\mathcal{L}$, and an algorithm for mapping the user history to this interest vocabulary.

Our approach has two phases: the modeling phase, and the inference phase. In the modeling phase we use query histories from multiple users to generate the vocabulary of interests, and train a machine learning model that maps collections of queries to labels in our vocabulary. In the inference phase, we apply our labeling algorithm to user query histories to obtain a labeling of the users in our interest vocabulary. We now discuss the details of the two phases.

3.1 Modeling User Interests

The modeling phase takes as input a collection $\mathcal{Q} = \{Q_1, ..., Q_m\}$ of query histories of m users, and produces a vocabulary of interest labels $\mathcal{L} = \{\ell_1, ..., \ell_K\}$, and a model $\mathcal{M}$ that assigns interest labels to collections of queries. This phase can be decomposed into three steps: First, we cluster the individual query histories in order to extract *themes*; Then we use the produced clusterings to generate the label vocabulary. When available, we also augment the interest vocabulary with advertiser provided interest labels; Finally, we train a machine learning model that maps themes into the label vocabulary. The model itself is trained using data obtained *automatically* from the clusters. The pipeline of these three steps is shown in Figure 2.

[2]http://www.stanford.edu/class/msande239/

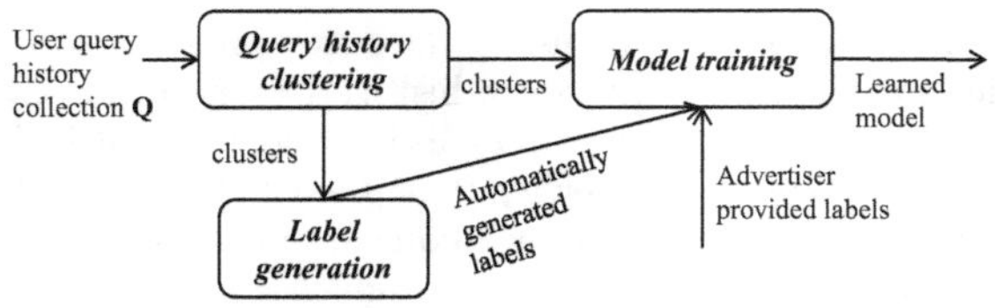

Figure 2: Modeling phase pipeline.

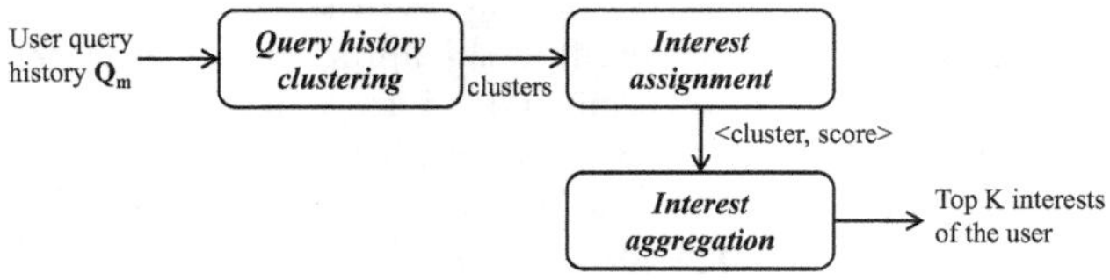

Figure 3: Inference phase pipeline.

Query History Clustering: Users express their interests in their search queries, but not necessarily in a temporally and syntactically coherent way. Queries pertaining to wildly different interests are interleaved over short intervals of time, while queries that refer to the same interest recur over the span of weeks, months, or even years, each time slightly mutated, using different terms and touching different aspects. As a first step towards extracting interests from query histories, we organize queries of individual users into *themes*: semantically coherent clusters that are potentially related to the same interest. We extract these themes by clustering the user history. For our clustering, we use a similarity measure that captures the semantic correlation between queries, as this is observed over the query histories of millions of users. We discuss our similarity measure, and clustering algorithm in detail in Section 4.1.

Formally, given the history Q_u of an individual user u, the query history clustering step produces a clustering $C_u = \{c_1, ..., c_{T_u}\}$, where each cluster of queries $c \in C_u$ corresponds to a semantically coherent theme that is candidate for capturing an interest. Given a collection of user query histories $\mathcal{Q} = \{Q_1, ..., Q_m\}$ the output of the clustering step is a collection of clusterings $\mathcal{C} = \{C_1, ..., C_m\}$, one for each individual user.

Label Generation: The clustering step does a good job in bringing together queries that are semantically related, and organizing the user query history into themes. Manual inspection reveals some clearly defined interests: an long-term engagement in online gaming, a prolonged search for a new house, or a long-standing quest for medical advice. These groups of queries make intuitive sense to a human observer, but they are not actionable for advertisers who cannot afford to go through millions of query clusters to find the ones that are of interest to their campaign. We thus need a concise way to describe the interests we observe. Using the themes we have identified, we will extract a set of interest labels, which will define the vocabulary with which advertisers can select the users they are interested in.

The label extraction process identifies key terms that can be used for labeling query clusters of individual users. It then aggregates these terms over the full history collection to identify terms that pertain to a large number of users. These terms will define the interest label vocabulary. We describe the details of this process in Section 4.2. In summary, given the collection of clusterings $\mathcal{C}$ output from the history clustering step, the label generation step will produce an interest label vocabulary $\mathcal{L} = \{\ell_1, ..., \ell_K\}$ that describes the space of possible interests of a search user.

Optionally, we can also incorporate advertiser-provided interest labels to the label set, thus allowing the advertisers to dynamically modify the set of interest labels. In Section 5.3, we show the performance of our system when advertiser-provided interest labels such as "webkinz" and "lego" are included.

Model training: We observed that the themes extracted from the clustering step align well with intuitively defined interests, and we used this fact to create our interest vocabulary $\mathcal{L}$. Given a new user u, with query history Q_u, which is clustered into a set of themes C_u, we want to be able to map these themes into the space of interest labels $\mathcal{L}$. In this step we train a discriminative model $\mathcal{M}$ that performs this task: given a cluster of queries c, it produces a probability distribution $P(\ell|c)$ over the interest labels $\ell \in \mathcal{L}$.

In order to train the model we need training data: clusters that are labeled within our label vocabulary $\mathcal{L}$. We obtain this data automatically from the clustering collection $\mathcal{C}$ we produced in the clustering step.

In summary, in the model training step, we take as input the interest vocabulary $\mathcal{L}$ produced in the label generation step, and the clustering collection $\mathcal{C}$ produced in the clustering step, and we produce a machine learning model $\mathcal{M}$ that maps a cluster of queries c into the label vocabulary $\mathcal{L}$. We describe the details of this step in Section 4.3.

3.2 Inferring User Interests

At the inference phase, given a user u, with query history Q_u, we will assign a set of labels $L_u \subseteq \mathcal{L}$ from the vocabulary of labels $\mathcal{L}$ produced in the modeling phase. This phase can be decomposed into three steps: the history clustering step, the interest assignment step, and the interest aggregation step. The pipeline for the inference procedure is shown in Figure 3.

Query History Clustering: In this step we extract the main themes in the query history of the user, using the same clustering techniques that we described in the modeling phase, which we describe in detail in Section 4.1. Given the input history Q_u we produce a clustering $C_u = \{c_1, ..., c_{T_u}\}$, where each cluster $c \in C_u$ corresponds to a theme in the user history.

Interest Assignment: In this step we apply the machine learning model $\mathcal{M}$ that we trained in the modeling phase to the clustering C_u. For every cluster $c \in C_u$, we obtain a probability distribution over the label set $\mathcal{L}$. That is, for each label $\ell \in \mathcal{L}$, we obtain the probability $P(\ell|c)$ that the cluster c should be labeled with label ℓ.

Interest Aggregation: Given the clustering C_u and the probability distributions $P(\ell|c)$ defined for each cluster c, we can aggregate them in a number of ways to obtain the consolidated user interest profile. In our case, we associate the user u with the set of labels L_u that have probability $P(\ell|c)$ above a certain threshold θ_p (set to 0.75 in our experiments), for some cluster $c \in C_u$. While being simple, the experimental results indicate that this aggregation scheme is robust and works well in practice. It is possible to exploit a variety of other signals for weighting the probability scores of the clusters such as the cluster size, the time interval over which the queries were asked, etc., but we leave this as potential problem for future investigation.

4. MODELING USER INTERESTS

We will now describe in details the three steps of the modeling phase: query history clustering, label generation, and model training.

4.1 Query History Clustering

An interest manifests itself in the query history over multiple queries that cover different aspects of the interest. For example, a user who has an interest in "football" will pose multiple queries about different football teams, NFL, or game schedules. All these queries are thematically related around the interest "football". Identifying such groups of thematically related queries poses the challenge of defining a suitable similarity measure between queries. Typical syntactic similarity measures such as Jaccard coefficient or edit distance are not sufficient, since they do not capture the diversity in the way people query about a topic. Queries like "wedding gown" and "floral arrangements" are semantically close under a "wedding" interest, yet far apart under any measure of textual similarity. Temporal affinity is a popular method for capturing such semantic correlations: related queries are likely to appear close in the user history. There is considerable amount of work in partitioning a user history into *sessions*, temporally coherent clusters of queries [4, 7, 10]. However, temporal coherence does not always guarantee thematic coherence: thematically diverse interests may be interleaved over a short period of time. Conversely, a thematically coherent interest may span several days, weeks or months in the history of a user. Therefore, sessions do not necessarily capture interests fully and accurately.

Although temporal affinity is not sufficient to capture interests in a single user history, when aggregating millions of user histories, it provides a strong signal for semantic similarity. This idea has been previously explored to extract correlations between queries for tasks such as query suggestions and query reformulations [23, 3]. In our approach we will use temporal co-occurrence of queries over multiple user histories in order to define semantic similarity between *terms*. We will then use this measure of similarity to group queries into clusters, which capture themes in the user history, and are candidates to be mapped to user interests.

Formally, let $\mathcal{Q}$ denote a collection of user histories. A user history Q_u is a sequence $Q_u = \langle (q_1, t_1), ..., (q_{n_u}, t_{n_u}) \rangle$ of query, time-stamp pairs (q_i, t_i), where query q_i was posed at time t_i. We partition the query history into *sessions* using the usual 30-minute timeout rule: a timeout of more than 30 minutes between two queries defines the beginning of a new session. The session contains the set of queries between two timeouts. Formally, a session is a maximal subset $S \subseteq Q_u$ of the query history, such that for any two query-timestamp pairs $(q_i, t_i), (q_j, t_j) \in S$, $|t_i - t_j|$ is less than 30 minutes.

Let $\mathcal{S}$ denote the set of all sessions defined over the history collection $\mathcal{Q}$. Each session $S \in \mathcal{S}$ can be thought of as a bag of words, $S = \{w_1, ..., w_k\}$, consisting of all the terms of the queries contained in S. Let $P(w_i, w_j)$ be the number of sessions where words w_i and w_j occur together. Let N be the total number of co-occurrences, that is, $N = \Sigma_i \Sigma_j P(w_i, w_j)$.

For a pair of terms (w_i, w_j) we define the co-occurrence frequency $f(w_i, w_j)$ as the fraction of co-occurrences that contain both terms w_i and w_j. That is, $f(w_i, w_j) = \frac{P(w_i, w_j)}{N}$. Similarly, for a term w_i, we define the *frequency* $f(w_i)$ of term w_i to be the fraction of co-occurrences that contain term w_i. That is, $f(w_i) = \frac{\Sigma_j P(w_i, w_j)}{N}$.

In order for two terms to be similar we would like them to have high co-occurrence frequency. However, high co-occurrence frequency by itself is not sufficient to determine similarity. Terms that have high frequency on their own are likely to participate in pairs with high co-occurrence frequency. For example, queries "facebook" and "google" are prominent in the search logs, and they exhibit high co-occurrence frequency with each other and with other terms, yet this does not imply semantic similarity. To normalize for this effect, we divide the co-occurrence frequency with the probability that the two terms co-occur in the same session by chance. This ratio, or more precisely the log of this ratio, is the *point-wise mutual information* (PMI) between the two terms, a commonly used similarity measure in text mining and natural language processing [6]. Formally, it is defined as follows:

$$\mathrm{PMI}(w_i, w_j) = \log \frac{f(w_i, w_j)}{f(w_i) f(w_j)}$$

A known drawback of PMI is that it favors rare co-occurrences. Two terms that appear only once in the the query histories in the same session, have the highest possible PMI. This is undesirable, since we would like the pair of terms to have some support in order to be deemed similar. We address this issue by using the discounted PMI (dPMI) measure [15]:

$$\mathrm{dPMI}(w_i, w_j) = \mathrm{PMI}(w_i, w_j) \frac{f(w_i, w_j)}{f(w_i, w_j) + 1/N} \frac{\min\{f(w_i), f(w_j)\}}{\min\{f(w_i), f(w_j)\} + 1/N}$$

Given the similarity measure between terms, we can extend it to queries, or collection of queries. We represent those as bags of terms. Given two bags of terms $X = \{x_1, ..., x_{k_x}\}$ and $Y = \{y_1, ..., y_{k_y}\}$, we define their similarity as follows:

$$\mathrm{sim}(X, Y) = \frac{1}{|X||Y|} \sum_{(x,y) \in X \times Y} \mathrm{dPMI}(x, y)$$

That is, the similarity of the two bags of terms is the average dPMI similarity of the pairs of terms in the cross-product between the two bags.

Note that a collection of terms may contain the same term multiple times. According to our similarity definition this term will appear multiple times in the sum, and thus contribute more to the similarity. This follows the intuition that terms that are frequent should have more impact on the similarity of the collection of queries. It is also possible that X and Y share a term w. In this case we need to define a measure of similarity of a term to itself. We compute this using the definition of PMI, where we define $f(w, w) = f(w)$. Therefore, we have:

$$\mathrm{PMI}(w, w) = \log \frac{1}{f(w)}$$

This definition captures nicely the intuition that two collections that share a rare term (*e.g.*, "aquarium") are more similar than two collections that share a frequent term (*e.g.*, "facebook").

Note that our final query similarity measure makes use of both semantic and syntactic similarity between queries. Semantic similarity is explicitly introduced by using the temporal co-occurrence of terms, while syntactic similarity is a side benefit of reducing the similarity of queries to comparisons between terms.

Equipped with a similarity measure between queries and sets of queries, we can now apply any standard clustering algorithm for grouping the queries into interests. We opt for hierarchical agglomerative clustering. The algorithm proceeds iteratively, starting with a set of singleton clusters each consisting of a single query, and at each iteration it merges the clusters with the highest similarity. It continues until the similarity of the most similar pair drops below a predefined threshold.

Therefore, given a collection of m user query histories $\mathcal{Q} = \{Q_1, ..., Q_m\}$, we have obtained a collection of m clusterings $\mathcal{C} = \{C_1, ..., C_m\}$. A cluster $c \in C_u$ in the clustering of user u is a set of queries that are thematically related, and are candidates for defining an interest of user u. In the following section, we will show how we generate the interest labels from the clusterings $\mathcal{C}$, and then label the clusters in C_u with the appropriate interest label.

4.2 Label Generation

In the label generation step, we exploit the collection of clusterings $\mathcal{C}$ that we obtained in the clustering step to automatically generate a rich set of terms that can serve as the vocabulary $\mathcal{L}$ of interest labels.

Given the collection $\mathcal{C}$, we first perform a pruning step to remove clusters with number of distinct queries below a certain threshold (set to 30 in our experiments). Such clusters are too small to capture a prevalent interest of the user. Let $\mathcal{C}_p$ denote the new clustering collection. For each cluster $c \in \mathcal{C}_p$ we produce a set T_c containing the top-q most frequent terms, where $q = 5$ in our experiments (we exclude stop words, *etc.*). These top frequently-occurring terms represent a "synopsis" of the cluster, capturing the underlying "theme" of its queries. Let $T = \cup T_c$ denote the union of all terms that are among the most frequent terms T_c of at least one cluster, for at least one user. We keep as our label set $\mathcal{L}$ the terms in T that appear in the query history of at least θ_u users, where $\theta_u = 100$ in our experiments. That is, our label set consists of terms that appear as a theme for at least 100 users. We also do minimal human inspection to remove certain labels that do not correspond to interests (*e.g.*, "map" and "store"), and canonicalize certain synonymous terms (*e.g.*, "recipes" and "recipe").

Table 1 shows a subset of the 300 labels that were generated using this approach. We can see that the labels cover a wide spectrum of interests, and at different levels of granularity. For instance, while a label like "games" tends to be more encompassing, a label such as "basketball" is more specific. There are subtle variants of similar kind of interests, *e.g.*, "food", "recipes", "baking" and "dining", to name a few. There are also time bounded interests such as "wedding" and "roofing". Furthermore, these interest labels are of high value to the advertisers. To verify this, we performed the following check: we obtained the top 1,000 unigram advertising bid terms (in terms of the revenue that they generate in a major sponsored search engine), and we computed the overlap with the list of generated interest labels. It turns out that 12.5% of these 1,000 top advertising terms are actually included in our list.

It is important to note that our approach is not restricted to using these automatically-generated interest labels. Any list of interest labels provided by the advertisers can be used, as long as it contains terms that appear in the query clusters. In Section 5.3, we experimentally show the effectiveness of our approach not only in the scenario of automatically-generated labels but also in the case of additional labels provided by the advertisers.

4.3 Model Training

Given the label set $\mathcal{L} = \{\ell_1, ..., \ell_K\}$, in this step we train a machine learning model $\mathcal{M}$ which given a cluster c, produces the probability $P(\ell|c)$ that the cluster c belongs to the interest described by label ℓ, for every label $\ell \in \mathcal{L}$. We use a multiclass logistic regression model parameterized by $\mathbf{W}$ to compute $P(\ell|c)$. The parameter matrix $\mathbf{W}$ is a collection of weight vectors $\{\mathbf{w}_k\}$, one for each label $\ell_k \in \mathcal{L}$ such that each component w_{jk} measures the relative importance of the jth feature for predicting k^{th} label. The multiclass logistic regression learns a mapping from the feature vector of c, denoted by $\mathbf{z}(c)$ to the label y, using the following softmax logistic function:

$$P(\ell_k|c) = P(y = \ell_k|\mathbf{z}(c), \mathbf{W}) = \frac{\exp{(b_k + \mathbf{z}(c) \cdot \mathbf{w}_k)}}{1 + \sum_{j=1}^{K} \exp{(b_j + \mathbf{z}(c) \cdot \mathbf{w}_j)}} \quad (1)$$

where b_j $(1 \leq j \leq K)$ are bias terms.

In our setting, the feature vector $\mathbf{z}(c)$ corresponds to a summary constructed from the cluster, c. In particular, we used lexical features consisting of all unigrams (terms) appearing in the queries in the cluster. We then converted them to boolean features representing the presence or absence of these unigrams. We did not consider the frequency of occurrence of these terms as that would require that the clusters are normalized for many factors such as number of queries in the cluster, number of unigrams in the cluster, *etc.* In fact, our experimental evaluation shows that these simple binary features perform effectively.

The weight vector in Equation 1 is learned from a labeled data set $\mathcal{D} = \{(\mathbf{x}^1, y^1), \ldots, (\mathbf{x}^n, y^n)\}$, where each pair $(\mathbf{x}^j, y^j)$ corresponds to the feature extracted from a cluster and its corresponding interest label. In particular, $\mathbf{W}$ is learned so as to maximize the conditional log-likelihood of the labeled data:

$$\mathbf{W}^* = \arg\max_{\mathbf{W}} \sum_{j=1}^{n} \log P(y^j = \ell_k|\mathbf{x}^j, \mathbf{W}) \quad (2)$$

Labeled data for training: Manual construction of a labeled training set can be too expensive and time-consuming. Our approach enables an effective way to obtain large amounts of *automatically* labeled training data. For some label $\ell \in \mathcal{L}$, let $\mathcal{C}_\ell$ denote the set of clusters, from any clustering $C_u \in \mathcal{C}$, such that for all $c \in \mathcal{C}_\ell$, $\ell \in T_c$, that is, the label ℓ is one of the top terms in the cluster c. We treat the clusters in $\mathcal{C}_\ell$ as positive examples for the label ℓ, and we use this data to train our model. In order for our approach to be successful, we need clusters in $\mathcal{C}_\ell$ to be homogenous, with highly frequent terms being semantically related. We manually evaluated the clusterings for their homogeneity and we confirmed that this is indeed the case. The homogeneity of the clusters follows from the way we have constructed our similarity function to capture the semantic similarity of terms.

Note that our approach generalizes naturally to the case that the set of labels we want to train against is provided from some external source (*e.g.,* provided by the advertisers). Let $\mathcal{L}'$ denote this provided set of labels. For each label $\ell' \in \mathcal{L}'$ we can use the process described above to obtain the set $C_{\ell'}$ of clusters that have ℓ' in their top terms. Then we can train our model against these externally provided labels. We experiment with this case in Section 5.3.

5. EXPERIMENTAL EVALUATION

We now report the results of a large-scale, end-to-end evaluation that we performed on our system. In Section 5.1, we present the experimental setup. In Section 5.2, we describe our methodology and metrics for evaluating on advertising data. Finally, in Section 5.3, we present our key findings.

5.1 Experimental Setup

We now provide the details of the data and parameters used for the different components of our system. The clustering algorithm uses the similarity measure defined in Section 4.1, which relies on a discounted PMI computation for unigram pairs over user sessions. We computed discounted PMI over the sessions of 2.2 million users over 16 months of queries from the query log of the Bing search engine. We used the standard definition of session, where a session consists of all consecutive queries until there is a period of 30 minutes inactivity [4].

To create the set of interest labels, we ran the clustering algorithm on 580,000 users. To ensure good quality keywords, we constrained ourselves to clusters with at least 30 queries. As a result, we obtained 1,042,729 clusters mapped to their top-5 keywords. We aggregated this mapping by counting for each keyword the number of users who have at least one cluster that is mapped to the keyword. We then produced a list of all keywords that are associated to at least 100 users; after removing stop-words, plurals etc, this resulted in 5,500 keywords. The size of this list was manageable enough to be processed editorially in order to detect highly frequent terms related to interests. After editorial processing, we obtained a list of 332 interest labels. To verify that these interest labels are of high value to the advertisers, we performed the following check: we obtained the top 1,000 unigram advertising bid terms in terms of the revenue that they generate in a major sponsored search engine, and we computed the overlap with our list of interest labels. It turns out that 12.5% of these 1,000 top advertising terms are actually captured by our list. This indicates that the interest labels are, indeed, monetizable.

We note that the creation of a meaningful taxonomy, or class system, is an extremely hard undertaking that merits its own scientific field. Complete automation is nearly impossible, and probably not desirable, since introducing some human intuition can improve the quality significantly. Our approach simplifies the vocabulary creation process significantly, by offering a manageable set of labels for the data analyst to process. Processing is also simplified, consisting mostly of filtering out uninteresting or very specific terms. This is a considerably easier task compared to deriving such class labels from scratch. More importantly, the produced labels capture the underlying trends in the data, they can be updated dynamically as query histories get updated, and they come together with training data.

The Model Training component used the clustering of 120,000 users to create 116,839 (user,cluster,label) training examples. The classifier uses lexical features: we used a feature vector consisting of 56,983 binary features (these features correspond to unigrams that appeared in at least 20 queries among the 120,000 users). A logistic regression model was learned using these training examples.

At inference time, the Interest Aggregation component mapped users to the labels for which they had at least one cluster with classification score above a threshold. Unless otherwise stated, we used threshold $\theta_p = 0.75$. As we explain in the next section, the system was tested on 150,000 users using 16 month of query activity. Running the system at this scale was enabled by our implementation on large-scale Map-Reduce distributed data processing system.

5.2 Evaluation on Advertising data

The main goal of this evaluation is to study the effectiveness of our interest-aware audience selection system. Our hypothesis is that users who match advertiser-specified interests are (on average) more likely to click on ads related to the interest than the users currently selected via keyword match.

User click probability. Let A denote a set of ads, e.g., the set of ads in a specific advertising campaign, or all the ads related to a specific interest. Let U denote the set of users that are candidates to be shown the ads in A, and let $U^A \subseteq U$ denote the set of users that are actually impressed with at least one ad from the set A. Also let $C^A \subseteq U^A$ denote the subset of these users that clicked on at least one of the ads that they were impressed. We define the user click probability of the set A *with respect to the user set* U as follows:

$$P_U(A) = \frac{C^A}{U^A}$$

That is, $P_U(A)$ is the fraction of users being impressed with ads from A, that actually clicked on at least one ad from the set A.

This metric is reminiscent of the standard notion of click-through rate (CTR)[3] which, like user click probability, is also a ratio between clicks and impressions. However, CTR is the probability that, given an impression of an ad, the ad will be clicked, while user click probability is the probability that given a *user* who is impressed an ad, the user will at some point click on the ad. Although related, the two metrics capture different information. We believe that user click probability metric fits nicely with the goal of audience selection, which is to select users to whom to impress advertisements.

Now, let U_ℓ denote a set of users tagged with an interest label ℓ. Also, let A_ℓ denote a set of ads that are related to the interest ℓ (we discuss later how we obtain this set). The user click probability $P_{U_\ell}(A_\ell)$ is the probability that a user who is assigned the interest label ℓ will click on an ad related to the interest ℓ. Therefore, mathematically, our hypothesis is that on average $P_{U_\ell}(A_\ell) > P_U(A_\ell)$, that is, users associated with interest ℓ are more likely to click on an ad related to ℓ, than users drawn from the general population of all users U who are impressed with the ad.

[3]http://www.stanford.edu/class/msande239/

To test our hypothesis, we used the sponsored search logs of the Bing search engine for a 2-month period, which does not overlap with the time period used to compute user interests[4]. For each label ℓ in the vocabulary $\mathcal{L}$, we applied our algorithm to the set of users U in the 2-month query log, and we generated a subset of users $U_\ell \subseteq U$ that were assigned this label. Next, for each label ℓ we need to obtain a set of ads A_ℓ that are related to interest ℓ. It is not immediate how to obtain such a set, since currently, advertisers do not provide interest labels, and thus there exists no test set of ads labeled with interest labels that we could use for the evaluation. We tackle this problem by making the following approximation: we use the readily available, existing bid terms from advertisers as a proxy for interest labels. More specifically, let a be an ad, and let B_a denote the set of all bid keywords associated with this ad. We say that ad a is labeled with interest label ℓ if $\ell \in B_a$. We define the set A_ℓ as the set of ads that are labeled with the label ℓ.

Given the set of ads A_ℓ, we use $U_\ell^{A_\ell}$ to denote the subset of users from U_ℓ that are impressed an ad in A_ℓ. Ideally, we would like to have control over the set $U_\ell^{A_\ell}$ in our experiments. However, since we do not have such control, we define $U_\ell^{A_\ell} = U_\ell \cap U^{A_\ell}$, i.e., the subset of users labeled with ℓ, that are impressed an ad from A_ℓ in the existing logs. The set $C_\ell^{A_\ell}$ of users tagged with the interest label ℓ that clicked on the ads in A_ℓ is defined similarly. The user click probability of A_ℓ with respect to set U is $P_U(A_\ell) = |C^{A_\ell}|/|U^{A_\ell}|$ while the user click probability with respect to U_ℓ is $P_{U_\ell}(A_\ell) = |C_\ell^{A_\ell}|/|U_\ell^{A_\ell}|$.

To make it more concrete, consider the following example. We have a set of four users $U = \{Alice, Bob, Cathy, David\}$, and a set of three ads $A = \{a_1, a_2, a_3\}$. Advertisement a_1 is tagged with bid keywords B_1 ={ "casino", "hotel"}, a_2 with keywords B_2 = {"vegas", "casino" }, and a_3 with keywords B_3 = {"vegas", "hotel"}. In our logs, Alice is shown ads $\{a_1, a_2, a_3\}$, Bob is shown ads $\{a_2, a_3\}$, Cathy is shown ads $\{a_1, a_3\}$ and David is shown ad $\{a_3\}$. Alice clicked on ads a_1 and a_2, Bob clicked on a_3, and Cathy and David did not click on any of the ads.

Suppose now that our interest label ℓ is "casino", and that our algorithm tagged users $U_\ell = \{Alice, Bob, David\}$ with the interest label ℓ. We have that $A_\ell = \{a_1, a_2\}$, and $U^{A_\ell} = \{Alice, Bob, Cathy\}$ is the set of users that were impressed with an ad in A_ℓ. The set of users tagged with the label ℓ that are also impressed with an ad in A_ℓ is $U_\ell^{A_\ell} = \{Alice, Bob\}$. Only Alice clicked on an ad related to the interest ℓ, therefore, $C^{A_\ell} = C_\ell^{A_\ell} = \{Alice\}$. The user click probability with respect to the set of all users U is $P_U(A_\ell) = |C^{A_\ell}|/|U^{A_\ell}| = 1/3$ while the user click probability with respect to the set of users U_ℓ that we tagged with the interest ℓ is $P_U(A_\ell) = |C_\ell^{A_\ell}|/|U_\ell^{A_\ell}| = 1/2$. Therefore, in our example, among the users impressed with an ad in A_ℓ there is a 33% probability for one of them to click on an ad, while this probability increases to 50% when a user is drawn from the set of users tagged with the interest label ℓ.

User coverage. We also consider a measure of coverage which is defined as the fraction of users who are assigned an interest profile (set of labels) of a minimum given size. The goal is to show that a large fraction of users get assigned

[4]We further restricted the users to "high engagement" users, as determined by the rules of the search engine company.

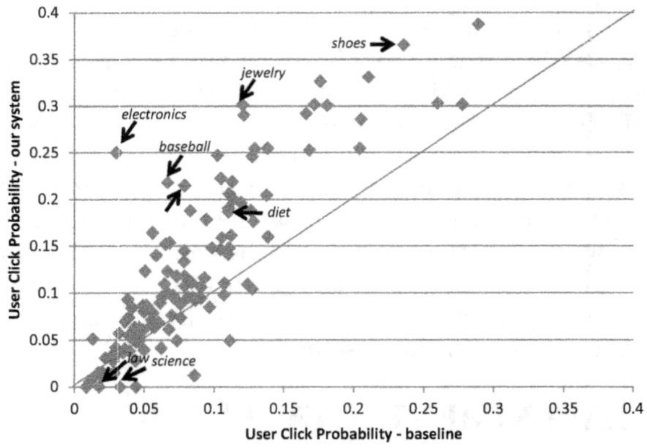

Figure 4: Scatter plot of User Click Probability of baseline vs. our system.

interest labels. Let U be the universe of users considered in an experiment (in our case, the users in the 2-month snapshot of the sponsored search logs). Let V_k be the users in U that are assigned a profile consisting of at least k labels by the interest-aware system. Then, the measure *user coverage for profile of size k* is defined as follows:

$$UserCoverage_k = \frac{|V_k|}{|U|}$$

Recall that in our system, we only keep the labels whose classification score for some cluster is above a classification threshold. Thus, there is a clear tradeoff between user coverage and user click probability. A high user coverage means that more users will be assigned interest labels, but this may come at the expense of retrieving "poor-quality" users who might not click on ads.

5.3 Key Findings

We now discuss the main results from our experiments.

Effect on user click probability. We first compare the user click probability of our system against that of the baseline, for every label ℓ for which there were at least 30 impressed ads in the 2 month time period that we considered for the advertising data (126 labels in total). In Figure 4, we present a scatter plot of the user click probability of the two alternatives we consider for every label ℓ. The x-axis corresponds to the user click probability $P_U(A_\ell)$ of the baseline system, and the y-axis corresponds to the user click probability $P_{U_\ell}(A_\ell)$ of our system. We can observe that the points for most labels lie above the diagonal (more precisely, for 97 out of 120 labels). This means that our system outperforms the baseline for 81% of the labels.

To get an understanding of the performance for individual interest labels, we indicate on Figure 4 some labels for which we do particularly well, and some labels for which the baseline outperforms our approach. For example, we have large gains for labels such as "baseball" and "jewelry" which represent permanent (or long-term) interests of users, and for long term tasks such as "wedding". Arguably, considering entire histories to make a determination of the user interests helps for these long-term interests. Some of the worst performing labels for our system are broad, high-level interests which do not necessarily lead to higher user click probabilities. Examples include terms such as "science" and "law".

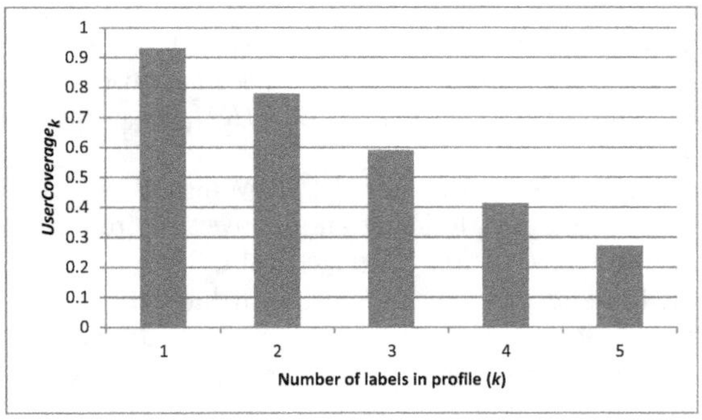

Figure 5: User Coverage for our interest-aware system.

To get an aggregated view of the results, we computed the average user click probability over all labels l. For our system, the average user click probability is 0.131; for the baseline, it is 0.087. This represents a 50.5% increase over the baseline. We used a one-tailed t-test, and verified that this difference is statistically significant with 95% confidence, thus establishing our hypothesis that on average it is more likely for a user who is tagged with an interest label to click on an ad related to that interest than a user drawn from the general population.

Our results demonstrate that given an interest of the advertiser, our technique produces an audience that has increased probability of clicking to an ad related to that interest. Of course, this audience must be of significant size. That is, $U_\ell^{A_\ell}$, the labeled users to whom the ads related to ℓ are impressed, should be a sizeable fraction of U^{A_ℓ} all the users to whom an ad related to ℓ were impressed. In our experiments $U_\ell^{A_\ell}$ is on average 10% of U^{A_ℓ}, indicating that we capture a sizeable fraction of impressed users.

Effect on user coverage. Since, in our system, a profile consists of all labels above a classification threshold, users may get profiles of different sizes (in terms of the number of labels), or even no profile at all. We measured user coverage for different minimum profile sizes for our interest-aware system. In Figure 5, we give size k of the profile in terms of number of labels on the x-axis; and the user coverage for profiles that have at least k labels, $UserCoverage_k$, on the y-axis. We can observe that the coverage is as high as 0.93 and 0.78 for histories with at least 1 and 2 labels respectively. It remains at reasonable levels even for histories of size at least five (0.27). This implies that the number of users retrieved by our system is significant for the different labels.

Sensitivity to classification threshold. We also performed a sensitivity analysis of the classification score threshold θ_p. In particular, we considered different instantiations of our system, where we varied the classification threshold θ_p and measured the corresponding average user click probability. The results are shown in Figure 6. We can observe that the average user click probability is not overly sensitive to the classification threshold: for classification threshold

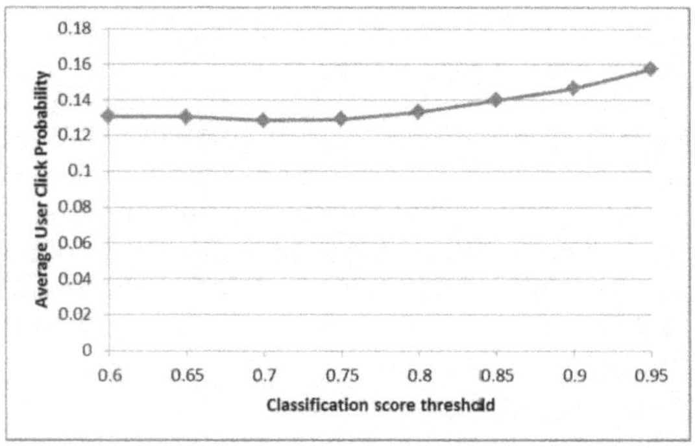

Figure 6: Average User Click Probability for different classification score thresholds.

Interest	*Baseline*	*Interest-aware*
Vegas	0.181	**0.301**
Disney	0.205	**0.286**
Hawaii	0.071	**0.097**
Lego	0.128	**0.176**
Webkinz	0.049	**0.061**

Table 2: Performance on advertiser-provided interests. The first column shows the User Click Probability of the Baseline, while the second column the User Click Probability of our method.

$\theta_p = 0.95$ it is 0.158, decreasing gently to 0.130 for threshold $\theta_p = 0.6$.

Enabling advertisers to extend the vocabulary of interests. So far, we have presented results on a set of interest labels derived from the clusters themselves (Label Generation component). However, our system is by no means restricted to that list: it enables advertisers to flexibly provide new interest labels and add them to the interest label set. To show that this is possible, we performed an experiment where we added some highly monetizable interests to the list of labels, and then performed the same evaluation as before but with the extended list. In particular, we added three popular tourist destinations (Vegas, Disney, and Hawaii), and two popular toys (Lego and Webkinz). We show the results on Table 2. We can observe that our system outperforms the baseline on the five interests. This means that click-through rate increases for interests that are flexibly added by the advertisers to the interest vocabulary.

6. CONCLUSIONS

In this paper, we presented a system for direct interest-aware audience selection. Our system takes the query histories of search engine users as input, extracts their interests, and describes them with interpretable labels that enable advertisers to easily target users.

We showed the effectiveness of our approach through a large-scale evaluation using advertising data. The results indicate that our system associates users to interest labels that are highly useful for advertisers to better target relevant users. Our system can lead to an increase in user click probability of over 50% compared to the baseline system.

We are planning to extend our work in multiple directions. Extensions include employing additional signals such as clicked URLs and timestamps, and studying the effect of interests on conversion rates, in addition to clicks. One particularly interesting direction involves building upon the output of the clustering algorithm to infer a "time signature" for different types of interests, based on the distribution over time of the queries in an interest cluster. This can enable us to better understand the nature of users interests. For instance, one may expect that the time signature of a time-bounded task such as planning a wedding would be different from that of a more permanent interest such as gardening.

Acknowledgements.

We would like to thank Patrick Pantel, Michael Gamon, and Maria Christoforaki for their insightful feedback. We would also like to thank Josh Bonis and Gil Lapid Shafriri for providing support and access to multiple resources needed for this project.

7. REFERENCES

[1] A. Ahmed, Y. Low, M. Aly, V. Josifovski, and A. J. Smola. Scalable distributed inference of dynamic user interests for behavioral targeting. In *KDD*, pages 114–122, 2011.

[2] E. Bakshy, D. Eckles, R. Yan, and I. Rosenn. Social influence in social advertising: evidence from field experiments. In *Proceedings of the 13th ACM Conference on Electronic Commerce*, EC '12, pages 146–161, New York, NY, USA, 2012. ACM.

[3] P. Boldi, F. Bonchi, C. Castillo, D. Donato, A. Gionis, and S. Vigna. The query-flow graph: model and applications. In *CIKM*, pages 609–618, 2008.

[4] L. Catledge and J. Pitkow. Characterizing browsing strategies in the world-wide web. In *WWW*, pages 1065–1073, 1995.

[5] Y. Chen, D. Pavlov, and J. F. Canny. Large-scale behavioral targeting. In *KDD*, pages 209–218, 2009.

[6] K. Church and P. Hanks. Word association norms, mutual information, and lexicography. In *ACL*, pages 22–29, 1989.

[7] D. He, A. Göker, and D. J. Harper. Combining evidence for automatic web session identification. *Information Processing and Management*, 38:727–742, 2002.

[8] H. Hwang, H. W. Lauw, L. Getoor, and A. Ntoulas. Organizing user search histories. *IEEE Transactions on Knowledge and Data Engineering*, 24(5):912–925, 2012.

[9] J. Jaworska and M. Sydow. Behavioural targeting in on-line advertising: An empirical study. In *WISE*, pages 62–76, 2008.

[10] R. Jones and K. L. Klinkner. Beyond the session timeout: automatic hierarchical segmentation of search topics in query logs. In *CIKM*, pages 699–708, 2008.

[11] A. Kotov, P. N. Bennett, R. W. White, S. T. Dumais, and J. Teevan. Modeling and analysis of cross-session search tasks. In *SIGIR*, pages 5–14, 2011.

[12] K. Liu and L. Tang. Large-scale behavioral targeting with a social twist. In *CIKM*, pages 1815–1824, 2011.

[13] Q. Mei, K. Klinkner, R. Kumar, and A. Tomkins. An analysis framework for search sequences. In *CIKM*, pages 1991–1994, 2009.

[14] S. Pandey, M. Aly, A. Bagherjeiran, A. Hatch, P. Ciccolo, A. Ratnaparkhi, and M. Zinkevich. Learning to target: what works for behavioral targeting. In *CIKM*, pages 1805–1814, 2011.

[15] P. Pantel and D. Lin. Discovering word senses from text. In *KDD*, pages 613–619, 2002.

[16] B. Piwowarski, G. Dupret, and R. Jones. Mining user web search activity with layered bayesian networks or how to capture a click in its context. In *WSDM*, pages 162–171, 2009.

[17] F. J. Provost, B. Dalessandro, R. Hook, X. Zhang, and A. Murray. Audience selection for on-line brand advertising: privacy-friendly social network targeting. In *KDD*, pages 707–716, 2009.

[18] F. Radlinski and T. Joachims. Query chains: learning to rank from implicit feedback. In *KDD*, pages 239–248, 2005.

[19] M. Richardson. Learning about the world through long-term query logs. *ACM Trans. Web*, 2:21:1–21:27, 2008.

[20] E. Sadikov, J. Madhavan, L. Wang, and A. Y. Halevy. Clustering query refinements by user intent. In *WWW*, pages 841–850, 2010.

[21] S. K. Tyler, S. Pandey, E. Gabrilovich, and V. Josifovski. Retrieval models for audience selection in display advertising. In *CIKM*, pages 593–598, 2011.

[22] J. Yan, N. Liu, G. Wang, W. Zhang, Y. Jiang, and Z. Chen. How much can behavioral targeting help online advertising? In *WWW*, pages 261–270, 2009.

[23] Z. Zhang and O. Nasraoui. Mining search engine query logs for query recommendation. In *WWW*, 1039-1040.

Influence Propagation in Adversarial Setting: How to Defeat Competition with Least Amount of Investment

Shahrzad Shirazipourazad, Brian Bogard, Harsh Vachhani, Arunabha Sen
School of Computing, Informatics and Decision Systems Engineering
Arizona State University
Tempe, AZ 85287
{sshiraz1, bbogard, hvachhan, asen}@asu.edu

Paul Horn
Department of Mathematics
Harvard University
Cambridge, MA 09322
phorn@math.harvard.edu

ABSTRACT

It has been observed that individuals' decisions to adopt a product or innovation are often influenced by the recommendations of their friends and acquaintances. Motivated by this observation, the last few years have seen a number of studies on influence maximization in social networks. The primary goal of these studies is identification of k most influential nodes in a network. A major limitation of these studies is that they focus on a non-adversarial environment, where only one player is engaged in influencing the nodes. However, in a realistic scenario multiple players attempt to influence the nodes in a competitive fashion. The proposed model considers a competitive environment where a node that has not yet adopted an innovation, can adopt only one of the several competing innovations and once it adopts an innovation, it does not switch. The paper studies the scenario where the first player has already chosen a set of k nodes and the second player, with the knowledge of the choice of the first, attempts to identify a smallest set of nodes (excluding the ones already chosen by the first) so that when the influence propagation process ends, the number of nodes influenced by the second player is larger than the number of nodes influenced by the first.

The paper studies two propagation models and shows that in both the models, the identification of the smallest set of nodes to defeat the adversary is NP-Hard. It provides an approximation algorithm and proves that the performance bound is tight. It also presents the results of extensive experimentation using the collaboration network data. Experimental results show that the second player can easily defeat the first with this algorithm, if the first utilizes the node degree or closeness centrality based algorithms for the selection of influential nodes. The proposed algorithm also provides better performance if the second player utilizes it instead of the greedy algorithm to maximize its influence.

CIKM'12, October 29–November 2, 2012, Maui, HI, USA.

Categories and Subject Descriptors

F.2.2 [**Analysis of Algorithms and Problem Complexity**]: [Non-numerical Algorithms and Problems]

General Terms

Algorithms, Experimentation, Performance

Keywords

Social Networks, Influence Maximization, Adversarial Environment

1. INTRODUCTION

It has been widely observed in various studies in social sciences and economics that an individuals' decision to adopt a product, behavior or innovation is often influenced by the recommendations of their friends and acquaintances. Motivated by this observation, the last few years have seen a number of studies on influence maximization problem in social networks [2, 3, 4, 6, 7, 11, 13]. One major goal of several of these studies is identification of k *most influential nodes* in a network. A product manufacturer may want to identify the k most influential nodes in the network, as she may want to incentivize these nodes to buy the new product by providing free samples to them, on the expectation that once these nodes are convinced about the quality of the product, they will recommend it to their friends on the social network and encourage them to buy the product. This set of k nodes, being the most influential on the network, will have the largest impact on convincing the rest of the nodes about the quality of the product. Since the manufacturer has a fixed budget for advertising, she can provide free samples only to a limited number of nodes in the network. The size of the advertising budget determines the value of the parameter k.

It may be noted that most of the studies on influence propagation are geared toward a *non-adversarial environment*, where only one manufacturer (player) is attempting to influence the nodes of a social network to buy her product. However, in a realistic market scenario, most often there exists multiple players, each attempting to sell their competing products or innovations. For example, just as Coke attempts to convince customers in an emerging market about the quality of their beverage, its main competitor, Pepsi, also does the same. Both the competitors have only a finite advertisement budget and both of them want to derive the greatest benefit out of their advertising campaign. The goal of both the players often is to capture a share of this emerging market that is larger than its competition.

The non-adversarial influence propagation models consider scenarios where a user (a node u in a social network graph $G = (V, E)$) adopts (or does not adopt) an innovation based on how her acquaintances have adopted the innovation. In these models each node u in the social network graph is in one of the following two states: (i) u has adopted innovation A, and (ii) u has not adopted innovation A but u is *open to the idea of adoption*. One can visualize such a scenario by coloring the nodes of the social network graph with *red* if they have adopted the innovation A and with *white* if they have not adopted A yet, but are open to the idea of adopting A in the future. As the diffusion process progresses with time, by observing changing color of the nodes of the graph one can infer if innovation A is being adopted by the members of the social network. Although, this paper focus on influence propagation in social networks, conceptually, the scenario is identical for spread of any *contagion* through a network - be it *spread of diseases* through a *human contact network* or *spread of worms* through the Internet.

The influence (contagion) propagation models can be divided into three distinct classes:

- Class I: Non-adversarial
- Class II: Adversarial with passive adversary
- Class III Adversarial with active adversary

The problems in classes I and II can be stated as follows:

- Class I: How to identify a set of k initial (seed) nodes, so that once they are *influenced/infected*, they will infect the largest number of uninfected nodes in the network?
- Class II: Given that a subset of the nodes is already *influenced/infected*, how to identify a set of k uninfected nodes, so that when they are *immunized*, they will have the largest impact in preventing the uninfected nodes from being infected.

In most of the influence propagation models, influence propagates in a step-by-step fashion and as such there is a notion of time step (or propagation step) involved. The expected number of nodes influenced at the end of time step D is at most the expected number of nodes influenced at the end of time step $D + 1$. In other words, expected number of nodes influenced at the end of time step D is a *non-decreasing* function of D.

The Class I influence propagation problem considered in [11] may be viewed to have three dimensions, (i) the number of seed nodes activated at the beginning (*budget or cost of influence*), (ii) the expected number of activated nodes at the end of propagation (*impact or coverage of initial seed nodes*), and (iii) *time steps* for propagation. The objective of the influence maximization problem considered in [11], is to *maximize the coverage subject to a budget constraint but without any constraint on the number of time steps.*

The Class I problem considered in [11] can be stated in the following way: "Which k white nodes should be colored red initially, so that the largest number of white nodes turn to red at the end of propagation process?". The Class II problems can be stated in the following way: "Given that some nodes are already colored red, which k white nodes should be colored blue, so that this set of nodes will have the largest impact in preventing the white nodes from turning red.

In Class I, there is no notion of an *adversary*. The red nodes are trying to convert all the white nodes into red nodes and there is no agent that is actively trying to prevent this conversion. The Class II, although it has a notion of an adversary (i.e., the blue nodes) which is trying to slow down (or stop) white-to-red conversion, at best this agent can be viewed as a *passive adversary*, because its goal is to prevent white-to-red conversion, and it is not engaged in white-to-blue conversion. This gives rise to Class III, a truly adversarial scenario, where the red agent is trying to convert all the white nodes into red, while the blue agent is trying to convert all the white nodes into blue. In this case, the blue agent can be viewed as an *active adversary* of the red agent.

The Class III models the scenario where a node u is being actively encouraged by an adversary not only *not to adopt the innovation* but also *to adopt a competing innovation.* In this case, each node u in the social network graph can be in one of following three states: (i) u has adopted innovation A , (ii) u has adopted innovation B, and (iii) u has not adopted any innovation A or B but is open to the idea of adopting either one of them. This adversarial scenario can be viewed as a classic case of a strategic conflict game between the proponent(s) and the opponent(s) of adoption of an innovation and a game is won by the proponent(s) if u decides to adopt the innovation A.

This paper studies a Class III scenario where two vendors (players) are trying to sell their competing products by influencing the nodes of a social network. The goal of both the players is *to have a market share that is larger than its competition.* It considers the scenario where the first player (P_1) has already chosen the k nodes to have a large influence (coverage) on the social network. The second player is aware of the first player's choice and the goal of the second player (P_2) is to *identify a smallest set of nodes (excluding the ones already chosen by the first player) so that the number of nodes influenced by the second player will be larger than the number of nodes influenced by the first player within D time steps.* In other words, the objective of the problem is to *minimze the cost subject to the constraint that the coverage of the second player is larger than the coverage of the first player within D time steps.* Since the goal of the second player is to win the "game" (i.e., to have a larger coverage or market share), with influencing (incentivizing) as few nodes as possible, the problem under study in this paper is referred to as the "Winning with Minimum Investment" (WMI) problem. In [3], the authors study a similar problem belonging to class III. However, the objective of the problem studied in [3] is different from the one being studied in this paper. The goal of the second player in the problem studied in [3] is not to defeat the first player with least amount of investment, but to maximize its own influence.

Using the same two influence propagation models introduced in [3], the contributions of the paper may be listed as follows:

- Introduction of a new influence propagation problem in an adversarial setting where the goal of the second player is to defeat the first within D time steps and least amount of cost (i.e., number of seed nodes)
- NP-Hardness proof for the problem under both the influence propagation models
- Approximation algorithm for the problem with a tight performance bound.
- Experimental evaluation of the Approximation algorithm with collaboration network data

Experimental results show that utilizing the proposed algorithm, the second player can easily defeat the first, if the first player utilizes the node degree or closeness centrality based algorithms for the selection of the initial (seed) nodes. The proposed algorithm also provides better performance for the second player if she utilizes it instead of the algorithm to maximize influence proposed in [3], in the sense that it requires selection of a fewer number of seed nodes to defeat the first player.

The rest of the paper is organized as follows. The section II summarizes related work on influence propagation. The section III describes the propagation models used in the paper in detail. The sections IV, V and VI discuss the problem statement, computational complexity and approximation algorithm results respectively. The results of experimental evaluation is presented in section VII and section VIII concludes the paper.

2. BACKGROUND AND RELATED WORK

The studies on identification of influential nodes in a social network were triggered by a paper authored by Domingos and Richardson [6]. They introduced the notion of "network value" of a node in a social network and using a Markov random field model where a joint distribution over all node behavior is specified, computed the network value of the nodes. Kempe, Kleinberg and Tardos followed up the work in [6] by providing new models derived from mathematical sociology and interacting particle systems [11]. They made a number of important contributions by providing approximation algorithms for maximizing the spread of influence in these models by utilizing the *submodularity* property of the objective functions. In addition to providing algorithms with provable performance guarantee, they also presented experimental results on large collaboration networks. Their experimental results showed that their greedy approximation algorithm significantly out-performed the node selection heuristics based on *degree centrality* and *distance centrality* [18].

The approximation algorithm proposed in [11] is compute-intensive. Accordingly, several researchers approached the issue of scalability from different directions. Chen et. al. in [4] provided improvement of the original greedy algorithm of [11] and proposed a *degree discount* heuristic to improve influence spread. Mathioudakis in [13] introduced the notion of *sparsification of influence networks* and presented an algorithm, SPINE, to compute the "backbone" of the influence network. Utilizing SPINE as a pre-processing step for the influence maximization problem, they showed that computation on the sparsified model provided significant improvements in terms of speedup without compromising accuracy. Wang *et. al.* in [17] considered the influential node identification problem in a mobile social network and presented a two step process, where in the first step, communities in the social network are detected and in the second step a subset of communities is selected to identify the influential nodes. Experimental results with data from large real world mobile social network showed that their algorithm performed an order of magnitude faster than the state-of-the-art greedy algorithm for finding the top-k influential nodes. A simulated annealing (SA) based algorithm for finding the top-k influential nodes was presented in [10]. It has been reported in [10], that using data from four real networks, the SA based algorithm performed 2-3 orders of magnitude faster than the state-of-the-art greedy algorithm.

In addition to attempts to address the scalability issue of the greedy algorithm in [11], efforts on variations of the original problem formulation and also the computation model is underway in the research community. In [7] two new problem formulations are provided. In the first formulation, the goal is to minimize the cost, subject to the constraint that coverage exceeds a minimum threshold ν without any constraint on the number of time steps. The goal of the second formulation is to minimize the number of time steps, subject to a budget constraint k and a coverage constraint ν. For the first version of the problem, the authors provide a simple greedy algorithm and show that it provides a bicriteria approximation. For the second version, they show that even bicriteria or tricriteria approximations are hard under several conditions. In [1], the authors argue that a user (a node in the social network) may be influenced by positive recommendations from a group of friends (neighbors in the network) but that does not necessarily imply that she will adopt the product herself. However, she may pass on her positive impression about the product to another group of friends. Clearly, such a model departs from the model considered in [11]. The authors in [1] consider an "adoption maximization" problem instead of "influence maximization" problem and present both analytical and experimental results for the new problem. The authors in [12] argue that a limitation of the traditional influence analysis technique is that they only consider positive relations (agreement, trust) and ignore the negative relations (distrust, disagreement). Moreover, the traditional techniques also ignore *conformity* of people, i.e., an individual's inclination to be influenced. The paper studies the interplay between influence and conformity of each individual and computes the influence and conformity indices of individuals. The authors in [5] suggest an alternate way of measuring the influencing capability of an individual on her peers, through the individuals *reach* within the social network for certain *actions*.

All the references discussed in the last three paragraphs pertain to the class I (non-adversarial) problems as defined in the previous section. Results on study of class II problems (adversarial with passive adversary) is presented in [8]. It focuses on identification of *blockers*, the nodes that are most effective in blocking the spread of a dynamic process through a social network, and reports that simple local measures such as the degree of a node are good indicators of its effectiveness as a blocker. The blocker identification problem has been extensively studied in the public health community, where the goal is to stop or slow down progress of an infectious disease by immunizing a small set of key individuals in the community.

As indicated in the previous section, the WMI problem studied in this paper belongs to Class III (adversarial with active adversary). Unfortunately, there exists only a handful of studies on problems belonging to Class III. Bharathi *et. al.* were one of the earliest to study a Class III problem [2]. They proposed a mathematical model for diffusion of multiple innovations in a network, an approximation algorithm with a $(1-1/e)$ performance guarantee for computing the best response to an opponent's strategy. In addition they prove that the "price of competition" of the game is at most 2. While game theoretic framework was utilized for deriving the results in [2], Carnes *et al.* used an algorithmic framework to study a Class III problem [3]. Their research primarily extends the problem studied in [11] from the Class I domain to the Class III domain. They study the follower's perspective (i.e., the player who entered the market after the first player) and investigate how a follower can maximize her influence in the network with a limited budget, given that the first player has already entered the market and influenced a certain number of key individuals (nodes in the network). They prove that the influence maximization problem for the second player is NP-complete and provide an approximation algorithm that is guaranteed to produce a solution within 63% of the optimal. Adversarial models in evolutionary game dynamics was studied by Istrate em et al. in [9].

In all the problems discussed in [2, 3] once a node adopts an innovation (i.e., changes its color from white to red or white to blue), it is not allowed to change its color, i.e., the model precludes the possibility of an individual changing her mind. However, the model considered by Nowak *et al.* in [16] there are only red and blue nodes (no white nodes) and the model allows a node to change its color from red to blue and vice-versa. Although this model was developed to capture a biological phenomenon involving viruses and cells, this model can be equally effective in capturing the phenomenon of the spread of ideas and behaviors in human population. Using evolutionary game theoretic and evolutionary graph theoretic techniques, the authors establish fundamental laws that govern choices of competing players regarding strategies.

3. INFLUENCE PROPAGATION MODELS

A number of influence propagation models for the non-adversarial scenario have been proposed in the literature [11]. Among these, the *Linear Threshold Model (LTM)* and the *Independent Cascade Model (ICM)* have drawn most attention in the research community. As indicated earlier, the literature on influence propagation in adversarial scenario with active adversaries is very sparse [2, 3]. Bharati *et al.* in [2] and Carnes *et al.* in [3] have studied influence propagation in adversarial scenario with active adversaries, and have proposed two different models for it. Both of these two models are generalizations of the Independent Cascade Model. The model proposed in [2] is suitable for a multi-player scenario, whereas the model proposed in [3] is for two competing players. Bharati *et al.* in [2] study the problem from a game-theoretic perspective and focus on finding best response strategies for the players. Carnes *et al.* on the other hand study the problem from an algorithmic perspective. Since this paper studies the problem with only two competing players, the models proposed in [3] are more relevant for this study than the one proposed in [2]. Accordingly, the influence propagation models of [3] are used here. Since these models, *Distance-based Model* (DBM) and *Wave-propagation Model* (WPM), are generalization of the ICM, the paper first discusses ICM and then DBM and WPM.

3.1 Independent Cascade Model

The social network is modeled as a graph $G = (V, E)$, where each node represents an individual. Each individual may either be *active* (i.e., has adopted innovation) or *inactive*. A node can switch from an inactive state to an active state but cannot switch back in the other direction. The propagation process from the perspective of an inactivate node $v \in V$ can be described in the following way: With passage of time, more and more of v's neighbors become active and this may cause v to become active at some time step. The activation of v in turn may trigger activation of some of v's inactive neighbors. In the ICM model there exists a set of nodes $V' \subset V$ that are active (seed nodes) initially and the rest of the nodes are inactive. Influence propagation unfolds in discrete steps following a randomized process. When a node v first becomes active in time step d, it has a single chance to activate each of its inactive neighbors w with probability $p_{v,w}$ at time step $d+1$. If v succeeds, w become active at $d+1$. However, if v fails, it doesn't get another chance to turn w active. The process of conversion of nodes from the inactive to the active state continues, till no further activation is possible. Since v influences w with probability $p_{v,w}$, the $v-w$ edge is considered active with probability $p_{v,w}$. The set of active edges is denoted by E_a.

3.2 Generalized ICM for Adversarial Scenario

The ICM can be adapted to handle adversarial scenario by allowing the nodes to be in one of the following three states - (i) active by adopting innovation A, (ii) active by adopting innovation B, and (iii) inactive. We use the notation I_A and I_B to indicate the initial adopters (seed nodes) of technologies A and B respectively. The nodes in the set $V-(I_A \cup I_B)$ are the nodes that are inactive initially. The sets I_A and I_B are disjoint, i.e., $I_A \cap I_B = \emptyset$. Just as in ICM, an active node v may influence each one of its inactive neighbors w with probability $p_{v,w}$. However, in an adversarial scenario, an inactive node w, may be in a situation where one of its active neighbor v attempts to influence w with innovation A, whereas another active neighbor u attempts to influence w with innovation B. In order to deal with this situation, the authors in [3] proposed two new models - (i) Distance-based Model, and (ii) Wave-propagation Model. The models specify the probability with which the node w will be influenced, when its active neighbors attempt to influence w with two competing technologies. The GICM operates on a random subgraph of the social network graph $G = (V, E)$, where each edge is included independently with probability $p_{v,w}$. The details of these two models are described in the following two subsections.

3.3 Distance-based Model

Suppose that $d_u(I, E_a)$ denotes the shortest path distance from the node u to the node set I where $I = I_A \cup I_B$ along the active edges in the edge set E_a. If u is not connected to any node of I using only the active edges E_a, then $d_u(I, E_a) =$

∞. Let $\nu_u(I_A, d_u(I, E_a))$ and $\nu_u(I_B, d_u(I, E_a))$ be the number of nodes in I_A and I_B respectively, at distance $d_u(I, E_a)$ from u along edges in E_a. The probability that node u adopts innovation $i \in \{A, B\}$ when maximum number of propagation steps is D is denoted by $P_i(u|I_A, I_B, E_a, D)$ and is computed in the following way:
if $d_u(I, E_a) \leq D$,
$P_i(u|I_A, I_B, E_a, D) = \frac{\nu_u(I_i, d_u(I,E_a))}{\nu_u(I_A, d_u(I,E_a)) + \nu_u(I_B, d_u(I,E_a))}$;
otherwise, it is zero.

In this model the expected number of nodes which adopt $i \in \{A, B\}$ will be computed in the following way:

$$\sigma_j(I_A, I_B, D) = \mathbb{E}\left[\sum_{u \in V} P_i(u|I_A, I_B, E_a, D)\right]$$

where $j = 1$ if $i = A$; else $j = 2$ and the expectation is over the set of active edges.

3.4 Wave-propagation Model

In this model, in step $d < D$ all nodes that are at distance $d-1$ from some node in I have adopted technology A or B and all nodes that are farther than $d-1$ from I have not adopted any technology yet(where the distance is measured with respect to active edges). Every node at distance d from I chooses one of its neighbors at distance $d-1$ from I independently at random and adopt the same technology as its neighbor. For every node u, S denotes the set of neighbors of u that are closer to I than u; i.e., their distance from I is $d_u(I, E_a) - 1$. In this model $P_i(u|I_A, I_B, E_a, D)$, the probability that node u adopts innovation $i \in \{A, B\}$ in at most D steps, is computed as follows:
If $d_u(I, E_a) \leq D$,
$P_i(u|I_A, I_B, E_a, D) = \frac{\sum_{v \in S} P_i(v|I_A, I_B, E_a, D)}{|S|}$;
otherwise, it is zero.

In this model the expected number of nodes which adopt $i \in \{A, B\}$ will be computed in the following way:

$$\sigma_j(I_A, I_B, D) = \mathbb{E}\left[\sum_{u \in V} P_i(u|I_A, I_B, E_a, D)\right]$$

where $j = 1$ if $i = A$; else $j = 2$ and the expectation is over the set of active edges.

4. PROBLEM STATEMENT

The WMI problem can be stated informally as follows: Given a diffusion model and the information that a subset of network nodes I_A have already adopted innovation A marketed by player P_1, what is the fewest number of nodes should player P_2 (marketing innovation B) target so that by the end of D time steps, the number of nodes that adopt innovation B will exceed the number of nodes that adopt innovation A? If $\sigma_1(I_A, I_B, D)$ and $\sigma_2(I_A, I_B, D)$ denote the expected number of nodes that adopt innovations A and B respectively within D time steps, the objective of the WMI problem is to

$$\begin{array}{ll} & \text{minimize } |I_B| \\ \texttt{subject to} & \sigma_2(I_A, I_B, D) > \sigma_1(I_A, I_B, D) \end{array}$$

5. COMPUTATIONAL COMPLEXITY

In this section, we prove that WMI problem is NP-hard for both propagation models.

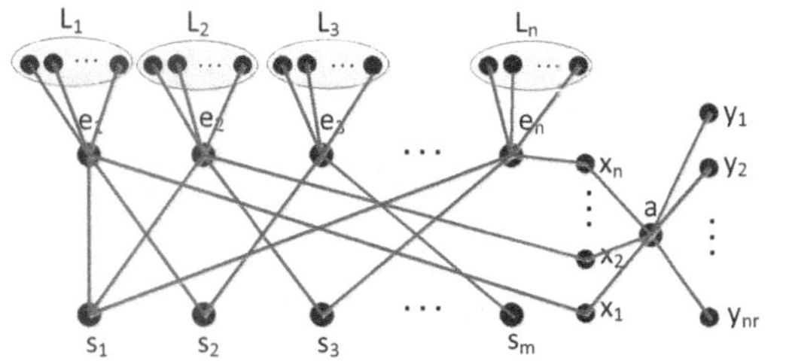

Figure 1: Graph $G = (V, E)$ of WMI instance in set cover reduction

5.1 Distance-based Model

Decision version of WMI: Is there a set I_B where $|I_B| \leq M$ and $\sigma_2(I_A, I_B, D) > \sigma_1(I_A, I_B, D)$?

THEOREM 1. *WMI is NP-hard for the distance-based model.*
Proof: In order to prove that WMI is NP-hard when diffusion is based on distance based model, we reduce the NP-compete *Set Cover* problem to WMI. The decision version of the *Set Cover* problem is defined in the following way: A ground set of elements $S = \{e_1, e_2, \ldots, e_n\}$, a collection of sets $C = \{s_1, s_2, \ldots, s_m\}$ such that $s_i \subseteq S$ and a positive integer $K \leq |C|$ are given. The question is whether there exists a collection $Q \subseteq C$ that covers all the elements in S and $|Q| \leq K$.

Given an instance of set cover problem we construct an instance of WMI. We compute $G = (V, E)$ in the following way. For every element $e_i \in S$ we add a node e_i and for every set $s_j \in C$ we add a node s_j to V. We add an edge (e_i, s_j) to E for every e_i and s_j if $e_i \in s_j$. Also, we add a node a and nodes $x_1, \ldots, x_n$ to V. Then, for every e_i we add edges (a, x_i) and (x_i, e_i) to E. Moreover, for every e_i we add a set of r nodes, $L_i = \{l_{i,j} | 1 \leq j \leq r\}$ to V and we connect them directly to e_i. We identify the value of r later in the proof. Finally, we add $n \times r$ additional nodes, $y_1, \ldots, y_{n \times r}$, to V and edges $(y_t, a), 1 \leq t \leq n \times r$ (Fig. 1). We consider that all edges are active; i.e., $p_{u,v} = 1$ for all edges in E. We assign $D = 4$ equal to the diameter of the graph G, $M = K$ and $I_A = \{a\}$.

Now, we show that the set cover problem has a solution if and only if there is a set $I_B \subseteq V - I_A$ such that $|I_B| \leq M$ and $\sigma_2(I_A, I_B, D) > \sigma_1(I_A, I_B, D)$. First we consider that there is a collection $Q \subseteq C$ that covers S and $|Q| \leq K$. Then I_B includes all nodes s_j corresponding to the sets in Q. In this case, all e_i will be at distance one from I_B and two from I_A. So, all e_i and the nodes in L_i will adopt I_B with probability one. Moreover, the nodes $s_j \notin I_B$ are two hops away from I_B while 3 hops away from I_A. Hence, all nodes s_j will adopt I_B. Therefore, we have $\sigma_2(I_A, I_B, D) = m + n(1 + r)$; so, $\sigma_2(I_A, I_B, D) > \sigma_1(I_A, I_B, D)$.

Next, we show that if there is no collection Q of size K that covers all elements then there is no set $I_B \subseteq V - I_A$ of size M where $\sigma_2(I_A, I_B, D) > \sigma_1(I_A, I_B, D)$. Considering that set cover does not have a solution, there should be at least one e_i whose distance from I_B cannot be one; so, there is an e_i and consequently nodes in L_i that choose A with the probability at least $\frac{1}{K+1}$ and the probability that they choose B is at most $\frac{K}{K+1}$. Also, at most K nodes from $x_1, \ldots, x_n$ can be at distance less than or equal to 1 from I_B. Hence $n - K$ of them will adopt A with probability one. Therefore, we have

$\sigma_2(I_A, I_B, D) \leq m + (n-1)(1+r) + \frac{K}{K+1}(r+1) + K$ and $\sigma_1(I_A, I_B, D) \geq 1 + nr + n - K + \frac{1}{K+1}(r+1)$. We choose r in our instance large enough such that $r > \frac{(m+2K-2)(K+1)+K-1}{2}$. Then we have $1+nr+n-K+\frac{1}{K+1}(r+1) > m+(n-1)(1+r) + \frac{K}{K+1}(r+1) + K$; so $\sigma_2(I_A, I_B, D) < \sigma_1(I_A, I_B, D)$.

5.2 Wave Propagation Model

THEOREM 2. *WMI is NP-hard for the wave propagation model.*

Proof: Similar to Theorem 1, we reduce decision version of *Set Cover* problem to decision version of WMI when wave propagation model is used for diffusion. We construct an instance of WMI in the same way as in Theorem 1. The only change that should be made to this instance is the value of r which will be computed later.

We need to show that the set cover problem has a solution if and only if there is a set $I_B \subseteq V - I_A$ such that $|I_B| \leq M$ and $\sigma_2(I_A, I_B, D) > \sigma_1(I_A, I_B, D)$. First we consider that there is a collection $Q \subseteq C$ that covers S and $|Q| \leq K$. Then I_B includes all nodes s_j corresponding to the sets in Q. Similar to the proof of Theorem 1 we have $\sigma_2(I_A, I_B, D) = m + n(1+r)$; so, $\sigma_2(I_A, I_B, D) > \sigma_1(I_A, I_B, D)$.

Next, we show that if there is no collection Q of size K that covers all elements then there is no set $I_B \subseteq V - I_A$ of size M where $\sigma_2(I_A, I_B, D) > \sigma_1(I_A, I_B, D)$. Considering the construction of G and the fact that set cover does not have a solution , there should be at least one e_i whose distance from I_B cannot be one or smaller. Since the node x_i connected to this e_i will have probability 1 to accept A and the maximum number of nodes in first hop neighborhood of e_i that are at distance one from $I_A \cup I_B$ is $m+1$, there is an e_i and consequently nodes in L_i that choose A with the probability at least $\frac{1}{m+1}$ and the probability that they choose B is at most $\frac{m}{m+1}$. Also, at most K nodes from $x_1, \ldots, x_n$ or $y_1, \ldots, y_{n\times r}$ can be at distance less than or equal to 1 from I_B. Hence $n(r+1) - K$ of them will adopt A with probability one. Therefore, we have $\sigma_2(I_A, I_B, D) \leq m + (n-1)(1+r) + \frac{m}{m+1}(r+1) + K$ and $\sigma_1(I_A, I_B, D) \geq 1 + n(r+1) - K + \frac{1}{m+1}(r+1)$. We choose r in our instance large enough such that $r > \frac{m^2}{2} + K(m+1) - \frac{3}{2}$. Then we have $1 + n(r+1) - K + \frac{1}{m+1}(r+1) > m + (n-1)(1+r) + \frac{m}{m+1}(r+1) + K$; so $\sigma_2(I_A, I_B, D) < \sigma_1(I_A, I_B, D)$.

6. APPROXIMATION ALGORITHM

Since we proved that finding the optimal solution for WMI is hard, in this section we propose a greedy algorithm called $GWMI$. In this algorithm either of the two propagation models discussed before can be used as the diffusion process.

Let $\omega(I_A, I_B, D)$ be $(\sigma_2(I_A, I_B, D) - \sigma_1(I_A, I_B, D))$. We define F_i to denote the amount of increase in the value of ω when node i is added to I_B; i.e., $F_i = \omega(I_A, I_B \cup \{i\}, D) - \omega(I_A, I_B, D)$. Initially I_B is empty. Hence, $\omega(I_A, I_B, D) \leq 0$. The algorithm executes through iterations and in each iteration node $i \in V - I_A$ with the maximum F_i is selected. The steps of the algorithm $GWMI$ has been shown in Algorithm 1.

Algorithm 1 GWMI

Input: $G = (V, E)$, I_A, D
Output: I_B
while $\omega(I_A, I_B, D) \leq 0$ **do**
  for every node $i \in V - (I_A \cup I_B)$ **do**
    Compute F_i
  end for
  Select node j with maximum F_j
  $I_B = I_B \cup \{j\}$
end while
return I_B

In [11], it is mentioned that computing the exact value of $\sigma_1(I_A, \emptyset, D)$ efficiently is an open question. Similarly, there is no known way to compute $\sigma_1(I_A, I_B, D)$, $\sigma_2(I_A, I_B, D)$ in both propagation models efficiently. However, by sampling the active sets we can get a close approximation with high probability. Given I_A, I_B and a set of active edges E_a, computation of σ_1 and σ_2 in both propagation models has $O(n^3)$ time complexity since it needs computation of single all-pairs shortest paths. Given I_A, I_B and input graph G, using sampling, we can then approximate σ_1 and σ_2 to within $(1+\gamma)$ for any $\gamma > 0$ where the running time depends on $1/\gamma$ [3].

6.1 Upper Bound Computation

THEOREM 3. *GWMI has a* $\log n$ *approximation ratio.*
Proof. Let I_B^t be the set of B's initial adopters selected by $GWMI$ at step t. Initially, I_B is empty and $\omega(I_A, I_B^0, D) = -\sigma_1(I_A, \emptyset, D)$. In every iteration t, the nodes in the optimal set of B's initial adopters, I_B^{opt}, will make $\omega(I_A, I_B^{t-1} \cup I_B^{opt}, D)$ positive. We denote the size of I_B^{opt} by OPT and the size of the solution of $GWMI$ by H. Therefore, There will be at least one node in $V - \{I_A \cup I_B^{t-1}\}$ that increases $\omega(I_A, I_B^{t-1}, D)$ at least by $\frac{|\omega(I_A, I_B^{t-1}, d)|}{OPT}$. Let, v_t be the node selected by $GWMI$ at iteration t. Then, $F_{v_t} \geq \frac{|\omega(I_A, I_B^{t-1}, D)|}{OPT}$. Therefore, for $t < H$ we have

$$|\omega(I_A, I_B^t, D)| \leq |\omega(I_A, I_B^{t-1}, D)| - \frac{|\omega(I_A, I_B^{t-1}, D)|}{OPT}$$

$$\leq |\omega(I_A, I_B^0, D)|(1 - \frac{1}{OPT})^t$$

Also, we know that $|\omega(I_A, I_B^0, D)| = \sigma_1(I_A, \emptyset, D) \leq n$. Hence we have

$$|\omega(I_A, I_B^t, D)| \leq n(1 - \frac{1}{OPT})^t \leq ne^{\frac{-t}{OPT}}.$$

Since adding a node to I_B will increase $\omega(I_A, I_B, D)$ at least by one, we need to find the smallest t that $|\omega(I_A, I_B^t, D)| < 1$. Then adding at most one more node will make $\omega(I_A, I_B, D)$ positive. Therefore, $H \leq 1 + OPT \ln n$. We note that this proof holds for both propagation models.

6.2 Lower Bound Computation

We now give a construction giving the lower bound for GWMI when distance-based propagation model is used. Let X and Y be disjoint sets of $\frac{n}{2}$ vertices and $G(n, 3/4)$ be the Erdős-Renyi random graph on $X \cup Y$ with $p = 3/4$.

We take two new vertices u and v, connect u to all vertices of X and v to all vertices of Y. Now, we add a disjoint star S with $n+2$ leaves and connect the center of the star to u and v. This yields our graph G (Fig. 2).

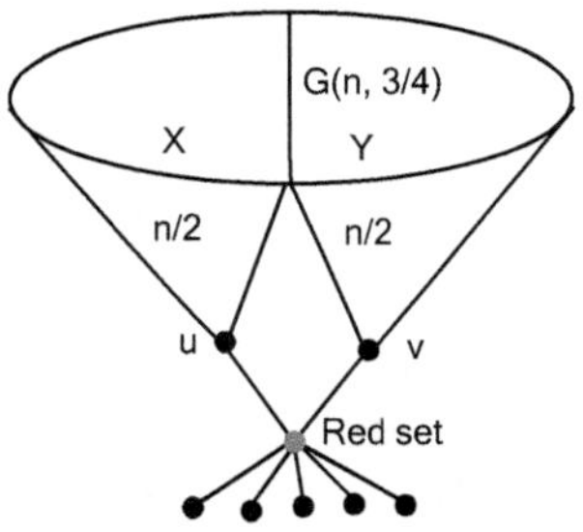

Figure 2: Construction of G.

We consider that the center of the star is the only initial adopter of A (red node), and $p_{u,v}$ is uniform and it is 1 for all the edges of G and $D = 3$. An optimal set of initial adopters of B (initial blue nodes) includes u, v and any of the leaves of S. We claim that the greedy algorithm $GWMI$ will select $\Omega(\log n)$ vertices with high probability, assuming n is large enough.

In order to prove this we first state a technical lemma giving a condition that G satisfies with high probability. Let $S \subseteq X \cup Y$. We say S is *fair* if

1. $|X \setminus \partial(S)| = (1/4)^{|S|}\frac{n}{2} + O(n^{3/4})$ and $|Y \setminus \partial(S)| = (1/4)^{|S|}\frac{n}{2} + O(n^{3/4})$.

where $\partial(S)$ is the set of one hop neighbors of vertices in S.
We claim the following lemma, whose proof we defer:

LEMMA 4. *With probability $1 - o(1)$ every set $S \subset X \cup Y$ with $|S| < \frac{1}{100}\ln(n)$ is fair. Furthermore, the induced graph on $X \cup Y$ has diameter 2, every vertex in Y is at distance at most 2 from u and every vertex in X is at distance at most 2 from v.*

Assuming Lemma 4 we prove the lower bound. In particular we prove the following: The greedy algorithm selects at least $\frac{1}{100}\ln n$ vertices from $X \cup Y$. We proceed by induction. At the first step, the greedy algorithm has to choose between a vertex in $X \cup Y$, one of u or v, or one of the vertices in the star. Selecting a vertex in the star will cause the number of blue vertices to increase by one and red vertices to decrease, a net change of two. Selecting u (or resp. v) will increase blue (and decrease red) by a total of $1 + \frac{n}{2} + \frac{n}{4}$; since every vertex in X will be at distance 1 from a blue vertex and every vertex in Y will be at distance 2 from both u and the red vertex if u is selected. On the other hand, by fairness, if a vertex x in $X \cup Y$ is selected; the increase in blue is at least $\frac{3n}{4} + \frac{n}{8} + O(n^{3/4})$; since $\frac{3n}{4} + O(n^{3/4})$ vertices are at distance 1 from x and the other $\frac{n}{4} + O(n^{3/4})$ are at distance 2 from both x and the red vertex. Therefore the greedy algorithm will select from $X \cup Y$ at the first time.

Now suppose that the greedy algorithm has selected from $X \cup Y$ a total of $k < \frac{1}{100}\ln n$ times. Let B denote the selected set, and $X' = X \setminus \partial(B)$ and $Y' = Y \setminus \partial(B)$. Every vertex in $X' \cup Y'$ is at distance two from all k blue vertices, and hence they are currently blue with probability $\frac{k}{k+1}$. Furthermore by fairness X' and Y' are both of size $(1/4)^k\frac{n}{2} + O(n^{3/4})$.

Again, the greedy algorithm must choose: If u (or similarly v) is chosen, then increase is at most

$$1 + \frac{1}{k+1}|X'| + \frac{1}{(k+1)(k+2)}|Y'| \qquad (1)$$
$$= \frac{1}{k+1}(1/4)^k\frac{n}{2} + \frac{1}{(k+1)(k+2)}(1/4)^k\frac{n}{2} + O(n^{3/4}).$$

On the other hand, if a vertex x in $X' \cup Y'$ is chosen, the increase is at least

$$\frac{1}{k+1}|\partial(x) \cap X'| + \frac{1}{k+1}|\partial(x) \cap Y'| \qquad (2)$$
$$+ \frac{1}{(k+1)(k+2)}|X' \cup Y' \setminus \partial(X)|$$
$$= 2 \cdot \frac{1}{k+1} \cdot \frac{3}{4}(1/4)^k\frac{n}{2} + \frac{1}{(k+1)(k+2)}(1/4)^{k+1}\frac{n}{2} + O(n^{3/4});$$

therefore, (2) - (1) is positive and hence the vertex in $X' \cup Y'$ will be chosen as desired. We note that this construction is for sufficiently large n and $(1/4)^k n >> n^{3/4}$.

PROOF OF LEMMA 4. Let $S \subset X \cup Y$, with $|S| < \frac{1}{100}\ln n$. Then

$$\mathbb{E}[|X \setminus \partial S|] = (1/4)^{|S|}(|X| - |X \cap S|) = (1/4)^{|S|}\frac{n}{2} + O(\ln n).$$

Let $X_S = |X \setminus \partial S|$. Chernoff bounds imply that

$$\mathbb{P}(|X_S - \mathbb{E}[X_S]| > n^{3/4}) \le \exp(-\Omega(\frac{n^{3/2}}{\mathbb{E}[X_S]})) \le \exp(-\Omega(n^{1/2})).$$

Bounds for $|Y \setminus \partial S|$ follow similarly. On the other hand there are at most

$$\sum_{i=1}^{\frac{1}{100}\ln n} \binom{n}{i} \le \frac{1}{100}\ln(n) \cdot n^{\ln n},$$

sets S. Thus union bounds imply every set is fair with probability $1 - \exp(-\Omega(n^{1/2}))$.

Note that the expected number of common neighbors between x and y in $X' \cup Y'$ is $\frac{9n}{16}$, and Chernoff bounds plus union bounds imply every pair x and y is of distance 2 (and in fact has $(1 - o(1))\frac{9n}{16}$ common neighbors). Likewise, u and a vertex in Y have $\frac{3n}{8}$ expected neighbors and Chernoff bounds imply that every pair has $(1 + o(1))\frac{3n}{8}$ common neighbors. Likewise, for v and vertices in X. A union bound over all events completes the proof. □

7. SIMULATION

In this section we evaluate the performance of our approximation algorithm, $GWMI$, on a real network data set. It has been suggested in [15] that the co-authorship graphs are representative of typical social networks. As such, we use the real collaboration network data set of the scientists posting preprints on the high-energy theory archive at www.arxiv.org, 1995-1999 [14]. This network has 8361 nodes (authors) and 15751 edges. The largest connected component has 5835 number of nodes (authors) and maximum distance between the nodes in a connected component is 19.

Our experiments were conducted on a high performance computer which is a 5K processor Dell Linux Cluster. The program is parallelized with OpenMP, optimized with Intel compiler and was executed on an 8 core compute node. The cores in the node have equal access to a common pool of shared memory. Each node is comprised of 2.66/2.83 GHz processors, 8MB cache, 16GB memory and 8 cores. Since our experiments required execution of the algorithm on a large number of instantiation of a social network (the graphs were different as their set of active edges were different), we used OpenMP for parallelization of the graph instances for the simulation with one data set.

In the first set of experiments we evaluate the performance of GWMI algorithm against the results obtained from the heuristics based on node degree and closeness centrality. These heuristics are most often used in social networks to identify most influential nodes [11]. We also compare performance of GWMI with the greedy algorithm proposed in [3] for selection of seed nodes for the second player P_2. In our model the first player P_1 is trying to market product A and the second player P_2 is trying to market product B. Since WMI problem is NP-hard and the input data set is large, computation of the optimal solution within a reasonable amount of time is unlikely. It may be noted that there is no known way of computing the exact value of $\sigma_1(I_A, I_B, D)$ and $\sigma_2(I_A, I_B, D)$ efficiently [11]. Accordingly, we use sampling of the active edge sets to obtain close approximation of $\sigma_1(I_A, I_B, D)$, $\sigma_2(I_A, I_B, D)$ with high probability. As in the experiments reported in papers [11, 3], we assign the edge probabilities to be 0.1. In all the experiments we use WPM as the diffusion model.

The node degree based heuristic selects the nodes in the decreasing order of their degrees and the closeness centrality based heuristic selects the nodes in the increasing order of their average distance to other nodes. The distance between two nodes that are not in the same connected component is taken to be n, where n is number of nodes in the network. In the greedy algorithm proposed in [3], in every iteration the node that increases $\sigma_2(I_A, I_B, D)$ the most is selected. We refer to this algorithm as *Second Player Influence Maximization* (SPIM) algorithm. In these experiments, maximum number of propagation steps is taken to be 10, i.e., $D = 10$. In the experiments, the player P_1 used node degree based heuristic to select its k initial adopters. In our experiments, the size of initial adopters of A is varied from 20 to 100. The results of this set of experiments using the WPM is shown in Fig. 3. The Fig. 3 shows that all five sizes of the initial adopters of A (20, 40, 60, 80, 100), the GWMI algorithm required the fewest number of initial adopters of B necessary to defeat A's influence at the end of time step 10. The legend Degree-Degree in Fig. 3 denotes that both the players are using the node degree based heuristics to select the initial adopters. Similarly,the legend Degree-GWMI denotes that while P_1 is using the node degree based heuristics to select the initial adopters, P_2 is using the GWMI algorithm to do the same.

The Figs. 4 and 5 show the coverage (i.e., the number of nodes influenced at the end of 10 time steps) for players P_1 and P_2 respectively. Although the GWMI algorithm does not make an effort to minimize the coverage of P_1, it may be observed from the Fig. 4, the coverage of P_1 is less if P_2 uses GWMI instead of SPIM. Thus P_2 is better off using GWMI instead of SPIM, if in addition to be able to defeat P_1 with least investment (i.e., initial adopters), P_2 wants to have a smaller market share for P_1. The Fig. 5 shows the coverage of P_2 at the end of ten time steps. It may be observed from the Fig. 5, that at all five data points the coverage for P_2 is highest when she uses the SPIM algorithm. This is not surprising as the stated goal of SPIM is to maximize P_2's coverage (influence). However, this figure may be somewhat misleading because it does not provide the information pertaining to the number of initial adopters required by the SPIM algorithm to achieve the higher coverage. By its stated objective, the number of initial adopters required by GWMI to defeat P_1 cannot be higher than the the number of initial adopters required by SPIM. Once this is factored in, and we compute the coverage per initial adopter, we find that the coverage per initial adopter of the SPIM algorithm is very close to that of the GWMI algorithm. This is shown in Fig. 6.

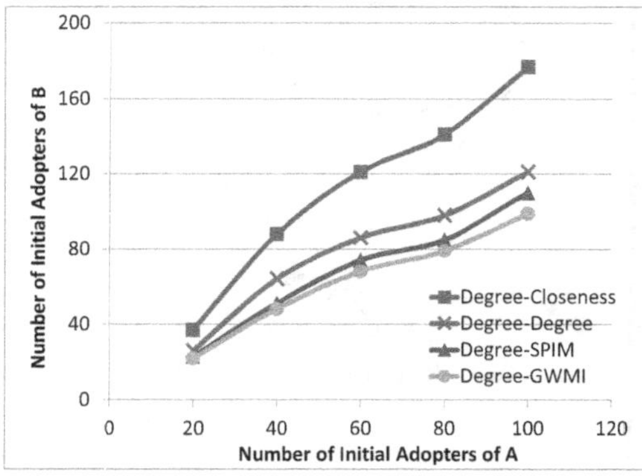

Figure 3: Number of initial adopters of B for different values of $|I_A|$

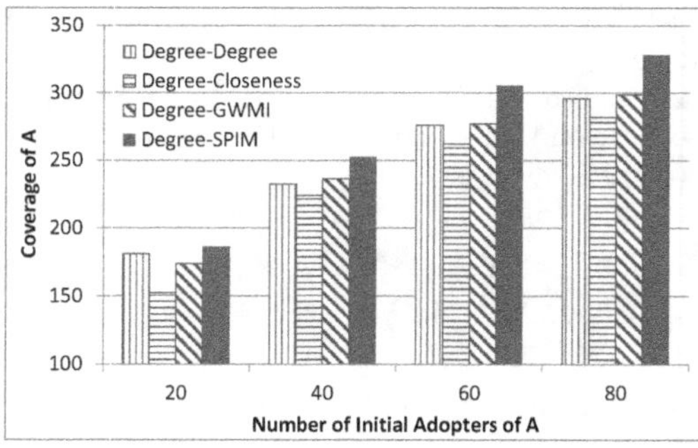

Figure 4: Expected number of nodes adopting A after 10 propagation steps

From Fig. 3 it is clear that the node degree and centrality based heuristics and the SPIM algorithm require a larger number of initial adopters of B to beat A than is needed by the *GWMI* algorithm. While this is a negative aspect of SPIM (cost), it also has a positive aspect in the sense that at the end of ten time steps, it also secures a larger coverage for B (benefit). We compute the additional benefit provided by the additional initial adopters. Let $I_{B(X)}$ be the smallest set of initial adopters of B that is required by algorithm X to defeat A and $\sigma_{2(X)}$ be the expected number of nodes that adopt B after D propagation steps. Here X can be node-degree or centrality based heuristic or the SPIM algorithm. In the case, $(\sigma_{2(X)} - \sigma_{2(GWMI)})$ indicates the additional benefit and $(|I_{B(X)}| - |I_{B(GWMI)}|)$ indicates the additional cost. In this case, $(\sigma_{2(X)} - \sigma_{2(GWMI)})/(|I_{B(X)}| - |I_{B(GWMI)}|)$ indicates the average market share gain of B with each additional initial adopter when using algorithm

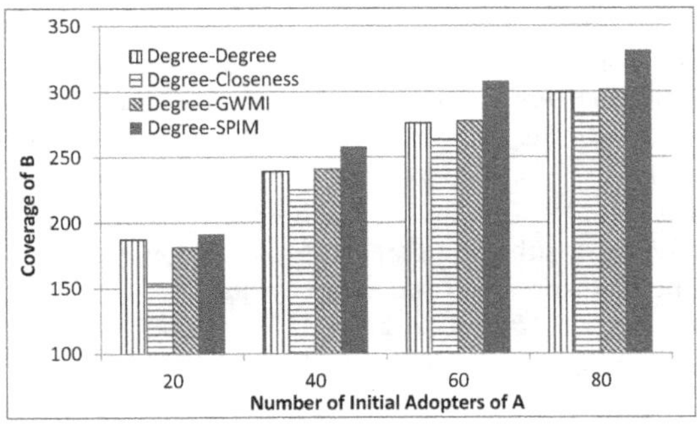

Figure 5: Expected number of nodes adopting B after 10 propagation steps

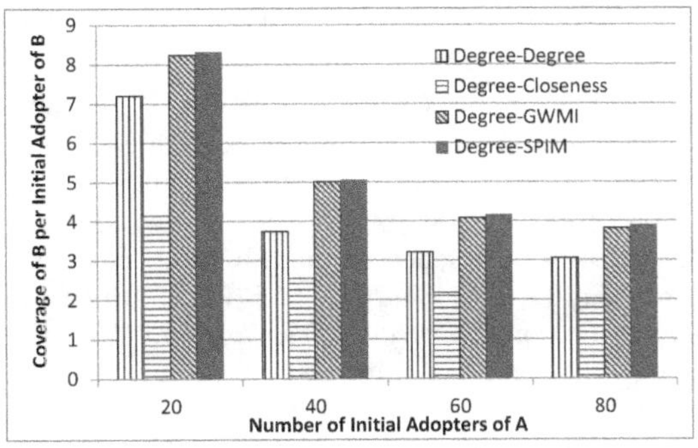

Figure 6: Expected number of nodes adopting B per initial adopter of B after 10 propagation steps

X. The Fig. 7 depicts the results for the heuristics and SPIM. The negative gains are not shown. It may be observed from Fig. 7 that the average market share gain of B with each additional initial adopter diminishes with increase of the number of initial adopters of A, when it uses the SPIM algorithm.

While the stated objective of P_2 is to have a larger market share than P_1 with the fewest number of initial adopters, it may also have two other unstated objectives - (i) to have a large $\sigma_{2(X)}$ and (ii) a small $\sigma_{1(X)}$ for all X ($\sigma_{1(X)}$ be the expected number of nodes that adopt A after D time steps). Therefore while considering the benefit of the additional initial adopters, we can consider not only $(\sigma_{2(X)} - \sigma_{2(GWMI)})$

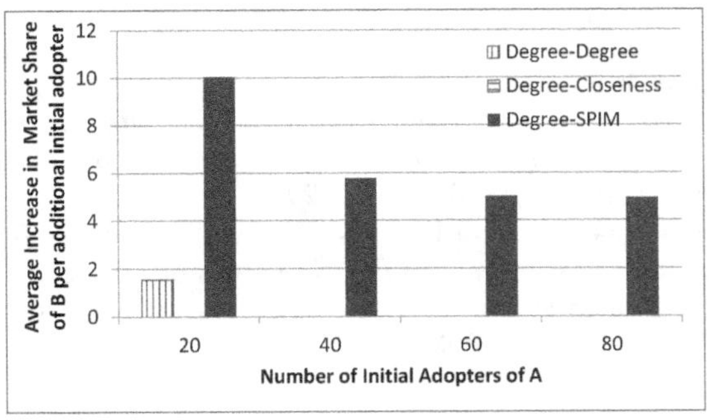

Figure 7: Average market share increase that innovation B can capture per additional initial adopter with respect to $GWMI$

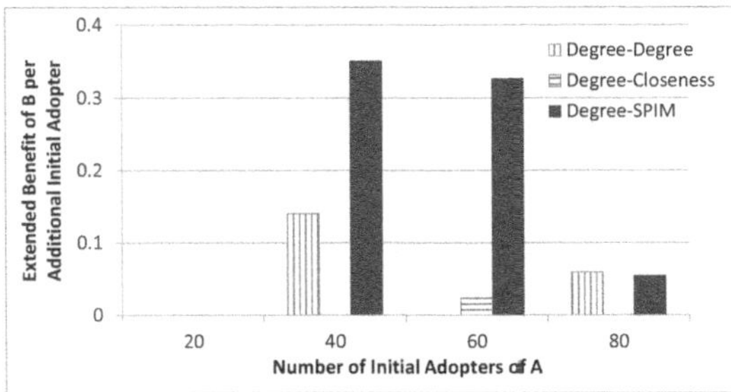

Figure 8: Extended benefit that B can capture per additional initial adopter with respect to $GWMI$

but also $(\sigma_{1(GWMI)} - \sigma_{1(X)})$. It introduces a notion of *extended benefit* by combining these two factors in the following way: $(\sigma_{2(X)} - \sigma_{2(GWMI)}) - (\sigma_{1(GWMI)} - \sigma_{1(X)})$. With this notion of *extended benefit*,

$$\frac{((\sigma_{2(X)} - \sigma_{2(GWMI)}) + (\sigma_{1(GWMI)} - \sigma_{1(X)}))}{|I_{B(X)}| - |I_{B(GWMI)}|}$$

indicates the average market share gain of B with each additional initial adopter when using algorithm X. The Fig. 8 depicts the results for the heuristics and SPIM. It may be observed from Fig. 7 that when extended benefit is considered, the average market share gain of B with each additional initial adopter diminishes even more drastically with increase of the number of initial adopters of A, when it uses the SPIM algorithm. Moreover, the gain of each additional initial adopter is smaller than 1 and implies that the additional adopter is not worth its cost.

In the second set of experiments we investigate different strategies for selection of initial adopters of A when P_2 uses $GWMI$. The strategies that we consider for selection of initial adopters of A includes the greedy algorithm proposed in [11] and heuristics based on node degree and closeness centrality. In these experiments WPM is used as diffusion model and $D = 10$.

Fig. 9 depicts the results of these experiments. We observe that the closeness-centrality based heuristic performs poorly in comparison to other two algorithms. This is true because the number of initial adopters of B that it needs to defeat A's overall influence (coverage) is much smaller than the size of initial adopters of A. More specifically, for closeness-centrality based heuristic, for $|I_A|$ values greater than 60, the number of initial adopters of B is less than 50% of $|I_A|$. This set of results show that if the influence maximization algorithm (IM) proposed in [11] is used for the selection of I_A, it forces P_2 to select a large set for I_B in order to be able to defeat P_1 within D time steps.

8. CONCLUSION

In this paper we have introduced a new influence propagation problem in an adversarial setting where the goal of the second player is to defeat the first within D time steps and least cost, measured in terms of the number of seed nodes. Considering two different influence propagation models, we provided the NP-Hardness proof for the problem and an approximation algorithm with a tight performance bound. In addition, we evaluated the performance of the approximation algorithm with collaboration network data.

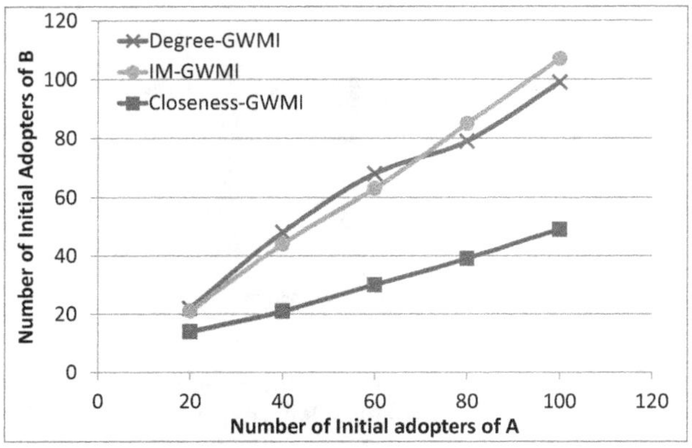

Figure 9: Size of initial adopters of B for different values of $|I_A|$

We can envisage at least two new directions of research with this problem. In the first direction, P_2 is not aware of P_1's choice. In the second direction, back and forth transition of the nodes between two competing products is allowed.

9. ACKNOWLEDGMENTS

The research was supported in part by a grant to the Center for the Study of Religion and Conflict at Arizona State University (N00014-09-1-0815). The award was funded through the Office of the Secretary of Defense Minerva program, and managed out of the Office of Naval Research. The content is solely the responsibility of the authors and does not necessarily represent the views of the Office of Naval Research. In addition, it was also supported in part by the DTRA grant HDTRA1-09-1-0032 and the AFOSR grant FA9550-09-1-0120.

10. REFERENCES

[1] S. Bhagat, A. Goyal, and L. V. Lakshmanan. Maximizing product adoption in social networks. In *Proceedings of the fifth ACM international conference on Web search and data mining*, WSDM '12, pages 603–612, 2012.

[2] S. Bharathi, D. Kempe, and M. Salek. Competitive influence maximization in social networks. In *Proceedings of the 3rd international conference on Internet and network economics*, WINE'07, pages 306–311, 2007.

[3] T. Carnes, C. Nagarajan, S. M. Wild, and A. van Zuylen. Maximizing influence in a competitive social network: a follower's perspective. In *Proceedings of the ninth international conference on Electronic commerce*, ICEC '07, pages 351–360, 2007.

[4] W. Chen, Y. Wang, and S. Yang. Efficient influence maximization in social networks. In *Proceedings of the 15th ACM SIGKDD International Conference on Knowledge Discovery and Data Mining*, KDD '09, pages 199–208, 2009.

[5] K. Dave, R. Bhatt, and V. Varma. Modelling action cascades in social networks. 2011.

[6] P. Domingos and M. Richardson. Mining the network value of customers. In *Proceedings of the seventh ACM SIGKDD international conference on Knowledge discovery and data mining*, KDD '01, pages 57–66, 2001.

[7] A. Goyal, F. Bonchi, L. V. S. Lakshmanan, and S. Venkatasubramanian. Approximation analysis of influence spread in social networks. *arXiv:1008.2005v4*, 2011.

[8] H. Habiba, Y. Yu, T. Y. Berger-Wolf, and J. Saia. Finding spread blockers in dynamic networks. In *Proceedings of the Second international conference on Advances in social network mining and analysis*, SNAKDD'08, pages 55–76, 2010.

[9] G. Istrate, M. V. Marathe, and S. S. Ravi. Adversarial models in evolutionary game dynamics. In *Proceedings of the twelfth annual ACM-SIAM symposium on Discrete algorithms*, SODA '01, pages 719–720, 2001.

[10] Q. Jiang, G. Song, C. Gao, Y. Wang, W. Si, and K. Xie. Simulated annealing based influence maximization in social networks. 2011.

[11] D. Kempe, J. Kleinberg, and E. Tardos. Maximizing the spread of influence through a social network. In *Proceedings of the ninth ACM SIGKDD international conference on Knowledge discovery and data mining*, KDD '03, pages 137–146, 2003.

[12] H. Li, S. S. Bhowmick, and A. Sun. Casino: towards conformity-aware social influence analysis in online social networks. In *Proceedings of the 20th ACM international conference on Information and knowledge management*, CIKM '11, pages 1007–1012, 2011.

[13] M. Mathioudakis, F. Bonchi, C. Castillo, A. Gionis, and A. Ukkonen. Sparsification of influence networks. In *Proceedings of the 17th ACM SIGKDD international conference on Knowledge discovery and data mining*, KDD '11, pages 529–537, 2011.

[14] M. Newman. *http://networkdata.ics.uci.edu/data/hep-th/*.

[15] M. E. J. Newman. The structure of scientific collaboration networks. *Proceedings of the National Academy of Sciences of the United States of America*, 98(2):404–409, 2001.

[16] M. A. Nowak, C. E. Tarnita, and T. Antal. Evolutionary dynamics in structured populations. *Philosophical Transactions of the Royal Society B: Biological Sciences*, 365(1537):19–30, 2010.

[17] Y. Wang, G. Cong, G. Song, and K. Xie. Community-based greedy algorithm for mining top-k influential nodes in mobile social networks. In *Proceedings of the 16th ACM SIGKDD international conference on Knowledge discovery and data mining*, KDD '10, pages 1039–1048, 2010.

[18] S. Wasserman and K. Faust. *Social Network Analysis: Methods and Applications.* Number 8 in Structural analysis in the social sciences. Cambridge University Press, 1 edition, 1994.

Large-scale Item Categorization for e-Commerce

Dan Shen*
dianping.com
No. 492 AnHua Rd
Shanghai, China
dan.shen@dianping.com

Jean-David Ruvini
eBay Research Labs
2145 Hamilton Avenue
San Jose, CA 95032, USA
jruvini@ebay.com

Badrul Sarwar†
eBay Research Labs
2145 Hamilton Avenue
San Jose, CA 95032, USA
bsarwar@ebay.com

ABSTRACT

This paper studies the problem of leveraging computationally intensive classification algorithms for large scale text categorization problems. We propose a hierarchical approach which decomposes the classification problem into a coarse level task and a fine level task. A simple yet scalable classifier is applied to perform the coarse level classification while a more sophisticated model is used to separate classes at the fine level. However, instead of relying on a human-defined hierarchy to decompose the problem, we we use a graph algorithm to discover automatically groups of highly similar classes. As an illustrative example, we apply our approach to real-world industrial data from eBay, a major e-commerce site where the goal is to classify live items into a large taxonomy of categories. In such industrial setting, classification is very challenging due to the number of classes, the amount of training data, the size of the feature space and the real-world requirements on the response time. We demonstrate through extensive experimental evaluation that (1) the proposed hierarchical approach is superior to flat models, and (2) the data-driven extraction of latent groups works significantly better than the existing human-defined hierarchy.

Categories and Subject Descriptors

H.3.2 [**Information Storage**]: Record classification

General Terms

Algorithms, Performance, Experimentation

Keywords

Classification, Text

1. INTRODUCTION

Online commerce has gained a lot of popularity over the past decade. Large online consumer-to-consumer (C2C) marketplaces such as eBay.com and Amazon.com, feature a very large and long-tail inventory with millions of *items* (product offers) entered into the marketplace every day. To structure and manage items effectively and help buyers find them easily, these web sites often organize items into a taxonomy of fine-grained categories. For instance, the eBay category structure has approximately 20,000 leaf categories which cover almost all of the goods that can be legally traded in the world.

Item categorization is fundamental to many aspects of an item life cycle for e-commerce sites. A correct categorization of items is essential for tasks such as extracting relevant item-specific metadata or attributes, assigning category specific rules for listing policy enforcement, charging insertion and final value fees, determining reasonable shipping and handling fees and so on. Moreover, the quality of item categorization plays a significant role in subsequent customer facing applications such as search, product recommendation, trust & safety, product catalog building, and seller utilities. A correct item categorization system is also essential for user experience as it helps determine the relevant presentation logic in surfacing the items to users through search and browsing.

Item categorization can be formulated as a supervised classification problem where the categories are the target classes and the features are the words composing some textual description of the items. Text classification has been well studied in recent years. Classification algorithms such as Naïve Bayes [14], K-Nearest-Neighborhood (kNN) [28], Decision Tree (DT) [1], Support Vector Machines (SVM) [11] and Maximum Entropy(ME) [16] have demonstrated satisfactory empirical results in various domains of text classification. However, the computational complexity involved in some of the state-of-the-art learning algorithms is well beyond linear with respect to the numbers of training examples, features, or classes. For an e-commerce site like eBay the item categorization problem translates into a supervised classification with 20,000+ target classes. A recent study of eBay's categorization problem describes a supervised method that is trained using several million items and approximately 3 million unique features. The system classifies several millions of newly listed items on-the-fly everyday into these 20,000+ classes (see [21] for more details). The computational complexity may arise due to polynomial variable selection, e.g., to compute information gain in decision tree based learning, or iterative optimization algorithms, such as in maximum entropy or SVM learning. The scale of the classification problem on e-commerce web sites

*Work done while the author was at eBay Research Labs.
†Corresponding author

CIKM'12, October 29–November 2, 2012, Maui, HI, USA.

requires algorithms capable of processing huge volume of training data in reasonable time, capable of handling large number of classes and also capable of making fast real-time predictions.

In this paper, we describe a novel approach to leverage computationally demanding classification algorithms on very large datasets. We don't use any pre-existing hierarchy but rather learn a new hierarchy automatically from the data. The basic idea is to 1) group classes into disjoint sets called *latent groups* and 2) to decompose the classification task into two classification tasks, coarse level classification and fine level classification. The coarse level classifier is responsible for classifying items into one latent group while the fine level classifiers (typically one such classifier per latent group) are responsible for assigning items to the right class in a given latent group. In other words, our approach consists in using a simple classifier to make coarse-grained classification and a sophisticated classifier to make fine-grained distinctions.

Clearly, one key element of this approach is the way these latent groups are identified. Given the scale of the classification task at hand, it is very impractical to manually construct them and we propose a data-driven solution to discover them automatically. Furthermore, our approach aims at minimizing inter latent group similarity while maximizing intra latent group similarity[1]. This is very important as low inter latent group similarity makes coarse level classification relatively easy and allows the use of a simple and scalable machine learning algorithm. High intra latent group similarity makes fine level classification relatively harder but, because latent groups comprise only a subset of the classes and involve a much smaller volume of data, more sophisticated algorithms can be leveraged for this second classification task.

Comparing with the flat classification approach which treats classes separately, our decomposition of the classification problem has the following advantages:

- The constraints on the choice of learning algorithm are largely alleviated since the numbers of training samples, features, and classes are considerately reduced in the fine level classification step. Sophisticated machine learning algorithms, which cannot be directly applied for flat item classification due to their computational complexity, can now be leveraged.

- The decomposition approach can lead to more problem-specialized feature selection and hence more accurate classifier. Intuitively, many locally predictive features are not useful discriminators in the flat approach. For instance, a word like *case* is not very discriminative globally since it occurs within so many different classes. But at fine level classification time, it may play a crucial role to differentiate between cell phone devices and some of their accessories. As an example, we have empirically shown that the word *case* is the most indicative feature to assign the item "*Leather Cover Case for Verizon Motorola RIZR Z6tv*" to the category "*Cell Phones & PDAs → Cell Phone & PDA Accessories*" rather than the incorrect category "*Cell Phones & PDAs → Cell Phones & Smartphones*".

[1]This notion of similarity will be defined later. For now one can assume it is a function of the similarity of the training samples belonging to these groups.

In the remainder of this paper, we first review related work and then we describe the 3 components of our approach, namely how we discover the latent groups, the coarse level classifier and the fine level classifier. Finally, we present experimental results on real large-scale e-commerce data.

2. RELATED WORK

Many websites organizes categories into a concept hierarchy or taxonomy. Some notable examples are the International Patent Classification (IPC) schema, the Web catalogs created by Yahoo!, the Open Directory Project (ODP), Amazon.com, eBay.com and most recently the Wikipedia subject hierarchy. A lot of results have been published around leveraging pre-existing concept hiearchies for classification. For instance, Koller and Sahami [12] applied a "gates-and experts" strategy to a small hierarchy using naive Bayes as local classifier, and demonstrated advantages over flat models on a small feature space. Weigend et al. [23] transformed a category hierarchy into a neural network, and multiplicatively combined output probabilities from each level to yield a final classification decision. On a Reuters benchmark dataset, they reported a 5% improvement in average precision by the hierarchical model over the flatten model. Dumais and Chen [6] showed that a hierarchical approach leveraging SVM as a local classifier is particularly suited for web page classification. To better exploit the semantic relationship embedded in a hierarchy, McCallum et al. [15] studied a statistical technique called "shrinkage" to smooth parameter estimates along a hierarchy. Some recent work [3, 26, 4] leveraged the hierarchical structure by developing a tree-induced loss function from a learning theoretical perspective. Readers interested in hierarchical classification may refer to Sillas and Freitas [22] for an extensive survey of this litterature.

Our approach for solving a large text classification problem consists in reformulating it into a two levels (coarse level and fine level) hierarchical classification problem. However, it ignores pre-existing hierarchical information (or any sort of pre-defined parent-child relationship between the categories) and does not belong to this trend of research. Also, while this prior work is methodologically appealing, the data and category collection under study is still relatively small and well organized compared with many real-world commercial applications. For instance, the dataset used by Dumais and Chen [6] contains only 370597 training samples, which is relatively small according to nowadays e-commerce standards.

The idea of simplifying a classification problem by modifying the output space (i.e. the target classes) is not new. Pairwise decomposition [10], one-vs-all decomposition [18] and error correcting output codes [5] are well known examples. However, these methods have a high training time because they require to learn many binary classifiers over most of the training data; have a long classification time because they require to query all these classifiers; and are thus not suitable for large scale classification problems. Kumar et al. [13], and later Bengio et al. [2], proposed algorithms to break down a classification problem into smaller problems by learning a tree structure over the set of classes. Kumar et al. used a clustering algorithm based on Fisher's discriminant to cluster training examples in disjoint groups and thus induce a partitioning of the classes. Although the classification process of this approach is orders of magnitude faster than previous work, the training process is computationally expensive as it requires to solve many clustering problems. Bengio et al. solution to large scale classification does not involve clustering the training samples but rather uses the confusion matrix of a surrogate one-vs-all classifier as a proxy to estimate class similarity. Two classes are assumed to be similar if there are highly confused together by the surrogate classifier. A spectral clustering algorithm where the edges of the similarity graph are weighted by the class confusion probabilities is then used to group similar classes together. Although theoretically very appealing, Bengio et al. approach leads to an accuracy comparable (and actually worse on one of their datasets) to the accuracy of the flat one-vs-all solution.

Large-scale classification problems have received increased attention in the recent years. Liu et al. [27] conducted a thorough analysis of the behavior of the SVM algorithm with respect to a large-scale classification task and found that its performance is "still far from satisfactory". Xue et al. [8] proposed an interesting two stage strategy called "deeped classification". Whenever a document needs to be classified, the most similar documents in the training set are retrieved using a search approach and the classification task is reduced to the classes these documents belong to. In the second stage, a classifier is trained on these classes and used to eventually classify the document. The main drawback of this approach is that a specific classifier is trained for each document to classify, considerably slowing down the classification process.

In contrast to the approaches mentioned in this section, our solution has a fast training and classification process; allows us to use any off-the-self classification algorithm to separate classes that tend to be highly confused with each other; and leads to improved accuracy as will be shown in the next sections.

3. METHODS

In order to achieve item classification for a very large number of target classes, we propose to decompose the classification problem into smaller problems. This is achieved by grouping classes into mutually exclusive "latent groups" and performing a two stage classification process. First, a coarse level classifier assigns an item into one of the latent groups; second, a fine level classifier assigns a specific class within the latent group. This section describes in details how these three steps are carried out.

3.1 Latent groups discovery

The key element of our approach is obviously how the latent groups of classes are built. Ideally, these groups should be such that similar classes are grouped together and classes that are not similar belong to different groups, so that a simple classifier can be used to separate groups while a sophisticated algorithm may be applied to separate classes within each group.

One way to measure similarity between classes is through the similarity of the training samples that belong to these classes. As mentioned in section 2, this is the approach followed by [13] who used a clustering algorithm to cluster training examples in disjoint groups and thus induce a partitioning of the classes. However, clustering is a hard and computationally expensive process.

As in [2], our approach consists of leveraging the confusion matrix of a classification algorithm to approximate the similarity of classes. More precisely, following the intuition that categories that are hard to separate by a classification algorithm may actually be similar, we approximate the similarity of two classes by the probability of the classifier to incorrectly predict one of the categories when the correct label is the other category. In practice, class confusion probabilities are estimated empirically by (1) training a flat classifier on all the classes and (2) applying the classifier on a development data set. This classifier can be any classifier but, as we will explain below, we recommend using the exact same algorithm for coarse level classification. More formally, the confusion probability between two categories $\mathrm{Conf}(c_1, c_2)$ is defined as follows:

$$\mathrm{Conf}(c_1, c_2) = \frac{\sum_{t: f_s(t) \neq f_m(t), f_s(t) \in \{c_1, c_2\}, f_m(t) \in \{c_1, c_2\}} (1)}{\sum_{t: f_s(t) \in \{c_1, c_2\}, f_m(t) \in \{c_1, c_2\}} (1)},$$

where, $f_s(t)$ is the class of item t and $f_m(t)$ is the class predicted by the model. It is clear that the distance measure is specialized for the task and reflects the difficulty of making a distinction between two classes.

Once the confusion probabilities have been estimated, we use a graph algorithm to generate problem-specific latent groups. We represent the relationship among classes using an undirected graph ($G = (V, E)$), where the set of vertices V is the set of all the classes and E is the set of all edges. Two vertices are connected by an edge if the confusion probability $\mathrm{Conf}(c_1, c_2)$ is greater than a given threshold α (to be discussed later).

If the actual confusion probability of every pair of classes was known, one could formulate the latent group discovery problem as finding all maximum cliques, a clique being defined as a set of vertices any two of which are adjacent. However, and this is a key observation, because the confusion probabilities are estimated using a finite development set, all possible class confusions may not be observed and our graph may lack some edges. As a consequence, we formalize the latent group discovery problem as finding dense subgraphs [9], that is, sets of vertices highly connected with each other, which turns out to be a much easier problem than the *NP-complete* clique problem.

We approximate the dense subgraph enumeration problem using an efficient two steps algorithm we devised specifically for this purpose. The first step consists of randomly imposing a direction to all the edges of our undirected confusion graph. Second, once the graph is directed, we formulate the subgraph enumeration problem as a strongly-connected components enumeration problem. A directed graph or subgraph is called strongly connected if there is a path from each vertex in the graph to every other vertex. We use a well known and efficient algorithm from Tarjan [24] to list all the strongly connected components.

Randomly imposing a direction to edge may seem arbitrary but it practically leads to a good approximation of dense subgraphs. This is due to the fact that the denser a subgraph, the higher the probability that a path between any two nodes exists. However, the sensitivity of the performances of our approach to the algorithm used to identidy the latent groups is a very interesting question and on-going research work.

Algoritm 1 below summarizes the latent group discovery process.

Algorithm 1 Algorithm for latent group discovery

Input: i) Set of categories $\mathcal{C} = \{c_1, c_2, ..., c_n\}$
ii) a threshold value α

Output: Set of dense subgraphs $\mathcal{G} = \{g_1, g_2, ..., g_m\}$ that forms a latent group

1: Train a Classifier $\mathcal{H}$ on all flat classes.
2: Compute pair-wise confusion probabilities $\text{Conf}(c_i, c_j)$ between classes.
3: Build the confusion graph, $G = (V, E)$
4: Apply the input threshold α to remove loosely connected edges.
5: Run a dense subgraphs approximation algorithm to find a set of dense subgraphs $\{g_1, g_2, ..., g_m\}$ each dense subgraph forms a latent group $\mathcal{G}$.

The parameter α controls the size of the latent groups. Higher values of α induce smaller latent groups and thus reduce the computational complexity at the fine classifier level. But classes within these groups are likely to be very similar and harder to separate. The right value for this parameter is problem specific and can be found using a development set.

3.2 Coarse level classification

Once classes have been clustered into latent groups, the coarse level classifier can be trained. The coarse level classifier is responsible for classifying items into one latent group. For this classifier, each latent group is a class (in the machine learning sense) and the training set is the union of the samples of all the classes belonging to that group.

Any scalable classifier can be used at the coarse level and the Naïve Bayes algorithm or the k-Nearest-Neighborhood algorithm are good candidates. However, we recommend using the exact same classifier that was used to estimate the confusion probabilities during the latent group discovery process (see Section 3.1) so that no re-training is needed.

3.3 Fine level classification

The fine level classifiers are dedicated to separating classes within latent groups and are responsible for the final classification, that is assigning a class to an item (as opposed to the coarse level classifier which assigns a latent group). There is one fine level classifier per latent group. Each category in a latent group is a target class for this multi-class classifier.

The dimensionality reduction obtained by training each fine level classifier on a latent group, whose size can be controlled empirically by using the α parameter described in Section 3.1, allows using a sophisticated and computationally demanding algorithm for fine level classification.

The next sections shows, through experiments on real data, that decomposing the classification tasks into coarse level and fine level subtasks, leads to significantly higher classification accuracy.

4. EXPERIMENTS

This section presents experimental results on a real dataset. The goal of this empirical study is to address the following research questions:

- How does the state-of-the-art text classification technologies perform on the large-scale item categorization on e-commerce site?
- Does the item classification task benefit from the hierarchical category structure typically available at e-commerce sites? In other words, we want to compare the performance of flat classification with hierarchical classification models.
- Does the proposed coarse level - fine level method bring any performance gains over the flat classification or more conventional hierarchical classification models?

In the following, we describe the dataset used for these experiments, the algorithms we compared and finally discuss the results.

4.1 Dataset

We collected a sample data from the eBay.com e-commerce site for this experiment.

eBay organizes items (product offers) into a six-level category structure similar to a topic hierarchy, where there are 39 top-level nodes called *meta categories*, and more than 20,000 bottom-level nodes called *leaf categories*. The hierarchy is designed and maintained by human experts. Table 1 shows the leaf category distribution on the hierarchy. It can be observed that the leaf categories are highly skewed over the nodes at higher levels. For the nodes at the first three levels (*Level 1*, *Level 2* and *Level 3*), there can be hundreds or thousands of leaf categories under a node. Our task is to categorize items into the most relevant leaf categories, that is to solve a 20,000+ class classification problem.

An item is typically listed in one category, although it is possible that the item might be suitable for multiple categories by nature. Furthermore, eBay has a very large and complex hierarchical taxonomy in which the topic nodes almost cover all of the goods in the world. The category nodes are not guaranteed to be mutually exclusive with each other, although the hierarchy was designed by human experts and has been extensively refined over the past years. Some of ambiguous leaf categories are even across meta categories, such as:

1. Clothing, Shoes & Accessories → Men's Shoes
2. Sporting Goods → Outdoor Sports → Camping & Hiking → Clothing, Shoes & Accessories → Shoes → Men

Although it seems at first sight that the inventory listed in these categories should be very different, many type of shoes can be listed in both categories and sellers use both categories interchangeably.

The distribution of items over leaf categories exhibits high skewness and heavy-tail nature, as shown in Figure 1. 86.9% of the categories (the head) only containing less than 1,000 items per category, while 1% of the categories (the tail) with more than 10K items per category account for 51.7% of the items. As a consequence, a large portion of the categories

Level	Top nodes	Leaf Nodes within a top node		
		Avg	Max	Min
Level 1 (meta)	39	547.1	4526	3
Level 2	487	43.8	793	1
Level 3	4346	4.9	495	1
Level 4	13904	1.5	80	1
Level 5	19942	1.1	35	1
Level 6 (leaf)	21337	1	1	1

Table 1: Distribution of categories in eBay topic hierarchy. Level 1 represents the "meta" categories and level 6 represents the "leaf" categories

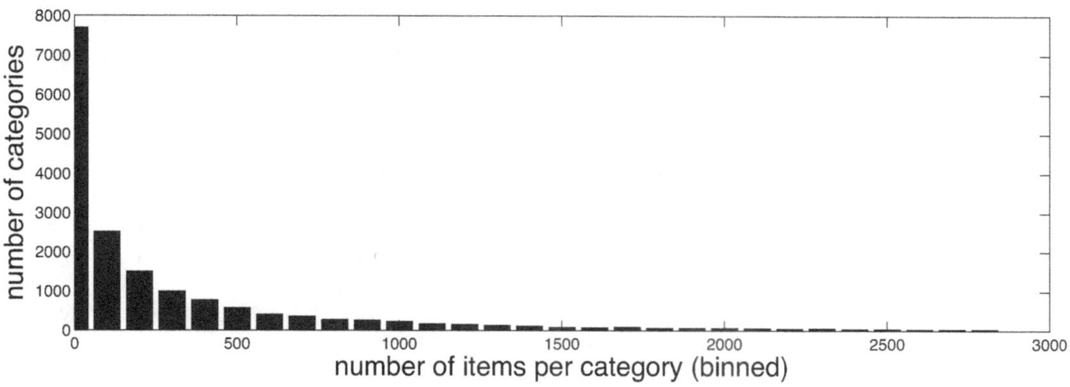

Figure 1: Distribution of items over eBay leaf categories. eBay categories exhibit high skewness with the vast majority of categories holding little inventory.

still suffers from data sparseness in spite of a huge inventory on the whole. The lack of training data for the corresponding classes may adversely affect the performance of machine learning algorithms which require adequate labeled documents for each class to learn reliable statistics. Moreover, many algorithms tend to behave poorly on unbalanced training sets as they tend to favor strongly predominant classes.

It is dauntingly expensive to label items manually for such a large number of categories. To alleviate this problem we tap into the expertise of millions of savvy eBay sellers and use the high volume of existing item inventory labeled by sellers as the proxy of ground-truth labels, under the assumption that items successfully sold have been placed into appropriate categories by sellers. Although the assumption does not always hold, it avoids the otherwise very expensive human labeling, and serves as a good approximation. However, the reduction in cost of human labeling comes at the expense of a quality drop of the training data. We observed, using editorial validation, that approximately 15% of the time the label provided by the seller is incorrect. This error rate in label approximation can give a loose upper bound of actual prediction error, based on observed experimental results.

When a seller lists an item on eBay, he or she is asked to write a title to briefly describe the item. Once the title is entered, the site suggests proper categories for the seller to choose from. So the item categorization is only based on the title words. Unlike typical free text documents, eBay limits the length of item title to a maximum of 50 characters (about 10 words on average), which in many cases is inadequate to describe an item precisely. For example, the following item title does not contain enough information to decide the most appropriate category.

Title: 9.5 White Gold Ring with .25 Carat Diamond Stones Band

- Jewelry & Watches → Men's Jewelry → Rings → Diamond
- Jewelry & Watches → Fine Jewelry → Fine Rings → Diamond
- Jewelry & Watches → Fashion Jewelry → Rings

Furthermore, the quality of titles varies a lot on the eBay site. Some inexperienced or malicious sellers give inaccurate or fraudulent titles, which makes our data set even noisier.

One important criterion for any large-scale production system is scalability. As an item categorization system for a popular e-commerce site, the model needs to be trained offline with hundreds of millions items, and then make online prediction in real-time for an incoming item. There are four million to twenty millions items listed daily on eBay. For the experiment presented here, we randomly collected a sample of 83 million items sold over a three month period of time. We ensured that even the smallest classes have some examples. For testing we used several millions of item sold a few days after the training period.

Although we cannot share the exact dataset we used due to legal reasons, very similar data is publicly available on eBay web site and through eBay Developers API [2].

[2]See `https://www.x.com/developers/ebay/` for details.

Level	Top nodes	Leaf Nodes within a top node		
		Avg	Max	Min
Balanced Splitting	4659	4.6	50	1

Table 2: Balanced splitting for the *hier-ebay-struc* baseline model.

4.2 Algorithms

4.2.1 Preprocessing

In data preprocessing step, item titles are first tokenized, and then punctuation is removed. A small stop-word list is used to omit the most common words. Furthermore, we observe that (1) numbers are indicative to distinguish between *single sale* and *whole sale* categories, and (2) prepositions, such as *with* and *for*, are useful to distinguish between *product* and *accessory* categories. Therefore, contrary to other text classification tasks, we keep numbers and prepositions in titles.

Our training set has more than 3 millions unique words after the preprocessing. We use unigrams of title words as features.

4.2.2 Coarse level classifier

For the coarse level classifier we use the K-Nearest-Neighbor (kNN) algorithm but applied feature selection to reduce the feature space.

We employ information gain (IG) as selection criteria which showed promising results in other text classification tasks [29]. We select the top 10% features with the highest IG. The optimal number of features was cross-validated in a foregoing study under a similar setting [21, 20]. There are 322,792 features in the coarse level.

We choose K-Nearest-Neighbor (kNN) algorithm as the coarse level classifier because of its great scalability, linear computational complexity, robustness to data sparseness and skewed category distribution [28], and interpretable category predictions which is especially important for a practical system.

KNN is based on a lazy learning method in which no explicit training process is required and all computation is deferred until classification. It classifies a test instance based on its closest training instances in the feature space. Given a test item, the kNN classification performs two steps: (1) find the k nearest neighbors among the items in training set, and then (2) perform a majority voting amongst the k neighbors to identify the category candidates. We use cosine values of two vectors to measure the similarity between items. The number of neighbors k is dynamically decided as follows: for an item to classify, the neighbors are fetched greedily first in descending order of similarity until the similarity score of a neighbor is below a threshold. The threshold is set as half of the score of the first neighbor. Next, the item is assigned to the class with the majority votes of its k nearest neighbors. The nearer neighbors are supposed to contribute more in the voting than the more distant ones. We have investigated various voting schema in our experiments, and finally used the reciprocal of the rank position to weight the neighbors. The voting function is a generalization of linear interpolation as follows:

$$score(t, c_i) = \sum_{t_j \in \mathrm{KNN}(t)} \frac{1}{R(t_j)} y(t_j, c_i)$$

where, KNN(t) indicates the set the k nearest neighbors of the item to classify t; $R(t_j) = \{1, 2, ..., k\}$ is the rank position of the neighbor t_j; $y(t_j, c_i) \in \{0, 1\}$ is the classification for the training item t_j with respect to the class c_i ($y = 1$ for $t_j \in c_i$, otherwise, $y = 0$). This paper does not aim to report rigorous exploration of the optimal settings for the parameter k, neighbor weighting or voting function in the kNN model. The setting introduced above, however, performed the best in our preliminary experiments of kNN-based flat classification.

The kNN classifier is often considered a slow classifier as intensive computation is needed at classification time to retrieve the neighbors. However, modern search engines make it possible to fetch and sort neighbors in milliseconds and have rendered kNN perfectly suitable for large scale classification problems. For instance, our production implementation of kNN using eBay search engine is able to classify an item in less than 100 ms in spite of a large number of classes and training samples.

4.2.3 Fine level classifier

For the fine level classifier we experimented with the Support Vector Machine (SVM) [25] algorithm. We do not apply feature selection for fine level classification as the feature space in latent groups is much smaller than the overall feature space.

Extensive empirical comparisons on text classification [19, 28] have shown that SVMs achieve excellent state-of-the-art performance.

SVMs construct a binary classifier that predicts whether an instance $\vec{x}$ is positive or negative, where the instance is represented as a feature vector. In the case of linearly separable instances, the decision $f(x) = sgn(\vec{w} \cdot \vec{x} + b)$ is made based on a separating hyperplane $\vec{w} \cdot \vec{x} + b = 0$ ($\vec{w} \in \mathcal{R}^n, b \in \mathcal{R}$). The goal of SVMs is to find the optimal hyperplane that separates the positive and negative training instances with a maximal margin, by solving a dual quadratic programming problem. Given a set $\mathcal{T}$ of training data and corresponding label pairs $(x_i, y_i), i = 1, \ldots, m$, where $x_i \in R^n$ and $y_i \in \{1, -1\}$, SVMs essentially solve the following optimization problem:

$$min_{w,b,\xi} \; \frac{1}{2} w^T w + C \sum_{i=1}^{m} \xi_i$$

$$\text{subject to } y_i(w^T \phi(x_i) + b) \geq 1 - \xi_i \text{ and } \xi_i \geq 0$$

Here x_i are the training vectors and $C > 0$ is the budget parameter, a penalty for the error term. In case of linearly non-separable data SVMs project the instances from the original space $\mathcal{R}^n$ to a higher dimensional space $\mathcal{R}^N$ based on a kernel function $K(\vec{x_1}, \vec{x_2}) = \Phi(\vec{x_1}) \cdot \Phi(\vec{x_2})$. This is commonly referred to as the *kernel-trick*, which makes it possible to find a linearly separable hyperplane in the projected high dimensional space.. A kernel function has the form $K(x_i, x_j) = \phi(x_i)^T \phi(x_j)$ and projects the input data x_i into a higher dimensional feature space $\phi(x_i)$. Although there are a number of kernels, in practice most often a linear

Classification Models	Top 1	Top 2	Top 5
flat-NB	64.4	77.1	87.3
flat-kNN	71.8	81.5	88.5
hier-ebay-struc	72.2	81.6	88.0
KNN-SVM	**75.4**	**83.8**	**89.9**

Table 3: Precision of various classification methods when top 1, 2 and 5 categories are returned. The classification methods are flat multinomial NB, flat k-nearest neighbor, hierarchical classifier leveraging eBay category structure and our proposed algorithm *k*NN-SVM.

kernel or radial basis function (RBF) kernels are used. They have the following form:

- linear kernel : $K(x_i, x_j) = x_i^T x_j$.
- RBF kernel : $K(x_i, x_j) = exp(-\gamma||x_i - x_j||^2), \gamma > 0$.

For our fine level classifier, we employed a highly efficient implementation of SVM with linear kernel, LibLinear [7]. This package also supports multi-class classification using one-vs-all strategy.

4.3 Baselines

We evaluated our proposed algorithm (**kNN-SVM**) against three different baselines, namely a flat kNN classifier (*flat-kNN*), a flat multinomial Naive Bayes (*flat-NB*) and a hierarchical classifier leveraging eBay category structure (*hier-ebay-struc*). We describe the baseline methods below.

- *Flat-kNN* is an implementation of the kNN classifier. As described in section 4.2.2, we use information gain (IG) as feature selection method, employ a production search engine for initial candidate selection, and finally use cosine similarity and dynamic neighbor selection for nearest neighbor voting.

- The multinomial NB classifier (*flat-NB*) is a good choice especially for large-scale online classification mainly because of its great scalability. Many previous work [14] reported that it performs quite well empirically. Smoothing plays an important role in NB training to alleviate the problems caused by data sparseness and unbalanced distribution. Since Shen et al. [21] reported quite promising results of the Dirichlet Priors (DP) smoothing in a similar task, we adopt DP smoothing ($\mu = 1000$) in the *flat-NB* model. One notorious drawback of NB classifier though, is that it may produce poorly calibrated probability estimation.

- The third baseline, *hier-ebay-struc*, performs hierarchical classification using the existing six-level topic structure at eBay. The large number of eBay categories makes it hard to train an iteration-based second-level classifier efficiently and accurately, such as DT, SVM or ME. On the other hand, lower levels (*Level 4* and *Level 5*) contain too many nodes to train the first level classifier effectively, e.g., *Level 4* has 13,904 nodes and *Level 5* has 19,942 nodes. To optimize the performance of the hierarchical classification, we propose a balanced splitting method to extract a small number of high-level nodes under which leaf categories distribute more or less evenly. The balanced splitting works as follows. We search on the entire hierarchical tree as in depth-first search (DFS). Once a non-leaf node (internal node) contains less than 50 leaf categories, we extract the internal node as a high-level node, and remove the path from root to the extracted node from further consideration. After exhausting the entire hierarchical tree, the extracted high-level nodes are mutually exclusive and spanning all leaf categories. The row "Balanced splitting" in Table 2 shows the number of high-level nodes (4659 nodes) and the distribution of the leaf categories over these internal nodes. This approach is easy to implement and heavily relies on the existing hierarchy. *hier-ebay-struc* uses this balanced splitting hierarchy. We first apply kNN model, the same as the *flat-kNN* model, to classify items into top-level nodes, and then apply a SVM model to further classify the items into one of the leaf categories.

Flat-kNN serves as a proxy for one-vs-all classification. Unfortunately we have not been able to scale SVM to our classification problem.

4.4 Results

The item classification system is evaluated using the usual precision metric defined as the fraction of items of the test for which the classifier recovered the correct class label. However, because some applications of item classification on e-commerce require to present several alternatives to the users, we are also interested in measuring accuracy when 2 and 5 classes are returned. This requires the fine level classifiers to return a ranked list of classes instead of a single prediction. For the various classifiers we tested, the ranking is obtained using the confidence score returned by the classifier. In the case of SVM, Platt's scaling [17] was used to obtain such confidence score. For the purpose of measuring accuracy when more than one class is returned, the classifier is considered correct when the gold standard (i.e the category picked by the seller when the item was listed on the site) is one of the returned classes. In the following "Top 1", "Top 2" and "Top 5" denotes the accuracy when 1, 2 and 5 classes are returned respectively.

Table 3 shows the overall accuracies of the flatten classification models (*flat-NB*, *flat-kNN*), the hierarchical classification models (*hier-ebay-struc* and our proposed approach (*KNN-SVM*). At all three recall levels ("Top 1", "Top 2" and "Top 5"), our approach performs the best in terms of accuracy. For "Top 1" in particular, it outperforms *flat-kNN* and *hier-ebay-struc* by about 3.6 percentage points, 3.2 percentage points, and the edge over *flat-NB* is 11 percentage points.

As for the conventional text classification models, *flat-kNN* significantly outperforms *flat-NB* by 7.4 percentage points for "Top 1". This gives the insight that the instance-based learning method, i.e. kNN, might be more suitable

1.	Cell Phones & PDAs → Cell Phone & PDA Accessories Electronics → iPod & MP3 Accessories → Cases
2.	Video Games → Wholesale Lots → Accessories Video Games → Accessories
3.	Jewelry & Watches → Loose Beads → Crystal Crafts → Beads & Jewelry Making → Beads, Pearls & Charms → Beads
4.	Books → Textbooks, Education Books → Nonfiction
5.	Sports Mem, Cards → Fan Shop → Cards → Football Sports Mem, Cards → Fan Shop → Autographs-Original → Football-NFL → Trading Cards
6.	Business & Industrial → Restaurant & Catering → Commercial Kitchen Equipment → Food Preparation Equipment → Food Processors Home & Garden → Inside the Home → Kitchen, Dining & Bar → Small Kitchen Appliances → Food Processors

Table 4: Examples of the category pairs which are frequently misclassified by the flatten classification model *flat-kNN*

Model	First level classification		Second level classification			
	Number of Nodes	Top 1	Number of leafs per node			Top 1
			Avg	Max	Min	
hier-ebay-struc	4659	79.8	4.6	50	1	72.2
KNN-SVM	6494	86.1	3.3	45	1	73.0

Table 5: Number of categories and accuracy for two level hierarchical classification models.

for classifying heterogeneous and short texts, i.e. the items on eBay. One conclusion we can draw here is that data sparseness penalizes *flat-NB* severely while it does not affect *flat-kNN* in the same fashion.

Another interesting finding is that the hierarchical classification model *hier-ebay-struc* does not show significant improvement over the flatten classification model *flat-kNN*. A later manual inspection of the items misclassified by *flat-kNN* suggests one explanation for this—the error cases from *flat-kNN* are beyond adjacent leaf categories on the category structure. This violates one prerequisite of hierarchical classification that it requires satisfactory classification accuracy at the top level and tackles the difficulty of classifying very confusing categories at lower levels. Table 4 shows examples of 6 category pairs which are most frequently misclassified by the flatten classification model *flat-kNN*. It is can be observed that some of the error cases are even across meta categories. Thus in the hierarchical model *hier-ebay-struc*, this type of errors will be made on the top level, which cannot be recovered by SVM models at the lower levels due to algorithmic design.

We now attempt to answer the third question concerning our proposed two level classification with latent group approach. The experiments show that our approach is significantly better than the conventional hierarchical model *hier-ebay-struc*. In Table 5 we show the detailed performance comparison between two hierarchical classification models. For *KNN-SVM*, classes are grouped into 6494 latent groups and each latent group contains 3.3 classes on average. For the top level classification, *KNN-SVM* performs better than *hier-ebay-struc* by 6.3 percentage points, although the number of categories is more than that in *hier-ebay-struc*. It indicates the latent group generation method we proposed in this paper captures class similarities properly, groups the most similar classes effectively, and ultimately ensures satisfactory performance on the top level classification. Table 6 further illustrates some examples of leaf categories within a latent group. It is obvious that the leaf categories in this latent group are actually hard to distinguish from each other despite some of them are quite far away in the eBay hierarchy structure.

Finally, the main motivation of this research is to leverage computationally demanding classification algorithms on very large datasets. The mere fact that we are able to leverage SVM (as a fine level classifier) and achieve higher classification accuracy on a problem where a flat SVM does not scale is a very significant step in that direction. But speed of execution is also a very important criterion in term of scalability and we now show that the goal is achieved on that front as well. The training time of *KNN-SVM* which includes training the kNN coarse level classifier (i.e. indexing the training sample using the search engine), estimating class confusion probabilities, running the dense subgraph enumeration algorithm and training the fine level classifier is about 3 hours for the setting of this experiment using a 10 thread implementation. The classification time of *KNN-SVM* is 520ms per item (for our research prototype, the production implementation taking only 100ms per item). This was measured on a 16 core x86 processor operating at 2.3 Ghz with 128Gb of memory. Table 7 shows a comparison with the multinomial NB classifier and the K-Nearest-Neighbor algorithm. Although *KNN-SVM* is slower than the flat classifiers, it is remarkably fast given the problem involves more than 20,000 classes and 83 million training samples.

1. Clothing, Shoes & Accessories → Men's Accessories → Backpacks, Bags & Briefcases → Duffle, Gym Bags
2. Clothing, Shoes & Accessories → Unisex Clothing, Shoes & Accs → Unisex Accessories → Bags & Backpacks → Backpacks & Bookbags
3. Clothing, Shoes & Accessories → Unisex Clothing, Shoes & Accs → Unisex Accessories → Bags & Backpacks → Duffle, Gym Bags
4. Clothing, Shoes & Accessories → Women's Handbags & Bags → Duffle & Gym Bags
5. Computers & Networking → Computer Accessories → Laptop Cases & Bags → Backpacks
6. Travel → Luggage

Table 6: Example of leaf categories in a latent group. Latent groups are discovered automatically using a graph algorithm. Our algorithm discovers latent group that spans three different meta categories namely, "Clothing, Shoes & Accessories", "Computers and Networking", and "Travel".

Classification model	Training (h)	Classification (ms)
flat-NB	0.66	20
flat-kNN	1	360
KNN-SVM	3	520

Table 7: Training speed (in hours) and classification speed (in millisecond) of two flat models and our two levels approach.

5. CONCLUSION

Item categorization, which can be formulated as a supervised text classification problem, is a fundamental technical challenge for e-commerce sites such as eBay. But the number of classes, the volume of the training data and the size of the feature space make the use of computationally intensive algorithms impractical for large scale deployment. In this paper, we proposed a novel and practical approach that allows leveraging off-the-shelf text classification algorithm by automatically grouping similar classes into latent groups using a dense subgraph enumeration algorithm and decomposing the problem into a coarse level classification task and a fine level classification task. The coarse level classifier is responsible for assigning a latent group while the fine level classifiers are responsible for assigning a class within a latent group. Experiments on large scale real data from eBay show that our approach significantly outperforms other known approaches while maintaining a very practical speed of execution.

For future work we are particularly interested in exploring the sensitivity of this two-levels approach in terms of classification accuracy with respect to the coherence of the latent groups i.e., the method used for enumerating the dense subgraphs.

6. ACKNOWLEDGMENTS

Authors are grateful to Rajyashree Mukherjee, Suresh Raman, Niraj Kothari, Chelly Yan and Wallace Mann for fruitful discussions about this research and for engineering assistance in deploying our algorithm into the production classification system. Thanks to Chih-Jen Lin for useful comments. Also thanks to the anonymous reviewers for providing us with important suggestions.

7. REFERENCES

[1] C. Apté, F. Damerau, and S. M. Weiss. Automated learning of decision rules for text categorization. *ACM Trans. Inf. Syst.*, 12:233–251, 1994.

[2] S. Bengio, J. Weston, and D. Grangier. Label embedding trees for large multi-class tasks. In *Advances in Neural Information Processing Systems (NIPS)*, 2010.

[3] L. Cai and T. Hofmann. Hierarchical document categorization with support vector machines. In *Proc. of the 13th ACM International Conference on Information and Knowledge Management(CIKM)*, pages 78–87, 2004.

[4] O. Dekel, J. Keshet, and Y. Singer. Large margin hierarchical classification. In *Proc. of the 21st International Conference on Machine Learning(ICML)*, pages 27–34, 2004.

[5] T. G. Dietterich and G. Bakiri. Solving multiclass learning problems via error-correcting output codes. *Artificial Intelligence Research*, 2:263–286, 1995.

[6] S. T. Dumais and H. Chen. Hierarchical classification of web content. In *Proc. of the ACM SIGIR Conference on Research and Development in Information Retrieval*, pages 256–263, 2000.

[7] R. E. Fan, K. W. Chang, C. J. Hsieh, X. R. Wang, and C. J. Lin. Liblinear: A library for large linear classification. *Journal of Machine Learning Research*, pages 1871–1874, 2008.

[8] Q. Y. G.-R. Xue, D. Xing and Y. Yu. Deep classification in large-scale text hierarchies. In *Proc. of the 31st International ACM SIGIR Conference on Research and Development in Information Retrieval*, pages 619–626, 2008.

[9] A. V. Goldberg. Finding a maximum density

subgraph. Technical Report UCB/CSD-84-171, EECS Department, University of California, Berkeley, 1984.

[10] T. Hastie and R. Tibshirani. Classification by pairwise coupling. *Annals of Statistics*, 26:451–471, 1998.

[11] T. Joachims. Text categorization with support vector machines: Learning with many relevant features. In *Proc. of the 10th European Conference on Machine Learning(ECML)*, pages 137–142, 1998.

[12] D. Koller and M. Sahami. Hierarchically classifying docuemnts using very few words. In *Proc. of the 14th International Conference on Machine Learning(ICML)*, pages 171–178, 1997.

[13] S. Kumar, J. Ghosh, and M. M. Crawford. Hierarchical fusion of multiple classifiers for hyperspectral data analysis. *Pattern Analysis and Applications*, 5:210–220, 2002.

[14] A. Macallum and K. Nigam. A comparison of event models for naive bayes text classification. In *Proc. of the AAAI-98 Workshop on Learning for Text Categorization*, 1998.

[15] A. McCallum, R. Rosenfeld, T. Mitchell, and A. Y. Ng. Improving text classification by shrinkage in a hierarchy of classes. In *Proc. of the 15th International Conference on Machine Learning(ICML)*, pages 359–367, 1998.

[16] K. Nigam, J. Lafferty, and A. McCallum. Using maximum entropy for text classification. In *Proc. of IJCAI-99 Workshop on Machine Learning for Information Filtering*, pages 61–67, 1999.

[17] J. C. Platt. Probabilistic outputs for support vector machines and comparisons to regularized likelihood methods. In *ADVANCES IN LARGE MARGIN CLASSIFIERS*, pages 61–74. MIT Press, 1999.

[18] R. Rifkin and A. Klautau. In defense of one-vs-all classification. *Machine Learning Research*, 5:101–141, 2004.

[19] F. Sebastiani. Machine learning in automated text categorization. *ACM Computing Surveys (CSUR)*, 34:1–47, 2002.

[20] D. Shen, J. Ruvini, M. Somaiya, and N. Sundaresan. Item categorization in the e-commerce domain. In *Proc. of The 20th ACM International Conference on Information and Knowledge Management (CIKM)*, 2011.

[21] D. Shen, J. D. Ruvini, R. Mukherjee, and N. Sundaresan. A study of smoothing algorithms for item categorization on e-commerce sites. In *Proc. of The Ninth International Conference on Machine Learning and Applications(ICMLA)*, 2010.

[22] C. N. Silla and A. A. Freitas. A survey of hierarchical classification across different application domains. *Data Mining and Knowledge Discovery*, 22:31–72, 2011.

[23] A. S.Weigend, E. D.Wiener, and J. O. Pedersen. Exploiting hierarchy in text categorization. *Information Retrieval*, pages 193–216, 1999.

[24] R. Tarjan. Depth-first search and linear graph algorithms. *SIAM Journal on Computing*, 1(2):146–160, 1972.

[25] V. N. Vapnik. *Statistical Learning Theory*, 1998.

[26] K. Weinberger and O. Chapelle. Large margin taxonomy embedding with an application to document categorization. *Advances in Neural Information Processing Systems*, pages 1737–1744, 2008.

[27] T. yan Liu, Y. Yang, H. Wan, H. jun Zeng, Z. Chen, and W. ying Ma. Support vector machines classification with a very large-scale taxonomy. *SIGKDD Explorations*, 7:2005, 2005.

[28] Y. Yang and X. Liu. A re-examination of text categorization methods. In *Proc. of the ACM SIGIR Conference on Research and Development in Information Retrieval*, pages 42–49, 1999.

[29] Y. Yang and J. O. Pedersen. A comparative study on feature selection in text categorization. In *Proc. of the 14th International Conference on Machine Learning(ICML)*, pages 412–420, 1997.

Matching Product Titles using Web-based Enrichment

Vishrawas Gopalakrishnan*
Suny Buffalo
Buffalo, NY
vishrawa@buffalo.edu

Suresh Iyengar
Yahoo Labs
Bangalore, India
supartha@yahoo-inc.com

Amit Madaan*
TheFind, Inc
Mountain View, CA
amadaan@thefind.com

Rajeev Rastogi*
Amazon
Bangalore, India
rastogi@amazon.com

Srinivasan Sengamedu*
Komli Labs
Bangalore, India
shs@komli.com

ABSTRACT

Matching product titles from different data feeds that refer to the same underlying product entity is a key problem in online shopping. This matching problem is challenging because titles across the feeds have diverse representations with some missing important keywords like brand and others containing extraneous keywords related to product specifications. In this paper, we propose a novel *unsupervised* matching algorithm that leverages web search engines to (1) *enrich* product titles by adding important missing tokens that occur frequently in search results, and (2) compute *importance scores* for tokens based on their ability to retrieve other (enriched title) tokens in search results. Our matching scheme calculates the Cosine similarity between enriched title pairs with tokens weighted by their importance scores. We propose an optimization that exploits the templatized structure of product titles to reduce the number of search queries. In experiments with real-life shopping datasets, we found that our matching algorithm has superior F1 scores compared to IDF-based cosine similarity.

Categories and Subject Descriptors

H.3.3 [**Information Storage and Retrieval**]: Information Search and Retrieval

General Terms

Algorithms

Keywords

Web-based enrichment, Entity resolution

*Work done while at Yahoo Labs, Bangalore

CIKM'12, October 29–November 2, 2012, Maui, HI, USA.

1. INTRODUCTION

Consumers are increasingly turning to online shopping sites (e.g., shopping.yahoo.com, shopping.bing.com) to research products prior to making buying decisions. These sites leverage data from multiple sources that include aggregator sites (e.g., PriceGrabber, CNET), merchant sites (e.g., buy.com, amazon.com) containing sales offers, reviews sites (e.g., epinions.com, newegg.com) containing reviews and ratings information, and auction sites (e.g., eBay, Amazon marketplace). The sites consolidate the specifications, prices, ratings, and reviews information for each product present in the various source data feeds, and present a unified view of each product to the user. Thus, the sites allow users to compare prices offered by different vendors for a product or browse through reviews for a product from different web sites.

A key challenge to providing a unified product view is matching records for the same product from different data feeds. This record matching problem has been extensively studied in the literature under different names like record linkage [13], duplicate detection [12, 20], entity resolution [2, 1], and merge/purge [14]. Much of this previous work has focused on matching records with multiple overlapping attributes. The general approach is to first compute similarity scores for each attribute using traditional similarity metrics like Jaccard similarity, Cosine similarity, edit distance, etc. [17, 12], and then combine these attribute-level similarity scores to derive record-level matching scores using unsupervised and supervised techniques. However, as discussed below, prior approaches may not work well in our product record matching scenario.

In our product setting, records in the different data feeds may have heterogeneous schemas and thus contain diverse sets of attribute values. For example, sales offer feeds from merchants may contain information about prices but not reviews, while a feed from a blogging or a product forum site may contain ratings and reviews information but not prices. Furthermore, even if these attributes are present, their values for the same product may vary widely across feeds making them unreliable to use for matching. This is because different vendors may price the same product very differently; similarly, product reviews across feeds may be written by diverse users with disparate viewpoints and writing styles. In the absence of universally agreed upon unique product identifiers between the various information providers, the only attribute that uniquely identifies a product and that is consistently present in all the feeds is *product title*. So in this paper, we rely on product titles for matching records in the different data feeds.

A product title is a short unstructured textual description that uniquely identifies a product. Previous work has used similarity metrics like Jaccard similarity, Cosine similarity, edit distance, etc. for determining the similarity between string-valued attributes like person names or addresses. However, different feeds may use diverse product title representations for the same product. Consequently, traditional string similarity metrics may not work well for matching product titles.

Consider the 3 product title pairs from product aggregators PriceGrabber and CNET in rows (a)-(c) of Table 1. The pair of titles in row (a) are different representations of the same camera product with model number "d200". The brand name "nikon" is missing in Title 1 while Title 2 does not contain relevant descriptive keywords like "digital slr camera" and other product specifications. Even though the two titles correspond to the same product, the Jaccard similarity between their token sets (using white space as delimiter) is only $\frac{1}{22} = 0.045$. In contrast, the pair of titles in row (b) correspond to different camera models but have a much higher Jaccard similarity of 0.125. Now, based on the title pairs in rows (a) and (b), it may be tempting to declare two titles as matching if they have identical model numbers. However, besides the obvious difficulty of identifying a wide range of model number formats within titles, this strategy will not work in many cases. For instance, the two titles in row (c) have the same model number but they represent different products. Specifically, Title 2 corresponds to a camera while Title 1 refers to its accessory – a camera battery charger.

Clearly, traditional similarity metrics like Jaccard similarity fare very poorly at the task of detecting matching product titles – the first matching title pair in Table 1 has a much lower similarity score compared to the other two non-matching pairs. The problem with simple Jaccard similarity is that it treats all tokens equally. However, as we saw earlier, tokens like model number are more important and thus should be assigned a higher weight. A popular weight assignment method in the IR literature [17] is *Inverse Document Frequency* (IDF) – it assigns each token w a weight of $I_w = \log \frac{N}{N_w}$ where N is the the total number of records in the feeds and N_w is the number of records that contain token w. The Cosine similarity metric (with IDF token weights) between a pair t, t' of titles is then given by $\frac{\sum_{w \in (t \cap t')} I_w^2}{\sqrt{\sum_{w \in t} I_w^2}\sqrt{\sum_{w \in t'} I_w^2}}$. We show the Cosine similarity scores for the title pairs in the final column of Table 1 (the IDF scores are computed over a corpus of 30M product titles obtained from PriceGrabber). As can be seen, taking IDF weights into account, the Cosine similarity score of the matching title pair in row (a) increases but is still much below the similarity scores for non-matching titles in rows (b) and (c).

One of the main reasons for the poor performance of the Cosine similarity metric is that product titles for the same entity across feeds have fairly diverse representations. Some titles could be missing important tokens like brand (e.g., "nikon" in Title 1 of row (a)), while others may contain extraneous tokens corresponding to product specifications that are not critical for identifying the product (e.g., Title 1 in row (a)). This hurts the similarity score of the matching title pair in row (a). Furthermore, in some instances, IDF weights do not accurately capture the importance of tokens. In Table 2, we show the IDF weights (in parenthesis) assigned to tokens belonging to the titles in Table 1.

As can be seen, in Title 1 of row (a), several extraneous tokens like "3872" and "2592" are assigned higher weights than the model number "d200". Similarly, in Title 1 of row (c), important tokens like "charger", "2800mah" and "rechargeable" that describe the battery charger accessory are assigned low weights compared to the model number "fe140". A shortcoming of IDF is that it assigns a single weight to each token proportional to the inverse of its global frequency in the feeds independent of the context. Essentially, IDF does not take into account the relevance of a token to its product title context when computing its weight.

To overcome the above-mentioned challenges associated with using traditional similarity metrics to match product titles, we leverage the web. Our approach to matching product titles involves three key steps: (1) *Enrich* each product title by filling in missing tokens that frequently occur in the broader context of the product title, (2) Compute an *importance score* for each token in the enriched product title based on its power to identify the underlying product, and (3) Match enriched titles with tokens weighted by their importance scores. We use web search engines in the first two steps to determine an expanded context for each product title in order to enrich it, and to compute importance scores. Web search engines allow us to efficiently sift through billions of pages to identify the most relevant web pages for a product.

Our main contributions can be summarized as follows:

1) We present an end-to-end system architecture for matching product titles with varying formats. The system is completely unsupervised, and performs a sequence of tasks starting with enrichment of product titles and computation of token weights, followed by matching the potentially co-referent enriched title pairs.

2) We propose a method for enriching product titles with (missing) keywords that appear frequently in the context defined by search engine results.

3) We assign an importance score to each token in the enriched title based on its ability to retrieve other tokens (of enriched title) in search results. Our matching algorithm calculates the Cosine similarity between enriched title pairs with tokens weighted by their importance scores.

4) We propose an optimization for reducing the number of calls to the search engine. Our optimization predicts approximate enrichments and importance scores for a product title based on past enrichments for similar-structured product titles.

5) In experiments with real-life shopping datasets, our matching algorithm achieves higher F1 scores compared to IDF-based Cosine similarity. Furthermore, our enrichment and importance score prediction optimizations reduce the number of search queries significantly without adversely impacting matching accuracy.

Table 1: Matching and non-matching product titles.

#	Title 1 (PriceGrabber)	Title 2 (CNET)	Jaccard Similarity	Cosine Similarity
(a)	d200 10.2 megapixel digital slr camera body with lens kit - 18 mm - 135 mm (2.5" lcd - 7.5x optical zoom - 3872 x 2592 image)	nikon d200	0.045	0.19
(b)	dcr-ip55 handycam (2.5"" hybrid lcd)	sony handycam dcr-sx41 (red)	0.125	0.27
(c)	fe-140 digital camera battery charger replacement for 4 aa nimh 2800mah rechargeable batterie	olympus fe-140	0.07	0.47

Table 2: IDF scores for product title tokens.

#	Title 1 (PriceGrabber)	Title 2 (CNET)
(a)	*d200(10.2)* 10.2(8) megapixel(8.5) digital(6.3) slr(9.4) camera(6.6) body(5.7) with(2.6) lens(6.1) kit(3.9) 18(4) mm(6.9) mm135(15.6) 2.5"(5.7) lcd(6.8) 7.5x(12.6) optical(6.8) zoom(7.8) *3872(12.6)* *2592(12.2)* image(6.9)	nikon(9.5) d200(10.2)
(b)	dcrip55(13.7) handycam(11.3) 2.5""(5.7) hybrid(7.8) lcd(6.8)	sony(8) handycam(11.3) dcrsx41(16.5) red(4)
(c)	*fe140(15.6)* digital(6.3) camera(6.6) battery(5.6) *charger(6.7)* replacement(4.9) for(2.6) 4(3.7) aa(8.5) nimh(9.5) *2800mah(11)* *rechargeable(8.5)* batterie(5.6)	olympus(10) fe140(15.6)

2. MATCHING SYSTEM OVERVIEW

The input to our matching system consists of a pair of data feeds D_1, D_2, each containing product title records. Each record contains a variable length string that represents the title of a unique product. For a product title record t, we abuse notation a bit and use t to also denote the set of tokens (using space as delimiter) in t. Our system outputs matching product title pairs from the two data feeds that refer to the same underlying product entity.

As we saw earlier, product titles contained in data feeds are unstructured and have diverse formatting conventions – some may be missing important keywords while others may contain redundant keywords that are not required for identifying the product. This makes the task of matching product title pairs extremely challenging. Our matching system consists of four main components: (1) Enrichment, (2) Importance score computation, (3) Blocking, and (4) Pairwise matching. Below, we describe the high-level functionality of each component, deferring the presentation of algorithmic details to the next section.

(1) *Enrichment.* The enrichment module enriches product titles by adding relevant tokens like brand or product line that may be previously absent. It leverages web search engines to determine the broader context for a product title t, and then augments the title with high-frequency tokens in the context to get the enriched title $E(t)$.

(2) *Importance score computation.* Each token w belonging to an enriched title $E(t)$ is assigned an importance score $I_t(w)$ based on its power to identify the underlying product entity. This is computed based on the search results obtained by pairing each enriched title token w with the remaining tokens. $I_t(w)$ is proportional to the number of enriched title tokens retrieved in these results.

(3) *Blocking.* The enriched feeds $E(D_1), E(D_2)$ containing the enriched product titles with token importance scores are input to the blocking module. Comparing every pair of enriched titles to see if they match is extremely inefficient especially for large feeds containing hundreds of thousands of records. The blocking module uses prefix filtering [6] to prune away enriched title pairs that cannot possibly match.

(4) *Pairwise matching.* A subset of the enriched title pairs $E(t)$, $E(t')$ (returned by blocking) are compared, and output if they are found to match. More specifically, if the Cosine similarity between the titles with tokens weighted by their importance scores exceeds a pre-specified threshold, then titles t and t' are declared to be a matching pair.

The enrichment and importance score computation modules are the most expensive from a computational perspective – as they repeatedly invoke the search engine to enrich the product titles and calculate token weights. In Section 4, we propose an optimization to reduce the overall number of web search queries for enrichment and importance score calculation. Our optimization predicts enrichments and importance scores for product titles based on previously computed enrichments and importance scores for product titles with similar structure/templates.

3. ALGORITHMS

In the following subsections, we describe the algorithms at the core of the four components of our matching system.

3.1 Enrichment

The enrichment module is responsible for filling in missing relevant tokens in the product title. Our enrichment solution described in Algorithm 1 achieves this by first determining the expanded context for the product title, and then adding to the title frequently occurring tokens in the context.

Algorithm 1 uses the web to determine the broader context for an entity given its product title. The web is a vast repository of documents containing information on virtually every possible entity or topic, from the very esoteric to the

Algorithm 1 Enrich

Input: Product title t, support threshold τ;
Output: Enriched title $E(t)$;

Get top-K web search result titles $t_1, \ldots, t_K$ by issuing t as query;
For each token w, let $freq(w)$ be the number of distinct titles t_i that contain w;
/* Compute high-frequency tokens */
Let $w_1, w_2, \ldots, w_q$ be tokens with $freq(w_j) > \tau$ arranged in decreasing order of $freq(w_j)$;
Let j be the index for which $freq(w_j) - freq(w_{j+1})$ is maximum;
High-frequency tokens $h = \{w_1, \ldots, w_j\}$;
$E(t) = t \cup h$;
return $E(t)$;

Algorithm 2 Compute_Importance_Scores

Input: Enriched title $E(t)$, support threshold τ;
Output: Token importance scores $I_t(w)$;

for each token $w \in E(t)$ **do**
  $I_t(w) = 0$;
  for each token $w' \in (E(t) - \{w\})$ **do**
    Get top-K web search result titles $t_1, \ldots, t_K$ by issuing the keyword pair $w\ w'$ as query;
    for each token $w'' \in (E(t) - \{w, w'\})$ **do**
      Let $freq(w'')$ be the number of distinct titles t_i that contain w'';
      if $freq(w'') > \tau$ **then** $I_t(w) = I_t(w) + 1$;
    end for
  end for
end for
return $\{I_t(w) : w \in E(t)\}$;

extremely common. For product entities, the web contains dedicated pages containing product information like title, price, description, reviews, ratings etc. in a wide range of web sites like Wikipedia, and aggregator sites like PriceGrabber, CNET, Amazon, Yahoo!, MSN, etc. These sites contain mentions of product entities in a variety of different formats. Thus, we can use the different representations of a given entity on the web, and also the keywords that occur in the vicinity of entity references within web pages to establish the extended context for the entity.

The key question, of course, is how to sift through the billions of pages on the web to locate the most relevant pages with mentions of a product entity. This is exactly the task that web search engines are good at. Given a query with a subset of keywords describing a unique product, search engines return the top web pages related to the product. To surface the most relevant pages for a given query, search engines exploit a range of signals like font, size, and position of query keywords within a page, presence of query keywords in anchor text for the page, PageRank, query and page categories (e.g., electronics, music, apparel), etc.

Search engines assign a ranking to the returned web pages with the ranking algorithm designed to place the most relevant pages at the top. Consequently, in our work, we only consider the top-K results returned by the search engine since these are very likely to contain most of the highly relevant product pages. For each result of a query, the search engine interface returns the page URL, title, and a short summary comprising a few sentences from the page containing query terms.

Our enrichment procedure starts by invoking the search engine interface with the product title t as the search query. It then considers the titles t_i of the top-K results returned by the search engine as the expanded context for the underlying product entity. Finally, it uses the high-frequency tokens in the context to enrich the input title t. To identify the high-frequency tokens, Algorithm 1 considers the tokens w with frequency $freq(w)$ greater than the support threshold τ and clusters them into two sets such that the minimum gap in frequencies between the two sets is maximized. The tokens in the cluster with the higher frequencies are then considered to be the high-frequency tokens h. Note that clustering helps to separate the more relevant tokens with higher frequencies from the less relevant ones which are pruned. The final enriched title $E(t)$ is then obtained by adding the high-frequency tokens in h to the title t.

In our experiments, we found that selecting $K = 20$ and $\tau = 0.2$ gave enrichments with the best matching performance. Also, in our implementation, we shrunk the gap $freq(w_j) - freq(w_{j+1})$ in the frequencies of tokens w_j and w_{j+1} by a factor $(0.9)^j$ – this further biased token selection towards higher frequencies and increased relevance.

Table 3 shows the enrichments for the product titles in Table 1 – the new keywords that are added to the enriched titles are shown in bold. As can be seen, the enriched representations now contain important tokens like brand (e.g., "nikon", "sony") that were previously missing.

3.2 Importance Score Computation

Not all tokens in an enriched title are equally important – clearly, certain tokens like model number are more important than others. Intuitively, a token in an enriched title is important if it is critical for identifying the underlying product entity. For example, in Title 1 in row (a) of Table 1, the model number "d200" is more important than "zoom" or "2592" since it plays a bigger role in identifying the product. Consequently, we assign importance scores to tokens based on their identification power.

The main question then is: how do we measure the identification power of a token? For this, we rely on web search. A key observation here is that the enriched product title contains several relevant keywords for describing (and uniquely identifying) the corresponding product. As a result, if the search results for a token contain many repetitions of keywords in the enriched title, then the results are very likely for the underlying product and we can conclude that the token has high identification power. Thus, the number of repeatedly appearing enriched title keywords in the web search results for a token is a good proxy for its identification power.

In practice, however, individual tokens can be ambiguous, causing search results to span the diverse meanings for the token. So to disambiguate queries, we pair each token w with other tokens w' in the enriched title, and consider the number of frequently occurring title tokens in the web search results of all the pairs as a measure of importance of the token w. Algorithm 2 describes our procedure for computing importance scores for the tokens of an enriched title $E(t)$. Notice that when computing the importance score $I_t(w)$ for

Table 3: Enriched product titles and importance scores.

#	Enriched Title 1 (PriceGrabber)	Enriched Title 2 (CNET)	Cosine Similarity
(a)	**nikon**(35) *d200(69)* 10.2(55) megapixel(54) digital(23) slr(60) camera(34) body(35) with(26) lens(33) kit(17) 18(31) mm(20) mm135(2) 2.5"(19) lcd(35) 7.5x(93) optical(44) zoom(42) *3872(58) 2592(38)* image(14)	nikon(1) d200(1)	0.36
(b)	**sony**(2) dcrip55(9) handycam(6) 2.5""'(5) hybrid(5) lcd(4)	sony(2) handycam(3) dcrsx41(7) rec(4)	0.18
(c)	*fe140(22)* digital(21) camera(21) battery(7) *charger(14)* replacement(11) for(8) 4 aa(15) nimh(24) *2800mah(27) rechargeable(20)* batterie(16)	olympus(1) fe140(1)	0.25

token $w \in E(t)$, we only consider tokens w'' in $E(t)-\{w,w'\}$ that frequently occur in the search result titles for keyword pair w w'. This is because the search result titles for query w w' will most likely contain the keywords w and w' irrespective of how important tokens w or w' are; however, if the result titles also repeatedly contain other keywords from $E(t)-\{w,w'\}$, then it is a strong indication that either token w or w' or both are important.

Traditional IR approaches use IDF scores to capture the importance of tokens. The basic premise is that rare words in a corpus have high identification power, and so are more important. Thus, IDF assigns each token a single score that is inversely proportional to its global frequency in the corpus. In our experiments, we found that IDF usually assigns high scores to important tokens like model number. However, there are also instances when it assigns high scores to redundant keywords like "2592" (in row (a) of Table 2) because they are rare and low scores to important keywords like "charger" (in row (c) of Table 2). A general drawback of IDF is that it assigns each token a single score based only on global context independent of the co-occurring keywords in the token's local product title context. Furthermore, IDF score computation requires a base corpus, and token scores can vary depending on the choice of corpus.

Our importance score computation approach is very different from the IDF approach. For each token, we directly estimate its identification power by measuring the overlap between its local product title context and web search results, and use the degree of overlap as a measure of the token's importance. Thus, our approach computes importance scores taking into account only local contextual information for each product title and web search results – this has multiple consequences: (1) Our approach does not require a base corpus and is not sensitive to the choice of corpus, and (2) A token can have multiple importance scores depending on the local product title context that it appears in.

The importance scores computed by our approach for tokens in enriched product titles are shown in parenthesis in Table 3. As can be seen, in Title 1 of row (a), the model number "d200" with high identification power is also assigned a high importance score while the less relevant tokens like "zoom" and "2592" are assigned much lower importance scores. Similarly, important tokens like "charger" and "2800mah" in Title 1 of row (c) are also assigned high scores relative to the model number "fe140". In contrast, IDF assigns high scores to tokens "3872" and "2592" relative to the model number "d200" (see row (a) of Table 2). Also, "charger" and "2800mah" are assigned low IDF scores of 6.7 and 11 compared to the model number "fe140" which is assigned an IDF score of 15.6 (see row (c) of Table 2). Thus, our importance scores capture the significance of a token in a product title better than IDF scores.

Algorithm 3 MATCHING_PAIRS

Input: Titles t, t', support threshold τ, similarity threshold γ;
Output: Match/No match;

$E(t) =$ ENRICH(t,τ);
$\{I_t(w)\} =$ COMPUTE_IMPORTANCE_SCORES$(E(t),\tau)$;
$E(t') =$ ENRICH(t',τ);
$\{I_{t'}(w)\} =$ COMPUTE_IMPORTANCE_SCORES$(E(t'),\tau)$;
if $\frac{\sum_{w\in(E(t)\cap E(t'))} I_t(w)\cdot I_{t'}(w)}{\sqrt{\sum_{w\in E(t)} I_t(w)^2}\sqrt{\sum_{w\in E(t')} I_{t'}(w)^2}} > \gamma$ **then**
  return match;
else
  return no-match;
end if

Observe that Algorithm 2 issues a search query for every keyword pair w w', where $w' \in E(t)-\{w\}$, when computing the importance score $I_t(w)$ for token w. This can result in a large number of calls to the search engine which can get computationally expensive. One way to reduce the number of queries is to randomly select a subset of tokens E' from $E(t)-\{w\}$, and then issue queries for only keyword pairs w w' where $w' \in E'$. The importance score $I_t(w)$ for w is then computed by summing up the number of times tokens from $E(t)-\{w,w'\}$ frequently occur in the search results for the random queries.

3.3 Blocking

Comparing every pair of enriched titles to see if they match can be prohibitively expensive for large data feeds containing hundreds of thousands of records. Clearly, titles whose enrichments have no tokens in common cannot possibly match, and we can skip comparing such title pairs. The blocking module uses prefix filtering techniques [6] that look for overlap among small filtered prefixes of the titles to generate potentially matching title pairs.

3.4 Pairwise Matching

Algorithm 3 describes our matching algorithm to determine whether two product titles t and t' represent the same entity or not. Our matching procedure calculates the Cosine similarity between the two enriched titles with importance scores as token weights. The titles are a declared to be a match if their similarity exceeds the similarity threshold γ.

Table 3 shows the similarity scores between enriched title pairs using our matching approach. Compared to traditional IDF-based similarity between the original product titles (see Table 1), our matching algorithm returns higher similarity scores for matching titles (in row (a)) and lower scores for non-matching titles (in rows (b)-(c)). Moreover, observe that the similarity scores for matching titles are greater than those for non-matching titles, thus allowing the matching title pairs to be distinguished from the non-matching ones.

4. OPTIMIZATIONS

Issuing queries to the search engine and subsequently processing the search results to compute product title enrichments and importance scores is the most expensive step in our matching solution. In this section, we propose an optimization to reduce the number of search engine invocations.

Frequently, within a data feed, there are groups of product titles with very similar structure. For example, product titles for the same product line in Table 4 share a common template with the only difference being the model number. Now, within a group of similar-structured titles, if a sufficient number of titles have already been enriched, then we can use these enrichments to predict approximate enrichments for the remaining titles in the group. Similarly, we can leverage previously calculated importance scores for enriched titles to predict approximate importance scores for new enrichments. This is the key idea underlying our optimization that predicts enrichments and importance scores for product titles.

Algorithm 4 describes our procedure for predicting the enrichment and importance scores for a given input title t. The procedure starts by using Jaccard similarity (with threshold λ) to identify a subset S of previously enriched titles that are similar to t. Note that the subset S can be efficiently retrieved by indexing the entire set T of enriched titles and using prefix filtering techniques described in [6]. Now, if S contains very few titles (less than δ), then we simply compute the enrichment and importance scores using Algorithms 1 and 2 instead of trying to predict them. Else, we find the tokens F that consistently and frequently occur in the enrichments of the similar titles in S – clearly, these are very likely to also belong to the enrichment for t and so we add these to t to obtain its enrichment $E(t)$. These frequent tokens in the enrichments cover brand names and generic keywords like camera, etc. Observe that some of the tokens in F may not occur in the titles themselves. For each token w in F, we set its importance score $I_t(w)$ to the average of its importance scores $I_{t'}(w)$ for titles $t' \in S$. Furthermore, to overcome the variations in token importance scores across titles, we normalize scores by dividing each token score by the maximum score in the title.

Now, certain discriminating tokens like model numbers will not be frequent in the enrichments, and thus will not be in F. In order to predict importance scores for these (infrequent) tokens in $E(t) - F$, we introduce the notion of landmark tokens – these are basically tokens in t that occur frequently in the titles in S. We store landmark tokens in the set L. For each token w occurring in a title $t' \in S$, we construct a signature $sig_{t'}(w)$ based on w's distance from the landmark token set. More specifically, the signature $sig_{t'}(w)$ consists of pairs $(w', dist_{t'}(w, w'))$ for each landmark token w'. Here, $dist_{t'}(w, w')$ is the distance (in terms of tokens) of w from w' in the sequence-of-tokens representation for t'.

Algorithm 4 PREDICT

Input: Title t, set T of enriched titles, their enrichments $E(t')$, and normalized token importance scores $I_{t'}(w)$;
Input: Threshold parameters λ, δ, σ, μ;
Output: Predicted enrichment $E(t)$, importance scores $I_t(w)$;

$S = \{t' : t' \in T \wedge \text{JACCARDSIM}(t, t') > \lambda\}$;
if ($|S| < \delta$) **then return** $\emptyset$, $\emptyset$;

/* Compute enrichment */
Let $E(S) = \{E(t') : t' \in S\}$;
Let $freq(w, E(S))$ = frequency of token w in $E(S)$;
$F = \{w : freq(w, E(S)) \geq \mu\}$;
$E(t) = F \cup t$;

/* Predict importance scores for tokens in F */
for all tokens $w \in F$ **do**
  $I_t(w) = \text{avg}\ \{I_{t'}(w) : w \in E(t') \wedge t' \in S\}$;
end for

/* Predict importance scores for tokens in $E(t) - F$ */
Let $freq(w, S)$ = frequency of token w in S;
$L = \{w : w \in t \wedge freq(w, S) \geq \sigma\}$;
for all titles $t' \in S$ **do**
  for all tokens $w \in t'$ **do**
    $sig_{t'}(w) = \{(w', dist_{t'}(w, w')) : w' \in L\}$;
  end for
end for
for all tokens $w \in (E(t) - F)$ **do**
  $sig_t(w) = \{(w', dist_t(w, w')) : w' \in L\}$;
  $I_t(w) = \text{avg}\ \{I_{t'}(w') : w' \in t' \wedge t' \in S \wedge sig_{t'}(w') \approx sig_t(w)\}$;
end for
return $E(t), \{I_t(w) : w \in E(t)\}$;

Table 4: Product titles along with importance scores.

#	Product Title	Importance Scores
(a)	sony cybershot dsct20 black	0.4 0.6 1 0.8
(b)	sony cybershot dsch10 black	0.4 0.6 1 0.8
(c)	sony cybershot dsct2 blue	0.4 0.6 1 0.8

Note that $dist_{t'}(w, w')$ is negative if w occurs to the left of landmark token w' in the title t', and positive if it occurs to the right. In case w' does not belong to t', then $dist_{t'}(w, w')$ is ∞.

Now, since titles in S and t follow the same template, tokens of the same type (e.g., model number, color) occur in similar positions across the titles and will thus have near-identical signatures. As a result, even though an individual token w in $E(t) - F$ is not frequent in the enrichments, w's signature will be frequent due to tokens of the same type as w in other titles. Furthermore, these tokens belonging to other titles in S, of the same type and with near-identical signatures as w, will also have similar importance scores as w. Thus, we can predict the importance score of token $w \in (E(t) - F)$ by averaging the importance scores of tokens belonging to $t' \in S$ with very similar signatures (that agree on the distances to most of the landmark tokens).

EXAMPLE 1. *Consider a new product title t = "sony cybershot dscw80 black" and let the product titles in Table 4 be the set S of titles similar to t. Let the enriched product titles be the same as the raw product titles. Furthermore, let the importance scores for the four tokens in each title be 0.4, 0.6, 1 and 0.8 as shown in Table 4. For support threshold $\mu = 2$, the frequent tokens F in the enrichments are {"sony", "cybershot", "black"}. Thus, the enriched title $E(t) = F \cup t$ = {"sony", "cybershot", "dscw80", "black"}. The importance scores for tokens in F are computed by averaging their importance scores across the enrichments. Thus, the importance scores (shown in parenthesis) for tokens in F are: "sony" (0.4), "cybershot" (0.6), and "black" (0.8). Next, we show how the importance score for token "dscw80" in $E(t) - F$ is calculated. For $\sigma = 2$, the landmark tokens L are {"sony", "cybershot", "black"} – these are the frequent tokens in the titles in S. Now, the signature for token "dscw80" in t is {("sony", 2), ("cybershot", 1), ("black", -1)}. The tokens "dsct20" and "dsch10" in their respective titles (in rows (a) and (b)) have the same signature. Thus, the importance score for token "dscw80" is 1 which is the average of the scores for tokens "dsct20" and "dsch10".* □

5. EXPERIMENTS

In this section, we present a detailed evaluation of our proposed enrichment, importance score computation, and optimization algorithms.

Datasets: We use two datasets in our experiments.

- **Abt-Buy dataset**[1]**:** This contains 1081 products from Abt and 1092 product titles from Buy. The matching quality for this dataset is also evaluated in [16].
- **PG-CNET dataset:** This is a smaller dataset containing 340 matching camera and appliance product titles from PriceGrabber and CNET. The ground truth is generated using MPN-UPC values, if available. For those products that did not have the MPN-UPC value, matching pairs are identified manually.

Evaluation Metrics: We use the popular F1 score measure to evaluate the matching quality. To characterize the effectiveness of enrichment prediction, we define two metrics: *Enrichment Prediction Coverage (EPC)* and *Enrichment Prediction Quality (EPQ)*. *EPC* is the fraction of titles for which enrichments as well as importance scores are predicted, and *EPQ* is the average Cosine similarity between the actual and the predicted importance score vectors over predicted titles. Observe that the cost savings in search queries (defined as the fractional decrease in search queries issued to get the enrichments and the importance scores) is equal to *EPC*. Also, *EPQ* measures the similarity between the actual and the predicted importance scores.

Schemes Compared: We evaluate the matching quality for the following two schemes:

- **IDF:** We use the Cosine similarity between raw titles with the IDF weighting scheme as the baseline for comparison.
- **EN+IMP:** This is our matching algorithm with enriched titles and importance scores. We set the default values for the number of search results K and support threshold τ (in Algorithms 1 and 2) to 20 and 0.2 respectively.
- **EN+IMP(Opt):** This is our EN+IMP algorithm with enrichment prediction (Algorithm 4).

We use the Bing Search API for the search results. Furthermore, we perform blocking as discussed in Section 3.3 for all the above three schemes. Our experimental results demonstrate that (1) our web-based enrichments and importance scores improve the matching quality compared to IDF-based Cosine similarity, and (2) the search query volume reduces substantially with our proposed enrichment prediction scheme.

5.1 Matching quality of IDF vs EN+IMP

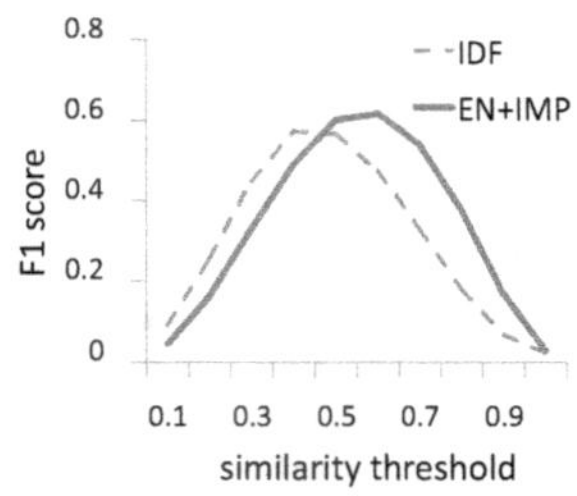

(a) Abt-Buy

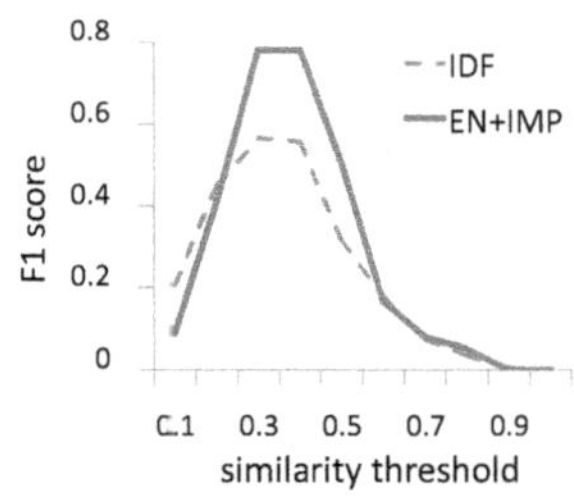

(b) PG-CNET

Figure 1: Matching quality of IDF vs EN+IMP.

The graphs in Figure 1 show the F1 scores for the IDF and EN+IMP schemes as the similarity threshold (parameter γ in Algorithm 3) is varied. As can be seen from the figure, our EN+IMP matching scheme with web-based enrichments and importance scores outperforms IDF-based matching. For instance, for the Abt-Buy dataset, IDF performs the best at $\gamma = 0.4$ with an F1 score of 0.57, as compared to our EN+IMP scheme which achieves a higher F1 score of 0.62 at $\gamma = 0.6$. The difference in F1 scores is much higher in the PG-CNET dataset, with IDF having its highest F1 score of 0.57 at $\gamma = 0.3$, as compared to 0.78 with our EN+IMP scheme.

Also, an important point to note here is that our method is completely unsupervised. The F1 scores obtained with our scheme, specifically for the Abt-Buy dataset, are comparable to the scores presented in [16], obtained using supervised techniques. The PG-CNET dataset performs better than the Abt-Buy dataset, mainly because the product titles in PG-CNET are more ambiguous than the Abt-Buy titles – missing key tokens and presence of extraneous words.

Table 5 compares the normalized scores assigned by IDF and EN+IMP to important keywords for a few example product titles. For a given product title, the brand name and model number are the representative tokens and are expected to get high scores. As can be seen, the IDF scores for brand names are significantly lower than the importance scores computed by EN+IMP. This is because brand names like Cannon and Samsung despite being important appear in many product titles, and so get assigned low IDF scores. Also, model number terms get higher importance scores compared to IDF scores most of the times.

[1]Available at `http://dbs.uni-leipzig.de/en/research/projects/object_matching/fever/benchmark_datasets_for_entity_resolution`

Table 5: Normalized scores for brand name and model number in IDF and EN+IMP.

Product title	Brand (IDF)	Brand (EN+IMP)	Model (IDF)	Model (EN+IMP)
Canon Yellow Ink Cartridge - Yellow - **CLI8Y**	0.17	0.42	0.52	0.72
Canon Black Ink Cartridge - Black - **PG40BK**	0.20	0.47	0.64	0.68
Toshiba SD-P91S Portable DVD Player	0.37	0.42	0.75	0.68
Samsung LN40A650 40' LCD TV	0.26	0.43	0.61	0.62

Table 6: F1 scores with varying number of web results (K) for Abt-Buy.

similarity threshold	$K=5$	$K=10$	$K=20$	$K=25$
0.3	0.329	0.325	0.328	0.324
0.4	0.503	0.492	0.490	0.479
0.5	0.609	0.595	0.600	0.587
0.6	0.614	0.616	**0.617**	0.601
0.7	0.530	0.540	0.542	0.542

5.2 Parameter sensitivity analysis for EN-IMP

We perform a series of experiments to identify the optimal parameter settings for our algorithms. In this section, we present the parameter sensitivity results for the Abt-Buy dataset. The number of web results for each query (K) and support threshold (τ) are two important parameters in our matching scheme (Algorithms 1 and 2). Enrichments and importance scores are computed based on the search results fetched. The support threshold should not be high so as to miss some important keywords; and at the same time it should not be very low to allow erroneous keywords.

Table 6 shows the F1 matching scores with varying number of web results (K) for similarity match thresholds (γ) between 0.3 and 0.7. As can be seen, we obtain the highest F1 score at $K = 20$. Figure 2 shows the F1 scores for different values of support threshold (τ). Setting τ to 0.2 gives the best F1 score. So we set $K = 20$ and $\tau = 0.2$ in all our experiments. In general, we found that the matching quality of EN+IMP to be more sensitive to the support threshold (τ), as opposed to the number of search results (K). However, K plays an important role in limiting the number of results processed.

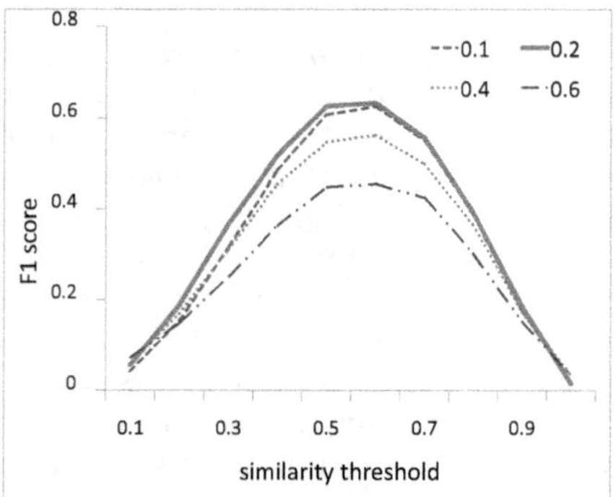

Figure 2: Varying support threshold τ for Abt-Buy.

5.3 Enrichment prediction results

Reducing the number of web searches is an important component of our matching scheme. In this section, we present a detailed evaluation of our enrichment prediction algorithm EN+IMP(Opt). We perform enrichment prediction in a batch setting. Here we use an initial seed set of (randomly selected) titles and their enrichments (B), and use this seed set for predicting enrichments and importance scores for the rest of the corpus. Recall that EPC captures the cost savings in the number of search queries and EPQ measures the quality of prediction - we compute these metrics for the non-seed titles. We also evaluate the effect of seed set size $|B|$ on EPC and EPQ. In our experiments, we set the default value of |B| for the Abt-Buy and PG-CNET datasets to 1000 and 133 respectively.

5.3.1 *Matching quality with enrichment prediction*

The graphs in Figure 3 compare the matching quality of EN+IMP with enrichment prediction to IDF, for both the datasets. From the graph 3(a), we observe that the EN+IMP(Opt) does marginally better than the IDF scheme, for the Abt-Buy dataset. The difference in performance is higher for the PG-CNET dataset, as seen from the graph 3(b). The highest F1 score with IDF is 0.57 as compared to 0.61 with EN-IMP(Opt). Furthermore, the EPC value is 0.8 implying that enrichments were predicted for 80% of remaining titles. This shows that with our prediction schemes based on the templatized structure of product titles, we can reduce the number of web searches significantly while preserving matching quality. One important observation to make here is the prediction algorithm does well if the initial seed set of titles is diverse and covers various title templates. We have not focussed on this batch selection problem. However, random selection of the seed set does ensure good coverage for frequently occurring title templates.

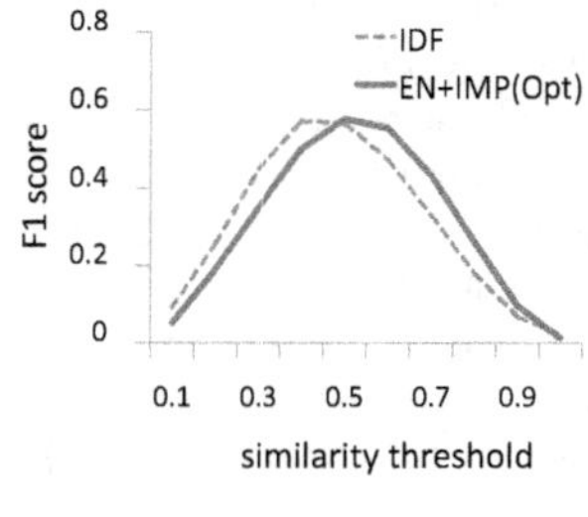

(a) Abt-Buy

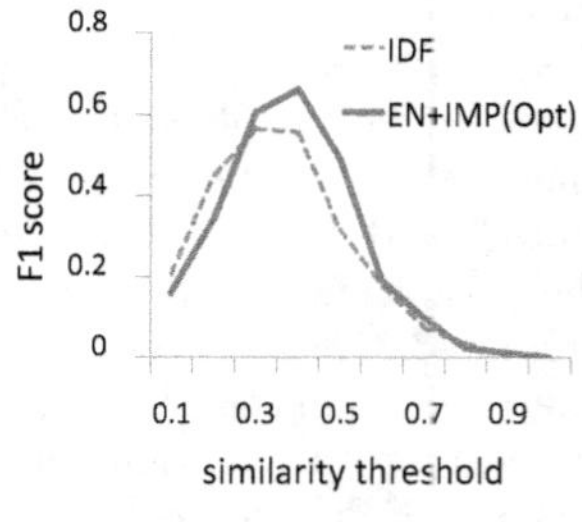

(b) PG-CNET

Figure 3: Match quality with prediction.

5.3.2 *Parameter sensitivity analysis for enrichment prediction*

Table 7 shows the EPC, EPQ values and the corresponding highest F1 score in the setting where we vary $|B|$ for the Abt-Buy dataset. Observe that, with a batch size of 1000, EPC and EPQ values are 0.87 and 0.89 respectively,

Table 7: EPC-EPQ values with highest F1 score for different $|B|$ for Abt-Buy.

$\|B\|$	EPC	EPQ	Highest F1 score
250	0.86	0.87	0.46
500	0.92	0.86	0.53
750	0.93	0.83	0.56
1000	0.87	0.89	**0.59**

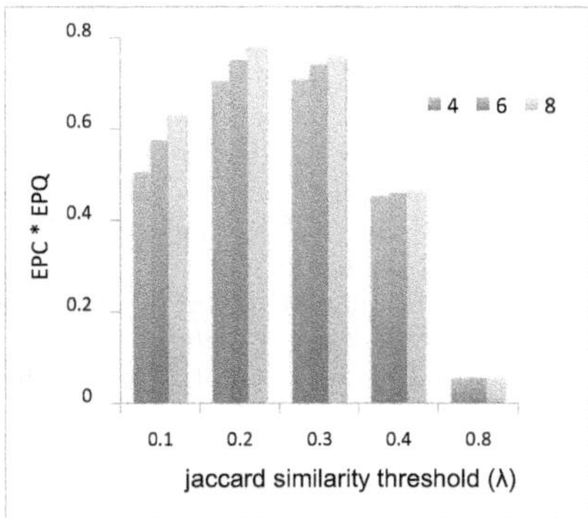

Figure 4: EPC*EPQ for varying λ and $\mu = 4, 6, 8$ for Abt-Buy.

which implies that the coverage and quality of enrichment prediction are high. A batch size of 1000 and an EPC of 0.87 implies that with an initial seed set size of 1000, we could predict 87% of the remaining enrichments/importance scores. The F1 score achieved in this setting is 0.59, which is more than that of IDF which has a highest score of 0.57.

For a batch size of 1000, we analyze the sensitivity of two important parameters, support size μ and Jaccard similarity threshold λ (Algorithm 4). Figure 4 shows the EPC * EPQ values for different values of μ and λ. We want both EPC and EPQ values to be high; a high EPC value implies that we have predicted a high number of enrichments and a high EPQ value implies that the quality of prediction is high. As we can see, a support size μ of 8 performs the best at all thresholds. This can be attributed to better quality enrichment predictions at higher μ values. We further analyze the EPC and EPQ values for $\mu = 8$ to find an optimum value for λ. For $\mu = 8$, Figure 5 shows EPC and EPQ as a function of the Jaccard similarity threshold (λ). EPC values decrease with an increase in λ value, whereas enrichment quality EPQ increases. Observe that, a threshold value λ of 0.3 strikes a good balance between enrichment prediction coverage and quality, for the Abt-Buy dataset.

Table 8 gives an example of the importance scores with enrichment prediction. The predicted scores are very close to the actual scores; thus the Cosine similarity between the actual and the predicted scores (EPQ) is close to 1.

6. RELATED WORK

The problem of matching records has been extensively studied in the literature – [12] and [11] present comprehensive surveys of research work in the area. Prior research on matching has primarily focused on three aspects: (1) similarity functions for matching individual attribute values, (2) unsupervised and supervised techniques for matching records containing multiple attributes, and (3) blocking methods for determining record pairs to match.

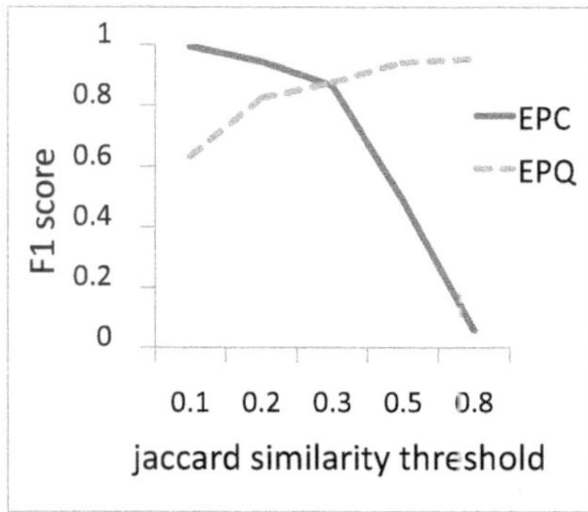

Figure 5: EPC vs EPQ with $\mu = 8$ for Abt-Buy.

Table 8: Example of enrichment prediction.

Token	Actual Score	Predicted Score
sony	0.4	0.41
cybershot	0.6	0.68
dscw80	1.0	0.99
black	0.8	0.70
EPQ	1.000	0.996

Developing robust similarity metrics for attribute comparison is essential since the input data to the matching process is often noisy (e.g., due to spelling errors) and/or in different formats (e.g., phone numbers with and without '-'). There is a large body of work on approximate string similarity measures like edit distance or Cosine similarity applied to IDF-weighted string tokens, q-grams, etc. [12, 17, 5].

Existing matching approaches use attribute-level similarity measures as the basic building block, and can be either unsupervised or supervised. Unsupervised methods combine attribute-level similarity scores to define record-level similarity which is then compared with a fixed threshold to identify matching records. In the supervised approach, labeled record pairs with attribute similarity values as features are used to train a classifier. The trained classifier is then used to predict whether a new record pair matches or not. In essence, one can view the classifier as learning record-level similarity measures from attribute-level ones. A detailed evaluation of the matching performance of existing unsupervised and supervised techniques on two real-world product datasets is presented in [16]. In general, the authors find that conventional approaches result in low matching quality for product entities with supervised techniques (with multiple attributes) performing the best.

To handle continuously arriving product offers from merchants, [3] uses a voted perceptron classifier for online learning of similarity functions. In other work, [20] uses active learning to reduce classifier training data requirements. Finally, since running classifiers on all record pairs is expensive, blocking techniques are used to reduce the number of record pairs that enter into the matching phase. [9] contains a recent survey on the use of indexing techniques for blocking.

The focus of our work is not on record-level matching or blocking, but rather on devising a good attribute-level similarity function for product titles. Our matching algorithm improves upon traditional Cosine similarity with IDF weights by leveraging the web to enrich product titles and assign token weights.

The enrichment step of our matching solution is closely related to previous work on query expansion [18], although the primary goal of query expansion is to improve recall as opposed to matching quality. Given the widespread prevalence, efficiency, and relevance of web search engines, there has been a growing trend to exploit search engines for tasks such as word similarity computation [10], query classification [4], extracting model numbers from titles [21], etc. Matching is no exception and recently there has been interest in leveraging web search engines (or more generally, the web corpus) for the matching problem. For instance, [21] uses web search for author name disambiguation. It augments the author name with associated information (like co-author, institution, etc.) and uses the search results of the augmented query for disambiguation. [19] also employs web search engines to compute context vectors for short text snippets that are then used to determine similarity. Weights for tokens in the context vectors, however, are still computed using IDF.

[7, 8] explore the use of web data for identifying discriminating token subsets (called "IDTokenSets") of comprehensive title strings in a reference entity table. These IDTokenSets are then matched with candidate strings in documents in order to disambiguate entity mentions. The papers propose efficient techniques for deriving IDTokenSets: [7] uses web search while [8] employs a web corpus. Both [7, 8] assume the existence of a reference entity table with comprehensive title strings containing the most relevant tokens to identify an entity, and possibly extraneous tokens. However, this is a strong assumption and may not hold in practice – as shown in Table 1, important tokens like brand may be missing from product title strings. Observe that we also leverage web search results in our work, but to compute enrichments and token importance scores as opposed to IDTokenSets.

[15] considers the problem of matching unstructured offers to structured product descriptions. Tokens in the offer that match attribute values in the product are tagged with attribute names, and a feature vector is constructed based on the similarity between attribute values. The similarity function is then learned by training a logistic regression classifier using the features. Note that our matching algorithm is completely unsupervised and does not require training data. Moreover, our focus in this paper is on matching unstructured product title pairs, and our approach does not require product specification tables.

7. CONCLUSIONS

In this paper, we have proposed two novel ideas to tackle the matching problem for product titles: enrichment of titles with essential missing tokens and importance score computation that takes context into account. Both ideas leverage the web corpus effectively through web search engines. To reduce repeated invocation of search engines, we also presented a technique for predicting enrichments and importance scores. This exploits the templatized structure of product titles. The experimental results demonstrate that the proposed techniques are effective and outperform the widely used IDF technique with higher F1 scores. Enrichment prediction reduces search queries significantly while retaining matching effectiveness over IDF. Our experimental results validate our approach for product titles having distinctive tokens like brand name and model number (product titles of cameras and appliances). We plan to extend this approach to other domains like apparel, toys, software product titles (e.g., from the Amazon-Google dataset [16]) which may not contain representative tokens.

8. REFERENCES

[1] O. Benjelloun, H. Garcia-Molina, D. Menestrina, Q. Su, S. E. Whang, and J. Widom. Swoosh: a generic approach to entity resolution. *VLDB Journal*, 18(1), 2009.

[2] I. Bhattacharya and L. Getoor. Collective entity resolution in relational data. *ACM TKDD*, 1(1), 2007.

[3] M. Bilenko, S. Basu, and M. Sahami. Adaptive product normalization: Using online learning for record linkage in comparison shopping. In *ICDM*, 2005.

[4] A. Z. Broder, M. Fontoura, E. Gabrilovich, A. Joshi, V. Josifovski, and T. Zhang. Robust classification of rare queries using web knowledge. In *SIGIR*, 2007.

[5] S. Chaudhuri, K. Ganjam, V. Ganti, and R. Motwani. Robust and efficient fuzzy match for online data cleaning. In *SIGMOD*, 2003.

[6] S. Chaudhuri, V. Ganti, and R. Kaushik. A primitive operator for similarity joins in data cleaning. In *ICDE*, 2006.

[7] S. Chaudhuri, V. Ganti, and D. Xin. Exploiting web search to generate synonyms for entities. In *WWW*, 2009.

[8] S. Chaudhuri, V. Ganti, and D. Xin. Mining document collections to facilitate accurate approximate entity matching. In *VLDB*, 2009.

[9] P. Christen. A survey of indexing techniques for scalable record linkage and deduplication. *IEEE TKDE*, 2011.

[10] R. L. Cilibrasi and P. M. B. Vitanyi. The google similarity distance. *IEEE TKDE*, 2007.

[11] C. F. Dorneles, R. GonÃğalves, and R. dos Santos Mello. Approximate data instance matching: a survey. *Knowledge and Information Systems*, 2011.

[12] A. K. Elmagarmid, P. G. Ipeirotis, and V. S. Verykios. Duplicate record detection: A survey. *IEEE TKDE*, 2007.

[13] I. P. Fellegi and A. B. Sunter. A theory for record linkage. *Journal of the American Statistical Association*, 64(328), 1969.

[14] M. A. Hernandez and S. J. Stolfo. Real-world data is dirty: Data cleansing and and the merge/purge problem. *Data Mining and Knowledge Discovery*, 2(1), 1998.

[15] A. Kannan, I. E. Givoni, R. Agrawal, and A. Fuxman. Matching unstructured product offers to structured product specifications. In *KDD*, 2011.

[16] H. Kopcke, A. Thor, and E. Rahm. Evaluation of entity resolutoin approaches on real-world match problems. *PVLDB*, 3(1), 2010.

[17] C. Manning, P. Raghavan, and H. Schutze. *Introduction to Information Retrieval.* Cambridge University Press, 2008.

[18] M. Mitra, A. Singhal, and C. Buckley. Improving automatic query expansion. In *SIGIR*, 1998.

[19] M. Sahami and T. Heilman. A web-based kernel function for measuring the similarity of short text snippets. In *WWW*, 2006.

[20] S. Sarawagi and A. Bhamidipaty. Interactive deduplication using active learning. In *SIGKDD*, 2002.

[21] Y. F. Tan, M.-Y. Kan, and D. Lee. Search engine driven author disambiguation. In *JCDL*, 2006.

Scalable Clustering of Signed Networks Using Balance Normalized Cut

Kai-Yang Chiang
Dept. of Computer Science
University of Texas at Austin
kychiang@cs.utexas.edu

Joyce Jiyoung Whang
Dept. of Computer Science
University of Texas at Austin
joyce@cs.utexas.edu

Inderjit S. Dhillon
Dept. of Computer Science
University of Texas at Austin
inderjit@cs.utexas.edu

ABSTRACT

We consider the general k-way clustering problem in signed social networks where relationships between entities can be either positive or negative. Motivated by social balance theory, the clustering problem in signed networks aims to find mutually antagonistic groups such that entities within the same group are friends with each other. A recent method proposed in [13] extended the spectral clustering algorithm to the signed network setting by considering the signed graph Laplacian. This has been shown to be equivalent to finding clusters that minimize the 2-way signed ratio cut. In this paper, we show that there is a fundamental weakness when we directly extend the signed Laplacian to the k-way clustering problem. To overcome this weakness, we formulate new k-way objectives for signed networks. In particular, we propose a criterion that is analogous to the normalized cut, called balance normalized cut, which is not only theoretically sound but also experimentally effective in k-way clustering. In addition, we prove that these objectives are equivalent to weighted kernel k-means objectives by choosing an appropriate kernel matrix. Employing this equivalence, we develop a multilevel clustering framework for signed networks. In this framework, we coarsen the graph level by level and refine the clustering results at each level via a k-means based algorithm so that the signed clustering objectives are optimized. This approach gives good quality clustering results, and is also highly efficient and scalable. In experiments, we see that our multilevel approach is competitive to other state-of-the-art methods, while it is much faster and more scalable. In particular, the largest graph we have considered in our experiments contains 1 million nodes and 100 million edges — this graph can be clustered in less than four hundred seconds using our algorithm.

Category: I.5.3 - Computing Methodologies - Pattern Recognition - Clustering
General Terms: Algorithms, Experimentation
Keywords: Clustering, Signed Networks, Social Balance Theory, Signed Graph Kernels

CIKM'12, October 29–November 2, 2012, Maui, HI, USA.

1. INTRODUCTION

Social network analysis has gained considerable attention in recent years. These networks can be modeled as graphs with nodes and edges, where nodes indicate individual actors and edges indicate the relationships between actors. In many real social networks, there are not only positive relationships but also negative relationships. For example, online news and review websites such as *Epinions* and *Slashdot* allow users to approve or denounce others. These kinds of networks can be modeled as *signed networks* where a positive relationship is denoted by a positive edge weight while a negative relationship is denoted by a negative edge weight.

It has been shown that signed networks tend to have a particular structure that is derived by the fact that relationships between entities tend to follow so-called "balanced" patterns in signed networks [3, 9]. Motivated by social balance theory, the clustering problem in signed networks is to find antagonistic clusters such that entities within the same cluster have a positive relationship with each other and entities between different clusters have a negative relationship with each other. While much research on graph clustering has been conducted on unsigned graphs which contain only positive relationship information, it is yet to be explored how many existing clustering algorithms can be extended to signed networks. In particular, since the goal of clustering changes when we consider signed networks, existing unsigned clustering methods cannot be directly applied to signed graph clustering.

Due to the massive size of real networks, scalability is an important issue. For unsigned networks, several scalable clustering algorithms have been proposed based on the multilevel framework [7, 11]. However, to the best of our knowledge, there is no scalable multilevel clustering algorithm for signed networks.

In this paper, we formulate new k-way objectives for signed networks based on social balance theory. In particular, we propose a criterion that is analogous to the normalized cut, called balance normalized cut, which is not only theoretically sound but also experimentally effective in k-way clustering. Furthermore, we show that these objectives are equivalent to a general weighted kernel k-means objective. Using this equivalence, we develop a fast multilevel clustering algorithm for signed networks. In this multilevel algorithm, clustering can be optimized level by level very efficiently.

The following are the contributions of our paper:

- We formulate new k-way objectives and kernels for signed networks, and compare them with the signed graph Laplacian considered in [13]. We also show a fundamental weakness of the signed graph Laplacian in k-way clustering problems.

- We show that our new k-way objectives are mathematically equivalent to a general weighted kernel k-means objective. Using this equivalence, we show that the graph clustering objectives of signed networks can be optimized by using a kernel k-means like algorithm.
- Employing the equivalence between k-way graph clustering and weighted kernel k-means objectives, we develop a fast and scalable multilevel clustering algorithm for signed networks. Our multilevel clustering algorithm is comparable in accuracy to other state-of-the-art methods while it is much faster and more scalable.

This paper is organized as follows. In Section 2, we briefly review some related work, and in Section 3, we state some preliminaries. In Section 4, we show a weakness of the signed graph Laplacian and introduce our new k-way objectives and kernels for signed networks. Also, we prove the equivalence between these objectives and a general weighted kernel k-means objective. In Section 5, we embed our algorithm into a multilevel framework, and explain our multilevel clustering algorithm for signed networks. We show our experimental results in Section 6, and state our conclusions in Section 7.

2. RELATED WORK

The clustering problem in signed networks can be dated back to the 1950s. Cartwright and Harary [3, 9] introduced the notion of social balance. They defined balanced triads, and showed that a network which follows the balance notion can be clustered into two perfect antagonistic groups. This balance notion was generalized by Davis [4], who defined the concept of a weakly balanced network, and showed that a network can be partitioned into k antagonistic groups if it is weakly balanced. In Section 3.3, we formally state balance theory and weak balance theory.

Motivated by (weak) balance, many researchers have tried to develop algorithms for clustering signed networks. For example, Doreian et al. [8] proposed a local search strategy which is similar to the Kernighan-Lin algorithm [12]. Yang at el. [17] proposed an agent-based method which basically conducts a random walk on the graph. Anchuri at el. [1] proposed hierarchical iterative methods that solve 2-way frustration and signed modularity objectives using spectral relaxation at each hierarchy. On the other hand, Nikihil at el. also consider the signed graph clustering problem, though their formulation is motivated by correlation clustering [2]. They proposed two approximation algorithms and proved approximation bounds. Different from these works, our work starts with considering k-way signed cut and association objectives which directly measure the quality of clusters. Thereafter, we obtain k clusters by globally optimizing these signed objectives.

The most relevant work to ours is a spectral method proposed by Kunegis et al. [13], who showed that a signed version of the 2-way ratio-cut problem can be solved by considering the so-called signed graph Laplacian. However, there is a fundamental weakness when we directly extend the signed Laplacian to the k-way clustering problem, which we will discuss in detail in Section 4.1.

Another state-of-the-art framework for signed graph clustering is based on a low rank model proposed by Hsieh et al. [10]. They observe that matrix completion on signed networks can be thought as recovering the missing structure of the network. Thus, in this framework they first complete the network and derive low rank factors (for example, top k eigenvectors) as representations of the signed network. Afterward, they run k-means on the low rank factors to derive the clustering. We will compare this state-of-the-art approach with our proposed multilevel clustering algorithm in Section 6.

Scalability is always an important issue for graph clustering algorithms. For unsigned networks, many scalable graph clustering algorithms make use of a multilevel framework, such as Metis [11] and Graclus [7]. In the multilevel framework, the input graph is repeatedly coarsened level by level until the graph size becomes small enough. An initial clustering is then performed on the coarsest graph. Finally, the clustering result is refined as the graph is uncoarsened level by level. Furthermore, Dhillon et al. [7] showed that a weighted graph clustering objective is mathematically equivalent to a general weighted kernel k-means objective, and utilizing this equivalence into the multilevel framework can make the clustering procedure very efficient. However, the algorithms used in [7] cannot be directly applied to signed networks, and the modifications are not trivial either.

3. PRELIMINARIES

In this paper, we use capital letters to denote matrices, lowercase bold letters to denote vectors, and lowercase italics to denote scalars. We use $x_c(i)$ to denote the ith element of the vector $\mathbf{x}_c$ when the vector has a subscript; otherwise, we use x_i to denote the ith element of the vector $\mathbf{x}$.

In this section, we first review spectral clustering of unsigned networks in Section 3.1. In Section 3.2, we introduce weighted kernel k-means which has been shown to be effective in optimizing graph cut objectives of unsigned networks. In Section 3.3, we state some basic concepts for signed networks. Finally, in Section 3.4, we introduce a state-of-the-art spectral method that solves a 2-way signed network clustering problem.

3.1 Graph Cuts on Unsigned Networks

Let us consider k-way clustering on unsigned networks. One of the most popular approaches to solving this problem is to consider some objective, such as graph association or graph cuts, that quantifies the quality of clusters, and derive a clustering result by maximizing or minimizing the objective function. Here are some well-known objectives:

- **Ratio Association objective** aims to maximize the number of edges within clusters relative to the size of the cluster, where the size of a cluster is defined as the number of nodes it contains. Precisely, the ratio association objective may be written as:
$$\max_{\{\mathbf{x}_1,\dots,\mathbf{x}_k\}\in I}\left(\sum_{c=1}^{k}\frac{\mathbf{x}_c^T A\mathbf{x}_c}{\mathbf{x}_c^T\mathbf{x}_c}\right),$$
where A is the network's adjacency matrix, and the constraint $\{\mathbf{x}_1,...,\mathbf{x}_k\}\in I$ means $\{\mathbf{x}_1,...,\mathbf{x}_k\}$ is a k-cluster indicator set. Formally, an indicator set $\{\mathbf{x}_1,...,\mathbf{x}_k\}$ is defined as a set of k vectors $\mathbf{x}_1\ldots\mathbf{x}_k$, such that:
$$x_c(i)=\begin{cases}1, & \text{if node } i\in\pi_c,\\ 0, & \text{otherwise,}\end{cases}$$
with $|\pi_c|>0$, where π_c denotes the cth cluster.
- **Ratio Cut objective** aims to minimize the number of edges between different clusters relative to the size of

the cluster. It is known that the number of edges across clusters can be captured by the graph Laplacian of A. More precisely, let D be the diagonal degree matrix of A, i.e. $D_{ii} = \sum_{j=1}^{n} A_{ij}$, then the graph Laplacian is defined by $L = D - A$. The ratio cut objective is:

$$\min_{\{\mathbf{x}_1,\ldots,\mathbf{x}_k\}\in I} \left(\sum_{c=1}^{k} \frac{\mathbf{x}_c^T L \mathbf{x}_c}{\mathbf{x}_c^T \mathbf{x}_c} \right). \tag{1}$$

- **Normalized Association** and **Normalized Cut objectives** also consider within-cluster edges and between-cluster edges, respectively. However, these objectives are normalized by the volume of each cluster rather than the number of nodes in each cluster. The volume of a cluster is defined as the sum of degrees of nodes in the cluster. It has been shown that these two normalized objectives are equivalent, i.e.,

$$\max_{\{\mathbf{x}_1,\ldots,\mathbf{x}_k\}\in I} \left(\sum_{c=1}^{k} \frac{\mathbf{x}_c^T A \mathbf{x}_c}{\mathbf{x}_c^T D \mathbf{x}_c} \right) \equiv \min_{\{\mathbf{x}_1,\ldots,\mathbf{x}_k\}\in I} \left(\sum_{c=1}^{k} \frac{\mathbf{x}_c^T L \mathbf{x}_c}{\mathbf{x}_c^T D \mathbf{x}_c} \right). \tag{2}$$

In addition, under the special case $k = 2$, the ratio cut objective (1) is equivalent to the following problem:

$$\min_{\mathbf{x}} \left(\mathbf{x}^T L \mathbf{x} \right), \tag{3}$$

where the 2-class indicator $\mathbf{x}$ has the following form:

$$x_i = \begin{cases} \sqrt{|\pi_2|/|\pi_1|}, & \text{if node } i \in \pi_1, \\ -\sqrt{|\pi_1|/|\pi_2|}, & \text{if node } i \in \pi_2, \end{cases}$$

with $|\pi_1|, |\pi_2| > 0$. See [5] for detailed proof.

Note that all the above formulated problems are NP-hard problems [15]. In practice, these problems are usually solved with spectral relaxation, which is known as spectral clustering [16]. Specifically, if we consider the relaxed problems by dropping the combinatorial constraint $\{\mathbf{x}_1, \ldots, \mathbf{x}_k\} \in I$, then the top k eigenvectors will yield the optimal solution. One way to round $\{\mathbf{x}_1, \ldots, \mathbf{x}_k\}$ to a valid indicator set, we treat each $[x_1(i), x_2(i) \ldots x_k(i)]$ as a k-dimensional vector for $1 \le i \le n$, and do k-means clustering on these n vectors.

Though spectral clustering works quite well in practice, it suffers a scalability issue since computing eigenvectors can be costly. In particular, the normalized objective usually squeezes the spectrum of the matrix to a small range, which makes the computation much more expensive due to the smaller eigengaps.

3.2 Weighted Kernel K-means

Weighted kernel k-means is a generalized version of k-means [7]. Given a set of vectors $\mathbf{v}_1 \ldots \mathbf{v}_n$, the weighted kernel k-means objective is defined as follows:

$$\min_{\pi_1\ldots\pi_k} \sum_{c=1}^{k} \sum_{\mathbf{v}_i\in\pi_c} w_i \|\phi(\mathbf{v}_i) - \mathbf{m}_c\|^2, \tag{4}$$

where w_i is a nonnegative weight of each vector $\mathbf{v}_i$, ϕ is a non-linear mapping, and $\mathbf{m}_c$ is the weighted centroid of π_c which is defined by:

$$\mathbf{m}_c = \frac{\sum_{\mathbf{v}_i\in\pi_c} w_i \phi(\mathbf{v}_i)}{\sum_{\mathbf{v}_i\in\pi_c} w_i}.$$

Like the traditional k-means algorithm, weighted kernel k-means computes the closest centroid for every node, and

Algorithm 1: Weighted Kernel k-means

Input: $\mathbf{v}_1 \ldots \mathbf{v}_n$: data vectors, K: kernel matrix, k: number of clusters, $\{\pi_c\}_{c=1}^{k}$: initial clustering, t: maximum number of iterations.

Output: $\{\pi_c\}_{c=1}^{k}$: final clustering

- Initialize $\tau = 0$.
- **Do**
  1. For each $\mathbf{v} = \mathbf{v}_1 : \mathbf{v}_n$ and $c = 1 : k$, compute $D(\mathbf{v}_i, \mathbf{m}_c)$ using Equation (5).
  2. Compute C^* for each $\mathbf{v}$ defined by: $C^*(\mathbf{v}_i) := \arg\min_c D(\mathbf{v}_i, \mathbf{m}_c)$.
  3. Reform the clustering defined by: $\pi_c = \{\mathbf{v}_j \mid C^*(\mathbf{v}_j) = c\}$.
  4. $\tau = \tau + 1$.

  While not converged and $\tau < t$

assigns the node to the closest cluster. After all the nodes are considered, the centroids are updated. Given the Kernel matrix K, where $K_{ji} = <\phi(\mathbf{v}_j), \phi(\mathbf{v}_i)>$, the distance between $\phi(\mathbf{v}_i)$ and $\mathbf{m}_c$, denoted as $D(\mathbf{v}_i, \mathbf{m}_c)$, can be simplified as follows:

$$D(\mathbf{v}_i, \mathbf{m}_c) = K_{ii} - \frac{2\sum_{j\in c} w_j K_{ji}}{\sum_{j\in c} w_j} + \frac{\sum_{j\in c}\sum_{l\in c} w_j w_l K_{jl}}{(\sum_{j\in c} w_j)^2}. \tag{5}$$

This procedure is summarized in Algorithm 1.

It has been shown that all the objectives stated in Section 3.1 are equivalent to the weighted kernel k-means objective by choosing appropriate kernels [7]. Therefore, we can use the weighted kernel k-means algorithm to attempt to optimize these graph clustering objectives without computing eigenvectors.

3.3 Signed Networks and Social Balance

A signed network can be represented as an adjacency matrix A that describes relationships between entities. Formally, the adjacency matrix A is defined as follows:

$$A_{ij} \begin{cases} > 0, & \text{if relationship of } (i,j) \text{ is positive,} \\ < 0, & \text{if relationship of } (i,j) \text{ is negative,} \\ = 0, & \text{if relationship of } (i,j) \text{ is unknown.} \end{cases}$$

We can break A into its positive part A^+ and negative part A^-. Formally, $A^+_{ij} = \max(A_{ij}, 0)$ and $A^-_{ij} = -\min(A_{ij}, 0)$. By this definition, we have $A = A^+ - A^-$. For convenience, in the remaining part of this paper, we will use the term "network" as an abbreviation of *signed* network unless we specify it is unsigned. In addition, similar to the convention in spectral clustering, we will focus our discussion on undirected signed networks, i.e., A is symmetric.

The most prevailing theory related to signed networks is *social balance.* The intuition of social balance can be interpreted as "a friend of my friend is my friend", "an enemy of my friend is my enemy", and "an enemy of my enemy is my friend". We say that a graph is *balanced* if any part of the graph does not violate this intuition. It is known that if the network is balanced, then it has a clusterable global structure:

THEOREM 1 (BALANCE THEORY [3, 9]). *A network is balanced iff (i) all of its edges are positive, or (ii) nodes can be clustered into two groups such that edges within groups are positive and edges between groups are negative.*

In addition, Davis [4] proposed a weaker notion of balance, called weak balance, that generalizes social balance. They relax the balanced relationships by allowing an enemy of one's enemy to still be an enemy. Under such relaxation, they show that a network which satisfies weak balance rules can be clustered as follows:

THEOREM 2 (WEAK BALANCE THEORY [4]). *A network is weakly balanced iff (i) all of its edges are positive, or (ii) nodes can be clustered into k groups such that edges within groups are positive and edges between groups are negative.*

We then say that a network is k-weakly balanced iff it can be divided into k antagonistic groups.

Motivated by Theorem 2, we now formally state the k-way clustering problem in signed networks as follows. Given a signed network, we are asked to partition the network into k clusters such that most edges within clusters are positive and most edges between clusters are negative. In addition, to avoid partitioning where most clusters contain only a few nodes, we prefer that clusters are of substantial size/volume. A similar desire occurs in unsigned network clustering when we consider normalized cut as the criterion [15].

3.4 Clustering via Signed Laplacian

Recently, Kunegis et al. [13] proposed a spectral method for clustering of signed graphs by defining a signed graph Laplacian. Let $\bar{D}$ be the diagonal absolute degree matrix, i.e., $\bar{D}_{ii} = \sum_{j=1}^{n} |A_{ij}|$, then the signed Laplacian $\bar{L}$ is defined in [13] to be $\bar{D} - A$. The signed Laplacian $\bar{L}$ is always positive semidefinite by the fact that $\forall \mathbf{x} \in \mathbb{R}^n$,

$$\mathbf{x}^T \bar{L} \mathbf{x} = \sum_{(i,j)} |A_{ij}|(x_i - \text{sgn}(A_{ij}) x_j)^2 \geq 0. \tag{6}$$

Now let us define k-way ratio cut for signed networks. Given a signed network G, we define k-way ratio cut to be equal to the sum of positive edge weights of edges that lie between different clusters and the sum of negative edge weights of all edges lie within the same cluster, normalized by each cluster's size as in (1) (also see (13) in Section 4.1).

In [13], it has been shown that the 2-way signed ratio cut objective can be formulated as an optimization problem with a quadratic form:

$$\min_{\mathbf{x}} \left(\mathbf{x}^T \bar{L} \mathbf{x} \right), \tag{7}$$

where the 2-class indicator $\mathbf{x}$ has the following form:

$$x_i = \begin{cases} \frac{1}{2}(\sqrt{|\pi_2|/|\pi_1|} + \sqrt{|\pi_1|/|\pi_2|}), & \text{if node } i \in \pi_1, \\ -\frac{1}{2}(\sqrt{|\pi_2|/|\pi_1|} + \sqrt{|\pi_1|/|\pi_2|}), & \text{if node } i \in \pi_2, \end{cases}$$

with $|\pi_1|, |\pi_2| > 0$. This objective has a similar form to the original unsigned ratio cut objective (3). However, by examining (7), we can verify that only negative edges within the same cluster ($A_{ij} < 0$ and $x_i = x_j$) and positive edges between clusters ($A_{ij} > 0$ and $x_i \neq x_j$) will contribute to the objective function. See [13] for more details.

4. SIGNED GRAPH CUTS AND KERNELS

In this section, we propose new criteria and objectives, including graph association and cut, for general k-way signed graph clustering. We can derive the signed graph kernel corresponding to each objective. In addition, we show that we can use the weighted kernel k-means algorithm to optimize these objectives, by selecting the proper kernel matrix.

4.1 k-way Signed Objectives for Clustering

Before we introduce our proposed objectives, we show why the signed Laplacian is hard to extend to the k-way clustering problem. While the signed Laplacian can be properly used in 2-way clustering, it is not clear how we can extend this definition to general k-way clustering. One intuitive solution is to directly extend (7) to the following k-way objective:

$$\min_{\{\mathbf{x}_1,\ldots,\mathbf{x}_k\} \in I} \left(\sum_{c=1}^{k} \frac{\mathbf{x}_c^T \bar{L} \mathbf{x}_c}{\mathbf{x}_c^T \mathbf{x}_c} \right). \tag{8}$$

However, unlike in unsigned networks, this direct extension suffers a weakness. To explain this weakness more clearly, let us first consider the unsigned ratio cut. We can observe that we use different representation for indicators ($\mathbf{x}$ in (3) and $\{\mathbf{x}_1, ..., \mathbf{x}_k\}$ in (1)) for 2-way objective and k-way objective. This generalization is valid because based on a 2-way objective (3) with well-defined indicator $\mathbf{x}$, we can properly generalize it to k-way objective (1) by selecting another appropriate representation for indicator set $\{\mathbf{x}_1, ..., \mathbf{x}_k\}$, such that the cut criterion remains the same. Similarly, now given a 2-way signed ratio cut objective (7), we aim to find an appropriate setting of the indicator set $\{\mathbf{x}_1, ..., \mathbf{x}_k\}$, such that the k-way objective (8) with such setting also minimizes the signed ratio cut. Nevertheless, the following theorem proves that this generalization is hopeless no matter how we choose as our indicators $\{\mathbf{x}_1, ..., \mathbf{x}_k\}$:

THEOREM 3. *There does not exist any representation of $\{\mathbf{x}_1, ..., \mathbf{x}_k\}$ such that the objective (8) minimizes the general k-way signed ratio cut (defined in Section 3.4).*

PROOF. Recall that to define a proper representation of $\{\mathbf{x}_1, ..., \mathbf{x}_k\}$, we need to pick two representatives $a, b \in \mathbb{R}$, $a \neq b$, $x_c(i) = a$ if $i \in \pi_c$ and $x_c(i) = b$ if $i \notin \pi_c$, such that the objective (8) minimizes the signed ratio cut.

To begin with, we rewrite the k-way objective (8) by plugging (6) into it as follows:

$$\min_{\{\mathbf{x}_1,\ldots,\mathbf{x}_k\} \in I} \left(\sum_{c=1}^{k} \frac{1}{|\pi_c|} \sum_{(i,j)} |A_{ij}|(x_c(i) - \text{sgn}(A_{ij}) x_c(j))^2 \right). \tag{9}$$

We can prove the theorem by showing that no matter how we choose a, b, we will incorrectly punish some favorable clustering patterns when minimizing (9).

First we argue that b must be 0. This is because when two nodes, i and j, are both not in π_c, we will never know whether i and j are in the same cluster or not by only seeing information about $\mathbf{x}_c$. Therefore, in this case, we have to assign $x_c(i) = x_c(j) = 0$ to ensure a zero penalty, or otherwise we may possibly penalize some patterns that conform to weak balance.

However, given $b = 0$, any $a \neq 0$ cannot make the objective (9) correctly minimize signed ratio cut. To see this, consider that $i \in \pi_c$ and $j \notin \pi_c$, in which case we should put penalty only when $\text{sgn}(A_{ij}) = 1$. However, any fixed choice of a will lead to a penalty regardless of $\text{sgn}(A_{ij})$. Thus, no matter how we select a, b, we will always punish some desirable clustering patterns. This proves the impossibility of a direct generalization of signed ratio cut objective by using (8). □

Notice that the above proof, however, does not apply if we restrict $k = 2$. If there are only two clusters, $i, j \notin \pi_c$ implies that i, j are in the other cluster simultaneously. In this case, we can directly punish this clustering assignment if $\text{sgn}(A_{ij}) = -1$. Therefore, under the special case $k = 2$, the first argument that b needs to be 0 in the proof is no longer valid. However, for general $k > 2$, b needs to be 0 as shown in the proof. This condition precludes the direct extension of the signed Laplacian to the k-way clustering problem.

To fix this basic theoretical flaw, we now propose alternate objectives that (i) follow the weak balance clusterability stated in Theorem 2, and (ii) are valid for general k-way clustering.

- **Positive/Negative Ratio Association**:
  In positive ratio association, we aim to maximize the number of positive edges within each cluster relative to cluster's size. The objective can be written as:
  $$\max_{\{\mathbf{x}_1,\ldots,\mathbf{x}_k\}\in I} \left(\sum_{c=1}^{k} \frac{\mathbf{x}_c^T A^+ \mathbf{x}_c}{\mathbf{x}_c^T \mathbf{x}_c} \right) \tag{10}$$
  Alternatively, we can also minimize the number of negative edges within each cluster relative to the cluster's size. This negative ratio association criterion corresponds to:
  $$\min_{\{\mathbf{x}_1,\ldots,\mathbf{x}_k\}\in I} \left(\sum_{c=1}^{k} \frac{\mathbf{x}_c^T A^- \mathbf{x}_c}{\mathbf{x}_c^T \mathbf{x}_c} \right) \tag{11}$$
- **Positive/Negative Ratio Cut**:
  In addition to within-cluster criteria, between-cluster criteria can also be considered. We define a positive ratio cut objective by minimizing the number of positive edges between clusters:
  $$\min_{\{\mathbf{x}_1,\ldots,\mathbf{x}_k\}\in I} \left\{ \sum_{c=1}^{k} \frac{\mathbf{x}_c^T (D^+ - A^+) \mathbf{x}_c}{\mathbf{x}_c^T \mathbf{x}_c} = \sum_{c=1}^{k} \frac{\mathbf{x}_c^T L^+ \mathbf{x}_c}{\mathbf{x}_c^T \mathbf{x}_c} \right\} \tag{12}$$
  where D^+ is the diagonal degree matrix of A^+. The negative ratio cut can also be defined similarly.
- **Balance Ratio Cut/Association**:
  We now combine both cut and association criteria together to obtain a balance criterion. According to Theorem 2, we prefer to partition nodes such that the number of positive edges between clusters and the number of negative edges within each cluster are both minimized. Thus, we define the balance ratio cut as a combination of positive ratio cut (12) and negative ratio association (11) as follows:
  $$\min_{\{\mathbf{x}_1,\ldots,\mathbf{x}_k\}\in I} \left(\sum_{c=1}^{k} \frac{\mathbf{x}_c^T A^- \mathbf{x}_c}{\mathbf{x}_c^T \mathbf{x}_c} + \lambda \frac{\mathbf{x}_c^T L^+ \mathbf{x}_c}{\mathbf{x}_c^T \mathbf{x}_c} \right),$$
  where λ is a weighting parameter. In the following we set $\lambda = 1$ for the case where within-cluster criterion is as important as between-cluster criterion. The balance ratio cut can thus be further simplified as follows:
  $$\min_{\{\mathbf{x}_1,\ldots,\mathbf{x}_k\}\in I} \left(\sum_{c=1}^{k} \frac{\mathbf{x}_c^T (D^+ - A) \mathbf{x}_c}{\mathbf{x}_c^T \mathbf{x}_c} \right). \tag{13}$$
  While this objective is almost the same as (8) except that the matrix in the quadratic form $D^+ - A$ changes to $\bar{D} - A$, this definition resolves the weakness of the signed Laplacian defined in [13]. In Section 6, we will show that clusters derived from solving (13) will be better than those derived from solving (8), which reconfirms our analysis.

  Of course, we can derive another balance criterion by considering the maximization problem. Following the same flow, we can define balance ratio association as combination of negative ratio cut and positive ratio association with equal weight. This objective can be derived as follows:
  $$\max_{\{\mathbf{x}_1,\ldots,\mathbf{x}_k\}\in I} \left(\sum_{c=1}^{k} \frac{\mathbf{x}_c^T (D^- + A) \mathbf{x}_c}{\mathbf{x}_c^T \mathbf{x}_c} \right). \tag{14}$$
- **Balance Normalized Cut**:
  Similar to clustering tasks in unsigned networks, we can also consider the objectives normalized by cluster volume instead of by the number of nodes in the clusters. For example, we can extend (13) to balance normalized cut as follows:
  $$\min_{\{\mathbf{x}_1,\ldots,\mathbf{x}_k\}\in I} \left(\sum_{c=1}^{k} \frac{\mathbf{x}_c^T (D^+ - A) \mathbf{x}_c}{\mathbf{x}_c^T \bar{D} \mathbf{x}_c} \right), \tag{15}$$
  Balance normalized association can also be derived from (14) in the same way.

  As an analogy to normalized cut and association in unsigned networks, these two objectives hold a similar equivalence in (2). This nice property is summarized by the following theorem:

THEOREM 4. *Minimizing balance normalized cut is equivalent to maximizing balance normalized association.*

PROOF. Consider the objective (15), we have:

$$\begin{aligned}
(15) &\equiv \max_{\{\mathbf{x}_1,\ldots,\mathbf{x}_k\}\in I} \left(k - \sum_{c=1}^{k} \frac{\mathbf{x}_c^T (D^+ - A) \mathbf{x}_c}{\mathbf{x}_c^T \bar{D} \mathbf{x}_c} \right) \\
&\equiv \max_{\{\mathbf{x}_1,\ldots,\mathbf{x}_k\}\in I} \left(\sum_{c=1}^{k} \frac{\mathbf{x}_c^T \left(\bar{D} - (D^+ - A)\right) \mathbf{x}_c}{\mathbf{x}_c^T \bar{D} \mathbf{x}_c} \right) \\
&\equiv \max_{\{\mathbf{x}_1,\ldots,\mathbf{x}_k\}\in I} \left(\sum_{c=1}^{k} \frac{\mathbf{x}_c^T (D^- + A) \mathbf{x}_c}{\mathbf{x}_c^T \bar{D} \mathbf{x}_c} \right),
\end{aligned}$$

by the fact that $\bar{D} = D^+ + D^-$. Thus, (15) is equivalent to maximizing balance normalized association. □

4.2 Solving Signed Objectives via Weighted Kernel K-means

One way to solve the signed cut/association objectives is to use spectral relaxation as traditional spectral clustering does. However, as described in Section 3.1, this approach fails to scale to very large networks due to computational issues. Thus, we now argue that similar to unsigned network clustering, we can use k-means like algorithm to optimize the objectives, by showing the following theorem:

THEOREM 5 (EQUIVALENCE OF OBJECTIVES). *For any signed cut or association objective, there exists some corresponding weighted kernel k-means objective (with properly chosen kernel matrix), such that these two objectives are mathematically equivalent.*

PROOF. We prove this by showing that both weighted kernel k-means objective and signed cut/association objectives can be represented as trace maximization problems. We will also show that given a signed objective, we can construct the kernel matrix such that the corresponding weighted kernel k-means objective is equivalent to the signed objective.

First we consider the weighted kernel k-means objective (4). As proved in [7], this objective can be rewritten as the following trace maximization problem:

$$\max_{Y} \operatorname{trace}\left(Y^T W^{1/2} K W^{1/2} Y\right), \tag{16}$$

where Y is an (weighted) indicator matrix, W is the diagonal weight matrix for the nodes, and K is the kernel matrix.

Now we show how to derive the corresponding trace maximization given the graph cut/association objectives in Section 4.1. Generally, every objective can be written in the following form:

$$\sum_{c=1}^{k} \frac{\mathbf{x}_c^T \acute{K} \mathbf{x}_c}{\mathbf{x}_c^T W \mathbf{x}_c}, \tag{17}$$

where W is some diagonal weight matrix, and the goal is to either maximize or minimize (17).

First, we represent the problem as a maximization problem. We use the following equivalence when the original problem is a minimization problem:

$$\begin{aligned}
\min_{\{\mathbf{x}_1,\ldots,\mathbf{x}_k\}\in I} \sum_{c=1}^{k} \frac{\mathbf{x}_c^T \acute{K} \mathbf{x}_c}{\mathbf{x}_c^T W \mathbf{x}_c} &\equiv \max_{\{\mathbf{x}_1,\ldots,\mathbf{x}_k\}\in I} \left(k - \sum_{c=1}^{k} \frac{\mathbf{x}_c^T \acute{K} \mathbf{x}_c}{\mathbf{x}_c^T W \mathbf{x}_c}\right) \\
&\equiv \max_{\{\mathbf{x}_1,\ldots,\mathbf{x}_k\}\in I} \sum_{c=1}^{k} \frac{\mathbf{x}_c^T (W - \acute{K}) \mathbf{x}_c}{\mathbf{x}_c^T W \mathbf{x}_c} \\
&\equiv \max_{\{\mathbf{x}_1,\ldots,\mathbf{x}_k\}\in I} \sum_{c=1}^{k} \frac{\mathbf{x}_c^T \tilde{K} \mathbf{x}_c}{\mathbf{x}_c^T W \mathbf{x}_c}, \qquad (18)
\end{aligned}$$

Next, we enforce the positive semi-definiteness on $\tilde{K}$ in (18) by the fact that:

$$\begin{aligned}
\max_{\{\mathbf{x}_1,\ldots,\mathbf{x}_k\}\in I} \sum_{c=1}^{k} \frac{\mathbf{x}_c^T \tilde{K} \mathbf{x}_c}{\mathbf{x}_c^T W \mathbf{x}_c} &\equiv \max_{\{\mathbf{x}_1,\ldots,\mathbf{x}_k\}\in I} \left(\sigma k + \sum_{c=1}^{k} \frac{\mathbf{x}_c^T \tilde{K} \mathbf{x}_c}{\mathbf{x}_c^T W \mathbf{x}_c}\right) \\
&\equiv \max_{\{\mathbf{x}_1,\ldots,\mathbf{x}_k\}\in I} \sum_{c=1}^{k} \frac{\mathbf{x}_c^T (\sigma W + \tilde{K}) \mathbf{x}_c}{\mathbf{x}_c^T W \mathbf{x}_c}. \qquad (19)
\end{aligned}$$

Therefore, every problem in form (18) can be rewritten as:

$$\max_{\{\mathbf{x}_1,\ldots,\mathbf{x}_k\}\in I} \left(\sum_{c=1}^{k} \frac{\mathbf{x}_c^T \hat{K} \mathbf{x}_c}{\mathbf{x}_c^T W \mathbf{x}_c}\right), \tag{20}$$

where $\hat{K}$ is a kernel matrix. This is because we can always choose some sufficiently large σ in (19) such that $\hat{K} = \sigma W + \tilde{K}$ is positive semi-definite.

Finally, (20) is in fact equivalent to a trace maximization problem since:

$$\begin{aligned}
(20) &\equiv \max_{\mathbf{y}_1 \cdots \mathbf{y}_k} \sum_{c=1}^{k} \frac{\mathbf{y}_c^T (W^{-1/2} \hat{K} W^{-1/2}) \mathbf{y}_c}{\mathbf{y}_c^T \mathbf{y}_c} \\
&\equiv \max_{Y} \operatorname{trace}\left(Y^T W^{1/2} (W^{-1} \hat{K} W^{-1}) W^{1/2} Y\right), \qquad (21)
\end{aligned}$$

where $Y \in \mathbb{R}^{n \times k}$, whose c^{th} column is also the normalized indicator $\tilde{\mathbf{y}}_c$ for cluster π_c, i.e. $\tilde{\mathbf{y}}_c = \mathbf{y}_c / \sqrt{(\mathbf{y}_c^T \mathbf{y}_c)}$.

Hence, by choosing the kernel matrix to be $K = W^{-1} \hat{K} W^{-1}$, (21) is equivalent to (16). This proves the theorem. □

This equivalence implies that we can define some implicit kernel matrix $\hat{K}$ given a signed cut/association objective by choosing a proper σ. In addition, running weighted kernel k-means with $W^{-1}\hat{K}W^{-1}$ as the input kernel matrix is equivalent to optimizing the corresponding signed cut/association objective, since both of them optimize the same trace maximization problem.

To explain how to derive the corresponding signed graph kernel more clearly, we take balance normalized cut (15) as an example. With the notations in the proof, the objective is to minimize (17) with $\acute{K} = D^+ - A$ and $W = \bar{D}$. By (18), we can rewrite it as a maximization problem by setting $\tilde{K} = W - \acute{K} = \bar{D} - (D^+ - A)$. The problem is further equivalent to (20) by setting $\hat{K} = \sigma W + \tilde{K} = \sigma' \bar{D} - (D^+ - A)$. This becomes our balance normalized cut kernel, since we can always choose a large enough σ' such that $\hat{K}$ is positive semi-definite. Also, by (21), if we set another kernel matrix K as $W^{-1}\hat{K}W^{-1} = \sigma' \bar{D}^{-1} - \bar{D}^{-1}(D^+ - A)\bar{D}^{-1}$, and use K as the input of weighted kernel k-means, we can optimize balance normalized cut efficiently.

5. MULTILEVEL APPROACH FOR LARGE-SCALE SIGNED GRAPH CLUSTERING

In Section 4.2, we have seen that there are two general approaches to optimize signed graph clustering objectives - spectral clustering and weighted kernel k-means algorithm. Typically, k-means based algorithm is more efficient and scalable than spectral clustering. However, k-means algorithm is also easier to be trapped into qualitatively poor local optima. In this section, we will use a popular multilevel framework which allows kernel k-means based algorithms to converge to better local optima.

Our approach can be viewed as a generalization of Graclus [7] for the signed network setting. The multilevel approach is a divide-and-conquer method that includes three phases: coarsening, base clustering and refinement.

5.1 Coarsening Phase

In the coarsening phase, given the input graph G_0, we generate a series of graphs $G_1 \ldots G_\ell$, such that $|V_{i+1}| < |V_i|$ for all $0 \leq i < \ell$. Given a graph G_i, the coarsened graph G_{i+1} is generated as follows: At the beginning every node is unmarked. We then visit each node in a random order, and try to merge two nodes in G_i into one supernode in G_{i+1} with the following strategy: If the node, say x, is already marked then we skip it. Otherwise, we consider all of x's unmarked neighbors y, and select the one such that the edge weight A^i_{xy} is the largest (where A^i is the adjacency matrix of G_i). We then merge x and y as a supernode z, and all the neighbors of x and y are added to neighbors of z. We mark both x and y. If all neighbors of x are marked, then we simply mark x and do not merge it into any node. After all nodes are visited, the supernodes and non-merged nodes become the vertex set of G_{i+1}.

The matching strategy is quite intuitive since the larger the edge weight between x and y, the more likely that x and y are in the same cluster. There can be some variants of the matching strategy such as visiting nodes ordered by their positive degree and so on.

5.2 Base Clustering Phase

When the original graph is coarsened to a small enough graph, we can directly perform clustering on the coarsest graph G_ℓ. We take two kinds of approaches to do base clustering on G_ℓ: Minimize balance normalized cut of A^ℓ with spectral relaxation, or perform unsigned graph clustering on $A^{\ell+}$ using region-growing algorithm as in Metis [11].

Here are some pros and cons between these two approaches. Considering balance normalized cut using spectral relaxation usually gives a better initialization, but it could be slow if G_ℓ is still very large. The latter might occur if the original network is power-law so that the size reduction at each level might not be significant. On the other hand, the region-growing algorithm used in Metis is very efficient since it requires no eigenvector computation. However, since this method does not consider signed edges in G_ℓ, it is possible to derive a base clustering result such that both positive and negative edges are dense within clusters. This problem is not critical, however, since we will refine the clustering results with consideration of signed edges in the refinement phase. Therefore, for the base clustering method, we use Metis on $A^{\ell+}$ in our experiments.

5.3 Refinement Phase

After we derive the base clustering result in G_ℓ, we run the refinement algorithm to derive clustering results in $G_{\ell-1}$, $G_{\ell-2}$, ..., G_0. Thus, given a clustering result in G_i, the goal is to get a clustering result in G_{i-1}. To do this, we first project the clustering result in G_i to G_{i-1} as the initial clusters. In other words, for $x \in \pi_c$ in G_i, all the nodes in G_{i-1} which were merged to x at the coarsening phase are assigned to π_c. After having the initial clusters, we refine the clustering result by running weighted kernel k-means. As shown in Theorem 5, we can choose a suitable kernel of A^i such that optimizing the weighted kernel k-means objective is equivalent to optimizing the appropriate signed graph criterion. In our implementation, we choose balance normalized cut kernel as our kernel matrix. Notice that since at each level i we have a good initialization by projecting the clustering from level $i-1$, weighted kernel k-means usually converges quickly.

The quality of clusters is dominated by the local optimal of the weighted kernel k-means objective. To make the clustering result better, we can use a local search strategy, which allows k-means to converge to a better local optimal. We incorporate this local search strategy with the standard batch k-means algorithm. Basically, we alternatively run the batch k-means and incremental k-means at each refinement level. More details of this ping-pong procedure can be found in [6].

5.3.1 *Choosing the Kernel Matrix*

In Theorem 5 we have seen that we can choose a sufficiently large σ to construct a kernel matrix K. However, in practice, if σ is too large, it makes the k-means algorithm harder to escape a poor local optimal. As a result, the clustering result could be bad. On the other hand, a small σ which does not make K positive semi-definite can still be used for k-means algorithm since K might still possibly provide a pretty accurate distance measurement. Observing this fact, we develop a procedure for finding an appropriate σ for K.

We begin with some small σ and derive a corresponding K as the input of our ping-pong procedure. This K could be effective for distance measurement in k-means even if it is not positive semi-definite. However, it is also possible that k-means algorithm cannot converge with such K due to the lack of positive definiteness. If we observe lack of convergence, we change K by increasing σ and repeat the ping-pong procedure.

On the other hand, if no move occurs in batch k-means, it might be a signal that the σ is too large to make k-means jump out from the local optimal. So, in this case, we change K by decreasing σ and repeat the ping-pong procedure. We do not change σ in other cases.

5.3.2 *Computational Issues*

Now let us discuss the computational complexity of our k-means based refinement procedure. In Algorithm 1, the bottleneck of computation is to compute the weighted distance $D(\mathbf{v}_i, \mathbf{m}_c)$ for every pair (i, c). If we observe the weighted distance formula in Equation (5), the first term K_{ii} is a constant for fixed i, so we only need to compute last two terms when reassigning nodes to clusters. Now consider the balance normalized cut kernel $K = \sigma\bar{D}^{-1} - \bar{D}^{-1}D^+\bar{D}^{-1} + \bar{D}^{-1}A\bar{D}^{-1}$. We notice that the first two terms in K are diagonal matrices, which only contribute values for all K_{ii}, so that $K_{ij} = (\bar{D}^{-1}A\bar{D}^{-1})_{ij}$ for all $i \neq j$. By substituting these to (5) and simplifying all expressions, we have:

$$D(\mathbf{v}_i, \mathbf{m}_c) \propto \begin{cases} -\frac{2\sum_{j\in c} A_{ij}}{w_i \sum_{j\in c} w_j} + \alpha_c, & \text{if } i \notin \pi_c, \\ -\frac{2(\sum_{j\in c} A_{ij} + \sigma w_i - D^+_{ii})}{w_i \sum_{j\in c} w_j} + \alpha_c, & \text{if } i \in \pi_c, \end{cases} \tag{22}$$

where α_c is a constant for fixed c:

$$\alpha_c = \frac{\sum_{j,l\in c} A_{jl} + \sum_{j\in c}(\sigma w_j - D^+_{jj})}{(\sum_{j\in c} w_j)^2}.$$

Therefore, when running weighted kernel k-means in Algorithm 1, we can first compute and store each α_c in $O(m)$ time, where m is the number of edges in the network. After that, for each node we compute $D(\mathbf{v}_i, \mathbf{m}_c)$ for each c using (22), which takes $O(m + nk)$ time. Finally it takes additional $O(n)$ time to compute $C^*(\mathbf{v}_i)$. If the number of iterations is t, the time complexity of Algorithm 1 is only $O(t(m + nk))$. The same time complexity can be derived similarly for incremental k-means.

We can furthermore make refinement stage more efficient by only considering refinement on boundary nodes. Specifically, at each level, we only refine nodes that have neighbors in different clusters in initial clustering. Considering only boundary nodes usually leads to a similar clustering result to one derived by considering all nodes, but this makes the whole procedure much faster.

6. EXPERIMENTAL RESULTS

In the first part of this section, we demonstrate the effectiveness of the graph objectives and kernels proposed in Section 4.1. In the second part, we show that the multilevel approach is faster than other state-of-the-art methods, and it yields satisfactory clustering results. In addition, we show that our approach is scalable to networks with millions of nodes and edges.

6.1 Graph Kernels

We now compare the graph objectives and kernels proposed in Section 4.1. In particular, we show that the proposed balance ratio cut and balance normalized cut kernels are effective in solving the k-way clustering problem.

Criteria and Kernels. In Section 4, we showed that each proposed objective corresponds to a kernel by repre-

Criterion	Kernel
Signed Laplacian	$\sigma I - \bar{L}$
Normalized Signed Laplacian	$\sigma \bar{D}^{-1} + \bar{D}^{-1} A \bar{D}^{-1}$
Positive Ratio Association	$\sigma I + A^+$
Positive Ratio Cut	$\sigma I - L^+$
Ratio Association	$\sigma I + A$
Balance Ratio Cut	$\sigma I - (D^+ - A)$
Balance Normalized Cut	$\sigma \bar{D}^{-1} - \bar{D}^{-1}(D^+ - A)\bar{D}^{-1}$

Table 1: Criteria and kernels considered in experiments.

senting the objective as in (19). Now we select the following kernels for comparison: Positive Ratio Association (**PosRatioAssoc**), Ratio Association (**RatioAssoc**), Positive Ratio Cut (**PosRatioCut**), Balance Ratio Cut (**BalRatioCut**) and Balance Normalized Cut (**BalNorCut**) as representatives of our proposed methods, and Signed Laplacian (**SignLap**), Normalized Signed Laplacian (**NorSignLap**) as the current state-of-the-art spectral methods [13]. We summarize these kernels in Table 1. For each kernel, we properly choose the smallest σ such that K is positive semi-definite, by computing the spectrum of the matrix.

Experimental Setup and Metrics. To compare the effectiveness of each kernel, we create some synthetic networks with the following procedure. We begin with a complete 5-weakly balanced network A_{com}, in which group sizes are $100, 200, \ldots 500$ respectively. We then uniformly sample some entries from A_{com} to form a weakly balanced network A, with two parameters: sparsity s and noise level ϵ. The sparsity s represents the percentage of edges sampled from A_{com}, and the noise level ϵ specifies the probability of flipping the sign of an edge when sampling. Afterwards, we consider each kernel and its corresponding objective in (19), and derive the clustering using spectral clustering. When we perform spectral clustering, we run k-means ten times with different initializations and select the one that gives us the smallest objective value since a bad initialization of k-means might influence the clustering result.

To evaluate a clustering result (or an indicator set $\{\mathbf{x}_1, ..., \mathbf{x}_k\}$ in other words), we first consider the following objective value:

$$\sum_{c=1}^{k} \frac{\mathbf{x}_c^T A^- \mathbf{x}_c + \mathbf{x}_c^T L^+ \mathbf{x}_c}{\mathbf{x}_c^T W \mathbf{x}_c}. \tag{23}$$

We call (23) the ratio objective if $W = I$ and normalized objective if $W = \bar{D}$. Both objectives measure the degree of imbalance of clusters, with size or volume normalization. Typically, if the underlying kernel is ratio normalized, we use ratio objective to measure the clustering result; otherwise, we use normalized objective to measure the clustering result. Note that the normalized objective is upper bounded by k. In addition, since we also have the "real" clustering as the ground truth in the synthetic datasets, we can calculate the error rate of clustering based on the ground truth. Specifically, we calculate the percentage of misclassified edges if we apply the clustering to A_{com}. We consider an edge to be misclassified if the edge is a between-cluster edge and it is positive, or if the edge is a within-cluster edge and it is negative. The precise definition of error rate is:

$$\sum_{c=1}^{k} \frac{\mathbf{x}_c^T A_{com}^- \mathbf{x}_c + \mathbf{x}_c^T L_{com}^+ \mathbf{x}_c}{n^2},$$

where n is the number of nodes in A_{com}. To make the comparison fair, all results are averaged over ten times trials.

Results. In the first experiment, we sample from A_{com} with different sparsity levels and a fixed $\epsilon = 0$, i.e., no noise. Since in most cases we expect a network to be sparse, we zoom in the range of sparsity $s \in [4 \times 10^{-3}, 10^{-1}]$. The results are shown in Figure 1. A lower error rate and objective implies a more effective method. We can see that PosRatioAssoc, NegRatioAssoc and PosRatioCut, which only consider one of positive or negative criterion, perform worse than others. This confirms that both positive and negative relationships are essential when we cluster signed networks. Furthermore, we see that BalRatioCut and BalNorCut outperform SignLap and NorSignLap under every sparsity level, and the difference becomes significant when a graph becomes more sparse. This is also not surprising since SignLap and NorSignLap are not optimizing the desired clustering patterns when $k = 5$, as explained in Theorem 3.

In the second experiment, we fix the sparsity at 10^{-2} and increase noise level ϵ from 0 to 0.5. The results are shown in Figure 2. Here we observe that for $\epsilon < 0.17$, BalRatioCut and BalNorCut still give the lowest error rate, but their error rates go higher for larger ϵ. However, if we see in Figures 2b and 2c, we observe that their objectives are still quite small compared with others. The possible reason is that when noise level goes too high, antagonistic clusters are no longer significant. In such case, ground-truth clusters cannot be captured by minimizing these objectives.

In summary, we see that BalRatioCut and BalNorCut are very effective in k-way clustering and improve the state-of-the-art signed Laplacian based methods.

6.2 Multilevel Clustering

We now show that the quality of results using the multilevel clustering method discussed in Section 5 is comparable to recent state-of-the-art methods. Furthermore, multilevel clustering is much faster than other methods, so it can scale up to large-scale signed networks. We have implemented our multilevel clustering algorithm in C++. In refinement phase, we use balance normalized cut kernel for weighted kernel k-means, since it gives us the most favorable result as shown in Section 6.1. For efficiency, we do not apply local search strategy and we only consider boundary nodes in refinement phase (See Section 5.3 for details). Similarly, to make a fair comparison, all results are averaged over ten trials.

Methods. To compare our multilevel clustering with other existing state-of-the-art methods, we consider the normalized signed Laplacian (**NorSignLap**) [13]. In addition, we also consider two more approaches, **MC-SVP** and **MC-MF**, which are based on the low rank model proposed in [10]. MC-SVP uses SVP to complete the network and runs k-means on k eigenvectors of the completed matrix to get the clustering result. while MC-MF completes the network using matrix factorization and derives two low rank factors $U, H \in \mathbb{R}^{n \times k}$, and runs k-means on both U and H. We then select the clustering that gives us smaller normalized balance cut objective. See [10] for more details.

Results. First we see the quality of clustering results. Using the same procedure conducted in Section 6.1, we create some networks sampled from a complete 10-weakly balanced network, in which each group contains $1,000$ nodes. We fix $\epsilon = 0$, and compare the objective and error rate of each method under different sparsity. To make the comparison

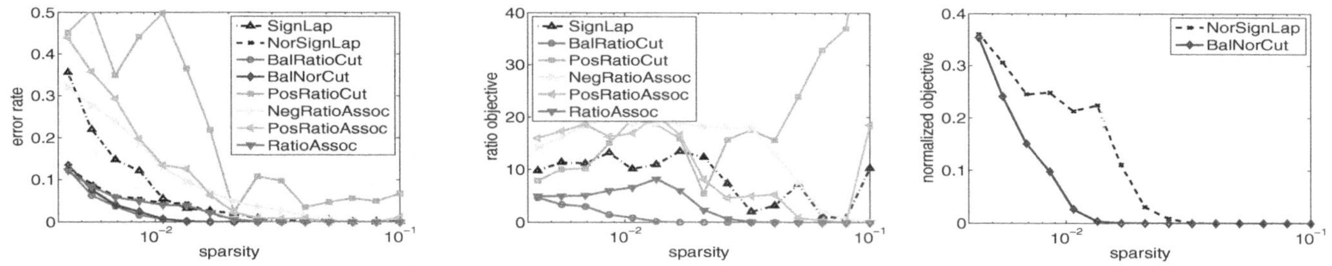

(a) Error rate (b) Ratio objective: $W = I$ in (23) (c) Normalized objective: $W = \bar{D}$ in (23)

Figure 1: Spectral clustering results using different kernels on weakly balanced networks, with different sparsity.

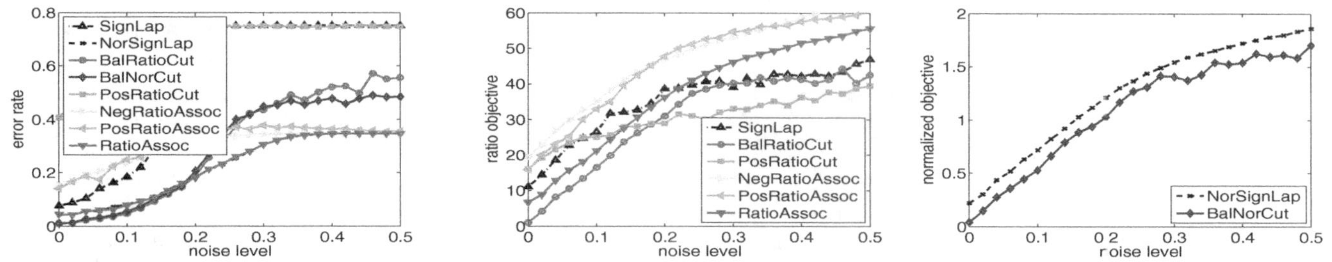

(a) Error rate (b) Ratio objective: $W = I$ in (23) (c) Normalized objective: $W = \bar{D}$ in (23)

Figure 2: Spectral clustering results using different kernels on weakly balanced networks, with different noise levels.

clearer, here we consider the balance normalized objective for all methods. The result is shown in Figure 3. As a graph becomes more sparse, MC-MF and MC-SVP perform worse than NorSignLap and multilevel clustering. However, MC-MF requires much less running time than NorSignLap. We will discuss timing details issue in the next subsection. In addition, the multilevel clustering outperforms other state-of-the-art methods in most cases. It usually achieves the lowest error rate and normalized objective.

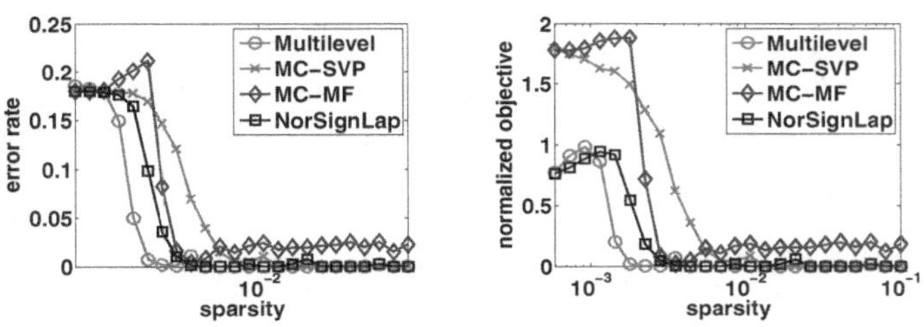

(a) Error rate (b) Normalized objective

Figure 3: Clustering results for multilevel clustering and other state-of-the-art methods on weakly balanced networks, with different sparsity.

Now let us compare the efficiency of different methods. We consider A_{com} to be a large balanced network, which contains 20 groups, with 50,000 nodes in each group. By choosing a proper sparsity, we randomly sample some edges from A_{com} to form A with desired number of edges. We then measure the running time required for each clustering algorithm under different A. Both NorSignLap and MC-SVP are too costly to apply on this large-scale network, since both of them require eigenvectors computation of top k eigenvectors. Therefore, here we only compare the multilevel algorithm with MC-MF method. While we report the running time of whole procedure for multilevel clustering, we only report the time for computing two factors U and H for MC-MF. Thus, the MC-MF time we report is just an under-estimate of the real clustering time, since we ignore the time for doing k-means clustering on U and H. To solve matrix factorization efficiently, we implement alternating least squares (ALS) algorithm in C++ with MKL library, and run ALS iterations 3 times to derive U and H. In practice, ALS usually needs more than 3 iterations to obtain converged U and H, which will take more time than we report.

The running time of the multilevel clustering and MC-MF is shown in Figure 4. We can see that the multilevel clustering is faster than MC-MF even if we only consider the time for matrix factorization procedure of MC-MF. In particular, we can obtain the clustering result of a 20-weakly balanced network, with 1M nodes and 100M edges (so, sparsity $= 10^{-4}$), in only 398.77 seconds. We further plot the clustering result of this network in Figure 5. By reordering nodes based on clustering result, we can see A^+ becomes nearly block-diagonal while A^- is pretty dense in the between-cluster part. This reconfirms that our multilevel algorithm is both efficient and effective.

Finally, we apply our multilevel clustering algorithm to large-scale real networks considered by Leskovec et al. [14], in which the authors argue that there are no significant (two) nearly antagonistic groups, though local structure in these networks tends to be balanced. We now extend the consideration from balance to weak balance, and examine whether there exist k nearly antagonistic groups in these networks. We first make the network symmetric by considering $\text{sgn}(A+A')$, and take the largest connected component as the input of the multilevel clustering algorithm. We then obtain several clustering results by considering k from 3 to 30. Since we do not have the ground truth of clustering in real networks, we can only compute the "empirical" error rate on A, i.e., the percentage of misclassified edges in A under such clustering.

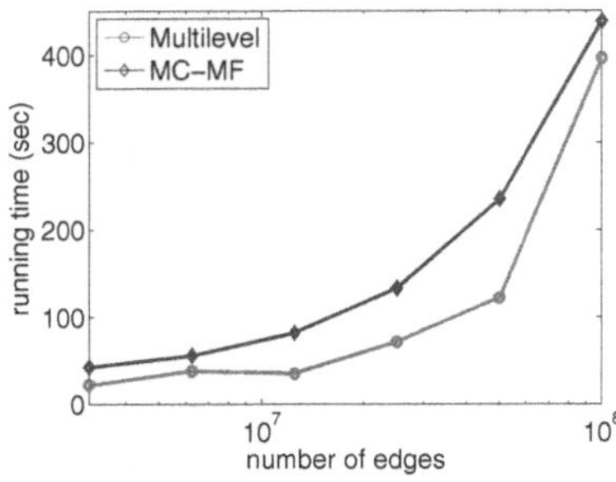

Figure 4: Running time of multilevel clustering and MC-MF on weakly balanced networks, with 1 million nodes and 100 million edges. For MC-MF we report the time to solve matrix factorization only, while in multilevel clustering we report the time for the whole procedure.

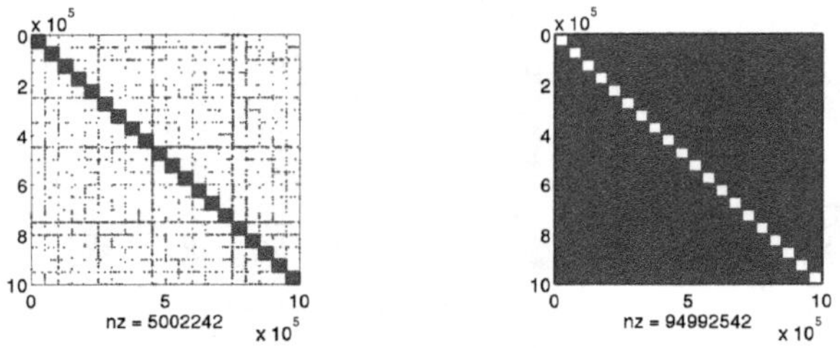

Figure 5: Clustering result of a 20-weakly balanced network, with 1M nodes and 100M edges. We see that most positive edges are within clusters and most negative edges are between clusters. The normalized objective of this clustering is 0.032, which is much smaller than 20.

We find the empirical error rate for each k is very close to each other, so we report the average error rate for each dataset, which is summarized in Table 2. Similar to the observation in [14], the empirical error rates of k-way clustering result are trivially achievable (by putting all nodes into one cluster). This implies that we can hardly find significant k nearly antagonistic groups in these networks even if we extensively consider weak balance.

7. CONCLUSIONS

In this paper, we study the k-way clustering problem in signed networks. We first find that the state-of-the-art signed graph kernels, (normalized) signed Laplacian, suffer from a weakness when we apply them to the k-way clustering problem. Thus, we propose some new signed cut and association objectives and kernels. In particular, we show one of our proposed objectives, balance normalized cut, is both theoretically sound and experimentally effective. Furthermore, we prove that our proposed objectives are mathematically equivalent to the weighted kernel k-means objective. Based on this equivalence, we propose a multilevel clustering algorithm, which is competitive to recent state-of-the-art methods in terms of the quality of the clustering result, while it is much more efficient and scalable.

	Epinions	Slashdot	Wikipedia
# of nodes	119,070	82,052	7,064
# of edges	1,403,138	994,052	200,590
% of + edges	0.8321	0.7641	0.7855
error rate	0.1679	0.2369	0.2186
avg time (sec)	9.860	6.830	0.450

Table 2: Multilevel clustering results on large-scale real networks. The (empirical) error rate is the percentage of misclassified edges for $k = 3$ to 30; the above results support observation in [14] that these networks do not have significant clustering structure.

Acknowledgments: This research was supported by NSF grants CCF-0916309, CCF-1117055 and DOD Army grant W911NF-10-1-0529.

8. REFERENCES

[1] P. Anchuri and M. Magdon-Ismail. Communities and balance in signed networks: A spectral approach. *IEEE/ACM ASONAM*, 2012.

[2] N. Bansal, A. Blum, and S. Chawla. Correlation clustering. *Machine Learning*, 56:89–113, 2004.

[3] D. Cartwright and F. Harary. Structure balance: A generalization of Heider's theory. *Psychological Review*, 63(5):277–293, 1956.

[4] J. A. Davis. Clustering and structural balance in graphs. *Human Relations*, 20(2):181–187, 1967.

[5] I. S. Dhillon. Co-clustering documents and words using bipartite spectral graph partitioning. In *KDD*, 2001.

[6] I. S. Dhillon, Y. Guan, and J. Kogan. Iterative clustering of high dimensional text data augmented by local search. In *ICDM*, pages 131–138, 2002.

[7] I. S. Dhillon, Y. Guan, and B. Kulis. Weighted graph cuts without eigenvectors: A multilevel approach. *IEEE Trans. on Pattern Analysis and Machine Intelligence*, 29(11):1944–1957, 2007.

[8] P. Doreian and A. Mrvar. A partitioning approach to structural balance. *Social Networks*, 18(21):149–168, 1996.

[9] F. Harary. On the notion of balance of a signed graph. *Michigan Mathematical Journal*, 2(2):143–146, 1953.

[10] C.-J. Hsieh, K.-Y. Chiang, and I. S. Dhillon. Low rank modeling of signed networks. In *KDD*, 2012.

[11] G. Karypis and V. Kumar. A fast and high quality multilevel scheme for partitioning irregular graphs. *SIAM Journal on Scientific Computing*, 20(1):359–392, 1999.

[12] B. W. Kernighan and S. Lin. An efficient heuristic procedure for partitioning graphs. *Bell system technical journal*, 49(1):291–307, 1970.

[13] J. Kunegis, S. Schmidt, A. Lommatzsch, J. Lerner, E. W. D. Luca, and S. Albayrak. Spectral analysis of signed graphs for clustering, prediction and visualization. In *SDM*, pages 559–570, 2010.

[14] J. Leskovec, D. Huttenlocher, and J. Kleinberg. Predicting positive and negative links in online social networks. In *WWW*, pages 641–650, 2010.

[15] J. Shi and J. Malik. Normalized cuts and image segmentation. *IEEE Trans. on Pattern Analysis and Machine Intelligence*, 2000.

[16] U. von Luxburg. A tutorial on spectral clustering. *Statistics and Computing*, 17(4), 2007.

[17] B. Yang, W. Cheung, and J. Liu. Community mining from signed social networks. *IEEE Trans. on Knowledge and Data Engineering*, 19(10):1333–1348, 2007.

Maximum Margin Clustering on Evolutionary Data

Xuhui Fan,
Longbing Cao, Xia Cui
Advanced Analytics Institute
Faculty of Engineering and
Information Technology
University of Technology
Sydney, Australia
Xuhui.Fan@student.uts.edu.au

Lin Zhu
Institute of Image Processing
and Pattern Recognition
Shanghai Jiao Tong University,
Shanghai, China
wxzhulin@yahoo.com.cn

Yew-Soon Ong
School of Computer
Engineering
Nanyang Technological
University
asysong@ntu.edu.sg

ABSTRACT

Evolutionary data, such as topic changing blogs and evolving trading behaviors in capital market, is widely seen in business and social applications. The time factor and intrinsic change embedded in evolutionary data greatly challenge evolutionary clustering. To incorporate the time factor, existing methods mainly regard the evolutionary clustering problem as a linear combination of *snapshot cost* and *temporal cost*, and reflect the time factor through the *temporal cost*. It still faces accuracy and scalability challenge though promising results gotten. This paper proposes a novel evolutionary clustering approach, evolutionary maximum margin clustering (e-MMC), to cluster large-scale evolutionary data from the maximum margin perspective. e-MMC incorporates two frameworks: *Data Integration* from the data changing perspective and *Model Integration* corresponding to model adjustment to tackle the time factor and change, with an adaptive label allocation mechanism. Three e-MMC clustering algorithms are proposed based on the two frameworks. Extensive experiments are performed on synthetic data, UCI data and real-world blog data, which confirm that e-MMC outperforms the state-of-the-art clustering algorithms in terms of accuracy, computational cost and scalability. It shows that e-MMC is particularly suitable for clustering large-scale evolving data.

Categories and Subject Descriptors

I.2.6 [**Artificial Intelligence**]: Learning; I.5.3 [**Pattern Recognition**]: Clustering.

Keywords

Maximum Margin Clustering; Evolutionary data.

1. INTRODUCTION

Evolutionary data is ubiquitous, such as social networking data and capital market trading information, and is increasing exponentially with the widespread development and emergence of business and social applications. The key challenge of learning evolutionary data lies on its evolution nature with time development, for instance, the change of topics in blogging or the adjustment of trading behaviors [3]. Evolutionary clustering is a topic aiming at segmenting such time-varied data [4].

A critical factor in evolutionary data is the time factor t. It affects the accuracy, consistency and robustness of evolutionary clustering algorithms when the data presents dynamics in attribute values or interactions between data objects at different time points. This is much more challenging when learning a large scale of evolutionary data. A typical approach is to verify the modeling performance between data in a historical time window and the data currently learned, and to apply techniques like weighting to adjust the learning objective function.

Typical evolutionary clustering includes agglomerative clustering, k-means clustering [4], and spectral clustering [6]. For all these proposed approaches, the time factor t is involved as a smoothness control term in adjusting the clustering performance of the current data against that of historical one. It usually divides the objective function into two parts: *snapshot cost* (CS) defining the clustering quality of the current data, and *temporal cost* (CT) verifying the shift from historical records to current ones. It is reported that this can achieve rather promising outcomes, especially on the small size of data sets. They also face real-world data challenges, for example, the existing k-means evolutionary clustering algorithms suffer from complicated situations such as non-spherical datasets, and evolutionary spectral clustering algorithms perform unsatisfactorily on data with tens of thousands of objects.

This paper proposes a novel evolutionary clustering approach, Evolutionary Maximum Margin Clustering (e-MMC), for clustering evolutionary data. Unlike identifying centers of clusters in k-means evolutionary clustering in the common Euclidean Space or spectral clustering in Eigenspace, we employ the Maximum Margin Clustering (MMC) [20] algorithm to seek a hyperplane that best separates the data distribution in a pre-defined kernel space. This is motivated by the advantage of MMC through obtaining the maximum margin between two clusters to segment all possible clusters for a higher accuracy [20, 21] and even better computational performance [18]. e-MMC is challenged by identifying proper mechanisms for (1) incorporating the time influence into the MMC clustering process to obtain a time-smoothed data partition, and (2) tackling the large scale evolutionary data.

We incorporate the time factor into MMC and handle the time smoothness problem through two frameworks: *data integration* (DI) and *model integration* (MI). *Data integration* regards the historical data as the required records and measures the performance of the MMC-oriented margin partition on both current data and historical data with different weights. *Model integration* considers both the current data partition cost and the margin change in

CIKM'12, October 29–November 2, 2012, Maui, HI, USA.

terms of time. We employ an optimization strategy similar to the cutting plane MMC [23] to conduct e-MMC both efficiently and effectively. Three e-MMC based clustering algorithms are then proposed for evolutionary clustering. To the best of our knowledge, e-MMC is the first evolutionary version of the Maximum Margin Clustering algorithm to cluster the evolutionary data from the margin perspective, and can deal with the label assignments under the evolutionary framework adaptively.

We further verify the e-MMC approach, the two proposed frameworks, and the three algorithms through substantial experiments on synthetic dataset, UCI data and real-world blog data. Compared to the four baseline clustering algorithms, experimental results have shown that e-MMC can cluster evolutionary data with better accuracy, improved computational performance and scalability. It shows that e-MMC has a great potential for clustering large-scale evolutionary data, which is of high demand in the real world.

The rest of this paper is organized as follows. Section 2 introduces the related work on evolutionary clustering and MMC. Preliminaries and notations are introduced in Section 3. The evolutionary MMC approach and its two frameworks are described in Section 4. More discussion and analysis about them are available in Section 5. Extensive experimental evaluation is performed in Section 6. Section 7 concludes the work and discusses future work.

2. RELATED WORK

In contrast to static data set, various formats of non-static data set appear in business and social applications [2], such as social network linkage data and topic change in online news update, as well as behavioral data [3, 17]. Various effective methods have been put forward to tackle different characteristics of the evolving data, such as data stream clustering focusing on the one-scanned data [9, 1], and incremental clustering concentrating on updating the cluster parameters [10, 14, 16].

Focusing on the data attribute's evolving behavior, evolutionary clustering was first put forward by [4], where a framework was also defined for formulating the problem. Through exemplified algorithms of the bottom-up evolutionary hierarchical clustering and the evolutionary k-means clustering, they break the objective function into two parts: one focusing on the current data, and the other addressing the historical adjustment; both reaches satisfactory results on both current and historical data sets. In [6, 7], the two compositions are further extended to spectral clustering, enabling it to address more sophisticated situations. Both of the methods achieve successful results in capturing the evolving behaviors under some cases. However, according to their capacity of handling data size, data with larger than tens of thousands of objects would be challenging for them to process. What is more, both algorithms automatically assign the same label to current and previous time stamps in each data set. In practice, data objects often change so as to be associated with different labels during the evolution. This requests an adaptive way to assign labels.

Recently, [20] proposed Maximum Margin Clustering (MMC), which is inspired by the idea of Support Vector Machine (SVM). Similar to SVM, MMC also aims at seeking the maximum margin solution during unsupervised learning. This is to achieve the maximum margin between two clusters among all the possible cluster constitution. Experiments in [20, 21] show that MMC can achieve better performance on the clustering results, especially in the clustering accuracy. [18] further generalizes the MMC algorithm and reduces the corresponding computational load.

A most recent work in [11] involves MMC on time series data. It employs the MMC Algorithm to cluster a set of non-overlapping time series segments to overcome the intractable inference in generative models. However, it only segments time series data, without considering the data time evolving and there is no test on the large data scale case.

3. PRELIMINARIES

3.1 Notations

Here the evolutionary data is specialized by a discrete time factor t, and is denoted as $\{\boldsymbol{X}_t, t = 1, \cdots, T\}$. We use $\boldsymbol{X}_t = \{\boldsymbol{x}_{1,t}, \cdots, \boldsymbol{x}_{n,t}\} \in R^d$ to denote the whole n data points with d dimensions at time t. $\{\phi(\boldsymbol{x}_{i,t}), i = 1, \cdots, n\}$ are related to the corresponding kernel space used in our Maximum Margin Clustering framework, the same as used in Support Vector Machine, with Kernel matrix $K_t = \{k_{ij,t}\}^{n\times n} = \{\phi(\boldsymbol{x}_{i,t})\phi(\boldsymbol{x}_{j,t})\}^{n\times n}$. For a given similarity matrix, a Cholesky decomposition [13] of the kernel matrix $\boldsymbol{K} = \hat{\boldsymbol{X}}\hat{\boldsymbol{X}}^T$ is computed, and $\phi(\boldsymbol{x}_i)$ is taken as the corresponding set $(\hat{\boldsymbol{X}}_{i,1}, \cdots, \hat{\boldsymbol{X}}_{i,n})^T$.

3.2 Maximum Margin Clustering

Maximum Margin Clustering (MMC) [20, 21] is inspired by the idea of Support Vector Machine (SVM), a widely used classification method in machine learning.

Briefly speaking, SVM aims at finding an optimal hyperplane in a pre-defined kernel space $\{\mathcal{F} : \phi(\boldsymbol{x}) \in \mathcal{F} | \boldsymbol{\omega}\phi(\boldsymbol{x}) + b = 0\}$ that can best separate the data points with different labels $\{y_i\}_{i=1}^n$. Defining $\{\phi(\boldsymbol{x}_i)\}_{i=1}^n$ as the kernel coordinators of $\{\boldsymbol{x}_i\}_{i=1}^n$, C as the balancing parameter of the slack variables $\{\xi_i\}_{i=1}^n$, SVM seeks the optimal values of $\boldsymbol{\omega}, b, \xi$ for the optimization problem below:

$$\begin{aligned} \min_{\boldsymbol{\omega},b,\xi} \quad & \frac{1}{2}\boldsymbol{\omega}^T\boldsymbol{\omega} + \frac{C}{n}\sum_{i=1}^n \xi_i \\ s.t. \quad & y_i(\boldsymbol{\omega}^T\phi(\boldsymbol{x}_i) + b) \geq 1 - \xi_i; \\ & \xi_i \geq 0 \quad i = 1, \cdots, n. \end{aligned} \tag{1}$$

With its success in real applications, MMC extends SVM to the unsupervised case, i.e., $\{y_i\}_{i=1}^n$ is unknown. That is to say, the goal of MMC is to find a labeling set $\{y_i\}_{i=1}^n$ that generates the largest margin among all the potential label assignments. More formally, the problem is defined as:

$$\begin{aligned} \min_{\boldsymbol{y}\in\{-1,+1\}^n} \min_{\boldsymbol{\omega},b,\xi} \quad & \frac{1}{2}\boldsymbol{\omega}^T\boldsymbol{\omega} + \frac{C}{n}\sum_{i=1}^n \xi_i \\ s.t. \quad & y_i(\boldsymbol{\omega}^T\phi(\boldsymbol{x}_i) + b) \geq 1 - \xi_i; \\ & \xi_i \geq 0 \quad i = 1, \cdots, n; \\ & -l \leq \boldsymbol{e}^T\boldsymbol{y} \leq l \end{aligned} \tag{2}$$

where $l \geq 0$ is a constant controlling the clustering's balance and $\boldsymbol{e}$ is the all-one vector.

Comparing to SVM (Equation (1)), the only difference lies in the variables needed to be solved. MMC (Equation (2)) includes the label assignments $\{y_i\}_{i=1}^n$, while the SVM assumes to have the prior information. The label assignment in MMC makes it complicated to achieve the solutions.

The Cutting Plane MMC (CPMMC) Algorithm [23] is a recently proposed method to solve the MMC problem (Equation (2)) both efficiently and effectively. It is based on constructing a sequence of successively tighter relaxation of Equation (2); and during each of the intermediate tasks, a Wolfe dual form is utilized in the constrained concave-convex procedure.

In this paper, we use an optimization strategy similar as the CPMMC implementation to conduct MMC on evolutionary data. The details of its implementation are in [23] and Appendix A.

3.3 Evolutionary Data

Evolutionary data is closely related to stream data and incremental data. However, it differs from them since evolutionary data embeds data change as a major concern.

As in [4, 6], the evolutionary clustering clusters the current and historical data under the same clustering mechanism, although with a different weight in the objective cost function. A better performance of the cost function is expected to happen on both data sets rather than one of them only. This fact is embodied through the cost function by two compositions: *snapshot cost (CS)* measuring the proposed partition cost on the current data, and *temporal cost (CT)* scaling the temporal smoothness on historical data or historical partitions. More formally, the cost function for evolutionary clustering is defined as a linear combination of *CS* and *CT*, with a tuning parameter $\alpha (0 \leq \alpha \leq 1)$:

$$Cost = \alpha \cdot CS + (1 - \alpha) \cdot CT \tag{3}$$

The larger α value, the more focus we put on the current data partition effect.

In [6, 7], evolutionary clustering is extended to the spectral clustering. Two frameworks called Preserving Cluster Quality (PCQ) and Preserving Cluster Membership (PCM) are proposed. Instead of taking the so-called "inter-cluster" cost as the cost function, the current partition cost function of evolutionary spectral clustering is set as the graph cut result, and the evaluation criterion of the historical data partition is categorized into the graph cut result on historical data in PCQ and partition shift from historical data to current data in PCM.

4. EVOLUTIONARY MMC FRAMEWORK

4.1 Basic Principle

Motivated by the evolutionary clustering strategies proposed in [4, 6], two novel Maximum Margin Clustering-based evolutionary frameworks are introduced to separate the evolving data distribution by a required hyperplane. More specifically, in order to avoid the confusion of different performance targets, we define two new evolutionary approaches: *snapshot margin(SM)* and *integration relaxation(IR)* to replace the *snapshot cost* and *temporal cost* in [4], respectively. The weighted linear combination function is defined to take both of the historical and current data into consideration.

$$\begin{aligned} &\text{Current Margin} = \alpha \cdot SM + (1 - \alpha) \cdot IR \\ &SM, IR \text{ subject to some pre-defined constraints} \end{aligned} \tag{4}$$

Here, *SM* is formulated as the process of seeking objects with the maximum margins: $SM = \frac{1}{2}\boldsymbol{\omega}^T\boldsymbol{\omega} + C \cdot \sum_{i=1}^{n} \xi_i$, while *IR* mainly considers the cost of incorporating historical records. Under the special case of $\alpha = 1$ with the initial constraints, the problem is converted into the common two-cluster MMC problem.

In this paper, we propose two novel frameworks corresponding to two different *IR* representatives. In the first framework, historical factor is represented by the historical data, termed *Data Integration (DI)*. *DI* utilizes the historical data and compares with the current data for data change and clustering performance variation. The data evolving behaviors in *DI* are categorized into *cohort data evolving* of the whole data set and *individual data evolving* of a single data object. The former captures the variation process of the whole data set, while the latter handles the particular movement of each data point. The second framework is named as *Model Integration* (MI) which focuses on margin evolving.

Figure 1 clearly depicts the structure of our proposed frameworks for MMC-based evolutionary clustering. Two frameworks are proposed from different points of view while encountering evolutionary data. One from the *data integration* perspective, which further handles two scenarios *cohort data evolving* and *individual data evolving* respectively. The other reflects *model integration.*

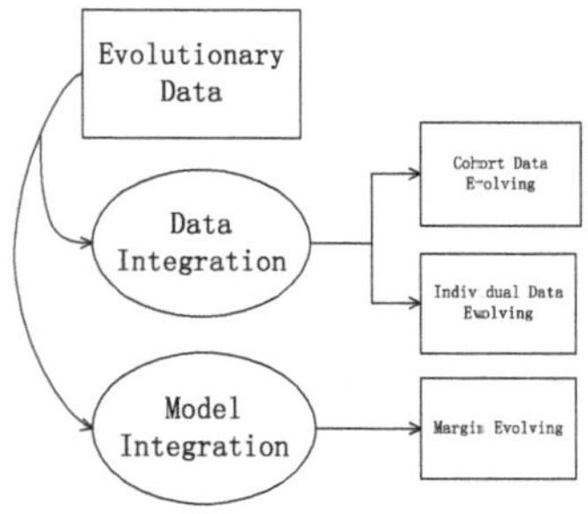

Figure 1: The evolutionary-MMC frameworks

4.2 Data Integration (DI)

In *data integration*, historical data is incorporated to represent the influence of time factor t. To simplify the algorithm, we mainly employ the data set of the current time t and that of the previous time $t-1$ to represent the whole data. A tuning parameter is set to differentiate the importance of the current and previous data sets.

By treating the data evolving behaviors from different perspectives, we deploy our framework into two different directions: *cohort data evolving* (CDE) in cohort analysis and *individual data evolving* (IDE) in individual observation. Below we explain them in detail.

4.2.1 Cohort Data Evolving(CDE)

In *cohort data evolving* (CDE), we treat the moving behavior of the whole data set as an evolving characteristic of the whole data set. This is reflected through the metrics such as mean and variation measuring the cluster shifting triggered by the evolution of its belonging data points. With this mechanism, each feasible solution in the MMC solution set is constrained by the specific time point. By denoting the MMC problem at time t as J_t and the *Integration Relaxation* (IR) as the MMC problem at time $t-1$, the CDE problem is simplified as:

$$\min_{\boldsymbol{y}, \boldsymbol{\omega}, b} \alpha \cdot J_t + (1 - \alpha) \cdot J_{t-1} \tag{5}$$

According to the annotation for MMC in Equation (2), we specify our current margin problem (Equation (5)) as:

$$\begin{aligned} \min_{\boldsymbol{y}_t, \boldsymbol{y}_{t-1} \in \{-1,+1\}^n} \min_{\boldsymbol{\omega}, b, \boldsymbol{\xi}_t, \boldsymbol{\xi}_{t-1}} & \frac{1}{2}\boldsymbol{\omega}^T\boldsymbol{\omega} + \alpha \cdot \frac{C}{n}\sum_{i=1}^{n} \xi_{i,t} \\ & + (1 - \alpha) \cdot \frac{C}{n}\sum_{i=1}^{n} \xi_{i,t-1} \\ & s.t. y_{i,t-1}(\boldsymbol{\omega}^T\phi(\boldsymbol{x}_{i,t-1}) + b) \geq 1 - \xi_{i,t-1}; \\ & \xi_{i,t-1} \geq 0, i = 1, \cdots, n; \\ & y_{i,t}(\boldsymbol{\omega}^T\phi(\boldsymbol{x}_{i,t}) + b) \geq 1 - \xi_{i,t}; \\ & \xi_{i,t} \geq 0, i = 1, \cdots, n. \end{aligned} \tag{6}$$

While the tuning parameter α satisfies $\alpha = 1 - \alpha$, Equation (6) conveys a quite straightforward solution that seeks a margin to best separate the current data from historical data. Otherwise, the slack variables are scaled according to its time stamp, leading to different weights in the solving process.

We employ the similar techniques in [23] to solve Equation (6). According to the results in [23]'s result, problem (6) is equally transformed into the following problem by eliminating the label $\{y_i\}_{i=1}^n$ temporally:

$$\begin{aligned} \min_{\boldsymbol{\omega},b,\boldsymbol{\xi}_t,\boldsymbol{\xi}_{t-1}} \quad & \frac{1}{2}\boldsymbol{\omega}^T\boldsymbol{\omega} + \alpha \cdot \frac{C}{n}\sum_{i=1}^{n}\xi_{i,t} \\ & + (1-\alpha)\cdot\frac{C}{n}\sum_{i=1}^{n}\xi_{i,t-1} \\ s.t. \quad & |\boldsymbol{\omega}^T\phi(\boldsymbol{x}_{i,t-1}) + b| \geq 1 - \xi_{i,t-1}; \\ & \xi_{i,t-1} \geq 0, i = 1, \cdots, n; \\ & |\boldsymbol{\omega}^T\phi(\boldsymbol{x}_{i,t}) + b| \geq 1 - \xi_{i,t}; \\ & \xi_{i,t} \geq 0, i = 1, \cdots, n. \end{aligned} \tag{7}$$

To solve problem (7), we employ the same cutting plane strategy in [23]. Starting from an initialized constraint set Ω, we iteratively select the most violated label assignment $\boldsymbol{c} \in \{0,1\}^n$. Then we using a constraint concave convex procedure (CCCP) to optimize the solution until the pre-defined tolerable error contains the current most violated label assignment.

The Wolfe Dual form of the transformed CCCP problem is essential in the CCCP solving procedure. For simplicity, we show the related Wolfe Dual form and put it in Appendix B.1.

4.2.2 Individual Data Evolving(IDE)

In *individual data evolving* (IDE), we track the attribute change of each data point during the evolution. To make it clearer, we name the i-th data point from time t to $t-1$ as "time-paired data points" $\{\boldsymbol{x}_{i,t}, \boldsymbol{x}_{i,t-1}\}_{i=1}^n$. The following effective method is then proposed to find the structure of these "time-paired data points".

In respect to this time relation, the constraints of each time-paired data point have been shared (on ξ_i) here, reflected through the problem formalization that each time-paired data point employs the same slack variables. We again employ the tuning parameter α to unequally weight the data points at time points t and $t-1$, and thus convert the problem to the following:

$$\begin{aligned} \min_{\boldsymbol{y}\in\{-1,+1\}^n}\min_{\boldsymbol{\omega},b,\boldsymbol{\xi}} \quad & \frac{1}{2}\boldsymbol{\omega}^T\boldsymbol{\omega} + \frac{C}{n}\sum_{i=1}^{n}\xi_i \\ s.t. \quad & y_{i,t-1}(\boldsymbol{\omega}^T\phi(\boldsymbol{x}_{i,t-1}) + b) \geq 1 - \frac{1}{1-\alpha}\cdot\xi_i; \\ & y_{i,t}(\boldsymbol{\omega}^T\phi(\boldsymbol{x}_{i,t}) + b) \geq 1 - \frac{1}{\alpha}\cdot\xi_i; \\ & \xi_i \geq 0, i = 1, \cdots, n. \end{aligned} \tag{8}$$

Here *IR* does not have an explicit expression on the problem formalization; however, its influence reflects on the constraints. By this strategy, *IR* automatically chooses a slack variable that could cover the other's among the historical time point $t-1$ and the current time stamp t for all $i \in \{1, \cdots, n\}$.

Similar strategy as in *cohort data evolving* is used here to approximate problem (8). We put its Wolfe dual form in Appendix B.2 for consistency.

4.3 Model Integration (MI)

In *Model Integration*, historical records are mapped to previous hyperplane required in the learning. We target on a more stable margin result to keep the clustering result consistent. Also as predicted, a smaller shift is always preferable.

Firstly, *margin distance (md)* at time point t is introduced to better describe this shift. The *margin distance* is defined as the distance of i-th object to the required hyperplane:

$$md_{i,t} = \boldsymbol{\omega}_t\phi(\boldsymbol{x}_{i,t}) + b_T, i = 1, \cdots, n. \tag{9}$$

Here we should note that $\{md_{i,t}\}_{i=1}^n$ could be negative.

Further, we define the *margin shift (ms)* as the whole objects' difference between the current margin distance ($md_{i,t}$) and the previous margin distance ($md_{i,t-1}$).

$$ms = \sum_{i=1}^{n}(md_{i,t} - md_{i,t-1}) \tag{10}$$

Figure 2 illustrates the above concepts. M_{t-1} is the resulted hyperplane at the previous time point $t-1$. M_t^1 and M_t^2 are the two newly obtained hyperplanes without considering the historical records. $\boldsymbol{x}_1$ and $\boldsymbol{x}_2$ are two data points distributed in different clusters. Each is associated with margin distances $d_{1,t-1}, d_{1,t}^1, d_{1,t}^2$ and $d_{2,t-1}, d_{2,t}^1, d_{2,t}^2$ corresponding to margins M_{t-1}, M_t^1, M_t^2, represented in dash line, solid line and dash dot line in the figure. As a result, we can easily obtain $\sum_{i=1}^2(d_{i,t}^1 - d_{i,t-1}) < \sum_{i=1}^2(d_{i,t}^2 - d_{i,t-1})$. If the performance of M_t^1 and M_t^2 on partitioning the current data is nearly the same, we should choose M_t^1 as the current margin according to Equations (9) and (10). It is also noticed that the variation of M_t^1 is smaller than that of M_t^2 compared to M_{t-1}.

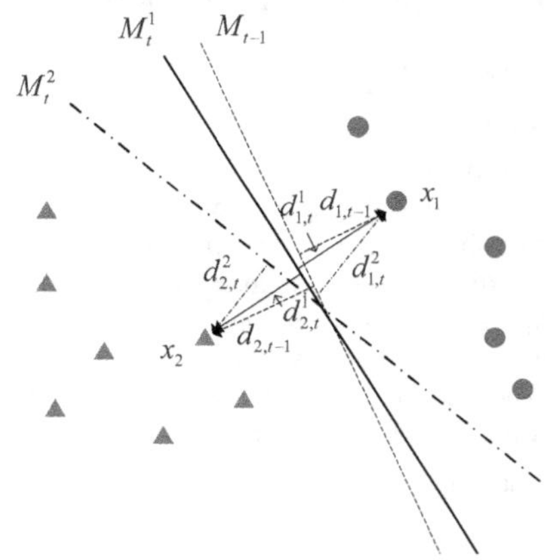

Figure 2: Model integration

In our *model integration (MI)* framework, *integration relaxation (IR)* in Equation (4) is the so-called *margin shift (ms)*. By incorporating the *IR* into the objective function, MI is formalized as:

$$\begin{aligned} \min_{\boldsymbol{y}\in\{-1,+1\}^n}\min_{\boldsymbol{\omega},b,\boldsymbol{\xi}} \quad & \frac{1}{2}\boldsymbol{\omega}^T\boldsymbol{\omega} + \frac{C}{n}\sum_{i=1}^{n}\xi_i + \alpha\cdot\sum_{i=1}^{n}\|\boldsymbol{\omega}_t\phi(\boldsymbol{x}_i) \\ & + b - (\boldsymbol{\omega}_{t-1}\phi(\boldsymbol{x}_i) + b_{t-1})\|_2^2 \\ s.t. \quad & y_i(\boldsymbol{\omega}^T\phi(\boldsymbol{x}_{i,t}) + b) \geq 1 - \xi_i; \\ & \xi_i \geq 0 \qquad i = 1, \cdots, n. \end{aligned} \tag{11}$$

Here α is the tuning parameter as usual.

Due to the complexity of the problem-solving of Equation (11), we use an approximation of *IR* to simplify it. More specifically, *IR* is separated into two terms: ω-penalty and b-penalty.

$$\min_{y\in\{-1,+1\}^n} \min_{\omega,b,\xi} \frac{1}{2}\omega^T\omega + \frac{C}{n}\sum_{i=1}^{n}\xi_i + \alpha\cdot\sum_{i=1}^{n}|\omega\phi(\boldsymbol{x}_i) - \omega_{t-1}\phi(\boldsymbol{x}_i)|_2^2 + \alpha\cdot|b-b_{t-1}|_2^2 \quad (12)$$
$$s.t. \quad y_i(\omega^T\phi(\boldsymbol{x}_i)+b) \geq 1-\xi_i;$$
$$\xi_i \geq 0 \quad i=1,\cdots,n.$$

The Wolfe dual form of this problem is given in Appendix B.3, with its further solution process in Appendix A.

4.4 Evolutionary MMC(e-MMC)

Inspired by the CPMMC Algorithm [23, 24, 19], we propose our algorithm for MMC-based evolutionary clustering both efficiently and effectively. As mentioned in Section 3, we need to provide a Wolfe dual form of the transformed problem during its problem solving process. The evolutionary Maximum Margin Clustering (e-MMC) algorithm is described in Algorithm 1.

Algorithm 1 Evolutionary Maximum Margin Clustering (e-MMC)

Require: violation parameter C; balance parameter l; error ε; parameter α;historic records ω_{t-1}, b_{t-1} or $\{\phi(\boldsymbol{x}_{i,t-1})\}_{i=1}^n$; current kernel coordinator $\{\phi(\boldsymbol{x}_{i,t})\}_{i=1}^n$ initialized ω_0, b_0; initialized constraints set $\Omega=\emptyset$
Ensure: resulted data label $\{y_{i,t}\}_{i=1}^n$,$\{y_{i,t-1}\}_{i=1}^n$

```
choose a proper framework: CDE, IDE, MI;
select the most violated constraint c according to [23]
while (1/n) Σ_{i=1}^n c_i − (1/n) Σ_{i=1}^n c_i |ω^T φ(x_i) + b| > ξ + ε do
    Ω = Ω ∪ c
    use quadratic programming technique to iteratively solve the
    Wolfe Dual form of the selected framework until converged
    update ω, b
    select the most violated constraint c
end while
return corresponding hyperplane parameter {ω, b}
```

Details of the CPMMC method can be checked in Appendix A.

5. ANALYSIS AND EXTENSION

5.1 Comparison and Analysis

Here we re-formulate the original MMC problem from the *loss function* perspective to make a better comparison of the two strategies in the *data integration* framework.

$$\min_{y\in\{-1,+1\}^n} \min_{\omega,b} \frac{1}{2}\omega^T\omega + C\cdot Loss \quad (13)$$

where *Loss* (different from *IR* as *IR* has constraints) is a pre-defined hinge loss function in the original MMC problem.

$$Loss = \sum_{i=1}^{n}\max\{0, 1-y_i(\omega^T\phi(\boldsymbol{x}_i)+b)\} \quad (14)$$

One advantage of $Loss$ is that this form exists without the introduction of the object's slack variables $\{\xi_i\}_{i=1}^n$.

Our CDE strategy is a linear combination of this original *Loss* at time stamps t and $t-1$.

$$Loss = \sum_{i=1}^{n}Loss_i = \sum_{i=1}^{n}[\alpha\cdot\max\{0,1-y_{i,t}(\omega^T\phi(\boldsymbol{x}_{i,t})+b)\} + (1-\alpha)\cdot\max\{0,1-y_{i,t-1}(\omega^T\phi(\boldsymbol{x}_{i,t-1})+b)\}] \quad (15)$$

The *Loss function* of IDE is in the form as:

$$Loss = \sum_{i=1}^{n}\max\{0, \alpha\cdot(1-y_{i,t}(\omega^T\phi(\boldsymbol{x}_{i,t})+b)), (1-\alpha)\cdot(1-y_{i,t-1}(\omega^T\phi(\boldsymbol{x}_{i,t-1})+b))\} \quad (16)$$

From the above *Loss function* analysis, we can easily obtain a deep understanding of the different evolutionary strategies incorporating the time factor t. In CDE, the hinge loss of the data cohort in different time stamps $(t, t-1)$ is linearly combined to form the whole loss, whereas the data violation in IDE is expressed through paired data object's comparison.

In the MI framework, the *margin shift* is used to smoothen the change of the model, where the change of label assignments can be regarded as another penetration point. Therefore, the difference between the current partition and historical partition is calculated to measure the continuity and robustness trend of evolutionary clustering. The time factor influence can be defined as:

$$df = \sum_{i=1}^{n}|y_{i,t}-y_{i,t-1}|^2 \quad (17)$$

As we know, the signum function $sgn(\cdot)$ value of *margin distance* is the label prediction result both in SVM and MMC. Thus, the difference led by various data point allocations can be calculated as:

$$df = \sum_{i=1}^{n}|\mathrm{sgn}(\omega_t\phi(\boldsymbol{x}_i)+b_t) - \mathrm{sgn}(\omega_{t-1}\phi(\boldsymbol{x}_i)+b_{t-1})|_2^2 \quad (18)$$

The function $sgn(\cdot)$ is inconvenient to be calculated during the derivation. We thus approximate the solution with the following relaxation function:

$$df = \sum_{i=1}^{n}|(\omega_t\phi(\boldsymbol{x}_i)+b_t) - (\omega_{t-1}\phi(\boldsymbol{x}_i)+b_{t-1})|_2^2 \quad (19)$$

Note that *df* is the same as *margin shift* in the second framework in Section 4, which shares the same representation under this strategy.

Based on the above analysis, it is clear that *data integration* focuses on data consistency during the evolutionary clustering procedure with the historical data; whereas the *model integration* aims at margin consistency, which is more related to the existed historical maximum margin.

5.2 Object Inserting and Removing

During the data evolutionary procedure, the inserting and removing of data objects are different natural phenomena.

In the *data integration* framework, we fix the problem through the *Loss function* expression. More specifically, inserting and removing objects are regarded as a single term in calculating the object loss, i.e., $Loss_i = \alpha\cdot\max\{0,1-y_{i,T}(\omega^T\phi(\boldsymbol{x}_{i,T})+b)\}$ for a coming object i and $Loss_i = (1-\alpha)\cdot\max\{0,1-y_{i,T-1}(\omega^T\phi(\boldsymbol{x}_{i,T-1})+b)\}$ for a disappearing object i.

Another case is the *margin consistency* framework. An average value of the whole *margin distance* is calculated for those disappearing object's *margin distance*.

6. EXPERIMENTAL EVALUATION

The experimental evaluation is conducted on three types of datasets, which are grouped into synthetic dataset, UCI-benchmarking datasets [8] and NEC blog dataset [22]. All datasets are preprocessed by normalizing each feature on each dimension into the interval [0, 1]. Furthermore, the clustering process of the algorithms is repeated for 50 times at each setting. All experiments were run on a computer with Intel Xeno (R) CPU 2.53-GHz, Microsoft Windows 7 with algorithms coded in Matlab.

6.1 Baseline and Experimental Settings

Our proposed methods are compared with four baseline algorithms to verify our algorithm performance: k-means clustering on accumulated historical data (ACC), k-means clustering on current individual data (IND), spectral evolutionary clustering with preserving cluster quality (PCQ) and the one with preserving cluster membership (PCM).

Parameters in these algorithms are set accordingly. In ACC and IND, we use the random initialization strategy to start the clustering; Euclidean distance and the RBF function $f(d) = \exp(-\frac{d^2}{2\delta^2})$ are used to construct the similarity matrix, and parameter δ ranges from 0.1 to 2.

Moreover, to accelerate the spectral clustering calculation and to better capture the similarity matrix, we employ the recently proposed spectral clustering implementation [5]. On the k-means clustering implementation, we directly use the existed function in the Matlab implementation toolbox.

In our algorithms, unless specified, the tuning parameter α is set to be 0.7 for all comparison algorithms.

6.2 Performance Metrics

For fair comparison, we use the k-means clustering cost function km-cost to measure the clustering performance of our proposed methods and the above baseline evolutionary clustering methods.

$$km\text{-cost} = \alpha \cdot \sum_{j=1}^{c_t} \sum_{i=1}^{C_{j,t}} \|\boldsymbol{x}_{i,t} - \frac{\sum_{l=1}^{C_{j,t}} \boldsymbol{x}_{l,t}}{C_{j,t}}\|^2 + (1-\alpha) \cdot \sum_{j=1}^{c_{t-1}} \sum_{i=1}^{C_{j,t-1}} \|\boldsymbol{x}_{i,t-1} - \frac{\sum_{l=1}^{C_{j,t-1}} \boldsymbol{x}_{l,t-1}}{C_{j,t-1}}\|^2 \tag{20}$$

where $\{C_j, j = 1, \cdots, c\}$ are the resultant cluster assignments given by the comparison methods, c is the cluster number and α is a pre-defined parameter tuning the importance weight between the *snapshot cost* and *temporal cost*. Obviously, the smaller the values are, the better the clustering performance is.

Besides the km-cost criterion, we also use the NMI (normalized mutual information) to study the performance of the clustering algorithms in the synthetic data learning, which is defined as:

$$NMI = \frac{\sum_{i=1}^{c} \sum_{j=1}^{c} \log(\frac{N \cdot n_{ij}}{n_i n_j})}{\sqrt{\sum_{i=1}^{c} n_i \log(\frac{n_i}{N}) \sum_{i=1}^{c} n_j \log(\frac{n_j}{N})}} \tag{21}$$

where n_{ij} is the number of agreements between clusters i and j, n_i is the number of data points in cluster i, n_j is the number of data points in cluster j, and N represents the number of data points in the whole dataset.

6.3 Experiments on Synthetic Data

6.3.1 Synthetic Dataset

In this experiment, we first adopt a synthetic dataset to investigate the performance of our proposed methods, where the dataset is derived from the same generation algorithm as that in [6]. 1500 2-dimensional data points are initially generated as described in Figure 3, with two Guassian Distributions generating 750 data points at locations [3, 5] and [3, 1] respectively. We then disturb the positions of data points by adding different noises to the origin points sequentially along the time line to simulate the data evolving process. To represent each cluster's individual evolving trend, the noisy points are set to be generated by uniform distributions with different parameters in different original clusters.

Figure 3 shows the data point distribution and its evolving appearance at time points $t-1$ and t. We set the evolving direction as $\Delta_1 = (0.5, -0.5)$ for the upper cluster and $\Delta_2 = (-0.5, 0.5)$ for the lower cluster, both scaling in 0.5 unity.

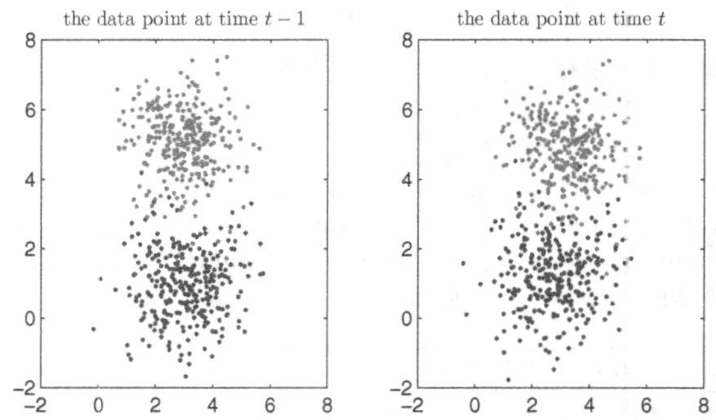

Figure 3: Data evolving

6.3.2 Clustering Result Comparison

A trial study on the synthetic evolutionary data is reported in Table 1. The synthetic data setting is provided above and we keep on adding the evolving noise to the previous data in 12 iterations. The boldface numbers in each column denote the best two values in correspondence to both km-cost and NMI value.

From Table 1, we can easily see that our e-MMC algorithms (CDE, IDE and MI) produce the smallest km-cost values during the time period from $t = 1$ to $t = 12$, comparing to that of the four baseline algorithms. For the NMI value, although PCQ and PCM are better than e-MMC algorithms in first three instances, e-MMC algorithms obtain better performance in the rest nine time stamps. Both ACC and IND cannot achieve a satisfied result in this study.

6.3.3 Evolving Range Study

We also conduct the evolving range learning. The experimental settings are almost the same as above, except the difference of the size of uniform distribution added to the data points. We set the uniform distribution size ranging from 0.1 to 1, and then observe the km-cost under these different situations. Figure 4 shows the detailed results. Since *CDE* and *IDE*'s value are approximate the same, their value lines overlap mostly.

From Figure 4, we can see that the km-cost grows with the increase of the range value. This is due to a larger diversity of the data set associated with a larger evolving range. Also, we can see that e-MMC algorithms can always obtain the smallest value from all the situations. This shows robustness of the proposed three e-MMC methods.

6.3.4 Computational Time Analysis

Figure 5 displays the running time of our methods against that of the baselines algorithms.

t scales in ms (margin shift) unity. It shows that our proposed methods CDE, IDE and MI can manipulate the data size at at least the million level. They runs much efficiently than the existed spectral evolutionary clustering, especially in large scale data. Although they are not as fast as the k-means implementations *ACC* and *IND*,

Table 1: Synthetic data experimental performance

Time	criteria	$t=1$	$t=2$	$t=3$	$t=4$	$t=5$	$t=6$	$t=7$	$t=8$	$t=9$	$t=10$	$t=11$	$t=12$
CDE	KM-cost	**5.630**	**5.591**	**5.576**	**5.642**	**5.810**	**6.047**	**6.376**	**6.685**	**6.936**	**7.191**	**7.407**	**7.538**
	NMI	0.794	0.707	0.629	0.589	0.606	0.643	**0.714**	**0.785**	**0.854**	**0.907**	**0.956**	**0.983**
IDE	KM-cost	**5.630**	**5.590**	**5.575**	**5.639**	**5.806**	**6.046**	**6.376**	**6.685**	**6.935**	**7.191**	**7.407**	**7.538**
	NMI	0.796	0.707	0.633	**0.602**	**0.610**	**0.647**	**0.717**	**0.795**	**0.854**	**0.906**	**0.957**	**0.987**
MI	KM-cost	5.635	5.592	5.580	5.642	5.810	6.051	6.380	6.697	6.937	7.201	7.417	7.538
	NMI	0.799	0.699	0.652	**0.600**	**0.608**	**0.645**	0.713	0.790	0.851	0.896	0.957	0.987
PCQ	KM-cost	5.649	5.614	5.589	5.648	5.812	6.060	6.393	6.703	6.950	7.211	7.415	7.540
	NMI	**0.815**	**0.736**	**0.644**	0.589	0.598	0.637	0.711	0.786	0.837	0.890	0.94	0.973
PCM	KM-cost	5.653	5.627	5.595	5.666	5.833	6.075	6.419	6.742	6.963	7.223	7.431	7.544
	NMI	**0.826**	**0.757**	**0.659**	0.593	0.580	0.621	0.675	0.736	0.815	0.867	0.932	0.968
ACC	KM-cost	5.683	5.657	5.620	5.663	5.833	6.075	6.425	6.750	6.963	7.222	7.431	7.544
	NMI	0.756	0.688	0.602	0.583	0.573	0.619	0.668	0.730	0.812	0.872	0.928	0.968
IND	KM-cost	5.681	5.653	5.631	5.681	5.826	6.080	6.399	6.705	6.953	7.210	7.420	7.540
	NMI	0.754	0.662	0.586	0.573	0.616	0.629	0.703	0.742	0.812	0.892	0.928	0.979

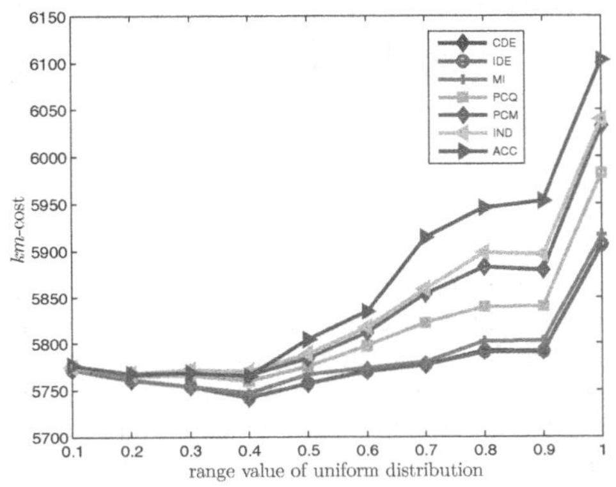

Figure 4: Uniform distribution performance

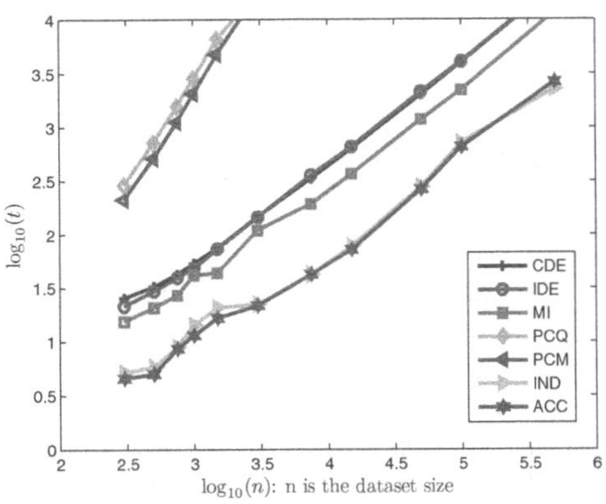

Figure 5: Running time

according to the previous experiments, our methods reach better clustering results than *ACC* and *IND*.

6.4 Experiments on Real World Data

In this section, we present outcomes on the UCI-benchmarking data sets and an NEC Blog data set.

6.4.1 UCI Data

First, we use a bunch of UCI data sets to test the performance of the three e-MMC methods CDE, IDE and MI. Each cluster in the datasets is set a fixed direction for adding the uniform distribution to simulate the evolving behavior of the data. Since the data attributes change randomly making it hard to determine each data point's belonging clusters, we use the km-cost rather than NMI to verify the performance. Table 2 displays our testing results. The boldface value in each row denotes the best in correspondence to the km-cost.

As we can see, our proposed three methods CDE, IDE and MI reach the best values in every dataset. This shows the clear advantage of the e-MMC approach compared to the baseline algorithms.

6.4.2 NEC Blogs Data

Here we further test the performance of our proposed evolutionary-MMC (e-MMC) frameworks on social network learning. We conduct experiments on a real Blog data set, which was collected by an NEC in-house blog crawler and had been used in [6, 15, 22] for evaluation. It contains 148,681 entry-to-entry links among 407 blogs during 15 months, with a set of 303 blogs focusing on technology theme and a set of 104 blogs on politics in accordance with their contents.

Before using this Blog data set, we first pre-process the linked data by aggregating data in months 6 and 7 into the 6th time step, data in months 8-10 into the 7th time step, and data in months 11-15 into 8th time step. This is because the linked data entries reduced sharply as the data include less blogs towards the end of the time period. The links in each time step of data are shown in Table 3.

Table 3: Blog links in each time step

Time step	1	2	3	4	5	6	7	8
Link number	822	877	681	640	606	888	723	762

Figures 6, 7 and 8 depict the performance of our proposed methods CDE, IDE and MI compared to the baseline methods PCQ,

Table 2: km-cost on UCI datasets ($\times 10^2$)

	CDE	IDE	MI	PCQ	PCM	ACC	IND
$\mathbf{digits_{1,2}}$	**25.44**	25.46	25.51	25.58	25.55	25.50	25.62
$\mathbf{digits_{1,3}}$	24.07	**24.06**	24.11	24.28	24.18	24.30	24.19
$\mathbf{vowel_{1,2}}$	**1.204**	1.208	1.225	1.240	1.294	1.216	1.213
$\mathbf{satellite_{1,2}}$	40.19	**40.02**	40.39	40.46	40.46	40.44	40.41
breast	**4.989**	5.032	5.016	5.315	5.464	5.471	5.315
diabetes	**3.970**	3.971	4.012	4.200	4.213	4.222	4.202
liver	0.798	**0.797**	0.800	0.812	0.821	0.820	0.814
$\mathbf{pendigits_{0,1}}$	**21.74**	21.75	21.79	21.74	21.83	21.87	21.78

PCM, ACC and IND in terms of km-cost, *snapshot cost* and *historical cost.*

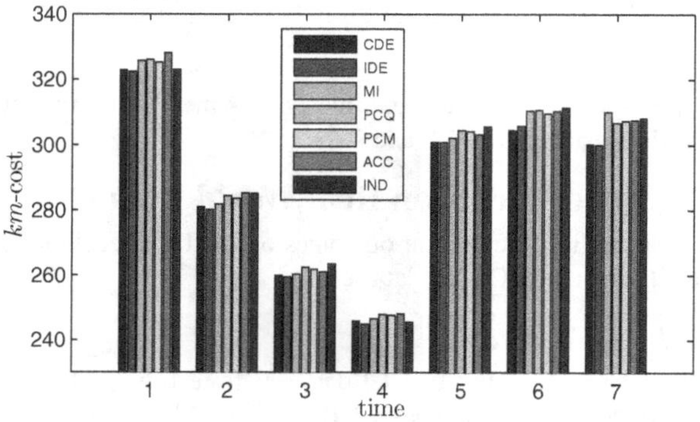

Figure 6: km**-cost**

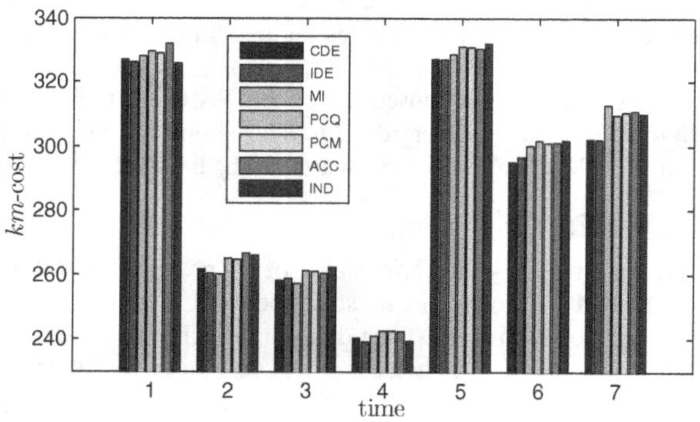

Figure 7: ***Snapshot cost***

From Figures 6-8, we can see the proposed e-MMC methods always achieve better km-cost compared to the baseline algorithms. *MI* does not always perform perfectly on the time steps 6 and 7, this is due to that the outcomes are subject to the aggregation method.

7. CONCLUSIONS AND FUTURE WORK

Evolutionary data is ubiquitous in business and social applications. Maximum margin clustering (MMC) has demonstrated its power in achieving better accuracy by seeking maximum margin between two clusters. As the first work in the field, this paper has proposed the evolutionary MMC, and two corresponding frameworks, *data integration* and *margin consistency*, as well as three clustering algorithms for adapting MMC to learn unsupervised data.

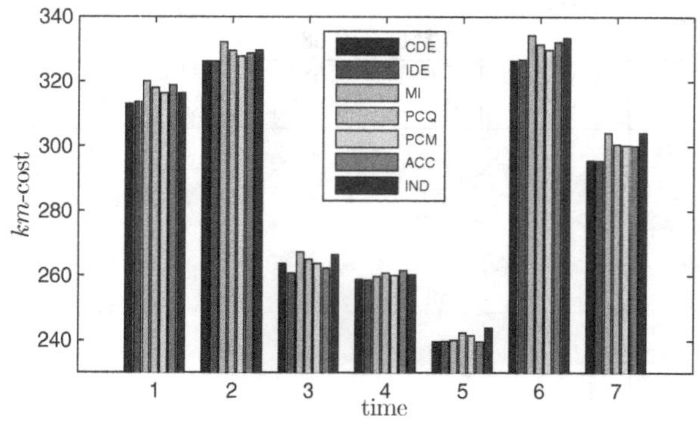

Figure 8: ***Historic cost***

The design nicely incorporates time information into maximum margin learning. We have conducted substantial experiments on synthetic, UCI and real-life blog data to compare the accuracy, computation and scalability of our proposed three algorithms with four baseline algorithms. The outcomes clearly show that the proposed evolutionary MMC and the subsequent algorithms outperform the baselines in terms of achieving better accuracy, and are effective in tackling large scale of unlabeled data.

We are now working on expanding the evolutionary MMC to multiple cluster applications, towards multi-cluster maximum margin clustering algorithms on learning evolutionary data.[3][2][17]

8. ACKNOWLEDGEMENTS

This work is sponsored in part by Australian Research Council Discovery Grants (DP1096218) and ARC Linkage Grant (LP100200774). We appreciate the comments and help provided by Xiaodong Yue and Yiling Zeng.

9. REFERENCES

[1] C. Aggarwal, J. Han, J. Wang, and P. Yu. A framework for clustering evolving data streams. In *Proceedings of the 29th international conference on Very large data bases-Volume 29*, pages 81–92. VLDB Endowment, 2003.

[2] L. Cao. *Data mining for business applications.* Springer-Verlag New York Inc, 2008.

[3] L. Cao, Y. Ou, P. S. Yu, and G. Wei. Detecting abnormal coupled sequences and sequence changes in group-based manipulative trading behaviors. In *ACM SIGKDD*, KDD '10, pages 85–94, New York, NY, USA, 2010. ACM.

[4] D. Chakrabarti, R. Kumar, and A. Tomkins. Evolutionary clustering. In *Proceedings of the 12th ACM SIGKDD international conference on Knowledge discovery and data mining*, pages 554–560. ACM, 2006.

[5] W. Chen, Y. Song, H. Bai, C. Lin, and E. Chang. Parallel spectral clustering in distributed systems. *Pattern Analysis and Machine Intelligence, IEEE Transactions on*, (99):1–1, 2010.

[6] Y. Chi, X. Song, D. Zhou, K. Hino, and B. Tseng. Evolutionary spectral clustering by incorporating temporal smoothness. In *Proceedings of the 13th ACM SIGKDD international conference on Knowledge discovery and data mining*, pages 153–162. ACM, 2007.

[7] Y. Chi, X. Song, D. Zhou, K. Hino, and B. Tseng. On evolutionary spectral clustering. *ACM Transactions on Knowledge Discovery from Data (TKDD)*, 3(4):17, 2009.

[8] A. Frank and A. Asuncion. UCI machine learning repository, 2010.

[9] S. Guha, N. Mishra, R. Motwani, and L. O'Callaghan. Clustering data streams. In *Foundations of computer science, 2000. proceedings. 41st annual symposium on*, pages 359–366. IEEE, 2000.

[10] C. Gupta and R. Grossman. Genic: A single pass generalized incremental algorithm for clustering. In *Proceedings of the SIAM International Conference on Data Mining*, pages 137–153, 2004.

[11] M. Hoai and F. De la Torre. Maximum margin temporal clustering. In *Proceedings of International Conference on Artificial Intelligence and Statistics*, 2012.

[12] J. Kelley. The cutting-plane method for solving convex programs. *Journal of the Society for Industrial and Applied Mathematics*, 8(4):703–712, 1960.

[13] A. LH21. The cholesky decomposition. *LINPACK: users' guide*, (8), 1979.

[14] Y. Li, J. Han, and J. Yang. Clustering moving objects. In *Proceedings of the tenth ACM SIGKDD international conference on Knowledge discovery and data mining*, pages 617–622. ACM, 2004.

[15] Y. Lin, Y. Chi, S. Zhu, H. Sundaram, and B. Tseng. Analyzing communities and their evolutions in dynamic social networks. *ACM Transactions on Knowledge Discovery from Data (TKDD)*, 3(2):8, 2009.

[16] H. Ning, W. Xu, Y. Chi, Y. Gong, and T. Huang. Incremental spectral clustering with application to monitoring of evolving blog communities. In *SIAM Int. Conf. on Data Mining*, pages 261–72, 2007.

[17] Y. Song, L. Cao, X. Wu, G. Wei, W. Ye, and W. Ding. Coupled behavior analysis for capturing coupling relationships in group-based market manipulations. In *ACM SIGKDD*, 2012.

[18] H. Valizadegan and R. Jin. Generalized maximum margin clustering and unsupervised kernel learning. *Advances in Neural Information Processing Systems*, 19:1417, 2007.

[19] F. Wang, B. Zhao, and C. Zhang. Linear time maximum margin clustering. *Neural Networks, IEEE Transactions on*, 21(2):319–332, 2010.

[20] L. Xu, J. Neufeld, B. Larson, and D. Schuurmans. Maximum margin clustering. *Advances in neural information processing systems*, 17:1537–1544, 2004.

[21] L. Xu and D. Schuurmans. Unsupervised and semi-supervised multi-class support vector machines. In *Proceedings of the 20th national conference on Artificial intelligence - Volume 2*, AAAI'05, pages 904–910. AAAI Press, 2005.

[22] T. Yang, Y. Chi, S. Zhu, Y. Gong, and R. Jin. Detecting communities and their evolutions in dynamic social networksŮa bayesian approach. *Machine learning*, 82(2):157–189, 2011.

[23] B. Zhao, F. Wang, and C. Zhang. Efficient maximum margin clustering via cutting plane algorithm. In *The 8th SIAM International Conference on Data Mining*, pages 751–762, 2008.

[24] B. Zhao, F. Wang, and C. Zhang. Efficient multiclass maximum margin clustering. In *Proceedings of the 25th international conference on Machine learning*, pages 1248–1255. ACM, 2008.

APPENDIX

A. CPMMC IMPLEMENTATION

[23][19] formulate the Maximum Margin Clustering problem as

$$\begin{aligned} \min_{\boldsymbol{\omega},b,\boldsymbol{\xi}} \quad & \frac{1}{2}\boldsymbol{\omega}^T\boldsymbol{\omega} + \frac{C}{n}\sum_{i=1}^{n}\xi_i \\ s.t. \quad & |\boldsymbol{\omega}^T\phi(\boldsymbol{x}_i) + b| \geq 1 - \xi_i; \\ & \xi_i \geq 0, i = 1, \cdots, n. \end{aligned} \tag{22}$$

They proved that without the cluster-balance constraint, the solution to problem (22) is identical to problem (2) and made use of the *cutting plane* method[12] to solve the problem. However, since the problem is nonconvex with respect to $\boldsymbol{\omega}$, they first transformed it into a constraint concave convex procedure(CCCP).

One key step in the CCCP procedure is the below *quadratic programming*(QP) problem:

$$\begin{aligned} & \min_{\boldsymbol{\omega},b,\boldsymbol{\xi}} \frac{1}{2}\boldsymbol{\omega}^T\boldsymbol{\omega} + C\xi \\ & s.t. \xi \geq 0 \\ & \quad -l \leq \sum_{i=1}^{n}(\boldsymbol{\omega}^T\phi(\boldsymbol{x}_i) + b) \leq l \\ & \quad \forall \mathbf{c} \in \Omega : \frac{1}{n}\sum_{i=1}^{n} c_i - \xi - \frac{1}{n}\sum_{i=1}^{n} c_i \\ & \quad \cdot \operatorname{sign}(\boldsymbol{\omega}_t^T\phi(\boldsymbol{x}_i) + b_t)[\boldsymbol{\omega}^T\phi(\boldsymbol{x}_i) + b] \leq 0 \end{aligned} \tag{23}$$

This problem could be solved in polynomial time, the Wolfe dual of problem is introduced to solve the problem more efficiently.

$$\begin{aligned} \max_{\lambda\geq 0,\mu\geq 0} \quad & -\frac{1}{2}\sum_{k=1}^{|\Omega|}\sum_{l=1}^{|\Omega|}\lambda_k\lambda_l\boldsymbol{z}_k^T\boldsymbol{z}_l + (\mu_1 - \mu_2)\sum_{k=1}^{||\Omega|}\lambda_k\hat{\boldsymbol{x}}^T\boldsymbol{z}_k \\ & -\frac{1}{2}(\mu_1 - \mu_2)^2\hat{\boldsymbol{x}}^T\hat{\boldsymbol{x}} - (\mu_1 + \mu_2)l + \sum_{k=1}^{|\Omega|}\lambda_k\|\boldsymbol{c}_k\|_1 \\ s.t. & \sum_{k=1}^{|\Omega|}\lambda_k \leq C; \\ & (\mu_1 - \mu_2)n - \sum_{k=1}^{|\Omega|}\frac{\lambda_k}{n}c_{ki} \cdot \operatorname{sign}(\boldsymbol{\omega}_t^T\phi(\boldsymbol{x}_i) + b_t) = 0. \end{aligned} \tag{24}$$

Here the definition of $\|\boldsymbol{c}_k\|_1, \boldsymbol{z}_k, \hat{\boldsymbol{x}}$ is the following for simplicity of the problem statement:

$$\|\boldsymbol{c}_k^1\|_1 = \frac{1}{n}\sum_{i=1}^{n} c_{ki}$$
$$\boldsymbol{z}_k^1 = \frac{1}{n}\sum_{i=1}^{n} c_{ki}\text{sign}(\boldsymbol{\omega}_t^T\phi(\boldsymbol{x}_i)+b_t)\phi(\boldsymbol{x}_i); \tag{25}$$
$$\hat{\boldsymbol{x}} = \sum_{i=1}^{n}\phi(\boldsymbol{x}_i).$$

The above dual form of the (QP) problem solving will continue until $\{\lambda_i\}_{i=1}^n, \mu$ converge. Details of the notations and algorithm solving could be checked in the original paper[23].

Attached is the detail CPMMC Algorithm.

Algorithm 2 Cutting Plane Maximum Margin Clustering[23]

Require: violation parameter C;
balance parameter l; initialized $\boldsymbol{\omega}_0, b_0$;error ε;
initial constraints set $\Omega = \emptyset$.

Ensure: resulted data label $\{y_i\}_{i=1}^n$

select the most violated constraint $\boldsymbol{c}$
while $\frac{1}{n}\sum_{i=1}^n c_i - \frac{1}{n}\sum_{i=1}^n c_i|\boldsymbol{\omega}^T\phi(\boldsymbol{x}_i)+b| > \xi + \varepsilon$ **do**
  $\Omega = \Omega \cup \boldsymbol{c}$
  use quadratic programming to iteratively solve the Wolfe Dual form (Eq. (24)) of CCCP problem until converged
  update $\boldsymbol{\omega}, b, \xi$
  select the most violated constraint $\boldsymbol{c}$
end while
return corresponding hyperplane parameter $\{\boldsymbol{\omega}, b\}$

B. VARIOUS WOLFE DUAL FORMS

Appendixes B.1-B.3 are the basic Wolfe dual forms required in [23] to employ the Cutting Plane Approximation, in correspondence to each proposed objective function.

B.1 Cohort Data Evolving

Under the *cohort data evolving* method, the problem can be transformed into the following Wolfe dual form:

$$\max_{\lambda^1\ge 0,\lambda^2\ge 0,\mu\ge 0} -\frac{1}{2}\sum_{k=1}^{|\Omega|}\sum_{m=1}^{|\Omega|}(\lambda_k^1\lambda_m^1\boldsymbol{z}_k^{1T}\boldsymbol{z}_m^1 + 2\lambda_k^1\lambda_m^2\boldsymbol{z}_k^{1T}\boldsymbol{z}_m^2$$
$$+\lambda_k^2\lambda_m^2\boldsymbol{z}_k^{2T}\boldsymbol{z}_m^2) + (\mu_1-\mu_2)\sum_{k=1}^{|\Omega|}\hat{\boldsymbol{x}}^T(\lambda_k^1\boldsymbol{z}_k^1 + \lambda_k^2\boldsymbol{z}_k^2)$$
$$-\frac{1}{2}(\mu_1-\mu_2)^2\hat{\boldsymbol{x}}^T\hat{\boldsymbol{x}} - (\mu_1+\mu_2)l$$
$$+\sum_{k=1}^{|\Omega|}(\lambda_k^1\|\boldsymbol{c}_k^1\|_1 + \lambda_k^2\|\boldsymbol{c}_k^2\|_1)$$
$$s.t. \sum_{k=1}^{|\Omega|}\lambda_k^1 \le \alpha\cdot C; \sum_{k=1}^{|\Omega|}\lambda_k^2 \le (1-\alpha)\cdot C;$$
$$(\mu_1-\mu_2)(n_1+n_2) - \sum_{k=1}^{|\Omega|}\frac{\lambda_k^1}{n_1}\sum_{i=1}^{n_1}c_{ki}\cdot\text{sign}(\boldsymbol{\omega}_t^T\phi(\boldsymbol{x}_i)$$
$$+b_t) - \sum_{k=1}^{|\Omega|}\frac{\lambda_k^2}{n_2}\sum_{i=n_1+1}^{n_1+n_2}c_{ki}\cdot\text{sign}(\boldsymbol{\omega}_t^T\phi(\boldsymbol{x}_i)+b_t) = 0. \tag{26}$$

Here the definitions of $\|\boldsymbol{c}_k^1\|_1, \|\boldsymbol{c}_k^2\|_1, \boldsymbol{z}_k^1, \boldsymbol{z}_k^1, \hat{\boldsymbol{x}}$ are below, for the simplicity of the problem statement:

$$\|\boldsymbol{c}_k^1\|_1 = \frac{1}{n_1}\sum_{i=1}^{n_1}c_{ki}; \|\boldsymbol{c}_k^2\|_1 = \frac{1}{n_2}\sum_{i=n_1+1}^{n_1+n_2}c_{ki};$$
$$\boldsymbol{z}_k^1 = \frac{1}{n_1}\sum_{i=1}^{n_1}c_{ki}\text{sign}(\boldsymbol{\omega}_t^T\phi(\boldsymbol{x}_i)+b_t)\phi(\boldsymbol{x}_i);$$
$$\boldsymbol{z}_k^2 = \frac{1}{n_2}\sum_{i=n_1+1}^{n_1+n_2}c_{ki}\text{sign}(\boldsymbol{\omega}_t^T\phi(\boldsymbol{x}_i)+b_t)\phi(\boldsymbol{x}_i), k=1,\ldots,|\Omega|;$$
$$\hat{\boldsymbol{x}} = \sum_{i=1}^{n_1+n_2}\phi(\boldsymbol{x}_i). \tag{27}$$

B.2 Individual Data Evolving

Under the *individual data evolving* method, the Wolfe Dual form is represented as:

$$\max_{\lambda\ge 0,\mu\ge 0}\frac{1}{1+2\beta}[-\frac{1}{2}\sum_{k=1}^{|\Omega|}\sum_{l=1}^{|\Omega|}\lambda_k\lambda_l\boldsymbol{z}_k^T\boldsymbol{z}_l + (\mu_1-\mu_2)\sum_{k=1}^{||\Omega|}\lambda_k\hat{\boldsymbol{x}}^T\boldsymbol{z}_k$$
$$-\frac{1}{2}(\mu_1-\mu_2)^2\hat{\boldsymbol{x}}^T\hat{\boldsymbol{x}}] - (\mu_1+\mu_2)l + \sum_{k=1}^{|\Omega|}\lambda_k\|\boldsymbol{c}_k\|_1$$
$$s.t. \sum_{k=1}^{|\Omega|}\lambda_k \le C;$$
$$(\mu_1-\mu_2)n - \sum_{k=1}^{|\Omega|}\frac{\lambda_k}{n}c_{ki}\cdot\text{sign}(\boldsymbol{\omega}_t^T\phi(\boldsymbol{x}_i)+b_t) = 0. \tag{28}$$

where $\boldsymbol{z}_k, \hat{\boldsymbol{x}}, \|\boldsymbol{c}_k\|_1$ are the same as in Equation (25).

B.3 Model Integration

Due to the computational complexity, we take an approximation of the objective function and select the $\boldsymbol{\omega}$-penalty term into consideration. After the similar transformation as above, we get the following Wolfe dual formulation:

$$\max_{\lambda\ge 0,\mu\ge 0}\frac{1}{1+2\beta}[-\frac{1}{2}\sum_{k=1}^{|\Omega|}\sum_{l=1}^{|\Omega|}\lambda_k\lambda_l\boldsymbol{z}_k^T\boldsymbol{z}_l + (\mu_1-\mu_2)\sum_{k=1}^{||\Omega|}\lambda_k\hat{\boldsymbol{x}}^T\boldsymbol{z}_k$$
$$-\frac{1}{2}(\mu_1-\mu_2)^2\hat{\boldsymbol{x}}^T\hat{\boldsymbol{x}}] + (\frac{2\beta}{1+2\beta}\boldsymbol{\omega}_{T-1}^T\hat{\boldsymbol{x}} - l)\mu_1$$
$$-(\frac{2\beta}{1+2\beta}\boldsymbol{\omega}_{T-1}^T\hat{\boldsymbol{x}} + l)\mu_2 - \sum_{k=1}^{|\Omega|}\lambda_k(\frac{2\beta}{1+2\beta}\boldsymbol{\omega}_{T-1}^T\boldsymbol{z}_k - \|\boldsymbol{c}_k$$
$$s.t. \sum_{k=1}^{|\Omega|}\lambda_k \le C;$$
$$(\mu_1-\mu_2)n - \sum_{k=1}^{|\Omega|}\frac{\lambda_k}{n}c_{ki}\cdot\text{sign}(\boldsymbol{\omega}_t^T\phi(\boldsymbol{x}_i)+b_t) = 0. \tag{29}$$

where $\boldsymbol{z}_k, \hat{\boldsymbol{x}}, \|\boldsymbol{c}_k\|_1$ are the same as in Equation (25)), and β is defined as:

$$\beta = \alpha\cdot\sum_{i=1}^{n}\|\phi(\boldsymbol{x}_i)\|_2^2 \tag{30}$$

Document-Topic Hierarchies from Document Graphs

Tim Weninger Yonatan Bisk Jiawei Han
University of Illinois at Urbana-Champaign
{weninge1, bisk1, hanj}@illinois.edu

ABSTRACT

Topic taxonomies present a multi-level view of a document collection, where general topics live towards the top of the taxonomy and more specific topics live towards the bottom. Topic taxonomies allow users to quickly drill down into their topic of interest to find documents. We show that hierarchies of documents, where documents live at the inner nodes of the hierarchy-tree can also be inferred by combining document text with inter-document links. We present a Bayesian generative model by which an explicit hierarchy of documents is created. Experiments on three document-graph data sets shows that the generated document hierarchies are able to fit the observed data, and that the levels in the constructed document hierarchy represent practical groupings.

Categories and Subject Descriptors

I.2.6 [**Artificial Intelligence**]: Learning; G.3 [**Probability and Statistics**]: Probabilistic algorithms, Nonparametric statistics

General Terms

Algorithms, Experimentation

Keywords

hierarchical clustering, Bayesian generative models, topic models, model evaluation

1. INTRODUCTION

As the number of online resources and Web documents continues to increase, the need for better organizational structures that guide readers towards the information they seek increases. Hierarchies and taxonomies are invaluable tools for this purpose. Taxonomies are widely used in libraries via the Library of Congress System or the Dewey Decimal System, and hierarchies were a fixture of the early World Wide Web; perhaps the most famous example being the Yahoo search engine, which is actually an acronym for Yet Another Hierarchical Officious Oracle. These hierarchical systems were developed because their effectiveness at topical organization and their logarithmic depth allowed users to quickly find the relevant documents they were searching for.

Unfortunately, taxonomy curation of documents, articles, books, etc. is mostly a manual process, which is only possible when the number of curated documents is relatively small. This process becomes increasingly impractical when the number of documents grows to Web-scale. This has motivated research towards automatically inducing document taxonomies from the data [1, 4, 14, 5, 6, 19]. Most of the existing techniques rely on a single type of data – usually text. The problem with text-only hierarchy induction is that words often have multiple meanings. For example, the words "worm" and "bug" have very different meanings in the contexts of biology and computer science. Therefore without proper context proper taxonomy induction can be difficult.

Most document repositories contain linkages between the document creating a *document-graph*. These links provide proper context to the terms in each document. Document-graphs are especially common in nonfiction and scientific literature, where citations are viewed as inter-document links. The World Wide Web can be considered to be a single, very large document-graph, where Web pages represent documents and hyperlinks link documents.

Web sites, in particular, are a collection of documents with a very specific and purposeful organizational structure. Web sites are often specifically designed to guide the user from the entry page, *i.e., homepage*, to progressively more specific Web pages. Similarly, scientific literature can be categorized into a hierarchy of increasingly specific scientific topics by their citation links, and encyclopedia articles can be categorized into a hierarchy of increasingly specific articles by their cross references. Thus, we assert that most document-graphs contain a hidden document hierarchy.

In this paper we draw a specific distinction between a *hierarchy* and a *taxonomy*. We define a taxonomy to be a classification of objects into increasingly finer granularities, where each non-leaf node is a conceptual combination its children. A biological taxonomy is a great example of this definition because a classified species, say homo sapiens (*i.e.*, humans), can only be placed at a leaf in the taxonomy; the inner nodes, *e.g.*, primate, mammal, animal, do not declare new species, rather they are conceptual agglomerations of species. Furthermore, each species is described by its path through the taxonomy. For example, homo sapiens, can be described as primates, as mammals and as animals (among others). A hierarchy, on the other hand, is an arrangement of objects where some objects are considered to be *above*, *below* or *at the same level as* others. This necessarily means that objects of a hierarchy live at the internal nodes.

Strictly speaking, most existing models infer taxonomies. The goal of this paper is to construct document hierarchies from a document-graph using document text and inter-document links. For

CIKM'12, October 29–November 2, 2012, Maui, HI, USA.

these purposes *above*, *below* or *at the same level as* refers to the topical granularity of the documents. In other words, given a document graph with an explicitly identified root, such as a Web site homepage, we aim to learn a document-hierarchy which best captures the conceptual hierarchy of the document-graph. This problem poses three technical challenges:

1. **Inducing document topic mixtures**. We propose learning a document hierarchy where the internal (non-leaf) nodes of the hierarchy are documents. In such a hierarchy, parent documents consist of topics that are more general than their children. This requires that we view a parent document as a mixture of the topics contained within its children, and children documents should topically fit underneath their selected parent. We present the *Hierarchical Document-Topic Model* (HDTM) which generates a course-to-fine representation of the text information, wherein high-level documents live near the top of the hierarchy, and low-level, more specific documents live at the leaves.

2. **Selecting document placement**. Placement of a document within the hierarchy drives the topic mixing. Because links between edges hint at the context of and relationship between documents, we constrain the document placement in the induced hierarchy by their edges within the original document-graph. In other words, if an edge exists in the induced hierarchy, then it must also exist in original document-graph. Unlike existing models, such as hLDA [3], that select topic paths using the nested Chinese Restaurant Process (nCRP), we perform document placement based on a stochastic process resembling random walks with restart (RWR) over the original document-graph. The use of a stochastic process over the document-graph frees the algorithm from rigid parameters. Furthermore, the adoption of RWR stochastic process over nCRP allows documents to live at non-leaf nodes, and frees the algorithm from the depth parameter of hLDA.

3. **Analysis at Web site-scale**. In most document-graph collections, the number of edges grows quadratically with the number of nodes. This limits the scalability of many topic diffusion algorithms [20, 10]. Fortunately, document hierarchies are represented as trees, wherein the number of edges scales linearly with the number of documents.

The remainder of this paper is organized as follows. In Section 2 we review the related literature with specific attention paid to distinctions between similar generative models. In Section 3 we discuss the intuition behind hierarchy induction from document-graphs. Our proposed model is described in Section 4. In Section 5 we perform quantitative experiments on three data sets, as well as a large qualitative exploration based on thousands of human judgments. We find that our model constructs document hierarchies that are coherent with respect to their textual topics and conform to the graphical representation of the underlying document-graph.

2. RELATED WORK

There has been a substantial amount of previous work on hierarchical clustering of documents. The first approaches were called agglomerative clustering, which used greedy heuristics such as single-link or complete-link [29]. Dendrograms are often the output of such clustering techniques, in which the root node is split into a series of branches that terminate with a single document at each leaf. Ho, *et al.*, point out that manually-curated hierarchies like the Open Directory Project[1] are typically flatter and contain fewer inner nodes than agglomerative clustering techniques produce [14]. Other hierarchical clustering algorithms include top-down processes which iteratively partition the data [31], incremental methods like COBWEB [9], CLASSIT [11], and other algorithms optimized for hierarchical text clustering.

The processes that typically define most hierarchical clustering algorithms can be made to fit in a probabilistic setting that build bottom-up hierarchies based on Bayesian hypothesis testing [13]. On the other hand, most recent work uses Bayesian generative models to find the most likely explanation of observed text and links. The first of these hierarchical generative models was hierarchical latent Dirichlet allocation (hLDA). In hLDA each document sits at a leaf in a tree of fixed depth as illustrated in Figure 1(a). The document is represented by a mixture of multinomials along the path through the tree from the document to the root. Documents are placed at their respective leaf nodes by the nested Chinese restaurant process (nCRP).

NCRP is a recursive version of the standard Chinese Restaurant Process (CRP), which progresses according to the following analogy: An empty Chinese restaurant has an infinite number of tables, and each table has an infinite number of chairs. When the first customer arrives he sits in the first chair at the first table with probability of 1. The second customer can then chose to sit at an occupied table with probability of $\frac{n_i}{\gamma+n-1}$ or sit at a new, unoccupied table with probability of $\frac{\gamma}{\gamma+n-1}$, where n is the current customer, n_i is the number of customers currently sitting at table i, and γ is a parameter that defines the affinity to sit at a previously occupied table following a rich get richer scheme.

The nested version of the CRP extends the original analogy as follows: At each table in the Chinese restaurant are cards with the name of another Chinese restaurant. When a customer sits at a given table, he reads the card, gets up and goes to that restaurant, where he is reseated according to the CRP. Each customer visits L restaurants until he is finally seated and is able to each. This process creates a stochastic tree with a width determined by the γ parameter of a fixed depth L. This process has also been called the Chinese Restaurant Franchise because of this analogy [4].

Adams, *et al.* proposed a hierarchical topic model called tree structured stick breaking (TSSB), illustrated in Figure 1(c), wherein documents can live at internal nodes, rather than exclusively at leaf nodes. However, this process involves chaining together conjugate priors which makes inference more complicated, and it also does not make use of link data.

Other work along this line include hierarchical labeled LDA (hLLDA) by Petinot *et al.* [22] hLLDA, as well as fixed structure LDA (fsLDA) by Reisinger and Pasca [25] which modify hLDA by fixing the hierarchical structure and learning hierarchical topic distributions. The hierarchical pachinko allocation model(hPAM), shown in Figure 1(b), produces a directed acyclic graph (DAG) of a fixed depth allowing for each internal (non-document) node to be represented a mixture of more abstract, *i.e.*, higher level, topics [19].

In network-only data, community discovery is the process of finding self-similar group, or clusters. The SHRINK algorithm creates hierarchical clusters by identifying tightly-knit communities and by finding disparate clusters by looking for hubs and other heuristics [16]. The focus of this paper is more on probabilistic models to generate hierarchies, rather than heuristic approaches. Clauset, *et al*, discover dendrograms by Monte Carlo sampling;

[1] `http://www.dmoz.org`

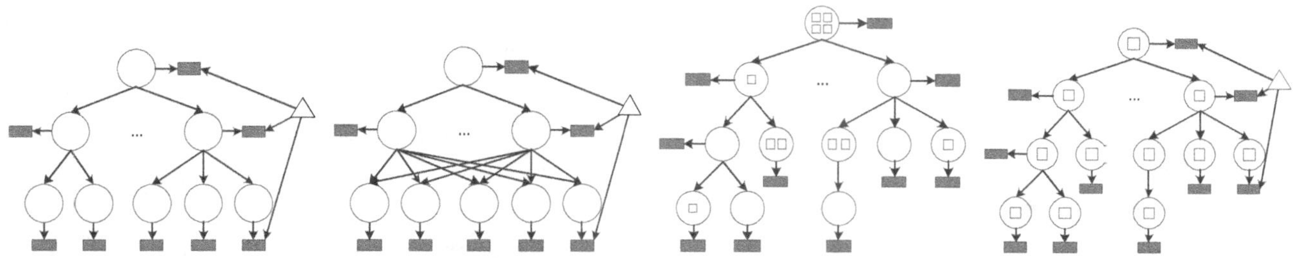

(a) hLDA, TopicBlock (b) hPAM (c) TSSB (d) HDTM, fsLDA

Figure 1: Generative structures in related work. Circles and squares represent topics and documents respectively. Each topic has a multinomial over words (gray boxes), and a separate distribution over levels for each path (white triangles).

however, dendrograms poorly represent the manually curated hierarchies and taxonomies that we are pursuing [7].

In this paper we merge document text and inter-document links into a single model. This assumes that the words and their latent topics fit within the link structure of the graph, and that the graph structure explains topical relationships between interlinked documents. Topic Modeling with Network Structure (TMN), regularizes a statistical topic model with a harmonic regularizer based on the graph structure in the data; the result is that topic proportions of linked documents are similar to each other [18]. However, hierarchical information is not discovered nor can be easily inferred from this model.

Other work on generative models that combine text and links include: a probabilistic model for document connectivity [8], the Link-PLSA-LDA and Pairwise-Link-LDA methods [21], the Latent Topic Model for Hypertext (LTHM) method [12], role discovery in social networks [17], the author-topic-model [26], and others. The above models operate by encoding link probability as a discrete random variable or a Bernoulli trial that is parameterized by the topics of the documents. The relational topic model (RTM) builds links between topics, where observed links are given a very high likelihood [6]; although the paper is titled *hierarchical* relational models for topical networks, the RTM model does not build a topic or document hierarchy. The TopicBlock model combines the non-parametric hLDA and stochastic block models [15] to generate document taxonomies from text and links [14]; however, TopicBlock does not permit documents to reside at non-leaf nodes of the tree hierarchy.

In contrast to the previous work, our model builds a hierarchy of documents from text and inter-document links. In our model, each node in the hierarchy contains a single document, and the hierarchy's width and depth is not fixed.

3. HIERARCHIES OF DOCUMENTS

In the previous work, document hierarchies were not actually hierarchies of documents in the literal sense. Instead, leaf nodes of the hierarchy contains the actual, literal documents, and internal nodes contained increasingly more general topics about the ancestor documents. See Figure 1 for a brief comparison of model outputs. In this paper we require inner nodes, which in previous work are made of word multinomial distributions, to be literal documents. This requires an assertion that *some documents are more general than others*. This section explores this assertion through examples and a review of similar assertions made in previous research.

3.1 Web sites as document hierarchies

A Web site G can be viewed as a directed graph with Web pages as vertices V and hyperlinks as directed edges E between Web pages $v_x \rightarrow v_y$ – excluding inter-site hyperlinks. In most cases, designating Web site entry page as the root r allows for a Web site to be viewed as a rooted directed graph. Web site creators and curators purposefully organize the hyperlinks between documents in a topically meaningful manner. As a result, Web documents further away from the root document typically contain more specific topics than Web documents graphically close to the root document.

For example, the Web site at the University of Illinois in Urbana-Champaign, shown in Figure 2 contains a root Web document (the entry page), and dozens of children Web documents. Even with a very small subset of documents and edges, the corresponding Web graph is quite complicated and messy. A breadth first traversal of the Web graph starting with the root node is a simple way to distill a document hierarchy from the Web graph. Unfortunately, we shall see that a fixed breadth-first hierarchy cannot account for many of the intricacies of real world Web graphs.

For explanation purposes we define four types of hyperlink edges in a Web site: (1) parent-to-child links, (2) upward links, (3) shortcuts, and (4) cross-topic links. Parent-to-child links direct the user from one Web page to a more topically specific Web page; *e.g.*, a hyperlink from `../engineering` to `cs.illinois.edu` is a parent-to-child hyperlink because computer science is topically more specific than engineering. Upward links are hyperlinks that reference a more general document; *e.g.*, there may exist a hyperlink from `cs.illinois.edu` to `illinois.edu` because the computer science department would like to reference the fact that it belongs to the university. Shortcut links are hyperlinks that skip from very general Web documents to very specific Web documents as a way of featuring some specific topic; *e.g.*, if a computer science professor wins a prestigious award or grant, his Web page may be linked to from the news section of the root Web page. Cross topic links are hyperlinks that move across topical subtrees; *e.g.*, the college of media may reference some working relationship with the athletic department by creating a hyperlink between the two Web pages.

Because our goal is to infer the document hierarchy, we are, in a sense, trying to find parent-to-child links. In the event that there is more than one parent-to-child link to a particular Web page, our goal is to find the best topical fit for each Web document in the inferred hierarchy.

Web researchers and practitioners have used the hyperlink structure to organize Web documents for many years. The PageRank and HITS algorithms are two of the most famous examples of information propagation through links. Specifically, PageRank uses the model of a random Web surfer (*i.e.* random walker), who randomly follows hyperlinks over the Web. A current measure of a Web page's authority corresponds to the probability that a random surfer lands upon that Web page. In our model, we assert that

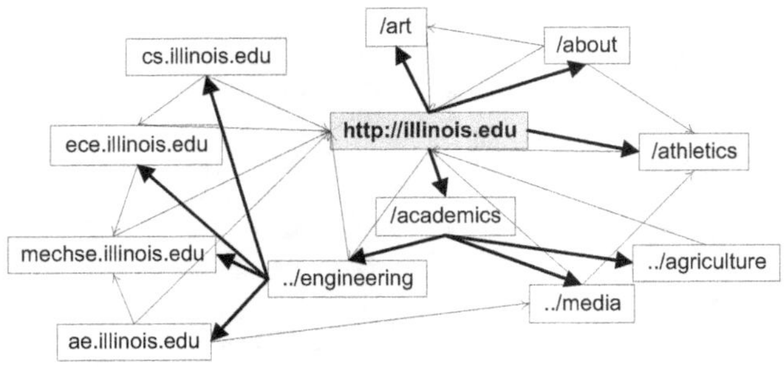

Figure 2: Truncated Web site graph of the University of Illinois Urbana-Champaign. Bold lines represent edges stochastically selected by the RWRH process

PageRank's notion of authority corresponds to topical generality. That is, Web pages with a high random surfer probability are likely to be topically more general than others.

3.1.1 Term propagation in Web sites

Plenty of previous works in the information retrieval domain use document-graph structure to enrich document features for improved retrieval performance. We find that some of the intuition behind these previous works are helpful in framing our generative model.

A limitation of the random walker model is that it only looks at the graphical structure of the Web. The word distributions found in each document are clearly an important factor to consider when generating Web hierarchies. Previous work by Song, *et al.* [27] and Qin, *et al.* [24] show that a given Web page can be enriched by propagating information from its children. Their relevance propagation model modifies the language distribution of a Web page to be a mixture of itself and its children according to the formula:

$$f'(w;d) = (1+\alpha)f(w;d) + \frac{(1-\alpha)}{|Child(d)|}\sum_{c\in Child(d)} f(w;c),$$

where $f(w;d)$ is the frequency of term w in Web page d before propagation, $f'(w;d)$ is frequency of term w in Web page d after propagation, c is a child page of d in the sitemap $\mathcal{T}$, and α is a parameter to control the mixing factor of the children. This propagation algorithm assumes that the sitemap, $\mathcal{T}$, is constructed ahead of time using URL features of the Web pages in a particular Web site.

Note that $f'(w;d)$ is a pseudo frequency count that is unsmoothed. The goal of previous works was to perform Web information retrieval, wherein they used BM25-type functions to normalize and smooth the language distribution. For illustration purposes, lets smooth the term distribution using Dirichlet prior smoothing [30]. The $f'(w;d)$ from above is used in place of the usual $c(w;d)$.

$$p_\mu(w;d) = \frac{f'(w;d) + \mu p(w|C)}{|d|' + \mu},$$

where C is the distribution over all terms in V, μ is the smoothing parameter, and the length is modified by the propagation algorithm to be $|d|' = (1+\alpha)|d|$.

As a result of the upward propagation p_μ of the root document (Web site entry page) contains all of the words from all of the Web pages in the Web site. The most probable words are those that occur most frequently and most generally across all documents, and are thus propagated the most.

In traditional topic hierarchy models (hLDA, TopicBlock, etc.), the root topic contains a distribution of all of the most general topic words in the document collection.

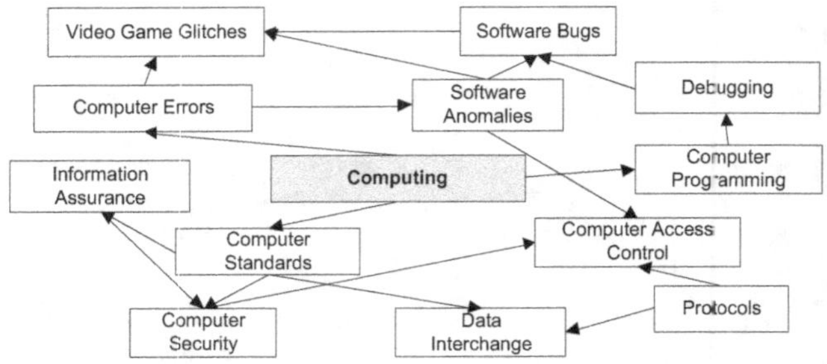

Figure 3: Truncated portion of the Wikipedia category subgraph rooted at the node COMPUTING.

p_μ $\alpha=.5$	hLDA $\gamma=1$	HDTM $\gamma=0.95$
illinois	illinois	illinois
computer	computer	computer
science	science	science
university	graduate	graduate
department	research	research
urbana	university	university

Table 1: Comparison of most probable words in top document (in p_μ), and in root topic of hLDA and HDTM

As a small, preliminary example, Table 1 shows the top six most probable words in the top document (via text propagation) and in root topics of hLDA and HDTM of the computer science department's Web site at the University of Illinois at Urbana-Champaign[2]. We see that the most probable words from the sitemap based Web document hierarchy is very similar to the most probable words in the most general topic of hLDA. This small example reinforces our intuition that certain Web sites have a hidden hierarchical topical structure.

In the previous term propagation work, the sitemaps were constructed ahead of time using URL heuristics. Our goal is to learn the document hierarchy automatically and in conjunction with the topical hierarchy.

3.2 Other document hierarchies

Documents from many different collections exist in hidden hierarchies. While technically a Web site, Wikipedia documents and categories form a unique document graph. Wikipedia categories are especially interesting because they provide a type of ontology wherein categories have more specific sub-categories and more general parent-categories. Most Wikipedia articles are are represented by at least one category description; this allows for users to drill down to relevant articles in a very few number of clicks by browsing the category graph. A partial example of the Wikipedia category graph is shown in Figure 3.

Bibliographical networks may also be hierarchically structured. In a bibliographic network, papers or authors (wherein each author could be a collection of documents) are represented by nodes and each citation is represented by an edge in the graph.

4. MODEL DESCRIPTION

We treat the problem of inferring the document hierarchy as a learning problem akin to finding the single, best parent for each

[2] `http://cs.illinois.edu`

document-node. Unlike previous algorithms, which discover latent topic taxonomies, the hierarchical document-topic model (HDTM) finds hidden hierarchies by selecting edges from a set of possible edges in the document graph. This section presents a detailed description of the model. A plate diagram of the generative process is shown in Figure 5.

We begin with a document graph $G = \{D, E\}$ of documents D and edges E. Each document is a collection of words, where a word is an item in a vocabulary. The basic assumption of HDTM and similar models is that each document can be generated by randomly mixing words from among topics. Distributions over topics are represented by z, which is a multinomial variable with an associated set of distributions over words $p(w|z, \beta)$, where β is a Dirichlet hyper-parameter. Document-specific mixing proportions are denoted by the vector θ. Parametric-Bayes topic models also include a K parameter that denote the number of topics, wherein z is one of K possible values and θ is a K-D vector. HDTM does not require a K parameter as input. Instead, in HDTM there exist $|G|$ topics, one for each graph node, and each document is a mixture of the topics on the path between itself and the root document.

In basic LDA, a single document mixture distribution is $p(w|\theta) = \sum_{i=1}^{K} \theta_i p(w|z = i, \beta_i)$. The process for generating a document is (1) choose a θ of topic proportions from a distribution $p(\theta|\alpha)$, where $p(\theta|\alpha)$ is a Dirichlet distribution; (2) sample words from the mixture distribution $p(w|\theta)$ for the θ chosen in step 1.

HLDA is an extension of LDA in which the topics are situated in a hierarchy T of fixed depth L. The hierarchy is generated by the nested Chinese restaurant process (nCRP) which essentially represents θ as an L-dimensional vector, defining an L-level path through T from root to document. Because of the nCRP process, every document lives at a leaf and the words in each document are a mixture of the topic-words on the path from it to the root.

4.1 Random Walks with Restart at Home

Because the nCRP process forces documents to the leaves in the hierarchy T, HDTM replaces nCRP with a slightly modified version of random walk with restart (RWR) called random walk with restart at home (RWRH). In traditional RWR, a walker begins by selecting a random starting point. With probability $(1 - \gamma)$ the walker randomly walks to a new, connected location or chooses to restart his walk at a random location with probability γ, where γ is called the restart probability[3].

In HDTM, the root node is fixed, either as the entry page of a Web site, or by some other heuristic. Therefore, for the purposes of hierarchy inference, we force the random walker to start and restart at the root node *i.e., at home*. Forcing the random walker to restart at the root is similar to, but not the same as, finding the personalized PageRank score [2] between the root node and every document-node in the hierarchy.

Let $deg(u)$ be the outdegree of document u in G. Consider a random walker visiting document d at time t. In the next time step, the walker chooses a document v_i from among u's outgoing neighbors $\{v|u \to_T v\}$ in the hierarchy T uniformly at random. In other words, at time $t+1$, the surfer lands at node $v_i \in \{v|u \to_T v\}$ with probability $1/deg(u)$. If at any time, there exists an edge $k \in \{v|u \to_G v\}$, *i.e*, an edge between the current node u and the target node k in the original graph G, then we record the probability of that new path possibility for later sampling. Alg. 1 describes this process algorithmically. This procedure allows for new paths from the root $r \rightsquigarrow k$ to be probabilistically generated based on the current hierarchy effectively allowing for documents to migrate up,

[3]Most related works denote the restart probability as α, however, this would be ambiguous with the Dirichlet hyper-parameter α.

Algorithm 1: Random Walk with Restart at Home

```
input  : Path Probs. P, Current Node u, Target k, Weight w
globals: Graph G, Hierarchy T, Restart Prob. γ
output : P

foreach v_i ∈ T.Ch(u) do                    /* child of u in T */
    if v_i ≠ k then
        w ← w + log( (1−γ) / len(T.Ch(u)) );
        RWRH (P, v_i, k, w);                /* Recurse */

if u →_G k then                     /* Edge u to k exists in G */
    P.Put(u, w);
```

down and through the hierarchy during sampling. The bold edges in Figure 2 show an example of edges stochastically selected by the RWRH process.

4.2 Generating document paths

Because a document hierarchy is a tree, each document-node can only have a one parent. Selecting a path for a document d in the graph G is akin to selecting a parent $u = Pa(d)$ (and grandparents, etc.) from $\{d|u \to_G d\}$ in the document graph G. HDTM creates and samples from a probability distribution over each documents' parent, where the probability of document u being the parent of d is defined as:

$$\prod_{k=0}^{\text{dep}_T(d)-1} \frac{1-\gamma}{\text{deg}_T(d_k)},$$

where d_k is the walkers current position at time k, $\text{dep}_T(d)$ is the depth of d in T, and $\text{deg}_T(d_k)$ is the outdegree of d_k in T. In other words, the probability of landing at d is the product of the emission probabilities from each document in the path through T from r to d.

The modified random walker function assigns higher probabilities to parents that are at a shallower depth than those at deeper positions. This is in line with the intuition that flatter hierarchies are easier for human understanding than deep hierarchies [14]. Simply put, the restart probability γ controls how much resistance there is to placing a document at successive depths.

Algorithmically, we infer document hierarchies by drawing paths $\mathbf{c}_d$ from the r to the document d. Thus, the documents are drawn from the following generative process:

1. Each document $d \in G$ is assigned a topic $\beta_d \sim \text{Dir}(\eta)$:
2. For each document $d \in G$:
    (a) Draw a path $\mathbf{c}_d \sim \text{RWRH}(\gamma)$
    (b) Draw an L-dimensional topic proportion vector θ from $\text{Dir}(\alpha)$, where $L = \text{len}(\mathbf{c}_d)$.
    (c) For each word $n \in \{1, \ldots, N\}$:
        i. Choose topic $z_{d,n}|\theta \sim \text{Mult}(\theta_d)$.
        ii. Choose word $w_{d,n}|\{z_{d,n}, \mathbf{c}_d, \boldsymbol{\beta}\} \sim \text{Mult}(\beta_{\mathbf{c}_d, z_{d,n}})$, where $\beta_{\mathbf{c}_d, z_{d,n}}$ is the topic in the zth position in $\mathbf{c}_d$.

In this generative process hierarchical nodes represent documents *and* topics, where internal nodes contain the shared terminology of its descendants.

Like in earlier models, there is statistical pressure in the posterior to have more general terms in topics towards the root of the hierarchy. This is because every path in the hierarchy includes the

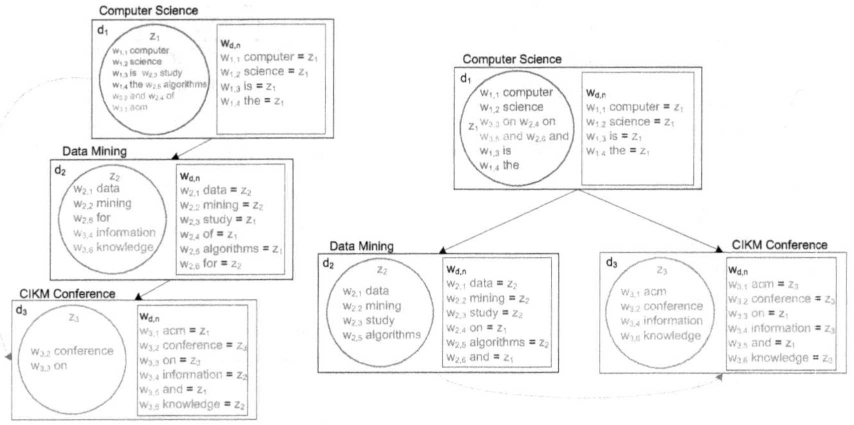

Figure 4: Illustration of two HDTM samples of the same data. Each node in the hierarchy contains a document and an associated topic. During the generative process, general terms are more likely to be found in topics near the root and vice versa.

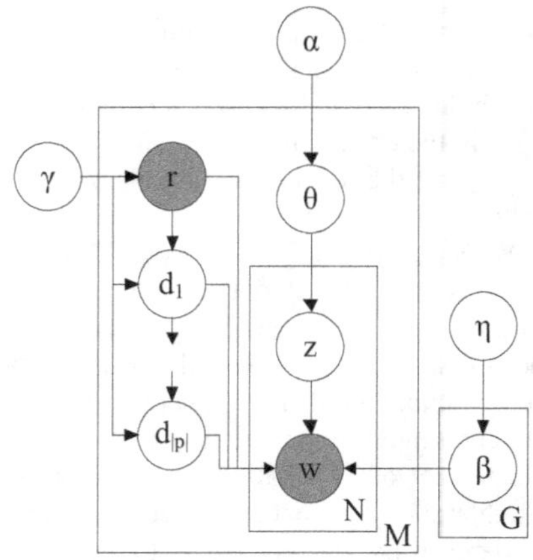

Figure 5: Graphical model illustration

root node and there are more paths through nodes at higher levels than through nodes at lower levels. As we move down the tree, the topics, and therefore the documents, become more specific.

Hyperparameters also play an important role in the shape and character of the hierarchy. The α parameter affects the smoothing on topic distributions, and the η parameter affects the smoothing on word distributions. The γ parameter is perhaps the most important parameter because it affects the depth of the hierarchy. Specifically, if γ is set to be large (*e.g.*, $\gamma = 0.95$) then resulting hierarchy shallow. Low values (*e.g.*, $\gamma = 0.05$) may result in deep hierarchies, because there is a smaller probabilistic penalty for each step that the random walker takes.

4.3 Inference

Exact inference on this model is intractable, so we must use a approximation technique for posterior inference. The Gibbs sampling algorithm is ideal in this situation because it simultaneously allows exploration of topic distributions and potential graphical hierarchies.

The variables needed by the Gibbs sampler are: $w_{d,n}$, the nth word in document d; $z_{d,n}$, the assignment of the nth word in document d; and $c_{d,z}$, the topic corresponding to document at the zth level. The θ and β variables are integrated out forming a collapsed Gibbs sampler.

The sampling is performed in two parts: (1) given the current level allocations of each word $z_{d,n}$ we sample the path $c_{d,z}$, (2) given the current state of the hierarchy, we sample $z_{d,n}$.

4.3.1 Sampling document paths

The first Gibbs sampling step is to draw a path from each document to the root through the graph. The sampling distribution for a path c_d is

$$\begin{aligned} &p(c_d|\mathbf{c}_{-d}, \mathbf{z}, \mathbf{w}, \eta, \gamma) \\ &\quad \propto p(c_d, \mathbf{w}_d|\mathbf{c}_{-d}, \mathbf{z}, \mathbf{w}_{-d}, \gamma, \eta) \\ &\quad = p(\mathbf{w}_d|\mathbf{c}, \mathbf{z}, \mathbf{w}_{-}d, \eta)p(c_d|\mathbf{c}_{-d}) \end{aligned} \tag{1}$$

where $\mathbf{w}$ is the count of terms in document d, and $\mathbf{w}_{-d}$ are the words without document d.

The second term represents the probability of drawing the path $c_{d,k}$ to document d at depth k from the RWRH process. Recall that each node has an emission probability of $1/\text{deg}_T(d)$, and a restart probability of γ. We define the probability recursively:

$$\begin{aligned} &p(c_{d,k}|\mathbf{c}_{-d}, c_{d,1:(k-1)}) \\ &\quad = \prod_{k=0} \frac{1-\gamma}{\text{deg}_T(d_k)} \end{aligned} \tag{2}$$

In other words, the probability of reaching d is equal to the probability of a random walker with restart probability γ being at document d at time k.

The first term represents the word distribution:

$$\begin{aligned} &p(\mathbf{w}_d|\mathbf{c}, \mathbf{w}_{-d}, \mathbf{z}, \eta) \\ &\quad = \prod_{k=1}^{\max(\mathbf{z}_d)} \frac{\Gamma(\sum_w \#[\mathbf{c}_{-d,k} = c_{d,k}, \mathbf{w}_{-d} = w] + V\eta)}{\prod_w \Gamma(\#[\mathbf{c}_{-d,k} = c_{d,k}, \mathbf{w}_{-d} = w] + \eta)} \\ &\qquad \frac{\prod_w \Gamma(\#[\mathbf{z} = k, \mathbf{c}_k = c_{d,k}, \mathbf{w} = w] + \eta)}{\Gamma(\sum \#[\mathbf{z} = k, \mathbf{c}_k = c_{d,k}, \mathbf{w} = w] + V\eta)} \end{aligned} \tag{3}$$

where $\max(\mathbf{z}_d)$ is the maximum depth of the current hierarchy state.

4.3.2 Sampling word levels

Given the current state of all the variables, the sampler must first pick an assignment z for word n in document d. The sampling distribution of $z_{d,n}$ is

$$\begin{aligned} &p(z_{d,n}|\mathbf{c}, \mathbf{z}, \mathbf{w}, \eta, \gamma) \\ &\quad \propto p(w_{d,n}, z_{d,n}|\mathbf{c}, \mathbf{z}_{-(d,n)}, \mathbf{w}_{-(d,n)}, \eta, \gamma) \\ &\quad = p(w_{d,n}|\mathbf{c}, \mathbf{z}, \mathbf{w}_{-(d,n)}, \eta)p(z_{d,n}|\mathbf{z}_{d,-n}, \mathbf{c}, \gamma) \end{aligned} \tag{4}$$

where $\mathbf{z}_{d,-n} = \{z_{d,\cdot}\} \setminus z_{d,n}$ and $\mathbf{w}_{-(d,n)} = \{w\} \setminus w_{d,n}$. The first term is a distribution over word assignments:

$$\begin{aligned} &p(w_{d,n}|\mathbf{c}, \mathbf{z}, \mathbf{w}_{-(d,n)}, \eta) \\ &\quad \propto \#[\mathbf{z}_{-(d,n)} = z_{d,n}, \mathbf{c}_{z_{d,n}} = c_{d,z_{d,n}}, \mathbf{w}_{-(d,n)} = w_{d,n}] + \eta \end{aligned} \tag{5}$$

which is the η-smoothed frequency of seeing word $w_{d,n}$ in the topic at level $z_{d,n}$ in the path c_d.

The second term is the distribution over levels

$$p(z_{d,n} = k|\mathbf{z}_{d,-n}, \mathbf{c}, \gamma) = \left(\prod_{j=1}^{k-1} \frac{1-\gamma}{\deg_T(d_{j-1})} \frac{\#[\mathbf{z}_{d,-n} > j]}{\#[\mathbf{z}_{d,-n} \geq j]}\right) \times \frac{1-\gamma}{\deg_T(d_{k-1})} \frac{\#[\mathbf{z}_{d,-n} = k]}{\#[\mathbf{z}_{d,-n} \geq k]}, \quad (6)$$

where we denote $\#[\cdot]$ as the number of elements in the vector which satisfy the given condition. We abuse notation in Eq. 6 so that the product from $j = 1$ to $k - 1$ combines terms representing nodes at the jth level in the path $\mathbf{c}$ down to the parent of d_k, and the second set of terms represents document d_k at level k. The $>$ symbol in Eq. 6 refers to terms representing all ancestors of a particular node, and $\geq$ refers to the ancestors of a node including itself.

5. EXPERIMENTS

This section describes the method and results for evaluating our model. We show quantitative and qualitative analysis of the hierarchical document-topic model's ability to learn accurate and interpretable hierarchies of document graphs. Our main evaluations explore the empirical likelihood of the data and a very large case study wherein human judges are asked to evaluate the constructed hierarchies.

5.1 Data

We evaluate HDTM on three corpora: the Wikipedia category graph, the Computer Science Department Web site at the University of Illinois, and a bibliographic network.

	Wikipedia	CompSci Web site	Bib. Network
root	Computing	cs.illinois.edu	Ponte, SIGIR [23]
documents	609	1,078	4,713
tokens	5,570,868	771,309	43,345
links	2,014	63,052	8,485
vocabulary	146,624	15,101	3,908

Table 2: Comparison of most probable words in top document (in p_μ) and in root topic (in hLDA)

The Wikipedia dataset has been used several times in the past for topic modeling purposes [12, 14]. Gruber *et al.*, crawled 105 pages starting with the article on the NIPS conference finding 799 links. Ho *et al.* performed a much larger evaluation of their TopicBlock model using 14,675 document with 152,674 links; however, they truncated each article to only the first 100 terms and limited the vocabulary to the 10,000 most popular words. Our Wikipedia dataset is a crawl of the *category* graph of Wikipedia, beginning at the category COMPUTING. In Wikipedia each category has a collection of articles and a set of links to other categories; however, categories don't typically have text associated with them, so we considered the text of each article associated with a particular category as the category's text. For example, the category INTERNET includes articles, INTERNET, HYPERLINK, WORLD WIDE WEB, ETC. In total we constructed a graph of 609 categories from 6,745 articles. The category graph is rather sparse with only 2,014 edges between categories, but has vocabulary size of 146,624 with 5,570,868 total tokens. We did not perform any stopword removal or stemming.

We chose a computer science department Web site as the second data set because it a rooted Web graph with familiar topics. By inferring the document hierarchy, we aim to find the organizational structure of the computer science department. Our intuition is that Web sites reflect the business organization of the underlying entity; thus we expect to find a subtrees consisting of courses, faculty, news, research areas, etc. at high levels, and specific Web pages at lower levels in the hierarchy. We crawled the Web site starting at the entry page and captured 1,078 Web pages and 63,052 hyperlinks. In total there were 15,101 unique terms from 771,309 tokens.

The bibliographic network consists of documents and titles from 4,713 articles from the SIGIR and CIKM conferences. There exist 3,908 terms across 43,345 tokens in the document collection. In this collection, links include citations between papers within the CIKM and SIGIR conferences. Citations between documents were provided by the authors of the ArnetMiner project [28], and is not complete. A SIGIR 1998 paper by Ponte and Croft [23] was chosen to be the root document because, in our records, it had the most in-collection citations.

5.2 Quantitative Analysis

HDTM has some distinct qualities that make apples to apples comparison difficult. Because HDTM is the first model to generate document hierarchies based on graphs, there is nothing to *directly* compare against. However, some of the models in the related work perform similar tasks, and so we perform comparisons when we are able.

The related works typically perform quantitative evaluation by measuring the log likelihood on held out data or by performing some other task like link prediction, etc. Log likelihood analysis looks at the goodness of fit on held out data. Unfortunately, we are not able to "hold out" any of our documents for testing, because each document, especially a first or second level document, is very important to the resulting hierarchy. Removing certain documents might even cause the graph to separate, which would make hierarchy inference impossible. For quantitative evaluation, we borrow the setup from [3] by comparing the states of each models' Gibbs sampler with the highest log complete likelihood.

We perform quantitative experiments on HLDA [3], TopicBlock [14], TSSB [1], and fsLDA [25]. The fixed structure in fsLDA is determined by a breadth first iteration over the document graph because URL heuristics were found to be unreliable. Hyper-parameters are the default unless otherwise specified. The depth of HLDA and TopicBlock is 4.

In all cases, a Gibbs sampler was run for 5,000 iterations; 2000 iterations were discarded as burn-in. Figure 5(a) shows the log complete likelihood for each sample. We ran the the Gibbs sampling algorithm on HDTM for various values of γ, and Figure 6 shows the best cumulative log complete likelihood for each of the tested values of γ.

Interestingly, Figure 5(b) shows that higher likelihood values are strongly correlated with hierarchies of deeper average depth; Figure 5(c) finds that the same is true for hierarchies of deeper maximum depth.

Figure 6 shows that HDTM with $\gamma = 0.05$ achieved the best likelihood score, and HDTM with $\gamma = 0.95$ achieved the worst likelihood score.

Table 3 shows the results of the different algorithms on the three data sets. The TopicBlock and TSSB clearly infer models with the best likelihood. The remaining algorithms, including HDTM, have mixed results.

5.2.1 Discussion

In order to properly understand the results captured in Table 3, recall that log probability is a metric on the *fit* of the observations on the configuration of the model. The original work on LDA [4] found that likelihood increases as the number of topics

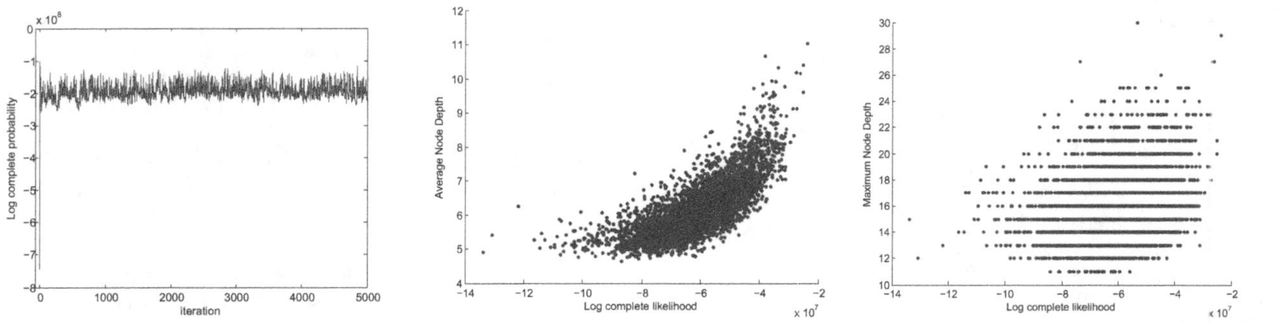

(a) The complete log likelihood

(b) Log complete likelihood and corresponding average node depth. High likelihood corresponds with hierarchies of high average depth.

(c) Log complete likelihood and corresponding maximum node depth. High likelihood corresponds with hierarchies of high maximum depth.

Figure 5: Analysis of Likelihood Scores for 5,000 iterations of the Gibbs sampler run on the CompSci collection.

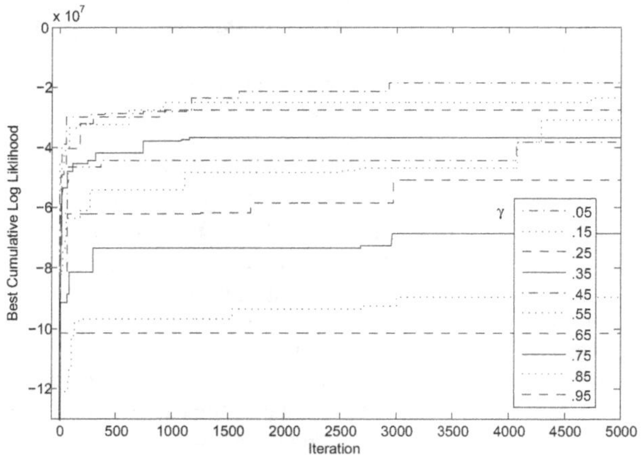

Figure 6: Best cumulative log complete likelihood for each tested γ value. Lower γ values result in deeper hierarchies.

	CompSci Web site	Wikipedia	Bib. Network
HDTM $\gamma = 0.05$	-1.8570	-148.071	-0.4758
HDTM $\gamma = 0.95$	-9.2412	-148.166	-0.5183
HLDA $\gamma = 1.0$	-8.5306	-50.6732	-8.5448
TopicBlock $\gamma = 1.0$	**-0.2404**	-2.9827	**-0.4192**
TSSB $k = 10$	-0.5689	**-0.0336**	-0.4655
fsLDA	-48.9149	-149.622	-0.6602

Table 3: Log complete likelihood results of the best sample from among 5,000 Gibbs iterations. Values are $\times 10^6$. Higher values are better. Best results are in bold.

increases. Along those lines, Chang, *et al.* demonstrated that more fine grained topics, which appear in models with a larger number of topics have a lower interpretability, despite having higher likelihood scores. Simply put, there exists a negative correlation between likelihood scores and human interpretability.

Applying these lessons to our experiments recall that HDTM has as many topics as there are documents, and non-root document topics are mixtures of the topics on the path to the root. Also recall that HLDA, TopicBlock and TSSB all generate a large number of latent topics. In HLDA and TopicBlock, there are infinitely many topics/tables in the nCRP. Practically speaking, the number of topics in the final model is much larger than the number of documents (conditioned on the γ parameter). In TSSB, the topic generation is said to be an interleaving of two stick breaking processes; practically, this generates even larger topic hierarchies. The fsLDA algorithm has as many topics as there are in hLDA, however, the fsLDA hierarchy is not redrawn during Gibbs iterations to fit the word distributions resulting in a lower likelihood.

Similarly, Figures 5(b) and 5(c) show that deeper hierarchies have higher likelihood scores. This is because long document-to-root paths, found in deep hierarchies, are able to provide a more fine grained fit for the words in the document resulting in a higher likelihood.

Therefore, we contend that the better likelihood values of HLDA, TopicBlock and TSSB are due to the larger number of topics that these models infer. A better way to evaluate model accuracy is by some external task or by manually judging the coherence of the topics.

5.3 Qualitative Analysis

To measure the coherence of the groupings, we modify the *word intrusion* task developed by Chang *et al* [6] to create the *document intrusion* task. In this task, a human subject is presented with a randomly ordered set of eight document titles. The task for the human judge is to find the intruder, that is, which document is out of place or does not belong. If the set of documents without the intruder document all make sense together, then the human judge should easily be able to find the intruder. For example, given a set of computer science documents with titles {`systems`, `networking`, `databases`, `graphics`, `Alan Turing`}, most people, even non-computer scientists, would pick `Alan Turing` as the intruder because the remaining words make sense together – they are all computer science disciplines.

For the set {`systems`, `networking`, `RAM`, `Minesweeper`, `Alan Turing`}, identifying a single intruder is more difficult. Human judges, when forced to make a choice, will choose an intruder at random, indicating that the grouping has poor coherence.

To construct a set of document titles to present to the human judge, we first select a grouping from the hierarchy at random (discussed in Sec. 5.3.1), and select 7 documents at random from the grouping. If the there are fewer than 7 documents available in the selected grouping, then we select all of the documents available; groupings of size less than 4 are thrown out. In addition to these documents, an intruder document is selected at random from among the entire collection of documents minus the documents in the test group. Titles are then shuffled and presented to the human judges.

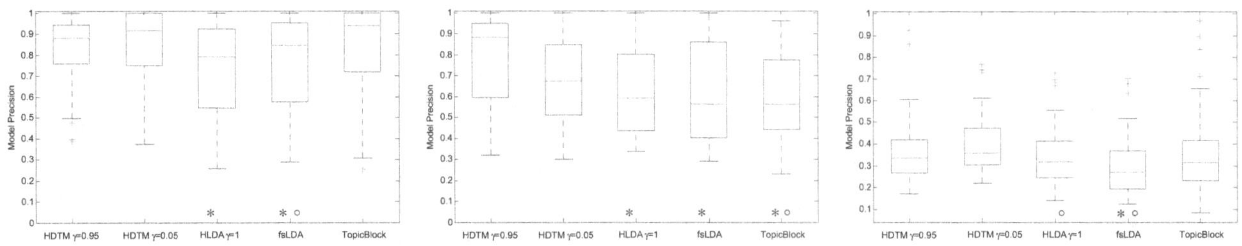

(a) CompSci Web site (b) Wikipedia (c) Bib. Network

Figure 7: The model precision for five models on three document-graph collections. Higher is better. $*$ and $\circ$ represents statistical significance from HDTM $\gamma = 0.95$ and $\gamma = 0.05$ respectively.

1 / 5	LANGUAGE REVIVAL	BILINGUAL EDUCATION	LINGUISTIC PURISM	CLASSICAL PHILOLOGISTS
2 / 5	ANDROID SOFTWARE	MOBILE BUSINESS SOFTWARE	VIDEO GAME JOURNALISM	FREE MOBILE SOFTWARE
3 / 5	LIBRARY AUTOMATION	POINTING-DEVICE TEXT INPUT	MULTI-TOUCH	AUDITORY DISPLAYS
4 / 5	SPREADSHEET SOFTWARE	INDIC COMPUTING	ONLINE SPREADSHEETS	SPREADSHEET FORMATS
5 / 5	NETWORK ACCELERATION	COMPUTER HARDWARE TUNING	COPY PROTECTION	COMPUTER OPTIMIZATION

Figure 8: Illustration of the intruder detection task from the Wikipedia collection, wherein human judges are presented with a set of document titles and asked to select the document that does not belong.

5.3.1 Comparison Models

In preparation for human judgments, we construct a hierarchy from the mode of sampled hierarchies. Specifically, at every 20th sample (*i.e.* Gibbs lag = 20), the parent of each document is recorded. After the Gibbs iterations are complete, each document is endowed by the parent that it saw in the most samples.

Extracting document groupings for evaluation is slightly different for each model. HDTM and fsLDA store a document at each node in the hierarchy. We select a grouping by first picking a document at random, and then choosing its siblings. TopicBlock and HLDA store documents at the leaves of the taxonomy, which often include several documents. We select a grouping from these models by first picking a document at random, and then choosing the other documents in the leaf-topic.

The hierarchies that the TSSB model constructed allowed multiple documents to live at inner nodes, We were unsuccessful in our attempts to evaluate groupings on inner nodes with more than 4 documents. We also tried to find nodes with 4 or more siblings, however, the hierarchies that were generated were too sparse to find practical groupings. Thus we were unable to provide human judges with TSSB groupings.

Each document-graph collection had different types of labels presented to the judges. The CompSci web site collection was labeled by the Web Page title and URL; the Wikipedia collection was labeled by the category title as shown in Figure 8; the bibliography network was labeled by the title of the paper.

5.3.2 Analyzing human judgments

The intruder detection tasks described above were offered on Amazon Mechanical Turk. No specialized training is expected of the judges. 50 tasks were created for each dataset and model combination; each user was presented with 5 tasks at a time at a cost of \$0.07 per task. Each task was evaluated by 15 separate judges. In order to measure the trustworthiness of a judge, we selected 5 easy tasks, *i.e.*, groupings with clear intruders, and created gold answers.

- A Language Modeling Approach to Information Retrieval [the, a, retreval, information, for, of, language]
  - Combining Multiple Classifiers for Text Categorization
    - Probabilistic combination of text classifiers using reliability indicators: models and results
      - Parameterized generation of labeled datasets for text categorization based on a hierarchical directory
      - Using bayesian priors to combine classifiers for adaptive filtering.
        - On-line spam filter fusion.
          - Spam filtering for short messages.
          - Relaxed online SVMs for spam filtering.
        - Robustness of adaptive filtering methods in a cross-benchmark evaluation.
          - Generalizing from relevance feedback using named entity wildcards.
  - Predicting the Cost-Quality Trade-Off for Information Retrieval Queries
  - Organizing structured web sources by query schemas: a clustering approach.
  - Information Retrieval as Statistical Translation.
    - Cross-lingual relevance models.
      - A search engine for historical manuscript images.
      - A method for transferring retrieval scores between collections with non-overlapping vocabularies.
    - Evaluating a Probabilistic Model for Cross-Lingual Information Retrieval.
      - Stemming in the language modeling framework.
      - Translating unknown queries with web corpora for cross-language information retrieval.
        - Mining translations of OOV terms from the web through cross-lingual query expansion.
      - Probabilistic structured query methods.
        - Addressing the lack of direct translation resources for cross-language retrieval.
          - Triangulation without translation.
        - Ambiguous queries: test collections need more sense.
    - Bayesian extension to the language model for ad hoc information retrieval.
    - Comparing cross-language query expansion techniques by degrading translation resources.
      - Measuring pseudo relevance feedback & CLIR.
      - Cross-lingual query suggestion using query logs of different languages.
    - Statistical cross-language information retrieval using n-best query translations.
      - Study of cross lingual information retrieval using on-line translation systems.
      - Using the web for automated translation extraction in cross-language information retrieval.
        - Bootstrapping dictionaries for cross-language information retrieval.
        - Detection and translation of OOV terms prior to query time.
  - and 16 others

Figure 9: Constructed hierarchy of bibliographic network with HDTM $\gamma = .95$. Words at the root document represent the most probable words in the root topic. Most probable words for other documents are not shown due to space constraints.

Judges who did not answer 80% of the gold answers correctly are thrown out and not paid. In total our solicitation attracted 31,494 judgments, across 14 models of 50 tasks each. Of these, 13,165 judgments were found to be from trustworthy judges.

We measure the *model precision* based on how well the intruders were detected by the judges. Specifically, if the intruder word w_k^m is from model m and task k, and $i_{k,j}^m$ is the intruder selected by the human judge j on task k in model m then

$$\text{MP}_k^m = \sum_J \mathbb{1}(i_{k,j}^m = w_k^m)/J.$$

where $\mathbb{1}(\cdot)$ is the indicator function and J is the number of judges. The model precision is basically the fraction of judges agreeing with the model.

Figure 7 shows boxplots of the precision for the four models on three corpora. In most cases, HDTM performs the best. As in [6], the likelihood scores do not necessarily correspond to human judgments. This is probably because the RWRH function essentially constrains the flexibility of the word sampler to operate only over explicit paths in the rooted graph. Paired, two-tailed t-tests of statistical significants ($p < 0.05$) performed between HDTM $\gamma = 0.95$ and $\gamma = 0.05$ and the other models are represented by $*$ and $\circ$ in Figure 7 respectively.

The bibliography network data had relatively low precision scores. This is probably because it was more difficult for the judges, who were probably not computer scientists, to differentiate between the topics in research paper titles. Figure 9 shows a small portion of the document hierarchy for the bibliographic network dataset constructed with HDTM $\gamma = .95$. The root document has 20 children in the hierarchy despite having 145 in-collection links. The remaining 120 documents live deeper in the hierarchy because HDTM has determined that they are too specific to warrant a first level position, and have a better fit in one of the subtrees.

Recall that each document is associated with the topics from itself to the root, where the root is a single, general topic. The seven most probable terms at the root level are also shown adjacent to the root's title in Figure 9. We see that these terms, like in HLDA and TopicBlock, are terms that are general to the entire collection.

6. CONCLUSIONS

We have presented hierarchical document-topic model (HDTM), a Bayesian generative model that creates document and topic hierarchies from rooted document graphs. We hypothesized that document graphs, such as Web sites, Wikipedia and bibliographic networks contain a hidden hierarchy, and we show corollaries to this intuition in language model propagation literature. Unlike most previous work, HDTM allows documents to live at non-leaf nodes in the hierarchy, which requires a new path sampling technique we call Random Walk with Restart at Home. An interesting side-effect of the random walker adaptation is that the path sampling step, Eq. 1, is much faster than the nCRP because RWRH only creates a sampling distribution for the parents of a document, whereas the nCRP process creates a sampling distribution over all possible paths in the taxonomy.

We performed several quantitative experiments comparing HDTM with related models. We conclude, as others have before us, that likelihood scores are a poor indicator of hierarchy interpretability, especially when the number of topics are different between comparison models. We performed a large qualitative case study which showed that the cohesiveness of the document groupings generated by HDTM were statistically better than many of the comparison models despite the poor likelihood scores.

7. ACKNOWLEDGMENTS

We thank Qirong Ho for his helpful discussion, the developers of the Mallet toolkit, as well as Rob Rutenbar and Abner Guzmán Rivera for their initial guidance. This work is funded by an NDSEG Fellowship to the first author. The third author is supported by NSF IIS-09-05215, U.S. Air Force Office of Scientific Research MURI award FA9550-08-1-0265, and by the U.S. Army Research Laboratory under Cooperative Agreement Number W911NF-09-2-0053 (NS-CTA).

8. REFERENCES

[1] R. P. Adams, Z. Ghahramani, and M. I. Jordan. Tree-Structured Stick Breaking for Hierarchical Data. In *NIPS*, pages 19–27, 2010.

[2] B. Bahmani, A. Chowdhury, and A. Goel. Fast Incremental and Personalized PageRank. *PVLDB*, 4(3):173–184, 2010.

[3] D. M. Blei, T. L. Griffiths, and M. I. Jordan. Hierarchical Topic Models and the Nested Chinese Restaurant Process. *Journal of the ACM*, 57(2):1–30, 2010.

[4] D. M. Blei, A. Y. Ng, and M. I. Jordan. Latent dirichlet allocation. *The Journal of Machine Learning Research*, 3:993–1022, Mar. 2003.

[5] A. Chambers, P. Smyth, and M. Steyvers. Learning concept graphs from text with stick-breaking priors. In *NIPS*, pages 334–342, 2010.

[6] J. Chang and D. M. Blei. Relational Topic Models for Document Networks. *Annals of Applied Statistics*, 4(1):121–150, 2010.

[7] A. Clauset, C. Moore, and M. E. J. Newman. Hierarchical structure and the prediction of missing links in networks. *Nature*, 453(7191):98–101, May 2008.

[8] D. A. Cohn and T. Hofmann. The Missing Link - A Probabilistic Model of Document Content and Hypertext Connectivity. In *NIPS*, pages 430–436, 2000.

[9] D. H. Fisher. Knowledge Acquisition Via Incremental Conceptual Clustering. *Machine Learning*, 2(2):139–172, Sept. 1987.

[10] T. Furukawa, Y. Matsuo, I. Ohmukai, K. Uchiyama, and M. Ishizuka. Extracting Topics and Innovators Using Topic Diffusion Process in Weblogs. In *ICWSM*, 2008.

[11] J. H. Gennari, P. Langley, and D. Fisher. Models of incremental concept formation. *Artificial Intelligence*, 40(1-3):11–61, Sept. 1989.

[12] A. Gruber, M. Rosen-Zvi, and Y. Weiss. Latent Topic Models for Hypertext. In *UAI*, pages 230–239, 2008.

[13] K. A. Heller and Z. Ghahramani. Bayesian hierarchical clustering. In *ICML*, pages 297–304, New York, New York, USA, Aug. 2005.

[14] Q. Ho, J. Eisenstein, and E. P. Xing. Document hierarchies from text and links. In *WWW*, page 739, New York, New York, USA. Apr. 2012.

[15] P. W. Holland, K. B. Laskey, and S. Leinhardt. Stochastic blockmodels: First steps. *Social Networks*, 5(2):109–137, 1983.

[16] J. Huang, H. Sun, J. Han, H. Deng, Y. Sun, and Y. Liu. SHRINK. In *CIKM*, page 219, New York, New York, USA, Oct. 2010.

[17] A. McCallum, A. Corrada-Emmanuel, and X. Wang. Topic and Role Discovery in Social Networks. In *IJCAI*, pages 786–791, 2005.

[18] Q. Mei, D. Cai, D. Zhang, and C. Zhai. Topic modeling with network regularization. In *WWW*, pages 101–110, New York, New York, USA, Apr. 2008.

[19] D. Mimno, W. Li, and A. McCallum. Mixtures of hierarchical topics with Pachinko allocation. In *ICML*, pages 633–640, New York, New York, USA, June 2007.

[20] R. Nallapati, D. A. McFarland, and C. D. Manning. TopicFlow Model: Unsupervised Learning of Topic-specific Influences of Hyperlinked Documents. In *AISTATS*, volume 15, pages 543–551, 2011.

[21] R. M. Nallapati, A. Ahmed, E. P. Xing, and W. W. Cohen. Joint latent topic models for text and citations. In *SIGKDD*, pages 542–550, New York, New York, USA, Aug. 2008.

[22] Y. Petinot, K. McKeown, and K. Thadani. A hierarchical model of web summaries. In *ACL*, pages 670–675, June 2011.

[23] J. M. Ponte and W. B. Croft. A language modeling approach to information retrieval. In *SIGIR*, pages 275–281, New York, New York, USA, Aug. 1998.

[24] T. Qin, T.-Y. Liu, X.-D. Zhang, Z. Chen, and W.-Y. Ma. A study of relevance propagation for web search. In *SIGIR*, page 408, New York, New York, USA, Aug. 2005.

[25] J. Reisinger and M. PaÅ§ca. Latent variable models of concept-attribute attachment. *ACL*, pages 620–628, Aug. 2009.

[26] M. Rosen-Zvi, T. L. Griffiths, M. Steyvers, and P. Smyth. The Author-Topic Model for Authors and Documents. In *UAI*, pages 487–494, 2004.

[27] R. Song, J.-R. Wen, S. Shi, G. Xin, T.-Y. Liu, T. Qin, X. Zheng, J. Zhang, G.-R. Xue, and W.-Y. Ma. Microsoft Research Asia at Web Track and Terabyte Track of TREC 2004. In *TREC*, 2004.

[28] J. Tang, J. Zhang, L. Yao, J. Li, L. Zhang, and Z. Su. ArnetMiner. In *SIGKDD*, page 990, New York, New York, USA, Aug. 2008.

[29] P. Willett. Recent trends in hierarchic document clustering: A critical review. *Information Processing & Management*, 24(5):577–597, Jan. 1988.

[30] C. Zhai and J. Lafferty. A study of smoothing methods for language models applied to information retrieval. *ACM TOIS*, 22(2):179–214, Apr. 2004.

[31] Y. Zhao, G. Karypis, and U. Fayyad. Hierarchical Clustering Algorithms for Document Datasets. *Data Mining and Knowledge Discovery*, 10(2):141–168, Mar. 2005.

Improving Document Clustering Using Automated Machine Translation

Xiang Wang
Dept. of Computer Science
University of California, Davis
Davis, CA 95616
xiang@ucdavis.edu

Buyue Qian
Dept. of Computer Science
University of California, Davis
Davis, CA 95616
byqian@ucdavis.edu

Ian Davidson
Dept. of Computer Science
University of California, Davis
Davis, CA 95616
davidson@cs.ucdavis.edu

ABSTRACT

With the development of statistical machine translation, we have ready-to-use tools that can translate documents from one language to many other languages. These translations provide different yet correlated views of the same set of documents. This gives rise to an intriguing question: can we use the extra information to achieve a better clustering of the documents? Some recent work on multiview clustering provided positive answers to this question. In this work, we propose an alternative approach to address this problem using the constrained clustering framework. Unlike traditional Must-Link and Cannot-Link constraints, the constraints generated from machine translation are dense yet noisy. We show how to incorporate this type of constraints by presenting two algorithms, one parametric and one non-parametric. Our algorithms are easy to implement, efficient, and can consistently improve the clustering of real data, namely the Reuters RCV1/RCV2 Multilingual Dataset. In contrast to existing multiview clustering algorithms, our technique does not need the compatibility or the conditional independence assumption, nor does it involve subtle parameter tuning.

Categories and Subject Descriptors

H.3.3 [**Information Search and Retrieval**]: Clustering

Keywords

Document clustering, constrained spectral clustering, machine translation

1. INTRODUCTION

1.1 Motivation

Automated Machine Translation (MT) [17] allows documents written in one language to be translated into other languages at very low cost. The field has made great strides recently and many online tools, such as Google Translate and Microsoft Translator, have been made available. This gives rise to an intriguing question: *can machine translation help us to achieve better clustering of documents?*

This problem has been recently explored from the multiview learning perspective [3,15,16] and positive results have been reported. In the multiview learning framework, each original document and its translation are treated as two views of the same data object. Multiview learning makes the assumption that the two views are *compatible* and *conditionally independent* [7], thus combining them will lead to a better classification or clustering. However, in reality there is no principled way to check the validity of these assumptions. Another limitation of the existing multiview clustering techniques is that their performance is sensitive to parameter tuning, which relies heavily on the prior knowledge on the relative quality of each particular view.

An alternative approach we shall explore to incorporating machine translation into document clustering is constrained clustering [5]. The basic idea of constrained clustering is to convert side information into Must-Link and Cannot-Link pairwise constraints; then the constraints are enforced on the original dataset to help improving the clustering. Traditionally, the constraints are assumed to be **accurate but sparse**: "accurate" means that they come from domain experts or ground truth, thus they are definite and correct; "sparse" means only a small amount of constraints are incorporated, given acquiring them in practice is costly.

However, the constraints generated from machine translation are **dense but noisy**: "dense" means that we have access to large amounts of constraints with no cost or very low cost; "noisy" means that the constraints are noisy and may not necessarily reflect the ground truth clustering. As a result, existing constrained clustering algorithms cannot be directly applied to our problem. A new algorithm is needed to properly incorporate this type of constraints so that it can 1) fully exploit the useful information in the massive constraint set; 2) ignore constraints that are inaccurate and excessive; and 3) not be easily over-constrained as most constrained clustering algorithms are [9].

1.2 Our Contribution

We show how to incorporate massive amounts of noisy side information into spectral clustering and demonstrate that this approach outperforms multiview techniques for MT aided document clustering. We choose a spectral formulation for two reasons: 1) spectral clustering has been proven effective on high-dimensional data, particularly text [6], and 2) by converting the two views into two graphs with the same

CIKM'12, October 29–November 2, 2012, Maui, HI, USA.

set of nodes we can transfer knowledge between two heterogeneous feature spaces (languages) in a principled manner. Our objective function extends earlier work by Wang and Davidson [21]. Their work was limited to clusterings for $K = 2$ and used a sparse constraint matrix generated from domain experts or ground truth labeling. In our problem setting, the constraint matrix is generated from another graph. As a result, the constraint matrix we use is guaranteed to be positive semi-definite. This difference enables us to extend the formulation in [21] from 2-way partition to K-way partition, and to propose a parametric as well as a non-parametric solution. As compared to existing work in MT aided document clustering, our algorithm has several unique benefits:

- As compared to the multiview techniques, the effectiveness of our algorithm does not rely on the compatibility or the conditional independence assumptions.
- It is easy to implement, efficient, and produces deterministic output.
- It does not require prior knowledge on the dataset, nor does it involve complicated parameter tuning.

Our contribution to the field is to propose a spectral clustering formulation that can handle dense but noisy constraints. We also show:

1. Our method is able to improve the clustering on the Reuters RCV1/RCV2 Multilingual Dataset. The improvement is consistent and significant (99% confidence level, see Table 3 and Figure 2).
2. Our approach outperforms many existing multiview spectral clustering techniques (see Table 3 and Figure 2).
3. Our approach yields improvements in the vast majority of trials with randomly sampled documents (see Figure 3). This is pragmatically very important given most practitioners only have one dataset (sample) to work with and **average** performance gain is not sufficient.
4. Our algorithm can be extended to other applications and datasets where the side information is dense and not always accurate.

The remainder of the paper is organized as follows: Section 2 provides some background knowledge on spectral clustering and the constrained spectral clustering formulation proposed in [21]; we present our algorithm in Section 3; we test our algorithm on real data in Section 4 and compare it to existing techniques; related work is discussed in Section 5; we discuss future directions and conclude the paper in Section 6.

2. PRELIMINARIES

To make this paper self-contained, we provide some background knowledge and also introduce notations that will be used throughout the rest of the paper (also summarized in Table 1).

Table 1: Notations

Notation	Meaning
$\mathcal{G}$	An undirected (weighted) graph
A	The affinity matrix
D	The degree matrix
I	The identity matrix
$\bar{L}$	The normalized graph Laplacian
$\bar{Q}$	The normalized constraint matrix
K	The number of clusters
N	The number of nodes
$\mathbf{v}, V$	The relaxed cluster indicator vector(s)

2.1 Spectral Clustering

We first introduce the formulation and notation for spectral clustering. Readers who are familiar with the topic can skip to Section 2.2.

Given a graph $\mathcal{G}$ with N nodes, A is the affinity matrix of $\mathcal{G}$. A is symmetric and nonnegative. D is the degree matrix of $\mathcal{G}$:

$$D_{ij} = \begin{cases} \sum_{k=1}^{N} A_{ik} & \text{if } i = j \\ 0 & \text{if } i \neq j \end{cases}.$$

$L = D - A$ is the graph Laplacian of $\mathcal{G}$, and $\bar{L} = D^{-1/2} L D^{-1/2}$ is called the *normalized* graph Laplacian [20].

The objective function for the normalized min-cut problem is (after relaxation):

$$\begin{aligned} \operatorname*{argmin}_{\mathbf{v} \in \mathbb{R}^N} \quad & \mathbf{v}^T \bar{L} \mathbf{v}, \\ \text{s.t.} \quad & \mathbf{v}^T \mathbf{v} = 1, \ \mathbf{v} \perp D^{1/2} \mathbf{1}. \end{aligned} \tag{1}$$

Shi and Malik [18] showed that the optimal solution to Equation (1) is the second smallest eigenvector of $\bar{L}$.

For K-way partition, the objective becomes

$$\begin{aligned} \operatorname*{argmin}_{V \in \mathbb{R}^{N \times K}} \quad & tr(V^T \bar{L} V), \\ \text{s.t.} \quad & V^T V = I. \end{aligned} \tag{2}$$

tr is the matrix trace. The optimal solution to Equation (2) is the top-K smallest eigenvectors of $\bar{L}$, and the clustering assignment is derived from applying K-means to the rows of V [20].

2.2 Constrained Spectral Clustering

Next we briefly summarize the constrained spectral clustering formulation proposed in [21].

Let $Q \in \mathbb{R}^{N \times N}$ be a relaxed constraint matrix. Q is symmetric and

$$Q_{ij} \begin{cases} > 0 & i \text{ and } j \text{ belong to the same cluster} \\ < 0 & i \text{ and } j \text{ belong to different clusters} \\ = 0 & \text{unknown} \end{cases}.$$

Given a cut $\mathbf{v}$, the objective is to minimize its cost on $\bar{L}$ and to lower bound its satisfaction on Q with a parameter α. Specifically:

$$\begin{aligned} \operatorname*{argmin}_{\mathbf{v} \in \mathbb{R}^N} \quad & \mathbf{v}^T \bar{L} \mathbf{v}, \\ \text{s.t.} \quad & \mathbf{v}^T \bar{Q} \mathbf{v} \geq \alpha, \\ & \mathbf{v}^T \mathbf{v} = 1, \ \mathbf{v} \perp_{\bar{L}} D^{1/2} \mathbf{1}. \end{aligned} \tag{3}$$

Algorithm 1: The parametric version of our algorithm (csp-p)

Input: $\bar{L}$, $\bar{Q}$, α, K;
Output: $\mathbf{u}$;
Solve the generalized eigenvalue problem $\bar{L}\mathbf{v} = \lambda\bar{Q}\mathbf{v}$;
Let $\mathcal{V} = \{\mathbf{v}_i\}_{i=1}^N$ be the set of all generalized eigenvectors;
for $i = 1$ **to** N **do**
  if $\mathbf{v}_i^T\bar{Q}\mathbf{v}_i < \alpha$ **then**
    Remove $\mathbf{v}_i$ from $\mathcal{V}$;
  end
end
$V \leftarrow [\,]$;
for $i = 1$ **to** K **do**
  $\mathbf{v}^* = \operatorname{argmin}_{\mathbf{v}\in\mathcal{V}} \mathbf{v}^T\bar{L}\mathbf{v}$;
  Remove $\mathbf{v}^*$ from $\mathcal{V}$;
  $V \leftarrow [V, \mathbf{v}^*]$;
end
return $\mathbf{u} \leftarrow Kmeans(V, K)$;

Equation (3) can be solved by introduce the Karush-Kuhn-Tucker conditions [14]. The solution is among the eigenvectors of the following the generalized eigenvalue problem:

$$\bar{L}\mathbf{v} = \lambda(\bar{Q} - \alpha I)\mathbf{v}.$$

After removing all negative eigenvectors (which fail to satisfy the lower bound α), the one that minimizes $\mathbf{v}^T\bar{L}\mathbf{v}$ is the solution.

This formulation has several limitations: 1) it is for 2-way clustering instead of K-way; 2) setting the cut-off threshold α requires prior knowledge; and 3) it is unclear if it can handle huge amounts of constraints. In Section 3, we will adapt this formulation to our problem and address these limitations.

3. OUR ALGORITHM

In this section, we present our constrained spectral clustering algorithm for MT aided document clustering. The objective function we use is derived from Equation (3). But unlike earlier work, since the constraint matrix Q in our problem setting is obtained from a distance metric, it is guaranteed to be positive semi-definite (PSD). We first show how to construct the graph Laplacian and the constraint matrix in the document clustering setting; then we extend Equation (3) from 2-way partition to K-way partition (Equation (5)); we further develop a non-parametric version of the formulation (Equation (7)); efficient solutions are provided for both objectives (Algorithm 1 and 2).

3.1 Graph and Constraint Construction

Given a set of N documents, after standard tf-idf indexing and normalization, they can be represented by a set of d-dimensional vectors: $\{\mathbf{x}_i \in \mathbb{R}^d : \|\mathbf{x}_i\| = 1, i = 1, \ldots, N\}$. Let $X = [\mathbf{x}_1, \ldots, \mathbf{x}_N]$, then

$$A = X^T X$$

is an $N \times N$ cosine similarity matrix and A is positive semi-definite.

In our problem setting, given a set of documents and their translation, we can construct two similarity matrices, $A^{(1)}$

Algorithm 2: The non-parametric version of our algorithm (csp-n)

Input: $\bar{L}$, $\bar{Q}$, K;
Output: $\mathbf{u}$;
Solve the generalized eigenvalue problem $\bar{L}\mathbf{v} = \lambda\bar{Q}\mathbf{v}$;
Let $\mathcal{V} = \{\mathbf{v}_i\}_{i=1}^N$ be the set of all generalized eigenvectors;
$V \leftarrow [\,]$;
for $i = 1$ **to** K **do**
  $\mathbf{v}^* = \operatorname{argmin}_{\mathbf{v}\in\mathcal{V}} \frac{\mathbf{v}^T\bar{L}\mathbf{v}}{\mathbf{v}^T\bar{Q}\mathbf{v}}$;
  Remove $\mathbf{v}^*$ from $\mathcal{V}$;
  $V \leftarrow [V, \mathbf{v}^*]$;
end
return $\mathbf{u} \leftarrow Kmeans(V, K)$;

and $A^{(2)}$, one for each language. We use $A^{(1)}$ as the affinity matrix of the graph, which is equivalent to A in the constrained spectral clustering formulation. We use $A^{(2)}$ as the constraint matrix, which is equivalent to Q in the constrained spectral clustering formulation. The interpretation of $A^{(2)}$ is: the greater $A^{(2)}_{ij}$ is, the more likely document i and j are considered to belong to the same cluster.

Let $D^{(i)}$ be the degree matrix of $A^{(i)}$, $i = 1, 2$. We have:

$$\begin{aligned} \bar{L} &\triangleq I - (D^{(1)})^{-1/2}A^{(1)}(D^{(1)})^{-1/2}, \\ \bar{Q} &\triangleq (D^{(2)})^{-1/2}A^{(2)}(D^{(2)})^{-1/2}. \end{aligned} \tag{4}$$

Note that as long as $A^{(1)}$ and $A^{(2)}$ are guaranteed to be PSD, other similarity functions and preprocessing techniques can be freely used. For example, instead of cosine similarity, we can use a Gaussian kernel. We can also apply various dimensionality reduction techniques to improve the quality of the similarity matrix.

3.2 Objective Function

Given $\bar{L}$ and $\bar{Q}$, we first present a parametric formulation for constrained spectral clustering. It is a natural extension of Equation (3) from 2-way to K-way partition. Our objective function is:

$$\begin{aligned} \operatorname*{argmin}_{\mathbf{v}_i \in \mathbb{R}^N|_{i=1}^K} \quad & \sum_{i=1}^K \mathbf{v}_i^T \bar{L}\mathbf{v}_i, \\ \text{s.t.} \quad & \mathbf{v}_i^T\bar{Q}\mathbf{v}_i \geq \alpha, \forall i, \\ & \mathbf{v}_i^T\mathbf{v}_i = 1, \ \forall i, \\ & \mathbf{v}_i \perp_{\bar{L}} \mathbf{v}_j, \forall i \neq j. \end{aligned} \tag{5}$$

α is the only parameter in this objective. It serves as a cut-off threshold. Any cut $\mathbf{v}$ that fails to satisfy (in the relaxed sense) at least α constraints in $\bar{Q}$ will be rejected. For the remaining cuts, which are called *feasible cuts* [21], the top-K ones with the lowest cost on $\bar{L}$ will be chosen. To guarantee the existence of at least K feasible cuts to choose from, when setting the value of α, we require:

$$\alpha \in [0, \lambda_K(\bar{Q})], \tag{6}$$

where $\lambda_K(\bar{Q})$ is the K-th largest eigenvalue of $\bar{Q}$. Note that since $\bar{Q}$ is PSD in our problem setting, if α is set to 0, any $\mathbf{v} \in \mathbb{R}^N$ is a feasible cut.

Given that Equation (6) is satisfied, raising the threshold α will reduce the range of the feasible cuts that we can choose from. As a result, the final partition will be more biased towards the constraint matrix $\bar{Q}$. Similarly, lowering the threshold α will give the algorithm more freedom to choose cuts that are favored by the graph $\bar{L}$. Therefore, in practice, the choice of α is determined by our preference between $\bar{L}$ and $\bar{Q}$. If we have confidence that $\bar{Q}$ is more accurate, then we should set α to a larger value; and vice versa.

Next we present an alternative objective which is non-parametric. To get rid of the cut-off threshold α, we consider the following cost-satisfaction ratio for any cut $\mathbf{v}$:

$$f(\mathbf{v}) \triangleq \frac{\mathbf{v}^T\bar{L}\mathbf{v}}{\mathbf{v}^T\bar{Q}\mathbf{v}}.$$

Since $\bar{Q}$ is now guaranteed to be PSD, we have

$$f(\mathbf{v}) \in [0, \infty), \forall \mathbf{v} \in \mathbb{R}^N.$$

The goal of constrained spectral clustering is to maximize $\mathbf{v}^T\bar{Q}\mathbf{v}$ and minimize $\mathbf{v}^T\bar{L}\mathbf{v}$, which is equivalent to minimize $f(\mathbf{v})$. Therefore $f(\mathbf{v})$ becomes a unified measure for the quality of the cut $\mathbf{v}$: smaller $f(\mathbf{v})$ means better cut.

Formally, the non-parametric version of our objective is:

$$\begin{aligned} \underset{\mathbf{v}_i \in \mathbb{R}^N|_{i=1}^K}{\operatorname{argmin}} \quad & \sum_{i=1}^{K} \frac{\mathbf{v}_i^T\bar{L}\mathbf{v}_i}{\mathbf{v}_i^T\bar{Q}\mathbf{v}_i}, \\ \text{s.t.} \quad & \mathbf{v}_i^T\mathbf{v}_i = 1, \ \forall i, \\ & \mathbf{v}_i \perp_{\bar{L}} \mathbf{v}_j, \forall i \neq j. \end{aligned} \tag{7}$$

3.3 Efficient Solutions

We first show how to solve the non-parametric objective in Equation (7). Consider the generalized eigenvalue problem:

$$\bar{L}\mathbf{v} = \lambda\bar{Q}\mathbf{v}. \tag{8}$$

Since both $\bar{L}$ and $\bar{Q}$ are Hermitian and PSD, we will have N real generalized eigenvectors [4], and they are the critical points for the generalized Rayleigh quotient [11]

$$\frac{\mathbf{v}^T\bar{L}\mathbf{v}}{\mathbf{v}^T\bar{Q}\mathbf{v}}. \tag{9}$$

Consequently, the solution to Equation (7) is the top-K generalized eigenvectors from Equation (8) that minimize the Rayleigh quotient in Equation (9). The full algorithm is presented in Algorithm 2.

On the other hand, the solution to Equation (5) is similar to that in [21]. We first solve the generalized eigenvalue problem

$$\bar{L}\mathbf{v} = \lambda(\bar{Q} - \alpha I)\mathbf{v},$$

and the non-negative eigenvectors are the feasible cuts. For efficiency consideration, in our implementation, we simply solve Equation (8), and choose eigenvectors associated with eigenvalues that are no smaller than α. This allows us to only solve the generalized eigenvalue problem once, and reuse the eigenvectors for multiple α values. The algorithm for the parametric objective in Equation (5) is summarized in Algorithm 1.

3.4 An Illustrative Example

In Figure 1 we illustrate how our approach can improve over clustering using a single view. The dataset consists of 1200 documents on 6 topics originally written in English and their translation into French. We plot the top-6 eigenvectors (each color corresponds to one eigenvector). The y-axis is the entry values of the eigenvectors. Due to the sparsity of the feature space, for spectral clustering using a single view, we observe a couple of "spikes" among the top eigenvectors (Figure 1(a) and (b)), which are trivial cuts that separate a small number of outlying documents from the rest. Including these trivial cuts will inevitably harm the quality of the final partition. In contrast, when we combined the two views together using our approach, the two views rejected the trivial cuts proposed by each other, and reached agreement on 6 eigenvectors that are more informative (Figure 1(c)). As a result, the quality of the final partition is substantially improved.

Note that Figure 1 is just one among many cases where our approach could help improve the clustering. It could be still effective even when there are no trivial cuts involved.

3.5 Remarks

3.5.1 *Algorithm Complexity*

The runtime for our algorithm is dominated by that of solving the eigenvalue problem in Equation (8). Therefore, the complexity of our algorithm is on par with spectral clustering in big-O notation, which is $O(KN^2)$ for dense matrices and $O(KM)$ for sparse matrices, M be the number of non-zeros entries.

3.5.2 *Direction of Knowledge Transfer*

The process of enforcing the constraint matrix $\bar{Q}$ to the graph $\bar{L}$ can be viewed as the transfer of knowledge. From Equation (5) we can see that the transfer is asymmetric. Therefore, given the original view and the translated view, we need to decide which view should be used to construct $\bar{Q}$ and which view should be used to construct $\bar{L}$. The role of the constraint matrix $\bar{Q}$ is to select N' feasible cuts from the N generalized eigenvectors ($N' \ll N$); the role of the graph Laplacian is to select K min-cuts from the N' feasible cuts. Therefore, $\bar{Q}$ plays a more critical role than $\bar{L}$ does. If the quality of $\bar{Q}$ is very poor, it will rule out eigenvectors that lead to good cuts; and once those cuts are ruled out, $\bar{L}$ will not be able to recover them. On the other hand, if the quality of $\bar{Q}$ is very high, it will select a set of good feasible cuts for $\bar{L}$ to choose from.

Consequently, in practice we should use the better view to construct the constraint matrix. Although such prior knowledge is not always available, according to our observation on real data, the original (language) view usually has better quality. Therefore in our experiments, $\bar{Q}$ is always constructed from the original documents and $\bar{L}$ is always constructed from the translation.

4. EMPIRICAL STUDY

In this section, we empirically study the performance of our algorithm on real-world data and compare it to existing techniques. We aim to answer the following questions:

1. **Effectiveness:** Is our algorithm able to improve the clustering quality by using machine translation?

2. **Consistency:** Is the performance gain of our algorithm consistent over a range of diverse data samples?

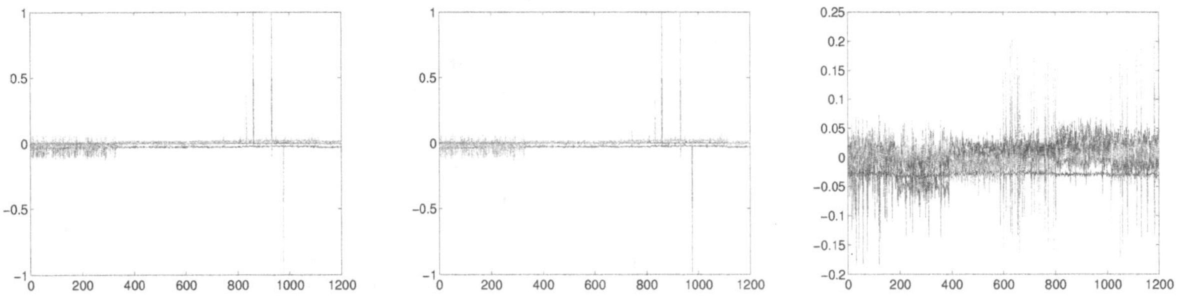

(a) Original (b) Translation (c) Original+Translation

Figure 1: An illustrative example to show how our algorithm can utilize the extra view to achieve better clustering. In each plot we show the top-6 eigenvectors from spectral clustering (x-axis are documents, y-axis are the corresponding eigenvector entry values). The "spikes" in (a) and (b) are trivial cuts suggested by the two views individually, which could cause a bad final partition. After combining the two views using our approach, these trivial cuts are ruled out in (c), which in turn leads to a better partition.

Table 2: Dataset Statistics

Language	#docs	#words
English	18,758	21,531
French	26,648	24,839
German	29,953	34,279
Spanish	12,342	11,547
Italian	24,039	15,506

Topics	#docs	Percentage
C15	18,816	16.84%
CCAT	21,426	19.17%
E21	13,701	12.26%
ECAT	19,198	17.18%
GCAT	19,178	17.16%
M11	19,421	17.39%

3. **Comparison:** Does our algorithm outperform existing techniques?

4.1 Methodology

4.1.1 Dataset

We used the Reuters RCV1/RCV2 Multilingual Dataset introduced by [3]. This dataset has been used by previous work [13, 15, 16] to evaluate the performance of multiview spectral clustering algorithm. The dataset contains documents originally written in five different languages, namely English (EN), French (FR), German (GR), Spanish (SP) and Italian (IT). Each document, originally written in one language, was translated to the other four languages using the Portage system [19]. The documents are categorized into six different topics. The statistics of the dataset is summarized in Table 2. More detail can be found on the dataset homepage [1].

The dataset is provided in the form of tf-idf vectors. We did not apply additional preprocessing to the data. No dimensionality reduction technique was applied. We used cosine similarity to construct the graphs.

4.1.2 Evaluation metrics

We used two common evaluation metrics to measure the quality of clustering, namely Adjusted Rand Index (ARI) [12] and Normalized Mutual Information (NMI). Both of them indicate the similarity between a given clustering and the ground truth partition: higher value means better clustering; 1 means perfect match.

Note that the dataset we chose is a very difficult dataset to work with. Even the state-of-the-art techniques can only achieve moderate clustering accuracy on this dataset [15,16]. The results we report in Section 4.2 may seem low, but they are consistent with the numbers reported by previous work.

4.1.3 Algorithm Implementations

We implemented both the parametric (`csp-p`) and the non-parametric (`csp-n`) version of our algorithm[1]. For the parametric version, we always set

$$\alpha \leftarrow \lambda_{2K}(\bar{Q}),$$

where $\lambda_{2K}(\bar{Q})$ is the $2K$-th largest eigenvalue of $\bar{Q}$. In other words, we provide $2K$ feasible cuts and $\bar{L}$ will choose the top-K with the lowest costs.

We also implemented five baseline algorithms in MATLAB to compare with:

- `orig`: Spectral clustering using the original view only.
- `trans`: Spectral clustering using the translated view only.
- `kersum`: The kernel summation method for multiview spectral clustering, which performs spectral clustering on the weighted sum of the two views' kernels. Previous study [8] showed that this approach works very well in practice, even in comparison to much more sophisticated multiview learning techniques. We used equal weights for the two views in our experiments.
- `mrw`: The mixing random walk algorithm proposed in [22], which finds the stationary distribution of a mixing random walk in both graphs. We used equal weights for the two views in our experiments.
- `co-reg`: The co-regularization multiview spectral clustering algorithm proposed in [16]. We implemented

[1]The MATLAB code is available by contacting the authors.

the centroid based version and used the centroids to compute final clustering. This algorithm has one parameter, which is the weight for the regularizer. We set it to 0.01 in our experiments, as suggested in the original paper.

4.1.4 Task Description

We first pick a language pair, say EN-FR, which means documents that are originally written in English along with their French translation. To maximize the diversity between the data samples we use, in each trial we randomly sample 1200 documents, which is less than 10% of all available documents. We have 100 trials for each language pair. We apply our algorithm and the baseline algorithms to the sample and partition it into $K = 6$ clusters. We measure the resultant clusterings using both ARI and NMI. Since the last step of spectral clustering involves the K-means algorithm, in each trial, we repeat K-means algorithm 100 times with 100 random seeds and report the average performance.

For all language pairs, we report the average performance (Table 3), aggregated results over 100 trials (Figure 2), and the performance of each individual trial (Figure 3).

4.2 Results and Analysis

Since we have 5 different languages, there are 20 possible original-translation language combinations. We show our results on 8 pairs, namely English to French (EN-FR), German (EN-GR), Italian (EN-IT), Spanish (EN-SP), and German to English (GR-EN), French (GR-FR), Italian (GR-IT), and Spanish (GR-SP). The conclusions we draw from these 8 pairs also hold for the other 12 pairs.

First we give an overview of the results in terms of average performance. In Table 3, we report the average ARI of 7 different algorithms on 8 different language pairs. Our approach (`csp-p`) shows consistent and significant (99% confidence level) improvement over the clustering on the original view only (`orig`) for all language pairs. Also, for all language pairs, `csp-p` has the highest average ARI.

More detailed results are reported in Figure 2, with box plots for all 7 algorithms and 8 language pairs, in terms of ARI and NMI, respectively. Besides of showing the advantage of our approach (`csp-p`), as we have seen in Table 3, Figure 2 illustrates the diversity of the data samples we used in different trials. Some data samples were easier to cluster and others more difficult. This demonstrates that the effectiveness of our approach is not limited to a certain data distribution or a certain language.

Note that the performance of our non-parametric approach (`csp-n`) is not as good as the parametric one (`csp-p`). This is expected because `csp-n` uses zero prior knowledge. On the other hand, as shown in Table 3, `csp-n` managed to outperform `orig` on all 8 language pairs. It also outperformed the multiview competitors on several language pairs. This result is non-trivial considering the approach is completely parameter-free.

To further demonstrate the consistency and reliability of our approach over different random samples, in Figure 3, we show the trial by trial breakdown of the performance gain of our approach (`csp-p` and `csp-n`) over the clustering on the original view only (`orig`), as measured by ARI. We can see that for 800 random trials over 8 different language pairs, our algorithm achieved positive gain in most cases, and it rarely caused large performance loss. This means our approach is reliable in practice. Practitioners can apply our approach to a dataset, with peace of mind that it is very likely that our algorithm will improve the result, and it is very unlikely that our algorithm will lead to a great performance loss.

5. RELATED WORK

Recent work in the multiview learning literature studied the potential of using automated machine translation to improve both document classification [2, 3] and clustering [13, 15, 16]. Given a set of documents, their translation in another language is modeled as a second view. These multiple views are considered as partial observations of the same set of data objects. When properly combined, these views will complement each other and improve the resultant classification or clustering. Several multiview learning algorithms have been proposed and tested on the same Reuters RCV1/RCV2 Multilingual Dataset [3] as we used in this paper. Empirical results confirmed the helpfulness of machine translation. Note that the effectiveness of multiview learning is based on the assumption that the views are compatible and conditionally independent [7]. There is no practical way to validate either assumption for a specific sample.

In this work, we adopted an alternative approach, namely constrained clustering [5]. In contrast to the multiview formulation, constrained clustering does not make assumption about the underlying distribution of the data. Traditional constrained clustering algorithm cannot be directly applied to our problem because they can only deal with sparse and accurate constraints. If the number of constraints increases, or incorrect constraints are introduced, the clustering algorithm will be over-constrained [9]. It is also difficult to choose a small set of helpful constraints [10].

Wang and Davidson [21] proposed a spectral formulation for constrained clustering, which suits our problem setting well because it can incorporate soft constraints. Instead of enforcing each and every constraint given, they use a user-specified parameter to lower bound the number of satisfied constraints. As a result, noisy and incorrect constraints can be ignored by the final clustering. The difference between our work and theirs is that they considered sparse constraints generated from ground truth or domain experts, whereas our constraints are dense, generated from a distance metric. Furthermore, the constraint matrix we use is always PSD. As a result, we are able to extend their objective to K-way partition, and develop a new non-parametric solution to the problem.

The focus of this work is to show how to use machine translation to improve document clustering. We assume that the translations of documents are readily available. Technical detail of statistical machine translation [17] is not considered, although it is expected that better translation will lead to greater performance gain.

6. CONCLUSION AND FUTURE WORK

Automated Machine Translation offers the ability to supplement existing document representations with additional information. Previous work has explored using this additional information in a multiview clustering setting with some success. In this work, we take an alternative approach of encoding the additional information as constraints. This is a challenging problem since existing constrained clustering algorithms expect a small number of constraints generated

Table 3: Average ARI of 7 Algorithms on 8 Language Pairs

	orig	trans	kersum	mrw	co-reg	csp-p	csp-n
GR-EN	0.276	0.261	0.303	0.296	0.303	**0.314**	0.289
GR-FR	0.277	0.250	0.284	0.279	0.274	**0.303**	0.281
GR-IT	0.279	0.301	0.294	0.286	0.303	**0.304**	0.287
GR-SP	0.274	0.224	0.280	0.273	0.271	**0.293**	0.276
EN-FR	0.168	0.163	0.195	0.172	0.174	**0.203**	0.194
EN-GR	0.171	0.149	0.192	0.172	0.167	**0.197**	0.192
EN-IT	0.168	0.170	0.178	0.161	0.183	**0.184**	0.179
EN-SP	0.169	0.163	0.180	0.164	**0.182**	**0.182**	0.175

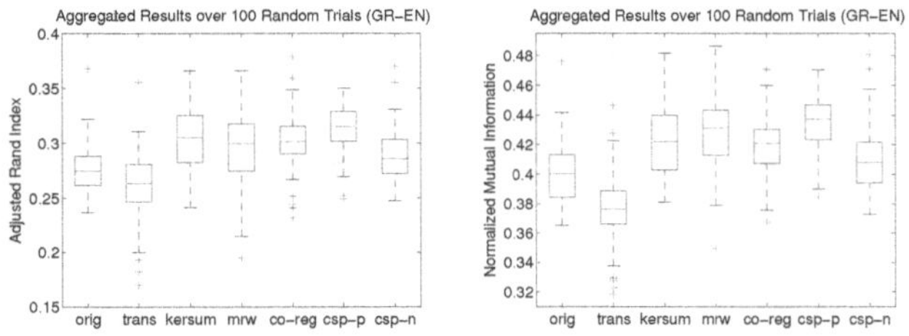

(a) GR-EN

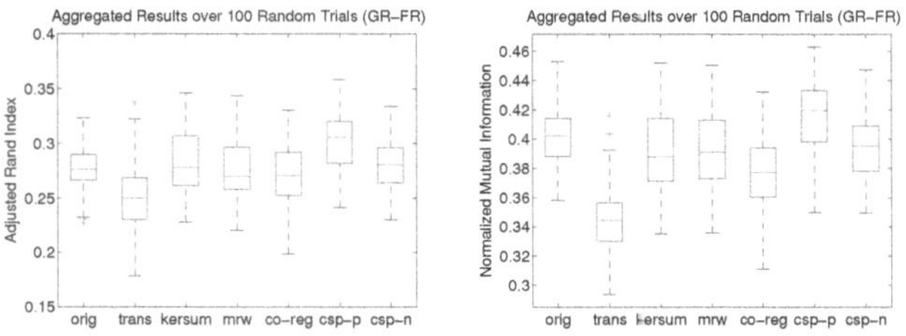

(b) GR-FR

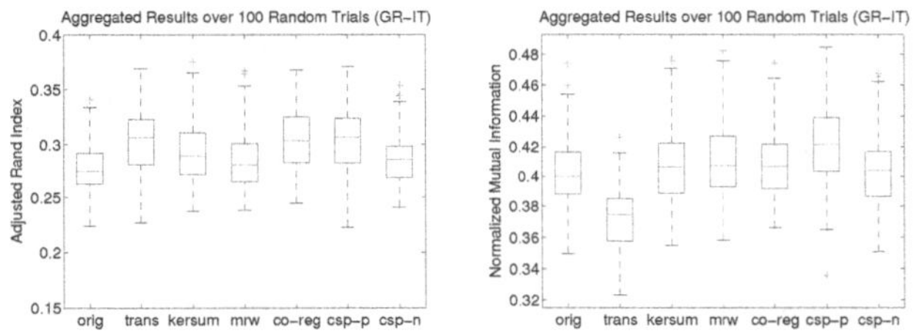

(c) GR-IT

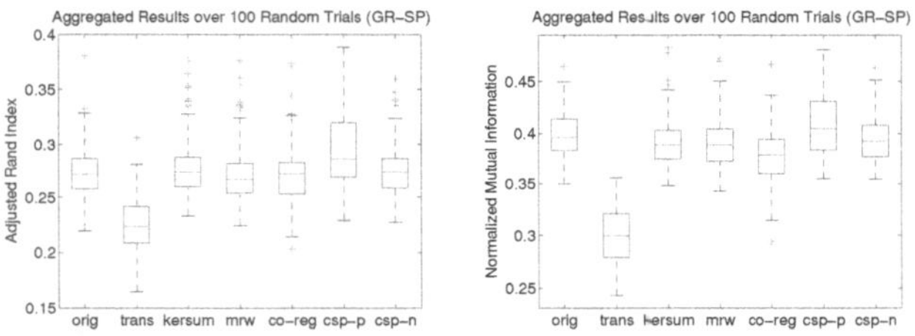

(d) GR-SP

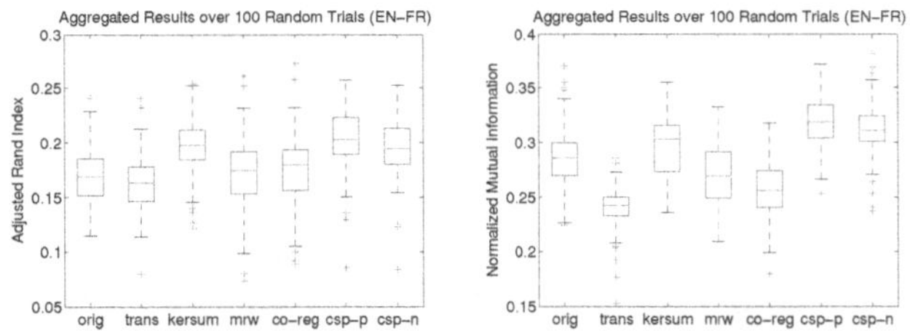

(e) EN-FR

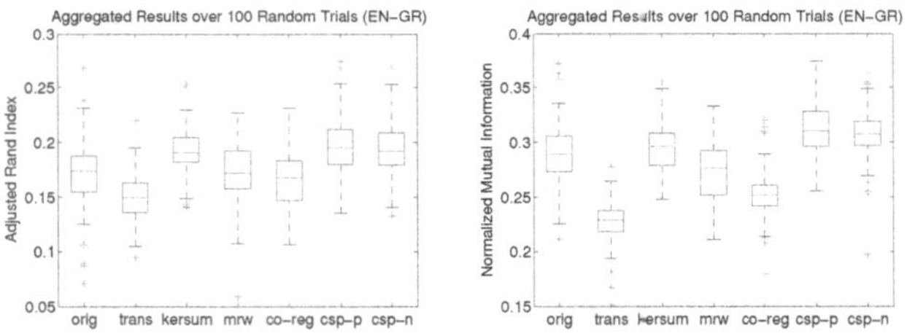

(f) EN-GR

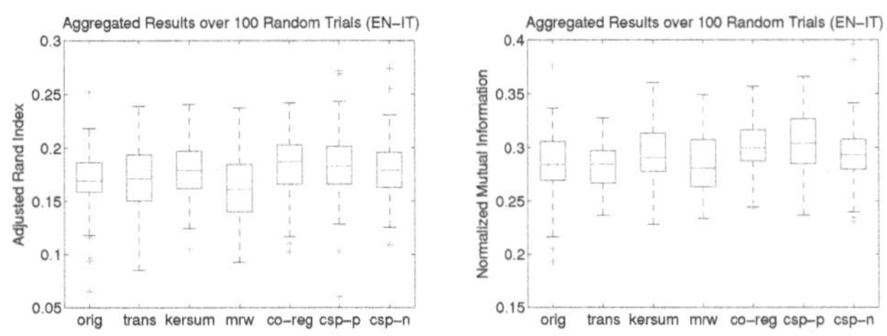

(g) EN-IT

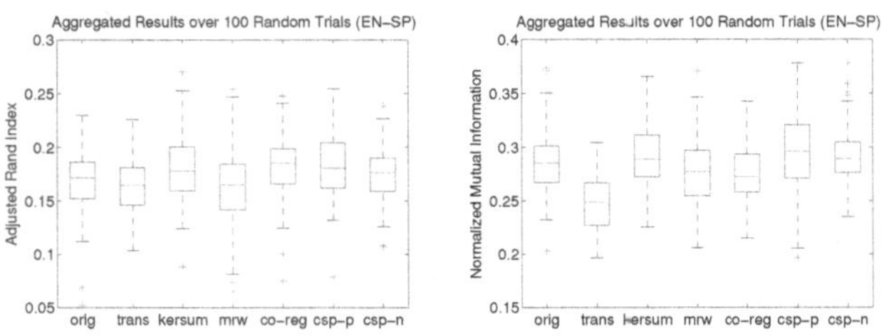

(h) EN-SP

Figure 2: The box plot for 8 language pairs, 100 random trials each. Results are evaluated in terms of both ARI and NMI. Our technique (`csp-p`) consistently and significantly improves over the clustering on the original view (`orig`), and outperforms the competitors.

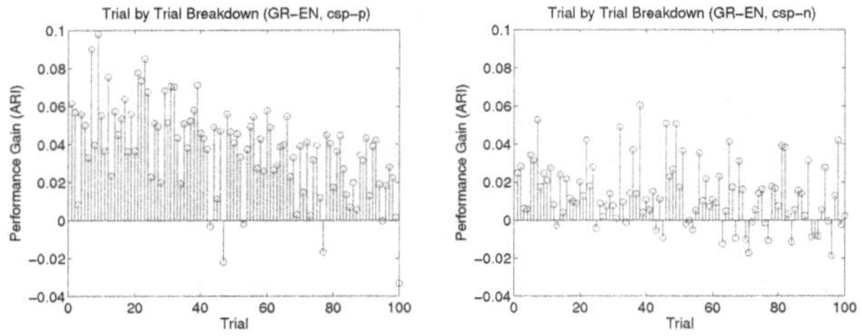

(a) GR-EN

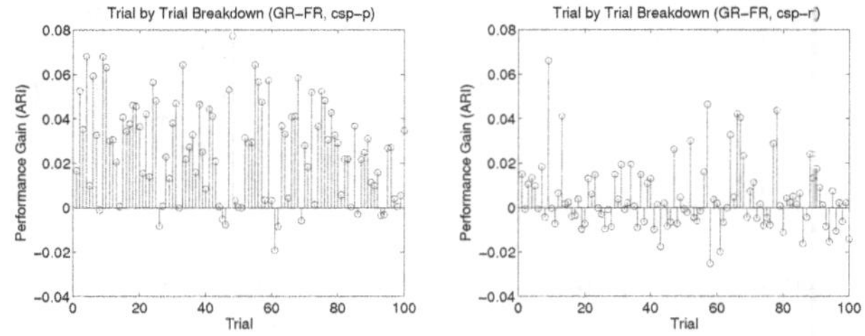

(b) GR-FR

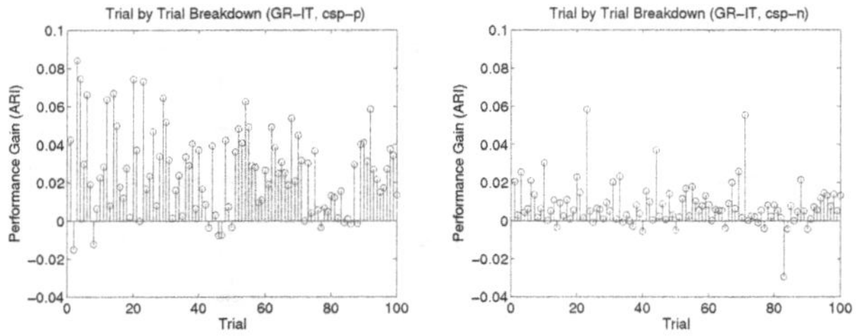

(c) GR-IT

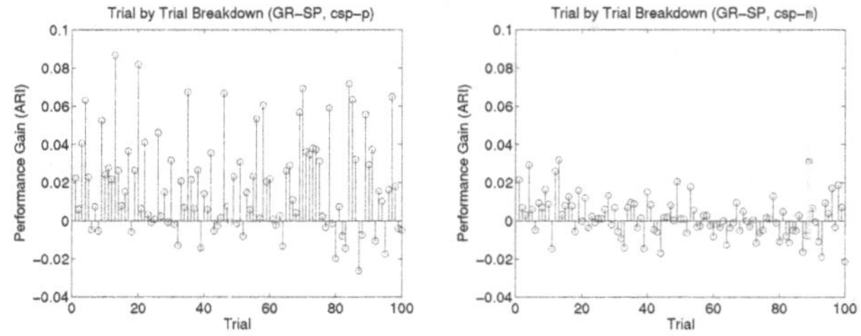

(d) GR-SP

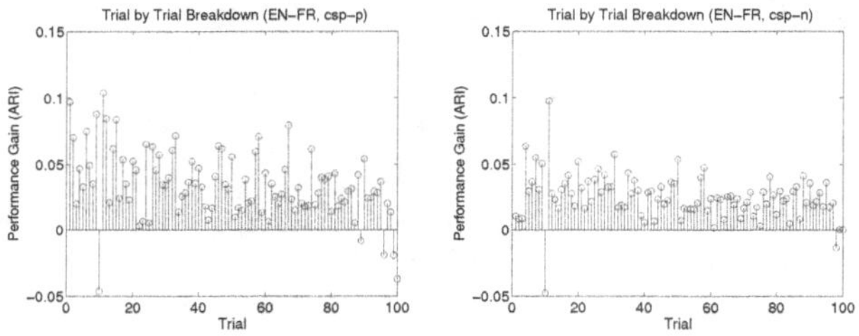

(e) EN-FR

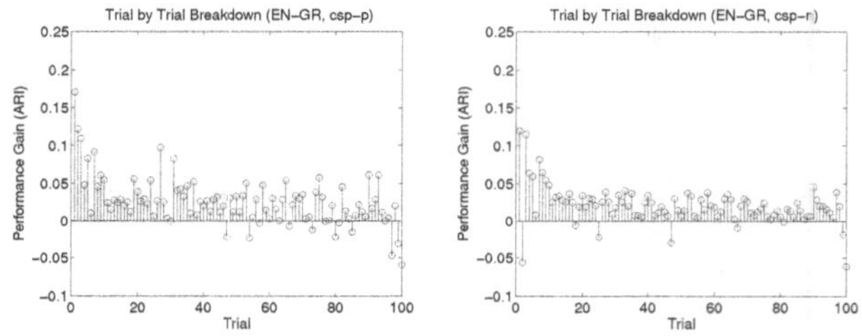

(f) EN-GR

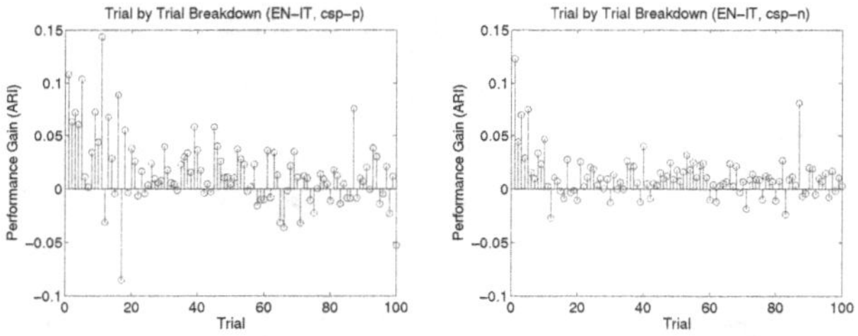

(g) EN-IT

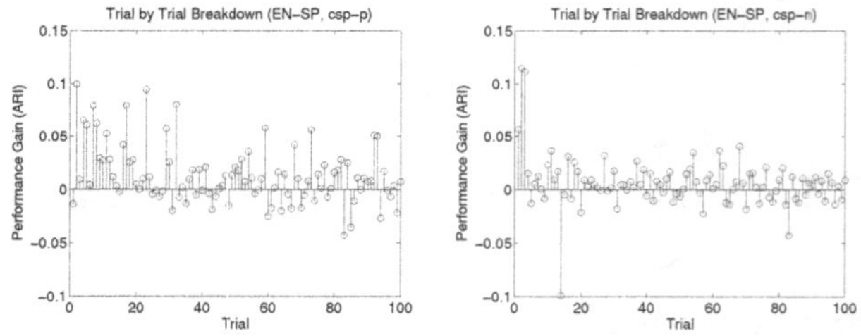

(h) EN-SP

Figure 3: The trial by trial breakdown of the performance gain of our technique (`csp-p` and `csp-n`) over the baseline (`orig`) on all 8 language pairs. Our technique not only achieved positive performance gain in average, but also in most of the individual trials.

from the ground truth or domain experts, whereas MT produces dense and potentially inaccurate information. We proposed two algorithms that can be viewed as an extension of spectral clustering to encode many noisy constraints without being over-constrained and with the ability to ignore constraints. We showed with real data that our approach is effective (it improves the clustering using a single view (language), see Table 3), consistent (since it can ignore poor side information, see Figure 2 and 3), and outperforms other comparable techniques (see Table 3).

It is important to remember that existing work on multi-view clustering [15] showed that the performance gain from using more than two views is marginal. Our future work will revisit this question by clustering using constraints generated from multiple translated views. Also, in this work we showed that adding constraints from translations does not hurt the clustering (since our approach ignores harmful constraints). However, an important problem we hope to address is determining *a priori* how much the translation will improve the clustering. This will help address the problem: "Which language should we translate into?"

7. ACKNOWLEDGMENTS

We gratefully acknowledge support of this research via ONR grants N00014-09-1-0712 Automated Discovery and Explanation of Event Behavior, N00014-11-1-0108 Guided Learning in Dynamic Environments and NSF Grant NSF IIS-0801528 Knowledge Enhanced Clustering.

8. REFERENCES

[1] Reuters RCV1/RCV2 multilingual dataset: `http://multilingreuters.iit.nrc.ca/ReutersMultiLingualMultiView.htm`

[2] M.-R. Amini and C. Goutte. A co-classification approach to learning from multilingual corpora. *Machine Learning*, 79(1-2):105–121, 2010.

[3] M.-R. Amini, N. Usunier, and C. Goutte. Learning from multiple partially observed views - an application to multilingual text categorization. In *NIPS*, pages 28–36, 2009.

[4] Z. Bai, J. Demmel, J. Dongarra, A. Ruhe, and H. van der Vorst, editors. *Templates for the solution of Algebraic Eigenvalue Problems: A Practical Guide.* SIAM, Philadelphia, 2000.

[5] S. Basu, I. Davidson, and K. Wagstaff, editors. *Constrained Clustering: Advances in Algorithms, Theory, and Applications.* Chapman & Hall/CRC, 2008.

[6] M. W. Berry, editor. *Survey of text mining: clustering, classification, and retrieval.* Springer, 2004.

[7] A. Blum and T. M. Mitchell. Combining labeled and unlabeled data with co-training. In *COLT*, pages 92–100, 1998.

[8] C. Cortes, M. Mohri, and A. Rostamizadeh. Learning non-linear combinations of kernels. In *NIPS*, pages 396–404, 2009.

[9] I. Davidson and S. S. Ravi. Identifying and generating easy sets of constraints for clustering. In *AAAI*, pages 336–341, 2006.

[10] I. Davidson, K. Wagstaff, and S. Basu. Measuring constraint-set utility for partitional clustering algorithms. In *PKDD*, pages 115–126, 2006.

[11] R. Horn and C. Johnson. *Matrix analysis.* Cambridge Univ. Press, 1990.

[12] L. Hubert and P. Arabie. Comparing partitions. *Journal of Classification*, 2:193–218, 1985.

[13] Y.-M. Kim, M.-R. Amini, C. Goutte, and P. Gallinari. Multi-view clustering of multilingual documents. In *SIGIR*, pages 821–822, 2010.

[14] H. Kuhn and A. Tucker. Nonlinear programming. *ACM SIGMAP Bulletin*, pages 6–18, 1982.

[15] A. Kumar and H. D. III. A co-training approach for multi-view spectral clustering. In *ICML*, pages 393–400, 2011.

[16] A. Kumar, P. Rai, and H. D. III. Co-regularized multi-view spectral clustering. In *NIPS*, pages 1413–1421, 2011.

[17] A. Lopez. Statistical machine translation. *ACM Comput. Surv.*, 40(3), 2008.

[18] J. Shi and J. Malik. Normalized cuts and image segmentation. *IEEE Trans. Pattern Anal. Mach. Intell.*, 22(8):888–905, 2000.

[19] N. Ueffing, M. Simard, S. Larkin, and J. H. Johnson. NRC's PORTAGE system for WMT 2007. In *ACL-2007 Second Workshop on SMT*, pages 185–188, 2007.

[20] U. von Luxburg. A tutorial on spectral clustering. *Statistics and Computing*, 17(4):395–416, 2007.

[21] X. Wang and I. Davidson. Flexible constrained spectral clustering. In *KDD*, pages 563–572, 2010.

[22] D. Zhou and C. Burges. Spectral clustering and transductive learning with multiple views. In *ICML*, pages 1159–1166, 2007.

Right-Protected Data Publishing with Hierarchical Clustering Preservation

Michail Vlachos
IBM Research - Zurich

Aleksander Wieczorek
Poznan University of Technology, Poland

Johannes Schneider
IBM Research - Zurich

ABSTRACT

The emergence of cloud-based storage services is opening up new avenues in data exchange and data dissemination. This has amplified the interest in right-protection mechanisms to establish ownership in case of data leakage. Current right-protection technologies, however, rarely provide strong guarantees on the dataset utility after the protection process. This work presents techniques that explicitly address this shortcoming and provably preserve the outcome of certain mining operations. In particular, we take special care to guarantee that the outcome of hierarchical clustering operations remains the same before and after right protection. We encode data ownership using watermarking principles. In the process, we derive fundamental bounds on the distortion incurred by the watermarking. We leverage our theoretical analysis to design fast algorithms for right protection without exhaustively searching the vast design space.

Categories and Subject Descriptors

H.3.3 [**Information Search and Retrieval**]: Clustering

Keywords

Watermarking, Distortion Estimation

1. INTRODUCTION

Data exchange and data sharing have become an inherent part of business and academic efforts. Both practices encourage scientific enquiry, ease validation of research efforts and maximize transparency. As such, data sharing and data publishing are recognized as important productivity catalysts in diverse research efforts. To offer a concrete example, it is widely recognized that initiatives such as the human genome project [1] that advocated data sharing lead to "rapid scientific breakthroughs that otherwise would not have occurred" [1]. Recently, even fields that viewed data sharing through a negative prism (e.g., banking industry), have promoted the establishment of consortia to ease data exchange [6]. Owing to the high availability of cloud-based services in the near future, similar initiatives are projected to experience a surge in demand, as attested in many recent studies [11, 17, 10].

Data owners, nonetheless, need also maintain principal rights over the shared datasets, datasets which in many cases have been obtained after laborious procedures. This work presents a protection mechanism that can deliver detectable evidence on the legal ownership of a shared dataset, without compromising its usability for a class of mining operations. To achieve this, we guarantee that important distance-based relationships between the dataset objects remain unaltered.

We embed ownership evidence using watermarking techniques. Watermarking has emerged over the years as a successful method for establishing data progeny. It has been used extensively in many multimedia applications, on image, video, and audio data. Traditional watermarking techniques focus on a single data object and are not tailored for preserving relationships between multiple objects. In that sense, our technique augments and strengthens existing watermarking methodologies. Our goal is two-fold: to guarantee right-protection and, at the same time, preserve the original relationships between the dataset objects. Having accomplished this, any learning or retrieval task that depends on the preserved structural properties will remain undistorted even after the watermark application.

In this work, we explicitly show how to **preserve hierarchical clustering** (HC). HC is a popular knowledge extraction tool, because it can visually communicate the similarity between objects and groups of objects. Because of its descriptive power and ease of implementation it is a valuable tool in many disciplines, including:

- Biology and Bioinformatics, for the construction of phylogenetic trees between species [16].
- Natural Sciences, for the taxonomic categorization of plants or animals based on their similarity to previously categorized objects [23].
- Business Analytics and Marketing, for performing customer-base segmentation and aiding the discovery of common customer profiles [28].

Our objective is to maximize the knowledge we can garner from the watermarked data. Here, we give provable guarantees of identical outcome for HC algorithms on the original and watermarked dataset. To achieve this we provide a **theoretical analysis** of the distance distortion due

[1]`http://scientificdatasharing.com/about/`

CIKM'12, October 29–November 2, 2012, Maui, HI, USA.

to watermarking. We derive tight bounds on the expansion/contraction of distances caused by multiplicative watermarking techniques. We exploit these results to engineer **fast watermarking variants** that drastically prune the parameter search space, compared to the exhaustive algorithms.

2. OVERVIEW OF OUR APPROACH

Our goal is to discover how to right-protect a dataset so that the dendrogram resulting from the hierarchical clustering after the right protection is isomorphic to the one on the original data (see Fig. 1). This translates into studying with what watermark *intensity* to protect the dataset so that important parts of the dataset graph are not distorted. We study how to achieve this goal for both single- and complete-linkage hierarchical clustering.

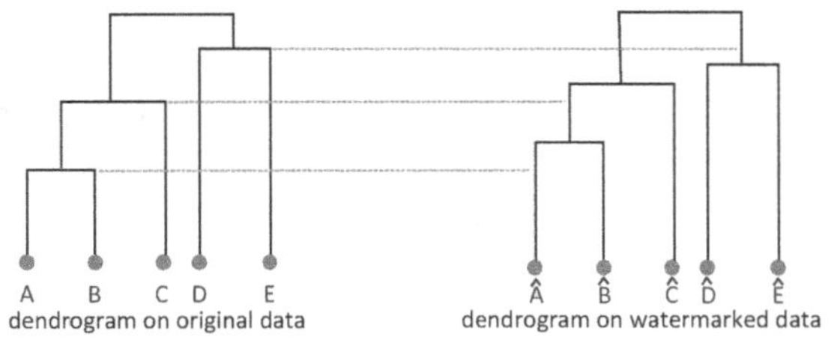

Figure 1: Our goal is to guarantee 'isomorphic' dendrograms before and after right-protection

It is essential to discover the maximum watermark intensity for right protection. This provides assurances of better detectability and hence security for the right-protection scheme. Therefore, we first study how (Euclidean) distances between the objects are distorted as a parameter of the watermark embedding strength. This provides insight into designing fast variants of our algorithms that still guarantee hierarchical clustering preservation, but operate significantly faster than the exhaustive algorithms.

Our paper is structured as follows: First, we describe how right-protection can be materialized via a spread-spectrum watermarking approach. We also show how to detect the watermark. Subsequently, we study the distortion of distances due to watermarking. We describe single- and complete-linkage algorithms and the necessary conditions to preserve them post-watermarking. We provide a theorem that gives tight lower and upper bounds on the distance distortion. We use it to design faster HC-preservation algorithms that are based on the bounds derived. Finally, we provide a comprehensive set of experiments, and we review the related work.

3. RIGHT PROTECTION THROUGH WATERMARKING

We describe first how watermarking mechanisms can embed a secret key (watermark) on a collection of objects. We demonstrate the techniques for 2D sequence data (image contours, trajectories, etc). We later demonstrate how to detect the watermark using a correlation filter.

3.1 Watermark Embedding

Assume an object represented as a vector of complex numbers $x = \{x_1, \ldots, x_n\}$, where $x_k = a_k + b_k i$ (i is the imaginary unit, $i^2 = -1$), and where the real and imaginary parts, a_k and b_k respectively, describe the coordinates of the k-th point of object x on the imaginary plain. Such a model can describe data trajectories or even image contour data which capture coordinates of a shape perimeter, as shown later in Figure 10.

We adapt a spread-spectrum approach [7]. This embeds the watermark across multiple frequencies of each object and across multiple objects of the dataset. As such, it renders the removal of the watermark particularly difficult without substantially compromising the data utility. An object x is mapped into the frequency domain using its complex Fourier descriptors $X = \{X_1, \ldots, X_n\}$. The mapping from the space domain to the frequency domain is described by the normalized discrete Fourier transform, $DFT(x)$, and its inverse, $IDFT(X)$. Every coefficient X_j can be expressed as a function of its *magnitude* δ_j and *phase* ϕ_j as $X_j = \delta_j e^{\phi_j i}$. The watermark constitutes a piece of *secret information* to be hidden inside each sequence. In our approach, we consider the watermark to be a vector $W \in \{-1, 0, +1\}^n$, which is embedded in all objects of the dataset.

DEFINITION 3.1. *(Watermark Embedding (W,p)) Given are a sequence $x \in \mathbb{C}^n$ with corresponding set of Fourier descriptors X, a watermark $W \in \mathbb{R}^n$ and power $p \in [0,1]$, which specifies the intensity of the watermark. A* ***multiplicative watermark embedding*** *(W,p) generates a watermarked sequence $\widehat{x}$ by replacing the magnitudes of each Fourier descriptor of x with a watermarked magnitude $\widehat{\delta_j}$ while not altering the phases, specifically:*

$$\widehat{\delta_j} = \delta_j \cdot (1 + pW_j) \ \ , \text{ and } \widehat{\phi_j} = \phi_j$$

Using the modified magnitudes $\widehat{\delta_j}$ and the original phases ϕ_j, we can revert from the frequency domain to the space domain and obtain the watermarked sequence using the inverse discrete Fourier transform. An overview of the methodology described is given in Fig. 2.

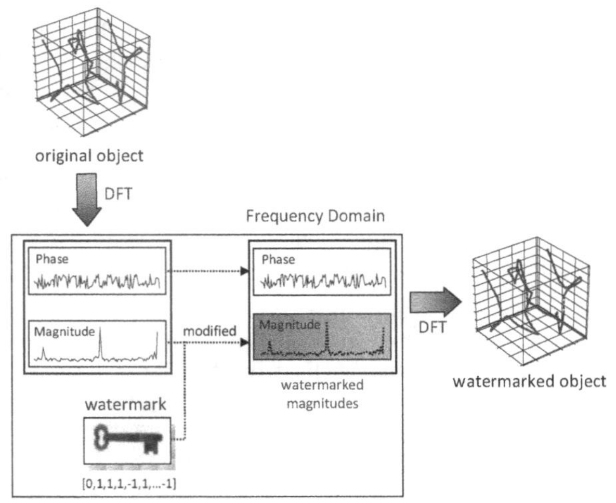

Figure 2: Overview of the right-protection process.

The robustness of the watermark embedding depends on the choice of coefficients. We embed the watermark in the coefficients that exhibit, on average over the dataset, the largest Fourier magnitudes. This makes the removal of the watermark difficult; masking it out (e.g. by noise addition) would mean that important frequencies of the dataset will be distorted. This would diminish the dataset utility. Fig. 3 shows the reconstruction of a shape from a dataset when approximated using the highest-energy coefficients. It is apparent that the high-energy coefficients capture important characteristics of the dataset.

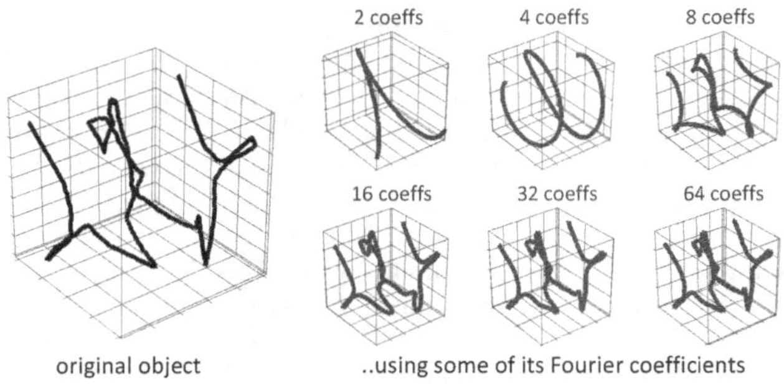

Figure 3: Object reconstruction for different number of Fourier coefficients that contain the highest energy.

Watermark Choice: Given dataset $\mathcal{D}$ and an even integer $2 \leq l \leq n$, we focus on the following class of watermarks:

DEFINITION 3.2. *(Class of watermarks $\mathcal{W}_l(\mathcal{D})$ with l non-zero elements, compatible with dataset $\mathcal{D}$)* The class of watermarks with l non-zero elements, compatible with dataset $\mathcal{D}$, *denoted by $\mathcal{W}_l(\mathcal{D})$, is the set of all $W \in \{-1, 0, +1\}^n$ that satisfy:*

$$W_j = \begin{cases} 0 & \text{if} \quad j = 1 \quad \text{(DC component)} \\ \{-1, 1\} & \text{if} \quad \mu_j(\mathcal{D}) \text{ is among the } l \text{ largest } \mu_{i \neq 1}(\mathcal{D}) \\ 0 & \text{otherwise} \end{cases} \tag{1}$$

as well as $\sum_{j=1}^{n} W_j = 0$.

Note that in the above definition we do not embed any part of the watermark in the first Fourier descriptor, X_1 (also called the DC component), but leave it intact. The DC component captures the center of mass of object x and is therefore highly susceptible to translational attacks. For example, if a part of the watermark were embedded on the DC component of an object then a simple translation would shift the center of mass of the object, thus rendering this part of the watermark useless without affecting the general shape of the object at all.

In summary, we embed the watermark in the magnitudes of the Fourier descriptors and leave the phases unchanged; we leave the DC component intact, and we watermark the Fourier descriptors with the largest average magnitudes.

Resilience to transformations: By construction, our right-protection mechanism provides resilience to geometric data transformations, such as rotation, translation, and scaling. Global object rotation is an intelligent attack because it distorts all coordinates of the objects, but pairwise distances remain the same. However, rotation in the frequency domain affects *only the phases* but not the magnitudes. Our watermark being embedded in the magnitude space will remain unaffected. Similarly, global translation of all objects only distorts the DC component, in which no part of the watermark was embedded. Scaling attacks can be addressed simply by normalizing all objects/sequences appropriately before watermark detection.

3.2 Watermark Detection

We measure the probability of existence of a watermark by evaluating the correlation between a tested watermark and the right-protected dataset. Measuring directly the correlation between the watermark and the magnitudes of Fourier descriptors may prove ineffective. The reason being that the original level of the average of magnitudes acts as background noise, masking the embedded watermark we seek to detect. We address this issue by explicitly recording the bias of average magnitudes before embedding the watermark, and removing it before the detection. We also record this bias vector along with the watermark W, and both are used jointly as the key.

For a dataset $\mathcal{D} = \{x^{(1)}, \ldots, x^{(|\mathcal{D}|)}\}$, we denote as $\delta_j^{x^{(i)}}$ the magnitude of the jth Fourier descriptor of object $x^{(i)}$ before watermarking. The average of the magnitudes of the jth Fourier descriptor across all objects in $\mathcal{D}$, denoted as $\mu_j(\mathcal{D})$, is given by

$$\mu_j(\mathcal{D}) := \frac{1}{|\mathcal{D}|} \sum_{i=1}^{|\mathcal{D}|} \delta_j^{x^{(i)}}. \tag{2}$$

We measure the correlation between a watermarked dataset $\widehat{\mathcal{D}}$ and watermark W as follows:

$$\chi(W, \widehat{\mathcal{D}}) := \left(\frac{\mu(\widehat{\mathcal{D}}) - \mu(\mathcal{D})}{\mu(\mathcal{D})} \right)^T W,$$

where the division is *element-wise*, excluding elements where $\mu_j(\mathcal{D}) = 0$. In other words, we remove the bias of average magnitudes before computing the correlation. The scheme enables a very effective detection of the watermark. We show briefly why; after elementary algebraic calculations, the correlation between a dataset watermarked with W and any other watermark W' is reduced to:

$$\chi(W', \widehat{\mathcal{D}}) \quad = pW^T W'$$

The quantity is maximized for $W' = W$, giving $\chi(W', \widehat{\mathcal{D}}) = pl$. So, for any $W' \neq W$, $\chi(W', \widehat{\mathcal{D}}) < \chi(W, \widehat{\mathcal{D}})$.

Recall that $\mu(\mathcal{D})$ is part of the watermark (key). This results in a very secure protocol. The reason being that a malicious attacker may try to discover the embedded key by probing different watermarks. However, the correlation depends on the vector $\mu(\mathcal{D})$, which the attacker has no way of knowing without access to the non-watermarked data.

4. HIERARCHICAL CLUSTERING PRESERVATION

Hierarchical clustering (HC) builds a nested hierarchy of groups of objects according to a given distance function. This nested hierarchy is called a dendrogram (see Fig. 1). A popular method of building a dendrogram is to use an agglomerative "bottom-up" approach: each data point starts in its own cluster, and pairs of clusters are merged iteratively until a single cluster remains. There exist different functions for evaluating the distance between clusters, leading to many variants of HC approaches, such as single- or complete linkage. We explain these in detail later on, and also show how to preserve them post-watermarking.

Our right-protection scheme operates in such a way that important object distances are preserved, leading to identical clustering structure irrespective of whether the data contains a watermark or not. It is important to strike a balance between security, i.e. detectability of the watermark, visual distortion of objects, and correctness of the clustering. Therefore, we seek to find the *maximum* embedding power p^* that does not distort the original dendrogram of the objects.

In certain cases, it may be possible to embed a watermark with high intensity and still maintain the dendrogram structure. This however, may lead to a visible distortion in an object's shape. Fig. 4 depicts how an object is distorted for increasingly larger watermark embedding powers. Therefore, in practice, we set an upper limit on the maximum allowed power, i.e., $p^* \in [p_{\min}, p_{\max}]$. In our experiments we used $p_{max} = 0.01$, therefore we allow up to 1% relative distortion. This assures that objects before and after watermarking will look virtually the same.

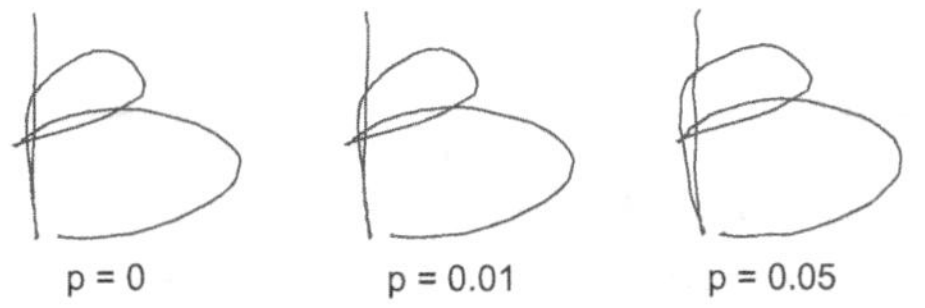

Figure 4: One object from a handwritten dataset (hand dataset) for different embedding powers of the watermark. Left: original object ($p = 0$). Middle: object distortion for $p = 0.01$. Right: object is more visibly distorted when the watermark is embedded with $p = 0.05$, corresponding to a 5% relative distortion.

Here, we study HC-preservation approaches that use the Euclidean distance between objects. We can also view pairwise relationships between objects as the edges of a complete graph. On this graph each edge $e = (x, y)$ connecting two objects x, y has weight (or length) equal to their distance $D(x, y)$. After right-protection, the edges of the dataset graph may change, because the new distance of objects x, y watermarked with power p will be $\widehat{D}_p(x, y)$. We want to ensure that important parts of the graph remain the same.

Note, also, that the function $\widehat{D}_p(x, y) = \sum_{j=1}^{n} \|(1 + pW_j)(X_j - Y_j)\|^2$ is a **parabola** with respect to the embedding power p (see Figure 7 for an example). We use this important observation to discover the appropriate lower or upper envelope of the parabolas, when we deal with single- or complete-linkage, respectively. More details on this will be provided later.

The next three definitions formalize the goal of hierarchical clustering preservation.

DEFINITION 4.1. *(Dendrogram) A dendrogram over $(\mathcal{D}, D)$ is a triplet (T, M, l) where T is a binary rooted tree, M : leaves$(T) \to \mathcal{D}$ is a bijection, and $l : V(T) \to \{0, \ldots, h\}$ (for some integer $h \geq 0$) such that (i) for every leaf node $u \in V(T), l(u) = 0$ and (ii) if $(u, v) \in E(T)$ then $l(u) > l(v)$.*

DEFINITION 4.2. *(Isomorphic Dendrograms) Dendrograms (T_0, M_0, l_0) and (T_1, M_1, l_1) are (order) isomorphic, if there exists a graph isomorphism $\phi : V(T_0) \to V(T_1)$ between the two trees T_0 and T_1, such that $\forall v, u \in V(T_0)$: $l_0(u) < l_0(v) \Leftrightarrow l_1(\phi(u)) < l_1(\phi(v))$.*

DEFINITION 4.3. *(Hierarchical Clustering Preservation Problem) Given a set of objects $\mathcal{D}$ and a range of feasible powers $[p_{\min}, p_{\max}]$, find the maximal embedding power p^* such that the dendrograms computed on $\mathcal{D}$ and $\widehat{\mathcal{D}}$ are isomorphic.*

4.1 Single-Linkage Clustering

Single-linkage hierarchical clustering operates as follows: initially each object belongs to its own cluster. The two clusters with the smallest distance are merged and the distances of the newly formed cluster to the old ones are updated. The process is repeated until only one cluster remains. The linkage function L that evaluates the distance between two clusters C_0 and C_1 is given by $L(C_0, C_1) := \min D(u, v)$, where $u \in C_0, v \in C_1$. Algorithm 1 gives a high-level description of the process. Note, that the naive algorithm requires $O(n^3)$ runtime, given n objects. More efficient algorithms exist in the literature that leverage additional data structures, such as priority queues or data structures for finding the *next-best-match*. These effectively reduce the runtime to $O(n^2)$. One such algorithm is SLINK [22].

Algorithm 1 Single-Linkage Algorithm

INPUTS: dataset $\mathcal{D}$
OUTPUT: Clustering $\mathcal{C}(i)$, $i \in [1, |\mathcal{D}|]$
$\mathcal{C}(1) := \mathcal{D}$ {Each object is its own cluster}
for $i = 1 \to |\mathcal{D}| - 1$ **do** {repeat until one cluster remains}
  Find clusters $M(i) := \{C_{m1}, C_{m2}\}$ of minimum distance $\{L(C_{m1}, C_{m2}) = \min_{C, C' \in \mathcal{C}(i)} L(C, C')\}$
  $\mathcal{C}(i+1) = \mathcal{C}(i) \setminus M(i) \cup \{C_{m1} \cup C_{m2}\}$ {Merge clusters}
end for

To guarantee that the dataset after watermarking yields the same dendrogram, we ensure that all mergers between clusters are the same, and that they are also executed in the same order. However, it is not important which objects between the clusters lead to the merger (i.e., which edge on the distance graph is shortest), as long as the same clusters are merged for both watermarked objects and non-watermarked objects. We wish to ensure that for every feasible watermark embedding power p the shortest edge is an edge between the two merged clusters and not between any other two clusters. Formally, if C_{m1} and C_{m2} are the clusters merged in the current step then:

$$p \text{ is feasible } \Leftrightarrow \forall i \text{ with } M(i) = \{C_{m1}, C_{m2}\} : \quad (3)$$

$$\min_{\substack{u \in C_{m1} \\ v \in C_{m2}}} \widehat{D}_p(u, v) \leq \min_{\substack{r \in C_1 \\ s \in C_2 \\ C_1 \neq C_2}} \widehat{D}_p(r, s)$$

To get the feasible powers p for a merger $M(i)$, defined by inequality (3), one must determine for every $p \in [p_{min}, p_{max}]$ whether the shortest distance is between the two merged clusters C_{m1} and C_{m2} or between any other two clusters. This is illustrated in Fig. 5. The two solid lines originating from $\widehat{C}$ represent graph edges between the two clusters. The three dashed lines from $\widehat{D}$ correspond to all graph edges in between any other two clusters. In terms of inequality (3), the solid edges belong to the left-hand side and the dashed edges to the right-hand side of the inequality.

Therefore, to discover the proper power p, we consider each edge $e = (x, y)$ on the distance graph and find the ranges of power p where the examined parabola $\widehat{D}_p(e)$ is smaller than all other relevant parabolas. All power ranges for which the current edge is not the smallest should be eliminated (see Fig. 6), because otherwise the dendrogram mergers will not happen in the same order.

Analytically, this boils down to finding the lower envelope of a set of parabolas. The lower envelope EN^l (see Figure

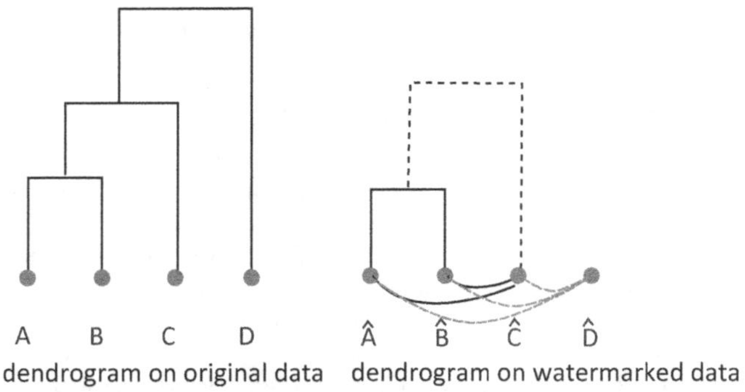

Figure 5: All relevant distances when computing the feasible powers to ensure the merger of clusters $\{\widehat{A}, \widehat{B}\}$ and $\widehat{C}$.

7) corresponds to a sequence of interleaving edges e of minimum distance and intersection points of the feasible powers p, i.e., $EN^l = (p_0 = p_{min}, e_0, p_1, e_1, p_2, e_2, ...e_m, p_{max})$, where $p_i \in [p_{min}, p_{max}]$ is an intersection point of e_i and e_{i+1}, i.e. $\widehat{D}_{p_i}(e_i) = \widehat{D}_{p_i}(e_{i+1})$. One might compute a separate lower envelope for all constraints on the left-hand side and right-hand side of inequality (3) and then compare the two envelopes to determine the feasible powers for a merger $M(i)$. It is somewhat simpler to just build a single parabola containing all parabolas from the left- and right-hand side of inequality (3). This is essentially what our Algorithm 2 does. We can achieve that very efficiently using the algorithm presented in [9] to compute the compound envelope.

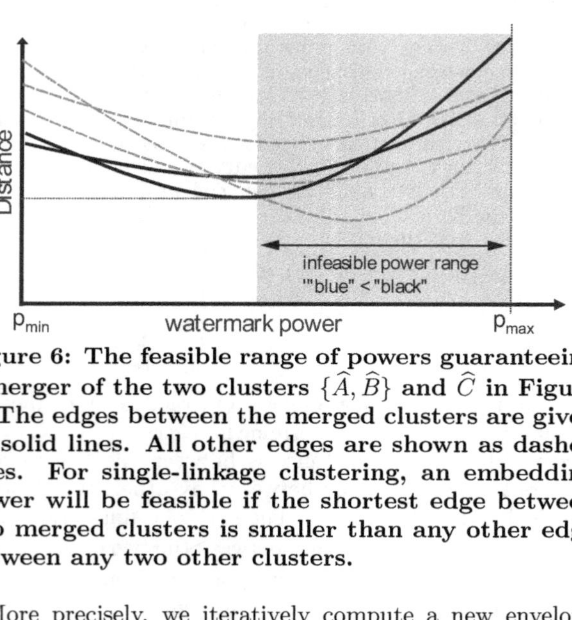

Figure 6: The feasible range of powers guaranteeing a merger of the two clusters $\{\widehat{A}, \widehat{B}\}$ and $\widehat{C}$ in Figure 5. The edges between the merged clusters are given by solid lines. All other edges are shown as dashed lines. For single-linkage clustering, an embedding power will be feasible if the shortest edge between two merged clusters is smaller than any other edge between any two other clusters.

More precisely, we iteratively compute a new envelope EN^l using all edges E in the prior envelope except the edges E' (line 8) that are between the previously merged clusters C_{m1} and C_{m2}. We go through all mergers (see line 5) in ascending order, i.e., let $M(i) = \{C_{m1}, C_{m2}\}$ be the merger currently considered. We compute the lower envelope EN^l according to [9] (line 9). Then we consider all edges $e \in E'$ that have been added to EN^l (line 10). If an edge e is not in the envelope then there are edges of smaller distance for every power $p \in [p_{min}, p_{max}]$. Thus, edge e has no influence on the feasible powers. It no longer has to be considered. If edge e is part of EN^l, say e corresponds to edge $e_j \in EN$, then the range of powers $[p_j, p_{j+1}]$ is feasible. This range $[p_j, p_{j+1}]$ is added to the set of feasible power ranges $pRanges(M(i))$. At the end of the algorithm (line 15), we compute the intersection of all $pRanges(M(i))$ to determine the maximum power p^* that yields the same mergers for watermarked and non-watermarked data.

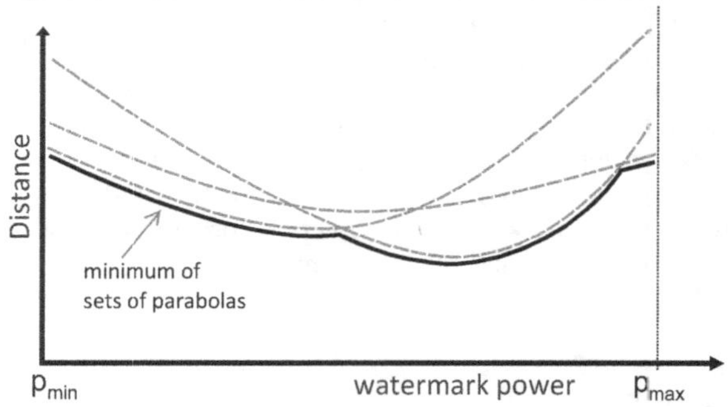

Figure 7: Dashed line shows the distance function $\widehat{D}_p(x, y)$ for an edge $e = (x, y)$. The solid line corresponds to the lower envelope, i.e., the minimum distance for every power p for a set of edges, e.g., between two clusters. For single-linkage clustering only the minimum distance is relevant.

Algorithm 2 Single-Linkage Preservation Algorithm

1: **INPUTS: dataset $\mathcal{D}$, watermark $W \in \mathcal{W}(D), p_{min}, p_{max}$**
2: **OUTPUT:** p^*
3: *den* $\leftarrow$ dendrogram on original data $\mathcal{D}$, e.g. using SLINK[22]
4: $E := \{(u, v) | u, v \in \mathcal{D}\}$ {set of all edges}
5: **for** $i = 1 \rightarrow |\mathcal{D}| - 1$ **do**
6: $\quad\mathcal{C} \leftarrow$ set of clusters before ith merger $M(i)$ in *den*
7: $\quad\{C_{m1}, C_{m2}\} \leftarrow$ clusters merged at ith merger $M(i)$ in *den*
8: $\quad E' \leftarrow \{(u, v) | u \in C_{m1}, C_{m2}\}$
9: $\quad EN^l :=$ lower envelope EN^l of edges E using [9]
10: $\quad$**for all** $e_j \in (E' \cap EN^l)$ **do** {edges between the merged clusters that are in the envelope}
11: $\quad\quad pRanges(M(i)) := pRanges(M(i)) \cup [p_j, p_{j+1}]$
12: $\quad$**end for**
13: $\quad E := E \setminus E'$ {Remove edges between merged clusters}
14: **end for**
15: $p^* = \max\{p \in \left(\bigcap_{1 \leq i < |\mathcal{D}|} pRanges(M(i))\right) \bigcap [p_{min}, p_{max}]\}$

Complexity: Construction of the Single-Linkage Dendrogram requires $O(|\mathcal{D}|^2)$ time [22]. Computation of the lower envelope using $O(|\mathcal{D}|^2)$ elements takes $O(|\mathcal{D}|^2 \log |\mathcal{D}|)$ using [9]. When computing the lower envelope EN^l, we become immediately see which edges $e \in E'$ are added between merged clusters, i.e. the intersection edges $E' \cap EN^l$ (line 10) does not add to the time complexity. Combining this, the outer for loop (line 5) takes time $O(|\mathcal{D}|^3 \log |\mathcal{D}|)$. Computing the intersections of feasible powers $pRanges(M(i))$ of individual mergers takes time $O(|\mathcal{D}|^2 \log |\mathcal{D}|)$: There are in total (for all $M(i)$ together) at most as many edges as intervals of feasible powers $[p_j, p_{j+1}]$, i.e., $O(|\mathcal{D}|^2)$. Sorting the power intervals in each $pRanges(M(i))$ according to the left end point and merging the different sorted intervals $pRanges(M(i))$ yields the time complexity.

4.2 Complete Linkage Clustering

Just like single-linkage, complete-linkage hierarchical clustering merges two clusters according to a different linkage function L. The distance L between two clusters of nodes

C_0 and C_1 is given by the maximal distance of a pair of nodes in distinct clusters, i.e. $L(C_0, C_1) := \max_{x \in C_0, y \in C_1} D(x, y)$. Therefore, we are not interested in the edges of smallest distance between clusters but in edges of maximum distance. This changes the (number of) relevant constraints significantly. Instead of a single constraint for each merger, a constraint for every pair of clusters is required. We define $M(i)$, $\mathcal{C}(i)$, EN in the same way as in the previous section.

$$p \text{ is feasible} \Leftrightarrow \forall i \text{ with } M(i) = \{C_{m1}, C_{m2}\}: \quad (4)$$
$$\forall C_1, C_2 \in \mathcal{C}(i), C_1 \neq C_2:$$
$$\max_{\substack{u \in C_{m1} \\ v \in C_{m2}}} \widehat{D}_p(u,v) \leq \max_{\substack{r \in C_1 \\ s \in C_2}} \widehat{D}_p(r,s)$$

Algorithm 3 for complete-linkage clustering preservation is more involved than Algorithm 2 for single-linkage. We have to deal with the min-max relationship due to the complete linkage criterion expressed in Inequalities (4), i.e., merge the two clusters with minimum maximum distance of two nodes. This requires to maintain a set of upper envelopes $\mathcal{EN}^u$, i.e. for each pair of clusters $C_1, C_2 \in \mathcal{C}$ there is an envelope $EN^u(C_1, C_2) \in \mathcal{EN}^u$. To get the minimal maximum distance, we compute a lower envelope EN^l for the edges in the upper envelopes.

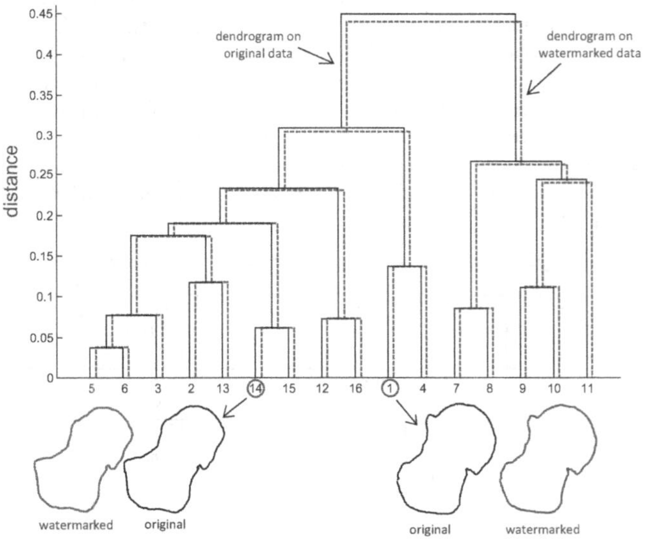

Figure 8: Preservation of complete-linkage dendrogram by watermarking (largest possible power $p = 0.0221$).

An overview of the process is given in Algorithm 3. Initially, a clustering of non-watermarked objects is computed using the CLINK algorithm [8]. We maintain a set of upper envelopes for any pair of clusters, i.e., $\mathcal{EN}^u := \{EN^u(C_1, C_2) | C_1, C_2 \in \mathcal{C}\}$. Computing the upper and lower envelope are equivalent problems, thus we can use [9] for lower envelopes with some adjustments[2]. Originally, when each object is a cluster, the upper envelope between two clusters is given by the edge between the two objects (line 4 of Algorithm 3). To get all feasible powers for merger $M(i) = \{C_{m1}, C_{m2}\}$ we compute a lower envelope EN^l consisting of the union of all edges contained in any upper envelopes $EN^u(C_1, C_2)$ of any pair $C_1, C_2 \in \mathcal{C}$. For any edge e_j between the merged clusters $\{C_{m1}, C_{m2}\}$ that is also in the lower envelope EN^l (line 12) we add the power range $[p_j, p_{j+1}]$ for which edge e_j is smallest to the feasible powers *pRanges*$(M(i))$. After a merger $M(i) = \{C_{m1}, C_{m2}\}$ all upper envelopes between pairs containing either C_{m1} or C_{m2} must be adjusted to keep $\mathcal{EN}^u$ up-to-date. We delete all upper envelopes of pairs involving any of two merged clusters C_{m1} or C_{m2} from $\mathcal{EN}^u$. Then a new upper envelope $EN^u(C_{m1} \cup C_{m2}, C)$ for each $C \in \mathcal{C}(i) \setminus \{C_{m1}, C_{m2}\}$ is added to $\mathcal{EN}^u$. After having gone through all mergers i in ascending order, we finally compute the intersection of all *pRanges*$(M(i))$ giving the maximum power p^*.

[2]e.g. in [9] Section 4, replace the lower envelope function $F(x) = \min_{i \leq n} p_i(x)$ by $F(x) = \max_{i \leq n} p_i(x)$. In Lemma 5 use $F_{i+1}(x) = \max(p_{i+1}(x), F_i(x))$

Algorithm 3 Complete-Linkage Preservation Algorithm

1: **INPUTS: dataset $\mathcal{D}$, watermark $W \in \mathcal{W}(D)$,** p_{min}, p_{max}
2: **OUTPUT:** p^*
3: *den* $\leftarrow$ dendrogram on original data $\mathcal{D}$, e.g. using CLINK[8]
4: $EN^u(u,v) := \{p_{min}, e = (u,v), p_{max}\}$ {upper envelope of one edge}
5: $\mathcal{EN}^u := \{EN^u(u,v) | u, v \in \mathcal{D}\}$ {set of upper envelopes}
6: **for** $i = 1 \rightarrow (|\mathcal{D}| - 1)$ **do**
7: $\quad \mathcal{C} \leftarrow$ set of clusters before ith merger $M(i)$ in *den*
8: $\quad \{C_{m1}, C_{m2}\} \leftarrow$ clusters merged at ith merger $M(i)$ in *den*
9: $\quad$ /*– Compute feasible powers *pRanges*$(M(i))$ –*/
10: $\quad$ Compute lower envelope EN^l consisting of all edges in the upper envelopes in $\mathcal{EN}^u$ using [9]
11: $\quad E' \leftarrow \{(u,v) | u \in C_{m1}, v \in C_{m2}\}$
12: $\quad$ **for all** $e_j \in (E' \cap EN^l)$ **do** {edges between the merged clusters that are in the envelope}
13: $\quad\quad$ *pRanges*$(M(i))$:= *pRanges*$(M(i)) \cup [p_j, p_{j+1}]$
14: $\quad$ **end for**
15: $\quad$ /*– Update upper envelopes $\mathcal{EN}^u$ –*/
16: $\quad$ Remove $\{EN^u(C_{m1}, C), EN^u(C_{m2}, C) | C \in \mathcal{C}\}$ from $\mathcal{EN}^u$
17: $\quad$ **for all** $C \in \mathcal{C} \setminus \{C_{m1}, C_{m2}\}$ **do**
18: $\quad\quad$ Compute envelopes for newly merged cluster $C_{m1} \cup C_{m2}$ and C to $EN^u(C_{m1} \cup C_{m2}, C)$
19: $\quad$ **end for**
20: **end for**
21: $p^* = \max\{p \in \left(\bigcap_{1 \leq i < |\mathcal{D}|} pRanges(M(i))\right) \bigcap [p_{min}, p_{max}]\}$

Complexity: Construction of the Complete-Linkage Dendrogram requires $O(|\mathcal{D}|^2)$ time [8]. Computation of the lower envelope EN^l using [9] (line 10) takes $O(|\mathcal{D}|^2 \log |\mathcal{D}|)$. When adding an edge $e \in E'$ to envelope EN^l, we become immediately aware whether the edge becomes part of EN^l (or is too large for all powers). Thus determining the edges between merged clusters that are part of the lower envelope, i.e. $E' \cap EN^l$, (line 12) causes no costs. In iteration i of the for-loop (line 6) there are $|\mathcal{D}| - i$ clusters remaining. Computing the upper envelopes $\mathcal{EN}^u$ requires deleting $O(|\mathcal{D}|)$ envelopes and adding at most $O(|\mathcal{D}|)$ upper envelopes. More precisely, the number of edges within upper envelope $EN^u(C_{m1} \cup C_{m2}, C)$ with $C \in \mathcal{C} \setminus \{C_{m1}, C_{m2}\}$ is given by $|C_{m1} \cup C_{m2}||C|$. Thus the total number is given by $|C_{m1} \cup C_{m2}| \sum_{C \in \mathcal{C}} |C|$. Each object is in exactly one cluster, i.e. $\sum_{C \in \mathcal{C}} |C| = |\mathcal{D}|$. Therefore, $|C_{m1} \cup C_{m2}| \sum_{C \in \mathcal{C}} |C| \leq |C_{m1} \cup C_{m2}||\mathcal{D}| \leq |\mathcal{D}|^2$. The algorithm in [9] runs in $O(|\mathcal{D}|^2 \log |\mathcal{D}|)$. Therefore the running time of the for-loop (line 6) is bounded by $O(|\mathcal{D}|^3 \log |\mathcal{D}|)$. Computing the intersections of feasible powers *pRanges*$(M(i))$ of individual mergers takes time $O(|\mathcal{D}|^2 \log |\mathcal{D}|)$ as for Algorithm 2.

5. FAST ALGORITHMS

Here we derive faster variants of the previous HC-preservation algorithms. They are based on a study of the distance distortion due to the multiplicative watermarking.

THEOREM 5.1. *For any two watermarked objects $\widehat{x}, \widehat{y} \in \widehat{\mathcal{D}}$, their Euclidean distance denoted as $D_p(\widehat{x}, \widehat{y})$ is lower and upper bounded by the Euclidean distance of the non-watermarked objects $x, y \in \mathcal{D}$ as follows:*

$$(1-p)D(x,y) \leq D_p(\widehat{x}, \widehat{y}) \leq (1+p)D(x,y)$$

The proof can be found in the Appendix. Fig. 9 illustrates it.

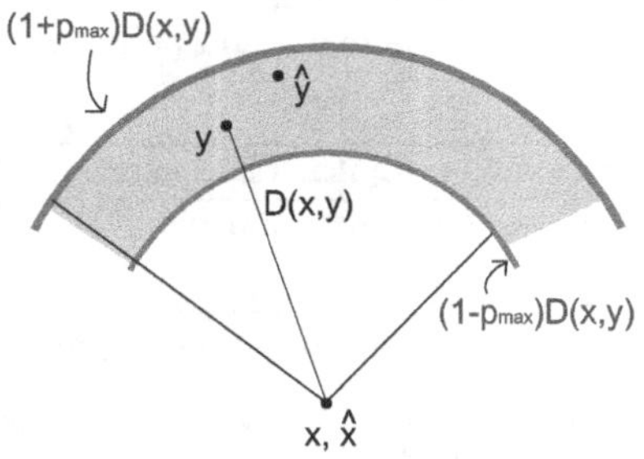

Figure 9: Two objects cannot get arbitrarily close or arbitrarily far after the watermark embedding. In this figure we represent objects as points for presentational purposes. To better illustrate the distortion bounds, objects $\widehat{x}, \widehat{y}$ are globally translated so that x and $\widehat{x}$ coincide.

We can exploit Theorem 5.1 to prune the search space while preserving the clustering structure. Namely, if for two edges e' and e'' we know that the upper bound for one of them is lower than the lower bound for the other, then those two edges will not intersect. Therefore, if for edges e' and e'' holds that:

$$(1+p_{\max})D(e') < (1-p_{\max})D(e'')$$

or

$$(1+p_{\max})D(e'') < (1-p_{\max})D(e')$$

then using Theorem 5.1 we can be sure that edge e' will be shorter than e'' (or e'' shorter than e', respectively) for any feasible power $p \in [0, p_{max}]$. Thus, there is no need to search for their intersection. After adding an edge e' to the lower envelope in Algorithm [9] (line 9 of Algorithm 2) we can therefore avoid computing the intersection of edges e' and e'' to update the envelope, i.e. figure out which edges to remove from the envelope due to the addition of e'. Indeed, the algorithm can avoid the computation for e' and e'' if:

$$\frac{1-p_{\max}}{1+p_{\max}} \leq \frac{D(e'')}{D(e')} \leq \frac{1+p_{\max}}{1-p_{\max}}$$

thus affecting significantly the number of quadratic inequalities to be solved.

In the experimental section that follows, we show that the use of lower- and upper-bounds on the watermarked distance can lead to reduction of the search space that ranges from one (1) to three (3) orders of magnitude.

6. EXPERIMENTAL EVALUATION

In this section, we evaluate the presented schemes. First, we verify that our right-protection methodology discovers the maximum watermarking power that correctly preserves the original dendrogram. Then, we compare the fast algorithms proposed in Section 5 to their exhaustive counterparts cf. Section 4, in terms of number of operations. We report major speed-ups. Finally, we assess the resilience of our scheme against a broad range of potential attacks: geometric distortions, resampling, etc.

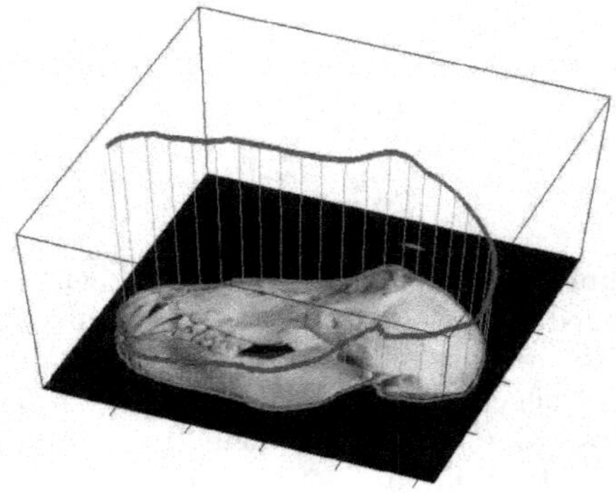

Figure 10: Image shapes can also be treated as two-dimensional sequences by extracting the perimeter of a shape.

We test our methods on datasets from various application areas: mobility data (taxi trajectories in Beijing [32, 33] and San Francisco [21]), financial data (stock prices in the NASDAQ stock market), video-tracking data, handwritten data, and image contour data from anthropology and natural sciences (the latter datasets were obtained from [15]). The characteristics of our datasets are summarized in Table 1. All experiments have been executed on a 2.16GHz Intel CPU with 3GB RAM.

Name	Data Type	Points/Object	Objects
nasdaq	Stock Prices	1000	500
taxiSF	Taxi Traj. SF	5000	516
taxiBeijing	Taxi Traj. Beijing	1411	1063
skulls	Image Contour	1500	16
fish	Image Contour	256	247
video1	Video-Tracking	1500	15
video2	Video-Tracking	500	23
hand	Handwritten	128	90

Table 1: Datasets used in the experiments.

6.1 Preservation of Distance Relations

Here we evaluate whether the single- and complete-linkage preservation algorithms discover the correct embedding power for the watermark so the dendrograms both on the original and the watermarked data remain isomorphic. This means that both the tree structure and the order of the merger points $M(i)$ are the same. A sample comparison of a dendrogram resulting from the complete linkage procedure of the original data and of the watermarked data was presented in Figure 8. In Figure 11 we show the distortion of the dendrogram that occurs when a watermark is embedded with power $p > p^*$. Indeed, even a slightly increased value of the power results in alterations in the resulting dendrogram. We report the maximal power p^* that the algorithms returned which resulted in all cases in total dendrogram preservation. The same maximal embedding power was returned by both exhaustive and fast variants of the algorithms. Table 2 summarizes our findings.

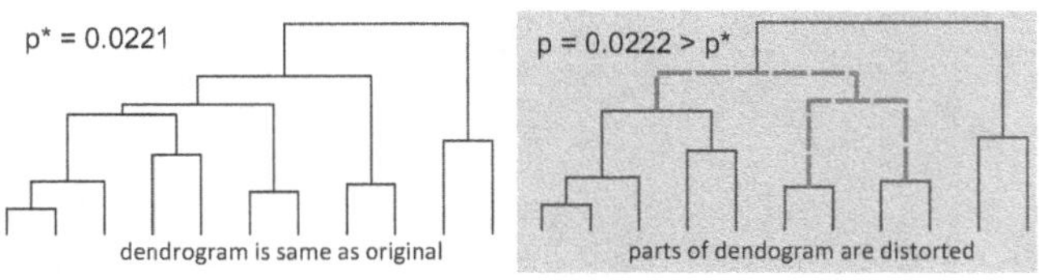

Figure 11: Dendrogram portion for the skulls dataset. Left: dendrogram for maximum discovered $p^* = 0.0221$ is same as original. Right: for even slightly larger $p = 0.0222$ the dendrogram changes.

Dataset	Single linkage p^*	Single linkage Pres.	Complete linkage p^*	Complete linkage Pres.
nasdaq	$0.77 \cdot 10^{-4}$	100%	$0.243 \cdot 10^{-3}$	100%
taxiSF	$0.47 \cdot 10^{-4}$	100%	$0.97 \cdot 10^{-4}$	100%
taxiBeijing	$0.4 \cdot 10^{-5}$	100%	$0.28 \cdot 10^{-4}$	100%
skulls	$0.1 \cdot 10^{-1}$	100%	$0.1 \cdot 10^{-1}$	100%
fish	$0.229 \cdot 10^{-3}$	100%	$0.122 \cdot 10^{-3}$	100%
video1	$0.39 \cdot 10^{-2}$	100%	$0.1 \cdot 10^{-1}$	100%
video2	$0.1 \cdot 10^{-1}$	100%	$0.1 \cdot 10^{-1}$	100%
hand	$0.2271 \cdot 10^{-2}$	100%	$0.116 \cdot 10^{-3}$	100%

Table 2: Maximal watermarking power p^* and the percentage of dendrogram preservation.

6.2 Comparison of Algorithms

Now we compare the efficiency of the fast dendrogram preservation algorithms. With the use of the lower- and upper-bounds on the distance distortion, the fast variants can eliminate many pairs of objects from examination. This reduction leads to solving fewer quadratic inequalities in the progress of the algorithm. We record exactly how many quadratic inequalities we need to solve with each algorithm. Note, that this is also a CPU-agnostic measure and therefore does not depend on any runtime optimization.

Table 3 summarizes the results of single-linkage preservation. The pruning efficiency is reported as the ratio of the number of inequalities solved by the exhaustive algorithms, compared to the fast algorithms. The use of the bounds on the distance distortion (Section 5) results in considerable speedup in terms of solved inequalities; up to 3 orders of magnitude. Table 4 reports the results of the same experiment for the case of complete-linkage preservation.

Dataset	Single-L	Fast Single-L	Pruning
nasdaq	22,039,601	16,854	**1,308**×
taxiSF	23,032,154	5,993	**3,843**×
taxiBeijing	214,304,616	161,305	**1,329**×
skulls	770	16	**48**×
fish	2,895,694	8,425	**344**×
video1	637	23	**28**×
video2	2,311	40	**58**×
hand	129,377	976	**133**×

Table 3: Number of quadratic inequalities solved for different datasets, single linkage ($p_{min} = 0$, $p_{max} = 0.01$).

Dataset	Complete-L	Fast Complete-L	Pruning
nasdaq	21,187,434	36,280	**584**×
taxiSF	28,667,907	91,039	**315**×
taxiBeijing	322,436,544	393,970	**818**×
skulls	770	14	**55**×
fish	2,618,789	9,552	**274**×
video1	646	29	**22**×
video2	2,260	54	**42**×
hand	126,953	1,113	**114**×

Table 4: Number of quadratic inequalities solved for different datasets, complete linkage ($p_{min} = 0$, $p_{max} = 0.01$).

6.3 Resilience to Attacks

Here, we test the resiliency to potential attacks of the right-protection scheme . We right protect the dataset by inserting a watermark with the maximum allowed embedding power that preserves the dendrogram (we test on the power that preserves single-linkage clustering). We measure how detectable is the embedded watermark under a series of attacks: addition of Gaussian noise in the space and in the frequency domain, up- and down-sampling, and geometric transformations (rotation, translation, scaling). Fig. 12 depicts the ROC curves representing true- versus false-positives rates. We also report the performance of a random baseline, that randomly classifies the dataset as having or not having the watermark embedded. Due to lack of space, we only report ROC curves for four datasets. However, the results for the remaining ones were very similar.

We observe that our detection method works very effectively. It is more than 4 orders of magnitude more effective than the random baseline. In addition, the graphs exhibit a large area under-the-curve, suggesting high detectability and therefore high resilience to attacks.

7. RELATED WORK

Watermarking is a steganographic technique used for establishing the ownership, with many applications in multimedia datasets [7], such as images [18], vector graphics [19], audio [4, 27] and video [24, 34]. Multimedia watermarking focuses on the protection of a *single* object whilst minimizing visual/audible distortions of the data. In contrast, our setting operates on a collection of objects and at the same time accounts for preservation of distance relations between objects. More importantly, our scenario incorporates additional constraints in the form of guaranteeing identical outputs, after watermarking, for a class of mining and learning algorithms based on hierarchical clustering.

Privacy-preserving techniques are also related to our work, because they also alter data but enforce different constraints. To achieve privacy-preservation two research paths are typically followed: a) protection through data alteration or masking, and b) protection through dataset partition. *Data alteration* can be achieved via noise addition [14, 13], condensation [2] or data transformation [5, 20]. Similar notions have also been used for watermarking databases [3, 25]. Contrary to the above approaches, we do not attempt to reconstruct the original data distribution but work *directly* on the perturbed data, while guaranteeing preservation of distance properties on them.

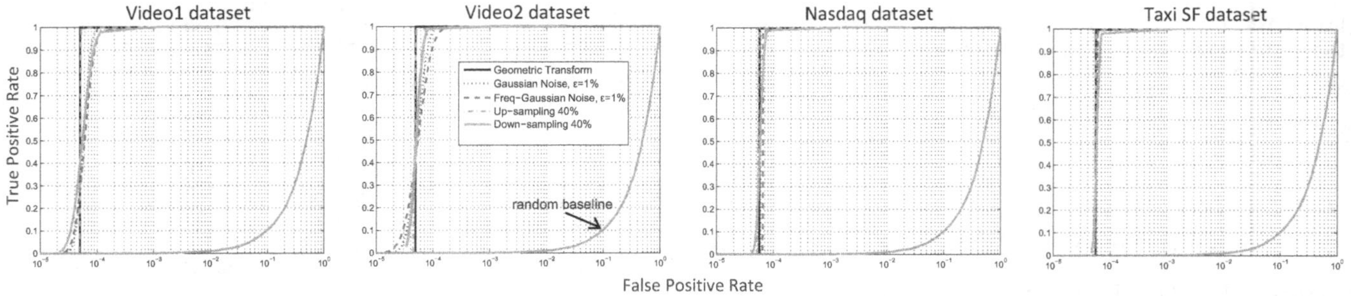

Figure 12: ROC curves for watermark detection corresponding to geometric transformations, noise addition, noise addition in the frequency domain, upsampling, and downsampling on different datasets.

Privacy-protection via *dataset partition* is achieved using horizontal or vertical data partitioning [29, 12, 30, 31]. Different portions of the data are distributed to different sites, and data exchange without leakage of private information becomes possible through cryptographic techniques (multi-party computation). The techniques in our approach are fundamentally different; the dataset is not dissected in portions, but is distributed as a whole.

Of relevance is also the work on watermarking streaming time-series [26]. Differently from our approach, they examine watermarking on a *single* numerical sequence, as opposed to considering a collection of sequences. We also aim at maintaining the original pairwise relationships and we consider resilience even under geometric data transformations (rotations, etc).

In summary, our setting presents additional challenges compared to traditional watermarking or privacy preservation techniques, because not only do we work directly on the perturbed data, but more importantly, we provide *provable guarantees* on preservation of distance properties. A right-protection scheme based on watermarking principles that preserved the Nearest Neighbor of objects was presented in [15]. We adopt the watermarking model of that work, but here we study the more elaborate case of hierarchical clustering preservation. In addition, we provide a thorough theoretical analysis on the distance distortion under a multiplicative watermarking process. We leverage the theoretical analysis, first presented in this work, to obtain fast versions of the exhaustive algorithms that we put forward, and we demonstrate substantial speed-up in all experiments, without any sacrifice in accuracy.

8. CONCLUSION

Right protection of a dataset presents an inherent engineering tradeoff: the protection should be strong enough to offer robustness of detection, but at the same time not so dominant to destroy the utility of the dataset for subsequent mining operations. We propose a watermarking technique that identifies an optimal compromise between the two conflicting factors. We design algorithms that find the maximum embedding power that guarantees preservation of hierarchical clustering operations on the modified dataset. The fast variants that we put forward can reduce the search space by more than 3000 times compared to the exhaustive algorithms, with no sacrifice in accuracy. Our analysis is generic and delivers great promise for a broader applicability for an extended class of distance-based mining operations, such as anomaly detection, classification and visualization.

9. REFERENCES

[1] The Human Genome Project. In *U.S. National Library of Medicine*, 2012.

[2] C. C. Aggarwal and P. S. Yu. A condensation approach to privacy preserving data mining. In *International Conference on Extending Database Technology*, pages 183–199, 2004.

[3] R. Agrawal and J. Kiernan. Watermarking relational databases. In *28th International Conference on Very Large Databases*, pages 155–166, 2002.

[4] P. Bassia and I. Pitas. Robust audio watermarking in the time domain. In *9th European Signal Processing Conference*, pages 25–28, 1998.

[5] K. Chen and L. Liu. Privacy preserving data classification with rotation perturbation. In *International Conference on Data Mining*, pages 589–592, 2005.

[6] E. Cope and G. Antonini. Observed correlations and dependencies among operational losses in the ORX consortium database. In *Journal of Operational Risk*, 2008.

[7] I. J. Cox, J. Kilian, F. T. Leighton, and T. Shamoon. Secure spread spectrum watermarking for multimedia. *IEEE Transactions on Image Processing*, 6(12):1673–1687, 1997.

[8] D. Defays. An efficient algorithm for a complete link method. *Comput. J.*, 20(4):364–366, 1977.

[9] O. Devillers and M. J. Golin. Incremental algorithms for finding the convex hulls of circles and the lower envelopes of parabolas. *Inf. Process. Lett.*, 56(3):157–164, 1995.

[10] I. M. Faniel and A. Zimmerman. Beyond the Data Deluge: A Research Agenda for Large-Scale Data Sharing and Reuse. In *Proc. of 6th International Digital Curation Conference*, 2010.

[11] R. Geambasu, S. D. Gribble, and H. M. Levy. CloudViews: Communal Data Sharing in Public Clouds. In *Proc. of HotCloud*, 2009.

[12] G. Jagannathan, K. Pillaipakkamnatt, and R. N. Wright. A new privacy-preserving distributed k-clustering algorithm. In *SIAM International Conference on Data Mining*, 2006.

[13] H. Kargupta, S. Datta, Q. Wang, and K. Sivakumar. On the privacy preserving properties of random data perturbation techniques. In *3rd IEEE International Conference on Data Mining*, pages 99–106, 2003.

[14] L. Liu, M. Kantarcioglu, and B. Thuraisingham. The

applicability of the perturbation model-based privacy preserving data mining for real-world data. In *6th IEEE International Conference on Data Mining*, pages 507–512, 2006.

[15] C. Lucchese, M. Vlachos, D. Rajan, and P. S. Yu. Rights protection of trajectory datasets with nearest-neighbor preservation. *The VLDB Journal*, 19(4):531–556, 2010.

[16] W. Ludwig and H.-P. Klenk. Overview: A phylogenetic backbone and taxonomic framework for prokaryotic systematics. In *Manual of Systematic Bacteriology*, pages 49–65, 2001.

[17] M. C. Mont, I. Matteucci, M. Petrocchi, and M. L. Sbodio. Enabling Data Sharing in the Cloud. In *HP Laboratories, Tech Report HPL-2012-22*, 2012.

[18] P. Moulin, M. E. Mihcak, and G.-I. Lin. An information-theoretic model for image watermarking and data hiding. In *IEEE International Conference on Image Processing*, pages 667–670, 2000.

[19] X. Niu, C. Shao, and X. Wang. A survey of digital vector map watermarking. *International Journal of Innovative Computing, Information and Control*, 2(6):1301–1316, 2006.

[20] S. Oliveira and O. Zaiane. Privacy preserving clustering by data transformation. In *18th Brazilian Symposium on Databases*, pages 304–318, 2003.

[21] M. Piorkowski, N. Sarafijanovoc-Djukic, and M. Grossglauser. A Parsimonious Model of Mobile Partitioned Networks with Clustering. In *The First International Conference on COMmunication Systems and NETworkS (COMSNETS)*, January 2009.

[22] R. Sibson. Slink: An optimally efficient algorithm for the single-link cluster method. *Comput. J.*, 16(1):30–34, 1973.

[23] J. V. Sickle. Using Mean Similarity Dendrograms to Evaluate Classifications. In *Journal of Agricultural, Biological and Environmental Statistics*, pages 370–384, 2001.

[24] D. Simitopoulos, S. A. Tsaftaris, N. V. Boulgouris, and M. G. Strintzis. Compressed-domain video watermarking of MPEG streams. In *IEEE International Conference on Multimedia and Expo*, volume 1, pages 569–572, 2002.

[25] R. Sion, M. Atallah, and S. Prabhakar. Rights protection for relational data. *IEEE Transactions on Knowledge and Data Engineering*, 16(12):1509–1525, 2004.

[26] R. Sion, M. J. Atallah, and S. Prabhakar. Rights Protection for Discrete Numeric Streams. *IEEE Transactions on Knowledge and Data Engineering*, 18(5):699–714, 2006.

[27] M. D. Swanson, B. Zhu, A. H. Tewfik, and L. Boney. Robust audio watermarking using perceptual masking. *Signal Processing*, 66(3):337–355, 1998.

[28] A. Z. V. Zabkar. Application of End-Users Market Segmentation using Statistical Methods. In *Advances in Methodology and Statistics (19)*, 2003.

[29] J. Vaidya and C. Clifton. Privacy-preserving k-means clustering over vertically partitioned data. In *9th ACM SIGKDD International Conference on Knowledge Discovery and Data Mining*, pages 206–215, 2003.

[30] H. Yu, X. Jiang, and J. Vaidya. Privacy-preserving SVM using nonlinear kernels on horizontally partitioned data. In *ACM Symposium on Applied Computing*, pages 603–610, 2006.

[31] H. Yu, J. Vaidya, and X. Jiang. Privacy-preserving SVM classification on vertically partitioned data. In *10th Pacific-Asia Conference on Knowledge Discovery and Data Mining*, pages 647–656, 2006.

[32] J. Yuan, Y. Zheng, X. Xie, and G. Sun. Driving with knowledge from the physical world. In *KDD*, pages 316–324, 2011.

[33] J. Yuan, Y. Zheng, C. Zhang, W. Xie, X. Xie, G. Sun, and Y. Huang. T-drive: driving directions based on taxi trajectories. In *GIS*, pages 99–108, 2010.

[34] W. Zhu, Z. Xiong, and Y.-Q. Zhang. Multiresolution watermarking for images and video. *IEEE Transactions on Circuits and Systems for Video Technology*, 9(4):545–550, 1999.

Appendix

Proof of Theorem 5.1: The squared Euclidean distance can be expressed in the time or frequency domain as: $D^2(x,y) = \|x - y\|^2 = \|X - Y\|^2$. The same objects x and y after watermarking with power p have distance:

$$\begin{aligned}\widehat{D}_p^2(x,y) &= \|\widehat{x} - \widehat{y}\|^2 = \|\widehat{X} - \widehat{Y}\|^2 = \sum_{j=1}^{n} \|\widehat{X_j} - \widehat{Y_j}\|^2 \\ &= \sum_{j=1}^{n} \|(1+pW_j)X_j - (1+pW_j)Y_j\|^2 \\ &= \sum_{j=1}^{n} \|(1+pW_j)(X_j - Y_j)\|^2\end{aligned}$$

However, because $W_j \in \{0,1,-1\}$, we get the following bounds:

$$\begin{aligned}\sum_{j=1}^{n} \|(1-p)(X_j - Y_j)\|^2 &\leq \widehat{D}_p^2(x,y) \leq \sum_{j=1}^{n} \|(1+p)(X_j - Y_j)\|^2 \\ \Leftrightarrow (1-p)^2\|X - Y\|^2 &\leq \widehat{D}_p^2(x,y) \leq (1+p)^2\|X - Y\|^2 \\ \Leftrightarrow (1-p)^2 D^2(x,y) &\leq \widehat{D}_p^2(x,y) \leq (1+p)^2 D^2(x,y)\end{aligned}$$

□

Tightness of Distance Bounds: The bounds are tight, i.e. there exist distinct data points x and y such that $(1-p)^2D^2(x,y) = \widehat{D}_p^2(x,y)$ and points x', y' such that $(1+p)^2D^2(x',y') = \widehat{D}_p^2(x',y')$. First, we show how to construct the subspace containing points X, Y to match the lower bound. Consider two points $X = (X_0, X_1, ...)$ and $Y = (Y_0, Y_1, ...)$ such that $X_j = Y_j$ for $W_j \in \{0,1\}$. All remaining coordinates j with $W_j = -1$ are arbitrary. This gives:

$$\begin{aligned}\widehat{D}_p^2(x,y) &= \sum_{j=1}^{n} \|(1+pW_j)(X_j - Y_j)\|^2 \\ &= \sum_{j=1, W_j \in \{0,1\}}^{n} \|(1+pW_j)(X_j - Y_j)\|^2 \\ &\quad + \sum_{j=1, W_j=-1}^{n} \|(1+pW_j)(X_j - Y_j)\|^2 \\ &= (1-p)^2 \sum_{j=1}^{n} \|(X_j - Y_j)\|^2 = (1-p)^2 D^2(x,y)\end{aligned}$$

The points X', Y' to reach the upper bound are constructed analogously: $X'_j = Y'_j$ for $W_j \in \{0,-1\}$ and arbitrary coordinates X_j, Y_j otherwise.

Metaphor: A System for Related Search Recommendations

Azarias Reda
University of Michigan
azarias@umich.edu

Yubin Park
University of Texas at Austin
yubin.park@utexas.edu

Mitul Tiwari
LinkedIn
mtiwari@linkedin.com

Christian Posse
LinkedIn
cposse@linkedin.com

Sam Shah
LinkedIn
samshah@linkedin.com

ABSTRACT

Search plays an important role in online social networks as it provides an essential mechanism for discovering members and content on the network. Related search recommendation is one of several mechanisms used for improving members' search experience in finding relevant results to their queries. This paper describes the design, implementation, and deployment of *Metaphor*, the related search recommendation system on LinkedIn, a professional social networking site with over 175 million members worldwide. Metaphor builds on a number of signals and filters that capture several dimensions of relatedness across member search activity. The system, which has been in live operation for over a year, has gone through multiple iterations and evaluation cycles. This paper makes three contributions. First, we provide a discussion of a large-scale related search recommendation system. Second, we describe a mechanism for effectively combining several signals in building a unified dataset for related search recommendations. Third, we introduce a query length model for capturing bias in recommendation click behavior. We also discuss some of the practical concerns in deploying related search recommendations.

Categories and Subject Descriptors

H.3.3 [**Information Systems**]: Information Search and Retrieval

General Terms

Algorithms, Design, Experimentation

Keywords

Query Suggestions, Recommender System, Log Analysis

1. INTRODUCTION

Search plays an important role in social networking sites such as LinkedIn as it provides an essential mechanism for discovering members and content on the network. By the time members have scrolled to the bottom of a search results page, it is reasonable to assume that they have not found what they are looking for, at least on the first page. This is when related search recommendations are most useful: they allow users to refine their searches or explore variants by providing alternate queries to their original search. Related search recommendations ("related searches") provide an important tool for improving members' search experience in finding relevant results to their queries and improving overall search engagement.

This paper describes *Metaphor*, the related searches system on LinkedIn. LinkedIn is a professional social networking site with over 175 million members worldwide, serving billions of searches every year. Search is particularly important in the professional context of the LinkedIn network, and represents one of the primary avenues for members and companies to find and connect with one another. Metaphor is an important addition to the set of tools used to guide members in their search experience. These related searches are displayed at the bottom of the search results page, as shown in Figure 1 for the query "Hadoop". In this paper, we will describe the design, implementation, and deployment of Metaphor—including scalability and practical considerations of mining billions of queries—that drives related search recommendations. At the time of writing, Metaphor has been in production for more than a year.

Metaphor builds on a number of signals and filters that capture several dimensions of relatedness in search activity, populating a unified dataset that drives related searches. Related searches are computed and periodically updated offline in batch as a series of Hadoop MapReduce [18] jobs, which handles parallelization.

There are four main signals that go into building the search recommendation dataset. The first signal is based on collaborative filtering [1]: analyzing what members search for together. Using sessionized search logs, we establish sets of related query pairs based on temporal proximity. Each member is allowed a limited number of votes in associating query terms with each other, and the system penalizes generally popular terms.

The second signal is based on a result-anchored relationship of query terms. Using search logs for queries and results, the system constructs a click graph for searches. This results in a bipartite graph from queries to search results, with a many-to-many relationship between the vertices. Unlike previous applications of click graphs for related searches [14, 29], our approach benefits from the personalized nature of search on social networks, and in particular LinkedIn, where results are largely ordered by degree distance in the social graph from the searcher. For a given query, there are often several clicks resulting from the search, and for a given search result, there are several queries that lead to the result being clicked. This graph reflects the collective click behavior of members. Using this graph, Metaphor generates related searches by anchoring on results that relate queries with each other. We call this signal a *query-result-query* signal.

CIKM'12, October 29–November 2, 2012, Maui, HI, USA.

The third signal leverages query term overlap. This is a commonly used approach in query suggestion on web search engines. We refine this approach to first identify terms within a query that have more significance to its meaning. Metaphor evaluates the frequency of terms in the query log, and how often the parts of the query occur together. When generic terms are used together with meaning-rich ones, the system identifies the terms that are more important to the query (for example, "Hadoop" in "Hadoop developer"). After priority of each term is established, Metaphor finds related queries that share important terms.

Related searches can help users to refine a given search query. For example, if a user searches for "Hadoop" to find Hadoop developers, we could suggest "Hadoop engineer" or "Hadoop developers", a refined query. The fourth signal in the recommendation pipeline helps with this problem by looking at the number of terms in a given query and its suggestions: suggestions with more terms are more likely to be refined queries. We built a statistical model for capturing click behavior on results based on recommendation length, which Metaphor uses as a bias to filter recommendations from the previous three signals.

After experimenting with recommendations from the individual signals on the production website for isolated evaluation, we settled on a step-wise union combination of related searches. In this approach, recommendations from collaborative filtering are backfilled with query-result-query recommendations and then partial overlapping recommendations. After each union step, we perform a length-biased filter based on our analysis of past clicks on recommendations.

Our evaluation shows that this approach results in 15% more clicks compared to collaborative filtering, the best signal in the ensemble, and a common technique for deriving such related search suggestions in large-scale production scenarios [24]. Metaphor scales to billions of queries and the recommendations can be computed using idle cluster resources.

The main contributions of this paper include:

- The description of the design, implementation, and deployment of a large-scale related search recommendation system that mines billions of queries,
- A mechanism for effectively combining several signals in building a unified dataset for search recommendation, and
- A novel approach of using query length for modeling click-through behavior and biasing search suggestions to reflect search intent

In addition, we enhanced signals to generate related searches, which included a variation of query-result-query click graph method and a partial matching technique that weighs in the specificity of each query term. Finally, we evaluated Metaphor by performing large-scale bucket or split tests involving millions of queries and members, an effective way of measuring the quality of a real recommendation system.

The rest of the paper is organized as follows. First, we discuss related work in Section 2. In Section 3 we describe the design principles, data flow behind Metaphor, and algorithms that comprise the various signals in the system. We then discuss the implementation and deployment of the system on the LinkedIn infrastructure in Section 4. We describe our evaluation and results in Section 5. Finally, we provide our conclusion and plans for future work in Section 6.

2. RELATED WORK

Related search recommendation has been an active area of research in the context of web search [9, 22, 25, 34, 41], and recently, e-commerce site search [24]. Metaphor is influenced by this research and by recommendation systems at large, and takes advantage of

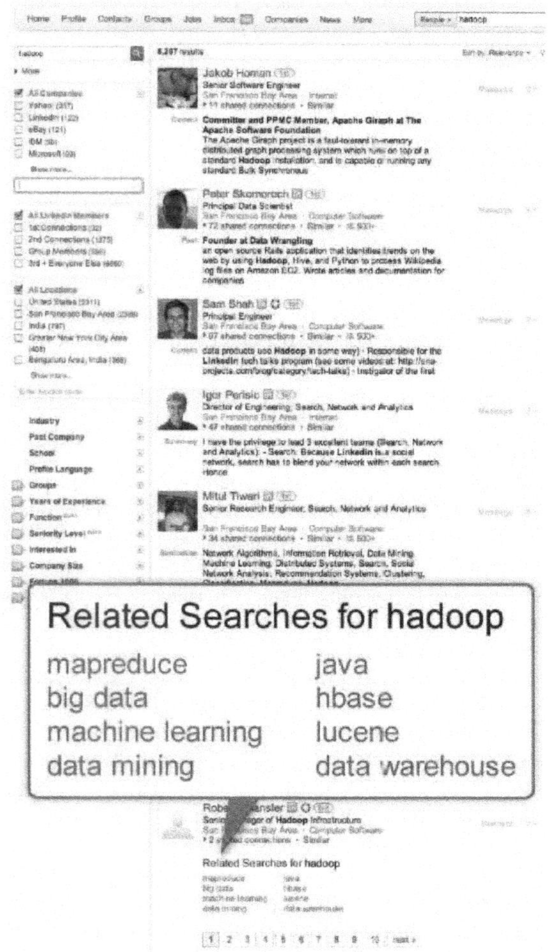

Figure 1: A screenshot of related searches in the context of a search for the query "Hadoop." The module shows a maximum of 8 results in a two-column layout and is available on every page of the search results.

some popular recommendation techniques such as collaborative filtering [36] in addition to utilizing click graphs and partial matches.

Collaborative filtering based recommender systems have been successfully applied for movie recommendations [8] and product recommendations in e-commerce sites [24]. In Metaphor, query relatedness is implicit in query logs unlike movie rating data or historical purchases. Implicit relatedness among queries based on user sessions has been used for search recommendation in the context of web search engines [10, 11, 22, 25, 41]. Recently, query-flow graphs [10, 11] have been utilized to compute similarity between a pair of queries using the transition probabilities between them. Fonseca et al. [22] generate related queries by mining web search query logs and identifying queries that co-occur in the same session, while Zhang and Nasraoui [41] proposed finding related queries based on session and content similarity measures. A collaborative filtering approach based on implicit relatedness among queries works well (see Section 5), and forms an important component of Metaphor. However, in the context of a social network, collaborative filtering fails to discover related queries performed by different members, and it can be effectively combined with other interesting signals that improve the overall performance of related search recommendation.

Utilizing clicked results for queries is another way of extracting related searches. Baeza-Yates et al. [7] introduced the idea of using clicks to infer related searches, which was then used to recommend queries by clustering searches leading to clicks on the same result. This approach was further developed to build an explicit bipartite graph with queries and results [4, 5, 14, 29]. The bipartite graph indirectly conveys the semantic relatedness of queries, which has been shown to be effective in search recommendation. Social networks provide a new context for click-based approaches that benefit from the underlying structure of members and the social graph. The personalized nature of search on LinkedIn, where results are largely ordered by degree distance, produces different results for different members, which often leads to different clicks for the same query. In aggregate, this allows us to discover diverse yet relevant recommendations. Furthermore, we have made several modifications to the algorithms and tailored them to the MapReduce framework as discussed in Section 3.

Partial matching techniques often can be found in query expansion research [15, 17, 38, 40]. Voorhees [38] shows lexically related words ameliorate mismatched vocabulary problems. Query refinement [26] and search shortcuts [13] are closely related to this concept. Our partial matching engine also suggests lexically overlapping queries to users. However, this process is significantly assisted by a prioritization step that identifies semantically important parts of a query. We utilize the frequency of terms and co-occurrence in the search log to rank the importance of terms within a query. This allows us to perform partial matches primarily based on terms that are essential to the query. We combine these approaches with a query length model that captures bias in recommendation click behavior. Based on statistical analysis of clicks on related searches, this length bias model is used to filter recommendations from the underlying signals. Although query length has been closely analyzed in the context of search characterization [3, 35], this is the first application of a length bias model in related search recommendation to the best of our knowledge.

Finally, ensemble methods such as bagging [12], boosting [32], stacking [39], and cascading [23] are widely studied in machine learning and statistics [20]. Some of these ensemble methods have been successfully applied in various recommendation scenarios such as movies [33] and music [21]. Most of these ensemble methods assume comparable performances in their base classifier engines, and expect overlap among datasets generated by each engine. However, each of our signals generates datasets with relatively small overlap and varied performance in different contexts. After experimenting with several alternatives, we devised a step-wise union model that combines the signals based on priority derived from empirical observations. As we will discuss in Section 5, this results in improved query coverage and clicks.

3. DESIGN

Metaphor is a data intensive system that relies on billions of queries in search activity logs to compute suggestions, which amounts to terabytes of search, result, and click data. This data is analyzed in building search recommendations based on a series of signals, notably correlating queries based on time, clicks, and the contents of the query string itself. Metaphor combines these underlying signals to generate a unified recommendation dataset for related searches. This section discusses these signals and the combination process in detail.

3.1 Collaborative Filtering

The first signal we use to generate related search recommendations is based on collaborative filtering techniques. The collaborative filtering based signal uses temporal locality between queries as the primary factor for relating searches; that is, searches correlated by time are considered related. This is enabled by query logs that give us access to the search behavior of members.

User	Query	Time (hh:mm)	Query pairs
John	q_1	17:04	(q_1, q_2), (q_1, q_3)
	q_2	17:06	(q_2, q_1), (q_2, q_3)
	q_3	17:07	(q_3, q_1), (q_3, q_2)
	q_4	20:52	-
Chris	q_5	21:34	(q_5, q_6)
	q_6	21:39	(q_6, q_5)
...			

Table 1: Query pairs based on temporal locality. q_4 is temporally distant from the other queries, thus it does not form a query pair. Note that each query pair is differently weighted according to the time between two queries.

Collaborative filtering in a social networking context can be enhanced by the strong sense of member identity as follows. We start by grouping together queries performed by the same member. We continue by identifying sessions within each member's search history using the inter-search time. We consider the member to have two sessions if the time elapsed between consecutive searches is above a threshold (currently set to 30 minutes). Using all the queries within a session, we form bidirectional (from, to) pairs of queries, which is a permutation rather than a combination. For each pair, we consider the time in between the two searches to assign a weight for the relationship between them. The farther apart the two searches are in the session, the lower the weight associated with the pair. Table 1 describes a brief example of the process.

Since some users often search for similar things, we would like to discount the impact of repeated searches across several sessions of the same user. We accomplish this by considering only one weight (the highest) for each unique pair that was generated by the same user. At the end of this process, we have each pair associated with a weight, with potentially many users having the same pair with different weights. This allows us to calculate a TF-IDF (term frequency, inverse document frequency) [6] score that will eventually be used for recommendations.

To compute the TF-IDF score, we first aggregate all identical pairs, with the final pair weight given as sum of the individual weights from each pair. The TF component in TF-IDF score for each pair is the final pair weight. The IDF component is important because it dampens queries that are generally popular, which end up forming pairs with a large number of other queries. If such queries are not appropriately dealt with, we would have them as recommendations for an unproportionally large number of queries. For example, President Barack Obama is an active member of the site and is regularly searched out of curiosity; this penalization prevents searches for him from being incorrectly correlated with other queries.

We use a variant of the Jones-Robertson IDF measure [31] for our application as given in Equation (1). For a query q:

$$\text{IDF}(q) = \log \frac{d \cdot (N - D(q) + 0.5)}{D(q) + 0.5} \quad (1)$$

In this case, N is the total number of pairs in the dataset, $D(q)$ is the number of pairs that contain query q and d is a dampening factor, which was tuned using offline precision/recall evaluation. The resulting TF-IDF score is used to generate recommendations from the collaborative filtering signal.

3.2 Query-result-query (QRQ)

The second signal we consider in constructing the related search dataset is relationship through member click activity. The basic idea

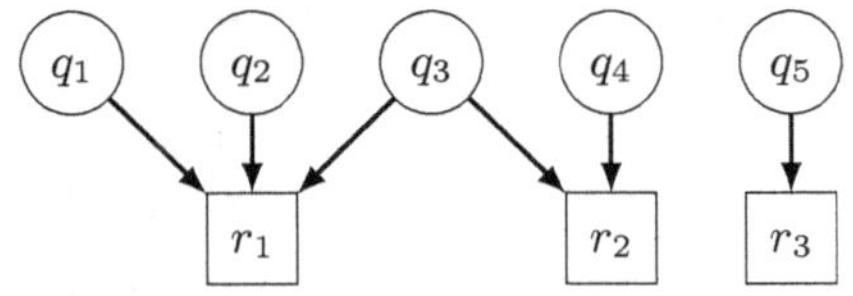

Figure 2: Query-result-query diagram. An arrow from q_i to r_j represents a click on result r_j for query q_i. Queries (q_1, q_2, q_3) are related through clicks on the same result r_1, and queries (q_3, q_4) are related through clicks on the result r_2.

in this signal is that by paying attention to similarity in click behavior for queries, we can discern some relatedness among queries. The LinkedIn search engine orders results largely by degree distance in the social graph from the searcher; thus, users searching for the same query will often get different results based on their social graph. Moreover, users are likely to be presented with intersecting result sets even as they are searching for different terms. This allows us to analyze click behavior from several members, and build relationships among different queries that prompt users to click on similar results. As a simple example, if several members searching for "Hadoop" and "MapReduce" end up clicking on similar results, then it might be a good idea to associate these searches in our related search recommendation. This allows us to recommend "Hadoop" in future searches of "MapReduce" and vice versa. Figure 2 shows the idea behind the query-result-query signal.

We begin data processing by identifying results that were clicked from the search results page in our logs. We then form (query, clicked-result) pairs by associating each query with the corresponding results that were clicked by the user. To prevent bias from a few members who often click on the same result, we document a pair only once per member. We then aggregate all similar pairs and attach a count to each unique pair, $C(q, r)$, which essentially describes the number of unique members who clicked on result r for query q.

The data processing then branches to two complementary components. On one hand, we aggregate all pairs with the same clicked-result r, say $G(r)$, and rank queries based on the pair count obtained in the previous step. With that goal in mind, we obtain $G'(r)$ from $G(r)$ with a few optimizations as follows. First, we remove clicked results that have too many unique inbound queries. Such results are too popular to form a meaningful relationship among the inbound queries. Second, we remove results that are clicked only for a single query since we require at least two queries to be related with each other. Finally, we sort the words in each query alphabetically, resulting in a bag of words model. This allows us to combine queries that would result in the same search result (for example, "Hadoop developer" and "developer Hadoop"). We define branching B as a measure that captures how many inbound branches a clicked result has. For a query q and a clicked result r, we define:

$$B(q, r) = \frac{C(q, r)}{\sum_{(q', r) \in G'(r)} C(q', r)} \quad (2)$$

In addition, we aggregate all pairs with the same query, and rank the results that were clicked for this query using the pair count. Let $K(q)$ represents all the clicks from query q across all searches. We obtain $K'(q)$ by the optimizations as described in the preceding paragraph. We define relevance R that captures how important a particular clicked result r was to a query q as follows:

$$R(q, r) = \frac{C(q, r)}{\sum_{(q, r') \in K'(q)} C(q, r')} \quad (3)$$

With both components—ranked queries and ranked clicks—available, we join the two datasets to infer relatedness among queries. For each result associated with a query, we identify a number of other queries that also lead to the result being clicked.

To combine these measures, we define a query-result-query (QRQ) score for related queries. For a given query q, a number of other queries $q_i, \ldots, q_j$ are related through a clicked result r. The QRQ score for each of those queries with respect to q is:

$$\text{score}(q, q_i) = \sum_r R(q, r) \cdot \log(1 + B(q_i, r)) \quad (4)$$

Here the sum is over each result r such that at least one member clicked on result r for queries q and q_i.

The intuition behind the QRQ score is that we consider both how important the result was to the query, and how important the potentially related query was to the result. From our empirical results, we find that we get better recommendations by emphasizing relevance over branching, hence the log scale for branching.

Finally, we deal with the issue of some queries that are generally more popular than others. Even with the measures taken to decrease bias, we find that certain queries can sometimes dominate recommendations because of their general popularity. To dampen those suggestions, we calculate TF-IDF scores, much in the way we did for collaborative filtering, using the QRQ score from above as the TF component, and the IDF component as computed in Section 3.1. We use these adjusted scores when generating recommendations for the query-result-query signal.

3.3 Partial Matches

The third signal we consider in building the related search recommendation set is the term overlap of queries (partial matching). Although the basic principle in this approach is straightforward, several adjustments must be made to obtain good recommendations. With millions of unique queries, term overlaps are rather common, and the difficulty is in identifying a set of queries that are "meaningfully" overlapping. To tackle this problem, we start out by grouping unique queries together and counting their occurrence. This results in pairs of form (query, count) that are used as input for further processing.

For each unique query, we then identify the tokens (terms) that make up the query. The tokenization process incorporates some optimizations. First, we remove stop words from the set that add little meaning to the query. In addition, we also remove very short tokens. While this can potentially remove some meaningful tokens, the optimization measurably improves overall relevance of the recommendations. Using the query pairs and their associated tokens, we generate a new set of tuples of the form (token, query, count). We then regroup the tuples using the tokens as key, which gives us a set of queries that share the token.

Given the volume of queries that share a token with each query, we make two important observations. The first is that not all tokens in the query are equally important to the query in question. For example, if we consider the query "Hadoop engineer", the term "Hadoop" is more important to the query than the term "engineer". Accordingly, it is more useful to make recommendations that look like "Hadoop developer" rather than "mechanical engineer", although both queries share a token with the original query. To measure importance of a token t in the query, we use a flavor of an inverse document frequency as follows:

$$\text{IDF}(t) = \log \frac{M - Q(t) + 0.5}{Q(t) + 0.5} \quad (5)$$

Here, M is the total number of unique queries and $Q(t)$ is the total number of queries that contain the token t. The more common a token is across different queries, the less significant we consider it for any one of them.

The other observation is that we can apply a similar principle to filter out queries that are generally popular. Therefore, the final scores we assign to potential recommendations depend on both how important the token is to the query, as well as how popular the other queries that are associated with the token are. For a given query, we first identify all the queries that share a token with it using the (token, query, count) tuple, and then score each potentially related query as a multiple of the token significance measure and the TF-IDF measure of the related query in the corpus of queries. We use this score to generate recommendations based on partial matches.

3.4 Length Bias

Related searches can help members refine a given query. If a member has a clear objective when searching, they might benefit from query suggestions for refinement as the initial query might not directly map to their desired result. For example, if a member searches for "Hadoop" to find Hadoop engineers, related searches can suggest refined keywords such as "Hadoop engineer" or "Hadoop developer". We refer to this type of query suggestions as "refined" queries.

We developed a statistical biasing engine based on LinkedIn members' overall behavior. The analysis of the click behavior on displayed recommendations suggests a feature that captures the properties of refined queries. From our analysis, the number of words in queries is related to refinement type of queries, where longer queries tend to be more refined. Furthermore, we observed that members often click suggested queries that are slightly longer than the original query, but not too much longer.

We call this behavior "drift," which translates to a members' click preference for slightly longer recommendations. The additive drift score, which models the drift behavior, depends on the length of the previous query and the next query. The new score S' is computed by adding the drift score δ to the original score S:

$$S' \leftarrow S + \lambda \cdot \delta \tag{6}$$

where λ controls the strength of the length bias module. Since the length bias drift takes an additive form with a control parameter λ, this bias term is flexible in combining with multiple signals. By setting λ larger, longer queries tend to receive a higher score. The value of λ is determined by A/B testing to capture members' preferences. The additive drift score δ is computed using a parameterized equation of the form:

$$\log(\delta|q_p) \propto -\frac{\| l(q_n) - (\alpha \cdot l(q_p) + \beta) \|^2}{l(q_p)} \tag{7}$$

where q_p and q_n are the previous query and the next query respectively, parameters α, β are greater than zero, and for a query q, function $l(q)$ returns the length of the query q. The parameters (α, β) in Equation (7) are estimated using search query logs. Table 2 illustrates how the length bias module affects the recommendation result for a query "Hadoop". The length bias lifts longer recommendations to higher rankings, resulting in more "refined" queries in top-N recommendations. Parameter estimation and experimental results will be further explained in Section 5.2.1.

3.5 Ensemble Approach

After generating related searches using the three separate signals and a length bias filter, the next step is to create a unified recommendation dataset that will be shown to members. To decide how to best combine signals together, we turned to empirical analysis. As we report in the evaluation section, we first segmented the LinkedIn population and ran the various signals individually on the website to get measures of performance. These measures include precision/recall, click-through rate, clicks, and coverage rate, as our evaluation will show.

Recommendations	Length	Score	L-bias	Total
HBase	1	23.21	0.70	23.91
Hadoop developer	2	20.30	4.26	24.56
Cloud computing engineer	3	11.30	3.49	14.79

Table 2: Effects of the length bias module when $\alpha = 1.4$, $\beta = 1.0$, and $\lambda = 5$. Scores and L-biases represent original scores and length bias drifts, respectively. Longer recommendations tend to attain higher rankings after the length bias adjustment; for example, "Hadoop developer", which was second in original scores, becomes the first recommendation. Note that parameters and terms are arbitrarily selected to illustrate the mechanism.

Our first model was based on binary classification of the three signals with respect to click-through, which was not successful: we find there is minimal overlap across the clicked recommendations for related search suggestions. This led us to analyze the general characteristics of recommendations that were generated from the signals. As we see in the evaluation, the overlap is relatively small not only in the clicked recommendations, but also in the actual datasets that were generated from the three signals.

The minimal overlap of suggestions allows us to consider a different approach—step-wise unionization—for combining recommendations. Since our individual analysis has given us information on relative performance of signals, we are able to prioritize signals in the step-wise union. Accordingly, we first backfill collaborative filtering results with query-result-query recommendations. This is then processed through the length-bias filter to promote potentially better recommendations. We then backfill the result set with partial match recommendations, and once again run the length bias filter. In each of the union steps, we take measures to remove duplicate or near duplicate recommendations using a threshold minimum edit distance between recommendations. When it is time to display related searches, we choose the top-N results from this union set.

3.6 Practical Considerations

As a system designed for public consumption from the beginning, we had to consider a number of practical issues before deploying it to end users. For example, we have a very strong profanity filter that conservatively removes potentially offensive terms from recommendations. We apply the filter in the query preparation phase before using queries as an input for any of the signals. In addition, we incorporate a mechanism to deal with common misspellings in recommendations: in our recommendation dataset for a given query, we look at all suggested queries that are within a threshold of edit distances (currently set to less than or equal to 2) from each other. All such recommendations are collapsed to the most common entry in the set, which often removes many of the misspellings and typos in the collection.

Another important consideration was language. LinkedIn is an international website translated in a multitude of languages. We bucket search queries by language, and related searches are computed on these buckets. As LinkedIn has strong identities, these buckets are determined from the locale of the member performing the search, which segments Metaphor's recommendations by language fairly well. This frees the system from performing language detection, which is difficult and often error-prone.

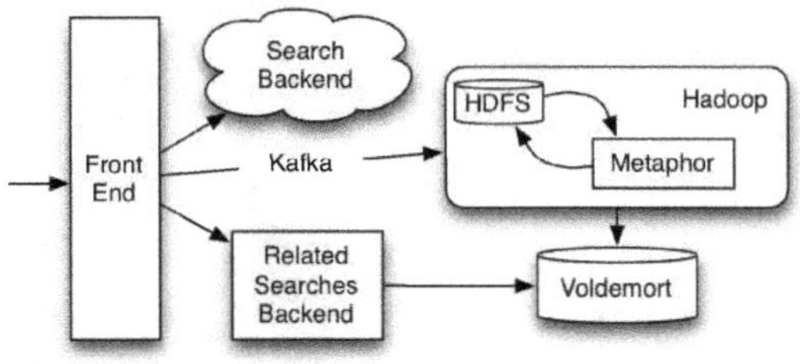

Figure 3: Dataflow in LinkedIn's production system. Tracking data is aggregated through Kafka, and after processing the data in Hadoop, related searches recommendations are stored in Voldemort to serve to end users.

Finally, LinkedIn uses a number of mechanisms to detect spam and tag suspicious accounts accordingly. Like all of our production systems, the related searches pipeline receives input from these spam filters to remove queries that were performed by tagged accounts.

4. IMPLEMENTATION

The Metaphor pipeline runs on Hadoop, an open source implementation of MapReduce [18]. MapReduce provides a framework for processing big datasets on a large number of commodity computers through a series of steps that partition and assemble data in a highly parallel fashion. It further simplifies the process of writing parallel programs by providing the underlying infrastructure, failure handling, and simple interfaces for programmers.

Figure 3 shows how data flows through Metaphor. Incoming query logs and other activity-based tracking data is aggregated from production services using Kafka [27], a publish-subscribe system for event collection and dissemination. This log data can be easily represented as a set of tuples, which is a natural fit for Hadoop's distributed computing paradigm. As of this writing, Kafka aggregates hundreds of gigabytes of data and more than a billion messages per day from LinkedIn's production systems.

Metaphor consists of a series of MapReduce jobs implemented in Java and Pig [30], a high-level scripting language on top of Hadoop. In total, there are over 50 such jobs, from initially pre-processing the query logs to computing and combining the requisite signals. Figure 4 shows a sketch of how data flows within these jobs.

There is some dependency among these jobs, where a job might require outputs from another job to continue. These dependencies are expressed using a workflow manager. Jobs such as query preparation need to be prioritized before all other jobs, while each individual signal can proceed independent of each other. In addition to dependency management, the workflow manager provides a set of useful services like resource locking, log collection, error reporting, simplified configuration, and job scheduling.

The pipeline scales well, as our evaluation shows (see Section 5.3), and handily processes the production data size of LinkedIn. Related searches need only be updated infrequently, meaning the computational cost can be amortized away by using idle cluster time. Once computed, the resulting recommendations are served to end users through Voldemort [37], an open-source key-value system, which is similar to Amazon's Dynamo [19].

5. EVALUATION

Iterative evaluation was an important part of the system development, and this section provides some of the characteristics and performance measures we used as we tuned related search recommendations. The first evaluation approach we used was an offline

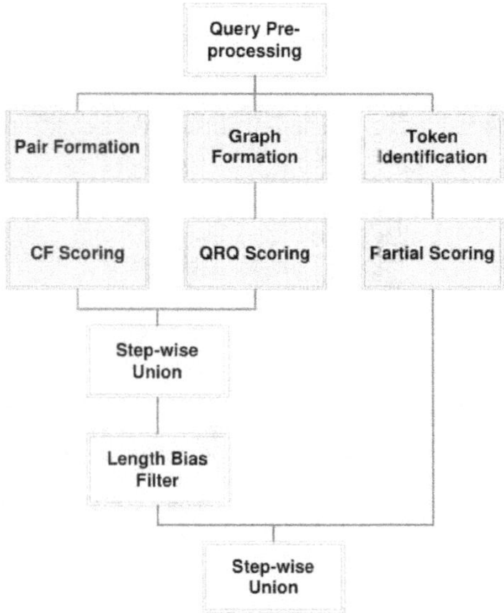

Figure 4: Dataflow in the Metaphor pipeline. Each stage consists of one or more MapReduce jobs that process loaded query and click data.

measure of precision/recall for the various signals in Metaphor. Second, we segmented the LinkedIn user base and conducted several A/B tests that were used to provide online measurements of performance. We used the results of these evaluations to derive the unified approach for the current recommendation set on production. Finally, we evaluated the runtime of the Metaphor pipeline.

Our evaluation answers the following questions:

- What is the performance of each of Metaphor's individual signals and its ensemble approach?
- What is the impact of length biasing?
- What is the system performance of the Metaphor pipeline and how does it scale?

5.1 Offline Evaluation

Offline evaluation provides a scientific and easily repeatable mechanism for establishing performance and tuning parameters. As a proxy for relevance, we measure the accuracy of predicting a member's future searches given their current search using precision and recall. In general, analysis of top-N recommendations shows that accuracy metrics such as precision/recall provide a better performance evaluation than error metrics [16].

We segment the query log into a training and test set. We start by generating the top-N recommendations for the training set from each signal of interest, where N is the number of recommendations that would be displayed to the user. To determine correctness in the test set, we use a moving time window of length K, which determines how far into the future from the current search we should consider in the member's search activity. This correct set is defined as the set of searches that were performed by the user in the following K minutes.

Precision and recall are defined as the mean of the average precision and recall, respectively, computed per member. A related search recommendation is relevant if the recommendation is in the correct set. Precision is the ratio of the number of relevant recommendations to the total number of recommendations N, while recall is the ratio of the number of relevant recommendations to the total number of searches in the correct set. This precision/recall measure

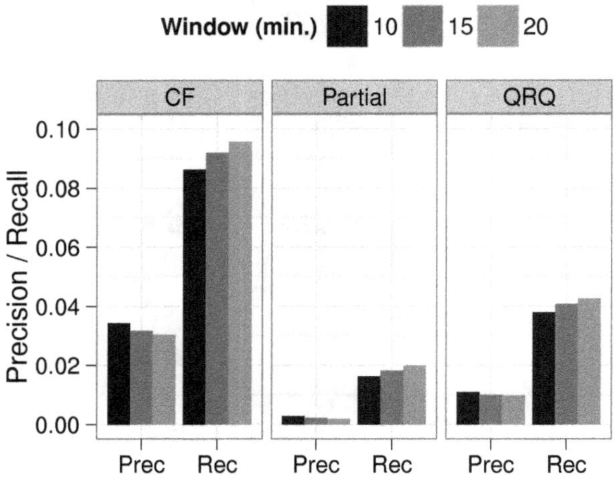

Figure 5: The mean average precision and recall measures for the top-10 recommendations as we vary the moving time window used to determine the correct set.

indicates how well the recommendations reflect members' future search activity in the next K minutes.

Admittedly, this captures only a narrow dimension of recommendation quality by introducing a strong visibility bias: without members having seen possible recommendations, the precision/recall measurement only tells us the ability of our signals to predict future search behavior, not the system's ability to find other novel or serendipitous searches. Thus, this measure is not necessarily a strong indicator of recommendation performance, but it provides a reasonable metric for fast, iterative offline evaluation.

Figure 5 shows a comparison of mean average precision and recall for collaborative filtering, partial matches, and query-result-query. The precision and recall values are rather low as there are very diverse searches on LinkedIn, making predicting future searches quite difficult. As expected, recall increases as we increase the time window K, while precision decreases. At all cutoffs, the collaborative filtering approach has an advantage in both precision and recall.

Figure 6 compares mean average precision and recall for Metaphor's union ensemble approach. To make comparisons easier, we show performance for a fixed recommendation size and time cutoff, with the window size K set to 10 minutes and a top-N of 10. The results are generalizable across other time window and top-N values: the precision and recall values for the union approach are less than the best performing signal, collaborative filtering. While this is initially surprising, our discussion of the online evaluation reveals why the union approach performs better in practice because of a higher coverage of queries.

Furthermore, we evaluate the utility of related searches beyond the metrics of precision and recall. While large gains in mean average precision are detectable to the user, nominal improvements remain inconclusive [2]. Moreover, precision and recall in this context simply captures the ability of the recommendation engines to predict future search behavior, and is thus an incomplete proxy for relevance. We would like a more robust measurement that more directly evaluates a perception of quality.

5.2 Online Evaluation

We performed several isolated tests of the various signals in our model on independent segments of the LinkedIn population, commonly known as A/B or bucket testing. When combined with

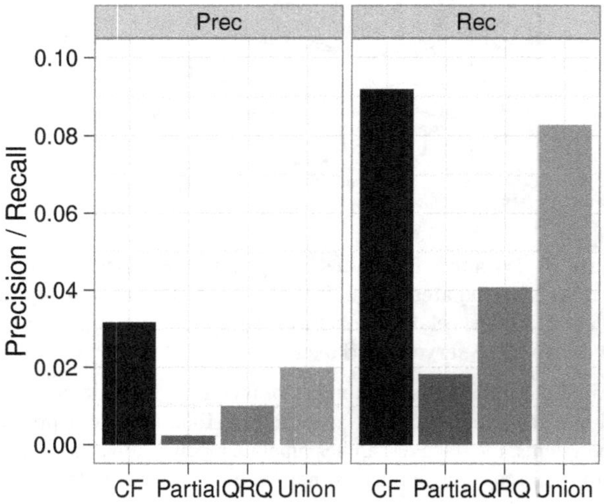

Figure 6: The precision/recall measures for the top-10 recommendations from the step-wise union-based ensemble approach. We use a 10 minute time window for the correct set.

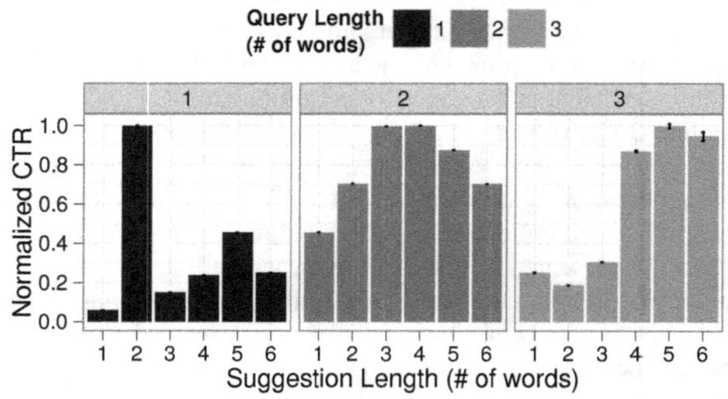

Figure 7: Suggestion length (# of words) compared to normalized CTRs for a given query length (# of words). Higher CTRs are exhibited for longer suggestions than the original query.

offline statistical analysis of recommendation signals, A/B tests allow a deeper understanding of user engagement. We focused on a few key metrics for this evaluation:

- *Coverage*. Not all typed queries have recommendations. The coverage rate is the fraction of queries that have recommendations for a given signal. The higher the coverage, the better members' experience if the recommendations are of high quality.
- *Impressions*. Impressions describe the number of times recommendations were displayed and are analogous to the trigger rate of the module on the search page. It does not make sense to track impressions at the per recommendation level (that is, 8 impressions as seen in Figure 1), as a member can at most click on one result.
- *Clicks*. Related searches recommendations might not always be useful to the user. A click by the user represents a vote that this particular recommendation is relevant.
- *Click-through rate (CTR)*. The click-through rate is the fraction of clicks over impressions.

For each of these measures, we took care to ignore page reloads and the browser back button to avoid incorrectly inflating the above metrics.

Related searches are not the main focus of the search result page (see Figure 1), but rather means for users to pivot to a more useful, novel, or serendipitous search. It is tempting to consider CTR as the sole basis for evaluation, but more careful consideration is needed. It would make sense to count each individual search *result* on the page as an impression—changing the number of results has a dramatic effect on the utility of the search—but for a small module on the bottom of the page (a maximum of 8 results in a two-column layout), absolute clicks is an additional important metric to consider as it encapsulates the notion of coverage as well as quality. As a pedagogical example, consider a recommender that has a single suggestion: it recommends "Hadoop" when given the typed query "MapReduce." Based on our query logs, this recommender would have a very high click-through rate, but very low coverage, a handful of clicks, and ultimately little usefulness. Simply put, increased clicks from users indicate the recommendations are more useful.

As part of our online evaluation, we generated four datasets to run split or A/B tests based on collaborative filtering, query-result-query, partial matches, and step-wise union as described in Section 3. We segmented the LinkedIn population into four separate buckets of 10% each, serving one dataset to one of the members buckets for 2 weeks. We first evaluate the effect of length biasing, then gauge Metaphor's ensemble approach.

5.2.1 Length Bias

In our initial analysis, we observe a key feature that is closely related to users' clicks. This feature is the length difference between clicked suggestions and typed queries. Figure 7 shows the CTRs, which are normalized by the highest CTR in the given query length. Somewhat surprisingly, the highest CTR appears on suggestions one term longer than the original query, indirectly suggesting that users tend to click more refined queries.

From our analysis, we observed that we can improve "future" CTRs by only showing refined queries. For example, suppose a user types a single word query, and we show only two word suggestions. This removes 21% of the total suggestions for a single word query, but increases the CTR by 23% ($p<0.01$). For two and three word queries, similar results are observed. Simply suggesting longer queries comparatively improves the CTR, but reduces coverage, impacting overall clicks and hurting performance.

Our length bias filter can be regarded as a concise formulation of this idea that utilizes users' query selection bias; in other words, we can softly adjust the length of the suggestions, as described in Section 3.4. From our A/B testing, the scale parameter λ is set as ≈ 20, which depends on the scale of the original score. Note that λ determines the strength of length bias as noted earlier. Equation (7) in Section 3.4 approximates the behavior in Figure 7, where $\alpha \approx 1.5$ and $\beta \approx 1$ is estimated by minimizing KL-divergence [28] between the parameterized equation and the observed CTR graph. Accordingly, we can reflect our users' length bias into the resultant query recommendation distributions with a simple maneuver, which would guarantee higher CTR values.

5.2.2 Ensemble Approach

Metaphor constructs three underlying signals for use in its recommendations. We observed that there was minimal overlap in the clicks among various signals. In other words, different queries seemed to be clicked for different recommendation approaches. This led us to analyze recommendation overlap in the underlying dataset for the various signals. Although there was a significantly higher number of recommendations for partial matches (about three times the volume of the other signals), this dataset was inflated by recommendations for tail queries that are not often searched for. As a result, the difference in the coverage of recommendations for the queries issued during our experiment was not that high.

Signal	Jaccard index
CF and Partials	0.36
CF and QRQ	0.27
Partials and QRQ	0.24

Table 3: Overlap of recommendation signals. The Jaccard index is a statistic for comparing the similarity between sets and is defined as: $J(A,B) = \frac{|A \cap B|}{|A \cup B|}$ for sets A and B. As shown in the table, there is little overlap between the Metaphor's various signals.

Signal	# of recommendations		
	1–4	5–8	>8
CF	74%	10%	16%
QRQ	62%	18%	20%
Partials	27%	7%	65%

Table 4: The number of results for each signal. Collaborative filtering and query-result-query have relatively few recommendations for a given typed query.

Table 3 captures the set similarity among signals using the Jaccard index between the recommendation datasets, which simply gives the ratio of the intersection to the union. That is, for sets A and B, $J(A,B) = \frac{|A \cap B|}{|A \cup B|}$. The results indicate minimal overlap across the various signals.

This suggests that we could combine recommendations in a step-wise union. To further understand the implications of using an ensemble, we looked at the depth of recommendations for each signal: Table 4 shows the number of recommendations for each signal. We found that collaborative filtering and query-result-query also have a small number of recommendations for each query (less than 4 suggestions for the majority of queries). Combined with low overlap, this means a step-wise union can safely capture recommendations from multiple methods.

To establish priority in our union approach, we looked at the individual performance of the signals. Figure 8 shows the normalized click, impression, and CTR for each individual approach. On average, recommendations from collaborative filtering receive almost twice as many overalls clicks and twice the CTR of partial matches and query-result-query-based recommendations. Naturally, Metaphor should show collaborative filtering-based results first if available. Query-result-query matches are the second best performing signal and should be shown second. Finally, recommendations based on partial matches should be shown.

We also A/B tested this step-wise union ensemble, the results of which are also shown in Figure 8 and validate this step-wise union ensemble approach. While the CTR of the union approach is virtually identical to collaborative filtering, coverage increases by over 20% in the union model. As Metaphor's suggestions are able to span more typed queries, the absolute number of clicks improves by about 15% compared to collaborative filtering ($p<0.01$), the best signal in the ensemble. These clicks represent increased engagement from users and are indicative of overall higher quality recommendations.

These results differ from our offline evaluation because of a visibility bias. In the absence of ground truth, the offline evaluation uses subsequent searches as its gold standard, which penalizes discoverability. Here, precision and recall are only capturing future search behavior and are not necessarily indicative of recommendation quality and engagement in a live system.

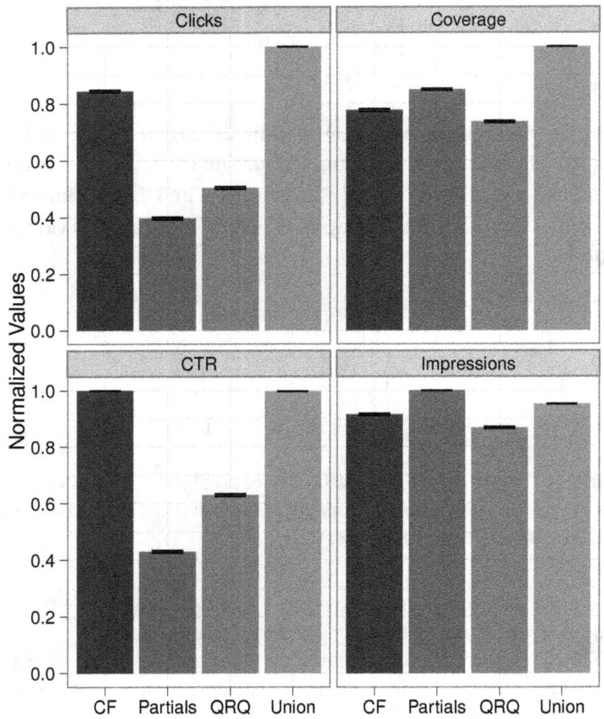

Figure 8: A/B results for clicks, coverage, CTR, and impressions with the individual signals and the union model. Each metric has been normalized to the maximum value within that metric.

5.3 Runtime Performance

Finally, we evaluated the runtime performance of the Metaphor pipeline. To understand the runtime behavior with respect to the number of input queries, we ran the pipeline on a Hadoop test cluster in isolation. This cluster consisted of 80 2x quad-core Nehalem-based Intel Xeon 5500 Sun Fire x4275 machines at 2.533 GHz with 24 GB RAM and 8x1 TB SATA drives configured in a 6:6 map:reduce ratio for a total of 480 available map and 480 available reduce slots. We ran several experiments by varying the number of input queries from 1 million to 3 billion and measured the completion time for the pipeline, as shown in Figure 9. Each experiment was run five times.

The pipeline scales quadratically due to the underlying nature of our algorithms. There are some optimizations that can be made. The partials signal is the most computationally intense as it generates more than 3 times the amount of output as the other signals. This signal could be computed asynchronously and refreshed less frequently than the rest of the pipeline.

More importantly, related search recommendations stay fresh for a relatively long period of time and can be refreshed rather infrequently. To test this, we segmented the LinkedIn user population into 3 A/B test buckets (10% each), refreshing recommendations at a weekly, biweekly, and monthly frequency for each respective bucket. Clicks and CTR were virtually indistinguishable between the weekly and biweekly refresh buckets, with a 1.2% drop in clicks ($p<0.01$) and a 2.1% drop in CTR ($p<0.01$) in the monthly refresh bucket. This makes intuitive sense: these recommendations only change at the introduction or shift in query terms, which moves at the speed of the change in the professional lexicon.

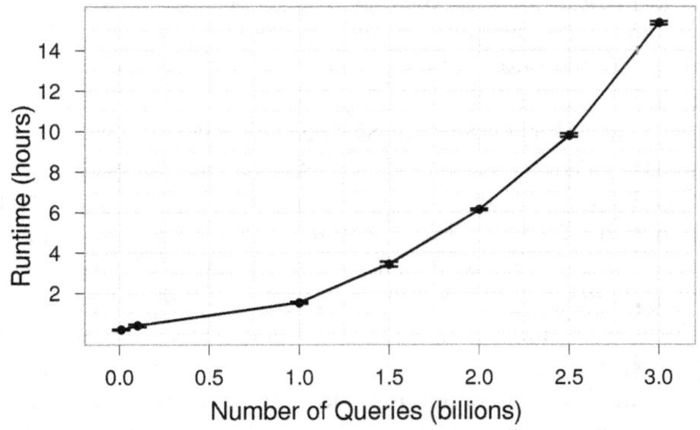

Figure 9: Runtime of the Metaphor pipeline while varying the size of the input query log. The pipeline was run on a dedicated 80-node Hadoop test cluster for 5 trials each.

In practice, the runtime of the pipeline is more than sufficient. Hadoop provides horizontal scalability so it is easy and cheap to add nodes, and due to the infrequent nature of this refresh, the computational cost is completely amortized away by using idle cluster resources.

6. CONCLUSIONS AND FUTURE WORK

This paper discussed the design, implementation and deployment of Metaphor, the related search recommendation system at LinkedIn. With millions of searches served every day, related search recommendation is an important addition to the suite of tools used at LinkedIn to improve member search experience. There are four main signals that went into building the recommendation dataset for Metaphor. One signal is based on collaborative filtering, and analyzes what members search for together based on temporal proximity. Another signal takes advantage of search personalization in the social network to derive relationships based on clicks. Additional signals look at partial matches among queries and the length differential between queries and suggestions for modeling click behavior. We use a step-wise union with priority for combining signals into an ensemble. Metaphor has been in production for more than a year.

We plan to work on two additional approaches to improve related search recommendations in the context of the social network. The first is to incorporate and evaluate a user feedback loop for displayed suggestions. A feedback loop can be useful because it allows us to experiment with new recommendations that would not otherwise have made it to the top-N suggestions displayed to the user. This can be done by replacing some of the recommendations with randomly selected choices from lower in the dataset. If a new replacement is clicked often, we can then promote it to a higher position in the recommendation list. Second, we also plan to work on personalizing related searches based on member searches and profiles, much like the core search experience that provides personalized results to members.

REFERENCES

[1] Gediminas Adomavicius and Alexander Tuzhilin. Toward the next generation of recommender systems: A survey of the state-of-the-art and possible extensions. *TKDE*, 17(6): 734–749, 2005.

[2] James Allan, Ben Carterette, and Joshua Lewis. When will

information retrieval be "good enough?". In *Proceedings of the SIGIR*, 2005.

[3] Avi Arampatzis and Jaap Kamps. A study of query length. In *Proceedings of the SIGIR*, 2008.

[4] Ricardo Baeza-Yates. Applications of web query mining. In *Proceedings of the ECIR*, 2005.

[5] Ricardo Baeza-Yates. Graphs from search engine queries. *LNCS*, 4362:1–8, 2007.

[6] Ricardo Baeza-Yates and Berthier Ribeiro-Neto. *Modern Information Retrieval.* Addison Wesley, 1999.

[7] Ricardo A. Baeza-Yates, Carlos A. Hurtado, and Marcelo Mendoza. Query recommendation using query logs in search engines. In *Proceedings of the EDBT Workshops*, 2004.

[8] James Bennett and Stan Lanning. The Netflix prize. In *KDD Cup and Workshop*, 2007.

[9] Sumit Bhatia, Debapriyo Majumdar, and Prasenjit Mitra. Query suggestions in the absence of query logs. In *Proceedings of the SIGIR*, 2011.

[10] Paolo Boldi, Francesco Bonchi, Carlos Castillo, Debora Donato, Aristides Gionis, and Sebastiano Vigna. The query-flow graph: model and applications. In *Proceedings of the CIKM*, 2008.

[11] Paolo Boldi, Francesco Bonchi, Carlos Castillo, Debora Donato, and Sebastiano Vigna. Query suggestions using query-flow graphs. In *Proceedings of the WSDM*, 2009.

[12] Leo Breiman. Bagging predictors. *Machine Learning*, 24(2): 123–140, 1996.

[13] Peter D. Bruza and Simon Dennis. Query reformulation on the internet: Empirical data and the hyperindex search engine. In *Proceedings of the RIAO*, 1997.

[14] Carlos Castillo, Claudio Corsi, Debora Donato, Paolo Ferragina, and Aristides Gionis. Query-log mining for detecting spam. In *Proceedings of the AIRWeb*, 2008.

[15] Paul A. Chirita, Claudiu S. Firan, and Wolfgang Nejdl. Personalized query expansion for the web. In *Proceedings of the SIGIR*, 2007.

[16] Paolo Cremonesi, Yehuda Koren, and Roberto Turrin. Performance of recommender algorithms on top-n recommendation tasks. In *Proceedings of the RecSys*, 2010.

[17] Hang Cui, Ji-Rong Wen, Jian-Yun Nie, and Wei-Ying Ma. Query expansion by mining user logs. *TKDD*, 15(4):829–839, 2003.

[18] Jeffrey Dean and Sanjay Ghemawat. MapReduce: simplified data processing on large clusters. In *Proceedings of the OSDI*, 2004.

[19] Giuseppe DeCandia, Deniz Hastorun, Madan Jampani, Gunavardhan Kakulapati, Avinash Lakshman, Alex Pilchin, Swaminathan Sivasubramanian, Peter Vosshall, and Werner Vogels. Dynamo: Amazon's highly available key-value store. *SIGOPS Oper. Syst. Rev.*, 41:205–220, 2007.

[20] Thomas G. Dietterich. Ensemble methods in machine learning. *LNCS*, 1857:1–15, 2000.

[21] Gideon Dror, Noam Koenigstein, Yehuda Koren, and Markus Weimer. Recommending music items based on the Yahoo! music dataset. In *KDD-Cup*, 2011.

[22] Bruno M. Fonseca, Paulo B. Golgher, Edleno S. de Moura, and Nivio Ziviani. Using association rules to discover search engines related queries. In *Proceedings of the LA-WEB*, 2003.

[23] João Gama and Pavel Brazdil. Cascade generalization. *Machine Learning*, 41:315–343, 2000.

[24] Mohammad Al Hasan, Nish Parikh, Byanit Singh, and Neel Sundaresan. Query suggestion for E-commerce sites. In *Proceedings of the WSDM*, 2011.

[25] Rosie Jones, Benjamin Rey, Omid Madani, and Wiley Greiner. Generating query substitutions. In *Proceedings of the WWW*, 2006.

[26] Reiner Kraft and Jason Zien. Mining anchor text for query refinement. In *Proceedings of the WWW*, 2004.

[27] Jay Kreps, Neha Narkhede, and Jun Rao. Kafka: A distributed messaging system for log processing. In *Proceedings of the NetDB*, 2011.

[28] Solomon Kullback and Richard A. Leibler. On information and sufficiency. *Ann. Math. Statist.*, 22(1):79–86, 1951.

[29] Qiaozhu Mei, Dengyong Zhou, and Kenneth Church. Query suggestion using hitting time. In *Proceedings of the CIKM*, 2008.

[30] Christopher Olston, Benjamin Reed, Utkarsh Srivastava, Ravi Kumar, and Andrew Tomkins. Pig Latin: a not-so-foreign language for data processing. In *Proceedings of the SIGMOD*, 2008.

[31] Stephen Robertson. Understanding inverse document frequency: On theoretical arguments for IDF. *Journal of Documentation*, 60(5), 2004.

[32] Robert E. Schapire. A brief introduction to boosting. In *Proceedings of the IJCAI*, 1999.

[33] Joseph Sill, Gábor Takács, Lester Mackey, and David Lin. Feature-weighted linear stacking. *CoRR*, abs/0911.0460, 2009.

[34] Yang Song, Dengyong Zhou, and Li-wei He. Query suggestion by constructing term-transition graphs. In *Proceedings of the WSDM*, 2012.

[35] Amanda Spink, Dietmar Wolfram, Major B. J. Jansen, and Tefko Saracevic. Searching the web: The public and their queries. *Journal of American Society for Information Science and Technology*, 2001.

[36] Xiaofei Su and Taghi M. Khoshgoftaar. A survey of collaborative filtering techniques. *Advances in AI*, 2009:4:1–4:19, 2009.

[37] Roshan Sumbaly, Jay Kreps, Lei Gao, Alex Feinberg, Chinmay Soman, and Sam Shah. Serving Large-scale Batch Computed Data with Project Voldemort. In *Proceedings of the FAST*, 2012.

[38] Ellen M. Voorhees. Query expansion using lexical-semantic relations. In *Proceedings of the SIGIR*, 1994.

[39] David H. Wolpert. Stacked generalization. *Neural Networks*, 5:241–259, 1992.

[40] Jinxi Xu and W. Bruce Croft. Query expansion using local and global document analysis. In *Proceedings of the SIGIR*, 1996.

[41] Zhiyong Zhang and Olfa Nasraoui. Mining search engine query logs for query recommendation. In *Proceedings of the WWW*, 2006.

Exploring Personal Impact for Group Recommendation

Xingjie Liu Yuan Tian Mao Ye Wang-Chien Lee
The Pennsylvania State University
State College, PA 16801, USA
{xzl106, yxt144, mxy177, wlee}@cse.psu.edu

ABSTRACT

Group activities are essential ingredients of people's social life. The rapid growth of online social networking services has greatly boosted group activities by providing convenient platform for users to organize and participate in such activities. Therefore, recommender systems, as a critical component in social networking services, now face new challenges in supporting group activities. In this paper, we study the *group recommendation* problem, i.e., making recommendations to a group of people in social networking services. We analyze the decision making process in a group to propose a *personal impact topic* (PIT) model for group recommendations. The PIT model effectively identifies the group preference profile for a given group by considering the personal preferences and personal impacts of group members. Moreover, we further enhance the discovery of personal impact with social network information to obtain an *extended personal impact topic* (E-PIT) model. We have conducted comprehensive data analysis and evaluations on three real datasets. The results show that our proposed group recommendation techniques outperform baseline approaches.

Categories and Subject Descriptors

H.3.3 [**Information Search and Retrieval**]: Information Filtering; J.4 [**Computer Applications**]: Social and Behavior Sciences

General Terms

Algorithms, Experimentation.

Keywords

Recommender Systems, Probabilistic Generative Model, Group Recommendation.

1. INTRODUCTION

Group activities are essential ingredients of people's social life. With recent development of social networking services, such as Facebook[1] and Meetup[2], organizing and participating in group activities (e.g., dining out, movie watching, vacations and parties) become very easy. As more and more people are willing to share their social relationships and activities online, new web services today need to target not only on individual users but also user groups. As a key technology in modern web services, recommender systems are now facing vigorous new demands and challenges in making recommendations for a group of people.

While making significant advances in the recommender system technology, most of the prior research studies in this topic area have focused on providing recommendations for individuals, which unfortunately can not be effectively applied for *group recommendations*, i.e., making recommendations for a group of people. Notice that a common idea behind recommender systems that make personalized recommendations for individuals is to discover users' preference profiles (either from user ratings or item text descriptions) in order to identify items that best match the profiles of targeted users. However, for group recommendations, we argue that a good recommender system not only needs to model users' individual preferences but also understands how a decision among group members is reached.

The pioneering researches on group recommendation have been dated back to MusicFX [14], a music recommender system built for gym users in 1998. Over these years, important findings and solutions have been reported in various studies on web/news pages [18], tourism [15], music [8], TV programs [25] and movies [17]. In this paper, we aim to study the problem of group recommendation, under the context of group activities in social events. Our research is unique from previous research in both of the problem and solution aspects.

- Problem aspect - Prior research studies on group recommendations [18, 17], mostly assume static groups which consist of stable membership (e.g., a movie interest group). In this study, we are targeting on "ad hoc" groups (e.g., people gathering for a dinner). In addition, different from [14, 17], where individual user's ratings or profiles are made available explicitly, we avoid such a strong assumption and consider only the group activity history.
- Solution aspect - Prior studies on group recommendation systems usually explore heuristics to apply some interesting strategies in recommendations, for example, PloyLens [17] adopts *least misery* (i.e., the least

[1]www.facebook.com
[2]www.meetup.com

CIKM'12, October 29–November 2, 2012, Maui, HI, USA.

satisfied user's preference) as the main strategy for its group recommendations. Aiming to better understand the latent factors behind group activities, in our study, we propose a probabilistic model to capture both of a user's own preference and her influence (termed as *personal impact*) to a group.

In this paper, we propose a probabilistic model, namely, the personal impact topic (PIT) model, for group recommendations. This model naturally captures the process in which an item is selected collectively by an ad hoc group. In this model, user preferences over items are abstracted into a number of latent topics. As such, each user's personal preference is modeled as a distinct distribution over all these topics, while each topic is expressed as a distinct distribution over all the items. Now a key issue is how an item is selected by a group of users, each of whom has her own preferences. While each group member may contribute to the group decision, we model the decision making process for an ad-hoc group with two key points. First, group decision on item selection follows the personal preferences of group members. Second, for a given item selection event (i.e., a decision on a group activity), a group member is probabilistically chosen to be a *group decision representative* (or representative for short)[3]. In this model, we introduce the personal impact parameter to control this process such that users with higher personal impact values shall have higher probabilities to serve as a group representative.

Our contributions can be summarized as follows:

- Group recommendation is essential in today's web services, especially in social networking systems that encourage various group activities. In this paper, we tackle a general group recommendation problem, where a group is formed in an ad hoc manner. In our study, we require only groups' item selection history (i.e., we do not need individuals' item selection history).
- We capture a group item selection process in a probabilistic model, called *personal impact topic* (PIT) model, that introduces the notion of personal impact to differentiate contributions of group members to a group decision. We perform statistical tests on real datasets to show that people do have different personal impacts in group decisions.
- Based on PIT model, we develop learning algorithms to learn personal impacts. Accordingly, we are able to use these parameters to construct group profiles from individual's user profile to make group recommendations. Additionally, we utilize social information as additional features to improve the personal impact estimations and thus further alleviate the potential problem of over-fitting.
- Finally, we evaluate our proposed group recommendation methods using three real dataset collected from whrrl.com and meetup.com. We consider three scenarios of group recommendations, i.e., Whrrl POI visit recommendation , Meetup tag selection recommendation and Meetup event venue selection recommendation. Experimental results show that our proposals significantly outperform the compared baselines.

[3]Please note that this representative is not designated as the decision maker but to denote the "probable source" of group decision made.

The rest of the paper is organized as follows. In Section 2, we review related works for both recommender systems designed for individual users as well as those for a group of users. In Section 3, we define the tackled group recommendation problem and provide some background for the proposed probabilistic models. The personal impact parameters are introduced in Section 4. Accordingly, we propose the personal impact topic (PIT) model to address the proposed recommender problem and extend the PIT model by exploring additional social features. In Section 5, we evaluate our proposed models using three datasets and conclude the paper in Section 6.

2. RELATED WORKS

Here, we review some related works, including general recommender systems, recommender systems for groups, and latent semantic models applied to recommender system.

Item recommender system: Item recommendation is an essential service for e-commerce and web services (e.g. netflix.com and amazon.com). The goal is to recommend a list of items that a targeted user may be interested in. Collaborative filtering and content-based techniques are two widely adopted approaches for recommender systems [1, 22]. Both of them discover users' personal profiles and utilize these profiles to find relevant items. Collaborative filtering techniques [7, 9, 21] automatically predict relevant items for a given user by referencing item rating information from other similar users. Content-based techniques [16] make recommendations by matching a user's personal profile to descriptive information of items. Although both techniques are complimentary to each other, collaborative filtering gains huge popularity among modern web services because it is easier to obtain item ratings explicitly (e.g. from movie rating by netflix.com) or implicitly (e.g. click information from amazon.com) from users than to collect interest descriptive information from users. Therefore, many techniques adopt the ideas of collaborative filtering. The classic *memory-based* collaborative filtering technique [19, 21] identifies a group of k users that have the most closed rating results with the targeted user, and merge ratings from these k users to find the top-N recommendations. However, there are several limitations for the memory-based CF techniques, such as when data are sparse and the common items are few, it is problematic to find similar users. To achieve better prediction performance and overcome shortcomings of memory-based CF algorithms, *model-based* CF approaches, including matrix factorization [6], clustering CF models [23], and latent semantic models [10], have been investigated.

Group recommender system: Group recommender systems make item recommendations for a user group. Existing group recommender systems have been applied in web/news pages [18], tourism [15], music [14, 8], and TV programs and movies [17, 25]. Generally speaking, two main approaches have been proposed for group recommendation [11]. The first one creates an aggregated profile for a group based on individual profiles of its group members and makes recommendations based on the aggregated group profile [14, 25]. The second approach *aggregates* the recommendation results for individual members into a single group recommendation list. In other words, recommendations (i.e., ranked item lists) for individual members are created independently and then aggregated into a joint group recommendation list [4], where the aggregation functions could be based on average or least misery strategies [13, 17]. However, the group recommendation system can go beyond simple strategies such as averaging or least misery. In fact, the group member's personality and social status may determine how much weight his preference would determine group selections. Intrigue [3] take roles of tourist group members into account to recommend places to visit, (such that children would follow their parents' plans). The group members' disagreement to candidate items are considered in the recommendation score function in [2]. In this paper, we introduce the notion of personal impact which differentiates the contribution of group members to a decision in a different way. Personal impacts are useful for constructing group profiles to make good recommendations for groups.

Probabilistic Latent Topic Models. Latent topic models analyze relationships between a set of documents and the words, and identify latent topics that are represented as distributions over words in a corpus. In [10], a probability topic model is proposed to recommend item for individual users. In [24], a latent topic model incorporating social influence has been proposed to make better item recommendations. Latent Dirichlet Allocation (LDA) [5], a well known latent semantic model for text summarization, adopts Dirichlet priors for document topic distributions and word distributions. The principle of LDA is applicable under the context of item recommendation by mapping document/word entities to user/item entities. As an extension to LDA, author topic (AT) model [20] analyze co-authored document text, and therefore discover each author's expertise and contributions to each co-authored documents. Our approach focus on group recommendation problem, and is related to LDA [5] and author topic model [20].

3. PRELIMINARY

In this section, we first formally define the group recommendation problem studied in this paper. Then we adopt a probabilistic modeling approach for document analysis, called author topic model, to serve as the basis for addressing the group recommendation problem.

3.1 Problem Definition

Let $U = \{u_1, u_2, \cdots, u_V\}$ be a set of V users, and $W = \{w_1, w_2, \cdots, w_M\}$ denote a set of M items. A history log of group-item selection can be written in the form of $\{\langle G_1, s_1\rangle, \langle G_2, s_2\rangle, \cdots \langle G_N, s_N\rangle\}$ where $G_n = \{u_i\}$ and $s_n = w_j$ denote an ad hoc group and the item selected by the group, respectively[4]. Let $\vec{G}$ collectively denote the N ad hoc groups and $\vec{s}$ be the collection of N selections made by them. $H = \langle \vec{G}, \vec{s}\rangle$ represents the history of all the N group-item pairs. Given H, the group recommendation problem is defined as to construct a ranked recommended list of items for a targeted group G_x, in accordance with the likelihood of the group to select those items.

We aim to adopt the collaborative filtering paradigm to address the group recommendation problem without requiring additional context information for users, groups or items. Also, we assume an input dataset of implicit ratings among groups and items in forms of clicks, tags, likes, checkins, etc, which are generally available in various web services, especially social networking systems.

The group recommendation problem defined above brings us several challenges. First, the groups are formed in ad hoc manner and usually ephemeral. For example, three friends may have dinner together and checkin the restaurant in a social network service. The user groups for such one-off social activities are usually not persistent, as different groups may be formed on another day. Thus, we do not treat these groups as pseudo users to apply single user recommendation techniques. There are very few item selections logged for each group, and some targeted group even has no previous history at all, leading to severe cold-start problem. Second, many services are group-centric which do not keep track of individual users' item selections/ratings. Thus, it requires a technique that would construct user preference profiles purely from group activities. Finally, how groups reach a decision to select an item is not well answered in previous studies. In [3, 2, 17, 25], group recommendations are made based on various strategies. In this study, we aim to model the impacts from different group members on group item selections, and then exploit such information in making recommendation for groups.

3.2 Extended Author Topic Model

To solve the group recommendation problem defined above, we need to address two issues: 1) how to profile preferences of individual users, and 2) how to model the group selection decision making process, given the preferences of its members. To address these issues, we propose to use the latent topic modeling approach which is known for achieving good recommendations even when dataset is sparse [10, 24]. Moreover, the model provides an interpretation of the item selection process.

Without loss of generality, we assume there are K latent topics $T = \{t_1, t_2, \cdots, t_K\}$, each of them represents a different multinomial distributions over items. Every topic can be considered as a soft-cluster of items, where items with higher probabilities in the same topic tend to be picked by similar groups. A user's preference is modeled as a mixture of topics, which is also a multinomial distribution. To model the group preference profile, we assume the preference profile is a mixture of the group members' preferences. Thus, we use an election process to describe this mixture. More specifically, for each item selection observation (logged as a historical transaction) , we assume a representative is probabilistically selected from the group. Then, the item is probabilistically picked based on this representative's personal preferences. Because every member has a chance to be elected as the representative, the overall probability of an item selected by the group can reflect the mixture of the group members' personal preferences.

While there is no prior latent topic model proposed for the group recommendation problem, we observe that the Author Topic (AT) model [20] proposed for document-authorship analysis may provide some hints as the authors of a paper naturally form a group. In the AT model, the creation of a document is modeled as follows. For each word in the document, an author is drawn from the document's author group. Next, a topic is selected following the author's topic distributions, and from the topic's word distributions, the word is selected. Each author's topic distribution and each topic's

[4]Note that it is possible that a group is duplicated (e.g. $G_x = G_y, (x \neq y)$). However, this situation is rare since there is quite a few item selection history for a distinct group.

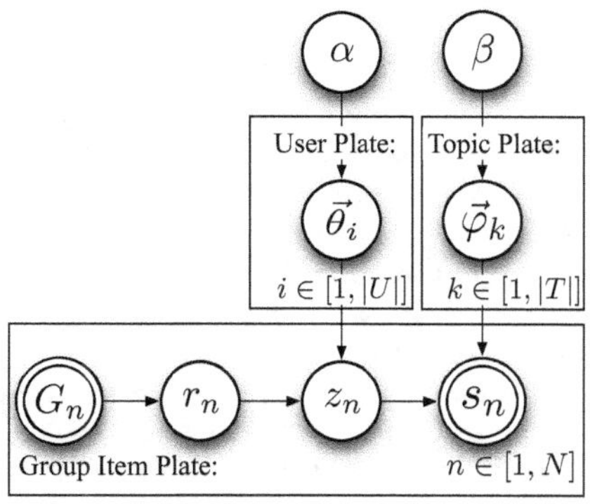

Figure 1: Author topic model under the group item selection context. G_n and s_n (in double circled nodes) represent the observed group and the selected item, respectively. r_n is the corresponding representative, and z_n is the generated topic.

word distribution are modeled as multinomial distribution with Dirichlet prior.

Through a careful analysis, we find that the above-described document generation process shares some similar properties with our group item selection that we envisage. More specifically, if we consider the authors of a document a group and items selected by this group collected as words of the document, we may potentially apply the AT model to the group item selection process (as depicted in the plate representation of an author topic model in Fig. 1). As shown, the nth group G_n generates the nth representative $r_n \in G_n$ following the uniform multinomial distribution. The latent topic z_n is then generated following the r_n's topic distribution, which is a multinomial distribution $\vec{\theta}_i$ following the Dirichlet prior $\mathcal{D}(\vec{\alpha})$. Finally, the item s_n is selected following the topic z_n's word distribution, which is also a multinomial distribution $\vec{\varphi}_k$ following the Dirichlet prior $\mathcal{D}(\vec{\beta})$.

Furthermore, in AT model, the latent variables $\vec{r}$ and $\vec{z}$ are learned from the observations of both $\vec{G}$ and $\vec{s}$. In group recommendation, we need to not only learn the latent variables, but also make prediction of s when a targeted group G is given. Here, we extend the AT model with a prediction function. Specifically, after the latent parameters $\vec{\theta}$ and $\vec{\varphi}$ are learned, the probability that a user u_i selects an item w_j can be derived as:

$$\mathrm{Pr}^{\mathrm{AT}}(w_j|u_i) = \sum_{k=1}^{|T|} \mathrm{Pr}(w_j|t_k) \cdot \mathrm{Pr}(t_k|u_i) = \sum_{k=1}^{|T|} \varphi_{j,k} \cdot \theta_{k,i} \quad (1)$$

Following the generative process in Fig. 1, each group representative is generated with equal probabilities. Thus an item s_n is accessed by a given group G_n with the following probability:

$$\begin{aligned}\mathrm{Pr}^{\text{E-AT}}(s_n = w_j|G_n) &= \sum_{\forall u_i \in G_n} \mathrm{Pr}(r_n = u_i|G_n) \cdot \mathrm{Pr}^{\mathrm{AT}}(w_j|u_i) \\ &= \sum_{\forall u_i \in G_n} 1/|G_n| \cdot \mathrm{Pr}^{\mathrm{AT}}(w_j|u_i)\end{aligned} \quad (2)$$

Eqn. (2) directly uses the AT model parameters to estimate the future group item selections. We call this recommendation method as Extended-AT (E-AT) model and use it as a baseline in this study.

4. PERSONAL IMPACT TOPIC MODEL

The E-AT model assumes that each group member has an equal probability to be a representative (see Eqn. (2)). In this section, we argue that group members have different impacts in group item selection decisions. Hence, we introduce the notion of *personal impact* parameter to model this difference. Accordingly, we propose a personal impact topic (PIT) model by incorporating the personal impacts to control the generation of group representatives. We also provide the model learning algorithm to infer personal impacts, topic distribution of users and item distributions of topics. Finally, to over-come the over-fitting problem when input dataset is sparse, we extend the PIT model by exploring additional social features.

4.1 Personal Impact

From our daily life experience, we may observe that many group activities are usually proposed and organized by some active people, while other participants mostly follow the agenda. Similarly, in decisions such as item selections, some group members may out-speak others in expressing their preferences (due to expertise, authority, or other personality factors) and thus have more influence on the decision. Therefore, the group selection decisions may reflect their opinions more than other indiscriminate group members. To quantify such influence, we introduce a latent variable of *personal impact* in our model to better capture how likely a user would influence a decision made within a group.

In our model, the personal impact of each individual user u_i can be abstracted as a positive numerical value γ_i, where a higher value indicates greater impact on a group's decisions. For $|U|$ users, we use $\vec{\gamma}$ to represent all the personal impacts. More specifically, γ_i reflects the *relative* probability to influence a group decision. In other words, the probability that a user is the representative of the group is:

$$\mathrm{Pr}(r_n = u_i|G_n) = \begin{cases} \frac{\gamma_i}{\sum_{\forall u_j \in G_n} \gamma_j} & \text{if } u_i \in G_n \\ 0 & \text{otherwise.} \end{cases} \quad (3)$$

In Eqn.(3), the probability for a group member $u_i \in G_n$ to be selected as a representative is proportional to his personal impact. Otherwise, a user has zero probability to be a representative if he does not belong to the group. Following this definition, Eqn. (2) in E-AT model assumes that group members have the same personal impact, i.e., $Pr(r_n = u_i|G_n) \equiv 1/|G_n|$, which is a strong assumption. Next, we introduce the personal impact topic (PIT) model and develop techniques to learn personal impacts from group item selection dataset.

4.2 Personal Impact Topic Model

Fig. 2 illustrates the personal impact topic (PIT) model in plate graph. In the figure, personal impact parameters are introduced in the user plate, one for each user. Thus, the group item selection process is composed as three steps: 1) representative $r_n = u_i$ is drawn from G_n according to group members' personal impacts in Eqn. (3), 2) representative u_i probabilistically selects a topic $z_n = t_k$ following his topic distribution $\vec{\theta}_i$, and then 3) the item s_n is probabilistically selected following t_k's item distribution $\vec{\varphi}_k$. Since users may have different personal impacts, the group representative selection is biased towards those with higher personal impacts. That is, people with higher personal impacts have higher

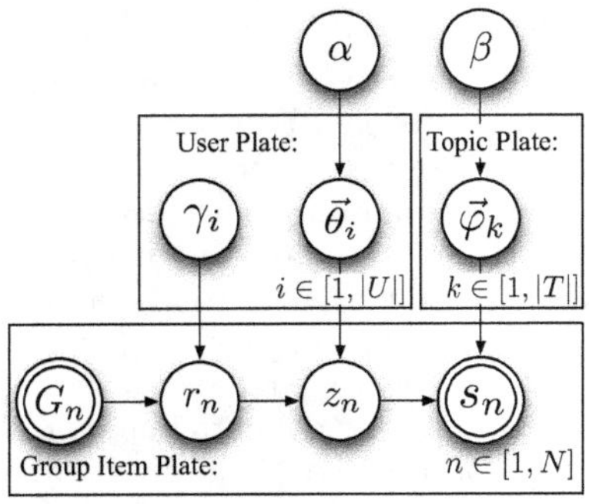

Figure 2: Personal Impact Topic (PIT) Model

probabilities to influence the group to select items following their preferences. For simplicity, we do not assume a Bayes prior for personal impacts in the PIT model.

4.3 PIT Model Parameter Inference

We adopt the Gibbs sampling method to infer model parameters as it provides fast and effective solutions to our model. Gibbs sampling is a MCMC method that samples latent variables based on the model's posterior distribution. We use $\vec{s}$ to represent all the items previously selected by groups $\vec{G}$, and the latent representatives and topics for those group-item pairs can be denoted as $\vec{r}$ and $\vec{z}$, respectively. Following the PIT model in Fig. 2, the posterior is:

$$\begin{aligned}&\Pr(\vec{r},\vec{z}|\vec{G},\vec{s},\vec{\gamma},\alpha,\beta)\\ &\propto \Pr(\vec{r}|\vec{G},\vec{\gamma})\cdot\Pr(\vec{z}|\vec{r},\alpha)\cdot\Pr(\vec{s}|\vec{z},\beta)\\ &=\prod_{n=1}^{N}\frac{\gamma_{r_n}}{\sum_{u_j\in G_n}\gamma_j}\cdot\prod_{i=1}^{|U|}\frac{B(\vec{C}^{UT}_{i,*}+\vec{\alpha})}{B(\vec{\alpha})}\cdot\prod_{k=1}^{|T|}\frac{B(\vec{C}^{TW}_{k,*}+\vec{\beta})}{B(\vec{\beta})}\end{aligned} \tag{4}$$

In Eqn. (4), $\vec{C}^{UT}$ represents a counting matrix where $\vec{C}^{UT}_{i,k}$ is the number of times that the kth topic is sampled for the ith user. Hence, $\vec{C}^{UT}_{i,*}$ denotes a vector of the ith user's sample topic counts. Similarly, $\vec{C}^{TW}_{k,*}$ is a vector of the kth topic's item counts. In Eqn. (4) the first term is the product of all the representative selection probabilities under the personal impacts. The second term is the joint probability of the respective users' selected topics. Because the Dirichlet prior is conjugate to the multinomial distribution of each users' topic selection, the joint probability can be simplified as $\frac{B(\vec{C}^{UT}_{i,*}+\vec{\alpha})}{B(\vec{\alpha})}$, where $B(\cdot)$ represents extended beta function. Similarly, the last term is the joint probability for each topic's item selections.

In order to sample the posterior probability, a Gibbs sampling method computes the full conditional probability for one single representative user and topic assignment $\langle r_n, z_n\rangle$ conditioned on all the other assignments $\vec{r}_{\neg n}, \vec{z}_{\neg n}$ as:

$$\begin{aligned}&\Pr(r_n=u_i,z_n=t_k|\vec{G},\vec{s},\vec{r}_{\neg n},\vec{z}_{\neg n},\vec{\gamma},\alpha,\beta)\\ &\propto\frac{\gamma_i}{\sum_{u_j\in G_n}\gamma_j}\cdot\frac{\vec{C}^{UT}_{i,k,\neg n}+\alpha}{\sum_{k'}(\vec{C}^{UT}_{i,k',\neg n}+\alpha)}\cdot\frac{\vec{C}^{TW}_{k,j,\neg n}+\beta}{\sum_{j'}(\vec{C}^{TW}_{k,j',\neg n}+\beta)}\end{aligned} \tag{5}$$

The subscript $\neg n$ indicates that the counting matrix or the sample vector *excludes* the nth sample of $\langle r_n, z_n\rangle$. The derivation of Eqn. (5) is similar to the AT model's posterior in [20], except that the first personal impact term. Eqn. (5) provides a method to sample $\langle r_n, z_n\rangle$ in a batch. Note that user profiles $\vec{\theta}$ and topic profiles $\vec{\varphi}$ are not presented in Eqn. (5). These two parameter spaces are integrated out to produce a simplified probability computation. The actual $\vec{\theta}$ and $\vec{\varphi}$ parameters are inferred from sampled $\vec{r}$ and $\vec{z}$ after the Gibbs sampling converges. Hence, this is called a *collapsed* Gibbs sampling method.

Although by repeatedly sampling $\vec{r}$ and $\vec{z}$, we can produce fairly good posterior samples, Eqn. (5) assumes the personal impacts $\vec{\gamma}$ are known and fixed. However, in our study, we also need to estimate personal impact values as well. To do this, we follow the maximum likelihood paradigm. The rationale is that after each round of Gibbs sampling, $\vec{r}$ is updated to reflect the new representative distributions. Thus personal impact parameters $\vec{\gamma}$ are also updated so that the likelihood of generating samples $\vec{r}$ is maximized. In particular, the likelihood of observing $\vec{r}$ given the groups $\vec{G}$ and personal impacts $\vec{\gamma}$ is:

$$\mathcal{L}(\vec{r}|\vec{\gamma},\vec{G})=\log\left(\prod_{n=1}^{N}\Pr(r_n|G_n)\right)=\sum_{n=1}^{N}\log\frac{\gamma_{r_n}}{\sum_{u_j\in G_n}\gamma_j} \tag{6}$$

To find the maximum likelihood estimation of $\vec{\gamma}$ from Eqn.(6), we adopt the gradient descent method. Specifically, by taking a derivative regarding to each γ_i, we have:

$$\frac{\partial\mathcal{L}(\vec{r}|\vec{\gamma},\vec{G})}{\partial\gamma_i}=\sum_{\forall r_n=u_i}\frac{1}{\gamma_i}-\sum_{\forall G_n,u_i\in G_n}\frac{1}{\sum_{\forall u_j\in G_n}\gamma_j} \tag{7}$$

First we initialize all the personal impacts $\vec{\gamma}$ to a default value 1, which indicates that all users are assumed to have equal impacts *when there are no observations.* By iteratively take steps proportional to the personal impact gradients (see Eqn. (7)), we are able to find a set of local optimal personal impact parameters $\hat{\vec{\gamma}}$ that fits the observations $\vec{r}$. Note that, by definition, the personal impacts $\vec{\gamma}$ should be non-negative. Thus, we introduce a positive number δ as the lower bound of personal impacts. That is, whenever a personal impact is made lower than δ, its value is set to δ (fixed to 0.1 in our experiments). As such, we avoid some overfitting effects by ensuring that every user has a positive probability to be selected as a representative.

To put everything together, the Gibbs sampling algorithm for PIT model inference can be presented in Algorithm 1. This algorithm does two things: 1) output a Gibbs sampling $\vec{r}$ and $\vec{z}$ that converge to the posterior distribution of Eqn. (4) and 2) output a maximum likelihood estimation of personal impacts $\hat{\vec{\gamma}}$ so that the representative sampling of $\vec{r}$ can be explained. The first part of Algorithm 1 from line 1 to 5 initializes the latent variable samples $\vec{r}$ and $\vec{z}$ by randomly drawing the users from the corresponding groups G_n and topics $1 \sim |T|$. During the initialization, the algorithm maintains two counting matrices $\vec{C}^{UT}$ and $\vec{C}^{TW}$. These two counting matrices are used to efficiently compute the sampling posterior as in Eqn. (5). From line 6, The transitions between successive states of the Markov chain result from repeatedly drawing $\langle r_n, z_n\rangle$ from their distributions conditioned on all other variables as in Eqn. (5). Also, after each iteration of $\vec{r}$, $\vec{z}$ sampling, we use the gradient descend method to fit $\vec{\gamma}$ in line 11.

After Algorithm 1 finishes, we obtain the samples of $\vec{r}$, $\vec{z}$ and the maximum likelihood estimation of personal impact

Algorithm 1: PIT model Gibbs sampling algorithm.

Input: Group Item Access History $\vec{G}, \vec{s}$, super-parameters: α, β, max_iter.
Output: Sampled $\vec{r}, \vec{z}$, personal impact $\vec{\gamma}$.

$\vec{\gamma} \leftarrow \vec{1}$;
for $n \leftarrow 1, 2, 3, \cdots, N$ **do**
  Sample user $r_n \leftarrow x \sim \text{Mult}(1/|G_n|)$;
  Sample topic $z_n \leftarrow y \sim \text{Mult}(1/|T|)$;
  Update counters $\vec{C}^{UT}$ and $\vec{C}^{TW}$;
for *iter* $\leftarrow 1, 2, 3 \cdots$ *max_iter* **do**
  for $n \leftarrow 1, 2, 3, \cdots, N$ **do**
    Remove r_n, z_n from counters $\vec{C}^{UT}$ and $\vec{C}^{TW}$;
    Sample representative r_n topic z_n block $r_n, z_n \sim \Pr(r_n, z_n | \vec{G}, \vec{s}, \vec{r}_{\neg n}, \vec{z}_{\neg n}, \vec{\gamma}, \alpha, \beta)$ following Eqn. (5);
    Update counters $\vec{C}^{UT}$ and $\vec{C}^{TW}$;
  Gradient descend fit $\hat{\vec{\gamma}}$ given $\vec{G}, \vec{r}$;
return $\vec{r}, \vec{z}$ and $\hat{\vec{\gamma}}$;

$\vec{\gamma}$. To infer the user and item profiles $\vec{\theta}$ and $\vec{\varphi}$, we have them following the Dirichlet distributions:

$$\begin{aligned} \Pr(\vec{\theta}_i | \vec{r}, \vec{z}, \alpha) &\sim \texttt{Dir}(\vec{C}^{UT}_{i,*} + \vec{\alpha}) \\ \Pr(\vec{\varphi}_k | \vec{r}, \vec{z}, \beta) &\sim \texttt{Dir}(\vec{C}^{TW}_{k,*} + \vec{\beta}) \end{aligned} \tag{8}$$

Usually, we only need to use the maximized probability estimation of these parameters, which can be written as

$$\begin{aligned} \hat{\theta}_{i,k} = \hat{\Pr}(t_k | u_i) &= \frac{\vec{C}^{UT}_{i,k} + \alpha}{\sum_{k'} (\vec{C}^{UT}_{i,k'}) + \alpha)} \\ \hat{\varphi}_{k,j} = \hat{\Pr}(w_j | t_k) &= \frac{\vec{C}^{TW}_{k,j} + \beta}{(\sum_{j'} (\vec{C}^{TW}_{k,j'}) + \beta)} \end{aligned} \tag{9}$$

Therefore, the probability for a targeted group G_x to select an item w_j is :

$$\begin{aligned} \hat{\Pr}^{\text{PIT}}(w_j | G_x, \hat{\vec{\theta}}, \hat{\vec{\varphi}}, \hat{\vec{\gamma}}) &\propto \sum_{\forall u_i \in G_x} \hat{\gamma}_i \cdot \left(\sum_{k=1}^{|T|} \hat{\theta}_{i,k} \cdot \hat{\varphi}_{k,j} \right) \\ &\propto \sum_{\forall u_i \in G_x} \hat{\gamma}_i \cdot \hat{\vec{\theta}}_i \cdot \hat{\vec{\varphi}}_j^{\,T} \end{aligned} \tag{10}$$

Eqn. (10) is then used to make item recommendations.

4.4 PIT Model Extension

In the previous section, we discussed the PIT model to exploit the differences of personal impacts in group item selections. Yet, since the PIT model introduces an additional parameter γ for each user, if the group-item dataset is sparse, learning personal impact parameters suffers from overfitting problems. More specifically, if a user u_i has only participated in very few group activities, then estimating personal impact γ_i using PIT model may not be practical. In this section, we explore the relationship between the personal impacts and other features (especially social network features). By including these related features to PIT model, we expect these additional data shall further alleviate the over-fitting problem and thus achieve more reliable group recommendations.

As shown in Fig. 3, we introduce another feature e_i as the evidence of the personal impact parameter. Consider e_i as a numerical observation feature for the user u_i, and personal impact γ_i is correlated with e_i. Candidates for this feature can be network degree, clustering coefficient, betweenness, page rank of the social network etc. Here, we studied the correlation between personal impact and social network degree as an example. In Fig. 4, we plot the personal impact parameters learned from PIT model against corresponding user social network degrees on the Whrrl dataset (dataset details can be found in Section 5.1). From this figure, although the personal impacts learned form PIT model may have overfitted values, users with higher personal impacts still are more likely to have larger social network degrees. Actually, the computed correlation between $\vec{\gamma}$ and $\vec{e}$ in this dataset is 0.596, and the slope of the red fitted line is 6.13.

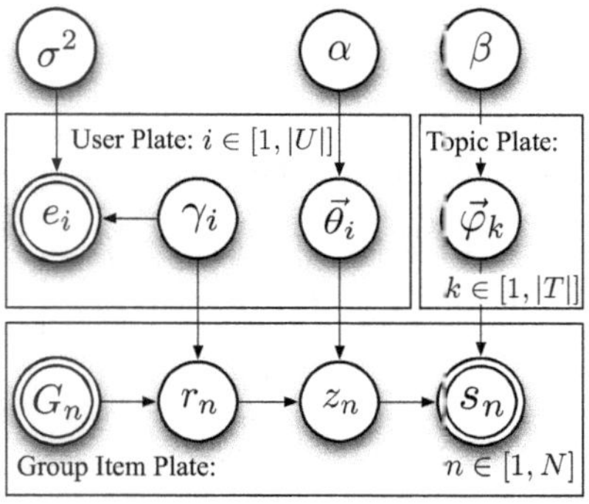

Figure 3: Extended Personal Impact Topic Model

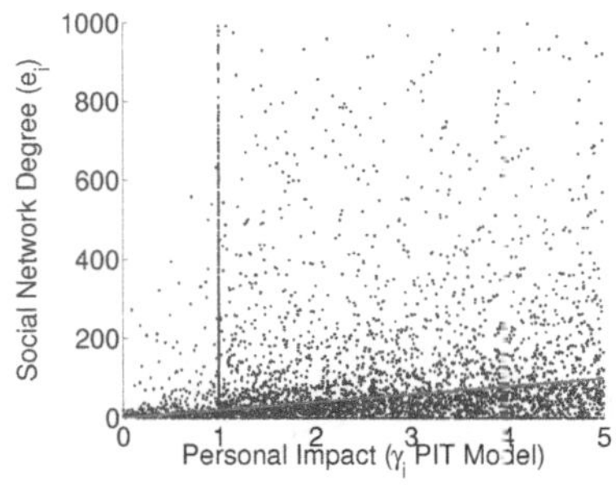

Figure 4: Personal Impacts vs. Degree distributions

To model the correlation between e_i and γ_i, we assume a linear model between them with Gaussian error, leaving other possible non-linear models to future works. Under our linear model assumption, the personal impact log likelihood can be expressed as:

$$\mathcal{L}(\vec{r}, \vec{e} | \vec{G}, \vec{\gamma}) = \sum_{n=1}^{N} \log \frac{\gamma_i}{\sum_{u_j \in G_n} \gamma_j} - \frac{1}{2} \sum_{i}^{|U|} (\frac{a + b\gamma_i - e_i}{\sigma})^2 \tag{11}$$

Under this log-likelihood, we not only need to estimate $\vec{\gamma}$ but also need to find the linear relation's parameter a and b. Because the correlation is modeled as linear, parameter a and b can be found the same as linear regression, but the gradient for each γ_i should be updated as:

$$\begin{aligned} \frac{\partial \mathcal{L}(\vec{r}, \vec{e} | \vec{G}, \vec{\gamma})}{\partial \gamma_i} &= \sum_{\forall r_n = u_i} \frac{1}{\gamma_i} - \sum_{\forall G_n, u_i \in G_n} \frac{1}{\sum_{\forall u_j \in G_n} \gamma_j} \\ &- \sum_{i}^{|U|} \frac{b(a + b\gamma_i - e_i)}{\sigma^2} \end{aligned} \tag{12}$$

By replacing Eqn. (7) with Eqn. (12), we incorperate the personal impact related evidence into the PIT model. Intuitively, the evidence value for each user gives a hint to his personal impact estimation. The inclusion of the personal impact evidence penalizes those personal impacts that deviate e_i more than σ away. Therefore, a smaller σ penalizes more the error in Eqn. (12), and therefore forces the learned personal impacts to be closer to the observed evidence. In this paper, we use empirical methods to determine a good selection of σ.

5. EVALUATION

In this section, we evaluate the proposed models with three real datasets, one collected from a location-based social network service whrrl.com and the other two from an event-based social network service meetup.com. We evaluate our proposed group recommendation models with three recommendation problems: 1) Whrrl group POI checkin recommendation, 2) Meetup group tag recommendation, and 3) Meetup event venue recommendation. These three recommendation problems have different data space and group-item selection behaviors, which reflect comprehensive performances of proposed approaches. For each dataset, we evaluate the proposed PIT model against the baseline methods. Since the Meetup datasets do not contain additional social network information, E-PIT model is only tested in Whrrl dataset.

5.1 Dataset Description

Whrrl.com is an online location-based social network that helps people to explore points-of-interests (POIs) (e.g. restaurants, movie theaters, parks etc). A group of people can checkin POIs and share the experiences via mobile devices. Given the group-POI checkin history, a recommendation task is to identify POIs that a target group has potential to visit. On the other hand, meetup.com is an online event-based social network that provides a platform for users to organize face-to-face social events. From the website, we collected two datasets that support two types of group recommendation problems. First, each meetup online group can specify some tags to represent common interests of group members, so we may recommend additional tags for groups based on existing ones. Second, to help people to organize social events at venues that fit participants' preferences on meetup.com, we may recommend event venues to users depending on event participations and past venue selections.

The datasets collected for these three group recommendation problems are summarized as in Table 1[5]. The first three rows show the total number of distinct users and groups, as well as the recommendation items (POIs, tags and venues). The fourth and fifth rows summarize average sizes of groups and how many groups each user participated in. Generally, smaller group sizes and more user-group participations lead to easier group recommendations. Finally, the sixth and seventh rows show how many items each *unique* group has selected, and how many selections each item received, respectively. The fewer items a group selects or the fewer group selections an item receives, the more sparse the dataset is, which results in more difficult recommendations. With different statistics on the three datasets, we are able to comprehensively test the proposed approaches in various application scenarios.

[5]Meetup dataset [12] can be downloaded from http://largenetwork.org/ebsn

5.2 Evaluated Recommendation Methods

CF	Neighborhood collaborative filtering methods. Treat each group members as equal.
LM-CF	Neighborhood collaborative filtering methods. Use least miserable strategy to merge individual users' recommendations.
E-AT	Extended author topic model, introduced in Section 3.2
PIT	Personal impact topic model, introduced in Section 4.3.
E-PIT	Extended personal impact topic model, introduced in Section 4.4.

Table 2: Evaluated Recommendation Methods

In Table 2, we summarize the recommendation methods evaluated in this paper. In addition to the E-AT, PIT, E-PIT models, we also introduce two memory-based collaborative filtering methods as the baselines, namely, the classic memory-based CF method [19] (CF) and the least miserable CF [17] (LM-CF). Since our datasets provide group-item pairs instead of user-item pairs, we first project a group-item pair $\langle G_n, s_n \rangle$ into user-item selection pairs $\{\langle u_i, s_n \rangle | \forall u_i \in G_n\}$. After applying memory-based CF to the projected dataset, we make recommendations for a target group by averaging group members' individual preference scores. LM-CF was studied in [17] as an important strategy to make group recommendations. LM-CF is similar to CF method, but when making recommendation to a target group, each item's lowest score from group members is used to make recommendations.

For each method, we randomly sample 20% group-item pairs from the entire dataset as validation dataset. The other 80% data are used as training data. We use recall as the evaluation metric. Therefore, for each top-n recommended items, we calculate

$$\texttt{recall} = \frac{\#\text{ of items that are included in top-}n\text{ recommendations}}{\#\text{ group-item pairs validated}} \quad (13)$$

Therefore, the recall of each recommendation method is the percentage of targeted group's selected items that are included within recommendations.

5.3 Evaluation Results

The first set of results on recall vs. number of recommendations are reported in Fig. 5. We fix the total number of topics K at 250, and vary the number of recommendations. As shown in Fig. 5, while the recall grows as the number of recommendations increases, PIT models achieve the best performance, followed by E-AT, and the CF approaches perform the worst. The results validate our proposed methods, in which the personal impacts of group members effectively improved recommendation results. CF and LM-CF fall behind others because these two methods not only ignore the difference among users, but also treat each group activity as a trivial union of individual behaviors per group member. By breaking up the group selection transactions into personal activities, the CF methods overlook the social indication in group activities. The extended author topic (E-AT) model considers each group as a whole, which effectively preserves the group's social information. It also

Whrrl POI		Meetup Group Tag		Meetup Event Venue	
Parameters	Value	Parameters	Value	Parameters	Value
# Users ($\|U\|$)	10,147	# Users ($\|U\|$)	124,047	# Users ($\|U\|$)	329,590
# Checkin Groups	34,338	# Online Groups	1,613	# Event Groups	115,634
# POIs ($\|W\|$)	15,940	# Tags ($\|W\|$)	2,118	# Venues ($\|W\|$)	47,606
Avg. Checkin Group Size	3.98	Avg. Group Size	97.64	Avg. Event Participants	10.75
Avg. Checkins for a User	13.48	Avg. Groups joined by a User	1.205	Avg. Events for a user	3.77
Avg. POI for a Group	1.21	Avg. Tags for a Group	4.92	Avg. Venues for an Event Group	1.03
Avg. Checkins for a POI	2.15	Avg. Groups for a Tag	3.74	Avg. Events for an Venues	2.43

Table 1: Data Set Summary

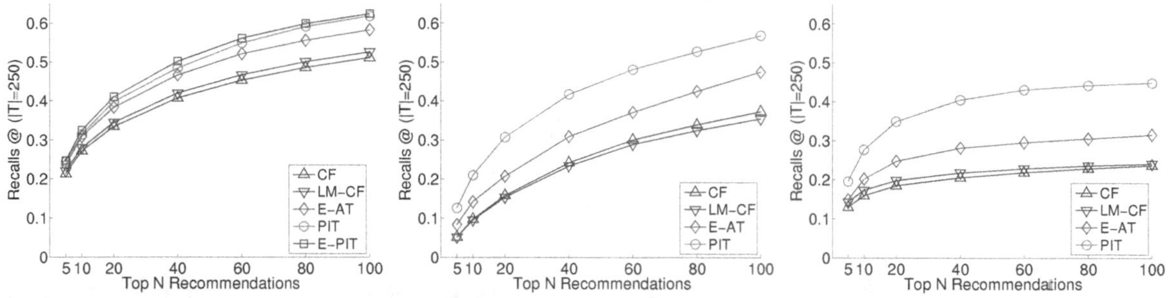

(a) Whrrl POI dataset (b) Meetup group tag dataset (c) Meetup event venue dataset

Figure 5: Recalls under # recommendations made (n)

utilizes Dirichlet prior to prevent over-fitting, thus obtains better results. However, since the E-AT model is not aware of the differences of personal impacts, every group member is treated the same while making prediction for a target group, which degrades the recommendation performance. By mining the personal impacts from group-item pair histories, our proposed PIT model improves the recommendation performance significantly. To further alleviate the over-fitting of personal impact parameters, our E-PIT model exploits social network degrees as an additional feature $\vec{e}$ to guide the personal impact estimation, and achieves the best result on the Whrrl dataset.

Fig. 6 illustrates the recall results when the number of recommendations is fixed at 80, and the number of topics varies. As CF and LM-CF do not involve topics, they have constant recalls. In Fig. 6 (a) and Fig. 6(c), when the number of topics increases, the recalls first increase and then flat out. This is because items in these two datasets have large data space (see row 3 of Table 1), a large number of topics can help to precisely differentiate the items. In Fig. 6 (b), because the number of tags (item space) is much smaller, the Figure shows that 100 topics are enough to model tags. In all three recommendation test cases, we can see that the proposed PIT and E-PIT models improve over the E-AT model by about 10%, and outperform the CF approaches by 15%-25%. These significant improvements demonstrated the effectiveness of our proposals.

5.4 Personal Impact Distribution and Significance

By learning the PIT and E-PIT models, we obtain a set of estimated personal impacts. One fundamental question that we need to answer is whether people do exhibit different personal impacts. Because only if most of people's personal impacts are significantly different from 1, the proposed PIT and E-PIT model can improve over E-AT model which assumes equal personal impacts.

In Fig. 7, the histograms of the learned personal impacts are plotted. Fig. 7(a) and Fig. 7(b) demonstrate learned personal impacts from PIT model and E-PIT model for the Whrrl POI checkin dataset, while Fig. 7(c) and Fig. 7(d) show personal impact distributions for the Meetup group tag and event venue dataset obtained from PIT model, respectively. In all four results, we can see that there are also a great portion of users with personal impacts close to 1. These users are either because 1) they have limited historical data to derive personal impacts, or 2) as their group representative probabilities are balanced, their personal impacts are indeed 1. Through careful examination of the data, we found that most of these users have extremely sparse historical information in the dataset (e.g., they have only participated in one group and involved in only one item selection, and the other group members are inactive as well). Hence, we are not able to differentiate the personal impact of such users from other group members. This result reflects the case that these users have equal impact on group decisions. By comparing Fig. 7(a) and Fig. 7(b), we can find that by introducing additional social network degree features, E-PIT model improves over the PIT model by reducing the number of users with personal impacts closed to 1 from 28% to 17%. Thus, we believe about 10% of ambiguous personal impacts can be refined after introducing the social network degree.

On the other hand, Fig. 7 demonstrate the rest of users' personal impacts distributed relatively evenly above and below the value of 1, meaning that some of them influence their group's decision more, while others influence much less. Interestingly, Fig. 7(c) shows a drop of the distribution on $[0.5, 1)$ and $(1, 2]$. The reason for this is that each of Meetup group selects an average of 4.92 tags. Based on our analysis, tags selected by one group are usually related. Thus, one user with the interest matching the group's tags may have multiple chances to be sampled as representatives. The personal impacts of these users are therefore boosted multiple times, leading to higher impact values. Meanwhile, users

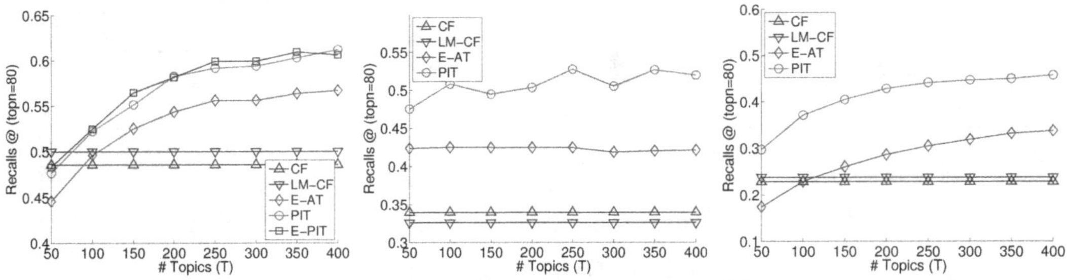

(a) Whrrl POI dataset (b) Meetup group tag dataset (c) Meetup event venue dataset

Figure 6: Recalls under # topics (T)

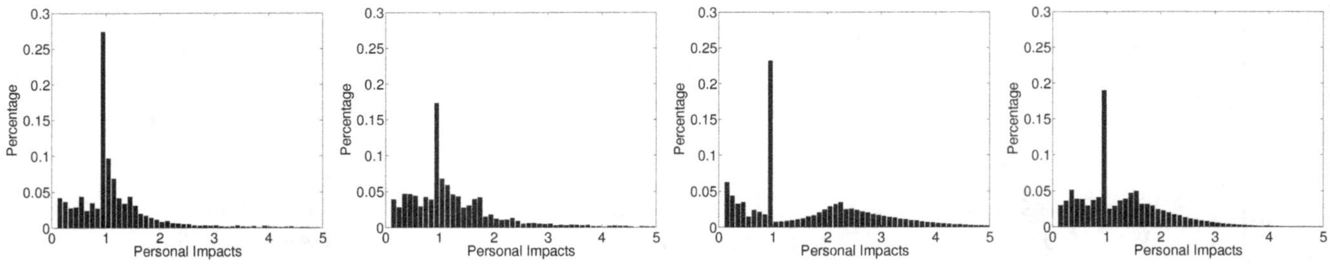

(a) Whrrl POI dataset (PIT Model) (b) Whrrl POI dataset (E-PIT Model) (c) Meetup group tag dataset (PIT Model) (d) Meetup event venue dataset (PIT Model)

Figure 7: Personal Impacts Learned from Dataset

who do not match the group preference profile tend to gain even lower personal impact values. The learned personal impacts thus deviate more from 1. Fig. 7(d) has similar trends as in Fig.7(a), which does not have extreme personal impacts as Fig. 7(c) does, because each social event group usually only selects one venue.

To statistically confirm that most users have their personal impact significantly deviate from 1, we applied a statistic test on a non-hypothesis that the personal impact values equal to 1 for all the users. Accordingly, for an arbitrary user u_i, the expected number of times that u_i is selected as representatives under this non-hypothesis is $E_i = \sum_{\forall G_n|u_i \in G_n} 1/|G_n|$. The observed times that u_i is selected as representatives is $O_i = \sum_{\forall r_n|u_i=r_n} 1$. Therefore, for each user, the p-value for his personal impact is the probability that a more extreme statistic value to O_i is observed. By taking this statistic test for each individual user's personal impact, we are able to find the percentage of users whose personal impacts are significantly not equal to 1 under the Type I error $\alpha = 0.05$. For these four results, the percentages are 56.4%, 68.0%, 50.7% and 61.0%, respectively. Thus, due to the limitation of our dataset size and user activities, we cannot show that all the users' personal impacts are significant other than 1. However, these results demonstrate that lots of users' personal impacts are indeed statistically significant, which proves our theory on utilizing personal impacts.

5.5 Topic Analysis

In this subsection, we conduct semantic investigations on the topics established by the proposed PIT model. In general, if the topics generated by the PIT model are semantically meaningful, we believe that the model is effective. Here, we show the analysis results with both location-centric data and text tag data.

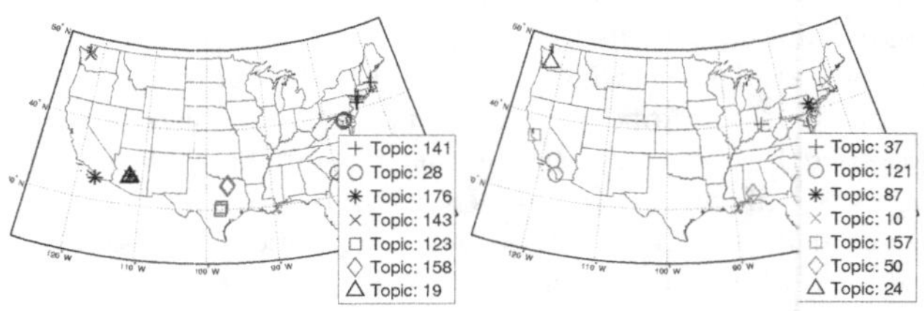

(a) Whrrl POI dataset (b) Meetup event venue dataset

Figure 8: Geographic distribution of sampled topics

Fig 8 depicts item geographic location distributions of 7 selected topics on the Whrrl dataset and the Meetup event venue dataset. Each topic is represented by locations of 5 items with the highest generating probabilities. In both datasets, we can observe that the items of the same topic locate close to each other. The reason is that location-related group activities such as checkins and offline events are usually constrained by spatial distance, and people tend to move within small geographic areas most of the time. Thus, the items selected in these group activities fall into such small geographic areas. These results demonstrate that the PIT model has good ability to extract topics from pure group-item selections.

In Table 3, we present a list of topics composed of text tags. Given a set of topics $T = t_k$ identified by the PIT model, we associate each user u_i with a topic that he/she is most interested in (i.e., t_k with the largest $Pr(t_k|u_i)$). Then we sort the topics by number of users they are associated with. Intuitively, the more users associated with the topic, the more popular the topic is. As shown in Table 3, each row represents a topic and we list the top three tags for each topic (w_j with highest $Pr(w_j|t_k)$). The most popular topic

# Users	Top 3 Tags
14,126	hiking, outdoors, outdoor recreation
6,850	business networking, business referral networking, business connection
6,279	dating and relationships, singles, newly single
6,248	active dogs, dog play groups, socializing dogs
6,186	photo, digital camera, photography workshops
......	
126	meeting new people, social network, women
119	personal growth, self-improvement, law of attraction
45	social network, women, Christian parent

Table 3: Meetup group tag dataset PIT model topics

is about hiking and outdoor activities, which matches our daily life experience that such activities are usually held on a group basis. It also indicates that people love to use online social network services to organize such outdoor events. Further, we find that more elaborated and specific tags attract more users, such as business networking, photography and dogs, and this indicates that people are willing to participate in group activities with focused topics. On the opposite, generic and vague tags like "meeting new people" degrades the model's ability of separating topics, and they are not as attractive to users. Therefore, we can conclude that our PIT model works well on identifying interesting topics.

6. CONCLUSION

As social group oriented services are growing rapidly in recent years, recommender systems need to adapt to this new trend to offer better service. This paper studies the group recommendation problem that aims at recommending items to ad hocly formed target groups. We proposed a probablistic *personal impact topic* (PIT) model to effectively address this problem. In the PIT model, we introduced the personal impact parameter to describe different influence of users on the group decision making process, and identify the recommended items by collectively consider users personal preferences and their personal influences. Therefore, we naturally capture the fact that influencial users have higher chances to affect group selection decisions. Under the general assumption that individual user preference profiles are not available, we designed a learning algorithm to inference the personal impacts and user preferences purely from group selection history. Furthermore, we exploit other social network features such as degree distributions to help refine the parameter inference in an extended PIT (E-PIT) model. Via comprehensive evaluations, we demonstrate that our proposed models bring great recommendation improvements over baseline approaches.

7. REFERENCES

[1] G. Adomavicius, G. Adomavicius, and A. Tuzhilin. Toward the next generation of recommender systems: A survey of the state-of-the-art and possible extensions. *IEEE TKDE*, 17(6):734–749, 2005.

[2] S. Amer-Yahia, S. B. Roy, A. Chawlat, G. Das, and C. Yu. Group recommendation: semantics and efficiency. *PVLDB*, 2:754–765, 2009.

[3] L. Ardissono, A. Goy, G. Petrone, M. Segnan, and P. Torasso. Intrigue: personalized recommendation of tourist attractions for desktop and hand held devices. *Applied Artificial Intelligence*, 17(8):687–714, 2003.

[4] L. Baltrunas, T. Makcinskas, and F. Ricci. Group recommendations with rank aggregation and collaborative filtering. In *RecSys*, pages 119–126, 2010.

[5] D. M. Blei, A. Y. Ng, and M. I. Jordan. Latent dirichlet allocation. *Journal of Machine Learning Research*, 3:993–1022, 2003.

[6] J. S. Breese, D. Heckerman, and C. Kadie. Empirical analysis of predictive algorithms for collaborative filtering. In *UAI*, pages 43–52, 1998.

[7] J. S. Breese, D. Heckerman, and C. M. Kadie. Empirical analysis of predictive algorithms for collaborative filtering. In *UAI*, pages 43–52, 1998.

[8] A. Crossen, J. Budzik, and K. J. Hammond. Flytrap: intelligent group music recommendation. In *IUI*, pages 184–185, 2002.

[9] D. Goldberg, D. Nichols, B. M. Oki, and D. Terry. Using collaborative filtering to weave an information tapestry. *CACM*, 35:61–70, 1992.

[10] T. Hofmann. Latent semantic models for collaborative filtering. *TOIS*, 22(1):89–115, 2004.

[11] A. Jameson and B. Smyth. The adaptive web. chapter Recommendation to groups, pages 596–627. 2007.

[12] X. Liu, Q. He, Y. Tian, W.-C. Lee, J. McPherson, and J. Han. Event-based social networks: Linking the online and offline social worlds. In *KDD*, 2012.

[13] J. Masthoff. Group modeling: Selecting a sequence of television items to suit a group of viewers. *UMUAI*, 14:37–85, 2004.

[14] J. F. McCarthy and T. D. Anagnost. Musicfx: an arbiter of group preferences for computer supported collaborative workouts. In *CSCW*, pages 363–372, 1998.

[15] K. McCarthy, M. Salamó, L. Coyle, L. McGinty, B. Smyth, and P. Nixon. Cats: A synchronous approach to collaborative group recommendation. In *FLAIRS*, pages 86–91, 2006.

[16] R. J. Mooney and L. Roy. Content-based book recommending using learning for text categorization. In *DL*, pages 195–204, 2000.

[17] M. O'Connor, D. Cosley, J. A. Konstan, and J. Riedl. Polylens: a recommender system for groups of users. In *ECSCW*, pages 199–218, 2001.

[18] S. Pizzutilo, B. De Carolis, G. Cozzolongo, and F. Ambruoso. Group modeling in a public space: methods, techniques, experiences. In *WSEAS*, pages 175–180, 2005.

[19] P. Resnick, N. Iacovou, M. Suchak, P. Bergstrom, and J. Riedl. Grouplens: an open architecture for collaborative filtering of netnews. In *CSCW*, pages 175–186, 1994.

[20] M. Rosen-Zvi, T. Griffiths, M. Steyvers, and P. Smyth. The author-topic model for authors and documents. In *UAI*, pages 487–494, 2004.

[21] B. Sarwar, G. Karypis, J. Konstan, and J. Riedl. Item-based collaborative filtering recommendation algorithms. In *WWW*, pages 285–295, 2001.

[22] X. Su and T. M. Khoshgoftaar. A survey of collaborative filtering techniques. *Advance in Artificial Intelligence*, pages 4:2–4:2, 2009.

[23] L. Ungar, L. Ungar, D. Foster, E. Andre, S. Wars, F. S. Wars, D. S. Wars, and J. H. Whispers. Clustering methods for collaborative filtering. In *AAAI Workshop on Recommendation Systems*, 1998.

[24] M. Ye, X. Liu, and W.-C. Lee. Exploring social influence for recommendation - a generative model approach. In *SIGIR*, 2012.

[25] Z. Yu, X. Zhou, Y. Hao, and J. Gu. Tv program recommendation for multiple viewers based on user profile merging. *UMUAI*, 16:63–82, 2006.

The Efficient Imputation Method for Neighborhood-based Collaborative Filtering

Yongli Ren, Gang Li, Jun Zhang and Wanlei Zhou
School of Information Technology
Deakin University, 221 Burwood Highway
Vic 3125, Australia
{yongli, gang.li, jun.zhang, wanlei}@deakin.edu.au

ABSTRACT

As each user tends to rate a small proportion of available items, the resulted *Data Sparsity* issue brings significant challenges to the research of recommender systems. This issue becomes even more severe for neighborhood-based collaborative filtering methods, as there are even lower numbers of ratings available in the neighborhood of the query item. In this paper, we aim to address the *Data Sparsity* issue in the context of the neighborhood-based collaborative filtering. Given the $(user, item)$ query, a set of key ratings are identified, and an auto-adaptive imputation method is proposed to fill the missing values in the set of key ratings. The proposed method can be used with any similarity metrics, such as the *Pearson Correlation Coefficient* and *Cosine*-based similarity, and it is theoretically guaranteed to outperform the neighborhood-based collaborative filtering approaches. Results from experiments prove that the proposed method could significantly improve the accuracy of recommendations for neighborhood-based Collaborative Filtering algorithms.

Categories and Subject Descriptors

H.4 [**Information Systems Applications**]: Miscellaneous; H.3.3 [**Information Storage and Retrieval**]: Information Search and Retrieval—*Information Filtering*

General Terms

Algorithms

Keywords

Imputation, Collaborative Filtering, Recommender Systems

1. INTRODUCTION

Recommender System attempts to automatically provide personalized recommendations based on the historical records of users' activities, and it is commonly constructed on the basis of *Collaborative Filtering* (CF) methods because of their insensitivity to the detailed features of users or items. In general, there are two types of collaborative filtering methods: the *neighborhood*-based method and the *model*-based method [1,10]. Although, a lot of research attention has been attracted to the *model*-based method, a lesson learned from the well-known *Netflix Competition* tells that *neighborhood*-based methods and *model*-based methods can explore very different levels of data patterns in the data set, therefore none of them can always output optimal results solely based on its own [3]. In this paper, we aim to address the data sparsity issue in the context of *neighborhood*-based method with theoretical analysis.

Neighborhood-based CF methods are generally based on the k nearest neighbor rule. Namely, its performance is highly affected by the selected nearest neighbors. However, there has been serious problems for practitioners trying to use this kind of method in areas where data is sparse. Specifically, *Data Sparsity* refers to insufficient information on a user's rating history, and the corresponding $user \times item$ rating matrix will thus become extremely sparse. When the data is prevailing with missing values, two like-minded users may not show any similarity. To overcome this problem for recommendation purposes, two major categories of approaches exist: one is to utilize more suitable similarity metrics to identify a better set of neighborhood [1, 5, 19]. The other approach is to design better aggregation methods which integrate the item ratings given by all the neighbors [6, 13]. It might be argued that a third category of approaches based on data imputation [5,16,23,25,26,28], to which this work belongs, has begun to emerge over the past couple of years. Among others, data imputation mainly involves selecting a set of $(user, item)$ pairs whose values are missing or unavailable in the $user \times item$ rating matrix, and filling them with imputed values before predicting the ratings for the active user. However, despite evidence of improved performance in the predictive accuracy, the research of imputation-based CF methods is still in its infancy. Issues such as *does all missing data possess the same importance to the recommendation purpose*, *how to select the most informative missing data to impute*, and *how to trade off the imputation benefit and error*, still largely remain unexplored.

In this paper, we propose an *Auto-Adaptive Imputation* (AutAI) method which can automatically identify a *key set* of missing data, and adaptively imputate them according to each individual user's rating history. Through this novel method, we can maximize the information contained in the neighborhood of the active user while minimizing the im-

CIKM'12, October 29–November 2, 2012, Maui, HI, USA.

putation error brought in. Inspired by Cover's [8] research on the nearest neighbor rule, which showed that the nearest neighbor contains at least 50% of the information in the infinite training set, we argue that not all missing data possesses equivalent information for a particular prediction, and some missing data is more informative than others. Then, we propose an auto-adaptive imputation method to identify the critical *key set* of missing data for each active user adaptively so as to impute the most informative missing data. Therefore, the proposed imputation method can lead to better recommendations in terms of accuracy, and we provide theoretical analysis on the performance benefit for the proposed AutAI method. On this basis, we propose a collaborative filtering algorithm by using the AutAI method from both user and item aspects (AutAI-Fusion).

The major contributions of this paper are as follows:

- We propose a novel imputation method (AutAI) to identify a *key set* of missing data for each rating prediction to address the problem of data sparsity.
- For the first time, we analyse the imputation-based methods from a theoretical perspective in the area of collaborative filtering.
- Based on the AutAI method, we propose a novel efficient collaborative filtering algorithm (AutAI-Fusion) by simultaneously considering both user activity and item popularity.
- We conduct a large set of experiments to examine the performance of the AutAI method on various similarity metrics, and to compare the proposed AutAI-Fusion algorithm with 6 state-of-the-art collaborative filtering algorithms, including other representative imputation-based algorithms.

The rest of the paper is organized as follows. We present the background in Section 2, define the *Auto Adaptive Imputation* (AutAI) method in Section 3, together with theoretical analysis about imputation benefit and error. Section 4 presents the experiment results, followed by conclusion in Section 5.

2. BACKGROUND AND RELATED WORK

In this section, we define the notations used in the paper, and we briefly recap the neighborhood-based method and the model-based method.

2.1 Notation

Let us assume $\mathcal{U} = \{u_1, u_2, \cdots, u_m\}$ be a set of m users, $\mathcal{T} = \{t_1, t_2, \cdots, t_n\}$ be the set of n items. For m users and n items, the *user* $\times$ *item* rating matrix $\mathcal{R}$ is represented as a $m \times n$ matrix. The *user* $\times$ *item* matrix $\mathcal{R}$ can be decomposed into row vectors: $\mathcal{R} = [\mathbf{u_1}, \mathbf{u_2}, \cdots, \mathbf{u_m}]^T$ and $\mathbf{u_i} = [r_{i1}, r_{i2}, \cdots, r_{in}]$, where T denotes *transpose*. The row vector $\mathbf{u_i}$ corresponds to the user u_i's rating information, and r_{ij} denotes the rating that user u_i gave to item t_j. $\mathcal{N}_k(u_x)$ denotes the set of user u_x's k nearest neighbors. $T_{xy} = \{t_i \in T | r_{xi} \neq \emptyset, r_{yi} \neq \emptyset\}$ denotes the set of items co-rated by both u_x and u_y. u_a denotes the active user for whom the recommendation is processing. t_s denotes the active item on which the recommendation is processing. $\bar{u}_a$ and $\bar{t}_s$ denote the average rating of user u_a and the average rating on item t_s, respectively.

2.2 Neighborhood-based CF

One of the pioneering works in *neighborhood-based Collaborative Filtering* was proposed by Paul Resnick [19]. This system, *GroupLens* utilizes users' ratings as input, then predicts how much the active user like an un-rated item. In general, the neighborhood-based Collaborative Filtering method is based on k nearest neighbors (KNN) rules. Its input is usually the entire *user* $\times$ *item rating* matrix $\mathcal{R}$. Two stages are involved in this process: *Neighbor Selection* and *Rating Aggregation*.

In the stage of *Neighbor Selection*, similarity could be evaluated between any two rows or any two columns in the *user* $\times$ *item* rating matrix, corresponding to the user-based approaches [5], or the item-based approaches [22]. It is clear that similarity measurements is one of the foundational problems in *collaborative filtering* methods. When the *user* $\times$ *item* rating matrix is sparse, this problem would be even more difficult. Several methods have been propoesd to address this problem. One way is to design better similarity metrics that tolerant the sparsity issue, e.g. the two popular metrics, *Pearson Correlation Coefficient* [19] and *Cosine-based Similarity* [1,5]. Another way is to tackle the sparsity issue directly through data imputation, such as *Default Voting* [5], *EMDP* [16] etc. We are going to discuss this part with more details in the following Section 2.4.

In the stage of *Rating Aggregation*, for any item t_s, all the ratings on t_s by users in the $N_k(u_a)$, will be aggregated into the predicted rating value $\hat{r}_{as}$ by user u_a [1]. The *weighted majority prediction* algorithm predicts the rating on new items based on a weighted sum of the users ratings on those items [11]. Hence the determination of a suitable set of weights becomes an essential problem here. While most conventional work relies on the similarity between users or items to determine the weight, *Data Sparsity* therefore affects this stage too.

2.3 Model-based CF

In contrast to the *Neighborhood-based CF* methods, the *Model-based collaborative filtering* algorithms attempt to construct a model from the given rating matrix, and utilize the model to predict ratings on new items. A wide range of machine learning techniques have been adopted: *supervised learning*, *unsupervised learning* and *matrix decomposition* etc. For supervised learning techniques, Su and Khoshgoftaar applied the *Belief Nets* to treat rating prediction as a multi-class classification problem [24]. For unsupervised learning techniques, Lemire and Maclachlan proposed the *slope one* algorithm, based on the *popularity differential* principle between items, which means user rating behaviour is influenced by both the user's rating style (e.g. the user's average rating) and items popularity (e.g. the average rating for an item) [14]. For matrix decomposition techniques, Billsus and Pazzani proposed to use the *Singular Value Decomposition* (SVD) to exploit the '*latent structure*' in user ratings [4]. This method could utilize information from users whose ratings are not correlated with the active user. Since then, many other SVD-based methods have been proposed, such as the *SVD++* method which combines the user's explicit and implicit feedbacks [12].

2.4 Data Sparsity and Imputation

Data Sparsity is one of the most challenging issues in recommendation techniques. Since users tend to rate only a small fraction of items in a system, the *user* $\times$ *item* rating matrix is usually very sparse, with a density of around 1% [22]. Furthermore, *Data Sparsity* may make the *neighborhood*-based CF methods incapable of finding neighbors and therefore fail to make accurate recommendations [17,22]. To overcome this problem, a number of methods have been proposed. One category of methods is to design some similarity measurement which can tolerate the sparsity in the recommendation field [9]. Another category is to design better aggregation methods which integrate the item ratings given by all neighbors [6,13]. The third category of these methods is to fill in the missing data by *imputation*, e.g. the *default voting* [5], the *smoothing method* [28], and the missing data prediction [16]. In this paper, we focus on the methods by using imputation.

Default Voting is a straight forward imputation-based method [5] which assumes default values for those missing ratings, such as exploiting average ratings by a small group of users as default ratings for other items in order to increase the size of the *co-rated item set* [7]. Xue et. al. proposed to use some machine learning methods to smooth all missing data in the *user* $\times$ *item* rating matrix [28]. Results from their experiment show that more accurate recommendations are obtained if imputing properly. Recently, Ma et. al. took the imputation confidence into consideration, and only filled in the missing data when it was confident to impute [16]. Specifically, they set a threshold to identify highly confident users, and only make a prediction about the missing data to users that have highly confident neighbors. This idea works well as it prevents poor imputation. However, their proposed EMDP algorithm treats all the missing data equally. Other previous imputation-related works focus on investigating various imputation techniques [23, 25, 26], e.g. the mean imputation, the linear regression imputation, the multiple imputation [21], and the predictive mean matching imputation [15].

Little work investigates *how to impute and which missing data should be imputed?* This question is interesting and of importance, since imputed data will bring in some imputation error as well as alleviating the sparsity issue. In this paper, we will investigate these questions, and propose an auto-adaptive imputation method that is presented in the following section.

3. AUTO-ADAPTIVE IMPUTATION BASED COLLABORATIVE FILTERING

In this section, we propose a new imputation method to effectively improve the performance of neighborhood-based collaborative filtering. Moreover, a theoretical analysis on the performance benefit of the proposed method is also provided. To our best knowledge, this work is the first one that analyses the imputation methods from a theoretical perspective in the area of collaborative filtering. Finally, by applying the proposed AutAI method, we, furthermore, propose a collaborative filtering framework by using AutAI form both user and item perspectives (AutAI-Fusion).

3.1 Formulation of Neighborhood-based CF

We first formulate the *neighborhood*-based CF using the probability theory [20]. The *neighborhood*-based CF provides recommendations by estimating how much the active user may like un-rated items, which is known as the *rating prediction* task. Given two variables, the user consuming history u and the available ratings r, the rating prediction task can be formulated as $\mu(u) = E(r|u)$, which is the expectation of dependent variable r given the independent variable u. For the recommendation purpose, it is interesting to estimate the value r_{as} on an un-rated item t_s for a singular independent variable value u_a. The estimator for u_a is then:

$$\hat{\mu}(u_a) = E(r_{as}|u_a). \tag{1}$$

From the perspective of probability theory, the observation values sampled at u_a can be used to estimate $\hat{\mu}(u_a)$.

However, there is no observation values at u_a in the context of collaborative filtering. To tackle this problem, certain similar users of u_a are selected and used to estimate $\hat{\mu}(u_a)$. This is the assumption of collaborative filtering: *similar users may have similar ratings on items.* Specifically, to estimate $\hat{\mu}(u_a)$, we can first select several *neighbors* of u_a, then treat the ratings of these neighbors as *samples* at u_a. Finally, we process the above estimation method as usual. This is the well-known k nearest neighbor estimator [10] (KNN):

$$\hat{\mu}(u_a) = E(r_{as}|u_a) = \frac{1}{k} \sum_{u_x \in \mathcal{N}_k(u_a)} r_{xs}, \tag{2}$$

where k is the number of selected neighbors, u_x is one of u_a's neighbors, $\mathcal{N}_k(u_a)$ is the set of k nearest neighbors, and r_{xs} is the rating of neighbor u_x on t_s. To further reduce the estimation bias, the KNN estimation usually apply the weighted average [2]:

$$\hat{\mu}(u_a) = E(r_{as}|u_a) = \frac{1}{\eta} \sum_{u_x \in \mathcal{N}_k(u_a)} w_{ax} r_{xs}, \tag{3}$$

where w_{ax} is the weight of neighbor u_x to u_a, and $\eta = \sum_{u_x \in \mathcal{N}_k(u_a)} w_{ax}$ is the normalizing factor. The weights reflect how close the neighbors are to u_a.

For neighborhood-based CF, the sparsity issue can lead to the critical problem of unreliable similarity since the similarity between two users is actually calculated using a very small set of co-rated items. The user relationship measured by the unreliable similarity cannot capture the overall relationship between two users [17]. Moreover, the similarities of an active user u_a to two users (u_x and u_y) are computed on two different sets of co-rated items, which results in incomparable similarities. Consequently, the performance of neighborhood-based CF is seriously affected by inaccurate similarities due to the sparsity issue.

3.2 A Novel Auto-adaptive Imputation Method

In this section, we propose a novel *Auto-Adaptive Imputation* (AutAI) method. To make a rating prediction on the active item t_s for the active user u_a, we argue that not all missing data in the *user* $\times$ *item* rating matrix possesses equivalent information for this rating prediction, and conversely there is a *key set* of missing data that are most informative for this particular prediction. Accordingly, this *key set* should be different for every prediction, even for the same user.

The proposed AutAI method can identify which missing data should be imputed automatically, with the imputed set determined adaptively according to a user's own rating history. Specifically, to make rating prediction on item t_s for user u_a, the imputed set is identified by two factors, the users related to u_a and the items related to t_s. We denote the related users as $\mathcal{U}_a$, and denote the related items as $\mathcal{T}_s$:

$$\mathcal{U}_a = \{u_{a'} | r_{a's} \neq \oslash\} \quad (4)$$

$$\mathcal{T}_s = \{t_i | t_i \subset [T_{aa'_1} \cup \cdots \cup T_{aa'_i} \cup \cdots \cup T_{aa'_l}]\}, \quad (5)$$

where $T_{aa'_i}$ is the co-rated item set between the active user u_a and $u_{a'_i} \in \mathcal{U}_a$, and $l = |\mathcal{U}_a|$. For example, suppose that the rating histories for two users u_a and $u_{a'}$ are represented as:

$$\mathbf{u_a} = [r_{a1}, \ 0, \ 0, \ r_{a4}, \ r_{a5}, \ 0, \ \cdots, \ r_{an}]$$

$$\mathbf{u_{a'}} = [r_{a'1}, \ r_{a'2}, \ 0, \ 0, \ r_{a'5}, \ 0, \ \cdots, \ 0],$$

where 0 indicates that the corresponding rating is missing. Then $T_{aa'} = [t_1, t_5, \cdots]$, since both user u_a and $u_{a'}$ have rated t_1, t_5 etc. Therefore, $\mathcal{T}_s$ is the union of $T_{aa'}$ over all $u_{a'} \in \mathcal{U}_a$. Furthermore, with respect to item t_s, we define the *key neighborhood* for the active user u_a as:

$$\mathcal{N}_{a,s} = \{r_{a'i} | u_{a'} \in \mathcal{U}_a, t_i \in \mathcal{T}_s\}, \quad (6)$$

where $r_{a'i}$ can either be an observing or missing rating. Normally, due to the sparsity of the *user* $\times$ *item* rating matrix, this selected *key neighborhood* is also sparse. We define all the missing data in this *key neighborhood* as the *key set* of missing data for the prediction $\hat{r}_{as}$. For each observing rating $r_{a'i}$ in $\mathcal{N}_{a,s}$, it plays a key role in the prediction for $\hat{r}_{as}$, as both user $u_{a'}$ and item t_i are highly related to $\hat{r}_{as}$. Even for the missing data in $\mathcal{N}_{a,s}$, they have equal importance for the prediction of $\hat{r}_{as}$. Please note that $\mathcal{N}_{a,s}$ is defined from the user's perspective, so we call this as the *user*-based *Auto-Adaptive Imputation* (*user*-based AutAI). After $\mathcal{N}_{a,s}$ is determined, for each missing data $r_{a'i}$ in $\mathcal{N}_{a,s}$, we use the following equation to impute its value:

$$\hat{r}_{a'i} = \bar{u}_{a'} + \frac{\sum_{u_x \in \mathcal{N}_k(u_{a'})} sim(u_{a'}, u_x) \times (r_{xi} - \bar{u}_x)}{\sum_{u_x \in \mathcal{N}_k(u_{a'})} sim(u_{a'}, u_x)}, \quad (7)$$

where $sim(u_{a'}, u_x)$ is the similarity between $u_{a'}$ and u_x as defined:

$$sim(u_{a'}, u_x) = \frac{\sum_{t_i \in T_{a'x}} (r_{a'i} - \bar{u}_{a'})(r_{xi} - \bar{u}_x)}{\sqrt{\sum_{t_i \in T_{a'x}} (r_{a'i} - \bar{u}_{a'})^2 \sum_{t_i \in T_{a'x}} (r_{xi} - \bar{u}_x)^2}}, \quad (8)$$

which is the *Pearson Correlation Coefficient* (PCC) between $u_{a'}$ and u_x [19]. Then, the imputed ratings in $\mathcal{N}_{a,s}$ can be put back to *user* $\times$ *item* rating matrix $\mathcal{R}$, and will be used for the rating prediction on item t_s for user u_a. It is clear that the missing data are imputed adaptively for user u_a on item t_s, and the *key set* of missing data is identified automatically from the user's perspective. The pseudocode of the *user*-based AutAI method is presented in Algorithm 1.

Similarly, AutAI can also work in an item-based manner. In this case, the *key neighborhood* for the active user u_a with respect to the active item t_s is defined as $\mathcal{N}'_{a,s} = \{r_{a'i} | u_x \in \mathcal{U}'_a, t_{s'} \in \mathcal{T}'_s\}$, where $\mathcal{T}'_s = \{t_{s'} | r_{as'} \neq \oslash\}$, $\mathcal{U}'_a = \{u_x | u_x \subset [U_{ss'_1} \cup \cdots \cup U_{ss'_i} \cup \cdots \cup U_{ss'_l}]\}$, $U_{ss'_i}$ denotes the set of users who rated both t_s and $t_{s'_i}$, and $l = |\mathcal{T}'_s|$. Consequently, the missing data in $\mathcal{N}'_{a,s}$ forms the *key set* of missing data in this item-based manner. Imputing this missing data is called the *item*-based *Auto-Adaptive Imputation* (*item*-based AutAI).

The imputed missing data in $\mathcal{N}_{a,s}$ contributes in two ways. Firstly, Cover [8]'s research on the nearest neighbor rule

Algorithm 1 Auto-Adaptive Imputation (AutAI)

Require: the user-item rating matrix $\mathcal{R}$. the active user u_a. the active item t_s.
Ensure: $\mathcal{R}'$: the imputed matrix $\mathcal{R}'$.
for each $u_x \in \mathcal{U}$ **do**
  for each $u_y \in \mathcal{U} \& u_y \neq u_x$ **do**
    calculate $sim(u_x, u_y)$ according to Eq. 8;
  end for
end for
$\mathcal{R}' \leftarrow \mathcal{R}$;
$\mathcal{U}_a \leftarrow \{u_{a'} | r_{a's} \neq \oslash\}$;
$\mathcal{T}_s \leftarrow \emptyset$;
for each $u_{a'} \in \mathcal{U}_a$ **do**
  $T_{aa'} \leftarrow \{t_i | r_{ai} \neq \oslash, r_{a'i} \neq \oslash\}$;
  $\mathcal{T}_s \leftarrow \mathcal{T}_s \cup T_{aa'}$;
end for
$\mathcal{N}_{a,s} \leftarrow \{r_{a'i} | u_{a'} \in \mathcal{U}_a, t_i \in \mathcal{T}_s\}$;
for each $r_{a'i} \in \mathcal{N}_{a,s}$ **do**
  if $r_{a'i} = \oslash$ **then**
    $\hat{r}_{a'i} \leftarrow \bar{u}_{a'} + \frac{\sum_{u_x \in \mathcal{N}_k(u_{a'})} sim(u_{a'}, u_x) \times (r_{xi} - \bar{r}_x)}{\sum_{u_x \in \mathcal{N}_k(u_{a'})} sim(u_{a'}, u_x)}$;
    $\mathcal{R}'(u_{a'}, t_i) \leftarrow \hat{r}_{a'i}$;
  end if
end for
return $\mathcal{R}'$;

shows that the nearest neighbor contains at least 50% of the information in the infinite training set. In this sense, the missing data in $\mathcal{N}_{a,s}$ contains much more information than the missing data outside of $\mathcal{N}_{a,s}$. So, imputing this missing data will bring in much more benefit compared to imputing other missing data. Moreover, imputation in this way will also bring in less associated imputation error. We provide a theoretical analysis on this point in the following section. Secondly, AutAI makes a further similarity measurement between each neighbor to the active user in the same $\mathcal{T}_s$ space. Based on the common assumption of the *neighborhood*-based CF algorithms that *if two users rated n items similarly, they tend to rate similarly on other items* [5, 22], this auto-adaptive imputation method makes the similarity measurement between the active user and any other neighbor on the same $\mathcal{T}_s$ items, rather than on the co-rated items between two users. Formally, we denote the similarity between two users u_a and u_x on imputed data as $sim'(u_a, u_x)$, which can be measured by any similarity metric, for example, its PCC-based version is formulated as:

$$sim'(u_a, u_x) = \frac{\sum_{t_i \in \mathcal{T}_s} (r_{ai} - \bar{u}_a)(r_{xi} - \bar{u}_x)}{\sqrt{\sum_{t_i \in \mathcal{T}_s} (r_{ai} - \bar{u}_a)^2 \sum_{t_i \in \mathcal{T}_s} (r_{xi} - \bar{u}_x)^2}}, \quad (9)$$

where $\bar{u}_x$ is the average rating of user u_x.

On the other hand, the imputed missing data in $\mathcal{N}'_{a,s}$ also contributes in a similar way to its counterpart in $\mathcal{N}_{a,s}$, so we will not list them separately. The similarity between two items, after applying the item-based AutAI, can be calculated in a similar way, and its PCC-based version is defined:

$$sim'(t_s, t_i) = \frac{\sum_{u_{a'} \in \mathcal{U}'_a} (r_{a's} - \bar{t}_s)(r_{a'i} - \bar{t}_i)}{\sqrt{\sum_{u_{a'} \in \mathcal{U}'_a} (r_{a's} - \bar{t}_s)^2 \sum_{u_{a'} \in \mathcal{U}'_a} (r_{a'i} - \bar{t}_i)^2}}, \quad (10)$$

where $\bar{t}_s$ is the average rating of item t_s.

3.3 Analysis on Auto-Adaptive Imputation

Why and how can the proposed AutAI method benefit the neighborhood-based CF? In this section, we attempt to answer this question from a theoretical perspective. Specifically, we study how the proposed AutAI method can help to select nearest neighbors more accurately. The analysis is conducted in the user-based AutAI, and it can be extended to the item-based AutAI in a straightforward manner.

Neighbor Selection determines the performance of the neighborhood based CF, which is based on the measured similarities among users [1, 2]. Let us consider a general case: suppose the active user u_a and two other users, u_x and u_y, have the following rating histories:

$$\begin{aligned}\mathbf{u_a} &= [r_{a1}, r_{a2}, \cdots, r_{ai}, \cdots, r_{al}]\\ \mathbf{u_x} &= [r_{x1}, \hat{r}_{x2}, \cdots, \hat{r}_{xi}, \cdots, \hat{r}_{xl}]\\ \mathbf{u_y} &= [r_{y1}, \hat{r}_{y2}, \cdots, r_{yi}, \cdots, \hat{r}_{yl}]\end{aligned}$$

where $\hat{r}_{xi}$ is the imputed rating on item t_i for u_x, and $l = |\mathcal{T}_s|$. According to Eq. 5, $\mathbf{u_a}$ contains the real ratings for u_a, but $\mathbf{u_x}$ contains both real ratings and imputed ratings. So, both $\mathbf{u_a}$ and $\mathbf{u_x}$ can be divided into two subsets: T_{ax} and $\mathcal{T}_s \setminus T_{ax}$, where T_{ax} denotes the co-rated item set between u_a and u_x, and $\mathcal{T}_s \setminus T_{ax}$ denotes the relative complement of T_{ax} in $\mathcal{T}_s$ [20]. Therefore, $\mathbf{u_a}$ and $\mathbf{u_x}$ can be represented as:

$$\begin{aligned}\mathbf{u_a} &= [\overbrace{r_{a(1)}, \cdots, r_{a(p)}}^{|T_{ax}|}, \overbrace{r_{a(p+1)}, \cdots, r_{a(l)}}^{|\mathcal{T}_s \setminus T_{ax}|}]\\ \mathbf{u_x} &= [\overbrace{r_{x(1)}, \cdots, r_{x(p)}}^{|T_{ax}|}, \overbrace{\hat{r}_{x(p+1)}, \cdots, \hat{r}_{x(l)}}^{|\mathcal{T}_s \setminus T_{ax}|}],\end{aligned}$$

where $p = |T_{ax}|$ and $l = |\mathcal{T}_s|$.

We measure the similarity between u_a and u_x by the distance in their item space. The distance on each item can be considered as an estimation for their similarity. The distance on item t_i is denoted as d_{t_i}. Then, the distance d_{ax} between u_a and u_x can be expressed by

$$d_{ax} = \begin{cases} d_{t_i}, & \text{if } r_{xi} \text{ is real rating,} \\ d_{t_i} + \varepsilon_i, & \text{if } r_{xi} \text{ is imputed,} \end{cases} \tag{11}$$

where $\varepsilon_i = r_{xi} - \hat{r}_{xi}$ denotes the imputation error on item t_i for user t_x, and $\hat{r}_{xi}$ denotes the imputed value.

In this study, for two users, we assume that the distance on any item is independent and identically distributed (i.i.d), and we adopt the normal distribution for theoretical analysis. Then, the Probability Density Function (PDF) [20, 29] of d_{t_i} is:

$$p(d_{t_i}) \sim \begin{cases} \mathcal{N}(\mu_1, \sigma_1^2), \text{ for } u_a \text{ and } u_x \\ \mathcal{N}(\mu_2, \sigma_2^2), \text{ for } u_a \text{ and } u_y \end{cases} \tag{12}$$

Similarly, we assume the imputation error ε on any item for any user is also independent and identically distributed (i.i.d), and its PDF is:

$$p(\varepsilon) \sim \mathcal{N}(\mu_\varepsilon, \sigma_\varepsilon^2), \tag{13}$$

Then, the distance d_{ax} between u_a and u_x is formulated as the expectation over all possible items, $d_{ax} = E(d_t)$. Practically, the expectation can be estimated by using the average of all observations, so,

$$d_{ax} = E(d_t) = \frac{1}{n}\sum_{i=1}^{n} d_{t_i}, \tag{14}$$

where n is the number of items taking into account when measuring d_{ax}. In the user-based AutAI method, this set of items is $\mathcal{T}_s$, and d_{ax}^{aai} denotes the distance d_{ax}. Considering $\mathcal{T}_s$ consists of two subsets, T_{ax} and $\mathcal{T}_s \setminus T_{ax}$, d_{ax}^{aai} is affected by items coming from both of them, and can be represented as:

$$\frac{1}{p}\sum_{i=1}^{p} d_{t_i} \text{ and } \frac{1}{q}\sum_{j=1}^{q} \hat{d}_{t_j},$$

where $p = |T_{ax}|$, $q = |\mathcal{T}_s \setminus T_{ax}|$, and $\hat{d}_{t_j} = d_{t_j} + \varepsilon_j$ represents the estimation from imputed values as defined in Eq. 11. Due to the existence of the imputation error ε, the similarity estimation coming from $\mathcal{T}_s \setminus T_{ax}$ has to take it into consideration. The *cumulative imputation error* for the estimation of d_{ax}^{aai} over $\mathcal{T}_s \setminus T_{ax}$ is:

$$\begin{aligned}\varepsilon_{aai} &= \frac{1}{q}\sum_{j=1}^{q} \hat{d}_{t_j} - \frac{1}{q}\sum_{j=1}^{q} d_{t_j}\\ &= \frac{1}{q}\left(\sum_{j=1}^{q}(d_{t_j} + \varepsilon_j) - \sum_{j=1}^{q} d_{t_j}\right)\\ &= \frac{1}{q}\sum_{j=1}^{q} \varepsilon_j.\end{aligned} \tag{15}$$

Consequently, d_{ax}^{aai} in AutAI is represented as the calculation based on real ratings plus the *cumulative imputation error* ε_{aai}:

$$\frac{1}{l}\sum_{i=1}^{l} d_{t_i} \text{ and } \varepsilon_{aai} = \frac{1}{q}\sum_{j=1}^{q} \varepsilon_j,$$

where $l = |\mathcal{T}_s|$. According to Eq. 13 and Eq. 15, ε_{aai} is also normal, and its PDF is:

$$p(\varepsilon_{aai}) \sim \mathcal{N}(\mu_\varepsilon, \frac{\sigma_\varepsilon^2}{q}), \tag{16}$$

where $q = |\mathcal{T}_s \setminus T_{ax}|$. Normally, due to $|\mathcal{T}_s \setminus T_{ax}| \gg 1$, $\frac{\sigma_\varepsilon^2}{q}$ is much smaller than σ_ε^2. For example, in *MovieLens* data set, $mean(|\mathcal{T}_s \setminus T_{ax}|) = 85.08$, which means the order of magnitude of $\frac{\sigma_\varepsilon^2}{q}$ is around two orders of magnitude less than σ_ε^2. Namely, ε_{aai} actually varies little around its mean value, and its variance can be ignored comparing with its initial distribution ε. Consequently, the measurement of d_{ax}^{aai} over $\mathcal{T}_s$ is defined:

$$d_{ax}^{aai} = E(d_t) = \frac{1}{l}\sum_{i=1}^{l} d_{t_i} + \mu_\varepsilon, \tag{17}$$

where $l = |\mathcal{T}_s|$. According to Eq. 12, Eq. 13 and Eq. 17, we obtain that:

$$p(d_{ax}^{aai}) \sim \mathcal{N}(\mu_1 + \mu_\varepsilon, \frac{\sigma_1^2}{l}). \tag{18}$$

Similarly, the PDF of the distance between u_a and u_y in AutAI, d_{ay}^{aai}, is:

$$p(d_{ay}^{aai}) \sim \mathcal{N}(\mu_2 + \mu_\varepsilon, \frac{\sigma_2^2}{l}). \tag{19}$$

We define the *distance divergence* ψ between the distance of two users u_x and u_y to the active user u_a as:

$$\psi = d_{ax} - d_{ay}, \tag{20}$$

which determines their order to the active user. It is well-known that the *confidence interval* (CI) can be used to indicate the reliability of an estimation [20], and it has been widely used in the research of neighborhood-based models [2]. Therefore, in this study, we apply CI to measure the reliability of the estimation of ψ. CI is a range of values that quantify the uncertainty of the estimation, and a narrow CI means high precision [20]. According to Eq. 18 and Eq. 19, the $100(1-\alpha)\%$ confidence interval for ψ in AutAI can be formulated as follows:

$$\begin{aligned} CI(\psi_{aai}) &= ((\mu_1+\mu_\varepsilon)-(\mu_2+\mu_\varepsilon)) \\ &\quad \pm z_{\alpha/2}\sqrt{\frac{\frac{\sigma_1^2}{l}}{l}+\frac{\frac{\sigma_2^2}{l}}{l}} \\ &= (\mu_1-\mu_2)\pm z_{\alpha/2}\sqrt{\frac{\sigma_1^2}{l^2}+\frac{\sigma_2^2}{l^2}}, \end{aligned} \tag{21}$$

where $z_{\alpha/2}$ is a standard normal variate which is exceeded with a probability of $\alpha/2$. We define $\sigma_{\psi_{aai}}$ as the standard error of ψ_{aai}:

$$\sigma_{\psi_{aai}} = \sqrt{\frac{\sigma_1^2}{l^2}+\frac{\sigma_2^2}{l^2}}. \tag{22}$$

Please note the width of $CI(\psi_{aai})$ is proportional to $\sigma_{\psi_{aai}}$.

Now, let us consider conventional neighborhood-based CF, the measurement of the distance between u_a and u_x, d_{ax}^{knn}, is estimated over T_{ax}, which is:

$$d_{ax}^{knn} = E(d_t) = \frac{1}{p}\sum_{i=1}^{p} d_{t_i}, \tag{23}$$

where $p = |T_{ax}|$. According to Eq. 12 and Eq. 23, we have

$$p(d_{ax}^{knn}) \sim \mathcal{N}(\mu_1, \frac{\sigma_1^2}{p_1}), \tag{24}$$

where $p_1 = |T_{ax}|$. Similarly, d_{ay}^{knn}, the distance between u_a and u_y in conventional neighborhood-based CF, also follows the normal distribution, and its PDF is:

$$p(d_{ay}^{knn}) \sim \mathcal{N}(\mu_2, \frac{\sigma_2^2}{p_2}), \tag{25}$$

where $p_2 = |T_{ay}|$. Therefore, according to Eq. 24 and Eq. 25, the $100(1-\alpha)\%$ confidence interval for ψ_{knn}, ψ in neighborhood based CF approaches, is:

$$\begin{aligned} CI(\psi_{knn}) &= (\mu_1-\mu_2)\pm z_{\alpha/2}\sqrt{\frac{\frac{\sigma_1^2}{p_1}}{p_1}+\frac{\frac{\sigma_2^2}{p_2}}{p_2}} \\ &= (\mu_1-\mu_2)\pm z_{\alpha/2}\sqrt{\frac{\sigma_1^2}{p_1^2}+\frac{\sigma_2^2}{p_2^2}}, \end{aligned} \tag{26}$$

where $z_{\alpha/2}$ is a standard normal variate which is exceeded with a probability of $\alpha/2$. $\sigma_{\psi_{knn}}$ is the standard error of the estimated ψ_{knn}:

$$\sigma_{\psi_{knn}} = \sqrt{\frac{\sigma_1^2}{p_1^2}+\frac{\sigma_2^2}{p_2^2}}, \tag{27}$$

where $p_1 = |T_{ax}|$ and $p_2 = |T_{ay}|$. And the width of $CI(\psi_{knn})$ is proportional to $\sigma_{\psi_{knn}}$.

According to Eq. 5, it is clear that $l = |\mathcal{T}_s| \geq |T_{ax}| = p_1$ and $l = |\mathcal{T}_s| \geq |T_{ay}| = p_2$. For example, in the benchmark dataset *MovieLens*, $mean(|\mathcal{T}_s|) = 103.47$, and $mean(|T_{ax}|) = 18.4$. Together with Eq. 22 and Eq. 27, we obtain:

$$\sigma_{\psi_{aai}} \leq \sigma_{\psi_{knn}} \tag{28}$$

with equality if and only if $|\mathcal{T}_s| = |T_{ax}|$ and $|\mathcal{T}_s| = |T_{ay}|$, which is not valid when facing the data sparsity issue in the field of collaborative filtering. Furthermore, according to Eq. 21 and Eq. 26, one can see that the $CI(\psi_{aai})$ is narrower than or equal to $CI(\psi_{knn})$, since $\sigma_{\psi_{aai}}$ is smaller than or equal to $\sigma_{\psi_{knn}}$. Based on the above theoretical analysis, we can conclude that the proposed AutAI method can effectively improve the performance of the neighborhood-based CF through more accurate nearest neighbor selections by using a sparse rating matrix in a novel way.

3.4 Rating Prediction

For the purpose of recommendation, we propose a new rating prediction algorithm, an Auto-Adaptive Imputation algorithm for both users and items (AutAI-Fusion), which can simultaneously take the user activity and the item popularity into account. Specifically, we apply the AutAI method for both users and items, and combine the predictions using a linear function.

To take users activity into consideration, we first perform a user-based AutAI imputation as described in Eq. 6, then make prediction as follows. The prediction for r_{as} in this user-based manner is calculated as:

$$\hat{r}_{as}^{u} = \bar{u}_a + \frac{\sum_{u_x\in\mathcal{N}_k(u_a)} sim'(u_a,u_x)\times(r_{xs}-\bar{u}_x)}{\sum_{u_x\in\mathcal{N}_k(u_a)} sim'(u_a,u_x)}, \tag{29}$$

where $\bar{u}_a$ is the average rating of u_a, and $sim'(u_a, u_x)$ is defined in Eq. 9.

Similarly, to take item popularity into consideration, we do an item-based AutAI imputation as described in Section 3.2, then the prediction for r_{as} in this item-based manner is calculated as:

$$\hat{r}_{as}^{i} = \bar{t}_s + \frac{\sum_{t_i\in\mathcal{N}_k(t_s)} sim'(t_s,t_i)\times(r_{ai}-\bar{t}_i)}{\sum_{t_i\in\mathcal{N}_k(t_s)} sim'(t_s,t_i)}, \tag{30}$$

where $\bar{t}_s$ is the average rating of t_s, and $sim'(t_s, t_i)$ is defined in Eq. 10.

After imputing and predicting from both user and item respectively, the final prediction for r_{as} in the proposed AutAI-Fusion algorithm is calculated as:

$$\hat{r}_{as} = \lambda\hat{r}_{as}^{u} + (1-\lambda)\hat{r}_{as}^{i}. \tag{31}$$

A similar fusion strategy is performed in [16, 27]. The parameter λ determines to what extent the final prediction is based on user-based AutAI or item-based AutAI imputation prediction. When $\lambda = 1$, the prediction is completely generated by taking user activity to perform an AutAI-based prediction. On the other hand, when $\lambda = 0$, the prediction is totally estimated by taking item popularity to perform an AutAI-based prediction. The value for λ can be determined by doing cross-validation, which we will discuss further in the experiment section.

4. EXPERIMENT

In this section, we conduct several experiments to answer the following questions:

1. How does the proposed AutAI method perform with various similarity metrics? For this point, we employ two well-known similarity metrics in the field of collaborative filtering, the *Pearson Correlation Coefficient* (PCC) [19] and the *Cosine*-based similarity (COS) [5]. To achieve a fair comparison, we perform this experiment in a user-based manner. Namely, we only do AutAI imputation from the perspective of users (the user-based AutAI), and do the prediction based on Eq. 29. Then we compare it with the user-based collaborative filtering algorithm.

2. How does the proposed AutAI-Fusion algorithm compare with other imputation-based CF algorithms? For this question, we compare the proposed AutAI-Fusion algorithm with other state-of-the-art *imputation*-based algorithms, including the well-known *EMDP* [16], the *SCBPCC* method [28], *Default Voting* (Default Voting) [5], and two traditional collaborative filtering algorithms, the user-based algorithm [19] and the item-based CF algorithm [22], and one model-based algorithm, the *Slope One* algorithm [14]. Please note that EMDP is an imputation-based algorithm by fusing the user-based CF algorithm and the item-based CF algorithm.

3. How does the parameter λ affect the performance of the proposed AutAI-Fusion algorithm? Since the proposed AutAI method take either user activity or item popularity into consideration, the parameter λ balance how much the prediction comes from the user-based AutAI and the item-based AutAI. We examine AutAI-Fusion's performance in accuracy by varying λ from 0 to 1.

4.1 Experimental Setup

The data set we experiment with is the popular benchmark data set *MovieLens* [1], which has been widely used in CF research [16, 18, 27, 28]. *MovieLens* includes around 1 million ratings collected from 6,040 users on 3,900 movies.

To evaluate the performance thoroughly, we extract a subset of 2000 users from *MovieLens* who rated at least 30 movies, and further we set up several different experimental configurations. Specifically, we split the selected subset into two sets, the Training set and the Test set. The size of the Training set varies from the first 500, 1000 and 1500 users, and are denoted as M_{500}, M_{1000} and M_{1500} respectively. The remaining 500 users are treated as the Test set. For each of the active user within the Test set, we alter the number of rated items provided from 10, 20 to 30, which are represented as $Given_{10}$, $Given_{20}$ and $Given_{30}$, respectively. This protocol is widely used in Collaborative Filtering research [16, 27, 28]. Furthermore, we also apply the *All-But-One* configuration, in which we randomly select one single rating for each user in the data set, then try to predict its value when observing all the other ratings the user has given.

4.2 Evaluation Metric

For consistency with other literatures [16, 27, 28], we apply the *Mean Absolute Error* (MAE) as the measurement metric, which is defined as:

$$MAE = \frac{\sum_{(a,s)\in X} |r_{as} - \hat{r}_{as}|}{|X|}, \quad (32)$$

where r_{as} is the true rating given by user u_a on item t_s, $\hat{r}_{as}$ is the predicted rating, X denotes the test data set, and $|X|$ represents its size. A smaller MAE value means better performance.

[1]http://www.grouplens.org/

Table 1: MAE comparison on different similarity measurement metrics on the *Given* Data set. (A smaller value means better performance)

Training Users		PCC	AutAI+PCC	COS	AutAI+COS
M_{500}	$Given_{10}$	0.7925	**0.7788**	0.7855	**0.7726**
	$Given_{20}$	0.7663	**0.7530**	0.7663	**0.7513**
	$Given_{30}$	0.7546	**0.7404**	0.7561	**0.7406**
M_{1000}	$Given_{10}$	0.7802	**0.7713**	0.7853	**0.7663**
	$Given_{20}$	0.7594	**0.7464**	0.7672	**0.7437**
	$Given_{30}$	0.7491	**0.7348**	0.7563	**0.7333**
M_{1500}	$Given_{10}$	0.7764	**0.7670**	0.7854	**0.7630**
	$Given_{20}$	0.7581	**0.7423**	0.7687	**0.7397**
	$Given_{30}$	0.7487	**0.7309**	0.7585	**0.7293**

Table 2: MAE comparison on different similarity measurement metrics on the *All-But-One* Data set. (A smaller value means better performance)

Training Users	PCC	AutAI+PCC	COS	AutAI+COS
All-But-One	0.7477	**0.6910**	0.7652	**0.6932**

4.3 Performance with Different Similarity Metrics

In order to evaluate the performance of AutAI, we use the proposed AutAI method on two state-of-the-art similarity metrics in Collaborative Filtering [1, 10, 16, 27, 28], the PCC and the COS. We implement 4 algorithms in the user-based manner, namely the user-based PCC algorithm, user-based COS algorithm, and user-based AutAI with PCC and COS, respectively. Then, we compare their prediction performance, in which the number of neighbors is set to 30. We examine AutAI performance on all the experiment configurations, including *Given* and *All-But-One* data sets.

The results on the *Given* and *All-But-One* data sets are shown in Table 1 and Table 2, respectively. The results show that AutAI achieves significant improvements on both similarity metrics in all experiment configurations. This indicates that the proposed AutAI method works well and robustly in different sparsity situations. Specifically, on the *Given* data set, the number of given ratings for the active user is restricted to 10, 20 or 30, which suppresses the effectiveness of AutAI, as AutAI determines the *key set* of missing data to fill in according to the rated items by this user as shown in Eq. 6. However, AutAI can still significantly outperform the user-based CF on all the *Given* data sets. On the *All-But-One* data set, AutAI achieves even larger improvements on both PCC and COS metrics as shown in Table 2. For PCC, the MAE is reduced from 0.7477 to 0.6910 by 7.58%, and for COS, it is reduced from 0.7652 to 0.6932 by 9.41%. This is mainly because there is no limitation to users' rating history, so AutAI can fully work in this natural setting.

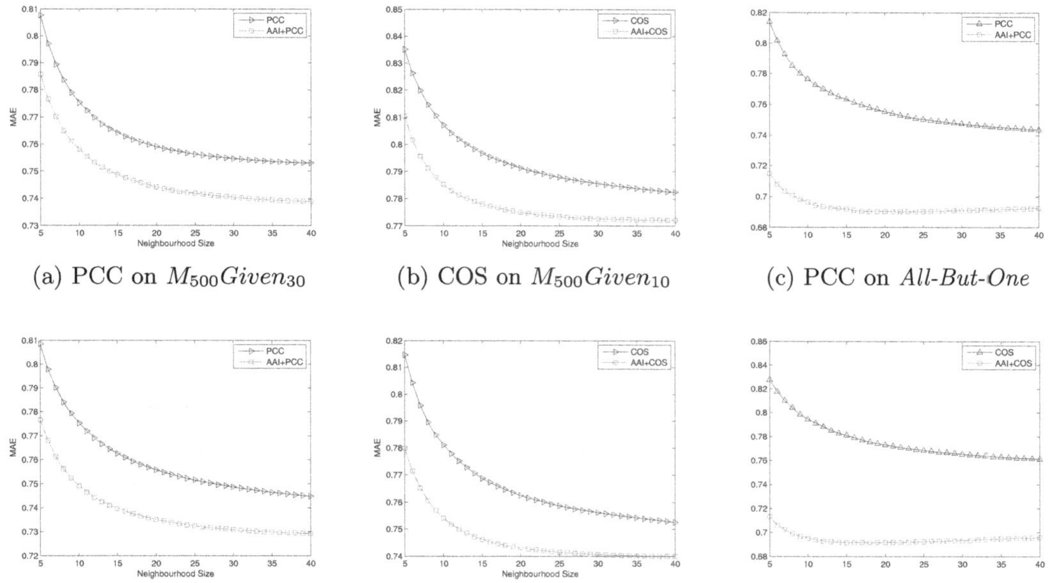

(a) PCC on $M_{500}Given_{30}$ (b) COS on $M_{500}Given_{10}$ (c) PCC on *All-But-One*

(d) PCC on $M_{1500}Given_{30}$ (e) COS on $M_{500}Given_{30}$ (f) COS on *All-But-One*

Figure 1: Sensitivity to the Size of Neighborhood

Table 3: Paired-t-test for MAE on the *Given* Dataset and the *All-but-one* Dataset

	Paired-t statistics		
Methods	df	t	*p*-value
AutAI+PCC vs. PCC	9	4.0137	0.0030
AutAI+COS vs. COS	9	4.8512	0.0009

Moreover, in order to examine AutAI's performance thoroughly, we vary the number of neighbors from 5 to 40 so as to examine its sensitivity to the neighborhood size. In this paper, we report results on $M_{500}Given_{30}$ and $M_{1500}Given_{30}$ for PCC, results on $M_{500}Given_{10}$ and $M_{500}Given_{30}$ for COS, and results on *All-But-One* data sets for both PCC and COS in Fig. 1. We can observe that the neighborhood size does affect the performance. The AutAI method outperforms its counterpart across all neighborhood sizes from 5 to 40 on all data sets. This indicates that the AutAI method identifies the neighborhood relationship more accurately as we demonstrate in Section 3.3, and therefore, achieves better performance across all neighborhood sizes.

The two-tailed, paired t-test with a 95% confidence level has been applied to evaluate the performance of AutAI on both similarity metrics. The results show that the difference of performance with and without AutAI is statistically significant. The detailed paired-t statistics are shown in Table 3.

4.4 Comparison with Other Methods

In this section, we examine the proposed AutAI-Fusion algorithm by comparing it with other state-of-the-art *imputation*-based algorithms, including the *default voting* (Default Voting) method [5], the EMDP method [16], and the SCBPCC meth-od [28], and two traditional collaborative filtering algorithms, the *user-based* CF (UPCC) and the *item-based* CF (IPCC), and one model-based algorithm, the *Slope One* algorithm [14]. For fair comparison, we set λ and K with the values used in [28], but they may not lead to the best performance. Specifically, the parameters in SCBPCC are set as $\lambda = 0.35$, and the cluster number $K = 20$. All the parameters in EMDP are set as used in [16], namely $\lambda = 0.7, \gamma = 30, \delta = 25, \eta = \theta = 0.4$. Please note that EMDP is an imputation-based algorithm by fusing the user-based CF algorithm and the item-based CF algorithm. The parameter λ in our algorithm is set to 0.4.

Table 4: MAE comparison with other methods on the *Given* Data set. (A smaller value means better performance)

Training users	Methods	$Given_{10}$	$Given_{20}$	$Given_{30}$
M_{500}	AutAI-Fusion	**0.7579**	**0.7387**	**0.7298**
	EMDP	0.7724	0.7573	0.7421
	SCBPCC	0.7837	0.7633	0.7550
	Default Voting	0.7762	0.7594	0.7513
	UPCC	0.7925	0.7663	0.7546
	IPCC	0.7927	0.7613	0.7493
	Slope One	0.7704	0.7455	0.7341
M_{1000}	AutAI-Fusion	**0.7488**	**0.7298**	**0.7211**
	EMDP	0.7602	0.7440	0.7301
	SCBPCC	0.7784	0.7602	0.7499
	Default Voting	0.7776	0.7614	0.7535
	UPCC	0.7802	0.7594	0.7491
	IPCC	0.7673	0.7402	0.7293
	Slope One	0.7601	0.7374	0.7263
M_{1500}	AutAI-Fusion	**0.7445**	**0.7256**	**0.7172**
	EMDP	0.7548	0.7383	0.7264
	SCBPCC	0.7792	0.7587	0.7506
	Default Voting	0.7812	0.7659	0.7580
	UPCC	0.7764	0.7581	0.7487
	IPCC	0.7572	0.7315	0.7214
	Slope One	0.7581	0.7355	0.7246

The results on the *Given* data sets are shown in Table 4. Clearly, it is observed that AutAI-Fusion outperforms all of the other 6 algorithms on all configurations. Specifically,

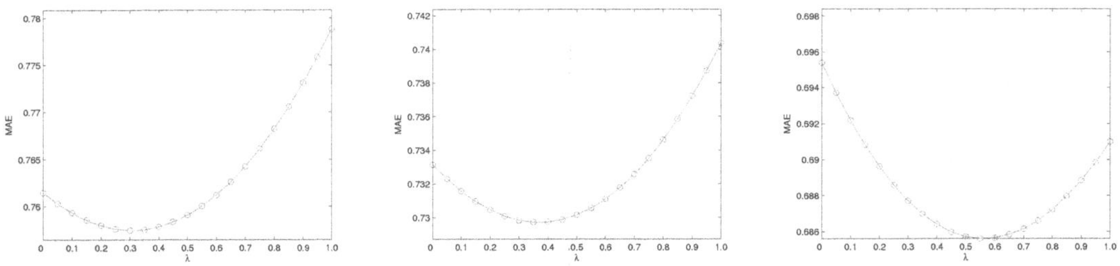

(a) M_{500} $Given_{10}$ (b) M_{500} $Given_{30}$ (c) *All-But-One*

Figure 2: Impact of Parameter λ on MAE

Table 5: MAE comparison with other methods on the *All-But-One* Data set. (A smaller value means better performance)

Training Users	AutAI-Fusion	EMDP	SCBPCC	Default Voting	UPCC	IPCC	Slope One
All-But-One	**0.6864**	0.7244	0.7613	0.7954	0.7477	0.7056	0.7164

Table 6: Paired-t-test for MAE on the *Given* Dataset and the *All-but-one* Dataset

	Paired-t statistics		
Methods	df	t	p-value
AutAI-Fusion vs. EMDP	9	5.5460	0.0004
AutAI-Fusion vs. SCBPCC	9	7.2837	< 0.0001
AutAI-Fusion vs. Default Voting	9	4.5898	0.0013
AutAI-Fusion vs. UPCC	9	10.3010	< 0.0001
AutAI-Fusion vs. IPCC	9	5.3386	0.0005
AutAI-Fusion vs. Slope One	9	4.6457	0.0012

on the $M_{500}Given10$ data set, although all imputation-based methods, AutAI-Fusion, EMDP, SCBPCC and Default Voting, achieve a better performance than UPCC and IPCC, AutAI-Fusion achieves the largest improvement. This trend is obvious on all data sets as shown by the figures in bold in Table 4. This indicates that when the training set is small and the rating history of users is limited, AutAI-Fusion can still identify the most determinant missing values to fill in, in order to identify more appropriate relationships among neighbors. On the *All-But-One* data set as shown in Table 5, AutAI-Fusion obtains even better results than all compared algorithms by achieving a much smaller MAE 0.6864. This is mainly because there is no limitation to the rating history of users, and also because AutAI can work more efficiently in this natural configuration. Table 6 lists the paired-t test statistics (with a 95% confidence level) between AutAI-Fusion and these algorithms, and it is clear that the differences between the performance of AutAI-Fusion and that of other methods are statistically significant.

4.5 Impact of Parameter

As we discussed in Section 3.4, we introduced a parameter λ to balance the prediction from the user-based AutAI and the item-based AutAI, to simultaneously consider both the activity of users and the popularity of items. We conducted several experiments to determine the impact of λ to the proposed AutAI-Fusion algorithm. Specifically, we vary the λ value from 0 to 1 with an increasing step of 0.05. We report the results on $M_{500}Given_{10}$, $M_{500}Given30$, and *All-But-One* data sets in Fig. 2.

When $\lambda = 0$, the prediction totally depends on the item-based AutAI imputation; when $\lambda = 1$, the prediction fully depends on the user-based AutAI imputation. Results on the *Given* data sets show that when there are few training users or few ratings of the active user, item-based AutAI can achieve significant improvement compared to user-based AutAI. For example, on data sets $M_{500}Given_{10}$ and $M_{500}Given30$ as shown in Fig. 2a and Fig. 2b, the performance of AutAI-Fusion with $\lambda = 0$ is better than its performance with $\lambda = 1$. This is because a limited user rating history suppresses the effectiveness of user-based AutAI. However, AutAI-Fusion achieves an even better performance with $\lambda = 0.4$. On the other hand, Fig. 2c shows that user-based AutAI and item-based AutAI achieve a similar performance on the *All-But-One* configuration, which indicates that in a natural situation there is no big difference between them. Yet, on all configurations, it is clear that better accuracy can be obtained by combining imputations from users and items.

5. CONCLUSION

In this paper, we treat each rating given by a user on an item as an observation for the predictions on this item to other users, which matches the theory of nearest neighbor rules [2, 8]. From this point of view, we define the notation of the *key set* of missing data for the rating prediction, and propose AutAI, a method to automatically and adaptively identify these key missing data for each prediction from both the user and the item perspective. Theoretical and empirical analysis show that imputation based on this *key set* of missing data leads to a more accurate identification of neighborhood relationships. Therefore, the AutAI-based algorithm can make more accurate predictions than neighborhood-based CF algorithms, including other imputation-based algorithms. To the best of our knowledge, no previous work has studied the theoretical analysis for imputation-based CF methods like this paper has. Therefore, the proposed AutAI method guarantees to work regardless of whichever similarity metric is applied. Moreover, we also propose an AutAI-Fusion algorithm based on the AutAI method to make predictions by taking user activity and item popularity into consideration. The experiment results show that: (1) the proposed AutAI method can identify neighbors more accurately, and (2) the proposed AutAI-Fusion algorithm can achieve better predictions in terms of accuracy.

6. REFERENCES

[1] G. Adomavicius and A. Tuzhilin. Toward the next generation of recommender systems: A survey of the state-of-the-art and possible extensions. *IEEE transactions on knowledge and data engineering*, 17(6):734–749, 2005.

[2] N. S. Altman. An Introduction to Kernel and Nearest-Neighbor Nonparametric Regression. *The American Statistician*, 46(3):175, Aug. 1992.

[3] R. M. Bell and Y. Koren. Lessons from the Netflix Prize Challenge. *SIGKDD Explorations*, 9(2):75–79, 2007.

[4] D. Billsus and M. Pazzani. Learning collaborative information filters. In *Proceedings of the Fifteenth International Conference on Machine Learning*, volume 54, page 48, 1998.

[5] J. Breese, D. Heckerman, C. Kadie, and Others. Empirical analysis of predictive algorithms for collaborative filtering. In *Proceedings of the 14th conference on Uncertainty in Artificial Intelligence*, pages 43–52, 1998.

[6] L. M. D. Campos, J. M. Fernández-luna, J. F. Huete, and M. A. Rueda-morales. Measuring Predictive Capability in Collaborative Filtering. In *Proceedings of the 3rd ACM Conference on Recommender Systems*, pages 313–316, 2009.

[7] S. Chee, J. Han, and K. Wang. Rectree: An efficient collaborative filtering method. *Data Warehousing and Knowledge Discovery*, pages 141–151, 2001.

[8] T. Cover. Estimation by the nearest neighbor rule. *IEEE Transactions on Information Theory*, pages 50–55, 1968.

[9] C. Desrosiers and G. Karypis. A Novel Approach to Compute Similarities and Its Application to Item Recommendation. In *Proceeding of PRICAI 2010*, pages 39–51, 2010.

[10] C. Desrosiers and G. Karypis. *Chapter 4 A comprehensive Survey of Neighborhood-based Recommendation Methods*, chapter 4, pages 107–144. Springer US, Boston, MA, 2011.

[11] S. a. Goldman and M. K. Warmuth. Learning binary relations using weighted majority voting. *Machine Learning*, 20(3):245–271, Sept. 1995.

[12] Y. Koren. Factorization meets the neighborhood: a multifaceted collaborative filtering model. In *SIGKDD 2008*, pages 426–434. ACM, 2008.

[13] M. Larson and A. Hanjalic. Exploiting User Similarity based on Rated-Item Pools for Improved User-based Collaborative Filtering. In *Proceedings of the 3rd ACM Conference on Recommender Systems*, pages 125–132, 2009.

[14] D. Lemire and A. Maclachlan. Slope one predictors for online rating-based collaborative filtering. In *In SIAM Data Mining (SDM'05)*, volume 05, 2005.

[15] R. Little. Missing-data adjustments in large surveys. *Journal of Business & Economic Statistics*, 6(3):287–296, 1988.

[16] H. Ma, I. King, and M. R. Lyu. Effective missing data prediction for collaborative filtering. In *SIGIR 2007*, pages 39–46, New York, New York, USA, 2007. ACM Press.

[17] M. R. Mclaughlin and J. L. Herlocker. A Collaborative Filtering Algorithm and Evaluation Metric that Accurately Model the User Experience. *Proceeding of SIGIR 2004*, 2004.

[18] Y. Ren, G. Li, and W. Zhou. Learning Rating Patterns for Top-N Recommendations. In *Proceeding of The IEEE/ACM International Conference on Social Networks Analysis and Mining (ASONAM 2012)*, 2012.

[19] P. Resnick, N. Iacovou, M. Suchak, P. Bergstrom, and J. Riedl. GroupLens : An Open Architecture for Collaborative Filtering of Netnews. In *ACM Conference on Computer Supported Cooperative Work*, pages 175–186, 1994.

[20] G. K. B. Richard A. Johnsom. *Statistics: Principles and Methods.* John Wiley and Sons, 6 edition, 2009.

[21] D. Rubin. Multiple imputation for nonresponse in surveys. *New York, USA: John Wiley & Sons*, 1987.

[22] B. Sarwar, G. Karypis, J. Konstan, and J. Reidl. Item-based collaborative filtering recommendation algorithms. In *Proceedings of the 10th international conference on World Wide Web*, pages 285–295. ACM, 2001.

[23] X. Su and R. Greiner. A Mixture Imputation-Boosted Collaborative Filter. *Artificial Intelligence*, pages 312–317, 2008.

[24] X. Su and T. Khoshgoftaar. Collaborative Filtering for Multi-class Data Using Belief Nets Algorithms. In *2006 18th IEEE International Conference on Tools with Artificial Intelligence (ICTAI'06)*, pages 497–504. Ieee, Nov. 2006.

[25] X. Su, T. Khoshgoftaar, and R. Greiner. Imputed Neighborhood Based Collaborative Filtering. In *Web intelligence 2008*, volume 1, pages 633–639. IEEE, 2008.

[26] X. Su, T. M. Khoshgoftaar, X. Zhu, and R. Greiner. Imputation-boosted collaborative filtering using machine learning classifiers. *Proceedings of the 2008 ACM symposium on Applied computing - SAC '08*, (2):949, 2008.

[27] J. Wang, A. P. de Vries, and M. J. T. Reinders. Unifying user-based and item-based collaborative filtering approaches by similarity fusion. In *SIGIR 2006*, pages 501–208, New York, New York, USA, 2006. ACM Press.

[28] G.-R. Xue, C. Lin, Q. Yang, W. Xi, H.-J. Zeng, Y. Yu, and Z. Chen. Scalable collaborative filtering using cluster-based smoothing. In *SIGIR 2005*, pages 114–121, New York, New York, USA, 2005. ACM Press.

[29] J. Zhang, Y. Xiang, Y. Wang, W. Zhou, Y. Xiang, and Y. Guan. Network Traffic Classification Using Correlation information. *IEEE Transaction on Parallel and Distributed Systems*, 2012.

Multi-Faceted Ranking of News Articles using Post-Read Actions*

Deepak Agarwal
LinkedIn
Mountain View, CA
dagarwal@linkedin.com

Bee-Chung Chen
LinkedIn
Mountain View, CA
bchen@linkedin.com

Xuanhui Wang
Facebook
Menlo Park, CA
xuanhui@fb.com

ABSTRACT

Personalized article recommendation is important for news portals to improve user engagement. Existing work quantifies engagement primarily through click rates. We suggest that quality of recommendations may be improved by exploiting different types of "post-read" engagement signals like sharing, commenting, printing and e-mailing article links. Specifically, we propose a multi-faceted ranking problem for recommending articles, where each facet corresponds to a ranking task that seeks to maximize actions of a particular post-read type (e.g., ranking articles to maximize sharing actions). Our approach is to predict the probability that a user would take a post-read action on an article, so that articles can be ranked according to such probabilities. However, post-read actions are rare events — enormous data sparsity makes the problem challenging. We meet the challenge by exploiting correlations across different post-read action types through a novel locally augmented tensor (LAT) model, so that the ranking performance of a particular action type can be improved by leveraging data from all other action types. Through extensive experiments, we show that our LAT model significantly outperforms a variety of state-of-the-art factor models, logistic regression and IR models.

Categories and Subject Descriptors: H.3.3 [Information Storage and Retrieval]: Information filtering

General Terms: Algorithms

Keywords: Multi-faceted, post-read, tensor model

1. INTRODUCTION

Publishing links to news articles has become important to facilitate information discovery on the Web. Users visiting a news website do not have a specific objective in mind and simply want to be informed about news stories that are important to them, or learn about topics of their interest. Quality of recommended links is crucial to ensure good user engagement in both short and long terms. But the explicit signals about what the user truly wishes to see is typically weak. Thus, it is important to consider a broad array of complementary indicators of users' interests — novel techniques which can effectively leverage these weak signals are desired.

The primary indicator of user engagement used in most existing work is click-through rate or CTR, i.e., the probability that a user would click an article when a link to the article is displayed, and articles are usually ranked to optimize for it [6, 2, 12]. We argue that merely using CTR to rank news articles is not sufficient since user interaction with online news has become multi-faceted. Users no longer simply click on news links and read articles — as shown in Figure 1, they can share it with friends, tweet about it, write and read comments, rate other users' comments, email the link to friends and themselves, print the article to read it thoroughly offline, and so on. These different types of "post-read" actions are indicators of deep user engagement from different facets and can provide additional signals for news recommendations. We will use *facet* and *post-read action type* interchangeably. For example, news articles can be ranked for individual facets based on the predicted action rates. We can also consider using combinations of both CTR and those post-read action rates together to blend news articles so that such a ranking can be potentially useful for users not only clicking on the articles, but also sharing or commenting them after reading.

However, to the best of our knowledge, little prior work provides a thorough analysis of these post-read actions and our understanding of them is very limited. For example, how indicative is the CTR of an article to those post-read actions? Do users in different age groups have different preferences for those post-read action types? How difficult is it to predict the post-read action rates? To answer these questions, we collected and analyzed a large dataset from an major online news portal. Interestingly, we found that post-read actions are mostly orthogonal to CTR. For example, the kinds of articles that users like to share are quite different from those they like to read, suggesting two distinct types of users' news consumption: private reading and public sharing. A good news recommendation system should provide ranking capabilities for both. Furthermore, our analysis shows that different users prefer different post-read actions but the signal-to-noise ratios of those post-read actions are much lower than clicks, suggesting the need for advanced modeling techniques.

*This work was conducted when all authors were affiliated with Yahoo!

CIKM'12, October 29–November 2, 2012, Maui, HI, USA.

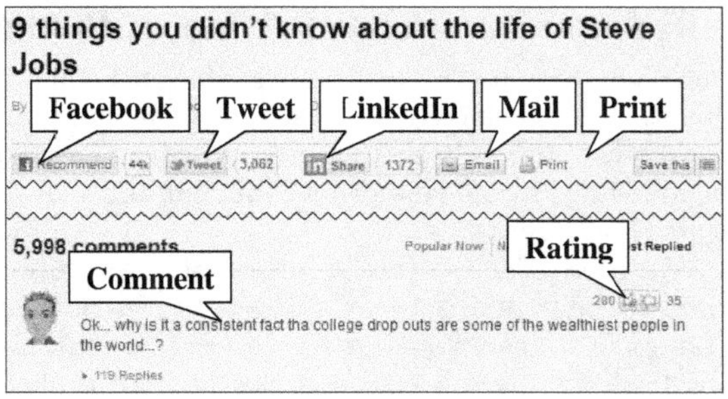

Figure 1: Illustration of post-read actions

The main challenges in modeling post-read actions are due to data sparsity which is more severe than the sparsity of CTR estimation because a post-read action can only happen after a user clicks. To our knowledge, little work in news recommendation has considered the use of such signals despite the availability of post-read behavioral data on many online news sites. In fact, an increasing number of users are using social media to actively promote/demote news articles through their circles and are freely expressing their opinions through comments. The focus of this paper is on machine learning techniques that can mitigate data sparsity and provide reliable estimates of post-read action rates that is essential to incorporate such signals into news recommendation.

Fortunately, our analysis also shows positive correlations among different types of post-read actions. Exploiting such correlations helps in borrowing or transferring information across action types and thus reduce data sparsity. We model such correlations among post-read action types through a tensor product of latent factors of a user, an item (i.e., article) and an action type. The tensor product is further augmented by local user and item factors that are specific to the action type, in order to capture unique patterns in the action type.

Our contributions are as follows: (1) Our data analysis in Section 2 unveils interesting post-read behavior that has not been reported in the literature. (2) Based on the analysis, we propose a new problem of predicting the probabilities that a user would take actions of different types after reading an article, which provide a principled approach to ranking articles according to different action types (i.e., facets). (3) To solve the problem, we propose a novel Locally Augmented Tensor model (LAT) in Section 3 that effectively exploits the correlations in noisy and sparse post-read data. (4) We then empirically show that LAT outperforms a variety of state-of-the-art matrix factorization methods, logistic regression and baseline IR models in Section 4. These contributions open the door to effective use of multi-faceted ranking to improve news recommendation on websites.

2. EXPLORATORY DATA ANALYSIS

We study post-read behavior based on data collected from a major news site in the US that has millions of visitors on a monthly basis. Although this does not represent the entire news reading population in the US and elsewhere in the world, it has a large enough market share to study online news consumption behavior in the US. The site provides various functionalities for users to act after reading an article. Figure 1 shows a portion of a typical news article page. On top are links/buttons that allow a user to share articles on

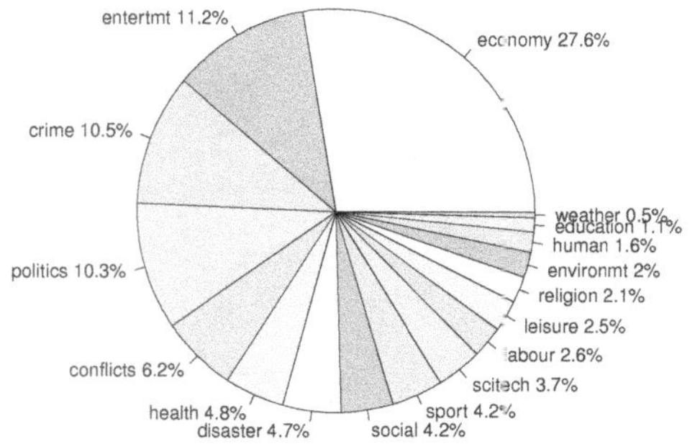

Figure 2: Distribution of news articles over categories

various social media websites such as Facebook, Twitter and LinkedIn. The user can also share the article with others or herself via email or by printing a hard copy. At the bottom portion of the page, the user can leave comments on the article or rate other users' comments by thumb-up or thumb-down votes.

In addition to links/buttons that facilitate post-read actions, most article pages on this site publish a module that recommends interesting article links. This module is an important source to create page views on the site and hence recommends article links that maximize overall click-through rates. To estimate the CTR of each article unbiasedly, a small portion of the user visits are shown a random list of articles and the CTR estimated from this small portion of traffic is used to perform our CTR analysis.

2.1 Data

Source of Data: The data used in our analysis was collected from Feb to May in 2011. We collected two kinds of data — (1) all article page views on the news site to study post-read actions (these page views are generated via clicks on links to news articles published by the site on the web); and (2) click logs from the module as described earlier. To distinguish link views on the module from page views of news article pages (after clicking article links), we shall refer to the former as "linkview" while the latter is referred to as "pageview". For instance, using this terminology, pre-read article click-through rate (CTR) is computed as the number of clicks divided by the number of linkviews on the module and post-read Facebook share rate (FSR) is computed as the number of sharing actions divided by the number of pageviews. Post-read action rates of other types can be computed similarly. *We focus on the following post-read actions: Facebook share, email, print, comment, and rating.* Note that LinkedIn and Tweeter sharing actions are very rare in the period of our data.

Data Diversity: We selected articles that were shown on the module and were clicked at least once, received at least one comment and one post-read action type out of Facebook share, email and print. This gives us approximately 8K articles that were already classified into a hierarchical directory by the publishers. We use the top three levels of the hierarchy in our analysis. The first level of the hierarchy has 17 categories; the distribution of article frequency in these categories is shown in Figure 2. As evident from this figure, news articles published on the site are diverse in nature and provides a good source to study user interaction with online news. We also obtain user demographic information which

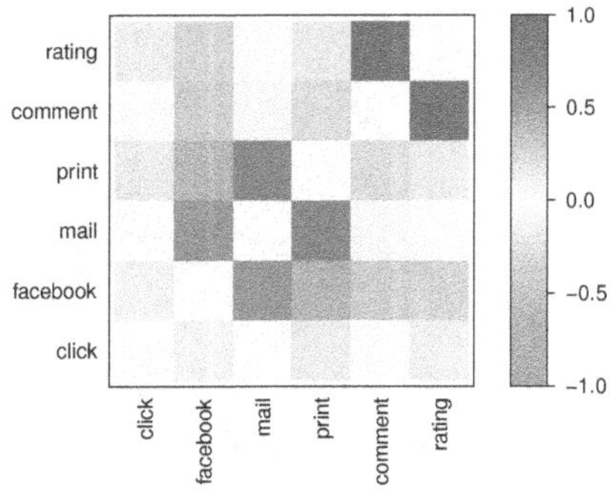

Figure 3: Correlation between different action types (diagonals cells are not of interest)

includes age, gender and geo-location (identified through IP address). All user IDs are anonymized. In total, we have hundreds of millions of pageview events in our data which are sufficient for us to estimate the post-read action rates.

2.2 Pre-Read vs Post-Read

In this section, we investigate the relationship between pre-read clicks and post-read actions. For example, is a highly clicked article also highly shared or commented by users? For each article, we compute the article's overall click-through rate (CTR) on the module and post-read action rates of different types. In Figure 3, we show the correlation between clicks and other actions types using Pearson's correlation (the left most column or the bottom row). We observe very low correlation between click rates and other post-read action rates. We also computed the correlations after stratifying articles by categories and found that the correlations are still very low. This lack of correlation is perhaps not surprising: clicks are usually driven by user's topical interest in certain articles versus others, while post-click behaviors are inherently conditioned on clicks and hence topical interest. Thus, ranking articles using CTR and other post-click indicators would likely lead to different rankings. For instance, if the goal of a news website is to maximize CTR but also ensure a certain minimum number of sharing actions, then the ranking method should take both CTR and share rates into consideration.

2.3 Correlations among Post-Read Actions

In Figure 3, we also show all pairwise Pearson's correlations among post-read action types, computed using article-level action rates. We observe positive correlations among various post-read action types; Mail has high correlation with Facebook and print, but not with comment and rating. There is high correlations among Facebook, mail, and print. Not surprisingly, comment and rating are also highly correlated. These provides evidence of being able to leverage correlations among post-read action types to improve post-read action prediction.

A word of caution: it is not necessary that correlations will hold when the data is disaggregated at the (user, item) level since our data is observational and subject to various sources of bias. It is not possible to study correlations at the (user, item) level through exploratory analysis due to lack of replicates; we will study this problem rigorously through a modeling approach described in Section 3. The exploratory analysis is shown to provide a flavor of our data and to gain some insights at an aggregate level.

2.4 Read vs. Post-Read: Private vs. Public

We now compare users' reading behavior with their post-read behavior. Specifically, is post-read behavior uniform across different article types or user types? Does Joe, a typical young male from California comment and share most of the articles he reads?

To understand this, we use a vector of the fractions of pageviews in different article categories to represent the reading behavior. One can think of this vector as a multinomial probability distribution over categories; i.e., the probability that a random pageview is in a given category. Similarly, post-read behavior of an action type is represented as a vector of fractions of post-read actions of that type in different categories. To compare a post-read behavior vector with the reading behavior vector, we compute the element-wise ratio between the two vectors. Figure 4(a) shows these ratios on the log-scale using the top 10 most viewed categories, where the categories are ordered according to the numbers of pageviews they received (highest on the left). All the sample sizes are sufficiently large (with at least tens of thousands of post-read actions) to ensure statistical significance. To help understand this plot, let us consider the green color (i.e., negative value) in the (mail, conflicts) cell for instance. It indicates that a typical user is more likely to read an article about conflicts than email it. In general, if post-read action behavior of users were the same as reading behavior or uniform across news types, the ratios (on log-scale) should be all close to 0. Obviously this is not the case for all action types as we see both "hot" and "cold" cells in the plot.

Some interesting tidbits. Users are more likely to read articles about crime, politics and conflicts than to share them with friends via email or on Facebook; they are more likely to read about disaster and science & technology but reluctant to comment on them. When it comes to science and religion, they are eager to share more. They are also more open to leave comments and engage in discussions in a public forum on matters of politics.

We observe an interesting pattern in news consumption: Reading news articles is a private activity, while sharing (Facebook and mail) or expressing opinions (comment and rating) on articles is a public activity and there is difference in a typical user's public and private activity. Users tend to share articles that earn them social prestige and credit but they do not mind clicking and reading some salacious news in private.

2.5 Variation in Post-Read Action Rates at Different Resolutions

The previous subsection showed interesting differences in read and post-read behavior across different article types. In this section, we study variation in post-read action rates by slicing and dicing the data at different resolutions. We note that analysis at some coarse resolution for data obtained through a non-randomized design may not reveal the entire picture; ideally such inferences should be drawn after adjusting for data heterogeneity at the finest, i.e, (user, item) resolution. It is impossible to study variation at this fine resolution through exploratory analysis due to lack of replicates. Our goal in this section is to study variation at resolutions where enough replicates exist. Such an analysis also provide insights into the hardness of predicting action rates and whether sophisticated modeling at fine resolutions is even necessary. For instance, if all science articles behave

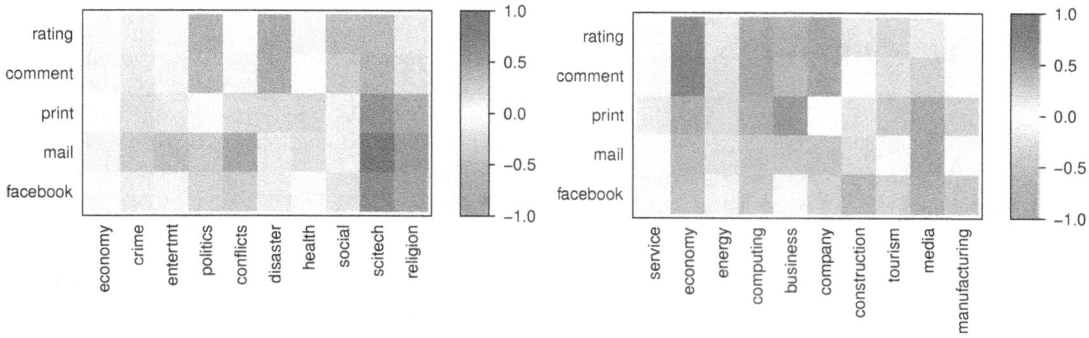

(a) On top level categories

(b) On subcategories of economy

Figure 4: Difference between pageview and post-read actions. This also shows variation of post-read action rates of different types by article categories

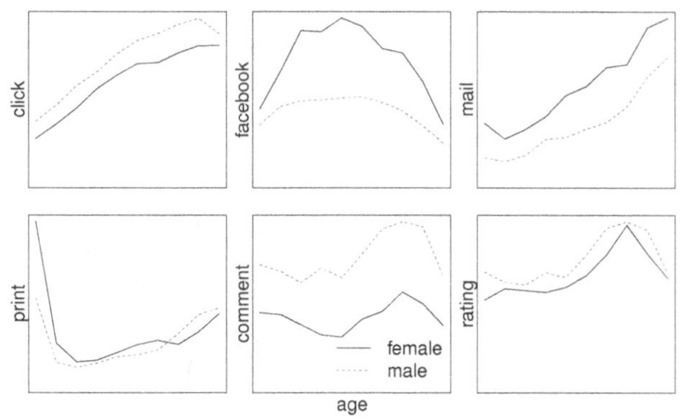

Figure 5: Post-read action rate variation over age-gender segments

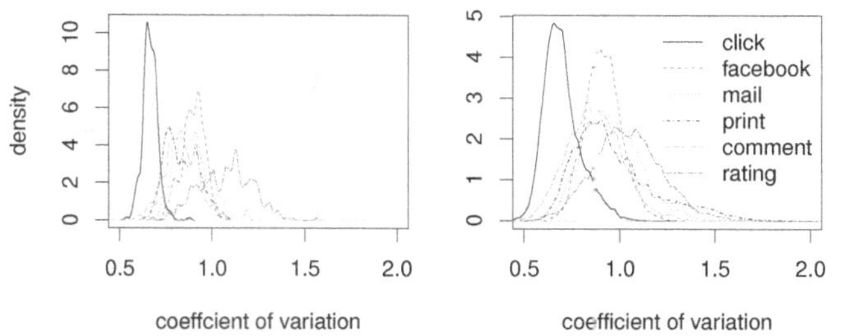

(a) on article categories

(b) categories × age-gender

Figure 6: Density of coefficient of variation

similarly, it is not necessary to model data at the article level within the science category.

Variation across article categories: To study variation in post-read action rates across article categories, we compute the ratio between the category-specific post-read action rates (i.e., #actions in the category divided by #pageviews in the category) and the global action rate (i.e., total #actions divided by total #pageviews) using the top 10 most viewed categories for each action type. Interestingly, this is exactly what Figure 4(a) and Figure 4(b) show. As we noted earlier, there is variation in action rates at this resolution as evident from the "hot" and "cold" cells.

Variation across user segments: We segment users by age and gender and show post-read action rates for the two genders across different age-groups in Figure 5. Once again we see variation. Some interesting observations: Facebook share rates are highest among young and middle aged users. Users in older age groups tend to mail more but young users tend to share more on Facebook. We see females to have surprisingly high share rates and male users tend to comment more on articles. We also include pre-read click actions in this figure and observe that users in older age groups tend to click more; males across all age-groups are more active clickers than females.

Variation within categories and segments: We now dig deeper and analyze variation at the article resolution after stratifying our data by article categories and user segments. High within-category/segment variations at the article level indicate excessive heterogeneity with categories and segments and suggest the need to model the rates at finer resolutions. To study such variation, we leverage the coefficient of variation defined as σ/μ, where σ is the standard deviation of article action rates within a given category (or category × user segment) and μ is the average article action rate in the category (or category × user segment). σ/μ is a positive number; smaller values indicate less variation. In general, values above 0.2 are indicative of high variation.

In Figure 6(a) and Figure 6(b), we show the distribution of coefficient of variation with respect to article categories and the cross-product of categories with user age-gender. From these two figures, we can see that all post-read actions have much larger coefficients of variation than click. This means that although there is variation in average post-read behavior across categories and user segments, the variation at the article resolution within each such stratum is high making it difficult to predict article post-read action rates than article click rates based on the category information. Comparing the two figures, we can see that adding user features helps little in terms of reducing coefficients of variation indicating that stratification by user segments does not help in explaining article level variation within each category. Perhaps users with a given (age, gender) segments have different news consumption behavior at the article level.

Our exploratory analysis suggests that predicting post-read actions of any type is harder than estimating CTR. We also see that while using features like article category and user demographics are useful, there is heterogeneity at the article and user resolution that has to be modeled. We also see evidence of positive correlations among post-read action types; it is interesting to study if such correlations can make the estimation task any better. We explore such an approach by modeling all post-read action types simultaneously at the finest (user, item) resolution in section 3.

3. POST-READ ACTION PREDICTION

Because post-read actions have low correlations with clicks, rankings of articles according to CTR would be likely to be different from rankings of articles according to different post-read action rates. It is useful for news portals to have rankings according to different criteria, in order to enrich user experience or serve users depending on the criteria that they prefer. As a first step, here we study how to effectively rank articles for each post-read type, and defer the problem of how to effectively combine rankings of different types to improve user experience to future work.

In this section, we present our locally augmented tensor (LAT) model for predicting users' post-read rates, based on which articles can be ranked. Given a user, an item (i.e., article) and a post-read action type (e.g., comment, Facebook share), we want to predict the probability that the user would take the action after reading the item. The main challenges are:

- *Data sparsity:* Post-read actions are rare events. Most users only have single-digit post-read actions in a month in our dataset. If we further breakdown actions by types, data becomes sparser.
- *Diverse behavior across action types:* As we saw in Section 2, users behave differently for different action types. For example, the kinds of articles that users like to share are quite different from those they like to comment on.

To handle data sparsity, an attractive approach is to appropriately pool the action data of a user from all types, so that the action data of one type can be used to improve the prediction performance for another type. However, naive ways of pooling action data that ignore the differences between action types may lead to poor performance, especially for our sparse post-read data.

Problem definition: Consider an online news system with M users, N items and K post-read action types. Let y_{ijk} denote whether user i takes a post-read action of type k on item j. If the user takes the action, $y_{ijk} = 1$; if the user reads the item and does not take the action, $y_{ijk} = 0$; if the user does not read the item, y_{ijk} is unobserved. We also call y_{ijk} the observation or response of user i to item j of type k. Each user is associated with a feature vector (e.g., age, gender, geo-location). Each item is also associated with a feature vector (e.g., content categories, words and entities in the item). Because i always denotes a user and j always denotes an item, we slightly abuse our notations by using $\boldsymbol{x}_i$ to denote the feature vector of user i and $\boldsymbol{x}_j$ to denote the feature vector of item j. Given user features, item features and a set of training observations, our goal is to predict the response of a set of (user, item, action type) triples that do not appear in the training data.

We model the data using variants of factor models. We begin with a review of baseline matrix factorization models and then extend them to address the above challenges.

3.1 Baseline Factor Models

Matrix factorization is a popular method for predicting user-item interaction. User-item interactions can be represented through a $M \times N$ matrix $\mathbf{Y}$, where the value y_{ij} of the $(i,j)^{th}$ entry is the response of user i to item j. Notice that this is a matrix with many unobserved (i.e., missing) entries because a user typically does not interact with many items. The main idea of matrix factorization is to obtain two low rank matrices $\mathbf{U}_{M\times F}$ and $\mathbf{V}_{N\times F}$ such that $\mathbf{Y}$ is close to the product $\mathbf{UV}'$ measured in terms of a loss function $l(\mathbf{Y}, \mathbf{UV}')$ (e.g. squared-error, logistic). Here F is much smaller than M and N. Such a decomposition enables us to predict the unobserved entries in the response matrix.

Each row $\boldsymbol{u}_i$ of matrix $\mathbf{U}$ is called the factor vector of user i, representing his/her latent profile. Similarly, each row $\boldsymbol{v}_j$ of matrix $\mathbf{V}$ represents the latent profile of item j. Intuitively, the inner product $\boldsymbol{u}_i'\boldsymbol{v}_j$ is a measure of similarity between the profiles of user i and item j, representing how much i likes j. It is common to also add a bias term α_i for each user i to represent his/her average response to items, and a bias term β_j for each item j to represent its popularity. Then, the response y_{ij} of user i to item j is predicted by $\hat{y}_{ij} = \alpha_i + \beta_j + \boldsymbol{u}_i'\boldsymbol{v}_j$.

Let $\ell\ell(y,x) = -\log(1+\exp\{-(2y-1)x\})$ denote the logistic log-likelihood for a binary observation y. The loss function is given by

$$l(\mathbf{Y}, \mathbf{UV}') = -\sum_{\text{observed } (i,j)} \ell\ell(y_{ij}, \hat{y}_{ij}) \qquad (1)$$

Optimizing the loss function in Equation 1 tends to give estimates that overfit sparse data since the number of parameters is too large even for small values of F. It is customary to impose penalty (regularization) to avoid overfitting, the most commonly used penalty is to constrain the L_2 norm of parameters. Thus, we obtain parameter estimates by minimizing

$$l(\mathbf{Y}, \mathbf{UV}') + \frac{1}{2\sigma_\alpha^2}\sum_i \alpha_i^2 + \frac{1}{2\sigma_\beta^2}\sum_j \beta_j^2 + \frac{1}{2\sigma_u^2}\sum_i ||u_i||^2 + \frac{1}{2\sigma_v^2}\sum_j ||v_j|| \qquad (2)$$

where the σ^2s are tuning constants. Stochastic gradient descent (SGD) is a popular method to perform such optimization. However, our models involve several tuning constants that are hard to estimate using procedures like cross-validation. Further, SGD also requires tuning learning rate parameters. Thus, we pursue a different estimation strategy for fitting our models by working in a probabilistic framework and using a Monte-Carlo Expectation Maximization (MCEM) procedure. The MCEM approach we follow is both scalable and *estimates all parameters automatically* through the training data.

3.2 Probabilistic Modeling Framework

Observation model: Matrix factorization can also be interpreted in a probabilistic modeling framework [18]. The given y_{ij}s are the observations, based on which we want to estimate the unobserved latent factors α_i, β_j, $\boldsymbol{u}_i$ and $\boldsymbol{v}_j$. For numerical response, it is common to use a Gaussian model.

$$y_{ij} \sim N(\alpha_i + \beta_j + \boldsymbol{u}_i'\boldsymbol{v}_j,\ \sigma_y^2),$$

where $N(\mu, \sigma^2)$ denote a Gaussian distribution with mean μ and standard deviation σ^2. For binary response, it is common to use a logistic model.

$$y_{ij} \sim \mathit{Bernoulli}(p_{ij}) \text{ and } \log\frac{p_{ij}}{1-p_{ij}} = \alpha_i + \beta_j + \boldsymbol{u}_i'\boldsymbol{v}_j.$$

For ease of exposition, we use $y_{ij} \sim \alpha_i + \beta_j + \boldsymbol{u}_i'\boldsymbol{v}_j$ to denote that y_{ij} is predicted based on $\alpha_i + \beta_j + \boldsymbol{u}_i'\boldsymbol{v}_j$ either using the Gaussian model or the logistic model.

Regression priors: Although $\boldsymbol{u}_i$ and $\boldsymbol{v}_j$ are low dimensional, there are still a large number of factors to be estimated from sparse data, which can similarly lead to overfitting. A common approach is to shrink the factors toward zero; i.e., if a factor is not supported by enough data, it's estimated value should be close to zero. When features are available, we can achieve better performance by shrinking the factors toward values predicted by features [1], instead of zero. For example, if user i has very few activities in the training data, instead of ensuring $\boldsymbol{u}_i$ to be close to zero, we predict $\boldsymbol{u}_i$ using a regression function $G\boldsymbol{x}_i$, where G is the regression coefficient matrix learned from training data through linear regression. Notice that $\boldsymbol{u}_i$ is a vector; thus, G is a matrix, instead of a vector. If features are predictive, then we can obtain good $\boldsymbol{u}_i$ estimates even for users without any training data. Specifically, we assume the following priors.

$$\begin{aligned} \alpha_i &\sim N(\boldsymbol{g}'\boldsymbol{x}_i, \sigma_\alpha^2), & \boldsymbol{u}_i &\sim N(G\boldsymbol{x}_i, \sigma_u^2), \\ \beta_i &\sim N(\boldsymbol{d}'\boldsymbol{x}_j, \sigma_\beta^2), & \boldsymbol{v}_j &\sim N(D\boldsymbol{x}_j, \sigma_v^2). \end{aligned}$$

Training and prediction: We defer the training algorithm to Section 3.4. Here, we note that this model is a generative model that specifies how the observations y_{ij} are generated according to the latent factors α_i, β_j, $\boldsymbol{u}_i$ and $\boldsymbol{v}_j$, which in turn are generated according to the prior parameters ($\boldsymbol{g}$, G, $\boldsymbol{d}$, D and the σ^2s). Given a set of observations, we first obtain the maximum likelihood estimate (MLE) of the prior parameters. Then, based on the MLE of prior parameters and the observations, we obtain the posterior mean of α_i, β_j, $\boldsymbol{u}_i$ and $\boldsymbol{v}_j$, which then can be used to predict the response of an unseen (i, j) pair by $\alpha_i + \beta_j + \boldsymbol{u}_i'\boldsymbol{v}_j$.

Baseline models: Two straightforward ways of applying matrix factorization to our problem are as follows:

- *Separate Matrix Factorization (SMF):* Treat observations of K action types as K separate matrices and apply factorization [1] to each of them independently:

$$y_{ijk} \sim \alpha_{ik} + \beta_{jk} + \boldsymbol{u}_{ik}'\boldsymbol{v}_{jk}.$$

- *Collapsed Matrix Factorization (CMF):* Collapse observations of all types into a single matrix and apply factorization [1] to it:

$$y_{ijk} \sim \alpha_i + \beta_j + \boldsymbol{u}_i'\boldsymbol{v}_j,$$

  where the right hand side does not depend on type k.

Notice that SMF is a strong baseline because for users and items with large number of training samples, their factors can be estimated accurately. For users and items without much training data, their factors can still be predicted by features. Compared to CMF, SMF has K times more factors to be estimated from data and is more sensitive to data sparsity. Although CMF is less sensitive to data sparsity, it ignores the behavioral differences across different action types, which may lead to bias and poor performance.

3.3 Locally Augmented Tensor Model

We now introduce the locally augmented tensor (LAT) model, which addresses data sparsity through tensor factorization, augmented with SMF to model the residuals locally for each action types. We first specify the model and then discuss how it works.

Model specification: The action y_{ijk} that user i takes on item j of type k is modeled as:

$$y_{ijk} \sim \alpha_{ik} + \beta_{jk} + \langle \boldsymbol{u}_i, \boldsymbol{v}_j, \boldsymbol{w}_k \rangle + \boldsymbol{u}_{ik}'\boldsymbol{v}_{jk}, \tag{3}$$

where $\langle \boldsymbol{u}_i, \boldsymbol{v}_j, \boldsymbol{w}_k \rangle = \sum_\ell \boldsymbol{u}_i[\ell]\, \boldsymbol{v}_j[\ell]\, \boldsymbol{w}_k[\ell]$ is the tensor product of three vectors $\boldsymbol{u}_i$, $\boldsymbol{v}_j$ and $\boldsymbol{w}_k$, and $\boldsymbol{u}_i[\ell]$ denotes the ℓth element in vector $\boldsymbol{u}_i$. The intuitive meaning of the factors are as follows.

- α_{ik} is the type-specific bias of user i.
- β_{jk} is the type-specific popularity of item j.
- $\langle \boldsymbol{u}_i, \boldsymbol{v}_j, \boldsymbol{w}_k \rangle$ measures the similarity between user i's global profile $\boldsymbol{u}_i$ and item j's global profile $\boldsymbol{v}_j$ weighted by a type-specific weight vector $\boldsymbol{w}_k$. These profiles are called global because they are not type-specific. Note that this weighted inner product (i.e., tensor product) imposes a constraint when we try to use it to approximate the observations y_{ijk}. Specifically, it may not be flexible enough to accurately model post-read actions when there is diverse behavior across action types. However, this constraint in the parametrization helps to avoid overfitting when data is sparse.
- $\boldsymbol{u}_{ik}'\boldsymbol{v}_{jk}$ also measures the similarity between user i and item j for type k and is more flexible than the tensor product. Thus, the residuals that the tensor product does not capture can be captured by this inner product of type-specific user factor $\boldsymbol{u}_{ik}'$ and item factor $\boldsymbol{v}_{jk}$.

To contrast the global factors $\boldsymbol{u}_i, \boldsymbol{v}_j$, we call the type-specific factors $\boldsymbol{u}_{ik}, \boldsymbol{v}_{jk}$ *local factors.* Since we augment the tensor product with the inner product of local factors, the resulting model is called the locally augmented tensor model. The priors of the factors are specified as follows.

$$\alpha_{ik} \sim N(\boldsymbol{g}_k'\boldsymbol{x}_{ik} + q_k\alpha_i,\ \sigma_{\alpha,k}^2), \quad \alpha_i \sim N(0,1) \tag{4}$$

$$\beta_{jk} \sim N(\boldsymbol{d}_k'\boldsymbol{x}_{jk} + r_k\beta_j,\ \sigma_{\beta,k}^2), \quad \beta_j \sim N(0,1) \tag{5}$$

$$\boldsymbol{u}_{ik} \sim N(G_k\boldsymbol{x}_i,\ \sigma_{uk}^2 I), \quad \boldsymbol{v}_{jk} \sim N(D_k\boldsymbol{x}_j,\ \sigma_{vk}^2 I), \tag{6}$$

$$\boldsymbol{u}_i \sim N(\boldsymbol{0},\ \sigma_{u0}^2 I),\ \boldsymbol{v}_j \sim N(\boldsymbol{0},\ \sigma_{v0}^2 I),\ \boldsymbol{w}_k \sim N(\boldsymbol{0}, I), \tag{7}$$

where $\boldsymbol{g}_k$, q_k, $\boldsymbol{d}_k$, r_k, G_k and D_k are regression coefficient vectors and matrices similar to those discussed in Section 3.1. These regression coefficients are to be learned from data and provide the ability to make predictions for users or items that do not appear in training data. The factors of these new users or items will be predicted based on their features through regression.

Training and prediction: Given training data $\boldsymbol{y} = \{y_{ijk}\}$, the goal of the training process is to learn the latent factors $\boldsymbol{\eta} = \{\alpha_{ik}, \beta_{jk}, \alpha_i, \beta_j, \boldsymbol{u}_i, \boldsymbol{v}_j, \boldsymbol{w}_k, \boldsymbol{u}_{ik}, \boldsymbol{v}_{jk}\}$ and prior parameters $\boldsymbol{\Theta} = \{\boldsymbol{g}_k, \boldsymbol{d}_k, q_k, r_k, G_k, D_k, \text{the } \sigma^2\text{s}\}$ (which consists of regression coefficients and variances) from the data $\boldsymbol{y}$. The training algorithm will be given later. After training, given an unobserved (user i, item j, action type k) triple, we predict the response as follows. If both user i and item j have some type-k observations in the training data, we just use their learned factors to make a prediction as $\alpha_{ik} + \beta_{jk} + \langle \boldsymbol{u}_i, \boldsymbol{v}_j, \boldsymbol{w}_k \rangle + \boldsymbol{u}_{ik}'\boldsymbol{v}_{jk}$. If user i appears in the training data but has no type-k observation (α_i and $\boldsymbol{u}_i$ are available from training but not α_{ik} and $\boldsymbol{u}_{ik}$), then we first predict α_{ik} as $\boldsymbol{g}_k'\boldsymbol{x}_{ik} + q_k\alpha_i$ and $\boldsymbol{u}_{ik}$ as $G_k\boldsymbol{x}_i$, and then use Equation 3 to predict the response y_{ijk}. Other cases can be handled in a similar manner.

Relation to prior work – SMF and BST: If we set α_i, β_j, $\boldsymbol{u}_i$, $\boldsymbol{v}_j$ and $\boldsymbol{w}_k$ to zero, we obtain the SMF model (defined in Section 3.1). If we set $\boldsymbol{u}_{ik}$ and $\boldsymbol{v}_{jk}$ to zero, we obtain the bias-smoothed tensor (BST) model proposed in [4] for a multi-context comment-rating prediction problem:

$$y_{ijk} \sim \alpha_{ik} + \beta_{jk} + \langle \boldsymbol{u}_i, \boldsymbol{v}_j, \boldsymbol{w}_k \rangle .$$

Although LAT is a conceptually simple combination of SMF and BST, it significantly improves the ranking performance over SMF and BST (see Section 4), and also impose a model training challenge. Notice that LAT has many latent factors and parameters to be learned. It may be sensitive to overfitting. However, because of the regularization provided by the priors (Equation 4 to 7), overfitting can be prevented when the prior variances are appropriately learned.

3.4 Training Algorithm

Since SMF, CMF and BST are special cases of LAT, we only discuss the training algorithm for LAT. Based on Equations 3 to 7, the joint log-likelihood of $\boldsymbol{y}$ and $\boldsymbol{\eta}$ given $\boldsymbol{\Theta}$ is

$$\begin{aligned}
\log \Pr(\mathbf{y}, \boldsymbol{\eta} \mid \boldsymbol{\Theta}) = &\text{ some constant } + \textstyle\sum_{ijk} \ell\ell(y_{ijk}, \hat{y}_{ijk}) \\
&- \tfrac{1}{2} \textstyle\sum_{ik} \left(\log \sigma^2_{\alpha,k} + (\alpha_{ik} - \boldsymbol{g}'_k \boldsymbol{x}_{ik} - q_k \alpha_i)^2 / \sigma^2_{\alpha,k} \right) - \tfrac{1}{2} \sum_i \alpha_i^2 \\
&- \tfrac{1}{2} \textstyle\sum_{jk} \left(\log \sigma^2_{\beta,k} + (\beta_{jk} - \boldsymbol{d}'_k \boldsymbol{x}_{jk} - r_k \beta_j)^2 / \sigma^2_{\beta,k} \right) - \tfrac{1}{2} \sum_j \beta_j^2 \\
&- \tfrac{1}{2} \textstyle\sum_{ik} \left(F \log \sigma^2_{u,k} + \| \boldsymbol{u}_{ik} - G_k \boldsymbol{x}_i \|^2 / \sigma^2_{u,k} \right) - \tfrac{1}{2} \sum_k \| \boldsymbol{w}_k \|^2 \\
&- \tfrac{1}{2} \textstyle\sum_{jk} \left(F \log \sigma^2_{v,k} + \| \boldsymbol{v}_{jk} - D_k \boldsymbol{x}_j \|^2 / \sigma^2_{v,k} \right) \\
&- \tfrac{1}{2} \textstyle\sum_i (F \log \sigma^2_u + \| \boldsymbol{u}_i \|^2 / \sigma^2_{u0}) - \tfrac{1}{2} \sum_j (F \log \sigma^2_v + \| \boldsymbol{v}_j \|^2 / \sigma^2_{v0}),
\end{aligned}$$

where $\hat{y}_{ijk} = \alpha_{ik} + \beta_{jk} + \langle \boldsymbol{u}_i, \boldsymbol{v}_j, \boldsymbol{w}_k \rangle + \boldsymbol{u}'_i \boldsymbol{v}_j$. The goal of training is to obtain MLE of $\boldsymbol{\Theta}$; i.e.,

$$\arg\max_{\boldsymbol{\Theta}} \Pr(\boldsymbol{y} \mid \boldsymbol{\Theta}) = \arg\max_{\boldsymbol{\Theta}} \int \Pr(\boldsymbol{y}, \boldsymbol{\eta} \mid \boldsymbol{\Theta}) \, d\boldsymbol{\eta},$$

which can be obtained using the MCEM algorithm [3]. The MCEM algorithm iterates between an E-step and an M-step until convergence. Let $\hat{\boldsymbol{\Theta}}^{(t)}$ denote the current estimated value of the set of prior parameters $\boldsymbol{\Theta}$ at the beginning of the tth iteration.

- **E-step:** We take expectation of the complete data log likelihood with respect to the posterior of latent factors $\boldsymbol{\eta}$ conditional on the observed training data $\boldsymbol{y}$ and the current estimate of $\boldsymbol{\Theta}$; i.e., compute

  $$f_t(\boldsymbol{\Theta}) = E_{\boldsymbol{\eta} \sim \Pr(\boldsymbol{\eta} \mid \boldsymbol{y}, \hat{\boldsymbol{\Theta}}^{(t)})} [\log \Pr(\boldsymbol{y}, \boldsymbol{\eta} \mid \boldsymbol{\Theta})]$$

  as a function of $\boldsymbol{\Theta}$, where the expectation is taken over the posterior distribution of $(\boldsymbol{\eta} \mid \boldsymbol{y}, \hat{\boldsymbol{\Theta}}^{(t)})$, which is not in closed-form, thus, approximated by Monte Carlo mean through Gibbs sampling.
- **M-step:** We maximize the expected complete data log likelihood from the E-step to obtain updated values of $\boldsymbol{\Theta}$; i.e., find $\hat{\boldsymbol{\Theta}}^{(t+1)} = \arg\max_{\boldsymbol{\Theta}} f_t(\boldsymbol{\Theta})$.

Note that the actual computation in the E-step is to generate sufficient statistics for computing $\arg\max_{\boldsymbol{\Theta}} f_t(\boldsymbol{\Theta})$, so that we do not need to scan the raw data every time when we need to evaluate $f_t(\boldsymbol{\Theta})$. At the end, we obtain the MLE of $\boldsymbol{\Theta}$ modulo local maximums and Monte Carlo errors. We can then use the estimated $\hat{\boldsymbol{\Theta}}$ to obtain the posterior mean of the factors $(\boldsymbol{\eta} \mid \boldsymbol{y}, \hat{\boldsymbol{\Theta}})$ again through Gibbs sampling. See [1] for an example of such an MCEM algorithm.

Computational complexity: We use a Gibbs sampler in the E-step, which is actually highly parallelizable. Take user and item factors for example. Conditional on global factors $\boldsymbol{u}_i, \boldsymbol{v}_j$, the local factors $\boldsymbol{u}_{ik}, \boldsymbol{v}_{jk}$ for each action type can be sampled in parallel since they are only connected to each other through the global factors. When sampling local factors for each action type, we note that given v_{jk}s, the u_{ik}s are conditionally independent and can be sampled in parallel (similar assertion holds for v_{jk}s). Conditional on local factors, the global factors can also be sampled efficiently since the $\boldsymbol{u}_i$s and $\boldsymbol{v}_j$s are conditionally independent. The complexity of sampling a factor vector is at most $O(F^3)$ and since F is typical small, the E-step is computationally efficient. The major computation in the M-step involves fitting standard linear regressions, which can also be parallelized. Thus, our MCEM algorithm is computationally efficient. We note that this training algorithm is similar to [4, 1] and logistic response can be handled by variational approximation [10]. Thus, we omit the details and will provide links to our code and detailed derivations.

4. EXPERIMENTS

We evaluate the models presented in Section 3 using post-read data collected from a major online new site. We collected post-read actions from 13,739 users, each of whom has at least 5 actions for at least one facet, to 8,069 items, each of which received at least one post-read action for each type. As a result, we obtain 2,548,111 post-read action events, where each *event* is identified by (user, facet, item). If the user took an action on the item in the facet, the event is positive or *relevant* (meaning that the item is relevant to the user in the facet); if the user saw the item but did not take an action in the facet, the event is negative or *irrelevant*. In this setting, it is natural to treat each (user, facet) pair as a *query*; the set of events associated with that pair defines the set of items to be ranked with relevance judgments coming from user actions. Notice that it is difficult to use editorial judgments in our setting since different users have different preferences for their news consumption.

Evaluation metrics: We use mean precision at k (P@k) and mean average precision (MAP) as our evaluation metrics, where mean is taken over the test (user, facet) pairs. P@k of a model is computed as follows: For each test (user, facet) pair, we use the model predictions to rank the items seen by the user in that facet and compute the precision at rank k, and then average the precision numbers over all the test pairs. MAP is computed in the similar way. To help comparison among different models, we define *P@k Lift* and *MAP Lift* over SMF of a model as the lift in P@k and MAP of the model over the SMF model, which is a strong baseline defined in Section 3.1. Take P@k for example; if P@k of a model is A and P@k of SMF is B, then the lift is $\frac{A-B}{B}$.

Experimental setup: We create a training set, a tuning set and a test set as follows. For each user, we randomly select one facet in which he/she took some action and put all of the events associated with this (user, facet) pair into set $\mathcal{A}$ (for tuning and testing). The rest of the (user, facet) pairs form the *training set*. Different facets may be selected for different users. Recall that each (user, facet) pair represents a query as in standard retrieval tasks. We then put 1/3 of set $\mathcal{A}$ into the *tuning set* and the rest 2/3 into the *test set*. The tuning set is used to select the number of latent dimensions of the factor models (i.e., the numbers of dimensions of $\boldsymbol{u}_i, \boldsymbol{v}_j, \boldsymbol{w}_k, \boldsymbol{u}_{ik}, \boldsymbol{v}_{jk}$). Notice that the EM-algorithm

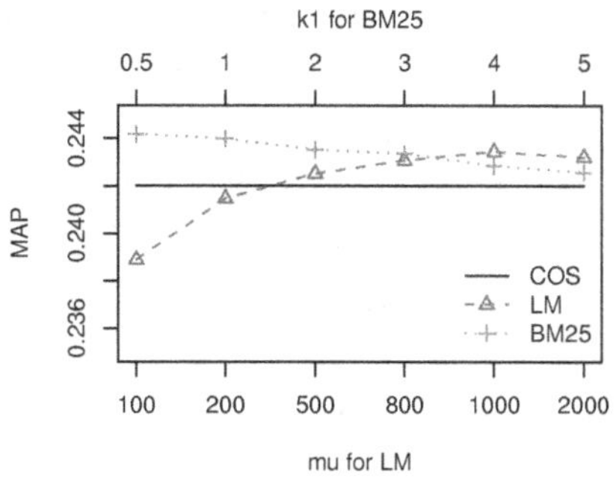

Figure 7: Performance of different IR models

used in our paper automatically determines all the model parameters except for the number of latent dimensions. For each model, we only report the test-set performance of the best number of dimensions selected using the tuning set.

The user features used in our experiments consist of age, gender and geo-location identified based on users' IP addresses. We only consider logged-in users; their user IDs are anonymized and not used in any way. The item features consists of article categories tagged by the publishers and the bag of words in the article titles and abstracts.

Models: We compare there classes of models:
(1) Latent factor models:

- *LAT:* Locally augmented tensor model (Section 3.3).
- *BST:* Bias-smoothed tensor model, which is a special case of LAT (Section 3.3).
- *SMF:* Separate matrix factorization (Section 3.1).
- *CMF:* Collapsed matrix factorization (Section 3.1).

Note that, for our experimental setup, a test event (user i, item j, facet k) has no training data to determine factor vector $\boldsymbol{u}_{ik}$ directly, but it will be predicted based on user features $\boldsymbol{x}_{ik}$. However, it is not the case for $\boldsymbol{v}_{jk}$, because events of item j in facet k may appear in training data. We also note that the Gaussian version gives better MAP values on the tuning set than the logistic version; so, we report the performance of the Gaussian version.
(2) Logistic regression: This model called *Bilinear* uses the user features $\boldsymbol{x}_i$ and item features $\boldsymbol{x}_j$ to predict whether a user would take an action on an item. Specifically,

$$y_{ijk} \sim \boldsymbol{x}_i' W_k \boldsymbol{x}_j,$$

where W_k is the regression coefficient matrix for facet k. Notice that this model has a regression coefficient for every pair of an individual user feature and an individual item feature, which is fitted using Liblinear [8] with L_2 regularization, where the regularization weight is selected using 5-fold cross-validation.
(3) IR models: We also consider a set of baseline IR models. For these models, we build a user profile based on the training data by aggregating all the text information of the items on which the user took positive actions. We treat such user profiles as queries and then use different retrieval functions to rank the items. The IR models include:

- *COS:* Vector space model with cosine similarity.
- *LM:* The Dirichlet smoothed language model [23].
- *BM25:* The best variant of Okapi retrieval methods [17].

Performance of IR Models: We first compare the baseline IR models in Figure 7. In this figure, we vary parameter μ for LM and parameter k_1 for BM25. The other two parameters are set at the recommended default values $k_3 = 1000$ and $b = 0.75$ in all the experiments. From this figure, we can see that both LM and BM25 can outperform COS, but the difference is not large. In the following, we use the BM25 with $k_1 = 1$ as the IR model to compare with other learning-based methods.

Table 1: Overall performance of different models

Model	Precision P@1	P@3	P@5	MAP
LAT	**0.3180**	**0.2853**	**0.2648**	**0.3048**
BST	0.2962	0.2654	0.2486	0.2873
SMF	0.2827	0.2639	0.2469	0.2910
Bilinear	0.2609	0.2472	0.2350	0.2755
CMF	0.2301	0.2101	0.2005	0.2439
BM25	0.2256	0.2247	0.2207	0.2440

Table 2: Paired t-test result. Note that smaller level values represent stronger significance.

Comparison	Significance level
LAT > BST	0.05 (P@1), 10^{-4} (P@3, P@5, MAP)
Rest	10^{-4} (all metrics)
BST ≈ SMF	insignificant
BST > Bilinear	10^{-3} (all metrics)
SMF > Bilinear	0.05 (P@1), 10^{-3} (P@3, P@5, MAP)
BST > CMF SMF BM25	10^{-4} (all metrics)
Bilinear > CMF BM25	10^{-3} (all metrics)
CMF ≈ BM25	insignificant

Overall performance: The precision-recall curves averaged over all (user,facet) pairs in the test data of different models are shown in Figure 8(a), and P@1, P@3, P@5 and MAP are reported in Table 1. Notice that as k increases, the precision drops. It is because post-read actions are rare events; many users do not have 3 or 5 post-read actions in the test set. For example, if a user only had one action and saw at least five items in the test set, his/her P@5 is at most 1/5. To test the significance of the performance difference between two models, we look at P@k and MAP for each individual (user, facet) pair and conduct paired t-test for the two models over all test (user, facet) pairs. The test result is shown in Table 2. In particular, LAT significantly outperforms all other models. We find that the difference between BST and SMF and the difference between CMF and BM25 are insignificant.

We defer the comparison between LAT, BST and SMF to the breakdown analysis below. Here, we note that Bilinear outperforms CMF because CMF completely ignores the behavioral differences among action types. The fact that Bilinear outperforms CMF shows that user and item features have some predictive power, but compared to SMF, these features are not sufficient to capture the behavior of individual users or items. We also note that BM25 is one of the worst performing models probably because it is the only model without supervised learning.

Breakdown by facets: In Table 3, we break the test data down by facets and report P@1 for different models; the results for other metrics are similar. Here, we focus on the comparison between LAT, BST and SMF. Starting with BST vs. SMF, we see that BST outperforms SMF for the

Table 3: P@1 broken down by Facets

Model	Facet				
	Comment	Thumb	Facebook	Mail	Print
LAT	**0.3477**	**0.3966**	**0.2565**	0.2069	**0.2722**
BST	0.3310	0.3743	0.2457	0.1936	0.1772
SMF	0.2949	0.3408	0.2306	**0.2255**	0.2532
Bilinear	0.2837	0.2947	0.2328	**0.2255**	0.1709
CMF	0.2990	0.2905	0.1638	0.1114	0.1203
BM25	0.2726	0.3198	0.1509	0.1061	0.0886

first three facets but underperforms for the last two facets. We note that the first three facets have more events in our dataset than the last two. The advantage of BST over SMF is that it has global factors; thus, the training actions in one facet are utilized to predict the test actions in other facets through the correlation among facets. However, BST is less flexible than SMF. In particular, it is not flexible enough to capture the differences among facets; thus, it is forced to fit some facets better than others. As expected, it fits the actions in facets with more data better than those with less data. LAT addresses this problem by adding facet-specific factors ($\boldsymbol{u}_{ik}$ and $\boldsymbol{v}_{jk}$) to model the residuals of BST. As can be seen, LAT uniformly outperforms BST. It also outperforms SMF except for Mail. The fact that SMF and Bilinear have the same performance for Mail suggests the difficulty of using latent factors to improve accuracy. Since LAT has more factors than SMF, it has a higher chance of overfitting.

Breakdown by user activity levels: In Figure 8(b) and 8(c), we break test users down by their activity levels in terms of the numbers of post-read actions that they took in the training data. Here, our focus is also on comparing LAT and BST to SMP. Each curve represent the P@1 Lift or MAP Lift of each model over the SMF model as a function of the user activity level specified on the x-axis. As can be seen, LAT almost uniformly outperforms all other models. For users with low activity levels (0-5), there is almost no difference between LAT, BST and SMF because they all lack data and the predictions are mostly based on features. For users who took 5-50 post-read actions, we see the largest advantage of using LAT.

Perceived differences among facets: In Table 4, we show some examples of the result of multi-faceted news ranking. On the top half of the table, we show top-ranked articles for an average user. On the bottom half, we show top-ranked articles for males with ages between 41 and 45. From this table, we can see that different facets have very different ranking results. For example, in the Facebook and Mail facets, many health-related articles are highly ranked. But for the Comment facet, political articles are usually preferred. Furthermore, if we compare the males in the middle age with the overall population, we also see notable differences. For example, although both populations have health-related articles in the Mail facet, middle-age males tend to mail more cancer-related articles. These differences confirm the need for personalized multi-facet ranking and our proposed method can address this need in a principled way.

5. RELATED WORK

Algorithmic news recommendation has received considerable attention recently. Traditional recommendation approaches include content-based filtering and collaborative filtering techniques [25, 19, 11]. These techniques have been successfully applied to applications like movie or product recommendation [19, 14]. In particular, matrix factorization based collaborative filtering, which belongs to the family of latent factor models, have achieved the state-of-the-art accuracy [11]. Recently, these methods have been adapted for news recommendation. For example, [9] studied information novelty using content-based methods. In [6], collaborative filtering was leveraged in an online news recommendation system. Hybrid approaches which combine both content-based and collaborative methods are also studied in news recommendation recently [13]. In the news domain, the existing work mainly ranks articles using clicks as the metric. Some recent work starts looking into other metrics such as social sharing [5]. To the best of our knowledge, little prior work has studied the news recommendation in a multi-faceted view, which becomes natural along with the popularity of Web 2.0. In our work, we define facets according to post-read actions and provide detailed analysis which shows the importance of multi-faceted news ranking. Furthermore, a novel matrix factorization based method to jointly model multi-type post-read actions is proposed.

Our work is related to faceted search [22, 24, 7]. The goal of faceted search is to use facet metadata of a domain to help users narrow their search results along different dimensions. In the most recent TREC Blog track 2009 [15], a special track of "faceted blog distillation" is initiated and the task of this track is to find results relevant to a single facet of a query such as "opinionated" articles in the blog collection. In these types of work, facets are metadata related to contents. The facets in our definition are based on user post-read actions and our multi-faceted ranking is to help users quickly get interesting news articles according to their preferred actions. Thus our work provides a novel angle to define facets.

The technique used in our paper is closely related to latent factor models such as matrix factorization or tensor decomposition. For example, singular value decomposition (SVD) based methods [11], tensor-based methods [16], and collaborative competitive filtering [21] all belong to this family. All these methods did not consider post-read actions. In particular, our technique is related to the collective matrix factorization (CMF) [20] and bias-smoothed tensor (BST) model [4]. As compared in our experiments, our models are better than these existing ones in exploring the correlations among different post-read facets.

6. CONCLUSION

Jointly mining and modeling post-read actions of multiple types has not been previously studied in the literature. We conducted a rigorous study on post-read behavior on a major news portal with action types like facebook share, commenting, rating that users engage in after reading an article. Through data analysis, we found some interesting patterns in news consumption when it comes to read and post-read behavior. Reading articles is private, post-read behavior like sharing and commenting are more public. Users tend to differ in interesting ways in their public and private behavior when interacting with news. We found positive correlations among different action types and were able to exploit these through a tensor product of global user, item and facet factors — the facet factors capture the correlations by a low-rank approximation. The tensor product is augmented using local factors to capture the local residuals to improve rank-

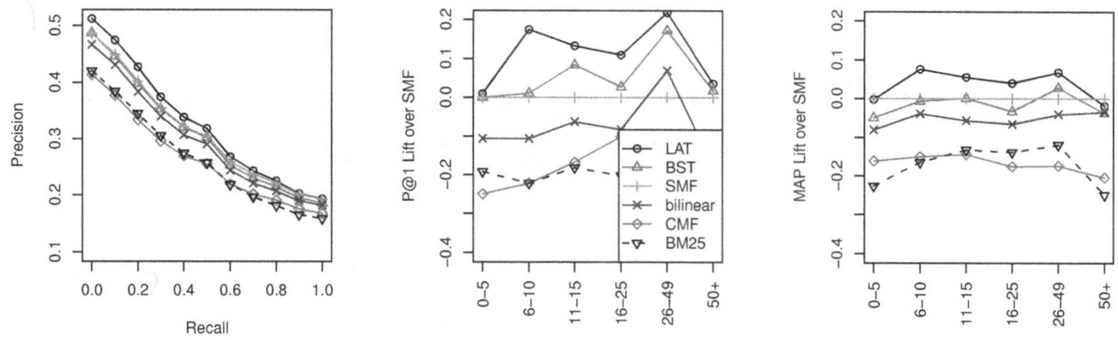

(a) Precision-recall curves (b) P@1 by user activity levels (c) MAP by user activity levels

Figure 8: Performance of different models

Facebook	Mail	Comment
Overall population		
US weather tornado Japan disaster aid	Teething remedies pose fatal risk to infants	US books Michelle Obama
Eight ways monsanto is destroying our health	US med car seats children	US Obama immigration
Teething remedies pose fatal risk to infants	Super women mom soft wins may live longer	US exxon oil prices
New zombie ant fungi found	Tips for a successful open house	Harry Reid: republicans fear tea party
Indy voters would rather have Charlie Sheen ...	Painless diabetes monitor talks to smartphone	Obama to kick off campaign this week
For male at age 41 to 45		
Oxford English dictionary added new words	Richer white women more prone to melanoma	Israel troubling tourism
US exxon oil prices	Obesity boost aggressive breast cancer in older women	Israel palestinians
Children make parents happy eventually	US med car seats children	USA election Obama
Qatar Saudi politics Internet	Are coffee drinkers less prone to breast cancer	US books Michelle Obama
Lawmakers seek to outlaw prank calls	Short course of hormone therapy boosts prostate cancer	Levi Johnston to write memoir

Table 4: Examples of multi-faceted news ranking. Only the titles of the news articles are shown.

ing performance of post-read action types. This opens the door to incorporate post-read engagement behavior in creating new products/modules on news sites online. We plan to explore such possibilities in the future.

7. REFERENCES

[1] D. Agarwal and B.-C. Chen. Regression-based latent factor models. In *KDD*, 2009.

[2] D. Agarwal, B.-C. Chen, P. Elango, N. Motgi, S.-T. Park, R. Ramakrishnan, S. Roy, and J. Zachariah. Online models for content optimization. In *NIPS*, 2008.

[3] J. Booth and J. Hobert. Maximizing generalized linear mixed model likelihoods with an automated monte carlo EM algorithm. *J.R.Statist. Soc. B*, 1999.

[4] B.-C. Chen, J. Guo, B. Tseng, and J. Yang. User reputation in a comment rating environment. In *KDD*, 2011.

[5] P. Cui, F. Wang, S. Liu, M. Ou, S. Yang, and L. Sun. Who should share what?: item-level social influence prediction for users and posts ranking. In *SIGIR*, 2011.

[6] A. S. Das, M. Datar, A. Garg, and S. Rajaram. Google news personalization: scalable online collaborative filtering. In *WWW*, 2007.

[7] S. T. Dumais. Faceted search. In *Encyclopedia of Database Systems*. 2009.

[8] R.-E. Fan, K.-W. Chang, C.-J. Hsieh, X.-R. Wang, and C.-J. Lin. Liblinear: A library for large linear classification. *JMLR*, 2008.

[9] E. Gabrilovich, S. T. Dumais, and E. Horvitz. Newsjunkie: providing personalized newsfeeds via analysis of information novelty. In *WWW*, 2004.

[10] T. S. Jaakkola and M. I. Jordan. Bayesian parameter estimation via variational methods. *Statistics and Computing*, 2000.

[11] Y. Koren. Factorization meets the neighborhood: a multifaceted collaborative filtering model. In *KDD*, 2008.

[12] L. Li, W. Chu, J. Langford, and R. E. Schapire. A contextual-bandit approach to personalized news article recommendation. In *WWW*, 2010.

[13] L. Li, D. Wang, T. Li, D. Knox, and B. Padmanabhan. Scene: a scalable two-stage personalized news recommendation system. In *SIGIR*, 2011.

[14] G. Linden, B. Smith, and J. York. Amazon.com recommendations: Item-to-item collaborative filtering. *IEEE Internet Computing*, 7(1), 2003.

[15] C. Macdonald, I. Ounis, and I. Soboroff. Overview of the trec 2009 blog track. 2009.

[16] S. Rendle, Z. Gantner, C. Freudenthaler, and L. Schmidt-Thieme. Fast context-aware recommendations with factorization machines. In *SIGIR*, 2011.

[17] S. E. Robertson, S. Walker, S. Jones, M. M.Hancock-Beaulieu, and M. Gatford. Okapi at TREC-3. In D. K. Harman, editor, *The Third Text REtrieval Conference (TREC-3)*, 1995.

[18] R. Salakhutdinov and A. Mnih. Bayesian probabilistic matrix factorization using markov chain monte carlo. In *ICML*, 2008.

[19] B. M. Sarwar, G. Karypis, J. A. Konstan, and J. Riedl. Item-based collaborative filtering recommendation algorithms. In *WWW*, 2001.

[20] A. P. Singh and G. J. Gordon. Relational learning via collective matrix factorization. In *KDD*, 2008.

[21] S.-H. Yang, B. Long, A. J. Smola, H. Zha, and Z. Zheng. Collaborative competitive filtering: learning recommender using context of user choice. In *SIGIR*, 2011.

[22] K.-P. Yee, K. Swearingen, K. Li, and M. Hearst. Faceted metadata for image search and browsing. In *CHI*, 2003.

[23] C. Zhai and J. Lafferty. A study of smoothing methods for language models applied to ad hoc information retrieval. In *SIGIR*, 2001.

[24] L. Zhang and Y. Zhang. Interactive retrieval based on faceted feedback. In *SIGIR*, 2010.

[25] Y. Zhang and J. Koren. Efficient bayesian hierarchical user modeling for recommendation system. In *SIGIR*, 2007.

A Decentralized Recommender System for Effective Web Credibility Assessment

Thanasis G. Papaioannou, Jean-Eudes Ranvier, Alexandra Olteanu and Karl Aberer
School of Computer and Communication Sciences
École Polytechnique Fédérale de Lausanne (EPFL)
1015 Lausanne, Switzerland
Email: firstname.lastname@epfl.ch

ABSTRACT

An overwhelming and growing amount of data is available online. The problem of untrustworthy online information is augmented by its high economic potential and its dynamic nature, e.g. transient domain names, dynamic content, etc. In this paper, we address the problem of assessing the credibility of web pages by a decentralized social recommender system. Specifically, we concurrently employ i) item-based collaborative filtering (CF) based on specific web page features, ii) user-based CF based on friend ratings and iii) the ranking of the page in search results. These factors are appropriately combined into a single assessment based on adaptive weights that depend on their effectiveness for different topics and different fractions of malicious ratings. Simulation experiments with real traces of web page credibility evaluations suggest that our hybrid approach outperforms both its constituent components and classical content-based classification approaches.

Categories and Subject Descriptors

H.3.3 [**Information Storage & Retrieval**]: Information Search & Retrieval

General Terms

Theory

Keywords

collaborative filtering, social networks, similarity metrics

1. INTRODUCTION

People employ online information more and more in their everyday lives for shopping, business, social life, relationships, etc. However, the overwhelming amount of online content as well as the great economic potential involved in influencing people's knowledge render the problem of web credibility assessment a non-trivial one. Credibility is a rather subjective term depending on multiple factors, such as information authenticity, authority, objectivity, freshness and topic coverage [12]. Authors of non-credible online content employ dynamic web page content, easy domain name changes and web link graph modifications to hide their traces and appear at a high position in the ranking of the search results, i.e. web spamming.

Several approaches, e.g. [13, 18], have been proposed that combine different page content features to assess credibility with limited effectiveness. Since many users perceive high ranking position of a page in the search results as high credibility, reordering the search results based on page credibility would greatly facilitate people's access to credible information. To this end, several approaches [2, 6] have been proposed against web spamming. Also, some system initiatives have arisen, such as Google+ "+1" button[1] or Facebook[2] "like" button, in order to evaluate credibility of web pages based on user ratings. However, as these approaches collect ratings that are subject to data mining, valid privacy concerns are raised by the users that may deter participation to these systems.

In this paper, we propose a decentralized privacy-friendly social recommender system for web page credibility assessment. Our recommendation scheme for credibility assessment of a web page includes a user-based collaborative filtering component for taking into account the user ratings for the page, an item-based collaborative filtering component for considering the content-based features of the page and a third component that is based on the ranking of the page in the search results. To the best of our knowledge, none of the existing approaches combines these aspects in a generic way. Along the way of the content-based component description, we define new versions of existing similarity measures that are convenient for the different content features employed. Moreover, our approach is generic-enough to include additional web page features. The different components of the recommendation scheme are combined in a weighted average, while the weights are properly updated to reflect the effectiveness of each individual component for credibility assessment. In this decentralized social network, friends should be opportunistically added, so that ratings exist for a large number of web pages. Since malicious users may infiltrate into the social network, we propose a friend banishment approach that progressively expels them. We verify the effectiveness of our recommendation scheme by simulation experiments with two real corpus of web page

CIKM'12, October 29–November 2, 2012, Maui, HI, USA.

[1]http://www.google.com/+1/button/
[2]http://www.facebook.com

credibility assessments, while assuming the presence of varying fractions of malicious users in the social network. Finally, we implemented a working prototype of the proposed system and our design choices were validated in practice.

The remainder of this paper is organized as follows: In Section 2, we overview our system for credibility assessment. In Section 3, we present our multi-component approach for web page credibility assessment. In Section 4, we explain how to determine the weights of our multi-component recommendation scheme and then in Section 5, we describe our banishment scheme for malicious friend exclusion from the recommendation algorithm. In Section 6, we present our prototype system implementation, while in Section 7, we experimentally evaluate our web page credibility assessment based on two page corpus. In Section 8, we overview the related work and finally, in Section 9, we conclude our work.

2. SYSTEM DESIGN

In our system, users are connected to each other on a Peer-to-Peer (P2P) overlay. A P2P node resides in a plug-in at the user browser. The user inserts queries in the web search engine and the plug-in fetches the search results, assesses the credibility of the 100 top-ranked pages according to our credibility estimation scheme (described in the next section) and modifies the ranking of the search results accordingly. The user is able to assign a binary vote to any page that she visits or sees in the search results, i.e. $\{-1, 1\}$. Each user rating for a page is stored at a local database. Periodically, batches of user ratings are broadcasted to all user friends. Upon receiving a rating for a web page from a friend, the rating is stored at the local database and it is employed for credibility evaluation in subsequent web searches. The overall architecture of our approach is shown in Figure 1.

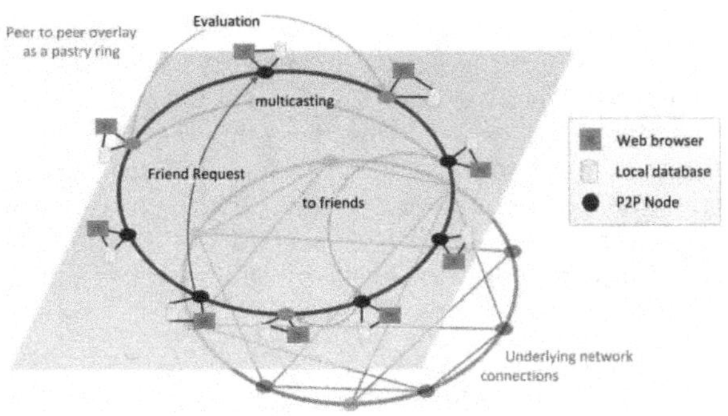

Figure 1: Overview of our system.

3. RECOMMENDATION SCHEME

In our system, users are connected to their friends in the "social graph", while pages can be implicitly linked with other pages based on their content-based similarity in a "content-similarity graph" or explicitly linked with other pages based on their incoming/outgoing links in the web, as depicted in Figure 2. Also, note that a user may rate or edit/own a web page. Based on the different semantics of the node associations in each graph, we derive a separate credibility assessment by each graph for a web page under evaluation and later we combine them into a single credibility assessment. In the social component, the credibility assessment is based on the recommendations of the friends in the social graph. Moreover, we evaluate the credibility of the user friends by evaluating the consistency of their recommendations with those of the user herself and banish them according to the approach of Section 5. In the content component, we evaluate credibility of a page based on its content-based similarity with other pages. Lastly, in the search-ranking component, we evaluate the credibility of the page based on its associations in the web graph. We describe these components for credibility evaluation and their combination in the following subsections.

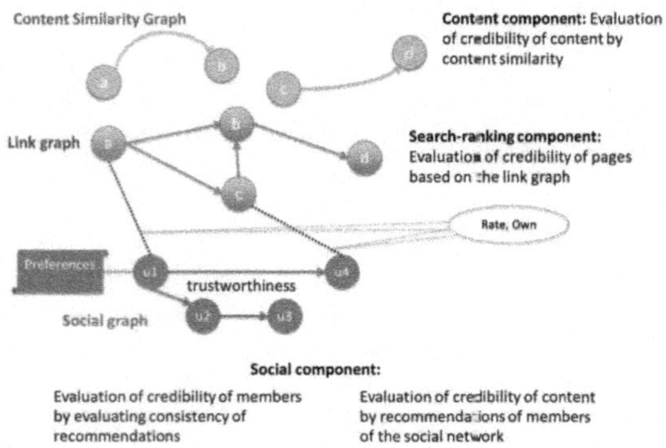

Figure 2: Our recommendation scheme.

3.1 Social Component

The social component ρ_u estimates the credibility of a web page based on the ratings of the user friends for this page. It is calculated according to the user-based collaborative filtering algorithm introduced in [7], which is given by the formula below:

$$\rho_{u,j} = \overline{r_u} + \frac{\sum_{v \in U_{u,i}} (\overline{w}_{u,v}(r_{v,i} - \overline{r_v}))}{\sum_{v \in U_{u,i}} (\overline{w}_{u,v})}, \quad (1)$$

where $\overline{r_u}$ is the average rating over all ratings of user u, $\overline{w}_{u,v}$ is the similarity between user u and user v based on their ratings for mutually rated pages (given by the mean-adjusted Pearson correlation metric), $r_{v,i}$ is the rating of user v for the page i, $\overline{r_v}$ is the average rating over all ratings of user v, and $U_{u,i}$ is the "neighborhood" of user u defined as her k nearest friends in terms of $\overline{w}_{u,v}$. The mean-adjusted Pearson correlation for users u, v that mutually rated pages in $I = I_u \cap I_v$ is given by:

$$\overline{w}_{u,v} = \frac{\sum_{i \in I} (r_{u,i} - \overline{r_u}) * (r_{v,i} - \overline{r_v})}{\sqrt{\sum_{i \in I} (r_{u,i} - \overline{r_u})^2 * \sum_{i \in I} (r_{u,i} - \overline{r_u})^2}} \quad (2)$$

Note that Pearson correlation is not defined for $|I| = 1$ and when the standard deviation for the rating vector of one user is 0, i.e. $\sigma_{R_u} = 0$ or $\sigma_{R_v} = 0$, where R_u, R_v are the rating vectors of users u, v. In such a case, a very low positive standard deviation is assumed in the calculations. Only the top-k most similar friends are considered in Eq. (1), which is referred to as the *neighborhood of the user* for this collaborative filtering algorithm.

3.2 Content Component

This component assesses the credibility of the web page based on content-based features, such as semantic ones (e.g. category, entities, keywords etc.), NLP ones (sentiments, subjectivity, etc.), syntactic ones (part-of-speech tag multiplicities, punctuation marks, spelling errors, etc.), advertisements, page layout, etc. The credibility of a page is calculated by the item-based collaborative filtering [16] approach is used, which is defined as follows:

$$\rho_{c,i} = \frac{\sum_{j \in I_u} s_{i,j} \times r_{u,j}}{\sum_{j \in I_u} |s_{i,j}|}, \quad (3)$$

where I_u is the set of pages rated by u, $s_{i,j}$ is the similarity between pages i and j, and $r_{u,j}$ is the rating of user u for page j. Notice that only the pages rated by user u are considered in the item-based algorithm, as opposed to considering pages rated by friends as well. This is done in order for the user to have "personalized" means to assess the credibility of the page as she can be assumed to assign maximum trust to her own ratings. Moreover, we do not use the ratings of different users for calculating the similarity between pages, proposed by [16]. The calculation of the page similarity depends on the specific content features employed, as described in the following paragraphs. Only the top-k most similar pages are considered in Eq. (3), which is referred to as the *neighborhood of the page* for this collaborative filtering algorithm.

Syntactic and lexical features.

The syntactic features that we consider include part-of-speech and punctuation marks, while the lexical ones include text complexity and spelling errors. Part-of-speech feature extraction refers to the categorization of the page content to different word categories, e.g. nouns, verbs, adjectives, adverbs, based on their definition and their context. Text complexity defined in [8] is given by the entropy of different words in the text of the web page. Each of these features is single-valued, and thus, we can compare two different pages based on their corresponding feature vectors A, B, by using the cosine similarity, defined as follows:

$$\cos(\theta) = \frac{A \cdot B}{||A|| \times ||B||} = \frac{\sum_{i=1}^{n} A_i \times B_i}{\sqrt{\sum_{i=1}^{n} A_i^2} \times \sqrt{\sum_{i=1}^{n} B_i^2}} \quad (4)$$

Semantic features.

We employed as semantic features the page category, the entities, the keywords and the informativeness of the keyword to the page content. For comparing two pages based on their entities and keywords, we propose a Jaccard-like similarity, as explained below. The Jaccard similarity metric $J_{A,B}$ between pages A and B is given by:

$$J_{A,B} = \frac{A \cap B}{A \cup B}, \quad (5)$$

where $A \cap B$ is the set of elements in A and B that are strictly equal to each other and $A \cup B$ is the union of all elements. However, the requirement for strict equality between entities or keywords between pages is very restrictive. Thus, we relax this requirement and use a normalized Levenshtein[3] distance for comparing strings between pages. Specifically, the distance $\hat{L}_a(B)$ of a keyword/entity a in page A from page B is given by:

$$\hat{L}_a(B) = \min_{b \in B} \frac{L(a,b)}{\max\{length(a), length(b)\}}, \quad (6)$$

where $L(a,b)$ is the Levenshtein distance between strings a and b, and $length(.)$ provides the length of its string parameter. This function expresses the closest normalized distance of a keyword/entity a in page A with any of the keywords/entities in page B and takes values in $[0,1]$. Otherwise, it would not be obvious to select the keywords/entities based on which two pages would have to be compared. The Jaccard-like similarity $\hat{J}_{A,B}$ of two pages A, B is defined by the formula below:

$$\hat{J}_{A,B} = \frac{\sum_{a \in A}(1 - \hat{L}_a(B))}{\sum_{a \in A}(1 + \hat{L}_a(B))} \quad (7)$$

$\hat{J}_{A,B}$ takes values in $[0,1]$ and it is a loose version of the intersection (i.e. common characteristics) over the union (i.e. all characteristics) ratio of Eq. (5). Indeed, the numerator in Eq. (7) is the sum of similarities among keywords/entities between two pages, while the denominator expresses the summed distance between the pages.

The page category (elsewhere referred to as category cohesion [8]) refers to the proximity of a page to a specific category based on the frequency of appearance of its terms to the pages of various categories, e.g. sports, politics, religion, entertainment, etc. The page category was only used to evaluate the effectiveness of restricting the comparison between pages the same category, assuming no similarity between pages of different categories.

The informativeness of a keyword to the page (calculated by the $tf * idf$ metric in [8]) is also considered in page similarity. In the $tf * idf$ metric, tf is the term frequency, while idf is the inverse document frequency that measures how common is the term across all documents. The lower the informativeness of a keyword to the page where it belongs, the less significant it should be for comparing the page to another one. Therefore, we define an informativeness weight $m_{a,b}$ for the distance between two keywords/entities a and b belonging to pages A and B respectively, as the minimum of their informativeness to their corresponding pages, i.e.:

$$m_{a,b} = \min\{tf * idf(a), tf * idf(b)\}, \quad (8)$$

We integrate the keyword informativeness in the normalized Levenshtein distance of Eq. 6 as follows:

$$\hat{J}'_{A,B} = \frac{\sum_{a \in A}(1 - \hat{L}_a(B)) m_{a,\hat{b}}}{\sum_{a \in A}(1 + \hat{L}_a(B)) m_{a,\hat{b}}}, \quad (9)$$

where $\hat{b} = \arg\min_{b \in B} \frac{L(a,b)}{\max\{length(a), length(b)\}}$.

NLP features.

Two pages can very similar in terms of keywords and entities, but they may have different sentiments (i.e. positive/negative opinions) associated with them. Therefore, we also consider the sentiment associated with each keyword/entity (as provided by tools, such as LingPipe[4] and AlchemyAPI[5]) in the page similarity. The sentiment associated to a keyword/entity takes values in $[-1,1]$, where -1

[3]Levenshtein (or edit) distance between strings a, b is the number of single character edits (i.e. insertion, deletion, substitution) in order for string a to transform to b.

[4]http://alias-i.com/lingpipe/

[5]http://www.alchemyapi.com/

means totally negative, 1 means totally positive and 0 means neutral sentiment. For two keywords/entities a, b, we define the *sentiment similarity* $\varphi_{a,b}$ by the formula below:

$$\varphi_{a,b} = 1 - |sentiment(a) - sentiment(b)| \quad (10)$$

Note that $\varphi_{a,b}$ again takes values in $[-1, 1]$. We integrate sentiment similarity into Eq. (9) and we define the combined Jaccard-like similarity metric $\hat{J}^*_{A,B}$ between pages based on their keywords/entities, including their informativeness (or relevance) to the page and their sentiment, by the formula below:

$$s_{A,B} \equiv \hat{J}^*_{A,B} = \frac{\sum_{a\in A}(1-\hat{L}_a(B))m_{a,\hat{b}}\varphi_{a,\hat{b}}}{\sum_{a\in A}(1+\hat{L}_a(B))m_{a,\hat{b}}}, \quad (11)$$

where $\hat{b} = \arg\min_{b\in B} \frac{L(a,b)}{\max\{length(a),length(b)\}}$. In Eq. (11), we multiply the pages similarity by the sentiments similarity to make sure that pages with opposite sentiments would have opposite ratings. Note that in Eq. (11) $s_{a,b}$ appears only in the numerator. This is due to the definition of the similarity as a Jaccard-like one: the numerator expresses the summed similarity between pages, while the denominator expresses the union of compared terms. Therefore, the maximum sentiment (i.e. 1) is implicitly considered in the denominator. The complexity of the combined Jaccard-like similarity metric is $O(n^2)$, where n is the maximum number of keywords/entities per page. To this end, proactive calculation of this metric for potentially-targetted pages is foreseen for adequately fast online web credibility assessment.

3.3 Search-Ranking Component

The search ranking component estimates the credibility of a web page based on the page ranking in the search results. According to [13], many people tend to believe that a higher ranking in the search results means a higher credibility, which is not always true. Even worse, spammers exploiting this belief, have targeted the ranking mechanisms of popular search engines with relative success [2, 6]. In general, page ranking algorithm employ the link associations among pages and page popularity, which we deem as important features for assessing credibility. Our search-ranking component employs the ranking of the page in the search results as a credibility metric. This can be done by using directly the Google PageRank metric normalized by its maximum value as a credibility score, i.e. $\rho_{g,i} = pagerank(i)/\max_j\{pagerank(j)\}$. Another approach would be to estimate the page credibility rating based on its search ranking by a Zipf distribution, i.e. $\rho_{g,i} = \frac{1/k^s}{\sum_{j=1}^{N}(1/j^s)}$ for a page i in the kth position of the search results, where $s > 0$ is an exponent characterizing the steepness of the distribution.

3.4 Aggregate estimation

Each individual component of the recommendation scheme described above provides a (potentially different) estimation of the credibility rating that should be assigned to the web page under credibility evaluation. These credibility estimates can be presented to the user individually; this choice would be transparent to the user and she would be able to conclude on the page credibility given all information. However, individual assessment by the different components may be conflicting to each other and they may confuse the user. A simple alternative would be to provide the user with the average of the estimated ratings of the individual components as the credibility assessment. A criticism on this choice would be that not all components are so influential for assessing the credibility of specific categories or so informative for specific users. To this end, we assign a different weight to each individual component for credibility assessment and calculate the estimated overall credibility rating, as follows:

$$\rho_i = \omega_u\rho_{u,i} + \omega_c\rho_{c,i} + \omega_g\rho_{g,i}, \quad (12)$$

where $\rho_{u,i}$, $\rho_{c,i}$, $\rho_{g,i}$ are the estimated ratings for page i based on the social component, the content component and the search results ranking component, and ω_u, ω_c, ω_g are the respective weights of these components in the aggregate credibility estimation. These weights satisfy that $\omega_u + \omega_i + \omega_g = 1$ and they are properly set, so as to reflect the significance that has to be put to the individual components of the credibility estimation of the web page, as explained in the following section.

4. ADAPTIVE WEIGHT UPDATE

A natural question on the aggregate credibility estimation is how to properly determine the weights of the different components of the recommendation mechanism, so as to maximize its effectiveness for credibility assessment of different web pages. For different pages, different aspects may be more dominant than others for the estimation of the page credibility, e.g. for scientific pages content-based recommendation may be preferable than community-based one, while for music-related pages the social component could be much more useful than others. To this end, we maintain different credibility component weights per page category at each user.

Also, as explained in [5], different aspects of the web page affect differently its perceived credibility by different users and the prominence of these aspects in the web page determines the estimated page credibility. In other words, the a posteriori (i.e. after visiting it) credibility assessment of a web page by a user is rather subjective. We respect this inherent subjectivity by maintaining individual credibility component weights per page category at the user premises.

We propose that the weight of each credibility assessment component, given a history of s agreements of the posterior credibility assessment by the user with the prior recommendation of the respective component of the web credibility mechanism out of t recommendations in total, is updated according to the following Beta-distribution-based reputation formula [9]

$$\omega = \frac{s'}{t'}, \quad (13)$$

where $s' = \beta s + \mathbb{1}(agreement)$ and $t' = \beta t + 1$, while $\mathbb{1}(.)$ is the indicator function, *agreement* denotes the consistency of the a priori credibility estimation of the new web page by the credibility component with the a posteriori credibility assessment by the user, and $0 \leq \beta \leq 1$ a discount factor for past credibility assessments. This weight updating approach guarantees convergence of each weight to the mean effectiveness of its respective credibility component per page category, as opposed to asymmetric TCP-like approaches (i.e. additive increase upon agreement, multiplicative decrease upon disagreement). The discount factor β is chosen, so as to reflect the dynamic effectiveness that may arise for a credibility component, i.e. for relatively stable effectiveness β should be close to 1 and vice versa. Note that after updating the weights based on Eq. (13), the weights are normalized so that they sum up to 1.

Recall that the contacts of the user in the social network are not necessarily trusted friends, as the social network has to opportunistically expand to large user communities, in order to effectively collect ratings for arbitrary web pages. Thus, the community composition may dynamically change; more malicious users may infiltrate the neighborhood of a target user, while certain pages may become targets of malicious ratings. On the other hand, the effectiveness of the content and the search-ranking components are assumed to be rather stable. Thus, a low discount factor (e.g. $\beta \sim 0.6$) can be chosen for the social credibility component, while a high one (e.g. $\beta \sim 0.9$) can be used for the content and the search-ranking components. However, although the overall ineffectiveness of the social component can be captured by the described weight updating approach, malicious ratings are still taken into account in the credibility assessment. We deal with this issue in the next section.

5. FRIEND BANISHMENT

As the social network of the user may opportunistically increase, malicious users may become part of the user neighborhood in the user-based collaborative filtering algorithm for a web page. In such a case, the weight of the social component will reflect its ineffectiveness according to the weight updating approach described in the previous section. However, given the low weight of the social credibility component, the overall credibility estimation will not be able to benefit from the social credibility component, while the malicious ratings will still be included in the credibility evaluation of future web pages. To this end, we propose a *friend banishment* mechanism that is inspired by [14], as explained below. A user maintains for each friend j a local variable $nd_j \geq 0$ for the number of disagreements with her and a banishment period $bp_j \geq 0$. After visiting a page, the user u compares her credibility evaluation $\hat{r}$ to the rating r_j for this page of every user j that is *eligible* to be part of her collaborative-filtering neighborhood (i.e. most similar users) for this page and updates nd_j, bp_j as follows:

- If $\hat{r} = r_j$, then $bp_j = \max\{bp_j - 1, 0\}$ and $nd_j = nd_j - y$, where $y > 0$ is a certain *forgiveness* factor.
- If $\hat{r} \neq r_j$, then $nd = nd_j + x$ and $bp_j = bp_j + b^{nd_j}$, where $b > 1$ is the base of the banishment period and determines the *harshness* of the punishment for disagreement.

In the user collaborative-filtering neighborhood for a page are only considered her top-k most similar friends that are not currently banished (i.e. those with banishment period equal to 0). All users anticipated in the construction of the neighborhood for a page are considered eligible and their nd_j, bp_j values are updated, as already explained. This approach considerably limits the number of users whose banishment values have to be updated per web page visit. This banishment mechanism satisfies two desirable properties: i) it quickly excludes altogether malicious users, ii) it allows the consideration of the credibility assessment of people that only occasionally disagree with the user.

6. IMPLEMENTATION

Our recommendation mechanism has been implemented as a Firefox add-on. The interactions with the browser are made through Javascript, while computation-intensive operations and network communications are handled using Java, in order to benefit from its multithreading capabilities.

The peer to peer overlay management is made by a Java implementation of the peer-to-peer overlay Pastry [15]. Pastry is used to manage social relationships among friends in a decentralized manner (i.e. friend list is stored locally and managed through Pastry messages) and to exchange their evaluations.

All the data manipulated by the mechanism is stored locally in an embedded H2 SQL database[6] and then used to compute the credibility evaluations. The database is structured using the following tables:

- Document: Represents a page that has been evaluated and the collection of its single-valued features.
- Entity: Represents an entity defined in a page, its relevance and its sentiment.
- Keyword: Represents a keyword defined in a page, its relevance and its sentiment.
- Evaluation: Contains the evaluations of pages made by friends of the user and the user himself.
- User: Contains the list of the friends of the user.

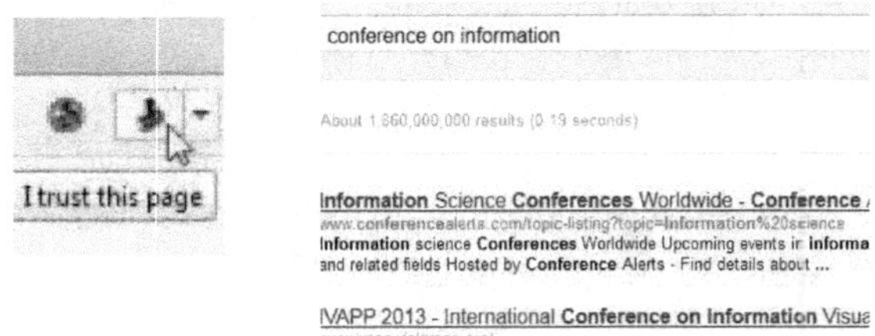

(a) (b)

Figure 3: (a) User interface in Firefox navigation bar. (b) Initial results returned for a query.

As we can see in Figure 3(a), the user interface is mainly composed of two buttons to rate the displayed page and a contextual menu (Figure 4(a)) to evaluate pages referenced by a link, i.e. without visiting the page.

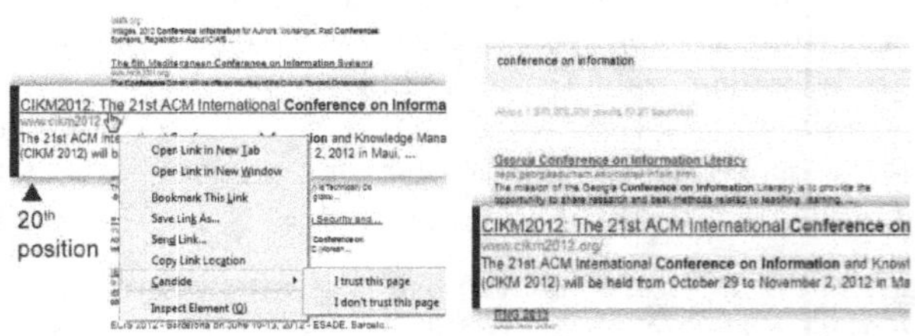

(a) (b)

Figure 4: (a) Evaluation of the page by the user via the contextual menu. (b) Modified results.

A typical use case would be to query a search engine (in our case Google) for "conference on information". Assume that the initial ordering of the results places the CIKM 2012 website outside of the top 10 results (Figure 3(b)). If the user thinks that the website is credible and relevant to her

[6]http://www.h2database.com

query, she can manually rate the page as credible (Figure 4(a)). Upon resubmission of the same query by the user or her friends, her evaluation will be taken into account and the website will appear in the top results (Figure 4(b)). Notice that if her friends have already rated this page or if she has rated pages with similar content, the ordering of the results would also be affected accordingly.

7. EVALUATION

7.1 Simulation setup

Content-based component.

In order to assess the performance of our content-based component for web credibility evaluation, we compare our collaborative filtering approach to a machine learning approach (executed in Weka 3[7]). The Support Vector Machine (SVM) classifier is known for having good performance, in general, and thus we employ it as a base comparison against content-based collaborative filtering. We use a leave-one-out cross-validation to evaluate the performance of both approaches. This method consists in testing each page of the corpus independently, while training the model with the rest of the corpus.

Social component.

The social component requires several users that exchange their ratings. Although in the Reconcile data set (see Subsection 7.2) different users rate the same page, the Microsoft corpus provides only one credibility evaluation per document. We handle this issue by simulating multiple virtual users who rate pages from the Microsoft corpus, according to different behavioral types. We consider two types of behavioral profiles for the virtual users: A trustworthy profile according to which the user rates the pages with their corresponding ratings in the Microsoft data set. A malicious profile according to which the user rates most of the pages correctly except a specific subset of the corpus, namely the target pages, which represent the pages that the malicious user evaluates oppositely to the evaluation in the Microsoft data set. In our experiment, we gradually increase the percentage of malicious users and see how the weighted average and the social component react to these malicious users.

In practice, to simulate this multi-user environment, we create 100 users and, for each of them, we randomly select 100 pages across all categories to be stored in her history of visited pages; thus, we populate the neighborhoods of the collaborative filtering algorithm and avoid cold-start effects. Another 100 randomly selected pages are evaluated by each user for training her component weights and obtaining an optimal weighted average for each category. The Beta-distribution-based reputation formula for updating the weights is parameterized using $\beta = 0.6$, while the component weights are initially equal to $\frac{1}{3}$. Finally, 50 random trustworthy users randomly select one unvisited page from the subset of pages targeted by the malicious users and evaluate it with their social-based, content-based and search-ranking-based web credibility components. The weighted average of the component recommendations provide the credibility assessment for the web page. This prediction is finally compared with the ground truth represented by the Microsoft evaluation.

[7]http://www.cs.waikato.ac.nz/ml/weka/

Banishment system.

In order to assess the usefulness of the banishment approach, three different banishment configuration are tested: a) No banishment, in which case there is no penalty for a friend that provides a rating that is different than the user's a posteriori evaluation. b) Temporary banishment according to the approach of Section 5 with both base and initial exponent equal to 2. c) Lifetime banishment, which implies that if a friend provides an inaccurate rating, her ratings will not be used by the user for any future web credibility assessments.

7.2 Data sets

In order to evaluate the system, we use two different data sets: a) The Microsoft one that contains a single evaluation per page and b) the Reconcile one with fewer pages, but with the advantage of multiple evaluations per page. We describe these data sets in detail below.

Microsoft corpus.

This corpus comes from a study performed by Microsoft as part of [17]. It contains a set of 1000 pages belonging to 5 categories, namely: health, politics, environmental science, celebrities, personal finance.

Using Google zeitgeist[8], the authors in [17] were able to define for each topic, the 5 most popular queries performed on Google. Finally, each query has been provided to a search engine and the first 40 URLs for these queries have been used, i.e. 40 URLs x 5 queries x 5 topics = 1000 URLs. The original corpus has been provided with the credibility rating for each page given as a 5-point Likert-scale evaluation, with 0 denoting that the page is not credible at all, while 5 denoting high credibility.

The whole corpus has been entirely evaluated by one of the researchers. Then, several subsequent researchers as well as experts evaluated a subset of this corpus and verified that these evaluations are correlated to the initial rating. For convenience in the credibility evaluation, the ratings of this corpus have been transformed into a binary system, i.e. ratings 4 and 5 have been mapped to 1, ratings 1 and 2 have been mapped to -1, while ratings with 3 Likert points have been considered as neutral and extracted from the corpus. Thus, we end up with a corpus of 773 pages with binary credibility ratings.

Reconcile corpus.

This corpus has been created by researchers of the Polish Japanese Institute of Information Technology (PJIIT) of Warszawa in the framework of the Reconcile project. It is an aggregation of the evaluations of 90 students of PJIIT that have rated 9 web pages each from a corpus of 85 polish documents (all related to health topics).

The pages have been evaluated on a Likert 6 point scale but for the purpose of our experiments, as in the Microsoft corpus, each evaluation have been transformed to a binary scale, i.e. -1 (for ratings 0, 1 and 2) and 1 (for ratings 3, 4 and 5). This corpus allows us to evaluate the social component of our approach with real user evaluations instead of artificial ones by virtual users of different static behaviors.

7.3 Results

We first experimentally find the content features that maximize the effectiveness of our item-based collaborative filter-

[8]http://www.google.com/zeitgeist/

ing (CF) algorithm. At the same time, we verify the correctness of our CF content-based credibility evaluation approach by comparing its effectiveness with a machine learning (ML) classifier, namely SVM. As depicted in Figures 5, 6, 7, where we compare the precision and recall of CF and ML approaches per category of the Microsoft corpus for different feature sets, employing syntactic and lexical features has similar or better performance, as compared to using semantic ones. Also, as illustrated in Figures 5, 6, 7, our approach is a valid credibility assessment approach as the precision and recall of the CF algorithm are very close to those of ML for all different feature sets. Moreover, as depicted in Table 1, the area-under-the-(ROC)-curve (AUC) for the CF approach is higher than that of the ML one when the syntactic features are employed for all page categories, as opposed to using all features. Therefore, for simplicity in the computations and without loss of generality, in the rest of the experiments we only employed the syntactic and the lexical features in the content-based component. However, the AUC values in Table 1 are still not high enough. This means that our content component cannot perform adequately well when individually employed.

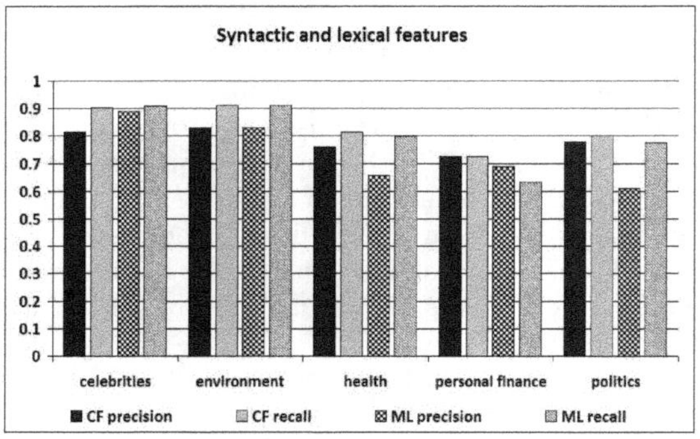

Figure 5: Syntactic and lexical features: Content component (CF) vs. SVM classification (ML).

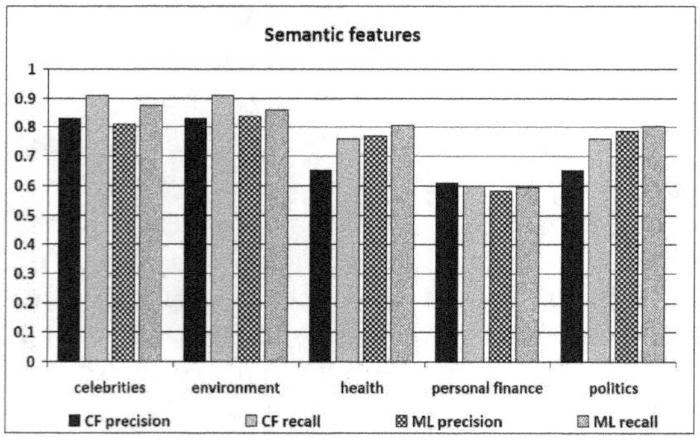

Figure 6: Semantic features: Content component (CF) vs. SVM classification (ML).

Indeed, combining the 3 components of our recommendation scheme by simple average, we vastly improve the performance of the content component when individually employed, as illustrated in Figure 8. In this experiment, we artificially varied the percentage of the malicious users in the population from 0 to 100; our recommendation scheme remains highly effective for fewer than 70% malicious users in the population.

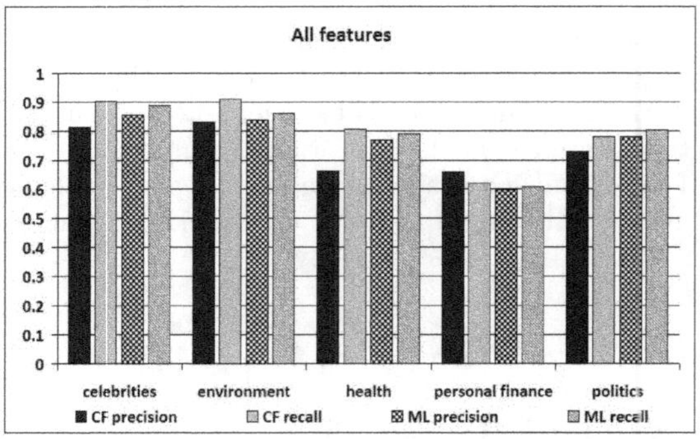

Figure 7: All features: Content component (CF) vs. SVM classification (ML).

Category	CF(a)	ML(a)	CF(b)	ML(b)
Celebrities	0.746	0.568	0.808	0.556
Environment	0.605	0.5	0.5	0.501
Health	0.675	0.491	0.409	0.601
Pers. Finance	0.755	0.567	0.638	0.58
Politics	0.776	0.495	0.796	0.586

Table 1: AUC of content component (CF) vs. SVM classification (ML) for different page categories when (a) only syntactic and lexical or (b) all content features are employed.

Since simply averaging the estimated ratings of the components of our recommendation scheme, one could argue that there is no need for finding the appropriate weights per page category. However, comparing Figures 9 and 10, we observe that different recommendation components can perform differently per page category: in this example, for the category "celebrities", the content component performs equally or better than the search-ranking one, and vice versa for the category "finance". Also, note that the relative performance of the social component depends on the fraction of malicious friends in the system. Therefore, a normalized weight approximating the relative performance of each component per category needs to be found.

As depicted in Figure 11, the weighted average component aggregation outperforms the simple average aggregation in terms of precision and recall when the component

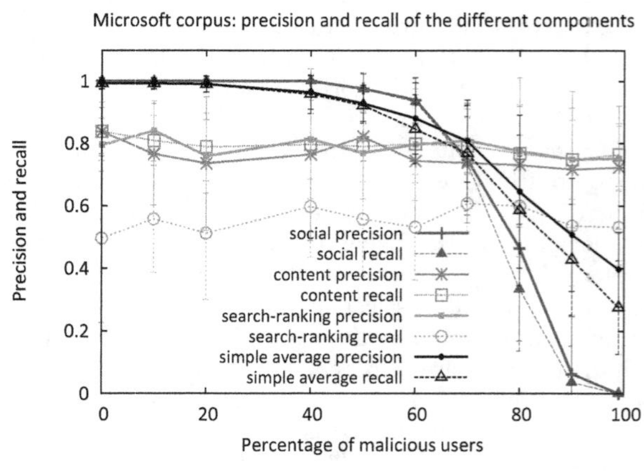

Figure 8: Microsoft corpus: Effectiveness of different components of the recommendation scheme for increasing fraction of malicious friends.

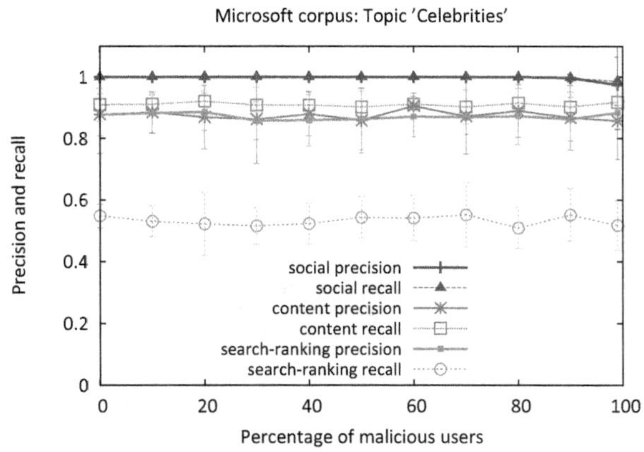

Figure 9: Microsoft corpus: Performance of different components for the category "celebrities". The content component has higher recall and almost equal precision as compared with the search-ranking component.

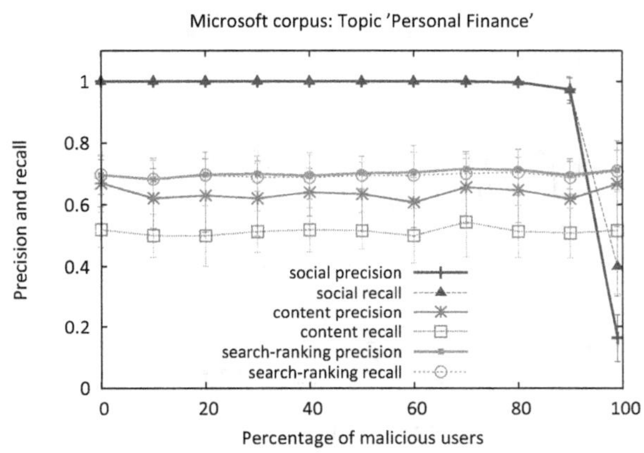

Figure 10: Microsoft corpus: Performance of different components for the category "finance". The search-ranking component has higher precision and recall than the content component.

weights are calculated according to the approach of Section 4. Similarly for the Polish corpus, we can easily see that the weighted average of the 3 components using different weights per category achieves higher effectiveness as compared to their simple average, both in terms of precision (cf. Figure 12) and of recall (cf. Figure 13).

Finally, we evaluate the effectiveness of our banishment mechanism for excluding the malicious users from the credibility assessment, while including all trustworthy ones at the same time. As depicted by Figures 14, 15, banishment increases the performance of our recommendation scheme for the Microsoft corpus, as compared to no banishment (cf. Figure 11). This was expected, since in this corpus, any disagreement in the credibility evaluation (cf. Section 5) means the discovery of a malicious user that has to be banned. However, as depicted in Figure 16 (as compared to Figure 12), lifetime banishment deteriorates the effectiveness of our recommendation scheme for honest -but occasionally subjective- friends, as is the case for the Reconcile corpus.

8. RELATED WORK

There is significant amount of related work in the literature dealing directly or indirectly with web credibility assessment. A number of them deal with defining web credibility and the main features involved in its assessment [12, 4, 13, 17, 18]. Kapoun in [12] perceived credibility as a journalism quality depending on accuracy of information, authority of the source, objectivity, currency and topic coverage. Fogg in [5] added in those factors the impact of prominence of different page features on personalized credibility perception.

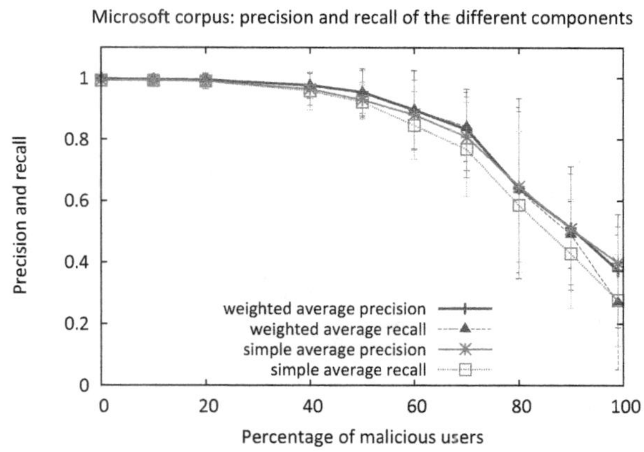

Figure 11: Microsoft corpus: Effectiveness of component weight updating per page category vs. simple average.

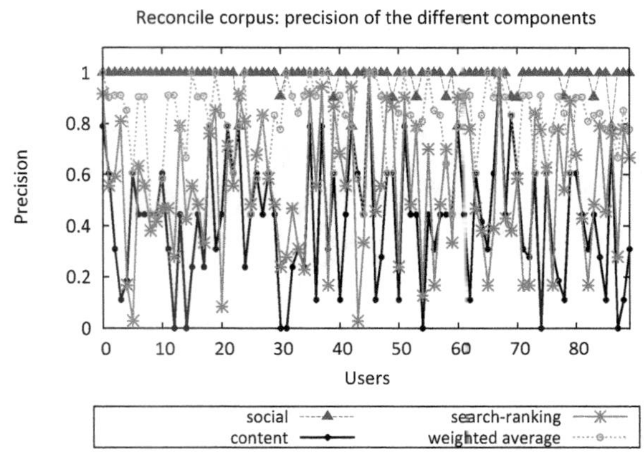

Figure 12: Reconcile corpus: Precision of different components for different users.

Closer to our work, several approaches have been proposed for enhancing the search results with page credibility information [13, 17, 18]. Nakamura *et al.* [13] developed a system prototype augmenting the search results for each page with three attributes, namely topic majority (i.e. number of retrieved pages sharing same topic with the target page), the topic coverage and the locality of supporting pages ((i.e. pages linked to each search result). Schwarz *at al.* in [17] additionally take a social aspect by visualizing a different set of attributes, including the overall web page popularity, the popularity among experts, the location origin of the page hits, any awards or certifications of the page and the PageRank metric. However, both approaches in [13] and [17] had limited effectiveness for improving the page credibility assessment. Yamamoto *et al.* in [18] proposed an iterative approach based on which users evaluate the importance of different visualized page aspects in their credibility assess-

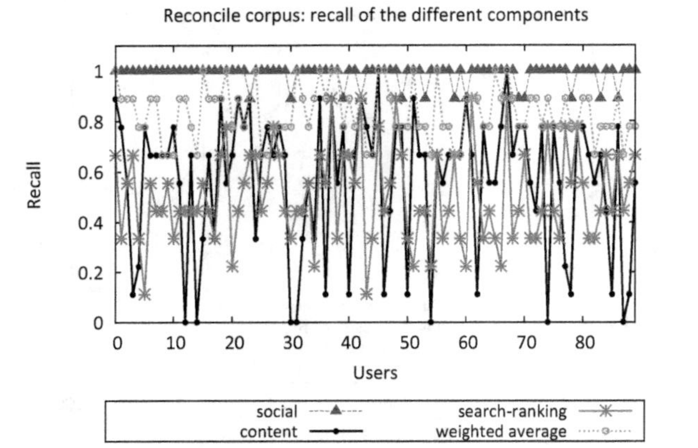

Figure 13: Reconcile corpus: Recall of different components for different users.

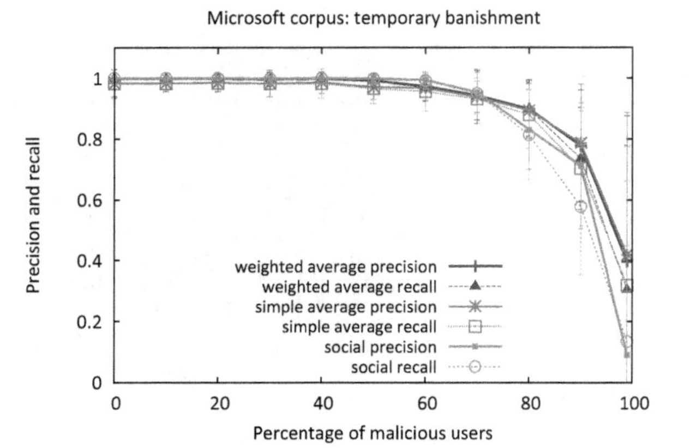

Figure 14: Microsoft corpus: Credibility assessment with temporary friend banishment upon wrong evaluation.

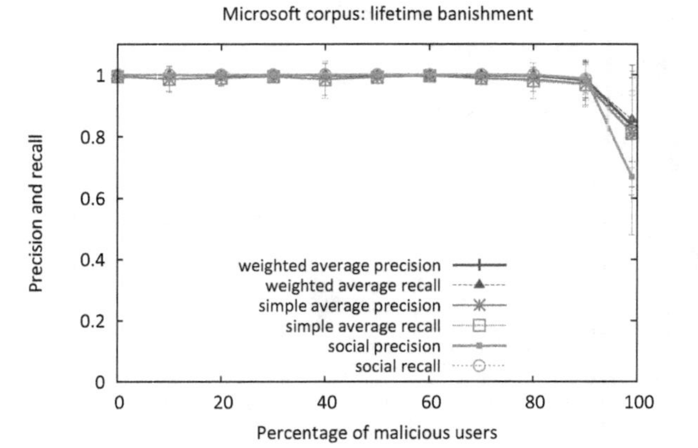

Figure 15: Microsoft corpus: Credibility assessment with lifetime friend banishment upon one wrong evaluation.

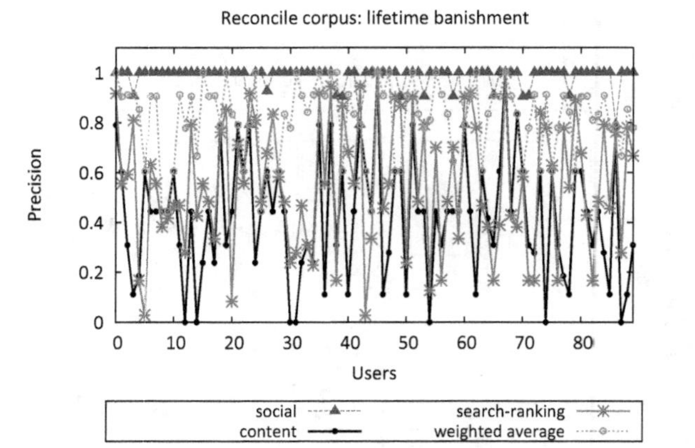

Figure 16: Reconcile corpus: Precision of credibility assessment with temporary friend banishment upon wrong evaluation. The effectiveness does not drop significantly due to the unfair banishments of honest friends that occasionally disagree.

ment, the system updates their significance in the credibility estimation and the search results are re-ranked. The visualized page aspects in [18] were the referential importance, the social reputation, the content typicality, the topic coverage, the freshness and the update frequency. Our system also takes into account the user feedback for updating the weights of the components of the recommendation scheme and for the banishment of friends from future credibility evaluations.

Additional approaches attempt automatic credibility evaluation based on the aggregation of different sets of features. For example, type of website, date of update, sentiment analysis and PageRank metric are utilized in [1], while information commonality, source independence, prestige of the source and experience with the source have been considered in [11]. However, none of these approaches employs a holistic approach such as ours to the problem of credibility assessment that combines a social-based, a content-based and a link-based component. Note that additional features that fall in the semantic scope of these three components can also be integrated in our approach.

Also, the robustness of web page ranking algorithms has been studied in [2, 6]. Both works study the resilience of web page ranking algorithms against web spam via link structure and credibility analysis. The use of trust and reputation mechanisms to minimize the influence of adversarial attacks in ranking systems has also attracted much effort [10]. Also, [6] uses reputation-based trust management techniques to improve the robustness of ranking systems, yet with little analysis on the impact of trust mechanisms to the adversarial cost for strategic manipulation of the system. Our multi-component recommendation scheme is less sensitive to link spamming by properly updating the component weight and by banishing the malicious users.

Collaborative filtering techniques are used in [3, 19] to weight ratings in trust estimation proportionally to the similarity of preferences between the agent who computes the estimate and the raters. Only ballot stuffing and positive discrimination are dealt with in [3] for adversaries constituting up to 10% of the population, as opposed to our approach that deals effectively with higher fractions of malicious friends.

As already mentioned, there are some system initiatives towards higher web page credibility by employing a socially-informed component. A popular one is the inclusion of the Facebook "like" button in a web page. When someone "likes" a page, this information is attached to the page and the total number of likes is displayed in the page. However, although useful for web page credibility assessment, this approach mostly measures the popularity of a web page. Another similar approach is the "+1" button of Google+. According to this mechanism, a user can positively rate a certain page and this information can be shared with her friends or everyone. This information is integrated with the PageRank algorithm (in a proprietary way) and ideally results to a personalized ranking of web search results. The same idea with Google+ was employed in the search engine SearchWinds[9], which is now integrated into Microsoft Bing search engine[10]. Initially, all pages are assumed to be credible and their credibility is updated based on ratings by the members of the search engine. However, these approaches enjoyed only limited user adoption so far, partially because of user privacy concerns, as the user ratings can also be employed for data mining purposes. Our recommendation scheme could be integrated to Google+ or Bing for ranking the search results, while our decentralized system facilitates user adoption.

9. CONCLUSION

In this paper, we proposed a decentralized recommendation system for credibility evaluation. Our recommendation scheme employs a social-based, a content-based and a search-ranking based component, which are combined in a weighted average. The weights are properly adjusted to reflect the effectiveness of each individual component for credibility assessment. Moreover, our approach is robust against malicious ratings; we proposed a mechanism that bans a friend from the user neighborhood for an adequate number of web page credibility evaluations according to its malicious or not nature. Our simulation results with 2 real data corpus of web page credibility evaluations suggest that our approach is promising. As a future work, we plan to integrate into the item-based component the semantic distance between pages based on the page category and a certain category ontology.

Acknowledgments

This work was partially funded by the grant *Reconcile: Robust Online Credibility Evaluation of Web Content* from Switzerland through the Swiss contribution to the enlarged EU.

10. REFERENCES

[1] S. Aggarwall and H. V. Oostendorp. An attempt to automate the process of source evaluation. In *Proc. of the Int. Conference on Advances in Computer Engineering*, July 2011.

[2] J. Caverlee, S. Webb, L. Liu, and W. B. Rouse. A parameterized approach to spam-resilient link analysis of the web. *IEEE Trans. Parallel Distrib. Syst.*, 20(10):1422–1438, 2009.

[3] C. Dellarocas. Immunizing online reputation reporting systems against unfair ratings and discriminatory behaviour. In *Proc. of the ACM EC*, New York, NY, USA, 2000.

[4] B. J. Fogg. Prominence-interpretation theory: explaining how people assess credibility online. In *Proc. of the CHI*, New York, NY, USA, 2003.

[5] B. J. Fogg, J. Marshall, O. Laraki, A. Osipovich, C. Varma, N. Fang, J. Paul, A. Rangnekar, J. Shon, P. Swani, and M. Treinen. What makes web sites credible?: a report on a large quantitative study. In *Proc. of the CHI '01*, New York, NY, USA, 2001.

[6] Z. Gyongyi, H. Garcia-Molina, and J. Pedersen. Combating web spam with trustrank. In *Proc. of the VLDB*, 2004.

[7] J. L. Herlocker, J. A. Konstan, A. Borchers, and J. Riedl. An algorithmic framework for performing collaborative filtering. In *Proc. of the ACM SIGIR*, SIGIR '99, New York, NY, USA, 1999.

[8] C.-F. Hsu, E. Khabiri, and J. Caverlee. Ranking comments on the social web. In *Proc. of the CSE*, Washington, DC, USA, 2009.

[9] A. Jøsang, S. Hird, and E. Faccer. Simulating the effect of reputation systems on e-markets. In *Proc. of the 1st International Conference on Trust Management*, Berlin, Heidelberg, 2003.

[10] A. Jøsang, R. Ismail, and C. Boyd. A survey of trust and reputation systems for online service provision. *Decis. Support Syst.*, 43(2):618–644, 2007.

[11] A. L. Kaczmarek. Automatic evaluation of information credibility in semantic web and knowledge grid. In *WEBIST*. INSTICC Press, 2008.

[12] J. Kapoun. Teaching undergrads web evaluation: A guide for library instruction. *College and Research Library News*, 59(7), July/August 1998.

[13] S. Nakamura, S. Konishi, A. Jatowt, H. Ohshima, H. Kondo, T. Tezuka, S. Oyama, and K. Tanaka. Trustworthiness analysis of web search results. *LNCS*, 4675:38–49, 2007.

[14] T. G. Papaioannou and G. D. Stamoulis. An incentives' mechanism promoting truthful feedback in peer-to-peer systems. In *Proc. of the CCGRID '05*, Washington, DC, USA, 2005.

[15] A. Rowstron and P. Druschel. Pastry: Scalable, decentralized object location and routing for large-scale peer-to-peer systems. In *Proc. of the IFIP/ACM International Conference on Distributed Systems Platforms (Middleware)*, Heidelberg, Germany, November 2001.

[16] B. Sarwar, G. Karypis, J. Konstan and J. Riedl. Item-based collaborative filtering recommendation algorithms. In *Proc. of the WWW '01*, New York, NY, USA, 2001.

[17] J. Schwarz and M. Morris. Augmenting web pages and search results to support credibility assessment. In *Proc. of the CHI*, New York, NY, USA, 2011.

[18] Y. Yamamoto and K. Tanaka. Enhancing credibility judgment of web search results. In *Proc. of the CHI*, New York, NY, USA, 2011.

[19] G. Zacharia, A. Moukas, and P. Maes. Collaborative reputation mechanisms in electronic marketplaces. In *Proc. of the HICSS*, Washington, DC, USA, 1999.

[9]http://www.searchwinds.com

[10]http://www.bing.com

Towards an Effective and Unbiased Ranking of Scientific Literature through Mutual Reinforcement

Xiaorui Jiang
Key Lab of Intell. Inf. Processing
Inst. of Comput. Technol., CAS
Beijing, 100190, China
xiaoruijiang@kg.ict.ac.cn

Xiaoping Sun
Key Lab of Intell. Inf. Processing
Inst. of Comput. Technol., CAS
Beijing, 100190, China
sunxp@kg.ict.ac.cn

Hai Zhuge*
Key Lab of Intell. Inf. Processing
Inst. of Comput. Technol., CAS
Beijing, 100190, China
zhuge@ict.ac.cn

ABSTRACT

It is important to help researchers find valuable scientific papers from a large literature collection containing information of authors, papers and venues. Graph-based algorithms have been proposed to rank papers based on networks formed by citation and co-author relationships. This paper proposes a new graph-based ranking framework MutualRank that integrates mutual reinforcement relationships among networks of papers, researchers and venues to achieve a more synthetic, accurate and fair ranking result than previous graph-based methods. MutualRank leverages the network structure information among papers, authors, and their venues available from a literature collection dataset and sets up a unified mutual reinforcement model that involves both intra- and inter-network information for ranking papers, authors and venues simultaneously. To evaluate, we collect a set of recommended papers from websites of graduate-level computational linguistics courses of 15 top universities as the benchmark and apply different methods to estimate paper importance. The results show that MutualRank greatly outperforms the competitors including PageRank, HITS and CoRank in ranking papers as well as researchers. The experimental results also demonstrate that venues ranked by MutualRank are reasonable.

Categories and Subject Descriptors

H.3.3 [**Information Search and Retrieval**]: Retrieval models.

General Terms

Algorithms, Experimentation.

Keywords

Mutual reinforcement, iterative ranking, time distortion

1. INTRODUCTION

Researchers and students new in a particular area often feel at a loss when facing an ocean of papers published year after year. Researchers often need to answer the following questions. "Which classical papers in a particular area are the most influential and valuable to read for building consolidated background knowledge? Which papers and researchers are worth being paid attention to so as to catch up recent advance? And which venue is the most suitable for one to publish so as to maximize personal capacity?" Of all the three questions, the former two are more difficult to answer because of the huge numbers of papers and researchers. For example, many digital libraries like DBLP[1] and CiteSeer[2] contain paper metadata such as authors and venues, but it is hard for people to manually extract a series of important papers or authors for a given area.

To rank authors, papers and journals, citation count information has long been used, e.g., [6] [9] and [15] for journal ranking, h-index [7] for researcher ranking and citation count for paper ranking. But only using citation count based metrics for evaluation is still a controversial issue as most of these methods do not consider the network structure of literature information available. Recently, graph-based methods have been developed for literature ranking [3] [5] [13] [19] [23-24] [27]. They model a literature collection as a network and apply iterative computation over the adjacency matrix of the network to achieve a converged ranking vector for objects, just as PageRank over Web pages [2]. Most of these works focus on only one type of network, which limits their effectiveness in ranking objects. Recent works begin to consider multiple networks for ranking [4] [18] [21] [25-26]. For example, one of the most relevant research CoRank combines the citation network and the corresponding co-authorship network to achieve better ranking results for both authors and documents [26].

However, current research still does not fully leverage the available information of a general literature dataset which contains papers, authors and venues. All of the previous works on ranking papers and authors only utilize the paper and/or author metadata. But venue information is also important for ranking because we often assign reasonable importance values to new papers in prestigious venues with few citations and to young scientists with few collaborators. Besides, previous works assign only one type of importance values to each type of objects. But in many cases, different types of objects may, in nature, play different roles in a network and thus have different kinds of importance values. In the meanwhile, how to evaluate different ranking methods is still a problem. There lacks a common standard for ranking performance evaluation. Citation counts and future downloads are two predominant metrics widely adopted in previous research. However, we

* Corresponding author

[1] http://www.informatik.uni-trier.de/~ley/db.

[2] http://citeseer.ist.psu.edu.

argue that it is researcher who is the most appropriate for judging the relevance of papers and importance of authors. Thus any reasonable ranking algorithm should return many papers that are highly recommended by domain experts when user needs are taken into consideration.

To overcome these limitations, we propose a new ranking framework, MutualRank, which employs mutual reinforcement relationships across networks of papers, researchers and venues to achieve a more synthetic and reasonable ranking of papers, authors and venues simultaneously. The intuition of mutual reinforcement is that a higher value of x will lead to a higher value of y and vice versa. For instance, HITS [10] can be viewed as a mutual reinforcement process between authority and hub values of nodes. Mutual reinforcement is a ubiquitous phenomenon in real-world networks and has already been successfully studied and used in several works, e.g., the preferential attaching model depicts the features of complex networks in physical world [1]. It is also widely found that high degree nodes in social networks tend to link to other high degree networks [16]. In real applications, mutual reinforcement can be used for finding specific patterns. Jensen et al. use reinforcement relationships to mine significant places: places visited by authoritative users are significant and users visiting significant places gain authorities [8].

Compared to viewing ranking iteration as a random walk process, it is more instructive to take it as a reinforcement process. In MutualRank, three basic networks are constructed to capture the intra-network influences between papers, authors and venues respectively. Moreover, mutual reinforcement information across these networks are defined as follows: a paper which is written by an important researcher and published in a prestigious venue should be ranked high; a researcher who publishes highly ranked papers on prestigious venues gains personal importance; and a venue where important researchers publish highly ranked papers will be prestigious. Based on inter-network mutual reinforcement relationships, we integrate all these networks into one unified ranking framework to find important papers, authors and venues simultaneously. A synthetic transition matrix is then built for the iterative computation of ranks of different objects.

2. DATASETS AND BASIC DATA MODEL

2.1 Datasets

This paper uses the ACL (Association of Computational Linguistics) Anthology Network (AAN)[3] [20] dataset for evaluating ranking algorithms (the latest version till March 2011). AAN consists of all the metadata of ACL Anthology, a collection of papers published in journals and conferences hosted by the ACL. The dataset contains 18041 papers published in 273 venues and authored by 14386 researchers. From the AAN dataset we can obtain the authors, publication venue and reference list of a paper.

For joint conferences such as ACL-COLING 2006, we treat the corresponding published papers as being published in more than one venue. For example, the paper "P06-1001" belongs to both ACL'2006 and COLING'2006. If a conference accepts papers other than long, regular or full papers, we construct a new venue X-Companion for those papers in this conference, where X stands for the conference name. For example, there are two venues for the annual conference of ACL: ACL for full papers and ACL-Companion for short and student papers.

2.2 Scientific Literature Ranking Benchmark

For ranking papers. To evaluate the results of paper ranking, we collect papers from the reading lists of graduate-level courses in natural language processing or computational linguistics of top universities, and record the number of times each paper is recommended as the basic benchmark dataset *BenchP*. We discard those reading lists focusing only on a limited number of subareas of computational linguistics and only include those with an extensive coverage of the whole area. If a paper in the AAN dataset is on k universities' reading lists, i.e., receives k recommendations, its importance is k. If a paper receives recommendations from more universities, it is regarded as more relevant and more important in the area of computational linguistics.

In 218 papers collected from 15 universities, 181 are recommended once, 28 are recommended twice, 6 papers receive 3 recommendations, and the rest 3 papers occur 4, 7 and 8 times respectively on the reading lists. We believe the established benchmark well reflects the consensus of the research community because: (1) the benchmark papers are all recommended by prestigious researchers from world famous universities including MIT, CMU, Stanford, Cornell etc.; (2) although most papers has only one recommendation, the fact of winning recommendation is still an indicator of influence to a certain degree; (3) the benchmark set is consistent with the reference section of many survey papers and standard text books such as "Speech and Language Processing".

For ranking researchers. We construct two different benchmark collections for researchers. The first benchmark *BenchR1* is constructed from *BenchP*. If an author has at least 2 papers in *BenchP*, the author is put in *BenchR1*. There are in total 46 researchers in *BenchR1*. Four researchers are each recommended 16, 13, 8 and 7 times. Five occur on the reading lists 6 times. Six researchers win 5 and another six researchers get 4 recommendations. Each of the remaining 25 researchers gets 3 recommendations. The second benchmark collection for researchers *BenchR2* consists of the first 100 top-cited authors of AAN.[4]

2.3 Basic Data Model

We build three basic types of networks from the AAN dataset: Paper Influence Network (PIN), Research Influence Network (RIN) and Venue Influence Network (VIN). Figure 1 gives an example of the network construction.

Network of papers. We construct the PIN based on the citation relationship. For each paper p_i in AAN, we add a corresponding node i to PIN. If paper p_i cites another paper p_j, we add an edge (i, j) to PIN. PIN is un-weighted.

Network of researchers. We use citation relationships to build the weighted directed RIN. For each researcher r_i in AAN, we add a node i to RIN. If r_i has a paper that cites another paper authored by r_j, we add an edge (i, j) to RIN. The weight on RIN edges is assigned as follows. Let

$$Cite(p_k, p_l) = \begin{cases} 1 & \text{paper } p_k \text{ cites } p_l \\ 0 & \text{otherwise} \end{cases} \quad (1)$$

[3] http:// clair.si.umich.edu/clair/anthology/

[4] http://clair.si.umich.edu/clair/anthology/rankings.cgi

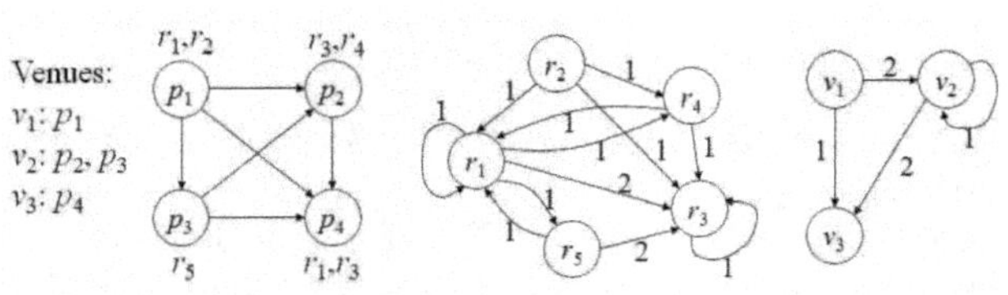

(a) Metadata and PIN (b) RIN (c) VIN

Figure 1. Construction of RIN and VIN from PIN.

and $P(r_i)$ be the set of papers written by researcher r_i. The weight of edge (i, j) in RIN is set as

$$w_{RIN}(i,j) = \sum_{p_k \in P(r_i), p_l \in P(r_j)} Cite(p_k, p_l) . \quad (2)$$

The other type of researcher network is the Researcher Collaboration Network (RCN). RCN is a weighted undirected network. If two researchers r_i and r_j have coauthored at least one paper, there is an edge (i, j) in RCN. The weight of edge (i, j) in RCN is set as

$$w_{RCN}(i,j) = \left| P(r_i) \cap P(r_j) \right| . \quad (3)$$

Different from CoRank, we use RIN rather than RCN for ranking researchers. The motivation behind RCN is that the collaboration with an important researcher on some papers will raise the importance of researcher him/herself. However, we argue that if papers of a researcher are highly cited, we are confident that he/she is influential because his/her ideas may inspire a lot of other researchers in their own work. In Section 4, we will show that performances are slightly improved by substituting RIN for RCN. It should be noted that our framework is flexible enough for incorporating different ways of modeling researcher network.

Network of venues. We construct the VIN to incorporate venue information. VIN is a weighted directed network such that if a paper p_k published on venue v_i has another paper p_l published on venue v_j on its reference list, then there is an edge (i, j) in VIN. Let $P(v_i)$ be the set of papers published in v_i. Then the weight of edge (i, j) in VIN is set as follows. Let $P(v_i)$ be the set of papers published in v_i. Then the weight of edge (i, j) in VIN is set as

$$w_{VIN}(i,j) = \sum_{p_k \in P(v_i), p_l \in P(v_j)} Cite(p_k, p_l) . \quad (4)$$

3. MUTUALRANK MODEL

Before delving into the details of MutualRank, we first make a preliminary study of the limitations of two classic ranking algorithms, PageRank and HITS, on ranking papers and discuss the causes of these limitations. Typically, similar phenomena appear in simply applying these algorithms on RIN (resp. VIN) for ranking researchers (resp. venues). The results obtained in this section well motivate the proposed MutualRank method.

3.1 Studies on PageRank and HITS

3.1.1 Results of PageRank

Table 1 lists the PageRank results that match *BenchP*. We only show the results from the top 100 answers returned by each algorithm. The matched ranking result of a paper is given in the format "o_p:*pname*[c_p]", where o_p is the ranked order, c_p is the recommendation count in *BenchP*, and *pname* is the paper id used in ACL anthology. For example, "4:J90-2002[1]" means that the paper J90-2002 is ranked 4th by PageRank and is recommended once in *BenchP*. "7:J93-2003[7]" is ranked 7th by PageRank and is recommended by 7 times in *BenchP*. Relevant papers published in the 1990s and 1980s are represented in boldface and italic respectively in Table 1

The Problem of Time Distortion. In PageRank, paper ranks are transferred from one paper to the other through the citing relationships. Thus, papers published in earlier years will inevitably gain higher ranks than new papers. This phenomenon is clearly reflected by Table 1. In all the 19 results, only 3 are published after year 2000 (P02-1040, A00-2018 and J02-3001). This contradicts to our experience that researchers not only read old classic papers but also pay much attention to recent papers to keep up with the fast-changing research fronts. We call this problem as *time distortion.*

Table 1. Relevant Papers in top-100 PageRank Results

4:J90-2002[1]	29:P02-1040[2]	**70:J93-2006[1]**
7:J93-2003[7]	**33:P97-1003[3]**	75:J02-3001[2]
8:J86-3001[1]	40:A00-2018[1]	**84:P98-2127[1]**
12:J96-1002[2]	**49:J95-4004[1]**	**88:P97-1023[1]**
13:J92-4003[1]	**54:J96-2004[1]**	96:P02-1053[1]
18:J88-1003[1]	**60:P95-1026[4]**	
25:W96-0213[2]	**65:C96-2141[1]**	

3.1.2 Results of HITS

We use a randomized version of HITS (RHITS) from [17] in this study because RHITS typically returns the same results with the HITS by Kleinberg [10] and is more easy to formulate and analyze in our context. RHITS can be formalized as follows. Let **P** be the adjacency matrix corresponding to PIN and $\hat{\mathbf{P}}$ is the corresponding transition matrix obtained by normalizing each row of **P**. Similar to PageRank, random jump (aka. teleportation) is incorporated by rewriting the transition matrix $\hat{\mathbf{P}}$ into $\overline{\mathbf{P}}$ as follows:

$$\overline{\mathbf{P}} = \lambda(\hat{\mathbf{P}} + \mathbf{d}_r \frac{\mathbf{e}}{n_p}) + (1-\lambda)\frac{\mathbf{e}\mathbf{e}^T}{n_p} , \quad (5)$$

where n_P is the number of papers in PIN, $\mathbf{d_r}$ is an n_P-dimensional vector indicating which row of $\hat{\mathbf{P}}$ is zero, **e** is an n_P-dimensional identity vector and (1-λ) is the dangling factor controlling the probability in which the rank of a paper is evenly distributed onto every paper in the network. Similarly, $\mathbf{P}^T$ is rewritten into $\overline{\mathbf{P}^T}$.

Let **paut** and **phub** be the authority and hub vectors of papers in PIN. We formulate RHITS using a similar way as SALSA [12] which models the ranking process as two independent random walks as in Eq. (6–7).

$$\mathbf{paut}^{(t)} = \overline{\mathbf{P}}^T \mathbf{phub}^{(t-1)} \quad (6)$$

$$\mathbf{phub}^{(t)} = \overline{\mathbf{P}^T}^T \mathbf{paut}^{(t-1)} \quad (7)$$

Shown in Table 2, RHITS overcomes the problem of PageRank to some extent. (1) RHITS returns more relevant papers than PageRank. (2) 20 out of total 27 returned papers are in year after 2000. The second point is due to the mutual reinforcement nature of HITS. Unlike PageRank where ranks flow uni-directionally from new papers to old papers (forward flow), RHITS has the mechanism to let the ranks of old papers flow back to new papers (backward flow). Therefore, new papers have much higher probabilities for being authoritative in RHITS than in PageRank. But Table 2 also shows that RHITS overestimate the values of new papers. Firstly, no papers in the 1980s are returned by HITS although many pioneering work in computational linguistics are done during this period. Secondly, it misses many important papers in the 1990s, the decade of statistical natural language processing which greatly boost the prosperity of the area and incubates many applications and new research problems in the new century. However, RHITS only returns 7 papers in this period.

In conclusion, RHITS performs better than PageRank in ranking on PIN because RHITS assigns two different kinds of paper ranks and the two types of ranks mutually reinforce each other to alleviate time distortion. Thus, mutual reinforcement may play an important role in improving ranking precision. However, the fact that RHITS may overestimate new papers is in fact another type of time distortion. It means that using PIN only for ranking papers may inevitably suffer from time distortion. All these findings lead us to develop a new ranking method.

Table 2. Relevant Papers in top-100 RHITS Results

1:P02-1040[2]	29:A00-2018[1]	**58:W96-0213[2]**
4:J93-2003[7]	30:P03-1054[2]	59:P06-1096[1]
7:P05-1033[1]	33:P07-1019[1]	60:P05-1012[1]
9:J04-4002[2]	38:N04-1021[1]	75:D07-1090[2]
14:C96-2141[1]	40:P05-1074[2]	77:E06-1032[1]
24:J96-1002[2]	49:P05-1074[1]	79:P01-1030[2]
26:J90-2002[1]	51:D07-1091[1]	85:P06-1055[3]
27:N06-1014[1]	52:P05-1022[2]	**89:J92-4003[1]**
28:W06-1606[1]	**57:P97-1003[3]**	97:J04-2003[1]

3.2 Mutual reinforcement in the dataset

We develop the MutualRank framework for ranking papers, researchers and venues simultaneously. The MutalRank algorithm employs mutual reinforcement relationships between papers, researchers and venues to improve the precision of recommending valuable papers. In MutualRank, the importance measures of different objects are as follows:

- **paut(p_i):** Authority of a paper p_i;
- **psnd(p_i):** Soundness of a paper p_i;
- **rimp(r_j):** Importance of a researcher r_j;
- **vprs(v_k):** Prestige of a venue v_k.

Authority **paut**(p_i) depicts whether this paper is of high influence and promotes research advancements in its corresponding area. Soundness **psnd**(p_i) describes whether this paper grounds itself on a thorough study of major previous works. Authority and soundness correspond to the authority and hub values in the traditional HITS algorithm. We use soundness instead of hub to make the semantics of this importance measure clearer in our context. Low authority implies that this paper is somewhat less important or inspiring. High soundness indicates that this paper might be a good reference for background knowledge of a particular area.

For each paper p_i published in venue v_k and each researcher r_j authoring p_i, the mutual reinforcement relationships are as below:

(1) If a researcher r_j is important, a paper p_i of r_i will receive high authority and high soundness, i.e., **paut**(p_i) $\propto$ **rimp**(r_j) if $p_i \in P(r_j)$, and if a paper p_j is of high authority and high soundness, the researchers r_i authoring p_j receives high importance, i.e., **rimp**(r_j) $\propto$ **paut**(p_i) and **rimp**(r_j) $\propto$ **psnd**(p_i) if $p_i \in P(r_j)$.

(2) For a paper p_i published in venue v_k, p is of high rank if v_k is prestigious and v_k gains more prestige if p is ranked high, i.e., **paut**(p_i) $\propto$ **vprs**(v_k), **psnd**(p_i) $\propto$ **vprs**(v_k), **vprs**(v_k) $\propto$ **paut**(p_i), and **vprs**(v_k) $\propto$ **psnd**(p_i).

(3) Similarly, for a researcher r_j authoring some papers in venue v_k, we have **rimp**(r_j) $\propto$ **vprs**(v_k) and **vprs**(v_k) $\propto$ **rimp**(r_j).

To compute the ranks of objects we need to consider both intra-network relationships and inter-network relationships.

3.3 Intra-network ranking model

Intra-network ranking iteration is modeled by using PIN, RIN and VIN respectively. The classical PageRank is applied to RIN and VIN. To compensate the biases of PageRank and RHITS towards old and new papers respectively and improve ranking on PIN, we derive the First-Order HITS as follows.

In traditional HITS in Eq. (6)–(7), $\mathbf{paut}^{(t+1)}$ only relies on $\mathbf{psnd}^{(t)}$ and $\mathbf{psnd}^{(t+1)}$ only relies on $\mathbf{paut}^{(t)}$. We call this **Zero-Order HITS**, which means **paut** (resp. **psnd**) does not inherit its historical values directly. The name is borrowed from notations of Markovian processes. However, in **First-Order HITS**, **paut** (resp. **psnd**) also inherits a portion of its historical values directly (Eq. (8)–(9)). More specifically, $\mathbf{paut}^{(t+1)}$ inherits $\xi\mathbf{paut}^{(t)}$ from its nearest historical value, while the remaining comes from $\mathbf{psnd}^{(t)}$, i.e., $(1-\xi)\overline{\mathbf{P}}^{\mathrm{T}}\mathbf{psnd}^{(t)}$. Similarly, a ξ portion of $\mathbf{psnd}^{(t+1)}$ comes from $\xi\mathbf{psnd}^{(t)}$, while the remaining is reinforced by $\mathbf{paut}^{(t)}$, i.e., $(1-\xi)\overline{\mathbf{P}^{\mathrm{T}}}^{\mathrm{T}}\mathbf{paut}^{(t)}$.

$$\mathbf{paut}^{(t+1)} = \xi\mathbf{paut}^{(t)} + (1-\xi)\overline{\mathbf{P}}^{\mathrm{T}}\mathbf{psnd}^{(t)} \tag{8}$$

$$\mathbf{psnd}^{(t+1)} = \xi\mathbf{psnd}^{(t)} + (1-\xi)\overline{\mathbf{P}^{\mathrm{T}}}^{\mathrm{T}}\mathbf{paut}^{(t)} \tag{9}$$

Eq. (8) and (9) can be rewritten into the following matrix equation,

$$\mathbf{r}^{(t+1)} = \mathbf{M}_1^{\mathrm{T}}\mathbf{r}^{(t)}, \tag{10}$$

where $\mathbf{r} = [\mathbf{paut}^{\mathrm{T}}, \mathbf{psnd}^{\mathrm{T}}]^{\mathrm{T}}$ and

$\mathbf{M}_1 = \begin{bmatrix} \xi\mathbf{\Lambda}_1 & (1-\xi)\overline{\mathbf{P}} \\ (1-\xi)\overline{\mathbf{P}^{\mathrm{T}}} & \xi\mathbf{\Lambda}_1 \end{bmatrix}$ where $\mathbf{\Lambda}_1$ is n_P-dimensional identity matrix.

$\mathbf{M}_1$ is a transition matrix corresponding to a Markovian process. $\mathbf{M}_1$ is *irreducible* because there is only one communicating class in $\mathbf{M}_1$ as for each pair $\langle i, j\rangle$, i and j reaches each other. $\mathbf{M}_1$ is *aperiodic* because there exists self-loops in the transition matrix. And $\mathbf{M}_1$ is clearly also a *stochastic* matrix. So according to Frobenius theorem [11], **r** calculated in Eq. (10) converges to the principle eigenvector of $\mathbf{M}_1$ with the principle eigenvalue being 1.

3.4 Inter-network ranking model

For incorporating the mutual reinforcement relationships between different networks, 3 undirected networks are constructed: Paper-Researcher Network (PRN), Paper-Venue Network (PVN) and Researcher-Venue Network (RVN). They are constructed as follows: If a researcher r_i has written a paper p_j published in venue v_k,

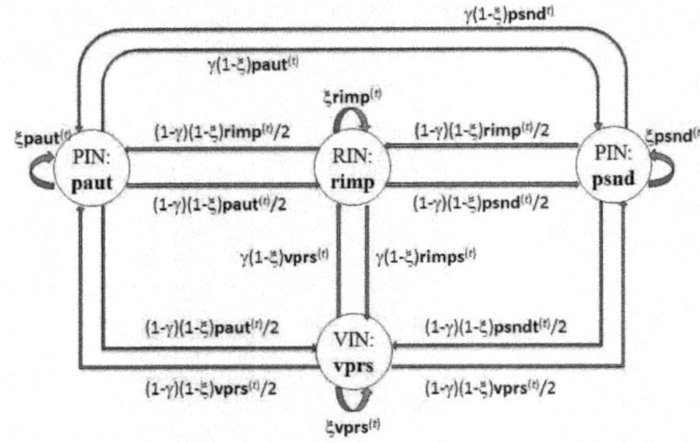

Figure 2. Mutual reinforcement relationships between paut, psnd, rimp and vprs.

we add an edge (i, j) to PRN, an edge (j, k) to PVN and an edge (i, k) to RVN. Then, we obtain two transition matrices for each of the above three networks as follows.

Let **PR** (resp. **RP**) be the adjacency matrix from PIN (resp. RIN) to RIN (resp. PIN). We have

$$\mathbf{RP}(i,j)=\mathbf{PR}(j,i)=\begin{cases}1 & \text{edge } (i,j) \text{ is in PRN}\\ 0 & \text{otherwise}\end{cases}. \tag{11}$$

Let **PV** and **VP** be the adjacency matrices coupling PIN and VIN together. We have

$$\mathbf{PV}(i,k)=\mathbf{VP}(k,i)=\begin{cases}1 & \text{edge } (i,k) \text{ is in PVN}\\ 0 & \text{otherwise}\end{cases}. \tag{12}$$

Finally, **RV** and **VR** are the adjacency matrices between RIN and VIN and we have

$$\mathbf{RV}(j,k)=\mathbf{VR}(k,j)=\begin{cases}1 & \text{edge } (j,k) \text{ is in RVN}\\ 0 & \text{otherwise}\end{cases}. \tag{13}$$

3.5 The unified iterative model

Now we have totally 9 adjacency matrices from the 6 networks which capture intra-network ranking iteration and inter-network mutual reinforcement. Similar to Eq. (5), we create the corresponding intra-network transition matrices $\overline{\mathbf{P}}$, $\overline{\mathbf{R}}$, $\overline{\mathbf{V}}$ and inter-network transition matrices $\overline{\mathbf{PR}}$, $\overline{\mathbf{RP}}$, $\overline{\mathbf{PV}}$, $\overline{\mathbf{VP}}$, $\overline{\mathbf{RV}}$ and $\overline{\mathbf{VR}}$. Thus, we can couple the First-Order HITS on PIN and PageRank on RIN and VIN into a unified framework as follows (see Figure 2 for illustration). Taking initial vectors of **paut, psnd, rimp** and **vprs** as inputs, the trilateral mutual reinforcement process updates these vectors at each iteration as follows.

1. Value of **paut** at time t reinforces values of **paut, psnd, rimp** and **vprs** at time t+1. $\xi\mathbf{paut}^{(t)}$ is reserved for $\mathbf{paut}^{(t+1)}$ in First-Order HITS on PIN. The remaining $(1-\xi)\mathbf{paut}^{(t)}$ is divided into three parts, one part is $\gamma(1-\xi)\mathbf{paut}^{(t)}$ and the other two parts are both $(1-\gamma)(1-\xi)\ \mathbf{paut}^{(t)}/2$ and $(1-\gamma)(1-\xi)\mathbf{paut}^{(t)}/2$. The first part $\gamma(1-\xi)\mathbf{paut}^{(t)}$ is used for reinforcing $\mathbf{psnd}^{(t+1)}$. The second and third parts are for $\mathbf{rimp}^{(t+1)}$ and for $\mathbf{vprs}^{(t+1)}$ respectively.
2. Value of **psnd** at time t reinforces values of **paut, psnd, rimp** and **vprs** at time t+1. Similarly, a portion $\xi\mathbf{psnd}^{(t)}$ is inherited by $\mathbf{psnd}^{(t+1)}$. The remaining $(1-\xi)\mathbf{psnd}^{(t)}$, divided into 3 parts $\gamma(1-\xi)\mathbf{psnd}^{(t)}$, $(1-\gamma)(1-\xi)\mathbf{pnd}^{(t)}/2$ and $(1-\gamma)(1-\xi)\mathbf{psnd}^{(t)}/2$, are for reinforcing $\mathbf{paut}^{(t+1)}$, $\mathbf{rimp}^{(t+1)}$ and $\mathbf{vprs}^{(t+1)}$ respectively.
3. For **rimp** at time t to reinforce **paut, psnd, rimp** and **vprs** at time t+1, a fraction $\xi\mathbf{rimp}^{(t)}$ is used in PageRank on RIN. The remaining $(1-\xi)\mathbf{rimp}^{(t)}$ is divided into 3 parts, $\gamma(1-\xi)\mathbf{rimp}^{(t)}$, $(1-\gamma)(1-\xi)\mathbf{rimp}^{(t)}/2$ and $(1-\gamma)(1-\xi)\mathbf{rimp}^{(t)}/2$. They are used to reinforce $\mathbf{vprs}^{(t+1)}$, $\mathbf{paut}^{(t+1)}$ and $\mathbf{psnd}^{(t+1)}$ respectively. $\mathbf{vprs}^{(t)}$ is processed in a way similar to $\mathbf{rimp}^{(t)}$.

To summarize, MutualRank is formulated in Eq. (14)–(17).

$$\begin{aligned}\mathbf{paut}^{(t+1)} &= \xi\mathbf{paut}^{(t)}+\gamma(1-\xi)\overline{\mathbf{P}}^{\mathrm{T}}\mathbf{psnd}^{(t)}\\ &+\frac{(1-\gamma)}{2}(1-\xi)\overline{\mathbf{RP}}^{\mathrm{T}}\mathbf{rimp}^{(t)}+\frac{(1-\gamma)}{2}(1-\xi)\overline{\mathbf{VP}}^{\mathrm{T}}\mathbf{vprs}^{(t)}\end{aligned} \tag{14}$$

$$\begin{aligned}\mathbf{psnd}^{(t+1)} &= \gamma(1-\xi)\overline{\mathbf{P}^{\mathrm{T}}}^{\mathrm{T}}\mathbf{paut}^{(t)}+\xi\mathbf{psnd}^{(t)}\\ &+\frac{(1-\gamma)}{2}(1-\xi)\overline{\mathbf{RP}}^{\mathrm{T}}\mathbf{rimp}^{(t)}+\frac{(1-\gamma)}{2}(1-\xi)\overline{\mathbf{VP}}^{\mathrm{T}}\mathbf{vprs}^{(t)}\end{aligned} \tag{15}$$

$$\begin{aligned}\mathbf{rimp}^{(t+1)} &= \frac{(1-\gamma)}{2}(1-\xi)\overline{\mathbf{PR}}^{\mathrm{T}}\mathbf{paut}^{(t)}+\frac{(1-\gamma)}{2}(1-\xi)\overline{\mathbf{PR}}^{\mathrm{T}}\mathbf{psnd}^{(t)}\\ &+\xi\overline{\mathbf{R}}^{\mathrm{T}}\mathbf{rimp}^{(t)}+\gamma(1-\xi)\overline{\mathbf{VR}}^{\mathrm{T}}\mathbf{vprs}^{(t)}\end{aligned} \tag{16}$$

$$\begin{aligned}\mathbf{vprs}^{(t+1)} &= \frac{(1-\gamma)}{2}(1-\xi)\overline{\mathbf{PV}}^{\mathrm{T}}\mathbf{paut}^{(t)}+\frac{(1-\gamma)}{2}(1-\xi)\overline{\mathbf{PV}}^{\mathrm{T}}\mathbf{psnd}^{(t)}\\ &+\gamma(1-\xi)\overline{\mathbf{RV}}^{\mathrm{T}}\mathbf{rimp}^{(t)}+\xi\overline{\mathbf{V}}^{\mathrm{T}}\mathbf{vprs}^{(t)}\end{aligned} \tag{17}$$

Eq. (14)–(17) can be rephrased as follows:

$$\mathbf{r}^{(t+1)}=\mathbf{M}^{\mathrm{T}}\mathbf{r}^{(t)}, \tag{18}$$

where $\mathbf{r} = [\mathbf{paut}^{\mathrm{T}}, \mathbf{psnd}^{\mathrm{T}}, \mathbf{rimp}^{\mathrm{T}}, \mathbf{vprs}^{\mathrm{T}}]^{\mathrm{T}}$,

$$\mathbf{M}=\begin{bmatrix}\xi\mathbf{\Lambda}_1 & \gamma(1-\xi)\overline{\mathbf{P}^{\mathrm{T}}} & \frac{(1-\gamma)}{2}(1-\xi)\overline{\mathbf{PR}} & \frac{(1-\gamma)}{2}(1-\xi)\overline{\mathbf{PV}}\\ \gamma(1-\xi)\overline{\mathbf{P}} & \xi\mathbf{\Lambda}_1 & \frac{(1-\gamma)}{2}(1-\xi)\overline{\mathbf{PR}} & \frac{(1-\gamma)}{2}(1-\xi)\overline{\mathbf{PV}}\\ \frac{(1-\gamma)}{2}(1-\xi)\overline{\mathbf{RP}} & \frac{(1-\gamma)}{2}(1-\xi)\overline{\mathbf{RP}} & \xi\overline{\mathbf{R}} & \gamma(1-\xi)\overline{\mathbf{RV}}\\ \frac{(1-\gamma)}{2}(1-\xi)\overline{\mathbf{VP}} & \frac{(1-\gamma)}{2}(1-\xi)\overline{\mathbf{VP}} & \gamma(1-\xi)\overline{\mathbf{RV}} & \xi\overline{\mathbf{V}}\end{bmatrix} \tag{19}$$

and $\mathbf{\Lambda}_1$ is a diagonal matrix with each $\mathbf{\Lambda}_{i,i} = 1$ ($i = 1, \ldots, n_P$).

The $(2n_P+n_R+n_V)\times(2n_P+n_R+n_V)$ dimensional matrix **M** is a transition matrix corresponding to a Markovian process. Similar to Eq. (10), it is easy to verify that **M** is an *irreducible*, *aperiodic* and *stochastic* matrix. So **r** converges to the principle eigenvector of **M** with principle eigenvalue of 1. Given initial values of **r**, MutualRank iteratively updates **r** until the convergence criterion $\|\mathbf{r}\|_1 \leq \varepsilon$ is met for some small ε. The initial values of **paut, psnd, rimp** and **vprs** are set to $\mathbf{e_p}/(2n_P+n_R+n_V)$, $\mathbf{e_p}/(2n_P+n_R+n_V)$, $\mathbf{e_r}/(2n_P+n_R+n_V)$, and $\mathbf{e_v}/(2n_P+n_R+n_V)$ respectively, where $\mathbf{e_p}$, $\mathbf{e_r}$ and $\mathbf{e_v}$ are n_P-, n_R- and n_V-dimensional unit vectors respectively.

4. EXPERIMENTAL EVALUATION

4.1 Evaluation Metrics

In evaluation, we do not use the traditional IR metric *Precision-at-k* [14] because there exists a partial order between paper and researcher pairs. What's more, each benchmark paper has a recommendation count and our design of evaluation metric should reflect this information which cannot be reflected by *Precision-at-k*. Meanwhile, it is also hard to employ *Normalized Discounted Cumulative Gain* (NDCG@*k*) in our context although NDCG@*k* is almost a de facto metric for ranking evaluation beyond binary relevance. This is because we are estimating the importance of papers in the whole computational linguistics area, and even for human, it is very difficult to judge the levels of relevance. The performance metric we use is called *Recommendation Intensity*. Let *P* be the list of top-*k* returned papers. For each paper *p* in *P*, the *recommendation intensity of p at k*, denoted as *RI(p)@k*, is defined as

$$RI(p)@k = \begin{cases} c_p / \log(c_p) + (1 - o_p / k) & p \in \text{BenchP} \\ 0 & p \notin \text{BenchP} \end{cases}. \quad (20)$$

where c_p is the number of recommendations of *p* in *BenchP* and o_p is the ranked order of *p* in *P*. Eq. (20) means that if a paper *p* has larger recommendation counts (with larger c_p) and is ranked higher (with smaller o_p), then its recommendation intensity *RI(p)@k* is higher. $\log(c_p)$ is a controlling factor for preventing a few papers with extremely high recommendation counts from dominating the value of recommendation intensity of the whole result set. $(1-o_p/k)$ is to reflect the fact that a returned relevant result *p* (i.e. *p* is also in *BenchP*) is more useful if *p* is ranked higher in *P*. This is because users tend to look at only the first several items in the returned result list. Thus, the higher the rank of a relevant paper is, the more chances it has to be read by the user. *Recommendation intensity of P at k*, denoted as *RI(P)@k*, is defined as

$$RI(P)@k = \sum\nolimits_{p \in P, o_p \le k} RI(p)@k . \quad (21)$$

The bigger *RI(P)@k* is, the better a ranking method is. *RI(P)@k* is an extension to *Precision-at-k*. In fact, if we ignore recommendation counts, *RI(P)@k* degenerates to *Precision-at-k*. Recommendation intensity is also used for ranking researchers. Based on *BenchR1*, for each researcher *r* in the top-*k* result list *R*, *recommendation intensity of r at k* is defined as

$$RI_1(r)@k = \begin{cases} c_r / \log(c_r) + (1 - o_r / k) & r \in BenchR1 \\ 0 & r \notin BenchR1 \end{cases}, \quad (22)$$

where c_r is the recommendation count of *r* in *BenchR1* and o_r is the order of *r* in *R*. The *recommendation intensity of R at k* is

$$RI_1(R)@k = \sum\nolimits_{r \in R, o_r \le k} RI_1(r)@k . \quad (23)$$

For evaluation using *BenchR2*, if a researcher *r* is the o_r-th one on the top-*k* result list *R* and the g_r-th in BenchR2, then

$$RI_2(r)@k = \begin{cases} 1 + (o_r - g_r) / k & r \in BenchR2 \\ 0 & r \notin BenchR2 \end{cases}, \quad (24)$$

and $RI_2(R)@k$ is defined as to $RI_1(R)$.

We compare MutualRank with PageRank, RHITS and CoRank using the above benchmark datasets and metrics. CoRank works on both PIN and RCN. CoRank is rephrased as follows,

$$\mathbf{r} = \begin{bmatrix} (1-\gamma)\overline{\mathbf{P}}^{n} & \gamma\overline{\mathbf{RP}}(\overline{\mathbf{PRRP}})^{l} \\ \gamma\overline{\mathbf{RP}}(\overline{\mathbf{PRRP}})^{l} & (1-\gamma)\overline{\mathbf{R}}^{m} \end{bmatrix}^{\mathrm{T}} \mathbf{r} , \quad (25)$$

where $\mathbf{r} = [\mathbf{prnk}^{\mathrm{T}}, \mathbf{rimp}^{\mathrm{T}}]^{\mathrm{T}}$, $\mathbf{prnk}^{\mathrm{T}}$ and $\mathbf{rimp}^{\mathrm{T}}$ are the rank vectors for papers and researchers respectively. The superscripts *l* is the number of times a random surfer does inter-network walk, and *m* and *n* denote the number of intra-network random walks.

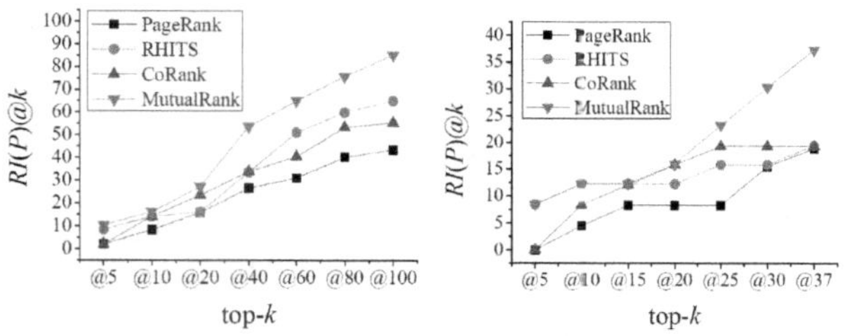

(*a*) *#recommend* ≥ 1 (*b*) *#recommend* ≥ 2

Figure 3. Recommendation intensity curves of different methods on ranking papers.

4.2 Results for Ranking Papers

We first demonstrate how MutualRank compensate the problem of time distortion compared to PageRank and RHITS. Table 3 lists the relevant returned results of MutualRank under parameter settings that $\xi = 0.5$, $\gamma = 0.5$, $\lambda = 0.85$ and $\varepsilon = 1\text{e-}5$. Out of the top-100 results returned by MutualRank, 36 are verified as relevant according to *BenchP*. (1) Out of the 36 relevant results, 16 papers (in boldface) are published in the 1990s and 17 papers (in normal font) come from the 2000s which demonstrates that MutualRank not only accurately identifies the contributions of the last decade of the 20th century to the development of statistical natural language processing, but also assigns enough importance to the new century where many practical applications flourish, many new research problems emerge and the progresses in NLP are ever faster than before, armed with the promising tools developed and together with the boom of web science. To better catch up this, readers can refer to Table 5 and verify that all the top-15 papers published in the 1990s are indeed amongst the most influential papers through the years. (2) MutualRank returns extra papers of high recommendations that are lost by RHITS, e.g. P95-1026[4] and W02-1011[3] etc.

Table 3. Relevant Papers in top-100 MutualRank Results

2:J93-2003[7]	**24:P95-1026[4]**	63:J01-4004[1]
3:J86-3001[1]	25:P03-1054[2]	*66:J88-1003[1]*
4:P02-1040[2]	**26:P97-1003[3]**	68:J00-3003[1]
5:J96-1002[2]	**27:J95-2003[1]**	**72:H94-1028[1]**
8:J90-2002[1]	30:W02-1011[3]	*73:P87-1022[1]*
13:J92-4003[1]	33:W02-1001[2]	**76:C96-2141[1]**
15:J96-2004[1]	38:P02-1053[1]	79:P06-1055[3]
17:A00-2018[1]	43:P05-1022[2]	80:J01-2001[3]
18:J95-4004[1]	45:N03-1028[1]	82:P05-1012[1]
19:J02-3001[2]	**47:J98-1004[1]**	**86:J93-2006[1]**
21:P98-2127[1]	52:P05-1033[1]	**89:J94-2001[2]**
23:W96-0213[2]	58:J04-4002[2]	95:P02-1035[1]

Note: $\xi = 0.5$, $\gamma = 0.5$, $\lambda = 0.85$ and $\varepsilon = 1\text{e-}5$.

Figure 3 shows the results of ranking papers. For Figure 3(a), we compare the results of each competitor algorithm with *BenchP*. For Figure 3(b), we use a subset of papers in *BenchP* with at least two recommendations. To obtain the results in Figure 3, we set the parameters as follows, (i) for MutualRank $\xi = 0.5$, (ii) for

Table 5. Top-15 papers returned by MutualRank and their ranks by other competitors

MR	Title	AAN ID	Rank by #cite	CR	PR	HITS
1	Building A Large Annotated Corpus Of English: The Penn Treebank	J93-2004	1 (775)	5	6	17
2	The Mathematics Of Statistical Machine Translation: Parameter Estimation	J93-2003	2 (615)	6	7	4
3	Attention Intentions And The Structure Of Discourse	J86-3001	8 (343)	7	8	**1079**
4	Bleu: A Method For Automatic Evaluation Of Machine Translation	P02-1040	3 (591)	14	29	1
5	A Maximum Entropy Approach To Natural Language Processing	J96-1002	7 (344)	8	12	24
6	A Systematic Comparison Of Various Statistical Alignment Models	J03-1002	5 (473)	**58**	**71**	5
7	A Stochastic Parts Program And Noun Phrase Parser For Unrestricted Text	A88-1019	16 (234)	1	1	**291**
8	A Statistical Approach To Machine Translation	J90-2002	29 (189)	3	4	26
9	Minimum Error Rate Training In Statistical Machine Translation	P03-1021	4 (475)	42	**64**	2
10	Moses: Open Source Toolkit for Statistical Machine Translation	P07-2045	10 (325)	**102**	**195**	6
11	Statistical Phrase-Based Translation	N03-1017	6 (436)	**60**	**83**	3
12	The Berkeley FrameNet Project	P98-1013	19 (220)	21	31	**267**
13	Class-Based N-Gram Models Of Natural Language	J92-4003	28 (193)	9	13	**89**
14	Accurate Methods For The Statistics Of Surprise And Coincidence	J93-1003	20 (218)	27	46	**103**
15	Assessing Agreement On Classification Tasks: The Kappa Statistic	J96-2004	32 (179)	30	54	**247**

Note: PR stands for PageRank.

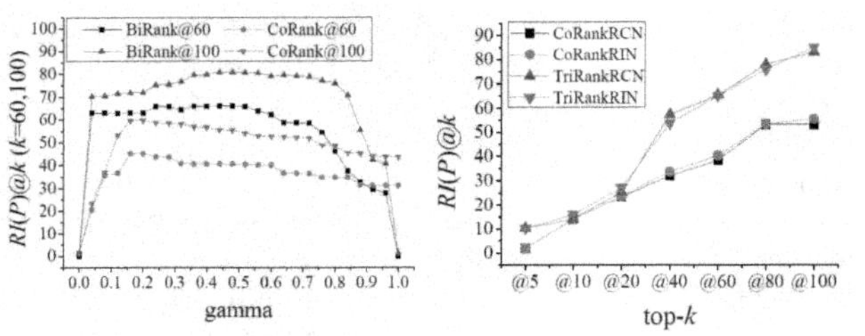

(*a*) Parameters (*b*) Network models

Figure 4. Parameters and network models on ranking performance (BiRank: MutualRank without venue information; TriRank: MutualRank with venue information).

CoRank, $m = 2$, $n = 2$, $l = 1$ (parameters that obtain the best performances in the original paper [26]), and (iii) for both $\gamma = 0.5$. Results show that MutualRank has the best performance. Taking MutualRank and RHITS for example, there are 20 MutualRank-only relevant papers (those benchmark papers that are only recommended by MutualRank) on the top-100 result list and among them 5 are recommended more than twice. There are only 11 RHITS-only papers and only 2 of them are recommended more than twice. As MutualRank applies HITS-style ranking on PIN, the results verify that using different types of importance values for certain objects does improve ranking performance.

An interesting observation is that, although RHITS uses PIN only, it sometimes performs even better than CoRank, e.g. when $k \geq 40$ in Figure 3(a) and $k \leq 15$ in Figure 3(b). After investigating the results of both algorithms we find that RHITS returns more relevant results than CoRank and some RHITS-only papers have high recommendation counts in *BenchP*. A possible explanation is that CoRank uses PageRank for ranking in PIN which fails to reflect the soundness of the paper and thus still biases towards old papers to some extent. The time distortion of CoRank can also be seen from the CR column of Table 5. High rank papers are still mostly old papers and ranks of papers after 2000 are relatively lower. An extreme example is P07-2045 (shadowed in Table 5). Although it is ranked 10th by MutualRank and receives 325 citations in less than 4 years, it is only ranked 102th and 195th by CoRank and PageRank respectively.

To understand why MutualRank wins, we take a deep look at the relevant results. We see from Table 4 that, besides more relevant papers by MutualRank, most common (highly recommended) relevant results are ranked higher in MutualRank than in CoRank except for the papers in italic (Notice that these papers are published in earlier years). There are also 15 MutualRank-only results where 6 papers are recommended more than 2 times in *BenchP*.

Table 4. Shared Relevant Papers of MutualRank and CoRank

Paper id	#rec	Rank		Paper id	#rec	Rank	
		MR	CR			MR	CR
J93-2003	7	2	6	*W96-0213*	*2*	*23*	*15*
J86-3001	1	3	7	P95-1026	4	24	49
P02-1040	2	4	14	*P97-1003*	*3*	*26*	*23*
J96-1002	2	5	8	W02-1011	3	30	75
J90-2002	*1*	*8*	*3*	W02-1001	2	33	77
J92-4003	*1*	*13*	*9*	P02-1053	1	38	61
J96-2004	1	15	30	*J88-1003*	*1*	*66*	*19*
A00-2018	1	17	25	*H94-1028*	*1*	*72*	*50*
J95-4004	1	18	32	*C96-2141*	*1*	*76*	*64*
J02-3001	2	19	62	*J93-2006*	*1*	*86*	*67*
P98-2127	1	21	68				

Note: MR stands for MutualRank and CR stands for CoRank.

Figure 4 shows the results of MutualRank under different different parameter settings and network models. We include CoRank for comparison with γ varying from 0 to 1 with parameter step of 0.02 (see Eq. (25)). To see how researcher and venue information helps improve ranking performance, we fix γ in MutualRank to 0.5 and vary ξ from 0 to 1 with parameter step of 0.02. For a fairer comparison, we do not use venue information. MutualRank thus degenerates to BiRank in Figure 4(a). In both MutualRank and CoRank, parameter γ governs how much information outside the PIN is incorporated for improving ranking. The larger γ is, the more researcher information is used. When $\gamma = 0$ CoRank degenerates to PageRank and MutualRank degenerates to First-Order

Table 7. Comparisons between different rankings of 8 well-known venues

	Venue Rank								Correlation				
	CL	ACL	COLING	EMNLP	NAACL	EACL	HLT	IJCNLP	AM	MR	H1	H2	Avg_Correl
AM	1	2	3	5	4	6	7	8	1.00	0.81	0.88	0.86	0.89
MR	**3**	1	2	4	6	7	*5*	8	0.81	1.00	**0.64**	0.83	0.82
H1	1	2	5	4	4	6	8	7	0.88	0.64	1.00	0.88	0.85
H2	2	1	4	3	6	5	7	8	0.86	0.83	0.88	1.00	0.89

Note: AM – ArnetMiner; MR – MutualRank; H – Human judgments; Avg_Correl – Average correlation with the other three rankings; CL – The Computational Liguistics journal

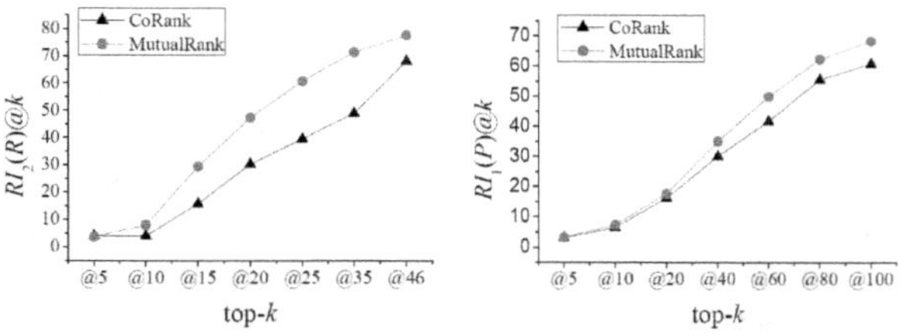

(a) *BenchR1* (b) *BenchR2*

Figure 5. Recommendation intensity curves of different methods on ranking researchers.

HITS. γ = 1 means that, loosely speaking, paper rank in both MutualRank and CoRank is the aggregated importance of its authors. As is expected, when γ increases from 0 to 1, ranking performances of both MutualRank and CoRank increase. This means adding metadata information such as research (or venue) influence network indeed improves ranking of papers. This performance gain peaks at some points (around γ = 0.46 for MutualRank and γ = 0.20 for CoRank) and turns to decrease when γ becomes too large. The results in Figure 4(a) show that using First-Order HITS instead of PageRank on PIN helps improve ranking performance a lot. Figure 4(b) shows the influence of network model on recommendation intensity, where both γ and ξ are fixed to 0.5. We compare two versions of MutualRank and two versions CoRank. On the whole, performances using RIN is slightly better RCN.

To get an intuitive understanding of MutualRank, we list the top-15 papers returned by MutualRank and its competitors in Table 5. We include the ranks by CoRank, PageRank, RHITS and #cite (citation count) for comparison. It is clear that the ranks given by MutualRank are quite reasonable. We also see how severely PageRank and RHITS bias towards old and new papers respectively (see the boldfaced items). The results of CoRank are in a sense close to PageRank. The IDs of papers are given so that interested readers can find them on the AAN website for more information.

4.3 Results for Ranking Researchers

For ranking researchers, we compare MutualRank to CoRank. The recommendation intensity curves in Figure 5 show that MutualRank outperforms CoRank by at most 53.8% under *BenchR1* and 19.7% under *BenchR2*.

Taking *BenchR2* for example, in the top-10 results returned by MutualRank, two matches *BenchR2*. They are $r_{(5)}$ = 'Della Pietra, Vincent J.' and $r_{(10)}$ = 'Manning, Christopher D.', but none of CoRank's top-10 results matches *BenchR2*. Moreover, compared to CoRank results, most MutualRank ranks are closer to their benchmark orders. For example, the top 4 researchers in *BenchR2* 'Och, Franz Josef', 'Ney, Hermann', 'Koehn, Philipp' and 'Marcu, Daniel' are ranked 24th, 19th, 50th and 16th by MutualRank and 45th, 11th, 65th, and 39th by CoRank respectively.

Table 6 shows the top-15 researchers by MutualRank with their benchmark and CoRank ranks. The columns "Rank in *BenchR1*" and "Rank in *BenchR2*" are in the form of o_r (*#rec*) and *r* (*#cite*), respectively, where o_r is the order of *r* in the benchmark, *#rec* and *#cite* are the number of recommendations in *BenchR1* and number of incoming citations in *BenchR2* respectively. Two lines in boldface are exact match of *BenchR2* by MutualRank. Exact match by *BenchR1* is italicized. The symbol '-- (--)' means that the returned researcher is not in *BenchR1*.

Table 6. Top-15 researchers returned by MutualRank

MR	Researcher Name	CR	Rank in *BenchR1*	Rank in *BenchR2*
1	Church, Kenneth Ward	1	-- (--)	19 (2667)
2	Marcus, Mitchell P.	9	-- (--)	12 (3411)
3	Pereira, Fernando	10	-- (--)	15 (3070)
4	Brill, Eric	26	22 (3)*	35 (1829)
5	***Della Pietra, Vincent J.***	***12***	***5 (6)***	***5 (3978)***
6	Joshi, Aravind K.	3	-- (--)	30 (2065)
7	McKeown, Kathleen R.	2	-- (--)	33 (1956)
8	Hovy, Eduard	8	-- (--)	24 (2327)
9	Grishman, Ralph	6	-- (--)	31 (2023)
10	Manning, Christopher D.	22	2 (13)	6 (3915)
11	**Mercer, Robert L.**	**4**	10 (5)	**11 (3453)**
12	Della Pietra, Stephen A.	15	10 (5)	10 (3549)
13	Collins, Michael John	21	10 (5)	7 (3909)
14	Johnson, Mark	13	5 (6)	17 (2908)
15	Yarowsky, David	17	22 (3)*	23 (2335)

4.4 Results for Ranking Venues

Although it is difficult to give a consolidated quantitative metric for verifying venue ranking, the results show that the top venues returned by MutualRank conform to our common knowledge on conference and journal reputations. Among all the 273 venues, the top 10 are $v_{(1)}$ = ACL, $v_{(2)}$ = COLING, $v_{(3)}$ = CL, $v_{(4)}$ = EMNLP, $v_{(5)}$ = HLT, $v_{(6)}$ = NAACL, $v_{(7)}$ = wDSANL, $v_{(8)}$ = ANLP, $v_{(9)}$ = CoNLL, and $v_{(10)}$ = EACL. wDSANL is a shorthand for 'Workshop on Speech and Natural Language' and CL stands for 'Journal of Computational Linguistics'. Following are some other reputed conferences including $v_{(11)}$ = LREC, $v_{(14)}$ = MU, $v_{(16)}$ = IJCNLP, $v_{(18)}$ = NLG, $v_{(19)}$ = wSMT, $v_{(20)}$ = VLC. MU is short for the 'Message Understanding Conference', NLG stands for 'International Conference on Natural Language Generation', wSMT stands for 'Workshop on Statistical Machine Translation' and VLC abbreviates 'Workshop on Very Large Corpora'.

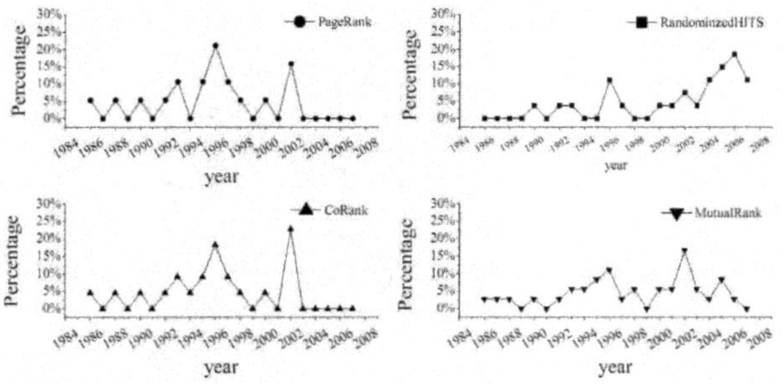

Figure 6. Distribution of relevant returned papers (k = 100)

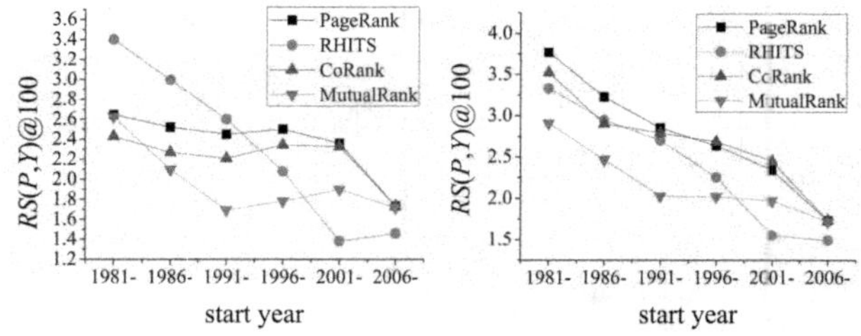

(a) Curves of relevant papers (b) Curves of returned papers

Figure 7. Recommendation sensitivity curves of different methods on ranking papers (k = 100).

To make a qualitative investigation, we compare our results with the 2008 conference ranks given by ArnetMiner[5] [22] and 2 human evaluations (H1 and H2 in Table 7) of 8 well-known venues, and analyze the correlations between these four rankings. As Table 7 shows, the four rankings are highly correlated with each other. The only significant difference lies between MR and H1, where the correlation coefficient of 0.64 is not high enough to be consistent. With in-depth investigation of H1 and MR, we found the problem lies in the following points. Firstly, in MutualRank, a joint conference such as HLT-NAACL is split into two different venues. Such a way assigns extra prestige to less-prestigious conferences, that is HLT in this context. We are unable to distinguish between jointly held conferences using AAN metadata only. Secondly, the Journal of Computational Linguistics is by all means the most prestigious venue to NLP researchers. However, in MutualRank it is ranked lower than ACL and COLING because the latter two conferences have far more papers published every year and so their aggregated prestige is higher.

Very interestingly in MutualRank, ACL-Companion (12th), COLING-Companion (13th), HLT-Companion (15th) and NAACL-Companion (17th) all have high prestige too. This phenomenon reveals that, on one hand, researchers often focus on the most influential conferences and thus even the short or demo papers published in these conferences gain many citations, and on the other hand, it is more attractive to important researchers for publishing their short or demo papers on these prestigious conferences. Moreover, MutualRank returns some well-known workshops too, e.g., $v_{(21)}$ = wDAD (SIGDIAL Workshop on Discourse And Dialogue), $v_{(23)}$ = BioNLP (a series of workshops on Natural Language Processing in Biology and Biomedicine).

4.5 Time Distributions

Finally, we study the time distributions of returned papers of different ranking algorithms. Figure 6 shows the yearly distributions of the relevant papers in the top-100 papers returned by different algorithms. (1) From the chart we can see that two peaks around year 1996 and 2002 can be identified by PageRank, CoRank and MutualRank but the RHITS algorithm has an obvious bias towards new papers after 2000 year. Bias here means favoring certain years or year ranges. PageRank has a strong bias towards older papers and older papers receive citations more easily than new papers. CoRank and MutualRank are less biased in this sense. (2) Around each of these two peaks, MutualRank has a slowly-increasing and slowly-decreasing slope, which is much close to the real development process of a booming area while PageRank and CoRank has sharper busts at the two peaks. From the above, we argue that MutualRank not only captures the booming of statistical natural language in the 1990s but also shows enough respect of the flourishing development in the new century.

To make a deeper investigation of the problem of time distortion identified in Section3.1.1, we define a new metric *recommendation sensitivity* for ranking papers. Given a year range $Y = [y_s, y_e]$ and a paper list P returned by some ranking algorithm, for each year $y \in Y$, let $pub(y)@k$ and $pub(Y)@k$ be the percentages of papers in P that are published in year y and in year range Y respectively. Let $\overline{pub(y)@k} = \sum_{y \in Y} pub(y)@k / |Y|$. The *recommendation sensitivity of P at k*, denoted as $RS(P)@k$, is defined as

$$RS(Y)@k = \sum_{y \in Y} -dev(y)@k \cdot \log\left(dev(y)@k\right) , \qquad (26)$$

where $dev(y)@k = \left| pub(y)@k - \overline{pub(y)@k} \right|$. If $dev(y)@k = 0$, the corresponding *log*-element in Eq. (7) is set to 0. Recommendation sensitivity measures how biased the yearly distribution of returned papers during a year range is. Big recommendation sensitivity means that the yearly distribution of the returned papers has very sharp peaks, i.e. biasing towards certain periods. What's more, we can see how recommendation sensitivity changes during different periods by choosing different start years of the year ranges with fixed end year and drawing the recommendation sensitivity curves corresponding to the year ranges. Figure 7 shows the recommendation sensitivity curves (RSC) of different methods, where we fix the end year as 2010 and vary the start year from 1981 to 2006 with step = 5. Figure 7(a) shows the RSCs of relevant papers, i.e. the top-100 papers that match *BenchP*, while Figure 7(b) illustrates the RSCs of the top-100 papers returned by different algorithms. Parameters of different ranking algorithms are just set as in Figure 3. An unbiased and fair ranking algorithm should have both small recommendation sensitivity values in different year ranges and a flat RSC in the whole time period.

From Figure 7(a), we see that RHITS is very time-sensitive. The sharp slope reflects the fact that RHITS heavily biases towards new papers. By contrast, PageRank and CoRank are relatively not that sensitive. However, the sharp slope from year 2001 to 2006 reveals that PageRank and CoRank both bias towards old papers. On the contrary, the smaller values and flatter slop of MutualRank RSC from year 1986 to 2010 demonstrate that MutualRank is not only less sensitive to changes in year range but also less biased

[5] http://v1.arnetminer.org/page/conference-ranking/html/NLP.html

towards papers of certain time periods. There are two more points about MuturalRank RSC worth note. (1) The sharp slope from 1981 to 1986 shows that MutualRank returns few papers which are too old. (2) The flat slope from year 2001 to 2006 reveals the fact that MutualRank does not omit some important recent papers as PageRank and CoRank do. To sum up, MutualRank is the most unbiased method for ranking papers. Similar observations can be found in Figure 7(b). The point reserving attention is that, unlike in Figure 7(a), PageRank and CoRank also have sharp slopes from year 1981 to 1986 and from year 1986 to 1991. This is understandable because in the early days fewer papers are published every year, so all the methods have fewer returned results in these years (Note that these returned papers are not necessarily relevant with respect to *BenchP*).

5. CONCLUSION

This paper proposes a new framework MutualRank towards an unbiased ranking of papers. MutualRank employs the mutual reinforcement relationships between papers, researchers and publication venues to fairly rank papers of certain time periods, as well as researchers and venues. It models the intra- and inter-network rankings in a unified way and computes the ranking vectors of papers, researchers and venues in an iterative fashion. Using the manually collected benchmark datasets for papers and researchers, we show through experiments that MutualRank outperforms state-of-the-art competitors including PageRank, Randomized HITS and CoRank in the following aspects: (1) MutualRank returns more relevant highly-ranked papers and researchers, and (2) results of MutualRank are more unbiased. The MutualRank rankings of venues are verified to be reasonable. We also present a detailed discussion on the problem of time distortion in ranking papers and propose methods for judging biases of ranking.

In the future work, we will study the convergence properties of the ranking algorithms, establish a better benchmark, and consider more indicators for evaluation such as awards for ranking papers and researchers and social factors. The idea of MutualRank can be also applied to other network resource ranking scenarios where multiple heterogeneous sub-networks are interwoven with different node types and edge semantics. For example, in a heterogeneous social network where friend network, email network, collaboration network and affiliation network co-exist, mutual reinforcement information can be modeled to help ranking nodes in a synthetic way.

6. ACKNOWLEDGEMENT

This work was partially supported by National Science Foundation of China (No.61075074 and No.61070183), Natural Science Foundation of Chongqing (No.cstc2012jjB40012), and the Key Discipline Fund of National 211 Project (Southwest University: NSKD11013). We thank Dr. Yang Liu for annotating venue rankings. Thanks also go to Dr. Jianmin Yao for venue ranking annotation and helpful discussions and comments.

7. REFERENCES

[1] Barabási, A.-L. and Albert, R. 1999. Emergence of Scaling in Random Networks. *Science*, 286: 509–512.

[2] Brin, S., and Page, L. 1998. The anatomy of a large-scale hypertextual Web search engine. *Comput. Netw. ISDN Syst.*, 30, 1-7, (Apr. 1998) 107–117.

[3] Chen, P., Xie, H., Maslov, S., and Redner, S. 2007. Finding scientific gems with Google's PageRank algorithm. *J. Informetrics*, 1, 1 (Jun. 2007), 8–15.

[4] Das, S., Mitra, P., and Lee Giles, C. 2011. Ranking Authors in Digital Libraries. In *Proc. JCDL'11*, 251–254.

[5] Ding, Y., Yan, E., Frazho, R., and Caverlee, J. 2009. PageRank for Ranking Authors in Co-citation Networks. *J. Am. Soc. Inf. Sci. Technol.*, 60, 11 (Jun. 2009), 2229–2243.

[6] Garfield, E. 1972. Citation analysis as a tool in journal evaluation. *Science*, 178, 60 (Nov. 1972), 471–479.

[7] Hirsch, J. E. 2005. An index to quantify an individual's scientific research output. *Proc. Natl. Acad. Sci.*, 102, 46 (Nov. 2005), 16569–4.

[8] Jensen, C. S., Cao, X., and Cong, G. 2010. Mining Significant Semantic Locations from GPS Data. In *Proc. VLDB*, 3, 1–2 (Sep. 2010), 1009–1020.

[9] Katerattanakul, P., Han, B., and Hong, S. 2003. Objective quality ranking of computing journals. *Commun. ACM*, 46, 10 (Oct. 2003), 111–114.

[10] Kleinberg, J. M. 1999. Authoritative Sources in a Hyperlinked Environment. *J. ACM.* 46, 5 (Sep. 1999), 604–632.

[11] Lefebvre, M. 2006. *Applied Stochastic Processes*. Springer.

[12] Lempel, R., and Moran, S. 2001. SALSA: The Stochastic Approach for Link-Structure Analysis. *ACM Trans. Internet Tech.* 19, 2 (Apr. 2001), 131-169.

[13] Li, X., Liu, B., and Yu, P. 2008. Time Sensitive Ranking with Application to Publication Search. In *Proc. ICDM'08*, 893–898.

[14] Manning, C. D., Raghavan, R., and Schütze, H. 2008. *Introduction to Information retrieval*. Cambridge University Press.

[15] Nerur, S., Sikora, R., Mangalaraj, G., and Balijepally, V. 2005. Assessing the relative influence of journals in a citation network. *Commun. ACM*, 48, 11 (Nov. 2005), 71–74.

[16] Newman, M. E. J. 2002. Assortative Mixing in Networks. *Phys. Rev. Lett.*, 89, 20: 208701–5.

[17] Ng, A. Y., Zheng, A. X., and Jordan, M. I. 2001. Stable Algorithms for Link Analysis. In *Proc. SIGIR'01*, 258–266.

[18] Ng, M. K., Li, X., and Ye, Y. 2011. MultiRank: co-ranking for objects and relations in multi-relational data. In *Proc. KDD'11*, 1217–1225.

[19] Radicchi, F., Fortunato, S., Markines, B., and Vespignani, A. 2009. Diffusion of scientific credits and the ranking of scientists. *Phys. Rev. E*, 80, 5 (Nov. 2009), 056103–12.

[20] Radev, D. R., Muthukrishnan, P., and Qazvinian, V. 2009. The ACL Anthology Network. In *Proc. NLPIR4DL'09*, 54–61.

[21] Sayyadi, H., and Getoor, L. 2009. FutureRank: Ranking Scientific Articles by Predicting their Future PageRank. In *Proc. SDM'09*. 533–544.

[22] Tang, J., Zhang, J., Yao, L., Li, J., Zhang, L., and Su, Z. 2008. ArnetMiner: extracting academic social networks. In *Proc. KDD'08*. 990–998.

[23] Walker, D., Xie, H., Yan, K.-K., and Maslov, S. 2007. Ranking scientific publications using a model of network traffic. *J. Stat. Mech.*, 7 (Jun. 2007), 06010–9.

[24] Yan, E., and Ding, Y. 2009. Applying centrality measures to impact analysis: A coauthorship network analysis. *J. Am. Soc. Inf. Sci. Technol.* 60, 10 (Oct. 2009), 2107–2118.

[25] Yan, S., and Lee, D.-W. 2007. Toward Alternative Measures for Ranking Venues: A Case of Database Research Community. In *Proc. JCDL'07*, 235–244.

[26] Zhou, D., Orshanskiy, S. A., Zha, H., and Lee Giles, C. 2007. Co-Ranking Authors and Documents in a Heterogeneous Network. In *Proc. ICDM'07*, 739–744.

[27] Zhuge, H., and Zhang, J. 2010. Topological Centrality and Its e-Science Applications. *J. Am. Soc. Inf. Sci. Technol.*, 61, 9 (May 2010), 1824–1841.

A Math-Aware Search Engine for Math Question Answering System

Tam T. Nguyen, Kuiyu Chang, and Siu Cheung Hui
Nanyang Technological University
50 Nanyang Avenue, Singapore 639798
nguy0080@e.ntu.edu.sg, {askychang, asschui}@ntu.edu.sg

ABSTRACT

We propose a math-aware search engine that is capable of handling both textual keywords as well as mathematical expressions. Our math feature extraction and representation framework captures the semantics of math expressions via a Finite State Machine model. We adapt the passive aggressive online learning binary classifier as the ranking model. We benchmarked our approach against three classical information retrieval (IR) strategies on math documents crawled from *Math Overflow*, a well-known online math question answering system. Experimental results show that our proposed approach can perform better than other methods by more than 9%.

Categories and Subject Descriptors

H.3.3 [**Information Storage and Retrieval**]: Information Search and Retrieval

General Terms

Algorithms, Performance

Keywords

math document retrieval, math-aware search engine, learning to rank

1. INTRODUCTION

Math question answering (Q&A) systems deal with mathematical questions and answers embedded in math documents. A math document can contain both textual data and math expressions.Major online Math Q&A systems such as *Math Overflow* are constantly monitored and updated by their online user community. Therefore, an up-to-date and effective *math-aware search system* is essential for users to find the latest math documents. This system must support searching based on both keywords and math expressions. Although there are many conventional keyword-based search engines available for searching textual documents, to the best of our knowledge, there exist no publicly-available math-aware search engine for math Q&A systems.

Wolfram research hosts a public computation knowledge search engine called Wolfram *Alpha* [1], which can parse simple math queries and expressions. It is not a search engine per se, but more of a computational engine *Mathematica*[2]. For example, *Alpha* will compute and return the numerical result of a math expression like $e^{\sin 20}$, in addition to providing its alternate form and continuous fraction representation. For math related search queries like "Riemann", *Alpha* returns a brief biographical summary of Bernhard Riemann the Mathematician, including his full name, date of birth/death, etc. What it will not do is return a list of relevant documents like conventional Web search engines. Although this system does not require huge amount of storage for operation, it is not really an all-purpose search engine since it returns largely the computational results and/or knowledge from a few selected common topics instead of Web pages crawled from the entire Internet. For instance, if we search for "iphone5", *Alpha* will respond with the message, "development of this topic is under investigation" even though "iphone5" is a very popular term [3]. On the other hand, *Alpha* understands search queries of stock symbols and also geographical entities such as "Los Angeles".

Another approach to tackle the problem is to extend text search systems for math search. In the preprocessing phase, math expressions are simply converted to textual data, after which classical information retrieval (IR) techniques are applied for retrieval, as was previously reported in *Mathdex* [18] and *MathWebSearch* [12, 14]. Developing math search systems in this way is fast and simple, but their performance depends heavily on the fidelity of the conversion from symbolic math expressions to textual representations.

To overcome the above limitations, we propose a novel approach for math-aware search, which comprises two steps: (1) extract meaningful math index terms based on the semantically rich *MathML* format; (2) apply the learning-to-rank approach to improve the accuracy of the ranking process.

1.1 A Motivating Example

A question posted by user *"Alejandro Erickson"* from the Math Overflow system is shown below. The question belongs to the probability category.

[1]http://www.wolframalpha.com
[2]http://www.wolfram.com/mathematica
[3]as of August 2012, prior to the actual product launch date.

CIKM'12, October 29–November 2, 2012, Maui, HI, USA.

> **Title**: Formulate edge length problem as convex optimization problem
>
> **Content**: I want to use convex optimization to describe a problem in computational geometry. Let $E = (E_1, E_2, \ldots, E_m)$ be a sequence of line segments in the plane, where E_1 and E_m may be points and the rest are non-degenerate segments. A *critical path* on E is a selection of points $(p_1, p_2, \cdots, p_m)$ with $p_i \in E_i$ with edges $e_i = (p_i, p_{i+1})$ such that (1) all e_i has the same length l and (2) no other selection of points results in a path with edges that are not longer than l and some that are shorter.
>
> Find the critical path using convex optimization (if it exists). Can you use the convex optimization problem to show that the solution is unique? ...

To provide a search facility for questions like this, one can ignore math expressions and simply deploy a conventional keyword-based search engine. However, users could also be interested in finding math documents containing a particular math expression. In this case, conventional search engines fail miserably. For one, it cannot handle mathematical expressions in the query. Second, it does not know that a+b is semantically equivalent to x+y. These are just two of the many limitations of the simple approach. We shall discuss more in the following section.

1.2 Our Key Contributions

The key contributions of this paper are summarized below.

- We propose a two-view representation format for math documents.
- We propose a new math *feature extraction* algorithm for math expressions.
- We propose a novel *matching model* for math document retrieval, which utilizes both math and text index terms in a balanced manner.
- We propose a new learning-to-rank algorithm in a *ranking model* for improving the ranking of the search results.

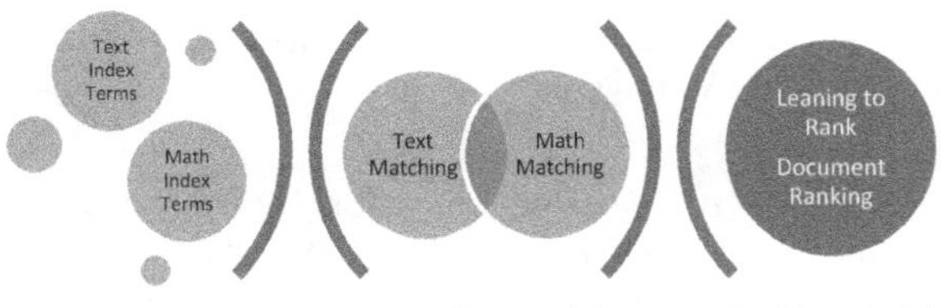

Figure 1: Math-Aware Search Engine Framework.

Figure 1 shows the proposed math-aware search engine framework. The idea is to extract and index text and math terms independently in two separate inverted indexes. A user query is first matched against both the math and text inverted indexes to retrieve an initial set of unranked candidates based on the intersection of matching documents in both the math and text query terms. A continuously learning *ranking model* assign scores to each document in this candidate set. Figure 2 shows the graphical user interface of the search engine, in which the user-friendly graphical equation editor CODECOGS allows math expressions to be entered effortlessly. The CODECOGS[4] editor converts user entered math expressions automatically into our preferred LaTeX storage format.

2. RELATED WORK

There exists several math-aware retrieval systems such as MathFind [19], ActiveMath [15], Wolfram Formula Search[5], Wikipedia Formula Search[6], Whelp [1], Mathdex [18], and MathWebSearch [12, 14]The vast majority of these systems are developed based mainly on conventional text retrieval techniques, which treats math expressions as textual data.

Since text retrieval based math search systems follow more or less the same principles, we will only review a few representative math search systems in this section. In the MathFind system [19], Munavalli and Miner encoded math expressions into a sequence of textual data called math fragments. In this approach, math expressions are preprocessed and converted into the corresponding *MathML* format [2]. Similarly, Nguyen et al. [21] extracted math features from *MathML* and used Formal Concept Analysis as the formula search mechanism. To index math expressions and support sub-expression search, Miner and Munavalli [18] defined math n-grams, where each math token is considered a *1*-gram. For instance, "a+b" has three 1-grams, i.e., 'a', 'b', and '+'. To search for math expressions, a query is decomposed into n-grams. The indexes are then searched for each n-gram in the query. Similarly, Libbrecht and Melis [15] proposed the ActiveMath Search Tool, which was built on top of Apache Lucene[7]. In the ActiveMath Search Tool, math data are represented in the OMDoc [13] format. They are subsequently converted into tokens and indexed using the Lucene text search engine.

Wolfram Formula Search[8] is another math search system that was developed by Wolfram Research. Wolfram Formula Search allows users to search for formulas from its formula compendium of math functions via the Web. Its database contains more than three hundred thousand formulas classified into 14 categories. The formula search engine provides a friendly interface for users to explore the vast collection of formulas. However, although Wolfram Formula Search engine provides semantic search, it only supports search queries based on predefined constants, operations, and function names. For example, it understands common constants like e, π, etc., and operations including sum, product, etc., appearing anywhere in a formula.

For the past few years, many learning-to-rank algorithms have been proposed to improve the ranking of search results. Some adapted binary classification algorithms such as Perceptron and its variants [4]. In [9], Gao et al. applied the Perceptron algorithm to learn the ranking function. Although the Perceptron algorithm is elegant and fast, it performs poorly on datasets that are not linearly separable. To overcome this limitation, Crammer et al. [7] proposed the Passive Aggressive (PA) algorithm, which uses large margin optimizations. Improved versions of PA include Confidence-Weighted (CW) Linear Classification [8] and Passive-Aggressive Mahalanobis (PAM) [20]. In the

[4]http://www.codecogs.com/latex/about.php
[5]http://functions.wolfram.com/formulasearch
[6]http://shinh.org/wfs/
[7]http://lucene.apache.org
[8]http://functions.wolfram.com/formulasearch

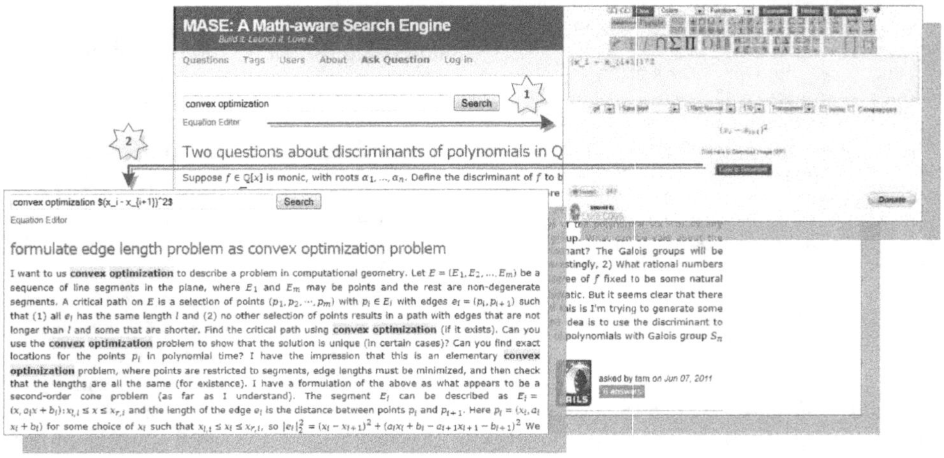

Figure 2: Math-Aware Search Engine.

realm of batch learning, the SVM algorithm [6, 26] has also been applied to the ranking problem. However, for dynamic systems like math Q&A systems, where math questions are posted every minute, an online learning algorithm is more desirable as it can incrementally update itself whenever new data is added. Therefore, in this research, we extend and apply the PA algorithm to learn the document ranking function.

3. MATH DOCUMENT PREPROCESSING

Math documents can be significantly more complex than textual documents; it can involve math expressions that are sequence sensitive in two dimensions, e.g., matrices, fractions, nested forms. Conventional text retrieval methods, which typically throw away the linear sequence information in text, are thus extremely poorly suited to process math documents. Therefore, new retrieval methods must be devised to effectively handle math documents. We introduce our math document format and feature extraction approach in this section.

3.1 Math Document Representation

Mathematical markup languages play an important role in the development of math search systems. It affects the storage and techniques for the processing of math expressions. There are several common mathematical markup languages: LaTeX, *ASCIIMath*[9], *OMDoc* [13], *OpenMath* [5] and *MathML* [2]. The content-oriented LaTeX markup language has been commonly used by many researchers, especially mathematicians, for document processing. ASCIIMath markup is a simpler variant of the LaTeX markup language [25], which is often used as a format for specifying math expression queries for math-aware search systems. Math expressions represented using ASCIIMath markup are easy to store as it mainly uses *ASCII* characters to represent the math expressions. However, the disadvantage of ASCIIMath is that its data representation is not well-structured, thereby requiring additional processing time to parse and extract math expressions. OMDoc and OpenMath are two other less popular standards for the semantic-oriented representation of math or expressions.

Among the various format, the MathML markup of W3C is the most popular, and is currently used by many math search engines for the presentation and storage of math expressions [15, 17, 19]. There are two variants of MathML: MathML content markup and MathML presentation markup. Among the two markup representations, MathML content markup is commonly used for the processing of math expressions as it contains richer semantic content than the MathML presentation markup.

Despite the advantages of MathML, our system uses the LaTeX markup as the storage and user interface language for entering queries. This is because LaTeX markup has a significantly smaller storage footprint than MathML. More importantly, LaTeX markup has a large user base and is more intuitive for users to enter arbitrary math expressions online. In fact, open source Javascript display engines like MathJax[10] and ASCIIMath can parse LaTeX markups and render the corresponding graphical math expressions on the web browser.

Moreover, during the feature extraction step, we transform our LaTeX queries and documents into MathML, which are easier for machines to analyze. Listing 1 shows an example question in LaTeX format, comprising the title and content of the example question from Section 1.

Listing 1: An Example Question in LaTeXformat.

```
Formulate edge length problem as convex
    optimization problem

I want to use convex optimization to describe a
    problem in computational geometry. Let $E = (E
    _1, E_2,\ldots , E_m) $ be a sequence of line
    segments in the plane, where $E_1$ and $E_m$
    may be points and the rest are non-degenerate
    segments. A \emph{critical path} on $E$ is a
    selection of points $(p_1,p_2,\cdots ,p_m)$
    with $p_i\in E_i$ with edges $e_i=(p_i,p_{i
    +1})$ such that (1) all $e_i$ has the same
    length $l$ and (2) no other selection of
    points results in a path with edges that are
    not longer than $l$ and some that are shorter
    ...
```

[9]http://www1.chapman.edu/~jipsen/mathml/asciimath.html

[10]http://www.mathjax.org

3.2 Math Feature Extraction

Due to the existence of both semantic and structural information, the preprocessing step for math expressions is more complex than that of text documents. For the purpose of math search, math features should be representative enough to reflect the underlying characteristics of each math expression. We thus extract math features as follows:

- Content MathML conversion. Convert math expressions into Content MathML format.
- Math feature extraction. Extract math features by traversing the Content MathML tree.

To convert math expressions from LaTeX, we use the *SnuggleTeX* library[11]. We first convert math expressions from LaTeX to the representation MathML format, then we use cascading stylesheets to map the representation MathML to content MathML. Listing 2 shows an example of the content MathML for the math expression $(x+y)^2$.

Once the expression is converted into content MathML, we use XML tree traversal to extract the math features. In this paper, we only use two kinds of features, namely single and combination features. Single features are used to express constant numbers, variable names, function names, etc. On the other hand, combination features refer to combinations of math operators and operands.

Listing 2: MathML Content Markup of $(x+y)^2$.

```
<apply>                 % apply operator
   <power/>             % power operator
   <mfence>
      <apply>           % apply operator
         <plus/>        % plus operator
         <ci>x</ci>     % variable (ci) x
         <ci>y</ci>     % variable (ci) y
      </apply>
   </mfence>
   <cn>2</cn>           % constant (cn) 2
</apply>
```

Take the sub-expression $x+y$ in Listing 2 as an example, based on the content MathML data, we have four single features, namely *ci*, *plus*, *cix*, and *ciy*, where *ci* stands for a variable and *cix* stands for a variable named x. We also have one combination feature *pluscixciy*, where *plus* stands for the operator + and *pluscixciy* stands for operator + applied to two operands x and y.

4. DATA MODEL

In this section, we define two types of index terms, namely text and math. These two types of index terms collectively form our math-aware search engine.

Definition 1 (Text Index Term). *Let n be the number of index terms in the system. Denote each text index term by t_i, and the set $T = \{t_1, \ldots, t_n\}$ contains all text index terms.*

Definition 2 (Math Index Term). *Let m be the number of math index terms in the system. Each math index term m_j is an element of the math feature set. Let $M = \{m_1, \ldots, m_m\}$ be the set of all math index terms.*

[11]http://www2.ph.ed.ac.uk/snuggletex

Let $\mathbb{D} = \{\mathbf{d}_1, \mathbf{d}_2, \ldots, \mathbf{d}_k\}$ and $\mathbb{Q} = \{\mathbf{q}_1, \mathbf{q}_2, \ldots, \mathbf{q}_l\}$ be a collection of k math documents and a set of l user queries, respectively. The math-aware IR problem aims to determine a *ranking function* score : $\mathbb{D} \times \mathbb{Q} \mapsto \mathbb{R}$, which defines an ordering among documents based on the queries via a *framework* F. This framework considers all math documents and queries. For example, in text IR, the framework F is typically the vector space of document and query points, with the ranking function determined by cosine similarity.

In this section, we formally define the query and ranking models for math Q&A search based on the vector space model. The proposed approach is an extension of the vector space model for conventional text IR.

4.1 Matching Model

In this section, we formally define math documents and queries in the math-ware search engine, where the data consists of both text and math expressions. The search engine should index both types of data simultaneously.

Definition 3 (Math Predicate). *A math predicate is defined as p_i if the math index term m_i appears in a document $\mathbf{d}_j$. In other words, $\mathbf{d}_j$ satisfies p_i if $\mathbf{d}_j$ contains the math index term m_i.*

Definition 4 (Math Specification). *A math specification $P = p_1 \wedge p_2 \wedge \ldots \wedge p_s$ specifies a subset of documents $\mathbb{D}_P \subset \mathbb{D}$, where $\mathbf{d}_i \in \mathbb{D}_P$, if $\mathbf{d}_i$ satisfies P.*

Definition 5 (Math Document). *A math document $\mathbf{d}_j \in \mathbb{D}$ is determined by a vector $\mathbf{d}_j = (d_{1j}, \ldots d_{nj})$ and a math specification P_j, where $d_{ij} \geq 0$. If the text index term t_i appears in document $\mathbf{d}_j$, then $d_{ij} > 0$; otherwise, $d_{ij} = 0$. Thus P_j is the corresponding math specification satisfied by document $\mathbf{d}_j$.*

Definition 6 (Math Query). *A query in a math question answering system, $\mathbf{q} = \mathbf{q}_t|\mathbf{q}_m$, is comprised of two parts: a keyword query $\mathbf{q}_t \subset T$ and a math expression query $\mathbf{q}_m \subset M$. The keyword query $\mathbf{q}_t$ is a list of keywords and the math expression query $\mathbf{q}_m$ is a list of math expressions.*

For the math query $\mathbf{q} = \mathbf{q}_t|\mathbf{q}_m$, suppose that $\mathbf{q}_t = \{t_1, \ldots, t_i\}$ and $\mathbf{q}_m = \{m_1, \ldots, m_j\}$ corresponds to math specification P, the unranked result $\mathbf{q}(\mathbb{D})$ denotes the subset of documents that satisfies P, and those that contain all the terms in $\mathbf{q}_t$ as follows:

$$\mathbf{q}(\mathbb{D}) = \sigma_P(\mathbb{D}) \cap \sigma_{t_1}(\mathbb{D}) \cap \ldots \cap \sigma_{t_i}(\mathbb{D})$$

where the selection function $\sigma_{t_i}(\mathbb{D}) = \{\mathbf{d}_j | t_i \in \mathbf{d}_j \wedge \mathbf{d}_j \in \mathbb{D}\}$.

4.2 Ranking Model

4.2.1 A Straightforward Approach

Now, we define the ranking of the result of $\mathbf{q}$. We start by presenting a generic representation of the conventional ranking function for keyword queries. We then extend it into the math document ranking function.

Given a query $\mathbf{q}$ and a document $\mathbf{d} \in \mathbb{D}$, a conventional ranking function $f(\cdot)$ takes as argument statistics from $\mathbf{q}$, $\mathbf{d}$, and computes a score of $\mathbf{d}$ with respect to $\mathbf{q}$ as follows:

$$\text{score}(\mathbf{q}, \mathbf{d}) = f(\mathbf{q}_t, \mathbf{q}_m, \mathbf{d})$$

For example, $tf \times idf$ weighting [16, 23] is a well-known ranking model. Among its variants, the pivoted normalization formula is one of the best performing vector space models, and is widely used in many text search systems. Specifically, it is defined as

$$\text{score}(\mathbf{q}, \mathbf{d}) = \sum_{t \in \mathbf{q}} \frac{1 + \ln(1 + tf(t, \mathbf{d}))}{(1-s) + s \cdot \frac{len(\mathbf{d})}{|\mathbb{D}|}} \cdot tf(t, \mathbf{q}) \cdot ln \frac{|\mathbb{D}| + 1}{df(t, \mathbb{D})}$$

where $len(\mathbf{d})$ is the length of document $\mathbf{d}$, $|\cdot|$ denotes the set cardinality function, $tf(t, \mathbf{d})$ is the term frequency of term t in document $\mathbf{d}$, $df(t, \mathbb{D})$ is the document frequency of term t in the document collection $\mathbb{D}$, and s is a parameter.

We note that the scoring function depends on the number of documents. Therefore, we revise this scoring function for ranking math document search results as follows:

$$\text{score}(\mathbf{q}, \mathbf{d}) = \sum_{t \in \mathbf{q}} \frac{1 + \ln(1 + tf(t, \mathbf{d}))}{(1-s) + s \cdot \frac{len(\mathbf{d})}{|\mathbb{D}_P|}} \cdot tf(t, \mathbf{q}) \cdot ln \frac{|\mathbb{D}_P| + 1}{df(t, \mathbb{D}_P)}$$

4.2.2 Ranking Passive Aggressive Algorithm

In this section, we describe the Ranking Passive Aggressive algorithm in details based on the Passive Aggressive algorithm [7]. Let $(\mathbf{x}_t, y_t)_{t=1,T}$ be a sequence of examples, Crammer et al. proposed the PA algorithm, which learns the weight $\mathbf{w}$ of a linear prediction function $f(\mathbf{x}) = \mathbf{w} \cdot \mathbf{x}$ based on the following optimization problem:

$$\begin{aligned} \mathbf{w}_{t+1} = \quad & \underset{\mathbf{w} \in \mathbb{R}^n}{\text{argmin}} \quad \frac{1}{2} \parallel \mathbf{w} - \mathbf{w}_t \parallel^2 \\ \text{s.t.} \quad & \ell(\mathbf{w}; (\mathbf{x}_t, y_t)) = 0 \end{aligned} \tag{1}$$

where ℓ is the Hinge loss function.

We adapt the Passive Aggressive algorithm to learn-to-rank by training on pairs of instances. A correct classification corresponds to ranking a pair so that the more relevant instance is scored higher and vice versa.

We know that math and text features are extracted from different data types and therefore should be treated differently. We can apply the cascade ranking model [24], where one type of data is used to rank documents at each stage of a multi-stage ranking procedure. However, in practice, this approach may not be practical because math questions do not always contain math expressions. Therefore, we propose another approach that combines math and text data as follows. Let $\mathbf{a}_t \in \mathbb{R}^k$ and $\mathbf{b}_t \in \mathbb{R}^l$ be the math and text vectors representing the document $\mathbf{d}_t \in \mathbb{R}^n$, respectively, where $k + l = n$. The simplest way is to concatenate the math and text data as follows:

$$\mathbf{d}_t = (\eta \mathbf{a}_t, (1 - \eta)\mathbf{b}_t)$$

where $\eta \in [0, 1]$ weighs the relative importance of the text and math data.

Remark $\eta = 0$ means that we ignore math expressions in the math document. If $\eta = 1$, we only rank the search result based on the math expressions and ignore the text data. Normally, η will be assigned values between 0 and 1. If we treat math and text data as equals, then $\eta = 0.5$. If $\eta < 0.5$, we consider text data to be more important than math data, and vice versa.

Let the feature score vector of a document $\mathbf{d}_t \in \mathbb{R}^n$ and query $\mathbf{q}$ be defined as follows:

$$\phi_t = (f_1(\mathbf{d}_t, \mathbf{q}), \ldots, f_n(\mathbf{d}_t, \mathbf{q}))$$

The goal is to learn the weight vector $\mathbf{w}$ of the following scoring function.

$$\text{score}(\phi_t, \mathbf{w}) = \mathbf{w} \cdot \phi_t \tag{2}$$

Suppose that R and N denote relevant and non-relevant feature score vectors. Then the feature score vectors of relevant and non-relevant documents to the query $\mathbf{q}$ are defined as ϕ_t^R and ϕ_t^N, respectively. Let $(\phi_t^R, \phi_t^N)_{t=1,T}$ be a sequence of training examples. We should have $\mathbf{w} \cdot \phi_t^R \geq \mathbf{w} \cdot \phi_t^N$ because the score of the relevant document to the query should be greater than that of the non-relevant document. For the Ranking Perceptron [9], the weight vector $\mathbf{w}_{t+1}$ is learnt on each round t as follows:

$$\mathbf{w}_{t+1} = \mathbf{w}_t + \tau(\phi_t^R - \phi_t^N)$$

where τ is a constant learning rate. Similar to the Perceptron algorithm, the Ranking Perceptron algorithm is very sensitive to the learning rate, and also works poorly on non-linearly separable data.

To overcome this problem, we introduce a new Hinge loss function,

$$\ell((\phi_t^R, \phi_t^N); \mathbf{w}) = \max\left\{0, 1 - (\mathbf{w} \cdot \phi_t^R - \mathbf{w} \cdot \phi_t^N)\right\},$$

which penalizes the difference of the two scores if the score of the non-relevant document is greater than that of the relevant document, with respect to the query. We then derive a soft margin optimization problem by introducing a slack variable ξ as follows:

$$\begin{aligned} \mathbf{w}_{t+1} = \quad & \underset{\mathbf{w} \in \mathbb{R}^n \wedge \mathbf{w} \succeq 0}{argmin} \frac{1}{2} \parallel \mathbf{w} - \mathbf{w}_t \parallel^2 + C\xi \\ \text{s.t.} \quad & 1 - (\mathbf{w} \cdot \phi_t^R - \mathbf{w} \cdot \phi_t^N) \leq \xi; \quad \xi \geq 0 \end{aligned} \tag{3}$$

where C is an aggressiveness parameter.

Proposition 1. *The optimization problem (3) has the closed-form solution as follows:*

$$\mathbf{w}_{t+1} = \mathbf{w}_t + \tau_t(\phi_t^R - \phi_t^N)$$

where the learning rate τ_t has the form

$$\tau_t = \min\left\{C, \frac{1 - (\mathbf{w}_t \cdot \phi_t^R - \mathbf{w}_t \cdot \phi_t^N)}{(\phi_t^R - \phi_t^N)^2}\right\}.$$

Algorithm 1 summarizes the *Ranking Passive Aggressive* algorithm.

Algorithm 1 Ranking Passive Aggressive Algorithm

Input:
  C = positive aggressiveness parameter
Output:
  None
Process:
  Initialize $\mathbf{w}_1 \leftarrow \mathbf{0}$;
  for $t = 1, 2, \ldots$ **do**
    Receive feature score vectors $\phi_t^R \in \mathbb{R}^n$ and $\phi_t^N \in \mathbb{R}^n$
    Suffer loss $\ell_t \leftarrow \max\left\{0, 1 - (\mathbf{w}_t \cdot \phi_t^R - \mathbf{w}_t \cdot \phi_t^N)\right\}$
    if $\ell_t > 0$ **then**
      Set $\tau_t \leftarrow \min\left\{C, \frac{1 - (\mathbf{w}_t \cdot \phi_t^R - \mathbf{w}_t \cdot \phi_t^N)}{(\phi_t^R - \phi_t^N)^2}\right\}$
      Update $\mathbf{w}_{t+1} \leftarrow \mathbf{w}_t + \tau_t(\phi_t^R - \phi_t^N)$
    end if
  end for

Let ϕ_t^R and ϕ_t^N be the feature score vectors of the relevant and non-relevant documents for query $\mathbf{q}$, respectively. Let $\mathbf{w}_t$ be the weight vector of the Ranking Passive Aggressive algorithm on round t. We say that the proposed algorithm makes a mistake if $\mathbf{w}_t \cdot \phi_t^R < \mathbf{w}_t \cdot \phi_t^N$. The total number of mistakes made by the proposed algorithm is bounded as shown in Preposition 2. The proofs of Prepositions 1 and 2 are given in the Appendix.

PROPOSITION 2. *Let $(\phi_t^R, \phi_t^N)_{t=1,T}$ be a sequence of examples, where $\phi_t^R \in \mathbb{R}^n$ and $\phi_t^N \in \mathbb{R}^n$ for all t. Then for any weight vector $\mathbf{u} \in \mathbb{R}^n$ and its loss $\ell_t^* = \ell((\phi_t^R, \phi_t^N); \mathbf{u})$, the number of mistakes made by the Ranking Passive Aggressive algorithm is bounded by*

$$\max\left\{\frac{1}{C}, \max_{t=1,T}(\phi_t^R - \phi_t^N)^2\right\}\left(\parallel \mathbf{u} \parallel^2 + 2C\sum_{t=1}^{T}\ell_t^*\right)$$

4.2.3 Adding Metadata to Math Question Retrieval

In math question answering system, math questions typically contains additional metadata such as user rating, number of views, number of answers, etc. The metadata can be very useful for improving ranking results, faceted search, and personalization [3]. The question is how to combine the document content and its metadata to answer a user's information need. To address this, we have to first choose a suitable set of metadata. For instance, user may prefer to see the most popular and/or answered questions. Moreover, he could also be looking for questions that have already been answered by other users. In each of these two scenarios, the number of views and answers are useful information for re-ranking the search results.

To retrieve documents based on user ratings, Zhang et al. [27] proposed a simple IR technique, which considers thumbs-up and thumbs-down as a term in the document. They came up with a scoring function, which is the ratio of the number of thumbs-up (n^+) to the number of thumbs-down (n^-). However, in practice systems like Math Overflow only store the difference ($n^+ - n^-$) between these two user ratings. Therefore, the above technique cannot be directly applied. In order to overcome this limitation and consider other kinds of metadata, we propose another IR approach, which is based on the $tf \times idf$ ranking model.

Since users want to retrieve "good" math questions, e.g., questions with thumbs-up, questions with many views, questions with several answers, questions with highly-rated answers, and questions with high reputation, we can embed this need into a virtual query $\mathbf{v}$ comprising metadata. The scoring function of this query is defined as follows:

$$score(\mathbf{d}_t, \mathbf{v}) = \sum_{w \in \mathbf{v}} \frac{1 + \ln(1 + \mathbf{m}_t(w))}{(1-s) - s\frac{len(\mathbf{m}_t)}{avg(len(\mathbf{m}_t))}} \quad (4)$$

where $\mathbf{m}_t$ is the metadata of document $\mathbf{d}_t$.

Let the scoring function between document $\mathbf{d}_t$ and query $\mathbf{q}$ be defined as in Equation (2). The overall scoring function is then defined as the linear combination of the query and virtual-query scoring functions, $score(\mathbf{d}_t, \mathbf{q})$ and $score(\mathbf{d}_t, \mathbf{v})$, as

$$score(\mathbf{d}_t, \mathbf{q}, \mathbf{v}) = \alpha \cdot score(\mathbf{d}_t, \mathbf{q}) + (1-\alpha) \cdot score(\mathbf{d}_t, \mathbf{v}) \quad (5)$$

where $\alpha \in [0, 1]$ determines the relative importance of content and metadata for document $\mathbf{d}_t$. The advantage of this approach is that we are able to determine the metadata score beforehand and update it whenever users update the metadata.

5. EXPERIMENTAL RESULTS

5.1 Experimental Testbed

The major obstacle to evaluating math search is that we do not have a standard benchmark dataset like for other more common IR tasks. Also, it is hard to compare our proposed approach with other systems such as MathFind and Wolfram Function Search because they are either unavailable or inaccessible.

Therefore, we build our own math search dataset by crawling and downloading 31,288 math questions and answers (or math documents for short) from the Math Overflow online question answering system. Each math document can have one or more of the 20 categorical label. We parsed and converted the math documents from HTML into the *Text REtrieval Conference (TREC)*[12] XML format. We also manually generated 30 queries in the TREC format. Each query has a set of relevant and non-relevant documents determined manually.

5.2 Experimental Setup

Each document is identified by a numerical document ID. All math documents are indexed using standard inverted index techniques with stop-word removal based on the English stop-word list provided by *Terrier Information Retrieval Platform* [22]. The total number of index terms is 29,745.

To learn the ranking function, all math documents and queries are processed and converted into $tf \times idf$ [16] vectors. The feature score vectors are calculated based on these documents and queries. The feature score vectors (consisting of more than 1000 vectors) are used to train the Ranking Perceptron and Ranking PA algorithms.

After training with cross validation, we obtained an optimal weight vector $\mathbf{w}$, which is used to determine the scores of all retrieved math documents. Since other math-aware search systems only focus on math feature extraction and apply classical IR techniques, we only compared our approach against standard retrieval methods such as BM25 [11], InL2, and $tf \times idf$, where InL2 stands for "Inverse Document Frequency with Laplace after-effect and normalization 2" [10]. While BM25 and $tf \times idf$ are established IR techniques, the InL2 model was only proposed recently. For the $tf \times idf$ ranking model, we applied the straightforward approach describe in Section 4.2.1.

5.3 Math Feature Extraction Evaluation

In this section, we evaluate the proposed math feature extraction approach by comparing the retrieval precision on the math expressions with and without math feature extraction. The procedure is as follows:

- Extract all math expressions from the Math Overflow dataset to create a math-only dataset, called Math Expression dataset.
- Generate a textual math feature set, where the math expressions are treated as normal text.

[12]http://trec.nist.gov/

Table 1: **Textual Math and Math Feature Properties.**

	Textual Math	Math Feature	N-Gram
# Unique Terms	2959	6060	7145
Avg. DocLen	40.25	13.46	65.55
Avg. PLLen	25.53	8.63	28.01
Avg. QT (ms)	62.20	53.80	78.80

- Generate a math feature set, where math features are extracted as described in Section 3.2.
- Generate an n-gram feature set as described in [18].
- Conduct the experiments on these three feature sets and compare their performances.

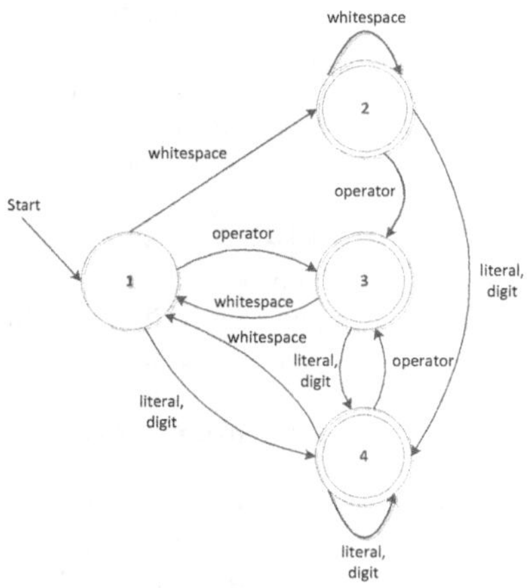

Figure 3: FSM for extracting Textual Math Features.

A finite state machine (FSM) as shown in Figure 3 is used to extract textual math features, where whitespace stands for invisible characters, end-of-stream characters, and delimiters such as space, tab, comma, etc. Operator refers to common math operators such as plus, minus, power, etc. Literal includes characters from the set 'a' to 'z' and 'A' to 'Z'. Digit refers to numbers '0' to '9'. The FSM accepts a math expression as a sequence of characters, on which it extracts math operators, math variables, function names, and constant numbers. Specifically, at state 2, it skips a whitespace. At state 3, it extracts the operator. Upon termination at state 4, it returns a variable, a function name, or a constant number.

The properties of all three feature sets are summarize in Table 1. We counted the number of unique terms and calculated the average *document length* (DocLen) and average *posting list length* (PLLen), where the document length is determined based on the number of index terms in the document (i.e., math expressions). While the number of unique terms represents the size of the *lexicon*, the average posting list length indicates the number of documents associated with a term in the inverted index. These two major factors impact the performance of a search system in terms of *query time* (QT) and accuracy.

Note that the total number of unique terms in the math feature set is greater than that of the textual math feature set. However, the average document length and posting list length of the math feature set are smaller than those of the textual math feature set. This implies that the math feature set is less uniform and therefore more discriminative than the textual math feature set.

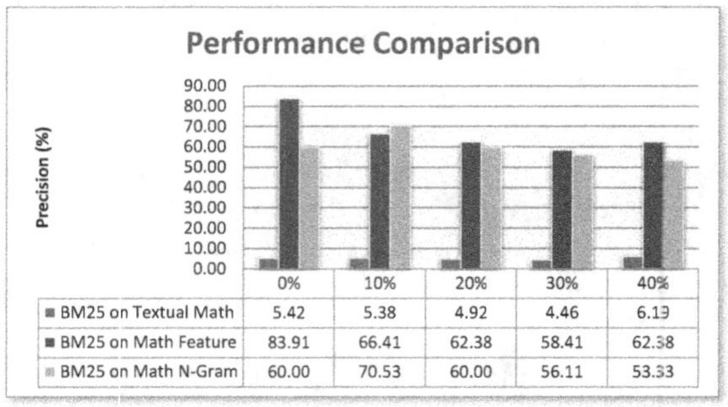

Figure 4: Performance Comparison on the Math Expression Dataset.

To verify the above claim, we carried out a retrieval experiment and compared the IR performance on both feature sets. Figure 4 shows the precision at different recall values on the three feature sets. In this experiment, the popular ranking method BM25 was applied. We see that BM25 does not work well on the textual math dataset. Its max precision on this set is 6% at 40% recall. On the other hand, its precision on the math feature set and n-gram set is significantly larger. Even in the worst case, the math feature set's precision is improved by more than 53%. This result confirms that math feature extraction is essential for an effective math-aware search engine, compared to the simplistic textual math set. Besides, the math feature set gave better precision than n-gram for all levels of recall greater than 10%, which makes it the practical feature choice.

5.4 Ranking Algorithm Evaluation

We trained both the Ranking Perceptron and Ranking PA algorithms on the feature score vectors. We then compared their performance by using the standard cumulative error rate, which is the ratio of mistakes made by the online learning algorithm over the total number of examples observed to-date. In this experiment, the performance of the Ranking PA algorithm and the Ranking Perceptron algorithm [9] is evaluated on the Math Overflow dataset.

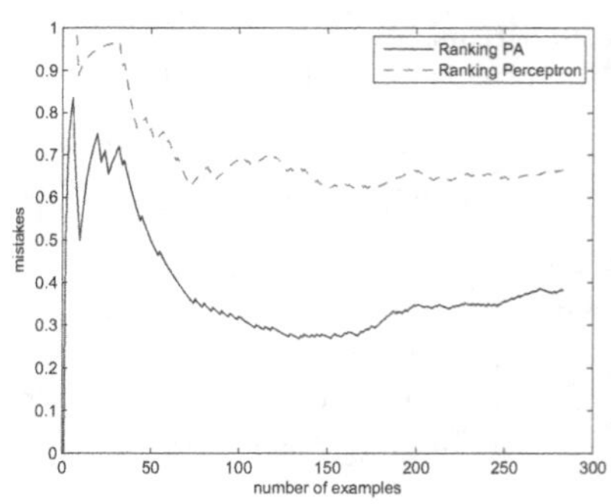

Figure 5: Cumulative Error Rate for Math Overflow Datatset.

Figure 5 shows the cumulative error rates of both the

Table 2: **Metadata Properties (* using Equation (4)).**

	Rate	#Ans	#Views	Ans Rate	Score*
Min	-3	0	14	-4	2.9215
Max	93	121	21606	86	27.2277
Avg	5.9049	1.9146	498.2342	5.8395	14.8662

Ranking Perceptron and Ranking PA algorithms on the Math Overflow dataset. Compared to the Ranking Perceptron algorithm, the proposed Ranking PA algorithm consistently achieved a lower cumulative error rate than the Ranking Perceptron algorithm. This shows that the proposed algorithm is effective in improving the online ranking function learning. Hence, in the ranking process, if the weight of the Ranking PA is utilized, the retrieval precision will be improved compared to that of the Ranking Perceptron algorithm. More experimental results shall confirm this claim in the next section.

5.5 Retrieval Performance Evaluation

For the Ranking PA algorithm, we used cross validation to choose the optimal parameter C. Then, we used the optimal solution/weight to rank retrieved documents based on the scoring function (5) of Section 4.2.3. We also evaluated the Ranking Perceptron algorithm. In this experiment, we used both text and math feature sets, where the text features were extracted using an English tokenizer with stop-word removal and the math features were extracted as described in Section 3.2. Moreover, the metadata of each question is extracted to calculate the score. We determined the optimal trade-off parameter α in Equation (5) to be around 0.958. This means that content largely rules over metadata. The properties of the metadata of all questions are shown in Table 2.

Figure 6 shows the performance comparison between our proposed approach and other methods. The retrieval precision of each method is compared at recall levels of 0%, 10%, and 20%. The experimental results show that the Ranking PA algorithm consistently outperformed other methods. Its precision is at least 9% better than other methods at 0% and 10% recall levels. In the worst case, the improvement is more than 7% at 20% recall. We did not further evaluate higher recall levels because the precision have fallen to way less than 50% to be of practical significance.

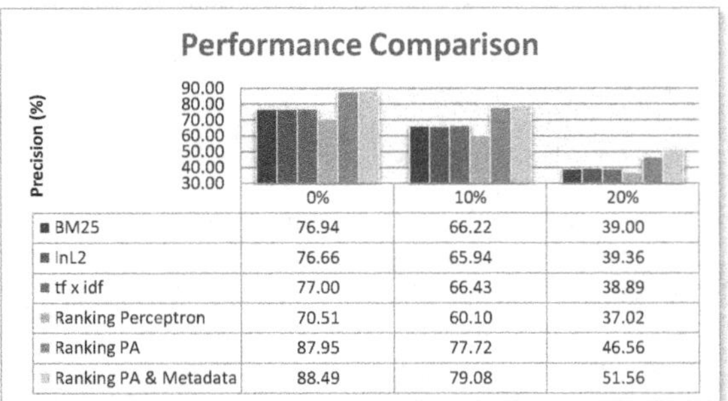

Figure 6: Performance Comparison on the Math Overflow Dataset.

Compared with other methods, the straightforward approach $tf \times idf$ is slightly better. The improvement is nearly 1%. Hence, term weighting method alone is not good enough to rank highly structured data such as math expressions. In this case, the learning-to-rank algorithm should be applied to improve the performance of the search system. In this experiment, the Ranking PA has been shown to be an elegant solution for this problem. If we take into account the metadata, the performance is just marginally improved. This improvement is nearly 5% at 20% recall but declines gradually with decreasing recall levels.

6. CONCLUSION

In this paper, we proposed a new approach to math-aware search engine, which consists of two major steps: feature extraction and learning-to-rank. In feature extraction, we proposed a new method for math expression feature extraction based on the content MathML format. To learn the score function, we formulated and derived an online optimization problem. We then derive a closed-form solution, leading to our Ranking PA algorithm. In addition, we derived the mistake bound of the Ranking PA algorithm.

Moreover, we crawled the Math Overflow question answering system and generated a new dataset for math document retrieval. Our Math Overflow dataset is a big dataset, which has more than 30,000 math documents. It is very useful for math document retrieval evaluation in general and can be downloaded from project.mosuma.net. We evaluated our proposed ranking approach and benchmarked it against other baseline techniques on the Math Overflow dataset. The experimental results show that the proposed approach performs better than the runner-up by more than 9%. Although we evaluated our proposed approach on the math question answering dataset, it is possible to apply it to other kinds of math document retrieval.

Acknowledgements

This research was supported in part by Singapore Ministry of Education's Academic Research Fund Tier 2 grant ARC 9/12 (MOE2011-T2-2-056).

7. REFERENCES

[1] A. Andrea, G. Ferruccio, C. C. Sacerdoti, T. Enrico, and Z. Stefano. A content based mathematical search engine: Whelp. In *TYPES*, pages 17–32, 2004.

[2] R. Ausbrooks, S. Buswell, S. Dalmas, S. Devitt, A. Diaz, R. Hunter, B. Smith, N. Soiffer, R. Sutor, and S. Watt. Mathematical markup language (mathml) version 2.0, 2000.

[3] P. N. Bennett, K. El-Arini, T. Joachims, and K. M. Svore. Sigir '11 workshop report: Enriching information retrieval, 2011.

[4] H. Block. The perceptron: A model for brain functioning. *Rev. Modern Phys.*, 34:123–135, 1962.

[5] S. Buswell, O. Caprotti, D. P. Carlisle, M. C. Dewar, M. Gaetano, and M. Kohlhase. *The Open Math standard version 2.0*. 2004.

[6] Y. Cao, J. Xu, T.-Y. Liu, H. Li, Y. Huang, and H.-W. Hon. Adapting ranking svm to document retrieval. In *Proceedings of the 29th annual international ACM SIGIR conference on Research and development in information retrieval*, SIGIR '06, pages 186–193, New York, NY, USA, 2006. ACM.

[7] K. Crammer, O. Dekel, J. Keshet, S. Shalev-Shwartz, and Y. Singer. Online passive-aggressive algorithms. *Journal of Machine Learning Research*, pages 551–585, 2006.

[8] M. Dredze, K. Crammer, and F. Pereira. Confidence-weighted linear classification. In *ICML '08: Proceedings of the 25th international conference on Machine learning*, pages 264–271, New York, NY, USA, 2008. ACM.

[9] J. Gao, H. Qi, X. Xia, and J.-Y. Nie. Linear discriminant model for information retrieval. In *Proceedings of the 28th annual international ACM SIGIR conference on Research and development in information retrieval*, SIGIR '05, pages 290–297, New York, NY, USA, 2005. ACM.

[10] R. Guillén. Gir with language modeling and dfr using terrier. In *Proceedings of the 9th Cross-language evaluation forum conference on Evaluating systems for multilingual and multimodal information access*, CLEF'08, pages 822–829, Berlin, Heidelberg, 2009. Springer-Verlag.

[11] K. S. Jones. Index term weighting. *Information Storage and Retrieval*, 9(11):619 – 633, 1973.

[12] A. Kohlhase and M. Kohlhase. Reexamining the mkm value proposition: From math web search to math web research. In *Calculemus '07 / MKM '07: Proceedings of the 14th symposium on Towards Mechanized Mathematical Assistants*, pages 313–326, Berlin, Heidelberg, 2007. Springer-Verlag.

[13] M. Kohlhase and I. Sucan. A search engine for mathematical formulae. In J. Calmet, T. Ida, and D. Wang, editors, *AISC '06: Proceedings of 8th International Conference on Artificial Intelligence and Symbolic Computation*, pages 241–253. Springer-Verlag, 2006.

[14] M. Kohlhase and I. A. Sÿucan. A search engine for mathematical formulae. In *Proc. of Artificial Intelligence and Symbolic Computation, number 4120 in LNAI*, pages 241–253. Springer, 2006.

[15] P. Libbrecht and E. Melis. Methods to access and retrieve mathematical content and activemath. In *ICMS '06: In Proceeding of the 2nd International Congress on Mathematical Software*, 2006.

[16] C. D. Manning, P. Raghavan, and H. Schütze. *Introduction to Information Retrieval*. Cambridge University Press, 2008.

[17] B. R. Miller and A. Youssef. Augmenting presentation mathml for search. *MKM '08: Proceedings of the 7th International Conference on Mathematical Knowledge Management*, pages 536–542, 2008.

[18] R. Miner and R. Munavalli. An approach to mathematical search through query formulation and data normalization. In *Calculemus '07 / MKM '07: Proceedings of the 14th symposium on Towards Mechanized Mathematical Assistants*, pages 342–355, Berlin, Heidelberg, 2007. Springer-Verlag.

[19] R. Munavalli and R. Miner. Mathfind: a math-aware search engine. In *SIGIR '06: Proceedings of the 29th annual international ACM SIGIR conference on Research and development in information retrieval*, pages 735–735, New York, NY, USA, 2006. ACM.

[20] T. T. Nguyen, K. Chang, and S. C. Hui. Distribution-aware online classifiers. In T. Walsh, editor, *IJCAI*, pages 1427–1432. IJCAI/AAAI, 2011.

[21] T. T. Nguyen, S. C. Hui, and K. Chang. A lattice-based approach for mathematical search using formal concept analysis. *Expert Systems with Applications*, 2011.

[22] I. Ounis, G. Amati, V. Plachouras, B. He, C. MacDonald, and D. Johnson. Terrier information retrieval platform. *Advances in Information Retrieval*, 3408:517–519, 2005.

[23] A. Singhal. Modern information retrieval: a brief overview. *Bulletin of the IEEE Computer Society Technical Committee on Data Engineering*, 24:2001, 2001.

[24] L. Wang, J. Lin, and D. Metzler. A cascade ranking model for efficient ranked retrieval. In *Proceedings of the 34th international ACM SIGIR conference on Research and development in Information Retrieval*, SIGIR '11, pages 105–114, New York, NY, USA, 2011. ACM.

[25] A. S. Youssef. Roles of math search in mathematics. In J. M. Borwein and W. M. Farmer, editors, *MKM '06: Proceedings of the 5th International Conference on Mathematical Knowledge Management*, pages 2–16, Berlin Heidelberg, 2006. Springer-Verlag.

[26] Y. Yue, T. Finley, F. Radlinski, and T. Joachims. A support vector method for optimizing average precision. In *Proceedings of the 30th annual international ACM SIGIR conference on Research and development in information retrieval*, SIGIR '07, pages 271–278, New York, NY, USA, 2007. ACM.

[27] D. Zhang, R. Mao, H. Li, and J. Mao. How to count thumb-ups and thumb-downs?: an information retrieval approach to user-rating based ranking of items. In *Proceedings of the 34th international ACM SIGIR conference on Research and development in Information Retrieval*, SIGIR '11, pages 1223–1224, New York, NY, USA, 2011. ACM.

APPENDIX

Here, we prove Proposition 1 as follows:

PROOF. We define the Lagrangian of the optimization problem as follows:

$$\begin{aligned}\mathcal{L} = & \frac{1}{2} \parallel \mathbf{w} - \mathbf{w}_t \parallel^2 + C\xi - \lambda\xi \\ & + \tau(1 - \xi - (\mathbf{w} \cdot \phi_t^R - \mathbf{w} \cdot \phi_t^N)) \\ = & \frac{1}{2} \parallel \mathbf{w} - \mathbf{w}_t \parallel^2 + (C - \lambda - \tau)\xi \\ & + \tau(1 - (\mathbf{w} \cdot \phi_t^R - \mathbf{w} \cdot \phi_t^N)\end{aligned} \tag{6}$$

where $\lambda \geq 0$ and $\tau \geq 0$ are the Lagrangian multipliers.

Setting the partial derivatives of $\mathcal{L}$ with respect to the weight $\mathbf{w}$ to zero, we have,

$$\begin{aligned}& 0 = \frac{\partial \mathcal{L}}{\partial \mathbf{w}} = \mathbf{w} - \mathbf{w}_t - \tau(\phi_t^R - \phi_t^N) \\ & \Rightarrow \mathbf{w} = \mathbf{w}_t + \tau(\phi_t^R - \phi_t^N)\end{aligned} \tag{7}$$

Setting the partial derivatives of $\mathcal{L}$ with respect to weight ξ to zero, we have,

$$0 = \frac{\partial \mathcal{L}}{\partial \xi} = (C - \lambda - \tau) \Rightarrow \lambda + \tau = C \tag{8}$$

Substituting (7) and (8) into (6), we have,

$$\mathcal{L} = -\frac{1}{2}\tau^2(\phi_t^R - \phi_t^N)^2 + \tau(1 - (\mathbf{w}_t \cdot \phi_t^R - \mathbf{w}_t \cdot \phi_t^N)) \tag{9}$$

Setting the partial derivatives of $\mathcal{L}$ with respect to weight τ to zero, we have,

$$0 = \frac{\partial \mathcal{L}}{\partial \tau} = -\tau(\phi_t^R - \phi_t^N)^2 + 1 - (\mathbf{w}_t \cdot \phi_t^R - \mathbf{w}_t \cdot \phi_t^N)$$

$$\Rightarrow \tau = \frac{1 - (\mathbf{w}_t \cdot \phi_t^R - \mathbf{w}_t \cdot \phi_t^N)}{(\phi_t^R - \phi_t^N)^2}$$

We have $\lambda + \tau = C$ and $\lambda \geq 0$. Therefore, we can conclude that $0 \leq \tau \leq C$, which concludes the proof. □

Next, we prove Proposition 2 as follows:

PROOF. We have

$$\begin{aligned}&\sum_{t=1}^{T} \| \mathbf{w}_t - \mathbf{u} \|^2 - \| \mathbf{w}_{t+1} - \mathbf{u} \|^2 \\ &= \| \mathbf{w}_1 - \mathbf{u} \|^2 - \| \mathbf{w}_{T+1} - \mathbf{u} \|^2 \\ &= \| \mathbf{u} \|^2 - \| \mathbf{w}_{t+1} - \mathbf{u} \|^2 \leq \| \mathbf{u} \|^2\end{aligned} \tag{10}$$

We also have

$$\begin{aligned}&\| \mathbf{w}_t - \mathbf{u} \|^2 - \| \mathbf{w}_{t+1} - \mathbf{u} \|^2 \\ &= \| \mathbf{w}_t - \mathbf{u} \|^2 - \| \mathbf{w}_t + \tau_t(\phi_t^R - \phi_t^N) - \mathbf{u} \|^2 \\ &= -\tau_t^2(\phi_t^R - \phi_t^N)^2 + 2\tau_t(\mathbf{w}_t - \mathbf{u}) \cdot (\phi_t^R - \phi_t^N) \\ &= \tau_t\Big(2\ell_t - \tau_t(\phi_t^R - \phi_t^N)^2 - 2\ell_t^*\Big)\end{aligned} \tag{11}$$

where $\ell_t = \ell((\phi_t^R, \phi_t^N); \mathbf{w}_t)$.

Based on (10) and (11), we can conclude that

$$\sum_{t=1}^{T} \tau_t\Big(2\ell_t - \tau_t(\phi_t^R - \phi_t^N)^2 - 2\ell_t^*\Big) \leq \| \mathbf{u} \|^2 \tag{12}$$

Recall that $\tau_t(\phi_t^R - \phi_t^N)^2 \leq \ell_t$, substituting it into (12), we have,

$$\sum_{t=1}^{T} \tau_t \ell_t \leq \| \mathbf{u} \|^2 + 2C \sum_{t=1}^{T} \ell_t^* \tag{13}$$

If the Ranking PA algorithm makes a mistake on round t, we have $\ell_t \geq 1$. We also have $\tau_t = \min\Big\{C, \frac{\ell_t}{(\phi_t^R - \phi_t^N)^2}\Big\}$. Therefore, $\tau_t \ell_t \geq \min\Big\{C, \frac{1}{\max_{t=1,T}(\phi_t^R - \phi_t^N)^2}\Big\}$

Let M be the number of mistakes made by the Ranking PA algorithm, we have,

$$\sum_{t=1}^{T} \tau_t \ell_t \geq \min\Big\{C, \frac{1}{\max_{t=1,T}(\phi_t^R - \phi_t^N)^2}\Big\} M \tag{14}$$

Substituting (14) into (13), we have,

$$\min\Big\{C, \frac{1}{\max_{t=1,T}(\phi_t^R - \phi_t^N)^2}\Big\} M \leq \| \mathbf{u} \|^2 + 2C \sum_{t=1}^{T} \ell_t^*$$

which concludes the proof. □

Contextualization using Hyperlinks and Internal Hierarchical Structure of Wikipedia Documents

Muhammad Ali Norozi
Department of Computer and Information Science
Norwegian University of Science and Technology
Trondheim, Norway
mnorozi@idi.ntnu.no

Paavo Arvola
School of Information Sciences
University of Tampere
Tampere, Finland
paavo.arvola@uta.fi

Arjen P. de Vries
Interactive Information Access
Centrum Wiskunde & Informatica
Amsterdam, The Netherlands
arjen@cwi.nl

ABSTRACT

Context surrounding hyperlinked semi-structured documents, externally in the form of citations and internally in the form of hierarchical structure, contains a wealth of useful but implicit evidence about a document's relevance. These rich sources of information should be exploited as contextual evidence. This paper proposes various methods of accumulating evidence from the context, and measures the effect of *contextual* evidence on retrieval effectiveness for document and focused retrieval of hyperlinked semi-structured documents.

We propose a re-weighting model to *contextualize* (a) evidence from citations in a query-independent and query-dependent fashion (based on Markovian random walks) and (b) evidence accumulated from the internal tree structure of documents. The *in-links* and *out-links* of a node in the citation graph are used as external context, while the internal document structure provides internal, within-document context. We hypothesize that documents in a *good* context (having strong contextual evidence) should be *good* candidates to be relevant to the posed query, and vice versa.

We tested several variants of contextualization and verified notable improvements in comparison with the baseline system and gold standards in the retrieval of full documents and focused elements.

Categories and Subject Descriptors

H.3.3 [**Information Storage and Retrieval**]: Information Search and Retrieval—*retrieval models*; H.3.4 [**Information Storage and Retrieval**]: System and Software—*performance evaluation*; H.2.1 [**Database Management**]: Logical Design—*data models*; E.1 [**Data**]: Data structures—*trees*; E.5 [**Data**]: Files—*organization/structure*

Keywords

XML retrieval, Semi-structured data, Structural indices, Schema agnostic search, Contextualization, Re-weighting, Random walks

1. INTRODUCTION

Focused or element retrieval addresses the possiblity to utilize the hierarchical structure of documents, and hence return the most specific (and exhaustive) text units, rather than returning only full documents. One problem with this approach is that the retrieval units have varying length in textual content, as the size of elements varies with the level in the hierarchy (see Figure 3); the leaf element or descandent elements have less textual evidences than their ancestors. This scant textual evidence makes matching those small text units, such as paragraphs, hard. As a consequence, although they are what the users (might) require, they are considered less relevant by the focused retrieval systems, only because they have too few textual content, hence too little evidence to be ranked higher for the posed user query. Fortunately, this scant textual evidence can be alleviated significantly by a method called *Contextualization* [16].

Contextualization is a mechanism to estimate the relevance of a given structural text or document unit with information obtainable from - besides the unit itself - the surrounding structural text or document units, i.e., from the context of the unit [16]. With contextualization, we assume that context of a retrievable unit gives hints about the relevance of the retrievable unit (can be document or element retrieval). Hence, it is expected in contextualization that context of a retrievable unit gives hints about the relevance of the retrievable unit.

In this study, we incorporate the idea of random walk together with contextualization on citation structure of documents and internal hierarchical structure of XML document. The approach is inspired by the random surfer model of [5, 10] over XML documents and relational databases respectively, as well as the contextualization model for XML retrieval developed by Arvola et al. [4]. The hypothesis is that contextualization together with random surfer (or walk) model will improve search effectiveness over considering retrieval units in isolation.

Until recently, the importance of contextualization (based on hierarchical relationships of element) has been studied in several settings [1, 2, 4, 19, 22, 23, 25]. Even in a schema-agnostic environment, it has been found that by contextualizing the scores of the surrounding components, such as, parents, ancestors or siblings in the scoring function of the element itself, the overall precision and recall of the focused retrieval system improves [4]. In document retrieval, the hyperlink structure of documents (i.e., inlinks and outlinks) provides both a wider *context* and a wider *semantics* to the content. This far-reaching context and semantics should possibly be used to boost or reduce the documents retrieval scores. Without using the structural information (citations graph), the search system would simply ignore the documents containing a wealth of implicit information in its context as irrelevant to the query topic in question. Contextualization based on the bibliographic structure of scientific documents has been shown a promising direction in [22].

The models proposed in this research paper are experimentally evaluated using the semantically annotated Wikipedia XML Collection from INEX [26], both at the granularity of a document (document retrieval) and at the XML element level (focused retrieval). We have applied several variants of contextualization, and the results are in-line with the proposed theory about the effectiveness of contextualization. The results obtained, on both document (article level) and focused retrieval (paragraph level) tasks, exhibit clear improvements over a strong and competitive baseline system – itself based on data fusion over all INEX 2009 submitted runs (see Section 3), and already achieving a performance higher than any INEX 2009 official run.

Summarizing, the contributions of this study include:

- Contextualization of the citation structure of hyperlinked documents, with random walks as a theoretically sound foundation (Section 2.1).
- Contextualization of the hierarchical structure of documents, using the same random walk model (Section 2.2).
- Developing a competitive focused retrieval system baseline based on data fusion and constructing a test setting for evaluating the retrieval of small textual units, i.e., paragraphs (Section 3).
- Experimental validation (Section 4) of the ideas proposed, using citation (Section 2.1), hierarchical (Section 2.2) and hybrid contextualization (Section 2.3) within the random walk framework.
- Evaluation of the use of citation and hierarchical information on the large semantically annotated Wikipedia XML corpora [3, 8, 11, 13, 26] (Section 4.1).

Section 5 concludes and highlights future work.

2. CONTEXTUALIZATION MODELS

Contextualization is a method of exploring the features in the context of a retrievable unit [4]. In document retrieval, in turn, this means combining the evidences from a document and its context using different but plausible combination functions. The context of a document (i.e., *contextualizing* documents) consists of other documents which point-to or are pointed-to by the document in question (*contextualized* document, P2), see Figure 1. The context of an element in focused retrieval and in this study consists of all the ancestors of the element in question. We use random walks to induce a similarity structure over the documents based on their bibliographic relationships, and over the elements based on the containment and reverse-containment relationships (element, sub-element and vice versa). Hence, these relationships affect the weight each contextualizing document or element has in contextualization. A contextualization model is a re-scoring scheme, where the basic score, usually obtained from a fulltext retrieval model, of a contextualized document or element is re-enforced by the weighted scores of the contextualizing documents or elements.

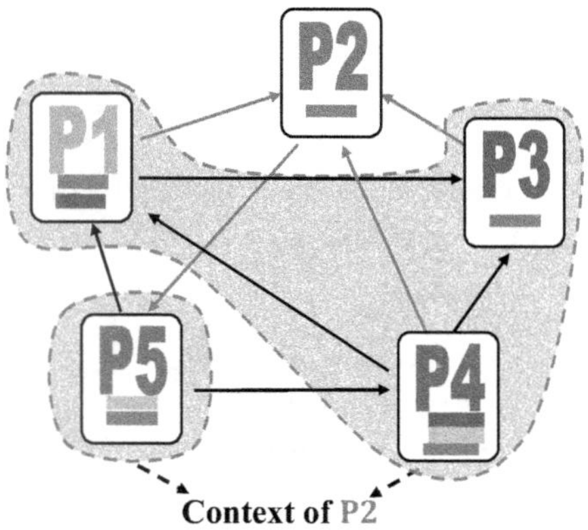

Figure 1: Citation structure of 5 documents and context of P2

The premise is that *good context* (identified by random walk and contextualization) provides evidence that a document in document retrieval and an element in focused retrieval is a good candidate for a posed query and therefore documents and elements should be contextualized by their bibliographically similar documents and hierarchically similar elements respectively. Good context is an *evidence* that should be used to deduce that a document or an element is a good candidate for the posed query.

In Section 2.1 we will explain the idea of contextualization based on citation structure, in Section 2.2 we elaborate on contextualization based on the internal hierarchical structure of XML document (see XML document in Figure 2) and in Section 2.3 we present a contextualization model based on first the citation contextualization and then hierarchical contextualization.

2.1 Citation Contextualization

There are enough empirical and intuitive support for the premise that a good document in citation graph is good because it contains references to alot of good documents, and more importantly, a good document is good if it is contained in a good document as a reference (recursive definition) [13, 17, 20]. But here, the question is, can the evidences, lying loosely in the context surrounding the contextualized document, be intelligently materialized? Fortunately, the answer is yes, later in the section we will show a formalism that can be used to materialize and then utilize the contextual evidences for improving retrieval effectiveness.

Previous work [1, 4] presents a contextualization model where a binary vector represents the relevant context (a part of) a document. Here, we extend that work to use probabilistic infomation derived from a random walk over the citation structure. A random walk on the citation structure of the documents independent or dependent of a query topic will populate the contextualization vector with the probablisties that indicate *authority* of a document in the network of citations.

An alternative way to conceive the intuition behind the random walk model here is, to consider that authority and relevance information flows in the bibliographic structure of documents in the same fashion as that of the HITS model [17]. The authority flows in the bibliographic structure of documents until an equilibirium is established which specifies that a document is authoritative if it is referenced by authoritative documents [20].

The bibliographic network of documents (for example, Figure 1) can be represented in matrix notation by adjacency matrix $\mathbf{A}$ such that:

$$\mathbf{A_{ij}} = \begin{cases} 1 & \text{if there is a link from page } P_i \text{ to } P_j \\ \varepsilon & \text{if } \mathbf{A_{ij}} = 0 \text{ and there is a link from page } P_j \text{ to } P_i, \\ & 0 < \varepsilon \ll 1 \\ 0 & \text{otherwise} \end{cases}$$

The reverse edge ε, very small value, is added to ensure a unique solution to the system of linear Equations 1. For Figure 1 the corresponding adjacency matrix $\mathbf{A}$ can be:

$$\mathbf{A} = \begin{pmatrix} 0 & 1 & 1 & \varepsilon & \varepsilon \\ \varepsilon & 0 & \varepsilon & \varepsilon & 1 \\ \varepsilon & 1 & 0 & \varepsilon & 0 \\ 1 & 1 & 1 & 0 & \varepsilon \\ 1 & \varepsilon & 0 & 1 & 0 \end{pmatrix}$$

The random walk probabilities are then obtained by iteratively solving the following system of linear equations[1]:

$$g^k = \mathbf{A^T} \, \mathbf{A} g^{k-1} \tag{1}$$

Here g^k is the proposed contextualization vector, and k is the number of iterations. The matrix $\mathbf{A^T} \, \mathbf{A}$ constructed this way would lead to a *unique* solution to the system of linear Equations 1 [17].

2.1.1 Query independent and query-dependent walks

A *query independent random walk* is conducted on the entire bibliographic structure of the documents, irrespective of any query. This walk primarily captures the authoritativeness of documents in the collection. The adjacency matrix $\mathbf{A}$ becomes quite huge for the citation structure of Wikipedia collection ($2,668,160 \times 2,668,160$, see Section 4.1). The contextualization vector g^k depicts the scores of each document in the massive citation graph for the entire collection iteratively calculated using Equation 1.

A *query dependent random walk* is conducted on the rather smaller subset of the citation graph, corresponding to a specific query topic in question. Adjacency matrix $\mathbf{A}$ is in this case considerably smaller then the query-independent walk. The contextualization vector g^k depicts the stationary distribution of random walk (scores of documents) specific to a query. The focused subgraph can be constructed from the output of per topic output of fusion run, which can be used to iteratively produce set of documents that are most likely considered to be relevant to the query topic. The Base-set S_q (which is used to form $\mathbf{A}$) can be obtained by growing query results (Root-set R_q); which includes any document that pointed to by a document in Root-set R_q, and any document that points to a document in R_q, i.e., inlinking and outlinking documents from root-set R_q respectively.

2.1.2 Combination function

We now give a tailored re-ranking function CR, which allows the contextualizing scores to be added to the basic scores. The function can be formally defined as follows:

$$\begin{aligned} CR(x, f, C_x, g^k) &= (1-f) \cdot BS(x) + \\ & f \cdot \frac{\sum_{y \in C_x} BS(y) \cdot g^k(y)}{\sum_{y \in C_x} g^k(y)} \end{aligned} \tag{2}$$

where

- $BS(x)$ is the basic score of contextualized document x (text-based score, e.g., $tf \cdot idf$). Documents occurring more than one times in the resultset, will get the basic score as the mean of the basic scores of all the occurences (which we observed in experiments after testing with the other options, like sum, best and worst basic scores).
- f is a parameter which determines the weight of the context in the overall scoring
- C_x is the context surrounding the contextualizing document x, i.e., $C_x \subseteq (inlinks(x) \cup outlinks(x))$, $\subseteq$, because we are only considering the set of inlinks and / or outlinks of x in the retrieved documents, not all the inlinks and outlinks of x.
- $g^k(y)$ is the contextualization vector which gives the authority weight of y, the contextualizing documents of x.

We can have several variants of the combination function of Equation 2, as discussed in forthcoming Sections below.

2.1.3 Context as the authority

Do documents cited a lot, or documents containing more in-links or authoritative documents form a good context? Let's assume that the context function C_x in Equation 2 only contextualize based on the in-links. In this case the argument would be: $C_x \subseteq inlinks(x)$. The set C_x only contains the in-links of the contextualizing document. The inlinks of a document x corresponds to its column in the adjacency matrix $\mathbf{A}$. For example, the inlinks of document $P2$ in the Figure 1 correspond to the non-zero cells of column 2 in the adjacency matrix $\mathbf{A}$.

Section 4 presents experiments with two variants of contextualization:

1. *first* based on random walk conducted on query independent adjacency matrix $\mathbf{A}$ (the entire bibliographic graph, see Section 2.1.1) and
2. *second* based on query dependent random walk on adjacency matrix $\mathbf{A}$ (the base-set).

We have experimented with both of the approaches, see Section 4. In addition to the two variants, a third variant combines the query independent and query dependent random walk into a combination function:

$$\begin{aligned} CR(x, f, C_x, g^k_{qi}, g^k_{qd}) = (1-f) \cdot BS(x) + \\ f \cdot \alpha \cdot \frac{\sum_{y \in C_x} BS(y) \cdot g^k_{qi}(y)}{\sum_{y \in C_x} g^k_{qi}(y)} + \\ f \cdot (1-\alpha) \cdot \frac{\sum_{y \in C_x} BS(y) \cdot g^k_{qd}(y)}{\sum_{y \in C_x} g^k_{qd}(y)} \end{aligned} \tag{3}$$

[1] Finding the dominant Eigenvector of the system of linear equations, corresponding to the dominant eigenvalue, which is 1 in this case [20].

```
<article xmlns:xlink="http://www.w3.org/1999/xlink/">
 <header><title>Wiki markup</title><id>42</id>
   <revision>
    <timestamp>2006-10-05 14:22</timestamp>
   </revision>
   <categories>
    <category>Markup languages</category>
   </categories>
 </header>
 <body>
  <section><st>Introduction</st>
   <p><b>Wiki markup</b> is used in
    <link xlink:href="../Wi/Wikipedia.xml"
    xlink:type="simple">Wikipedia</link>.</p>
  </section>
  <section><st>Language Components</st>
   <list>
    <entry>tables</entry>
    <entry>lists</entry>
    <entry>and a lot more</entry>
   </list>
  </section>
  <section><st>See also</st>
   <weblink xlink:href="htt://www.wikipedia.org">
   www.wikipedia.org</weblink>
  </section>
 </body>
</article>
```

Figure 2: XML document

where

- $g^k_{qi}(y)$ is the contextualization vector which gives the authority weight of the contextualizing documents of x based on query independent walk.
- $g^k_{qd}(y)$ is the contextualization vector which gives the authority weight of the contextualizing documents of x based on query dependent walk.
- α is the parameter moderating the share of contextualization from query independent and query dependent.

2.1.4 Context for a better content description

The existence of inlinks for contextualized document is certainly a positive indication, but outlinks also happen to occur in the contextualized document's context. By linking to another document, the author implicitly includes the outlinking document in its document context. Inlinks together with outlinks provide a much wider context for the contextualized document. Combination functions, Equations 2 and 3 remain the same, only the interpretation of the contextualization function changes now to: $C_x \subseteq (inlinks(x) \cup outlinks(x))$. The set C_x now contains the inlinks and outlinks of the contextualizing document, containing the query term. The outlinks of a document x correspond to its row in the adjacency matrix $\mathbf{A}$. For example, the outlinks of document $P2$ in the Figure 1 corresponds to the non-zero cells of row 2 in the adjacency matrix $\mathbf{A}$.

2.2 Hierarchical Contextualization

Hierarchical contextualization model has been studied before in different settings in XML retrieval [1, 4, 16, 19, 25, 27]. In hierarchical contextualization we tend to utilize the intrinsic structure within the XML document. The represen-

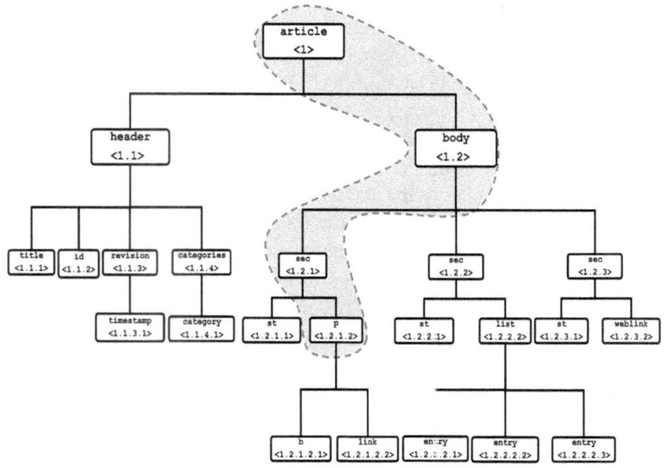

Figure 3: XML Graph of Figure 2 with context of element ⟨1.2.1.2⟩ (dewey encoding)

tation of documents in XML aims to follow the established structure of documents, i.e., an academic book is typically composed of ⟨**chapters**⟩, ⟨**sections**⟩, ⟨**subsections**⟩ etc., tags. This organization of document gives an intuitive starting point for manipulating text passages at the established hierarchy levels of text documents.

With contextualization on hierarchical structure of documents we aim to rank higher an element in a good context than an identical element in a not so good context within the document. In Figure 2 the ⟨**article**⟩, ⟨**section**⟩ and ⟨**subsection**⟩ form different levels of context for a paragraph ⟨p⟩. Hence the paragraph can be viewed in context of ⟨**subsection**⟩, ⟨**section**⟩ or the ⟨**article**⟩. While the root element ⟨**article**⟩ possesses no context.

In hierarchical contextualization the weight of the element is modified by the basic weights of its contextualizing elements. Each element in the context of the contextualized element, should possess an impact factor. An higher impact factor shows the importance of the contextualizing element and vice versa. The role and relation of contextualizing element are operationalized by giving the element a contextualizing weight. A contextualization vector is defined to capture the impact factor of each contextualizing element, and this contextualization vector is represented by a g function, in a similar way as it is defined in citation contextualization.

The important research question here is: which types of element context help to improve retrieval effectiveness? More specifically which types of context serves our purpose, which is, to boost the ranking of contextualized element in good context and vice versa. Sigurbjörnsson et al. (2004) [27] argued that by taking the root level only (i.e., ⟨**article**⟩ element in the example case) as a context improves the overall retrieval. Camps (2007) [25] later also found that the use of article as a contextual information clearly helps to improve retrieval effectiveness. Arvola et al. (2005) [1] uses a binary value to include or exclude different element types in hierarchy from the context. Ogilvie and Callan (2005) [23] utilizes the children of the element to smooth up the parents (smooth up tree). The smoothing up method in their hierarchical modeling is quite similar to contextualization. In it they contextualize the scores of individual keywords instead of whole elements. In the vertical contextualization approach again by Arvola et al. (2011) [4] the impact or strength of the contextualization is adjusted with a help of different parameters. Instead of considering only a specific element as a context or using the children to smooth up the parent element or using a parameter to find the impact of each of the units in the context, we propose a generalized mechanism based on the Markovian Random walk principle.

The tree-structure of the XML document is considered as a graph. Myriad of random surfers traverse the XML graphs. In particular, at any time step a random surfer is found at an element and either (a) makes a next move to the sub-element of the existing element by traversing the containment edge, or (b) makes a move to the parent-element of the existing element, or (c) jumps randomly to another element in the XML graph. As the time goes on, the expected percentage of surfer at each node converges to a limit the dominant eigenvector of the XML graph. This limit provides the impact or strength of each element in the context of the contextualized element in the form of g function. We consider all the ancestors of the contextualized element in contextualization; where the contextualization vector g identifies the importance of each of the unit of context (see Equation 4).

Contextualization model formulated in this way, is independent of the basic weighting scheme of the elements and it could be applied on the top of any query language and retrieval systems. We have applied the contextualization model on the top of the baseline system which is the result of fusion from the INEX 2009 offically submitted runs by the participants (see Section 3.2).

In the experiments we evaluated the retrieval effectiveness at different granularity levels. We mainly tested, retrieval effectiveness at article level ($\langle$`article`$\rangle$ element), and at paragraph level ($\langle$`p`$\rangle$ element); a brief intuition is explained in Section 3.3. The most improvements in retrieval are observed when $\langle$`p`$\rangle$ elements are retrieved. The primary reason is because paragraph has the most context (hierarchical depth) and most specific element in context (see Figure 3).

2.2.1 Combination Function

The re-ranking function based on the random walk principle described earlier can be formally defined as follows:

$$CR(x, f, C_x, g^k) = BS(x) + f \cdot \frac{\sum_{y \in C_x} BS(y) \cdot g^k(y)}{\sum_{y \in C_x} g^k(y)} \quad (4)$$

where

- $BS(x)$ is the basic score of contextualized element x (text-based score, e.g., $tf \cdot ief$)
- f is a parameter which determines the weight of the context in the overall scoring.
- C_x is the context surrounding the contextualizing element x, i.e., $C_x \subseteq ancestors(x)$, $\subseteq$, because only the context containing the query terms are considered.
- $g^k(y)$ is the generalized contextualization vector based on random walk, which gives the authority weight of y, the contextualizing elements (ancestors) of x in XML graph.

2.3 Hybrid Contextualization

Hybrid or twofold contextualization is when the externally accumulated evidences re-enforce the evidence accumulated from within the hyperlinked and hierarchical XML documents. In this approach we first select the best documents based on the citation contextualization (Section 2.1) and later retrieve the most relevant and most specific context from the XML hierarchy using the hierarchical contextualization. The re-ranking functions are the same as before, first we use the re-ranking function, Equation 2 and later we use Equation 4 for better contextualization.

Contextualization with the hybrid approach provided the most benefit in the retrieval effectiveness, based on our empirical studies (see Section 4).

3. TEST BED AND BASELINE SYSTEM

In order to study the effect of contextualization on focused and element levels, we need a suitable baseline and a test bed with adequate evaluation methods. Next, in Section 3.1 we introduce the test bed, then in Section 3.2 a baseline system based on data fusion is introduced and examined briefly in Section 3.4 with the evaluation procedure of Section 3.3.

3.1 Test collection

The outcome of the present study relates to the Initiative of Evaluation for XML retrieval INEX [11] and the test bed provided by it. INEX is a forum for the evaluation of XML and focused retrieval offering a test collection with topics and corresponding relevance assessments, as well as various evaluation metrics. Aside evaluating element retrieval, passage retrieval evaluation is also supported in INEX. In this study we use the data provided by the 2009 INEX ad-hoc track. The track has 68 topics with character-wise relevance assessments, and the test collection, English Wikipedia, covers around 2.66 million XML marked articles and 50.7 Gigabytes of XML marked data [26].

This large, semantically marked-up, Wikipedia collection has been used in INEX since 2009 and is still in use. The reason for using the INEX 2009 test topics (instead of 2010) is the larger variety of elements in the participants' results. This is mainly because of the existence of the thorough task, where elements are retrieved regardless of overlap, i.e., in the results a section and its sub elements, paragraphs, may be retrieved within the same results [11]. The large variety of elements is a necessity for a data fusion of results, which our baseline system is based on.

3.2 Baseline System

Contextualization is independent of basic scoring method, thus we are able to implement the baseline system quite freely. In this study, we use a fusion run as our baseline system for which 159 element runs out of total 173 runs from the INEX 2009 participants was used. The remaining 13 were not element runs, i.e., they contained ranges of fragments or file-offset-lengths (FOL) as retrievable units and were omitted from the fusion. In addition, in order to avoid noise, we made a decision to remove 61 runs having an extensive number of non-existing elements. Thus, a total of 98 runs from the participants of all tasks (best-in-context, relevant-in-context, focused, fetch and browse) of the ad-hoc track were used in fusion.

The runs were fused using an acknowledged method called the reciprocal rank. The method has been found effective in document retrieval [6]. In it, every element (item) in each of the result list (candidate run) is given a score based on its ranking and the fused score for an element is the sum of their ranked scores per topic. A fusion score for an element e is calculated as follows.

$$RRScore(e,q) = \sum_{r \in R} \frac{1}{k + rank(r,e,q)} \quad (5)$$

where

- R is the set of runs (rankings)
- and $rank(r,e,q)$ returns the rank of element e as a result of query q in run r.
- If e is not in the ranking, $rank(r,e,q)$ is not defined and the outcome of $\frac{1}{k+rank(r,e,q)}$ is 0.
- The parameter k is for tuning.

Before addressing the effectiveness of such approach as a baseline system, we introduce shortly our evaluation approach, which aims at measuring performance of very focused elements only.

3.3 Evaluation methodology

One of the key issues in semi-structured retrieval is the handling of overlap in results. A partial solution has been introduced not to accept structurally overlapping elements in the results. Still non-overlapping elements of various granularities are accepted, so that retrieval of e.g., a whole section instead of its smaller descendants separately leads to different result list than returning the descendants as individual elements. Measuring these kinds of result lists has led to numerous, typically quite complex and unintuitive metrics [9, 15, 24]. The aim of these metrics is not only to measure the matching of the text content, but also the selection of granularity level at various situations. Unfortunately, retrieving elements of various granularity levels has an uncontrolled effect on the evaluation results and has led to bizarreness in the true evaluation results, and favouring systems retrieving large elements over focused ones [4]. Thus, as a criticism, deciding the right granularity level is based on the laboratory environment (especially metrics) rather than on true user needs.

Elements low in a hierarchy are focused answers to a query and possess more context and thus supposedly benefit more on contextualization. In order to study the effect of contextualization especially on those small and focused elements, and to exclude the effect of element granularity level selection on evaluation results, we use granulation [4], where specific types of elements are pre- selected in the collection. The search is focused on those elements only. For that purpose also the underlying recall base needs to be pruned so that only those selected elements are involved (see Fig 4(a)). Obviously, a semi-structured collection can be granulated in numerous ways. In this study, we focus on two types of granulations: full document granulation and a granulation containing paragraphs (⟨p⟩-elements) only. To put it short, the former is for document retrieval and the latter is paragraph retrieval. The paragraph level elements are very frequent in the collection (on average 274 relevant paragraphs per topic) and a list containing such elements may provide satisfactory and focused answers. It is worth mentioning that, Crouch et al. [7] had similar setting and used the paragraph as the basic index node. One obvious use case for paragraph retrieval is snippet retrieval.

In terms of structural query language NEXI (strict interpretation) [28, 29], we use the following queries *//article* (., *about*("*query−expr*")) and *//p* (., *about*("*query−expr*")) for full document and focused runs respectively. The "*query−expr*" stands for the title field bag-of-words query of a topic.

In the full document approach only root elements (i.e. articles) are considered in the result lists and in the focused run, only elements having the name (⟨p⟩). The corresponding runs are made by pruning the fusion results by basically taking out everything else but the lines corresponding to the structural conditions (i.e., ⟨`article`⟩ and ⟨p⟩). In other words, the paragraph list is a sub list of the fusion run. Corresponding recall base is made for paragraph list. The full document recall base is provided by the initiative. The fusion run contains every element retrieved by the participants. The pool was constructed from the paragraph granulation by analyzing the FOLs in the recall base against the submitted paragraphs. Out of the full set of runs used, 46 runs did contain paragraphs. So the paragraph result list is a fusion of those runs.

3.4 Thoughts of competitiveness of the baseline system

Next, we aim to give an insight of the baseline system we want to improve using contextualization in next section. In order to avoid over tuning of the baseline system, we refer only to results, which are achieved using basic values only and leave the further analysis of the data fusion of element results for later studies. Thus, our baseline system is the bare format of reciprocal rank, i.e., $k = 0$. In other words, an element at the first rank of any run yields basically the score of 1 and the second yields 0.5, third 0.33 and so on.

At article level granulation, i.e., full document retrieval, the fusion run outperforms all reported official full document runs of INEX having the MAP as high as 0.4141. The best official INEX full document run yielded at the level of 0.3578 (UamsTAbi100 by the University of Amsterdam) [11]. The granulation of the run is made so that only results rows with */article*[1] are considered. Similarly, at paragraph level any result row ending with */p*[*n*] is considered (n is positive integer). We did the same granulation for every 46 INEX run and compared the results with ours. Early precision was used in comparison at paragraph level for two reasons. First, the granulation results in a subset of the result, so the result list may be short. Second, early precision is in line with the nature of focused retrieval.

The runs of the Technical University of Queensland (qtau) yielded the best early precision figures, especially a run called ANTbigramsThorough. Figure 4(b) represents the recall base sizes per topic at paragraph level and the number of retrieved paragraphs of the ANTbigramsThorough run. In 21 topics the number of retrieved paragraphs of the run outnumbers the number of relevant paragraphs, so a fair comparison can be made using $r-precision$ score for those topics. Accordingly, the $r-precision$ score for the run ANTbigramsThorough is 0.2779 and for the baseline fusion 0.3479. Based on these figures, we can say that the fusion approach is competitive. Next, we apply contextualization for the fusion and see if there still is room for improvements.

4. EXPERIMENTAL EVALUATION

We now experimentally evaluate the propositions presented in this paper. First, we lay down the experimental settings. Later, we present some empirical evidence that our ranking models return intuitive results both on document and focused retrieval. We then evaluate the retrieval effectiveness of our models againts the competitive baseline systems

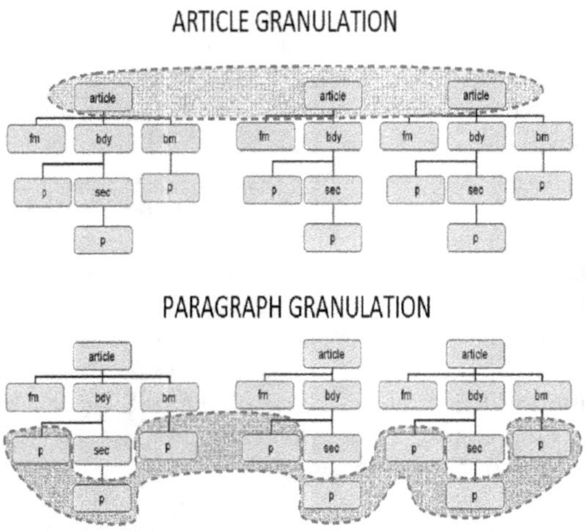

(a) Granulating the recall-base at article and paragraph levels.

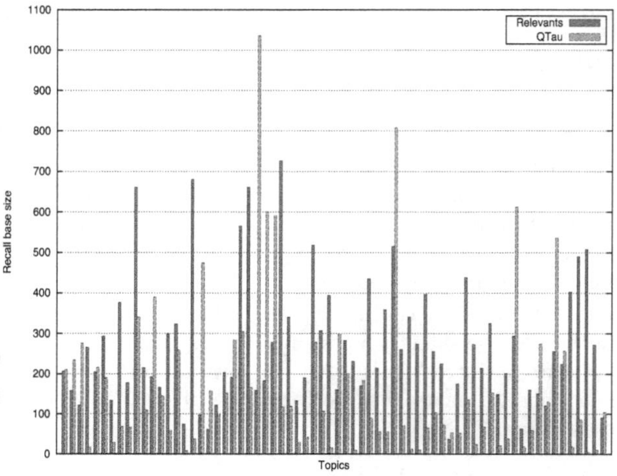

(b) Recall base sizes per topic

Figure 4: Granulating overall recall-base (a) and recall-base sizes for QTau baseline (b).

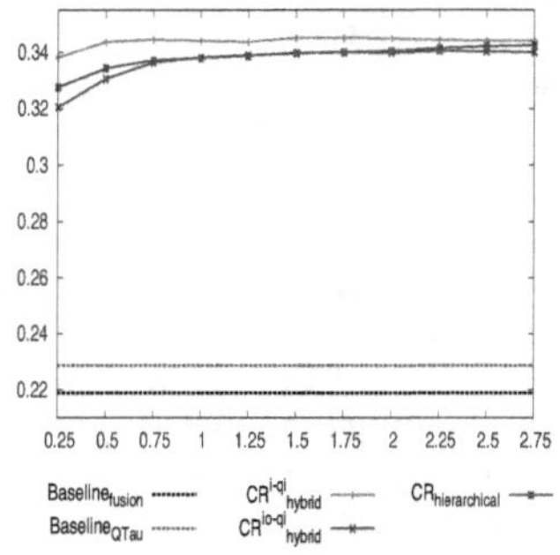

(a) MAP for different f

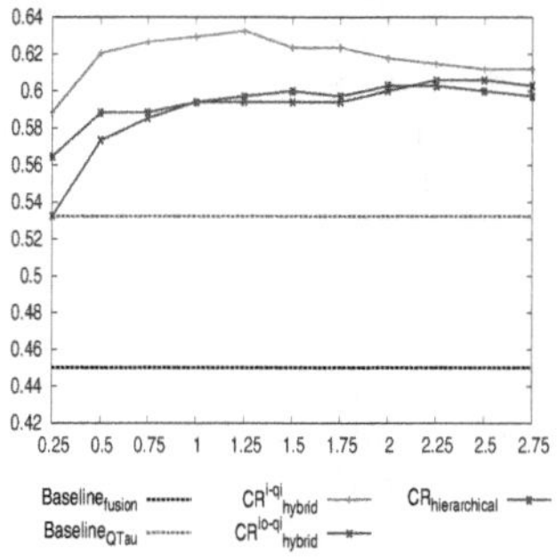

(b) P@5

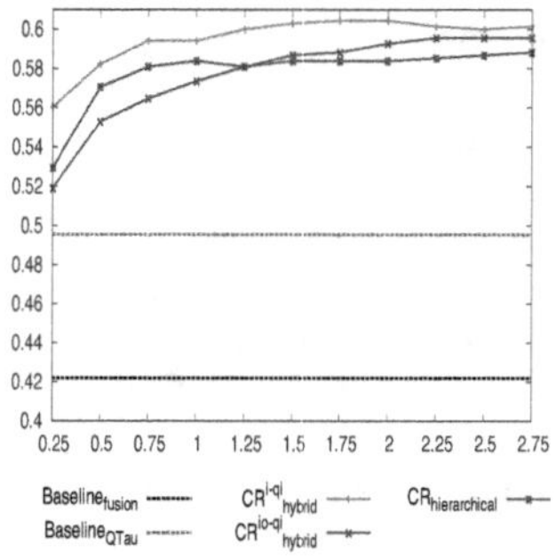

(c) P@10

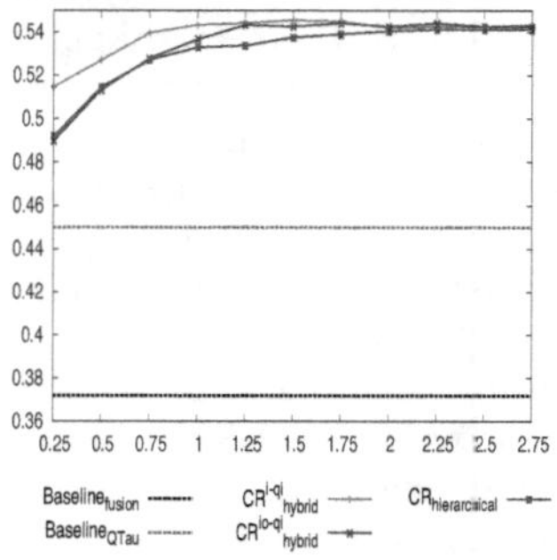

(d) P@20

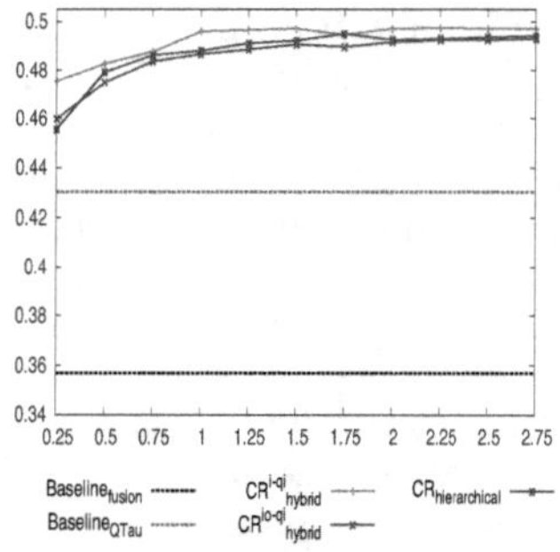

(e) P@30

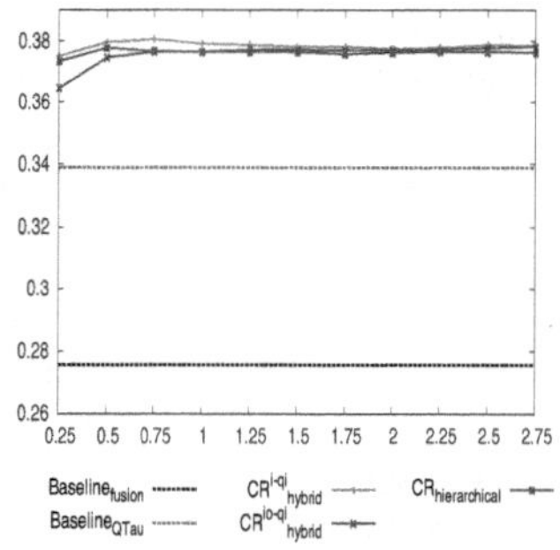

(f) P@100

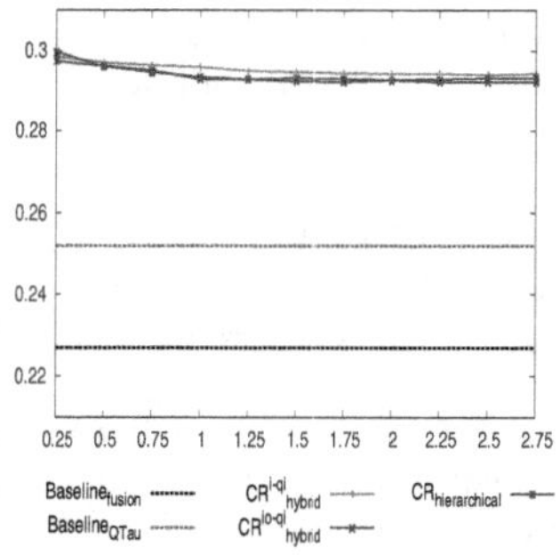

(g) P@200

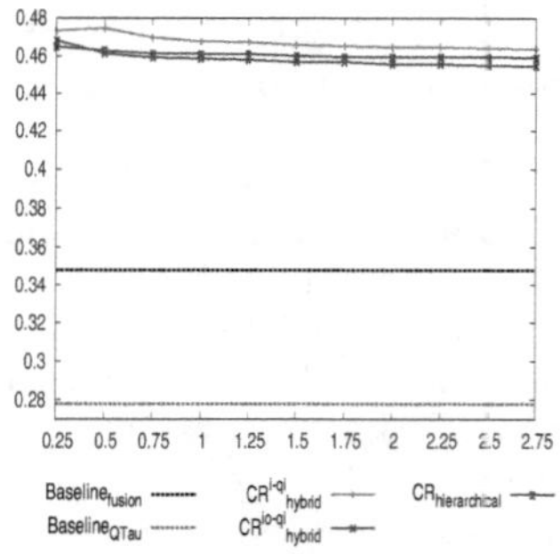

(h) rPrecision

Figure 5: Trends for different measures at different context force f for focused retrieval task (paragraph level)

that were introduced in Section 3. Finally, we relate the empirical evidence with the theoretical claims.

4.1 Experimental Settings

The proposed approaches are evaluated using the Wikipedia test collection, described in Section 3.1. The choice of experimenting with the Wikipedia collection is for the following reasons. First, XML documents in Wikipedia 2009 collection has a very deep internal hierarchical structure, containing overall about 32 thousand different tags [26]. Second, Wikipedia has quite a huge number of inter-document references (in the form of citations). Finally because Wikipedia collection is quite big and extensively assessed test bed used over the years at INEX [3, 11] and at other evaluation forums.

The 2.66 million semantically marked XML documents contain a total of around 135 million citations (links), which were extracted by parsing each of the documents in the collection. We use the resultant gigantic citations graph for experimentation with the citations and hybrid contextualization (Sections 2.1 and 2.3). The computation of the contextualization vector g^k from Equation 1 for the large Wikipedia collection was quite extensive, however this process is performed offline. The linear system of Equations 1 is usually solved iteratively, using the well known *Power method* [18]. The convergence of power method is accelerated using a technique called *Extrapolation* [2]. At the query

[2]Extrapolation is a technique for constructing new data points (dominant eigenvector) outside a discrete set of known data points (known values during each iteration of

time, we combine the iteratively computed random walk scores and the basic scores based on the proposed methods (Equation 3).

In the forth coming sections we will present empirical evidence that the contextualization vector g^k together with the citation contextualization model, produces intuitive overall retrieval effectiveness (see Tables 2 and 1).

For hierarchical contextualization we index the collection and use the dewey encoding to capture the internal tree structure of the XML documents (as shown in the example, Figure 3). This way each element in the document possess a unique index within the document, and together with document's unique id, this becomes unique for the entire collection. The tree structure of XML documents are converted into a matrix, and random walk is performed on this matrix, as it is described in Section 2.1. In this case also the contextualization vector g^k from Equation 4 is computed offline for each and every XML documents in Wikipedia collection. This suggests that computing g^k vector is feasible for a reasonably large XML document collections. Again, at the query time, the scores from g^k vector and basic scores are combined to produce an overall ranking score, using Equation 4.

Focused Retrieval									
Method	f	MAP	P5	P10	P20	P30	P100	P200	rPrec
Baseline (Fusion)	–	.2189	.4500	.4221	.3721	.3569	.2757	.2269	.3479
Baseline ($QTau$)	–	.2286	.5324	.4956	.4500	.4304	.3388	.2522	.2779
$CR_{hierarchical}$	.25-2.75	**.3425**$^{\blacktriangle *}$	**.6029**$^{\blacktriangle *}$	**.5882**$^{\blacktriangle *}$	**.5412**$^{\blacktriangle *}$	**.4951**$^{\blacktriangle *}$	**.3778**$^{\blacktriangle *}$	**.2996**$^{\blacktriangle *}$	**.4649** $^{\blacktriangle *}$
$CR^{i-qi}_{citations}$	.025-1.75	.2423$^{\triangle +}$	.4912$^{\blacktriangle}$	.4500$^{\triangle}$	.3897$^{\triangle}$	.3755$^{\triangle}$	.2915$^{\triangle}$	.2465$^{\triangle}$	**.3811**$^{\triangle *}$
$CR^{io-qi}_{citations}$	.025-1.75	.2207	.4588$^{\triangle}$	.4206	.3750	.3578	.2765	.2288	**.3548**$^{\triangle *}$
CR^{i-qi}_{hybrid}	.25-2.75	**.3451**$^{\blacktriangle *}$	**.6324**$^{\blacktriangle *}$	**.6044**$^{\blacktriangle *}$	**.5456**$^{\blacktriangle *}$	**.4971**$^{\blacktriangle *}$	**.3806**$^{\blacktriangle *}$	**.2986**$^{\blacktriangle *}$	**.4746**$^{\blacktriangle *}$
CR^{io-qi}_{hybrid}	.25-2.75	**.3404**$^{\blacktriangle *}$	**.6059**$^{\blacktriangle *}$	**.5956**$^{\blacktriangle *}$	**.5441**$^{\blacktriangle *}$	**.4931**$^{\blacktriangle +}$	**.3782**$^{\blacktriangle *}$	**.2974**$^{\blacktriangle *}$	**.4615**$^{\blacktriangle *}$

Table 1: Ret. performance for focused retrieval $^{\blacktriangle *}$ = stat. significant than both the Fusion and QTau baselines runs at p < 0.01 (1-tailed t-test), and $^{\triangle +}$ = stat. significant at p < 0.05 respectively.

Document Retrieval								
Method	f	MAP	P5	P10	P20	P30	P100	P200
Baseline (Fusion)	–	.4141	.6618	.5853	.5029	.4554	.2949	.2126
Baseline ($UAmst$)	–	.3578	.6500	.5397	.4515	.3961	.2635	.1898
$CR_{hierarchical}$	.25-2.75	.4142*	.6618*	.5853*	.5029*	.4559*	.2949*	.2126*
$CR^{i-qi}_{citations}$	.025-1.75	.4186*	**.6706**$^{\triangle *}$	.5853*	**.5118**$^{\triangle *}$	**.4618**$^{\triangle *}$	.2965*	.2153*
$CR^{io-qi}_{citations}$	.025-1.75	.4159*	**.6706**$^{\triangle *}$	.5853*	.5051*	.4583*	.2951*	.2129*
CR^{i-qi}_{hybrid}	.25-2.75	**.4194**$^{\triangle *}$	**.6706**$^{\triangle *}$	.5853*	**.5125**$^{\triangle *}$	**.4608**$^{\triangle *}$	.2965*	.2148*
CR^{io-qi}_{hybrid}	.25-2.75	.4139	.6676*	.5779*	.5044*	.4549*	.2944*	.2126*

Table 2: Retrieval performance for document retrieval (article level).

4.2 Results

We have tested five different retrieval methods based on the propositions (Sections 2.1, 2.2, 2.3) and three different baseline systems (Section 3).

- Baseline systems
  - Fusion run, $Baseline_{fusion}$.
  - University of Queensland run, which performed best on paragraph level, $Baseline_{QTau}$.
  - University of Amsterdam run, which performed best on article level, $Baseline_{UAmst}$.
- Hierarchical contextualization, $CR_{hierarchical}$
- Citation contextualization
  - Query independent - inlinks context, $CR^{i-qi}_{citations}$
  - Query independent - inlinks and outlinks context, $CR^{io-qi}_{citations}$
- Hybrid Contextualization
  - Query independent - inlinks context, CR^{i-qi}_{hybrid}
  - Query independent - inlinks and outlinks context, CR^{io-qi}_{hybrid}

power method) and using the properties of Markov chain; $\lambda_1 = 1$ (dominant eigenvalue) [14, 21].

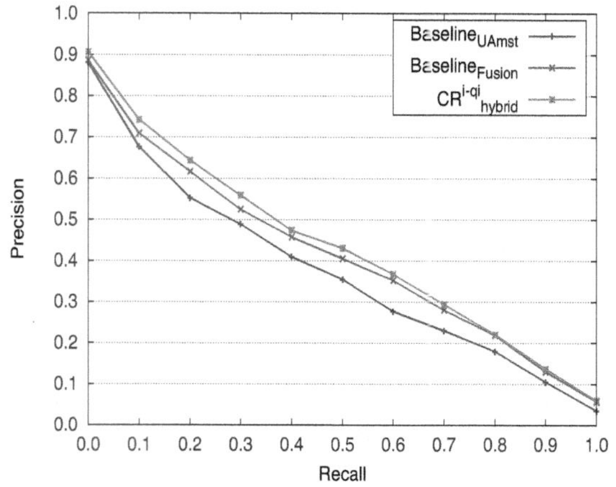

Figure 6: Precision - recall performance for document retrieval (article)

We did not report results on citation contextualization based on query-dependent random walk, as the preliminary experimental analysis showed not enough or desirable retrieval gains, apparently because of the definition of citations or links in the Wikipedia collection. Hence, we omit query-dependent citation contextualization from evaluations, and therefore investigate the usefulness of this approach in our future studies.

As defined earlier, contextualization has two general dimensions - the magnitude of contextualization (contextualization force) and the impact of each contextualizing element. The impact of each contextualizing factor is identified automatically with random walk principle, in contrast to the earlier studies [1, 4]. While, the contextualization force has to be parameterized. For each proposed contextualization model, we tuned the contextualization force and report the values leading to best overall performance. In our parameterization process we found: (i) the optimal values of contextualization force f in citation contextualization (from Equation 2) lies in: ($f \in \{0.025, 0.055, 0.10, 0.25, 0.50, 0.75, 1.00, 1.25, 1.50, 1.75\}$); (ii) and in hierarchical contextualization (from Equation 4) $f \in \{0.25, 0.50, 0.75, 1.00, 1.25, 1.50, 1.75, 2.00, 2.25, 2.50, 2.75\}$.

These optimal values for f are obtained by using cross-validation technique[3]. We did 68-fold cross-validation (or complete cross-validation in our case) - by randomly partitioning the collection into 68 training and test samples based on the number of assessed topics. Of the 68 samples, a single sample is retained as the validation set for testing, and remaining 67 samples are used as training set. The cross-validation process is repeated 68 times (for each fold), with each of 68 samples used exactly only once as validation set.

[3]Cross-validation is a technique for assessing how the results of a statistical analysis will generalize to an independent data set. It is mainly used in settings where the goal is prediction, and one wants to estimate how accurately a predictive model will perform in practice.

These 68 independent or unseen samples are then combined to produce a single or a set of estimations for the parameter f.

Figures 5 illustrate the behaviour of the methods as we change the optimal values of f parameter, from Equations 2, 3 and 4, on precision-oriented measures. As can be visually observed, the proposed methods out-perform notably all the baseline systems, Fusion, QTau and UAmst (Figure 6).

Table 1 and 2 show the overview of the retrieval performance of our approaches against the baselines for focused (paragraph level) and document (article level) retrieval tasks. All the proposed contextualization models improves the performance over the baselines. The improvements are statistically significant (1-tailed t-test at $p < 0.01$ and $p < 0.05$) on $rPrecision$, $P@5$, $P@10$, $P@20$, $P@30$ and so on (Figures 5). The improvements overall are surprisingly good on both focused and document retrieval.

The best overall results among the proposed methods are obtained with CR^{i-qi}_{hybrid} and $CR_{hierarchical}$, in terms of highest mean average precision, $r-precision$ and precision at N values. Documents with many and important inlinks have a higher probability of being relevant [12, 13] and hence in contextualization their role is considerable and fruitful, which is also verified in our experiments. We conclude that, context from citations, hierarchical structure of documents and their hybrid indeed improve the retrieval effectiveness, and the improvements are in-line with the theoretical anticipations.

4.3 Discussion

Contextualization is a re-ranking model utlizing the context of the relevant retrievable unit for improving the overall retrieval. We studied context from three different but related perspectives; (i) external perspective (based on citations) (ii) internal perspective (hierarchical structure) and (iii) hybrid perspective (external and internal perspective). The common thread among the three ways of contextualization is the use of the graph structure originated from the documents citation structure externally and hierarchical structure internally. We hypothesized that context gathered from graph structure of documents (from within and outside), influence the retrieval effectiveness. The experiments validated the hypothesis that utilizing the context actually enhances the retrieval of information on article and paragraph granularity levels. The results obtained in this study are inline with the earlier work on use of hyperlinked and hierarchical tree (graph) structure of documents [5, 10, 12, 17] and the role of contextualization [1, 4, 19, 22, 23, 25]. However, none of these works exploits evidence accumulated from the link structure of documents with random walk as a contextual evidence.

The authority score 'in isolation' can identify the importance of each node in the graph formed from either citations or hierarchical structure of documents. The usefulness of these authority scores in isolation (not in context) has been studied well over the years [5, 10, 17]. The novelty of this study is the utilization these useful sources of information not 'in isolation' but 'in contextualization'. That means, to use the importance score of each document or element as an impact factor for identifying how essential is the role of this document or element in context. A retrievable unit (document or element) with strong context must be boosted higher in ranking than the retrievable unit with less strong context. Extensive experimentation validated this view point.

5. CONCLUSIONS AND FURTHER WORK

We have presented an in-depth study into the use of context from citations and hierarchical structure information, in order to improve retrieval performance on document and focused retrieval tasks. To the best of our knowledge, this is the first study that takes context into account by mixing two perspectives (a) the context from the citation structure of documents, and (b) the context from the hierarchical structure of semi-structured documents. The approaches presented are generic and can be applied to different test collections and baseline systems. Evidence is collected in a systematic way, from the surrounding context of both the document itself and the element to be ranked, in document and focused retrieval respectively. In this paper, XML documents are used as a sample case of semi-structured documents. These documents have an hierarchical structure, which is often represented in a form of tree. However, the approaches could also be applicable for other generic structured (or semi-structured) test collections (e.g., Linked Data, RDF, etc.), where the structure may be represented as a general graph (with cycles). The proposed methods are particularly suited for collections that carry more types of evidence than just textual information. The importance of each single unit in the context is identified by a Markovian random walk. Most of the proposed methods are tested and found to be significantly better than the baseline system, which had an overall performance that was already better than any run submitted to INEX 2009. The proposed methods both boost the rankings of the documents in good context and degrade the rankings of documents in not so good context.

The effectiveness of random walks to materialize the context has been evaluated in five different settings. We have found that the context from in- and out-links as well as a document's hierarchical structure can indeed improve retrieval results. Given that the citation structure of Wikipedia collection does not necessarily form a sound bibliographic semantics, because, (a) two documents can cite each other at the same time (A cites B and B cites A), without temporal ordering, (b) the link structure in Wikipedia is a (possibly weak) indicator of relevance [12] in isolation. Yet, when applying contextualization using weights obtained with the random walk principle, this information is found to be significantly plausible, both theoretically and empirically. Bibliographical structure of scientific documents could lead to even better results, as their citation structure characterizes stronger semantics, and possibly a stronger indicator of relevance. Nevertheless, we consider our experiments on the Wikipedia test collection sufficiently promising to consider different types of evidence in future work. Specifically, we would like to investigate the effects of context derived from tweet mentions that may help improve retrieval from video collections. There are also several other venues for future work, for instance, experimenting with different granularity levels than just article and paragraph levels – identify the importance of each granularity level(s) and possibly automatically boost 'important' ones more than other 'not so important' granularity levels. The sequential document ordering, often referred to as the document order, where text passages follow each other in sequence, one after the other, could also be considered as a second dimenion of the structural context within the random walk paradigm. Finally, graph-based methods for results list fusion may be naturally included in our current approach, where we applied random walks over result lists obtained from a separate fusion phase.

6. ACKNOWLEDGEMENTS

This study was supported by Academy of Finland under grant #140315.

7. REFERENCES

[1] P. Arvola, M. Junkkari, and J. Kekäläinen. Generalized Contextualization Method for XML Information Retrieval. In *Proc. of the 14th ACM International Conference on Information and Knowledge Management (CIKM)*, pages 20–27. ACM, 2005.

[2] P. Arvola, J. Kekäläinen, and M. Junkkari. The Effect of Contextualization at Different Granularity Levels in Content-oriented XML Retrieval. In *Proc. of the 17th ACM Conference on Information and Knowledge Management (CIKM)*, pages 1491–1492. ACM, 2008.

[3] P. Arvola, S. Geva, J. Kamps, R. Schenkel, A. Trotman, and J. Vainio. Overview of the INEX 2010 ad-hoc track. *Comparative Evaluation of Focused Retrieval*, pages 1–32, 2011.

[4] P. Arvola, J. Kekäläinen, and M. Junkkari. Contextualization Models for XML Retrieval. *Info. Processing & Management*, pages 1–15, 2011.

[5] A. Balmin, V. Hristidis, and Y. Papakonstantinou. ObjectRank: Authority-based Keyword Search in Databases. In *Proc. of the 13th International Conference on Very Large Data Bases-Volume 30*, pages 564–575. VLDB Endowment, 2004.

[6] G. Cormack, C. Clarke, and S. Buettcher. Reciprocal rank fusion outperforms condorcet and individual rank learning methods. In *Proc. of the 32nd international ACM SIGIR conference on Research and development in information retrieval*, pages 758–759. ACM, 2009.

[7] C. Crouch, D. Crouch, N. Kamat, V. Malik, and A. Mone. Dynamic element retrieval in the Wikipedia collection. *Focused Access to XML Documents*, pages 70–79, 2008.

[8] S. Geva, J. Kamps, R. Schenkel, and A. Trotman. INEX 2010 Workshop Pre-proceedings. 2010.

[9] N. Gövert, N. Fuhr, M. Lalmas, and G. Kazai. Evaluating the effectiveness of content-oriented XML retrieval methods. *Information Retrieval*, 9(6): 699–722, 2006.

[10] L. Guo, F. Shao, C. Botev, and J. Shanmugasundaram. XRANK: Ranked Keyword Search over XML Documents. In *Proc. of the 2003 ACM SIGMOD International Conference on Management of Data*, pages 16–27. ACM, 2003.

[11] W. Huang, S. Geva, and A. Trotman. Overview of the INEX 2009 link the wiki track. *Focused Retrieval and Evaluation*, pages 312–323, 2010.

[12] J. Kamps and M. Koolen. The Importance of Link evidence in Wikipedia. *Advances in Information Retrieval*, pages 270–282, 2008.

[13] J. Kamps and M. Koolen. Is Wikipedia Link Structure Different? In *Proc. of the Second ACM International Conference on Web Search and Data Mining*, pages 232–241. ACM, 2009.

[14] Kamvar, S.D. and Haveliwala, T.H. and Manning, C.D. and Golub, G.H. Extrapolation methods for accelerating PageRank computations. *In Proc. of the 12th Int. Conf. on WWW*, pages 261–270, 2003.

[15] G. Kazai and M. Lalmas. eXtended Cumulated Gain Measures for the Evaluation of Content-oriented XML Retrieval. *ACM Transactions on Information Systems (TOIS)*, 24(4):503–542, 2006.

[16] J. Kekäläinen, P. Arvola, and M. Junkkari. Contextualization. *Encyclopedia of Database Systems*, pages 174–178, 2009.

[17] J. Kleinberg. Authoritative Sources in a Hyperlinked Environment. *Journal of the ACM (JACM)*, 46(5): 604–632, 1999.

[18] D. Lay. *Linear Algebra and its Applications.* Addison-Wesley Reading, Mass, 1994.

[19] Y. Mass and M. Mandelbrod. Component Ranking and Automatic Query Refinement for XML Retrieval. *Advances in XML IR*, pages 1–18, 2005.

[20] M. Norozi. IR Models and Relevancy Ranking. Master's thesis, University of Oslo, 2008.

[21] M. Norozi. Faster ranking using extrapolation techniques. *International Journal of Computer Vision and Image Processing (IJCVIP)*, 1(3):35–52, 2011.

[22] M. Norozi, A. de Vries, and P. Arvola. Contextualization from the Bibliographic Structure. In *Proc. of the ECIR 2012 Workshop on Task-Based and Aggregated Search (TBAS2012)*, page 9, 2012.

[23] P. Ogilvie and J. Callan. Hierarchical Language Models for XML Component Retrieval. *Advances in XML IR*, pages 269–285, 2005.

[24] B. Piwowarski and G. Dupret. Evaluation in (XML) information retrieval: expected precision-recall with user modelling (EPRUM). In *Proc. of the 29th Annual International ACM SIGIR Conference on Research and Development in IR*, pages 260–267. ACM, 2006.

[25] G. Ramirez Camps. *Structural Features in XML Retrieval.* PhD thesis, SIKS, the Dutch Research School for Information and Knowledge Systems., 2007.

[26] Schenkel, R. and Suchanek, F.M. and Kasneci, G. YAWN: A Semantically Annotated Wikipedia XML Corpus. *Proc. of GIFachtagung für Datenbanksysteme in Business Technologie und Web BTW2007*, 103 (Btw):277–291, 2007.

[27] B. Sigurbjörnsson, J. Kamps, and M. De Rijke. An Element-based Approach to XML Retrieval. In *INEX 2003 Workshop Proc.*, pages 19–26, 2004.

[28] A. Trotman and M. Lalmas. Strict and vague interpretation of XML-retrieval queries. In *Proc. of the 29th Annual International ACM SIGIR Conference on Research and Development in IR*, pages 709–710. ACM, 2006.

[29] A. Trotman and B. Sigurbjörnsson. Narrowed Extended Xpath I (NEXI). *Advances in XML IR*, pages 533–549, 2005.

Understanding Book Search Behavior on the Web

Jin Young Kim
Dept. of Computer Science
University of Massachusetts
Amherst, MA 01003
jykim@cs.umass.edu

Henry Feild
Dept. of Computer Science
University of Massachusetts
Amherst, MA 01003
hfeild@cs.umass.edu

Marc-Allen Cartright
Dept. of Computer Science
University of Massachusetts
Amherst, MA 01003
irmarc@cs.umass.edu

ABSTRACT

With the increased availability of e-books and digitized book collections, more users are searching the web for information about books. There are many online digital libraries containing book, author and subject data, which are accessed via internal search services as well as external web sites, such as Google. Although this is a common yet complex information-seeking behavior involving multiple search systems with different characteristics, little is known about how users find information in this scenario.

In this work, we analyze web-based book search behavior using three months of logs from the Open Library, a globally accessible digital library. Our study encompasses the user behavior on web search engines and the digital library, unlike previous work which focused on institution-level digital libraries. Among our findings are (1) query characteristics and session-level behaviors are drastically different between internal and external searchers; (2) the field usage is different based on the modes of interaction—keyword search, advanced search interface and faceted filtering; (3) users go through with more iterations of faceted filtering than query reformulation. To facilitate future research on book search, we also create a book search test collection based on the log data. We then perform an evaluation of several retrieval methods, finding that field-based retrieval models have advantages over document-based models.

Categories and Subject Descriptors

H.3.3 [**Information Storage and Retrieval**]: Information Search and Retrieval—*search process*

General Terms

Algorithms, Design, Experimentation, Human Factors

Keywords

Query log analysis, user modeling, book search

CIKM'12, October 29–November 2, 2012, Maui, HI, USA.

1. INTRODUCTION

Books are the most widely used archival form of knowledge and entertainment, and searching over them and related information like authors, subjects, and publishers is a popular activity on the web. There are many online digital libraries that collect, organize, and offer information about books and if a user wants to access this content, they can do it in several ways. One way is to visit the digital library website directly and browse or search using the internal search interface. Alternatively, provided the digital library's content can be crawled, then web search engines (WSEs) are another avenue for finding book-related content. We consider web-based book search that pertains to digital libraries that are searchable by WSEs.

There are several characteristics that make book search on the web particularly interesting from an information retrieval perspective. First, users can use a domain-specific search engine (i.e., the internal digital library search service), a generic WSE, or a combination of both to find relevant information. Second, there is rich metadata associated with books, authors, and other book-related entities, which have implications for the design of a ranking algorithm that uses such structural evidence. Third, the existence of metadata also allows the implementation of interaction methods such as field operators, advanced search interfaces, and faceted filtering for book search, all of which are offered by most digital libraries.

Given these characteristics, there are many complexities regarding users' book search behavior on the web. While previous work [4, 12] investigated user behavior within a digital library or within a web search engine, we know of no work that studies the behavior of users searching for books across both WSEs and digital libraries. Scale is another aspect by which previous analyses of book search behavior are limited, in that most work studied institution-level digital libraries with limited user bases.

To better understand the complex task of web-based book search, we present a large-scale analysis of book search behavior across WSEs and the Open Library,[1] a freely available digital library that serves users from across the world. The log consists of 18 million records spanning 8 million user sessions and the last three months of 2010.

In our analysis, we focus on internal and external search behavior separately. Our decision is motivated by the extreme differences in behavior we found between them, as well as the number of variables unique to each, such as the search interface. We also study the use of various field-based inter-

[1] http://www.openlibrary.org

action methods within the library website, finding that the field usage is different based on the modes of interaction—keyword search, advanced search, and faceted filtering.

Based on these findings, we provide recommendations that can significantly influence the design of a book search system from both the interface and ranking perspectives. While we focus on book search behavior in this work, our findings are generalizable to most web catalogs that rely on WSEs as a primary entry point, and provide various interaction methods based on rich metadata.

To evaluate retrieval models for book search in a realistic setting, we then create a test collection based on a year-long sample of Open Library log data. We perform a comprehensive evaluation of relevant retrieval methods, and find that the effective use of field structure is critical for retrieval performance. We plan to release the data set for future research on book search.

The rest of this paper is organized as follows. We provide an overview of related work in the next section. Then we introduce the search environment and data set methods we used in Section 3. We then present the results of our analysis in Section 4. Finally, the process of test collection generation and the results of retrieval experiments are presented in Section 5.

2. RELATED WORK

There are three primary areas of related work: user behavior analysis on digital libraries, search behavior analysis on the web and other domains, and book retrieval development.

Analyzing user behavior over digital libraries is an important problem in the library and information science community. Blummer et al. [2] provide a detailed survey. Jones et al. [5] analyzed a digital library log, focusing on the use of operators and search options in queries. They also examined patterns in query construction and refinement. Kules et al. [9] performed a task-based evaluation of faceted search interfaces in a library catalog using eye-tracking devices, finding that faceted search plays a major role in exploratory search and affects searcher tactics, including the reduction of query reformulations.

More recently, Niu et al. [12] investigated people's faceted search behavior over two library catalogs, concluding that users incorporate faceted filtering as part of their information-seeking process, and that the use of facets depend on how facets are ordered, and whether faceted filtering is allowed before entering a query. Guo et al. [4] proposed a Markovian user interaction model, which we adapt to model user session behavior.

Domain-specific search behavior has been studied in the context of searching for people on the web [16], biomedical information seeking [10], blog search [11], and so on. Weerkamp et al. [16] analyzed a large-scale log of people search on the web, providing detailed statistics at the level of queries, sessions and users. Lin et al. [10] examined the relationship between initial search results and the overall utility of interaction, finding that similarity-based browsing tool helps in the case of poor initial retrieval results. Mishne et al. [11] focused on the analysis of blog search behavior, finding that blog searches typically include named entities of interests.

The INEX Book Track workshop[2] has held a number of book retrieval tasks in recent years, with the most relevant to this work being the 2010 Best Books to Reference task [6] and the 2011 Social Search for Best Books task [7]. The Social Search task dataset includes 2.8 million book metadata records from Amazon Books, augmented with user generated information from LibraryThing.[3] Search topics were extracted from LibraryThing forums in which users ask for recommendations. In contrast, our test collection aims to evaluate retrieval models using actual user queries and judgments generated from click data.

3. ENVIRONMENT AND DATA SET

In this section, we describe the search environment and the data set we used. We first describe the Open Library—the environment in which we observe user behavior—followed by several definitions used throughout this paper. We then describe the data set collected from the Open Library users, how we prepared the data, and the limitations of our analysis.

3.1 Open Library

The Open Library (OL) is a community-curated, open access digital library. An Internet Archive[4] initiative, the goal of the OL is to have one web page per book ever published along with the corresponding subject and author data.

The OL provides several features for searching and exploring the stored book records. An example book search result page is shown in Figure 1. At the top right of every page is a search box with an advanced search interface that appears on page at the click of a link

The search box, labeled (1) in the figure, supports several search operators, most notably quotes and field operators.[5] While WSEs also provide several operators including field operators, the OL supports field operators based on book metadata (e.g., *title:*, *author:*), unlike WSEs, which provide domain-independent operators (e.g., *site:*, *inurl:*).

The advanced search interface, labeled (2), includes: title, author, ISBN, subject, place, person, and publisher. The interface also provides an option to perform a full-text search. This search box and associated advanced search interface only searches over books, although users can also access author names linked in the results list. As with the search operators, the OL's advanced search interface features are domain specific, unlike the advanced options of general WSEs.

At the top of the search page is a set of sorting options, labeled (3): sort by relevance (the default), the number of editions a book has, and publication date (ascending and descending order). When a book search is conducted, a set of filters are presented on the right side of the screen, labeled (4) in the figure.

Filters available in the OL include: e-books versus non-e-books, authors, subjects, people, places, times, first published dates, publishers, and languages. These narrow the results by filtering them based on the selected criteria. For example, clicking the "History" facet under the subjects filter will restrict the results list to only books that fall into the "History" category. Note that filters can only be applied

[2]`https://inex.mmci.uni-saarland.de/tracks/books/`
[3]`http://www.librarything.com/`
[4]`http://www.archive.org`
[5]`http://openlibrary.org/search/howto`

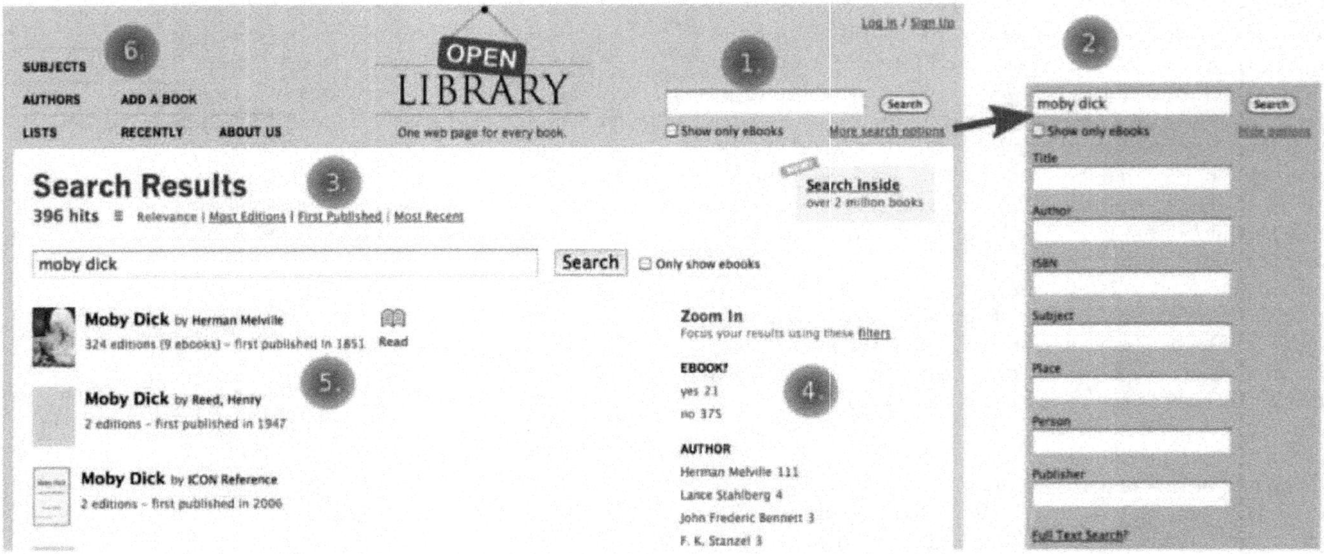

Figure 1: An example book search. The red circles are annotations highlight, in order, (1) the book search box, (2) the advanced book search interface (displays when "More search options" is clicked), (3) the available sorting options, (4) the filters available for book search, (5) the links available for each result, and (6) additional verticals.

after an initial book search by clicking one of the links on the right side of the results page.

A book search retrieves a list of *work* pages, where a work is a collection of book editions. Each work in the results (an example is labeled (5) in the figure) includes a link to that work's page and a link to the author. If there is an electronic version of the book available, a link titled "Read" appears to the left of the result. A work page, e.g., "Moby Dick", consists of a description of the book and a list of the known editions. If any of the editions are available in full text, as e-books, or via library loan, the appropriate links are displayed.

On the top left of every page is a set of verticals, labeled (6): subjects, authors, and lists. Subjects contain sets of books with shared heading information and are broken into several categories: subjects, places, people, and times. Authors are self explanatory. Lists are user-generated and contain a set of books.

3.2 Definitions

We will use the following definitions throughout this work:

Object types: books, works, authors, and subjects. The OL differentiates between a *work* and a *book*. A *book* represents a specific edition. A *work* refers to all of the editions of a given book. The OL's book search actually searches over works. The page for a given work shows a listing of all the editions for that work. A *subject*, as described in Section 3.1, is a collection of works that share common heading information. In addition, *authors* can be searched and are linked with both books and works.

SERP-clicks. A *SERP-click*, short for search engine results page click, signifies that a user arrived at the current page via a link on a search result page, either from an internal or external search engine.

User. We consider the combination of an IP address and the access date (e.g., *111.111.111.111/December 15, 2010*) to identify a user. Due to the instability of IP address assignments, we do not group actions from a single IP address over more than a 24 hour period.

Session. A session contains all actions from a user such that the duration between any two adjacent events is no greater than 30 minutes.

External vs. Internal session. An *external* session is a session in which the first event is an external query. Any session that is not an external session is internal.

Query. We use the term *query* to refer to a set of user inputs to search for information. A query issued to a WSE is a *keyword query* that can optionally include search operators. A query in the OL can be any combination of three elements described in Section 3.1: a *keyword query*, which refers to the text a user entered into the search box including search operators; a *structured query*, which refers to user input to one or more advanced search fields; and lastly, a set of *filters*.

External vs. Internal query. A search that is initiated from outside of the OL domain, e.g., from the Google search engine, is called an *external query*. A search that was initiated from an OL search interface is called an *internal search*.

Search operator. A search operator is any portion of a keyword query that invokes special instructions to the retrieval system. For example, using quotes around phrases or specifying an advanced search feature like *title:moby dick*.

3.3 Data Set & Preparation

The analysis presented here is based on the Apache server logs from the OL web servers from October through December 2010. The log contains roughly 18 million records. The log format[6] includes, among other information, the URL re-

[6]The full Apache log format is a slight modification of the NCSA extended/combined log format, the description of which can be found here: `http://httpd.apache.org/docs/2.2/mod/mod_log_config.html`

quested, the time of a request, and the referrer URL (when available).

In preparing the data for analysis, we converted the chronologically ordered Apache logs into a more readable user session format. User identifiers were created by concatenating the IP address and the date (day, month, and year)—as mentioned before, this helps avoid the ambiguity of associating the same user with an IP address over a prolonged period of time, since the IP address may have been reassigned. We demarcate session breaks with 30 minutes of inactivity between consecutive events [15]. All events were grouped by user and session.

4. ANALYSIS OF SEARCH BEHAVIOR

In this section, we present our analysis of book search behavior. We first introduce how we structure our analysis exploring behavior at the query, session, and user levels, and major goals within each. We then present analysis results for each level.

4.1 Framework of Analysis

The overarching goal of our analysis is to understand how users find books and book-related information on the web. Figure 2 illustrates the major steps of user interactions for book-related search assumed in this paper. One way users can begin their interaction is from within the digital library (e.g., by typing the URL into the address bar), and using the internal search engine to find the relevant content, possibly with multiple iterations of query formulation and faceted filtering.

Alternatively, users can arrive from an external search engine that leads to either the digital library homepage or a content page directly, from which users can continue their interaction with the digital library. Since it is plausible that users entering from WSEs might have different intents from the those starting their interaction from within, we hypothesize that user behaviors between the former group and the latter group are different.

Compared to the user interaction models assumed in previous work, this model allows users to start their interaction from both the inside and outside the digital library, and multiple modes of interaction once they enter the library. While we focus on book search behavior with the Open Library in this work, the proposed interaction model is generalizable to most web catalogs that rely on WSEs as a primary entry point, and provides various interaction methods based on rich domain-specific metadata.

Since *users* search books over one or more *sessions*, each of which is composed of one or more *queries* or steps of information-seeking, we structure our analysis into three levels of granularity: queries, sessions and users. We outline our expectations for each of these next.

4.1.1 Query-level Analysis

Queries form a unit of a user's expression of an information need, and therefore it is critical to understand the characteristics of queries in our analysis. As we assume that users can search from inside or outside of the digital library, each presenting a different search environment, we distinguish between internal and external queries. As digital libraries provide a rich set of interaction methods, internal queries can be a keyword query, a structured query (using search operators or the advanced search interface), a set of filtering conditions, or any combination thereof.

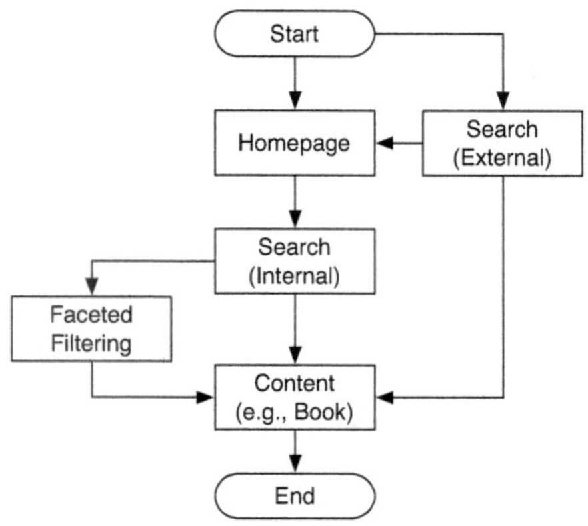

Figure 2: The sequence of user interaction for book-related search assumed in this paper.

Given these diverse classes of queries, the goal of our query-level analysis is to understand how internal and external queries differ in terms of length, the use of operators, and other aspects. For internal queries, we want to understand the use of search operators, the advanced search interface, and filtering conditions; we would like to know how frequently these different query types are used. Finally, since we hypothesize that field-level metadata plays a critical role in book-related searches, we analyze the usage of different metadata fields for each interaction method.

4.1.2 Session-level Analysis

While queries provide a glimpse of how users express their information needs, a more complete understanding of search behavior requires the inspection of the interaction between the user and the system as a whole. Analyzing user behavior at the level of sessions, defined as a series of system-user interaction with a single goal,[7] allows us to look at how users combine internal and external search and interaction methods, like filtering, to accomplish their goal.

Since we hypothesize that users starting from within the digital library have different intents from the those arriving via a WSE, we make a distinction between internal sessions (starting from within the digital library) and external sessions (starting from the referral of a WSE). We first compare the statistics of internal and external sessions, and analyze how users' navigation behavior in internal sessions differ from external sessions. Finally, since the internal search engine provides both advanced search and filtering interfaces, we analyze users' query reformulation behavior within internal sessions.

4.1.3 User-level Analysis

Moving beyond stand-alone sessions, we want to understand the habits of users across multiple sessions. As defined in Section 3.2, we identify users by a combination of IP address and the date on which activity is logged. Thus, activity from the same IP address on two different days is interpreted as coming from two distinct users. This means

[7]As noted in the definition of *session* in Section 3.2, we approximate user goal boundaries using a 30 minute timeout between adjacent user interactions.

Table 1: The distribution of SERP click counts for different object types in internal vs. external queries.

Source	works	books	authors	subjects	Total
External	575,291	8,634,914	1,094,050	46,737	10,350,992
Internal	413,775	8,123	133,829	69,260	624,987

Table 2: The distribution of search types for internal queries.

works (metadata)	works (full-text)	authors	subjects
1,006,487	18,113	75,141	80,096

that user-level statistics are only ever computed over a single day. For user-level analysis, we are interested in how often users search internally and externally, how consistent their use of internal versus external search is between sessions, and general statistics, like the average number of sessions, queries, and SERP clicks per user.

4.2 Query-level Analysis Results

Here we present the results for our query-level analysis. We first present the overall query statistics, and the results on search operator and method usage. We then provide a detailed analysis of how fields are used in keyword queries (both implicitly and explicitly by operators), queries from the advanced search interface, and faceted filtering conditions.

4.2.1 *Query Statistics*

We first compare the volume of internal and external searches. Note that we compare over SERP clicks as opposed to search requests here in following analyses, since we only have SERP clicks and the corresponding queries for external searches.

Table 1 shows the distribution of SERP click counts for different object types. Clicks from external searches account for 94% of all SERP clicks, and it is clear that clicks from internal searches exhibit very different patterns from external searches. While it is natural that *work* clicks overwhelm *book* clicks for internal searches, since internal SERPs link to *works*, it is interesting that *book* clicks substantiate a vast majority of external clicks. It might be due to the fact that search engines favor indexing book over work pages, or users looking for books tend to click on results with 'books' rather than 'works' in the URL.

The OL provides vertical search over books, authors, and subjects and provides the option to search over the full-text or only metadata (the default) for book search. Table 2 shows the distribution over these search verticals and options for internal queries. The two columns on the left denote the count of book searches based on metadata vs. full-text contents—the option which is accessible from advanced search interface, and the right columns show statistics about the other verticals.

It is interesting that full-text search accounts for only 1.8% of metadata-based search, even after considering that users need to enter the advanced interface to do so. We revisit this issue in the following section. Also, the search volume over authors and subjects each is less than 10% of book searches. Based on the statistics above, we focus on the analysis of metadata-based book search in what follows.

Table 3: Statistics of query lengths and operator usage for internal and external searches.

Source	length	quote	plus	minus	field	count
External	4.24	2.95%	0.09%	0.08%	0.02%	8,634,914
Internal	2.31	0.55%	0.01%	0.01%	0.27%	413,775

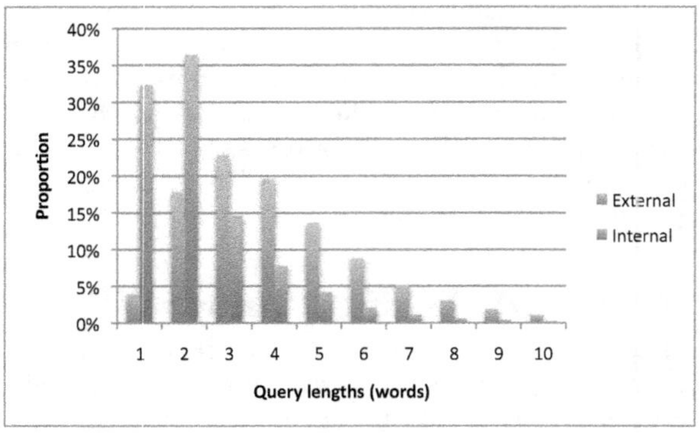

Figure 3: The distribution of query length (number of terms) based on source.

4.2.2 *Search Feature Usage*

Here we analyze how various search features supported by the internal and external search engines are used by book searchers. We first compare query length and the operator usage statistics for internal versus external searches in Table 3. Internal search queries are significantly shorter (2.31 words) than those from external search engines (4.24 words). The distribution of query lengths is shown in Figure 3. It is clear that the bulk of external queries are in the 2–4 word range, while internal queries contain 1–2 words.

Analyzing queries from both sources suggests the increase in query length for external searches is due in part to an abundance of book title searches, though we will see additional explanations in the coming sections. As for the operator usage shown in Table 3, while most operators are used more frequently for external queries, field operators are more common in internal searches. Note that the internal search engine provides field operators corresponding to book-level metadata, which may account for this difference.

While the user can only submit typed queries to external search engines, the internal search engine provides additional field-based search features via the advanced search interface and faceted filtering. It also supports options to specify whether users want results that only contain works with available e-books, or to change the sorting order of initial results (by the number of editions, oldest or newest in terms of publication date). Here, we looked at how frequently these search features are used for internal queries.

The results in Table 4 show that other search features such as the advanced search interface (advIF), faceted filtering and sorting by other criteria are all used more frequently than any search operators, including field operators (we include field operator usage for comparison). The use of these rich interaction methods may attribute to the discrepancy in query lengths between internal and external queries, since

Table 4: Statistics of search feature use in internal searches.

field	advIF	facets	e-book	sort
0.27%	2.41%	9.59%	32.59%	0.76%

Table 5: Correlation of keyword query length and search feature use for internal searches.

quote	field	advIF	facets
0.044	-0.011	-0.269	-0.082

these methods can be used instead of entering additional terms in a query.

As for search options, it turns out that filtering results to show only books with available e-books is a very popular activity (33% of book searches), which stands in stark contrast with the dearth of full-text search (1.7% of total book searches). Sorting of initial search results was used for 0.8% of internal queries (3,592 queries), and the most popular sorting orders were by the most recent first (64%), the least recent first (27%) and the number of editions (9%). From this we can infer that recency can be a important feature for the book search ranking algorithm.

To verify the hypothesis that the use of advanced search methods reduces the length of queries, we investigate the Spearman's rank correlation between query length and search method use for internal searches. The results in Table 5 show that the use of search features have a negative correlation with the length of keyword queries, except in the case of the *quote* operator. The trend is most conspicuous with the use of the advanced search interface and faceted filtering, which provide field-based interactions that complement keyword queries. The positive correlation of query length and the quote operator can be explained by considering that many people submit queries consisting of quoted book titles or author names, which are typically longer than average keyword queries.

4.2.3 Field Usage

Users can specify field-specific search terms in their keyword query or via the advanced search interface, but they can also restrict results to those with specific field values via filtering. In the previous section, we found that the field operators and field-based interaction methods are often used for internal searches. Here we investigate the use of fields more closely.

Table 6 compares the field use in search operators and the advanced search interface across all internal queries. While *title* and *authors* are popular in both search methods, *isbn* and *subject* are used mostly with the advanced search interface.

Previously in Table 4, we found that faceted filtering is by far the most frequently used search method. Table 7 shows the frequency of field usage for faceted filtering. While *title* and *authors* are still popular, *publisher* and *language* are used with disproportionately high frequency compared to other methods. The high use of the *language* filter is partly explained by the fact that corresponding search operator and advance interface field do not exist, whereas *publisher* field is available for other search methods.

Overall, the statistics reveals an interesting trend: the use of metadata fields is different based on the mode of interaction. For instance, it is plausible that people do not realize that they can use operators such as *isbn:* and *subject:*. Also, some field values (e.g., *publisher*) may be hard to type in, yet easy to click on. As will be discussed further in Section 4.5, this finding has implications for the search interface design,

Table 8: Average duration and action count for sessions from external and internal entry point.

Entry Point	duration (sec.)	actions	total sessions
External	69	1.75	7,516,990
Internal	262	3.79	286,587

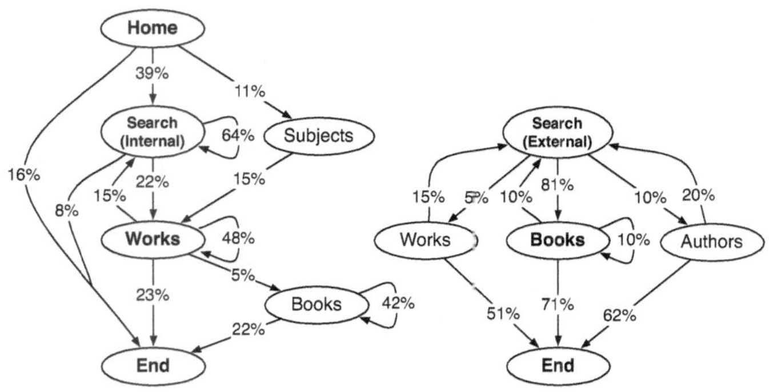

Figure 4: Markov model of navigation behavior for sessions started from the homepage (left), and started from the Google search engine (right).

many of which present fields in the same order regardless of the modes of interaction.

4.3 Session-level Analysis Results

Here we present the results of our session-level analysis. We first present overall session statistics from our data set and analyze user navigation behavior captured in page-to-page transitions conditioned on entry point. We then shift our focus to query reformulation behavior, which includes query reformulation and faceted filtering.

4.3.1 Session Statistics

Table 8 shows the session statistics from our data according to the point of entry. Session lengths are measured in duration and the count of user actions recorded. We find that external sessions are only half as long compared to internal sessions, and the difference is more significant in duration than in the action count.

We also looked at the distribution of action counts for external and internal sessions, where we found that about 90% of external sessions have fewer than 3 actions, whereas 70% of internal sessions consist of up to 3 actions. Consistent with previous results, users from external search engines tend to engage in brief search activities than those who start the interaction from within the website.

4.3.2 Analysis of Navigation Behavior

Previous work used Markov models to characterize user behavior in the context of email systems [3] and institution-level library systems [4]. To analyze the difference in user behavior between between externally and internally started sessions, we built a Markov model of navigation behavior, mostly following the methodology described in [4]. We first filtered sessions by a representative starting point for both internal sessions (homepage) and external sessions (Google), and then calculated the transition probability from each of page type to other page types.

The results in Figure 4 show the navigation patterns for

Table 6: **Statistics of field use via search operators and the advanced search interface, as a ratio within all internal queries.**

	title	author	isbn	subject	place	person	publisher
Operator	0.110%	0.110%	0.020%	0.030%	0.005%	0.001%	0.010%
Adv. I/F	0.490%	0.800%	0.890%	0.300%	0.030%	0.006%	0.060%

Table 7: **Statistics of field usage for faceted filtering, as a ratio within all internal queries.**

author	subject	person	place	time	publish_year	publisher	language
3.16%	2.75%	0.35%	0.59%	0.23%	0.43%	2.28%	1.34%

internal and external sessions, where the edge labels denote the probability that users move from one page to another. For instance, users starting from the *Home* page move into a *search* page with a probability of 39%. Note that we only show transitions with a minimum occurrence of 5%.

For internal sessions, a typical user enters the *search* page, and then visits a *work* page before leaving the website. It is typical that users re-visit the *search* page to reformulate a query or visit another *work* page. Some users diverge into a *subject* page to reach a *work* page, or visit a *book* page to find the information about a specific edition, though this happened rather infrequently. For external sessions, most users directly enter a *book* page, and then exit the website. Fewer than 20% of users enter the site via an *author* or *work* page.

There are several noticeable differences in navigation patterns between internal and external sessions. First, interactions in internal sessions show greater diversity with lower transition probabilities between major pages, whereas external sessions mostly include a single *book* page visit. This explains why external sessions are substantially shorter than internal sessions. Second, the most visited page types are vastly different between internal and external sessions and reflect the dominate result type for each source: Internal sessions mostly finish on a *work* page, whereas external sessions typically only include visits to *book* pages.

4.3.3 *Analysis of Query Reformulation Behavior*

The previous section explored user behavior as a whole, focusing on the difference between internal and external sessions. Since we found that internal sessions typically involve many query reformulations, filtering and other operations, here we investigate the patterns of query reformulation. Note that our query reformation include adding and removing a filtering condition. We built a Markov model of query reformulation by calculating the transition probability from one query behavior to another. The difference from the previous section is that each state of the model represents the form of reformulation taken by the user.

The results in Figure 5 illustrates the transitions between major reformulation actions. Note that we conflated the state of a session ending and a new query formulation to reduce visual clutter. While most users follow up a new query by ending their session or issuing a completely different query (87%), about 5% of users add a filtering condition, and another 7% reformulate the original query by adding or removing terms.

Once users add a filtering condition or reformulate their query, they tend to engage in the interaction by adding or deleting filtering conditions, or by reformulating the query again. The transition probabilities between faceted filtering actions were greater than those between query reformulation actions, which shows that users go through more iterations of faceted filtering than query reformulation.

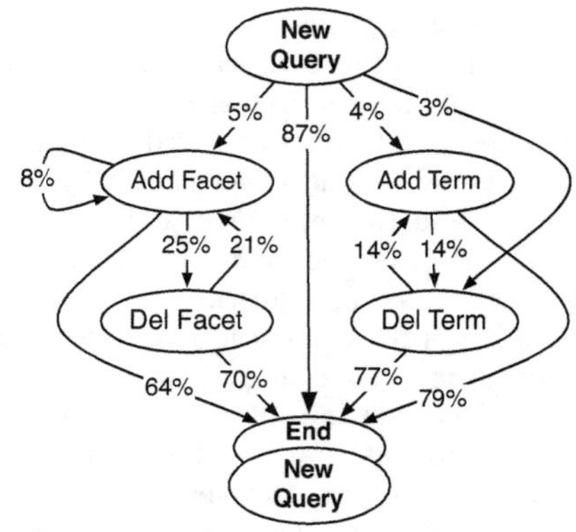

Figure 5: **Markov model of query behavior for sessions started from the internal pages.**

Table 9: **User-level statistics from the October–December 2010 Open Library logs.**

User counts	All Users	Users with >1 query	Users with >1 session
Total	8,728,077	2,015,013	582,947
Start all sessions from the OL homepage	322,441	135,117	8,765
Start *no* sessions from the OL homepage	8,373,609	1,857,640	542,155
Conduct only internal searches	1,014,483	159,013	50,945
Conduct only external searches	6,758,948	1,371,633	267,840
Average counts/user			
Actions	2.03	4.25	5.48
Queries	1.34	2.90	3.11
Internal queries	0.14	0.57	0.44
External queries	1.21	2.33	2.67
SERP clicks	1.35	2.88	3.13
Sessions	1.10	1.37	2.54

4.4 User-level Analysis

In this section, we present the results of our user-level analysis. We first characterize the behavior of Open Library users in terms of the session starting point and the type of searches they perform. We then explore the generation of book suggestions using user-level session data.

4.4.1 *User Statistics*

Table 9 shows a summary of the user-level statistics. Each of the three columns describes a different subset of the data. The *All users* column covers all users. The *Users with >1 query* column is the subset of users that entered more than one internal or external search, which includes 23% of all users. Finally, the *Users with >1 session* column describes the subset of users that engaged in two or more sessions and includes approximately 7% of all users.

The first several rows give counts of users that meet the specified criteria. The second and third rows describe how consistent users are across sessions in terms of how they begin their session—either from starting from the OL homepage or a different page, including SERP clicks for external searches. Only 4% of all users begin all of their sessions from the OL homepage, while almost all other users begin all their sessions from somewhere else. Of users conducting at least two sessions, the vast majority—93%—start from somewhere other than the homepage in every session, while only 1.5% consistently start from the homepage, and 5.5% start at least one session from the homepage, and one from a different page.

The next two rows indicate the number of users that exclusively submitted queries either internally or externally across their sessions. Users are more consistent in searching externally, though this drops significantly for users engaging in more than one session, while inconsistency dominates. This suggests that many users rely on a mix of internal and external searching.

The bottom half of the table describes average event counts. As expected, users conducting multiple sessions tend to enter more queries. However, the ratio of internal to external searches is the highest for users who enter multiple queries, but who do not necessarily conduct multiple sessions: 0.24 versus 0.16 (users with multiple sessions) and 0.12 (all users). This is possibility explained by users entering the site via an external search and then performing a follow-up internal query.

Most users seem interested in the OL's content and not its search service. It is difficult to discern by only looking at the log data why users with multiple sessions prefer external searching—it could be that they are looking for other media in addition to book records, like Wikipedia pages, book reviews, or shopping sites like Amazon. In this case, using a WSE makes more sense. However, it may also be due to other aspects of users' online experiences. For example, external WSEs may be used as a shortcut—plugging a query into the default search box built into the browser and clicking on a link takes much less effort than navigating to the OL web site and entering the query there. Without an in depth user study, we can only speculate.

4.4.2 Extracting Book Suggestions

In addition to user-level statistics, we investigate the possibility of extracting book suggestions from the user-level. Table 10 shows a sample of four frequently clicked books (in bold) and the five most commonly co-occurring book clicks associated with each. For example, users who click on the book *1984* also click on *Animal Farm* and *Brave New World.* Surprisingly, *Pride and Prejudice* co-occurs frequently with slightly more antiquated classics, a grouping that would be unlikely using genre and publication era meta data alone. These initial results, based on a limited sample of data, suggest recommendations are a promising application of co-occurring book clicks.

4.5 Implications of Findings

The analyses presented in earlier sections have many implications for improving book search on the web. First, since search sessions typically span both internal and external search engines, a coordination between internal and external search is necessary to maximize user benefit. Second, the importance of metadata was stressed in both query formulation and the use of advanced search features, like filtering. In what follows, we provide specific design recommendations for both external WSEs and the Open Library's internal search engine.

Table 10: A sample of some of the most frequently co-occurring book clicks at the user-level.

Pride and Prejudice	**1984**
Chapman's Homer	Animal Farm
Odyssey	Brave New World
Don Quixote	The Hobbit
Divina commedia	The Call of the Wild
Faust: A Tragedy	The Great Gatsby

The Right Stuff	**Little women**
The right stuff	Wuthering Heights
Ascent	Pride and Prejudice
Omon Ra	Through the looking-glass
Man on the Moon	Gulliver's travels
Now and Forever	A Christmas Carol

4.5.1 External Search Engines

The proliferation of web search means that it functions as a entry point for many types of information-seeking and our analysis demonstrates that the same holds true of book search. However, the distinctive characteristics of book search do not seem to be taken into account by WSEs. Assuming that book-related queries can be classified with reasonable accuracy, there are two major ways in which we believe WSEs can better serve book searchers.

First, WSEs could allow field-based access of library catalogs. While services such as the Open Library use metadata with many fields, supporting the interaction (field operator, advanced UI or faceted filtering) based on the key fields across common across most library sites would be beneficial for users. And second, since a large fraction of internal searches included filtering results to only show those with available e-books, WSEs might consider including shortcuts to e-books next to Open Library results when available.

4.5.2 Internal Search Engines

Our analysis has several implications for design choices to the Open Library search engine and the site as a whole. While we only analyzed data from the Open Library, there is no reason these design recommendation could not be applied to similar digital libraries, or online catalogues in general. First, given the importance of fields in user's information-seeking process, field-level metadata should be exploited for ranking, query suggestions, and other purposes. The results from our retrieval experiments in Section 5.3 also support this argument. The analysis in Section 4.2.2 also showed that users consider recency an important ranking criteria.

Second, consider that most users are directed to an Open Library book page from an external WSE, after which they leave the site, sometimes performing another external search. To prevent users from leaving, the Open Library needs to present an easy-to-use feature that external WSEs do not have. We believe one such feature is a list of book recommendations presented on each book and work page. As we saw in Section 4.4.2, even with three months of data and a simple recommendation algorithm, the suggestions seem

Table 11: Statistics of the queries in the training and test collections.

Collection	Train Count	Train Avg. Length	Test Count	Test Avg. Length
Internal-Works	704	2.00	686	2.02
Internal-Authors	697	1.70	646	1.65
External-Books	9,758	3.44	9,911	3.45
External-Authors	115	2.84	105	2.65

useful. Extending this to multiple years of data and some additional information, such as dwell time and whether users tried to download the e-book or buy it from a linked vendor, should produce higher quality recommendations.

5. RETRIEVAL EXPERIMENTS

In this section, we present retrieval experiments using a test collection created from the Open Library log data. We first describe how we created test collection, and then experimental settings including the methods we compared, followed by the experimental results.

5.1 Building a Test Collection

Here we describe the process of building a test collection out of queries and click data. We first describe how we collected a reasonable set of queries, and then how we eliminated the position biases from click data.

5.1.1 Query Cleaning

To build a training and test collection, we first cleaned all the queries and aggregated their clicks over a year's worth of data (1.9 billion records). Cleaning entailed removing consecutive whitespace, non alpha-numeric characters, and converting all characters to lower case. Two queries were considered the same if they shared the same source (i.e., internal versus external searches), general key word phrase, advanced interface queries, and search facets. We ignored all queries with user-defined operators in the general keyword query, e.g., "title: moby dick" and queries with facets. We then broke these into two groups a training set Tr and a testing set Te.

Within each set, we broke queries and document clicks down into one of the following groups: internal searches over works (IW), internal searches over authors (IA), external searches over books (EB), and external searches over authors (EA). A query may belong to one or more of these groups, though the relevance judgments are specific to the object type (books or author).

We further filtered out queries without a sufficient number of clicks so as to not be overwhelmed with the data tail (too few total clicks) or the uninteresting queries where the same result is always clicked. Sufficiency required there be at least two distinct clicked documents of that object type (e.g., books) and a total of 30 or more clicks between the documents within that group. Table 11 shows the statistics of the queries built by the procedure described above.

5.1.2 Click De-biasing

Previous research has shown clicks to be biased by the presentation rank, and thus are not well suited for relevance judgments. To mitigate this for the internal queries, we followed the background subtraction model introduced by Agichtein et al. [1].

The process is as follows: first, we established an expected relative click frequency model over the queries—for each query, we calculated the proportion of clicks made at each rank, then averaged each rank's relative click frequency across all queries. Because rankings are not available in the Apache logs, we used the rankings of the current system as a surrogate. For each group in the training set, we generated a background model using all the queries with a sufficient number of clicks and a random sample of queries without. For each group in the testing set, we took the corresponding training background model and added the relative click frequencies the test queries with sufficient clicks.

Table 12: The list of fields indexed.

Category	Field
title	title, series, edition
author	authors, bio
subject	subjects, subject-people, subject-places
time	publish-date, death-date
place	publish-places, publish-country
person	personal-name, alternate-names
publisher	publishers

Table 13: Record counts for the training and test collections.

Collection	Record Count
Works	15,032,815
Books	24,359,019
Authors	6,730,812

Once the background models were established, we de-biased queries in the training and testing sets by subtracting the background model from each query's relative click frequencies. After the subtraction, a result with a de-biased click frequency greater than 0 was normalized on a graded scale from 1 to 5. This was then used as the relevance judgment for that query-document pair.

To quantify the effectiveness of the de-biasing, we randomly sampled 20 queries from the internal book and author test sets, gathered the records that were marked relevant in either the biased or de-biased implicit relevance qrels, pooled the top 10 results from each of the three retrieval systems, and manually assessed each record. Using the explicit relevance judgments as the gold standard, we calculated the accuracy of the binarized biased and de-biased implicit relevance judgments. We found that de-biasing greatly increases the the accuracy for internal book search from 0.29 to 0.54.

Note that this de-biasing model assumes that users view internal search results, which are available by crawling the OL search results for the queries within our set. For external queries, due to the difficulty in obtaining ranking information for the variety of external search engines, we decided not to de-bias their clicks. Instead, if a document is clicked, it is counted as relevant.

5.2 Experimental Settings

Here we describe settings for our retrieval experiments. During indexing, no stemming was applied, and no stopwords were eliminated. Table 12 lists the indexed fields and their categories corresponding to the fields in Table 6. Table 13 provides the number of records contained in each of the collections. All experiments were conducted with a modified version of the Galago retrieval system.[8]

Since our goal in retrieval experiments is to provide results for well-established baseline retrieval models, we exper-

[8]http://www.lemurproject.org/galago.php

Table 14: Retrieval results (MAP).

Internal queries	*QL*	*MFLM*	*BM25F*
Works	0.1866	0.1913	0.2041
Authors	0.4114	0.4311	0.4277

External queries	*QL*	*MFLM*	*BM25F*
Books	0.5568	0.5268	0.5924
Authors	0.3151	0.3224	0.3282

Table 15: Retrieval results (P@5).

Internal queries	*QL*	*MFLM*	*BM25F*
Works	0.3000	0.2040	0.2120
Authors	0.1867	0.1972	0.2012

External queries	*QL*	*MFLM*	*BM25F*
Books	0.1880	0.2360	0.2840
Authors	0.1644	0.1584	0.1624

iment with the query-likelihood language model (QL) [14], the mixture of field language models (MFLM) by Ogilvie and Callan [13], and the 2004 TREC Hard track version of the BM25F model by Robertson et al. [17]. A detailed descriptions of these models can be found in [8].

Each model is tuned using training queries within each group. MFLM has each language model weight tuned independently, and for BM25F, the order of tuning for the parameters is: $K_1 \rightarrow B_f \rightarrow W_f$. All field-level parameters are tuned by iterative line search.

5.3 Experimental Results

Tables 14 and 15 list the mean average precision (MAP) and precision at rank 5 (P@5) of the systems, respectively. Internal book queries were run over *works* while the external book queries were run over *books*—this reflects the click-through behavior we observed in the logs. The results are consistent with a recent evaluation of structured document retrieval models [8], where field-based models showed advantages over document-based models.

Another interpretation is that the results tend to improve as the amount of parameterization increases (from left-to-right in the tables). We hypothesize that the high number of fields in these sets provides opportunity for fine-grained tuning, which is what the additional parameters provide in a model such as BM25F.

Finally, MAP results tend to be higher than the corresponding P@5 values, indicating that while the experimental models can effectively retrieve relevant documents, they have difficulties in getting them consistently into the top 5 results.

6. CONCLUSIONS

In this work, we analyze web-based book search behavior using three months of logs from the Open Library. We find that the query characteristics and session-level behaviors are drastically different between internal and external searchers. We also study the use of various field-based interaction methods within library website, finding that the field usage is different based on the modes of interaction—keyword search, advanced search interface, faceted filtering. We make numerous design recommendations for both web search engines and digital libraries.

In addition to the behavior analysis, we also took the first steps towards developing a viable test collection based on the Open Library metadata record and query log data. We also perform evaluations of several well-known retrieval methods. We are in the process of preparing to release this test collection, so that it can be used by researchers to further improve systems that provide book search capabilities.

An avenue of future work includes implementing the recommendations we made here in a large-scale digital library service. By selectively exposing the new features to user traffic in a controlled manner, we expect to uncover the degree to which our suggestions make a difference in the digital library user experience.

7. ACKNOWLEDGMENTS

This work was supported in part by the Center for Intelligent Information Retrieval, in part by UMass NEAGAP fellowship, and in part by NSF grant #IIS-0910884. Any opinions, findings and conclusions or recommendations expressed in this material are those of the authors and do not necessarily reflect those of the sponsor.

References

[1] E. Agichtein, E. Brill, S. Dumais, and R. Ragno. Learning user interaction models for predicting web search result preferences. In *Proc. of SIGIR '06*, pages 3–10, 2006.

[2] B. A. Blummer. A literature review of academic library web page studies. *Journal of Web Librarianship*, 1(1):45, 2007.

[3] D. Elsweiler, S. Mandl, and L. Azzopardi. Evaluating personal information management behaviour using markov models. In *Wissensmanagement*, pages 280–288, 2009.

[4] Q. Guo. Modeling user interactions for automatic library search evaluation: Preliminary results. In *Proc. of the JCDL'08*, 2008.

[5] S. Jones, S. J. Cunningham, R. Mcnab, and S. Boddie. A transaction log analysis of a digital library. *Int. Journal on Digital Libraries*, 3:152–169, 2000.

[6] G. Kazai, M. Koolean, J. Kamps, A. Doucet, and M. Landoni. Overview of the inex 2010 book track. In *INEX 2010 Workshop Proceedings*, 2011.

[7] G. Kazai, M. Koolean, J. Kamps, A. Doucet, and M. Landoni. Overview of the inex 2011 book track. In *INEX 2011 Workshop Proceedings*, 2012. To appear.

[8] J. Kim and W. B. Croft. Retrieval experiments using pseudo-desktop collections. In *Proc. of CIKM*, CIKM '09, pages 1297–1306, 2009.

[9] B. Kules, R. Capra, M. Banta, and T. Sierra. What do exploratory searchers look at in a faceted search interface? In *Proc. of JCDL*, JCDL '09, pages 313–322, 2009.

[10] J. Lin and M. D. Smucker. How do users find things with pubmed?: towards automatic utility evaluation with user simulations. In *Proc. of SIGIR*, SIGIR 08, pages 19–26, 2008.

[11] G. Mishne and M. Rijke. A study of blog search. In *Proc. of ECIR '06*, pages 289–301, 2006.

[12] X. Niu and B. M. Hemminger. Beyond text querying and ranking list: how people are searching through faceted catalogs in two library environments. In *Proc. of ASIS&T*, ASIS&T '10, pages 29:1–29:9, 2010.

[13] P. Ogilvie and J. Callan. Combining document representations for known-item search. In *Proc. of SIGIR*, SIGIR '03, pages 143–150, New York, NY, USA, 2003. ACM.

[14] J. M. Ponte and W. B. Croft. A language modeling approach to information retrieval. In *Proc. of SIGIR*, SIGIR '98, pages 275–281, New York, NY, USA, 1998. ACM.

[15] F. Radlinski and T. Joachims. Query chains: learning to rank from implicit feedback. In *Proc. of KDD '05*, pages 239–248. ACM, 2005.

[16] W. Weerkamp, R. Berendsen, B. Kovachev, E. Meij, K. Balog, and M. de Rijke. People searching for people: Analysis of a people search engine log. In *Proc. of SIGIR*, pages 45–54. ACM, ACM, July 2011.

[17] H. Zaragoza, N. Craswell, M. Taylor, S. Saria, and S. Robertson. Microsoft Cambridge at TREC-13: Web and HARD Tracks. In *Proc. of TREC*, TREC '04, 2004.

Temporal Corpus Summarization Using Submodular Word Coverage

Ruben Sipos
Dept. of Computer Science
Cornell University
Ithaca, NY 14853 USA
rs@cs.cornell.edu

Adith Swaminathan
Dept. of Computer Science
Cornell University
Ithaca, NY 14853 USA
adith@cs.cornell.edu

Pannaga Shivaswamy
Dept. of Computer Science
Cornell University
Ithaca, NY 14853 USA
pannaga@cs.cornell.edu

Thorsten Joachims
Dept. of Computer Science
Cornell University
Ithaca, NY 14853 USA
tj@cs.cornell.edu

ABSTRACT

In many areas of life, we now have almost complete electronic archives reaching back for well over two decades. This includes, for example, the body of research papers in computer science, all news articles written in the US, and most people's personal email. However, we have only rather limited methods for analyzing and understanding these collections. While keyword-based retrieval systems allow efficient access to individual documents in archives, we still lack methods for understanding a corpus as a whole. In this paper, we explore methods that provide a temporal summary of such corpora in terms of landmark documents, authors, and topics. In particular, we explicitly model the temporal nature of influence between documents and re-interpret summarization as a coverage problem over words anchored in time. The resulting models provide monotone sub-modular objectives for computing informative and non-redundant summaries over time, which can be efficiently optimized with greedy algorithms. Our empirical study shows the effectiveness of our approach over several baselines.

Categories and Subject Descriptors

H.3.3 [**Information Storage and Retrieval**]: Information Search and Retrieval—*Retrieval models*

General Terms

Design, Theory

Keywords

summarization, temporal, submodular

CIKM'12, October 29–November 2, 2012, Maui, HI, USA.

1. INTRODUCTION

From news and blogs to twitter feeds, and from research papers to patents, we are accumulating unprecedented amounts of text in digital form. Advances in storage technology have allowed us to maintain complete records of these text streams, and information retrieval research has developed excellent tools for accessing individual documents in the resulting collections. However, our ability to analyze and interpret archives on a macroscopic level is still limited. Macroscopic questions one may ask about a collection range from the creation of a timeline of influential documents or authors, to the automatic summarization of the main chains of discussion.

To answer such macroscopic questions about a corpus of text documents, we draw upon methods from document summarization (see [14]). Instead of summarizing a single (or small number of) individual documents using extracted sentences, we aim to summarize a collection using extracted documents, authors, or keywords. This shift implies substantial differences in what constitutes a meaningful summary. In particular, time is more important for the creation of corpus summaries than it is for conventional summaries, and we argue that corpus summaries should reflect the influence that a document or author had on the future development of the collection. Therefore, our summaries take the form of timelines, where components of a summary are defined with respect to intervals or points of time.

More specifically, we formulate several variants of the corpus summarization problem. First, we seek to identify k documents that had the largest influence on the content of the corpus. Second, for each point in time, we seek to identify those documents that were most influential for that time. Third, we similarly identify the most influential authors for each time-point. And fourth, we identify key phrases at each time-point that were influential and represent a coherent segment of the corpus.

All four corpus-summarization problems will be formulated as coverage problems, where we approximate coverage of abstract concepts through coverage of words in time. For conventional summarization and diversified retrieval, coverage approaches [21, 28, 16, 23, 19] and, more generally, submodular summarization methods [10] represent the state of the art. In particular, they provide an elegant model of the relevance/redundancy trade-off inherent in all summarization problems. The key technical challenge for the problem of corpus summarization is the ability to model time-points and time-intervals effectively, without sacrificing the computational approximation guarantees that the greedy algorithm provides for submodular function maximization [13, 8]. Our approach models the fact that different ideas have varied novelty, and that the influence of an idea changes over time. An important feature of our approach is that it does not rely on observed or inferred link structure between documents, but requires only the time-stamped document text. This makes our approach applicable to a wide range of corpora for which citation information is not available or not reliable. Furthermore, it allows us to use citation information as "ground truth" for quantitative evaluation. On three scientific corpora, we perform such evaluations, compare to several baselines and find that our methods provide qualitatively interesting results.

2. RELATED WORK

Our approach in this paper is based on the idea of extractive summarization; in this approach, a summary is created by selecting smaller units (i.e. sentences) [3, 23, 10]. Corpus summarization has similarities to extractive document summarization: instead of a document to summarize, we have a corpus and instead of selecting sentences, we select entire documents. Extractive summaries can be obtained by maximizing the coverage of words over the corpus. This idea has been used both in document summarization [23] and information retrieval [28]. While existing approaches focused on covering words as a proxy for concepts, we extend the notion to identify documents from a corpus that had substantial influence on the future development of the corpus. This gives us a more versatile framework than, say, selecting sentences based on time-dependent event weights [25].

There are several approaches that deal with the corpus as a whole in an attempt to improve its accessibility. Recommender systems strive to suggest what to read next based on past behavior and personal preferences [7] or on a query set consisting of example papers [6]. A related approach uses collaborative filtering and/or content filtering [24]. The goal of recommender systems, broadly, is to suggest documents based on a query; the goal of our work is to understand how a corpus evolved over time and which authors, papers and key-words demonstrated their influence during the evolution.

There has been previous work on modelling and visualizing text corpora. On the macro level, we can describe a corpus in terms of topics [2]. There has also been work [4] which show trends in topics, indicating the main turning points. A different approach considers intra-corpus relations and describes influence between documents [18]. The disadvantage of these approaches is that the units being summarized (e.g. documents) and being visualized (e.g. turning points) are distinct objects. Bridging this disconnect is an important aim for summarization systems since providing an explicit guide in the visualization (e.g. by providing the influential documents in the corpus) helps a user become familiar with the novel content in a corpus.

Temporal text mining [20] is another popular area of research. There has been work [1] which views a news topic as a sequence of events and selects those events that are relevant and novel to form the summary. Further, timelines of events can be created [27, 22] which show the major developments in a news topic. There is also work on event threading [12] where events are not viewed as a flat hierarchy of topics; these approaches model the dependencies between events. In addition, temporal features can also be used when doing document summarization [9] to improve the performance. Our work implicitly models sequences of events over time, but always presents explicit examples that highlight influential contributions. The main insight of this work is that explicitly modelling the temporal context in which words appear in documents provides a simple and very effective approximation to the flow of ideas in a corpus.

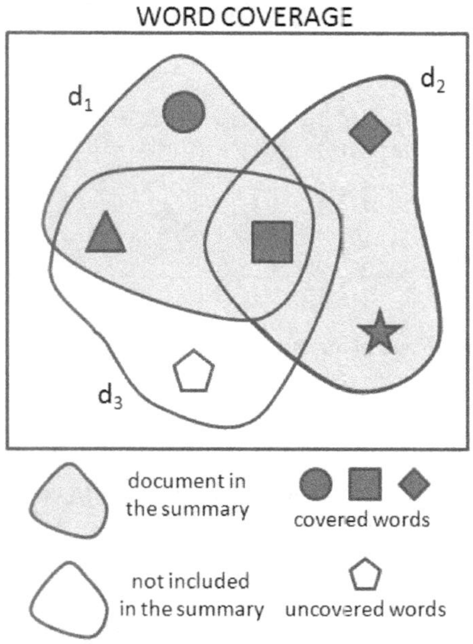

Figure 1: Illustration of word-coverage objective.

3. SUMMARIZATION AS COVERAGE

In this paper, we explore several variants of the corpus summarization problem, providing a temporal summary of the corpus in terms of landmark papers, authors and key-phrases. All approaches are formulated as maximum coverage problems, which have been found to provide elegant and effective methods for conventional summarization and diversified retrieval problems [10, 28, 21]. We start by reviewing the coverage-based summarization idea in the remainder of this section, and then extend it to corpus summarization in Section 4.

3.1 Information Coverage as Word Coverage

Coverage-based summarization methods make a direct analogy between a summary covering the information content in the object to be summarized, and maximum coverage problems as defined in theoretical computer science [8]. The key assumption of coverage-based summarization methods is that coverage of words can be used as a proxy for the coverage of information content. By achieving a good coverage over words, the word coverage approach aims to select a summary which covers different topics. In this way, coverage-based summarization methods elegantly avoid redundancy and promote diversity.

While document summarization involves selecting a diverse set of sentences from it, the idea can be naturally extended to corpus summarization by selecting a diverse set of documents that maximizes coverage. In this approach, every word in a document has a weight associated with it, indicating how important it is to cover this word in the summary. These document weights are either determined through a heuristic [10] or learned [19]. Documents are selected so that the total weight of the covered words is maximized; this is illustrated in Figure 1. In this example we want to select at most two documents out of three and each covered word has unit weight. We see that by selecting d_1 and d_2 we achieve the best score of the summary, since we cover the maximum number of words.

Formally, let $U = \{d_1, d_2, \ldots\}$ be the set of all documents in the corpus, where each document is represented as a bag of words.

Algorithm 1 for greedy submodular function maximization.

$S^* \leftarrow \emptyset$
$A \leftarrow U = \{d_1, ...\}$
while $A \neq \emptyset$ **and** $|S^*| < k$ **do**
  $z \leftarrow \arg\max_{d \in A} F(S^* \cup \{d\}) - F(S^*)$
  $S^* \leftarrow S^* \cup \{z\}$
  $A \leftarrow A \backslash \{z\}$
end while

The word coverage objective function, for any $S \subseteq U$, is defined as follows:

$$F(S) = \sum_{w} \theta(w) \max_{d \in S} \phi(d, w), \tag{1}$$

where, $\phi(d, w)$ represents the weight of a word w in the document d. One common choice of ϕ is the TFIDF score [17]. Moreover $\theta(w)$ is the weight for the word w depending on our belief of the word's importance.

3.2 Optimization via Greedy Algorithm

With the objective function defining the score of a summarization S, corpus summaries are constructed by finding the set S with the highest score $F(S)$. To obtain a summary we have to solve the following optimization problem:

$$S^* = \arg\max_{S \subseteq U} F(S). \tag{2}$$

An important property that enables the fast and accurate solution of this optimization problem lies in the structure of $F(S)$. It is well known that the coverage objective $F(S)$ is monotone (i.e. $|S'| \geq |S| \implies F(S') \geq F(S)$) and submodular [8].

DEFINITION 1. *Given a set U, a function $f : 2^U \rightarrow \mathbb{R}$ is submodular iff for all $u \in U$ and all sets S and T such that $S \subseteq T \subseteq U$, we have,*

$$f(S \cup \{u\}) - f(S) \geq f(T \cup \{u\}) - f(T).$$

Submodular functions have a property that says that adding u to a subset s of t increases f at least as much as adding it to t. While maximizing monotone sub-modular functions is NP-hard [11], it is known that the greedy Algorithm 1 achieves a $1 - 1/e$ approximation to the optimum solution for any linear budget constraint [10, 8]. Further, this algorithm provides a $1-1/e$ approximation for any monotone submodular scoring function. The algorithm starts with an empty summary. In each step, a document is added to the summary that results in the maximum relative increase of the objective. The algorithm terminates when the budget k is reached.

4. CORPUS SUMMARIZATION

While submodular summarization approaches have been very successful for conventional summarization problems, we argue that corpus summarization should not only optimize coverage of information content, but also reflect which documents and authors were important in the development of the corpus. In particular, we aim to include influence between documents into the summarization objective.

To illustrate the difference between a conventional summarization problem and the type of corpus summarization we envision, consider a corpus consisting of research papers covering two decades of a particular field. In such a scenario, conventional word-based coverage approaches would pick several (non-redundant) survey papers, or papers that otherwise touch on a lot of different areas, since their union will tend to cover the largest subset of words in the corpus. However, while these survey papers are indeed a good summary of the content, this selection will not provide any information about how the corpus developed over time, what papers opened new areas of activity, and which authors influenced the direction of the field. In the subsequent sub-sections, we show how the conventional coverage-based approach can be extended to provide summaries that not only optimize information content, but also reflect influence and importance of individual documents and authors.

To achieve this goal, the remainder of this section shows how to (a) incorporate time into the summarization problems, (b) formulate the summarization objective in terms of influence, and (c) show how corpora can be summarized not only through landmark documents, but also through influential authors and key-phrases.

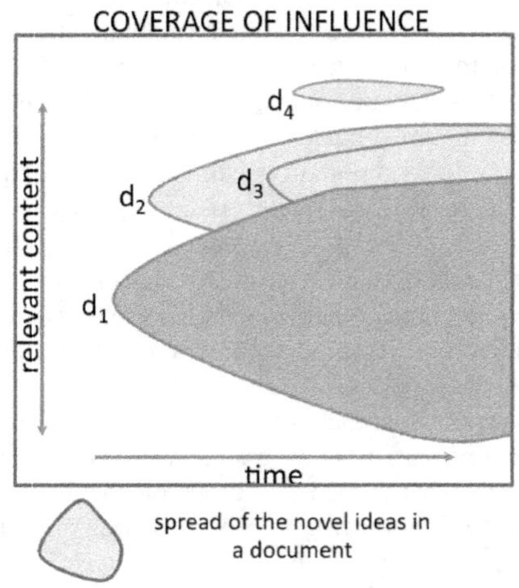

Figure 2: Illustrating the coverage function for revealing influential documents.

4.1 Summarization through Influential Documents

We now explore how the word-based coverage objective can be extended to summarize a corpus through a non-redundant set of influential documents. A pictorial illustration is shown in Figure 2, indicating how influential documents introduce ideas that increasingly cover the content of documents observed in later years. To get to an operational formalization of influence in the coverage model, we start with the following properties:

Spread: An influential document contains ideas that spread to other documents. The more an idea spreads, the greater is its influence. Note that this aspect of influence requires us to include a notion of time into the coverage objective, since ideas can only spread forward in time.

Novelty: A document should only be credited for generating influence with respect to some idea, if this idea was first proposed in that document. If an earlier document already contained that idea, influence should be credited to that earlier document. Note that this can be quite different from citation-based impact measures, which may credit influence to review papers or other papers that popularize an existing idea.

To capture *novelty* in the word-based coverage approach, we redefine $\phi(d, w)$ in the coverage objective (1). Intuitively, we do not want to give document d credit for an idea – as represented by its word distribution – if there already exist older documents d', $t(d') < t(d)$ that already cover this idea. $t(d)$ denotes the year of publication of the document d. More formally, let $\mathcal{N}(d)$ denote the k-nearest neighbors (for example, based on cosine similarity) of the document d among all the documents published before it, then we capture the novel contribution of a document as

$$\nu(d, w) = \max\left\{0, \min_{d' \in \mathcal{N}(d)} \{\phi(d, w) - \phi(d', w)\}\right\}. \quad (3)$$

In order to capture *spread* in the coverage objective, we enlarge the set of objects that need to be covered to word-time pairs w_y for all words w and years y. This allows the coverage objective to make a distinction between covering the word w in a year y and covering the same word in year y'. Formally, we generalize $\theta(w)$ in (1) and make it dependent on time, where each $\theta(w, y)$ separately defines how important word w is for the given time y. We say that the importance of a word w in year y is determined by the sum of the TFIDF scores of the documents in year y:

$$\theta(w, y) = \sum_{d:t(d)=y} TFIDF(d, w). \quad (4)$$

Other weighting schemes can work here too (e.g. per-year inverse document frequencies) because our model is oblivious to the precise choice of θ (as long as it well represents the spread). Note that this allows us to model that some documents cover a word in certain years, but not in others. In particular, we say that a document d only covers a word in those years that are later than its publication date $t(d)$. This allows us to formulate the objective for finding influential papers as follows:

$$F(S) = \sum_w \sum_y \theta(w, y) \max_{d \in S, y > t(d)} \nu(d, w). \quad (5)$$

The above objective multiplies the novel aspect of a word in a paper with how important a word is in the future years. Intuitively, the score is large when the set of selected documents S contains documents with high novelty scores as well as a high influence in the future. We therefore maximize the above objective using the greedy Algorithm 1.

Note that this approach will not tend to select survey papers unlike the word coverage approach for two reasons. First (and most importantly), a survey paper will have a low novelty score since it is mostly based on previous work. Second, usually survey papers are written after a field is well developed, hence it does not cover all those documents that appeared before it in (5).

The key feature that differentiates our model from related coverage-based approaches is the insight that modelling the temporal context in which words appear (and not just the within-document context) can provide a strong signal for summarization tasks. We achieve this by not just using words as proxy for ideas in a coverage objective, but anchor words at specific time-points to gauge the influence. Additionally, modelling novelty helps us correctly attribute impact and avoids the pitfalls of citation-based impact measures.

4.2 Timelines of Document Influence

The previous section showed how the coverage objective can be extended to focus on influential papers, producing summaries that are organized by the publication date of the influential documents. However, dual to such summaries, we may also ask the following question: for each year y, what are the documents that most influenced the content of this year? This is illustrated in Figure 3.

In the following subsection, we formulate a coverage objective that identifies the k documents that had the most influence in a year

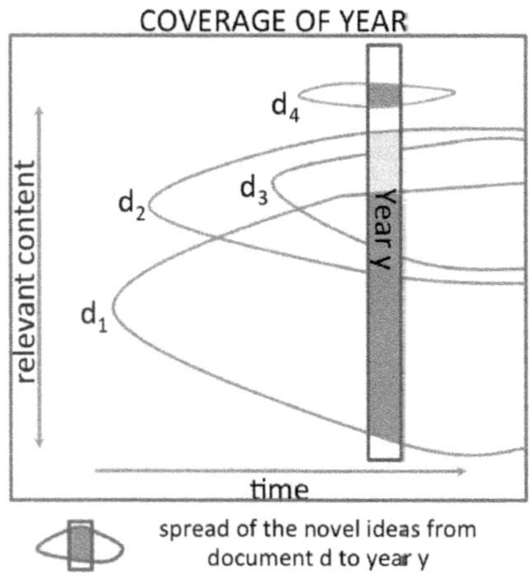

Figure 3: Illustrating the influence of documents in a particular year.

(for every year). Intuitively, a document d influences a year y, if it was published before year y, i.e. $t(d) < y$, and the novel ideas from d have substantial coverage in year y. Instead of selecting documents independent of year as in the previous section, we now allow our method to select an influential document to cover a particular year y. This means that our optimization problem now selects from a universe of document-year pairs $U_y = \{(d_i, y_i), ...\}$. Here d_i is any document from the corpus, and y_i is any year such that $y_i > t(d_i)$. This leads to the following objective which we seek to maximize.

$$F(S) = \sum_w \sum_y \theta(w, y) \max_{\substack{(d, y_d) \in S \\ y = y_d > t(d)}} \nu(d, w). \quad (6)$$

Similar to (5), the above objective multiplies the novelty score of word w in a document d with the importance of the word for a year y. However, (6) allows picking a different set of documents for each year y_i.

It is easy to see that $F(S)$ in (6) decomposes into a set of independent optimization problems – one for each year. We may therefore solve the following subproblem separately for each year and concatenate the solution for each year to obtain the solution of the original problem. Formally,

$$F_y(S_y) = \sum_w \theta(w, y) \max_{d \in S_y, y > t(d)} \nu(d, w). \quad (7)$$

Each of the above objectives is monotone submodular and can be solved using the greedy Algorithm 1.

4.3 Timelines of Author Influence

Analogous to selecting documents that had a large influence on a given year, we can also ask which authors were most influential. It is easy to extend the optimization problem from the previous section so that it selects influential authors. Denote with $d(a)$ the documents in the corpus that were authored by author a. The universe of items to select from now consists of author-year pairs $U_y = \{(a_i, y_i), ...\}$. Selecting an author a_i for year y_i implies that all documents the author wrote before year y_i get selected. This leads to the following objective,

$$F(S) = \sum_w \sum_y \theta(w, y) \max_{\substack{(a, y_a) \in S \\ d \in d(a) \\ y = y_a > t(d)}} \nu(d, w). \quad (8)$$

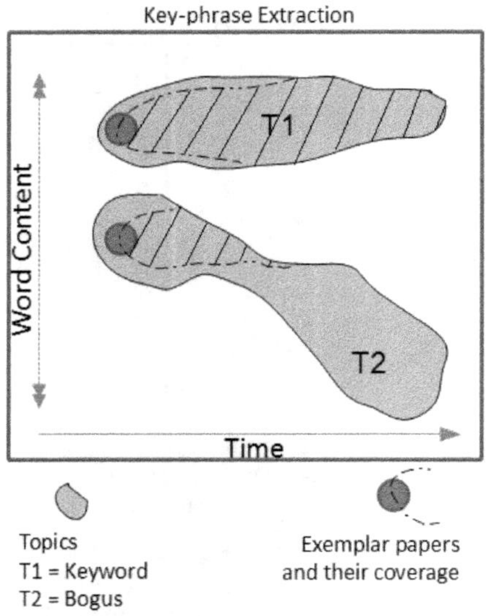

Figure 4: Illustrating the difference in word distributions over time between a bogus term and a genuine keyword.

which again can be broken into independent optimization problems for each year.

4.4 Summarizing Timelines with Key-Phrases

Summaries in terms of documents and authors still require the user to read through some documents from the collection. We now explore whether timelines of influence can be summarized through key-phrases. In particular, we aim to identify the points in time when new and influential ideas – as represented by a key-phrase – entered the collection.

While we already have operational definitions of novelty and influence, we still need to define what makes a key-phrase a good representative of an idea. We conjecture that a key-phrase that represents an idea well will be accompanied by stable word distribution over the years. For instance, documents that mention the phrase "HITS algorithm" will probably also mention several words related to that idea, whereas documents mentioning "Related work" need not have such a coherent set of overlapping words. The keyphrase T1 in Figure 4 is an example of a good key-phrase, since documents that contain T1 also share many other words. On the other hand, a key-phrase that is not a good representative of an idea may occur in documents talking about a variety of different ideas. T2 in Figure 4 is an example of a bad key-phrase.

We formalize this definition of key-phrases as follows. Define the universe of elements to choose from, $U = \{(p, y), \dots\}$, where p is a candidate key-phrase and y denotes the year when the key-phrase became influential. Let the subset of the corpus that mentions a candidate key-phrase p be D_p. Intuitively, we wish to associate with (p, y) a representative document $d^* \in D_p$ which was published in year y and which was the most influential document in the subsequent development of D_p. According to our conjecture, for a bogus keyphrase, the associated d^* will achieve very poor coverage of the word content observed in documents of D_p that were published after y, while influential keyphrases will have a document that covers the associated stable word distribution very well. Following (4), we model the importance of covering a word

---

Algorithm 2 for greedy submodular function maximization with budget constraint.

$S^* \leftarrow \emptyset$
$A \leftarrow U = \{p_1, \dots\}$
$z^* \leftarrow \underset{p \in A | C(p) < k}{\arg\max} \; F(\{p\})$
while $A \neq \emptyset$ **and** $C(S^*) < k$ **do**
  $z \leftarrow \underset{p \in A}{\arg\max} \dfrac{F(S^* \cup \{p\}) - F(S^*)}{C(p)}$
  $S^* \leftarrow S^* \cup \{z\}$
  $A \leftarrow A \backslash \{z\}$
end while
if $F(S^*) < F(z^*)$ **then**
  return z^*
else
  return S^*
end if

---

in D_p as $\theta(w, y)^p$. More precisely,

$$\theta(w, y)^p = \sum_{d \in D_p : t(d) = y} TFIDF(d, w).$$

$$d^*(p, y) = \underset{d \in D_p : t(d) = y}{\arg\max} \sum_w \sum_{y' > y} \theta(w, y')^p \nu(d, w).$$

With this d^* for each element in U, we can formulate the objective

$$F(S) = \sum_w \sum_y \max_{\substack{(p_i, y_i) \in S \\ y = y_i}} \nu(d^*(p_i, y_i), w) \theta(w, y)^{p_i}. \quad (9)$$

Again, the objective decomposes into independent sub-problems for each year, and we can rewrite it for each year y as,

$$F_y(S) = \sum_w \max_{(p_i, y_i) \in S, y_i = y} \nu(d^*(p_i, y_i), w) \theta(w, y)^{p_i}. \quad (10)$$

Unlike in the previous optimization problems, we now associate a cost $C(p, y) = |\{d \in D_p : t(d) = y\}|$ with each element of S. This is done to encourage associating a key-phrase with the point in time when it begins to gain popularity. The number of documents published in a year mentioning a key-phrase is used as a proxy for the maturity of an idea. The optimization problem is,

$$S_y{}^* = \underset{S \subset U}{\arg\max} F_y(S)$$
$$\text{subject to} \quad \sum_{(p,y) \in S} C(p, y) \leq K.$$

This formulation is an instance of the budgeted coverage problem with a linear cost constraint, and the greedy Algorithm 2 is $(1 - 1/\sqrt{e})$ optimal [10, 8].

4.5 Alternate Formulation using Global Optimization and Adaptive Budget

For simplicity, so far we have decomposed the timeline-generating optimization problems into independent sub-problems, one for each year. This was possible since we imposed a cardinality constraint for each year. However, we can also define a global optimization problem across all years that constrains the maximum amount of content covered in each year. This results in a summary that will choose more documents from years that actually contain more interesting information. Formally, We change the global objective from (6) into

$$F(S) = \sum_w \sum_y \min\{F_y(S_y), \tau F_y(U_y)\}, \quad (11)$$

where the parameter τ determines how much relative word content per year we want to cover, $F_y(S_y)$ is as defined in (7) and U_y is the whole universe for year y. This global $F(S)$ is also monotone submodular and can be solved using the greedy Algorithm 1. Whereas earlier we had a cardinality constraint parameter k to set for each year, we have to set one global parameter τ (setting it higher results in more detailed summary) and one global k (higher values result in longer summary) now.

5. EXPERIMENTS

In this section, we empirically evaluate our proposed models on publicly available datasets. We first describe the datasets and then present the results of our experiments along with evaluation metrics. The experimental results show the advantage of our approaches compared to other baselines in addition to good qualitative results.

5.1 Datasets

We used three corpora containing research publications for evaluating our proposed approaches. The Neural Information Processing Systems (NIPS) corpus contains 1955 published papers over a span of 14 years. Similarly, the Association for Computational Linguistics (ACL) corpus [15] contains 18041 papers published in a number of conferences over a span of 39 years. We also collected the set of papers published in the proceedings of SIGIR and CIKM conferences over the years available from CiteSeer. This corpus contains 2097 papers published over a span of 18 years (the last year being 2007). In all cases, we associate each document (paper) with its publication year and limit ourselves to 12 consecutive years ending at the year before last (the citation graph is also constrained only to those years). Since we compute novelty of a document based on the nearest neighbors from the past, we also used the year immediately before our subset for this purpose in the subsequent experiments. The last year is skipped because it does not have any citations from the future. We did not use the early years in ACL and SIGIR-CIKM corpus because they contain significantly less papers and citations compared to other years.

All datasets include citation graphs which we use for evaluation purposes, however our method does not require citation information and could thus be easily applied to other document collections. Note that the citation graphs are sparse as they do not include references to and from the papers outside the corpus. The NIPS collection has 1512, the ACL collection has 82892 and the SIGIR-CIKM collection has 1750 citations between papers inside the corpus. In addition to regular research papers, NIPS corpus also contains meta documents representing volume indices. We removed such documents manually since they are very easy to spot. We also pruned the words and retained only those words which occurred at least twice in a document and in at least three documents in the corpus. This simple heuristic removed a lot of noise introduced by the OCR system, and allowed us to meaningfully interpret influence. We represent every document by the TFIDF score (computed on the whole corpus) of the words contained in it after pruning, and normalize the resulting document vector to unit length. To compute the nearest neighbor in the past (to determine novelty), we use the cosine similarity between the document vectors. We do not require the exact nearest neighbors, and in case of a very large corpus, approximate methods to find similar documents can be employed to sidestep the quadratic time complexity of this step.

5.2 Influential Documents

The word coverage approach (from Section 3) obtains a summary by maximizing the word coverage. In Section 4.1 we argued that influential documents have novel ideas which subsequently spread through the corpus. In this experiment, we select the most influential papers based on our objective (5) which captures novelty of a document and its sphere of influence, and compare it with those selected by the simple word coverage objective (1). Since there is no standard way of measuring the influence of a paper, we resort to the citation structure available in the corpora. To quantitatively evaluate whether the selected papers were indeed influential, we compute the total citation count for the set of papers (i.e., the number of times these papers were cited by documents in the corpus) selected by any algorithm. There have been several criticisms of citation-based impact measures and some effort [5, 26] addresses them. However, for a comparative study, we believe citation counts are the least biased choice in this setup.

To provide a point of comparison for the coverage based approaches, we considered several baselines. The simplest baseline was to randomly select documents until the budget was reached (*random*). Another baseline that we considered was to select the most prolific authors in the conference (in terms of number of accepted papers) and then select the required number of papers from the union of their papers (*authors*). More concretely, we first rank the authors according to the number of papers in the collection they authored. Next, we pick the 10 most prolific authors. Finally, we sample uniformly at random with replacement from the set of authored papers the same number of papers for each author. We also computed the upper bound on the total citation count possible for a selection by selecting papers with the highest observed citation inlinks in the corpus (*bound*).

We selected 100 documents from the NIPS, SIGIR-CIKM and ACL corpus that maximize the respective objective function. Our experiments presented here are using unigrams as the elements in the universe. However, our methods can use other types of elements (e.g. bigrams formed from consecutive words, for which we observed a similar trend in the results). The results of this experiments are provided in Table 1. We also provide standard error of these results; they were estimated from the citation count on 10 re-runs of 70% subsampling of the corpus.

From the table, it is clear that our approach (*infl. papers*) gets significantly higher citations compared to the word-coverage approach (*word cover*) in all corpora. Moreover, finding influential papers is computationally cheap (with running time linear in the size of the corpus multiplied by the number of selected papers if we do not count the preprocessing step of computing nearest neighbors for novelty score) and, for example, takes a few seconds for the NIPS corpus on a standard desktop computer.

method	NIPS	ACL	SIGIR-CIKM
Random	64 (4.6)	422 (41)	84 (7.9)
Authors	115 (4.0)	1097 (49)	86 (4.8)
Word Cover	92 (2.7)	799 (170)	96 (5.2)
Infl. Papers	196 (12.8)	1842 (111)	217 (14.5)
Bound	521 (11.0)	9787 (143)	815 (13.5)

Table 1: Total citations obtained by the papers selected for influential documents and baselines using unigrams. All results use 1-NN for novelty score. The values in parentheses indicate standard error.

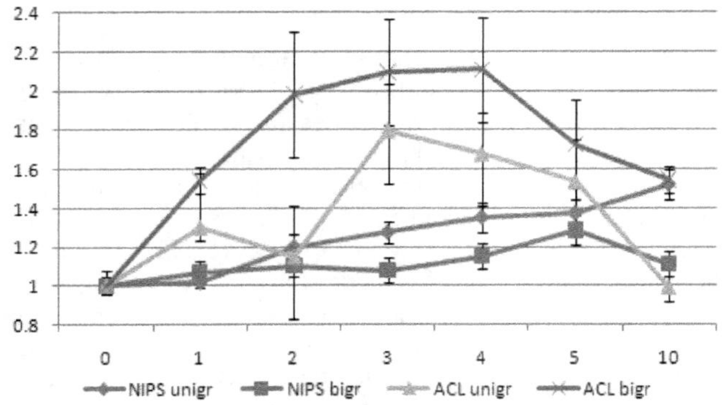

Figure 5: Comparison of results of word coverage approach when using different values of k (number of nearest neighbors for computing novelty score) on NIPS and ACL corpus for unigrams and bigrams. The horizontal axis represents the value of k and the vertical axis relative performance (number of citations) when compared to not using the novelty score (i.e. $k = 0$).

5.3 Impact of Using Novelty Score

Our approach uses the novelty score (introduced in Section 4.1, Eq. (3)) to credit a document for an idea only if it was the first one proposing it. Novelty is captured by considering k nearest neighbors in the past and subtracting their word weights (clipping at 0 to prevent negative values) from the current document. In this subsection we explore the impact of choosing different values of parameter k.

Results for the word coverage approach on NIPS and ACL (as examples of two slightly different behaviors) using unigrams or bigrams as elements in the universe are presented in Figure 5 . We would expect word coverage to improve when using novelty scores because the coverage most likely does not choose the initial (highly cited) paper but some later one with better coverage (e.g. a derivative paper that also incorporates some other ideas). This intuition is confirmed by our results showing that using more neighbors improves the score as we incorporate more and more information about novelty. After a point we can see that performance starts dropping again because we are subtracting too much content.

Almost all coverage approaches benefit from using 1-NN, but increasing k only improves performance for word coverage approach. We believe that using 1-NN helps because it mimics a language background model and penalizes frequent non-content words, while increasing k above that does not bring significant benefits because we already model temporal behavior with the choice of our model.

5.4 Timelines of Document Influence

In this sub-section, we evaluate our approach to create timelines of document influence and compare it against several other baselines. For each NIPS, ACL and SIGIR-CIKM corpus, we select 10 documents per year.

Again, we considered the random baseline (*random*) and the 10 most prolific authors (*authors*). The authors baseline is constructed as follows: first create a union of all papers by 10 authors with the highest number of accepted papers, and for each year select 10 documents randomly from this union (with replacement) published on or before this year. We computed the upper bound on the citations (*bound*) by selecting papers with highest citation count in a given year (i.e. we count only citations occurring in that particular year) – we call this the *current citations*.

We evaluate the selections based on the citation network as before. In the previous section, our evaluation was based on the total number of citations a paper obtained. However, in this section, it is based on the current citations. To select a timeline of influential papers, we select papers that have maximum influence in a particular year (for each year). So, to quantitatively evaluate the selections, if a paper is selected as influential in the year y, we count the number of citations it gets in the year y (i.e. only citations from papers citing it in this year count) and then sum them across all years.

Results for this experiment are summarized in Table 2. We can see that *random* baseline and *authors* have inferior performance compared to our approach (*timeline*). Note that the gap between our approach (*timeline*) and the *bound* is larger than in the influential papers experiment. We believe this is due to *timeline* being an inherently harder problem – not only do we have to find influential papers but we also have to specify exactly when were they influential (as the evaluation metric counts only citations from papers citing in that selected year). Our approach to constructing timelines is fast to compute (time complexity is linear in the number of years, papers selected and corpus size) and, e.g., takes less than 3 seconds on the NIPS corpus on a standard desktop computer.

method	NIPS	ACL	SIGIR-CIKM
Random	14 (1.4)	85 (11)	11 (1.2)
Authors	14 (1.2)	84 (14)	7 (1.0)
Timeline	60 (3.0)	190 (14)	30 (1.9)
Bound	269 (3.0)	3316 (11)	367 (4.1)

Table 2: Current citations (i.e. number of citations from papers citing in that particular year) obtained by the papers selected for timeline and baselines using unigrams as elements of the universe. All results are for 10 re-runs of 70% subsampling and using 1-NN for novelty score. The values in parentheses indicate standard error.

5.5 Timelines of Author Influence

In this section, we conducted experiments based on the objective proposed in Section 4.3 to select timelines of Author Influence. Instead of selecting papers we now consider meta-documents describing authors and construct a timeline showing which authors were important and when. In addition to this, for each selected author we constrain the corpus to that author's papers and find the most influential ones (including their timeframe of prominence).

We present a visualization of the results for NIPS corpus in Figure 6. By just looking at the plot it is easy to gain some insight into the development and content of the corpus. Features such as some authors having an influence throughout the whole corpus (e.g. Jordan, Sejnowski) are easy to spot. We can also see that some authors have had more influence only in specific timeframes (e.g. Hinton in the early years and Smola in the later years). In addition, looking at the selection of an author's most influential papers gives us insight into what topics they usually write about.

Although there are quantitative metrics which might be used to judge the output of the system to pick influential authors (e.g. *H-index*), note that we require these metrics to be computed for the timeframe of the collection only. Given the very sparse citation graph, using only observed intra-collection citations is expected to be a noisy signal. Qualitative results clearly indicate good performance of our approach and we feel that any simple adaptation of existing measures would not give a significantly better insight.

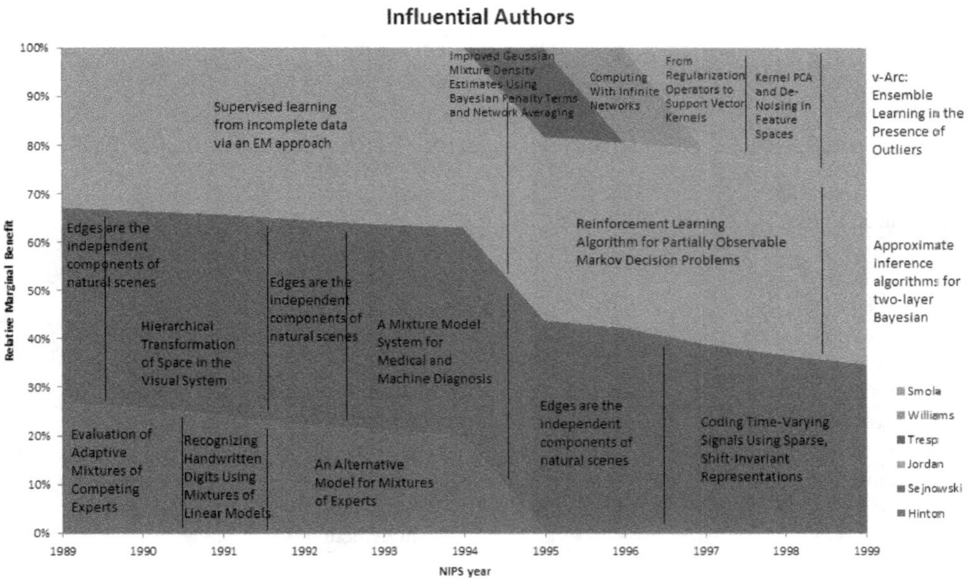

Figure 6: An example of applying our framework to select the most important authors and the most important papers for the given authors using our framework. In each of 11 consecutive years of NIPS we selected three authors and then we selected that author's most influential paper in a particular year. The width of the author's slice (relative marginal benefit) represents the importance relative to other selected authors (which is computed as decrease in objective score if we remove that author from the collected set).

5.6 Key-phrase Extraction

With the formulation described in 4.4, we ran experiments to find prominent key-phrases in each of the scientific corpora. For the set of candidate key-phrases, we considered trigrams and bigrams that occurred in at least 0.2% of the documents in the respective corpus. Moreover, if a trigram is admitted to the set of candidate key-phrases, the constituent bigrams are not considered as candidates. This is a simple heuristic that recognizes that the lexical unit for phrases is usually a trigram or bigram and greedily prefers trigrams. More sophisticated ways to determine the set of candidates are possible, say independently running a Part-Of-Speech tagger and considering only noun phrases. The number of candidate key-phrases using this heuristic rule is 3035 for the NIPS corpus, 8139 for the SIGIR-CIKM corpus and 4687 for the ACL corpus. The fewer number of candidates in the ACL corpus is explained by the fact that requiring the document frequency of bigrams or trigrams to be 0.2% of a much larger corpus is a more restrictive filter.

We lack ground truth key-phrases to evaluate the output of our system; also, it is hard to quantitatively judge the quality of an influential key-phrase's associated timestamp. We therefore estimate the average citations in the collection of documents that mentions a key-phrase as a measure of its quality. Concretely, for a key-phrase p and the subset of the corpus D_p that mentions it,

$$Score(p) = \sum_{d \in D_p; d' \in D_p; d' \neq d} Cite(d \leftarrow d') / |D_p|$$

where $Cite(d \leftarrow d')$ indicates that document d is cited by d'. We optimized the objective in Section 4.4 for each year with a budget of 3, and collected the set of all unique key-phrases. The reported scores for this approach (presented as *TimeCov* in Table 4) are the sum of $Score(p)$ for each unique collected key-phrase p. As a point of comparison, we also report the number of unique key-phrases collected as *Count*. A simple baseline for this experiment would be to pick the most frequent key-phrases occurring in the corpus in each year: this approach is hindered by the frequent occurrence of redundant phrases. For instance, "neural network" in the NIPS corpus,"natural language" in the ACL corpus and "information retrieval" in the SIGIR-CIKM corpus appear in such an overwhelming majority of documents over all the years as to drown out other informative candidates. This baseline is reported as *MostFreq* in our results. Another approach we compare with is to pick candidates that optimize the $Score$ directly in each year; this can be interpreted as an upper bound for this evaluation metric. We also provide the collected candidates from the coverage approach and one that optimizes the $Score(t)$ directly for the SIGIR-CIKM corpus in Table 3. Several informative phrases that come from diverse areas of research covered in SIGIR and CIKM get selected in the coverage approach. Furthermore, a visualization of the key-phrases over years for the NIPS corpus is shown in Fig. 7. Area of the shaded region corresponding to a term represents the fraction of documents observed in the corpus in that year that mention that particular term.

	NIPS		ACL		SIGIR-CIKM	
Method	Count	Score	Count	Score	Count	Score
MostFreq	13	2.13	20	34.33	20	7.41
TimeCov	17	4.68	77	116.92	29	12.28
Bound	13	6.09	96	124.10	29	18.82

Table 4: Quantitative results of keyphrase extraction.

6. CONCLUSIONS

This paper presented a submodular framework for temporal corpus summarization. We extended the notion of word coverage and asserted that summaries cover important concepts by covering associated words over a time interval. A timeline of influential documents, or authors, or coherent key phrases was constructed using

Year	Coverage		CiteScore	
	Keyword	Marginal Influence	Keyword	Marginal Influence
1995	relevant document query expansion	17.240 5.464	information retrieval singular value training set	20.0 5.0 5.0
1996	search engine semantic indexing lsi filtering system	8.228 6.034 2.818	speech recognition block size	3.5 2.0
1997	web search training data language model	11.853 7.871 6.760	retrieval system test collection	5.0 5.0
1998	language model retrieval model learning algorithm	5.411 4.799 4.024	summarization system naive bayes unjudged document	8.0 7.0 6.0
1999	language model	12.358	general english pearson correlation	10.0 5.0
2000	clustering result document model cori algorithm	4.354 3.130 2.645	cumulative gain expansion term event detection	8.0 4.0 4.0
2001	cross-language information user information hits algorithm	4.897 3.450 3.044	smoothing method topic distillation	14.5 7.0
2002	training example term dependency input stream	2.099 1.868 1.698	translation disambiguation hoc retrieval	3.0 3.0
2003	query language feature selection document clustering	2.509 1.779 1.751	image feature finding expert novelty detection	5.0 5.0 4.0
2004	training image inverted index element retrieval	1.887 1.413 1.100	regularized logistic regression label information web browser	3.0 3.0 3.0
2005	xml retrieval	3.926	existing retrieval function new system index construction	3.0 2.0 2.0

Table 3: The list of key-phrases for SIGIR-CIKM selected by the greedy algorithm solving the budgeted coverage problem with budget of 3 and by optimizing the citation score.

our approach, providing concrete suggestions for further and more detailed exploration of the corpus contents. Our approach leveraged both the novelty of a document as well as its influence in the development of the corpus and relied only on word features; in particular, it does not require a citation structure to infer influence across time. Therefore it is applicable to any textual collection which provides timestamped documents. Our optimization objectives used monotone submodular functions to trade-off relevance and redundancy elegantly, and were solved using an efficient greedy algorithm with a constant factor approximation guarantee. We empirically demonstrated that our approach performs better than several baselines using citation based performance measures and provided qualitative timelines for a few scientific corpora.

7. ACKNOWLEDGEMENTS

This research was funded in part through NSF Awards IIS-0812091, IIS-0905467, and IIS-1217686.

8. REFERENCES

[1] J. Allan, R. Gupta, and V. Khandelwal. Temporal summaries of new topics. In *SIGIR*, pages 10–18, New York, NY, USA, 2001. ACM.

[2] D. M. Blei, A. Y. Ng, and M. I. Jordan. Latent dirichlet allocation. *Journal of Machine Learning Research*, 3:993–1022, Mar. 2003.

[3] J. Carbonell and J. Goldstein. The use of mmr, diversity-based reranking for reordering documents and producing summaries. In *SIGIR*, pages 335–336, New York, NY, USA, 1998. ACM.

[4] C. C. Chen and M. C. Chen. Tscan: a novel method for topic summarization and content anatomy. In *SIGIR*, pages 579–586, New York, NY, USA, 2008. ACM.

[5] P. Chen, H. Xie, S. Maslov, and S. Redner. Finding scientific gems with google's pagerank algorithm. *Journal of Informetrics*, 1(1):8 – 15, 2007.

[6] K. El-Arini and C. Guestrin. Beyond keyword search: discovering relevant scientific literature. In *KDD*, pages 439–447, New York, NY, USA, 2011. ACM.

[7] K. El-Arini, G. Veda, D. Shahaf, and C. Guestrin. Turning down the noise in the blogosphere. In *KDD*, pages 289–298, New York, NY, USA, 2009. ACM.

[8] S. Khuller, A. Moss, and J. S. Naor. The budgeted maximum coverage problem. *Information Processing Letters*, 70(1), 1999.

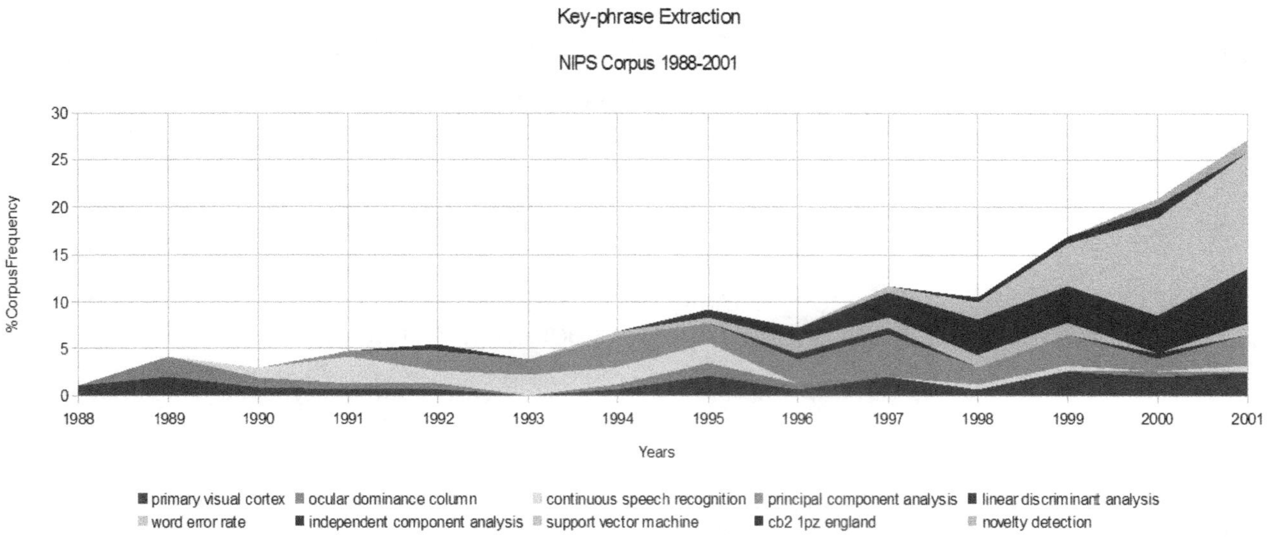

Figure 7: A timeline showing the evolution of the key-phrases selected by the coverage approach in the NIPS corpus.

[9] J.-M. Lim, I.-S. Kang, J.-H. Bae, and J.-H. Lee. Sentence extraction using time features in multi-document summarization. In *Information Retrieval Technology*, volume 3411 of *Lecture Notes in Computer Science*, pages 82–93. Springer Berlin / Heidelberg, 2005.

[10] H. Lin and J. Bilmes. Multi-document summarization via budgeted maximization of submodular functions. In *HLT*, pages 912–920, Stroudsburg, PA, USA, 2010. Association for Computational Linguistics.

[11] R. McDonald. A study of global inference algorithms. In *Lecture Notes in Computer Science*, 2007.

[12] R. Nallapati, A. Feng, F. Peng, and J. Allan. Event threading within news topics. In *CIKM*, pages 446–453, New York, NY, USA, 2004. ACM.

[13] G. L. Nemhauser, L. A. Wolsey, and M. L. Fisher. An analysis of approximations for maximizing submodular set functions. *Mathematical Programming*, 14:265–294, 1978.

[14] A. Nenkova and K. McKeown. Automatic summarization. *Foundations and Trends in Information Retrieval*, 5(2-3):103–233, 2011.

[15] D. R. Radev, P. Muthukrishnan, and V. Qazvinian. The ACL anthology network corpus. In *Proceedings, ACL Workshop on Natural Language Processing and Information Retrieval for Digital Libraries*, Singapore, 2009.

[16] K. Raman, T. Joachims, and P. Shivaswamy. Structured learning of two-level dynamic rankings. In *CIKM*, 2011.

[17] G. Salton and C. Buckley. Term weighting approaches in automatic text retrieval. Technical report, Cornell University, Ithaca, NY, USA, 1987.

[18] B. Shaparenko and T. Joachims. Information genealogy: Uncovering the flow of ideas in non-hyperlinked document databases. In *KDD*, pages 619–628, 2007.

[19] R. Sipos, P. Shivaswamy, and T. Joachims. Large-margin learning of submodular summarization methods. In *EACL*, 2012.

[20] I. Subašić and B. Berendt. From bursty patterns to bursty facts: The effectiveness of temporal text mining for news. In *ECAI*, pages 517–522, Amsterdam, The Netherlands, The Netherlands, 2010. IOS Press.

[21] A. Swaminthan, C. Metthew, and D. Kirovski. Essential pages. In *Technical Report, MSR-TR-2008-15*, Microsoft Research, 2008.

[22] R. Swan and J. Allan. Automatic generation of overview timelines. In *SIGIR*, pages 49–56, New York, NY, USA, 2000. ACM.

[23] H. Takamura and M. Okumura. Text summarization model based on maximum coverage problem and its variant. In *EACL*, pages 781–789, Stroudsburg, PA, USA, 2009. Association for Computational Linguistics.

[24] R. Torres, S. M. McNee, M. Abel, J. A. Konstan, and J. Riedl. Enhancing digital libraries with techlens+. In *Proceedings of the 4th ACM/IEEE-CS joint conference on Digital libraries*, JCDL '04, pages 228–236, New York, NY, USA, 2004. ACM.

[25] M. Wu, W. Li, Q. Lu, and K.-F. Wong. Event-based summarization using time features. In *Proceedings of the 8th International Conference on Computational Linguistics and Intelligent Text Processing*, CICLing '07, pages 563–574, Berlin, Heidelberg, 2007. Springer-Verlag.

[26] E. Yan and Y. Ding. Weighted citation: An indicator of an article's prestige. *Journal of the American Society for Information Science and Technology*, 61(8):1635–1643, 2010.

[27] R. Yan, X. Wan, J. Otterbacher, L. Kong, X. Li, and Y. Zhang. Evolutionary timeline summarization: a balanced optimization framework via iterative substitution. In *SIGIR*, pages 745–754, New York, NY, USA, 2011. ACM.

[28] Y. Yue and T. Joachims. Predicting diverse subsets using structural SVMs. In *ICML*, pages 271–278, 2008.

TCSST: Transfer Classification of Short & Sparse Text Using External Data

Guodong Long, Ling Chen, Xingquan Zhu, Chengqi Zhang
QCIS*, University of Technology Sydney, Australia
Guodong.Long@student.uts.edu.au,
{Ling.Chen, Xingquan.Zhu, Chengqi.Zhang}@uts.edu.au

ABSTRACT

Short & sparse text is becoming more prevalent on the web, such as search snippets, micro-blogs and product reviews. Accurately classifying short & sparse text has emerged as an important while challenging task. Existing work has considered utilizing external data (e.g. Wikipedia) to alleviate data sparseness, by appending topics detected from external data as new features. However, training a classifier on features concatenated from different spaces is not easy considering the features have different physical meanings and different significance to the classification task. Moreover, it exacerbates the "curse of dimensionality" problem. In this study, we propose a transfer classification method, TCSST, to exploit the external data to tackle the data sparsity issue. The transfer classifier will be learned in the original feature space. Considering that the labels of the external data may not be readily available or sufficiently enough, TCSST further exploits the unlabeled external data to aid the transfer classification. We develop novel strategies to allow TCSST to iteratively select high quality unlabeled external data to help with the classification. We evaluate the performance of TCSST on both benchmark as well as real-world data sets. Our experimental results demonstrate that the proposed method is effective in classifying very short & sparse text, consistently outperforming existing and baseline methods.

Categories and Subject Descriptors

H.3.1 [**Information Storage and Retrieval**]: Content Analysis and Indexing; I.2.7 [**Artificial Intelligence**]: Natural Language Processing—*text analysis*; I.2.6 [**Artificial Intelligence**]: Learning

*QCIS: centre for Quantum Computation & Intelligent Systems

CIKM'12, October 29–November 2, 2012, Maui, HI, USA.

General Terms

ALGORITHMS, PERFORMANCE, EXPERIMENTATION

Keywords

Short & Sparse Text Mining, Classification, Transfer Learning, Wikipedia, External Data

1. INTRODUCTION

Text categorization, one of the most important tasks of text mining, has been studied intensively in the past decade. Various algorithms (e.g. Naive Bayes, Maximum Entropy) have been applied to text classification and proved to be effective on different benchmark datasets (e.g. 20Newsgroups, Reuters-21578). Due to the rapid advancement of information technologies and web applications, there has been an increasingly large amount of *short & sparse text* data available online, such as micro-blogs, web search snippets, forum messages and product reviews etc. Consequently, mining short & sparse text to derive high quality knowledge will benefit many information retrieval and web applications.

Briefly, short & sparse text refers to a data set where each text instance is short, consisting of from a dozen words to a few sentences. Moreover, two instances usually do not share enough word co-occurrence. These new features render traditional text mining tools ineffective, motivating the development of novel methodologies. For example, for the research tasks of measuring similarity between short texts and clustering short texts, methods have been proposed to overcome the data sparsity by expanding original data with information or context extracted from external data, such as the query results returned by search engines [14] and the online data repositories (e.g. Wikipedia) [2].

For the task of classifying short & sparse text, although limited work has been done in this area, the proposed methods [12][16] similarly resort to external or auxiliary data to deal with the data sparseness problem. For instance, Phan et al. [12] proposed to mine hidden topics from a very large external data collection, and represent each text instance as a vector of words and topics. Then, one classifier was trained on concatenated features from two spaces. The main limitations of the method are: 1) the original features of words and the detected topics are not comparable as they have different physical interpretations and, therefore, different contributions to the classification task. It may not be appropriate to directly concatenating features from different spaces to train a classifier; 2) appending detected topics as new features will increase the dimension of the data, exacerbating the "curse of dimensionality" problem. Hence, in this paper, we aim to construct a classification model for short & sparse text by using external data and dealing with original feature space.

In particular, we propose a method called, **T**ransfer **C**lassification of **S**hort & **S**parse **T**ext (TCSST), which uses transfer learning to exploit the external data to aid the classification for short & sparse text. It is usually assumed by traditional transfer classification that, while there is only a very small set of labeled data in the new target domain, there are plenty of labeled data in the old source domain. Therefore, traditional transfer classification focuses on leveraging the labeled data in the source domain to learn an effective classifier for the target domain. However, for the problem of short & sparse text classification, the external data is typically acquired through querying search engines or crawling online data repositories. It can't be expected that there are plenty of data in the external domain with labels readily available. Therefore, TCSST focuses on exploiting both labeled and unlabeled data in the external domain to construct the classification model for the short & sparse text. We develop novel strategies to allow TCSST to efficiently and iteratively select from the large set of unlabeled external data a subset where the data are very likely to be useful in the transfer classification. The selected data will be used to train the transfer classifier together with other labeled training data.

The main contributions of the work is summarized as follows.

- We proposed a novel short & sparse text classification method which uses transfer learning to exploit the external data and deals with features in the original space.
- We developed novel strategies to leverage both labeled and unlabeled data in the source domain to construct a high quality classification model for the target domain.
- We evaluated the performance of the proposed method on both benchmark and real-world data sets, comparing against baseline and the state-of-the-art approaches.

The rest of this paper is organized as follows. In Section 2, we review existing research on short & sparse text data mining. The problem definition of the transfer classification of short & sparse text data and the proposed method, TCSST, are discussed in details in Section 3. In Section 4, we provide the results of the experiments evaluating the performance of the proposed method. Finally, we summarize the work and discuss the future study in Section 5.

2. RELATED WORK

In this section, we review related research in the areas of short & sparse text mining, from similarity measure to clustering and classification.

Semantic similarity measure between short texts (e.g. words and named entities) has long been an integral part of information retrieval and natural language processing. Existing research can be generally divided into two categories: knowledge-based approaches and corpus-based approaches [10]. The former usually finds the relationship between words using some external lexical database (e.g. WordNet); while the latter frequently identifies the similarity degree by resorting to the information derived from large corpora. For corpus-based approaches, the two representative approaches to obtain large text collection are querying search engines and crawling online data repositories. For example, Bollegala et al. [3] used search engines to obtain enriched context data for measuring similarity between words. Similarly, Sahami and Heilman [14] measured the similarity between short text snippets by leveraging the search engines to acquire greater context. Yin and Meek [18] further improved the work [14] by introducing a web-relevance similarity measure and using a machine learning approach. Gabrilovich and Markovitch [6] computed semantic relatedness by representing the meaning of any text as a vector of Wikipedia concepts.

Clustering short text has attracted growing interests in recent years. Most of the existing research similarly relies on auxiliary data to overcome the data sparseness. For example, Banerjee et al. [2] tried to improve the clustering accuracy for short text by enriching their representation with additional features from Wikipedia. Hu et al. [7] proposed a hierarchical three-level structure to tackle the data sparsity problem and reconstruct the corresponding feature space with the integration of multiple semantic knowledge bases – Wikipedia and WordNet. Recently, Jin et al. [8] proposed to cluster short text messages via transfer learning from auxiliary long text data. While we similarly use transfer learning to exploit the auxiliary data, we focus on a different text mining task – text categorization.

The short and sparse feature pose similar challenges to the task of text categorization. The insufficient word cooccurrence renders traditional techniques such as "Bag-Of-Words" limited. Likewise, existing methods mainly exploit external data to expand the original data. In [16], Sriram et al. proposed to use a small set of features extracted from the author's profile and text to classify *tweets* – microblogs provided by Twitter. Sun et al. [17] used semantic analysis to extract concept information from Wikipedia to deep classify short text. Phan et al. [12] proposed to mine hidden topics from crawled Wikipedia corpus as new features and simply train a classifier from the augmented and combined feature space. However, it may not be appropriate to train a classifier on incomparable features with different physical meanings, and consequently different significance to the classification task. It also results in the increase of data dimensions. In our work, we study a different method – transfer learning – to exploit the external data, such that the classifier is trained in original feature space.

3. THE PROPOSED METHOD

In this section, we first formally define the problem of transfer classification of short & sparse text data. Next, we describe the framework of our proposed method, which is followed by the details of the algorithms.

3.1 Problem Definition

Similar to the existing research in short & sparse text mining, we consider exploiting external data (e.g. Wikipedia) for classifying short & sparse text (details of crawling relevant Wikipedia documents will be discussed in Section 4). Therefore, we have text data from two domains: the short & sparse domain χ^s and the external domain χ^e.

In particular, let $\chi^s = \{x_1^s, x_2^s, \ldots, x_m^s\}$ be the set of text

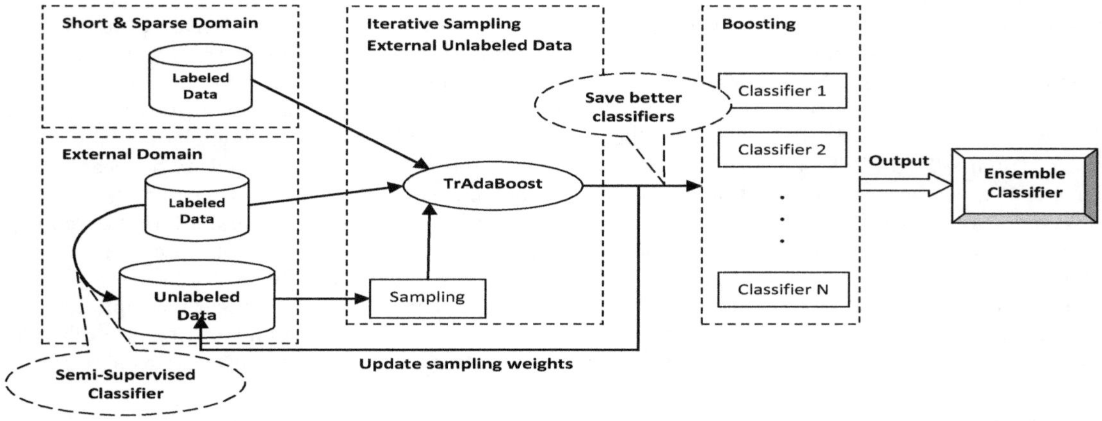

Figure 1: The framework of TCSST.

instances in the short & sparse domain, $\chi^e = \{x_1^e, x_2^e, \ldots, x_n^e\}$ be the set of instances in the external domain, and $\mathcal{C}=\{c_1, c_2, ..., c_k\}$ be the set of category labels. The instances in χ^s are divided into two disjoint subsets: the labeled subset $\mathcal{T}^s = \{(x_i^s, c(x_i^s))\}$ and the unlabeled subset $\mathcal{S}^s = \{(x_i^s)\}$, where $x_i^s \in \chi^s$ and $c(x_i^s) \in \mathcal{C}$. Similarly, χ^e is composed of the labeled subset $\mathcal{T}^e = \{(x_j^e, c(x_j^e))\}$ and the unlabeled subset $\mathcal{S}^e = \{(x_j^e)\}$, where $x_j^e \in \chi^e$ and $c(x_j^e) \in \mathcal{C}$. Then, **the problem of transfer classification of short & sparse text data is**: given a small number of labeled short & sparse text data $\mathcal{T}^s \subset \chi^s$, a small number of labeled external data and a large number of unlabeled external data $\chi^e = \mathcal{T}^e \cup \mathcal{S}^e$, the objective is to learn a classifier $H_{\chi^s \to \mathcal{C}}$ that minimizes the prediction error on the set of unlabeled short & sparse text $\mathcal{S}^s \subset \chi^s$.

There are two major issues that differentiate our problem from traditional transfer classification. Firstly, we focus on dealing with the short & sparse text data. Secondly, we aim to exploit both labeled and unlabeled data in the external domain, while traditional transfer classification leverages only the labeled data in the source domain to help with the classification in the target domain. The reason we try to exploit the unlabeled external data is motivated by the situation in the real-world application. For instance, given a set of labeled short & sparse text, we managed to crawl relevant documents from Wikipedia using carefully selected seeds. However, the labels of the crawled documents may not be readily available, or may be assigned very crudely. In this case, it is only affordable to manually label a very small number of documents in the external domain. Therefore, the proposed method will be practically useful if the unlabeled external data is made good use of to construct a high quality classification model for the short & sparse text data.

3.2 The Framework of TCSST

The framework of our proposed method, Transfer Classification of Short & Sparse Text (TCSST), is shown in Figure 1.

The input data is a small set of labeled short & sparse text. From online data repositories, we should be able to gather a large collection of relevant documents as external data, among which only a small set is labeled. Certainly, without considering the unlabeled external data $\mathcal{S}^e$, existing transfer classification method (e.g. TrAdaBoost [4]) can be employed directly to consider only the labeled data, $\mathcal{T}^s \subset \chi^s$ and $\mathcal{T}^e \subset \chi^e$, to learn a classifier for the short & sparse text. However, due to the insufficient number of labeled external data, the improvement brought by the traditional transfer classification might be limited. Therefore, TCSST aims to further exploit the unlabeled external data.

Intuitively, we can first predict labels for unlabeled external data, using some semi-supervised classification algorithm, in consideration of the limited number of labeled data in the external domain. Then, traditional transfer classification can be applied straightforwardly by treating all external data (with known or predicted labels) as training data.

However, as will be shown in our experiments in Section 4, this straightforward method fails to train a classifier of high quality. Sometimes its performance is even worse than the one using only the labeled external data (referred to as the *base classifier* hereafter). This is because there are too much noise in the unlabeled external data with predicted labels. Therefore, rather than including all unlabeled external instances into the transfer classification, we devise an iterative sampling process to allow TCSST to select a small set of unlabeled external data in each round. The selected unlabeled external data, with predicted labels, will be used together with other labeled data to train a transfer classifier. Each unlabeled external instance is associated with sampling probability, which will be updated in each round to reflect the importance of the instance to the transfer classification. Subsection 3.6 describes the details of the sampling process. Basically, an unlabeled external instance will be more likely to be sampled if it is regarded to be more useful in the transfer classification. If the learned transfer classifier works better than the base classifier, the classifier will be saved. As shown in the Figure 1, the output of TCSST is an ensemble classifier consisting of all intermediate classifiers better than the base classifier.

The main steps of TCSST are outlined as follows.

1. Predict labels for unlabeled external data (Subsection 3.4);
2. Assign initial sampling probabilities for unlabeled external data (Subsection 3.6) ;
3. Sample a set of unlabeled external data to train a

transfer classifier (Subsection 3.5), together with labeled external data and labeled short & sparse data;

4. Save or discard the transfer classifier depending on its performance and update the sampling probabilities for unlabeled external data (Subsection 3.6);
5. Go back to step 3 or output the boosting classifier on saved classifiers (Subsection 3.7).

3.3 Data Preparation

Today, Wikipedia has been known as the richest online encyclopedia which includes a huge number of documents in various topics. Since Wikipedia covers a lot of concepts and domains, it is reasonable to extract parts of Wikipedia documents to form an external dataset related to the target domain.

To collect data from Wikipedia, we prepare various seed crawling keywords from different class domains. The simplest method is utilizing the class name as the seed keywords. For example, in our five-class dataset, we utilize five class names (Human, Natural, Social, Physical, Financial) as crawling keywords. Furthermore, if the class labels are inconsistent or irrelevant to instances context, we can generate some keywords from the context information by common sense. For example, Phan et al. [12] generated seventy keywords for classification task. We crawl the seed's corresponding Wikipedia page and follow the outgoing hyperlinks to acquire related pages. Each crawling transaction is limited by the maximum depth of hyperlink (usually 4).

After downloading the pages, we would like to assign labels for these pages. Intuitively, for each seed, we can assign class label by manual, and assign the same label to the seed' related pages. However, this method has two limitations. Firstly, different seeds may share same related pages. Secondly, as the hyperlink depth increasing, the content of related pages are surprisingly different to the original seed page. Consider the limitations above, we manually assign labels for part of documents, and leave others as unlabeled data.

3.4 Semi-supervised Classification

In order to use the unlabeled external data in the transfer classification framework, we first predict labels for unlabeled external data. Considering the limited number of labeled external data, we choose to use semi-supervised classification instead of supervised classification. In particular, we use the Naive Bayes based self-training approach [19], while any semi-supervised classification algorithm should be workable here. The basic idea of self-training is to train firstly a classifier with the small amount of labeled data. The classifier is then used to classify the unlabeled data. Typically the most confident unlabeled data, together with their predicted labels, are added to the training set. The classifier is re-trained and the procedure repeated.

To avoid the over-fitting problem, we add a bagging framework on classifiers trained by the self-training at each iteration, and output an ensemble classifier $H(x)$ as the final classifier of semi-supervised learning.

$$H(x) = arg\min_{c_k \in \mathcal{C}} \sum_i (|h_i(x) - c_k|) \tag{1}$$

where $x \in \mathcal{S}^e \subset \chi^e$, and h_i is the classifier trained at the ith iteration of the semi-supervised learning.

3.5 Transfer Classification

According to the categorization of transfer learning in [11], our task of classifying short & sparse text using external data belongs to the category of *inductive transfer learning*. Different types of inductive transfer learning methods have been proposed, such as the feature representation based transferring [13] and the parameter based transferring [5]. In our work we adopt the *instance based transferring*, which provides a more flexible framework to allow us to include unlabeled external data instances afterward.

In particular, we borrow the framework of TrAdaBoost [4], which is a representative instance based transferring classification method. It extends from AdaBoost [15] that aims to boost the accuracy of a weak learner by carefully adjusting the weights of training instances and learn a classifier accordingly. Similar to AdaBoost, TrAdaBoost iteratively increases the weights for instances from the target domain (e.g. short & sparse domain) if they are wrongly predicted, expecting that the subsequent classifiers built will be tweaked in favor of the instances misclassified by previous classifiers. For instances in the source domain (e.g. external domain), the weights of wrongly predicted instances will be decreased, because it is regarded that these instances are most dissimilar to those in the target domain, exerting less impact on the classification.

In particular, the weight of instances in the target domain is updated as follows.

$$w_i^{(t+1)} = w^{(t)} * (\frac{1-\epsilon_t}{\epsilon_t})^{|h_t(x_i)-c(x_i)|}, \epsilon < 1/2 \tag{2}$$

where x_i is the ith labeled instance in the target domain, ϵ_t is the tth classifier's average lost over the target domain, and $|h_t(x_i) - c(x_i)|$ represents the tth classifier's lost on the instance x_i.

For wrongly predicted instances in the source domain, the weight is decreased based on the maximal iteration number, N, and the size of the data set n.

$$w_i^{(t+1)} = w^{(t)} (\frac{1}{1+\sqrt{2 \ln n/N}})^{|h_t(x_i)-c(x_i)|} \tag{3}$$

Classifiers trained from iterations 0 to $N/2$ are supposed to filter dissimilar instances in the source domain. Hence, TrAdaBoost finally outputs an ensemble classifier which is a weighted combination of the classifiers trained from iteration $N/2$ to N.

$$H(x) = arg\min_{c_k \in C} \sum_{t=\lceil N/2 \rceil}^{N} ((\log \frac{1-\epsilon_t}{\epsilon_t}) * |h_t(x) - c_k|) \tag{4}$$

where $\log \frac{1-\epsilon_t}{\epsilon_t}$ is the weight of the classifier h_t.

3.6 Sampling Unlabeled External Data

Recall that, due to the small number of labeled external data, TCSST aims to exploit the large set of unlabeled external data to boost the transfer classification. In particular, TCSST first predicts labels for unlabeled external data and then iteratively selects a small set of unlabeled external data, with predicted labels, to learn the transfer classifier together with the other training data (i.e. the labeled external data and labeled short & sparse data). In this subsection, we describe the strategies TCSST uses to sample unlabeled external data.

The basic idea is that, the more likely an instance is useful in the transfer classification, the more possible it will be sampled. To implement the idea, we assign a *sampling probability* to each unlabeled instance in the external domain. Given an instance $x_i \in \mathcal{S}^e \subset \chi^e$, an initial sampling probability $\rho(x_i)^0$ will be assigned. We first describe how to update $\rho(x_i)^{t+1}$ based on $\rho(x_i)^t$. We will revisit the point to discuss how to assign the initial sampling probability $\rho(x_i)^0$ later.

As introduced in Subsection 3.5, TrAdaBoost updates the weights for training instances in the external domain after each iteration. In particular, the weight of an instance will be decreased if it is regarded to be less useful in the transfer classification (i.e. Eq. 3). We will use the by-product of TrAdaBoost to update the sampling probability for unlabeled external data. First, a set of unlabeled external instances $\mathcal{P}^0 = \{x_1, x_2, \ldots, x_p\} \subset \mathcal{S}^e$ is selected, based on some initial sampling probabilities, to be included in TrAdaBoost. Each instance x_i will be assigned a sequence of weights respectively in the N iterations of TrAdaBoost $< w_i^{(0)}, w_i^{(1)}, \ldots, w_i^{(N)} >$. We define the final weight of the instance, ω_i, as the sum of the weights assigned in the iterations from $\lceil N/2 \rceil$ to N where the classifiers start to converge.

$$\omega_i = \sum_{t=\lceil N/2 \rceil}^{N} w_i^{(t)} \tag{5}$$

Let the final weights of the instances in $\mathcal{P}^0$ be $< \omega_1, \omega_2, \ldots, \omega_p >$. We normalize the weights by setting ω_i to $\omega_i / \sum_{j=1}^{p} \omega_j$ such that $\omega_i \in (0, 1)$. Then, we update the sampling probability for each unlabeled external instance as follows.

$$\rho(x_i)^{(t+1)} = \begin{cases} \omega_i * \rho(x_i)^{(t)}, & \text{if } x_i \in \mathcal{P}^{(t)} \\ \rho(x_i)^{(t)}, & \text{otherwise} \end{cases} \tag{6}$$

For an unlabeled instance that has been selected in the tth round, if it turns out to be useful in the transfer classification (e.g. the weight ω_i is high), Eq. 6 will decrease (because $\omega_i < 1$) its sampling probability less significantly. Otherwise, its weight ω_i will be low and its sampling probability will be decreased more significantly. If an unlabeled instance has not been selected in the t-th round, its sampling probability will not be decreased. That is, an unsampled instance will have more chances to be selected.

We now discuss how to assign the initial sampling probability $\rho(x_i)^{(0)}$ for each unlabeled external data. Since we have a large collection of unlabeled external data, if starting from a set $\mathcal{P}^0$ consisting of instances that are not useful in the transfer classification, it may require more rounds of iterative sampling to find useful data to boost the classification. Therefore, instead of assigning equal sampling probabilities to all unlabeled external data, we assign higher sampling probabilities to instances which are more likely to be useful. In particular, we learn a base classifier by running TrAdaBoost on labeled short & sparse text (e.g. $\mathcal{T}^s$) and labeled external text (e.g. $\mathcal{T}^e$) only. Based on the results of the base classifier, we can similarly compute the final weight for each labeled external instance, $\omega(x_j)$, using Eq. 5 and normalize to make sure $\omega(x_j)$ ranges between 0 and 1. Next, given an unlabeled external instance $x_i \in \mathcal{S}^e$, we measure its similarity with every labeled external instance $x_j \in \mathcal{T}^e$. If it is more similar to a high quality labeled external instance, its initial sampling probability will be higher. That is,

$$\rho(x_i)^{(0)} = \sum_{x_j \in \mathcal{T}^e} sim(x_i, x_j) * \omega(x_j) \tag{7}$$

where $sim(x_i, x_j)$ is the similarity between two text instances and the cosine similarity measure is adopted here.

Algorithm 1 Transfer Classification of Short & Sparse Text

input
 $\mathcal{T}^s, \mathcal{T}^e, \mathcal{S}^e$, M - size of $\mathcal{P}$, MAX_ITERATION
output
 $H(x)$ - the TCSST classifier

```
1: TrAdaBoost(T^s, T^e) /*learn the base classifier h_0(x)*/
2: For each x_i ∈ S^e, assign ρ(x_i)^(0) as Eq. 7
3: Let t = 0, H = ∅
4: while t<MAX_ITERATION do
5:    Sample S^e to generate P^(t)
6:    h_t(x) =TrAdaBoost(T^s, T^e, P^(t))
7:    if α_t > α_0 then
8:       H = H ∪ {h_t(x)} /*α_i is n-fold cross-validation
         accuracy of h_i*/
9:    end if
10:   t= t+1
11:   For each x_i ∈ S^e, update ρ(x_i)^(t) as Eq. 6
12: end while
13: H(x) = argmin_{c_k∈C} Σ_{i=1}^{|H|} (α_i * |h_i(x) − c_k|)
```

3.7 Boosting From Saved Classifiers

As aforementioned, TCSST iteratively samples a set of unlabeled external instances with predicted labels, together other labeled training data to learn a transfer classifier. If the learned classifier performs better than the base classifier which uses labeled training data only, the learned classifier will be saved. The final output of TCSST is an ensemble classifier combining all saved classifiers. We use the n-fold cross-validation accuracy over the training data as the voting weight of each saved classifier $h_i(x)$. Then, the output classifier $H(x)$ of TCSST is,

$$H(x) = arg\min_{c_k \in C} \sum_i (\alpha_i * |h_i(x) - c_k|) \tag{8}$$

where α_i is the n-fold cross validation accuracy of the i-th saved classifier.

The pseudo code of TCSST is given in Alg. 1. Firstly, we learn a base classifier by training TrAdaBoost on labeled training data (line 1), based on which we assign initial sampling probabilities to unlabeled external data (line 2). Then, an iterative process is started by sampling a subset of unlabeled external data $\mathcal{P}^{(t)}$ (line 5), which will be used to train the t-th transfer classifier $h_t(x)$ (line 6). If the performance of the t-th classifier is better than the base classifier $h_0(t)$, $h_t(x)$ will be saved (lines 7-9). Based on the results of t-th classifier, the sampling probabilities of unlabeled external instances are updated (line 11). The final classifier is a weighted combination of saved classifiers (line 13).

4. PERFORMANCE STUDY

In this section, we evaluate the performance of TCSST. We describe first the data sets used in our experiments. Then, the methods used to be compared with TCSST will

Table 1: Data set constructed from 20-Newsgroup

Data Set	Short & Sparse D.	External D.
rec vs talk	rec.autos rec.motorcycles talk.politics.guns talk.politics.misc	rec.sport.baseball rec.sport.hockey talk.politics.mideast talk.religion.misc

Table 2: Statistics of the two data sets

	Benchmark Data	NRM Data
Size of χ^s	3669	189
Size of χ^e	3561	1137
Sparse degree	99.93% $\longrightarrow$ 99.98%	99.92%
Vocabulary size $\|V\|$	15254	6112
Number of classes	2	5

be discussed. Finally, we show the results of different types experiments.

4.1 Datasets

We evaluate the performance of TCSST on a benchmark data set as well as a real-world data set.

For the benchmark data set, we consider the well-known 20newsgroup data [9], which has been frequently used for evaluating and comparing different transfer learning algorithms for text classification. The 20newsgroup is a text collection of approximately 20,000 news-group documents, which are partitioned across 20 different newsgroups nearly evenly. In our study, we generate a data set from two top categories, *rec* and *talk*, one as positive and the other as negative. We then split the data in the two categories based on their sub-categories. Table 1 shows the specific sub-category based splitting strategy that divides the data into two domains. The splitting strategy ensures that the documents in the two domains are different but related, since they are under different sub-categories while same top categories. The task is to classify top categories. Since we focus on dealing with the classification of short & sparse text, we make one of the domains (the one in the second column of Table 1) to be sparse, by randomly deleting features for instances. The other domain (i.e. the third column of Table 1) then serves as the external domain. In our experiments, we will vary the parameter – the percentage of features deleted from each instance – to generate sparse domains with different sparse degrees, and evaluate classification models on the generated sparse data sets. The second column of Table 2 summarizes some statistics of the benchmark data set. The top two numbers are the sizes of the short & sparse domain and the external domain respectively. The third number is the sparse degree of the short & sparse domain, which is defined as follows. Let M be a matrix representation of the short & sparse domain χ^s such that m_{ij} is non-zero if the i-th instance contains the j-th word. Then, the sparse degree of χ^s is defined as the ratio of zero elements to all elements in M.

$$Sparse\_degree(\chi^s) = \frac{|\{m_{ij}|m_{ij} = 0\}|}{|\chi^s| * |V|} \quad (9)$$

where $|V|$ is the vocabulary size. Thus, the higher the sparse degree, the more sparse the data.

We also use a real-world data set to evaluate the classification models. The data was collected from participatory workshops that were held to assess the capacity of natural resource managers, such as landholders and graziers, to adapt to natural resource changes. Participants were invited to comment from five indicators: *human*, *social*, *natural*, *physical* and *financial*. Each comment thus is a short & sparse text instance, belonging to one of the five categories. To obtain relevant external data, we follow the strategy used in [12] to crawl Wikipedia documents. We use the five class labels as the seed keywords. For each seed keyword, we ran JWikiDocs [1] to download the corresponding Wikipedia pages. We also crawled the relevant pages by following outgoing hyperlinks, with the maximal depth of hyperlink as 3. We crawled overall 1137 relevant documents from Wikipedia. After removing HTML tags, noisy text and links, stop words, the statistics of the real-world data set are reported in the third column of Table 2. We refer to this data set as NRM Data and make it available online [1].

4.2 Compared Methods

We compare the performance of TCSST against the following methods.

- Supervised Classification. This method uses only the small set of labeled short & sparse text $\mathcal{T}^s \subset \chi^s$ as the training data to learn a classifier. It serves as the baseline approach. In particular, we use Random Tree as the classification model and refer to this method as *Random Tree*.

- Traditional Transfer Classification. This method uses only the small set of labeled short & sparse text $\mathcal{T}^s \subset \chi^s$, and the small set of labeled external data $\mathcal{T}^e \subset \chi^e$ as the training data to learn a transfer classifier. In particular, we use TrAdaBoost as the classification model, and RandomTree as the weak learner used by TrAdaBoost. Note that, TCSST is an ensemble classifier which combines multiple TrAdaBoost classifiers. To enable a fair comparison, we randomly generate the same number of TrAdaBoost classifiers using $\mathcal{T}^s \cup \mathcal{T}^e$ only, and then boost from the set of TrAdaBoost classifiers. We refer to the algorithm as *Ensemble-TrAdaBoost*.

- Feature Augmented Classification. This is the state-of-the-art method proposed in [12], which augments the feature vector with topics detected from large collection of external data. We refer to this method as *LDA-Classification*.

- TCSST without sampling. This is the method which simultaneously includes all of the unlabeled external data $\mathcal{S}^e \subset \chi^e$, together with other labeled data $\mathcal{T}^s \cup \mathcal{T}^e$, to train the TrAdaBoost classifier. Similarly, the weak learner used by TrAdaBoost is RandomTree. We refer to method as *TCSST-No-Sampling*.

Similar to Ensemble-TrAdaBoost and TCSST-No-Sampling, we consistently use RandomTree as the weak learner of TrAdaBoost for TCSST.

[1]JWikiDocs: http://jwebpro.sourceforge.net

Table 3: **Accuracy of TCSST and other methods on the benchmark data**

Percentage of removed features	Classifier	5% labeled short sparse data	10% labeled short sparse data	15% labeled short sparse data	20% labeled short sparse data
90 %	Random Tree	53.9171 %	56.7847 %	57.9801 %	60.3508 %
	Ensemble-TrAdaBoost	58.4065 %	62.1435 %	66.8512 %	66.8512 %
	LDA-Classification	50.7497 %	58.4066 %	59.1630 %	60.2287 %
	TCSST-No-Sampling	56.7604 %	60.1473 %	63.9788 %	66.4339 %
	TCSST	**61.5127 %**	**66.4648 %**	**68.9003 %**	**71.3215 %**
95 %	Random Tree	51.6638 %	52.4735 %	54.4758 %	56.3420 %
	Ensemble-TrAdaBoost	54.4062 %	56.3427 %	58.4514 %	59.9336 %
	LDA-Classification	46.4033 %	55.5250 %	55.5675 %	57.8508 %
	TCSST-No-Sampling	**56.1102 %**	56.7464 %	58.5123 %	59.2643 %
	TCSST	55.9811 %	**59.6654 %**	**60.3719 %**	**63.3174 %**

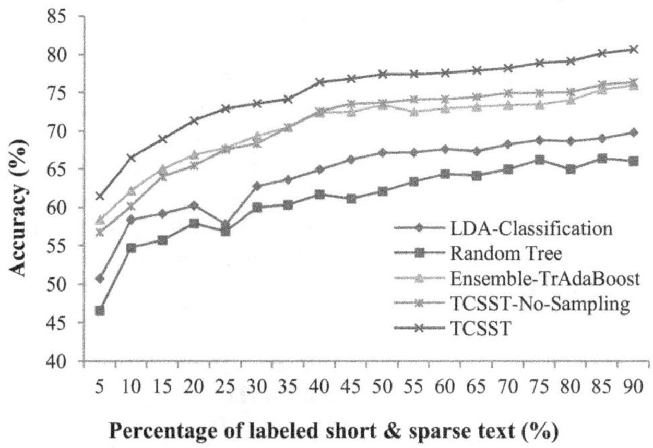

(a) Variation of the size of labeled short & sparse text

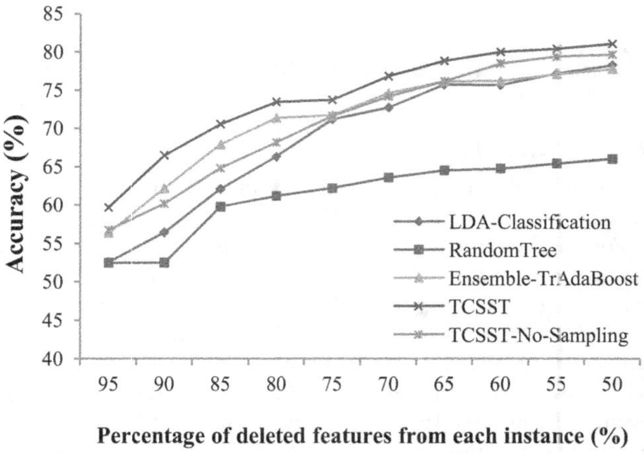

(b) Variation of the sparse degree

Figure 2: Comparison of TCSST and other methods along a wide range of data variation.

4.3 Experimental Results

4.3.1 Comparison between algorithms.

Firstly, we compare the performance of TCSST against the other methods on the benchmark data set. We vary the parameter, percentage of features deleted from instances, from 90% to 95% to generate two sparse domains, while the external domain is not changed. The results of the classifiers mentioned in Subsection 4.2 as well as those of TCSST on the two data sets are shown in Table 3. In this set of experiments, we respectively set the percentage of labeled data in the short & sparse domain as 5%, 10%, 15% and 20%. For Ensemble-TrAdaBoost, TCSST-No-Sampling and TCSST, the percentage of the labeled external data is set to 10%. For TCSST, in each round, 20% of unlabeled external data is selected to be included in the training data.

For Ensemble-TrAdaBoost, TCSST-No-Sampling and TCSST, the number of iterations used by TrAdaBoost is set to 40. For Ensemble-TrAdaBoost and TCSST, the number of TrAdaBoost classifiers is set to 20. For LDA-Classification, 100 topics are detected from the sparse domain and the external domain.

All results listed in Table 3 are generated from 10-fold cross validation. It can be observed that TCSST outperforms all of the other four algorithms in nearly every setting. Comparing Random Tree and Ensemble-TrAdaBoost, we notice that transfer learning using external data improves the classification using labeled sparse data only. Comparing Ensemble-TrAdaBoost and LDA-Classification, it shows that transfer classification which deals features in the original space is better than the existing approach which trains one classifier by concatenating features from different spaces. For TCSST-No-Sampling, we observe that its performance is not stable. It works better than Ensemble-TrAdaBoost sometimes (and better than TCSST once), and worse than Ensemble-TrAdaBoost some other times. This might be caused by the noise in the large set of unlabeled external data. Therefore, the experimental results demonstrate the superiority of TCSST.

While Table 3 lists the accuracy results of the classification algorithms at a few settings of the two parameters: the percentage of labeled short & sparse text and the percentage of features deleted from each instance, Figure 2 plots the performance trend of each method along a wide range variations of the two parameters. Figure 2 (a) shows the results when the percentage of labeled short & sparse text is varied from 5% to 90% while the percentage of features deleted is set to 90%. It can be observed that TCSST clearly and consistently outperforms other methods along the whole variation range. Figure 2 (b) shows the results when the percentage of features deleted from each instance is varied from 95% to 50%, while the percentage of labeled short & sparse text data is 10%. Again, TCSST improves over all of the other four algorithms, while the improvement margin decreases when the data becomes less sparse.

Table 4: Accuracy of TCSST and other methods on the NRM data

Classifier	50% labeled short sparse data
Random Tree	32.8042 %
Ensemble-TrAdaBoost	42.1053 %
LDA-Classification	46.0317 %
TCSST-No-Sampling	44.5089 %
TCSST	**50.8772** %

The results of the algorithms on the NRM data is shown in Table 4. For Ensemble-TrAdaBoost, TCSST-No-Sampling and TCSST, the number of labeled data in the external domain is set to be the same as the number of labeled data in the short & sparse domain (i.e. $50\% * 189 = 95$). For TCSST, in each round, twice of the number of labeled data in the external domain is selected to be included as training data (i.e. $95 * 2 = 190$). The other settings of each classifier are same as in the previous experiment. Again, TCSST achieves the best performance on the real-world data.

4.3.2 *Parameter Influence on TCSST*

We also conduct experiments to evaluate the influence of parameters on the performance of TCSST. In particular, we vary the two parameters: the percentage of labeled external data and the size of the unlabeled external data selected in each round. The results are shown in Figures 3 (a) and (b) respectively. The experiments were run on the benchmark data set where the sparse domain is generated by deleting 90% of features from instances. For both experiments, the percentage labeled short & sparse text data is 20%.

For Figure 3 (a), we vary the percentage of labeled external data from 5% to 50% and set the size of unlabeled external data selected in each round to be 20%. It can be observed the performance of TCSST will be better given more labeled external data. The results can be understood intuitively.

For Figure 3 (b), we vary the size of the unlabeled external data selected in each round from 5% to 50%, and set the percentage labeled external data to be 10%. We notice that, when the parameter increases, that is, more unlabeled external data is selected in each round, the performance of TCSST will decrease slightly. This is probably because when more unlabeled external data is selected in each round, some noise is introduced.

4.3.3 *Iterations vs Accuracy of TCSST*

We further carry out experiments by varying the number of MAX_ITERATION in the Algorithm 1. That is, the number of iterative sampling process. We are interested in finding out how many iterations it takes before TCSST's accuracy becomes stable.

We run the experiment on the benchmark data set where the sparse domain is generated by deleting 90% of features from each instance. The percentage of labeled short & sparse text is 20%, the percentage of labeled external data is 10% and the size of unlabeled external data selected in each round is 20%. The experimental results are shown in Figure 4. It can be observed from the figure that TCSST becomes stable approximately when the MAX_ITERATION reaches 20. Given the large set of unlabeled external data, we believe the result is quite promising. It indicates that our strategies of starting with a good initial set $\mathcal{P}^{(C)}$ of unlabeled external data, and updating sampling probabilities based on the usefulness of unlabeled instances are effective.

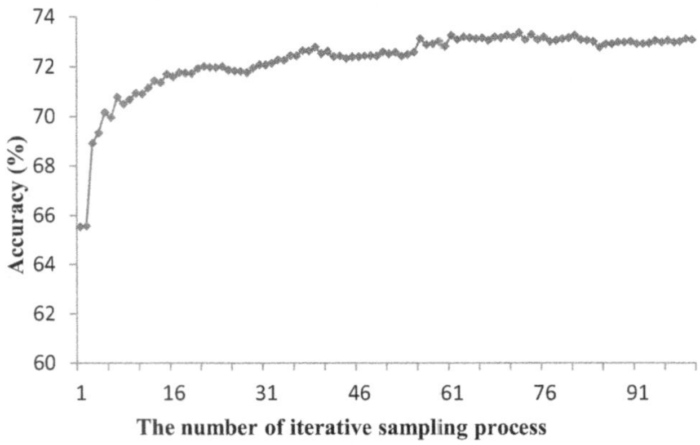

Figure 4: Iterations vs Accuracy of TCSST w.r.t. MAX_ITERATION.

4.3.4 *Computational Complexity of TCSST*

TCCST's computational performance is related to three factors: C - weak classifier's complexity, N - number of iteration for training classifier in TrAdaBoost, and M - number of iteration for sampling in TCCST. The computational complexity of TCSST is $O(MNC)$.

Accurately the three factors above are not independent. For example, the weak classifier's complexity C is usually related to the training data scale which influences the selection of TrAdaBoost iteration number N. Furthermore, the N decides the external data sampling size (S) which empirically choose $10\% - 20\%$ of N. Obviously, the S acts as the learning rate to induce the TCCST's sampling iteration M.

5. CONCLUSIONS & FUTURE WORK

In this paper, we proposed a novel method, TCSST, which classifies short & sparse text by using transfer learning to exploit the external data. Motivated by the situation that there may not be enough labeled external data, TCSST leverages both labeled and unlabeled external data for transfer classification. In order to avoid the noise in the large set of unlabeled external data, TCSST uses an iterative sampling process to include only a subset of high quality unlabeled external data, with predicted labels, in each round into the training data, rather than including all unlabeled external instances into the training data in a batch. The experimental results demonstrate the effectiveness of the iterative sampling process and the strategies to allow the selection of

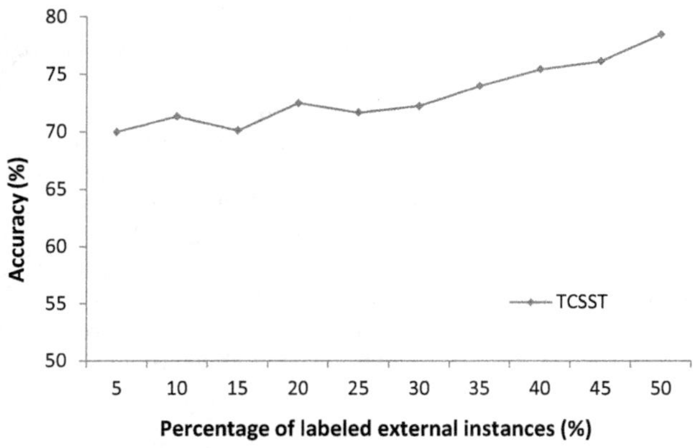

(a) Variation of the size of labeled external instances

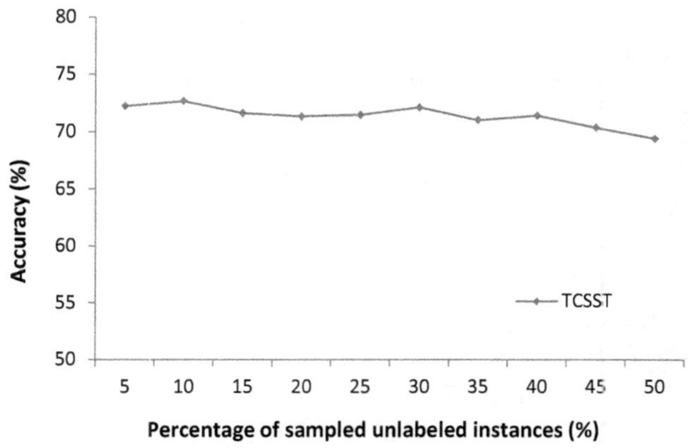

(b) Variation of the size of sampled unlabeled external instances

Figure 3: Parameter influence on TCSST.

external instances that are more likely to be useful. Compared with baseline as well as the existing methods, TCSST presents superior performance across benchmark and real-world data sets.

While TCSST borrows the framework of TrAdaBoost, which focuses on transferring the knowledge of instances, there are other types of inductive transfer learning, such as transferring knowledge of feature representations, transferring knowledge of parameters, and transferring relational knowledge [11]. As ongoing research, we will study how to employ other types of inductive transfer learning frameworks to classify short & sparse text using a small set of labeled external data and a large set of unlabeled external data, or using only a large set of unlabeled external data.

6. ACKNOWLEDGMENTS

This work was supported, in part, by the Australian Research Council (ARC) Linkage Project under Grant No. LP120100566, Discovery Project under Grants No. DP1093762, and the NSW Department of Environment, Climate Change and Water (DECCW).

7. REFERENCES

[1] Natural resource manager capacity accessment data. In *http://sourceforge.net/projects/tcsst/*.

[2] S. Banerjee, K. Ramanathan, and A. Gupta. Clustering short texts using wikipedia. In *Proc. ACM SIGIR*, 2007.

[3] D. Bollegala, Y. Matsuo, and M. Ishizuka. Measuring semantic similarity between words using web search engines. In *Proc. WWW*, 2007.

[4] W. Dai, Q. Yang, G.-R. Xue, and Y. Yu. Boosting for transfer learning. In *Proc. ICML*, 2007.

[5] T. Evgeniou and M. Pontil. Regularized multi-task learning. In *Proc. KDD*, 2004.

[6] E. Gabrilovich and S. Markovitch. Computing semantic relatedness using wikipedia-based explicit semantic analysis. In *Proc. IJCAI*, 2007.

[7] X. Hu, N. Sun, C. Zhang, and T.-S. Chua. Exploiting internal and external semantics for the clustering of short texts using world knowledge. In *Proc. CIKM*, 2009.

[8] O. Jin, N. N. Liu, K. Zhao, Y. Yu, and Q. Yang. Transferring topical knowledge from auxiliary long texts for short text clustering. In *Proc. CIKM*, 2011.

[9] K. Lang. Newsweeder: Learning to filter netnews. In *Proc. ICML*, 1995.

[10] R. Mihalcea, C. Corley, and C. Strapparava. Corpus-based and knowledge-based measures of text semantic similarity. In *Proc. AAAI*, 2006.

[11] S. J. Pan and Q. Yang. A survey on transfer learning. *IEEE TKDE*, 22(10):1345–1359, 2010.

[12] X.-H. Phan, L.-M. Nguyen, and S. Horiguchi. Learning to classify short and sparse text & web with hidden topics from large-scale data collections. In *Proc. WWW*, 2008.

[13] R. Raina, A. Battle, H. Lee, B. Packer, and A. Ng. Self-taught learning: Transfer learning from unlabeled data. In *Proc. ICML*, 2007.

[14] M. Sahami and T. D. Heilman. A web-based kernel function for measuring the similarity of short text snippets. In *Proc. WWW*, 2006.

[15] R. E. Schapire, Y. Freund, P. Bartlett, and W. S. Lee. Boosting the margin: A new explnation for the effectiveness of voting methods. In *Proc. ICML*, 1997.

[16] B. Sriram, D. Fuhry, E. Demir, H. Ferhatosmanoglu, and M. Demirbas. Short text classification in twitter to improve information filtering. In *Proc. SIGIR*, 2010.

[17] X. Sun, H. Wang, and Y. Yu. Towards effective short text deep classification. In *Proc. SIGIR*, 2011.

[18] W. Yih and C. Meek. Improving similarity measures for short segments of text. In *Proc. AAAI*, 2007.

[19] X. Zhu. Semi-supervised learning literature survey. In *http://pages.cs.wisc.edu/~jerryzhu/pub/ssl_survey.pdf*, 2008.

The Generalized Dirichlet Distribution in Enhanced Topic Detection

Karla Caballero*
UC, Santa Cruz
Santa Cruz CA, USA
karla@soe.ucsc.edu

Joel Barajas
UC, Santa Cruz
Santa Cruz CA, USA
jbarajas@soe.ucsc.edu

Ram Akella
UC, Santa Cruz
Santa Cruz CA, USA
akella@soe.ucsc.edu

ABSTRACT

We present a new, robust and computationally efficient Hierarchical Bayesian model for effective topic correlation modeling. We model the prior distribution of topics by a Generalized Dirichlet distribution (GD) rather than a Dirichlet distribution as in Latent Dirichlet Allocation (LDA). We define this model as GD-LDA. This framework captures correlations between topics, as in the Correlated Topic Model (CTM) and Pachinko Allocation Model (PAM), and is faster to infer than CTM and PAM. GD-LDA is effective to avoid over-fitting as the number of topics is increased. As a tree model, it accommodates the most important set of topics in the upper part of the tree based on their probability mass. Thus, GD-LDA provides the ability to choose significant topics effectively. To discover topic relationships, we perform hyper-parameter estimation based on Monte Carlo EM Estimation. We provide results using Empirical Likelihood (EL) in 4 public datasets from TREC and NIPS. Then, we present the performance of GD-LDA in ad hoc information retrieval (IR) based on MAP, P@10, and Discounted Gain. We discuss an empirical comparison of the fitting time. We demonstrate significant improvement over CTM, LDA, and PAM for EL estimation. For all the IR measures, GD-LDA shows higher performance than LDA, the dominant topic model in IR. All these improvements with a small increase in fitting time than LDA, as opposed to CTM and PAM.

Categories and Subject Descriptors

H.3.3 [**Information Storage and Retrieval**]: Information Search and Retrieval—*Document Filtering*; G.3 [**Probability and Statistics**]: Statistical Computing

General Terms

Algorithms, Experimentation

Keywords

Statistical Topic Modeling, Document Representation

*Main contact.

1. INTRODUCTION

Topic modeling has been widely studied in Machine Learning and Text Mining as an effective approach to extract latent topics from unstructured text documents. The key idea underlying topic modeling is to use term co-occurrences in documents to discover associations between those terms. The development of Latent Dirichlet Allocation (LDA) [3, 8] enabled the rigorous prediction of new documents first time. Consequently, variants and extensions of LDA have been an active area of research in topic modeling. This research has 2 main streams in document representation: 1) The exploration of super and subtopics as in Pachinko Model Allocation (PAM) [9, 10]; and 2) the correlation of topics [2, 9, 10]. However, despite the improvement of these approaches over LDA, they are rarely used in applications that handle large datasets, such as Information Retrieval. Major gaps in these models include: modeling correlated topics in a computationally effective manner; and a robust approach to ensure good performance for a wide range of document numbers, vocabulary size and average word length per document.

In this paper we develop a new model to meet these needs. We use the Generalized Dirichlet (GD) distribution as a prior distribution of the document topic mixtures, leading to GD-LDA. We show that the Dirichlet distribution is a special case of GD. As a result, GD-LDA is deemed to be a generalized case of LDA. Our goal is to provide a more flexible model for topics while retaining the conjugacy properties, which are desirable in inference. The features of the GD-LDA model include: 1) An effective method to represent sparse topic correlations in natural language documents. 2) A model which handles global topic correlations with time complexity $O(KW)$, adding minimal computational cost respect to LDA. This results in a fast and robust approach compared to CTM and PAM. 3) A hierarchical tree structure that accommodates the most significant topics, based on probability mass, at the upper levels allowing us to reduce the number of topics efficiently. Note that GD is a special case of Dirichlet Trees [13, 5]. This distribution has been used previously in topic modeling to add domain knowledge to the probability of words given a topic [1]. In contrast, we use the GD distribution to model topic correlations. Thus, this approach is complementary to GD-LDA.

To validate our model, we use Empirical Likelihood (EL) in four data sets with different characteristics of document length, vocabulary size, and total number of documents. GD-LDA outperforms CTM, PAM and LDA consistently in all the datasets. In addition, we test the performance of GD-LDA in adhoc Information Retrieval, obtaining superior

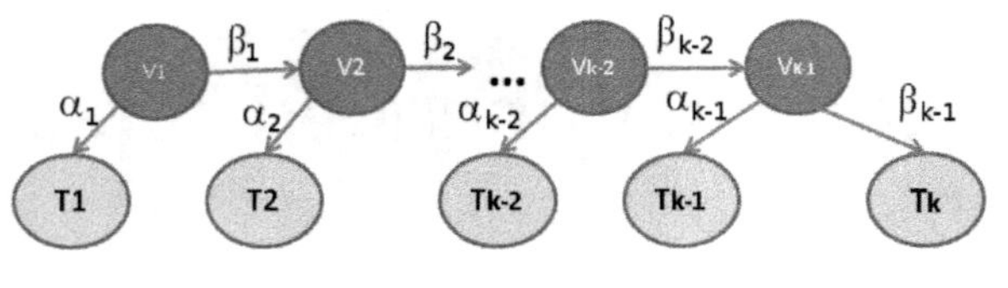

Figure 1: Tree structure of the GD distribution.

results to those in the literature. We show a significant difference in running times between GD-LDA, CTM and PAM which makes GD-LDA as viable as LDA for large data sets.

This paper is organized as follows: In section 2, we present the definition and features of the GD distribution. We will use this definition to develop the methodology of the GD-LDA model. Section 3 depicts our proposed approach with the proper derivations. Validation criteria, experimental settings, and results are presented in section 4. Finally the discussion and conclusion are presented in section 5.

2. THE GENERALIZED DIRICHLET DISTRIBUTION

2.1 Properties and Intuition

The Generalized Dirichlet (GD) distribution was introduced by Connor and Mosimann in [4]. The GD distribution is motivated by the limitations of the Dirichlet distribution in modeling covariances. In the case of the Dirichlet distribution, all the entries of the random vector must share a common variance, and they must sum to one. When we use the Dirichlet distribution as a prior for the multinomial distribution we have only one degree of freedom, the total prior sample size, to incorporate our confidence in the prior knowledge. As a consequence, we can not add individual variance information for each entry of the random vector. In addition, all entries are always negatively correlated. In other words, if the probability of one entry increases each of the other probabilities must either decrease or remain the same to sum to one. Despite these limitations, the Dirichlet distribution is widely used given that this is a conjugate prior of the multinomial distribution.

The GD distribution allows us to sample each entry of the random vector of proportions from independent Beta distributions. This independence is the key property that provides more flexibility than the Dirichlet distribution. Formally this distribution is defined as:

$$p(\theta|\alpha,\beta) = \prod_{j=1}^{K-1} \frac{\Gamma(\alpha_j+\beta_j)}{\Gamma(\alpha_j)\Gamma(\beta_j)} \theta_j^{\alpha_j-1}(1-\theta_1-\cdots-\theta_j)^{\eta_j} \quad (1)$$

where $\theta_1+\theta_2+\ldots+\theta_{K-1}+\theta_K = 1$, $\eta_j = \beta_j - \alpha_{j+1} - \beta_{j+1}$ for $1 \leq j \leq K-2$ and $\eta_{K-1} = \beta_{K-1} - 1$.

To illustrate the properties of the GD distribution we define $Z_1 = \theta_1$ and $Z_k = \theta_k/V_k$ for $k = 2, 3, \ldots, K-1$ where $V_k = 1-\theta_1-\cdots-\theta_{k-1}$. Let T_k be the discrete random variable with multinomial distribution with parameter $\theta_1 \ldots \theta_K$ for K different categories. We start at node V_1, and at this node we sample T_1 with probability Z_1 and V_2 with probability $1-Z_1$. Conditional on V_2, we sample T_2 with probability Z_2 and V_3 with probability $1-Z_2$. In the general case, conditional on V_k, we sample T_k with probability Z_k and V_{k+1} with probability $1-Z_k$ for $k = 1 \ldots K-1$. If we now add a prior Beta distribution with parameters α_k, β_k for each conditional Binomial distribution of the nodes V_k, we have a GD distribution where this set of Beta distributions is conjugate to the set of Binomial distributions.

$$Z_k \sim Beta(\alpha_k, \beta_k) \quad T_k \sim Bin(Z_k, N_k) \text{ for } N_k = N - \textstyle\sum_{i<k} T_i \quad (2)$$

where N is the total number of observations and N_k is the number of observations remaining from previous categories in the tree[20].

The GD distribution is a special case of the Dirichlet Tree distribution [13, 5] where a cascade hierarchy is employed in the generative process of the distribution. To interpret the parameters of the GD distribution we refer to its tree representation shown in Fig 1. Conditional on V_k, α_k is the sample size assigned to the discrete output T_k, and β_k is the sample size assigned to the next level in the tree. If β_k is too small compared to α_k, we could discard the rest of the tree. This is a desirable property as it facilitates dimensionality reduction in the number of topics. By setting $\beta_k = \alpha_{k+1} + \beta_{k+1}$, $\beta_{K-1} = \alpha_K$, we obtain a Dirichlet distribution. This is why GD distribution "generalizes" the Dirichlet distribution [4]. Although a general Dirichlet Tree structure that is inferred by data is highly appealing, in practice this structure determines the number and properties of the parameters to fit. Thus, the tree must be fixed before inferring the model [13, 14]. A key property of the GD cascade structure is that it facilitates topic reduction. This is because the tree can be pruned based on the conditional probability of going to the following level.

The GD distribution is a conjugate prior distribution to the Multinomial distribution, then we can integrate out the parameter of the Multinomial distribution leading to:

$$p(T|\alpha,\beta) = \int p(T|\theta)p(\theta)d\theta = \prod_{k=1}^{K-1} \frac{\Gamma(\alpha_k+\beta_k)}{\Gamma(\alpha_k)\Gamma(\beta_k)} \prod_{k=1}^{K-1} \frac{\Gamma(\alpha'_k)+\Gamma(\beta'_k)}{\Gamma(\alpha'_k+\beta'_k)} \quad (3)$$

where $\alpha'_k = \alpha_k + T_k$, $\beta'_k = \beta_k + T_{k+1} + \ldots + T_K$. The ability to estimate this integral in closed form is crucial for GD-LDA model because this enables us to perform Gibbs sampling. This is the product of Beta-Binomial distributions for Z_k independent random variables. As a result, this expression is factorized into independent ratios of Gamma functions , which allows us to find the Maximum Likelihood Estimation (MLE) of α, β in a simple manner (independently) which is not the case of the Dirichlet distribution.

2.2 Covariances: Properties and Constraints

In natural language documents, most of the times only a few topics co-occur leading to sparse topic correlations [19]. This implies that a very few random topics may suffice, rather than the full joint distribution including all the topics.

When considering useful distributions for topic modeling, a desirable feature is to model only a few topics in a document. For instance, the topic *domestic politics* could frequently co-occur with *middle east politics* and *health care reform*. This implies that if we observe *domestic politics*, the conditional probabilities of observing *middle east politics* and *health care reform* will increase. However, if a document contains *domestic politics* and *middle east politics*, it could very rarely contain *health care reform*.

GD has the computational advantage of only having $2K-1$ parameters. This also implies that the distribution covariances are constrained. The question is whether it is possible that these constraints imply that only a few topics co-occur

Algorithm 1 GD-LDA Generative Model

```
for topic k ← 1 to K do
   draw φ_k ~ Dir(γ)
end for
for document j ← 1 to D do
   draw θ_j ~ GenDir(α, β)
   for word w ← 1 to N_j do
      draw z_wj ~ Mult(θ_j)
      draw w|z_wj = k ~ Mult(φ_k)
   end for
end for
```

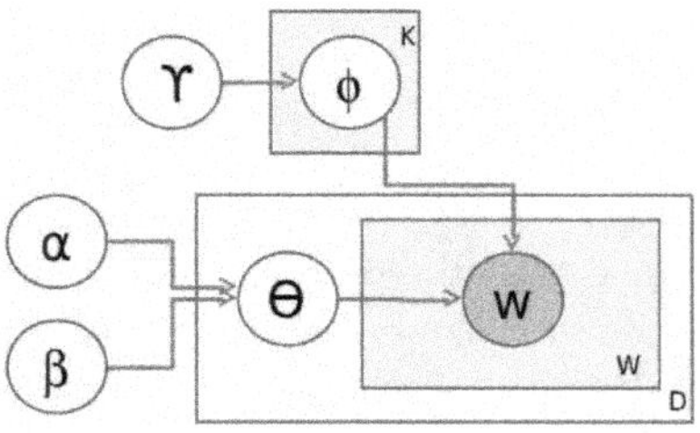

Figure 2: Graphical Model for GD-LDA. α and β are vectors of size $K-1$ where K is the number of topics. γ is a vector of size V (vocabulary size).

in a document. In this respect, the covariance properties described in Appendix A.1, particularly the third one, indicate that the covariances are dependent on the expected value of two topics, then several covariances might be close to zero if the right hand side ratio is small. This is an important feature of the GD distribution which we propose to exploit in topic modeling. A detailed discussion of the covariance constraints of GD distribution is provided in Appendix A.

3. GD-LDA: METHODOLOGY

In this section, we depict the parameter estimation process to fit the GD as a prior distribution for topics. We show that GD-LDA can be computed with a computational cost similar to that of LDA. Fig 2 shows the graphical model for GD-LDA and its generative model is described in Algorithm 1. We follow a Monte Carlo Expectation Maximization (MCEM) approach to fit our model. Conditional on the hyper-parameters, we develop a Gibbs sampling approach to infer the topic assignments to each word in the corpus. Then, assuming that the topic assignment expectations as given, we optimize the hyper-parameters of the model.

3.1 Notation

Let K be the number of topics, D the number of documents, and V the vocabulary size. We use the indices: i to denote a word or term index in the vocabulary, k to denote a specific topic, j to refer to a document, and w to identify a specific observed word. $N_{i,k}$ defines the number of observed words which correspond to term i and have been assigned to topic k. $N_{j,k}$ is the frequency of topic k in document j. We refer to $p(w, z|\cdot)$ as the joint probability of all the words w in the corpus and their topic assignments z. γ represents a vector of size V. α and β are vectors of size $K-1$.

3.2 Model and Gibbs Sampling

We define the joint probability associated with the graphical model defined in Fig 2 with joint distribution:

$$p(w, z|\alpha, \beta, \gamma) = p(w|z, \gamma)p(z|\alpha, \beta) \tag{4}$$

This expression allows us to decompose the problem into two hierarchical models that can be treated and optimized separately based on these conditional probabilities. The probability of words given topics is:

$$p(w|z, \gamma) = \int_{\phi} p(w|\phi, z)\, p(\phi|\gamma, z)\, d\phi = \prod_{k=1}^{K} \frac{\Gamma(\sum_{i=1}^{V} \gamma_i)}{\prod_{i=1}^{V} \Gamma(\gamma_i)} \frac{\prod_{i=1}^{V} \Gamma(\gamma_i - N_{k,i})}{\Gamma(\sum_{i=1}^{V} (\gamma_i - N_{k,i}))} \tag{5}$$

For the probability of topics, we have a GD prior distribution for the topic mixtures in each document which is assumed to be Multinomial. Thus we have:

$$p(z|\alpha, \beta) = \int_{\theta} p(z|\theta)\, p(\theta|\alpha, \beta)\, d\theta = \prod_{j=1}^{D} \prod_{k=1}^{K-1} \frac{\Gamma(\alpha_k + \beta_k)}{\Gamma(\alpha_k)\Gamma(\beta_k)} \prod_{k=1}^{K-1} \frac{\Gamma(\alpha_k^j) + \Gamma(\beta_k^j)}{\Gamma(\alpha_k^j + \beta_k^j)} \tag{6}$$

where $\alpha_k^j = \alpha_k + N_{j,k}$, $\beta_k^j = \beta_k + N_{j,k+1} + ... + N_{j,K}$.

The topic assignments z are not observed. Then, we define a Gibbs sampling method to infer z as follows:

$$p(z_{wj} = k|z^{\neg wj}, \alpha, \beta, \gamma) = \frac{p(w|z, \gamma)p(z|\alpha, \beta)}{p(w|z^{\neg wj}, \gamma)p(z^{\neg wj}|\alpha, \beta)} \tag{7}$$

Here, $z^{\neg wj}$ represents the topic assignments for all the words except the word w from document j. This analysis leads us to the following distributions for Gibbs sampling:

$$\frac{p(w|z, \gamma)}{p(w|z^{\neg wj}, \gamma)} \propto \frac{N_{i,k}^{\neg wj} + \gamma_i}{\sum_{i=1}^{V} \left(N_{i,k}^{\neg wj} + \gamma_i\right)} \tag{8}$$

$$\frac{p(z|\alpha, \beta)}{p(z^{\neg wj}|\alpha, \beta)} \propto \begin{cases} \dfrac{\alpha_k + N_{j,k}^{\neg wj}}{\alpha_k + \beta_k + \sum_{l=1}^{K} N_{j,l}^{\neg wj}}, & k = 1 \\ \dfrac{\alpha_k + N_{j,k}^{\neg wj}}{\alpha_k + \beta_k + \sum_{l=k}^{K} N_{j,l}^{\neg wj}} \displaystyle\prod_{m=1}^{k-1} \dfrac{\beta_m + \sum_{l=m+1}^{K} N_{j,l}^{\neg wj}}{\alpha_m + \beta_m + \sum_{l=m}^{K} N_{j,l}^{\neg wj}} & 1 < k < K \\ \displaystyle\prod_{m=1}^{K-1} \dfrac{\beta_m + \sum_{l=m+1}^{K} N_{j,l}^{\neg wj}}{\alpha_m + \beta_m + \sum_{l=m}^{K} N_{j,l}^{\neg wj}} & k = K \end{cases} \tag{9}$$

In LDA, the topic distribution depends on α_k alone for the current topic k. Intuitively, if a new sample is assigned to a topic k in LDA, there is no effect on the sampling distribution of other topics. However, if a new sample is assigned to a topic k in GD-LDA, it will affect other topics through the evaluation of the product in Eq 9. The impact of this assignment will depend on the parameters α, β.

Sampling from the distribution in Eq 9 results in a high computational cost due to the cumulative product defined there. Since this distribution is not standard, we need to estimate its normalization constant. To perform this task with a computational cost comparable to collapsed Gibbs sampling in LDA [8], we compute the cumulative product for each $k > 1$ iterations and pass it to the next iteration of the evaluation. This is illustrated in Algorithm 2. From this pseudo code, $O((2K+1)W)$ operations are required for each Gibbs sampling draw for the whole corpus, where W is the total number of words. Thus, the time complexity for each iteration is $O(KW)$ as in the case of LDA [15]. This complexity is possible due to the cascade structure of the GD

Algorithm 2 GD-LDA Gibbs Sampling

$cumFactor \leftarrow 1,\ k \leftarrow 1$

$CDF[k] \leftarrow \frac{\alpha_k + N_{j,k}^{\neg wj}}{\alpha_k+\beta_k+\sum_{l=1}^{K} N_{j,l}^{\neg wj}} \times \frac{N_{i,k}^{\neg wj}+\gamma_i}{\sum_{i=1}^{V}\left(N_{i,k}^{\neg wj}+\gamma_i\right)}$

for $k \leftarrow 2$ to $K-1$ **do**

  $cumFactor \leftarrow cumFactor \times \frac{\beta_{k-1}+\sum_{l=k}^{K} N_{j,l}^{\neg wj}}{\alpha_{k-1}+\beta_{k-1}+\sum_{l=k-1}^{K} N_{j,l}^{\neg wj}}$

  $CDF[k] \leftarrow CDF[k-1] + cumFactor \times \frac{\alpha_k + N_{j,k}^{\neg wj}}{\alpha_k+\beta_k+\sum_{l=1}^{K} N_{j,l}^{\neg wj}} \times \frac{N_{i,k}^{\neg wj}+\gamma_i}{\sum_{i=1}^{V}\left(N_{i,k}^{\neg wj}+\gamma_i\right)}$

end for

$CDF[K] \leftarrow CDF[K-1] + cumFactor \times \frac{N_{i,K}^{\neg wj}+\gamma_i}{\sum_{i=1}^{V}\left(N_{i,K}^{\neg wj}+\gamma_i\right)}$

distribution, which facilitates the calculation of the cumulative factor in Algorithm 2. In contrast, the time complexity of a Gibbs draw for PAM depends on the number of super-topics, S, and sub-topics K as $O(SKW)$ [11]. The general recommendation is to set $S = K/2$[1] leading to $O(K^2W)$.

3.3 Parameter Estimation

Previous research has assumed uniform priors for the topic mixtures θ and the vocabulary distribution for topics ϕ without estimating them (constant values for α and γ) [8]. Wallach *et al.* in [16] concludes that parameter estimation with asymmetric Dirichlet prior probability of topics provides an improvement in the fitting. In GD-LDA, we estimate the parameters α, β of the GD distribution to discover topic correlations. We estimate the parameters for the prior distribution of words given topics γ. Ideally, we should maximize the likelihood $p(w|\alpha, \beta, \gamma)$ for observations w and hyper-parameters α, β, γ directly. Unfortunately, this distribution is intractable for this model. To solve this issue, we augment the likelihood to $p(w, z|\alpha, \beta, \gamma)$ and use Monte Carlo Expectation Maximization (MCEM) [18]. Conditional on hyper-parameters α, β, γ, we use Gibbs sampling to estimate the posterior topic assignment distribution for each word (E-step). Then, given the expected topic assignments and words, we optimize $p(w, z|\alpha, \beta, \gamma)$ (M-step). Algorithm 3 describes these iterations.

To fit γ, we maximize the joint distribution described in Eq 5 conditional on the expected topic assignments, $\overline{z} = E(z|\alpha, \beta, \gamma)$, estimated from Gibbs sampling. Then we have the following optimal function:

$$\gamma^{new} = \arg\max_{\gamma} \prod_{k=1}^{K} \frac{\Gamma(\sum_{i=1}^{V}\gamma_i)}{\prod_{i=1}^{V}\Gamma(\gamma_i)} \frac{\prod_{i=1}^{V}\Gamma(\gamma_i + \overline{N}_{k,i})}{\Gamma(\sum_{i=1}^{V}(\gamma_i + \overline{N}_{k,i}))} \tag{10}$$

where: $\overline{N}_{k,i} = f(\overline{z})$

We follow the Newton-based approach proposed by Minka in Eqs 56-60 of [12]. Here, we have a DCM distribution to fit from K observed vectors of dimension V. To initialize the search, we use the method of moments based on the observed proportions $p_{k,i} = \overline{N}_{k,i}/\sum_{i=1}^{V}\overline{N}_{k,i}$.

Similarly, we estimate the parameters of the GD distribution by maximizing the joint distribution:

$$\alpha^{new}, \beta^{new} = \arg\max_{\alpha,\beta} \prod_{j=1}^{D}\prod_{k=1}^{K-1} \frac{\Gamma(\alpha_k+\beta_k)}{\Gamma(\alpha_k)\Gamma(\beta_k)} \prod_{k=1}^{K-1} \frac{\Gamma(\alpha_k^j)+\Gamma(\beta_k^j)}{\Gamma(\alpha_k^j+\beta_k^j)} \tag{11}$$

[1] $K/2$ super-topics is the recommendation by Mallet toolbox, `http://mallet.cs.umass.edu/`

Algorithm 3 Monte Carlo EM

Start with an initial guess for α, β, γ and z
repeat
  Run Gibbs Sampling using Eqs. 8 and 9
  Find Expected value for topic assignments $E(z|\alpha, \beta, \gamma) = \overline{z}$
  Choose γ to maximize complete Likelihood Eqs 56-60 in [12]
  Choose α, β that maximize complete Likelihood using Eq 27
until convergence of α, β, γ
Choose topic assignments z^* with highest probability
Set $\alpha^* = \alpha, \beta^* = \beta, \gamma^* = \gamma$
return $\alpha^*, \beta^*, \gamma^*, z^*$

where $\alpha_k^j = \alpha_k + \overline{N}_{j,k}$, $\beta_k^j = \beta_k + \overline{N}_{j,k+1} + ... + \overline{N}_{j,K}$.

We develop a Newton-based method in Appendix B. To initialize the search, we use the method of moments based on the conditional beta distributions from the tree representation of the GD distribution [21]. The proportions $p_{k,i} = \overline{N}_{k,i}/\sum_{i=1}^{V}\overline{N}_{k,i}$ are employed for this initialization.

One key component of this optimization is that each pair α_k, β_k is optimized separately. Thus, the time complexity for this optimization is linear in time with K. Parameter fitting in PAM is performed using the method of moments due the high model complexity and computational cost of the optimization [10, 11]. In addition, the number of parameters to fit for CTM and PAM is K^2 [2] [19], assuming $K/2$ super-topics for PAM. As a result, these methods are highly prone to over-fitting, as many parameters are being fit.

3.4 Predictive Distributions

Given the optimal parameters (α^*, β^*) obtained from Algorithm 3, and the word-topic observations (w, z) the predictive distribution for document j, $\hat{\theta}_j$, is estimated as:

$$\hat{\theta}_{jk} = \begin{cases} \frac{\alpha_k^* + \overline{N}_{j,k}}{\alpha_k^* + \beta_k^* + \sum_{l=1}^{K}\overline{N}_{j,l}}, & \text{if } k = 1 \\ \frac{\alpha_k^* + \overline{N}_{j,k}}{\alpha_k^* + \beta_k^* + \sum_{l=k}^{K}\overline{N}_{j,l}} \times \prod_{m=1}^{k-1} \frac{\beta_m^* + \sum_{l=m+1}^{K}\overline{N}_{j,l}}{\alpha_m^* + \beta_m^* + \sum_{l=m}^{K}\overline{N}_{j,l}} & \text{if } 1 < k < K \\ \prod_{m=1}^{K-1} \frac{\beta_m^* + \sum_{l=m+1}^{K}\overline{N}_{j,l}}{\alpha_m^* + \beta_m^* + \sum_{l=m}^{K}\overline{N}_{j,l}} & \text{if } k = K \end{cases} \tag{12}$$

for the topics $k = 1 \dots K$ and the documents $j = 1 \dots D$.

The predictive distribution for the probability of words given topics, $\hat{\phi}_k$ is estimated as follows [8]:

$$\hat{\phi}_{ki} = \frac{\overline{N}_{i,k} + \gamma_i^*}{\sum_{i=1}^{V}(\overline{N}_{i,k} + \gamma_i^*)} \tag{13}$$

Notice that the probability of topics $\hat{\theta}_j$ is document dependent. On the other hand, the probability of words given their topic $\hat{\phi}_k$ is topic dependent. This implies that for an unseen document, we need to estimate its predictive distribution of topics while the probability of words given their topics remains the same.

4. EXPERIMENTAL RESULTS

4.1 Validation

The main challenge to validate statistical topic models is the lack of reliable observed topic labels for each word of a corpus. The standard approach is to estimate the likelihood of held-out data [17]. In addition, model performance in a

Algorithm 4 EL Estimation for model M

```
for s ← 1 to N_s do
    Sample document d_s with mixture θ_s given model M
    Find p(w = i|θ_s, φ̂, M) = Σ_{k=1}^{K} θ_{sk} φ̂_{ki} for i = 1, ..., V
end for
Set logEL= 0
for t ← 1 to D_t do
    Find p(d_t|d_s, M) = Π_{w_t=1}^{N_t} p(w_t|θ_s, φ̂, M)
    Find p(d_t|M) = (1/N_s) Σ_{s=1}^{N_s} p(d_t|d_s, M)
    Update logEL=logEL+Log(p(d_t|M))
end for
return logEL
```

supervised task has also been used [22]. Here, we validate the GD-LDA performance addressing these two forms. We estimate the likelihood of completely unseen documents using Empirical Likelihood, and we compare the performance of topic models in the ad hoc Information Retrieval as developed in [19].

4.1.1 Empirical Likelihood (EL)

There has been a debate about the evaluation of topic models with methods ranging from the harmonic mean of complete likelihood for topic assignments, to perplexity and empirical likelihood. As discussed in [17], perplexity falls into the category of document completion where a portion each document must be observed to estimate the likelihood of the remaining content. Similarly, a "left to right" evaluation has been proposed to estimate the probability of words in a test document incrementally [17]. For validation, we use Empirical Likelihood (EL) criterion. Our intent is to predict the likelihood of fully unseen documents. We do not use perplexity or "left to right" evaluation because they are based on the word order inside the document, in contrast to "bag of words". In addition, EL has been shown to be a more pessimistic approximation for the probability of held-out documents than "left to right" method [17].

We estimate EL as described in [11]. Here, we generate a set of pseudo documents, θ_s using the estimated prior topic distribution of the model being tested using training data. Then, a word distribution is estimated for each θ_s based on $\hat{\phi}$. This is used to estimate the probability of seeing the test set. We define this process by means of Algorithm 4. Here, D_t represents the number of documents for a test set, d_t is the document $t = 1, \ldots, D_t$, w_t are the N_t words of d_t, and N_s is the number of pseudo documents given model M. We use the generative approach based on the conditional Beta distributions of the tree representation for GD as in Fig 1. The main limitation of EL estimation is that the number of pseudo documents should be sufficiently large to cover the parameter space of θ given the trained model. Then, N_s determines the accuracy of the approximation.

4.1.2 Ad hoc Retrieval

Information Retrieval represents a hard problem where the gains of new models are often small or nil. This application represents a good test of the power of our approach. We compare the performance of different topic models in ad hoc Information Retrieval (IR). We use the approach proposed in [19] and incorporate our model by replacing the LDA model described in the method. Based on the predictive distribution estimators for topics $\hat{\phi}$, and for each document $\hat{\theta}_j$, we provide a topic-based language model for each document, $P_{TM}(w|\theta_j)$, as follows:

Table 1: Features of the datasets analyzed. Mean document includes the 95% interval

Dataset	NIPS	NYT	APW	OHSUMED
# documents	1840	5553	14657	196404
# unique terms	13649	11229	18471	38900
Mean doc. length	1322 ± 274	274 ± 132	169 ± 76	186 ± 36

Table 2: Number of Gibbs samples per EM iteration

MCEM iteration	1-4	5-6	7-8	9	10
Burn-in Samples	10	15	20	40	50
Gibbs Samples	50	100	200	500	700

$$P_{TM}(w|\hat{\theta}_j, \hat{\phi}) = \sum_{k=1}^{K} P(w|z = k, \hat{\phi}_k) P(z = k|\hat{\theta}_j) \quad (14)$$

This is augmented with the maximum likelihood estimate for the language model based on document terms D_j, $P_{ML}(w|D_j)$, and for the language model based on the corpus C, $P_{ML}(w|C)$, leading to:

$$P_{IR}(w|D_j, \hat{\theta}_j, \hat{\phi}) = \lambda \left(\frac{N_j}{N_j + \mu} P_{LM}(w|D_j) + \frac{\mu}{N_j + \mu} P_{ML}(w|C) \right) + (1 - \lambda) P_{TM}(w|\hat{\theta}_j, \hat{\phi}) \quad (15)$$

where μ is a smoothing parameter, N_j is the number of words in document j, and λ is a parameter for the linear combination. Therefore, the ranking function for query Q with terms q is given by:

$$P(Q|D_j, \hat{\theta}_j, \hat{\phi}) = \prod_{q \in Q} P_{IR}(w = q|D_j, \hat{\theta}_j, \hat{\phi}) \quad (16)$$

We use the parameter values: μ=1000, λ=0.7. These are the values recommended in [19].

4.2 Experimental Settings

We use 4 different datasets to test our model. NIPS conference papers dataset[2] which contains long documents (8-10 pages). Two news datasets, NYT and APW, obtained from TREC-3. These collections contain shorter documents (1 page) with different vocabulary size. A fourth dataset, OHSUMED from TREC-9, consists of abstracts from medical papers. In contrast to the other datasets, the number of documents is much larger (more than ten times). Table 1 shows the features of these datasets. We remove standard stop words and perform stemming in all datasets.

We test 4 variants of the GD-LDA algorithm. In two of these cases we fix the value of γ and optimize the parameters α and β as in Algorithm 3 based on two variants: 1) using the empirical expected topic assignments $\bar{z}$ [18], *GD-LDA Fixed Gamma Mean*; and 2) using the empirical mode z^* [7] in the M-step, *GD-LDA Fixed Gamma Max*. In the other two cases, we optimize all the three parameters (α,β and γ) based on the expected topic assignments, *GD-LDA Mean*, and the topic assignment mode *GD-LDA Max*.

We compare GD-LDA, LDA with parameter optimization, CTM and PAM. For LDA, we use our own implementation. We follow the collapsed Gibbs sampling approach [8], with asymmetric Dirichlet prior distributions for both, the probability of words given a topic, and for the probability of topics. These parameters are optimized as discussed by authors in [6]. For optimization, we follow the Newton-based approach proposed by Minka in Eqs 56-60 [12]. For both

[2]Available at: `http://cs.nyu.edu/~roweis/data.html`

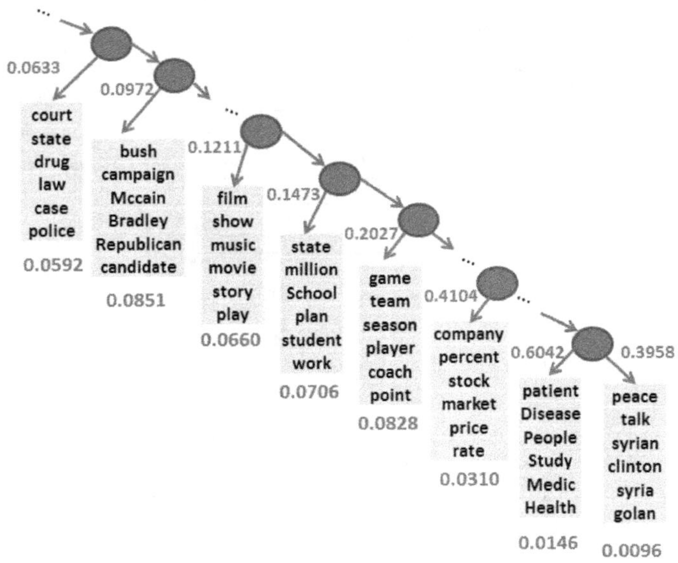

Figure 3: Qualitative example of GD-LDA for the NYT dataset with 20 topics. Probability of topics: marginal probability as defined by Eq 18 (red), conditional probability given the parent node as defined by Eq 22 (blue).

GD-LDA and LDA, we set a maximum of 1,000 Newton iterations for parameter optimization. The schedule of the Gibbs sampling is detailed in Table 2. We initialize the values $\alpha_k = 2/K$ for $k = 1, \ldots, K-1$, and $\beta_{K-1} = 2/K$ in GD-LDA to obtain the special case of Dirichlet distribution; we start with LDA as prior model, and allow the data to adapt the model in the MCEM iterations to the more general GD. For CTM[3], we use the default settings with parameter estimation: a maximum of 1,000 EM iterations with convergence of 10^{-5} and maximum of 20 variational iterations with a convergence rate of 10^{-6}. For PAM[4] we use 1000 Gibbs samples and $K/2$ super topics. This implementation supports multi-threading; to enable a fair comparison we use only one thread. We modify the implementation to obtain the fitted parameters since they are not provided by default. For EL estimation, we perform 10-fold cross-validation and we sample $N_s = 10,000$ pseudo documents.

4.3 Results

4.3.1 Qualitative Results

Fig 3 shows a qualitative example of GD-LDA in the NYT dataset. The figure represents the empirically estimated probability of topics for a subset of the topics. Each box represents a topic and the terms displayed are the ones with highest posterior predictive probability $\hat{\phi}_k$. Given the fitted GD-LDA model, we calculate the point estimate of the total probability for each topic (in blue) and its conditional probability given a parent node (red). Here, conditional on the current node, we move deeper into the tree or observe a word from the topic at that level. As we move down into the tree, the conditional probability of picking the left hand topic increases since the probability mass of the remaining topics is less. This is a desirable property which facilitates

[3]We use the CTM implementation provided by Blei at `http://www.cs.princeton.edu/~blei/ctm-c/`.

[4]We use the implementation provided by Mallet `http://mallet.cs.umass.edu/`.

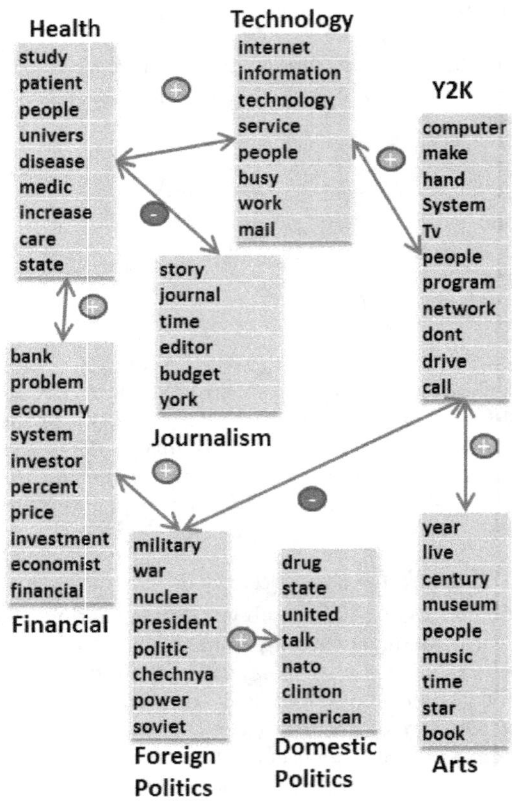

Figure 4: Correlation graph of a subset of topics inferred by GD-LDA for the NYT dataset with 30 topics.

dimensionality reduction. If this probability is *large* compared with the probability of exploring further the tree, we can discard the remaining tree.

Fig 4 shows some of the positive and negative correlations between different topics inferred by GD-LDA. We observe that *Health* is positively correlated with *Technology* and *Financial*. *Y2K* is positively correlated with *Technology* and *Arts* but negatively correlated with *Foreign Politics*. Note that by default LDA assumes negative correlations, thus the main value of topic correlated models is to discover positive correlations. Fig 5(a) shows the decomposition of a *sports* document from the NYT dataset into topics using PAM with 10 super-topics and 20 sub-topics, CTM and GD-LDA with 20 topics. This shows that CTM and GD-LDA assign a high probability to a single topic (sports). On the other hand, PAM provides 3 sub-topics and most of the super-topics with a significant probability mass. This is not desirable since an important objective with topic modeling is to cluster documents based on the topic mixture. Fig 5(b) shows a comparison between CTM and GD-LDA for a document about the *Y2K* problem and *airport functionality*. We observe that GD-LDA provides better segmentation of the document based on the topics proportions and content.

In addition, we calculate the distribution of the number of significant topics in a document. We rank the topics based on their topic probability mass in each document. Then, we estimate the number of topics which accounts for 95% of this probability mass. Fig 6 shows the distribution of this number of topics inferred by LDA, CTM, PAM, and GD-LDA. For PAM, we consider the number of sub-topics. Here, we observe that CTM favors high number of topics for

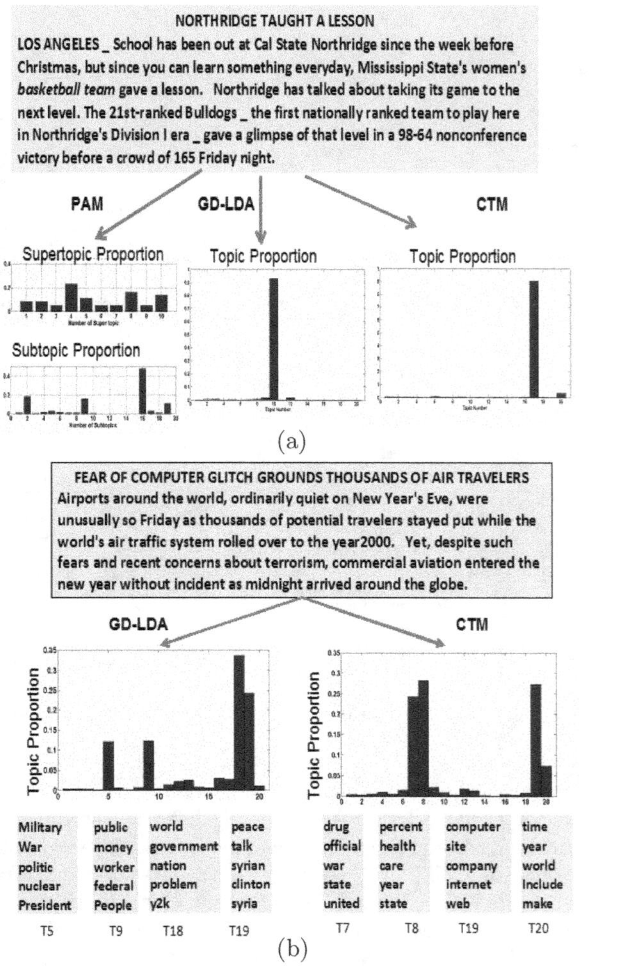

Figure 5: Qualitative comparison of the topic distribution for two documents from the NYT dataset. (a) From left to right: PAM, CTM, and GD-LDA (b) From left to right: GD-LDA and CTM

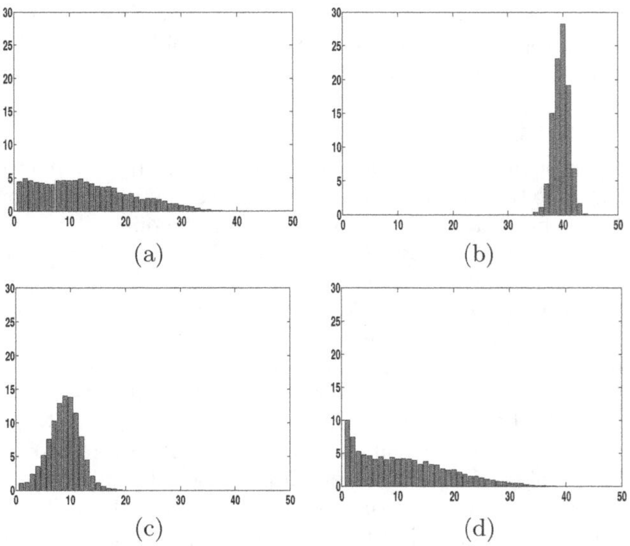

Figure 6: Distribution of the number of significant topics per document for the APW corpus inferred by: (a)LDA, (b)CTM, (c)PAM, and (d)GDLDA using $K = 50$ topics. X-axis is number of topics per documents and Y-axis is the percentage of documents in the corpus.

each documents which introduces noise when the goal is to characterize documents as in Information Retrieval. In PAM the number of topics per document is highly dependent of the number of super topics used. In order to handle topic correlation sparsity, PAM prunes the relationships between a super topic and subtopics [11]. This reduces the amount of correlations that can be modeled. In contrast, GD-LDA favors smaller number of topics per documents and without any constraint in the inference. The key property for this behavior is the cascade structure of the distribution. As discussed in section 2.2, this validates empirically the intuition of few significant topics for natural language documents, and sparse correlations.

4.3.2 Empirical Likelihood Results

Fig 7 shows EL estimations for the 4 variants of GD-LDA, CTM, PAM and LDA with asymmetric prior and parameter optimization in the four datasets. For the NIPS dataset, LDA is not shown since its predictive likelihood is extremely low. Similarly, PAM performance for the OHSUMED dataset is not shown for the same reason. The CTM model would not run for the OHSUMED dataset (mid-size dataset) based on the number of documents and vocabulary size.

We observe that optimizing γ has a low impact as more data becomes available. Conceptually, a prior distribution represents the prior knowledge with a given sample size. Consequently adding more data decreases the impact of the prior information. This is consistent with the conclusions discussed in [16]. We then compare the use of the topic assignments, $\bar{z}$ (posterior mean), and the topic assignment mode, z^* (maximum a posteriori MAP). We find that *GD-LDA mean* performs better, when the number of documents and the vocabulary size are relatively small (NIPS dataset). In contrast, *GD-LDA Max* shows the highest performance for the other datasets, Fig 7(b)-(d). In particular, this method performance is clearly superior for all the topics when tested for the largest dataset (OHSUMED). *GD-LDA Mean* requires fewer topics to achieve a superior performance compared to LDA, CTM and PAM. Moreover, EL decreases more smoothly than these methods. It also remains fairly constant when the number of topics attains a high value.

An important difference between the datasets analyzed is the average document length and number of unique terms. The worst performance of CTM, as well as PAM, is found in the case of APW dataset. This dataset has a larger vocabulary size, and significantly shorter documents than NIPS dataset, where both CTM and PAM show a similar performance to that of *GD-LDA Mean*. This suggests over-fitting by CTM where a full topic covariance matrix is estimated, and by PAM where a matrix of K subtopics by $K/2$ supertopics is estimated. In addition, PAM uses the method of moments, instead of optimization, for parameter estimation. This is a limitation of PAM when EL based evaluation is performed since the fitted parameters do not optimize the likelihood. As discussed in section 4.3.1, CTM favors larger number of topics for each document than the other methods. This behavior introduces noise in EL because correlations are sparse, and only a few topics are present in natural language documents.

4.3.3 Ad hoc Information Retrieval Results

We show the application of GD-LDA in ad hoc IR using the OHSUMED dataset. As discussed above, we use the ap-

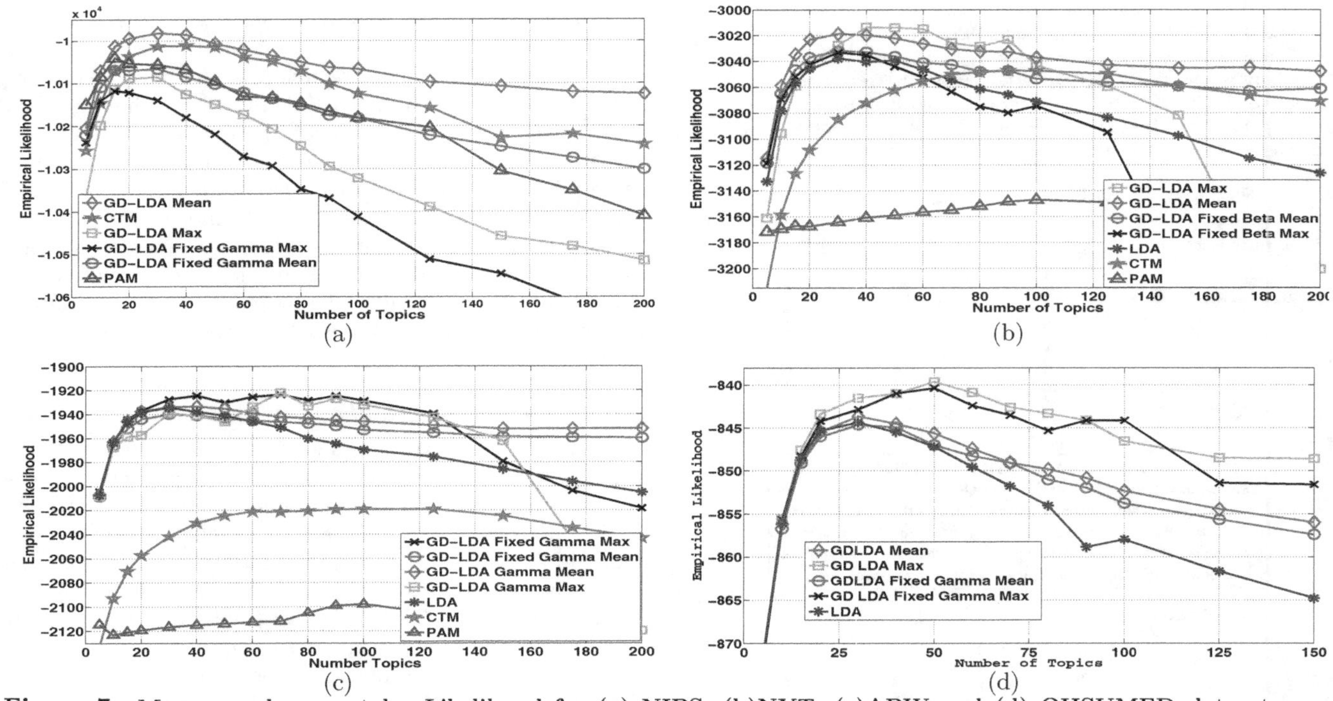

Figure 7: Mean per-document log-Likelihood for (a) NIPS, (b)NYT, (c)APW and (d) OHSUMED datasets as a function of the number of topics.

Table 3: Results of ad hoc IR using GDLDA, LDA and PAM models using K topics for the OHSUMED dataset

Model	K	P@10	MAP	DG
GD-LDA	50	**0.502**±0.06	**0.496**±0.06	**0.790**±0.07
LDA	50	0.470±0.06	0.470±0.06	0.780±0.08
PAM	50	0.434±0.06	0.439±0.05	0.671±0.04
GD-LDA	75	0.470±0.06	**0.491**±0.06	0.742±0.04
LDA	75	0.470±0.06	0.461±0.06	0.741±0.04
PAM	75	0.431±0.06	0.438±0.05	0.651±0.03

proach from [19] as a benchmark for comparison. We train the *GD-LDA Max* using $K = 50$ and $K = 75$ topics, and compare its performance with LDA and PAM. We use standard IR measures: Precision at 10 (P@10), Mean Average Precision (MAP) and Discounted Gain (DG), to compare these methods. The OHSUMED dataset is considered to be a medium size dataset in the IR literature. This contains 63 topical queries with 35,000 relevant labels.

We have not modified the retrieval model of [19] to exploit the power of the new GD-LDA model. Despite this, the performance improvement for all the measures is significant as we observe in Table 3. Here, the best performance is for $K = 50$ topics, where EL estimation peaks in Fig 7(d). For this case, there is agreement between the adhoc IR and EL performance. Respect to LDA, GD-LDA shows improvement of: **6.3%** for P@10, **5.5%** for MAP, and **1.1%** for DG. Note that PAM shows lower performance than LDA in IR for all the measures. This is consistent with the IR performance of PAM reported in [22].

4.3.4 Computational Cost Comparison

One advantage of GD-LDA over CTM and PAM is that its computational complexity is linear in the number of topics. This is not the case for CTM and PAM which scale quadratically with the number of topics. As discussed in section 3, GD-LDA should add minimal computational cost to LDA. Fig 8 shows the computational time in minutes to fit the model for LDA, CTM, PAM and GD-LDA in the datasets we consider. A non-linear increase in time is observed after 50 topics for CTM in NYT and APW datasets, and after 80 topics in NIPS dataset. We observe that the computational cost of PAM grows quadratically after 20 topics. In general, the computational cost of GD-LDA is comparable to that of LDA and is less than CTM and PAM. This is a significant advantage since GD-LDA provides a more flexible model structure when compared with LDA. Moreover, variances and a number of covariances are modeled more effectively, and with minimal increase in computational cost. This property makes GD-LDA more suitable than CTM or PAM for larger scale applications, such as IR.

4.3.5 Choosing the Number of Topics

An open problem is how to select the optimal number of topics to train a model. In general, an exhaustive experimentation needs to be performed to select the optimal number of topics. Due to the tree structure of the GD distribution, GD-LDA tends to accommodate the most relevant topics, based on probability mass, at the upper levels of the tree.

Fig 9 shows the cumulative probability vs the number of topics of the expected topic mixture of documents given the fitted parameters for GD-LDA and CTM. We observe that GD-LDA favors a smaller number of topics. Notice that, after a certain number of topics, the expected contribution of the remaining ones is not significant. This prevents GD-LDA from over-fitting. When comparing GD-LDA with CTM, we observe that CTM favors uniform topic mixtures in each document. Thus, if we fit CTM for larger number of topics, we would observe the same linear behavior as seen in graphs from Fig 9. This prevents CTM from discarding any topic easily or suggesting an optimal topic range as opposed to GD-LDA. In addition, this behavior makes CTM less effective in handling over-fitting.

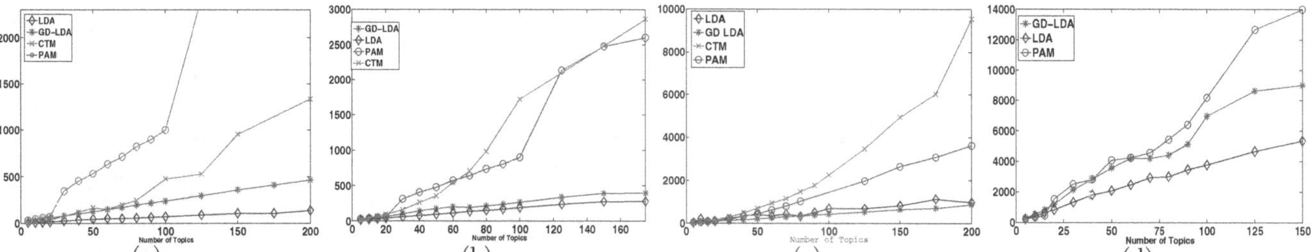

(a) (b) (c) (d)

Figure 8: Average running times in minutes of CTM, GD-LDA and LDA for: (a) NIPS, (b) APW, (c) NYT, (d) OHSUMED. x-axis represents the number of topics. All the experiments were performed using a Quad Intel machine with 2.5GHz with 8GB of memory.

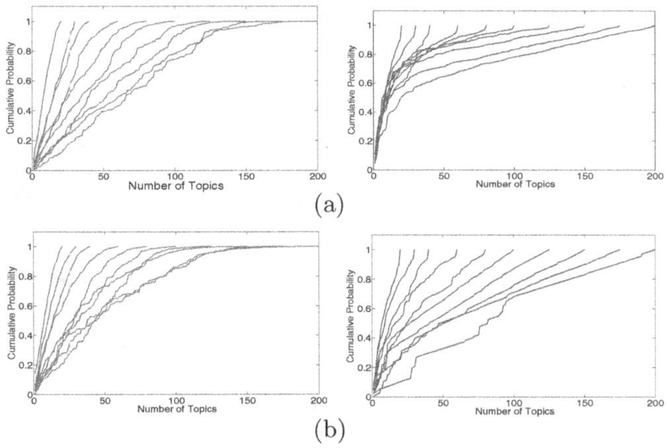

Figure 9: Cumulative distribution of the topic mixtures based on the fitted prior distribution parameters. From left to right GD-LDA and CTM for: (a) NIPS and (b) APW. The distributions are shown for $\{20, 30, 40, 60, 80, 100, 125, 150, 175, 200\}$ topics.

5. DISCUSSION AND CONCLUSION

We have introduced the use of the GD distribution in probabilistic topic modeling. The advantages of the GD over the Dirichlet distribution, and the benefits when compared with the estimation of the full covariance matrix in CTM have been described. The apparent constraints on covariances in GD actually results in modeling better sparse topic correlations in natural language documents, as our empirical validation indicates. This results in better performance in empirical likelihood and IR measures. We have developed an efficient Gibbs sampling model which uses the conjugacy property of GD with the Multinomial distribution. We have demonstrated that the running time of GD-LDA is comparable to LDA and less than CTM and PAM. This provides a model computationally competitive and with better performance than these methods.

We have shown that the impact of optimizing the vocabulary parameter γ decreases when the vocabulary size and the number of documents in the corpus is large. Due to the tree structure of the GD distribution, GD-LDA proves to be powerful in handling over-fitting with a large number of topics as its performance remains fairly high even when the number of topics is increased. This is not the case for CTM, PAM, and LDA. As a consequence, we can reduce the number of topics, by using the conditional probability of the remaining topics when we are moving down into the tree. A natural extension of the model is to allow the tree structure to be fitted. A direction of improvement is to modify the Dirichlet tree to have a comparable notion of subtopics and super topics as in PAM with the same conjugacy and computational cost as GD-LDA.

We have shown that the use of GD-LDA in adhoc IR increases the performance significantly, in contrast to earlier incorporations of topic models. Future directions include the use of topic mixture instead the probability of words in the ranking function. In addition, we plan to explore the impact of GD-LDA in Interactive Information Retrieval.

6. ACKNOWLEDGEMENTS

This work is partially funded by CONACYT grant 207751 and CONACYT-MEXUS grant 194880.

7. REFERENCES

[1] D. Andrzejewski, X. Zhu, and M. Craven. Incorporating domain knowledge into topic modeling via dirichlet forest priors. In *ICML*, pages 25–32, 2009.

[2] D. Blei and Lafferty. Correlated topic models. *NIPS*, 18:147–154, 2006.

[3] D. Blei, A. Ng, and M. Jordan. Latent dirichlet allocation. *Journal of Machine Learning*, 3:993–1022, 2003.

[4] R. J. Connor and J. E. Mosimann. Concepts of independence for proportions with a generalization of the dirichlet distribution. *Journal of American Statistics*, 64:194–206, 1969.

[5] S. Y. Dennis. A bayesian analysis of tree-structured statistical decision problems. *Journal of Statistical Planning and Inference*, 53(3):323–344, 1996.

[6] G. Doyle and C. Elkan. Accounting for burstiness in topic models. *Proceedings of the 26th ICML*, 2009.

[7] C. Elkan. Clustering documents with an exponential family approximation of the dirichlet compound multinomial distribution. *In Proceedings of 23rd ICML*, 2006.

[8] T. Griffiths and M. Steyvers. Finding scientific topics. *Proceedings of the NAS*, 101(6):5228–5235, 2004.

[9] W. Li, D. Blei, and A. McCallum. Nonparametric Bayes pachinko allocation. In *23rd UAI Conference*, 2007.

[10] W. Li and A. McCallum. Pachinko allocation: Dag-structured mixture models of topic correlations. In *Proceedings of ICML 06*, pages 577–584, 2006.

[11] W. Li and A. McCallum. Pachinko allocation: Scalable mixture models of topic correlations. *Journal of Machine Learning*, 2008. Submitted.

[12] T. P. Minka. Estimating a dirichlet distribution. 2003.

[13] T. P. Minka. The dirichlet-tree distribution. 2004.

[14] B. Null. The nested dirichlet distribution: Properties and applications. *Submitted*, 2008.

[15] I. Porteous, D. Newman, A. Ihler, A. Asuncion, P. Smyth, and M. Welling. Fast collapsed gibbs sampling for latent dirichlet allocation. *Proceedings of the KDD 2008*, 2008.

[16] H. Wallach, D. Mimno, and A. McCallum. Rethinking lda: Why priors matter. In *NIPS 22*, pages 1973–1981. 2009.

[17] H. M. Wallach, I. Murray, R. Salakhutdinov, and D. Mimno. Evaluation methods for topic models. In *Proceedings of ICML '09*, pages 1105–1112, 2009.

[18] G. C. G. Wei and M. A. Tanner. A Monte Carlo Implementation of the EM Algorithm and the Poor Man's Data Augmentation Algorithms. *Journal of the American Statistical Association*, 85:699–704, 1990.

[19] X. Wei and W. B. Croft. Lda-based document models for ad-hoc retrieval. *In Proceedings SIGIR 2006*, 2006.

[20] T.-T. Wong. Generalized dirichlet distribution in bayesian analysis. *Applied Mathematics and Computation*, 97:165–181, 1998.

[21] T.-T. Wong. Parameter estimation for generalized dirichlet distributions from the sample estimates of the first and the second moments of random variables. *Comput. Stat. Data Anal.*, 54(7):1756–1765, 2010.

[22] X. Yi and J. Allan. Evaluating topic models for information retrieval. *In Proceedings CIKM*, 2008.

APPENDIX

A. FIRST AND SECOND MOMENTS OF THE GD DISTRIBUTION

We derive the first and second moments of the GD distribution based on the tree representation of Eq 2. We write:

$$\theta_1 = Z_1 \quad \theta_k = Z_k(1-\theta_1-\cdots-\theta_{k-1}) = Z_k \prod_{m=1}^{k-1}(1-Z_m) \tag{17}$$

Let $S_k = E(Z_k)$, $R_k = E(Z_k^2)$. Since Z_k's are independent:

$$E(\theta_k) = S_k \prod_{m=1}^{k-1}(1-S_m), \quad E(\theta_k^2) = R_k \prod_{m=1}^{k-1}(1-2S_m+R_m) \tag{18}$$

Similarly for the crossproducts where $k < j$:

$$\begin{aligned} E(\theta_k\theta_j) &= E\left\{Z_k\left[\prod_{m=1}^{k-1}(1-Z_m)\right] Z_j \left[\prod_{m=1}^{j-1}(1-Z_m)\right]\right\} \\ &= E\left\{\left[\prod_{m=1}^{k-1}(1-Z_m)^2\right] Z_k(1-Z_k)\left[\prod_{m=i+1}^{j-1}(1-Z_m)\right] Z_j\right\} \\ &= \left[\prod_{m=1}^{k-1}(1-2S_m+R_m)\right](S_k-R_k)\left[\prod_{m=i+1}^{j-1}(1-S_m)\right] S_j \end{aligned} \tag{19}$$

Therefore, we have for the variance and covariance:

$$\begin{aligned} Var(\theta_k) &= R_k\left[\prod_{m=1}^{k-1}(1-2S_m+R_m)\right] - S_k^2\prod_{m=1}^{k-1}(1-S_m)^2 \\ &= R_k E(V_k^2) - S_k^2(E(V_k))^2 \end{aligned} \tag{20}$$

$$\begin{aligned} &Cov(\theta_k,\theta_j) = S_j\left[\prod_{m=i+1}^{j-1}(1-S_m)\right] \\ &\left\{(S_k-R_k)\prod_{m=1}^{k-1}(1-2S_m+R_m) - (S_k-S_k^2)\prod_{m=1}^{k-1}(1-S_m)^2\right\} \\ &= \left[E(\theta_j)/E(V_{k+1}^2)\right]\left[S_k Var(V_k) - Var(\theta_k)\right] \end{aligned} \tag{21}$$

for $k = 1,\ldots,K$ in Eq 20, and for $k = 1,\ldots,K-1$ and $j = k+1,\ldots,K$ in Eq 21. We estimate S_k, R_k based on the independent Beta distributions of Z_k. From the moment generating function for the Beta distribution we have:

$$S_k = \frac{\alpha_k}{\alpha_k+\beta_k} \quad R_k = \frac{\alpha_k(\alpha_k+1)}{(\alpha_k+\beta_k)(\alpha_k+\beta_k+1)} \quad k = 1,\ldots,K \tag{22}$$

where $\alpha_K = 1, \beta_K = 0$ [4]. Note that the variances and the expected value are not constrained.

A.1 Covariance Properties of GD Distribution

Three key properties can be derived from Eqs 20-22:

1. For $j > k$, $Cov(\theta_k,\theta_j) > 0$ if and only if $Var(V_k) > Var(\theta_k)$. Thus, $Cov(\theta_k,\theta_j) > 0$ if and only if the summation of the first $k-1$ θ's varies more than θ_k
2. For $j > 1$, $Cov(\theta_1,\theta_j) = -Var(\theta_1)E(\theta_j)/E(1-\theta_1) < 0$ since θ_1 is at the root level of the tree
3. For $j > k+1$, $Cov(\theta_k,\theta_j) = Cov(\theta_k,\theta_{k+1})E(\theta_j)/E(\theta_{k+1})$. Thus, $Cov(\theta_k,\theta_j)$ at deeper levels of the tree will have the same sign as $Cov(\theta_k,\theta_{k+1})$

The GD distribution models the $Cov(\theta_k,\theta_{k+1})$ for consecutive tree levels without constraints. The covariances for deeper levels in the tree $Cov(\theta_k,\theta_j), j > k+1$ are constrained. Since θ_1 is used as base category, it is always negatively correlated with the other categories. This is a typical constraint of the Logistic Normal distribution used in CTM[2]. The GD distribution constrains the sign of $Cov(\theta_k,\theta_j)$ to be the same as that of $Cov(\theta_k,\theta_{k+1})$ for $j > k+1$. These constraints imply that probability of co-occurrence of these topics is very small.

B. MAXIMIZATION OF α AND β FOR GD

To estimate the parameters of the GD distribution, the log-likelihood of Eq. 6 is optimized using the Newton method.

$$\begin{aligned} L(\alpha,\beta) = &\sum_{j=1}^{D}\sum_{k=1}^{K-1}\log\Gamma(\alpha_k+\beta_k) - \sum_{k=1}^{K-1}(\log\Gamma(\alpha_k)+\log\Gamma(\beta_k)) \\ &+\sum_{k=1}^{K-1}\left(\log\Gamma(\alpha_k^j)+\log\Gamma(\beta_k^j)\right) - \sum_{k=1}^{K-1}\log\Gamma(\alpha_k^j+\beta_k^j) \end{aligned} \tag{23}$$

By taking the derivative with respect to α, β we have:

$$\begin{aligned} \frac{\partial L(\alpha,\beta)}{\partial\alpha_k} &= D\Psi(\alpha_k+\beta_k) - D\Psi(\alpha_k) + \sum_{j=1}^{D}\Psi(\alpha_k^j) - \sum_{j=1}^{D}\Psi(\alpha_k^j+\beta_k^j) \\ \frac{\partial L(\alpha,\beta)}{\partial\beta_k} &= D\Psi(\alpha_k+\beta_k) - D\Psi(\beta_k) + \sum_{j=1}^{D}\Psi(\beta_k^j) - \sum_{j=1}^{D}\Psi(\alpha_k^j+\beta_k^j) \end{aligned} \tag{24}$$

Recall that $\alpha_k^j = \alpha_k + \overline{N}_{j,k}$, $\beta_k^j = \beta_k + \overline{N}_{j,k+1} + \ldots + \overline{N}_{j,K}$. Notice that the derivative of $L(\alpha,\beta)$ with respect to α_k just depends on α_k and β_k as opposed to the Dirichlet distribution. For the second derivative we have:

$$\begin{aligned} \frac{\partial^2 L(\alpha,\beta)}{(\partial\alpha_k)^2} &= D\Psi'(\alpha_k+\beta_k) - D\Psi'(\alpha_k) + \sum_{j=1}^{D}\Psi'(\alpha_k^j) - \sum_{j=1}^{D}\Psi'(\alpha_k^j+\beta_k^j) \\ \frac{\partial^2 L(\alpha,\beta)}{(\partial\beta_k)^2} &= D\Psi'(\alpha_k+\beta_k) - D\Psi'(\beta_k) + \sum_{j=1}^{D}\Psi'(\beta_k^j) - \sum_{j=1}^{D}\Psi'(\alpha_k^j+\beta_k^j) \\ \frac{\partial^2 L(\alpha,\beta)}{\partial\alpha_k\partial\beta_k} &= D\Psi'(\alpha_k+\beta_k) - \sum_{j=1}^{D}\Psi'(\alpha_k^j+\beta_k^j) \\ \frac{\partial^2 L(\alpha,\beta)}{\partial\alpha_k\partial\alpha_l} &= 0, \qquad \frac{\partial^2 L(\alpha,\beta)}{\partial\beta_k\partial\beta_l} = 0 \quad \text{for } l \neq k \end{aligned} \tag{25}$$

Therefore, the Hessian matrix can be written as:

$$H(\alpha,\beta) = \text{block-diag}\left[H_1(\alpha_1,\beta_1),\ldots,H_{K-1}(\alpha_{K-1},\beta_{K-1})\right] \tag{26}$$

where H_k is the Hessian matrix for α_k, β_k. Following a similar logic as in the case of a Dirichlet distribution described in Eqs (56-60) of [12], we have the following Newton iteration:

$$\begin{aligned} &\alpha_k^{new} = \alpha_k - \left(H_k^{-1}g_k\right)_1, \qquad \beta_k^{new} = \beta_k - \left(H_k^{-1}g_k\right)_2 \\ &q_{11}^k = \sum_{j=1}^{D}\Psi'(\alpha_k^j) - D\Psi'(\alpha_k), \qquad q_{22}^k = \sum_{j=1}^{D}\Psi'(\beta_k^j) - D\Psi'(\beta_k), \\ &a_k = \frac{g_1^k/q_{11}^k + g_2^k/q_{22}^k}{b_k^{-1} + (q_{11}^k)^{-1} + (q_{22}^k)^{-1}}, \qquad b_k = D\Psi'(\alpha_k+\beta_k) - \sum_{j=1}^{D}\Psi'(\alpha_k^j+\beta_k^j) \\ &\left(H_k^{-1}g_k\right)_l = \frac{g_l^k - a_k}{q_{ll}^k} \qquad \text{for } l = 1,2 \end{aligned} \tag{27}$$

where $g_1^k = dL(\alpha,\beta)/d\alpha_k$ and $g_2^k = dL(\alpha,\beta)/d\beta_k$ from Eq 24.

Modeling Topic Hierarchies with the Recursive Chinese Restaurant Process

Joon Hee Kim, Dongwoo Kim, Suin Kim, and Alice Oh
Department of Computer Science
Korea Advanced Institute of Science and Technology
Daejeon, Republic of Korea
{joon.kim,dw.kim,suin.kim}@kaist.ac.kr, alice.oh@kaist.edu

ABSTRACT

Topic models such as latent Dirichlet allocation (LDA) and hierarchical Dirichlet processes (HDP) are simple solutions to discover topics from a set of unannotated documents. While they are simple and popular, a major shortcoming of LDA and HDP is that they do not organize the topics into a hierarchical structure which is naturally found in many datasets. We introduce the recursive Chinese restaurant process (rCRP) and a nonparametric topic model with rCRP as a prior for discovering a hierarchical topic structure with unbounded depth and width. Unlike previous models for discovering topic hierarchies, rCRP allows the documents to be generated from a mixture over the entire set of topics in the hierarchy. We apply rCRP to a corpus of New York Times articles, a dataset of MovieLens ratings, and a set of Wikipedia articles and show the discovered topic hierarchies. We compare the predictive power of rCRP with LDA, HDP, and nested Chinese restaurant process (nCRP) using held-out likelihood to show that rCRP outperforms the others. We suggest two metrics that quantify the characteristics of a topic hierarchy to compare the discovered topic hierarchies of rCRP and nCRP. The results show that rCRP discovers a hierarchy in which the topics become more specialized toward the leaves, and topics in the immediate family exhibit more affinity than topics beyond the immediate family.

Categories and Subject Descriptors

G.3 [**Probability and Statistics**]: Nonparametric Statistics; H.3.3 [**Information Storage and Retrieval**]: Information Search and Retrieval—*clustering*; I.2.6 [**Artificial Intelligence**]: Learning

Keywords

Hierarchical Topic Modeling, Bayesian Nonparametric models

CIKM'12, October 29–November 2, 2012, Maui, HI, USA.

1. INTRODUCTION

Probabilistic topic models [5, 20] are important tools for discovering the latent semantic patterns in various data including text [11, 13], users [12, 24] and movie ratings [18]. A major limitation of these basic topic models and many of their extensions is that they discover topics in flat structures without organizing them into groups or hierarchies. This is a significant limitation because in many domains, topics can be naturally organized into hierarchies where the root topic of each hierarchy is the most general topic, and the topics become more specific toward the leaves. Consider, for example, the domain of movies, where there are genres (e.g., *action*) and sub-genres (e.g., *martial arts*)[1]. One branch of the tree may have the genre *action* as a topic, and children topics *martial arts* and *James Bond series*, and another branch may have the genre *comedy* and as children *slapstick* and *black comedy*. A user with preferences, then, should be allowed to be associated with both the *action* topic to indicate that his preferences span a wide variety of action movies, as well as the *black comedy* sub-genre to indicate that his preferences for comedy are limited to that sub-genre.

There have been previously proposed topic models that look at correlations among the topics [4] and hierarchical topic structure [2, 16], but these models do not fully exhibit the following three characteristics of an intuitive and flexible topic structure. First, the number of topics should be unbounded, and an optimal number should be automatically determined by the model. Second, topics should be structured in a hierarchy of unbounded depth from general to specific, and similar topics should form groups within the hierarchical structure. Third, a document should be composed of multiple topics from anywhere in the hierarchy of topics, not just a single topic, the topics of a single path, or the topics at the bottom of the hierarchy. Detailed comparisons with other related models will be presented in the next section.

We propose a novel prior, recursive Chinese restaurant process (rCRP), and a hierarchical topic model with rCRP as a prior that can handle such flexible hierarchical topic modeling. The topic hierarchies found by rCRP are consistent with the general intuition that the topics start out quite general at the root level and become more specialized toward the leaves. Additionally, the topics within the immediate family (i.e., a parent topic and its direct children) are much more similar than the topics outside the family boundary. This characteristic of the topic hierarchy is more natural and fitting for many domains where each data point

[1] http://visual.ly/complete-list-film-sub-genres

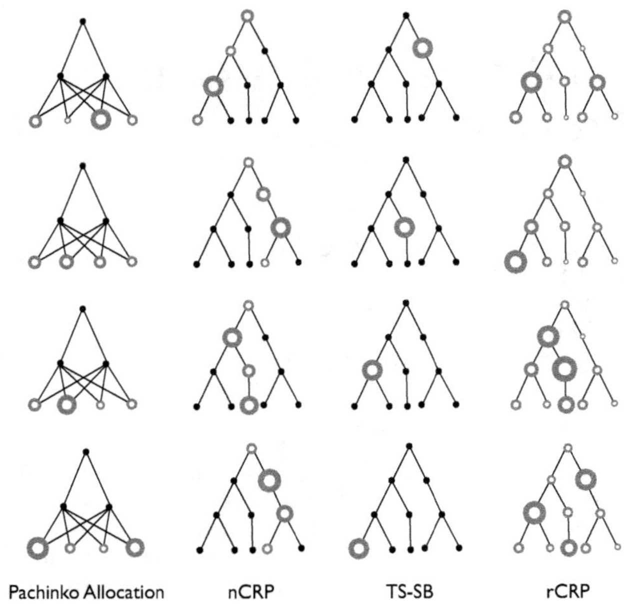

Figure 1: In PAM [14], a document is modeled as a distribution over the topics at the leaves of the topic hierarchy. In nested CRP [2], a document is modeled as a distribution over a single path from the root to the leaf node. In TS-SB [1], a document is modeled by a single node of the tree. In rCRP, a document has a distribution over all of the nodes of the hierarchy.

is best explained by a variety of topics, general to specific and placed anywhere within the hierarchy. In addition to the flexibility of the model, rCRP outperforms LDA, HDP, and nCRP [2] on the predictive metric of heldout likelihood.

The rest of this paper is organized as follows. In Section 2, we discuss existing hierarchical topic models and how they differ from rCRP. In Section 3, we describe our model with the novel nonparametric prior, the recursive Chinese restaurant process. In Section 4, we present a Markov chain Monte Carlo inference algorithm for approximating the posterior probability. In Section 5, we describe the three datasets used for experiments and visualize the topic hierarchies found for those datasets. We also compare our model against LDA, HDP, and nCRP on heldout likelihood. In Section 6, we propose two new metrics for quantifying the characteristics of a topic hierarchy and show the results of our model and nCRP. In Section 7, we conclude the paper with discussions and future directions.

2. TOPIC HIERARCHIES

Two classes of previously proposed models address hierarchical structures: ones that cluster each of the documents into the nodes of the hierarchy [9, 17, 23], and ones that place each of the topics into the nodes of the hierarchy [2, 14, 16]. Within the latter class of models, none are flexible enough to accommodate the intuition that a document exhibits multiple topics, and those topics can come from anywhere in the hierarchy of topics, from the general root-level topic down to the most specific leaf node topic, and along any path of the tree.

The different assumptions of the related models, pachinko allocation model (PAM) [14, 16], nested Chinese restaurant process (nCRP) [2], tree-structured stick-breaking process (TS-SB) [1], as well as our rCRP model are illustrated in Figure 1. The figure shows the topic assignments for four fictitious documents highlighting the different assumptions of the four models. Each of the rows is a document, modeled by each of the four models in the columns. The different sized thick circles represent proportions of the document generated by a topic represented by that node. PAM [14] is a generalization of the LDA that enables learning of topics in a form of a directed acyclic graph. In [16], the model is further extended to explicitly identify the word distribution of super-topics and sub-topics. PAM and its extension assume that the documents are generated by only the leaf node topics. The nCRP [2] extends the original CRP representation and constructs a tree-structured hierarchy of topics. This model assumes that a topic is represented by a path from the root to a particular leaf node, and each document is generated by a single path. TS-SB [1] can be used to discover a hierarchy of mixture components with each data point belonging to a component. This model assumes that each document is generated by only a single node which has its unique topic distribution. Our proposed model with recursive CRP (rCRP) as a nonparametric prior enables a document to have a distribution over the entire topic tree.

3. RECURSIVE CHINESE RESTAURANT PROCESS

Chinese Restaurant Process (CRP) is a stochastic process that generates an exchangeable partition of data points. Due to its flexibility and extendability, CRP is widely used in nonparametric topic models. One of the most widely used model is hierarchical Dirichlet process mixture model [20]. It combines two levels of CRP to construct a mixture model of grouped data. The second level CRP partitions data points into homogeneous groups, while the first level CRP associates each group with a mixture component.

Our model also employs two levels of partitioning process. However, we discover the hierarchical structure of the mixture components by replacing the first level CRP with a new stochastic process called recursive Chinese Restaurant Process (rCPR). In rCRP, mixture components are organized in an infinite tree, and each group of data points can be associated with any node in the tree. As in [20], second level CRP is used to partition data points into groups.

With this setting, we propose a nonparametric Bayesian model that is capable of uncovering the hierarchical structure of the mixture components. In Section 3.1 we present the metaphor and notations, and review CRP. In Section 3.2 we provide a detailed description of rCRP. In Section 3.3 we formalize the generative process of our model.

3.1 Table Assignment with CRP

We maintain most of the basic assumptions and metaphors used in previous nonparametric probabilistic models as they have been proven to have strong explanatory power over data. A document is represented as a restaurant, and words are represented as customers in the restaurants. Words that convey homogeneous semantic theme are grouped together as customers of similar taste sit at the same table. A dish is chosen for each table from the global menu of dish tree,

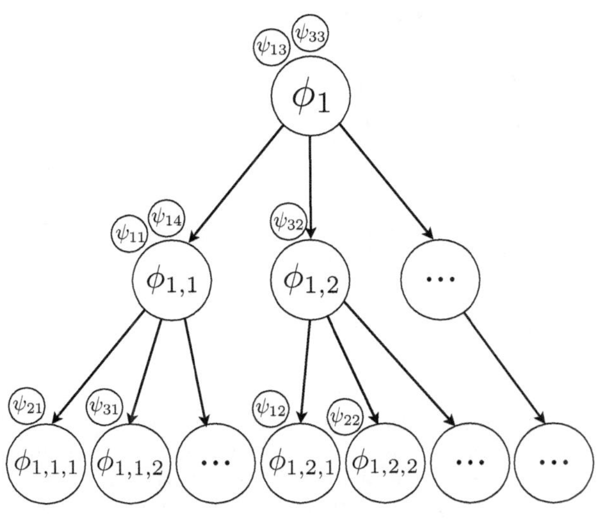

(a) First (menu) level rCRP

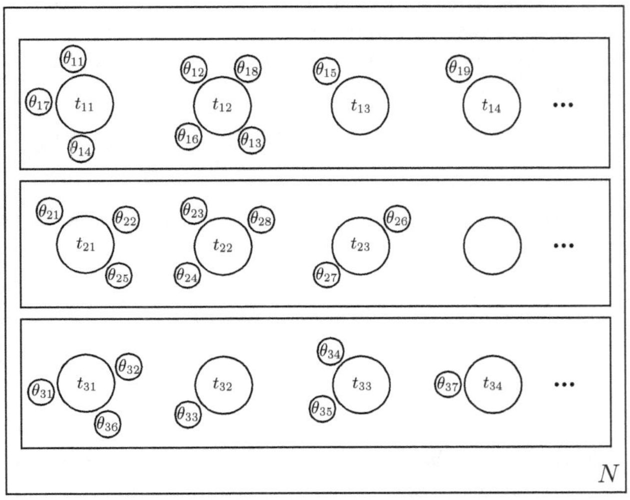

(b) Second (customer) level CRP

Figure 2: Our proposed model consists of two levels of partitioning process. In the diagram, ϕ represents a dish, ψ represents a table, and θ represents a customer. The first level rCRP associates each table to a dish. The second level CRP associates each customer to a table.

which corresponds to topic assignment for each group of words. In our proposed model, the assignment of each customer to a table is determined by CRP. The association between tables and dishes is governed by rCRP.

CRP is a stochastic process that generates a random partition of discrete data. The table assignment probability distribution for a particular customer is as follows. The first customer always sits on the first table. The ith customer sits on a table depending on a draw from the following distribution

$$p(t^{th} \text{ table} \mid \text{previous assignments}) = \frac{n_t}{\alpha + i - 1} \quad (1)$$

$$p(\text{new table} \mid \text{previous assignment}) = \frac{\alpha}{\alpha + i - 1} \quad (2)$$

where n_t is the number of customers already sitting at t^{th} table of the restaurant, and α is a parameter governing the likelihood of choosing of a new table.

3.2 Dish Assignment with recursive CRP

rCRP is an extension to CRP that assumes an infinite tree structure of the mixture components. Sticking to the metaphor, rCRP assigns a dish from the global menu for each table. The menu is an infinite tree of dishes unbounded in both branching factor and height. Indexing dishes in the infinite tree is nontrivial, as the number of potential dishes is uncountably infinite whereas the number of integers used for ordinary indexing scheme is only countably infinite. Therefore we utilize the index set of strings of integers. The root dish has an index of 1. Let k be an index string of a particular dish on the menu, i'th child of dish ϕ_k is named $\phi_{k,i}$. This is visualized in Figure 2(a).

To find a dish for a particular table, we perform a recursive search beginning from the root dish. Let ϕ_k be the dish that is currently under examination. Then we make one of the three choices. The recursive search stops only when the first choice is made.

1. Choose ϕ_k
2. Choose one of the existing child dish of ϕ_k
3. Create a new child dish of ϕ_k, and choose it

We introduce the notations that will be used in the formal definition of the conditional probability of dish assignment. Let n_{jtk} be the number of customers at table t of restaurant j eating dish k. We replace an index with dot to signify that the count is marginalized. For example, $n_{jt\cdot}$ is the number of customers at table t of restaurant j, and $n_{j\cdot k}$ is the number of customers at restaurant j eating dish k. We use m_{jk} to count the number of tables at restaurant j serving dish k. Likewise, $m_{j\cdot}$ is the number of tables at restaurant j, and $m_{\cdot k}$ is the total number of tables serving dish k at any restaurant. Finally, we use $M_{\cdot k}$ to denote the cumulative counts of $m_{\cdot k}$ summed over for all dishes that are descendants of ϕ_k including ϕ_k itself. The need for this cumulative counts is illustrated shortly.

Now we formalize the probability of three choices. To find the dish for table t in restaurant j, we perform recursive search from the root dish. Let ϕ_k be the current dish, then we draw from the following distribution

$$\begin{aligned} p(\phi_k|\text{previous tables}) &= \frac{m_{\cdot k}^{-jt}}{M_{\cdot k}^{-jt} + \gamma^n} \\ p(\phi_{k'}|\text{previous tables}) &= \frac{M_{\cdot k'}^{-jt}}{M_{\cdot k}^{-jt} + \gamma^n} \\ p(\phi_{k_{\text{new}}}|\text{previous tables}) &= \frac{\gamma^n}{M_{\cdot k}^{-jt} + \gamma^n} \end{aligned}$$

where $\phi_{k'}$ is a direct descendent of ϕ_k, and ϕ_{new} is a new child dish of ϕ_k.

Dishes are equivalent to topic distributions used in the generation of documents, and each dish is drawn from a level-specific Dirichlet distribution. Let ϕ_k be the dish indexed by k, then it is generated as follows:

$$\phi_k \sim Dir(\beta^{\delta(k)}),$$

where $\delta(k)$ is a depth of current dish. We use $\beta^{\delta(k)}$ as a prior of Dirichlet distribution. Because symmetric Dirichlet distribution generates more sparse distribution with small values of parameter, we can expect more sparse topics with increasing depth of k when β is less than one.

3.3 Generative Process

We employ the two stages of generative process as described in Section 3.1 and Section 3.2. Now we formally describe the generative process.

Topic Tree Generation The measure G_{tree} of the global topic tree is drawn from the rCRP.

$$G_{tree} \sim rCRP(\alpha)$$

Document Generation G_j, the topic distribution of jth document, is distributed according to G_{tree}. θ_{ji} denotes the topic of ith word in the jth document, and x_{ji} denotes the word generated from the topic.

$$\begin{aligned} G_j &\sim DP(G_{tree}) \\ \theta_{ji} &\sim G_j \\ x_{ji} &\sim F(\theta_{ji}) \end{aligned}$$

4. POSTERIOR INFERENCE

In this section, we develop a Markov Chain Monte Carlo algorithm for posterior sampling of table and dish assignments. Generally, computing an exact posterior of DP and its related models is intractable. Several approaches have been employed to compute the approximate posterior. Possible approaches include (1) a Pólya urn scheme based on the marginalization of unknown infinite-dimensions [15, 7], (2) a truncation approximation which limits the complexity of the model from infinite dimensions to finite dimensions [10], (3) a variational inference which converts inference algorithms into optimization problems [3, 21]. In this work, we employ the Pólya urn scheme by incorporating the CRP metaphor for approximate inference.

Before we discuss the posterior inference algorithm, let us define variables of interest. x_{ji} indicates the ith observed word of jth document, and θ_{ji} denotes the topic of x_{ji}. ϕ_k is an atom of G_{tree}. ψ_{jt}, which denotes the topic of tth table in the jth document, is an atom of G_j. Note that each θ_{ji} is associated with one ψ_{jt} since the topic assigned to x_{ji} must correspond to the topic assigned to the table in which x_{ji} is seated. Likewise, each ψ_{jt} is associated with one ϕ_k.

For the posterior inference, we marginalize out ϕ_k, ψ_{jt}, and θ_{ji}. Therefore we need to sample the assignment relationship between these variables rather than sampling the quantities of variables themselves. For this purpose, we introduce two index variables. t_{ji} is the index variable of tables such that $\psi_{jt_{ji}} = \theta_{ji}$, and k_{jt} is the index variable of topics such that $\phi_{k_{jt}} = \psi_{jt}$.

First we write out the conditional density of x_{ji} given dish k in the inference steps for convenience. Each x_{ji} is drawn from some ϕ_k, and ϕ_k is drawn from its level distribution, $\text{Dir}(\beta^{|k|})$. Therefore, by marginalizing out ϕ_k, we can simply compute the conditional density. Letting $\mathbf{x}_k = \{x_{j'i'}; k_{jt_{j'i'}} \in \Lambda(k)\}$, the conditional density of x_{ji} only depends on the other $\mathbf{x}_k$ already assigned to that dish and its decendents, and can be computed as follows

$$\begin{aligned} p(x_{ji}|\mathbf{x}^{-ji}, \mathbf{t}, \mathbf{k}) &= \frac{p(x_{ji}, \mathbf{x}^{-ji}|\mathbf{t}, \mathbf{k})}{p(\mathbf{x}^{-ji}|\mathbf{t}, \mathbf{k})} \\ &= \frac{\int p(x_{ji}|\phi_k) \prod_{x_{j'i'}}^{\mathbf{x}_k} p(x_{j'i'}|\phi_k) p(\phi_k|\beta_k) d\phi_k}{\int \prod_{x_{j'i'}}^{\mathbf{x}_k} p(x_{j'i'}|\phi_k) p(\phi_k|\beta_k) d\phi_k}. \end{aligned}$$

We can further simplify the above equation by utilizing the Dirichlet-multinomial conjugacy as

$$p(x_{ji}|\mathbf{x}^{-ji}, \mathbf{k}) = \frac{\sum_{\{j'i';x_{j'i'} \in \mathbf{x}_k\}} 1[x_{j'i'} = x_{ji}] + \beta^{|k|}}{\sum_{\{j'i';x_{j'i'} \in \mathbf{x}_k\}} 1 + V\beta^{|k|}},$$

where V is the size of the vocabulary. With the Pólya urn based sampling scheme, we can efficiently sample from the above distribution by marginalizing out unknown infinite dimensional distributions. Thus, our variables of interest are index variable of tables and dishes, namely t_{ji}, and k_{jt}. It is natural to sample table t_{ji} before sampling dish k_{jt} with the CRF metaphor, so we start with sampling t_{ji}.

Sampling t The conditional distribution of t_{ji} given x_{ji} is proportional to the number of customers sitting at table t times the probability of x_{ji} being observed under table t, which can be written as

$$p(t_{ji} = t|rest) \propto \begin{cases} n_{jt}^{-ji} \times p(x_{ji}|\mathbf{x}^{-ji}, \mathbf{t}^{-ji}, t_{ji} = t, \mathbf{k}) \\ \alpha \times p(x_{ji}|\mathbf{x}^{-ji}, \mathbf{t}^{-ji}, t_{ji} = t_{\text{new}}, \mathbf{k}), \end{cases}$$

where the probability of sitting at a new table can be found by marginalizing over all available dishes.

$$\begin{aligned} &p(x_{ji}|\mathbf{x}^{-ji}, \mathbf{t}^{-ji}, t_{ji} = t_{\text{new}}, \mathbf{k}) \\ &= \sum_{k \in K} \frac{m_{\cdot k}}{m_{\cdot\cdot} + \gamma} p(x_{ji}|\mathbf{x}^{-ji}, \mathbf{t}, \mathbf{k}) \\ &+ \frac{\gamma}{m_{\cdot\cdot} + \gamma} p(x_{ji}|\mathbf{x}^{-ji}, \mathbf{t}, \mathbf{k}_{\text{new}}) \end{aligned}$$

Sampling k The posterior sampling of k_{jt} involves a sequence of search along the menu tree. We begin from the root dish and move down along the tree until we find the dish. Suppose we want to sample a dish for customers at table t in restaurant j. We perform a recursive search beginning from the root dish as illustrated in Algorithm 1. The conditional probability of k_{jt} is the prior probability of

Algorithm 1 Sampling k_{jt} by recursive algorithm

```
function samplingK(k_current)
k_next ~ p(k_jt = k|t, k^{-jt}, k_current)
if k_next = k_current then
  return k
else if k_next = child of k_current then
  k_current ← k_next
  return samplingK(k_current)
else if k_next = new child of k_current then
  add node k_next into tree
  k_current ← k_next
  return samplingK(k_current)
end if
```

k times the likelihood of $\mathbf{x}_{jt}$ being observed under dish k. The prior depends on k. If $k = k_{\text{current}}$, it is proportional to the number of tables serving dish k. Otherwise, it is proportional to the number of tables serving dish k or any of its descendants.

$$p(k_{jt} = k | t, k^{-jt}, k_{\text{current}}) \propto \begin{cases} m_{.k}^{-jt} \times p(\mathbf{x}_{jt} | \mathbf{x}^{-jt}, \mathbf{t}, \mathbf{k}) \text{ if } k = k_{\text{current}} \\ M_{.k}^{-jt} \times p(\mathbf{x}_{jt} | \mathbf{x}^{-jt}, \mathbf{t}, \mathbf{k}) \text{ if } k = \text{a child of } k_{\text{current}} \\ \gamma^{n} \times p(\mathbf{x}_{jt} | \mathbf{x}^{-jt}, \mathbf{t}, \mathbf{k}) \text{ if } k = \text{a new child of } k_{\text{current}}. \end{cases}$$

Sampling k_{jt} is important as it potentially changes the membership of all data sitting at table t and leads to a well-mixed MCMC.

Estimating ϕ For the rest of this paper and the experiments, we estimate $\hat{\Phi}$ with a Maximum a posteriori (MAP) estimator.

5. EXPERIMENTS

We fit our rCRP model to discover and analyze the hierarchical topic structures in both synthetic and real data sets. We chose not only text data but also user-movie ratings data to show the generality of our model with respect to the type of data.

5.1 Datasets

5.1.1 Synthetic Data

We generated a synthetic corpus that consists of 1,000 documents each having 1,000 word tokens. We used a three-level topic tree where the root topic has a uniform distribution over the entire vocabulary. Topics at the second level are distributed over the terms in each of the columns. Topics at the third level have full probability concentrated at a single term from the column of its parent. The topic assignment process is performed by the two-level CRP and rCRP as described in Section 3.

5.1.2 Real Data

New York Times The corpus consists of 1.8 million articles published between January 1, 1987 and June 19, 2007 [2]. We randomly sampled 10,000 articles. We removed non-alphabetic characters and single-character words.

MovieLens The MovieLens dataset is a collection of movie ratings from 71,567 users on 10,681 movies. Users rated the movies on a scale of 1 to 5. We turned each user into a document made up of movies that he/she rated as 4 or 5. After this process, the dataset is equivalent to a text corpus consisting of 71,567 documents with 10,681 unique words.

Wikipedia Contemporary Art The WikiArt corpus consists of 3,600 web pages crawled by taking two hops from the Wikipedia Contemporary Art page[3].

In both New York Times and Wikipedia, we applied porter stemming algorithm. We also removed words that occur too infrequently (less than 1%), and too frequently (more than 20%) in terms of the document frequency. These data statistics are illustrated in Table 1.

5.2 Topic Tree Visualization

We visualize the result of inferring topic hierarchy from the synthetic data in Figure 3. The model successfully recovers the original structure and topics. The first and second level topics are almost identical to the original topics. The third level topics show some noise, however most noise words in a topic are accounted by its direct parent topic.

[2]http://archive.ics.uci.edu/ml/

[3]en.wikipedia.org/wiki/Painting#Contemporary_art

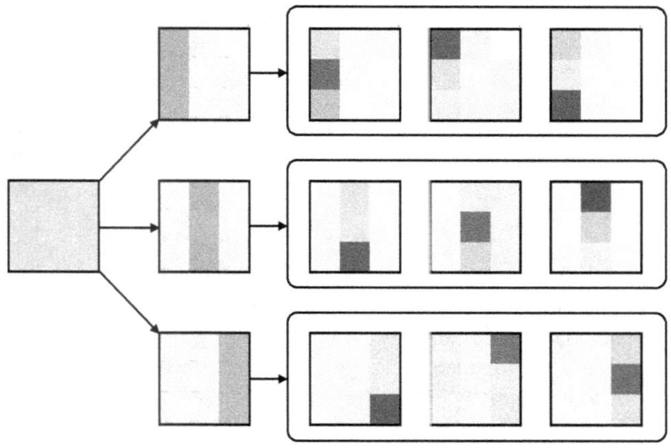

Figure 3: Topic tree inferred from synthetic data. Each cell corresponds to a single word, and is shaded with intensity proportional to the probability of each word in the topic. The first and second level topics are almost identical to the original topics. There exist some noise in the third level topics. However, they are accounted by its direct parent.

Figure 4: An example user from our MovieLens data. This user watched movies from the topics of Horror and Family from the genre level, and the topics of Action Thriller and Crime Thriller from the sub-genre level.

Figure 5 shows the topic trees inferred from NYTimes, MovieLens, and Wikipedia. Each topic tree is too large to fit in the space provided, so we take a subtree from each tree to illustrate the important points of the discovered topic hierarchies. Each topic is represented by the top ten highest probability words in that topic, and words with probability lower than 0.001 are not shown.

The root topic of each tree contains the most frequently used words in each corpus, and as we move down the tree, topics become more specialized. For example, in the topic tree of the NYTimes dataset, the **Economy** topic is followed by topics about **Technology**, **Stocks**, **Prices**, and **Labor**. For the MovieLens dataset, the root topic represents the generally popular movies, the movies with the most number of high ratings such as *Star Wars* and *Forest Gump*. One level down from the root, we can see the movies being clustered into genres such as **Family, Horror, and Classics**, and the **Horror** movie topic is separated into the more typical **Horror** movies and movies in the **Zombie** sub-genre. As with any hierarchical taxonomy, some parts of the structure are arguable, for example, whether the **Drama** topic should be a subtopic of **Family** or vice versa. Such arguable anomalies in the topic trees discovered by our model reflect the unique characteristics of the data.

Table 1: Data statistics

	Documents	Unique Terms	Ave Doc Length
Synthetic	1,000	9	1,000
New York Times	10,000	6,841	1,886
MovieLens	71,567	10,681	56
Wikipedia	3,600	6,386	445

The rCRP model allows each document to have a topic distribution over the entire topic tree. For example, using the topic tree in Figure 5(a), a user with high ratings for "Toy Story" and "Hellraiser" can be interpreted to be interested in both the **Disney** topic and the **Horror** topic. We show, in figure 4, an example user from our data whose topic proportion includes **Horror, Family, Action Thriller**, and **Crime Thriller**, with the movie titles that belong to those topics. Although the vanilla LDA and HDP models allow this, such flexible assignment of document-topic assignments is rare in models of topic hierarchies, and this shows that our model better reflects the nature of the hierarchical topic structure than previously proposed models.

5.3 Heldout likelihood

Heldout likelihood, widely used as a comparative evaluation metric in topic modeling (cf. [5]), evaluates how well the trained model explains the heldout data. Heldout likelihood is defined as log-likelihood of the heldout data given the trained model. Formally,

$$L = \log p(W_{\text{heldout}} | M_{\text{trained}})$$

where W_{heldout} is the heldout data and M_{trained} is the trained model. We use ten-fold cross validation.

We compare heldout likelihoods of our model with the baselines of LDA, HDP, and nCRP [4]. The result is shown in Figure 6. A model with higher explanatory power produces higher heldout likelihood. Note that the result of LDA with the optimal number of topics is very close to that of the HDP, which is natural because the HDP is designed to find the optimal number of topics for LDA. Figure 6 shows that rCRP model outperforms LDA, HDP, and nCRP which confirms the intuition that the flexible hierarchical topic structure of rCRP explains the data better than the topic structures of HDP and nCRP.

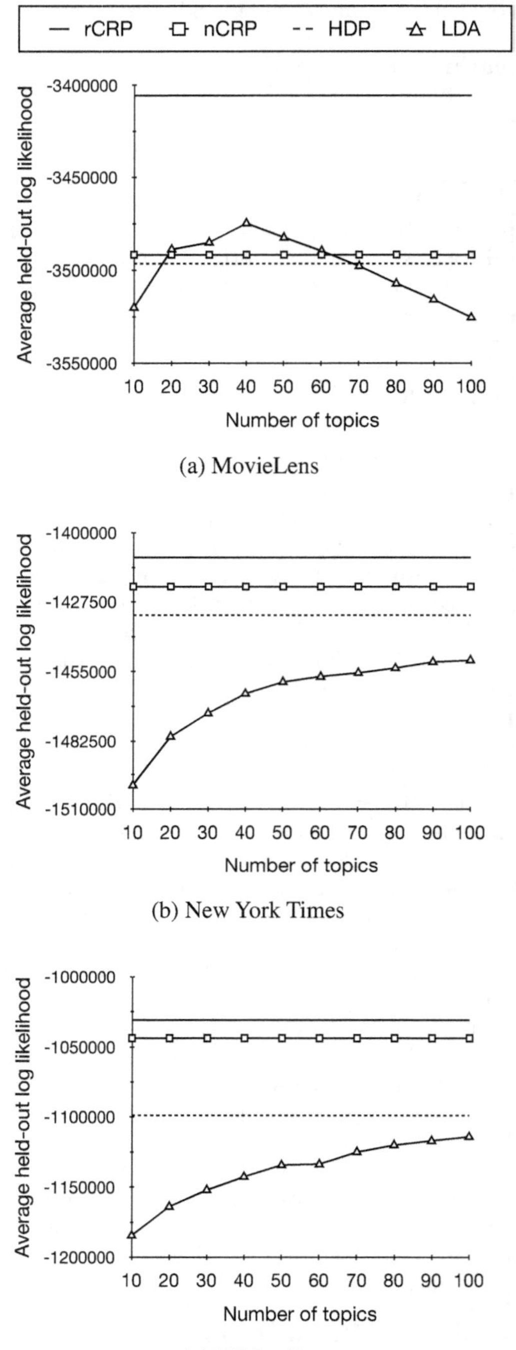

(a) MovieLens

(b) New York Times

(c) Wikipedia

Figure 6: Heldout likelihoods of LDA, HDP, and rCRP for the three datasets. A higher value indicates that the model can explain better the heldout data.

6. HIERARCHY ANALYSIS

A topic model is commonly evaluated by either directly calculating the perplexity or likelihood of held-out data [22], or applying the result to related tasks such as document classification or recommendation [5]. To our knowledge, however, there is no commonly used evaluation metric for measuring the goodness of a topic hierarchy. We suggest two fundamental characteristics of a topic hierarchy and propose concrete evaluation metrics. We then use these metrics to quantitatively compare the characteristics of the topic trees discovered by our model and by nCRP.

6.1 Topic Specialization

Studies on human semantic processing [6] find that in concept trees, the most general semantic category is placed at the top of the tree, and more specific categories toward

[4]http://www.cs.princeton.edu/ blei/downloads/hlda-c.tgz

(a) MovieLens

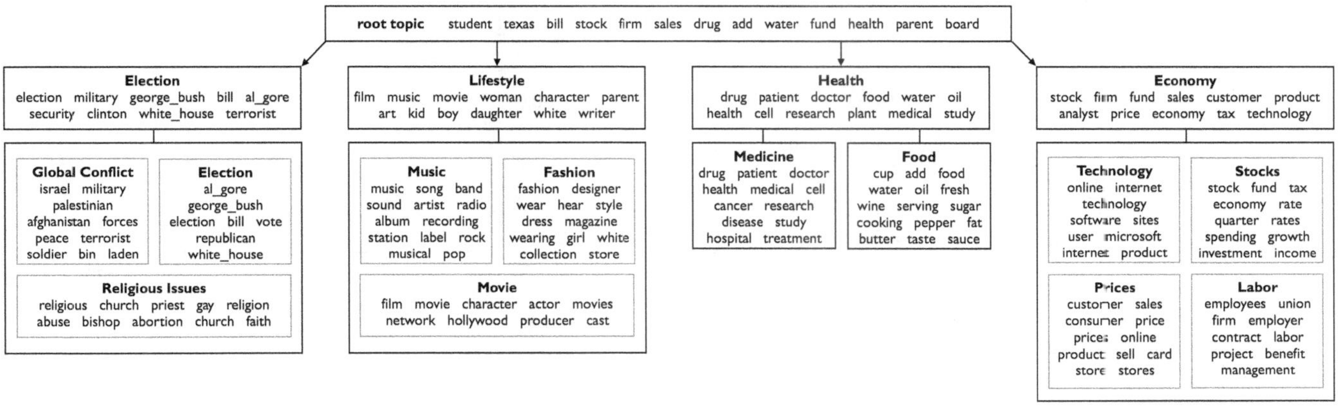

(b) New York Times

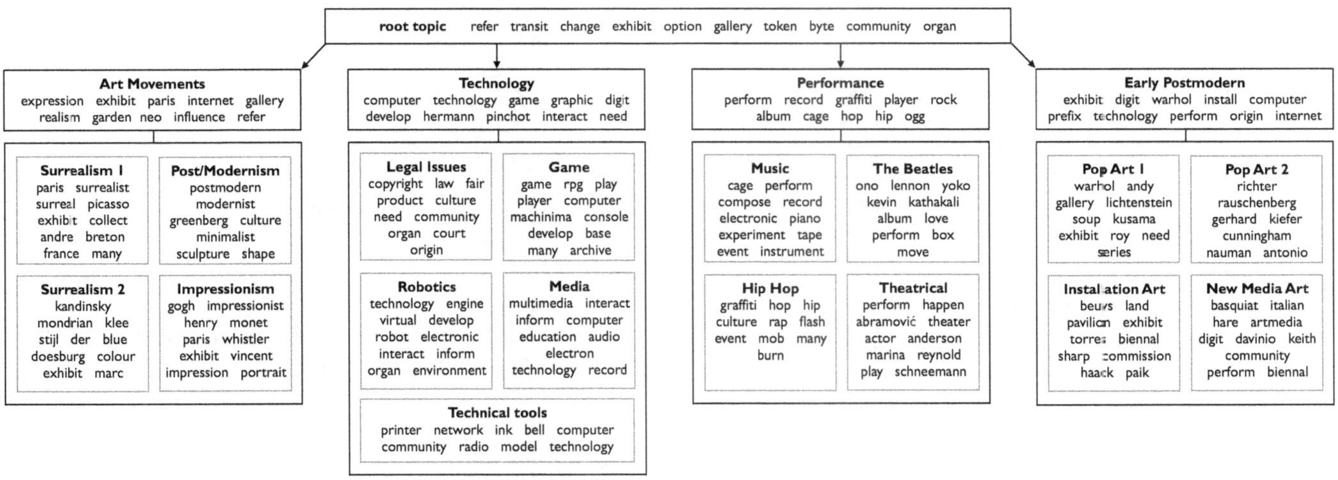

(c) Wikipedia

Figure 5: Topic trees inferred from each dataset. The bold labels at the top of the topics are manually chosen for better readability.

the leaves. We assume the hierarchy of topics should follow this general principle and propose a metric to quantify the general-to-specific characteristic. We name this *topic specialization* and compute it by the semantic distance of a topic from the norm as defined below.

Let ϕ_{Norm} be the norm topic such that the probability of generating a particular word x_i is proportional to the frequency of x_i in the entire corpus. Formally, let $freq(x_i)$ be the frequency of word x_i in the entire corpus, V be the set of entire vocabulary, and β be the smoothing factor. ϕ_{Norm} is a topic such that for each word x_i,

$$p(x_i|\phi_{\text{Norm}}) = \frac{freq(x_i) + \beta}{\sum_{j \in V} freq(x_j) + \beta|V|}.$$

As ϕ_{Norm} represents the word distribution of the entire corpus, we consider it to be the most general topic. For each topic ϕ_k, we measure how much it has drifted away from ϕ_{Norm} by measuring the cosine distance between the two. Formally, let $\Delta(\phi_k)$ be the topic specialization of topic ϕ_k then

$$\Delta(\phi_k) = 1 - \frac{\phi_k \cdot \phi_{\text{Norm}}}{|\phi_k||\phi_{\text{Norm}}|}$$

In rCRP, since customers at each table always visit the root topic first, the semantic distance between ϕ_{Norm} and ϕ_{Root} is zero.

We calculate and average the topic specialization of all topics at each level. From the definition of Δ, a higher value indicates that the topic has drifted farther away from ϕ_{Norm}, which implies that the topic has become more specialized. Figure 7 illustrates the concept of this topic specialization score, where we can see that the topic-word multinomial is near uniform for the root topic and becomes increasingly sparse toward the leaf topic.

In Figure 8, we summarize the topic specialization scores of rCRP and nCRP. In rCRP, topics at the second, third and fourth levels become increasingly more specialized. In nCRP, the general trend is the same, but the pattern is not so pronounced as the topics at all levels appear to be quite specialized. We conjecture this is because nCRP assumes that a document is generated only by the topics in a single path of the hierarchy, so all of the topics must be more specialized to explain the data well. On the other hand, the topics discovered by rCRP do not have that restriction, so the model can focus more on finding an appropriate hierarchy of increasingly more specialized topics, as shown in the topic trees in Figure 5.

6.2 Hierarchical Affinity

Another important characteristic we expect to find from a hierarchical structure of topics is *hierarchical affinity*. That is, topics that descend from ϕ_k must be more similar to ϕ_k than topics that descend from other topics. For clarity, we only use topics at the second level as the parent topics, and topics at the third level as the children topics, and compute the hierarchical affinity among them. Figure 9 illustrates this concept of hierarchical affinity, where the topic-word multinomial for the **Lifestyle** topic is similar to its children topics **Music** and **Movie** but quite different from its non-children topic **Stocks**.

Let ϕ_k be a topic at the second level, and let $\lambda(k)$ be the index set of all topics that have ϕ_k as a direct parent. Also let $\bar{\lambda}(k)$ be the index set of all topics at third level

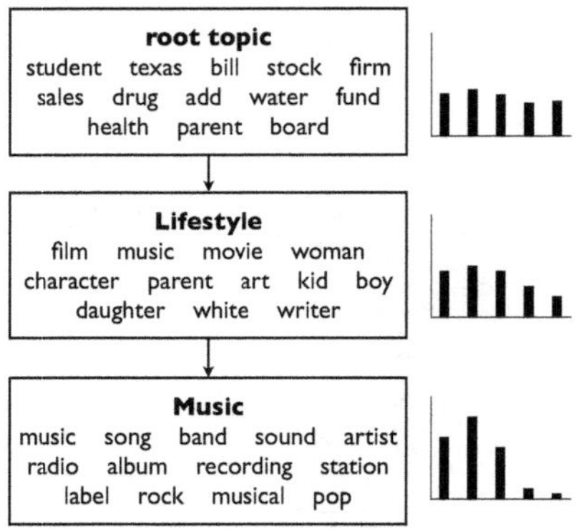

Figure 7: Topic specialization. The topic-word multinomial is near uniform for the root topic and becomes increasingly sparse toward the leaf topic.

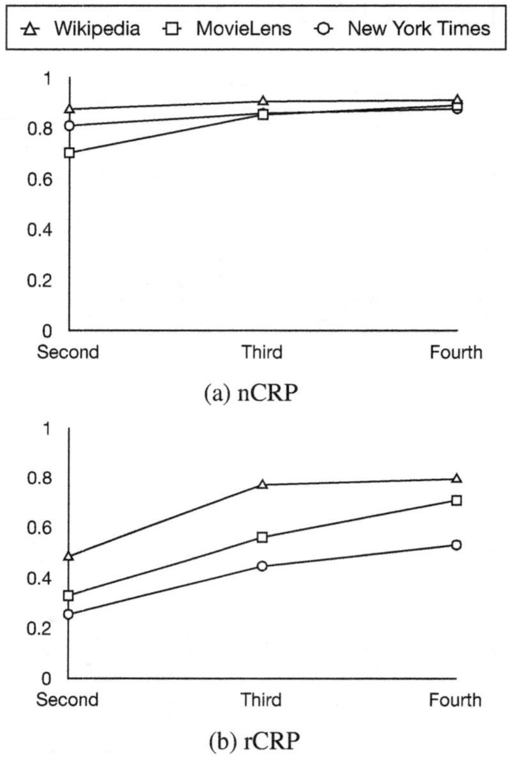

Figure 8: Topic specialization scores of rCRP and nCRP. This shows the characteristic of rCRP to find general topics at the root and increasingly more specialized topics toward the leaves.

that do not have ϕ_k as a direct parent. In other words, $\lambda(k)$ are children of ϕ_k and $\bar{\lambda}(k)$ are non-children of ϕ_k. To measure the hierarchical affinity, we compare the average cosine similarity between ϕ_k and all topics in $\lambda(k)$ against the average cosine similarity between ϕ_k and all topics in $\bar{\lambda}(k)$.

We compute this hierarchical affinity for all topics at the second level and compare the results for rCRP and nCRP. The results are illustrated in Figure 10. For all three data sets, rCRP clearly shows stronger hierarchical affinity for

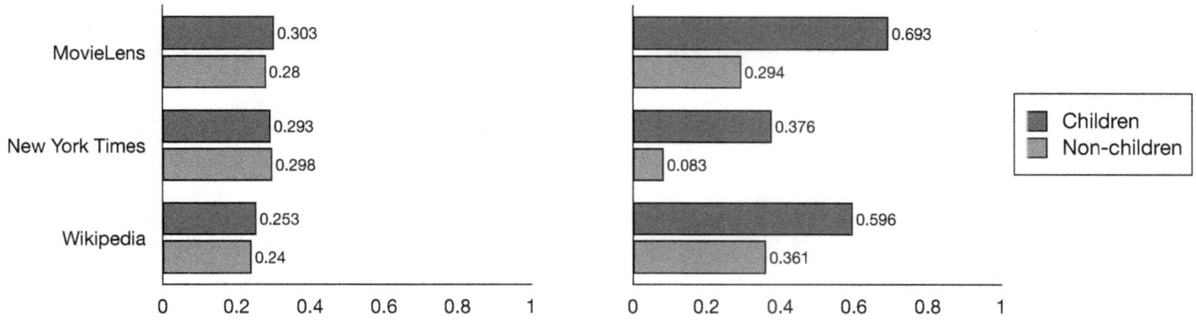

(a) nCRP (b) rCRP

Figure 10: Hierarchical Affinity. The average cosine similarity between topics at second and their direct children is compared against their non-children topics. A higher affinity score means that the topics are more similar. For all three data sets, rCRP shows stronger hierarchical affinity for children topics compared to the non-children topics, but nCRP shows similar affinity for children and non-children.

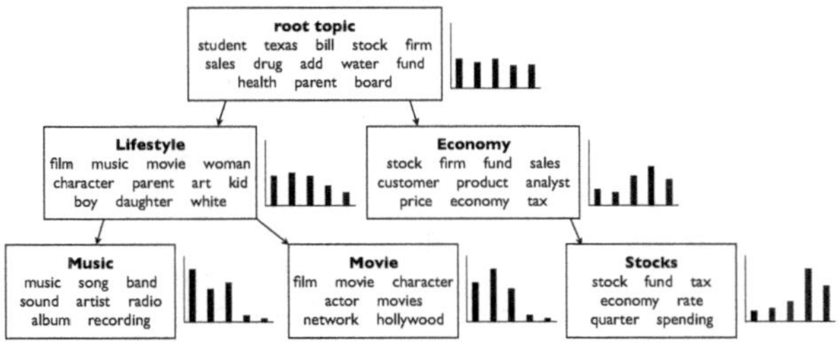

Figure 9: Hierarchical Affinity. Topics that form parent-child relationship show greater similarity in their word distribution than topics that are distant in the topic tree.

children topics compared to the *non-children* topics. However, in nCRP the affinity scores are not different for *children* compared to *non-children*.

7. DISCUSSION

We developed the recursive Chinese Restaurant Process, a new nonparametric prior that captures the hierarchical nature of mixture components. We used the rCRP to construct a nonparametric topic model that infers the hierarchical structure of topics from discrete data. We applied our model to two text corpora and a user ratings dataset and visualized the inferred topic trees to show how our model can find intuitive hierarchical topic structures. We identified topic specialization and hierarchical affinity as two important characteristics of a hierarchical topic structure, and we suggested and tested evaluation metrics to quantify them. We also showed that our model outperformed LDA, HDP, and nCRP in terms of heldout likelihood.

Our model for discovering topic hierarchies with the recursive Chinese restaurant process describes a natural procedure of finding a mixture component in a tree-structured way. This intuitive representation facilitates further extensions to our proposed model. One can relax the assumption that each table is assigned a single dish, and devise the Indian Buffet Process [8] in with topics are in a hierarchical structure. The proposed model can also be deployed in various applications that rely on the latent structure of general-to-specific themes. An example would be recommendations based on collaborative filtering, extending our results with the movie ratings data, or social network search based on topics [19].

8. ACKNOWLEDGEMENTS

This research was supported by Basic Science Research Program through the National Research Foundation of Korea (NRF) funded by the Ministry of Education, Science and Technology (2011-0026507).

9. REFERENCES

[1] R. Adams, Z. Ghahramani, and M. Jordan. Tree-structured stick breaking for hierarchical data. *Advances in Neural Information Processing (NIPS)*, 23, 2010.

[2] D. Blei, T. Griffiths, M. Jordan, and J. Tenenbaum. Hierarchical topic models and the nested chinese restaurant process. *Advances in Neural Information Processing Systems*, 16, 2003.

[3] D. Blei and M. Jordan. Variational inference for dirichlet process mixtures. *Bayesian Analysis*, 1(1):121–144, 2006.

[4] D. Blei and J. Lafferty. Correlated topic models. In *Advances in Neural Information Processing Systems*, 2006.

[5] D. Blei, A. Ng, and M. Jordan. Latent dirichlet allocation. *The Journal of Machine Learning Research*, pages 993–1022, Jan 2003.

[6] A. Collins and E. Loftus. A spreading-activation theory of semantic processing. *Psychological Review*, 82(6):407, 1975.

[7] M. Escobar and M. West. Bayesian density estimation and inference using mixtures. *Journal of the American Statistical Association*, pages 577–588, 1995.

[8] T. Griffiths and Z. Ghahramani. Infinite latent feature models and the indian buffet process. *Advances in Neural Information Processing Systems*, 18:475, 2006.

[9] K. Heller and Z. Ghahramani. Bayesian hierarchical clustering. In *Proceedings of the 22nd international conference on Machine learning*, pages 297–304, 2005.

[10] H. Ishwaran and L. James. Approximate dirichlet process computing in finite normal mixtures. *Journal of Computational and Graphical Statistics*, 11(3):508–532, 2002.

[11] M. Jeong and I. Titov. Multi-document topic segmentation. In *Proceedings of the 19th ACM International Conference on Information and Knowledge Management*, 2010.

[12] N. Kawamae. Latent interest-topic model: finding the causal relationships behind dyadic data. In *Proceedings of the 19th ACM International Conference on Information and Knowledge Management*, 2010.

[13] D. Kim and A. Oh. Accounting for data dependencies within a hierarchical dirichlet process mixture model. In *the Proceedings of the 20th ACM Conference on Information and Knowledge Managment*, 2011.

[14] W. Li and A. McCallum. Pachinko allocation: Dag-structured mixture models of topic correlations. In *Proceedings of the 23rd International Conference on Machine Learning*, pages 577–584, 2006.

[15] S. MacEachern. Estimating normal means with a conjugate style dirichlet process prior. *Communications in Statistics-Simulation and Computation*, 23(3):727–741, 1994.

[16] D. Mimno, W. Li, and A. McCallum. Mixtures of hierarchical topics with pachinko allocation. In *Proceedings of International Conference on Machine Learning*, 2007.

[17] R. Neal. Density modeling and clustering using dirichlet diffusion trees. *Bayesian Statistics*, 7:619–629, 2003.

[18] T. Rubin and M. Steyvers. A topic model for movie choices and ratings. In *Proceedings of International Conference on Cognitive Model*, 2009.

[19] J. Tang, S. Wu, B. Gao, and Y. Wan. Topic-level social network search. In *Proceedings of the 17th ACM SIGKDD International Conference on Knowledge Discovery and Data Mining*, pages 769–772, 2011.

[20] Y. Teh, M. Jordan, M. Beal, and D. Blei. Hierarchical dirichlet processes. *Journal of the American Statistical Association*, Jan 2006.

[21] Y. Teh, K. Kurihara, and M. Welling. Collapsed variational inference for hdp. *Advances in Neural Information Processing Systems*, 20:1481–1488, 2008.

[22] H. M. Wallach, I. Murray, R. Salakhutdinov, and D. Mimno. Evaluation methods for topic models. *Proceedings of the 26th International Conference on Machine Learning*, 2009.

[23] C. Williams. A mcmc approach to hierarchical mixture modelling. *Advances in Neural Information Processing Systems*, 12:680–686, 2000.

[24] G. Zheng, J. Guo, L. Yang, S. Xu, S. Bao, Z. Su, D. Han, and Y. Yu. A topical link model for community discovery in textual interaction graph. In *Proceedings of the 19th ACM International Conference on Information and Knowledge Management*, 2010.

Two-part Segmentation of Text Documents

Deepak P[1] Karthik Visweswariah[1] Nirmalie Wiratunga[2] Sadiq Sani[2]
[1]IBM Research - India, Bangalore, INDIA
[2]School of Computing, Robert Gordon University, Aberdeen, Scotland, UK
{deepak.s.p|v-karthik}@in.ibm.com {n.wiratunga|s.a.sani}@rgu.ac.uk

ABSTRACT

We consider the problem of segmenting text documents that have a two-part structure such as a problem part and a solution part. Documents of this genre include incident reports that typically involve description of events relating to a problem followed by those pertaining to the solution that was tried. Segmenting such documents into the component two parts would render them usable in knowledge reuse frameworks such as Case-Based Reasoning. This segmentation problem presents a hard case for traditional text segmentation due to the lexical inter-relatedness of the segments. We develop a two-part segmentation technique that can harness a corpus of similar documents to model the behavior of the two segments and their inter-relatedness using language models and translation models respectively. In particular, we use separate language models for the problem and solution segment types, whereas the inter-relatedness between segment types is modeled using an IBM Model 1 translation model. We model documents as being generated starting from the problem part that comprises of words sampled from the problem language model, followed by the solution part whose words are sampled either from the solution language model or from a translation model conditioned on the words already chosen in the problem part. We show, through an extensive set of experiments on real-world data, that our approach outperforms the state-of-the-art text segmentation algorithms in the accuracy of segmentation, and that such improved accuracy translates well to improved usability in Case-based Reasoning systems. We also analyze the robustness of our technique to varying amounts and types of noise and empirically illustrate that our technique is quite noise tolerant, and degrades gracefully with increasing amounts of noise.

Categories and Subject Descriptors

I.2.7 [**Artificial Intelligence**]: Natural Language Processing—*Text Analysis, Language Models*

Keywords

Text, Segmentation, Language Models, Translation Models

1. INTRODUCTION

Experience reports are prepared in various contexts for various purposes. An example is a bug report in software development which describes a sequence of events starting from events that characterize the occurence of the bug, and events involving fixing of the bug. Incident reports in other scenarios comprise descriptions of a temporal sequence of events, some of which characterize the cause of the incident, followed by those that describe the way the incident was dealt with. A real incident report from an airline company is shown below:

A Nexen employee checked his rebreather unit and found it to be past its "Service Due Date". He alerted the other passengers and they found the same situation with their re-breather units. All the units were promptly changed by the heliport staff and the flight proceeded as normal.

Of this, the first two sentences describe the (symptoms of the) incident, and the third indicates how the incident was resolved. In many cases, however, the events describing the *problem* and those describing the *solution* could be interleaved, especially at the boundaries. In clinical diagnosis, medical transcriptionists maintain diagnosis reports; these often have a similar two-part structure with a symptoms part and a diagnosis part.

School reports continuing difficulties with repetitive questioning. Obsession with cleanness on a daily basis. Inability to relate this well in the classroom. Asperger disorder. Obsessive compulsive disorder.

In the above sample medical transcription report (from MTSamples[1]), the first three sentences talk about symptoms whereas the remaining indicate diagnosis. In most cases where the diagnosis is complete, the two-part structure is very apparent. Root-cause Analysis (RCA) reports generated from service delivery organizations also have a two part structure (problem and solution).

Though such reports are mostly used currently for auditing and tracking purposes, it is easy to see that they provide a wealth of information that could be exploited in knowledge reuse systems such as Case-Based Reasoning[2]. CBR systems make use of problem-solution repositories to find possible solutions to new problems. For a newly posed problem, similar problems are retrieved from the repository and the solutions associated with them are deemed to be usable for the new problem. For example, a CBR system that uses symptom-diagnosis cases would respond to a new symptom report with historical diagnoses of similar symptoms and could help a medical practicioner arrive at a better/faster conclusion regarding the diagnosis. Depending on the complexity of the problems and solutions, linguistic processing would have to be performed to be able to choose/adapt the solutions of similar problems for us-

[1]http://www.mtsamples.com/
[2]http://en.wikipedia.org/wiki/Case-based_reasoning

age to solve the new problem. The CBR framework provides a powerful platform to exploit such experience and incident reports once they are partitioned into the problem and solution (or similar) components. Problem-solution partitioning is useful beyond CBR too; such paritioning enables better retrieval by usage of translation models [24].

In this paper, we address the problem of segmenting experience/incident reports into problem and solution parts. We will see that this is a hard case for traditional text segmentation approaches that typically rely on inter-segment *dissimilarity*; this is because the problem and solution parts may have significantly similar vocabulary due to being talking about related incidents. Towards solving our two-part segmentation problem, *we develop a technique that harnesses the availability of a set of similar incident reports to build language models (that learn the nature of problem and solution parts using statistical techniques) and translation models (that learn the correlation between words in the problem and those in the solution) that are then used to identify problem and solution segments.* We call our technique as Correlation and Cohesion Driven Segmentation (*CCS*). Our specific contributions are as follows:

- We propose a novel technique, *CCS*, that exploits a collection of similar two-part text documents to segment them.
- We present an empirical evaluation that depicts the superiority of our technique over state-of-the-art methods on segmentation quality by large and statistically significant margins.
- Further, we empirically illustrate that such improved segmentation by *CCS* leads to better solution qualities in a CBR system and that the *CCS* technique is robust to small amounts of noise in the input text.

Section 2 presents an overview of related work. We define our problem in Section 3 and present our approach in Section 4. Our experimental validation comprises Section 5 and we conclude in Section 6.

2. RELATED WORK

Segmenting experience/incident reports to problem and solution segments (or similar segmentation, e.g., cause-effect, symptoms-diagnosis) is a special case of the text segmentation problem [3]. Text segmentation involves splitting text into topical segments; the number or nature of the segments are usually not known a priori. Unsupervised text segmentation techniques may use domain-independent assumptions such as lexical cohesion [9] and/or domain dependent features such as cue words [7]. We briefly review text segmentation methods and knowledge reuse techniques that work on problem-solution data.

Text Segmentation, the problem of splitting text into *lexically coherent* or *topical* segments, started getting attention with the *TextTiling* algorithm [9]. Subsequent works focussed on using word repetetions [20], semantic networks [14], deep semantic features such as presence of co-reference across a candidate segment boundary [18] and hidden markov models [23] whereas segmental semi-markov models have been exploited for a related task of change-point detection [8]. A recent text segmentation algorithm, APS [12], uses affinity propagation to identify segment assignments. In contrast to the above approaches that deal with one document at a time, [15] present an approach that makes use of a collection of similar documents to segment individual documents better. *We will compare the approach that we develop against APS, TextTiling and [15].*

Using Problem-Solution Repositories: Case-based reasoning [13] or CBR relates to the theory and practice of reusing knowledge available as question-answer (or problem-solution) pairs; a problem-solution pair is referred to as a *case* in CBR parlance. CBR systems maintain a repository of cases, and respond to a new problem with solutions derived from those of problems related/similar to the new problem. Research in CBR focusses on improving the mechanisms to *retrieve* similar problems, *reuse* their solutions by adapting to solve the new problem, *revise* the adapted solution based on the new problem, and *retain* the new solution by storing it in the repository. In addition to the large recent interest in textual CBR [16, 2, 10], there has been a good amount of work in improving retrieval in textual question answer repositories [24, 11] of late, mostly from the information retrieval community. Usage of translation models to model question-answer vocabulary correlations was first explored in [6]. [24] builds a translation model using the question set and the answer set as a parallel corpus and uses it to conceptually 'expand' a new question before posing it to a retrieval system. Apart from being beneficial to knowledge reuse, such segmentation would help more traditional scenarios such as the task of a corporate knowledge-author who seeks to look through incident reports to identify and document new and interesting problems and their solutions.

3. PROBLEM DEFINITION

We now define the problem formally. Given a set $\mathcal{D}$ of n documents (e.g., incident/experience reports) of a similar nature, $\mathcal{D} = \{\mathcal{D}_1, \mathcal{D}_2, \ldots, \mathcal{D}_n\}$, with document $\mathcal{D}_i$ comprising of l_i words that we denote as $[w_{i\,1}, \ldots, w_{i\,l_i}]$, we want to identify a vector $\mathcal{Z}$, of n values $[z_1, z_2, \ldots, z_n]$ such that the segmentation of every document $\mathcal{D}_i$ into the two segments,

$$[w_{i\,1}, \ldots, w_{i\,z_i}], [w_{i\,(z_i+1)}, \ldots, w_{i\,l_i}]$$

approximates as closely as possible the actual segmentation of the document $\mathcal{D}_i$ into its two inherent segments (e.g., problem and solution, symptoms and diagnosis etc.) that we will generically refer to as problem and solution segments from hereon. For every document $\mathcal{D}_i$, we will limit our search space to only those values of z_i that are sentence boundaries. In other words, we will ensure that sentences are not broken since it is not very natural to have parts of the sentence in the problem segment and the remaining in the solution. $dom(z_i)$ denotes all possible values of segmentation points (i.e., all segmentation points that are at a sentence boundary) for $\mathcal{D}_i$.

4. OUR APPROACH

In this section, we outline our approach for two-part segmentation of documents in a corpus of similar documents. We start by outlining certain assumptions that we use and go on to describe our approach in detail.

4.1 Assumptions

Our approach is based on some assumptions, some of which are well-known. At the risk of re-stating some of the obvious, we list the assumptions:

- **Separation:** We assume that problem and solution segments are reasonably well-separated. Such smoothness assumptions are at the core of most text segmentation approaches and is hence not novel. In particular, the worst case for our approach would be one where the problem and solution sentences are interleaved fully and the best case would be one where there is a contiguous sequence of problem sentences and another contiguous sequence of solution sentences, in the document.

- **Segment Ordering:** Unlike most other segmentation approaches, we assign a label to the segment (as either a problem or solution segment), and want to be able to reason across common segments across documents. To enable such reasoning, *we assume that the relative ordering of the two segments across documents in the corpus is reasonably consistent*. We argue that this assumption is not very restrictive since events are often described in chronological fashion in incident reports, and the events that are part of the problem typically precede those that form the solution. In other scenarios such as diagnosis reports, the symptoms are mostly described before the diagnosis.

- **Similar Problems have Similar Solutions:** The assumption that similar problems have similar solutions is the foundational principle for case-based reasoning [1]. At the word-level, this translates to the presence of correlations between certain words in the problem and certain others in the solution. We will use translation models to identify and use such correlations and use them in our segmentation algorithm.

- **Intra-segment Lexical Cohesion:** That sentences within the same segment have a higher likelihood of being lexically similar is a heavily used assumption in text segmentation literature (as seen in Section 2). Since we use a notion of a segment being either problem of solution, we extend the assumption to say that segments of the same type have a higher likelihood to be similar, *across documents*. We use language models to tap this assumption.

As in the case of any statistical/learning technique, we do not require each of the above assumptions to hold in an absolute sense; minor aberrations that do not throw the statistics haywire are typically easily tolerated. In Section 5.7, we will empirically evaluate the performance of our technique in datasets where some of these assumptions do not fully hold.

4.2 Correlation and Cohesion Driven Segmentation (CCS)

We now describe our approach, Correlation & Cohesion Driven Segmentation (CCS), that exploits the correlation between words in the problem and solution, to arrive at a segmentation of incident reports (or similar text documents) into problem and solution parts. Our approach is fully unsupervised and has no apriori knowledge of problem and solution behavior or the nature of correlatedness between them. CCS relies on the following premises that are based on assumptions in Section 4.1.

- A good segmentation of each of the documents can be used to learn problem and solution segment behavior well. Well-learnt solution and problem segment behavior can be used to derive a good segmentation.

- A good segmentation of each of the documents can be used to capture inter-segment word correlations better. Once the inter-segment word correlations are captured well, they could be used to derive a good segmentation.

We use the popular IBM Model 1 [4] translation model to learn word correlations across segments, and a unigram language model [22] to model behavior of segment types. We first describe the generative model for text documents that we use in our segmentation technique. We then outline an objective function and followed by the CCS approach which is basically an EM algorithm that optimizes the objective function.

4.2.1 The Generative Model

Consider a unigram problem language model $\mathcal{P}$, a unigram solution language model $\mathcal{S}$ and an IBM Model 1 translation model, $\mathcal{T}$, that models translation probabilities from problem words to solution words. The unigram language models for problems and solutions are multinomial distributions of words that would favor words that occur more in problems and solutions respectively. The translation model is intuitively a 2-d associative array with $\mathcal{T}[w][v]$ being directly related to the probability of the word v occuring in the solution whenever w is seen to occur in the problem; for consistency with previous literature on translation models, we will use $\mathcal{T}(v|w)$ to refer to this probability. Further, $\mathcal{T}(.|w)$ refers to the multinomial distribution of words with their value indicating the probability of occurence whenever w occurs in the problem.

Using such a set of models $\{\mathcal{P}, \mathcal{S}, \mathcal{T}\}$, our generative model that generates a document $\mathcal{D}_i$ having the first z_i words in the problem and the remaining $(l_i - z_i)$ words in the solution, works as follows:

1. For $j, 1 \leq j \leq z_i$,
   (a) Choose $w_{i\,j} \sim Mult(\mathcal{P})$
2. For $j, z_i < j \leq l_i$,
   (a) Choose $r \sim U(0,1)$
   (b) If $r < \lambda$,
      i. Choose $w_{i\,j} \sim Mult(\mathcal{S})$
   (c) Else,
      i. Choose $w_{i\,j} \sim Avg(Mult(\mathcal{T}(.|w_{i\,1})), \ldots, Mult(\mathcal{T}(.|w_{i\,z_i})))$

Informally, the z_i words (those belonging to the problem part) are sampled from the problem language model. The remaining $(l_i - z_i)$ words that are associated with the solution are then sampled from the solution langauge model with a probability of λ and from the average of the multinomial translation model distributions corresponding to each problem word with a probability of $(1 - \lambda)$.

Table 1: Example Report Document

Disk full reported.
Some files were deleted to resolve the issue.

Illustrative Example: Consider a hypothetical two sentence document from an IT helpdesk-like scenario, as given in Table 3. Let the segmentation point be the one that splits it into these two sentences, the first sentence being the problem and the second being the solution. Now, among the words $\{$*files, deleted, resolve, issue*$\}$ in the solution, it is intuitively likely that *resolve* and *issue* have high probabilities under the solution language model, especially if $\mathcal{D}$ is a dataset of IT helpdesk reports. On the other hand, *files* and *deleted* are likely to be better supported by the translation model that is conditioned on very related words such as *disk* and *full* that already appear in the problem part. This intuition of the dual origin of solution words is factored into the generative model by allowing it to sample solution words from either the solution language model or the combination of the translation model distributions that are conditioned over the chosen problem words.

Probability Computation: Under the generative framework outlined above, the probability of generating a document $\mathcal{D}_x$ of which the first z_x words belong to the problem, given the models $\mathcal{P}, \mathcal{S}, \mathcal{T}$ is denoted as follows:

$$p(\mathcal{D}_x, z_x|\mathcal{P}, \mathcal{S}, \mathcal{T}) = \prod_{1\leq i\leq z_x} \mathcal{P}(w_{x\,i}) \quad \times$$

$$\prod_{z_x<i\leq l_x}(\lambda\,\mathcal{S}(w_{x\,i})+(1-\lambda)\,avg\{\mathcal{T}(w_{x\,i}|w_{x\,1}),..,\mathcal{T}(w_{x\,i}|w_{x\,z_x})\})$$

where $\mathcal{P}(w)$ denotes the probability associated with w in the multinomial model $\mathcal{P}$. For each of the problem words, the probability of the word according to the problem language model is used in the product formulation. The solution word's contribution to the product, similar to that in the generative model, is modeled as a weighted sum of its probability from the solution language model and the average of its probabilities from the multinomial translation model distributions for each of the z_x problem words.

For a document corpus $\mathcal{D}$ and a segmentation vector $\mathcal{Z}$ (Ref. Sec 3), the probability of the $[\mathcal{D}, \mathcal{Z}]$ combination given the models $\{\mathcal{P}, \mathcal{S}, \mathcal{T}\}$ is then estimated as a product of the probabilities of the separate $(\mathcal{D}_i, z_i)$ combinations:

$$L(\mathcal{P}, \mathcal{S}, \mathcal{T}; \mathcal{D}, \mathcal{Z}) = p(\mathcal{D}, \mathcal{Z}|\mathcal{P}, \mathcal{S}, \mathcal{T}) = \prod_{\mathcal{D}_i\in\mathcal{D}} p(\mathcal{D}_i, z_i|\mathcal{P}, \mathcal{S}, \mathcal{T})$$

4.2.2 The Objective Function and EM Overview

For a set of documents $\mathcal{D}$, we can now estimate the models $\{\mathcal{P}, \mathcal{S}, \mathcal{T}\}$ that are most likely to generate the document set. Towards this intent, our objective function that is to be maximized denotes the maximum likelihood estimate of the models.

$$L(\mathcal{P}, \mathcal{S}, \mathcal{T}; \mathcal{D}) = p(\mathcal{D}|\mathcal{P}, \mathcal{S}, \mathcal{T})$$

Since the segmentation vector $\mathcal{Z}$ is unknown, the maximal likelihood estimate is calculated by marginalizing over all possible values of $\mathcal{Z}$ (i.e., all possible segmentation points over all documents).

$$p(\mathcal{D}|\mathcal{P}, \mathcal{S}, \mathcal{T}) = \sum_{\mathcal{Z}'\in domain(\mathcal{Z})} p(\mathcal{D}, \mathcal{Z}'|\mathcal{P}, \mathcal{S}, \mathcal{T})$$

$$= \prod_{\mathcal{D}_i\in\mathcal{D}} \sum_{z\in dom(z_i)} p(\mathcal{D}_i, z|\mathcal{P}, \mathcal{S}, \mathcal{T})$$

We will use an iterative EM formulation [5] to find the maximum likelihood estimate outlined above. Each iteration is a sequence of two high-level steps, the E and M steps, that are summarized as follows:

- **E-step:** In the E-step, we use the current estimates of the language and translation models to compute the posterior probability of each segmentation point, for every document. At the document corpus level, this translates to determining the posteriors associated with each possible value of the segmentation vector $\mathcal{Z}$.
- **M-step:** The M-step re-builds the language and translation models in accordance with the posterior probabilities of various values of $\mathcal{Z}$.

In addition to the high-level steps outlined above, the E and M steps involve more detailed processing, especially, those corresponding to estimating whether solution words in each document were derived from the language or translation model and using them in re-estimating the models. We describe these steps in greater detail in respective sections.

4.2.3 E-Step

According to our generative model and the objective function derived from it, the maximum likelihood estimates of the models may be obtained if the following are known:

- The correct segmentation point for each document, $\mathcal{D}_i$
- Information as to the source of each of the solution word in the solution part of $\mathcal{D}_i$ i.e., whether it came from the solution language model or the translation language model

However, none of these information is available to us. Thus, in the E-step, we estimate this information using the current estimates of language and translation models. For each segmentation point in a document $\mathcal{D}_i$, we estimate the probability of that being the correct segmentation point. Similarly, for each such segmentation point, we estimate the probabilities that each solution word is derived from either of the sources. These estimates are then used in the M-step to rebuild the language and translation models, as we will show in the next section. We will use θ as a shorthand to denote the set $\{\mathcal{P}, \mathcal{S}, \mathcal{T}\}$ for notational convenience, whenever appropriate. The estimated values for every $(\mathcal{D}_i, z')$ pair, where z' denotes any possible segmentation point for $\mathcal{D}_i$, are:

- $p(z'|\mathcal{D}_i, \theta)$: This denotes the posterior probability of the segmentation point z' according to the language and translation models for the document $\mathcal{D}_i$.
- Every word w in the solution part of $\mathcal{D}_i$ according to the segmentation point z' could have been derived from either the solution language model or the translation model. We determine these separate probabilities:
  - $p(Source = \mathcal{S}|w, \mathcal{D}_i, z', \theta)$ represents the probability that w in the solution part of $\mathcal{D}_i$ (according to the segmentation point z') was derived from the solution model.
  - $p(Source = \mathcal{T}|w, \mathcal{D}_i, z', \theta)$ analogously denotes the probability of the source being the translation model. Since the source needs to be either $\mathcal{S}$ or $\mathcal{T}$, these two values would always sum to 1.0.

Estimating Segmentation Point Posteriors: The posterior probability of each candidate segmentation point z' in a document $\mathcal{D}_i$ is obtained easily by conditioning the distribution $p(\mathcal{D}_i, z'|\theta)$ (computed as shown in Section 4.2.1) over the document $\mathcal{D}_i$:

$$p(z'|\mathcal{D}_i, \theta) = \frac{p(\mathcal{D}_i, z'|\theta)}{\sum_{z\in dom(z_i)} p(\mathcal{D}_i, z|\theta)}$$

Estimating Posteriors for Solution Word Source: The probability of the language model and translation model generating a given solution word w are assessed separately as follows:

$$p(\mathcal{S}, w|\mathcal{D}_i, z', \theta) = \lambda \times \mathcal{S}(w)$$

$$p(\mathcal{T}, w|\mathcal{D}_i, z', \theta) = (1-\lambda)\times avg\{\mathcal{T}(w|p)|p \in problem(\mathcal{D}_i, z')\}$$

The above construction is derived from the generative framework; λ is the relative weighting used in Section 4.2.1 whereas

$problem(\mathcal{D}_i, z')$ denotes the set of words in the problem when the document $\mathcal{D}_i$ is split at the segmentation point z'. The above two values when conditioned over w, give the posterior probabilities of the word w being generated from either sources.

$$p(Source{=}\mathcal{S}|w, \mathcal{D}_i, z', \theta){=}\frac{p(\mathcal{S}, w|\mathcal{D}_i, z', \theta)}{p(\mathcal{S}, w|\mathcal{D}_i, z', \theta) + p(\mathcal{T}, w|\mathcal{D}_i, z', \theta)}$$

$$p(Source = \mathcal{T}|w, \mathcal{D}_i, z', \theta) = 1.0 - p(Source = \mathcal{S}|w, \mathcal{D}_i, z', \theta)$$

4.2.4 M-Step

In the M-Step, we use the segmentation point posteriors and solution word souce assessments from the E-step to (re-)estimate the language and translation models.

Estimating the Language Models: We start with an overview on generating unigram language models. Let $\mathcal{V}_1 = [\{w_1 = 0.8, w_2 = 0.3\}, 0.4]$ and $\mathcal{V}_2 = [\{w_1 = 1.2\}, 0.5]$ denote two conceptual documents; the first one contains the word w_1 with a frequency of 0.8 and w_2 with a frequency of 0.3 whereas the second one contains just one word w_1 with a frequency of 1.2. The second entry in each document representation is meant to represent the weight associated with the document; in this case, the weights for the documents are seen to be 0.4 and 0.5 respectively. Though documents do not have fractional word frequencies in reality, our statistical estimates can accomodate such fractional frequencies and weights. The unigram language model derived out of a collection of such documents is a multinomial distribution where the value corresponding to any word w is computed as follows:

$$\mathcal{L}(w) = \frac{\sum_{\mathcal{V}_i} weight(\mathcal{V}_i)\ freq(\mathcal{V}_i, w)}{\sum_{w'} \sum_{\mathcal{V}_i} weight(\mathcal{V}_i)\ freq(\mathcal{V}_i, w')}$$

where w' is any word in the vocabulary and the $weight(.)$ and $freq(.,.)$ functions denote the document weight and document-specific word frequency respectively. In a language model generated from $\mathcal{V}_1$ and $\mathcal{V}_2$, the value corresponding to w_1 would be:

$$\mathcal{L}(w) = \frac{0.4 * 0.8 + 0.5 * 1.2}{(0.4 * 0.8 + 0.5 * 1.2) + (0.4 * 0.3)} = 0.8846$$

For each segmentation point z' for every $\mathcal{D}_i$, let $Prob(\mathcal{D}_i, z')$ and $Sol(\mathcal{D}_i, z')$ denote the set of words in the problem and solution parts respectively. We generate one conceptual document each for the problem and solution part (denoted as $\mathcal{V}_{\mathcal{P}}(.)$ and $\mathcal{V}_{\mathcal{S}}(.)$ respectively) as follows:

$$\mathcal{V}_{\mathcal{P}}(\mathcal{D}_i, z') = [\{w = 1.0|w \in Prob(\mathcal{D}_i, z')\}, p(z'|\mathcal{D}_i, \theta)]$$

$$\mathcal{V}_{\mathcal{S}}(\mathcal{D}_i, z') =$$

$$[\{w{=}p(Source{=}\ \mathcal{S}|w, \mathcal{D}_i, z', \theta)|w \in Sol(\mathcal{D}_i, z')\}, p(z'|\mathcal{D}_i, \theta)]$$

Informally, the problem document is simply the collection of problem words in $Prob(\mathcal{D}_i, z')$ with the document weight being the posterior probability of the segmentation point. The solution document is also weighted by the posterior probability of the segmentation point; however, unlike the problem case, each word in the solution document has a frequency that is determined by the probability of it being generated by the solution model. Each document $\mathcal{D}_i$ thus generates as many problem and solution documents as there are possible segmentation points (i.e., $|dom(z_i)|$) in it. The

Alg. 1 ***CCS***

Input. $\mathcal{D}$, a set of documents
Output. $\mathcal{Z}$, a vector denoting the segmentation

1. *Segment documents in* $\mathcal{D}$ *using state-of-the-art techniques to initialize* $\mathcal{Z}$
2. *Estimate the models* $\mathcal{P}$, $\mathcal{S}$ and $\mathcal{T}$ *using* $\mathcal{Z}$
3. *while* ($p(\mathcal{D}|\mathcal{P}, \mathcal{S}, \mathcal{T})$ *has not yet converged)*
4. **E-Step:** *Estimate the segmentation point posterior probabilities and solution word source probabilities*
5. **M-Step:** *Re-estimate the language and translation models using the E-step probabilities*
6. $\forall \mathcal{D}_i \in \mathcal{D}$
   $z_i = \underset{z \in dom(z_i)}{\operatorname{argmax}}\ p(\mathcal{D}_i, z|\mathcal{P}, \mathcal{S}, \mathcal{T})$
7. return $\mathcal{Z}$

problem documents collection is used to estimate $\mathcal{P}$ whereas $\mathcal{S}$ is generated from the collection of solution documents; these are models in conformance with the estimates derived in the E-step.

Estimating the translation model: The translation model represents the correlation between words in the problems and those in the solutions. Towards this, it makes use of a corpus of document pairs such as below:

$$[\{w_1 = 0.8, w_2 = 0.4\}, \{w_1 = 0.2, w_3 = 0.6\}, 0.8]$$

The example above denotes a document pair as a 3-tuple, with the first element denoting the frequencies of words in the problem part, second denoting the frequencies of words in the solution part whereas the third element denotes the weight assigned to the document pair. Towards estimating the translation model, we create one such 3-tuple for each $(\mathcal{D}_i, z')$ pair as follows:

$$[\{w = 1.0|w \in Prob(\mathcal{D}_i, z')\},$$

$$\{w{=}p(Source = \mathcal{T}|w, \mathcal{D}_i, z', \theta)|w \in Sol(\mathcal{D}_i, z')\}, p(z'|\mathcal{D}_i, \theta)]$$

Analogous to the language model case, each document would generate as many 3-tuples as there are segmentation points. The collection of such 3-tuples are then used to learn a translation model which would then be in accordance with the E-step estimates. In particular, we use the weighted document pairs to derive an IBM Model 1 using a straightforward adaptation of the EM algorithm from [4]; we do not delve into the finer details of the translation model training process since that is tangential to the focus of this paper.

4.2.5 The CCS Algorithm

The CCS algorithm is outlined in Algorithm 1. We start in Line 1 by initializing the $\mathcal{Z}$ vector according to the segmentation derived from a state-of-the-art segmentation algorithm (e.g., APS [12], [15] or TextTiling [9]); we will use APS to initialize the segmentation in our experiments (Ref. Section 5.4). Segmentations by generic text segmentation algorithms, however, do not necessarily generate exactly two segments per document; we use a post-processing step (in Line 2) to convert any multi-segmentation to a two-part segmentation by retaining only the most appropriate segment switch for each document, as determined using a TextTiling-style estimation[3]. The models are built using the initialized $\mathcal{Z}$ and an iterative sequence of

[3]TextTiling estimates the score of each sentence boundary to be a

Table 2: Datasets and Sizes

Dataset	#Docs	#Sents per doc	#Words per doc
visa	511	4.22	49.75
health	433	5.98	72.61
agri	229	5.10	70.38
loan	514	4.90	61.88
tourism	134	4.79	60.95
railways	268	4.51	50.57
telecom	103	4.70	47.48
web	109	4.08	49.27

E-step (Ref. Section 4.2.3) and M-step (Ref. Section 4.2.4) operations follow. We run this sequence of steps until no more changes occur to the objective function in Section 4.2.2, or for 20 iterations, whichever is fewer.

When the iterations are complete, we set the segmentation point for each document as that which maximizes the probability of generating that document, according to the final estimates of the language and translation models. These form the $\mathcal{Z}$ vector that is then output as the final segmentation for the documents. Since there is no apriori evidence to guess the relative importance of the solution language model and the translation model in generating solution words, we weigh them equally by setting $\lambda = 0.5$ in our approach. In the remainder of this paper, unless mentioned otherwise, *CCS* refers to this setting of λ.

Time Complexity: Consider a corpus of n documents with a vocabulary of size m, each document having an average of l sentences or w words. Calculating the posterior probabilities in the E-step costs $\mathcal{O}(lnw^2)$. The M-step operations of learning the translation models (using k iterations) and language models costs $\mathcal{O}(k(nw^2 + m))$ and $\mathcal{O}(nw + m)$ respectively. For k' iterations of *CCS*, the total time taken, hence, is of the order of $\mathcal{O}(k'nw^2(k + l) + k'km)$.

5. EXPERIMENTAL EVALUATION

We now describe our experimental study where we compare the CCS algorithm against the state of the art algorithms. We describe the datasets, evaluation measures and baseline algorithms followed by a detailed description of our extensive experimentation.

5.1 Datasets

In the absence of any available segmented incident report data (to the best of our knowledge), we use various datasets that were collected as part of a recent IR task and are publicly available[4]. We selected 8 domains from the training dataset preferring those domains that comprise verbose descriptions of problems and associated solutions. These datasets, unlike typical experience/incident reports, often have a first person narrative in the problem part (e.g., *I have been in need of a career switch to something related to networking and have a UK work visa*), and a slightly instructional narrative at the solution part (e.g., *Most UK companies look for a work visa that is valid for beyond one year*). It may be noted that such style differences between segments are advantageous for all text segmentation techniques (including baselines); since *CCS* is not tapping such style differences explicitly, we argue that it is kosher to attribute its improved performance with respect to the baselines mostly to the *CCS* formulation. The style differences may be captured in the intra-segment lexical cohesion assumption to some extent; while lexical cohesion of segments at the document level is used by all the baselines that we compare against, *CBA* (Ref. Sec 5.3) exploits the lexical cohesion of the same segment type across documents in the corpus. The various datasets (named by their domains) are listed in Table 2 and example problem-solution pair is given in Table 3. The documents in our datasets are seen to have 4-6 sentences and 45 to 70 words, on an average. We collate the problem and solution part to create a single document, and run the segmentation algorithms on them; the quality of segmentation is then evaluated with respect to the actual segment boundary (which is known, since the collation of parts to arrive at the single document was performed by us).

5.2 Evaluation Measures

We now outline the various evaluation measures that we use in our empirical study:

WindowDiff: We primarily use the well-known segmentation evaluation measure, *WindowDiff* [19], to evaluate segmentation quality. *WindowDiff* can be conceptually thought of as moving a sliding window simultaneously over the two segmentations (the created, and the ground truth), capturing the differences in the number of segment boundaries at each step, and then aggregating it across the entire document to arrive at a single measure of segmentation agreement. Consider two segmentations $\mathcal{Z}_1$ and $\mathcal{Z}_2$ of a document comprising of l sentences; the *WindowDiff* metric is computed as follows:

$$WD(\mathcal{Z}_1, \mathcal{Z}_2) = \frac{\sum_{1 \leq i \leq (l-w+1)} f(\#SB(\mathcal{Z}_1, i, w), \#SB(\mathcal{Z}_2, i, w))}{l - w + 1}$$

where $\#SB(\mathcal{Z}, i, w)$ counts the number of segment boundaries according to the segmentation $\mathcal{Z}$ among the w sentences from the ith sentence in the document, and $f(.,.)$ is a function that returns 1 if the two arguments are equal, and 0 otherwise. w is typically chosen as half of the average segment size. The *WindowDiff* values are then averaged across documents in the corpus. It may be noted that *WindowDiff is a penalty measure with lower values indicating better agreement among the segmentations compared.*

P_K**:** This metric [3], the precursor to *WindowDiff*, is very similar to the latter in using a sliding window type approach. Instead of counting the number of segment boundaries within a sliding window for each segmentation, P_K checks whether the two ends of the window are in the same segment. For a window, in cases where the segmentations disagree in terms of the membership of the sentences in the two ends, a penalty of 1.0 is added to the numerator. These are then averaged across sliding windows and documents similar to that in the *WindowDiff* measure.

Diff: *WindowDiff* and P_K are metrics that can handle segmentations that segment documents into any number of segments. However, our problem deals with choosing just one segmentation boundary for each document, where it would be segmented into two parts. *Diff* is a simple measure that measures the distance between the boundaries chosen in the segmentations that are compared. For example, for a document in question, if $\mathcal{Z}_1$ chooses a segmentation point beyond the z_1^{th} sentence and z_2 denotes the choice by $\mathcal{Z}_2$, the $Diff(\mathcal{Z}_1, \mathcal{Z}_2)$ is estimated as $abs(z_1 - z_2)$, with $abs(.)$ denoting the absolute value. This is a very intuitive measure since it gives the number of sentences that a segmentation is *off* by, when compared with the ground truth.

segmentation point and uses a threshold to designate all points that have a higher assessed score as segmentation points. In our adaptation to derive a two-part segmentation from a multi-segmentation, we simply choose that candidate among the multiple segmentation points that scores best (according to the TextTiling estimate), as the only segmentation point.

[4]http://www.isical.ac.in/ clia/faq-retrieval/faq-retrieval.html

Table 3: Example Problem & Solution from *loan*

My home was appraised by VA and now I am having problems with its condition. Since the appraisal is an inspection of the property, I think the VA should be able to help me with the problems.
Although the VA fee appraiser must view the property from both the exterior and interior to determine its overall condition, the appraisal process is not intended to be an "inspection" of the property. ...

CBR Usability Measures: Since our eventual goal is to aid knowledge reuse, we also illustrate the improvements achieved on a CBR system that uses the CCS segmented dataset with respect to the one that uses other segmentations; in particular, we use the max and tot [17] metrics; more details are in Section 5.5.

Statistical Significance: We also present results of statistical significance on various measures using randomization tests [21] with a p-value of < 0.05. A technique being statistically significant over another with a p-value of < 0.05 suggests that the probability that the former achieved superior results by mere chance is less than 0.05; such statistical significance tests are becoming standard practice in evaluating retrieval systems[5].

5.3 Baseline Approaches

TextTiling [9] (TT): Among the earliest algorithms for text segmentation, TextTiling relies on lexical frequency and distributional information to identify segment boundaries. This uses the cosine similarity between two blocks of text, one before and another after each candidate segment boundary, to determine whether a segment boundary be placed at the location. We adapt *TextTiling* by forcing it to choose only one segment boundary per document. This is trivial since *TextTiling* scores each sentence boundary; instead of using a threshold to choose possibly multiple candidate sentence boundaries as segmentation points, we simply choose the single sentence boundary with the best score as the segmentation point.

Clustering-based Approach [15] (CBA): This, unlike most other algorithms in literature, is similar to *CCS* in the usage of knowledge across a corpus of similar text documents to segment each document. It clusters sentences across documents to arrive at sentence clusters, which are then clustered using spatial similarity (in the documents that contain them) to arrive at larger clusters called *representative segments*. Each document is then segmented using such *representative segments*. We adapt this approach by running the spatial-similarity based clustering until only two *representative segments* remain. Under such a setting, given a corpus with two segment types that manifest in many documents in the corpus, the clustering process in *CBA* is expected to produce one representative segment per segment type. This representative segment model, due to being built across documents, enables *CBA* to use corpus level signatures per segment type to segment each document; such a corpus-level modeling of segment types is something that algorithms that deal with one document at a time are incapable of doing. Even with two representative segments, CBA could produce multipe segment boundaries; in such case, we use *TextTiling* type scoring of such segment boundaries to choose the best segment boundary as the segmentation point.

APS [12]: In this recent algorithm, each basic unit (e.g., sentence) is treated as a data point. Similarities between data points are estimated using lexical measures unless provided by other means. An iterative message passing based on the affinity propagation formulation is then run, until coherent segments (sets of basic units) emerge. This approach could generate segmentations that have more than two segments per document. Similar to earlier scenarios, for such cases, we choose the best segment break from among them using a *TextTiling* style evaluation.

[5]http://faculty.vassar.edu/lowry/ch4pt1.html

Table 4: WindowDiff Evaluation

Dataset	TT	CBA	APS	$CCS_{\mathcal{L}}$	CCS
visa	0.307	0.483	<u>0.216</u>	0.158	**0.085**$\star$
health	0.379	0.309	<u>0.302</u>	0.106	**0.030**$\star$
agri	0.329	0.419	<u>0.200</u>	0.135	**0.052**$\star$
loan	0.369	0.402	<u>0.261</u>	0.223	**0.042**$\star$
tourism	0.373	0.398	<u>0.215</u>	0.188	**0.079**$\star$
railways	0.341	0.380	<u>0.213</u>	0.138	**0.015**$\star$
telecom	0.374	0.380	<u>0.276</u>	0.269	**0.186**$\star$
web	0.366	0.480	<u>0.213</u>	0.147	**0.018**$\star$
Average	0.355	0.406	<u>0.237</u>	0.170	**0.063**

5.4 Segmentation Quality Evaluation

5.4.1 *WindowDiff Evaluation*

For each technique, we assess the segmentation generated using the *WindowDiff* measure when compared against the ground truth segmentation, and present the results in Table 4. *WindowDiff* being a penalty measure, the technique scoring lesser is considered as being better. Among the two types of models that *CCS* uses, the language and translation models, the former is more intuitive since it stems from the intra-segment lexical cohesion assumption that is central to most text segmentation algorithms. The language model representation of each segment type is analogous to the representative segment representation in the *CBA* approach. Towards illustrating the value of the usage of the translation model over and above the language models, we include the results of the *CCS* variant that uses only language models. This corresponds to setting $\lambda = 1.0$ in the *CCS* approach; we refer to this variant as $CCS_{\mathcal{L}}$ and include the results derived from it in Table 4.

The results table presented in Table 4 illustrates the effectiveness of the *CCS* formulation. The best among the baseline approaches is indicated by an underline. *APS* is seen to outperform the other baselines significantly, and was thus chosen to initialize the $\mathcal{Z}$ vector in Line 1 of Algorithm 1. *CCS* beats the baselines by large margins (the best number for each dataset is indicated in boldface) and also fares much better than $CCS_{\mathcal{L}}$ on each dataset; this illustrates that the translation models help improve the segmentation considerably over and above the usage of language models alone.

Statistical Significance ($p < 0.05$): Those entries of *CCS* that were found to be statistically significant over the corresponding entries of each of the other techniques (including CCS_L) are marked with a $\star$. A seen from the Table, *CCS* performance is statistically significant over every technique on each dataset.

5.4.2 P_K *and Diff Evaluation*

We now analyze the performance of the techniques on the P_K and *Diff* penalty measures. Since the general trends were similar to the *WindowDiff* evaluation with *APS* outperforming the other baselines, we present a comparison between *CCS* and *APS* herein.

As seen from Figure 1, *CCS* is able to bring down the P_K values down by upto three times than that of *APS*. When averaged across datasets, *APS* and *CCS* were seen to score 0.27 and 0.09 respec-

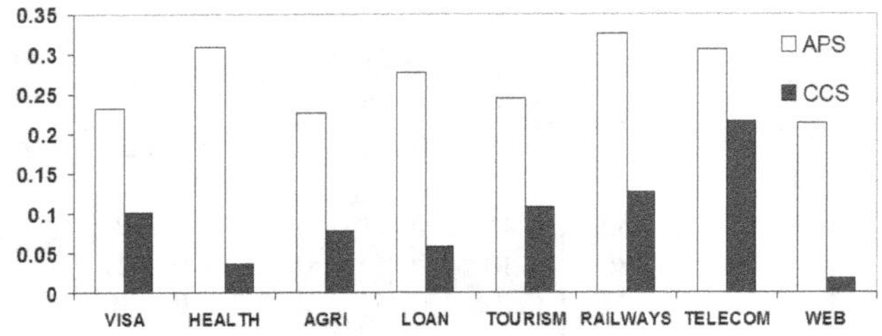

Figure 1: *APS* and *CCS* on the P_K Measure

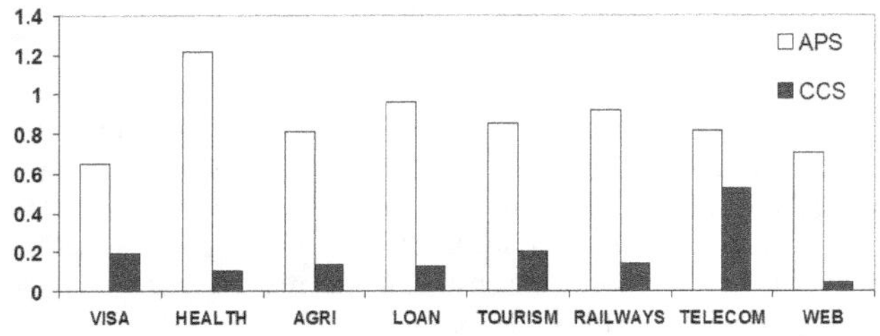

Figure 2: *APS* and *CCS* on the *Diff* Measure

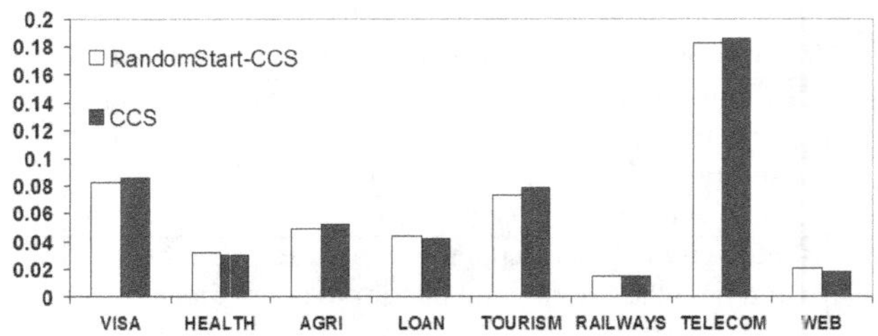

Figure 3: *CCS* initialization Analysis

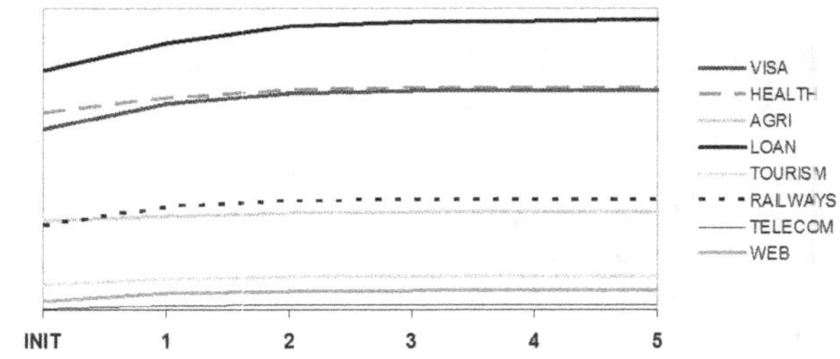

Figure 4: *CCS* Objective Function Across Iterations

tively. These results were seen to be statistically significant on each dataset at a p-value of less than 0.05. The efficacy of *CCS* over *APS* was seen to be much more pronounced under the *Diff* measure with the techniques scoring 0.19 and 0.87 respectively. The chart appears in Figure 2. Informally, the *CCS* segmentation was off from the ground truth by 0.19 sentences on an average, whereas the *APS* segmentation points were seen to be as much as 0.87 sentences away from the ground truth segmentation. Under the *Diff* measure too, the *CCS* performance was seen to be statistically significant over *APS*.

5.5 CBR Usability Evaluation

Though more accurate segmentation would intuitively be expected to deliver a better performance when used in a CBR system, we use a more direct measure to quantify the actual improvement. The *tot* measure [17] uses a leave-one-out style evaluation by posing each problem against the repository and measures the similarity between the top-k retrieved solutions against its own (which are known) using cosine similarity. Much like the configuration used in [17], we use cosine similarity as a proxy for the usability of the solution and set k=3. *tot* then denotes the denotes the total usability of the top-k solutions that are retrieved. The *tot* measure is to be understood as a lower bound on the usability, since the cosine similarity cannot model polysemy, and linguistic processing that could help rendering the retrieved solution more appropriate. The *tot* (for which, a higher value indicates better performance, unlike *WindowDiff*) value across the datasets for the *APS* and *CCS* techniques is presented in Table 5. As usual, the best measure is shown in boldface and *CCS* segmentation is seen to yield a better CBR system consistently, providing an average of **7%** gains across datasets. Similar results were obtained on the *max* measure [17] also. Much like in Table 4, we indicate statistically significant results by a $\star$; from Table 5, it is observed that the usability improvements achieved by *CCS* are statistically significant over *APS* on 5 datasets at a p-value < 0.05.

Table 5: CBR Usability Evaluation (*tot* measure)

Dataset	APS	CCS
visa	0.238	**0.252**$\star$
health	0.268	**0.296**$\star$
agri	0.394	**0.395**
loan	0.369	**0.404**$\star$
tourism	0.161	**0.162**
railways	0.546	**0.612**$\star$
telecom	0.202	**0.227**$\star$
web	0.236	**0.246**
Average	0.302	**0.324**

5.6 CCS Specific Analysis

5.6.1 CCS Initialization Analysis

Since we use the best-performing baseline, *APS*, to initialize the segmentation for the *CCS* technique (in line 1 in Algorithm 1), part of the credit for the good performance of the latter is likely to be due to the performance of *APS*. In this section, we analyze the robustness of the *CCS* formulation by subjecting it to a scenario where a good initialization is not available. In particular, we provide a random initialization of $\mathcal{Z}$ for *CCS* to start processing. Somewhat surprisingly, the randomly initialized *CCS* variant was seen to be highly competetive with that of the *APS* initialization. The *WindowDiff* measures are plotted in Figure 3; it is seen that the performance is nearly identical with minor variations. This shows that the *CCS* technique is extremely robust and can easily recover from bad initializations. However, a good initialization is likely to be more critical while working with datasets of longer documents that may span dozens of sentences each.

5.6.2 CCS Convergence

Due to the EM formulation, the value of the objective function outlined in Section 4.2.2 is bound to monotonically improve with each iteration. We now analyze the trends of the objective function values across EM iterations; Figure 4 plots the objective function

Table 6: Translation Model Samples from *railways*

Problem Word	*cancel*	*duplicate*	*delivery*
Correlated Solution Words	*tdr*	*deducted*	*letter*
	etktcanc	*misplaced*	*authority*
	slip	*authentic*	*authorization*
	printed	*genuineness*	*cities*

values in the Y-axis against the number of iterations in the X-axis. As expected, large gains are achieved between the initialization and the first iteration with the gains becoming smaller in subsequent steps. More importantly, the objective function is seen to stabilize very fast with the gains becoming marginal beyond the third iteration, on every dataset. Thus, *CCS* may be terminated beyond the third iteration in case of a need to optimize on computational expense, since the segmentations are likely to have been relatively stabilized.

5.6.3 Example Translation Model Estimates

Having shown that the usage of translation models in the *CCS* formulation leads to substantially more accurate segmentations, we now present a few sample translation model correlations to illustrate the kind of correlations that are learnt by it. We focus on the *railways* dataset, documents within which mostly start with descriptions of specific scenarios in relation to ticketing and traveling in the Indian Railway network, followed by steps to overcome such situations[6]. We pick three words that are commonly found in problem parts in the *railways* dataset based on a cursory glance through the dataset; these are *cancel*, *duplicate* and *delivery*. For each chosen problem word, we mine for the top-10 solution words that are correlated with it, and present a sample from them in Table 6.

We briefly outline intuitions as to why the correlations in Table 6 may be meaningful. **cancel** was found to be associated with situations involving ticket cancellation, for which remedies included resorting to one of the *tdr* or *etktcanc* cancellation processes provided by the railway. The third option, that of walking in to the counter for cancellation involves procuring a cancellation *slip* or *printing* it from the internet. Another common circumstance of interest is related to fetching a **duplicate** ticket. Towards getting this done, one needs to report that the ticket has been *misplaced* and produce ID proofs to assert the *authenticity* or *genuineness* of the request. Issuance of a duplicate ticket often involves *deduction* of a prescribed fee too. When tickets are booked online, Indian Railways provides an option of mailing a printed ticket to the passenger through courier. **delivery** of such tickets often is often problematic with common problems being unavailability of the passenger at the address location or due to the railways not providing delivery service in certain *cities*. The former problem is often easily resolved by leaving an *authorization letter* with someone who is available at the address provided for delivery.

5.7 Evaluation of Robustness to Noise

Unlike *APS* and other approaches that segment each document independently, *CCS* uses models created out of the entire corpus to segment each document. This, as illustrated above, leads to significant improvements in segmentation accuracy. However, it also implies that noise in a few documents in the corpus could affect the

[6]The choice of dataset was also partially motivated by the domain knowledge of one of the authors; such considerations are inevitable is because understanding and making sense of word pairs is a fairly knowledge intensive process.

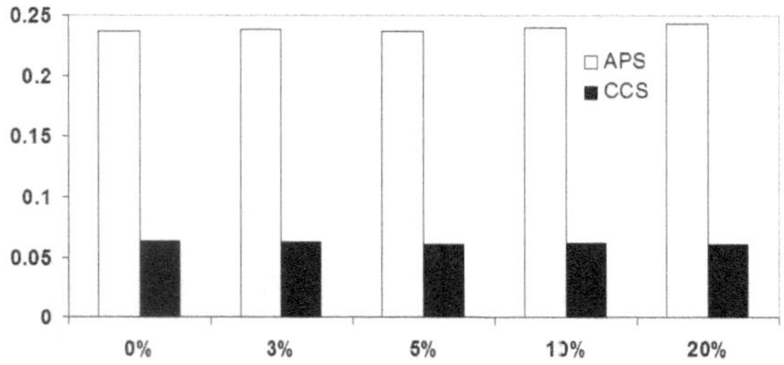

Figure 5: *WindowDiff* under varying levels of *Sentence Swapping*

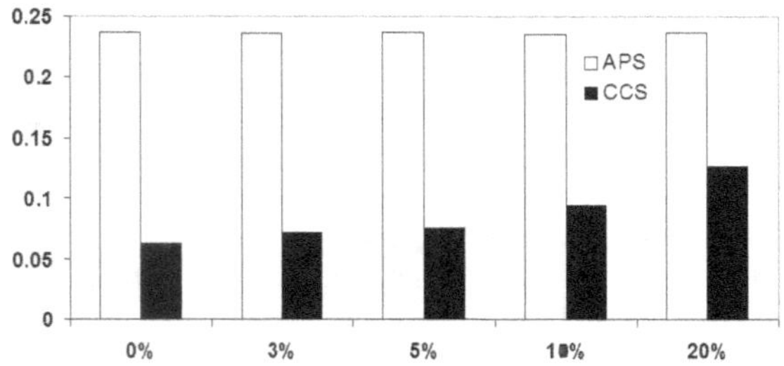

Figure 6: *WindowDiff* under varying levels of *Segment Swapping*

segmentation of even non-noisy documents in the corpus. In this section, we evaluate the robustness of *CCS* to two different kinds of noise to which incident reports are susceptible.

5.7.1 Interleaving at Boundaries

Incident reports often follow a chronological order of narration; however, an initial solution step could be followed by an incident that discovers something more about the problem, leading to a violation of the assumption of clear separation between the segments. To evaluate the robustness of *CCS* to this kind of noise, we inject such perturbation in a few documents by swapping the positions of sentences on either side of the true segment boundary (i.e., by making the last sentence in the problem segment as the first statement in the solution segment and vice versa); we call such noise as *Sentence Swapping*. We let *CCS* operate on the corpus that contains varying fractions of such noisy documents, and evaluate the performance with respect to *APS* on the *WindowDiff* measure. In accuracy evaluation using the *WindowDiff* measure, we consider only the *non-noisy* documents since the real segmentation for the noisy documents is not well-defined (due to the swapping).

We illustrate the *WindowDiff* evaluation in Figure 5. *APS* is not affected by the presence of noisy documents since it operates on a per-document level and the noisy documents are not considered in the *WindowDiff* computation as indicated above. More importantly, it is interesting to note that *CCS* performance is also seen to be very stable across varying fractions of noisy documents in the corpus; we show values for upto 20% noise (in the X-axis) in the chart.

5.7.2 Segment Ordering

Certain authors could violate the convention of segment ordering (e.g., problem segment followed by solution) and may use the opposite ordering. The presence of a few documents with the opposite ordering in the collection is detrimental to techniques like *CCS* that operate at the corpus level. Towards evaluating effects of such noise, we swap the ordering of problem and solution segments in a few documents (i.e., *Segment Swapping*). As in the earlier case, we evaluate the performance on corpora containing varying fractions of such noisy documents. Unlike *Sentence Swapping*, the boundaries are well defined even in the case of noisy documents since whole segments are swapped.

While *APS* is unaffected by such noise due to the per-document formulation, *CCS* is empirically seen to be fairly sensitive to swapping of whole segments in documents in the collection. It may be seen from the *WindowDiff* evaluation in Figure 6 that *CCS* degrades from 0.06 to 0.13 when the fraction of noisy documents is increased to up to 20%. However, even at 20% noise, *CCS* is seen to perform twice as better as *APS*, and is hence, still remains the preferred technique.

6. CONCLUSIONS AND FUTURE WORK

We outlined the two-part text segmentation problem to segment documents such as incident reports that contain problem and solution segments. Accurate identification of problem solution segments is critical towards making the knowledge in incident reports and diagnosis reports available to knowledge reuse systems. This problem, however, poses an unfriendly scenario to traditional text segmentation algorithms due to the relatedness of the segments. We outlined an iterative technique, *CCS*, that models the behavior of problem and solution segments and word-correlations across them in a corpus of similar documents, and exploits such modeling to arrive at more accurate segmentations. The *CCS* generative model formulates each document as being generated by initially sampling words from a problem language model, followed by choosing words from either the solution language model or a translation model conditioned on the words already chosen for the problem part. Our empirical study over a large collection of datasets establish that *CCS* provides vast and statistically significant improvements (on the *WindowDiff* measure) over state-of-the-art techniques, including techniques that use corpus-wide knowledge. Such improvements in segmentation accuracy are seen to reflect as improved solution usability in Case-based Reasoning systems. We have further shown that our technique can recover from not-so-good initializations, is reasonably noise-tolerant, and degrades very gracefully with increasing noise in the dataset. In short, we have established the utility of corpus-wide statistics and inter-segment word correlation in two-part text document segmentation, whenever a corpus of similar documents are available.

Since higher order language models (e.g., 2-gram, 3-gram etc.) and translation models (IBM Models 2 and beyond) are designed to rectify some of the drawbacks with the first order models, harnessing them to improve text segmentation would be an interesting future work. In this work, we have exploited the correlatedness of two segments; generalizing this into a framework that could detect and exploit word correlations in scenarios where any number of segments may be expected in a document, would be a useful extension to this work and a logical next step.

7. REFERENCES

[1] A. Aamodt and E. Plaza. Case-based reasoning: Foundational issues, methodological variations, and system approaches. *AI Commun.*, 7(1):39–59, 1994.

[2] I. Adeyanju, N. Wiratunga, R. Lothian, and S. Craw. Applying machine translation evaluation techniques to textual cbr. In *ICCBR*, pages 21–35, 2010.

[3] D. Beeferman, A. Berger, and J. Lafferty. Statistical models for text segmentation. *Mach. Learn.*, 34:177–210, February 1999.

[4] P. F. Brown, J. Cocke, S. A. D. Pietra, V. J. D. Pietra, F. Jelinek, J. D. Lafferty, R. L. Mercer, and P. S. Roossin. A statistical approach to machine translation. *Comput. Linguist.*, 16:79–85, June 1990.

[5] A. P. Dempster, N. M. Laird, and D. B. Rubin. Maximum likelihood from incomplete data via the em algorithm. *JOURNAL OF THE ROYAL STATISTICAL SOCIETY, SERIES B*, 39(1):1–38, 1977.

[6] A. Echihabi and D. Marcu. A noisy-channel approach to question answering. In *ACL*, pages 16–23, 2003.

[7] J. Eisenstein and R. Barzilay. Bayesian unsupervised topic segmentation. In *EMNLP*, pages 334–343, 2008.

[8] X. Ge and P. Smyth. Segmental semi-markov models for change-point detection with applications to semiconductor manufacturing, 2000.

[9] M. A. Hearst. Multi-paragraph segmentation of expository text. In *ACL*, pages 9–16, 1994.

[10] K. Jayanthi, S. Chakraborti, and S. Massie. Introspective knowledge revision in textual case-based reasoning. In *ICCBR*, pages 171–185, 2010.

[11] J. Jeon, W. B. Croft, and J. H. Lee. Finding semantically similar questions based on their answers. In *SIGIR*, 2005.

[12] A. Kazantseva and S. Szpakowicz. Linear text segmentation using affinity propagation. In *EMNLP*, pages 284–293, 2011.

[13] J. L. Kolodner. An introduction to case-based reasoning. *Artif. Intell. Rev.*, 6(1):3–34, 1992.

[14] H. Kozima. Text segmentation based on similarity between words. In *ACL*, pages 286–288, 1993.

[15] K. Kummamuru, D. P, S. Roy, and L. V. Subramaniam. Unsupervised segmentation of conversational transcripts. In *SDM*, pages 834–845, 2008.

[16] M. Lenz, A. Hübner, and M. Kunze. Textual cbr. In *Case-Based Reasoning Technology, From Foundations to Applications*, pages 115–138, 1998.

[17] D. P, S. Chakraborti, and D. Khemani. More or better: on trade-offs in compacting textual problem solution repositories. In *CIKM*, pages 2321–2324, 2011.

[18] R. J. Passonneau and D. J. Litman. Discourse segmentation by human and automated means. *Computational Linguistics*, 23(1):103–139, 1997.

[19] L. Pevzner and M. A. Hearst. A critique and improvement of an evaluation metric for text segmentation. *Computational Linguistics*, 28(1):19–36, 2002.

[20] J. C. Reynar. An automatic method of finding topic boundaries. In *ACL*, pages 331–333, 1994.

[21] M. D. Smucker, J. Allan, and B. Carterette. A comparison of statistical significance tests for information retrieval evaluation. CIKM, pages 623–632, New York, NY, USA, 2007. ACM.

[22] F. Song and W. B. Croft. A general language model for information retrieval. CIKM, pages 316–321, New York, NY, USA, 1999. ACM.

[23] P. van Mulbregt, I. Carp, L. Gillick, S. Lowe, and J. Yamron. Text segmentation and topic tracking on broadcast news via a hidden markov model approach. In *ICSLP*, 1998.

[24] X. Xue, J. Jeon, and W. B. Croft. Retrieval models for question and answer archives. In *SIGIR*, pages 475–482, 2008.

On the Design of LDA Models for Aspect-based Opinion Mining

Samaneh Moghaddam
School of Computing Science
Simon Fraser University
Burnaby, BC, Canada
sam39@cs.sfu.ca

Martin Ester
School of Computing Science
Simon Fraser University
Burnaby, BC, Canada
ester@cs.sfu.ca

ABSTRACT

Aspect-based opinion mining, which aims to extract aspects and their corresponding ratings from customers reviews, provides very useful information for customers to make purchase decisions. In the past few years several probabilistic graphical models have been proposed to address this problem, most of them based on Latent Dirichlet Allocation (LDA). While these models have a lot in common, there are some characteristics that distinguish them from each other. These fundamental differences correspond to major decisions that have been made in the design of the LDA models. While research papers typically claim that a new model outperforms the existing ones, there is normally no "one-size-fits-all" model. In this paper, we present a set of design guidelines for aspect-based opinion mining by discussing a series of increasingly sophisticated LDA models. We argue that these models represent the essence of the major published methods and allow us to distinguish the impact of various design decisions. We conduct extensive experiments on a very large real life dataset from Epinions.com (500K reviews) and compare the performance of different models in terms of the likelihood of the held-out test set and in terms of the accuracy of aspect identification and rating prediction.

Categories and Subject Descriptors

I.7.0 [**Document and Text Processing**]: General; G.3 [**Mathematics of Computing**]: Probability and Statistics—*statistical computing, multivariate statistics*

General Terms

Algorithms, Design, Experimentation

Keywords

aspect-based opinion mining, latent dirichlet allocation, variational methods, aspect identification, rating prediction

1. INTRODUCTION

Other people's opinions have always been an important piece of information during the decision-making process when buying a new product. Today people like to make their opinions available to strangers via the Internet. As a result, the Web has become an excellent source for gathering consumer opinions. As online commerce activity continues to grow, the role of online reviews is expected to become increasingly important [18]. Epinions,Amazon, and Cnet,are examples of the most important Web resources containing such opinions.

However, reading all product reviews to make a good decision is a time-consuming job. Reading different and possibly even contradictory opinions written by different reviewers may even make customers more confused. While some of the reviewing websites ask reviewers to express an overall rating (as stars) for the reviewed item, focusing on just overall ratings will not be sufficient for a user to make decision. These needs have inspired a new line of research on mining online product reviews, which is *aspect-based opinion mining*. Aspect-based opinion mining aims to extract major aspects of a product and to predict the rating of each aspect from the product reviews. Aspects are attributes or components of products (e.g., 'LCD', 'battery life', etc. for a digital camera) and ratings are the intended interpretation of user satisfaction in terms of numerical values. Aspects and ratings clearly provide more detailed information than the overall rating and help users to make better decisions [23]. Aspect-based opinion mining is not only very useful for potential customers to know the opinions of other users before they use a service or purchase a product, but also crucial for businesses to find consumer opinions on their products and services [16]. These techniques can also provide valuable sources of information for other applications, e.g. advertising methods, recommendation systems, etc.

In the last decade several probabilistic models have been proposed to address the problem of aspect-based opinion mining (e.g., [26, 30, 2, 29, 10, 19, 6, 15, 15]). Most of these models are based on Latent Dirichlet Allocation (LDA) which is typically used in topic modeling. While these models have a lot in common, there are some characteristics that distinguish them from each other. In the following we point out some of the main distinctive features:

- Modeling words using one latent variable vs. having separate latent variables for aspects and ratings.
- Modeling all words of the reviews vs. modeling only opinion phrases.
- Modeling the dependency between aspects and ratings vs. modeling them independently.

CIKM'12, October 29–November 2, 2012, Maui, HI, USA.

- Using only review texts as input vs. also using additional input data, e.g. a review's overall rating.

These features correspond to major decisions that must be made in the design of an LDA model. While research papers typically claim that a new model outperforms the existing ones and demonstrate this with experiments on some data sets, there is normally no "one-size-fits-all" model. However, in the literature it is normally not shown why and in which scenarios a model performs better than another one. For example, let us consider a proposed model A generating all words which considers the dependency between aspects and their ratings and takes the overall rating of reviews as an additional observed variable. The comparison of model A with the basic LDA model on a dataset with a large number of reviews per product shows better performance of model A. The problem with this experimental evaluation is that it does not reveal whether the better performance of model A is due to the dependency assumption between aspects and ratings or due to the additional observed data. It is also not clear whether model A still performs better for another dataset containing products with few reviews.

We argue that the best choice for some design decision may depend on other design decisions and on the content and the size of the dataset. So, in this paper we do not propose yet another LDA model for the problem of aspect-based opinion mining, but we present design guidelines for such models. To derive these guidelines, we discuss a series of increasingly sophisticated probabilistic graphical models based on LDA. We start with the basic LDA model and then gradually extend the model by adding latent and observed variables as well as dependencies. The discussed models are as follows:

- LDA: The basic LDA model proposed in [1] which learns general topics of reviews using all words of the training reviews.
- S-LDA: An extension of LDA where the model learns both aspects and ratings from reviews.
- D-LDA: Extension of S-LDA considering the dependency between aspects and their ratings.
- PLDA: The basic LDA model which learns general topics of reviews from opinion phrases.
- S-PLDA: An extension of PLDA where the model learns both aspects and ratings from phrases.
- D-PLDA: An LDA-based model learning aspects and their corresponding ratings from opinion phrases while considering the dependency between the aspects and ratings.

We argue that these six models represent the essence of the major published methods and allow us to tease apart the impact of various design decisions. For example, the comparison of S-LDA and S-PLDA against D-LDA and D-PLDA shows whether the dependency of aspects and ratings improves the performance, independent from the type of observed data (all words or opinion phrases).

Since there is no benchmark dataset for the problem of aspect-based opinion mining, current works have been evaluated on different data sets. However, one dataset may have products with only few reviews, while the products of another dataset may have been selected to have at least a few hundred reviews. We crawled the well-known reviewing website, Epinions.com, and built a very large dataset containing 505,978 reviews about 94,792 products from 257 different product categories. We made the dataset publicly available for research purposes[1]. We evaluate the performance of the six models in terms of the likelihood of a held-out test set. To measure the impact of the training set size, we perform experiments for different subsets of products with different numbers of reviews. We also evaluate the accuracy of the models in aspect identification and rating prediction (precision, recall, and mean squared error) on a labeled dataset and find a strong correlation between model perplexity and accuracy.

As a novel technical contribution, we present a method for extracting opinion phrases based on grammatical relations provided by a dependency parser. This technique promises to generate opinion phrases more accurately than current methods that consider only syntactic properties such as the proximity of words.

The remainder of the paper is organized as follows. The next section is devoted to related work. Section 3 introduces the problem statement and discusses our contributions. Section 4 presents different LDA models for the considered problem. Section 5 describes the inference and estimation techniques for the presented models. The proposed technique for extracting opinion phrases is discussed in 6. In Section 7 we report the results of our experimental evaluation. Finally, Section 8 concludes the paper with a summary of our design guidelines and the discussion of future work.

2. RELATED WORK

The problem of aspect-based opinion mining has recently attracted increasing attention. As a result, there are several lines of related works on this problem. Most of the early works on this problem are feature-based approaches (e.g., [8, 17, 22]). These approaches normally apply some constraints on high-frequency noun phrases to identify product aspects. As a result they usually produce too many non-aspects and miss low-frequency aspects [6]. In addition, feature-based approaches require the manual tuning of various parameters which makes them hard to port to another dataset [21].

Latent variable models overcome these limitations by automatically learning the model parameters from the data. Some of the proposed models are based on Hidden Markov Model (HMM) [28, 10], Conditional Random Field (CRF) [13, 3], and Latent Semantic Association [19, 6, 5]. However, most of the current models are based on Latent Dirichlet Allocation (LDA), e.g., [26, 25, 30, 2, 11, 29, 27, 12, 14, 15, 7]. Since the focus of our paper is LDA-based models, in the following we will only discuss the most recent and most important LDA-based models presented in the literature for the problem of aspect-based opinion mining.

Titov et al. [26, 25] propose a model, based on LDA, for extracting aspects from reviews. They consider two types of topics for each review: global topics, which correspond to global properties of the product (e.g., product brand) and local topics which are related to the product aspects. Their proposed model assumes that each corpus has a certain dis-

[1] `http://www.sfu.ca/~sam39/Datasets/EpinionsReviews/`

tribution of global topics and each review has a distribution of local topics. Each word of a review is generated by sampling a topic from one of these distributions. An indicator variable is used to select the type of topic for each word.

An LDA-based model for jointly identifying aspects and sentiments is proposed in [30]. The model assumes that all of the words in a sentence are generated from a single topic. It also considers different word distributions for aspects, sentiments, and background words and leverages Part-Of-Speech (POS) tags of words (using indicator variables) to separate them. The authors of [2, 11] also assume that all words in a single sentence are generated from one topic and apply LDA at the sentence level to extract product aspects. The model presented in [11] is further extended to extract sentiments related to each aspect. In this model, each review has a distribution over sentiments and each sentiment has a distribution over aspects. For each sentence of a review, the model first draws a sentiment from the sentiment distribution and then an aspect is sampled conditioned on the selected sentiment. Each words of the sentence is then generated based on the selected aspect and sentiment.

The authors of [27] propose an LDA-based model to jointly identify aspects, their ratings, and the weight placed on each aspect by the reviewer. As input the model takes all words of reviews about a product and the overall ratings assigned by reviewers to that product. Each word of a review is generated by sampling an aspect from the learned distribution. The word and the aspect together generate the rating of the aspect. Finally, the aspect weights are sampled from a normal distribution and the overall rating of review is generated based on the weighted sum of all the aspect ratings.

The authors of [12] propose an LDA-based model for identifying aspects, sentiments, and their ratings. The model assumes that each review has a distribution over aspects and another distribution over sentiments. To generate each word of a review, an aspect and a sentiment are first chosen from the corresponding distributions. Then a word is generated conditioned on both aspect and sentiment. The rating of each sentiment is also computed using a normal linear model learned by the overall rating of review. The model further captures the dependencies between the syntactic class of aspects and sentiments. The syntactic class of a word is chosen based on the POS tag of that word and the POS tag of the previous word.

Zhan's model [29] is defined on opinion phrases (see Section 3.1 for definition). They apply a set of POS patterns on the review text to extract nouns and related adjectives as opinion phrases. Then the basic LDA model is applied at the sentence level to extract topics from opinion phrases. Each topic of this model is a pair of head term and modifier. The model presented in [21] also learns from opinion phrases, which are extracted from frequent nouns and adjectives. This model assumes the dependency between aspects and ratings. To generate each opinion phrase, an aspect is first chosen from a Dirichlet distribution. Then a rating is selected conditioned on the aspect. Finally, a head term and a modifier are generated based on the selected aspect and rating, respectively.

There are also some works [14, 15, 7] proposing LDA-based models for extracting topics and their polarity from documents. While these works did not talk about aspects and rating specifically, their model can be applied on reviews for identifying aspects and their ratings. The generative assumption of the model proposed in [14] is as follows: To generate a word of a document, a topic is first selected and the word polarity (positive or negative) is then sampled depending on the chosen topic. Finally, a word is generated conditioned on both topic and polarity. The authors further extend this model by considering the dependency of word polarity on the local context. For example, if two words are connected using 'and', their ratings are considered the same.

The authors of [15, 7] assume that each document has a specific distribution over the polarity of words and there is a specific topic distribution for each polarity (positive and negative) which is independent from the documents (global topic distribution). To generate a word, the proposed model first chooses the polarity of word form the document specific polarity distribution. Then it selects a topic from the global topic distribution conditioned on the selected polarity. Finally, a word is generated conditioned on the selected topic and polarity.

3. PROBLEM DEFINITION

In this section we first define the basic terminologies we will use in this paper. Then we formulate the problem statement and discuss our contributions.

3.1 Problem Statement

Review: A review contains a sequence of words describing opinions of reviewer regarding a specific item (e.g. product or service).

Aspect: An aspect (also called product feature [8]) is an attribute or component of the product that has been commented on in a review, e.g. 'battery life', 'zoom', 'shutter lag', etc. for a digital camera.

Sentiment: Sentiment is a linguistic term which refers to the direction in which a concept or opinion is interpreted [16]. We use sentiment in a more specific sense as an opinion about an aspect which is usually expressed by an adjective. For example, 'great' is a sentiment for the aspect 'picture quality' in the sentence "It has great picture quality".

Opinion Phrase: An opinion phrase $< h, m >$ is a pair of head term h and modifier m [19]. Usually the head term is a candidate aspect, and the modifier is a corresponding sentiment expresses some opinion towards the aspect, e.g. <LCD, blurry>, <screen, inaccurate>, etc.

Rating: A sentiment can be classified in n-level orientation scale. Sentiment orientation is an intended interpretation of the user satisfaction in terms of numerical values [21]. Polarity is a two-level orientation scale. In this scale a sentiment is either positive or negative. Most of the reviewing websites use five-level orientations, presented by stars in the range from 1 to 5 which is called rating.

Aspect-based Opinion Mining: Given a set of reviews for product P, the task is to identify the k major aspects of P and to predict the rating of each aspect for P.

3.2 Our Contributions

As discussed in the introduction section, our goal is to present a set of design guidelines for LDA models for learning aspects and their ratings from reviews. We focus on the following design choices:

- Is it better to have separate latent variables for aspects and ratings?

- Is it better to assume dependency between ratings and aspects?
- Is it better to learn from bag-of-words or preprocess the reviews and learn from opinion phrases?
- Which preprocessing technique for extracting opinion phrases works best?
- Does the answer to the above questions differ for products with few reviews and products with many reviews?

We start our investigation with the basic LDA model [1] and then gradually extend the model by considering different probabilistic assumptions. In summary we discuss five LDA-based models with various underlying assumptions for our problem: *S-LDA* extends LDA by assuming the review is generated by a set of aspects and their ratings. *D-LDA* adds the dependency between aspects and their ratings. *PLDA* learns one latent variable from opinion phrases. *S-PLDA* learns both aspects and their corresponding ratings from opinion phrases. Finally, *D-PLDA* learns aspects and ratings from opinion phrases while considering the dependency between the generated aspects and ratings.

We also present a novel technique for extracting opinion phrases from reviews based on dependency parsing. Different from current preprocessing methods which are mainly based on syntactic properties our technique is based on the semantic relationships between words. We conduct extensive experiments on a real life dataset from Epinions.com, and based on the results we propose a set of design guidelines for LDA models for aspect-based opinion mining.

4. LDA MODELS FOR ASPECT-BASED OPINION MINING

In this section, we first briefly discuss the basic LDA model for the problem of aspect-based opinion mining. Then we introduce a series of models based on LDA making different probabilistic assumptions.

4.1 LDA

Latent Dirichlet Allocation (LDA) is a generative probabilistic model of a corpus [1]. The basic idea is that documents are represented as mixtures over latent topics where topics are associated with a distribution over the words of the vocabulary. Figure 1 shows the graphical model of this model. Following the standard graphical model formalism, nodes represent random variables and edges indicate possible dependency. Shaded nodes are observed random variables and unshaded nodes are latent random variables. Finally, a box around groups of random variables is a 'plate' which denotes replication. The outer plate represents reviews and the inner plate represents words. D and N denote the number of product reviews and the number of words in each review, respectively. In our domain, LDA assumes the following generative process:

1. Sample $\theta \sim Dir(\alpha)$.
2. For each word w_n, $n \in \{1, 2, ..., N\}$
   (a) Sample a topic $z_n \sim Mult(\theta)$
   (b) Sample a word $w_n \sim P(w_n|z_n, \beta)$, a multinomial distribution conditioned on the topic z_n.

Translating this process into a joint probability distribution results in the following expression:

$$P(\boldsymbol{z}, \boldsymbol{w}, \theta|\alpha, \beta) = P(\theta|\alpha) \prod_{n=1}^{N} [P(z_n|\theta) P(w_n|z_n, \beta)] \quad (1)$$

The key inference problem is to compute the posterior distribution of the latent variables given a review:

$$P(\boldsymbol{z}, \theta|\boldsymbol{w}, \alpha, \beta) = \frac{P(\boldsymbol{z}, \boldsymbol{w}, \theta|\alpha, \beta)}{P(\boldsymbol{w}|\alpha, \beta)} \quad (2)$$

Since this distribution is intractable to compute (due to the coupling between θ and β), variational inference is used to approximate this distribution [1]. We will explain the inference and estimation techniques in Section 5.

Some of the current works [2, 30, 26, 25] apply this model on reviews to extract topics as product aspects. In [2] and [30], the model has been used at the sentence level. The authors of [30] further improve the model by considering different word distributions for aspects, ratings, and background words. In [26, 25] the basic LDA model is improved by considering different topic distributions for local and global topics and is applied at the document level.

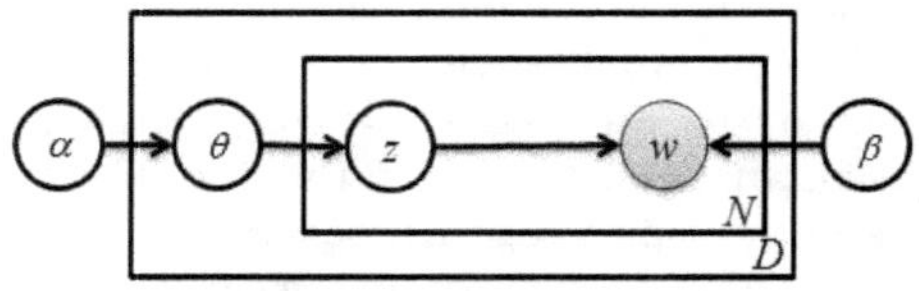

Figure 1: LDA

4.2 S-LDA

The second model replaces the one latent variable for topics by two separate variables for aspects and ratings. We call this model Separate-LDA (S-LDA). For every aspect/rating pair, θ contains the probability of generating that combination of aspect and rating. The variable θ is sampled once per review. After sampling θ, the latent variables a_n and r_n are sampled independently (conditional independency), and then a word w_n is sampled conditioned on the sampled aspect and rating (Figure 2). The joint probability distribution of this model is as follows:

$$P(\boldsymbol{a}, \boldsymbol{r}, \boldsymbol{w}, \theta|\alpha, \beta) = P(\theta|\alpha) \prod_{n=1}^{N} [P(a_n|\theta) P(r_n|\theta) P(w_n|a_n, r_n, \beta)] \quad (3)$$

A model similar to S-LDA has been proposed in [12], learning two Dirichlet distributions (one for aspects and one for sentiments) per review. While that model further considers the syntactic dependency between words and is more an LDA-HMM model, the generation of words conditioned on both aspects and ratings is the same as the generative process of S-LDA.

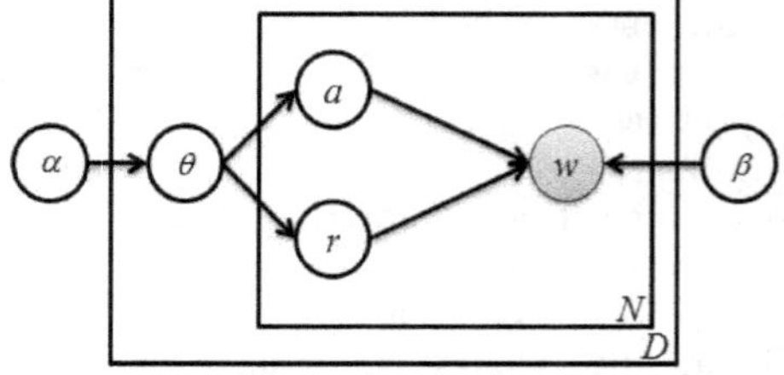

Figure 2: S-LDA

4.3 D-LDA

Dependency-LDA (D-LDA) also models the dependency between the latent aspects and ratings while learning from a bag-of-words model of reviews (Figure 3). The joint probability distribution of D-LDA considers this dependency:

$$P(\boldsymbol{a}, \boldsymbol{r}, \boldsymbol{w}, \theta|\alpha, \beta, \omega) = P(\theta|\alpha) \prod_{n=1}^{N} [P(a_n|\theta)P(r_n|a_n, \omega)P(w_n|a_n, r_n, \beta)] \quad (4)$$

Several models similar to D-LDA have been proposed in the literature [14, 15, 7, 27, 11]. The model presented in [14] further considers the dependency of the rating from the local context. The model proposed in [15] (further extended in [7]) assumes the dependency of the selected aspect from the sampled rating, i.e., the opposite direction of the dependency. The authors of [11] also make the same assumption as [15] and apply the model at the sentence level to extract aspects and ratings.

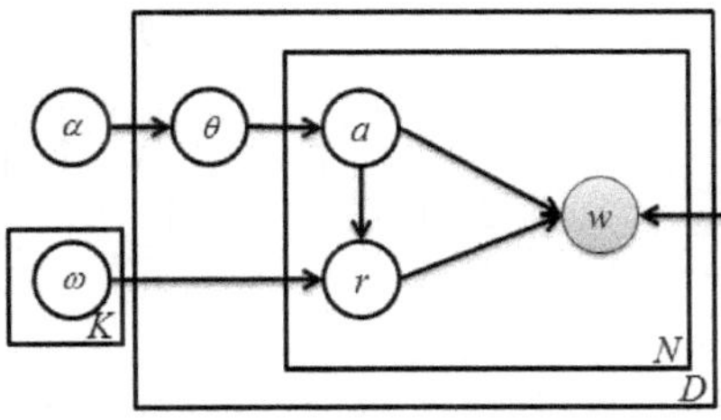

Figure 3: D-LDA

4.4 PLDA

While LDA assumes a bag-of-words model, Phrases-LDA (PLDA) assumes a bag-of-phrases model of product reviews (Figure 4). A review is preprocessed into a bag-of-opinion-phrases $< h_n, m_n >$ which leads to two observed variables h_n (head term) and m_n (modifier). Translating this process into a joint probability distribution results in the expression:

$$P(\boldsymbol{z}, \boldsymbol{h}, \boldsymbol{m}, \theta|\alpha, \beta, \pi) = P(\theta|\alpha) \prod_{n=1}^{N} [P(z_n|\theta)P(h_n, m_n|z_n, \beta, \pi)] \quad (5)$$

In [29] a similar model is applied on opinion phrases to extract topics from reviews. While the generation of opinion phrases in [29] is the same as the generative process of PLDA, their model further assumes that each sentence of the review is related to only one topic.

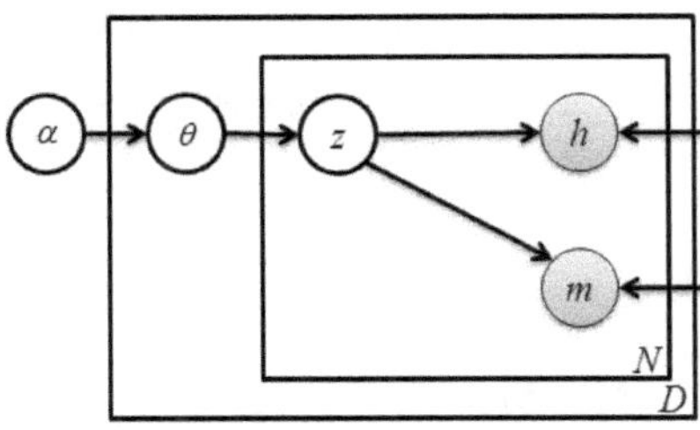

Figure 4: PLDA

4.5 S-PLDA

Compared to PLDA, the S-PLDA model introduces a separate rating variable which is conditionally independent from the aspect. In this model a review is assumed to be generated by first choosing a value of θ, and then repeatedly sampling N aspects and ratings as well as opinion phrases $< h_n, m_n >$ conditioned on the chosen value of θ. Similar to S-LDA, θ represents the aspect/rating pairs and for every pair, α contains the probability of generating that combination of aspect and rating (Figure 5). The joint probability distribution of S-PLDA is as follows:

$$P(\boldsymbol{a}, \boldsymbol{r}, \boldsymbol{h}, \boldsymbol{m}, \theta|\alpha, \beta, \pi) = P(\theta|\alpha) \prod_{n=1}^{N} [P(a_n|\theta)P(r_n|\theta)P(h_n|a_n, \beta)P(m_n|r_n, \pi)] \quad (6)$$

$P(h_n|a_n, \beta)$ and $P(m_n|r_n, \pi)$ are multinomial distributions conditioned on the aspect a_n and rating r_n, respectively. The same model is presented in [21] as a comparison partner.

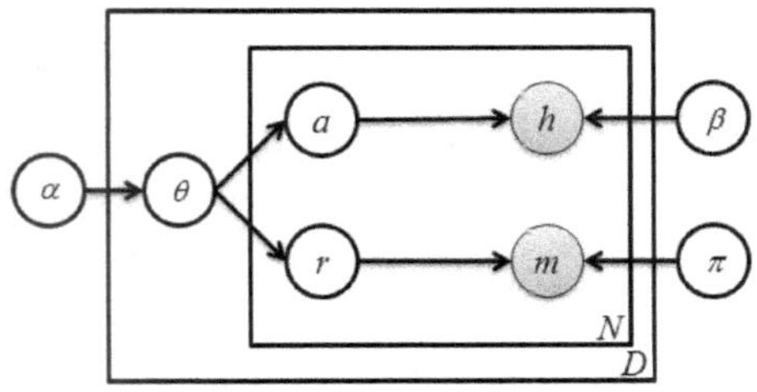

Figure 5: S-PLDA

4.6 D-PLDA

Similar to the step from S-LDA to D-LDA, compared to S-PLDA, the D-PLDA model adds the dependency between ratings and aspects. There are various options for dependencies between the two latent variables and the two observed variables. We assume that modifiers depend on the aspect and the rating. To illustrate the importance of this dependency, consider the following opinion phrases: 'low LCD resolution' and 'low price'. The modifier 'low' expresses a negative opinion for the head term 'LCD resolution', while it is a positive opinion for 'price'. On the other hand, we assume that the rating of an aspect does not affect the choice of a head term for that aspect.

D-PLDA can be viewed as generative process that first generates an aspect and subsequently generates its rating. In particular, for generating an opinion phrase, this model first generates an aspect a_n from an LDA model. Then it generates a rating r_n conditioned on the sampled aspect a_n. Finally, a head term h_n is drawn conditioned on a_n and a modifier m_n is generated conditioned on both the aspect a_n and rating r_n (Figure 6). D-PLDA specifies the following joint distribution:

$$P(\boldsymbol{a}, \boldsymbol{r}, \boldsymbol{h}, \boldsymbol{m}, \theta|\alpha, \omega, \beta, \pi) = P(\theta|\alpha) \prod_{n=1}^{N} [P(a_n|\theta)P(r_n|a_n, \omega)P(h_n|a_n, \beta)P(m_n|a_n, r_n, \pi)] \quad (7)$$

In [21] a similar model is presented. D-PLDA generates the modifier conditioned on both aspect and rating, but in [21] only the selected rating generates the modifier.

5. INFERENCE AND ESTIMATION

Computing the posterior distribution of the latent variables for the LDA models is intractable. Blei et al. [1] proposed to obtain a tractable lower bound by modifying the

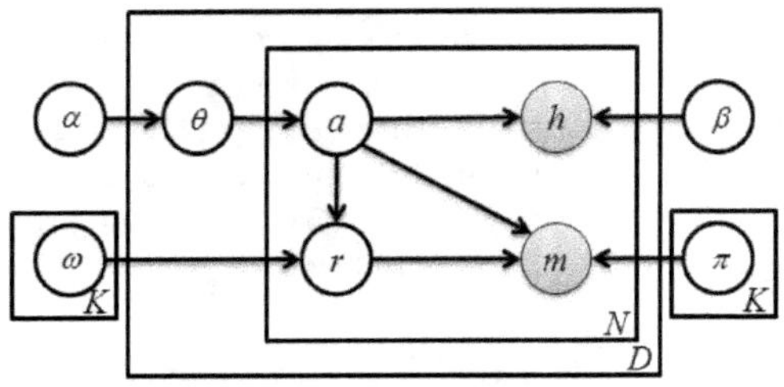

Figure 6: D-PLDA

graphical model through considering a variational Dirichlet parameter for generating θ and a variational multinomial parameter for generating each latent variable. In a good approximation, the KL-divergence between the variational distribution and the true posterior will be minimum. So, by setting the derivative of the KL-divergence with respect to variational parameters equal to zero, the update equations can be obtained. Using Variational Estimation-Maximization (EM) technique [1], a lower bound on the posterior probability can be obtained.

Regarding the computational complexity, each iteration of variational inference for the basic LDA requires $O(Nk)$ operations [1] where k is the number of topics. According to the variational inference algorithms, S-LDA and D-LDA require $O(5Nk)$, PLDA and S-PLDA require $O(2Nk)$, and D-PLDA require $O(6Nk)$ operations for each iteration. As stated in [1], the number of iterations required for a single document is on the order of the number of words in the document. This means that the total number of operations for the LDA models is roughly on the order of $O(N^2k)$.

When working with conditional distributions, over-fitting is always a serious problem [1]. A new review is very likely to contain words that did not appear in any of the reviews in a training corpus. Maximum likelihood estimate of the model parameters assign zero probability to such words, and so zero probability to new reviews. Smoothing is a standard approach to dealing with this problem [1]. We smooth all the parameters which depend on the observed data by assigning positive probability to all vocabulary terms whether or not they are observed in the training set.

Finally, when estimating model parameters using maximum likelihood estimation, it is possible to increase the likelihood by adding parameters, which may however result in over-fitting. Since our goal is to compare the average performance of different models, we perform our experiments for different values of k. Note that, before applying the models on reviews, we first apply the Porter Stemmer algorithm [24] and then remove stop words using a standard lists of stop words[2].

6. EXTRACTION OF OPINION PHRASES

Bag-of-words is a popular representation of documents in text processing. In the area of aspect-based opinion mining most of the current works [2, 30, 26, 25, 12, 14, 15, 7, 27, 11] adopt this representation of reviews. However, it is not clear whether representing a review as a bag of words is sufficient for this problem. Some of the recent works [29, 21] propose to preprocess the product reviews to extract opinion phrases and present LDA models that generate only opinion phrases. These works typically use some simple parsing techniques to extract pairs of frequent noun and nearest adjective, or use POS patterns, e.g. "[adjective] [noun]", "[noun] [verb] [adjective]", etc.

In this section, we present a novel method for extracting opinion phrases based on the Stanford Dependency parser [20], which is a parser widely used in the area of text mining. A dependency parser determines the semantic relationships between words and promises to generate opinion phrases more accurately than methods that consider only the proximity of words. Dependency parsers provide a simple description of the grammatical relationships in a sentence. In the following, we briefly explain the grammatical relations [20] we use:

- Adjectival complement (*acomp*): An adjectival phrase which functions as the complement, e.g., "The automode works amazing" parsed to 'acomp(works, amazing)'.
- Adjectival modifier (*amod*): An adjectival phrase that serves to modify the meaning of a noun phrase, e.g., "It has a wide screen" parsed to 'amod(screen, wide)';
- "And" conjunct (*conj_and*): A relation between two elements connected by the coordinating conjunction "and", e.g., "The LCD is small and blurry" parsed to 'conj_and(small, blurry)'.
- Copula (*cop*): A relation between the complement of a copular verb and the copular verb, e.g., "The batteries are ok" parsed to 'cop(ok, are)'.
- Direct object (*dobj*): A noun phrase which is the object of the verb, e.g., "I like the auto-focus" parsed to 'dobj(like, auto-focus)'.
- Negation modifier (*neg*): A relation between a negation word and the word it modifies, e.g., "The shutter lag is'n fast" parsed to 'neg(fast, n't)'.
- Noun compound modifier (*nn*): A noun that serves to modify the head noun, e.g., "The shutter lag is'n fast" parsed to 'nn(lag, shutter)'.
- Nominal subject (*nsubj*): A noun phrase which is the syntactic subject of a clause, e.g., "The zoom is disappointing" parsed to 'nsubj(disappointing, zoom)'.

We employ these grammatical relations to define a set of dependency patterns for extracting opinion phrases. In the following we list the extraction patterns (N indicates a noun, A an adjective, V a verb, h a head term, m a modifier, and $< h, m >$ an opinion phrase). Table 1 shows some examples of how these patterns are used for extracting opinion phrases.

1. $amod(N, A) \rightarrow < N, A >$
2. $acomp(V, A) + nsubj(V, N) \rightarrow < N, A >$
3. $cop(A, V) + nsubj(A, N) \rightarrow < N, A >$
4. $dobj(V, N) + nsubj(V, N') \rightarrow < N, V >$
5. $< h_1, m > + conj\_and(h_1, h_2) \rightarrow < h_2, m >$
6. $< h, m_1 > + conj\_and(m_1, m_2) \rightarrow < h, m_2 >$
7. $< h, m > + neg(m, not) \rightarrow < h, not + m >$
8. $< h, m > + nn(h, N) \rightarrow < N + h, m >$
9. $< h, m > + nn(N, h) \rightarrow < h + N, m >$

[2]http://ir.dcs.gla.ac.uk/resources/linguistic_utils/stop_words

Table 1: Dependency patterns for extracting opinion Phrases

Sentence	Dependency Relations	Patrn.	Opinion Phrases
This camera has great zoom and resolution.	amod(zoom,great), conj_and(zoom,resolution)	1, 5	<zoom,great>, <resolution,great>
It comes with small and rechargeable batteries.	amod(batteries,rechargeable), conj_and(small,rechargeable)	1, 6	<batteries,rechargeable>, <batteries,small>
The camera case looks nice.	acomp(looks,nice),nsubj(looks,case),nn(case,camera)	2, 8	<camera case,nice>
I love the picture quality.	dobj(love,picture),nsubj(love,I),nn(quality,picture)	4, 9	<picture quality,love>
The screen is wide and clear.	cop(wide,is),nsubj(wide,screen),conj_and(wide,clear)	3, 6	<screen,wide>, <screen,clear>
The battery life is not long.	cop(long,is),nsubj(long,life),nn(life,battery),neg(long,not)	3,8,7	<battery life,not long>

7. EXPERIMENTS

As discussed in the introduction, there is still no benchmark dataset for the problem of aspect-based opinion mining. Since our goal is to compare the performance of different LDA models for products with different numbers of reviews, we have built a very large real life dataset by crawling Epinions.com. In the next subsections, we first briefly describe our dataset and then present a qualitative and quantitative evaluation of the LDA models. For qualitative analysis we compare the top words obtained by different models. For the quantitative analysis we measure the performance of the models in terms of test set likelihood.

7.1 Dataset

We built a crawler to extract product reviews from the well-known reviewing website Epinions.com. The dataset contains 505,978 reviews about 94,792 products from 257 product categories (e.g., camcorder, cellular phone, digital camera, Mp3 player, etc.). Note that, in aspect-based opinion mining, since both aspects and ratings are product-specific, one model is learnt per product. Out of 94,792 products, 49,324 products have only one review which makes it impossible to train and test, so these products were removed.

Table 2: Statistics of the Dataset

Subset	#Products	#Rev./Product
$1 < \#Rev. <= 10$	36,166	3
$10 < \#Rev. <= 50$	7,886	19
$50 < \#Rev. <= 100$	869	67
$100 < \#Rev. <= 200$	368	137
$200 < \#Rev.$	179	341

To the best of our knowledge, the impact of the size of the training dataset has not been evaluated in the literature on aspect-based opinion mining. To do so, we define five subsets of products with different numbers of reviews. The first subset contains products with at least 2 and at most 10 reviews. We also consider subsets of products with more than 10 and less than 50 reviews, between 50 and 100 reviews, from 100 to 200 reviews, and more than 200 reviews. For each subset of products, Table 2 shows the number of products in that subset and the average number of reviews per product. In the following sections we present evaluation results for each subset of products as the average of the results for the products of that subset.

7.2 Qualitative Evaluation

To perform a qualitative evaluation, we select a product from the digital camera category that has 166 reviews. Table 3 shows the top (most probable) words/phrases extracted by different models for this product. We also compare the performance of models learning from phrases (PLDA, S-PLDA, and D-PLDA) using different preprocessing techniques:

- Frequent noun technique: Pairs of frequent nouns and nearest adjectives [21].
- POS patterns: Pairs of nouns and adjectives extracted using POS patterns [29].
- Dependency patterns (introduced in Section 6)

By comparing the top words of the first three models, we observe that the extracted words are almost the same, i.e., S-LDA and D-LDA do not perform better than the basic LDA. Comparing the extracted phrases using frequent noun technique and POS patterns, we see that the frequent noun technique is not that promising since there are some frequent phrases which are not relevant (e.g., <time, hard> and <pictur, mani>) and there are lots of opinion phrases which are not frequent (e.g., <pictur, good> and <displai, nice>). It is also shown that often the extracted phrases based on dependency patterns are more informative, e.g., <qualiti, amaz>, <view find, love>, and <photo qualiti, high>.

7.3 Quantitative Evaluation

If the necessary ground truth is available, the performance of a model can be evaluated by measures such as accuracy, precision and recall. However, in large data sets such as our Epinions dataset ground truth is typically not available. In such cases, a standard approach for the evaluation of graphical models is comparing the likelihoods of a held-out test set. We hold out 10% of the reviews for testing purposes and use the remaining 90% to train the model. As is standard for LDA models [1, 29, 21], we computed the *perplexity* of the held-out test set for all models for various numbers of aspects, $k = \{5, 10, 15, 20, 25\}$. Since the relative results are similar for different values of k, we choose $k = 15$ for our discussion. The perplexity is monotonically decreasing in the likelihood of the test data, and a lower perplexity score indicates better performance. More formally, for a test set of N reviews, the perplexity is defined as [1]:

$$perplexity(R_{test}) = exp\{-\frac{\sum_{d=1}^{D} \log P(\mathbf{w}_d)}{\sum_{d=1}^{D} N_d}\} \quad (8)$$

Table 3: Top words/phrases extracted by different LDA Models

Prep.	Model	Top words/phrases extracted for a digital camera (stemmed)
N/A	LDA	good, pictur, digit, resolut, set, disk, great, time, shot, featur
	S-LDA	featur, zoom, disk, good, pictur, set, shot, resolut, camera, floppi
	D-LDA	bright, time, resolut, good, disk, set, great, digit, shot, camera
Freq. nouns	PLDA	<pictur,mani>,<resolut,high>,<time,hard>,<camera,digit>,<disk,floppi>
	S-PLDA	<time,hard>,<drive,floppi>,<resolut,mani>,<camera,digit>,<featur,good>
	D-PLDA	<resolut,high>,<camera,digit>,<drive,floppi>,<usb,easi>,<disk,hard>
POS patrn.	PLDA	<usag,normal>,<price,high>,<drive,floppi>,<pictur,good>,<featur,sever>
	S-PLDA	<pictur,good>,<effect,special>,<displai,nice>,<life,long>,<printer,great>
	D-PLDA	<batteri,dead>,<resolut,mani>,<camera,digit>,<pictur,good>,<featur,offer>
Dep. patrn.	PLDA	<displai,nice>,<zoom,optic>,<effect,mani>,<pictur,good>,<reolut,high>
	S-PLDA	<resolut,high>,<qualiti,amaz>,<printer,compat>,<displai,nice>,<zoom,optic>
	D-PLDA	<photo qualiti,high>,<zoom,optic>,<storag capac,unlimit>,<printer,compat>,<viewfind,love>

For models learning from opinion phrases, $P(\boldsymbol{w}_d)$ is being replaced by $P(\boldsymbol{h}_d, \boldsymbol{m}_d)$. While perplexity is a well-established measure for comparing LDA models, it is not clear how perplexity relates to the accuracy of aspect identification and rating prediction. To this end, we use a well-known public dataset with ground truth used in [8, 9, 4] (with 314 reviews of 5 products) to analyze the correlation between model perplexity and accuracy of these tasks. Table 4 shows the average precision and recall of aspect identification, the Mean Squared Error (MSE) of rating prediction and the perplexity of different models on this dataset averaged over all products.

Table 4: Evaluation on Labeled Dataset

Model	Precision	Recall	MSE	Perplexity
S-LDA	0.54	0.51	1.25	813.11
LDA	0.54	0.52	1.22	795.72
D-LDA	0.58	0.55	1.18	748.26
PLDA	0.81	0.73	0.96	587.82
S-PLDA	0.83	0.73	0.93	335.02
D-PLDA	0.87	0.78	0.85	131.80

We observe a strong correlation of the perplexity and precision, recall, and MSE. All three accuracy measures improve monotonically with improving (decreasing) perplexity. Extrapolating these results to the much larger Epinions dataset, for which we have no ground truth, we argue that the perplexity results reported in our quantitative evaluation provide a good indication of the relative accuracy of aspect identification and rating prediction for the compared models.

7.3.1 Comparing Preprocessing Techniques

We compare the perplexity of models learning from opinion phrases for different preprocessing techniques. As the baselines we use pairs of one frequent noun and one adjective [21] and phrases generated from POS patterns [29].

Which preprocessing technique for extracting opinion phrases works best? To answer this question, Table 5 presents the average perplexity of different models using different preprocessing techniques. The results indicate that using POS patterns for extracting opinion phrases is more effective than the frequent noun technique. However, it is unclear whether this better performance is due the infrequency of some of the opinion phrases or because of the inaccuracy of extracted frequent phrases. Table 5 also demonstrates that our proposed technique based on dependency parsing clearly and consistently outperforms the other preprocessing techniques for all subsets of products. This confirms our hypothesis that exploiting the semantic relationship between words pays off for extracting opinion phrases.

7.3.2 Evaluation of LDA Models

In this section we compare the performance of the discussed models to answer the key design questions stated in the introduction. Figure 7(a) shows the perplexity of all models for different subsets of products. The perplexity of the models learning from opinion phrases are given for preprocessing using dependency patterns, which performs best according to Table 5. Figure 7 compares only products with at least 10 reviews, similar to the literature. At the end of this section, we also discuss the models' performance for products with less than 10 reviews.

Is it better to have separate latent variables for aspects and ratings? To answer this question, we compare the performance of LDA vs. S-LDA (Figure 7(b)), and also PLDA vs. S-PLDA (Figure 7(c)). It turns out that having separate latent variables for aspects and ratings cannot improve the performance of a model having only one observed variable (i.e., using the bag-of-words model). As a result, the performance of LDA and S-LDA are almost the same. However, S-PLDA outperforms PLDA thanks to the separate aspect and rating variables generating head terms and modifiers, respectively.

Is it better to assume dependency between ratings and aspects? Here we compare the perplexity of S-LDA vs. D-LDA (Figure 7(d)) and also S-PLDA vs. D-PLDA (Figure 7(e)). The higher perplexity of D-LDA compared to S-LDA demonstrates that increasing model complexity while keeping the observed data fixed decreases the performance of the model. However, the comparison of D-PLDA and S-PLDA indicates that assuming the dependency between ratings and aspects improves the performance of a model that generates opinion phrases.

Is it better to learn from bag-of-words or preprocess the reviews and learn from opinion phrases? To address this question, we compare three pairs of models: LDA vs. PLDA (Figure 7(f)), S-LDA vs. S-PLDA (Figures 7(g)), and D-LDA vs. D-PLDA (Figure 7(h)). The only difference between these pairs of models is generation of words vs. generation of opinion phrases. Except for products with more

Table 5: Perplexity of the LDA models using different preprocessing techniques

Preprocessing	Frequent nouns			POS patterns			Dependency patterns		
Subset of Products	PLDA	S-PLDA	D-PLDA	PLDA	S-PLDA	D-PLDA	PLDA	S-PLDA	D-PLDA
$1 < \#Rev. <= 10$	11834.99	11824.35	11740.95	7735.32	7679.10	7650.67	5463.80	5422.24	5413.66
$10 < \#Rev. <= 50$	6724.61	6129.57	5829.33	4573.20	4124.06	3847.92	3438.19	2937.36	1975.35
$50 < \#Rev. <= 100$	3024.59	2243.22	1882.91	2734.58	1912.88	1381.86	1998.42	1514.71	592.40
$100 < \#Rev. <= 200$	1885.52	1511.47	660.96	1753.39	1328.77	411.94	1481.00	1038.25	164.19
$200 < \#Rev.$	1337.93	1165.88	406.27	1301.00	1066.89	353.73	1284.19	879.29	142.37

than 200 reviews, LDA performs better than PLDA, showing that extracting opinion phrases does not help if only one latent variable is used to generate both head terms and modifiers. Comparing S-LDA and S-PLDA, we observe that for products with more than 50 reviews S-PLDA achieves a lower perplexity (better performance), while for products with fewer reviews it performs poorer. Finally, D-PLDA performs significantly better than D-LDA in all of the product subsets, showing the advantage of learning from opinion phrases rather than bag-of-words when modeling aspects, ratings, and their dependency.

Does the answer to the above questions differ for products with few reviews and products with many reviews? Here, we discuss the performance of the LDA models for products with less than 10 reviews. Since products of this subset have only 3 reviews on average (see Table 2), learning a proper model is very difficult. As Table 6 shows, the basic LDA model outperforms the more complex models for these products, demonstrating that neither preprocessing nor model complexity can improve the performance of LDA. Thus, the best design choices are very different for products with many reviews and for those with few reviews.

Table 6: Perplexity of products with $\#Rev. <= 10$

LDA	S-LDA	D-LDA	PLDA	S-PLDA	D-PLDA
4413.6	4567.2	4729.3	5463.8	5422.2	5413.6

8. CONCLUSION

Aspect-based opinion mining, which aims to extract aspects and their corresponding ratings from online product reviews, provides very useful information for users to make their purchase decision. LDA-based models are considered to be state-of-the-art for aspect-based opinion mining. Realizing that there is no "one-size-fits-all" model that always outperforms all other models, in this paper we developed a set of design guidelines. We conducted extensive experiments on a very large real life dataset from Epinions.com (500K reviews) and compared the performance of different models in terms of the likelihood of the held-out test set. Based on our experimental results, we formulate the following guidelines for the design of LDA models for aspect-based opinion mining:

- When learning from bag-of-words, having separate latent variables for aspects and ratings cannot improve the performance of a model. However, when learning from opinion phrases, it does help to consider two latent variables for generating head terms and modifiers.
- When learning from opinion phrases and having separate latent variables for aspect and rating, assuming their dependency improves the performance.
- When separate latent variables are assumed for aspects and ratings, using preprocessing techniques can improve the performance.
- Using dependency patterns consistently achieves the best performance for extracting opinion phrases.
- For products with few reviews, the basic LDA model outperforms the more complex models. For products with many reviews, the model learning aspects and ratings from opinion phrases with dependency assumption performs best.

This paper suggests several directions for future research, such as investigating different factors for improving the model performance for products with only few reviews. Another direction is exploring the impact of different additional input sources (e.g. review's overall rating) on the performance of the models.

9. REFERENCES

[1] D. M. Blei, A. Y. Ng, and M. I. Jordan. Latent dirichlet allocation. *J. Mach. Learn. Res.*, 2003.

[2] S. Brody and N. Elhadad. An unsupervised aspect-sentiment model for online reviews. In *HLT '10*.

[3] Y. Choi and C. Cardie. Hierarchical sequential learning for extracting opinions and their attributes. In *ACL '10*.

[4] X. Ding, B. Liu, and P. S. Yu. A holistic lexicon-based approach to opinion mining. In *WSDM '08*.

[5] H. Guo, H. Zhu, Z. Guo, and Z. Su. Domain customization for aspect-oriented opinion analysis with multi-level latent sentiment clues. In *CIKM '11*.

[6] H. Guo, H. Zhu, Z. Guo, X. Zhang, and Z. Su. Product feature categorization with multilevel latent semantic association. In *CIKM '09*.

[7] Y. He, C. Lin, and H. Alani. Automatically extracting polarity-bearing topics for cross-domain sentiment classification. In *HLT '11*.

[8] M. Hu and B. Liu. Mining and summarizing customer reviews. In *KDD '04*.

[9] M. Hu and B. Liu. Mining opinion features in customer reviews. In *AAAI'04*.

[10] W. Jin, H. H. Ho, and R. K. Srihari. Opinionminer: a novel machine learning system for web opinion mining and extraction. In *KDD '09*.

[11] Y. Jo and A. H. Oh. Aspect and sentiment unification model for online review analysis. In *WSDM '11*.

[12] H. Lakkaraju, C. Bhattacharyya, I. Bhattacharya, and S. Merugu. Exploiting coherence for the simultaneous discovery of latent facets and associated sentiments. In *SDM '11*.

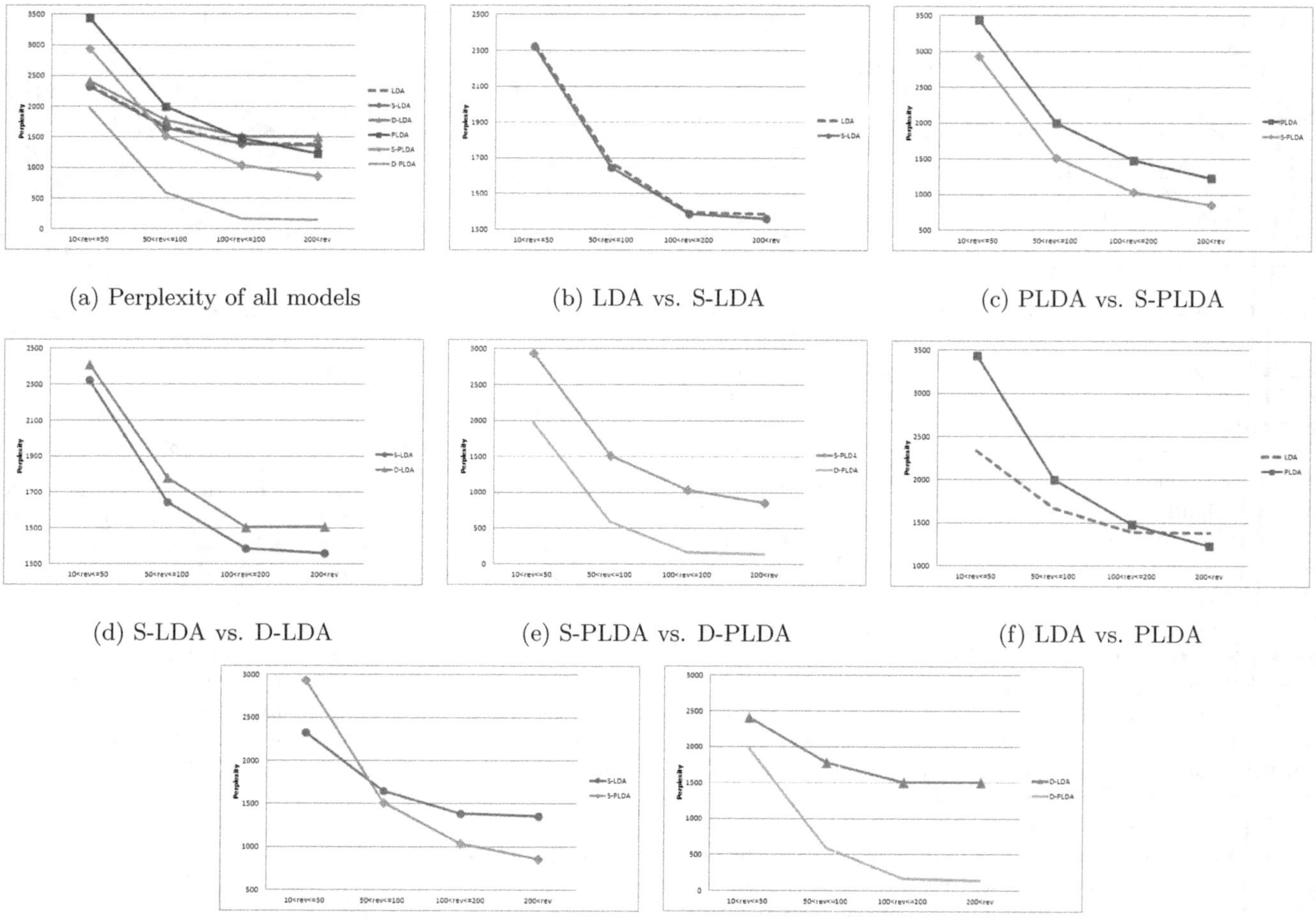

(a) Perplexity of all models (b) LDA vs. S-LDA (c) PLDA vs. S-PLDA

(d) S-LDA vs. D-LDA (e) S-PLDA vs. D-PLDA (f) LDA vs. PLDA

(g) S-LDA vs. S-PLDA (h) D-LDA vs. D-PLDA

Figure 7: Perplexity comparisons for different subsets of products

[13] F. Li, C. Han, M. Huang, X. Zhu, Y.-J. Xia, S. Zhang, and H. Yu. Structure-aware review mining and summarization. In *COLING '10*.

[14] F. Li, M. Huang, and X. Zhu. Sentiment analysis with global topics and local dependency. In *AAAI '10*.

[15] C. Lin and Y. He. Joint sentiment/topic model for sentiment analysis. In *CIKM '09*.

[16] B. Liu. *Web Data Mining: Exploring Hyperlinks, Contents, and Usage Data*, chapter 11. Springer, 2007.

[17] B. Liu, M. Hu, and J. Cheng. Opinion observer: analyzing and comparing opinions on the web. In *WWW '05*.

[18] Y. Lu, P. Tsaparas, A. Ntoulas, and L. Polanyi. Exploiting social context for review quality prediction. In *WWW '10*.

[19] Y. Lu, C. Zhai, and N. Sundaresan. Rated aspect summarization of short comments. In *WWW '09*.

[20] B. M. Marie-Catherine de Marneffe and C. D. Manning. Generating typed dependency parses from phrase structure parses. In *LREC '06*.

[21] S. Moghaddam and M. Ester. ILDA: interdependent LDA model for learning latent aspects and their ratings from online product reviews. In *SIGIR '11*.

[22] S. Moghaddam and M. Ester. Opinion Digger: an unsupervised opinion miner from unstructured product reviews. In *CIKM '10*.

[23] S. Moghaddam, M. Jamali, and M. Ester. ETF: Extended Tensor Factorization model for personalizing prediction of review helpfulness. In *WSDM '12*.

[24] M. F. Porter. An algorithm for suffix stripping. *Readings in information retrieval*, 1997.

[25] I. Titov and R. McDonald. A joint model of text and aspect ratings for sentiment summarization. In *ACL-HLT '08*.

[26] I. Titov and R. McDonald. Modeling online reviews with multi-grain topic models. In *WWW '08*.

[27] H. Wang, Y. Lu, and C. Zhai. Latent aspect rating analysis without aspect keyword supervision. In *KDD '11*.

[28] T.-L. Wong, L. Bing, and W. Lam. Normalizing web product attributes and discovering domain ontology with minimal effort. In *WSDM '11*.

[29] T.-J. Zhan and C.-H. Li. Semantic dependent word pairs generative model for fine-grained product feature mining. In *PAKDD '11*.

[30] W. X. Zhao, J. Jiang, H. Yan, and X. Li. Jointly modeling aspects and opinions with a maxent-lda hybrid. In *EMNLP '10*.

Predicting Query Performance for Fusion-Based Retrieval

Gad Markovits
gadm@tx.technion.ac.il

Anna Shtok
annabel@tx.technion.ac.il

Oren Kurland
kurland@ie.technion.ac.il

Faculty of Industrial Engineering and Management, Technion — Israel Institute of Technology
Haifa 32000, Israel

David Carmel
IBM Research lab
Haifa 31905, Israel
carmel@il.ibm.com

ABSTRACT

Estimating the effectiveness of a search performed in response to a query in the absence of relevance judgments is the goal of query-performance prediction methods. Post-retrieval predictors analyze the result list of the most highly ranked documents. We address the prediction challenge for retrieval approaches wherein the final result list is produced by *fusing* document lists that were retrieved in response to a query. To that end, we present a novel fundamental prediction framework that accounts for this special characteristics of the fusion setting; i.e., the use of intermediate retrieved lists. The framework is based on integrating prediction performed upon the final result list with that performed upon the lists that were fused to create it; prediction integration is controlled based on inter-list similarities. We empirically demonstrate the merits of various predictors instantiated from the framework. A case in point, their prediction quality substantially transcends that of applying state-of-the-art predictors upon the final result list.

Categories and Subject Descriptors: H.3.3 [Information Search and Retrieval]: Retrieval models

General Terms: Algorithms, Experimentation

Keywords: query-performance prediction, fusion

1. INTRODUCTION

The effectiveness of retrieval methods often varies across queries [35, 15]. Thus, the ability to automatically infer which queries are more difficult for a retrieval method than others can be very important. These observations motivated a large body of work on predicting query performance [5]; that is, estimating the effectiveness of a search performed in response to a query in the absence of relevance judgments.

Pre-retrieval predictors [18, 16] analyze the query expression and utilize corpus-based statistics. By definition, then, their prediction is not based on the ranking at hand, the effectiveness of which is the goal of prediction. Post-retrieval predictors [9, 5], on the other hand, analyze also the *result list* of the most highly ranked documents. Hence, they often yield prediction quality that (substantially) transcends that of pre-retrieval predictors [5].

We address the challenge of post-retrieval query performance prediction for *fusion*-based retrieval [14, 8]. The goal is predicting the effectiveness of a document list that is produced by fusing (merging) a few lists that were retrieved, from the same corpus, in response to the query.

The motivation for addressing the challenge just mentioned is twofold. First, fusion methods post effective retrieval performance on average [8]; e.g., when fusing lists retrieved by using different query and document representations or retrieval methods [8]. Furthermore, although fusion-based retrieval was shown to somewhat improve retrieval-performance robustness across queries [2], we empirically show that commonly used fusion methods still suffer from substantial performance variance. Hence, predicting which queries are more difficult for fusion-based methods than others is motivated by the same reasons that drove forward work on query-performance prediction in general.

The second factor motivating the pursue of the query-performance prediction challenge for fusion-based retrieval is the unique characteristics of this retrieval paradigm. Specifically, we address the following question, which to the best of our knowledge, has not been been tackled before: *Can using information induced from the intermediate results of the fusion-based retrieval process (i.e., the document lists that are fused) in addition to that which is the focus of previous work on post-retrieval prediction (i.e., that induced from the final result list) help improve prediction quality?*

We present a novel probabilistic query-performance prediction framework for fusion-based retrieval that addresses the question stated above. The framework is based on integrating prediction performed upon the final result list, the effectiveness of which is the goal of prediction, with that employed over the lists that are fused; prediction integration is controlled by using inter-list similarity measures. The underlying idea is that lists that are similar — with respect to the documents they contain and their ranking — should have similar performance. We instantiate various predictors from the framework by varying the prediction-integration approach, the single-list predictors employed, and the inter-list similarity measure used.

CIKM'12, October 29–November 2, 2012, Maui, HI, USA.

Empirical evaluation performed with several tracks of TREC, and with various fusion methods applied to runs submitted to these tracks, attests to the merits of our prediction approach. For example, the prediction quality of the predictors we derive substantially transcends that of applying state-of-the-art post-retrieval predictors upon the final result list.

Our main contributions can be summarized as follows.

1. Previous work on post-retrieval prediction [5] focuses on analyzing the final — and single retrieved — result list. In contrast, our prediction framework targets the unique characteristics of the fusion-based retrieval process; specifically, by integrating prediction based on the final result list with that based on the intermediate lists fused to create it.

2. Empirically demonstrating the substantial merits of our prediction approach; specifically, with respect to the (standard) practice of applying prediction only upon the final result list. Furthermore, our approach is shown to be highly effective in predicting query performance for a variety of fusion methods.

2. RELATED WORK

There is a large body of work on query-performance prediction [5]; specifically, on devising post-retrieval predictors that analyze properties of the result list of top-retrieved documents. For example, clarity-based predictors [9] measure the divergence of a model induced from the result list from that of the corpus. Other prediction methods measure different notions of the robustness of the result list [37, 33, 39, 3, 40]. Some predictors analyze the retrieval scores of documents in the result list [13, 40, 27, 11, 12, 31].

The prediction methods mentioned above analyze the properties of a single retrieved list. In contrast, our prediction framework predicts the effectiveness of the final result list by analyzing both its properties and those of the lists that were fused to create it. We use adaptations of some previously proposed predictors [9, 40, 31] for single-list-based prediction in our framework.

Query-performance predictors were used to improve fusion effectiveness [4, 28]. Specifically, predictors were applied upon the lists that are fused so as to weigh them in the fusion process. In contrast, our goal is to predict the effectiveness of the final document list that is the result of fusion.

The similarity between the final result list and the intermediate lists fused to create it was used as a predictor in its own right for the effectiveness of the intermediate lists [32, 3, 13]. In contrast, our methods predict the effectiveness of the final result list; specifically, by using the inter-list similarities to control the integration of prediction applied upon the intermediate lists and upon the final result list.

Some recent work [20] showed that several post-retrieval predictors [9, 13, 40, 30, 31] essentially rely on the following principle. Given a result list, the effectiveness of which we want to predict, a pseudo effective and/or ineffective "reference" document lists are created; then, the similarity between the reference lists and the result list at hand serves for prediction. In contrast, our goal is to predict the effectiveness of a result list that was produced by fusing several given result lists. To that end, we propose a novel probabilistic prediction framework wherein inter-list similarities serve a specific role.

There is recent work [21] that derives the prediction principle mentioned above, of using reference lists, in a probabilistic manner. In contrast to our approach, prediction applied directly upon the final result list, which we empirically show to be highly important for the fusion setting we address here, is not integrated in the proposed model. In fact, the fundamental predictor we present, which serves for deriving various predictors, can be viewed as a generalized form of the reference-list-based prediction model presented in this work [21].

3. PREDICTION FRAMEWORK

Throughout this section we assume that the following have been fixed. A query q, a corpus of documents $\mathcal{C}$; and, m document lists, $L_1, \ldots, L_m$, each of which contains n documents that were retrieved from $\mathcal{C}$ by *some* retrieval method in response to q.

Suppose that *some* fusion method [8] was employed over the retrieved lists to produce a final result list, L_{res}, of n documents. Our goal is to predict the effectiveness of L_{res} with respect to the information need expressed by q in the absence of relevance judgments.

The query-performance prediction framework that we present does not assume knowledge of the fusion method, nor knowledge about the retrieval methods used to create the lists $L_1, \ldots, L_m$. Hence, the framework is quite general and yields high quality prediction for various fusion methods as we show in Section 4. Yet, in Section 3.5 we discuss the connection between the prediction framework and a specific family of fusion approaches.

The prediction framework is based on utilizing *some* post-retrieval query-performance predictor $\mathcal{P}_{base}$. The predictor $\mathcal{P}_{base}$ operates upon q and a document list L that was retrieved in response to q; corpus-based information can also be utilized. The prediction value assigned by $\mathcal{P}_{base}$, denoted $\mathcal{P}_{base}(L;q)$, is an estimate for the effectiveness of L with respect to q. In Section 3.4 we discuss several adaptations of previously proposed predictors that we use for $\mathcal{P}_{base}$.

We can state the prediction goal as that of estimating, in the absence of relevance judgments, $p(L_{res}|q)$, i.e., the probability that L_{res} satisfies the information need expressed by q. The resultant estimate reflects the presumed effectiveness of L_{res}. Following previous work on post-retrieval query-performance prediction [5], we can apply $\mathcal{P}_{base}$ *directly* upon L_{res}, so as to derive an estimate for $p(L_{res}|q)$. This is the **Direct** predictor:

$$\mathcal{P}_{Direct}(L_{res};q) \stackrel{def}{=} \mathcal{P}_{base}(L_{res};q). \tag{1}$$

However, we would like to exploit the special characteristics of the fusion-based retrieval setting to potentially improve prediction quality; that is, utilize also information induced from the lists $L_1, \ldots, L_m$ that were fused to produce L_{res}. A case in point, if many of these lists are predicted to be highly effective, and L_{res} is not very different — in the documents it contains and their ranking — from these lists, then the effectiveness predicted for L_{res} should be high.

Accordingly, we use the lists $L_1, \ldots, L_m$ as proxies for L_{res} in estimating its effectiveness. Specifically, we can write

$$p(L_{res}|q) = \sum_{L_i} p(L_{res}|q, L_i)p(L_i|q). \tag{2}$$

Equation 2 is based on the premise that the effectiveness of L_{res} can be predicted (estimated) using a mixture of estimates (predictions) used for the effectiveness of the lists (L_i) that were fused to create it. In what follows we further develop Equation 2 and present a variety of predictors that can be derived based on this premise. Later on, specifically in Section 3.5, we discuss the formal connections between some of the derived predictors and a specific family of fusion methods (namely, linear models). Yet, we hasten to point out that in Section 4 we show that the proposed predictors post high prediction quality for a variety of fusion approaches, among which is a highly effective non-linear method.

We estimate $p(L_{res}|q, L_i)$ in Equation 2 using a linear mixture governed by a free parameter λ: $(1-\lambda)\hat{p}(L_{res}|q) + \lambda\hat{p}(L_{res}|L_i)$;[1] here and after, $\hat{p}(x)$ denotes an estimate for $p(x)$. Applying some probabilistic algebra, and assuming that $\hat{p}(L_i|q)$ is a probability distribution over the lists L_i (i.e., $\sum_{L_i} \hat{p}(L_i|q) = 1$), yields the following generic prediction approach

$$\mathcal{P}_{Gen}(L_{res}; q) \stackrel{def}{=} (1-\lambda)\hat{p}(L_{res}|q) + \lambda \sum_{L_i} \hat{p}(L_{res}|L_i)\hat{p}(L_i|q); \quad (3)$$

$\hat{p}(L|q)$ is an estimate for the probability that the list L satisfies the information need expressed by q. Thus, the resultant prediction for the effectiveness of L_{res} is based on integrating a direct estimate for its effectiveness ($\hat{p}(L_{res}|q)$) with estimates for the effectiveness of the lists L_i from which it was fused ($\hat{p}(L_i|q)$); these estimates are weighted by L_i's "association" with L_{res} ($\hat{p}(L_{res}|L_i)$).

3.1 Deriving specific predictors

To instantiate specific prediction methods from Equation 3, we use the prediction value $\mathcal{P}_{base}(L; q)$ for the estimate $\hat{p}(L|q)$. To estimate the association between L_{res} and L_i ($\hat{p}(L_{res}|L_i)$), we use an inter-list similarity measure, $sim(\cdot, \cdot)$. We discuss two similarity measures in Section 3.2.[2] The resultant **AMean** predictor instantiated from Equation 3, which is based on an arithmetic mean of (weighted) prediction values, is defined as

$$\mathcal{P}_{AMean}(L_{res}; q) \stackrel{def}{=} (1-\lambda)\mathcal{P}_{base}(L_{res}; q) + \lambda \sum_{L_i} sim(L_i, L_{res})\mathcal{P}_{base}(L_i; q).$$

Setting $\lambda = 0$ amounts to the Direct predictor from Equation 1. Higher values of λ result in increased importance attributed to prediction based on the lists L_i.

As an alternative to the arithmetic-mean-based approach employed by AMean, we explore the **GMean** predictor that is based on a *form* of a geometric mean:[3]

$$\mathcal{P}_{GMean}(L_{res}; q) \stackrel{def}{=} \mathcal{P}_{base}(L_{res}; q)^{(1-\lambda)} \Big(\prod_{L_i} sim(L_i, L_{res})\mathcal{P}_{base}(L_i; q)\Big)^{\lambda}.$$

Consequently, if L_{res} or any of the lists L_i is predicted by $\mathcal{P}_{base}$ to be of very low effectiveness, the resultant prediction value is lower for GMean than for AMean as GMean is more "conservative". Similar considerations motivated the use of the GMAP effectiveness evaluation metric [36] (i.e., the geometric mean of per-query average precision values) as a conservative alternative to MAP (the arithmetic mean).

3.2 Inter-list similarity measures

There is a wide variety of inter-list similarity measures that can be used in the prediction methods presented above. Here, we study two measures that attribute more importance to documents at high ranks of the lists than to those at low ranks. This is because retrieval effectiveness, the goal of prediction, is often measured, as will be the case in Section 4, using metrics that are heavily affected by top ranks (e.g., average precision). The first inter-similarity measure that we use, **KL**, utilizes rank information, is asymmetric, and only considers the most highly ranked documents in the list. The second measure, **Cosine**, uses retrieval scores, is symmetric, and considers all documents in the list.

The KL measure. Let $\mathcal{C}_{init} \stackrel{def}{=} \bigcup_i L_i$ denote the *set* of documents in the lists that are fused. We use $p_L(\cdot)$ to denote the representation of L as a probability distribution over $\mathcal{C}_{init}$. To induce $p_L(\cdot)$, we follow a previous proposal [3]. Specifically, let d_r ($\in L$) be the document at rank r of L. ($r = 1$ is the highest rank.) Then, $p_L(d_r) \stackrel{def}{=} \frac{1}{2c}(1 + \frac{1}{r} + \frac{1}{r+1} + \cdots + \frac{1}{c})$, where c is a cutoff parameter. For d that is at rank r of L with $r > c$, or that is not in L, $p_L(d)$ is set to 0. The similarity between lists L_i and L_j is defined based on the asymmetric KL divergence measure: $sim_{KL}(L_i, L_j) \stackrel{def}{=} \exp(-KL\left(p_{L_i}(\cdot) \,\middle|\middle|\, p_{L_j}(\cdot)\right))$ [3].

The Cosine measure. The second inter-list similarity measure is based on a vector-space representation of L, denoted $\vec{L}$, defined over $\mathcal{C}_{init}$. Specifically, the l'th component of the vector $\vec{L}$ is set to the score of document d_l ($\in \mathcal{C}_{init}$) if d_l appears in L and to 0 otherwise. The cosine is used as a symmetric inter-list similarity measure: $sim_{Cosine}(L_i, L_j) \stackrel{def}{=} \cos(\vec{L_i}, \vec{L_j})$.

3.3 A uniform inter-list similarity measure and alternative prediction-aggregation methods

To study the merits of differentially weighting the prediction values assigned to the lists L_i based on their similarity with L_{res}, we devise variants of the AMean and GMean

[1] A somewhat conceptually similar estimation technique, and consequent derivation, were used in work on cluster-based retrieval [19].

[2] Normalizing the similarity measure to yield a probability distribution showed no empirical merit in terms of prediction quality. We also note that the base predictors used in Section 3.4, as the vast majority of previously proposed predictors [5], do not induce probability distributions. Hence, while our framework is probabilistic, it is instantiated using estimates that are not probability distributions.

[3] GMean is the geomtric mean of the prediction value assigned to L_{res} and the *weighted* prediction values assigned to the lists L_i. We do not use the geometric mean of the latter (i.e., use the inter-list similarity values for the exponent of the prediction values) as doing so turned out to yield worse prediction quality than that attained by GMean as defined here. We also note that GMean cannot be directly derived from Equation 3 as opposed to AMean.

methods that use a uniform inter-list similarity measure; i.e., the similarity between L_i and L_{res} is not accounted for. Specifically, we study the **UniAMean** predictor:

$$\mathcal{P}_{UniAMean}(L_{res};q) \stackrel{def}{=} (1-\lambda)\mathcal{P}_{base}(L_{res};q) + \frac{\lambda}{m}\sum_{L_i}\mathcal{P}_{base}(L_i;q); \quad (4)$$

and, the **UniGMean** predictor[4]:

$$\mathcal{P}_{UniGMean}(L_{res};q) \stackrel{def}{=} \mathcal{P}_{base}(L_{res};q)^{(1-\lambda)}\prod_{L_i}\mathcal{P}_{base}(L_i;q)^{\frac{\lambda}{m}}; \quad (5)$$

m is the number of lists.

The methods presented above assign a prediction value that is based on the aggregation of the prediction values for all the lists that are fused. To consider the alternative of using the prediction for only "representative" lists, we upper-bound the prediction value assigned by UniAMean in Equation 4 using the **UniMax** predictor:

$$\mathcal{P}_{UniMax}(L_{res};q) \stackrel{def}{=} (1-\lambda)\mathcal{P}_{base}(L_{res};q)+\lambda\max_{L_i}\mathcal{P}_{base}(L_i;q); \quad (6)$$

and lower-bound it using the **UniMin** predictor:

$$\mathcal{P}_{UniMin}(L_{res};q) \stackrel{def}{=} (1-\lambda)\mathcal{P}_{base}(L_{res};q)+\lambda\min_{L_i}\mathcal{P}_{base}(L_i;q). \quad (7)$$

3.4 Base predictors

The last step for instantiating predictors using the methods described above is defining the predictor $\mathcal{P}_{base}$ that operates on a document list L. However, most previously proposed post-retrieval predictors were devised for specific retrieval methods [5]; in fact, most state-of-the-art predictors were shown to be effective when the retrieval was based on surface-level document-query similarities (e.g., [9, 13, 40, 17, 30, 31]). Here, we have to employ $\mathcal{P}_{base}$ upon lists $L_1, \ldots, L_m$ that were retrieved by *some* retrieval methods that may not be those for which previous predictors were designed for; and, upon L_{res} which is created using a fusion method. Thus, we use some recently proposed adaptations [31] of three (highly) effective post-retrieval predictors that operate on a list (L) retrieved by *some* method. In what follows we use $s(d;L)$ to denote the (non-negative) score of document d in L. For the lists L_i that are fused, we normalize the original retrieval scores so they sum to 1; $s(d;L)$ is the normalized retrieval score in this case. (See Section 4.1 for further details.) The predictors we present focus on $L^{[k]}$, the k highest ranked documents in L; k is a free parameter.

Clarity. Clarity measures the focus of a retrieved list L with respect to the corpus by computing the divergence between their induced language models [9]. The higher the divergence, the more distant the models are; and, L is presumed to be more effective.

The (relevance) language model utilized by Clarity, which is induced from L, is based on a language-model-based retrieval used to create L. Here, we use Clarity for the general retrieved list case. Let $w(d;L)$ be a weight assigned to document d with respect to a list L in which it appears. Then, the relevance model $R_{L^{[k]}}$ induced from $L^{[k]}$ is defined by: $p(t|R_{L^{[k]}}) \stackrel{def}{=} \sum_{d\in L^{[k]}} p(t|d)\frac{w(d;L)}{\sum_{d'\in L^{[k]}} w(d';L)}$; t is a term in the vocabulary; $p(t|d)$ is the probability assigned to t by a language model induced from d. (Language model induction details are provided in Section 4.1.) Clarity is the KL divergence between the relevance model and the (unsmoothed) corpus language model ($p(\cdot|\mathcal{C})$):

$$Clarity(q;L) \stackrel{def}{=} KL\left(p(\cdot|R_{L^{[k]}}) \,\middle|\middle|\, p(\cdot|\mathcal{C})\right). \quad (8)$$

We use two variants of Clarity. The first, **sClarity**, weighs document d by its retrieval score in L: $w_{sClarity}(d;L) \stackrel{def}{=} s(d;L)$. The **rClarity** measure, as in previous proposals [10, 13], weighs d using a linearly decreasing function of its rank r ($\leq k$) in L; specifically, $w_{rClarity}(d;L) \stackrel{def}{=} 2(k+1-r)$.

WIG. The WIG predictor is based on the premise that high retrieval scores at top ranks of the list, specifically, with respect to that of the corpus, indicate effective retrieval [40]. WIG was proposed in the markov random field (MRF) retrieval framework [25]; and, was also shown to be effective for predicting the effectiveness of a language-model-based retrieval [30]. Here, for the case of a list retrieved by *some* method, we use for prediction the mean of retrieval scores of the highest ranked documents [31][5]:

$$WIG(q;L) \stackrel{def}{=} \frac{1}{k}\sum_{d\in L^{[k]}} s(d;L). \quad (9)$$

We note that the corpus retrieval score cannot be used, as opposed to the original implementation of WIG [40], since we do not have knowledge of the retrieval method used to create L; or, it might be created by fusion as is the case for L_{res}. While the corpus retrieval score originally served to ensure inter-query compatibility of prediction values due to lack of inter-query compatibility of retrieval scores, here retrieval scores in the lists L_i are sum-normalized to $[0,1]$.[6]

NQC. The NQC predictor measures the standard deviation of retrieval scores of top-retrieved documents [31]. It was argued that increased standard deviation amounts to potentially reduced *query drift* in the result list; and hence, implies improved retrieval effectiveness [31]. While the argument was based on the assumption that retrieval scores reflect document-query surface-level similarities, we use NQC for a list retrieved by *some* method [31]. Specifically, let

[4]UniGMean is the geometric mean of (i) the prediction value assigned to L_{res}, and (ii) the geometric mean of the prediction values assigned to the lists L_i.

[5]The original WIG measure also employs query-length normalization [40]. This normalization is important for inter-query compatibility of retrieval scores in the MRF and language modeling frameworks. We found that such normalization hurts the prediction quality when using lists retrieved by *some* method (e.g., TREC runs) as is the case here.

[6]Sum-normalization of the fusion scores in L_{res} degraded prediction quality for the different predictors, and hence was not used here and after.

$\mu \stackrel{def}{=} \frac{1}{k}\sum_{d\in L^{[k]}} s(d;L)$ be the mean score in $L^{[k]}$, then[7]

$$NQC(L;q) \stackrel{def}{=} \sqrt{\frac{1}{k}\sum_{d\in L^{[k]}} (s(d;L)-\mu)^2}. \quad (10)$$

3.5 On the connection between the prediction framework and (specific) fusion methods

Suppose that the final result list, L_{res}, contains a single document, d. Then, using Equation 3 with $\lambda = 1$ yields

$$\mathcal{P}_{Gen}(d;q) \stackrel{def}{=} \sum_{L_i} \hat{p}(d|L_i)\hat{p}(L_i|q). \quad (11)$$

That is, the predicted (estimated) relevance of d to q is determined based on d's association with the lists L_i ($\hat{p}(d|L_i)$), wherein the association is weighted by the predicted effectiveness of L_i ($\hat{p}(L_i|q)$). If $\hat{p}(d|L_i)$ is based on d's retrieval score (or rank) in L_i, then we attain the general form of linear fusion functions [14, 34]. For example, the commonly used CombSUM method [14], which is one of the fusion approaches used for the evaluation presented in Section 4, is based (in spirit) on using d's normalized score in L_i for $\hat{p}(d|L_i)$ and a uniform estimate for $\hat{p}(L_i|q)$ — i.e., considering the L_i's to be equi-effective.

Thus, we see that the proposed prediction framework can conceptually be viewed as a generalization (including a geometric-mean-based form), and adaptation, of the basic linear fusion principle to the prediction task. Yet, the framework utilizes not only information induced from the lists that are fused, as is the (natural) case in the fusion-based retrieval process, but also information from the final result list (L_{res}); specifically, if $\lambda < 1$. (See Equation 3.) This is an important fundamental difference, among others, that rises due to the inherent difference between the prediction and fusion (retrieval) tasks.

4. EVALUATION

4.1 Experimental setup

For experiments we use the ad hoc tracks of TREC3 and TREC8, the Web tracks of TREC9 and TREC10, and the robust track of TREC12. Thus, a variety of query sets and corpora (newswire and Web) serves for evaluation.

We randomly sample $m = 5$ runs from *all* those submitted to a track and that contain at least 100 documents as results for each query. The $n = 100$ highest ranked documents for a query in a run serve as one of the 5 lists L_i to be fused[8]. We repeat this runs-sampling process 20 times and report the average prediction quality of each predictor over the samples. Statistically significant differences of prediction quality are determined using the two-tailed paired t-test computed at a 95% confidence level with respect to the 20 samples.

To measure prediction quality, we follow common practice [5]. That is, we compute Pearson's correlation between the values assigned by a predictor to the queries in a track, and the true average precision (AP at cutoff 100) values for these queries — determined using TREC's relevance judgments — attained by the fusion method at hand.

Fusion methods. Fusion methods that utilize retrieval scores require inter-list score compatibility. Therefore, we normalize the retrieval score of a document in a list with respect to the sum of all scores in the list. As before, we use $s(d;L_i)$ to denote the resultant normalized retrieval score of document d in L_i; if $d \notin L_i$, we set $s(d;L_i) \stackrel{def}{=} 0$. In what follows, $F_x(d)$ denotes the score assigned to d by a fusion method x.

The **CombSUM** linear fusion method [14] scores d by the sum of its retrieval scores: $F_{CombSUM}(d) \stackrel{def}{=} \sum_{L_i} s(d;L_i)$. **CombMNZ** [14, 22], which is a non-linear fusion method, further rewards documents that appear in many lists: $F_{CombMNZ}(d) \stackrel{def}{=} \#\{L_i : d \in L_i\}F_{CombSUM}(d)$.

The **Borda** method [38], in contrast to CombSUM and CombMNZ, considers only rank information. Specifically, d is scored by the number of documents not ranked higher than it in the lists. Formally, if $d \in L$, we use $r(d;L)$ to denote d's rank in L. (The rank of the top most document is 1.) Then, d's Borda score is: $F_{Borda}(d) \stackrel{def}{=} \sum_{L_i:d\in L_i} \#\{d' \in L_i : r(d';L_i) > r(d;L_i)\}$. The **RRF** fusion method [6], which was shown to be effective, also relies only on ranks: $F_{RRF}(d) \stackrel{def}{=} \sum_{L_i:d\in L_i} \frac{1}{\nu + r(d;L_i)}$, where $\nu = 60$ [6].

Base predictors, free parameters, and reference comparisons. We follow previous recommendations with regard to effective free-parameter settings for the Clarity predictor [30]. Specifically, for all predictors that use the rClarity and sClarity measures, we set k, the cutoff at which the relevance model is computed, to $n = 100$, the number of documents in the list; the language models of documents from which the relevance model is constructed are not smoothed; and, the number of terms used is 100. For predictors that use the WIG and NQC measures, k, the number of most highly ranked documents considered by these measures, is set to a value in $\{5, 10, 25, 50, 100\}$.[9]

The interpolation parameter λ (see Equation 3) is set to a value in $\{0, 0.1, \ldots, 1\}$. The cutoff parameter c used for computing inter-list similarity with the KL approach is set to 20 following previous recommendations [3].

For predictors — both those proposed here and the reference comparisons — that incorporate free parameters, i.e., k and/or λ, we first set the free parameters to values optimizing prediction quality over the query set for a track. Thus, we start by using all prediction methods with their free parameters set to (generally) effective values. This practice enables to study the influence on prediction quality of various aspects (e.g., the inter-list similarity measure used, and the approach employed for aggregating prediction values) when the effect of free-parameter values is ameliorated. Then, in

[7]As is the case for WIG, the original NQC measure normalizes retrieval scores with respect to that of the corpus [31]. In contrast, here we cannot use corpus-based normalization of retrieval scores, but the scores in the lists L_i are sum normalized.

[8]We use 100 rather than 1000 documents as results for each query, as fusion methods are most effective when the number of documents in the lists that are fused is relatively small [34]. We use the 100 documents most highly ranked by the fusion method for the final result list L_{res}.

[9]NQC's prediction of the effectiveness of a *TREC run* is better when retrieval scores are not normalized, while that of WIG is better when retrieval scores are normalized [31]. However, as some of the fusion methods employed require score normalization, retrieval scores in the runs are always normalized as described above.

	TREC3		TREC8		TREC9		TREC10		TREC12	
	MAP	σ(AP)	MAP	σ(AP)	MAP	σ(AP)	MAP	σ(AP)	MAP	σ(AP)
CombSUM	.195	.153	.244	.218	.176	.165	.175	.151	.242	.217
CombMNZ	.196	.153	.241	.214	.182	.175	.175	.149	.239	.215
Borda	.189	.152	.235	.211	.188	.182	.180	.156	.243	.218
RRF	.197	.155	.238	.212	.189	.182	.182	.155	.243	.218
Best Run	.209	.165	.252	.223	.192	.189	.164	.142	.240	.221
Worst Run	.068	.078	.100	.126	.066	.091	.093	.116	.140	.169

Table 1: Retrieval performance of the fusion methods: the mean of AP (MAP) values, and their standard deviation (σ(AP)), computed over the queries in a track. The best and worst runs are selected from the 5 that are fused according to MAP. Numbers represent averages over the 20 samples of 5 runs.

Section 4.2.5 we perform an in-depth study of the effect of free-parameter values on prediction quality. In Section 4.2.6 we present the prediction quality of our methods, and that of the reference comparisons, when free-parameter values are set using a train set of queries.

The Direct predictors, which manifest the common practice of applying post-retrieval predictors upon the final result list, serve as our reference comparisons. This comparison sheds light on whether integrating prediction employed upon the lists that are fused with prediction performed upon the final result list — the underlying idea of our approach — can improve over using only the latter.

Analysis of retrieval performance. As noted in Section 1, the main factor driving the development of query-performance prediction methods is the significant variability of retrieval performance across queries [35, 15]. We now turn to study this variability for the fusion methods. In comparison, we present the variability for the best and worst (MAP) performing runs among the 5 fused. Specifically, we report the MAP, which is the mean of the average precision (AP) values attained for the queries, and, their standard deviation. The numbers are reported in Table 1 and represent averages over the 20 samples of 5 runs.

We see that in most cases, both the MAP and the standard deviation of AP posted by the fusion methods are somewhat lower than those posted by the best-performing run. Yet, they are much higher than those posted by the worst-performing run, which can be quite ineffective as suggested by its MAP. Furthermore, the standard deviation of AP for the fusion methods, as well as for the best run, is very high. These results show that fusion methods, as other retrieval approaches, post performance that can substantially vary across queries.

In the evaluation presented below we focus on predicting the query-performance of CombMNZ. CombMNZ is a standard baseline in many reports on fusion approaches [22, 23, 1, 26, 24, 29]. In Section 4.2.4 we study the effectiveness of our predictors for the other fusion methods.

4.2 Experimental results

4.2.1 Main result

Our first order of business is studying the general effectiveness of our prediction framework; specifically, that of the two main prediction methods, AMean and GMean. To that end, and unless otherwise specified, we use the KL inter-list similarity measure, as it will be shown in Section 4.2.2 to outperform the Cosine measure. As noted above, we focus on predicting the query-performance of the CombMNZ fusion method. Table 2 presents our main result. The numbers

$\mathcal{P}_{base}$	Predictor	TREC3	TREC8	TREC9	TREC10	TREC12
WIG	Direct	.586	.642	.385	.444	.570
	AMean	**.664**^{d}	.687	<u>**.465**</u>^{d}	<u>**.501**</u>^{d}	<u>**.634**</u>^{d}
	GMean	.659^d	<u>**.711**</u>^{d}	.446^d	.485^d	.626^d
NQC	Direct	.549	.630	.352	.446	.555
	AMean	.684^d	.630	.364^d	.446	.570
	GMean	<u>**.685**</u>^{d}	**.673**^{d}	**.416**^{d}	**.446**	**.582**^{d}
sClarity	Direct	.484	.423	.089	.054	.385
	AMean	**.586**^{d}	**.614**^{d}	**.290**^{d}	**.316**^{d}	**.543**^{d}
	GMean	.576^d	.595^d	.211^d	.251^d	.518^d
rClarity	Direct	.479	.357	.072	.027	.332
	AMean	**.608**^{d}	**.602**^{d}	**.287**^{d}	**.326**^{d}	**.541**^{d}
	GMean	.594^d	.578^d	.211^d	.256^d	.506^d

Table 2: Main result table. The prediction quality of the AMean and GMean methods. Prediction quality, here and after, is measured by Pearson correlation with the ground-truth retrieval performance. (Refer to Section 4.1 for details.) CombMNZ serves for the fusion method, and the KL inter-list similarity measure is used. The best result per track and a base predictor is boldfaced. Underline marks the best result for a track; 'd' marks a statistically significant difference with Direct.

in Table 2, and those in all the following tables and graphs, represent prediction quality measured using Pearson's correlation. (Refer back to Section 4.1 for details.)

We first observe in Table 2 that when using the base predictors alone upon the final result list (Direct), WIG is the best-performing method. NQC outperforms both variants of Clarity, which can be quite ineffective for the Web tracks (TREC9 and TREC10). Yet, even in these cases, using the Clarity measures in our AMean and GMean methods can yield relatively effective prediction. Recall that, originally, WIG [40] and NQC [31] were devised for retrieval methods utilizing surface-level document-query similarities. Here we see that their adapted variants, which were discussed in Section 3.4, yield relatively high prediction quality when employed upon the final result list (Direct) that is the result of fusion. This finding is novel to this study.

Perhaps the most important observation based on Table 2 is that the AMean and GMean predictors outperform the Direct predictor in a vast majority of the relevant comparisons (base predictor × track); most of the improvements are substantial and statistically significant. This finding attests to the merits of the underlying idea of our prediction framework — integrating prediction based on the final result list (Direct) with that based on the intermediate lists that are fused to create it. In comparing AMean and GMean we see that the former is more effective than the latter when using

$\mathcal{P}_{base}$	Predictor	TREC3	TREC8	TREC9	TREC10	TREC12
WIG	Direct	.586	.642	.385	.444	.570
	UniAMean	$\mathbf{.711}^d$	.642	$.396^d$	.452	$.582^d$
	AMean (KL)	$.664^d_u$	**.687**	$\underline{\mathbf{.465}}^d_u$	$\underline{\mathbf{.501}}^d_u$	$\underline{\mathbf{.634}}^d_u$
	AMean (Cos)	$.655^d_u$	$.682^d_u$	.389	.448	$.580^d$
	UniGMean	$\underline{\mathbf{.717}}^d$	$.681^d$	$.423^d$	$.460^d$	$.592^d$
	GMean (KL)	$.659^d_u$	$\underline{\mathbf{.711}}^d$	$\mathbf{.446}^d_u$	$\mathbf{.485}^d_u$	$\mathbf{.626}^d_u$
	GMean (Cos)	$.594_u$	$.666^d$	$.414^d$	.451	$.574_u$
NQC	Direct	.549	.630	.352	.446	.555
	UniAMean	$.655^d$	.630	.356	.446	.560
	AMean (KL)	$.684^d_u$	.630	$\mathbf{.364}^d_u$	**.451**	**.570**
	AMean (Cos)	$\mathbf{.711}^d_u$	**.645**	.352	.446	.561
	UniGMean	$\mathbf{.695}^d$	$.666^d$	$.402^d$	**.453**	$\mathbf{.583}^d$
	GMean (KL)	$.685^d$	$.673^d$	$\mathbf{.416}^d$	.446	$.582^d$
	GMean (Cos)	$.667^d_u$	$\mathbf{.678}^d$	$.391^d$	.446	$.571^d_u$

Table 3: Prediction quality of using the various inter-list similarity measures. ('Cos' stands for 'Cosine'.) The best result per track in a AMean/GMean block is boldfaced; the best result per track is underlined. 'd' and 'u' mark statistically significant differences with Direct and with using a uniform similarity measure (the Uni predictors), respectively. CombMNZ is the fusion method.

WIG and Clarity for base predictors, while the reverse holds when using NQC.

Using the base predictors in AMean and GMean yields relative prediction-quality patterns similar to those of using these alone upon the final result list (Direct); that is, WIG (almost always) outperforms NQC which outperforms both Clarity variants. Hence, in the evaluation below we mainly focus on using WIG and NQC for base predictors. Indeed, the best prediction quality for a track in Table 2 is always attained by either a WIG-based or a NQC-based predictor. Specifically, using WIG in AMean yields the best prediction quality for 3 out of the 5 tracks.

4.2.2 *Inter-list similarity measures*

We next compare the prediction quality of using the KL, Cosine, and uniform inter-list similarity measures. Table 3 reports the prediction quality numbers.

We can see in Table 3 that in most relevant comparisons (base predictor × track × AMean/GMean) the KL measure yields prediction quality that is better than that of using the Cosine and uniform measures. (The main exception is the comparison with UniGMean for NQC.) Furthermore, KL yields more statistically significant improvements over Direct. The superiority of KL over the uniform measure, which is in quite a few cases (specifically, for WIG) statistically significant, attests to the merits of differentially weighting the prediction values for the lists that are fused based on their similarity to the final result list.

We also see in Table 3 that using WIG in AMean, with the KL measure, yields prediction quality that is, in general, highly effective with respect to that of the other predictors; specifically, the prediction quality is the best for 3 out of the 5 tracks as was the case in Table 2.

The Cosine measure is often less effective than the uniform measure; yet, both yield prediction quality that transcends that of Direct in almost all cases; sometimes, the improvements are statistically significant. All in all, these findings demonstrate the effectiveness of our framework when applied with different inter-list similarity measures.

$\mathcal{P}_{base}$	Predictor	TREC3	TREC8	TREC9	TREC10	TREC12
WIG	Direct	.586	.642	.385	.444	.570
	UniAMean	$.711^d$	.642	$.396^d$	.452	$.582^d$
	UniGMean	$\underline{\mathbf{.717}}^d$	$\underline{\mathbf{.681}}^d$	$\underline{\mathbf{.423}}^d$	$\underline{\mathbf{.460}}^d$	$\underline{\mathbf{.592}}^d$
	UniMin	$.590^d$	.642	.390	.446	.571
	UniMax	$.610^d$	.652	.385	.445	.580
NQC	Direct	.549	.630	.352	.446	.555
	UniAMean	$.655^d$	.630	.356	.446	.560
	UniGMean	$\mathbf{.695}^d$	$\mathbf{.666}^d$	$\mathbf{.402}^d$	.453	$\mathbf{.583}^d$
	UniMin	$.612^d$	.643	.391	**.455**	.559
	UniMax	$.584^d$	.630	.352	.446	.555

Table 4: Using the minimal and maximal prediction values (UniMin and UniMax) vs. using the mean of all prediction values (UniGMean and UniAMean). Boldface: the best result per track in a block of a base predictor. Underline: the best result per track. 'd' marks a statistically significant difference with Direct. CombMNZ serves for the fusion method.

4.2.3 *Comparing prediction-aggregation methods*

Insofar, we focused on two approaches for aggregating the prediction values assigned to the lists that are fused and to the final result list; i.e., those based on the arithmetic (AMean) and geometric (GMean) mean. We now compare these with the methods that integrate the prediction value assigned to the final result list with the minimal and maximal prediction values for the lists that are fused (UniMin and UniMax, respectively). As UniMin and UniMax utilize the uniform similarity measure, we use UniAMean and UniGMean for the comparison.

We see in Table 4 that UniMin and UniMax outperform the Direct predictor in several cases. However, these predictors are almost always outperformed — often, quite substantially — by AMean and GMean. This exemplifies the benefit in utilizing the mean prediction value for the lists that are fused with respect to using the minimal and maximal prediction values.

4.2.4 *Prediction for additional fusion methods*

The evaluation presented thus far focused on predicting query performance for the CombMNZ fusion method. In Table 5 we present the prediction quality of our AMean and GMean predictors for the CombSUM, Borda, and RRF fusion methods in addition to CombMNZ. (Refer back to Section 4.1 for details.) WIG and NQC serve as the base predictors and KL serves as the inter-list similarity measure.

Table 5 shows that AMean and GMean outperform the Direct predictors in most relevant comparisons (base predictor × track × fusion method); specifically, across fusion methods. The best prediction quality (boldfaced numbers) attained for Borda and RRF, which use rank information for fusion, is almost always higher than that obtained for CombSUM and CombMNZ, which utilize retrieval scores.

Thus, we see that our prediction approach is effective for different fusion methods whether they are based on retrieval scores (CombSUM and CombMNZ) or ranks (Borda and RRF) and whether they are linear (CombSUM, Borda and RRF) or not (CombMNZ). Furthermore, we see that the conceptual connection between our prediction approach and linear fusion methods, which was discussed in Section 3.5, does not necessarily imply that prediction quality is better for linear fusion methods. For example, the best prediction

$\mathcal{P}_{base}$	Predictor	TREC3 CombMNZ	TREC3 CombSUM	TREC3 Borda	TREC3 RRF	TREC8 CombMNZ	TREC8 CombSUM	TREC8 Borda	TREC8 RRF	TREC9 CombMNZ	TREC9 CombSUM	TREC9 Borda	TREC9 RRF
WIG	Direct	.586	.613	.582	.570	.642	.638	.564	.560	.385	.403	.414	.420
	AMean	**.664**^{d}	**.665**^{d}	**.656**^{d}	**.662**^{d}	.687	.682	.689^d	.687^d	**.465**^{d}	**.481**^{d}	.461^d	.466^d
	GMean	.659^d	**.665**^{d}	.652^d	.657^d	**.711**^{d}	**.707**^{d}	**.716**^{d}	**.714**^{d}	.446^d	.469^d	**.489**^{d}	**.493**^{d}
NQC	Direct	.549	.597	.584	.544	.630	.594	.596	.588	.352	.309	.418	.421
	AMean	.684^d	.681^d	.682^d	.687^d	.630	.594	.601	.612	.364^d	.310	.420^d	.421
	GMean	**.685**^{d}	**.695**^{d}	**.702**^{d}	**.698**^{d}	**.673**^{d}	**.634**	**.695**^{d}	**.688**^{d}	**.416**^{d}	**.405**^{d}	**.471**^{d}	**.477**^{d}

$\mathcal{P}_{base}$	Predictor	TREC10 CombMNZ	TREC10 CombSUM	TREC10 Borda	TREC10 RRF	TREC12 CombMNZ	TREC12 CombSUM	TREC12 Borda	TREC12 RRF
WIG	Direct	.444	.436	.459	.449	.570	.599	.523	.525
	AMean	**.501**^{d}	**.504**^{d}	**.516**^{d}	**.509**^{d}	**.634**^{d}	**.636**^{d}	.633^d	.637^d
	GMean	.485^d	.478^d	.502^d	.494^d	.626^d	.623^d	**.639**^{d}	**.640**^{d}
NQC	Direct	.446	.394	.470	**.466**	.555	.567	.530	.527
	AMean	**.451**	.394	.472^d	**.466**	.570	.567	.563^d	.592^d
	GMean	.446	**.396**	**.480**	**.466**	**.582**^{d}	**.574**	**.643**^{d}	**.627**^{d}

Table 5: Predicting the query-performance of additional fusion methods (CombSUM, Borda and RRF). The best result per track, base predictor, and a fusion method, is boldfaced; 'd' marks a statistically significant difference with the Direct predictor; KL serves for the inter-list similarity measure.

quality attained when using NQC in AMean is always higher for CombMNZ than for CombSUM.

4.2.5 *Effect of free-parameter values*

The AMean and GMean prediction methods incorporate two free parameters: k, the number of highest ranked documents in a list — both for the lists used for fusion and for the final result list — that are considered by the base predictor employed; and, λ, which controls the balance between using prediction based on the final result list and that based on the lists that are fused.

Insofar, k and λ were set to values that yield optimal prediction quality for a predictor for a track's query set. (For the Direct predictors, k was set to optimize prediction quality.) In Figure 1 we present the effect on prediction quality of varying their values when WIG and NQC serve for the base predictors and KL is used for the inter-similarity measure. While CombMNZ serves for the fusion method, we note that the patterns presented are the same for the other fusion methods. When studying the effect of varying the value of k we set λ to its optimal value and vice versa.

The effect of k. We see in Figure 1 that the prediction quality of using WIG as a base predictor is relatively stable when varying the value of k.[10] Optimal prediction quality is obtained when k is set to a relatively small value. The latter observation is in accordance with findings about using WIG to predict the effectiveness of a single retrieved list [40]. The prediction quality of using NQC monotonically rises with increasing values of k, until optimal prediction quality is attained for $k = 100$. This finding is in line with those about using NQC to predict the effectiveness of a single retrieved list [31]. Finally, we observe that the effect of varying the value of k is quite consistent across tracks and between using AMean and GMean.

The effect of λ. Recall from Equation 3 that $\lambda = 0$ amounts to relying only on the prediction employed upon the final result list; and, increasing the value of λ results in more weight put on the predicted effectiveness of the lists that are fused.

When using WIG as the base predictor, whether in AMean or in GMean, the optimal prediction quality is almost always attained for $\lambda = 1$; i.e., not using the prediction performed upon the final result list, and relying only on the predicted effectiveness of the lists fused to create it. This is a striking observation as the goal of prediction is the effectiveness of the final result list. Thus, this finding re-echoes the importance of using prediction performed upon the lists that are fused so as to predict the effectiveness of the final result list — a key principle in our framework.

When using NQC as the base predictor, we see that the prediction quality patterns change between AMean and GMean. For AMean the patterns are not consistent across tracks, while for GMean the optimal prediction quality is often attained for $\lambda \in \{0.1, 0.2\}$. Thus, automatically setting λ's value for a prediction method and a query (and/or a corpus) is an important future venue to explore.

Finally, we see that the prediction quality for the Web tracks (TREC9 and TREC10) is consistently lower than that for the tracks using newswire corpora (TREC3, TREC8, and TREC12). This finding echoes those in previous reports about the query-performance prediction task for a single retrieved list being highly challenging for the WT10g corpus and its accompanying queries [17]. This corpus and queries were the ones used in TREC9 and TREC10.

4.2.6 *Learning free-parameter values*

As already noted, the free parameters (k and/or λ) of all predictors (ours and the reference comparisons) were set at the above to values that yield optimal prediction quality per track's query set. This practice enabled to study the impact of various aspects of prediction (e.g., the inter-list similarity measure, the aggregation method for prediction values, the fusion method used for retrieval) while ameliorating effects of free-parameter values. In Section 4.2.5 we explored the effects of the free-parameter values on prediction quality.

Our goal now is studying the prediction quality when free-parameter values are set using a held-out query set. We randomly split the queries for a track into two equal-sized folds, train and test. Then, the values of the free param-

[10]This also holds when k approaches 100, the number of documents in a list. For $k = 100$, WIG's prediction value for each of the 5 lists that are fused is $\frac{1}{100}$ (see Equation 9). In this case, prediction is based on that performed upon L_{res}, and on L_{res}'s similarity with the 5 lists.

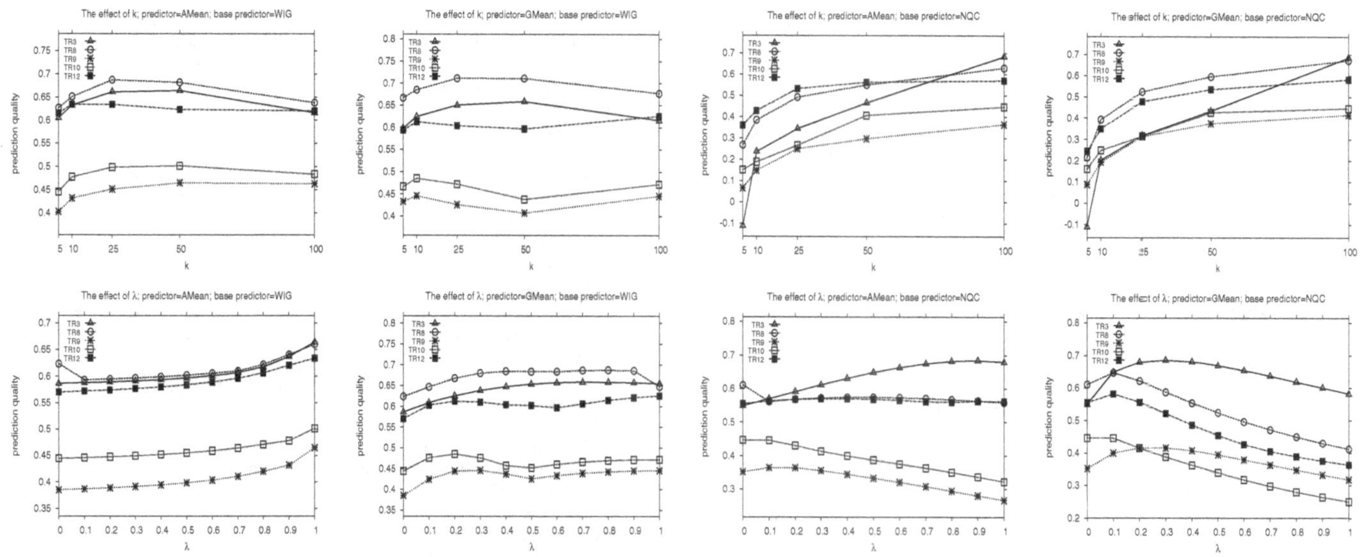

Figure 1: The effect on the prediction quality of AMean and GMean of varying the values of k (first row) and λ (second row); $\lambda = 0$ amounts to the Direct predictor that uses the base predictor only upon the final result list; WIG (two leftmost figures) and NQC (two rightmost figures) are used for base predictors. The KL inter-similarity measure is used in all cases. CombMNZ is the fusion method. 'TR' stands for TREC.

$\mathcal{P}_{base}$	Predictor	TREC3	TREC8	TREC9	TREC10	TREC12
WIG	Direct	.603 (.108)	.661 (.096)	.388 (.104)	.444 (.113)	.640 (.072)
	AMean	**.613** (.092)	<u>**.685**</u> (.089)	**.453**^{d} (.111)	**.478** (.117)	<u>**.643**</u> (.061)
	GMean	.604 (.100)	.662 (.101)	.442^d (.120)	.470 (.125)	.630 (.073)
NQC	Direct	.057 (.237)	.592 (.129)	.211 (.140)	.299 (.152)	.500 (.107)
	AMean	<u>**.656**</u>^{d} (.118)	**.636** (.124)	.303^d (.140)	.415 (.137)	**.601**^{d} (.078)
	GMean	.624^d (.145)	.613 (.140)	**.341**^{d} (.164)	**.431**^{d} (.139)	.600^d (.080)
sClarity	Direct	.400 (.102)	.526 (.132)	**.320** (.168)	.074 (.140)	.494 (.087)
	AMean	**.565**^{d} (.095)	**.598**^{d} (.095)	.285 (.132)	**.293**^{d} (.117)	**.560**^{d} (.077)
	GMean	.541^d (.121)	.571^d (.112)	.214^d (.158)	.219^d (.131)	.528^d (.090)
rClarity	Direct	.387 (.106)	.494 (.127)	**.308** (.165)	.054 (.139)	.415 (.085)
	AMean	**.588**^{d} (.097)	**.595**^{d} (.093)	.276^d (.131)	**.302**^{d} (.118)	**.559**^{d} (.077)
	GMean	.562^d (.119)	.559^d (.112)	.209^d (.153)	.217^d (.124)	.513^d (.089)

Table 6: Prediction quality when using a train query set for setting the values of free parameters of the predictors. Numbers in parentheses indicate the standard deviation of prediction quality over the 30 test sets of queries. CombMNZ serves for the fusion method, and KL serves for the inter-list similarity measure. Boldface marks the best result for a track and a base predictor. The best result in a column is underlined. Statistically significant differences with Direct are marked with 'd'.

eters that yield optimized prediction quality over the train fold are used for all queries in the test fold. We repeat this procedure 30 times, to avoid irregularities rising from a single random split, and report for each predictor its average prediction quality and its standard deviation over the 30 test folds. (Recall that the evaluation of prediction quality for any query set is based on 20 random samples of 5 runs.) The prediction quality numbers are presented in Table 6 when using the CombMNZ fusion method and the KL inter-list similarity measure. Note that the reported numbers are not necessarily comparable to those presented above. A case in point, the evaluation here is based on average prediction quality for 30 samples of half of the queries in the track, while that above was based on all queries per track.

We see in Table 6 that in a vast majority of the relevant comparisons (4 base predictors × 5 tracks), our AMean and GMean predictors outperform the Direct predictor. Furthermore, the prediction quality of AMean and GMean is statistically significantly better than that of Direct in 12 and 13 relevant comparisons, respectively, out of the entire 20. These findings, again, attest to the importance of integrating prediction performed upon the lists that are fused with prediction performed upon the final result list (Direct) — the core principle of our prediction framework.

A specific interesting observation is with regard to using NQC over TREC3, and sClarity and rClarity over TREC10. In these cases, the prediction quality of Direct, which is based only on the final result list, is extremely low. This is in part due to the fact that effective free-parameter values do not necessarily generalize across queries in this case. Yet, the prediction quality of using the base predictors in our AMean and GMean predictors can be quite higher, and to a statistically significant degree.

Another observation that we make based on Table 6 is that the standard deviation of the prediction quality of the AMean predictors is almost always lower than that of Direct. We note that while AMean and GMean incorporate two free parameters (k and λ), Direct incorporates only one (*k*). The standard deviation for GMean is in most relevant comparisons higher than that for AMean, yet in quite a few relevant comparisons it is still lower than that of Direct. These findings attest to the improved robustness of the prediction quality of our framework, as measured over different query sets, with respect to that of the Direct predictors.

All in all, we see that our prediction framework is effective and quite robust with respect to the Direct predictors when setting free-parameter values using a train query set.

5. CONCLUSIONS AND FUTURE WORK

We addressed the query-performance prediction task for retrieval methods that are based on fusion of retrieved lists. Specifically, we presented a novel prediction framework that integrates prediction performed upon the final result list with that performed upon the lists that are fused to create it; inter-list similarity measures control the integration. The framework is generic in that it does not assume knowledge of the methods used to retrieve the lists that are fused, nor of the fusion method employed. Empirical evaluation demonstrated the merits of our approach.

We plan to explore whether the framework can be improved by exploiting knowledge of the fusion method employed. Furthermore, we intend to study whether the framework can be used for effective *meta fusion*; i.e., fusing result lists produced by different fusion methods based on the lists' predicted effectiveness.

Acknowledgments We thank the reviewers for their helpful comments. This paper is based upon work supported in part by the Israel Science Foundation under grant no. 557/09, by IBM's Ph.D. fellowship and SUR award, and by Google's and Yahoo!'s faculty research awards. Any opinions, findings and conclusions or recommendations expressed in this material are the authors' and do not necessarily reflect those of the sponsors.

6. REFERENCES

[1] J. A. Aslam and M. Montague. Models for metasearch. In *Proceedings of SIGIR*, pages 276–284, 2001.

[2] J. A. Aslam and M. H. Montague. Metasearch consistency. In *Proceedings of SIGIR*, pages 386–387, 2001.

[3] J. A. Aslam and V. Pavlu. Query hardness estimation using Jensen-Shannon divergence among multiple scoring functions. In *Proceedings of ECIR*, pages 198–209, 2007.

[4] N. Balasubramanian and J. Allan. Learning to select rankers. In *Proceedings of SIGIR*, pages 855–856, 2010.

[5] D. Carmel and E. Yom-Tov. *Estimating the Query Difficulty for Information Retrieval.* Synthesis Lectures on Information Concepts, Retrieval, and Services. Morgan & Claypool Publishers, 2010.

[6] G. V. Cormack, C. L. A. Clarke, and S. Büttcher. Reciprocal rank fusion outperforms condorcet and individual rank learning methods. In *Proceedings of SIGIR*, pages 758–759, 2009.

[7] W. B. Croft, editor. *Advances in Information Retrieval: Recent Research from the Center for Intelligent Information Retrieval.* Number 7 in The Kluwer International Series on Information Retrieval. Kluwer, 2000.

[8] W. B. Croft. Combining approaches to information retrieval. In Croft [7], chapter 1, pages 1–36.

[9] S. Cronen-Townsend, Y. Zhou, and W. B. Croft. Predicting query performance. In *Proceedings of SIGIR*, pages 299–306, 2002.

[10] S. Cronen-Townsend, Y. Zhou, and W. B. Croft. A language modeling framework for selective query expansion. Technical Report IR-338, Center for Intelligent Information Retrieval, University of Massachusetts, 2004.

[11] R. Cummins. Predicting query performance directly from score distributions. In *Proceedings of AIRS*, pages 315–326, 2011.

[12] R. Cummins, J. M. Jose, and C. O'Riordan. Improved query performance prediction using standard deviation. In *Proceedings of SIGIR*, pages 1089–1090, 2011.

[13] F. Diaz. Performance prediction using spatial autocorrelation. In *Proceedings of SIGIR*, pages 583–590, 2007.

[14] E. A. Fox and J. A. Shaw. Combination of multiple searches. In *Proceedings of TREC-2*, 1994.

[15] D. Harman and C. Buckley. The NRRC reliable information access (RIA) workshop. In *Proceedings of SIGIR*, pages 528–529, 2004.

[16] C. Hauff, D. Hiemstra, and F. de Jong. A survey of pre-retrieval query performance predictors. In *Proceedings of CIKM*, pages 1419–1420, 2008.

[17] C. Hauff, V. Murdock, and R. Baeza-Yates. Improved query difficulty prediction for the web. In *Proceedings of CIKM*, pages 439–448, 2008.

[18] B. He and I. Ounis. Inferring query performance using pre-retrieval predictors. In *Proceedings of SPIRE*, pages 43–54, 2004.

[19] O. Kurland and L. Lee. Corpus structure, language models, and ad hoc information retrieval. In *Proceedings of SIGIR*, pages 194–201, 2004.

[20] O. Kurland, A. Shtok, D. Carmel, and S. Hummel. A unified framework for post-retrieval query-performance prediction. In *Proceedings of ICTIR*, pages 15–26, 2011.

[21] O. Kurland, A. Shtok, S. Hummel, F. Raiber, D. Carmel, and O. Rom. Back to the roots: A probabilistic framework for query-performance prediction. In *Proceedings of CIKM*, 2012.

[22] J. H. Lee. Combining multiple evidence from different properties of weighting schemes. In *Proceedings of SIGIR*, pages 180–188, 1995.

[23] J. H. Lee. Analyses of multiple evidence combination. In *Proceedings of SIGIR*, pages 267–276, 1997.

[24] D. Lillis, F. Toolan, R. W. Collier, and J. Dunnion. Probfuse: a probabilistic approach to data fusion. In *Proceedings of SIGIR*, pages 139–146, 2006.

[25] D. Metzler and W. B. Croft. A Markov random field model for term dependencies. In *Proceedings of SIGIR*, pages 472–479, 2005.

[26] M. Montague and J. A. Aslam. Condorcet fusion for improved retrieval. In *Proceedings of CIKM*, pages 538–548, 2002.

[27] J. Pérez-Iglesias and L. Araujo. Standard deviation as a query hardness estimator. In *Proceedings of SPIRE*, pages 207–212, 2010.

[28] D. Sheldon, M. Shokouhi, M. Szummer, and N. Craswell. Lambdamerge: merging the results of query reformulations. In *Proceedings of WSDM*, pages 795–804, 2011.

[29] M. Shokouhi. Segmentation of search engine results for effective data-fusion. In *Proceedings of ECIR*, pages 185–197, 2007.

[30] A. Shtok, O. Kurland, and D. Carmel. Using statistical decision theory and relevance models for query-performance prediction. In *Proccedings of SIGIR*, pages 259–266, 2010.

[31] A. Shtok, O. Kurland, D. Carmel, F. Raiber, and G. Markovits. Predicting query performance by query-drift estimation. *ACM Transactions on Information Systems*, 30(2):11, 2012.

[32] I. Soboroff, C. K. Nicholas, and P. Cahan. Ranking retrieval systems without relevance judgments. In *Proceedings of SIGIR*, pages 66–73, 2001.

[33] V. Vinay, I. J. Cox, N. Milic-Frayling, and K. R. Wood. On ranking the effectiveness of searches. In *Proceedings of SIGIR*, pages 398–404, 2006.

[34] C. C. Vogt and G. W. Cottrell. Fusion via linear combination of scores. *Information Retrieval*, 1(3):151–173, 1999.

[35] E. M. Voorhees. Overview of the TREC 2004 Robust Retrieval Track. In *Proceedings of TREC-13*, 2004.

[36] E. M. Voorhees. The TREC 2005 robust track. *SIGIR Forum*, 40(1):41–48, 2006.

[37] E. Yom-Tov, S. Fine, D. Carmel, and A. Darlow. Learning to estimate query difficulty: including applications to missing content detection and distributed information retrieval. In *Proceedings of SIGIR*, pages 512–519, 2005.

[38] H. P. Young. An axiomatization of Borda's rule. *Journal of Economic Theory*, 9:43–52, 1974.

[39] Y. Zhou and W. B. Croft. Ranking robustness: a novel framework to predict query performance. In *Proceedgins of CIKM*, pages 567–574, 2006.

[40] Y. Zhou and W. B. Croft. Query performance prediction in web search environments. In *Proceedings of SIGIR*, pages 543–550, 2007.

Back to the Roots: A Probabilistic Framework for Query-Performance Prediction

Oren Kurland[1]
kurland@ie.technion.ac.il

Anna Shtok[1]
annabel@tx.technion.ac.il

Shay Hummel[1]
hummels@tx.technion.ac.il

Fiana Raiber[1]
fiana@tx.technion.ac.il

David Carmel[2]
carmel@il.ibm.com

Ofri Rom[1]
ofri.rom@gmail.com

1. Faculty of Industrial Engineering and Management, Technion, Haifa 32000, Israel
2. IBM Research Lab, Haifa 31905, Israel

ABSTRACT

The query-performance prediction task is estimating the effectiveness of a search performed in response to a query when no relevance judgments are available. Although there exist many effective prediction methods, these differ substantially in their basic principles, and rely on diverse hypotheses about the characteristics of effective retrieval. We present a novel fundamental probabilistic prediction framework. Using the framework, we derive and explain various previously proposed prediction methods that might seem completely different, but turn out to share the same *formal* basis. The derivations provide new perspectives on several predictors (e.g., Clarity). The framework is also used to devise new prediction approaches that outperform the state-of-the-art.

Categories and Subject Descriptors: H.3.3 [Information Search and Retrieval]: Retrieval models

Keywords: query-performance prediction

1. INTRODUCTION

The query-performance prediction task has attracted a lot of research attention [4]. The goal of this task is to estimate the effectiveness of a search performed in response to a query when there is a lack of relevance judgments. The prediction can be performed before retrieval using the query and corpus-based information [19, 16]. Post-retrieval prediction, on the other hand, also uses information induced from the result list of the most highly ranked documents [4].

Although there exists abundance of effective prediction methods, these often rely on substantially different principles. More specifically, various predictors are based on completely different hypotheses with respect to what results in effective retrieval. For example, some post-retrieval prediction methods rely on the premise that a result list that exhibits high *clarity* with respect to the corpus indicates effective retrieval [10, 1, 11, 5, 18]. Other prediction methods assume that effective retrieval should be manifested in a result list that is robust with respect to query perturbations [37, 42], document perturbations [36, 41], and retrieval method perturbations [2]. Another class of prediction methods is based on various analyses of retrieval scores in the result list [35, 14, 42, 30, 12, 13].

Given the large variety of prediction approaches, and the underlying hypotheses on which they are based, a few questions arise. The most fundamental one is whether there is a unified formal basis (framework) that can help explain various prediction methods and techniques. A related, albeit more specific, question is "what formal aspects of prediction are shared by seemingly different prediction approaches?". The operational question that naturally emerges is whether a formal analysis of the prediction task can give rise to new (effective) prediction approaches.

To address the questions stated here, we present a novel query-performance prediction framework that is based on fundamental probabilistic IR principles. We establish the framework by starting with a basic question that has not been explicitly addressed in previous work on prediction: "What is the probability that *this* result list is relevant to *this* query?". This question is a generalization to the document-list case of the core question of probabilistic retrieval [33, 22, 27]: "What is the probability that *this* document is relevant to *this* query?".

The framework we present sets the first *formal* grounds for integrating pre-retrieval and post-retrieval prediction methods. We show that these two paradigms target different, yet complementary, *formal* aspects of prediction. Empirical evaluation demonstrates the merits of their integration.

We use the framework to explain and derive various post-retrieval predictors that might seem at first glance to rely on completely different hypotheses and use different principles. For example, we derive (explain) the *Clarity* predictor [10]. This derivation provides a novel perspective about the actual property of the result list that Clarity quantifies. Furthermore, we use the framework to show that some predictors that are based on the result-list robustness notion [37, 36, 41, 42] and on analysis of the retrieval-scores distribution [14], implicitly share the same formal basis for prediction.

Our framework also provides a formal ground to using, for prediction, measures of query-independent properties of the result list (e.g., cohesion and dispersion); and, to integrating

CIKM'12, October 29–November 2, 2012, Maui, HI, USA.

these with query-dependent measures that are the focus of most previously proposed predictors.

The proposed framework not only provides new insight into existing predictors, it also gives rise to novel prediction approaches. Some of these outperform state-of-the-art methods, as shown by experiments conducted with a large variety of TREC corpora (including ClueWeb).

To summarize, our main contributions are twofold. The first, and perhaps most important, is on the formal side. The prediction framework that we present sets unifying formal grounds for a variety of prediction methods that might seem to be completely different. The formal analysis also results in novel insights about existing, and commonly used, prediction methods and the connections between them. The second contribution is using the framework to devise new prediction approaches that outperform state-of-the-art.

2. RELATED WORK

Pre-retrieval query-performance predictors [19, 29, 25, 16, 39, 28] analyze the query expression, often using corpus-based information. Post-retrieval predictors also use information induced from the result list of the most highly ranked documents [10, 1, 35, 37, 11, 5, 36, 2, 14, 42, 18, 30, 31, 7, 12, 13]. As noted above, the framework we present sets *formal* probabilistic grounds to the integration of pre-retrieval and post-retrieval prediction. We empirically show that the integration yields prediction quality that transcends the state-of-the-art. Furthermore, we show that the framework provides a *unified* formal basis that can be used to explain (derive), and provide new perspectives for, many previously proposed post-retrieval predictors.

A recently proposed framework [21] explains several post-retrieval predictors. The idea is that an effective result list is that which is similar to some pseudo effective list and dissimilar to a pseudo ineffective list. Our framework is shown to provide a formal probabilistic basis for this framework. Furthermore, our framework accounts for prediction aspects not accounted for by this framework [21]. (See Section 3.1.3 for a discussion.) Our framework also provides novel views of predictors such as Clarity [10] and WIG [42], which substantially depart from those previously proposed [21].

A conceptual framework for predicting *query difficulty* [5] is based on measuring similarities between the result list, the query, and the corpus. Our framework provides formal grounds to several aspects of this framework; and, helps explain several prediction methods and techniques that do not naturally fit in this framework; e.g, those using reference document lists [37, 36, 41, 14, 42].

A prediction framework [31], based on statistical decision theory, uses multiple re-rankings of the result list and their estimated effectiveness. We show that our framework provides probabilistic grounds for the underlying prediction principle of this framework. Furthermore, we use our framework to explain predictors that cannot be explained in terms of this approach [31]; e.g., Clarity [10] and WIG [42]. In addition, the integration of pre-retrieval and post-retrieval prediction that emerges in our framework was not addressed.

Notions of result list cohesion (dispersion) [37, 36] were argued to be correlated to some extent with retrieval effectiveness. We show that the *formal* prediction aspect targeted by measures of this query-independent result list property is complementary to that targeted by measures of query-dependent properties; the latter are the focus of most post-retrieval predictors. We also demonstrate the empirical merits of the integration of these two types of measures.

Integrating predictors using a linear interpolation of prediction values was employed with either pre-retrieval predictors [15] or post-retrieval predictors [36, 14, 42, 31]. In contrast, our framework provides formal grounds to the integration of different *types* of predictors which target different *formal* aspects of prediction; namely, pre-retrieval and post-retrieval prediction, and prediction based on query-independent and query-dependent measures of result list properties. Prediction integration as that proposed in previous work can be used in our framework (e.g., for improving pre-retrieval prediction quality) to potentially further improve overall prediction quality. We leave the exploration of this direction for future work.

3. PREDICTION FRAMEWORK

The query-performance prediction task is stated as estimating the effectiveness of a ranking induced by retrieval method $\mathcal{M}$ over a corpus of documents $\mathcal{D}$ in response to query q in lack of relevance judgments [4].

Our first key observation is that the goal of prediction can be stated, in probabilistic terms, as answering the question:

What is the probability that <u>this</u> result list ($\mathcal{D}_{res}$), of the most highly ranked documents, is relevant to <u>this</u> query (q)?

We focus on the result list and its ranking, rather than address the entire corpus ranking, as this is also the focus of the most commonly used evaluation measures (e.g., average precision, precision at top ranks, and NDCG). Furthermore, the question just stated is a generalization to the document list case of the question posed by Sparck Jones et al. [33] with respect to a single document: "What is the probability that *this* document is relevant to *this* query"? This question directly connects to the probability ranking principle [26] that states that maximal retrieval effectiveness is attained if documents are ranked by their relevance probabilities. The question serves as the basis for the probabilistic retrieval approach [33] and was used for a parallel derivation of the language modeling approach [22, 27].

3.1 Probabilistic prediction

In what follows we use the question stated above as the basis for developing our prediction framework. Let r be the event of relevance. The query-performance prediction task is, then, estimating $p(r|q, \mathcal{D}_{res})$, which can be written as

$$p(r|q, \mathcal{D}_{res}) = \frac{p(\mathcal{D}_{res}|q, r)p(r|q)}{p(\mathcal{D}_{res}|q)}. \quad (1)$$

The probability $p(\mathcal{D}_{res}|q)$ does not depend on relevance, but rather on the likelihood of retrieving $\mathcal{D}_{res}$ in response to q by the given retrieval method $\mathcal{M}$. As a case in point, if document-query surface-level similarities are used for retrieval, it is likely that $\mathcal{D}_{res}$ is composed of documents containing many occurrences of query terms. Furthermore, an estimate for $p(\mathcal{D}_{res}|q)$ can serve as a normalization factor to ensure the compatibility of prediction values across retrieval methods. However, as the evaluation of prediction quality in prior work was based on fixing the retrieval method (and varying the queries) [4], such normalization was not called for. Accordingly, the expression

$$\mathcal{P}_{base}(\mathcal{D}_{res}; q) \stackrel{def}{=} p(\mathcal{D}_{res}|q, r)p(r|q) \quad (2)$$

from Equation 1 reflects the core prediction task. It turns out, as we show below, that $\mathcal{P}_{base}(\mathcal{D}_{res}; q)$ is the basis for numerous query-performance prediction methods that might seem at first glance to be completely different and/or based on different hypotheses with regard to the characteristics of effective retrieval. We further show how new prediction approaches can be devised based on $\mathcal{P}_{base}(\mathcal{D}_{res}; q)$. Finally, we note that if $\mathcal{D}_{res}$ contains a single document, then the prediction task modeled in Equation 2 is based on estimating the likelihood of the document given the query. This is the basis of the probabilistic approach to retrieval [33].

3.1.1 Integrating pre- and post- retrieval prediction

Estimating the prior probability of relevance to q in Equation 2, $p(r|q)$, is (in spirit) the goal of pre-retrieval prediction methods that operate prior to retrieval time [19, 16]. Indeed, pre-retrieval predictors quantify this *query difficulty* notion using information induced only from q and the corpus.

The probability $p(\mathcal{D}_{res}|q, r)$ is the likelihood of the result list $\mathcal{D}_{res}$ given that a relevance event happens for q; i.e., the probability that $\mathcal{D}_{res}$ is *the* list that provides information pertaining to q. This is the list-based generalization of the document likelihood principle used in probabilistic retrieval [33]. Estimating the list likelihood is the implicit goal of post-retrieval predictors.

Hence, our second key observation is that while by design, post-retrieval predictors use result-list-based information in addition to the information used by pre-retrieval predictors (the query and the corpus), the two types of predictors target different formal aspects of prediction; that is, the prior probability of relevance to a query (pre-retrieval) and the likelihood of a result list given relevance to the query (post-retrieval). To the best of our knowledge, Equation 1, and consequently Equation 2, set the first *formal* grounds to integrating pre-retrieval and post-retrieval prediction. We demonstrate the empirical merits of the integration in Section 4. In what follows we focus on $p(\mathcal{D}_{res}|q, r)$, i.e., post-retrieval prediction.

3.1.2 Post-retrieval prediction

Our third key observation is that $p(\mathcal{D}_{res}|q, r)$ can be estimated by using documents in $\mathcal{D}_{res}$ as $\mathcal{D}_{res}$'s proxies. We use $\hat{p}(\cdot)$ to denote an estimate for $p(\cdot)$. Let $p(d|q, r)$ be the probability that d is *the* document relevant to q; i.e., d's likelihood [33]. If we set $\hat{p}(d|q, r) \stackrel{def}{=} 0$ for $d \notin \mathcal{D}_{res}$, i.e., a document not in the result list is not considered relevant; and, $\sum_{d_i \in \mathcal{D}_{res}} \hat{p}(d_i|q, r) = 1$ holds, that is, $\hat{p}(d_i|q, r)$ is a probability distribution over $\mathcal{D}_{res}$, and more generally, over the corpus $\mathcal{D}$, then we can define the following:[1]

$$\hat{p}(\mathcal{D}_{res}|q, r) \stackrel{def}{=} \sum_{d_i \in \mathcal{D}_{res}} \hat{p}(\mathcal{D}_{res}|d_i, r)\hat{p}(d_i|q, r). \quad (3)$$

Assuming that $\hat{p}(r|d_i)$ (the prior probability for d_i's relevance), $\hat{p}(d_i)$ (the prior probability for d_i), and $\hat{p}(\mathcal{D}_{res})$ (the prior probability for the result list) are uniformly distributed, and since $\hat{p}(\mathcal{D}_{res}|d_i, r) = \frac{\hat{p}(d_i|\mathcal{D}_{res}, r)\hat{p}(r|\mathcal{D}_{res})\hat{p}(\mathcal{D}_{res})}{\hat{p}(r|d_i)\hat{p}(d_i)}$, Equation 3 then yields a generic post-retrieval predictor:

$$\mathcal{P}_{generic}(\mathcal{D}_{res}; q) \stackrel{def}{=} \hat{p}(r|\mathcal{D}_{res}) \sum_{d_i \in \mathcal{D}_{res}} \hat{p}(d_i|\mathcal{D}_{res}, r)\hat{p}(d_i|q, r). \quad (4)$$

Devising an estimate for the probability that $\mathcal{D}_{res}$ is relevant regardless of a specific query, $\hat{p}(r|\mathcal{D}_{res})$, is the implicit goal of several post-retrieval prediction methods. For example, some predictors are based on the premise that result list cohesion indicates effective retrieval, wherein cohesion can be quantified by the list radius [5] and its clustering tendency [36][2]. Conversely, a diversified result list might be considered as more likely to cover different aspects of the underlying information need, and thereby assumed to be relevant [5]. Hence, in Section 4 we empirically contrast the two hypotheses of list cohesion versus list dispersion as indicators for list relevance.

The summation in Equation 4 is of the weighted document likelihood values in $\mathcal{D}_{res}$ ($\hat{p}(d_i|q, r)$); d_i's weight is based on the strength of its "association" with $\mathcal{D}_{res}$ given that the latter is relevant ($\hat{p}(d_i|\mathcal{D}_{res}, r)$). For example, $\hat{p}(d_i|\mathcal{D}_{res}, r)$ can be based on the probability that d_i is generated from a language model induced from $\mathcal{D}_{res}$. We next show how Equation 4 can be used to explain additional predictors.

Explaining WIG. Let the document-list association strength in Equation 4, $\hat{p}(d_i|\mathcal{D}_{res}, r)$, be a uniform distribution over $\mathcal{D}_{res}$; i.e., each document in $\mathcal{D}_{res}$ is considered as its equi-important representative. Then, the average document likelihood score in $\mathcal{D}_{res}$, $\frac{1}{k}\sum_{d_i \in \mathcal{D}_{res}} \hat{p}(d_i|q, r)$, where k is the number of documents in $\mathcal{D}_{res}$, is used for prediction. This is perhaps the most direct manifestation of the probability ranking principle; that is, a result list with documents for which the probability for relevance is high is considered effective (relevant).[3] Furthermore, this prediction principle is the basis of the weighted information gain (WIG) predictor [42]. WIG measures the difference between the average retrieval score in the list and that of the corpus. The divergence from the corpus retrieval score serves to ensure inter-query compatibility of prediction values.

Explaining Clarity. As mentioned above, list-cohesion measures (e.g., radius) were suggested in prior work as performance predictors [5, 36]. These implicitly serve for the estimate $\hat{p}(r|\mathcal{D}_{res})$, of the result list relevance prior, in Equation 4. An alternative approach to measuring cohesion is using the corpus. That is, if a model of the result list is distant from that of the corpus, which can be viewed as a pseudo non-relevant document, then the list is considered focused; hence, the retrieval is presumed to be effective. This is the hypothesis underlying the Clarity prediction method [10].

However, the method used to compute Clarity *explicitly* depends on the query [10]. Thus, Clarity, *in implementation*, cannot be considered as an estimate for $p(r|\mathcal{D}_{res})$. Rather, Clarity turns out to be an estimate for the summation in Equation 4 as we show below.

[1] As is standard in work on mixture models, Equation 3 is based on an independence assumption; specifically, $\mathcal{D}_{res}$ is independent of q given d_i and r; i.e., we "back off" from $\mathcal{D}_{res}$ to its proxies (d_i).

[2] In implementation, the query is used when computing query-based inter-document similarities [36]. We come back to this point later on.

[3] In the probabilistic retrieval framework [33], for example, ranking is based on document likelihood values.

In Appendix A we show that the standard approach of computing Clarity can be (re-)written as:

$$\mathcal{P}_{Clarity}(\mathcal{D}_{res}; q) = \sum_{d_i \in \mathcal{D}_{res}} \hat{p}(d_i|q, r)\big(Sim(d_i, \mathcal{D}_{res}) - Sim(d_i, \mathcal{D})\big); \quad (5)$$

$Sim(d_i, X)$, where X is either $\mathcal{D}_{res}$ or $\mathcal{D}$, is the similarity (based on the cross entropy measure) between a language model induced from d_i and that induced from X.

Hence, Clarity is a special case of the generic predictor from Equation 4 with a uniform $\hat{p}(r|\mathcal{D}_{res})$. That is, Clarity is a weighted sum of document likelihood values, which in the language modeling case represent normalized query-likelihood values. (See Appendix A for details.) The document-list association strength ($\hat{p}(d_i|\mathcal{D}_{res}, r)$) is estimated in the Clarity case, as is shown in Equation 5, using the corpus-regularized similarity between the document and the result list; the corpus-based regularization downplays the effect of general non-query-related aspects when computing similarity to the list.

Thus, we attained the following novel perspective about Clarity. Suppose that the retrieval at hand, whose effectiveness we want to predict, uses the language-model-based surface-level similarity between documents and the query. This is the case for the query likelihood [32] and KL retrieval [23] methods that are commonly used in work on using Clarity for prediction. Hence, the induced ranking is essentially based on the document likelihood scores defined in Appendix A (i.e., normalized query-likelihood scores). Then, by Equation 5, a result list for which the highest ranked documents are similar to the entire list — wherein similarity is corpus regularized — is presumed to be effective (relevant).

3.1.3 Using reference lists

Equation 3 served as the basis for deriving the generic post-retrieval prediction approach presented in Equation 4. The underlying idea was to use documents in $\mathcal{D}_{res}$ as its proxies for estimating the result list likelihood, $p(\mathcal{D}_{res}|q, r)$. An alternative type of a proxy for $\mathcal{D}_{res}$ is a *reference document list* [37, 41, 14, 42, 31]. Formally, a similar formulation to that in Equation 3 that uses a set S_{ref} of reference document lists (denoted $\mathcal{D}_{ref}$) is:

$$\mathcal{P}_{ref}(\mathcal{D}_{res}; q) \stackrel{def}{=} \sum_{\mathcal{D}_{ref} \in S_{ref}} \hat{p}(\mathcal{D}_{res}|\mathcal{D}_{ref}, r)\hat{p}(\mathcal{D}_{ref}|q, r). \quad (6)$$

Thus, the relevance of $\mathcal{D}_{res}$ is estimated based on its association with the reference lists, $\hat{p}(\mathcal{D}_{res}|\mathcal{D}_{ref}, r)$, where $\mathcal{D}_{ref}$ is weighted by its presumed relevance, $\hat{p}(\mathcal{D}_{ref}|q, r)$. As we discuss below, Equation 6 sets the probabilistic formal grounds to quite a few predictors. These predictors differ by the choice of reference lists and inter-list association measure.

Explaining QF and autocorrelation. Devising the estimate $\hat{p}(\mathcal{D}_{ref}|q, r)$ is a prediction problem in its own right, which is not addressed by most predictors that utilize reference lists [37, 41, 2, 14, 42]. For example, the query feedback (QF) predictor [42] uses the overlap at top ranks between $\mathcal{D}_{res}$ and a (single) list $\mathcal{D}_{ref}$ for $\hat{p}(\mathcal{D}_{res}|\mathcal{D}_{ref}, r)$; $\mathcal{D}_{ref}$ is retrieved from the corpus using a (relevance) language model induced from $\mathcal{D}_{res}$. However, the presumed relevance of $\mathcal{D}_{ref}$, $\hat{p}(\mathcal{D}_{ref}|q, r)$, is not accounted for. Thus, it is not surprising that QF was found to be a highly effective predictor for the effectiveness of the reference result list ($\mathcal{D}_{ref}$) and not only to that of the original result list ($\mathcal{D}_{res}$) [31]. Indeed, this finding can be formally explained using Equation 6. That is, the effectiveness (relevance) of the reference list $\mathcal{D}_{ref}$ can be estimated using $\mathcal{D}_{res}$ as its proxy, by switching their roles in Equation 6. (The inter-list association estimate, overlap at top ranks, is symmetric.)

Autocorrelation [14] is another example of a predictor that does not account for the presumed relevance of a single reference list used for prediction. The reference list, $\mathcal{D}_{ref}$, is obtained by re-ranking $\mathcal{D}_{res}$ using score regularization; and, Pearson correlation between retrieval scores serves for $\hat{p}(\mathcal{D}_{res}|\mathcal{D}_{ref}, r)$. In Section 4 we show that the autocorrelation predictor does not only predict the effectiveness of $\mathcal{D}_{res}$, as originally reported, but also the effectiveness of $\mathcal{D}_{ref}$. This finding provides further support to the prediction principle presented in Equation 6.

Other predictors that use reference lists without accounting for their presumed relevance include those using query perturbations [37], document perturbations [41], and retrieval method perturbations [2, 14], to induce reference lists.

Explaining additional prediction approaches. The UEF predictor [31] does estimate the presumed relevance of the reference lists used. Specifically, each reference list is created by re-ranking $\mathcal{D}_{res}$ using a relevance language model. The presumed relevance of the reference list is estimated using previously proposed predictors. Thus, while UEF is based on statistical decision theory, it can be directly explained by Equation 6.

A prediction framework recently proposed [21] relies on the premise that the result list $\mathcal{D}_{res}$ is relevant to the extent that it is similar to a pseudo relevant result list and dissimilar to a pseudo non-relevant result list. The framework was used to explain several post-retrieval predictors. In contrast to the framework we present in this work, this framework does not arise from a probabilistic analysis of the prediction task. Moreover, it does not account for several formal aspects of prediction that emerged in the development of our framework. These include integrating pre-retrieval and post-retrieval prediction and integrating query dependent and independent measures of result list properties. Yet, in Appendix B we show that Equation 1, which served as the basis for deriving our framework, can be used to provide formal probabilistic grounds to this framework [21].

4. EVALUATION

We present an empirical exploration of three formal aspects that emerged in the development of our prediction framework. These give rise to new prediction methods and shed new light on existing ones.

We study the merits of the integration of pre-retrieval and post-retrieval prediction in Section 4.2.1. In Section 4.2.2 we explore the use of measures of query-independent properties — specifically, cohesion and dispersion — of the result list for prediction. Finally, in Section 4.2.3 we focus on using reference lists for prediction. We begin by describing the experimental setup we used for evaluation in Section 4.1.

4.1 Experimental setup

Table 1 presents the eight TREC-based experimental settings used for evaluation. TREC5 and ROBUST are composed primarily of newswire documents. WT10G is a small

Collection	Data	Num Docs	Topics
TREC5	Disks 2,4	524,929	251-300
ROBUST	Disks 4,5-CR	528,155	301-450, 601-700
WT10G	WT10g	1,692,096	451-550
GOV2	GOV2	25,205,179	701-850
Clue09	ClueWeb (Category B)	50,220,423	1-50
Clue09+SpamRm	ClueWeb (Category B)	50,220,423	1-50
Clue10	ClueWeb (Category B)	50,220,423	51-100
Clue10+SpamRm	ClueWeb (Category B)	50,220,423	51-100

Table 1: TREC settings used for experiments.

Web collection that contains some pages of low quality (e.g., spam). GOV2 is a much larger Web collection that is a crawl of the .GOV domain and hence contains mainly well edited pages. We also use the ClueWeb corpus (category B) [6], which is a large scale noisy Web collection, with the queries used in TREC 2009 (Clue09) and TREC 2010 (Clue10).

Retrieval effectiveness for ClueWeb can be significantly influenced by spam documents [8]. Thus, in what follows we explore the potential effects of spam on query-performance prediction. Specifically, we also perform evaluation where documents "suspected" as spam that are initially highly ranked are removed from the result list. To that end, we scan the initial ranking from top to bottom and remove documents that are assigned by Waterloo's spam classifier [8] a score below 50 [8, 3], until 1000 documents are accumulated. The score reflects the presumed percentage of documents in the ClueWeb English collection (category A) that are "spammier" than the document at hand. Clue09+SpamRm and Clue10+SpamRm denote the resulting (ranked) corpora for Clue09 and Clue10, respectively.

The titles of TREC topics serve as queries. We applied Porter stemming and stopword removal, using the INQUERY list, to documents and queries using the Lemur/Indri toolkit[4].

To measure prediction quality, we follow the standard practice in work on query-performance prediction [4]. Specifically, we report the Pearson correlation between the prediction values assigned by a predictor to the set of queries per setting, and the ground-truth average precision (AP@1000) values for these queries; the ground truth is determined based on TREC's relevance judgments.[5] Statistically significant differences of prediction quality (between Pearson correlations) are determined at the 95% confidence level [34].

As in many previous reports of work on predicting query performance [10, 11, 41, 14, 16, 30, 17, 31], we use the query likelihood (QL) model [32] for the retrieval method. The goal of the predictors we study is to estimate the retrieval effectiveness of this standard language-model-based retrieval approach. The QL retrieval score assigned to document d in response to query q is $Score_{QL}(q;d) \stackrel{def}{=} \log \prod_{q_i \in q} p(q_i|d)$, where $p(w|d)$ is the probability assigned to term w by a language model induced from d; q_i is a query term. Unless otherwise stated, we use Dirichlet-smoothed unigram language models with the smoothing parameter set to 1000 [38].

Post-retrieval predictors. We use the Clarity [10], query feedback (QF) [42], and weighted information gain (WIG) [42] predictors in the following. These methods represent the three classes of post-retrieval prediction approaches mentioned in Section 1; these include, measuring the clarity of the result list with respect to the corpus (Clarity), quantifying the robustness of the result list (QF), and analyzing properties of retrieval scores in the result list (WIG). WIG and QF were shown to yield state-of-the-art prediction quality [42, 40, 31]. In Section 4.2.3 we address the autocorrelation predictor [14], which uses regularized retrieval scores.

The predictors just mentioned, as other previously proposed post-retrieval predictors, do not provide *direct* estimates for the likelihood of the result list. (Refer back to Equation 2 and the accompanying discussion.[6]) Rather, the assigned prediction values are correlated with this likelihood as implied by the attained prediction quality. We hasten to point out, however, that the purpose of using these predictors in the evaluation to follow is exploring aspects and principles that emerged in the development of our framework; specifically, the integration of different *types* of prediction approaches, namely, pre-retrieval and post-retrieval methods and query-independent and query-dependent measures of properties of the result list; and, the use of reference lists for prediction. Devising novel predictors that provide direct estimates for the result list likelihood, and using them in our framework, is left to future work.

The post-retrieval predictors analyze the result list $\mathcal{D}_{res}$ of the k documents that are the highest ranked by the QL retrieval method. The Clarity predictor [10] measures the KL divergence between a relevance language model $R_{\mathcal{D}_{res}}$ induced from $\mathcal{D}_{res}$ and a language model induced from the corpus. (See Appendix A for details.) The QF prediction value [42] is the number of documents that are both among the ν_{QF} highest ranked by the QL method and among the ν_{QF} highest ranked by retrieval performed over the corpus using the relevance model $R_{\mathcal{D}_{res}}$; ν_{QF} is a free parameter. The prediction value of WIG is $\frac{1}{\sqrt{|q|}} \frac{1}{k} \sum_{d \in \mathcal{D}_{res}} (Score_{QL}(q;d) - Score_{QL}(q;\mathcal{D}))$, where $|q|$ is the number of terms in q; i.e., the (query-length normalized) difference between the average retrieval score in $\mathcal{D}_{res}$ and that of the corpus[7].

One of the goals of the exploration we present in Section 4.2 is to study whether *formal* aspects of prediction that emerged in the framework described above can be used to devise prediction methods that outperform state-of-the-art predictors. Hence, we use highly optimized versions of Clarity, QF, and WIG as baselines. Specifically, we set the free parameters of each of these predictors to values maximizing prediction quality per setting. All three predictors rely on k, the number of documents in the result list; QF also depends on ν_{QF}. For all settings, except for those for ClueWeb, the value of k is selected from $\{5, 10, 50, 100, 150, 200, 300, 500, 700, 1000, 2000, 3000, 4000, 5000\}$. For ClueWeb we use a slightly more moderate range of values to alleviate the computational effort: $k \in \{5, 10, 50, 100, 150, 200, 300, 500, 700,$

[4]www.lemurproject.org

[5]Prediction-quality patterns similar to those we report are observed if Kendall's-τ is used for evaluation [4]. Actual numbers are omitted to avoid cluttering the presentation.

[6]There is work on estimating average precision directly from score distributions [12]. The proposed estimates are still surrogates for estimates for the result list likelihood.

[7]The corpus $\mathcal{D}$ is represented by the unsmoothed language model induced from the concatenation of the documents it contains; concatenation order has no effect, as we use unigram language models. While WIG's original implementation was with the Markov Random Field model [42], it was noted [42, 40] and shown [31] that WIG is highly effective for predicting the effectiveness of the query likelihood model.

	TREC5	ROBUST	WT10G	GOV2	Clue09	Clue09+SpamRm	Clue10	Clue10+SpamRm
SumIDF	0.053	0.287	0.162	0.281	0.618	0.620	0.202	0.201
AvgIDF	0.208	0.466	0.149	0.266	0.211	0.161	0.175	0.227
MaxIDF	0.269	0.486	0.134	0.294	0.409	0.357	0.233	0.252
SumVarTF.IDF	0.049	0.266	0.269	0.328	0.631	0.637	0.267	0.273
AvgVarTF.IDF	0.203	0.428	0.282	0.360	0.365	0.293	0.247	0.309
MaxVarTF.IDF	0.180	0.443	0.406	0.372	0.590	0.528	0.312	0.341
Clarity	**0.431**	0.522	0.432	0.456	0.105	−0.016	−0.147	−0.077
SumIDF∧Clarity	0.170	0.392	0.270	0.368	**0.687***	**0.643***	0.156*	0.225*
AvgIDF∧Clarity	0.310	0.527	0.287	0.367	0.254	0.157	0.093*	0.174*
MaxIDF∧Clarity	0.345	**0.545**	0.265	0.383	0.457*	0.365*	0.149*	0.222*
SumVarTF.IDF∧Clarity	0.187	0.358	0.358	0.420	0.667*	0.623*	**0.207***	**0.289***
AvgVarTF.IDF∧Clarity	0.341	0.482	0.401	**0.459**	0.338*	0.228*	0.139*	0.224*
MaxVarTF.IDF∧Clarity	0.300	0.483	**0.450**	0.447	0.555*	0.458*	0.206*	0.270*
QF	0.447	0.500	0.483	0.566	0.516	0.616	0.393	0.483
SumIDF∧QF	0.388	0.505	0.487	0.502	0.675*	**0.767***	0.496	0.674*
AvgIDF∧QF	0.444	0.602*	0.423	0.518	0.499	0.443	0.520*	0.559*
MaxIDF∧QF	**0.489**	**0.613***	0.482	0.554	0.604	0.595	0.537*	0.610*
SumVarTF.IDF∧QF	0.366	0.496	**0.511**	0.527	**0.689***	0.751*	0.524*	**0.684***
AvgVarTF.IDF∧QF	0.409	0.586*	0.432	0.561	0.557	0.488	0.538*	0.579*
MaxVarTF.IDF∧QF	0.390	0.578*	0.496	**0.574**	0.651*	0.643	**0.557**	0.603*
WIG	**0.297**	0.550	0.376	**0.486**	0.507	0.498	**0.415**	**0.468**
SumIDF∧WIG	0.133	0.425	0.314	0.362	0.611*	0.606*	0.233	0.260
AvgIDF∧WIG	0.222	0.540	0.218	0.348	0.246	0.225	0.240	0.302
MaxIDF∧WIG	0.270	**0.572**	0.261	0.381	0.406	0.385	0.288	0.332
SumVarTF.IDF∧WIG	0.138	0.391	0.404	0.427	**0.677***	**0.666***	0.277	0.305
AvgVarTF.IDF∧WIG	0.239	0.508	0.334	0.432	0.409	0.372	0.287	0.352
MaxVarTF.IDF∧WIG	0.226	0.524	**0.431**	0.465	0.587	0.546	0.333	0.372

Table 2: Integrating pre-retrieval and post-retrieval prediction. The best result per setting in a block of a post-retrieval predictor is boldfaced. The best result in the entire setting (column) is underlined. '*' marks a statistically significant difference with using the post-retrieval predictor alone.

1000}. For all settings, ν_{QF}, the additional free parameter of QF, is set to values in $\{5, 10, 50, 100, 150, 200, 300, 500, 700, 1000\}$. Following previous recommendations [31], the number of terms used by the relevance model, $R_{\mathcal{D}_{res}}$, which is utilized by Clarity and QF, is set to 100; and, language models of documents from which the relevance model is constructed are not smoothed (i.e., a maximum likelihood estimate is used).

4.2 Experimental results

4.2.1 Integrating pre- and post- retrieval prediction

Using Equation 2 we showed that pre-retrieval and post-retrieval prediction methods target different, yet complementary, formal aspects of prediction. Hence, we now turn to study whether their integration can yield prediction quality that transcends that of using each alone. To the best of our knowledge, this is the first such empirical study.

For post-retrieval predictors we use the optimized Clarity, QF and WIG methods described above. For pre-retrieval prediction we use two sets of methods, each based on a different type of statistics computed for a query term. The first set, referred to as IDF [10, 19, 16], uses the inverse document frequency (IDF) value of a query term. The second set of pre-retrieval predictors, denoted VarTF.IDF [39], uses the variance of the TF.IDF value of a query term in documents across the corpus in which it appears. Predictors based on VarTF.IDF were shown to substantially outperform other pre-retrieval predictors [16]; and, to outperform highly effective post-retrieval predictors for Clue09 [17].

To aggregate the statistics for the query terms, we use the sum, average, and maximum operators. Accordingly, we study the SumIDF, AvgIDF, MaxIDF, SumVarTF.IDF, AvgVarTF.IDF, and MaxVarTF.IDF predictors. If X is a pre-retrieval predictor and Y is a post-retrieval predictor, we use X∧Y to denote their integration, attained by the multiplication of prediction values following Equation 2.

In what follows we focus on the question of whether the prediction quality of a highly optimized post-retrieval predictor can be improved if integrated, *as is*, with pre-retrieval predictors. Our experiments show that the prediction quality of the *integration* of pre-retrieval and post-retrieval prediction can be further improved, as expected, by optimizing the free-parameter values of the post-retrieval predictors to that end. (The pre-retrieval predictors do not incorporate free parameters.) Actual numbers are omitted due to space considerations and as they convey no additional insight.

Our first observation based on Table 2, which is in line with previous reports [4], is that all post-retrieval predictors, when used alone, almost always outperform all pre-retrieval predictors, when used alone, for TREC5, ROBUST, WT10G and GOV2. For the ClueWeb settings, the pre-retrieval predictors can in some cases outperform the post-retrieval predictors. This finding generalizes that presented in a recent report for (only) the Clue09 setting [17].

Evidently, spam removal for ClueWeb can have considerable (positive or negative) effect on prediction quality. We see in Table 2 that in most cases the prediction quality of the predictors for Clue09+SpamRm is lower than that for Clue09, while the prediction quality for Clue10+SpamRm is superior to that for Clue10; the prediction quality differences can be quite substantial.

Perhaps the most important observation with regard to Table 2 is the following. In quite a few cases, the integration of pre-retrieval and post-retrieval prediction can yield prediction quality that much transcends that of each, even

	TREC5	ROBUST	WT10G	GOV2	Clue09	Clue09+SpamRm	Clue10	Clue10+SpamRm
d-dispersion	0.082	0.253	0.158	−0.228	−0.338	−0.082	−0.327	−0.328
d-cohesion	−0.084	−0.257	−0.149	0.244	0.153	−0.136	−0.097	−0.104
e-dispersion	−0.033	0.139	0.159	−0.100	0.324	0.349	0.391	0.396
e-cohesion	0.028	−0.138	−0.157	0.094	−0.274	−0.323	−0.339	−0.326
Clarity	0.431	**0.522**	0.432	0.456	0.105	−0.016	−0.147	−0.077
d-dispersion∧Clarity	0.313	0.490	0.418	0.066	−0.229	−0.056	−0.284	−0.248
d-cohesion∧Clarity	**0.522**	0.460	0.327	**0.471**	0.130	−0.139	−0.110	−0.118
e-dispersion∧Clarity	0.404	**0.522**	**0.455**	0.447	**0.353***	**0.215***	**0.095***	**0.155***
e-cohesion∧Clarity	0.454	0.518	0.395	0.446	−0.148	−0.154	−0.301	−0.232
QF	0.447	0.500	0.483	**0.566**	0.516	0.616	0.393	0.483
d-dispersion∧QF	**0.504**	**0.528***	**0.496**	0.445	0.465	**0.697**	0.292	0.373
d-cohesion∧QF	0.368	0.447	0.432	0.544	0.527	0.014	−0.038	−0.021
e-dispersion∧QF	0.448	0.503	0.492	0.565	**0.569***	0.679*	**0.495***	**0.549***
e-cohesion∧QF	0.444	0.496	0.473	0.565	0.450	0.508	0.253	0.367
WIG	0.297	**0.550**	0.376	0.486	0.507	0.498	0.415	0.468
d-dispersion∧WIG	0.248	0.539	0.359	0.183	0.128	0.293	−0.091	−0.049
d-cohesion∧WIG	0.294	0.481	0.298	**0.550**	0.430	−0.006	−0.069	−0.072
e-dispersion∧WIG	0.281	**0.550**	**0.394**	0.463	**0.525**	**0.514**	**0.471**	**0.521**
e-cohesion∧WIG	**0.313**	0.547	0.349	0.500	0.293	0.410	0.104	0.183

Table 3: Integrating query-independent result list measures of cohesion and dispersion with the post-retrieval predictors that utilize query-dependent list properties; '*' marks statistically significant differences between the integration and using the post-retrieval predictor alone. The best result per setting in a block of a post-retrieval predictor is boldfaced; the best result in the entire setting (column) is underlined.

in cases where the former is far less effective than the latter; the improvements over using post-retrieval prediction alone are often statistically significant for the ClueWeb settings. For example, QF is the most effective among the three post-retrieval predictors, when these are used alone, for 6 out of the 8 experimental settings. Yet, the best prediction quality reported in the QF block in the table (boldfaced numbers), and more generally, for an entire setting (underlined numbers), is always attained when integrating QF with a pre-retrieval predictor. Furthermore, the prediction quality of the integration in these cases is often much better than that of QF, although QF's prediction quality is often substantially better than that of the pre-retrieval predictor with which it is integrated. Specifically, MaxIDF∧QF and SumVarTF.IDF∧QF turn out to be highly effective predictors. For Clarity and WIG, the best prediction quality is attained when integrating them with a pre-retrieval predictor in 7 and 4 out of the 8 experimental settings, respectively.

All in all, these findings attest to the complementary nature of pre-retrieval and post-retrieval prediction that formally emerged in Equation 2.

4.2.2 *List cohesion versus list dispersion*

The generic post-retrieval predictor in Equation 4 uses a query-independent estimate for the effectiveness (relevance) of the result list ($\hat{p}(r|\mathcal{D}_{res})$). This estimate plays a complementary formal role to that addressed by the query-dependent estimates used in most post-retrieval prediction methods. Thus, following Equation 4, we turn to study the potential merits of integrating the measures of query-independent and query-dependent properties of the result list.

We contrast two hypotheses. The first is that high cohesion of the result list attests to reduced *query drift* [36], and hence, to improved retrieval. The second is that list dispersion might indicate increased cover of query aspects, and thereby imply effective retrieval [5]. We employ two measures that quantify list cohesion and dispersion: the diameter of the list, adapted in spirit from [5], and the list entropy, a variant of a measure proposed in [20].

List diameter. We define the result list ($\mathcal{D}_{res}$) diameter as

$$dim(\mathcal{D}_{res}) \stackrel{def}{=} -\frac{1}{k(k-1)} \sum_{d_i, d_j \in \mathcal{D}_{res}; d_i \neq d_j} Sim(d_i, d_j);$$

$Sim(d_i, d_j) \stackrel{def}{=} -KL\left(p(\cdot|d_i) \,\middle|\middle|\, p(\cdot|d_j)\right)$ is the negative KL divergence between the (unsmoothed) language model induced from d_i and the (smoothed[8]) language model induced from d_j. Increased KL divergence corresponds to a larger difference between language models (i.e., weaker inter-document similarity); accordingly, $\mathcal{D}_{res}$ is of greater diameter and consequently assumed to be less coherent (more dispersed). We use **d-cohesion** and **d-dispersion** to refer to $\frac{1}{dim(\mathcal{D}_{res})}$ and $dim(\mathcal{D}_{res})$, respectively, that reflect the presumed extent of cohesion and dispersion, respectively.

List entropy. Let $Cent(\mathcal{D}_{res})$ be the (arithmetic) centroid of language models of documents in $\mathcal{D}_{res}$: $p(w|Cent(\mathcal{D}_{res})) \stackrel{def}{=} \frac{1}{k}\sum_{d \in \mathcal{D}_{res}} p(w|d)$, where $p(w|d)$ is the probability assigned to term w by an unsmoothed language model induced from d. We "clip" $Cent(\mathcal{D}_{res})$ by using the 100 terms w to which it assigns the highest probability, and re-normalize to yield a probability distribution. (As noted in Section 4.1, the same clipping practice was employed to the relevance model used by the Clarity and QF predictors.)

We define the entropy of the result list $\mathcal{D}_{res}$ as the entropy of its centroid:

$$H(\mathcal{D}_{res}) \stackrel{def}{=} -\sum_{w} p(w|Cent(\mathcal{D}_{res})) \log p(w|Cent(\mathcal{D}_{res})).$$

Low entropy amounts to the term distribution in $\mathcal{D}_{res}$ being focused around a few terms, which potentially implies increased list cohesion; conversely, high entropy might indicate increased list dispersion. We use **e-cohesion** and **e-dispersion** to refer to $\frac{1}{H(\mathcal{D}_{res})}$ and $H(\mathcal{D}_{res})$, respectively,

[8]The document language model is Jelinek-Mercer smoothed [38] with a 0.1 weight assigned to corpus-based term counts.

which are measures of $\mathcal{D}_{res}$'s presumed cohesion and dispersion, respectively.

To integrate the query-independent list cohesion (dispersion) measures with the optimized query-dependent post-retrieval predictors (Clarity, QF and WIG), we multiply their assigned values following Equation 4. The cohesion (dispersion) measures are computed for the $k = 100$ highest ranked documents. (Using the top-50 documents yields similar prediction quality.) Table 3 presents the prediction quality numbers. ($\wedge$ indicates that a list cohesion (dispersion) measure is integrated with a predictor.)

We can see in Table 3 that in most cases, the query-independent result-list cohesion (dispersion) measures yield very low prediction quality when used alone. The main exception is the e-dispersion measure, which yields somewhat higher prediction quality for the ClueWeb settings. This finding echoes those from previous work [20] about list dispersion being a potential signal for effective retrieval in the noisy Web setting.

We also see in Table 3 that for 7 out of the 8 experimental settings, the best prediction quality (underlined) is attained by integrating a dispersion measure (d-dispersion or e-dispersion) with a post-retrieval predictor. For all (optimized) post-retrieval predictors, Clarity, QF and WIG, the best prediction quality (boldfaced) is almost always obtained when integrated with a dispersion measure rather than when used alone. The improvements over using the post-retrieval predictor alone can be substantial (e.g., for the ClueWeb settings) and statistically significant (e.g., for e-dispersion$\wedge$Clarity and e-dispersion$\wedge$QF over the ClueWeb settings). In most cases, integrating a post-retrieval predictor with the entropy-based dispersion measure (e-dispersion) outperforms using the post-retrieval predictor alone and integrating the predictor with the diameter-based dispersion measure (d-dispersion).

The findings presented above support the merits of the integration of measures of query-independent and query-dependent result list properties that formally emerged in Equation 4. Specifically, quantifying list dispersion by measuring its term-distribution entropy, and integrating this measure with optimized post-retrieval predictors, yields prediction quality that can substantially transcend that of using the predictors alone.

It is important to note that our findings do not contradict those in previous work [36] with regard to increased list cohesion being an indicator for effective retrieval. Specifically, cohesion was shown to be an effective indicator when measured in a *query-dependent* manner utilizing document-query similarities [36]. In contrast, we measure cohesion using query-independent estimates.

4.2.3 Using reference lists for prediction

We presented the fundamental approach of using reference lists for prediction in Equation 6:

$$\mathcal{P}_{ref}(\mathcal{D}_{res}; q) \stackrel{def}{=} \sum_{\mathcal{D}_{ref} \in S_{ref}} \hat{p}(\mathcal{D}_{res}|\mathcal{D}_{ref}, r)\hat{p}(\mathcal{D}_{ref}|q, r).$$

The relevance of $\mathcal{D}_{res}$ to q is estimated based on its association with reference lists $\mathcal{D}_{ref}$ ($\hat{p}(\mathcal{D}_{res}|\mathcal{D}_{ref}, r)$), where each $\mathcal{D}_{ref}$ is weighted by its presumed relevance to q ($\hat{p}(\mathcal{D}_{ref}|q, r)$). As discussed in Section 3, this prediction paradigm underlies several predictors [37, 41, 14, 42, 31]. However, many of these predictors do not estimate, and consequently utilize, the presumed relevance of $\mathcal{D}_{ref}$ [37, 41, 14, 42].

	RefList(Uni)	RefList(Clarity)	Clarity
TREC5	0.414	**0.459**	0.431
ROBUST	0.520	**0.562**^{c}	0.522
WT10G	0.415	0.418	**0.432**
GOV2	0.377	**0.486**^{u}	0.456
Clue09	−0.06	0.019	**0.105**
Clue09+SpamRm	**0.121**	0.039	−0.016
Clue10	**−0.079**	−0.175	−0.147
Clue10+SpamRm	**0.047**	−0.054	−0.077

Table 4: Using reference lists for prediction. 'c' and 'u' mark statistically significant differences with Clarity and RefList(Uni), respectively. Best result in a row is boldfaced.

To further explore the merits, or lack thereof, of the reference-lists-based prediction paradigm, when using both the association between $\mathcal{D}_{res}$ and $\mathcal{D}_{ref}$ and the estimated relevance of $\mathcal{D}_{ref}$ to q, we study the following novel simple predictor, henceforth referred to as **RefList**.

In the empirical evaluation presented thus far, we used the QL retrieval method to induce the corpus ranking used to create the result list $\mathcal{D}_{res}$. The document language model smoothing parameter value was set to 1000. (See Section 4.1.) To create reference lists, $\mathcal{D}_{ref}$, we *re-rank* $\mathcal{D}_{res}$ using the QL method with the smoothing parameter set to values in $\{100, 200, 500, 800, 1500, 2000, 3000, 4000, 5000, 10000\}$. Thus, we get that S_{ref} contains 10 reference lists that are created by varying the document (language) models.

We set the estimate for the association strength of $\mathcal{D}_{res}$ and $\mathcal{D}_{ref}$ ($\hat{p}(\mathcal{D}_{res}|\mathcal{D}_{ref}, r)$) to Pearson's correlation between the retrieval scores of the documents. The estimate for the presumed relevance of $\mathcal{D}_{ref}$ to q ($\hat{p}(\mathcal{D}_{ref}|q, r)$) is set to either the Clarity value of $\mathcal{D}_{ref}$ (**RefList(Clarity)**) or to $\frac{1}{10}$ (**RefList(Uni)**). We employ the predictors upon a result list, $\mathcal{D}_{res}$, of $k = 150$ documents. The relevance model used by Clarity is constructed as described in Section 4.1. As a reference comparison, we use the *optimized* Clarity predictor used above and for which the value of k was tuned. Thus, the RefList predictors are *underoptimized* with respect to the Clarity baseline. We hasten to point out that RefList can also be optimized with respect to k and predictors other than Clarity can be used by RefList to estimate the relevance of $\mathcal{D}_{ref}$. Nevertheless, our goal here is to focus on the underlying principles of using reference lists for prediction rather than devise the most effective predictor. The prediction quality numbers are presented in Table 4.

We see in Table 4 that RefList(Clarity) improves — often substantially, although statistically significantly in a single case — over RefList(Uni) for all non-ClueWeb settings (TREC5, ROBUST, WT10G, and GOV2). This finding provides some support to the importance of using an estimate for the presumed relevance of the reference list. We also see that RefList(Clarity) substantially outperforms Clarity for 3 out of these 4 settings, and statistically significantly so for ROBUST, although RefList(Clarity) is *underoptimized* with respect to Clarity. These results support the merits of using reference lists for prediction, even if the reference lists are created using a very simple approach as we employ here.

Table 4 shows that for the ClueWeb settings, the RefList predictors and the optimized Clarity predictor yield very low prediction quality. This could be attributed to the noisy na-

		TREC5	ROBUST	WT10G	GOV2	Clue09	Clue09+SpamRm	Clue10	Clue10+SpamRm
QF	$\mathcal{D}_{res}$	0.447	0.500	**0.483**	0.560	0.516	**0.616**	0.393	0.483
	$\mathcal{D}_{ref}$	**0.467**	**0.594**	0.482	**0.643**	**0.605**	0.543	**0.445**	**0.574**
autocorrelation	$\mathcal{D}_{res}$	0.277	0.347	0.328	0.417	**0.235**	0.505	**−0.021**	**0.213**
	$\mathcal{D}_{ref}$	**0.287**	**0.427**	**0.399**	**0.442**	0.105	**0.538**	−0.080	0.064

Table 5: The prediction quality of QF and autocorrelation. Prediction quality is measured by the success in predicting the effectiveness of the result list at hand ($\mathcal{D}_{res}$, as originally proposed) and that of the reference list used ($\mathcal{D}_{ref}$). The best result in a column within a block of a predictor is boldfaced.

ture of the corpus-based term counts (e.g., due to spam) that affects Clarity computation and the smoothing of document language models which is very important in the RefList predictors. (See [20] for an additional explanation about Clarity's low prediction quality for ClueWeb.) We found that using Clarity (alone) with "term clipping" [18] yields a somewhat improved prediction for Clue09 and Clue09+SpamRm but not for Clue10 and Clue10+SpamRm.

On the symmetry in using reference lists. As noted in Section 3.1.3, the QF [42] and autocorrelation [14] predictors use a single reference list. However, both predictors do not use an estimate for the presumed relevance of the reference list. Hence, these predictors are based solely on the association between $\mathcal{D}_{res}$ and $\mathcal{D}_{ref}$ ($\hat{p}(\mathcal{D}_{res}|\mathcal{D}_{ref}, r)$). Thus, if we swap the roles of $\mathcal{D}_{res}$ and $\mathcal{D}_{ref}$ in Equation 6, and given that the inter-list association measure for both predictors is symmetric, we should get that the predictors do not only estimate the effectiveness of $\mathcal{D}_{res}$, but also that of $\mathcal{D}_{ref}$. This hypothesis was shown to hold for QF in some previous work [31], but the ClueWeb settings were not used. Hence, we (re-)examine the hypothesis for QF; and, we present a novel study of the hypothesis for autocorrelation.

We use the optimized QF predictor described in Section 4.1. The optimization was with respect to the prediction quality for the effectiveness of $\mathcal{D}_{res}$, which is computed (as is the case for $\mathcal{D}_{ref}$) as at the above; that is, by Pearson correlation with the true AP@1000. We also use an optimized autocorrelation predictor. Specifically, the number of nearest neighbors considered when constructing the graph [14] is selected from $\{5, 10, 50\}$ (a document is included in the set of its own nearest neighbors); and, k, the number of documents in $\mathcal{D}_{res}$ (and $\mathcal{D}_{ref}$) is selected from $\{50, 100\}$ to optimize prediction quality for $\mathcal{D}_{res}$ with respect to AP@k.[9] Accordingly, we report the prediction quality of autocorrelation for both $\mathcal{D}_{res}$ and $\mathcal{D}_{ref}$ with respect to AP@k. We do not use AP@1000 since autocorrelation is based on re-ranking $\mathcal{D}_{res}$ rather than ranking the entire corpus.

We see in Table 5 that in most settings QF and autocorrelation post high prediction quality for the effectiveness of the reference list ($\mathcal{D}_{ref}$); often, the prediction quality transcends that for the original result list ($\mathcal{D}_{res}$). Both QF [42] and autocorrelation [14] were originally stated as targeting the effectiveness of $\mathcal{D}_{res}$ and they were optimized to this end as described above. Hence, these findings — which are novel for autocorrelation — support the hypothesis stated above with regard to predictors using a single reference list without utilizing an estimate for its presumed relevance. That is, prediction is essentially performed for the effectiveness of both the result list and the reference list. These findings further support the underpinning of the reference-list-based prediction approach from Equation 6.

[9]We used a language-model-based inter-document similarity measure rather than a vector-space-based measure as in the original proposal [14].

5. CONCLUSIONS AND FUTURE WORK

We presented a novel probabilistic query-performance prediction framework. The importance of the framework is threefold. First, setting common formal grounds to various previously proposed prediction methods that might seem to rely on completely different principles and hypotheses. Second, providing new insights about commonly used prediction methods such as Clarity and the connections between them. Third, giving rise, based on formal arguments, to new prediction approaches that were empirically shown to improve over the state-of-the-art. Integrating various prediction types that emerged in our framework using additional approaches — e.g., machine-learning-based techniques — is a future venue we intend to explore.

Acknowledgments We thank the anonymous reviewers, and Yuval Nardi, for their comments. This paper is based upon work supported in part by the Israel Science Foundation under grant no. 557/09, by IBM's Ph.D. fellowship and SUR award, by Google's and Yahoo!'s faculty research awards, and by Miriam and Aaron Gutwirth Memorial Fellowship. Any opinions, findings and conclusions or recommendations expressed here are the authors' and do not necessarily reflect those of the sponsors.

6. REFERENCES

[1] G. Amati, C. Carpineto, and G. Romano. Query difficulty, robustness, and selective application of query expansion. In *Proc. of ECIR*, pages 127–137, 2004.

[2] J. A. Aslam and V. Pavlu. Query hardness estimation using Jensen-Shannon divergence among multiple scoring functions. In *Proc. of ECIR*, pages 198–209, 2007.

[3] M. Bendersky, W. B. Croft, and Y. Diao. Quality-biased ranking of web documents. In *Proc. of WSDM*, pages 95–104, 2011.

[4] D. Carmel and E. Yom-Tov. *Estimating the Query Difficulty for Information Retrieval.* Synthesis Lectures on Information Concepts, Retrieval, and Services. Morgan & Claypool Publishers, 2010.

[5] D. Carmel, E. Yom-Tov, A. Darlow, and D. Pelleg. What makes a query difficult? In *Proc. of SIGIR*, pages 390–397, 2006.

[6] C. L. A. Clarke, N. Craswell, and I. Soboroff. Overview of the TREC 2009 Web track. In *Proc. of TREC*, 2009.

[7] K. Collins-Thompson and P. N. Bennett. Predicting query performance via classification. In *Proc. of ECIR*, pages 140–152, 2010.

[8] G. V. Cormack, M. D. Smucker, and C. L. A. Clarke. Efficient and effective spam filtering and re-ranking for large web datasets. *CoRR*, abs/1004.5168, 2010.

[9] W. B. Croft and J. Lafferty, editors. *Language Modeling for Information Retrieval.* Number 13 in Information Retrieval Book Series. Kluwer, 2003.

[10] S. Cronen-Townsend, Y. Zhou, and W. B. Croft. Predicting query performance. In *Proc. of SIGIR*, pages 299–306, 2002.

[11] S. Cronen-Townsend, Y. Zhou, and W. B. Croft. A language modeling framework for selective query expansion. Technical Report IR-338, Center for Intelligent Information Retrieval, University of Massachusetts, 2004.

[12] R. Cummins. Predicting query performance directly from score distributions. In *Proc. of AIRS*, pages 315–326, 2011.

[13] R. Cummins, J. M. Jose, and C. O'Riordan. Improved query performance prediction using standard deviation. In *Proc. of SIGIR*, pages 1089–1090, 2011.

[14] F. Diaz. Performance prediction using spatial autocorrelation. In *Proc. of SIGIR*, pages 583–590, 2007.

[15] C. Hauff, L. Azzopardi, and D. Hiemstra. The combination and evaluation of query performance prediction methods. In *Proc. of ECIR*, pages 301–312, 2009.

[16] C. Hauff, D. Hiemstra, and F. de Jong. A survey of pre-retrieval query performance predictors. In *Proc. of CIKM*, pages 1419–1420, 2008.

[17] C. Hauff, D. Kelly, and L. Azzopardi. A comparison of user and system query performance predictions. In *Proc. of CIKM*, pages 979–988, 2010.

[18] C. Hauff, V. Murdock, and R. Baeza-Yates. Improved query difficulty prediction for the web. In *Proc. of CIKM*, pages 439–448, 2008.

[19] B. He and I. Ounis. Inferring query performance using pre-retrieval predictors. In *Proc. of SPIRE*, pages 43–54, 2004.

[20] S. Hummel, A. Shtok, F. Raiber, O. Kurland, and D. Carmel. Clarity re-visited. In *Proc. of SIGIR*, 2012. Poster.

[21] O. Kurland, A. Shtok, D. Carmel, and S. Hummel. A unified framework for post-retrieval query-performance prediction. In *Proc. of ICTIR*, pages 15–26, 2011.

[22] J. Lafferty and C. Zhai. Probabilistic relevance models based on document and query generation. In Croft and Lafferty [9], pages 1–10.

[23] J. D. Lafferty and C. Zhai. Document language models, query models, and risk minimization for information retrieval. In *Proc. of SIGIR*, pages 111–119, 2001.

[24] V. Lavrenko and W. B. Croft. Relevance-based language models. In *Proc. of SIGIR*, pages 120–127, 2001.

[25] J. Mothe and L. Tanguy. Linguistic features to predict query difficulty. In *ACM SIGIR 2005 Workshop on Predicting Query Difficulty - Methods and Applications*, 2005.

[26] S. E. Robertson. The probability ranking principle in IR. *Journal of Documentation*, pages 294–304, 1977.

[27] T. Rölleke and J. Wang. A parallel derivation of probabilistic information retrieval models. In *SIGIR*, pages 107–114, 2006.

[28] F. Scholer and S. Garcia. A case for improved evaluation of query difficulty prediction. In *Proc. of SIGIR*, pages 640–641, 2009.

[29] F. Scholer, H. E. Williams, and A. Turpin. Query association surrogates for web search. *JASIST*, 55(7):637–650, 2004.

[30] A. Shtok, O. Kurland, and D. Carmel. Predicting query performance by query-drift estimation. In *Proc. of ICTIR*, pages 305–312, 2009.

[31] A. Shtok, O. Kurland, and D. Carmel. Using statistical decision theory and relevance models for query-performance prediction. In *Proccedings of SIGIR*, pages 259–266, 2010.

[32] F. Song and W. B. Croft. A general language model for information retrieval (poster abstract). In *Proc. of SIGIR*, pages 279–280, 1999.

[33] K. Sparck Jones, S. Walker, and S. E. Robertson. A probabilistic model of information retrieval: development and comparative experiments - part 1. *Information Processing and Management*, 36(6):779–808, 2000.

[34] J. H. Steiger. Tests for comparing elements of a correlation matrix. *Psychological Bulletin*, 87(2):245–251, 1980.

[35] S. Tomlinson. Robust, Web and Terabyte Retrieval with Hummingbird Search Server at TREC 2004. In *Proc. of TREC-13*, 2004.

[36] V. Vinay, I. J. Cox, N. Milic-Frayling, and K. R. Wood. On ranking the effectiveness of searches. In *Proc. of SIGIR*, pages 398–404, 2006.

[37] E. Yom-Tov, S. Fine, D. Carmel, and A. Darlow. Learning to estimate query difficulty: including applications to missing content detection and distributed information retrieval. In *Proc. of SIGIR*, pages 512–519, 2005.

[38] C. Zhai and J. D. Lafferty. A study of smoothing methods for language models applied to ad hoc information retrieval. In *Proc. of SIGIR*, pages 334–342, 2001.

[39] Y. Zhao, F. Scholer, and Y. Tsegay. Effective pre-retrieval query performance prediction using similarity and variability evidence. In *Proc. of ECIR*, pages 52–64, 2008.

[40] Y. Zhou. *Retrieval Performance Prediction and Document Quality*. PhD thesis, University of Massachusetts, 2007.

[41] Y. Zhou and W. B. Croft. Ranking robustness: a novel framework to predict query performance. In *Proc. of CIKM*, pages 567–574, 2006.

[42] Y. Zhou and W. B. Croft. Query performance prediction in web search environments. In *Proc. of SIGIR*, pages 543–550, 2007.

APPENDIX

A. CLARITY

Clarity is defined as the KL divergence between a relevance language model $R_{\mathcal{D}_{res}}$ constructed from $\mathcal{D}_{res}$ and a language model $p(\cdot|\mathcal{D})$ induced from the corpus [10]:

$$\mathcal{P}_{Clarity}(\mathcal{D}_{res};q) \stackrel{def}{=} \sum_{w} p(w|R_{\mathcal{D}_{res}}) \log \frac{p(w|R_{\mathcal{D}_{res}})}{p(w|\mathcal{D})}; \quad (7)$$

w is a term in the vocabulary. $R_{\mathcal{D}_{res}}$ is a linear mixture of language models of documents in $\mathcal{D}_{res}$ [24]:

$$p(w|R_{\mathcal{D}_{res}}) \stackrel{def}{=} \sum_{d_i \in \mathcal{D}_{res}} p(w|d_i)p(d_i|q,r); \quad (8)$$

$p(w|d_i)$ is the probability assigned to w by a language model induced from d_i; and, $p(d_i|q,r) \stackrel{def}{=} \frac{p(q|d_i,r)}{\sum_{d' \in \mathcal{D}_{res}} p(q|d',r)}$ is d_i's normalized query-likelihood when using uniform distributions for $p(r|d)$ and $p(d)$, where $d \in \mathcal{D}_{res}$.[10]

Using $R_{\mathcal{D}_{res}}$'s definition from Equation 8 in Equation 7, and applying arithmetic manipulation, we get that:

$$\mathcal{P}_{Clarity}(\mathcal{D}_{res};q) = \sum_{d_i \in \mathcal{D}_{res}} p(d_i|q,r) \Big(\sum_{w} p(w|d_i) \log p(w|R_{\mathcal{D}_{res}}) - \sum_{w} p(w|d_i) \log p(w|\mathcal{D}) \Big).$$

We define the similarity between d_i and X ($\mathcal{D}_{res}$ or $\mathcal{D}$) as the minus cross entropy between their induced language models: $Sim(d_i, X) \stackrel{def}{=} \sum_w p(w|d_i) \log p(w|X)$, with $p(w|\mathcal{D}_{res}) \stackrel{def}{=} p(w|R_{\mathcal{D}_{res}})$. Thus, Clarity is:

$$\mathcal{P}_{Clarity}(\mathcal{D}_{res};q) = \sum_{d_i \in \mathcal{D}_{res}} p(d_i|q,r) \big(Sim(d_i, \mathcal{D}_{res}) - Sim(d_i, \mathcal{D}) \big). \quad (9)$$

B. EXPLAINING A PREVIOUSLY PROPOSED PREDICTION FRAMEWORK

Applying log odds, which is a monotonic transformation, upon Equation 1 yields:

$$\log O(r|q,\mathcal{D}_{res}) \stackrel{def}{=} \log \frac{p(r|q,\mathcal{D}_{res})}{p(\bar{r}|q,\mathcal{D}_{res})} = \log p(\mathcal{D}_{res}|r,q)p(r|q) - \log p(\mathcal{D}_{res}|\bar{r},q)p(\bar{r}|q); \quad (10)$$

$\bar{r}$ is the non-relevance event.

Suppose we estimate $p(\mathcal{D}_{res}|r,q)$ and $p(\mathcal{D}_{res}|\bar{r},q)$ based on $\mathcal{D}_{res}$'s similarity with a (pseudo) relevant and non-relevant document lists, respectively; and, use a uniform relevance prior, $p(r|q) = p(\bar{r}|q) = \frac{1}{2}$. Then, we obtain the prediction principle underlying the framework proposed in [21].

[10]While the common notation used in the language modeling framework does not include an explicit relevance event indicator, here we follow Lafferty and Zhai [22] and use it.

Learning to Rank for Robust Question Answering

Arvind Agarwal*
Department of Computer Science
University of Maryland
College Park, MD 20742 USA
arvinda@cs.umd.edu

Hema Raghavan
IBM T. J. Watson Research Center
Yorktown Heights, NY 10598 USA
hraghav@us.ibm.com

Karthik Subbian†
University of Minnesota
Minneapolis, MN 55455 USA
karthik@cs.umn.edu

Prem Melville
IBM T. J. Watson Research Center
Yorktown Heights, NY 10598 USA
pmelvil@us.ibm.com

Richard D. Lawrence
IBM T. J. Watson Research Center
Yorktown Heights, NY 10598 USA
ricklawr@us.ibm.com

David C. Gondek
IBM T. J. Watson Research Center
Yorktown Heights, NY 10598 USA
dgondek@us.ibm.com

ABSTRACT

This paper aims to solve the problem of improving the ranking of answer candidates for factoid based questions in a state-of-the-art Question Answering system. We first provide an extensive comparison of 5 ranking algorithms on two datasets – from the Jeopardy quiz show and a medical domain. We then show the effectiveness of a cascading approach, where the ranking produced by one ranker is used as input to the next stage. The cascading approach shows sizeable gains on both datasets. We finally evaluate several rank aggregation techniques to combine these algorithms, and find that Supervised Kemeny aggregation is a robust technique that always beats the baseline ranking approach used by Watson for the Jeopardy competition. We further corroborate our results on TREC Question Answering datasets.

Categories and Subject Descriptors

H.3.3 [**Information Search and Retrieval**]: Information filtering, Retrieval models

General Terms

Algorithms

Keywords

Ranking, Question-answering, Rank-aggregation

*The part of this work was done during the internship at IBM T. J. Watson Research Center, Yorktown Heights, NY

†The work was done during the employment at IBM T. J. Watson Research Center, Yorktown Heights, NY.

CIKM'12, October 29–November 2, 2012, Maui, HI, USA.

1. INTRODUCTION

Question answering (QA) is the task of finding an exact answer to a user's natural language question. In February, 2011, the IBM Watson QA system beat human grand champions in the game of Jeopardy!, marking a major milestone in QA research. This was made possible by great advances in all stages of the QA system pipeline, including question analysis, search, hypothesis generation, and hypothesis scoring. One of the key steps at the end of this pipeline is ranking the candidate answers produced by weighing all the evidence extracted and scored in support of each answer. In Watson, this task is solved by using a Machine Learning approach, where a model is built based on a set of training questions with known answers, and then used to score new question-answer pairs. This task can be viewed as a special case of rank-learning, and as such recent advances in learning to rank [6] may be effectively applied here. In this paper, we provide an extensive study of different approaches to ranking candidate answers as applied to QA.

Most recent advances in learning to rank have been driven by web search [8]. While the task of ranking candidate answers in QA is similar to document-retrieval, there are some key differences: (1) Instead of relevance, which can be multi-graded in search, we just have binary relevance judgments, corresponding to the right or wrong answer. (2) The data has high class imbalance. While search datasets also tend to have a high ratio of irrelevant to relevant documents, in the case of QA, there is typically only one correct answer. (3) Search systems are typically evaluated on an entire ranked list or the top 10 results produced, using metrics such as ERR, NDCG, and MAP. However, in most QA systems the desired goal is to get the top-ranked answer right [15, 36]. As such Precision@1 becomes the primary metric to optimize.

The above distinctions make answer-ranking in QA a special case of the learning to rank problem, and observations made in the context of document retrieval may not hold. This paper makes the following contributions: (1) To the best of our knowledge this is the first work that provides an extensive comparison of several approaches to learning to rank, applied specifically to answer-ranking in open-domain QA (Jeopardy), as well as in the highly specialized domain of medicine. (2) We show how results can be improved using a cascading approach, where the rankings produced by one ranker are provided as inputs to another. Such a cascading approach not only gives better performance, but also speeds up runtime prediction. (3) We demonstrate how multiple rankers can be

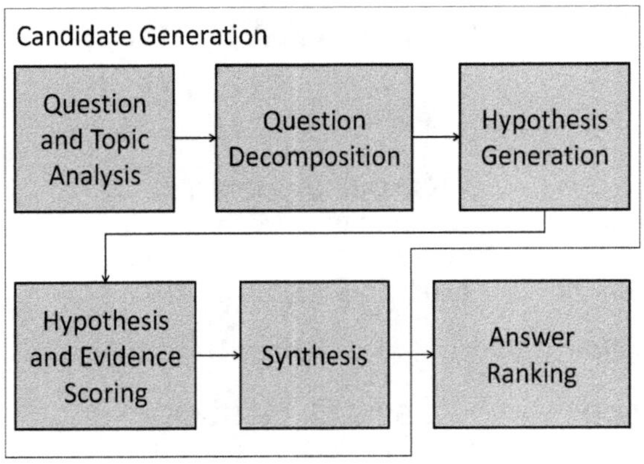

Figure 1: Overview of Watson

effectively combined using rank aggregation techniques stemming from the Social Choice Theory literature. As will be seen later in our experiments, in one dataset, logistic regression performs best, while in other, LambdaRank perform best; and a combined system performs better than any individual ranker in both cases. (4) In practice, since it is hard to find a single ranker that performs best on all datasets, our proposed system is a practical solution to this problem of having to rely on one ranker. Our system does not rely on any single best ranker, rather combines different rankers and gives the best of all. (5) The final system proposed in this paper is both efficient and robust, giving improvements of 3.4 and 2.2% points in Precision@1, over the algorithm used by Watson on the Jeopardy and Medical task respectively. We show similar improvements in performance on publicly available TREC QA datasets.

We believe our work furthers the state-of-the-art in Open Domain QA by showing how learning to rank (LETOR) can be effective for the task. At the time of running the TREC QA tasks which ended in 2007, pointwise classification methods like logistic regression and Maximum Entropy Models were state of the art for the final answer selection component [19, 27, 32]. Many advances in Machine Learning for Information Retrieval tasks have been made since then. We provide an extensive comparison of several approaches of LETOR and Rank Aggregation for QA and improve over the baseline Watson system built for Jeopardy. Given the renewed interest in QA with Jeopardy, Siri and the DARPA BOLT Program[1], this work establishes a baseline for future QA research. We emphasize that improvements on Jeopardy are significant because the system was worked on for several years and obtaining improvements has not been trivial.

2. ANSWER RANKING IN WATSON

We begin by providing an overview of the Watson QA system. Watson answers questions by first analyzing the question, generating candidate answers, and then collecting evidence over its text and knowledge base resources supporting or refuting those answers. For each answer, individual pieces of evidence are scored by an ensemble of answer scorers, yielding features capturing the degree to which evidence justifies or refutes an answer. Most features provide some measure of how justified the answer is for the question according to evidence in text passages or knowledge base information. However, there are also scores representing question-level features which indicate information about the question (for instance the answer type specified by the question) as well as answer-level features (for instance the popularity of an answer). An example of a *high recall* score is a measure of the weighted overlap between terms in a question and a passage. In contrast, an example of a *high precision* score is a measure of the alignment of grammatical and semantic relationships between the question and passage using a graphical abstraction.

Finally, these features are used to rank candidate answers, based on the likelihood the answer is correct. Crafting successful strategies for resolving thousands of answer scores into a final ranking would be difficult, if not impossible, to optimize by hand; so Watson was designed to learn over existing questions and their correct answers. From a Machine Learning perspective, a training/test instance here, is a feature vector presenting evidence for or against a question-answer pair being correct. Fig. 1 shows an overview of the Watson system pipeline. In this paper, we only focus on the final stage of ranking candidate answers. For a longer description of the machine learning component of Watson the reader is referred to [17].

Architecturally, Watson provides a confidence estimation framework which uses a common data model for registration of answer scores and performs machine learning over large sets of training data in order to produce models for answer ranking and confidence estimation. While the ranking component is critical for *deploying* a full question answering system, it is also essential for *developing* the system. Developers working on any aspect of the system, from candidate generation to answer scoring, must evaluate the system-wide impact of their component on end-to-end question answering performance. This development methodology requires performing thousands of experiments requiring retraining of the system to assess the impact of every potential change. This drives the need for machine learning which is computationally efficient, to allow for rapid experimentation, and which is highly automatic, to achieve valid results without requiring manual parameter tuning or specialist knowledge of machine learning algorithms to perform each experiment. This approach allows developers to focus on optimizing performance of their component and entrust to the framework the assessment and proper combination of the component's scores for the end-to-end question answering task.

3. EXPERIMENTAL METHODOLOGY

We now describe our datasets and evaluation approach.

3.1 Datasets

We evaluate our system on two datasets – Jeopardy and Medical. The questions and correct answers for the Jeopardy dataset are obtained from historical records of the American TV quiz show, Jeopardy. In Watson, answer candidates are generated by searching for hypotheses through several sources like Wikipedia, the Bible, IMDB, ebooks on Project Gutenberg, using the INDRI[29] search engine. NLP techniques are used to understand the focus and category of a question, find the lexical answer type, and finally narrow down on an answer-candidate in the retrieved passages. Details of the techniques used for answer-candidate generation can be found elsewhere [15, 13].

The Medical dataset was obtained from a Jeopardy-like competition held by the American College of Physicians called the *Doctor's Dilemma*. The underlying content being searched in this case includes several medical content sources such as: ACP Medicine, Merck Manual of Diagnosis and Therapy and MKSAP (a study

[1]`http://bit.ly/vViNIG`

	Jeopardy		Medical	
	Train	Test	Train	Test
No. of questions	9337	2961	909	607
Avg. no. of candidates per question	220	223	244	241
Avg. no. of correct answers per question	1.30	1.20	1.57	1.77

Table 1: Dataset statistics

guide from ACP). Several candidate answers are generated per question using a system similar to Watson but which had been adapted for the medical domain [14].

Although the original datasets contain questions which do not have a correct answer in the candidate set, in our experiments, as in [31], we only consider those questions that have at least one correct answer. Table 1 shows a summary of the data.

For both datasets several hundred features are extracted as described in the previous section. There are 547 features in the Jeopardy dataset and 323 in the Medical dataset. We refer the reader to the references for a detailed description of the NLP components. The focus of this paper is to study the effectiveness of various algorithms on ranking the candidate answers. An example question in the Medical dataset is *PULMONOLOGY: Diagnosis associated with "egg shell" calcification of intrathoracic lymph nodes.* Watson produces candidate answers such as *Sarcoidosis*, *Silicosis* and *Lymphadenopathy*. Our task is to correctly rank these answers, so that the correct answer(s) (*Silicosis*) is placed at the top of the list. In all experiments in this work, the feature set is kept constant and the goal is to evaluate algorithms for ranking.

3.2 Evaluation Measures

The output of our system is a *ranked list* of candidate answers for each question. However, for most QA tasks we only get credit for selecting one correct response – for instance, in the Jeopardy! challenge a contestant is only allowed to give one answer. As such, our primary evaluation metric is Precision@1 (P@1), which measures the percentage of questions for which the top-ranked answer is correct.

In some domains, such as Medical QA, there can be more than one correct answer – for instance, two valid diagnoses for the same symptoms. In order to evaluate this setting, we also measure Normalized Discounted Cumulative Gain [20] at rank K ($K = 5, 10$). NDCG@K looks at the top-K candidate answers, and assigns a higher weight to a correct answer that is ranked higher than one that is ranked lower. NDCG@K is computed as:

$$NDCG@K = \frac{1}{Q}\sum_{q=1}^{Q}\frac{DCG_q}{IdealDCG_q}, \quad (1)$$

where Q is the total number of queries, and

$$DCG_q = \sum_{i=1}^{K}\frac{2^{y_{qi}}-1}{\log_2(1+i)} \quad (2)$$

y_{qi} is the relevance level of candidate answer i for query q. $IdealDCG$ is simply DCG with the ideal ranking. While P@1 only looks at the top-ranked response, NDCG provides a finer granularity for evaluation, rewarding algorithms for having a higher rank for a correct answer, even if it is not at the top of the list. All metric numbers in this paper are reported in %.

4. LEARNING TO RANK

Over the last decade, learning to rank methods have been effectively applied to information retrieval tasks. These methods aim at learning a model that given a query and a set of relevant documents, finds the appropriate ranking of documents according to their relevancy. A question answering task is similar to the information retrieval task i.e., a question is simply a query and a set of candidate answers is analogous to a set of relevant documents. The goal is now to find the appropriate ranking of these candidate answers according to their correctness. There have been numerous learning to rank methods developed, which can be divided into three main categories: pointwise methods, pairwise methods, and listwise methods.

Pointwise methods treat the ranking problem as a standard classification or a regression task. These methods assume that each question-answer pair has either (a) a numerical or ordinal (rank) score associated with it or (b) a relevance label in one of two or more classes. The objective in the former formulation is to find a model that predicts this score correctly through ordinal regression methods [10]. In the latter case, the problem is reduced to classification and can be solved by methods such as SVMs or logistic regression [25].

Pairwise methods like FRank [34], SVMRank [21], RankNet [5], RankBoost [16] aim to learn the pairwise preference of candidate answers rather than their absolute rank. The intuition behind these approaches is that in information retrieval one cares about metrics like NDCG and MAP which reward a system for a ranking of results as opposed to an absolute prediction of relevance, and modeling preferences is closer to that final objective. In these ranking methods, given a ranked set of candidate answers for a query, preferences expressing that one answer is preferred over the other are constructed from each pair of answers. More specifically, each pair of candidate answers is given a binary label $\{+1, -1\}$ based on if the first answer in the pair has a higher rank than the second answer. This construction transforms the original ranking problem into a binary classification problem of predicting these pairwise preferences. The goal is now to learn a binary classifier that minimizes the number of incorrectly ordered pairs. A total ordering of candidates is inferred from the predicted pairwise preferences.

Listwise methods operate on the entire list of candidate answers. Unlike pointwise and pairwise methods where a loss based on the rank of the individual candidate answer or of a pair is minimized; in listwise methods, a direct loss (an appropriate evaluation measure defined by the user) is minimized between the true ranks of the list and the estimated ranks of the list. These methods are the most sophisticated and have been shown to outperform the other two types of methods for information retrieval tasks [28]. Many of these methods allow for the optimization of the final metric relevant to the application. Examples of listwise methods are LambdaRank [28], Coordinate-Ascent [24], AdaRank [37], ListNet [7] and [40].

In this work, we compare the following representative learning to rank methods for each of the 3 categories, applied to the task of question-answering. We emphasize here that these different rankers were selected based their ease of availability and implementation, and also based on their ability to run on a large dataset.

Logistic Regression (LR) is a binary classification method giving a score that is a probability of relevance, and is therefore a natural as well as effective choice for question-answering tasks [27, 19] including for Watson for the Jeopardy challenge [13, 35]. It is a pointwise method, and simply minimizes the logistic loss between the true label of an answer and the estimated label (represented as a real value). At the test time, it assigns a probability of relevance to each candidate answer which can be sorted to get the appropriate

Dataset	LR	Rank Boost	Ada-Rank	Coord-Ascent	Lambda Rank
Jeopardy	69.0	62.8	55.3	-	66.9
	80.9	76.3	71.2	-	79.0
Medical	43.3	39.2	33.4	28.8	39.2
	54.6	51.7	44.0	41.4	52.0

Table 2: Performance of different learning to rank methods. Top entry in each cell is P@1 while bottom is NDCG@10.

ranking. Although logistic regression has not received much attention in the information retrieval task because of the other sophisticated learning to rank methods, it has been successfully used in the question answering task e.g. Watson system, to rank answers. The team working on the Watson system has consistently found logistic regression to beat other point-wise methods and logistic regression was used in the final Jeopardy game[17].

RankBoost [16] is a pairwise ranking method based on boosting. RankBoost first constructs the pairs (as would be done for any pairwise method) based on the preference order, and assigns each pair a label +1 if the first answer is ranked higher than the second, and -1 if the second answer is ranked higher that the first; and transforms the ranking task into a binary classification task. RankBoost then applies the boosting algorithm on this classification task. It starts with equal weights assigned to all pairs, and in each round, uses weak rankers to reassign the weights. The pairs that are correctly ranked are given lower weights while those incorrectly ranked are given higher weights. In the end, a linear combination of these weak rankers is used for the final ranking.

AdaRank [37] is similar to RankBoost except that it is a listwise approach. The weak rankers in AdaRank are learned by directly optimizing ranking measures such as NDCG or MAP, unlike in RankBoost, where a pairwise loss is minimized.

Coordinate-Ascent is a listwise method proposed by [24]. It is a linear feature-based method that directly optimizes the ranking measure using the well-known optimization method i.e., coordinate ascent. Optimization is performed cyclically, optimizing one parameter at-a-time while keeping others fixed.

LambdaRank [28] is a listwise method based on the pairwise ranking method, RankNet [5]. LambdaRank is based on the idea that in order to learn a model the actual value of the loss function is not needed, in fact only the gradient of the loss function is sufficient. Once a gradient is known, it can be used with standard optimization methods e.g. gradient descent to minimize the original cost function. An intuitive technique is used to compute the gradient for different evaluation measures like NDCG and MAP and is used to learn the model.

Note that our datasets are relatively large (~4GB, both train and test) and some methods, such as SVMRank [21] took more than a day to train on the smaller (Medical) dataset, and were therefore discarded for this study.

As a sanity check of our implementations, we experimented and found that all rankers (except logistic regression, as it is unsuitable for multivalued data) were quite competitive when evaluated on the Yahoo! dataset provided as a part of a recent learning to rank challenge [8].

4.1 Experiments

We evaluated the performance of the different learning to rank methods on the Jeopardy and Medical datasets. For logistic regression, we used the implementation in WEKA [18]. For RankBoost, Coordinate-Ascent, and AdaRank, we used RankLib [11]; where AdaRank and Coordinate-Ascent optimized P@1. For LambdaRank, we used our own implementation, written to optimize NDCG (as it cannot directly optimize P@1). For all rankers, we used the default hyperparameters suggested by authors, without any tuning.

Results are presented in Table 2 for two metrics P@1 (top entry in each cell), and NDCG@10 (bottom). Given its computational complexity, Coordinate-Ascent did not terminate on Jeopardy (after 2 days), and as such we only present its results on the smaller dataset (Medical). We see that despite being the simplest, the pointwise method logistic regression performs best on both datasets and on both metrics, followed by LambdaRank and RankBoost. This behavior is in contrast to the one noted by the information retrieval community, where listwise methods usually outperform pairwise methods, and pairwise methods outperform pointwise methods [28]. This could be the case for the following reasons: (1) Pointwise methods may be desirable in this degenerate case of learning to rank, where we only have binary relevance and mostly just 1 correct answer amongst many incorrect answers. We will see in the next section, that the other rankers often outperform logistic regression when there is less of a class imbalance. (2) The features generated over the years of Watson development were tested with logistic regression. So there might be an inherent bias in feature generation and selection in favor of logistic regression. This ordering in performance is not what we expect in general – as we have independently verified by applying the above rankers on web search data.

In the section, we will provide a mechanism that will not only improve on each of these results, but also speed up the training time, allowing us to fill in the missing entries corresponding to Coordinate-Ascent in Table 2.

5. PRUNING

As discussed previously Question Answering for factoid questions is a high accuracy task and one is typically interested in providing one (or very few) precise answers. Matveeva et al. ([23]) showed that training a learning to rank algorithm (Rank-Net in their case) using the top N results from an initial ranking helped improve precision at the top of the ranked list for web-search. In this section we study the impact of restricting the training set for the learning to rank algorithms to the top N candidates determined by the baseline Logistic Regression trained on all the training data. The idea behind such a pruning technique is that if the first stage is reasonably accurate, the re-ranking phase can focus on improving the precision at high ranks. The motivation is different from active learning or boosting where the most difficult examples are added to the training set in subsequent training phases.

In the experiments in this section we train a base logistic regression using all training data. A new model is trained using the top N answers for each query. For each such model trained we test its performance on the top N candidates as ranked by the base logistic regression on the test data. We repeat this procedure for all rankers including logistic regression and the results are shown in Figure 2.

From the figure, all rankers including logistic regression show significant improvements due to pruning on Jeopardy. When $N = 5$, logistic regression achieves a P@1 of 72.2% which is a *statistically significant* improvement compared to the baseline model's P@1 of 69.0%. When $N = 5$, the performance of LambdaRank (P@1=71.8%) is on par with that of logistic regression and their performances are statistically indistinguishable.

On the medical data all rankers show improvements in going from using all the data to pruning at 50. Unlike Jeopardy however, all the rankers achieve their peak performance at different pruning thresholds. LambdaRank peaks at $N = 20$ and further pruning seems to hurt its performance. To understand this effect, we list the Success@K metric for the two datasets for the base Logistic Regression model. The Success@K metric is the percentage of queries for which a relevant result exists in the top-K results. While on the Jeopardy data, even for $K = 5$ the base Logistic Regression model achieves 90% success, on the Medical data this value sharply drops after $K = 20$. We suspect that the quality of the initial ranker is a factor that determines the extent of pruning that can be done for a corpus. The impact of pruning on other metrics like NDCG was similar to P@1.

We also experimented with using the models trained on the top N candidates to re-score the *entire* test data but found that our approach of pruning the test data was slightly better. Such pruning of data for training and testing the second pass rankers has the advantage of speeding both train and test times allowing us to use more complex rankers that might not be feasible on a large dataset. For example, while we were unable to run Co-ordinate Ascent on the entire Jeopardy data, pruning the results to $N = 50$ allowed us to evaluate and use this ranker. An additional advantage of pruning is that it reduces the class bias and therefore allows one to benefit from more sophisticated learning to rank methods, an observation also made in [35]. In our experiments, we have observed (see Figure 2) that in case of full data, pointwise methods such as logistic regression outperform pairwise and listwise methods, but when the data is pruned, listwise methods e.g., LambdaRank start to take over.

K	Jeopardy	Medical
50	98.31%	94.39%
30	97.46%	90.44%
20	96.55%	87.80%
10	94.25%	80.23%
5	90.74%	71.82%

Table 3: Success@K for the baseline ranker, on the two corpora

In the next section, we will improve on these results even further by combining these different rankers which will be the output of our final ranking system.

6. RANK AGGREGATION

The performance of individual rankers vary significantly across different datasets and training set sizes, as seen in Fig. 2. This suggests that instead of relying on the single best ranker, it may be better to combine all rankers to produce a more robust and accurate ranking. Since individual rankers produce an ordering of elements, and not a pointwise score that can be meaningfully aggregated, we can leverage approaches to aggregating rankings that have been studied in Social Choice Theory, and successfully applied to meta-search [12].

We begin by formally defining the rank aggregation task. Given a set of entities S, let V be a subset of S; and assume that there is a total ordering in V. We are given r individual rankers $\tau_1, ..., \tau_r$ who specify their order preferences of the m candidates, where m is size of V, i.e., $\tau_i = [d_1, ..., d_m], i = 1, ..., r$, if $d_1 > ... > d_m, d_j \in V, j = 1, ..., m$. If d_i is preferred over d_j we denote that by $d_i > d_j$. Rank aggregation function ψ takes input orderings from r rankers and gives τ, which is an aggregated ranking order. If V equals S, then τ is called a *full list* (total ordering), otherwise it is called a *partial list* (partial ordering).

All commonly-used rank aggregation methods, satisfy one or more of the following desirable *goodness* properties: Unanimity, Non-dictatorial Criterion, Neutrality, Consistency, Condorcet Criterion and Extended Condorcet Criterion (ECC) [1]. We will primarily focus on ECC, defined below:

Algorithm 1 Supervised Kemeny Ranking (SKR)

Input: $\tau_i = [\tau_{i1}, ..., \tau_{im}], \forall i = 1, ..., r$, ordered arrangement of m candidates for r rankers.
$w = [w_1, ..., w_r]$ – where w_i is the weight of ranker i
$\mu = [\mu_1, ..., \mu_m]$ – initial ordered arrangement of m candidates
k – the number candidates to consider in each ranker's preference list ($k \leq m$)
Output: τ – rank aggregated arrangement of candidates in decreasing order of relevance

1. Initialize majority table $M_{i,j} \Leftarrow 0, \forall i, j = 1, ..., m$
2. For each ranker $p = 1$ to r
3. For each candidate $i = 1$ to k-1
4. For each candidate $j = i + 1$ to k
5. $M_{\tau_{pi}, \tau_{pj}} \Leftarrow M_{\tau_{pi}, \tau_{pj}} + w_p$
6. Quick sort μ, using M_{μ_i, μ_j}. If $M_{\mu_i, \mu_j} - M_{\mu_j, \mu_i} > 0$ then μ_i is greater than μ_j. If $M_{\mu_i, \mu_j} - M_{\mu_j, \mu_i} = 0$ then μ_i is equal to μ_j. If $M_{\mu_i, \mu_j} - M_{\mu_j, \mu_i} < 0$ then μ_i is less than μ_j.
7. Return τ

DEFINITION 1. *The Extended Condorcet Criterion [33] requires that if there is any partition $\{C, R\}$ of S, such that for any $d_i \in C$ and $d_j \in R$ a majority of rankers prefer d_i to d_j, then the aggregate ranking τ should prefer d_i to d_j.*

The ECC property is highly desirable in our domain, as it eliminates the possibility of inferior candidates in a ranking to affect the choice between superior candidates. In other words, it offers the property of Independence of Irrelevant Alternatives. Additionally, ECC is a relaxed form of Kemeny optimal aggregation (defined below), where the partition C and R are arranged in the "true" order, but not necessarily the elements within partitions C and R. In addition to the desirable theoretical properties, ECC proves to be very valuable in ranking in practice [12, 30], as is further corroborated in our experiments.

We will focus on two classical rank aggregation techniques in this paper: Borda and Kemeny, described below:

Borda Aggregation: In Borda aggregation [4] each candidate is assigned a score by each ranker. The score for a candidate is the number of candidates below it in each ranker's preferences. The Borda aggregation is the descending order arrangement of the average Borda score for each candidate averaged across all ranker preferences. Though Borda aggregation satisfies neutrality, monotonicity, and consistency, it does not satisfy the Condorcet Criterion [38] and ECC. In fact, it has been shown that no method that assigns weights to each position and then sorts the results by applying a function to the weights associated with each candidate satisfies the Extended Condorcet Criterion [12]. This includes pointwise classifiers like logistic regression. This motivates the use of order-based methods for rank aggregation that do satisfy ECC.

Kemeny Aggregation: A Kemeny optimal aggregation [22] is an aggregation that has the minimum number of pairwise disagreements with all rankers, i.e., a choice of τ that minimizes:

$$K(\tau, \tau_1, ..., \tau_r) = \frac{1}{r} \sum_{i=1}^{r} k(\tau, \tau_i);$$

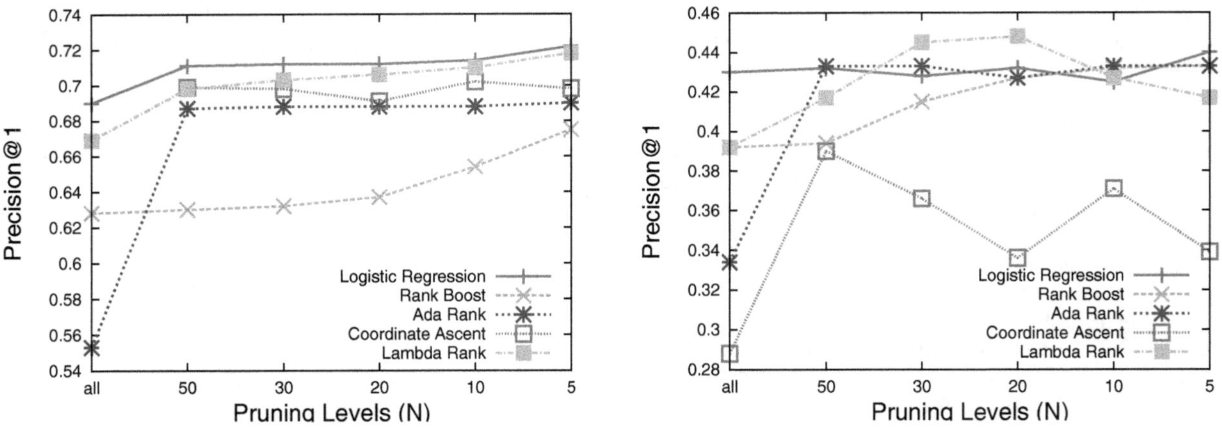

Figure 2: Performance (P@1) for various pruning levels (N) for Jeopardy (left) and Medical (right) datasets.

Datasets	Rankers						Aggregation					
							Unsupervised			Supervised		
	LR	Rank Boost	AdaRank	Coord Ascent	Lambda Rank	Mean	Borda	Kemeny	Kemeny Top-k	Borda	Kemeny	Kemeny Top-k
Jeopardy	72.2	67.5	69.0	69.8	71.8	70.1	72.2	72.3	72.0	72.0	**72.4**	**72.4**
(pruned@5)	82.3	80.2	80.9	81.0	82.2	81.3	82.3	82.3	82.1	82.3	**82.4**	**82.4**
Medical	43.2	42.7	42.7	33.6	44.8	41.4	43.3	44.0	43.8	44.0	**45.5**	**45.5**
(pruned@20)	54.7	53.6	54.6	48.0	**55.7**	53.3	55.0	54.9	54.9	55.3	**55.7**	**55.7**

Table 4: Performance of rank-aggregation methods along with the learning to rank methods on Medical and Jeopardy data. The top entry in each cell is Precision@1, while the bottom is NDCG@10. The best results for each setting are presented in bold.

where the function $k(\sigma, \tau)$ is the *Kendall tau* distance measured as $|\{(i,j)|i<j, \sigma(i)>\sigma(j), \text{but } \tau(i)<\tau(j)\}|$, where $\sigma(i)$ is used to denote the position of i in ranking σ.

Kemeny aggregation satisfies neutrality, consistency, and the Extended Condorcet Criterion. Kemeny optimal aggregation also has a good maximum likelihood interpretation [39]. Suppose there is an underlying "correct" ordering σ of S, and each order $\tau_1, ..., \tau_r$ is obtained from σ by swapping pairs of elements with some probability less than $1/2$. That is, the τ's are "noisy" versions of σ. A Kemeny optimal aggregation of $\tau_1, ..., \tau_r$ is one (not necessarily unique) that is maximally likely to have produced the τ's.

While Kemeny aggregation is optimal in the sense described above, computing a Kemeny aggregation is NP-Hard for $r \geq 4$ [12]. So in practice, we use an approach that produces a 2-approximation of Kemeny optimal aggregation, referred to as Approximate Kemeny in [30]. The Approximate Kemeny can be described simply as a Quick Sort on elements using the majority precedence relation $\succ$ as a comparator, where $d_i \succ d_j$ if the majority of input rankings has ranked d_i before d_j. In [30], Approximate Kemeny is shown to satisfy the ECC property. Unless otherwise specified, we will use *Kemeny* to refer to this approximation in the rest of the paper.

Instead of using total orderings provided by each ranker, we can use partial orderings (for a subset of candidates). Since identifying relevant candidates at the top of the list is more important, we use partial orderings corresponding to the top k candidates for each ranker. In our experiments, we use the top-ranked 50% of candidates for each ranker, and refer to this variant as *Kemeny Top-k*.

Supervised Rank Aggregation: Kemeny and Borda aggregation, being motivated from Social Choice Theory, strive for *fairness* and hence treat all rankers as equally important. However, fairness is not a desirable property in our setting, since we know that some individual rankers perform better than others in answer-ranking. If we knew *a priori* which rankers are better, we could leverage this information to produce a better aggregate ranking. In fact, given the ordering of a (validation) set of candidates, we can estimate the performance of individual rankers and use this to produce a better ranking on a new set of candidates.

In order to accommodate such supervision, *Supervised Kemeny Ranking* [30] extends Approximate Kemeny aggregation to incorporate weights associated with each input ranking. The weights correspond to the relative utility of each ranker; so for our experiments we use weights proportional to the P@1 computed on the training set. The pseudo-code for Supervised Kemeny Ranking is presented in Algo. 1. Analogously to the unsupervised setting, we use *Supervised Kemeny Top-k* to refer to SKR with k set to 50% of m.

As in SKR, for *Supervised Borda* (See Algo. 2), we incorporate performance-based (Precision@1) weights in Borda aggregation by taking weighted averages of Borda scores instead of simple averages. A similar approach to supervised Borda was used in [2].

6.1 Experiments

Given the 5 base rankers as inputs, we compare the 6 rank aggregation methods described above. Since we are trying to establish if rank aggregation can further improve results, we pick the pruning setting with the best individual ranker performance, i.e. pruning at 20 for Medical and 5 for Jeopardy. The results of these experiments are presented in Table 4. Following Matveeva et al. ([23]), any metric@K for datasets pruned@N when $K > N$, was computed by appending the datasets with the next $K - N$ examples from the unpruned but ranked data. For example, we appended Jeopardy pruned@5 with the 5 next examples from the logistic regression

Algorithm 2 Supervised Borda

Input: $\tau_i = [\tau_{i1}, ..., \tau_{im}], \forall i = 1, ..., r$, ordered arrangement of m candidates for r rankers.
$w = [w_1, ..., w_r]$ – where w_i is the weight for ranker i
Output: τ – rank aggregated arrangement of candidates in decreasing order of importance

1. Initialize $\beta_i \Leftarrow 0, \forall i = 1, ..., m$, β_i is the borda score of candidate i
2. For each ranker $p = 1$ to r
3. For each candidate $i = 1$ to m
4. $\beta_i \Leftarrow \beta_i + ((m - i + 1)w_p)$
5. Sort β_i in descending order, such that $\tau = [d_1, ..., d_m], \beta_{d_i} \geq \beta_{d_j}, \forall i, j = 1, ..., m, i \neq j$
6. Return τ

pruning step to compute NDCG@10. This is reasonable for an application where K results must be shown. In addition to individual ranker performance, we also present the mean performance across rankers. It is clear from the results that all rank aggregation techniques perform better than the mean performance of rankers, both in terms of P@1 and NDCG@10. While better than the mean, the unsupervised aggregation techniques are outperformed by the best single ranker. Additionally, note that the best individual ranker is different for each corpus; while it is logistic regression for Jeopardy, it is LambdaRank for Medical. So in the absence of hindsight, it is always beneficial to use rank aggregation for more robust results, with lower variance.

The unsupervised aggregation techniques implicitly assume all rankers are equally valuable; as such the performance of the best ranker may be pulled down by other rankers. However, by incorporating performance-based weights for each ranker, Supervised Kemeny Ranking is able to do even better than the best individual rankers in terms of P@1 without loss on NDCG@10. Since we are already aggressively pruning to the top 20 and top 5 in these datasets, further focusing on the top 50% of these candidates, as done in Kemeny Top-k does not improve results. Also Borda, the weaker aggregation technique, is not competitive even with supervision. See [30] for a deeper analysis of Kemeny versus Borda.

Based on these results, we recommend always using multiple base rankers and supervised rank aggregation, rather than relying on the best individual ranker.

7. DISCUSSION

Figure 3 shows our proposed system with its different stages. The initial set of candidates are ranked by logistic regression and then the top N candidates are re-ranked by different rankers. The output of the rankers is aggregated and the top K results as seen fit for the application are shown to the user. Since logistic regression and the different re-rankers use the same feature-set in our setup and only the top N (20 or less) candidates are re-ranked, the overhead due to the additional stages is minimal.

Table 5 summarizes the performance of our proposed system in comparison with the baseline logistic regression. We also report two new metrics in this table: RR@5 and RR@10. The reciprocal rank (RR) is the average of the reciprocal of the rank at which the first correct answer is found. RR@K limits the ranked list per question to K. All metrics show improvement on both datasets. P@1

Metrics	Jeopardy		Medical	
	Base-line	Supervised Kemeny (Pruned @5)	Base-line	Supervised Kemeny (Pruned @ 20)
P@1	69.0	<u>72.4</u>	43.3	45.5
NDCG@5	79.3	<u>80.8</u>	50.5	51.3
NDCG@10	80.9	<u>82.4</u>	54.6	<u>55.7</u>
RR@5	77.9	<u>80.0</u>	53.6	54.8
RR@10	78.4	<u>80.5</u>	54.7	<u>56.2</u>

Table 5: Supervised Kemeny vs baseline. An underline indicates significance with a paired t-test at the 0.05 level.

on Medical is significant at the 0.1 level (p=0.09) and NDCG@10 and RR@10 are significant at the 0.05 level. For our Medical application, the P@1 improvement of 2.2% points is substantial in practice. However, it appears that our test set was not large enough to establish statistical significance here. On the larger Jeopardy test set, all metrics show significant improvements even at the 0.01 level. Our final system therefore always shows improvement regardless of the performance of the individual rankers, and thus an application developer can use it as a black box without evaluating individual rankers. Rank aggregation therefore provides for a robust system combination strategy that we hope to test on other domains that Watson can be applied to.

8. ADDITIONAL EXPERIMENTS ON TREC DATA

In addition to our application domains of Jeopardy! and Medical, we also ran experiments on the publicly-available TREC Question Answering datasets. The TREC tracks have largely focused on factoid questions e.g. "What is David Lee Roth's birthday?" We used data from the TREC 8-10 and TREC 12 evaluations [36] available at the NIST website (http://trec.nist.gov/data/qamain.html). We only considered questions that had at least one candidate answer from the first pass retrieval stage, giving a total of 1,128 questions of which 794 were randomly partitioned into the training set and the remaining 334 made the test set. On average both the training and test sets contain 2 correct answers per question from about 93 candidate answers retrieved from the initial retrieval.

In addition to the features used for the Jeopardy! dataset, 3 domain adaptation changes were made: first, the question analysis component was modified to address the differences in question formats between Jeopardy! and TREC. Second, we included Ephyra [26] and PIQUANT [9] question answer systems' static type based candidate generation components. Third, we included the AQUAINT corpus, the 3 GB news wire corpus used in TREC evaluation, in our searches. The domain adaptation resulted in 6 new features over those that were used on Jeopardy. Previous work [15] has shown the competitiveness of these additional features on top of the Jeopardy features for the TREC task.

Table 6 shows the performance of individual rankers with a pruning setting of 50. The learning to rank methods are quite competitive on both P@1 and NDCG@10 with LambdaRank equaling the performance of logistic regression on P@1 and Coordinate-Ascent being slightly better. All aggregation methods show improvement over the mean performance of individual rankers. As before, we see that the best performance is produced by Supervised Kemeny Ranking, both in terms of P@1 and NDCG@10. Table 7 compares Supervised Kemeny with a pruning threshold of 50 to the baseline logistic regression trained on all candidates. The results show that we achieve consistent improvements over the baseline on 5 differ-

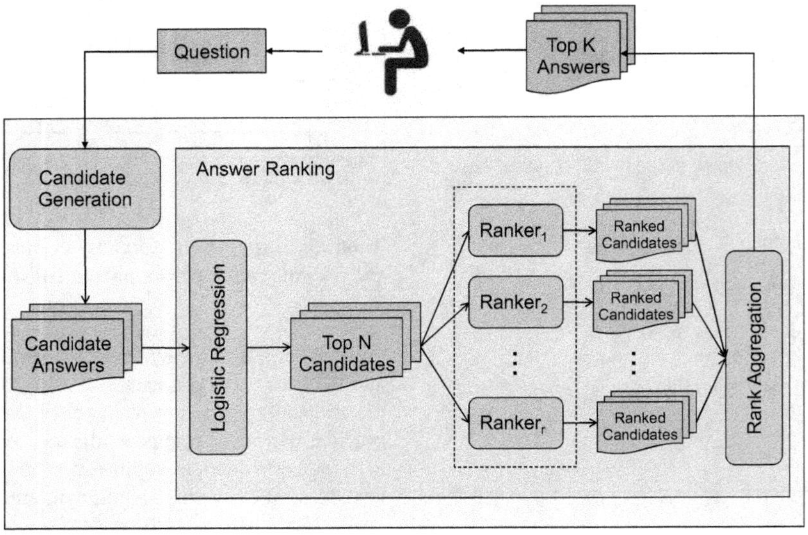

Figure 3: Our system pipeline.

Metrics	TREC	
	Base-line	Supervised Kemeny (Pruned @50)
P@1	65.9	66.8
NDCG@5	66.6	67.2
NDCG@10	70.6	71.1
RR@5	73.8	74.8
RR@10	74.4	75.4

Table 7: Supervised Kemeny vs baseline on TREC data.

ent metrics. In additional experiments on testing different pruning settings we find that, while Supervised Kemeny improves over the baseline, it is not always the approach with the highest performance. However, the best performance, in general, is still achieved by one of the rank aggregation approaches.

9. RELATED WORK

Related work in the area of QA and learning to rank has been already introduced at various points. In this section we compare our work with relevant work in learning to rank for QA. Although learning to rank methods have extensively been applied to web search, the application to QA has been limited. In fact, to the best of our knowledge, Verberne et al. ([35]) is the only work where learning to rank methods have actually been applied to the QA task with the focus on the learning component – unlike others [3, 31] where the focus has been on feature generation. Although similar in spirit, Verberne et al. only study the behavior of various learning to rank methods on the QA task; while in this work, we not only study this behavior, but also provide a robust multi-stage system that is able to improve over the results obtained by simply applying learning to rank methods. Additionally, their work was restricted to *why* questions while we work on *factoid* questions. We note that our findings from the ranking stage of this multi-stage system corroborate the observations of Verberne et al., that pairwise and listwise methods are not always superior to pointwise methods.

10. CONCLUSION

We have presented a multistage approach to learning to rank candidate answers in a QA system. The final system proposed is efficient and robust, giving significant improvements over the state-of-the-art Watson baseline, both in open-domain QA as well as in the specialized discipline of Medicine. Our approach is also easily extensible, in that, many more base rankers may be added to our aggregation, which may lead to further improvements. While we evaluated our methods on candidate answers generated by Watson, the results are applicable to any QA system, and may be more broadly applicable to other rank-learning tasks.

11. ADDITIONAL AUTHORS

Additional authors: James Fan(IBM T. J. Watson Research Center, email: `fanj@us.ibm.com`).

12. REFERENCES

[1] K. Arrow. Social choice and individual values. New Haven: Cowles Foundation, 2nd Edition 1963.

[2] J. A. Aslam and M. Montague. Models for metasearch. In *Proceedings of the International ACM SIGIR conference on Information Retrieval*, pages 276–284, 2001.

[3] M. Bilotti, J. Elsas, J. Carbonell, and E. Nyberg. Rank learning for factoid question answering with linguistic and semantic constraints. In *Proceedings of the ACM International Conference on Information and Knowledge Management*, pages 459–468, 2010.

[4] J. Borda. Memoire sur les elections au scrutin. In *Histoire de l'Academie Royale des Sciences*, 1781.

[5] C. Burges, T. Shaked, E. Renshaw, A. Lazier, M. Deeds, N. Hamilton, and G. Hullender. Learning to rank using gradient descent. In *Proceedings of the International Conference on Machine learning*, pages 89–96, 2005.

Datasets	Rankers						Aggregation					
							Unsupervised			Supervised		
	LR	Rank Boost	AdaRank	Coord Ascent	Lambda Rank	Mean	Borda	Kemeny	Kemeny Top-k	Borda	Kemeny	Kemeny Top-k
TREC	65.0	62.6	65.9	66.2	65.0	64.9	65.3	65.9	66.5	65.6	**66.8**	**66.8**
(pruned@50)	70.1	66.4	70.6	70.4	69.9	69.5	70.4	70.6	70.7	70.6	**71.5**	71.1

Table 6: Performance of rank-aggregation methods along with the learning to rank methods on TREC. The top entry in each cell is Precision@1, while the bottom is NDCG@10. The best results for each metric are presented in bold.

[6] C. J. C. Burges, K. M. Svore, P. N. Bennett, A. Pastusiak, and Q. Wu. Learning to rank using an ensemble of lambda-gradient models. In *Journal of Machine Learning Research*, pages 253–35, 2011.

[7] Z. Cao, T. Qin, T. Liu, M. Tsai, and H. Li. Learning to rank: from pairwise approach to listwise approach. In *Proceedings of the International Conference on Machine learning*, pages 129–136, 2007.

[8] O. Chapelle and Y. Chang. Yahoo! learning to rank challenge overview. *the Journal of Machine Learning Research - Proceedings Track*, 14:1–24, 2011.

[9] J. Chu-Carroll, P. A. Duboué, J. M. Prager, and K. Czuba. Ibm's piquant ii in trec 2005. In *TREC*, 2005.

[10] K. Crammer and Y. Singer. Pranking with ranking. In *Advances in Neural Information Processing Systems 14*, pages 641–647, 2001.

[11] V. Dang. Ranklib - a library of ranking algorithms. `http://www.cs.umass.edu/~vdang/ranklib.html`.

[12] C. Dwork, R. Kumar, R. Naor, and D. Sivakumar. Rank aggregation methods for the web. In *the International World Wide Web Conference*, pages 613–622, 2001.

[13] D. Ferrucci. Building watson: An overview of the deepQA project. `http://techtalks.tv/talks/54458/`, 2011.

[14] D. Ferrucci, A. Levas, S. Bagchi, D. Gondek, and E. Mueller. Watson: Beyond Jeopardy! *Artificial Intelligence (to appear)*, 2012.

[15] D. A. Ferrucci, E. W. Brown, J. Chu-Carroll, J. Fan, D. Gondek, A. Kalyanpur, A. Lally, J. W. Murdock, E. Nyberg, J. M. Prager, N. Schlaefer, and C. A. Welty. Building watson: An overview of the deepqa project. *AI Magazine*, 31(3):59–79, 2010.

[16] Y. Freund, R. Iyer, R. Schapire, and Y. Singer. An efficient boosting algorithm for combining preferences. *The Journal of Machine Learning Research*, 4:933–969, 2003.

[17] D. C. Gondek, A. Lally, A. Kalyanpur, J. W. Murdock, P. A. Duboue, L. Zhang, Y. Pan, Z. M. Qiu, and C. Welty. A framework for merging and ranking of answers in deepqa. *IBM Journal of Research and Development*, 56(3.4):14:1 -14:12, may-june 2012.

[18] M. Hall, E. Frank, G. Holmes, B. Pfahringer, P. Reutemann, and I. H. Witten. The weka data mining software: an update. *SIGKDD Explorations Newsletter*, 11(1):10–18, 2009.

[19] A. Ittycheriah and S. Roukos. IBM's statistical question answering system - trec-11. In *Proceedings of the Text REtrieval Conference*, 2001.

[20] K. Järvelin and J. Kekäläinen. Cumulated gain-based evaluation of ir techniques. *ACM Transactions on Information Systems*, 20(4):422–446, 2002.

[21] T. Joachims. Optimizing search engines using clickthrough data. In *Proceedings of the eighth ACM SIGKDD international conference on Knowledge discovery and data mining*, pages 133–142, 2002.

[22] J. Kemeny. Mathematics without numbers. In *Daedalus*, volume 88, pages 571–Ű591, 1959.

[23] I. Matveeva, C. Burges, T. Burkard, A. Laucius, and L. Wong. High accuracy retrieval with multiple nested ranker. In *Proceedings of the International ACM SIGIR conference on Information Retrieval*, pages 437–444, 2006.

[24] D. Metzler and B. Croft. Linear feature-based models for information retrieval. *Information Retrieval*, 10(3):257–274, 2007.

[25] R. Nallapati. Discriminative models for information retrieval. In *Proceedings of the International ACM SIGIR conference on Information Retrieval*, pages 64–71, 2004.

[26] S. Nico, J. Ko, J. Betteridge, M. Pathak, E. Nyberg, E, and G. Sautter. Semantic extensions of the ephyra qa system for trec 2007. In *TREC-07*, 2007.

[27] J. Prager, E. Brown, A. Coden, and D. Radev. Question-answering by predictive annotation. In *Proceedings of the International ACM SIGIR conference on Information Retrieval*, pages 184–191, 2000.

[28] C. Quoc and V. Le. Learning to rank with nonsmooth cost functions. In *Proceedings of the Advances in Neural Information Processing Systems 19*, pages 193–200, 2007.

[29] T. Strohman, D. Metzler, H. Turtle, and W. B. Croft. Indri: a language-model based search engine for complex queries. In *Proceedings of the International Conference on Intelligent Analysis*, 2005.

[30] K. Subbian and P. Melville. Supervised rank aggregation for predicting influence in networks. In *Proceedings of the IEEE International Conference on Social Computing*, 2011.

[31] M. Surdeanu, M. Ciaramita, and H. Zaragoza. Learning to rank answers to non-factoid questions from web collections. *Computational Linguistics*, 37(2):351–383, 2011.

[32] J. Suzuki, Y. Sasaki, and E. Maeda. Svm answer selection for open-domain question answering. In *Proceedings of the 19th international conference on Computational linguistics - Volume 1*, COLING '02, pages 1–7, Stroudsburg, PA, USA, 2002. Association for Computational Linguistics.

[33] M. Truchon. An extension of the condorcet criterion and kemeny orders. In *J. Eco. Lit.*, 1998.

[34] M. Tsai, T. Liu, T. Qin, H. Chen, and W. Ma. Frank: a ranking method with fidelity loss. In *Proceedings of the International ACM SIGIR conference on Information Retrieval*, pages 383–390, 2007.

[35] S. Verberne, H. van Halteren, D. Theijssen, S. Raaijmakers, and L. Boves. Learning to rank for why-question answering. *Information Retrieval*, 14(2):107–132, 2011.

[36] E. M. Voorhees. Overview of the TREC 2003 question answering track. pages 54–68, 2003.

[37] J. Xu and H. Li. Adarank: a boosting algorithm for

information retrieval. In *Proceedings of the International ACM SIGIR conference on Information Retrieval*, pages 391–398, 2007.

[38] H. Young and A. Levenglick. A consistent extension of condorcet's election principle. In *SIAM Journal on Applied Mathematics*, volume 25, pages 163–177, 1978.

[39] H. P. Young. Condorcet's theory of voting. In *American Political Science Review*, volume 82, pages 1231–1244, 1998.

[40] Y. Yue, T. Finley, F. Radlinski, and T. Joachims. A support vector method for optimizing average precision. In *Proceedings of the International ACM SIGIR conference on Information Retrieval*, pages 271–278, 2007.

Learning to Rank By Aggregating Expert Preferences

Maksims N. Volkovs
University of Toronto
40 St. George Street
Toronto, ON M5S 2E4
mvolkovs@cs.toronto.edu

Hugo Larochelle
Université de Sherbrooke
2500 boul. de l'Université
Sherbrooke, QC J1K 2R1
hugo.larochelle@usherbrooke.ca

Richard S. Zemel
University of Toronto
40 St. George Street
Toronto, ON M5S 2E4
zemel@cs.toronto.edu

ABSTRACT

We present a general treatment of the problem of aggregating preferences from several experts into a consensus ranking, in the context where information about a target ranking is available. Specifically, we describe how such problems can be converted into a standard learning-to-rank one on which existing learning solutions can be invoked. This transformation allows us to optimize the aggregating function for any target IR metric, such as Normalized Discounted Cumulative Gain, or Expected Reciprocal Rank. When applied to crowdsourcing and meta-search benchmarks, our new algorithm improves on state-of-the-art preference aggregation methods.

Categories and Subject Descriptors

H.3.3 [**Information Storage and Retrieval**]: Information Search and Retrieval—*Retrieval models*; I.2.6 [**Artificial Intelligence**]: Learning

General Terms

Algorithms, Experimentation

Keywords

Preference Aggregation, Meta-search, Crowdsourcing

1. INTRODUCTION

Preference aggregation is the problem of combining multiple preferences over objects into a single consensus ranking. This problem is crucially important in many applications, such as information retrieval (IR), collaborative filtering and crowdsourcing. Across various domains, the preferences over objects are expressed in many different ways, ranging from full and partial rankings to arbitrary comparisons. For instance, in meta-search an issued query is sent to several search engines and the (often partial) rankings returned by them are aggregated to generate more comprehensive ranking results. In crowdsourcing, tasks often involve assigning ratings to objects or pairs of objects ranging from images to text. The ratings from several users are then aggregated to produce a single labelling of the data.

Research in preference aggregation has largely concentrated on unsupervised aggregation, where the ground truth ranking is unknown and the aim is to produce an aggregate ranking that satisfies the majority of the observed preferences. However, many of the recent aggregation problems are amenable to supervised learning, as ground truth ranking information is available. For example, in meta-search the documents retrieved by the search engines are often given to annotators who assign relevance labels to each document. The relevance labels provide ground truth preference information about the documents i.e., the documents with higher relevance labels are to be ranked above those with lower relevance. Similarly, in crowdsourcing, a domain expert typically labels a subset of the data shown to the "crowd". These labels are then used to evaluate the quality of annotations submitted by each worker. In these settings aggregating methods that aim to satisfy the majority often lead to suboptimal results, since the majority preference can often be wrong. In meta-search for instance, many of the search engines are likely to return incorrect results for difficult long-tail queries, and we expect high quality rankings only from a few search engines that were specifically optimized for these queries. Consequently, we need the aggregating function to be able to "specialize" and infer when to use the majority preference and when to concentrate only on a small subset of preferences. The specialization property is impossible to achieve with unsupervised preference aggregation techniques. There is thus an evident need to develop an effective supervised aggregation method that is able to fully utilize the labeled data.

In this paper we address this problem by developing a general framework for supervised preference aggregation. Our framework is based on a simple yet powerful idea of transforming the aggregation problem into a learning-to-rank one. This transformation makes it possible to apply any learning-to-rank method to optimize the parameters of the aggregating function for the target metric. Experiments on a crowdsourcing task from TREC2011 [17] and meta-search tasks with Microsoft's LETOR4.0 [20] data sets show that our model significantly outperforms existing aggregation methods.

CIKM'12, October 29–November 2, 2012, Maui, HI, USA.

2. PREFERENCE AGGREGATION

A typical supervised preference aggregation problem consists of N training instances where for each instance n we are given a set of M_n items. We also have a set of K "experts" and each expert k generates a list of preferences for items in each instance. The preferences can be in the form of full or partial rankings, top-T lists, ratings, relative item comparisons, or combinations of these. All of these forms can be converted to a set of *partial pairwise preferences*, which in most cases will be neither complete nor consistent. Moreover, for each instance n we are also given a set of ground truth preferences over the items. The goal is to learn an aggregating function which takes expert preferences as input and produces an aggregate ranking that maximally agrees with the ground truth preferences.

In this work we concentrate on the rank aggregation instance of this problem from the information retrieval domain. However, the framework that we develop is general and can be applied to any supervised preference aggregation problem in the form defined above. In information retrieval the instances correspond to queries $\mathbf{Q} = \{q_1, ..., q_N\}$ and items to documents $\mathbf{D}_n = \{d_{n1}, ..., d_{nM_n}\}$, where M_n is the number of documents retrieved for q_n. For each query q_n the experts' preferences are summarized in a rank matrix $\mathbf{R}_n$, where $\mathbf{R}_n(i,k)$ denotes the rank assigned to document d_{ni} by the expert $k \in \{1, .., K\}$. Note that the same K experts rank items for all the instances, so K is instance independent. Furthermore, $\mathbf{R}_n$ can be sparse, as experts might not assign ranks to every document in $\mathbf{D}_n$; we use $\mathbf{R}_n(i,k) = 0$ to indicate that document d_{ni} was not ranked by expert k. The sparsity arises in problems like meta-search where q_n is sent to K different search engines and each search engine typically retrieves and ranks only a portion of the documents in $\mathbf{D}_n$. The ground truth preferences are expressed by the relevance levels $\mathbf{L}_n = \{l_{n1}, ..., l_{nM_n}\}$ which are typically assigned to the documents by human annotators.

A ranking of documents in $\mathbf{D}_n$ can be represented as a permutation of $\mathbf{D}_n$. A permutation π is a bijection $\pi : \mathbf{D}_n \rightarrow \{1, ..., M_n\}$ mapping each document d_{ni} to its rank $\pi(d_{ni}) = j$, and $d_{ni} = \pi^{-1}(j)$. Given the training queries the goal is to create an aggregating function such that, given a set of documents $\mathbf{D}$ with relevance levels $\mathbf{L}$ and ranking matrix $\mathbf{R}$ retrieved for a new query q, the aggregate ranking π produced by the function has maximal agreement with $\mathbf{L}$.

Normalized Discounted Cumulative Gain (NDCG) [14] is typically used to evaluate the agreement between the aggregate permutation and the relevance levels. Given the aggregate permutation π, relevances $\mathbf{L}$, and truncation level $T \leq M$, NDCG is defined as:

$$NDCG(\pi, \mathbf{L})@T = \frac{1}{G_T(\mathbf{L})} \sum_{i=1}^{T} \frac{2^{\mathbf{L}(\pi^{-1}(i))} - 1}{\log(i+1)} \qquad (1)$$

where $\mathbf{L}(\pi^{-1}(i))$ is the relevance level of the document in position i in π and $G_T(\mathbf{L})$ is a normalizing constant.

In contrast to the learning-to-rank problem where each document is represented by a fixed length, query dependent, and typically heavily engineered feature vector, in rank aggregation the rank matrix $\mathbf{R}$ is the only information available to train the aggregating function. Additionally this matrix is typically very sparse. Hence there is no fixed length document description, as is required by most supervised methods. To overcome this problem we convert the rank matrix into a pairwise preference matrix and demonstrate that through this conversion the rank aggregation problem

	EXPERTS		
d1	2	7	0
d2	0	0	1
d3	10	5	0
d4	0	15	3

(a) $\mathbf{R}$

	d1	d2	d3	d4
d1	0	0	0	0.28
d2	0	0	0	0
d3	0.12	0	0	0.41
d4	0	0	0	0

(b) $\mathbf{Y}_2$

Figure 1: (a) An example rank matrix R where 4 documents are ranked by 3 experts. Note that in meta-search the rank for a given document can be greater than the number of documents in R. (b) The resulting pairwise matrix $\mathbf{Y}_2$ for expert 2 (second column of R) after the ranks are transformed to pairwise preferences using the log rank difference method.

can be cast into a learning-to-rank one which is well explored with many developed approaches readily available.

2.1 Pairwise Preferences

Given the $M_n \times K$ ranking matrix $\mathbf{R}_n$ our aim is to convert it into K $M_n \times M_n$ pairwise matrices $\mathbf{Y}_n = \{\mathbf{Y}_{n1}, ..., \mathbf{Y}_{nK}\}$, where each $\mathbf{Y}_{nk}$ expresses the preferences between pairs of documents based on the expert k. To convert $\mathbf{R}_n$ to $\mathbf{Y}_n$ we use a transformation of the form $\mathbf{Y}_{nk}(i.j) = g(\mathbf{R}_n(i,k), \mathbf{R}_n(j,k))$. In this work we experiment with three versions for g that were proposed by Gleich & Lim [12]:

1. **Binary Comparison**

   The rank magnitude is ignored:

   $$\mathbf{Y}_{nk}(i,j) = I[\mathbf{R}_n(i,k) < \mathbf{R}_n(j,k)]$$

   here $I[x]$ is an indicator function evaluating to 1 if x is true and to 0 otherwise.

2. **Rank Difference**

   Here the normalized rank difference is used:

   $$\mathbf{Y}_{nk}(i,j) = I[\mathbf{R}_n(i,k) < \mathbf{R}_n(j,k)] \frac{\mathbf{R}_n(j,k) - \mathbf{R}_n(i,k)}{\max(\mathbf{R}_n(:,k))}$$

   Normalizing by the maximum rank assigned by the expert k ($\max(\mathbf{R}_n(:,k))$) ensures that the entries of $\mathbf{Y}_{nk}$ have comparable ranges.

3. **Log Rank Difference**

   This method uses the normalized log rank difference:

   $$\mathbf{Y}_{nk}(i,j) = I[\mathbf{R}_n(i,k) < \mathbf{R}_n(j,k)] \frac{\log(\mathbf{R}_n(j,k)) - \log(\mathbf{R}_n(i,k))}{\log(\max(\mathbf{R}_n(:,k)))}$$

In all cases both $\mathbf{Y}_{nk}(i,j)$ and $\mathbf{Y}_{nk}(j,i)$ are set to 0 if either $\mathbf{R}_n(j,k) = 0$ or $\mathbf{R}_n(i,k) = 0$ (missing ranking). Non-zero entries $\mathbf{Y}_{nk}(i,j)$ represent the strength of the pairwise preference of d_{ni} over d_{nj} expressed by expert k. Figure 1 shows an example ranking matrix and the resulting pairwise matrix after the ranks are transformed to pairwise preferences using the log rank difference method. Note that preferences in the form of ratings and top-N lists can easily be converted into

Table 1: A summary of notation.

Variable	Description
$\mathbf{Q} = \{q_1, ..., q_N\}$	input queries
$\mathbf{D}_n = \{d_{n1}, ..., d_{nM_n}\}$	documents for q_n
$\mathbf{L}_n = \{l_{n1}, ..., l_{nM_n}\}$	relevance levels for q_n
$\mathbf{R}_n(i, k)$	ranking for d_{ni} by expert k
$\mathbf{Y}_n = \{\mathbf{Y}_{n1}, ..., \mathbf{Y}_{nK}\}$	pairwise representation of $\mathbf{R}_n$
$\psi(d_{ni})$	feature vector for d_{ni}
$f(\psi(d_{ni}), \mathbf{W})$	scoring function
$\mathbf{S}_n = \{s_{n1}, ..., s_{nM_n}\}$	scores given by f to D_n

$\mathbf{Y}_{nk}$ using the same transformations. Moreover, if pairwise preferences are observed, we simply skip the transformation step and fill the entries $\mathbf{Y}_{nk}(i, j)$ directly. Table 1 summarizes the notation used throughout this paper.

Working with pairwise comparisons has a number of advantages, and models over pairwise preferences have been extensively used in areas such as social choice [10], information retrieval [16, 5], and collaborative filtering [22, 12]. First, pairwise comparisons are the building blocks of almost all forms of evidence about preference and subsume the most general models of evidence proposed in literature. A model over pairwise preferences can thus be readily applied to a wide spectrum of preference aggregation problems and does not impose any restrictions on the input type. Second, pairwise comparisons are a relative measure and help reduce the bias from the preference scale. In meta-search for instance, each of the search engines that receives the query can retrieve diverse lists of documents significantly varying in size. By converting the rankings into pairwise preferences we reduce the list size bias emphasizing the importance of the relative position.

3. RELEVANT WORK

Relevant previous work on rank aggregation can be divided into two categories: permutation-based and score-based. In this section we briefly describe both types of models.

3.1 Permutation-Based Models

Permutation based models work directly in the permutation space. The most common and well explored such model is the Mallows model [24]. Mallows defines a distribution over permutations and is typically parametrized by a central permutation σ and a dispersion parameter $\phi \in (0, 1]$; the likelihood of a ranking matrix $\mathbf{R}$ under this model is given by:

$$P(\mathbf{R}_n|\phi, \sigma_n) = \prod_{k=1}^{K} \frac{1}{Z(\phi, \sigma_n)} \phi^{-d(\mathbf{R}_n(:,k), \sigma_n)}$$

where $d(\mathbf{R}(:, k), \sigma_n)$ is a distance between the ranking given by the expert k and the σ_n. For rank aggregation problems inference in this model amounts to finding the aggregate permutation σ_n that maximizes the likelihood of the observed rankings $\mathbf{R}$. However, finding the most likely permutation is typically very difficult and in many cases is intractable [25]. A number of extensions of the Mallows model, e.g., [28, 22, 18, 19], have also recently been explored.

Another disadvantage of these models is that they are difficult to adapt to the fully supervised rank aggregation problem considered here. The dispersion parameter ϕ and the parameters that define the distance function d are typically estimated via maximum likelihood with σ_n clamped to the ground truth ranking. This learning procedure cannot be used to optimize a particular target metric, such as NDCG.

3.2 Score-Based Models

In score-based approaches the goal is to learn a set of real valued scores (one per document) $\mathbf{S}_n = \{s_{n1}, ..., s_{nM_n}\}$ which are then used to sort the documents. Working with scores avoids the discontinuity problems of the permutation space.

A number of heuristic score-based methods for rank aggregation have been proposed. For example, BordaCount [1], Condorcet [26] and Reciprocal Rank Fusion [8] derive the document scores by averaging (weighted) ranks across the experts or counting the number of pairwise wins. In statistics a popular pairwise score model is the Bradley-Terry [4] model:

$$P(\mathbf{R}_n|\mathbf{S}_n) = \prod_{k=1}^{K} \prod_{i \neq j} I[\mathbf{R}_n(i, k) < \mathbf{R}_n(j, k)] \frac{e^{s_{ni}}}{e^{s_{ni}} + e^{s_{nj}}}$$

where $\frac{\exp(s_{ni})}{\exp(s_{ni}) + \exp(s_{nj})}$ can be interpreted as the probability that document d_{ni} beats d_{nj} in the pairwise contest. Note that the scores do not depend on the expert k and thus represent the consensus preference expressed by the experts. In logistic form the Bradley-Terry model is very similar to another popular pairwise model, the Thurstone model [29]. Extensions of these models include the Elo Chess rating system [11], adopted by the World Chess Federation FIDE in 1970, and Microsoft's TrueSkill rating system [9] for player matching in online games, used extensively in Halo and other games. The popular learning-to-rank model RankNet [5] is also based on this approach. The Bradley-Terry model was later generalized by Plackett and Luce to a model for permutations [23, 27]. A Bayesian framework was also recently introduced for the Plackett-Luce model by placing a Gamma prior on the selection probabilities [13].

Recently, factorization approaches have been developed to model the joint pairwise matrix [12, 15]. There the pairwise matrices are aggregated into a single matrix $\mathbf{Y}_n^{tot} = \sum_{k=1}^{K} \mathbf{Y}_{nk}$ which is then approximated by a low rank factorization such as: $\mathbf{Y}_n^{tot} \approx \mathbf{S}_n \mathbf{e}^T - \mathbf{e}\mathbf{S}_n^T$. The resulting scores $\mathbf{S}_n$ are used to rank the documents.

Finally, a supervised score-based rank aggregation approach based on a Markov Chain was recently introduced [21]. In this model the authors use the ground truth preferences to create a pairwise constraint matrix and then learn a scoring function such that the produced aggregate rankings satisfy as many pairwise constraints as possible. The main drawbacks of this approach are that it is computationally very intensive requiring constrained optimization (semidefinite programming), and it does not incorporate the target IR metric into the optimization.

In general, none of the models mentioned above take the target metric into account during the optimization of the aggregating function. To the best of our knowledge no such approach has been developed.

4. SUPERVISED FRAMEWORK

In this section we describe our supervised framework for preference aggregation. To simplify notation, for the remainder of this section, we drop the query index n and work with a general query q with M documents $\mathbf{D} = \{d_1, ..., d_M\}$, relevance labels $\mathbf{L} = \{l_1, ..., l_M\}$ and ranking matrix $\mathbf{R}$ that has been converted to a set of pairwise matrices $\mathbf{Y} = \{\mathbf{Y}_1, ..., \mathbf{Y}_K\}$ using one of the techniques mentioned earlier.

The main idea behind our approach is to summarize the relative preferences for each document across the K experts by a fixed length feature vector. This transforms the preference aggregation problem into a learning-to-rank one, and any of the standard methods can then be applied to optimize the aggregating function for the target IR metric such as NDCG. In the next section we describe an approach to extract the document features.

4.1 Feature Extraction

Given the rank matrix $\mathbf{R}$ and the resulting pairwise matrix $\mathbf{Y}_k$ for expert k (as shown in Figure 1), our aim is to convert $\mathbf{Y}_k$ into a fixed length feature vector for each of the documents in $\mathbf{D}$. Singular Value Decomposition (SVD) based approaches for document summarization such as Latent Semantic Indexing are known to produce good descriptors even for sparse term-document matrices. Another advantage of SVD is that it requires virtually no tuning and can be used to automatically generate the descriptors once the pairwise matrices are computed. Because of these advantages we chose to use SVD to extract the features. For a given $M \times M$ pairwise matrix $\mathbf{Y}_k$ the rank-p SVD factorization has the form:

$$\mathbf{Y}_k \approx \mathbf{U}_k \mathbf{\Sigma}_k \mathbf{V}_k'$$

where $\mathbf{U}_k$ is an $M \times p$ matrix, $\mathbf{\Sigma}_k$ is an $p \times p$ diagonal matrix of singular values and $\mathbf{V}_k$ is an $M \times p$ matrix. The full SVD factorization has $p = M$, however, to reduce the noise and other undesirable artifacts of the original space most applications that use SVD typically set $p \ll M$. Reducing the rank is also an important factor in our approach as pairwise matrices tend to be very sparse with ranks significantly smaller than M.

Given the SVD factorization we use the resulting matrices as features for each document. It is important to note here that *both* $\mathbf{U}$ and $\mathbf{V}$ contain useful document information since $\mathbf{Y}_k$ is a pairwise document by document matrix. To get the features for document d_i and expert k we use:

$$\psi(d_i, \mathbf{Y}_k) = [\mathbf{U}_k(i,:), \text{diag}(\mathbf{\Sigma}_k), \mathbf{V}_k(i,:)] \quad (2)$$

here $\mathbf{U}_k(i,:)$ and $\mathbf{V}_k(i,:)$ are the i'th rows of $\mathbf{U}_k$ and $\mathbf{V}_k$ respectively and $\text{diag}(\mathbf{\Sigma}_k)$ is the main diagonal of $\mathbf{\Sigma}_k$ represented as a $1 \times p$ vector. Note that the $\text{diag}(\mathbf{\Sigma}_k)$ component is independent of i and will be the same for all the documents in $\mathbf{D}$. We include the singular values to preserve as much information from the SVD factorization as possible. The features $\psi(d_i, \mathbf{Y}_k)$ summarize the relative preference information for d_i expressed by the expert k. To get a complete view across the K experts we concatenate together the features extracted for each expert:

$$\psi(d_i) = [\psi(d_i, \mathbf{Y}_1), ..., \psi(d_i, \mathbf{Y}_K)] \quad (3)$$

Each $\psi(d_i, \mathbf{Y}_k)$ contains $3p$ features so the entire representation will have $3Kp$ features. Moreover, note that since both K and p are fixed across queries this representation

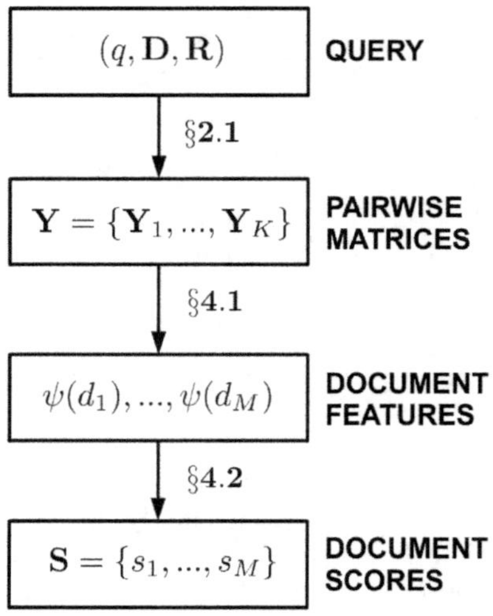

Figure 2: The flow diagram for the feature-based preference aggregation approach. (1) The ranking matrix R is converted to a set of pairwise matrices Y. (2) SVD is used to extract document features from each pairwise matrix $\mathbf{Y}_k$. (3) The learned scoring function is applied to the features to produce the scores for each document. The scores are then sorted to get the aggregate ranking.

will have the *same* length for every document in each query. We have thus created a fixed length *feature representation* for every document d_i, effectively transforming the aggregation problem into a standard learning-to-rank one. During training our aim is now to learn a scoring function $f : \mathbb{R}^{3Kp} \rightarrow \mathbb{R}$ which maximizes the target IR metric such as NDCG. At test time, given a new query q' with rank matrix $\mathbf{R}'$, we (1) convert $\mathbf{R}'$ into a set of pairwise matrices $\mathbf{Y}' = \{\mathbf{Y}_1', ..., \mathbf{Y}_K'\}$; (2) extract the document features using rank-p SVD; and (3) apply the learned scoring function to get the score for every document. The scores are then sorted to get the aggregate ranking. This process is shown in Figure 2. The feature representation allows us to fully utilize the available labeled training data to optimize the aggregating function for the target metric, which is not possible to do with the existing aggregation methods.

It is worth mentioning here that the SVD factorization of pairwise matrices has been used in the context of preference aggregation (see [12] for example). However, previous approaches largely concentrated on applying SVD to fill the missing entries in the joint pairwise matrix $\mathbf{Y}^{tot} = \sum_{k=1}^{K} \mathbf{Y}_k$ and then use the completed matrix to infer the aggregate ranking. Our approach on the other hand uses SVD to compress each pairwise matrix $\mathbf{Y}_k$ and produce fixed length feature vector for each document.

4.2 Learning the Scoring Function

Given the document features extracted via the SVD approach our goal is to use the labeled training queries to optimize the parameters of the scoring function for the target IR metric. The main difference between the introduced feature-based rank aggregation approach and the typical learning-to-rank setup is the possibility of missing features. When a given document d_i is not ranked by the expert k the row

$\mathbf{Y}_k(i,:)$ and column $\mathbf{Y}_k(:,i)$ will both be missing (i.e., 0). To account for this we modify the conventional linear scoring function to include a bias term for each of the K experts:

$$f(\psi(d_i), \mathbf{W}) = \sum_{k=1}^{K} w_k \cdot \psi(d_i, \mathbf{Y}_k) + I[\mathbf{R}(i,k) = 0]b_k \quad (4)$$

where $\mathbf{W} = \{w_k, b_k\}_{k=1}^{K}$ is the set of free parameters to be learned with each w_k having the same dimension as $\psi(d_i, \mathbf{Y}_k)$, and I is an indicator function. The bias term b_k provides a base score for d_i if d_i is not ranked by expert k. The weights w_k control how much emphasis is given to preferences from expert k. It is important to note here that the scoring function can easily be made non-linear by adding additional hidden layer(s) as done in conventional multilayer neural nets. In the form given by Equation 4 our model has a total of $(3p+1)K$ parameters to be learned. We can use any of the developed learning-to-rank approaches to optimize $\mathbf{W}$; in this work we chose to use the LambdaRank method. We chose LambdaRank because it has shown excellent empirical performance recently winning the Yahoo! Learning To Rank Challenge [7]. We briefly describe LambdaRank here and refer the reader to [6] and [5] for a more extensive treatment.

LambdaRank learns pairwise preferences over documents with emphasis derived from the NDCG gain found by swapping the rank position of the documents in any given pair, so it is a listwise algorithm (in the sense that the cost depends on the sorted list of documents). Formally, given a pair of documents (d_i, d_j) with $l_i \neq l_j$, the target probability that d_i should be ranked higher than d_j is defined as:

$$P_{ij} = \begin{cases} 1 & \text{if } l_i > l_j \\ 0 & \text{otherwise} \end{cases}$$

The model's probability is then obtained by passing the difference in scores between d_i and d_j through a logistic:

$$\begin{aligned} Q_{ij} &= \frac{1}{1 + \exp(-(f(\psi(d_i), \mathbf{W}) - f(\psi(d_j), \mathbf{W})))} \\ &= \frac{1}{1 + \exp(-(s_i - s_j))} \end{aligned}$$

The aim of learning is to match the two probabilities for every pair of documents with different labels. To achieve this a cross entropy objective is used:

$$O_q = -\sum_{l_i > l_j} P_{ij} \log(Q_{ij})$$

This objective weights each pair of documents equally thus placing equal importance on getting the relative order of document correctly both at the top and at the bottom of the ranking. However, most target evaluation metrics including NDCG are heavily concentrated on the top of the ranking. To take this into account the LambdaRank framework uses a smooth approximation to the gradient of a target evaluation measure with respect to the score of a document d_i, and we refer to this approximation as λ-gradient. The λ-gradient for NDCG is defined as the derivative of the cross entropy objective weighted by the difference in NDCG obtained when a pair of documents swap rank positions:

$$\lambda_{ij} = |\Delta NDCG@M(s_i, s_j)| \frac{\partial O_q}{\partial s_i - s_j}$$

Algorithm 1 Learning Algorithm

Input: $\{(q_1, \mathbf{D}_1, \mathbf{L}_1, \mathbf{R}_1), ..., (q_N, \mathbf{D}_N, \mathbf{L}_N, \mathbf{R}_N)\}$
Parameters: learning rate η
initialize weights: $\mathbf{W}$
for $n = 1$ **to** N **do** {feature extraction: §4.1}
  from $\mathbf{R}_n$ compute $\mathbf{Y}_n = \{\mathbf{Y}_{n1}, ..., \mathbf{Y}_{nK}\}$
  for $i = 1$ **to** M_n **do**
    compute features $\psi(d_{ni})$
  end for
end for
repeat {scoring function optimization: §4.2}
  for $n = 1$ **to** N **do**
    calculate query cross entropy objective:
    $O_{q_n} = \sum_{l_{ni} > l_{nj}} \log(1 + e^{s_{nj} - s_{ni}})$
    compute λ-gradients: $\nabla \mathbf{W} = \sum_i \lambda_{ni} \frac{\partial s_{ni}}{\partial \mathbf{W}}$
    update weights: $\mathbf{W} = \mathbf{W} - \eta \nabla \mathbf{W}$
  end for
until convergence
Output: $\mathbf{W}$

Thus, at the beginning of each iteration, the documents are sorted according to their current scores, and the difference in NDCG is computed for each pair of documents by keeping the ranks of all of the other documents constant and swapping only the rank positions for that pair (see [6] for more details on λ calculation). The λ-gradient for document d_i is computed by summing the λ's for all pairs of documents (d_i, d_j) for query q:

$$\lambda_i = \sum_{j: l_j \neq l_i} \lambda_{ij}$$

The $|\Delta NDCG|$ factor emphasizes those pairs that have the largest impact on NDCG. Note that the truncation in NDCG is relaxed to the entire document set to maximize the use of the available training data.

To make the learning algorithm more efficient the document features can be precomputed a priori and re-used throughout learning. This significantly reduces the computational complexity at the cost of additional storage requirement of $O(M_n K p)$ for each query q_n. The complete stochastic gradient descent learning procedure is summarized in Algorithm 1.

5. CROWDSOURCING EXPERIMENTS

Our approach is primarily designed for supervised preference aggregation problems where sufficient expert preference data is available to learn a feature-based model for each expert. However, to further examine the utility of the proposed method we also conducted experiments on the crowdsourcing problem where very limited preference data is typically available for each expert.

For crowdsourcing experiments we use the dataset from Task 2 of the TREC2011 Crowdsourcing Track[1] [17]. The dataset is a collection of binary (relevant or not relevant) judgements from 762 workers for 19,033 documents. The documents are split into 100 topics and for each topic ground truth or "gold" labels are provided for a subset of the documents. The topics in this task can be thought of as queries in the traditional search problem. For each topic n the judgements for the documents are represented as a matrix $\mathbf{R}_n$

[1] https://sites.google.com/site/treccrowd/home

Table 2: TREC2011 crowdsourcing dataset NDCG results. The NDCG values in this and other tables were multiplied by 100.

	N@1	N@2	N@3	N@4	N@5	N@6	N@7	N@8	N@9	N@10
Condorcet	42.00	50.00	49.28	49.87	49.04	49.53	49.35	50.34	52.16	51.41
Majority vote	59.00	64.00	62.80	63.95	63.96	64.45	64.93	66.34	66.46	64.83
LR-consensus	70.00	72.00	70.80	69.56	69.85	69.47	68.86	68.79	68.83	66.79
LR-labeled	80.00	79.50	77.46	75.63	74.10	73.80	73.29	73.18	72.78	71.13
LR-unlabeled	**83.00**	**82.00**	**80.80**	**78.76**	**77.94**	**76.77**	**75.93**	**75.34**	**75.36**	**73.37**

where each entry $\mathbf{R}_n(i,k)$ is either 1 (relevant), -1 (not relevant) or 0 (not observed). The ground truth (gold) labels $\mathbf{L}_n$ are available only for a subset of the documents under each topic and are given by one of two values: 1 = relevant and 0 = not relevant. There are a total of 2275 gold labels: 1275 relevant and 1000 not relevant. The aim is to use the worker judgements to accurately rank the documents under each topic (note that this is a different problem from the Task 2 in TREC2011 where the goal was to predict each document's relevance label). To evaluate the models we created 5 random splits of topics into 60/20/20 sets for training/validation/testing. The results shown for each model are the average test set results for the five folds. For each topic the models are evaluated using only those documents for which the gold labels are available.

Across all topics the data contains 89,624 judgements and each document is judged by 5 workers on average. Moreover, out of the 762 workers 547 have less than 40 judgements so the dataset is very imbalanced with the majority of judgements coming from a small subset of the workers. Given the label sparsity there is not enough preference data to learn an accurate feature-based model for each worker. Instead of extracting preference features for every worker, we used a hybrid approach. Separate features were extracted for workers that had 500 or more preferences in the training set, there were around 20 such workers in each fold. Preferences for all the other workers were combined into a single preference matrix for which we extracted an additional set of features. Using $\mathbf{\Gamma}_{500}$ to denote the set of workers that have 500 or more preferences in the training set we can write the complete feature vector as:

$$\psi(d_{ni}) = \{\psi(d_{ni}, \mathbf{Y}_k) \mid k \in \mathbf{\Gamma}_{500}\} \cup \psi(d_{ni}, \mathbf{Y}_n^{<500}) \quad (5)$$

where $\mathbf{Y}_n^{<500}$ is given by $\mathbf{Y}_n^{<500} = \sum_{k \notin \mathbf{\Gamma}_{500}} \mathbf{Y}_{nk}$. The hybrid approach allows us to learn accurate feature-based models for those workers that have enough preferences in the training data and combine these models with a consensus-based model for workers with few training ratings. Each pairwise matrix was computed using the binary comparison approach (see Section 2.1) since it is the only suitable approach for binary judgements.

5.1 Results

We conducted experiments with three versions of the LambdaRank model. The first model, which we refer to as LR-consensus, did not use the per-worker features and only used features from the SVD factorization of the combined matrix $\mathbf{Y}_n^{tot} = \sum_{k=1}^{K} \mathbf{Y}_{nk}$. This model thus does not take the individual worker preferences into account and ranks only based on consensus features. The second model, LR-labeled, uses the individual worker features as per equation Equation 5 but the features were computed using preferences only for the documents that had ground truth labels. The last model, LR-unlabeled, included the preferences for the unlabeled documents during feature computation. Through cross validation we found that setting $p = 1$ (SVD rank) gave the best performance which is expected considering the sparsity level of the pairwise matrices $\mathbf{Y}$. For all settings, LambdaRank was run for 200 iterations with a learning rate of 0.01, and validation NDCG@10 was used to choose the best model.

We compare our feature based model with the condorcet and the majority vote approach which was shown to work well on the related TREC2011 Task 2 [3]. Table 2 shows test NDCG (N@T) at truncations $1 - 10$. From the table it is seen that all LambdaRank models significantly outperform the majority vote baseline on the ranking task. It is also seen that the consensus based model LR-consensus performs significantly worse than the models that take the individual worker preferences into account. This indicates that ranking based on consensus alone leads to suboptimal performance, as we further demonstrate in the meta-search experiments in the next section. Finally, we see that using features computed from preferences for only the labeled documents (LR-labeled) does not perform as well as using all the preferences (LR-unlabeled). The LR-unlabeled model performs significantly better than the LR-labeled at all truncations. This indicates that preferences from the unlabeled documents do contain useful information and should be included during the feature extraction. This can be especially relevant when the number of labeled documents and/or preferences is small which is the case here.

6. META-SEARCH EXPERIMENTS

For our meta-search experiments we use the LETOR4.0 benchmark datasets. These data sets were chosen because they are publicly available, include several baseline results, and provide evaluation tools to ensure accurate comparison between methods. In LETOR4.0 there are two meta-search data sets, MQ2007-agg and MQ2008-agg. MQ2007-agg contains 1692 queries with 69,623 documents and MQ2008-agg contains 784 queries and a total of 15,211 documents. Each query q_n contains a ranking matrix $\mathbf{R}_n$ with partial expert rankings of the documents under that query. There are 21 experts in MQ2007-agg and 25 experts in MQ2008-agg. In this setting the experts correspond to the search engines to which the query was submitted. In addition, in both data sets, each document is assigned one of three relevance levels: 2 = highly relevant, 1 = relevant and 0 = irrelevant. Finally, each dataset comes with five precomputed folds with 60/20/20 splits for training/validation/testing. The results shown for each model are the averages of the test set results for the five folds. The MQ2007-agg dataset is approximately 35% sparse, meaning that for an average query the ranking

Table 3: MQ2008-agg and MQ2007-agg results; all differences between LambdaRank and the best baseline are statistically significant.

	NDCG					Precision					
	N@1	N@2	N@3	N@4	N@5	P@1	P@2	P@3	P@4	P@5	MAP
MQ2008-agg											
BordaCount	23.68	28.06	30.80	34.32	37.13	29.72	30.42	29.38	29.75	29.03	39.45
CPS-best	26.52	31.38	34.59	37.63	40.04	31.63	32.27	32.27	31.66	30.64	41.02
SVP	32.49	36.20	38.62	40.17	41.85	38.52	36.42	34.65	32.01	30.23	43.61
Bradley-Terry	38.05	39.24	40.77	41.79	42.62	44.77	39.73	36.26	33.19	30.28	44.35
Plackett-Luce	35.20	38.49	39.70	40.49	41.55	41.32	38.96	35.33	32.02	29.62	42.20
Condorcet	35.67	37.39	39.11	40.50	41.59	40.94	37.43	34.73	32.08	29.59	42.63
RRF	38.77	40.73	43.48	45.70	47.17	44.89	41.32	38.82	36.51	34.13	47.71
LR-I	40.22	43.94	46.33	48.30	50.16	46.94	44.00	41.45	38.52	36.28	49.54
LR-R	40.90	42.75	45.83	47.93	49.68	47.45	42.92	41.20	38.77	36.22	49.26
LR-logR	**42.81**	**44.53**	**47.02**	**49.00**	**50.69**	**48.85**	**44.13**	**41.84**	**39.09**	**36.50**	**50.32**
MQ2007-agg											
BordaCount	19.02	20.14	20.81	21.28	21.88	24.88	25.24	25.69	25.80	25.97	32.52
CPS-best	31.96	33.18	33.86	34.09	34.76	38.65	38.65	38.14	37.19	37.02	40.69
SVP	35.82	35.91	36.53	37.16	37.50	41.61	40.28	39.50	38.88	38.10	42.73
Bradley-Terry	39.88	39.86	40.40	40.60	40.91	46.34	44.65	43.48	41.98	40.95	43.98
Plackett-Luce	40.63	40.39	40.26	40.71	40.96	46.93	45.10	43.09	42.32	41.09	43.64
Condorcet	37.31	37.63	38.03	38.37	38.66	43.26	42.14	40.94	39.85	38.75	42.56
RRF	41.93	42.66	42.42	42.73	43.13	48.70	47.20	44.84	43.52	42.52	46.72
LR-I	46.13	**46.76**	**46.71**	**46.87**	**47.28**	52.90	**51.39**	**49.33**	**47.80**	**46.66**	50.05
LR-R	45.02	45.40	45.68	45.87	46.12	51.83	50.36	48.88	47.25	45.98	49.55
LR-logR	**46.30**	46.18	46.46	46.56	47.02	**53.19**	51.04	49.26	47.48	46.29	**50.39**

matrix is missing 35% of its entries. MQ2008-agg is significantly sparser, with $\sim 65\%$ entries missing.

The goal is to use the rank lists to infer an aggregate ranking of the documents for each query which maximally agrees with the held-out relevance levels. To evaluate this agreement, in addition to NDCG (N@T), we also compute Precision (P@T) and Mean Average Precision (MAP) [2]. MAP only allows binary (relevant/not relevant) document assignments, and is defined in terms of average precision (AP). For an aggregate ranking π, and relevance levels $\mathbf{L}$, AP is given by:

$$AP(\pi, \mathbf{L}) = \frac{\sum_{t=1}^{M} P@t * \mathbf{L}(\pi^{-1}(t))}{\sum_{t=1}^{M} \mathbf{L}(\pi^{-1}(t))} \tag{6}$$

where $L(\pi^{-1}(t))$ is a relevance label for document in position t in π; and $P@t$ is the precision at t:

$$P@t = \frac{\sum_{i=1}^{t} \mathbf{L}(\pi^{-1}(i))}{t} \tag{7}$$

MAP is then computed by averaging AP over all queries. To compute P@t and MAP on the MQ-agg datasets the relevance levels are binarized with 1 converted to 0 and 2 converted to 1 (as per LETOR4.0 evaluation guidelines). All presented NDCG, Precision and MAP results are averaged across the test queries and were obtained using the evaluation script available on the LETOR4.0 website[2].

6.1 Results

To investigate the properties of our approach we conducted extensive experiments with various versions of the model. We experimented with binary, rank difference, and log rank difference methods to compute the pairwise matrices (see Section 2.1) and refer to these models as LR-I, LR-R and LR-logR respectively. Through cross validation we found that setting $p = 1$ (SVD rank) gave the best performance. For all settings, LambdaRank was run for 200 iterations with a learning rate of 0.01, and validation NDCG@10 was used to choose the best model.

We compare the results of our model against the best methods currently listed on the LETOR4.0 website, namely the BordaCount model and the best of the three CPS models (combination of Mallows and Plackett-Luce models) on each of the MQ-agg datasets. We also compare with the established meta-search standards Condorcet and Reciprocal Rank Fusion (RRF) as well as the Bradley-Terry and Plackett-Luce models and the SVD-based method SVP. The above models cover all of the primary leading approaches in the rank aggregation research except for the Markov Chain model [21]. We were unable to compare with this method because it is neither publicly available nor listed as one of the baselines on LETOR, making standardized comparison impossible.

The NDCG and Precision results for truncations 1-5 as well as MAP results are shown in Table 3. From the table we see that all versions of the LambdaRank model significantly outperform the other aggregation methods, improving by as much as 5 NDCG points over the best baseline on each of the MQ-agg datasets. The results on the MQ2008-agg which is more than 65% sparse demonstrate that features extracted by the SVD approach are robust and generalize well even in the sparse setting. From the table we also see that the binary and log rank transformations lead to the best performance, with LR-logR significantly outperforming the other LambdaRank models on MQ2008-agg and having comparable performance to LR-I on MQ2007-agg.

To investigate the utility of representing each expert's preferences with a separate set of features we ran experiments with a combined approach. For each query q_n we combined all pairwise preference matrices into a single ma-

[2]research.microsoft.com/en-us/um/beijing/projects/letor/

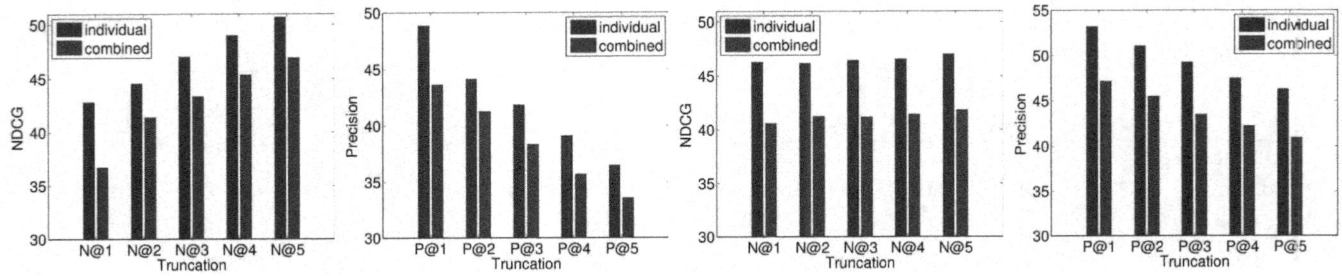

(a) NDCG, MQ2008-agg (b) Precision, MQ2008-agg (c) NDCG, MQ2007-agg (d) Precision, MQ2007-agg

Figure 3: Test NDCG@1-5 and Precision@1-5 results for LR-logR trained on SVD features extracted from each $\mathbf{Y}_{nk}$ (individual), versus LR-logR trained on SVD features extracted only from the joint preference matrix $\mathbf{Y}_n^{tot}$ (combined).

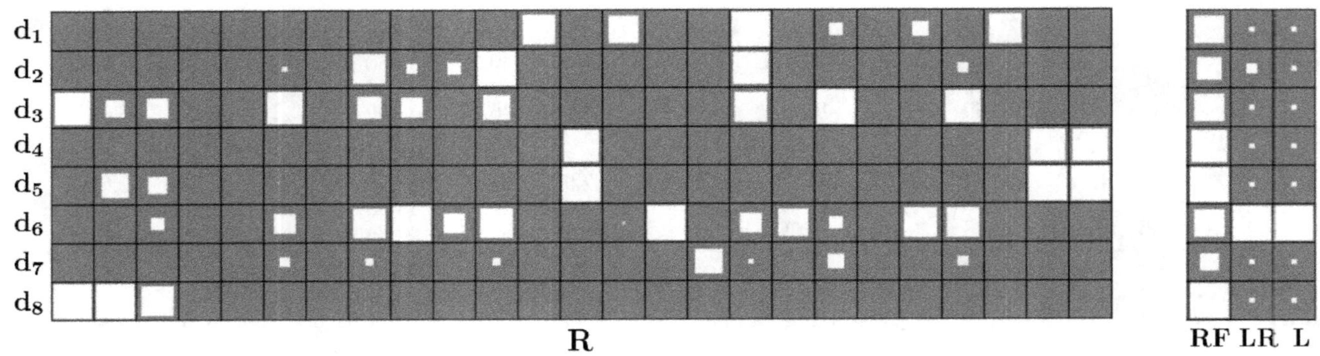

Figure 4: The matrix on the left shows the expert ranking matrix R for a test query in Fold 1 of the MQ2008-agg dataset. 8 documents $\{d_1, ..., d_8\}$ were retrieved for this query and the normalized expert rankings are represented by white squares. The size of each square reflects the preference strength, so that large squares correspond to high rankings (strong preference). Missing rankings are represented by empty cells. The matrix on the right shows the normalized scores for each document produced by the Reciprocal Rank Fusion (RF) and the LR-logR (LR) models, as well as the ground truth relevance levels (L). Note that only d_6 is relevant to this query.

trix $\mathbf{Y}_n^{tot} = \sum_{k=1}^{K} \mathbf{Y}_{nk}$ and trained the LR-logR model on the SVD features from $\mathbf{Y}_n^{tot}$ only. Note that this model has no information about the individual expert preferences. We refer to this model as "combined" and compare it to the full model which uses SVD features from each $\mathbf{Y}_{nk}$ referred to as "individual". The results for the two datasets are shown in Figure 3. From the figure we see that the individual model significantly outperforms the combined one on both datasets. The performance of the combined model is comparable to the best baseline consensus method, the Reciprocal Rank Fusion. This is not surprising since $\mathbf{Y}_n^{tot}$ summarizes the consensus preference across the agents, and without access to the individual preferences the ranker can only learn to follow the consensus. Note however, that the gain from using the individual expert features is very significant which further supports the conclusion that specialization is very important for the supervised preference aggregation.

Figure 4 further demonstrates the importance of specialization. The figure shows the expert ranking matrix together with the scores produced by the Reciprocal Rank Fusion and LR-logR for an example test query from MQ2008-agg. From the the ground truth relevance levels (**L**) it is seen that only document d_6 is relevant to this query. However, from the ranking matrix we see that the experts express strong net preference for documents d_1, d_4, d_5 and d_8, whereas the preferences for d_6 are mixed with many positive and negative preferences. The Reciprocal Rank Fusion is a consensus-based approach and as such ranks documents d_1, d_4, d_5 and d_8 above d_6 with NDCG@1-4 of 0. Other consensus-based methods produce similar rankings. LR-logR on the other hand, is able to ignore the consensus and concentrate on a small subset of the preferences, placing d_6 on top and producing a perfect ranking. Moreover, note that the scores for the other documents produced by the LR-logR are significantly lower than the score for d_6, so the model is confident in this ranking. The query shown in Figure 4 is an example of a difficult query (often these correspond to long-tail queries) where the majority of experts generate incorrect preferences. For these queries the aggregated rankings produced by the consensus-based methods will also be incorrect. Our feature-based supervised approach is able to fix this problem through specialization. By examining the queries in both MQ2008-agg and MQ2007-agg we found that both datasets contain a number of such queries and that our approach performs significantly better on those queries than all of the consensus-based baselines.

7. CONCLUSION

We presented a fully supervised rank aggregation framework. Our approach transforms the rank aggregation problem into a supervised learning-to-rank one. The transformation is based on feature summarization of pairwise preference matrices. To compute the features we employ a low-rank SVD factorization. The extracted features allow us to use any supervised learning-to-rank approach to learn the aggregating function. This in turn allows us to optimize the aggregating function for any target IR metric. Experimental results with LambdaRank as the learning-to-rank approach show that our method outperforms the existing methods on supervised aggregation tasks. The improvements are especially significant on difficult queries where the majority of preferences are wrong. Future work includes investigating other ways of producing effective fixed length representations from full/partial preferences.

8. REFERENCES

[1] J. A. Aslam and M. Montague. Models for metasearch. In *Proceedings of the International ACM SIGIR Conference on Research and Development in Information Retrieval*, pages 276–284, 2001.

[2] R. Baeza-Yates and B. Ribeiro-Neto. *Information Retrieval.* Addison-Wesley, 1999.

[3] P. N. Bennett, E. Kamar, and G. Kazai. MSRC at TREC 2011 Crowdsourcing Track. In *To Appear in Proceedings of the Text Retrieval Conference*, 2011.

[4] R. Bradley and M. Terry. Rank analysis of incomplete block designs. I. The method of paired comparisons. *Biometrika*, 39:324–345, 1952.

[5] C. J. C. Burges. From RankNet to LambdaRank to LambdaMART: An overview. Technical Report MSR-TR-2010-82, Microsoft Research, 2010.

[6] C. J. C. Burges, R. Rango, and Q. V. Le. Learning to rank with nonsmooth cost functions. In *NIPS*, 2007.

[7] O. Chapelle, Y. Chang, and T.-Y. Liu. The Yahoo! learning to rank challenge, 2010.

[8] G. V. Cormack, C. L. A. Clarke, and S. Büttcher. Reciprocal rank fusion outperforms condorcet and individual rank learning methods. In *Proceedings of the International ACM SIGIR Conference on Research and Development in Information Retrieval*, 2009.

[9] P. Dangauthier, R. Herbrich, T. Minka, and T. Graepel. TrueSkill through time: Revisiting the history of chess. In *Proceedings of the Neural Information Processing Systems*, 2007.

[10] H. A. David. *The method of paired comparissons.* Hodder Arnold, 1988.

[11] A. E. Elo. *The rating of chess players: Past and present.* Acro Publishing, 1978.

[12] D. F. Gleich and L.-H. Lim. Rank aggregation via nuclear norm minimization. In *Proceedings of the ACM SIGKDD Conference on Knowledge Discovery and Data Mining*, pages 60–68, 2011.

[13] J. Guiver and E. Snelson. Bayesian inference for Plackett-Luce ranking models. In *Proceedings of the International Conference on Machine Learning*, pages 377–384, 2009.

[14] K. Jarvelin and J. Kekalainen. IR evaluation methods for retrieving highly relevant documents. In *Proceedings of the ACM SIGIR Conference on Research and Development in Information Retrieval*, pages 41–48, 2000.

[15] X. Jiang, L.-H. Lim, Y. Yao, and Y. Ye. Statistical ranking and combinatorial hodge theory. *Mathematical Programming*, 127:203–244, 2011.

[16] T. Joachims. Optimizing search engines using clickthrough data. In *Proceedings of the ACM SIGKDD Conference on Knowledge Discovery and Data Mining*, pages 133–142, 2002.

[17] G. Kazai and M. Lease. TREC2011 Crowdsourcing Track, 2011.

[18] A. Klementiev, D. Roth, and K. Small. Unsupervised rank aggregation with distance-based models. In *Proceedings of the International Conference on Machine Learning*, pages 472–479, 2008.

[19] G. Lebanon and J. Lafferty. Cranking: Combining rankings using conditional probability models on permutations. In *Proceedings of the International Conference on Machine Learning*, pages 363–370, 2002.

[20] T. Liu, J. Xu, W. Xiong, and H. Li. LETOR: Benchmark dataset for search on learning to rank for information retrieval. In *ACM SIGIR Workshop on Learning to Rank for Information Retrieval*, 2007.

[21] Y.-T. Liu, T.-Y. Liu, T. Qin, Z.-M. Ma, and H. Li. Supervised rank aggregation. In *Proceedings of the International Conference on World Wide Web*, pages 481–489, 2007.

[22] T. Lu and C. Boutilier. Learning Mallows models with pairwise preferences. In *Proceedings of the International Conference on Machine Learning*, 2011.

[23] R. D. Luce. *Individual choice behavior: A theoretical analysis.* Wiley, 1959.

[24] C. L. Mallows. Non-null ranking models. *Biometrika*, 44:114–130, 1957.

[25] M. Meila, K. Phadnis, A. Patterson, and J. Bilmes. Consensus ranking under the exponential model. In *Proceedings of the Uncertainty in Artificial Intelligence Conference*, 2007.

[26] M. Montague and J. A. Aslam. Condorcet fusion for improved retrieval. In *Proceedings of the International ACM CIKM Conference on Information and Knowledge Management*, 2002.

[27] R. Plackett. The analysis of permutations. *Applied Statistics*, 24:193–302, 1975.

[28] T. Quin, X. Geng, and T.-Y. Liu. A new probabilistic model for rank aggregation. In *Proceedings of the Neural Information Processing Systems*, pages 681–689, 2010.

[29] L. L. Thurstone. The method of paired comparisons for social values. *Journal of Abnormal and Social Psychology*, 21:384–400, 1927.

Learning to Rank Duplicate Bug Reports

Jian Zhou and Hongyu Zhang
School of Software, Tsinghua University
Beijing 100084, China
zhoujian1286@yahoo.com.cn, hongyu@tsinghua.edu.cn

ABSTRACT
For a large and complex software system, the project team could receive a large number of bug reports. Some bug reports could be duplicates as they essentially report the same problem. It is often tedious and costly to manually check if a newly reported bug is a duplicate of an already reported bug. In this paper, we propose *BugSim*, a method that can automatically retrieve duplicate bug reports given a new bug report. BugSim is based on learning to rank concepts. We identify textual and statistical features of bug reports and propose a similarity function for bug reports based on the features. We then construct a training set by assembling pairs of duplicate and non-duplicate bug reports. We train the weights of features by applying the stochastic gradient descent algorithm over the training set. For a new bug report, we retrieve candidate duplicate reports using the trained model. We evaluate BugSim using more than 45,100 real bug reports of twelve Eclipse projects. The evaluation results show that the proposed method is effective. On average, the recall rate for the top 10 retrieved reports is 76.11%. Furthermore, BugSim outperforms the previous state-of-art methods that are implemented using SVM and $BM25F_{ext}$.

Categories and Subject Descriptors
D.2.7 [**Software Engineering**]: Distribution, Maintenance, and Enhancement–*Restructuring, reverse engineering, and reengineering;* H.3.1 [**Information Storage and Retrieval**]: Content Analysis and Indexing.

Keywords
Bug reports, duplicate bug retrieval, duplicate documents, software maintenance, learning to rank.

1. INTRODUCTION
With the rapid development of information technology, software systems are getting more and more complex. Although a range of measures have been taken to assure software quality, in reality released software systems still contain bugs. For a large-scale, widely-used software system, the project team could receive a large number of bug reports over time. For example, 49,422 bugs were reported for the Eclipse projects in 2010, in average 135 bugs every day. Software bugs are typically maintained by a bug tracking system such as BugZilla[1], which stores the reported bug reports and tracks their status. After a bug report is created by the bug tracking system, the project team could retrieve it, examine it, verify it, and assign it to a developer to work on.

CIKM'12, October 29–November 2, 2012, Maui, HI, USA.

The bug reporting process is essential an uncontrolled, distributed process. Users and testers at different sites can report bugs whenever they encounter them. Therefore, often some bug reports are duplicates because they actually describe the same problem. For example, among all Eclipse bugs reported in 2010, 3799 of them are duplicates. Studies also show that as many as 36% of bug reports could be duplicates or invalid [1]. The existence of duplicate bug reports can exacerbate the already high cost of software maintenance, and can even lead to wasted maintenance efforts (imaging a developer spends days on verifying and debugging a bug, and finally realizes that the same problem has been reported before by a different user and fixed by another developer).

To reduce software maintenance effort, users/developers are required to check whether a new bug report is a duplicate of an existing one or not before reporting/handling a new bug. As the number of bug reports maintained by a bug tracking system could be very large, a manual process could be tedious and error-prone. In recent years, researchers have proposed automated methods for detecting duplicate bug reports. Given a new bug report, these methods analyze the existing bug reports stored in a bug track system, and return the top *N* related bug reports using certain information retrieval techniques. For example, [20] uses a SVM-based discriminative model to compute the probability of two bug reports being duplicate and then retrieval the top *N* most similar bug reports as the candidate duplicate bug reports. [21] uses an extended BM25F model to retrieve related bug reports.

In this paper, we propose *BugSim*, a duplicate bug retrieval method based on the concept of *learning to rank*. We first collect a training set, which consists of triples (*bug, dup bug, non-dup bug*), where *dup bug* represents a duplicate of the *bug, non-dup bug* represents a non-duplicate of the *bug*. We then create a ranking model to rank the *dup bug* higher than the *non-dup bug*. To construct the ranking model, we identify 9 textual and statistical features of bug reports, and learn the weights of the features by applying the stochastic gradient descent algorithm over the training dataset. For a new bug report, we retrieve and rank the duplicate bug reports using the trained model.

We evaluate our method using more than 45,100 real bug reports of twelve Eclipse projects. The evaluation results show that the proposed method is effective. The recall rates for the top 10 retrieved reports are above 61%, with an average of 76.11%.

[1] http://www.bugzilla.org/

Furthermore, BugSim outperforms the previous SVM-based method by 15.41% and the $BM25F_{ext}$-based method by 3.71% on the recall rate of the top 10 results.

The organization of the paper is as follows. In Section 2, we describe the background of this work. In Section 3, we describe the proposed BugSim approach. Section 4 describes our experimental design, and Section 5 shows and discusses the experimental results. Section 6 gives the threats to validity. We discuss the related work in Section 7 and conclude the paper in Section 8.

2. BACKGROUND

2.1 Duplicate Bug Reports

During software testing and maintenance, a large number of bugs could be discovered and reported. Different users/testers may report the same problem at different time, thus causing duplicate bug reports. Figure 1 gives an example of duplicate bug reports. Bug #214445[2] and Bug #214451[3] are real bug reports for the Eclipse project. Each bug report contains a *summary* and a *description*, and is written in natural language. We can see that the two bug reports contain many similar words such as *select*, *value*, *filter*, *table*, etc. Usually, duplicate bug reports exhibit high degree of text similarity as they report the same problem. Therefore, information retrieval (IR) techniques can be applied to help developers detect duplicate bug reports.

Bug #214445, reported by ysun, on 2008-01-06

Summary: <Select value...>cannot select any value.

Description: <Select value...>cannot select any value [00].

Step:1. New a report. 2. Add a data source and dataset. 3. Add a table. 4. Add a filter/map/highlight. 5. Select a column and open the select value dialog. 6. Select one value and click OK.

Actual result: Nothing value is selected.

Bug #214451 , reported by Wen Lin, on 2008-01-07

Summary: Select value in table filter condition panel does not take any effect.

Description: Select value in table filter condition panel does not take any effect...

Step to reproduce: 1. New a table binding to a dataset in a report. 2. Add a filter in filters panel. 3. Set a filter condition as row "xxx" not equal to a value; select this value from select value panel.

Expect result: The value selected by user should be set to the condition combo.

Actual result: The select value operation does not take any effect.

Figure 1. An example of duplicate bug reports

2.2 Duplicate Bug Report Detection

Recently, researchers have proposed some IR-based methods for automated retrieval of duplicate bug reports. A general process of these methods is shown in Figure 2. The existing bug reports are stored at a repository managed by a bug tracking system. These bug reports are first preprocessed (including tokenization, stemming, and stop words removal). The features of the bug report are extracted and used to construct a retrieval model. When a new bug report arrives, the retrieval model compares its features to the features of the existing reports stored in the repository. The existing reports are then ranked according to their similarities to the new bug report, and are returned to the users. The users can examine the top N returned results and mark if the new bug report is a duplication.

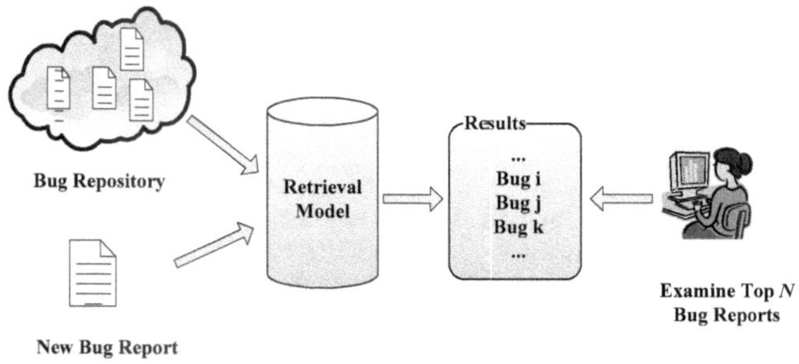

Figure 2. A general process for duplicate bug detection

The differences among the existing duplicate bug report detection methods are mainly in the types of features being selected and in the information retrieval techniques being applied. In this section, we briefly introduce two major state-of-art methods:

SVM:

In [20], the authors proposed a SVM-based discriminative model to determine how likely two bug reports are duplicates. They organize the existing bug reports as a list of buckets, where each bucket contains a set of confirmed duplicate bug reports. Pairs of duplicate and non-duplicate bug reports can be extracted from the buckets and used for training the model. As a bug report consists of two textual fields: summary and description, they identify three bags of words: summary, description, and both (summary + description). For each bag, an *idf* measure is computed, so there are three types of *idf* (*idf*-summary, *idf*-description, and *idf*-both). The total number of *idf* combinations is 27 for each pair of bug. Each *idf* combination is considered as a feature. They also consider bigrams besides unigrams, therefore making the total number of features 54. After identifying the features, they then build a SVM-based discriminative model, which can produce a probability of two bug reports being duplicates of each other. When a new bug report comes, the trained model is applied to retrieve a ranked list of candidate reports of which the new bug is likely a duplicate. Once developers confirm a duplication, the new bug report is placed into the corresponding bucket. Otherwise, a new bucket is created for the new bug.

$BM25F_{ext}$:

In [21], the authors proposed to use $BM25F_{ext}$, an extended BM25F model [17], to measure the textual similarity between two bug reports. They also organize the existing bug reports as a list of buckets and pairs of duplicate and non-duplicate bug reports are used for model training. They consider bug reports as structural documents that are composed of two fields (summary and description) with different degrees of importance, thus applying a BM25F model for structured document retrieval. Also, they consider using the entire bug report as a query, therefore they extend the BM25F model to incorporate the effect of long query. For a document d and a query q, the score of their extended model $BM25F_{ext}$ is computed as follows:

[2] https://bugs.eclipse.org/bugs/show_bug.cgi?id=214445

[3] https://bugs.eclipse.org/bugs/show_bug.cgi?id=214451

$$BM25F_{ext}(d,q) = \sum_{t \in d \cap q} IDF(t) \times \frac{TF_D(d,t)}{k_1 + TF_D(d,t)} \times W_Q$$

$$\text{, where } W_Q = \frac{(k_3+1) \times TF_Q(q,t)}{k_3 + TF_Q(q,t)}$$

$$TF_Q(q,t) = \sum_{f=1}^{k} w_f \times occurrences(q[f],t) \quad (1)$$

$$TF_D(d,t) = \sum_{f=1}^{k} \frac{w_f \times occurrences(d[f],t)}{1 - b_f + b_f \times \frac{length_f}{average\_length_f}}$$

, where f represents a field (either bug summary or bug description). For each field f, $length_f$ is the length of the field, $average\_length_f$ is the average length of f across all documents in the corpus, w_f is the field weight, and b_f is a scaling parameter ($0 \leq b_f \leq 1$). IDF is the inverse document frequency and TF is the term frequency. k_1 and k_3 are tuning parameters that control the effect of term frequency. Unlike the classic BM25F function, $BM25F_{ext}$ considers the weight of terms in queries by introducing an additional parameter k_3.

In [21], the authors also propose a retrieval function called REP. In REP, they identify seven features of bug reports, including textual similarity computed using $BM25F_{ext}$ and several categorical related features. The weight of each feature is tuned using the gradient descent algorithm. Finally, the reports in all buckets are ranked by the weighted sum of feature scores and are returned to developers. However, many of the categorical features (such as bug priority, buggy component, type, and version) may be unknown at the time of reporting bug, especially to end users. Therefore, we only consider the $BM25F_{ext}$ model in this paper.

2.3 Learning to Rank

As a relative new form of statistical learning, learning to rank techniques have received much attention in recent years. Learning to rank is a supervised (or semi-supervised) learning method, which learns a model from ordered objects in a training set and uses the model to rank unknown objects.

The information retrieval (IR) problem can be transformed as the problem of ranking. All documents in the corpus are ranked according to their relevancy to the query, highly relevant documents should be ranked higher than the irrelevant ones. Learning to ranking algorithms such as RankBoost [8], RankSVM [10], and RankNet [4] construct pairs between documents and use machine learning technique to minimize the number of disordered pairs. These algorithms are often called pairwise approaches and have been applied to retrieve documents [4, 5, 13]. More recently, researchers also proposed Listwise approaches [6, 28, 29], which aim to directly minimize the loss function defined on a list of objects.

In our approach, we treat existing bug reports stored in a bug tracking system as documents and a newly arrived bug report as a query. We design methods to retrieve duplicate bug reports by using learning to rank techniques. We apply the pairwise approach, as it is difficult to obtain the complete order of duplicate bug reports, but it is easier to know the partial orders between two bug reports.

3. THE PROPOSED METHOD

3.1 Overall Structure

In this section, we present a method called *BugSim* for ranking duplicate bug reports for a software project. Figure 3 shows an overall structure of BugSim. Following [20], we organize the existing bug reports as a list of buckets, where each bucket contains a set of confirmed duplicate bug reports. A bug report cannot belong to any two buckets thus each bucket is distinct. If a bug does not have duplicates, it corresponds to a bucket that only contains itself.

From the buckets, we collect a training set consisting of triples (*bug, dup bug, non-dup bug*), where *dup bug* represents a duplicate of the *bug, non-dup bug* represents a non-duplicate of the *bug*. We first identify features of bug reports and propose a similarity function to measure the similarities between two bug reports based on these features. Based on the training set, we then construct a retrieval model, which ranks the *dup bug* higher than the *non-dup bug* and minimizes the loss function.

Given a new bug report, the retrieval model can rank the existing bug reports according to the similarity function, and present the ranked results to users as candidate duplicate bug reports. If the new bug report does not belong to any existing bucket, a new bucket is created for this bug. Otherwise, the bug is assigned to the bucket where the duplicate bug report is.

In the following subsections, we describe the feature selection, the model training, and the ranking processes in more details.

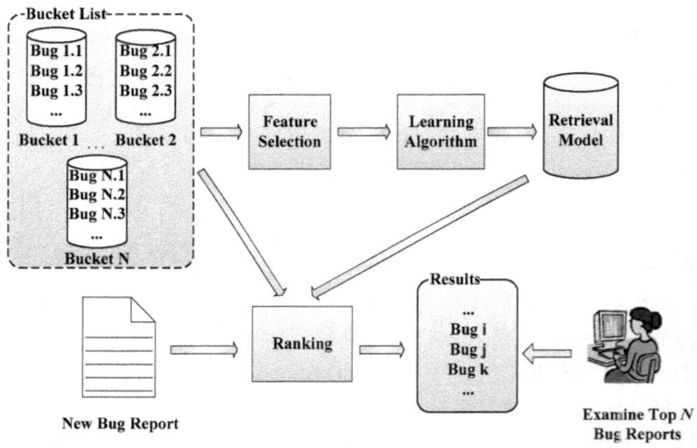

Figure 3. An overall structure of BugSim

3.2 Feature Selection

As described in Section 2, a bug report consists of two parts: summary and description. Inspired by the work on discriminative models for information retrieval [16], we identify 9 features based on bug summary and bug description as shown in Table 1. These features use statistics such as the word count and *idf* (inverse document frequency) and their combinations. We use these features to discriminate the bug reports.

In Table 1, S_1 and D_1 represent the summary and descriptions of a bug report B_1, respectively. S_2 and D_2 represent the summary and descriptions of a bug report B_2, respectively. $idf_s(w)$ represents the *idf* (Inverse Document Frequency) value of a word w over the summaries of all existing bug reports. $idf_D(w)$ represents the *idf* value of a word w over the descriptions of all existing bug reports. $c(w,D_2)$ represents the number of times the word w appears in D_2. $|D_2|$ means the length of D_2. $|C_D|$ means the total number of unique words that appear in the descriptions of all existing bug reports. $c(w,C_D)$ means the number of times the word w appears in the descriptions of all existing bug reports.

Table 1. The identified features between two bug reports

#	Feature	#	Feature
1	$\sum_{w \in S_1 \cap S_2} idf_S(w)$	2	$\frac{\lvert S_1 \cap S_2 \rvert}{\lvert S_1 \cup S_2 \rvert}$
3	$\sum_{w \in S_1 \cap D_2} \log(c(w,D_2)+1)$	4	$\sum_{w \in S_1 \cap D_2} \log(\frac{c(w,D_2)}{\lvert D_2 \rvert}+1)$
5	$\sum_{w \in S_1 \cap D_2} \log(\frac{c(w,D_2)}{\lvert D_2 \rvert} \times idf_D(w)+1)$	6	$\sum_{w \in S_1 \cap D_2} idf_D(w)$
7	$\sum_{w \in S_1 \cap D_2} \log(\frac{c(w,D_2)}{\lvert D_2 \rvert} \times \frac{\lvert C_D \rvert}{c(w,C_D)}+1)$	8	$\sum_{w \in S_1 \cap D_2} \log(\frac{\lvert C_D \rvert}{c(w,C_D)}+1)$
9	$VSMScore(D_1,D_2)$		

Feature 1 describes the *idf* values of the words that are common to the summary of the two bug reports. Feature 2 describes the similarity between the summary of the two bug reports (measured in terms of the number of common words). Feature 3 describes the number of times words used in the summary of B_1 appearing in the descriptions of B_2. Feature 4 describes the frequency of words used in the summary of B_1 appearing in the descriptions of B_2. Feature 5 gives the multiplication of the term frequency and the *idf* values (*tf* * *idf*). Feature 6 gives the *idf* values of words that are used in both the summary of B_1 and the descriptions of B_2. Feature 7 describes the weights of words that are used in both the summary of B_1 and the descriptions of B_2, in the entire document collection. Feature 8 describes the inverse collection frequency of words that are used in both the summary of B_1 and the descriptions of B_2. Feature 9 gives the text similarity of the two bug reports, measured using VSM (Vector Space Model). For some features, the *log* function is used to dampen the effects of large numbers.

Based on the identified features, we define a metric *BugSim* for measuring the similarity between two bug reports B_1 and B_2 as follows:

$$BugSim(B_1,B_2) = \sum_{i=1}^{\#feature} w_i f_i^{B_1,B_2} \tag{2}$$

In (2), f_i represents the ith feature; w_i represents the weight of the ith feature. Higher *BugSim* values indicate higher similarity between the two bug reports.

3.3 Learning the Model

To apply (2), 9 weights should be given. It is difficult to obtain the values of these weights subjectively. In our approach, we adopt a learning process to tune these weights.

In our training set, each instance is a triple (*bug, dup bug, non-dup bug*), where *dup bug* represents a duplicate of the *bug, non-dup bug* represents a non-duplicate of the *bug*. Clearly, if we want the *dup bug* to be ranked higher than the *non-dup bug,* the followings should hold:

$$BugSim(bug, dup\ bug) > BugSim(bug, non\text{-}dup\ bug) \tag{3}$$

We also utilize the Fidelity loss function (F_{ij}) [25] to measure the cost of the *BugSim* on an instance *I*:

$$F_{ij} = 1 - \left(\left[P_{ij}^* \times (\frac{e^{o_{ij}}}{1+e^{o_{ij}}}) \right]^{\frac{1}{2}} + \left[(1-P_{ij}^*) \times (\frac{1}{1+e^{o_{ij}}}) \right]^{\frac{1}{2}} \right)$$
$$\text{where } o_{ij} = BugSim(bug, non\text{-}dup\ bug) - BugSim(bug, dup\ bug) \tag{4}$$

In (4), P^*_{ij} is the target probabilities that sample i is to be ranked higher than sample j. In the case of duplicate bug detection, duplicate bug reports should be always ranked higher than non-duplicate ones. So equation (4) can be simplified as follows:

$$F_{ij} = 1 - (\frac{1}{1+e^{o_{ij}}})^{\frac{1}{2}} \tag{5}$$

The Fidelity loss function was originally a distance metric in physics and was recently used by [25] in the probabilistic ranking framework. It has been shown that the Fidelity loss function exhibits properties that are helpful for ranking. From (5) we can see that the value of F_{ij} increases when o_{ij} increases.

To better differentiate *dup bug* and *non-dup bug*, the values of w_i should be chosen in such a way that the Fidelity loss function is minimized. To obtain the optimal values of w_i, we apply the stochastic gradient descent algorithm [15]. The stochastic gradient descent algorithm iterates N time. In each iteration, for each instance in the training set, the algorithm adjusts each weight as follows:

$$w_i = w_i - \eta \times \frac{\partial F_{ij}}{\partial w_i}(I) \tag{6}$$

, where η is the tuning rate, which is usually a very small number such as 0.001. After N iterations, the w_i values that lead to the minimum F_{ij} value are the optimal weight values. In (6), the partial derivative of the Fidelity loss function with respect to w_i is derived as follows:

$$\frac{\partial F_{ij}}{\partial w_k} = \frac{\partial F_{ij}}{\partial o_{ij}} \times \frac{\partial o_{ij}}{\partial w_k} = \frac{\partial(1-(1+e^{o_{ij}})^{-1/2})}{\partial o_{ij}} \times \frac{\partial o_{ij}}{\partial w_k} = \frac{1}{2}(1+e^{o_{ij}})^{-3/2} \times e^{o_{ij}} \times \frac{\partial o_{ij}}{\partial w_k}$$
$$\frac{\partial o_{ij}}{\partial w_k} = \frac{\partial(BugSim(bug,non\text{-}dup\ bug) - BugSim(bug,dup\ bug))}{\partial w_k} = f_k^{bug,non\text{-}dup\ bug} - f_k^{bug,dup\ bug} \tag{7}$$

In summary, Figure 4 shows the algorithm we used to perform training. The algorithm includes two parts: the selection of training instances and the learning of weights.

3.4 Ranking for New Bug Reports

After the ranking model is trained, we can use it for duplicate bug report retrieval. When a new bug report arrives, BugSim computes the similarity between a new bug report and a bucket, which is the maximum similarity value between the new bug report and all the existing bug reports in the bucket. To compute the similarity between the new report and an existing one, BugSim first extracts the features between them (as described in Section 3.2), and then calculates the similarity using equation (2). BugSim ranks all the buckets by their similarity values to the new report. For each bucket, the most similar bug report is presented to the users. The users can then check if the new bug is a duplicate of a bug in the top N list. If it is a duplicate, it is inserted into the bucket that contains the bug it duplicates to. If it is not a duplicate bug, a new bucket is created for the new bug report.

TRAINING (*Buckets, S*)

Buckets: The list of buckets that contain duplicate bug reports.

S: The size of the training set

// Training set selection

1. Initialize the training set *T*
2. Randomly select two bug reports from the *Buckets* that contain more than one bug reports, and label them as *bug* and *dup bug.*
3. Randomly select a bucket that is different from the bucket that contains the *bug,* and randomly select one bug, label it as *non-dup bug*
4. Create a triple *I(bug, dup bug, non-dup bug)*, and add it into *T.*
5. Repeat the steps 2-4 until the size of *T* reaches *S.*

// Learning weights

6. Applying the stochastic gradient descent algorithm on *T* to tune the weight *w* of each feature
7. Return the tuned weights *w*

Figure 4. The training algorithm

4. EVALUATION

4.1 Dataset

To evaluate the effectiveness of the proposed approach, we choose the Eclipse[4] projects as our subject. Eclipse is an open source community whose projects are focused on building extensible software development platforms and frameworks. Software tools produced by the Eclipse projects are very popular and have millions of users worldwide[5]. The bugs reported against Eclipse are stored and tracked by the BugZilla tool[6]. Like in other projects, users who would like to post an Eclipse bug report are encouraged to check whether it has been posted already[7].

In our evaluation, we investigate 12 relatively independent projects (categories) in Eclipse, as shown in Table 1. These projects contain 45,170 bugs reported from January 1, 2008 to December 31, 2008. Among the 45,170 bugs, 2,949 are duplicates. Following the previous work [21], we construct a small training set, which contains total 5,863 bugs and 200 duplicate bugs (from 2008-01-01 to 2008-02-22). The remaining data is used as the testing dataset.

We use Java to implement the research prototype. The experiments are carried out on a Windows 2008 Server R2 with Intel Xeon(R) CPU E5506@2.13GHz and 8G memory.

Table 2. The Eclipse dataset

Project	Training Set		Test Set	
	#Duplicate Bugs	#Bugs	#Duplicate Bugs	#Bugs
Eclipse IDE			928	9872
Eclipse Foundation			63	1497
DataTools			29	699
Tools			365	5257
BIRT			203	2989
RT	200	5863	472	4702
DSDP			52	1321
TPTP			83	905
WebTools			226	3641
STP			3	129
Modeling			99	3239
Technology			226	5056

4.2 Research Questions

RQ1: How effective is BugSim?

RQ1 evaluates the effectiveness of our approach described in Section 3. To answer RQ1, we evaluate BugSim on the projects described in Table 2. We use the training set to train a ranking model, following the algorithm described in Figure 4. For each bug report in the testing set, BugSim retrieves the candidate duplicate bug reports and returns a ranked list to users. The performance of retrieval is measured using the recall rate and the MRR metrics.

RQ2: Can BugSim outperform the related methods?

RQ2 compares the proposed method with the two major related methods that are described in Section 2.2:

- SVM [20]: We use the *libsvm* tool[8] as the SVM implementation. Following [20], we identify 54 features to build a discriminative model on the training set. Once the model is created, we use it to determine the probability of a bug being a duplicate of the other.
- $BM25F_{ext}$ [21]: We use the parameters given in [21] to build a $BM25F_{ext}$-based model. $BM25F_{ext}$ is an extension of BM25F as described in Section 2.2. We use it to calculate the textual similarity between two bug reports and rank the candidate duplicate bugs according to the similarity values.

RQ3: Does the Fidelity loss function outperform the related RNC loss function?

4 http://www.eclipse.org/

5 http://www.numberof.net/number-of-eclipse-users/

6 https://bugs.eclipse.org/bugs/

7 http://wiki.eclipse.org/FAQ_How_can_I_search_the_existing_list_of_bugs_in_Eclipse%3F

8 Libsvm: http://www.csie.ntu.edu.tw/~cjlin/libsvm.

In our approach, we use the Fidelity function as the loss function. Other loss functions could be also adopted in learning to rank approaches. In RankNet [4], a pairwise cross entropy loss function is used to penalize ordering error, which is defined as:

$$C_{ij} = -P_{ij}^{*}O_{ij} + \log(1 + e^{O_{ij}}) \tag{8}$$

The above loss function is also used in [21, 23] and is referred to as the RNC function. This RQ compares the effectiveness of the Fidelity function with that of the RNC function.

4.3 Evaluation Metrics

We evaluate the performance of BugSim using the following metrics:

- Recall@*N*: The percentage of bug reports whose relevant duplicates can be detected in the top *N* (*N* = 1, 5, 10, 20) of the returned results. A better duplicate bug retrieval method should allow users to identify more duplicate bug reports by examining less number of bug reports. Thus, the higher the metric value, the better the retrieval performance.
- MRR (Mean Reciprocal Rank), which is a statistic for evaluating a process that produces a list of possible responses to a query [26]. The reciprocal rank of a query is the multiplicative inverse of the rank of the first relevant answer. The mean reciprocal rank is the average of the reciprocal ranks of results of a set of queries *Q*:

$$MRR = \frac{1}{|Q|}\sum_{i=1}^{|Q|}\frac{1}{rank_i} \tag{9}$$

The higher the MRR value, the better the retrieval performance. Note that MRR is equal to MAP (Mean Average Precision), when only the first relevant answer is considered.

5. EVALUATION RESULTS

5.1 Results of RQs

RQ1: How effective is BugSim?

Table 3 shows the performance of BugSim on 12 projects, when recall rate is concerned. For the STP project, BugSim can successfully rank all its three duplicate bug reports as top 1 (the first returned result). Therefore its Recall@1 is 1. For the Eclipse IDE project, it has 9872 bugs and 928 of them are duplicates. Using BugSim, 45.58% duplicate bug reports can be detected at top 1, 71.77% can be detected within top 10, and 76.51% can be detected within top 20. For all the projects, the Recall@1 values are above 33% (with an average of 49.48%), the Recall@10 values are above 61% (with an average of 76.11%), and the Recall@20 values are above 67% (with an average of 82.03%). These results are considered satisfactory.

Table 3 also shows the performance of BugSim measured in terms of MRR. For the STP and Modeling projects, the MRR values exceed 0.7. For the rest of the projects, the MRR values are above 0.42.

In general, the evaluation results show that BugSim is effective in retrieving duplicate bug reports. It can allow developers detect duplicate bug reports by examining a small number of bug reports. The effort spent on bug handling can be reduced.

Table 3. The performance of BugSim

Project	Recall @1	Recall @5	Recall @10	Recall @20	MRR
BIRT	38.92%	66.01%	70.94%	80.30%	0.5054
DataTools	41.38%	68.72%	82.76%	86.21%	0.5434
DSDP	40.38%	76.92%	78.85%	82.69%	0.5515
Eclipse Foundation	44.44%	68.25%	76.19%	84.13%	0.5576
Eclipse IDE	45.58%	64.55%	71.77%	76.51%	0.5447
Modeling	71.72%	85.86%	88.89%	91.92%	0.7636
RT	33.26%	51.91%	61.23%	67.58%	0.4274
STP	100%	100%	100%	100%	1
Technology	46.02%	66.37%	73.01%	80.97%	0.5574
Tools	52.05%	72.33%	78.90%	84.93%	0.6148
TPTP	36.14%	56.63%	62.65%	73.49%	0.4564
WebTools	43.81%	61.50%	68.14%	75.66%	0.5226
average	*49.48%*	*69.92%*	*76.11%*	*82.03%*	*0.5871*

RQ2: Can BugSim outperform the related methods?

Table 4 shows the comparison between BugSim and SVM and $BM25F_{ext}$ based methods, when MRR is concerned. BugSim performs better than the SVM-based discriminative model on all experimental projects. The MRR values SVM achieves are between 0.32 and 0.73, with an average of 0.45. The improvements of BugSim over SVM range from 4.87% to 76.47%, with an average of 31.49%.

Table 4. The comparison between BugSim and the related work (MRR)

		SVM		$BM25F_{ext}$	
Project	BugSim	MRR	%impr.	MRR	%impr.
BIRT	0.5054	0.3159	60.03%	0.4763	6.11%
DataTools	0.5434	0.4378	24.12%	0.5068	7.23%
DSDP	0.5515	0.4883	12.94%	0.5431	1.54%
Eclipse Foundation	0.5576	0.4678	19.21%	0.4897	13.86%
Eclipse IDE	0.5447	0.3987	36.62%	0.5211	4.53%
Modeling	0.7636	0.7282	4.87%	0.7772	-1.75%
RT	0.4274	0.3265	30.93%	0.3870	10.43%
STP	1.0000	0.5667	76.47%	0.8333	20.00%
Technology	0.5574	0.4002	39.29%	0.5146	8.32%
Tools	0.6148	0.4666	31.77%	0.5744	7.03%
TPTP	0.4564	0.3710	22.99%	0.4438	2.84%
WebTools	0.5226	0.3901	33.96%	0.5264	-0.72%
average	*0.5871*	*0.4465*	*31.49%*	*0.5495*	*6.84%*

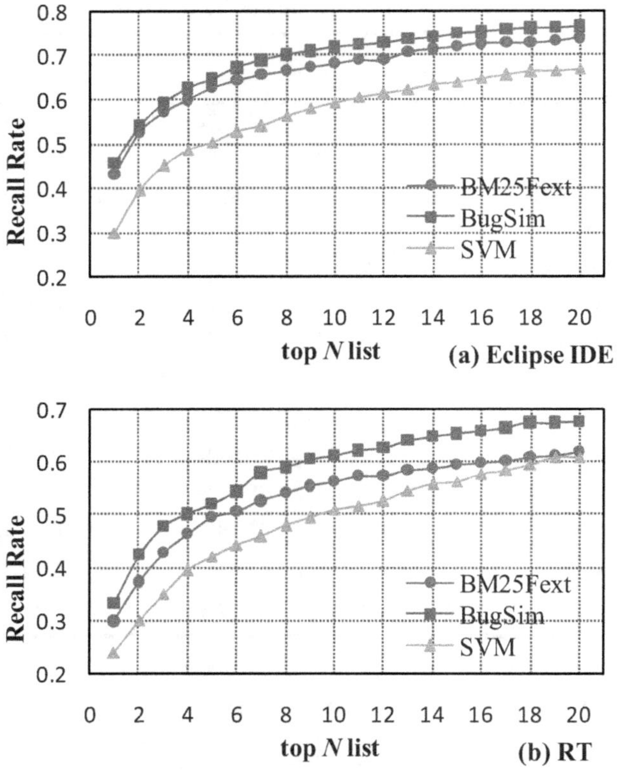

Figure 5. The comparisons between BugSim and the related work on Eclipse IDE and RT projects

BugSim also outperforms $BM25F_{ext}$ on 10 projects. The improvement is from 1.5% to 20%. BugSim only performs slightly worse than $BM25F_{ext}$ on two projects (1.7% and 0.7%, respectively). The average improvement of BugSim over $BM25F_{ext}$ is 6.84%. We also conduct a paired t-test and the result confirms that BugSim performs statistically significantly better than $BM25F_{ext}$, at the significance level 0.05 (with p value 0.017).

We also find that BugSim outperforms SVM and $BM25F_{ext}$, when performance is measured in terms of recall rate. For example, Figure 5 shows the results on Eclipse IDE and RT projects, at different top *N* lists. For the two projects, BugSim improves the SVM method by 14.15% – 53.26% and 9.75% – 29.00%, respectively, and improves $BM25F_{ext}$ by 2.59% – 5.47% and 4.49% – 12.00%, respectively. Table 5 gives the details on the percentage of improvement BugSim over SVM and $BM25F_{ext}$ on Recall@10 values, for all experimental projects. The average improvement of BugSim over SVM and $BM25F_{ext}$ is 15.41% and 3.71%, respectively.

RQ3: Does the Fidelity loss function outperform the related loss functions?

Figure 6 shows the impact of two different loss functions (Fidelity loss and RNC) on BugSim. Fidelity loss outperforms RNC when recall rate is concerned. For example, on the Eclipse IDE project, Fidelity loss function leads to 14.89% – 31.37% higher recall values than RNC. On the RT project, Fidelity loss function leads to 18.05% – 31.34% higher recall values than RNC.

Similarly, Fidelity loss function also outperforms RNC when the effectiveness is measured in terms of MRR (Figure 7). Fidelity loss leads to 4.07% – 27.78% higher MRR values on 10 projects. On STP and DSDP projects, the two loss functions obtain similar performance. A paired t-test confirms that the results are statistically significant, at the significance level 0.05(with p value 0.0002).

Table 5. The comparison between BugSim and the related work (Recall@10)

Project	Bug-Sim	SVM		$BM25F_{ext}$	
		Recall@10	%impr.	Recall@10	%impr.
BIRT	70.94%	50.74%	39.81%	67.98%	4.35%
DataTools	82.76%	62.07%	33.33%	75.86%	9.10%
DSDP	78.85%	71.15%	10.82%	75%	5.13%
Eclipse Foundation	76.19%	73.02%	4.34%	73.02%	4.34%
Eclipse IDE	71.77%	59.38%	20.87%	68.10%	5.39%
Modeling	88.89%	80.81%	10.00%	86.87%	2.33%
RT	61.23%	50.85%	20.41%	56.36%	8.64%
STP	100%	100%	0.00%	100%	0.00%
Technology	73.01%	57.52%	26.93%	70.80%	3.12%
Tools	78.90%	69.32%	13.82%	76.16%	3.60%
TPTP	62.65%	59.04%	6.11%	61.45%	1.95%
WebTools	68.14%	57.52%	18.46%	69.03%	-1.29%
average	*76.11%*	*65.95%*	*15.41%*	*73.39%*	*3.71%*

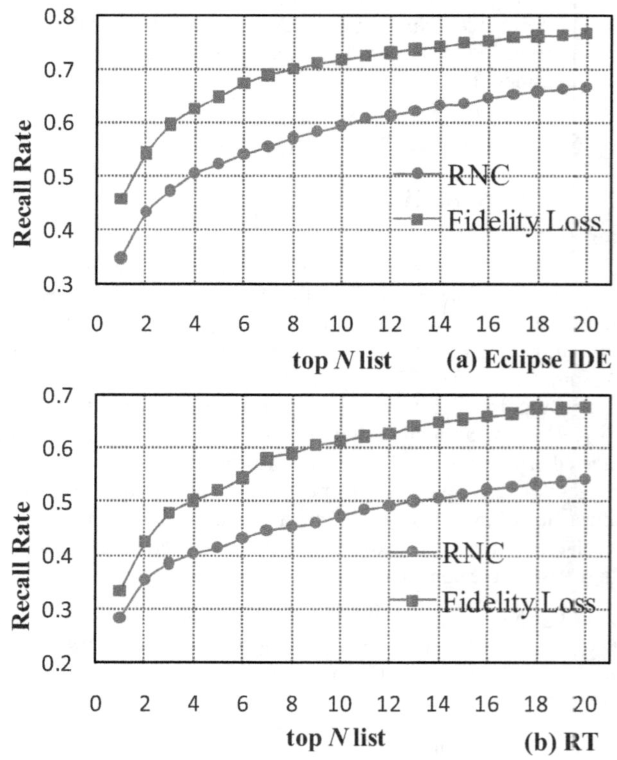

Figure 6. The impact of Fidelity Loss and RNC functions on BugSim (recall rate)

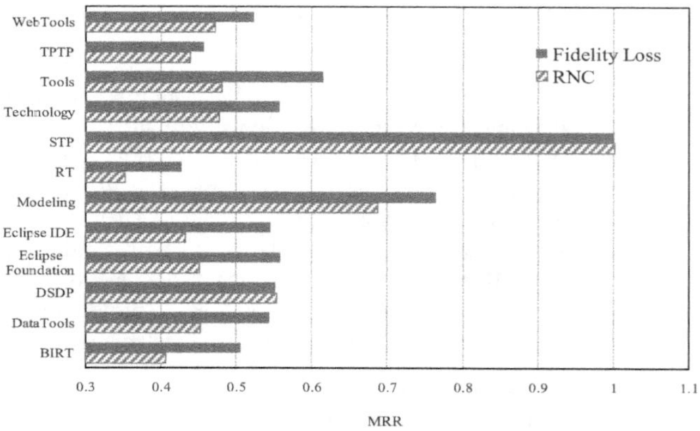

Figure 7. The impact of Fidelity Loss and RNC functions on BugSim (MRR)

5.2 Discussions

5.2.1 Why does BugSim perform better?

In Section 5.1, we have shown that BugSim outperforms SVM and $BM25F_{ext}$ based methods for detecting duplicate bug reports. We have identified the following major differences between BugSim and the two previous methods:

1) Feature selection: Inspired by the work on discriminative models for information retrieval [16], BugSim uses a much richer feature set that consists of both text similarity feature (feature 9 in Table 1) and statistical features (features 1-8 in Table 1). The statistical features consider both bug summary and bug description. Generally, a bug summary is short and a bug description is more detailed. Therefore, we treat a summary as a query and descriptions as documents, and identify features (features 3-8) to measure the similarity between a bug summary and a description. To measure the similarity of two bug summaries, we use two features (features 1-2) based on the *idf* value and the overlap of common words. To measure the similarity between two bug descriptions, we use a VSM model. In this way, we use different metrics to measure the similarity between different aspects of bug reports. We should note that in [21], the authors also identified several categorical features of bug reports, such as bug priority, buggy component, type, version, etc. The retrieval performance could be further improved by 2% (in terms of MRR) if these features are considered [21]. However, in real settings the values of these features could be unknown at the time of reporting bug, especially to end users. Therefore, in our work, we only consider the text similarity between two bug reports, which can be derived from natural language text only and is independent of bug tracking tools or processes.

2) Learning method: BugSim is essentially a pairwise learning to rank method. The previous SVM work [20] is based on classification of pairs of bug reports and can be considered as a form of pointwise learning to rank method. As pointed out by [14], the pointwise approach assumes relevance is absolute and query independent, which may bring bias to the training model. Also, BugSim utilizes the Fidelity loss function, while the previous $BM25F_{ext}$ work used the RNC loss function. As discussed in [25], Fidelity loss function possesses several new properties that are helpful for ranking (e.g., having a finite upper bound that is necessary for conducting query-level normalization) and therefore improves ranking performance.

5.2.2 The missing cases

Although our experiments show that BugSim can effectively retrieve duplicate bug reports, it may still fail to identify some duplicate bug reports. BugSim assumes that duplicate bug reports have high degree of text similarity, which is a valid assumption for most of duplicate bug reports. However, we found that some duplicate bug reports may use different words to describe the same problem. For example, when reporting the problem of a software crash, different reporters may use different words such as "exception", "crash", "failure", "error", "down", etc. Currently BugSim does not consider the semantic similarity among words. Therefore, it may treat these reports as dissimilar texts.

Another reason of missing cases is that some bug reports are very brief, as the users did not spend much time on writing detailed problem scenarios. This also causes difficulty in statistical analysis. We will address these two issues in our future work and to further improve the performance of the proposed approach.

5.2.3 Comparison to the Fingerprint-based methods

BugSim and the related methods (such as the SVM-based discriminative model and the $BM25F_{ext}$ model) basically detect near-duplicate documents by comparing the text similarity between pairs of bug reports using information retrieval techniques. Another major approach to the detection of similar documents is a technique known as *fingerprinting*, which represents and compares documents using compact values computed by certain hash functions. Examples of Fingerprint-based methods include Shingling [3, 9] and SimHash [7, 9, 19].

We compare the performance of BugSim to that of SimHash on the Eclipse projects. The results are shown in Figure 8. The MRR values of SimHash are ranging from 0.15 to 0.57 (with an average of 0.29), while the MRR values of BugSim are ranging from 0.43 to 1.00 (with an average of 0.59). A paired t-test also confirms the statistical significance ($p = 0.00$). Clearly, BugSim is more capable of detecting duplicate bug reports than SimHash. According to the literature, SimHash is effective in detecting duplicate web pages at a very large scale [9]. The duplicate web pages are identical/near-identical web pages stored at different locations. While in the cases of bug reports, although duplicate bug reports describe the same problem, they could differ in the detailed natural language descriptions.

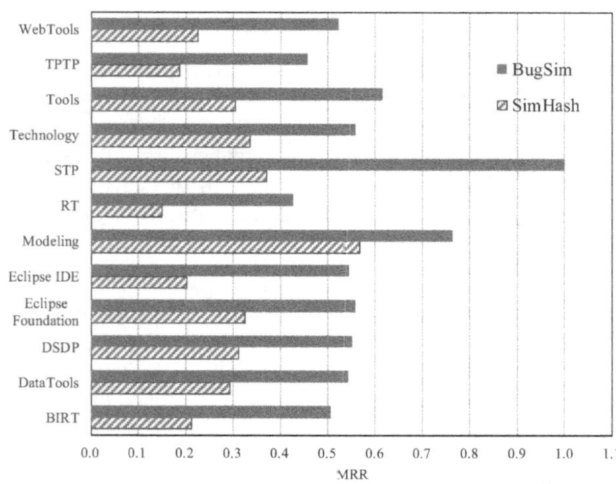

Figure 8. The comparison between BugSim and SimHash (MRR)

6. THREATS TO VALIDITY

There are potential threats to the validity of our work:

- The performance of our approach relies on bug report quality. A "bad" bug report could cause misclassification of the bug report. If a bug report does not provide enough information, or provides misleading information, the performance of BugSim is adversely affected.
- The dataset used in our experiments is collected from the Eclipse open source projects. We need to evaluate the performance of the proposed method on more types of projects, especially on commercial projects. This remains as an important future work.
- In our experiments, we evaluate BugSim on 45,100+ real bug reports of twelve Eclipse projects. We assume that the number of bug reports for a software system is limited. If the scale of a bug repository is very large (say consisting of millions of bug reports), the performance of BugSim could be affected. However, in real projects the number of bugs in a single software system is usually limited.

7. RELATED WORK

7.1 Duplicate document detection

Duplicate documents are often found in large corpus. Many researchers have proposed methods for detecting duplicate or near-duplicate documents. For example, Broder et al. [3] used word sequences (shingles) and a clustering algorithm to efficiently detect near-duplicate web pages. Brin et al. [2] proposed to use word sequences to detect copyright violations. Theobald et al. [24] proposed SpotSig, an algorithm for extracting and matching signatures for near duplicate detection in large Web crawls. Sood and Loguinov [19] used SimHash [7] to detect similar document pairs in large-scale collections.

The above methods are based on documents' fingerprints. Hoad and Zobel [11] also experimented with information retrieval based method for identifying versioned and plagiarized documents. They proposed several term-weight based similarity measures (called identity measures) to rank similar documents. Their experiments on two document collections showed that both the identity measures and the fingerprint-based methods can identify duplicate documents, and in general identity measures outperform fingerprint-based methods in terms of accuracy.

In this work, we focus on a special form of documents – bug reports. Unlike duplicate web pages or plagiarized documents, duplicate bug reports are not identical. The scale of bug reports for a software system is usually much smaller than the scale of a Web corpus. We identify statistical features of bug reports and apply learning to rank techniques to detect duplicate bug reports.

7.2 Duplicate bug detection

Recently, some researchers have proposed methods for detecting duplicate bug reports. We have already discussed and compared the SVM-based discriminative method and the $BM25F_{ext}$ method in previous sections. Runeson et al. [18] also treated bug reports as text documents and applied the Vector Space Model to retrieve duplicate bug reports. They computed a term's weight as *1+log(frequency)*, and applied three measures (cosine measure, dice coefficient, and Jaccard coefficient) to measure text similarity. Their experiments on Sony Ericsson mobile systems showed that about 40% of the duplicates could be found. Sun et al. [20] found that their SVM-based discriminative method outperforms Runeson et al.'s method.

Wang et al. [27] proposed to detect duplicate bug reports using both natural language text and execution information. However, their approach is limited in that not all bug reports come with runtime program execution information. Jalbert and Weimer [12] built a classifier to detect duplicate bug reports. They used bug reports' surface features, text similarity metrics, and graph clustering algorithms to identify duplicate documents. Their evaluation on 29,000 bug reports from the Mozilla project showed that 8% of duplicate reports can be successfully detected.

Recently, Sureka and Jalote [22] proposed to use n-grams based features to characterize a bug report. Their experiment on Eclipse projects showed that their approach is able to detect duplicate bug reports with reasonable accuracy. They randomly selected 1100 duplicate Eclipse bug reports and found that their approach can achieve Recall@10 value 21% and Recall@20 value 25%. Sun et al. [21] reported that their $BM25F_{ext}$ method outperforms Sureka and Jalote's method.

As described in previous sections, BugSim outperforms the existing state-of-art SVM and $BM25F_{ext}$ based methods (therefore other related methods described above). On Eclipse projects, the Recall@10 values BugSim achieves are between 61% and 100%.

8. CONCLUSIONS AND FUTURE WORK

Although quality control measures have been taken, in reality, software systems contain bugs. For a large-scale, widely-used software system, the project team could receive a large number of bug reports over time. The existence of duplicate bug reports could greatly increase software maintenance efforts. In this paper, we have proposed *BugSim*, a duplicate bug retrieval method based on learning to rank techniques. BugSim constructs a training set by assembling pairs of duplicate and non-duplicate bug reports. A training model is built using textual and statistical features of bug reports and a similarity function based on these features. Our experiments on 12 Eclipse projects show that BugSim is effective in retrieving duplicate bug reports. The recall rates for the top 10 retrieved reports are above 61%, with an average of 76.11%. Our method also outperforms the related state-of-art methods (SVM and $BM25F_{ext}$).

In the future, we will consider the semantic similarity between bug reports, aiming to further improve the performance of the proposed approach. We will evaluate the proposed approach on industrial projects. We also plan to integrate our approach into an existing bug tracking system.

ACKNOWLEDGEMENTS

This research is supported by the NSFC grant 61073006, and the Tsinghua University project 2010THZ0. We thank the authors of [21] for providing us the tool and the Eclipse dataset used in their experiments.

REFERENCES

[1] J. Anvik, L. Hiew, and G. C. Murphy. 2006. Who should fix this bug? In *Proceedings of the 28th international conference on Software engineering* (ICSE '06). Pages: 361-370.

[2] S. Brin, J. Davis, and H. Garcia-Molina. 1995. Copy detection mechanisms for digital documents. In *Proc. ACM SIGMOD Annual Conference*. Pages: 398-409.

[3] A. Z. Broder, S.C. Glassman, M.S. Manasse, and G. Zweig. 1997. Syntactic Clustering of the Web. In *Proc. 6th International World Wide Web Conference.* Pages: 393-404.

[4] C. Burges, T. Shaked, E. Renshaw, A. Lazier, M. Deeds, N. Hamilton, and G. Hullender. 2005. Learning to rank using gradient descent. In *Proceedings of the 22nd international conference on Machine learning* (ICML '05). Pages: 89-96.

[5] Y. Cao, J. Xu, T-Y Liu, H. Li, Y. Huang, and H-W Hon. 2006. Adapting ranking SVM to document retrieval. In *Proceedings of the 29th annual international ACM SIGIR conference on Research and development in information retrieval* (SIGIR '06). Pages: 186-193.

[6] Z. Cao, T. Qin, T-Y Liu, M-F Tsai, and H Li. 2007. Learning to rank: from pairwise approach to listwise approach. In *Proceedings of the 24th international conference on Machine learning* (ICML'07). Pages: 129-136.

[7] M. S. Charikar. 2002. Similarity estimation techniques from rounding algorithms. In *Proceedings of the thirty-fourth annual ACM symposium on Theory of computing* (STOC '02). Pages: 380-388.

[8] Y. Freund, R. Iyer, R. E. Schapire, and Y. Singer. 2003. An efficient boosting algorithm for combining preferences. *J. Mach. Learn. Res. 4* (December 2003). Pages: 933-969.

[9] M. Henzinger. 2006. Finding near-duplicate web pages: a large-scale evaluation of algorithms. In *Proceedings of the 29th annual international ACM SIGIR conference on Research and development in information retrieval* (SIGIR '06). Pages: 284-291.

[10] R Herbrich, T. Graepel, and K. Obermayer. Large margin rank boundaries for ordinal regression. *Advances in Large Margin Classifiers* (2000). Volume: 88, Issue: 2, Publisher: MIT Press, Pages: 115-132.

[11] T. C. Hoad and J. Zobel. Methods for identifying versioned and plagiarized documents. *Journal of the American Society for Information Science and Technology* (2003). Volume 54, Issue 3, pages 203–215.

[12] N. Jalbert and W. Weimer. 2008. Automated Duplicate Detection for Bug Tracking Systems. In *Proceedings of the International Conference on Dependable Systems and Networks* (DSN '08). Pages: 52-61.

[13] T. Joachims. 2002. Optimizing search engines using click through data. In *Proceedings of the eighth ACM SIGKDD international conference on Knowledge discovery and data mining* (KDD '02). Pages: 133-142.

[14] T-Y Liu. 2009. Learning to Rank for Information Retrieval. *Foundations and Trends in Information Retrieval.* Vol. 3: No 3. Pages: 225–331.

[15] T. M. Mitchell. *Machine Learning*. New York: McGraw -Hill, 1997. Pages: 88-95.

[16] R. Nallapati. 2004. Discriminative models for information retrieval. In *Proceedings of the 27th annual international ACM SIGIR conference on Research and development in information retrieval* (SIGIR '04). Pages: 64-71.

[17] S. Robertson, H. Zaragoza, and M. Taylor. 2004. Simple BM25 extension to multiple weighted fields. In *Proceedings of the thirteenth ACM international conference on Information and knowledge management* (CIKM '04). Pages: 42-49.

[18] P. Runeson, M. Alexanderson, O. Nyholm. 2007. Detection of Duplicate Defect Reports Using Natural Language Processing. In *Proceedings of the 29nd ACM/IEEE International Conference on Software Engineering* (ICSE '07). Pages: 499-510.

[19] S. Sood and D. Loguinov. 2011. Probabilistic near-duplicate detection using simhash. In *Proceedings of the 20th ACM international conference on Information and knowledge management* (CIKM '11). Pages: 1117-1126.

[20] C. Sun, D. Lo, X. Wang, J. Jiang, and S-C. Khoo. 2010. A discriminative model approach for accurate duplicate bug report retrieval. In *Proceedings of the 32nd ACM/IEEE International Conference on Software Engineering* (ICSE '10). Pages: 45-54.

[21] C. Sun, D. Lo, S-C. Khoo, and J. Jiang. 2011. Towards more accurate retrieval of duplicate bug reports. *In Proc. Automated Software Engineering* (ASE'11). Pages: 253 – 262.

[22] A. Sureka and P. Jalote. 2010. Detecting duplicate bug report using character n-gram-based features. In *Proceedings of the 2010 Asia Pacific Software Engineering Conference*. Pages: 366–374.

[23] M. Taylor, H. Zaragoza, N. Craswell, S. Robertson, and C. Burges. 2006. Optimisation methods for ranking functions with multiple parameters. In *Proceedings of the 15th ACM international conference on Information and knowledge management* (CIKM '06). Pages: 585-593.

[24] M. Theobald, J. Siddharth, and A. Paepcke. 2008. SpotSigs: robust and efficient near duplicate detection in large web collections. In *Proceedings of the 31st annual international ACM SIGIR conference on Research and development in information retrieval* (SIGIR '08). Pages: 563-570.

[25] M-F. Tsai, T-Y. Liu, T. Qin, H-H. Chen, and W-Y. Ma. 2007. FRank: a ranking method with fidelity loss. In *Proceedings of the 30th annual international ACM SIGIR conference on Research and development in information retrieval* (SIGIR '07). Pages: 383-390.

[26] E.M. Voorhees. 1999. Question Answering Track Report. In *Proceedings of the 8th Text Retrieval Conference.* Pages: 77–82.

[27] X. Wang, L. Zhang, T. Xie, J. Anvik, and J. Sun. 2008. An approach to detecting duplicate bug reports using natural language and execution information. In *Proceedings of the 30th international conference on Software engineering* (ICSE '08). Pages: 461-470.

[28] F. Xia, T-Y. Liu, J. Wang, W. Zhang, and H. Li. 2008. Listwise approach to learning to rank: theory and algorithm. In *Proceedings of the 25th international conference on Machine learning* (ICML '08). Pages: 1192-1199.

[29] J. Xu and H. Li. 2007. AdaRank: a boosting algorithm for information retrieval. In *Proceedings of the 30th annual international ACM SIGIR conference on Research and development in information retrieval* (SIGIR '07). Pages: 391-398.

A Model-based Approach for RFID Data Stream Cleansing

Zhou Zhao and Wilfred Ng
The Hong Kong University of Science and Technology
Clear Water Bay, Kowloon, Hong Kong
{zhaozhou, wilfred}@cse.ust.hk

ABSTRACT

In recent years, RFID technologies have been used in many applications, such as inventory checking and object tracking. However, raw RFID data are inherently unreliable due to physical device limitations and different kinds of environmental noise. Currently, existing work mainly focuses on RFID data cleansing in a static environment (e.g. inventory checking). It is therefore difficult to cleanse RFID data streams in a mobile environment (e.g. object tracking) using the existing solutions, which do not address the data missing issue effectively.

In this paper, we study how to cleanse RFID data streams for object tracking, which is a challenging problem, since a significant percentage of readings are routinely dropped. We propose a probabilistic model for object tracking in a mobile environment. We develop a Bayesian inference based approach for cleansing RFID data using the model. In order to sample data from the movement distribution, we devise a sequential sampler that cleans RFID data with high accuracy and efficiency. We validate the effectiveness and robustness of our solution through extensive simulations and demonstrate its performance by using two real RFID applications of human tracking and conveyor belt monitoring.

Categories and Subject Descriptors

H.2 [**Information Systems**]: Database Management

General Terms

Algorithms, Design, Experimentation

Keywords

Probabilistic Algorithms, Uncertainty, Data Cleaning

1. INTRODUCTION

RFID (Radio Frequency IDentification) technologies have been widely applied in many areas such as supply chains and warehouse management owing to its low cost and non-intrusive tracking techniques [6, 11]. However, raw RFID data are inherently unreliable due to physical device limitations and different kinds of environmental noise.

Most previous approaches for cleaning RFID data are rule-based inference algorithms [3, 10, 12, 18]. Although the methods arising from these approaches could be simple and fast, their accuracy is rather low. Currently, probabilistic model based approaches were proposed to cleanse RFID data and it can be shown that such approaches are better than those using rule-based algorithms [7]. Many model-based approaches [5, 17, 4, 7] also propose formal models for different RFID applications and cleanse data under the framework of *Expectation Maximization* or *Sampling*.

To clean RFID data collected from a mobile environment, we focus on the following three major issues:

- **Data Missing.** The read rate for RFID data in the real-world is often in the range of 60-70%, which means over one third of the data are missing [15, 9]. This poses a great challenge for mobile data cleansing because sometime, there is no observation of tracking objects.
- **Large Volume of Data.** The RFID data collected from mobile environment are always in quantity and arriving in high speed. Since these arriving data cannot be stored in the databases, we have to cleanse the data based only on current observation.
- **Real Time Inference.** Many RFID applications need the current locations of tracking objects in real time. For example, an elderly caring system monitors any abnormal behavior of an elderly and needs to inform a paramedic in real time.

There have already been some papers addressing RFID data cleansing by using probabilistic inference [5, 17, 4, 7]. However, none of them considers all the above issues.

In this paper, we study the problem of cleaning the RFID data streams in a mobile environment that causes large missing rate. The underlying idea of our approach for dealing with the data missing issue is to make use of the historic data of the tracking objects. Historic observations are able to provide some evidence to assist the location inference under the current timestamp. This paper presents a probabilistic model for RFID tracking objects in a mobile environment. Then a Bayesian inference based algorithm is proposed to sequentially clean the collected RFID data. Our model based approach is suitable for cleansing the RFID data stream in the mobile environment, our model takes advantage of the

CIKM'12, October 29–November 2, 2012, Maui, HI, USA.

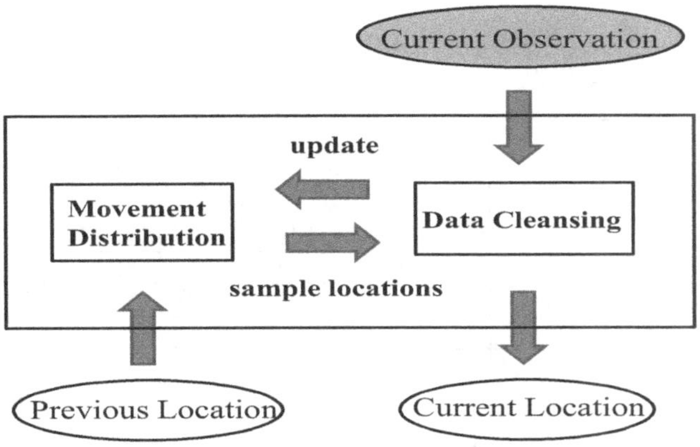

Figure 1: General RIFD Data Cleansing Process

spatiotemporal correlation of tracking objects. The general cleansing process for RFID data streams is depicted in Figure 1. Our model considers the movement of tagged objects in order to reduce the uncertainty of a missed reading.

Contributions. We mainly improve the utility of RFID data. We propose a probabilistic model to clean the RFID data collected in a mobile environment. We take advantage of the spatiotemporal correlation of tracking objects to tackle the missed reading problem. Specifically, we make the following contributions.

- We propose a probabilistic model for RIFD data stream cleansing in a mobile environment.
- We devise a sequential sampler to clean RFID data with high accuracy and efficiency.
- We employ extensive simulations to evaluate the robustness of our model and evaluate the effectiveness on two real RFID data, such as human tracking and conveyor belt monitoring.

This paper is organized as follows. Section 2 introduces the preliminary knowledge of RFID data and formulates the problem. Section 3 surveys the related work while Section 4 introduces a baseline algorithm to this problem. Section 5 then presents our model and states the sampling algorithm for cleansing data. Section 6 presents the experimental results and we conclude the paper in Section 7.

2. BACKGROUND

In this section, we introduce some background knowledge of RFID technologies and the notations used in our subsequent discussion of RFID data cleansing. Then, we formulate the problem of cleansing RFID data streams.

2.1 Preliminary Knowledge

RFID Technology. RFID is an electronic tagging and tracking technology designed to provide non-line-of-sight identification. The typical installment of RFID consists of three components: readers, antennae and tags. RFID readers communicate with tags using antennae. The antenna interrogates nearby tags by sending out an RF signal. Tags in the detection field respond to antenna by their unique identifier codes [16].

An acquisition of tags by an antenna in a static environment is composed of several reading iterations. Table 1 illustrates an example of an acquisition of 10 reading iterations by the antenna Ant_0. *Resp* denotes the number of responses received by the antenna during this acquisition. The reader rate is defined as the ratio of *Resp* to the total reading iterations sent by the antenna. For example, the read rate of tag "3008 33B2 DDD9 06C0 0000 0013" detected by Ant_0 is $\frac{7}{10}$ in Table 1.

TagID	Resp	AntID
3008 33B2 DDD9 06C0 0000 0013	7	Ant_0
3008 33B2 DDD9 06C0 0000 0012	6	Ant_0
3008 33B2 DDD9 06C0 0000 0005	2	Ant_0

Table 1: Tag Reading List for 10 Reading Iterations by Ant_0

Read Rate Distribution. We investigate the geographical read rate distribution of antennae by RFID readers and tags. The model of reader is Alien ALR-9900+[1] and the brand of RFID tag is Gen2 ALN-9640 "Squiggle" Inlay[2]. We put the RFID reader in the center of the room, then divide the area of the room into grids and put tags in the center of each grid. The RFID reader carries out the acquisitions for 15 minutes. The read rate distribution found is shown in Figure 2.

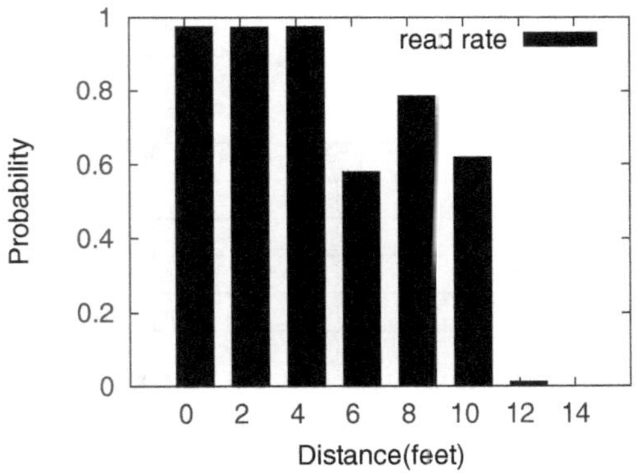

Figure 2: Read Rate Distribution

The read rate distribution plays an important role in RFID data cleansing such that the grids can be associated with detection probability. For example, Figure 2 shows that tags in the grids eight feet away from the antenna have a probability of 80% of being detected. The detection region is 12 feet in Figure 2.

We are also able to observe that the read rate may not always decay due to physical device limitations and different kinds of environmental noise, which is described by some specific curves, such as the *sigmoid* function [17]. In this paper, we employ grid-based discrete probability distribution to model the read rate deterioration. The grid size can be set according to the physical device and effect of environmental noise. We set the grid size to two feet for this work.

RFID Tracking. In a mobile environment, RFID antennae autonomously carry out reading iterations for moving

[1] http://www.alientechnology.com/products/index.php
[2] http://www.alientechnology.com/tags/index.php

TagID	Time	Resp	AntID
3008 33B2 DDD9 06C0 0000 0013	57:06.5	1	Ant_0
3008 33B2 DDD9 06C0 0000 0005	57:06.5	1	Ant_0
3008 33B2 DDD9 06C0 0000 0012	57:06.5	1	Ant_1
3008 33B2 DDD9 06C0 0000 0013	57:06.5	1	Ant_1

Table 2: Tag Reading List

tags during the tracking period and record the received responses by *Resp* at each timestamp.

We now give an example of a tag reading list in a mobile environment in Table 2. The *Resp* records the response of tags by 0 or 1. RFID antennae carry out one reading iteration at each 500ms. At 57:06.5, the tag "3008 33B2 DDD9 06C0 0000 0013" is detected by Ant_0 (first row) and Ant_1 (second row) simultaneously in Table 2. The tags not shown in Table 2 are considered missing at this timestamp.

2.2 Basic Concepts and Notations

DEFINITION 1. *The observed reading O is represented by a binary matrix which records the received response of tracking objects by antennae.*

The observed reading O is a binary matrix of two dimensions: tracking objects and antennae. Each entry in the matrix (i.e. o_{ik}) records the received response of object i by Ant_k which can be 0 or 1. Table 3 shows an example of the observed reading O. For instance, the response of object 1 (obj_1) is received by Ant_1(i.e. $o_{11} = 1$). We denote O^t to be the observed reading from the RFID data streams at the t-th timestamp.

	Ant_1	Ant_2	Ant_3	Ant_4
obj_1	1	0	0	0
obj_2	0	1	0	0
obj_3	1	0	0	0
...	...	...	...	...

Table 3: Observed Reading Matrix

As aforementioned, the tracking area is divided into grids. We represent the whole collection of grids as Z and denote each grid by z. The detection region of antenna can be said to be a set of grids with a positive read rate, denoted as R_k. The read rate distribution of Ant_k can be represented as $p(z|R_k)$ which is zero for $z \notin R_k$.

DEFINITION 2. *Given the observed reading O and a grid z, the posterior read rate $p(O|z)$ is the probability of the tracking objects as in the grid z.*

The relationship between observed readings and the posterior read rate can be categorized into four cases:

- If $o_{ik} = 0$ and $z \notin R_k$, then $p(o_{ik}|z) = 1$.
- If $o_{ik} = 0$ and $z \in R_k$, then $p(o_{ik}|z) = 1 - Pr(z|R_k)$.
- If $o_{ik} = 1$ and $z \notin R_k$, then $p(o_{ik}|z) = 0$.
- If $o_{ik} = 1$ and $z \in R_k$, then $p(o_{ik}|z) = Pr(z|R_k)$.

If obj_i is detected by Ant_k, then it must be at some grid z where $z \in R_k$. On the other hand, if obj_i is not detected by Ant_k, then it has a probability of $1-p(z|R_k)$ to be considered as a missed reading.

Table 4: Summary of Notations

Notation	Meaning
O	Observed Reading
L	Collection of Continuous Locations
Z	Collection of Discrete Grids
C	Grid Capacity
o_i	Observed Reading of obj_i
o_{ik}	Detection of obj_i by Ant_k
y_{it}	Location of obj_i at Time t
z_{it}	Grid of obj_i at Time t
$p(O\|z)$	Posterior Read Rate

2.3 Problem Definition

Using the notations given in Table 4, we define the problem of cleansing RIFD data streams in the mobile environment below.

DEFINITION 3. *Given a series of observed readings O^t where $t \in \{1, \ldots, T\}$, posterior read rate $p(O^t|z)$, we aim to find out which grid z the tracking objects are located in at each timestamp during the tracking period T.*

3. RELATED WORK

RFID data cleansing has attracted a lot of attention in the database community, which can be roughly classified into two categories: *rule-based inference* and *probabilistic inference*.

The rule-based inference algorithms for RFID data cleansing [3, 10, 12, 18, 8] were proposed in an early stage. These algorithms are directly applied to an RFID data stream or after the RFID data has been persisted. Examples of rules used are assigning the item to the first antenna which has identified it [12]. Another work from [18] assumes that the most recent data is correct and assigns the item to the last antenna that identified it. The item is assigned to the antenna with the most readings in [10]. The methods in the mentioned work are fast, but they also generate a lot of wrong predictions. Their accuracy and general performance do not outperform the probabilistic inference algorithm [7].

Recently, probabilistic inference algorithms were introduced as a new way of carrying out RFID data cleansing. The work in [13, 14] enabled declare query over RFID data streams of probabilistic events. The work [17] proposed to cleanse RFID data stream with reference objects such as shelves. The work [4] studied how to inference the containment relationship of tagged objects.

The most recent work [5] studied the RFID data cleansing problem and built a probabilistic model by taking capacity constraints of a location into consideration. A *Metropolis-Hasting* sampler based on the posterior read rate was proposed to infer the hidden variables in the model in order to get the locations of tagged objects. The experiments validate its performance in the static environment.

However, none of these data cleansing algorithms addresses the data missing problem arising from the RFID applications in a mobile environment such as object tracking, which involves a significant missing rate of the collected RFID data. Thus, we focus on studying how to cleanse such RFID data in a mobile environment. By taking capacity constraints [5] and data missing issues into consideration, we develop a new probabilistic model for object tracking.

4. BASELINE ALGORITHM

In this section, we first present a baseline algorithm (referred to as *BL*) for this problem. Our proposed algorithm considers the location inference at each timestamp independently and utilizes the posterior read rate to clean the RFID data streams. We only need to take the current RFID readings O^t and posterior read rate $p(O|z)$ into consideration. Then we infer the grids of tracking objects at time t. Formally, we denote a set of J location states $LS^0, LS^2, \ldots, LS^{J-1}$ to represent the possible grids in which the tracking objects are. The main procedure of *BL* is illustrated as the following three phases:

Initialization. The initial location state LS^0 of tracking objects are generated randomly. That is, for each tagged object, we select a grid to denote its location. Figure 3(a) is an example of the initial location state. Six grids are sampled for four objects in LS^0. The obj_1 in the first row is assigned to grid 1.

$$\begin{pmatrix} 1 & 0 & 0 & 0 & 0 & 0 \\ 1 & 0 & 0 & 0 & 0 & 0 \\ 0 & 1 & 0 & 0 & 0 & 0 \\ 0 & 0 & 1 & 0 & 0 & 0 \end{pmatrix} \qquad \begin{pmatrix} 1 & 0 & 0 & 0 & 0 & 0 \\ 0 & 1 & 0 & 0 & 0 & 0 \\ 0 & 1 & 0 & 0 & 0 & 0 \\ 0 & 0 & 0 & 1 & 0 & 0 \end{pmatrix}$$

(a) LS^0 (b) LS^1

Figure 3: Location States

Update. For the current location state LS^j, we generate its neighboring state by applying a uniform distribution to it. For example, we have six grids of one dimension in Figure 3(a). The obj_4 is in grid 3 in LS^0 and the neighbors of grid 3 are grid 2 and grid 4. By using the uniform distribution, the possible grids for obj_4 in the next iteration are grids 2,3 and 4 with equal probability $\frac{1}{3}$. Figure 3(b) shows an example of LS^1 which is a neighboring location state of LS^0.

Selection. Suppose we denote the current location state as LS^j and its neighboring state as LS^{j+1}. We proceed to decide whether the neighboring state is accepted as the next state or rejected. By the known posterior read rate, the neighboring state LS^{j+1} is accepted with the probability $\frac{p(O^t|LS^{j+1})}{p(O^t|LS^j)}$. The probability $p(O^t|LS^{j+1})$ is the posterior read rate of state LS^{j+1} which can be factorized by

$$p(O^t|LS^{j+1}) = \prod_i p(o_i^t|LS_i^{j+1}) \tag{1}$$

where o_i^t is the RFID readings for obj_i at time t and LS_i^{j+1} is the sampled grid for obj_i. For example, in Figure 3(b), LS_3^1 is the third row(i.e. [0 1 0 0 0 0 0]). Finally, we get a set of location states for tracking objects in $\mathcal{S}$.

By considering the capacity of locations, the sampling process would become more effective and efficient. Suppose each grid has a capacity of C objects, then we are able to prune these location states directly by summing up their columns (i.e. $\sum_k LS_{ik}^{j+1} > C$).

Although it is feasible to clean RFID data streams, we may not be able to get high accuracy because of the missing data problem. In a mobile environment, there may be missed readings of tracking objects at some time due to physical device limitations and environmental noise. Under the missed reading scenario, the posterior read rate is not able to validate the quality of the sampled location state. Then the result of the baseline algorithm may be random and sharply deviates from the true location. We propose to make use of the spatial-temporal correlation of the tracking objects to tackle this problem.

5. ADAPTIVE CLEANSING MODEL

In this section, we present our *Adaptive Cleansing* model (referred to as *AC*). First, we introduce the general idea of our model. Second, we present the detail of our generative process. Third, we explain how to estimate the parameter.

5.1 General Idea

As aforementioned, the returned location states of *BL* are very uncertain for a significant missed reading of RFID data. Intuitively, to reduce any uncertainty, new constraints for cleansing RFID data are needed. For example, if we know the upper bound of the moving speed of some tracking object (i.e. radius of R grids), then we can sample its next possible locations with R grids.

One simple approach is to use a fixed radius R as the upper bound of the moving speed of tracking objects. The initial location state at time t is sampled from previous inferred locations by assuming a uniform distribution (i.e. $Uni(0, R)$). Thanks to the moving radius, the sampled location states becomes more effective such that the uncertainty is reduced. However, it is difficult to set the value of R. If R is too large, the returned location states are still very uncertain. On the other hand, if R is too small, then it fails to sample the correct location state and the accuracy of the algorithm becomes very low.

We propose a probabilistic model for the generation of the RFID data streams by considering its spatio-temporal correlation. The graphical representation of the adaptive cleansing model is given in Figure 4. We adopt the common motion model *Normal Distribution* [17] to generate the movement of tracking objects, denoted as θ. Formally, the location state at time t(i.e.L^t) is generated by the previous location and the motion model, denoted as $p_\theta(L^t|L^{t-1})$.

5.2 Generative Process

We now illustrate the generative process to produce the observed RFID readings $O^1, \ldots, O^T$ of tracking objects, given the posterior read rate. We denote a set of parameters $\varphi = \{\nu, \eta, \alpha, \beta\}$ as hyper parameters of our model. The procedure of generative process is outlined in Algorithm 1.

Algorithm 1 Generate Observed RFID Reading

Input: a set of tracking objects *obj*, a set of antennae and posterior read rate
Output: observed RFID reading O

```
Choose λ ~ Ga(α, β), μ ~ N(ν, (ηλ)^{-1})
for t = 1 → T do
    for For each object obj_i do
        (a) Choose motion model θ_i ~ N(μ_i, λ_i)
        (b) Choose location l_it ~ p_θi(l_i(t-1))
        (c) Locate the grid z covering location l_it
        (d) Generate o_i^t by posterior read rate p(O|z)
    end for
end for
```

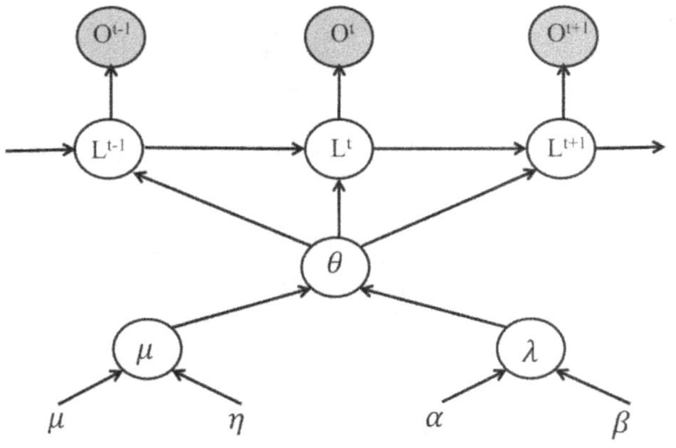

Figure 4: A Graphical Representation of The Adaptive Cleansing Model (AC)

5.2.1 *Generating* μ, λ

In order to generate motion model θ, we need to determine the average move parameter μ and the inverse variance λ.

We first sample λ from a Gamma distribution (i.e. $Ga(\lambda|\alpha, \beta)$). Given the sampled λ, we sample μ from a Normal distribution (i.e. $N(\mu|\nu, (\eta\lambda)^{-1})$). The joint distribution of μ, λ is given by

$$\begin{aligned} p(\mu, \lambda|\varphi) &= N(\mu|\nu, (\eta\lambda)^{-1})Ga(\lambda|\alpha, \beta) \\ &\propto \lambda^{\frac{1}{2}} \exp[-\frac{\eta_0\lambda}{2}(\mu-\mu)^2]\lambda^{\alpha-1}\exp(-\lambda\beta) \\ &= \frac{1}{Z}\lambda^{(\alpha-\frac{1}{2})}\exp\{-\frac{\lambda}{2}[\eta(\mu-\nu)^2+2\beta]\} \quad (2) \end{aligned}$$

where Z is the normalization factor of Equation 2.

5.2.2 *Generating* θ, L^t

Given the average movement μ_i and inverse variance λ_i of obj_i, we sample the location l_{it} from the motion model by $p_{\theta_i}(l_{it}|l_{i(t-1)})$. The location of all tracking objects is given by $L_t = [l_{it}]$.

5.2.3 *Generating* O^t

Given the current location for tracking object obj_i (i.e. l_{it}), the observed reading O_i^t of obj_i is generated from the posterior read rate by

$$\begin{aligned} p(O_i^t|l_{it}) &= \prod_k p(o_{ik}^t|l_{it}) \\ &= \prod_k p(o_{ik}^t|z) \quad (3) \end{aligned}$$

where k is an indication of the antennae and z is the grid covering the location l_{it}. $p(o_{ik}^t|z)$ is the posterior read rate of grid z. The current observed reading of all tracking objects is given by $O^t = [o_i^t]$.

Given the set of hyper-parameters $\varphi = \{\nu, \eta, \alpha, \beta\}$, we factorize the log likelihood of our model using the conditional independence assumption encoded in Figure 4.

$$\begin{aligned} \mathcal{L}(\varphi; O) &= \log p(O|\varphi) \\ &= \log \prod_{t=1}^{T} \prod_{obj_i} p(\theta_i|\varphi)p_{\theta_i}(l_{it}|l_{i(t-1)})p(o_i^t|l_{it}) \quad (4) \end{aligned}$$

5.3 Sequential Inference

The model in Figure 4 can be generalized as a kind of sequential probabilistic models [1]. *Particle Filter* [2] is a well known algorithm that solves sequential inference problems. However, it is difficult to apply this algorithm to our model inference problem because not only do we need to infer the hidden variables $L^1, L^2, \ldots, L^T$, but we also have to deduce the hyper model parameters $\{\nu, \eta, \alpha, \beta\}$.

We now devise a new sequential inference algorithm based on *Particle Filter* to solve the problem. Formally, we denote a set of samples (termed *particles* in the literature) at time t using $s_t^1, s_t^2, \ldots, s_t^J$, which is a hypothesis about the location of tracking objects. For the ease of the presentation, we use a particle as a location state in this section (i.e. a particle and a location state are interchangeable terms).

The set of initial particles $s_0^1, \ldots, s_0^J$ can be obtained from BL. The sequential procedure of our algorithm is:

- *Sampling.* For each particle s_{t-1}^j, we generate a new particle s_t^j from $p_\theta(s_t^j|s_{t-1}^j)$ where p_θ is the movement distribution of tracking objects.

- *Weighting.* We compute a particle weight as follows:

$$w_t^j = Bw_{t-1}^j \cdot \frac{p(O^t|s_t^j)}{p_\theta(s_t^j|s_{t-1}^j)} \quad (5)$$

  where B is a constant with respect to *j-th* particle, chosen so that $\sum_j w_t^j = 1$. $p(O^t|s_t^j)$ is the posterior read rate probability of particle s_t^j.

- *Re-sampling.* We sample the obtained particles to reproduce the highest weight ones. Each new particle is sampled from a set of old ones with replacement. The sampling probability of the particle is equal to its weight.

- *Re-estimating.* We compute the hyper model parameters by the obtained samples. The movement between two particles s_t^j and s_{t-1}^j can be denoted as $d^j = s_t^j - s_{t-1}^j$. Then m movements are sampled with probability proportional to $w_t^j w_{t-1}^j$, denoted as $D = \{d^1, \ldots, d^m\}$. The hyper parameter at time t (i.e.φ_t) is updated by φ_{t-1} and sampled movements D.

Now, we discuss how to estimate the hyper parameters sequentially. Then we discuss the location inference output of the tracking objects.

Recall the generating distribution for μ and λ by Equation 2, we set the generating distribution condition on φ_t to be equal to on D, φ_{t-1} as:

$$\begin{aligned} p(\mu, \lambda|\varphi_t) &= p(\mu, \lambda|D, \varphi_{t-1}) \\ &\propto Pr(\mu, \lambda|\varphi_{t-1})Pr(D|\mu, \lambda, \varphi_{t-1}) \\ &= Pr(\mu, \lambda|\varphi_{t-1})p(D|\mu, \lambda) \\ &\propto \lambda^{(\alpha_t-\frac{1}{2})}\exp\{-\frac{\lambda}{2}[\eta_t(\mu-\nu_t)^2+2\beta_t]\} \quad (6) \end{aligned}$$

where the updating schema for parameters φ_{t-1} by Equations 7, 8, 9 and 10.

$$\alpha_t = \alpha_{t-1} + \frac{m}{2} \quad (7)$$

$$\beta_t = \beta_{t-1} + \frac{1}{2}\sum_{i=1}^{m}(d_i - \overline{d})^2 + \frac{\eta_{t-1}m(\overline{d} - \nu_{t-1})^2}{2(\eta_{t-1} + m)} \quad (8)$$

$$\nu_t = \frac{\eta_{t-1}\nu_{t-1} + m\overline{d}}{\eta_{t-1} + m} \quad (9)$$

$$\eta_t = \eta_{t-1} + m \quad (10)$$

where $\overline{d}$ is the average movement of D. The derivation is according to the Bayesian rule and the details can be found in the Appendix. The time complexity of parameter re-estimation is $O(m)$.

The inference output of our model is a probability distribution of locations of tracking objects at any given time. Given a set of samples which are associated with their weights, the probability distribution of the locations is given by

$$p(z_t|O^t) = \sum_{j=1}^{J} w_t^j \mathbf{1}_{\{s_t^j \in z_t\}}. \quad (11)$$

where $\mathbf{1}_{a \in b}$ is an indicator function that is 1 if and only if the location of sample s_t^j is in the grid z_t. The grid z_t with the highest posterior probability is returned as the inference location of tracking object at time t.

5.4 Inference Algorithm

Now, we introduce our sequential inference algorithm for RFID data streams. Given particles s_{t-1}, model parameters φ_{t-1} at time $t-1$ and observed reading at time t, the algorithm re-estimates the model parameter and outputs a set of particles $\mathcal{S}_t$ at time t. Using particles $\mathcal{S}_t$, we are able to output objects' locations inference by Equation 11. The procedure of the algorithm is given by Algorithm 2 below:

Algorithm 2 Inference Algorithm(s_{t-1},φ_{t-1},O^t)

Input: $\mathcal{S}_{t-1}$: a set of particles at time $t-1$;φ_{t-1}: model parameters;O^t observed reading
Output: $\mathcal{S}_t$: a set of particles at time t;φ_t: current model parameters;

1: set $\mathcal{S} \leftarrow \emptyset$
2: **for** $j = 1 \rightarrow J$ **do**
3: **repeat**
4: particle $s_t^j \sim$ proposal distribution $p_\theta(s_t^j|s_{t-1}^j)$
5: **until** s_t^j subject to capacity constraint
6: weight $w_t^j = Cw_{t-1}^j \cdot \frac{p(O^t|s_t^j)}{p_\theta(s_t^j|s_{t-1}^j)}$
7: Add s_t^j to $\mathcal{S}$
8: **end for**
9: Re-sample J samples from $\mathcal{S}$ with replacement by their weights and add to $\mathcal{S}_t$
10: Compute movements D by $\mathcal{S}_t$ and $\mathcal{S}_{t-1}$
11: Re-estimate model parameter φ_t from D and φ_{t-1} by Equation 7, 8, 9 and 10.
12: **return** set $\mathcal{S}_t$ and parameter φ_t

The algorithm samples J qualified particles subject to capacity constraints from Line 3 to Line 5. Next, it associates sampled particles with weights at Line 6. It re-samples these particles to produce particles with the highest weights, denoted as $\mathcal{S}_t$, at Line 9. Then it re-estimates the model parameter φ_t at time t from D and φ_{t-1} by Equations 7, 8, 9 and 10 at Line 11. Finally, the algorithm produces a set of particles $\mathcal{S}_t$ and model parameters φ_t at time t.

Table 5: Default Values

Parameters	Values
z(Number of grids)	1500 (grids)
o(Number of objects)	50 (objects)
t(Number of timestamps)	100 (seconds)
c(capacity of grid)	4 (objects)
r(Number of grid by antenna)	5 (grids)
v(Moving speed of objects)	2 (feet per second)
δ(speed variance)	0.5
Missing rate	0.1

6. EXPERIMENT

We implement the proposed algorithms and study their efficiency and effectiveness using both real and synthetic data sets. The synthetic experimental evaluation is designed to investigate the robustness of our algorithm. All algorithms are implemented using Java. The experiments are performed in a Linux box with an 8-core Intel(R) Xeon(R) CPU X5450 3.00GHz and 16GB memory.

6.1 Synthetic Experiment

Synthetic Data Generation. We calibrate the read rate distribution of the synthetic data generator by posterior read rate collected from a static environment. We set the size of a grid to one square foot. The detection range of antenna is five grids. There is one grid overlapping in the detection range of two antennae. The size of tracking area is set to 1500 grids which is large enough for indoor environment. The movements of tracking objects are generated from *Normal Distribution* with *mean* two feet per second and *standard variance* 0.5. Other default values of the generator can be found in Table 5.

Measurement. We define *TopK* accuracy to measure the effectiveness of the proposed algorithms. The inference output of the proposed algorithms is a probability distribution of locations. The locations with the top K highest probabilities are selected as the inference result. The *TopK* accuracy is defined as the ratio of the number of correct cases in the inference result to the number of inference cases. The formula of *TopK* accuracy is given by

$$TopKAccuracy = \frac{\#\text{ of correct cases}}{\#\text{ of objects} \times \#\text{ of timestamp}} \quad (12)$$

where the number of correct cases increases as K becomes large. In this experiment, we evaluate the effectiveness of the algorithms using Top1, Top2 and Top3 accuracy.

We compare the effectiveness and efficiency of *BL* with our proposed algorithm on five issues: (1) missing rate of RFID reading, (2) tracking time of the objects, (3) capacity constraint of the grid, (4) moving speed of the objects and (5) detection range of the antenna. The experimental result shows that our proposed algorithm is very robust.

Effect of Missing Rate. Figures 5(a), (b) and (c) illustrate the Top1,Top2 and Top3 accuracy of our algorithm on different missing rates (i.e. 0.1, 0.2, 0.3, 0.4 and 0.5),

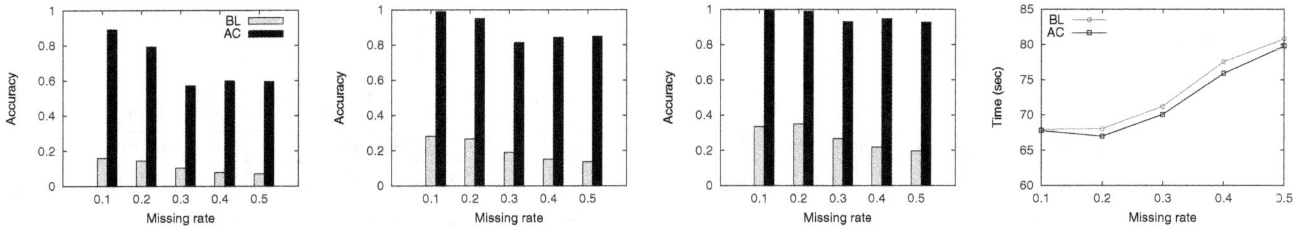

(a) Top1 (b) Top2 (c) Top3 (d) Running time

Figure 5: Effect of Missing Rate

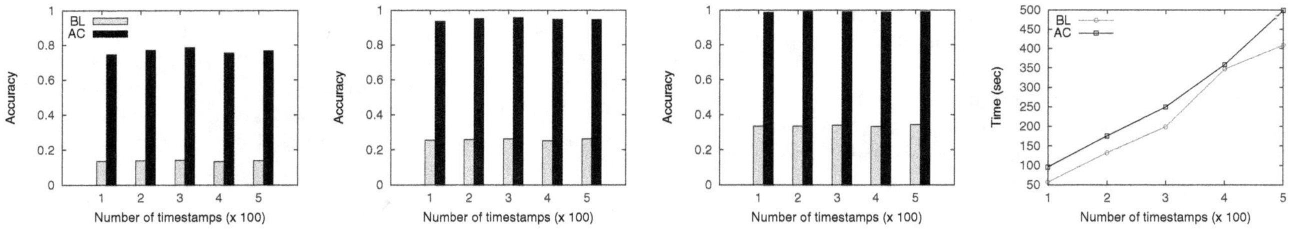

(a) Top1 (b) Top2 (c) Top3 (d) Running time

Figure 6: Effect of Tracking Time

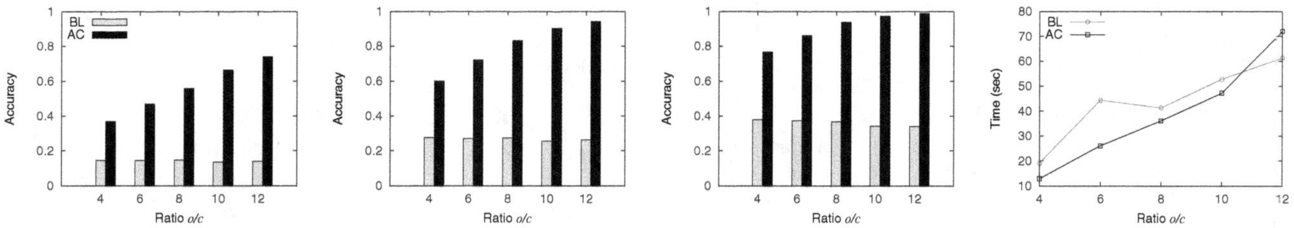

(a) Top1 (b) Top2 (c) Top3 (d) Running time

Figure 7: Effect of Objects by Capacity

respectively. For example, the missing rate 0.1 means that ten percentage of the RFID readings are missing during the tracking period.

As the missing rate increases, the inference accuracy of the algorithms deteriorates. However, the accuracy of the algorithm AC deteriorates slowly and outperforms the BL algorithm for all missing rates because our algorithm is able to capture the current movement of tracking objects in order to make the samples closer to the real moves. From Figure 5(a), we could observe that the algorithm AC has high $Top1$ accuracy when the missing rate is above 0.3, the common missing rate for RFID data. The $Top2$ accuracy shown in Figure 5(b) shows that AC has 80% inference correctness among these missing rates. The cost of the running time of our algorithm is slightly more efficient than BL, as shown in Figure 5(d). When the missing rate increases, it is difficult for BL to get qualified samples because the data uncertainty increases. However, our algorithm is able to utilize the estimated parameters to sample qualified particles in order to reduce the data uncertainty and improve the efficiency of the algorithm.

Effect of Tracking Time. We investigate the inference accuracy of the algorithm over different tracking time period to illustrate the robustness of our algorithm. Figures 6(a) to (c) demonstrate the Top1 to Top3 inference accuracy of our algorithm over different time periods in sec (i.e. 100, 200, 300, 400 and 500), respectively. We are able to observe that the inference accuracy of our algorithm is very stable, as shown in Figure 6. The Top2 accuracy of our algorithm reaches 90% for all the time periods in Figure 6(b). We could conclude that the inference accuracy of our algorithm does not decrease when we increase the tracking time period. So our algorithm is capable of cleaning RFID data streams in a satisfactory manner. The accumulated running time of the algorithms is given in Figure 6(d). The running time increases linearly. The time cost of location inference at one timestamp is less than one second which is very efficient.

Effect of Objects by Capacity. We study the effect of location capacity on our algorithm using a proposed ratio called *objects by capacity*. The *objects by capacity* is a ratio of the number of tracking objects by the location capacity. This constraint becomes stricter when we increase the number of tracking objects or reduce the location capacity. The strict constraint is able to prune many false positive candidate location states. For example, the location state can be considered to be invalid if it violates the constraint, no matter how high its probability is. Given the default grid capacity 4, we increase the number of tracking objects linearly. Figures 7(a) to (c) show the Top1 to Top3 accuracy result of our algorithm on different ratio of *objects by capacity* (i.e. 4,

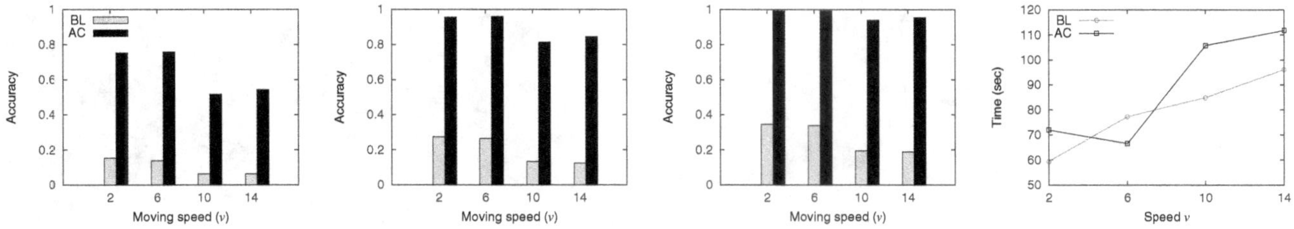

(a) Top1 (b) Top2 (c) Top3 (d) Running time

Figure 8: Effect of Moving Speed

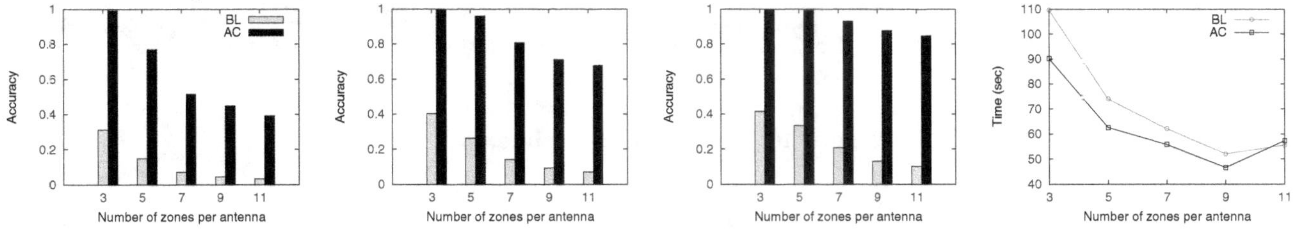

(a) Top1 (b) Top2 (c) Top3 (d) Running time

Figure 9: Effect of Grids per Antenna

6, 8, 10 and 12), respectively. The inference accuracy of our algorithm increases dramatically, as shown in Figure 7. The performance of our algorithm can be improved by *objects by capacity*. For example, the Top1 accuracy is below 40% when *objects by capacity* is set to 4 and it reaches 75% when the ratio set to 12 in Figure 7(a). The running time of the algorithms increases linearly, as shown in Figure 7(d).

Effect of Moving Speed. We investigate the inference accuracy of our algorithm by varying the speed of the tracking objects in (feet/s) (i.e.2, 6, 10 and 14). The inference accuracy of the algorithms decreases when we increase the moving speed, as shown in Figure 8. The sampling range of each move becomes larger as the moving speed increases. However, the inference accuracy of our algorithm only decreases slightly. The parameters of our model can be estimated by the sequential inference algorithm on the observed data. Then our model is able to capture the moving of tracking objects in order to make a better location inference.

Effect of Grids per Antenna. We study the effect of the density of antennae deployed by varying the number of grids managed by antenna (i.e. 3 ,5 ,7, 9 and 11 zones per antenna) in Figure 9. The inference accuracy decreases when we increase the grids managed by antenna (i.e. we decrease the density of antennae), as shown in Figures 9(a), (b) and (c). There are two reasons for this happening. First, the uncertainty of the observed readings increases when we assign more grids to the antenna. For example, suppose that the antenna only manages one grid. If the readings show that the tracking object is read by that antenna, we then know the object must be in that grid. If the antenna manages more grids, we only know the object is in one of its grids. Secondly, if the antenna manages more grids, the missing rate of the readings would increase because the read rate of the zones which are far away from the antenna is very low. Our algorithm is able to deal with this problem, since our algorithm is able to take the spatial-temporal correlation of the tracking objects which is very useful for reducing data uncertainty and coping with high missing rate.

The running time of the algorithm decreases first when the number of antennae is reduced. The algorithm only needs to process fewer antennae. Then the running time of the algorithm increases when we further increase the number of grids per antenna, as shown in Figure 9(d). This is because it is difficult to get qualified samples when the uncertainty of data raises.

Through this experiment, we could conclude that our algorithm is very effective and more efficient than the *BL* algorithm on decaying with data uncertainty and missing issues. Our algorithm is based on a probabilistic model which takes the spatial-temporal consideration of tracking objects in order to reduce data uncertainty. Using the proposed sequential inference approach, our algorithm cleans the current RFID data in the streams and it only depends on the previous location states and estimated model parameters. Our algorithm is efficient enough to clean RFID data streams with high speed. The robustness of our algorithm is also evaluated through various issues.

6.2 Real Experiment

In this section, we evaluate the performance of the algorithms on different applications using two real datasets: human tracking and conveyer monitoring. We give a brief description of data collection and result analysis of human tracking and conveyor monitoring using our algorithm.

6.2.1 Real Data: Human Tracking

We evaluate the performance of our algorithm on the application of human tracking in this section. We use two *Alien* RFID readers and seven antennae in an indoor area. We divide the indoor area into 20 grids of two feet long. The capacity constraint of each grid is two in this experiment. We ask five undergraduate students to hold an RFID tag each and move inside this area. We ask the students

(a) Human Tracking (b) Conveyor Monitoring (c) Transport Shuttle

Figure 10: Setting of Experiments

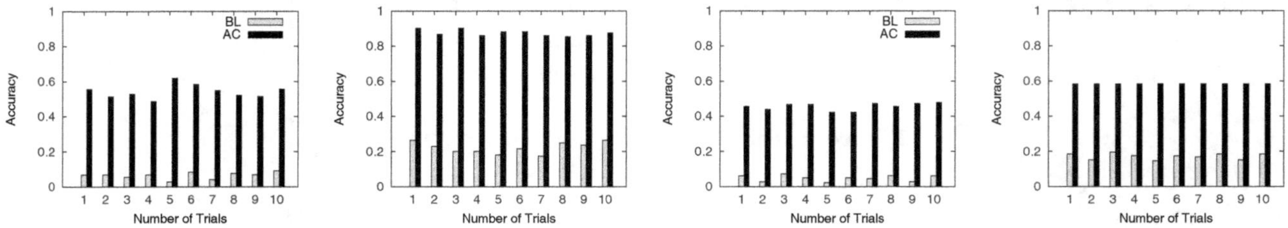

(a) Top1 (b) Top3 (c) Top1 (d) Top3

Figure 11: Experiments on Real Datasets

to start at different grids inside this area. Then we record the RFID reading of these students for 40 seconds using autonomous mode of RFID readers. At the same time, we ask other students to record the actual grids of the tagged students passed during the tracking period as the ground truth of this experiment. Finally, we repeat this experiment 10 times. The deployment of antenna of this experiment can be found in Figure 10(a). Figures 11(a) and (b) illustrate the inference accuracy of our algorithm on 10 trials. We observe that our algorithm has more than 50% correctness in $Top1$ inference accuracy and 80% in $Top3$.

6.2.2 Real Data: Conveyor Monitoring

We validate the performance of our algorithm on the application of conveyor monitoring. We deploy four antennae on a Bocsh conveyor {`http://www.bosch.com/worldsite_startpage/en/default.aspx`}, as shown in Figure 10(b). We program the Bocsh conveyor to ask the transport shuttle to run on a predefined path at a constant speed. The whole path is 18 meters and we divide it into 18 grids of one meter long. The tagged objects are put in a transport shuttle, as shown in Figure 10(c). We consider the location of the transport shuttle as the location of the tracking objects. The ground truth of the movement of tagged objects is calculated based on the speed of transport shuttle and predefined path. We repeat this experiment 10 times. Each time, we start the transport shuttle at the same grid.

The inference accuracy of the algorithms can be found in Figures 11(c) and (d). We observe that the $Top1$ inference accuracy of our algorithm is more than 40% in Figure 11(c) which is much better than the BL algorithm. The inference accuracy reaches nearly 60% in Figure 11(d). The inference accuracy of this experiment is slightly lower than that of human tracking because the material of conveyors made of metal increases the false reading rate of the RFID antennae.

7. CONCLUSION

In this paper, we study the problem of cleaning RFID data streams in a mobile environment. To tackle the problem of significant missing rate, we propose a probabilistic model for RFID object tracking. Then a sequential inference algorithm is devised for inferring the hidden variables of our proposed probabilistic model. The sequential inference algorithm produces the inferred locations of tracking objects and incrementally re-estimates the model parameters in an efficient way. To evaluate the effectiveness and robustness of our proposed algorithm, we investigate its performance on various issues in the synthetic experiment. We also validate our algorithm on real data: human tracking and conveyor monitoring. The results of our algorithm on real data demonstrate the effectiveness of our algorithm to clean RFID data streams.

8. ACKNOWLEDGEMENTS

We thank the help from the UROP project student Gary Zhijun Zhang at HKUST for collecting the data used in our experiments. This work is partially supported by HKUST RFID Center under grant numbers ITP/022/02LP and SSRI08RGC, and RGC GRF under grant number HKUST 617610.

9. REFERENCES

[1] M. Arulampalam, S. Maskell, N. Gordon, and T. Clapp. A tutorial on particle filters for online nonlinear/non-gaussian bayesian tracking. *Signal Processing, IEEE Transactions on*, 50(2):174–188, 2002.

[2] C. Bishop and S. S. en ligne). *Pattern recognition and machine learning*, volume 4. springer New York, 2006.

[3] C. Bornhövd, T. Lin, S. Haller, and J. Schaper. Integrating automatic data acquisition with business processes experiences with sap's auto-id infrastructure. In *Proceedings of the Thirtieth international conference on Very large data bases-Volume 30*, pages 1182–1188. VLDB Endowment, 2004.

[4] Z. Cao, C. Sutton, Y. Diao, and P. Shenoy. Distributed inference and query processing for rfid tracking and monitoring. *Proceedings of the VLDB Endowment*, 4(5):326–337, 2011.

[5] H. Chen, W. Ku, H. Wang, and M. Sun. Leveraging spatio-temporal redundancy for rfid data cleansing. In *Proceedings of the 2010 international conference on Management of data*, pages 51–62. ACM, 2010.

[6] D. Delen, B. Hardgrave, and R. Sharda. Rfid for better supply-chain management through enhanced information visibility. *Production and Operations Management*, 16(5):613–624, 2007.

[7] L. Ferreira Chaves, E. Buchmann, and K. Böhm. Finding misplaced items in retail by clustering rfid data. In *Proceedings of the 13th International Conference on Extending Database Technology*, pages 501–512. ACM, 2010.

[8] H. Gonzalez, J. Han, and X. Shen. Cost-conscious cleaning of massive rfid data sets. In *Data Engineering, 2007. ICDE 2007. IEEE 23rd International Conference on*, pages 1268–1272. IEEE, 2007.

[9] S. Jeffery, G. Alonso, M. Franklin, W. Hong, and J. Widom. A pipelined framework for online cleaning of sensor data streams. In *Data Engineering, 2006. ICDE'06. Proceedings of the 22nd International Conference on*, pages 140–140. IEEE, 2006.

[10] S. Jeffery, M. Garofalakis, and M. Franklin. Adaptive cleaning for rfid data streams. In *Proceedings of the 32nd international conference on Very large data bases*, pages 163–174. VLDB Endowment, 2006.

[11] W. Ng. Developing rfid database models for analysing moving tags in supply chain management. *Conceptual Modeling-ER 2011*, pages 204–218, 2011.

[12] J. Rao, S. Doraiswamy, H. Thakkar, and L. Colby. A deferred cleansing method for rfid data analytics. In *Proceedings of the 32nd international conference on Very large data bases*, pages 175–186. VLDB Endowment, 2006.

[13] C. Ré, J. Letchner, M. Balazinksa, and D. Suciu. Event queries on correlated probabilistic streams. In *Proceedings of the 2008 ACM SIGMOD international conference on Management of data*, pages 715–728. ACM, 2008.

[14] C. Ré, J. Letchner, M. Balazinksa, and D. Suciu. Event queries on correlated probabilistic streams. In *Proceedings of the 2008 ACM SIGMOD international conference on Management of data*, pages 715–728. ACM, 2008.

[15] L. Sullivan. Rfid implementation challenges persist, all this time later. *Information Week*, 2005.

[16] F. Thiesse and F. Michahelles. An overview of epc technology. *Sensor Review*, 26(2):101–105, 2006.

[17] T. Tran, C. Sutton, R. Cocci, Y. Nie, Y. Diao, and P. Shenoy. Probabilistic inference over rfid streams in mobile environments. In *Data Engineering, 2009. ICDE'09. IEEE 25th International Conference on*, pages 1096–1107. IEEE, 2009.

[18] F. Wang and P. Liu. Temporal management of rfid data. In *Proceedings of the 31st international conference on Very large data bases*, pages 1128–1139. VLDB Endowment, 2005.

10. APPENDIX

We give the derivation of model parameter re-estimation and show that the model parameter can be incrementally estimated.

Given a set of movements D and model parameter φ_{t-1}, we want to estimate model parameter φ_t at time t. Suppose that we have estimated model parameter φ_t, the the posterior distribution of μ and λ can be written as $Pr(\mu, \lambda|\varphi_t)$ which is equal to the posterior distribution given movements D and model parameter φ_{t-1}. The formula of this equation is given by

$$
\begin{aligned}
Pr(\mu,\lambda|\varphi_t) &= Pr(\mu,\lambda|D,\varphi_{t-1}) \\
&\propto Pr(\mu,\lambda|\varphi_{t-1})Pr(D|\mu,\lambda,\varphi_{t-1}) \\
&= Pr(\mu,\lambda|\varphi_{t-1})Pr(D|\mu,\lambda) \\
&\propto \lambda^{(\alpha_t-\frac{1}{2})}\exp\{-\frac{\lambda}{2}[\eta_t(\mu-\nu_t)^2+2\beta_t]\} \\
&\propto \lambda^{(\alpha_{t-1}-\frac{1}{2})}\exp(-\frac{\lambda}{2}[\eta_{n-1}(\mu-\mu_{t-1})^2+2\beta_{t-1}]) \\
&\quad \cdot\lambda^{\frac{m}{2}}\exp(-\frac{\lambda}{2}\sum_{j=1}^{m}(d_j-\mu)^2) \\
&= \lambda^{(\alpha_{n-1}+\frac{m}{2}-\frac{1}{2})}\exp(-\frac{\lambda}{2}R)
\end{aligned}
$$

where $R = \eta_{t-1}(\mu-\mu_{t-1})^2 + \sum_{j=1}^{m}(d_j-\mu)^2 + 2\beta_{t-1}$. It is clear that α_t is equal to $\alpha_{t-1} + \frac{m}{2}$. Then we study how to assign other model parameters. We first separate the second term in R(i.e. $\sum_{j=1}^{m}(d_j-\mu)^2$) into two components, as shown below:

$$\sum_{i=1}^{m}(d_j-\mu)^2 = m(\mu-\bar{a})^2 + \sum_{j=1}^{m}(d_j-\bar{d})^2$$

Then we rearrange R as:

$$
\begin{aligned}
R &= \eta_{t-1}(\mu-\mu_{n-1})^2 + m(\mu-\bar{d})^2 + \sum_{j=1}^{m}(d_j-\bar{d})^2 + 2\beta_{t-1} \\
&= (\eta_{t-1}+m)(\mu-\mu_t)^2 + 2\beta_t
\end{aligned}
$$

where we derive

$$
\begin{aligned}
\beta_t &= \beta_{t-1} + \frac{1}{2}\sum_{j=1}^{m}(d_j-\bar{d})^2 + \frac{\eta_{t-1}m(\bar{d}-\mu_{t-1})^2}{2(\eta_{n-1}+m)} \\
\eta_t &= \eta_{t-1}+m \\
\mu_t &= \frac{\eta_{t-1}\mu_{t-1}+m\bar{d}}{\eta_{t-1}+m}.
\end{aligned}
$$

What is the IQ of your Data Transformation System?

Giansalvatore Mecca[1] Paolo Papotti[2] Salvatore Raunich[3] Donatello Santoro[1,4]

[1] Università della Basilicata – Potenza, Italy
[2] Qatar Computing Research Institute (QCRI) – Doha, Qatar
[3] University of Leipzig – Leipzig, Germany
[4] Università Roma Tre – Roma, Italy

ABSTRACT

Mapping and translating data across different representations is a crucial problem in information systems. Many formalisms and tools are currently used for this purpose, to the point that developers typically face a difficult question: "what is the right tool for my translation task?" In this paper, we introduce several techniques that contribute to answer this question. Among these, a fairly general definition of a data transformation system, a new and very efficient similarity measure to evaluate the outputs produced by such a system, and a metric to estimate user efforts. Based on these techniques, we are able to compare a wide range of systems on many translation tasks, to gain interesting insights about their effectiveness, and, ultimately, about their "intelligence".

Categories and Subject Descriptors: H.2 [Database Management]: Heterogeneous Databases

General Terms: Algorithms, Experimentation, Measurement.

Keywords: Data Transformation, Schema Mappings, ETL, Benchmarks.

1. INTRODUCTION

The problem of translating data among heterogeneous representations is a long-standing issue in the IT industry and in database research. The first data translation systems date back to the seventies. In these years, many different proposals have emerged to alleviate the burden of manually expressing complex transformations among different repositories.

However, these proposals differ under many perspectives. There are very procedural and very expressive systems, like those used in ETL [18]. There are more declarative, but less expressive schema-mapping systems. Some of the commercial systems are essentially graphical user-interfaces for defining XSLT queries. Others, like data-exchange systems, incorporate sophisticated algorithms to enforce constraints and generate solutions of optimal quality. Some systems are inherently relational. Others use nested data-models to handle XML data, and in some cases even ontologies.

In light of this heterogeneity, database researchers have expressed a strong need to define a unifying framework for data translation and integration applications [16, 6]. In fact, it would be very useful, given a task that requires to translate some input instance of a *source* schema into an output instance of the *target* schema, to have a common model to answer the following fundamental question: *"what is the right tool for my translation task?"*

Answering this question entails being able to compare and classify systems coming from different inspirations and different application domains. For this purpose, several benchmarks have been proposed [3, 29]. In this paper, we concentrate on an ambitious task that has not been addressed so far, i.e., we aim at measuring the *level of intelligence* of a data transformation system, in order to base the comparison upon this measure.

In our vision, the level of intelligence of the internal algorithms of a tool can be roughly defined as *the ratio between the* quality *of the outputs generated by the system, and the* amount of user effort *required to generate them*. In other terms, we want to measure, for each system, how much effort it takes to obtain results of the highest possible quality.

To make this rather general intuition more precise, we need several tools: (i) a notion of data-transformation system that is sufficiently general to capture a wide variety of the tools under exam, and at the same time tight enough for the purpose of our evaluation; (ii) a definition of the quality of a data translation tool on a mapping scenario; (iii) a definition of the user-effort needed to achieve such quality.

1.1 Contributions

We develop several techniques that contribute to give an answer to the question above.

(i) We introduce a very general definition of a *data-transformation system*, in terms of its input-output behavior; differently from earlier approaches that have focused their attention on the actual specification of the transformations, we see a system as a black box receiving as input some specification of the mapping task and an instance of the source schema, and producing as output an instance of the target schema; then, we analyze the system in terms of this input-output function.

(ii) We define the notion of *quality* of a data transformation tool on a given scenario as the *similarity* of the output instance wrt the *expected instance*, i.e., the "right" solution that the human developer expects for a given input. Notice that we allow nested data models and XML data, and therefore measuring the quality of an output imposes to compare two different trees, notoriously a difficult problem, for which high-complexity techniques are usually needed. We show, however, that for the purpose of this evaluation it is possible to define an elegant and very efficient similarity measure that provides accurate evaluations. This comparison technique is a much needed contribution in this field, since it is orders of magnitude

CIKM'12, October 29–November 2, 2012, Maui, HI, USA.

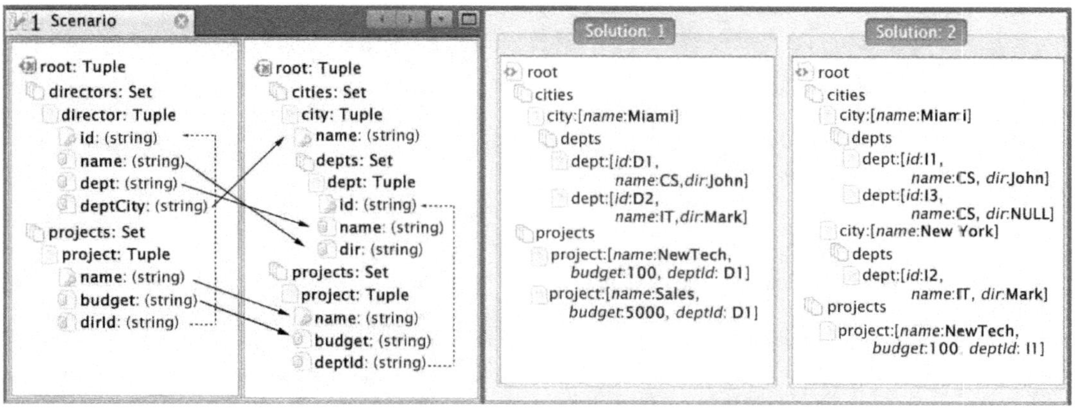

Figure 1: Sample Scenario in the GUI of an Open-Source Mapping System

faster than typical edit-distance measures, and scales up to large instances. In addition, it concretely supports the mapping improvement process, since it returns detailed feedback about mismatches between the two trees. By doing this, it helps users in understanding why their mapping is faulty, and proves much more effective than simple yes/no measures used in previous benchmarks.

(iii) Transformation systems typically require users to provide an abstract specification of the mapping, usually through some graphical user interface; to see an example, consider Figure 1, which shows the graphical specification of a mapping scenario. The figure shows the source and target schema with a number of *correspondences* used to provide a high-level specification of the mappings, as it is common in this framework. Based on the mapping specification, given a source instance the system generates an output, i.e., a target instance such as the ones shown on the right. Despite the fact that different tools have usually different primitives to specify the transformations, it is still possible to abstract the mapping specification as a *labeled input graph*; our estimate of the user effort is a measure of the size of an encoding of this graph inspired by the minimum description length principle in information theory [19]. We believe that this measure approximates the level of user effort better than previous measures that were based on point-and-click counts [3].

(iv) We develop a working prototype of our techniques, and use it to conduct a comprehensive evaluation of several data transformation systems. In this evaluation, we are able to gain a deeper insight about data transformation tools that exist on the market and in the research community, based on a novel graphical representation, called *quality-effort* graphs. More specifically, we fix a number of representative scenarios, with different levels of complexity, and different challenges in terms of expressive power. Then, we run the various tools on each scenario with specifications of increasing efforts, and we measure the quality of the outputs. The introduction of quality-effort graphs is a major contribution of this paper: it allows us to derive several evidences about how much intelligence the internal algorithms of a tool put into the solution, i.e., how fast the quality of solutions increases with respect to the increasing effort.

We want to make it clear that our primary goal is not comparing transformation systems in terms of expressiveness, as it has been done in previous benchmarks [3]. In fact, our approach has been conceived to be applicable to a wide variety of tools, which, as we discussed above, have rather different inspiration and goals. For example, in our evaluation, we consider both schema-mapping systems and ETL tools. It is well known that ETL tools are by far more expressive than schema-mapping systems, since they allow for a number of operations like pivoting, aggregates, rollups [18] that are not natively supported by other systems in our evaluation. As a consequence, in any application scenario in which these primitives are needed, the developer has very little choice. However, there are a number of transformation tasks for which tools of different kinds are indeed applicable, and therefore it makes sense to compare their level of effectiveness in carrying out these specific tasks. In fact, this work represents a concrete investigation of the trade-offs between declarative and procedural approaches, a foundational problem in computer science.

Using the framework proposed in this paper, we conduct a systematic evaluation of data transformation tools. We strongly believe that this evaluation provides precious insights in the vast and heterogeneous world of transformation systems, and may lead to a better understanding of its different facets.

- On one side, it may be the basis for a new and improved generation of benchmarks that extend the ones developed so far [3, 29]. Besides providing a better guide to data architects, this would also help to identify strong and weak points in current systems, and therefore to elaborate on their improvements.
- In this respect, our framework represents an advancement towards the goal of bringing together the most effective features of different approaches to the problem of data translation. As an example, it may lead to the integration of more sophisticated mapping components into ETL workflows [9].
- Finally, as it will be discussed in the following sections, it provides a platform for defining test scenarios for data exchange systems, another missing component in the mapping ecosphere.

1.2 Outline

The paper is organized as follows. Section 2 introduces the notion of a transformation system. The quality measure is introduced in Section 3, its complexity in Section 4. User efforts are discussed in Section 5. We introduce ways to define a scenario and to select gold standards in Section 6. Experiments are reported in Section 7. Related works are in Section 8, conclusions in Section 9.

2. TRANSFORMATION SYSTEMS

In our view, a *data-transformation system* is any tool capable of executing *transformation scenarios* (also called *mapping scenarios* or *translation tasks*). Regardless of the way in which transformations are expressed, in our setting these scenarios require to translate instances of a source schema into instances of a target schema.

The transformation system is seen as a black box, of which we are only interested in the input-output behavior, as shown in Figure 2.

For the purpose of our evaluations, we fix a set of *translation tasks*. A *translation task* is defined in terms of a quadruple $\{S, T, I_S, I_e\}$, where: (i) S is the source schema; (ii) T is the target schema; (iii) I_S is an input instance, i.e., a valid instance of S; (iv) I_e, the *expected output*, is an instance of T generated by applying the desired transformation to I_S.

Notice that the source and target schema may be either explicit, or implicit, as it happens in many ETL tasks. To better express the intended semantics of the transformation, it is possible that also some specification of the mapping, M_e, is given, in a chosen language. This, however, is not to be intended as a constraint on the way in which the transformation should be implemented, but rather as a means to clarify to developers the relationship between the expected output, I_e, and the input, I_S, in such a way that $I_e = M_e(I_S)$.

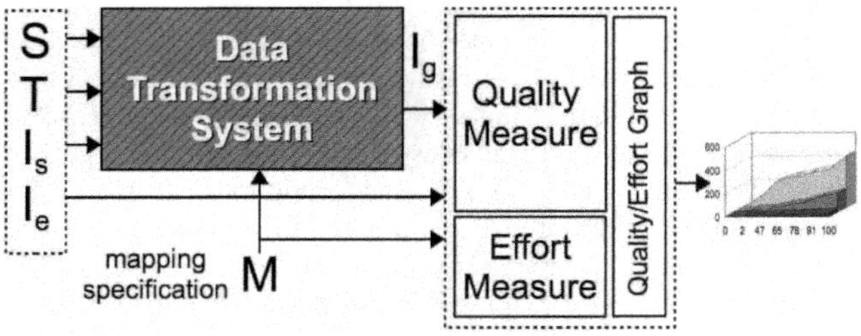

Figure 2: Architecture of the Evaluation Framework

We want to emphasize the high level of generality with which the various components of the architecture have been chosen.

First, as it was discussed in the previous section, we encode the behavior of a system in terms of its input-output function. By doing this, we allow ample space to the different formalisms that are commonly used to express the semantics of the transformation and the mapping specification, M_e; it is in fact perfectly fine to specify the mapping as a query Q in a concrete query language – say XQuery – as STBenchmark does [3]. As an alternative, the transformation can be expressed as a set of embedded dependencies (tgds and egds) [10], as it happens in schema-mapping and data-exchange works. To be even more general, it is also possible to assume that a procedural specification of the mappings is provided, as it happens in some ETL tools.

Second, we are not constraining the primitives offered by the systems under evaluation, nor the way in which users express the transformation. This can be done through a GUI, or – going to the opposite extreme – even by manually writing a query in an executable query language.

Finally, the data model according to which S and T are constructed is a generic one. For the purpose of this paper, we adopt a nested-relational data model, as it will be detailed in the following Section, that provides a uniform representation for most of the structures typically found in concrete data models – primarily relational and, to some extent, XML. However, as it will be clear in the following Section, any data model based on collections, tuples of attributes and relationships is compatible with our framework.

A distinctive feature of our approach is that we assume that a "gold standard", I_e, has been fixed for each scenario. We discuss in detail how this can be done in Section 6. For the time being, we want to emphasize that this is the basis of our evaluation. More specifically, as shown in Figure 2, assume a translation task $\{S, T, I_S, I_e\}$ is given, and we need to evaluate a transformation system *TS*. We proceed as follows:

- we use the primitives offered by *TS* to express the desired transformation; this gives us a specification M - possibly in a different formalism or query language wrt the expected one, M_e - that is supposed to have the same input-output behavior;
- we run M on the input instance, I_S, to generate the output, a target instance I_g;
- then, we measure the quality achieved by the system by comparing I_g to our expected output, I_e. If $I_g = I_e$, then *TS* achieves 100% quality on that specific translation task. Otherwise, the quality achieved by *TS* is the measure of the similarity between I_g and I_e;
- once the quality has been measured, we use the techniques in Section 5 to measure the user-effort, and generate the quality-effort graph.

3. THE QUALITY MEASURE

As discussed in the previous Section, our idea is to evaluate the quality of a tool by measuring the similarity of its outputs wrt a fixed, expected instance that has been selected in advance using one of the methods that will be introduced in Section 6.

Since we adopt a nested relational data model, our instances are trees, as shown in Figure 1. While there are many existing similarity measures for trees, it is important to emphasize that none of these can be used in this framework, for the following reasons:

(i) We want to perform frequent and repeated evaluations of each tool, for each selected scenario, and for mapping specifications of different complexity. In addition, we want to be able to work with possibly large instances, to measure how efficient is the transformation generated by a system. As a consequence, we cannot rely on known tree-similarity measures, like, for example, edit distances [7], which are of high complexity and therefore would prove too expensive.

(ii) The problem above is even more serious, if we think that our instances may be seen as graphs, rather than trees, as it will be discussed in the following paragraphs; we need in fact to check key/foreign-key references that can be seen as additional edges among leaves, thus making each instance a fully-fledged graph. Graph edit distance [13] is notoriously more complex than tree edit distance.

(iii) Even if we were able to circumvent the complexity issues, typical tree and graph-comparison techniques still would not work in this setting. To see this, consider that it is rather frequent in mapping applications to generate synthetic values in the output – these values are called *surrogate keys* in ETL and *labeled nulls* in data-exchange. In Figure 1, values $D1, D2, I1, I2, I3$ are of this kind. These values are essentially placeholders used to join tuples, and their actual values do not have any business meaning. We therefore need to check if two instances are identical up to the renaming of their synthetic values. We may say that we are rather looking for a technique to check *tree or graph isomorphisms* [12], rather than actual similarities.

It can be seen that we face a very challenging task: we need to devise a new similarity measure for trees that is efficient, and at the same time precise enough for the purpose of our evaluation.

In order to do this, we introduce the following key-idea: since the instances that we want to compare are not arbitrary trees, but rather the result of a transformation, we expect them to exhibit a number of regularities; as an example, they are supposedly instances of a fixed nested schema that we know in advance. This means that we know: (a) how tuples in the instances must be structured; (b) how they should be nested into one another; (c) in which ways they join via key-foreign key relationships.

We design our similarity metric by abstracting these features of the two trees in a set-oriented fashion, and then compare these features using precision, recall and ultimately F-measures to derive the overall similarity. In the following paragraphs, we make this intuition more precise.

3.1 Data Model

We fix a number of *base data types*, τ_i – e.g., string, integer, date etc. – each with its domain of values, $dom(\tau_i)$, and a set of *attribute labels*, $A_0, A_1 \ldots$. A *type* is either a base type or a *set* or *tuple* complex type. A *set type* has the form $\mathsf{set}(A : \tau)$, where A is a label and τ is a tuple type. A *tuple type* has the form $\mathsf{tuple}(A_0 : \tau_0, A_1 : \tau_1, \ldots, A_n : \tau_n)$, where each A_i is a label and each τ_i is either a base type or a set type. A *schema* is either a set or a tuple type. Notice that schemas can be seen as (undirected) trees of type nodes. In the following, we will often blur the distinction between a schema and the corresponding tree.

Constraints may be imposed over a schema. A *constraint* is either a functional dependency or an inclusion constraint – i.e., a foreign key – defined in the usual way [1]. Both schemas in Figure 1 are constructed according to this data model. It can be seen that the source schema is relational, the target schema is nested.

Let us first formalize the notion of an *instance* of a schema in our data model, as a tree that may contain constants and *invented values*. More specifically, for each base type, τ_i, we consider the constants in the corresponding domain $dom(\tau_i)$. We also consider a countable set of special values, NULLS, typically denoted by $N_0, N_1, N_2 \ldots$ that are called *placeholders* – but in other terminologies have been called *labeled nulls* and *surrogates* – which we shall use to invent new values into the target when required by the mappings. An instance of the base type, τ_i, is a value in $dom(\tau_i) \cup$ NULLS. Instances of base types are also called *atomic values*.

Instances of a tuple type $\mathsf{tuple}(A_0 : \tau_0, A_1 : \tau_1, \ldots, A_n : \tau_n)$ are (unordered) tuples of the form $[A_0 : v_0, A_1 : v_1, \ldots, A_n : v_n]$, where, for each $i = 0, 1 \ldots, n$, v_i is an instance of τ_i. Instances of a set type $\mathsf{set}(A : \tau)$ are finite sets of the form $\{v_0, v_1, \ldots, v_n\}$ such that each v_i is an instance of τ. An instance of a schema is an instance of the root type. Sample instances can be found in Figure 1 ($D1, D2, I1, I2, I3$ are placeholders); from those examples it should be apparent that, like schemas, also instances can be seen as undirected trees. In the following, we shall often refer to tuple nodes in an instance simply as "tuples".

As it is common in nested data model, we assume a *partitioned normal form (PNF)* [26], i.e., at each level of nesting we forbid two tuples with the same set of atomic values. In light of this, we also forbid tuples whose atomic values are all placeholders.

3.2 Identifiers

Given a mapping scenario as defined in Section 2, we consider the target schema, T, and the expected solution, I_e. The features we associate with a target instance are *tuple* and *join identifiers*.

Tuple identifiers are string encodings of paths going from the root to tuple nodes. To introduce them, we shall first introduce a function $\mathsf{enc}()$ that we recursively apply to nodes. Given a node n in an instance tree, I, we denote by $\mathsf{father}(n)$ the father of n, if it exists; for the root node, n_{root}, $\mathsf{father}(n_{root})$ is a special, dummy node, $\perp$ such that $\mathsf{enc}(\perp)$ equals the empty string. Then, the $\mathsf{enc}()$ function is defined as follows:

- if n is an instance of a set node $\mathsf{set}(A : \tau)$, then $\mathsf{enc}(n) = \mathsf{enc}(\mathsf{father(n)}).A$;
- if n is an instance of a tuple node $[A_0 : v_0, A_1 : v_1, \ldots, A_n : v_n]$, then $\mathsf{enc}(n) =$
  $\mathsf{enc}(\mathsf{father(n)}).[A_{i_0} : \mathsf{enc}(v_{i_0}), \ldots, A_{i_k} : \mathsf{enc}(v_{i_k})]$
  where $v_{i_0} \ldots v_{i_k}$ are the atomic values in the tuple, and A_{i_0}, $\ldots A_{i_k}$ appear in lexicographic order;
- if n is an instance of a base type τ, then $\mathsf{enc}(n) = value(n)$, where $value(n)$ equals n if n is a constant in $dom(\tau)$, or the string *null* if n is a placeholder in NULLS.

Join identifiers are strings encoding the fact that the same placeholder appears multiple times in an instance. More specifically, given two tuples t_1, t_2 in an instance with atomic attributes A, B, respectively, they are said to be *joinable* over attributes A, B if the same placeholder N appears as the value of attribute A in t_1 and of attribute B in t_2. If $t_1 = t_2$, i.e., we consider the same tuple twice, then we require that $A \neq B$, i.e., A and B must be different attributes.

We are now ready to define the identifiers associated with an instance. Given an instance I of the target schema T, we define two different sets of strings associated with I. The *tuple ids*:

$$\mathsf{tids}(I) = \{\mathsf{enc}(t) \mid t \textit{ is a tuple node in } I\}$$

and the *join ids*:

$$\mathsf{jids}(I) = \{\mathsf{enc}(t_1).A = \mathsf{enc}(t_2).B \mid t_1, t_2 \textit{ are tuples in } I \textit{ joinable over } A, B \textit{ and } \mathsf{enc}(t_1).A, \mathsf{enc}(t_2).B \textit{ appear in lexicographic order}\}$$

Tuple and join identifiers for the instances in Figure 1 are reported in Figure 3. It is worth noting that the computation of tuple identifiers requires special care. As it can be seen in the figure, we keep the actual values of placeholders out of our identifiers, in such a way that two instances are considered to be identical provided that they have the same tuples and the same join pairs, regardless of the actual synthetic values generated by the system.

3.3 Instance Quality

Based on these ideas, whenever we need to compute the quality of a solution generated by a system, I_g, we compare I_g to the expected output, I_e by comparing their identifiers. More specifically: we first compute the tuple and join ids in I_e, $\mathsf{tids}(I_e)$, $\mathsf{jids}(I_e)$. Then, we compute the actual ids in I_g, $\mathsf{tids}(I_g)$, $\mathsf{jids}(I_g)$, and measure their precision and recall wrt to $\mathsf{tids}(I_e)$, $\mathsf{jids}(I_e)$, respectively, as follows:

$$p_{tids} = \frac{|\mathsf{tids}(I_g) \cap \mathsf{tids}(I_e)|}{|\mathsf{tids}(I_g)|} \qquad r_{tids} = \frac{|\mathsf{tids}(I_g) \cap \mathsf{tids}(I_e)|}{|\mathsf{tids}(I_e)|}$$

$$p_{jids} = \frac{|\mathsf{jids}(I_g) \cap \mathsf{jids}(I_e)|}{|\mathsf{jids}(I_g)|} \qquad r_{jids} = \frac{|\mathsf{jids}(I_g) \cap \mathsf{jids}(I_e)|}{|\mathsf{jids}(I_e)|}$$

As it is common, to obtain the distance between I_g and I_e, we combine precisions and recalls into a single *F-measure* [31], by computing the harmonic means of the four values as follows:

$$\mathsf{distance}(I_g, I_e) = 1 - \frac{4}{\frac{1}{p_{tids}} + \frac{1}{r_{tids}} + \frac{1}{p_{jids}} + \frac{1}{r_{jids}}}$$

Figure 3 reports the values of precision and recall and the overall F-measure for our example.

We want to emphasize the fact that our technique nicely handles placeholders. Consider for example instance $I_e = \{R(a, N_1), S(N_1, b)\}$, where a, b are constants, and N_1 is a placeholder. Any instance that is identical to I_e up to the renaming of placeholders –

A) Tuple Ids:
gid1 = cities.[*name*:Miami]
gid2 = cities.[*name*:Miami].depts.[*dir:John, id*:null, *name*:CS]
gid3 = cities.[*name*:Miami].depts.[*dir:Mark, id*:null, *name*:IT]
gid4 = projects.[*budget:100, deptId:null, name*:NewTech]
gid5 = projects.[*budget:5000, deptId:null, name*:Sales]

A) Join Ids:
gid2.id-gid4.deptId
gid2.id-gid5.deptId

Tuple Ids: Pr.=0.5 Rec.=0.6
Join Ids: Pr.=1 Rec.=0.5
F-Measure = 0.6 D = 0.4

B) Tuple Ids:
gid1'=cities.[*name*:Miami]
gid2'=cities.[*name*:Miami].depts.[*dir:John, id*:null, *name*:CS]
gid3'=cities.[*name*:Miami].depts.[*dir:null, id*:null, *name*:CS]
gid4'=cities.[*name*:New York]
gid5'=cities.[*name*:New York].depts.[*dir:Mark, id*:null, *name*:IT]
gid6'=projects.[*budget*:100, *deptId*:null, *name*:NewTech]

B) Join Ids:
gid2'.id-gid6'.deptId

Figure 3: Comparing instances. Instance A is the expected output, B is the generated output

like, for example, $I_e = \{R(a, N_2), S(N_2, b)\}$ – has distance 0 wrt I_e. On the contrary, instances with different constants, and/or additional/missing tuples, are considered different and have distance greater than 0.

Notice also that our approach also allows us to easily detect the actual differences with respect to the expected output, i.e., tuples/surrogates that were expected and were not generated, and unexpected tuples/surrogates. Consider for example tuple ids; we define the set of *missing tuples* and the set of *extra tuples* as follows (here $-$ is the set-difference operator):

$$\mathsf{missingTuples}(I_g, I_e) = \mathsf{tids}(I_e) - \mathsf{tids}(I_g)$$
$$\mathsf{extraTuples}(I_g, I_e) = \mathsf{tids}(I_g) - \mathsf{tids}(I_e)$$

Similarly for *missing joins* and *extra joins*:

$$\mathsf{missingJoins}(I_g, I_e) = \mathsf{jids}(I_e) - \mathsf{jids}(I_g)$$
$$\mathsf{extraJoins}(I_g, I_e) = \mathsf{jids}(I_g) - \mathsf{jids}(I_e)$$

When reported to users, these sets represent a precious feedback, since they clearly point out what are the tuples and surrogates that cause mismatches between the expected solution and the one generated by a system. In other words, our similarity measure provides two different comparison indicators: the first one is a number measuring the overall similarity of the two instances; the second one is a detailed list of "edits" (tuple additions, tuple deletions, surrogate replacements) that should be applied to the instances to make them equal. In this respect, it is very similar to a traditional edit distance measure, as it will be discussed in Section 4.

4. COMPLEXITY AND EXPRESSIBILITY

Since our quality measure is based on the idea of comparing instances, we believe it is important to explore its relationship to other known tree-comparison techniques. As we have already noticed, the problem we deal with is at the crossroads of two different problems: the one of computing tree similarity (like, for example, tree edit distances), and the one of detecting graph isomorphisms (due to the presence of placeholders). In this section, we establish a number of results that relate the complexity and expressibility of our framework to those of other known techniques. In particular, we show that our technique is orders of magnitude faster than some of the known alternatives.

Assume that we need to compare two instances, of n_1, n_2 nodes, t_1, t_2 tuple nodes, and p_1, p_2 placeholders, respectively. Notice that $t_i < n_i, p_i < n_i$. Usually $p_i \ll n_i$. On the contrary, while the number of tuples is strictly lower than the number of nodes, for large instances t_i is of the same order of magnitude as n_i, since tuples in sets are the primary factor of multiplicity for the instance tree. Therefore, in the following, we shall approximate t_i by n_i. Let us call n the maximum value of n_1, n_2. To establish a complexity bound, let us analyze the various steps of the algorithm.

(i) As a first step, our algorithm computes tuple identifiers. This can be done by visiting the instance and keeping track of the labels and identifiers of the visited nodes. This step has therefore a cost of $O(n_1 + n_2)$ and generates $t_1 + t_2$ identifiers.

(ii) Then, we generate join pairs. For each placeholder, during the visit we also keep track of the identifiers of the tuples it appears in. To generate join pairs, we need to combine these identifiers in all possible ways. If we call o_{max} the maximum number of occurrences of a placeholder in one of the instances, we generate $n_{max} = \binom{o_{max}}{2}$ identifiers at most for each placeholder. Note that o_{max} is usually quite low, in the order of 2 or 3; moreover, it typically depends on the mapping and it is independent from n. As a consequence, we shall approximate the number of join identifiers by $O(p_1 + p_2)$.

(iii) Finally, in order to compare the two instances and compute the quality measure, we need to intersect the two identifier sets. To do this, we can use a sort-merge algorithm, with a cost of $O(t_1 log(t_1) + t_2 log(t_2))$ to compare tuple identifiers, and $O(p_1 log(p_1) + p_2 log(p_2))$ to compare join identifiers. Since, as discussed above, $p_i \ll n_i$ and we can approximate t_i by n_i, we have a total cost of $O(n_1 log(n_1) + n_2 log(n_2))$. The overall time cost is therefore lower than $O(n log(n))$.

We are interested in comparing this bound with those of other comparison techniques. In order to do this, we shall discuss two different cases.

Case 1: General Case Let us first discuss the case in which the two instances may contain placeholders. In this case, we find it useful to formalize the relationship between our instances, which we have defined in Section 3 as undirected trees, and their graph counterpart. Given a schema T, and an instance I of T, the *instance graph* associated with I contains all nodes and edges in I. In addition it contains an additional edge between each pair of distinct leaf nodes labeled by the same placeholder N.

Based on this, we are not looking for *identical* instance graphs, but rather *isomorphic* instance graphs, i.e., instance graphs that are identical up to the renaming of placeholders. We say that two instance graphs G_1, G_2 are *isomorphic* if there is a bijective mapping, h, between the nodes of G_1 and G_2 such that: (i) for each pair of nodes n_1, n_2 in G_1 there exists an edge between n_1 and n_2 if and only if there exists and edge between $h(n_1)$ and $h(n_2)$ in G_2; (ii) in addition, the mapping h preserves the labels of non-placeholder nodes, i.e., if n is labeled by a constant v, then also $h(n)$ is labeled by v. We can state the following soundness property for our algorithm:

THEOREM 4.1. *Given two instances* I_1, I_2, *then* $\mathsf{distance}(I_1, I_2) = 0$ *if and only if the corresponding instance graphs* G_1, G_2 *are isomorphic.*

Notice that the general problem of computing graph isomorphisms is known to be in *NP*, and only high complexity algorithms are currently known for its solution [12]. This makes these techniques hardly applicable in practice. Our technique, on the contrary, runs with an $O(nlog(n))$ time bound, and therefore easily allows the comparison of large instances. The improvement in the complexity bound is not surprising, since the problem we concentrate on is a simplified variant of the general graph-isomorphism problem. It is, however, remarkable that for this specific instance of the problem such a significant speed-up is achievable.

Case 2: Absence of Placeholders It is interesting to evaluate the performance of our algorithm also in the case in which instances do not contain placeholders. In this case, the instance graph coincides with the instance tree, and the notion of isomorphism degrades into the usual one of equality. It would therefore be possible to apply one of the known tree-similarity algorithms, like, for example, tree-edit distances, to compute the quality of solutions.

The tree-edit distance measures the similarity of a tree T_1 with respect to a tree T_2 by counting the number of operations that are needed to transform T_1 into T_2. In our framework, we concentrate on two operations: node insertions and node deletions. We call these $insert(T_1, T_2)$, $delete(T_1, T_2)$.

In order to state our result, we need to introduce an additional data structure, called the *tuple-reduced tree* associated with an instance I. The latter is obtained by taking the induced subtree of I corresponding to set and tuple nodes, and then by relabeling tuple nodes by the corresponding tuple identifiers in I. In essence, such subtree is obtained by discarding nodes corresponding to atomic attributes, and by embedding their values into tuple labels (Figure 1 shows the tuple-reduced trees of the two instances).

We can state the following result, which shows that our algorithm correctly computes the tree edit distance of tuple-reduced trees.

THEOREM 4.2. *Given two instances I_1, I_2 without placeholders, then* $\mathsf{distance}(I_1, I_2) = 0$ *if and only if the corresponding tuple-reduced trees T_1, T_2 are identical. Moreover, the set of extra tuples (missing tuples) detected by the algorithm is equal to the set of node insertions (node deletions, respectively) computed by the tree-edit distance over T_1, T_2, i.e.,* $\mathsf{missingTuples}(T_1, T_2) = insert(T_1, T_2)$, $\mathsf{extraTuples}(T_1, T_2) = delete(T_1, T_2)$.

Notice that the best algorithms [7] to compute edit distances have an upper bound of $O(n_1 n_2)$. Better bounds can be achieved for ordered trees, but this is clearly not the case we consider, since we do not assume any order of appearance of tuples inside sets. Our bound improves this for the particular instance of the problem we concentrate on. Other works [4] have reported bounds similar to ours, but, unlike ours, results computed by these algorithms cannot be related to tree edit distances.

5. ESTIMATING USER EFFORTS

Now that we have formalized our quality metric, we need to introduce a way to measure user efforts. This is needed in order to compute our quality-effort graphs.

Previous works have used point-and-click counts to do this [2]. However, click-counts are often unreliable since they are heavily influenced by GUI layout choices and, even more important, by the level of expertise of users. On the contrary, to estimate user-efforts, we measure the complexity of the mapping specification by means of an information-theoretic technique. We model the specification complexity as an *input graph* with labeled nodes and labeled edges. This model is general enough to cover a very broad range of approaches to data transformations.

More precisely, the *input graph* is an undirected graph $G = (N, E)$, where N is a set of nodes, and E is a set of edges. Nodes are partitioned in two groups: *schema nodes*, and *additional nodes*. Given a graphical specification of a transformation, we build the corresponding input-graph as follows: (i) every element in the source and target schemas is a schema node in the graph; (ii) arrows among elements in the GUI become edges among nodes in the graph; (iii) a tool may provide a library of graphical elements – for example to introduce system functions – that are modeled as additional nodes in the graph; (iv) extra information entered by the user (e.g., manually typed text) is represented as labels over nodes and edges.

We report in Figure 4 the input-graph for a sample scenario specified using a commercial mapping system (this scenario will be discussed in Section 6.1). In this example there are 31 nodes for the source and target schemas; arrows are drawn among schema nodes to specify logical correspondences. The white boxes are graphical elements on the GUI that specify functions used to manipulate source values; there are 5 functions in this scenario that generate additional nodes in the graph.

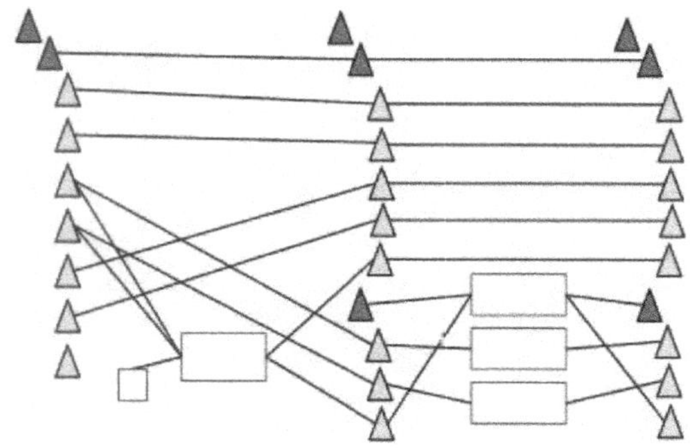

Figure 4: Sample input graph.

We measure the size of such graphs by encoding their elements according to a *minimum description length* technique [19], and then by measuring the size in bits of such description, with the following algorithm:

- as a first step, we assign a unique id to each node in the graph, and compute the minimum number of bits, b_n, needed to encode node ids. Our example uses a total of 36 nodes, so that we need 6 bits for their encoding. Therefore $b_n = 6$ bits;

- next, we measure the size of the encoding of nodes in the graph; the source and target schema nodes are considered as part of the input and therefore are not counted in the encoding. On the contrary, we encode the additional function nodes. To do this, we build an encoding of the corresponding function, by assigning a binary id to each function in the library. Based on the size of the library of functions provided by the tool (approximately 150), every function node in our example requires an additional 8 bits for its encoding; therefore, encoding additional nodes requires $5 * (6 + 8)$ bits;

- then, we measure the encoding of edges; each edge in the graph is encoded by the pair of node ids it connects, with a cost of $2b_n$ bits; in our example, the graph contains 26 edges (without labels) that we shall encode by $2 * 6$ bits;

- finally, node and edge labels are treated as arbitrary strings, and therefore are encoded in ASCII; in this example, one of the graph nodes must be labeled by a single char, for which we need 8 bits.

The specification complexity is therefore given by the following sum of costs: $(5 * (6 + 8)) + (25 * (2 * 6)) + (6 + 8) = 384$ bits. With the same technique we are able to measure the size of the specification needed by different systems, and compare efforts.

We want to stress that this representation is general enough to accomodate very different visual paradigms. To give another example, consider Figure 5. It shows the input graph for a complex ETL workflow. In the graph, each oval represents a workflow step. The schemas and intermediate recordsets used in the various steps are encoded as nodes, with their correspondences as edges.

Our abstraction can also be used to model purely textual queries. In this case, the input graph degenerates into a single node, labeled with the textual specification of the query.

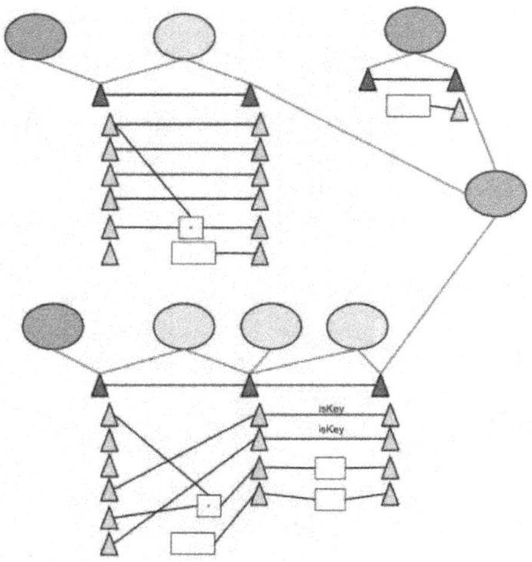

Figure 5: Input graph for an ETL workflow.

6. DESIGNING SCENARIOS

Based on the techniques introduced in Sections 3 and 5, we have conducted a comprehensive experimental evaluation based on several transformation scenarios. Before getting to the details of these experimental results, we want to discuss how it is possible to design scenarios in this framework.

Designing a scenario amounts to choosing a source and target schema, and an input-output function, i.e., a set of source instances given as inputs, and a set of target instances considered as expected outputs, i.e., as the gold standard. It can be seen that the critical point of this process consists in deciding what the expected output should be when some input is fed to the system.

6.1 Selecting the Gold Standard

In this respect, our approach is very general, and allows one to select expected outputs in various ways. It is in principle possible to craft the expected output by hand.

A more typical way – as it was done, for example, in [2] – would be to express the input-output function as a query Q written in a concrete query language, say SQL or XQuery. In this case, for a given input I_S, the expected output would be $I_e = Q(I_S)$. For more complex workflows, one would need to choose a reference system, design the transformation using the system, compute the result, and take this as the expected output.

This approach has the disadvantage of forcing designers to express all of the details of the intended transformation, thus leaving very limited space to explore the variants supported by alternative tools. As an example, it requires to devise a precise strategy to generate surrogates – for example by using Skolem functions [17].

Data exchange theory [10, 11] represents an elegant alternative. More precisely, it provides a clean theoretical framework to state two essential elements of the description of a scenario: (a) a semantics of the transformation in terms of logical expressions; (b) a clear notion of optimal solution for each mapping scenario and source instance.

A mapping is specified using dependencies, expressed as logical formulas of two forms: *tuple-generating dependencies* (tgds) and *equality-generating dependencies* (egds). *Source-to-target tgds* (s-t tgds) are used to specify which tuples should be present in the target based on the tuples that appear in the source. *Target tgds* and *target egds* encode foreign-key and key constraints over the target.

As an example, consider the *vertical partition* scenario of ST-Benchmark [2]. This scenario takes a single, non-normalized table, *SourceReaction*, and splits it into two tables, *Reaction, ChemicalInfo*, joined via a key-foreign key reference. In doing this, it introduces a surrogate key.[1] Notice that the input graph in Figure 4 refers exactly to this scenario.

The intended transformation can be formally expressed in data exchange as follows:

$$m_1.\ \forall e,n,d,q,c,o,r: \mathit{SourceReaction}(e,n,d,q,c,o,r) \rightarrow \exists F: \mathit{Reaction}(e,n,c,o,F) \wedge \mathit{ChemicalInfo}(d,q,F)$$

$$t_1.\ \forall e,n,c,o,f: \mathit{Reaction}(e,n,c,o,f) \rightarrow \exists D,Q: \mathit{ChemicalInfo}(D,Q,f)$$

$$e_1.\ \forall d,q,f,f': \mathit{ChemicalInfo}(d,q,f) \wedge \mathit{ChemicalInfo}(d,q,f') \rightarrow (f = f')$$

Here, m_1 is a *source-to-target tgd* that states how the target tables should be materialized based on the source data. Dependency t_1 is a *target tgd* stating the referential integrity constraint over the target tables. Finally, e_1 is a *target egd* expressing the fact that the first two attributes are a key for the *ChemicalInfo* table. Notice how, by using existential variables, the tgds express the requirement that a placeholder is used to correlate the target tables, without actually providing any technical details about its generation.

A data exchange problem may have multiple solutions on a given source instance, with different degrees of quality. The *core universal solution* [11] is the "optimal" one, since, informally speaking, it is the smallest among the solutions that preserve the mapping. A nice property of the core solution is that there exist polynomial algorithms [11, 15, 30], some of which have been proven to be very scalable [23] to generate the core.

In light of this, a natural way to design scenarios would be to express the semantics of the transformation as a set of logical dependencies, and to pick the core universal solution as the expected output for a given source instance. In our experiments, whenever this was possible, we used this approach. We want, however, to remark that this is not the only alternative, as discussed above, nor it is imposed by the method.

6.2 Test Scenarios

This discussion suggests another promising facet of our evaluation technique. In fact, it shows that it can be used as the basis for a *regression-test tool* for schema-mapping systems whose algorithms are under development. Suppose, in fact, that we need to test the algorithms of a new system, currently under development. We may proceed as follows: (a) fix a set of mapping scenarios expressed as sets of logical dependencies; (b) use an existing system – for example [21, 22] or [30] – to generate the core universal solution; (c) run the system under evaluation to generate the output, and measure its distance from the expected output. Then, in case of errors, use the feedback to correct the translation algorithms.

In essence, this is an alternative evaluation process with respect to the one that we have discussed so far, in which there is less emphasis on quality-effort trade-offs, and more on correctness. To the best of our knowledge, this is the first proposal towards the development of test tools for schema-mapping systems.

7. EXPERIMENTAL RESULTS

The techniques presented in the paper have been implemented in a working prototype using Java; the prototype has been used to perform a large experimental evaluation. To start, we show how the proposed quality measure scales well up to very large instances and outperforms existing techniques. Then, we use our framework to compare several data-translation systems on a common set of scenarios and discuss the results. All the experiments have been

[1] We are actually considering a variant of the original scenario in [3] that has no key constraints.

conducted on a Intel Xeon machine with four 2.66Ghz cores and 4 GB of RAM under Linux.

7.1 Scalability of the Quality Measure

To test the scalability of our quality measure on instances of large size, we used the instance provided for the *Unnesting* scenario in STBenchmark [3]. The original instance contains 2.2 millions nodes and has a size of 65 MB. We generated a modified version of the same file by randomly introducing errors, in such a way that the original and the modified instance had a similarity of 90% according to our quality metrics. Then, we extracted smaller subtrees from this complete instance, in order to obtain a pool of instances of increasing size, varying from a few hundreds to 2 million nodes.

Since the nesting scenario does not require the generation of surrogates, we were able to compare experimentally our measure against an implementation of a tree-edit distance algorithm for ordered trees [5]. We tested ordered instances because of the lack of implementations of the tree edit-distance algorithm for unordered ones. We remark, however, that in the general case of unordered trees the complexity of the tree edit-distance computation is even higher.

We compared times of execution to compute our quality measure, the tree edit-distance on the original trees, and the tree edit-distance on the more compact tuple-reduced trees introduced in Section 4. We call this hybrid measure TED-TRT.

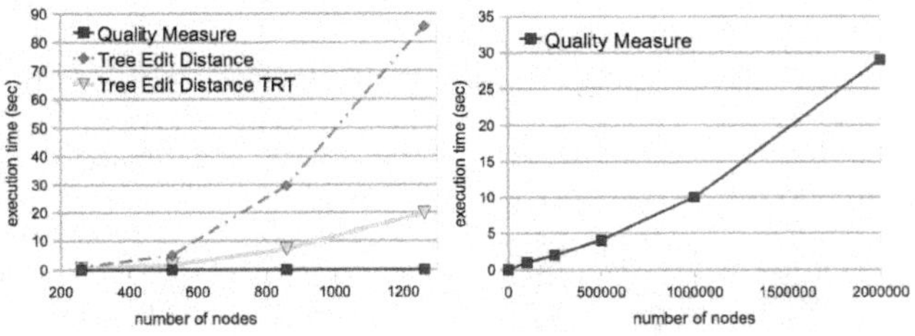

Figure 6: Execution times with files of increasing size.

Figure 6 summarizes the experimental results in terms of execution times and instance sizes. We experimentally confirmed the results reported in Section 4. More specifically, as stated in Theorem 4.2, the distance measured using our quality measure was identical to the one measured using the TED-TRT distance. In addition, the computation was orders of magnitude faster. In the graph on the left hand side, we show the comparison of our measure against the tree edit-distance on small instances. On the right, we show times only for our quality measure, since the tree edit-distance implementation did not scale to large instances. On the contrary, our comparison algorithm scaled nicely: it computed the distance between two files of approximately 65 MB in less than 30 seconds, thus confirming the low complexity bound established in Section 4.

7.2 Comparison of the Systems

In the spirit of evaluating representative systems from different perspectives, we have included the following tools: (i) an open-source schema-mapping research prototype [21, 22]; (ii) a commercial schema-mapping system; (iii) a commercial ETL tool.

In addition, to discuss the relationship of our technique to ST-Benchmark, we have also evaluated the performances of a different schema-mapping tool [25] on some of the scenarios. It is worth mentioning that we also considered the idea of including in our evaluation the open-source OpenII data integration tool [28]. We found out that, while promising, the data translation module of the current version of OpenII is still in a rather preliminary state, and therefore decided to exclude it from the evaluation.

To conduct the evaluation, we selected twelve transformation tasks from the literature, with different levels of complexity. The selected tasks can be roughly classified in three categories:

(i) basic mapping-operations, taken from STBenchmark [3]: *Copy* (Cp), *Denormalization* (Dn), *Vertical Partition* (VP), *Key Assignment* (KA), *Value Management* (VM), and *Nesting* (Ne);

(ii) advanced mapping operations, taken from [23, 21]: *Minimization* (Mi), *Fusion* (Fu), *Nested Keys* (NK); these scenarios require the management of more complex target constraints wrt those above;

(iii) typical ETL tasks: *Aggregation* (Ag) is a simplified version of the *line* workflow from an ETL benchmark [29], while *AccessLog* (AL) and *CreditCards* (CC) are taken from the http://cloveretl.com/-examples Web page.

Of these twelve scenarios, five required the introduction of surrogates; two use nested models, the others are relational. For each scenario we have identified the gold standard, that is, the desired target solution for the given translation task and source instance. As discussed in Section 6, expected solutions were identified in such a way that they contained no unsound or redundant information [11]. Then, we tried to generate the expected output with each of the tools, and measured efforts and quality.

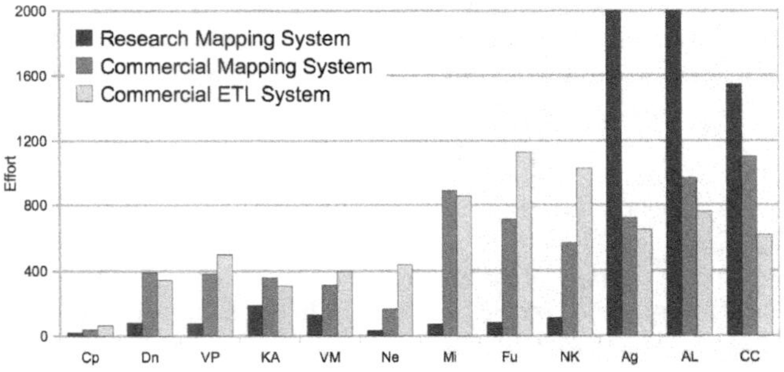

Figure 7: Effort needed by the systems to obtain 100% quality in the various scenarios.

Notice that the three tools under exam use fairly different strategies to compute the transformations: the research mapping systems generate SQL or XQuery code, the commercial mapping system typically generates XSLT, while the ETL workflow requires the internal engine in order to produce results. Nevertheless, our general view of the transformation process permits their comparison. We also want to mention that, while it is not in the scope of this paper to compare the systems in terms of scalability, all of the systems in our experiments scaled well to large instances

Results are shown in Figure 7 and 8. More specifically, Figure 7 reports the effort needed by the various systems to obtain 100% quality in the various scenarios, while Figure 8 shows the quality-effort graphs. There are several evidences in the graphs that we want to highlight. Let us first look at Figure 7. As a first evidence, we note that the research mapping tool required considerably less effort than the commercial counterparts on the basic and advanced mapping tasks. On these tasks, the ETL tool was the one requiring the highest effort to compute the requested transformations. However, we also note that the situation is reversed for the ETL-oriented tasks. Notice how the commercial mapping system had intermediate performances. This suggests that these tools are progressively evolving from the schema-mapping ecosphere into fully-fledged ETL tools.

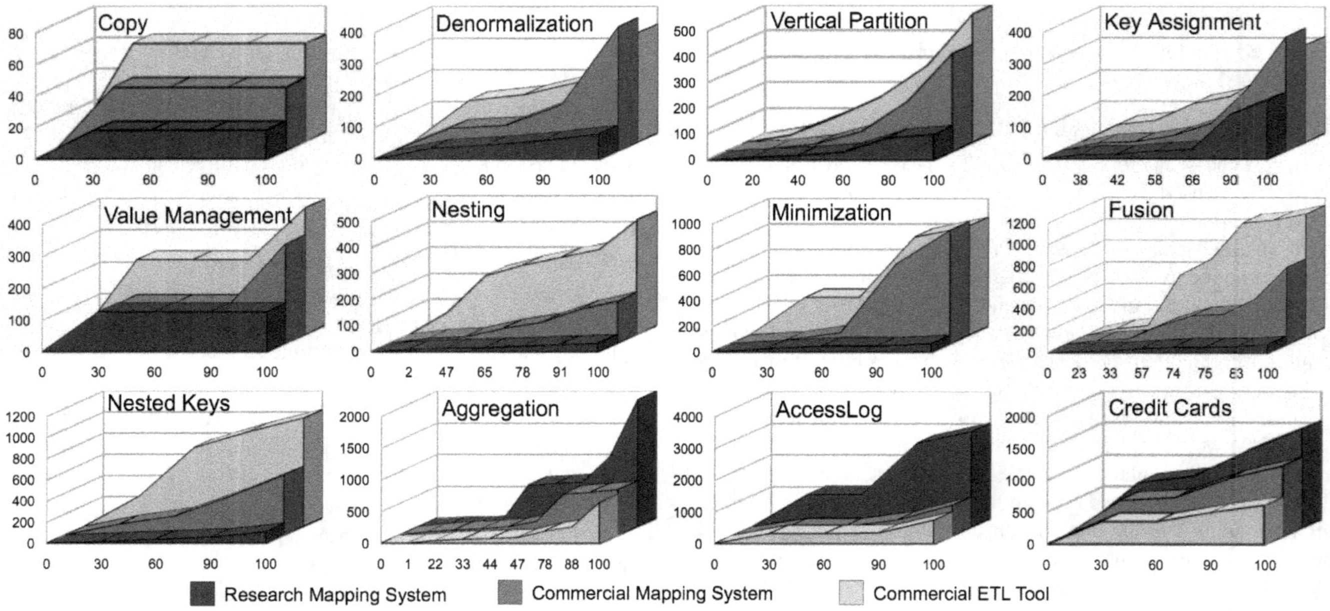

Figure 8: Quality-effort graphs. For each scenario, the smaller the area, the higher is the IQ of a transformation tool.

To get more insights about this, let us look at the quality-effort graphs in Figure 8. The Figure shows how much effort is needed to get a certain level of quality with a given system. Recall that one of our aims is that of measuring the "level of intelligence" of a tool, as its quality/effort ratio. From the graphical viewpoint, this notion of IQ can be associated with the area of the graph delimited by the effort-quality function: such area can be taken as a measure of the progressive effort needed by a tool to achieve increasing levels of quality in one experiment. The smaller the area, the higher is the IQ of a system.

We can observe that the research mapping tool handles in a more natural way some complex operations, like nesting values or data fusion and redundancy removal. But, as soon as the task at hand becomes more procedural, like in the key-assignment scenario or when typical ETL-like operations such as aggregations are required, this advantage becomes less visible or it is completely lost. This is apparent in the *Aggregation*, *AccessLog*, and *CreditCard* scenarios – three rather typical data warehousing transformations. For these tasks, while the effort needed to compute the transformation in commercial systems was in line with those of previous scenarios, in the case of the research mapping tool the cost was enormously increased by the need of manually changing the generated SQL code in order to introduce the needed aggregates. In fact, there is no declarative way of expressing aggregates in data exchange yet.

In fact, our experiments confirm the intuition that the sophisticated declarative algorithms introduced in recent years in schema-mappings research may really provide some advantage in terms of productivity to the data architect. However, this advantage is somehow confined to the typical scope of applicability of schema-mappings. When users want to deal with more complex scenarios, i.e., transformations requiring a rather fine-grained manipulation of values, the adoption of more procedural paradigms brings some advantages.

We strongly believe that these results clearly confirm the need for a new strategy for developing data-transformation tools, which brings together the best of both worlds, in the spirit of [9]. While the expressive power of procedural ETL tools is necessary to properly handle the wide range of transformations that a data architect typically faces, still there are a variety of mapping tasks – ranging from conjunctive queries, data-fusion and instance minimization, to management of functional dependencies and nested constraints – for which research mapping tools provide building blocks that may represent a very powerful addition to commercial transformation systems.

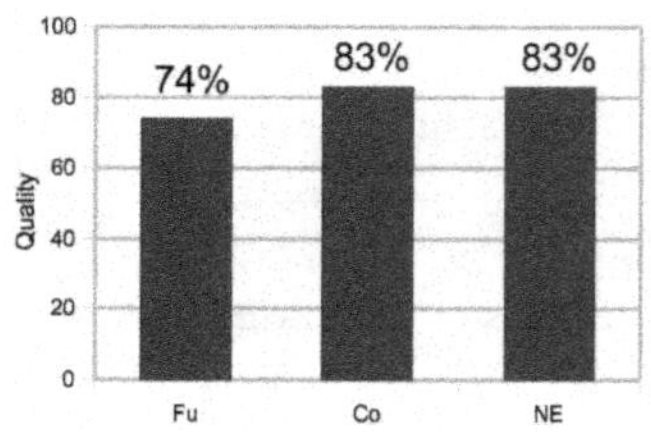

Figure 9: Comparison to STBenchmark.

As a final remark, we think it is useful to put in perspective the results reported in [3] using STBenchmark. STBenchmark uses a coarse-grained yes/-no style of evaluation to measure the performance of a mapping system on a given scenario. Our technique gives a better understanding of the performances of a system, especially in those cases in which it is not capable of fully capturing the semantics of a transformation.

We considered the mapping algorithm used in the STBenchmark evaluation [25], and evaluated its performance on three advanced mapping scenarios. The table in Figure 9 shows the maximum quality that we were able to obtain with such a system by using the GUI only, i.e., without manually changing the SQL or XQuery code (operation, which, as discussed has very high costs in our metrics). It can be seen that in three of the scenarios the system failed to achieve 100% quality. Differently from the yes/no output of STBenchmark, our comparison technique provided a detailed account of the results obtained by the algorithm in these cases. This is a further evidence that our evaluation framework may help to improve the design of benchmarks, and to gain better insights about the effectiveness and limitation of tools.

8. RELATED WORKS

Data translation tasks in enterprise settings are very often tackled using *Extraction-Transform-Load* (or *ETL*) tools, where transformations are defined by using sequences of building blocks in a rather procedural fashion. Representative examples of ETL systems can be found on the market (e.g., Oracle Warehouse Builder or IBM Information Server) (www.oracle.com/technetwork/developer-tools/warehouse, www-01.ibm.com/software/data/integration) and in the open-source community (e.g., Clover ETL or Talend Open Studio) (www.cloveretl.com, www.talend.com).

Different generations of research mapping systems have been developed in the last ten years. A first generation of schema-mapping systems [24, 25] has been followed first by an intermediate generation [30, 23], focused on the quality of the solutions, and then by a second generation [21, 22], which is able to handle a larger class of scenarios. In addition, Altova Mapforce and Stylus Studio (www.altova.com/mapforce, www.stylusstudio.com) are examples of commercial mapping systems.

Several works have studied the issue of quality in mapping-systems with a different focus, either to check desirable properties [27], or to rank alternative mappings [8].

The analysis of the information-integration and business-intelligence market is the subject of a large number of studies by business consulting firms [14]. However, these reports are centered around features and functionalities of the various systems, and do not rely on a quality evaluation metric such as the one developed in this paper. Closer to our approach, there exist some early benchmarks, designed both for ETL tools [29, 32, 20] and schema-mapping systems [3], which provide a basis for evaluating systems in the respective areas only. They mainly concentrate on expressibility, by introducing representative, small scenarios [3, 29], or on the efficiency evaluation [20]. With respect to measuring user efforts, existing solutions (such as [3]) rely on a simple metric based on the count of user actions (e.g., the number of clicks and the number of typed characters) in defining the transformation. Their main limitation, however, is that they fail in answering the main question addressed in this paper.

9. CONCLUSIONS

In this paper, we introduce a number of novel techniques that significantly improve the ones used in previous works. Our quality measure, coupled with the information-theoretic effort measure, enables the introduction of a new tool, called quality-effort graph, to study the effectiveness of a data transformation system.

This evaluation framework provides a clear perception of the level of intelligence of a data transformation tool, and ultimately measures how productive it is for a given scenario. For the specific problem of data-translation, it represents a concrete measure of the trade-off between declarative and procedural approaches.

In addition, we have shown that the technique is very scalable, despite the fact that we deal with a rather difficult problem, i.e., comparing possibly isomorphic graph-like structures.

We believe that this technique sheds some light on the right approach to solve data-integration problems: transforming and integrating data is a multi-faceted problem that requires a combination of state-of-the-art techniques, bringing together the expressibility of ETL tools and the declarative algorithms of schema-mapping research. Coupling together these approaches is a challenging but very promising research problem.

Acknowledgments The authors would like to thank Angela Bonifati and Yannis Velegrakis for the many helpful discussions on the subject of this paper.

10. REFERENCES

[1] S. Abiteboul, R. Hull, and V. Vianu. *Foundations of Databases*. Addison-Wesley, 1995.

[2] B. Alexe, W. Tan, and Y. Velegrakis. Comparing and Evaluating Mapping Systems with STBenchmark. *PVLDB*, 1(2):1468–1471, 2008.

[3] B. Alexe, W. Tan, and Y. Velegrakis. STBenchmark: Towards a Benchmark for Mapping Systems. *PVLDB*, 1(1):230–244, 2008.

[4] N. Augsten, M. Bohlen, and J. Gamper. Approximate Matching of Hierarchical Data Using pq-Grams. In *VLDB*, pages 301–312, 2005.

[5] A. Bernstein, E. Kaufmann, C. Kiefer, and C. Bürki. SimPack: A Generic Java Library for Similiarity Measures in Ontologies. Technical report, Department of Informatics, University of Zurich, 2005.

[6] P. A. Bernstein and S. Melnik. Model Management 2.0: Manipulating Richer Mappings. In *SIGMOD*, pages 1–12, 2007.

[7] P. Bille. A Survey on Tree Edit Distance and Related Problems. *TCS*, 337:217–239, 2005.

[8] A. Bonifati, G. Mecca, A. Pappalardo, S. Raunich, and G. Summa. Schema Mapping Verification: The Spicy Way. In *EDBT*, pages 85 – 96, 2008.

[9] S. Dessloch, M. A. Hernandez, R. Wisnesky, A. Radwan, and J. Zhou. Orchid: Integrating Schema Mapping and ETL. In *ICDE*, pages 1307–1316, 2008.

[10] R. Fagin, P. Kolaitis, R. Miller, and L. Popa. Data Exchange: Semantics and Query Answering. *TCS*, 336(1):89–124, 2005.

[11] R. Fagin, P. Kolaitis, and L. Popa. Data Exchange: Getting to the Core. *ACM TODS*, 30(1):174–210, 2005.

[12] F. Fortin. The Graph Isomorphism Problem. Technical report, Department of Computer Science, University of Alberta, 1996.

[13] X. Gao, B. Xiao, D. Tao, and X. Li. A Survey of Graph Edit Distance. *Pattern Analysis & Application*, 13:113–129, 2010.

[14] Gartner. Magic Quadrant for Data Integration Tools. http://www.gartner.com/technology/, 2011.

[15] G. Gottlob and A. Nash. Efficient Core Computation in Data Exchange. *J. of the ACM*, 55(2):1–49, 2008.

[16] L. M. Haas. Beauty and the Beast: The Theory and Practice of Information Integration. In *ICDT*, pages 28–43, 2007.

[17] R. Hull and M. Yoshikawa. ILOG: Declarative Creation and Manipulation of Object Identifiers. In *VLDB*, pages 455–468, 1990.

[18] R. Kimball and J. Caserta. *The Data Warehouse ETL Toolkit*. Wiley and Sons, 2004.

[19] D. MacKay. *Information Theory, Inference, and Learning Algorithms*. Cambridge University Press, 2003.

[20] T. A. Majchrzak, T. Jansen, and H. Kuchen. Efficiency evaluation of open source etl tools. In *SAC*, pages 287–294, 2011.

[21] B. Marnette, G. Mecca, and P. Papotti. Scalable data exchange with functional dependencies. *PVLDB*, 3(1):105–116, 2010.

[22] B. Marnette, G. Mecca, P. Papotti, S. Raunich, and D. Santoro. ++SPICY: an opensource tool for second-generation schema mapping and data exchange. *PVLDB*, 4(11):1438–1441, 2011.

[23] G. Mecca, P. Papotti, and S. Raunich. Core Schema Mappings. In *SIGMOD*, pages 655–668, 2009.

[24] R. J. Miller, L. M. Haas, and M. A. Hernandez. Schema Mapping as Query Discovery. In *VLDB*, pages 77–99, 2000.

[25] L. Popa, Y. Velegrakis, R. J. Miller, M. A. Hernandez, and R. Fagin. Translating Web Data. In *VLDB*, pages 598–609, 2002.

[26] M. A. Roth, H. F. Korth, and A. Silberschatz. Extended Algebra and Calculus for Nested Relational Databases. *ACM TODS*, 13:389–417, October 1988.

[27] G. Rull Fort, F. C., E. Teniente, and T. Urpí. Validation of Mappings between Schemas. *Data and Know. Eng.*, 66(3):414–437, 2008.

[28] L. Seligman, P. Mork, A. Halevy, K. Smith, M. J. Carey, K. Chen, C. Wolf, J. Madhavan, A. Kannan, and D. Burdick. OpenII: an Open Source Information Integration Toolkit. In *SIGMOD*, pages 1057–1060, 2010.

[29] A. Simitsis, P. Vassiliadis, U. Dayal, A. Karagiannis, and V. Tziovara. Benchmarking etl workflows. In *TPCTC*, pages 199–220, 2009.

[30] B. ten Cate, L. Chiticariu, P. Kolaitis, and W. C. Tan. Laconic Schema Mappings: Computing Core Universal Solutions by Means of SQL Queries. *PVLDB*, 2(1):1006–1017, 2009.

[31] C. J. Van Rijsbergen. *Information Retrieval*. Butterworths (London, Boston), 1979.

[32] L. Wyatt, B. Caufield, and D. Pol. Principles for an etl benchmark. In *TPCTC*, pages 183–198, 2009.

On the Foundations of Probabilistic Information Integration

Fereidoon Sadri
Department of Computer Science
University of North Carolina at Greensboro
Greensboro, NC 27402, USA
f_sadri@uncg.edu

ABSTRACT

Information integration has been a subject of research for several decades and still remains a very active research area. Many new applications depend or benefit from large scale integration. Examples include large research projects in life sciences, need for data sharing among government agencies, reliance of corporations on business intelligence (which requires data integration from many heterogeneous sources), and integration of information on the web. The importance of information integration *with uncertainty* has been observed in recent years. Frequently, information from multiple sources are uncertain and possibly inconsistent. Further the process of integration often depends on approximate schema mappings, another source of uncertainty. An integration system is useful only to the extent that the information it produces can be trusted. Hence, providing a measure of certainty for integrated information is of crucial importance in many important applications.

In this paper we study the problem of integration of uncertain information. We present a simple and intuitive approach to the representation and integration of uncertain information from multiple sources, and show that our integration approach coincides with a recent formalism for uncertain information integration. We extend the model to probabilistic possible-worlds, and show certain unintuitive constraints are imposed upon probabilities of possible-worlds of sources. In particular, we show the probabilities of possible worlds of a source are not independent, rather, they are dependent on probabilities of other sources. We study the problem of determining the probabilities for the result of integration. Finally, we present a practical approach to relaxing probabilistic constraints in integration.

Categories and Subject Descriptors

H.2 [**Database Management**]: [Miscellaneous]

General Terms

Theory

Keywords

Information integration, uncertain data, probabilistic data.

CIKM'12, October 29–November 2, 2012, Maui, HI, USA.

1. INTRODUCTION

Information integration has been a subject of research for several decades, and despite significant progress, in particular in recent years, it still remains a very active research area [24, 28]. Many new applications depend or benefit from large scale integration. Examples include large research projects in life sciences (such as biological and astronomy research), need for data sharing among government agencies, reliance of corporations on business intelligence (which requires data integration from many heterogeneous sources), and integration of information on the web [25]. The importance of information integration *with uncertainty* has been observed in recent surveys on information integration [24, 28, 34, 35]. The following quote is from [28]:

> While in traditional database management managing uncertainty and lineage seems like a nice feature, in data integration it becomes a necessity.

Frequently, information from multiple sources are uncertain and possibly inconsistent. Further the process of integration often depends on approximate schema mappings, another source of uncertainty. An integration system is useful only to the extent that the information it produces can be trusted. Hence, providing a measure of certainty for integrated information is of crucial importance in many important applications.

In this paper we study the problem of integration of uncertain information. Our contributions include:

- We study the problem of uncertain information integration using the possible-worlds model and present a simple and intuitive approach to representation and integration of uncertain information from multiple sources.
- We show that our integration approach coincides with a recent formalism for uncertain information integration [2].
- We extend the model to probabilistic possible-worlds, and show certain unintuitive constraints are imposed upon probabilities of possible-worlds of sources. In particular, we show the probabilities of possible worlds of a source are not independent, rather, they are dependent on probabilities of other sources. We study the problem of determining the probabilities for the result of integration. Finally, we present a practical approach to relaxing probabilistic constraints in integration.

This paper is organized as follows. We start with a motivating example in Section 2, and discuss issues involved in uncertain information integration. Then we revisit the well-known possible-worlds framework for uncertain information in Section 3. We introduce a simple and intuitive logical representation of possible worlds, and present an algorithm for information integration using this representation (Sections 3.2 and 3.3), and show the correspondence of integration using logical representation with integration based on the concept of *superset containment* of [2] (Section 3.4). In Section 4 we extend the integration framework to probabilistic possible worlds model, and show that certain restrictive constraints are imposed on the probabilities assigned by sources to their possible worlds. Then we study the problem of determining the probabilities for the result of integration, and present a practical approach to relaxing probabilistic constraints in integration (Section4.2). We review related work in Section 5 and present conclusions and future work in Section 6.

2. A MOTIVATING EXAMPLE

EXAMPLE 1. *Consider information sources S1 and S2 containing data about student registrations. Source S1 states that Bob is taking CS100 or CS101 (but not both). Source S2 states that Bob is taking CS101 or CS 102 (but not both). How do we integrate the information from S1 and S2?*

This is a very simple example, yet, as we will see, certain questions arise when we attempt the integration. First, let us look at how the information in sources S1 and S2 are represented. The *possible worlds* model [1] has been widely accepted as the conceptual model of uncertain information. In this model, the information represented by each source is (conceptually) considered as a set of database instances, each instance being a *possible* state of the real world. In our example, each database instance for source S1 consists of a single relation. The possible worlds of S1 are shown in Figure 1. Possible worlds of S2 are similar and are shown in Figure 2.

student	course
Bob	CS100

D1

student	course
Bob	CS101

D2

Figure 1: Possible Worlds of source S1

student	course
Bob	CS101

D3

student	course
Bob	CS102

D4

Figure 2: Possible Worlds of source S2

In practice, a compact representation, such as probabilistic databases [11, 12] or U-Relational Model [3], is chosen that avoids enumerating all possible worlds, and, hopefully, permits efficient information integration and query processing. We will not address the issue of compact representation in this paper. Rather, we concentrate our discussion on the fundamental problems of information integration. Interested readers are referred to [44, 45] for a detailed discussion regarding representations of uncertain data and their properties.

2.1 How to Integrate?

When integrating information from multiple sources with definite data, the usual approach is to form the union of corresponding relations from the sources. For example, if S3 stated that Bob is (definitely) taking CS100 and S4 stated that Bob is (definitely) taking CS102, then the integration would state that Bob is taking both CS100 and CS102. Let us apply the union approach to uncertain case. A pairwise union of possible worlds of S1 and S2 in our first example yields the following four possible worlds:

student	course
Bob	CS100
Bob	CS101

student	course
Bob	CS100
Bob	CS102

student	course
Bob	CS101

student	course
Bob	CS101
Bob	CS102

Figure 3: A Possible Result of Integrating Sources S1 and S2

Is this the correct answer to integrating S1 and S2? As we will see, in some cases it is although there are many cases where it is not the correct answer.

2.2 Two Scenarios

Scenario 1. John and Jane are talking about fellow student Bob. John says "I am taking CS100 and CS101 and Bob is in one of them, but I am not sure which one." Note that John's statement coincides with source S1. Namely, Bob is taking CS100 or CS 101 (but not both).

Jane says "I am taking CS101 and CSC102 and Bob is in one of them, but I am not sure which one." Jane's statement coincides with source S2.

How do we integrate John's and Jane's statements? Intuitively, the combination of John and Jane's statements indicate that Bob is either taking CS101, or he is taking both CS100 and CS102. If we compare this with the four possible worlds of Figure 3 which were obtained by pairwise union operation, we note that the first and fourth possible worlds are ruled out. This is due to the fact that John's statement implies Bob is not in both CS100 and CS101, ruling out the first possible world. Similarly, Jane's statement implies Bob is not in both CS101 and CS102, ruling out the fourth possible world. Note that these observations, that John's statement implies that Bob is not in both CS100 and CS101 and Jane's statement implies that Bob is not in both CS101 and CS102 are evident from the possible worlds representations (Figures 1 and 2).

Scenario 2. Andy and Amy are talking about fellow student Bob. Andy says "I am taking CS100, CS101, and CS102 and Bob is in either CS100 or CS101 but not in both." Note that Andy's statement coincides with source S1. Additionally, his statement implies that Bob is not taking CS102. This fact is *not* evident from the possible worlds representation (Figure 1). Amy's statement is the same as Jane's statement. It coincides with source S2.

In this case, the integration is that Bob is in CS101. The first and last possible worlds in the pairwise union are ruled out as in the previous scenario. Additionally, the second possible world in the pairwise union is ruled out by Andy's statement as well.

3. POSSIBLE-WORLDS MODEL REVISITED

The examples of previous section, in particular Scenario 2, demonstrate that the "pure" possible worlds model is not sufficient for information integration applications. In this section we explore an extension to the possible worlds model that makes it better suited for integration.

3.1 Possible Worlds plus Tuple Set

The model used in [2] adds the set of all tuples to the pure possible worlds model. The following definition is taken from [2]. Note that, for simplicity, each database is assumed to contain a single relation scheme. We adopt the same assumption. Extension to the usual case is straightforward.

DEFINITION 1. (UNCERTAIN DATABASE). *An* uncertain database *U consists of a finite set of tuples $T(U)$ and a nonempty set of possible worlds $PW(U) = \{D_1, \ldots, D_m\}$, where each $D_i \subseteq T(U)$ is a certain database.* ■

The addition of the tuple-set makes it possible to represent some negative information that is not possible to represent in the pure possible-worlds model. For example, consider Scenario 2 in Section 2.2. Recall that Andy's statement implies that Bob is not taking CS102. While this information can not be represented in the pure possible-worlds model (Figure 1), adding that corresponding tuple-set contains (Bob, CS102) makes this information explicit (that Bob is not taking CS 102). We explain this further below.

3.2 Propositional Logic Representation

In this section we present a logical representation of possible-worlds with tuple-set model that helps clarify the semantics and expressive power of this model.

Given an uncertain database U, we assign a propositional variable x_i to each tuple $t_i \in T(U)$. We define the formula f_j corresponding to a possible world D_j, and the formula f corresponding to the uncertain database U as follows:

DEFINITION 2. (FORMULA CORRESPONDING TO AN UNCERTAIN DATABASE). *Let D_j be a database in the possible worlds of uncertain Database U. Construct a formula as the conjunction of all variables x_i where the corresponding tuple t_i is in D_j, and the conjunction of $\neg x_i$ where the corresponding tuple t_i is not in D_j. That is,*

$$f_j = \bigwedge_{t_i \in D_j} x_i \bigwedge_{t_i \notin D_j} \neg x_i$$

The formula corresponding to the uncertain database *U is the disjunction of the formulas corresponding to the possible worlds of U. That is,*

$$f = \bigvee_{D_j \in PW(U)} f_j$$

EXAMPLE 2. (FORMULA CORRESPONDING TO AN UNCERTAIN DATABASE). *Consider our Scenario 1 in Section 2.2. John's statement was captured in the possible-worlds representation of Figure 1. In this case, the tuple set for source S1 (John) consists of two tuples, {(Bob, CS100), (Bob, CS101)} Let variable x_1 and x_2 correspond to each of these tuples, respectively. Then the formula for the first possible world, second possible world, and the database are, respectively, $x_1 \wedge \neg x_2$, $\neg x_1 \wedge x_2$, and $(x_1 \wedge \neg x_2) \vee (\neg x_1 \wedge x_2)$.*

Now consider Scenario 2. The difference in this case is Andy's knowledge regarding CS102. Here, the tuple set for Andy's information consists of three tuples, *{(Bob, CS100), (Bob, CS101), (Bob, CS102)}. Let x_1, x_2, x_3 correspond to these three tuples. Then the formula corresponding to the uncertain database representing Andy's statement is $(x_1 \wedge \neg x_2 \wedge \neg x_3) \vee (\neg x_1 \wedge x_2 \wedge \neg x_3)$. This is despite the fact that the pure possible worlds representation of Andy's statement is the same as the representation of John's statement in Scenario 1 (Figure 1).*

3.3 Integration Using Logical Representation

Let $S_1, \ldots, S_n$ be sources containing (uncertain) databases $U_1, \ldots, U_n$. Let the propositional formulas corresponding to $U_1, \ldots, U_n$ be $f_1, \ldots, f_n$. We obtain the formula f corresponding to the uncertain database resulting from integrating $U_1, \ldots, U_n$ by conjuncting the formulas of the databases: $f = f_1 \wedge \cdots \wedge f_n$.

EXAMPLE 3. (INTEGRATION USING LOGICAL REPRESENTATION). *Consider Scenario 1 of Section 2.2. Uncertain database corresponding to John's statement is represented by formula $(x_1 \wedge \neg x_2) \vee (\neg x_1 \wedge x_2)$ (see Example 2). Similarly, the uncertain database corresponding to Jane's statement is represented by formula $(x_2 \wedge \neg x_3) \vee (\neg x_2 \wedge x_3)$, where x_3 corresponds to tuple (Bob, CS102). The integration is obtained as*

$$((x_1 \wedge \neg x_2) \vee (\neg x_1 \wedge x_2)) \wedge ((x_2 \wedge \neg x_3) \vee (\neg x_2 \wedge x_3)) = (\neg x_1 \wedge x_2 \wedge \neg x_3) \vee (x_1 \wedge \neg x_2 \wedge x_3)$$

which corresponds to possible world databases of Figure 4. Note that the result is consistent with our intuition in Scenario 1: Based on statements by John and Jane, Bob is either taking CS101, or he is taking both CS100 and CS102.

student	course
Bob	CS101

student	course
Bob	CS100
Bob	CS102

Figure 4: Possible Worlds of Scenario 1

In contrast, consider Scenario 2. The uncertain database corresponding to Andy's statement is represented by $(x_1 \wedge \neg x_2 \wedge \neg x_3) \vee (\neg x_1 \wedge x_2 \wedge \neg x_3)$ (Example 2). The integration in this case is obtained as

$$((x_1 \wedge \neg x_2 \wedge \neg x_3) \vee (\neg x_1 \wedge x_2 \wedge \neg x_3)) \wedge ((x_2 \wedge \neg x_3) \vee (\neg x_2 \wedge x_3)) = (\neg x_1 \wedge x_2 \wedge \neg x_3)$$

corresponding to the (in this case, definite) database consisting only of the first database in Figure 4. Again, the result is consistent with our intuition in Scenario 12: Based on statement by Andy and Amy, Bob is taking CS101. ■

3.4 Equivalence of Integration Using Logical Representation and Superset-Containment Integration

In this section we show that our integration approach coincides with a recent formalism for uncertain information integration [2]. First, we review some definitions from [2].

DEFINITION 3. (SUPERSET-CONTAINMENT) *Consider uncertain databases U_1 and U_2. We say that U_2* superset-contains *U_1, denoted $U_1 \sqsubseteq_S U_2$, if and only if:*

- *$T(U1) \subseteq T(U_2)$, and*
- *$PW(U_1) \supseteq \{W \cap T(U1) \mid W \in PW(U_2)\}$*

The following definition is a simplified version of a definition in [2]. We have restricted the definition to identity views and queries, and have concentrated on superset containment.

DEFINITION 4. (CONSISTENT MEDIATED DATABASE) *The set of sources $S = \{S_1, \ldots, S_m\}$ with (uncertain) databases $U_1, \ldots, U_n$ is* consistent *if and only if there exists an uncertain database M such that:*

- $PW(M) \neq \phi$
- $U_i \sqsubseteq_S M$ *for all* $i = 1, \ldots, m$

M is called a consistent mediated database *for S (under superset containment).* ■

Intuitively, a consistent mediated database is a possible integration of the sources. Note that we are assuming each source database consists of a single uncertain relation, and the mediated database is also a single uncertain relation.

EXAMPLE 4. (CONSISTENT MEDIATED DATABASE) *Consider sources S1 and S2 of Figures 1 and 2. It is easy to verify that the database of Figure 4 is indeed a mediated database of S1 and S2 under scenario 1. Note that tuple sets for the sources and for the mediated database are, respectively, T_1 = {(Bob, CS100), (Bob, CS101)}, T_2 = {(Bob, CS101), (Bob, CS102)}, and T_M = {(Bob, CS100), (Bob, CS101), (Bob, CS102)}.* ■

A set of uncertain sources can have many consistent mediated databases. We are interested in a mediated database (which we call the integrated database) that contains all the information implied by sources and nothing more.

DEFINITION 5. (INTEGRATED DATABASE) *Given a set of sources $S = \{S_1, \ldots, S_m\}$, their* integrated database *is a consistent mediated database M for S such that for every consistent mediated database M' for S, $M \sqsubseteq_S M'$.*

Now we will prove that the notions of integration using logical formulas and that of integration using superset containment (Definition 5) coincide.

In the following, let $S_1, \ldots, S_m$ be sources with (uncertain) databases $U_1, \ldots, U_m$. Let the propositional formulas corresponding to $U_1, \ldots, U_m$ be $f_1, \ldots, f_m$. The logical integration results in the uncertain database M with the formula $f_M = f_1 \wedge \cdots \wedge f_m$ (Section 3.3). There is a special case where f_M obtained as above is *false*. In this case the sources are inconsistent and no consistent mediated database exists. Henceforth, we concentrate on the case where $f_M \neq$ *false*.

LEMMA 1. *Let $S = \{S_1, \ldots, S_m\}$ be a set of uncertain sources, and M their integration using logical formulas. Then M is a consistent mediated database for S.*

Proof. *We need to show that $PW(M) \neq \phi$ and $U_i \sqsubseteq_S M$ for all $i = 1, \ldots, m$. The first condition is satisfied for consistent sources since f_M represents at least one world. For the second condition, we should show*

- $T(U_i) \subseteq T(M)$ *for all* $i = 1, \ldots, m$, *and*
- $PW(U_i) \supseteq_S \{W \cap T(U_i) \mid W \in PW(M)\}$ *for all* $i = 1, \ldots, m$.

Consider the form of $f_M = f_1 \wedge \cdots \wedge f_m$. Each f_k has the form

$$f_k = \bigvee_{D_j \in PW(U_k)} \left(\bigwedge_{t_i \in D_j} x_i \bigwedge_{t_i \notin D_j} \neg x_i \right)$$

It follows that f_M, after expansion, is the disjunction of conjunctive terms that have the form

$$\left(\bigwedge_{t_i \in D_j^1} x_i \bigwedge_{t_i \notin D_j^1} \neg x_i \right) \wedge \ldots \wedge \left(\bigwedge_{t_i \in D_j^m} x_i \bigwedge_{t_i \notin D_j^m} \neg x_i \right)$$

Where $D_j^1, \ldots, D_j^m$ are databases in the possible worlds of $U_1, \ldots, U_m$, respectively. Each of these conjunctive terms will be false if for one variable x, both x and $\neg x$ appear in the term. Otherwise, it will have variables corresponding to all tuples in $T(U_1) \cup \cdots \cup T(U_m)$, and it represents one possible world in the logical integration. Since M is nonempty, it follows that $T(M) = T(U_1) \cup \cdots \cup T(U_m)$. Hence, $T(U_i) \subseteq T(M)$ for all $i = 1, \ldots, m$.

Further, if a conjunctive term as above is not false, then it is easy to verify that the possible world corresponding to the conjunction, when restricted to tuples in $T(U_k)$, is represented exactly by the formula

$$\bigwedge_{t_i \in D_j^k} x_i \bigwedge_{t_i \notin D_j^k} \neg x_i$$

and hence is equal to $D_j \in PW(U_k)$. It follows that $PW(U_k) \supseteq_S \{W \cap T(U_k) \mid W \in PW(M)\}$ for all $k = 1, \ldots, m$. ■

THEOREM 1. *Let $S = \{S_1, \ldots, S_m\}$ be a set of uncertain sources, and M their integration using logical formulas. Then M is the integrated database for S.*

Proof. *By Lemma 1 M is a consistent mediated schema for S. We need to prove for every consistent mediated database M' for S, $M \sqsubseteq_S M'$.*

Since M' is a consistent mediated database, we have $U_i \subseteq_S M'$ for all $i = 1, \ldots, m$. Then $T(U_i) \subseteq T(M')$ for all $i = 1, \ldots, m$, and $T(U_1) \cup \cdots \cup T(U_m) \subseteq T(M')$. But in Lemma 1 we showed that $T(M) = T(U_1) \cup \cdots \cup T(U_m)$. It follows that $T(M) \subseteq T(M')$.

It remains to show that $PW(M) \supseteq \{W \cap T(M) \mid W \in PW(M')\}$. Assume the contrary. That is, there exists $W \in PW(M')$ such that $W \cap T(M) \notin PW(M)$. On the other hand, since M' is a consistent mediate database, every uncertain database U_i should have a (regular) relation D_{j_i} such that $D_{j_i} = W \cap T(U_i)$. It is easy to see that the logical construction of the integrated database, when applied to the logical formulas of D_{j_i}, $i = 1, \ldots, m$, generates the logical formula for $W \cap T(M)$. Hence $W \cap T(M) \in PW(M)$, contradiction. ■

4. BEYOND POSSIBLE WORLDS: ADDING PROBABILITIES

We extend the possible-worlds model by associating a probability distribution with each uncertain database:

DEFINITION 6 (PROBABILISTIC UNCERTAIN DATABASE). *A probabilistic uncertain database U consists of a finite set of tuples $T(U)$, a nonempty set of possible worlds $PW(U) = \{D_1, \ldots, D_m\}$, where each $D_i \subseteq T(U)$ is a certain database with a probability p_i, $0 \leq p_i \leq 1$. Further, $\sum_{i=1}^{m} p_i = 1$.* ■

Given a probabilistic uncertain database U with $PW(U) = \{D_1, \ldots, D_m\}$, it is convenient to associate a probabilistic *event* e_i with each possible world D_i. Intuitively, e_i represents the event where the value of the uncertain database U

is equal to D_i. Then, the probability of e_i, $P(e_i) = p_i$. We can make the following observations:

- Each world in the set of possible worlds for a source is exclusive of other worlds for the same source. Hence, we have $P(e_i \mid e_j) = 0$ for all $j \neq i$, where $P(e \mid e')$ represents the conditional probability of event e given event e'.
- Given sources $S_1, \ldots, S_n$, with probabilistic uncertain databases $U_1, \ldots, U_n$, let $PW(U_i) = \{D_{i_1}, \ldots, D_{i_{m_i}}\}$. Each possible world of the integration of $U_1, \ldots, U_n$ corresponds to the conjunction of possible worlds, one from each source. That is, if e_{i_j} is the event associated with possible world D_{i_j} of U_i, then a possible world in the integration corresponds to the event

$$e_{1_i} \wedge e_{2_j} \wedge \cdots \wedge e_{n_l}$$

for some $1 \leq i \leq m_1$, $1 \leq j \leq m_2$, ..., $1 \leq l \leq m_n$.
- In the integration, depending on the contents of the sources, two worlds from different sources may be inconsistent. This can be detected using the formulas corresponding to the two worlds, when the conjunction of the two formulas is false. An example was discussed in Example 3. Let the events corresponding to two inconsistent worlds be e_{i_j} and e_{l_k}. Then we have $P(e_{i_j} \mid e_{l_k}) = P(e_{l_k} \mid e_{i_j}) = 0$.
- Note that if two of the worlds forming the integration corresponding to $e_{1_i} \wedge e_{2_k} \wedge \cdots \wedge e_{n_l}$ are inconsistent, then $P(e_{1_i} \wedge e_{2_k} \wedge \cdots \wedge e_{n_l}) = 0$. This is because $P(e_{i_j} \wedge e_{l_k}) = P(e_{i_j} \mid e_{l_k}) \times P(e_{l_k}) = 0$ for any two inconsistent events e_{i_j} and e_{l_k}.

We present an example to demonstrate that probabilities associated with possible worlds of different sources need to satisfy certain constraints. We will generalize this observation in Section 4.1 further below.

EXAMPLE 5. *Consider Scenario 1 of Section 2.2. Possible worlds of the sources are shown again for convenience (Figures 5 and 6). Possible worlds of the integration were shown in Figure 4 (see Example 3).*

student	course
Bob	CS100

D1

student	course
Bob	CS101

D2

Figure 5: Possible Worlds of source S1

student	course
Bob	CS101

D3

student	course
Bob	CS102

D4

Figure 6: Possible Worlds of source S2

Let the events associated with possible worlds $D1, \ldots, D4$ be $e_1, \ldots, e_4$, respectively. We have the following equations:
$P(e_1) + P(e_2) = 1$
$P(e_3) + P(e_4) = 1$
$P(e_1 \mid e_2) = P(e_2 \mid e_1) = 0$
$P(e_3 \mid e_4) = P(e_4 \mid e_3) = 0$

Further, by Example 3, we know e_1 and e_3 are inconsistent, and so are e_2 and e_4. Hence
$P(e_1 \mid e_3) = P(e_3 \mid e_1) = 0$
$P(e_2 \mid e_4) = P(e_4 \mid e_2) = 0$

Our goal is to compute $P(e_1 \wedge e_3)$, $P(e_1 \wedge e_4)$, $P(e_2 \wedge e_3)$, and $P(e_2 \wedge e_4)$ in terms of $P(e_1)$, $P(e_2)$, $P(e_3)$, and $P(e_4)$.

It is easy to verify that $P(e_1 \wedge e_3) = P(e_1 \mid e_3) \times P(e_3) = 0$. Similarly, $P(e_2 \wedge e_4) = P(e_2 \mid e_4) \times P(e_4) = 0$. The only possible worlds in the integration with nonzero probabilities correspond to $e_1 \wedge e_4$ and $e_2 \wedge e_3$. These possible worlds were shown in Figure 4.

Some Observations

First, we note that e_1 and e_2 are complementary events since they are mutually exclusive and $P(e_1) + P(e_2) = 1$. So, we can write $e_1 = \neg e_2$ and vice-versa. Similarly, e_3 and e_4 are complementary. Hence, we have $P(e_3) = P(e_3 \wedge e_1) + P(e_3 \wedge e_2)$. But $P(e_3 \wedge e_1) = 0$ as discussed above. So, we get $P(e_3) = P(e_3 \wedge e_2) = P(e_2 \wedge e_3) = P(e_2 \mid e_3) \times P(e_3)$. It follows that $P(e_2 \mid e_3) = 1$. Similarly, we can show $P(e_3 \mid e_2) = 1$, $P(e_1 \mid e_4) = 1$, and $P(e_4 \mid e_1) = 1$.

Finally, since $P(e_3) = P(e_3 \wedge e_2) = P(e_3 \mid e_2) \times P(e_1)$ and $P(e_3 \mid e_2) = 1$, we obtain $P(e_2) = P(e_3)$. We can also obtain $P(e_1) = P(e_4)$ in a similar fashion.

This is a very interesting result. It shows that probabilities associated with possible worlds D_1 and D_2 of source 1 have to be the same as probabilities associated with worlds D_4 and D_3 of source 2. Let's recall our Scenario 1: The information that Bob is taking CS100 or (xor) CSC101 was given by John, and the information that Bob is taking CS101 or (xor) CSC102 was given by Jane. The restriction that probabilities associated with possible worlds D_1 and D_2 of source 1 have to be the same as probabilities associated with worlds D_3 and D_4 of source 2 means that If John assigns probabilities, say, 40% and 60%, to his statements, then Jane also has to assign exactly the same probabilities to her two statements (40% that Bob is taking CS102, and 60% that Bob is taking CS101). This is highly counter intuitive. We will generalize this observation, which we will call probabilistic consistency constraint, *in the next section.*

Let's assume for now that indeed $P(e_1) = P(e_4)$ and $P(e_2) = P(e_3)$. Then it becomes easy to obtain the probabilities of the possible worlds in the integration:
$P(e_1 \wedge e_4) = P(e_1 \mid e_4) \times P(e_4) = P(e_4)$, *and*
$P(e_2 \wedge e_3) = P(e_2 \mid e_3) \times P(e_3) = P(e_3)$

To summarize, For Scenario 1: $P(e_1 \wedge e_3) = 0$, $P(e_1 \wedge e_4) = P(e_1) = P(e_4)$, $P(e_2 \wedge e_3) = P(e_2) = P(e_3)$, and $P(e_2 \wedge e_4) = 0$. ■

4.1 Probabilistic Consistency Constraints

Given the possible world sets of two information sources S and S', we use a bi-partite graph G to represent the consistency relation between the worlds of the sources. Let the possible world set of S be $\{D_1, \ldots, D_k\}$, and the possible world set of S' be $\{D'_1, \ldots, D'_{k'}\}$. Graph G has $k + k'$ nodes corresponding to possible world sets $\{D_1, \ldots, D_k\}$ and $\{D'_1, \ldots, D'_{k'}\}$. There is an edge between D_i and D'_j if the formulas $f(D_i)$ and $f(D'_j)$ corresponding to these worlds are mutually satisfiable. That is, $f(D_i) \wedge f(D'_j) \neq$ *false*. (See Section 3.2 regarding logical representation of possible worlds.) We call G the *possible-worlds consistency graph* (or *consistency graph* for short) of S and S'.

In the following, we overload possible world symbol D (or D') to also represent the event corresponding to D (or D')

(Section 4) as well as the node corresponding to D (or D') in the consistency graph G. The actual meaning will be clear from context.

We will prove the following:

- If a node D (or D') has no edges connected to it, then $P(D)$ (or $P(D')$) must be zero.
- Connected components of G are *complete* bi-partite graphs.
- Let G_1 be a connected component of G. Let N and N' denote the nodes of G_1 corresponding to the possible worlds of sources S and S', respectively. Then
$$\sum_{D_i \in N} P(D_i) = \sum_{D'_j \in N'} P(D'_j)$$
- As a special case, if D and D' are connected in G, and not connected to any other node, then $P(D) = P(D')$. We had this case in Example 5.

THEOREM 2. *Let G be the consistency graph of sources S and S'. Let G_1 be a connected component of G. Then G_1 is a complete bi-partite graph.*

Proof: *We will show that if there is a path between nodes D and D' in G, where D and D' correspond to possible worlds of S and S', respectively, then there must be an edge between D and D'.*

Assume there is a path between D and D') but there is no edge (D, D'). Since there is no edge (D, D'), then $f(D)$ and $f(D')$ are not mutually satisfiable. That means there is a variable t such that one formula has t and the other has $\neg t$ in their conjuncts. Without loss of generality, assume $f(D)$ has t. Hence, (1) there is a tuple t in D (recall that a variable represents a tuple), (2) t is not in D', and (3) t is in the tuple set of S'.

The path between D and D' consists of a sequence of alternating nodes D_is and D'_js such that $D = D_1$, $D'_k = D'$, and the following edges are in G:

(D_i, D'_i) *for* $i = 1, \ldots, k$, *and*

(D'_i, D_{i+1}) *for* $i = 1, \ldots, k-1$.

Since t is in $D = D_1$ and edge (D_1, D'_1) exists, then t must also be in D'_1. Similarly, since edge (D'_1, D_2) exists, then t must also be in D_2. In a similar way we can show t must be in all possible worlds along this path, including D'. This provides a contradiction to the assumption that $\neg t$ is in $f(D')$. ■

THEOREM 3. *Let G_1 be a connected component of G. Let N and N' denote the nodes of G_1 corresponding to the worlds of sources S and S', respectively. Then*
$$\sum_{D_i \in N} P(D_i) = \sum_{D'_j \in N'} P(D'_j)$$

Proof: *Let k and k' be the number of possible worlds for S and S', respectively. We have*
$$P(D_i) = \sum_{j=1}^{k'} P(D_i \wedge D'_j)$$

If $D_i \in N$, then $P(D_i \mid D_j)$ and $P(D_i \wedge D_j)$ are both zero for $D_j \notin N'$. So, for a node $D_i \in N$, we have
$$P(D_i) = \sum_{D'_j \in N'} P(D_i \wedge D'_j)$$

It follows that
$$\sum_{D_i \in N} P(D_i) = \sum_{D_i \in N} \sum_{D'_j \in N'} P(D_i \wedge D'_j)$$

Similarly, we can show, for a node $D'_j \in N'$,
$$P(D_j) = \sum_{D_i \in N} P(D_i \wedge D'_j)$$

and hence,
$$\sum_{D'_j \in N'} P(D'_j) = \sum_{D_i \in N} \sum_{D'_j \in N'} P(D_i \wedge D'_j)$$

Theorem follows. ■

EXAMPLE 6. *Consider the possible worlds of two sources shown in Figures 7 and 8.*

student	course
Bob	CS100

D1

student	course
Bob	CS100
Bob	CS101

D2

student	course
Bob	CS101

D3

Figure 7: Possible Worlds of source One

student	course
Bob	CS100

D'1

student	course
Bob	CS100
Bob	CS201

D'2

student	course
Bob	CS201

D'3

student	course
Bob	CS201
Bob	CS202

D'4

Figure 8: Possible Worlds of source Two

The consistency graph G for these sources is shown in Figure 9. Note that G has two connected components: G_1 consists of nodes D_1, D_2, D'_1, D'_2 and G_2 consists of nodes D_3, D'_3, D'_4. Note that these connected components are complete bipartite graphs. According to Theorem 3, we must have $P(D_1) + P(D_2) = P(D'_1) + P(D'_2)$, and $P(D_3) = P(D'_3) + P(D'_4)$.

The result of integration will consist of 6 possible-worlds relations, corresponding to compatible pairs of possible worlds from the two sources, namely, (D_1, D'_1), (D_1, D'_2), (D_2, D'_1), (D_2, D'_2), (D_3, D'_3), and (D_3, D'_4). It is shown in Figure 10. We will discuss the problem of determining probabilities of possible-worlds relations of the integration in the next section. ■

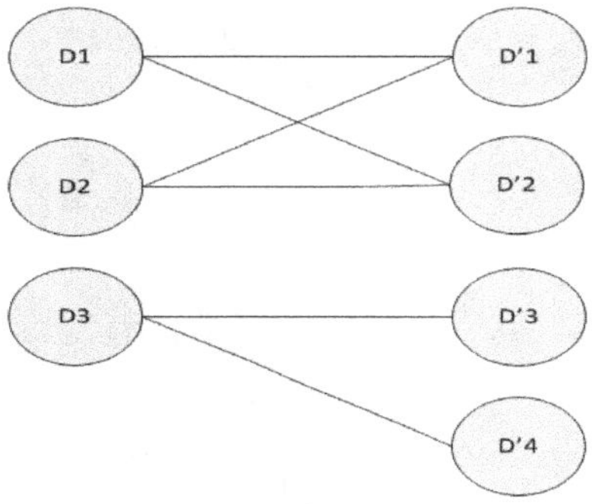

Figure 9: Consistency Graph for Example 6

student	course
Bob	CS100

(D1,D'1)

student	course
Bob	CS100
Bob	CS201

(D1,D'2)

student	course
Bob	CS100
Bob	CS101

(D2,D'1)

student	course
Bob	CS100
Bob	CS101
Bob	CS201

(D2,D'2)

student	course
Bob	CS101
Bob	CS201

(D3,D'3)

student	course
Bob	CS101
Bob	CS201
Bob	CS202

(D3,D'4)

Figure 10: Result of integration of sources One and Two

4.2 Determining the Probabilities for the Result of Integration

In the integration of probabilistic uncertain databases, the goal is to obtain the probabilities of the possible worlds of the integration in terms of the probabilities of individual worlds (p_{i_j}'s, or, equivalently, $P(e_{i_j})$'s). In other words, we would like to obtain

$$P(e_{1_i} \wedge e_{2_k} \wedge \cdots \wedge e_{n_l})$$

in terms of $P(e_{i_j})$'s for all possible values of i, k, ..., and l. We discussed a simple case in Example 5. If worlds D and D' are connected in the consistency graph, and not connected to any other nodes, then (1) $P(D) = P(D')$ and (2) $P(D \wedge D') = P(D) = P(D')$ (note that we are overloading the symbol D to mean a possible world, the node in the consistency graph corresponding to the possible world D, and the event corresponding to the possible world D.) This case corresponds to simple connected components in the consistency graph, those with only two nodes.

We face two difficulties in determining the probabilities of possible worlds in the integration in the general case:

- How to determine the probabilities of possible worlds resulting from the integration of pairs of worlds in a connected component with more than two nodes?
- How to deal with violations of probabilistic consistency constraints?

In this section we discuss approaches to address these difficulties. First, we concentrate on the case where probabilistic consistency constraints are satisfied. The following lemma follows the proof of Theorem 3.

LEMMA 2. *Let G be the consistency graph of sources S and S', and G_1 be a connected component of G. Let the nodes of G_1 consist of nodes N corresponding to source S and N' corresponding to source S'. Then*

$$\sum_{D_i \in N} \sum_{D'_j \in N'} P(D_i \wedge D'_j) = \sum_{D_i \in N} P(D_i) = \sum_{D_j \in N'} P(D_j)$$

Note that each $D_i \wedge D'_j$ corresponds to a possible world in the integration. In other words, we know the sum of the probabilities of possible worlds resulting from the integration corresponding to each connected component of the consistency graph. ■

It is easy to extend the observation from Example 5 regarding connected components with only two nodes to the case where N or N' (in Lemma 2) is a single node. For example, if $N = \{D\}$ is a single node, then $P(D \wedge D'_j) = P(D'_j)$ for all $D'_j \in N'$. However, if neither N nor N' is a single node, then, in the absence of additional information, there are multiple (infinite) possibilities for the probabilities of the possible worlds in the integration (see Example 7). We can use the following approaches to compute the probabilities of possible worlds in the integration.

- Additional information can be used to pinpoint the probabilities of integrated possible worlds. One such information is the conditional probabilities of the form $P(D \mid D')$ for possible worlds in the same connected component of the consistency graph of the two sources.
- In the absence of any other information we adapt some heuristics to distribute the known sum of the probabilities over individual possible worlds in the integration (see Example 7).

EXAMPLE 7. *Consider Example 6. Let's assume the probabilities of possible worlds of sources S and S' are $P(D_1) = 0.3$, $P(D_2) = 0.5$, $P(D_3) = 0.2$, $P(D'_1) = 0.35$, $P(D'_2) = 0.45$, $P(D'_3) = 0.05$, and $P(D'_4) = 0.15$. Note that these probabilities satisfy the probabilistic consistency constraints $P(D_1) + P(D_2) = P(D'_1) + P(D'_2)$, and $P(D_3) = P(D'_3) + P(D'_4)$.*

The consistency graph for S and S' was shown in Figure 9. It has two connected components. The second component satisfies the special case where N is a single node. So, we can easily determine the probabilities of two of the possible worlds in the integration: $P(D_3 \wedge D'_3) = P(D'_3) = 0.05$ and $P(D_3 \wedge D'_4) = P(D'_4) = 0.15$.

The first connected component of the consistency graph gives rise to possible worlds corresponding to $D_1 \wedge D'_1$, $D_1 \wedge D'_2$, $D_2 \wedge D'_1$, and $D_2 \wedge D'_2$. We have four unknowns. We have four equations too but they are not independent:

$P(D_1 \wedge D'_1) + P(D_1 \wedge D'_2) = P(D_1)$,
$P(D_2 \wedge D'_1) + P(D_2 \wedge D'_2) = P(D_2)$,
$P(D_1 \wedge D'_1) + P(D_2 \wedge D'_1) = P(D'_1)$,
$P(D_1 \wedge D'_2) + P(D_2 \wedge D'_2) = P(D'_2)$.

Given one more equation, we will be able to determine the four probabilities. An attractive possibility is the knowledge of a conditional probability. For example, let $P(D_1 \mid D'_1) = 0.6$. *Then we get* $P(D_1 \wedge D'_1) = 0.21$, $P(D_1 \wedge D'_2) = 0.09$, $P(D_2 \wedge D'_1) = 0.14$, *and* $P(D_2 \wedge D'_2) = 0.36$.

In the absence of any additional knowledge, we can incorporate some heuristics to provide the probabilities of possible worlds in the integration. One possibility is to distribute the sum (0.8 in our example) according to the pairwise product of probabilities of underlying possible worlds (0.105, 0.135, 0.175, and 0.225 in our example). We obtain the following values for our example: $P(D_1 \wedge D'_1) = 0.13125$, $P(D_1 \wedge D'_2) = 0.16875$, $P(D_2 \wedge D'_1) = 0.21875$, *and* $P(D_2 \wedge D'_2) = 0.28125$. *Note that this distribution corresponds to the assumption*

$$P(D1 \mid D'1) = \frac{P(D_1)}{P(D_1) + P(D_2)} \quad \blacksquare$$

Next, we consider the second difficulty: How to cope with violations of probabilistic consistency constraints? A strict approach would be to declare the sources as inconsistent and deem integration impossible. But in many applications, probabilities associated with possible worlds are approximate, and may represent some *degree of belief* rather than a strict mathematical probability. Rather than dismissing the sources' assessment completely when their probabilities violate some probabilistic constraint, we should try to provide approximate probabilities for possible worlds in the integration. The following example demonstrates a promising approach.

EXAMPLE 8. *Consider Example 5 again. The consistency graph corresponding to this example has two connected components:* (D_1, D_4) *and* (D_2, D_3), *where* D_1 *and* D_2 *are possible worlds of source 1 and* D_3 *and* D_4 *are possible worlds of source 2.*

Assume probabilities 40% and 60% for possible worlds of source 1, and 70% and 30% for the possible worlds of source 2. That is $P(D_1) = 0.4$, $P(D_2) = 0.6$, $P(D_3) = 0.7$, $P(D_4) = 0.3$. *Note that probabilistic consistency constraints are violated. That is,* $P(D_1) \neq P(D_4)$ *and* $P(D_2) \neq P(D_3)$. *We showed that* $P(D_1 \wedge D_4)$ *must be equal to* $P(D_1)$ *and* $P(D_4)$ *(and also* $P(D_1) = P(D_4)$*). But that is not satisfied here. So,* intuitively, *what is the best probability to associate with* $P(D_1 \wedge D_4)$*? Source 1 says it must be 40%, while source 2 says it is 30%. One possible choice is the average of the two values, 35%. This corresponds to the first possible world of the integration in Figure 4. Similarly, we use the average of 60% and 70%, namely 65%, for the probability of the second possible world of the integration in Figure 4.* ■

The following is the generalization of our heuristics:

Consider each connected component of the consistency graph independently. The probabilistic consistency constraint is that the sum of probabilities of the possible worlds corresponding to the first source is equal to the sum of probabilities of the possible worlds corresponding to the second source. If they are not equal, we use the average of the two values. Then we will distribute this value into probabilities for each "edge" of the connected component (note that an edge represents the integrated possible world that is the union of the two possible worlds represented by the nodes of that edge).

5. RELATED WORK

Information integration and modeling and management of uncertain information have been active research areas for decades, with both areas receiving significant renewed interest in recent years (for example, some recent publications in these areas include [2, 3, 4, 7, 10, 12, 15, 16, 17, 19, 20, 23, 24, 26, 28, 31, 39, 41, 42, 44, 45, 46, 47] Research on information integration with uncertainty, on the other hand, is quite recent [2, 18, 19, 20, 21, 34, 35]. In the following we review some of related research in these areas.

We start with a fundamental work on information integration with uncertainty [2]. The focus of this work is on the foundations for local-as-view information integration when the sources contain uncertain data. To our knowledge, this is the first work that enhances the well-known possible-worlds model with tuple sets, a concept that proves critical for information integration applications. They introduce fundamental concepts of equality and superset containment, consistency, and correct and strongest correct answer to queries. They prove that for superset containment, an uncertain database instance exists that gives the strongest correct answer to any query. We have chosen this instance as the formalism for the integration of uncertain databases, and provide a conceptually simpler algorithm to compute it. [2] also contains studies of complexities of checking consistency and evaluating queries in this model.

Most of the other research on information integration with uncertainty deal with the issue of uncertain schema mapping. Schema matching/mapping is a key step in information integration. Significant research has been spent on automated schema mapping (for example, [5, 6, 13, 14, 27, 29, 32, 33, 36, 37, 40, 48]). Automated schema mapping generates uncertain mappings and hence the study of uncertain mappings is important for information integration.

In [18, 19] authors argue that data integration systems should handle uncertainty at three levels: Semantic mappings, translation of keyword queries to structured queries, and data. They introduce the concepts of by-table and by-tuple probabilistic schema mappings. In by-table semantics, all tuples of a given table use the same mapping to the mediated schema, whereas in the by-tuple semantics, each tuple may use a different mapping. [9, 18, 19] present query complexity and algorithms for query processing over inexact schema mappings, as well as algorithms for efficiently computing top-k answers to queries.

A study and survey of uncertainty in data integration is presented in [34, 35]. They introduce a generic data integration process in terms of *wrapping*, *matching* and *merging* operations, and identify critical points for uncertain information integration. They demonstrate the importance of handling uncertainties produced by the matching process, and introduce approaches to improve the matching phase. They also present a survey of a number of data integration methods that explicitly deal with uncertainty.

The authors of [21] concentrate on another dimension of using probabilistic information in information integration. Their goal is "to improve the performance of a mediator system by obtaining answers to queries as fast as possible." They consider three types of probabilistic information: (1) degree of overlap between collections in the mediated schema, (2) degree of coverage of each information source, and (3) degree of overlap between information sources (such as when a source is a *view* of another source.) They propose algorithms to order access to information sources using probabilistic information and study their performances.

Management of uncertainty in XML schema matching and efficient query processing in this context has been studied in [22]. Authors present approaches to improve the efficiency of generating, storing, and querying possible mappings.

Information integration from uncertain XML sources is studied in [20]. The underlying model for uncertain XML is the ProTDB probabilistic XML model of [38], and the integration system uses the *Semantic Model* approach of [7, 8, 30, 43]. It introduces the *lineage-encoding* relational model for the mediated schema which makes it possible to capture the uncertainties in the ProTDB-style probabilistic XML sources, and presents query processing and probability calculation algorithms for this framework.

6. CONCLUSIONS

We studied the problem of information integration from multiple sources with uncertain data. We reviewed the possible-worlds approach to the modeling of uncertain information, presented an intuitive logical representation of possible-worlds information, and presented an algorithm for uncertain information integration using the logical representation. We also showed that our integration approach coincides with a recent formalism for uncertain information integration. Then we extended the approach to probabilistic possible-worlds, and showed certain probabilistic consistency constraints are imposed upon possible-worlds of information sources in the integration. We studied the problem of determining the probabilities for the result of integration, and presented a practical approach to probabilistic information integration based on relaxation of probabilistic constraints.

Our work has established a formal model for the integration of information from sources containing uncertain data, including probabilistic information about sources contents. To be practical, uncertain information should be presented using a compact representation rather than an enumeration of the possible-worlds. Future work includes selecting an efficient representation (such as the probabilistic relation of [12]) and designing efficient algorithms for integration of uncertain information in the selected representation.

7. REFERENCES

[1] Serge Abiteboul, Paris C. Kanellakis, and Gösta Grahne. On the representation and querying of sets of possible worlds. In *Proceedings of ACM SIGMOD International Conference on Management of Data*, pages 34–48, 1987.

[2] Parag Agrawal, Anish Das Sarma, Jeffrey D. Ullman, and Jennifer Widom. Foundations of uncertain-data integration. *Proceedings of International Conference on Very Large Databases*, 3(1):1080–1090, 2010.

[3] Lyublena Antova, Thomas Jansen, Christoph Koch, and Dan Olteanu. Fast and simple relational processing of uncertain data. In *Proceedings of IEEE International Conference on Data Engineering*, pages 983–992, 2008.

[4] Lyublena Antova, Christoph Koch, and Dan Olteanu. 10^{10^6} worlds and beyond: Efficient representation and processing of incomplete information. In *Proceedings of IEEE International Conference on Data Engineering*, pages 606–615, 2007.

[5] Zohra Bellahsene, Angela Bonifati, and Erhard Rahm, editors. *Schema Matching and Mapping*. Springer, 2011.

[6] Philip A. Bernstein and Sergey Melnik. Model management 2.0: manipulating richer mappings. In *Proceedings of ACM SIGMOD International Conference on Management of Data*, pages 1–12, 2007.

[7] Dongfeng Chen, Rada Chirkova, Maxim Kormilitsin, Fereidoon Sadri, and Timo J. Salo. Query optimization in XML-based information integration. In *Proceedings of International Conference on Information and Knowledge Management*, pages 1405–1406, 2008.

[8] Dongfeng Chen, Rada Chirkova, Fereidoon Sadri, and Timo J. Salo. Query optimization in information integration, December 2010. Submitted for publication.

[9] Reynold Cheng, Jian Gong, David W. Cheung, and Jiefeng Cheng. Evaluating probabilistic queries over uncertain matching. In *Proceedings of IEEE International Conference on Data Engineering*, pages 1096–1107, 2012.

[10] Nilesh N. Dalvi, Christopher Ré, and Dan Suciu. Probabilistic databases: diamonds in the dirt. *Communications of the ACM*, 52(7):86–94, 2009.

[11] Nilesh N. Dalvi and Dan Suciu. Efficient query evaluation on probabilistic databases. In *Proceedings of International Conference on Very Large Databases*, pages 864–875, 2004.

[12] Nilesh N. Dalvi and Dan Suciu. Efficient query evaluation on probabilistic databases. *The VLDB Journal*, 16(4):523–544, 2007.

[13] Robin Dhamankar, Yoonkyong Lee, AnHai Doan, Alon Y. Halevy, and Pedro Domingos. iMAP: Discovering complex mappings between database schemas. In *Proceedings of ACM SIGMOD International Conference on Management of Data*, pages 383–394, 2004.

[14] Hong Hai Do and Erhard Rahm:. COMA - a system for flexible combination of schema matching approaches. In *Proceedings of International Conference on Very Large Databases*, pages 610–621, 2002.

[15] AnHai Doan and Alon Y. Halevy. Semantic integration research in the database community: A brief survey. *AI Magazine*, 26(1):83–94, 2005.

[16] AnHai Doan, Natalya F. Noy, and Alon Y. Halevy. Introduction to the special issue on semantic integration. *SIGMOD Record*, 33(4):11–13, 2004.

[17] Xin Luna Dong, Laure Berti-Equille, and Divesh Srivastava. Integrating conflicting data: The role of source dependence. *PVLDB*, 2(1):550–561, 2009.

[18] Xin Luna Dong, Alon Halevy, and Cong Yu. Data integration with uncertainty. In *Proceedings of International Conference on Very Large Databases*, pages 687–698, 2007.

[19] Xin Luna Dong, Alon Y. Halevy, and Cong Yu. Data integration with uncertainty. *The VLDB Journal*, 18(2):469–500, 2009.

[20] Ala A. Eshmawi and Fereidoon Sadri. Information integration with uncertainty. In *Proceedings of*

International Database Engineering and Applications, IDEAS, pages 284–291, 2009.

[21] Daniela Florescu, Daphne Koller, and Alon Y. Levy. Using probabilistic information in data integration. In *Proceedings of International Conference on Very Large Databases*, pages 216–225, 1997.

[22] Jian Gong, Reynold Cheng, and David W. Cheung. Efficient management of uncertainty in xml schema matching. *The VLDB Journal*, 21(3):385–409, 2012.

[23] Todd J. Green, Gregory Karvounarakis, Nicholas E. Taylor, Olivier Biton, Zachary G. Ives, and Val Tannen. ORCHESTRA: facilitating collaborative data sharing. In *Proceedings of ACM SIGMOD International Conference on Management of Data*, pages 1131–1133, 2007.

[24] Laura M. Haas. Beauty and the beast: The theory and practice of information integration. In *Proceedings of International Conference on Database Theory*, pages 28–43, 2007.

[25] Alon Halevy and Chen Li. Information integration research: Summary of NSF IDM workshop breakout session. `http://www2.cs.washington.edu/nsf2003/final-reports/information integration breakout summary.pdf`, September 2003.

[26] Alon Y. Halevy, Naveen Ashish, Dina Bitton, Michael J. Carey, Denise Draper, Jeff Pollock, Arnon Rosenthal, and Vishal Sikka. Enterprise information integration: successes, challenges and controversies. In *Proceedings of ACM SIGMOD International Conference on Management of Data*, pages 778–787, 2005.

[27] Alon Y. Halevy, Zachary G. Ives, Dan Suciu, and Igor Tatarinov. Schema mediation for large-scale semantic data sharing. *The VLDB Journal*, 14(1):68–83, 2005.

[28] Alon Y. Halevy, Anand Rajaraman, and Joann Ordille. Data integration: The teenage years. *Proceedings of International Conference on Very Large Databases*, pages 9–16, 2006.

[29] Mauricio A. Hernández, Paolo Papotti, and Wang Chiew Tan. Data exchange with data-metadata translations. *Proceedings of the VLDB Endowment*, 1(1):260–273, 2008.

[30] Laks V. S. Lakshmanan and Fereidoon Sadri. Interoperability on XML data. In *Proceedings of the International Semantic Web Conference (ISWC)*, pages 146–163, 2003.

[31] Chen Li, Jia Li, and Qi Zhong. Raccoon: A peer-based system for data integration and sharing. In *Proceedings of IEEE International Conference on Data Engineering*, page 852, 2004.

[32] Jayant Madhavan, Philip A. Bernstein, AnHai Doan, and Alon Y. Halevy. Corpus-based schema matching. In *Proceedings of IEEE International Conference on Data Engineering*, 2005.

[33] Jayant Madhavan, Philip A. Bernstein, and Erhard Rahm. Generic schema matching with Cupid. In *Proceedings of International Conference on Very Large Databases*, pages 49–58, 2001.

[34] Matteo Magnani and Danilo Montesi. Uncertainty in data integration: current approaches and open problems. In *Proceedings of VLDB Workshop on Management of Uncertain Data*, pages 18–32, 2007.

[35] Matteo Magnani and Danilo Montesi. A survey on uncertainty management in data integration. *ACM Journal of Data and Information Quality*, 2(1), 2010.

[36] Sergey Melnik, Atul Adya, and Philip A. Bernstein. Compiling mappings to bridge applications and databases. In *Proceedings of ACM SIGMOD International Conference on Management of Data*, pages 461–472, 2007.

[37] Sergey Melnik, Philip A. Bernstein, Alon Y. Halevy, and Erhard Rahm. Supporting executable mappings in model management. In *Proceedings of ACM SIGMOD International Conference on Management of Data*, 2005.

[38] Andrew Nierman and H. V. Jagadish. ProTDB: Probabilistic data in XML. In *Proceedings of International Conference on Very Large Databases*, pages 646–657, 2002.

[39] Dan Olteanu, Jiewen Huang, and Christoph Koch. SPROUT: Lazy vs. eager query plans for tuple-independent probabilistic databases. In *Proceedings of IEEE International Conference on Data Engineering*, pages 640–651, 2009.

[40] Erhard Rahm and Philip A. Bernstein. A survey of approaches to automatic schema matching. *The VLDB Journal*, 10(4):334–350, 2001.

[41] Christopher Re, Nilesh N. Dalvi, and Dan Suciu. Efficient top-k query evaluation on probabilistic data. In *Proceedings of IEEE International Conference on Data Engineering*, pages 886–895, 2007.

[42] Patricia Rodríguez-Gianolli, Maddalena Garzetti, Lei Jiang, Anastasios Kementsietsidis, Iluju Kiringa, Mehedi Masud, Renée J. Miller, and John Mylopoulos. Data sharing in the Hyperion peer database system. In *Proceedings of International Conference on Very Large Databases*, pages 1291–1294, 2005.

[43] Fereidoon Sadri. Local as view information integration in the semantic model approach. In *Proceedings of IEEE International Conference on Information Reuse and Integration (IRI)*, pages 148–153, 2011.

[44] Anish Das Sarma, Omar Benjelloun, Alon Y. Halevy, Shubha U. Nabar, and Jennifer Widom. Representing uncertain data: models, properties, and algorithms. *The VLDB Journal*, 18(5):989–1019, 2009.

[45] Anish Das Sarma, Omar Benjelloun, Alon Y. Halevy, and Jennifer Widom. Working models for uncertain data. In *Proceedings of IEEE International Conference on Data Engineering*, page 7, 2006.

[46] Prithviraj Sen and Amol Deshpande. Representing and querying correlated tuples in probabilistic databases. In *Proceedings of IEEE International Conference on Data Engineering*, 2007.

[47] Nicholas E. Taylor and Zachary G. Ives. Reliable storage and querying for collaborative data sharing systems. In *Proceedings of IEEE International Conference on Data Engineering*, pages 40–51, 2010.

[48] Ling-Ling Yan, Renée J. Miller, Laura M. Haas, and Ronald Fagin. Data-driven understanding and refinement of schema mappings. In *Proceedings of ACM SIGMOD International Conference on Management of Data*, pages 485–496, 2001.

GPU Acceleration of Probabilistic Frequent Itemset Mining from Uncertain Databases

Yusuke Kozawa[1]
kyusuke@kde.cs.tsukuba.ac.jp

Toshiyuki Amagasa[1,2]
amagasa@cs.tsukuba.ac.jp

Hiroyuki Kitagawa[1]
kitagawa@cs.tsukuba.ac.jp

[1] Graduate School of Systems and Information Engineering, University of Tsukuba

[2] Institute of Space and Astronautical Science, Japan Aerospace Exploration Agency

ABSTRACT

Uncertain databases have been widely developed to deal with the vast amount of data that contain uncertainty. To extract valuable information from the uncertain databases, several methods of frequent itemset mining, one of the major data mining techniques, have been proposed. However, their performance is not satisfactory because handling uncertainty incurs high processing costs. In order to address this problem, we utilize GPGPU (General-Purpose computation on GPU). GPGPU implies using a GPU (Graphics Processing Unit), which is originally designed for processing graphics, to accelerate general purpose computation. In this paper, we propose a method of frequent itemset mining from uncertain databases using GPGPU. The main idea is to speed up probability computations by making the best use of GPU's high parallelism and low-latency memory. We also employ an algorithm to manipulate a bitstring and data-parallel primitives to improve performance in the other parts of the method. Extensive experiments show that our proposed method is up to two orders of magnitude faster than existing methods.

Categories and Subject Descriptors

H.2.8 [**Database Management**]: Database Applications—*Data mining*

General Terms

Algorithms, Performance

Keywords

GPGPU, Uncertain Databases, Frequent Itemset Mining

1. INTRODUCTION

The problem of uncertain data management has attracted a great deal of attention due to the inherent uncertainty in the real world. For example, when analyzing purchasing behavior of customers using RFID sensors, there may be incorrect sensor readings due to errors. In addition to this, uncertain data take place in many situations. Major sources of the uncertainty are limitations of equipment, privacy concerns, or statistical methods such as forecasting. To deal with such uncertain data, *uncertain databases* have recently been developed by many researchers [1, 6, 7, 19, 20].

In the area of uncertainty data management, the application of frequent itemset mining or association rule mining [2] to uncertain databases is one of the major research issues, and there have been a number of algorithms [6, 7, 19, 20]. In fact, frequent itemset mining is a part of association rule mining, and is known to be more computationally intensive than subsequent association rule mining. More than that, frequent itemset mining from uncertain databases is different from conventional one [2, 3, 10] in the sense that we need to take into account uncertainty. The existing methods suffer from performance problems due to the fact that extra costs for dealing with uncertainty, such as probability computation, is needed and this another process is often highly time-consuming. It is thus necessary to accelerate this process in order to handle large uncertain databases.

To this end, GPGPU (General-Purpose computation on Graphics Processing Unit) is an attractive solution. GPGPU has recently been an interesting research subject in the field of high performance computing as well as many other fields [8, 9, 11, 12, 13, 17, 21]. GPGPU implies using a GPU (Graphics Processing Unit), which is a processor originally designed for processing graphics, to accelerate general purpose computation. The GPU can simultaneously process many data with high parallelism compared to CPUs because it has many SIMD (Single Instruction, Multiple Data) cores (tens to hundreds). Hence, growing number of researchers are trying to exploit the processors for various purposes, such as database processing and data mining. The architecture of these SIMD cores is inherently suitable for processes that employ one instruction on multiple data in parallel. As a result, the GPU has difficulty to deal with a procedure with many conditional branches. Therefore, it is one of typical technical challenges to develop an algorithm to make the best use of the SIMD architecture.

In fact, there have been few works using GPGPU to accelerate frequent itemset mining from uncertain databases, other than our previous work [13]. However, the previous approach has some limitations:

- It performs a fairly large number of unnecessary probability computations.

CIKM'12, October 29–November 2, 2012, Maui, HI, USA.

- It does not fully utilize several kinds of memories on the GPU.
- It only focuses on accelerating probability computations, resulting in poor performance on some datasets.

In this paper, we propose a method for frequent itemset mining from uncertain databases using GPGPU. Our work aims to overcome the above limitations. To remove the unnecessary computations, we employ a filter primitive [12]. Besides, to further optimize the computations, we use a tree-based approach with low-latency memory on the GPU. We also propose an algorithm to efficiently manipulate a bit-string by using GPU intrinsic functions. In addition, data-parallel primitives are utilized to increase speeds of the other parts of the existing approach. Extensive experiments show that our proposed method is up to two orders of magnitude faster than existing approaches.

The remainder of this paper is organized as follows. Section 2 defines the problem and describes the pApriori algorithm [19]. In Section 3, we briefly introduce GPGPU and data-parallel primitives. In Section 4, we propose a method for processing pApriori using GPGPU. Section 5 evaluates the performance of the proposed scheme. Section 6 shortly reviews related work, and in Section 7 we conclude and mention future work.

2. PROBABILISTIC FREQUENT ITEMSET MINING

First, we define the conventional (non-probabilistic) frequent itemsets in Section 2.1, and then extend the problem for uncertain databases in Section 2.2. Our definition basically follows [19]. In Section 2.3, we describe the pApriori algorithm, which was proposed by Sun *et al.* [19].

2.1 Frequent Itemsets

Let I denote a set of all items. A set of items $X \subseteq I$ is called an *itemset* and a k-itemset means an itemset that contains k items. A pair of ID and an itemset is called a *transaction* T.[1] A *transaction database* $\mathcal{T}$ is defined as a set of transactions. Given a transaction database $\mathcal{T}$ of size (the number of transactions) n and an itemset X, the *support* of X, which is denoted by $sup(X)$, is defined as the number of transactions in $\mathcal{T}$ that include X. An itemset X is called a *frequent itemset*, if $sup(X) \geq \texttt{minsup}$, where `minsup` is a support threshold given by users.

2.2 Probabilistic Frequent Itemsets

A transaction database $\mathcal{T}$ is called an *uncertain transaction database* (UTDB) $\mathcal{U}$, when each transaction in $\mathcal{T}$ has an *existential probability* that indicates the probability that the transaction exists in $\mathcal{T}$. Table 1 shows an example of a UTDB, which represents purchase records of some customers. For example, *game* and *music* is purchased together with the probability 0.8.

A UTDB is often interpreted with the possible world semantics [19, 20]. Under this notion, a UTDB generates a set of *possible worlds*, each of which contains a combination of transactions in the UTDB. For instance, the UTDB in Table 1 produces 16 possible worlds such as $\emptyset$, $\{T_1\}$, $\{T_2\}$, $\{T_3\}$, $\{T_4\}$,, $\{T_1, T_2\}$, etc. Each world is also associated with an existential probability that is the product of the probabilities of the world's transactions. In Table 1, a world $\{T_1\}$ has the probability that the transaction T_1 exists and T_2, T_3, and T_4 do not exist, i.e., $0.8 \cdot (1-0.7) \cdot (1-0.9) \cdot (1-0.5) = 0.012$.

[1]In this paper, a *transaction* is used to mean the *itemset* of the transaction for the set-theoretic inclusion relation.

Table 1: A UTDB.

ID	Itemset	Prob.
T_1	{game, music}	0.8
T_2	{music, video}	0.7
T_3	{game}	0.9
T_4	{game, music, video}	0.5

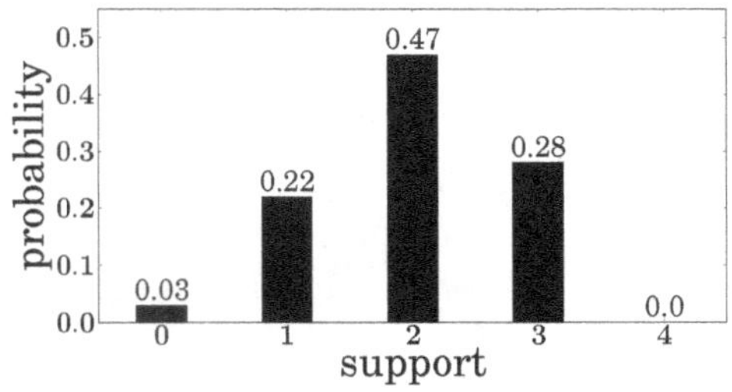

Figure 1: The SPMF of an itemset {music}.

In this interpretation, the support of an itemset X varies with each world and becomes a random variable. The probability mass function of the support is called a *support probability mass function* (SPMF), denoted by f_X. In particular, $f_X(k)$ is the probability that $sup(X) = k$, where k is an integer that $sup(X)$ can take, i.e., $k \in [0, |\mathcal{U}|]$. For example, Figure 1 illustrates $f_{\{\text{music}\}}$ in the UTDB in Table 1. In principle, $f_{\{\text{music}\}}(k)$ can be calculated by summing the probabilities of the worlds where the support of {music} is equal to k.

An itemset X is called a *probabilistic frequent itemset* (PFI), if

$$P(sup(X) \geq \texttt{minsup}) = \sum_{k=\texttt{minsup}}^{|\mathcal{U}|} f_X(k) \geq \texttt{minprob}, \quad (1)$$

where $\texttt{minprob} \in (0, 1]$ is a probability threshold given by users. In other words, a PFI is an itemset whose support is greater than or equal to `minsup` with a probability at least `minprob`. For example, when $\texttt{minsup} = 2$ and $\texttt{minprob} = 0.5$ with the UTDB in Table 1, the itemset {music} is a PFI, because

$$\begin{aligned} P(sup(\{\text{music}\}) \geq \texttt{minsup}) &= f_{\{\text{music}\}}(2) + f_{\{\text{music}\}}(3) \\ &= 0.47 + 0.28 \\ &= 0.75 > \texttt{minprob} \end{aligned}$$

Having defined a UTDB and PFI, the problem addressed in this paper is defined as follows. This problem is called *Probabilistic Frequent Itemset Mining* (PFIM).

Problem. Given a UTDB $\mathcal{U}$, `minsup`, and `minprob`, extract all PFIs from $\mathcal{U}$.

2.3 pApriori Algorithm

The Apriori algorithm, which was originally proposed by Agrawal *et al.* [3], is a well-known algorithm for association rule mining. Sun *et al.* [19] proposed pApriori that adapts

Apriori to uncertain transaction databases. The pApriori algorithm can be divided into two procedures:

1. Generating a set of *candidate* k-itemsets $\mathcal{C}_k$ from a set of $(k-1)$-PFIs $\mathcal{L}_{k-1}$
2. Extracting a set of k-PFIs $\mathcal{L}_k$ from $\mathcal{C}_k$

The pApriori algorithm continues these procedures alternately with incrementing k by one until no additional PFIs are detected. Note that, in the beginning of the algorithm, k's value is one and each candidate 1-itemset is an itemset whose element is merely one item in $\mathcal{U}$. Finally, the pApriori algorithm returns all the PFIs extracted from $\mathcal{U}$.

2.3.1 Generating Candidates

The procedure of generating candidate itemsets can be separated into two phases. The first phase is a merging phase and the second phase is a pruning phase.

In the merging phase, it is verified that two $(k-1)$-PFIs, X and Y, are *joinable*, that is, X and Y satisfy $X.item_1 = Y.item_1 \wedge \ldots \wedge X.item_{k-2} = Y.item_{k-2} \wedge X.item_{k-1} < Y.item_{k-1}$, where $X.item_i$ denotes the ith item of X in a certain order. If X and Y are joinable, a candidate k-itemset is created as the union of X and Y, and is stored in a set of candidate k-itemsets $\mathcal{C}_k$.

In the pruning phase, the following lemma is used in order to prune the candidates [19].

LEMMA 1 (ANTI-MONOTONICITY). *If an itemset X is a PFI, then any itemset $X' \subset X$ is also a PFI.*

The contraposition of this lemma yields that if any itemset $X' \subset X$ is not a PFI, then the itemset X is not a PFI either. Hence a candidate k-itemset can be pruned out when any size-$(k-1)$ subset of the candidate is not contained in a set of $(k-1)$-PFIs $\mathcal{L}_{k-1}$. If the candidate can be pruned out, it is deleted from $\mathcal{C}_k$.

2.3.2 Extracting Probabilistic Frequent Itemsets

In order to reveal whether or not an itemset X is a PFI, the SPMF of X needs to be computed and assigned to Equation 1. Since the number of possible worlds is exponentially large, a naïve solution to compute SPMFs is considered to be intractable. To address this problem, Sun *et al.* proposed two algorithms, a dynamic programming approach and a divide and conquer approach. Here, we only describe the latter algorithm because it is shown to be more efficient and more suitable for GPGPU.

The algorithm takes a UTDB $\mathcal{U}$ and an itemset X as its inputs, and returns the SPMF of X. If $\mathcal{U}$ contains only one transaction, it just computes the SPMF and returns the result. If $\mathcal{U}$ contains two or more transactions, it horizontally partitions $\mathcal{U}$ into two UTDBs ($\mathcal{U}_1$ and $\mathcal{U}_2$), and recursively applies the same algorithm to them. Having finished the computation for $\mathcal{U}_1$ and $\mathcal{U}_2$, the algorithm combines the resulting SPMFs into one SPMF and returns it as output. The point here is that two SPMFs are efficiently combined into one by convolution [19]. Although a naïve algorithm of the convolution has $O(n^2)$ time complexity, it can be improved to $O(n \log n)$ time complexity with the Fast Fourier Transform (FFT) algorithm.

2.3.3 Pruning

Owing to the high computational complexity of SPMF computations, it is desirable to prune infrequent itemsets without computing the SPMFs. Let $cnt(X)$ be the number of transactions that contain an itemset X in a UTDB $\mathcal{U}$ regardless of the existential probabilities. In addition, let $esup(X)$ be the expected support of X. With these two values, Sun *et al.* proved two lemmas [19]. By using these lemmas, candidates can be pruned in $O(|\mathcal{U}|)$ time.

LEMMA 2. *If $cnt(X) <$ `minsup`, then an itemset X is not a PFI.*

LEMMA 3. *Let $\mu = esup(X)$ and $\sigma = (\texttt{minsup} - \mu - 1) / \mu$. Then, X is not a PFI if,*

- $\sigma \geq 2e - 1$ *and* $2^{-\sigma\mu} < \texttt{minprob}$, *or*
- $0 < \sigma < 2e - 1$ *and* $\exp(\frac{-\sigma^2\mu}{4}) < \texttt{minprob}$.

3. GPGPU

GPGPU (General-Purpose computation on GPU) implies using a GPU (Graphics Processing Unit), which is a coprocessor originally designed for graphics processing, to accelerate general-purpose computation [8, 9, 11, 12, 13, 17, 21]. The GPU has recently been paid much attention from numerous researchers and developers as a many-core processor, because of its high performance, low price, and low power consumption, compared to CPUs. The GPU contains multiple SIMD processors, each of which is called a *Streaming Multiprocessor* (SM), and one SM consists of many processing units, each of which is called a *Streaming Processor* (SP).

3.1 CUDA

When developing GPGPU applications, the most common framework is CUDA[2] provided by NVIDIA. CUDA enables developers to write a program with the C programming language. CUDA provides fine-grained parallelism by spawning tens of thousands of lightweight threads. These threads are grouped together into multiple *thread blocks* (or *blocks* in short). Threads within a block are allocated to a same SM and can cooperate, sharing a local memory of the SM. The blocks compose a *grid*, which is generated for one process on the GPU.

Meanwhile, the GPU has several kinds of memories. The largest memory on the GPU is called *global memory*. For instance, NVIDIA Tesla C2050 has a global memory of 3GB. This memory can be accessible from all threads of GPU, and has a high bandwidth and a high access latency. In addition, the GPU contains another type of memory called *shared memory*, which is shared by all threads in a block and can be used to exchange data among the threads. The size of the shared memory is small, while the access latency is much lower than the global memory. To use these memories appropriately is one of the most important points in order to reach GPU's peak performance.

3.2 Data-Parallel Primitives

In this subsection, we describe data-parallel primitives on the GPU [11, 12, 23]. These primitives are highly optimized for the GPU, and can be used as building blocks to implement other operations.

[2] `http://www.nvidia.com/object/cuda_home_new.html`

3.2.1 Reduce

A *reduce* operation takes an array of n elements $[a_0, a_1, ..., a_{n-1}]$ and a binary associative operator $\oplus$, and returns the value $a_0 \oplus \cdots \oplus a_{n-1}$. If the binary operator is addition, the reduce operation computes the sum of the array. To implement the reduce primitive, we adopt the tree-based approach described in [23].

3.2.2 Scan

A *scan*, also known as *prefix sum*, operation takes an array of n elements $[a_0, a_1, ..., a_{n-1}]$ and a binary associative operator $\oplus$ with identity I, and returns the array $[I, a_0, a_0 \oplus a_1, ..., a_0 \oplus a_1 \oplus \cdots \oplus a_{n-2}]$. This operation is a useful building block for other primitives and many algorithms [12, 24]. We adopt the implementation from GPU Computing SDK[3].

4. GPU ACCELERATION OF PFIM

Although the above mentioned pApriori algorithm achieved an efficient way of probabilistic frequent itemset mining, even better performance is desirable when dealing with huge databases. To this end, we aim at improving performance of the pApriori algorithm exploiting the massive parallelism of a GPU.

We now describe a method for probabilistic frequent itemset mining using GPGPU. Here, we assume that items in transactions are denoted as integer values from zero to $|I|-1$. After transferring necessary data from a CPU to the GPU, this method runs entirely on the GPU. In Section 4.1, we explain data layouts on the GPU. Then, Sections 4.2 and 4.3 describe algorithms for generating candidate itemsets and extracting PFIs, respectively.

4.1 Data Layout on the GPU

We represent a UTDB $\mathcal{U}$ using two (1-dimensional) arrays on the GPU: an array of itemsets in transactions and an array of existential probabilities. For the first array, we use the ELL format, which is a format for representing sparse matrices. It is known that this format is well-suited to the GPU's architectures [5]. In the ELL format, an M-by-N sparse matrix with at most K nonzeros per row is stored as a dense M-by-K array of nonzeros and an array of column indexes. When considering itemsets of transactions in a UTDB as a matrix, each element contains merely one or zero. Therefore, we can represent the itemsets by storing only the latter array. In this case, K is the maximum size of transactions.

For example, the UTDB in Table 1 can be represented as arrays shown in Figure 2. In the figure, game, music, and video are denoted as 0, 1, and 2, respectively. Each row of the first array represents the itemset of a transaction. Since the length of each row is the maximum size of transactions, shorter rows are padded with a sentinel denoted as X. We use the number of items $|I|$ as the sentinel in our implementation. The second array just stores existential probabilities corresponding to the transactions. Note that the first array is stored in column-major order, i.e., the array is laid out in linear memory as 0, 1, 0, 0, 1, 2, X, 1, X, and so on. This layout enables the GPU to *coalesce* multiple memory accesses into one transaction when processing inclusion check that is described in Section 4.3.1.

[3]http://developer.nvidia.com/gpu-computing-sdk

$$(1)\begin{bmatrix} 0 & 1 & \mathrm{X} \\ 1 & 2 & \mathrm{X} \\ 0 & \mathrm{X} & \mathrm{X} \\ 0 & 1 & 2 \end{bmatrix} \qquad (2)\begin{bmatrix} 0.8 \\ 0.7 \\ 0.9 \\ 0.5 \end{bmatrix}$$

Figure 2: A UTDB on a GPU.

Algorithm 1 Extracting PFIs.

for all C in $\mathcal{C}_k$ **in parallel do**
  // Section 4.3.1
  Inclusion check of C
end for
for each C in $\mathcal{C}_k$ **do**
  // Section 4.3.2
  Pruning C
  // Section 4.3.3
  Filtering transactions
  // Section 4.3.4
  Computing the SPMF of C
end for

Meanwhile, we use an array of integers to represent itemsets. A k-itemset is stored in an integer array of k elements. Let now $\mathcal{S}_k$ be a set of k-itemsets, which corresponds to k-PFIs or candidate k-itemsets. Then, $\mathcal{S}_k$ is stored in an integer array of $k \cdot |\mathcal{S}_k|$ elements in the following way. The first itemset in $\mathcal{S}_k$ is stored in the array from 0 to $k-1$ elements, and the second itemset is stored in the array from k to $2 \cdot k - 1$ elements. In other words, the ith itemset occupies the elements from $(i-1) \cdot k$ to $i \cdot k - 1$.

4.2 Generating Candidates

The algorithm to generate candidates is similar to that of pApriori, although the details are different to adapt to GPGPU.

First, it allocates an integer array on the GPU that can store all candidate itemsets, i.e., an array of $k \cdot \binom{|\mathcal{L}_{k-1}|}{2}$ elements, where $\mathcal{L}_{k-1}$ is a set of $(k-1)$-PFIs. Then, it checks in parallel that pairs in $\mathcal{L}_{k-1}$ are joinable. If X_i and X_j are joinable, where X_i is the ith PFI in $\mathcal{L}_{k-1}$, they are combined into a candidate k-itemset, and the candidate stored in the array at an index corresponding to i and j. This index can be computed as $(|\mathcal{L}_{k-1}| - 1) \cdot i - i \cdot (i+1)/2 + j - 1$. If X_i and X_j are not joinable, -1 is assigned to the array at the index to indicate that the candidate is not a PFI. In the pruning phase, if it is confirmed that $\mathcal{L}_{k-1}$ does not contain any size-$(k-1)$ subset of the candidate, -1 is assigned to the array at the index of the candidate as before.

By allocating the array that stores all the candidate k-itemsets, we can generate the candidate itemsets with a few conditional branches in parallel.

4.3 Extracting PFIs

Algorithm 1 shows the procedure to extract PFIs that comprises four steps: inclusion check, pruning, filtering, and SPMF computation. Note that inclusion check is processed in parallel for all candidates and the other steps are taken for each candidate. The following sections describe these four steps one by one.

4.3.1 Inclusion Check

It is necessary to compute an SPMF in order to judge whether a candidate X is a PFI. To compute the SPMF, we firstly need to check whether each transaction in a UTDB $\mathcal{U}$ includes the candidate X. Here, we call this process *inclusion check* of the candidate X in the UTDB $\mathcal{U}$. In fact, a straight forward implementation of inclusion check using iterative loops with conditional branching deteriorates the performance, because GPUs cannot execute such codes in parallel due to the architecture's limitation. Although latest GPUs support parallel execution of conditional branching, it is more desirable to investigate a method that can be executed efficiently on GPUs.

First, $|\mathcal{C}_k|$ arrays of $|\mathcal{U}|$ elements need to be prepared in order to store the results of inclusion checks, where $\mathcal{C}_k$ is a set of candidate k-itemsets. Since the arrays only holds one or zero, it is wasteful to represent the result of each transaction as one integer element. In addition, as the number of candidates is increasing, the arrays get larger and larger. As a result, the size of the arrays may exceed a capacity of the global memory. Therefore, we store the results to 4-byte integers arrays as bitstrings, thereby reducing the number of necessary elements to $\lceil |\mathcal{U}| \ / \ 32 \rceil \cdot |\mathcal{C}_k|$.

In the inclusion check, each block on the GPU deals with 32 transactions and each thread in a block checks $|\mathcal{C}_k|/B$ candidates, where B is the number of threads in one block. In other words, one thread conducts the inclusion checks of $|\mathcal{C}_k|/B$ candidates with regard to 32 transactions, and stores these 32 binary values into one element of the resultant arrays. We allocate one thread to 32 transactions so that the thread can store the results to the arrays without a lock because each element of the resultant arrays is considered as a 4-byte integer. Besides, transactions that are accessed from a block are transferred to the shared memory before the inclusion checks, because the transactions are shared by threads in the block and are read multiple times. Furthermore, since the threads read consecutive addresses on the global memory thanks to the column-major order, these accesses are coalesced into fewer memory reads. and the transfers can be done fast.

For each candidate, each thread judge whether transactions include the candidate by linear search. Linear search enables threads in a block to read same data on the shared memory at the same time. These memory accesses are broadcasted to all the threads and thus take only one access time, resulting in quite fast memory reads. A bit corresponding to the transaction is set to one, if a transaction includes all items in the candidate; otherwise the bit is set to zero.

Optimization. In the case of $k > 1$, it is not necessary to scan the whole database by reusing the inclusion check results for $k-1$. In this case, we borrow the idea from [8]. The inclusion check of a candidate k-itemset X is processed as bitwise AND operations between two $(k-1)$-PFIs that are used to create the candidate X. For example, the inclusion check of {game, music} can be computed as bitwise AND operations between the two arrays of the inclusion checks of {game} and {music}. This method substantially reduces accesses to the global memory and make inclusion checks run much faster.

Algorithm 2 Decode a bitstring.

Input: integer x

1: nls = `__popc(x)` // the number of bits set to one
2: acc = −1 // accumulating the position of the first set bit to maintain an index
3: **for** i = 0 to nls − 1 **do**
4: pos = `__ffs(x)`
5: acc = acc + pos
6: *do some operation using* acc *as an index*
7: x = x >> pos
8: **end for**

4.3.2 Pruning

Having finished inclusion check, the next step is to prune the candidates out. As explained in Section 2.3.3, pruning requires computing *cnt* and *esup*.

$cnt(X)$ means the number of transactions which include the candidate X. This value can be computed by summing the numbers of bits set to one in the array of the inclusion check of X. For this computation, the reduce primitive (Section 3.2.1) is utilized. Meanwhile, $esup(X)$ means the expected number of $sup(X)$, which can be computed by summing all existential probabilities of transactions that include the candidate X. We also use the reduce primitive for this computation. However, the reduce primitive cannot be applied directly, because the elements in the arrays of inclusion checks are bitstrings. It is thus necessary to get indexes of the transactions encoded in the bitstrings.

To this end, we exploit two GPU intrinsic functions, `__ffs` and `__popc` [21]. `__ffs` takes an integer and returns the position of the first (least significant) set bit. `__popc` takes an integer and returns the number of bits that are set to one in the binary representation. Combining these functions, an algorithm to decode a bitstring can be written as pseudocode in Algorithm 2. This algorithm enables us to work only with bits set to one. Since `__ffs` returns the position of the first set bit, an index of the first transaction in a bitstring that contain the candidate is obtained at the first iteration. Then, some operation is done with *acc* as an index, and x is shifted right by *pos* bits to make the first set bit disappear. The algorithm repeats these operations `__popc`(x) (the number of bits set to one in x) times.

Actually, the computation of *cnt* requires only the number of bits that are set to one. Hence, there is no need to use this algorithm and using `__popc` is enough. In the case of *esup*, on the other hand, the indexes of the transactions are necessary for addressing existential probabilities. For each bitstring, the existential probabilities corresponding to the transactions in the bitstring are summed at line 6 in Algorithm 2. The results of `__popc` and the summed probabilities are handed to the reduce primitives as input arrays with the addition operator.

If the candidate is determined to be pruned by evaluating Lemmas 2 and 3, the procedure to extract PFIs continues to a next candidate; otherwise it proceeds to the next step.

4.3.3 Filtering

To compute the SPMF of a candidate X, it is sufficient to use the transactions that include X, and the other transactions can be ignored because these transactions do not contribute to the SPMF. To discard the unnecessary transactions, we use the filter primitive that is described in [12].

We firstly decode the array of the inclusion check of X by using Algorithm 2, and store the result to an array of $|\mathcal{U}|$ elements. The elements of this array are *flags* indicating whether transactions include the candidate. Then, the scan operation is applied to the *flags* array with the addition operator and the result is stored in another array. This array holds *indexes* of the non-filtered transactions. These *flags* and *indexes* arrays are used in the next step to initialize SPMFs.

4.3.4 SPMF Computation

Since the computation of an SPMF is the most computationally intensive part of the pApriori algorithm, we must carefully parallelize this computation.

First, we allocate an array of $4 \cdot 2^{\lceil \log_2 |cnt(X)| \rceil}$ elements, denoted by F_X, to store first SPMFs. In other words, the number of elements is 4 multiplied by the next power of two of $cnt(X)$. Then, each GPU thread computes the SPMF of X in a UTDB consisting of one transaction, by referring the precomputed *flags* and *indexes* arrays in the last step. For the ith transaction of the input UTDB, *indexes*[i] is the position for storing the SPMF to the output array, if *flags*[i] is 1. The thread stores the computed SPMF to the array F_X, so that the SPMF occupies four elements of F_X. The reasons that the size of F_X is $4 \cdot 2^{\lceil \log_2 |cnt(X)| \rceil}$ is as follows:

1. The number of SPMFs in F_X must be the power of two in order to combine the SPMFs into one SPMF with repeated convolutions.
2. Each area of an SPMF must be able to accommodate a convoluted SPMF, which has three elements after the first convolution.
3. Making the size of each SPMF the power of two is beneficial to the performance of FFT [22].

To make the size of SPMFs the power of two and larger than three, zero padding (padding extra elements with zero) is carried out. Then, the convolutions of two adjacent SPMFs on F_X are computed, by performing Fast Fourier Transform (FFT), computing the pairwise products of the two transformed SPMFs, and performing inverse FFT (IFFT) on the multiplied one.

For the FFT and IFFT, we use CUFFT, which is the CUDA FFT library [22]. The CUFFT library provide a simple interface for computing parallel FFTs on an NVIDIA GPU. The performance of any transform size that can be factored as $2^a \cdot 3^b \cdot 5^c \cdot 7^d$ (where a, b, c, and d are non-negative integers) is optimized in the CUFFT library. In particular, the library achieves the best performance when transforming the 2^a size. We can also use batch execution that is a feature of CUFFT, by storing the SPMFs in one array with the same size,

The two operations (zero padding and convolutions) continue until the number of SPMFs becomes one. Finally, the SPMF is stored in the array $F_X[0]$ to $F_X[cnt(X)]$.

Figure 3 illustrates one iteration plus zero padding of the SPMF computation of $f_{\{\text{music}\}}$ in Table 1. f_X^i denotes the SPMF of {music} in a UTDB consisting of the ith transaction that include {music}. The first element of f_X^i is the value of $f_{\{\text{music}\}}^i(0)$ and the second element shows $f_{\{\text{music}\}}^i(1)$. The shaded area indicates the elements that are updated with a previous operation. It can be seen that two convoluted SPMFs are obtained after IFFT. Note that

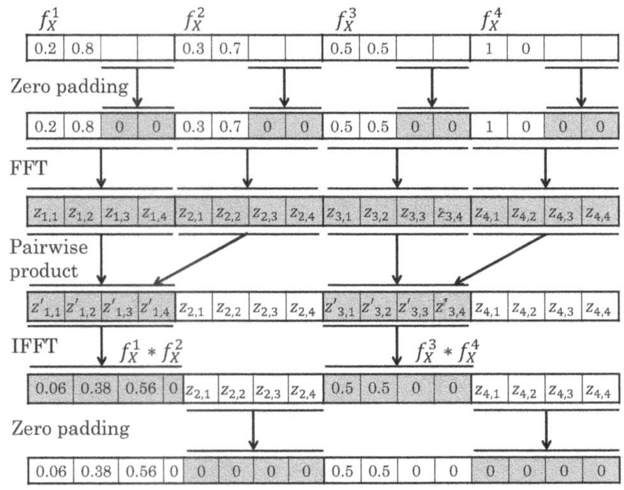

Figure 3: One iteration of SPMF computation.

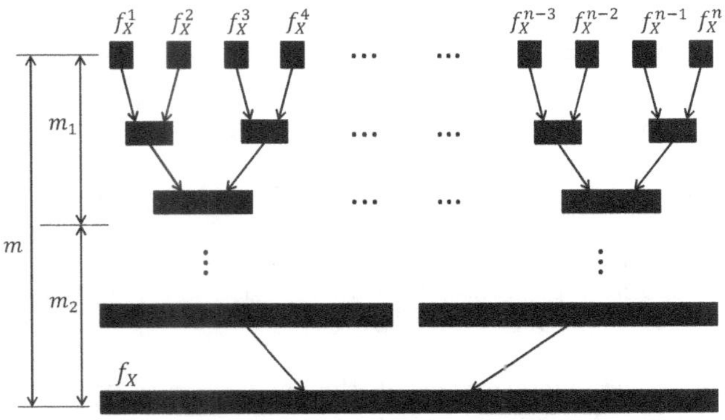

Figure 4: A tree structure of SPMF computation.

IFFT is only performed on half of the SPMFs and the other half is padded with zero, thereby enabling next convolutions to take SPMFs of a power-of-two size.

Optimization. The SPMF computation process is represented as a tree structure in Figure 4. A node means an SPMF and its size indicates the size of the SPMF. In the figure, n denotes the number of first SPMFs, $2^{\lceil \log_2 |cnt(X)| \rceil}$, and m denotes the height of the tree, $\log_2 n = \lceil \log_2 |cnt(X)| \rceil$.

The SPMF computation begins from the leaf nodes. By executing convolutions repeatedly, the sizes of the SPMFs are gradually increasing and the number of SPMFs is decreasing. That is, in the beginning of the computation, there are many small SPMFs to be convoluted. Since these SPMFs do not get so large in the first a few levels, the convolutions can be computed on the shared memory of a GPU. Therefore, we consider dividing the SPMF computation into two phases, m_1 level phase and m_2 level phase in Figure 4. In the first phase, the convolutions are directly computed entirely on the shared memory. In the second phase, we use the previously explained algorithm to compute the convolutions.

Table 2: Characteristics of datasets.

Dataset	Type	# of items	Avg. size of transactions	# of transactions	Density	Probability distribution
connect	real	129	43	67,557	33%	$\mathcal{U}(0,1)$
Accidents	real	468	33.8	340,183	7.2%	$\mathcal{N}(0.5,0.02)$
T40I10D100K	synthetic	942	39.6	100,000	4.2%	$\mathcal{U}(0,1)$
T25I10D500K	synthetic	7558	25.0	499,960	0.33%	$\mathcal{N}(0.8,0.01)$

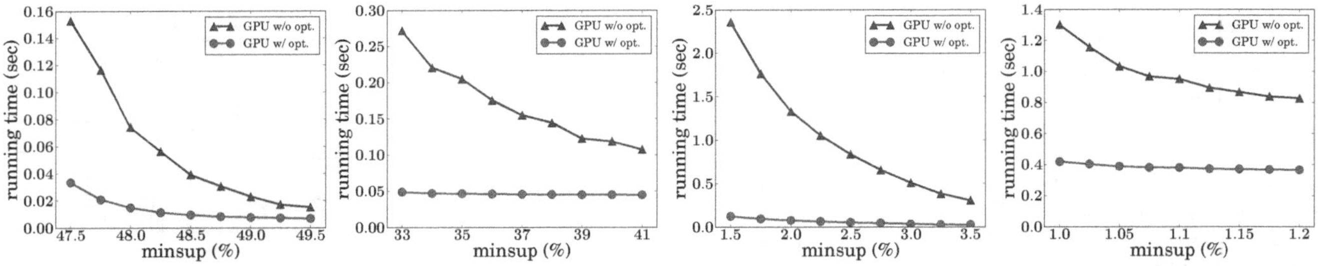

(a) connect (b) Accidents (c) T40I10D100K (d) T25I10D500K

Figure 5: Impact of optimization for inclusion check on performance.

5. EXPERIMENTS

5.1 Experimental Setup

We have implemented our approach using CUDA 4.1 and conducted experiments on a NVIDIA C2050, which has 14 SMs each of which consists of 32 SPs with 1.15 GHz and has a global memory of 3GB. We have also run the pApriori algorithm on a Intel Xeon E5620 CPU (2.40 GHz) with memory of 4GB.

We have used four datasets for the experiments. Table 2 summarizes characteristics of the datasets. The density of a dataset is computed as the average length of transactions divided by the number of items.

The first dataset *connect* and second dataset *Accidents* are real datasets that are accessible on Frequent Itemset Mining Implementations (FIMI) Repository[4]. connect is the densest one in the four datasets. For connect, existential probabilities are given by a uniform distribution between 0 and 1. For Accidents, existential probabilities are randomly drawn from a normal distribution with mean 0.5 and variance 0.02. The default values of `minsup` are 48% and 35% respectively.

The third and fourth datasets, called *T40I10D100K* and *T25I10D500K* respectively, are synthetic datasets generated by IBM data generator[5]. T25I10D500K is the sparsest one in the four datasets. Existential probabilities for each dataset are given by a uniform distribution between 0 and 1, and a normal distribution with mean 0.8 and variance 0.01 respectively. `minsups` are set to be 2.0% and 1.0% for each dataset if not specified.

For all the datasets, the default value of `minprob` is 0.5.

5.2 Experimental Results

We have conducted extensive experiments to evaluate several parts of our GPU-based method. Sections 5.2.1 through 5.2.3 show the results for each part of the GPU-based pApriori algorithm, namely, inclusion check, pruning, and SPMF computation, and Section 5.2.4 shows the result for the whole method. For all the experiments, we omit the results when changing `minprob` because it does not quite affect running times.

5.2.1 *Performance of Inclusion Check*

In these experiments, we evaluate the impact of the optimization scheme (described in Section 4.3.1) for inclusion check on the performance. Figures 5(a), 5(b), 5(c), and 5(d) depict running times with varying `minsup`, which is the percentage of the size of dataset. In the graphs, `GPU w/ opt.` plots the running times that are measured with the optimized method, and `GPU w/o opt.` plots the running times without the optimization. We have not compared our GPU-based method with the CPU-based method, because the CPU-based method carry out inclusion check and pruning at the same time and thus it is difficult to compare these two methods directly.

By applying the optimization, we achieve 3–19x speedups on all the datasets. As decreasing the value of `minsup`, the optimized method gains more and more performance improvements. This behavior is because a small value of `minsup` makes the number of candidates large and then inclusion check must handle numerous candidates. In particular, when `minsup` is 1.5 % on T40I10D100K, `GPU w/ opt.` outperforms `GPU w/o opt.` by a factor of 19.2.

5.2.2 *Performance of Pruning*

We also compare the two pruning methods, with and without Algorithm 2 (denoted by `GPU w/ Alg.2` and `GPU w/o Alg.2` respectively). `GPU w/o Alg.2` simply loops 32 times to manipulate each bit. Figures 6(a), 6(b), 6(c), and 6(d) illustrates running times vs. `minsup` on the four datasets. We have not compared our GPU-based method with the CPU-based method for the same reason in the previous section.

From the figures, it can be said that if a dataset is dense, then the performance of Algorithm 2 degrades, and if a dataset is sparse, the algorithm is beneficial to performance. For example, `GPU w/ Alg.2` is about 1.2 times slower than `GPU w/o Alg.2` on connect and Accidents. On the other

[4]`http://fimi.cs.helsinki.fi/`

[5]`http://miles.cnuce.cnr.it/~palmeri/datam/DCI/datasets.php`

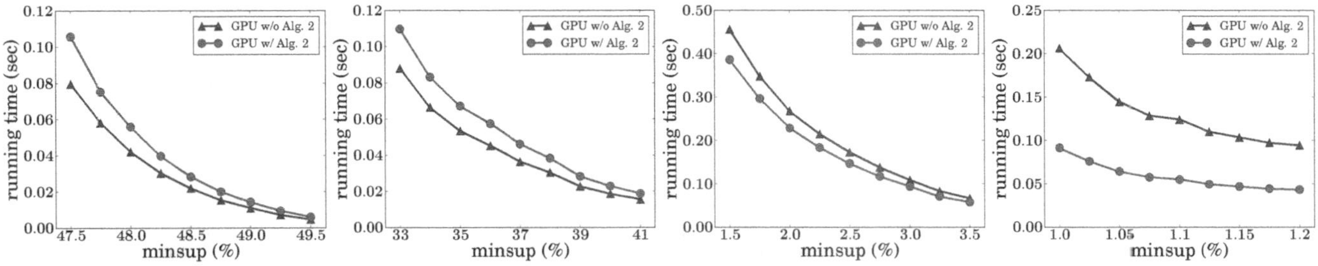

(a) connect (b) Accidents (c) T40I10D100K (d) T25I10D500K

Figure 6: Impact of Algorithm 2 on performance.

Table 3: SPMF Computation times.

Dataset	k	CPU (ms)	GPU (ms) w/o filtering	GPU (ms) $m_1 = 0$	GPU (ms) $m_1 = 8$	Overall speedup
connect	1	376	6.88	5.91	3.78	99.5
	5	281	6.87	4.70	2.97	94.6
Accidents	1	1990	28.2	26.2	18.6	107
	5	1341	28.2	16.2	12.8	105
T40I10D100K	1	22.9	6.94	0.94	0.57	40.2
	2	12.1	6.94	0.78	0.47	25.7
T25I10D500K	1	20.5	28.2	0.99	0.62	33.1
	5	16.2	28.2	0.92	0.58	27.9

hand, on T40I10D100K and T25I10D500K, `GPU w/ Alg.2` achieves better performance. In particular, this method is about 2 times faster than `GPU w/o Alg.2` on T25I10D500K. The reason for this behavior can be explained as follows: The efficiency of Algorithm 2 depends on the number of bits set to one in an input integer. If most of the bits are set to on, the algorithm performs a number of wasteful instructions compared to simple loops. In contrast, the algorithm can only process necessary bits with fewer instructions when few bits are set to one.

5.2.3 *Performance of SPMF Computation*

We have measured running times of SPMF computation on the four datasets. Table 3 summarizes the results that are computed as the average of the measured times for each value of k. The `w/o filtering` column shows the results without the filtering method described in Section 4.3.3. The $m_1 = 0$ and $m_1 = 8$ columns means the results with filtering and setting m_1 in Figure 4 to the respective value. $m_1 = 0$ indicates the method that uses no shared memory and computes SPMFs entirely on global memory. On the other hand, $m_1 = 8$ implies exploiting the shared memory. In our preliminary experiments with varying m_1, $m_1 = 8$ has achieved the best performance.

The `w/o filtering` method much improves the performance on connect and Accidents. By contrast, the performance gain on T40I10D100K is modest, and moreover it is slower than the CPU-based method on T25I10D500K. The cause for such results is that the method processes all the transactions that include a large number of unnecessary ones. For instance, T25I10D500K has about 500,000 transactions, although the number of essential ones for SPMF computations is nearly 15,000. In fact, by filtering the transactions, we obtain substantial speedups as shown in the $m_1 = 0$ column. In particular, filtering increases the speeds by a factor of 28 on T25I10D500K. Furthermore, applying filtering makes the SPMF computations for larger itemsets faster because the number of discarded transactions increases as k gets larger.

In addition, the method to utilize shared memory ($m_1 = 8$ column) further increases the speed by a factor of 1.5. Finally, our method achieves about 100x speedups on connect and Accidents, and 25–40x speedups on T40I10D100K and T25I10D500K. The reason for the difference between the speedup ratios is considered as follows: The time complexity for computation of f_X is $O(cnt(X)\log^2(cnt(X)))$, i.e., dependent on $cnt(X)$ [19]. Furthermore, the bigger the value of $cnt(X)$ is, the larger the size of SPMFs is. In our cases, the value of $cnt(X)$ is likely to be high on connect (about 65,000) and Accidents (between 200,000 and 300,000), and low on T40I10D100K and T25I10D500K (between 10,000 and 15,000). Hence, GPU's high parallelism is fully utilized on connect and Accidents to compute large FFTs. On the other hand, the SPMF computation is not a quite computationally intensive task on T40I10D100K and T25I10D500K. Consequently, we achieve the speedups but not to the extent on connect and Accidents.

5.2.4 *Performance of PFIM*

We compare three methods for probabilistic frequent itemset mining: the pApriori algorithm (`CPU`), our GPU-based method (`GPU`), and a GPU-based method of [13] (`GPU-MUD`). The running times vs. `minsup` on the four datasets are shown in Figures 7(a), 7(b), 7(c), and 7(d). Breakdowns of our method's running times are illustrated in Figure 8 as well.

Figures 7(a) and 7(b) depict the results on connect and Accidents, respectively. `GPU` is two orders of magnitude faster than `CPU`, and outperforms `GPU-MUD` by a factor of 3 to 5. The speedup of PFIM directly reflects that of SPMF computation, because the SPMF computations dominate the overall running times as shown in Figure 8.

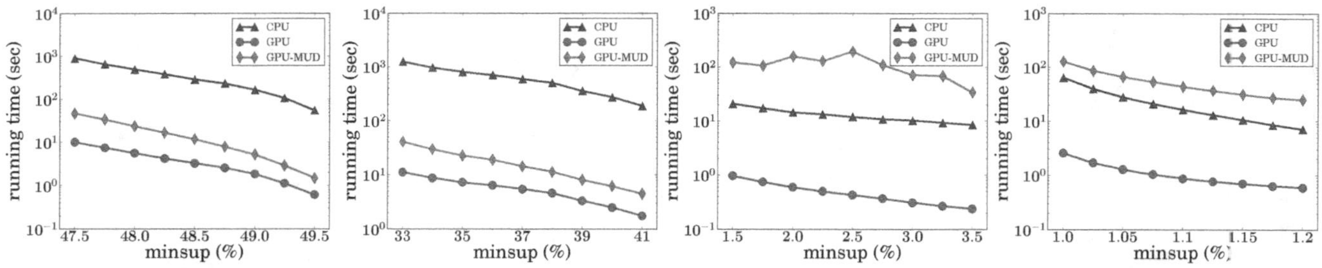

(a) connect (b) Accidents (c) T40I10D100K (d) T25I10D500K

Figure 7: Running times of probabilistic frequent itemset mining.

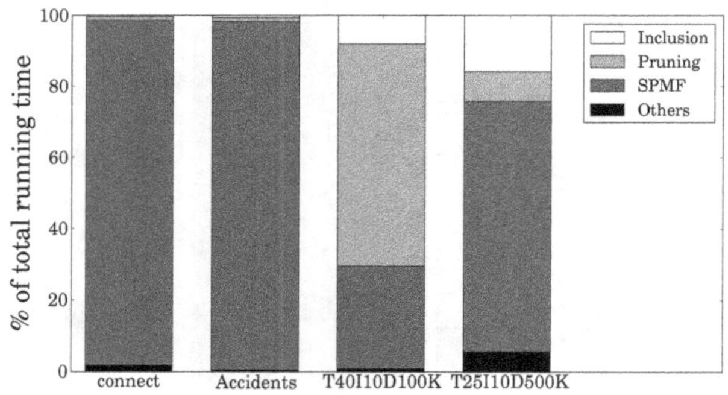

Figure 8: Running time breakdowns.

Figures 7(c) and 7(d) illustrate the results on T40I10D100K and T25I10D500K, respectively. On these two datasets, `GPU` is up to 35 times faster than `CPU`, and achieves considerable speedups compared with `GPU-MUD`. In particular, when `minsup` is 2.5% on T40I10D100K, the speedup ratio is 451. This performance gain is caused by the optimization of inclusion check and pruning, where `GPU-MUD` uses naïve methods. Meanwhile, since the SPMF computation does not dominates the running times on these two datasets as shown in Figure 8, the speedup ratios of PFIM are about the middles between those of SPMF computation and inclusion check and/or pruning.

6. RELATED WORK

In this section, we briefly review related work on frequent itemset mining, probabilistic frequent itemset mining, and GPGPU (General-Purpose computation on GPU).

6.1 Frequent Itemset Mining

The association rule mining problem was firstly introduced by Agrawal *et al.* [2]. Frequent itemset mining can be considered as the first step for association rule mining. To accelerate this step, many efficient algorithms were developed. In such algorithms, there are two major algorithms, Apriori [3] and FP-growth [10].

Parallelization of these algorithms has been widely studied in many literatures [4, 18, 16, 15, 14]. Agrawal *et al.* [4] presented three parallel algorithms, based upon Apriori on a shared-nothing architecture, that explore several tradeoffs such as computation, communication, and synchronization. Parthasarathy *et al.* [18] parallelized the Apriori algorithm that uses hash trees. They developed a parallel implementation on a shared-memory multi-processor, taking into account load balancing, data locality, and false sharing. Liu *et al.* [16] proposed a cache-conscious FP-array to improve the spatial locality of FP-growth, and a lock-free dataset tiling approach to fully utilize a modern multi-core processor. Li *et al.* [15] designed a parallel algorithm of FP-growth on a massive computing environment using MapReduce. More recently, Özkural *et al.* [14] introduced a data distribution scheme that divides the frequent itemset mining task in a top-down manner, and developed two parallel algorithms based on this data distribution scheme.

6.2 Probabilistic Frequent Itemset Mining

While the above mentioned parallel algorithms work well for the conventional *certain* transaction databases, they cannot effectively process frequent itemset mining from uncertain databases, which gains increasing importance in order to handle data uncertainty. There is a lot of work for modeling, querying, and mining such uncertain data (see a survey by Aggarwal *et al.* [1] for details and more information).

To mine frequent itemsets with taking into account the uncertainty, a number of methods have been proposed [7, 6, 19, 20]. Chui *et al.* [7] proposed the U-Apriori algorithm that computes the expected support of itemsets by summing up all itemset probabilities. Later, Bernecker *et al.* [6] found that the use of expected support may result in missing important itemsets. Instead, they consider the probability that an itemset is frequent. While [6, 7] deal with the uncertain data model that assume each item in transactions is associated with a confidence value, which is called *attribute-uncertainty model*, Sun *et al.* [19] consider the *tuple-uncertainty model*, where each transaction has an existential probability. Wang *et al.* [20] proposed a model-based approach to accelerate probability computations for both the attribute-uncertainty model and tuple-uncertainty model.

6.3 GPGPU

GPGPU is another hot research topic and has been paid attention from database community as well as high performance computing researchers. Govindaraju *et al.* [9] presented GPUTeraSort that used a GPU as a co-processor to sort databases with billions of records. He *et al.* [11] developed a set of data-parallel primitives, and implemented several relational join algorithms for GPGPU, using the primitives as building blocks. In [12], He *et al.* extended the primitives, implemented other relational operators, developed cost models for CPU-GPU coprocessing, and finally presented a CPU-GPU hybrid method. Additional information of GPGPU can be found in a survey by Owens *et al.* [17].

Frequent itemset mining from "certain" databases on GPU was studied by Fang *et al.* [8]. They proposed two approaches, a GPU-based method and a CPU-GPU hybrid method, for the GPU with massive SIMD parallelism. The GPU-based method utilized bitstrings and bit operations for fast support counting, running entirely on the GPU. The hybrid method adopted the trie structure on CPU and counted supports on GPU.

Our previous work [13] proposed an approach for probabilistic frequent itemset mining using GPGPU. This approach has some limitations and our work aims to overcome them. To this end, we decompose the procedure extracting PFIs into four steps and then optimize each step for GPU. In particular, we employ the ELL format instead of the CSR format, which is used in [13], a bitstring-based method, data-parallel primitives such as reduce and scan, and a tree-based approach.

7. CONCLUSION

This paper proposed a method for probabilistic frequent itemset mining using GPGPU based on the pApriori algorithm. The main idea is to accelerate SPMF computations by employing a filter primitive and tree-based approach with low-latency memory on the GPU. We also presented an algorithm to efficiently manipulate a bitstring and utilized a reduce primitive to achieve high parallelism. We have implemented our method using CUDA and compared the performance with the original pApriori algorithm and our previous GPU-based approach. We observe that our method outperforms the pApriori algorithm by a factor of two orders of magnitude on a non-sparse dataset, and by a factor of 35 on sparse datasets. In addition, the experiments show that our new GPU-based approach runs considerably faster than the previous one, on sparse datasets in particular.

As future work, we plan to extend our method to multi-GPU system, which utilizes multiple GPUs.

8. ACKNOWLEDGMENTS

This work is supported in part by JSPS KAKENHI Grant Number 24240015 and the HA-PACS Project for advanced interdisciplinary computational sciences by exa-scale computing technology.

9. REFERENCES

[1] C. C. Aggarwal and P. S. Yu. A Survey of Uncertain Data Algorithms and Applications. *TKDE*, 21(5), 2009.

[2] R. Agrawal, T. Imielinski, and A. Swami. Mining Association Rules between Sets of Items in Large Databases. *SIGMOD*, 1993.

[3] R. Agrawal and R. Srikant. Fast Algorithms for Mining Association Rules. In *VLDB*, 1994.

[4] R. Agrawal and J. C. Shafer. Parallel Mining of Association Rules. *TKDE*, 8(6), 1996.

[5] N. Bell and M. Garland. Implementing Sparse Matrix-Vector Multiplication on Throughput-Oriented Processors. In *SC*, 2009.

[6] T. Bernecker, H.-P. Kriegel, M. Renz, F. Verhein, and A. Zuefle. Probabilistic Frequent Itemset Mining in Uncertain Databases. In *KDD*, 2009.

[7] C.-K. Chui, B. Kao, and E. Hung. Mining Frequent Itemsets from Uncertain Data. In *PAKDD*, 2007.

[8] W. Fang, M. Lu, X. Xiao, B. He, and Q. Luo. Frequent Itemset Mining on Graphics Processors. In *DaMoN*, 2009.

[9] N. K. Govindaraju, J. Gray, R. Kumar, and D. Manocha. GPUTeraSort: High Performance Graphics Co-processor Sorting for Large Database Management. In *SIGMOD*, 2006.

[10] J. Han, J. Pei, and Y. Yin. Mining Frequent Patterns without Candidate Generation. In *SIGMOD*, 2000.

[11] B. He, K. Yang, M. Lu, N. K. Govindaraju, Q. Luo, and P. V. Sander. Relational Joins on Graphics Processors. In *SIGMOD*, 2008.

[12] B. He, M. Lu, K. Yang, R. Fang, N. K. Govindaraju, Q. Luo, and P. V. Sander. Relational Query Coprocessing on Graphics Processors. *ACM Trans. Database Syst.*, 34(4), 2009.

[13] Y. Kozawa, T. Amagasa, and H. Kitagawa. Fast Frequent Itemset Mining from Uncertain Databases using GPGPU. In *MUD*, 2011.

[14] E. Özkural, B. Uçar, and C. Aykanat. Parallel Frequent Item Set Mining with Selective Item Replication. *TPDS*, 22(10), 2011.

[15] H. Li, Y. Wang, D. Zhang, M. Zhang, and E. Y. Chang. PFP: Parallel FP-Growth for Query Recommendation. In *RecSys*, 2008.

[16] L. Liu, E. Li, Y. Zhang, and Z. Tang. Optimization of Frequent Itemset Mining on Multiple-Core Processor. In *VLDB*, 2007.

[17] J. D. Owens, D. Luebke, N. Govindaraju, M. Harris, J. Krüger, A. E. Lefohn, and T. J. Purcell. A Survey of General-Purpose Computation on Graphics Hardware. In *Computer Graphics Forum*, 2007.

[18] S. Parthasarathy, M. J. Zaki, M. Ogihara, and W. Li. Parallel Data Mining for Association Rules on Shared-Memory Systems. *Knowledge and Information Systems*, 3(1), 2001.

[19] L. Sun, R. Cheng, D. W. Cheung, and J. Cheng. Mining Uncertain Data with Probabilistic Guarantees. In *KDD*, 2010.

[20] L. Wang, R. Cheng, S. D. Lee, and D. W. Cheung. Accelerating Probabilistic Frequent Itemset Mining: A Model-Based Approach. In *CIKM*, 2010.

[21] NVIDIA. CUDA C Programming Guide. `http://developer.download.nvidia.com/compute/DevZone/docs/html/C/doc/CUDA_C_Programming_Guide.pdf`, 2012.

[22] NVIDIA. CUFFT Library User Guide. `http://developer.download.nvidia.com/compute/DevZone/docs/html/CUDALibraries/doc/CUFFT_Library.pdf`, 2012.

[23] M. Harris. Optimizing Parallel Reduction in CUDA. `http://developer.download.nvidia.com/compute/cuda/2_2/sdk/website/projects/reduction/doc/reduction.pdf`, 2007.

[24] M. Harris. Parallel Prefix Sum (Scan) with CUDA. `http://developer.download.nvidia.com/compute/cuda/2_2/sdk/website/projects/scan/doc/scan.pdf`, 2009.

Completeness of Queries over SQL Databases

Werner Nutt
Free University of Bozen-Bolzano
Dominikanerplatz 3
39100 Bozen, Italy
nutt@inf.unibz.it

Simon Razniewski
Free University of Bozen-Bolzano
Dominikanerplatz 3
39100 Bozen, Italy
razniewski@inf.unibz.it

ABSTRACT

Data completeness is an important aspect of data quality. We consider a setting, where databases can be incomplete in two ways: records may be missing and records may contain null values. We (i) formalize when the answer set of a query is complete in spite of such incompleteness, and (ii) we introduce table completeness statements, by which one can express that certain parts of a database are complete. We then study how to deduce from a set of table-completeness statements that a query can be answered completely.

Null values as used in SQL are ambiguous. They can indicate either that no attribute value exists or that a value exists, but is unknown. We study completeness reasoning for the different interpretations. We show that in the combined case it is necessary to syntactically distinguish between different kinds of null values and present an encoding for doing that in standard SQL databases. With this technique, any SQL DBMS evaluates complete queries correctly with respect to the different meanings that nulls can carry. We study the complexity of completeness reasoning and provide algorithms that in most cases agree with the worst-case lower bounds.

Categories and Subject Descriptors

H.2.7 [**Database Management**]: Database Administration

Keywords

Data Quality, Data Completeness, Metadata Management

1. INTRODUCTION

Decisions in business, politics and administration are taken on the basis of an ever increasing supply of information. To make the right decision, it is crucial to know how reliable the underlying data is. Often, data from diverse backgrounds are combined, which originate independently and according to different policies. As a consequence, the quality of the data may largely vary.

CIKM'12, October 29–November 2, 2012, Maui, HI, USA.

Aspects of data quality concern accuracy, currency, correctness, and similar issues [3]. In settings such as manual data insertion or data integration, completeness of data plays a key role [15]. Many approaches aim to improve data quality by inspecting and transforming concrete data. For instance, there is a wealth of techniques to detect and eliminate duplicate records. To deal with data completeness, such approaches have limited applicability: by inspecting data it is hard to detect whether or not something is missing.

Consider as a driving example the management of school data in a school district, which motivated the technical work reported here. The schools in the district are largely autonomous in the way they run their business: although the district provides a central database for administering data about students, teachers and the like, the schools can choose to what extent to use this system. As a consequence, on many topics data is incomplete, which becomes a problem when statistics about the schools are needed. While in principle, those statistics could be generated by queries over the database, the administration does not know whether or not it can trust the answers. In particular, if an item does not show up in a query result, or has the value null in an attribute, it is unclear whether that item does not have the property queried for in reality, or relevant data were just not submitted. The administration has some knowledge as to what data individual schools put into the central database. The question is how such metadata can be utilized to judge whether it is complete and thus can be trusted.

The first researcher to address this question was Motro who formalized completeness of databases and queries [14]. Halevy introduced statements, by which one can express that certain parts of a database are complete and raised the question how to use such statements to infer query completeness [12]. Recently, Razniewski and Nutt provided a general solution to this problem, including a technique to design algorithms and a comprehensive study of the complexity [16]. All this work considered only incompleteness in the form of missing records. In practice however, incompleteness in the form of *null* values is at least the same important. To take into account nulls we extend in this work previous formalisms by refining the granularity of completeness descriptions.

A problem with *null*s as used in standard SQL databases is their ambiguity, as those *null*s may mean both that an attribute value exists but is unknown, or that no value applies to that attribute. The established models of null values, such as Codd, v-, and c-tables [13], avoid this ambiguity by concentrating on the aspect of unknown values. In this work, we consider the ambiguous standard SQL *null* values [5], because those are the ones used in practice.

In this paper, we define a formal framework to study reasoning about the completeness of query answers over databases with *null* values and missing records. In Section 2, we introduce a school database as running example. Sections 3 formalizes databases with null values, incomplete databases and completeness statements. Section 4 presents the reasoning for simple, uniform meanings of null values, while in Section 5 we point out the limitations when combining the different meanings. Section 6 shows how the different meanings of nulls can be made explicit in standard SQL databases, while Sections 7 shows that reasoning is possible in that case. Section 8 discusses the reasoning for queries under bag semantics, Section 9 the complexity of reasoning, and Section 10 related work.

2. EXAMPLE: SCHOOL DATABASE

Our running example is that of a school database, which contains, inter alia, the following two tables:

- `student` (`name`, `classCode`, `homeTown`)
- `class` (`code`, `formTeacher`, `profile`)

The `student` table stores for each student the name, the class and the home town. Because we assume that the school is situated in a remote area, some students do not belong to any class but are taught at home. This would be indicated by a *null* value for the `classCode` attribute. It may also happen that there is no entry for the `homeTown` attribute, because the student did not provide this information or the secretary did not enter the data yet.

The `class` table stores the classes of the school. For each class, it stores its code, its form teacher and its profile, such as arts, science or similar. The `formTeacher` attribute may be *null*, because the decision of forming a class may have been taken before assigning the form teachers, or because the secretary may have forgotten to insert the form teacher. The profile attribute can be *null*, because some classes do not have a special profile.

3. FORMALISATION

In the following, we introduce standard notations about databases with null values and query evaluation, and introduce the notions of partial databases, query completeness and table completeness that we use in reasoning about completeness.

3.1 Relational Databases

A database *schema* is a set of relation symbols Σ each with an arity. In the following, we assume the schema to be fixed. We assume an infinite set of constants *dom* including a special symbol $\perp$ for null values.

For a relation R with arity n, an *atom* is an expression $R(t_1, \ldots, t_n)$, where $t_1 \ldots t_n$ are either elements of *dom* or variables. A database instance D is a finite set of ground atoms. We sometimes refer to the atoms in an instance as facts. A *condition* is a set of atoms.

A *conjunctive query* is written as $Q(\bar{x}) \leftarrow L$, where L is a condition and $\bar{x}$ is a tuple of variables, each occuring also in L. We call L the *body* of Q, the variables in $\bar{x}$ the *distinguished variables* and the other variables in L the *nondistinguished variables*. Given a conjunctive query $Q(\bar{x}) \leftarrow L$ and an instance D, an answer to Q is a tuple $\alpha\bar{x}$, where α is an assignment of values to variables such that $\alpha L \subseteq D$. The set of all answers to Q over D is written as $Q^s(D)$. Similarly, we define $Q^b(D)$ as the bag of anwers that contains as many copies of a tuple as there are assignments returning it. We say that Q is evaluated under set or bag semantics, respectively, if we refer to the set or bag of answers. We drop the superscripts s, b if they are not important or clear from the context.

A conjunctive query is *linear*, if its body does not contain any relation symbol twice. It is *minimal*, if no atom can be removed from its body without changing the semantics of the query (cf. [4]).

3.2 Null Values

Nulls are a common form in which incompleteness is manifested in real-world databases. Null values mainly have two meanings:

- an attribute value exists, but is *unknown*;
- an attribute value does not exist, the attribute is thus *not applicable*.

In database theory, unknown values are represented by so-called *Codd nulls,* which are essentially existentially quantified first-order variables. A relation instance with Codd nulls, called a *Codd table*, represents the set of all regular instances that can be obtained by instantiating those variables with non-null values. [1]. For a conjunctive query Q over an instance with Codd nulls, say D_{Codd}, one usually considers *certain answer* semantics [1]: the result set $Q_{\text{cert}}(D_{\text{Codd}})$ consists of those tuples that are in $Q(D')$ for every instantiation D' of D_{Codd}. The set $Q_{\text{cert}}(D_{\text{Codd}})$ can be computed by evaluating Q over D_{Codd} while treating each occurrence of a null like a different constant and then dropping tuples with nulls from the result. Formally, using the notation

$$Q(D)^{\downarrow} := \{\, \bar{t} \in Q(D) \mid \bar{t} \text{ does not contain nulls} \,\}, \quad (1)$$

this means $Q_{\text{cert}}(D_{\text{Codd}}) = Q(D_{\text{Codd}})^{\downarrow}$.

The null values supported by SQL ("SQL nulls" in short) have a different semantics than Codd nulls. Evaluation of first order queries follows a three-valued semantics with the additional truth value *unknown*. For a conjunctive query Q, we say that y is a *join variable* if y occurs at least twice in the body of Q and a *singleton variable* otherwise. If D_{SQL} contains facts with null values, then under SQL's semantics the result of evaluating $Q(\bar{x})$ over D_{SQL} is

$$Q_{\text{SQL}}(D_{\text{SQL}}) = \{\, \alpha\bar{x} \mid \alpha \text{ maps no join variable to nulls} \,\}. \quad (2)$$

To see this, note that a twofold occurrence of a variable y is expressed in an SQL query by an equality between two attributes, which evaluates to *unknown* if a null is involved.

Recently, Franconi and Tessaris [11] have shown that the SQL way to evaluate queries over instances with nulls captures exactly the semantics of attributes that are not applicable. To make this more precise, suppose that R is an n-ary relation with attribute set $X := \{\, A_1, \ldots, A_n \,\}$. If each attribute in an R-tuple can be null, then R can be seen as representing for each $Y \subseteq X$ a relation R_Y with attribute set Y. In this perspective, an instance of R with tuples containing nulls represents a collection of 2^n instances of the relations R_Y, where a tuple t belongs to the instance R_Y iff the entries in t for the attributes in Y are not null. In other words, null values are padding the positions that do not correspond to attributes of R_Y.

Example 1. Consider the query Q that asks for all classes whose form teacher is also form teacher of a class with arts as profile, which we write as $Q(c_1) \leftarrow \texttt{class}(c_1, t, p), \texttt{class}(c_2, t, \text{'arts'})$, and the instance $D = \{\, \texttt{class}(1a, \perp, \text{'arts'}) \,\}$. If we interpret $\perp$ as Codd-null, then $(1a) \in Q_{\text{Codd}}(D)$. If we evaluate Q under the standard SQL semantics, we have that $(1a) \notin Q_{\text{SQL}}(D)$.

Suppose we know that class 1a has a form teacher. Then whoever the teacher of that class really is, the class has a teacher who teaches a class with arts as profile and the the first interpretation is correct. If no teacher exists, the second interpretation is correct.

Note that certain answer semantics and SQL semantics are not comparable in that the former admits more joins, while the latter allows for nulls in the query result. Later on we will show how for complete queries we can compute certain answers from SQL answers by simply dropping tuples with nulls.

We will say that a tuple with nulls representing an unknown but existing value is an *incomplete tuple*, since this nulls indicate the

D^i	
class	student
(1a, Smith, arts)	(John, 1a, Chester)
(2b, Rossi, ⊥)	(Mary, ⊥, Hampton)
	(Paul, 2b, Westfield)

D^a	
class	student
(1a, Smith, arts)	(John, 1a, Chester)
(2b, Rossi, ⊥)	(Mary, ⊥, Hampton)

Table 1: Partial database with restricted facts

D^i	
class	student
(1a, Smith, arts)	(John, 1a, Chester)
(2b, Rossi, science)	(Mary, 2b, Hampton)
	(Paul, 2b, Westfield)

D^a	
class	student
(1a, Smith, arts)	(John, 1a, ⊥)
(2b, Rossi, ⊥)	(Mary, 2b, Hampton)

Table 2: Partial database with incomplete facts

absence of existing values. We say that a tuple where nulls represent that no value exists is a *restricted tuple*, because only the not-null values in the tuple are related to each other. When modeling databases with null values, we will initially not syntactically distinguish between different kinds of null values and assume that some atoms in an instance contain the symbol ⊥.

3.3 Partial Databases

When stating that data is incomplete, one must have a conceptual complete reference. We model partial databases in the style of Levy [12] as pairs $\mathcal{D} = (D^i, D^a)$ of database instances: D^i, the *ideal* state, with complete information, and D^a, the *available* state, which contains possibly less information. In general, both D^i and D^a may contain facts with nulls.

In an application, the state stored in a DBMS is the available state, which represents only a part of the facts that hold in reality. The facts holding in reality constitute the ideal state, which however is unknown. (Later on we will assume that we have some meta-information about the extent to which the available state captures the ideal state.)

We formalize that the available database contains less information than the ideal one using the concept of dominance: Let $R(\bar{s})$ and $R(\bar{t})$ be atoms that possibly contain nulls. Then $R(\bar{s})$ is *dominated* by $R(\bar{t})$, written $R(\bar{s}) \preceq R(\bar{t})$, if $R(\bar{s})$ is the same as $R(\bar{t})$, except that $R(\bar{s})$ may have nulls where $R(\bar{t})$ does not. An instance D is *dominated* by an instance D', written $D \preceq D'$, if each fact in D is dominated by some fact in D'.

Proposition 1 (Monotonicity) *Let Q be a conjunctive query and D, D' be database instances with nulls. Suppose that D is dominated by D'. Then $Q_{\text{cert}}(D) \subseteq Q_{\text{cert}}(D')$ and $Q_{\text{SQL}}(D) \preceq Q_{\text{SQL}}(D')$.*

A *partial database* (or PDB for short) is a pair of database instances (D^i, D^a) such that D^a is dominated by D^i. We say that $\mathcal{D} = (D^i, D^a)$ is a *simple* partial database if $D^a \subseteq D^i$ and neither D^i nor D^a contains a null value. Completeness reasoning for simple partial databases has been studied in [16]. We say that $\mathcal{D}$ is a partial database *with restricted facts* if $D^a \subseteq D^i$. Note that in this case the ideal state may contain nulls and that every fact in the available state must appear in the same form in the ideal state. Thus, a null in the position of an attribute means that the attribute is not applicable and nulls are interpreted the way SQL does. The pair (D^i, D^a) is a partial database *with incomplete facts* if D^i does not contain any nulls and D^a is dominated by D^i. In this case, there are no nulls in the ideal state, which means that all attributes are applicable, while the nulls in the available state indicate that attribute values are unknown. Therefore, those nulls have the same semantics as Codd nulls.

Example 2. Recall the school database from our running example, defined in Section 2. In Table 1 we see a partial database with restricted facts for this scenario. All null values appearing in the available database mean that no value exists for the corresponding attributes. The `class` table shows that no profile hass been assigned to class 2b and that Mary is an external student not belonging to any class.

In contrast, Table 2 shows a partial database with incomplete facts. Here, null values in the available database mean that a value exists but is unknown. So, class 1a has form teacher, but we do not know who. Class 2b has a profile, but we do not now which. John has a hometown, but we do not no from where he comes.

Observe that in both kinds of partial databases, some facts, such as the one about Paul being a student, can be missing completely.

In practice, null values of both meanings will occur at the same time, which may lead to difficulties if they cannot be distinguished.

3.4 Query Completeness

Data are accessed by posing queries. The core question we pursue in our work is whether a database has sufficient information to answer a query, that is, whether a query is *complete*. Intuitively, if we can infer from some meta-information that a query is complete, we know that the answer we receive over the available database at hand is the same as the one we would get when querying the ideal database. In other words, the available database contains all the data that is relevant for calculating the query answer, so one can trust the result that one gets.

We write $\mathit{Compl}^s(Q)$ and $\mathit{Compl}^b(Q)$, respectively, to indicate that Q is complete under set or bag semantics. We now define when such a *query completeness* (QC) statement is satisfied by a partial database.

If $\mathcal{D} = (D^i, D^a)$ is a simple partial database (i.e., without nulls), then $\mathcal{D} \models \mathit{Compl}^s(Q)$ if and only if $Q^s(D^i) = Q^s(D^a)$, and $\mathcal{D} \models \mathit{Compl}^b(Q)$ if and only if $Q^b(D^i) = Q^b(D^a)$ (cf. [14]).

If D contains nulls, then $Q^s(D)$ and $Q^b(D)$ depend on whether we interpret those as Codd or as SQL nulls.

Suppose $\mathcal{D}$ is a PDB with incomplete facts. Then nulls are interpreted as Codd nulls and queries are evaluated under certain answer semantics. While D^a may contain nulls, D^i does not and $Q_{\text{cert}}(D^i) = Q(D^i)$. We therefore define

$$\mathcal{D} \models_{\text{inc}} \mathit{Compl}^*(Q) \quad \text{iff} \quad Q^*(D^i) = Q^*_{\text{cert}}(D^a) \tag{3}$$

where $* \in \{s, b\}$. That is, the tuples returned by Q over D^i are also returned over D^a if nulls are treated according to certain answer semantics. Conversely, that every null-free tuple returned over D^a is also returned over D^i follows by mononoticity from the fact that $D^a \preceq D^i$ (Proposition 1).

Suppose that $\mathcal{D}$ is a PDB with restricted facts. Then nulls are interpreted as SQL nulls and queries are evaluated under SQL semantics. For $* \in \{ s, b \}$ we define

$$\mathcal{D} \models_{\text{res}} Compl^*(Q) \quad \text{iff} \quad Q^*_{\text{SQL}}(D^i) = Q^*_{\text{SQL}}(D^a). \tag{4}$$

Again, the crucial part is that tuples returned by Q over D^i are also returned over D^a if nulls are treated according to SQL semantics, while the converse inclusion holds due to monotonicity.

Example 3. The query $Q_{\text{art\_students}}(n) \leftarrow \texttt{student}(n, c, h), \texttt{class}(c, t, \text{'arts'})$ asks for the names of students in classes with arts as profile. Over D^i in Table 2 it returns the singleton set {(John)} and over D^a as well. Therefore, $Q_{\text{art\_students}}$ is complete over that partial database.

In contrast, $Q_{\text{homes}}(h) \leftarrow \texttt{student}(n, c, h)$ is not complete over this database, because it returns {(Chester), (Hampton), (Westfield)} over the ideal database but only {(Hampton), $(\bot)$} over the available one.

3.5 Table Completeness

We use *table completeness* (TC) statements to specify that parts of a table are complete. A table completeness statement, written $Compl(R(\bar{s}); P; G)$, has three components: (i) a relational atom $R(\bar{s})$, (ii) a set of numbers $P \subseteq \{1, \ldots, arity(R)\}$, and (iii) a condition G. The numbers in P are interpreted as attribute positions of R. For instance, if R is the relation `student`, then $\{1, 3\}$ refers to the attributes `name` and `hometown`.

Let $C = Compl(R(\bar{s}); P; G)$ be a TC statement and $\mathcal{D} = (D^i, D^a)$ an incomplete database. An atom $R(\bar{u}) \in D^i$ is *constrained by* C if there is an assignment α such that $\bar{u} = \alpha\bar{s}$, $R(\alpha\bar{s}) \in D^i$, and $\alpha G \subseteq D^i$. An atom $R(\bar{u}') \in D^a$ is an *indicator for* $R(\bar{u})$ *wrt* C if $\bar{u}[P] = \bar{u}'[P]$, where $\bar{u}[P]$ is the projection of $\bar{u}$ onto the positions in P. We say that C *is satisfied by* $\mathcal{D}$ if for every atom $R(\bar{u}) \in D^i$ that is constrained by C there is an indicator $R(\bar{u}') \in D^a$.

Note that this type of TC statements extends the ones in [12] and [16] in that it allows one to state the completeness of projections of tables.

Example 4. In our school scenario, the TC statement

$$Compl(\texttt{student}(n, c, h); \{1, 2\}; \texttt{class}(c, t, \text{'arts'})) \tag{5}$$

states, intuitively, that the available database contains for all students of classes with arts as profile the name and the class. However, the student's hometown need not be present. Over the ideal database in Example 2, the fact student(John, 1a, Chester) is constrained by the statement (5). Any fact student(John, 1a, $\bot$), student(John, 1a, Chester) or student(John, 1a, Clayton) in D^a would be an indicator. In the database in Table 2 the first fact is present, and therefore Statement (5) is satisfied over it.

The semantics of TC statements can also be expressed using rule notation like the one that is used for instance for tuple-generating dependencies (TGDs) (see [7]). As a preparation, we introduce two copies of our signature Σ, which we denote as Σ^i and Σ^a. The first contains a relation symbol R^i for every $R \in \Sigma$ and the second contains a symbol R^a. Now, every incomplete database (D^i, D^a) can naturally be seen as a $\Sigma^i \cup \Sigma^a$-instance. We extend this notation also to conditions G. By replacing every occurrence of a symbol R by R^i (resp. R^a), we obtain G^i (resp. G^a) from G. Similarly, we define Q^i and Q^a for a query Q. With this notation, $(D^i, D^a) \models Compl(Q)$ iff $Q^i(D^i) = Q^a(D^a)$.

We associate to each TC statement $C = Compl(R(\bar{s}); P; G)$ a rule ρ_C. For instance, to Statement (5) we associate the rule

$$\texttt{class}^i(c, t, \text{'arts'}), \texttt{student}^i(n, c, h) \rightarrow \exists h'. \texttt{student}^a(n, c, h').$$

To simplify our notation, we assume that the projection positions P are the first k positions of R and that $\bar{s}$ has the form $(\bar{s}', \bar{s}'')$, where $\bar{s}'$ has length k and $\bar{s}''$ has length $arity(R) - k$. Then ρ_C is

$$G^i, R^i(\bar{s}', \bar{s}'') \rightarrow \exists \bar{z}. R^a(\bar{s}', \bar{z}),$$

where $\bar{z}$ is a tuple of distinct fresh variables that has the same lenght as $\bar{s}''$. Clearly, for every TC statement C, an incomplete database satisfies C in the sense defined above if and only if it satisfies the rule ρ_C in the classical sense of rule satisfaction.

Note, that our definition of when a TC statement is satisfied takes into account null values. Regarding nulls in D^a, we treat nulls like non-null values and consider their presence sufficient to satisfy an existential quantification in the head of a TC rule.

Nulls in D^i, however, have to be taken into account when evaluating the body of a rule. Since nulls in the ideal database always represent the absence of a value, we always interpret the rules that we associated with TC statements under SQL semantics.

3.6 Reasoning

As usual, a set C of TC statements *entails* completeness of a query Q (we write $C \models Compl(Q)$) if every partial database that satisfies all statements in C also satisfies $Compl(Q)$.

While TC statements are a natural way to describe completeness of available data ("These parts of the data are complete"), query completeness captures requirements for data quality ("For these queries we need complete answers"). Thus, in the following we investigate how to decide whether a set of TC statements entails query completeness (TC-QC entailment).

4. REASONING FOR SPECIFIC NULLS

In this section we discuss reasoning for databases where the meaning of nulls is unambiguous. In 4.1, we assume that nulls always mean that a value is missing but exists, while in 4.2, we assume that nulls mean that a value is inapplicable. For both cases we give decidable characterizations of TC-QC entailment. Moreover, we show that evaluation under certain answer and under SQL semantics lead to the same results for minimal complete queries.

4.1 Incomplete Facts

We suppose we are given a set of TC statements C and a conjunctive query Q, which is to be evaluated under set semantics. We say that C entails $Compl^s(Q)$ over PDBs with *incomplete facts*, written

$$C \models_{\text{inc}} Compl^s(Q), \tag{6}$$

iff for every such PDB $\mathcal{D}$ we have that

$$\mathcal{D} \models C \quad \text{implies} \quad \mathcal{D} \models_{\text{inc}} Compl^s(Q).$$

To decide property (6), we will derive a characterization that can be effectively checked.

To this end we introduce for every set C of TC statements a transformation T_C that, intuitively, maps an instance D to the least informative instance $T_C(D)$ such that $(D, T_C(D)) \models C$. Let $C = Compl(\,R(\bar{s}', \bar{s}''); P; G\,)$ be a TC statement, where wlog $\bar{s}'$ consists of the terms in the positions P. We define the query Q_C by the rule

$$Q_C(\bar{s}', \bar{\bot}) \leftarrow R(\bar{s}', \bar{s}''), G. \tag{7}$$

This means, given an instance D, the query Q_C returns for every α satisfying the condition $R(\bar{s}', \bar{s}''), G$, a tuple $(\alpha\bar{s}', \bar{\bot})$ that consists of the projected part $\alpha\bar{s}'$ and is padded with $\bot$s for the positions projected out. We then define

$$T_C(D) := \{ R(\bar{t}) \mid \bar{t} \in Q_C(D) \} \tag{8}$$

and $T_C(D) := \bigcup_{C \in \mathcal{C}} T_C(D)$.

Intuitively, for a database instance D^i and a TC statement C, the function T_C calculates the minimal information that any available database D^a must contain in order that (D^i, D^a) together satisfy C. Observe that every atom in $T_C(D)$ is an indicator for some $R(\bar{u})$ in D wrt C. This is the case because every fact in $T_C(D)$ is created as an indicator for some fact in D constrainted by C. Observe also that in general, $T_C(D)$ may contain more facts than D, because several TC statments may constrain the same atom and therefore several indicators are produced.

Example 5. Consider the TC statement C defined in Example 4 as $Compl(\texttt{student}(n, c, h); \{1, 2\}; \texttt{class}(c, t, \text{'arts'}))$. The corresponding query is $Q_C(n, c, \bot) \leftarrow \texttt{student}(n, c, h), \texttt{class}(c, t, \text{'arts'})$. For the partial database in Table 2, $Q_C(D^i)$ is $\{(John, 1a, \bot)\}$ and hence $T_C(D^i) = \{\texttt{student}(John, 1a, \bot)\}$, which is the minimal information that any available database must contain to satisfy together with D^i the TC statement C.

The following proposition formalizes the intuition about T_C.

Proposition 2 *Let D be a database instance without nulls and let $\mathcal{D}_0$ be the partial database $(D, T_C(D))$. Then*

1. *$T_C(D)$ is dominated by D,*
2. *$\mathcal{D}_0$ is a PDB with incomplete facts, and*
3. *$\mathcal{D}_0 \models C$.*

Moreover, if D' is another instance such that (D, D') is a PDB with incomplete facts that satisfies C, then D' dominates $T_C(D)$.

Similar to a database instance, the body of a conjunctive query is a set of atoms, to which we can apply the transformation T_C if we view the variables as constants. The following characterization of TC-QC-entailment over PDBs with incomplete facts says that completeness of Q wrt. C can be checked by evaluating Q over $T_C(L)$.

Theorem 3 *Let $Q(\bar{x}) \leftarrow L$ be a conjunctive query and C be a set of table completeness statements. Then*

$$C \models_{\text{inc}} Compl^s(Q) \quad \textit{iff} \quad \bar{x} \in Q_{\text{cert}}(T_C(L)).$$

Proof. "$\Rightarrow$" By Proposition 2, $(L, T_C(L))$ is a PDB with incomplete facts that satisfies C. Thus, by assumption, $(L, T_C(L)) \models_{\text{inc}} Compl^s(Q)$, which implies $Q^s(L) = Q^s_{\text{cert}}(T_C(L))$. The identity from L to L is a satisfying assignment for Q over L, from which it follows that $\bar{x} \in Q(L)$, and hence $\bar{x} \in Q_{\text{cert}}(T_C(L))$.

"$\Leftarrow$" Suppose that $\bar{x} \in Q_{\text{cert}}(T_C(L))$. We show that $C \models_{\text{inc}} Compl^s(Q)$. Let $\mathcal{D} = (D^i, D^a)$ be a PDB with incomplete facts that satisfies C and suppose that $\bar{d} \in Q^s(D^i)$. We show that $\bar{d} \in Q^s_{\text{cert}}(D^a)$ (the converse holds because of the dominance of D^a by D^i).

Given that there is an assignment δ such that $\delta L \subseteq D^i$ and $\delta\bar{x} = \bar{d}$ we construct an assignment δ' such that $\delta' L \subseteq D^a$ and $\delta'\bar{x} = \bar{d}$. To define δ', we specify how it maps atoms of L to D^a.

Let A be an atom in L. Since $\bar{x} \in Q_{\text{cert}}(T_C(L))$, there is a homorphism θ from L to $T_C(L)$ such that $\theta\bar{x} = \bar{x}$. Let $B' = \theta A \in T_C(L)$. By construction of $T_C(L)$, there is a TC-statement $C = Compl(B; P; G)$ such that $(B, G) \subseteq L$ and B' has been constructed as indicator for B wrt. C. Since $\delta L \subseteq D^i$, we have $(\delta B, \delta G) \subseteq D^i$. Clearly, δB is constrained by C over $\mathcal{D}$. Since $\mathcal{D} \models C$, there is an indicator atom $\tilde{B}$ for δB in D^a. Defining that $\delta' A := \tilde{B}$, the mapping δ' proves that $\bar{d}$ is also in $Q(D^a)$ and hence that the query is complete. □

The idea of the theorem is the following: To check whether completeness of a query Q is entailed by a set of TC statements C, we perform a test over a prototypical database: Considering the body of the query as an ideal database, we test whether the satisfaction of the TC statements C implies that there is also enough information in any available database to return the tuple of the distinguished variables $\bar{x}$. If that is the case, then also for any other tuple found over an ideal database, there is enough information in the available database to compute that tuple again.

Example 6. Consider again the query from Example 3, which is $Q_{\text{art\_students}}(n) \leftarrow \text{student}(n, c, h), \text{class}(c, t, \text{'arts'})$. Suppose we are given TC statements $C_1 = Compl(\texttt{class}(c, t, p); \{1, 2, 3\}; true)$ and $C_2 = Compl(\texttt{student}(n, c, h); \{1, 2\}; \texttt{class}(c, t, p))$, which state that complete facts about all classes are in our database, and that for all students from art classes the name and the class attribute are in the database. When we want to find out whether C_1 and C_2 imply that query $Q_{\text{art\_students}}$ returns a complete answer, we proceed according to Theorem 3 as follows:

1. We take the body of the query $Q_{\text{art\_students}}$ as a prototypical test database: $L = \{\texttt{student}(n, c, h), \texttt{class}(c, t, p)\}$.
2. We apply the functions T_{C_1} and T_{C_2} to L to generate the minimum information that can be found in any available database if the TC statements are satisfied: $T_{C_1}(L) = \{\texttt{class}(c, t, p)\}$ and $T_{C_2}(L) = \{\texttt{student}(n, c, \bot)\}$.
3. We evaluate $Q_{\text{art\_students}}$ over $T_{C_1}(L) \cup T_{C_2}(L)$. The result is $\{(n)\}$.

The tuple (n) is exactly the distinguished variable of $Q_{\text{art\_students}}$. Therefore, we conclude that C_1 and C_2 entail query completeness under certain answer semantics.

We will discuss the complexity of reasoning in Section 9. At this point we only remark that the reasoning is in NP for conjunctive queries, since all that needs to be done is query evaluation, first of the TC rules in order to calculate $T_C(L)$, second of Q, in order to check whether $\bar{x} \in Q(T_C(L))$. Also, for conjunctive queries without self-joins the reasoning can be done in polynomial time.

So far we have assumed that nulls in the available database are treated as Codd nulls and that queries are evaluated under certain answer semantics. Existing DBMSs, however, implement the SQL semantics of nulls, which is more restrictive, as it does not allow for joins involving nulls, and thus leads to fewer answers. In the following we will show that SQL semantics gives us the same results as certain answer semantics for a query Q, if Q is complete and minimal.

In analogy to "$\models_{\text{inc}}$", we define for a PDB with incomplete facts $\mathcal{D} = (D^i, D^a)$ that $\mathcal{D} \models_{\text{inc,SQL}} Compl^s(Q)$ if and only if $Q^s(D^i) = Q^s_{\text{SQL}}(D^a)^{\downarrow}$. Moreover, we write $C \models_{\text{inc,SQL}} Compl^s(Q)$ if and only if $\mathcal{D} \models_{\text{inc,SQL}} Compl^s(Q)$ for all PDBs where $\mathcal{D} \models C$. Intuitively, "$\models_{\text{inc,SQL}}$" is similar to "$\models_{\text{inc}}$", with the difference that queries over D^a are evaluated as by an SQL database system.

We show that query completeness for this new semantics can be checked in a manner analogous to the one for certain answer semantics in Theorem 3. The proof is largely similar.

Lemma 4 *Let $Q(\bar{x}) \leftarrow L$ be a conjunctive query and C be a set of table completeness statements. Then*

$$C \models_{\text{inc,SQL}} Compl^s(Q) \quad \textit{iff} \quad \bar{x} \in Q_{\text{SQL}}(T_C(L)).$$

Now, suppose that the conjunctive query Q is minimal (cf. [4]). Then Q returns a result over $T_C(L)$ only if each atom from L has an indicator in $T_C(L)$. The next lemma shows that it does not matter whether the nulls in $T_C(L)$ are interpreted as SQL or as Codd nulls.

Lemma 5 *Let C be a set of TC statements and $Q(\bar{x}) \leftarrow L$ be a minimal conjunctive query. Then*

$$\bar{x} \in Q_{\mathrm{SQL}}(T_C(L)) \quad \textit{iff} \quad \bar{x} \in Q_{\mathrm{cert}}(T_C(L)).$$

Combining Theorem 3 and Lemmas 4 and 5 we conclude that for minimal conjunctive queries that are known to be complete, it does not matter whether one evaluates them under certain answer or under SQL semantics.

Theorem 6 *Let $\mathcal{D} = (D^i, D^a)$ be an incomplete database with incomplete facts, let C be a set of TC statements, and let $Q(\bar{x}) \leftarrow L$ be a minimal conjunctive query. If $C \models_{\mathrm{inc}} Compl^s(Q)$ and if $\mathcal{D} \models C$ then $Q^s_{\mathrm{cert}}(D^a) = Q^s_{\mathrm{SQL}}(D^a)^{\downarrow}$.*

It follows that for complete queries we also get a complete query result when evaluating them over standard SQL databases.

Example 7. Consider again the query $Q_{\mathrm{art\_students}}$ from Example 3, where $Q_{\mathrm{art\_students}}(n) \leftarrow \mathtt{student}(n, c, h), \mathtt{class}(c, t, \text{'arts'})$, and the TC statements C_1 and C_2 from Example 6 that entailed query completeness over PDBs with incomplete facts. Since $Q_{\mathrm{art\_students}}$ has no self-joins it is clearly minimal, and hence over the available database of any PDB that satisfies C_1 and C_2 we can evaluate it under set semantics and will get a complete query result.

4.2 Restricted Facts

We now move to PDBs with restricted facts. Recall that in this case a null in a fact indicates that an attribute is not applicable. Accordingly, a PDB with restricted facts is a pair (D^i, D^a) where both the ideal and the available database may contain nulls, and where the available is a subset of the ideal database ($D^a \subseteq D^i$).

Again, we suppose that we are given a set of TC statements C and a conjunctive query $Q(\bar{x}) \leftarrow L$, which is to be evaluated under set semantics. Similar to the case of incomplete facts, we say that *C entails $Compl^s(Q)$ over PDBs with restricted facts*, written

$$C \models_{\mathrm{res}} Compl^s(Q), \tag{9}$$

iff for every such PDB $\mathcal{D}$ we have that

$$\mathcal{D} \models C \quad \text{implies} \quad \mathcal{D} \models_{\mathrm{res}} Compl^s(Q).$$

We will derive a characterization of (9) that can be effectively checked. We reuse the function T_C defined in Equation (8).

Proposition 7 *Let D be an instance that may contain nulls and let $\mathcal{D}_1 = (D \cup T_C(D), T_C(D))$. Then*

1. *$\mathcal{D}_1$ is a PDB with restricted facts;*
2. *$\mathcal{D}_1 \models C$.*

Moreover, if D' is another instance such that $(D \cup D', D')$ is a PDB with restricted facts that satisfies C, then D' dominates $T_C(D)$.

In contrast to databases with incomplete facts, nulls can now appear in the output of queries over the ideal database, and therefore must not be ignored in query answers over the available database. Recent results in [11] imply that for queries over databases with restricted facts, evaluation according to SQL's semantics of nulls returns correct results.

The characterization of completeness entailment is different now because Q's body L is no more a prototypical instance for Q to retrieve an answer $\bar{x}$. Since the ideal database may now contain nulls, we must consider the case that variables in L are mapped to $\perp$ when Q is evaluated over D^i.

We first present a result for *boolean* queries, that is, for queries where the tuple of distinguished variables $\bar{x}$ is empty, and for *linear* (or self-join free) queries, that is, queries where no relation symbol occurs more than once.

A variable y in a query $Q(\bar{x}) \leftarrow L$ is a *singleton* variable, if it appears only once in L. Recall that only singleton variables can be mapped to $\perp$ when evaluating Q under SQL semantics. Let $L^{\perp}$ and $\bar{x}^{\perp}$ be obtained from L and $\bar{x}$, respectively, by replacing all singleton variables with $\perp$.

Theorem 8 *Let $Q(\bar{x}) \leftarrow L$ be a boolean or linear conjunctive query and C be a set of table completeness statements. Then*

$$C \models_{\mathrm{res}} Compl^s(Q) \quad \textit{iff} \quad \bar{x}^{\perp} \in Q_{\mathrm{SQL}}(T_C(L^{\perp})).$$

The theorem reduces completeness reasoning in the cases above to conjunctive query evaluation. We conclude that deciding TC-QC entailment wrt databases with restricted facts is in PTIME for linear and NP-complete for arbitrary boolean conjunctive queries.

For general conjunctive queries, which may have distinguished variables, evaluating Q over a single test database obtained from L is not enough. We can show, however, that it is sufficient to consider all cases where singleton variables in L are either null or not. A *null version* of L is a condition obtained from L by replacing some singleton variables with $\perp$. We represent null versions of L as instantiations γL, where γ is a substitution that replaces some singleton variables of L with $\perp$ and is the identity otherwise.

Theorem 9 *Let $Q(\bar{x}) \leftarrow L$ be a conjunctive query. Then the following are equivalent:*

- *$C \models_{\mathrm{res}} Compl^s(Q)$;*
- *$\gamma\bar{x} \in Q_{\mathrm{SQL}}(T_C(\gamma L))$, for every null version γL of L.*

The theorem says that instead of just one prototypical case, we have to consider several now, because query evaluation for databases with nulls is more complicated: while the introduction of nulls makes the satisfaction of TC statements and the query evaluation more difficult, it also creates more possibilities to retrieve null as a result (see [10]).

The above characterisation can be checked by a Π^P_2 algorithm: in order to verify that containment does not hold, it suffices to guess one null version γL and then show that $\gamma\bar{x}$ is not in $Q(T_C(\gamma L))$, which is an NP task.

5. AMBIGUOUS NULLS

So far we have assumed that nulls have one of two possible meanings, standing for unknown or for non-existing values. In this section we discuss completeness reasoning in the presence of one syntactic null value, which can have three possible meanings, the previous two plus indeterminacy as to which of those two applies. This is the typical usage of nulls in SQL.

We model PDBs for this case as pairs $\mathcal{D} = (D^i, D^a)$, where both instances, D^i, D^a, may contain $\perp$ and each tuple in D^a is dominated by a tuple in D^i. We assume that queries are evaluated as in SQL, since we cannot tell which nulls are Codd-nulls and which not. For a query Q and $* \in \{ s, b \}$ we define

$$\mathcal{D} \models_{\mathrm{ambg}} Compl^*(Q) \quad \text{iff} \quad Q^*_{\mathrm{SQL}}(D^i) = Q^*_{\mathrm{SQL}}(D^a). \tag{10}$$

Different from the case where nulls stand for unknown values, we may not drop nulls in the query result over the available database, because they might carry information (absence of a value).

We observe that without further restrictions on the PDBs, for many queries there is no way to conclude query completeness from table completeness.

Proposition 10 *There exists a PDB $\mathcal{D}$ with ambiguous nulls and a query Q, such that $\mathcal{D}$ satisfies any set of TC statements but $\mathcal{D}$ does not satisfy $Compl^s(Q)$.*

Proof. Let $\mathcal{D}$ be with $D^i = \{\, \texttt{student}(\text{Mary}, 2\text{a}, \text{Chester}) \,\}$ and $D^a = \{\, \texttt{student}(\text{Mary}, 2\text{a}, \text{Chester}), \texttt{student}(\text{Mary}, \bot, \text{Chester}) \,\}$. Clearly, $\mathcal{D}$ satisfies all possible TC statements, because $D^a \subseteq D^i$. But query $Q_{\text{classes}}(c) \leftarrow \texttt{student}(n, c, h)$ is not complete over $\mathcal{D}$, because $Q^s(D^i) = \{\, (2a) \,\}$ while $Q^s(D^a) = \{\, (2a), (\bot) \,\}$. □

Inspecting $\mathcal{D}$ in the proof above more closely, we observe that the two facts in D^a are dominated by the same fact in the ideal database. Knowing that, we can consider the second fact in D^a as redundant: it does not add new information about Mary. This duplicate information leads to the odd behaviour of $\mathcal{D}$ wrt completeness: while all information from the ideal database is also in the available database, $Q(D^a)$ contains an additional fact with a null.

Sometimes, such duplicates occur naturally, e.g., when data from different sources is integrated. In other scenarios, however, redundancies are unlikely because objects are identified by keys, and only non-key attributes may be unknown or non-applicable.

In a school database, it can happen that address or birth place of a student are unknown. In contrast, it is hard to imagine that one may want to store a fact $\texttt{student}(\bot, \bot, \text{Chester})$, saying that there is a student with unknown name and class living in Chester.

Keys alone, however, are still not sufficient:

Example 8. Suppose we are given a partial database with $D^i = \{\texttt{student}(\text{Mary}, 2\text{a}, \text{Chester}), \texttt{student}(\text{Paul}, 2\text{a}, \text{Hampton})\}$ and $D^a = \{\, \texttt{student}(\text{Mary}, 2\text{a}, \text{Chester}), \texttt{student}(\textit{Paul}, \bot, \text{Hampton}) \,\}$. Observe that there are no redundant tuples in D^a. The TC statement $Compl(\texttt{student}(n, c, h);\ \{\, 2 \,\};\ \textit{true})$, which says that all classes from D^i are also in D^a, is satisfied over this PDB. One might believe that over a PDB satisfying this statement the query Q_{classes}, defined above, is complete, as it is the case for PDBs with incomplete facts or with restricted facts. However, query evaluation returns that $Q^s_{\text{classes}}(D^i) = \{\, (2\text{a}) \,\}$ while $Q^s_{\text{classes}}(D^a) = \{\, (2\text{a}), (\bot) \,\}$.

The problem with ambiguous nulls is that while all information needed for computing a query result may be present in the available database, it is not clear how to treat a null in the query answer. If it represents an unknown value, we can discard it because the value will still be there explicitly. But if it represents that no value exists, it should also show up in the query result.

Therefore, we conclude that one should disambiguate the meaning of null values. In the next section we propose how to do this in an SQL database.

6. MAKING NULL SEMANTICS EXPLICIT

Nulls in an available database can express three different statements about a value: absence, presence with the concrete value being unknown, and indeterminacy which of the two applies. As seen in Section 5, this ambiguity makes reasoning impossible. To explicitly distinguish between the three meanings of nulls in an SQL database, we present an approach that adds an auxiliary boolean attribute to each attribute that possibly has nulls as values.

student		
name	...	code
Sara		2a
John		$\bot_{\text{uk}}$
Mary		$\bot_{\text{n/a}}$
Paul		$\bot_{\bot}$

student			
name	...	hasCode	code
Sara		*true*	2a
John		*true*	$\bot$
Mary		*false*	$\bot$
Paul		$\bot$	$\bot$

Table 3: Making the semantics of nulls explicit

Example 9. Consider relation $\texttt{student}(\texttt{name}, \texttt{code}, \texttt{hometown})$. Imagine a student John for whom the attribute `code` is null because John attends a class, but the information was not entered into the database yet. Imagine another student Mary for whom `code` is null because Mary is an external student and does not attend any class. Imagine a third student Paul for whom `code` is null because it is unknown whether or not he attends a class. We mark the different meanings of nulls by symbols $\bot_{\text{uk}}$ (unknown but existing value), $\bot_{\text{n/a}}$ (not applicable value) and $\bot_{\bot}$ (indeterminacy), but remark that in practice, in an SQL database, all three cases would be expressed using syntactically identical null values.

We can distinguish them, however, if we add a boolean attribute `hasCode`. For John, the value of `hasCode` would be *true*, expressing that the tuple for John has a code value, which happens to be unknown, indicated by the $\bot$ for `code`. For Mary, `code` would have the value *false*, expressing that the attribute `code` is not applicable. For Paul, the `hasCode` attribute itself would be $\bot$, expressing that nothing is known about the actual value. Table 3 shows a `student` instance with explicit types of null, on the left using three nulls, on the right with a single null and the auxiliary attribute.

In general, for an attribute `attr` where we want to disambiguate null values, we introduce a boolean attribute `hasAttr`. We refer to `hasAttr` as the *sign* of `attr`, because it signals whether a value exists for the attribute, no value exists, or whether this is unknown.

Note that if `hasAttr` is *false* or $\bot$, then `attr` must be $\bot$. This can be enforced by an SQL check constraint.

As seen earlier, in general SQL semantics does not fully capture the semantics of unknown nulls as it may miss some certain answers. We will show in Theorem 12, that our encoding can be exploited to compute answer sets for complete queries by joining attributes with nulls according to SQL semantics and then using the signs to drop tuples with unknown and indeterminate nulls.

7. REASONING FOR DIFFERENT NULLS

In the previous section we showed how to implement a syntactic distinction of three different meanings of null values in SQL databases. In this section we discuss how to reason with these three different nulls.

An instance D with the three different kinds of nulls represents an infinite set of instances D' that can be obtained from D by (i) replacing all occurrences of $\bot_{\text{uk}}$ with concrete values and (ii) replacing all occurrences of $\bot_{\bot}$ with concrete values or with $\bot_{\text{n/a}}$.

As usual, the set of *certain answers* of a query Q over D consists of the tuples that are returned by Q over all such D' and is denoted as $Q_{\text{cert}}(D)$.

It is easy to see that a tuple $\bar{d}$ is in $Q_{\text{cert}}(D)$ iff the only nulls in $\bar{d}$ are $\bot_{\text{n/a}}$ and there exists an assignment α such that (i) $\bar{d} = \alpha\bar{x}$, (ii) $\alpha L \subseteq D$, (iii) α does not map join variables to $\bot_{\text{n/a}}$ or $\bot_{\bot}$, and (iv) no two occurrences of a join variable are mapped to different occurences of $\bot_{\text{uk}}$. Intuitively, this means that we have to treat $\bot_{\text{uk}}$ as Codd null and the other nulls as SQL nulls.

We say that a partial database $\mathcal{D} = (D^i, D^a)$ contains *partial facts* if (i) the facts in D^i may contain the null $\bot_{n/a}$, (ii) the facts in D^a may contain all three kinds of nulls, and (iii) each fact $R(\bar{t}) \in D^a$ is *dominated* by a fact $R(\bar{t}')$ in D^i in the sense that for any position p

- if $\bar{t}[p] = \bot_{n/a}$, then also $\bar{t}'[p] = \bot_{n/a}$,
- if $\bar{t}[p] = \bot_{uk}$, then $\bar{t}'[p]$ is a value from the domain *dom*,
- if $\bar{t}[p] = \bot_{\bot}$, then $\bar{t}'[p]$ is $\bot_{n/a}$ or in *dom*,
- if $\bar{t}[p] = d$ for a value $d \in dom$, then also $\bar{t}'[p] = d$.

We then say that a query is complete over a database $\mathcal{D} = (D^i, D^a)$ with partial facts, if $Q(D^i) = Q_{\text{cert}}(D^a)$, and write $\mathcal{D} \models_{3\bot} Compl(Q)$.

Satisfaction of TC-statements is not affected by these changes, as D^i contains only nulls $\bot_{n/a}$, which indicate restricted facts that can be treated according to SQL semantics.

Example 10. Consider the available database D^a that contains the three facts $\texttt{class}(1a, \bot_{uk}, \text{'arts'})$, $\texttt{class}(2b, \bot_{n/a}, \text{'arts'})$ and $\texttt{class}(3c, \bot_{\bot}, \text{'arts'})$. Also, consider the query from Example 1 that asks for all classes whose form teacher is also form teacher of an arts class, written as $Q(c_1) \leftarrow \texttt{class}(c_1, t, p_1), \texttt{class}(c_2, t, \text{'arts'})$.

Then similar to before, the only tuple in $Q_{\text{cert}}(D^a)$ is $(1a)$, because since the teacher of that class is unknown but existing, it holds in any complete database that the class 1a has a teacher that also teaches an arts class (1a again). The tuples 2b and 3c do not show up in the result, because the former has no form teacher at all ($\bot_{n/a}$), while the latter may or may not have a form teacher.

A first result is that TC-QC entailment over PDBs with partial facts is equivalent to entailment over PDBs with restricted facts:

Theorem 11 *Let Q be a conjunctive query and C be a set of TC statements. Then*

$$C \models_{3\bot} Compl^s(Q) \quad \textit{iff} \quad C \models_{\text{res}} Compl^s(Q).$$

Proof. (Sketch) "$\Rightarrow$" Trivial, because PDBs with restricted facts are PDBs with partial facts that contain only the null value $\bot_{n/a}$.

"$\Leftarrow$" Assume, $C \not\models_{3\bot} Compl^s(Q)$. Then there is a PDB with partial facts $\mathcal{D}$ such that $\mathcal{D} \models C$, but $\mathcal{D} \not\models_{3\bot} Compl^s(Q)$. We construct a PDB $\mathcal{D}_0$ with restricted facts that also satisfies C, but does not satisfy $Compl^s(Q)$. Let $D_0^a = D^a[\bot_{uk}/\bot_{n/a}, \bot_{\bot}/\bot_{n/a}]$ be the variant of D^a where $\bot_{uk}$ and $\bot_{\bot}$ are replaced by $\bot_{n/a}$, and let $D_0^i = D^i \cup D_0^a$.

The additional facts in D_0^i do not lead to violations of TC statements, since they are dominated by facts in D^i, thus, $\mathcal{D}_0 \models C$. However, $Q(D_0^a) \subseteq Q(D^a)$, since changing nulls to $\bot_{n/a}$ makes query evaluation more restrictive, and $Q(D^i) \subseteq Q(D_0^i)$ due to monotonicity. Hence, $Q(D_0^a) \subsetneq Q(D_0^i)$, that is, $\mathcal{D}_0 \not\models_{\text{res}} Compl^s(Q)$. □

Also, we define the query evaluation $Q(D)^{\Downarrow}$ as $Q(D)$ without all tuples containing $\bot_{uk}$ or $\bot_{\bot}$.

Similar to a database with incomplete facts only, it holds that query answering for minimal queries that are complete does not need to take into account certain answer semantics but can safely evaluate the query using standard SQL semantics:

Theorem 12 *Let $\mathcal{D} = (D^i, D^a)$ be an incomplete database with partial facts, Q be a minimal conjunctive query and C be a set of table completeness statements. If $C \models_{3\bot} Compl^s(Q)$ and $\mathcal{D} \models C$ then $Q_{\text{cert}}^s(D^a) = Q_{\text{SQL}}^s(D^a)^{\Downarrow}$.*

8. QUERIES UNDER BAG SEMANTICS

Bag semantics is the default semantics of SQL queries, while set semantics is enabled with the DISTINCT keyword. As the next example shows, for relations without keys reasoning about query completeness under bag semantics may not be meaningful.

Example 11. Consider the partial database with incomplete facts $\mathcal{D} = (D^i, D^a)$, where $D^i = \{\texttt{student}(\text{Mary}, 2a, \text{Chester})\}$ and $D^a = \{\texttt{student}(\text{Mary}, 2a, \text{Chester}), \texttt{student}(\text{Mary}, \bot, \text{Chester})\}$. Since it is a priori not possible to distinguish whether the fact containing $\bot$ is redundant, the boolean query $Q() \leftarrow \texttt{student}(n, c, h)$ that is just counting the number of students is not complete, because the redundant tuple in the available database leads to a miscount.

As tuples with nulls representing unknown values can introduce redundancies, we require that keys are declared for PDBs with incomplete facts, with one ambiguous null or with partial facts. Only for partial databases with restricted facts keys are not necessary, because there the available database is always a subset of the ideal one and hence no redundancies can appear.

Formally, for a relation R with arity n, a *key* is a subset of the attribute positions $\{1, \dots, n\}$. Wlog, we assume that the key attributes are the first $k(R)$ attributes, where k is a function from relations to natural numbers. An instance D *satisfies the key* of a relation R, if (i) no nulls appear in the key positions of facts and (ii) no two facts have the same key values, that is, if for all $R(\bar{t})$, $R(\bar{t}') \in D$ it holds that $\bar{t}[1..k(R)] = \bar{t}'[1..k(R)]$ implies $\bar{t} = \bar{t}'$, where $\bar{t}[1..k(R)]$ denotes the restriction of $\bar{t}$ to the positions $1..k(r)$.

Table completeness statements that do not talk about all key attributes of a key are not useful for deciding the entailment of query completeness under bag semantics, because, intuitively, they cannot assure that the right multiplicity of information is in the available database. We say that a TC statement $Compl(R(\bar{x}); P; G)$ is *key-preserving*, if $\{1..k(R)\} \subseteq P$. In the following, we only consider TC statements that are key-preserving.

We develop a characterization for TC-QC entailment that is similar to the one for set semantics. However now, we need to ensure that over a prototypical database not only query answers but assignments are preserved, because a query answer tuple can be produced by different assignments. So if an assignment is missing, the multiplicity of a tuple in the result is incorrect. As a consequence, a set of TC statements may entail completeness of a query Q for set semantics, but not for bag semantics.

Example 12. The relation $\texttt{lnCourse(student,language)}$ stores the language courses that students take. Consider the query $Q_{\text{nr\_for\_french}}(n) \leftarrow \texttt{lnCourse}(n, l), \texttt{lnCourse}(n, \text{'french'})$, which counts for each student that attends French, how many language courses he attends. Under set semantics, $Q_{\text{nr\_for\_french}}$ is complete if D^a contains all facts about French courses, which is expressed by $C_{\text{french}} = Compl(\texttt{lnCourse}(n, \text{'french'}); \{1, 2\}; true)$. To test completeness for set semantics, we apply T_C to the query body L, which results in $T_C(L) = \{\texttt{lnCourse}(n, \text{'french'})\}$, since the first body atom is not constrained by C_{french}. Evaluating $Q_{\text{nr\_for\_french}}$ over $T_C(L)$ returns (n), which shows set completeness.

But this does not entail that $Q_{\text{nr\_for\_french}}$ is complete under bag semantics. The PDB $(L, T_C(L))$ is a counterexample: it satisfies C and we can evaluate $Q_{nr\_for\_french}$ over L two times, while over $T_C(L)$ just once. If Paul takes French and Spanish according to D^i, it is clearly not sufficient to only have the fact about French in D^a when we want to count how many courses Paul takes!

We therefore modify the test criterion in Theorem 8 in two ways.

For a query $Q(\bar{x}) \leftarrow L$, the tuple $\bar{w}$ of *crucial variables* consists of the variables that are in $\bar{x}$ or occur in key positions in L. For any two assignments α and β that satisfy L over a database D, we have that α and β are identical if they agree on $\bar{w}$. Thus, the crucial variables determine both, the answers of Q and the multiplicities with which they occur. We associate to Q the query $\breve{Q}(\bar{w}) \leftarrow L$ that has the same body as Q, but outputs all crucial variables. Consequently,

Q is complete under set semantics if and only if $\bar{Q}$ is complete under set semantics. The first modification of the criterion will consist in testing $\bar{Q}$ instead of Q.

A direct implication of the first modification is that we need not consider several null versions γL of L as in Theorem 9. The reason for doing so was that a null $\perp = \alpha x$ in the ouput of Q over γL could have its origin in an atom γA in γL such that x does not occur in A, but another variable, say y is instantiated to $\perp$. Now, the query $\bar{Q}$ passes the test for set completeness only if an atom in L is mapped to an atom with the same key values. Thus, a variable x cannot be bound to a null $\perp = \gamma y$. Hence it suffices to consider just the one version $L^\perp$ where all singleton variables are mapped to null. By the same mapping, $\bar{w}^\perp$ is obtained from $\bar{w}$.

The second modification is due to the possibility that several TC statements constrain one fact in D^i und thus T_C generates several indicators. Since we assumed TC statements to be key-preserving, these indicators all agree on their key positions. However, in some non-key position one indicator may have a null while another one has a non-null value. So, $T_C(L^\perp)$ may not satisfy the keys. This can be repaired by "chasing" $T_C(L^\perp)$ (cf. [1]).

The function *chase* takes a database D with nulls as input and merges any two R-facts A', A'' that have the same key values into one R-fact A as follows: the value of A at position p, denoted $A[p]$ is $A'[p]$ if $A'[p] \neq \perp$ and is $A''[p]$ otherwise. Clearly, if C is key-preserving and D satisfies the keys, then $chase(T_C(D))$ also satisfies the keys. Intuitively, *chase* condenses information by applying the key constraints. Obviously, *chase* runs in polynomial time.

We now are ready for our characterization of completeness entailment under bag semantics, which is similar, but slightly more complicated than the one in Theorem 8.

Theorem 13 *Let $Q(\bar{x}) \leftarrow L$ be a conjunctive query and C be a set of key-preserving TC statements. Then*

$$C \models_{3\perp} Compl^b(Q) \quad \text{iff} \quad \bar{w}^\perp \in \bar{Q}(chase(T_C(L^\perp))).$$

Since the criterion holds for incomplete databases with three different nulls, it holds also for the special cases where only one type of null values is present (restricted or incomplete facts).

Notably, it also holds for partial databases with one ambiguous null, because when keys are present and TC statements guarantee that all mappings are preserved, no additional nulls can show up in the query result.

9. COMPLEXITY OF REASONING

We now discuss the complexity of inferring query completeness from table completeness. We define TC-QC$_\star$ as the problem of deciding whether under $\star$-semantic for all partial databases $\mathcal{D}$ it holds that $\mathcal{D} \models C$ implies that $\mathcal{D} \models Compl(Q)$. We will find that for all cases considered in the paper, the complexity of reasoning is between NP and Π_2^P:

Theorem 14 (Complexity Bounds)

1. TC-QC$^s_{\text{inc}}$ *is NP-complete;*
2. TC-QC$^s_{\text{res}}$ *is NP-hard and in Π_2^P;*
3. TC-QC$^s_{3\perp}$ *is NP-hard and in Π_2^P;*
4. TC-QC$^b_{3\perp}$ *is NP-complete.*

Proof. NP-hardness in all four cases can be shown by a reduction of containment of Boolean conjunctive queries, which is known to be NP-complete [4]. We sketch the reduction for (1)–(3), the one for (4) being similar. Suppose we want to check whether $Q() \leftarrow L$ is contained in $Q'() \leftarrow L'$. Let P be a new unary relation. Consider the query $Q_0() \leftarrow P(a), L$ and the TC statement $C_0 = Compl(P(a); \{1\}; L')$. Let C consist of C_0 and the statement that R is complete for every relation R in L. Then it follows from Theorems 3, 8 and 11 that $C \models_* Compl^s(Q)$, where $* \in \{\text{inc}, \text{res}, 3\perp\}$, if and only if $P(a) \in T_C(L)$, $P(a) \in T_C(L^\perp)$, and $P(a) \in T_C(L^\perp)$, respectively. The latter three conditions hold iff $P(a) = T_{C_0}(P(a), L)$, which holds iff Q is contained in Q'.

Problem 1 is in NP, because according to Theorem 3 to show that the entailment holds, it suffices to construct $T_C(L)$ by guessing assignments that satisfy sufficiently many TC statements in C over L, and to guess an assignment that satisfies Q over $T_C(L)$ such that the tuple $\bar{x}$ is returned.

Problem 2 is in Π_2^P, because according to the characterization in Theorem 9, to show that entailment does not hold, it suffices to guess one null version γL of the body of Q and show that $\gamma\bar{x}$ is not in $Q(chase(T_C(\gamma L)))$, which is an NP task.

Problem 3 is in Π_2^P for the same reason.

Problem 4 is in NP, because we do not consider different nullversions of L but only one. The remaining argument is the same as for Problem 1, since one needs to show that $\bar{x}^\perp$ is in $T_C(L^\perp)$, which is an NP task. □

Partial database class	Query semantics: set semantics	Query semantics: bag semantics & databases with keys
no nulls	NP-complete	NP-complete
incomplete facts	NP-complete	NP-complete
restricted facts	NP-hard, in Π_2^P	NP-complete
partial facts	NP-hard, in Π_2^P	NP-complete

Table 4: Complexity of TC-QC entailment

Reasoning becomes easier for special cases of queries:

Theorem 15 (Special Cases) *Let $* \in \{\text{inc}, \text{res}, 3\perp\}$. Then*

1. TC-QC$^s_*$ *and* TC-QC$^b_*$ *are in PTIME for linear queries;*
2. TC-QC$^s_*$ *is NP-complete for boolean queries.*

Proof. Regarding Claim 1, the most critial case is $* = \text{res}$. For linear queries under bag semantics, observe that the criterion in Theorem 13 can be checked in polynomial time. First, there is only one choice to map an atom in a query Q_C to an atom in $L^\perp$ (the one with the same relation). Second, $chase(T_C(L^\perp))$ can be computed in polynomial time. Lastly, the evaluation of $\bar{Q}$ over the chase result is in PTIME, because an atom in $\bar{Q}$ can be mapped in only one way.

Note that for linear queries under set semantics, we only need to consider one null version $L^\perp$ because a binding for an output term can only come from one position.

The lower bounds of Claim 2 follow from Theorem 14, the upper bounds from Theorem 14 for inc, and from Theorems 8 and 11 for res and $3\perp$, since evaluation of conjunctive queries is in NP. □

In Table 4 we summarize our complexity results for TC-QC entailment over databases with nulls. Notably, if we have keys then under bag semantics the complexity does not increase with respect to databases without null values. For queries under set semantics, it remains open whether the complexity of reasoning increases from NP to Π_2^P for databases with restricted facts and with 3 null values.

10. RELATED WORK

Since the introduction of null values in relational databases [5], there has been a long debate about their semantics and the correct implementation. In particular, the implementation of nulls in

SQL has led to wide criticism and numerous proposals for improvement (for a survey, see [19]). Much work has been done on the querying of incomplete databases with missing but existing values [2, 17], while only recently, Franconi and Tessaris showed that SQL correctly implements null values that stand for inapplicable attributes [11]. It was observed early on that different syntactic null values in databases would allow to capture more information [6], but these ideas did not reach application.

Query completeness over incomplete databases was first studied by Motro [14]. He investigated query completeness as an aspect of query integrity, and introduced the notion of partially incomplete and incorrect databases as databases that can both miss facts that hold in the real world and contain facts that do not hold there, but do not contain null values. He described partial completeness in terms of *query completeness* (QC) statements under set semantics. To infer completeness of a query from a set of queries known to be complete, he would search for a conjunctive rewriting of the given query in terms of the complete queries. This solution is correct, but not complete, as later results on query determinacy show [18].

Halevy [12] suggested *local completeness* statements, which we call table completeness (TC) statements, as an alternate formalism for asserting partial completeness of an incomplete database without nulls. The main problem he addressed was how to derive query completeness from table completeness (TC-QC reasoning). However, his approach led only to a decision procedure applicable to trivial cases.

Fan and Geerts [8] discussed the problem of query completeness in the presence of master data. Their work is not directly comparable to the one presented here because in addition to the different setting it always considers a database instance. In follow-up work, they considered incomplete data also in the form of missing, but existing values [9], which they represented by *c-tables* [13].

Recently, Razniewski and Nutt picked up Levy's problem of TC-QC entailment over databases that can miss records [16]. They showed that TC-QC entailment is decidable if conjunctive queries with comparisons are used for formulating TC and QC statements and analysed the complexity of the problem in detail for queries under bag semantics, set semantics and aggregate queries, finding complexities ranging from PTIME to Π_2^P.

11. CONCLUSION

Although null values are an important aspect of incompleteness in relational databases, they were not supported by formalisms for reasoning about data completeness. We generalized partially complete databases, table completeness and query completeness statements as in [12, 16] so that one can describe incompleteness in the form of both missing records and missing values.

Our approach addresses two challenges. First, if a table contains nulls, it may be that not entire rows, but only the columns of some rows are complete. To describe such a situation, we refined table completeness statements so that they can refer to projections of parts of tables. Second, null values as used in practice are ambiguous (unknown, not applicable, indeterminate). To resolve such ambiguities, we proposed an encoding for SQL databases that makes diffent kinds of nulls explicit. We then developed techniques to infer the completeness of conjunctive queries from such refined statements for different semantics of nulls and assessed the complexity of the reasoning task.

While SQL's query evaluation is generally not correct for nulls that represent missing values, we showed that for a minimal complete query correct query answers can be calculated from the SQL query result by dropping tuples with unknown and indeterminate nulls.

In this work, we focussed on conjunctive queries without built-in predicates like inequalities or disequalities. Treatment of built-in is orthogonal to the one of nulls, so that our results can be extended to them, using the techniques in [16]. Similarly, as aggregate queries are computed on top of non-aggregate queries, our results can also be extended in this direction.

Acknowledgements

This work was partially supported by the ESF project 2-299-2010 "SIS - Wir verbinden Menschen", and the European commission FP7 project ICT-2009.4.2 "TERENCE".

12. REFERENCES

[1] Serge Abiteboul, Richard Hull, and Victor Vianu. *Foundations of Databases*. Addison-Wesley, 1995.

[2] Serge Abiteboul, Paris C. Kanellakis, and Gösta Grahne. On the representation and querying of sets of possible worlds. *Theor. Comput. Sci.*, 78(1):158–187, 1991.

[3] Carlo Batini and Monica Scannapieco. *Data Quality: Concepts, Methodologies and Techniques*. Springer, 2006.

[4] Ashok K. Chandra and Philip M. Merlin. Optimal implementation of conjunctive queries in relational data bases. In *STOC*, pages 77–90, 1977.

[5] Edgar F. Codd. Understanding relations (installment #7). *FDT – Bulletin of ACM SIGMOD*, 7(3):23–28, 1975.

[6] Edgar F. Codd. Missing information (applicable and inapplicable) in relational databases. *SIGMOD Record*, 15(4):53–78, 1986.

[7] Ronald Fagin, Phokion Kolaitis, Renée Miller, and Lucian Popa. Data exchange: Semantics and query answering. In *Proc. ICDT*, pages 207–224, 2003.

[8] Wenfei Fan and Floris Geerts. Relative information completeness. In *PODS*, pages 97–106, 2009.

[9] Wenfei Fan and Floris Geerts. Capturing missing tuples and missing values. In *PODS*, pages 169–178, 2010.

[10] Carles Farré, Werner Nutt, Erneste Tenient, and Toni Urpí. Containment of conjunctive queries over databases with null values. In *ICDT*, pages 389–403, 2007.

[11] Enrico Franconi and Sergio Tessaris. On the logic of SQL nulls. In *AMW*, 2012.

[12] Alon Y. Halevy. Obtaining complete answers from incomplete databases. In *Proc. VLDB*, pages 402–412, 1996.

[13] Tomasz Imieliński and Witold Lipski, Jr. Incomplete information in relational databases. *J. ACM*, 31, 1984.

[14] Amihai Motro. Integrity = Validity + Completeness. *ACM TODS*, 14(4):480–502, 1989.

[15] Felix Naumann, Johann C. Freytag, and Ulf Leser. Completeness of integrated information sources. *Inf. Syst.*, 29, 2004.

[16] Simon Razniewski and Werner Nutt. Completeness of queries over incomplete databases. In *VLDB*, 2011.

[17] Raymond Reiter. A sound and sometimes complete query evaluation algorithm for relational databases with null values. *J. ACM*, 33(2):349–370, 1986.

[18] Luc Segoufin and Victor Vianu. Views and queries: Determinacy and rewriting. In *PODS*, pages 49–60, 2005.

[19] Ron van der Meyden. Logical approaches to incomplete information: A survey. In *Logics for Databases and Information Systems*, pages 307–356, 1998.

Being Picky—Processing Top-K Queries with Set-Defined Selections*

Aleksandar Stupar
Saarland University
Saarbrücken, Germany
astupar@mmci.uni-saarland.de

Sebastian Michel
Saarland University
Saarbrücken, Germany
smichel@mmci.uni-saarland.de

ABSTRACT

Focusing on the top-K items according to a ranking criterion constitutes an important functionality in many different query answering scenarios. The idea is to read only the necessary information—mostly from secondary storage—with the ultimate goal to achieve low latency. In this work, we consider processing such top-K queries under the constraint that the result items are members of a specific set, which is provided at query time. We call this restriction a set-defined selection criterion. Set-defined selections drastically influence the pros and cons of an id-ordered index vs. a score-ordered index. We present a mathematical model that allows to decide at runtime which index to choose, leading to a combined index. To improve the latency around the break even point of the two indices, we show how to benefit from a partitioned score-ordered index and present an algorithm to create such partitions based on analyzing query logs. Further performance gains can be enjoyed using approximate top-K results, with tunable result quality. The presented approaches are evaluated using both real-world and synthetic data.

Categories and Subject Descriptors

H.3.1 [**Information Storage and Retrieval**]: Content Analysis and Indexing; H.3.3 [**Information Storage and Retrieval**]: Information Search and Retrieval

Keywords

top-K query processing, index partitioning

1. INTRODUCTION

Reporting on ranked results is essential in many applications. Not only does it provide an ordered view on the data, according to some criteria, but it also allows users to focus on a few important results instead of inspecting hundreds or thousands of result items. Research on top-K query processing investigates how only the top portion of a hypothetically full ranking can be computed without full execution of the query—accessing only data items that are elementary for the final result (cf., [23] for an overview).

Id	Attr1	Attr2	Attr3	Attr4	Attr5	Attr6
1	34.1	15.2	13.7	34.1	7.2	23.1
2	38.1	32.8	22.6	21.6	15.2	4.5
3	11.5	11.8	27.0	39.1	24.0	3.5
4	8.5	24.0	5.2	18.2	14.3	24.1
5	21.3	3.4	9.6	22.4	10.2	11.5

Figure 1: Top-K query with set-defined selection.

In this work, we consider set-defined selections, where the items of interest are—by whatever means—identified upfront and represented in the query as a set of item ids. In addition, the query specifies the ranking attribute of interest and the result set size referred to as parameter K. Figure 1 gives an example: *Attr4* is the attribute used to rank; the set {2, 4} restricts the result to id=2 or id=4. In case of a top-1 query with descending ordering, the result would be the tuple with id=2, which has a score of 21.6.

This problem setup is very generic and occurs in many different scenarios: Set defined selections occur frequently between independent Web services that offer different views on the same data items—like in case of Linked Open Data (LOD) portals, where different datasets capture different aspects of (the same) entities. For instance, US-born computer scientists are identified based on a knowledge base [2] and subsequently ranked based on the number of publications obtained from DBLP[13].

Our research has originally been motivated by our prior work on proposing suitable songs as soundtracks for images [33], where images are uploaded through a smartphone app. It is based on a large index containing information about one million songs, where each song is described by a numeric attribute of how good it fits to a specific sample image. A query consists of a query image and the selection set, which in this case is simply the list of songs installed on a user's smartphone. The sample images (that correspond to attributes in Figure 1) are extracted by sampling movies. The index is 120GB big and contains information for 50 sampled movies and one million known songs—to provide enough diversity in both audio and visual dimensions. At query time, though, only the songs the user possesses are relevant for the top-K results.

*This work has been supported by the Excellence Cluster on Multimodal Computing and Interaction (MMCI).

The size of the selection set drastically influences the design of an ideal index: When the selection set contains a small number of ids, the query is efficiently answered using an index on the id attribute. In case the selection set contains most of the ids, the best performance is reached by reading the ids from the score-sorted lists.

To be able to choose the appropriate index at query time, we develop cost models for both data organizations. Still, as we will see, the *latency around the break even point* (the point of same performance for both indices) is the main cause of a sub-optimal performance. We show how this latency can be decreased by partitioning the data based on query logs.

1.1 Problem Formulation

Given a relation R over the attributes $\{id, A_1, ..., A_N\}$, in which id is the unique identifier of an item (e.g., real world entity, document, video, image). The attributes A_i describe properties of an item and are numeric (integer or floating point numbers).

DEFINITION 1. *A top-K selection query is defined by the triple (K, A_i, S), that is, the size of the result ranking K, the attribute used for ranking A_i, and a set $S \subseteq dom(id)$. The task is to efficiently compute those ids that have the K largest values for attribute A_i among all ids that appear in R and the query specific set S. The result is ordered by attribute A_i (w.l.o.g. in descending order).*

That means, a top-K query with set-defined selection can be expressed as a traditional top-K query over the subset of relation R that is given by the selection $\sigma_{id \in S} R$.

A SQL-like notation for this kind of query would look like

SELECT id, A_i **FROM** R
WHERE id **IN** S
ORDER BY A_i **LIMIT** K

where A_i is any of the numerical attributes of R. In this work, the case of a query specifying exactly one numerical attribute is considered.

1.2 Contribution and Outline

We consider the problem of efficiently processing top-K queries where the results are constrained upfront to a specified set of ids. To the best of our knowledge, this problem has not been addressed before.

In this paper, we make the following contributions:

(i) we investigate the trade-offs between id- and score-ordered indices and present a cost model that allows to pick the right index at query time (Section 3),

(ii) we propose means to benefit from a partitioned score-ordered index and show how to create such partitions using query logs (Section 4),

(iii) where approximate answers are acceptable, our algorithm can enjoy an even larger gain in latency with provided estimates for the result quality (Section 5),

(iv) we report on the results of a performance evaluation using real-world and synthetic data (Section 6).

2. RELATED WORK

There is a large body of existing work in the area of processing top-K queries, ranging from database systems [27, 23, 8], over distributed systems [9, 29], to information retrieval [16, 34, 14, 1]. Among the most prominent approaches are the so called *threshold algorithms* [15, 20, 16], which aggregate scores from score-sorted lists, while maintaining a threshold used for an early termination.

Ranking join results based on aggregated scores obtained from multiple tables (i.e., top-K join processing) and embedding such ranking concepts in a query optimizer have been addressed in [22, 36]. If we ignore the ranking criterion in our setup (and, hence, want to retrieve all items), our problem consist of computing an, so called, index join (i.e., a join involving lookups in an index for at least one involved table). Then, the problem is to identify the *break-even point* between index lookups (e.g., a B+ tree) vs. a full table scan—for which standard textbook solutions based on cost models exist [19]. With the top-K ranking requirement, however, this "index join" has not been considered yet.

For general top-K join queries [22, 36], our studies can be of use for the direct access to the base tables in a *rank-aware* query plan.

Using query logs (i.e., historic workloads) with the aim of tuning a system's performance is encountered frequently [31, 21, 35, 12]. Applications where the workload is used to improve performance vary from index defragmentation [31], over cache replacement [35] to range queries [21]. Query logs have been used in [12] with the aim to reduce the number of distributed partitions by allocating tuples that are frequently used together to the same partition. In our index organization, the graph based approach proposed in [12] is used for data partitioning.

The work in [38, 37], supports selection criteria on multiple categorical attributes (e.g., producer = 'Ford' and production_year=2011). The mentioned approaches extend the well known principle of *data cubes for data warehousing* [11] to incorporate ranking functionality. Clearly, we can not materialize data cubes for all combinations of selection sets.

Retrieving the top-K documents that contain a certain phrase can be transformed into a top-K query with range selection using data structures such as suffix trees. Data structures and algorithms for processing top-K queries with range selection, also known as top-K *color queries*, have been proposed in [30, 24]. It is obvious that representing set-defined selections as multiple range selections is not appropriate.

In traditional information retrieval problems, the part of the data to look at is determined by query terms, not upfront by a set of documents. A notable exception is the work by Singh et al. [32] on efficient enterprise search, where the results are restricted based on the file access rights. Knowing all access rights upfront with a clear grouping in a small number of disjunctive groups renders this problem different from the problem we address here. Another exception is the work by Bast et al. [4, 5] on auto-completion search where a query is executed while a user enters it to the search box. However, the work does not consider ranking documents, hence, early termination techniques can not be applied.

3. INDICES & COST MODEL

Considering a relation R with attributes $\{id, A_1, \cdots, A_N\}$, for each pair of attributes (id, A_i) two basic indices can be created:

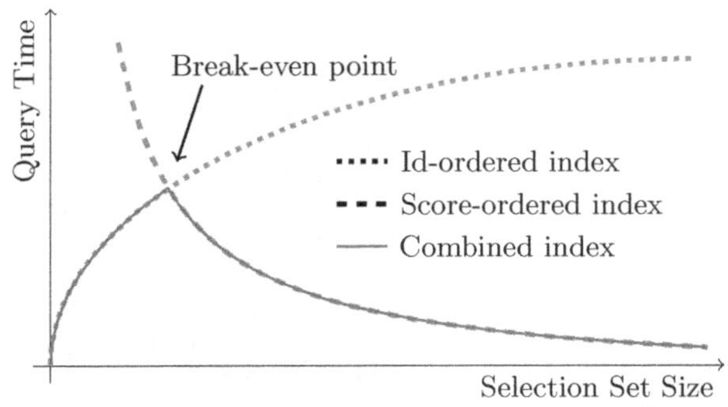

Figure 2: Characteristic performances of id-ordered index, score-ordered index, and the ideal combined index.

- an index on the *id* attribute (called **id-ordered index**)
- an index on the numerical attribute A_i (called **score-ordered index**)

The id attribute are assumed to be *densely populated in sequential order*, such that the position of a score on the disk can be calculated directly from the id value. Hence, only scores need to be stored—not the ids themselves. If the ids are not sequential, existing techniques based on B+ trees (cf., e.g., [19]) can be used for indexing. We adapt a *column-store data layout* where the relation R is stored on disk in a per-attribute fashion (not row-by-row).

Both index organizations come with advantages and disadvantages: The id-ordered index is ideal if the size of the query set is rather small, resulting in a small number of index lookups. In contrast, the scored-ordered index is ideal if the size of the query set is large, such that K items out of the query set are found very early when scanning the sorted list on disk.

To benefit from both sweet spots at the same time, a cost model is required to decide at query time which index to use. We optimize for low query response time, which is modeled as

$$t = c_1 + c_2 \times D_b$$

where D_b is the size of the data read from disk and c_1 and c_2 are constants which *minimize the squared error* on real-world measurements. The intuition is that c_2 represents the data transfer time, while c_1 approximates the time needed for a random access to disk. To keep the analysis tractable, we ignore influences of distributions of ids and scores, and, hence, treat the size of the selection set and the value of K (specified in the query) as the main ingredients for the amount of data read from disk. The latter is represented in number of disk blocks, as the access to disk is naturally done in a block-based manner.

For the **id-ordered index**, Equation 1 is used to estimate the number of disk blocks read, D_b. N represents the total number of tuples in the index, b is the number of tuples stored in a single disk block, and P_b is the probability that a single block is going to be read.

$$D_b = \frac{N}{b} P_b; \quad P_b = 1 - \overline{P_b}; \quad \overline{P_b} = \frac{\binom{N-b}{|q|}}{\binom{N}{|q|}}$$

$$\Rightarrow D_b = \frac{N}{b}\left(1 - \frac{\binom{N-b}{|q|}}{\binom{N}{|q|}}\right) \tag{1}$$

The probability P_b is the probability of reading one or more ids from a single block and is inverse to the probability $\overline{P_b}$ that a block is not going to be read. This probability is approximated by all possible combinations of ids from all blocks without the ids from one block, $N - b$, falling into a query of size $|q|$, divided by all possible combination of all ids, N, falling into query of size $|q|$. This probability approximation assumes independence between ids when they are chosen into a query. This, however, does not affect the precision of the estimate as tuple ids (determining the disk position) are assigned independently of their co-occurrences in the queries (no id reassignment).

For the **score-ordered index**, Equation 2 is used to estimate disk blocks read (D_b). Here, b is the number of tuples in one disk block, K is the number of requested results, and P is the portion of the index to be read. The probability that an id just read from disk is contained in the selection set is estimated as $\frac{|q|}{N}$, where $|q|$ is the number of ids in the selection set and N is the total number of ids in the index. The expectation of a geometric distribution with this *hit probability*, i.e., $\frac{N}{|q|}$, gives us the portion of the index needed to be read to find one id that is contained in the selection set. As K ids are needed for the final result, the portion size for one id is then multiplied by K. The total number of blocks is given as the ceiling of the ratio between the index portion and the bock size.

$$D_b = \left\lceil \frac{1}{b} \times P \times K \right\rceil; \; P = \frac{N}{|q|}; \Rightarrow D_b = \left\lceil \frac{N}{b \times |q|} \times K \right\rceil \tag{2}$$

Once the query is submitted to the system, the execution-time estimates are calculated and the index with the smaller execution time is used to answer the query. This procedure is totally hidden from the application layer: it appears as one index that combines the best of two index organizations. We call this index **combined index**. With an ideal cost model at hand, the combined index has a performance as illustrated in Figure 2.

4. PARTITIONED INDEX ORGANIZATION

The above model provides a solid mechanism to identify the best index to use. In fact, experiments show that it is (almost) perfect. On the other hand, the characteristics of the underlying indices lead to a degenerated performance of the combined index around the break-even point (cf., Figure 2).

The above cost model reveals a way to improve runtime beyond the point of simply choosing the right index: The index size in terms of number of tuples stored, has a strong influence on the query response time, while the query features themselves can not be influenced.

Thus, the main idea of a partitioned index is to organize the original index into multiple chunks, such that a large fraction of queries is answered by reading only from one of them. This has a high potential: partitioning the score-ordered index into m parts lowers the query answering time by a factor of m (the number of blocks read from the disk would be m times smaller).

The large score-ordered index is chopped up in a set of non-overlapping partitions. Each partition is organized as a score-ordered index. The decision which tuples to put together in a partition is done using a graph-based clustering approach.

To fully harness such a partitioning, we check at query time whether the selection set is

i) **entirely contained** in one partition,

ii) **mostly contained** in one partition,

iii) **distributed** between many partitions.

Answering a query in the first case is done using only the selected partition, while the second case requires a lookup of missing tuples using the id-ordered index. In the third case the query is answered using the combined index.

To determine if the partitioned index should be used for query answering, we employ the cost models introduced in Section 3. If one partition captures the entire selection set, only the model for the partitioned index is used, which essentially is the model for a score-ordered index, where the index size is adjusted accordingly.

In case not all of the ids from the selection set are found in one partition, the intersection size is used to estimate the query response time of the partitioned index. The number of the remaining ids (which are not covered by the partition) is used to estimate the lookup cost of the scores in the id-ordered index. The sum of the two estimates is used as a final response time estimate in case of this *mixed access* to the partitioned and the id-ordered index.

4.1 The Partition Selection Phase

To determine the partition which contains the largest subset of the selection set, data structures for computing set intersections are required. A bit-set structure is created for each partition, where each id is represented by one bit. The bit indicates whether or not the id is contained in the partition. This representation is exact (no false positives, no false negatives).

First, we consider the case when these bit set structures are kept in main memory, and then we focus on the case when they are stored on the disk with compact sketches used to decide which partition to access on disk.

Bits Sets in Main Memory

Bit sets in main memory allow a fast calculation of the intersection between the query selection set and each of the partitions in the index. *Only the partition with the largest intersection is used*, in case the time estimate using this partition is less than the time estimate for the combined index. Otherwise the query is answered using the combined index. This cost assessment is easy to achieve as the available bit sets give precise (exact) numbers of the contained and missing ids in a partition.

Bits Sets on Disk

If the bit sets do not fit in main memory, reading them from disk would in most cases consume more time than answering a query using the combined index. Our solution to this problem keeps only compact sketches [17, 3, 7] of partitions in main memory and the full sketch information on disk in the header of the corresponding partition. At query time, these sketches are used to determine the most promising partition to access by estimating the intersection size between partitions and the query selection sets. The accuracy of this estimation can be tuned using sketch specific parameters. In this work, KMV sketches (k-Minimum Values) [3] are used.

The structure for the partitioned index with sketches is shown in Figure 3: The bit set structure for a given partition is located on the disk at the beginning of the partition itself. This is done such that once the bit set is read—and it tells that the partition is useful—the reading of the actual partition content can continue without an additional disk seek.

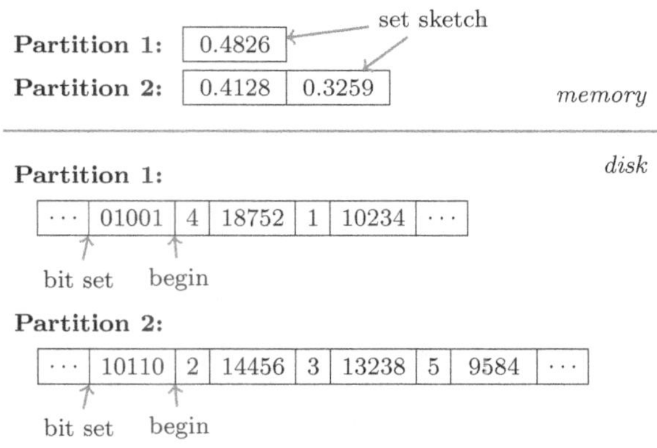

Figure 3: Partitioned index structure with sketches

Having only rough sketches of the partition contents in main memory requires changes to the querying algorithm. First, the most promising partition is identified using sketches. Then, the bit set for this partition is read and used to calculate the exact intersection size between the partition and the selection set. This information is then used to estimate if the selected partition is beneficial for answering the query.

It is important to avoid accessing a partition on disk that turns out to be of little use once the bit set is inspected. To limit these wrong decisions, made by the estimation inaccuracy of the sketches, a partition is identified as promising only if we are highly confident that it will be useful for the query optimization later on. The problem with sketches is that comparing a huge list of ids with a relatively small selection set often results in an empty intersection. We identify a partition to be useful, if and only if the intersection with the selection set is estimated to be larger than zero and there is no other partition for which the estimate is non zero.

In case partitioned indices are created for multiple attribute pairs of the same relation (e.g., (id,A_1), (id, A_2),...), the content of the partitions will be the same for all of them. Hence, bit sets describing the partitions are materialized only once—they are shared to reduce the overhead.

4.2 Index Partitioning

The problem of data partitioning is formulated as follows: given selection sets from a query log, create m **disjoint data partitions** such that the probability of finding a randomly selected pair of ids from a randomly selected selection set in a single partition is maximized. The partitions should further be approximately equal in size. Determining the optimal number of partitions is not trivial: A large number of ideal partitions (i.e., each selection set is completely found in one partition) would decrease the runtime. However, increasing the number of partitions would increase the error introduced by the partitioning, that means, less and less queries could be answered by a single partition. In this work, we determine the optimal number of partitions experimentally (cf., Section 6).

For partitioning, we employ a technique used in recent work on data partitioning in distributed database systems, by Curino et al. [12]. The basic idea of their approach, coined Schism, is to create a graph based on a database workload (query logs). The vertices of the graph are tuples with edges connecting frequently co-occurring tuples in the transactions. The edge weight is given by the number of transac-

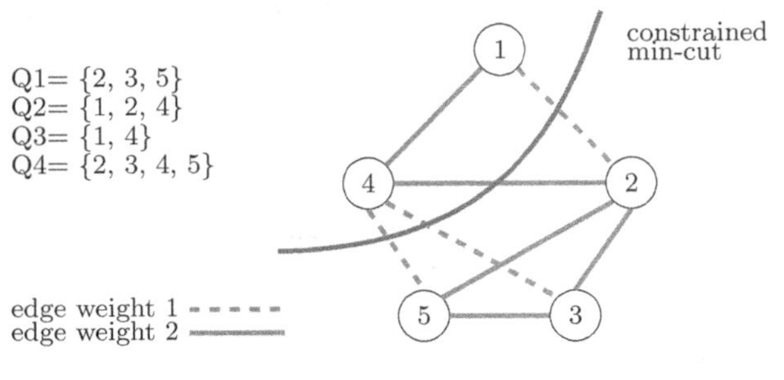

Figure 4: Graph based data partitioning

tions in which two connected tuples occur together. Once the graph is constructed, the actual partitioning is done *using constrained k-way graph partitioning.*

An example of the graph data partitioning, with a query log of four queries, is shown in Figure 4. We see that the vertices 1 and 4 are connected with an edge with weight 2 as they occur together in two queries (Q2 and Q3), while the vertices 4 and 5 are connected with an edge of weight 1 as they have only one query in common (Q4). Using the constrained k-way graph partitioning, we obtain the following two partitions: (1, 4) and (2, 3, 5).

This way, each query contributes $\frac{(|q|-1)(|q|-2)}{2}$ edges to the graph, where $|q|$ is the size of the query selection set. To avoid a quadratic explosion, in particular for queries with larger selection sets, we introduced *edge sampling*. For each of the ids in the given selection set, 10 randomly selected ids from the same set are used to create edges between them, rather than using all of the other ids. This way we get $10 \cdot |q|$ edges for each query, while preserving the density in the graph.

The basic assumption behind index partitioning is that selection sets are clustered in a meaningful way. Although this might not hold in general, selection sets are usually coherent in a semantic way (e.g., most people possess songs from mainly one genre).

Constrained k-way graph partitioning is NP-complete, but there exist efficient and accurate approximation techniques. In this work, we are using the software package METIS [25, 28], a freely available software library that offers approximate constrained k-way partitioning based on multilevel coarsening techniques.

5. APPROXIMATE QUERY ANSWERING

Given the partitioned index organization, even higher performance gains can be achieved by returning approximate top-K results instead of the exact ones. By approximate top-K results, we refer to the case when the selected partition does not cover all of the ids from the selection set. The missing ones could be retrieved based on the id-ordered index, but this is not done now. Hence, there is a risk that some of the missing ids would contribute to the actual top-K result, in which case the returned result is not exact. Although such approximations bring performance gains, without a quantification of the expected error, such approximate results are in most cases not acceptable, as the result quality can arbitrarily vary.

5.1 Tunable Expected Precision

Approximate results are often very acceptable, but only up to a point where the precision is still above a certain level, for instance, above 80%. With precision we refer to the fraction of the returned top-K results which are also in the hypothetically exact result.

In the following, we derive an estimate for the results quality provided by the approximate query answering algorithm. Using this estimate at query time enables us to fall back to the exact query answering mode, in case this expected result quality is below the specified minimum threshold.

We describe the probability distribution of the precision as a binomial distribution with "success probability" p_h. This p_h is the probability that an id is found in the partition, given that it is in the selection set and also a true top-K element. Note that, due to the nature of the partitions and the retrieval algorithm, p_h is the same as the probability that a retrieved top-K element is a true top-K element.

The estimated precision is then given by the expectation of the binomial distribution, divided by the size of the results,

$$P(X \leq x) = \sum_{i=0}^{\lfloor x \rfloor} \binom{K}{i} {p_h}^i (1-p_h)^{K-i}$$

$$prec = \frac{E[X]}{K} = \frac{p_h \times K}{K} = p_h$$

where K is the size of the results (K in top-K) and hit probability is p_h.

The success (or hit) probabilty p_h can be written as

$$p_h = P(id \in F | id \in S, id \in topK)$$

with F representing the partition and S representing the selection set. Applying Bayes' theorem and assuming *conditional independence* between an id being found in the top-K results and the id being found in partition, given that it is in the selection set, we can derive

$$p_h = P(id \in F | id \in S)$$

Applying the definition of conditional probability and using $P(X,Y) = P(X)P(Y) + cov(X,Y)$ for Bernoulli random variables, we obtain:

$$p_h = \frac{P(id \in F)P(id \in S) + cov(id \in F, id \in S)}{P(id \in S)}$$

Estimating that $P(id \in F) = \frac{|F|}{N}$ and that $P(id \in S) = \frac{|S|}{N}$ (where N is the total number of tuples), together with the covariance estimation $cov(id \in F, id \in S) = \frac{|F \cap S|}{N} - \frac{|F||S|}{N^2}$, gives us:

$$p_h = \frac{\frac{|F|}{N}\frac{|S|}{N} + \frac{|F \cap S|}{N} - \frac{|F||S|}{N^2}}{\frac{|S|}{N}} = \frac{|F \cap S|}{|S|}$$

This shows that the precision is estimated as the size of intersection between the selection set and partition, divided by the selection set size. For instance, if there are 90% of the selection set contained in the queried partition, we estimate the precision to be 90%.

To get an accurate precision estimate, we use the exact intersection size using the partition bit sets that are read from the disk once the partition is selected based on the sketches.

6. EXPERIMENTAL EVALUATION

We implemented the described indexing techniques and algorithms in Java 1.6 using direct access to the disk by a JNI (Java Native Interface) connection to routines written in C. The direct IO access uses the `O_DIRECT` flag in the libraries provided by the operating system. One disk block is kept cached in main memory while data is read from the disk. As a direct access to the disk is used, the size and the speed of the main memory was of negligible influence to our measurements.

All experiments are conducted on a Linux machine (Ubuntu 11.04 64bit with kernel version 2.6.32-28) with a Intel Xeon W3530 CPU (2.8GHz, 8MB cache, 4 cores (8 threads)). The local disk used is a 3Gb/s Barracuda 7200.12 SATA (7200 rpm, 32 MB cache, avg. latency 4.16 ms, random read seek time: 8.5 ms). The routines are executed using Java SE runtime version 1.6 64-bit, with C routines compiled using gcc version 4.4.3.

Prerequisites: To estimate the query response time, the cost models (Section 3) need to know the block size. This, however, depends on how much the disk is actually reading ahead with each access to the physical disk. In our case, we measured a size of 896 KB.

Real-world Dataset

As for the real-world dataset we get back to the problem that originally motivated our research. With Picasso [33] we have developed an approach to suggest songs, out of a user provided collection, to pictures submitted by a user to our system. We analyzed the Million Song Dataset [6] which contains low-level feature descriptors of one million songs. This way we need only the title of a user's mp3 and can recommend songs out of this set, for a given picture. A user provided set of songs is interpreted as a selection set.

In addition, 50 movies are processed and analyzed resulting in approximately 10,000 movie snapshots. Fitness information between each song and each movie snapshot is calculate and stored. With 4 bytes for an id and 4 bytes for the score encoding, the total size of the indexed information is around 120GB for both id-ordered and score-ordered indices.

We extended the 1 million songs to 14 million songs to account for a more realistic total count of songs in the world. This approximation is based on the overlap between the user profiles (i.e., sets of songs in users' collections) we received and the list of songs in the free base [18] database. The scores for those artificially added songs are generated from the distribution of scores for the songs in the million songs dataset.

For one index entry, the score in case of the id-ordered index and both the score and id in case of the score-ordered index are stored—which sums up to 12 bytes in total. As one tuple needs one bit in the partition bit set, the size of the bit set for one partition is 12×8 (= 96) smaller than the combined index size of one column (e.g., movie snapshot). As bit sets are the same for all columns, only one copy per partition is kept. In our case of 10,000 columns, thus, the required space for the bit set information of one partition is a factor of 960,000 smaller than the whole combined index (relation). When the bit sets are stored on disk, we used 28,000 minimum values in the KVM-sketch (each value is of 4 bytes size) for each partition, rendering the signature for one partition 60,000 times smaller than the combined index size of one column. As an illustration: with only 1 GB of main memory used and 10 partitions one can index 5.85 TB of data on disk using sketches.

Queries: We use 150 user profiles, i.e., sets of songs, obtained through our iPhone app PicasSound. The profiles are anonymized and do not contain any personal information. Each of those profiles represents one selection set that we use as the top-10 query in this study. We execute each query ten times and the average runtime is reported for that query. Each execution is accessing disk (no caching), which is a direct consequence of direct IO usage. The distribution of the selection set sizes for the iPhone queries is shown in Figure 5.

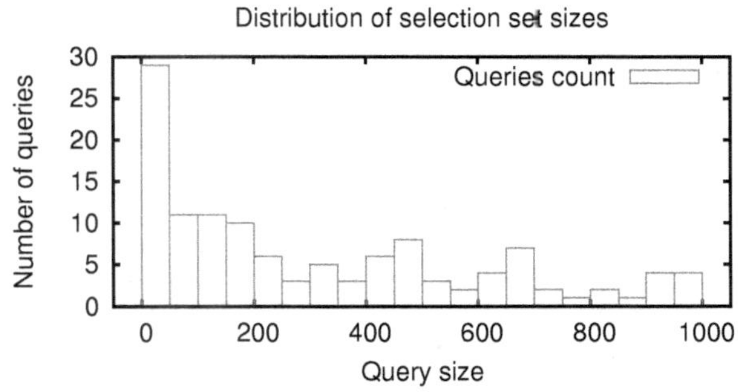

Figure 5: Distribution of selection set sizes

Partitioning: as 150 queries obtained from iPhone users are not enough for both testing and partitioning purposes and in particular to also show that the partitioning can be done on different but semantically related data, we use publicly available data [10] from last.fm [26] for the partitioning. This dataset contains the most-listened-to artists for 360,000 last.fm users. Although this dataset contains artists rather than individual songs, we partition the artists and then assign songs to the partition which contains the corresponding artist. The partitioning of the artists is done as described in Section 4.2, where the top artists of one user are considered as a query used in graph creation.

As the partitioning dataset and the query dataset have different sources, we measured that around 82% of the artists present in the queries are also contained in the partitioning dataset. We removed song ids from the queries' selection sets if they were not contained in the partitioning set.

Synthetic DataSet

For the synthetic dataset, we use the same song collection with the same scores used in the real-world dataset, but create synthetic queries for execution and queries used in the partitioning process. This allows varying the query clustering density to study its effect on the performance of the partitioned index. To create the artificial clustering, ids are randomly split into 10 groups (artificial clusters). Then, we generate queries based on these groups.

We distinguish three types of queries: (i) all ids from the selection set are found in one cluster (ii) ids are split between two clusters and (iii) ids are uniformly spread between all clusters. Based on the ratio between these types of queries, we create three query logs for partitioning and testing purposes. The first query log, named "best" contains 80% of type (i) queries, 10% of type (ii) queries, and 10% of type (iii) queries. The second query log, named "middle", contains 60% type (i), 20% type (ii), and 20% of type (iii) queries. Finally, the third, named "worst" query log contains 40% type (i), 30% type (ii), and 30% of type (iii) queries.

Queries: 200 queries for testing purposes were generated for each of the query log types with selection size uniformly distributed between 10 and 1000. Each query is generated by randomly selecting ids from one, two, or all artificial clusters. For instance, the "best" query log has 80% queries for which ids are selected from one randomly selected artificial cluster.

Partitioning: 20,000 queries for each of the query log

types are generated, with the selection size uniformly distributed between 10 and 500.

6.1 Model Verification

First, we experimentally evaluate the accuracy of the runtime estimates obtained by the models proposed in Section 3. We use the songs dataset and create top-20 queries with uniformly selected ids in the selection set.

First, we measure the effect of the table size (in terms of number of tuples) on the runtime of the score-ordered index. The results are shown in Figure 8(a): we distinguish three index sizes, 14 million tuples, 7 million tuples, and 3.5 million tuples. We can see that the runtime drops almost by a factor of two when decreasing the index by a factor of two. This shows that the runtime is proportional to the number of tuples stored in the index as proposed by the model (cf., Equation 2). The effects of changing K in the top-K queries on the runtime using the score-ordered index is shown in Figure 8(b). We observe that a larger value of K increases the runtime proportionally, which is again in accordance to the model. After fitting the c_1 and c_2 parameters, we see that the estimated values are almost a perfect fit to the measured values, see Figure 8(d).

The effects of the table size on id-ordered index are shown in Figure 9(a), where we see that the runtime is proportional to the table size. This plot also reveals small anomalies for small query sizes, in which case the 7 million songs index is performing better than the 3.5 million songs index. This together with the sudden decrease in runtime for 14 million songs at query size 200 is most likely the effect of the disk's adaptive read-ahead strategy. Figure 9(d) shows that the values estimated the model are very close to the measured ones.

Figure 9(b) shows that the parameter K has no effect on the runtime for id-ordered index. This is also in accordance to our model (cf., Equation 1).

The quartiles of multiple runtime measurements on the score-ordered index (Figure 8(c) and the id-ordered index (Figure 9(c)) are shown for 14 million songs and $K = 20$. We see that the runtimes have low variance, which means that time estimates are good in general, not only on average.

Overall, we see that the proposed models give a good estimate of the runtime for both indices. It is important to note that they do not have to be perfect in estimating the absolute runtimes, rather we need them to provide a reasonable decision of which index is better suitable to answer a query. To get a better understanding of this, we study the performance of the combined index which highly depends on the runtime estimates. The results for the real-world dataset are shown in Figure 6. We observe that the combined index performs almost optimally, choosing the right index for almost all of the queries, with only a couple of misses around the break-even point where the difference in runtime of the id- and score-ordered indices is negligible.

6.2 Exact Top-K Retrieval

We report on the results for the partitioned index evaluation, when the index is used to retrieve the exact top-K results. We measure the runtime of the partitioned index on the real-world dataset with 10 partitions, when the bit sets are in main memory (Figure 7(a)) and when they are on disk (Figure 7(b)). The selection set size is shown on the x-axis, while the y-axis shows the runtime in milliseconds. We summarize these results in Figure 10, where query sizes are grouped into ranges of size 50. For a better readability, we do not use histogram plots (with bars). In case some other representation is used in the plots it will be explicitly stated and explained. As expected, when the selection set size is small, the id-ordered index provides an efficient query answering. On the other hand, if the selection set size is large, the query can be processed more efficiently with the score-ordered index. Around the break-even point between these two indices, the partitioned index can greatly improve performance, as shown in Figure 10. We observe that the latency for queries of sizes between 50 and 100 drops down more than 140ms with bit sets in main memory and around 70ms for queries of size between 100 and 150. When the bit sets are kept on disk, the performance of the partitioned index is slightly worse than with bit sets in main memory, which is expected as reading bit sets from disk causes additional latency.

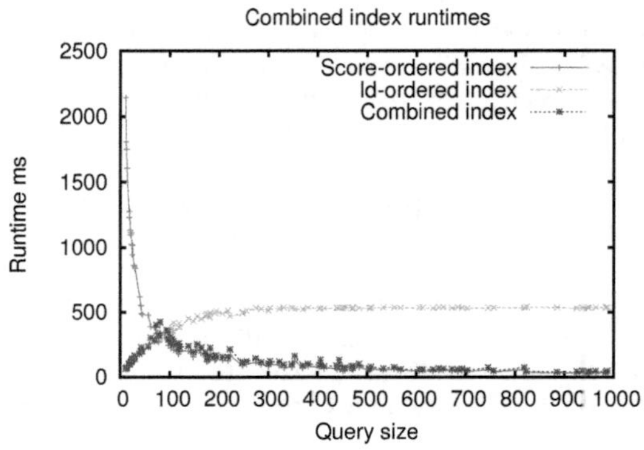

Figure 6: Runtime combined index

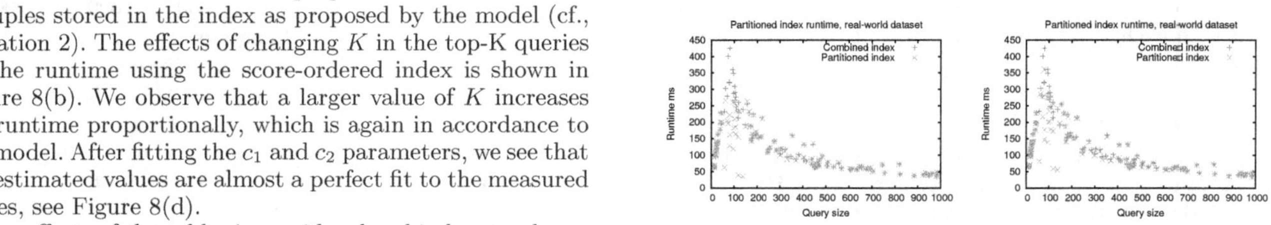

Figure 7: Partitioned index runtime (a) bitsets in main memory (b) bitsets on disk

To study the implications of using different numbers of partitions on the performances of the partitioned index, we show results for 4, 6, 8, and 10 partitions. The runtime improvements (difference between combined and partitioned index) in terms of milliseconds for different numbers of partitions are shown in Table 1 and Table 2. Table 1 reports on the runtime when the bit sets are kept in main memory, while Table 2 reports on the case when the bit sets are stored on disk. As the improvements were measured for queries with selection set size between 50 and 150, as seen in Figure 10, we report only on these. As we can see from these tables, some numbers of partitions perform better than the others. We can also see that we have a comparable improvements even if we are not using the optimal number of partitions, rendering our approach robust to changes in the number of partitions used.

Figures 11 and 12 show runtime experiments for the partitioned index on the synthetic dataset. Figure 11 shows the runtimes when the bit sets are kept in main memory and Figure 12 shows the runtime when bit sets are kept on disk. As expected, the runtimes are high for the worst synthetic

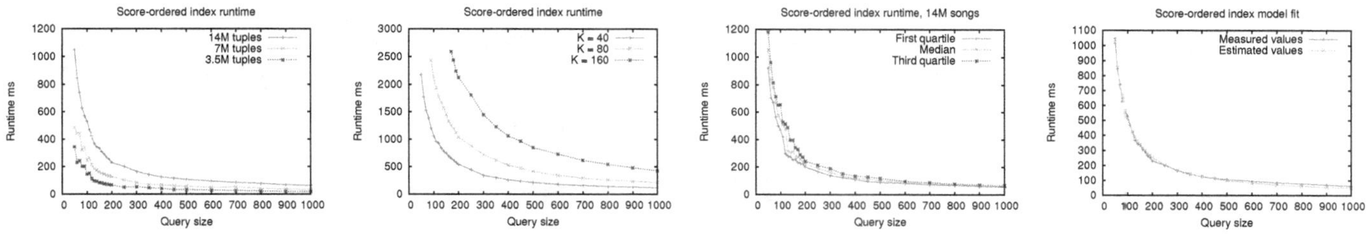

Figure 8: Score-ordered index runtime (a) table size varied (b) K in top-K varied (c) runtime quartiles (d) model fit

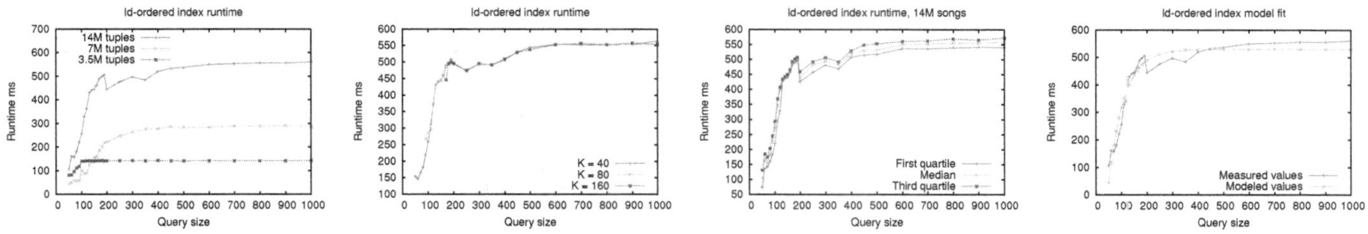

Figure 9: Id-ordered index runtime (a) table size varied (b) K in top-K varied (c) runtime quartiles (d) model fit

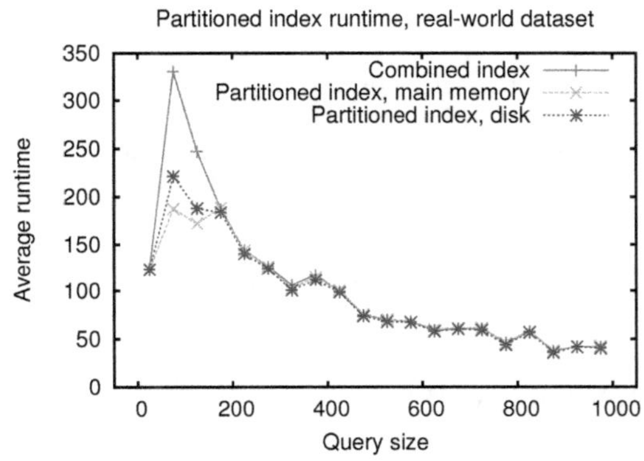

Figure 10: Partitioned index runtime, ten partitions

	Number of partitions			
Query size	4 part.	6 part.	8 part.	10 part.
0-50	0	0	0	0
50-100	112	130	145	142
100-150	82	97	59	75
...	0	0	0	0

Table 1: Runtime improvment (ms), bit sets in memory

	Number of partitions			
Query size	4 part.	6 part.	8 part.	10 part.
0-50	0	0	0	0
50-100	50	87	119	109
100-150	40	47	47	60
...	0	0	0	0

Table 2: Runtime improvment (ms), bitsets on disk

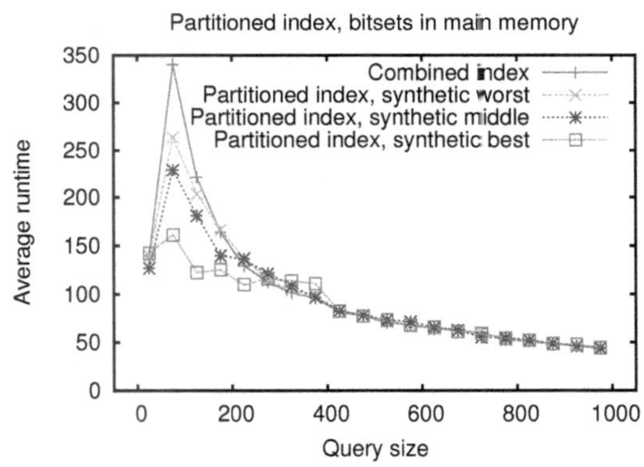

Figure 11: Synthetic dataset, bitsets in main memory

dataset and get smaller with the middle dataset and are smallest for the best synthetic dataset. We can see that the gain for the worst dataset, when the bit sets are kept on disk, is tiny, almost nonexistent. However, when the bit sets are kept in main memory, there is a gain for even the worst setup. Comparison between keeping bitsets in main memory and on disk is shown in Figure 13(a) for best synthetic dataset and in Figure 13(b) for worst synthetic dataset.

6.3 Approximate Top-K Retrieval

We have measured the runtime for the approximate querying, with and without guarantees, using the real-world dataset, shown in Figure 14. We see that the average runtime for the approximate querying without guarantees is much lower than for the variant with guarantees, e.g., for query sizes between 100 and 150 average runtime without guarantees is 83 milliseconds while runtime with guarantees is 140 milliseconds. This of course comes with the cost of decreased in precision shown in the same Figure 14. We used a requested precision of 80% for querying with guarantees in this case, which resulted in average precision around 95%.

Varying the requested (minimum) precision from 60% to 90% for approximate querying with guarantees is shown in Figure 15. We see that the precision drops down when the requested precision is lowered. Lowering the requested precision results also in lower runtimes, as reported in Figure 15.

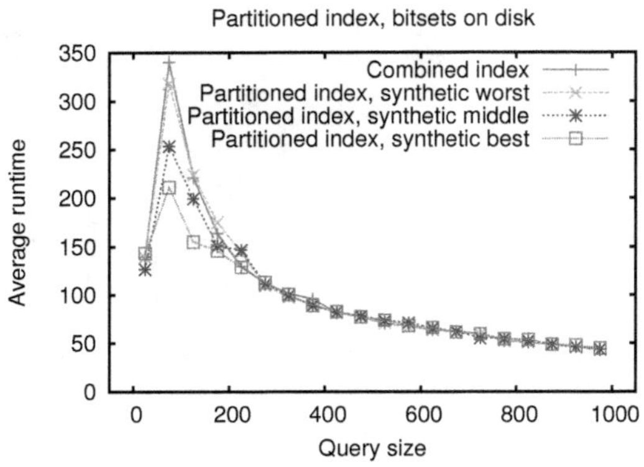

Figure 12: Synthetic dataset, bitsets on disk

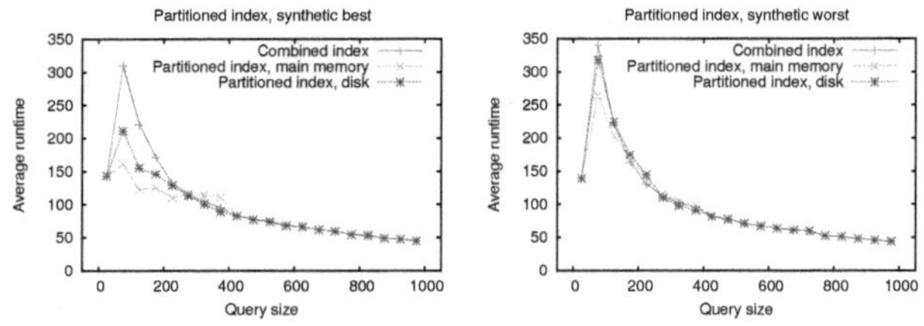

Figure 13: Partitioned index runtime (a) synthetic best (b) synthetic worst

The results of the approximate querying without guarantees over synthetic data are shown in Figure 16. As expected, the runtime for best synthetic dataset is lowest, the middle synthetic dataset has medium runtime, and the worst setup incurs the highest runtime. We see that even for the worst synthetic dataset, the improvement in runtime over the combined index is still high (up to 105 ms). As the modeling in these three cases has little control over the precision, it varies independently of the synthetic dataset use (Figure 16).

Approximate querying with guarantees and a requested precision of 90% over synthetic data results in an average precision close to 100%, independently of the dataset used, cf., Figure 17. This emphasizes once more the influence of the requested precision over the actually observed result precision. The measured runtime is again as expected. It is lowest for the best synthetic dataset, highest for the worst dataset, and medium for the middle one, cf., Figure 17.

7. CONCLUSION

In this work, we addressed the problem of finding the top-K items out of a global index, where the choice of result items is restricted to a query-dependent subset. This problem is very fundamental: it appears in cases of distributed services on the Web (e.g., linked open data) or at the source layer of rank-aware query processing in databases, etc. To our knowledge, we are the first to consider this problem, which is completely different from common top-K aggregation queries in the literature. Our approach is based on a careful analysis of the pros and cons of an id- vs. a score-ordered index. We derived a cost model to choose the most suitable of these indices at runtime. We devised a way to benefit from a partitioned data organization and investigated the influences of an approximate query answering. The conducted performance evaluation, based on real-world as well as synthetically generated data, revealed that the cost model is (almost) perfect in deciding which index to choose. While the combined index is, hence, almost optimal, we saw that based on data partitioning, the performance around the break-even point can still be drastically improved. We further saw that the derived estimate for the result quality—in case of approximate query answering—provides a robust and intuitive mechanism to trade off result quality for runtime performance.

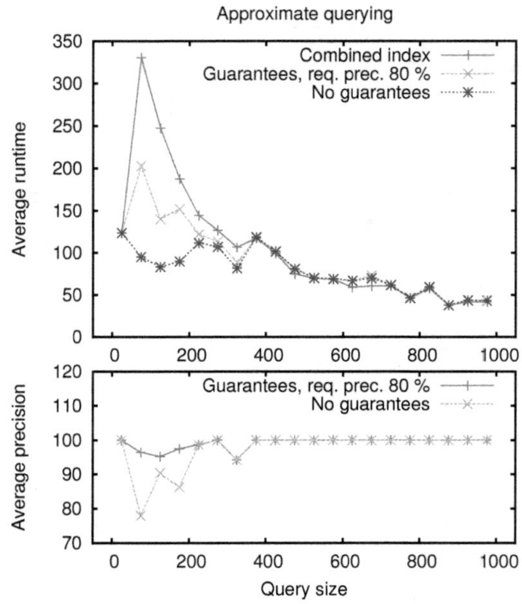

Figure 14: Approximate querying, real-world dataset

8. REFERENCES

[1] V. N. Anh, O. de Kretser, and A. Moffat. Vector-space ranking with effective early termination. In *SIGIR*, 2001.

[2] S. Auer, C. Bizer, G. Kobilarov, J. Lehmann, R. Cyganiak, and Z. G. Ives. Dbpedia: A nucleus for a web of open data. In *ISWC/ASWC*, 2007.

[3] Z. Bar-Yossef, T. S. Jayram, R. Kumar, D. Sivakumar, and L. Trevisan. Counting distinct elements in a data stream. In *RANDOM*, 2002.

[4] H. Bast and I. Weber. Type less, find more: fast autocompletion search with a succinct index. In *SIGIR*, 2006.

[5] H. Bast and I. Weber. The completesearch engine: Interactive, efficient, and towards ir& db integration. In *CIDR*, 2007.

[6] T. Bertin-Mahieux, D. P. Ellis, B. Whitman, and P. Lamere. The million song dataset. In *Proceedings of the 12th International Conference on Music Information Retrieval ISMIR*, 2011.

[7] A. Z. Broder, M. Charikar, A. M. Frieze, and M. Mitzenmacher. Min-wise independent permutations (extended abstract). In *STOC*, 1998.

[8] N. Bruno, S. Chaudhuri, and L. Gravano. Top-k selection queries over relational databases: Mapping strategies and performance evaluation. *ACM Trans. Database Syst.*, 2002.

[9] P. Cao and Z. Wang. Efficient top-k query calculation in distributed networks. In *PODC*, 2004.

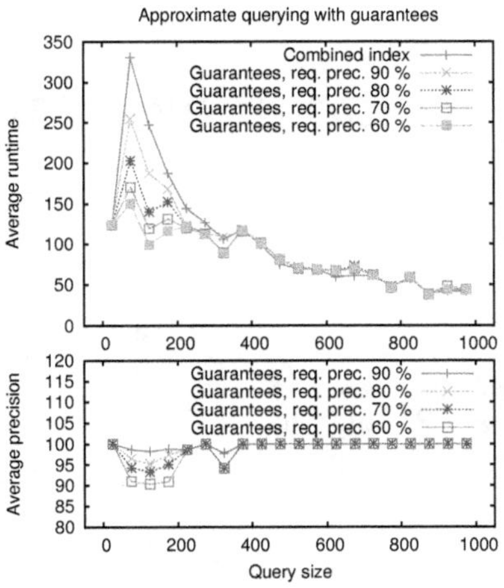

Figure 15: Approximate querying, real-world dataset

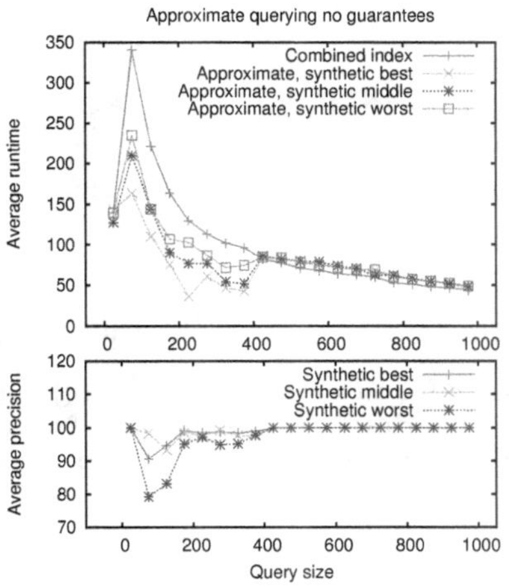

Figure 16: Approximate querying no guarantees, synthetic dataset

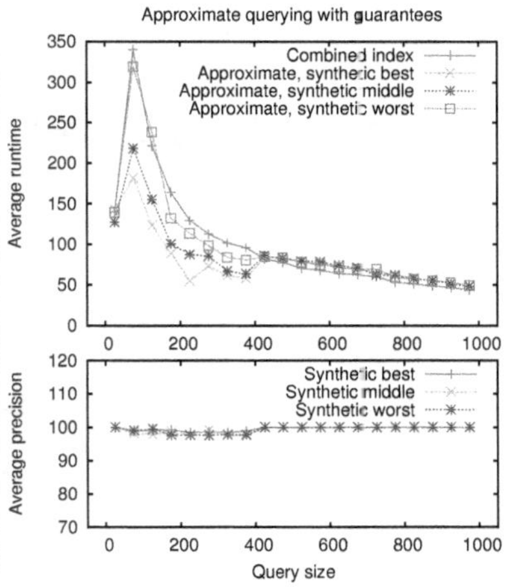

Figure 17: Approximate querying with guarantees req. prec 90%, synthetic dataset

[10] O. Celma. *Music Recommendation and Discovery in the Long Tail*. Springer, 2010.

[11] S. Chaudhuri and U. Dayal. An overview of data warehousing and olap technology. *SIGMOD Record*, 1997.

[12] C. Curino, Y. Zhang, E. P. C. Jones, and S. Madden. Schism: a workload-driven approach to database replication and partitioning. *PVLDB*, 2010.

[13] DBLP - The DBLP Computer Science Bibliography. `http://www.informatik.uni-trier.de/~ley/db/`.

[14] S. Ding and T. Suel. Faster top-k document retrieval using block-max indexes. In *SIGIR*, 2011.

[15] R. Fagin. Combining fuzzy information from multiple systems. *J. Comput. Syst. Sci.*, 1999.

[16] R. Fagin, A. Lotem, and M. Naor. Optimal aggregation algorithms for middleware. *J. Comput. Syst. Sci.*, 2003.

[17] P. Flajolet and G. N. Martin. Probabilistic counting algorithms for data base applications. *J. Comput. Syst. Sci.*, 1985.

[18] Freebase. `http://www.freebase.com/`.

[19] H. Garcia-Molina, J. D. Ullman, and J. Widom. *Database Systems: The Complete Book*. Prentice Hall Press, 2008.

[20] U. Güntzer, W.-T. Balke, and W. Kießling. Optimizing multi-feature queries for image databases. In *VLDB*, 2000.

[21] S. Idreos, M. L. Kersten, and S. Manegold. Database cracking. In *CIDR*, 2007.

[22] I. F. Ilyas, W. G. Aref, and A. K. Elmagarmid. Supporting top-k join queries in relational databases. *VLDB J.*, 2004.

[23] I. F. Ilyas, G. Beskales, and M. A. Soliman. A survey of top-k query processing techniques in relational database systems. *ACM Comput. Surv.*, 2008.

[24] M. Karpinski and Y. Nekrich. Top-k color queries for document retrieval. In *SODA*, 2011.

[25] G. Karypis and V. Kumar. A fast and highly quality multilevel scheme for partitioning irregular graphs. *SIAM Journal on Scientific Computing*.

[26] Last FM. `http://www.last.fm`.

[27] C. Li, K. C.-C. Chang, I. F. Ilyas, and S. Song. Ranksql: Query algebra and optimization for relational top-k queries. In *SIGMOD Conference*, 2005.

[28] METIS - Serial Graph Partitioning and Fill-reducing Matrix Ordering. `www.cs.umn.edu/~metis`.

[29] S. Michel, P. Triantafillou, and G. Weikum. Klee: A framework for distributed top-k query algorithms. In *VLDB*, 2005.

[30] S. Muthukrishnan. Efficient algorithms for document retrieval problems. In *SODA*, 2002.

[31] V. R. Narasayya, H. Park, and M. Syamala. Automatic workload driven index defragmentation. *PVLDB*, 2011.

[32] A. Singh, M. Srivatsa, and L. Liu. Efficient and secure search of enterprise file systems. In *ICWS*, 2007.

[33] A. Stupar and S. Michel. Picasso - to sing, you must close your eyes and draw. In *SIGIR*, 2011.

[34] M. Theobald, G. Weikum, and R. Schenkel. Top-k query evaluation with probabilistic guarantees. In *VLDB*, 2004.

[35] X. Wang, T. Malik, R. C. Burns, S. Papadomanolakis, and A. Ailamaki. A workload-driven unit of cache replacement for mid-tier database caching. In *DASFAA*, 2007.

[36] M. Wu, L. Berti-Equille, A. Marian, C. M. Procopiuc, and D. Srivastava. Processing top-k join queries. *PVLDB*, 2010.

[37] D. Xin and J. Han. P-cube: Answering preference queries in multi-dimensional space. In *ICDE*, 2008.

[38] D. Xin, J. Han, H. Cheng, and X. Li. Answering top-k queries with multi-dimensional selections: The ranking cube approach. In *VLDB*, 2006.

Finding Top k Most Influential Spatial Facilities over Uncertain Objects

Liming Zhan   Ying Zhang   Wenjie Zhang   Xuemin Lin

School of Computer Science & Engineering
The University of New South Wales, Sydney NSW 2052, Australia
{zhanl, yingz, zhangw, lxue}@cse.unsw.edu.au

ABSTRACT

Uncertainty is inherent in many important applications, such as location-based services (LBS), sensor monitoring and radio-frequency identification (RFID). Recently, considerable research efforts have been put into the field of uncertainty-aware spatial query processing. In this paper, we study the problem of finding top k most influential facilities over a set of uncertain objects, which is an important spatial query in the above applications. Based on the *maximal utility principle*, we propose a new ranking model to identify the top k most influential facilities, which carefully captures influence of facilities on the uncertain objects. By utilizing two uncertain object indexing techniques, R-tree and U-Quadtree, effective and efficient algorithms are proposed following the *filtering and verification* paradigm, which significantly improves the performance of the algorithms in terms of CPU and I/O costs. Comprehensive experiments on real datasets demonstrate the effectiveness and efficiency of our techniques.

Categories and Subject Descriptors

H.2.8 [**DATABASE MANAGEMENT**]: Database Applications—*Spatial databases and GIS*

General Terms

Algorithms, Performance

Keywords

Spatial, uncertain

1. INTRODUCTION

Bichromatic reverse nearest neighbor (BRNN) query has been extensively studied as an important spatial operator ever since it was introduced in [10] due to a wide spectrum of applications such as decision support, profile-based marketing, resource allocation, etc. Informally, given a set $\mathcal{F}$ of facilities (e.g., gas station, supermarket) and a set of $\mathcal{O}$ of objects (e.g., car, person), the influence of a facility F can be evaluated by the number of objects whose nearest neighbors are F. Intuitively, it is desirable to identify the most influential facilities for various reasons such as resource allocation and decision making. Motivated by this, some existing work [20] proposed efficient algorithms to identify the influential facilities, in which they assume the location of an object or facility is precisely described by a spatial point. As shown in Figure 1(a), we can calculate the influence score (e.g., the number of reverse nearest neighbors) for each facility, where F_1, F_2 and F_3 have scores 1, 2 and 0 respectively. Nevertheless, in many applications the location of an object may be uncertain due to various reasons such as data randomness and incompleteness, the limitation of measuring equipment, delay or loss of data updates and privacy preservation. Following are two example applications.

In some warehouse management systems, the RFID tags are attached to the items and their current locations can be obtained by RFID readers. Since the RFID reading may be noisy due to the sensitivity of the low cost readers to various environmental factors such as interference from nearby metal objects and contention among tags, the location of an object may be modeled as an uncertain object which is described by multiple instances. For instance, in Figure 1(b), the item A may appear at two positions a_1 and a_2 with the same probability. The facilities in Figure 1(b) represent the dispatching points for various items. Suppose an item will be delivered to the closest dispatch point. For a proper resource (e.g., labor, truck) allocation, the manager may want to know the k dispatching points with the highest influences (workload).

Another example application is the location based service (LBS). The location of a mobile user can be described as an uncertain object, since her/his location may be derived based on the nearest contour lines of users possible location regarding the nearby towers. In Figure 1(b), the mobile users are uncertain objects and supermarkets correspond to the facilities. Suppose that users tend to visit the nearby supermarket, it is meaningful to find the top k most promising supermarkets, i.e., supermarkets which influence the largest number of users.

Challenges. Motivated by the above examples, it is desirable to study the problem of finding top k most influential facilities over uncertain objects. The challenges are twofold.

Firstly, unlike the traditional spatial database in which an object only contributes to the influence score of one facility[1], it is non-trivial to evaluate the influence of a facility because of the existence of multiple instances. As shown in Figure 1(b), the uncertain object A may be influenced by both F_2 and F_3. Therefore, when we rank the influences of the facilities, it is desirable to propose new model to capture the uncertainty of the uncertain objects.

In the paper, we follow the popular *possible world semantics* (See Section 3.1 for a formal definition), and the influence of each facility is modeled as a influence score distribution. The definition

[1]Suppose the ties are broken arbitrarily if there are multiple nearest facilities for an object.

CIKM'12, October 29–November 2, 2012, Maui, HI, USA.

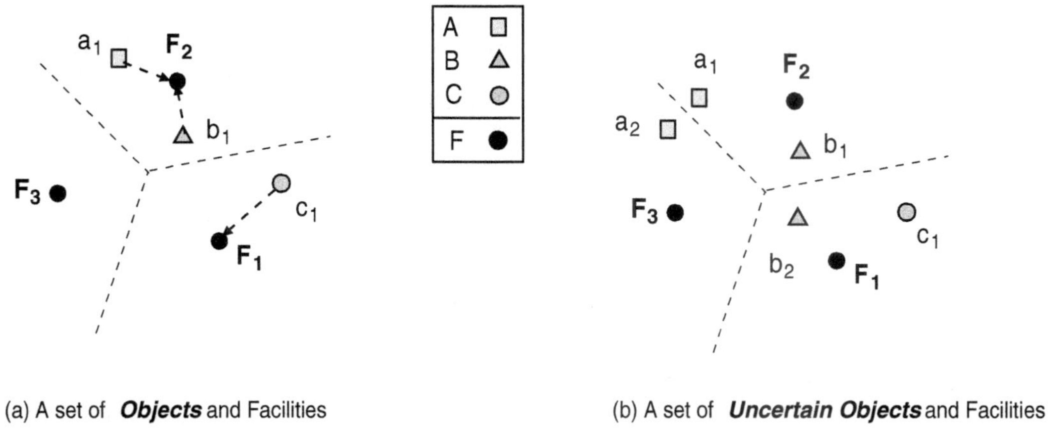

Figure 1: Motivation Example

of *influence score* of a facility in each possible world is exactly the same as the traditional BRNN query since only one instance occurs for each uncertain object in a possible world. Then we apply the **maximal utility principle** to rank the facilities. The maximal utility principle [14] has been widely used in various applications such as economic, finance and mathematics, and it selects the one with **highest expected score** as the optimal solution among a set of score distributions.

The second challenge is the efficiency of the algorithm. Computing the top k most influential facilities over uncertain objects is much more complicated than that of traditional objects (points). Although in Section 3 we show that our new model can avoid enumerating all possible worlds, the computation cost is still expensive if we conduct the calculation in a straightforward way due to the existence of multiple instances of uncertain objects. Therefore, in the paper, assuming the uncertain regions of uncertain objects are organized by R-tree which is the most popular indexing technique used for uncertain objects in the literature, we propose an efficient algorithm following the *synchronized* R-tree traversal paradigm. Moreover, based on a recent uncertain indexing technique [24], namely U-Quadtree, we further significantly improve the performance of the algorithm in terms of CPU and I/O costs.

Contributions. Our contribution can be summarized as follows.

- Based on the *maximal utility principle*, we propose a new model to evaluate the influences of the facilities over a set of uncertain objects.
- Efficient R-tree and U-Quadtree based algorithms are presented following the *filtering and verification* paradigm. Novel pruning techniques are proposed to significantly improve the performance of the algorithms by reducing the number of uncertain objects and facilities in the computation.
- Comprehensive experiments demonstrate the effectiveness and efficiency of our techniques.

Organization of the paper. The remainder of the paper is organized as follows. Section 2 presents the related work in the paper. Then, we formally define the problem of top k most influential facilities over uncertain objects, and introduce some preliminary work in Section 3. In Section 4, we propose our efficient algorithms based on R-tree and U-Quadtree respectively. Results of comprehensive performance studies are presented in Section 5. Finally, Section 6 concludes the paper.

2. RELATED WORK

In the last decade, a lot of work has been done in the field of uncertain data processing and management. Since our work focus on the top k query of influential facilities over uncertain data, we briefly introduce the existing work on uncertain data processing and influential facilities query.

2.1 Influential Facilities Computation

Bichromatic reverse nearest neighbor query is first introduced by Korn *et al.* in [10]. Given a set $\mathcal{F}$ of facilities and a set $\mathcal{O}$ of objects, the influence of a facility F can be measured by the number of objects whose nearest neighbors is F. As one of its natural extension, the problem of finding top k influential facilities (TkIS), is proposed in [20]. Instead of computing the set of BRNNs for a given set of facilities, it returns the top k facilities with highest number BRNNs (influences). They provide novel pruning techniques based on a new metric called $minExistDNN$, and found the top k most influential facilities by browsing trees once systematically. Furthermore, [9] found k locations from a set of candidate locations with the largest influence values according to a set of customers. On the other hand, the problem of optimal-location is studied in [21, 19] , aiming to find optimal area or location to set up a new facility such that it can attract the greatest number of facilities.

2.2 Uncertain Data Processing

With the emergence of many recent important and novel applications involving uncertain data, there has been a great deal of research attention dedicated to this field. Particularly, top k queries are important in analyzing uncertain data. Unlike a top k query over certain data which returns the k best alternatives according to a ranking function, a top k query against uncertain data has inherently more sophisticated semantics. Soliman et al [16] first relate top k queries with uncertain data. They define two types of important queries - U-Top$k$ and U-kRank, regarding discrete cases. The first one returns a set of k records which as a whole have the highest probability to be the top k results in all possible worlds, while the second one retrieves k ordered records where the i-th record has the highest probability of ranking in the i-th position among all possible worlds. Following, a large amount of work has been dedicated to top k queries with different semantics such as PT-k [8], Global-top k [22], expected rank top k [5] and unified top k [11] semantics.

Meanwhile, many spatial query techniques have been extended to solve uncertain problem. Nearest neighbor (NN) query over uncertain data is one of the most flourishing topic. Cheng *et al.* [4]

is the first to tackle the probabilistic nearest neighbor (PNN) query, whose aim is to determine probabilistic candidates for the nearest neighbor of a given target along with corresponding probability values. Zhang *et al.* [23] employ a rank based approach to process probabilistic kNN query, where k closest objects are returned according to their expected ranks. Cheema *et al.* [3] formalize PRNN query that is to retrieve the objects from the uncertain data that have higher probability than a given threshold to be the RNN of an uncertain query object. [12], [1] also propose techniques to solve PRNN queries over uncertain data. Moreover, some indexing techniques are proposed for uncertain data such as R-tree [15], U-tree [17] and U-Quadtree [24].

2.3 Influential Facilities over Uncertain data

To our best knowledge, Zheng *et al.* [25] is the only existing work which studies the problem of finding top k most influential facilities over uncertain objects. They assume that each object is characterized by multiple instances, and the facilities remain deterministic, and adopt the *expected rank* as the ranking function to define the order of the facilities with probabilistic influences. The definition is that given a set of facilities S, a set of uncertain objects U, a query region Q, and a natural number k, the uncertain top k influential facility query returns the top k facilities in Q according to the *expected rank semantics* [5]. Based on attribute-uncertain model, an uncertain object may be influenced by multiple facilities instead of one as the deterministic case, so they use PRNN search to get the probability mass function (pmf) of the influence of a facility, and then compute expected rank of a facility across all possible worlds. They propose a general filter-refine style approach which includes efficient PRNN search, effective pruning schemes and divide-and-conquer based refinement to obtain the query result.

3. BACKGROUND

We present problem definition and necessary preliminaries in this section. For references, notations frequently used in the paper are summarized in Table 1.

Notation	Definition
U	an uncertain object
F	the facility or facility entry
u	instance of the uncertain object
n	number of uncertain objects
m	number of instances per uncertain object
$I^+ (I^-)$	upper(lower) bound of *expected score*
E	entry of R-tree
NND	Nearest Neighbor Distance
$nnd\_min(R_1, R_2)$	the minimal NND between rectangles R_1 and R_2
$nnd\_max(R_1, R_2)$	the maximal NND between rectangles R_1 and R_2
T, t	object tuple
$T.e$	entry associated with T
$T.\mathcal{F}$	the facilities which may influence the object associated with T
λ	pruning threshold for *expected score*

Table 1: The summary of notations.

3.1 Problem Definition

A point (instance) x referred in the paper, by default, is in a d-dimensional numerical space. Given two points x and y, the distance between them is denoted by $d(x, y)$. Euclidian distance metric is employed in the paper, and the techniques developed in the paper can be easily extended to other metric distances. In the paper, we focus on the bichromatic nearest neighbor search. Given a set $\mathcal{F}$ of facilities (points) and the nearest neighbor of an object point x (x is not a facility) is its nearest facility, denoted by $NN(x)$; that is, $d(x, NN(x)) = \min\{d(x, F)|F \in \mathcal{F}\}$. Without loss of generality, we assume the nearest neighbor of a point x ($NN(x)$) is unique.

Uncertain Objects. An uncertain object can be described either *continuously* or *discretely*. In this paper, we focus on *discrete case*. Note that we can discretize a continuous probability density function (PDF) of an uncertain object by sampling methods. In the *discrete cases*, an uncertain object consists of a set $\{u_1, u_2, \ldots, u_m\}$ of instances (points) where for $1 \le i \le m$, u_i occurs with the probability p_{u_i} ($p_{u_i} > 0$), and $\sum_{i=1}^{m} p_{u_i} = 1$. For an uncertain object U, U_{mbr} denotes the minimal bounding rectangle (MBR) of the instances of U.

Note that, in the paper, we assume the facilities are represented by points because usually their locations can be obtained precisely.

The possible world semantics. Given a set of uncertain objects $\{U_1, U_2, \ldots, U_n\}$, a possible world $W = \{u_1, u_2, \ldots, u_n\}$ is a set of instances sequentially sampled from each object. Assume the uncertain objects are independent to each other, and the probability of W to appear is $Pr(W) = \prod_{i=1}^{n} p_{u_i}$. Let $\mathcal{W}$ denote the set of all possible worlds, then $\sum_{W \in \mathcal{W}} Pr(W) = 1.0$.

EXAMPLE 1. *In Figure 2(a), $\mathcal{F}$ consists of three facilities F_1, F_2 and F_3, and there are three uncertain objects A, B and C. Both A and B have two instances with the same occurrence probability (0.5), while C has only one single instance c_1 with $p_{c_1} = 1.0$. Consequently, there are totally 4 possible worlds in this example, where $W_1 = \{a_1, b_1, c_1\}$, $W_2 = \{a_1, b_2, c_1\}$, $W_3 = \{a_2, b_1, c_1\}$, $W_4 = \{a_2, b_2, c_1\}$ and the probability of each possible world is 0.25. Particularly, the possible world W_1 is illustrated in Figure 2(b).*

For each possible world W, let $s(F, W)$ denote the influence score of the facility F regarding W, which is the number of reverse nearest neighbors of F in W; In the paper, for each facility F, we use S_F to represent the influence score distribution of F, where $Pr(S_F = v) = \sum_{W \in \mathcal{W} \wedge s(F,W)=v} Pr(W)$.

EXAMPLE 2. *In Figure 2(b), we have $s(F_1, W) = 1$, $s(F_2, W) = 2$ and $s(F_3, W) = 0$. Figure 2(c) illustrates the score distributions of F_1, F_2 and F_3. For facility F_1, we have $Pr(S_{F_1} = 1) = 0.5$, $Pr(S_{F_1} = 2) = 0.5$. Similarly, $Pr(S_{F_2} = 0) = 0.25$, $Pr(S_{F_2} = 1) = 0.5$, $Pr(S_{F_2} = 2) = 0.25$, $Pr(S_{F_3} = 0) = 0.5$ and $Pr(S_{F_3} = 1) = 0.5$.*

The influence score distribution of a facility F (S_F) is a random variable, and hence we can apply the **maximal utility principle** to rank the facilities. The maximal utility principle [14] is one of the most popular models to select the one with **highest expected score** as the optimal solution among a set of score distributions. In the paper, the *expected influence score* of a facility F, denoted by $I(F)$, is defined as follows.

$$I(F) = \sum_{W \in \mathcal{W}} s(F, W) \times Pr(W) \quad (1)$$

As the number of possible worlds grows exponentially regarding the number of uncertain objects in $\mathcal{U}$ and the number of instances in each uncertain objects, it is cost-inhibitive to apply Equation 1 straightforwardly by enumerating all possible worlds. Therefore, we will find an alternative of Equation 1 which can be derived with reasonable computational cost.

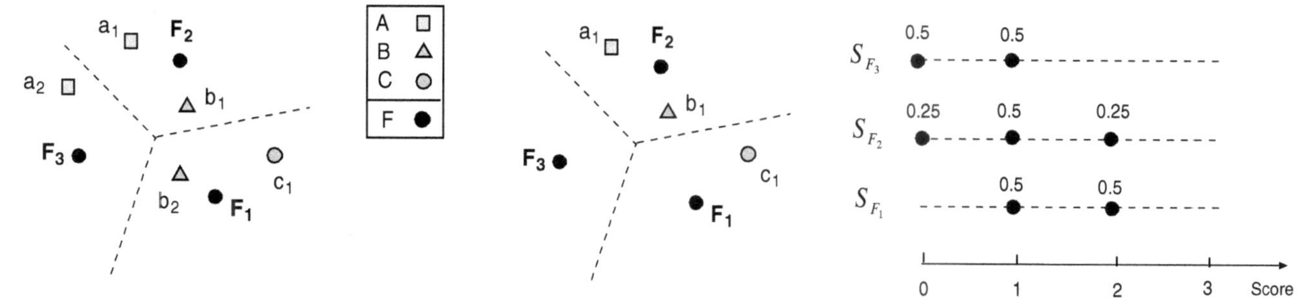

(a) A set of Uncertain Objects and Facilities (b) A possible world (c) Influence score distributions of the facilities

Figure 2: Example for the Problem Definition

Let $NN(U, W)$ denote the nearest neighbor (facility) of U in the possible world W, and $\sigma(NN(U, W) = F) = 1$ if the facility F is the nearest neighbor of U in the possible world W, and $\sigma(NN(U, W) = F) = 0$ otherwise. Since we assume the uncertain objects are independent to each other, Equation 1 can be rewritten as follows.

$$\begin{aligned} I(F) &= \sum_{W \in \mathcal{W}} (\sum_{U \in \mathcal{U}} \sigma(NN(U, W) = F)) \times Pr(W) && (2) \\ &= \sum_{U \in \mathcal{U}} Pr(NN(U) = F) && (3) \\ &= \sum_{U \in \mathcal{U}} \sum_{u \in U \wedge NN(u) = F} p_u && (4) \end{aligned}$$

, where $Pr(NN(U) = F)$ is the probability that F is the nearest neighbor of U, i.e., $Pr(NN(U) = F) = \sum_{u \in U \wedge NN(u) = F} p_u$ and $NN(u)$ is the nearest neighbor of the instance (point) u.

Equation 4 implies that we can avoid enumerating all possible worlds since we can independently compute $Pr(NN(U) = F)$ (i.e., nearest neighbor probability) for each uncertain objects. Our empirical study shows that even a naive implementation of the Equation 4 can outperform the existing work which follows the *expected rank* model.

In the light of *maximal utility principle*, we aim to find the k facilities with highest *expected influence scores*, which is formally described below.

Problem Statement. Given a set of uncertain object $\mathcal{O}$ and a set of facility $\mathcal{F}$, find the k facilities with the highest *expected influence scores*. We assume the number of facilities $|\mathcal{F}| \geq k$, and ties are broken arbitrarily.

3.2 Expected Score vs Expected Rank

In [25], Zheng *et* al. propose the *expected rank* based ranking model to evaluate the influence of the uncertain objects. For a given facility F, its *expected rank*, denoted by $er(F)$, is calculated as follows.

$$er(F) = \sum_{W \in \mathcal{W}} r(F, W) \times Pr(W) \quad (5)$$

, where $r(F, W)$ is the rank of F in the possible world W. Then the k facilities with highest ranks are retrieved.

Given a possible world W, the rank of a facility $(r(F, W))$, is calculated based on its influence score (i.e., $s(F, W)$) as well as influence scores of other facilities, while the *expected score* computation is independent to other facilities. This implies that the *expected rank* based ranking model is much more complicate than the *expected score* based model. As shown in [25], we may have to enumerate all possible worlds in the worse case, which is cost-inhibitive in practise. Therefore, although novel pruning techniques are proposed to significantly improve the performance, the computational cost of the algorithm is still expensive due to the high complexity of the ranking model.

As mentioned in [5], the *expected score* based ranking approach does not satisfy the *value invariance* property, which implies that the ranking results of the *expected rank* model and the *expected score* model may be different if there are some inconsistent extreme scores in the possible worlds. For instance, a facility F has extremely high score in a few of the possible worlds such that its rank is boosted by this extreme value. Nevertheless, under our problem setting, for each possible world we have $\sum_{F \in \mathcal{F}} s(F, W) = n$ where n is the number of uncertain objects, and hence it is unlikely to have facilities with inconsistent extreme scores. This is confirmed in our empirical study which shows that two models have almost the same top k results but new algorithms proposed in the paper are much more efficient (up to one order of magnitude faster) due to the simplicity of our new ranking model and efficiency of pruning techniques.

3.3 Preliminaries

Various indexing techniques have been proposed to organize uncertain objects. In the paper, we apply R-tree and U-Quadtree based indexing techniques to facilitate the *expected influence score* computation. Note that the R-tree based indexing technique is the most widely used approach in the literature to index uncertain objects [15], and U-Quadtree is the most recent indexing technique to support range search on uncertain objects.

Indexing uncertain objects by R-tree

Given an uncertain object U, we use U_{mbr} to denote the minimal bounding rectangle (MBR) of the instances of U. Figure 4 illustrates the basic idea of the R-tree based indexing approach where the MBRs of the uncertain objects are indexed by R-tree [7]. As to each uncertain object, an *aggregate* R-tree is employed to organize the instances where the aggregate value of each intermediate entry is the probability mass of the instances in the entry.

Indexing Uncertain Objects by U-Quadtree

A quadtree [6] is a space partitioning tree data structure in which a d-dimensional space is recursively subdivided into 2^d regions (cells). In [24], the instances of an uncertain object U are organized by a *summary*, denoted by S_U, which consists of a set of entries $\{e\}$, where each entry records the object id ($e.oid$), the cell of the quadtree ($e.cid$) and the probability mass of instances allocated on this cell ($e.p$). The entries of the uncertain objects are organized by a $B+$ tree where the cell ids are key values, which are

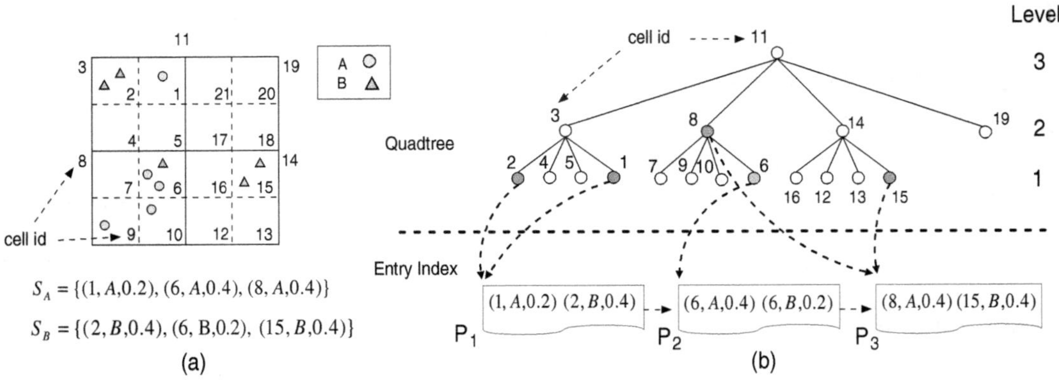

Figure 3: U**-Quadtree**

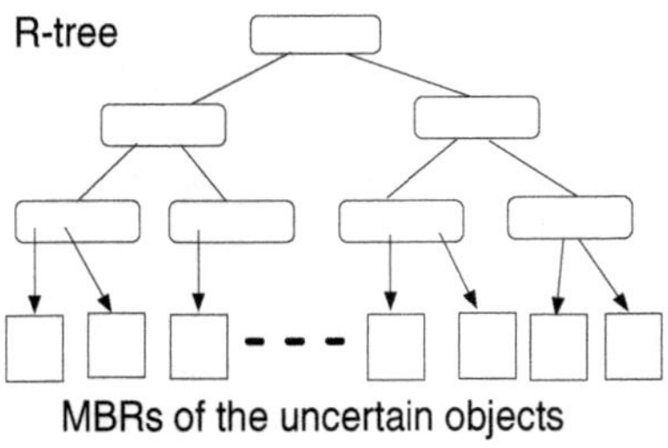

Figure 4: R**-tree based Indexing**

generated based on Hilbert curve. Figure 3 illustrates an example of the U-Quadtree.

EXAMPLE 3. *In Figure 3(a), objects A and B have 5 instances each and all instances have the same occurrence probability* (0.2). *The height of the quadtree* (h) *is* 3 *and the ids of the cells are labeled. We may have* $S_A = \{(1, A, 0.2), (6, A, 0.4), (8, A, 0.4)\}$ *and* $S_B = \{(2, B, 0.4), (6, B, 0.2), (15, B, 0.4)\}$.

Note that the summary of an object *is not unique* as an instance x can be assigned to any cell which *contains* x. In [24], a novel indexing construction algorithm is proposed to effectively build U-Quadtree based on the cost model. Moreover, the instances of each uncertain object are also organized by an aggregate R-tree in [24].

4. APPROACH

In this section, we investigate efficient algorithms to compute the top k most influential facilities based on their *expected influence scores*. Section 4.1 presents a straightforward implementation of the algorithm. Assuming the uncertain objects are organized by R-tree, Section 4.2 improves the performance of the algorithm following the *filtering and verification* paradigm. By taking advantage of an enhanced uncertain object indexing technique, U-Quadtree, Section 4.3 further improves the performance of the *filtering* and the *verification* algorithms.

In the paper, we assume facilities are organized by R-tree since it is one of the most popular index techniques in commercial spatial databases. Nevertheless, our techniques developed in the paper can be easily extended to other hierarchical spatial indexing techniques.

4.1 Naive Algorithm

Algorithm 1 illustrates a naive implementation of the algorithm to compute the nearest neighbor probability of each instance regarding all facilities following Equation 4. For each instance of an uncertain object, a nearest neighbor query [13] is issued to find its nearest facility F and the *expected score* of F is increased by the occurrence probability of the instance.

Algorithm 1: Naive Algorithm(S_U, S_F, k)

Input : k, Uncertain object set S_U, Facility set S_F
Output: Top k most influential facilities

```
for each U ∈ S_U do
    for each instance u ∈ U do
        for find nearest facility F ∈ S_F do
            I(F) := I(F) + p_u;
Return top k facilities with highest expected score;
```

Although we do not need to explore all possible worlds following the *expected score semantics*, the performance of the algorithm is not scalable to the number of instances and facilities because the instances of all objects are accessed in Algorithm 1 and the *expected scores* are calculated for all facilities, which leads to high CPU and I/O costs.

4.2 R-tree based Algorithm

To address the scalability issue in the above naive algorithm, in this subsection, we propose the R-tree based algorithm following the *filtering and verification* paradigm. More specifically, based on the MBRs of the uncertain objects, which are organized by R-tree, we can come up with the lower and upper bounds of the *expected influence scores* of the facilities in the *filtering* phase. Then some facilities can be pruned based on the widely used top k filtering conditions; that is, a facility F will be eliminated from candidate set if there are a set $\mathcal{Q}$ of k other facilities such that $I^+(F) < I^-(F')$ for any facility F' in $\mathcal{Q}$, where $I^+(F)$ ($I^-(F)$) denotes the upper (lower) bound of *expected score* for the facility F. In the *refinement* phase, we only need to explore the instances of the uncertain objects which may contribute to the *expected scores* of the facilities in the candidate set.

In the paper, we assume the MBRs of the uncertain objects and facilities are organized by an aggregate R-tree $R_{\mathcal{O}}$ and a R-tree $R_{\mathcal{F}}$ respectively. We first introduce some notations used in the paper.

DEFINITION 1. *Nearest Neighbor Distance (NND). Given a set of facilities $\mathcal{F}$, the distance between a point x and its nearest neighbor F is the nearest neighbor distance of x regarding $\mathcal{F}$, denoted by $nnd(x, \mathcal{F})$. In [20], effective method is proposed to compute the minimal and maximal nearest neighbor distances between two rectangles. In the paper, we use $nnd_{min}(R_1, R_2)$ to denote the minimal nearest neighbor distance between two rectangles R_1 and R_2; that is, for any point x in R_1, its nearest neighbor distance regarding a set of facilities $\mathcal{F}$ contained by R_2 is not smaller than $nnd_{min}(R_1, R_2)$, i.e., $nnd(x, \mathcal{F}) \geq nnd_{min}(R_1, R_2)$. With the same rationale, we have $nnd_{max}(R_1, R_2)$ where $nnd(x, \mathcal{F}) \leq nnd_{max}(R_1, R_2)$.*

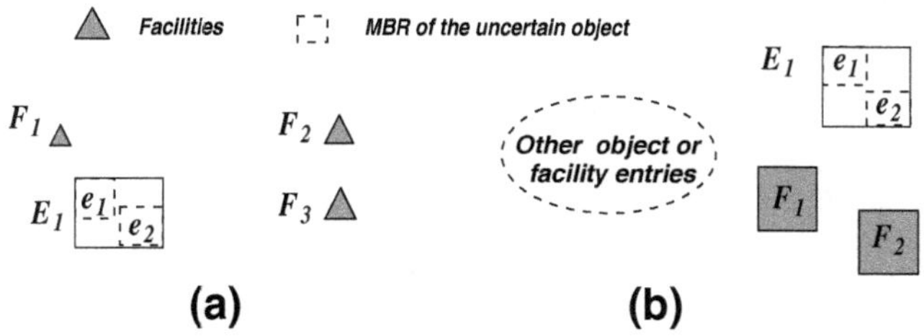

Figure 6: Motivation Example

To enable computing the *expected scores* of the facilities in a level by level fashion, we introduce the concept of object tuple and facility tuple so that the *expected score* of a group of facilities or uncertain objects can be updated or pruned at the same time.

DEFINITION 2. *Object Tuple (T). An object tuple T is employed to maintain the information used for the NND computation of a set of uncertain objects in an entry e. Particularly, $T.e$ is the object R-tree entry (intermediate entry or data entry) associated with T, and $T.\mathcal{F}$ is a set of facility R-tree entries (intermediate entry or data entry) which may contribute to the NND computation of the objects in $T.e$.*

EXAMPLE 4. *In Figure 5, there are four uncertain objects U_1, U_2, U_3 and U_4, and their MBRs are kept in data entries $\{e_1, e_2, e_3, e_4\}$. Suppose the object tuple T refers to the entry E_1, then we have $T.e = E_1$ and $T.\mathcal{F} = \{F_1, F_2, F_3\}$ where F_1, F_2, F_3 are facilities entries which may contribute to the NND computation of the object associated with T.*

Whenever there is no ambiguity, we use F to denote an entry in the facility R-tree. We use $I^-(F)$ and $I^+(F)$ to denote the lower and upper bounds of the *expected score* of F. Note that F may represent an intermediate entry which contains a set of facilities.

R-tree based Filtering

Motivation

The basic idea of the filtering algorithm is to conduct the *NND* computation on the high level entries of $R_\mathcal{O}$ and $R_\mathcal{F}$ such that we do not need to compute the *NND* regarding each individual object and facility, and hence improve the performance of the algorithm in terms of CPU and I/O costs.

In Figure 5, let T refer to the entry E_1 and $T.\mathcal{F} = \{F_1, F_2, F_3\}$. We can remove F_2 and F_3 from $T.\mathcal{F}$ since the maximal *NND* between E_1 and F_1 ($nnd\_max(E_1, F_1)$) is smaller than the minimal *NND* from E_1 to F_2 and F_3 ($nnd\_min(E_1, F_1)$ and ($nnd\_min(E_1, F_3)$)) , which implies that none of the facilities in F_2 and F_3 can contribute to the *NND* computation of the objects in E_1 and hence $T.\mathcal{F} = \{F_1\}$. Similarly, we have $T.\mathcal{F} = \{F_2, F_3\}$ when $T.e$ refers to E_2. Moreover, let λ be the k-th largest lower bounds of the *expected scores* for the facility entries seen so far, we do not need to further explore the entries since none of the facilities in the entry can be top k influential facilities. In the paper, we say a facility entry F is *disabled* if $I^+(F) < \lambda$.

Besides the facility entries, we can also *prune* object entries in the paper. In Figure 6(a), we have $T.e = E_1$ and $T.\mathcal{F} = \{F_1, F_2, F_3\}$. Suppose F_1 is a data entry, i.e., F_1 corresponds to a single facility, and the maximal *NND* between F_1 and E_1 is smaller than the minimal *NND* from E_1 to F_2 and F_3, then we can increase $I^-(F_1)$ by $agg(E_1)$ where $agg(E_1)$ is the number of uncertain objects in E_1. Clearly, we do not need to further explore the uncertain objects in E_1 and E_1 is marked as *disabled*. On the other hand, as shown in Figure 6(b), suppose all facility entries in $T.\mathcal{F}$ are *disabled* (shown as grey rectangles in the example), we can also prune E_1 since objects in E_1 only contribute to the *expected scores* of the non-promising facilities.

Algorithm 2: *R-tree based Filtering*($R_\mathcal{O}$, $R_\mathcal{F}$, k)

```
Input  : R_O : the aggregate R-tree for uncertain objects,
         R_F : the R-tree for facilities, k
Output : C : a set of candidate facilities,
         S : objects need to be further explored
1  C := ∅; S := ∅; Q := ∅; λ = 0;
2  generate a new tuple T;
3  T.e ← the root of R_O ;
4  e_f ← the root of R_F ;
5  T.F ← e_f; I^-(e_f) := 0 ; I^+(e_f) := # objects in R_O ;
6  push T into FIFO queue Q ;
7  while Q is not empty do
8      T ← pop the head of Q ;
9      if T.e is data entry and all facility entries in T.F are data
       entries then
10         S := S ∪ T ;
11     else
12         for each child entry e' of T.e do
13             generate a new object tuple t for e' where t.e := e' ;
14             for each facility entry F in T.F do
15                 if F is not disabled then
16                     for each child entry e_f of F do
17                         t.F := t.F ∪ e_f;
18                         I^-(e_f) := I^-(F); I^+(e_f) := I^+(F) ;
19             d_max := min{nnd_max(t.e, e_f) } for all e_f in t.F ;
20             for each facility entry e_f in t.F do
21                 if nnd_min(t.e, e_f) > d_max then
22                     t.F := t.F − e_f ;
23                     I^+(e_f) := I^+(e_f) − agg(t.e) ;
24                 if I^+(e_f) < λ then
25                     Disable F;
26             if t.F contains exactly one data entry e_f then
27                 I^-(e_f) := I^-(e_f) + agg(t.e) ;
28                 Update λ; Disable t;
29             if all facilities in t.F are disabled then
30                 Disable t ;
31             if t is not disabled then
32                 Push t to the tail of Q ;
33 C ← facilities with I^+(F) ≥ λ ;
34 return S, C
```

Algorithm

Algorithm 2 illustrates the details of the R-tree based *filtering* algorithm on $R_\mathcal{O}$ and $R_\mathcal{F}$, which follows the *synchronized* R-tree traversal paradigm used in spatial joins. A FIFO queue (Q) is employed to keep object tuples, and the first object tuple is initialized by the roots of $R_\mathcal{O}$ and $R_\mathcal{F}$ (Lines 2-5). For each object tuple T popped from Q, Line 10 puts the object tuple T to $\mathcal{S}$ which keeps the objects need to be further explored in the *refinement* phase **if** all entries in $T.e$ and $T.\mathcal{F}$ are *data* entries. Otherwise, Line 13 generates an object tuple t for each child entry of $T.e$ [2]. Then for each facility entry in $T.\mathcal{F}$, we put all of its child entries $\{e_f\}$ to $t.\mathcal{F}$ if it is not marked as *disabled*. Meanwhile, $I^-(e_f)$ and $I^+(e_f)$ are set by its parent entry in Line 18. Line 19 calculates the maximal *NND* from $T.e$ to facility entries in $t.\mathcal{F}$, denoted by d_{max}. For each facility entry e_f in $t.\mathcal{F}$, we exclude e_f from $t.\mathcal{F}$ if $nnd\_min(t.e, e_f) > d_{max}$ and decrease $I^+(e_f)$ by $agg(t.e)$

[2] In the case that $T.e$ is a data entry, we simply set $t.e = T.e$ at Line 13. The same strategy goes for facilities in Line 16.

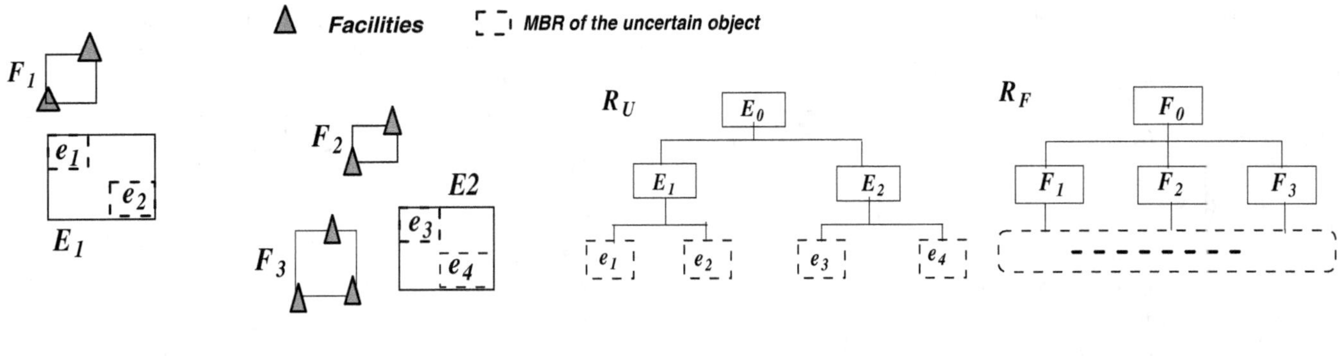

Figure 5: Motivation Example

(Line 20-23). Recall that $agg(t.e)$ is the number of uncertain objects in $t.e$. The facility entry e_f will be pruned in Line 25 if its upper bound of the *expected score* is smaller than λ. In Line 26-28, we increase $I^-(e_f)$ by $agg(t.e)$ and do not further explore uncertain objects in $t.e$ (i.e., prune t) if e_f is the only **data** entry in $e.\mathcal{F}$. In Line 29-30, we prune the object tuple t if all of the facilities in $t.\mathcal{F}$ are non-promising facilities. Line 32 pushes the object tuple t to Q if it is not *disabled*. Finally, Algorithm 2 terminates when Q is empty, and the facilities surviving the *filtering* phase ($\mathcal{C}$) will be returned as well as the object tuples in $\mathcal{S}$.

R-tree based Refinement

After the *filtering* phase, we need to explore the instances of the uncertain objects in $\mathcal{S}$ such that we can come up with the top k influential facilities in the *refinement* phase. Algorithm 3 illustrates the framework of the *refinement* procedure. For each object tuple T in $\mathcal{S}$, we apply the function **Refinement** to refine the *expected scores* of the facilities in the candidate set. Note that we do not need to process T if all facilities in $T.\mathcal{F}$ are marked as *disabled*. Finally we have $I(F) = I^-(F)$, and the k facilities with the highest *expected scores* are retrieved.

Algorithm 3: ***R-tree based Refinement***($\mathcal{C}, \mathcal{S}, k$)

```
Input   : C : the candidate facilities,
          S : the objects tuples,
          k
Output  : I : the top k influential facilities
1 I := ∅; ;
2 for each object tuple T in S do
3   | if all facilities in T.F are disabled then
4   |   Goto Line 2;
5   | U ← the uncertain object associated with T.e ;
6   | Refinement( root of R_U, T.F);
7 I ← k facilities with the highest I⁻(F) values ;
8 return I
```

In the following, we first discuss the access orders at Line 2 of Algorithm 3 , then present the function **Refinement** at Line 6.

Access Order. Intuitively, we should put high priority to the objects which contribute to the facilities with large upper bounds of the *expected scores* since they are more likely to be the top k influential facilities, and hence leads to a tighter *expected score* threshold λ, i.e., better pruning power. In the paper, an object tuple T is sorted by the largest upper bounds of *expected scores* for facilities in $T.\mathcal{F}$. Our empirical study shows this strategy outperforms others alternatives such as the random order and ordering by the size of $T.\mathcal{F}$, i.e., the number of facilities which may influence the uncertain objects associated with $T.e$.

Refinement Algorithm. Algorithm 4 is used to update the *expected scores* of the facilities by exploring the instances kept in an aggregate R-tree entry e. It is similar to the R-tree based filtering algorithm (Algorithm 2) except that: (i) In Algorithm 2, both object entry and facility entry are drilled down in a level by level fashion, while in Algorithm 4 only the object entries are expanded since we already reach the bottom of the facility R-tree in the *filtering* phase. (ii) At Line 7, 10, 18 and 22 of Algorithm 4, $p(e)$ represents the probability mass of the instances in the aggregate R-tree entry e.

Algorithm 4: **Refinement**($e, \mathcal{F}$)

```
Input   : e : the R-tree entry,
          F : a set of facilities
Output  : Updated F
1  Q := ∅; T.e := e ; T.F := F;
2  push T to Q;
3  while Q is not empty do
4    | T ← pop the head of Q ;
5    | if T.e is a data entry then
6    |   | Find the nearest facility F in T.F ;
7    |   | I⁻(F) := I⁻(F) + p(T.e) ;
8    |   | Update λ ;
9    |   | for other facility F' in T.F do
10   |   |   | I⁺(F') := I⁺(F') − p(T.e) ;
11   |   |   | Disable F' if I⁺(F') < λ ;
12   | else
13   |   | for each child entry e' of T.e do
14   |   |   | t.e ← e' ;
15   |   |   | t.F := T.F ;
16   |   |   | d_max := min{nnd_max(T.e, F) | F ∈ T.F} ;
17   |   |   | for facility F in t.F with nnd_min(T.e, F) > d_max
     |   |   | do
18   |   |   |   | I⁺(F) := I⁺(F) − p(t.e);
19   |   |   |   | remove F from t.F ;
20   |   |   |   | Disable F if I⁺(F) < λ ;
21   |   |   | if There is only one facility F in t.F then
22   |   |   |   | I⁻(F) := I⁻(F) + p(t.e) ;
23   |   |   |   | Update λ ;
24   |   |   | else
25   |   |   |   | Push t on the tail of Q ;
26 return F , λ
```

4.3 U-Quadtree based Algorithm

Observe that the performance of R-tree technique is poor when the sizes of the MBRs of the uncertain objects are not very small because it is not effective to capture the instance distribution of an uncertain object by a single MBR. In [24], Zhang *et al.* propose a novel indexing structure based on the quadtree such that a good tradeoff can be achieved between the filtering cost and refinement cost.

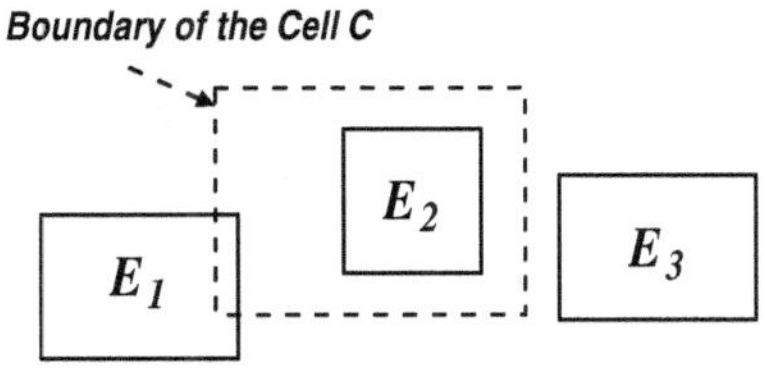

Figure 7: Containment Example

Suppose the uncertain objects are organized by U-Quadtree and the instances of each uncertain object are kept in an aggregate R-tree, in this subsection, we present efficient U-Quadtree based algorithm to identify the top k influential facilities.

U-*Quadtree based Filtering*

As the U-Quadtree is also a hierarchical spatial tree structure, Algorithm 2 can be modified to support the *filtering* procedure. Recall that the MBR of an uncertain object U is kept for R-tree index, while an uncertain object U is described by a summary S_U in U-Quadtree which consists of a set of entries where each entry is represented by its corresponding cell in the quadtree and the probability mass of the instances assigned to the cell. Therefore, in Line 10 of Algorithm 2, an object tuple is kept in $\mathcal{S}$ if it is a cell at the lowest level and all facilities in $T.\mathcal{F}$ are data entries. Moreover, for an object tuple T, $T.e$ corresponds to a cell c which maintains the entries of the uncertain object summaries assigned to c, and $T.\mathcal{F}$ records the facility entries which may influence the instances of the uncertain objects associated with c. When $I^-(e_f)$ ($I^+(e_f)$) is increased (decreased), instead of $agg(T.e)$ the probabilities sum of all entries on c (i.e., $T.e$) will be used.

U-*Quadtree based Refinement*

We first introduce the *containment* relationship between a cell c and an entry E in our algorithm description. The cell c *fully contains* the entry E if all points in the MBR of E are contained by the boundary of c. If c does not *fully contain* E but some points in the MBR of E are contained by the boundary of c, then c *partially contains* E. Otherwise, there is no containment relationship between c and E. For instance, in Figure 7, E_2 is *fully contained* by c and E_1 is *partially contained* by c.

Algorithm 5 illustrates the details of the U-Quadtree based refinement algorithm. For each uncertain object U survived in the *filtering* phase, we issue a set of window queries to update the *expected scores* of the facilities in $\mathcal{F}$. More specifically, a FIFO queue Q is employed to keep entries in the aggregate R-tree of the uncertain object U (R_U), which is initialized by the root of R_U. For an entry e in the R_U, we will invoke the function **Refinement if** it is *fully contained* by c. Otherwise, the child entries of e are pushed to Q **if** e is *partially contained* by c. Note that a *data* entry will either be *fully contained* by c or have no containment relationship with c. Finally, we have $I(F) = I^-(F)$, and the k facilities with the highest *expected scores* are returned.

5. EXPERIMENT

In this section, we present results of a comprehensive performance study to evaluate the efficiency and scalability of the proposed techniques in the paper. Following algorithms are evaluated.

- **Naive** The naive implementation proposed in Section 4.1.
- **RTKIS** The technique based on R-tree proposed in Section 4.2.
- **UQuadTKIS** The technique based on U-Quadtree proposed in Section 4.3.

Algorithm 5: U-***Quadtree based Refinement*** ($\mathcal{C}$, $\mathcal{S}$, k , λ)

```
Input  : C : the candidate facilities,
         S : the objects need to further explore,
         k
Output : I : the top k influential facilities
I := ∅; ;
for each uncertain object U in S do
    for each cell c associated with U do
        Q := ∅; Q ← root of R_U ;
        while Q is not empty do
            e ← pop the head of Q ;
            if MBR of e is fully contained by the cell c then
                Refinement( e , F) ;
            else if MBR of e is partially contained by the cell c
            then
                for each entry e' of e do
                    Push e' to the tail of Q ;
I ← k facilities with the highest I^-(F) ;
return I
```

- **UTKIS** The technique presented in [25].

Datasets. Three real spatial datasets, namely CA, USA and RT, are used to evaluate our techniques. CA and USA contain $62K$ and $200K$ 2-dimensional points representing locations in the Los Angeles and the United States respectively which are available at [2]. The two datasets are separated into several groups of data respectively, and we choose one group of data with 996 points as the facilities and the other group of data with $21,050$ points to represent the centers of uncertain objects from CA as default dateset, whose distributions are showed in Figure 8. RT is obtained from the R-tree-Portal [18] with cultural landmarks and populated places in North America. The number of uncertain objects in USA and RT are $20,287$ and $24,493$ respectively. By default, around 1000 facilities are chosen from corresponding datasets. In our experiment, all dimensions are normalized to domain [0, 10000], and the uncertain region of the uncertain object is a circle with expected radius r_u varying from 20 to 300 with default value 60. There are m instances for each uncertain object and the expected m varies from 100 to 500 with default value 200. Therefore, the total number of instances in default dataset is $4,210,000$. The instances of an uncertain object follow popular distributions Normal(N) and Uniform(U) where Normal(N) distribution serves as default instance distribution.

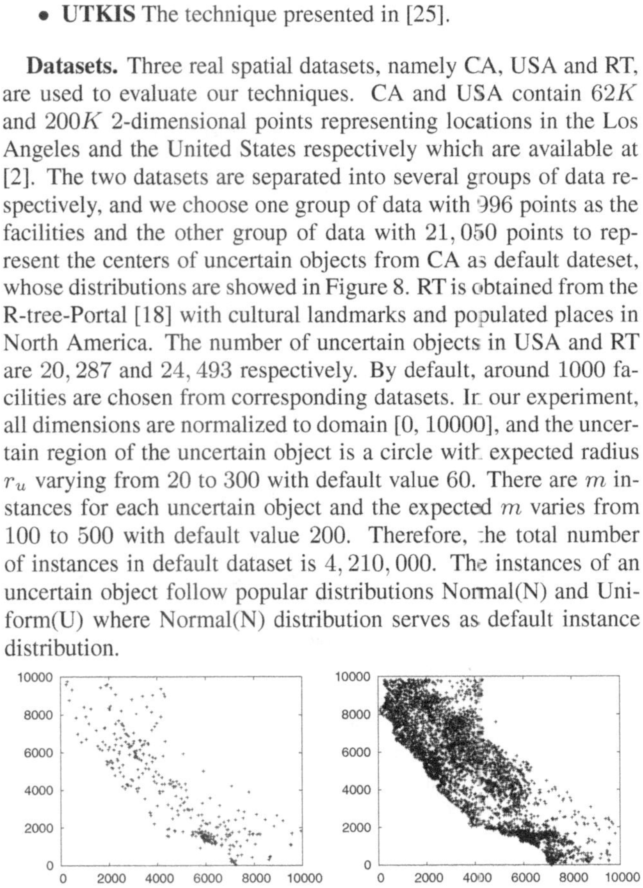

(a) *Facilities* (b) *Objects*

Figure 8: Data distribution

All algorithms proposed in this paper are implemented in standard C++ with STL library support and compiled with GNU GCC. Experiments are run on a PC with Intel Xeon 2.40GHz dual CPU and 4G memory running Debian Linux. The disk page size is fixed to 4096 bytes and the capacity of the entry page (f) is set to 512. In the paper, we evaluate the I/O performance of the algorithms by measuring the number of uncertain objects explored, i.e., uncertain objects whose aggregate R-tree are loaded in main memory.

Query response time is recorded to evaluate the efficiency of the algorithms, which contains the CPU time and the I/O latency.

Table 2 lists parameters which may have an impact on our performance study. In our experiments, all parameters use default values unless otherwise specified.

Notation	Definition (Default Values)
h	height of U-Quadtree (9)
r_u	radius of uncertain object region (60)
n	number of uncertain objects ($20K$)
m	number of instances per object (200)
f	number of facility ($1K$)

Table 2: Parameter settings

5.1 Performance Tuning

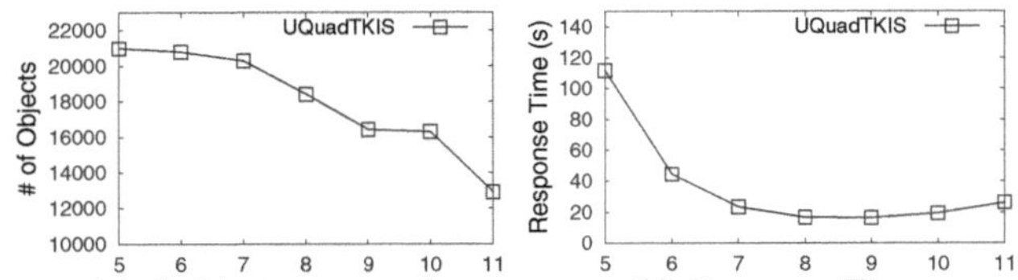

(a) *# objects accessed* (b) *Response Time*

Figure 9: Diff. U-Quadtree Height

The performance of UQuadTKIS is effected by the height (h) of the U-Quadtree. As expected, Figure 9(a) shows that number of objects visited in the *refinement* phase drops when h increases due to the larger size of uncertain object summaries. Nevertheless, UQuadTKIS becomes less efficient for larger h when $h > 9$, which implies that the algorithm cannot pay-off the larger index size when $h > 9$. In the following experiments, h is set to 9.

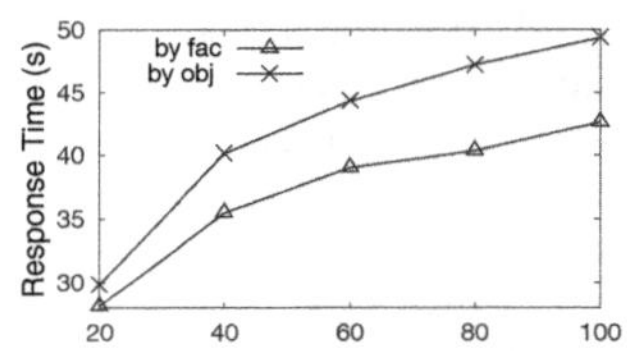

Figure 10: Access Order

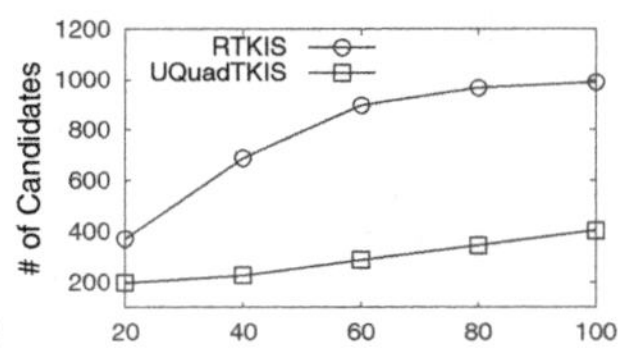

Figure 11: Candidate Size

Figure 10 reports the effectiveness of different access order strategies in R-tree based *refinement* algorithm where the sizes of the radius grow from 20 to 100. Particularly, "by fac" denotes the facilities *expected score* based access order strategy used in Algorithm 2, and "by obj" stands for the object based strategy, i.e., accessing in decreasing order of the number of facilities associated with each object. It is shown that our facility based strategy always outperform the object based strategy.

We evaluate the *filtering* effectiveness of RTKIS and UQuadTKIS in Figure 11 by measuring the number of candidates (facilities) after *filtering* phase. The performance of both algorithms degrade against the growth of r_u. UQuadTKIS significantly outperforms RTKIS since more resources are allocated to the U-Quadtree to capture the distribution of the instances of the uncertain objects.

5.2 Performance Evaluation

Comparing Different Ranking models. Figure 12 evaluates the similarity of different ranking models (*expected rank* and *expected score*) on three datasets CA, USA and RT respectively, which shows the scatter-plot of the ranks of 100 facilities. Particularly, each point in the scatter-plot represents a facility where x-axis and y-axis record the rank of objects based on *expected rank* model and

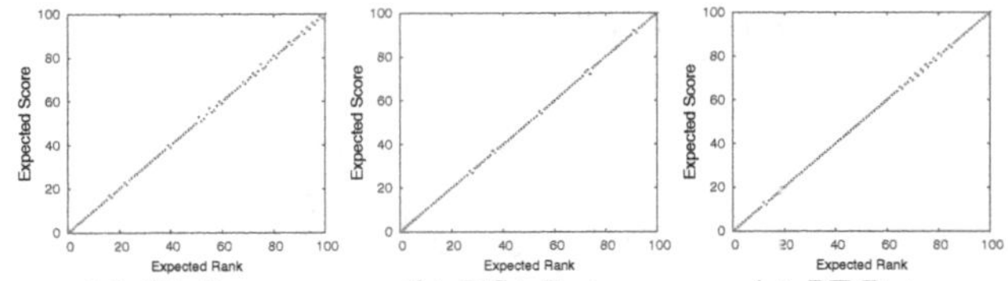

(a) *CA Data* (b) *USA Data* (c) *RT Data*

Figure 12: Result comparison

expected score model respectively. It is shown that all points line up along the diagonal, and the maximal difference of the ranks for a facility is only 2 in Figure 12 , which indicates that the results of two models are almost the same.

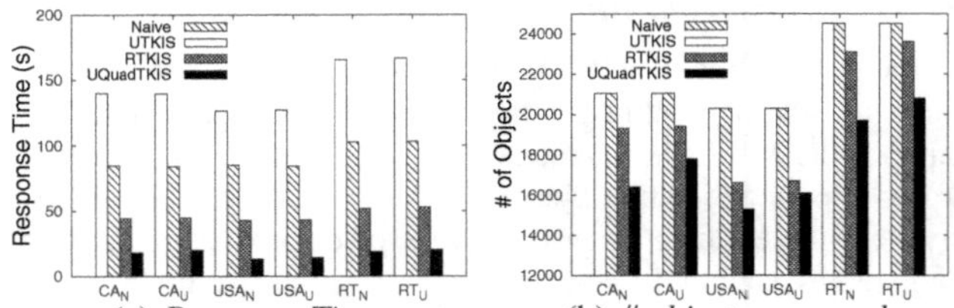

(a) *Response Time* (b) *# objects accessed*

Figure 13: Impact of Data Distributions

Impact of Data Distribution. Figure 13 reports the response time and the number of uncertain objects accessed of the algorithms against different data distributions where CA_N represent the dataset in which the centers of uncertain objects are from CA and the instances of each uncertain object follow the Normal(N) distribution. It is reported that UQuadTKIS significantly outperforms other algorithms under all data distributions, and UTKIS ranks the last due to the high complexity of the *expected rank* model. Particularly, on CA_N dataset, The response times of four algorithms (UQuadTKIS, RTKIS, Naive and UTKIS) are 17.8, 44.28, 84 and 140 seconds respectively. They are 20.14, 52.85, 103 and 166.2 seconds respectively on RT_U dataset.

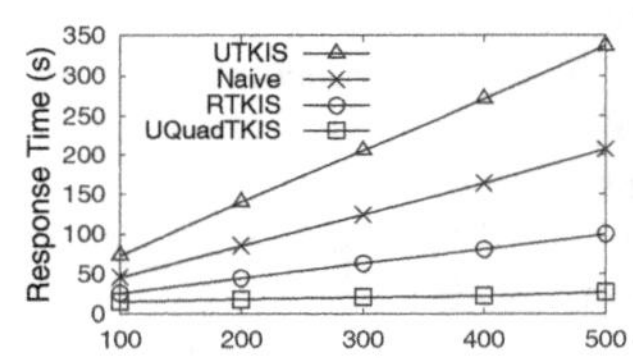

Figure 14: Diff. m

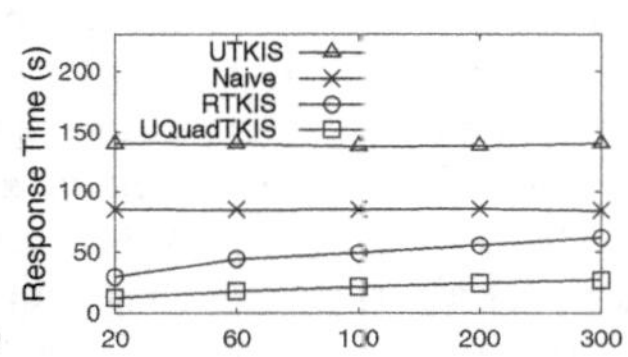

Figure 15: Diff. r_u

Impact of the number of instances (m). We evaluate the response time of the algorithms as a function of the number of instances (m) in each uncertain object which varies from 100 to 500. Clearly, the refinement cost increases in *refinement* phase when m grows. Figure 14 shows that UQuadTKIS has the best scalability against m, followed by RTKIS, Naive and UTKIS.

Impact of the radius(r_u). Figure 15 investigates the performance of four algorithms as a function of the radius size which various from 20 to 300. It is shown that the scalability of UQuadTKIS is better than that of RTKIS regarding the growth of r_u.

Impact of the number of facilities and objects. We also evaluate the impact of the number of facilities as well as the number of objects against four algorithms, where the number of facilities grows from 200 to 1000, and the number of objects varies from 10,000 to 50,000. Figure 16 and Figure 17 show that UQuadTKIS have the best scalability among four algorithms.

Impact of k . In the last set of experiments, we evaluate the response time and the number of I/O accesses against various k val-

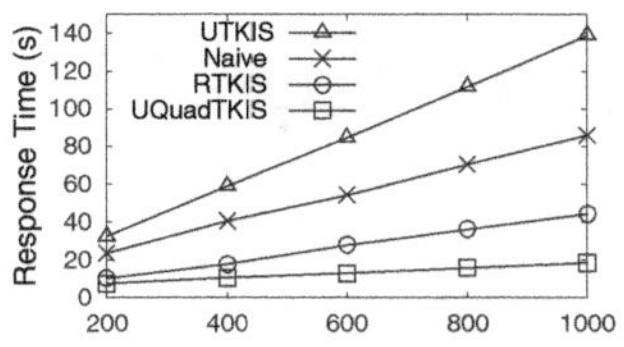

Figure 16: Diff. #facilities

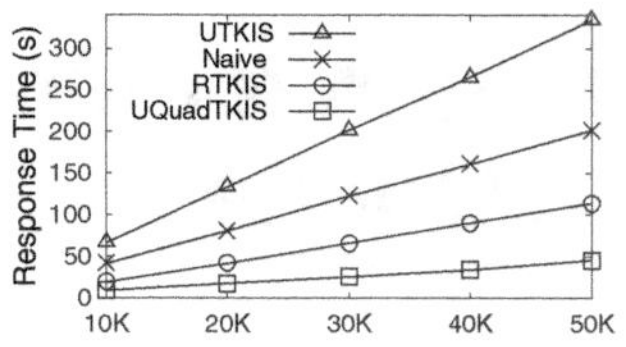

Figure 17: Diff. # objects

ues in Figure 18, which indicates that the performance of all algorithms are not very sensitive to the k value.

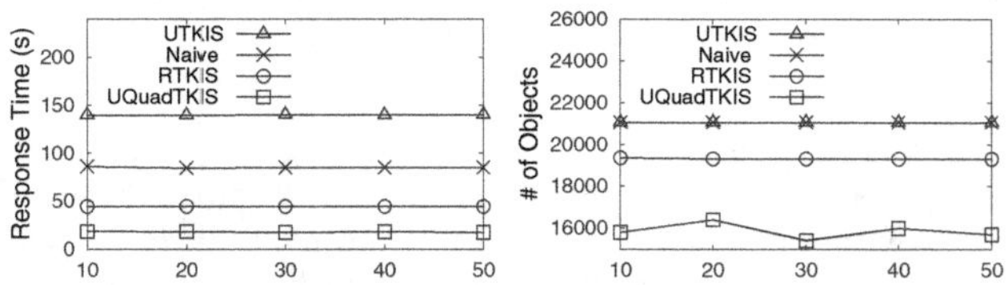

(a) *Response Time* (b) *# objects accessed*

Figure 18: Diff. k

Summary. As a short summary, our comprehensive performance study shows that our ranking model has very similar ranking result with that of *expected rank* model, while the efficiency of the algorithms under our ranking model is much better. Even a naive implementation can outperform UTKIS Algorithm which follows the *expected rank* model. The experiments also show the effectiveness and efficiency of the *filtering* and *refinement* algorithms proposed in the paper based on R-tree and U-Quadtree. The overall performance of the U-Quadtree based algorithm (UQuadTKIS) always outperforms the R-tree based one (RTKIS) under various experiment settings because more sophisticated indexing structure is employed in UQuadTKIS.

6. CONCLUSION

In this paper, we investigate the problem of finding top k most influential facilities over a set of uncertain objects. Based on a new ranking model, we develop two effective and efficient algorithms by utilizing two uncertain objects indexing techniques, R-tree and U-Quadtree respectively. A set of pruning techniques are proposed in the paper to significantly improve the performance of the *filtering* and *refinement* algorithms. Our experiments convincingly demonstrate the effectiveness and efficiency of our techniques.

Acknowledgement. Ying Zhang is supported by ARC DP110104880 and UNSW ECR grant PS27476. Wenjie Zhang is supported by ARC DP120104168 and DE120102144. Xuemin Lin is supported by ARC DP0987557, ARC DP110102937, ARC DP120104168 and NSFC61021004.

7. REFERENCES

[1] T. Bernecker, T. Emrich, H.-P. Kriegel, M. Renz, S. Zankl, and A. Züfle. Efficient probabilistic reverse nearest neighbor query processing on uncertain data. *PVLDB*, 4(10):669–680, 2011.

[2] U. C. Bureau. `http://www.census.gov/geo/www/tiger`.

[3] M. A. Cheema, X. Lin, W. Wang, W. Zhang, and J. Pei. Probabilistic reverse nearest neighbor queries on uncertain data. *IEEE Trans. Knowl. Data Eng.*, 22(4):550–564, 2010.

[4] R. Cheng, D. V. Kalashnikov, and S. Prabhakar. Querying imprecise data in moving object environments. *IEEE Trans. Knowl. Data Eng.*, 16(9):1112–1127, 2004.

[5] G. Cormode, F. Li, and K. Yi. Semantics of ranking queries for probabilistic data and expected ranks. In *ICDE*, pages 305–316, 2009.

[6] R. A. Finkel and J. L. Bentley. Quad trees: A data structure for retrieval on composite keys. *Acta Inf.*, 4:1–9, 1974.

[7] A. Guttman. R-trees: A dynamic index structure for spatial searching. In *SIGMOD Conference*, pages 47–57, 1984.

[8] M. Hua, J. Pei, W. Zhang, and X. Lin. Ranking queries on uncertain data: a probabilistic threshold approach. In *SIGMOD Conference*, pages 673–686, 2008.

[9] J. Huang, Z. Wen, J. Qi, R. Zhang, J. Chen, and Z. He. Top-k most influential locations selection. In *CIKM*, pages 2377–2380, 2011.

[10] F. Korn and S. Muthukrishnan. Influence sets based on reverse nearest neighbor queries. In *SIGMOD Conference*, pages 201–212, 2000.

[11] J. Li, B. Saha, and A. Deshpande. A unified approach to ranking in probabilistic databases. *VLDB J.*, 20(2):249–275, 2011.

[12] X. Lian and L. Chen. Efficient processing of probabilistic reverse nearest neighbor queries over uncertain data. *VLDB J.*, 18(3):787–808, 2009.

[13] A. Papadopoulos and Y. Manolopoulos. Performance of nearest neighbor queries in r-trees. In *ICDT*, 1997.

[14] M. Shaked and J. G. Shanthikumar. *Stochastic Orders and Their Applications*. Academic Press, 1994.

[15] S. Singh, C. Mayfield, S. Prabhakar, R. Shah, and S. E. Hambrusch. Indexing uncertain categorical data. In *ICDE*, pages 616–625, 2007.

[16] M. A. Soliman, I. F. Ilyas, and K. C.-C. Chang. Top-k query processing in uncertain databases. In *ICDE*, pages 896–905, 2007.

[17] Y. Tao, R. Cheng, X. Xiao, W. K. Ngai, B. Kao, and S. Prabhakar. Indexing multi-dimensional uncertain data with arbitrary probability density functions. In *VLDB*, pages 922–933, 2005.

[18] Y. Theodoridis. The r-tree-portal. `http://www.rtreeportal.org`, 2003.

[19] R. C.-W. Wong, M. T. Özsu, A. W.-C. Fu, P. S. Yu, L. Liu, and Y. Liu. Maximizing bichromatic reverse nearest neighbor for lp -norm in two- and three-dimensional spaces. *VLDB J.*, 20(6), 2011.

[20] T. Xia, D. Zhang, E. Kanoulas, and Y. Du. On computing top-t most influential spatial sites. In *VLDB*, pages 946–957, 2005.

[21] D. Yan, R. C.-W. Wong, and W. Ng. Efficient methods for finding influential locations with adaptive grids. In *CIKM*, pages 1475–1484, 2011.

[22] X. Zhang and J. Chomicki. On the semantics and evaluation of top-k queries in probabilistic databases. In *ICDE Workshops*, pages 556–563, 2008.

[23] Y. Zhang, X. Lin, G. Zhu, W. Zhang, and Q. Lin. Efficient rank based knn query processing over uncertain data. In *ICDE*, pages 28–39, 2010.

[24] Y. Zhang, W. Zhang, Q. Lin, and X. Lin. Effectively indexing the multi-dimensional uncertain objects for range searching. In *EDBT*, 2012.

[25] K. Zheng, Z. Huang, A. Zhou, and X. Zhou. Discovering the most influential sites over uncertain data: A rank based approach. *Knowledge and Data Engineering, IEEE Transactions on*, PP(99):1, 2011.

Efficient Safe-Region Construction for Moving Top-K Spatial Keyword Queries

Weihuang Huang† Guoliang Li† Kian-Lee Tan‡ Jianhua Feng†
†Department of Computer Science and Technology, Tsinghua National Laboratory for Information Science and Technology (TNList), Tsinghua University, Beijing, China
‡Department of Computer Science, School of Computing, National University of Singapore , Singapore
huangwh10@mails.thu.edu.cn; {liguoliang,fengjh}@tsinghua.edu.cn; tankl@comp.nus.edu.sg

ABSTRACT

Many real-world applications have requirements to support moving spatial keyword queries. For example a tourist looks for top-k "**seafood restaurants**" while walking in a city. She will continuously issue moving queries. However existing spatial keyword search methods focus on static queries and it calls for new effective techniques to support moving queries efficiently. In this paper we propose an effective method to support moving top-k spatial keyword queries. In addition to finding top-k answers of a moving query, we also calculate a *safe region* such that if a new query with a location falling in the safe region, we can directly use the answer set to answer the query. To this end, we propose an effective model to represent the safe region and devise efficient search algorithms to compute the safe region. We have implemented our method and experimental results on real datasets show that our method achieves high efficiency and outperforms existing methods significantly.

Categories and Subject Descriptors

H.2.8 [**Database Applications**]: Spatial databases

General Terms

Algorithms, Design, Experimentation, Performance

Keywords

Moving Top-k Spatial Keyword Queries, Safe Region

1. INTRODUCTION

Location based services (LBS) have attracted significant attention from both industry and academic communities in recent years, thanks to the modern mobile phones and new Internet technologies. Many existing systems provide users with location-aware search experiences based on users' location which can be easily gotten from GPS devices equipped in modern mobile phones.

Recently there are many studies on location based services and most of them address the spatial keyword search problem [9, 4, 2, 7], which, given a set of spatio-textual objects with a location and textual description (e.g., points of interest and geo-tagged documents) and a top-k spatial keyword query with a location and a set of keywords, finds top-k relevant answers. However they focus primarily on static queries and cannot support moving queries efficiently. Notice that many real-world applications have requirements to support moving spatial keyword queries. For example, a housewife is driving to a supermarket and may want to find the top-3 "**car parking places**" near the supermarket. Since she is driving, her query location is continuously changing. As another example, a tourist looking for the top-2 "**seafood restaurants**" while walking in a city will require a moving query. Although we can extend existing methods to support moving queries by repeatedly issuing multiple queries, these methods have the following limitations. First, it increases the communication cost between the client (the user who issues the query) and the server (the system that provides the search service), and also wastes the bandwidth in transmission. Second, it aggravates the system burden due to issuing multiple repeated queries.

To address this problem, in this paper we emphasize on efficiently supporting moving top-k spatial keyword queries. We adopt a client-server model. The client is moving and continuously issues a spatial keyword query to the server. The server returns the top-k answers of the query, as well as a **safe region** of the answer set (We will formally define the safe region in Section 2). Then before the client issues a new query at another location, it will first check whether the new location is still in the **safe region**. If yes, it can reuse the answer set; otherwise the client needs to issue a query with the new location to the server. Obviously our method not only avoids unnecessary communication cost but also reduces the system burden. Notice that although Wu et al. [17] studied the moving top-k spatial keyword query, they used an ad-hoc ranking function (see Section 2). In contrast, we use a widely adopted ranking function [2, 11].

Different from existing studies [2, 4] which focus on computing the answer set of a query, we emphasize on how to compute the safe region. There are several research challenges. First, how to represent the safe region? Traditional studies on spatial data (without textual description) use Voronoi diagrams to represent the safe region, which can be pre-computed and materialized for efficient online query processing. However safe region in our problem depends on query keywords and cannot be materialized. To address this issue, we propose an effective representation model in Section 3. Second, how to compute the safe region? For a query issued to the server, we need to find its answer set

CIKM'12, October 29–November 2, 2012, Maui, HI, USA.

and compute the safe region simultaneously. Thus the time for computing the safe region cannot be large. To address this issue, we develop efficient algorithms in Section 4. To summarize, we make the following contributions.

- We propose an effective model to represent the safe region of a moving top-k spatial keyword query.
- We devise efficient incremental algorithms to efficiently compute the safe region.
- We develop effective pruning techniques to reduce the computation time on the server and the verification time on the client.
- Experimental results show that our method achieves high efficiency and outperforms existing methods.

The rest of the paper is organized as follows. We first formulate our problem in Section 2. A model to represent the safe region is discussed in Section 3. We devise efficient algorithms to compute the safe region in Section 4. Section 5 extends our techniques to support moving top-k queries. We conduct experimental results in Section 6 and review related work in Section 7. Section 8 concludes the paper.

2. PRELIMINARY

2.1 Problem Formulation

We adopt a client-server model. The server contains a set of spatio-textual objects, O. Each object $o \in O$ contains a location o_s and textual description o_t, denoted by $o = (o_s, o_t)$. In the paper we consider two-dimensional space, and use x-coordinate $o_s.x$ and y-coordination $o_s.y$ to denote a location o_s. We use a set of terms to denote o_t. The client is moving and continuously issues a top-k spatial keyword query q to the server. Query q consists of a query location q_s, a set of keywords q_t, and an integer k to restrict the result size, denoted by $q = (q_s, q_t, k)$. For ease of presentation, we first define the answer of a top-k spatial keyword query.

DEFINITION 1 (TOP-k SPATIAL KEYWORD QUERY). *Given an object set O and a query q, the answer of a top-k spatial keyword query is a subset of O, $\mathcal{A}$, such that*

(1) The size of $\mathcal{A}$ is k, i.e., $|\mathcal{A}| = k$, and

(2) $\forall o^* \in \mathcal{A}, \forall o \in O - \mathcal{A}, \texttt{score}(q, o^*) \leq \texttt{score}(q, o)$,

where `score` *is a ranking function to evaluate the relevance between a query and an object. The smaller the value is, the more relevant is the object to the query. We will define the ranking function in Section 2.2.*

For example, there is a dataset O as shown in Figure 1 and a top-k spatial keyword query $q = ((0.515, 0.294), \{\texttt{Chinese}, \texttt{restarant}\}, 1)$. We can get $\mathcal{A} = \{o_4\}$ under the ranking function defined in Section 2.2. If $k = 2$ with the same q_s and q_t, then the answer set $\mathcal{A} = \{o_4, o_9\}$.

For a moving top-k spatial keyword query q, in addition to finding the answer set $\mathcal{A}$, we also need to find a *safe region* for query q. Note that the safe region depends on the keyword set q_t and k, and we denote it by $\mathcal{R}(q_t, k)$. For a query $q' = (q'_s, q_t, k)$ with a new location q'_s, if $q'_s \in \mathcal{R}(q_t, k)$, the answer set of q' is the same as that of q. Thus we can use the answer set $\mathcal{A}$ to answer q'. If the context is clear, $\mathcal{R}(q_t, k)$ and $\mathcal{R}$ are used interchangeably. Next we formally define the safe region $\mathcal{R}$.

DEFINITION 2 (SAFE REGION). *Given an object set O and a query q, the safe region of query q is*

$$\mathcal{R} = \{q'_s | \forall o^* \in \mathcal{A}, \forall o \in O - \mathcal{A}, \texttt{score}(q', o^*) \leq \texttt{score}(q', o)\},$$

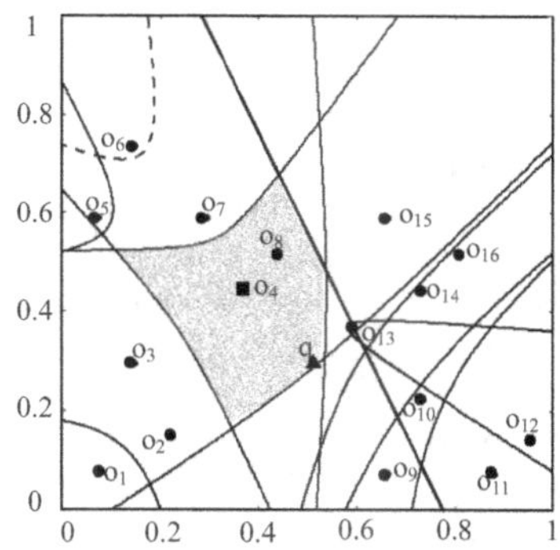

Figure 1: Dataset(k_1:`Chinese`,k_2:`Franch`,k_3:`restarant`, k_4:`seafood`,k_5:`pastry`, numbers in brackets are tf)

where $q' = (q'_s, q_t, k)$ and q'_s is any location.

For example, in Figure 1, the shadow region in the center is the safe region for $q_t = \{\texttt{Chinese}, \texttt{restarant}\}$ and $k = 1$.

Then based on the answer set $\mathcal{A}$ and the safe region $\mathcal{R}$, we define the answer of a moving top-k spatial keyword query.

DEFINITION 3. *(Moving Top-k Spatial Keyword Query) Given an object set O and a moving top-k spatial keyword query $q = (q_s, q_t, k)$. As the query is moving, for each new location q'_s, its answer is $\langle \mathcal{A}, \mathcal{R} \rangle$, where $\mathcal{A}$ is the top-k result set of $q' = (q'_s, q_t, k)$ and $\mathcal{R}$ is the corresponding safe region.*

In the client-server model, for a query q, the client first checks whether $q_s \in \mathcal{R}$. If yes, $\mathcal{A}$ is the answer of query q; otherwise the client submits the query q to the server which returns the answer set and the safe region of the query. In our example in Figure 1, the server will return the answer set $\mathcal{A} = \{o_4\}$ and a safe region $\mathcal{R}$ (shaded in the Figure). Next the client updates its location and checks whether it is still in $\mathcal{R}$. If yes, $\{o_4\}$ is still the answer; otherwise the answer changes and the client issues a new query to the server.

Existing studies [2] focus on top-k spatial keyword queries and they propose efficient algorithms to compute the answer set $\mathcal{A}$. In this paper we emphasize on how to compute the safe region $\mathcal{R}$ and address the research challenges as discussed in Section 1.

2.2 Ranking Function

Given a query q and an object o, to compute their ranking score $\texttt{score}(q, o)$, we combine their spatial proximity between o_s and q_s, denoted by $\texttt{dist}(o_s, q_s)$, and their textual relevancy between o_t and q_t, denoted by $\texttt{text}(o_t, q_t)$. The ranking function is defined as follows.

$$\texttt{score}(q, o) = \alpha \cdot \texttt{dist}(q_s, o_s) + (1 - \alpha) \cdot (1 - \texttt{text}(q_t, o_t)) \quad (1)$$

where α is a tuning parameter to trade-off the importance between the spatial distance and textual relevancy. Notice that in the ranking function, we normalize $\texttt{dist}(q_s, o_s)$ and $\texttt{text}(q_t, o_t)$ to $[0, 1]$ using their possible maximum values. In the paper, we use the Euclidean distance (function `dist`) to compute the spatial distance (`dist`) between two locations, and adopt the well-known TFIDF function to evaluate the textual relevancy (`text`) as follows.

$$\texttt{text}(q_t, o_t) = \sum_{t \in q_t} (\mathsf{tf}(t, o_t) \times \mathsf{idf}(t)) \quad (2)$$

where $\mathsf{tf}(t, o_t)$ is the term frequency of term t in o_t and $\mathsf{idf}(t)$ is the inverse document frequency of term t, i.e., the ratio of the number of objects in O to that of objects whose textual descriptions contain t. For ease of presentation, if the context is clear, we use $\texttt{text}(q_t, o_t)$ and $\texttt{text}(q, o)$, and $\texttt{dist}(q_t, o_t)$ and $\texttt{dist}(q, o)$ interchangeably.

For the example in Figure 1, assume $\alpha = \frac{2}{3}$. $\texttt{dist}(q, o_1) = 0.49$, $\texttt{text}(q, o_1) = 0.1$, and $\texttt{score}(q, o_1) = 0.63$; $\texttt{dist}(q, o_4) = 0.21$, $\texttt{text}(q, o_4) = 0.75$ and $\texttt{score}(q, o_4) = 0.22$; $\texttt{dist}(q, o_9) = 0.27$, $\texttt{text}(q, o_9) = 0.85$ and $\texttt{score}(q, o_9) = 0.23$. The top-1 answer is $\{o_4\}$ and the top-2 answer is $\{o_4, o_9\}$.

Notice that our ranking function is widely adopted in existing studies [2, 11]. Although Wu et al. [17] studied the moving top-k spatial keyword query problem, they used a very ad-hoc ranking function as defined below.

$$\mathsf{rank}(q, o) = \frac{\texttt{dist}(q, o)}{\texttt{text}(q, o)}. \quad (3)$$

Obviously our ranking function is more general. We will discuss how to support their ranking function and experimentally compare with their method in Section 6.

3. REPRESENTATION MODEL FOR TOP-1 QUERIES

In this section, we first introduce a concept *dominant region* in Section 3.1, and then based on the definition we discuss how to represent the safe region in Section 3.2.

3.1 Dominant Region

Given a query q and two objects, o^* and o, the *dominant region* of o^* to o is a region such that if q is in the region, o^* is a better answer than o, as defined below.

DEFINITION 4. *Given a query $q = (q_s, q_t, k)$, the dominant region of o^* to o is:*

$$D_{o^*,o} = \{q'_s | \mathit{score}(q', o^*) \leq \mathit{score}(q', o)\} \quad (4)$$

where $q' = (q'_s, q_t, k)$.

For example, in Figure 1, the dominant region of o_4 to o_6 is the region outside the dashed line. That is if a query q is in the region, o_4 is a better answer than o_6.

Next we deduce how to represent the dominant region. We first introduce two notations.

$$\begin{aligned} \Delta d &= \texttt{dist}(q', o^*) - \texttt{dist}(q', o), \\ \Delta t &= \frac{1-\alpha}{\alpha}\left(\texttt{text}(q', o^*) - \texttt{text}(q', o)\right). \end{aligned} \quad (5)$$

Based on Equation 1, $\texttt{score}(q', o^*) \leq \texttt{score}(q', o)$ if and only if $\Delta d \leq \Delta t$. Thus we have $D_{o^*,o} = \{q'_s | \Delta d \leq \Delta t\}$, according to Definition 4. Based on the relationship between Δt and $\texttt{dist}(o^*, o)$, we can determine the shape of the dominant region as follows (also shown in Table 1 and Figure 2).

Case 1: $\Delta t \geq \texttt{dist}(o^*, o)$. Based on the triangle inequality, $\Delta d = \texttt{dist}(q', o^*) - \texttt{dist}(q', o) \leq \texttt{dist}(o^*, o)$. If $\Delta t \geq \texttt{dist}(o^*, o)$, $\Delta d \leq \Delta t$ is always true, thus the dominant region is the whole plane.

Case 2: $\Delta t < -\texttt{dist}(o^*, o)$. Based on the triangle inequality, $-\texttt{dist}(o^*, o) \leq \Delta d = \texttt{dist}(q', o^*) - \texttt{dist}(q', o)$. If $\Delta t < -\texttt{dist}(o^*, o)$, $\Delta d \leq \Delta t$ is always false, thus the dominant region is empty.

Case 3: $\Delta t = -\texttt{dist}(o^*, o)$. Based on Case 2, only the points on the half-line starting from o^* and with direction from o to o^* (denoted by $\mathcal{H}_{o^*,\overrightarrow{oo^*}}$) satisfy $-\texttt{dist}(o^*, o) \leq \Delta d \leq \Delta t = -\texttt{dist}(o^*, o)$, thus the dominant region is half-line $\mathcal{H}_{o^*,\overrightarrow{oo^*}}$.

Table 1: Dominant Region

Cases	Dominant Region
$\Delta t \geq \texttt{dist}(o^*, o)$	whole plane
$\Delta t = -\texttt{dist}(o^*, o)$	half-line $\mathcal{H}_{o^*,\overrightarrow{oo^*}}$
$\Delta t < -\texttt{dist}(o^*, o)$	empty
$\Delta t = 0$	half-plane ($III \cup IV$ in Figure 2)
$0 < \Delta t < \texttt{dist}(o^*, o)$	outside $\mathcal{H}_o$ ($II \cup III \cup IV$ in Figure 2)
$-\texttt{dist}(o^*, o) < \Delta t < 0$	inside $\mathcal{H}_{o^*}$ (IV in Figure 2)

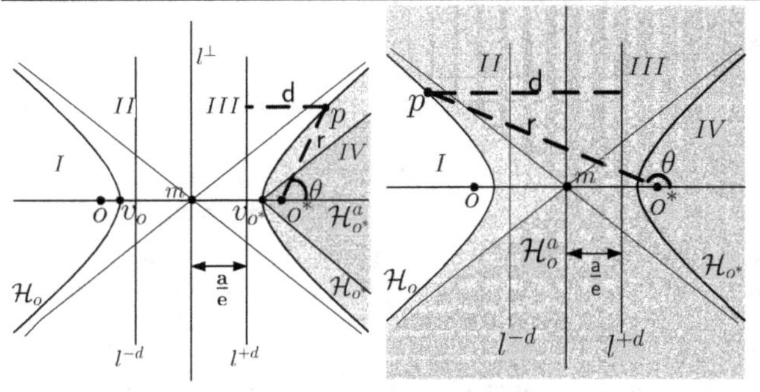

(a) -$\texttt{dist}(o^*, o) < \Delta t < 0$ (b) $0 < \Delta t < \texttt{dist}(o^*, o)$

Figure 2: Dominant Region

Case 4: $\Delta t = 0$. Obviously the locus of $\Delta d = 0$ is the perpendicular bisector of segment $\overline{o^*o}$ which partitions the space into two half planes. The dominant region for $\Delta d \leq \Delta t$ is the half plane that contains o^*.

Case 5: $0 < \Delta t < \texttt{dist}(o^*, o)$. The locus of points satisfying $|\Delta d| = |\texttt{dist}(q, o^*) - \texttt{dist}(q, o)| = |\Delta t|$ is a hyperbola with o^* and o as its two focuses as proved in Lemma 1. Let $\mathcal{H}$ denote the hyperbola satisfying $|\Delta d| = |\Delta t|$, $\mathcal{H}_{o^*}$ denote the branch nearby the focus o^* (i.e., satisfying $\Delta d = -\Delta t$), and $\mathcal{H}_o$ denote the branch nearby the focus o (i.e., satisfying $\Delta d = \Delta t$). $\mathcal{L}^\perp$ is the perpendicular bisector of segment $\overline{o^*o}$. $\mathcal{L}^\perp$, $\mathcal{H}_{o^*}$, $\mathcal{H}_o$ divide the plane into four regions I, II, III, IV, as shown in Figure 2. Obviously in this case, the dominant region for $\Delta d \leq \Delta t$ is the region outside $\mathcal{H}_o$ (i.e., region $II \cup III \cup IV$ in Figure 2).

Case 6: $-\texttt{dist}(o^*, o) < \Delta t < 0$. Similar to Case 5, the dominant region for $\Delta d \leq \Delta t$ is the region inside $\mathcal{H}_{o^*}$ (i.e., region IV in Figure 2).

LEMMA 1. *If $0 < \Delta t < \mathit{dist}(o^*, o)$ or $-\mathit{dist}(o^*, o) < \Delta t < 0$, the locus of points satisfying $|\Delta d| = |\Delta t|$ is a hyperbola with o^* and o as its two focuses. The locus of points satisfying $\Delta d = \Delta t$ is the branch $\mathcal{H}_o$ and that for $\Delta d = -\Delta t$ is the branch $\mathcal{H}_{o^*}$.*

PROOF. Due to space constraints, we omit all proofs. □

As illustrated in Figure 2, $\mathcal{H}$ is the hyperbola derived from o^* and o. m is the the center of $\mathcal{H}$, i.e., the midpoint of segment $\overline{o^*o}$. Next we give the basic parameters and their values of hyperbola $\mathcal{H}$.

Focuses : o^* and o.

Vertices : The two nearest points located at the two branches: v_o^* in $\mathcal{H}_{o^*}$ and v_o in $\mathcal{H}_o$.

Semi-focal Length : The distance from one focus to the center, denoted by c. $\mathsf{c} = \frac{dist(o^*,o)}{2}$.

Semi-major Length : The distance from one vertex to the center, denoted by a. $\mathsf{a} = \frac{1}{2}|\Delta t|$.

Eccentricity : The parameter determines the shape of a curve (for all conic curves), denoted by e. $\mathsf{e} = \frac{\mathsf{c}}{\mathsf{a}}$.

3.2 Safe Region

In this section, we discuss how to represent the safe region. Given a query q, suppose its top-1 answer is o^*. Based on the definition of the dominant region, obviously the safe region is the intersection of the dominant region of o^* to all other objects, i.e., $\mathcal{R} = \bigcap_{o \neq o^*} D_{o^*,o}$ as formalized in Lemma 2.

LEMMA 2. *Given a query q, suppose its top-1 answer is o^*. $\mathcal{R} = \bigcap_{o \neq o^*} D_{o^*,o}$.*

In this way, after finding the top-1 answer o^*, we compute the dominant region of o^* to each object $o \in O - \{o^*\}$. Then we compute the intersection of these dominant regions. Notice that the safe region is always not empty and q_s is in $\mathcal{R}$ as formalized in Lemma 3.

LEMMA 3. *For a query q, the safe region $\mathcal{R}$ is always not empty and q_s is in $\mathcal{R}$.*

Some readers may find that in Case 3 ($\Delta t < -\texttt{dist}(o^*, o)$), the dominant region is empty. Interestingly, we can prove that for the best answer o^*, there is no such case, that is, $\Delta t \geq -\texttt{dist}(o^*, o)$.

LEMMA 4. *Given a query q and its best answer o^*, for any object $o \in O - \{o^*\}$, $\Delta t \geq -\texttt{dist}(o^*, o)$.*

Next we discuss how to represent the safe region. Recall the different shapes of the dominant regions. It is easy to represent planes, half-planes, and half-lines. However it is not easy to represent a hyperbola. A hyperbola is a type of conic section. In a Cartesian coordinate system, it is usually represented by a second-degree polynomial or a matrix. However it is very expensive to use such methods and it is also inefficient to compute the intersection. To address this issue, we introduce two alternative methods.

Using Polygons to Approximate a Hyperbola: Since the distance between a hyperbola and its asymptotes tends to 0 when they approach infinity, we can use asymptotes to approximate hyperbola.

For the dominant region inside $\mathcal{H}_{o^*}$ (the shaded region in Figure 2(a)), consider the two half-lines starting from the vertex v_{o^*} with directions the same as the two asymptotes. Let $\mathcal{H}^a_{o^*}$ denote the region inside the two half-lines (the shaded polygon region in Figure 2(a)). Obviously $\mathcal{H}^a_{o^*}$ is in the dominant region and we use it to approximate the region inside $\mathcal{H}_{o^*}$. Similarly for the dominant region outside $\mathcal{H}_o$ (the shaded region in Figure 2(b)), consider the two half-lines starting from the center m with directions the same as the two asymptotes. Let $\mathcal{H}^a_o$ denote the region outside the two half-lines (the shaded polygon region in Figure 2(b)). Obviously $\mathcal{H}^a_o$ is in the dominant region and we use it to approximate the region outside $\mathcal{H}_o$.

Using Polar Coordinates to Denote Hyperbola: We propose to use the polar coordinate to represent a hyperbola. Consider two objects o and o^*. Suppose the corresponding dominant region $D_{o^*,o}$ is a hyperbola, denoted by $\mathcal{H}$. Let $\mathcal{H}_{o^*}(\mathcal{H}_o)$ denote the branch nearby o^* (o). Let l^{+d} and l^{-d} denote the two directrices. We construct a coordinate system where the origin is the midpoint between o and o^*, and the x-axis is the line passing o and o^*, the y-axis is the perpendicular bisector of segment between o^* and o. The distance from $l^{+d}(l^{-d})$ to y-axis is $\frac{\mathsf{a}}{\mathsf{e}}(-\frac{\mathsf{a}}{\mathsf{e}})$.

Consider any point p in branch $\mathcal{H}_{o^*}$. Let $\mathsf{d} = \texttt{dist}(p, l^{+d})$ denote the distance from p to directrix l^{+d} and $\mathsf{r} = \texttt{dist}(p, o)$. We have $\frac{\mathsf{r}}{\mathsf{d}} = \frac{\texttt{dist}(p,o)}{\texttt{dist}(p,l^{+d})} = \mathsf{e}$, where $\mathsf{e} = \frac{\mathsf{c}}{\mathsf{a}}$ is the eccentricity as discussed in Section 3.1. Let θ denote the angle between $\overrightarrow{o^*p}$ and x-axis. We have $p.x = \mathsf{r} * \cos\theta + \mathsf{c}$. As $\mathsf{d} = p.x - \frac{\mathsf{a}}{\mathsf{e}}$, we have $\mathsf{d} = \mathsf{r} * \cos\theta + \mathsf{c} - \frac{\mathsf{a}}{\mathsf{e}}$. Thus $\frac{\mathsf{r}}{\mathsf{r}*\cos\theta+\mathsf{c}-\frac{\mathsf{a}}{\mathsf{e}}} = \mathsf{e}$. We can deduce that

$$\mathsf{r} = f(\theta) = \frac{\mathsf{a}(\mathsf{e}^2 - 1)}{1 - \cos\theta * \mathsf{e}}.$$

where $-\arccos(\frac{1}{\mathsf{e}}) \leq \theta \leq \arccos(\frac{1}{\mathsf{e}})$.

In this way, we can use this polar coordinate representation to denote $\mathcal{H}_{o^*}$. Similarly for the other branch $\mathcal{H}_o$,

$$\mathsf{r}' = f'(\theta) = \frac{\mathsf{a}(1 - \mathsf{e}^2)}{1 + \cos\theta * \mathsf{e}},$$

where $\pi - \arccos(\frac{1}{\mathsf{e}}) \leq \theta \leq \pi + \arccos(\frac{1}{\mathsf{e}})$.

Similarly we can also use the polar coordinate to represent the plane, half-planes, and half-lines. The key to use polar coordinate to represent plane, half-planes or half-lines is to use it to represent lines. Considering line s, we draw its perpendicular $s^{\perp}$ from o^*. s and $s^{\perp}$ intersect at f. For any point p on s, the distance from o^* to p can be represented as $\mathsf{r} = \frac{\texttt{dist}(o^*,f)}{\cos\theta}$, where θ is the angle between lines o^*p and o^*f. Note that we need to transfer the coordinate. In the polar coordinate, the new origin is o^*. For all other objects, the origin is always o^*. We need to prove that o^* is in $\mathcal{A}$.

LEMMA 5. *Given a query q, if o^* is the best answer, the location of o^* must be in the safe region $\mathcal{R}$.*

To compute the intersection among multiple polar equations, we use a piecewise function in a polar coordinate with the origin of o^*. The safe region can be represented by

$$f^1(\theta)[\theta_1 \leq \theta < \theta_2], f^2(\theta)[\theta_2 \leq \theta < \theta_3], \cdots, f^m(\theta)[\theta_m \leq \theta < \theta_1].$$

4. COMPUTATION OF Safe Region

In this section we study how to calculate the safe region.

4.1 Framework

A naive method to compute the safe region is to first calculate the dominant regions of o^* to all other objects and then compute their intersection. To improve the performance, we propose an effective pruning technique. The basic idea is as follows. Consider two objects o_i and o_j. If $D_{o^*,o_i} \subseteq D_{o^*,o_j}$, we can prune D_{o^*,o_j} since $\mathcal{R} \subseteq D_{o^*,o_i} \cap D_{o^*,o_j} = D_{o^*,o_i}$. Notice that it is usually hard to determine whether $D_{o^*,o_i} \subseteq D_{o^*,o_j}$. To utilize this idea, we propose an alternative method. Consider a region $\mathcal{R}' \supseteq \mathcal{R}$. For any object o, if $\mathcal{R}' \subseteq D_{o^*,o}$, we can prune object o since $\mathcal{R} \subseteq \mathcal{R}' \subseteq D_{o^*,o}$ and object o will not affect the safe region.

To achieve our goal, there are two challenges. The first one is how to find such $\mathcal{R}'$. The second one is how to check whether $\mathcal{R}' \subseteq D_{o^*,o}$. To address the first challenge, we propose an incremental computation method. First, we initialize the safe region $\mathcal{R}'$ as the minimum bounding rectangle of all points. Next for each object o, we compute $D_{o^*,o}$. If $\mathcal{R}' \subseteq D_{o^*,o}$, we prune object o; otherwise we update $\mathcal{R}' = \mathcal{R}' \cap D_{o^*,o}$.

Next we discuss how to check $\mathcal{R}' \subseteq D_{o^*,o}$. We introduce two functions. As $o^* \in \mathcal{R}'$, let $d_{max} = \texttt{MaxBD}(o^*, \mathcal{R}')$ denote the maximum distance from o^* to *any point* in $\mathcal{R}'$. Given an object o, let $d_{min}(o) = \texttt{MinBD}(o^*, D_{o^*,o})$ denote the minimum distance from o^* to the *boundary* of $D_{o^*,o}$. Notice that if $d_{min}(o) \geq d_{max}$, we have $\mathcal{R}' \subseteq D_{o^*,o}$ as formalized in Lemma 6, and thus we can prune object o.

LEMMA 6. *Given a region $\mathcal{R}' \supseteq \mathcal{R}$ and object o, if $d_{min}(o) \geq d_{max}$, $\mathcal{R}' \subseteq D_{o^*,o}$.*

Given an object o, next we discuss how to compute the function $d_{min}(o) = \texttt{MinBD}(o^*, D_{o^*,o})$.

Case 1: $\Delta t \geq \texttt{dist}(o^*, o)$. $D_{o^*,o}$ is the whole plane, and $\texttt{MinBD}(o^*, D_{o^*,o})$ is the minimal distance from o^* to the boundary of the plane;

Case 2: $0 < \Delta t < \texttt{dist}(o^*, o)$. $d_{min}(o)$ is the distance from o^* to the left vertex and $\texttt{MinBD}(o^*, D_{o^*,o}) = \texttt{c} + \texttt{a} = \frac{\texttt{dist}(o^*,o)+|\Delta t|}{2} = \frac{\texttt{dist}(o^*,o)+\Delta t}{2}$;

Case 3: $\Delta t = 0$. $D_{o^*,o}$ is a half-plane, and $\texttt{MinBD}(o^*, D_{o^*,o})$ is $\frac{\texttt{dist}(o^*,o)}{2}$;

Case 4: $-\texttt{dist}(o^*, o) < \Delta t < 0$. $d_{min}(o)$ is the distance from o^* to the right vertex and $\texttt{MinBD}(o^*, D_{o^*,o}) = \texttt{c} - \texttt{a} = \frac{\texttt{dist}(o^*,o)-|\Delta t|}{2} = \frac{\texttt{dist}(o^*,o)+\Delta t}{2}$;

Case 5: $\Delta t = -\texttt{dist}(o^*, o)$. $\texttt{MinBD}(o^*, D_{o^*,o}) = 0$.

Case 6: $\Delta t < -\texttt{dist}(o^*, o)$. There will be no such case as formalized in Lemma 4.

As shown in Figure 1, $\texttt{MinBD}(o_4, D_{o_4,o_3}) = \frac{\texttt{dist}(o_4,o_3)+\Delta t}{2} = 0.153$, $\texttt{MinBD}(o_4, D_{o_4,o_{15}}) = \frac{\texttt{dist}(o_4,o_{15})}{2} = 0.164$.

Here we discuss how to compute MaxBD $(o^*, \mathcal{R}')$. Let $\mathcal{I} = \{I_1, I_2, \cdots, I_m\}$ denote the intersections in $\mathcal{R}'$ among dominant regions $D_{o^*,o}$ for each object o that has been added into $\mathcal{R}'$ (also including the intersections with the boundary of the whole plane and the four vertexes of the plane if they are in the region). We have $\texttt{MaxBD}(o^*, \mathcal{R}') = \max_{I_t \in \mathcal{I}} \texttt{dist}(o^*, I_t)$ as stated in Lemma 7. We can easily compute the intersections using the polar coordinate.

LEMMA 7. *Given a region $\mathcal{R}'$ computed in the incremental algorithm, we have*

$$d_{max} = \texttt{MaxBD}(o^*, \mathcal{R}') = \max_{I_t \in \mathcal{I}} \texttt{dist}(o^*, I_t).$$

To facilitate the pruning, we access objects in ascending order sorted by d_{min}(o). If $d_{min}(o) \geq d_{max}$, we can prune all objects after object o. Based on this idea, we introduce our framework to compute the safe region and the pseudo-code is shown in Figure 1. We first initialize $\mathcal{R}$ as the whole plane and d_{max} (line 3-4). Then we sort the objects by $d_{min}(o)$ and create a priority queue (line 5). We dequeue and get the object o with the minimal value. If $d_{min}(o) \geq d_{max}$, the algorithm terminates (line 8); otherwise we update $\mathcal{R}$ and d_{max} (line 10-11).

For example, in Figure 1, to get the safe region of the query, we initialize $\mathcal{R}'$ as the whole plane and d_{max} as the distance from o_4 to the top-right corner of $\mathcal{R}$, i.e., $d_{max} = 0.84$. Then we calculate MinBD $(o, D_{o_4,o})$ for every $o \in O - \{o_4\}$ and insert o into the priority queue $\mathcal{Q}$ in order. The first element in $\mathcal{Q}$ is o_7 with $d_{min}(o_7) = 0.12 < d_{max}$. We dequeue it and update $\mathcal{R}' = \mathcal{R}' \cap D_{o_4,o_7}$. d_{max} is still 0.84 as the top-right corner is still the farthest point to o_4. Next we process objects $o_3, o_{15}, o_{14}, o_9, o_{13}$ in the same way and get $d_{max} = 0.27$. For the next object o_{10}, since

Algorithm 1: SENSE-NoIndex(O, q)

```
   Input: O: A collection of objects
          q: A query
   Output: Safe Region R
1  begin
2  |  o* = the best answer for query q;
3  |  R = the whole plane bounding objects o ∈ O ;
4  |  d_max = MaxBD(o*, R) ;
5  |  Sort object o in O based on MinBD(o*, D_{o*,o}), and
   |  build a priority queue Q with the sorted objects;
6  |  while Q is not empty do
7  |  |  o = Q.dequeue () ;
8  |  |  if d_min(o) ≥ d_max then break;
9  |  |  else
10 |  |  |  R = R ∩ D_{o*,o} ;
11 |  |  |  d_max = MaxBD(o*, R) ;
12 end
```

Figure 3: Sense (No-Index) Algorithm (Safe-region construction for moving spatial keyword queries)

$d_{min}(o_{10}) = 0.28 > d_{max}$, the algorithm terminates. Thus we only compute the dominant regions for 6 objects and prune the other 9 objects.

4.2 Using Indexes to Improve Our Method

It is usually time-consuming to compute d_{min}(o) for all objects since there may be large numbers of objects. To address this issue, we utilize spatial structures to alleviate the problem. Without loss of generality, we use the IR-tree [2] as an example, which is the state-of-the-art index to answer top-k spatial keyword queries. Our method can be easily extended to support other indexing structures.

IR-tree incorporates inverted indexes into R-tree nodes. For each leaf node, in addition to keeping a set of objects in the minimum bounding rectangle (MBR) of this node, for each keyword contained in these objects, it also maintains an inverted list of objects in the node that contain the keyword. For each internal node, besides keeping a set of objects under this node, for each keyword, it also maintains an inverted list which keeps a list of its children which contain the keyword. Figure 4 shows the IR-tree structure.

The basic idea to use the spatial index to do pruning is as follows. Each IR-tree node n contains a group of objects under this node. We can estimate the lower bound of the dominant regions of objects under this node. If the estimated dominant region covers $\mathcal{R}'$, we can prune the whole subtree. As the IR-tree uses a hierarchical structure, we can prune many unnecessary nodes. Next we discuss the details.

Given a node n, we define the minimal bound distance for node n and object o^*, denoted by $\texttt{MinBD}(o^*, n)$. If $\texttt{MinBD}(o^*, n) \leq \min\{\texttt{MinBD}(o^*, D_{o^*,o}) | o \text{ is an object under node } n\}$, we have *if $\texttt{MaxBD}(o^*, \mathcal{R}) \leq \texttt{MinBD}(o^*, n)$, we can prune node n.* This is because for each object o under node n, we have $\texttt{MaxBD}(o^*, \mathcal{R}) \leq \texttt{MinBD}(o^*, D_{o^*,o})$ as $\mathcal{R}$ is inside $D_{o^*,o}$. Then we discuss how to define the function $\texttt{MinBD}(o^*, n)$.

Let $\textsf{mindist}(o^*, n)$ and $\textsf{maxdist}(o^*, n)$ respectively denote the minimal and maximal distance from node o^* to the MBR of node n. Let n_t denote the set of terms under this node. Notice that for each term t in n_t, its term frequency is the largest term frequency of objects under this node and its inverse document frequency is still idf(t). Let $\Delta t_{min} = \frac{1-\alpha}{\alpha}(\texttt{text}(q', o^*) - \texttt{text}(q', n_t))$. For each object o under node n, we have

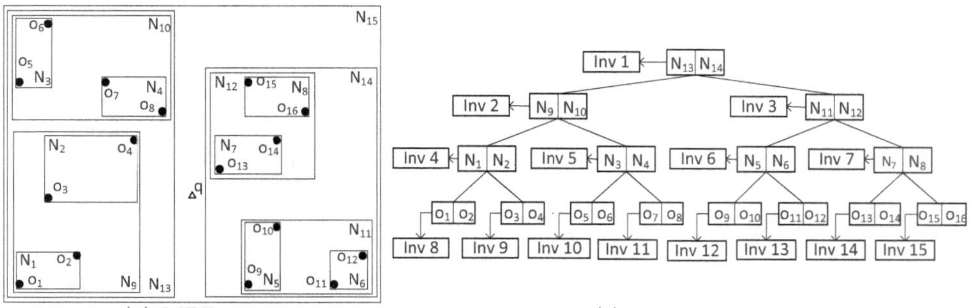

(a) MBRs (b) IR-tree

	Inv 1	Inv 2	···
k_1	N_{13}, N_{14}	N_9, N_{10}	···
k_2	N_{13}, N_{14}	N_9, N_{10}	···
k_3	N_{13}, N_{14}	N_9, N_{10}	···
k_4	N_{13}, N_{14}	N_9, N_{10}	···
k_5	N_{13}, N_{14}	N_9, N_{10}	···

	Inv 8	Inv 9	Inv 10	···
k_1	o_1	o_3, o_4	o_6	···
k_2	o_1, o_2	o_4	o_6	···
k_3	o_1	o_3, o_4	o_5	···
k_4	o_1, o_2	o_4	o_6	···
k_5	o_2	o_3	o_5, o_6	···

(c) Inverted Files

Figure 4: IR-tree

(1) $\mathsf{mindist}(o^*, n) \leq \mathtt{dist}(o^*, o) \leq \mathsf{maxdist}(o^*, n)$; and

(2) $\Delta t \geq \Delta t_{min}$ where $\Delta t = \frac{1-\alpha}{\alpha}(\mathtt{text}(q', o^*) - \mathtt{text}(q', o))$.

Based on these two notations, we can define $\mathtt{MinBD}(o^*, n)$ as follows.

Case 1: $\Delta t_{min} \geq \mathsf{maxdist}(o^*, n)$. $\mathtt{MinBD}(o^*, n)$ is the minimal distance from o^* to the boundary of the whole plane, denoted by D_{min}.

Case 2: $0 < \Delta t_{min} < \mathsf{maxdist}(o^*, n)$.

$$\mathtt{MinBD}(o^*, n) = \min(\frac{\mathsf{mindist}(o^*, n) + \Delta t_{min}}{2}, D_{min}).$$

Case 3: $\Delta t_{min} = 0$. $\mathtt{MinBD}(o^*, n) = \min(\frac{\mathsf{mindist}(o^*, n)}{2}, D_{min})$.

Case 4: $-\mathsf{mindist}(o^*, n) < \Delta t_{min} < 0$.

$$\mathtt{MinBD}(o^*, n) = \min(\max(0, \frac{\mathsf{mindist}(o^*, n) + \Delta t_{min}}{2}), D_{min}).$$

Case 5: $\Delta t_{min} < -\mathsf{mindist}(o^*, n)$. $\mathtt{MinBD}(o^*, n) = 0$.

LEMMA 8. *Given an object o^* and a node n, the above-defined function MinBD (o^*, n) satisfies MinBD(o^*, n)$\leq \min\{$MinBD$(o^*, D_{o^*,o}) | o$ is an object under node $n\}$.*

We can prove that $\mathtt{MinBD}(o^*, n) \leq \min\{\mathtt{MinBD}(o^*, D_{o^*,o}) | o$ is an object under node $n\}$. Based on this function, we can use indexes to prune nodes (groups of objects) and propose an index-based method. The pseudo-code is shown in Figure 5. We first initialize $\mathcal{R}$ and d_{max} similar to the non-index algorithm (line 3-4) and create an empty priority queue $\mathcal{Q}$ (line 5). Then we insert the root of the IR-tree in to $\mathcal{Q}$ (Line 6). We dequeue the top element n in $\mathcal{Q}$ until $\mathtt{MinBD}(o^*, n) \geq d_{max}$ (line 8). If $\mathtt{MinBD}(o^*, n) \geq d_{max}$, the algorithm terminates (line 9) since all dominant regions of remaining objects contain the safe region. If n is a node, we get each of its children n', calculate its dominant region $D_{o^*,n}$ and $d_{min}(n')$, and insert n' into $\mathcal{Q}$ with its corresponding $d_{min}(n')$ (line 10-13). If n is an object, we update $\mathcal{R}$ using the intersection between $\mathcal{R}$ and its dominant region (line 15) and also update d_{max} (line 16).

4.3 Cache-based Improvement

Note that before finding the safe region $\mathcal{R}$, we must compute the answer set $\mathcal{A}$. When computing $\mathcal{A}$, we have already traversed the IR-tree and visited some nodes and objects. To compute the safe region, we may still need to visit some of these nodes and objects. For example, in Figure 4, nodes N_{13}, N_{14}, N_{15} will be visited twice. More importantly, to compute the answer set and the safe region, we use the same keyword set. Based on these observations, we can cache some information to avoid unnecessary computation and facilitate the safe region computation. To this end, we cache the following information.

Algorithm 2: SENSE-Index(O, q)

Input: O: A collection of objects
q: A query
Output: Safe Region $\mathcal{R}$

1 **begin**
2 o^* = the best answer for query q;
3 $\mathcal{R}$ = the whole plane bounding all $o \in O$;
4 $d_{max} = \mathtt{MaxBD}(o^*, \mathcal{R})$;
5 $\mathcal{Q}$ = an empty priority queue ;
6 Build an IR-tree and insert *root* into $\mathcal{Q}$;
7 **while** *$\mathcal{Q}$ is not empty* **do**
8 $n = \mathcal{Q}$.dequeue () ;
9 **if** $d_{min}(n) \geq d_{max}$ **then** break;
10 **if** *n is a node* **then**
11 **for** *each child n' of n* **do**
12 $d_{min}(n') = \mathtt{MinBD}(o^*, n')$;
13 Insert n into $\mathcal{Q}$ with $d_{min}(n')$;
14 **else**
15 $\mathcal{R} = \mathcal{R} \cap D_{o^*,n}$;
16 $d_{max} = \mathtt{MaxBD}(o^*, \mathcal{R})$;
17 **end**

Figure 5: Sense (Index) Algorithm

(1) Inverted lists: When visiting a node, the answer computation step needs to load the inverted lists of query keywords. In the safe region computation step, we may still use such inverted lists, and thus we can cache them

(2) Keyword MBR: In order to get $\mathtt{MinBD}(o^*, n)$ for a node n, we have to use $\mathsf{mindist}(o^*, n)$ (and $\mathsf{maxdist}(o^*, n)$). The most direct way is to use the object which is nearest (and farthest) to o^*. However this method is inaccurate since some objects in the MBR may contain no query keyword and this kind of objects will not affect the safe region. To improve the accuracy, for a visited node in the answer computation step, we compute and store the MBR that contain at least one keyword, called *keyword MBR*. We use the keyword MBR to estimate the spatial information of this node.

(3) Score bounds: For a visited node in the answer computation step, for each node we can cache its virtual textual information n_t and Δt.

Thus during the answer computation step, we cache the above information. Then in the safe region computation step, we can utilize such information for pruning and thus can improve the efficiency. The cache-based method has the following two advantages. First, as IR-tree is a disk-based structure, it is expensive to access nodes multiple times from the disk and the cache-based method can reduce the number of disk accesses. Second, we can estimate the dominant region for each object more accurately.

4.4 Discussions

Checking Safe Region in the Client: In the client, we need to check whether the current location is in a safe region. As we use a piecewise function to represent a safe region, it is very efficient to do the checking as follows. Assume the current location is q'_s, $\mathcal{A} = \{o^*\}$ and $\mathcal{R} = f^i(\theta)[\theta_i \le \theta < \theta_{i+1}](1 \le i \le m, \theta_{m+1} = \theta_1)$. First, we compute θ' for q'_s which is the angle from line o^*q' to the x-axis. Suppose $\theta' \in [\theta_j, \theta_{j+1}), 1 \le j \le m$. We calculate $r = f^j(\theta')$ which is the distance from o^* to the boundary of $\mathcal{R}$ with this angle. Therefore, if $\texttt{dist}(o^*, q'_s) \le r$, q'_s is inside $\mathcal{A}$, and thus o^* is still the best answer. Otherwise, the client should send a new query to the server.

Supporting other functions: Our framework can be extended to support the ranking function in Equation 3 which was used in [17]. Different from our ranking function, the shape of the safe region of this function is composed of circles and lines. We can extend our techniques to compute the dominant region and the safe region. Notice that in their work, they only use polygons to approximate circles and they cannot find the exact safe region. However we can use the polar coordinate to efficiently compute the exact safe region. Due to space constraints, we omit the details.

5. EXTENDING OUR TECHNIQUES TO SUPPORT TOP-K QUERIES

In this section, we extend our techniques to support top-k queries. We propose an intersection-based method in Section 5.1 and an approximate method in Section 5.2.

5.1 Intersection-based Method

To compute the safe region for a top-k query, an intuitive way is to first compute the safe region for each object $o^* \in \mathcal{A}$ to the object set $O - \mathcal{A}$ (denoted by $\mathcal{R}_{o^*,O-\mathcal{A}}$) and then compute their intersection ($\mathcal{R} = \cap_{o^* \in \mathcal{A}} \mathcal{R}_{o^*,O-\mathcal{A}}$). We can compute $\mathcal{R}_{o^*,O-\mathcal{A}}$ by intersecting the dominant region of o^* to every object $o \in O - \mathcal{A}$. Thus we have $\mathcal{R} = \cap_{o^* \in \mathcal{A}}(\cap_{o \in O-\mathcal{A}} D_{o^*,o})$ as stated in Lemma 9.

LEMMA 9. *Given a query q and its answer set $\mathcal{A}$, the safe region can be computed as:*

$$\mathcal{R} = \cap_{o^* \in \mathcal{A}}(\cap_{o \in O-\mathcal{A}} D_{o^*,o}). \quad (6)$$

For example, in Figure 6(a), assume $k = 2$. The shaded regions respectively denote $\mathcal{R}_{o_4,O-\{o_9\}}$, $\mathcal{R}_{o_9,O-\{o_4\}}$, and the safe region for $\{o_4, o_9\}$. Obviously the safe region of $\{o_4, o_9\}$ is the intersection of $\mathcal{R}_{o_4,O-\{o_9\}}$ and $\mathcal{R}_{o_9,O-\{o_4\}}$.

Based on Lemma 9, for each object o^* in $\mathcal{A}$, we first compute $\mathcal{R}_{o^*,O-\mathcal{A}}$ and then intersect $\mathcal{R}_{o^*,O-\mathcal{A}}$ for every o^* in $\mathcal{A}$. For the no-index based algorithm (Algorithm 1), we can easily compute $\mathcal{R}_{o^*,O-\mathcal{A}}$ by replacing O with $O - \mathcal{A}$. For the index-based algorithm (Algorithm 2), during the traversal of the indexing structure, if we encounter an object in $\mathcal{A}$, we just ignore the object. If we encounter a node, we use the same method, regardless of whether the node contains an object in $\mathcal{A}$. The main reason is as follows. If we prune a node n, all objects under the node cover the safe region. Thus we can use the two algorithms to support top-k queries.

For example in Figure 6(a), consider $\mathcal{A} = \{o_4, o_9\}$. We first compute the safe region for o_4, i.e., $\mathcal{R}_{o_4,O-\{o_4,o_9\}}$. Different from finding the safe region for top-1 answer, we do not need to compute D_{o_4,o_9}. Then, based on the safe region for o_4, we traverse the IR-tree again to compute $\mathcal{R}_{o_9,O-\{o_4,o_9\}}$. The intersection between $\mathcal{R}_{o_4,O-\{o_4,o_9\}}$ and $\mathcal{R}_{o_9,O-\{o_4,o_9\}}$ is the safe region.

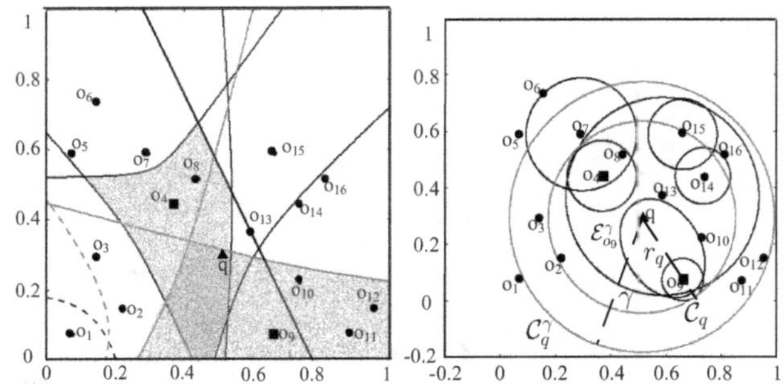

(a) Intersection-based (b) Approximate method

Figure 6: Supporting top-k queries

Next we discuss how to compute the intersection of regions $\mathcal{R}_{o^*,O-\mathcal{A}}$ for $o^* \in \mathcal{A}$. As each region is composed by a set of hyperbolas, it is expensive to compute the intersection. Although we use the polar coordination, different regions have different origins and we have to transfer coordinates. To alleviate this problem, we use a polygon to approximate the region as follows. For each curve of the region, if it is convex, we use the segment between its two end points to approximate it; if the curve is concave, we use tangents inside the safe region to approximate it. Notice that if we use the index-based algorithm, this method needs to access the index k times. If k is large, the performance will be poor. To address this issue, we propose an alternative method. The basic idea is to compute the intersection during the traversal of the index, we only access the index once. Before introducing our idea, we first define the dominant region of an answer set $\mathcal{A}$ to an object $o \notin \mathcal{A}$.

DEFINITION 5. *Given a query $q = (q_s, q_t, k)$, the dominant region of $\mathcal{A}$ to o ($o \notin \mathcal{A}$) is:*

$$D_{\mathcal{A},o} = \{q'_s | \forall o^* \in \mathcal{A}, score(q', o^*) \le score(q', o)\}, \quad (7)$$

where $q' = (q'_s, q_t, k)$.

Obviously $\mathcal{R} = \cap_{o \notin \mathcal{A}} D_{\mathcal{A},o}$. Based on this concept, we propose two incremental algorithms. For the no-index method, we only need to use $D_{\mathcal{A},o}$ to replace $D_{o^*,o}$. For the index-based method, besides replacing $D_{o^*,o}$ with $D_{\mathcal{A},o}$ for an object o, we need to redefine how to prune an object o (node n). As o^* may not be in $\mathcal{R}$, we need to reselect a location which must be in $\mathcal{R}$. Based on Lemma 3, q must be in $\mathcal{R}$. Thus we use $\texttt{MinBD}(q, D_{\mathcal{A},o})$ and $\texttt{MaxBD}(q, \mathcal{R})$ to do pruning. We can easily deduce a lower bound of the distance from q to the boundary of $D_{\mathcal{A},o}$ based on the triangle inequality, i.e., we set $\texttt{MinBD}(q, D_{\mathcal{A},o}) = \texttt{MinBD}(o^*, D_{\mathcal{A},o}) - \texttt{dist}(o^*, q)$. $\texttt{MaxBD}(q, \mathcal{R})$ is the maximal distance from q to the boundary of $\mathcal{R}$. Then, we can use our framework to compute the safe region. As $D_{\mathcal{A},o}$ and $\mathcal{R}$ are complex regions composed by a set of hyperbolas, it is expensive to compute the region. To address this issue, we use polygons to approximate the regions as described in Section 3.

For example, in Figure 6(a), the dashed lines represent the boundary of D_{o_4,o_1} and D_{o_9,o_1} respectively and their intersection is $D_{\mathcal{A},o_1}$. In the intersection method, we compute the safe region first for o_4 and then for o_9. Instead, our incremental method first computes $D_{\mathcal{A},o}$ for $o \notin \mathcal{A}$, and then calculates their intersection to get the safe region.

5.2 Approximate Method

The previous methods compute the *global* safe region, and in this section we compute a *local* safe region (denoted by $\tilde{\mathcal{R}}$) which is a subset of the exact *global* safe region ($\mathcal{R}$). As the client's locations are usually not far away from the current query, we can use the local safe region to approximate the safe region. This method has a big advantage that it is very efficient to compute the local safe region and outperforms the methods in Section 5.1. Next we discuss the details.

We can transfer our ranking function in Equation 1 into the following form:

$$\texttt{score}(q, o) = \alpha \times \big(\texttt{dist}(q, o) + \frac{1-\alpha}{\alpha} \cdot (1 - \texttt{text}(q, o))\big).$$

In this way we can model each object o as a circle $\mathcal{C}_o$ with center o and radius of $r_o = \frac{1-\alpha}{\alpha}(1 - \texttt{text}(q, o))$. Then,

$$\texttt{score}(q, o) = \alpha\big(\texttt{dist}(q, o) + r_o\big).$$

Let $r_q = \max\{\texttt{dist}(q, o^*) + r_{o^*} | o^* \in \mathcal{A}\}$ and $\mathcal{C}_q$ denote the circle centered at q and radius of r_q. For an object $o^* \in \mathcal{A}$, we have $\texttt{score}(q, o^*) \leq \alpha r_q$, which is equivalent to $\texttt{dist}(q, o^*) + r_{o^*} \leq r_q$, thus $o^* \in \mathcal{A}$ if and only if the circle $\mathcal{C}_{o^*}$ are inside $\mathcal{C}_q$. Similarly an object $o \in O - \mathcal{A}$ if and only if the circle $\mathcal{C}_o$ are not inside $\mathcal{C}_q$.

Then suppose the client moves to location q'. Let $\mathcal{C}_{q'}$ denote the circle centered at q' and radius of $r_q - \texttt{dist}(q, q')$. As $\mathcal{C}_{q'}$ is inside $\mathcal{C}_q$, for each object $o^* \in \mathcal{A}$, if $\mathcal{C}_{o^*}$ is inside $\mathcal{C}_{q'}$, o^* is still a top-k answer of q'. $\mathcal{C}_{o^*}$ is inside $\mathcal{C}_{q'}$ if and only if

$$\texttt{dist}(o^*, q') + r_{o^*} \leq r_q - \texttt{dist}(q, q'),$$

which can be written as

$$\texttt{dist}(o^*, q') + \texttt{dist}(q, q') \leq r_q - r_{o^*}. \tag{8}$$

Obviously the locus of such points is an ellipse with q and o^* as the two focuses, denoted by $\mathcal{E}_{o^*} = \{q'_s | \texttt{dist}(o^*, q') + \texttt{dist}(q, q') \leq r_q - r_{o^*}\}$. Obviously $\mathcal{E} = \cap_{o^* \in \mathcal{A}} \mathcal{E}_{o^*}$ is a local safe region, that is if $q' \in \mathcal{E}$, $\mathcal{A}$ is still the answer set. Since $q \in \mathcal{E}$ as stated in Lemma 10, $\mathcal{E}$ is not empty.

LEMMA 10. *Given a query q and its answer set $\mathcal{A}$, $\mathcal{E}$ is not empty and $q \in \mathcal{E}$.*

We can use the polar coordinate to represent an ellipse. As q is in each ellipse, we can take q as the origin of the polar coordinate and thus can efficiently compute the intersection of the k ellipses. Due to space constraints, we omit the details about how to use polar coordinates to compute the intersection. As the local safe region is small, we can enlarge it as follows. Based on Equation 8, if r_q increases, the eclipse $\mathcal{E}_{o^*}$ will become larger and so will region $\mathcal{E}$. Thus we can increase r_q to enlarge the safe region as follows (Figure 6(b)).

Let $\gamma = r_q + \triangle$ and $\mathcal{C}_q^\gamma$ denote the circle centered at q and radius of γ. We compute the ellipse $\mathcal{E}_{o^*}^\gamma = \{q'_s | \texttt{dist}(o^*, q') + \texttt{dist}(q, q') \leq \gamma - r_{o^*}\}$, and region $\mathcal{E}^\gamma = \cap_{o^* \in \mathcal{A}} \mathcal{E}_{o^*}^\gamma$. Obviously $\mathcal{E} \subseteq \mathcal{E}^\gamma$. Obviously $\mathcal{A}$ dominates the objects outside $\mathcal{C}_q^\gamma$. Since there may be other objects involved in $\mathcal{C}_q^\gamma - \mathcal{C}_q$, we need to determine whether $\mathcal{A}$ dominates these objects. Let $\mathcal{C}_q^\gamma - \mathcal{C}_q$ denote the set of objects whose corresponding circles inside circle $\mathcal{C}_q^\gamma$ but not inside $\mathcal{C}_q$ and $D_{\mathcal{A}, \mathcal{C}_q^\gamma - \mathcal{C}_q}$ denote the dominant region of $\mathcal{A}$ to $\mathcal{C}_q^\gamma - \mathcal{C}_q$ which is $\cap_{o^* \in \mathcal{A}} D_{o^*, \mathcal{C}_q^\gamma - \mathcal{C}_q}$. Let $\tilde{\mathcal{R}}^\gamma = \mathcal{E}^\gamma \cap D_{\mathcal{A}, \mathcal{C}_q^\gamma - \mathcal{C}_q}$. We can take $\tilde{\mathcal{R}}^\gamma$ as a local safe region since $\tilde{\mathcal{R}} \subseteq \mathcal{R}$ as formalized in Lemma 11.

LEMMA 11. *For any γ, we have*
(1) $\tilde{\mathcal{R}}^\gamma = \mathcal{E}^\gamma \cap D_{\mathcal{A}, \mathcal{C}_q^\gamma - \mathcal{C}_q} \subseteq \mathcal{R}$, and
(2) If γ is ∞, $\tilde{\mathcal{R}}^\gamma = \mathcal{R}$.

There are two challenges. The first one is how to compute $D_{\mathcal{A}, \mathcal{C}_q^\gamma - \mathcal{C}_q}$. We can find the objects in $\mathcal{C}_q^\gamma$-$\mathcal{C}_q$ using any spatial index structures (which is the objects with distance to q between γ and r_q). Then based on these objects, we can efficiently compute $D_{\mathcal{A}, \mathcal{C}_q^\gamma - \mathcal{C}_q}$ based on the non-index based algorithm. The second one is how to select γ. If γ is small, the local safe region is small, and the client queries have large probabilities outside the region. If γ is large, there will be more objects in $\mathcal{C}_q^\gamma - \mathcal{C}_q$, and it will take more time to compute $D_{\mathcal{A}, \mathcal{C}_q^\gamma - \mathcal{C}_q}$. Thus it is a tradeoff to select an appropriate γ. We can determine the value based on the client moving speed (e.g., m meter/per second). If we expect the query location to be still in the safe region after s seconds, we set $\gamma = r_q + k * m * s$.

6. EXPERIMENT

We implemented our proposed techniques and compared with the state-of-the-art method MSK [17]. We used disk-based IR-tree [2] as the index to compute the answers and safe regions. We fixed the page size at 4KB. We used two real spatial data sets composed of POIs in California and Beijing. The details are listed in Table 2. We randomly generated 100 query trajectories and each query had 2-5 keywords. Each trajectory consisted 1,000 points and the distance between two consecutive points were 100 meters. All the experiments were implemented in Java and conducted on a Linux server with Intel(R) Xeon(R) 2.27GHz CPU and 4GB RAM.

Table 2: Data Sets

data set	# of objects	# of distinct keywords	avg # of keywords per object
California	544,906	132,552	7.39
Beijing	1,056,770	93,543	4.52

6.1 Evaluation of Cache-based Technique

In this section, we evaluate the cache-based technique. We implemented two algorithms, SENSE-Index without cache and SENSE-index with cache, where we used the incremental intersection methods. Figure 7 shows the results. We can see that the cache-based technique can significantly improve the performance. For example, on the California dataset, when $k = 20$, the cache-based time reduces the time from 1228 milliseconds to 55 milliseconds. This is because we can reduce large numbers of IOs by using cached information.

6.2 Evaluation of Computing Algorithms

We first evaluate our different methods to compute the safe region. We implemented tree algorithms, intersection based method (SENSE-INTERSECTION), incremental intersection-based method (SENSE-INCREINTERSECTION), and approximate-based method (SENSE-APPROXIMATE). Figure 8 shows the experimental results. We can see that SENSE-INCREINTERSECTION and SENSE-APPROXIMATE outperform SENSE-INTERSECTION. This is because SENSE-INTERSECTION has to traverse the IR-tree k times. If $k = 1$, SENSE-INCREINTERSECTION and SENSE-INTERSECTION achieved nearly the same performance. SENSE-APPROXIMATE was better than the other two methods as it reduces the number of dominant regions and estimates the safe regions using smaller numbers of dominant regions. As SENSE-INCREINTERSECTION is always better than SENSE-INTERSECTION, next we only compare SENSE-INCREINTERSECTION and SENSE-APPROXIMATE.

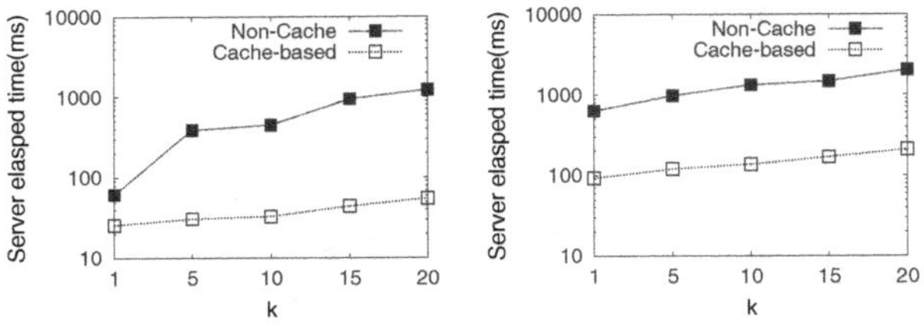

(a) California (b) Beijing

Figure 7: Evaluation on cache-based technique

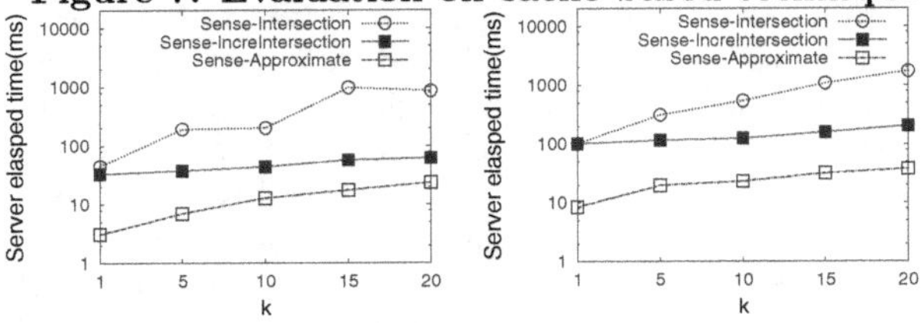

(a) California (b) Beijing

Figure 8: Evaluation of computing model on server

6.3 SENSE-INCREINTERSECTION vs. SENSE-APPROXIMATE

We further compare SENSE-INCREINTERSECTION and SENSE-APPROXIMATE in terms of average server elapsed time, average client elapsed time, average communication cost (bytes) and the update frequency which is the ratio of the number of queries issued to the server to the total number of queries. The client issued a query for each point in a trajectory. For SENSE-APPROXIMATE, to calculate $\mathcal{A}$ and $\mathcal{R}$, we set $s = 1000$. Figure 9 shows the results by varying k. Due to the space constraints, we only show the results on the California dataset. On the Beijing dataset, we got similar results. We can see that SENSE-APPROXIMATE took less server time as it uses an approximate method to compute the safe region. Although SENSE-APPROXIMATE involved more client time, it only took about 0.006 milliseconds which is negligible. SENSE-APPROXIMATE involved more communication overhead since it needs to intersect hyperbolas and ellipses which results in more vertexes. SENSE-APPROXIMATE had larger update frequency as it estimated the safe region which is much smaller than the real safe region.

To further compare the two methods, we evaluate the server time and communication cost in a time window (We do not compare the client time as it is negligible). In our experiments, the time windows is 10 minutes. We compared the total server elapsed time to answer the queries in the window. Figure 10 shows the results. We can see that SENSE-APPROXIMATE took less server time than SENSE-INCREINTERSECTION, especially for larger k values. This is because SENSE-APPROXIMATE estimates the safe regions and reduces the computation time. SENSE-APPROXIMATE involved nearly the same communication overhead with SENSE-INCREINTERSECTION, especially for a large k. This is because our approximate method has better approximation ratio for larger k, since it enlarges the space for larger k.

6.4 Comparison with state-of-the-art method

As the state-of-the-art method MSK [17] only supports the ad-hoc ranking function as discussed in Section 2.2, we extend SENSE-INCREINTERSECTION to support the same ranking function and compare with it. Figure 11 shows the results by varying k. We can see that our method significantly outperforms MSK in terms of server time, client time, and communication cost. The main reason is as follows. For server time, we use polar coordinates to represent the safe

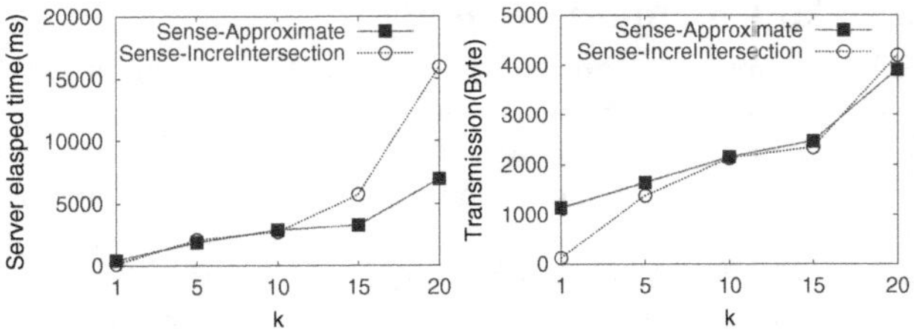

(a) Server Time (b) Communication Cost

Figure 10: Sense-IncreIntersection vs. Sense-Approximate (for 10 minutes, California)

region, which is much more efficient than the approximate based method. For the communication cost, MSK needs to return some objects to avoid involving false negatives. That is also why the client time of MSK is much larger than SENSE: besides checking whether the current location is in safe region, the client has to examine every returned objects. SENSE and MSK nearly achieve the same update frequency as they generate similar safe region. The only difference is that MSK approximates the safe regions using polygons and our method computes the exact ones. Figure 12 shows the results by varying velocity. We can see that our method still significantly outperforms MSK in terms of the server time, client time, and communication cost.

7. RELATED WORK

There have been many studies on spatial keyword search [9, 7, 22, 19, 18, 10, 13, 1, 3, 21]. Felipe et al. [4] addressed a k-nearest-neighbor problem which returns k objects that contain the query keywords and are near to the query location. They proposed IR^2-tree by adding signature files to R-tree nodes. Cong et al. [2] proposed the IR-tree which can support IR-based ranking functions. Zhou et al. [22] and Hariharan et al. [7] studied range-based spatial keyword search, which, given a rectangle and a set of keywords, finds all relevant answers that are located in the rectangle. Zhang et al. [19] studied collective keyword search, which finds a set of objects that contain all the query keywords. Lu et al. [10] studied reverse spatial and textual k nearest neighbor search. Li et al. [9] studied direction-aware search by considering directions. Obviously these problems are different from ours.

Wu et al. [17] studied moving spatial keyword search. However they only supported ad-hoc ranking functions (Section 2.2). Instead our method adopts a general ranking function. When we adapted our method to support their functions, our method significantly outperforms their approach in terms of both efficiency and communication cost.

Continuous queries have attracted much attention with the popularity of location-based services. For a continuous query, the query position was moving while the objects can be static [15, 14, 16] or moving [6, 8, 5]. We consider the former case. To avoid repeatedly issuing queries, the safe region based method was proposed [20, 12]. However these studies only considered spatial information and did not take into account textual descriptions.

8. CONCLUSION

In this paper we have studied the moving top-k spatial keyword search problem. For each query submitted to the server, besides generating top-k answers we also constructed its safe region. We proposed to use hyperbolas to represent the safe region. To efficiently calculate the safe region, we devised effective pruning techniques and utilized index-

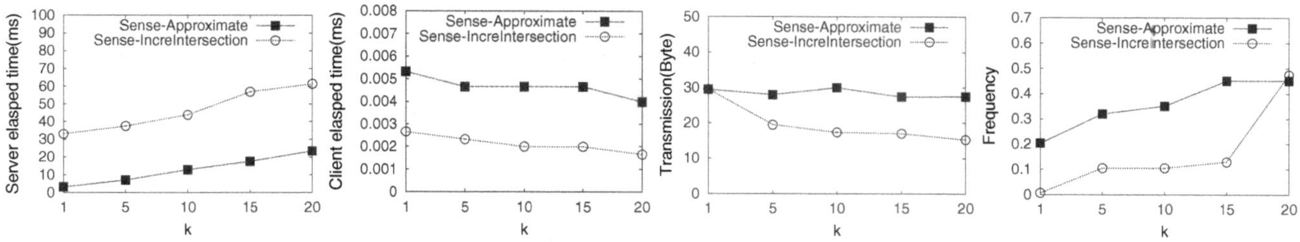

(a) Server Elapsed Time (b) Client Elapsed Time (c) Communication Cost (d) Update Frequency

Figure 9: Sense-IncreIntersection vs. Sense-Approximate (varying k, California)

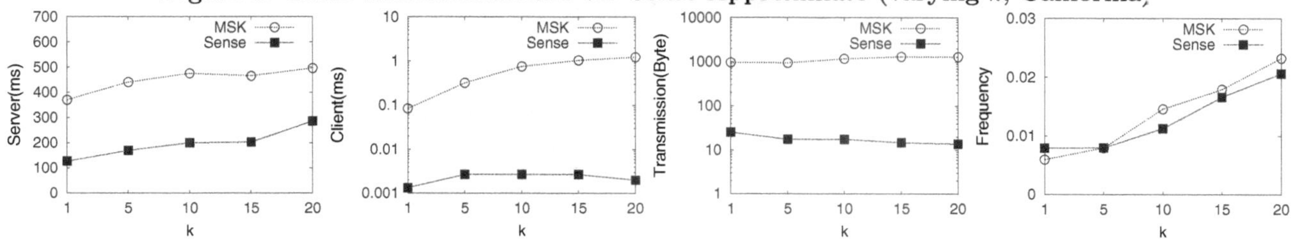

(a) Server Elapsed Time (b) Client Elapsed Time (c) Communication Cost (d) Update Frequency

Figure 11: Comparison with state-of-the-art method (varying k, California)

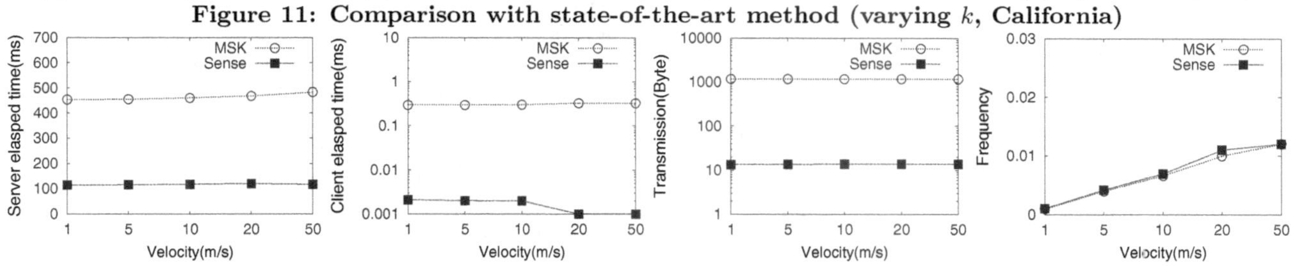

(a) Server Elapsed Time (b) Client Elapsed Time (c) Communication Cost (d) Update Frequency

Figure 12: Comparison with state-of-the-art method (varying velocity, California)

ing structures to improve the performance. We also developed incremental algorithms to efficiently compute the safe region. We have implemented our proposed techniques and experimental results show that our method significantly outperforms state-of-the-art approaches.

Acknowledgement. This work was partly supported by the National Natural Science Foundation of China under Grant No. 61003004, National Grand Fundamental Research 973 Program of China under Grant No. 2011CB302206, and a project of Tsinghua University under Grant No. 20111081073, and the "NExT Research Center" funded by MDA, Singapore, under Grant No. WBS:R-252-300-001-490.

9. REFERENCES

[1] Y.-Y. Chen, T. Suel, and A. Markowetz. Efficient query processing in geographic web search engines. In *SIGMOD Conference*, pages 277–288, 2006.

[2] G. Cong, C. S. Jensen, and D. Wu. Efficient retrieval of the top-k most relevant spatial web objects. *PVLDB*, 2(1):337–348, 2009.

[3] J. Fan, G. Li, L. Zhou, S. Chen, and J. Hu. Seal: Spatio-textual similarity search. *PVLDB*, 5(9):824–835, 2012.

[4] I. D. Felipe, V. Hristidis, and N. Rishe. Keyword search on spatial databases. In *ICDE*, pages 656–665, 2008.

[5] B. Gedik and L. Liu. Mobieyes: Distributed processing of continuously moving queries on moving objects in a mobile system. In *EDBT*, pages 67–87, 2004.

[6] B. Gedik, K.-L. Wu, P. S. Yu, and L. Liu. Motion adaptive indexing for moving continual queries over moving objects. In *CIKM*, pages 427–436, 2004.

[7] R. Hariharan, B. Hore, C. Li, and S. Mehrotra. Processing spatial-keyword (sk) queries in geographic information retrieval (gir) systems. In *SSDBM*, page 16, 2007.

[8] H. Hu, J. Xu, and D. L. Lee. A generic framework for monitoring continuous spatial queries over moving objects. In *SIGMOD Conference*, pages 479–490, 2005.

[9] G. Li, J. Xu, and J. Feng. Desks: Direction-aware spatial keyword search. In *ICDE*, pages 459–470, 2012.

[10] J. Lu, Y. Lu, and G. Cong. Reverse spatial and textual k nearest neighbor search. In *SIGMOD Conference*, pages 349–360, 2011.

[11] B. Martins, M. J. Silva, and L. A. Ribeiro. Indexing and ranking in geo-ir systems. In *GIR*, pages 31–34, 2005.

[12] S. Nutanong, R. Zhang, E. Tanin, and L. Kulik. The v*-diagram: a query-dependent approach to moving knn queries. *PVLDB*, 1(1):1095–1106, 2008.

[13] S. B. Roy and K. Chakrabarti. Location-aware type ahead search on spatial databases: semantics and efficiency. In *SIGMOD Conference*, pages 361–372, 2011

[14] Z. Song and N. Roussopoulos. K-nearest neighbor search for moving query point. In *SSTD*, pages 79–96, 2001.

[15] Y. Tao and D. Papadias. Time-parameterized queries in spatio-temporal databases. In *SIGMOD Conference*, pages 334–345, 2002.

[16] Y. Tao, D. Papadias, and Q. Shen. Continuous nearest neighbor search. In *VLDB*, pages 287–298, 2002.

[17] D. Wu, M. L. Yiu, C. S. Jensen, and G. Cong. Efficient continuously moving top-k spatial keyword query processing. In *ICDE*, pages 541–552, 2011.

[18] B. Yao, F. Li, M. Hadjieleftheriou, and K. Hou. Approximate string search in spatial databases. In *ICDE*, pages 545–556, 2010.

[19] D. Zhang, Y. M. Chee, A. Mondal, A. K. H. Tung, and M. Kitsuregawa. Keyword search in spatial databases: Towards searching by document. In *ICDE*, pages 688–699, 2009.

[20] J. Zhang, M. Zhu, D. Papadias, Y. Tao, and D. L. Lee. Location-based spatial queries. In *SIGMOD Conference*, pages 443–454, 2003.

[21] R. Zhong, J. Fan, G. Li, K.L.. Tan, and L. Zhou. Location-Aware Instant Search. In *CIKM*, 2012.

[22] Y. Zhou, X. Xie, C. Wang, Y. Gong, and W.-Y. Ma. Hybrid index structures for location-based web search. In *CIKM*, pages 155–162, 2005.

Monochromatic and Bichromatic Reverse Nearest Neighbor Queries on Land Surfaces

Da Yan, Zhou Zhao and Wilfred Ng
The Hong Kong University of Science and Technology
Clear Water Bay, Kowloon, Hong Kong
{yanda, zhaozhou, wilfred}@cse.ust.hk

ABSTRACT

Finding *reverse nearest neighbors* (RNNs) is an important operation in spatial databases. The problem of evaluating RNN queries has already received considerable attention due to its importance in many real-world applications, such as resource allocation and disaster response. While RNN query processing has been extensively studied in Euclidean space, no work ever studies this problem on land surfaces. However, practical applications of RNN queries involve terrain surfaces that constrain object movements, which rendering the existing algorithms inapplicable.

In this paper, we investigate the evaluation of two types of RNN queries on land surfaces: *monochromatic RNN* (MRNN) queries and *bichromatic RNN* (BRNN) queries. On a land surface, the distance between two points is calculated as the length of the shortest path along the surface. However, the computational cost of the state-of-the-art shortest path algorithm on a land surface is quadratic to the size of the surface model, which is usually quite huge. As a result, surface RNN query processing is a challenging problem.

Leveraging some newly-discovered properties of Voronoi cell approximation structures, we make use of standard index structures such as an R-tree to design efficient algorithms that accelerate the evaluation of MRNN and BRNN queries on land surfaces. Our proposed algorithms are able to localize query evaluation by accessing just a small fraction of the surface data near the query point, which helps avoid shortest path evaluation on a large surface. Extensive experiments are conducted on large real-world datasets to demonstrate the efficiency of our algorithms.

Categories and Subject Descriptors

H.2.8 [**Database Management**]: Database Applications—*Spatial databases and GIS*

Keywords

Reverse nearest neighbor, land surface, terrain

1. INTRODUCTION

Recent technological advances in remote sensing have made available high resolution terrain data of the entire Earth surface. As a result, many online Earth visualization platforms emerge, such as "Google Earth™" and "Bing Maps for Enterprise". Other examples involving geo-realistic rendering of surfaces include computer games such as "Counter-Strike" and "Call of Duty". However, these applications focus mainly on the rendering of land surfaces rather than the processing of spatial queries on them.

Due to the ubiquity of high resolution terrain data, it is becoming more and more important to develop geographic information systems (GISs) that support efficient query processing on land surfaces. Such systems would enable many novel and useful applications in the terrain context.

The shortest path problem has been studied on land surfaces by many works such as [5, 6, 7, 8], and the best-known exact algorithm is *Chen and Han's algorithm*, which takes $O(n^2)$ time on a surface model of size n. Recently, several works [1, 2, 3, 4] begin to study k-nearest neighbor (k-NN) queries on land surfaces, which is termed *surface k-NN* (SkNN) queries.

We call a *reverse nearest neighbor* (RNN) query on land surfaces as a *surface RNN* (SRNN) query, which, to our knowledge, has not been studied before. There are two popular types of RNN queries in the literature:

- Given a data point set O and a query point q, a *monochromatic reverse nearest neighbor* (MRNN) query finds all the data points $o \in O$ that have q as their nearest neighbor (NN).
- Given a site point set S, a data point set O and a query point $q \in S$, a *bichromatic reverse nearest neighbor* (BRNN) query finds all the data points $o \in O$ that are closer to q than any other point in S.

SRNN queries have many real world applications. For example, *bichromatic* SRNN (BSRNN) queries are important in the domain of disaster response: when a disaster (e.g. earthquake/tsunami) happens, the transportation system may stop functioning, and thus rescue teams have to find ways within the disaster area, instead of using the blocked/damaged roads, to save the lives of the suffered. In this case, a victim should be reached by the rescue team nearest to him/her, and therefore, it is important for the rescue teams to keep track of their RNNs among the victims. Other applications of BSRNN queries include supply distribution during military operations, and wild animal rescue in nature reserves.

Besides BSRNN queries, *monochromatic* SRNN (MSRNN) queries are also useful in many application domains, such as outdoor activities and military operations. Consider the activity of mountaineering: in order to keep the mountaineers safe, it is important for each member to keep track of his/her RNNs among all the other mountaineers, so that if a member encounters an accident such as a landslide, he/she can get help from his/her nearest neighbor who tracks him/her (e.g. through GPS devices). Similar situations happen in

CIKM'12, October 29–November 2, 2012, Maui, HI, USA.

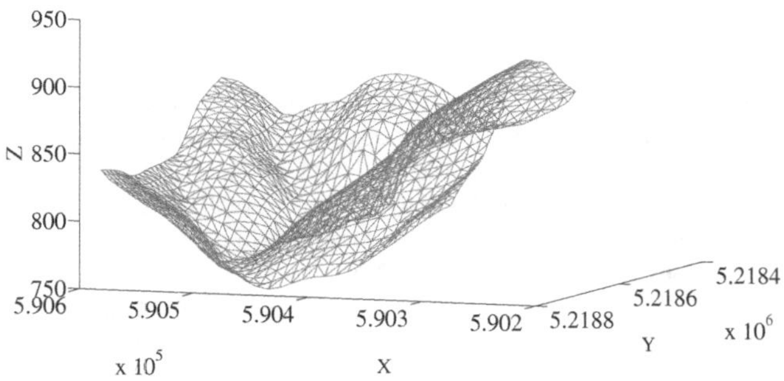

Figure 1: Triangular Irregular Network (TIN)

military operations, where a troop would reinforce one of its reverse nearest neighbor troop if that troop suffers severe casualty.

In this paper, we study RNN queries on land surfaces, including both MSRNN and BSRNN queries. Unlike traditional RNN queries, the evaluation of SRNN queries is more challenging due to the following two reasons:

- **The size of the surface model data is huge.** Unlike query processing in the Euclidean space, queries on land surfaces also involve the environmental data (i.e. the surface model) besides the object data. A land surface is usually represented by the *Triangulated Irregular Network* (TIN) model [1, 4], a mesh derived from the *Digital Elevation Model* (DEM) of sampled ground positions at regularly spaced interval (cf. Figure 1). The surface data are usually collected with high resolution, e.g. terrain data with 10m sampling interval can be easily accessed from [25]. As a result, a typical land surface data contains at least millions of TIN vertices.
- **Finding shortest surface path is computationally expensive.** The best-known algorithm for exact shortest surface path computation is *Chen and Han's algorithm*, which takes $O(n^2)$ time on a terrain data with n triangular faces. It is reported in [3] that, for some moderately large areas (a few square kilometers), *Chen and Han's algorithm* may take tens of minutes on a modern PC machine to compute a shortest surface path. The poor scalability of *Chen and Han's algorithm* poses a challenge for SRNN query processing, since the definition of RNNs on land surfaces is based on the shortest surface path distances.

As a result, efficient SRNN query evaluation requires that (1) the shortest surface path computation should be avoided whenever possible, by efficient pruning methods; and that (2) only a small fraction of the surface data near the query point should be accessed, so that shortest surface path computations are done on a small surface.

To achieve these two goals, we adopt the Voronoi cell [24] approximation structures (i.e. tight/loose cells) to accelerate SRNN query processing. The concepts of tight/loose cells are first proposed in [1] for processing SkNN queries. The algorithms of [1] achieve significant pruning power when answering SkNN queries, by using several properties of the relationship between a cell and a query points, which we call the *cell-point properties*.

However, the *cell-point properties* along are not sufficient for answering SRNN queries. We discover several (non-trivial) properties of the relationship between two cells, termed the *cell-cell properties*, which is essential in SRNN query processing. Furthermore, our MSRNN algorithm requires the loose cell of the query point, but [1] only gives an offline algorithm that computes the loose cells of all data points together. Therefore, we also study how to efficiently compute the loose cell of the query point online.

While [1] designs a cell index dedicated to SkNN query processing, we find that its algorithm may not return the exact kNNs, due to a flawed cell-cell property it assumes. Therefore, we do not follow that indexing methods, but rather use standard index structures such as R-tree in our algorithms. Extensive experiments on large real-world datasets have demonstrated the efficiency of our algorithms for MSRNN and BSRNN queries.

The rest of the paper is organized as follows. We formally define MSRNN and BSRNN queries in Section 2. In Section 3, we review the concept of tight/loose cells, as well as the *cell-point properties*. Our cell indexing method is explained in Section 4, where we also present the algorithm of surface NN query processing using the index. In Section 5, we prove two new *cell-cell properties* and present our algorithm for NN queries among the data objects (rather than the query point), which is a fundamental operation in our MSRNN algorithm. Our online algorithm for constructing tight/loose cells is introduced in Section 6, and our algorithms for MSRNN and BSRNN queries are described in Section 7. Extensive experiments are conducted in Section 8 on large real-world datasets to verify the efficiency of our algorithms. Finally, we review the related work in Section 9, and conclude the paper in Section 10.

2. MSRNN & BSRNN QUERIES

A land surface can be regarded as a continuous function that assigns every point (x, y) on a horizontal plane to a unique z-coordinate value. The TIN model is the most popular model to represent a land surface, which is constructed from the sampled ground positions at regularly spaced intervals, by Delaunay triangulation [24], to form a set of non-overlapping triangles whose vertices are these sampled points. We call the graph defined by the sampled vertices and the edges of the triangles as the *model network*. Figure 1 shows a piece of land surface represented by the TIN model, where the red lines correspond to the edges of the *model network*.

Before presenting the formal definition of SRNN queries, let us first define some distance metrics between two points on the TIN model, as well as the corresponding notations.

DEFINITION 1. *Let p_1 and p_2 be two points on a land surface.*

- *The **surface distance** between p_1 and p_2, denoted $d_S(p_1, p_2)$, is the length of the shortest path connecting p_1 and p_2 along the surface.*
- *The **Euclidean distance** between p_1 and p_2, denoted $d_E(p_1, p_2)$, is the length of the straight line connecting p_1 and p_2.*
- *The **network distance** between **vertices** p_1 and p_2, denoted $d_N(p_1, p_2)$, is the length of the shortest path connecting p_1 and p_2 along the model network.*

It is obvious that for any two given vertices p_1 and p_2 on a land surface,

$$d_E(p_1, p_2) \leq d_S(p_1, p_2) \leq d_N(p_1, p_2), \quad (1)$$

where the second inequality is because the shortest network path is also a path along the surface. Therefore, the *Euclidean distance* and the *network distance* are the lower bound and the upper bound of the *surface distance*, respectively.

Now, we are ready to formally define SRNN queries:

DEFINITION 2 (MSRNN). *Given a data point set O and a query point q on a land surface, a **monochromatic surface reverse nearest neighbor** (MSRNN) query finds all the data points $o \in O$ such that $\forall o' \in O - \{o\}, d_S(o, q) \leq d_S(o, o')$.*

DEFINITION 3 (BSRNN). *Given a site point set S, a data point set O and a query point $q \in S$ on a land surface, a* ***bichromatic surface reverse nearest neighbor*** *(BSRNN) query finds all the data points $o \in O$ such that $\forall s \in S - \{q\}, d_S(o,q) \leq d_S(o,s)$.*

3. TIGHT CELL & LOOSE CELL

Voronoi diagram [24] is a powerful tool for processing NN queries. Given a set O of data objects, a Voronoi diagram divides the space into disjoint cells, where each cell belongs to one object. If a query point q falls into the Voronoi cell of object $o \in O$, then o is guaranteed to be the NN of q among all objects in O.

Many algorithms have been proposed for computing Voronoi diagrams in 2D Euclidean space, among which the most commonly used one is Fortune's plain-sweep algorithm [24], whose time complexity is $O(n \log n)$ with $n = |O|$.

However, as pointed out by [1], it is very expensive to construct the exact Voronoi diagram on a land surface. Therefore, [1] proposes two approximation structures of Voronoi cells that can be computed without the necessity of shortest surface path evaluation:

DEFINITION 4 (TIGHT CELL). *Given a data point set O on a land surface S, the tight cell of a data object $o \in O$, denoted as $TC(o)$, is a polygon area around o, defined by $TC(o) = \{q \in S \mid d_N(o,q) \leq d_E(o',q), \forall o' \in O - \{o\}\}$.*

DEFINITION 5 (LOOSE CELL). *Given a data point set O on a land surface S, the loose cell of a data object $o \in O$, denoted as $LC(o)$, is a polygon area around o, defined by $LC(o) = \{q \in S \mid d_E(o,q) \leq d_N(o',q), \forall o' \in O - \{o\}\}$.*

Note that we can always assume an object $o \in O$ to be on a vertex, since otherwise, we can split the face that the object is on as three faces by connecting the three face vertices to o.

We can rewrite the definitions of tight and loose cells in the following equivalent forms:

$$\begin{aligned} TC(o_i) &= \{q \in S \mid d_N(o_i,q) \leq d_E(o_k,q), \\ &\quad o_k = \arg\min_{o_j \in O - \{o_i\}} d_E(o_j,q)\} \quad (2) \\ LC(o_i) &= \{q \in S \mid d_E(o_i,q) \leq d_N(o_k,q), \\ &\quad o_k = \arg\min_{o_j \in O - \{o_i\}} d_N(o_j,q)\}. \quad (3) \end{aligned}$$

Figure 2 shows the tight and loose cells of 6 objects (o_1 to o_6) on a surface, where the blue cells are the tight cells of the objects in them, and the green (purple) cell is the loose cell of o_1 (o_6).

Next, we review the cell-point properties proposed in [1], which are necessary in both the SkNN and our SRNN query processing.

Summary of cell-point properties. Let us use $NN_S(q \mid O)$ to denote the surface nearest neighbor of q among the data objects in O. Note that if $q \in O$, then $q = NN_S(q \mid O)$. Theorem 1 summarizes the cell-point properties that correspond to Properties 1 to 4 in [1], the proof of which can be found therein.

THEOREM 1. *Given a set of objects $O = \{o_1, o_2, \ldots, o_n\}$ on a land surface, the following statements hold:*

1. *If a query point $q \notin O$ is within $TC(o_i)$, then $o_i = NN_S(q \mid O)$.*
2. *If a query point $q \notin O$ is outside $LC(o_i)$, then o_i is guaranteed not to be $NN_S(q \mid O)$.*
3. *All the edges of the tight cells are also the edges of the loose cells.*
4. *If $o_i = NN_S(q \mid O)$, then the shortest surface path from q to o_i is within $LC(o_i)$.*

4. CELL INDEXING

In this section, we first point out a problem with the existing cell index for SkNN query processing [1], which explains why we do not follow that framework for indexing. Instead, we propose to index the loose cells of all data objects by an R-tree, which is used to answer surface NN and SRNN queries. Finally, we present an algorithm of surface NN query processing using the index.

Problem with the existing SkNN algorithm. Based on Statement 3 in Theorem 1, [1] defines the neighbors of an object $o \in O$ as $NL(o) = \{o' \in O - \{o\} \mid TC(o')$ and $LC(o)$ have common edges$\}$. For example, in Figure 2, $NL(o_1) = \{o_2, o_3, o_4, o_5\}$.

For each data object $o \in O$, its neighbor list $NL(o)$ is stored with o in the cell index of [1], and used to find the k NNs incrementally on the surface. However, the underlying property of that incremental algorithm (Property 6 in [1]) is based on the following statement:

If o_i and o_j are not neighbors, then $LC(o_i) \cap LC(o_j) = \emptyset$, and thus a point m on the shortest surface path between o_j and a point q within $LC(o_i)$ should exist outside both $LC(o_i)$ and $LC(o_j)$.

Nevertheless, this claim is not proved in [1], and in fact, it is not correct. One counterexample is given by Figure 2: although $o_6 \notin NL(o_1)$, we have $LC(o_6) \cap LC(o_1) \neq \emptyset$; moreover, the shortest surface path between o_6 and o_1 is totally within $LC(o_6) \cup LC(o_1)$.

Therefore, the incremental method is not guaranteed to be correct even when k goes from 1 to 2. This result is not surprising since Voronoi cells are dedicated to 1-NN queries.

In order to study how frequently the claim is breached in general, we randomly generate an object set O on a fraction of the Eagle Peak land surface dataset [25], and check how many objects $o_i \in O$ has its loose cell $LC(o_i)$ overlapping with that of a non-neighbor object $o_j \notin NL(o_i)$, by using the following approach.

We bulk-load an R-tree T_{LC} from the loose cells $\{LC(o) \mid o \in O\}$ using the Sort-Tile-Recursive (STR) algorithm [10]. For each object $o_i \in O$, we find the set of objects $C = \{o_j \in O - \{o_i\} \mid LC(o_j) \cap LC(o_i) \neq \emptyset\}$ by an intersection query on T_{LC} with query window $LC(o_i)$. Then, for each $o_j \in C$, we check whether $LC(o_i) \cap TC(o_j) \neq \emptyset$. If $o_j \in NL(o_i)$, we know that $LC(o_i)$ and $TC(o_j)$ have common edges and thus $LC(o_i) \cap TC(o_j) \neq \emptyset$. Otherwise, we find a breach of the claim.

The experimental results are surprising: we find that 70% to 80% of the objects in O breach of the claim (which is very high), and the larger the object set size $|O|$, the smaller the breach frequency.

Cell index. While the tight/loose cells of the data objects provide great pruning power in surface NN and SRNN query processing, cell construction is time-consuming. As a result, they are usually pre-computed offline, and organized by a spatial index.

We have shown that the neighbor information maintained by the cell index of [1] is no longer useful for correctly answering SkNN queries. Fortunately, only 1-NN queries are necessary in SRNN query processing, and therefore, we do not adopt the index structure of [1], but rather use the R-tree T_{LC} over all the object loose cells as the cell index, which has already been used in breach checking.

The R-tree T_{LC} is sufficient for answering surface NN and SRNN queries. We now present our algorithm for surface NN queries, namely Algorithm 1, which makes use of T_{LC}.

Algorithm for finding $\mathbf{NN_S(q \mid O)}$. According to Statements 2 and 4 in Theorem 1, we can use Algorithm 1 to find $NN_S(q \mid O)$ for a query point $q \notin O$. Specifically, we first issue a point intersection query on the R-tree T_{LC} to find the objects whose loose cells contain q (Line 1). If there is only one such object o (Line 2), this implies that $\forall o' \in O - \{o\}$, $LC(o')$ does not contain q, and according to Statement 2 in Theorem 1, only o has chance to be $NN_S(q \mid O)$, which is returned in Line 4. In fact, we have

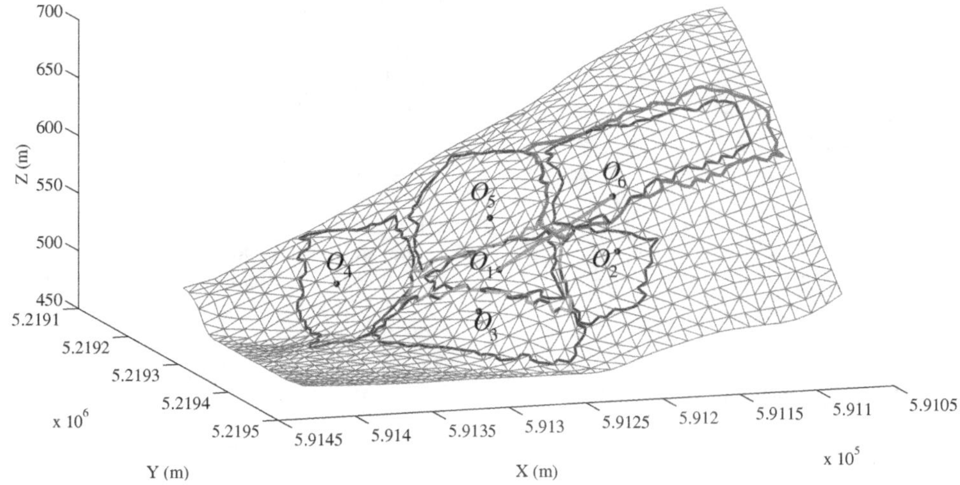

Figure 2: Tight Cells & Loose Cells

Algorithm 1 *QO-NN*(q, O, T_{LC})

Input: query point $q \notin O$; object set O; R-tree T_{LC} bulk-loaded from $\{LC(o) \mid o \in O\}$
Output: $NN_S(q \mid O)$

1: Find the object set $C = \{o \in O \mid q$ is within $LC(o)\}$ by a point intersection query on T_{LC} with query point q
2: **if** $|C|$=1 **then**
3: $\{C = \{o\}\}$
4: **return** o
5: $min \leftarrow \infty$, $o_{min} \leftarrow NULL$
6: **for each** $o \in C$ **do**
7: Invoke *Chen and Han's algorithm* to compute $d_S(o, q)$ on $LC(o)$
8: **if** $d_S(o, q) < min$ **then**
9: $min \leftarrow d_S(o, q)$
10: $o_{min} \leftarrow o$
11: **return** o_{min}

$q \in TC(o)$ in this case. Otherwise, we check all the candidates $o \in C$ and return the one with the smallest shortest surface path length (Lines 5 to 11). Note that we compute $d_S(o, q)$ on $LC(o)$ rather than on the whole surface, and therefore the shortest surface path between q and o found on $LC(o)$ may not be the global shortest surface path. However, according to Statement 4 in Theorem 1, we are able to find the shortest surface path to $NN_S(q \mid O)$, which guarantees the correctness of Algorithm 1.

5. OBJECT NN QUERIES

In this section, we study object NN queries: Given an object $o \in O$, find its nearest neighbor in O on the surface, i.e. $NN_S(o \mid O - \{o\})$. As we shall see, an object NN query is a fundamental operation in our MSRNN algorithm in Section 7.

Cell-cell properties. Before describing our algorithm for processing object NN queries, we first present two underlying *cell-cell properties* which guarantee the correction of our algorithm.

Theorem 2 prunes all the objects whose loose cells do not intersect with $LC(o)$, from being $NN_S(o \mid O - \{o\})$.

THEOREM 2. *Any object* $o' \in O$ *that satisfies* $LC(o) \cap LC(o') = \emptyset$ *cannot be* $NN_S(o \mid O - \{o\})$.

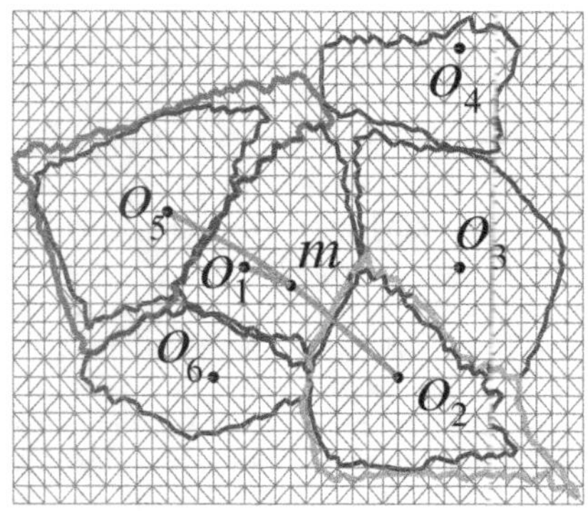

Figure 3: Illustration of the Proof of Theorem 2

PROOF. Let us illustrate the idea by Figure 3, where o_2 corresponds to o in Theorem 2, and o_5 corresponds to o'. In Figure 3, the green (purple) cell is $LC(o_2)$ ($LC(o_5)$).

Since $LC(o) \cap LC(o') = \emptyset$, a point m on the shortest path between o and o' (the orange path in Figure 3) should exist outside both $LC(o)$ and $LC(o')$.

Since m is outside of $LC(o')$, according to Definition 5, we know that $\exists o'' \in O - \{o'\}$, $d_E(o', m) > d_N(o'', m)$. We now prove that $\exists o'' \in O - \{o', o\}$, $d_E(o', m) > d_N(o'', m)$.

We prove by contradiction. If o is the only object in $O - \{o'\}$ that satisfies $d_E(o', m) > d_N(o, m)$, then $\forall o'' \in O - \{o', o\}$, $d_E(o', m) \leq d_N(o'', m)$. Since $d_E(o', m) > d_N(o, m) \geq d_E(o, m)$, we have $d_N(o', m) \geq d_E(o', m) > d_E(o, m)$ and $\forall o'' \in O - \{o', o\}$, $d_E(o, m) < d_E(o', m) \leq d_N(o'', m)$. Therefore, we obtain $\forall o'' \in O - \{o\}, d_E(o, m) < d_N(o'', m)$. According to Definition 5, this implies that m is inside $LC(o)$, which contradicts our assumption of m.

Now that we know $\exists o'' \in O - \{o', o\}$, $d_E(o', m) > d_N(o'', m)$ (in Figure 3, o_1 corresponds to o''), we have $d_S(o', m) \geq d_E(o', m) > d_N(o'', m) \geq d_S(o'', m)$. Thus, $d_S(o', o) = d_S(o', m) + d_S(m, o) > d_S(o'', m) + d_S(m, o) \geq d_S(o'', o)$, which implies that o'' is closer to o than o', i.e. $o' \neq NN_S(o \mid O - \{o\})$. □

Theorem 2 provides the candidates of $NN_S(o \mid O - \{o\})$ for further refinement. To find the exact $NN_S(o \mid O - \{o\})$ among the candidates, we have to invoke *Chen and Han's algorithm* to compute the lengths of shortest surface paths from o to these candidates.

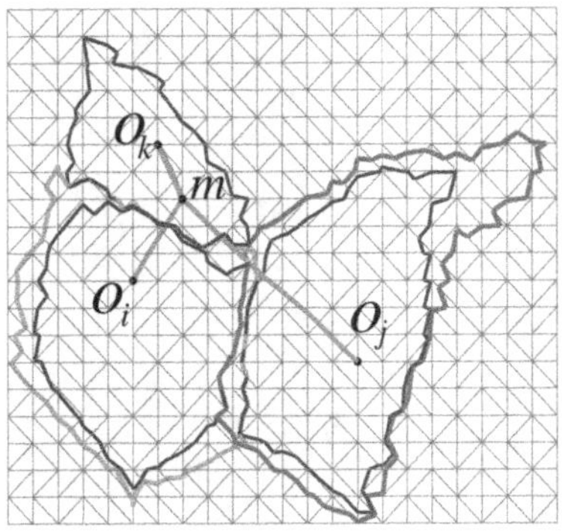

Figure 4: Illustration of the Proof of Theorem 3

Algorithm 2 *OO-NN*(o, O, T_{LC})

Input: query point $o \in O$; object set O; R-tree T_{LC} bulk-loaded from $\{LC(o) \mid o \in O\}$
Output: $d_S(o, NN_S(o \mid O - \{o\}))$

```
Find the set C = {o' ∈ O − {o} | LC(o') ∩ LC(o) ≠ ∅} by
  an intersection query on T_LC with query window LC(o)
min ← ∞
for each o' ∈ C do
    Invoke Chen and Han's algorithm to compute d_S(o, o') on
      LC(o') ∪ LC(o)
    if d_S(o, o') < min then
        min ← d_S(o, o')
return min
```

Since the time cost of *Chen and Han's algorithm* is quadratic to the number of triangular faces, we would like to evaluate the shortest surface paths on a small fraction of the surface, which is made possible by the following theorem:

THEOREM 3. *If* $o_j = NN_S(o_i \mid O - \{o_i\})$, *then the shortest surface path from* o_j *to* o_i *is within* $LC(o_j) \cup LC(o_i)$.

PROOF. Let us prove by contradiction. Note that $LC(o_j)$ must intersect with $LC(o_i)$ according to Theorem 2. Suppose that a point m on the shortest path between o_j and o_i exists that is outside both $LC(o_j)$ and $LC(o_i)$ (see Figure 4).

Since m is outside of $LC(o_j)$, according to Definition 5, we have $\exists o_k \in O - \{o_j\}$, $d_E(o_j, m) > d_N(o_k, m)$. We now prove that $\exists o_k \in O - \{o_i, o_j\}$, $d_E(o_j, m) > d_N(o_k, m)$.

We prove by contradiction. If o_i is the only object in $O - \{o_j\}$ that satisfies $d_E(o_j, m) > d_N(o_i, m)$, then $\forall o_k \in O - \{o_i, o_j\}$, $d_E(o_j, m) \leq d_N(o_k, m)$. Since $d_E(o_j, m) > d_N(o_i, m) \geq d_E(o_i, m)$, we have $d_N(o_j, m) \geq d_E(o_j, m) > d_E(o_i, m)$ and $\forall o_k \in O - \{o_j, o_i\}$, $d_E(o_i, m) < d_E(o_j, m) \leq d_N(o_k, m)$. Therefore, we have $\forall o_k \in O - \{o_i\}, d_E(o_i, m) < d_N(o_k, m)$. According to Definition 5, this implies that m is inside $LC(o_i)$, which contradicts our assumption of m.

Now that we know $\exists o_k \in O - \{o_i, o_j\}$, $d_E(o_j, m) > d_N(o_k, m)$ (see Figure 4), we have $d_S(o_j, m) \geq d_E(o_j, m) > d_N(o_k, m) \geq d_S(o_k, m)$. Thus, $d_S(o_j, o_i) = d_S(o_j, m) + d_S(m, o_i) > d_S(o_k, m) + d_S(m, o_i) \geq d_S(o_k, o_i)$, which implies that o_k is closer to o_i than o_j, contradicting the assumption $o_j = NN_S(o_i \mid O - \{o_i\})$ in the theorem. □

Algorithm for finding $\mathbf{NN_S(o \mid O - \{o\})}$. Our MSRNN query processing only requires to compute the surface distance between an object $o \in O$ and its surface nearest neighbor in O, i.e. $NN_S(o \mid O - \{o\})$. According to Theorems 2 and 3, we can use Algorithm 2 to compute this distance. Note that Algorithm 2 can be easily extended to find $NN_S(o \mid O - \{o\})$ by tracking the object with minimum current distance.

Since the computation of $d_S(o, NN_S(o \mid O - \{o\}))$ for objects $o \in O$ is a basic operation in our MSRNN query processing, one method is to pre-compute the value for each object $o \in O$. However, unlike Algorithm 1 which may not require any shortest surface path computation, Algorithm 2 requires to perform this expensive computation for $|C|$ times. Thus, the pre-computation phase takes a long time and is only worthwhile for those applications where the object set O is static and they are frequently queried. In our implementation, $d_S(o, NN_S(o \mid O - \{o\}))$ is computed online.

Intersection judgement. Algorithm 1 requires a point intersection query on R-tree T_{LC}, and if the query point q is found to be within the minimum bounding box (MBR) of a leaf node entry corresponding to $LC(o)$, a refinement step is required to check whether q is within the polygon $LC(o)$. Note that all the intersection judgements can be done simply on the xy-plane, without considering the z-coordinate values. We regard q as being within a polygon P even if q is on the boundary of P.

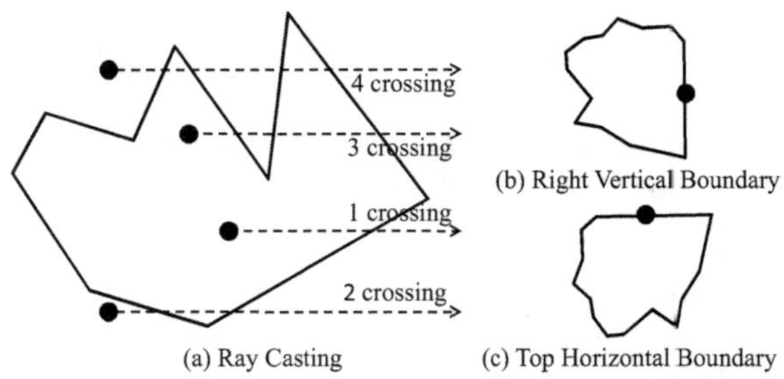

Figure 5: Illustration of the Ray Casting Algorithm

To determine whether a point q is within a polygon P, we use the *ray casting algorithm.* The method counts the number of times the horizontal ray extending to the right of q crosses a polygon boundary edge. If this number is even, the point is outside; otherwise, the point is inside. Figure 5(a) illustrates the idea of the *ray casting algorithm.* However, due to the *edge crossing rules* of the algorithm, a point on a right or top edge is considered outside, and therefore we check these special cases (e.g. the cases shown in Figures 5(b) and (c)) to ensure the correctness of intersection judgement.

Algorithm 2 requires an intersection query on R-tree T_{LC} with a polygon window win, and if the MBR of win is found to intersect with the MBR of a leaf node entry corresponding to $LC(o)$, a refinement step is needed to check whether polygon $LC(c)$ intersects with win.

The general problem of determining whether two polygons P_1 and P_2 intersect cannot be answered by simply checking whether there exists a vertex of P_1 that is within P_2 (see Figure 6(a)), and requires more advanced techniques such as the *Bentley-Ottmann algorithm* [24].

However, both win and $LC(o)$ in our problem are loose cells, whose boundary must have a vertex on an edge of the *model network* whenever it crosses the edge (see Section 6). Therefore, we have the following theorem:

THEOREM 4. *Two loose cells* LC_1 *and* LC_2 *intersect with each other, if and only if, there exists a vertex of* LC_1 *that is within* LC_2.

PROOF. Suppose that part of the edge de of LC_1 is inside LC_2 but both d and e are outside of LC_2, then de crosses at least two

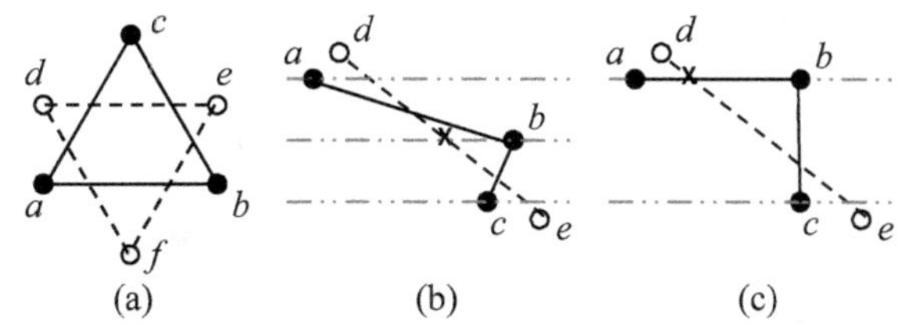

Figure 6: Polygon Intersection

edges of LC_2, such as edges ab and bc in Figures 6(b) and (c). Let us call a horizontal or vertical line of model network edges as a model line. Note that there are two possible cases: (1) If b is not collinear with a and c on a model line, then there exist at least 3 model lines between a and c (see Figure 6(b)) and de must cross the model line in between. (2) If b is collinear with a (or c) on a model line as shown in Figure 6(c), then de must cross the model line of ab (or bc). Thus, in either case, there is another vertex on de, contradicting the fact that de is an edge of LC_1. □

Note that we can use the *ray casting algorithm* described before to determine whether a vertex of LC_1 is within LC_2.

6. CELL CONSTRUCTION

In this section, we present our approach for cell construction, which is important due to the following reasons. (1) In order to accelerate SRNN query processing, we need to pre-compute $TC(o)$ and $LC(o)$ for all $o \in O$. Recall that we also need to bulk-load an R-tree T_{LC} from the loose cells $LC(o)$. (2) Our MSRNN algorithm requires to obtain the loose cell of the query point online.

The work of [1] proposes to compute the tight/loose cells by contracting/expanding the Voronoi cells of the object set O in 3D Euclidean space. However, it is not easy to compute the 3D Voronoi cells and then to map them onto the surface. Besides, this approach constructs the cells of all objects in O at once, and cannot support efficient cell evaluation for an individual point q, which is a fundamental operation in our MSRNN algorithm.

Therefore, we propose to construct the cells of a point online, by a breadth-first traversal of the faces starting from that point. We first describe the data structures relevant cell construction.

Vertex inverted index. We build an inverted index I_{faces} where each entry corresponds to a vertex v of the TIN model. Each entry of I_{faces} has format $\langle v, L(v)\rangle$, with $L(v)$ being the list of all the faces whose vertices include v. For example, in Figure 7, the list $L(b)$ contains six faces marked by 1 to 6.

One usage of I_{faces} is to get the seeding faces for our breadth-first cell construction algorithm, and the other usage is to obtain the gluing relationships of faces, which are required as part of the input to *Chen and Han's algorithm*. Referring to Figure 7 again, suppose that we want to obtain the face next to Face 6 by the edge ab. This can be done by first computing $L(a) \cap L(b) = \{5, 6\}$ and then picking the face that is not itself (i.e. Face 5). For a face on the

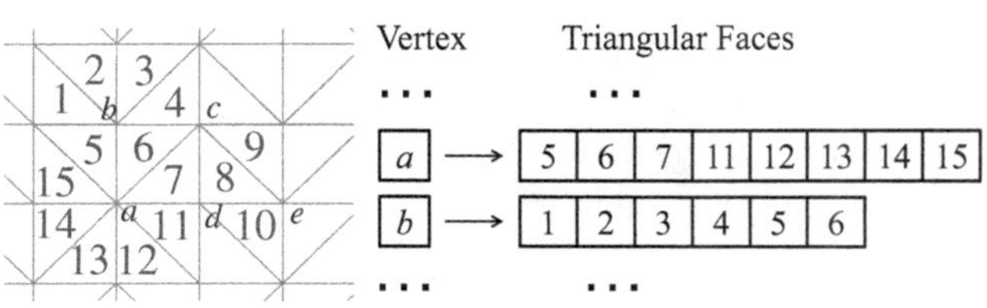

Figure 7: Vertex Inverted Index for Faces

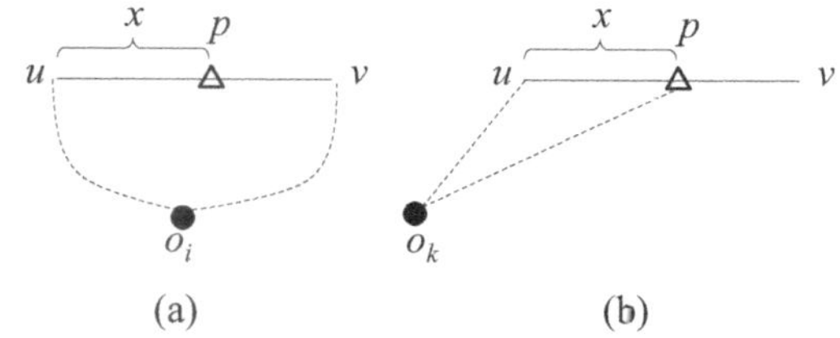

Figure 8: Exact Cell Vertex Computation

boundary of the land surface, its neighboring face along a boundary edge does not exist, and we denote it by $NULL$.

The above approach requires two I_{faces} look-ups (i.e. two I/O operations) to get one neighboring face of a given face. An alternative method is to pre-compute the three neighboring faces of each face in the TIN model, so that only one I/O operation is required to obtain all the three neighboring faces for a given face. We do not adopt this alternative to avoid the additional space overhead.

Tight cell vertex computation. Let us consider how to find the vertices of $TC(o_i)$. Given a vertex v of the model network, let o_k be the NN of v among $O - \{o_i\}$ in the Euclidean space, i.e. $o_k = \arg\min_{o_j \in O - \{o_i\}} d_E(o_j, v)$. We bulk-load an R-tree T_O from the object points in O beforehand, so that o_k can be found by a best-first NN search [12] using query point v, where object o_i is filtered out during the R-tree traversal.

To decide whether v is within $TC(o_i)$, according to Equation (2), we need to compute and compare $d_N(o_i, v)$ and $d_E(o_k, v)$. If $d_N(o_i, v) \leq d_E(o_k, v)$, we say that vertex v is on o_i's side, denoted as $v \dashv o_i$; otherwise, we say that $v \not\dashv o_i$.

For an edge uv of the model network, if $u \dashv o_i$ and $v \not\dashv o_i$, then $d_N(o_i, u) \leq d_E(o_k, u)$ and $d_N(o_i, v) > d_E(o_k, v)$, and therefore there must exist at least one *split point* s on uv such that $d_N(o_i, s) = d_E(o_k, s)$. The split point s is a vertex of $TC(o_i)$.

There can be more than one *split point* on an edge uv, which can be found by solving a quartic equation. Consider a point p on edge (u, v) with $|up| = x$. From Figure 8(a) we can see that $d_N(o_i, p) = \min\{d_N(o_i, u) + x, d_N(o_i, v) + (|uv| - x)\}$ is a piecewise linear function of x with at most 2 pieces. In Figure 8(b), by Cosine law, we can obtain $d_E(o_k, p)^2 = d_E(o_k, u)^2 + x^2 - 2 \cdot d_E(o_k, u) \cdot x \cdot \cos\angle o_k uv$. Thus, we can solve the equation $d_N(o_i, s)^2 = d_E(o_k, s)^2$ to compute split points s.

The work of [1] mistakenly assumes that at most one split point s exists on an edge uv. To avoid the complication of solving quartic equations, we follow their assumptions by finding a split point inside the exact $TC(o_i)$. Although cells computed in this way are not the exact ones, they do not influence the correctness of SRNN evaluation, but just slightly reduce the pruning power of the cells, due to the following intuitive principle:

Making the tight cells smaller and the loose cells larger than the exact ones does not influence the correctness of the cell properties.

We compute the split point s on an edge as follows. Consider face $\triangle def$ in Figure 9, where $e \dashv o_i$ and $f \not\dashv o_i$. We compute the split point s on ef as follows: Let us denote $x = |fs|$, we compute s by solving the equation

$$d_E(o_k, f) + x = (|ef| - x) + d_N(o_i, e) \qquad (4)$$

The solution is $x = (|ef| + d_N(o_i, e) - d_E(o_k, f))/2$, and the coordinate of s is computed as $\overrightarrow{Os} = \overrightarrow{Of} + x \cdot \overrightarrow{fe}$. We now prove that all the *split points* we compute is inside $TC(o_i)$: the R.H.S. of Equation (4) equals $d_N(o_i, s)$, and the L.H.S. is at least $d_E(o_k, s)$, which implies that $d_N(o_i, s) \leq d_E(o_k, s)$, or s is inside $TC(o_i)$.

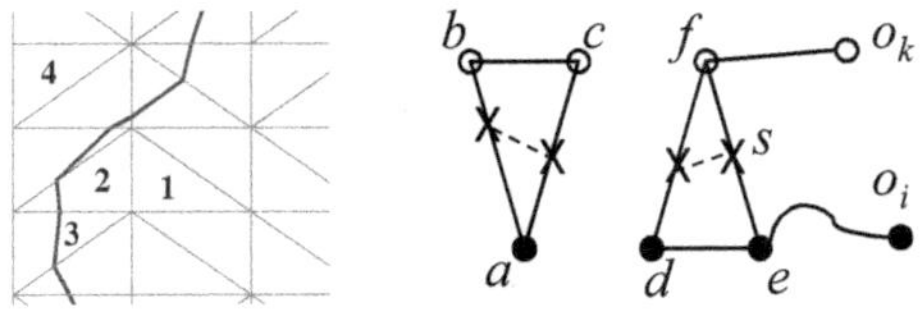

Figure 9: Relaxed Cell Vertex Computation

The work of [1] differentiates 4 possible cases for a face: (1) all three vertices are on o_i's side (e.g. Face 1 in Figure 9), in which case the face is totally contained in $TC(o_i)$; (2) all three vertices are not on o_i's side (e.g. Face 4 in Figure 9), in which case the face is totally outside of $TC(o_i)$; (3) only one vertex is on o_i's side (e.g. Face 3 in Figure 9), in which case two split points can be computed as illustrated by face $\triangle abc$ in Figure 9; (4) two vertices are on o_i's side (e.g. Face 2 in Figure 9), in which case two split points can be computed as illustrated by face $\triangle def$ in Figure 9. In the last two cases, a cell edge of $TC(o_i)$ is defined by the two split points. We also adopt this approach in our implementation.

Loose cell vertex computation. The vertices computation for $LC(o_i)$ is similar but more tricky. Given a vertex v of the model network, let $o_k = \arg\min_{o_j \in O-\{o_i\}} d_N(o_j, v)$. According to Equation (3), to decide whether v is within $LC(o_i)$, we need to compute and compare $d_E(o_i, v)$ and $d_N(o_k, v)$.

Due to the large size of the TIN *model network* (typically with millions of vertices) and the object set O, it is not practical to find o_k by evaluating $d_N(o_j, v)$ for all $o_j \in O - \{o_i\}$. Besides, since the computation of $LC(o_i)$ works in a breath-first manner, the network distance computation for different vertices v can be shared rather than done individually, so as to utilize the locality property.

Our approach of network distance computation when evaluating $LC(o_i)$ is as follows. We maintain a pool of partial results obtained from the Dijkstra algorithm for different source vertices $o_k \in O - \{o_i\}$ during the computation of $LC(o_i)$. Whenever a network distance computation $d_N(o_k, v)$ is required, we check whether the partial result of o_k exists in the pool: (1) if the partial result exists, we check whether $d_N(o_k, v)$ is already available. If it is available, it is returned directly; otherwise, we continue to run the Dijkstra algorithm until $d_N(o_k, v)$ is computed. (2) if the partial result does not exist, we create and initialize a new partial result for o_k, run Dijkstra until $d_N(o_k, v)$ is computed, and add the partial result to the pool.

Our approach is efficient since only a small number of partial results are kept in the pool. To see this, consider the example in Figure 10, where vertex c of face $\triangle abc$ is being evaluated. Note that o_{k5} is so far from o_i that $d_E(o_{k5}, c) > d_N(o_{k3}, c)$, thus $d_N(o_{k5}, c)$ is even larger and o_{k5} can be safely pruned. In general, if $d_E(o_\ell, v)$ is found to be larger than $\min_{o_j}\{d_N(o_j, v)\}$ (named *upper bound*) for all checked objects o_j, then o_ℓ can be pruned.

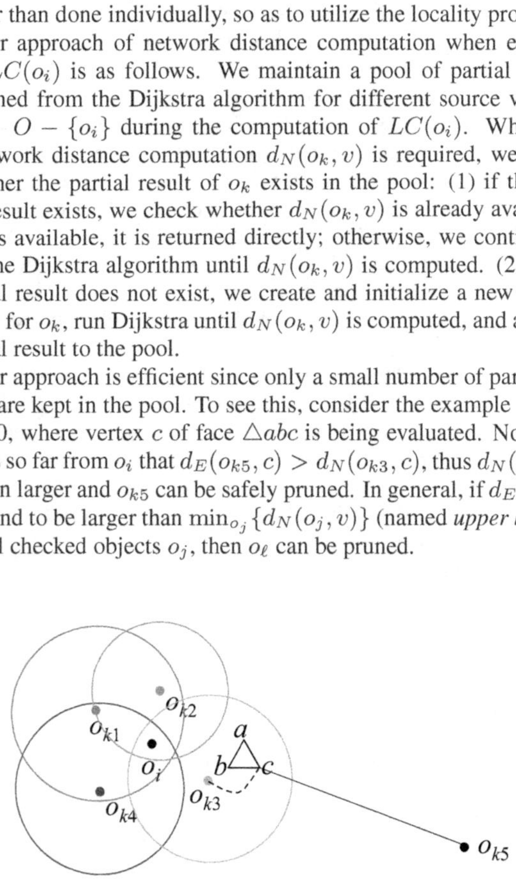

Figure 10: Pruning Candidates of o_k

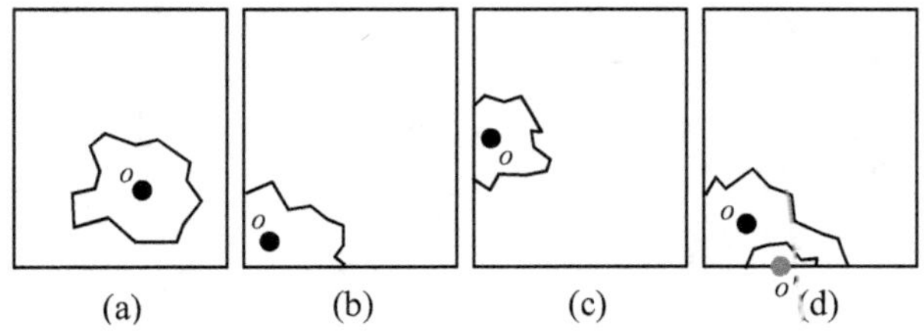

Figure 11: Boundary Cells

To get a tight *upper bound* in the very beginning, we find the nearest neighbor of v among objects in $O - \{o_i\}$ in the Euclidean space, say o_n, using the object R-tree index T_O mention before, and initialize the upper bound as $d_N(o_n, v)$.

The split point computation is similar to that of $TC(o_i)$.

Breath-first cell edge collection. To collect all the edges of $TC(o_i)$ and $LC(o_i)$, we check the faces in a breadth-first manner, starting from o_i. Specifically, we first initialize a queue Q with the faces whose vertices contain o_i, which can be obtained by looking up $L(o_i)$ from I_{faces}. Then, whenever Q is not empty, we fetch the next face in Q, check the three face vertices, and evaluate split points for $TC(o_i)$ and $LC(o_i)$ on the face. If at least one vertex is on o_i's side in terms of $LC(o_i)$, we add the non-visited neighboring faces (if exists) to Q; otherwise, we know that the face is totally outside of $LC(o_i)$ and we do not further expand faces.

Recall that during this process, we maintain a pool of partial Dijkstra results for different source vertices o_k. Since $LC(o_i)$ covers only a very small fraction of the whole surface, we can expect that objects far away from o_i will never require a network distance computation to a vertex on a traversed face. Thus, the pool is kept small (usually less than 10 source objects), and even for those source objects in the pool, the Dijkstra algorithm is run on just a small fraction of the whole surface, as illustrated by the circles in Figure 10.

Boundary cells. For most of the cells, the edges collected form a closed curve (see Figure 11(a)), and thus the polygon cell can be easily constructed. However, there are cases where the edges form one open curve (see Figures 11(b) and (c)), and additional edges or vertices from the boundary of the surface are required to form the polygon cell. To decide which side of the curve is inside, we check whether object o is in the resulted polygon. In our experiments, we also find other rare cases such as the one shown in Figure 11(d). Therefore, for all the other cases, we set $TC(o)$ to be the point o and $LC(o)$ to be the MBR of the collected split points.

7. SRNN QUERY PROCESSING

7.1 MSRNN Query Processing

Given an object set O and a query point q on a land surface, a MSRNN query returns the set of objects $\{o \in O \mid NN_S(o \mid O \cup \{q\} - \{o\}) = q\}$. Equivalently, an object o is the MSRNN of q, if and only if

$$d_S(o, NN_S(o \mid O - \{o\})) \geq d_S(o, q). \quad (5)$$

To obtain the MSRNN candidates, we compute $LC(q)$ among the set $O \cup \{q\}$ online using our breadth-first cell construction algorithm described in Section 6, with an important additional operation: whenever we obtain a split point s for the loose cell $LC(q)$ on edge uv, according to Equation (3) we have

$$d_E(q, s) = d_N(o, s),\ o = \arg\min_{o_i \in O} d_N(o_i, s), \quad (6)$$

and we collect o into the MSRNN candidate set C. The following theorem guarantees that the MSRNNs of q must be in C.

Algorithm 3 Finding the MSRNNs of Query Point q

1: $MRNN \leftarrow \emptyset$
2: Compute $LC(q)$ among $O \cup \{q\}$ and collect candidates to set C
3: **for each** $o \in C$ **do**
4:   **if** $LC(o) \cap LC(q) \neq \emptyset$ **then**
5:     $d_S(o, NN_S(o \mid O - \{o\})) \leftarrow$*OO-NN*$(o, O, T_{LC})$
6:     Invoke *Chen and Han's algorithm* to compute $d_S(o, q)$ on $LC(o) \cup LC(q)$
7:     **if** $d_S(o, NN_S(o \mid O - \{o\})) \geq d_S(o, q)$ **then**
8:       $MRNN \leftarrow MRNN \cup \{o\}$
9: **return** $MRNN$

THEOREM 5. *Any object $o \notin C$ in O cannot be q's MSRNN.*

PROOF. Note that the polygon $LC(q)$ computed in the context of $O \bigcup \{q\}$ is the same as the polygon $LC(q)$ computed in the context of $C \bigcup \{q\}$. Therefore, for any point v outside $LC(q)$, it holds that $\exists o_c \in C$, $d_E(q, v) > d_N(o_c, v)$.

For an object $o \notin C$ in O, it must be outside of $LC(q)$ according to the definition of loose cells, and therefore $\exists o_c \in C$, $d_E(q, o) > d_N(o_c, o)$. Thus $d_S(q, o) \geq d_E(q, o) > d_N(o_c, o) \geq d_S(o_c, o) \geq d_S(o, NN_S(o \mid O - \{o\}))$, and according to Equation (5), o cannot be an MSRNN. □

Algorithm 3 shows our algorithm for MSRNN queries. In Line 2, we first compute the MSRNN candidate set C by evaluating $LC(q)$ among $O \cup \{q\}$ using the breadth-first approach. We filter out those candidates o that satisfy $LC(o) \cap LC(q) = \emptyset$ in Line 4. This is because, according to Theorem 2, any point $p \in O \cup \{q\}$ that satisfies $LC(o) \cap LC(q) = \emptyset$ cannot be $NN_S(o \mid O \cup \{q\} - \{o\})$, where $LC(o)$ is computed in the context of $O \cup \{q\}$, denoted as $LC(o \mid O \cup \{q\})$. Note that the $LC(o)$ in Algorithm 3 is the pre-computed one in the context of O, i.e. $LC(o \mid O)$. According to Definition 5, it can be easily proved that $LC(o \mid O \cup \{q\}) \subseteq LC(o \mid O)$. Therefore, if Line 4 finds that $LC(o \mid O) \cap LC(q) = \emptyset$, then $LC(o \mid O \cup \{q\}) \cap LC(q) = \emptyset$ and q cannot be $NN_S(o \mid O \cup \{q\} - \{o\})$.

For each non-pruned candidate o, we compute $d_S(o, NN_S(o \mid O - \{o\}))$ in Line 5 using the object NN query described in Section 5, compute $d_S(o, q)$ in Line 6, and then determine whether o is an MSRNN of q by checking Equation (5) in Line 7. Note that in Line 6, we only need to evaluate the shortest surface path on $LC(o \mid O) \cup LC(q)$ ($\supseteq LC(o \mid O \cup \{q\}) \cup LC(q)$) according to Theorem 3.

If $d_S(o, NN_S(o \mid O - \{o\}))$ is pre-computed for all $o \in O$, Algorithm 3 only require one shortest surface path computation. Otherwise, it needs to compute several shortest surface paths.

7.2 BSRNN Query Processing

To process BSRNN queries, we pre-compute the cells for all sites $s \in S$ and bulk-load an R-tree T_{LC} from $\{LC(s) \mid s \in S\}$. During cell construction, an R-tree T_S is bulk-loaded for nearest neighbor queries when computing the cells. Besides, we also bulk-load an R-tree T_O for range queries used in the BSRNN query processing.

Algorithm 4 shows our algorithm for BSRNN queries. According to Statement 2 in Theorem 1, only those objects within $LC(q)$ have chance to be BSRNNs, and they are obtained as the candidate set C in Line 2. For each candidate o, if it is within $TC(q)$, it is guaranteed to be a BSRNN of q according to Statement 1 in Theorem 1. Otherwise, we find the nearest site to o in Line 7 and check whether it is q in Line 8 to determine whether o is a BSRNN.

The algorithm can also support BSRNN queries on a moving object set O, by maintaining T_O as a TPR*-tree [23].

Algorithm 4 Finding the BSRNNs of Query Site q

1: $BRNN \leftarrow \emptyset$
2: Perform a range query on T_O with query window $LC(q)$ to find the object set $C = \{o \in O \mid o \text{ is within } LC(q)\}$
3: **for each** $o \in C$ **do**
4:   **if** o is within $TC(q)$ **then**
5:     $BRNN \leftarrow BRNN \cup \{o\}$
6:   **else**
7:     $nn \leftarrow$*QO-NN*(o, S, T_{LC})
8:     **if** $nn = q$ **then**
9:       $BRNN \leftarrow BRNN \cup \{o\}$
10: **return** $BRNN$

8. EXPERIMENTS

In this section, we evaluate the performance of our algorithms for MSRNN and BSRNN queries on two large real-world datasets downloaded from [25]: Eagle Peak (Eagle) and Bearhead (BH), which have also been used in previous studies such as [1] and [2]. The statistical information of the datasets is given in Table 1.

Table 1: Statistics of Real Datasets

	Number of Vertices	Number of Faces
Eagle Peak	1,381,481	2,762,693
Bearhead	1,318,844	2,637,538

We use the most recent implementation of *Chen and Han's algorithm* [9] for surface shortest path computation. All our programs are written in JAVA, and the executable program of [9] is called on the localized surface regions for surface shortest path computation.

The pre-computation of the index structures, such as the vertex inverted index I_{faces} and the loose cell R-tree T_{LC}, are carried out on a public Linux server with eight 3GHz Intel Xeon X5450 CPU and 32GB memory. All the experiments on queries are done on a computer with 3GHz Intel Core2 Duo E8400 CPU and 2GB memory, where the huge *model network* and all the index structures are disk-based.

Let $G = (V, E)$ be the model network, we define object (site) density as $|O|/|V|$ ($|S|/|V|$). We test our algorithms with different object densities. For each density configuration, we randomly generate 100 query points and run our algorithms with each query point. All the reported measures are averaged on the 100 runs.

8.1 Results of Index Construction

The operation of breadth-first cell construction for all objects $o \in O$ dominates the time cost of the index construction phase. Figure 12(a) shows the number of source objects whose partial Dijkstra results is in the pool when computing $TC(o)$ and $LC(o)$ averaged over all the objects in O, with varying object density. We can see from Figure 12(a) that, as object density increases, the pool size also increases. The pool size is usually around 7 to 8, which verifies the effectiveness of our Euclidean distance based pruning of network distance computation.

Figure 12(b) shows the time of constructing cells for all the objects $o \in O$, with varying object density. We can see from the figure that the cell construction time increases almost linearly with the increment of object density. This is because, given a specific surface data, object number is proportional to object density.

8.2 Results of NN Queries

In this set of experiments, we evaluate the performance of our algorithm for surface NN queries (Algorithm 1). Recall that no

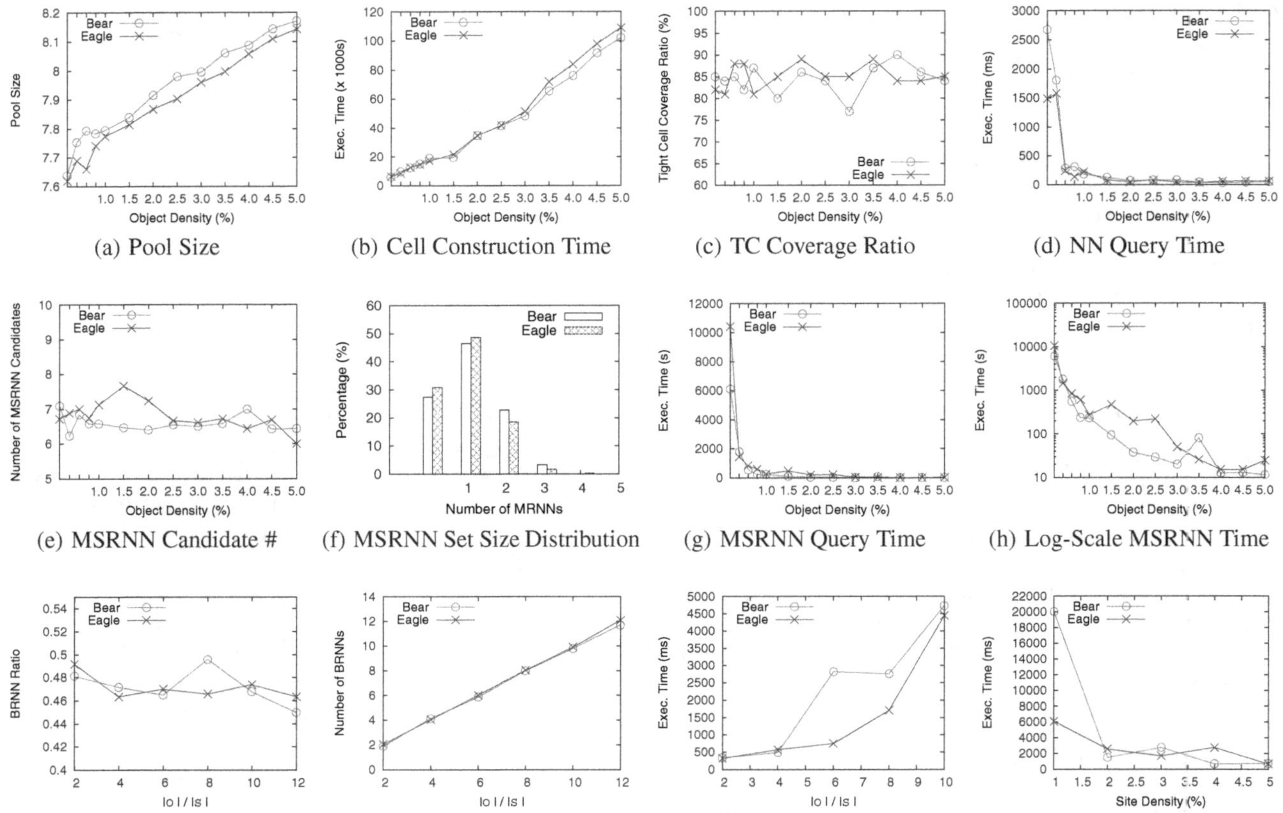

(a) Pool Size (b) Cell Construction Time (c) TC Coverage Ratio (d) NN Query Time

(e) MSRNN Candidate # (f) MSRNN Set Size Distribution (g) MSRNN Query Time (h) Log-Scale MSRNN Time

(i) LC BSRNN Ratio (j) Number of BSRNNs (k) BSRNN Time ($\rho = 3\%$) (l) BSRNN Time ($|O|/|S| = 8$)

Figure 12: Experimental Results

shortest surface path computation is necessary if query point q falls within the tight cell of some object. For each object density, we count the number of such queries, denoted N, among the 100 NN queries tested. The ratio $N/100$ is called the *Tight Cell Coverage Ratio* (TCCR). Figure 12(c) shows the TCCR with varying object density, where around 80% to 90% NN queries do not need to invoke *Chen and Han's algorithm*. Figure 12(d) shows the average NN query processing time with varying object density. The query processing time is long (1 to 3 seconds) for sparse object distribution, due to the large areas of loose cells which act as input to *Chen and Han's algorithm*.

8.3 Results of MSRNN Queries

In this set of experiments, we evaluate the performance of our algorithm for MSRNN queries (Algorithm 3). Recall that Algorithm 3 performs MSRNN candidate filtering in the beginning in Line 2. Figure 12(e) shows the average number of candidates with varying object density, where we can see that there are usually 6 to 7 candidates and the trend is not sensitive to object density. We also find that the MSRNN count distribution is not sensitive to object density. Figure 12(f) shows the MSRNN count distribution over all the MSRNN queries we tested, where almost half of the query points have exactly one MSRNN, very few of the query points have four MSRNNs, and no query point has over four MSRNNs.

Figure 12(g) shows the average MSRNN query processing time with varying object density. The query processing time is quite long for sparse object distribution, due to the large areas of loose cells which act as input to *Chen and Han's algorithm*.

To further clarify the trend of query time, we plot the curves in log-scale in Figure 12(h), where we can see that the performance of our algorithm is good for reasonably large object densities ($\geq$3%).

8.4 Results of BSRNN Queries

In this set of experiments, we evaluate the performance of our algorithm for BSRNN queries (Algorithm 4). For each site density, we generate object sets of different sizes, and for each object set, we perform 100 BSRNN queries.

The objects that fall in $TC(q)$ are guaranteed to be q's BSRNNs. Let the percentage of BSRNNs among the objects in $LC(q) - TC(q)$ be termed the *BSRNN ratio*. Figure 12(i) shows the *BSRNN ratio* when $|O|/|S|$ varies. The results are averaged over experiments with different site densities, since *BSRNN ratio* is insensitive to site density. We can see that around 45% to 50% of the objects that fall in region $LC(q) - TC(q)$ are q's BSRNNs.

The average number of BRNNs of a query point is also found to be insensitive to site density. On the other hand, it is sensitive to $|O|/|S|$, as Figure 12(j) shows. This is within the expectation, since each site $s \in S$ has to serve $|O|/|S|$ objects on average.

Figure 12(k) shows the average BSRNN query processing time on the site set S with site density 3%, when $|O|/|S|$ varies. The query processing time increases when $|O|/|S|$ increases. This is because, as $|O|/|S|$ becomes larger, more objects tend to fall in the region $LC(q) - TC(q)$, and therefore more NN queries are required to check whether each candidate object is q's BSRNN.

Figure 12(l) shows the average BSRNN query processing time for different site densities, when $|O|/|S| = 8$. The query time increases as site density decreases. This is because smaller site densities implies larger areas of loose cells, which not only implies larger input region to *Chen and Han's algorithm*, but also higher chance that an object falls in region $LC(q) - TC(q)$.

9. RELATED WORK

The concept of RNN is first introduced in [13]. Since then, many algorithms have been proposed for finding RNNs in the Euclidean space. Algorithms for MRNN query processing include SAA [14], TPL [15], Finch [20], Influence Zone [21]. Algorithms for BRNN query processing include [18] and [19]. [22] studies RNN queries in road networks.

Studies on finding shortest surface paths date back to the 80s to 90s, when a series of exact and approximation algorithms are proposed. The most efficient exact algorithms include the one proposed in [7] with $O(n^2 \log n)$ time complexity, and *Chen and Han's algorithm* [8] with $O(n^2)$ time complexity, where n corresponds to the number of triangles in the TIN model. *Chen and Han's algorithm* is later implemented in [9].

Recently, [5] proposes an approximate algorithm with $O(\log n + \sqrt{n})$ time complexity, by treating the surface paths on the *non-rough* areas as straight lines, and [6] studies the problem of finding shortest paths with slope constraint and develops the *surface simplification* technique to reduce the model complexity, so as to reduce the time complexity of finding shortest paths.

As for the research on surface k-NN queries, [2] and [3] first propose a filter and refinement strategy to answer SkNN queries on multi-resolution terrain models. However, this approach can neither guarantee accuracy nor provide the shortest surface paths to the nearest neighbors. An exact solution to the SkNN problem is proposed in [1], where approximations of *Voronoi cells* are constructed to prune unnecessary shortest surface path computation and to localize the shortest path computation. In this paper, we also make use of these *Voronoi Cell* approximation structures for the same purposes. Although the concept of *Voronoi diagram* is only related to 1-NN, [1] claims that its approximation structures can be used in an incremental manner to answer k-NN queries for arbitrary k. Unfortunately, as we have discussed in Section 4, the correctness of the algorithm relies on an unproved statement, which is, however, flawed. [4] studies the problem of continuously monitoring the k nearest neighbors of a fixed query point when the objects on the surface are moving.

10. CONCLUSION

In this paper, we investigate how to process RNN queries on land surfaces. Specifically, we study *monochromatic SRNN* queries and *bichromatic SRNN* queries. Our SRNN algorithms are based on several newly-discovered properties of the Voronoi cell approximation structures, and are able to localize the query evaluation by accessing just a small fraction of the surface data near the query point. The majority of the objects that cannot be the SRNNs of the query point are pruned by our cell properties. Furthermore, we propose a new online cell construction algorithm which is essential to our MSRNN algorithm, and is efficient due to our smart approach for computing network distances. Extensive experiments on large real-world datasets demonstrate the efficiency of our algorithms.

11. ACKNOWLEDGEMENTS

This work is partially supported by RGC GRF under grant number HKUST 618509.

12. REFERENCES

[1] C. Shahabi, L.-A. Tang and S. Xing. "Indexing Land Surface for Efficient kNN Query". In *VLDB*, 2008.

[2] K. Deng, X. Zhou, H. T. Shen, K. Xu and X. Lin. "Surface k-NN Query Processing". In *ICDE*, 2006

[3] K. Deng, X. Zhou, H. T. Shen, Q. Liu, K. Xu and X. Lin. "A Multi-Resolution Surface Distance Model for k-NN Query Processing". In *VLDB Journal*, 17(5):1101–1119, 2008.

[4] S. Xing, C. Shahabi and B. Pan. "Continuous Monitoring of Nearest Neighbors on Land Surface". In *VLDB*, 2009.

[5] S. Xing and C. Shahabi. "Scalable Shortest Paths Browsing on Land Surface". In *ACM GIS*, 2010.

[6] L. Liu and R. C.-W. Wong. "Finding Shortest Path on Land Surface". In *ACM SIGMOD*, 2010.

[7] J. S. B. Mitchell, D. M. Mount and C. H. Papadimitriou. "The Discrete Geodesic Problem". In *SIAM J. Comput.*, 16(4):647–668, 1987.

[8] J. Chen and Y. Han. "Shortest Paths on a Polyhedron". In *SoCG*, 1990.

[9] B. Kaneva and J. O'Rourke. "An Implementattion of Chen & Han's Shortest Paths Algorithm". In *CCCG*, 2000.

[10] S. T. Leutenegger, J. M. Edgington and M. A. Lopez. "STR: A Simple and Efficient Algorithm for R-tree Packing". In *Technical Report, Institute for Computer Applications in Science and Engineering*, 1997.

[11] N. Roussopoulos, S. Kelly and F. Vincent. "Nearest Neighbor Queries". In *SIGMOD*, 1995.

[12] G. R. Hjaltason and H. Samet. "Distance Browsing in Spatial Databases". In *ACM TODS*, 24(2), June 1999, pp. 265–318.

[13] F. Korn and S. Muthukrishnan. "Influence Sets Based on Reverse Nearest Neighbor Queries". In *SIGMOD*, 2000.

[14] I. Stanoi, D. Agrawal and A. El Abbadi. "Reverse Nearest Neighbor Queries for Dynamic Databases". In *ACM SIGMOD Workshop on Research Issues in Data Mining and Knowledge Discovery*, 2000.

[15] Y. Tao, D. Papadias and X. Lian. "Reverse kNN Search in Arbitrary Dimensionality". In *VLDB*, 2004.

[16] M. L. Yiu, D. Papadias, N. Mamoulis and Y. Tao. "Reverse Nearest Neighbors in Large Graphs". In *TKDE*, 2006.

[17] M. A. Cheema, W. Zhang, X. Lin, Y. Zhang and X. Li. "Continuous Reverse k Nearest Neighbors Queries in Euclidean Space and in Spatial Networks". In *VLDB Journal*, 2011.

[18] I. Stanoi, M. Riedewald, D. Agrawal, and A. E. Abbadi. "Discovery of Influence Sets in Frequently Updated Databases". In *VLDB*, 2001.

[19] T. Xia, D. Zhang, E. Kanoulas and Y. Du. "On Computing Top-t Most Influential Spatial Sites". In *VLDB*, 2005.

[20] W. Wu, F. Yang, C.-Y. Chan and K.-L. Tan. "Finch: Evaluating Reverse k-Nearest-Neighbor Queries on Location Data". In *PVLDB*, 2008.

[21] M. A. Cheema, X. Lin, W. Zhang and Y. Zhang. "Influence Zone: Efficiently Processing Reverse k Nearest Neighbors Queries". In *ICDE*, 2011.

[22] D. Taniar1, M. Safar, Q. T. Tran, W. Rahayu and J. H. Park. "Spatial Network RNN Queries in GIS". *The Computer Journal*, 2010.

[23] Y. Tao, D. Papadias and J. Sun. "The TPR*-Tree: An Optimized Spatio-Temporal Access Method for Predictive Queries". In *VLDB*, 2003.

[24] M. D. Berg, O. Cheong, M. V. Kreveld and M. Overmars. "Computational Geometry: Algorithms and Applications". *Springer-Verlag New York Inc.*, 2008.

[25] `http://data.geocomm.com`

Pay-as-you-go Maintenance of Precomputed Nearest Neighbors in Large Graphs

Tom Crecelius
Max Planck Institute for Informatics
Saarbrücken, Germany
tcrecel@mpi-inf.mpg.de

Ralf Schenkel
Saarland University
Saarbrücken, Germany
schenkel@mmci.uni-saarland.de

ABSTRACT

An important building block of many graph applications such as searching in social networks, keyword search in graphs, and retrieval of linked documents is retrieving the transitive neighbors of a node in ascending order of their distances. Since large graphs cannot be kept in memory and graph traversals at query time would be prohibitively expensive, the list of neighbors for each node is usually precomputed and stored in a compact form. While the problem of precomputing all-pairs shortest distances has been well studied for decades, efficiently maintaining this information when the graph changes is not as well understood. This paper presents an algorithm for maintaining nearest neighbor lists in weighted graphs under node insertions and decreasing edge weights. It considers the important case where queries are a lot more frequent than updates, and presents two approaches for transparently performing necessary index updates while executing queries. Extensive experiments with large graphs, including a subset of Twitter's user graph, demonstrate that the overhead for this maintenance is small.

Categories and Subject Descriptors

E.1 [**Data Structures**]: Graphs and networks; G.2.2 [**Discrete Mathematics**]: Graph Theory—*Graph algorithms*

Keywords

shortest paths, incremental APSD, databases

1. INTRODUCTION

1.1 Motivation

An increasing amount of applications need to manage large graphs with millions of nodes and billions of edges. Examples include user graphs in social networks such as Facebook, Myspace, or Twitter, knowledge graphs in large knowledge bases such as DBPedia or YAGO, or keyword search in large databases. A common problem that many applications need to solve is accessing transitive neighbors of a specific node ordered by increasing distance, which is a key building block of algorithms for aggregated search in social networks [4, 24], explorative search of connections in knowledge bases [17], or retrieval in linked documents [13].

CIKM'12, October 29–November 2, 2012, Maui, HI, USA.

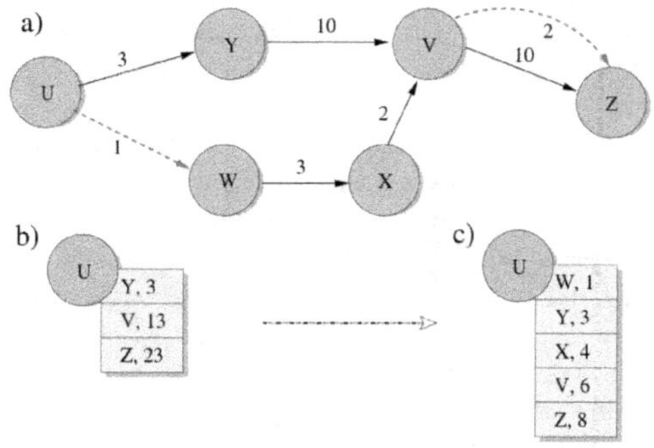

Figure 1: Example graph: A single inserted edge at U changes its entire nearest neighbor list and a decreased edge weight at V affects almost the entire graph because of changes in shortest paths for all predecessor nodes of Z.

For small graphs that fit into main memory, incrementally retrieving neighbors of a node can be efficiently implemented by running Dijkstra's algorithm [10]. However, this is not a valid option for large, disk-resident graphs as each access to a node corresponds to one disk access. For static graphs that do not change, a more efficient solution is to precompute, for each node, the distance to all other nodes (known as all-pairs shortest distance problem), and store this list of nodes in increasing order of distance. While precomputing this information can be expensive for large graphs, it is an offline, one-time operation. Accessing all neighbors of a node now requires only a few disk accesses to load this list.

This solution, however, turns prohibitively expensive when the graph changes over time. When a new edge from a node u is inserted or the weight of an existing edge starting at a node v is decreased, i.e., the distance to the edge's destination node is reduced, the precomputed nearest neighbor list of u or v, respectively, needs to be recomputed: new nodes may have appeared in that list or the distance of already connected nodes may have decreased. Figure 1a) depicts an example graph and 1b) the corresponding initial neighbor list for node u. The dashed lines indicate two graph updates: a new edge with weight 1 is inserted at node u and the weight of the edge starting at v is reduced from 10 to 2. As a consequence, nodes w and x are now connected with u through the new edge and appear as additional entries in u's neighbor list. Furthermore, the path to v and z through the new edge is now shorter than the previously existing shortest path (i.e. the distance to v and z changed from 13 and 23 to 6 and 8, respectively), and, hence, the corresponding entries in u's nearest neighbor list need to be updated as shown in Figure 1c). Moreover, the nearest neighbor lists of *all nodes preceding an updated node* v may have to be recomputed as a new edge or changed weight may affect the distances from these nodes to any node reachable through that edge. In our example the distance to node z changes indeed for all other nodes in the graph due to the decreased weight of the edge starting at v.

This problem, known as dynamic all-pairs shortest paths (APSP), has been intensively studied in the literature for only inserting / decreasing or deleting / increasing of edge weights in graphs or both (see Section 2 for an overview). However, this existing work focuses on maintaining in-memory data structures for graphs that fit into main memory, and therefore cannot be applied for large, disk-resident graphs. Additionally, the proposed algorithms attempt to update all affected precomputed information as soon as a new edge is inserted. In most applications, this proactive update is not needed, as some lists may not be queried for a long time, and additional updates in the future may happen before such a query arrives.

This paper proposes an algorithm for incrementally maintaining precomputed nearest-neighbor lists under edge addition and decreasing edge weights that defers updates of the lists as long as possible, namely to the point where a query attempts to read an entry from such a list that is not up to date. Any query that does not touch updated edges will efficiently read the precomputed list of neighbors. We provide two alternative versions of the algorithm. The first version maintains neighbor lists by merging complete neighbor lists at query time. The second version incrementally merges lists while processing a query, reading a variable number of entries from each list. Our algorithm has been developed with friendship graphs of social networks in mind where the insertion of friendship connections is much more frequent than their deletion. Moreover, we are aiming at operations on graphs that introduce "better" paths, not operations that reduce the quality of existing paths. We evaluate our proposed algorithms with two excerpts of real social networks.

1.2 Notation

We consider a sequence $G^0 \dots G^T$ of *directed weighted graphs* with a constant set V of nodes and a varying set of edges E^t and edge weights. $G^t = (V, E^t)$ does not contain any self edges. For each edge $e = (v_i, v_j) \in E^t$, there is an edge weight $w^t(e) \geq 0$. We consider the special case where two consecutive graphs G^t and G^{t+1} in the sequence differ by applying exactly one *edge update* on a single node u. We define an edge update for a node u at time $t+1$ as an operation applied on u in G^t such that either

- the weight of an edge starting at u in G^t has been decreased in G^{t+1}, i.e., $w^t(e) > w^{t+1}(e)$ for exactly one edge $e = (u, v)$ with $u, v \in V$ and $w^t(e') = w^{t+1}(e')$ for all other edges $e' \neq e$, or
- a single edge not existing in G^t has been added to u in G^{t+1}, i.e., $\exists! \ e = (u, v) : E^{t+1} = E^t \cup e \ with \ e \notin E^t$, $G^t = (V, E^t)$, $G^{t+1} = (V, E^{t+1})$ and $u, v \in V$.

Note: The restriction to a constant set of nodes has been made only to ease discussion. The retrieval of nearest neighbors for newly added nodes without edges is trivial as there are no neighbors at all. Hence, those nodes are not important when moving from G^t to G^{t+1}. However, as soon as there is a new edge for such a node, the problem description complies to the one mentioned above.

The distance along a path is defined as the aggregation of the weight of all edges on the path. The choice of edge weights depends on the application. For social networks, a number of proposals for measuring relationship strengths exist [24, 27].

We compute the weight of a path $p = (v_1, \dots, v_n)$ in G^t as

$$w^t(p) = \sum_{i=1}^{n-1} w^t(v_i, v_{i+1})$$

and define the weight of an arbitrary pair of nodes u and v in G^t as

$$w^t(u, v) = \min_{p=(u=v_1,\dots,v_n=v)} w^t(p)$$

Note that other notions of path weights can be incorporated in this model as well, for example maximization or the product of edge weights (if edge weights are between 0 and 1), which would correspond to transitive relationship strengths in social networks.

1.3 Problem Statement

For a given node u, we want to access the descendants v of u in graph G^t in ascending order of $w^t(u, v)$. We denote this operation as $query^t(u)$, where t corresponds to the the most up-to-date time with respect to the occurrence of updates. Hence, we are always interested in the most up-to-date nearest neighbors of a node, and no historical queries are possible or allowed. A query that retrieves only the first k descendants of u is denoted as $query^t(u, k)$.

For a node u, let denote $t(u)$ the time where all edge updates that occurred at a time $t' \leq t(u)$ have already been applied on u, such that u is up-to-date with respect to $G^{t(u)}$. We assume that we have already precomputed nearest neighbor lists for each node u, represented as lists $L(u)$ of u's descendants v in the graph $G^{t(u)}$ and sorted in ascending order of $w^{t(u)}(u, v)$.[1] Hence, each list for a node u is correct with respect to the node's specific time $t(u)$. We further assume that we know, for each node u, the edge updates that have been occurring for u since time $t(u)$, i.e. u's newly added or modified descendants since $t(u)$.

This paper aims at answering queries of the form $query^t(u)$ at time $t \geq t(u)$ by sequentially reading available precomputed information and, at the same time, updating this precomputed information on the fly when necessary.

Example. Assume that Figure 1a) depicts the initial graph G^0 at time 0 when neglecting the edges visualized as dashed lines. The corresponding precomputed list for node u at time $t(u) = 0$ is shown in Figure 1b). At time 1, the new edge $e_1(u, w)$ with weight 1 is added and at time 2, the weight of the edge $e_2 = (v, z)$ decreases from 10 to 2. Moreover, for each other node in G, there's also a precomputed list (not shown in the figure) for time 0 (or any later time 1 or 2). A $query^t(u)$ with $t = 2$ aims at retrieving u's descendants at time 2 and, equally, at updating u's list $L(u)$ by considering updated information about directly connected edges to u and by propagating updated information from lists $L(v)$ of descendants v while they are sequentially discovered in $L(u)$. The resulting nearest neighbor list is shown in Figure 1c).

2. RELATED WORK

The majority of work on indexing graphs has focused on compactly storing reachability information. Here, the proposed approaches include 2-hop covers [6, 25], 3-hop covers[15, 16], and storing tree- and non-tree edges of a graph separately [26]. Only a few proposals exist for efficiently updating such an index [3, 25].

Efficiently representing distances in such a compact index is a difficult problem, and mainly two classes of solutions have been proposed: adding distance information to 2-hop covers [2, 5, 6, 25], and building a shortest-path index by storing multiple BFS trees [28]. Gubichev et al [14] use path sketches to compute approximate distances and shortest paths between two nodes. Only [25] considers the problem of incremental index maintenance.

The problem of maintaining all-pairs shortest path information under certain classes of graph updates (like increasing or decreas-

[1]Imagine our algorithm is used not before the memory footprint of the graph reaches a certain threshold or the global recomputation of the graph exceeds a certain amount of time.

ing edge weights) is also an active topic in the algorithms community [1, 9, 12, 21, 8, 18, 23]. Here, solutions usually focus on graphs that fit in main memory. King [18] proposes a fully dynamic algorithm for APSP in directed graphs with integer edge weights bounded by b, which requires constant time to determine the distance between two arbitrary nodes. It provides amortized cost of $O(n^2\sqrt{bn})$ for a series of updates in a graph with n nodes [19], and it can be modified to retrieve neighbors of a node in ascending order of distance. Frigoni et al. [12] propose an algorithm for fully dynamic APSP in directed graphs with real weights; here, the amortized complexity of an update is $O(m \cdot \log n)$ in a graph with n nodes and m edges. Demetrescu and Italiano [9] experimentally compare several algorithms for the dynamic all-pair shortest path problem, namely [8, 18, 23] on random and real-world graphs of up to 3,000 nodes. Unlike these proposals, our method assumes that the graph is too big to store in memory and needs to be kept on disk, so traversing the graph as these methods do is not viable here. To the best of our knowledge, Meyer's work [21] is the only that considers graphs stored on external memory; however, it does not precompute any information, but performs a BFS traversal of the graph to determine node distances.

The problem of incremental maintenance of precomputed transitive closures and distances in databases was considered in [11, 22]. They update the complete set of precomputed information after a new edge was inserted or an existing edge was deleted. It is incremental in the sense that it does not need to recompute from scratch, but can modify the existing information. In contrast, our proposed approach is also incremental, but considers only a subset of the precomputed information affected by an update, and defers maintenance to the point where queries access information that is potentially out-of-date.

3. ALGORITHMIC OVERVIEW

3.1 Data Structures

We will make use of the following data structures:

- **L(u)** For each node u, $L(u)$ is the list of u's descendants in graph $G^{t(u)}$ in ascending order of distance and is initially precomputed and stored on secondary storage. Each entry in list $L(u)$ is a pair (v, w), representing a shortest path from u to node v with weight w.
  We use the short-cut notation $L(u, v)$ to refer to the weight w of a path from u to v stored in $L(u)$. For notational simplicity, we assume that $L(u, v) = \infty$ when there is no path from u to v. Moreover, $L(u)$ provides the operations $\textsc{pos}(u, v)$, denoting the position of v in $L(u)$, and $\textsc{replace}(v, w')$, which replaces the entry (v, w) in $L(u)$ with (v, w') or adds it when there is no such entry.
  The operations $\textsc{pos}(u, v)$, $\textsc{replace}(v, w)$ and $L(u, v)$ only consider prefixes of lists $L(u)$ which have already been traversed and, thus, are available in main memory. Hence, finding or replacing entries is cheap.
- **t(u)** For a node u, the in-memory timestamp $t(u)$ keeps the time when $L(u)$ was last updated.
- **tp(u)** The timestamp validity pointer $tp(u)$ is an offset into $L(u)$ and points to the position up to which all nearest neighbors are guaranteed to be correctly identified with respect to the timestamp $t(u)$.
- **OP(u)** The in-memory set $OP(u)$ keeps for each node u the set of edge updates for u that have not yet been applied on u since $t(u)$. Entries are triples (v, w', t) where v is the target node of the updated edge, w' the updated weight for the edge (u, v) and t the time when the update occurred. For multiple updates of the same edge since $t(u)$, only the latest update is stored in $OP(u)$. Whenever an entry is read from $OP(u)$, it is immediately removed and the corresponding main memory is freed.

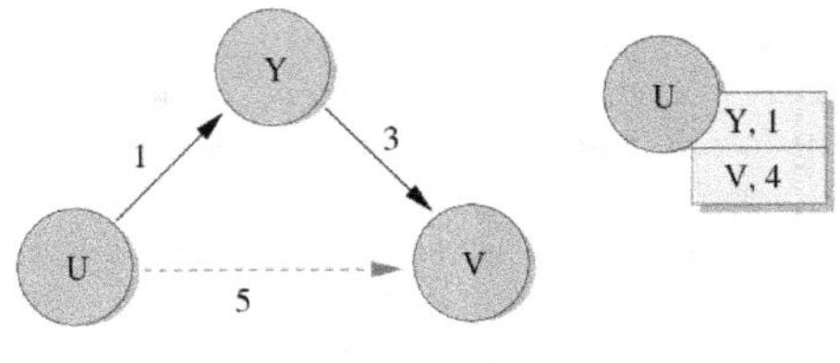

Figure 2: Example graph showing that a weight of an indirect path is lower than the one of a new edge update (the dashed line).

Initially, all $L(u)$ are precomputed for G^0, $t(u) = 0$, $tp(u)$ points to the end of $L(u)$, and $OP(u) = \emptyset$. The precomputed lists are stored on disk and loaded in batches when they are accessed. Therefore, $\textsc{replace}(v, w')$ requires a special handling: Assume that the in-memory prefix of $L(u)$ does not contain an entry for v and there is a new edge (u, v) which is applied during the query processing and inserted by $\textsc{replace}(v, w')$. Since $L(u)$ is sorted in ascending order of distance, all entries already read from disk have a lower weight than the remaining ones on disk. However, this is not necessarily true for a new edge (u, v). The weight w' of such an edge might actually be higher than the one of an indirect path from u to v whose edges are summing up to a smaller value $w < w'$ and which is already stored in the part of $L(u)$ still on disk. An example for this scenario is given in Figure 2. The indirect path from u over y to v has a lower weight $w = 1 + 3$ than the weight $w' = 5$ of the new direct edge (u, v).

Further assume that only the first entry of $L(u)$ is already in memory. Hence, when $\textsc{replace}(v, w')$ is called for $L(u)$, the in-memory part of $L(u)$ does not contain v, but the disk-based part contains an entry with a lower weight than the one of the new edge. We therefore buffer the new entry for v to $L(u)$ in memory and merge it with entries loaded in the next batches from disk, keeping only the entries with smallest weight if a node appears more than once. We remember the last weight $max(u)$ that has been read from disk for $L(u)$, and load the next batch from disk when reading an in-memory entry with an higher weight than $max(u)$.

3.2 Base Algorithm

Our algorithm framework builds on the following principles. Edge updates are not included in the precomputed lists when they happen but delayed to the last possible point, which is when they have an effect on the result of a query. We then process them in an on-the-fly manner during processing the query. To achieve this, a query $query^t(u)$ reads the precomputed list $L(u)$ until it encounters an added or modified edge; in that case, just the necessary updates are incorporated into the precomputed data structures.

Our base algorithm $\textsc{Neighbors}(u, k)$ for processing a query $query^t(u, k)$, shown in Listing 1, uses two core operations, $\textsc{Update}$ and $\textsc{Merge}$:

- $\textsc{Update}(u)$: This method incorporates all edges updates in $OP(u)$ into $L(u)$, but does not deal with transitive paths that may have changed due to the modified edges.
- $\textsc{Merge}(u, v)$: This method takes care of transitive paths from u to other nodes passing through v by connecting paths starting at v. In this way, updates located at even distant nodes propagate to u.

We will later introduce two different implementations for these two methods. The base algorithm successively determines the closest k

```
NEIGHBORS(u, k)
L ← ∅ ; i ← 0
if OP(u) ≠ ∅ then UPDATE(u)
R(u).RESET
while (v ← R(u).NEXT) ≠ NL
    do
        L[i] ← v ; i ← i + 1
        if i = k then Break
        if OP(v) ≠ ∅ then UPDATE(v)
        if NEEDS-MERGE(u, v) then MERGE(u, v)
        if i > tp(u) then tp(u) ← i
return L
```

```
NEEDS-MERGE(u, v)
return t(u) < t(v) or (pos(u, v) ≥ tp(u) and t(v) > 0))
```

Listing 1: Base algorithm for retrieving nearest neighbors of a node

neighbors of u. It first updates u itself to include any modified edges in $L(u)$ and then sequentially traverses $L(u)$, accomplishing update and merge operations for each seen node if necessary. An update of a node v, i.e., including new or modified edges of v into $L(v)$ that it does not yet include, is needed if and only if $OP(v)$ is not empty. The algorithm uses an operator $R(u)$ to sequentially read entries from $L(u)$ with operations NEXT for reading the next entry from the list and RESET for resetting the operator to the beginning of the list. The implementation of this operator depends on the implementation of UPDATE and MERGE; we will explain it later when discussing the two implementations.

The function NEEDS-MERGE(u, v) (also shown in Listing 1) determines if there are paths from u through v that are shorter than those already included in $L(u)$. This decision is made based on the timestamps of u and v and the timestamp validity pointer $tp(u)$. A merge is necessary if one of the two following conditions holds:

1. Whenever $t(v)$ is greater than $t(u)$, v must have seen some more recent updates than u, so there could be shorter paths through v created by these updates.
2. As soon as we reach $tp(u)$ in $L(u)$, we do not know if subsequent entries in $L(u)$ are correct (checks for update and merge are applied only to entries prior to $tp(u)$), so every node v that we encounter with $t(v) > 0$ (i.e., that had at least one update since we built the index) may introduce shorter paths.

Before returning the k nearest neighbors, $tp(u)$ can be safely increased to k as those are guaranteed to be correct.

Note: Only for ease of presentation, NEIGHBORS(u, k) computes the best k neighbors of u before returning the results. We introduce the algorithm in this way for a clearer pseudo code. It is, however, simple to change it to an operator-based architecture where results can be polled one at a time, analogous to the usage of the $R(u)$ operator to read from $L(u)$.

We will now introduce two implementations of this framework, a static combination of lists and an incremental approach, that differ only in their implementation of UPDATE, MERGE, and the NEXT method of the operator $R(u)$.

4. EAGER PROPAGATION APPROACH

Our first approach, coined *Eager Propagation (EAP)*, eagerly updates $L(u)$ while traversing it by propagating all available information from modified lists of descendant nodes when they are encountered. It maintains the invariant that an edge update is either stored in $OP(u)$ or its effects are included in $L(u)$. We now explain how UPDATE and MERGE are implemented in *EAP*.

```
UPDATE(u)
maxTS ← max{t|(v, w', t) ∈ OP(u)}
foreach (v, w', t) ∈ OP(u)
    do
        if w' < L(u, v)
            then L(u).REPLACE(v, w')
                MERGE(u, v)
t(u) ← maxTS ; tp(U) ← 0 ; OP(u) ← ∅
```

Listing 2: Implementation of UPDATE in *EAP*

```
MERGE(u, v)
foreach x ∈ L(v)
    do
        if L(u, v) + L(v, x) < L(u, x)
            then L(u).REPLACE(x, L(u, v) + L(v, x))
t(u) ← max{t(u), t(v)} ; tp(u) ← pos(u, v) + 1
```

Listing 3: Implementation of MERGE in *EAP*

4.1 EAP.UPDATE

Listing 2 shows the UPDATE(u) method in *EAP*. It iterates over all edge updates in $OP(u)$. For each such edge update (v, w', t) at time t and weight w' of edge (u, v), it checks if v's current weight w in $L(u)$ is larger, and replaces the entry in this case with the new one. (This includes the case when v is not yet included in $L(u)$ since $L(u, v) = \infty$ then.) If we modify the entry for v, we call MERGE(u, v) to take care of transitive paths through v. Finally, we set the timestamp $t(u)$ of u to the highest timestamp of any of the edge updates, and reset the timestamp validity pointer $tp(u)$ to the beginning of the list.

4.2 EAP.MERGE

All nodes x in $L(v)$ are connected to u through v and their distance from u is at most $L(u, v) + L(v, x)$ if that path is also a shortest path. The purpose of MERGE(u, v) (shown in Listing 3) is (a) to identify all nodes x in $L(v)$ that are either not yet contained in $L(u)$ or whose current weight in $L(u)$ is bigger than $L(u, v) + L(v, x)$, and (b) to replace those nodes in $L(u)$ accordingly. When the two lists are merged, we increase the timestamp $t(u)$ of u to the highest timestamp of both nodes. We set u's timestamp validity pointer $tp(u)$ to the next entry following v in $L(u)$.

4.3 EAP.NEXT

Implementing the operator to read from $L(u)$ is very simple with *EAP* since (1) any edge update is integrated directly into $L(u)$, and (2) it can take place only after the last position read in $L(u)$. Therefore, the NEXT method of the operator $R(u)$ simply needs to keep track of the current reading position and increases it with each call, reading the entry at that position in $L(u)$. (Remember that we may have to first load further entries from disk depending on the weight of that entry before we can return it, see the discussion about REPLACE(v, w') in Section 3.)

4.4 Problems and Improvements of EAP

The *EAP* approach needs to fully load from disk all lists that are merged with $L(u)$, so it comes with big performance penalties when these lists are huge and loaded from a slow storage backend. This is the price we need to pay to ensure that we read the correct entries no matter how far we read into $L(u)$, and this is also the case when we write the updated $L(u)$ back to disk after the query.

Unfortunately, this is true even if we usually read only a few neighbors in each query. However, if it is possible to limit the maximal number of neighbors that any query can read, we can considerably improve performance. Denoting this limit by $maxk$, MERGE(u, v) needs to consider only the first $maxk$ entries of the list since no query will ever access more entries. In fact, it is even enough to consider at most $maxk - pos(u, v)$ entries since the entries up to v in $L(u)$ will not be affected anyway. We could additionally stop merging when the resulting distances are not smaller than the $maxk$'s current entry of $L(u)$.

5. LAZY PROPAGATION APPROACH

The *EAP* approach from Section 4 and especially its implementation of the MERGE operation needs to access complete precomputed lists. As lists are often very long and queries access only small prefixes of them, it often causes way more work than necessary. We now present the *Lazy Propagation (LAP)* approach that merges lists on the fly as entries are read, improving performance especially for queries that read only a small number of results. The main differences to *EAP* are as follows:

- UPDATE(u) considers all edge updates from $OP(u)$ but does not immediately modify $L(u)$. Instead, the target nodes of updated edges are added to a priority queue $PQ(u)$ with the edges' weights as keys. The queue keeps possible candidates for the next node to return.
- MERGE(u, v) considers transitive paths from u through v. In contrast to *EAP*, $L(v)$ is not completely merged into $L(u)$ but only its first entry x is added to the priority queue $PQ(u)$ together with its weight that is computed as $L(u, v)+L(v, x)$.

The invariant that the *LAP* approach maintains is the following: For all nodes u, any edge that was modified or added since $L(u)$ was created is either stored in $OP(u)$, has an entry in $PQ(u)$, or its effects are fully integrated into the current version of $L(u)$.

LAP uses the following data structure in addition to those mentioned in Section 3.1:

- **PQ(u)** The priority queue $PQ(u)$ is actually a mergeable min-heap[7] that stores entries of the form (v, x) where v is a node and x is either v or a node from $L(v)$. An entry is uniquely identified and can be retrieved by its first component, in this case v. The key of such an entry denotes the weight w of the shortest path from u to x through v. Among the standard operations of such a data structure, we make use of ADD(v, x, w) to add entry (v, x) with key w, and EXTRACT-MIN to extract the current entry with minimal key. We extend the data structure by operations CONTAINS(v) to test if it contains an entry for v, and by REMOVE(v) to remove the entry for v.

Whenever the list $L(u)$ is read, the corresponding priority queue $PQ(u)$ is read from disk, too; correspondingly, after flushing an updated $L(u)$ back to disk, the current content of $PQ(u)$ is flushed to disk as well.

We will now explain UPDATE and MERGE for the *LAP* approach.

5.1 LAP.UPDATE

The implementation of UPDATE(u) in *LAP* is shown in Listing 4. This method considers all edge updates in $OP(u)$. For each edge update (v, w', t) in $OP(u)$, it adds an entry (v, v) with key w' to $PQ(u)$, removing any existing entry for v, if the weight of the new or updated edge (u, v) yields a lower path weight than any existing

```
UPDATE(u)
maxTS ← max{t|(v, w', t) ∈ OP(u)}
foreach (v, w', t) ∈ OP(u)
    do
        if w'(v) < L(u, v)
            then if PQ(u).CONTAINS(v)
                    then PQ(u).REMOVE(v)
                 PQ(u).ADD(v, v, w')
t(u) ← maxTS ; tp(U) ← 0 ; OP(u) ← ∅
```

```
MERGE(u, v)
R(v).RESET
x ← R(v).NEXT
if PQ(u).CONTAINS(v)
  then PQ(u).REMOVE(v)
PQ(u).ADD(v, x, L(u, v) + L(v, x))
t(u) ← max{t(u), t(v)} ; tp(u) ← pos(u, v) + 1
```

Listing 4: Implementation of UPDATE and MERGE in *LAP*

path from u to v. As depicted in Figure 2, an indirect path can have a lower weight than a new, direct edge.

The entry in $PQ(u)$ represents all shortest paths from u over v to nodes which are not yet known, hence, the paths currently end at v; we do not need to consider $L(v)$ at this point since we first need to deal with v itself. Next, we set the timestamp $t(u)$ of u to the newest timestamp of all new or modified edges for u, and set the timestamp validity pointer to the beginning of the list.

5.2 LAP.MERGE

MERGE(u, v) considers transitive paths from u to descendants of v taken from $L(v)$. In *LAP*, we do not directly merge the two lists, but use the priority queue. We first reset $R(v)$, the iterator on $L(v)$, and read the list's first node x, the closest neighbor of v. We now add the entry $(v, x, L(u, v)+L(v, x))$ to $PQ(u)$, representing the fact that x is the closest node that can be reached from u through any path through v with a weight $L(u, v)+L(v, x)$. As in *EAP*, we set the timestamp $t(u)$ of u to the maximum of the timestamps of u and v, and move the timestamp validity pointer $tp(u)$ right after the position of v in $L(u)$ since the correct node at this position is either already in place or exists in $PQ(u)$.

5.3 LAP.NEXT

Unlike the *EAP* approach where UPDATE(u) and MERGE(u, v) were expensive and NEXT was cheap, the majority of the work is now done in the NEXT operation (shown in Listing 5). As the timestamp validity pointer indicates the validity of entries in $L(u)$, we can immediately return the current entry from $L(u)$ as long as the read position is below $tp(u)$. The framework makes sure that we never read beyond $tp(u)$ without first updating $L(u)$, so this cannot happen. The only nontrivial case is when we are reading exactly at the position where $tp(u)$ points to. In this case, we have to identify the best candidate in $PQ(u)$ that is not yet part of the already read segment of $L(u)$, and read either this or the current entry in $L(u)$ at position $tp(u)$, depending on their weights. Identifying the best node from all candidates in $PQ(u)$ requires the following tasks:

1. Remove from $PQ(u)$ the current head triple (v, x, w) with the top candidate node x with weight w for a path from u to x over v.
2. If w is not smaller than the weight at the current reading posi-

```
R(u).NEXT
▷ pos: current reading position
pos ← pos + 1
if (pos) = tp(u)
  then (v, x, w) ← PQ(u).EXTRACT-MIN
       while pos(u, x) < tp(u) or x = u
           do QUEUENEXT(u, v, x)
              (v, x, w) ← PQ(u).EXTRACT-MIN
       if (v, x, w) = NL
         then return L(u)[pos]
       (y, z) ← L(u)[pos]
       if L(u)[pos] = NL or w > z
         then L(u).REPLACE(x, w)
              QUEUENEXT(u, v, x)
         else PQ(u).add(v, x, w)
       tp(u) ← tp(u) + 1
return L(u)[pos]
```

```
QUEUENEXT(u, v, x)
if NEEDS-UPDATE(x)
  then UPDATE(x)
if NEEDS-MERGE(v, x)
  then MERGE(v, x)
x ← R(v).NEXT
PQ(u).ADD(v, x, L(u, v) + L(v, x))
```

Listing 5: Implementation of NEXT in *LAP*

tion of $L(u)$, put it back to $PQ(u)$ and return the node from $L(u)$.

3. Otherwise, identify the next neighbor of v by reading from $L(v)$ and put it into $PQ(u)$; note that this may require updating and merging that node to reflect any updates not yet in $L(v)$.
4. Next, check if the current candidate x has already be seen in $L(u)$ at an earlier position with a lower weight. In that case, it is ignored, and we continue with step 1.
5. Check if x is equal to u. If so, we found a path with a cycle back to u, which we ignore by continuing with step 1.
6. Finally, we return x as this is the correct next neighbor of u.

5.4 Resolving Cycles

5.4.1 *Why cycles cause problems*

In *EAP*, we merge complete lists or list prefixes of fixed size into the list $L(u)$ of a queried node u. Cycles in the graph could therefore never cause problems. In *LAP*, however, we are considering several lists at the same time, trying to bring them up to date through UPDATE and MERGE operations. We illustrate the problem now with a very simple example with just two nodes.

Assume there are only two nodes a and b that do not have any edges in G^0, so both $L(a)$ and $L(b)$ are empty. Now we add edges $a \rightarrow b$ and $b \rightarrow a$ with weights $w_b = 1$ and $w_a = 3$, so a and b are mutual closest neighbors. Next, we query node a to retrieve $L(a)$. Our algorithm first updates a with the new edge to b by putting $(b, b, 1)$ into $PQ(a)$ (in UPDATE(a)), which will be at the head of $PQ(a)$ since it is the only entry. Thus, when our algorithm identifies the first neighbor of a by calling $R(a)$.NEXT, it will find b as top candidate in $PQ(a)$ and retrieves $(b, 1)$ as a result. Furthermore, it creates an entry in $PQ(a)$ for b containing b's nearest neighbor. Since a is b's nearest neighbor, this results in an entry $(b, a, 1 + 3)$ in $PQ(a)$. However, to identify that a is b's nearest neighbor, the same procedure as just described for a is executed for b, too. Hence, $PQ(b)$ finally contains the single entry $(a, b, 3 + 1)$. The scenario is depicted in Figure 3.

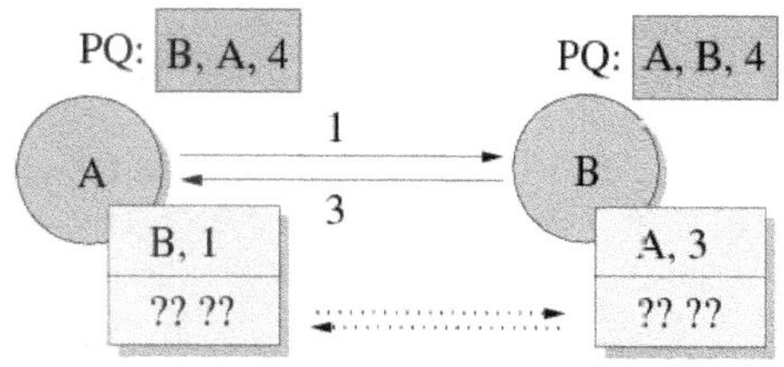

Figure 3: Example: cyclic graph. The next entry in PQ of each node cannot be processed because of the cycle.

The problem with cycles becomes obvious when trying to find the next neighbor of a. Then, the entry at the head of $PQ(a)$ is fetched, which is $(b, a, 4)$. As a is obviously not a valid neighbor, our algorithm tries to queue b's next neighbor. However, when trying to find b's next neighbor, we end up in the same situation as with a: the candidate for b's next neighbor is a's next neighbor. Hence, we are stuck in a cycle. Once such a cycle is identified, it is simple to break: as there are no other candidates left, each list ends at the current entry and there are no more next neighbors of a and b. The situation can get more complex when more nodes and longer lists are involved. We will now first describe how to detect cycles, and then how to break them.

5.4.2 *Detecting Cycles*

Identifying a cycle is rather simple. For a given query, we remember all nodes u for which the method QUEUENEXT(u, v, x, y) (see Listing 5) is called in a global data structure, e.g. a HashSet. When the method returns, we remove u from the data structure again. If u calls that method to queue a next entry from some other node's list and that node is already included in the data structure, we have identified a cycle.

5.4.3 *Breaking Cycles*

We mainly need to take care when extracting the current best entry from $PQ(u)$. If (v, x, w) is extracted from $PQ(u)$ and x belongs to a cycle, then we remove the entry and proceed to the next entry in $L(v)$ by calling QUEUENEXT(u, v, x), inserting it in $PQ(u)$ afterwards. We repeat this step until a candidate is found in $PQ(u)$ that does not belong to a cycle, or $PQ(u)$ is empty. When there is no more entry in $L(v)$, it is discarded from $PQ(u)$ and we repeat until a valid entry is found or $PQ(u)$ is empty.

5.5 Extension of LAP

Whenever $L(u)$ is loaded from disk for querying it, the corresponding priority queue $PQ(u)$ needs to be loaded and initialized as well. Especially when one of the previous queries read many entries of $L(u)$, this queue can be large, and it would be very expensive to open the lists for all nodes that have entries in $PQ)(u)$. Luckily, this is not necessary at the beginning but only when the queue entry for a node is pulled from the queue for the first time. To see why this is correct, assume that $PQ(u)$ contains an entry (v, x, w) when loaded from disk. This means that (1) v is contained in $L(u)$ since it is a descendant of u, (2) x is a descendant of v, (3) $L(u, v) \leq w$, and (4) all nodes in $L(v)$ up to x are already contained in $L(u)$. If any node in $L(v)$ up to x has seen a change since $PQ(u)$ was written to disk, this will be detected while traversing

$L(u)$, and necessary UPDATE and MERGE operations will be issued. When the entry for v is polled from $PQ(u)$, $L(v)$ is opened and read, ignoring any entries already seen. If the weight for x has decreased since $PQ(u)$ was written, it has already been seen in previous steps and will be ignored. Therefore, the serialized version of $PQ(u)$ on disk does not need to include the current candidate from each list, but simply entries of the form (v, w), where v is the note from whose list $L(v)$ entries are merged, and w is the last weight read from that list. Here, w serves as a threshold for opening the actual list $L(v)$ when running subsequent queries on $L(u)$.

6. EXPERIMENTAL EVALUATION

6.1 Setup

We evaluate our algorithm on excerpts of the following two social networks:

- **LT**: A combined corpus retrieved by two subsequent partial crawls of the user graph of the social book catalog LibraryThing, provided by the authors of [24]. It includes $7,793$ connected users and $28,853$ friendship edges (derived from explicit friends and users marked as having interesting libraries). Edge weights are defined as the Dice coefficient of the two users' tag sets.
- **Twitter**: A complete crawl of the user graph of the microblogging service Twitter which was used in [20]. It includes approximately 41 million users and 1.4 billion edges. As we did not have access to the tweets of the users, edge weights were assigned randomly from a uniform distribution.

Nodes in each graph are represented by integers. To form the initial graph G^0, we randomly removed edges according to the following pattern: For nodes with more than two edges, we removed 30% of the edges; for nodes with two edges, we removed one of them, and for nodes with only a single edge, we removed that edge for 50% of the nodes. We built the initial lists $L(u)$ for each node u using Dijkstra's algorithm and stored them in an Oracle database with appropriate indexes. The database runs on a Windows 2003 server with two dual-core AMD Opteron 2218 processors at 2.4 GHz and 32GB of main memory and a large network-attached disk array. All experiments, implemented in Java, were done on a Linux desktop PC with 4GB main memory and a 4-core Intel i5 650 CPU at 3.2GHz. Since the runtime costs are dominated by I/O accesses, the speed of the CPU is not crucial: in our single threaded experiments, a single core was barely used. For the bigger data set of Twitter, the total memory consumption of our algorithm reaches only 2.1GB after processing over 2 million queries.

Our algorithm is evaluated in the following way: We mix queries with updates at a fixed ratio (denoted as *upd-ratio* in the charts), i.e., after a fixed number of queries, one of the initially removed edges is added to the graph. A query retrieves the *top-k* nearest neighbors of a randomly chosen node. The order for adding edges was selected randomly once and is the same for all experiments.

For the evaluation, we measured the number of performed MERGE operations (#MRG), opened lists (#OL), the total number of list entries retrieved by sequential accesses (#SA) to the database, and the wall clock runtimes (RT) for each query. We report the results in charts where the x-axis denotes the number of the queries and the y-axis denotes the performance result. Additionally, the charts contain the moving average over intervals of 1000 queries, while only considering queries in the interval that indeed achieved a result set of *top-k*=200. Thus, quickly answered queries for nodes with no or only a few neighbors are neglected for the average computation.

6.2 Results for EAP on LT

Figure 4a shows the wall-clock runtimes (RT) and Figure 4b the number of sequential accesses (#SA) with the *EAP* approach. In total 63,572 queries were executed and every 100 queries one update was applied to the graph. The runtimes are not affected too much from #MRG and #OL (for *EAP*, #MRG=#OL) but mostly from #SA. In worst case, when each of the *top-k* friends is found in different lists by different merge operations, at most 200 lists are opened with *top-k*=200. Indeed, from the results in Figure 4c it is evident that EAP opens around 180 lists per query on average. This shows that the graph is tightly connected and a single update already influences many shortest path distances.

Furthermore, from Figures 4a and 4b it is evident that the runtimes are I/O-bound and increase rapidly with the number of read list entries. It takes over $20s$ to sequentially read around $60k$ entries from the involved friendship lists. The number of sequential reads is so large since the lists of transitive neighbors involved in a merge operation are long and, by the characteristics of *EAP*, have to be completely read during a MERGE operation.

Restricting Merge Operations to max-k.

Figures 4d–4i depict the results when merge operations are restricted to *max-k* entries. In each of the experiments *max-k* is set equal to a constant *top-k* value of 200 while the update ratio varies between 1 update per 1 and 100 queries. Depending on the update ratio, $17,438$ or $218,910$ queries were executed.

It can be observed that the different update ratios have only little effect on RT and #SA. For a query with an update ratio $1/1$, the maximum values for RT and #SA is $693ms$ or 2925 sequential accesses to the DB, respectively, and with an update ratio of $1/100$, the maximum value for RT is $723ms$ and 2130 for #SA. RT being slightly higher in the latter case although #SA being lower was most likely caused by network latency issues during the experiments. The average RT and #SA is fairly similar for both update ratios, too. The same is true for an update ratio of $1/10$, therefore, the charts are omitted. The drop in RT and #SA in Figures 4d and 4g after $8,456$ happens because all available edge updates have been applied to the graph at that time and, finally, the performance further improves when there are no more updates for a large number of queries. These experiments demonstrate that the modified *EAP* approach can handle different update loads and benefits quickly from long periods without updates.

Additionally, we evaluated the performance for an increased value of *max-k*=500 and an unchanged value of *top-k*=200 with 1 update per 100 queries (Figures 4f and 4i). As expected, RT and #SA increase because a larger prefix of the lists needs to be merged. However, the average RT/#SA keeps fairly stable at around $850ms$ and 2800 sequential accesses to the DB.

Even though one might expect for *max-k*=200 that there have to be 200 times 200 #SA for *max-k* opened lists and merge operations, this is usually not the case. Once a prefix of a list has been retrieved from the DB, it is kept in main memory until the end of the query and is reused whenever involved in another MERGE operation. For this reason, the relatively low #SA values also show that the graph is tightly connected. For tightly connected graphs, even a single update affects many shortest path distances. However, as shown, the amount of expensive I/O for retrieving the *top-k* nearest neighbors is still low with our algorithm. #SA could be further reduced and, thus, RT could be further improved when lists are cached for several queries.

6.3 Results for LAP

With our *LAP* approach, RT and #SA depend on the number of

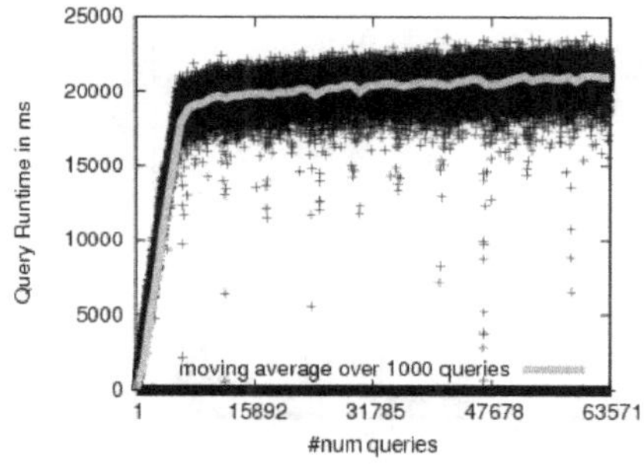

(a) EAP: RT, upd-ratio 1/100

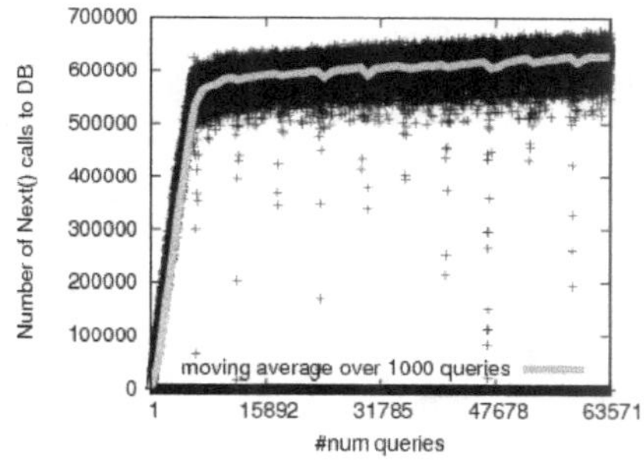

(b) EAP: #SA, upd-ratio 1/100

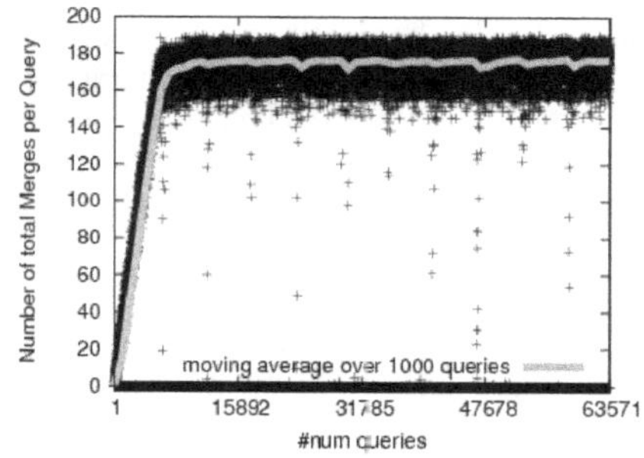

(c) EAP: #MRG, upd-ratio 1/100

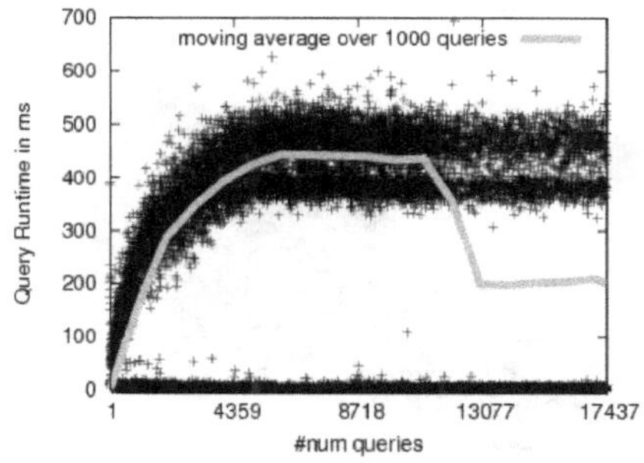

(d) EAP: RT, upd-ratio 1/1, *max-k*=200

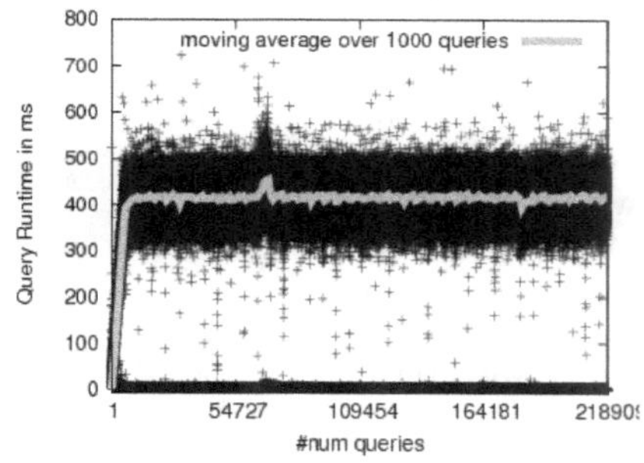

(e) EAP: RT, upd-ratio 1/100, *max-k*=200

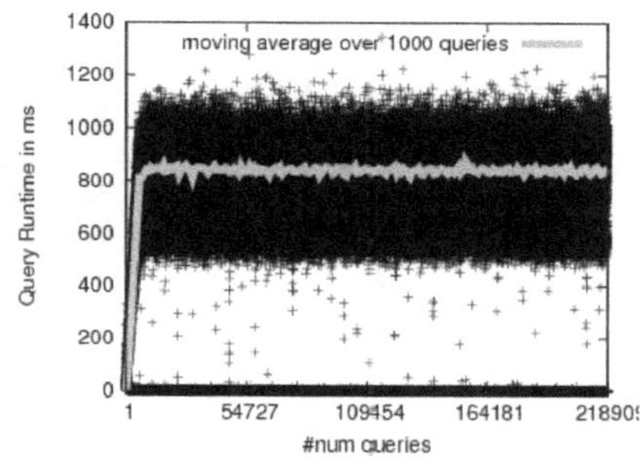

(f) EAP: RT, upd-ratio 1/100, *max-k*=500

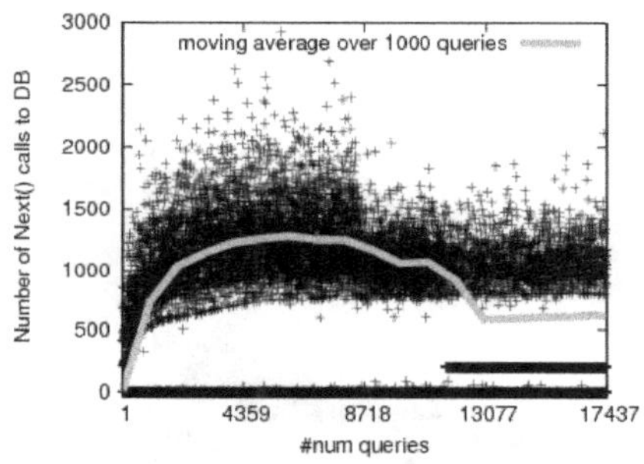

(g) #EAP: SA, upd-ratio 1/1, *max-k*=200

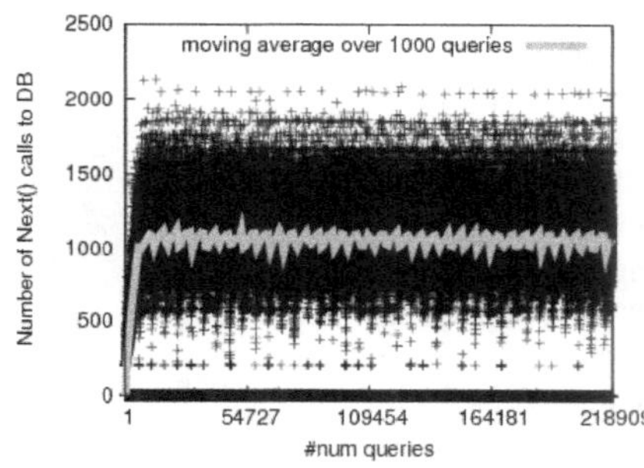

(h) EAP: #SA, upd-ratio 1/100, *max-k*=200

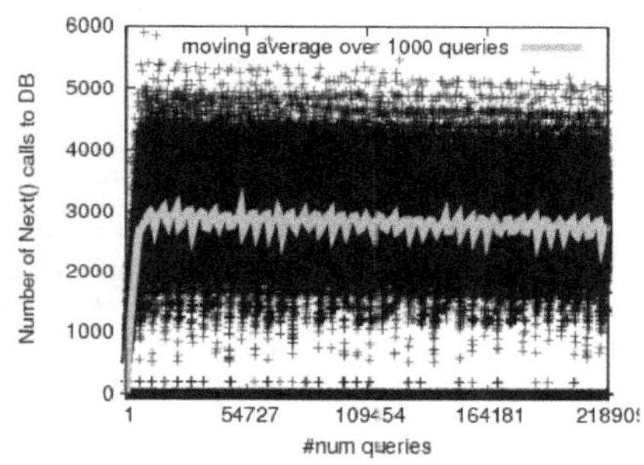

(i) EAP: #SA, upd-ratio 1/100. *max-k*=500

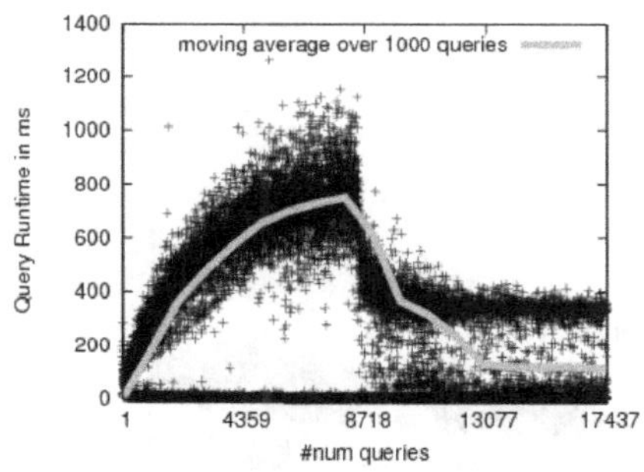

(j) LAP: RT, upd-ratio 1/1

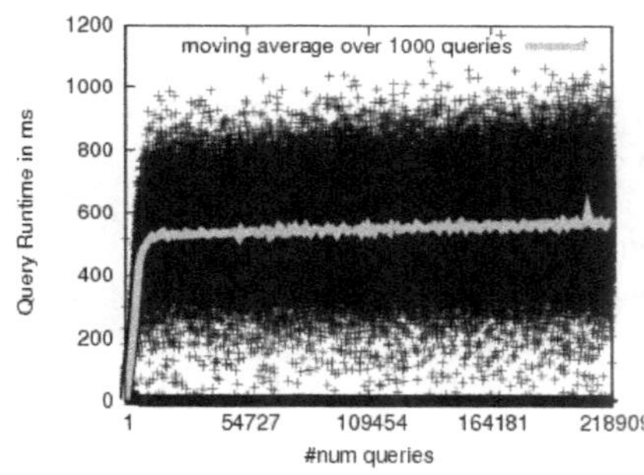

(k) LAP: RT, upd-ratio 1/100

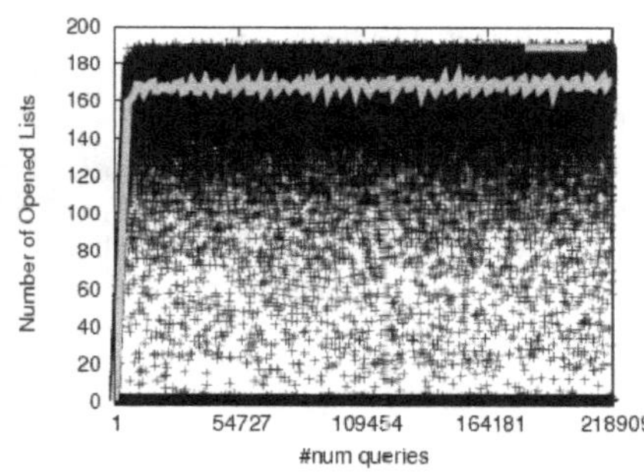

(l) LAP: #OL, upd-ratio 1/100

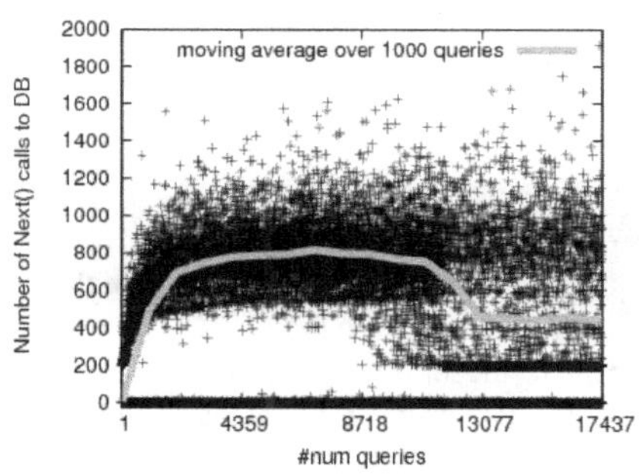

(m) LAP: #SA, upd-ratio 1/1

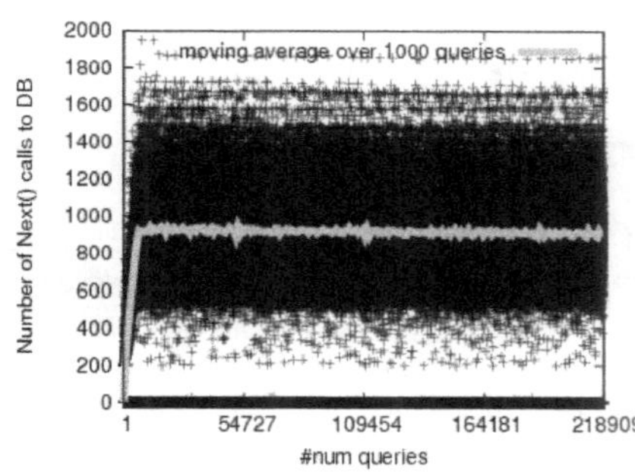

(n) LAP: #SA, upd-ratio 1/100

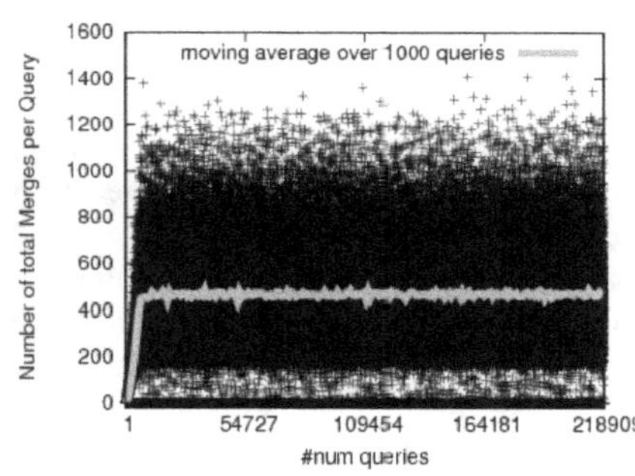

(o) LAP: #MRGs, upd-ratio 1/100

Figure 4: *EAP and LAP on LT*: Runtime (RT) and Sequiential Accesses (#SA) measure, *top-k*=200, Update Ratio: 1 update per 1 and 100 queries.

opened lists and number of merge operations as only single list entries are merged on demand. Therefore, in the following #OL and #MRG are visualized by charts, too. Although *LAP* is able to answer queries for any number of neighbors, *top-k*=200 remains fixed in order to compare the results with *EAP*.

Results on LT (in comparison with EAP).

Figures 4j–4o show the results for *LAP* with the update ratio varying again between 1 update per 1 and 100 queries. The total number of submitted queries depends on the update ratio but is kept equal to the numbers as used with *EAP*.

From Figures 4j and 4k we can see that the average RT is slightly worse than the one for *EAP* with *max-k*=200 (but better than with *max-k*=500). However, the average #SA has improved. It also can be observed that *LAP* is more sensitive to the update ratio. For lower update ratios, both RT and #SA improves. This becomes visible in Figures 4j and 4m after 8,456 queries when all edge updates have been applied. The drop in RT and #SA results in a better performance than *EAP*. Experiments with an update ratio 1/10 confirm this observeration (charts are ommitted for lack of space).

Figure 4n shows that #SA is fairly low, although #MRG (Figure 4o) is much higher than in *EAP* (Figure 4c) while the same number of lists have to be opened (#OL). The reason is that more MERGE operations have to be applied until all updated entries from other lists are merged in. Remember: only a single entry is read with a call of MERGE. In addition, since #SA is lower as in the *max-k*=200 case of our *EAP* approach, it also shows that indeed, in average, shorter prefixes of lists have to be read until the *top-k* nearest nodes can be correctly identified.

There are two reasons why the average RT per query is higher in *LAP* despite of lower #SA. First, maintaining the queue of candidates causes additional costs—again the dominating factor is I/O, not CPU time. Second, although the queue of candidates is small (no more than *top-k* nodes can be candidates), it is initialized with each query by fetching each single candidate from DB. A more efficient maintenance that allows to retrieve the lists with only one access to the DB could reduce the costs of maintenance.

Comparison From the experiments we can see that *LAP* performs equally well as *EAP* which limits queries to a fixed maximum *max-k* (better than *max-k*=500, worse than *max-k*=200). The *LAP* approach has no such limit and is able to correctly identify any amount of results and allows for queries for a variable number of neighbors. Hence, it can perfectly benefit from cases where the number of requested neighbors varies across queries. Moreover, *LAP* benefits more from time intervals with low update ratios.

Results on Twitter.

Since the reduced Twitter graph, achieved by removing the edges for re-insertion as described in the beginning of this section, is still large and the global computation of all nearest neighbor lists by an in-memory algorithm impossible on our server, we did not precompute the transitive lists of neighbors for each user. Instead, we considered a reduced graph by randomly picking a node with 20 outgoing edges and performing a breadth-first search on the link structure of the graph. For each node found, we precomputed the list of its nearest 1000 neighbors. In this way, we precomputed the 1000 nearest neighbors for $2,427,523$ connected nodes.

Since the number of nodes is large, it takes a huge number of queries, as shown in our experiments, until the effects of updates propagate through the graph and cause the runtimes to increase. In the begin, our algorithm has almost nothing to do and just can sequentially read the first *top-k* entries of $L(u)$ because the nearest neighbors have not yet changed. In contrast, a global recomputation of the whole graph as soon as an edge update arrives would not be feasible as no query could be correctly answered in that time and the costs for recomputing all lists are high.

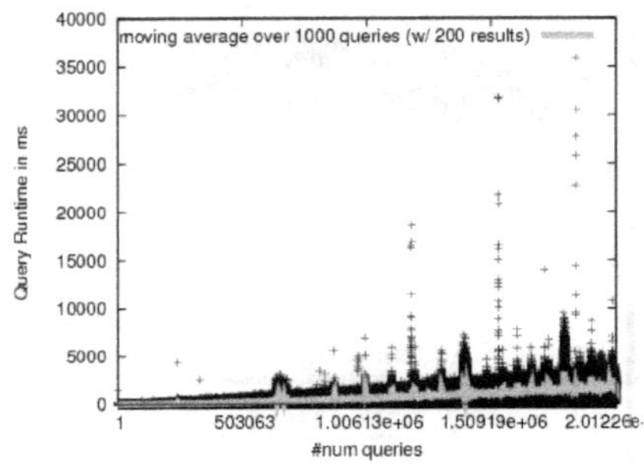

(a) RT, upd-ratio 1/100

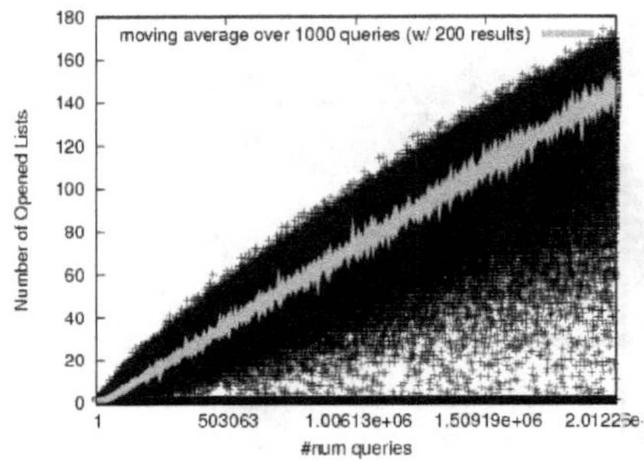

(b) #OL, upd-ratio 1/100

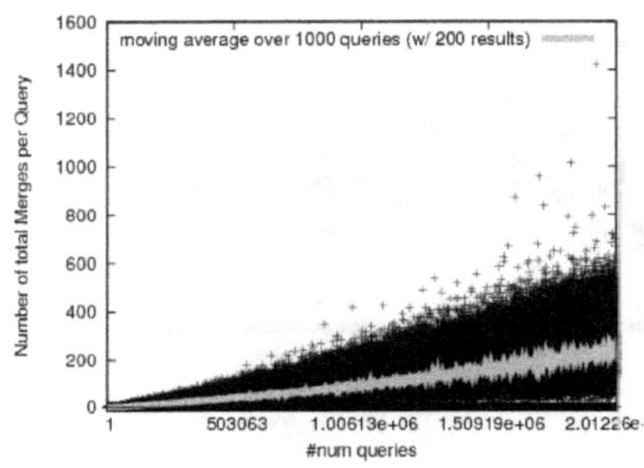

(c) #MRGs, upd-ratio 1/100

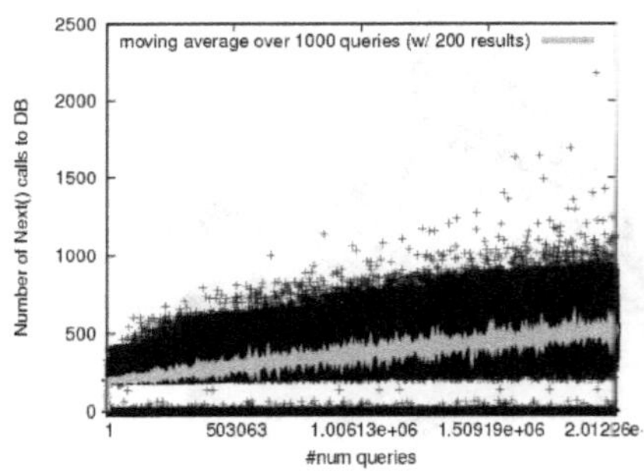

(d) #SA, upd-ratio 1/100

Figure 5: *LAP Approach on Twitter*: *top-k*=200, Update Ratio: 1 update per 100 queries.

Figures 5a–5d show the result for over 2 million queries on Twitter. It can be observed that in general RT increases linearly over time with rare peaks; no such peaks can be observed for the I/O related measures #SA, #MRG, and #OL. One explanation for this odd behavior is that the experiments ran for weeks until over 2 Million queries had been processed. It is likely that these peaks in RT are network-related. In addition, it turned out that the database needs to perform on average more than 3 accesses to the disk storage for each sequential read of a list entry. This can explain the relatively high runtimes on Twitter, even though #MRG, #OL and #SA are—even after 2 million queries—are much lower than for any other experiment on the smaller data set LT. In fact, since the I/O load on Twitter in terms of accesses etc. is actually lower than on LT, the runtime RT should be lower, too. We attribute this to the rather slow speed of the attached disk storage.

In retrospect, the choice of a relational database for storing the precomputed lists has turned out to be suboptimal. With appropriate data structures allowing to retrieve chunks of list entries at one shot, we expect to achieve much better runtimes. Further improvements could be achieved by caching lists in main memory.

7. CONCLUSIONS AND OUTLOOK

This paper presented a framework for incremental maintenance of precomputed nearest neighbors in graphs under edge insertions and decreasing edge weights. The two instantiations of the framework, *EAP* and *LAP*, can deal with large, disk-resident graphs up to millions of nodes. *EAP* can further exploit an upper bound for the number of neighbors to retrieve, while *LAP* does not need such an upper bound but achieves an equally good performance. Both approaches support a large variety of update ratios, up to extreme situations where the number of updates and queries are similar.

Our future work will consider improving the performance of the storage backend by moving to a dedicated list storage instead of a relational database. We will further attempt to evaluate our methods with realistic update loads. Furthermore, we will work towards methods for supporting increasing of edge weights and edge deletions.

8. REFERENCES

[1] S. Baswana, R. Hariharan, and S. Sen. Improved decremental algorithms for maintaining transitive closure and all-pairs shortest paths. In *STOC*, pages 117–123, 2002.

[2] P. Bouros, S. Skiadopoulos, T. Dalamagas, D. Sacharidis, and T. K. Sellis. Evaluating reachability queries over path collections. In *SSDBM*, pages 398–416, 2009.

[3] R. Bramandia, B. Choi, and W. K. Ng. Incremental maintenance of 2-hop labeling of large graphs. *IEEE Trans. Knowl. Data Eng.*, 22(5):682–698, 2010.

[4] D. Carmel, N. Zwerdling, I. Guy, S. Ofek-Koifman, N. Har'El, I. Ronen, E. Uziel, S. Yogev, and S. Chernov. Personalized social search based on the user's social network. In *CIKM*, pages 1227–1236, 2009.

[5] J. Cheng and J. X. Yu. On-line exact shortest distance query processing. In *EDBT*, pages 481–492, 2009.

[6] E. Cohen, E. Halperin, H. Kaplan, and U. Zwick. Reachability and distance queries via 2-hop labels. In *SODA*, pages 937–946, 2002.

[7] T. H. Cormen, C. E. Leiserson, R. L. Rivest, and C. Stein. *Introduction to Algorithms, Third Edition*. The MIT Press and McGraw-Hill Book Company, 2009.

[8] C. Demetrescu and G. F. Italiano. A new approach to dynamic all pairs shortest paths. *J. ACM*, 51(6):968–992, 2004.

[9] C. Demetrescu and G. F. Italiano. Experimental analysis of dynamic all pairs shortest path algorithms. *ACM Transactions on Algorithms*, 2(4):578–601, 2006.

[10] E. W. Dijkstra. A note on two problems in connexion with graphs. *Numerische Mathematik*, 1:269–271, 1959.

[11] G. Dong, L. Libkin, J. Su, and L. Wong. Maintaining transitive closure of graphs in SQL. *Int. Journal on Information Technology*, 5:1–23, 1999.

[12] D. Frigioni, A. Marchetti-Spaccamela, and U. Nanni. Fully dynamic shortest paths in digraphs with arbitrary arc weights. *J. Algorithms*, 49(1):86–113, 2003.

[13] J. Graupmann, R. Schenkel, and G. Weikum. The SphereSearch engine for unified ranked retrieval of heterogeneous XML and web documents. In *VLDB*, pages 529–540, 2005.

[14] A. Gubichev, S. Bedathur, S. Seufert, and G. Weikum. Fast and accurate estimation of shortest paths in large networks. In *CIKM*, pages 499–508, 2010.

[15] R. Jin, Y. Xiang, N. Ruan, and D. Fuhry. 3-HOP: a high-compression indexing scheme for reachability query. In *SIGMOD*, pages 813–826, 2009.

[16] R. Jin, Y. Xiang, N. Ruan, and H. Wang. Efficiently answering reachability queries on very large directed graphs. In *SIGMOD*, pages 595–608, 2008.

[17] G. Kasneci, F. M. Suchanek, G. Ifrim, M. Ramanath, and G. Weikum. NAGA: Searching and ranking knowledge. In *ICDE*, pages 953–962, 2008.

[18] V. King. Fully dynamic algorithms for maintaining all-pairs shortest paths and transitive closure in digraphs. In *FOCS*, pages 81–91, 1999.

[19] V. King and M. Thorup. A space saving trick for directed dynamic transitive closure and shortest path algorithms. In *COCOON*, pages 268–277, 2001.

[20] H. Kwak, C. Lee, H. Park, and S. Moon. What is Twitter, a social network or a news media? In *WWW*, pages 591–600, 2010.

[21] U. Meyer. On dynamic breadth-first search in external-memory. In S. Albers and P. Weil, editors, *STACS*, volume 1 of *LIPIcs*, pages 551–560. Schloss Dagstuhl - Leibniz-Zentrum fuer Informatik, Germany, 2008.

[22] C. Pang, G. Dong, and K. Ramamohanarao. Incremental maintenance of shortest distance and transitive closure in first-order logic and sql. *ACM Trans. Database Syst.*, 30(3):698–721, 2005.

[23] G. Ramalingam and T. W. Reps. An incremental algorithm for a generalization of the shortest-path problem. *J. Algorithms*, 21(2):267–305, 1996.

[24] R. Schenkel, T. Crecelius, M. Kacimi, S. Michel, T. Neumann, J. X. Parreira, and G. Weikum. Efficient top-k querying over social-tagging networks. In *SIGIR*, pages 523–530, 2008.

[25] R. Schenkel, A. Theobald, and G. Weikum. Efficient creation and incremental maintenance of the hopi index for complex xml document collections. In *ICDE*, pages 360–371, 2005.

[26] S. Trißl and U. Leser. Fast and practical indexing and querying of very large graphs. In *SIGMOD*, pages 845–856, 2007.

[27] R. Xiang, J. Neville, and M. Rogati. Modeling relationship strength in online social networks. In *WWW*, pages 981–990, 2010.

[28] Y. Xiao, W. Wu, J. Pei, W. W. 0009, and Z. He. Efficiently indexing shortest paths by exploiting symmetry in graphs. In *EDBT*, pages 493–504, 2009.

Spatial Influence vs. Community Influence: Modeling the Global Spread of Social Media

Krishna Y. Kamath, James Caverlee, Zhiyuan Cheng
Department of Computer Science and Engineering
Texas A&M University
College Station, TX 77843
{kykamath, caverlee, zcheng}@cse.tamu.edu

Daniel Z. Sui
Department of Geography
Ohio State University
Columbus, OH 43210
sui.10@osu.edu

ABSTRACT

In this paper we seek to understand and model the global spread of social media. How does social media spread from location to location across the globe? Can we model this spread and predict where social media will be popular in the future? Toward answering these questions, we develop a probabilistic model that synthesizes two conflicting hypotheses about the nature of online information spread: (i) the spatial influence model, which asserts that social media spreads to locations that are close by; and (ii) the community affinity influence model, which asserts that social media spreads between locations that are culturally connected, even if they are distant. Based on the geospatial footprint of 755 million geo-tagged hashtags spread through Twitter, we evaluate these models at predicting locations that will adopt hashtags in the future. We find that distance is the single most important explanation of future hashtag adoption since hashtags are fundamentally local. We also find that community affinities (like culture, language, and common interests) enhance the quality of purely spatial models, indicating the necessity of incorporating non-spatial features into models of global social media spread.

Categories and Subject Descriptors

H.3.4 [**Information Storage and Retrieval**]: Systems and Software—*Information networks*

General Terms

Algorithms, Experimentation

Keywords

social media, information diffusion models, virtual communities

1. INTRODUCTION

Users generate and consume a great deal of content on the Internet every day in the form of videos, blogs, tweets, and so on. YouTube, for example, streams more than 4 billion videos everyday, with 60 hours of new content uploaded every minute [21]. As users consume and share this content, some of it tends to gain traction and become popular resulting in viral videos, trending hashtags, popular blogs, and so forth. These phenomena have attracted a considerable amount of recent research to study the dynamics of the adoption of social media [3, 12, 16, 18, 22].

Of particular importance is the geospatial spread of social media. For example, how did videos captured on smartphones during the Arab Spring spread across the globe? Are there key locations that promoted the spread of these videos? As the Arab Spring has become increasingly part of the US's social conscious, do we see key US locations impacting the propagation of videos today? Answering these questions is extremely challenging, and so as a beginning step we study in this paper the dynamics of social media adoption across geographical locations. Concretely, we formalize the problem of predicting the global spread of social media as the *location subset selection problem*. That is, as a particular item (e.g., video, image) begins to propagate can we predict the locations where it will soon become popular? For example, observing a video which is gaining traction in Qatar, can we predict locations in Europe where the video is soon going to become popular?

Previous work in the area of information (content) diffusion and influence propagation have tended to focus on the pathways of diffusion through social and information networks, e.g., [11, 13, 14, 15, 17, 26]. Complementary to these efforts, we focus on the geospatial connections that impact the spread of social media, and so we abstract from the interaction network layer to consider fine-grained locations and their connections to other locations. Towards modeling the global spread of social media, we develop a probabilistic model that synthesizes two conflicting hypotheses about the nature of online information spread:

- **Distance matters**. As encapsulated by Tobler's first law of geography [24] which asserts that all things being equal, closer places are more alike, whereas distance places are more unalike. In the context of social media spread, Tobler's first law of geography would suggest that locations that are close to each other should be more likely to adopt similar online behaviors (e.g., viewing a YouTube video, posting the same hashtag).
- **"Distance is dead"** [5]. The second hypothesis claims that since online interactions are freed from geospatial constraints, mere proximity is no guarantee toward adopting similar online behavior. In this setting, long-distance links formed through common online community may be more predictive. For example, tech communities in Austin, San Francisco, and Seattle may be tightly linked through their common interest in similar YouTube videos, whereas more geographically close locations may share little in common.

Based on the first hypothesis, we develop the *spatial influence model*, which asserts that the adoption of a particular user activity in a nearby location has a stronger influence on a target location than

CIKM'12, October 29–November 2, 2012, Maui, HI, USA.

whether that same activity was adopted at a more distant location. In other words, distance matters. Based on the second hypothesis, we develop the *community affinity influence model*, which asserts that locations that share a similar community affinity, regardless of distance from each other, are more likely to influence one another. While there are many ways to measure community affinity, we propose two methods: (i) the first considers communities to be close to each other if they share similar activities regardless of *when* they adopt these activities, for example tech communities in Austin and San Francisco reading similar articles on thehackernews.com; and (ii) the second considers communities close to each other if they tend to adopt similar activities in sync, like a video becoming popular in New York and Boston around the same time. Note that both the spatial influence model and the community affinity influence model are developed completely orthogonal to the underlying social network and are based solely on the geospatial distribution of user activities, meaning that estimating flows of influence from one person to another are not necessary. We test these models in the context of the geospatial footprint of 755 million geo-tagged hashtags spread through Twitter. We find that while the spatial influence model has a higher impact than the community affinity influence model in predicting the spread, its combination with community affinity influence model gives the best performance, suggesting that both distance and community are key contributors to social media spread.

The rest of the paper is organized as follows. We start by describing related works in Section 2. In Section 3, we describe our dataset and measure geo-spatial properties of social media propagation. In Section 4, we formally define the location subset selection problem and present the spatial influence and community affinity models. Finally, in Section 5, we define the metrics to compare these models and evaluate the performance of these models before concluding in Section 6.

2. RELATED WORK

Our work presented here builds on two lines of research: Twitter information diffusion and geo-spatial analysis of social media.

Information Diffusion on Twitter: There have been several papers studying the general properties of Twitter as a social network and in analyzing information diffusion over this network [12, 16, 17, 26]. Continuing in this direction most papers related to hashtags have focused their attention on understanding the propagation of hashtags on the network. For example, in [22] the authors studied factors for hashtag diffusion and found that repeated exposure to a hashtag increased the chance of it being reposted again, especially if the hashtag is contentious. An approach grounded in linguistic principles has been to study the property of hashtag creation, use, and dissemination in [7]. In related research, approaches based on linear regression have been used to predict the popularity of hashtags in a given time frame in [25]. Because of the semantic nature of hashtags and the variety of ways in which it is used to convey information about a tweet, there have been some papers which have used hashtags to solve problems like sentiment detection [9], topic tracking on twitter streams [19], and so forth.

Geo-spatial Analysis of Social Media: The emergence of location-based social networks like Foursquare, Gowalla, and Google Latitude has motivated large-scale geo-spatial analysis [23, 20]. Some of the earliest research related to geo-spatial analysis of web content were based on mining geography specific content for search engines [10]. More recently in [1] the authors analyzed search queries to understand the spatial distribution of queries and understand their geographical centers. On Twitter, geo-spatial analysis has focused on inferring geographic information from tweets like predicting user locations from tweets [6] and spatial modeling to geolocate objects [8]. Similar analysis to infer user's location on Facebook based on their social network has been studied in [2]. A recent paper dealt with the spatial analysis of Youtube videos [4] . In this work the authors were able to observe the highly local nature of videos based on the propagation patterns of Youtube videos.

3. MEASURING THE GEOSPATIAL PROPERTIES OF SOCIAL MEDIA

In this section we first present notation for measuring social media spread with an eye toward developing models of this spread. Then we highlight the experimental setting – Twitter-based hashtags – and examine the geospatial properties of hashtag spread. Our goal is to study questions like: Does distance impact whether social media (hashtags, in this case) is shared between two locations? Does distance impact the timing of hashtag adoption? How predictable is the spread of a hashtag over a geographic area? Do early observations indicate whether a hashtag will spread compactly or be widely diffused over a large spatial area?

3.1 Preliminaries

Let M be the set of user activities of interest – for example, an activity could correspond to a click on a web link, a view of a Web video, sharing of a link on Facebook, posting a particular hashtag on Twitter, and so on. Suppose we have divided the globe into a set of distinct locations L (say by overlaying a mesh dividing the globe into squares of 0.001 degrees latitude by 0.001 degree longitude). Every activity is associated with some subset of locations in which the activity has been observed. For example, based on the IP address, a view of a Web video can be traced back to an approximate latitude and longitude. Similarly, many social media services and smartphones support GPS-enabled tagging of user activities. By discretizing time into regular intervals (say, into 5 second increments), we can express the set of occurrences of an activity $m \in M$ in a particular location $l \in L$ at time t as $o_l^m(t)$. For example, o_l^m may represent 10 clicks of a Web video m in the past minute, where each click originates in a particular neighborhood l.

Now, suppose we have observed all occurrences of an activity up to some critical time t_s. Then we can define the set of **observed occurrences** (O_l^m) of m at a single location l as:

$$O_l^m = \bigcup_{t=0}^{t_s} o_l^m(t) \tag{1}$$

and the **total observed occurrences** set O^m across all locations in L as:

$$O^m = \bigcup_{l \in L} O_l^m$$

We denote the set of unique hashtags observed in l as M_l.

3.2 Experimental Setting: Hashtags

To measure the geospatial properties of social media, we focus our attention on one type of globally observed user activity – the posting of hashtags on Twitter. Twitter hashtags are prefixed with a # and mostly serve as tags to the corresponding tweet. Users tag their tweets for different purposes. For example, some are event driven like #ripstevejobs, and #fukushima, while some are mostly for fun like #bestsportsrivalry and #ifyouknowmeyouknow.

We collected a sample of around ~755 million geo-tagged tweets containing ~10 million unique hashtags from Twitter using the Twitter Streaming API from February 1 to November 30, 2011. Each tweet in this sample is tagged with a latitude and longitude indicating the location of the user at the time of the posting. All $<$ `hashtag`, `time`, `latitude`, `longitude` $>$ tuples corresponding to a particular hashtag are considered as a single activity of interest. Together all hashtags give us the set of all activities M.

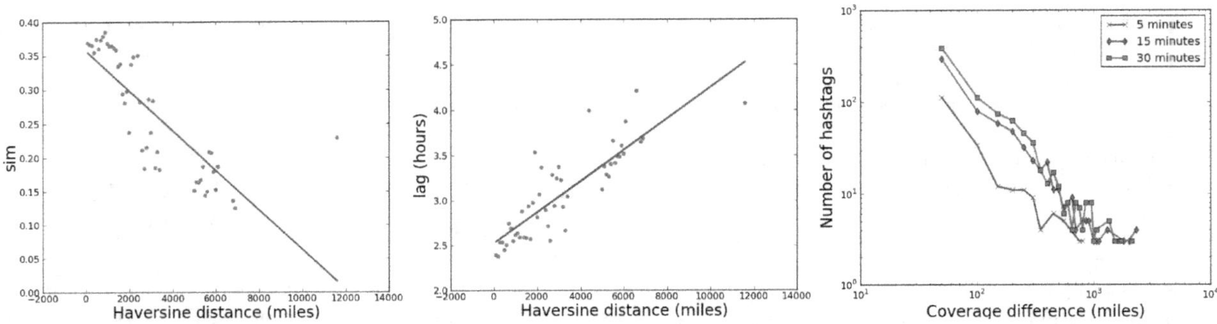

(a) Hashtag sharing versus distance (b) Hashtag adoption lag versus distance (c) Early indication of coverage.

Figure 1: Geospatial properties of hashtags. (a) shows correlation between location similarity and distance. We see that similarity between location decreases with increasing distance. (b) shown correlation between hashtag adoption lag and distance. We see that adoption lag increases with increasing distance. (c) comparison between early and late coverage for call hashtags. A power law indicates that most hashtags have a small difference between early and late coverage values.

We round latitudes and longitudes to their nearest tenth values, which overlays a mesh dividing the globe into locations (L). To avoid sparsely represented hashtags, we consider only hashtags with at least 5 occurrences in a location and consider only hashtags with at least 250 total occurrences across all locations. Since some hashtags may have begun their Twitter life before the first day of our sample (February 1) while others may have continued on after the last day (November 30), we consider both February and November as buffer months. Hence, we capture the full lifecycle of hashtags starting on or after March 1 and ending by October 31, which focuses our study to hashtags which have both their birth and death within the time of study (and as a result, removes cyclical hashtags like "#ff" and "#nofollow"). We additionally divide the set of all hashtags into two sets: a training set based on hashtags from March to August; and a test set based on September to October. Hashtags that start in training but continue into test are ignored. In this way, the training set contains 1466 complete hashtag propagations and the test set contains 515.

3.3 Geospatial Properties of Hashtags

Toward informing the development of models of social media spread, we study three geospatial properties of hashtags: (i) sharing versus distance, (ii) adoption lag versus distance, and (iii) the predictability of spread.

Hashtag Sharing versus Distance: We first seek to understand the relationship of the distance between locations on the commonality of hashtags adopted in locations. Do we find that distance has no impact on whether a hashtag is shared between two locations? We define the distance between two locations using the Haversine distance, which is commonly used to measure the distance between locations based on the spherical shape of the Earth (as compared to Euclidian distance)[1]. In essence, the Haversine maps from latitude-longitude pairs to distance: $\mathcal{D} : \mathbb{R}^2 \times \mathbb{R}^2 \rightarrow \mathbb{R}$. $H : L \times L \rightarrow \mathbb{R}_{\geq 0}$.

Given two locations, we measure their hashtag "similarity" using the Jaccard coefficient between the sets of hashtags observed at each location:

$$sim_{hashtag}(l_1, l_2) = \frac{M_{l_1} \cap M_{l_2}}{M_{l_1} \cup M_{l_2}}$$

where recall M_l is the the set of unique hashtags observed in l. Locations that have all hashtags in common have a similarity score of 1.0, while those that share no hashtags have a score of 0.0. The relationship between hashtag similarity and distance is plotted in Figure 1(a). We see a strong correlation ($\rho = -0.8$), suggesting that the more distant two locations are, the less alike they are. We also note that, though the similarities are high for most location pairs that are close to each other, there are some location pairs (above the blue line) where this doesn't hold true. Presumably, these outliers are linked by some other factors (language, culture), which we shall explore in the community affinity model shortly.

Hashtag Adoption Lag versus Distance: We additionally can measure the lag between two locations by measuring how close in time did the two locations adopt the same hashtag. Locations that adopt a common hashtag at the same time are more similar (and have a smaller lag) than are two locations that are farther apart in time (with a greater lag). Letting M_l be the set of unique hashtags observed in l and t_l^m be the time of first occurrence of m at l, we can define the hashtag adoption lag of two locations as:

$$lag_{adoption}(l_1, l_2) = \frac{1}{|M_{l_1} \cap M_{l_2}|} \sum_{m \in M_{l_1} \cap M_{l_2}} |t_{l_1}^m - t_{l_2}^m|$$

where the adoption lag measures the mean temporal lag between two locations for hashtags that occur in both the locations. A lower value for this measure indicates that common hashtags appear to reach both the locations around same time. We see in Figure 1(b) a positive correlation ($\rho = 0.86$), suggesting that locations that are close in spatial distance tend also to be close in temporal distance (e.g., they adopt hashtags at approximately the same time). Locations that are more spatially distant tend to adopt hashtags at much greater lags with respect to each other. As in the case of hashtag sharing, we see many location pairs having low lags despite being quite distant from each other, suggesting some other mechanism is at work.

Predictability of Spread: Finally, we measure the predictability of the "spread" of hashtag over a geographic area through its *coverage*. Coverage measures the mean Haversine distance for all occurrences of a hashtag from its geographic midpoint:

$$C(O^m) = \frac{1}{|O^m|} \sum_{o \in O^m} \mathcal{D}(o, G(O^m))$$

where we define the geographic midpoint[2] for a set of occurrences as a function $G : O \rightarrow \mathbb{R}^2_{\geq 0}$, where the first dimension is the

[1] For a fuller treatment, we refer the interested reader to http://en.wikipedia.org/wiki/Haversine_formula

[2] http://www.geomidpoint.com/

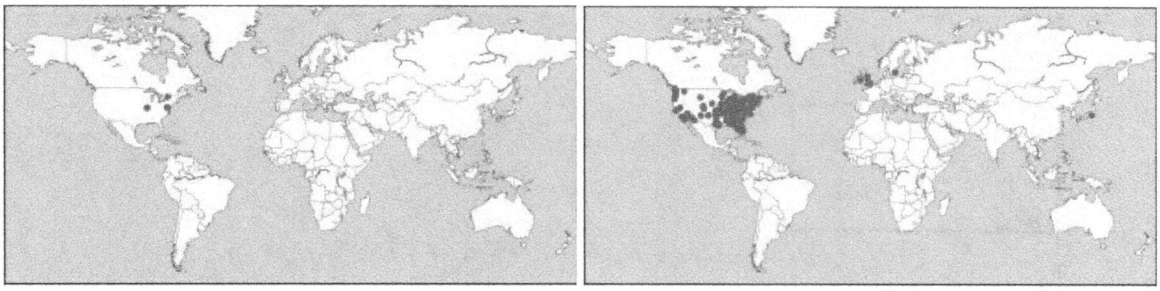

(a) (b)

Figure 2: #cnndebate after 5 minutes (left) and 2 hours (right)

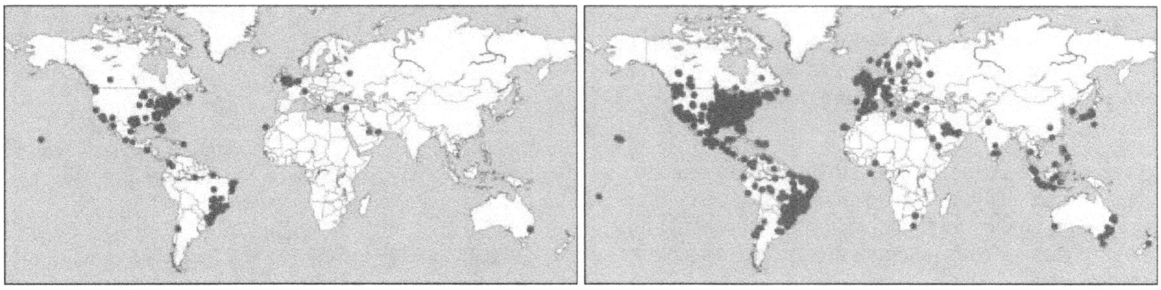

(a) (b)

Figure 3: #ripstevejobs after 5 minutes (left) and 2 hours (right)

latitude and the second is the longitude of the midpoint. The calculation of geographic midpoint is similar to calculating the midpoint on a plane for a set of 2-dimensional points, but as in the case of Haversine distance, the geographic midpoint is calculated by considering the effects of Earth's spherical shape. A hashtag localized to a specific areas has a small coverage, while a universal hashtag has a larger coverage. To illustrate, consider the two hashtags #cnndebate and #ripstevejobs. Figure 2(b) shows the propagation of #cnndebate – corresponding to the Republican Presidential debate – after 2 hours. We see that the hashtag is mostly local to the United States and has a coverage of 743.32 miles. In contrast, Figure 3(b) shows the propagation of #ripstevejobs after 2 hours, resulting in a coverage of 3120.96 miles, indicating a global footprint.

To understand the predictability of spread, we measure the distribution of differences between the coverage for hashtags after they have completely propagated and coverage after the hashtag has propagated for a smaller time interval. For three initial periods – of 5 minutes, 15 minutes, and 30 minutes – we plot the difference between the coverage at this early time of a hashtag's propagation and the coverage after the completion of the hashtag's entire lifespan. We observe in Figure 1(c) that most hashtags have a small coverage difference, indicating that the final coverage of hashtag propagations can be accurately estimated early in its lifecycle. And the predictability of coverage increases as the length of the initial period increases (from 5 to 30 minutes); that is, as more evidence is accumulated over the beginning stages of a hashtag, the final coverage differs by less.

Continuing the example of #cnndebate and #ripstevejobs, we see in Figure 2 and Figure 3 that occurrences observed early in a hashtag's lifecycle (in this case, after just 5 minutes) are good indicators of later occurrences (in this case, measured after 120 minutes).

Based on these three geospatial properties, we observe:

1. In most cases, pairs of locations that are close to each other tend to share common hashtags and adopt them around the same time, compared with locations that are distant.
2. Many distant location pairs, though, exhibit similar patterns of "closeness" in that they share hashtags and have a low hashtag adoption lag, suggesting some additional factor is "bending space" to link the two locations.
3. Finally, the spread predictability analysis suggests that early occurrences of a hashtag are good indicators of the relative coverage of a hashtag's future spread (either compact or widely diffuse).

4. MODELING HASHTAG SPREAD

Based on these observations, we next turn to the challenge of developing models of hashtag spread. Specifically we develop and evaluate the *spatial influence model* – in which nearby locations strongly influence hashtag adoption – and the *community influence model* – in which "similar", though perhaps distant, locations strongly influence hashtag adoption. The intuition behind both approaches is that locations influence each other, and that the future spread of a hashtag is guided by this mutual influence.

4.1 Problem Setting

To formalize the development of such hashtag spread models and to provide an experimental grounding for evaluating the quality of such models, we focus on the problem of selecting future locations that will adopt a hashtag based on the partial evidence of the hashtag's propagation up until that time. We call this the *location subset selection problem.* That is, as a particular social media begins to propagate can we predict the locations where it will soon arrive and become popular? For example, observing a video which is gaining traction in Qatar, can we predict locations in Europe where the video is soon going to become popular? The models developed for tackling this problem are an important and necessary step for

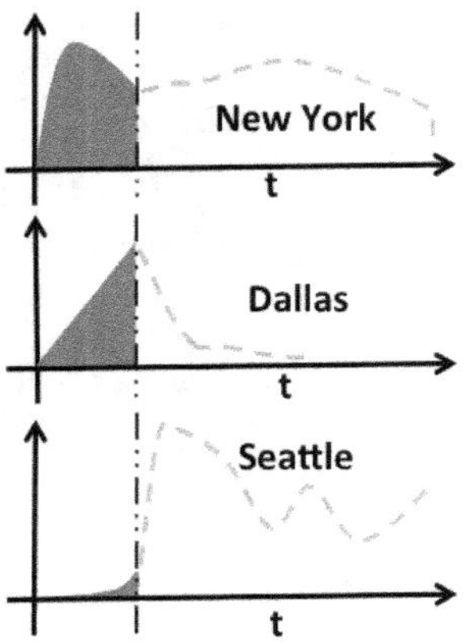

Figure 4: Based on the observed postings of a hashtag up to some time t_s (the vertical dotted line), can we predict which locations will post the most hashtags in the future?

supporting content localization, geo-advertising, fraud detection, and other social media analytics. It is particularly important that such models robustly predict the spread of social media while it is still developing (e.g., a video is going viral, a meme is becoming increasingly popular).

Recall the **total observed occurrences** set O^m across all locations in L ($O^m = \bigcup_{l \in L} O_l^m$) introduced in Section 3.1. In practice, these observed activities will vary by location. Early adopting locations may encompass many postings of a hashtag (or views of a Web video, ...), while later adopting locations will have few or no postings of a hashtag (or views of a video, ...), especially in the early moments of a hashtag's rise to popularity. Based on this state up to some time t_s, can we select some subset of locations $S \in L$ such that these locations are likely to observe many occurrences of the user activity.

For example, consider the three locations – New York, Dallas and Seattle – shown in Figure 4 and suppose a particular hashtag has been posted from each location. Based on the observed hashtag postings up to some time t_s (the vertical dotted line), can we predict which locations will post the most hashtags in the future? Toward this goal, we can express the occurrences of the activity *after the critical time* t_s as the unknown future set of **unobserved occurrences**:

$$U_l^m = \bigcup_{t=t_s+1}^{\infty} o_l^m(t) \tag{2}$$

where U_l^m is the set of occurrences of m observed in location l after time t_s. We can additionally express the **total unobserved occurrences** set U^m across all locations in L as:

$$U^m = \bigcup_{l \in L} U_l^m$$

Together, the total occurrences of an activity throughout its lifetime is $O^m \cup U^m$. Now, suppose for some subset of locations $S \subseteq L$, we measure the count of the total unobserved occurrences of an activity in this subset as U_S^m:

$$U_S^m = \sum_{l \in S} |U_l^m|$$

We can then formulate the task of selecting the best k locations at some critical time t_s as the **location subset selection problem**:

DEFINITION 4.1. ***(Location Subset Selection Problem):*** *Given an integer k, the location subset selection problem for a user activity m at time t_s is the problem of predicting top-k locations which will have the highest number of unobserved occurrences for m.*

$$\mathcal{M}(m, L) = S_{t_s}^m = \underset{\{S \subseteq L \mid |S|=k\}}{\arg\max} \; U_S^m$$

where, $\mathcal{M} : M \times L^{|L|} \rightarrow L^k$, defined as subset selection model, takes a user activity and the set of all locations as input and returns a subset of locations of cardinality k.

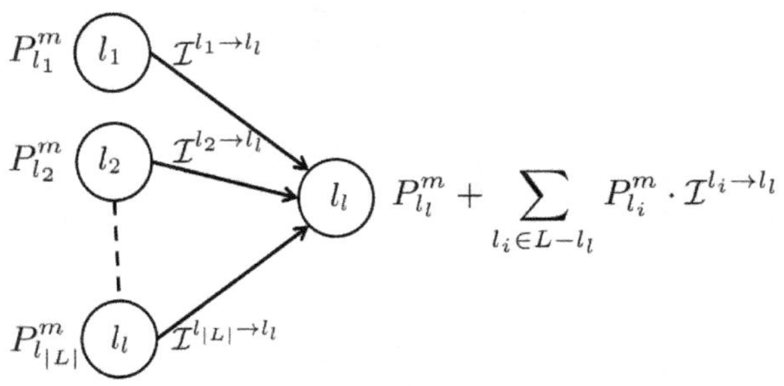

Figure 5: General spatial influence model.

The challenge for identifying the best choice of locations $S_{t_s}^m$ at time t_s is difficult because the future occurrences set for all locations, U^m, is available only after the complete evolution of the activity of interest. Hence, we must predict which locations are the best. Of course, determining the best choice of locations is simpler the longer the decision point is delayed (since many bursting and trending phenomenon will have run their course, saturating its locations), but of less value. The question is whether the best set of locations $S_{t_s}^m$ can be identified for some time t_s close to the activity's first observed occurrence.

4.2 Modeling Spread: Spatial Influence vs. Community Influence

With the problem statement in mind as well as our observations of the geospatial spread of hashtags, we now propose location influence based models for geo-spatial spread. The intuition behind our approach is that locations influence each other. And given a hashtag distribution, the future propagation of this hashtag is guided by this mutual influence between locations. The influence exerted by a location on another could be based either on proximity between locations or on the culture, language, and common interests shared by these locations. We measure this influence using an influence metric $\mathcal{I}^{l_i \rightarrow l_j}$ which has a range of $[0, 1]$ and represents the influence location l_i has on l_j such that the higher the value of this metric, then the greater is the influence exerted by l_i on l_j.

So given a hashtag m, the spread model for an influence metric $\mathcal{I}^{l_i \rightarrow l_j}$ is defined as:

$$\mathcal{M}_{\text{Spread}}(m, L) = \underset{\{S \subseteq L \mid |S|=k\}}{\arg\max} \sum_{l \in S} \left(P_l^m + \sum_{l_i \in L - l} P_{l_i}^m \cdot \mathcal{I}^{l_i \rightarrow l} \right)$$

where, $P_l^m = \frac{|O_{l_i}^m|}{|O^m|}$ is the probability of observing user activity m in l, estimated based on m's propagation until t_s and the expression within the parenthesis calculates the total effective influence exerted at this location to generate m. This concept is shown in Figure 5, where the location l_l gets influenced by all the locations and the effective influence on it is calculated as shown above. The spread model relies on the third observation that early occurrences of a hashtag are good predictors of future coverage. Hence, in this expression we use the probability of observing m in l to modify l's influence while calculating the effective influence. In this way the spread model, $\mathcal{M}_{\text{Spread}}$, selects a subset of the most influenced locations with the belief that this influence will make these locations adopt hashtags in future.

Using the spread model as framework, we now describe two general approaches – the spatial influence model and the community affinity model – that build on the observations made in Section 3.

4.2.1 Spatial Influence Model

The spatial influence model is based on our first observation in Section 3.3 that tells us that distance between locations influences what hashtags are shared and when they are shared. So, we define the spatial influence metric, $\mathcal{I}^{l_j \to l_i}_{\text{Spatial}}$, as:

$$\mathcal{I}^{l_j \to l_i}_{\text{Spatial}} = \frac{\alpha^{-H(l_i, l_j)}}{\sum_{l_i \in L} \alpha^{-H(l_i, l)}}$$

where, the numerator exponentially decays l_i's influence on l as a function of their Haversine distance and the denominator normalizes this influence so that $\sum_{l \in L} \mathcal{I}^{l \to l_i}_{\text{spatial}} = 1.0$. The parameter α controls the rate of influence decay. A higher value for α decreases influence from a point at a higher rate and a lower value for alpha (> 1.0) decreases influence at a lower rate. Using the this influence metric we define the spatial influence model as:

$$\mathcal{M}_{\text{Spatial}}(m, L) = \underset{\{S \subseteq L \mid |S|=k\}}{\arg\max} \sum_{l \in S} \left(P^m_l + \sum_{l_i \in L-l} P^m_{l_i} \cdot \mathcal{I}^{l_i \to l}_{\text{Spatial}} \right) \tag{3}$$

To illustrate, consider an example of a hashtag that occurs only in Houston. Now given an option between Austin and San Francisco, the model as defined in (3) picks Austin since it is much closer to Houston than San Francisco.

A real world example of modeling propagations using the spatial influence model for the hashtag #ripstevejobs is shown in Figure 6. We predicted the future distribution of this hashtag using the spatial influence model based solely on its initial (first 5 minutes) distribution. The comparison between the predicted and actual distribution is shown in Figure 6(a) and Figure 6(b) respectively. We observe that the relative distribution (indicated by color) and its values (indicated by scale) are very close to each other.

4.2.2 Community Affinity Influence Model

Of course, distance is not the only factor that impacts the spread of a hashtag, as we observed in Section 3.3 (second observation). Hence, we now propose the community affinity influence models for capturing non-distance links between locations like culture, language, and common community interest. Concretely, we define two influence metrics to model community affinity based on their common usage of hashtags.

- **Transmitting Influence**: Using temporal proximity, we observe that if a hashtag is observed at a particular location, then it will soon be observed in other related locations as well. To model the degree to which a location can impact other locations temporally, we define the transmitting score, $\mathcal{T}$, as:

$$\mathcal{T}_{l_j \to l_i} = \frac{|\{m \mid t^m_{l_j} > t^m_{l_i} \;\; \forall m \in M_{l_i} \cap M_{l_j}\}|}{|M_{l_i}|}$$

  where, the numerator is the number of hashtags that occurred in l_1 before l_2. So, when all hashtags occurring in l_1 have occurred in l_2 and all before occurring in l_2, the transmitting score for l_1 transmitting a hashtag to l_2 - $P_t(l_2|l_1) = 1.0$. Using this we define the transmitting influence as:

$$\mathcal{I}^{l_j \to l_i}_{\text{Trans.}} = \frac{\mathcal{T}_{l_j \to l_i}}{\sum_{l \in L} \mathcal{T}_{l \to l_i}} \tag{4}$$

  A value for $\mathcal{I}^{l_j \to l_i}_{\text{Trans.}}$ is in the range $[0, 1]$, with 0 indicating l_j doesn't transmit anything to l_i and 1.0 indicating l_j is the only location influencing l_i and it gets all of its hashtags after l_j.

- **Sharing Influence**: Similar to transmitting influence, we use content-related proximity to model the impact a location can have on nearby locations, using the sharing score:

$$\mathcal{S}_{l_j \to l_i} = \frac{|M_{l_i} \cap M_{l_j}|}{|M_{l_i}|}$$

  This function measures the probability that l_i observes the same hashtags as l_j. Using this we define the sharing influence as:

$$\mathcal{I}^{l_j \to l_i}_{\text{Share}} = \frac{\mathcal{S}_{l_j \to l_i}}{\sum_{l \in L} \mathcal{S}_{l \to l_i}} \tag{5}$$

  A value for $\mathcal{I}^{l_j \to l_i}_{\text{Share}}$ is in the range $[0, 1]$, with 0 indicating l_j doesn't share anything with l_i and 1.0 indicating l_j is the only location the influencing l_i and all hashtags that have occurred in l_i have occurred in l_j.

As in the case of the spatial influence model, we can use these two community affinity influence metrics to generate a model as:

$$\mathcal{M}_{\text{Trans.}}(m, L) = \underset{\{S \subseteq L \mid |S|=k\}}{\arg\max} \sum_{l \in S} \left(P^m_l + \sum_{l_i \in L-l} P^m_{l_i} \cdot \mathcal{I}^{l_i \to l}_{\text{Trans.}} \right)$$

which models spread using transmitting influence, and,

$$\mathcal{M}_{\text{Share}}(m, L) = \underset{\{S \subseteq L \mid |S|=k\}}{\arg\max} \sum_{l \in S} \left(P^m_l + \sum_{l_i \in L-l} P^m_{l_i} \cdot \mathcal{I}^{l_i \to l}_{\text{Share}} \right)$$

which models spread using sharing influence.

To give a bit more insight into these two models, we constructed two directed graphs over the hashtag dataset – one graph for transmitting and other for sharing influence – with locations as nodes and the influence scores calculated using these functions as edge weights. In this graph, a cluster represents a collection of nodes (locations) that are close to each other, where closeness is defined either temporally (via transmitting influence) or based on content (via sharing influence). If the functions models location relationships correctly, then nodes that are close to each other in terms of distance should be in the same cluster (observation 1) and, nodes that are culturally similar should be the same cluster (observation 2). The results from this experiments are shown in Figure 7(a) and Figure 7(b), where every cluster is represented with a different color. In both these figures we can verify the two observations. Most locations which are close to each other are in the same cluster and some locations that are culturally similar, like the locations between English speaking parts of Western Europe and United States, and French speaking parts of Brazil and France, are in the same cluster.

4.2.3 Combining the Two Models

We can also combine the spatial and community affinity models by first defining an effective influence score:

$$Score(l) = P^m_l + \sum_{l_i \in L-l} P^m_{l_i} \cdot (\beta \cdot \mathcal{I}^{l_i \to l}_{\text{Spatial}} - (1-\beta) \cdot \mathcal{I}^{l_i \to l}_{\text{Transmit}}) \tag{6}$$

where, β decides the weight assigned to each model and then using to model spread as:

$$\mathcal{M}_{\text{Spatial + Transmit.}}(m, L) = \underset{\{S \subseteq L \mid |S|=k\}}{\arg\max} \sum_{l \in S} Score(l)$$

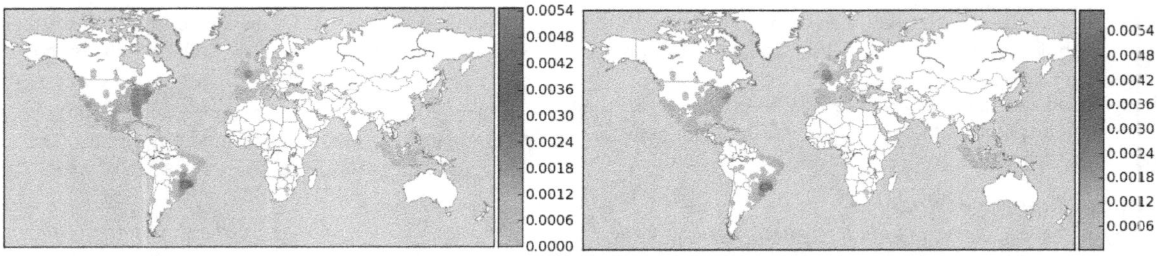

(a) Predicted (estimated using spatial influence model after 5 minutes) (b) Actual (real distribution after 2 hours of propagation)

Figure 6: Example of using spatial influence model for the hashtag #ripstevejobs

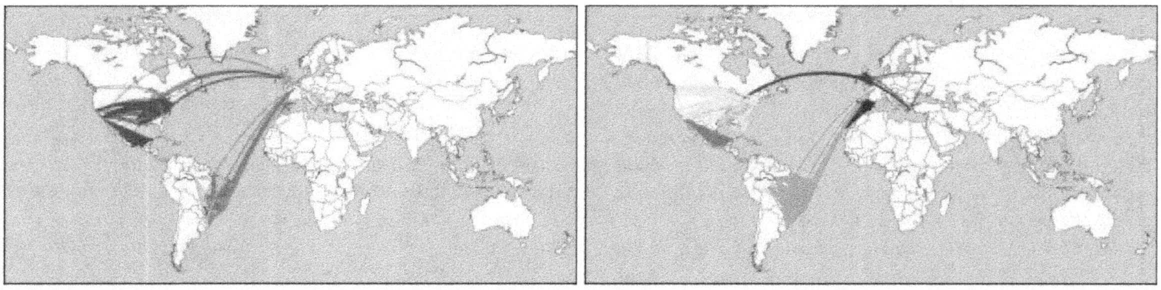

(a) Transmitting Probability (b) Sharing Probability

Figure 7: Clusters of related locations based on the transmitting and sharing probability functions.

We can define a similar model using sharing influence instead of transmitting influence as done above.

5. EXPERIMENTS

In this section, we compare the quality of the proposed location selection approaches against three baseline approaches. We introduce metrics for measuring the quality of a selection approach, investigate the proposed approaches with respect to these quality metrics and identify the best approach to solve the location selection problem.

5.1 Baseline Approaches

In addition to the three geo-spatial approaches introduced in this paper, we also consider three alternatives:

Random Selection: In this simplest approach, we randomly select k locations as the target subset, from the set of locations where the hashtag has occurred prior to t_s. The main drawback of this approach is that locations are selected without regard for the number of hashtags observed. In addition, since the target subset is selected based solely on a hashtag's propagation, the locations outside this set will never be selected. Hence, if the hashtag has occurred in fewer than k locations, then the target subset contains always fewer than k locations.

Greedy Selection: A natural improvement over random selection is a greedy approach, in which locations are selected based on the notion that a hashtag is going to continue to be used in locations where it is currently popular. Concretely, the greedy approach ranks locations based on the observed occurrence count of the hashtag: $|O_l^m|$. The intuition is that a hashtag that is popular in New York at location subset selection time is going to stay popular in the future as well. As in the random selection approach, it is possible that a hashtag might not have propagated to k locations, in which case we pick all the locations resulting in a subset with cardinality lesser than k.

Selection Based on Linear Regression: In this approach, we solve the location subset selection problem using a linear regression model. The idea behind this approach is to learn a model that can predict the unobserved occurrences for a hashtag given occurrences observed until the location subset selection time. Let M be the training hashtag set described in Section 3.2. Using M we first define the matrix X for observed occurrences as shown below:

$$X_i = \begin{pmatrix} 1 & \frac{|O_1^i|}{|O^i|} & \frac{|O_2^i|}{|O^i|} & \cdots & \frac{|O^i_{|L|}|}{|O^i|} \end{pmatrix} \quad \forall i \in [1, |M|]$$

$$X = \left(\frac{|O_j^i|}{|O^i|}\right)_{|M|\times 1+|L|} = \begin{pmatrix} X_1 & X_2 & \cdots & X_{|M|} \end{pmatrix}^T$$

where, each row in this matrix corresponds to a hashtag in the training hashtag set. Similar to X, we define the unobserved matrix Y using unobserved occurrences.

$$Y_j = \begin{pmatrix} \frac{|U_j^1|}{|U^1|} & \frac{|U_j^2|}{|U^2|} & \cdots & \frac{|U_j^{|M|}|}{|U^{|M|}|} \end{pmatrix}^T \quad \forall j \in [1, |M|]$$

$$Y = \left(\frac{|U_j^i|}{|U^i|}\right)_{|M|\times|L|} = \begin{pmatrix} Y_1 & Y_2 & \cdots & Y_{|L|} \end{pmatrix}$$

Using these matrices, we define Y as a linear function of X, $Y = X\beta + \mathcal{E}$, where, β is the $(|L| \times |L|)$ parameters matrix and $\mathcal{E}$ is the $(|L| \times |M|)$ matrix of error terms. Every column, β_l, in β models the relationships of a location l with the rest of locations and can be estimated by linear regression using the equation, $Y_l = X\beta_l + \mathcal{E}_l$, where $\mathcal{E}_l$ is the error column for l, in $\mathcal{E}$. We for a new hashtag m we can determine the top-k locations using:

$$\mathcal{M}_{\text{Lin. Reg.}}(m, L) = \underset{\{S\subseteq L \mid |S|=k\}}{\arg\max} \sum_{l\in S} \left(\hat{\beta_{l0}} + \sum_{i=1}^{|L|} \hat{\beta_{l_i}} \frac{|O_i^m|}{|O^m|}\right)$$

where, the expression in the parenthesis estimates probable occurrence distribution in locations for m.

Approach	Accuracy	Impact	Impact Diff.
Random	0.256	0.343	0.739
Greedy	0.296	0.372	0.76
Lin. Regression	0.328	0.241	0.626
Sharing Infl.	0.266	0.264	0.666
Transmitting Infl.	0.242	0.253	0.654
Spatial Infl.	0.373	0.309	0.685
Transmitting Infl. + Spatial Infl.	0.407	0.393	0.78
Sharing Infl. + Spatial Infl.	**0.421**	**0.403**	**0.789**

Table 1: Comparing the predictive models ($t_s = 5$ minutes, $k = 3$). The approach combining the community influence approach with spatial influence approach (*sharing influence* + *spatial influence*) performs the best.

5.2 Evaluation Metrics

We denote the best possible location subset that can be selected at t_s as $S_{t_s}^{m\star}$ ($S_{t_s}^m$ with a $\star$ on top). To evaluate the performance of the approaches proposed in this paper, we define three metrics:

Accuracy: This metric measures the similarity between the approximate subset, determined using our approaches, and the exact location subset that is determined after the completion of hashtag propagation. This measure is similar to other set comparison metrics like the Jaccard index. It is defined as:

$$Accuracy = \frac{S_{t_s}^{m\star} \cap S_{t_s}^m}{k}$$

where, k is cardinality of $S_{t_s}^m$. If the sets are identical, the accuracy is 1.0, and 0.0 if they are disjoint.

Impact: While accuracy measures the similarity between the sets, it doesn't measure the effect of selecting a particular subset over another. For example, it is possible that two disjoint sets of locations observe same number of occurrences after they are selected, resulting in the same impact. Hence, we also consider the subset **impact**, which measures the percentage of hashtag occurrences that were observed in the approximate location subset. It is defined as:

$$Impact = \frac{U_{S_{t_s}^m}^m}{|O^m \cup U^m|}$$

where, the numerator is the number of occurrences that were observed in $S_{t_s}^m$, after it was selected, and the denominator is the total number of occurrences of the hashtag. The impact value ranges from 0.0 to 1.0, with 0.0 signifying no impact, while 1.0 signifying maximum impact.

Impact Difference: If a hashtag is distributed uniformly across large number of locations, then the best impact for a given k might be small. In this case, the performance of an approach will be measured as low, even if it selects the best set. Hence, we can also measure the subset **impact difference** that measures the difference between the impact for the best subset and the approximate subset. It is defined as:

$$Impact\ Difference = 1 - \frac{U_{S_{t_s}^{m\star}}^m - U_{S_{t_s}^m}^m}{|O^m \cup U^m|}$$

Like the other two metrics, the lower the value of difference the better is the approach. A value of 1.0 signifies the impact is identical while a value of 0.0 indicates the subset has no impact at all.

5.3 Evaluating the Models

We now evaluate the performance of location subset selection approaches using the metrics defined in the previous section. We first evaluate the performance of the approaches for a fixed value of location selection time t_s and subset cardinality k. We then evaluate the performance of these approaches by varying the time used to select location subsets. Similarly, we then evaluate the performance of the approaches for different sizes of location subsets.

Experimental Setup: For our experiments we use two hashtag sets: (i) Training hashtag set, and (ii) Test hashtag set. The hashtag sets are extracted from Twitter hashtag propagations as described in Section 3.2. Techniques that require prior hashtag propagations (linear regression, sharing and transmitting influence) use the training hashtag set to build their models. For the spatial influence model, we set $\alpha = 1.01$.

We use the test hashtag set to evaluate the performance of the approaches. Given a hashtag from the test set, to evaluate an approach-metric pair, we replay the hashtag's propagation. At location subset selection time, we select location subset using this approach and then continue with the remaining propagation of the hashtag. At the end of this hashtag's propagation, we measure performance of the approach using this particular metric. We do this for all hashtags in the test set and calculate the mean score for this metric-approach pair. This experiment is done for a given value of t_s and k. We set $\beta = 0.5$ in (6) giving equal weight to both approaches.

Comparing the Models: We begin by fixing the selection time for each approach as 5 minutes (i.e., $t_s = 5$) and the number of locations to selects as 3 (i.e., $k = 3$). How well do the approaches predict future locations given only evidence of the first 5 minute's of a hashtag's lifetime? We report the results across all approaches for accuracy, impact, and impact difference in Table 1. Recall that accuracy measures the similarity between subsets selected by our approaches and the best subset; impact measures the actual percentage of occurrences observed in the locations; and impact difference measures the percentage difference between the best impact and the impact achieved using one of the approaches.

First, we observe that the approach combining the community influence approach with spatial influence approach (*sharing* + *spatial*) performs the best, with an accuracy of 42%, and impact of 40%, and an impact difference of 79%. Interestingly, we observe that approaches based on the spatial influence model tend to perform much better than approaches that use only historical hashtag propagations (e.g., linear regression). For example, the accuracy of the *spatial influence*, of *transmitting* + *spatial*, and of *sharing* + *spatial* is higher in all cases than all other approaches. We see similar strong results for the combined approaches (*transmitting* + *spatial*, and of *sharing* + *spatial*) as compared to all other approaches. Surprisingly, the community influence-based approaches alone (e.g., *sharing* and *transmitting*) perform the worst, even worse than the random and greedy approaches.

These results are significant because they illustrate the impor-

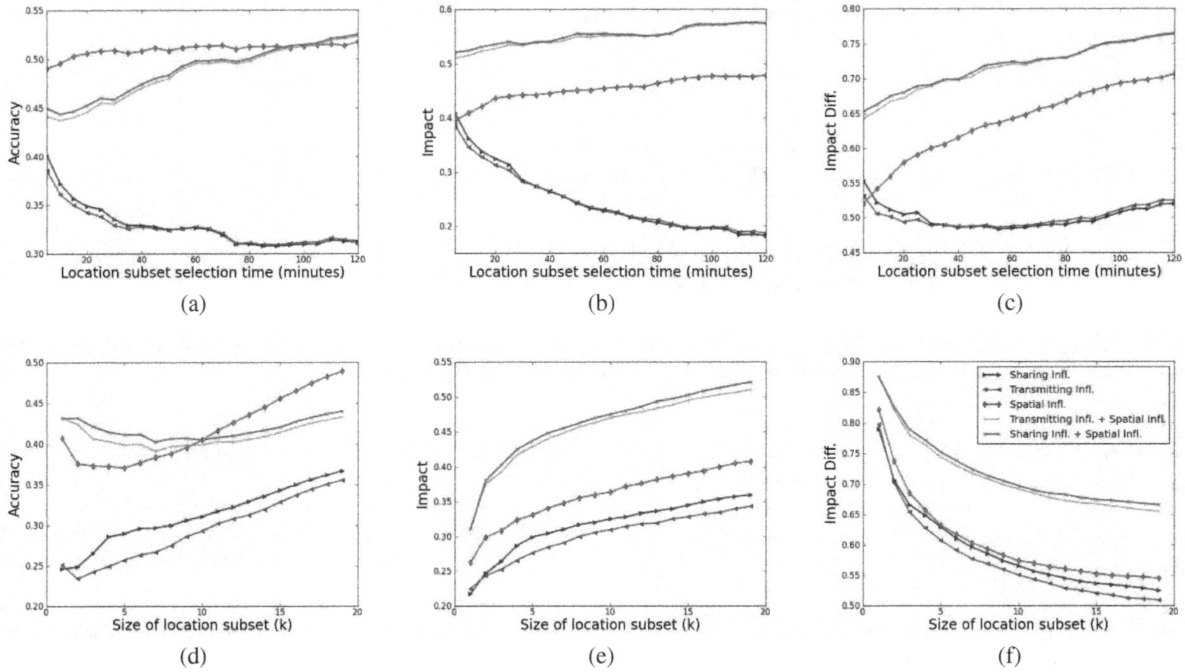

Figure 8: (Color) Varying the selection time (top) and varying the number of locations predicted (bottom).

tance of prioritizing the spatial influence model over the community affinity models, but also the combined power of incorporating community affinity into the spatial influence model for the best overall performance. Selecting future locations that will adopt a hashtags with very little knowledge of how a hashtag is going to propagate is a difficult problem. Based on these results, the performance achieved by the model that combines sharing probability with coverage probability is very encouraging. Most popular hashtags spread for several hours, but this model can identify 40% of all future occurrences of a hashtag within 5 minutes of the hashtag's first appearance. Also, the quality of locations selected by this model is high, as the locations it selected came close to 79% of the best performing locations.

Varying the Selection Time: What if we increase the time until the models have to make a prediction? That is, if we allow the hashtags to propagate for even longer, what impact does this have on the predictive ability of the models as they have access to additional evidence? Hence, we next varied the location subset selection time (t_s) from 5 minutes to 2 hours, keeping the k fixed at 20. We evaluated each approach for each selection time (e.g., after 5 minutes since a hashtag's first appearance, after 10 minutes, and so on up to 120 minutes) as shown in the top row of Figure 8. We plot the affect of varying the selection time against the five approaches, showing accuracy in Figure 8(a), impact in Figure 8(b), and impact difference in Figure 8(c).

We see that across all metrics, the approaches that use both sharing and transmitting influence coupled with spatial influence (the purple and light blue curves) improve with the increase in location selection time. As the time to select locations increases, each approach can observe a longer lifespan of a hashtag's propagation, leading to stronger evidence for making better predictions. In contrast, the community affinity approaches alone (*sharing* and *transmitting*, in blue and green) degrade in quality as the selection time increases (with a slight uptick for impact difference after 80 minutes). These results further confirm the importance of the spatial influence models as the single strongest predictor of hashtag spread.

An interesting result we observe in this figure is the performance of approach that uses spatial influence alone to select locations. We observe that the curve (red-diamonds) corresponding to this approach stays relatively constant irrespective of the value of t_s. This approach selects locations just based on spatial influence and hashtag distribution, hence a constant accuracy indicates that the probability scores for locations remain same irrespective of t_s, i.e., the overall probability distribution for a hashtag calculated after 5 minutes is similar to its probability distribution calculated after 2 hours. This result further strengthens our assessment, in Section 3.3, that early coverage for a hashtag is a good indicator of its final coverage.

Confirming the results from our previous experiment, we find that approaches that use the spatial influence model in concert with a community affinity model perform the best.

Varying the Number of Predictions: Finally, we evaluate the performance of each approach by varying the number of locations each predicts. Hence, we vary the cardinality k from 1 to 20, while fixing the selection time at 5 minutes, as shown in the bottom row of Figure 8. Across all three metrics – accuracy in Figure 8(d), impact in Figure 8(e), impact difference in Figure 8(f) – we again see the strong performance of the spatial influence models, both for the spatial model along (*spatial*) as well as the model incorporating community affinity into the spatial model (*transmitting + spatial* and *sharing + spatial*). As the number of locations increases, we see the accuracy of all approaches increase since each selects more top locations correctly. We also see an improvement in impact for all the approaches, with increasing cardinality. This result is straightforward since increasing the number of locations implies a higher number of occurrences are observed, which in turn increases the impact. But, the magnitude and rate for improvement of impact varies for all the approaches, with all the approaches that use spatial influence model showing greater impact than approaches that use community affinities only. This result is similar to the results observed in Figure 8(b). Finally, we observe that increasing the cardinality results in a decrease in impact difference for all approaches.

5.4 Summary of Results

Based on this experimental study, we find that:

- First, **distance does matter**. As shown in Table 1, we found that the spatial influence model – based on Tobler's first law of geography – is the single most important explanation of future hashtag adoption. Distance matters mostly because hashtags are fundamentally a *local phenomena*. Hashtags typically occur in an originating location and subsequently in nearby neighboring locations.
- Second, we additionally discovered that though the community affinity influence model alone performs worse than the spatial influence mode, **in combination** with the spatial influence model we can achieve the best fit for future hashtag adoption. This combination indicates that community affinities (like culture, language, and common interests) are a secondary factor

6. CONCLUSION

In this paper, we have begun an investigation of the global spread of social media. We have studied the geo-spatial properties of a collection of 755 million geo-tagged tweets and found that (i) pairs of locations tend to share common hashtags and adopt them around the same time, compared with locations that are distant; (ii) many distant location pairs, though, exhibit similar patterns of "closeness" in that they share hashtags and have a low hashtag adoption lag, suggesting some additional factor is "bending space"' to link the two locations; and (iii) the early occurrences of a hashtag are good indicators of the relative coverage of a hashtag's future spread (either compact or widely diffuse). Based on these observations, we developed two complementary models of hashtag spread – the spatial influence model and the community affinity influence models – and studied their effectiveness at predicting locations that will adopt hashtags in the future. We conclude that **distance does matter** as the single most important explanation of future hashtag adoption since hashtags are fundamentally local. We also find that community affinities (like culture, language, and common interests) enhance the quality of purely spatial models, indicating the necessity of adequately incorporating non-spatial features into models of global social media spread.

In our continuing work, we are interested in augmenting the developed models – that consider only the geo-spatial properties of hashtags – with additional evidence of the content of the hashtags (e.g., since politics-related social media may spread differently than sports-related social media) and with the underlying social network. Recall that the study in this paper has been completely orthogonal to the underlying social network and how social contagion affects hashtags spread. As part of this continuing work, we are interested in linking these geospatial diffusion models to these related efforts.

7. ACKNOWLEDGMENTS

This work was supported in part by NSF grant IIS-1149383, DARPA grant N66001-10-1-4044 and a Google Research Award. Any opinions, findings and conclusions or recommendations expressed in this material are the author(s) and do not necessarily reflect those of the sponsors.

8. REFERENCES

[1] L. Backstrom, J. Kleinberg, R. Kumar, and J. Novak. Spatial variation in search engine queries. WWW '08.

[2] L. Backstrom, E. Sun, and C. Marlow. Find me if you can: improving geographical prediction with social and spatial proximity. WWW '10.

[3] C. Bauckhage. Insights into internet memes. ICWSM' 11.

[4] A. Brodersen, S. Scellato, and M. Wattenhofer. Youtube around the world: geographic popularity of videos. WWW '12.

[5] F. Cairncross. *The death of distance: How the communications revolution is changing our lives*. Harvard Business School Press, Boston, 2001.

[6] Z. Cheng, J. Caverlee, and K. Lee. You are where you tweet: a content-based approach to geo-locating twitter users. CIKM '10.

[7] E. Cunha, G. Magno, G. Comarela, V. Almeida, M. A. Gonçalves, and F. Benevenuto. Analyzing the dynamic evolution of hashtags on twitter: a language-based approach. LSM '11.

[8] N. Dalvi, R. Kumar, and B. Pang. Object matching in tweets with spatial models. WSDM '12.

[9] D. Davidov, O. Tsur, and A. Rappoport. Enhanced sentiment learning using twitter hashtags and smileys. COLING '10.

[10] J. Ding, L. Gravano, and N. Shivakumar. Computing geographical scopes of web resources. VLDB '00.

[11] M. Gomez Rodriguez, J. Leskovec, and A. Krause. Inferring networks of diffusion and influence. In *Proceedings of the 16th ACM SIGKDD international conference on Knowledge discovery and data mining*, KDD '10.

[12] B. A. Huberman, D. M. Romero, and F. Wu. Social Networks that Matter: Twitter Under the Microscope. *Social Science Research Network Working Paper Series*, Dec. 2008.

[13] D. Kempe, J. Kleinberg, and E. Tardos. Maximizing the spread of influence through a social network. KDD '03.

[14] D. Kempe, J. Kleinberg, and É. Tardos. Influential nodes in a diffusion model for social networks. In *IN ICALP*, 2005.

[15] G. Kossinets, J. Kleinberg, and D. Watts. The structure of information pathways in a social communication network. KDD '08.

[16] H. Kwak, C. Lee, H. Park, and S. Moon. What is twitter, a social network or a news media? WWW '10.

[17] K. Lerman and R. Ghosh. Information contagion: an empirical study of the spread of news on digg and twitter social networks. *CoRR*, 2010.

[18] J. Leskovec, L. Backstrom, and J. Kleinberg. Meme-tracking and the dynamics of the news cycle. KDD '09.

[19] J. Lin, R. Snow, and W. Morgan. Smoothing techniques for adaptive online language models: topic tracking in tweet streams. KDD '11.

[20] A. Noulas, S. Scellato, C. Mascolo, and M. Pontil. An empirical study of geographic user activity patterns in foursquare. ICWSM' 11.

[21] A. Oreskovic. Huffington post: Youtube video views hit 4 billion per day, Jan. 2012.

[22] D. M. Romero, B. Meeder, and J. Kleinberg. Differences in the mechanics of information diffusion across topics: idioms, political hashtags, and complex contagion on twitter. WWW '11.

[23] S. Scellato, A. Noulas, R. Lambiotte, and C. Mascolo. Socio-spatial properties of online location-based social networks. ICWSM' 11.

[24] W. Tobler. A computer movie simulating urban growth in the detroit region. *Economic Geography*, 46(2), 1970.

[25] O. Tsur and A. Rappoport. What's in a hashtag?: content based prediction of the spread of ideas in microblogging communities. WSDM '12.

[26] J. Yang and J. Leskovec. Modeling information diffusion in implicit networks. ICDM' 2010.

TUT: A Statistical Model for Detecting Trends, Topics and User Interests in Social Media

Xuning Tang
College of Information Science and Technology
Drexel University
Philadelphia, PA, USA
xt24@drexel.edu

Christopher C. Yang
College of Information Science and Technology
Drexel University
Philadelphia, PA, USA
chris.yang@drexel.edu

ABSTRACT

The rapid development of online social media sites is accompanied by the generation of tremendous web contents. Web users are shifting from data consumers to data producers. As a result, topic detection and tracking without taking users' interests into account is not enough. This paper presents a statistical model that can detect interpretable trends and topics from document streams, where each trend (short for trending story) corresponds to a series of continuing events or a storyline. A topic is represented by a cluster of words frequently co-occurred. A trend can contain multiple topics and a topic can be shared by different trends. In addition, by leveraging a Recurrent Chinese Restaurant Process (RCRP), the number of trends in our model can be determined automatically without human intervention, so that our model can better generalize to unseen data. Furthermore, our proposed model incorporates user interest to fully simulate the generation process of web contents, which offers the opportunity for personalized recommendation in online social media. Experiments on three different datasets indicated that our proposed model can capture meaningful topics and trends, monitor rise and fall of detected trends, outperform baseline approach in terms of perplexity on held-out dataset, and improve the result of user participation prediction by leveraging users' interests to different trends.

Categories and Subject Descriptors

H.2.8 [**Database Management**]: Database Applications – Data Mining

General Terms

Algorithms, Experimentation

Keywords

Topic, Trend, User Interest, Evolution, Modeling.

1. INTRODUCTION

Different from the age of Web 1.0, nowadays web contents are mainly generated by web users. To catch the pulse of a rapidly changing world, it is critical to model the evolution of topics and users' interests over time in a streaming fashion. Therefore, given a document corpus, the goal of this work is proposing a model to discover trending stories and their representative vocabularies, to detect topics and their evolutions, to classify each individual document to a trending story, and to understand web users' interests toward the identified trending stories. This will bring great opportunities for news/blog recommendation, personalized search, and marketing.

From a statistical point of view, a topic is a cluster of words frequently co-occurred. For instance, news articles about "European sovereign debt crisis" might contain topics such as finance, trading, election and foreign relationship. Similarly, news articles about "Withdrawal of U.S. military force" might involve topics such as election, foreign relationship, military and homeland security. In this paper, we consider "European sovereign debt crisis" and "Withdrawal of U.S. military force" in the examples above as two **trending stories** (**trend for short**). Different trending stories can share one or more topics. Specifically, a trend can be a series of continuous events or a storyline, which can rise or fall over time. In addition, as it was evidenced in many online social media sites, users' interests play an important role to the generation of web contents. Users interested in a specific trend have more motivation to contribute their opinions, observations or thoughts to online social media sites. Therefore, we consider user interests in this paper as their interests toward trends instead of topics. To illustrate trend, topic and user interest, figure 1 below shows three different trends (trend I, trend II and trend III). For each trend, we plot its volume (y-axis) over 4 consecutive time intervals (x-axis). Each trend may contain different topics indicated by different colors. A topic can be shared by different trends. In addition, in different time interval, the portion of a given topic inside a trend can be different too. Last but not least, for each trend, users are ranked according to their interests to this trend within each time interval.

Most of the existing works regarding topic detection and tracking employed either generative approaches or clustering-based techniques. These methods retrieved topics as bags of words and captured the potential relationships between topics according to their word-based similarities, e.g. using KL-Divergence to quantify topic similarities when each topic was represented by a distribution of words [9, 11]. However, the topic evolution result obtained by these approaches is hard to interpret, as each ongoing trend might contain multiple topics and each topic can be shared by many different trends. For instance, 2012 NCAA tournament and 2012 UEFA Champions League are two completely different trends, although the news articles about NCAA tournament and the news articles about UEFA Champions League share several common topics such as Sports, Commercial Promotion and Security. By merely knowing the rise or fall of a specific topic, for example security topic, without knowing which trend the topic belongs to, readers will find it difficult to capture the major trending stories. Some most recent works tried to address this

CIKM'12, October 29– November 2, 2012, Maui, HI, USA.

problem by introducing the concept of "trend"[9] (or "story" [1]). Generally speaking, Kawamae introduced a trend class variable into his Trend Analysis Model (TAM), where each document belongs to a trend and each trend has a probability distribution over topics and words. Unfortunately, the number of trends in TAM is fixed over time and needs to be predefined, which might be difficult in real-world application. Furthermore, to our best knowledge, none of the existing topic detection and tracking works has incorporated dynamic user interests into their models. Different from the previous works which extracted topics from news articles or scientific literatures, our focus is to detect dynamic trends and topics from user-generated contents in online social media. As a result, user interests must be taken into consideration. In addition, incorporating user interests into topic model might help the model to better generalize to unseen data.

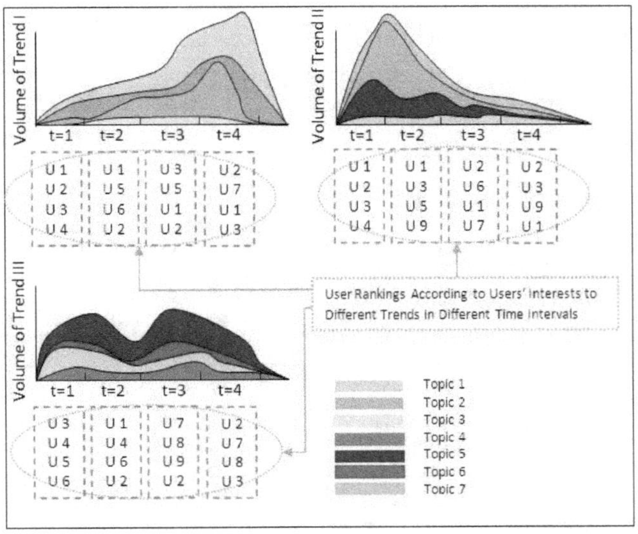

Figure 1. Illustration Example of Concepts about Trend, Topic and User Interest

In this paper, we propose a new probabilistic generative model to simulate the generation process of both web contents and users' participations in a unified framework. In our model, we use a latent variable to represent the trend label of each document which has benefits including: a) a document corpus can be well organized and navigated easily as documents within a corpus are classified according to their trend label; b) a detected trend can roughly represent a storyline or a series of continuous events which increases its interpretability; c) the word distribution of a given trend shows the signature terms of this trend which, to some extent, can be used to label a trend; d) each word can be generated by a background topic, a trend-specific background topic or one of the general topics shared by the whole corpus. In addition, our proposed model can determine the appropriate number of trends automatically in a document corpus by incorporating a RCRP. Last but not least, compared to existing works, another distinct feature of our model is that users' participations are modeled simultaneously during the generation process. It provides the opportunities of offering applications such as news recommendation, personalized search etc.

In the next section, we review some existing works about topic detection and tracking. We pay particular attention to two models, RCRP and TAM, which motivate our model and serve as baseline in the experiment section.

2. LITERATURE REVIEW

In the past decade, topic modeling has attracted many research efforts from both academia and industry. A topic consists of a cluster of words frequently co-occurred. Given a corpus, a topic model can distinguish words with different semantic meanings and extract hidden topics. Hofmann [8] proposed the PLSI model given the assumption that each document contains different topics and each word is generated by one of these topics. Blei et al. [4] proposed the LDA model which used a Dirichlet prior to solve the over-fitting problem which makes the model more flexible. As further extensions, Rosen-Zvi et al. proposed the author-topic model [13], and McCallum et al. proposed the author-recipient-topic-model [10]. Recently, Liu et al. [18] developed a Bayesian hierarchical approach to perform topic modeling and author community discovery in a unified framework. However, all these works only investigated static topics or users without considering their evolutions.

Beyond static topic modeling, other researchers of Topic Detection and Tracking (TDT) extend topic modeling to take into account of their evolutions. Some researchers studied TDT problem by using generative models. In Mei and Zhai's work [11], text streams were partitioned into intervals. They employed a probabilistic mixture model to infer topics within each interval and discovered their evolutionary transitions using KL-divergence. Wang and McCallum [17] proposed a Topic-Over-Time model (TOT) to generate topics. Each generated topic was associated with a continuous distribution over time. AlSumait et al presented an online version LDA model which automatically captures the thematic patterns and identifies emerging topics of text stream[3]. Similarly, Blei and Lafferty [5] designed a Dynamic Topic Model (DTM) by using Gaussian time series and logistic normal topic proportion models. Qi et al proposed to make use of citations to extract evolutionary relationships between topics [6]. However, none of these TDT models takes user information into consideration which is critical for modeling user-generated contents in online communities. Lin et al. [7] proposed to model topic evolution along with the burstiness of user interest. However, they modeled topics using a PLSI-like approach which suffered from the over-fitting problem.

Other than using generative models, some other research works rely on clustering approach to detect evolving topics. Each cluster corresponds to a set of documents with a focused theme. Morinaga and Yamanishi [12] treated documents as an incoming stream and then used a finite mixture model to cluster documents by maximizing their posterior probability. They also applied the theory of dynamic model selection to detect emerging topics indicated by changes of the mixture model. Schult and Spiliopoulou [14] proposed to use clustering approach to identify emerging and persistent taxonomy or ontology for documents. Shahaf et al introduced a novel method and a set of measurements to construct an information map, namely as metro map, to capture the connections of articles and provide structured summaries of information[15]. Recently, Ahmed and Xing extended the Chinese Restaurant Process to Recurrent Chinese Restaurant Process which can be used for evolutionary clustering for document corpus [2]. Concretely, the RCRP is formally defined as:

$$\theta_{t,i} | \{\theta_{t-1,.}\}, \theta_{t,1:i-1}, \alpha, G_0 \sim \frac{1}{N^{(t-1)} + i - 1 + \alpha} \times \left[\sum_{k \in I_{t-1}} \left(n_{k,t-1} + n_{k,t}^{(i)}\right) \delta(\phi_{k,t}) + \sum_{k \in I_t^{(i)} - I_{t-1}} \left(n_{k,t}^{(i)}\right) \delta(\phi_{k,t}) + \alpha G_0 \right]$$

where $\theta_{t,i}$ is a parameter of a likelihood function $F(\theta_{t,i})$ which generates an observation i at time t, $o_{t,i}$. The equation above can be illustrated by a RCRP metaphor. Assuming that customers entered a restaurant in a given day are not allowed to stay beyond this day, at the end of day $t-1$, the owner of the restaurant records on each table the dish served on this table and the number of customers who shared it. When the ith customer $c_i^{(t)}$ enters this restaurant at day t, he can pick a non-empty table k that already has $n_{k,t}^{(i)}$ customers at day t before $c_i^{(t)}$ comes in with probability $\frac{n_{k,t-1}+n_{k,t}^{(i)}}{N^{(t-1)}+i-1+\alpha}$ and use the dish $\phi_{k,t}$. If this table did not exist at day $t-1$, $n_{k,t-1}$ equals to 0. Otherwise, $n_{k,t-1}$ equals to the number of customers who sit on this table at day $t-1$. Alternatively, he can pick an empty table that nobody is sitting on at day t but $n_{k,t-1}$ customers sit on at day $t-1$ with probability $\frac{n_{k,t-1}+n_{i,k}^{(t)}}{N^{(t-1)}+i-1+\alpha}$ and then order a dish $\phi_{k,t}$, where $n_{i,k}^{(t)}$ equals to 0 in this case. Finally, he can pick an empty new table with probability $\frac{\alpha}{N^{(t-1)}+i-1+\alpha}$ and order a new dish based on G_0. We emphasis the RCRP here since it is used as an important component in our proposed model later.

Recently, Ahmed et al. proposed a new model, namely Storyline, which extended the traditional LDA model by incorporating the RCRP [1]. Storyline model combines the power of evolutionary clustering and topic modeling. Therefore it can simultaneously group articles into storylines and identify prevalent topics. The Storyline model has distinctive differences to our proposed model in several aspects: 1) Our model captures user interests toward detected trends while Storyline completely neglect user information; 2) Compared to Storyline, our model uses a switch variable to control topic selection; 3) The generation process of topics in Storyline model and our proposed model are also substantially different. Last but not least, Kawamae proposed a Trend Analysis Model (TAM) which extends the TOT model and introduces a latten trend class variable into each document [9]. As shown in Figure 2, in TAM, each document is assigned to a trend, c, according to a multinomial distribution ψ. Given a trend class c, for each token w_i in this document, a topic is chosen based on a multinomial distribution θ_c. At the same time, a switch variable r_i is sampled. According to the value of r_i, token w_i can be generated based on either a background topic, a trend-related background topic or one of Z topics. By introducing the concept "trend" into the model, some words can be generated directly from the trend class rather than from topics, which helps to model the generation process of the corpus more precisely. Further, relationships between trend and topic are also modeled. However, TAM model has a few limitations as follows: 1) the number of trend is difficult to predefine for practical problems, 2) the model is unsuitable for processing document stream and 3) valuable user information in online social media is completely neglected.

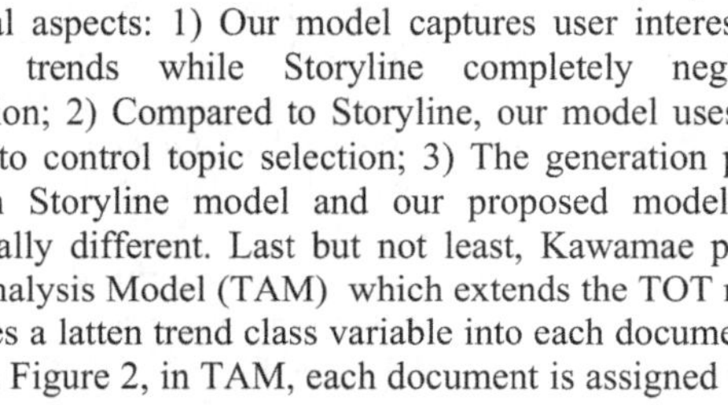

Figure 2. Trend Analysis Model

3. Topic-User-Trend Model (TUT)

In this section, we introduce our Topic-User-Trend model (TUT) to detect evolving topics and trends, and discover users' interests. This model depicts the generation process of web contents and user participations in a unified framework. By estimating this model, we can identify the major trends discussed by users in online social media, learn the topical structure of web contents, and understand users' interests to the detected trends.

Table 1. Notations

E^t, e_d^t	Trend labels of all documents in time interval t, the trend label of document d of time interval t
P, P_u	All users , the user u
Z, z_{d_i}	All topics , the topic of the ith word in document d
W, w_{d_i}	All words , the ith word in document d
X, x_{d_i}	All switch variables , the switch variable of the ith word in document d
α	α is a concentration parameter
$\gamma, \eta, \beta, \iota, \epsilon$	parameters of Dirichlet priors
ϕ_z	the multinomial distribution of words specific to topic z
Ω_e	the multinomial distribution of users specific to trend e
θ_e	the multinomial distribution of topics specific to trend e
φ_e	the multinomial distribution of words specific to trend e
μ_d	the multinomial distribution of switch variables specific to document d
$N^{(t)}$	total number of documents in time interval t
$n_i^{(t)}, n_{-d,i}^{(t)}$	number of documents assigned to trend i in time interval t, number of documents assigned to trend i in time interval t except for document d
$K_{d,x=0,1,2}$	number of word tokens assigned to switch x = 0/1/2 in document d
$M_{z,w}$	number of times that word w is assigned to topic z
$N_{e,w}$	number of times that word w is assigned to trend e
$L_{e,z}$	number of times that topic z is assigned to trend e
$C_{e,u}$	number of times that user u is assigned to trend e

3.1 Formulation of Topic-User-Trend Model

Topic-User-Trend model (TUT) is designed based on a real generation process of content terms and users. In online social media, we consider each document (e.g. a thread, a post, or a chain of retweet) as a collaborative contribution by its participants. In addition, it's the trend itself, rather than the topics, that encourages the participation of users. For instance, although threads of NCAA tournament and threads of UEFA Champions League share common topics such as Sports, Commercial Promotion and Security, college basketball fans may participate more in the threads related to 2012 NCAA basketball tournament rather than the threads related to 2012 UEFA Champions League.

In this work, we divide a time axis into several non-overlapping time intervals. Within each time interval, when a new document arrives, we first model the generation process of its trend label by a RCRP. Once the trend label of this new document is determined, users' interests play an important role to decide whom this new document will attract. In addition, depending on the trend label of this document, we model the generation process of its content terms by a variation of LDA model. Specifically, we assume that the generation of each content term is influenced by one of the three factors: 1) a general background topic, 2) a trend-specific background topic (e.g. 2012 NCAA basketball tournament or 2008 U.S. Presidential Election). and 3) topics shared by the whole corpus (e.g. economy topic, sport topic or military topic). Terms that are topic-unrelated but widely exist in the corpus have a higher chance coming from the general background topic. In addition, each trend may contain some signature terms serving as the trend-specific background terms. At last, similar to LDA model, the entire corpus shares a mixture of |Z| different topics. We adopt a switch variable to control the influence of these three factors in content term generation. It's important to note that the number of topics, |Z|, is predefined and fixed while the number of trends is theoretically countable infinity in our model. Different trends can share common topics. Our proposed model is shown in Figure 3. The meanings of notations in Fig. 3 are listed in Table 1.

As shown in Fig. 3(a), TUT model is a time-dependent model. Each component represents the generation process of documents in a time interval. Fig. 3(b) shows the detail of the TUT model in the tth time interval. Within time interval t, the trend label e_d^t of document d is sampled by a RCRP. If e_d^t is a new trend, a new distribution over users ($\Omega_{e_d^t}$), a new distribution over topics ($\theta_{e_d^t}$) and a new distribution over words ($\varphi_{e_d^t}$) are drawn for this new trend. Otherwise, the existing $\Omega_{e_d^t}$, $\theta_{e_d^t}$ and $\varphi_{e_d^t}$ will be used. Let $|U_d|$ equal to the number of users participated in document d, the user list of d is generated by repeating the sampling process $|U_d|$ times based on a trend-user distribution $\Omega_{e_d^t}$. Each word w_{d_i} is drawn either from the general background topic or the trend-specific background topic or one of |Z| topics shared by the whole corpus. As mentioned, a switch variable x_{d_i} is drawn first from a multinomial distribution for word w_{d_i} to control its generation process. If $x_{d_i} = 0$, w_{d_i} is drawn from the general background topic. If $x_{d_i} = 1$, w_{d_i} is drawn from the trend-specific background topic, $\varphi_{e_d^t}$, which consists of the signature terms of trend e_d^t. If $x_{d_i} = 2$, a topic z_{d_i} is first sampled from the trend-topic distribution $\theta_{e_d^t}$, and then the word w_{d_i} is drawn according to the topic. Overall, the generation process of users and words in the TUT model can be described as follows:

For each time interval t from 1 to T:

1. Draw 1+|Z| multinomial distributions ϕ_z from prior γ, one for each topic (a general background topic and Z topics)
2. Draw |D| multinomial distribution μ_d from prior ϵ, one for each document
3. Draw |E| multinomial distributions Ω_e, θ_e and φ_e from prior η, β and ι respectively, one for each existing trend

For each document d of time interval t:

A. Draw a trend label e_d^t from RCRP
B. If e_d^t is a new trend, Draw multinomial distributions Ω_e, θ_e and φ_e from prior η, β and ι respectively for this new trend
C. Draw $|U_d|$ users from multinomial distribution $\Omega_{e_d^t}$

For each word token w_{d_i} in document d:

Draw switch variable x_{d_i} from multinomial μ_d
if $x_{d_i} = 0$
i. Draw word w_{d_i} from multinomial ϕ_{bg}
else if $x_{d_i} = 1$
i. Draw word w_{d_i} from multinomial $\varphi_{e_d^t}$
else if $x_{d_i} = 2$
i. Draw topic z_{d_i} from multinomial $\theta_{e_d^t}$
ii. Draw word w_{d_i} from multinomial $\phi_{z_{d_i}}$

3.2 Inference and Learning

Several methods have been developed to estimate the latent variables in a probabilistic graphical model. Among them, Gibbs sampling often yields relatively simple algorithm for high-dimensional data model. In the Gibbs sampling schema, Markov chain is constructed for simulating the generation processes of terms and users. The transition between successive states in the Markov chain is achieved by repeatedly sampling topic and trend for each observed term and user based on its conditional probability. We first provide the joint distribution and then derive conditional probabilities for trend label and topics respectively in section 3.2.1 and 3.2.2.

For simplicity, we use Δ_t to denote all hidden variables of the tth time interval and O_t to denote all observations of the tth time interval including words and users. Instead of finding a global optimization of $\{\Delta_t\}_{t=1}^{T}$, given the whole observation sequence $\{O_1, O_2, \ldots, O_T\}$, our goal is to find greedy optimization configuration as did in [16]. Specifically, we assume that we only observe O_{t-1} and O_t. We want to maximize the posterior

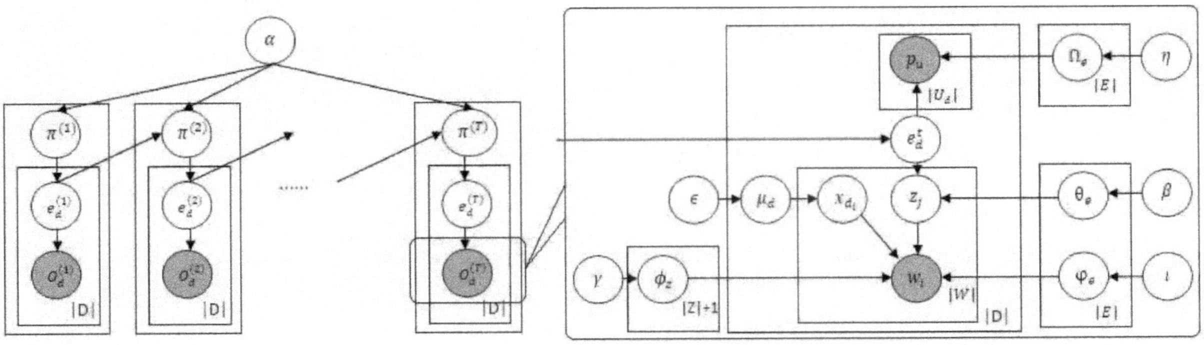

(a) (b)

Figure 3. Graphical Model of Topic-User-Trend Model

probability $\Pr(\Delta_t|\Delta^*_{t-1}, O_{t-1}, O_t)$, where Δ^*_{t-1} represents the optimal hidden variables estimated for time interval t-1. The justification is that, instead of observing the whole observation sequence $\{O_1, O_2, \ldots, O_T\}$ at the same time, it is more practical to assume that the data comes in a stream fashion and we update the model sequentially.

In the inference process, we need to first calculate the conditional distributions. As shown in the previous subsection, the joint distribution of the documents of time t is computed as:

$$\Pr(E^t, P, Z, W, X|E^{t-1}, \alpha, \gamma, \eta, \beta, \iota, \epsilon)$$
$$= \int\int\int\int\int \Pr(E^t, P, Z, W, X, \phi, \Omega, \theta, \varphi, \mu|E^{t-1}, \alpha, \gamma, \eta, \beta, \iota, \epsilon) d\mathcal{H}$$
$$= \int\int\int\int\int \prod_d^D [\Pr(e_d^t|E^{t-1}, E_{-d}^t, \alpha) \prod_u^{U_d} \Pr\left(P_u\middle|\Omega_{e_d^t}\right)$$
$$\times \prod_i^{N_d} (\Pr(x_{d_i}|\mu_d) \Pr(z_{d_i}|\theta_{e_d^t}) \Pr(w_{d_i}|x_{d_i}, \phi_{z_{d_i}}, \varphi_{e_d^t}))]$$
$$\times \prod_d^D \Pr(\mu_d|\epsilon) \prod_z^Z \Pr(\phi_z|\gamma) \prod_e^{E^t} (\Pr(\Omega_e|\eta) \Pr(\theta_e|\beta) \Pr(\varphi_e|\iota))\, d\mathcal{H}$$

where $d\mathcal{H} = d\phi d\Omega d\theta d\varphi d\mu$. In the joint distribution above, multinomials $(\phi, \Omega, \theta, \varphi, \mu)$ can be adapted by the conjugate priors $(\gamma, \eta, \beta, \iota\, \epsilon)$ and then integrated out eventually. The conjugate priors can be predefined in this work. Therefore, we only need to estimate e_d^t, z_{di} and x_{di}. The sampling scheme consists of two steps. The first step is to sample the trend label, e_d^t, for a document d of time period d, $\Pr(e_d^t = e| \ldots)$. The second step is to sample the switch variable and the topic for each individual word in a document: $\Pr(x_{-di} = 0| \ldots), \Pr(x_{-di} = 1|e_d^t = i \ldots), \Pr(z_{-di} = k, x_{-di} = 2| \ldots)$. Details of the derivation of Gibbs sampling for TUT is given below.

3.2.1 *Trend Label Sampling*

For each document, we use the chain rule to obtain the conditional distribution to sample its trend label e_d^t. The sampling equation is defined as:

$$\Pr(e_d^t = e| \ldots)$$
$$\propto \left[\frac{\prod_u^U \Gamma(C_{e,u} + \eta_u)}{\prod_u^U \Gamma(C_{e,u\backslash d} + \eta_u)} \cdot \frac{\Gamma(\sum_u^U (C_{e,u\backslash d} + \eta_u))}{\Gamma(\sum_u^U (C_{e,u} + \eta_u))}\right] \times \left[\frac{\prod_z^Z \Gamma(L_{e,z} + \beta_z)}{\prod_z^Z \Gamma(L_{e,z\backslash d} + \beta_z)} \cdot \frac{\Gamma(\sum_z^Z (L_{e,z\backslash d} + \beta_z))}{\Gamma(\sum_z^Z (L_{e,z} + \beta_z))}\right] \times \left[\frac{\prod_w^W \Gamma(N_{e,w} + \iota_w)}{\prod_w^W \Gamma(N_{e,w\backslash d} + \iota_w)} \cdot \frac{\Gamma(\sum_w^W (N_{e,w\backslash d} + \iota_w))}{\Gamma(\sum_w^W (N_{e,w} + \iota_w))}\right]$$
$$\times \begin{cases} \dfrac{\alpha}{N^{(1)} - 1 + \alpha} & \textit{new event when time } t = 1 \\ \dfrac{n_{-d,e}^{(1)}}{N^{(1)} - 1 + \alpha} & \textit{existing event when time } t = 1 \\ \dfrac{\alpha}{N^{(t)} + N^{(t-1)} - 1 + \alpha} & \textit{new event when time } t > 1 \\ \dfrac{n_{-d,e}^{(t)} + n_e^{(t-1)}}{N^{(t)} + N^{(t-1)} - 1 + \alpha} & \textit{existing event when time } t > 1 \end{cases}$$

where $C_{e,u\backslash d}$ represents the number of times that user u is assigned to trend e, except in document d. Similarly, $L_{e,z\backslash d}$ represents the number of times that topic z is assigned to trend e, except in document d; $N_{e,w\backslash d}$ represents the number of times that word w is assigned to trend e, except in document d. The terms within the first square bracket measure the posterior probability of observing users in document d given the trend label $e_d^t = e$. Similarly, the term in the second and third square bracket measures the posterior probability of observing topics and trend-specific background words respectively given $e_d^t = e$. The terms behind the curly bracket denote the probability of assigning document d to trend e by following the RCRP [2]. When time t = 1 which means historical trend information is unavailable, the top half of the term is used ($\frac{\alpha}{N^{(1)}-1+\alpha}$ chance belonging to a new trend and $\frac{n_{-d,e}^{(1)}}{N^{(1)}-1+\alpha}$ chance belonging to an existing trend e) When time t > 1, the second half of the term is used ($\frac{\alpha}{N^{(t)}+N^{(t-1)}-1+\alpha}$ chance belonging to a new trend and $\frac{n_{-d,e}^{(t)}+n_e^{(t-1)}}{N^{(t)}+N^{(t-1)}-1+\alpha}$ chance belonging to an existing trend e)

3.2.2 *Switch Variable and Topic Sampling*

By using the chain rule again, for each word token, the posterior probability of adding word w_{d_i} in document d to background topic is derived as:

$$\Pr(x_{-di} = 0| \ldots)$$
$$\propto \frac{K_{d,0} + \epsilon_0 - 1}{\sum_x^X (K_{d,x} + \epsilon_x) - 1} \cdot \frac{M_{z=bg,w} + \gamma_w - 1}{\sum_w^W (M_{z,w} + \gamma_w) - 1}$$

where the first term measures the probability of having the switch variable equals to 0, and the second term measures the probability of generating w_{d_i} from the background topic.

Similarly, the posterior probability of adding word w_{d_i} in document d to trend i is derived as:

$$\Pr(x_{-di} = 1|e_d^t = i \ldots)$$
$$\propto \frac{K_{d,1} + \epsilon_1 - 1}{\sum_x^X (K_{d,x} + \epsilon_x) - 1} \cdot \frac{N_{e=i,w} + \iota_w - 1}{\sum_w^W (N_{e,w} + \iota_w) - 1}$$

where the first term measures the probability of having the switch variable equals to 1, and the second term measures the probability of generating w_{d_i} from the trend-specific background topic.

Similarly, the posterior probability of adding word w_{d_i} in document d to topic k is defined as:

$$\Pr(z_{-di} = k, x_{-di} = 2| \ldots)$$
$$\propto \frac{K_{d,2} + \epsilon_2 - 1}{\sum_x^X (K_{d,x} + \epsilon_x) - 1} \cdot \frac{L_{e,z=k} + \beta_k - 1}{\sum_z^Z (L_{e,z} + \beta_z) - 1} \cdot \frac{M_{z=k,w} + \gamma_w - 1}{\sum_w^W (M_{z,w} + \gamma_w) - 1}$$

where the first term measures the probability of having the switch variable equals to 2, the second term measures the probability of selecting topic k in trend e, and the third term measures the probability of generating w_{d_i} from topic k.

3.2.3 *Parameter Estimation*

Once the sampling processes converge based on the conditional distributions derived in sections 3.2.1 and 3.2.2, we can estimate the five parameters using the following equations:

$$\theta_{e,k} = \frac{L_{e,k} + \beta_k}{\sum_z^Z (L_{e,z} + \beta_z)},\ \phi_{z,w} = \frac{M_{z,w} + \gamma_w}{\sum_w^W (M_{z,w} + \gamma_w)},\ \varphi_{e,w} = \frac{N_{e,w} + \iota_w}{\sum_w^W (N_{e,w} + \iota_w)}$$
$$\mu_{d,x} = \frac{K_{d,x} + \epsilon_x}{\sum_x^X (K_{d,x} + \epsilon_x)},\ \Omega_{e,u} = \frac{C_{e,u} + \eta_u}{\sum_u^U (C_{e,u} + \eta_u)}$$

4. EXPERIMENT

In the previous section we introduced the TUT model, a new statistical model for topic and trend tracking and user interest discovery. In this section, we evaluate the effectiveness of our model with experiments on three different datasets. First of all, we conducted a qualitative analysis on the topics and trends detected by our model. Secondly, we compared our model to the Trend Analysis Model [9] on several different datasets by using perplexity and rate of convergence as measurements. Finally, we built a recommendation model to test if the trend-user distribution is effective to predict user participation.

4.1 Data sets

Data 1 (**DBLP Dataset**): We implemented a XML parser to extract bibliography data from DBLP. Our dataset contains 10 years (2001-2010) of research papers in conference proceedings including CIKM, KDD, WWW and SIGIR. Each document in this dataset corresponds to a publication where title, author list and year of publication were extracted to form the content, user list and timestamp respectively. We preprocessed the data by removing stop words, stemming, and filtering low frequency words and authors. Concretely, we obtained a total set of 4,631 documents and 1,627 users. We considered one year as the time interval. The training set includes documents from 2001 to 2009 and the test set consists of documents from 2010.

Data 2 (**Digg Dataset**): Digg (digg.com) is a social news website where users can post news, make comments, or vote up/down other users' posts/comments. In this experiment, we selected the 5 most popular news sources in Digg: CNN, BBC, NPR, The Washington Post, and Yahoo! News. We then built our dataset by using Digg open API to collect all posts as well as their comments from these five news sources during the period between March 1st 2011 and May 31st 2011. Each post and all of its comments were aggregated as a document in this dataset. Contents from both a post and its comments were combined to be the content of a document. The post initiator and all commenters were extracted to be a user list. The same pre-processing used for DBLP dataset was then applied. Accordingly, we obtained a total set of 9,894 documents and 2,356 users. We considered a week as the time interval. The training set includes the documents from March 1st 2011 to May 15th 2011 and the test set consists of the documents from May 16th 2011 to May 31st 2011.

Data 3 (**MySpace Dataset**): MySpace is one of the popular social networking sites which offers its registered users to start a new thread to discuss several topics or participate in a thread created by other users and make comments. In this study, we used a public data set available for workshop CAW 2.0 (http://caw2.barcelonamedia.org/). The original MySpace dataset provided by the workshop consists of threads from three different sub-forums: campus life, news & politics and movies. In our experiment, we used threads from news & politics sub-forum and movies sub-forum. The same pre-processing used for DBLP dataset was then applied. We transformed the original dataset to an input format of our model. Each thread and its comments were aggregated as a document in our dataset. Contents from both an initial post and its comments were combined as the content of a document. The post initiator and all commenters were extracted to be the user list. Accordingly, we obtained a total set of 3,886 documents and 1,373 users. The time range of our processed dataset spans from October 2007 to November 2008. Therefore, we considered a month as the time interval. The training set includes the documents from October 2007 to September 2008 and the test set consists of the documents from October 2008 to November 2008.

4.2 Case Study

In the first experiment, we conducted a qualitative analysis on the **MySpace dataset** to investigate the quality of the topics and trends detected by our proposed model. In order to produce a small example fitting this paper's size, we chose the number of topic $|Z|= 50$. We empirically set $\alpha = 1$ and let $\gamma = 0.1, \eta = 0.1, \beta = 0.5, \iota = 0.1, \epsilon_0 = 0.1, \epsilon_1 = 0.2$ and $\epsilon_3 = 0.7$. Table 2 shows an illustrative example of 10 different topics extracted from MySpace dataset of August 2008 by our proposed model. The top 10 words with the largest topic-word association were presented for each topic in table 2. The top 10 words in each topic in table 2 show clearly what each topic is about and how the topics are differentiated. For instance, topic 6 is about taxation and

Table 2. Discovered Topics from MySpace Dataset

Topic 0	Topic 3	Topic 6	Topic 11	Topic 14
Russia 0.0605	Georgia 0.1015	money 0.0142	US 0.0224	vote 0.0198
war 0.0157	Russian 0.0578	pay 0.013	Iraq 0.0224	election 0.0137
US 0.0139	Ossetia 0.0271	people 0.0107	war 0.0123	power 0.0129
country 0.0102	south 0.0242	job 0.0107	al 0.0114	party 0.0128
world 0.0098	Saakashvili 0.0130	wage 0.0100	force 0.0111	state 0.0122
American 0.0083	peace 0.0075	company 0.0098	military 0.0106	president 0.0098
Georgia 0.0078	army 0.0072	work 0.0082	Pakistan 0.0098	republican 0.0094
soviet 0.0072	attack 0.0070	market 0.0080	terrorist 0.0091	country 0.0086
state 0.0070	force 0.0066	tax 0.0080	fight 0.0090	govern 0.0084
military 0.0062	troop 0.0065	price 0.0078	Afghanistan 0.0088	democrat 0.0075
Topic 26	**Topic 32**	**Topic 39**	**Topic 40**	**Topic 49**
kill 0.0278	American 0.0277	finance 0.0203	Obama 0.0467	bank 0.0388
Afghanistan 0.0207	Bush 0.0141	US 0.0155	McCain 0.0380	bailout 0.0232
civilian 0.0203	world 0.0094	mortgage 0.0123	Palin 0.0171	hometown 0.0144
war 0.0142	US 0.0083	loan 0.0095	vote 0.0133	loan 0.0111
bomb 0.0108	debt 0.0068	fund 0.0092	campaign 0.0084	bail 0.0078
Taliban 0.0091	George 0.0055	asset 0.0087	Bush 0.0084	mortgage 0.0075
UN 0.0083	European 0.0052	fed 0.0085	republican 0.0072	north 0.0061
attack 0.0080	critic 0.0053	institute 0.0082	president 0.0069	street 0.0061
British 0.0080	leader 0.0045	govern 0.0076	democrat 0.0067	crisis 0.0056
news 0.0078	student 0.0045	treasury 0.0076	Barack 0.0064	Bush 0.0052

employment. Topic 11 is about military. Topic 39 is about finance and topic 14 is about campaign.

We further analyzed the detected trends by selecting three trends as examples and listing top 5 topics with the largest trend-topic association for each trend, as showed in table 3. These three trends were manually labeled by human annotator according to the content of the threads assigning to them and their top topic list. These three detected trends are: 2008 Georgia-Russia Crisis, 2008 Mortgage and Credit Crisis and 2008 U.S. Presidential Election. As shown in table 3, some topics were shared by these three trends. We highlighted a topic in blue if it was shared by two trends and highlighted a topic in red if it was shared by three trends. For example, from table 3, we noticed that topic 14 (campaign topic), was shared by all three trends. From our understanding, trend A (2008 Georgia-Russia Crisis) happened around the same time as trend C (2008 U.S. Presidential Election). At that moment, presidential candidates' attitude toward this crisis was critical to exhibit their experience and capability of dealing with foreign affair, which explains why threads of trend A involved in campaign topic. Similarly, 2008 Mortgage and Credit Crisis continued to worsen from March 2008, when the U.S. Government freed up $200 billion to support Fannie Mae and Freddie Mac mortgage giants, to September 2008, when Lehman Brothers investment bank declared bankruptcy and the U.S. Government bailed out AIG. As a result, threads of trend B (2008 Mortgage and Credit Crisis) unavoidably involved campaign topic which showed the American's hope for a new president to remedy the economic problems. Similarly, threads of trend C (2008 U.S. Presidential Election) shared topic 6 (taxation and employment) and topic 39 (finance) with trend B (2008 Mortgage and Credit Crisis), which is also reasonable because possible solutions to the Mortgage and Credit Crisis were very hot topic during the 2008 U.S. Presidential Election. To sum up, without modeling trends and their associated topics (as in the traditional topic modeling works), it is difficult for us to a gain comprehensive view of each trend and find out the connections among them through their common topics.

In addition, we measured the volume of threads in each trend in one year period and visualized their accumulated volume in Figure 4. X-axis in figure 4 represents timeline and y-axis of figure 4 indicates the accumulated percentage of volume of the whole dataset. Concretely, 2008 U.S. Presidential Election was the most eye-catching event which attracted lots of threads in MySpace between Oct 2007 and Oct 2008. This campaign involved several different issues including taxation, employment, finance, counter-terrorism, military and more. We observed two peaks of trend C (green area). The first peak happened around February 2008 which can be explained by the primaries and caucuses, especially on the Super Tuesday, 5 February 2008. The second peak happened when the Election Day was getting closer. Similarly, for the trend of 2008 Mortgage and Credit Crisis, its volume was close to zero before 2008 but became substantially larger since January 2008. As we know, the Mortgage and Credit Crisis continued to worsen since UBS reported an $18 billion write-down due to its exposure to the American real estate market in January 2008 and Fannie Mac reported $3.55 billion loss for the fourth quarter of 2007 in February 2008. The increase of trend B's volume also can be explained by the fact that the crisis became even worse and the U.S. Congress gave final message to multi-billion-dollar program and tried to address the crisis in July 2008. Further, trend A kept going upward which indicated the Georgia-Russia crisis was getting more and more intense, especially when the South Ossetia War broke out on 7 August, 2008.

Table 3. Top Topics of Each Discovered Trend

Trend	Popular Topic List
A. 2008 Georgia-Russia Crisis	0,3,26,14,40
B. 2008 Mortgage and Credit Crisis	6,32,14,39,49
C. 2008 U.S. Presidential Election	40,14,6,39,11

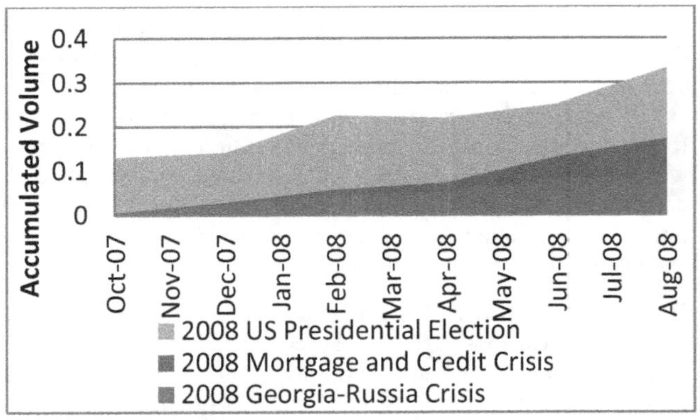

Figure 4. Accumulated Volume of Trends in MySpace Dataset

4.3 Quantitative Evaluation

In this section, we used perplexity as an evaluation metric to investigate the performance of our proposed model in 3 different datasets. For each dataset, we trained the model in its training set and computed its perplexity in the test dataset. Trend Analysis Model (TAM) [9] is employed as a benchmark. The major differences between TUT and TAM are: 1) TUT can automatically decide the number of trends while TAM needs human intervention to predefine the number of trends; 2) TAM is unsuitable for processing document streaming; and 3) TUT models the generation processes of contents and user participations in a unified framework while TAM neglects all user information.

4.3.1 Evaluation Criterion

Perplexity is a standard measure for evaluating the generalization performance of a probabilistic model. The value of perplexity reflects the ability of a model to generalize to unseen data. Specifically, in our case, perplexity reflects the ability of a model to predict words for unseen documents. The perplexity is monotonically decreasing in the likelihood of the test data, and is algebraically equivalent to the inverse of the geometric mean per-word likelihood. A lower perplexity score indicates better generalization performance. We follow [9] and define the perplexity score for a test set D_{test} as:

$$PPX(D_{test}) = \exp\left(-\frac{1}{W}\sum_{d=1}^{|D_{test}|}\sum_{w\in d}^{|d|}\log\left(\Pr\left(w_d\right)\right)\right)$$

where

$$\Pr(w_d) = \mu_{d,0}\phi_{bg,w} + \mu_{d,1}\varphi_{e_d,w} + \sum\nolimits_z^Z \mu_{d,2}\theta_{e_d,z}\phi_{z,w}$$

In the equation above, $\mu_{d,i}$ represents the probability of observing switch variable equals to i in document d, $\phi_{z,w}$ represents the probability of observing word w given topic z, $\varphi_{e_d,w}$ represents the probability of observing word w given trend e_d, and $\theta_{e_d,z}$ represents the probability of observing topic z given trend e_d. The probabilities $\phi_{bg,w}$, $\phi_{z,w}$, $\varphi_{e_d,w}$ and $\theta_{e_d,z}$ (when e_d is an existing trend in the training set) are learned from the training set, and $\mu_{d,0}$, $\mu_{d,1}$, $\mu_{d,2}$, $\varphi_{e_d,w}$ and $\theta_{e_d,z}$ (when e_d is a new trend in the test set) are estimated by a Gibbs sampling process on the test set.

4.3.2 Effect of Recurrent Chinese Restaurant Process

As mentioned in the literature review, TAM needs human intervention to predefine its number of trends |C|. However, in real world application, it's nontrivial to find out the optimal |C|. In addition, our proposed model can automatically decide the number of trends in a dataset without human intervention. In this sub-section, we first studied the performance of TUT on **Digg dataset**. For TUT model, we set $\alpha = 1$, $\gamma = 0.1, \eta = 0.1, \beta = 50/|Z|, \iota = 0.1, \epsilon_0 = 0.1, \epsilon_1 = 0.2$ and $\epsilon_3 = 0.7$. The experiment results were shown in figure 5. It's important to note that both TAM and TUT have fixed number of topics which needs to be predefined. Therefore, the x-axis in Figure 5 represents different numbers of topic, |Z|, from 50 to 300. Y-axis in Figure 5 represents the perplexity score in test set. TAM(5) denotes a TAM model with predefined number of trend |C|=5. TAM(10) denotes a TAM with |C|=10 and TAM(20) denotes a TAM with |C|=20. The number of trends determined automatically by TUT is around 11 (average number of 5 repeating experiments), so that we only tested TAM with |C| equaling to 5, 10 and 20. Figure 5 shows that TUT model achieved the lowest perplexity score across all settings of topic number comparing to TAM. We also observed that in TAM the perplexity score roughly increased with the value of |C| while TUT performed relatively stable. Last but not least, even though TAM(10) has a very close trend number to TUT in Digg dataset, TUT still outperformed TAM(10).

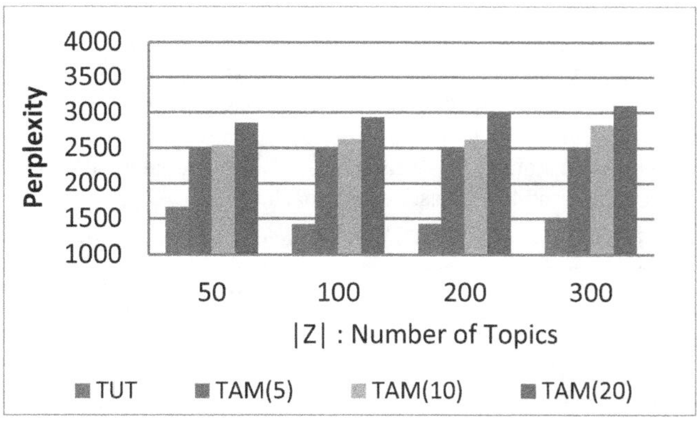

Figure 5. Perplexities over different # of topics for TUT and TAM model with different # of trend in Data 2

Furthermore, we compared the change of perplexity over iteration number during Gibbs sampling process. The results are shown in Figure 6. We set the number of topics, |Z|, to be 100 based on the following considerations: 1) all four models achieved decent performances when |Z| = 100; and 2) when |Z| = 100, it simplifies the result for clear visualization. From this figure, we observed that all these models are able to converge quickly. But given a similar starting point, there is a larger decrease for TUT's perplexity score comparing to TAM(5), TAM(10) and TAM(20)

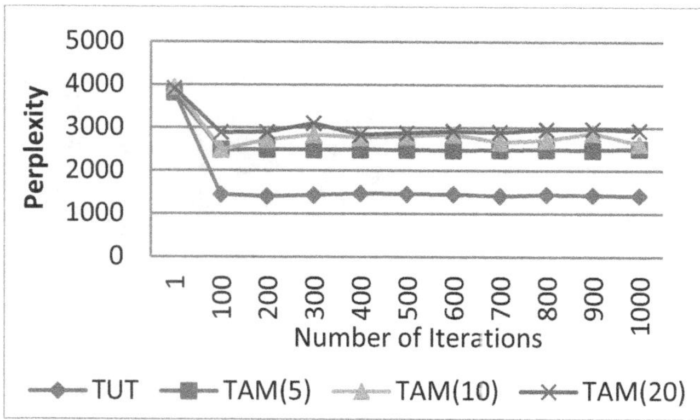

Figure 6. Perplexities over the number of iterations for TUT model and TAM model with different # of trend in Data 2

4.3.3 Performance of TUT in all other Datasets

Additionally, we compared the performance of TUT and TAM in the other two datasets. We repeated each model in each setting for five times and reported the average number. The experiment results were summarized in Figure 7 and Figure 8 respectively. For DBLP dataset, we predefined the number of trends for TAM to be 5, 10 and 20 respectively, because the average number of trends identified by our proposed model in test set equals to 11.5. We set $\alpha = 1$, $\gamma = 0.1, \eta = 0.1, \beta = 50/|Z|, \iota = 0.1, \epsilon_0 = 0.1, \epsilon_1 = 0.2$ and $\epsilon_3 = 0.7$. Similarly, we predefined the number of trends for TAM in MySpace dataset to be 5, 10 and 20 respectively since the average number of trends identified by our proposed model in MySpace's test set equals to 20.25. We set $\alpha = 0.1$, $\gamma = 0.1, \eta = 0.1, \beta = 50/|Z|, \iota = 0.1, \epsilon_0 = 0.1, \epsilon_1 = 0.2$ and $\epsilon_3 = 0.7$.

From both Fig. 7 and Fig. 8, we observed that our proposed TUT model consistently outperformed TAM in all settings of trend number and topic number. In addition, the perplexity scores of TUT were relatively stable comparing to TAM. As we know, the number of trends should be different in different time interval, but we predefined and fixed the number of trends for TAM according to the result of TUT, which might bring difficulties for TAM to generalize to the test dataset. However, even though TAM(10) has a very close number of trends to TUT in DBLP dataset, TUT still outperformed TAM(10). The same applies to TAM(20) in MySpace dataset. One possible explanation is that, modeling user participation, to some extent, might help TUT model to better generalize to the unseen dataset.

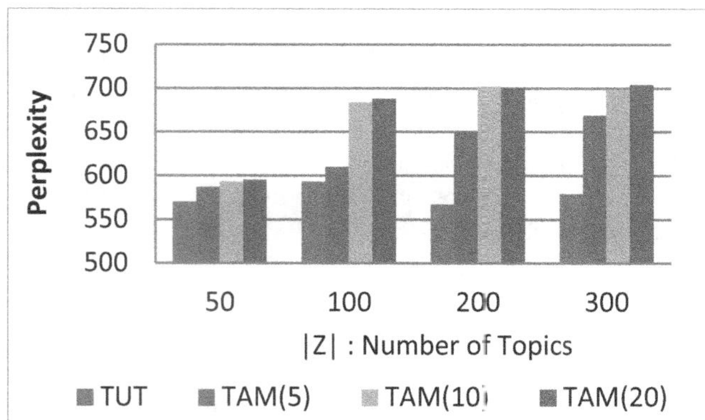

Figure 7. Perplexities over different number of topics for TUT and TAM model with different # of trend in Data 1

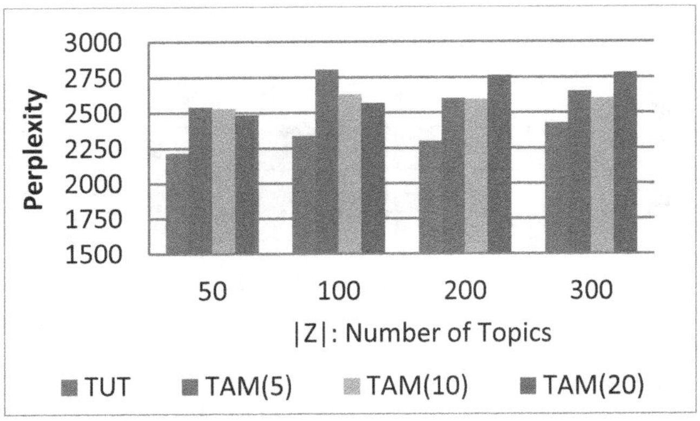

Figure 8. Perplexities over different number of topics for TUT and TAM model with different # of trend in Data 3

4.4 User Prediction

Modeling user interest is critical for news/blog recommendation and personalized search. One of the important outputs of TUT model is trend-user distributions, which can be considered as users' interests toward each detected trend. In this experiment, we evaluated the usefulness of the user interests to boost ranking for potential participant prediction. The experiment was conducted in **Digg dataset**. Generally speaking, we first trained a recommendation model based on the Digg dataset' training set. Then, for each document in its test set, we randomly removed 80% of the users and only withheld the other 20%. We then used the recommendation model to predict users and compared the result to the ground truth (the removed users). We first used a naïve ranking method as a baseline approach and then boosted the baseline by the user interests detected by our proposed model. Our goal is to show that, even though with a straightforward combination method, the detected user interests can boost the naïve ranking approach substantially.

Specifically, for the **naïve ranking approach**, we first constructed a bipartite graph based on the user-document relationships observed in the training dataset. The bipartite graph consists of nodes and edges. Each node represents either a Digg user or a document posted in Digg.com. All nodes representing users are on the left hand side while all nodes representing documents are on the right hand side. Each edge of the bipartite graph connects a user to a document which means that a user contributed to a document. Given this bipartite graph, the similarity between user i and j is defined by the Jaccard Index as: $Sim(i,j) = \frac{|C_i \cap C_j|}{|C_i \cup C_j|}$, where C_i represents the set of documents that user i participated. In this way, we calculated the similarity between every two users in the training set. Given a new document d in the test set and its 20% of withheld users, $\overline{P_d}$, we ranked all other users, excluding those in $\overline{P_d}$, based on $Pr\,(\overline{\overline{P_{d_i}}}|\overline{P_d}, \mathcal{g})$ defined as:

$$Pr\,(\overline{\overline{P_{d_i}}}|\overline{P_d}, \mathcal{g}) = \frac{\sum_{j \in \overline{P_d}} |Sim(i,j)|}{|\overline{P_d}|}$$

where $\overline{\overline{P_{d_i}}}$ represents a user i who does NOT exist in $\overline{P_d}$, and $\mathcal{g}$ represents a bipartite graph. The rationale of this naïve raking is that, if a user is very similar to those existing users of a given document, then this user is also likely to exist in this document. This naïve ranking method relying on user similarity will serve as the baseline approach in this experiment.

On the other hand, for our **boosted ranking method**, based on the trend-user distributions Ω that we obtained from the training set, we know which trends a user will be interested. By applying a trained TUT model to the test set, it automatically assign each document in the test set to a trend e. Since we already know users' interests toward each trend e, $\Omega_e = \{\Omega_{e,1}, \Omega_{e,2}, \dots, \Omega_{e,u}\}$ from the training set, the boosted ranking for user $\overline{\overline{P_{d_i}}}$ to document d, is then redefined as:

$$\Pr(\overline{\overline{P_{d_i}}}|\overline{P_d}, \mathcal{g}, e_d, \Omega_{e_d}) = w \times \Pr(\overline{\overline{P_{d_i}}}|e_d, \Omega_{e_d}) + (1-w) \times \Pr\,(\overline{\overline{P_{d_i}}}|\overline{P_d}, \mathcal{g})$$

where $\Pr(\overline{\overline{P_{d_i}}}|e_d, \Omega_{e_d})$ equals to $\Omega_{e_d,\overline{\overline{P_{d_i}}}}$, representing user i's interest to trend e_d and w denotes the weight to combine the baseline approach and user interests.

The experiment setup is as follows: 1) Using the training set, we constructed a user-thread bipartite graph and calculated user similarities; 2) Based on the user similarities computed in step 1, we applied the baseline ranking method to predict users for each document in the test set (results from the first two steps were used as baseline); 3) Using the training set again, we trained our TUT model to discover users' interests to trends; 4) We applied the trained TUT model to assign a trend label to each document in the test set; 5) For each document in the test set, since we knew its trend label from step 4 and also users' interests to each trend from step 3, we applied our boosted ranking method to predict its potential participants.

4.4.1 *Measurement*

We employed Precision@K as the evaluation measure in this experiment. Specifically, by using Precision@K, we consider the top-K list resulted by a recommendation method. Let $\boldsymbol{m}$ denotes the number of users that co-exist in the top-K list and the ground truth list of a document, Precision@k equals to $\boldsymbol{m/K}$. The higher the value, the better the performance of a recommendation method is.

4.4.2 *Result*

We empirically set weight w to 0.5. As shown in Table 4, our boosted ranking method consistently outperformed the naïve ranking from K=5 to K=30. The highlighted red figures within parentheses indicate the percentage of improvement of boosted rank comparing to the baseline approach.

Table 4. Precision@K of Baseline and Boosted Ranking

	P@5	P@10	P@15	P@20	P@25	P@30
Naïve Ranking	0.069	0.067	0.062	0.060	0.058	0.055
Boosted Ranking	0.081 (17%)	0.075 (12%)	0.074 (19%)	0.070 (17%)	0.068 (17%)	0.062 (12%)

5. CONCLUSION

In this paper, we proposed a Topic-User-Trend Model to simulate the generation process of user-generated web contents. By incorporating a latent variable "trend" and using RCRP to enable our model to decide automatically the appropriate number of trends in a document corpus and also taking users' interests into account, our proposed model is able to model the generation process of web contents in a more meaningful way. At the same time, our model achieves a better generalization performance than the TAM model in multiple test datasets. Besides, the user interests learned by our proposed model can be utilized for document recommendation, which substantially improved the performance of the naïve ranking method which relies on user similarity only. Thus far, our proposed model only considers users participated in a given document without taking their interactions into consideration. In the future work, we will incorporate the generation process of user relationships into our model. Moreover, we will further explore other opportunities to make use of the trend-user association for recommendation problems.

6. REFERENCES

[1] Ahmed, A., Ho, Q., Eisenstein, J., Xing, E., Smola, A. J. and Teo, C. H. 2011. Unified analysis of streaming news. Proceedings of the 20th international conference on World Wide Web (WWW'11) ACM 267-276.

[2] Ahmed, A. and Xing, E. 2008. Dynamic non-parametric mixture models and the recurrent chinese restaurant process. Proceedings of SDM 2008.

[3] AlSumait, L., Barbara, D. and Domeniconi, C. 2008. On-line LDA: Adaptive Topic Models for Mining Text Streams with Applications to Topic Detection and Tracking. Proceedings of the 2008 Eighth IEEE International Conference on Data Mining IEEE Computer Society 3-12.

[4] Blei, D., Ng, A. and Jordan, M. 2003. Latent dirichlet allocation. The Journal of Machine Learning Research. 3, 993-1022.

[5] Blei, D. M. and Lafferty, J. D. 2006. Dynamic topic models. Proceedings of the 23rd international conference on Machine learning Pittsburgh, Pennsylvania ACM 113-120. http://doi.acm.org/10.1145/1143844.1143859

[6] He, Q., Chen, B., Pei, J., Qiu, B., Mitra, P. and Giles, L. 2009. Detecting topic evolution in scientific literature: how can citations help? Proceeding of the 18th ACM conference on Information and knowledge management ACM 957-966.

[7] Hearst, M. A. and Pedersen, J. O. 1996. Reexamining the cluster hypothesis: scatter/gather on retrieval results. Proceedings of the 19th annual international ACM SIGIR conference on Research and development in information retrieval Zurich, Switzerland ACM 76-84. 10.1145/243199.243216

[8] Hofmann, T. 1999. Probabilistic latent semantic indexing. Proceedings of the 22nd annual international ACM SIGIR conference on Research and development in information retrieval ACM New York, NY, USA 50-57.

[9] Kawamae, N. 2011. Trend analysis model: trend consists of temporal words, topics, and timestamps. Proceedings of the fourth ACM international conference on Web search and data mining ACM 317-326.

[10] McCallum, A., Corrada-Emmanuel, A. and Wang, X. 2005. Topic and role discovery in social networks. Proceedings of the 19th international joint conference on Artificial intelligence Morgan Kaufmann Publishers Inc. 786-791.

[11] Mei, Q. and Zhai, C. 2005. Discovering evolutionary theme patterns from text: an exploration of temporal text mining. Proceedings of the eleventh ACM SIGKDD international conference on Knowledge discovery in data mining ACM New York, NY, USA 198-207.

[12] Morinaga, S. and Yamanishi, K. 2004. Tracking dynamics of topic trends using a finite mixture model. Proceedings of the tenth ACM SIGKDD international conference on Knowledge discovery and data mining Seattle, WA, USA ACM 811-816. http://doi.acm.org/10.1145/1014052.1016919

[13] Rosen-Zvi, M., Griffiths, T., Steyvers, M. and Smyth, P. 2004. The author-topic model for authors and documents. Proceedings of the 20th conference on Uncertainty in artificial intelligence Banff, Canada AUAI Press 487-494.

[14] Schult, R. and Spiliopoulou, M. 2006. Discovering emerging topics in unlabelled text collections. Lecture Notes in Computer Science. 4152, 353-366.

[15] Shahaf, D., Guestrin, C. and Horvitz, E. 2012. Trains of thought: generating information maps Proceedings of the 21st international conference on World Wide Web Lyon, France ACM 899-908.

[16] Sun, Y., Tang, J., Han, J., Gupta, M. and Zhao, B. 2010. Community evolution detection in dynamic heterogeneous information networks. Proceedings of the Eighth Workshop on Mining and Learning with Graphs ACM 137-146.

[17] Wang, X. and McCallum, A. 2006. Topics over time: a non-markov continuous-time model of topical trends. Proceedings of the 12th ACM SIGKDD international conference on Knowledge discovery and data mining ACM 424-433.

[18] Zeng, H.-J., He, Q.-C., Chen, Z., Ma, W.-Y. and Ma, J. 2004. Learning to cluster web search results. Proceedings of the 27th annual international ACM SIGIR conference on Research and development in information retrieval Sheffield, United Kingdom ACM 210-217. 10.1145/1008992.1009030

Predicting Aggregate Social Activities using Continuous-Time Stochastic Process

Shu Huang†, Min Chen‡, Bo Luo§, Dongwon Lee†

† College of IST, The Pennsylvania State University, University Park, PA, U.S.A.
‡ Department of AMS, Johns Hopkins University, Baltimore, MD, U.S.A.
§ Department of EECS, The University of Kansas, Lawrence, KS, U.S.A.

{shuang,dlee}@ist.psu.edu, minchen@jhu.edu, bluo@ku.edu

ABSTRACT

How to accurately model and predict the future status of social networks has become an important problem in recent years. Conventional solutions to such a problem often employ topological structure of the sociogram, i.e., friendship links. However, they often disregard different levels of *activeness* of social actors and become insufficient to deal with complex dynamics of user behaviors. In this paper, to address this issue, we first refine the notion of *social activity* to better describe dynamic user behaviors in social networks. We then propose a *Parameterized Social Activity Model (PSAM)* using continuous-time stochastic process for predicting aggregate social activities. With social activities evolving over time, PSAM itself also evolves and therefore dynamically captures the real-time characteristics of the current active population. Our experiments using two real social networks (Facebook and CiteSeer) reveal that the proposed PSAM model is effective in simulating social activity evolution and predicting aggregate social activities accurately at different time scales.

Categories and Subject Descriptors

H.1.0 [**Information Systems**]: Models and Principles; H.2.8 [**Database Management**]: Database Applications—*data mining*

Keywords

Aggregate Social Activity, Continuous-time Stochastic Process

1. INTRODUCTION

The intensive and highly diversified communications among people lead to complex social network infrastructure. With the emergence of online social networking sites and online communities, a lot of research have been conducted to help understand the complex social phenomena[9, 29]. Among social networking research areas, an important topic is to understand and predict the dynamics of user behaviors and interactions [26, 10, 4], as well as the establishment and evolution of social relationship [17, 18].

In conventional social networking research, social networks are usually represented by graphs, where vertices denote *social actors* and edges denote the *social relationships*. Therefore, the notion of social network evolution is mostly defined as the expansion of the social network graph. Different approaches have been proposed to analyze and predict social network evolution and information diffusion. They can be roughly grouped into three categories: static network mining [30], microscopic evolution prediction [22, 24], and structural analysis [14, 32]. In static network mining, structural patterns, such as power-law distribution and small-world phenomenon, are discovered by mining snapshots of networks. In microscopic evolution prediction, various models are proposed to simulate the social network growth at the micro scope. In structural analysis, a variety of structural features are investigated to explain and predict the evolution of the social graph.

However, approaches that are purely based on graph structures could be biased when social actors demonstrate different levels of *activeness*. In particular, highly active social actors make more contribution towards the interaction, expansion and functionality of the online society, while inactive and less-active members only contribute as "silent" nodes in the graph. Therefore, we would argue that the notion of *social interactions* is an important indicator in social network analysis. Let us look at an example.

Example 1: Figure 1 shows two real-world social groups extracted from Facebook [28]. In terms of friendship links, their structural evolution processes are very similar. The final states of their friendship-network structures are shown in Figures 1 (a) and (b), which appear to be similar as well. Therefore, if we apply pure structure-based analysis on the two groups, they are expected to demonstrate similar behaviors (e.g., information diffusion). However, social interactions (e.g., wall postings) within the two groups turn out to be quite different, as exhibited in Figures 1 (c) and (d). That is, members in one group frequently communicate in Facebook, while the other one is very silent. □

As we can see, it is impractical to predict social network activities only using social connections (i.e., social relation-

CIKM'12, October 29–November 2, 2012, Maui, HI, USA.

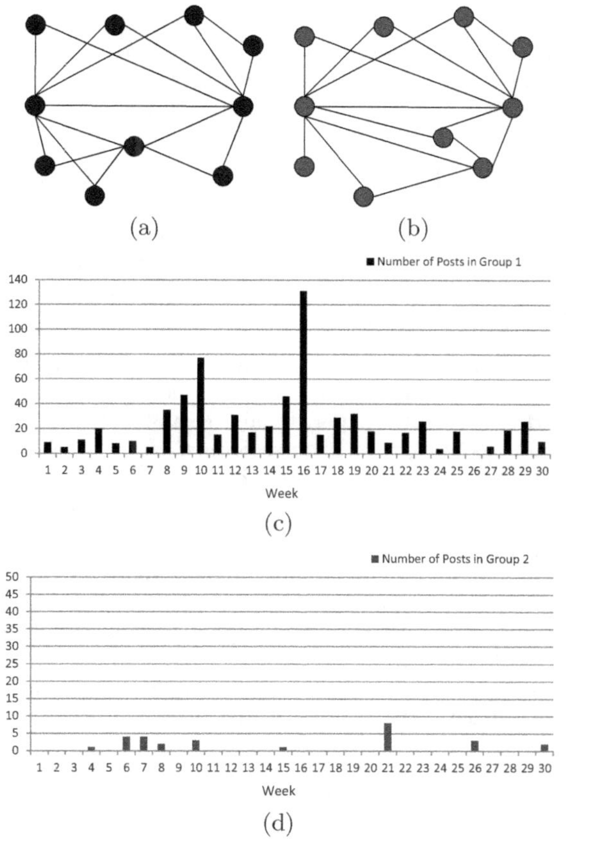

Figure 1: Example: two social groups with similar construction but different levels of interactions.

ships). As observed from Facebook data, a significant portion of the social network accounts are inactive, which causes purely structure-based evolution models to be less accurate. Moreover, compared with friendship links, *social activity* is a more meaningful indicator of *social dynamics* and *user behaviors* within social networks. In particular, social activities could be categorised into two types: *connective activities* and *interactive activities.* Connective activities (e.g., adding friends, subscripting, following) add new edges in the sociogram, and result in the expansion of social networks. Conventional research on social network evolution, which studies the development of the network structure, could be considered as the consequences of this type of activities. On the other hand, interactive activities, such as wall posting, poking and commenting, represent socialization interactions based on existing connections. This type of activities continuously contributes to the business value of social networking sites, and form the basis of online communities.

In this paper, we present a social activity predicting approach. By using a continuous-time stochastic process to simulate the social activity evolution, we address both the random impact from the environment and the tendency of evolution. At the same time, the model is parameterized with the current activity status, thus predictions are not purely based on historical information, but instead, based on the inherent characteristics and real-time observation of the social community. In addition, predictions made by our continuous-time stochastic model have an infinite future state space, i.e. numeric values instead of binary notions; therefore our model is advantageous in quantifying the activity evolution. Furthermore, the proposed approach could be applied on any arbitrary subset of users in a social network (to be elaborated), making the proposal very flexible. Finally, with comprehensive experiments on real-world social network data, the proposed method is shown to be effective and superior to baselines in predicting social activities.

Our major contributions in this paper are threefold:

(1) We introduce a social network evolution model based on social activity features, including both connective and interactive activities. This model better simulates and predicts the dynamics of social behaviors compared with purely structure-based models. The improved performance of the new model is demonstrated in experiments on real social networks.

(2) The parameters of the model also evolve with the day-to-day user activities in social communities. Therefore, the parameterized model is dynamic and accurately captures the active population in the network.

(3) The proposed model exploits aggregate interactions among a group of social network users. It is applicable to study an arbitrary subset of users, who are selected with diverse criterions. Such flexibility allows the model to be useful in a wide range of applications.

The rest of this paper is organized as follows: we introduce the problem and the background of continuous-time stochastic process in Sections 2 and 3. In section 4, we present the details of the parameterized social activity model. We show the experimental results in Section 5, discuss related works in Section 6, and finally conclude the paper in Section 7.

2. PROBLEM STATEMENT

2.1 Background

In this paper, we analyze and model a wide range of social behaviors in social networks, e.g., becoming a member, posting a message, adding a comment, inviting a friend, etc. We refer to such as *activity* in this paper. Further, an instance of such an activity is referred to as an *interaction.* For example, suppose we model an activity A_1 as "a member posting comments to others' walls in Facebook." If a member m_1 posts three comments on another member m_2's wall, it is said that m_1 and m_2 have three interactions.

User activities are very important in social network research, as they are basic indicators of user behaviors and social dynamics. Interactions among members also reveal the business value of social communities in multiple aspects. Meanwhile, the *realtime activeness* of social actors is also an important factor in the dynamic analysis and applications of social networks. For instance, in advertising, *ex-ante* knowledge to the status of the targeted social network will assist decision making and improve the profit; e.g. it is only worthwhile to advertise in active social groups that are potentially interested in the product/event. As another example, we can estimate the business potential of fans of college basketball teams by analyzing activities among fan groups, and inject advertisements when activities reach their peaks.

As we have introduced, social activities could be categorized into *connective activities* (i.e. establishing social connections) and *interactive activities* (i.e. information sharing and socialization). Despite much success in structural-based social network analysis, little work has been done in analyzing and predicting interactive activities such as wall postings. Meanwhile, in topology-based social network analysis, nodes and edges accumulate over time. However, this model does not explain the possible decrease of the active member population. Taking Facebook as an example, the active member population is not continuously increasing; instead, decrease and increase take place alternatively over time. Moreover, it is also challenging to simulate the influence of the environment on the social activity. The impact of the environment is usually random, which is hard to quantify and depict. Without quantifying the environment variables, it is difficult to predict the social activity accurately.

Intuitively, it is important to model both *individual activities* and *aggregate activities*. However, analysis of individual activities for all social network users may be impractical in many applications: (1) modeling and prediction at individual level could be biased due to the relatively large uncertainty and randomness. For instance, when we predict whether a user will reply to a message [13] or join a group [4], the likelihood is always low, i.e. users are always very unlikely to conduct any activity. Therefore, aggregate activity makes more sense as it represents collective user behaviors at a macro level, and the randomness on individuals offset each other. (2) It could be computationally too expensive to analyze every individual in the network. In particular, when we only expect aggregate results (e.g. the group of x users may post y messages in the next day), it is a waste to predict at individual level and then aggregate (e.g. predict the likelihood of posting a message for each user, and then compute the group-level aggregation).

In social network evolution, we observe that aggregate activities provide a good indication of social network status. Considering social activities from a macro scope, some activity features, such as the population of active members and the number of interactions, can serve to depict member activities. Meanwhile, activity features also imply future network evolution. Frequent member interactions usually indicate a growth of the social network, while low interactions may suggest a shrinking network. Therefore, social networks can be measured by incorporating a variety of activity features, and this measure can help predict future activities.

2.2 Problem Definition

In this paper, we aim at the problem of activity-based social behavior prediction. We emphasize the contribution of the active member interactions and exploit the activity features to predict social activities. Instead of the conventional sociogram that models users as nodes and friendship relationships as edges, we use the *social activity graph* that is formed by user interactions within a certain *time interval*. As we have introduced, types of interaction in a social network are highly diversified, e.g., adding a friend or posting on the wall in a friendship network, or collaborating on a publication in a co-authorship network. We formalize the concept of *social activity* (SA) as follows:

Definition 1 (Social Activity) *Given a subset M of the social network users (nodes), the social activities of M at time interval $[t_i, t_{i+1})$ is represented by a labeled graph $G(t_i) = (V_{t_i}, E_{t_i})$, where V_{t_i} is the vertex set and E_{t_i} is the edge set. Every vertex $v \in V_{t_i}$ corresponds to an individual who is involved in at least one activity on $[t_i, t_{i+1})$. An edge $e = \langle u, v\rangle, e \in E_{t_i}$ exists between a pair of vertex u and v if and only if u and v have at least one interaction of a preselected type of actions during the interval $[t_i, t_{i+1})$. The edge is labeled as the number of interactions between u and v during the interval.*

In the rest of the paper, we use *ISA* (interval-wise social activities) to denote social activity features within a time interval. With the definition, the membership is no longer permanent or cumulative. Only those who have activities at $[t_i, t_{i+1})$ are included in $G(t_i)$. Therefore, the membership and status of $G(t)$ is evolving over time.

The Problem. With the notions of social activity and social activity graph, we can ask many interesting questions. In particular, in this paper, we aim to answer the question: *how can we predict aggregate social activity at time t_{i+1} using social activities on the time up to t_i?*

Let N_{t_i} denote the social activity in a graph $G(t_i)$. Then, we can represent N_{t_i} in various ways: e.g. number of vertices $|V(t)|$ (i.e. number of active members), number of edges $|E(t)|$ (i.e. number of active pairs of users), or the number of interactions in the graph ($|I(t)|$), depending on the application. In the experiment, we examine all these three different measures in constructing and validating our parameterized social activity model.

Node selection. The proposed approach does not depend on the friendship network among users, hence, it could be applied on any arbitrary subset of users in a social network. In practice, nodes are selected based on the objective of the analysis/prediction, and the selection criteria could be structure-based (e.g. select the neighborhood of a seed user), attribute-based (e.g. select all the 2012 graduates of a school), content-based (e.g. select all users who have tweeted about New York Giants), or even activity-based (e.g. select the most active users in a community and analyze interactions between them). Theoretically, it is valid to select a subset of completely unrelated users. However, such selection makes no practical sense, since the interactions among selected users will be very sparse.

Solution overview. To quantify the influence of the environment and address the randomness, we make use of a continuous-time stochastic process, named *Wiener Process* (WP). With this tool, we derive a parameterized social activity evolution model, which takes into account the temporal change of the active population. By utilizing activity features, the proposed model dynamically fits the current network characteristics and accurately simulates the evolution of social activities. At last, the model generates a change rate distribution of the social activity status, based on which a prediction can be made.

3. PRELIMINARY: CONTINUOUS-TIME STOCHASTIC PROCESS

Due to the randomness in social dynamics, we seek to investigate the probability distribution of the ISA status N_t. As N_t is a continuous-time random variable, we simulate its evolution with a continuous-time stochastic process. A stochastic process is a process or system that evolves randomly but can be described by probability distributions. It is frequently used at macro scope to simulate the evolution of a random process. A continuous-time stochastic process is nowhere differentiable. To handle this property, stochastic calculus is developed with theoretical foundations and methods that are different from regular calculus.

In the evolution of a social network, N_t evolves with infinite future status, i.e. may take any numeric value. To address this property, we adopt the Wiener Process [16] as a component in our model. The Wiener Process (WP), also called Brownian Motion, is a fundamental and basic stochastic process. It is a key process to build other more complicated processes. WP is widely used in both pure and applied mathematics, in particular the Nobel-Prize-Winning result "Black-Scholes option pricing model" [16].

The definition of a Wiener Process $W(t)$ is as follows:

1. $W(0) = 0$.
2. $W(t)$ is almost surely continuous.
3. $W(t_2) - W(t_1)$ is a random variable for any $0 = t_0 < t_1 < t_2 < t_n$.
4. $W(t_2) - W(t_1)$ and $W(s_2) - W(s_1)$ are independent normal distributions that follows $N(0, \sqrt{t_2 - t_1}^2)$ and $N(0, \sqrt{s_2 - s_1}^2)$ respectively, when $[t_1, t_2]$ and $[s_1, s_2]$ do not overlap.

As a stochastic process, $W(t)$ is continuous but nowhere differentiable. Solving a continuous-time stochastic process involves some special properties, and the **quadratic variation** is the most important one. Denote $\prod = \{t_0, t_1, ...t_n\}$ as a partition of time interval $[0, T]$, and

$$||\prod|| = max_{j=0,...,n-1}(t_{j+1} - t_j),$$

The quadratic variation of $W(t)$ up to time T is defined as:

$$[W, W](T) = \lim_{||\prod||\to 0} \sum_{j=0}^{n-1} [W(t_{j+1}) - W(t)]^2 \tag{1}$$

where $0 = t_0 < t_1 < ... < t_n = T$. For all $T \geq 0$, $[W, W](T) = T$ almost surely [16]; in other words, *WP accumulates quadratic variation at rate one per unit time.* It can also be written as:

$$dW(t)dW(t) = dt \tag{2}$$

This property of quadratic variation distinguishes stochastic calculus from regular calculus. Consider a function $f(W(t))$, where $W(t)$ is a WP, according to equation (2), the differential of $f(W(t))$ is:

$$\begin{aligned} df(W(t)) &= f'(W)dW + \frac{1}{2}f''(W)dWdW \\ &= f'(W)dW + \frac{1}{2}f''(W)dt \end{aligned} \tag{3}$$

The equation above is different from what is obtained by regular calculus on regular functions. Any stochastic process that contains a WP inevitably inherits stochastic properties from the WP. As WP is a component in our parameterized evolution model, we will make use of stochastic calculus to generate the solution to our model.

By definition of WP, at time t_1, the expectation of future value of $W(t)$ equals the value of $W(t)$ at time t_1, i.e. $E[W(t_2)|F_{t_1}] = W(t_1)$ for any $0 \leq t_1 < t_2$, F_{t_1} represents the information at time t_1. This can be interpreted to mean that WP has no tendency to increase or decrease in the future. Although a WP is effective to simulate the influence of the environment, it does not indicate the long-term evolution tendency. Taking Facebook social network as an example, as Facebook becomes more popular, it has attracted more members and they are likely to have more intensive social activity. However, WP can not reflect this long-term evolution tendency, because the expectation of $W(t)$ equals its value at the evaluating time.

At the same time, a WP does not address the magnitude of randomness in the process. By definition, all WPs are considered equally volatile, because the standard deviation of the random increment $W(t_2) - W(t_1)$ is always $\sqrt{t_2 - t_1}$. If two stochastic processes with different volatility are both modeled by a WP, then on the same time interval $[t_1, t_2]$, their models will have the same standard deviation, which is not desirable.

For these two reasons, a WP by itself is insufficient to describe the evolution of N_t. Therefore, based on a WP, we propose a parameterized stochastic process model to simulate the evolution of ISA.

4. THE PARAMETERIZED SOCIAL ACTIVITY MODEL

4.1 Overview

By incorporating the Wiener Process, we propose the **Parameterized Social Activity Model (PSAM)** to simulate the social activity evolution over continuous-time. In this model, N_t is the random variable with the following observations and assumptions: (1) it evolves over continuous time; (2) the process is shaped by both the tendency of evolution factors and random shock from the environment, e.g. users' behavior patterns and environment shock; (3) the evolution tendency of N_t on any time interval $[t_i, t_{i+1}]$ can be considered determined by the information available at time t_i, and is independent from previous history. According to these observations, a continuous-time stochastic process is a proper simulation for N_t.

In evolution of the social activity, influential factors include both random impact from environment and characteristics of the active population. All this information is reflected within activity features of the social community. Incorporating WP as a component, the randomness of the process is addressed and quantified. At the same time, a variety of activity features are extracted as predicting variables(will be elaborated later). As a summary of influential factors, they enable parameterization of the model and resolve the insufficiency of WP. By incorporating them as predicting vector, N_t is dynamically simulated and predicted.

In PSAM, no distribution of social activity is assumed in advance. Meanwhile, the selection of social community is not subject to any restriction. As a component of the model, the WP makes sure the simulation is continuous-time and predictions can be made on any time point. The parameterization guarantees dynamics of the model, therefore the latest influential factors are addressed and included when making predictions.

4.2 Activity Feature Extraction

To measure member activities, we construct ISA over successive time intervals and extract a list of activity features out of it. They include not only the features indicating activity level of members, but also those related to the topology

Table 1: Activity features extracted from ISA

Features	Description
$\lvert V_t \rvert$	Number of active members in $G(t)$
$\lvert CV_t \rvert$	Cumulative number of active members by time t
ΔV_t	Difference between $\lvert V_t \rvert$ and $\lvert V_{t-1} \rvert$
$\lvert I_t \rvert$	Number of interactions in $G(t)$
$\lvert CI_t \rvert$	Cumulative number of activities by time t
ΔI_t	Difference between I_t and I_{t-1}
$\lvert E_t \rvert$	Number of edges in $G(t)$
$\lvert CE_t \rvert$	Cumulative number of edges by time t
ΔE_t	Difference between E_t and E_{t-1}
AI_t	Average number of interactions per each person in $G(t)$
AR_t	Average number of friends per each person in $G(t)$
CC_t	Average clustering coefficient in $G(t)$
AL_t	Average length of the shortest pathes in $G(t)$
D_t	Diameter across all vertices of $G(t)$

change[4]. Table 1 shows all the 14 activity features generated from the Facebook and Citeseer social networks.

In our datasets, the first 9 features evolves significantly over time, therefore they are rescaled by logarithm to handle the very large values. The rescale of features does not change the predicting accuracy of our model.

As a lot of activity features are used, they may introduce high dimensional parameters in the model construction later on. To keep the model simple, proper techniques (e.g. principle component analysis) could be employed to reduce the data dimension. Since this is not the main focus of our study, we do not present more details here.

With all activity features obtained, the results are plugged into the evolution model as predictors. Let s_j denote the j-th dimension extracted from activity features, m denote the total number of dimensions used, then the predictor vector at time t_i is $\vec{\lambda}_{t_i} = [s_{1t_i}, s_{2t_i}, ...s_{mt_i}]^T$.

4.3 The Parameterized Evolution Model

Let $\vec{\lambda}_t$ represent the predictor vector, N_t denotes the status of ISA. To describe the evolution of N_t, we derive a parameterized stochastic process with a drift and diffusion as follows:

$$dN_t = \gamma(\vec{\lambda}_t)N_t dt + \sigma(\vec{\lambda}_t)N_t dW(t) \qquad (4)$$

where t denotes the continuous time and $\vec{\lambda}_t$ is time-evolving. Both $\gamma(\vec{\lambda}_t)$ and $\sigma(\vec{\lambda}_t)$ are time-evolving parameters depending on $\vec{\lambda}_t$. $\gamma(\vec{\lambda}_t)N_t dt$ is the drift term, indicating the growth or shrinkage of active population. $\sigma(\vec{\lambda}_t)N_t dW(t)$ is the diffusion term, describing the uncertainty, e.g. the impact from the environment. $W(t)$ is a WP. Due to the existence of $W(t)$, N_t inherits the property of quadratic variation, and it is also continuous but nowhere differentiable.

Equation (4) not only describe the evolution tendency, but also address the magnitude of randomness in the process. As the coefficients σ and γ are parameterized with $\vec{\lambda}_t$, they allow the evolution model itself to evolve over time, and therefore reflect the latest characteristics of N_t.

The time-evolving coefficients make this model hard to work with. To solve this model, we make use of an approximated form. Denote $\prod = \{t_0, t_1, ...t_n\}$ as a partition of $[0, T]$ into intervals $[t_i, t_{i+1}]$, $0 \le i \le n-1$. Because the intervals are small, $\gamma(\vec{\lambda}_t)$ and $\sigma(\vec{\lambda}_t)$ can be treated as constant on each interval $[t_i, t_{i+1})$, as determined at time point t_i.

Let $0 \le \Delta t < t_{i+1} - t_i$ be the time increment, then on each interval $[t_i, t_{i+1})$, the equation (4) is approximated with the following format:

$$dN_{t_i+\Delta t} = \gamma(\vec{\lambda}_{t_i})N_{t_i+\Delta t}d\Delta t + \sigma(\vec{\lambda}_{t_i})N_{t_i+\Delta t}dW(\Delta t) \qquad (5)$$

where $\gamma(\vec{\lambda}_{t_i})$ and $\sigma(\vec{\lambda}_{t_i})$ are kept constant for any Δt. For simplicity, let $\aleph$ denote $N_{t_i+\Delta t}$, then equation (5) equals:

$$d\aleph = \gamma(\vec{\lambda}_{t_i})\aleph d\Delta t + \sigma(\vec{\lambda}_{t_i})\aleph dW(\Delta t) \qquad (6)$$

This yields:

$$\frac{d\aleph}{\aleph} = \gamma(\vec{\lambda}_{t_i})d\Delta t + \sigma(\vec{\lambda}_{t_i})dW(\Delta t) \qquad (7)$$

Because $\aleph$ has the property of quadratic variation, from equation (3), we obtain:

$$d\ln\aleph = \frac{d\aleph}{\aleph} + \frac{1}{2}(-\frac{1}{\aleph^2})d\aleph d\aleph \qquad (8)$$

It is then:

$$\frac{d\aleph}{\aleph} = d\ln\aleph + \frac{d\aleph d\aleph}{2\aleph^2} \qquad (9)$$

Plugging equation (9) into equation (7) yields:

$$d\ln\aleph + \frac{d\aleph d\aleph}{2\aleph^2} = \gamma(\vec{\lambda}_{t_i})d\Delta t + \sigma(\vec{\lambda}_{t_i})dW(\Delta t) \qquad (10)$$

Multiply equation (6) by itself, we obtain:

$$\begin{aligned} d\aleph d\aleph =& [\gamma(\vec{\lambda}_{t_i})\aleph d\Delta t + \sigma(\vec{\lambda}_{t_i})\aleph dW(\Delta t)]^2 \\ =& \gamma^2(\vec{\lambda}_{t_i})\aleph^2 d\Delta t d\Delta t + \sigma^2(\vec{\lambda}_{t_i})\aleph^2 dW(\Delta t)dW(\Delta t) \\ &+ 2\gamma(\vec{\lambda}_{t_i})\sigma(\vec{\lambda}_{t_i})\aleph^2 d\Delta t dW(\Delta t) \qquad (11) \end{aligned}$$

Note that, by calculus, $d\Delta t d\Delta t = d\Delta t dW(\Delta t) = 0$. Therefore, the above equation yields:

$$d\aleph d\aleph = \sigma^2(\vec{\lambda}_{t_i})\aleph^2 dW(\Delta t)dW(\Delta t) \qquad (12)$$

Furthermore, by *stochastic calculus* (equation (2)), equation (12) is then:

$$d\aleph d\aleph = \sigma^2(\vec{\lambda}_{t_i})\aleph^2 d\Delta t \qquad (13)$$

Then plugging equation (13) into equation (10), we obtain:

$$d\ln\aleph = [\gamma(\vec{\lambda}_{t_i}) - \frac{1}{2}\sigma^2(\vec{\lambda}_{t_i})]d\Delta t + \sigma(\vec{\lambda}_{t_i})dW(\Delta t) \qquad (14)$$

Integrating equation (14) on interval $[t_i, t_i + \Delta t]$, we have:

$$\ln\aleph = [\gamma(\vec{\lambda}_{t_i}) - \frac{1}{2}\sigma^2(\vec{\lambda}_{t_i})]\Delta t + \sigma(\vec{\lambda}_{t_i})W(\Delta t) + \ln N_{t_i} \qquad (15)$$

With $\aleph = N_{t_i+\Delta t}$ recovered, equation (15) becomes:

$$N_{t_i+\Delta t} = N_{t_i}exp\{[\gamma(\vec{\lambda}_{t_i}) - \frac{1}{2}\sigma^2(\vec{\lambda}_{t_i})]\Delta t + \sigma(\vec{\lambda}_{t_i})W(\Delta t)\}$$

Now denote $\mu(\vec{\lambda}_{t_i}) = \gamma(\vec{\lambda}_{t_i}) - \frac{1}{2}\sigma^2(\vec{\lambda}_{t_i})$, then:

$$\frac{N_{t_i+\Delta t}}{N_{t_i}} = exp\{\mu(\vec{\lambda}_{t_i})\Delta t + \sigma(\vec{\lambda}_{t_i})W(\Delta t)\} \qquad (16)$$

By definition of $W(t)$, its increment follows a normal distribution, i.e., $W_{t+\Delta t} - W_t \sim \text{Normal}(0, \sqrt{\Delta t}^2)$. Therefore, $\mu(\vec{\lambda}_{t_i})\Delta t + \sigma(\vec{\lambda}_{t_i})W(\Delta t) \sim \text{Normal}(\mu(\vec{\lambda}_{t_i})\Delta t, (\sigma(\vec{\lambda}_{t_i})\sqrt{\Delta t})^2)$. Then by definition of log-normal distribution, equation (16) implies:

$$\frac{N_{t_i+\Delta t}}{N_{t_i}} \sim \text{LogNormal}(\mu(\vec{\lambda}_{t_i})\Delta t, (\sigma(\vec{\lambda}_{t_i})\sqrt{\Delta t})^2) \qquad (17)$$

To focus only on the ending points of time intervals, make $\Delta t \rightarrow t_{i+1} - t_i$. Since N_t is continuous, $N^-_{t_{i+1}} = N_{t_{i+1}}$, therefore $N_{t_i+\Delta t} = N_{t_{i+1}}$. Note that the time interval to sample N_t is constant (e.g. daily). Without loss of generality, we take $t_{i+1} - t_i$ as the base unit to measure time, i.e. $\forall i, t_{i+1} - t_i \equiv 1$. Thus we obtain:

$$\frac{N_{t_i+1}}{N_{t_i}} \sim \text{LogNormal}(\mu(\vec{\lambda}_{t_i}), (\sigma(\vec{\lambda}_{t_i}))^2) \tag{18}$$

Define $X_{t_i} = N_{t_i+1}/N_{t_i}$, the change rate of N_t, the probability density function of X_{t_i} is then:

$$\begin{aligned} & f_{t_i}(X_{t_i}; \mu(\vec{\lambda}_{t_i}), \sigma(\vec{\lambda}_{t_i})) \\ =& \frac{1}{x\sigma(\vec{\lambda}_{t_i})\sqrt{2\pi}} exp(-\frac{(lnx - \mu(\vec{\lambda}_{t_i}))^2}{2\sigma(\vec{\lambda}_{t_i})^2}) \end{aligned} \tag{19}$$

The values of parameters $\mu(\vec{\lambda}_{t_i})$ and $\sigma(\vec{\lambda}_{t_i})$ both evolve with $\vec{\lambda}_{t_i}$. To estimate the parameters, we adopt a linear relation between μ and $\vec{\lambda}_{t_i}$, and an exponentially linear relation on σ and $\vec{\lambda}_{t_i}$. That is:

$$\mu(\vec{\lambda}_{t_i}) = \vec{\alpha}^T \begin{bmatrix} 1 \\ \vec{\lambda}_{t_i} \end{bmatrix} = \alpha_0 + \sum_{j=1}^{m} \alpha_j s_{jt_i} \tag{20}$$

$$\sigma(\vec{\lambda}_{t_i}) = exp(\vec{\beta}^T \begin{bmatrix} 1 \\ \vec{\lambda}_{t_i} \end{bmatrix}) = exp(\beta_0 + \sum_{j=1}^{m} \beta_j s_{jt_i}) \tag{21}$$

where $\vec{\alpha} = [\alpha_0, \alpha_1, ..., \alpha_m]^T$ and $\vec{\beta} = [\beta_0, \beta_1, ..., \beta_m]^T$ are the coefficient vectors of μ and σ respectively.

$\vec{\alpha}$ and $\vec{\beta}$ can be estimated with historical records, thus the parameterized model is partially determined. With a new ISA and activity features, the predictor vector $\vec{\lambda}_{t_i}$ takes new values, then a new distribution of X is generated by equation (19) to describe the evolution of N_t.

4.4 Prediction

Given a new ISA at time t_i, to predict its evolution, we start with the activity feature extraction. By applying the activity features to the parameterized evolution model, the current distribution of X can be generated. Then, according to the distribution, we calculate the upper and lower bound of the $1 - \alpha$ confidence interval. Based on the evolution model, we propose to predict the change rate at t_i as follows:

$$x_{t_i} = \frac{exp(\mu_{t_i} - \sigma_{t_i} q^*) + exp(\mu_{t_i} + \sigma_{t_i} q^*)}{2} exp(\mu_{t_i} + \frac{\sigma^2_{t_i}}{2})$$

where q^* is the $1 - \alpha/2$-quantile of the standard normal distribution. Here we take $\alpha = 0.1$.

As N_t can be measured by different aggregate variables, the prediction is made respectively. With the current status N_{t_i}, the future status $N_{t_{i+1}}$ is predicted as then:

$$N_{t_{i+1}} = [x_{t_i} N_{t_i}] \tag{22}$$

which is $x_{t_i} N_{t_i}$ rounded to the nearest integer. In this way, the evolution of ISA can be predicted.

5. EXPERIMENTAL VALIDATION

5.1 Set-Up

Dataset. The proposed Parameterized Social Activity Model (PSAM) is evaluated on 3 publicly-available datasets that

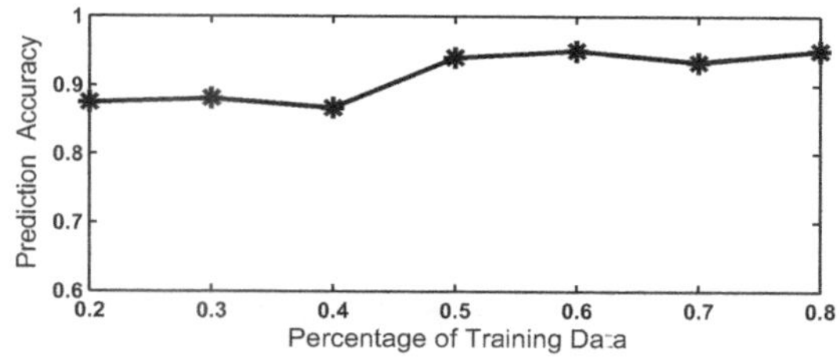

Figure 2: Accuracy of 90% Confidence interval of parameterized social activity model on Facebook friend-request dataset, when N(t)=|V(t)|

Table 2: Accuracy of 90% confidence interval of parameterized social activity model for 3 measures of social activity on Facebook friend-request dataset

	N=|I(t)|	N=|E(t)|	N=|V(t)|
Accuracy of 90% CI	0.95	0.933	0.95

represent different types of social activities: Facebook wall-post dataset [28], Facebook friend-request dataset [28], and Citeseer co-authorship dataset [15].

The Facebook datasets [28] are crawled from New Orleans regional network in Facebook. The friend-request dataset contains 905,565 records from 61,096 users over 850 days, while the wall-post dataset contains 875,993 posts between 46,952 users over 220 weeks (user attributes and textual content of wall posts are not available in the dataset). Each record is a tuple of $\langle UserID_1, UserID_2, Timestamp \rangle$. A record in the friend-request dataset denotes the time when $UserID_1$ adds $UserID_2$ as friend, while a record in the wall-post dataset indicates the time when $UserID_1$ posts on the wall of $UserID_2$. The Citeseer dataset contains 283,174 authors with 451,305 papers published from 1980 to 2005.

In the Facebook wall-post dataset, ISA is measured on a weekly basis, and activity features are extracted from them. The change rate is calculated with ISAs on every pairs of two successive weeks. In the Facebook friend-request dataset, to evaluate the predicting model on different time intervals, the interval of ISA is set to one day. For example, for the ground truth over 60 days, we construct 60 different ISAs and calculate a total of 60 change rates for them. In the Citeseer dataset, finally, the ISA and activity features are generated in a similar way. ISA is constructed with papers published every year and the corresponding authors. The change rate is then calculated with ISAs on every two successive years.

Feature selection. On each dataset, we extract 14 activity features as introduced in Table 1. After that, the *Principal Component Analysis (PCA)* is applied to eliminate the redundancy in the feature space, and to remove some noise. This also allows us to easily include more features into the framework without sacrificing performance. Then, top principal components with more than 80% of total data variation are used as the predicting vector.

Evaluation Metrics. To validate our method, we use the widely accepted evaluation metrics: Correlation and 90% Confidence Interval (CI). In particular, when we assume that the ground truth dataset is X and corresponding predicted dataset is Y, $\bar{x}$ and $\bar{y}$ denotes the mean values of X and Y respectively, and the correlation between X and Y is calcu-

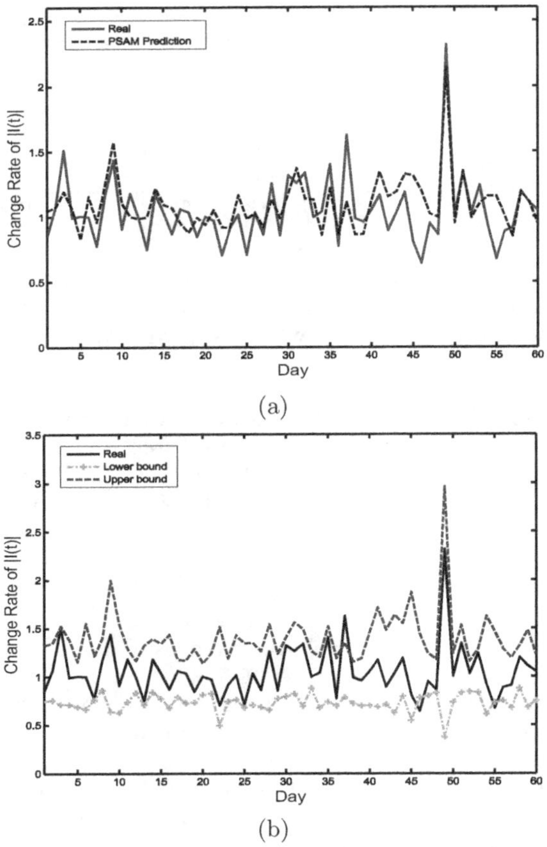

Figure 3: Comparison of parameterized social activity model prediction and ground truth on Facebook friend-request dataset over 60 days, $N(t) = |I(t)|$. (a): PSAM prediction and ground truth, (b): upper and lower bound of PSAM 90% CI with ground truth

lated as follows:

$$Corr(X,Y) = \frac{\sum(x-\bar{x})(y-\bar{y})}{\sqrt{\sum(x-\bar{x})^2\sum(y-\bar{y})^2}}$$

Baseline. Three baseline approaches are used for performance comparison with our PSAM model: linear regression (LR), cubic spline interpolation (CSI), and the average of ground truth of previous 5 ISAs (denoted as AVE).

5.2 Evaluation

In the experiments, we evaluate PSAM with one connective activity: friend-request on Facebook, and two interactive activities: wall-posting on Facebook and co-authorship on Citeseer. In particular, we evaluate PSAM on wall-posting data for the entire dataset as well as a subset of users. Meanwhile, we treat co-authorship as a dynamic and interactive activity – two scholars co-authoring a paper this year may or may not collaborate in next year. This is different from existing works on social network evolution, in which co-authorship links are "permanent" – once two scholars co-author a paper, they become co-authors permanently. Note that we are studying a different problem than network evolution – identifying active collaborations and predicting

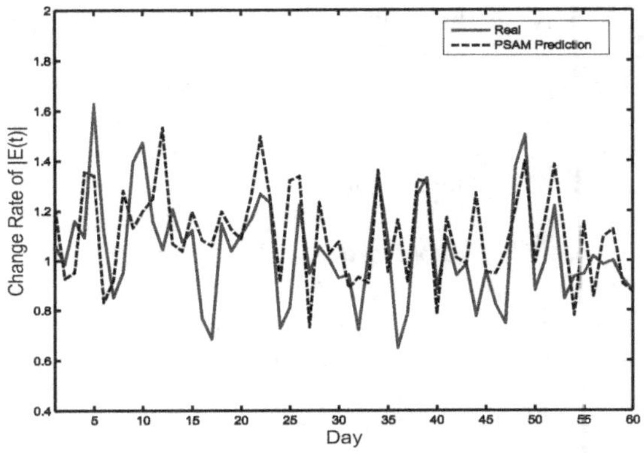

Figure 4: Comparison of parameterized social activity model prediction and ground truth on Facebook friend-request dataset, $N(t) = |E(t)|$

future collaborations. In this context, it is more reasonable to recognize the dynamics of co-authorship activities.

A. Facebook Friend-request Activity.

The Facebook dataset records daily friendship-requests for more than 2 years. As it is unnecessary to train and test the model for such a long period, we randomly select a subset of records on 300 successive days. In this experiment, we take three different measures of $N(t)$: $N(t) = |V(t)|$, $N(t) = |I(t)|$, and $N(t) = |E(t)|$. The parameterized evolution model is trained and tested against each measure.

The first group of experiments are conducted with $N(t) = |V(t)|$. To test the prediction accuracy, some of the records are randomly selected for training, and the rest for testing. We start by using 20% of the data for training (and 80% for testing), and gradually increase the portion of training data to 80% (hence, 20% for testing). Figure 2 shows the accuracy of 90%-CI with different percentages of training data (please note that the Y-axis starts at 0.6). Overall, the accuracy increases when we use more data for training. However, as shown in the figure, the PSAM approach has achieved 87.5% prediction accuracy even when only 20% of data (60 days) is used for training. The maximum accuracy is 95%, obtained when 80% of the data is used for training.

In the second group of experiments, the parameterized social activity model is compared with three baseline approaches on all measures of $N(t)$. With each measure, we compare our model prediction with the ground truth and measure the accuracy of 90% CI. Then the correlation of all methods with ground truth is evaluated.

First, when $N(t) = |I(t)|$, Figure 3(a) shows the comparison of PSAM prediction and ground truth on 60 random days. The model forecasts the up and down oscillation and predicts the change rate accurately, especially, for days 9, 28, 50 and 51. Figure 3(b) compares the upper and lower bounds of 90% CI with ground truth on the same days. A big burst of change rate 2.31 happens on day 49, i.e. an outlier. From Figure 3(a), we can see the model successfully predicts this burst. In Figure 3(b), the 90% CI covers this outlier without introducing a large variance. Among the 60 days, 57 data points falls into the 90% CI.

Overall the PSAM prediction is precise, though there are still a few points where predictions are not perfect. Considering the trade-off between the model usability and the

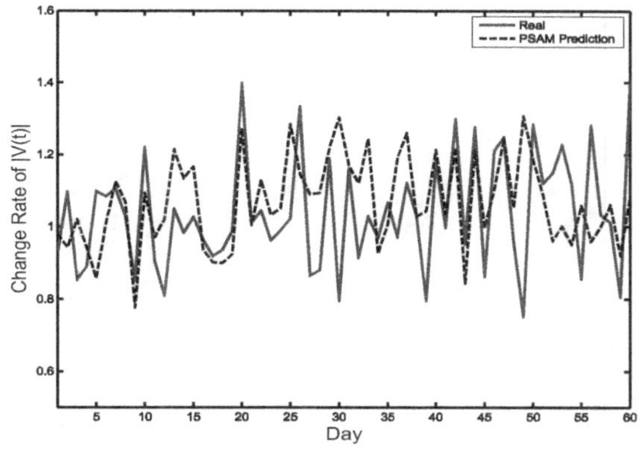

Figure 5: Comparison of parameterized social activity model prediction and ground truth on Facebook friend-request dataset, $N(t) = |V(t)|$

Table 3: Correlation of PSAM and 3 baseline methods against ground truth on Facebook friend-request dataset, when $N(t) = |V(t)|$, $|E(t)|$, and $|I(t)|$

Correlation	PSAM	LR	CSI	AVE
$N(t) = \|I(t)\|$	0.700	0.035	0.126	-0.671
$N(t) = \|E(t)\|$	0.515	0.059	0.222	-0.673
$N(t) = \|V(t)\|$	0.302	0.004	-0.026	-0.669

predicting accuracy, we suggest that 14 features are appropriate to ensure the simplicity as well as a high accuracy. For $N(t) = |E(t)|$ and $N(t) = |V(t)|$, the comparisons of PSAM prediction and ground truth on 60 random days are shown in Figure 4 and Figure 5 respectively. Comparing Figure 4 and Figure 5, we observe that the change rates of $|V(t)|$ and $|E(t)|$ evolve within the range $[0.75, 1.40]$ and $[0.65, 1.63]$ respectively, which are very close. The accuracy of 90% CI for the three social activity measures is shown in Table 2.

Finally, we compare PSAM with the baseline approaches. Table 3 illustrates the correlations of all methods with the ground truth, as $N(t)$ is measured by $I(t)$, $E(t)$, and $V(t)$. PSAM outperforms baselines with a high correlation. It has the highest correlation when predicting $I(t)$. From this group of experiments, it can be concluded that the PSAM makes effective and accurate prediction, even for outliers. The reason is that it is parameterized by the current activity features, which enables the model to incorporate the current network characteristics and therefore predict social activity accurately.

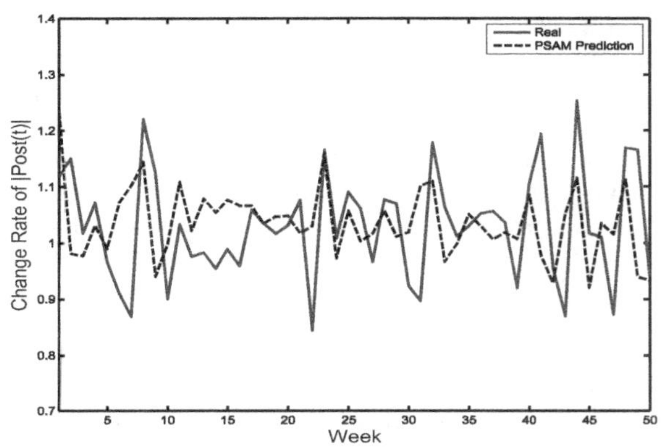

Figure 6: Comparison of parameterized social activity model prediction and ground truth on Facebook wall-post dataset over 50 weeks, $N = |Post(t)|$

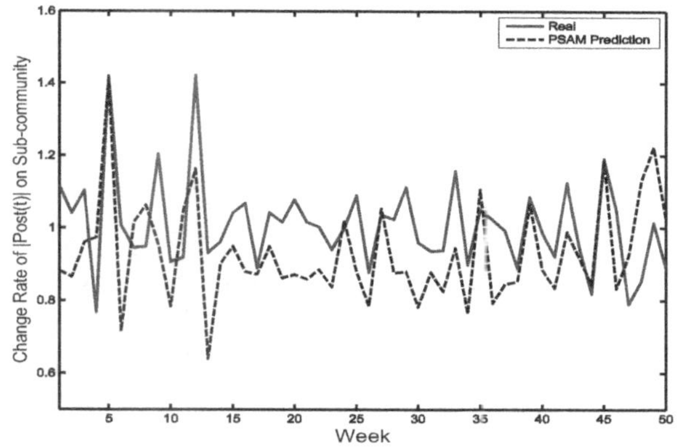

Figure 7: Comparison of PSAM prediction and ground truth on a 3000-user sub-community of Facebook wall-post data, $N = |Post(t)|$

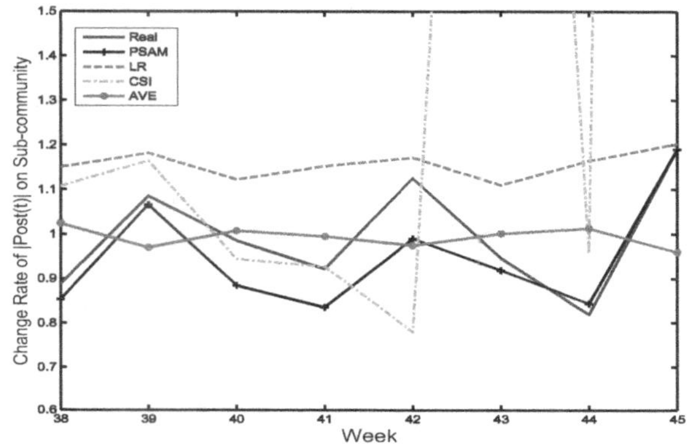

Figure 8: Details of PSAM prediction, baselines and ground truth from week 34 to week 42 in Figure 7

B. Facebook Wall-post Activity.

In the Facebook wall-post dataset, social activities are modeled as "posting on a friend's wall". We aim to predict the total number of posts in future, i.e. $N(t) = |Post(t)| = |I(t)|$. To demonstrate the effectiveness of the PSAM at different predicting intervals, the ISA interval on this dataset is set to be one week, instead of one day. We randomly select a period of 50 weeks for testing and use the rest 170 weeks for training. On this dataset, we evaluate the accuracy of PSAM, and compare it with three baselines.

Figure 6 shows the comparison of PSAM prediction and ground truth. The predictions generally match the up and down oscillation of ground truth. Some data points are accurately predicted, while others are not perfect yet. For the 50 weeks, the accuracy of 90% CI is 0.8, as shown in Table 4. Furthermore, to validate the performance of PSAM on arbitrary set of users, we choose 3,000 most active users from the wall-post dataset and try to predict the activities among them. In Figure 7, the PSAM prediction is compared with

Table 4: Accuracy of 90% confidence interval of PSAM on overall Facebook wall-post dataset and a subset of 3000 users

	Wall-post Overall	Wall-post Subset
Accuracy of 90% CI	0.8	0.94

Table 5: Correlation of PSAM and 3 baseline methods against ground truth on overall Facebook wall-post dataset and subset of 3000 users

Correlation	PSAM	LR	CSI	AVE
Overall	0.215	0.194	0.045	-0.197
Subset	0.481	0.291	0.138	-0.228

ground truth. We observe that the prediction accuracy is even better than that on the entire dataset. The accuracy of 90% CI is 0.94, as shown in Table 4.

Next, PSAM is evaluated against baselines on both overall wall-post dataset and the sub-community. To illustrate the performance of PSAM and baselines in detail, a section from week 38 to week 45 in the wall-post sub-community is enlarged in Figure 8. In this figure, we observe that the plot of LR is very flat and completely above the ground truth. For CSI, the predictions are far away from ground truth on some points, so they are not plotted in the figure. Predictions of AVE do not reflect ground truth on almost all points. Compared to baselines, predictions of PSAM are much more accurate. Table 5 shows the correlation of all methods against ground truth. Overall AVE is the worst among all methods and PSAM is the best. The correlation of PSAM on the subset is much higher than that on the overall dataset. It implies that PSAM may perform better on mid size communities.

C. Citeseer Co-authorship Activity.

As the Citeseer dataset only covers 25 years, relatively short for the time interval of ISA, overall dataset is used for both training and testing. Due to the page limit, we only show partial results of two measures: $N(t) = |I(t)|$ and $N(t) = |V(t)|$. Figure 9(a) shows the upper and lower bounds of 90% CI and ground truth on each year when $N(t) = |V(t)|$. In Figure 9(b), they are compared for $N(t) = |I(t)|$. Although the data set is small and the time interval of ISA is large, the 90% CI still has an accuracy of 0.82 for both measures. The prediction presents a good coverage of the ground truth. In all, the 90% CI of PSAM has more than 0.8 accuracy on all three datasets, which indicates that the model is effective to simulate the ISA evolution and applicable to predict various social activities. At the same time, PSAM is validated with different time intervals of ISA. Besides that, different measures of $N(t)$ also indicate that PSAM can make accurate prediction on multiple aspects and granularities.

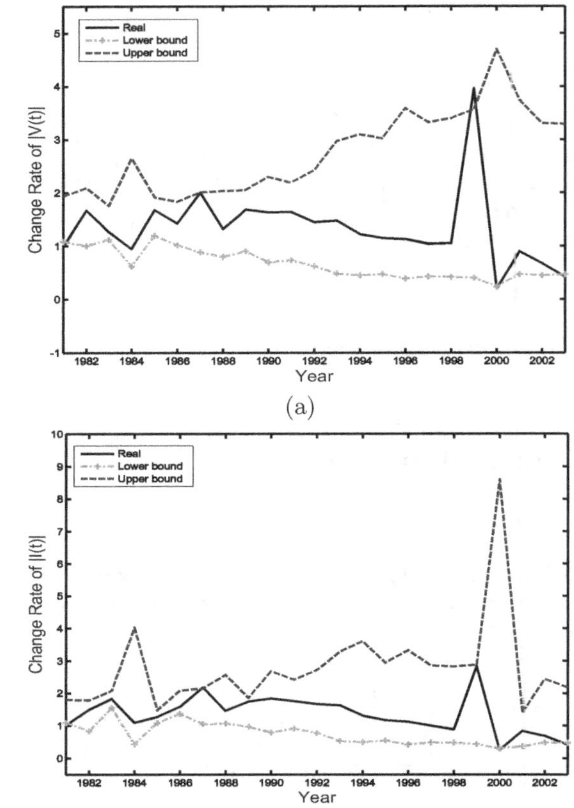

(a)

(b)

Figure 9: 90% CI of PSAM and ground truth on overall Citeseer data (a):$N(t) = |V(t)|$ **(b)** $N(t) = |I(t)|$

6. RELATED WORK

Social network evolution has been explored from different perspectives in recent years. They consider social networks formed in different environment: world-wide web, blogger networks, online friendship networks, academic co-authorship, etc. Existing works can be roughly categorized into three groups: static network mining, microscopic evolution prediction, and time-evolving structure analysis.

Some structural properties are discovered by mining the snapshots of the static network. The well-known small-world phenomenon is observed in [31]. A study on the web shows that its average diameter is small and the web forms a small-world network [2]. These studies revealed important properties but they were performed only on the static graphs.

The prediction of microscopic evolution pays more attention to the addition of new edges and new vertices [7]. The classic E-R model simulates the network growth when the edges between vertices are added randomly [12]. Different from that, preferential attachment of new vertices is proposed to capture the power-law degree distribution [5][11]. Another microscopic evolution model is proposed with nodes arriving at a pre-specified rate and selecting their lifetimes [20]. In [8], membership vectors of current members are used to address the co-evolution of the network topology and membership. Later, topological features and relations are explored to predict when a new link will appear [27].

More recent studies explore the state transition of individuals in a social network with a space of finite states. In [6], a model called NLDS, is presented to model the viral propagation and find out the epidemic threshold condition. Subsequently, to predict the popularity of news, a model based on the web site design is proposed to simulate voters' behavior [19]. These two models are only applicable to evolutions with countable future states. Different from them, the social activity evolution in our model has an infinite future state space. Therefore, our model can handel more situations on a broader perspective.

Time-evolving structure analysis focuses on the structural features and their evolution patterns [3]. The forest fire model [21] explains the densification and shrinking diameters over time. Different behavior scaling in degree distribution is analyzed on various online social networks [1] and the co-evolution of social and affiliation networks is addressed [33]. By analyzing a co-authorship network and a phone-call network, Palla et al. revealed some activity patterns and the influence of geographic locations [25]. In [23], researchers track the social events by studying the interplay between textual topics and network structures.

In these studies, the influence of structural properties is examined at the individual level and the measures of evolution are based on the cumulative additions of new vertices.

7. CONCLUSIONS AND FUTURE WORK

In this paper, we study and predict aggregate social activity with various measures. By observing that social connections are insufficient to determine a wide variety of user behaviors, we propose a continuous-time stochastic process to model the social activity evolution. The model is parameterized by activity features and integrates Wiener Process as a component, in order to address the randomness of the process and ensure dynamics therein. Experiments on three real datasets of different social activities reveal that our proposed parameterized social activity model (PSAM) can predict aggregate social activity accurately and outperforms other competing methods.

Many research issues are remaining for future work. We first plan to investigate other types of social activities in modeling and predicting future states of a social network. Second, while the accuracy of our proposed model is promising and superior to three baseline approaches, we will explore other ideas to improve the accuracy further.

8. ACKNOWLEDGEMENT

Both Shu Huang and Dongwon Lee were in part supported by NSF DUE-0817376 and DUE-0937891 awards. Bo Luo was partially supported by NSF OIA-1028098 award.

9. REFERENCES

[1] Y.-Y. Ahn, S. Han, H. Kwak, S. Moon, and H. Jeong. Analysis of topological characteristics of huge online social networking services. In *WWW*, 2007.

[2] R. Albert, H. Jeong, and A.-L. Barabasi. Diameter of the world-wide web. *Nature*, 401:130–131, 1999.

[3] S. Asur, S. Parthasarathy, and D. Ucar. An event-based framework for characterizing the evolutionary behavior of interaction graphs. In *KDD*, 2007.

[4] L. Backstrom, D. Huttenlocher, J. Kleinberg, and X. Lan. Group formation in large social networks: membership, growth, and evolution. In *KDD*, 2006.

[5] A.-L. Barabasi and R. Albert. Emergence of scaling in random networks. *Science*, 286:509–512, October 1999.

[6] D. Chakrabarti, Y. Wang, C. Wang, J. Leskovec, and C. Faloutsos. Epidemic thresholds in real networks. *ACM TISSEC.*, 10, January 2008.

[7] E. Cho, S. A. Myers, and J. Leskovec. Friendship and mobility: user movement in location-based social networks. In *KDD*, 2011.

[8] Y.-S. Cho, G. Steeg, and A. Galstyan. Co-evolution of selection and influence in social networks. In *AAAI*, 2011.

[9] D. Crandall, L. Backstrom, D. Cosley, S. Suri, D. Huttenlocher, and J. Kleinberg. Inferring social ties from geographic coincidences. *PNAS*, 2010.

[10] C. Danescu-Niculescu-Mizil, L. Lee, B. Pang, and J. Kleinberg. Echoes of power: language effects and power differences in social interaction. In *WWW*, 2012.

[11] E. Elmacioglu and D. Lee. Modeling idiosyncratic properties of collaboration networks revisited. *Scientometrics*, 80(1):195–216, July 2009.

[12] P. Erdös and A. Rényi. On random graphs. *Publicationes Mathematicae Debrecen*, 6:290, 1959.

[13] H. Fei, R. Jiang, Y. Yang, B. Luo, and J. Huan. Content based social behavior prediction: a multi-task learning approach. In *CIKM*, 2011.

[14] J. Huang, H. Sun, J. Han, H. Deng, Y. Sun, and Y. Liu. Shrink: a structural clustering algorithm for detecting hierarchical communities in networks. In *CIKM*, 2010.

[15] J. Huang, Z. Zhuang, J. Li, and C. L. Giles. Collaboration over time: characterizing and modeling network evolution. In *WSDM*, 2008.

[16] I. Karatzas and S. E. Shreve. Brownian motion and stochastic calculus. page 149. Springer, Aug. 1991.

[17] G. Kossinets and D. J. Watts. Empirical analysis of an evolving social network. *Science*, 311(5757):80–90, 2006.

[18] R. Kumar, J. Novak, and A. Tomkins. Structure and evolution of online social networks. In *Link Mining: Models, Algorithms, and Applications*, pages 337–357. Springer New York, 2010.

[19] K. Lerman and T. Hogg. Using a model of social dynamics to predict popularity of news. In *WWW*, 2010.

[20] J. Leskovec, L. Backstrom, R. Kumar, and A. Tomkins. Microscopic evolution of social networks. In *KDD*, 2008.

[21] J. Leskovec, J. Kleinberg, and C. Faloutsos. Graphs over time: densification laws, shrinking diameters and possible explanations. In *KDD*, 2005.

[22] C. W.-k. Leung, E.-P. Lim, D. Lo, and J. Weng. Mining interesting link formation rules in social networks. In *CIKM*, 2010.

[23] C. X. Lin, B. Zhao, Q. Mei, and J. Han. Pet: a statistical model for popular events tracking in social communities. In *KDD*, 2010.

[24] B. Meeder, B. Karrer, A. Sayedi, R. Ravi, C. Borgs, and J. Chayes. We know who you followed last summer: inferring social link creation times in twitter. In *WWW*, 2011.

[25] G. Palla, A.-L. Barabasi, and T. vicsek. Quantitative social group dynamics on a large scale. *Nature*, 2007.

[26] K. Radinsky, K. Svore, S. Dumais, J. Teevan, A. Bocharov, and E. Horvitz. Modeling and predicting behavioral dynamics on the web. In *WWW*, 2012.

[27] Y. Sun, J. Han, C. C. Aggarwal, and N. V. Chawla. When will it happen?: relationship prediction in heterogeneous information networks. In *WSDM*, 2012.

[28] B. Viswanath, A. Mislove, M. Cha, and K. P. Gummadi. On the evolution of user interaction in facebook. In *WOSN*, 2009.

[29] D. Wang, D. Pedreschi, C. Song, F. Giannotti, and A.-L. Barabasi. Human mobility, social ties, and link prediction. In *KDD*, 2011.

[30] X. Wang, L. Tang, H. Gao, and H. Liu. Discovering overlapping groups in social media. In *ICDM*, 2010.

[31] D. J. Watts and S. H. Strogatz. Collective dynamics of 'small-world' networks. *Nature*, 393(6684):440–442, 1998.

[32] S.-H. Yang, B. Long, A. Smola, N. Sadagopan, Z. Zheng, and H. Zha. Like like alike: joint friendship and interest propagation in social networks. In *WWW*, 2011.

[33] E. Zheleva, H. Sharara, and L. Getoor. Co-evolution of social and affiliation networks. In *KDD*, 2009.

Acquiring Temporal Constraints between Relations

Partha Pratim Talukdar*
Carnegie Mellon University
5000 Forbes Avenue
Pittsburgh, PA
ppt@cs.cmu.edu

Derry Wijaya*
Carnegie Mellon University
5000 Forbes Avenue
Pittsburgh, PA
dwijaya@cs.cmu.edu

Tom Mitchell
Carnegie Mellon University
5000 Forbes Avenue
Pittsburgh, PA
tom.mitchell@cs.cmu.edu

ABSTRACT

We consider the problem of automatically acquiring knowledge about the typical temporal orderings among relations (e.g., *actedIn*(person, film) typically occurs *before wonPrize* (film, award)), given only a database of known facts (relation instances) without time information, and a large document collection. Our approach is based on the conjecture that the narrative order of verb mentions within documents correlates with the temporal order of the relations they represent. We propose a family of algorithms based on this conjecture, utilizing a corpus of 890m dependency parsed sentences to obtain verbs that represent relations of interest, and utilizing Wikipedia documents to gather statistics on narrative order of verb mentions. Our proposed algorithm, GraphOrder, is a novel and scalable graph-based label propagation algorithm that takes transitivity of temporal order into account, as well as these statistics on narrative order of verb mentions. This algorithm achieves as high as 38.4% absolute improvement in F1 over a random baseline. Finally, we demonstrate the utility of this learned general knowledge about typical temporal orderings among relations, by showing that these temporal constraints can be successfully used by a joint inference framework to assign specific temporal scopes to individual facts.

Categories and Subject Descriptors

I.2.4 [**Artificial Intelligence**]: Knowledge Representation Formalisms and Methods; I.2.6 [**Artificial Intelligence**]: Learning; I.2.7 [**Artificial Intelligence**]: Natural Language Processing

General Terms

Algorithms, Experimentation

*Contributed equally.

CIKM'12, October 29–November 2, 2012, Maui, HI, USA.

Keywords

Knowledge Bases, Temporal Ordering, Temporal Scoping, Narrative Ordering, Graph-based Semi-Supervised Learning, Label Propagation

1. INTRODUCTION

Harvesting temporal knowledge from Web sources is an important research challenge [23]. Web search and Question Answering (QA) systems can benefit from having knowledge about entities, their relationships, and the time at which the relationships hold (i.e., their time scopes) [1]. A closely related task to time scoping is temporal ordering of relations. Instead of finding the temporal scopes of relation instances (or simply, facts), temporal ordering finds order (e.g., *before, simultaneous*, etc.) between facts. For example, while temporal scoping aims to infer that *presidentOf(Bill Clinton, USA)* was true during 1993 - 2001, temporal ordering at the relation level aims to infer that, for the same person, *wasBornIn(person, location)* happens *before presidentOf(person, country)*. Knowledge of temporal order can be useful for temporal scoping. For example, if we know that Al Gore's vice presidency was *simultaneous* with Bill Clinton's presidency, and if we know the time scope of Clinton's presidency, then we can infer the time scope of Gore's vice presidency.

We address the problem of inferring temporal ordering of relations at the macro (corpus) level: a novel, important, and unexplored problem. Previous research has mostly focused on temporal ordering at the micro level (i.e., sentence or intra-document level), and that too over verbs (or single-verb events). Instead of taking a verb-centric view, we aim to temporally order relations, where each relation may be expressed by different verbs in different sentences. For example, the $actedIn(person, film)$ relation can be expressed by the verbs *acted*, *starred*, and many others.

This paper explores the feasibility of inducing *typical* temporal orderings between relations based on the narrative order of inferred mentions of these relations, averaged across many documents. We define the narrative order of relation mentions in a document as the textual order of sentences that contain verbs expressing these relations. We explore the conjecture that narrative order is correlated with temporal order frequently enough (especially when aggregated across a large number of documents) for it to serve as a probabilistic training signal for learning the temporal order. Such conjecture is appropriate especially in documents that are each about an entity and the relations incident on the entity. In such document, relations are frequently mentioned around the entity in chronological order. Wikipedia is an example of a large and broad coverage corpus containing such documents.

Our temporal order of relations is related to structured sequences of participants and events in documents that have been called scripts [18] or narrative event chains [9], which are applied to or inferred from the narrative in the document. Since scripts are inherently temporal, e.g. restaurant script, employment script, or kidnapping script; we conjecture that narrative can also be useful for temporal ordering.

Our Contributions: We consider the problem of learning *typical* temporal ordering between *relations* (e.g., *actedIn*(person, film) happens *before* *wonPrize*(film, award)), given a database of macro-read facts (*relation instances*) such as Yago2 [12] without time information. We present GraphOrder, a graph-based label propagation algorithm for this task and demonstrate in our experiments that the narrative order of *mentions* of these relation instances (i.e., verbs expressing the relations), aggregated over a large number of documents, can be exploited as probabilistic training signals to infer the temporal ordering of the relations. We also mine syntactic information in the form of subject-verb-object triples from a large corpus of 890m dependency parsed sentences[1] and show how such information can be effectively used for finding these *relation mentions*. Through experiments on several domains of real-world datasets, we show the effectiveness of our method. We also propose CoTS$_{\text{Soft}}$, which extends a recent collective inference framework for temporal scoping [20], to handle soft temporal ordering constraints generated by GraphOrder. We incorporate our automatically acquired constraints into this framework and show the effectiveness of our learned temporal order constraints for temporal scoping of relation instances.

2. PROBLEM DEFINITION

Here we introduce our terminology and define the problem considered in this paper. We use the term *relation* to refer to any general typed binary relation r (e.g., *directed(person, film)* whose two arguments are of type *person* and *film*), and the term *relation instance* (or simply, *fact*) to refer to any instance of that relation (e.g., directed(George Lucas, Star Wars)). We say that a verb v expresses a relation r if mentions of v in documents frequently represent facts of relation r, with RelVerb(r, v) measuring the strength of this association. Default(r) is a function which returns a single default (or representative) verb (extracted from the *relation name*) which represents relation r. For example, Default(actedIn) = "act".

We use the term *narrative order* between verbs v_1 and v_2 within a document collection to refer to statistics about the sequence in which v_1 and v_2 are mentioned within the documents: we use NBefore(v_1, v_2) to measure how often v_1 occurs before v_2 in a text narrative, and use NSimultaneous(v_1, v_2) to measure how often v_1 occurs in the same sentence (i.e., simultaneously) as v_2 in the text narrative. We use the term *temporal order* between relations r_1 and r_2 to refer to the temporal sequence in which these relations occur in the real world. Specifically, we use TBefore$(\mathrm{r}_1, \mathrm{r}_2)$ to represent that facts of relation r_1 *typically* occur temporally before facts of r_2 involving at least one shared argument. Similarly, we use TSimultaneous$(\mathrm{r}_1, \mathrm{r}_2)$ to denote that facts of these two relations *typically* occur at the same time (i.e., there is a significant overlap between their temporal spans). We note that while TSimultaneous is a symmetric relation, TBefore is not. Our temporal orders are partial and uncertain (or soft). Given that many relations have only probabilistic temporal precedence, the non-negative values of TBefore$(\mathrm{r}_1, \mathrm{r}_2)$ and TSimultaneous$(\mathrm{r}_1, \mathrm{r}_2)$ are intended to capture a degree of confidence that increases monotonically with this probability. In this paper, we consider the following problem:

Problem Statement: Given (1) a set of typed binary relations R with one common argument type, which we shall refer to as the *domain*; (2) for each relation $r \in R$, a set of facts Q_r; and (3) an unlabeled text corpus C, where each document in the subset $D \subset C$ describes one instance from the *domain*; we would like to estimate the temporal relationship for each pair of relations in R, i.e., estimate values for TBefore$(\mathrm{r_i}, \mathrm{r_j})$, TSimultaneous$(\mathrm{r_i}, \mathrm{r_j}) \in \mathbb{R}_+$, $\forall r_i, r_j \in R$, where higher values represent higher confidence that the corresponding temporal relationship holds.[2]

Example: Let $R = \{actedIn(person, film), directed(person, film), wonPrize(film, award)\}$ be the set of typed binary relations, with common argument type *film*. Hence, *film* will also be the the domain in this case. Let the set of facts for each relation be as follows: $Q_{actedIn}$ = {(Tom Hanks, Forrest Gump)}, $Q_{directed}$ = {(Robert Zemeckis, Forrest Gump)}, and $Q_{wonPrize}$ = {(Forrest Gump, Academy Awards)}. Let D be a singleton set consisting of the Wikipedia page on the film "Forrest Gump", and let C be its superset consisting of additional documents sampled from a large text corpus such as [7]. Given these as input, we would like to determine the temporal relationship (i.e., estimate values for TBefore and TSimultaneous) for each pair of relations in R.

Please note that since our inputs do not consist of any labeled data with temporal orderings annotated (as in [17]), our proposed method is unsupervised with respect to this task.

3. METHOD

3.1 Overview

The central thesis behind the method introduced here is that: "*Statistics aggregated from a large number of documents about narrative orders of verbs representing two relations can serve as probabilistic training signals for learning the temporal order between the two relations.*"

Let us consider two relations incident on *film* instances: *directed* and *wonPrize*, whose default verbs are "directed" and "won," respectively. If in documents discussing *film* instances, we predominantly observe the narrative order *directed* $\rightarrow$ *won*, i.e., NBefore(*directed*, *won*) $\gg$ NBefore(*won*, *directed*), this should increase our estimate of TBefore(*directed*, *wonPrize*). In other words, NBefore(*directed*, *won*), which can be estimated directly from free text, can be exploited to estimate the unobserved TBefore(directed, wonPrize) (and similarly for TSimultaneous). Based on the thesis mentioned above, our proposed approach consists of three phases, which are outlined in Figure 1. We next describe each of these three phases.

[1]To the best of our knowledge, this is one of the largest parsed corpus ever used for temporal extraction task.

[2]$\mathbb{R}_+$ is the set of non-negative real numbers

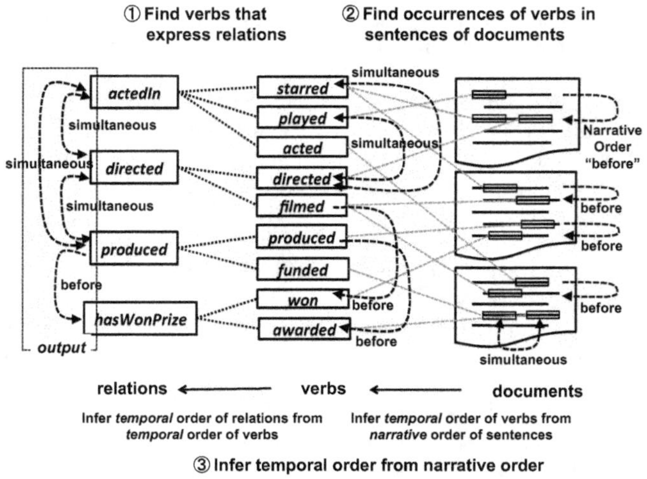

Figure 1: Outline of our proposed method which consists of three phases (see Section 3.1 for an overview). In the first phase, each relation is represented by a set of verbs (Section 3.2); in the second phase, the narrative order over verb mentions are estimated (Section 3.3); and in the final phase, the temporal order for each relation pair is estimated (Section 3.4).

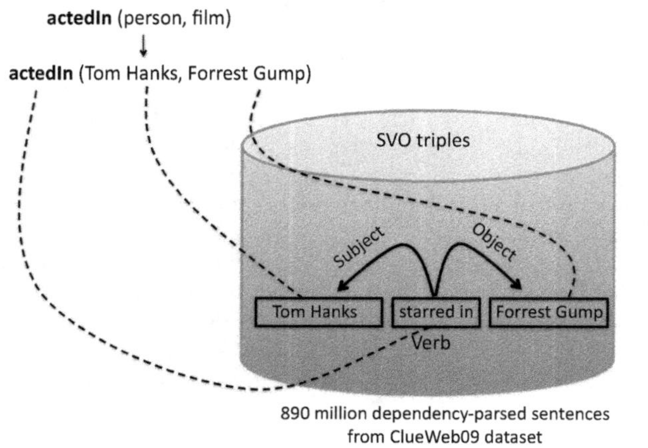

Figure 2: Finding verbs that express relations by mining a collection of subject-verb-object (SVO) triples extracted from 890m dependency parsed sentences (Section 3.2).

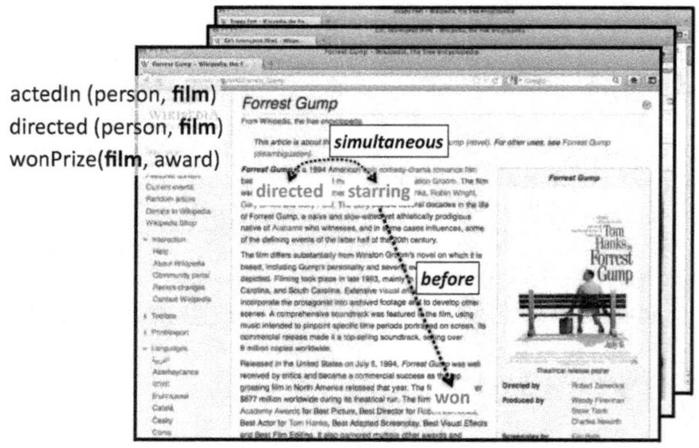

Figure 3: Narrative orders of verbs (e.g., *directed, starring, won*, etc.) in documents from the *film* domain (Section 3.3). Each document describes one instance (e.g., "Forrest Gump") from the domain (*film* in this case). These narrative orders provide guidance for learning temporal order of relations (e.g., *actedIn(person, film)*, *directed(person, film)*, *wonPrize(film, award)*) (Section 3.4).

3.2 Find Verbs that Express Relations

To identify verbs that express a particular relation r, we consider the given set of input facts Q_r representing known instances of relation r. Each fact $f \in Q_r$ is a triple, $\langle f_{a1}, f_{a2}, f_{rel}\rangle$ containing the values of the first argument, second argument, and the name of relation (in this case r), respectively. An example of a fact is ⟨Tom Hanks, Forrest Gump, actedIn⟩[3]. We draw on work on distributional similarity between verbs [10] and other means of grouping verbs that share the same lexical items in subject/object positions [6]. In particular, for each relation r we identify verbs whose mentions occur with subject/object pairs that match the known instances of relation r in Q_r.

More specifically, to identify the verbs associated with relation r (as illustrated in Figure 2), we use a large collection of Subject-Verb-Object (SVO) triples which can be compared to the facts Q_r about relation r. We construct this dataset of SVO triples by first parsing 50m Web documents (890m sentences, 16B tokens) using the MALT dependency parser [16], and then extracting SVO triples from these parsed sentences[4]. We aggregate all the SVO triples and count their frequency using Hadoop. This yields in a dataset with 114m triples, which we shall refer to as S.

[3]Alternatively, we also write it as actedIn(Tom Hanks, Forrest Gump)

[4]Details on the SVO triple extraction will appear in a longer version of this paper.

Fields within each tuple $s \in S$ can be accessed using the following: s_{sbj}, s_{obj}, s_{verb}, and s_{cnt}, which return the subject, object, verb, and the count of the tuple, respectively. To the best of our knowledge, this is one of the largest dependency parsed corpora that has ever been used in published research[5].

Let $S_v = \{s \mid s_{verb} = v,\ s \in S\}$ be the set of tuples in S with v as its verb. Also, let $U_S = \{u \mid |S_u| > 0\}$ be the set of unique verbs in S, and let U be the overall set of unique verbs under consideration. We have,

$$U = U_S \cup \{\text{Default}(r) \mid r \in R\} \tag{1}$$

We now compute RelVerb(r, v) to measure whether verb $v \in U$ expresses relation r as follows:

$$\text{RelVerb}(r, v) = \frac{I_1(r, v) + \sum_{f \in Q_r, s \in S_v} I_2(f, s) \times s_{cnt}}{\sum_{u \in U}\left[I_1(r, u) + \sum_{f \in Q_r, s \in S_u} I_2(f, s) \times s_{cnt}\right]} \tag{2}$$

where $I_1(r, u) = 1$ iff $\exists r \in R$ such that $u = \text{Default}(r)$, and 0 otherwise; and $I_2(f, s)$ is another indicator function which returns 1 whenever arguments of f and s match, i.e., $(f_{a1}, f_{a2}) = (s_{sbj}, s_{obj})$ or $(f_{a1}, f_{a2}) = (s_{obj}, s_{sbj})$, and 0 otherwise. We now define F_r, the set of verbs used to express relation r as follows,

$$F_{\delta,r} = \{v \in U \mid \text{RelVerb}(r, v) > \delta\}$$

where $\delta \in \mathbb{R}$ is a threshold, which is set to 0 for the experiments in this paper. Examples of the top-5 elements from the set $F_{\delta,actedIn}$ relation, are as follows: stars, features, 's, costars, starring. This suggests that this method is able to automatically discover meaningful verbs to express a given relation.

3.3 Estimating Narrative Order of Verbs

Once we find the set of verbs that express relations, we find mentions of these verbs in documents in D, as illustrated in Figure 3. Since each document in D is about a domain instance (Section 2), we make a simplifying assumption that verbs appearing in the same document are sharing the domain instance as subject/object argument. In the future, a dependency parse of sentences in the document can be used to find verbs sharing the same domain instance as subject/object.

We shall represent a document $d \in D$ as a sequence of sentences sorted as per the narrative order, with $|d|$ denoting the total number of sentences in the document, and $d_k (1 \leq k \leq |d|)$ returning the kth sentence in document d.

Now, for each sentence d_k, we compute the sentence score (SS) of each (r, v) pair mentioned in the sentence.

$$\text{SS}(d_k, r, v) = \frac{\text{VerbCount}(d_k, r, v)}{\sum_{r \in R, v \in U} \text{VerbCount}(d_k, r, v)} \tag{3}$$

where VerbCount(d_k, r, v) is the number of times verb v is used to express relation r in sentence d_k. This can be estimated by matching the arguments of v in d_k against Q_r, the set of facts from relation r. However, we shall make a simplifying assumption and increment verb count by 1 whenever we come across v in d_k, subject to the condition that $v \in F_{\delta,r}$ (increasing δ may improve precision of verbs expressing a relation, but may affect recall). The scoring in Equation 3 will discount scores for verbs which express a large number of relations.

We then define the narrative order scores for two verbs v_1 and v_2 in a document d as the sum of scores (SS) of v_1 and v_2 in all pairs of sentences for which v_1 is before v_2, and the sum of scores of v_1 and v_2 in all sentences where v_1 and v_2 both occur. We then aggregate these per-document narrative orders across all documents containing v_1 and v_2 by taking the average of these per-document scores as the final narrative order scores NBefore(v_1, v_2) and NSimultaneous(v_1, v_2) for the verbs v_1 and v_2.

We note that Rel-grams [2], a recently proposed semantic resource, may also be used to estimate NBefore, although it is less clear how this resource can be used to estimate NSimultaneous.

3.4 Estimating Temporal Order of Relations

Once we find narrative order of verbs as described in Section 3.3, we infer temporal order of relations expressed by these verbs using two methods. The first, Pairwise (Section 3.4.1), is a non-transitive method that determines the order for two relations r_i and r_j by making pairwise decisions. The other method, **GraphOrder** (Section 3.4.2), uses a novel graph-based label propagation algorithm to temporally order relations in a joint optimization, and also while taking transitivity into account.

Because we are the first to address the problem of temporally ordering relations, there are no existing techniques that we could compare to. In our experiments, we compare the resulting temporal order of relations to a random baseline inspired by [9], which addresses a related but different problem. We also use our non-transitive method, Pairwise, as baseline to compare to GraphOrder, our proposed transitive graph-based method.

3.4.1 *Pairwise Temporal Ordering of Relations*

We now define scores for the the temporal order relations TBefore and TSimultaneous as follows:

$$\text{TBefore}(r_i, r_j) = \frac{1}{Z} \sum_{u,v \in U} \text{RelVerb}(r_i, u) \times \text{NBefore}(u, v) \times \text{RelVerb}(r_j, v) \tag{4}$$

$$\text{TSimultaneous}(r_i, r_j) = \frac{1}{Z} \sum_{u,v \in U} \text{RelVerb}(r_i, u) \times \text{NSimultaneous}(u, v) \times \text{RelVerb}(r_j, v) \tag{5}$$

where $\text{TSimultaneous}(r_i, r_j) = \text{TSimultaneous}(r_j, r_i)$ and $Z = \text{TBefore}(r_i, r_j) + \text{TBefore}(r_j, r_i) + \text{TSimultaneous}(r_i, r_j)$ is the normalizing factor. As is evident from the equations above, the temporal ordering scores for a pair of relations are obtained by marginalizing over all the verb pairs used to express the two relations. We call this method Pairwise.

3.4.2 *GraphOrder: Collective Temporal Ordering of Relations*

The temporal ordering method described in previous section makes pairwise decision considering two relations at a time. However, it is conceivable that instead of ordering two relations at a time, a collective framework which looks at all relations at once could be useful. Transitivity is one such benefit that is possible in this collective ordering framework. For example, the pairwise method might infer that

[5]The SVO triples dataset is available from the authors on request.

TBefore(r_1,r_2) and TBefore(r_2,r_3) are true, but it might fail to identify that TBefore(r_1,r_3) is also true. However, if we considered all three relations at the same time, then it might be easier to establish the temporal relationship between r_1 and r_3. Although simple transitive closure would work well in case of hard orderings, it is not clear how such a closure could be computed with soft ordering constraints, as is the case in our setting, where there is inherent uncertainty in the inferred temporal orders. We note that the methods for inducing global ordering over soft orderings [5, 8] are not applicable in the current setting, as instead of a single global ordering, we are interested in finding the transitive closure over the soft orderings.

In order to overcome these challenges, we propose a novel graph-based label propagation algorithm GraphOrder, which is both parallelizable and scalable. We first create a graph $G = (X, E, W)$ whose vertices $X = R \cup U$ (see Equation 1), i.e., each vertex is either a relation or a verb. Edges in this graph consist of the following mix of directed and undirected edges[6]: (1) undirected edge between relation r and verb v with edge weight $W_{r,v}$ = RelVerb(r, v); (2) directed edge between verb v_i and v_j with W_{v_i,v_j} = NBefore(v_i, v_j); (3) undirected edge between verb v_i and v_j with W_{v_i,v_j} = NSimultaneous(v_i, v_j); (4) directed temporal order edge between relations r_i and r_j with W_{r_i,r_j} = TBefore(ri,rj); and (5) undirected temporal order edge between r_i and r_j with W_{r_i,r_j} = TSimultaneous(r_i,r_j). This graph is very similar to the one shown in Figure 1, except that there are no document nodes here. We have $E = E_D \cup E_U$ where E_D is the set of directed edges while E_U is the set of undirected edges.

We shall now inject each relation node $u \in R \subseteq X$ with a unique node specific label l_u. This seed information is stored in the initial label matrix Y with $Y_{u,l_u} = 1$. Each such relation specific label l_u has another temporally-after variant $\vec{l_u}$, which can be interpreted as follows: if another relation node $v \in R$ is assigned the label $\vec{l_u}$ with high score, then we should infer that there is a *before*(u, v) relationship between the two relations. Otherwise, a high l_u score on v should lead us to infer that there is a *simultaneous*(u, v). Following [19], we shall also have a none-of-the-above label, $\top$, which we shall use as an automatic threshold on the label scores. Let L be the total set of labels with total $|L| = 2 \times n + 1$ labels in it, where $|R| = n$ is the total number of relations.

In order to perform collective node classification and thereby infer temporal ordering among relations, our proposed algorithm, GraphOrder, optimizes the following objective function (Equation 6),

$$\begin{aligned}\min_{\{\hat{Y}_{u,l}\}} \quad & \mu_1 \sum_{u \in R} (Y_{u,l_u} - \hat{Y}_{u,l_u})^2 \\ & + \mu_2 \sum_{(u,v) \in E_D, l \in L} W_{u,v} \times (\hat{Y}_{u,l} - \hat{Y}_{v,\vec{l}})^2 \\ & + \mu_2 \sum_{(u,v) \in E_U, l \in L} W_{u,v} \times (\hat{Y}_{u,l} - \hat{Y}_{v,l})^2 \\ & + \mu_3 \sum_{x \in X, l \in L} (\hat{Y}_{u,l} - M_{u,l})^2 \qquad (6)\end{aligned}$$

where μ_1, μ_2, μ_3 are hyperparameters, and M is a regularization matrix, and $\hat{Y}_{u,l} \in \mathbb{R}$ is the output variable which measure the score of label l assigned to node u. The objective above is convex[7] and is similar in spirit to the QC criteria [3] and MAD [19] that tries to minimize difference between predicted and actual labels, with the critical distinction that the second term in this objective involves directed edges with transformed labels across the edge (l vs $\vec{l}$). We develop a Jacobi iteration-based iterative algorithm to solve this objective[7]. However, in order to handle the directed edges, whenever a label l is to be spread over the directed edge $(u, v) \in E_D$, instead of updating the score for label l on v, we transform the label and update the score for $\vec{l}$ on v. We iterate this process for a fixed number of iterations[8], after which the assigned labels are used to infer the temporal relations as described earlier in this section. The objective function and solution to the optimization problem are detailed in the Appendix (Section A and Section B).

The algorithm we propose above is novel as no previous label propagation algorithm has considered the situation when there is a need to transform labels during propagation. Also, this algorithm is essentially self-supervised as no external hand labeled data is necessary. As we will see in the experimental results in Figure 4, the proposed algorithm effectively combines these strategies for the task of temporal order acquisition.

4. EXPERIMENTS

4.1 Experimental Setup

We select entities in Yago2 [12] as our domain instances. We select relations in Yago2 that are incident on these entities to temporally *order* and their relation instances (facts) to temporally *scope*. Yago2 is a knowledge base containing entities and relations automatically extracted from the entities' Wikipedia infoboxes. For this reason, we choose Wikipedia as the source of our unlabeled corpus D. Each document in D is thus about an entity (i.e., contains the entity in its infobox). Although Wikipedia pages, being general purpose, may seem more chronological and thus better suit the assumption that narrative follows temporal order, we show in experiments that the choice of Wikipedia pages does not in fact trivialize the problem. There is enough variation in the narrative sequence of verb mentions in Wikipedia that we benefit from aggregation. We use Wikipedia pages without any special processing, omitting infoboxes, using only sentences in the page sorted by their narrative order in the page.

The relations we want to temporally order and whose instances we want to time scope are chosen from the domains: *albums*, *cricketers*, *films*, *footballers*, *novels*, *operas*, *plays*, *politicians*, and *songs*. For each domain, we select the top 25 relations that have at least one argument belonging to the domain, to temporally order (based on the number of relation instances/facts). We also select as *domain instances*, whose Wikipedia pages we use as our corpus D, the top 1000 Yago2 entities that participate the most in these relations. By doing so, we ensure that D contains a lot of information on the relations we want to temporally order. We define an argument of a relation as belonging to the domain *films* if it belongs to any Wikipedia category that ends with the word "_films": e.g. *wikicategory_1930s_crime_films*, etc.

[6]By directed, we refer to edges corresponding to NBefore and TBefore; and by undirected to edges corresponding to NSimultaneous and TSimultaneous orders.

[7]Please see appendix for details.

[8]Set to 10 iterations for the experiments in this paper

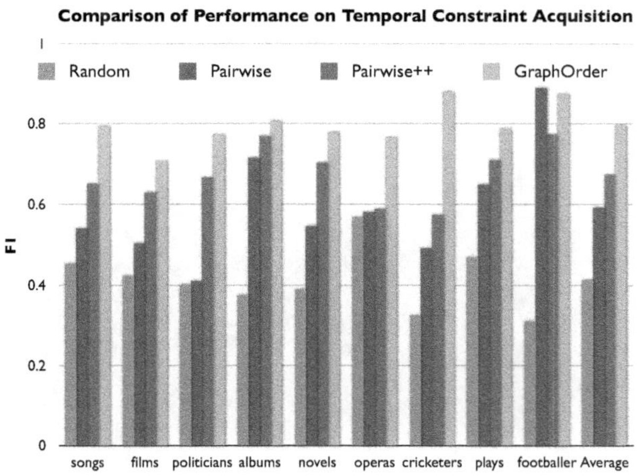

Figure 4: Comparison of performance of the temporal constraint acquisition methods discussed in the paper. We observe that the graph-based inference method GraphOrder (Section 3.4.2) (i.e., the rightmost bar) achieves the best performance on average.

For example, the top 5 relations selected for the domain *films* are *actedIn*, *wasCreatedOnDate*, *directed*, *created*, and *produced*. A lot of relations in Yago2 are biographical (birth, death) due to the nature of the infoboxes. We also notice that some entities are categorized incorrectly in Wikipedia, e.g., a *person* maybe categorized as *films*[9]. These may lead to irrelevant relations selected, e.g., *wasBornIn* for *films*.

4.2 Temporal Ordering Experiments

Following [9], we use a **random** baseline which generated 300 random sets of pairwise orderings for each domain. In each set, we generate the same number of orderings as that learned by GraphOrder (described below), and the performance is averaged across these 300 sets. As there are no existing methods that output temporal orders at the relation level, we use the methods that are based on Pairwise Temporal Ordering (Section 3.4.1): using default verbs only (**Pairwise**) or using also verbs derived from the SVO dataset (**Pairwise++**) as additional baselines. We compare these baselines to our proposed method **GraphOrder** (Section 3.4.2), which performs collective temporal ordering using label propagation-based inference over a graph consisting of constraints from the Pairwise++ system. We observe that GraphOrder converges quite fast (10 iterations are usually sufficient).

For each domain and each method, we obtain temporal orderings of relations and the scores of the orderings. Each ordering is between a pair of relations. For evaluation, for each domain and each method we create a directed acyclic graph (DAG) of the learned orderings, traversing over the orderings from the highest score to the lowest score, and adding an ordering to the DAG only if it does not conflict with previously added orderings.

Similar to temporal evaluation in [9], we hand identify a *gold standard* set of temporal orderings for each domain. All attempts were made to include every *before* and *simultaneous* relation that can exist between the relations for the domain or that could be deduced through transitivity rules. We ignore temporal orders of relations that are ambiguous to humans. For example, *isMarriedTo* and *actedIn*, one can be before or after the other at the relation-level. We evaluate each temporal ordering (i.e., each edge) in the DAG for correctness according to the gold standard. Precision is computed as the number of edges marked correct over the total number of edges marked unambiguous in the DAG. Since it is difficult to determine upfront the full set of valid temporal orderings, we decide to estimate the recall with respect to the largest number of correct edges returned by any one of the compared methods. Using precision and the estimated recall, we compute F1 (Figure 4).

Experimental results comparing these four systems are shown in Figure 4. We see that GraphOrder performs better than all three baselines on average and across all domains, showing the merit of our graph-based, unsupervised, macro learning of temporal orderings. On average, we observe a 38.4% improvement in F1 score over the random baseline for GraphOrder.

In Figure 4, we see that performance (F1) of Pairwise++ is higher than Pairwise on average and across all domains except in *footballers*. This indicates that adding verbs from SVO typically improves temporal ordering and demonstrates the benefits of having a more flexible representation of relations that involves multiple verbs. We see that the highest increase in performance is in *politicians*, in which we find the largest number of SVO verbs (118 verbs) to represent the relations. In contrast, we only obtain one verb from SVO: "had visited" that represents the *influences* relation in *footballers*. In this case, adding verbs from SVO does not help performance and may even degrade it if the verb found does not really express the relation, as in this case.

In Figure 4, we observe that performance of GraphOrder is higher than the non-transitive baselines (Pairwise++ and Pairwise). In terms of precision and estimated recall, we find that GraphOrder increases recall without hurting precision. On average, GraphOrder increases the number of correctly learned temporal orderings by 48.7% from that learned by Pairwise++ and this improves the F1 score by 12.2%. This shows how collective reasoning using label propagation can improve temporal ordering.

A few examples of temporal orders learned by GraphOrder in *politics* and in *films* are shown in Figure 5. As can be seen from the figure, in case of *politics*, the method is able to learn orderings pretty accurately: all relations happen after *wasBornIn*. In addition, a person must be a *citizen* of some country if he happens to *hold a political position*, and/or is *a leader* of something. We also notice that a *politician* or a *leader* must have an *influence* at least before he *dies*. In case of *films*, the method learns correctly that the process of *creating* a movie: *producing*, *directing*, *acting* must happen in the same period of time and all before the movie can *win* a prize. However, there are still questionable ordering such as *diedIn* before *hasWonPrize* (possibly winning an award posthumously), and mistake such as *wasBornIn* simultaneous *produced*. We note that all these orderings have scores attached to them which can be taken into account in any subsequent consumption of these constraints, as we do in temporal scoping (Section 4.4).

[9]http://en.wikipedia.org/wiki/Joseph_Kessel is a person that has a Wikipedia category: "Novels adapted into films"

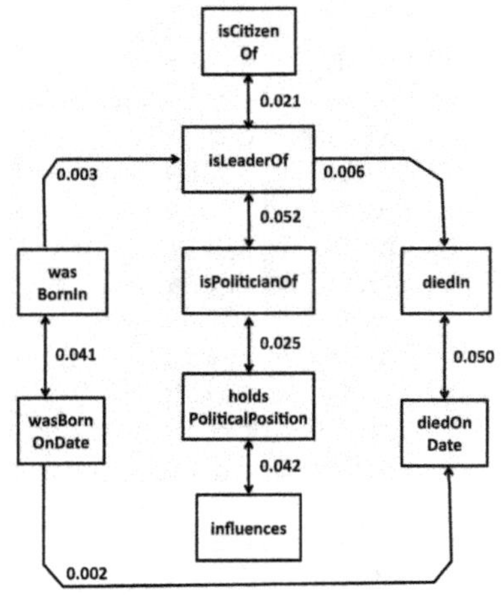

Figure 5: Examples of temporal orderings of relations in *politics* (left) and *films* (right) which were automatically learned by GraphOrder. Directed arrow indicates a *before* relation while each bi-directed arrow indicates a *simultaneous* relation. The score on each edge indicates the confidence of the temporal order.

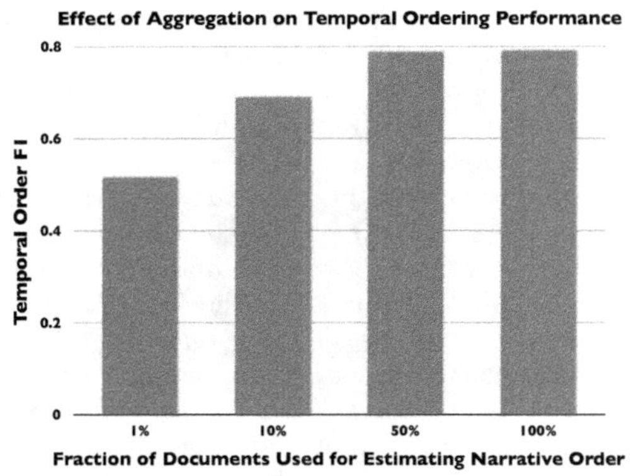

Figure 6: Performance of GraphOrder as the number of Wikipedia documents from which the narrative order of verbs are estimated is increased. We observe that the overall temporal ordering performance improves as increasing number of documents are used to estimate narrative order. All results are averaged over the 9 domains.

Domain	Constraint Source	Precision	Recall	F1
Films	None	55.6 (5.7)	49.9 (5.5)	52.6 (5.6)
	GraphOrder	71.0 (3.8)	62.3 (4.1)	66.4 (4.0)
	Manual	89.1 (5.6)	70.6 (3.3)	**78.8** (4.0)
Novels	None	53.4 (7.5)	37.5 (9.2)	43.8 (8.5)
	GraphOrder	67.2 (12.1)	44.4 (13.1)	**53.0** (12.7)
	Manual	60.8 (7.1)	41.4 (12.3)	48.8 (11.0)
Songs	None	31.0 (4.9)	16.5 (2.6)	21.5 (3.4)
	GraphOrder	60.0 (5.4)	26.9 (1.6)	**37.1** (2.4)
	Manual	43.5 (4.3)	20.8 (2.4)	28.1 (2.9)

Table 1: Results of temporal scoping experiment using the $\text{CoTS}_{\text{Soft}}$ framework, with different sources of inter-relation temporal ordering constraints: None (i.e., no such constraints used), constraints inferred by GraphOrder (Section 3.4.2), and manually encoded constraints. All results are averaged over five evaluation sets, with standard deviation indicated in brackets. For each domain, the setting with highest F1 score is marked in bold. See Section 4.4 for details.

4.3 Effect of Aggregation on Temporal Ordering

The goal in this section is to measure what effect aggregation of narrative order of verbs from a large number of Wikipedia documents has on final temporal ordering of relations. In Figure 6, we report the temporal ordering performance of GraphOrder, the best performing system from Section 4.2, as the fraction of Wikipedia documents from which narrative order of verbs are estimated is increased. All results are averaged across 9 domains. From Figure 6, we observe that performance improves sharply as the fraction of documents used is increased. This demonstrates the value of aggregation for temporal ordering. The results in Figure 6 suggest that a small number of documents (e.g., 1%) are not sufficient for optimal temporal ordering performance. This also suggests that the use of Wikipedia doesn't trivialize the problem as otherwise a small number of documents would have been sufficient for reliable estimation of narrative orders and thereby temporal order of relations. Instead, these results suggest that document specific inconsistencies can be overcome through aggregation across a large set of documents, resulting in improved temporal ordering performance.

4.4 Temporal Scoping Experiment

The experiments described above establish that GraphOrder, our proposed approach, can acquire knowledge of the *typical* temporal ordering between different relations. In this section we explore how useful these learned temporal constraints are, for the task of assigning specific temporal scope to individual facts (instances of these relations). In particular, we use an extended version of the CoTS system [20] to temporally scope facts from the Yago KB. CoTS is a joint inference ILP framework for temporal scoping that combines the rising and falling of counts of occurrences of facts in documents over time (as a signal to indicate the period of validity of the facts), with constraints about the facts (*si-*

multaneous, before or after temporal orders) to infer the temporal scope of facts (i.e., the interval of time when a fact is true). The original CoTS system [20] can only handle hard and unweighted constraints, which is not adequate in our case as the temporal ordering constraints learned by GraphOrder are soft and weighted in nature. In order to overcome these limitations, we present an extension of the CoTS system, which we shall refer to as $\text{CoTS}_{\text{Soft}}$.

$\text{CoTS}_{\text{Soft}}$ System: Let $x_{r,s,t} \in \{0,1\}$ be a binary variable with $x_{r,s,t} = 1$ whenever fact r from relation s is true at time t, and 0 otherwise. Let $z^b_{r,s,t} \in \{0,1\}$ be a binary variable with $z^b_{r,s,t} = 1$ indicating that fact s started to be true at time t. Similarly, $z^e_{r,s,t} = 1$ indicating that fact s ceased to be true at time t. Let $b(r,s,t)$ be our initial belief that fact s from relation r is true at time t. Now, given a temporal order TBefore(a, c) with score $q_{a,c}$, and two facts u and v from the relations a and c, respectively, $\text{CoTS}_{\text{Soft}}$ introduces the following constraint,

$$\sum_t t * z^e_{a,u,t} - \sum_t t * z^b_{c,v,t} - \xi_{a,u,c,v} \leq 0$$

where $\xi_{a,u,c,v} \in \{0,1\}$ is a binary *slack* variable which allows this constraint to be violated, but not without suffering a penalty of $q_{a,c}$ in the objective as we shall see shortly. Please note that $\text{CoTS}_{\text{Soft}}$ enforces this soft-constraint iff facts u and v have a shared argument entity. $\text{CoTS}_{\text{Soft}}$ also uses the CONSISTENCY constraints from [20] to make sure the z^b, z^e and x variables are consistent with one another at any given time. $\text{CoTS}_{\text{Soft}}$ uses the following set of inequalities to encode a TSimultaneous(a, c) ordering between the two facts u and v from above at any given time t.

$$\begin{aligned} x_{a,u,t} &\leq x_{c,v,t} + \xi_{a,u,c,v,t} \\ x_{c,v,t} &\leq x_{a,u,t} + \xi_{c,v,a,u,t} \end{aligned}$$

where $\xi_{a,u,c,v,t}$ and $\xi_{c,v,a,u,t}$ are binary slack variables. Let Δ be the set of all slack variables, with q_ξ representing the penalty associated with slack variable ξ. We now present the objective optimized by $\text{CoTS}_{\text{Soft}}$ subject to the constraints presented above.[10]

$$\max_{\{x_{r,s,t}\}} \sum_{r,s,t} b(r,s,t) * x_{r,s,t} - \gamma \times \sum_{\xi \in \Delta} q_\xi \times \xi$$

where γ is a hyperparamater which we set to 1 for all the experiments in this section. We use the Mosek[11] optimization package to solve this Integer Linear Program (ILP).

We now describe the experimental setup used to evaluate the usefulness of temporal orderings learned by GraphOrder. In this section, we experiment with three domains: *films*, *novels* and *songs*. For each domain, we obtain facts from the Yago2 KB as in previous sections, a subset of which is already temporally scoped. We split this subset into two parts, with the first set consisting 80% of the facts. We keep the temporal scopes of the first set fixed as prior knowledge, and use the $\text{CoTS}_{\text{Soft}}$ system to predict temporal scopes for the other set. We then compare predicted temporal scope with truth to compute precision, recall and F1. We repeat this process five times for each domain, generating a separate split each time. All results are averaged over these five runs. For each split, we evaluate temporal scoping performance of the $\text{CoTS}_{\text{Soft}}$ system when injected with inter-relation temporal ordering constraints obtained from three sources: (1) None (i.e., when no temporal ordering constraints are used); (2) temporal orders learned by GraphOrder in Section 4.2; and (3) manually crafted ordering rules. For all experimental runs, we required $\text{CoTS}_{\text{Soft}}$ to make point predictions (i.e., unit length temporal scopes). For each fact $r(a,b)$ we query the Gigaword corpus[12] with "*a AND b*" or "*a AND Default(r)*" if b is a date, to estimate $b(r,s,t)$. We perform all evaluations at the year granularity, and since Gigaword's coverage is limited to the period 1994-2008, we only consider facts which are true during this period.

Experimental results comparing these three ordering generators are presented in Table 1. For all three domains, we observe that GraphOrder leads to improvement in performance (F1) compared to when no constraints are used. Interestingly, constraints learned by GraphOrder outperforms manually crafted constraints in two out of the three domains. This might be due to the incomprehensiveness of the manual rule writing process leading to omission of certain useful orders, which were included in the orderings learned by GraphOrder.

Next, we evaluate whether the temporal orders learned by GraphOrder, along with $\text{CoTS}_{\text{Soft}}$, can be used to increase Yago2's temporal coverage, i.e., temporally scope Yago2 facts which are currently not scoped. We experiment with facts from the *films* domain (total 1831 facts), and fix all facts that are already temporally scoped (such as instances of *produced*). We then use the $\text{CoTS}_{\text{Soft}}$ system to temporally scope facts from the *actedin* relation, which are currently not scoped. Using random sampling-based manual evaluation of 100 facts, we observe a temporal scoping precision of 69.8%. Thus, we are able to increase Yago2's temporal coverage at a modest precision, showing the merit of learning temporal constraints by GraphOrder and using them for temporal scoping. A few examples of correct scoping are: 2001 for *actedIn*(Jason Biggs, American Pie 2); 1996 for *actedIn*(John Neville, High School High). Examples of an incorrect scoping is: 1998 for *actedIn*(Judy Davis, Deconstructing Harry) (correct: 1997).

5. RELATED WORK

Schank and Abelson [18] first proposed hand-coded scripts to describe frequently recurring social situations such as a visit to a restaurant. Our work is similar in spirit to scripts. However, instead of hand coding scripts, we automatically identify verbs that can express a relation, find sequence of these verbs in a document, and aggregate over similar sequences in a large number of documents to infer temporal order of relations expressed by the verbs.

We also draw from Chambers and Jurafsky's [9] automatic induction of script-like structure called narrative events chain. We use a related notion of protagonist (domain) overlap to relate the set of relations we temporally order. But we differ in that we use narrative order to serve as probabilistic training signals for learning temporal order; and use unsupervised method of temporal ordering instead of a supervised classifier. Also, their focus is to output the narrative chain of *verbs* in a document while ours is to output the

[10]Please note that even though we discuss only two types of constraints here, slack variable-based extensions of all the constraints in the CoTS system have been implemented inside $\text{CoTS}_{\text{Soft}}$. We refer the reader to [20] for a complete listing of these constraints.

[11]http://www.mosek.com/

[12]English Gigaword: http://bit.ly/KJMTYr

typical temporal order of *relations* over a large number of documents.

Fujiki et al. [11] investigated script acquisition by arranging first paragraphs of news articles based on their dates of issue. In contrast, we do not use such date of issue times to order paragraphs in documents, thus our method is applicable more widely even to documents without creation time. We also temporally order relations instead of just verbs.

Timely YAGO [22] harvests temporal facts using regular expressions in Wikipedia infoboxes, but is not applicable to arbitrary text. PRAVDA [21] harvests temporal facts using a combination of textual patterns and graph-based re-ranking techniques to extract facts and their temporal scopes at the same time. In contrast, our goal is to infer *typical* temporal order of *relations*, and not temporally scope individual facts. However, our experiments demonstrate that knowledge of typical temporal order can be effective in improving temporal scoping performance.

There are several algorithms for classifying temporal relations between events [15, 8, 24]; many of them trained on the TimeBank [17] dataset. Unlike these methods, we propose a self-supervised method for temporal ordering that does not require labeled data. While these previous works focused on temporal ordering of events with one verb per event, we temporally order relations that are represented by a group of verbs. To the best of our knowledge, there is no other work on temporal ordering of relations. However, these previous works are complementary in that their output can be used as additional verb ordering signals to augment our narrative order statistics.

Finally, CoTS [20] is a recently proposed system for temporally scoping relational facts which so far used manually edited temporal order constraints. While manual ordering is appealing, unfortunately it is not very scalable as in practice hundreds of relations, whose numbers are ever increasing, may need to be ordered. As demonstrated in Section 4, our automatically acquired, scalable temporal orderings can be a replacement for the current manual rules in CoTS. We also extend CoTS framework to $\text{CoTS}_{\text{Soft}}$ which can handle weighted constraints through the use of slack variables.

Learning to model ranked data from partial [13] and pairwise preferences [14] has been recently studied. While the pairwise orderings in [14] are unweighted, the orderings in GraphOrder are weighted. Also, these previous studies considered only one type of ordering relationship between two items (viz., whether one item is preferred over the other), while GraphOrder uses two ordering relationships, TBefore and TSimultaneous, to compare two items (relations in our case). More importantly, in contrast to these previous approaches, the goal in GraphOrder is *not* to learn a ranking model, but to expand an initial set of weighted pairwise temporal orderings by taking transitivity into account.

6. CONCLUSION

In this paper, we address the problem of learning typical temporal orderings over relations (e.g., learning that *directed(person, film)* typically occurs before *wonPrize(film, award)*). This problem is important because this type of knowledge can play a key role in assigning temporal scope to specific instances of these relations (e.g., to determine when the relation instance *wonPrize(Gone With The Wind, Academy Award)* occurred). We present both a method for acquiring this type of general ordering knowledge from distant supervision, and a method for using this knowledge to infer temporal scope for specific instances of these relations. To acquire this knowledge, we introduce GraphOrder, a novel graph-based collective label propagation method. Our approach is based on the assumption that relation mentions in sentences are often expressed by verbs, the assumption that narrative order of verbs correlates with the temporal order of the relations they represent, and the fact that temporal orderings are transitive. Our approach mines a corpus of 890m dependency parsed sentences to discover verbs that express relations of interest, and collects statistics about mentions of these verbs over a large number of documents. We show the effectiveness of our proposed method for learning temporal orders of relations, compared to non-transitive and random baselines. We also show the utility of this learned knowledge about temporal ordering, for the problem of assigning temporal scope to specific instances of these relations. In future work, we would like to explore alternative approaches of estimating narrative order. We would also like to extend the proposed algorithms to learning orderings when some relation arguments are instantiated, and believe the knowledge our current system learns can serve as useful priors for acquiring this information.

Acknowledgments

We thank Justin Betteridge (CMU) for help with parsing the corpus. We are thankful to Mosek[13] for their generous academic licensing; and to the anonymous reviewers for their constructive comments. This research has been supported in part by DARPA (under contract number FA8750-09-C-0179), Google, and Fulbright. Any opinions, findings, conclusions and recommendations expressed in this paper are the authors' and do not necessarily reflect those of the sponsors.

7. REFERENCES

[1] O. Alonso, M. Gertz, and R. Baeza-Yates. On the value of temporal information in information retrieval. In *ACM SIGIR Forum*, volume 41, pages 35–41. ACM, 2007.

[2] N. Balasubramanian, S. Soderland, Mausam, and O. Etzioni. Rel-grams: A probabilistic model of relations in text. In *Automatic Knowledge Base Construction and Web-scale Knowledge Extraction (AKBC-WEKEX 2012)*, 2012.

[3] Y. Bengio, O. Delalleau, and N. Le Roux. Label propagation and quadratic criterion. *Semi-supervised learning*, pages 193–216, 2006.

[4] S. P. Boyd and L. Vandenberghe. *Convex optimization*. Cambridge University Press, 2004.

[5] P. Bramsen, P. Deshpande, Y. Lee, and R. Barzilay. Inducing temporal graphs. In *Proceedings of EMNLP*, 2006.

[6] S. Brody. Clustering clauses for high-level relation detection: An information-theoretic approach. In *ACL*, 2007.

[7] J. Callan, M. Hoy, C. Yoo, and L. Zhao. Clueweb09 data set. *boston.lti.cs.cmu.edu*, 2009.

[8] N. Chambers and D. Jurafsky. Jointly combining implicit constraints improves temporal ordering. In *Proceedings of EMNLP*, 2008.

[9] N. Chambers and D. Jurafsky. Unsupervised learning of narrative event chains. *ACL*, 2008.

[13]Mosek ApS: http://mosek.com/

[10] T. Chklovski and P. Pantel. Verbocean: Mining the web for fine-grained semantic verb relations. In *Proceedings of EMNLP*, volume 4, pages 33–40, 2004.
[11] T. Fujiki, H. Nanba, and M. Okumura. Automatic acquisition of script knowledge from a text collection. In *Proceedings of EACL*, 2003.
[12] J. Hoffart, F. Suchanek, K. Berberich, E. Lewis-Kelham, G. De Melo, and G. Weikum. Yago2: exploring and querying world knowledge in time, space, context, and many languages. In *Proceedings of WWW*. ACM, 2011.
[13] G. Lebanon and Y. Mao. Non-parametric modeling of partially ranked data. *Journal of Machine Learning Research*, 9:2401–2429, 2008.
[14] T. Lu and C. Boutilier. Learning mallows models with pairwise preferences. *ICML*, 2011.
[15] I. Mani, M. Verhagen, B. Wellner, C. Lee, and J. Pustejovsky. Machine learning of temporal relations. In *Proceedings of ACL*, 2006.
[16] J. Nivre, J. Hall, J. Nilsson, A. Chanev, G. Eryigit, S. Kübler, S. Marinov, and E. Marsi. Maltparser: A language-independent system for data-driven dependency parsing. *Natural Language Engineering*, 13(02):95–135, 2007.
[17] J. Pustejovsky, P. Hanks, R. Sauri, A. See, R. Gaizauskas, A. Setzer, D. Radev, B. Sundheim, D. Day, L. Ferro, et al. The timebank corpus. In *Corpus Linguistics*, volume 2003, page 40, 2003.
[18] R. Schank, R. Abelson, et al. *Scripts, plans, goals and understanding: An inquiry into human knowledge structures*, volume 2. Lawrence Erlbaum Associates Hillsdale, NJ, 1977.
[19] P. P. Talukdar and K. Crammer. New regularized algorithms for transductive learning. *ECML*, 2009.
[20] P. P. Talukdar, D. Wijaya, and T. Mitchell. Coupled temporal scoping of relational facts. In *Proceedings of WSDM*, pages 73–82. ACM, 2012.
[21] Y. Wang, B. Yang, L. Qu, M. Spaniol, and G. Weikum. Harvesting facts from textual web sources by constrained label propagation. In *Proceedings of CIKM*, 2011.
[22] Y. Wang, M. Zhu, L. Qu, M. Spaniol, and G. Weikum. Timely yago: harvesting, querying, and visualizing temporal knowledge from wikipedia. In *Proceedings of EDBT*, 2010.
[23] G. Weikum, S. Bedathur, and R. Schenkel. Temporal knowledge for timely intelligence. *Enabling Real-Time Business Intelligence*, pages 1–6, 2011.
[24] K. Yoshikawa, S. Riedel, M. Asahara, and Y. Matsumoto. Jointly identifying temporal relations with markov logic. In *Proceedings of ACL*, 2009.

APPENDIX

A. GraphOrder OBJECTIVE IS CONVEX

We first reproduce the objective function minimized by the label propagation-based GraphOrder algorithm presented in Sec 3.2.2 (Equation 6), and write it as a sum of two functions as follows.

$$J(\{\hat{Y}_{ul}\}) = J_1(\{\hat{Y}_{ul}\}) + \mu_2 \times J_2(\{\hat{Y}_{ul}\})$$

where

$$\begin{aligned} J_1(\{\hat{Y}_{ul}\}) &= \mu_1 \sum_{u \in R} (Y_{u,l_u} - \hat{Y}_{u,l_u})^2 \\ &+ \mu_2 \sum_{(u,v) \in E_U, l \in L} W_{u,v} \times (\hat{Y}_{u,l} - \hat{Y}_{v,l})^2 \\ &+ \mu_3 \sum_{x \in X, l \in L} (\hat{Y}_{u,l} - M_{u,l})^2 \end{aligned}$$

where $\mu_1, \mu_2, \mu_3 \geq 0$ are hyperparameters and

$$J_2(\{\hat{Y}_{ul}\}) = \sum_{(u,v) \in E_D, l \in L} W_{u,v} \times (\hat{Y}_{u,l} - \hat{Y}_{v,\bar{l}})^2$$

From the construction of the graph, we have $W_{u,v} \geq 0$, i.e., all edge weights are non-negative. From the analysis in [19], we know that J_1 is a convex function. We also know that the non-negative weighted sum of two convex functions is also a convex function [4]. Putting all of these together, we shall be able to prove that J is convex if we can show that J_2 is a convex function.

We rewrite J_2 as the non-negative weighted sum of even smaller functions:

$$J_2(\{\hat{Y}_{ul}\}) = \sum_{(u,v) \in E_D, l \in L} W_{u,v} \times J_2'(\hat{Y}_{ul}, \hat{Y}_{v\bar{l}})$$

where $J_2'(\hat{Y}_{ul}, \hat{Y}_{v\bar{l}}) = (\hat{Y}_{u,l} - \hat{Y}_{v,\bar{l}})^2$.

Now, reusing the non-negative weighted sum property of convex functions once again, we can show that J_2 is convex if each $J_2'(\hat{Y}_{ul}, \hat{Y}_{v\bar{l}})$ is instead convex (please note that $W_{u,v} \geq 0, \ \forall u, v$). We shall prove that J_2' is indeed a convex function by showing that its Hessian is a Positive Semi-Definite (PSD) matrix.

After some algebra, we can show that the Hessian matrix of $J_2'(\hat{Y}_{ul}, \hat{Y}_{v\bar{l}})$ is $H_{2\times 2} = \begin{bmatrix} 2 & -2 \\ -2 & 2 \end{bmatrix}$ and that it is PSD as for any $x = [x_1 x_2]^T$, we have $x^T H x = 2(x_1 - x_2)^2 \geq 0$.

From this we conclude that $J_2'(\hat{Y}_{ul}, \hat{Y}_{v\bar{l}})$ is convex, which implies that J_2 is convex, and which in turn implies that J, i.e., the objective function function optimized by the GraphOrder is indeed convex.

B. SOLVING GraphOrder OBJECTIVE

In the previous section, we proved that the objective J minimized by GraphOrder is convex. Hence, the optimal solution is obtained by setting $\frac{\delta J}{\delta \hat{Y}_{u,l}} = 0, \ \forall u \in X, l \in L$. Following the analysis in [3], we develop a Jacobi iteration method and end up with the following iterative update, which updates the score for label l at node u at time instant $t+1$ as follows:

$$\hat{Y}_{u,l}^{(t+1)} = \frac{B_{u,l}^{(t)}}{B_{u,u}^{(t)}}$$

$$\begin{aligned} B_{u,l}^{(t)} &= \mu_1 \times S_{uu} \times I(l_u, l) \times Y_{u,l} + \\ &\mu_2 \times \sum_{v:(u,v) \in E_D} W_{u,v} \times \hat{Y}_{v,\bar{l}}^{(t)} + \\ &\mu_2 \times \sum_{v:(u,v) \in E_U} W_{u,v} \times \hat{Y}_{v,l}^{(t)} + \mu_3 \times M_{u,l} \end{aligned}$$

$$\begin{aligned} B_{u,u}^{(t)} &= \mu_1 \times S_{uu} \times I(l_u, l) + \mu_2 \times \\ &\sum_{v:(u,v) \in E_D} W_{u,v} + \mu_2 \times \sum_{v:(u,v) \in E_U} W_{u,v} + \mu_3 \end{aligned}$$

Above, S is a diagonal matrix with $S_{u,u} = p_u^{inj}$ when $u \in R$ (the set of relation nodes) and 0 otherwise, with p_u^{inj} set using the equations in Sec 2.2 of [19]; $I(l_u, l) = 1$ iff $u \in R$ and l is the node specific label for relation node u. While computing $\hat{Y}_{u,\bar{l}}^{(t+1)}$, we consider $l = \vec{l}$. This iterative process is updated until convergence or until a fixed number of iterations. We have found that the iterations usually converge with a small number of iterations. We also note that the iterative updates above can be easily parallelized in the MapReduce framework using Hadoop, and hence the optimization can be applied to large graphs.

Author Index

V1: pages 1-1014 **V2: pages 1015-1768** **V3: pages 1769-2792**

www.ingramcontent.com/pod-product-compliance
Lightning Source LLC
LaVergne TN
LVHW080100011026
849160LV00013B/1002
9781450320108